PENGUIN REFERENCE BOOKS

THE PENGUIN GUIDE TO COMPACT DISCS
YEARBOOK 2000/1

EDWARD GREENFIELD, until his retirement, in 1993, was for forty years on the staff of the *Guardian*, succeeding Neville Cardus as Music Critic in 1975. He still contributes regularly to the record column which he founded in 1954. At the end of 1960 he joined the reviewing panel of *Gramophone*, specializing in operatic and orchestral issues. He is a regular broadcaster on music and records for the BBC, not just on Radios 3 and 4 but also on the BBC World Service, latterly with his weekly programme, 'The Greenfield Collection'. In 1958 he published a monograph on the operas of Puccini. More recently he has written studies on the recorded work of Joan Sutherland and André Previn. He has been a regular juror on International Record awards and has appeared with such artists as Dame Elisabeth Schwarzkopf, Dame Joan Sutherland and Sir Georg Solti in public interviews. In October 1993 he was given a *Gramophone* Award for Special Achievement and in June 1994 received the OBE for services to music and journalism.

ROBERT LAYTON studied at Oxford with Edmund Rubbra for composition and with Egon Wellesz for the history of music. He spent two years in Sweden at the universities of Uppsala and Stockholm. He joined the BBC Music Division in 1959 and was responsible for Music Talks including such programmes as *Interpretations on Record*. He contributed 'A Quarterly Retrospect' to *Gramophone* magazine for thirty-four years and writes for the *BBC Music Magazine*, *International Record Review* and other journals. His books include studies of Berwald and Sibelius as well as a monograph on the Dvořák symphonies and concertos for the *BBC Music Guides*, of which he was General Editor for many years. His prize-winning translation of Erik Tawaststjerna's definitive five-volume study of Sibelius was completed in 1998. In 1987, Robert Layton was awarded the Sibelius Medal and in the following year made a Knight of the Order of the White Rose of Finland for his services to Finnish music. His other books include *Grieg: An Illustrated Life* and he has edited the *Guide to the Symphony* and the *Guide to the Concerto* (OUP).

IVAN MARCH is a former professional musician. He studied at Trinity College of Music, London, and at the Royal Manchester College. After service in the Central Band of the RAF, he played the horn professionally for the BBC and travelled with the Carl Rosa and D'Oyly Carte opera companies. He is a well-known lecturer, journalist and personality in the world of recorded music and acts as consultant to Squires Gate Music Ltd, an international mail order source for classical CDs (www.lprl.demon.co.uk). As a journalist he contributes to a number of record-reviewing magazines, including *Gramophone*, where he deals particularly with important reissues.

The Penguin Guide to Compact Discs Yearbook 2000/1
Completely revised and updated

Ivan March, Edward Greenfield and Robert Layton

Edited by Ivan March

PENGUIN BOOKS

PENGUIN BOOKS

Published by the Penguin Group
Penguin Books Ltd, 27 Wrights Lane, London W8 5TZ, England
Penguin Putnam Inc., 375 Hudson Street, New York, New York 10014, USA
Penguin Books Australia Ltd, Ringwood, Victoria, Australia
Penguin Books Canada Ltd, 10 Alcorn Avenue, Toronto, Ontario, Canada M4V 3B2
Penguin Books India (P) Ltd, 11, Community Centre, Panchsheel Park, New Delhi – 110 017, India
Penguin Books (NZ) Ltd, Private Bag 102902, NSMC, Auckland, New Zealand
Penguin Books (South Africa) (Pty) Ltd, 5 Watkins Street, Denver Ext 4, Johannesburg 2094, South Africa

Penguin Books Ltd, Registered Offices: Harmondsworth, Middlesex, England

This edition first published 2000
1

Set in 8/9.5 pt PostScript Monotype Times New Roman
Typeset, from material supplied, by Rowland Phototypesetting Ltd, Bury St Edmunds, Suffolk
Made and printed in Great Britain by Clays Ltd, St Ives plc

Contents

Foreword

The present Millennium *Penguin Guide to Compact Discs Yearbook* is essentially an extension of and supplement to our 1999 main volume. Altogether our combined survey of some 2,300 pages gathers together the very finest CDs issued over the last two decades, while discussing many more recent recorded performances that fail to measure up to that description.

The 1640 pages of our Main Volume represented the maximum number which it is feasible to bind securely in paperback format. Indeed, twenty-four hours before that book went to print in the late summer of 1999, the Editor had to cut some 70 pages of reviews (from composers S–Z) for which there was no room. These recordings have been reinstated in the present volume.

COMPOSERS NEW TO THE CURRENT *YEARBOOK*

Once again, our survey introduces a remarkable number of new composer entries, many of them names from the past almost completely forgotten until now, even though these musicians left us music of quality. One of the earliest is Reginaldus Libert, or Liebert (born *c.* 1430), whose Marian mass has the distinction of being one of the first to survive which includes settings of both the Ordinary and Proper. Among others are Alexander Agricola (*c.* 1446–1506), composer of French chansons, who left a celebrated setting of the famous *Fortuna desperata*, and the English composer Walter Frye (died 1475), whose Mass is held in the Brussels Bibliothèque, and being part of a manuscript including works by Du Fay and other contemporaries (a sure indication of its worth).

Naxos have provided us with the first comprehensive collection of the lute songs of Thomas Campion (1562–1620) and a no less valuable complete set of the twelve *Opus 3 Concerti grossi* of Francesco Manfredini (1684–1762), while two quite different groups of performances (from Fretwork on Virgin Veritas, and the Rose Consort on Naxos) show us that John Jenkins (1592–1678) wrote some remarkable consort music for viols in the generation before Purcell. Michel De la Barre (*c.* 1675–1745) had the title of *Flute de la chambre* at the Court of Louis XIV, and his Suites are among the first pieces written for the newly modelled transverse flute.

Among names associated with early keyboard music is the celebrated Elisabeth Jacquet de la Guerre (1665–1729), whose *Pièces de clavecin* established her as the first major female baroque composer for the keyboard, and Marc Roger Normand Couperin (1663–1734), the talented first cousin of François Couperin.

Johann Caspar Fischer (*c.* 1670–1746), whose *Musical Parnassus* established him as a major precursor of Bach, is matched by Johann Ludwig Krebs (1713–80), one of Bach's favourite pupils. Hearing his harpsichord music, one can understand his mentor's attributed description of him as the 'best Crawfish in the Brook', especially when one discovers the German translations of the words Krebs and Brook.

Turning to vocal music, there is a rewarding early setting – very like an oratorio – of the *Stabat Mater* by Emanuele D'Astorga (*c.* 1680–1757) on Hyperion, and we have some fine new recordings of the music of William Boyce (1711–79) – the Anthems, on CRD, and the *Ode for St Cecilia* as well as the remarkable *Secular Masque* on ASV.

Moving further on into the eighteenth century, we discover some delightful clarinet concertos from an Italian contemporary of Beethoven, Casimir Cartellieri (1772–1807), plus five delightful Haydnesque String quartets by Ignaz von Beck (1753–1803). A CPO collection further combines string quartets by three more female composers – Emilie Mayer (1812–1883), Fanny Mendelssohn (sister of Felix) and Maddelana Lombardini Sirmen – while Adalbert Gyrowetz (1763–1850), friend of both Haydn and Mozart, left some elegant and sparkling Bohemian symphonies.

We are also discovering that there was distinctive Russian music before Glinka. Dmitri Bortnyansky (1751–1825), born in the Ukraine, became Maestro di Cappella at the Court of Catherine the Great and gave us some fine, choral Sacred concertos.

Among collectable piano CDs is an outstanding Chandos recital from Míceál O'Rorke which immediately establishes the reputation of the London-born George Frederick Pinto (1785–1806). He died very young but left us three sonatas with an individual voice which not only show influences from Beethoven and Mozart, but even anticipate the piano writing of Schubert.

Moving on into the nineteenth century, we have an entertaining pair of Romantic piano concertos by Alexander Dreyschock and Theodor Kullak (both born in 1818), most persuasively played by Piers Lane on Hyperion. On MDG comes another, rather less individual piano concerto of the same period, coupled with a symphony, both by Felix Draeseke (1835–1913), while the Swedish composer, Adolf Lindblad (1801–78), who was better known as a song-writer, left us an engaging pair of Weberian symphonies. Richard Holl (1825–1904) was another (Dutch) symphonic composer, somewhat Schumannesque in style, but his works are capped by the four richly inventive Brahmsian symphonies of Friedrich Gernsheim (1839–1916).

A fair number of new names sit astride the nineteenth and early twentieth centuries, including Ernst Mielck (1877–99), a contemporary of Sibelius, who died sadly young, and two composers of highly individual piano music, Glauco Velasquez (1884–1914), born in Naples of a Brazilian mother, and the Russian, Georgy Catoire (1861–1926). Arthur Lourié (1892–1966) is another unfamiliar Russian name, as are the two Lithuanian composers, Mikalojus Konstantinas Ciurlionis (1875–1911), while the symphonist, Maximilian Steinberg (1883–1946), is mainly remembered as the teacher of Shostakovich.

The much more recognizable French composer, Lili Boulanger (1893–1918) brings music of real memorability, and equally worth seeking out are the three String quartets of Joseph Marx (1882–1964). He was a contemporary of Schoenberg who yet hated (and campaigned against) serial techniques, and his music has much of the voluptuous textural richness of that *fin de siècle* period of string writing before the Second Viennese School took over.

Joseph Achron (1886–1943) was yet another Russian-born composer (and virtuoso violinist). His *Hebrew melody* was a famous Heifetz encore, and it is good to discover (inexpensively on ASV Quicksilva) his more substantial music, including a fine violin sonata.

The very personable and cultivated flying Dutchman, Alexander Voormolen (1895–1980) is a real find. Unexpectedly, he is a kind of Netherlands' Lord Berners: his *Baron Hop suites* certainly take off, are full of geniality and wit, and sparklingly orchestrated. Equally enterprisingly, Chandos have also provided us with a coupling of symphonies by Londoner, Edgar Bainton (1880–1956) and Australian-born Hubert Clifford (1904–59), neither of them masterpieces, but both enjoyable in quite different ways.

Turning into the twentieth century proper, we encounter a whole host of new names: the Russian emigré, Nikolai Lopatnikoff (1903–76), Stefan Wolpe (1902–72), one of Webern's pupils, and Karl Amadeus Hartmann (1905–63) whose symphonies are very challenging, but satisfying for those who persevere. The symphonies of the American Paul Creston (1906–85) are a good deal more approachable, and certainly rewarding in equal measure.

Nino Rota (1911–79) is best known for his film scores, but we are discovering that, like Korngold, he also wrote enjoyable works for the concert hall, including several piano concertos and symphonies. The opposite is the case with Georges Auric (1899–

1983). He is not a newcomer to our pages, but his distinguished film scores are. They were written not only for Jean Cocteau, but more surprisingly for some of the most famous Ealing Studio comedies.

Friedrich Cerha, (born in 1926), remains a dedicated disciple of the Second Viennese School. Not so with many other names. Edgar Mayer (born 1969), double bass player as well as composer, has written a fine violin concerto which is unashamedly tonal, and a new generation of 'traditional' composers has moved away from serialism and back to melody, including Joan Trimble (born 1915), John Gardner (born 1917), Robert Docker (1918–92), and Stephen Frost (born 1959). The music of Sally Beamish (born 1956) is by no means 'easy listening', but well worth seeking out.

The American composer Joan Tower (born 1939) began as a serialist until she heard a performance of Messiaen's *Quartet for the end of time*. After that, she tells us, 'I felt like an acrobat – so I pulled out'. The brooding symphonic writing of the Yorkshireman Arthur Butterworth (born 1923) has no lack of forward thrust, and the Cornish seascapes evoked by Ruth Gipps (1921–99) are likewise full of colour and vitality, but while the symphonies of Norwegian Halvor Haug (born 1952) have genuine Nordic atmosphere, the writing is relatively static. However, there is no problem about movement, momentum and sparkle in the outstanding new ballet score, *Edward II* by John McCabe (born 1939), perhaps his finest work to date, full of colour and undoubtedly listener-friendly.

Two more of the most exciting of contemporary composers, who consistently make direct contact with the ordinary music-lover, and especially younger ears, are American: John Adams, who is not a new name in our pages, and Christopher Rouse, who makes his first appearance. As we go to press, Adams has scored an enormous popular success with the ENO production of his opera on an unlikely subject, *Nixon in China*. It is masterly, with neo-Romantic vocal lines that – like too little late-twentieth-century music – fall naturally for the voice. Appropriately Adams is currently represented by a ten-CD Nonesuch collection of his major orchestral and concertante works, and including operatic highlights not only from *Nixon in China*.

The output of Christopher Rouse has so far been less prolific, but he has already given us an amazingly original trombone concerto and an even more eloquent and ambitious five-movement flute concerto, dedicated to James Bulger, the English child horrifically murdered by two young boys. The intense anguish expressed in the work's slow movement provides one of the most moving threnodies in all contemporary music.

Samuel Barber is obviously not a new name to the Penguin Guide, but that of the astonishing young

American maestro, Marin Alsop certainly is. A shooting star in the firmament of conductors who is soon going to become very famous, she is a musician of enormous talent and interpretative skill. Her 'live' performances have a comparable electricity and depth of feeling with those of her mentor, Leonard Bernstein. It is she who conducts the excellent Colorado Symphony in Rouse's concerto for trombone, and with remarkable prescience, Naxos have put her in charge of their new coverage of all Barber's orchestral and concertante music. The first CD (with the RSNO) which includes the *First* and *Second Symphonies*, the *School for Scandal overture*, and a quite riveting acount of the *First Essay*, brings great intensity and excitement, and the Scottish orchestral players rise to the occasion, as do the Naxos engineers.

STANDARD REPERTOIRE

Bach to Byrd

In the year of the 150th anniversary of Bach's death, the flood of new issues and reissues has been overwhelming, and his most famous sons have not been neglected either. Johann Sebastian's orchestral and concertante music is now available in an almost unbelievable array of alternatives on both modern and period instruments. Among the newer keyboard issues, Angela Hewitt's highly imaginative and spontaneous account of the *Goldberg variations* (recorded in a single take), Maasaaki's Suzuki's *Two-* and *Three-part Inventions*, Trevor Pinnock's splendid new Hännsler set of the *Partitas*, and Bernard Roberts's *Well-tempered Klavier* stand out. In the field of organ music Kevin Bowyer, Ton Koopman and Christopher Herrick continue their complete surveys which are now supplemented by two classic sets from the past – from Helmut Walcha and Lionel Rogg.

The coverage of the cantatas is equally prolific. Suzuki's superb Japanese series with the Bach Collegium continues apace and remains the market leader, and he has now followed up with an equally fresh and beautifully sung recording of the *St Matthew Passion*. Rilling's excellent, more traditional Stuttgart cantata series is now three-quarters of the way towards completion, Koopman's Amsterdam survey continues on Erato, while John Eliot Gardiner and his Monteverdi Choir have begun a group of twelve recordings for DG Archiv, made at various European venues on ecclesiastical feast days during the anniversary year.

But perhaps the most striking new venture in this field is the highly successful recording of Bach's underrated *Missae breves* by the Purcell Quartet, with four splendid soloists who join together to form a surprisingly full-bodied chorus. Indeed, the quality of the singing combined with a warm

acoustic means that ears familiar with period performances will not crave a fuller choral texture. Certainly that is not a problem with the magnificent new recording from Jordi Savall and La Capella Reial de Catalunya of Heinrich Biber's *Missa Bruxellensis*, spectacularly recreating its first performance in Salzburg Cathedral just 300 years after its première in that same richly resonant venue.

Among the most recent recordings of Beethoven piano concertos, the new complete set by András Schiff with the Dresden State Orchestra under Haitink now takes its place as a first choice among performances on modern instruments, but there are also some splendid individual couplings, notably those taken from the BBC archives featuring Sir Clifford Curzon and Dame Myra Hess. And we must not forget a super-bargain two-disc Royal Longplayer reissue which includes the *Second* and *Third concertos* in inspired (1959) performances by Claudio Arrau (with Galliera and the Philharmonia) – two of the finest Beethoven performances he ever put on disc. They are paired with Hans Richter-Haaser's outstanding version of the *Fourth concerto* plus his *Emperor*, which is slightly less magnetic. But this remains an indispensable set.

The great Beethoven novelty is the recording of a transcription of the *Violin concerto* for clarinet and orchestra. Unlikely as that sounds, the result, when played by the highly sensitive Michael Collins, in partnership with Pletnev, is something of a revelation, while at super-budget price on Arte Nova, Alfredo Perl's complete recording of the thirty-two Beethoven *Piano sonatas* compares very favourably with sets from other more famous names. Similarly, the new Naxos recording of *Fidelio*, made in Hungary, conducted by Michael Halász, with Gösta Winberg as Florestan, and Inga Nielsen as Leonore represents something of an operatic triumph for that bargain label, and is strongly recommendable quite irrespective of its modest cost.

Another major achievement in the recording of previously little-known and seldom-performed repertoire is the complete set of Boccherini Symphonies by the German Chamber Academy Orchestra of Neuss directed by Johannes Goritzki. Their playing is polished and full of life and expressive vitality, and the music itself is revealed as being of consistently high quality.

Benjamin Britten is well represented both as composer and performer (again by courtesy of the BBC archives), but the current highlight of his discography must be the Chandos recordings of *Paul Bunyan* (in the much-admired 1999 Covent Garden production) and *Billy Budd*. Both are superbly conducted by Richard Hickox, and the latter is almost ideally cast, with Simon Keenlyside in the title role, Philips Langridge as Captain Vere, and John Tomlinson an unforgettable Claggart.

Georg Tintner has been continuing his highly

successful Naxos series of Bruckner Symphonies, while unexpectedly Nikolaus Harnoncourt has given us a really outstanding new version of the *Seventh*, gloriously played by the Vienna Philharmonic and given a 'live' Teldec recording of striking presence and realism. Also not to be missed is Mark Hamelin's new recording of the Busoni *Piano concerto* on Hyperion, easily the most convincing account this intractible work has ever received on disc. A further exploration of Buxtehude's chamber and keyboard music, continues to expand the reputation of this underrated composer, whom Bach so-admired, while Andrew Carwood's Cardinal odyssey through Byrd's vocal music moves forward apace on ASV, having now reached Volume 4. Happily, Davitt Moroney and Hyperion have combined to add a distinguished new integral survey of Byrd's keyboard music.

Chopin to Haydn

Prompted by the 150th anniversary of his death, DG have issued a complete Chopin Edition in seventeen volumes, and as – almost inevitably – the quality of the performances is uneven, it is good to report that they are all available separately. Jean-Yves Thibaudet has now completed his coverage of Debussy's piano music and the second Volume is as perceptively rewarding as the first, and beautifully recorded, to make this a clear first choice among modern recordings of this repertoire. Another CD which could be easily missed is a delightful Marco Polo collection of the various wind concertos by Donizetti, all played with great elegance and sparkle, while the fine new set of Dvořák's *Saint Ludmila* on Orfeo fills yet another gap in the catalogue.

Paul Daniel's splendid new recording of Anthony Payne's inspired completion of Elgar's *Third Symphony* comes as yet another feather in the Naxos cap, alongside Benjamin Frith's delightful performances of the Chopinesque *Nocturnes* of John Field (the first of a continuing series). But one of the two most remarkable bargains in our *Yearbook* comes as an EMI Virgin Bargain Double of string music, played with great ardour and warm expressive feeling by the London Chamber Orchestra. Included are Elgar's *Serenade*, and *Introduction and allegro*, together with *Serenades* by Dvořák, Suk, Tchaikovsky, plus Vaughan Williams's *Tallis* and *Greensleeves fantasias*, and *The lark ascending* with Christopher Warren-Green the highly sensitive soloist; it is he who directs the ensemble throughout.

Handel is well represented by fine new recordings of *Acis and Galatea* and *Alcina* (both from Harry Christophers), and Belart have reissued (at little more than the cost of one premium-priced CD) Boult's much-praised complete Decca *Messiah*, dating from the very end of the mono era. The soloists are the meltingly lovely Jennifer Vyvyan,

the rich-timbred Norma Proctor, the light-voiced George Maran, and the genially dramatic Owen Brannigan, with the LPO Choir and Orchestra singing and playing gloriously. The listener has initially to adjust to Boult's choice of tempi (relatively slow by today's standards) but, as Otto Klemperer once said to Walter Legge, 'You will get used to it'.

Another highly recommendable Virgin Double is of Kuijken's set of Haydn's *Paris Symphonies* with the OAE, while those preferring modern instruments can turn to the equally enjoyable (and underrated) recordings by Jeffrey Tate and the ECO on Royal Classics. But the jewel in the crown of new Haydn repertoire must be Hickox's recordings of the Masses, among the greatest of all the composer's late works. The performances are in every way worthy of them.

Ibert to Mozart

French chamber music is always a delight and the complete oeuvre of Ibert, offered on an Olympian Double is most recommendable, alongside the Nash Ensemble's comparable coverage of Poulenc on Hyperion. The two strongest Mahler recommendations are a 1977 BBC recording of *Das Lied von de Erde* conducted by Raymond Leppard, with Dame Janet Baker at her very peak partnered by John Mitchinson, and Sir Simon Rattle's new EMI Berlin Philharmonic recording of Deryck Cooke's revised performing edition of the *Tenth Symphony* which is in almost every respect an advance on his earlier Birmingham recording.

Massenet's opera *Werther* offers an alternative choice of the highly successful EMI team of Roberto Alagna, Angela Gheorghiu and Pappano, or a most enjoyable English language version with Dame Janet Baker as Charlotte. There is also an outstanding new set of the Mendelssohn *String quartets* on Naxos, played by the modern-instrument Aurora Quartet, while on Sony, L'Archibudelli give hardly less stimulating period performances of the two *String quintets*.

The Concerto Italiano directed by Rinaldo Alessandrini, continuing their series of Monteverdi madrigals, have reached Book VIII (*Madrigals of love and war*) and once again their performances, so full of Italianate colour and vitality, cannot be too highly praised, while Maria Cristina Kiehr has given us a ravishing anthology of Monteverdi's solo motets to match her superb earlier recital of the music of Barbara Strozzi.

Which brings us to Mozart and our bargain of bargains centring on Menuhin's much praised performances with the Lausanne Chamber Orchestra and (in the case of the symphonies) the admirable Sinfonia Varviso. We are offered the two *Flute concertos* and the *Flute and harp concerto* (with Samuel Coles and Naoko Yoshina), the finest of the three string *Divertimenti, in D major, K.136*, the *Serenata Notturna* and *Posthorn Serenade*, plus the six greatest late *Symphonies: Nos. 35–36* and *38–41*. All this music-making is of the highest calibre and, incredibly, the five CDs come in a slip-case for the cost of one premium-priced CD!

There are also some fine Mozart concerto pairings, notably from Richard Goode, but the most rewarding of all is a triptych: Daniel Barenboim's Teldec performances of Nos. 14, 15, and 16, K.449/451, with the Berlin Philharmonic, is a truly treasurable disc, one of Barenboim's really outstanding records of the last decade. No less remarkable is Nikolaus Harnoncourt's extremely vital coverage of Mozart's entire output of sacred vocal music on 13 Teldec CDs, with a starry team of soloists and choirs, and his own Vienna Concentus Musicus providing lively, expressive accompaniments, this is a major achievement. All the masses are here and the recording approaches the demonstration bracket throughout. The only minor disappointment is the *Requiem*, made before the others, where the sound is blurred by a too-resonant acoustic (not a problem elsewhere). But this problem is solved by the separate appearance of two excellent new versions of Mozart's final choral masterpiece, a fine traditional account from Abbado, and a vibrant period performance from the Tölz Boys' Choir, Swedish Radio Choir and Tafelmusik under Bruno Weil, using a brand new edition by H. C. Robbins Landon.

Puccini to Sullivan

Puccini is represented by an outstanding new recording of *La Bohème* on Decca again featuring Gheorghiu and Alagna, and conducted by Chailly, plus a thrilling new *Tosca* sung in English, with Jane Eaglen superb in the title role, and very well partnered by Dennis O'Neill as Cavaradossi, while from the Kirov Opera under Gergiev come definitve recordings of three Rimsky-Korsakov operas, hitherto little-known outside Russia, *Kashchey the Immortal*, *The Legend of the invisible city of Kitezh* and *The Tsar's bride*. The latest major enterprise from Opera Rara is the first really complete recording of Rossini's *Otello*, cast from strength, and admirably directed by David Parry.

Another of those records which could well slip by unnoticed, but which gives great pleasure, is Philippe Grafin's persuasive Hyperion triptych of the three Saint-Saëns *Violin concertos*, most engaging music, winningly presented. Similarly, Christoph Eschenbach's new set of the four Schumann *Symphonies*, with the North German Radio Orchestra might be missed, yet is considered by R. L. to be 'the best to have appeared in many years', while the new coupling of Schumann's *Piano concerto* and *Piano quintet* from Maria João Pires, Abbado and the C.O.E. and an instrumental group lead by Dumay is equally distinctive.

We are less sure about the Emersons' new DG set of the Shostakovich *String quartets*, dazzlingly played to be sure, and most realistically recorded. But these American players fail to penetrate to the very inner core of this often introspective music as tellingly as do the Borodin and Fitzwilliam Quartets.

Turning to Sibelius one immediately encounters a highly sensitive response from Osma Vänskä and the Lahti Symphony Orchestra (on BIS) to the original 1896 scores of the *Four Legends*, while Barbirolli's integral EMI Hallé set of the seven *Symphonies* and much orchestral music besides (all from the late 1960s), although uneven, has stood the test of time and will be welcomed by his admirers. Maazel's coupling of the *Fourth* and *Seventh Symphonies*, with *Tapiola* is another memorable reissue, rightly reissued in Decca's Legends series.

Standing out among a bonanza of new and re-issued recordings of the major orchestral works of Richard Strauss is Sarah Chang's remarkably fine EMI coupling of the lesser known *Violin concerto* and *Sonata*, in each case with Sawallisch as partner; and it is Sawallisch, a superb Straussian, who directs Bavarian forces in a CD digital première of the opera, *Friedenstag*, also well worth exploring, particularly as it comes complete on a single CD. Stravinky's early opera *Le Rossignol*, conducted by James Conlon with Natalie Dessay in the title role, and imaginatively coupled with *Renard*, is another outstanding novelty, while Rattle's riveting new set of Szymanowksi's *King Roger*, with Thomas Hampson, completes EMI's operatic hat-trick. But it is a much smaller label, Divine Arts, which enterprisingly offers the original (piano-accompanied), full-length 1866 version of Sullivan's *Cox and Box*, performed by members of the London Chamber Opera. The disc is appropriately dedicated to Arthur Jacobs, Sullivan's biographer, one of whose last acts before he died was to arrange for the recording's publication.

Tallis to Webern

Alistair Dixon's Chapelle du Roi have now reached Volume 4 of their complete recording of the glorious music of Thomas Tallis, while Hyperion's new bargain label, Helios, has reissued an enticing series from Harry Christophers and his Sixteen of the key Masses of John Taverner. In turn, Chandos have recorded *Fall and Resurrection*, the twentieth-century Tavener's contribution to the Millennium celebrations, in a powerfully atmospheric recording under Hickox.

Among many new additions to the Tchaikovsky discography, one orchestral record stands out, and is now one of the most attractive of all the reissues on the Penguin Classics label. George Szell's 1962 recording of Tchaikovsky's *Fourth Symphony* is in a class of its own. Apart from its physical excitement (especially in the finale), all four movements show how this great American conductor has rethought every detail of the score. The remastered Decca sound is superbly full and brilliant. Yet what makes this disc especially desirable is the fill-up, Karajan's early Vienna Philharmonic account of the *Romeo and Juliet fantasy overture*, which he never surpassed. There is also an extraordinary Stokowski reissue of the *Fourth Symphony* – his 1941 recording with the NBC Symphony Orchestra. It moves forward at an incredible speed throughout, as if the conductor had an express train to catch. Grotesquely rushed, it almost earns a special award for sheer perversity: however, the playing of the NBC strings in the frantic finale (which also has a small cut) has to be heard to be believed! So it remains a collector's item.

Chandos have also given us a complete recording by the BBC Philharmonic Orchestra of all Verdi's opera preludes and overtures, plus his underrated ballet music, sparkling with colour beneath the understanding baton of Edward Downes; while one of the most valuable of the Verdi recordings to come from the BBC sound archives is Giulini's remarkable 1967 *Requiem*, recorded at a Prom.

Appearing most appropriately on ASV's Gaudeamus logo come outstanding performances from Andrew Carwood's Cardinall's Musick of Victoria's *Missa Gaudeamus* and the even more astonishing *Missa pro victoria*, the composer's only mass written in nine parts, while the pick of the Vivaldi coverage is also vocal. Cecilia Bartoli's dazzling bravura exploration of his operatic arias and scenas is compiled from the composer's mostly forgotten works for the stage, and on the evidence of this brilliant collection undeservedly so.

Walton is admirably served by more Naxos enterprise, memorable couplings of the *Cello concerto* (Tim Hugh) and *Violin concerto* (Dong-Suk-Kang), and the 1921 *Piano quintet* and 1947 *String quartet* are equally impressive on the bows of the Maggini Quartet partnered by Peter Donohoe. There is also an outstanding reissue, (with greatly improved sound) of the composer's own EMI Philharmonia recordings of *Belshazzar's Feast* (with Donald Bell), and the *First Symphony*. Last but not least comes a collection of Webern's collected works on a six-CD DG set of great distinction.

CORNUCOPIA OF COLLECTIONS

Orchestral concerts and instrumental recitals

Collections are an essential part of any CD discography because (unlike the 78 era) shorter pieces cannot be presented alone, but have to be grouped with other works; and because a piece is short it does not mean that it is unimportant or uninspired. The trick is to make up a single-disc compilation which works as an overall concert or recital, and

yet also entices the listener to select works individually – so easy with a compact disc. A splendid example is Yan-Pascal Tortelier's Chandos programme with the BBC Philharmonic Orchestra of *'French bonbons'*, a delectable collection of orchestral lollipops which Sir Thomas Becham would have welcomed for its finesse, *joie de vivre* and sense of style, ranging from Offenbach's *La Belle Hélène* and Hérold's *Zampa overtures* to the *Gavotte* from Thomas's *Mignon*.

But there are multi-disc collections too, and most famous artists have their own 'Editions', some huge like Sony's coverage of Glenn Gould, Horowitz, Stern and Bruno Walter, RCA's Julian Bream Edition (with many discs now sadly deleted), the San Francisco recordings of Pierre Monteux, and the new Artur Rubinstein Collection on the same label. Other editions are, relatively speaking, more modest: those featuring Argerich, the organists Marie Claire Alain and Jennifer Bate, the Philips 'Art of Brendel', and the various surveys of the major recordings of Franz Brüggen, Pablo Casals, Kyung Wha Chung, Jacqueline Du Pré, Clara Haskil, Gustav Leonhardt, playing solo and with his Consort, Anne Sophie Mutter (with both classical and modern compilations), Itzak Perlman, Rostropovitch (including his Russian years), Sviatoslav Richter, (triply represented by Melodiya, Philips and Melodiya), and the Russian Piano School to which he belonged.

Among the most valuable of recent surveys are those of the multi-faceted art of Jordi Savall (both as a pioneering virtuoso of the bass viol and as imaginatively creative conductor of La Capella Reial de Catalunya), and a fine coverage of the Argo's outstanding analogue organ recordings of Dame Gillian Weir, now restored to the CD catalogue by Australian Decca.

Within the orchestral compilations Beecham is well represented, both by his early LPO recordings on 78s (given superb Dutton transfers), and his later sessions with the RPO, while through the enterprise of Australian Decca, Richard Bonynge's sparkling coverage with the ECO and LSO of eighteenth-century opera overtures and nineteenth-century ballet music is now available on CD for the first time and is soon to be issued in the UK.

Järvi's early Melodiya recordings, Karajan conducting the Berlin Philharmonic on EMI, and his even earlier Vienna Philharmonic sessions on Decca, serve to fill out the background of these conductors' recorded heritage, as does the representation of Mravinsky and the Leningrad Philharmonic, and of course Stokowski conducting a variety of orchestras, not only on RCA, but on other labels too. By comparison there is only a very modest coverage of Stokowski's successor in Philadelphia, Eugene Ormandy, appearing surprisingly, on Buddulph.

Artists not always given extended editions are

often featured in 'Portraits', usually single or double-CD anthologies, and these include the two trumpeters, Maurice André, and Håken Hardenburger (a superb collection), the great Russian pianist Emil Gilels, Marriner and his Academy, Stephen Hough, Julius Katchen, the Juilliard Quartet and Melos Ensemble, David and Igor Oistrakh, Perahia, Michaela Petri, Fritz Reiner, Sir Malcolm Sargent, George Szell, Toscanini, even the horn player, Barry Tuckwell.

The Ulsamer Collegium in partnership with the Edward Melkus Ensemble provide a remarkable survey of 'Dance music through the ages', while a sudden expansion of interest in twentieth-century British light orchestral music has brought a whole new range of outstanding anthologies demonstrating its ready tunefulness, led by those from Ronald Corp and the New London Orchestra on Hyperion, but including excellent contributions from the Royal Ballet Sinfonia on ASV and Naxos (among others).

Historical orchestral and instrumental recordings

Our coverage of orchestral and instrumental historical recordings is underpinned by two outstanding videos: *The Art of Conducting* and *The Art of the Piano*, supplemented by a valuable series of recorded telecasts by the Chicago Symphony Orchestra. Dating from as early as 1954, these feature conductors of the calibre of Monteux, Munch, Stokowski, Szell, and Paul Hindemith conducting his own music.

On CD, the historical instrumental section is led by Philips' ambitious coverage of the '*Great Pianists of the 20th Century*', masterminded by John Deacon. There are a hundred volumes altogether (each of two discs), and the coverage of this series begun in our main volume is here completed. Not everyone will agree with the choice of artists, and it seems to us that the glaring omissions of some names from the Philips roster is as remarkable as some of the inclusions. Equally controversial is the arbitrary decision to feature some pianists in more than one volume while others only have a single representation. Another of the snags is that of the repertoire included, too much of which is already in the catalogue. But generally speaking these generously filled, handsomely packaged and well-documented 'Duos' are good value for money.

Historical vocal recordings

The video, *The Art of Singing*, fascinating though it is, has less to offer the serious vocal collector than its orchestral and pianistic equivalents, while only Volume 3 (1926–1939) of EMI's extensive four-Volume historical coverage of '*The Record of Singing*' from the LP era is available on CD, enter-

prisingly published by Testament. Otherwise EMI's separate coverage of their historical vocal back-catalogue is inadequate, but it does include valuable (mostly single-disc) collections from the early recordings of Victoria de los Angeles and Jussi Bjoerling (including a four-CD set), plus recitals from Caruso, Boris Christoff (including five discs of Russian songs), Chaliapin, Sena Jurinac, John McCormack (including duets wth Elisabeth Rethberg and Lotte Lehmann), Joseph Schmidt and Georges Thill. The transfers are usually of high quality.

In consequence, the main historical coverage of vocal repertoire lies principally with two key labels, Romophone (at premium price) and Nimbus 'Prima voce' (at mid-price). Romophone usually concentrates on complete editions (from a given source) of a single singer. The straight CD transfers use modern technology to excellent advantage to reproduce as far as possible exactly what is on the original 78s, but often include a fair amount of backgound noise, rather than limit the range of the vocal timbre. Nimbus use a more controversial system of playing back the original 78s through a huge acoustic horn and re-recording them, often with remarkable success in terms of vocal naturalness, yet inevitably offering some limitation of the upper range. The Nimbus catalogue includes a very wide coverage, not only compiled under individual artists, but also collectively, in groups.

Obviously there is a great deal of duplication between the two labels and, as can be seen below, both have issues covering Battistini, Lucrezia Bori, Emma Eames, Flagstad, Galli-Curci, Gigli (very comprehensively), Martinelli, McCormack, Ernestine Schumann-Heinck, Marcella Sembrich, and Tetrazzini. Romophone also include Mario Ancona, Emmy Destinn, Mary Garden, Lotte Lehmann, Elisabeth Schumann, and Elizabeth Rethberg. Nimbus add in Bjoerling, Caruso, Chaliapin, Geraldine Farrar, Frieda Hempel (an outstanding disc), Maria Ivogun, Giuseppe de Luca, Melba, Lauritz Melchior, Cladio Muzio, Patti, Pinza, Ponselle, Schipa, Supervia, Tauber (with Lotte Schöne) and Lawrence Tibett.

Other vocal recordings

As with the orchestral and instrumental categories, the major labels offer 'Editions' featuring individual artists and specialist vocal groups, plus categories (such as the DG Archiv historical retrospective gathered together under the sobriquet 'Codex'). Standing out among the celebrations of individual artists is DG's 70th and 75th-birthday tributes to Dietrich Fischer-Dieskau totalling sixty-five CDs overall, while on Vanguard Alfred Deller's recorded legacy is nearly as generously represented on single discs.

EMI's Callas Edition is comprehensive, but again

not collected all together, and other singers like
Dame Janet Baker, Cecilia Bartoli, Emma Kirkby,
Christa Ludwig, Kenneth McKellar, Pavarotti,
Leontyne Price (including an eleven-disc set),
Schwarzkopf, Souzay, Rita Streich, Sutherland,
Tebaldi, and Bryn Terfel are all well represented.

Among the specialist groups in the field of early
music, the Anonymous Four, David Munrow's
Early Music Consort, and Hyperion's pioneering
coverage of the music of the twelfth to fifteenth

centuries by the Gothic Voices under Christopher
Page stand distinctively alongside the contribution
of the Tallis Scholars under Peter Phillips.

The gramophone's discography would be infinitely less comprehensive without its Collections,
and we are glad that at last we have found space to
cover them adequately.

Ivan March (Editor)

100 Great Recordings

A personal choice by the authors from the 1999 *Guide* and the Millennium *Yearbook*

Our selection endeavours to strike a balance between key repertoire and CDs from which one (or more) of the authors has derived special musical pleasure and satisfaction, and it is intended to be used in conjunction with the authors' more limited personal choice on p. xii of our main volume.

Please note that entries in the present *Yearbook* are marked **YB** and those from the 1999 main *Guide* **PG**; the relevant author's initials follow each choice.

BACH *Violin concertos 1–2; Double Violin concerto in D minor, BWV 1041/3; Chaconne* from *Unaccompanied Violin Partita No. 2, BWV 1004.* Yehudi Menuhin, Georges Enescu, Orchestre Symphonique de Paris, Enescu or Monteux. EMI mono CDH5 67201-2. **YB** (IM)
(Unaccompanied) *Violin Sonatas and Partitas 1–3, BWV 1001/6. Milstein.* DG 457 701-2 (2). **PG** (IM)
Partita (French overture) in B minor, BWV 831; Goldberg variations, BWV 988; Italian concerto, BWV 971; 4 Duets, BWV 802/5. Rosalyn Tureck ('*Great pianists*': Volume 94) Ph. 456 979-2 (2). **YB** (RL)
Mass in B minor, BWV 232. Argenta, Dawson, Fairfield, Knibbs, Kwella, Hall, Nichols, Chance, Collin, Stafford, Evans, Milner, Murgatroyd, Lloyd-Morgan, Varcoe, Monteverdi Choir, English Baroque Soloists, Gardiner. DG 415 514-2 (2). **PG** (EG)
BACH (trs. BUSONI) *Chorales.* LISZT *Concert paraphrases on Schubert Lieder.* MENDELSSOHN *Songs without words.* Murray Perahia. Sony SK 66511. **YB** (RL)
BACH/KUHNAU/ZELENKA *Magnificats.* Soloists, Bach Collegium, Japan, Masaaki Suzuki. BIS CD 1011. **YB** (RL)
BARBER *Symphonies 1–2, Opp. 9 & 19; First Essay for orchestra; The School for Scandal overture.* Royal Scottish National Orchestra, Marin Alsop. Naxos 8,559024. **YB** (IM)
BARTOK *Concerto for orchestra.* STRAVINSKY *The Rite of spring.* Concertgebouw Orchestra, Eduard van Beinum. Dutton Lab. mono CDK 1206. **YB** (RL)
Divertimento for strings. JANACEK. *Idyll; Suite for strings.* Norwegian Chamber Orchestra, Iona Brown. Chandos CHAN 9816. **YB** (RL/IM)
Piano music: *3 Burlesques, Op. 8c; 7 Esquisses, Op.9b; 10 Easy pieces; 15 Hungarian peasant dances; Improvisations on Hungarian peasant*

songs *Op. 20.* Zoltan Kocsis. Ph. 462 902-2. **YB** (RL)
BBC PHILHARMONIC ORCHESTRA, Yan Pascal Tortelier: '*French bonbons*': *Overtures:* ADAM *Si j'étais roi.* AUBER *Le cheval de bronze.* HEROLD *Zampa.* MAILLART *Les dragons de Villars.* THOMAS *Mignon* & *Gavotte.* OFFENBACH *La belle Hélène. Contes d'Hoffmann: Entr'acte & Barcarolle.* CHABRIER *Habanera; Joyeuse marche.* GOUNOD *Marche funèbre d'une marionette.* MASSENET *Thaïs: Méditation. Mélodie; Elégie. Les Erinnes: Tristess du soir. La vierge: Le dernier sommeil de la Vierge.* Chandos CHAN 9765. **YB** (IM)
BEETHOVEN *Piano concertos 2–3; 4–5 (Emperor).* Claudio Arrau; Hans Richter-Haaser, Philharmonia Orchestra, Galliera or Kertész. Royal Long Players DCL 705752 (2). **YB** (IM)
Violin concerto in D. MOZART *Violin concerto No. 5 in A (Turkish), K.219.* Wolfgang Schneiderhan, Berlin Philharmonic Orchestra, Jochum. DG 447 403-2. **PG** (IM)
Symphonies Nos. 3 (Eroica); 4 in B flat, Op. 60. Zurich Tonhalle Orchestra, David Zinman. Arte Nova 74321 59214-2. **PG** (EG)
Symphonies Nos. 6 (Pastoral); 4 in B flat. Columbia Symphony Orchestra, Bruno Walter. Sony SMK 64462. **PG** (IM)
(i) *String quartets 1, 9, 11, 12, 14–16;* (ii) *Violin sonata No. 3 in E flat, Op. 12/3.* (i) Busch Quartet; (ii) Adolf Busch, Rudolf Serkin. EMI mono CHS7 65308-2 (4). **PG** (RL)
Piano sonatas 1–32. Artur Schnabel. EMI mono CHS7 63765-2 (8). **PG** (RL)
(i) *Missa solemnis, Op. 123. Symphony No. 7 in A, Op. 92.* CHERUBINI *Anacréon overture.* MOZART *Symphony No. 35 in D (Haffner), K.385.* BBC Symphony Orchestra, Toscanini; (i) with Milanov, Thorborg, Von Pataky, Moscona, BBC Choral Society. BBC Legends BBCL 4016-2 (2). **YB** (RL)
Fidelio. Inga Nielsen, Gösta Winbergh, Kurt Moll, Alan Titus, Hungarian Radio Chorus, Esterházy Sinfonia, Michael Halász. Naxos 8.110054/55. **YB** (EG)
BENTZON *Symphonies Nos. 5 (Ellipser), Op. 61 & 7 (De tre versioner), Op. 83.* Aarhus Symphony Orchestra, Ole Schmidt. Dacapo 8.22411. **YB** (RL)
BERLIOZ *Roméo et Juliette, Op. 17.* Borodina, Moser, Miles, Bavarian Radio Chorus, Vienna Philharmonic Orchestra, Sir Colin Davis. Ph. 442 134-2 (2). **PG** (RL)

BIBER *Missa Bruxellensis*. Soloists, La Capella Reial de Catalunya, Les Concerts de Nations, Jordi Savall. Allia Vox AV 9808. **YB** (IM)

BRAHMS *Violin concerto in D*. Menuhin, Berlin Philharmonic Orchestra, Kempe. DVORAK *Violin concerto in A minor, Op. 53*. Krebbers, Amsterdam Philharmonic Orchestra, Kersjes. SIBELIUS *Violin concerto in D minor, Op. 47*. Emma Verhey, Netherlands Radio Philharmonia Orchestra, Hans Vonk. TCHAIKOVSKY *Violin concerto in D, Op. 35*. Vladimir Spivakov, Philharmonia Orchestra, Ozawa. Royal Long Players DCL 705742 (2). **YB** (IM)

Symphony No. 1 in C minor, Op. 68; Tragic overture, Op. 81; (i) *Alto rhapsody, Op.53*. Philharmonia Orchestra, Klemperer; (i) with Christa Ludwig, Philharmonic Chorus. EMI CDM5 67029-2. **PG** (IM)

Symphonies Nos. 2 in D; 3 in F. Columbia Symphony Orchestra, Bruno Walter. Sony SMK 64471. **PG** (IM)

BRITTEN *War Requiem; Ballad of heroes, Op. 14; Sinfonia da Requiem*. Heather Harper, Philip Langridge, John Shirley-Quirk, St Paul's Canterbury Choristers, London Symphony Chorus & Orchestra, Richard Hickox. Chandos CHAN 8983/4 (2). **PG** (EG)

Peter Grimes. Peter Pears, Claire Watson, James Pease, Jean Watson, Owen Brannigan, Royal Opera House Covent Garden Chorus & Orchestra, composer. Decca 414 577-2 (3). **PG** (EG)

BRUCKNER *Symphony No. 8 in C minor*. Vienna Philharmonic Orchestra, Karajan DG 427 611-2 (2). **PG** (RL)

CHOPIN *Nocturnes 1–19*. Artur Rubinstein (*'Rubinstein Edition'*: Volume 49). RCA 09026 63049-2 (2). **YB** (IM)

DEBUSSY *Syrinx. Bilitis* (arr. Lenski). *La plus que lente*. PROKOFIEV *Flute sonata, Op. 94*. (i) RAVEL *Chansons madécasses*. Emmanuel Pahud, Stephen Kovacevich, (i) with Katerina Karnéus, Truls Mørk. EMI CDC5 56982-2 **YB** (RL)

Piano music (complete). Jean-Yves Thibaudet. Volume I (including *Estampes; Pour le piano; Préludes, Books 1–2*) Decca 452 022-2 (2) **PG.** Volume II (including *Children's corner; Etudes, Books 1 & 2; Images, Books 1 & 2; Suite bergamasque*) Decca 460 247-2 (2). **YB** (IM)

DOHNANYI Piano music: *6 Concert études, Op.28; Pastorale; Ruralia hungarica, Op. 32a; Variations on a Hungarian folk song, Op. 29*. Markus Pawlik. Naxos 8.553332. **YB** (RL)

DONIZETTI *La fille du régiment*. Sutherland, Pavarotti, Sinclair, Malas, Coates, Royal Opera House Covent Garden Chorus and Orchestra, Bonynge. Decca 414 520-2 (2). **PG** (EG)

DVORAK *Cello concerto*. TCHAIKOVSKY *Variations on a rococo theme for cello and orchestra*. Rostropovich, Berlin Philharmonic Orchestra, Karajan. DG 447 413-2. **PG** (IM)

Symphony No. 5 in F, Op. 76; Othello overture, Op. 93; Scherzo capriccioso. Oslo Philharmonic Orchestra, Jansons. EMI CDC7 49995-2. **PG** (EG)

ELGAR (i) *Cello concerto;* (ii) *Sea pictures*. (i) Jacqueline du Pré; (ii) Dame Janet Baker, LSO, Barbirolli. EMI CDC5 56219-2. **PG** (EG)

Symphony No. 1 in A flat, Op. 55; Falstaff. LSO, composer. EMI mono CDM5 67296-2. **YB** (EG)

Symphony No. 3 (sketches elaborated by Anthony Payne). Bournemouth Symphony Orchestra, Paul Daniel. Naxos 8.554719. **YB** (RL/IM/EG)

'English string music': ELGAR (i; ii) *Introduction and allegro for strings;* (i) *Serenade for strings;* (iii) *Elegy, Op. 58; Sospiri, Op. 70*. (i) VAUGHAN WILLIAMS *Fantasia on Greensleeves;* (i; ii) *Fantasia on a theme of Thomas Tallis*. (i) Sinfonia of London; (ii) with Allegri Quartet; (iii) New Philharmonia Orchestra, Barbirolli. EMI CDM5 67240-2 [567264]. **YB** (IM)

(i) *The Dream of Gerontius;* (ii) *The Music Makers*. (i) Nicolai Gedda, Helen Watts, Robert Lloyd, Alldis Choir, LPO Choir, New Philharmonia Orchestra; (ii) Dame Janet Baker, LPO Choir, LPO, Boult. EMI CMS5 66540-2 (2). **PG** (IM)

GERSHWIN *Piano concerto in F; 'I got rhythm' variations; Rhapsody in blue; 2nd Rhapsody*. Wayne Marshall, Aalborg Symphony. Virgin/ EMI VMS5 61478-2. **YB** (IM)

Porgy and Bess. Willard White, Cynthia Haymon, Harold Blackwell, Cynthia Clarey, Damon Evans, Glydebourne Chorus, LPO, Rattle. EMI CDC7 49568-2 (3). **PG** (EG)

GODOWSKY *53 Studies based on the Etudes of Chopin, Opp. 10 & 25*. Marc-André Hamelin. Hyperion CDA 67411/2. **YB** (RL)

GRIEG *String quartets Nos. 1 in G minor, Op. 27; 2 in F* (unfinished). Chilingirian Quartet. Hyperion CDA 67117. **YB** (RL)

HANDEL *Messiah*. Arleen Augér, Anne Sofie von Otter, Michael Chance, Howard Crook, John Tomlinson, English Concert Chorus & Orchestra, Pinnock. DG 423 630-2 (2). **PG** (EG)

HAYDN *Piano concertos in F, G and D, Hob XVII:3, 4 & 11*. Leif Ove Andsnes, Norwegian Chamber Orchestra. EMI CDC5 56950-2. **YB** (RL)

Symphonies 82–7 (Paris). Orchestra of the Age of Enlightenment, Kuijken. Virgin Classics 2 x 1 Double VBD5 61659-2. **YB** (IM)

String quartets Nos. 75 in G; 76 in D minor (Fifths); 77 in C (Emperor), Op. 77/1–3. Lindsay Quartet. ASV Dig. CDDCA 1076. **YB** (IM)

HILDEGARD OF BINGEN *'Feather on the breath of God': Hymns and sequences*. Gothic Voices, Muskett, White, Page. Hyperion CDA 66039. **PG** (EG)

HINDEMITH *Kammermusik* (complete). Berlin Philharmonic Orchestra, Claudio Abbado. *Nos. 1* (with finale), *4 & 5*. EMI CDC5 56160-2 **PG.**

Nos. 2, 3, 6, & 7. EMI CDC5 56831-2. **YB** (RL)
HONEGGER. *Symphonies Nos. 2 for strings with trumpet obbligato; 3 (Symphonique liturgie).* STRAVINSKY *Concerto in D for strings.* Berlin Philharmonic Orchestra, Karajan. DG 447 435-2. **PG** (RL)

HOWELLS *Collegium regale: Te Deum and Jubilate; Office of Holy Communion; Magnificat and Nunc dimittis. Preces & Responses I & II; Psalms 121 & 122; Motet: Take him, earth, for cherishing. Rhapsody No. 3 (for organ), Op. 17.* Williams, Moore, King's College, Cambridge Choir, Decca 430 205-2. **PG** (EG)

Kenneth MCKELLAR'S Scotland: *'Sleeps the noon in the clear, blue sky'* (with accompaniments arr. and cond. Bob Sharples): Songs of the Hebrides (arr. Kennedy-Fraser); Folk songs from Scotland's heritage; Scottish popular songs. Australian Decca Double 844 840-2 (2). **YB** (IM)

MAHLER (i) *Symphony No. 4 in G;* (ii) *Lieder eines fahrenden Gesellen.* (i) Judith Raskin, Cleveland Orchestra, Szell; (ii) Frederica von Stade, LPO, Sir Andrew Davis. Sony SBK 46535. **PG** (IM)

Symphony No. 5 in C sharp minor. New Philharmonia Orchestra, Barbirolli. EMI CDM5 66910-2 [566962]. **PG** (EG/IM)

Symphony No. 10 in F sharp (revised performing edition by Deryck Cooke). Berlin Philharmonic Orchestra, Sir Simon Rattle. EMI CDC5 56972-2. **YB** (EG)

Kindertotenlieder; Lieder eines fahrenden Gesellen; 5 Rückert Lieder. Dame Janet Baker, Hallé Orchestra, or New Philharmonia Orchestra, Barbirolli. EMI CDM5 66981-2 [566996]. **PG** (EG)

MONTEVERDI *'Pianato della Madonna':* Motets for solo voice. MARINI *2 Sinfonias.* ATEGNATI *Ricercar.* MERULO *Toccata con minute.* Maria Cristina Kiehr, Concerto Soava, Jean-Marc Aymes. **YB** (IM)

MOZART (i) *Clarinet concerto in A, K.622;* (ii) *Clarinet quintet in A, K.581.* Thea King; (i) English Chamber Orchestra, Tate; (ii) Gabrieli Qt. Hyperion CDA 66199. **PG** (IM)

Flute concertos 1–2; Flute and harp concerto; Divertimento for strings No. 1 in D, K.136; 2 Marches, K.335; Serenades Nos. 6 (Serenata notturna), K.239; 9 (Posthorn), K.320; Symphonies Nos. 35 (Haffner); 36 (Linz); 38 (Prague); 39 in E flat, K.543; 40 in G min., K.550; 41 in C (Jupiter). Samuel Coles, Naoko Yoshino, ECO, Lausanne Chamber Orchestra or Sinfonia Varviso, Menuhin. Virgin Classics 5 x 1 VBD5 61678-2 (5). **YB** (IM)

Piano concertos Nos. 14 in E flat; 15 in B flat; 16 in D, K.449/51. Daniel Barenboim, Berlin Philharmonic Orchestra. Teldec/Warner 0630 16827-2. **YB** (IM)

Piano concertos Nos. 21 in C, K.467; 23 in A, K.488; Rondos Nos. 1–2, K.382 & K.386. Murray

Perahia, English Chamber Orchestra. Sony SMK 64128. **YB** (IM)

Masses 1–19 and complete sacred choral music. Soloists, Choruses, Vienna Concentus Musicus, Harnoncourt. Teldec/Warner 3984 21885-2 (13).

Requiem Mass (No. 19) in D minor (new edition by H. C. Robbins Landon) Soloists, Tölz Boys' Choir, Tafelmusic, Bruno Weil. Sony SK 60764. **YB** (IM)

Così fan tutte. Schwarzkopf, Ludwig, Steffek, Kraus, Taddei, Berry, Philharmonia Chorus & Orchestra, Karl Boehm. EMI CMS7 69330-2 (3). **PG** (EG)

OFFENBACH *Contes d'Hoffmann.* Sutherland, Domingo, Tourangeau, Bacquier, Lausanne Pro Arte Chorus. Suisse Romande Chorus and Orchestra, Bonynge. Decca 417 363-2 (2). (Highlights from the above recording available on Decca 458 234-2). **PG** (EG)

Mikhail PLETNEV playing Rachmaninov's piano: *'Hommage à Rachmaninov':* RACHMANINOV *Variations on a theme of Corelli, Op. 42; 4 Etudes-tableaux, Op. 39/5; Op. 44/6,8 & 9.* BEETHOVEN *Piano sonata No. 26 (Les Adieux), Op. 81a.* MENDELSSOHN *Andante cantabile and Presto agitato; Andante and Rondo capriccioso, Op. 14.* CHOPIN *Andante spianato et grande polonaise brillante, Op. 22.* DG 459 634-2. **YB** (RL)

PROKOFIEV *Violin concertos Nos. 1 in D, Op. 19; 2 in G minor, Op. 63.* STRAVINSKY *Violin concerto.* Kyung-Wha Chung, LSO, Previn. Decca 425 003-2. **PG** (EG)

PUCCINI (i) *La Rondine.* (ii) *Le Villi:* excerpts; Song: *Morir.* (i–iii) Roberto Alagna; (i) Angela Gheorghiu, Mula-Tchako, Matteuzzi; Rinaldi; (i–ii) London Voices, LSO, Pappano; (iii) Pappano (piano). EMI CDC5 56338-2. **PG** (EG)

PURCELL *Dido and Aeneas.* Dame Janet Baker, Herincx, Clark, Sinclair, St Anthony Singers, English Chamber Orchestra, Anthony Lewis. Decca 466 387-2. **PG** (EG)

RACHMANINOV *Piano concerto No. 2 in C minor, Op. 18; Rhapsody on a theme of Paganini, Op. 43.* Ashkenazy, LSO, Previn. Penguin Classics Decca 460 632-2. **PG** (IM)

(i) *Piano concerto No. 3 in D min. Op. 30. Elegy, Op.3/1; Polichinelle; Preludes: in C sharp min., Op. 3/2; in B flat, G minor, and E flat, Op. 23/2, 5, & 6; in G and G sharp minor, Op. 32/5 & 12.* Santiago Rodriguez; (i) with Lake Forest Symphony, Paul McRae. Elan CD 82412. **YB** (RL)

Symphony No. 2 in E minor, Op. 27; Vocalise, Op. 24/14l Aleko: Intermezzo & Women's dance. LSO, André Previn EMI CDM5 66982-2 [566997]. **YB** (EG)

Etudes-tableaux, Op. 39; Piano sonata No. 2 (1913 version). KREISLER *Liebeslied* (trs. Rachmaninov). Freddy Kempf. BIS CD 1042. **YB** (RL)

RAVEL *Piano concerto in G.* RACHMANINOV *Piano concerto No. 4 in G minor, Op. 40.* Michelangeli, Philharmonia Orchestra, Gracis. EMI CDM5 67238-2 [567258]. **YB** (IM)
ROYAL PHILHARMONIC ORCHESTRA, Sir Thomas Beecham: *'The RPO Legacy'*, Volume 1: BER-LIOZ *Le Corsaire overture.* SIBELIUS *Tapiola.* DEBUSSY *Printemps.* MUSSORGSKY *Khovanshchina: Dance of the Persian slaves.* BACH *Christmas oratorio: Sinfonia.* SMETANA *The Bartered Bride: Overture; Polka; Dance of the Comedians.* CHABRIER *Marche joyeuse.* Dutton Lab mono CDLX 7027. **YB** (RL)
SCHREKER *Ekkehard (symphonic overture), Op. 12; Fantastic overture, Op. 15; Der ferne klang; Nachstück. Prelude to a drama; Der Schatzgräber: Symphonic interlude. Valse lente.* BBC Philharmonic Orchestra, Vassily Sinaisky. Chandos CHAN 9797. **YB** (RL)
SCHUBERT *Symphonies Nos. 3 in D; 5 in B flat, 6 in C.* Royal Philharmonic Orchestra, Sir Thomas Beecham. EMI CDM5 66984-2 [5 66999]. **PG** (EG/IM/RL)
Graham Johnson Lieder Edition, Volume 25: (i) *Die Schöne Müllerin* (song cycle); (ii) with additional poems by Wilhelm Müller. Ian Bostridge, Graham Johnson; (ii) read by Dietrich Fischer-Dieskau. Hyperion CDJ 33025. **PG** (EG)
SCHUMANN *Fantasia in C, Op. 17.* Lieder: *Frühlingsnacht; Widmung* (trs. Liszt). LISZT *Concert paraphrases of Beethoven's An die ferne Geliebte; Mignon.* Chandos CHAN 9793. **YB** (RL)
Elisabeth SCHWARZKOPF sings operetta (with Philharmonia Chorus & Orchestra, Ackermann): Excerpts from: HEUBERGER *Der Opernball.* ZELLER *Der Vogelhändler.* LEHAR *Der Zarewitsch; Der Graf von Luxembourg. Giuditta.* Johann STRAUSS Jr *Casanova.* MILLOCKER *Die Dubarry.* SUPPE *Boccaccio.* SIECZYNSKY *Wien, du Stadt meiner Träume.* EMI CDM5 66989-2. **YB** (EG)
SCRIABIN *Symphony No. 3 (Le divin poème), Op. 43; Le poème de l'extase.* Russian National Orchestra, Mikhail Pletnev. DG 459 681-2. **YB** (RL)
SHOSTAKOVICH (i) *Symphony No. 15 in A, Op. 141;* (ii) *Piano sonata No, 2 in B minor, Op. 61.* (i) Philadelphia Orchestra, Eugene Ormandy; (ii) Emil Gilels. RCA 09026 63587-2. **YB** (RL)
SIBELIUS *Symphonies Nos. 4 in A minor, Op. 63; 7 in C, Op. 105; Pelléas et Mélisande suite, Op. 46; Swanwhite, Op. 54; Tapiola, Op. 112; The Tempest (incidental music): Dance of the nymphs* (with British and Finnish National anthems and speeches by Sir Thomas, including Beecham on Sibelius). RPO, Beecham. BBC Legends mono BBCL 4041-2 (2). **YB** (RL)
4 Legends, Op. 22 (with 1896 versions of Nos. 1 & 4 and alternative 1897 ending of No. 4). Lahti

Symphony Orchestra, Osmo Vänskä. BIS CD 1015. **YB** (RL)
STENHAMMAR *Serenade for orchestra, Op. 1.* BRAHMS *Serenade No. 1 in D, Op. 31.* Royal Stockholm Orchestra, Sir Andrew Davis. Finlandia/Warner 3984 25327-2. **YB** (RL)
STRADELLA *San Giovanni Battista.* Bott, Batty, Lesne, Edgar-Wilson, Huttenlocher. Musiciens de Louvre, Minkowski. Erato/Warner 2292 45739-2. **PG** (EG)
Richard STRAUSS *Four Last songs & Orchestral Lieder.* Elisabeth Schwarzkopf, Berlin Radio Symphony Orchestra or LSO, Szell. EMI CDM5 66908-2 [66960]. **PG** (EG)
Der Rosenkavalier. Schwarzkopf, Ludwig, Stich-Randall, Edelman, Waechter, Philharmonia Chorus & Orchestra, Karajan. EMI CDC5 56242-2 (3). **PG** (EG)
STRAVINSKY *Le rossignol.* Janine Micheau, Jean Giraudeaux, Geneviève Moizan, French Radio Chorus and Orchestra, André Cluytens. Testament mono SBT 1135. **PG** (RL)
Rita STREICH sings Waltzes and Arias by Johann STRAUSS Jr.; ARDITI; Josef STRAUSS; DELIBES; CZERNIK; MARCHESI; FLOTOW; GODARD; SUPPE; DVORAK; MEYERBEER and SAINT-SAENS: *Le rossignol et la rose.* VERDI *Lo spazzacamino (The chimney sweep).* DELL'ACQUA *Villanelle.* DG mono/stereo 457 729-2. **YB** (IM)
SULLIVAN *'The very best of Gilbert and Sullivan':* extracts from: *The Gondoliers; HMS Pinafore; Iolanthe; The Mikado; Patience; The Pirates of Penzance; Princess Ida; Ruddigore; The Sorcerer; Trial by Jury; The Yeomen of the Guard.* Soloists, D'Oyly Carte Opera Chorus, New SO; RPO; ROHCG O, Isadore Godfrey; Royston Nash; Sir Malcom Sargent. Decca Double 460 010-2 (2). **PG** (IM)
Joan SUTHERLAND *'Grandi Voci'* (with various orchestras & conductors): Arias from BELLINI *Norma; I Puritani.* DONIZETTI *Lucia di Lammermoor (Mad scene); Linda di Chamounix.* VERDI *Attila; Ernani; I vespri siciliani.* Decca 440 404-2. **PG** (EG)
SZYMANOWSKI (i) *King Roger;* (ii) *Symphony No. 4 (Sinfonia concertante for piano and orchestra), Op. 60.* (i) Hampson, Szmytka, Minkiewicz, CBSO Chorus & Youth Chorus; (ii) Andsnes; (i; ii) CBSO, Rattle. EMI CDS5 56823-2 (2). **YB** (RL)
TCHAIKOVSKY *Symphony No. 4 in F min., Op. 36;* (ii) *Fantasy overture Romeo and Juliet.* (i) LSO, Szell; (ii) Vienna Philharmonic Orchestra, Karajan. Decca Penguin Classics 460 655-2. **YB** (IM)
(i) *Symphony No. 6 in B minor (Pathétique), Op.74; Marche slave.* (ii) Piano music: *The Seasons* (complete); *6 Pieces, Op. 21; Sleeping Beauty* (excerpts; arr. Pletnev). Virgin Classics 2 x 1 VBD5 61636-2 (2). **PG** (IM/RL)

Introduction

As in previous editions, the object of *The Penguin Guide to Compact Discs Yearbook* is to give the serious collector a comprehensive survey of the finest recordings of permanent music on CD, irrespective of price. Although this is an independent publication, the *Yearbook* is meant to be used in conjunction with its companion *Penguin Guide to Compact Discs*, and the reader will find many references to the main *Guide* in the following pages.

What is new and important in the present volume is its extensive coverage of Collections of Orchestral, Chamber, Instrumental and Vocal music (including historical recordings) which we have called a 'Cornucopia' as it is by far the most comprehensive coverage of this vital area of recorded music ever attempted by us (or indeed any other Guide).

As many records are issued almost simultaneously on both sides of the Atlantic and use identical international catalogue numbers, this *Guide* should be found to be equally useful in Australia, Canada and New Zealand as it will in the UK and USA. The internationalization of repertoire and numbers now applies to almost all CDs issued by the major international companies and also by the smaller ones. Many European labels are imported in their original formats, both into Britain and the USA. Where recordings available in England are not issued in America (and vice versa), this will be indicated. Those CDs that are only available in England can be easily obtained by overseas collectors via the listed Web address, which is given on page xxv for this purpose.

The sheer number of records of artistic merit now available causes considerable problems in any assessment of overall and individual excellence. What is now very clear is that most major works are available in many recordings of comparable distinction, yet usually conveying different insights. While we always try and indicate a 'best buy', often referring to our Main Guide, the final choice will be subjective, and depends on a collector's personal reaction to the style of the performance as described by us, with perhaps an individual allegiance to the artists concerned.

We feel that it is a strength of our basic style to let our own conveyed pleasure and admiration (or otherwise) for the merits of an individual recording come over directly to the reader, even if this produces a certain ambivalence in the matter of such a final choice. Where there is disagreement between us (and this rarely happens), readers will find an indication of our different reactions in the text.

We have considered (and rejected) the use of initials against individual reviews, since this is essentially a team project. The occasions for disagreement generally concern matters of aesthetics, for instance in the manner of recording-balance, where a contrived effect may trouble some ears more than others, or in the matter of style, where the difference between robustness and refinement of approach appeals differently to listening sensibilities, rather than involving a question of artistic integrity. But over the years our views seem to grow closer together rather than to diverge; perhaps we are getting mellower, but we are seldom ready to offer strong disagreement following the enthusiastic reception by one of the team of a controversial recording, provided that the results are creatively stimulating. As performance standards have advanced, our perceptions of the advantages and disadvantages of performances of early music on original (as against modern) instruments seem fairly evenly balanced.

EVALUATION

Most major recordings issued today are of a high technical standard and offer performances of a quality at least as high as is experienced in the concert hall. In adopting a starring system for the evaluation of records, we have decided to make use of one to three stars. Brackets round one or more of the stars indicate some reservations about a recording's inclusion, and readers are advised to refer to the text. Brackets round all the stars usually indicate a basic qualification: for instance, a mono recording of a performance of artistic interest, where some allowances may have to be made for the sound-quality, even though the recording may have been digitally remastered.

Our evaluation system may be summarized as follows:

*** An outstanding performance and recording in every way.

** A good performance and recording of today's normal high standard.

* A fair or somewhat routine performance, well or reasonably well recorded.

Our evaluation is normally applied to the record as a whole, unless there are two main works or groups of works, and by different composers. In this case, each is dealt with separately in its appropriate place. In the case of a collection of shorter works, this may usually find its way into the Concerts or Recitals sections, unless each of these shorter works has a special individual interest.

ROSETTES

To certain special records we have awarded a Rosette: ✿.

Unlike our general evaluations, in which we have tried to be consistent, a Rosette is a quite arbitrary compliment by a member of the reviewing team to a recorded performance which, he finds, shows special illumination, magic, or a spiritual quality, or even outstanding production values, that place it in a very special class. Occasionally, a Rosette has been awarded for an issue that seems to us to offer extraordinary value for money, but that presupposes that the performance or performances are outstanding too. The choice is essentially a personal one (although often it represents a shared view) and in some cases it is applied to an issue where certain reservations must also be mentioned in the text of the review. The Rosette symbol is placed before the usual evaluation and the record number. It is quite small – we do not mean to imply an 'Academy Award' but a personal token of appreciation for something uniquely valuable. We hope that once the reader has discovered and perhaps acquired a 'rosetted' CD, its special qualities will soon become apparent. There are, of course, more of them now, for our survey has become a distillation of the excellence of CDs issued and reissued over a considerable time span.

DIGITAL RECORDINGS

Nearly all new compact discs are recorded digitally, but an increasingly large number of digitally remastered, reissued analogue recordings are now appearing, and we think it important to include a clear indication of the difference:

Dig. indicates that the master recording was digitally encoded;

Analogue/Dig. (or Dig./analogue) applies to a compilation where recordings come from mixed sources.

LISTINGS AND PRICE RANGES

Our listing of each recording assumes that it is in the premium-price category, unless it indicates otherwise, as follows:

(M) Medium-priced label

(B) Bargain-priced label

(BB) Super-bargain label

See below for differences in price structures in the UK and the USA.

LAYOUT OF TEXT

We have aimed to make our style as simple as possible. So, immediately after the evaluation and before the catalogue number, the record make is given, sometimes in abbreviated form. In the case of a set of two or more CDs, the number of units involved is given in brackets after the catalogue number. Cassette numbers, if they exist, are denoted by being given in *italic type*.

AMERICAN CATALOGUE NUMBERS

The numbers which follow in square brackets are US catalogue numbers, while the abbreviation [id.] indicates that the given number is used internationally, which is often the case. Even RCA has moved over to completely identical numbers, although a few earlier issues have an alphabetical prefix in the UK which is not used in the USA. Where a record is available in the USA but *not* the UK *it will appear in square brackets only*, and that applies especially to EMI's 'Red Line Classics', plus a number of Mercury issues which have been withdrawn outside the USA.

There are certain other small differences to be remembered by American readers. For instance, EMI use extra digits for their British compact discs; thus the British number CDM7 63351-2 becomes CDM 63351 in the USA (the -2 is the European indication that this is a compact disc). Prefixes can alter too. The British EMI forte and double fforte CZS5 68583-2 becomes CDFB 68583 in the USA; and Virgin Classics VBD5 61469-2 becomes CDVB 61469. We have taken care to check catalogue information as far as is possible, but as all the editorial work has been done in England there is always the possibility of error; American readers are therefore invited, when ordering records locally, to take the precaution of giving their dealer the fullest information about the music and recordings they want.

The indications (M), (B) and (BB) immediately before the starring of a disc refer primarily to the British CD, as pricing systems are not always identical on both sides of the Atlantic. But if we are aware of a difference in price for the American issue, that is indicated within the square brackets, e.g.:

(B) *** EMI CD-EMX 2055 [(M) id.].

This means that the disc is on a bargain label in the UK but is at mid-price in the USA.

When CDs are imported by specialist distributors into the USA, this again usually involves a price difference, e.g.:

(B) *** Decca Eclipse Dig. 448 710-2 [(M) id. import].

This means that the disc is on a bargain label in the UK and is a mid-priced import in the USA. (When mid-priced CDs on the smaller labels are imported into the USA, they often move up to the premium-price range.)

Where no American catalogue number is given, this does not necessarily mean that a record is not available in the USA; the transatlantic issue may not have been made at the time of the publication of this *Guide*. Readers are advised to check the current *Schwann* catalogue and to consult their local record store.

ABBREVIATIONS

To save space we have adopted a number of standard abbreviations in listing orchestras and performing groups (a list is provided below), and the titles of works are often shortened, especially where they are listed several times. Artists' forenames are sometimes omitted if they are not absolutely necessary for identification purposes. Also, we have not usually listed the contents of operatic highlights and collections.

We have followed common practice in the use of the original language for titles where it seems sensible. In most cases, English is used for orchestral and instrumental music and the original language for vocal music and opera. There are exceptions, however; for instance, the Johann Strauss discography uses the German language in the interests of consistency.

ORDER OF MUSIC

The order of music under each composer's name broadly follows the following system: orchestral music, including concertos and symphonies; chamber music; solo instrumental music (in some cases with keyboard and organ music separated); vocal and choral music; opera; vocal collections; miscellaneous collections. Within each group our listing follows an alphabetical sequence, and couplings within a single composer's output are *usually* discussed together instead of separately with cross-references. Occasionally and inevitably because of this alphabetical approach, different recordings of a given work can become separated when a record is listed and discussed under the first work of its alphabetical sequence. The editor feels that alphabetical consistency is essential if the reader is to learn to find his or her way about.

CATALOGUE NUMBERS

Enormous care has gone into the checking of CD catalogue numbers and contents to ensure that all details are correct, but the editor and publishers cannot be held responsible for any mistakes that may have crept in despite all our zealous checking. When ordering CDs, readers are urged to provide their record-dealer with full details of the music and performers, as well as the catalogue number.

DELETIONS

Compact discs regularly succumb to the deletions axe, and many are likely to disappear during the lifetime of this book. Sometimes copies may still be found in specialist shops, and there remains the compensatory fact that most really important and desirable recordings are eventually reissued, often costing less!

EMI's Special UK Import Service, which began in the UK in August 1995, means that the whole EMI international bargain catalogue is available to UK customers. CDs which are available only through this service are indicated with the abbreviation SIS. EMI suggest that dealers should be able to obtain these special import discs quite quickly, and such records will no longer cost more than those in the standard UK catalogue. This does not affect the American equivalent issue where indicated as available.

Polygram have now followed suit with their own import service, and these CDs are indicated with the abbreviation IMS. Polygram, however, do currently make a small extra charge for those discs which have to be obtained from Germany or Holland.

COVERAGE

As the output of major and minor labels continues to expand, it is obviously impossible for us to mention every CD that is available within the covers of a single book; this is recognized as a practical limitation if we are to update our survey regularly. Indeed, we have now to be very selective in choosing the discs to be included, and some good recordings inevitably fall by the wayside. There is generally a reason for omissions, and usually it is connected with the lack of ready availablity. However, we do welcome suggestions from readers about such omissions if they seem to be of special interest, although we cannot guarantee to include them in a future survey!

ACKNOWLEDGEMENTS

Our thanks are due to our zealous new Penguin copy editor, Helen Williams, who had her work cut out assembling the final copy, to which a huge number of last-minute additions had to be made. Paul Chaikowsky has now entered the fray as Assistant Editor, notably in the titling and retrieval of earlier material (connected with reissues), especially in the hectic period immediately before we sent off that final copy. Alan Livesey, Barbara Menard and Roy Randle all contributed to the titling – never an easy task, and especially complicated in the many anthologies involving a bouquet of different performers. Alan Livesey also cast an eagle eye over the proofs, in particular looking for mistakes in the musical listings, composers' dates and so on. Our team of Penguin proofreaders have once again proved themselves indispensable.

Grateful thanks also go to all those readers who write to us to point out factual errors and to remind us of important recordings which have escaped our notice.

The American Scene

CDs are much less expensive in the USA than they are in Great Britain and because of this (so we are told), many bargain recordings available in England are not brought into the USA by their manufacturers. This applies especially to the Polygram group, so that Decca Eclipse, DG Classikon and Philips Virtuoso labels have to be imported by the major US record stores and mail order outlets. What this means is that, while almost any recording mentioned in these pages will be available in the USA, if only as a specialist import, sometimes it will cost more than the buyer might reasonably expect.

Duos and Doubles, where available, remain at two discs for the cost of one premium-priced CD in both countries, and here US collectors have a price advantage. However, according to *Schwann*, many excellent lower-priced discs are not issued in the USA. Where a recording is of extra special interest American collectors can obtain it readily by mail order from England, through the listed Web site address given. However it will inevitably cost more than it would domestically.

From your many letters, and from visiting record stores in the USA, we know that our *Penguin Guide* is read, enjoyed and used as a tool by collectors on both sides of the Atlantic. We also know that some transatlantic readers feel that our reviews are too frequently orientated towards European and British recordings and performances. In concentrating on records which have common parlance in both Europe and the USA, we obviously give preference to the output of international companies, and in assessing both performers and performances we are concerned with only one factor: musical excellence. In a 400-year-old musical culture centred in Europe, it is not surprising that a great number of the finest interpreters should have been Europeans, and many of them have enjoyed recording in London, where there are four first-class symphony orchestras and many smaller groups at their disposal, supported by recording producers and engineers of the highest calibre. The early music period-instrument revolution is also centred in London, which seems to add another bias, which is not of our making.

However, the continuing re-emergence of earlier recordings by major American recording orchestras and artists is slowly redressing the balance. Our performance coverage in the present volume – helped by the huge proportion of reissued older records – certainly reflects the American achievement, past and present and particularly the 1930s, 1940s, 1950s and 1960s. Then, Koussevitzky was in Boston, Frederick Stock, and after him, Fritz Reiner were in Chicago; Mitropoulos, Bruno Walter and Bernstein directed the New York Philharmonic in its heyday, Stokowski and Ormandy were in Philadelphia, and George Szell was creating astonishing standards of orchestral virtuosity in Cleveland. At the same time, Heifetz and Horowitz, Piatigorsky, Rubinstein and Isaac Stern were carrying all before them in the instrumental field. With the current phenomenal improvements in transferring technology, we hope that increasing numbers of the recordings made by these great names from the past will enjoy the attention of the wider public.

Price Differences in the UK and USA

Retail prices are not fixed in either country, and various stores may offer even better deals at times, so our price structure must be taken as a guideline only. Premium-priced CDs cost on average approximately the same number of dollars in the USA as they do pounds in the UK. The Vanguard CD label (except for the 8000 Series, which retails at around $15) is now mid-price in both the USA and UK. Harmonia Mundi's Musique d' Abord label (prefix HMA) is described as budget – which it is in the UK – but the American list-price is $9.98.

Duos and Doubles, Delos Doubles, Double Deccas, double ffortes, Dyads, Finlandia 'Meet the Composer', Chandos 2-for-1 sets, Nimbus, Olympia, BMG/RCA 'twofers', Royal Long Players, Royal Classics, Warner Classics Ultimas where available (although they cost less west of the Atlantic) are two-for-the-cost-of-one premium-priced disc the world over. CDCFPD, and Carlton Doubles and the new Virgin Classics 2 x 1 Doubles are two-for-the-price-of-one mid-priced CD.

OTHER COMPARABLE PRICES IN THE UK AND USA

Here are comparative details of the other price-ranges:

(M) Mid-priced Series (sets are multiples of these prices)

Includes: ASV; Avid; BBCB; BBCM; Carlton 30366 series; Chandos (Collect; Enchant); Classic fM (UK only); CPO/EMI Operas (UK only); CRD; Decca/London including Classic Sound and Legends; DG (including Originals); Dutton CDEA (USA only); Dutton CDAX, CDCLP, CDK, CDLX (UK only); EMI (Classics, British music series, and Great Recordings of the Century); Erato/Warner (UK), Erato/WEA (USA); DHM; Hänssler Harmonia Mundi Musique d' Abord (USA), Suite; Mercury; Nimbus; Nimbus 'Prima Voce'; Pearl; Oiseau-Lyre; Philips; RCA Gold Seal, High Performance and Living Stereo; RCA Melodiya; Revelation; Sony; Supraphon, Teldec/Warner (UK), Teldec/WEA (USA); Unicorn UKCD; Vanguard; Virgin.

UK Under £10; more usually £9

USA Under $13; usually under $12

(B) Bargain-priced Series (sets are multiples of these prices)

Includes: Australian Decca Eloquence; Calliope Approche (UK only); Carlton (30367, 30368; more expensive: 30369, 30371); CfP; Debut; Decca Eclipse (UK only); DG Classikon (UK only); Dutton CDEA (UK only); Eminence (UK only); Harmonia Mundi Musique d' Abord (UK only); Penguin Classics; Solo; HMP; Hyperion Helios; Philips Virtuoso (UK only); Sony Essential Classics.

UK £5.50–£7.00

USA Under $7

(BB) Super-bargain Series

Includes: Arte Nova; Discover; Arts; ASV Quicksilva (UK only); DHM Baroque Esprit; Naxos; Polygram Belart; RCA Navigator (UK only); Royal Classics.

UK £5; some (including Navigator) cost slightly less

USA $5–$6

The Australian Scene

We have been fortunate in obtaining for review a number of recordings produced by the Australian branch of Universal Classics (which is responsible for the three key labels, Decca, DG and Philips). Under the artistic direction of its enterprising Australian Marketing and Repertoire Manager, Cyrus Meher-Homji, Australian Decca, DG and Philips have been making a series of local reissues of great interest. They are offered inexpensively and so – even if imported – remain reasonably priced.

Perhaps the most important are the collections, notably: those of eighteenth- and nineteenth-century overtures and ballet music conducted with great flair by Richard Bonynge; the complete '*Julius Katchen Edition*' already mentioned in our main *Guide*, of which the final volumes (7 & 8) are considered below; Dame Gillian Weir's remarkably extensive five-CD (originally Argo) coverage of organ music from the sixteenth through to the twentieth century, and a five-disc '*Art of Joan Sutherland*', which supplements the collections already available in the U.K. Also, and no less valuable, is a Decca Double compilation (taken from three LPs), of the folksongs of Scotland, and in particular the 'Songs of the Hebrides' as collected by Kennedy-Fraser, ravishingly sung by Kenneth McKellar.

In addition, on the budget Eloquence label, there are a number of single CDs of repertoire never before issued on CD, notably recordings conducted by Zubin Mehta from the vintage early years of his recording career. A true collector's item included in this fascinating series is an early Decca stereo collection of '*Children's classics*' offering a unique 1960 version of Prokofiev's *Peter and the wolf*,

narrated by Beatrice Lillie using an outrageous new version of the text by Bidrum Vabish. Readers are invited to guess who this pseudonym represents – no prizes offered. Kenneth McKellar then adds a bonus to this disc (which also features the Saint-Saëns *Carnival of the animals* with verses by Ogdon Nash) of a selection of nursery rhymes, sung with engaging simplicity, and backed by delightfully scored accompaniments from Bob Sharples.

The Australian sources for these records are:
  HMV Australia: Classical Department, Pitt Street Mall, Sydney, NSW 2000, Australia
  Tel.: +61 2 9221 2311
  Fax: +61 2 9221 1830
  Web-site: www.hmv.com.au
  Classical Mail Order Warehouse: Shop G6, Wesley Centre, Perth, Western Australia 6000, Australia
  Tel.: +61 8 9481 8184
  Fax: +61 8 9322 3507
  E-mail: clmailor@tpgi.com.au

All CDs reviewed in this section are featured on and can be purchased from this Australian website:
  www.buywell.com
For a complete catalogue of Australian titles please write to:
  Universal Classics Australia, PO Box 17, Millers Point, NSW 2000, Australia.

Readers in the U.K. should be able to obtain these CDs from:
  Seaford Music, 24 Pevensey Road, Eastbourne, Easy Sussex, BN 21 3 HP (Tel. 01323 732553).

An International Mail-order Source for Recordings in the UK

Readers are urged to support a local dealer if he is prepared and able to give a proper service, and to remember that obtaining many CDs involves expertise and perseverance. However, in recent years many specialist sources have disappeared and for that reason, if any difficulty is experienced in obtaining the CDs you want, we suggest the following mail-order alternative, which offers competitive discounts in the U.K., but also operates world-wide. Through this service, advice on choice of recordings from the Editor of *The Penguin Guide to Compact Discs* is always readily available to mail-order customers:

Squires Gate Music Centre Ltd (PG Dept)
Rear 13 St Andrew's Road South
St Annes on Sea, Lancashire FY8 1SX
UNITED KINGDOM

Tel.: (0)1253 782588; Fax: (0)1253 782985
Web-site address: www.lprl.demon.co.uk
E-mail address: sales@lprl.demon.co.uk

This organization patiently extends compact disc orders until they finally come to hand. A full guarantee of safe delivery is made on any order undertaken. Please write or fax for further details, or make a trial credit card order, by fax, e-mail or telephone.

❀ THE ROSETTE SERVICE

Squires Gate also offers a try-before-you-buy weekly loan service (within the UK only) so that customers can try out Rosetted recordings at home, plus a hand-picked group of some 3,000 recommended key-repertoire CDs, for a small charge, without any obligation to purchase. If a CD is subsequently purchased, it will be discounted and the trial charge waived. Full details sent on request. The Rosette service Catalogue can be accessed via the lprl Web site.

Squires Gate Music Centre also offers a simple regular mailing, listing a hand-picked selection of current new and reissued CDs, chosen by the Editor of the *Penguin Guide*, Ivan March. Regular customers of Squires Gate Music Centre, both domestic and overseas, receive the bulletin as available, and it is sent automatically with their purchases.

In addition customers sending a s.a.e. can receive a list of (often brand new) overstocks, covering a wide range of CD repertoire including deletions, which are available for purchase at approximately half-price (plus postage).

Abbreviations

AAM	Academy of Ancient Music	LOP	Lamoureux Orchestra of Paris
Ac.	Academy, Academic	LPO	London Philharmonic Orchestra
Amb. S.	Ambrosian Singers	LSO	London Symphony Orchestra
arr.	arranged, arrangement	(M)	mid-price CD
ASMF	Academy of St Martin-in-the-Fields	[(M) id. import]	mid-price; same catalogue number only available as an
(B)	bargain-price CD		import
(BB)	super-bargain-price CD	Mer.	Meridian
Bar.	Baroque	Met.	Metropolitan
Bav.	Bavarian	min.	minor
BBC	British Broadcasting Corporation	MoC	Ministry of Culture
		movt.	movement
BPO	Berlin Philharmonic Orchestra	N.	North, Northern
BRT	Belgian Radio & Television (Brussels)	nar.	narrated
		Nat.	National
Cal.	Calliope	NY	New York
CBSO	City of Birmingham Symphony Orchestra	O	Orchestra, Orchestre
		OAE	Orchestra of the Age of Enlightenment
CfP	Classics for Pleasure		
Ch.	Choir; Chorale; Chorus	O-L	Oiseau-Lyre
CO	Chamber Orchestra	Op.	Opera (in performance listings); opus (in music titles)
COE	Chamber Orchestra of Europe		
Col. Mus. Ant.	Musica Antiqua, Cologne	orch.	orchestrated
Coll.	Collegium	ORR	Orchestre Révolutionnaire et Romantique
Coll. Aur.	Collegium Aureum		
Coll. Voc.	Collegium Vocale	ORTF	L'Orchestre de la radio et télévision française
Concg. O	Royal Concertgebouw Orchestra of Amsterdam		
		Ph.	Philips
cond.	conductor, conducted	Phd.	Philadelphia
Cons.	Consort	Philh.	Philharmonia
DG	Deutsche Grammophon	PO	Philharmonic Orchestra
DHM	Deutsche Harmonia Mundi	Qt	Quartet
Dig.	digital recording	R.	Radio
E.	England, English	RLPO	Royal Liverpool Philharmonic Orchestra
ECCO	European Community Chamber Orchestra		
		ROHCG	Royal Opera House, Covent Garden
ECO	English Chamber Orchestra		
ENO	English National Opera Company	RPO	Royal Philharmonic Orchestra
		RSNO	Royal Scottish National Orchestra
Ens.	Ensemble		
ESO	English Symphony Orchestra	RSO	Radio Symphony Orchestra
Fr.	French	RTE	Radio Television Eireann
GO	Gewandhaus Orchestra	S.	South
HM	Harmonia Mundi France	SCO	Scottish Chamber Orchestra
Hung.	Hungaroton	Sinf.	Sinfonietta
[id.]	same record number for US and European versions	SIS	Special Import Service (EMI – UK only)
IMS	Import Music Service (Polygram – UK only)	SNO	Scottish National Orchestra
		SO	Symphony Orchestra
L.	London	Soc.	Society
LA	Los Angeles	Sol. Ven.	I Solisti Veneti
LCO	London Chamber Orchestra	SRO	Suisse Romande Orchestra
LMP	London Mozart Players	Sup.	Supraphon

trans.	transcription, transcribed	VPO	Vienna Philharmonic Orchestra
V.	Vienna	VSO	Vienna Symphony Orchestra
Van.	Vanguard	W.	West
VCM	Vienna Concentus Musicus	WNO	Welsh National Opera Company

Achron, Joseph (1886–1943)

Children's suite (for violin & piano; arr.Heifetz); Hebrew melody, Op. 33; Hebrew lullaby, Op. 35; Prelude, Op.13; Sonata for violin and piano, Op. 29; Stimmungen, Op.32; Suite (No. 1) en style ancien, Op. 21; Les Sylphides, Op. 18.
(BB) **(*) ASV Quicksilva Dig. CDQS 6235 [id.]. Miriam Kramer, Simon Over.

Born in Lodz, then part of Russia, Joseph Achron studied in St Petersburg with Auer, who taught Heifetz. He pursued a successful virtuoso career before emigrating to America in 1934, but was a prolific composer with a hundred or so works to his credit. Judging from the *Violin sonata No. 1* (1910) he was a composer of quality with a good feeling for large-scale structures. The sonata is strongly post-Romantic with touches of Franck and even early Scriabin, though in later years Debussy and Schoenberg cast their spell. It is obvious from the sonata alone that Achron is a far from negligible composer. Miriam Kramer and Simon Over prove accomplished advocates though Kramer's tone is not particularly big and, from hearing her play live, one knows that the rather close microphones do not do it full justice. Worth investigating, just the same.

Adam, Adolphe (1803–56)

Si j'étais roi: Overture.
*** Chandos Dig. CHAN 9765 [id.]. (i) Royal Liverpool PO Ch., BBC PO, Yan Pascal Tortelier (with Concert: *'French bonbons'* ***).

Tortelier's performance of this engaging overture is neatly pointed, stylishly played and splendidly recorded. It is part of an outstanding collection, which includes other similar works by Auber, Hérold, Offenbach and Thomas.

Adams, John (born 1947)

(i) *The Chairman dances*; (ii; iii) *Chamber symphony*; (i) *Christian zeal and activity; Common tones in simple time*; (iv; v; vi) *Violin concerto* (vii; vi) *El Dorado*; (viii; iii; ix) *Eros piano*; (viii; iii) *Fearful symmetries*; (i) *2 Fanfares for orchestra: Tromba lontana; Short ride in a fast machine*; (ii; iii; x) *Gnarly buttons*; (ii; iii) *Grand pianola music*; (i) *Harmonielehre*; (xi) *Hoodoo zephyr*; (vii; vi) *Lollapalooza*; (viii; iii) *Shaker loops*; (vii; vi) *Slonimsky's earbox. Instrumental music:* (xii) *John's Book of alleged dances. Vocal music:* (xiii) *Harmonium*; (xiv; viii; iii) *The Wound dresser*; (xv; viii; iii) *Arr. of 5 Songs by Charles Ives. Opera:* (xvi; vi) *The Death of Klinghoffer:* highlights. (xvii; iii) *I was looking at the ceiling and then I saw the sky*; (xviii) *Nixon in China: excerpts.*
(M)*** Nonesuch/Warner Dig. 7559 79453-2 (10) [id.]. (i) San Francisco SO, Edo de Waart; (ii) L. Sinfonietta; (iii) Composer; (iv) Gidon Kremer; (v) LSO; (vi) Kent Nagano; (vii) Hallé O; (viii) O of St Luke's; (ix) with Paul Crossley; (x) with Michael Collins; (xi) Composer (synthesizer); (xii) Kronos Qt; (xiii) San Francisco Ch., & SO; (xiv) with Sanford Sylvan; (xv) with Dawn Upshaw; (xvi) Soloists, Lyon Opera Ch. & O; (xvii) Soloists, Instrumental Ens.; (xviii) Soloists, Ch. & O of St Luke's, De Waart.

This impressive ten-CD box, with many of the performances directed by the composer himself (who is an excellent and persuasive advocate), gives an impressive survey of the achievement of John Adams. He is undoubtedly the leading American 'minimalist' composer and in his major works he has transformed the technique of minimalist extension of simple material far beyond the original boundaries envisaged by his contemporaries. As Simon Rattle has aptly commented: 'In almost all of his best pieces, there's a mixture of ecstasy and sadness – the catharsis at the end of *Harmonium*, or the still, sad, personal last Act of *Nixon in China*, or the middle movement of the *Violin concerto*. It has an immense sadness and depth at the centre of it'.

The obvious point of entry is *Grand pianola music*, scored for two pianos (John Alley and Shelagh Sutherland), three female voices as well as orchestra. Here, as Adams has told us, 'Beethoven and Rachmaninov soak in the same warm bath with Liberace, Wagner, the Supremes, Charles Ives, and Sousa'. The finale, *On the dominant divide*, seems custom-made for the Last Night of the Proms, with its 'flag-waving, gaudy tune, rocking back and forth between the pianos, amid ever increasing cascades of B flat major arpeggios'.

But you might also begin with the early *Shaker loops* with its tremolandos and trills, or the *Short ride in a fast machine*. Many of the other works here, including the *Chamber symphony* (inspired by Schoenberg), *Gnarly buttons* (a concertante work for the clarinet, the composer's own instrument) and the extraordinary cantata, *Harmonium*, are discussed in our main volume alongside the operas, *The Death of Klinghoffer* (in essence more an oratorio) and the piece inspired by the 1994 California earthquake, using for its title a quotation from one of its survivors.

But much else here is new to the catalogue, including the throbbing *Common tones in simple time* ('a pastoral with pulse'), and the infernally rhythmic *Lollapalooza*, dedicated to Simon Rattle. The title of the even more explosive *Slonimsky's earbox*, so obviously Stravinsky-oriented, also celebrates another Russian, the author of a *Thesaurus of Scales and Melodic Patterns*, whose influence Adams also acknowledges. By contrast *Eros piano* is a ruminative soliloquy, with distinct echoes of Messiaen. *Christian zeal and activity*, the earliest work here, which has an Ivesian flavour, exists as a framework for an actual revivalist sermon, taken from a radio broadcast.

Perhaps even more remarkable is *Hoodoo zephyr,* a work for synthesizer, inspired by travel in the deserts of California and Nevada. A 'hoodoo' is a sandstone outcropping that weirdly resembles a ghostly human form and its musical evocation has an extraordinary sonic range – from voices and orchestral simulations to electronic guitar – heard in 'a wash of harmonies that shimmer and oscillate like objects at midday on the broiling floor of a desert sink'. Finally, the orchestration of five famous Ives song-settings should not be forgotten, especially *At the River*, so beautifully sung by Dawn Upshaw.

The set is extensively documented and handsomely packaged, but the lack of track information with each individual disc and the complicated layout of the booklet, means that they are not easy to use together.

Violin concerto.
*** Telarc Dig. CD 80494 [id.]. Robert McDuffie, Houston SO, Christoph Eschenbach – GLASS: *Violin concerto* ***.

Robert McDuffie's performance of the Adams *Violin concerto* may not have the dazzling projection of Kremer's account on Nonesuch, but it is splendidly played and infinitely better balanced, so that the brilliance of the solo playing in the outer movements is in proper perspective with the orchestra, and the great *Chaconne* which forms the slow movement is no less movingly evocative. Moreover, the apt Glass coupling, equally well played, is a much better choice for coupling than the familiar *Shaker loops*.

Fearful symmetries; (i) *The wound dresser.*
*** Nonesuch/Warner 7559 79218-2 [id.]. O of St Luke's, Composer; (i) with Sanford Sylvan.

These are two of Adams's most powerful works, yet they are utterly different in mood and atmosphere. *Fearful symmetries*, to use the composer's own words, 'is cut from the same cloth as *Grand pianola music*, although it is more choreographic in feeling' and has been danced to by members of both the New York City Ballet and the Royal Ballet. In certain ways following on from Ives's *Central Park in the dark* 'it resembles one of those Soho night clubs with a heavy bouncer at the door; it mixes the weight and bravura of a big band with a glittering synthetic sheen of techno pop (samples and synthesizer) and the facility and finesse of a symphony orchestra'. The very opening with its rhythmic force

and vibrant wail of saxophones has the forceful motion of an American train. But the syncopations are increasingly dominant and after a section where the colours become more muted, even Ravelian, there is a wild climax before the mood finally quietens. The composer's performance is most exhilarating.

An even more distinct quotation of Ravelian texture comes towards the end of *The wound dresser* before the words 'Thus in silence in dream projections . . . I thread my way through the hospitals'. This is a very moving, elegiac setting (for baritone and orchestra) of Walt Whitman's poem, recalling the author's terrible experiences as a medic during the American Civil War. It is most touchingly sung by Sanford Sylvan and, partly but not entirely because of the music's delicacy of texture, every word is clear.

Nixon in China (highlights).
(M)*** Nonesuch/Warner Dig. 7559 79436-9 [id.]. Sanford Sylvan, Trudy Ellen Craney, James Maddalena, St Luke's Ch. & O, Edo de Waart.

It seemed an extraordinary idea to create an opera out of President Richard Nixon's greatest political gamble (which actually paid off) – his 1972 visit to China to establish a friendly relationship with the Communist regime and its leader Chou En-Lai. The complete recording is only available in the USA (Nonesuch 9177) but this set of highlights gives a good idea of Adams's score. His special brand of minimalism works magnetically and the music itself has a lyrical melodic flow absent from most post-Britten operas. The choral music is especially telling and Chou's banquet speech/aria is memorable, as is his wife's stirring soliloquy, which closes the selection. The singing is generally excellent, as is the recording. If you enjoy John Adams's music, this is well worth trying. A full translation is included.

Addinsell, Richard (1904–77)

Film music: *Blithe Spirit: Prelude & Waltz. Encore: Miniature overture* (both arr. Lane). *Fire over England: suite* (arr. Zalva). *Parisienne – 1885* (both arr. Lane). *The Passionate Friends: suite* (arr. Isaacs). *Scrooge: suite* (arr. S. Bernstein). *Southern Rhapsody* (arr. Lane); *South Riding: Prelude* (arr. Isaacs). *Waltz of the Toreadors: March and waltz* (arr. Lane). *WRNS March* (arr. Douglas).
(M) **(*) ASV Dig. CDWHL 2115 [id.]. Royal Ballet O, Kenneth Alwyn.

As we know from the *Warsaw concerto*, Richard Addinsell had a distinct melodic gift and it is heard at its best here in his early score for *Fire over England* (1937) and more especially in the suite of music from *Scrooge* (the definitive 1951 version with Alistair Sim). As the *Waltz* for *Blithe Spirit* and the brief *March* for *Waltz of the Toreadors* show, there are some deft inventions elsewhere, but their composer needed help from others to realize them orchestrally. All this music is slight, but it is very well played by the Royal Ballet Orchestra, affectionately and stylishly conducted by Kenneth Alwyn and very well recorded.

Agricola, Alexander (c. 1446–1506)

Songs: *Adieu m'amour* (3 versions); *A la mignonne de fortune; Allez, regretez; Ay je rien fet; Cecus non in dicat de coloribus; De tous bien plaine* (3 versions); *Et qui la dira; Fortuna desperata; Guarde vostre visage* (3 versions); *J'ay beau huer; S'il vous plaist; Soit loing ou pres; Sonnes muses melodieusement.*
(BB) *** Naxos Dig. 8.553840 [id.]. Unicorn Ensemble, Michael Posch.

Agricola was so highly regarded in his day that when he left the French court for Italy in the early 1470s an envoy was sent after him to insist on his return! His music is expressive but its structure and polyphony are quite complex, his polyphonic style nearer to Ockeghem than Josquin, while his musical personality is less individual than either. Nevertheless, these secular love songs (sung in medieval French) are full of interest, the more so as they are often presented with a mixed consort of voices and instruments sharing the polyphony, with close blending of the whole ensemble. The opening *A la mignonne* ('To the darling of fortune') is an intriguing example. Other items are sung unaccompanied, or by an accompanied soloist (*S'il vous plaist* by an accomplished counter-tenor) or are purely instrumental, with *De tous bien plaine* ('With all good things') offered in three different arrangements. The piece which gives the disc its title, the sombre *Fortuna desperata,* makes a powerfully sonorous conclusion, The presentation is scholarly, direct and appealing, the recording excellent, and the documentation could hardly be bettered, with full translations included.

Albéniz, Isaac (1860–1909)

Iberia (complete).
(M) **(*) DG Dig. 459 430-2 (2) [id.]. José María Pinzolas – GRANADOS: *Allegro de concierto* etc. **

DG's début for the young Spanish pianist José María Pinzolas comes at mid-price. His control of keyboard colour is impressive. He opens the *Evocación* very seductively, while later *Almeira* has a comparable sultry atmosphere. *El Puerto, El corpus en Sevilla* and *Rondeña* are all freshly presented and again the ear is taken by his articulation in *Triana* – and *El Albaicín* does not want for sparkle. But the four last pieces are less poised and his rubato in *Lavapiés* is not entirely convincing. He is well recorded, but Alicia de Larrocha remains first choice in this repertoire (Decca 417 887-2), although Martin Jones on Nimbus is also very impressive (see our main volume).

Piano sonatas 3–5; L'automne (valse).
(B) ** HM Musique d'abord HMA 1987007 [id.]. Albert Guinovart.

The three sonatas recorded here are all youthful and come from the mid 1880s. They have little in common with *Iberia* but they have a certain wistful charm and a high level of accomplishment as one would expect from so expert a pianist. They are derivative but likeable pieces, as is the charming *L'automne.* Albert Guinovart is a sympathetic advocate of these pieces but is let down by too reverberant an acoustic.

d'Albert, Eugen (1864–1932)

Die Toten Augen (complete).
*** CPO Dig. CPO 999 692-2 (2) [id.]. Dagmar Schellenberger, Anne Gjevang, Hartmut Walker, Lothar Odinius, Norbert Orth, Margaret Chalker, Olaf Bär, Dresden PO Ch. & O, Ralf Weikert.

Eugen d'Albert, born in the same year as Richard Strauss, is remembered for his opera, *Tiefland,* and very little else. An unsettled character, brought up and trained in Britain, who never decided which country he wanted to live in, and who married six times, d'Albert wrote 22 other operas, including this second-favourite, *Die Toten Augen* ('The Dead eyes').

It was first heard in Dresden under Fritz Reiner in 1916, a luscious piece set at the time of Christ, that defied the darkness of wartime. The central action is framed by a Prelude and Postlude in which a shepherd (beautifully sung here by the tenor, Lothar Odinius), meets another symbolic character, the Reaper (the celebrated Olaf Bär), and goes off in search of a lost sheep.

The central action, much more realistic, is then compressed into a single act, telling of a Roman official, Arcesius, whose wife, Myrtocle, is blind. She is cured by the intervention (offstage) of Christ, but as predicted by Christ the gift of sight proves a curse, bringing the disruption of her marriage and the murder of the handsome Galba whom she initially mistakes for her husband. In her love for Arcesius she opts to be blind again, with her 'dead eyes'.

The evocative pastoral sweetness of the prelude and postlude is set against the ripe German verismo style of the central action, with the character of

Mary Magdalene the main linking element, preaching the message of joy over finding a lost sheep. It could easily be a sickly story, but d'Albert with rich orchestration and surging melody carries it off impressively. This live recording of a concert performance, well-recorded, offers a persuasive account of the piece, with Dagmar Schellenberger powerful as Myrtocle, well-matched by the fine mezzo, Anne Gjevang, as Mary of Magdala. A rarity to recommend to those with a sweet tooth.

Albinoni, Tomaso (1671–1751)

(i) *12 concerti a cinque, Op. 5;* (ii) *12 Concerti a cinque, Op. 7.*

(B) **(*) Ph. Duo 464 052-2 (2) [id.]. (i) Pina Carmirelli, I Musici; (ii) Hanz Wätzig, Jürgen Abel, Heinz Klinge, Berlin CO, Negri.

Philips have now recoupled I Musici's Op. 5 (already available inexpensively on 442 688-2) with Negri's Op. 7, which meets strong competition, not only from I Musici, with Holliger and Bourge, but also the Camden/Georgiadis Naxos series (see our main volume). The playing in Berlin combines vitality and polish, but the balance is rather forward: the effect is vivid but the dynamic contrast is reduced. Also, Negri's direction with its strong, incisive rhythms lacks something in flexibility and resilience. Incidentally, Jeffrey Tate plays the harpsichord continuo in Op. 7.

Oboe concertos, Op. 7/1; Double oboe concertos, Op. 7/2 & 5; Op. 9/3 & 6; Concertos for strings, Op. 7/1 & 4; Op. 9/1 & 4; Sinfonia for strings.

*** Chandos Dig. CHAN 0602 [id.]. Anthony Robson, Catherine Latham, Coll. Musicum 90, Standage.

This is the missing CD from Simon Standage's original-instrument Chandos set combining the complete Op. 7 and Op. 9 concertos. The other two CDs are listed and discussed in our main volume (CHAN 0579 and CHAN 0610). The playing has both elegance and great vitality: it is more lively in effect than Hogwood's alternative version of Op. 9, and very freshly recorded.

Concerti a cinque, Op. 9/1–12.

*** O-L Dig. 458 129-2 (2) [id.]. Frank de Bruine, Alfredo Bernardi, Andrew Manze, AAM, Hogwood.

At last comes a separate complete set of Albinoni's splendid Op. 9 on original instruments, although the ear would hardly guess. String textures are smooth and pure, without a hint of acerbity and only the lightness and transparency confirm the authenticity. To tell the truth, the undoubted intimacy of effect is just a little cosy, and if you want something more athletic you must turn to Anthony Robson with Simon Standage's Collegium

Musicum 90 on Chandos, where the concertos of Op. 7 and Op. 9 are intermingled (see above and in our main volume).

However, the solo oboe playing of Frank de Bruine is very fine indeed – just listen to the *Adagio* of *No. 2 in D minor,* which is exquisitely played, as is the lively opening movement of *No. 11 in B flat* on the second disc. The lovely *Adagio* of *No. 11 in F* (for solo violin) is very like a Handel aria and here Andrew Manze is delightfully sweet-timbred. The *Double oboe concertos* also bring some splendidly nimble teamwork, and altogether this is most enjoyable set.

The bargain analogue alternatives on modern instruments by Pierlot, Toso and I Solisti Veneti (Erato/Ultima 3984 25593-2), or Ayo, Holliger and Bourgue with I Musici on a Philips Duo (456 333-2), are by no means completely upstaged and cost only half as much as the two-disc Oiseau-Lyre box.

Concertos for (solo) organ in B flat & F (arr. from Op. 2); Flute sonatas, Op. 4/2 & 6; Op. 6/6 & 7; Oboe sonata, Op. 6/2 Recorder sonata, Op. 6/5.

*** Meridian Dig. CDE 84400 [id.]. Badinage (with BACH: (Organ) *Fugue in C, BWV 946 after Op. 1/12).*

A lightweight but pleasing programme with some particularly deft playing on a slightly watery-sounding baroque flute (a copy of an eighteenth-century instrument) and some very agreeable organ interludes. These are all transcriptions, mostly from violin sonatas. Although it seems likely that Op. 4 is wrongly attributed to Albinoni, the music itself is very agreeable. Good, natural sound.

VOCAL MUSIC

12 Cantatas, Op. 4.

*** Etcetera Dig. KTC 2027 (2) [id.]. Barbara Schlick or Derek Lee Ragin, Nicholas Selo, Roderick Shaw.

Albinoni is much better known as an instrumental composer, but he was a fine singer as well as a string player, and he directed a celebrated singing academy in Venice. His *Twelve Cantatas,* Op. 4 were published in 1702. Characteristic pastoral works of their period, lightweight but with plenty of charm, they are written alternately for soprano and alto, with the even-numbered works given to the latter voice. On the whole, the most poignant music is allotted to the soprano voice, and the excellent Barbara Schlick responds appealingly. But Albinoni's expressive range is considerable and both soloists rise to the occasion. The continuo too is first class, with Nicolas Selo's beautifully focused and crisply rhythmic cello contribution a particular pleasure. The recording is excellent. Full translations are provided.

Alfvén, Hugo (1872–1960)

Symphony No. 3 in E, Op. 23; Legend of the Skerries, Op. 20; Swedish rhapsody No. 3 (Dalarapsodi), Op. 47.
(BB) **(*) Naxos Dig. 8.553729 [id.]. RSNO, Niklas Willén.

Symphony No. 3 in E, Op. 23; The Prodigal son: suite; Swedish rhapsody No. 3 (Dalarapsodi), Op. 47.
*** BIS Dig. CD 455 [id.]. Stockholm PO, Neeme Järvi.

Alfvén's *Third Symphony* is arguably one of his finest works (though there is a lot of Wagner in its *Andante*) and this sensitive, well-prepared performance by these Scottish players under Niklas Willén serves it well. Moreover it comes with equally good accounts of the *Dalarapsodi*, and the *Legend of the Skerries*. The acoustic is not as warm as in Järvi's cycle on BIS. All the same, given the general excellence of the playing, this Naxos disc is well worth the modest outlay.

Järvi's BIS CD is every bit as fine as its companions listed in our main volume and, in addition to the *Third Symphony* and the *Dalarapsodi*, brings the perennially popular suite from *The Prodigal son*. Excellent playing and recording of real quality. It is to be preferred to its Scottish alternative both in terms of performance and certainly as far as the recorded sound is concerned.

Alkan, Charles (1813–88)

Barcarolle, Op. 65/6; 12 Studies in minor keys, Op. 39/4, 5, 6, 7 (Symphonie), 12 (Le festin d'Esope); Grande sonate, Op. 33: 2nd movement (Quasi Faust) only.
(M) *** RCA High Performance 09026 63310 2 [id.]. Raymond Lewenthal – LISZT: *Hexameron* ***.

Raymond Lewenthal writes in the sleeve note: 'Everything about Charles-Valentin Alkan is strange: his life, his death, his music and its fate during his life and after his death. He was a misanthropic eccentric who maintained two dwellings to avoid visitors, was a great pianist who seldom played, was crushed to death by the Talmud, and he had an illegitimate son who kept in his apartment two apes and 121 cockatoos'. As a friend and rival of Chopin and Liszt, Alkan sought to outdo those masters with his wildly impractical virtuoso showpieces and for a century or more they were considered impossibly difficult, except by such a virtuoso pianist-composer as Busoni. Raymond Lewenthal made a speciality of Alkan, first by editing his music, then by performing it, and also by writing his biography. Lewenthal's passion for this music leaps out at you in these exciting perform-

ances, and the recording, dating from the mid 1960s, is excellent. Liszt's *Hexaméron* is an excellent bonus, and these recordings are worthy of RCA's High Performance label.

Alpher, David (born 20th Century)

Atlantic legend (for viola, cello & harpsichord); Returnings (for harp & piano); Tribute to Kerouac (for clarinet, tenor saxophone, piano & string bass); Elegy for a friend. Vocal: (i) Songs of transcendence.
** Ongaku Dig. 024-112 [id.]. Gallagher, Lutzke, Newton, Moor, Cohler, Radnofsky, Lynam; Composer (piano) (i) with Robert Honeysucker.

These pieces are light textured, direct and uncomplicated. The notes give no idea of the composer's date of birth and little of his career except that he is a native of Washington DC and studied at Bloomington, Indiana. The harmonies are greatly influenced by jazz; he is obviously a gifted musician and an accomplished pianist. There is a strong jazz component in his harmonic language, and some refinement of texture. Ultimately the idiom is civilized even if no strong individual voice asserts itself. (The notes contributed by the composer prompt a faint suspicion that this might be a 'vanity record', for Alpher is not mentioned in the generally comprehensive four-volume *American Grove*.)

Angulo, Eduardo (born 1954)

Guitar concerto No. 2 (El Alevín).
*** Guild Dig. GMCD 7176 [id.]. Rafael Jiménez, Bournemouth Sinf., Terence Frazor –
RODRIGO: *Concierto de Aranjuez*;
VILLA-LOBOS: *Guitar concerto*. ***

Angulo's *Concerto* is Mexican in inspiration and atmosphere. It is richly scored and the orchestral string tuttis have a glamorous melodic sweep to contrast with the more intimate solo writing. It has much in common with its famous Spanish coupling, with the slow movement at first pensive, then full-bloodedly romantic. The finale sparkles with Mexican dance rhythms, gaudy and gentle by turns. Rafael Jiménez is a highly sensitive and brilliant soloist and Terence Frazor and the Bournemouth Sinfonietta accompany him with both understanding and gusto. This is a highly spontaneous work of considerable popular appeal and it is very persuasively recorded here.

Arbeau, Thoinot (1520–1595)

Orchésographie (French popular dances).
(B) *** HM Musique d'abord HMA 1901052 [id.]. Broadside Band, Jeremy Barlow (with

John PLAYFORD: *English dancing master: 6 Dances ****).
** Arabesque Dig. Z 6514 [id.]. NY Renaissance Band, Sally Logemann.

Unlike Praetorius, Arbeau was not himself a composer and his collection of sixteenth-century dances, mostly galliards and branles, was part of a dissertation on dancing and its importance for the cultivated members of society, male and female alike. The tunes themselves are simply presented, giving the melody line only. One or two are familiar (*Ding dong merrily on high* appears as a branle), but all have plenty of character. The composer does offer some advice on instrumentation, but much editing and conjecture are required if they are to be brought fully to life. This the Broadside Band do admirably and Jeremy Barlow's choice of instrumentation is consistently ear-tickling. The performances are full of life and the recording excellent. For contrast Barlow offers half-a-dozen dances from John Playford's very similar collection, *The English dancing master*, which are equally personable and entertaining.

The New York Renaissance Band also uses a simple instrumental group, which includes krummhorns, shawms, pipes, a cornetto, recorders, viols, a Brittany bombarde, minstrel's harp and percussion, effectively varied between numbers. This is all pleasant enough and no doubt Arbeau would have approved of the sophistication of the playing and the intimate acoustic. However, at times one feels the musicians could have been more daring, and this is a much less attractive disc than its Harmonia Mundi competitor. The notes however are much more extensive, and include Arbeau's comments about some of the dances.

Arne, Thomas (1710–78)

Alfred (An English masque).
*** DHM/BMG Dig. 75605 51314-2 [id.].
    Jennifer Smith, Christine Brandes, David Daniels, Jamie MacDougall, Philh. Ch. & Bar. O, Nicholas McGegan.

Just as Elgar's *Coronation ode* of 1902 spawned 'Land of hope and glory', so Arne's English masque, *Alfred*, of 160 years earlier introduced 'Rule, Britannia', if in a slightly different form from what we hear on the Last Night of the Proms, with tenor and soprano soloists in alternation. First heard in London in 1745, the year of the Jacobite uprising, this story of King Alfred defying the Danes involves twenty-seven musical numbers, with simple, tuneful songs for the rustic characters and more elaborate arias for the royals. Nicholas McGegan in this brilliant American recording directs his period forces in fresh, resilient performances, with the counter-tenor David Daniels outstanding among the soloists.

Arnold, Malcolm (born 1921)

Anniversary overture; Beckus the Dandipratt overture; Flourish for orchestra, Op. 112; Peterloo overture, Op. 97; Philharmonic concerto; Symphony for strings, Op. 13; Water music, Op. 82b.
*** BMG/Conifer Dig. 75605 51298-2 [id.]. BBC Concert O, Vernon Handley.

A fascinating collection in that it includes four works otherwise not available on record. The short *Anniversary overture* was written to accompany a Hong Kong fireworks display: it is boisterous and tuneful. The *Flourish for orchestra* has a fine *nobilmente* tune framed by Waltonian brass, with bells thrown in for good measure. The *Symphony for strings* (another early work) is a real find. First performed in 1947 it has a characteristically jaunty theme in the first movement, but its atmosphere is for the most part unexpectedly plangent, with the central *Andante quasi allegretto* searchingly intense, followed by a powerful finale marked *feroce*, which is just the way the BBC Concert Orchestra plays it. The three-movement *Water music* shared with Handel's suites an intention of performance on a barge, but on the River Avon rather than the Thames. Originally scored for wind alone, it is heard here in a later orchestral version and its vivid scoring and colourful ideas have much in common with the *English dances*, especially the jubilant finale. The *Peterloo overture* is comparatively familiar, but the *Philharmonic concerto* is seldom heard. It was written in 1976 for the American bicentennial celebrations, and has both a melancholy central aria (opening on the viola) reflecting on the loss of life in the War of Independence, and a confident closing *Chaconne* to convey the ongoing strength of the New World. Overall this makes a most satisfying programme. Splendidly played and recorded, it was a happy idea to open with *Beckus the Dandipratt*, the early (1943) overture – a fascinating cross between Elgar's *Falstaff* and Richard Strauss's *Till Eulenspiegel* – which first established the composer's reputation, when it was memorably recorded on a Decca 78 disc conducted by Eduard van Beinum.

Symphony No. 5, Op. 74; The Belles of St Trinians (comedy suite); *Divertimento No. 2, Op. 75; Machines* (symphonic study); *Solitaire: Sarabande and Polka.*
**(*) Classico Dig. CLASSCD 294 [id.]. Munich SO, Douglas Bostock.

It is good to hear Malcolm Arnold's splendid *Fifth Symphony* being so idiomatically played in Munich by the excellent resident Symphony Orchestra conducted by Douglas Bostock. It is an impressive performance, with the slow movement treated elegiacally and the characteristic whimsical zest of the scherzo brightly caught, while the richly melodic reprise of the main theme of the slow movement in the finale has real ardour. Even so, Hickox's outstanding reading on Chandos is consistently emotionally gripping. His scherzo has an irresistibly heady momentum, while he is more penetrating in his more expansive account of the slow movement with the closing section a deeply moving threnody. The finale, too, has just that bit more sharpness of articulation and the return of the great Arnoldian melody at the close has *nobilmente* as well as passion. Bostock is at his finest in three of the other four works included, which are all first recordings. The *Divertimento* is a colourful triptych, with a lively *Chaconne* for finale, and there is much uninhibited fun in the early *St Trinian's* film score, where the Munich Orchestra let their hair down and obviously enjoy themselves. The touching *Sarabande* from *Solitaire* (one of Arnold's most beautiful tunes) and the audacious *Polka* are equally persuasive. Only the symphonic study, *Machines* gives cause for reservation. It was written in 1948 for a Central Office of Information propaganda film, 'Report on Steel', about the post-war nationalized steel industry. The performance is forceful, but needs just that bit more bite and propulsion.

Atterberg, Kurt (1887–1974)

(i) *Piano concerto in B flat minor, Op. 3*; (ii) *Violin concerto, Op. 7.*
*(*) Sterling CDS 1034-2 [id]. (i) Dan Franklin Smith; (ii) Christian Bergqvist; Gävle SO, B. Tommy Andersson.

The *Violin concerto* is an early work, written when Atterberg was twenty-six; the *Piano concerto* was started in 1927, but put to one side when he began work on the *Sixth Symphony* (the 'Dollar' symphony, so-called because it won the Schubert Centenary prize) and his opera, *Fanal*. The *Piano concerto* was finally finished in 1935. It is every Hollywood director's idea of a romantic piano concerto. The ideas range from the nondescript to the trite and, in the case of the finale, the breathtakingly banal. Dan Franklin Smith copes with its flamboyance and rhetoric with dazzling virtuosity. The *Violin concerto* is much better and has some poetic and imaginative moments though it is curiously shapeless. Good solo playing and enthusiastic orchestral support. The recording, however, is distinctly top-heavy and bass-light, and the balance gives Christian Bergqvist's tone a certain shrill wiriness.

Symphonies Nos. 1 in B min., Op. 3; 4 in G min. (Sinfonia piccola), Op. 14.
*** CPO Dig. CPO 999 639-2 [id]. Frankfurt RSO, Ari Rasilainen.

It is good to note the continuing interest in Atter-

berg, whose best works, for example the eloquent *Suite No. 3 for violin, viola and strings,* deserve the widest dissemination. The *First Symphony* (1909–11) was composed while he was still studying engineering and is naturally derivative, but none the worse for that. The *Fourth (Sinfonia piccola)* of 1918 is distinctly folksy but enjoyable, particularly in this committed performance. Those who invested in the Sterling CD of this coupling (see our main volume) will not need to make the change, but those coming to these symphonies for the first time, should opt for this newcomer. It is every bit as well played (better in fact) and has the advantage of superior recorded sound

Auber, Daniel (1782–1871)

Fra Diavolo (complete in Italian).
**(*) Warner Fonit 3984 27266-2 (2) [id].
Luciana Serra, Martine Dupuy, Dano Raffanti, Nelson Portella, Cambridge University Chamber Ch., Martina Franca Fest. O, Alberto Zedda.

First heard in Paris in 1830, *Fra Diavolo* was a popular repertory piece until well into the twentieth century. There was even a film adaptation with Laurel and Hardy taking the roles of the *buffo* servants, Giacomo and Beppo. The previous EMI recording offered the French text, sadly truncated, as the published score is incomplete. Here the scholar Alberto Zedda in this live festival performance offers the first recording of the Italian version as approved by the composer, with all the material preserved and with accompanied recitatives by Auber in place of dialogue. The result is substantially longer, and dramatically more convincing in presenting the picture of the flamboyant bandit hero who calls himself a marquis, and was nicknamed Brother Devil – Fra Diavolo.

Though the live recording, close and rather dry, brings odd balances and stage noises with occasional rough ensemble, the result is lively and involving, bringing out the winning lyricism of Auber's writing. In the title role, Dano Raffanti characterizes well, using a ringing tenor with flair and only occasional coarseness, relishing the challenge of the big arias. Luciana Serra has a touch of acid at the top of the voice, but this is a bright, agile soprano who brings out the charm in the role of the country-girl, Zerlina. Nelson Portella and Martine Dupuy, clear and firm, are well contrasted as the English Milord and Lady Pamela. An Italian libretto is provided but no translation.

Aulin, Tor (1866–1914)

Violin concerto No. 3 in C min., Op. 4.
(BB) **(*) Naxos Dig. 8.554287 [id]. Tobias

Ringborg, Swedish CO, Niklas Willén –
BERWALD: *Violin concerto;* STENHAMMAR: *2 Sentimental romances.***(*)

Tor Aulin was one of Stenhammar's closest collaborators and both were champions of Berwald, with whose 1820 *Concerto* the Aulin is coupled. It is a pleasing, well-crafted piece in the Brahms mould and well worth reviving. Apart from an early account by Christian Bergqvist on Musica Sveciae, this is its only representation on CD. A good performance with well-balanced recorded sound in a warm acoustic.

Auric, Georges (1899–1983)

Film scores: Suites from: *Caesar and Cleopatra; Dead of Night; Father Brown; Hue and cry* (overture); *The Innocents; It always rains on Sunday; The Lavender Hill Mob; Moulin Rouge; Passport to Pimlico; The Titfield Thunderbolt.*
*** Chandos Dig. CHAN 8774 [id.]. BBC PO, Rumon Gamba.

It is remarkable that a French composer should have provided the film scores for some of the most famous Ealing comedies, so British in every other respect. But Auric's delicacy of orchestral touch and feeling for atmosphere (together with his easy melodic gift) made him a perfect choice after his first flamboyant venture with Rank's *Ceasar and Cleopatra*. From the witty railway music of *The Titfield Thunderbolt* and the distinct menace of *Dead of Night*, Auric moved easily to the buoyantly spirited *Passport to Pimlico. The Innocents* (like Britten's opera based on Henry James's *The Turn of the Screw*) opens eerily with a boy-treble singing *O willow wally*, and a quietly sinister flute solo maintains the weird atmosphere. But it was *Moulin Rouge* that gave Auric his popular hit, with a charming Parisian waltz song (delicately sung here by Mary Carewe) that was understandably to be a remarkable commercial success. Most of the excerpts are short vignettes, but they make enjoyable listening when so well played and recorded.

Film scores (suites): *Orphée; Les Parents terribles; Ruy Blas; Thomas L'imposteur.*
*** Marco Polo Dig. 8.225066 [id.]. Slovak RSO, Adriano.

Jean Cocteau considered Auric 'his' composer, and the music recorded here was for films that were either directed by Cocteau, or for which he was the screenwriter. *Orphée* (1949) was a contemporary elaboration of the ancient myth of Orpheus, dealing with questions of death and immortality. The elements of fantasy and imagination that marked the film are reflected in the music: though scored for a large orchestra, it has a classical restraint and is most haunting throughout. Also included is Auric's arrangement of *Eurydice's lament* from Gluck's

opera – a lovely piquant bonus. For *Les Parents terribles* (1949), an alternately funny and tragic film in which the children are as neurotic as the parents, Auric dispenses with the strings and uses a large wind band, percussion, and piano: a short 'image musicale' has been assembled for this recording. France during the First World War is the backdrop for melodrama in *Thomas L'imposteur* (1964), of which the suite starts off in suitable military style. There is much variety of mood in this selection, one of the most memorable pieces being a wistful waltz for Clémence and Henriette. The longest suite here is that of *Ruy Blas* (1947) and for this swashbuckler, Auric had to compose straightforward and colourful music, which gave him plenty of scope for his own distinct brand of orchestration. Adriano has done sterling work on assembling these suites and securing first-class playing from the orchestra, and the recording is good too. Diverting though this music is, it tends to whet one's appetite for Auric's genuine orchestral and ballet music.

Avshalomoff, Aaron (1895–1964)

(i; ii) *Flute concerto;* (iii) *Symphony No. 1.*
** Marco Polo Dig. 8.225033 [id.]. (i) Nadine Asin; Moscow SO; (ii) Jacob Avshalomoff; (iii) David Avshalomoff.

(i; ii) *Piano concerto;* (iii) *Symphony No. 2; Elegy for strings.*
** Marco Polo Dig. 8.225035 [id.]. (i) Larissa Shilovskaya; Moscow SO; (ii) Jacob Avshalomoff; (iii) David Avshalomoff.

(i; ii) *Violin concerto;* (iii) *Hutungs of Peking* (tone poem); *Soul of the Ch'in* (ballet pantomime).
** Marco Polo Dig. 8.225034 [id.]. (i) Rodion Zamuruev; Moscow SO, (ii) David Avshalomoff; (iii) Jacob Avshalomoff.

Aaron Avshalomoff was brought up in the Chinese quarter of Nikolaievsk in Siberia and crossed into China at the outbreak of the Russian Revolution, bound for America. Despite the encouragement of Monteux and Stokowski and a commission from Koussevitzky, he found the lure of the Orient difficult to resist. He returned to China, making a living as a bookseller in Shanghai and composing prolifically. For some years he was also conductor of the Shanghai Symphony Orchestra. His *Violin concerto* is relentlessly pentatonic but is effectively laid out for the orchestra. The idiom recalls the Chinese cinema and the ideas escape memorability. Good playing and decent, though not spectacular, recording. The music on the companion discs is hardly more stimulating, although performances and sound are satisfactory.

Bach, Carl Philipp Emanuel
(1714–88)

(i) *Cello concertos: in A min., Wq.170, H.432; in B flat, Wq.171, H.436; in A, Wq.172, H. 436; Hamburg sinfonias, Wq. 183/1–4; Sinfonia in B min., Wq. 182/5.*
(BB) *** Virgin Classics 2 x 1 Dig. Double VBD5 61794-2 (2). OAE, Leonhardt; (i) with Anner Bylsma.

The cello concertos have alternative versions for both keyboard and flute, but they suit the cello admirably. Bylsma's expressive intensity communicates strongly, without ever taking the music outside its boundaries of sensibility, and these artists convey their commitment to this music persuasively. The allegros are full of life, and the slow movements are most eloquent, particularly the hauntingly volatile *Largo con sordini* of Wq. 172.

The *Hamburg sinfonias* (for woodwind and strings) are striking works, noted for their refreshing originality. Gustav Leonhardt's account of this second set is the one to have if you want them on period instruments. They are lively and alert, and distinguished by fine musical intelligence while the OAE are superbly in tune with this music, and convey both its vitality and expressive qualities to the full. A splendid bargain recommendation, although the BIS recording of the three *Cello concertos* by Hidemi Suzuki is special (● BIS CD 807 – see our main volume).

Harpsichord concertos in E, Wq. 14; in G, Wq. 43.
(M) *** CRD 3311 [id.]. Trevor Pinnock, E. Concert – J. C. BACH (arr. Mozart): *Harpsichord concerto ***.

The *E major Harpsichord concerto* is one of the most ambitious that C. P. E. Bach left us, with an expansive first movement, an intense slow movement with some fascinating chromatic writing and an exuberant finale. Trevor Pinnock and his English Concert (recorded before they moved on to the DG Archive label, but using original instruments) give admirable performances, nicely balancing the claims of modern ears and total authenticity. First-rate recording and a fascinating coupling.

Duo for 2 clarinets (Adagio & Allegro), H.636; 6 Sonatas forPianoforte, clarinet and bassoon, H.516–521; Flute sonatas (for flute and harpsichord): in E, H.506; in C, H.573; Oboe sonata (for oboe and continuo) in G min., H.549; Pastorale for oboe, bassoon and continuo.
*** CPO Dig. CPO 999 508-2 [id.]. Fiati con Tasto, Cologne.

This delightfully diverse cross-section of Carl Philipp Emanuel's chamber music for wind instruments could hardly be bettered as a source of exploration. The use of period instruments is expert, and

the *Flute sonatas* are engagingly perky and given attractively sprightly performances by Karl Kaiser, while Alfredo Bernadini's plaintive oboe timbre is as affecting in the sonatas as it is in the gentle *Pastorale* (a siciliano) in duet with a doleful bassoon. The felicitous interplay of the six *Sonatas for fortepiano, clarinet and bassoon* at times anticipates Mozart, and Harald Hoelden's fortepiano contribution here is as nicely judged as his harpsichord playing in the flute sonatas. The recording is very natural and gives a vivid projection to one-and-all.

Keyboard sonatas in B flat; in G, Wq.62/1–2; in F; in G; in A; in G min. Wq. 65/1, 5, 10–11.
** BIS Dig. CD 963 [id.]. Miklós Spányi (clavichord).

Miklós Spányi continues his exploration of the solo keyboard sonatas, now using a highly suitable clavichord (closely recorded). But once again, for all his keyboard dexterity, his eccentric little pauses consistently tend to interrupt the music's flow: sample the first movement of the *G minor Sonata*, with its sweeping runs, to experience this at its most wilful.

Keyboard sonatas for harpsichord: in E min., Wq.62/12, H.66; in E min., Wq.65/5, H.13; in B flat., Wq.65/20, H.51; for fortepiano: in B flat, Wq.65/44, K H.211; in C, Wq.65/47, H.248; in G, Wq.65/48, H.280.
**(*) Metronome Dig. MET CD 1032 [id.]. Carole Cerasi (harpsichord or fortepiano).

Carole Cerasi won the 1999 Gramophone Award for Baroque Music with her recording of the harpsichord suites of Elisabeth Jacquet de la Guerre (see below), so there is an element of disappointment here. In the *Harpsichord sonatas*, the resonance of the recording does not help her, but her very free musical line often brings a fussy effect. The opening *Allemande* of the *E minor Sonata, Wq.62/12* is an obvious example of her very free rubato, and the lively closing *Gigue* too, marvellously articulated as it is, needs a cleaner ouline, with the decorations less boldly done.

In the works played on the fortepiano it is the impulsiveness of Cerasi's approach that is daunting, with sudden *forte* accents and forward surges, especially well demonstrated in the finale of the *G major, Wq 65/48*. The preceding *Adagio* is more successful, but even here she seems determined to prove that C. P. E. Bach's music is quixotically temperamental.

Bach, Johann Christian (1735–82)

Harpsichord concerto in D (arr. by Mozart as K. 107/1).
(M) *** CRD 3311 [id.]. Trevor Pinnock, E. Concert – C. P. E. BACH: *Harpsichord concertos ***.

It seemed more sensible to list this work here as it tends to get lost in the Mozartean discography. In the early 1770s the teenage Mozart turned three sonatas by J. C. Bach into keyboard concertos, adding accompaniments and ritornellos as well as cadenzas. The first of the group makes an excellent coupling for the two fine C. P. E. Bach concertos.

Endimione (Serenata).
*(*) DHM/BMG Dig. 05472 77525-2 (2) [id.].
Jezovšek, Monoyios, Waschinski, Hering,
Cologne Vocal Ens., Capella Coloniensis,
Bruno Weil.

Described as a serenata, *Endimione*, first heard in London in 1772, is an opera in all but name. It is less extended than the Handel operas which were popular in London a generation earlier, though the lively opening overture is a formidable piece. The dozen arias and concluding duet to Act I plus two choruses, offer much delightful music, and it is a pity that the performance is flawed. The Capella Coloniensis favours an unreconstructed period style, rather abrasive in its string tone, not helped by the curiously focused recording which is slightly disembodied. Nor are the soloists ideal, though Ann Monoyios as the nymph Nice stands out for the silvery beauty of her singing. Vasiljka Jezovšek is lighter and brighter if not so secure, while the counter-tenor Jorg Waschinski as Amore is rather fluttery, as is the tenor Jorg Hering as Endimione, not helped by the recording.

Bach, Johann Sebastian (1685–1750)

Complete orchestral works and concertos

Brandenburg concertos Nos. 1–6, BWV 104–651; Concerto in F for 2 recorders and harpsichord, BWV 1057; Triple concerto in A min., for flute, violin, and harpsichord, BWV 1044 (8.554607/8); Harpsichord concertos Nos. 1–5, BWV 1052–6; in G min., BWV 1058; Triple harpsichord concertos Nos. 1–2, BWV 1063–4; Triple violin concerto in D, BWV 1064 (8.554604/5); Double harpsichord concertos Nos. 1–3, BWV 1060–2; Quadruple harpsichord concerto in A min., BWV 1065; Quadruple violin concerto in B min. (both arrangements of Vivaldi) (8.554606); Oboe d'amore concertos in D, BWV 1053; in A, BWV 1055; Oboe concertos in G min., BWV 1056; in D min., BWV 1059; Double concerto in C min. for oboe and violin, BWV 1060 (8.554602); Violin concertos Nos. 1 in A min., 2 in E, BWV 1041–2; in D min., BWV 1052; Double violin concerto in D min., BWV 1043 (8.554603); Orchestral suites Nos. 1–4,BWV 1066–9 (8.554609).

Complete (as above).
(BB) ** Naxos Dig. 8.508005 (8) [id.]. Soloists, Cologne CO, Helmut Müller-Brühl.

Helmut Müller-Brühl and his talented players give lively performances of all thirty-five works in this collection. Allegros tend to be fast, at times extremely so, as in the *Brandenburg concerto No. 3*, where one suspects that the players here have been influenced by their period-instrument colleagues from the same city, the Concerto Köln. Only occasionally do the fast speeds sound breathless, so agile is the playing of soloists and orchestra alike and so well sprung are the rhythms. Slow movements by contrast are broad and expressive, with the oboist, Christian Hommel, outstanding in the five concertos in the first volume, all of them reconstructions of works which have survived in harpsichord form. That includes not only the well-known *Double concerto for oboe and violin* (adapted from the *C minor Concerto for 2 harpsichords*) but four solo works from various sources. It may seem perverse that Volume 1 should feature merely reconstructions but that is among the most successful of the discs, not just because of Hommel's artistry, but because of the relatively unaggressive recording, with the oboe well to the fore.

Otherwise the recording balance, too often oppressively close, with harpsichord continuo cutting sharply through, brings the principal reservations over the set. The bright, edgy tone of the soloists in the *Violin concertos* disc detracts from what would otherwise be highly enjoyable performances of not only the three popular concertos, the *E major*, the *A minor* and the *Double concerto*, but a reconstruction of the *D minor Harpsichord concerto* for two violins. The *Brandenburg concertos*, brisk but only occasionally eccentrically so, bring some fine solo work, and the violas in No. 6 are beautifully tuned. The second disc offers two extra triple concertos, closely related, the *A minor*, BWV 1044 using the same three soloists as the *Fifth Brandenburg* and the *F major for two recorders and harpsichord*, transcribed from the *Fourth Brandenburg* (also on the same disc).

The three discs of concertos for one, two, three and four harpsichords also include transcriptions and reconstructions, mainly of violin works, plus the original Vivaldi four-violin concerto, RV 580, which Bach transcribed for four harpsichords. Where the orchestral tuttis tend to be very beefy, the harpsichords seem almost to be in another acoustic, far lighter, if with an abrasive 'birdcage twang'. The playing of the soloists is excellent, making the performances enjoyable none the less. The four *Orchestral suites*, fitted onto a single disc thanks to the omission of repeats in first movements, are rather different in style from the rest. They also suffer from the closeness of the sound, the more so when in the slow introductions to each work the strings adopt a squeezed tone – with no vibrato on long-sustained notes – in unreconstructed period style, a rather painful noise. Otherwise the performances follow a similar lively pattern to the rest. The eight discs come in a bargain package, but are also available separately.

Other recordings

Brandenburg concertos Nos. 1–6, BWV 1046–51.
(BB) ** Royal Long Players DCL 705692 (2).
    LPO, Boult.

Boult, when recording his lively set of *Brandenburgs* at the beginning of the 1970s, consciously turned back to the style of Bach-playing he knew at the turn of the century – 'to the smooth and solid expression given by a far larger orchestra than Bach could ever contemplate'. In fact by the standards of 1900 or even 1939 these are comparatively authentic performances, smoother at times than usual, but with lots of character, and not always using a big orchestra. Even so many will relish the full panoply of string tone in Nos. 3 and 6. The speeds are often on the fast side, but with fine solo playing and excellent recording there is a place for this individual set (especially at super-bargain price), which is clearly preferable to other 'big orchestra' versions by Karajan and Klemperer.

Brandenburg concertos Nos. 1–6, BWV 1046–51; Clavier concerto No. 5 in F minor, BWV 1056: Largo (only); (Solo) *Concerto in D minor, BWV 594* (after Vivaldi, Op. 3/11 arr. Cortot).
(M) (*) EMI mono CHS5 67211-2 [id.]. O. de l'Ecole Normale de Paris, Alfred Cortot.

Even at the time, Cortot's *Brandenburg Concertos* made in 1931–3 were pretty eccentric when put alongside say Boyd Neel or the wonderful set by the Busch Chamber Players. Of course there are many pianistic felicities, indeed many touches characteristic of the great pianist, including some hilarious eccentricities and gear changes. He takes a hop, skip and a jump in the middle of the main theme of the first movement of No. 2 and almost calls a halt at the end of the first paragraph of No. 6, only to make a forward spurt later on. He signals the ending of the first movement of No. 5, several bars ahead, by a long slowdown. Not really recommended except as a curiosity.

(i) *Brandenburg concertos Nos. 1–6, BWV 1046–51; Overture in B flat* (from *Cantata No. 194*); *Viola da gamba sonata in C, BWV 1027* (orch. Druce) (ii; iii) *Concerto for flute, violin and harpsichord, BWV 1044;* (ii) *Orchestral suites Nos. 1–4, BWV 1066–69.*
(M) ** Virgin/EMI Dig. VBD5 61726-2 (4). (i) Taverner Players, Parrott; (ii) Boston Early Music Festival O, Parrott; (iii) with Krueger, Stepner, Gibbons.

Andrew Parrott's two sets of recordings here, made four years apart, do not make ideal bedfellows. In the light-textured *Brandenburgs* from 1989 sometimes the speeds are so fast that resilience is lost and, with recording slightly distanced and not very sharply focused, the result is muddled. Parrott is also more severe than is a rival such as Pinnock and the English Concert over the question of vibrato. The squeezed style of the playing of sustained notes in slow movements is not easy on the ear, and the viola melody in the slow movement of No. 6 is very sour. However, there is a valuable supplement in works using comparable forces, the *Overture* from the *Cantata No. 104* and Duncan Druce's transcription of the *C major Viola da Gamba sonata*, for the same forces as Bach adopts in *Brandenburg No. 6*. For the *Orchestral suites*, Parrott directs one of the most talented American period-performance groups in exceptionally transparent and well-sprung readings with one instrument to a part and with the balance perfectly judged. Here one registers many details normally obscured, with dance rhythms made the more infectious. Christopher Krueger, the flautist in No. 2 is also an outstanding soloist in the *Triple concerto*, joined by Duncan Stepner on the violin and John Gibbons on harpsichord. There too textures are lightened in a small-scale reading, one instrument to a part. This makes a thoroughly rewarding new look at much recorded repertoire and we hope Virgin Classics will eventually decide to reissue this second pair of CDs separately as a 2 x 1 Double.

(i) *Clavier concertos Nos. 1 in D min., BWV 1052; 4 in A, BWV 1055; 5 in F min., BWV 1056;* (ii) *Triple clavier concertos Nos. 1 in D min., 2 in C, BWV 1063–4; Quadruple clavier concerto in A min., BWV 1065;* (iii) *Double violin concerto in D min., BWV 1043.*
(B) *** Erato/Warner Ultima Double 3984 26997-2 (2) [id.]. (i) Maria João Pires, Gulbenkian Foundation CO, Corboz; (ii) Anne Queffélec, Pascal Devoyon, Michel Dalberto, Jacques Gautier; (iii) Gérard Jarry, Pierre Amoyal; (i;ii) Paillard CO, Jean-François Paillard.

If you enjoy Bach played on the piano – and indeed in the multiple concertos, piano timbre can be clearer, less jangly than a clutch of harpsichords – then this set can be very strongly recommended, for it is excellently recorded throughout. In the three favourite solo concertos, Maria João Pires is a first-rate soloist. Her crisp and nimble fingerwork is a joy in the allegros and the orchestral strings will not sound too heavy, except to the most dedicated authenticists. The famous *Largo* of the *F minor Concerto* is exquisitely serene and the sound balance is fresh and believable. The concertos for three and four instruments are equally successful. The four soloists change around between each of them, but it is Michel Dalberto who leads the group in the *Quadruple concerto* (Bach's vivid transcription of Vivaldi's *Concerto in B minor* for four violins, from *L'Estro armonico*, Op. 3/10) and his opening is arresting. These are splendidly alive and spontaneous accounts with nicely judged espressivo in slow movements, and again they are very convincingly balanced and recorded. To cap the pleasures of this excellent anthology Gérard Jarry and Pierre Amoyal give an equally distinguished account of the famous *Double violin concerto* with the central *Largo* offering a most satisfying interplay between the two soloists. Again good sound.

Complete solo and multiple concertos

Harpsichord concertos: (i) *Nos. 1 in D min.; 2 in E; 3 in D; 4 in A; 5 in F min.; 6 in F; 7 in G min., BWV 1052-8;* (ii) *Double harpsichord concertos: Nos. 1 in C min.; 2 in C; 3 in C min., BWV 1060-62;* (i–iii) *Triple harpsichord concertos Nos. 1 in D min.; 2 in C, BWV 1063-4;* (i–vi) *Quadruple harpsichord concerto in A min., BWV 1065.* (i; v; vi) *Triple concerto for flute, violin and harpsichord, BWV 1044;* (vi; vii) *Double concerto for oboe and violin in C min., BWV 1060;* (vii) *Oboe d'amore concerto in A, BWV 1055;* (vi) *Violin concertos Nos. 1 in A min.; 2 in E;* (viii) *Double violin concerto in D min., BWV 1041/3.*
(b) *** DG Analogue/Dig. 463 725-2 (5) [id.]. E. Concert, Pinnock, with (i) Pinnock; (ii) Gilbert; (iii) Mortensen; (iv) Kraemer; (v) Beznosiuk; (vi) Standage; (vii) Reichenberg; (viii) Wilcock.

Pinnock's performances of the Bach *Harpsichord concertos* first appeared in 1981 and have dominated the catalogue ever since. In the solo concertos he plays with real panache, his scholarship tempered with excellent musicianship. Pacing is brisk, but to today's ears, used to period performances, the effect is convincing when the playing is so spontaneous, and the analogue sound bright and clear.

The Double, Triple and Quadruple concertos are digital and the combination of period instruments and playing of determined vigour certainly makes a bold effect. There is a bit more edge on the strings and everything is clearly laid out and forwardly projected. Outer movements emphasize the bravura of Bach's conceptions and, if slow movements could at times be more relaxed, those ears prepared to accept a hint of aggressiveness in the energetic musical flow will find these recordings as stimulating now as when they first appeared.

The transcribed concertos for flute, violin and harpsichord, for oboe and violin, and oboe d'amore are equally persuasive, both vigorous and warm with consistently resilient rhythms, while the Violin concertos are equally welcome. Rhythms are again crisp and lifted at nicely chosen speeds – not too fast for slow movements – and the solo playing here, led by Simon Standage is very stylish. Altogether this makes an impressive bargain package in DG's Collectors Edition, thoroughly recommendable to anyone wanting to obtain all this music economically, both in terms of space and financial outlay.

Complete harpsichord concertos

Complete harpsichord concertos, Volume 1: *Concertos No. 3 in D, BWV 1054; 5 in F min., BWV 1056;* (i) *Double concerto No. 3 in C min., BWV 1062. Brandenburg concerto No. 5 in D, BWV 1050.*
*** Chandos Dig. CHAN 0595 [id.]. Robert Woolley; (i) with Paul Nicholson; Purcell Qt.

Complete harpsichord concertos, Volume 2: *Concertos Nos. 2 in F, BWV 1053; 7 in E, BWV 1058;* (i) *Triple concerto No. 2 in C, BWV 1064;* (i; ii) *Quadruple concerto in A min., BWV 1065.*
*** Chandos Dig. CHAN 0611 [id.]. Robert Woolley; (i) with Paul Nicholson, Lawrence Cummings; (ii) John Toll; Purcell Qt.

Complete harpsichord concertos, Volume 3: *Concertos Nos. 4 in A, BWV 1055;* (i) *6 in F* (with 2 recorders), *BWV 1057;* (ii) *Double harpsichord concerto No. 1 in C min., BWV 1060;* (ii; iii) *Triple harpsichord concerto in D min., BWV 1063.*
*** Chandos Dig. CHAN 0636 [id.]. Robert Woolley; (i) with Marion Scott, Rachel Beckett; (ii) Paul Nicholson; (iii) Lawrence Cummings; Purcell Qt.

Complete harpsichord concertos, Volume 4: (i) *Concerto No. 1 in D min., BWV 1052;* (iii) *Double harpsichord concerto No. 2 in C, BWV 1061;* (ii; iii) *Triple concerto for flute, violin and harpsichord in A min., BWV 1044.*
*** Chandos Dig. CHAN 0641 [id.]. Robert Woolley; (ii) Paul Nicholson; (iii) Stephen Preston, Catherine Mackintosh; Purcell Qt.

The special feature of the new complete set on the Chandos Chaconne label is that the accompaniment is played on period instruments, with one instrument to each part. The warm ambience (which yet provides a naturally transparent sound picture) ensures that the result is neither thin nor emaciated; indeed the allegros sound striking, firm and full, and of course the balance with the harpsichord or harpsichords (modern copies of instruments made by Mietke) is just about ideal. The playing is of high quality, rhythmically fresh and pleasing, and Robert Woolley is most delicate in shaping the famous *Largo* of the *F minor Concerto*, and is hardly less appealing in the gentle *Siciliano* of the *E major*. The *F major Concerto*, BWV 1057 is of course another version of the *Brandenburg concerto No. 4* and the performance here underlines the colouristic parallels, with both the strings and recorders making the most of the busy contrapuntal finale, yet never dwarfing the soloist.

The *Double concerto in C*, BWV 1061 brings a

particularly successful solo interplay in the fugal finale (this work originated as a harpsichord duet without accompaniment), while the *Double concerto in C minor* is better known as the *D minor Double violin concerto*. Here the interchange of the slow movement is very successful but not (as Stephen Daw suggests in the notes) 'somehow more uplifting spiritually' than the original string concerto. The *Quadruple concerto* is another transcription, this time of Vivaldi's *Concerto for four violins*, Op. 3/10 and it works splendidly, with the harpsichords sounding vigorously robust without jangle. The *Fifth Brandenburg concerto* is an engagingly lithe and sprightly version of what was apparently Bach's very first concerto featuring a solo keyboard instrument, and even though it is an obbligato contribution it is very effective.

Bach also transcribed the *Triple concerto for flute, violin and harpsichord*. Its derivation is a keyboard *Prelude and fugue*, BWV 895, while the lovely slow movement, exquisitely registered here, was originally the second movement of an *Organ sonata*, BWV 527. Taken as a whole this set is very successful indeed, with the focus of multiple harpsichords clean and pleasing to the ear. The vitality and finesse of the playing give it claims to be placed alongside the Pinnock and Rousset versions, and in terms of recorded sound it is unsurpassed. The snag is that four separate full-priced CDs are involved, with an average of an hour's playing time on each.

Other recordings

(i) *Harpsichord concertos Nos. 1–8, BWV 1052–59;* (i; ii) *Double harpsichord concertos Nos. 1–3, BWV 1060–62;* (i, iii) *Triple harpsichord concertos Nos. 1–2, BWV 1063–64; Quadruple harpsichord concerto in A min., BWV 1065.* Solo pieces: (i) *Fantasia and fugue in A min., BWV 904; Italian concerto in F, BWV 971.*
(M) **(*) Virgin/EMI Dig. VBD5 61716-2 (4). (i) Bob van Asperen (ii) Gustav Leonhardt; (iii) Bernardt Klapprott, Marcello Bussi, Carsten Lohff; Melante Amsterdam.

Like Robert Woolley above, Bob van Asperen favours an accompaniment with one instrument to each part, basically using a string quartet, with a double bass added in BWV 1052–4, a pair of recorders in BWV 1057, violone and oboe in BWV 1059. But even more than in the Chandos performances one has an intimate sense of chamber music-making. Van Asperen's solo contribution is consistently nimble and has an appealingly graceful delicacy and for the most part the accompaniments from the Melante Amsterdam are lightly etched in, although sometimes in slow movements the bass seems just a little heavy and the *Andante* of BWV 1058 could be more imaginative. The recording balance is excellent. However, when one turns to

the *Double concertos*, where Gustav Leonhardt takes over the leading keyboard role, the effect is more robustly vigorous, and this applies equally to the *Triple* and *Quadruple concertos*. By their side, one feels a certain paleness about the solo concertos, even if they have no lack of character or style. But many collectors may find van Asperen's intimate approach exactly to their taste.

Harpsichord concerto No. 1 in D min., BWV 1052.
(**) Biddulph mono LHW 032 [id.]. Wanda Landowska, O, Eugène Bigot – HANDEL: *Concerto, Op. 4/6; Suite No. 15: Air and variations* (**(*)); HAYDN: *Concerto in D, Hob XVIII/11; Sonata No. 36 in C sharp min.: Minuet; German dance No. 5 (Ballo tedesco)* (***).

Landowska's account of the *D minor Concerto* won't be to all tastes, with a hefty accompaniment to match the weighty sound of her big Pleyel harpsichord. But in the *Andante* of the *Italian concerto* she at last lightens her registration. The transfers are obviously truthful, but the close sound is not ideal.

Harpsichord concertos Nos. 1 in D min., BWV 1052; 3 in D, BWV 1054; 6 in F, BWV 1057; (i) *Triple concerto for flute, violin and harpsichord, BWV 1044.*
**(*) Opus 111 Dig. 30-153 [id.]. Rinaldo Alessandrini, Concerto Italiano; (i) with Claudio Rufa, Francesca Vicari.

This is the first volume in yet another period-instrument survey, stimulating for its brisk allegros (the opening movement of No. 6 particularly so) and contrastingly grave slow movements. There is much to enjoy here, but not quite as much as in the Chandos set, with the lovely *Adagio* of the *Triple concerto* exuding less magic than in the performance by Paul Nicholson, Stephen Preston, and Catherine Mackintosh. The recording is excellent in all respects

Harpsichord concerto No. 3 in D, BWV 1054; Concerto for violin and oboe in C min., BWV 1060; Violin concertos in D min., BWV 1052; in G min., BWV 1056.
*** Virgin Veritas/EMI Dig. VC5 45361-2. Sergio Ciomei, Fabio Biondi, Alfredo Bernadini, Europe Galante.

In the hands of such fine players, these four works, all familiar and all reconstructed from other concertos, make a rewarding collection, casting new light on the music, when the performances are so freshly and warmly played (on period instruments) and beautifully recorded. The *Double concerto for violin and oboe* is a highlight, for Alfredo Bernadini's baroque oboe has a most appealing timbre and the balance with the violin is felicitous. The dialogue of the central *Adagio* is particularly pleasing and the finale buoyantly infectious. Fabio

Biondi, playing spiritedly and with easy virtuosity, then makes a good case for the two transcribed *Violin concertos* (arranged from keyboard concertos), and his expressive line in the two slow movements is also memorable. The *Adagio e piano sempre* of the *Harpsichord concerto* (taken from the *E major Violin concerto*) works surprisingly well on the keyboard.

Oboe d'amore concertos: in D, BWV 1053; in A, BWV 1055; Oboe concertos: in G min., BWV 1056; in D min., BWV 1059; Double concerto in C min. for oboe and violin, BWV 1060.
(BB) *** Naxos Dig. 8.554602 [id.]. Christian Hommel, Cologne CO, Helmut Müller-Brühl.

It is good that Naxos have made a separate issue of Christian Hommel's outstanding collection of concertos for oboe and oboe d'amore, all of them reconstructions of other works, but none the worse for that. The performances are first class, lively and sensitive and the recording, with the soloist balanced well in front, is excellent. A most enjoyable disc.

(i; ii, iii) *Violin concertos Nos. 1 in A min.; 2 in E; (i; ii; iv) Double violin concerto in D min., BWV. 1041–3; (i) Partita No. 2, BWV 1004: Chaconne.*
❋ (M) (***) EMI mono CDH5 67201-2. (i) Yehudi Menuhin; (ii) Orchestre Symphonique de Paris; (iii) cond. Georges Enescu; (iv) with Enescu (violin), cond. Monteux.

Menuhin's 78 r.p.m. recording of the *Double concerto* with Georges Enescu his partner (and teacher) and Monteux conducting, is legendary for its rapport and simple expressive beauty. It was recorded in Paris in 1932, the same year that Menuhin recorded the Elgar in London. The two solo concertos – with Enescu on the rostrum – followed in 1933 and 1936. They are hardly less remarkable, with a wonderful purity of line and natural expressive feeling. All these records were made when Menuhin was between sixteen and nineteen years of age and show (as did the Elgar in a quite different way) his unique instinctive musical vision, which came from within rather from outside influences. The famous *Partita* is hardly less impressive (see below). In the concertos the orchestral string sound is dry, the violins unflattered, but this expert remastering by Andrew Walter makes the very most of the original 78s, and so moving is the slow movement of the *Double concerto* that one quite forgets its early provenance. A Bach recording which should be in every collection.

Double violin concerto in D min., BWV 1043.
(M) *** RCA 09026 63531-2 [id.]. Heifetz, Friedman, London New SO, Sargent – BRAHMS: *Double concerto for violin and cello;* MOZART: *Sinfonia concertante in E flat, K. 364.****

It is good to have Heifetz's 1961 stereo recording of the *Double concerto* as a worthy successor to Menuhin's 78-r.p.m. version with Enescu. Sargent's tempi in the outer movements are brisk, but none the worse for that and the Elysian dialogue of the slow movement, with Heifetz's pupil Erick Friedman a natural partner, is hardly less inspired and much better recorded.

Orchestral suites Nos. 1–4, BWV 1066–9.
(B) ** Australian Decca Eloquence 458 169-2. Stuttgart CO, Münchinger.

Münchinger's way with these suites is hardly at the cutting edge of authentic practice, but these 1968 performances offer some first-class orchestral playing, undoubted vigour and expressive warmth, and they are beautifully recorded. This analogue set is preferable to Münchinger's later digital rerecordings in every way. However, first choice for the *Orchestral suites* on modern instruments rests with Marriner (Decca 430 378-2) and there is plenty of choice on period instruments (see our main volume).

CHAMBER MUSIC

The Art of fugue, BWV 1080.
**(*) Opus 111 Dig. 30-191 [id.]. Concerto Italiano, Rinaldo Alessandrini.
** Kontrapunkt Dig. 32259 [id.]. New Danish Saxophone Qt.

Rinaldo Alessandrini's approach to *The Art of fugue* is to seek out the underlying expressive and colouristic possibilities of the music itself, rather than emphasize its supreme contrapuntal interest and complexities. So after opening with strings, he scores each of the *contrapuncti* for different groups of wind and/or stringed instruments, allotting only the four *Canons* to the harpsichord. The result has distinct aural appeal, especially as the work proceeds, with *Contrapuncti 12* and *13* engagingly colourful dialogues involving flute, oboe da caccia, violin, viola, bassoon, cello and harpsichord. The performance ends as it begins, with the final, incomplete No. 15 given to a string quartet. Alessandrini's solution may not be conventional, nor appeal to pedagogues, but the playing (on baroque instruments) is full of life and easy to enjoy. The recording is clear within a pleasing ambience.

The New Danish Saxophone Quartet play Bach very spiritedly indeed and with a degree of rhythmic freedom that many will enjoy and others may not. They are excellent musicians, and have a finely blended sonority, while the part-writing is clearly presented. But in the end, the limited colour of four saxophones tells against the performance. For *aficionados* only.

(Unaccompanied) Cello suites Nos. 1–6, BWV 1007–12.

(B) *** Double Decca Dig. 466 253-2 (2) [id.].
Lynn Harrell.

If you are looking for larger than life, but intensely
personal performances of Bach's masterly *Cello
suites*, using the widest range of dynamic and espressivo, you must turn to Rostropovich (● EMI
CDS5 55363-2). But if you favour simple, but
deeply felt readings, clearly focused both musically
and in the actual recorded image, then Harrell's fine
performances will be found very satisfying. His
comparative spareness and restraint contrast
strongly with Rostropovich's more extrovert
manner, but rarely if ever is he guilty of understatement. The simple dedication of the playing, combined with cleanness of attack and purity of tone,
brings natural, unforced intensity, and in many ways
these readings might be compared with Milstein's
DG set of the *Unaccompanied Violin sonatas*. One
might disagree with the occasional tempo, but the
overall command is unassailable. The recording
quality, forward and real, yet aptly intimate in
acoustic, suits the performances admirably.

(Unaccompanied) *Cello suite No. 1 in G, BWV
1007.*
(M) (***) EMI mono CDM5 67008-2 [id.]. Pablo
Casals – BEETHOVEN: *Cello sonata No. 3;*
BRAHMS: *Cello sonata No. 2* (***).

The *G major suite* was recorded in 1938 and appeared along with the *Suite No. 6 in D major* as
Volume 7 of the HMV Bach Society Edition. It was
Casals who restored this repertoire to the concert
hall, and nobility shines through every bar. Of
course this has appeared along with the other suites
but duplication is worthwhile for the sake of its
companions.

*Flute sonatas Nos. 1–6, BWV 1030–35; in G min.,
BWV 1020; Partita in A min.* (for solo flute)*, BWV
1013; Trio sonatas in G* (for flute, violin and
continuo)*, BWV 1038; in G* (for 2 flutes and
continuo)*, BWV 1039; Suite in C min.* (for flute
and piano)*, BWV 997.*
(M)**(*) Hänssler Dig. CD 92.121 (2) [id.].
Jean-Claude Gérard, Azzaloni, Blumenthal,
Forchert, Formisano, Kleiner.

Jean-Claude Gérard is a fine player, especially impressive in the solo *Partita*, where he plays the
Sarabande with considerable expressive freedom.
But it seems curious that all this repertoire should
have been recorded (in 1999) with piano instead of
harpsichord, and using a bassoon continuo. This is
all very musical and pleasing enough in its way; but
if you want the six sonatas on a modern instrument,
then William Bennett's inexpensive ASV Quicksilva disc is the one to go for, with George Malcolm
providing a harpsichord continuo (CDQS 6108 –
see our main volume).

Music for lute-harpsichord or lute
*Suites Nos. 1–2, BWV 996–7; 3 (Prelude, fugue
and allegro in E flat), BWV 998; Fantasias and
fugues in B flat, BWV 907; in D, BWV 928;
Prelude and fantasia in C min., BWV 921–1121;
Prelude in C min., BWV 999.*
(M)*** Hänssler Dig. CD 92-109 [id.]. Robert Hill
(lute-harpsichord).

Bach's effects, as listed in his posthumous estate,
included two Lauten Werk (lute-harpsichords), and
it is thought that some of the music now included
in the repertoire of lutenists and guitar players was
intended for this instrument. Indeed, the *Suite in E
minor*, BWV 996 has the inscription 'Lautenwerck'
on its title page. But the instrument itself is obsolete.
We know that it had one, two or three keyboards,
used gut strings plucked simultaneously by several
jacks and quills, and reputedly possessed an uncannily effective lute stop. So the present instrument, built by Keith Hill in Manchester, Michigan,
USA, has had to be conjecturally reconstructed
from descriptions of instruments in use in Bach's
time. It features only one manual, authentically uses
damperless jacks; an ingenious jack-slide, worked
by a pedal, replaces the multiple system yet still
allows some of the effect of multi-plucking. Robert
Hill is a vivid and lively exponent of this experimental instrument; but, perversely, the works which
come off best are the *Fantasias and fugues* which are
less directly associated with the lute. The recording
could hardly be better managed, but the resonant,
undamped sound means that there is less delicacy of
texture than with performances of the three *Suites* on
lute or guitar. A fascinating collection none the less.

Viola da gamba sonatas Nos. 1–3, BWV 1027–9.
(M)*** Hänssler Dig. CD 92.124 [id.]. Hille Peri
(viola da gamba), Michael Behringer
(harpsichord).

This set stands alongside Jordi Savall's fine Virgin
Veritas disc for those with a taste for the authentic
gamba timbre. The performances are warmly sympathetic and alive. Peri's tone is full – not edgy – and
the balance with Behringer's excellently articulated
harpsichord-playing is good, the harpsichord a
shade backward but still coming through in a warm
but not clouding acoustic.

(i) *Viola da gamba sonatas Nos. 1–3, BWV 1027–
9 Preludes and fugues in D, BWV 850; in G, BWV
860; in G min., BWV 861.*
*** Signum Dig. SIGCD 024 [id.]. Alison Crum
(viola da gamba), Laurence Cummings
(harpsichord).

Yet another fine alternative set comes from Alison
Crum and Laurence Cummings. Here the harpsichord is very much in the picture, boldly played,
with plenty of life and vigour, by Laurence Cummings. But Alison Crum's firmly focused gamba is
never eclipsed and the balance overall is better than

that on the Hänssler CD. Moreover, Cummings offers sparkling performances of three keyboard *Preludes and fugues* as a bonus. They are placed to act as interludes between the viola da gamba sonatas. You have only to sample the infectious performance of the *G major Prelude* to find out how attractive they are.

(Unaccompanied) *Violin sonatas Nos. 1–3, BWV 1001, 1003 & 1005; Violin partitas Nos. 1–3, BWV 1002, 1004 & 1006.*

(M) (***) EMI mono EMI CHS5 67197-2 (2) [id.]. Yehudi Menuhin.

(B) **(*) EMI Double Fforte CZS5 73644-2 (2). Josef Suk.

**(*) Channel Classics Dig. CCS 12198 & 14498 [id.]. Rachel Podger.

(BB) ** Arte Nova Dig. 74321 67501-2 (2) [id.]. Rudolf Gähler (Bach bow).

It was the eighteen-year-old Yehudi Menuhin to whom (between 1934 and 1936) HMV entrusted the very first complete recording of the *Unaccompanied Sonatas* and *Partitas* and the young musician's remarkable accomplishment more than repaid the company's faith in him. The great *Chaconne* from BWV 1004 is one of most thrilling performances ever put on disc. Apparently Menuhin's famous teacher, Enescu, made him play the piece through three times in succession to test his stamina, and the playing here moves forward with commanding power. Yet on the way, with the concentration never slipping, Menuhin is able to relax and play more gently, with his eyes obviously still on that final resolution. Elsewhere the rich, vibrant tone and direct approach (with no swooning or lingering) must have astonished listeners of the time. The playing projects strongly in every bar and if the style is more unbending than we would expect today, there are movingly expressive moments, like the *Double* which follows the *Allamanda* of the *First B minor Partita*. Indeed Menuhin's integrity and bold emotional commitment are never in doubt – he feels every note of this music. What an astonishingly instinctive musician he was! The microphone is obviously very close, but the secure bowing can take such a scrutiny: the violin image is a little dry, yet is remarkably real and immediate.

Josef Suk's recording was made at Abbey Road in 1970 and it still sounds most real and vivid. At the time *Gramophone* magazine commented: 'As violin playing, it could not be bettered; it is what the instrument is all about'. True – and Suk is a superb artist – but his playing, although technically immaculate, is curiously self-conscious. There seems a tendency to over-inflate the music with broad tempi, and these are not the searching performances one expects in this repertoire. Milstein (DG 457 701-2) is far more satisfying, and both his and those of Végh (Audivis Valois V 4477) and

Grumiaux (Philips Duo 438 736-2) are among the finest post-Heifetz analogue versions, while Perlman heads the digital list (EMI CDS7 49483-2 – see our main volume).

Rachel Podger uses a period instrument, but her technique and intonation are secure, her tone is full and clean without scratchiness or edge. In the closing *Presto* of the *G minor Sonata,* and opening *Preludio* and the *Gavotte* of the *E major Partita*, her playing could hardly be more lithe and appealing. Only in slow movements is there a minor reservation about the linear style, with moments of minor tonal swelling slightly disturbing the phrasing. Try the opening of the famous *Chaconne*, which is otherwise very impressive, to see whether this is a problem. There is much to praise in this artist's simplicity of approach, and she is beautifully recorded, but in the last resort this cannot quite compete with the very finest versions.

Playing with a curved bow, Rudolf Gähler easily solves the problem of how to play the many chords in this greatest of all unaccompanied violin music. Where with a modern bow they have to be spread or arpeggiated, Gähler attacks the notes simultaneously, making them genuine chords. The spreading of chords was what even so dedicated a Bach scholar as Albert Schweitzer found hard to bear, and Gähler for many will prove an ideally warm and attractive interpreter. With such a bow one might have expected a period violin to be used, but Gähler opts for a modern-style instrument, used with a fair degree of vibrato. His intonation is firm and true, which adds to the beauty of the performance. Interpretatively he takes a direct view, avoiding expressive mannerisms. But his heavy accenting and bold, continuously full timbre (sounding almost like a pair of unison instruments) are unable to offer enough subtlety of dynamic or variety of tone for these performances to be really satisfying. In the great *Chaconne* from the *D minor Partita*, one needs more contrasts to clarify the expansive structure with its changes of mood, and when in the *Fugue* of the *C major Sonata* Gähler adopts a very measured speed (making the movement almost as long as the *D minor Chaconne*) one needs a keener sense of purpose as well as more varied timbre. None the less a substantial achievement, beautifully recorded.

Violin sonatas (for violin and harpsichord) *Nos. 1–6, BWV 1014–19; Sonatas for violin and continuo, BWV 1021 & 1023.*

(BB) **(*) Virgin Veritas/EMI Dig. VBD5 61650-2 (2). Holloway, Moroney, Sheppard.

In addition to the six *Sonatas for violin and harpsichord*, this set presents the two surviving *Sonatas for violin and continuo* (in the latter, Davitt Moroney uses a chamber organ), thus gathering together the complete accompanied violin chamber music known to be authentic. John Holloway has long experience in the early-music field: among his many accomplishments his work as a leader of the London Classical Players and of L'Ecole d'Orphée is widely admired. His undoubted sensitivity, ability and good taste have won him a wide following, but violin tone is as much a matter of personal taste as is the human voice. Some will find the actual sound he makes unpleasing: it is vinegary and at times downright ugly. Yet beauty is said to be in the eye – or ear – of the beholder, and those who take a different view will find him not wanting in artistry. Both Davitt Moroney and Susan Sheppard give excellent support, and the recording cannot be faulted in its clarity and presence. This can be recommended to those who know and admire this artist's playing. At bargain price, it is worth considering, though other versions are more persuasive in the *Violin sonatas, BWV 1014–19*.

Violin sonatas (for violin and harpsichord) *Nos. 1–6, BWV 1014–19*, with alternative version of *BWV 1019; Sonatas for violin and continuo, BWV 1021, 1023 & 1024; Toccata and fugue in D min., BWV 565* (arr. Manze for solo violin).
**(*) HM Dig. HMU 907250.51 (2) [id.]. Andrew Manze, Richard Egarr, Jaap ter Linden.

In these attractive and underrated *Violin sonatas* of Bach, Andrew Manze is nothing if not individual. Fast movements sparkle vivaciously – it is impossible to resist their infectious rhythmic buoyancy. Slow movements are gentle and searching, often played *sotto voce*, creating a withdrawn almost unearthly sense of repose, which perhaps is not quite what Bach intended, but is still very affecting. The balance with the harpsichord or continuo is excellent and both players make positive contributions, yet it is Manze who dominates. For some reason a gamba is also added to the first, *B minor Sonata*, BWV 1014 and it is curiously intrusive. We are offered alternative movements for BWV 1019 and the *Adagio* is typically ethereal. But the highlight of the collection is Manze's breathtaking paraphrase for solo violin of Bach's famous organ *Toccata and fugue in D minor*, BWV 565. Here Manze's timbre is sweet and full, whereas elsewhere at times it seems unnecessarily meagre, with touches of edginess.

Violin sonatas (for violin and harpsichord): (i) *Nos. 1–6, BWV 1014–19;* with alternative version of (ii) *BWV 1016*.
(M) (**) EMI mono CHS5 67203-2 (2). Menuhin; (i) Kentner (piano); (ii) Landowska (harpsichord).

In 1951 Menuhin found a sympathetic partner in Kentner and the most enjoyable movements in these sonatas are the simpler allegros (the finale of BWV 1015 or the second movement of BWV 1016 for instance) where Kentner follows the violin line with

great sensitivity. But generally – while the violin timbre is firm and full and the phrasing has an inherent musicality – Menuhin's line is rather stiff, as if at that stage in his career he was inhibited from being in any way romantically expressive in his approach to Bach, something which was to change a decade later when he recorded Bach's orchestral works and re-recorded violin concertos with the Bath Festival Orchestra. The alternative version of the *E major Sonata*, with harpsichord instead of piano, was recorded earlier, in 1944, and here Menuhin's style is slightly freer, more emotional. But Landowska follows the violin line less flexibly than Kentner. These sonatas are not deeply serious works, but often comparatively light-hearted and that is a quality which is seldom conveyed here. The recording balance is good, although the violin is obviously pretty near to the microphone. The CD transfers are excellent.

KEYBOARD MUSIC

The Art of fugue, BWV 1080; (i) *Musical offering, BWV 1079; The Well-tempered Clavier (48 Preludes & fugues), BWV 846–93.*
(M) *** HM Dig. HMX 2908084/90 [id.]. Davitt Moroney (harpsichord); (i) with Martha Cook, Janet See, John Holloway, Jaap ter Linden.

If you want all these works played on the harpsichord, and that a modern instrument built in 1980, this Harmonia Mundi mid-priced box is worth considering, for Davitt Moroney has imagination as well as scholarship. His *Art of fugue* commands not only the intellectual side of the work but also the aesthetic, and his musicianship is second to none. Moroney makes some alterations in the order of the various contrapuncti but he argues his case persuasively – and he is eminently well served by the engineers.

The *Musical Offering* is also very much dominated by one or two harpsichords, although Moroney is joined by flute and violin in the trio sonata and the violin also shares the second of the six regal canons. Again the recording is well balanced and natural.

In the *Well-tempered Clavier* the balance is rather close, the harpsichord image full-bodied and clear. Yet the effect is certainly tangible and realistic, and the perspective convincing. Moroney's thoughtful, considered approach is satisfying in its way, stylistically impeccable. Although the playing is less concentrated than Kenneth Gilbert on DG (413 439-2 – see our main volume), it will suit those who like a thoughtful, unostentatious approach to Bach, yet one that does not lack rhythmic resilience, or vitality.

Chromatic fantasia and fugue in D min., BWV 903; Italian concerto in F, BWV 971; Toccatas in

C min. & D, BWV 911–12; Well-tempered Clavier: Prelude and fugue No. 5 in D, BWV 850; (i) Double clavier concerto in C, BWV 1061.
(M) (**(*)) EMI mono CDH5 67210-2 [id.]. Artur Schnabel (piano); (i) with Karl Ulrich Schnabel, LSO, Boult.

These pioneering recordings (nearly all from the 1930s) are fascinating, for Schnabel's playing has a magnetism and authority, which made a strong case for playing Bach on the piano, even if the timbre is dry and bony. The *Chromatic fantasia* is magnetically wayward, the playing rhythmically uneven in the fugue as in the excerpt from the *Well-tempered Clavier*; the *Italian concerto* is strongly characterized, with a serene *Andante*, while the finale has irrepressible momentum. The most impressively poised playing comes in the two *Toccatas* and the *Double concerto*, where Artur Schnabel and Karl Ulrich are in total rapport (the thoughtful *Adagio* sounds remarkably spontaneous). The two pianists seem to be making music together in a different dimension from Boult's positive, crisply efficient accompaniment, which is not flattered by the scratchy string sound.

Concertos (for solo harpsichord) after Vivaldi, Nos. 1 in D (after Op. 3/9), BWV 972; 2 in C (after Op. 7/2), BWV 973; 4 in G min. (after Op. 4/6), BWV 975; 5 in C (after Op. 3/12), BWV 976; 7 in F (after Op. 3/3), BWV 978; 9 in G (after Op. 4/1), BWV 980; Italian concerto, BWV 971.
🟢 *** Erato/Warner Dig. 3984 25504-2 [id.]. Olivier Baumont (harpsichord).

We are more used to hearing Bach's transcriptions of Italian concertos on the organ, but these were intended for either a harpsichord or possibly an organ without pedals. In Olivier Baumont's hands they sound splendid on the harpsichord, full of vitality and vividly coloured. Baumont plays a modern French copy of a German harpsichord 'from the School of Silbermann' of 1735 and it has a particularly effective range of dynamic. He produces some splendidly dramatic staccato effects in the slow movement of Op. 4/6. The most famous *Italian concerto* is offered as an encore and how eloquently Baumont plays the slow movement. This collection is very enjoyable indeed.

English suites Nos. 1–6, BWV 806–11; French suites Nos. 1–6, BWV 812–7; Partitas Nos. 1–6, BWV 825–30.
(M) *** HM HMX 2908078.83 (6) [id.]. Kenneth Gilbert (harpsichord).

In the *English suites* and *Partitas*, Kenneth Gilbert uses a Couchet-Taskin of 1788 and is given first-class recording. In the *French suites*, he uses a 1636 Ruckers, rebuilt by Hemsch, and again the engineering is well judged so that the effect is clear and robust, the balance is forward but not excessively so. Gilbert's playing in the *English* and *French*

suites has a fine sense of style, the rubato flowing naturally and never self-conscious. He is inconsistent in the matter of repeats in the former, but that will not worry most collectors. In the latter there is an obvious feeling for the strongly rhythmic French style, yet his playing prevents any sense of rigidity. Tempi are well judged and ornamentation is discreet. The original issue of the *Partitas* involved a third CD, but now the whole set is encompassed by two, and there is no doubting the excellence of these performances, which in terms of scholarship and artistry have much to recommend them. Overall this box is good value.

English suite No. 2 in A min., BWV 807; Partita No. 2 in C min., BWV 826; Toccata in C min., BWV 911.
(M) *** DG 463 604-2 [id.]. Martha Argerich (piano).

Martha Argerich's playing provides a genuinely musical experience – alive, keenly rhythmic, but also wonderfully flexible and rich in colour. She is never didactic, her finger control is impressive, textures are always varied and clean, and there is an intellectual musical vitality here that is refreshing. She is very well recorded indeed, and this transfer on the DG's Originals label is very successful, even if the measure (50′) is not especially generous.

French suites Nos. 1–6, BWV 812–17; Suites in A min., BWV 818a; in E flat, BWV 819a.
(BB) *** Virgin Veritas 2 x 1 VBD5 61653-2 (2). Davitt Moroney (harpsichord).
(B) *** Decca Double Dig. 466 736-2 (2) [id.]. Christopher Hogwood (with *Allemande, BWV 819a*).

Davitt Moroney's set of the *French suites*, recorded in 1990, but now reissued as a Virgin Veritas superbargain Double, tends to sweep the board for those wanting these works played on the harpsichord. Not only on price grounds, but in comprehensiveness. Like Hogwood before him, Moroney plays two further suites, which are almost certainly authentic as they were included in a manuscript copy of the complete set made by Bach's pupil Heinrich Nikolas Gerber in 1725. For good measure Moroney also adds a recently discovered second *Gavotte* belonging to the original version of the *Suite No. 4 in E flat*. On artistic grounds too, these performances are very highly recommendable. Ornamentation may be individual, as is the addition of little galanteries, but Moroney is always convincing in what he does and the expressive content (notably in the *Sarabandes*) and the flexible spontaneity of his playing continually communicate a sense of 'live' music-making. Pacing is admirable and all repeats are included. He plays a modern harpsichord by John Phillips after Ruckers/Taskin and if you are careful not to set the volume level too high, the recording gives him a nice presence in a well-judged acoustic. It is a pity that the notes (including detailed comments by Moroney himself) have been truncated, but in all other respects the present reissue makes a splendid bargain.

Christopher Hogwood uses two harpsichords, a Ruckers of 1646, enlarged and modified by Taskin in 1780, and a 1749 instrument, basically the work of Jean-Jacques Goujon and slightly modified by Jacques Joachim Swanen in 1784. They are magnificent creatures and Hogwood coaxes superb sounds from them: his playing is expressive, and the relentless sense of onward momentum that disfigures so many harpsichordists (though not Moroney) is pleasingly absent. These performances have both style and character and can be recommended with some enthusiasm alongside Davitt Moroney; however that Virgin set has a modest price advantage.

Goldberg variations, BWV 988.
*** Hyperion Dig. CDA 67305 [id.]. Angela Hewitt (piano).
(M)*** Hänssler Dig. CD 92.112 (2) [id.]. Evgeni Koroliov (piano).
(M) *(**) Sony Great Performances Dig. SMK 64126 [id.]. Glenn Gould (piano).

Two new recordings of the *Goldberg variations* readily take their place at the top of the list of piano versions, alongside that of Tureck (● VAIA 1029) and András Schiff, which (on a mid-priced Penguin Classics disc, 466 214-2) still gives profound satisfaction. But Angela Hewitt, as always, has a totally individual approach. She made her recording in London's Henry Wood Hall – after five days of preparatory sessions – in a single take, and the effect has all the glowing spontaneity of a live performance. Her performance, as with her famous set of the *'48'* praised in our main volume (● CDA 67301/4), is totally pianistic, involving the widest range of dynamic contrast, variety of touch and colour. Within the Hyperion documentation comes a personal analysis of her approach to each variation and immediately in the first she describes what she calls 'the joyous tone that is characteristic of so much of this work'. Other adjectives include 'genial' to depict the *fughetta* of Variation 10, 'regal' for Variation 12, 'sublime' (Variation 13), 'grandiose' (Variation 16) and so on. She rightly regards the 'black pearl' Variation 25 as 'the greatest of all' and fully reveals its gentle, celestial beauty, yet she still finds the necessary reserves for the bravura of the brilliant following toccata. Variation 28 is captivating, and Variation 29 again bursts with virtuosity and energy. After the bold *Quodlibet* the return of the *Aria* on a magical half-tone reminds one of Tureck and there can be no higher praise. The Hyperion recording is first class in every way.

Otherwise, an extraordinarily powerful and auth-oritative new set from Evgeni Koroliov tends to dominate recent versions of this great work. He opens the *Aria* rather deliberately, but the performance immediately takes wing and his playing spontaneously gathers excitement as it proceeds. Though there is less variety of dynamic than with Hewitt, his splendidly clear articulation is a joy in itself and the shaping of each individual variation is compelling. The digital dexterity is remarkable (sample Variation 20), yet this is never virtuosity for its own sake. There are new insights here and many individual touches, with the reprise of the *Aria* at the close bringing a satisfying culmination. There is also at times some vocalization, but it is less intrusive than Glenn Gould's and such is the calibre of this playing that one willingly makes allowances. The bold style of the pianism is caught by the clear, forward recording.

Gould's stereo version of the *Goldberg variations* was one of the last records he made. In his earlier record he made no repeats; now he repeats a section of almost half of them and also joins some pairs together (6 with 7 and 9 with 10, for example). Yet, even apart from his vocalise, he does a number of weird things – fierce staccatos, brutal accents, and so on – that inhibit one from suggesting this as a first recommendation even among piano versions. As to whether it is a 'great recording', that is a matter for conjecture. It is certainly a unique version and with Gould nothing is either dull or predictable. The recording is, as usual with this artist, inclined to be dry and forward, which aids clarity.

Goldberg variations, BWV 988; Chromatic fantasia and fugue in D min., BWV 903; Italian concerto in F, BWV 971.
(M) (**(*)) EMI mono CDH5 67200-2. Wanda Landowska (harpsichord).

Wanda Landowska (in 1933) not only rediscovered and reintroduced Bach's complete *Goldberg variation* to the European musical public, but soon afterwards made its first recording, and this is it. She plays a large two-manual Pleyel and at times gives it a grand presence (as in the *Maestoso* of Variation 16), but for the most part her playing is quite restrained, delicate in nuance, and often thoughtfully expressive (Variations 21 and 25). At other times her virtuosity is very compelling (Variation 14) and her articulation a special pleasure (Variation 26). One has to remember she had to choose her own tempi (which are often quite different to what we expect today), for there was no precedent. She is not only convincing, but also – in spite of the fact that the recording was made on 78-r.p.m., a few variations at a time – leads the ear forward most spontaneously. The *Italian concerto* is understandably more robust, while the *Chromatic fantasia* shows just how fleet her fingers could be. The remastered recording sounds very well indeed, although the problem of slight 'wow' on sustained passages is not solved. But one readily adjusts when the playing is so magnetic.

15 2-Part Inventions, BWV 772–86; 15 3-Part Inventions, BWV 787–801.
*** BIS Dig. CD 1009 [id.]. Masaaki Suzuki (harpsichord).

Masaaki Suzuki, who has directed Bach's choral works and cantatas with great success on CD, here turns to the keyboard works with equal perception and skill. These *Inventions* can sound dry, but not in his hands. Neither are there those calculated interferences with the music's flow which some players mistake for flexibility. Here the playing is naturally spontaneous, fresh and alive, never didactic and rigid. Suzuki is one of the finest Bach exponents of our time and he is truthfully recorded. But be careful not to have the volume level too high.

Klavierbüchlein for W. F. Bach.
(M)**(*) Hänssler Dig. CD 92.137-2 (2) [id.].
Joseph Payne (harpsichord, clavichord, organ).

Joseph Payne has already given us an excellent organ set of the *33 Arnstadt chorale preludes* (HMA 1905158 – see our main volume). Now he combines organ, harpsichord and clavichord to survey another Yale autograph manuscript, dating from 1720, containing the sixty-three miniatures which form Bach's *Klavierbüchlein*. This pedagogical collection was compiled in Cöthen to provide a keyboard education for his oldest and favourite son. Like the companion notebook for Anna Magdalena, it provides fascinating insights into Bach's composing process, for after a series of engaging musical fragments, Bach features early versions of a number of the *Preludes* from the *Well-tempered Clavier*, of which the shorter version of the famous C major Prelude, BWV 846 is notable. These are presented with pleasing simplicity and vitality. Later a series of *Preambulums* and *Fantasias* turn out to be the *Two-* and *Three-part Inventions*, and here Payne's linear style is a little fussy. But he is generally a fine advocate, particularly in excerpts from suites by Telemann and Stölzel. The use of three different instruments introduces an appealing variety of colour. Not everything here is of equal interest, but there are quite a few items which tweak the ear, and the recording is exemplary.

Partitas Nos. 1–6, BWV 825–30.
(M) *** Hänssler CD 92.115 (2) [id.]. Trevor Pinnock (harpsichord).
*** Signum Dig. SIGD 012 (2) [id.]. Lucy Carolan (harpsichord).
(BB) *** Erato Ultima Double 3984 18167-2 (2) [id.]. Scott Ross (harpsichord).

Trevor Pinnock has recorded the six *Partitas* before for DG, but this new set is even finer. He uses a superb American copy of a Hemsch made by David Way in Stonington, Connecticut (with a particularly

effective mute stop). As before he plays these works with a keen sense of enjoyment and projects the music with enormous panache. The playing is arresting from the first bar (on both discs!) and the listener is quite bowled over, as the harpsichord is superbly recorded and given fine presence in a spaciously resonant acoustic. Indeed this is the only slight caveat, as the sound may seem a fraction over-resonant to some ears. Nevertheless playing of this calibre is impossible to resist, but those who have problems with the resonance can turn to the excellent Lucy Carolan, Scott Ross or Christophe Rousset.

Lucy Carolan's playing is as full of life as it is of imaginative touches. She is both commanding and scholarly, and her ready virtuosity and keen articulation in the *Gigues* are exhilarating. Yet her touch can also be appealingly delicate. To add variety of colour she uses a pair of harpsichords, both copies of early instruments. *Partitas Nos. 1, 3* and *6* are played on a copy of a Mietke, and *Partitas 2, 4* and *5* on a copy of a Goermans-Taskin instrument. Both are excellently recorded. Her readings give much pleasure and can be considered in the same breath as those of Christophe Rousset, our current primary recommendation (O-L 440 217-2 – see our main volume).

Scott Ross's set of the *Partitas* dates from 1989. He uses an unidentified but attractive instrument which is recorded with both warmth and clarity. He plays with enjoyable style and panache, and despite one or two minor points (in the *B flat Gigue* not every note speaks evenly and at times greater rhythmic freedom would be welcome), his readings are eminently competitive reissued as an Ultima Double. They make a good bargain alternative to Christophe Rousset.

Toccatas Nos. 1–7, BWV 910/916.
**(*) Lyrichord Dig. LEMS 8041 [id.]. Richard Troeger (clavichord).

Bach's *Toccatas*, which involve a good deal of virtuosity are usually played on the harpsichord, organ, or – often very effectively – on the piano. But hearing them played so fluently and musically on the more intimate clavichord, makes for an enjoyable diversity and Richard Troeger certainly phrases and articulates with character. The recording engineer, Garth Hobden, is also to be congratulated. He has not been tempted to put his microphones too close, and his comment that 'the clavichord is a quiet instrument, but it can fill a room with extraordinary resonanace' is borne out here, yet the instrument's essential intimacy is retained.

Trio sonatas Nos. 1–6, BWV 525/530 (arr. for 2 Lautenwerke).
*** Lyrichord Dig. LEMS 8045 [id.]. Shawn Leopard, John Paul.

In the excellent notes with this unusual Lyrichord disc, William Carragan makes a good case for performing these works on a pair of keyboard instruments. As he points out, when played on the organ the two melody parts are allotted to two different manuals, and usually registered slightly differently, the bass being given to the pedals. Bach is known to have possessed three Lautenwerke, but these instruments were lost, and the ones used here are modern reconstructions made following an eighteenth-century specification by Jacob Adlung.

They were both built by Anden Houben, using gut strings, primarily double strung. The one with a single keyboard is slightly brighter than its companion with a double keyboard, and their sound has something in common with both the lute and the clavichord, although with greater amplitude. (Both are pictured on the CD insert).

The performances here are highly musical and fluent and very well recorded, not too forwardly, and in a very pleasing acoustic. The intimate result certainly bears out Carragan's contention that the counterpoint is cleaner and more audible than when the music is heard on the organ. A thoroughly worthwhile issue for the special Bach year, which includes a fascinating essay on the problems of building these instruments by Anden Houben.

The Well-tempered Clavier (48 Preludes & fugues), BWV 846–93 (complete).
(B) *** Nimbus Dig. NI 5608/11 (4) [id.]. Bernard Roberts (piano).
(BB) ***Virgin Veritas Dig. VBD 561711-2(4). Bob van Asperen (harpsichord).
(M) (***) EMI mono CHS5 67214-2 (3) [id.]. Edwin Fischer (piano).
(**(*)) DG mono 463 305-2 (4) [id.]. Rosalyn Tureck (piano).

Bernard Roberts's Nimbus survey is plainer than Angela Hewitt's Hyperion piano version (● CDA 67301/4 – see our main volume), which is daringly adventurous in the use of dynamic rise and fall, and in exploring the full range of colour and feeling that is possible with a modern piano. But that is not to suggest that Roberts is unimaginative; indeed his survey is full of individual touches and insights. Speeds feel undistractingly right throughout and, as in his comparable set for Nimbus of the Beethoven piano sonatas, Roberts refuses to distract attention from the composer's argument with idiosyncratic gestures. That goes with the deepest concentration, bringing out the full power as well as the beauty with counterpoint consistently clarified. To confirm the recommendation the four discs come as a bargain offer. Those who find Hewitt's pianistic range and use of wide dynamic graduations not wholly in accordance with authentic baroque practice will surely find Roberts a stimulating alternative. He is certainly not lacking in scholarship or spontaneity

and he too is very well recorded. Those who have admired his Beethoven recordings will surely also want his '*Forty-eight*' and this is the version, superbly recorded, which for many will be a first choice.

Collectors wanting a complete modern harpsichord version will surely now choose the reissued mid-price 1989 Virgin Veritas set from Bob van Asperen. A pupil of Gustav Leonhardt, his account of the '*Forty-eight*' enshrines many of the finest of his master's qualities and outshines most of his rivals on CD. His playing is marked by consistent vitality, elegance and concentration: he plays every note as if he means it and is refreshingly unmetronomic without being too free. He plays a 1728 harpsichord by Christian Zell from the Hamburg Museum, which the engineers capture vividly. The acoustic is less resonant than with Gilbert on DG (our previous primary recommendation), which is an advantage, and with its price advantage van Asperen's set is very recommendable indeed.

Older collectors will recall Edwin Fischer's Bach with particular affection. His was the first ever '*Forty-eight*' to be put on shellac, being recorded in 1933–6. After more than six decades the sound is inevitably dated and the piano tone comparatively shallow but – make no mistake – there is nothing shallow about these interpretations, and the current remastering produces a crisp, clean timbre that suits this pianist's approach to Bach admirably. There is occasionally just a hint of swish at one or two side-ends, but this is never disturbing, and for the most part the background is commendably silent. Fischer has often been spoken of as an artist of intellect, but the approach here is never remote or cool. Moreover he produces a sense of line that is an unfailing source of musical wisdom and nourishment. Tempi are often brisk – witness the very first Prelude of Book I – but by no means always so, for Fischer can at times be ruminative, and he is always thoughtful as well as spontaneously commanding. The performance is economically laid out on three mid-price CDs, each accommodating close on 80 minutes. These discs are indispensable to the serious Bach collector and will give genuine refreshment.

Rosalyn Tureck's classic recording made in New York in the early 1950s, magnetic and concentrated, makes a welcome reappearance after too long in limbo. The dry mono sound and limited dynamic range tend to exaggerate the muscularity of the playing, but the tonal contrasts are still brought out strongly, at times echoing in sharp staccato a harpsichord sound. Tureck's Bach is always special; even so, it is disconcerting to find her adopting such idiosyncratically slow speeds for some of the most formidable fugues of Book 2, the one in G sharp minor for example, which for all Tureck's concentration becomes lethargic. And to reissue such a set at full-price seems an extraordinary gesture on DG's part.

The Well-tempered Clavier, Book I, Preludes and fugues Nos. 1–24, BWV 846–69.
*** BIS Dig. CD 813/4 [id.]. Masaaki Suzuki (harpsichord).
*** Meridian Dig. CDE 84384/5 [id.]. Julia Cload (piano).
*** Ongaku Dig. 024-113 (2) [id.]. Sergey Schepkin (piano).
(M) *** DG 463 601-2 (2) [id.]. Ralph Kirkpatrick (clavichord).

Suzuki only offers Book I so far, but lays claim to being first choice for a harpsichord version of the *'Forty-eight'*. His 2-manual instrument (by Willem Kroesbergen of Utrecht after an enlarged Ruckers) has a fine personality and is splendidly recorded. His pacing is admirably judged, his flexibility never sounds mannered and he brings Bach's great keyboard odyssey fully to life at every turn. A most satisfying achievement.

Julia Cload's new set also promises well, her pianistic style at times comparatively gentle (witness the very opening Prelude) but her control of dynamic follows Bach's underlying harmonic progressions very subtly. She can be both poetically reserved then suddenly extrovert and sparkling, and always remains faithful to the letter and spirit of this great work.

Sergey Schepkin immediately creates a more sharply focused, clearer style of articulation, still essentially pianistic, but with the extra bite of a 'plucked' keyboard instrument underlying his presentation. He is comparatively chimerical, and attractively so, with tempi in the Preludes (though not always the Fugues) often faster than with his colleagues. His articulation is crisp, the effect more extrovert than with Julia Cload. But there is no lack of expressive feeling. Indeed, the individuality of all these players is refreshing: even where two performances are essentially similar one senses a different musical personality behind the playing in this inexhaustible music.

It was a bold decision of Ralph Kirkpatrick to pioneer Book I on the clavichord (in the mid 1960s). Some of the *Preludes and fugues* seem better suited to this instrument, which is quite different from the piano, quieter and more intimate than the harpsichord, with a narrower dynamic range. Yet this does not seem a problem for Kirkpatrick, whose expressive powers are never in doubt, neither is his scholarship or musicianship, and he fully realizes the possibilities inherent in the use of his gentler instrument, which is very finely recorded, the sound admirably remastered for this undoubtedly fascinating and rewarding Originals reissue.

The title page of the documentation tells the listener: 'In accordance with the clavichord's naturally soft sound, a lower than normal listening level is recommended', a suggestion that must be followed if this performance is to make its proper effect. This is obviously not a first choice but a fascinating alternative for those collectors who already have a set on harpsichord or piano.

The Well-tempered Clavier, Book II: Preludes and fugue Nos. 25–48, BWV 870–93.
*** Ongaku Dig. 024-115 (2). Sergey Schepkin (piano).

Sergey Schepkin's survey of Book II arrived just as we were going to press and, if anything, proves even more stimulating than Book I. American collectors in particular need not hesitate to invest in both volumes. Schepkin's approach is bolder, more vibrant than that of Angela Hewitt, yet the range and variety of the playing is comparable, showing a constantly individual grasp of the essence of Bach's inspiration and the expressive range that lies beneath the surface of these apparently pedagogic exercises in polyphony.

This is immediately demonstrated by the first three *Preludes and fugues* of this second book. The *Prelude*, BWV 870 in C is reflective, the fugue almost aggressive in its sharply etched vitality which carries through to the moto perpetuo of the *C minor Prelude*; then the *C minor fugue* is gentle and thoughtful, which again carries through to the lovely *G major Prelude*. The following fugue is bright, buoyant, and crisp. The same diversity continues throughout, with the comparatively serene three-part *Fugue in F sharp* which opens the second disc followed by a sharply precise fugue. The piano is recorded forwardly and truthfully.

Keyboard transcriptions

Transcriptions (arr. Busoni): *Chorales: Ich ruf' zu dir, Herr Jesu Christ BWV 639; Nun freut euch, lieben Christen, BWV 734: Nun komm, der Heiden Heiland, BWV 659; Wachet auf, ruft uns die stimme, BWV 645.*
◉ *** Sony Dig. SK 66511 [id.]. Murray Perahia
– LISZT: *Concert paraphrases of Schubert Lieder*; MENDELSSOHN: *Songs without words.* ***

Murray Perahia knows how to make the piano sing as do few of his contemporaries and how to control pace. His pianism is impeccable in its polish and naturalness of flow, and there is a wonderful bloom about the sound he produces.

ORGAN MUSIC

Helmut Walcha DG Archiv series

The Art of the fugue, BWV 1080 (with Contrapunctus No. 18, completed Walcha); Allabreve, BWV 589; Chorale settings: BWV 645–650 (Schübler chorales), 651–664, 653b, 665–668a, 700, 709, 727, 733, 734, 736; Canonic

*variations on Vom Himmel hoch, BWV 769;
Canzona, BWV 588; Chorale partita (Sei
gegrüsset), BWV 768; Clavier-Übung, Part III
(Organ mass): Prelude & fugue, BWV 552 and
chorale settings, BWV 669–689; 4 Duets BWV
802–805; Fantasias: BWV 562, 572; Fantasias
and fugues, BWV 537, 542; Fugues: BWV 552/2,
578; Fugues on themes by Legrenzi and Corelli,
BWV 574, 579. Orgelbüchlein, BWV 599–644;
Pastorale, BWV 590; Passacaglia and fugue,
BWB 582; Preludes and fugues: BWV 531–536,
539, 541, 543–548, 550, 551; Toccatas and
fugues: BWV 538, 540, 564; Toccata, adagio and
fugue, BWV 565; Trio sonatas Nos. 1–6, BWV
525–530.*
(B) **(*) DG 463 712-2 (12) [id.]. Helmet Walcha
  (Organs at St. Laurenskerk, Alkmaar,
  Netherlands, and Saint-Pierre-le-Jeune,
  Strasburg).

It is good to see that DG have reissued Helmut
Walcha's pioneering stereo series, recorded between 1959 and 1971 as part of their bargain-priced
Collectors Edition. Even if by today's standards
Walcha's Bach style seems very relaxed and sometimes lacking in internal tension, his carefully calculated interpretations create a genuine sense of
organic unity, and a deeply musical sense of line
and phrase, which gains from felicitous registration
using highly suitable organs, splendidly recorded.

His distinguished version of *The Art of fugue* was
originally reviewed in Volume I of our hardback
Stereo Record Guide where we commented that the
registration is admirably varied, yet at all times
tasteful and restrained, with the contrasts in register
and timbre heightened by the spatial effect of the
stereo. The *Toccatas and fugues* certainly do not
lack bravura and, typical of Walcha's playing at its
most monumental, is the gigantic triptych of the
Toccata, adagio and fugue, a rigorous test of any
organist's technique. It is a work which Walcha
comes through with flying colours and the *Chorale
partita, Sei gegrüsset* is another expansive piece
that comes off very successfully.

The *Preludes and fugues* with their dignified
tempi, although seldom flamboyant, are dedicated
performances which allow every detail to come
through, with the E flat work, BWV 552, especially
impressive in its combination of majesty and clarity.
Among the shorter, more colourful pieces the silvery arpeggios of the *Fantasia in G,* BV 572 bring
a fine example of perceptive registration, and in
Walcha's hands the *Trio sonatas* are not treated
lightly but used to reflect the contrapuntal and
formal mastery of Bach's middle period.

*Chorale partita: Sei gegrüsset, Jesu gütig, BWV
768; Prelude and fugue in E flat, BWV 552; 6
Schübler chorales, BWV 646–50; Toccata and
fugue in D min., BWV 565; Trio sonata No. 1 in E
flat, BWV 525.*

(M) **(*) DG stereo/mono 457 704-2 [id.].
  Helmut Walcha (Schnitger organ of
  St Laurenskerk, Alkmaar).

DG have, on the whole, chosen well for a programme of 'Originals' to demonstrate the Bach
style of the famous German Bach scholar/organist
of the early LP era, Helmut Walcha. Even if modern
ears, used to Peter Hurford and Kevin Bowyer,
may find Walcha's approach rather slow and heavy,
especially at the close of the otherwise impressively
detailed *Chorale partita* and the massively conceived *Prelude and fugue*, the performance of the
famous *D minor Toccata and fugue*, although comparatively unflamboyant, is not dull. The *Trio
sonata* is engagingly registered, as are the steadily
presented *Schübler chorales*. The last four of these
are mono, but the ear hardly registers the difference
because of the high quality of DG's recording of
the magnificent Alkmaar organ.

Lionel Rogg Complete Harmonia Mundi series

Disc 1: (Early) *Preludes and fugues, BWV 531–5,
539, 549–50; Fugues, BWV 575–9.*

Disc 2: *Toccatas and fugues, BWV 538, 540, 566;
Toccata, adagio and fugue, BWV 564.*

Disc 3: *Allabreve, BWV 586; Canzone, BWV 588;
Chorale partitas, BWV 766–8; Pastorale, BWV
590.*

Discs 4 & 5: *Orgelbüchlein, BWV 599/644;
Chorales, BWV 653b, 720, 727, 734, 736–737.*

Disc 6: *Passacaglia and fugue, BWB 582;
Fantasias and fugues, BWV 537, 542; Fantasias,
BWV 562, 567; Chorale fuguettas BWV 696–699;
701, 703–4.*

Discs 7 & 8: *18 Leipzig chorale preludes, BWV
651–668; Chorale preludes, BWV 690–91, 695,
706, 709–713, 714, 717–718, 731, 738, 740.*

Disc 9: *Trio Sonatas Nos. 1–6, BWV 525/530;
Trio, BWB 583.*

Discs 10, 11 & 12: *Prelude, BWV 552; German
Organ Mass, BWV 669/688; Fugue, BWV 552; 6
Schübler chorales, BWV 645/650; Later Preludes
and fugues, BWV 536, 541, 543–8.*
(M) **(*) HM HMX 290772/83 (12) [id.]. Lionel
  Rogg (Silbermann organ, Arlesheim).

*Fantasias and fugues: in C min., BWV 537; in G
min., BWV 542; Passacaglia and fugue in C min.,
BWV 582; 6 Schübler chorales, BWV 645/650;
Toccata and fugue in C min., BWV 565.*
(M) **(*) HM HMX 295771 [id.] (from above).
  Lionel Rogg (Silbermann organ, Arlesheim).

Lionel Rogg made three surveys of Bach's organ
music and this is the second, originally published

in 1970. He followed on in the footsteps of DG's Walcha series, maintaining some of its scholarly sobriety yet clearly making progress towards the more volatile Bach style with which Peter Hurford on Decca was to transform the approach to Bach's organ music later in that decade. *Aficionados* will be glad to see that Rogg's complete set, as listed above, is available on CD; others will be content with the set of excerpts on a single disc.

The organ at Arlesheim is certainly a magnificent instrument, but is not quite as clear-textured (as recorded) as the Zurich organ on which Rogg recorded his previous series in the 1960s, issued on LP on the Bach and Oryx labels. The present instrument was carefully restored to its original pitch and timbre over a period from 1959 to 1962, when the pedal was strengthened, a weakness of the original registration, which is certainly not felt now. Indeed the new sound is ear-catching at the opening of the mighty *C minor Passacaglia and fugue*, with its sombre colouring and feeling of underlying reserves of power.

These big, expansive works admirably suited Rogg's measured style with its stateliness and gravity, and the performance has a cumulative effect, without ever being pressed forward. The famous *D minor Toccata and fugue* also sounds well, but this is not a work that responds so readily to Rogg's characterization – it needs rather more flair and flamboyance. The two *Preludes and fugues* too, could use rather more variety of approach, although the concentration is in no doubt. The *Schübler chorales* are the highlight of the recital and demonstrate Rogg's ready tapestry of baroque colouring (which was also so effective in the chorales, chorale partitas and variations), yet the cantus firmus always remains clear.

Ton Koopman Complete Teldec series

Volume 10: *Breitkopf (Kirnberger) chorales, BWV 694, 695a, 696–704, 709, 711–13, 715–18, 720–22, 724–7, 730–33, 735–6, 738–41, 743, 747, 749–50, 754–8, 762–5, 1085, BWV Anh. 49–50, 58; Other Chorales: Auf meinen lieben Gott (2 versions); Herr Christ, der einig Gottes Sohn; Ich ruf zu Dir, Herr Jesu Christ; Komm, heilger Geist, erfüll die Herzen* (all *BWV deest*). *** Teldec/Warner Dig. 3984 24828-2 (2) [id.].
Ton Koopman (Hans Heinrich Bader organ of St Walburgiskerk, Zutphen).

This is a convenient grouping of Bach's miscellaneous chorale preludes, simple chorale fantasias and fuguettas from a large group published by Breitkopf (around 1760), which are also named after one of Bach's pupils with whom their collection was associated – Johann Kirnberger. They are not a self-contained set (like the *Orgel-Büchlein*) but gather together a cross-section of Bach's works in this form, including many very early works from

the period before 1710, notably BWV 749, 750 and 756 which are probably Bach's first surviving compositions.

The *manueliter* chorales were written for small organs without pedals, while the *pedaliter* pieces are more ambitious, written for larger church organs. Ton Koopman creates his own order of performance, effectively alternating simpler and more elaborate settings. He also uses the widest possible range of registration, from piquant interplays as on the engaging opening *Allein Gott in der Höh sei Ehr*, BWV 711, to a richer treatment of the same chorale, BWV 717. Indeed he often places different settings of the same chorale in juxtaposition to diverting effect.

The polyphonic detail is very clear, with the cantus firmus always easily discernible, and this splendid organ with its vivid palette seems an ideal choice for such a programme, as many of the chorales are quite short and simple and need all the colour they can be given. The recording is first class in every way. Not to be played all at once, but rewardingly instructive to dip into.

Kevin Bowyer Nimbus series

Kevin Bowyer's projected complete coverage of Bach's organ music has been for the 1990s what Peter Hurford's was for the 1970s and 1980s. His playing is always both sensitive and wonderfully alive, and his Bach scholarship is never in doubt. He has chosen to produce a series of carefully planned recitals rather than grouping the works together in their respective genres, and Volume 4 (NI 5377), which earned a ✿ in our main volume, is a particularly attractive example, including the *Fantasia & imitatio*, BWV 563, a miscellany of *Fugues* plus a pair of *Toccatas*. Sensibly he has made an exception in the case of the so-called *Organ mass*, but adding other works to make up a two-CD set (NI 5561/2, another ✿ collection) and also in the case of the *Chorale Preludes*, see below.

Volume 10: *Leipzig chorale preludes Nos. 1–18, BWV 651–668a; 4 Early chorale settings: Wenn dich Unglück tut greifen an; Als Jesus Christus in der Nacht; Ach Gott, tu dich erbarmen; Wie nach einer Wasserquelle, BWV 1104, 1108–4;1199; Concerto No. 3 in C* (for solo organ) (after Vivaldi: *Concerto in D min., Op. 3/11, RV 565.) Fugue in A min., BWV 949.*
(B) *** Nimbus Dig. Double NI 5573/4(2) [id.].
Kevin Bowyer (Marcussen organ of Sct. Hans Kirke, Odense, Denmark).

As ever here, Bowyer's registration is consistently imaginative and he conveys the devotional mood of the gentler pieces unsanctimoniously. The rock-like opening *Fantasia on 'Komm, Heiliger Geist'* is followed by a gentler, more meditative setting of the same chorale with the following *An Wasserflüssen*

Babylon sublimely peaceful. The intricate texture of *Von Gott will ich nicht lassen* is splendidly clear and the contrasts of the three settings of *Nun komm der Heiden Heiland* are most effectively made – with the third ('in organo pleno, canto fermo in pedale'), which ends the first disc, vigorously exultant. Similarly, on the second CD, the three versions of both *Allein Gott in der Höh' sei Ehr* and *Jesus Christus, unser Heiland* are comparably resourceful. The final chorale, *Vor deinen Thron tret ich,* is reputed to have been dictated by Bach to his son, Carl Philipp, in the final days of his life: its mood of calm acceptance is beautifully evoked. The life-assertive *Fugue in A minor,* a jaunty early work, is then followed by four, more simple chorales, only recently discovered (also from Bach's youth) and the recital ends with an ebullient account of Bach's enthusiastic transcription of a familiar Vivaldi concerto. The recording of the Odense organ is first class.

Volume 11: *Canonic variations on 'Vom Himmel hoch', BWV 769; Chorale preludes, BWV 690, 691, 698, 702, 733, 743, 756; BWV Anh. 55, 60 & 70; 8 Chorale preludes from the Neumeister collection* (Yale manuscript), *BWV 957, 1092, 1096; 1111–13,1117–1;8 Fugue in B min. on a theme of Corelli, BWV 579; Prelude and fugue in C, BWV 943 & 953; Prelude and fugue in C min., BWV 546; in E min. (Wedge), BWV 548; Toccatas in C min., BWV 911; in E min., BWV 914; Trios in B min.* (arr. from *BWV 570); in D min., BWV 583.*
(B) *** Nimbus Dig. Double NI 5606/7(2) [id.].
    Kevin Bowyer (Marcussen organ of Sct. Hans Kirke, Odense, Denmark).

Volume 11, like Volume 10, is offered on a pair of CDs here, but each presents a separate recital, complete in itself. The first is prefaced by a pair of Bach's mightiest fugues, the *E minor* work organically whole, with the opening music of the fugue recapitulated without alteration at the close, the *C minor* with the two parts less integrated – the prelude tempestuous, the fugue more sombre but reaching a powerful culmination. In between come a series of more lightly registered pieces (even the *Canonic variations*). The second recital is framed by a pair of virtuoso *Toccatas* which Bowyer, recognizing as harpsichord originals, plays fluently and registers appropriately. Then come the simple early *Neumeister chorales,* where the organ's full colour palette is indulged. The *Prelude* and *Fugue in C* act as an intermission and are also delightfully presented, two independent but equally graceful works which fit well together. The recording like the playing is of very high quality.

Christopher Herrick Hyperion series

'Organ cornucopia': Chorale preludes, BWV 723, 741, 743, 747, 753–5, 758 (4 verses), 762, 764–5; *BWV Anh. 55; Concertos in G, BWV 571; in E flat, BWV 597; Fantasia in C, BWV 575; Fugues: in C, BWV 946; in C min., BWV 562; in D, BWV 580; Kleines harmonisches Labyrinth, BWV 591; Pedal-exercitium, BWV 598; Prelude and fugue in C, BWV 531; Prelude in C, BWV 567; Trio in G min., BWV 584.*
*** Hyperion Dig. CDA 67139 [id.]. Christopher Herrick (Metzler organ of Pfarrkirche, St Michael, Kaisten, Switzerland).

At its best, Christopher Herrick's Hyperion series is hardly less stimulating than Kevin Bowyer's for Nimbus, and it is equally superbly recorded. This organ in Kaisten has the strongest personality, and Herrick's registration for the chorales is strikingly rich in colour. *O Vater, allmächtiger Gott*, BWV 758 is given in four verses, each very brief, overall displaying an ear-tickling palette, with the pedals reserved for the final verse. The *Pedal-exercitium* brings an arresting opportunity for virtuoso footwork, and of the two solo Concertos, BWV 571 in G also features the pedals strongly, with a descending bass-scale in its *Chaconne* finale which is remarkably gripping here. The alternation of chorales and fugues certainly makes for a varied and aurally diverting 'cornucopia', for Bach's invention is inexhaustible. The strangely named and musically intangible *Kleines harmonisches Labyrinth* brings a further contrast near the end of this otherwise boldly presented recital which holds the listener from beginning to end.

36 Neumeister chorales.
*** Hyperion CDA 67215 [id.]. Christopher Herrick (Metzler organ of the Stadtkirche, Zofingen, Switzerland).

The original manuscript for the *Neumeister chorales* was a comparatively recent discovery, found in a collection at Yale University. Gottfried Neumeister's organ book contained eighty-two chorales by seven different composers and Professor Wolff (who made the discovery alongside the Yale music librarian, Harold Samuel) has not only confidently confirmed Bach's contribution, but also suggested the composition date for most of the settings as being between 1700 and 1708. The music itself has plenty of variety, for Bach's imagination in this field was inexhaustible, and Christopher Herrick is a very persuasive advocate on his fine Swiss organ. The music is admirably paced, and always spontaneously alive, while detail remains clear. But Stephen Westrop, the writer of the notes, sensibly suggests that the listener not attempt to play the collection as an integrated whole, but rather to 'dip in' and sample individual settings.

Other organ music

38 Neumeister chorales; 17 Rinck chorales; 5 Rudorff chorales.

(BB) ** Arte Nova Dig. 74321 31680-2 (3). Wilhelm Krumbach (Silbermann organ of Benedictine Monastery, Maurmünster in Elsass).

This three-disc Arte Nova set offers thirty-eight chorales from the recently discovered Yale University collection, adding to the *Neumeister chorales* (which have also been recorded, even more successfully, by Christopher Herrick). It also includes seventeen from the legacy of Christian Heinrich Rinck (1770–1846), court organist at Darmstadt, plus five more settings from the Rudorff collection, held in the Leipzig music library, which are also thought to belong to the same early period (i.e. 1703–4). Krumbach is not as imaginative a player as Herrick, but he uses a characterful organ and presents the chorales simply and where appropriate, robustly, with an expansive panoply of colour. He is well recorded and this inexpensive set is well worth its modest cost.

Orgelbüchlein: Chorale preludes, Nos. 1–46, BWV 599–644.
(M)**(*) Hänssler Dig. CD 92.094 [id.]. Wolfgang Zerer (organ of Martinkerk, Groningen).

Wolfgang Zerer's set of the *Orgelbüchlein* is of high quality, both in its colouristic range and its contrasts of mood and tempi. He can be vigorous and flamboyant when required (as in *In dir ist Freude*, BWV 615) but for the most part his presentation is intimate and effectively so, though he opens up the registration to use the full organ when needed. An enjoyable set, but we are still inclined to prefer Christopher Herrick's Hyperion recording (CDA 66756), which is that bit more imaginatively vivid.

VOCAL MUSIC

Complete cantatas Hänssler Rilling series

Cantatas Nos. 62: Nun komm, der Heiden Heiland; 63: Christen, ätzet diesen Tag; 64: Sehet, welch eine Liebes hat uns der Vater erzeiget.
(M)**(*) Hänssler CD 92.020 [id.]. Nielsen, Augér, Watts, Hamari, Laurich, Murray, Baldin, Kraus, Huttenlocher, Heldwein, Schöne, Gächinger Kantorei, Bach-Collegium, Stuttgart, Rilling.

Cantatas Nos. 65: Sie werden aus Saba alle kommen; 66: Erfreut euch, ihr Herzen; 67: Halt im Gedächtnis Jesum Christ.
(M)**(*) Hänssler CD 92.021 [id.]. Schreckenbach, Mitsui, Murray, Kraus, Huttenlocher, Heldwein, Gächinger Kantorei, Bach-Collegium, Stuttgart, Rilling.

Cantatas Nos. 68: Also hat Gott die Welt geliebt;

69: Lobe den Herrn, meine Seele; 70: Wachet! behet! betet! wachet!
(M)**(*) Hänssler CD 92.022 [id.]. Augér, Donath, Hamari, Gohl, Kraus, Harder, Huttenlocher, Schöne, Nimsgern, Gächinger Kantorei, Bach-Collegium, Stuttgart, Rilling.

Cantatas Nos. 71: Gott ist mein König; 72: Alles nur nach Gottes Willen; 73: Herr, wie du willt, so schicks mit mir; 74: Wer mich liebst, der wird mein Wort halten.
(M)**(*) Hänssler CD 92.023 [id.]. Grae, Augér, Schreiber, Donath, Gardow, Schwarz, Schreckenbach, Laurich, Senger, Kraus, Harder, Tuller, Huttenlocher, Schöne, Gächinger Kantorei, Bach-Collegium, Stuttgart, Rilling.

Cantatas Nos. 75: Die Elenden sollen essen; 76: Die Himmel erzählen die Ehre Gottes.
(M)**(*) Hänssler CD 92.024 [id.]. Reichelt, Augér, Gohl, Hamari, Watts, Kraus, Baldin, Kunz, Nimsgern, Gächinger Kantorei, Bach-Collegium, Stuttgart, Rilling.

Cantatas Nos. 77: Du sollst Gott, deinen Herren, lieben; 78: Jesu, der du meine Seele; 79: Gott der Herr ist Sonn, und Schild.
(M)**(*) Hänssler CD 92.025 [id.]. Donath, Augér, Hamari, Watkinson, Kraus, Baldin, Schöne, Huttenlocher, Gächinger Kantorei, Bach-Collegium, Stuttgart, Rilling.

Cantatas Nos. 80: Ein feste Burg ist unser Gott; 81: Jesus schläft, was soll ich hoffen?; 82: Ich habe genug.
(M)**(*) Hänssler CD 92.026 [id.]. Augér, Schreckenbach, Hamari, Harder, Kraus, Huttenlocher, Nimsgern, Gächinger Kantorei, Württemberg CO, Bach-Collegium, Stuttgart, Rilling.

Cantatas Nos. 83: Erfreute Zeit im neuen Bunde; 84: Ich bin vergnügt mit meinem Glücke; 85: Ich bin ein Guter Hirt; 86: Wahrlich, wahrlich, ich sage euch.
(M)**(*) Hänssler CD 92.027 [id.]. Augér, Watts, Schreckenbach, Kraus, Heldwein, Gächinger Kantorei, Bach-Collegium, Stuttgart, Württemberg CO, Rilling.

Cantatas Nos. 87: Bisher habt ich nichts gebeten in meinem Namen; 88: Siehe, ich will viel Fischer aussenden; 89: Was soll ich aus dir machen, Ephraim; 90: Es reisset euch ein schrecklich Ende.
(M)**(*) Hänssler CD 92.028 [id.]. Reichelt, Augér, Hamari, Gohl, Watts, Baldin, Kraus, Heldwein, Schöne, Huttenlocher, Nimsgern, Gächinger Kantorei, Bach-Collegium, Stuttgart, Rilling.

Cantatas Nos. 91: Gelobet seist du, Jesu Christ;

92: Ich habe in Gottes Herz und Sinn; 93: Wer nur den lieben Gott lässt walten.
(M)**(*) Hänssler CD 92.029 [id.]. Donath, Augér, Watts, Schreckenbach, Murray, Hamari, Baldin, Kraus, Huttenlocher, Heldwein, Schöne, Nimsgern, Gächinger Kantorei, Württemberg CO, Bach-Collegium, Stuttgart, Rilling.

Cantatas Nos. 94: Was frag, ich nach der Welt; 95: Christus, der ist mein Leben; 96: Herr Christ, der einge Gottessohn.
(M)**(*) Hänssler CD 92.030 [id.]. Donath, Augér, Paaske, Höffgen, Baldin, Kraus, Kunz, Heldwein, Schöne, Nimsgern, Gächinger Kantorei, Bach-Collegium, Stuttgart, Rilling.

Cantatas Nos. 97: In allen meinen Taten; 98: Was Gott tut, das ist wohlgetan; 99: Was Gott tut, Das ist wohlgetan.
(M) **(*) Hänssler CD 92.031 [id.]. Donath, Augér, Gardow, Hamari, Watts, Kraus, Harder, Heldwein, Huttenlocher, Bröcheler, Gächinger Kantorei, Bach-Collegium, Stuttgart, Rilling.

Cantatas Nos. 100: Was Gott tut, das ist wohlgetan; 101: Nimm von uns, Herr, du treuer Gott; 102: Herr, deine Augen schen nach, dem Glauben.
(M) **(*) Hänssler CD 92.032 [id.]. Augér, Hamari, Watts, Randova, Kraus, Baldin, Equiluz, Huttenlocher, Bröcheler, Schöne, Gächinger Kantorei, Bach-Collegium, Stuttgart, Rilling.

Cantatas Nos. 103: Ihr werdet weinen und heulen; 104: Du Hirte Israel, höre; 105: Herr, gehe nicht ins Gericht mit deinem Knecht.
(M) **(*) Hänssler CD 92.033 [id.]. Augér, Soffel, Watts, Schreier, Kraus, Heldwein, Schöne, Gächinger Kantorei, Bach-Collegium, Stuttgart, Rilling.

Cantatas Nos. 106: Gottes Zeist ist die allerbeste Zeit; 107: Was willst du dich betrüben; 108: Es ist euch gut, dass ich hingehe.
(M) **(*) Hänssler CD 92.034 [id.]. Csapo, Augér, Schwarz, Watkinson, Kraus, Baldin, Schreier, Schöne, Bröcheler, Huttenlocher, Gächinger Kantorei, Bach-Collegium, Stuttgart, Rilling.

Cantatas Nos. 109: Ich glaube, lieber, Herr; 110: Unser Mund sei voll Lachens; 111: Was mein Gott will, das gscheh allzeit.
(M) **(*) Hänssler CD 92.035 [id.]. Graf, Augér, Schreckenbach, Gardow, Watts, Equiluz, Baldin, Harder, Schöne, Huttenlocher, Gächinger Kantorei, Bach-Collegium, Stuttgart, Rilling.

Cantatas Nos. 112: Das Herr ist mein getreuer

Hirtl 113: Herr Jesu Christ, du höchstes Gut; 114: Ach, lieben Christen, seid Getrost.
(M) **(*) Hänssler CD 92.036 [id.]. Nielsen, Augér, Schnaut, Schreckenbach, Hamari, Baldin, Kraus, Equiluz, Heldwein, Tüller, Schöne, Gächinger Kantorei, Bach-Collegium, Stuttgart, Rilling.

Cantatas Nos. 115: Mache dich, mein Geist, bereit; 116: Du Friedefürst, Herr Jesu Christ; 117: Dei Lob 'und Ehr dem höchsten Gut.
(M) **(*) Hänssler CD 92.037 [id.]. Augér, Watts, Geor, Harder, Kraus, Schöne, Huttelocher, Schmidt, Gächinger Kantorei, Bach-Collegium, Stuttgart, Rilling.

Cantatas Nos. 119: Preise Jerusalem, Den Herrn; Gott, man lobet dich in der Stille; 121: Christum wir sollen loben schon.
(M) **(*) Hänssler CD 92.038 [id.]. Augér, Donath, Murray, Laurich, Soffel, Kraus, Schöne, Gächinger Kantorei, Bach-Collegium, Stuttgart, Rilling.

Cantatas Nos. 122: Das neugeborne Kinderlein; 123: Liebster Immanuel, Herzog der Frommen; 124: Meinen Jesum lass ich nicht; 125: Mit Fried und Freud ich fahr dahin.
(M) **(*) Hänssler CD 92.039 [id.]. Augér, Donath, Watts, Hoffgen, Kraus, Balden, Equiluz, Tüller, Huttenlocher, Schöne, Gächinger Kantorei, Bach-Collegium, Stuttgart, Rilling.

Cantatas Nos. 126: Erhalt uns, Herr, bei deinem Wort; 127: Herr Jesu Christ, wahr' Mensch und Gott; 128: Auf Christi Himmelfahrt allein; 129: Gelobet sei der Herr, mein Gott.
(M) **(*) Hänssler CD 92.040 [id.]. Augér, Watts, Schreckenbach, Kraus, Harder, Balden, Huttenlocher, Schöne, Gächinger Kantorei, Bach-Collegium, Stuttgart, Rilling.

Cantatas Nos. 130: Herr Gott, dich loben alle wir; 131: Aus der Tiefen rufe ich, Herr, zu dir; 132: Bereitet die Wege, bereitet die Bahn.
(M) **(*) Hänssler CD 92.041 [id.]. Graf, Augér, Schnaut, Watts, Kraus, Equiluz, Schöne, Gächinger Kantorei, Bach-Collegium, Stuttgart, Rilling.

Cantatas Nos. 133: Ich freue mich in dir; 134: Ein Herz, das seinen Jesum lebend weiss; 135: Ach Herr, mich armen Sünder.
(M) **(*) Hänssler CD 92.042 [id.]. Augér, Soffel, Watts, Baldin, Kraus, Huttenlocher, Gächinger Kantorei, Bach-Collegium, Stuttgart, Rilling.

Cantatas Nos. 136: Erforsche mich, Gott, und erfahre mein Herz; 137: Lobe den Herren, den mächtigen König der Ehren; 138: Warum betrübst di dich, mein Herz; 139: Wohl dem, der sich auf seinen Gott.

(M) **(*) Hänssler CD 92.043 [id.]. Augér,
Nielsen, Watts, Schreckenbach, Bollen,
Equiluz, Kraus, Baldin, Tüller, Huttenlocher,
Gächinger Kantorei, Bach-Collegium,
Stuttgart, Rilling.

*Cantatas Nos. 140: Wachet auf, ruft uns die
Stimme; 143: Lobe den Herrn, meine Seele; 144:
Nimm, was dein ist, und gehe him; 145: Ich lebe,
Mein Herze, zu deinem Ergötzen.*
(M) **(*) Hänssler CD 92.044 [id.]. Augér,
Cszapò, Cuccaro, Watts, Baldin, Kraus,
Huttenlocher, Schöne, Schmidt, Gächinger
Kantorei, Frankfurter Kantorei, Württemberg
CO; Bach-Collegium, Stuttgart, Rilling.

*Cantatas Nos. 146: Wir müssen durch viel
Trübsal; Herz und Mund und Tat und Leben.*
(M) **(*) Hänssler CD 92.045 [id.]. Augér,
Donath, Watts, Hoeffgen, Equiluz, Schöne,
Gächinger Kantorei, Frankfurter Kantorei,
Bach-Collegium, Stuttgart, Rilling.

*Cantatas Nos. 148: Bringet dem Herrn Ehre
seines Namens; 149: Man singet mit Freuden vom
Sieg; 150: Nach dir, Herr, verlanget mich; 151:
Süsser Trost, Mein Jesus kömmt.*
(M) **(*) Hänssler CD 92.046 [id.]. Augér,
Schreiber, Gamo-Yamamoto, Watts, Georg,
Jetter, Laurich, Equiluz, Baldin, Maus, Kraus,
Huttenlocher, Kunz, Gächinger Kantorei,
Frankfurter Kantorei, Bach-Collegium,
Stuttgart, Rilling.

*Cantatas Nos. 152: Tritt auf die Glaubensbahn;
153: Schau, lieber Gott, wie meine Feind; 154:
Mein Liebster Jesus ist verloren; 155: Mein Gott,
wie Lang ach lange.*
(M) **(*) Hänssler CD 92.047 [id.]. Augér,
Reichelt, Murray, Lerer, Kraus, Baldin,
Melzer, Schöne, Heldwein, Kunz, Gächinger
Kantorei, Bach-Collegium, Stuttgart, Rilling.

*Cantatas Nos. 156: Ich stehe mit einem Füss im
Grabe; 157: Ich lasse dich nicht, du segnest mich
denn; 158: Der Friede sei mit dir; 159: Sehet, wir
gehn hinauf gen Jerusalem.*
(M) **(*) Hänssler CD 92.048 [id.]. Laurich,
Hamari, Equiluz, Kraus, Baldin, Schöne,
Huttenlocher, Gächinger Kantorei, Figuralchor
der Gedächtniskirche, Bach-Collegium,
Stuttgart, Rilling.

*Cantatas Nos. 161: Komm, du susse Todesstunde;
162: Ach! ich sehe, itzt, da ich zur Hochzeit gehe;
163: Nur jedem das Seine; 164: Ihr, die ihr euch
von Christo nennet.*
(M) **(*) Hänssler CD 92.049 [id.]. Augér,
Wiens, Laurich, Rogers, Watts, Hamari,
Kraus, Equiluz, Harder, Schöne, Tüller,
Heldwein, Gächinger Kantorei, Frankfurter
Kantorei, Bach-Collegium, Stuttgart, Rilling.

We commented favourably on the first nineteen
CDs embracing *Cantatas 1–61*, plus a handful of
later discs of Helmut Rilling's Bach Cantata cycle
in our main volume, as a project to which readers
unresponsive to the sound world of period ensembles might turn. It emanates from the LP series
on which he embarked as long ago as 1969 and
which came to fruition in the early 1980s. They
were not always so easily available in Britain as
they were in the rest of Europe, and never enjoyed
the wide currency and *renommé* of the handsomely
produced cycle divided between Gustav Leonhardt
and Nikolaus Harnoncourt on Das Alte Werk
(Teldec), which in its LP format included miniature
scores from the *Neue Bach Gesamtausgabe*.

Rilling has the advantage of a wider range of solo
voices than the Teldec set and he uses female singers
rather than boys. Indeed, there are some twenty
different sopranos alone, among them the late-
lamented and much-loved Arleen Augér at her peak
in the period 1979–84, and two dozen mezzos and
contraltos including Marga Höffgen, Helen Watts
and Doris Soffel. Among the men are Peter Schreier,
Kurt Equiluz, who is frequently encountered in the
Leonhardt/Harnoncourt set, and Adalbert Kraus, a
Rilling regular, as well as Fischer-Dieskau in *Ich
habe genug* (BWV 82) (which he also recorded at
the beginning of his career with Karl Ristenpart and
then later with Karl Richter), as well as Siegmund
Nimsgern and Philippe Huttenlocher. Most of
Rilling's performances are with the Stuttgart
Gächinger Kantorei and the Stuttgart Bach-
Collegium, though on occasion he employs the
Württemberg Chamber Orchestra. As we indicated
in discussing earlier issues, the choral singing is
variable. It rarely falls below a certain standard but
at the same time seldom achieves real distinction.
Those wanting the warmer sonority of modern instruments will, of course, welcome this set, and
generally speaking, the instrumentalists are of high
quality. Rilling's treatment of recitative has
attracted some criticism and there are occasions
when he is a little rigid (albeit less so than Richter
can be). All in all, we have derived much satisfaction in either making or renewing our acquaintance
with this cycle, which will suit many readers in
search of a scholarly yet intelligently aware approach using a traditional sound world. It also has
the advantage of being complete – including some
cantatas omitted for various reasons from the Teldec
set. Documentation and transfers are eminently
satisfactory and so, too, is the price.

*Cantatas Nos. 208: Was mir behagt, ist nur die
muntre Jagd (Hunt cantata); 211: Schweigt stille,
plaudert nicht (Coffee cantata).*
(M)**(*) Hänssler Dig. CD 98.161 [id.]. Rubens,
Schäfer, Taylor, Quasthoff, Bach-Collegium,
Stuttgart, Rilling.

Cantatas Nos. 208: Was mir behagt, ist nur die

muntre Jagd (Hunt cantata); 209: Non sa che sia dolore
(M)**(*) Hänssler Dig. CD 92.065 [id.]. Rubens, Schäfer, Taylor, Quasthoff, Bach-Collegium, Stuttgart, Rilling.

Cantatas Nos. 210: O holder Tag, erwünschte Zeit (Wedding cantata); 211: Schweigt stille, plaudert nicht (Coffee cantata).
(M)**(*) Hänssler Dig. CD 92.066 [id.]. Rubens, Schäfer, Taylor, Quasthoff, Bach-Collegium, Stuttgart, Rilling.

Rilling recorded the *Hunt Cantata* (BWV 208) way back in 1965 with Helen Donath, Elizabeth Speiser and Jacob Stämfli. This newcomer with a distinguished line-up first appeared coupled with the *Coffee cantata* (BWV 211) at full price. It now reappears only three years later at mid-price. It is a lively, spirited account and he shares Thurston Dart's theory that the *First Brandenburg concerto's* opening movement was used as an opening sinfonia. Generally speaking these are serviceable accounts, more appropriately priced now than before, and should give pleasure. Sibylla Rubens gives a good account of herself in *Non sa che sia dolore,* and in the *Coffee cantata,* Christine Schäfer, James Taylor and Thomas Quasthoff do not disappoint. Not a first choice perhaps, but eminently dependable.

Complete cantatas Koopman Erato series

Volume VIII: *Cantatas Nos. 40; 46; 60; 64; 65; 77; 81; 83; 89; 89a; 90; 109; 167.*
*** Erato/Warner Dig. 3984 25488-2 (3) [id.]. Röschmann, Von Magnus, Bartosz, Dürmüller, Mertens, Amsterdam Bar. Ch. & O, Koopman.

This eighth volume in Ton Koopman's Bach survey with his Amsterdam Baroque forces brings twelve cantatas as well as the appendix to the *Cantata 89, Was soll ich aus dir machen, Ephraim?* Like its two immediate predecessors it is devoted to the first annual cycle of Leipzig cantatas from 1724–5. Generally speaking, these are instrumentally more polished and the choral singing more expert than the earlier issues in this series. Koopman still sticks to solo voices in the chorus of *Ich glaube, lieber Herr, hilf meinem* (BWV 109) but for the most part, the cantatas have the positive elements of earlier sets (light accents and well-ventilated textures) without too many of the negative ones (indifferent singing and all-too-brisk tempi). Of the soloists Dorothea Röschmann has a radiant and glorious quality that enhances the music's claims (try her in *Du sollst Gott, deinen Herren, lieben,* BWV 77. The recorded sound is of pleasing clarity.

Complete cantatas BIS Suzuki series

Cantatas Nos. 46: Schauet doch und sehet, ob irgendein Schmerz sei; 95: Christus, der ist mein Leben; 136: Erforsche mich, Gott, und erfahre mein Herz; 138: Warum betrübst du dich, Mein Herz.
*** BIS Dig. CD 991 [id.]. Midori Suzuki, Kai Wessel, Makoto Sakurada, Peter Kooy, Bach Collegium, Japan, Masaaki Suzuki.

Cantatas Nos. 105: Herr, gehe nicht ins Gericht mit deinem Knecht; 179: Siehe zu, dass deine Gottesfurcht nicht Heuchelei sei; 186: Arge dich, O Seele, nicht.
*** BIS Dig. CD 951 [id.]. Miah Persson, Robin Blaze, Makoto Sakurada, Peter Kooy, Bach Collegium, Japan, Masaaki Suzuki.

Masaaki Suzuki's survey of the Bach cantatas on BIS goes from strength to strength. It has the benefit of excellent soloists in Miah Persson, a Swedish soprano of real quality, and the tenor Makoto Sakurada. It seems invidious to single them out since both the counter-tenor, Robin Blaze, and Peter Kooy are hardly less impressive. *Herr, gehe nicht ins Gericht* (BWV 105) faces formidable competition but it more than withstands any comparison you might care to make. The balance does not place the soloists too far forward and the sound is as vivid, warm and clear as you could want.

Other cantata groupings

Cantatas Nos. (i) 6: Bleib' bei uns, denn es will Abend werden; (ii) 66: Erfreut euch, ihr Herzen.
*** DG 463 580-2 [id.]. (i) Bernarda Fink, Steve Davislim, Julian Clarkson; (ii) Michael Chance, Mark Padmore. Dietrich Henschel; Monteverdi Ch., Eng. Bar. Sol., Gardiner.

In 2000, the Bach year, John Eliot Gardiner, the Monteverdi Choir and English Baroque Soloists are performing Bach cantatas at various European venues on the ecclesiastically appropriate days of the year. Archive have abandoned their original plan to record all 198 cantatas which are being performed on this pilgrimage and have settled for a dozen. The present issue is the first, and brings the cantatas Bach composed for Easter Monday in 1724 (his first at Leipzig) and 1725 respectively. *Erfreut euch, ihr Herzen* (No. 66) is a re-working of a cantata written in 1719 for the birthday of Prince Leopold of Anhalt-Cöthen, but *Bleib' bei uns, denn es will Abend werden* was new and completely different in character. Generally impressive solo singing and eminently well-balanced recording. As always with Gardiner, the direction is crisp and cool, leaving some expressive depths unexplored, but this is an elegantly presented issue, though at 48 minutes, short on playing-time.

Cantatas for the Ascension, Advent, Christmas and Easter: (i) Ascension: *Nos. 11: Lobet Gott in seinen Reichen (Ascension oratorio); 43: Gott fähret auf mit Jauchzen; 44: Sie werden euch in*

den Bann tun; (ii) Advent: *Nos. 36: Schwingt freudig euch empor; 61: Nun komm, der Heiden Heiland; 62: Nun komm, der Heiden Heiland;* (iii) Christmas: *Nos. 57: Selig ist der Mann; 110: Unser Mund sei voll Lachens; 122: Das neugeborne Kindelein;* (iv) Easter: *No. 66: Erfreut euch, ihr Herzen; Easter oratorio, BWV 249.*
(M) ** HM Dig. HMX 2908070 (4) [id.]. (i; iv) Schlick, Patriasz, (i; ii) Prégardien; (i–iv) Kooy; (ii) Rubens; (ii; iii) Connolly; (iii) Jezovšek, Padmore; (iv) Wessel, Taylor; Ghent Collegium Vocale, Herreweghe.

On the whole, these are sympathetic and musical performances of well-chosen seasonal cantatas with good soloists, the only minor blot being the soprano and tenor duet in *Unser Mund sei voll Lachens,* where Vasiljka Jezovšek is insecure. However, generally the style of the music-making, although admirably refined, is a trifle wanting in the joy that this period of the Christian church calendar evokes. The account of the *Easter oratorio* is a different matter, as is its apt Easter cantata coupling, where both singers and players are very spirited and vividly recorded. Fortunately this disc is available separately (HMC 901513 – see our main volume).

Cantatas Nos. 28; 85; 90; 119; 140; 147.
(B) ** Erato/Warner Ultima 3984 28166-2 (2) [id.]. Friesenhausen, Lisken, Jelden, McDaniel, Scherler, Huber, Stämpfli, Wenk, Graf, Giebel, Hellman, Krebs, Heinrich Schütz Ch., Pforzheim CO, Fritz Werner.

Fritz Werner never had the same publicity machine behind him as Karl Richter in the 1960s, but between the late 1950s and early 1970s he recorded some sixty Bach cantatas for the Erato label. The present performances were recorded in 1963 (Nos. 90 & 147), 1965 (Nos. 28 & 119) and 1970 (Nos. 85 & 140), and serve as a reminder that the 1990s were not the sole arbiter of musical truth. Authenticity of feeling and humanity are every bit as important as period instruments. There are some distinguished solo contributions from Agnes Giebel and Helmut Krebs, particularly in BWV 147 (*In Herz und Mund und Tat und Leben*), and Georg Jelden, and some fine obbligato playing too from Maurice André in *Es reifet euch ein schrecklich Ende* (BWV 90). The Heinrich Schütz Chorale is not always as finely focused or vital as one would like but generally the set gives satisfaction. Werner is a stylist and this tells. The recordings are very good if not as wide ranging or as transparent in detail as modern sets.

Cantatas Nos. 35: Geist und Seele wird verwirret; 53: Schlage doch, gewünschte Stunde; 82: Ich habe genug.
(M) *** Harmonia Mundi Suite HMT 7901273 [id.]. René Jacobs, Ens. 415, Chiara Banchini.

Geist und Seele wird verwirret, BWV 35 comes

from 1726 and *Ich habe genug,* BWV 82 from the following year. Best known in its form for baritone and obbligato oboe, Bach reworked it in the 1730s, changing the key from C minor to E minor when he transcribed it for soprano, but reverting to C minor when he arranged it for a mezzo and replacing the oboe with a flute. The present performance uses an oboe, expertly played by Paul Dombrecht, and it finds the excellent René Jacobs in very good form. The playing of Ensemble 415 and Chiara Banchini is eminently spirited and stylish, and the opening concerto movement in *Geist und Seele wird verwirret* has a refreshing vigour. The fine one-movement *Schlage doch, gewünschte Stunde* BWV 53 – once attributed to Bach but now thought to be by Georg Melchior Hoffmann – is, as a result of its new attribution, scantily represented in the catalogue and is omitted from Rilling's survey on Hänssler. This enhances the claims of this excellently recorded mid-price issue, recorded in Saint-Martin-du-Mejan, Arles in 1987. Some find Jacobs's tone a little chilly but there is great intensity here.

Cantatas Nos. 35: Sinfonias (only); (i) 56: Ich will den Kreuzstab gerne tragen; 82: Ich habe genug; 158: Der Friede sei mit dir.
*** Decca Dig. 466 570-2 [id.]. (i) Matthias Goerne; Salzburg Bach Ch. & Camerata Academica, Norrington.

Matthias Goerne has so far concentrated on Schubert and Schumann, though he has taken part in some operatic projects – Braunfels's opera *Die Vögel* and Schreker's *Die Gezeichneten.* This is his first foray into Bach and very successful it is too. All three cantatas for bass are on the theme of death and the liberation it brings, and come from the same period, 1726–7. They were probably composed for the same singer. They are interspersed on this disc with two spirited instrumental sinfonias. As you would expect from a pupil of Fischer-Dieskau and Schwarzkopf, Goerne's feeling for and projection of words are impeccable and he invests both *Ich habe genug* and *Ich will den Kreuzstab* with great expressive eloquence. Norrington is sometimes given to exaggeration (some may find the pianissimo echo from the orchestra in Albrecht Mayer's wonderful oboe obbligato a little excessive) but for the most part he is supportive. The Decca balance places the voice rather close, perhaps to help the lower end of the register, but the sound is fresh and vivid. Impressive and satisfying accounts of these cantatas.

Cantatas Nos. 35: Geist und Seele wird verwirret; 169: Gott soll allein mein Herze haben; 170: Vergnügte Ruh', beliebte Seelenlust.
**(*) Finlandia/Warner Dig. 3984 25325-2 [id.]. Monica Groop, Ostrobothnian CO, Juha Kangas.

Monica Groop gives us three solo cantatas for alto (she herself is mezzo soprano), all dating from 1726. She is partnered by the Ostrobothnian Chamber Orchestra under Juha Kangas with the important organ obbligato parts played most expertly by Håkan Wikman. The orchestral playing is fresh and has a welcome liveliness, to which the recording engineer does justice. Ms Groop is in good voice though hers is commanding rather than moving singing. Not perhaps a first choice in these particular cantatas, though there is much that gives pleasure.

Cantatas Nos. 39: Brich dem Hungrigen dein Brot; 73: Herr, wie du willt, so schicks mit mir; 93: Wer nur den lieben Gott lässt walten; 105: Herr, gehe nicht ins Gericht mit deinem Knecht; 107: Was willst du dich Betrüben; 131: Aus der Tiefen rufe ich.
(B) **(*) Virgin/EMI Dig. VBD5 61721 (4).
    Barbara Schlick, Agnès Mellon, Gérard Lesne, Charles Brett, Peter Kooy, Ghent Collegium Vocale Ch. & O, Herreweghe – *Masses (Missae breves).* **(*)

These six cantatas seem to be quite arbitrarily chosen, but they are all among Bach's most rewarding works in this genre. With such a starry cast it is not surprising that the solo singing is of the very highest calibre, as is the instrumental playing (on period instruments), especially in the provision of obbligatos. The choral singing is stylishly sympathetic too, and these performances are all warmly enjoyable, with the single proviso that the resonant acoustic (as with the coupled *Missae breves*) takes the edge off the vocal projection and produces just a degree of blandness.

Cantatas Nos. 51: (i) *Jauchzet Gott in allen Landen* (complete); (ii) *68: Also hat Gott die Welt geliebt:* Aria: *Mein gläubiges Herz* (only); *199: Mein Herze schwimmt im Blut;* (iii) *202: Weichet nur, betrübte Schatten* (both complete); (ii) *208: Was mir behagt:* Recitative and Aria: *Schafe können sicher weiden* (only); (iv) STOLZEL, attrib. BACH: Aria: *Bist du bei mir.*
(M) (***) EMI mono CDH5 67206-2 [id.].
    Elisabeth Schwarzkopf, (i) Philh. O, cond. Peter Gellhorn; (ii) Thurston Dart; (iii) Concg. O, Klemperer; (iv) Gerald Moore.

EMI have gathered together a superb collection of Schwarzkopf's Bach recordings, made between 1946 (very fresh-toned in one of her first recordings with Walter Legge in Vienna from *Cantata No. 208* – the aria known in English as 'Sheep may safely graze') and 1958 (*Cantata No. 199*). The voice was consistently at its most radiant, though with a clear development revealed over those years. What is especially fascinating is the live recording which was taken from a performance of *Cantata No. 202* with Klemperer and the Concertgebouw, even more

vehement and characterful at generally faster speeds than in the more controlled studio recording made later the same year, 1957, and now issued on Testament. *Bist du bei mir*, long attributed to Bach, makes a delightful supplement, with Gerald Moore at the piano. Excellent transfers, though the Netherlands Radio recording with Klemperer is less full, if very atmospheric.

Cantatas Nos. 51: Jauchzet Gott in allen Landen; 82a: Ich habe genug; 84: Ich bin vergnügt mit meinem Glücke; 199: Mein Herze schwimmt im Blut; 202: Weichet nur (Wedding cantata); 209: Non sa che sia dolore.
(BB) *** Virgin Veritas 2 x 1 VBD5 61644-2 (2) [CDVB 61644]. Nancy Argenta, Ens. Sonnerie, Monica Huggett.

Here is an exceptional bargain. Nancy Argenta recorded these cantatas way back in the early 1990s and they have now been coupled on a two-CD set at super-budget price. Not only does she give us a radiantly brilliant account of *Jauchzet Gott in allen Landen*, one that belongs among the best, but also superb versions of both the *Wedding cantata* and *Non sa che sia dolore*. As is well known, Bach was particularly happy with *Ich habe genug* and scored it for other voices including soprano, transcribing the oboe obbligato for flute. Argenta's performance is arguably the finest we have in this form and in all six cantatas included in this package, the Ensemble Sonnerie and Monica Huggett give exemplary support. In every way a distinguished issue and not least in the quality of the recorded sound.

Cantatas Nos. 51: Jauchzet Gott in allen Landen (arr. W. F. Bach)*; 202: Weichet nur, betrübte Schatten; 210: O holder Tag, erwünschte Zeit.*
*** DG Dig. 459 621-2 [id.]. Christine Schäfer, Musica Antiqua Cologne, Goebel.

Christine Schäfer has made quite a name for herself in the last decade, not only in Rilling's Bach on the Hänssler label but in the Glyndebourne *Lulu*, and Hyperion's Schubert and Schumann song edition. Here in this handsomely presented volume, she couples two of Bach's wedding cantatas – *Weichet nur, betrübte Schatten* (BWV 202) and the less-frequently performed or recorded *O holder Tag, erwünschte Zeit* (BWV 210) – with the familiar *Jauchzet Gott in allen Landen*. Unusually this is given in Wilhelm Friedemann's arrangement which adds a second trumpet and timpani to Bach's trumpet, strings and continuo. In all three she is of radiant voice and delights us with her beauty of tone and virtuosity. Reinhard Goebel and his Musica Antiqua Cologne are spirited and vital, though there are times particularly in the closing *Alleluia* where the onward drive is somewhat unremitting. DG have provided one of their most expertly balanced recordings.

Cantatas Nos. 55: Ich armer Mensch, ich Sündenknecht; Meine seele rühmt und preist, BWV 189 (attrib. Georg Melchior Hoffmann); *Ich weiss, dass mein Erlöser lebt, BWV 160* (by Telemann); *Arias from Cantatas Nos. 5, 13, 26 and 102.*
*** Philips Dig. 442 786-2 [id.]. Peter Schreier, Kammerorchester Carl Philipp Emanuel Bach.

Peter Schreier, who directs from the larynx as it were, includes two tenor cantatas once numbered in the Bach canon but now attributed to others. *Meine seele rühmt und preist* is now thought to be by Georg Melchior Hoffmann (1679–1715), while *Ich weiss, dass mein Erlöser lebt* is now established as the work of Telemann. That leaves only one cantata (No. 55) for solo tenor as being *echt*-Bach. Schreier also includes solo arias from four other cantatas. The opening of the Telemann piece is particularly delectable and the whole work delights. Schreier sings and directs superbly, and the playing of the C. P. E. Bach Orchestra will give solace to readers with an aversion for period-instrument ensembles. Exemplary recording balance with plenty of warmth. The disc comes with excellent and authoritative notes from Malcolm Boyd.

Cantata Nos. 56: Ich will den Kreuzstab gerne tragen; 82: Ich habe genug.
(B) * Sony SBK 60373 [id.]. Max von Egmond, Koorschool St Bavo, Haarlem, Baroque O, Frans Brüggen.

These performances come from 1977 and offer some exemplary Bach singing from the splendid Max von Egmond. This originates from the Seon label and was also available for some time on RCA. However the recording is dryish and Frans Brüggen's direction is a shade ponderous. At less than 40 minutes this is not really competitive nowadays.

(i) *Cantatas Nos. 67: Halt'im Gedächtnis Jesum Christ; No. 130: Herr Gott, dich loben alle wir;* (ii; iii) *Masses (Missae breves): in F, BWV 233; in A, BWV 234;* (ii; iv) *in G min., BWV 235; in G, BWV 236.*
(B) **(*) Decca Double 466 754-2 (2) [id.]. (i) Ameling, Watts, Krenn, Krause, Lausanne Pro Arte Ch., OSR, Ansermet; (ii) Hickox Singers & O, Hickox; with (iii) Jenkins; (iii; iv) Eathorne, Esswood, Roberts; (iv) Langridge.

A rather arbitrary but tempting anthology. In Ansermet's accounts of *Cantatas Nos. 67* and *130*, the orchestra may not be the finest in the world (though the flute playing of André Pepin is certainly in that bracket), and they are hardly 'authentic' (though they are not particularly *Romantic* either), but there is plenty of character here. They are very well recorded, and offer much good singing. Hickox's mid 1970s performances bring more polished orchestral playing, fine singing and

excellent recording. *BWV 233* and *234* offer many beauties: the *A major Mass*, which draws on *Cantata 67* for its *Gloria*, is the more inspired, but it is hard to understand why all four of these works are relatively neglected. The two other *Masses, BWV 235* and BWV*236* are equally well performed, with the contribution of the choir shining out.

Cantatas Nos. 72: Alles nur nach Gottes Willen; 73: Herr, wie du willt, so schicks mit mir; 111: Was mein Gott will, das g'scheh allzeit; 156: Ich steh mit einem Fuss im Grabe.
*** DG Dig. 463 582-2 Joanne Lunn, Sara Mingardo, Julian Podger, Stephen Varcoe, E. Baroque Soloists, Monteverdi Ch., Gardiner.

For the third disc in his celebratory Bach cantata series, Gardiner has chosen four cantatas for the third Sunday after Epiphany. They would have been sung on a chilly morning immediately before the sermon, an hour into the service; in an intensely cold winter the choir was allowed to leave during the sermon! Bach, being a practical man, and conscious of the low temperature in the church, usually made his winter cantatas fairly short, so there is room for four on this CD.

From the very opening of No. 72, *Alles nur nach Gott Willen*, one is struck by the crisp lightness of the choral articulation which gives much pleasure, and one wonders if Bach was able to secure such clarity of enunciation from his own singers. The joyful opening chorus of No. 73, *Herr, wie du willt, so schicks mit mir* has a delightful oboe obbligato, and the oboe stays around to decorate the tenor aria which follows. BWV 111 begins with an even more impressive chorus, but here the double-dotting of the rhythm of the later contralto/tenor duet, for all the vitality it imparts, seems a bit exaggerated.

BWV 156 is perhaps the finest of the four, opening with a Sinfonia featuring a very beautifully played aria for solo oboe. The solo singing throughout is of a high standard, but refreshing as these performances are, one is less moved here than by the more expressive style found on Richter's older DG Archiv series, or indeed by Suzuki's period performances on BIS.

Cantatas Nos. 106: Gottes Zeit ist die allerbeste Zeit (Actus tragicus); 118: O Jesu Christ, meins Lebens Licht (2nd version); 198: Lass Fürstin, lass noch einen Strahl.
*** DG Dig. 463 581-2 [id.]. Argenta, Chance, Rolfe Johnson, Varcoe, Monteverdi Ch., E. Bar. Soloists, Gardiner.

Surprisingly, for this (second) instalment in the Gardiner Archiv series, DG have reissued a triptych first published a decade ago, in 1990, and still at full price. Nevertheless these are three of Bach's finest cantatas, all valedictory works. The performances are comparatively intimate. Indeed the whole record suggests a scale apt for a small chapel.

Cantatas Nos. 158: Der Friede sei mit dir; 203: Amore traditore. Arias and chorales: *Cantatas; Nos. 8: Aria: Doch weichet, ihr toilen; 13: Aria: Achzen und erbärmliche Weinen; Chorale: So sei nun Seele seine; 73: Aria: Herr, so du willt; 123: Recitative and aria: Kein Höllenfeind kann mich verschlingen . . . Lass, O Welt, mich aus Verachtung; 157: Aria: Ja, jan ich halte Jesum feste; Chorale: Meinen Jesum lass' ich nicht; 159: Aria: Es ist vollbracht; Chorale: Jesu, deine Passion is mir lauter Freunde.*

(M) *** EMI CDM5 67202-2. Dietrich Fischer-Dieskau, St Hedwig's Cathedral Ch., Schwalbé, Nicolet, Rampal, Koch, Poppen, Picht-Axenfeld, Veyron-Lacroix, BPO, Karl Forster.

An outstanding collection mostly from 1958 – it was first discussed in Volume II of our *Stereo Record Guide* – which has been out of the catalogue ever since. For its reissue EMI have added the secular cantata *Amore traditore* (with a nimble continuo provided by Irmgard Poppen and Edith Picht-Axenfeld), which dates from 1960, and the excerpts from Cantata No. 123, recorded a decade later. All in all, Fischer-Dieskau, in splendid voice (and looking very young in the 1958 sessions photograph), sings here two complete cantatas (No. 158 for the Feast of the Purification was included on the original LP), plus six individual arias, usually with accompanying chorale. Their range of pitch is wide, of emotion still wider, yet the great baritone proves time and time again that he is absolutely at home in this field. The choir and orchestra under Karl Forster give him excellent support and the list of obbligato soloists is full of star names: Aurèle Nicolet particularly fine in BWV 158 and Rampal no less impressive in the excerpt from BWV 123. The early stereo lends a convincingly spacious realism to what was already a finely balanced ensemble and the CD transfer is admirable. Full texts and translations are included.

Cantatas Nos. 199: Mein Herze schwimmt im Blut; 202: Weichet nur, Betrübte Schatten. Arias from *Cantatas Nos. 68; 208.*

*** Testament SBT 1178 [id.]. Elisabeth Schwarzkopf, Philh. O, Dart – MOZART: *Ch'io mi scordi di te?* (***)

Testament have here gathered together Schwarzkopf recordings made in 1955–8 that for various reasons were never published. Schwarzkopf and her husband, the great recording producer Walter Legge, were always hypercritical in assessing her performances but there were other, more likely reasons for non-issue, such as the absence of a suitable coupling or the possibility of a later recording. What is clear is the superb quality of the singing here, with Sidney Sutcliffe, the principal oboe of the Philharmonia, matching Schwarzkopf's

artistry in some of his obbligato solos. It is especially fascinating to compare the two versions (in German) of '*Sheep may safely graze*', recorded a year apart in 1957 and 1958 – the second one far more dramatic in the recitative, and generally more freely expressive. The version here of Cantata No. 199, recorded only two days before the one included on the EMI Références issue (see above), is also more romantically expressive at a rather broader speed, a change in the opposite direction. The poised Schwarzkopf predominates, but the vehement Schwarzkopf also repeatedly comes through vividly, directly reflecting the singer's strong, positive character. A wonderful bonus to Schwarzkopf's recorded legacy. Excellent transfers.

Christmas oratorio, BWV 248.

*** Decca 458 838-2 (2) [id.]. Catherine Bott, Michael Chance, Paul Agnew, Andrew King, Michael George, New L. Consort, Pickett.

Philip Pickett takes an intimate, relatively small-scale view of Bach's celebration of Christmas. Textures are transparent, and refinement is the keynote in the singing and playing of the Consort. Though that marks something of a contrast with the robust style of Pickett's performances of early music, this Bach performance too has plenty of vigour, with generally brisk speeds and sprung rhythms. The scale of performance is reflected in the refined singing of Paul Agnew as the Evangelist, but the soprano Catherine Bott, and the counter-tenor Michael Chance, are the soloists who stand out not just from the rest, but from most rivals in other versions. It is sad that Bach reserves the soprano just for the later cantatas. The tenor Andrew King is crisp and agile in his arias, and though Michael George is not as cleanly focused as he might be, his is a strong, sensitive contribution. Atmospheric recording, which sets the limited forces in a helpful acoustic. However, the joyful Gardiner DG version (with Rolfe Johnson and Anne Sofie von Otter (423 232-2)) and Suzuki's exceptionally fresh and alert version on BIS 941/2 marginally take pride of place over this newcomer.

Christmas oratorio: highlights.

(BB) ** Naxos Dig. 8.554508 [id.] (from complete recording with Kertesi, Nemeth, Mukk, Tóth, Hung. R. Ch., Failoni CO, Oberfrank).

This set of highlights comes from a 1992 recording on modern instruments (8.550428/30), where Oberfrank generally adopts the speeds and manner now associated with period instruments. Indeed, some of the conductor's speeds verge on the breathless. The excerpts include the famous opening chorus and a series of key arias and chorales. The recording is very good but exaggerates a slight unsteadiness in the soprano soloist Judith Nemeth. But this

71-minute selection is well managed and full translations are included.

(i) *Easter oratorio;* (ii) *Magnificat in D, BWV 243;* (i) *Cantata No. 4: Christ lag in Totesbanden;* (ii) *Cantata No. 11: Lobet Gott in seinen Reichen (Ascension cantata); Chorale: Nun ist das Heil und die Kraft* (from BWV 50).
(BB) ** Virgin Veritas 2 x 1 VBD5 61647-2 (2).
(i; ii) Van Evera, Trevor, Daniels, Kooy, Thomas; (ii) Kirkby, Tubb, Cable, Crook, Jochens, Charlesworth, Grant; Taverner Consort & Players, Parrott.

Both sets of performances here are on a small scale, as Andrew Parrott favours one voice to a part in choruses. The effect is undoubtedly refreshingly clear, for the singers are expert and the balance, even with Bach's exultant trumpets, is well managed. The solo singing is always good, often excellent, Caroline Trevor memorable in the alto solo *Esurientes implevit bonis* in the *Magnificat*. The instrumental support too is pleasingly fresh, with fine obbligato playing. But in the end the ear craves more weight. If one turns to Münchinger's splendid Stuttgart analogue Decca coupling of the *Easter oratorio* and *Magnificat* (466 420-2), there is a breadth and at times a spacious majesty altogether missing here.

Magnificat in D, BWV 243.
*** BIS Dig. CD 1011 [id.]. Miah Persson, Yukaria Nonoshita, Akira Tachikawa, Gerd Türk, Chiyuki Urano, Bach Collegium, Japan, Masaaki Suzuki – KUHNAU: *Magnificat in C;* ZELENKA: *Magnificats in C & D.* ***

Masaaki Suzuki's account of the *Magnificat* with his Japanese forces is quite exhilarating, and certainly among the most recommendable now available. He has good soloists, including the Swedish soprano Miah Persson and the German tenor Gerd Türk, as well as some impressive Japanese singers: the instrumental playing is of altogether outstanding quality. Ideal for those who don't now respond either to traditional modern-instrument performances or to authentic period orchestras, for Suzuki's players have the virtues of both: the warmth and vitality of the former and the clarity of the latter.

(i) *Masses (Missae breves): in F, BWV 233; in G, BWV 236. Trio sonata in C, transposed to D, BWV 529.*
*** Chandos Dig. CHAN 0653 [id.]. (i) Nancy Argenta, Michael Chance, Mark Padmore, Peter Harvey, Instrumental soloists; Purcell Qt.

Masses (Missae breves): in A, BWV 234; in G min., BWV 235.
*** Chandos Dig. CHAN 0642 [id.]. Susan Gritton, Robin Blaze, Mark Padmore, Peter Harvey, Purcell Qt.

There have been various fine modern-instrument

performances of these so-called Lutheran masses over the years, including Rilling's set below and those directed by Peter Schreier on Philips (438 873-2) praised in our main volume, as well as the fine earlier set under Hickox, now available within a generous and inexpensive Decca Double (see above). But these authentic period-instrument performances must now take pride of place.

Although the soloists provide the one-voice-to-a-part chorus, their voices blend so richly together that one is not conscious of any lack of body or contrast: indeed the effect is glorious, while in the F major work the vigorous trumpeting horns add to the joyfulness of the *Gloria* and *Cum Sancto Spiritu*. The solo singing is splendid, and the overall balance quite excellent. The first disc uses a *Trio sonata* to act as a kind of extended opening sinfonia, and very effectively too. This is the CD to try first, and you will surely want the other one also.

Masses (Missae breves): in F, BWV 233; in A, BWV 234; Kyrie eleison in F, BWV 233a.
(M)*** Hänssler CD 92.071 [id.]. Brown, Schäfer, Danz, Taylor, Quasthoff, Schöne, Gächinger Kantorei, Budapest Franz Liszt CO, Bach-Collegium, Stuttgart, Rilling.

Masses (Missae breves) in G min., BWV 235; in G, BWV 236; Sancti in C; D; G; D, BWV 237–8, 240–1; Christe eleison in G min., BWV 242; Credo in unum Deum, BWV 1081.
(M)*** Hänssler CD 92.072 [id.]. Oelze, Ziesak, Danz, Remmert, Prégardien, Quasthoff, Gächinger Kantorei, Bach-Collegium, Stuttgart, Rilling.

The masses on the first of the two Hänssler discs were recorded in the early 1990s and the *Kyrie in F,* BWV 233a in 1999. Similarly, on the second, the recording of the *G minor,* BWV 235 was made in 1992 and the remaining recordings in 1999. The Lutheran Mass as set by Buxtehude and his contemporaries consists only of a Kyrie and Gloria. These masses come from the late 1730s and in his 'Master Musician' study Malcolm Boyd notes their structural similarity but 'when and why Bach composed them are questions which remain unanswered'. They are parody masses, all drawing on Leipzig cantata movements from 1723–6. These are eminently well-recorded (and recommendable) accounts with fine singing from Christine Oelze and Christoph Prégardien.

Masses (Missae breves) in F; A; G min.; G, BWV 233–6; Sanctus in D, BWV 238.
(M) **(*) Virgin/EMI Dig. VBD5 61721 (4) [id.]. Agnès Mellon, Gérard Lesne, Howard Crook, Christoph Prégardien, Peter Kooy, Ghent Collegium Vocale Ch. & O, Herreweghe – *Cantatas 39; 73; 93; 105; 107; 131.* **(*)

Herreweghe's recordings of these four *Missae*

breves were originally issued as two separate CDs; they are now rather arbitrarily grouped with six cantatas (admirably sung), in a four-CD boxed set. The performances are authentic, quite spirited and certainly stylish. The snag – both here, and in the coupled cantatas – is the very resonant ecclesiastical acoustic, which while it provides a smooth freedom from period-instrument abrasiveness, also takes some of the edge off the choruses and detracts from the presence of the soloists. Even so the performances are warmly enjoyable.

Mass in B min., BWV 232 (i) (complete); (ii) (excerpts).
(M) (***) EMI mono CHS5 67207-2 (2) [id.]. (i) Schwarzkopf, Höffgen, Gedda, Rehfuss, V. Singverein, Philh. O, Karajan; (ii) Schwarzkopf, Ferrier, VSO, Karajan.

Karajan's 1952 recording of the *B minor Mass* was a pioneering set, and the freshness and clarity of the mono sound are astonishing in this excellent EMI transfer. It may seem odd that while the solo numbers were recorded in London, the choruses were recorded in Vienna with the Singverein Chorus and the Musikfreunde Orchestra. At the time, Walter Legge felt that there was no appropriate choir available in London, and the discrepancy of sound is hardly noticeable, if at all. With Schwarzkopf at her most radiant, the quartet of soloists, then still young, stands comparison with any rival since, and though characteristically for the time Karajan adopts a broad speed for the great opening *Kyrie*, the performance is the more remarkable for its period in the briskness and clarity in choruses like the *Gloria*, with the *Sanctus* exhilarating in its combination of freshness and weight, leading to a light, crisp *Osanna*.

The five fragmentary excerpts that come as a supplement, recorded at a rehearsal in 1950, are valuable not only because of Kathleen Ferrier's contribution alongside Schwarzkopf, but as a sample of the experimental work that was being promoted by the great engineer Anthony Griffith, but sadly not followed up till much later. Karajan's speeds in that 1950 rehearsal are a degree faster than in the studio recording of two years later.

Mass in B min., BWV 232.
(M) ** DG Double 459 460-2 (2) [id.]. Janowitz, Ludwig, Schreier, Kerns, Ridderbusch, V. Singverein, BPO, Karajan.
(M) *(*) RCA 09026 63529-2 (2) [id.]. Endich, Addison, Kopleff, Walker, Berberian, Robert Shaw Ch. and O, Shaw.

Unlike his earlier EMI set (see above), Karajan's 1974 performance is marked by his characteristic smoothness of Bach style – he conveys intensity, even religious fervour, but the sharp contours of Bach's majestic writing are often missing. The very opening brings an impressive first entry of the choir

on *Kyrie*, but then after the instrumental fugue the contrapuntal entries are sung in a self-consciously softened tone. But there is a strong sense of the work's architecture, and the highly polished surfaces do not obscure the depths of this music. The recording remains warm and rich in this latest, inexpensive CD transfer.

When released in 1960, this RCA version was a pioneering set at the cutting edge of authentic performance: a complement of five soloists, a small chorus and orchestra – quite different from the vast battery of musicians which was then the norm. Indeed, this set, which has not been available for years, has something of a cult following – even being issued on an unauthorized disc of highlights on Melodiya in the old USSR. From a modern point of view, it seems a dated approach to the score, though not with any interpretative extremes, except in its slow tempi, which will seem laboured for most listeners. However, it is well sung and played, the music unfolds naturally and, taken on its own terms, is acceptable. The most remarkable thing about this set is the recording: it is astonishingly full and vivid, with all the strands of the soloists, chorus and orchestra heard with amazing clarity – very authentic.

St John Passion, BWV 245.
(BB) ** Arte Nova Dig. 74321 67251-2 (2) [id.]. Helen Kwon, Ursula Ettinger, Lothar Odinius, Wolfgang Mowerla, Peter Lika, Europa ChorAkademie Bach Ens. Ch. & O, Joshard Daus.

Though the dramatic turba choruses are freshly done, recitatives are well paced and the women soloists are first rate, Joshard Daus as a Bach interpreter leans too far towards the ponderous old German tradition in chorales and big choruses. That is so even though the choir and orchestra are modest in size. Helen Kwon is outstanding among the soloists, unfazed by the slow speed for her first aria, *Ich folge dir*. Lothar Odinius is a fresh-toned Evangelist, untroubled by high tessitura, though he is ungainly in the first tenor aria. It does not help that the chorus is rather backwardly balanced. The two-for-the-price-of-one packages of Rotzsch on RCA Twofer (74321 49181-2), Jochum on Philips Duo (462 173-2) and, finest of all, Britten (in English) on a Decca Double (● 443 859-2) are far preferable bargain issues (see our main volume).

St Matthew Passion, BWV 244.
*** BIS Dig. CD 1000/1002 (3) [id.]. Gerd Türk, Peter Kooy, Nancy Argenta, Robin Blaze, Makoto Sakurada, Chiyuki Urano, Kirsten Sollek-Avella, Jun Hagiwara, Tetsuya Odagawa, Bach Collegium Japan Ch. & O, Masaaki Suzuki.
**(*) HM Dig. HMC 951676.68 (3) [id.]. Ian Bostridge, Franz-Josef Selig, Sibylla Rubens,

Andreas Scholl, Werner Güra, Dietrich Henschel, Schola Cantorum Cantate Domino, Ghent Coll. Vocale Ch. & O, Herreweghe.

Masaaki Suzuki follows up his outstanding Bach Collegium recordings with a fresh and beautifully sung reading of the most challenging of all Bach choral works. The light, crisp qualities which have shone from his previous recordings are present here too, with the choir bright and resilient, and with an outstanding team of soloists led by the free-toned Gerd Türk as the Evangelist, and with Nancy Argenta outstanding among the others. If the result is a little short on devotional intensity in the culminating sections of the work, that is partly the result of the rather close-up recording, with solo voices and orchestra not always cleanly separated. More seriously, the double choir in the great double-choruses at the beginning and end is more backwardly balanced than elsewhere, set behind the orchestra, so that the dramatic impact is lessened. Nonetheless, this remains a powerful achievement. Although the Gardiner recording (DG 427 648-2) will remain a first choice for many collectors, this is still a splendid alternative – a set to recommend to those who have been following this inspired Bach interpreter.

Herreweghe made his first recording of the St Matthew Passion in 1985, a fresh, eager performance with many fine solo contributions. This later version offers more-polished contributions from chorus and orchestra, a degree smaller in scale than before, and again the line-up of mainly young soloists is an impressive one. The set is well-worth hearing for the inspired singing of Ian Bostridge as the Evangelist, headily beautiful and finely detailed. Andreas Scholl too is superb in the alto numbers, singing with sensuously beautiful tone, not least in Erbarme dich. Werner Güra projects the tenor arias with clear, fresh tone, and the others follow a similar pattern of youthful freshness. It is a fine reading, beautifully paced, but those who are particularly fond of Herreweghe's earlier version may well feel that here polish and perfection have not been matched by spiritual intensity. The Harmonia Mundi set comes with an extra CD-ROM disc which helpfully provides a survey of the life of Bach and the background to the Passion linking it with musical excerpts.

Arrangements: Bach–Reger

(i) Orchestral suite No. 2 in B min. for flute and strings (with continuo by Max Reger); Bach–Reger suite in G min. (selected and arr. Reger); Aria: O Mensch, bewein dein Sünde gross.
*** MDG Dig. 321 0940-2 [id.]. Stuttgart CO, Dennis Russell Davies; (i) with Jean-Claude Gérard.

A fascinating collection. Reger stated that Bach 'is

the beginning and end of all music; all true progress is founded and rests on him'. So these arrangements are nothing if not respectful and the Aria (for strings) is very serious in its expansive serenity and certainly beautiful. Throughout there is a nineteenth-century amplitude. The Bach–Reger suite in G minor, which is made up of movements from the keyboard Partitas and English suites, is scored very like a typical set of Reger variations: the Courante which features oboe, flute and bassoon, may be anachronistic, but is very felicitous. The Stuttgart Orchestra plays very sympathetically (as does the excellent, nimble flautist) and Dennis Russell Davies seeks a performing style which Reger would have recognized. Excellent recording.

Arrangements: Bach–Stokowski and Bach–Ormandy

Arr. Stokowski: (i) Brandenburg concerto No. 5, BWV 1050; Chorale preludes: Ich ruf' zu dir, Herr Jesu Christ, BWV 177; Nun komm, der Heiden Heiland, BWV 62; Wir glauben all'einen Gott, BWV 437. Arr. Ormandy: (ii) Chorale: Wachet auf, ruft uns die Stimme, BWV 140; Passacaglia and fugue in C min., BWV 582; Toccata, adagio and fugue in C, BWV 564; Toccata and fugue in D min., BWV 565.
** Sony Heritage MH2K 62345 (2) [id.]. Phd. O, (i) Stokowski; (ii) Ormandy (with C. P. E. BACH: Concerto for orchestra (arr. Steinberg) **; J. C. BACH: 2 Sinfonias for double orchestra, Op. 18/1 & 3 *(*); W. F. BACH: Sinfonia in D min., F 65 **).

Stokowski's version of the Fifth Brandenburg is surprisingly restrained and detail comes through well. The three Chorale preludes are warmly expressive without emotional hyperbole. On the other hand, although Ormandy's arrangement and performance of the famous Toccata and fugue in D minor are not far removed from Stokowski's, his Toccata, Adagio and fugue is so flamboyant and freely romanticized, that not a great deal of Bach remains. The Passacaglia and fugue in C minor is very weightily done indeed, but with refined woodwind playing to provide contrast. It reaches a very powerful climax, but the full-blooded orchestration seems less apt than with a Stokowski arrangement. The outer movement allegros of the paired J. C. Bach Sinfonias are also rather heavy-going; the slow movements are more successful, as is the work by Wilhelm Friedemann, and Maximilian Steinberg's arrangement of C. P. E Bach, which has a delicately played central Andante. The Stokowski sound is first class, the Ormandy recordings are full-blooded and beefier. The pair of discs is handsomely presented, but the notes are primarily biographical, relating to the conductors rather than Bach.

Bach, Wilhelm Friedemann
(1710–84)

*Fantasias in C min., F2; A min., F23; 12
Polonaises, F12.*
** CPO Dig. CPO 999 501-2 [id.]. Harald Hoeren
(fortepiano).

Christophe Rousset (on the harpsichord) makes a
good deal more of the *C minor Fantasia* (HMA
1901305 – see our main volume) than Harald
Hoeren, who is more impressive in the A minor
work. That is perhaps the best thing on the disc
except for the *E minor Polonaise* (No. 10) which
is quite touchingly done. The E flat minor piece
(No. 8) is also thoughtfully presented. Otherwise
Hoeren dispatches these works directly and cleanly
without trying to make too much of them. They are
interesting in that apart from their metre they have
virtually nothing about their character to suggest
the Polish dance form. Good recording.

Bainton, Edgar (1880–1956)

Symphony No. 2 in D min.
*** Chandos Dig. CHAN 9757 [id.]. BBC PO,
Vernon Handley – CLIFFORD: *Symphony;*
GOUGH: *Serenade.* ***

Edgar Bainton was born in London and was a pupil
of Stanford. He taught at the conservatory at Newcastle upon Tyne, of which he became Principal in
1912. In 1934 he became director of the New South
Wales Conservatory in Sydney where he remained
until the end of his life. The *Symphony No. 2* is
exactly contemporaneous with the Hubert Clifford
work with which it is coupled. It is in one movement
but falls into a dozen or so short sections, all played
without a break. Its outlook is overtly romantic but
whereas Clifford's music has a stronger affinity
with, say, Bliss or Walton, Bainton is closer to
Arnold Bax. He certainly knows how to score and
although this symphony is uneven in quality of
ideas, there is a lot of it that is both inventive
and rewarding. A worthwhile and enterprising issue
with first-rate playing from the BBC Philharmonic
under Handley and excellent recording.

Miniature suite (for 2 pianos).
*** Olympia Dig. OCD 683 [id.]. Goldstone and
Clement – HOLST: *The Planets* (original
version); *Cotswolds Symphony: Elegy.* ELGAR:
Serenade in E min. *** (with BURY: *Prelude
and fugue in E flat* ***).

Edgar Bainton, Holst's contemporary and admirer,
wrote the first appreciative press review of Holst's
music in the London *Musical Opinion* in 1911. He
was a gifted composer himself, and his music is
now totally neglected, so it was a happy idea to
offer his charming *Miniature suite* as a coupling for

Holst's masterpiece. It is played and recorded most
persuasively. Frank Bury's *Prelude and fugue* is
equally well crafted, and makes an apt and enjoyable bonus. Bury's career was cut sadly short when
as a commando he was killed during the Battle of
Normandy in 1944.

Barber, Samuel (1910–81)

Adagio for strings, Op. 11.
(M) **(*) Penguin Classics Decca Dig. 460 656-2
[id.]. Baltimore SO, Zinman – BERNSTEIN:
Candide overture; West Side story dances
**(*); COPLAND: *Appalachian spring;
Fanfare.* ***

Zinman's account of the Barber *Adagio* is beautifully played, and richly and atmospherically
recorded, but the level of tension is not very high
and the effect is elegiac rather than passionate.

(i) *Adagio for strings; 2nd Essay for orchestra,
Op. 17; Medea's meditation and Dance of
vengeance, Op. 23a; The School for Scandal
Overture;* (ii) *Vanessa: Intermezzo;* (i; iii)
Andromache's farewell, Op. 39.
*** Sony Heritage MHK 62837 [id.]. (i) NYPO,
Schippers; (ii) Columbia SO, Schippers; (iii)
with Martina Arroyo (with (ii) MENOTTI:
Overture: Amelia al ballo; BERG: *Wozzeck:
Interlude;* D'INDY: *Fervaal: Introduction* ***).

This appealingly packaged Heritage reissue celebrates the work of the fine American conductor
Thomas Schippers, who died prematurely at the age
of forty-seven. It also makes an excellent Barber
anthology, with the New York Philharmonic
recordings originally compiled for the composer's
seventieth birthday. The programme features some
of his instantly memorable works, not only the
famous *Adagio* but other short orchestral pieces
including the catchy *School for Scandal overture.*
The original LP offered *Dover Beach,* but here
instead we are offered *Andromache's farewell,* with
text taken from Euripides' *The Trojan Women,* a
superb vehicle for Martina Arroyo at her finest. The
new transfers greatly improve on the old LPs, the
sound now full and atmospheric. Then, after
Menotti's buoyantly vivacious *Amelia al ballo
overture,* the pungency of Berg's *Wozzeck Interlude*
brings one up short, but balm follows with the
beautiful closing *Fervaal Introduction* of Vincent
d'Indy. Not surprisingly the documentation concentrates on Schippers's career but the music itself is
not neglected.

Violin concerto, Op. 14
*** Sony Dig. SK 89029 [id.]. Hilary Hahn,
St Paul CO, Hugh Wolff – MEYER: *Violin
concerto.* ***

Hilary Hahn, still only nineteen when she made this

recording, plays with characteristically sweet tone, immaculate technique and lyrical flair. She gives an outstanding performance of the Barber *Concerto*, at once romantic and thoughtful, bringing out heartfelt emotion without overplaying it. This is a work which has increasingly inspired fine recordings, and this one is distinctive both in using a chamber orchestra, making up in clarity for any loss of weight, and in offering the most unusual coupling, a warmly approachable work specially written for Hahn by the double-bass player and composer Edgar Meyer. The close balance for the soloist does not allow a genuine pianissimo, but otherwise this stands among the finest of all versions.

Symphonies Nos. 1, Op. 9; 2, Op. 19; Essay for orchestra No. 1; Overture: The School for Scandal, Op. 5.
✪ (BB) *** Naxos 8.559024 [id.]. RSNO, Marin Alsop.

As we have said in our Foreword, Marin Alsop is a shooting star in the firmament of international conductors. Before beginning this Naxos project to record all Barber's orchestral works, she had already made outstanding CDs of music by American contemporary composers, Christopher Rouse and Joan Tower (see below). Her performances of these two Barber symphonies are electrifying, while in the mellower *School for Scandal overture* with its endearing secondary theme, she creates a fizzing orchestral virtuosity yet shows a marvellous ear for detail, after the manner of her mentor, Leonard Bernstein.

The two symphonies are played with passionate commitment by the Scottish Orchestra and one can only wonder at their degree of excellence of ensemble in bravura writing with which they cannot have been familiar before coming under the spell of the Alsop baton. Their playing has great intensity and deep lyrical feeling. The account of the complete *Second Symphony* will surely confirm the reputation of a wartime work which the composer partly withdrew in despondency after its neglect. The *First Essay for orchestra* also generates a powerful atmosphere when played with such depth of feeling. With superbly spectacular recording this exciting collection is very strongly recommended, and especially to those who know little of this composer but his (justly) famous *Adagio for strings*.

Summer music.
(BB) **(*) Naxos Dig. 8.553851-2 [id.]. Michael Thompson Wind Quintet – HINDEMITH: *Kleine kammermusik* **(*); JANACEK: *Mládí* **(*); LARSSON: *Quattro tempi* **.

Barber's haunting *Summer music* is eminently well represented on CD but not at bargain price. The Michael Thompson Wind Quintet offer it with an enterprising choice of coupling, and give an ex-

pressive account. The recording has exemplary clarity, though the balance places the artists (and in particular the bassoon) rather too close to the microphone. The playing is wonderfully accomplished and sensitive but the balance does rob it of atmosphere.

Bartók, Béla (1881–1945)

Concerto for orchestra.
✪ (M) (***) Dutton Lab. mono CDK 1206 [id.]. Concg. O, Eduard van Beinum – STRAVINSKY: *The Rite of spring* (***).
(M) *(*) RCA High Performance 09026 63309-2 [id.]. Boston SO, Leinsdorf – KODALY: *Peacock variations* **.

Eduard van Beinum's recording with the incomparable Concertgebouw Orchestra of the Bartók *Concerto for orchestra* was for many collectors their entry into its world. Not having heard it since the early 1950s, it is astonishing how vivid is the work's impact. We have not been short of virtuoso performances of this wonderful score from Karajan, Solti, Haitink and others but in this account, virtuosity is just one component and does not draw attention to itself. Bartók's vision springs to life in an extraordinarily fresh way. If you feel a little tired of this piece, listen to van Beinum, for he renews one's enthusiasm for this score as do few others. The sound is quite astonishing in detail and sonority.

Leinsdorf's *Concerto for orchestra* returns freshly remastered on RCA's High Performance label, but still has little to recommend it. The orchestra plays well, often brilliantly, but there are moments of dullness, despite the sometimes driven quality of the orchestral response. There is none of the intensity and magic of Reiner's classic account, also on RCA – recorded earlier, but sounding even better (RCA 09026 61504-2).

Concerto for orchestra; Divertimento for strings.
*** BMG/Conifer Classics Dig 75605 51324-2 [id.]. RPO, Daniele Gatti.

Daniele Gatti's account of the *Concerto for orchestra* belongs up there with the best. It was generally underrated on its first appearance two years ago but the positive impression it made then has only grown. The orchestral playing is first class and Gatti gets phrasing of great imagination and subtlety of colouring. The central music has great atmosphere and sense of mystery, and the performance grips you from start to finish. There are many superb performances of this work (Reiner, Solti, Rattle, etc.) but none is better recorded than this beautifully realistic and finely balanced disc. The *Divertimento* is hardly less successful. Warmly recommended.

Concerto for orchestra; (i) The Miraculous Mandarin (complete ballet).

(BB) **(*) Virgin Classics 2 x 1 Dig. VBD5 61754-2 (2) [CDVB 61754]. (i) Dumont Singers; Melbourne SO, Iwaki – STRAVINSKY: *Agon; Petrushka* **(*).

Iwaki and the Melbourne Orchestra have an obvious advantage in presenting the complete *Miraculous Mandarin* ballet, not just the suite, as coupling for the *Concerto for orchestra*. The recording is excellent, spacious and full and the playing is finely pointed, but is often too well mannered for Bartók, lacking something in fierceness and excitement. However, not all listeners will find that a drawback and the ballet is generously cued. The coupling includes Stravinsky's rare *Agon* plus a vividly enjoyable account of *Petrushka*, so this is excellent value in its latest two-for-one format.

(i) *Piano concertos Nos. 1–2;* (ii) *2 Portraits, Op. 5.*
(M) *** DG Dig. 457 909-2 [id.]. (i) Pollini, Chicago SO; (ii) Minz, LSO; Abbado.

This DG concerto coupling celebrates an exuberant partnership between two of the most distinguished Italian musicians of the day. Virtuosity goes with a sense of spontaneity. Rhythms in fast movements are freely and infectiously sprung to bring out the bluff Bartókian high spirits. The vividly recorded Chicago Orchestra is in superb form and the CD transfer gives a new lease of life to the 1979 recording. The ear is then sweetened by Minz's warmth in the *Portraits*. This is an excellent recommendation in its own right, but most collectors will want all three piano concertos, for which they should turn to Schiff (Teldec 0630 13158-2), Kocsis (Philips 446 366-2) or, at mid-price, Anda (DG 447 399-2) or Ashkenazy (Decca 448 125-2). These alternatives are all discussed in our main volume.

Violin concertos Nos 1–2.
(BB) *** Naxos Dig. 8.554321 [id.]. György Pauk, Nat. Polish RSO (Katowice), Antoni Wit.

György Pauk is one of the most experienced interpreters of the Bartók *Violin concerto No. 2* and there are few violinists now before the public that bring a deeper understanding or greater authority to it. He plays both concertos with exemplary musicianship and is given very good support by the Polish National Radio Orchestra at Katowice. No one investing in this coupling need feel disappointed and the sound has great warmth and naturalness. A reminder, though, that Stern (Sony SMK 64502), and Kyung-Wha Chung with the Chicago Orchestra under Solti on Decca (425 015-2), are similarly coupled, at mid-price, and that there are other recordings of the individual concertos which are equally competitive. Though not a first choice, this offers value for money and gives musical satisfaction.

Divertimento for strings.
◉ *** Chandos Dig. CHAN 9816 [id.].

Norwegian CO, Iona Brown – JANACEK: *Idyll; Suite for strings.* *** ◉

Iona Brown continues her splendid series of key nineteenth- and twentieth-century string works with an arrestingly vibrant account of a piece that can sound dour, but here is life-enhancing. The first movement bounces in with superb rhythmic bite, while the atmospheric *Molto adagio* brings a haunting sense of desolation, without being itself desolate. The concentration of the playing is matched in the vigorous finale, which resolves tensions with its surge of more genial gypsy vigour, though the solo violin tells us not to take anything for granted. With playing of virtuosity and warmth, and demonstration-standard sound of great presence, this is unbeatable.

(i) *The Miraculous Mandarin* (complete ballet); *Divertimento for string orchestra;* (ii) *Sonata for 2 pianos and percussion.*
(M) *** Mercury 434 362-2 [id.]. (i) BBC SO (with BBC chorus); (ii) Geza Frid and Luctor Pons, LSO members; Antal Dorati.

The Miraculous Mandarin was always one of Dorati's favourite concert pieces and during his régime at the BBC in the early 1960s, he directed the orchestra in the ballet suite many times. Here he gives the complete score (at the time comparatively rare on record). The performance is as brilliant as anyone could want and the coupled *Divertimento*, apart from a perhaps too steady account of the finale, is interpreted with similar red-blooded Hungarian passion. The 1964 Mercury recording sounds marvellously full and vivid, not in the least dated. Whatever Dorati did not do for the BBC Orchestra, he certainly taught them to play Bartók with an idiomatic accent. The coupled account of the *Sonata for two pianos and percussion* is comparably red-blooded, and certainly spontaneous, if not as subtle as some in the central movement (partly the fault of the forward balance and the degree of resonance), but the boisterous finale has wit as well as bravura.

The Miraculous Mandarin (ballet suite).
(M) *** RCA High Performance 09026 63315-2 [id]. Chicago SO, Jean Martinon – HINDEMITH: *Nobilissima visione*; VARESE: *Arcana.* ***

Martinon's *Miraculous Mandarin* is brilliantly played, with this conductor's natural elegance giving the quieter passages of the score a chilling beauty, which is often quite haunting. The intelligent couplings are also recommendable and the recording, though it could be richer, certainly sounds better than it did on LP.

CHAMBER MUSIC

Contrasts for clarinet, violin and piano.
*** EMI Dig. CDC5 56816-2 [id.]. Michael

Collins, Chantal Juillet, Martha Argerich –
LISZT: *Concerto pathétique;* PROKOFIEV:
Quintet. *******

Like the companion pieces on this CD, this performance comes from live concerts at the Saratoga Arts
in 1998. The distinguished trio give as fine an account of Bartók's *Contrasts* as you are ever likely
to encounter on or off record. There have been many
good versions since Szigeti, Benny Goodman and
Bartók himself committed it to disc, but this must
be a first choice among them.

Rhapsody No. 1; Rumanian folk dances.
(*) Decca Dig. 455 488-2 (2) [id.]. Ida Haendel,
Vladimir Ashkenazy – ENESCU: *Violin sonata
No. 3;* SZYMANOWSKI: *Mythes.***(*);** with
Recital: '*The Decca years, 1940–1947*' (***).

Ida Haendel made these recordings when she was
in her seventies, and very remarkable they are too.
This is playing of the old, humane school, not being
afraid to phrase generously or of sounding old-
fashioned. Unusually, Vladimir Ashkenazy is rather
perfunctory in matters of dynamic nuance, as comparison with Haendel in the earlier recording of
the *Rumanian dances* will show (see the Recital
coupling).

These earlier discs are of much interest and include a rare partnership with Noel Mewton-Wood in
the Beethoven *G major Sonata*. Haendel's musical
personality is such that no readers should overlook
this issue, particularly in view of the companion
disc which brings some of the records she made
for Decca during and just after the war, expertly
restored in these transfers.

PIANO MUSIC

*3 Burlesques, Op. 8c; 7 Esquisses, Op. 9b; 10
Easy Pieces; 15 Hungarian Peasant Dances;
Improvisations on Hungarian Peasant Songs,
Op. 20.*
● ******* Ph. Dig./Analogue 462 902-2 [id.]. Zoltán
Kocsis.

Bartók playing doesn't come any better than this –
nor does piano recording. Some of these performances derive from a 1982 LP to which we accorded
a ●, and the performances have not lost an ounce
of their authority or subtlety with the passage of
years. It would be difficult to surpass the recordings:
the analogue piano sound still remains to our ears
state-of-the-art, and the 1998 recordings, the *Burlesques* and *Ten Easy Pieces*, match them perfectly.
A most satisfying issue.

*15 Hungarian peasant songs; 9 Little pieces; Out
of doors; Rumanian Christmas carols; Rumanian
folk dances; Sonata; Sonatina.*
** Chandos Dig. CHAN 9761 [id.]. Geoffrey
Tozer.

Far from negligible playing by Geoffrey Tozer and

very good recorded sound from the Chandos team.
Tozer has a very capable technique but his playing
offers prose rather than poetry and does not rivet
the listener's attention in the same way as does
Zoltán Kocsis on Philips, although his two companion Philips discs (● 434 104-2) and 442 016-2
bring different selections and do not include the
Sonata – see our main volume.

OPERA

Duke Bluebeard's Castle
(**(*)) Bluebell mono ABCD 075 [id.]. Birgit
Nilsson, Bernhard Sönnerstedt, Swedish Radio
O, Ferenc Fricsay – SCHIERBECK: *The Chinese
flute* (**(*)).

Bluebell offer a CD taken from a Swedish Radio
broadcast from 1953 with Nilsson, just poised to
make her name abroad, and Bernhard Sönnerstedt,
a wonderful baritone who never sought an international career – though he broadcast in Britain and
made some fine records in the late 1940s and early
1950s. Fricsay casts a powerful spell and gets wonderfully eloquent results. There are some cuts which
would rule it out of court were it not for the powerfully distilled and extraordinary atmosphere that
Fricsay evokes, and the superlative quality of both
soloists.

(i) *Duke Bluebeard's Castle;* (ii) *Cantata profana.*
(M) *** DG stereo/mono 457 756-2 [id.]. (i)
Hertha Töpper; (i; ii) Dietrich Fischer-
Dieskau; (ii) Helmut Krebs, Berlin RIAS Ch.,
St Hedwig's Cathedral Ch.; (i; ii) Berlin RSO,
Fricsay.

Fricsay also pioneered *Bluebeard's castle* in stereo
and his 1958 recording rightly won a *Grand Prix
du Disque*. The snag is that the performance was
again tactfully cut, so that it could fit onto a 12-inch
LP. But it certainly stands the test of time. Fischer-
Dieskau is a memorable Bluebeard, even if the
tone-quality of the voice is perhaps too heroic,
not quite sinister enough; for though Bluebeard is
hardly a conventional villain, a slightly darker hue
is preferable. Dieskau, needless to say, amply makes
amends with vividly dramatic vocal acting and his
Lieder-like attention to the meaning of the words
brings an added dimension. Herta Töpper never
made a better record than this: she is a superb Judith,
even if not always perfectly steady. The recording
is full and brilliant with voices and orchestra individually truthfully caught. However, the vivid remastering emphasizes the close balance of the
soloists, which is less than ideal. One thinks particularly of the moment when Bluebeard shows Judith
the broad acres of his dominion. Here the orchestral
fortissimo (recalling Vaughan Williams in its use
of block chords) has less impact than it should. But
despite this fault and despite the cuts, this remains
a fine achievement. For the reissue DG have coupled

Fricsay's arresting, indeed inspired, account of the remarkably original *Cantata profana*, recorded seven years earlier, with passionate contributions from both Helmut Krebs and the splendidly incisive chorus. Both recordings were made in the Jesus-Christus Kirche and such is the quality of the mono sound in the cantata that one hardly registers the absence of stereo. A worthy candidate for DG's series of Legendary Originals. Full translations are included.

Bax, Arnold (1883–1953)

Symphony No. 3; The Happy forest (symphonic poem).
(BB) *** Naxos Dig. 8.553608 [id.]. RSNO, David Lloyd-Jones

David Lloyd-Jones continues his admirable Bax series with a warmly idiomatic account of the *Third Symphony* of 1929, spacious in the long first movement and the meditative slow movement, defying any diffuseness of argument. That leads to a vigorous account of the main section of the finale and on to the tenderly beautiful epilogue. The playing of the Scottish National Orchestra is clear and refined, helped by the transparency of the recording, clarifying often thick textures. From earlier in Bax's career *The Happy forest*, described as a 'nature poem', provides a refreshing contrast in its youthful energy, tauter, less expansive.

Beach, Amy (1867–1944)

(i) *Piano concerto in C sharp min., Op. 45;* (ii) *Piano quintet in F sharp min., Op. 67.*
**(*) Arabesque Dig. Z 6738 [id.]. Joanne Polk; (i) ECO, Paul Goodwin; (ii) Lark Qt.

Amy Beach's *Piano concerto* (1898/9) is an expansive, warmly romantic work written in a post-Lisztian style, with pleasingly lyrical melodies which recall other composers including Grieg and, in the dramatic first movement, Dvořák. The work is autobiographical: all the themes are drawn from the composer's songs and are associated with key figures in her life. Her mother, a powerful, dominating figure of the composer's early life, is sympathetically characterized by the engagingly insistent moto perpetuo of the Scherzo, and it was her husband who wrote the poem of the song associated with the yearning slow movement *Lament*. This is briefly recalled in the waltzing finale, which not for the first time, recalls the lilting elegance of Saint-Saëns. In short, though its style is essentially eclectic, the composer's skill ensures that the concerto holds the listener's attention throughout, especially in a performance so lyrically sympathetic and sparkling as that by Joanne Polk, persuasively accompanied by Paul Goodwin and the ECO and

very well recorded. It was a pity, though understandable, that the chosen coupling was the ubiquitous *Piano quintet*. However, this is also passionately presented, with the lovely slow movement movingly done, though the balance here has the string quartet a shade too close and the acoustic lacks depth – those wanting the concerto will certainly not be disappointed at the quality of the performances of either work.

(i) *Piano quintet in F sharp min.,Op. 67; Piano trio in A min., Op. 50;* (ii) *Theme and variations for flute and string quartet.*
❀ Chandos Dig. CHAN 9752 [id.]. (i) Diana Ambache; (ii) Helen Keen; The Ambache.

Amy Beach's glorious 1908 *Piano quintet* with its passionately lyrical first movement and hauntingly beautiful *Adagio* is already available in a fine performance on ASV (CDDCA 932 – see our main volume), coupled with music by Rebecca Clarke. But this Chandos version from Diana Ambache and her group is even richer, more passionately involving, and the coupling with two other fine chamber works is more apt. The *Theme* for the *Flute variations* (1916) has a touching nostalgia, and with exquisite flute-playing from Helen Keen, this music comes over as equally deeply felt. With a brief scherzando *Presto leggiero* at its centre this is primarily gentle music, with a lighthearted closing *Allegro giocoso*. The *Piano trio* is a late work (1939), the opening movement delicate in the manner of Fauré, although rather more overtly romantic; the melancholy *Lento* (based on a Heine song setting) gives way to a lightweight scherzando, before returning to the closing *Lament*. The catchy finale might almost be a lively dance movement from Dvořák's American period, but the luxuriantly expansive centre-piece is all Beach's own. These are marvellous performances of three very highly rewarding works, superbly recorded.

Beamish, Sally (born 1956)

(i) *Cello concerto (River);* (ii) *Viola concerto;* (iii) *Tam Lin* (for oboe and orchestra).
*** BIS Dig. CD 971 [id.]. (i) Robert Cohen; (ii) Philip Dukes; (iii) Gordon Hunt; Swedish CO, Ola Rudner.

Sally Beamish was born in London and spent her early years playing the viola in the London Sinfonietta and other instrumental ensembles before turning to full-time composition in her early thirties. Since then she has rapidly built a formidable reputation as a thoughtful, positive composer. Each of these concertos demonstrates her clarity in creating textures at once transparent, complex and original. This is not easy music, but it repays repetition. The three works span the 1990s: *Tam Lin* comes from 1993 and is a scena for oboe and small orchestra including harp and percussion but no violins. It is based on a Scottish ballad in which the elfin knight, Tam Lin, is saved from damnation by the love of a girl, Janet. The *Viola concerto*, written two years later, brings a solo part which benefits from Beamish's string-playing background. The composer calls the work 'a personal response to the story of the Apostle Peter's denial of Christ' and casts the solo viola as Peter's voice, the horn being associated with Jesus. The three denials are punctuated by illustrations of Christ's trial in film-like contrasts. The four movements of the 1997 *Cello concerto* each illustrate poems from Ted Hughes's 'River' collection, with orchestral colourings suggested by the words. The music is consistently imaginative, with clean luminous textures which occasionally call Henze to mind, but with a distinct feeling for the natural world. The writing has diversity of texture and mood, it is eventful and holds the listener in its spell. Its acquaintance is well worth making, particularly in such fine performances and excellent recordings. Robert Cohen and Philip Dukes, the dedicatees who commissioned the cello and viola works respectively, give committed performances as does the oboist, Gordon Hunt, with distinctive plangent tone. Excellent support from the Swedish players, very well recorded, and made in Orebro, where Ms Beamish is composer-in-residence with the Swedish Chamber Orchestra.

Beck, Franz Ignaz (1734–1809)

Sinfonias in G min.; E flat; D min., Op. 3/3–5.
*** CPO Dig. CPO 999 390-2 [id.]. La Stagione, Frankfurt, Michael Schneider.

We have already discovered the earlier symphonies of the Mannheim composer Franz Ignaz Beck, on a thoroughly recommendable Naxos disc, played very impressively on modern instruments by the Northern Chamber Orchestra under Nicholas Ward (8.553790 – see our main volume). In spite of the low opus number, these are mature later works (especially the *G minor*, with the themes interrelated) and are very much in the Haydn *Sturm und Drang* style. They are all in four movements with bold allegros, rhythmically vital. The *D minor Sinfonia* is for strings alone, but the *E flat major*, which has a remarkably searching *Adagio*, uses the horns most effectively as soloists in the Minuet and Trio and in the closing section of the finale. The period performances here are aggressively full of gusto and vitality, the strings playing with an appropriate edge, but not lacking body in slow movements, creating a sound world very different from that on the Naxos collection.

Beecke, Ignaz von (1733–1803)

String quartets Nos. 9 in G; 11 in G; 16 in B flat, M.9, 11 and 16.
*** CPO Dig. CPO 999 509-2 [id.]. Arioso Qt.

Ignaz von Beecke is not to be confused with Franz Ignaz Beck above (although he was an almost exact contemporary). He began his career in the military, but later taught himself the harpsichord and became a virtuoso on that instrument, admired by Haydn and playing in duet with Mozart (in Frankfurt in 1790). Later he became a travelling court musical director, performing his own symphonies as well as those by others. Beecke's String quartets were less well known in his own time than his symphonies. They are finely crafted, cultivated works, which Haydn would surely not have been ashamed to own. The disarming warmth of the opening of the *G major*, M.11 (which is first on the disc) leads to a fine opening movement with two striking themes; the *Minuet* comes second and is equally personable, and after the elegant *Adagio* the finale is as spirited as you could wish. The *B flat Quartet* is in three movements, but is hardly less pleasing, with a songful *Adagio* marked *sotto voce*. The companion *G major* work brings a striking minor-key slow movement, opening with a grave slow fugue; the *Minuet* lightens the mood and prepares for a most engaging finale. All three works are thoroughly diverting when played with such warmth, vitality and finesse and this excellent quartet is very naturally recorded.

Beethoven, Ludwig van (1770–1827)

(i) *Piano concertos Nos. 1–5. Piano sonata No. 23 in F min. (Appassionata), Op. 57.*
*** Teldec/Warner Dig. 3984 26801-2 (1–2); 3984 26802-2 (3–4); 3984 26900-2. András Schiff, Dresden State O, Haitink (available separately).

(i) *Piano concertos Nos. 1–5. 32 Variations in C min., WoO 80.*
Ph. Dig. 464 142-2 (3) [id.]. Mitsuko Uchida; (i) Bavarian R SO or Concg. O, Kurt Sanderling.

Playing with exceptional clarity and incisiveness, András Schiff with ideal, equally transparent support from Haitink and the Dresden Staatskapelle offers one of the most refreshing, deeply satisfying Beethoven concerto cycles of recent years. While often choosing speeds on the fast side, Schiff never sounds rushed or breathless.

With brilliant articulation, using the pedal lightly, he lets one hear every note, not least counterpoint in the left hand – often obscured. Yet these are the opposite of miniature readings, for there is a biting strength in this spontaneous-sounding playing. The brightness of Schiff's tone may mean that in hushed passages such as the solos in the central *Andante* of No. 4 he is reluctant to use a veiled tone, but the singing cantabile of his playing is equally persuasive.

He crowns the cycle with a scintillating account of the *Emperor concerto*, electrifying from first to last, aptly coupled with the most heroic sonata of Beethoven's middle-period, the *Appassionata*, similarly presented with refreshing power and clarity. Clear, well-balanced sound to match. The discs are available separately.

Mitsuko Uchida is characteristically a thoughtful, often poetic Beethoven interpreter, most obviously at home in the earlier concertos – so much closer to Mozart – but finding ample power throughout, with weighty accompaniments from Sanderling and the two German orchestras involved. Some may find her spacious approach a little too relaxed, even in poetic slow movements, which in places sound a little self-conscious, but this set is a fine memento of a deeply committed artist, warmly recommended to her many admirers. The early *C minor Variations*, incisively performed, make an apt if rather ungenerous fill-up for the *Emperor*.

Piano concertos Nos. 1–5; Rondo in B flat, WoO 6; Piano concerto No. 4, Op. 58 (for piano and string quintet; reconstructed Hans-Werner Küthen); (i) *Choral fantasia, Op. 80. Symphony No. 2 in D* (arr. for piano, violin & cello).
*** DG Dig. 459 622-2 (4) [id.]. Robert Levin (fortepiano), ORR, Gardiner, with (i) Monteverdi Ch. and instrumental & vocal soloists.

Robert Levin's cycle of the five Beethoven piano concertos plus *Choral fantasia* – on balance the finest yet using fortepiano, despite flaws in the *Emperor* – is here collected in a four-disc box with the valuable bonus of two chamber arrangements. The first, already recorded a number of times, is a deft arrangement for piano trio made by Beethoven himself of his *Second Symphony*. The other is more intriguing – an arrangement only recently reconstructed – of the *Fourth Piano concerto* with the solo part modified by Beethoven and with the orchestral accompaniment neatly transcribed for string quintet. The result is all the more refreshing on period instruments.

Piano concerto No. 1 in C, Op. 15.
**(*) EMI Dig. CDC5 56974-2 [id.]. Martha Argerich, Concg. O, Heinz Wallberg – MOZART: *Piano concerto No. 25.*

Argerich's strongly characterized reading of the *First concerto* dates from October 1992, recorded live in the Concertgebouw, Amsterdam. This is playing white-hot with the inspiration of the moment, full of sparkle, even if her approach to the slow movement is on the cool side. The radio sound is good, even if it hardly matches the best studio

recordings, and the coughing of the audience is at times intrusive. A good coupling for the 1978 recording of the Mozart.

(i) *Piano concerto No. 1 in C, Op. 15. Overture Egmont; String quartet No. 16, Op. 135:* excerpts: *Lento; Vivace.* (arr. Toscanini).
(BB) (**) Naxos mono 8.110826 [id.]. (i) Ania Dorfman; NBC SO, Toscanini (with broadcast commentary by Ben Grauer).

Though this is one of the less generous historic issues of Toscanini by Naxos, it offers fizzing performances, generally more sympathetic than those on comparable RCA issues, all recorded at a single concert in November 1944. The sound is typically limited and dry, but has a satisfying body in tuttis, which makes it easier to listen to than many from this source. No one was more dramatic than Toscanini in the *Egmont overture*, with a lengthy pause before the final Victory hymn. Ania Dorfman, a Russian who settled in New York, was a pianist who – with her crisp, clean articulation and preference for fast speeds – matched Toscanini well, making the *First concerto* an exuberant expression of youthful high spirits, rather than an anticipation of the middle period. The two arrangements from Opus 135 were Toscanini party-pieces. (N.B.: The Naxos sleeve gets the indication wrong for the second of the movements from Opus 135. It's not the finale (as is suggested by the Naxos titling), but the *Vivace* Scherzo second movement, here presented after the third movement *Lento*, not before. What a confusion!)

Piano Concertos Nos. 1 in C, Op. 15; No. 4 in G, Op. 58.
(B) ** Australian Decca Eloquence Analogue/Dig. 466 707-2. Radu Lupu, Israel PO, Mehta.

The *First concerto* (recorded digitally) is a strikingly fresh account, with fast, resilient speeds – Lupu displaying both sparkle and sensitivity – with the slow-movement, dominated by the soloist, treated to a delicate lightness of touch. He is similarly magical in the *Fourth concerto*, though Mehta and his orchestra fail to quite match him in sensitivity. The recording in both concertos is good and well-balanced, though the Israel strings never sound particularly sweet. Certainly not a first choice, but Lupu's admirers will want to consider this.

Piano Concerto No. 2 in B flat, Op. 19; The Creatures of Prometheus: Overture and ballet music: Nos. 1–5, 8–10, 15, 16.
(B) **(*) Australian Decca Eloquence Analogue/ Dig. 466 681-2. Radu Lupu, Israel PO, Mehta.

Lupu's (digital) account of the *Second concerto* is as sparkling as the *First*, with the orchestra providing sympathetic, if not always refined support. The recording of the *Prometheus* ballet music (making its CD debut) dates from the late 1960s, and if anything sounds even fuller. The performance is strong and persuasive, especially in the little-known dance numbers: the piece for cello and harp is beautifully done, and the disc is well worth considering for this alone.

Piano concertos Nos. 2 in B flat, Op. 19; 3 in C min., Op. 37.
(b) *** Erato/Ultima Double 3984 28168-2 (2) [id.]. Till Fellner, ASMF, Marriner – *Mass in C; Meerstille und glücklich Fahrt.* *(*)

This was Till Fellner's recording début and his performances have uncommon freshness and perception, with both slow movements beautifully played. Marriner accompanies persuasively and even if the orchestra is less vividly caught than the soloist these are vital and enjoyable accounts, both highly recommendable. It is a pity that the coupling puts this Ultima reissue out of court.

(i) *Piano concertos Nos. 2 in B flat, Op. 19; 3 in C min., Op. 37; (ii) 4 in G, Op. 58; 5 in E flat (Emperor), Op. 73.*
⊕ (bb) *** Royal Long Players DCL 705752 (2) [id.]. (i) Claudio Arrau; (ii) Hans Richter-Haaser; Philh. O; (i) Galliera; (ii) Kertész.

The Rosette is for Arrau's two performances, dating from 1959, which must be among his very finest recordings. The interpretation of the *Second concerto* strikes an ideal balance between the work's Mozartean characteristics and Beethovenian character, although it looks forward rather than backward. The authoritative reading of the first movement (with splendid orchestral detail), Arrau's sensitive and imaginative playing of the beautiful *Adagio* and the crisp, saucy rhythms of the *Rondo* – all these are an unalloyed delight for the listener. The recording too is most naturally balanced, although the piano perspective alters slightly in the first movement cadenza. The first movement of the *C minor Concerto* has a spacious gravitas: there are no Mozartean echoes here, and again Arrau's reading is commanding from his very first entry. The *Largo*, wonderfully poised, is blissful in its sustained beauty and the finale, comparatively measured, is lyrically light-hearted. Both performances are enhanced by particularly fine playing from the Philharmonia under Galliera and the early stereo could hardly be more natural. This is a treasurable coupling: Arrau, for all his wisdom, seldom sounded as spontaneous as this in his later Beethoven recordings.

Richter-Haaser's hushed opening phrase of the *G major Concerto* is comparably memorable and although his reading has more of the grand manner than, say, Kempff's account, spontaneity breathes in every bar. The dialogue of the slow movement is not a dramatic argument (in the way of Ashkenazy and Solti), but more of a thoughtful conversation. It is intensely moving, while the finale provides a

combination of strength and sparkle. Again first-rate recording (from the early 1960s).

The *Emperor*, while by no means dull, is not on this level of intensity. Richter-Haaser gives an immaculate performance. One can barely fault a note. But there is less of the feeling of a live performance that makes No. 4 so very exciting. The approach is the same: the achievement less memorable, even if the difference is hard to pin down except in subjective statements. But three bull's-eyes out of four makes this an indispensable bargain. The *Emperor* has some beautiful playing in the slow movement and is by no means to be dismissed. The analogue recording is well up to standard.

Piano concertos Nos. 2 in B flat, Op. 19; 5 in E flat (Emperor), Op. 73.
(*(**)) BBC Legends mono BBCL 4028-2 [id.]. Dame Myra Hess, BBC SO, Sargent (includes interview with John Amis).

Recorded in the Royal Albert Hall at Prom performances, this issue in the BBC Legends series gives the most vivid idea of the dynamism and depth of Myra Hess as a Beethoven interpreter. As she herself says, in a delightful interview with John Amis which comes as a supplement, she hated recording – including all her existing recordings made in the studio; this live experience consistently makes clear the extra dimension in her playing when not so inhibited. The performance of the *Emperor*, recorded in 1957, is the more remarkable for the leonine quality of the performance. Her opening solo flourish promptly inspires the BBC Orchestra under Sargent to give an electrifying account of the tutti, before Dame Myra then launches into a vitally spontaneous reading which exploits the widest expressive range, at once heroic and poetic. The meditative intensity of the slow movement, rapt and refined, then leads to an exuberant account of the finale, with jollity the keynote. No. 2, recorded three years later, also brings a remarkable performance, with the orchestra under Sargent slack at first, but then responding to the high voltage of the soloist, fresh, poetic and youthfully urgent in the first movement, dedicated in the slow movement, and sparkling and witty in the finale. Alongside the performance of No. 4 which Dame Myra recorded with Toscanini (now on Naxos), this revolutionizes our ideas of a very great pianist, still at her peak as she reaches seventy. However, it is important to stress the considerable difference here in recording quality between Nos. 5 (1957) and 2 (1960). It is quite possible that the latter comes from a private off-air tape rather than a BBC mastertape. The sound is more opaque, has *very* limited frequency range and suffers from distortion.

Piano concerto No. 3 in C min., Op. 37; 32 Variations on an original theme in C min., WoO 80.

(B) **(*) Australian Decca Eloquence 466 690-2.
  Radu Lupu, LSO, Foster.

For the *Third concerto* in Lupu's Beethoven cycle
on the bargain Eloquence label, Australian Decca
have turned to his highly spontaneous early-1970s
version with the LSO under Lawrence Foster. True,
this performance is comparatively lightweight, but
many will find its more delicate approach appealing,
and the LSO playing is first class. It receives its CD
début here, where it is coupled to an outstanding set
of the *C minor Variations,* which has both eloquence and spontaneity.

(i) *Piano concertos Nos. 4 in G, Op. 58;* (ii) *5 in E
flat (Emperor).*
** Audite 95.459 [id.]. Clifford Curzon, Bav.
  RSO, Kubelik.

Clifford Curzon made these radio recordings of
Beethoven's last two concertos in February 1977,
some five years before he died. Though the piano
sound is rather clattery, and the orchestral textures
tend to be cloudy, the poetry and strength of Curzon
in Beethoven are clear enough, even if other, earlier
recordings reveal it more clearly. Passage work is
not always immaculate, and speeds are generally
broad – notably in the first movement of No. 4 –
but Kubelik is a warmly understanding partner,
readily matching his soloist.

Piano concerto No. 5 in E flat (Emperor).
*** BBC Legends BBCL 4020-2 [id.]. Clifford
  Curzon, BBC SO, Boulez – MOZART: *Piano
  concerto No. 26 (Coronation)* ***.

The partnership of the introspective Curzon and the
incisive Boulez may not seem a promising one, but
in this live performance recorded in 1971 at the
Royal Festival Hall the challenge between the two
brings electrifying results. Curzon is at his most
taut and incisive, while finding depths of poetry,
and Boulez proves a surprisingly sympathetic interpreter of Beethoven, matching his soloist in
subtle dynamic shading, while bringing home the
work's dramatic power. Full, forward recording.

*Piano concerto No. 5 (Emperor), Op. 73; Piano
sonatas Nos. 19 in G min., Op. 49/1; No. 20 in G,
Op. 49/2.*
(B) **(*) Australian Decca Eloquence 466 689-2.
  Radu Lupu, Israel PO, Mehta.

Lupu gives a performance of the *Emperor* which,
without lacking strength, brings a striking thoughtfulness and poetry even to the powerful first movement, with classical proportions made clear. The
slow movement has delicacy and fantasy, and the
finale easy exhilaration. Lupu is not matched in
distinction by either the orchestra or conductor,
but neither do they prevent one's enjoyment of an
unusual approach to Beethoven's masterpiece. The
two piano sonatas are superbly played and are fully
recommendable. The vintage Decca sound

throughout is impressive (though it can't make
those Israeli strings sound ideally sweet).

Piano concerto No. 5 in E flat (Emperor), Op. 73;
(i) *Choral fantasia in C min., Op. 80.*
(M) **(*) EMI CDM5 67329-2 [id.]. Barenboim,
  New Philh. O, Klemperer, (i) with John Alldis
  Ch.

Reissued as part of EMI's Klemperer Legacy, this
CD opens with the *Choral fantasia,* understandably
so as it is a magnificent account, the improvisatory
nature of the writing producing a performance of
exceptional life and spontaneity, very well balanced. The same partnership in the *Emperor* produces a reading which is individual to the point of
perverseness. Many collectors will resist it, but with
its dry style and measured speeds, coupled to a
remarkable degree of concentration from pianist
and conductor, it provides an astonishingly fresh
experience. The technical demands of the solo part,
the sheer power, are somehow brought out more
vividly, not less, when one has a pianist who, in
the best sense, has to struggle to be master – no
unthinking pile-driver, but a searching voyager. The
performance – with a number of unimportant
'fluff's unedited – has a striking sense of spontaneity. The new transfer of the 1967 Abbey Road
recording brings out a hint of harshness on the
massed strings, but the piano is admirably caught.

Violin concerto in D, Op. 61.
(M) *** DG 463 078-2 [id.]. Zukerman, Chicago
  SO., Barenboim – HAYDN: *Sinfonia
  concertante in B flat* ***.
(***) BBC Legends BBCL 4019-2 [id.]. Yehudi
  Menuhin, Moscow PO, David Oistrakh –
  MOZART: *Sinfonia concertante in E flat, K.364*
  (***).

(i) *Violin concerto in D, Op. 61;* (ii) *Romances
Nos. 1 in G, Op. 40; 2 in F, Op. 50.*
(M) *** Penguin Classics Ph. 460 647-2 [id.].
  Arthur Grumiaux; (i) Concg. O, Sir Colin
  Davis; (ii) New Philh. O, Edo de Waart.
**(*) Ph. Dig. 462 123-2 [id.]. Thomas Zehetmair,
  OAE, Frans Brüggen.

Arthur Grumiaux's beautiful, classical reading
coupled with equally persuasive accounts of the
two *Romances* now arrives in the Penguin Classics
series, complete with an introductory essay by John
Fortune. But unless this is essential, the same performances are available at bargain price on the
Philips Virtuoso label (420 348-2 – see our main
volume).

Zukerman's 1977 DG version is already available
as part of a DG Double, curiously joined to the
Brahms, Mendelssohn and Tchaikovsky concertos played by Milstein (see our main volume).
But Zukerman's Beethoven, spaciously conceived,
is well worth having in its own right and now

comes at mid-price attractively re-coupled with a fine performance of the Haydn B flat Sinfonia concertante.

In 1963, the Moscow Philharmonic Orchestra and Kyrill Kondrashin visited London's Royal Albert Hall and on 28 September, Yehudi Menuhin joined them in the Beethoven Violin concerto with no less than David Oistrakh conducting. (In the second half they reversed roles when Oistrakh was joined by his son Igor in the Mozart Sinfonia concertante under Menuhin's baton.) Menuhin recorded the Beethoven with Furtwängler twice and with both Klemperer and Silvestri, but there is something rather special about the present reading with Oistrakh, an artist whom he much loved. In a way it is his most serene and spontaneous account (the slow movement is seraphic), and those who treasure memories of the occasion will welcome its reincarnation in this BBC recording. Detail is not as analytical or wide-ranging as in commercial recordings of the period but it is warm and truthful.

The Zehetmair/Brüggen partnership is for authenticists only. The Romances are placed first and are far from romantic, with the G major very brisk and unbeguiling. So is the opening of the Concerto, with the timpani taps very dry, the orchestral exposition strongly accented, and dramatically gruff. It is as if Brüggen is not persuaded that this work is the epitome of radiant Beethoven lyricism, music above all to refresh the spirit. Zehetmair uses the first-movement cadenza, with timpani, favoured by Schneiderhan, but plays it as if it were by Paganini, and the great reprise of the main theme is all but thrown away in the closing pages. Fortunately the Larghetto relaxes more and Zehetmair's playing is often very beautiful, quite ethereal. Brüggen is merely supportive, and the bold gruffness returns to usher in the invigorating finale, again mirrored by the soloist in his cadenza. The sheer brilliance of this closing movement certainly adds to the individuality of a reading which is far from conventional, and certainly never dull. But overall there is a missing dimension. The recording is excellent.

(i) Violin concerto in D, Op. 61. Overtures: Consecration of the House, Op. 124; Leonore No. 3, Op. 72b.
(M) **(*) Sony SMK 63153 [id.]. (i) Stern; NYPO, Bernstein.

This reissue of Isaac Stern's performance on Sony shows the intense creative relationship established between this artist and Bernstein at an early peak in both their respective careers. Stern's reading has a tremendous onward flow with his personality strongly projected, yet (in spite of the forward balance of the soloist), Bernstein keeps the orchestra well in the picture and the energy of the music-making is compulsive. The caveat is that the close 1959 recording prevents any real pianissimo, but Sony has improved the original sound to an accept-

able level by modern standards. The two overtures make a good bonus.

Clarinet concerto in D (arr. Pletnev from Violin concerto, Op.61).
*** DG Dig. 457 652-2 [id.]. Michael Collins, Russian Nat. O, Pletnev – MOZART: Clarinet concerto.

For his long-awaited recording of the Mozart Clarinet concerto, Michael Collins, with the help of his friend, Mikhail Pletnev, offers the most challenging if controversial coupling, a daring transcription for the clarinet of the Beethoven Violin concerto. The conductor is quoted as saying that 'The clarinet needs more big works, and the Beethoven would certainly fill a gap'.

On this showing, one might well argue that the clarinet fits the music more comfortably than the piano, for which Beethoven himself provided a transcription. The point is that the warmth of Beethoven's lyricism is the more richly brought out in clarinet tone, not just in the slow movement – where Collins feels the advantages are greatest – but in the long first movement too. Sensibly, the cadenza (by Pletnev) is kept to a modest length, barely two minutes, predominantly lyrical, with fireworks only in the middle.

Apart from the obvious point that no double-stopping is possible on the clarinet, the main difference in the transcription involves downward octave transposition of the solo line over many sections in all three movements. Pletnev has managed it so deftly, that with passagework shifted to register comfortably for the clarinet, it consistently sounds natural, where getting the clarinet to play, like the violin, high up above the stave would have resulted in uncomfortable shrieking.

The wonder is that Collins makes light of all problems – not least of taking a breath in sustained passages – so that one readily can enjoy the music in a new way. Whatever reservations there may be about the transcription, here is music which provides a most satisfying coupling for the Mozart, warmly played and very well-recorded.

Overtures: The Consecration of the house, Op. 124; King Stephen, Op. 117; (i) Egmont (incidental music), Op. 84: excerpts.
(M) *** EMI CDM5 67335-2 [id.]. (i) Birgit Nilsson; Philh. O, or New Philh. O, Klemperer (with MENDELSSOHN: Overture: The Hebrides (Fingal's Cave), Op. 26; MOZART: Overtures: Don Giovanni; Die Entführung aus dem Serail; Le nozze di Figaro) ***.

It was a good idea of EMI to gather these overtures together as part of the Klemperer Legacy, for they are all outstanding performances. There is some really inspired playing in the Beethoven group. Even the trivial King Stephen is given strength and The Consecration of the house has seldom sounded so magnificent on record. The *Egmont* items too have an added dimension, with Birgit Nilsson at her most eloquent in *Die Trommel Gerühret* and *Freudvoll und Leidvoll*. The music portraying Clärchen's death is given a touching nobility. *Fingal's Cave*, too, is a magnificent performance, spacious and powerful, and his *Don Giovanni* stands out among the Mozart overtures; *Le nozze di Figaro* is also superbly played.

Overtures: Coriolan; Creatures of Prometheus; Egmont; Fidelio; Leonora 1–3; Ruins of Athens.
**(*) Virgin/EMI VCS5 45364-2 [id.]. Bremen German Chamber Philh. O, Daniel Harding.

In his first essay on disc in the classical repertory, Daniel Harding, still in his mid-twenties, gives strong, distinctive readings of eight Beethoven overtures. As the name of the Bremen orchestra suggests, these are performances on a chamber scale, which is emphasized by the recording, which does not try to boost the string tone, even when violins are exposed. With his chosen players Harding favours extreme speeds, with slow introductions very solemn and measured, leading to hectic allegros, which press home the drama of Beethoven's writing. Though all four overtures for *Fidelio* are included, as well as four others, it is a pity that *The Consecration of the house* was not included, if necessary with the omission of *The Ruins of Athens*.

Symphonies Nos. 1–9.
(B) *** DG 463 088-2 (5) [id.]. BPO, Karajan (with Janowitz, Rössel-Majdan, Kmentt, Berry, V. Singverein in No. 9).

DG are obviously well aware that Karajan's 1961–2 set is the most compelling of his Beethoven cycles, with only the hard-driven account of the *Pastoral* offering any reservations. Otherwise this remains a classic survey and the recording still sounds well. Now reissued yet again on five bargain CDs in DG's Collector's Edition, this is still eminently recommendable. The documentation is excellent.

Symphonies Nos. 2–4; 6 (Pastoral); 7–9 (Choral) Overture Leonora No. 3.
(M) ** EMI Dig./Analogue CDS5 56837-2 (8) [id.]. Munich PO, Celibidache (with Donath, Soffel, Jerusalem, Lika & Philharmonic Ch. in No. 9) – BRAHMS: *Symphonies 1–4; Variations on Haydn; German Requiem** (with SCHUMANN: *Symphony No. 2 **).

Sergiu Celibidache is the latest cult figure, and his followers will eagerly snap up his records in much the same way as do Furtwängler's admirers. Even so, to give us a Beethoven cycle (except for Nos. 1 and 5), and harness it to all four Brahms symphonies, the *Requiem* and the *Haydn Variations*, none of them available separately, is to strain even the most dedicated allegiance. Generally he is too

idiosyncratic to gain more than a guarded recommendation.

Symphony No. 4 in B flat, Op. 60.
*** Orfeo C 522 991 B [id.]. VPO, Karl Boehm –
    MAHLER: *Lieder eines fahrenden Gesellen;*
    SCHUMANN: *Symphony No. 4.* ***

Though this Orfeo issue may seem to offer a disconcertingly mixed bag of works, it vividly portrays the mastery of Karl Boehm in varied repertory. It brings out how this Salzburg Festival concert of August 1969 was electrifying from first to last. Though Boehm's studio recordings of Beethoven symphonies are impressive, they rarely offer so fiery a performance as this account of No. 4, bitingly intense in the fast movements with sharply rhythmic attack, and tender and sweet in the spacious slow movement.

Symphonies Nos. 5 in C min., Op. 67; 6 in F (Pastoral);Coriolan overture.
(BB) (*(*)) Naxos mono 8.110823 [id.]. NBC SO, Toscanini (with broadcast commentary by Gene Hamilton).

This 1939 account of Beethoven's *Fifth Symphony* has been well known from the days of 78s: a tough, urgent reading typical of Toscanini, a degree more sympathetic than his later NBC versions. The Naxos transfer is less full than those from RCA, and the same thin, often crumbly, sound also mars both the *Coriolan overture* (with the opening chords like bangs on a tin box) and this version of the *Pastoral*, also from Toscanini's 1939 Beethoven cycle, a fresh, urgently dramatic reading.

Symphony No. 7 in A, Op. 92 (see also under *Missa solemnis* below).

Symphony No. 7 in A, Op. 92; Egmont overture; Septet in E flat, Op. 20 (arr. Toscanini).
(BB) (*(*)) Naxos mono 8.110814 [id.]. NBC SO, Toscanini (with broadcast commentary by Gene Hamilton).

It was a favourite party piece of Toscanini to get his NBC Orchestra to play the Beethoven *Septet*, with the strings agile in parts designed for solo instruments. The sound in that is fuller and firmer than on the rest of the disc, where the thin crumbly recording which marks most of the Naxos transfers of Toscanini's 1939 Beethoven cycle spoils the impact of these searingly dramatic performances of both the *Egmont overture* and the *Seventh Symphony*, an interpretation broadly in line with his classic New York Philharmonic reading of three years earlier.

Symphonies Nos. (i) 7 in A, Op. 92; (ii) No. 8 in F, Op. 93; (iii) No. 9 (Choral) in D min., Op. 125.
(B) ** DG Double 459 463-2 (2) [id.]. (i) VPO;
    (ii) Cleveland O; (iii) Donath, Berganza,

Ochman, Stewart, Bavarian Radio SO; Kubelik.

Kubelik used as many orchestras as symphonies for his Beethoven cycle, so it is not surprising that the results were not uniformly impressive. The *Seventh Symphony*, with the VPO, is beautifully played and well recorded, but lacks the drama of his earlier account with the Bavarian RSO. The *Eighth Symphony* receives a robustly enjoyable performance in Cleveland, with the choice of tempi always well judged.

For the challenging *Ninth symphony*, Kubelik used his own Bavarian orchestra. It is a warm and understanding performance, rather than a monumental one; there is a Mendelssohnian lightness in the scherzo, and the slow movement is sunny as well as serene, leading on consistently to the high spirits of the finale. But there is a missing dimension of conveyed power and greatness here. The performances are well recorded (in the mid 1970s), but this reissue will be of primary interest to admirers of the conductor rather than the general collector.

Symphony No. 9 in D min. (Choral), Op. 125.
*** Testament SBT 1177 [id.]. Nordmo-Løvberg, Ludwig, Kment, Hotter, Philh. Ch. & O, Klemperer.

The previously unpublished live recording of Klemperer conducting Beethoven's *Ninth* on Testament is magnetic from beginning to end. The occasion at the Royal Festival Hall in November 1957 was the very first concert of the newly founded Philharmonia Chorus – the culmination of Klemperer's first Beethoven symphony cycle in London. He followed that up immediately by recording the *Ninth* in the studio with exactly the same forces, but in all four movements this live performance has an extra bite and intensity at marginally faster speeds. In every way it is preferable to the published EMI studio recording, when even the sound is both warmer and kinder to the voices.

(i) *Symphony No. 9 in D min. (Choral);* (i; ii) *Choral fantasia, Op. 80.*
(BB) (**) Naxos mono 8.110824 [id.]. NBC SO, Toscanini; with (i) Novotna, Thorborg, Peerce, Moscona, Westminster Ch.; (ii) Ania Dorfman.

In December 1939, Toscanini rounded off his Beethoven symphony cycle in New York with these apocalyptic performances of the *Ninth* and *Choral fantasia*. Though the sound is characteristically dry, and the first movement of the *Ninth* is almost painfully clipped and taut (more so than in Toscanini's RCA version of 1952), the atmosphere of a great occasion comes over vividly. Quite apart from the searing thrust and drama of Toscanini's approach to both works (bringing out the parallels between the two) it is good to have in the slow movement a keener impression than usual of Toscanini's ability

to mould phrases affectionately in hushed intensity. The soloists in the *Ninth* make a superb quartet, with the firm dark bass, Nicola Moscona, particularly impressive. Ania Dorfman's solo playing in the *Choral fantasia* is marked by a bright tone and diamond-clear articulation. The Naxos transfers, though very limited, have more body than most in this Toscanini series of 1939.

Symphony No. 9 in D min. (Choral), Op. 125; Fidelio: overture, Op. 72c.
(M) ** Sony SMK 63152 [id.]. Arroyo, Sarfaty, de Virgilio, Scott, Juilliard Ch., NYPO, Bernstein.

This was one of the best of Bernstein's Beethoven cycle. It offers a finely shaped first movement, which has genuine breadth and eloquence, a bitingly dramatic Scherzo that verges on the frenetic, a slow movement of considerable warmth, although with not quite enough inwardness and repose, and an intense and dramatic finale with some fine contributions from the soloists and chorus. The 1964 recording is better than it was on LP, but lacks sophistication. With the *Fidelio overture*, this CD makes a fair recommendation, but competition here is as hot as it can be.

CHAMBER MUSIC

(i; ii) *Cello sonatas Nos 1–5;* (ii; iii) *Horn sonata in F, Op. 17.*
(B) *** Decca Double Analogue/Dig. 466 733-2 (2) [id.]. (i) Harrell; (ii) Ashkenazy; (iii) Tuckwell.

The Harrell/Ashkenazy mid-1980s set of the *Cello sonatas* was a front runner at full price, with stiff competition. The superb digital recording helped – rich, perfectly balanced sound – but the performances are, of course, very fine too: they are unfailingly sensitive and alert, well thought out and yet seemingly spontaneous. The inclusion in this Double Decca issue of the *Horn sonata*, equally recommendable (from 1974), makes this a fine bargain, particularly for those who regard sound quality to be of importance.

Cello sonata No. 3 in A, Op. 69.
(M) (***) EMI mono CDM5 67008-2 [id.]. Pablo Casals, Otto Schulhof – BACH: (Unaccompanied) *Cello suite No. 1 in G, BWV 1007;* BRAHMS: *Cello sonata No. 2* (***).

Casals recorded the Beethoven sonatas with both Horszowski and Serkin but for the *A major sonata*, way back in 1930, he chose Otto Schulhof. He is a thoughtful pianist and their playing is wonderfully free from any of the glitz and glamour so prevalent nowadays. Schulhof is so natural, unforced and musical. This account has been out before in the EMI Référence series and the frail dry sound soon ceases to worry the experienced ear.

Clarinet trio in B flat, Op. 11.
(M) *** CRD 3345 [id.]. Nash Ens. (with
ARCHDUKE RUDOLPH OF AUSTRIA: *Clarinet
trio in B flat ***).

The Nash Ensemble's account of Beethoven's
Clarinet trio has a royal rarity as a coupling. Archduke Rudolph was a son of the Austrian Emperor.
But his claim to fame is as a pupil and friend of
Beethoven; he was a good enough pianist to take
part in the *Triple concerto* and he subscribed to the
fund that gave support to Beethoven after the onset
of his deafness. His *Clarinet trio* is incomplete: of
the closing rondo only a fragment survives and this
performance ends with the slow movement, a set of
variations on a theme by yet another prince, Louis
Ferdinand of Prussia. The music may be no great
shakes, but it is more than just a curiosity and its
inclusion on this mid-priced CD is welcome. The
playing is thoroughly persuasive, with some attractive pianism from the excellent Clifford Benson.
Much the same goes for the performance of the
Beethoven *Trio*, and though obviously not an indispensable issue, this is well worth investigating for
interest.

Piano trios Nos. 1 in E flat; 2 in G, Op. 1/1–2.
(BB) *** Naxos Dig. 8.550946 [id.]. Stuttgart
   Piano Trio.

*Piano trios Nos. 3 in C min., Op. 1/3; 8 in E flat,
WoO 38; 10 (Variations) in E flat, Op. 44. 12
(Allegretto) in E flat; Hess 48.*
(BB) **(*) Naxos Dig. 8.550947 [id.]. Stuttgart
   Piano Trio.

*Piano trios Nos. 5 in D (Ghost); 6 in E flat, Op.
70/1–2.*
(BB) *(*) Naxos Dig. 8.550948 [id.]. Stuttgart
   Piano Trio.

*Piano trios Nos. 7 in B flat (Archduke), Op. 97; 11
(Variations on 'Ich bin der Schneider Kakadu'),
Op. 121a.*
(BB) ** Naxos Dig. 8.550949 [id.]. Stuttgart Piano
   Trio.

The Naxos set of the Beethoven *Piano trios* was
recorded between 1989 and 1993. The performances have a good deal in common with those by
the Seraphim Trio in the same price range on Arte
Nova (74321 51621-2 – see our main volume), but
have the additional advantage of being available
separately. However, the Arte Nova set offers all
eleven works on four CDs, whereas the Stuttgart
series has already used that number of discs and is
not yet complete.
   The early Op. 1 set are very successful, played
with finesse and with a simplicity of style which is
very appealing. Slow movements have a pleasing
eloquence and there is plenty of vitality. The finale
of the *G major* is exhilarating and after the brio of
the opening movement of the *C minor*, the *Andante*

cantabile con variazioni is delightfully presented.
Then come some delectable runs from the excellent
pianist, Monika Leonhard, to tweak the ear in the
Trio of the following fast Minuet. The other early
Trio in E flat is persuasively done. The Stuttgart
players are good at characterizing variations: Op.
44 is particularly successful and rhythmically most
engaging.
   The first movement of the *Ghost trio* is very brisk
indeed, and the nervous intensity of the Stuttgart
players permeates the performance, although the
arrival of the 'Ghost' is eerily effective. The *E
flat Trio* is rather more relaxed and the central
movements are appealingly played. The finale,
however, is again pressed on rather too forcefully.
The performance of the *Archduke* is comparatively
mellow – not without character, but not really distinctive. The *Kakadu variations* come off well, and
the *Allegretto in B flat*, WoO 39 is pleasingly done.
Throughout the series the players are not helped by
the close microphones in the Clara Wieck Auditorium, but this seems more noticeable in the later
works. On the whole the Arte Nova set is the one
to go for.

*Septet in E flat, Op. 20; (i) Sextet in E flat, Op.
81b.*
(B) **(*) Ph. Virtuoso 426 091-2. BPO Octet
   (members); (i) with Manfred Klier.

An amiably refined performance from the excellent
Berlin Philharmonic group on Philips, with plenty
of life in the outer movements, but rather a solemn
view taken of the slow movement. The analogue
recording is excellent; many will like its warm
ambience. The *Sextet*, for two horns and string
quartet, is also very well played and recorded. But
first bargain-choice for the Septet remains with the
Vienna Octet on Decca Eclipse (448 232-2 – see
our main volume).

String quartets Nos. 1–16 (complete).
(BB) ** Arte Nova 74321 63637-2 (9) [id.].
   Alexander Qt.

String quartets Nos. 1 in F; 5 in A, Op. 18/1 & 5.
(BB) **(*) Arte Nova Dig. 74321 63673-2 [id.].
   Alexander Qt.

*String quartets Nos. 2 in G; 6 in B flat, Op. 18/2 &
6.*
(BB) ** Arte Nova Dig. 74321 49682-2 [id.].
   Alexander Qt.

*String quartets Nos. 7 in F (Razumovsky), Op. 59/
1; 10 in E flat (Harp), Op. 74.*
(BB) ** Arte Nova Dig. 74321 59224-2 [id.].
   Alexander Qt.

*String quartets Nos. 11 in F min, Op. 95; 12 in E
flat, Op. 127.*
(BB) **(*) Arte Nova Dig. 74321 63674-2 [id.].
   Alexander Qt.

String quartet Nos. 13 in B flat, Op. 130; Grosse fuge, Op. 133.
(BB) ** Arte Nova Dig. 74321 54455-2 [id.].
   Alexander Qt.

String quartets Nos. 14 in C sharp min., Op. 131; 16 in F, Op. 135.
(BB) *(*) Arte Nova Dig. 74321 63675-2 [id.].
   Alexander Qt.

String quartet No. 15 in A minor, Op. 132.
(BB) **(*) Arte Nova Dig. 74321 37312-2 [id.].
   Alexander Qt.

We discussed two of the San Francisco-based Alexander Quartet's Beethoven cycle (Opp. 18/3 and 4; Opp. 59/2 and 3) in our main volume. The remainder are much the same. Generally speaking their approach is selfless and dedicated; the readings are well thought through and distinguished by considerable tonal finesse. One or two individual observations: the first movement of the *F major Razumovsky) Quartet* (74321 59224-2) is very fast indeed, and they offer no exposition repeat. This is strange, as they had observed both repeats in the *E minor*. Good choice of tempo elsewhere, though some may find the finale too fast. In the *Harp Quartet*, Op. 74, tempi are better judged and they do observe the exposition repeat in the first movement. The balance is less forward than on Op. 59/1. The recorded sound is very bright: the Kodály Quartet on Naxos have the benefit of a warmer acoustic.

The *F minor Quartet*, Op. 95 (74321 63674-2) has a dramatic and concentrated first movement, though the slow movement has too little of the atmospheric contrast these artists might have achieved in other circumstances. Tempi are consistently well judged although there are moments of expressive emphasis that might strike some as a shade exaggerated. The leader's tone sounds a little hard in the Scherzo's trio. In the *E flat*, Op. 127, tempi are again intelligently chosen (the scherzando third movement could not be bettered), though there is a certain fierceness in tutti. The close balance does not rob the slow movement of its sense of mystery, which is a tribute to the tonal finesse these players command.

The great *A minor Quartet*, Op. 132 (74321 37312-2) was the first to be recorded, early in 1996, and it is undeniably impressive. Lovely pianissimo playing both in the opening and in the *Heiliger Dankegesang*, which has keen concentration. The *Alla marcia* is a bit too slow. Elsewhere tempi are expertly judged. One of the best in the set.

The *B flat Quartet* Op. 130 and the *Grosse fuge* (74321 54455-2) come off well. They are distinguished by fine musicianship and a technique which never draws attention to itself. They convey the sense of struggle and possess great lucidity of texture. The *C sharp minor Quartet*, Op. 131 (74321 63675-2) is less successful. In the fugal opening the

ethereal quality and sense of awe that you find in the greatest performances are missing. Their tempo, too, is just a bit too fast. Summing up, however good the playing, the sound is too bright and analytical. For a complete set in the bargain range better to stick with the Quartetto Italiano (Philips) or – though it is very much the second choice in this price level – the Alban Berg (EMI).

String quartets Nos. 1–16; Grosse fuge, Op. 133.
(B) *** EMI Analogue/Dig. CZS5 77606-2
   [66408] (7). Alban Berg Qt.
(B) *** Hyperion Helios Dig. CDH 55021/8 (8)
   New Budapest Qt.
(B) **(*) DG 463 143-2 (7) [id.]. Amadeus Qt.

The Alban Berg Quartet's performances are characterized by assured and alert playing, a finely blended tone and excellent attack; they generally favour brisk tempi in the first movements, which they dispatch with exemplary polish and accuracy of intonation. Occasionally a tendency to exaggerate dynamic extremes (Op. 59/3, for example) is evident which sounds self-conscious, but by any standards this is superb quartet playing. Other versions have displayed greater depth of feeling in this repertoire – including their own live performance cycle on the same label – but this well-packaged, beautifully recorded set (from 1978–83), at bargain price, is well worth considering.

The New Budapest Quartet offer fine performances, always intelligent, with many considerable insights. Throughout the cycle, their playing is distinguished by consistent (but not excessive) refinement of sonority, perfect intonation, and excellent ensemble and tonal blend. With first-class Hyperion recording they fully deserve three stars. If the very opening disc of Op. 18/1–2 lacks a little in vitality this is not a problem elsewhere. They are less searching than the Végh, the Talich and the Lindsays. At times one feels that they are somehow too clean and occasionally somewhat less than fully characterized. Yet this is always fully committed music-making with plenty of life, and as a super-bargain box (eight CDs for the price of five Helios discs offered in a slipcase) they are certainly well worth considering: overall the performances have more depth than those of their Amadeus competitors.

The Amadeus Quartet are at their very best in the Op. 18 *Quartets* where their mastery and polish are heard to excellent advantage. The smooth and beautifully balanced DG recording from the early 1960s disguises its age. In the middle-period and late quartets, their richly blended tone and refinement of balance are always in evidence and equally well caught by the DG engineers, but their playing does not always penetrate very far beneath the surface, particularly in the late quartets. There is some superb playing and immaculate ensemble in this cycle, which cannot help but give pleasure, but there are more searching accounts to be found. The set is now offered at bargain price in DG's Collector's Edition and is well documented.

String quartets Nos. 1–6, Op. 18/1–6.
(M) **(*) Calliope CAL 9633 (1–3); CAL 9634 (4–6). Talich Qt.

When they appeared in the 1980s, the Talich were the first set to accommodate all six of the Op. 18 quartets on two CDs. (At that time the rival sets by the Alban Berg (EMI) and the Melos (DG) ran to three.) They now resurface at mid-price. They have great directness and simplicity of utterance. They are refreshingly free from idiosyncracy and unconcerned with glamour and surface beauty, even if their accounts are not so inspired as they were later on in the cycle. Indeed, in one or two places they sound just a bit prosaic – the opening of the *C minor Quartet*, Op. 18/4 could have more fire and momentum. Mostly they find the right tempo and in the first movement of the *A major*, Op. 18/5 have a wonderful freshness and spontaneity. Incidentally, they omit the exposition repeat in the first movement of the *F major*, Op. 18/1 and in the *B flat*, Op. 18/6. Even if there are moments of prose, there is no lack of poetry elsewhere. Clean, present recording even if it is a bit on the dry side. Recommended but not in preference, say, to the Quartetto Italiano on Philips.

String quartets Nos. 4 in C min.; 5 in A, Op. 18/ 4–5; 13 in B flat, Op. 130.
(BB) **(*) Virgin Classics 2 x 1 Dig. VBD5 61748(2) [CDVB 61748] Borodin Qt.

For finesse and beauty of sound in Beethoven the Borodins are unmatched, even by the Alban Berg. In the early quartets the elegance and warmth of the playing are an undoubted pleasure. Indeed, it is difficult to resist the sweetness and elegance of Mikhail Kopelman's phrasing at the opening of the *A major*, and his tone at the opening of the Minuet is ravishing. One could say much the same of the playing of the great *Cavatina* of Op. 130, yet, eloquent as it is on the surface, the searching quality that Beethoven calls for is passed by. The *Grosse fuge* demands and receives great attack and gusto, and the energy and ensemble are technically remarkable, but one cannot help but feel that the players are even more in their element in the lighter, substituted finale, which is most winningly presented. The sound is very realistic, so at the modest price this set still offers much to enjoy.

String quartets Nos. 4 in C min., Op. 18/4; 14 in C sharp min., Op. 131.
* DG 459 611-2 [id.]. Hagen Qt.

A high-powered and aggressive account of the *C minor Quartet*, Op. 18/4. The Hagen Quartet get through the third movement in 3:06 minutes as opposed to the 4:29 minutes of the more thoughtful

and civilized Végh. The quartet is treated as a vehicle for the Hagen's virtuosity and is completely out of period. The *C sharp minor* is more acceptable and the fugue has concentration and a kind of eloquence, but everything is on the surface. Play the Végh and, for all the sniffs and one lapse of intonation, you are in a different world. The recording is excellent and very musically balanced.

String quartets Nos. 7 in F (Razumovky No. 1); 10 in E flat (Harp), Op. 74.
(B) ** DG Classikon 469 028-2 [id.]. Amadeus Qt.

Here is an inexpensive way of sampling the Amadeus style in a pairing of mid-period Beethoven quartets. Smoothness of timbre, immaculate ensemble and tonal blending are the hallmarks of this Quartet's style, but there is also an element of blandness. In the *Adagio* of the first *Razumovsky* the playing is undoubtedly concentrated, but one senses a missing dimension.

In the slow movement of the *Harp Quartet* the essential simplicity of Beethoven's cantilena is well conveyed, and certainly the Scherzo has bold attack. Yet the closing *Allegretto* with variations, seems calculated and lacking in genial humanity. The recording from the early 1960s has been immaculately transferred.

String quartets Nos. 8 in E min. (Razumovsky No. 2), Op. 59/2; 10 in E flat (Harp), Op. 74.
(BB) *** Naxos Dig. 8.550562 [id.]. Kodály Qt.

String quartets Nos. 9 in C (Razumovsky No. 3), Op. 59/3; 12 in E flat, Op. 127.
(BB) *** Naxos Dig. 8.550563 [id.]. Kodály Qt.

The last two issues in the Kodály Quartet's Beethoven cycle have a lot going for them. First, the Kodály have the benefit of very good recorded sound with a particularly good balance which reveals every strand in the texture. Secondly, the actual playing is very fine with judiciously chosen tempi and expertly moulded phrasing. No one getting either of these discs is likely to be disappointed. But competition is both stiff and legion. Curmudgeonly though it may seem to say it given their excellence, these performances do not have the distinction of those of the Quartetto Italiano.

String quartets Nos. 10 in E flat (Harp), Op. 74; 11 in F min., Op. 95; 16 in F, Op. 135.
**(*) Harmonia Mundi HMU 907254 [id.]. Eroica Qt.

We liked the Eroica Quartet's début recording, coupling the Mendelssohn quartets Opp. 13 and 14. They are dedicated musicians and have obviously thought long and hard about Beethoven. In these three quartets, tempi are generally well judged throughout, though some may find the *Allegretto* of the *F minor Quartet*, Op. 95 a bit too sedate. The Eroica do however understand that tempi are related to the pace with which the composer would have been familiar – walking or running pace, or the horse-driven carriage. Similarly the light and colours are related to natural daylight or candlelight. These are thought-provoking readings, but at the same time there is some ugly or vulnerable intonation here and there, most notably in the slow movement of the *F major*, Op. 135 and indeed the very opening of the *Harp*. Why, too, after the opening flourish in the *F minor*, Op. 95 does the violin linger slightly over the cadences, thus weakening the forward impetus? All the same this is an interesting and rewarding disc. The notes by David Watkins, the cellist here, are excellent and the disc is well filled, but both the cover and the contents page of the booklet erroneously refer to a quartet movement in B minor from 1817!

String quartet No. 11 in F min., Op. 95.
**(*) DG Dig. 457 615-2 [id.]. Hagen Qt. –
SCHUBERT: *String quartet No. 15.* ***

The Hagen Quartet bring plenty of dramatic intensity to the *F minor Quartet*, Op. 95: the first movement has great concentration, though it is fractionally too fast. Indeed, we can imagine many listeners finding all four movements on the brisk side (and perhaps even a mite aggressive). But there is much expressive power in, and a powerful musical intelligence behind, everything they do. The DG recording has exemplary warmth and clarity.

String trios Nos. 1 in E flat, Op. 3; 2 in G; 3 in D; 4 in C min., Op. 9/1–3; Serenade in D, Op. 8.
(B) *** DG Double 459 466-2 (2) [id.]. Italian String Trio.

These performances of Beethoven's delightful, if neglected, *String trios* date from the late 1960s and have long been admired. They are immaculately played accounts, full of vitality and vivid in sound. They stand alongside the equally fine accounts on Philips Duo with the Grumiaux Trio, which has the same charming *Serenade* as a bonus (456 317-2), and choice is a matter of taste: the Philips set is rather more mellow in performance and recording, but both are equally valid interpretations.

Violin sonatas Nos. 1–10 (complete).
(M) (***) DG mono 463 605-2 [id.]. Wolfgang Schneiderhan, Wilhelm Kempff.

Kempff's earlier mono set of the *Violin sonatas*, in which he is partnered by the estimable Schneiderhan, date from 1953. The combination of Schneiderhan's refinement and classical sense of poise with Kempff's concentration and clarity makes these performances highly competitive, even compared with Kempff's later set with Menuhin. Schneiderhan's playing has greater finish and his lyrical line sings sweet and true. One has only to sample the *Spring* or *Kreutzer Sonatas* to discover

the calibre of this partnership, spontaneous, dramatic, and full of insights, while Kempff's opening of the slow movement of the *C minor Sonata, Op. 30/2* is unforgettable, and his partner joins him in comparable rapt concentration. The recording obviously does not separate violin and piano as clearly as in the stereo set, but the internal balance could hardly be bettered and the sound is natural, with a particularly attractive piano image, fuller than Kempff sometimes received in later years. A worthy candidate for DG's Originals.

Violin sonatas Nos. 1–6.
**(*) EMI Double Fforte CZS5 73647-2 [CDFB 73647] (2). Pinchas Zukerman, Daniel Barenboim.

Violin sonatas Nos. 7–10.
**(*) EMI Double Fforte CZS5 73650-2 [CDFB 73650] (2). Pinchas Zukerman, Daniel Barenboim – TCHAIKOVSKY: *Trio.* *(**)

Zukerman and Barenboim, friends and colleagues, are both strong and positive artists and in their collaborations on record they have consistently struck sparks of imagination with each other. They do so here in these recordings (dating from 1972/3) yet there is a hint too that they may have been conscious of earlier criticism that their collaborations were too idiosyncratic. So these are very much central performances which, although not the most imaginative we have had, are a safe recommendation. At bargain price, in good sound, with an exciting performances of the Tchaikovsky *Piano trio* as a bonus, this is worth considering.

Violin sonatas Nos. 5 (Spring), Op. 24; 7, Op. 30/ 2; 9 (Kreutzer), Op. 47; Rondo in G, WoO 41.
(M) *** DG 463 175-2 (2) [id.]. Yehudi Menuhin, Wilhelm Kempff – TCHAIKOVSKY: *Violin concerto.* (**)

The Menuhin–Kempff partnership recorded all the Beethoven sonatas in Conway Hall, London in June 1970 and this two-CD set offers three of them in harness with a 1949 recording of the Tchaikovsky *Violin concerto* with Fricsay conducting. The *C minor*, Op. 30/2 and the *Rondo in G* occupy the first of the two discs and are placed immediately after the *Concerto* while the *Spring* and the *Kreutzer* occupy the second. If you have just bought the two sets issued last year (DG 459 433-2 and 459 436-2), you will obviously not want to duplicate for the sake of the Tchaikovsky concerto, for even though it is Menuhin's only recording of the work, it does not show him on his best form.

Violin sonata No. 9 in A (Kreutzer), Op. 47.
*** EMI Dig. CDC5 56815-2 [id.]. Itzhak Perlman, Martha Argerich – FRANCK: *Violin sonata.* ***

Perlman and Argerich, both big musical personalities, strike sparks off each other in this vividly characterful reading of the *Kreutzer*, recorded live at the Saratoga Performing Arts Center in 1998. Ensemble is not always immaculate, and audience noises intrude, but this playing could not be more vital, with the first movement fiery and dramatic, the slow movement warmly expressive, and the finale sparkily volatile. The recording, not as immediate as most of Perlman's studio recordings, gives a better idea than usual of his full range of dynamic and tone. Well coupled with a comparable reading of the Franck.

Wind music

Octet in E flat, Op. 103; Rondino in E flat, WoO 25; Septet in E flat, Op. 20 (arr. for wind nonet by Jirí Družecky).
*** EMI Dig. CDC5 56817-2 [id.]. Sabine Meyer Wind Ens.

The *Rondino* was Beethoven's alternative finale for the *Octet* Op. 103, an early work despite the late opus number. That delightful work for the typical Harmonie ensemble is well matched by the arrangement of the Op. 20 *Septet*. This was among Beethoven's most popular works of the time, and was treated to many different arrangements, including three for Harmonie wind band. This one from 1812, made by a leading composer of Harmoniemusik, adds a double-bassoon to the usual octet. In this dazzling performance (with Sabine Meyer astonishingly agile in the rapid triplets of the finale) it is just as attractive as the original. An outstanding disc, beautifully recorded, representing early Beethoven at his most winning.

SOLO PIANO MUSIC

Piano sonatas Nos. 1–32.
(B) ******* DG Dig. 463 127-2 (9) [id.]. Daniel Barenboim.

Spontaneity and electricity, extremes of expression in dynamic, tempo and phrasing, as well as mood, mark Barenboim's DG cycle, as they did his much earlier one for EMI. Some of the more extreme readings – such as the sleep-walking tempo for the finale of the *Waldstein* – have been modified to fall short of provocation or eccentricity. This time spontaneity is even more evident, though that means he has a tendency at times to rush his fences, particularly in the early sonatas, giving a hint of breathlessness to already fast speeds. That is exceptional, and so is the hint of technical stress. The first movement of the *Appassionata* is given with all his old flair, even more a vehicle for display thanks to dramatic extremes of light and dark. Conversely the second and third movements are now plainer and simpler. The plainness in the first movement of the *Moonlight* is disappointing, however, less poetic with little veiled tone; but the light, flowing finale of the *Tempest*, Op. 31, No. 2, is now more magically

Mendelssohnian than ever. All three movements of the *Waldstein* this time are more lyrical, and that applies to the late sonatas too, not just in slow movements but equally strikingly in the great fugal movements, where inner parts are brought out more clearly and warmly. Only in the final Adagio variations of Op. 111 does a hint of self-consciousness develop, thanks to agogic hesitations at a tempo even slower than before. The lyrical opening movement of Op. 101 *in A* is delectably done, flowing and simple. The role of such a cycle as this is not to set Barenboim's readings as though in amber, fixed for ever, but to act more nearly as a living document of a performer at a particular point in his career. The sound is full and spacious, more consistent than before. The CD transfers – taking the sonatas in consecutive order and on one less disc than Barenboim's earlier EMI set (see our main volume) – are of consistently high quality.

Piano sonatas Nos. 1–32; Diabelli variations, Op. 120.
(BB) ******* Arte Nova Dig. 74321 40740-2 (10) [id.]. Alfredo Perl.
Vol. 1: *Sonatas Nos. 1–3, Op. 2/1–3* (74321 27762-2); Vol. 2: *Nos. 4, Op. 7; 13–14 (Moonlight), Op. 27/1–2; 24, Op. 78* (74321 30459-2); Vol. 3: *Nos. 5–7, Op. 10/1–3; 26 (Les Adieux), Op. 81a* (74321 30460-2); Vol. 4: *Nos. 8 (Pathétique), Op. 13; 12 (Funeral march), Op. 26; 27, Op. 90; 28, Op. 101* (74321 27764-2); Vol. 5: *Nos. 9–10, Op. 14/1–2; 29 (Hammerklavier), Op. 106* (74321 37851-2); Vol. 6: *Nos. 11, Op. 22; 22, Op. 54; 23 (Appassionata), Op. 57; 25, Op. 79* (74321 39101-2); Vol. 7: *Nos. 15 (Pastoral), Op. 28; 19–20, Op. 49/1–2; 21 (Waldstein), Op. 53* (74321 34012-2); Vol. 8: *Nos. 16–17 (Tempest); 18, Op. 31/1–3* (74321 37311-2); Vol. 9: *Nos. 30–3, Opp. 109–111* (74321 39102-2); Vol. 10: *Variations on a waltz by Diabelli, Op. 120* (74321 27761-2).

The young Chilean pianist Alfredo Perl responds superbly to the challenge of a complete Beethoven sonata cycle, giving searching accounts of works both early and late, always fresh and spontaneous-sounding, consistently finding depths of concentration in the most demanding of Beethoven's slow movements. Particularly in the early sonatas, his manner is impulsive, often with allegros fast in a Schnabel manner, yet with technical problems masterfully solved and no fudging of detail. Slow movements by contrast are generally spacious, but not so exaggeratedly so that the music loses momentum or a sense of lyrical line. The cycle is splendidly rounded off in accounts of the late sonatas that transcend everything else, not least the *Hammerklavier*, where the slow movement has a sublime purity. The performance of the *Diabelli variations* is equally commanding and imaginative.

Overall Perl's readings are far more individual and characterful than those of his direct rival on super-bargain disc, Jenö Jandó on Naxos, yet never wilful. Like the Naxos set, this one offers the discs separately if required, where other cycles at super-bargain price, like Barenboim's on EMI or Bernard Roberts's on Nimbus, come simply as a package. The sound is first-rate, though inner textures are not always ideally clear, while Perl's use of the pedal is on the generous side, adding to the warmth of the readings, and this stands alongside the finest surveys of the Beethoven sonatas, irrespective of price.

Piano sonata No. 4 in E flat, Op. 7.
(M) * DG Analogue/Dig. 457 762-2 [id.].
    Michelangeli – SCHUBERT: *Piano Sonata in
    A min.* **; BRAHMS: *4 Ballades, Op. 10.* ***

This is a curiously aloof and detached reading of the Op. 7 *Sonata* – as if the artist is viewing the sonata's progress without ever involving himself in its evolution. Coupled with some superb Brahms and controversial Schubert, this CD is a curate's egg.

*Piano sonatas Nos. 5 in C min.; 6 in F; 7 in D,
Op. 10/1–3; 15 in D (Pastoral), Op. 28.*
*** EMI Dig. CDC5 56761-2 [id.]. Stephen
    Kovacevich.

In his ongoing Beethoven sonata cycle, that most thoughtful artist Stephen Kovacevich here offers one of his finest collections yet, with fresh and intense readings of four early sonatas, undisturbed by quirky mannerisms. The third of the Opus 10 sonatas is the first major masterpiece of the great cycle of thirty-two, with its dramatic first movement leading to the darkly tragic D minor slow movement. Not that Kovacevich misses Beethoven's wit and humour, whether in all three Opus 10 works or in Opus 28, the *Pastoral*, among the most amiable of all. Almost everything about this series has been touched with distinction, musically at any rate, and this newcomer is no exception. There is not the slightest trace of ego in this playing and a total dedication to Beethoven. One is tempted to say that this cycle is to our time what the Schnabel and Kempff sets were to theirs (and no praise could be higher), and the EMI engineers have got the sound right.

*Piano sonatas Nos. 11 in B flat, Op. 22; 12 in A
flat, Op. 26; 19 in G min.; 20 in G, Op. 49/1–2.*
*** Chandos Dig. CHAN 9755 [id.]. Louis Lortie.

Performances of vital and unfailing intelligence, which make one think afresh about the music itself. There is no trace of interpretative ego, just a natural musicianship placed at the composer's service. What we have heard so far of Lortie's Beethoven odyssey makes one feel that it is worth placing alongside Stephen Kovacevich's sonata cycle on EMI. It is certainly not inferior to it. The Chandos

recording is state-of-the-art and wonderfully natural. A most distinguished issue.

*Piano sonatas Nos. 15 in D (Pastoral), Op. 28;
17 in D min. (Tempest); 18 in E flat, Op. 31/2–3.*
(M) *(**) DG Dig. 463 079-2 [id.]. Emil Gilels.

Gilels's performances of the Op. 31 sonatas have excited universal acclaim and rightly so. In the D minor (No. 17) and E flat major (No. 18), there is enormous pianistic and musical distinction. It is a pity that the engineers placed the piano too forward; it sounds as though the listener is on the platform – bringing out the percussive qualities too much – but there is no doubting the impact of these readings. The snag with this CD is the very strange perform-ance of the *Pastoral*: a laboured, almost hectoring first movement, very deliberate in tempo and character, with little sense of flow and only oc-casional glimpses of the wisdom and humanity one associated with this great artist. But this CD is worth considering at mid-price for Op. 31/2–3.

*Piano sonatas Nos. 30 in E, Op. 109; 31 in A flat,
Op. 110; 32 in C min., Op. 111; Variations on a
theme of Diabelli, Op. 120; 6 Bagatelles, Op. 126;
11 Bagatelles, Op. 119; Ecossaise, WoO 86;
Klavierstücken, WoO 61 & 61a; Waltzes, WoO 80.*
(M) **(*) Audivis Naive-Classique NC 40001 (2).
    Jean-François Heisser.

These two CDs cover Beethoven's complete output for the keyboard during his last years, 1820–27. The French pianist, Jean-François Heisser, now in his early fifties, has the benefit of outstanding recording quality: the piano image is very lifelike with impressive detail and body, a firm bass and a jewel-like clarity at the top. The instrument is beautifully regulated and conditioned and expertly tuned.

Heisser is a thoughtful pianist, whose clear, pre-cise articulation commands admiration, and who radiates clarity of thought. There is a strong sense of musical purpose throughout and a refreshing absence of interpretative point-making. If he does not offer the insights of the very finest interpreters in this very demanding repertoire his performances are still distinctive, and the recorded sound is very much in the demonstration bracket.

Miscellaneous piano music

*Allegretto in C min., WoO 53; Allegretto, WoO
61; Allegretto quasi andante, WoO 61; Bagatelles,
WoO 52 & 56; in B flat, WoO 60; in C; 2
Bagatelles; Für Elise, WoO 59; 12 German
dances, WoO 8; 7 Ländler, WoO 11; 6 Ländler,
WoO 15; Minuet in C; 6 Minuets WoO 10.*
(BB) **(*) Naxos Dig. 8.553795 [id.]. Jenö Jandó.

*Allegretto in C min., H.69; Bagatelle in C
(Lustig-Traurig), WoO 54; Fantasia, Op. 77; 12
German dances, WoO 13; 7 Contredanses, WoO*

14; 6 Ecossaises, WoO 83; Fugue in C, H.64;
Minuet in E flat, WoO 82; Polonaise in C, Op. 89;
2 Preludes, Op. 39; Prelude in F min., WoO 55;
(Concert) Rondo in C, WoO 48; (Concerto) Finale
in C, H.65.
(BB) **(*) Naxos Dig. 8.553798 [id.]. Jenö Jandó.

It is always a joy to witness Beethoven relaxing.
This collection of shorter piano pieces may offer
no great music, but these chips from the master's
work-bench have a freshness and vitality that is
endlessly a delight. These are the first CDs in a
complete coverage of the *Bagatelles* and *Dances*.
Jenö Jandó is at his finest in the two *C minor
Allegrettos* and the *C major Rondo*, and he also
plays the famous *Für Elise* and the lesser-known
Lustig-Traurig persuasively. He opens the second
disc with an appropriately impulsive and enjoyable
account of the Op. 77 *Fantasia* which gives in its
ten-minute span a vivid idea of what a Beethoven
improvisation was like, quirky in its switches of
mood. Elsewhere his clear, direct manner certainly
evokes the spirit of Beethoven, although the dances
are not always coaxed as charmingly as they might
be. However, the set of six *Ecossaises* (in essence,
contredanses, and little to do with Scotland), which
have been inflicted on many a beginner, are rhythmically very jolly and emerge as an exhilarating
offering. The two *Preludes*, Op. 39 which as a
student exercise modulate through all the major
keys in turn, have their fascination too, as has the
solo arrangement of the final coda of the *Third
Piano concerto*, which buoyantly completes the
second disc. With playing fresh and clear, this is for
the most part a delightful supplement to Jandó's
ground-breaking cycle of Beethoven sonatas for
Naxos.

5 Variations in D on Arne's 'Rule, Britannia',
WoO 79; 6 Variations in F on an original theme,
Op. 34; 6 Variations in D on an original theme,
Op. 76; 7 Variations in F on 'Winter's Kind, willst
du ruhig schlafen?', WoO 75; 8 Variations in C
on Grétry's 'Un fièvre brûlante', WoO 72; 8
Variations in F on Süssmayer's 'Tändeln und
Scherzen', WoO 76; 10 Variations in B flat on
Salieri's 'La stessa, la stessissima', WoO 73.
*** DG Dig. 457 613-2 [id.]. Gianluca Cascioli.

Gianluca Cascioli recorded these variation sets in
1996–7 when he was still in his teens. He is an
immensely alert and intelligent player with a keen
wit and brilliant articulation. The engineers place
us a little too near the instrument so that his sforzati
may sound just a little too percussive but his refinement of colour and dynamics with delicacy of
touch is everywhere in evidence. He makes the most
of all these pieces and no one investing in this disc
is likely to be disappointed. These performances
were originally included in the mammoth DG Beethoven Edition Vol. 6, so readers who have that
eight-CD set will not want to duplicate. To others

it cannot be too strongly recommended and even if
the recording is brightly lit, it has striking clarity
and realism.

VOCAL MUSIC

Mass in C, Op. 86; Meeresstille und glückliche
Fahrt, Op. 112.
(B) *(*) Erato/Ultima Double 3984 28168-2 (2)
[id.]. Michael, Bizimeche-Eisinger, Schaeffer,
Brodard, Gulbenkian Ch. & O, Corboz –
Piano concertos Nos. 2–3. ***

On Erato the chorus sings with enthusiasm and
the soloists blend well if not showing any great
individuality. But the backward balance and the
lack of choral bite blunts the conductor's efforts.
The Gardiner version of this coupling on DG (435
391-2) is in every possible way superior.

(i) *Missa solemnis in D, Op. 123. Symphony*
No. 7 in A, Op. 92.
(**(*)) BBC Legends mono BBCL 4016-2 (2)
[id.]. (i) Milanov, Thorborg, Von Pataky,
Moscona, BBC Choral Soc.; BBC SO,
Toscanini – CHERUBINI: *Anacréon overture*
***; MOZART: *Symphony No. 35 in D*
(Haffner), K.385. (***)

Toscanini's visits to London in the 1930s, in order
to conduct the BBC Symphony Orchestra, resulted
each year in incandescent performances, culminating in this legendary May 1939 account of Beethoven's *Missa solemnis* with a formidable quartet
of soloists. This is a markedly broader, warmer
performance than the one from New York long
available on RCA, and the sound, though limited,
is satisfyingly full-bodied. The recordings of Beethoven's *Seventh* and Mozart's *Haffner*, similarly
warmer than his New York performances, date from
1935. Though the sound is crumbly at times, the
thrill of Toscanini in full flight is vividly conveyed.

OPERA

Fidelio (complete).
(BB) *** Naxos Dig. 8.660070/71 [id.]. Nielsen,
Winbergh, Moll, Titus, Lienbacher, Pecoraro,
Hungarian R. Ch., Nicolas Esterházy Sinf.,
Michael Halász.
** Teldec/Warner Dig. 3984 25249-2 (2) [id.].
Meier, Domingo, Pape, Struckmann, Isokoski,
Güra, German State Op. Berlin Ch. & O,
Barenboim.
(BB) (*(*)) Naxos mono 8.110054/55 [id.].
Flagstad, Maison, Kipnis, Huehn, Farell,
Laufkötter, Met. Op. Ch. & O, Bruno Walter.

The new Naxos *Fidelio* from Budapest is outstanding in every way. Using the excellent orchestra
which has already done a Beethoven symphony
cycle for Naxos, it offers a first-rate modern cast
incisively directed by Michael Halász, and very

well recorded, with the relative intimacy adding to
the impact and sense of drama. The cast is most
impressive, with singers consistently clear and
fresh. Inga Nielsen matches and even outshines her
earlier achievement in the title role of Strauss's
Salome on Chandos. Hers is an outstanding Leonore
with every note sharply focused, using the widest
tonal and dynamic range from bright fortissimo to
velvety half-tone. Few singers on disc in recent
years begin to rival her account of the *Abscheulicher*, ranging from venomous anger to radiant
tenderness. Gösta Winbergh makes a formidable
Florestan, with Alan Titus a firm, sinister Pizarro
and Kurt Moll a splendid Rocco. Only the Don
Fernando falls short with a voice too woolly to
focus cleanly. Even making no allowance for price,
this version is among the very finest to have arrived
in years, gaining in clarity and incisiveness from
the relatively small scale.

Barenboim's version developed from concert
performances he gave, not in Berlin, but in Chicago.
For an English-speaking audience he had Waltraud
Meier as Leonore providing spoken links between
numbers, rather than including the usual dialogue.
Here the links are provided in the booklet, and the
recording simply omits dialogue, except in passages
of accompanied melodrama. The other oddity is
that Barenboim prefers the magnificent *Leonore
No. 2* overture to the usual one for *Fidelio* and,
following what happened at the original 1805 production, reverses the order of the first two numbers,
with Marzelline's little aria coming first. Barenboim
is a dedicated Beethoven interpreter, but this is not
one of his most inspired recordings, disappointing
largely because of the casting. It is worth hearing
for Plácido Domingo's heroic account of the role
of Florestan, clean and incisive, if strained at times.
Waltraud Meier, originally a mezzo, becomes shrill
under pressure, notably at the top, the voice not quite
firm enough, and Soile Isokoski with her marked
vibrato is a matronly Marzelline. René Pape is an
excellent, firm Rocco, but Falk Struckmann is
wobbly and strained as Pizarro, and Kwangchul
Youn is a lightweight Fernando. Vocal flaws are all
the more apparent, as the recording balances the
voices well in front of the orchestra.

The second Naxos version, issued simultaneously with the new account from Budapest,
offers a historic radio recording of a live performance given in 1940 at the Metropolitan Opera in
New York with Bruno Walter conducting and
Kirsten Flagstad as Leonore. For many it will immediately be ruled out both by the limited, often
crumbly sound and by intrusive audience noises.
Yet listening through the distortion and interference
is not too difficult, when the performance under
Walter is urgently passionate at high voltage. The
idea of Walter as a mellow, reflective Beethoven
interpreter is completely contradicted. That the
voices are recorded very close may be oppressive,

but it adds to the power. Flagstad naturally dominates the performance vocally, even more vital than
in her Salzburg reading under Furtwängler (EMI).
Alexander Kipnis as Rocco and Herbert Janssen as
Don Fernando stand out among the rest, with the
others in the cast generally disappointing.

Bellini, Vincenzo (1801–35)

Sinfonias in C; D; E flat.
*** Koch Dig. 3-6733-2 [id.]. Krakau State PO,
Roland Bader – DONIZETTI: *Sinfonias*. ***

Bellini's *Sinfonias* are elegant, rather more serious
in mood and style than the Donizetti works with
which they are coupled. Each has a long, gracious
introduction. They have excellent ideas, well put
together, and secondary themes all have charm, as
indeed has the principal theme of the *C major*. All
three are very well played and recorded and this
collection is well worth exploring.

I Capuleti e i Montecchi (complete).
*** Teldec/Warner Dig. 3984 21472-2 (2) [id.].
Larmore, Hong, Groves, Aceto, Lloyd,
Scottish CO, Runnicles.

Donald Runnicles, born in Scotland but still neglected in Britain, here offers a fresh and sympathetic
reading of Bellini's 'Romeo and Juliet' opera with
an outstanding cast. The benefit of having the Scottish Chamber Orchestra instead of a full-blown
symphony orchestra is that the woodwind and brass
have a fairer balance against the strings. Though
the scale may be a degree smaller, the immediacy
of the sound adds to the impact. Jennifer Larmore is
warm, fresh and firm as Romeo, youthfully ardent.
Most remarkable of all is the Korean soprano Hei-
Kyung Hong as Juliet, at once pure and warm of
tone and passionate of expression, equally bringing
out the youthfulness of the heroine. As Tebaldo,
Paul Groves is clear and stylish, even though the
tone is not Italianate, and Robert Lloyd is a commanding Lorenzo. Though the competition is
strong, both from Muti on EMI (recorded live at
Covent Garden) and from Roberto Abbado on RCA
(with the benefit of offering the alternative Vaccai
ending on a third disc at no extra cost), the Teldec
set scores both in its casting and in the fullness of
sound.

Benjamin, Arthur (1893–1960)

*Brumas tunes; Chinoiserie; Elegiac mazurka;
Fantasies I–II; Haunted house; Jamaican rumba;
Let's go hiking; 3 New fantasies; Odds and ends
I–II; Pastorale, arioso and finale;
Romance-impromptu; Saxophone blues;
Scherzino; Siciliana; Suite.*
*** Tall Poppies Dig. TP 105 [id.]. Ian Munro.

Arthur Benjamin was born in Australia, but he studied at the Royal College of Music (where he later became a Professor of the piano). Apart from service in the Royal Flying Corps in the First World War and a period in Canada during the Second World War, he spent most of his life in England. His *Jamaican rumba* was the result of a professional examination visit there in 1938 and it soon became a world hit. He did not repeat that success, yet his other genre pieces here are full of attractive ideas and comparably catchy rhythmic invention, at times cool in the Jazz sense of the word (*Saxophone blues*), at others (the *Odds and ends* or the *Fantasies*, for instance) offering writing of charming, but indelible simplicity (sample the delectable *March* – the second of the *New fantasies*, or the third, *Drifting*). Benjamin's piano writing has the elegance and sophistication of the French School, and his 1926 *Suite* (with four of the five movements dedicated to contemporary musicians) is distinctly Ravelian, with obvious debts to *Le tombeau de Couperin*. The outer sections of the *Pastorale, arioso and finale* scintillate, and demand the utmost virtuosity. Ian Munro revels in the music's dashing bravura. Throughout he plays with great style and elegance and obvious affection. This is a wholly delightful recital with never a dull moment throughout its 78 minutes. And few CDs have more extensive notes about the music and also include a full composer biography. The recording is admirably natural. (If you find it difficult to obtain this CD – you can go direct to Tall Poppies, PO Box 373, Glebe, NSW 2037, Australia.)

Bennett, Robert Russell (1894–1981)

Abraham Lincoln (A likeness in symphonic form); Sights and sounds (An orchestral entertainment).
(BB) ** Naxos Dig. 8.5509004 [id.]. Moscow SO, William T. Stromberg.

Robert Russell Bennett, the orchestrator of many famous musicals, is best known on record for his Gershwin score, the *Symphonic picture of Porgy and Bess*, but he wrote much concert music of his own (having studied in the 1920s in Berlin and in Paris under Nadia Boulanger). The present two works were entered for a 1929 RCA Victor competition (the jury included Stokowski, Koussevitzky, and Frederick Stock). Bennett won, alongside Copland and Ernest Bloch. As might be expected both works show his great orchestral skill, but the quality of the invention does not match the vividly imaginative orchestral sounds. There are *longueurs* in the four-movement *Lincoln portrait* and the various American *Sights and sounds*, including *Union Station*, *Electric signs* and *Speed*, are little more than clever orchestral effects. Only the evocation of a *Night club*, with its saxophone riff, has anything approaching a memorable idea. The orchestral

playing and the commitment of the conductor cannot be faulted, neither can the recording. But the end result does not encourage repeated listenings.

Bentzon, Jørgen (1897–1951)

Divertimento for violin, viola and cello, Op. 2; Intermezzo for violin and clarinet, Op. 24; Sonatina for flute, clarinet and bassoon, Op. 7; Variazioni interrotti for clarinet, bassoon, violin, viola and cello, Op. 12; (i) *Mikrofoni No. 1, for baritone, flute, violin, cello and piano, Op. 44.*
**(*) Dacapo Dig. 8.224129 [id.]. Danish Chamber Players; (i) with Lars Thodberg Bertelsen.

Jørgen Bentzon was an interesting figure, an older cousin of Niels Viggo Bentzon and the flautist Johan. He was a gifted linguist and jurist. He studied composition with Nielsen and apart from devoting his time to composing and the Copenhagen Folke-Musikskole (a more informal music school than the Conservatoire, which had much in common with the *Volksmusikschule* movement in Germany), he held a senior civil-service post as Clerk of the Supreme Court. His music has a clean, fresh diatonic feel to it, though some of it sounds a bit manufactured. By far the best piece here is the *Mikrofoni*, Op. 44 though it is let down by the solo baritone, and by far the wittiest is the *Variazioni interrotti*.

Bentzon, Niels Viggo (1919–2000)

(i) *Piano concerto No. 4, Op. 96. 5 Mobiles, Op. 125.*
** Dacapo Dig. 8.224110 [id.]. (i) Anker Blyme; Aarhus SO, Ole Schmidt.

The veteran Danish composer Niels Viggo Bentzon is a direct descendant of J. P. E. Hartmann (1805–1900) and more distantly of Niels Gade. He is enormously prolific – a catalogue published in 1980 listed no fewer than 429 works, and he has not been idle since. There are at least twenty symphonies and as many piano sonatas, and fifteen piano concertos! The *Five Mobiles* is an inventive score but the *Fourth Piano concerto* is distinctly uneven in inspiration. Readers should try the two symphonies listed below, which are full of fantasy and invention.

Symphonies Nos. 5 (Ellipser), Op. 61; 7 (De tre versioner), Op. 83.
⊕ *** Dacapo Dig. 8.22411 [id.]. Aarhus SO, Ole Schmidt.

It would be idle to pretend that Niels Viggo Bentzon's creative hyperactivity is matched by consistency of inspiration. But the early symphonies from the *Second*, for piano and orchestra (1944), through to the *Seventh* (1953) are marvellously rich scores teeming with invention. His music offers real vision whose textures glow luminously. Both the *Seventh* and the *Fifth* have a sense of space and individuality (deriving from tonal composers Copland, Nielsen, Hindemith and Stravinsky). These records appeared on LP in the 1980s and the works wear well. It is no exaggeration to call the *Seventh* a masterpiece, an impressive study in thematic metamorphosis, whose techniques fascinated Holmboe at this time. Fine performances and recording.

Piano sonatas Nos. 3, Op. 44; 5, Op. 77; 9, Op. 104.
** Dacapo Dig. 8.224103 [id.]. Rodolfo Llambías.

Bentzon was a fine pianist and his output extends to some twenty or so piano sonatas as well as *The Well Tempered Clavier* – 24 Preludes and Fugues, Op. 409 – in all the tonalities. *Sonata No. 3* is an exceptionally fine work, not dissimilar to the sonatas of Tippett or the sole sonata of Robert Simpson, and inferior to neither. The composer recorded it in the days of 78s and later it was recorded by the Icelandic pianist Rognvaldur Sigurjonsson. Both took about sixteen minutes as opposed to Rodolfo Llambías's twenty-five! His approach is highly discursive and he lays bare all of No. 3's many beauties rather too lovingly. All the same, in the absence of any alternatives, these remarkable sonatas demand a hearing. Unfortunately the acoustic is over-reverberant.

Berg, Alban (1885–1935)

Lyric suite: 3 pieces; 3 Pieces for orchestra, Op. 6.
(M) *** DG 457 760-2 [id.]. BPO, Karajan – SCHOENBERG: *Variations;* WEBERN: *Passacaglia.* ***

Karajan's purification process gives wonderful clarity to Berg's often complex scores, with expressive confidence bringing out the romantic overtones. For those who resist Berg's style, Karajan's way is most likely to convert, for these are magnificently played and recorded accounts – superbly transferred on this DG Originals reissue.

Piano sonata, Op. 1.
(BB) *** Naxos Dig. 8.553870 [id.]. Peter Hill – SCHOENBERG: *Piano pieces; Suite;* WEBERN: *Variations, Op. 27.* ***

The Berg *Sonata* has enjoyed distinguished advocacy from Brendel, Perahia, Pollini and Glenn Gould among others. But Peter Hill's account on Naxos has more than just its bargain price to commend it. He is a pianist of proven intelligence and sensitivity and decently recorded. It comes with the Schoenberg piano music played with no less expertise and authority.

7 Early songs: Im Zimmer; Liebesode; Nacht; Die Nachtigall; Schifflied; Sommertage; Traumgekrönt.
*** Decca Dig. 466 720-2 [id.]. Barbara Bonney, Concg. O, Chailly – MAHLER: *Symphony No. 4 in G* **(*).

Barbara Bonney sounds even more spontaneous and warm in the seven early Berg songs (orchestrated by the composer) which come as a very generous coupling for Mahler's *Fourth Symphony,* and Chailly and the orchestra too sound a degree more involved than in the Mahler.

OPERA

Lulu (with orchestration of Act III completed by Friedrich Cerha).
(M) *** DG 463 617 (3) [id.]. Stratas, Minton, Schwarz, Mazura, Blankenheim, Riegel, Tear, Paris Op. O, Boulez.

Boulez was the first to unveil the full three-act structure of *Lulu* which was a revelation with few parallels. The third Act, musically even stronger than the first two, and dramatically essential in making sense of the stylized plan based on the palindrome, transforms the opera. Although it all ends with the lurid portrayal of Jack the Rippers's murder of Lulu – here recorded with hair-raising vividness – the nastiness of the subject is put in context, made more acceptable artistically.

The very end of the opera, with Yvonne Minton singing the Countess Geschwitz's lament, is most moving, though Lulu remains to the last a repulsive heroine. Teresa Stratas's bright, clear soprano is well recorded, and there is hardly a weak link in the cast. This is a historic issue, presenting an intensely involving performance of a work which is in some ways more lyrically approachable than *Wozzeck.* A fine candidate for DG's Originals packaging, with freshly improved remastered sound.

Wozzeck (complete).
(M) *** EMI Dig. CDS5 56865-2 (2) [id.]. Skovhus, Denoke, Olsen, Merritt, Blinkhof, Sacher, Hamburg State Op. Ch. & State PO, Ingo Metzmacher.

Ingo Metzmacher's live recording for EMI was made at the Hamburg State Opera, in a revolutionary production involving little scenery, with the orchestra on stage. The result is immediate and highly coloured, with Metzmacher drawing powerful, clean-textured playing from his orchestra, firmly establishing this as a high romantic work, whatever its modernist credentials. The casting is strong too, with Bo Skovhus singing with clean focus in the title role, and with Marie superbly sung by Angela Denoke. Hers is a warm, fresh, youthful-sounding voice, helping her to present Marie as sensuous on the one hand, tenderly affecting on the other, not least in the Bible-reading scene. Otherwise, the production on a bare stage seems to have encouraged each character to overact, Skovhus included, crudifying characterization at times, even while the results are exceptionally vivid, with the sense of a live performance consistently adding to the dramatic impact. The first two acts fit neatly on the first disc, leaving the relatively brief Act III on the second: EMI, in recognition, offers the set at mid-price.

Berkeley, Lennox (1903–89)

Concertino, Op. 49; Duo for cello and piano, Op. 81/1; Elegy for violin and piano, Op. 35/2; Introduction and allegro for solo violin, Op. 24; Oboe quartet, Op. 70; Petite suite for oboe and piano; Sextet, Op. 47; Toccata for violin and piano, Op. 33/3.
(M)*** Dutton Lab. Dig. CDLX 7100 [id.].
    Endymion Ens.

There have been relatively few new recordings of Lennox Berkeley's elegantly fashioned music. Grace and finesse seem to be qualities not greatly prized by today's world. The beguiling *Divertimento in B flat* is only available in one recording; the *Serenade for strings*, at one time often played, is now, relatively speaking, neglected, and the *First Symphony*, one of the composer's most deeply characteristic pieces, is not even listed in the catalogue. All the more praise to Dutton for temporarily abandoning their exemplary work in restoring great recordings of the past to commit this repertoire to disc. Berkeley's music is fastidiously crafted and musically rewarding, unpretentious, urbane and charming. The Endymion Ensemble do it proud and so does the natural and well-balanced recording.

Berlioz, Hector (1803–69)

Harold in Italy, Op. 16.
(B) **(*) Australian Decca Eloquence 466 907-2.
    Daniel Benyamini, Israel PO, Mehta – BLOCH: *Voice in the Wilderness* **(*).

(i) *Harold in Italy*; (ii) *Tristia: Méditation religieuse; La mort d'Ophélie; Marche funèbre pour la dernière scène de Hamlet, Op. 18. Les Troyens à Carthage: Prelude to Act II.*
(B) *** Ph. Virtuoso 416 431-2 [id.]. (i) Imai; (ii) John Alldis Ch.; LSO, Sir Colin Davis.

In addition to a noble account of *Harold* in which Nobuko Imai is on top form, this CD offers the *Tristia*, which includes the haunting *Funeral march for the last scene of Hamlet* given with chorus; this CD also offers the *Prelude* to the second Act of *Les Troyens*. The sound is natural and realistic, with impressive transparency and detail. Reissued on the Philips Virtuoso bargain label, this is formidable value.

Mehta draws sonorous playing from the Israeli orchestra and if the result is a little unrefined at times, the recording has the sort of brilliance and separation that one associates with Mehta's Los Angeles records. Its robust large-scale quality does not always suit the music, particularly when the solo viola is balanced too close, but the effect is certainly vivid. Though this is enjoyable – the *Pilgrim's march* is quite gripping, and there is great excitement in the finale – some of Berlioz's subtlety is missing. Nevertheless, a worthwhile bargain CD, especially in view of the interesting coupling.

Symphonie fantastique, Op. 14.
(*) BBC Legends BBCL 4018-2 [id.]. New Philh. O, Stokowski (with conversation with Deryck Cooke) – SCRIABIN: *Poème de l'extase.* *
(M) (***) Dutton Lab. mono CDK 1208 [id.]. Concg. O, Eduard van Beinum (with BEETHOVEN: *Creatures of Prometheus: Overture* (LPO)) – SCHUBERT: *Symphony No. 5* (***).
(M) **(*) Sony SMK 60968 [id.]. NYPO, Bernstein (with 'Berlioz takes a trip' – a talk on the *Symphonie fantastique* by Leonard Bernstein).

Symphonie fantastique, Op. 14; La damnation de Faust: Ballet des sylphes; Menuet des feux follets.
(M) **(*) DG 463 080-2 [id.]. BPO, Karajan.

A really high-voltage performance from Stokowski and the New Philharmonia Orchestra of the *Symphonie fantastique* recorded in 1968. The great conductor was eighty-six and in astonishing form. Although he also recorded it for Decca, the Berlioz masterpiece was a Stokowski rarity: he even told William Glock when he asked him to include it in a Prom programme earlier in the 1960s, that he thought Monteux or Paray would do it better. Though this would not be a first choice, every bar is stamped with personality. There are characteristic expressive exaggerations but everything rings true, and has conviction. The sound is acceptable, though not all the strands in the texture are ideally balanced. This comes together with an outstanding performance of *Le poème de l'extase* and a conversation between the great conductor and Deryck Cooke. However, it must be said that Stokowski's Decca Phase 4 version (448 955-2) is in every way superior, idiosyncratic perhaps, but electrifying and essentially true to the spirit of the music, with spectacular recording. Moreover, the Decca disc also offers an exquisite account of the *Danse des sylphes*, and is worth snapping up before it disappears under the deletions axe.

This is not Eduard van Beinum's *Symphonie fantastique* familiar from the early days of LPs, but the first post-war recording he made on six 78-r.p.m. shellac discs in 1947 which was quickly deleted to make room for it. *The Record Guide*, writing in

1951, regretting its deletion, called it the 'best of all' at the time – understandably so. Superbly cultured playing from this great orchestra and the recording is yet another tribute to Decca's post-war engineering.

One is in no doubt that Bernstein's talk was made in the Swinging Sixties (1968) with his description of the 'the first psychedelic symphony'. Yet he has a point and his comments are both compelling and informative – you understand why his magnetic personality introduced so many people to classical music. As for the performance: it is similarly compelling, emerging all the stronger on this, its CD début, with the 1963 recording sounding vivid and full. The virtuosity, especially in the last movement, is in no doubt and the only caveat is the rather unconvincing rubato in the first movement. This CD could make an excellent introduction for newcomers to this most Romantic of symphonies.

Opinions are divided about Karajan's 1975 performance of the *Symphonie fantastique*; it is certainly a compelling account with wonderful playing from the BPO. There is great intensity in the opening movement (without repeat), particularly in the hushed strings, with the orchestra bringing out many subtle nuances of detail. The two final movements are quite exciting (a minor 'clonk' is heard at the beginning of the finale) and the recording is very good. There is little doubt that other conductors have given us more exciting readings, but Karajan *aficionados* may respond to this 'refined approach'. The fill-ups are attractive but not so well recorded.

VOCAL MUSIC

Les nuits d'été (song cycle).
(M) *** Decca Legends 460 973-2 [id.]. Régine Crespin, SRO, Ansermet – RAVEL: *Shéhérazade* *** ✹ (with *Recital of French Songs* ***).

Régine Crespin's richness of tone, and a style which has an operatic basis, do not prevent her from bringing out the subtlety of detail in Berlioz's finest song cycle and, with Ansermet at his best accompanying brilliantly, this glowing performance is truly legendary – a *tour de force*. Moreover the Ravel coupling is even more inspired, and the superb new transfers enhance the listener's pleasure further.

Requiem mass, Op. 5.
(BB) *(*) Naxos Dig. 8.554494/5 [id.]. Michael Schade, Toronto Mendelssohn Ch. & Youth Ch., Elora Fest. O, Noel Edison.

The chief merits of this disappointing Naxos account of the Berlioz *Grande messe des morts* – a difficult work to hold together – are the singing of the Toronto Mendelssohn Choir, atmospherically recorded, and of the sweet-toned tenor, Michael Schade, in the *Sanctus*. Otherwise this is an under-

powered reading, lacking the biting intensity of rival versions, though the recording of the brass in the *Tuba mirum* section is rich and ripe.

Requiem mass (Grande messe des morts), Op. 5; Messe solennelle: Resurrexit. Tantum ergo. Veni creator (with BORTNYANSKY, arr. Berlioz: *Pater Noster; Adoremus*).
*** Decca Dig. 458 921-2 (2) [id.]. John Mark Ainsley, Montreal SO & Ch., Dutoit.

Following up his formidable series of major Berlioz recordings, Charles Dutoit here tackles the *Grande messe des morts*, with massive Montreal forces gloriously resonant and clearly defined in the Decca recording. The interpretation offers a powerful alternative to existing versions. As in *Les Troyens*, Dutoit favours speeds generally a degree or two more flowing than usual. The *Lacrymosa,* for example, with its offbeat jagged rhythms and surging melodic line sounds more like a chorus from that opera. The choral sound is beautifully integrated, with unrivalled weight in the climaxes thanks to the recording. Where the singing of the Montreal choir does not quite match that of the finest rival versions is in attack. This is a performance a degree more relaxed, less bitingly dramatic than those – comforting rather than disturbing – and at flowing, urgent speeds it is one which is held strongly together both in structure and argument. Thanks to the ripe and resonant recording, the sounds of the last trump in the *Dies irae* are magnificent, with massed brass and timpani exceptionally well defined, set vividly in a warm acoustic with clear focus and superb separation. The tenor soloist in the *Sanctus*, John Mark Ainsley, is sensitive rather than heroic, with the recording exaggerating the vibrato. The rare fill-ups are welcome, if not specially generous. The two pieces for women's choir – *Veni creator* unaccompanied, *Tantum ergo* with organ – reveal Berlioz at his simplest, touchingly so, as do the Bortnyansky arrangements. The *Resurrexit*, developed from the long-lost *Messe solennelle* which Sir John Eliot Gardiner revived, is the most relevant as well as the most ambitious piece here with its vision of the last trump, later modified for the *Requiem*. Among rival versions of that main work, the Previn still has very strong claims, more biting than Dutoit, altogether a superb performance and recording. It is now offered as a bargain two-disc package in EMI's Double Fforte series, with the very generous coupling of Previn's strongly symphonic account of the *Symphonie fantastique* (CZS5 69512-2). Yet on recording grounds Dutoit is a clear first choice among digital versions.

Berners, Lord (1883–1950)

The Triumph of Neptune (ballet): extended suite;
*Fantaisie espagnole; Fugue in C min.; 3
Morceaux; Nicholas Nickleby* (film music).
*** Olympia Dig. OCD 662 [id.]. RLPO, Barry
    Wordsworth.

Barry Wordsworth puts us in his debt by providing
a fine modern version of *The Triumph of Neptune*
and giving it in more complete form. While memories of Beecham remain undimmed (in his hands,
Cloudland and *The frozen forest* had a very special
character and elegance that sparkled through all the
surface noise), Wordsworth captures the character
of this music remarkably well. Moreover we have
other enjoyable (and valuable) repertoire: the *Trois
morceaux* and the *Fantaisie espagnole* are new to
the catalogue. They date from 1918 and are Gallic
in inspiration and sympathy, as their titles suggest,
and are attractively imaginative. Some commentators have drawn parallels with Satie: both were
renowned eccentrics and both had an irreverent
sense of humour, but Satie's vein of melancholy
went deeper and his awareness of pain was more
acute. The recording is good without being in the
demonstration class; detail is well defined and there
is plenty of body. Originally issued on EMI this
rather surprisingly reappears on the Olympia label
and is very welcome.

According to Roy Douglas, Berners almost certainly did not orchestrate his own music. Douglas
scored some of it himself and it seems possible that
Constant Lambert had a hand in the *Triumph of
Neptune*, and Hyam Greenbaum was responsible
for *Nicholas Nickleby* (both were on the musical
staff at Denham and friends of Muir Matheson), but
there is no definite knowledge in either case.

Bernstein, Leonard (1918–90)

*Candide overture; West Side story: symphonic
dances.*
(M) **(*) Penguin Classics Decca Dig. 460 656-2
    [id.]. Baltimore SO, Zinman – BARBER:
    Adagio for strings **(*); COPLAND:
    Appalachian spring; Fanfare. ***

Zinman's *Candide overture* is lively enough, but
the orchestral playing lacks the sheer exuberance of
Bernstein's own account, and the *West Side story
dances*, although very well played, similarly has
less rhythmic bite than the composer's own performance. The compensating factor is the richly
expansive Baltimore recording, which approaches
demonstration standard.

Serenade after Plato's Symposium.
*** DG 445 186-2 [id.]. Gidon Kremer, Israel PO,
    Composer – GLASS: *Violin concerto;* ROREM:
    Violin concerto. ***

It was an excellent idea for this fine benchmark
recording of Bernstein conducting one of his finest,
most thoughtful works, to be recoupled with two
other Kremer recordings of American concertos, if
of different vintage. The performance has already
been praised in our main volume, where it is differently coupled (at mid-price).

*Symphonies Nos. 1 (Jeremiah); 2 (The Age of
Anxiety); (i) Chichester psalms.*
(M) *** DG 457 757-2 [id.]. Israel PO, composer
    with; (i) Soloists of the Vienna Boys' Choir.

Bernstein's musical invention is always memorable, if at times a little too facile to match the
ambitiousness of his symphonic aim, but the compelling confidence of his writing often speaks of a
genius stretching himself to the limit. The *Jeremiah
Symphony* dates from his early twenties and ends
with a moving passage from *Lamentations* for the
mezzo soloist (here Christa Ludwig). As its title
suggests, the *Second Symphony* was inspired by the
poem of W. H. Auden, with the various movements
directly reflecting its more dramatic passages,
though no words are set to music in this purely
orchestral work. The *Chichester psalms* is one of the
most attractive choral works written in the twentieth
century: its jazzy passages are immediately appealing, as is the intrinsic beauty of the reflective
sequences. These live performances with the Israel
Philharmonic are not quite as polished or forceful
as those Bernstein recorded earlier in New York
(now on mid-price Sony), but the warmth of Bernstein's writing is fully conveyed in these excellent
recordings. With a playing time of just under 80
minutes, this DG Originals CD is exceptionally
good value.

Wonderful town.
*** EMI Dig. CDC5 56753-2 [id.]. Criswell,
    McDonald, Hampson, Barrett, Gilfry,
    L. Voices, Birmingham Contemporary Music
    Group, Rattle.

Wonderful town – written at high speed to meet a
five-week deadline early in 1953 – was one of
Leonard Bernstein's earliest successes, running for
two years on Broadway, but has unfairly tended to
be eclipsed by the later success of *West Side story*.
Here in a fizzing performance, starrily cast, Rattle
rights the balance in a performance at once vigorously idiomatic but also refined in the many lyrical
moments. Faced with what anyone else would regard as an impossible challenge, Bernstein with his
regular collaborators, Betty Comden and Adolph
Green, produced a winning adaptation of the play
My sister Eileen, later a film with Rosalind Russell.
The two characterful sisters finding their feet in the
big city are here brilliantly played by Kim Criswell
and Audra McDonald, not just charismatic as
actresses, but singing superbly. Thomas Hampson
as Robert just as commandingly bestrides the

conflicting problem of Broadway and the classical tradition, and Brent Barrett in the secondary role of Wreck delightfully brings in the cabaret tradition. Such numbers as 'Ohio', 'A little bit in love', 'Conversation piece' and 'Wrong note rag', rounded off with the big tune of 'It's love', can be appreciated for their full musical quality, with Rattle and his talented Birmingham group relishing the jazzy idiom. Bright, forward sound to match and a helpful booklet which gives the full text.

Berwald, Franz (1796–1868)

Violin concerto in C sharp min., Op. 2.
(BB) **(*) Naxos Dig. 8.554287 [id.]. Tobias Ringborg, Swedish CO, Niklas Willén –
AULIN: *Violin concerto No. 3;* STENHAMMAR: *2 Sentimental romances.* **(*)

The Berwald concerto is an early work, whose ideas are pleasing and mellifluous, very much in the Spohr tradition. Tobias Ringborg plays well, though he is not as spirited as was Tellefsen (EMI). Good recorded sound. The two Stenhammar pieces are rarities and sound persuasive in his hands. Apart from Christian Bergqvist's record on Musica Sveciae, this newcomer is the only current version of Tor Aulin's well-crafted *C minor Concerto.* A decent performance and good, well-balanced recorded sound.

Piano quintets Nos. 1 in C min.; 2 in A; Piano quintet in A: Larghetto & Scherzo only.
(BB) * Naxos Dig. 8.553970 [id.]. Bengt-Ake Lundin, Uppsala Chamber Soloists.

The two *Piano quintets* are both late works, composed in 1853 and 1857 respectively, with Berwald's pupil Hilda Thegerström in mind. It was the *Second Piano quintet in A major* that Berwald sent to Liszt with a warm dedication. The two additional movements have not been recorded before and were possibly intended for the *A major Quintet* which Berwald began in 1850 and subsequently discarded: when it first appeared in 1853, Berwald referred to the *C minor* as the Second. They are mellifluous works but are not well served here. The quartet itself falls short of distinction to put it mildly, though in both quintets the balance places the pianist in so dominant a position that they are masked. Those who have the Vienna Philharmonic version with Eduard Mrazek on Decca, better played and recorded, should stick with it or wait for something better.

Biber, Heinrich (1644–1704)

Battaglia; (Lute) Passacaglia in C min.; Partita VII for 2 viole d'amore and continuo; Violin sonata (Solo representativa) with continuo.
**(*) Teldec/Warner Dig. 3984 21464-2 [id.]. Il Giardino Armonico (with ZELENKA: *Fanfare;* ANON: *Tune for the woodlark;* ONOFRI: *Ricercare for viola da gamba & lute*) – LOCKE: *The Tempest.* **(*)

This collection opens with an impressive cavalry *Fanfare* by Zelenka and the emphasis is clearly to dramatize what is essentially a Biber sampler. The most impressive work here is the *Partita for two viole d'amore and continuo,* a powerful piece opening with a chimerical *Prelude,* and then after the usual dance movements concluding with a very fine *Arietta variata,* which is in essence a chaconne. It is very well played indeed. So too is the *Solo violin sonata representativa,* a much lighter piece whose main interest is an ingenious series of bird and animal imitations – nightingale, cuckoo, cock and hen and even a miaowing cat. If the Lute *Passacaglia* is rather pale, the familiar *Battle* sequence is just the opposite and suits the generally rather aggressive period-instrument style, closely recorded which is favoured here and which also affects the coupled music by Matthew Locke. Rather bitty, anyway.

12 Sonatae (Fidicinium sacro-profanum; Balletti lamentabili; (i) Passacaglia for solo violin; (ii; iii) Laetatus sum; (iii) Nisi Dominus; (ii) Serenada (der Nachtwächer).
*** Chandos Dig. CHAN 0605 (2) [id.]. (i) Catherine Mackintosh; (ii) Peter Harvey; (iii) Richard Wistreich; Augmented Purcell Qt.

The *Fidicinium sacro-profanum* probably appeared in 1682 as part of the celebrations of the 1100th anniversary of the founding of the Archdiocese of Salzburg. Biber's church sonatas were often performed at the opening and close of services, but also at key moments during their progress. They are characteristically inventive works varying between three and eight linked sections of considerable variety (rhythmic as well as melodic) and interest, very much the precursor of the concerto grosso. They are presented here with great freshness and give consistent pleasure. To add contrast the Purcell Quartet intersperse them with other key works: the solo *Nisi Dominus* (Richard Wistreich in excellent form) and the dramatic duet setting of *Laetatus sum,* which is equally stimulating. Later Peter Harvey returns as the Nightwatchman, singing against a winning pizzicato accompaniment. The famous *Battle* evocation is as impressive here as in any competing version. The second disc opens with the *Balletti lamentabili,* in which a haunting *Sonata* and a delicate closing *Lamenti* frame an *Allemande, Sarabande, Gavotte* and *Gigue,* all of which, for all their dance rhythms, maintain a mood of gentle melancholy. The programme ends with Biber's masterly *Passacaglia for solo violin,* which has a guardian angel engraved on the title page to add gravitas to a work which undoubtedly anticipates Bach's unaccompanied violin music. It is superbly played by Catherine Mackintosh. A splendid set, among the Purcell Quartet's finest achievements. The recording is very real indeed. The only disappointment is that there are no internal cues for the *Sonatas*.

12 Sonatae tam aris, quam aulis servientes.
*** Audivis Astrée Dig. E 8630 [id.]. Rare Fruits Council, Manfredo Karemer.
(B) ** Hyperion Helios CDH 55041 [id.]. Parley of Instruments, Roy Goodman and Peter Holman.

Biber's *Sonatae tam aris, quam aulis servientes* are among his most immediately attractive works, with their direct appeal comparable with the Bach *Brandenburgs*. They combine appealing expressive elements and great rhythmic vitality. This robustly extrovert new recording from the Rare Fruits Council is full of character, vividly colourful and alive. In about half the sonatas (Nos. 1, 4, 7, 10 and 12) the authentic string group of seven players plus continuo are joined by one or two trumpets and here the effect is quite spectacular. The works for strings alone, however, are splendidly full-bodied and colourful (helped by the liberal use of organ in the continuo). The energy and expressive vigour of the music-making here bubbles over, and this new Audivis Astrée set now takes pride of place over the (augmented) Purcell Quartet on Chandos mentioned in our main volume. Highly recommended.

Indeed, by the side of the Rare Fruits Council the much more intimate performances from the Parley of Instruments, sympathetically played as they are, sound rather pale. However, with the excellent Crispian Steele-Perkins the principal, the music springs vividly to life with the entry of the trumpets. The documentation is ambiguous about who is in charge: whether it is Roy Goodman, the lead violin, or Peter Holman, who plays the harpsichord, virginals and organ continuo. This Helios reissue is inexpensive but the Audivis Astrée disc is well worth the extra money.

VOCAL MUSIC

Missa Bruxellensis.
✪ *** Allia Vox Dig. AV 9808 [id.]. Soloists, La Capella Reial de Catalunya, Les Concerts des Nations, Jordi Savall.

Biber is fast emerging as one of the greatest and most original composers of the second half of the seventeenth century. This glorious festive *Missa Bruxellensis* – a late (perhaps final) work, dating from 1700 and until recently wrongly attributed to its manuscript copyist, Orazio Benevoli – surely represents the very peak of his achievement. It is scored for two eight-voice choirs, groups of wind, strings, trumpets, horns and trombones and a bass continuo of organs and bassoons. The disposition of the soloists, choristers and instruments in the

stalls, around the transept and in the cathedral choir was designed to add to the sense of spectacle, and the music is fully worthy of its ambitious layout. Its imaginative diversity, with continual contrasts between tutti and soli of great expressive power, shows the composer working at full stretch. The *Kyrie* opens in great splendour with the two antiphonal choirs and festive trumpets (*cornets à bouquin*). After the extended *Gloria* (the longest section) the *Credo* reintroduces the solo group – singing magnificently here – and soon expands into a full tutti, while the powerful *Sanctus* is as fine as almost any setting written before or since. The closing *Agnus Dei* has the soloists singing radiantly, but with piercing dissonance from Biber's extraordinary sustained suspensions, with the full forces then entering for the closing *Amen*. The performance here, superlatively recorded in the echoing, but never blurring, acoustics of Salzburg Cathedral, re-creates the work's première, and is truly inspired. There is not a weak link – the whole team of soloists are first class, the trumpets blaze, and the choral singing has great fervour. This marvellous disc cannot be too highly recommended.

Missa Salisburgensis.
**(*) Erato/Warner Dig. 3984 25506-2 [id.].
Soloists, Amsterdam Bar. Ch. & O, Koopman.

Koopman's version of Biber's spectacular score has the obvious merit of being recorded (during the 1998 Festival) in its original venue, Salzburg Cathedral. But in practice that is not such an advantage as it sounds, for the long reverberation period tends to blur the choral clarity and it also affects the brilliance of the trumpets (which Biber uses liberally). Koopman's spacious approach must also have been dictated by the problems of resonance and fine though his account is, it cannot match the superb DG version from the Gabrieli Consort and Musica Antiqua Cologne under Paul McCreesh (457 611-2 – see our main volume).

Bizet, Georges (1838–75)

L'Arlésienne: suites Nos. 1–2; Jeux d'enfants.
(B) *** Australian Decca Eloquence 460 505-2.
Cleveland O, Maazel – FRANCK: *Symphony* **.

(i) *L'Arlésienne suites Nos. 1–2;* (ii) *Symphony in C.*
(M) *** EMI CDM5 67231-2 [567259]. (i) RPO;
(ii) French Nat. RO; Beecham.
** HM Dig. HMC 901675 [id.]. Orquesta Ciudada de Granada, Josep Pons.

This is one of Maazel's very best recordings: the music glitters and sparkles, and the sound (from the late 1970s) is altogether outstanding. Maazel chooses fast tempi in the *L'Arlésienne* suites, though not so fast that they sound rushed, whilst the *Jeux d'enfants* is a delight, with some really delicate pianissimo playing from the Cleveland Orchestra. Unfortunately the coupling is not so outstanding (though still acceptable). Although Beecham and Dutoit are in a class of their own in *L'Arlésienne*, this Australian bargain CD will surely appeal to audiophiles.

Beecham's famous Bizet coupling now rightly reappears as one of EMI's 'Great Recordings of the Century'. His magical touch is especially illuminating in the two *L'Arlésienne suites*, and the early (1956) stereo gives the RPO woodwind striking luminosity yet plenty of body. The *Symphony* too sounds freshly minted. Although the playing here has slightly less finesse, its zest is in no doubt, especially in the finale, and the oboe soloist in the slow movement distinguishes himself.

Under Josep Pons the Orquesta Ciudada de Granada plays very well indeed. Rhythms are neatly pointed, wind solos sensitive. The *Adagietto* from *L'Arlésienne* is very touching. The *Symphony* is graceful and elegant, but until the finale the extra sparkle which carries Beecham's reading forward so infectiously is missing, and although well recorded, at full price this Harmonia Mundi CD is uncompetitive.

Symphony in C.
(M) ** Sony SMK 61830 [id.]. NYPO, Bernstein –
OFFENBACH: *Gaîté parisienne, etc.***; SUPPE:
Beautiful Galathea: overture. ***

Bernstein's 1963 performance of the *Symphony in C* brings much to enjoy. The finale, in particular, has tremendous brilliance, which is most infectious, and the slow movement is affectionately done. On the down side, the first movement lacks the charm it ideally needs and the recording sounds a bit glassy, though it is better than it was on LP.

Carmen (complete).
(BB) (*) Naxos mono 8.110001/2 [id.]. Swarthout, Kullman, Albanese, Warren, Met. Op. Ch. & O, Wilfrid Pelletier.

It would be hard to imagine a less French-sounding account of *Carmen* than this performance given live at the Met in New York in March 1941, and offered here in a raucous radio recording, close and boxy. What is valuable is to hear some of the principal stars of that great opera-house in their prime, even in repertory that hardly suited them. Gladys Swarthout is a great singer far too little represented on disc, and her magnificent contralto, firm and rich, is an instrument of wonder, particularly for us today in an age when genuine contraltos have given way to mezzos. The downside is that though musically her singing is masterly, her characterization is sketchy, rather like Margaret Dumont in a Marx Brothers movie pretending to be a voluptuous young gypsy. Licia Albanese, early in her career, already sounds too knowing, not innocent enough

for Micaela, with the tone not pure enough. Neither those two soloists, nor Leonard Warren as Escamillo, is helped by the closeness of the radio recording. Warren may have been a heroic performer, but the voice with its juddery vibrato too easily comes to sound woolly, not incisive enough for the bullfighter. Only the American tenor Charles Kullman survives the test well, singing with sensitivity and refinement, even if his is not the voice one would normally expect for Don José. The French Canadian Wilfred Pelletier belies his French training in a perfunctory account of the score, with the hard-pressed chorus almost comically unidiomatic. With so many excruciating French accents – and not a single French-speaking singer among the soloists – one wonders why they bothered to use the original language.

Carmen: highlights.
(B) ** Penguin Classics Decca 460 652-2 (from complete recording with Troyanos, Domingo, Van Dam; cond. Solti).

This 61-minute Penguin Classics selection (with its essay by Miriam Stoppard, but otherwise comparatively poorly documented) is a non-starter when compared with Decca's own compilation in the mid-price range (458 204-2), which includes 75 minutes of music, is handsomely packaged in a slipcase, and includes full translations!

Bliss, Arthur (1891–1975)

Piano sonata.
** Divine Art Dig. 2-5011 [id.]. Trevor Barnard –
BUSONI: *24 Preludes, Op. 37* **.

Arthur Bliss's *Piano sonata* comes from 1952 and was composed for Noel Mewton-Wood, whose tragic death took place the following year. Trevor Barnard will be remembered for his 1960s recording of the Bliss *Piano concerto* with Sir Malcolm Sargent and the Philharmonia. He played the *Sonata* to Bliss in the late 1950s who made some annotations and corrections in the printed score that are incorporated here. There is no current alternative of this well-argued and powerful work but collectors should note that the recording is distinctly monochrome and lacklustre. A qualified recommendation.

Bloch, Ernest (1880–1959)

Baal Shem.
(B) *** EMI Début Dig. CDZ5 73501-2 [id.]. Ittai Shapira, ECO, Charles Hazlewood – BRUCH: *Violin concerto No. 1 in G min. Op. 26* **; BUNCH: *Fantasy* **; SARASATE: *Zigeunerweisen.* **(*)

The EMI account of *Baal Shem* forms part of a début

recital by the twenty-four-year-old Israeli violinist
Ittai Shapira, designed to show off his artistry. A
gifted player, who is perhaps more at home in
this triptych than he is in the Bruch. A very fine
performance and very well recorded too.

(i) *Violin concerto; Hebrew suite for violin and
orchestra;* (ii) *Schelomo (Hebrew rhapsody).*
(M) ** Supraphon SU 3169-2 011 [id.]. (i) Hyman
   Bress, Prague SO, Rohan; (ii) André Navarra,
   Czech PO, Ančerl.

Szigeti's famous pre-war 78 set of the *Violin concerto* with Charles Munch and the Paris Conservatoire Orchestra so dominated the catalogues that it
inhibited others from venturing onto this territory
for the best part of three decades. Menuhin waited
until 1963 before recording it memorably with
Kletzki and the Philharmonia. Three years later
Hyman Bress recorded it in Prague with Jindřich
Roman, a recording which by the side of the
Menuhin seemed somewhat pale, and so indeed it
is. But it is also a thoughtful, ruminative account
well worth hearing and totally unforced. At the
time of writing the *Hebrew suite* is not otherwise
currently available in its orchestral form. André
Navarra's 1964 account of *Schelomo* is more high
voltage, albeit not so electrifying as its 78-r.p.m.
predecessor from Feuermann and Stokowski. Not a
first choice but those investing in these performances will find that there is musical satisfaction to
be had here.

Schelomo (Hebraic rhapsody).
(M) *** DG 457 761-2 [id.]. Fournier, BPO,
   Wallenstein – BRUCH: *Kol Nidrei*; LALO:
   Cello Concerto; SAINT-SAENS: Cello concerto
   No. 1. ***
** MDG Dig. MDG 0321 0215-2 [id.]. Ulrich
   Schmid, NW German PO, Dominique Roggen
   – HONEGGER: *Cello concerto.* **

Fournier is a bit too closely balanced in this fervent
performance, but the sound is very beautiful, and he
is excellently supported by the Berlin Philharmonic
under Wallenstein. Apart from the balancing of the
cello, the 1967 recording is excellent, and this DG
Originals CD, with its excellent couplings (conducted by Martinon), is well worth the asking price.

Bloch's impassioned *Schelomo* is well served on
CD, as a glance at our main volume will show.
Ulrich Schmid and the Nordwestdeutsche Philharmonie under the Swiss conductor Dominique
Roggen give a thoroughly idiomatic and well-
recorded performance. However, all its rivals offer
more generous couplings: at only 42 minutes'
playing time, this is not a viable recommendation.

Voice in the Wilderness (symphonic poem for
orchestra with cello obligato).
(B) **(*) Australian Decca Eloquence 466 907-2.
   Janos Starker, Israel PO, Mehta – BERLIOZ:
   Harold in Italy **(*).

Voice in the Wilderness is a rather diffuse piece
which at times sounds for all the world like the
sound-track of a Hollywood biblical epic, while at
others its textures are so vivid and imaginative that
such thoughts are promptly banished. Starker's is a
finely played account vividly recorded. Compared
with Rostropovich's or Feuermann's marvellously
full-blooded versions on 78s, Starker's partnership
with Mehta seems just a little lacking in intensity,
but there is little current competition on CD so
this is well worth considering if the coupling is
attractive.

3 Nocturnes for piano trio.
*** Simax Dig. PSC 1147 [id.]. Grieg Trio –
   MARTIN: *Piano trio on Irish folktunes*;
   SHOSTAKOVICH: *Piano trios.* ***

The three *Nocturnes* for piano trio come from 1924,
like the Martin *Trio on Irish folktunes* and the first
Shostakovich. The first *Nocturne* (*Andante*) finds
Bloch in Hebraic–Debussy mode, while the second
(*Andante quieto*) is more overtly romantic and less
interesting, though the Grieg Trio play it with much
feeling, as they do the final *Tempestuoso*. These
pieces are not otherwise currently available (except
on a rare label) and in any event it would be difficult
to better this account. The couplings further enhance
the value of this issue, arguably the best the Grieg
Trio have given us.

*Violin sonatas Nos. 1; 2 (Poème mystique);
Abodah (Yom Kippur melody); Melody; Suite
hébraïque.*
(BB) *** Naxos Dig. 8.554460 [id.]. Miriam
   Kremer, Simon Over.

Recordings of this repertoire are not legion and as
far as the *Second Sonata*, the *Poème mystique,* is
concerned, the only rival at less than full price is
Heifetz with Emanuel Bey. Neither of the sonatas
enjoys the favour it did in Bloch's lifetime. In
Miriam Kremer and Simon Over they have sympathetic advocates: both artists play with exemplary
taste and sensitivity, and Simon Over produces a
wonderful range of colour. So for that matter does
Ms Kremer, who has great refinement of tone. Good
recordings made at the Church of St Silas, Chalk
Farm, London, which have plenty of space round
the aural image.

Blow, John (1649–1708)

(i) *An ode on the death of Mr Henry Purcell.
Fugue in G min.; Grounds: in C min; in D min.;
Sonata in A; Suite in G.*
**(*) Virgin Veritas/EMI Dig. VC5 45342-2 [id.].
   (i) Gérard Lesne, Steven Dugardin; La
   Canzona – PURCELL: Songs and Duets: *Here
   let my life; In vain the am'rous flute; Music for
   a while; Sweetness of nature.* **(*)

Gérard Lesne and his fellow counter-tenor give a stylish performance of the touching *Ode* that John Blow wrote on the death of his brilliant pupil, Purcell. The style reflects that of the younger master, but it is good to identify the character of Blow himself more clearly in the instrumental pieces of his which punctuate the series of Purcell songs and duets. The recorder players of La Canzona are on the abrasive side, not helped by the close recordings, but this makes an attractive and illuminating disc.

Boccherini, Luigi (1743–1805)

Complete cello concertos

Cello concertos Nos. 1 in E flat, G.474; 2 in A, G.475; 3 in D, G.476; 5 in D, G.478.
(BB) *** Naxos Dig. 8.553572 [id.]. Tim Hugh, Scottish CO, Anthony Halstead.

Cello concertos Nos. 4 in C, G.477; 6 in D, G.479; 7 in G, G.480; 8 in C, G.481.
(BB) *** Naxos Dig. 8.553571 [id.]. Tim Hugh, Scottish CO, Anthony Halstead.

Naxos has now begun an impressive new series covering Boccherini's twelve cello concertos (the last was only discovered as recently as 1987). They are beautifully performed on modern instruments but with concern for period practice, and superbly recorded. But rather confusingly the listing on the two discs offered so far does not follow that of the 1969 Yves Gérard catalogue, instead using the numbers against which the works were originally published. Our listing above uses Gérard, so the collector must be careful to identify the contents of each CD by the Gérard numbers.

Volume 1 in the series (8.553571) is a winner of a disc, *No. 7 in G* is the work which provided the slow movement for Grützmacher's popular but highly inauthentic edition of the *B flat Concerto*. Tim Hugh's dedicated account of this lovely G minor movement is a high spot of this issue, with rapt, hushed playing not just from the soloist but also from the excellent Scottish Chamber Orchestra under Anthony Halstead. Hugh offers substantial cadenzas not just in the first movements of each work, but in slow movements and finales too, though none is as extended as the one in the G minor slow movement. The formula in all four works is similar, even though each has its individual delights, with strong, four-square first movements, slow movements that sound rather Handelian (that of the *D major*, G.479 is particularly memorable and galloping finales in triple time.

Volume 2 is only marginally less enticing. The remarkably extended opening movement of the *E flat major Concerto*, G.474 is again capped by an impressive cadenza, and the noble melody of the slow movement sings eloquently on Tim Hugh's bow. The *A major* is less ambitious, but the *D major*,

G.476 is made the more attractive by the flute sonority in the orchestra. The *D major*, G.478 has alternative Rondo finales, one a stately Minuet, but the follow-up in 4/4 time is much more lively and inventive. Tim Hugh and Anthony Halstead again make a stimulating partnership, and all four works spring to life appealingly.

Complete symphonies

Volume 1: Sinfonia in D, G.490; Sinfonia concertante in C for 2 violins and cello, Op. 7, G.491; Sinfonia with solo guitar in C, Op. 10/3, G.523.
*** CPO Dig. CPO 999 084-2 [id.]. Deutsche Kammerakademie, Neuss, Johannes Goritzki.

The early *Sinfonia in D*, G.490 originated as an (Italian) overture to a cantata, *La confederazione del Sabini con Roma*. Dating from 1765, it has a most engaging, dancing finale, while the charming central *Andante grazioso* was also featured in the *Cello concerto*, G.478. The *Sinfonia concertante*, G.491, first heard in Paris in 1768, is a wholly different matter – an ambitious work of considerable character and immediate appeal. It must have made a great impression at the time, for the first movement centres on a pair of solo violins, while the cello dominates the memorably bitter-sweet *Adagio* and the bucolic finale uses all three soloists plus boisterous orchestral horns.

The sinfonia with obbligato solo guitar is an arrangement of G.491 made some years later for the Marquis de Benevent, an amateur guitarist. The role is not demanding, and agreeable though this arrangement is, the original work is far more impressive.

Volume 2: Symphonies in D; in E flat; in C, Op. 12/1–3, G.503–5.
*** CPO Dig. CPO 999 172-2 [id.]. Deutsche Kammerakademie, Neuss, Johannes Goritzki.

Volume 3: Symphonies: in D min.; in B flat; in A, Op. 12/4–6, G.506–8.
*** CPO Dig. CPO 999 173-2 [id.]. Deutsche Kammerakademie, Neuss, Johannes Goritzki.

The Op. 12 symphonies of 1771 mark Boccherini's full entry into his own galant symphonic world, even if at times he is still thinking in terms of concertante writing, especially in Op. 12/3. Allegros are full of vigour, yet that melancholy element which is part of his musical personality is always apparent and immediately appears in the plaintive *Andantino* of the D major work, while its *Minuet amoroso* opens with cellos to remind us that the cello was the composer's own instrument. There is a charming flute solo in the Trio.

The *Maestoso* theme of the first movement of the E flat work brings characterful solo writing for horns, and the cellos are again heard in a solo role (even given cadenzas) while the central, sombre *Grave*, brings contrasting delicate scoring. Good cheer returns in the finale, with its siciliano rhythm and there are romantic echoes alongside its witty vigour.

The enticing Op. 12/3 in C major opens with, and is dominated throughout by, flutes, and its rather lovely *Andantino amoroso* brings shades of Gluck's *Orpheus*. Op. 12/4 only has three movements but is a particularly strong work, the vigour and drama of the outer movements (linked by the same slow, powerfully expressive introduction) offset by the delicate tracery of the gentle, brief *Andantino*. The extended finale, a remarkable fast Chaconne, again draws on Gluck, supposedly representing Hell as depicted in the latter's *Don Juan* ballet.

The following two symphonies, Opp. 12/5 and 6, are each in four movements. A solo flute leads in the opening movement of the *B flat major* and the flutes are again prominent throughout, while the graceful *Adagio* brings concertante passages for the horns. The *A major* is lightweight and elegant, although a touch of pathos enters with the *Grave* introduction to the vivacious finale.

Volume 4: *Symphonies in B flat; in E flat; in C; in D; in B flat, Op. 21/1–5, G.493–7.*
*** CPO Dig. CPO 999 174-2 [id.]. Deutsche Kammerakademie, Neuss, Johannes Goritzki.

Boccherini composed his Op. 21 set of 1775 during a congenial period of his life when he was living in Aranjuez, and this is reflected in their generally lighthearted manner. They are all three-movement works, elegant and tuneful, yet by no means lacking strength; the flutes frequently colour the scoring appealingly, as in the opening movement of the first of the set. The slow movements are usually dainty *Andantinos*, and the composer favours *dolce* and *con grazia* flavourings. Finales are usually vigorous, with bouncing energy; alternatively, those of the second and third of the set are gracious Minuets.

The second symphony in E flat, makes attractively bold use of hunting-horn effects in what is a very strong opening movement, and the touching *Andantino* features a solo violin, with flute obbligato. The third, fourth and fifth works of the set have vital, energetic opening movements, classical in feeling (one thinks at times of both Haydn and Mozart). The work in C major, has a highly characteristic, memorably plaintive *Larghetto sostenuto* dominated by a pair of solo cellos, while the slow movements of the *Fourth* and *Fifth* both have lovely main themes which might almost have come from the pen of Haydn.

The *Fourth* is also unusual in that Boccherini resourcefully repeats the attractive ideas of the first movement in the last. Even so the dancing finale of the *Fifth* is even more delightful. All these works are played with much warmth and energy, and this is a most attractive disc.

Volume 5: *Symphonies in A Op. 21/6, G.498; in D; in E flat; in A, Op. 35/1–3, G.509–11.*
*** CPO Dig. CPO 999 175-2 [id.]. Deutsche Kammerakademie, Neuss, Johannes Goritzki.

Volume 6: *Symphonies in F; in E flat; in B flat, Op. 35/4–6, G.512–14; in C, Op. 37/1, G.515.*
*** CPO Dig. CPO 999 176-2 [id.]. Deutsche Kammerakademie, Neuss, Johannes Goritzki.

The last of the Op. 21 series is in A and is richly scored, with aurally striking use of the highly crooked horns. The charmingly delicate *Andantino grazioso* leads naturally into the elegant finale – a Minuet without a Trio.

The Opus 35 group of 1782 marks a further step forward in maturity. They are all still three-movement works, but the scoring is more expansive, yet the ideas in the allegros are as invigorating as ever. The pensive mood of the strings in the *Andantino* of the first, D major work suggests an added seriousness, but the finale dances as gaily as ever.

The bold use of the horns is a feature of both the *E flat major* work and the *A major* which follows. The *Andante* of the former is Mozartean in its grace, but the latter brings dainty solo string writing which is pure Boccherini. Op. 35/6 has an unusual finale with a bold central Minuet with its robust trilling horn, framed by two vivacious Prestos.

The energetic first symphony of the Op. 37 set (one of the composer's most fertile works) is in four movements setting the pattern for the rest of the series. Its first movement returns to Boccherini's concertante style, with pairs of oboes, bassoons, flutes and a solo violin. The precise Minuet makes a foil for the colourful *Andante* with its plaintive oboe and cello solos, and the spirited monothematic finale brings a panoply of colour with chirping trills adding to the gaiety.

Volume 7: *Symphonies in D min.; in A, Op. 37/3–4, G.517–18; in C min., Op. 41, G.519.*
*** CPO Dig. CPO 999 177-2 [id.]. Deutsche Kammerakademie, Neuss, Johannes Goritzki.

By the time he wrote his Opus 37 symphonies in 1786/7 Boccherini was established as the director of the Duchess of Osuna's court orchestra in Madrid. These mature four-movement works are obviously Haydn-influenced, but the lively invention and rich scoring remains Boccherini's own. The repeated horn duo which opens the Minuet of Op. 37/2, for instance, is followed by a colourful woodwind interplay, while the *Andante amoroso* begins with a striking oboe solo.

The last work in this set of three uses the woodwind throughout as freely as the string groups. The horns shine through in the *A major* finale which, with its single striking theme, is reminiscent of the finale of Haydn's *Symphony No. 88*. Moreover the outer movements of the powerful C minor work,

Op. 41 (1788) have much in common with Haydn's *Sturm und Drang*, with a lovely *Pastorale* to give peaceful contrast. The bold Minuet even has a hint of the scherzo about it, and the woodwind trio makes a delightful contrast. This key work is one of the composer's most imaginative symphonies.

Volume 8: *Symphonies in D, Op. 42, G.520; in D, Op. 45, G.522; in D, G.500.*
*** CPO Dig. CPO 999 178-2 [id.]. Deutsche Kammerakademie, Neuss, Johannes Goritzki.

Boccherini's last two symphonies, Op. 42 and Op. 45 were written in 1789 and 1792 respectively, while the composer was in the employ of the King of Prussia. They are both first-class works, clearly following the pattern Haydn had established, but as ever with Boccherini, remain highly individual in colour. Op. 45, for instance, has a D minor introduction, and the *Andantino* soon introduces a solemn violin and bassoon duet, while in the Minuet the main theme is given to oboe and bassoon, and the horns dominate the trio. Another *Adagio* is used to open the vigorous finale. After this, G.500 is unduly simplistic and unadventurous, and more likely to be spurious than an early work wrongly catalogued. However, Goritzki makes the very most of its brief *Presto* finale, avoiding a sense of anticlimax.

28 Symphonies (complete).
(M) *** CPO Dig. CPO 999 401-2 (8) [id.]. Deutsche Kammerakademie, Neuss, Johannes Goritzki.

In this first complete survey of the Boccherini symphonies, Goritzki's achievement is remarkable. Himself a cellist, he shows a natural feeling for Boccherini's special combination of galant and classical styles, revealing the music's strengths rather than its weaknesses, making the most of its colour and revelling in its fecundity of invention and easy tunefulness. The playing – on modern instruments – of the German Chamber Academy Orchestra of Neuss is alert, polished and warmhearted, besides showing a nice feeling for Boccherini's delicate *Andantinos*, which are never sentimentalized. The recording is excellently balanced and has plenty of life and bloom. All the discs are available separately at premium-price, but the box comes at mid-price and is well worth considering.

Other recordings

Symphonies in C; in D min.; in A, Op. 37/1, 3 & 4, G.515, 517–18.
** Opus 111 Dig. OPS 30-168 [id.]. Academia Montis Regalis Bar. O, Luigi Mangiocavallo.

Symphonies in C; in D min.; in A, Op. 37/1, 3 & 4, G.515, 517–18; in D, Op. 42, G.520.
*** Hyperion Dig. CDA 66904 [id.]. L. Fest. O, Ross Pople.

In the mid 1990s, Hyperion embarked on a Boccherini series with Ross Pople directing lively, characterful and polished performances with his excellent chamber orchestra. As can be seen above, these are four attractive and mature works. The Hyperion sound is pleasingly fresh and open and this is a most enjoyable disc, but not necessarily preferable to the CPO series.

The Academia Montis Regalis play pleasingly enough on period instruments. These are fresh sprightly performances, with excellent solo wind-playing, which give pleasure, and the recording is good. The overall effect is more lightweight, but tuttis are less clearly focused than with the Hyperion versions and this disc, unlike any of its competitors, only offers three symphonies.

CHAMBER MUSIC

Quintet: La Ritirata di Madrid (Procession of the Night Watch in Madrid): orchestral version.
(M) *** DG 457 914-2 [id.]. BPO, Karajan – ROSSINI: *String sonatas.* **(*)

This colourful and original work, which sets out to evoke music heard in Madrid at night, responds wonderfully to the full Karajan treatment. The playing is glorious with sound to match, but it is also available, with better couplings, on one of DG's Originals (449 724-2) as a bonus for Respighi's *Pines* and *Fountains of Rome* – see our main volume.

String quartets: in C; in G min.; in A, Op. 32/4–6.
*** CPO Dig. CPO 999 202-2 [id.]. Nomos Qt.

These are three most attractive works, of Boccherini's best quality. All three slow movements are expressively potent, the *Andantino lentarello* of the *A major* is particularly searching and the following Minuet is hardly less striking. The Nomos is a first-class group, using modern instruments but in such a way as to provide textures which are fully blended and sweet yet avoiding nineteenth-century opulence. The recording is excellent.

VOCAL MUSIC

(i) *Stabat Mater* (original 1781 version); (ii) *String quintet in C min., Op. 31/4, G.328.*
**(*) HM Dig. HMC 901378 [id.]. (i) Agnès Mellon, Ens. 415, Chiara Banchini; (ii) Banchini, Gatti, Moreno, Dieltiens, Brugge.

Stabat Mater (1800 version).
*** Hyperion Dig. CDA 67108 [id.]. Susan Gritton, Sarah Fox, Susan Bickley, Paul Agnew, Peter Harvey, King's Consort, Robert King – D'ASTORGA: *Stabat Mater.* ***

Boccherini originally wrote his *Stabat Mater* in 1781 for solo soprano and strings. But, stimulated by the ongoing success of Pergolesi's famous 1736 setting of the same text, he revised the work in 1800 for two sopranos and a tenor, increasing its dramatic range and power.

The pure-voiced Agnès Mellon makes a gently touching case for the earlier version and she is expressively and authentically supported by the refined playing of Chiara Banchini and her four colleagues of Ensemble 415, who also give a sensitive account of the *String quintet* which acts as filler. If the effect of the vocal work with period-instrument accompaniment is comparatively restrained, many will enjoy the gently luminous sense of spirituality which pervades this Harmonia Mundi version, with the closing *Quando corpus morietur* gravely reflective and tender. The recording is very natural.

But Boccherini's ambitious revision is masterly in increasing the range and expressive power of the work. With first-class soloists, Robert King's performance is as moving as it is gripping in the more dramatic moments. Notable are the lovely soprano duets, so beautifully sung by Susan Gritton and Sarah Fox. Their voices blend angelically in *Eia, Mater, fons amoris*, contrasting with the dramatic trios with tenor (especially *Tui nati vulneratri*), and the closing *Quando corpus morietur* (another trio) is exquisitely managed. The apt coupling with a fine setting of the same text, written nearly a century earlier by an almost unknown Spanish composer, increases the value of this disc.

Boismortier, Joseph Bodin de (1689–1755)

6 Concertos for 5 flutes, Op. 15/1–6.
(BB) ** Naxos Dig. 8.553639 [id.]. Soloists of Concert Spirituel.

Although Boismortier's invention holds up well throughout these very 'samey' works – the first movement of No. 5 in A major is a good example – his predilection for block chords in slow movements means that the music has relatively little variety of colour. These excellent players blend and match their timbres expertly, often presenting a very homogenous sound, the effect emphasized by the close balance. A disc to recommend primarily to amateur flautists.

Borodin, Alexander (1833–87)

Symphonies Nos. 1 in E flat; 2 in B min.
(B) ** Ph. Virtuoso Dig. 422 996-2. Rotterdam PO, Gergiev.

Helped by the warmly resonant acoustics of their concert hall the Rotterdam Orchestra create rich, expansive textures in the *Andantes* of both symphonies, with a fine horn solo in the latter, and it is a pity that the conductor does not move the music on more. He could also be rhythmically more invigorating in outer movements, though he is by no

means dull; the Scherzos of both symphonies are very colourful in his hands, and here the warm ambience adds a good deal. However, there are better versions of both symphonies listed in our main volume.

Prince Igor: Overture and Polovtsian dances.
(BB) *** Virgin Classics 2 x 1 Dig. VBD5 61751-2 (2) [CDVB 61751]. Royal Philharmonic Liverpool Ch. & O, Mackerras – MUSSORGSKY: *Pictures at an exhibition; Night on the bare mountain* **; RIMSKY-KORSAKOV: *Scheherazade* **(*); TCHAIKOVSKY: *The Tempest.* ***

A splendid account of the *Prince Igor overture* from Mackerras, with the brilliant, jaggedly thrusting imitation in the allegro given plenty of bite, and the lyrical secondary melody glowingly phrased by principal horn and strings alike. The *Polovtsian dances* proceed with comparable brilliance and fervour, with the Royal Liverpool Philharmonic Choir producing an expansive lyrical tone and joining in the frenzy of the closing section with infectious zest. Excellent recording too, vivid and full; if only the Mussorgsky and Rimsky-Korsakov couplings had produced comparable electricity, this superbargain double would have been a world-beater. As it is it is good value.

Børresen, Hakon (1876–1954)

At Uranienborg or *Tycho Brahe's dream* (ballet);
(i) *Romance for cello and orchestra. The Royal Guest: Prelude.*
**(*) Marco Polo DaCapo Dig. 8.224105 [id.]. Aalborg SO, Owain Arwel Hughes; (i) with Henrik Brendstrup.

Those who responded to Hakon Børresen's symphonies reviewed in our main volume might consider the present disc. *The Royal Guest*, a one-act opera from 1919, was Børresen's greatest success and its *Prelude* whets the appetite. The twelve numbers that constitute the ballet *At Uranienborg* or *Tycho Brahe's dream*, composed in 1924, are a pleasing example of post-Bournonville ballet (far less cumbersome than the work's titles), and though some of the dances overstay their welcome, the idiom is pleasing. They are given a committed performance, as is the *Romance* played by Henrik Brendstrup and written in 1908 at the time of the *Second Symphony*. Owain Arwel Hughes and his Aalborg musicians sound as if they are enjoying themselves. Our recommendation must however carry a note of caution since the acoustic of the Aalborg hall is not ideal: the sound is tubby in climaxes and lacks transparency.

Bortnyansky, Dmitri (1751–1825)

Sacred concertos Nos. 1–9.
*** Chandos Dig. CHAN 9729 [id.]. Russian
    State Symphonic Capella, Valeri Polyansky.

Sacred concertos Nos. 10–16.
*** Chandos Dig. CHAN 9783 [id.]. Russian
    State Symphonic Capella, Valeri Polyansky.

Bortnyansky was born in the Ukraine but was soon
recruited for the Court Cappella at St Petersburg.
He studied with Galuppi – who had been court
composer of Catherine the Great – and while in
Italy composed three Italian operas. On his return
to Russia in 1779 he became Kapellmeister of the
Court Cappella where he remained for the rest of
his life. He began composing liturgical music in the
1780s and during the last years of Catherine's reign
the liturgy ended with these choral concertos. They
are more indebted to the Italian motet than to Byzantine traditions of chant but Bortnyansky wrote for
voices with consummate expertise and no mean
artistry. As Philip Taylor puts it in his notes, 'the
music unfolds according to its own laws [and] it is
the evolution of the melodic ideas and the way they
are distributed among the different voice registers
that give the concertos their entirely distinctive
character'.

The performances by the Russian State Symphonic Capella under Valeri Polyansky have great
eloquence and though there is a long period of
reverberation in the acoustic of both the Dormition
Cathedral, Smolensk and St Sophia's Cathedral,
Polotsk – where the recordings were made in 1989–
90 – the sound is beautifully focused. They have
taken some time to reach us but their welcome is
no less warm. Strongly recommended.

Boulanger, Lili (1893–1918)

*Faust et Hélène; Psaume 24; Psaume 130: Du
fond de l'abîme; D'un matin de printemps; D'un
soir triste.*
*** Chandos Dig. CHAN 9745 [id.]. Lynne
    Dawson, Ann Murray, Bonaventura Bottone,
    Neil MacKenzie, Jason Howard, CBSO Ch.,
    BBC PO, Yan Pascal Tortelier.

This is the first recording of Lili Boulanger's 1913
cantata, *Faust et Hélène*, which won the *Prix de
Rome*, and one can certainly see why it did. *Faust
et Hélène* is a major discovery. It has astonishing
beauty and a natural eloquence. Like *Psaum 26*, *Du
fond de l'abîme* and the other music on the disc
offers testimony to an altogether remarkable talent.
Small wonder that her more famous sister, Nadia
Boulanger, lost no opportunity to sing her praises
and promote her cause. There is a distinguished
team of soloists (Lynne Dawson and Bonaventura
Bottone in the cantata and Ann Murray in one of

the Psalms) and first-rate contributions from the
Birmingham Chorus and the BBC Philharmonic
under Yan Pascal Tortelier.

*Psaume 24; Psaume 130: Du fond de l'abîme; Pie
Jesu.*
🌓 **(*) BBC Legends BBCL 4026-2 [id.]. Janet
    Price, Bernadette Greevy, Ian Partridge, John
    Carol Case, BBC Ch., BBC SO, Nadia
    Boulanger – FAURE: *Requiem.* **(*) 🌓

Lili Boulanger died in her mid-twenties but not
before committing some remarkable music to paper
including the *Pie Jesu* composed not long before
her death and dedicated to her sister Nadia. In 1968
to mark the fiftieth anniversary of her death, the
BBC invited Nadia Boulanger to London to conduct
some of her work along with the Fauré *Requiem*
(Fauré was one of her teachers at the Paris Conservatoire) which she had conducted before in the
studio in the early years of the Third Programme.
She certainly conveys her fervour and belief in these
remarkable scores – and *Du fond de l'abîme* is a
work of astonishing originality and imagination.
Recorded at a live concert in the Fairfield Halls,
Croydon, the BBC engineers provide more than
acceptable sound. And though it is not as wide-
ranging or transparent as a modern recording, it is
more than serviceable and the balance is skilfully
done. A rather special musical document.

Boyce, William (1711–79)

12 Trio sonatas (1747).
**(*) Chandos Dig. CHAN 0648 (2) [id.].
    Collegium Musicum 90, Simon Standage.

Simon Standage and Collegium Musicum 90 offer
one instrument to a part throughout their set of
Boyce's 1747 *Trio sonatas*. The performances are
fresh and alive, the recording clean and clear and
(as we have commented earlier) the music seems
to get more and more attractive as it continues.
However, the competing set from Peter Holman,
with the Parley instrumental groups on Hyperion
(CDA 67151/2), is in almost every way preferable.
He alternates chamber and orchestral performances,
which provides much greater textural variety; moreover he includes three extra sonatas recently discovered in manuscript in the Cambridge Fitzwilliam
Museum.

*Anthems: By the waters of Babylon; I have surely
built thee an house; The Lord is King, be the
people never so impatient; O give thanks; O
praise the Lord; O where shall wisdom be found?;
Turn thee unto me; Wherewithal shall a young
man. Organ voluntaries Nos. 1; 4 & 7.*
(M) *** CRD Dig. CRD 3483 [id.]. New College
    Ch., Oxford, Edward Higginbottom; Gary
    Cooper.

We missed this valuable collection of anthems when it was first issued in 1992; now it reappears at mid-price and is even more welcome. Boyce is better known for his orchestral symphonies, but on the evidence of this collection, these five verse anthems and three others in a rather more ambitious ternary format, are all of high quality, broadly following a Purcellian tradition. The beautiful *By the waters of Babylon* is perhaps the finest of the latter, but the verse anthem, *I have surely built thee a house* is also very commanding, as is the opening *O where shall wisdom be found*. Three organ voluntaries are included to add variety, and with such strong well-integrated performances and excellent recording in a highly suitable acoustic, this can be truly recommended.

Ode for St Cecilia's Day.
*** ASV Dig. CDGAU 200 [id.]. Patrick
    Burrowes, William Purefoy, Andrew Watts,
    Richard Edgar-Wilson, Michael George, New
    College, Oxford, Ch., Hanover Band, Graham
    Lea-Cox.

Written in 1739 when he was still in his twenties, Boyce's *Ode for St Cecilia's Day* uses a text by his friend John Lockman, celebrating Apollo and the Muses as well as St Cecilia, patron saint of music. It is only at the very end that the saint herself appears in the last aria, sung in this performance (following the example of the original performance in Dublin) by a boy chorister, the fresh-voiced Patrick Burrowes. This has similar vigour to *The Secular masque*, recorded earlier by Graham Lea-Cox with the same choir and orchestra, with comparably lively results in the choruses, if with less distinguished singing from the soloists. Good atmospheric sound.

The Secular masque. Overtures: *Birthday Ode for George III* (1768); *King's Ode for the new year* (1772); *Ode for St Cecilia's Day.*
*** ASV Dig. CDGAU 176 [id.]. Judith Howarth,
    Kathleen Kuhlmann, Charles Daniels, Timothy
    Robinson, Stephen Varcoe, David Thomas,
    New College, Oxford Ch., Hanover Band,
    Graham Lea-Cox.

Written in the mid 1740s originally for private performance, *The Secular masque* represents Boyce at his freshest and most unbuttoned. Such a chorus as *'Tis better to laugh than to cry* in a rollicking 6/8 time captures the mood, with classical figures made earthy and human. So 'Diana's song' – which Boyce published separately – with elaborate horn parts, brims with rustic jollity, and is radiantly sung here by Judith Howarth. 'Mars's song', *Sound the trumpet, beat the drum* also has Boyce responding with engaging directness, vigorous and colourful.

This is an ode which draws inspiration from the example of Purcell as well as of Handel (still active when it was written) while establishing an open flavour of its own, very much in the style of the popular Boyce Symphonies. Each of the overtures here, including the one for the *Secular masque*, follow a similar form in two, three or four brief movements. Graham Lea-Cox draws lively performances from the Hanover Band, the choir and his excellent team of soloists. Warm, full sound.

Brahms, Johannes (1833–97)

Piano concertos Nos. 1 in D min., Op. 15; 2 in B flat, Op. 83.
** DG Dig. 457 837-2 (2) [id.]. Maurizio Pollini,
    BPO, Abbado.

DG have now paired together Pollini's two Brahms concertos, recorded live in 1997/8. Unlike the comparable Gilels set (which is at mid-price) there are no fill-ups. No. 1 is further handicapped by a balance which places the piano very forward in relation to the orchestra. The *Second concerto* is much more satisfactory in this respect: indeed the sound is very satisfactory. The performance too is of some distinction, but this set is poor value at premium price, and in any case Gilels and Jochum, who throw in the *Fantasias Op. 116* (DG 447 446-2), and Barenboim and Barbirolli, who offer the *Tragic overture* and *Haydn variations* (EMI CZS5 72649-2) are much to be preferred; while Stephen Hough gives keenly distinctive and deeply thoughtful readings of both concertos very inexpensively indeed on a Virgin Classics super-bargain Digital Double (VBD5 61412-2).

Piano concerto No. 2 in B flat, Op. 83.
(**(*)) Testament mono SBT 1170 [id.]. Edwin
    Fischer, BPO, Furtwängler – FURTWÄNGLER:
    Symphonic concerto: Adagio. (**)

The partnership of Edwin Fischer and Wilhelm Furtwängler produced inspired music-making, both in the 1943 wartime German radio recording of the Brahms concerto and in the slow movement from the conductor's own ambitious concerto, recorded in 1939. The sound in the Brahms is limited, but the piano is bright and clear, and the performance has such energy and warmth, rapt in the slow movement, that one readily forgives any flaws and intrusive audience noises.

(i) *Piano concerto No. 2 in B flat, Op. 83;* (ii)
Cello sonata in D (arr. of *Violin sonata in G,*
Op. 78).
**(*) Sony Dig. SK 63229 [id.]. Emanuel Ax;
    with (i) Boston SO, Haitink; (ii) Yo-Yo Ma.

The magisterial and autumnal *Second Piano concerto in B flat* from Emanuel Ax and the Boston Symphony under Bernard Haitink on Sony has tremendous breadth. It strikes the right balance between the rhapsodic and the symphonic, the seemingly improvisatory solo writing and the sinewy orchestral texture. Ax is a perceptive and thoughtful artist whose beautiful pianism impresses as does the eloquent orchestral playing. Memories of such partnerships as Gilels and Jochum on DG (439 466-2 or 447 446-2 paired with No. 1) are not banished, and the new recorded sound, though good, is not in the demonstration bracket. The fill-up, an arrangement by an unknown hand of the *G major Sonata* transposed to D major for cello is played with refinement but is hardly an urgent addition to the catalogue.

Violin concerto in D, Op. 77.
(BB) *** Royal Long Players DCL 705742 (2).
Yehudi Menuhin, BPO, Kempe – DVORAK; SIBELIUS; TCHAIKOVSKY: *Violin concertos.* ***

This super-bargain collection of 'Great violin concertos' includes four outstanding recordings and is alone worth its modest cost for Menuhin's performance of the Brahms with Kempe and the Berlin Philharmonic at the end of the 1950s – one of his supreme achievements in the recording studio. He was in superb form, producing tone of resplendent richness and the reading is also notable for its warmth and nobility. Kempe and the Berlin Philharmonic were inspired to outstanding playing – the oboe solo in the slow movement is particularly beautiful. The sound is remarkably satisfying and well balanced and the present transfer is wholly admirable.

Double concerto for violin and cello in A min.
(M) *** RCA 09026 63531-2 [id.]. Heifetz, Piatigorsky, RCA Victor SO, Wallenstein – J. S. BACH: *Double violin concerto in D min., BWV 1043*; MOZART: *Sinfonia concertante in E flat, K.364.***

Although Wallenstein is not as fine an accompanist as Ormandy, he provides a sympathetic backcloth for the 1960 Heifetz–Piatigorsky partnership which, even if it does not quite match Heifetz's earlier version with Feuermann, is still a strong, warm-hearted account with a strikingly brilliant finale. The 1960 recording, although a bit close, has been improved ,upon out of all recognition compared to the harsh quality of the LP, and there is certainly no lack of warmth here.

Hungarian dances Nos. 1–21 (complete).
**(*) Ph. Dig. 462 589-2 [id.]. Budapest Fest. O, Ivan Fischer.

Brahms arranged rather than composed the *Hungarian dances*, and only scored three of them himself, the other orchestrators include various names (notably Dvořák for the last three) and here also Ivan Fischer himself. His performances are warmly enjoyable and obviously have an authentic Hungarian underlay, including players of the 'gypsy violin' and cimbalom. But it is the gentler numbers

(Nos. 3 and 4, for instance), which come off best, and even here, for all the elegance of the playing, at times the rubato sounds just a trifle calculated. The recording is full and natural, but this does not alter our allegiance to the splendid Naxos set, also recorded in Budapest, which is sheer a delight from beginning to end. (● 8.550110 – see our main volume.)

Serenade No. 1 in D, Op. 11.
*** Finlandia/Warner Dig. 3984-25327-2 [id.]. Royal Stockholm PO, Sir Andrew Davis – STENHAMMAR: *Serenade for orchestra, Op. 31.* *** ●

Andrew Davis and the Stockholm Orchestra give a spirited account of Brahms's early masterpiece. His direction is as sympathetic as the players' response. The recording is very good even if the texture could be more transparent; the microphones do not always allow enough air round the wind textures, and some of the wind section are rather close. However, Stenhammar's early debt to Brahms (he was a noted exponent of the *D minor Concerto*) makes his glorious *Serenade* a logical and useful coupling, and this performance is very special.

Serenades Nos. 1 in D, Op. 11; 2 in A, Op. 16.
** Telarc Dig. CD 80522 [id.]. SCO, Mackerras.

Mackerras's performances of the two *Serenades* are curiously disappointing. They are short of the conductor's usual vigorous enthusiasm, and although they have affectionate touches and are well played, they lack the kind of 'live' spontaneity and warm geniality that makes Michael Tilson Thomas's performances on Sony so persuasive (SMK 60134). If you want a bargain coupling, D'Avalos with the Philharmonia on ASV Quicksilva makes a fine alternative (CDQS 6216).

Symphonies Nos. 1–4.
(M) *(*) Chandos Dig. CHAN 9776 (4) [id.]. LSO, Järvi.

During the late 1980s, Neeme Järvi had been among the most active of all recording conductors, with records appearing on many different labels and the quality has been astonishingly consistent, sounding not at all hasty and slapdash. By Järvi's standards, however, his Brahms cycle is a great disappointment, often fussy, sometimes wilful, with playing from the LSO which generally lacks that very quality that marks out most of his records: the sense of a genuine performance rather than a studio run-through. Added to that, the Chandos engineers' preference for a wide, reverberant acoustic, makes Brahms's heavy orchestral textures sound thick and vague, however great the richness and range of the recording. The lack of definition in the bass is particularly damaging in No. 1. The slackness of ensemble in the outer movements adds to the heaviness of approach and the middle movements are similarly heavy-handed and this criticism applies equally to No. 2. The first movement, taken relatively fast, is warmly lyrical, but lacks both tension and delicacy. The middle movements miss the charm of Brahms's inspiration and the finale, taken fast, sounds slapdash, with the lack of definition in the bass making the results even more muddled.

Järvi takes a broad view of No. 3 and the weight of the recording at the very start gives appropriate grandeur – before the thickening of texture which mars this series then obtrudes. Though he responds well to the lyricism, the end result is again too heavy-handed, often fussy, with the ensemble no better than in the rest of the series. His effortfulness at the start of No. 4 is similarly disappointing: the reservations about the previous symphonies apply equally here and it emerges as a none-too-careful studio run-through.

Originally, every symphony was coupled with a Schumann overture and these have now been removed, making each CD particularly ungenerous in playing time. Four for the price of two premium-price discs is hardly compensation, amid strong mid- and bargain-price competition. When Karajan's 1970s recordings with the Berlin Philharmonic are available on a DG Double (453 097-2) this Chandos set is a non-starter.

Symphony No. 1; Tragic overture.
(BB) ** Royal Classics ROY 6433. VPO, Barbirolli.

Symphonies Nos. 2 & 3.
(BB) ** Royal Classics ROY 6434. VPO, Barbirolli.

Symphony No. 4; Academic festival overture; Variations on a theme by Haydn (St Anthony chorale).
(BB) ** Royal Classics ROY 6435. VPO, Barbirolli.

Barbirolli recorded the four Brahms symphonies in 1967/8. His warmly expansive approach benefits from the sympathetic playing of the Vienna Philharmonic and the glowing Sofiensaal ambience. The orchestral ensemble is excellent for all his waywardness. This is immediately striking in No. 1, which remains a controversial, essentially lyrical reading of a work that has more inherent drama than Barbirolli seeks to find. He draws out the finale in particular, although he produces a surge of adrenalin in the closing pages. However, this same relaxed approach suits the golden *Second Symphony* admirably, with the similarly expansive recording and the ready response of the Viennese players. But to underpin a performance of the *Third* as slow as Barbirolli's demands the keenest concentration and although the playing of the VPO is again refined and warmly beautiful the tension is not maintained at a high enough level and the outer movements demand more thrust.

Alas the *Fourth* is the least satisfying of the cycle. The first movement seriously lacks momentum, and only in the slow movement does Barbirolli achieve the sort of intensity needed to carry his interpretation forward naturally without a feeling of self-indulgence. The *Academic festival overture,* too, needs much more sparkle, but the *Tragic overture,* which is similarly expansive, is full of vigour and the *Variations* at last reveal the conductor at his finest.

Symphonies Nos. 1–4; Tragic overture; Variations on a theme of Haydn.
(***) Testament mono SBT 3167 (3) [id.]. Philh. O, Toscanini.

The concerts here recorded preserve the two legendary occasions in the autumn of 1952 when, in a Brahms cycle at the Royal Festival Hall, Toscanini conducted the Philharmonia Orchestra on his one visit to London after the war. Stewart Brown of Testament is to be congratulated on untying the contractual knots which for almost fifty years have prevented the original EMI tapes from being issued. Then only six years old, the Philharmonia was already the front runner among London orchestras, and it is fascinating to compare these readings of the Brahms symphonies with those which Toscanini recorded in the same twelve months with the NBC Symphony Orchestra in New York. Where the New York performances, resonant and superbly drilled, have a hardness and rigidity with dynamic contrasts ironed out, the Philharmonia ones consistently bring a moulding of phrase and subtlety of rubato which bears out the regular Toscanini instruction to 'Sing!' And in contrast with most Toscanini recordings the hushed playing is magical.

These players, gathered as the best in Britain by Walter Legge, were plainly following every nuance of Toscanini's baton, whereas the New York players seem evidently to have forgotten how to respond to the finer subtleties of this notorious taskmaster among conductors. Though mono recordings made in the Royal Festival Hall are inevitably limited in range, the clarity and definition of this EMI recording, very different from pirated versions taken from the BBC broadcasts, quickly make one forget such limitations, with the crumble of the radio broadcast eliminated. One almost forgets the intrusive coughing. The glorious horn-playing of Dennis Brain has a rich bloom, and the timpani is thrillingly focused, arguably too prominent but very dramatic. Not only Brain's horn but the woodwind contributions of Gareth Morris on flute, Sidney Sutcliffe on oboe and Frederick Thurston on clarinet are markedly sweeter than their counterparts in Toscanini's own NBC Orchestra.

In contrast with his often abrasive contacts with BBC players in the 1930s, the Philharmonia sessions were consistently happy. At the end Toscanini said he wished he was ten years younger so as to make regular recordings with the Philharmonia. Alas, already aged eighty-five, he never returned. Even so, there are a couple of blips to note, which in context hardly matter. The chorale on trombones just after the great horn theme in the introduction to the finale of No. 1 brings a series of split notes, and the finale of No. 4 is disturbed by firecrackers let off by pranksters. Toscanini was completely unfazed, giving a magnificent reading, not just full of adrenalin in the drama of the movement but with a heart-stopping flute solo from Gareth Morris in the slow 3/2 variation. A set to restore Toscanini's unique reputation as a conductor without equal, when too many of his commercial discs give only a limited view of his mastery.

Symphonies Nos. 1–4; Variations on a theme by Haydn, Op. 56a; (i) *German Requiem.*
(M) ** EMI Dig./Analogue CDS5 56837-2 (8) [id.]. Munich PO, Celibidache; (i) with Arleen Augér, Philharmonic Ch. & Munich Bach Ch. (members) – BEETHOVEN: *Symphonies Nos. 2–4; 6 (Pastoral); 7–9 (Choral); Leonora overture No. 3 ** (with SCHUMANN: Symphony No. 2**).*

Sergiu Celibidache enjoys cult status in some quarters, but to box all four Brahms symphonies, the *Requiem,* the *Haydn Variations,* and couple them with Schumann's *Second Symphony* and an incomplete Beethoven cycle on eight CDs not available separately, puts a strain on even the most dedicated collector. Celibidache dwells on beauty of sound and refinement of texture. He is happy to pull phrases completely out of shape but inspired much devotion among many musicians, and to judge from these recordings audiences at these performances. He gave orchestras such as the Munich Philharmonic, the Stuttgart Radio and the Swedish Radio much tonal finesse but was seldom invited to direct any of the great European or American orchestras. In the Brahms *Haydn variations* he is lethargic and at times positively funereal.

(i) *Symphony No. 1 in C min., Op. 68;* (ii) *Academic festival overture;* (iii) *Alto rhapsody Op. 61.*
(M) (***) Dutton Lab. mono CDK 1210 [id.]. (i) Concg. O, Eduard van Beinum; (ii) LSO; (iii) Kathleen Ferrier, LPO Ch., LPO, both cond. Clemens Kraus.

All these recordings were made in the autumn of 1947 only two years after the end of the Second World War. In all, van Beinum made three recordings of the *First Symphony* – a second followed in 1951, also for Decca, and a third in 1958 on the Philips label. This earliest record has a great sense of spontaneity, and it is no surprise to learn from Alan Sanders's excellent note, that the first takes of all ten 78 rpm sides were used. Ferrier's classic record of the *Alto rhapsody* with the LPO and chorus

with Clemens Kraus, newly rehabilitated after the war, and his exemplary *Academic festival overture* come up splendidly and in this fine transfer leave no doubts as to the quality of Decca's post-war engineering.

Symphonies Nos. 2 in D Op. 73; 3 in F, Op. 90.
*** Simax Dig. PSC 1204 [id.]. Oslo PO, Jansons.

Jansons draws incandescent playing from his Oslo Philharmonic in outstanding versions of both symphonies. The refinement of the playing and the subtlety of Jansons' dynamic shading go with an approach which is at once direct and refreshing with generally steady speeds yet warmly expressive on detail. Whereas in No. 3 Jansons observes the exposition repeat in the first movement, in No. 2 he omits it, a justifiable decision when it is very much a question of proportion. These now stand among the very finest versions of both symphonies; a formidable addition to the Simax catalogue, recorded in full, well-detailed sound.

Symphony No. 3 in F, Op. 90.
(***) Testament mono SBT 1173 [id.]. Philh. O, Cantelli – MENDELSSOHN: *Symphony No. 4 (Italian).* (***)

Cantelli's 1955 version of Brahms's *Third,* justly famous in the mono LP era, is among the warmest, most glowing accounts ever put on disc, with Dennis Brain's glorious horn-playing, ripely recorded, crowning the whole incandescent performance. Sadly, in mono, it has been available only rarely in the years since 1955, making this superbly transferred reissue very welcome, particularly when the coupling is an equally unforgettable, previously unissued version of the Mendelssohn.

CHAMBER MUSIC

Cello sonatas Nos. 1 in E min., Op. 38; 2 in F, Op. 99; Songs without words: Feldeinsamkeit; Die Mainacht; Minnelied; Mondenschein; Nachtwandler; Sommerabend; Der Tod, das ist die kühle Nacht.
**(*) DG Dig. 459 677-2 [id.]. Mischa Maisky, Pavel Gililov.

Maisky has exceptional refinement of tone at his disposal as well as much expressive eloquence, and the engineers do him and his partner justice. His phrasing is at times tinged with affectation, and some will find him a bit gushing and oversweet. He emotes a bit too heavily in the seven song transcriptions. Recommended to Maisky's following rather than a wider constituency. First choice probably remains with Rostropovich and Serkin (DG 410 510-2), although Lynn Harrell and Stephen Kovacevich are also magnificent and commanding, and this HMV disc includes also Kovacevich's eloquent account of the *Handel variations* (EMI CDC5

56440-2). At mid-price Starker and Sebök rather sweep the field (Mercury 434 377-2).

Cello sonata No. 2 in F, Op. 99.
(M) (***) EMI mono CDM5 67008-2 [id.]. Pablo Casals, Mieczslaw Horszowski – BACH: (Unaccompanied) *Cello suite No. 1 in G, BWV 1007*; BEETHOVEN: *Cello sonata No. 3.* (***)

This celebrated 1936 Paris recording of the Brahms *F major sonata, Op. 99,* with Horszowski has had numerous incarnations, most recently on EMI Références, but its splendours do not fade. It remains one of the most moving accounts of this leonine score on disc.

Clarinet quintet in B min., Op. 115.
*** DG Dig. 459 641-2 [id.]. David Shifrin, Emerson Qt. – MOZART: *Clarinet quintet.****

David Shifrin's newest recording of the Brahms *Quintet* is outstandingly fine. He establishes a natural partnership with the Emersons and the outer movements, while warmly lyrical, are much more characterful and positive than in his earlier version. Yet the *Adagio* achieves a gentle, ruminative, almost improvisational quality. The recording is admirably balanced and the equally recommendable Mozart coupling has an appealing simplicity.

(i; ii) *Clarinet quintet in B min., Op. 115;* (i; iii) *Clarinet sonatas Nos. 1 in F min.; 2 in E flat, Op. 120/1–2;* (ii) *String quintet No. 2 in G, Op. 111.*
(B) **(*) Delos Dig. Double DE 3706 [id.]. (i) David Shifrin; (ii) Chamber Music Northwest; (iii) Carol Rosenberger (with SCHUMANN: *Fantasiestücke, Op. 73*).

David Shifrin's earlier, 1988 account of the *Clarinet quintet* has a glowing delicacy of feeling and is played with lovely tone and much warmth from the supporting Northwest string group. However, the mellow atmosphere persists throughout and although the performance is very easy to enjoy, there is too little difference of character between the four movements. One would have liked more bite and character from the strings, especially in the finale. This applies equally to the *G major Quintet,* where it is the lyrical warmth of the *Adagio* that remains in the memory. The two *Clarinet sonatas* are songful, have great warmth, and again Shifrin's richly lyrical phrasing gives much pleasure. He has fine support from Carol Rosenberger. These performances, less volatile than those of Ralph Manno and Alfredo Perl on Arte Nova (see below), are very satisfying in a quite different way, for Shifrin's tone is consistently beautiful. So are the three Schumann *Fantasy pieces,* especially the wistful opening number, which might well be another movement by Brahms.

(i) *Clarinet quintet in B min., Op. 115;* (ii) *Piano quintet in F min., Op. 34.*
(BB) *(*) Arte Nova Dig. 74321 30493-2 [id.]. (i)

Ralph Manno; (ii) Alfredo Perl; Paetsch, Cunz, Rohde, Schiefen.

In the *Clarinet quintet,* Ralph Manno's style is boldly romantic, but there is no lack of light and shade, especially in the lovely *Adagio.* The balance is good too. But in the *Piano quintet* the recording recedes into a very resonant acoustic and although Alfredo Perl leads strongly in the outer movements, detail is very blurred. In the *Andante* this lack of definition is even more serious. The Scherzo has splendid impetus, but the *Poco sostenuto* which opens the finale is again recessive. This is a pity as the performance overall offers much to enjoy.

(i) *Clarinet quintet in B min., Op. 115;* (ii) *String quintet No. 1 in F, Op. 88.*
** Nimbus Dig. NI 5515 [id.]. (i) Karl Leister; (ii) Brett Dean; Brandis Qt.

Good performances of both pieces on Nimbus by these distinguished instrumentalists, but the recording is rather two dimensional with little space round the artists. The sound is close and ill-ventilated, particularly in the *F major Quintet,* which is a great pity since there is a great deal to admire artistically including eloquent playing from Leister and the Brandis Quartet.

(i) *Clarinet quintet in B min., Op. 115;* (ii) *String quintet No. 2 in G, Op. 111*
** EMI Dig. CDC5 56759-2 [id.]. (i) Sabine Meyer; (ii) Hariolf Schlichtig; Alban Berg Qt.

Famous names do not always guarantee a great artistic experience, and few quartets have greater celebrity than the Alban Berg, while Sabine Meyer is one of EMI's more recent recording stars. She joins them for a good rather than outstanding account of the *Clarinet quintet* and there are more moving accounts to be had (including those by David Shifrin listed above), and more memorable versions of the *G major Quintet.*

Clarinet sonatas Nos. 1–2, Op. 120/1–2.
(BB) *** Arte Nova Dig. 74321 27767-2 [id.]. Ralph Manno, Alfredo Perl.

Ralph Manno has a succulent tone, highly suitable for Brahms. He establishes a strong partnership with Alfredo Perl and these volatile performances are full of imaginative light and shade. In the *F minor,* the slow movement is freely ruminative, the *E flat major* opens most persuasively and is equally strong on contrast. There is some most winning playing in the *Andante* and the brief finale is full of energy. The well-balanced recording is most realistic and vivid.

Clarinet/Viola sonata, Op. 120/2 (arr. for violin); *Hungarian Dances Nos. 2, 5, 8 & 9* (arr. Joachim).
*** Ph. Dig. 462 621-2 [id.] Akiko Suwana, Boris Berezovsky – DVORAK: *4 Romantic pieces, Op. 75, etc.*; JANACEK: *Violin sonata.* ***

This partnership brings two Tchaikovsky Competition prizewinners together: Akiko Suwana carried off the first prize for the violin at the same time as Boris Berezovsky won the piano first prize. Brahms's own transcription of the *Sonata*, Op. 120, No. 2 – originally written for clarinet or viola – brings eminently civilized music-making but the arrangement, though understandable when clarinet or viola recitals were rare, is hardly necessary when the gramophone has rendered the originals so readily accessible. However, this is distinguished playing, wholly natural and unforced. The recording is superb in every way.

Clarinet trio in A min., Op. 114.
*** RCA Dig. 09026 63504-2 [id.]. Michael Collins, Steven Isserlis, Stephen Hough – FRUHLING: *Clarinet trio;* SCHUMANN: *Märchenerzählungen; Träumerei.* ***

It would be hard to imagine a finer performance of the Brahms *Clarinet trio*, a work which quite unfairly has tended to be neglected in favour of the *Clarinet quintet*. All three of these fine young musicians are natural recording artists, never failing to sound spontaneously expressive on disc, always conveying the feeling of live music-making, so that their interchanges are magnetic. It makes an imaginative coupling having the Brahms masterpiece alongside the long-buried but delightful Frühling *Trio* and the arrangements of Schumann items for the same forces.

(i) *Clarinet trio in A min., Op. 114. Clarinet sonatas Nos. 1–2, Op. 120/1–2.*
*** Nimbus Dig. NI 5600 [id.]. Karl Leister, Ferenc Bognár; (i) with Wolfgang Boettcher.

Like the *Clarinet quintet* listed above, the Nimbus recording gives the artists rather less space round the aural image than we would like. All the same this is by no means as worrying in the *A minor Trio*, which Karl Leister and his two distinguished colleagues play with great expressive eloquence and artistry. These performances have warmth and all three artists phrase with great artistry and spontaneity.

Viola sonatas Nos. 1 in F min. 2 in E flat, Op. 120/ 1–2; (i) 2 Songs with viola, Op. 91.
*** RCA Dig. 09026 63293-2 [id.]. Yuri Bashmet, Mikhail Muntian.

The *Viola sonatas*, Op. 120 are more often heard in their original and more effective form for clarinet. They are superbly played by Yuri Bashmet, whose sumptuous tone and refined musicianship along with the expert support of Mikhail Muntian are persuasive. Finely poised and well-proportioned accounts, among the finest around, although Lars Anders Tomter and Leif Ove Andsnes are rather special and were given a ● in our main volume (Virgin/EMI VC7 59309-2).

String quartets Nos. 1 in C min.; 2 in A min., Op. 51/1–2.
(**(*)) Biddulph mono LAB [id.]. Busch Qt – SCHUMANN: *Violin sonata No. 2* (***) (with REGER: *Violin sonata No. 5, Op. 84: Allegretto* (***)).

The Busch recorded the *C minor Quartet*, Op. 51/1 for HMV in 1932, and for a long time this was the classic account of the work: so much so that the post-war *A minor*, Op. 51/2 (made in 1947 on four Columbia LXs when the ensemble were past their prime) came as a disappointment. There is no lack of insight but the playing is less polished. Busch and his colleagues were profound musicians and there is always something to learn from them despite the frail sound. Excellent transfers and interesting couplings.

String sextets Nos. 1 in B flat, Op. 18; 2 in G, Op. 36.
*** Signum Dig. SIGCD 013 [id.]. Hausmusik, London.

Hausmusik are dedicated to the performance of nineteenth-century music on the instruments of the time. These well-recorded accounts of the two Brahms *Sextets* do not readily compete with the Raphael Ensemble (Hyperion CDA 66276) or the distinguished team led by Isaac Stern (Sony S2K 45820) or indeed the ASMF Chamber Ensemble on Chandos (CHAN 9151). The instrumental timbre is lighter and more transparent, perhaps more suited to Mozart, for there is no lack of warmth. The sonority is less well upholstered and rich than in modern versions but tempi are well chosen and the playing is unfailingly sensitive and musical. It is a more than welcome addition to the catalogue but for most collectors will be a supplement rather than an alternative to the existing recommendations. Excellent notes by the Brahms scholar, Robert Pascall.

PIANO MUSIC

German Requiem, Op. 45 (arr. for piano, 4 hands).
(BB) ** Naxos Dig. 8.554115 [id.]. Silke-Thora Mattheis, Christian Köhn.

Brahms made the piano-duet arrangement of his great choral work for a projected performance (with soloists and choir) in London, but it works better than might be expected when played, as here, by two pianists without vocal support. Though the whole project may seem odd, what does come out from this warmly expressive performance is the spring-like lyricism of Brahms's writing. On the other hand, having piano tone alone does emphasize the fact that the work is predominantly slow. A curiosity, well recorded.

4 Ballades, Op. 10.
(M) *** DG Analogue/Dig. 457 762-2 [id.].

Michelangeli – SCHUBERT: *Piano Sonata in A min.***; BEETHOVEN: *Piano Sonata No. 4 in E flat, Op. 7.* *

A mixed programme of which the Brahms is the finest performance included. Michelangeli plays an instrument made in the 1910s, which produces a wonderfully blended tone and fine mellow sonority. The *Ballades* are given a performance of the greatest distinction, without the slightly aloof quality that sometimes disturbs his readings and the 1981 digital recording is excellent. The couplings are alas, not in the same league.

Variations on a theme of Schumann (trans. for 2 hands by Theodor Kirchner).
** Athene Minerva Dig. ATHCD 23 [id.].
Andreas Boyde – SCHUMANN: *Impromptus; Variations.***

Brahms published his variations on the so-called Schumann *Geister variations* for piano duet as Op. 23, and his friend, the composer Theodor Kirchner, transcribed it for solo piano. It comes as the make-weight for an intelligently planned Schumann recital by the German pianist Andreas Boyde. The playing is very convincing but the recording somewhat too close and shallow.

VOCAL MUSIC

Sacred motets: *Ach, arme Welt, du trügest mich, Op. 110; Es ist das Heil uns kommen her, Op. 29; O Heiland reiss die Himmel auf, Op. 74.*
**(*) Paraclete Press Dig. GDCG 107 [id.]. Gloria Dei Cantores, Elizabeth C. Patterson – MENDELSSOHN: *Motets.* **(*)

These three *a cappella* motets are used as an effective interlude in what is for the most part a more romantic collection of Mendelssohn's sacred settings. Brahms's way can be more austere: *Es ist das Heil,* for instance, owes a debt to Bach in its four-part chorale followed by a five-part fugue, where the part-writing could be more sharply delineated. But the other two works have a simple eloquence, which is well caught by these persuasively committed performances, beautifully recorded.

Lieder: *Agnes; Alte Liebe; Dein blaues Auge hält so still; Dort in den Weiden; 2 Gesänge, Op. 91; Gold überwiegt die Liebe; Immer leiser wird mein Schlummer; Der Jäger; Klage I–II; Die Liebende schreibt; Liebesklage des Mädchens; Liebestreu; Des Liebsten Schwur; Das Mädchen, Op. 85/3; Mädchenfluch, Op. 95/1; Mädchenlied. Op. 107/5; Das Mädchen spricht; 5 Ophelia Lieder; Regenlied; 6 Romanzen und Lieder, Op. 84; Salome; Sapphische Ode; Spanisches Lied; Der Schmied; Therese; Todessehnen; Die Trauernde; Vom Strande; Von waldbekränzter Höhe; Vorschneller Schwur; Wie melodien zieht; 8 Zigeunerlieder, Op. 103.*

(B) *** DG Double 459 469-2 (2) [id.]. Jessye Norman, Daniel Barenboim.

This double CD concentrates on Brahms's 'women's songs', taken from DG's complete Brahms Lieder survey, of which these were recorded in the early 1980s. Jessye Norman's tone is full and golden: it was this series which showed how much she had developed as an artist over the years. Her imagination even matches that of Fischer-Dieskau on the complete set, and no praise could be higher. Her voice is ideally suited to many of these songs, and if occasionally there is a hint of an over-studied quality, this is of little consequence considering the overall achievement. Barenboim's accompaniments are superb – he almost gives the impression of improvisation, and this contributes much to the success of this recital. The recording is excellent and this is a real bargain.

German Requiem, Op. 45 (new English adaptation by Robert Shaw).
*** Telarc Dig. CD 80501 [id.]. Janice Chandler, Nathan Gunn, Mormon Tabernacle Ch., Utah SO, Craig Jessop.

When Robert Shaw died in January 1999, he was on the point of recording with the forces here his new adaptation of the *German Requiem.* Telarc, instead of abandoning the project, decided to go ahead with the recording in tribute to Shaw as a great choir trainer, using the newly nominated choirmaster of the Tabernacle Choir, Craig Jessop, who had worked with Shaw on all the preparations. The result is a dedicated reading which for English-speaking listeners will communicate warmly, not least thanks to the extra immediacy of the words. The choir, which too often has been mushily recorded, here emerges far fresher than before, and the two soloists are both first-rate. Janice Chandler has a warm, creamy soprano, and Nathan Gunn has a youthfully clear baritone which he uses with finesse and passion. Full, warm sound, not always ideally transparent, but this remains a fully worthy tribute to Shaw.

Bretón, Tomás (1850–1923)

La Dolores (complete).
*** Decca Dig. 466 060-2 (2) [id.]. Matos, Domingo, Lanza, Beltrán, Pierotti, Liceu Grand Theatre Ch., Badalona Conservatoire Children's Ch., Barcelona SO, Antoni Ros Marbà.

With Plácido Domingo as a star attraction, working well as a member of a first-rate, stylish team, this set of a popular Spanish opera presents a formidable case for a genre which is seriously neglected outside Spain. Bretón may not be the most original of composers, a contemporary of Puccini who writes fluently in an undemandingly melodic style, but *La*

Dolores still makes enjoyable listening. With the melodramatic story confidently handled – including crowd choruses, such colourful genre pieces as a lively *Jota*, and echoes of popular repertory operas such as an offstage bullfight at the end of Act II – the result is rather like Mascagni in a plainer idiom. Ros Marbà conducts a lively performance, with Domingo in splendid voice. As the heroine of the title, Elisabete Matos is on the shrill side, but sings warmly and idiomatically, and Tito Beltrán is an impressive second tenor. Full-blooded sound to match.

Brian, Havergal (1876–1972)

Symphony No. 3 in C sharp min.
(B) **(*) Hyperion Helios CDH 55029 [id.].
  Andrew Ball, Julian Jacobson, BBC SO,
  Lionel Friend.

The *Third Symphony* began life as a concerto for piano; this perhaps explains the prominent role given to two pianos in the score. The work is full of extraordinarily imaginative and original touches, but the overall lack of rhythmic variety is a handicap. The playing of the BBC Symphony Orchestra under Lionel Friend is well prepared and dedicated, but the recording does not open out sufficiently in climaxes. Even so, this is well worth considering at Helios price.

Britten, Benjamin (1913–76)

An American overture; Ballad of heroes; The building of the house; Canadian carnival; (i) Diversions for piano (left-hand) and orchestra; Occasional overture; Praise we great men; Scottish ballad; Sinfonia da Requiem; Suite on English folk tunes: A time there was . . ; Young Apollo; (ii) 4 Chansons françaises.
(B) *** EMI Dig. CZS5 73983-2 (2) [CDZB
  573983]. (i) Peter Donohoe; (ii) Jill Gomez;
  CBSO Ch., CBSO, Rattle.

A valuable compilation from the various recordings of Britten's music, most of it rare, which Rattle has made over the years. It is good to have the *Diversions for piano (left-hand) and orchestra*, with Peter Donohoe as soloist – amazingly this was the first version in stereo – and the most cherishable item of all is the radiant performance given by Jill Gomez of the *Four Chansons françaises*, the remarkable and tenderly affecting settings of Hugo and Verlaine composed by the 15-year-old Britten. This fine collection is now all the more desirable at its new bargain price.

A time there was . . . (suite on English folk tunes), Op. 90; Lachrymae: Reflections on a song of Dowland (arr. for orchestra); *Prelude and fugue for 18 part string orchestra, Op. 29; Simple*

Symphony, Op. 4; Variations on a theme of Frank Bridge; Young person's guide to the orchestra, Op. 34. (i) Song cycles: *Les Illuminations, Op. 18; Nocturne, Op. 60;* (i; ii) *Serenade for tenor, horn and strings, Op. 31. Gloriana: Courtly dances. Peter Grimes: 4 Sea interludes.*
(B) **(*) Nimbus Dig. NI 1751 (3) [id.]. E. String
  O and ESO, William Boughton; with (i) Jerry
  Hadley; (ii) Anthony Halstead.

This inexpensive bargain box will seem to many collectors an admirable way of collecting Britten's key orchestral works plus the three major song cycles. In the latter Jerry Hadley is a dramatic and involving soloist. His is not far short of an operatic approach with the crystal clear projection of words and histrionic power of his singing compensating for some lack of subtlety in word colouring. *Les Illuminations* (in easily colloquial French) is strikingly fresh and spontaneous and in the *Nocturne*, which opens magnetically and evocatively, the orchestral playing is full of tension. Anthony Halstead's horn contribution in the *Serenade* is hardly less impressive. William Boughton shows himself a fine Britten advocate throughout and both the works for strings and those for full orchestra are most sympathetically played and certainly do not lack vitality. The recording (for the most part made in the Great Hall of Birmingham University) is outstandingly rich and resonant in a characteristic Nimbus way, while the powerful evocation of the *Peter Grimes Sea interludes* is enhanced by the acoustic of Birmingham's Symphony Hall – one of the first recordings to be made there. Excellent value.

Piano concerto, Op. 13.
*** EMI Dig. CDC5 56760-2 [id.]. Leif Ove
  Andsnes, CBSO, Järvi – ENESCU: *Legend for
  trumpet and piano;* SHOSTAKOVICH: *Piano
  concerto No. 1 in C min., Op. 35.* ***

Leif Ove Andsnes and Järvi *fils* were recorded at a live concert in Symphony Hall. Their account of this rewarding and brilliant concerto ranks along with the very best in the catalogue – including the classic Richter/Britten version (Decca 417 308-2). Andsnes has all the virtuosity the score calls for, plus the thoughtfulness and inner feeling required in the slow movement. First-rate sound.

(i) *Double concerto in B min. for violin, viola and orchestra. 2 Portraits for strings; Sinfonietta* (version for small orchestra); (ii) *Young Apollo* (for piano, string quartet and strings), *Op. 16.*
*** Erato/Warner Dig. 3984 25502-2 [id.]. (i)
  Gidon Kremer, Yuri Bashmet; (ii) Nikolai
  Lugansky; Hallé O, Kent Nagano.

Of the many works which Britten left in his bottom drawer to be discovered only after his death, none is more rewarding than this striking three-movement *Double concerto for violin and viola.* He wrote it in

1932 in the months leading up to his nineteenth birthday. Studying at the Royal College of Music, Britten was deflected from completing it in one go by a sudden urge to compose a piece with obvious echoes of Schoenberg – his *Sinfonietta* – also on this disc. What he left was the short score with indications of orchestration, which Colin Matthews had little difficulty in completing. Fascinatingly, it helps to explain what has long seemed the anomaly of the *Sinfonietta*. Though the chromatic writing in the *Double concerto* betrays something of the same influence, it is stylistically less radical than the *Sinfonietta*, warmer and more recognizably the work of Britten with its distinctive melodies and orchestration, both spare and striking. It receives a magnetic reading here from the two high-powered Russian soloists, with Kent Nagano and the Hallé Orchestra. The disc has other première recordings too. The *Sinfonietta* comes in a version that Britten made in America, for small orchestra rather than solo instruments; and there is the *Two Portraits*, written when Britten was sixteen, a vigorous, purposeful picture of a friend, and a reflective, melancholy one of himself, with the viola solo beautifully played by Bashmet. A revelatory disc.

(i; ii) *Lachrymae, Op. 48;* (ii; iii; iv) *Canticle No. 3: Still falls the rain, Op. 55;* (iii; v) *Our hunting fathers, Op. 8;* (ii; iii) *Who are these children?, Op. 84.*
(M) (**(*)) BBC Music mono/stereo BBCB 8014-2 [id.]. (i) Margaret Major; (ii) composer (piano); (iii) Peter Pears; (iv) Dennis Brain; (v) LSO, Britten.

This valuable issue in the BBC's 'Britten the Performer' series fills in two gaps in the list of his own works which he recorded – the early cantata *Our hunting fathers* and the extended, enigmatic viola piece, *Lachrymae*. Britten's Opus 8, *Our hunting fathers*, created something of a scandal when it was first performed, at the Norwich Festival in 1936, thanks to its anti-blood-sports theme, prompted by W. H. Auden. The composer in his interpretation here, biting and urgent to the point of violence in climaxes, reflects what he must have felt in writing the work. Pears is in superb voice too, focused sharply in this rather dry mono BBC studio recording of 1961. In *Lachrymae*, not so much a set of variations on the Dowland theme as a series of episodic reflections, the playing of Britten at the piano magnetizes the ear almost as in an improvisation, with the viola player Margaret Major characteristically warm in a beautifully sustained reading.

Britten and Pears recorded the late song cycle, *Who are these children?*, to words by the Scottish poet William Soutar, for Decca soon after it was first performed in 1971, but that recording has long been unavailable. With its clutch of brief nursery-rhyme settings in the Scots dialect, it may initially seem a relatively lightweight piece, but they only serve to intensify, by contrast, the darkness of the four, more substantial war-inspired songs. Again there is violence in this performance, with both Britten and Pears at their finest. It is good too to have this 1956 Aldeburgh Festival account of the *Canticle No. 3* with Dennis Brain as horn soloist, warm even in face of a dry acoustic. The big snag is the absence of texts – particularly serious in the case of the little-known Soutar poems.

Prelude and fugue for 18 part string orchestra, Op. 29; Simple Symphony, Op. 4; Variations on a theme of Frank Bridge.
(BB) *** ASV Quicksilva Dig. CDQS 6215 [id.].
    Northern Sinf., Richard Hickox.

Bargain hunters not wanting to stretch to the three-disc Nimbus set above might well turn to the triptych of string works on ASV's super-bargain Quicksilva label, which is notable for an outstandingly fine account of the *Frank Bridge variations*, which stands up well alongside not only the composer's own version, but also Karajan's superb mono Philharmonia account (❂ EMI CDM5 66601-2). Hickox's reading encompasses the widest range of emotion and style from the genial, exuberant bravura of the *Moto perpetuo* to the powerful intensity of the *Funeral march*. Although here the Northern Sinfonia double-basses fall short of the extraordinary weight of tone produced by Karajan's Philharmonia players, the passionate attack of the Northern Sinfonia violins more than compensates. The earlier parodies have a wittily light touch; throughout the string playing is enormously responsive, combining polish with eloquence, and the hauntingly atmospheric passage before the closing bars is full of tension. The rich string sonorities resonate powerfully in the glowing ambience of All Saints Quayside Church, Newcastle, and in the *Simple symphony* the reverberation recalls Britten's own famous account made in The Maltings. Hickox does not quite match the composer's gleeful rhythmic bounce in the *Playful pizzicato*, and his approach is less light-hearted than Britten's, but it remains a very compelling performance, with a strong as well as a *Boisterous bourrée* and strains of both *nobilmente* and passion in the *Sentimental sarabande*. The *Prelude and fugue* is comparably eloquent, although here the playing is marginally less assured. The recording is first class, with the bright upper range well supported by the firm bass.

Symphony for cello and orchestra, Op. 68.
*** Virgin/EMI Dig. VC5 45356-2 [id.]. Truls Mørk, CBSO, Sir Simon Rattle – ELGAR: *Cello concerto.* ***

This is the second recording Truls Mørk has made of the *Cello symphony*. He is completely attuned to the Britten sensibility playing with ardour and vision. Rattle gets a superb response from the

Birmingham players and the sound is state-of-the-art with particularly impressive depth and naturalness of perspective. The best account of the piece to have appeared for some years and highly recommended.

The Young person's guide to the orchestra (Variations and fugue on a theme of Purcell), Op. 34.
(M) **(*) Virgin/EMI VM5 61782-2 [id.]. Royal Liverpool PO, Libor Pešek – PROKOFIEV: *Peter and the wolf*; SAINT-SAENS: *Carnival of the animals.* ***
(M) (*) Sony SMK 60175 [id.]. Henry Chapin (narrator), NYPO, Bernstein – PROKOFIEV: *Peter and the wolf*; SAINT-SAENS: *Carnival of the animals.* *

Libor Pešek and the Royal Liverpool Philharmonic Orchestra give a detailed and brilliantly played account of Britten's *Young person's guide to the orchestra*. Tension is comparatively relaxed, but the closing fugue is lively and boldly etched.

For Bernstein's *Young person's guide*, the narration is confidently read by Master Henry Chapin. Alas, the script is embarrassingly patronizing (a fault which runs through this disc) and makes for unattractive listening. The 1961 recording is quite good, but this CD is not recommended.

CHAMBER MUSIC

(i) *Cello sonata in C, Op. 65*; (ii) *Elegy for solo viola*; (iii) *6 Metamorphoses after Ovid, for solo oboe, Op. 49*; (iv) *Suite for violin and piano, Op. 6.*
(B) *** EMI Dig. CZS5 73989-2 (2) [id.]. (i) Moray Welsh, John Lenehan; (ii) Paul Silverthorne; (iii) Roy Carter; (iv) Alexander Barantschick, John Alley – WALTON: *Piano quartet*, etc. ***.

In the *Cello sonata*, Moray Welsh and John Lenehan make no attempt to ape the famous Rostropovich account but instead choose their own approach which is thoughtful, ardent (especially in the central *Elegia*) and strong (as in the *Marcia* – very *echt*-Shostakovich) and highly spontaneous. The moto perpetuo finale has great energy and develops a vibrant intensity at the close, and the whole performance is vividly immediate. Paul Silverthorne gives a touchingly valedictory account of the *Elegy* and Roy Carter is rhapsodically free in the six piquant oboe miniatures, capturing their wistful innocence to perfection.

But perhaps the most remarkable of all is the compellingly alive account of the early *Suite for violin and piano*, written between 1934 and 1936. As if anticipating the *Cello sonata*, the five movements are beautifully contrasted, either full of imaginative vitality or, as in the *Lullaby* – marked *Lento tranquillo* – bringing a serene repose. Here

the result is quite ravishing. Throughout, the recordings, made in the Conway Hall, have a pleasing degree of resonance: the effect is present in the most natural way. At its new bargain price, and with a superb coupling, this is strongly recommended.

Suite for violin and piano, Op. 6.
(B) *** EMI Début CZS5 72825-2 [id.]. Rafal Zambrzycki-Payne, Carole Presland – GRIEG: *Violin sonata No. 3*; SZYMANOWSKI: *Violin sonata, Op. 9.* ***

Rafal Zambrzycki-Payne is a young Polish-born player who studied at the Menuhin School and later at the Royal Northern College in Manchester. He was nineteen when this recording was made, a year after he became the 1996 BBC 'Young Musician of the Year'. Unlike some Début releases which concentrate on pieces that serve more purpose as a visiting card for the artist than a useful addition to the catalogue, this makes good sense on both scores. The Britten is a rarity, and though there is a rival account, this has tremendous personality and life. What an imaginative and characterful piece it is! His partner Carole Presland is a superb player too. The Abbey Road recording is expertly balanced and sounds very natural. A most desirable disc.

(i) *2 Insect pieces; 6 Metamorphoses after Ovid, Op. 49*; (ii) *Phantasy, Op. 2*; (i) *Temporal variations.*
**(*) MDG Dig. MDG 3010925-2 [id.]. Gernot Schmalfuss; with (i) Mamiko Watanabe; (ii) Mannheim Qt members.

All of Britten's music for oboe has been recorded but there are few discs exclusively devoted to it. Gernot Schmalfuss plays it expertly and is excellently supported by the pianist Mamiko Watanabe and members of the Mannheim Quartet. Excellent recording, too, though it is not very realistically marketed – 46:47 minutes' playing time is rather short measure for a premium-price disc.

VOCAL MUSIC

Antiphon; Festival Te Deum; Hymn to St Cecilia; A Hymn of St Columba; Hymn to St Peter; Hymn to the Virgin; Jubilate Deo; Missa brevis; Rejoice in the lamb; Te Deum in C. (Organ) Prelude and fugue on a theme of Vittoria.
(BB) *** Naxos Dig. 8.554791 [id.]. St John's College Choir, Christopher Robinson.

This is among the freshest, most electrifying discs of Britten's choral music in the catalogue, a splendid follow-up to the St John's College Choir's outstanding disc of Howells' church music for Naxos. This collection of eleven choral works may omit the much-recorded *Ceremony of carols*, but as a result it gives a wider view of Britten's achievement in this area, with Barry Holden's excellent notes relating each work to the composer's career and his personal associations. The biting attack of these young singers is enhanced by refined recording which thrillingly brings out the wide dynamic contrasts. The *Prelude and fugue* for organ with its elaborate counterpoint is also brilliantly done. The booklet includes full texts.

Nocturne, Op. 60.
(M) **(*) BBC Music BBCB 8013-2 [id.]. Peter Pears, ECO, Britten – SHOSTAKOVICH: *Symphony No. 14.* **(*)

This vivid live performance of Britten's evocative song cycle on the theme of Sleep, recorded by the BBC at the Queen Elizabeth Hall in 1967, contrasts well with Britten and Pears's studio recording for Decca, made with the LSO in 1959 soon after the first performance. Pears here sounds warmer and sweeter, balanced a little backwardly and so set against a helpful ambience. The obbligato instrumentalists in each song, by contrast, are more closely balanced than in the Decca recording, adding to the impact of such a song as the Wordsworth with its terrifying timpani solo, superbly played by James Blades. Not just Blades but all the soloists here from the ECO are even more attuned to Britten's idiom than their LSO counterparts on Decca who, in tackling what was then a brand new work, are a degree less expressive. Sadly, no texts are included.

On this island; Folk-song arrangement: *The Salley Gardens.*
(M) *** BBC Music BBCB 8015-2 [id.]. Peter Pears, composer – SCHUBERT: *7 songs;* WOLF: *7 Mörike Lieder* *** (with ARNE: *Come away death; Under the greenwood tree;* QUILTER: *O mistress mine;* TIPPETT: *Come unto these yellow sands;* WARLOCK: *Take, o take those lips away;* ***).

Britten as accompanist in songs regularly conveyed a sense of spontaneity, as though improvising, and never more so than when playing for Pears in his own works. Britten's early song cycle set to poems by his friend W. H. Auden, is especially valuable, as he did not otherwise record it, and typically it brings a bitingly dramatic reading. Inspired performances of the Lieder by Schubert and Wolf, as well as the sharply contrasted Shakespeare settings by a wide range of British composers.

(i) *Our hunting fathers, Op. 8;* (ii) *Serenade for tenor, horn and strings, Op. 31;* (i) Folksong arrangements: *Oliver Cromwell; O waly, waly.*
**(*) EMI Dig. CDC5 56871-2 [id.]. Ian Bostridge; with (i) Britten Sinf., Daniel Harding; (ii) Marie Luise Neunecker, Bamberg SO, Ingo Metzmacher.

Ian Bostridge's radiantly lyrical tenor is ideally suited to the works which Britten wrote for Peter Pears, providing new insights, not merely copying. This superb version of the *Serenade* was originally coupled less aptly, and the early song cycle on an anti-blood-sports theme, *Our hunting fathers,* makes a welcome alternative. Though Bostridge gives a most illuminating account of the solos, bringing out the bite of the texts prepared by W. H. Auden, Daniel Harding's direction is beautifully textured at spacious speeds – but next to the venom of Britten's own urgent performance it seems a degree too relaxed.

OPERA

Billy Budd (complete).
*** Chandos Dig. CHAN 9826 (3 for 2) [id.]. Simon Keenlyside, Philip Langridge, John Tomlinson, Alan Opie, Bayley, Matthew Best, LSO Ch., LSO, Hickox.

Hickox's brilliant Chandos version of *Billy Budd,* with the finest cast of principals yet assembled for this powerful but difficult opera, was recorded immediately after a concert performance at the Barbican. That has helped Richard Hickox to heighten the dramatic impact of the piece, and above all to illustrate the conflict of good and evil which lies at the heart of the Melville-inspired story. Like the composer himself in his pioneering recording of 1967, Hickox uses the revised two-act score. Kent Nagano in his Erato version with the Hallé reverted to the original four-act score, including the muster scene on *HMS Indomitable* which Britten removed (goaded by the jibe that it was like Captain Corcoran's arrival in *HMS Pinafore*). Yet Hickox not only demonstrates the extra tautness of the revision, but also finds an extra emotional thrust, highlighting the inner conflict of Captain Vere as the officer forced to condemn Billy, the personification of good.

In Philip Langridge the role of Vere has found its most thoughtful interpreter yet, so that from the start his self-searching is the key element in the whole work. Far from the final monologue of Vere as an old man seeming to be a tailing-off, here it provides the most powerful conclusion, a cathartic resolution on the words: '*He has saved me and blessed me*'. Comparably magnetic is John Tomlinson's Claggart, the personification of evil, chillingly malevolent in every inflection, oily in face of authority. Equally, Simon Keenlyside as Billy gains over all rivals in the fresh, youthful incisiveness of the voice, movingly shaded down to a rapt half-tone for the lyrical monologue sung by Billy about to die. Helped by sound of spectacular quality, Hickox at marginally broader speeds conveys more mystery in reflective moments than even Britten himself did. His expansiveness means that the set spills over on to a third disc but with three discs for the price of two, that brings no disadvantage.

Paul Bunyan (complete).
*** Chandos Dig. CHAN 9781 (2) [id.]. Gritton,
Streit, Robinson, Egerton, Broadbent, White,
Coleman-Wright, Graham, Royal Opera Ch. &
O, Hickox.

The much-admired Covent Garden production, presented during the two years that the company was away from the Royal Opera House during rebuilding, was recorded live at the Sadler's Wells Theatre in 1999. Though there are intrusive stage noises, the Chandos sound vividly captures the dramatic atmosphere of this ballad opera with its witty libretto by W. H. Auden. More than ever, it seems inexplicable that this first of Britten's full-length stage works should have originally been so totally rejected, so full as it is of colourful, distinctive invention. Hickox directs a warmly idiomatic reading, which gains over the only previous version (from Philip Brunelle on Virgin, currently unavailable) in featuring such fine singers as Susan Gritton as Tiny, and Kurt Streit as Johnny Inkslinger. The Chandos sound is more open and atmospheric than the studio recording for Virgin, which yet in many ways gains from the closeness of the voices.

Bruch, Max (1838–1920)

Double piano concerto in A flat min., Op. 88a.
*** Chandos Dig. CHAN 9711 [id.]. Güher and
Süther Pekinel, Philh. O, Marriner –
MENDELSSOHN: *Double piano concerto in E;*
MOZART: *Double piano concerto in E flat,
K.365.* ***

The Max Bruch *Double concerto*, adapted from a suite for organ and orchestra, is an oddity of a work, of which the score was lost for some fifty years. It is well worth hearing in a performance as strong, sympathetic and well-recorded as this one, particularly when it is offered in unique and attractive couplings. The problem is the layout of movements, with an andante fugue leading to a second movement which also begins slowly, before launching into a relatively brief allegro. A warmly lyrical *Adagio* follows, the longest of the four movements, and finally, after a repeat of the ponderous opening motif of the whole work, the jolly finale belatedly helps to right the balance. With some attractive themes, it makes a welcome rarity, whatever its limitations.

Violin concerto No. 1 in G min., Op. 26.
(B) ** EMI Début Dig. CDZ5 73501-2 [id.]. Ittai
Shapira, ECO, Charles Hazlewood – BLOCH:
Baal Shem ***; BUNCH: *Fantasy* **;
SARASATE: *Zigeunerweisen.* **(*)

Ittai Shapira's account of the Bruch concerto forms part of a début recital. He is perhaps at his best in the Bloch *Baal Shem*, and the Sarasate *Zigeunerweisen*, the closing section of which comes off brilliantly.

Wonderfully talented though he is, this account of the *G minor Concerto* does not sweep all before it. He needs a little more sense of abandon, though Charles Hazlewood's rather steady, almost sedate tempi do not help.

(i) *Violin concerto No. 2 in D min., Op. 44.*
Symphony No. 3 in E, Op. 51.
*** Chandos Dig. CHAN 9738 [id.]. (i) Lydia
Mordkovitch; LSO, Hickox.

It was Bruch's fate never quite to match the exuberant lyricism of his ever-popular *First Violin concerto*, and it would be idle to pretend that the themes here are as instantly memorable. Yet in such warmly expressive, spaciously conceived readings as these, the coupling of symphony and concerto offers a welcome alternative to the general run of Bruch issues, concentrating on one genre or the other. In the *Third Symphony* Hickox takes an affectionate view of the work. Speeds are broad in the first three movements, markedly so in the *Adagio*, with the chorale theme spacious and dedicated. Bruch wrote this work while he was still Music Director of the Liverpool Philharmonic Society, and the surging theme which opens the finale has a hint of English folk-song. In the *Violin concerto No. 2*, Lydia Mordkovitch gives a raptly intense reading, making the long, slow first movement (in sonata form) into a deeply reflective meditation punctuated by virtuoso flurries, readily justifying her spacious speeds, and with ripe Chandos recording bringing out the warmth and bite of her bravura playing, often in thorny double-stopping.

(i) *Violin concerto No. 3 in D min., Op. 58.*
Symphony No. 1 in E flat, Op. 28.
*** Chandos Dig. CHAN 9784 [id.]. (i) Lydia
Mordkovitch; LSO, Hickox.

This follows the earlier Chandos issue with the same artists. This time the *Third Concerto* is the more substantial work. Written in 1891 when Bruch was professor of composition at the Berlin Music Academy when Joachim was director, it is roughly twice as long as either of the first two concertos, laid out spaciously on the lines of Beethoven or Brahms. The powerful opening, strongly rhythmic, at once establishes the contrast of manner and purpose, yet Bruch characteristically allows himself plenty of lyrical lingering, which inspires Lydia Mordkovitch to playing of rapt intensity down to magical pianissimos. The slow movement is the most typical of Bruch, again with Mordkovitch responding warmly to this hushed meditation, before the vigorous moto perpetuo finale. The *Symphony No. 1*, written soon after the popular *Violin concerto in G minor*, is also based on striking material, with the four movements including a Mendelssohnian *Presto* (prompting dazzling playing from the LSO) and a ripely lyrical slow movement. As in the earlier disc Hickox is a warmly expressive, but never self-indulgent interpreter, and the Chandos recording is full and atmospheric.

Kol Nidrei.
(M) *** DG 457 761-2 [id.]. Fournier, LOP, Martinon – BLOCH: *Schelomo;* LALO: *Cello concerto*; SAINT-SAENS: *Cello concerto No. 1.* ***

This is an excellent (1960) account, which sounds better in this DG Originals transfer than in previous incarnations. If the performance lacks the last degree of romantic urgency, it makes up for it in the beauty and style of Fournier's playing, and he is well supported by Martinon's Lamoureux Orchestra.

Moses (oratorio; complete).
*** Orfeo Dig. C 438 982 H [id.]. Michael Volle, Robert Gambill, Elizabeth Whitehouse, Bamberg Ch. & SO, Claus Peter Flor.

Written in 1895, Bruch's oratorio celebrating the story of Moses – as the composer said, from where Handel's *Israel in Egypt* leaves off – regularly recalls an earlier celebration in music of an Old Testament prophet, Mendelssohn's *Elijah*. The fresh, bright opening chorus leads on to a series of strong and colourful choruses. The story as outlined in the four sections – *On Sinai, The golden calf, The return of the scouts from Canaan* and *The promised land* – is then filled in with solos from the three characters – Moses a baritone, Aaron a tenor and The Angel of the Lord a soprano. The result may not be as vividly dramatic as *Elijah*, even when Moses returns from the mountain to find his people worshipping the golden calf, but in a warm and purposeful performance under a conductor with strong Mendelssohnian sympathies, it makes its mark, thanks also to striking melodic material. The Victorian optimism of the whole piece leads up to a final lament for Moses, which quickly turns into a chorus of joyful thanksgiving. Bright, clear, well-balanced sound.

Bruckner, Anton (1824–96)

Symphony No. 00 in F min. (Study Symphony); Symphony No. 4: Volkfest finale (1878).
(BB) *** Naxos Dig. 8. 554432 [id.]. RSNO, Georg Tintner.

It is good that Tintner, in his superb Bruckner cycle for Naxos, here fills in what might easily have been two gaps. The composer was thirty-nine when he completed this *F minor Symphony*, but he still regarded it as an experimental work. The thematic material may for the most part be untypical – in the first movement suggesting Mendelssohn or Weber – but the progressions and effects point forward to what we now recognise as fully Brucknerian, with

sharp contrasts and sudden changes of direction in the argument.

With excellent playing and recording – as in the rest of the series – Tintner could not be more persuasive, and as a welcome bonus he adds the very rare second version of the finale of the *Fourth Symphony*, which Bruckner entitled *Volkfest*, 'Festival of the People'. Strikingly different, particularly at the start, from the 1880 version of that movement generally performed, it is well worth hearing in a fine performance like this, even if it hardly displaces the usual version.

Symphony No. 1 in C minor (1866 version, revised Carragan); *Symphony No. 3 in D min.: Adagio* (1876).
(BB) *** Naxos Dig. 8.554430 [id.]. RSNO, Georg Tintner.

As with other symphonies in his mould-breaking Bruckner series for Naxos, Georg Tintner opts for the earliest version of the *Symphony No. 1*, antedating the so-called Linz version normally performed, which was in fact a revision made in 1877. The Bruckner scholar, William Carragan, using material assembled by Robert Haas in 1935, has restored what was originally heard at the performance conducted by the composer in Linz in 1868, a première which baffled listeners. The principal differences here are in the finale, which brings angular writing and orchestration more radical than in the revisions.

Tintner in his dedicated performance, with refined playing from the Scottish orchestra, amply justifies his choice, powerfully bringing out the bald originality of the writing. It is a performance which also lends support to Tintner's contention – well-explained in his note – that Schubert had a more profound influence on the work than Wagner. The generous makeweight also offers a rare text, a version of the slow movement of the *Symphony No. 3* unearthed by the Bruckner editor, Leopold Nowak, which was composed in 1876, between the original one of 1873 and the shortened one of 1877.

Again the intensity and refinement of the performance sustain the expansiveness compellingly. An essential disc not just for Brucknerians, reinforcing the high claims of Tintner's cycle, irrespective of price. Clear atmospheric sound, at once transparent and weighty in climaxes.

Symphony No. 3 in D min. (original version).
(BB) *** Naxos Dig. 8.553454 [id.]. RSNO, Georg Tintner.

Symphony No. 3 in D min.
(BB) *** Arte Nova Dig. 74321 651412-2 [id.]. Saarbrücken RSO, Skrowaczewski.

With characteristic boldness, Georg Tintner opts here to record the very rare first version of Bruckner's *Third symphony*, far more expansive than the final revised version normally heard. The score was lost for almost a century, and finally published only in 1977. Tintner masterfully holds the vast structure together, even though his speeds in the three expanded movements are daringly slow. The first movement alone lasts over half an hour, yet the concentration of the performance, with dynamic contrasts heightened, never falters for a moment, with playing from the Scottish Orchestra both powerful and refined. The slow movement too is rapt and dedicated, with pianissimos of breathtaking delicacy. The Scherzo is then fast and fierce, before the spacious account of the finale. Tintner in every way justifies his daring and revelatory choice of text. The notes include Tintner's own fascinating explanation of his choice.

Skrowaczewski, like Tintner, offers a super-budget version of the *Third,* which in both performance and recording rivals any more expensive version (1888). Unlike Tintner he opts for the usual text, following Bruckner's final reworking in his third version of the work. As in Skrowaczewski's other Bruckner recordings for Arte Nova, the playing of the Saarbrücken orchestra is strong and intense, with opulent sound to match. So the slow movement is sweet and warm in its lyrical flow, and the finale glows with resplendent brass.

Symphony No. 4 in E flat (Romantic).
(BB) *** Arte Nova Dig. 74321 72101-2 [id.]. Saarbrücken RSO, Skrowaczewski.

Skrowaczewski's reading of Bruckner's most popular symphony is characteristically strong and refined, with extreme dynamic contrasts heightened by the excellent recording, so that the crescendo at the start of the finale is exceptionally powerful. Only in the third movement Scherzo does he adopt a tempo at all out of the ordinary, challenging the horns in daringly fast hunting calls, which yet are finely disciplined.

Symphony No. 5 in B flat.
*** BBC Legends BBCL 4033-2 [id.]. BBCSO, Jascha Horenstein.

Horenstein's magisterial account of the *Fifth Symphony* with the BBC Symphony Orchestra has the advantage of relatively rich and vivid sound and comes from a 1971 Prom. It is an eloquent and compelling performance of a symphony which Horenstein – to the best of our knowledge – never recorded commercially.

Symphony No. 6 in A (ed. Nowak).
*** Decca Dig. 458 189-2 [id.]. Concg. O, Chailly
 – WOLF: *4 Goethe Lieder ***.*

Chailly's reading of the *Sixth Symphony* is at once refined and powerful at spacious speeds. The extreme pianissimo at the very start sets the mysterious mood, leading to a performance which is warmly emotional at every turn, without a trace of sentimentality. Chailly, more than most interpreters, presents this as perhaps the most original of the Bruckner symphonies, relying on the delicacy of the writing if anything more than the monumental weight typical of Bruckner. In the slow movement, as in the first, the extreme pianissimos have a breathtaking beauty, with the hushed, noble dedication of the strings at the opening contrasted with the poignancy of the oboe.

Chailly's pointing of rhythms in the Scherzo has a Mendelssohnian lightness, and in the finale too fantasy is set against Brucknerian power. The recording is of demonstration quality. The Decca engineers capture to great effect the glorious tonal opulence this great orchestra commands and the wonderful Concertgebouw acoustic in which they work. The Wolf songs, superbly sung with the composer's own orchestrations, make a valuable and generous fill-up.

Symphony No. 7 in E.
*** Teldec/Warner Dig. 3984 24488-2 [id.]. VPO, Harnoncourt.
**(*) Decca Dig. 466 574-2 [id.]. Berlin Radio SO, Riccardo Chailly.
(M) **(*) EMI CDM5 67330-2 [id.]. Philh. O, Klemperer (with RAMEAU: *Gavotte with variations **).*

Harnoncourt's outstanding performance of the *Seventh* was recorded live in the Sofiensaal and is one of his very finest records. The audience, obviously held in the spell of the music-making, is all but silent, and the sound is magnificent, the Viennese strings have a radiant sheen and the brass is gloriously sonorous. The performance could hardly be more compelling. Of course, it has its minor eccentricities, notably certain gruff brass tuttis (which work well with Bruckner, especially in the finale) and a curious separation of the notes of the main string theme of the slow movement. But one adjusts to this when the playing itself has such sustained tension and warmth, so that Harnoncourt can relax without ever losing the forward flow. The cymbal crash at the climax is omitted, but even this does not spoil its impact, and in the beautiful coda Harnoncourt draws out the resemblance in the valedictory overlapping horn parts to Wagner's *Das Rheingold.* The Scherzo is extremely vivid and (not surprisingly) rhythmically biting, yet bringing out the curiously Elgarian lyrical strain in the strings. Indeed, what is so striking about the reading overall is its appealing lyrical feeling, with its moments of gentle restraint. Yet the closing section is superbly controlled and the coda has never come off more effectively on record. This has to compete with Chailly and Karajan and Haitink, but it is very highly recommendable in its own right. Harnoncourt admirers need not hesitate.

We thought highly of Chailly's Bruckner *Seventh* when it first appeared in 1984, and ranked it among the finest of its period. There are so many superb *Seventh*s now in the catalogue that fine though it is, it perhaps no longer enjoys its old preeminence. It seems scarcely credible that Decca have chosen to reissue it at full price – small wonder the industry is in such dire straits!

We have always been divided in our view of Klemperer's Bruckner *Seventh*, beautifully played and recorded as it is. The first movement is slow, and although both here and in the second movement the tension is far from low, some listeners may find it difficult to concentrate to the end. The Scherzo goes well and in the finale Klemperer makes the lovely chorale melody glow most beautifully, but as an overall reading this can only be strongly recommended to keen Klemperer admirers, which in this instance include E. G., who finds much to admire in the performance. Certainly the new transfer of the 1960 Kingsway Hall recording is impressively full and natural. The Rameau *Gavotte*, recorded eight years later makes a piquant bonus, the manner far from authentic, but most winning when played with such elegance and finish.

Symphonies Nos. 7 (Ed. Haas); 8–9 (Ed. Nowak).
*(**) DG 445 471-2 (4) [id.]. Stuttgart SW RSO, Celibidache – SCHUBERT: *Symphony No. 5.***(*).*

Symphony No. 8 in C min. (ed. Nowak).
(M) *(*) EMI Dig. ZDCB5 56696-2 (2). Munich PO, Celibidache.

Celibidache's Bruckner is for the dedicated initiate rather than the true Brucknerian. For many this conductor is an exceptionally illuminating artist and for them the DG set, extremely well recorded at live performances, will be self-recommending and probably preferable to the Munich version of No. 8 on EMI, where, while he dwells lovingly on the admittedly many beauties, he does not really hold the structure together.

Celibidache's Stuttgart *Seventh* is nearly 7 minutes longer than Harnoncourt's version (they both appear to use the same edition), and it must be said that in the 24-minute slow movement one has to be very patient while waiting for the climax to arrive! Scherzi are lively enough and although on the whole the account of the *Eighth* is the most convincing of the three (with some beautiful pianissimo string playing in the third movement), Celibidache conveys a sense of apotheosis at the end of each work.

For all his dawdling to admire the ravishing scenery on the way, there is still a sense of an ongoing interpretation. The orchestral response is very impressive and one can imagine how in the concert hall the audience came under the conductor's spell. The set includes rehearsal sequences from *symphonies 7* and *8* and the coupled per-

formance of Schubert's *Fifth Symphony* also shows Celibidache in a favourable light.

Symphony No. 8 in C min. (ed Nowak).
(B) *** DG Classikon 463 263-2 [id.]. BPO, Jochum.

Jochum's earlier 1964 DG account of the *Eighth*, like the later EMI Dresden version uses the Nowak Edition, which involves cuts in the slow movement and finale. In addition he here more often presses the music on impulsively in both the outer movements and especially in his account of the *Adagio*, where the climax has great passion and thrust. (Compared with the EMI version his overall timing for the symphony is two minutes shorter.) The DG recording is rather less full-blooded, but cleaner in detail and very well balanced, and this bargain Classikon disc is worth any Brucknerian's money.

Symphonies Nos. 8 in C min.; 9 in D min.
(B) *** EMI Double fforte CZS5 73827-2 (2). Dresden State O, Eugen Jochum.

With the benefit of wide-ranging, full-blooded recording Jochum's Dresden version of the *Eighth*, the most searching and expansive of Bruckner symphonies, is a performance of incandescent warmth. In the great *Adagio,* Jochum may not build up the climaxes with such towering intensity as, for example, Karajan does, but his flexible, spontaneous-sounding style in Bruckner is here consistently persuasive from the mysterious opening of the first movement onwards. As in his earlier vesion for DG, Jochum opts for the Nowak edition, rather than the Haas with its amplification of the finale (preferred by both Karajan and Haitink). The quality is vivid for much of the time but the climaxes are not without a touch of harshness and a hint of congestion. The Dresden account of the *Ninth* is another splendid example of Jochum's art, with the strings made to sound weighty and sonorous by the Dresden acoustic. Jochum characteristically allows himself a wide degree of flexibility over tempi and here is again at his most convincing, giving an impression of spontaneity such as you would expect in the concert hall.

Symphony No.9 in D min. (original version).
*** RCA Dig. 74321 63244-2 [id.]. BPO, Günter Wand.

Günter Wand has recorded the *Ninth Symphony* twice before, once in the late 1980s with the Cologne Orchestra and then in 1994 with the North German Radio Orchestra in Lübeck Cathedral. Using what he describes as the 'original version', he now directs an incandescent performance which gains from being recorded not only live (in September 1998) but with the Berlin Philharmonic. The concentration is unremitting, with tension maintained through the stillest pianissimos, and the opulence of the Berlin players, most strikingly with the strings and brass, gives one a satisfying cushion of sound throughout, with climaxes of shattering weight. The recording-balance is relatively close, so marginally reducing the contrast of pianissimos. Tiny things may go wrong (some ugly wind intonation at 10'45" into the slow movemement) but they are few and unlikely to worry most listeners. Although Wand does not displace the likes of Walter, Karajan and Jochum (see our main volume), he brings the same sense of authority and wisdom to this extraordinary score and he is certainly superbly recorded.

Symphony No.9 in D min. (ed. Nowak).
(BB) *** Naxos Dig. 8.554268 [id.]. RSNO,
   Georg Tintner.
(**) BBC Legends mono BBCL 4034-2 (2) [id.].
   Hallé O, Sir John Barbirolli – MAHLER:
   Symphony No. 7 (**).

Like others in his Bruckner series Georg Tintner's Naxos recording of the *Ninth Symphony* is a match in every way for the finest rival versions, whatever the price. The refinement of pianissimos brings out the full mystery of the massive outer movements, while the delicate fantasy of the Scherzo is brilliantly touched in at high speed, with a touch of wildness. The final *Adagio* builds up in exultation: this may not have been planned as the finale, but here it becomes the most deeply satisfying conclusion. The playing of the Royal Scottish National Orchestra is superb, with recording at once transparent and refined as well as weighty.

Barbirolli's account of the *Ninth* with the Hallé Orchestra comes from a 1966 Promenade concert and has much finer recorded sound than his valuable reading of the Mahler *Seventh*. Sir John does not exactly linger, and his first movement is at times quite rushed. Though there is that individual Barbirolli intensity, this does not show him at his best.

Symphony No. 9 in D min.; Adagio for string orchestra (3rd movt of *String quintet*, arr. Stadlmair).
*** Decca Dig. 458 964-2 [id.]. Leipzig GO,
   Blomstedt.

Blomstedt's *Ninth Symphony* with the Gewandhaus Orchestra strikes us as every bit as fine as his account of the *Sixth*. The orchestral playing is no less tonally sumptuous than the Concertgebouw for Chailly in the same symphony and the recording is magnificent. Blomstedt lays out the terrain with great clarity, the vistas with which we are presented have an awesome grandeur and, as always with this conductor, there is nobility. There is perhaps a certain want of the mystery that you find in Karajan (DG 429 904-2) and Jochum (DG 427 345-2) while Bruno Walter was at his very best in his Sony recording of this work (SMK 64483). But Blomstedt stands high on the current list of recommendations

and his issue offers a useful fill-up in the shape of a transcription by Hans Stadlmair of the slow movement of the *String quintet* for full strings.

Bunch, Kenji (born 1973)

Fantasy for violin and orchestra
(B) ** EMI Début Dig. CDZ5 73501-2 [id.]. Ittai
   Shapira, ECO, Charles Hazlewood – BLOCH:
   *Baal Shem ***; BRUCH: *Violin concerto
   No. 1 in G min., Op. 26 **; SARASATE:
   Zigeunerweisen. **(*)

This piece forms part of a début recital. It was written for this gifted player, who is described by the composer as playing a Joachim-like role in its gestation. It would be unkind to press the parallel with Brahms further, for this is a very thin, amorphous piece – quite sub-Bloch.

Burgon, Geoffrey (born 1941)

(i) *The Calm; Merciless beauty;* (ii) *A vision.*
*** ASV Dig. CDDCA 1059 [id.]. (i) James
   Bowman; (ii) Neil Jenkins.

Geoffrey Burgon seems to have a special feeling for the counter-tenor voice and he also has a natural gift for melody, which is consistently present in the first group of songs here, *Merciless beauty.* Here the alto voice blends so closely with the orchestra that James Bowman seems an integral part of the texture, within semi-voluptuous scoring not unlike Canteloube's Auvergne settings. All these seven songs are about love, but the most striking is the title number (a setting of Chaucer) while the closing *Campionesque for Anna* matches the opening *Western wind* in its languorously exotic line. The tenor cycle *A vision* offers settings of John Clare (1793–1864) and pictures the countryside seen through the eyes of a sensitive farm-worker poet. These songs are generally more restrained and reflectively touching, especially the closing *Where the ash tree weaves.* An interlude, *Voices from the calm* (originally a ballet score), offers instrumental writing, with the counter-tenor voice again laminated in, and is no less evocative in feeling. The closing *Voices from the calm,* a dream couplet by Walt Whitman (which also inspired the ballet), returns to voices – overlapping vocal lines. All the performances are warmly sensitive and beautifully recorded in an ideally warm ambience.

Busoni, Ferruccio (1866–1924)

Piano concerto.
*** Hyperion Dig. CDA 67143 [id.]. Marc-André
   Hamelin, CBSO, Mark Elder.

Lasting an hour and a quarter, with a male chorus

joining in for the finale, Busoni's *Piano concerto* is arguably the most formidable in his repertory – the outpouring of a composer who was also a great virtuoso pianist. In a laboured performance it can seem a bore, a white elephant, but in such an inspired reading as Hamelin's it emerges as a genuine Everest of a work. The challenge it presents has already sparked off an impressive list of recordings, but Hamelin's is the finest yet. Over the last few years his recordings for Hyperion have alerted us to one of the most thrilling of today's pianists, totally unfazed by the most hair-raising technical problems, using his technique not just to make us marvel but also to reveal deeper qualities.

Even before the piano enters, the opening tutti, four-minutes long, establishes the rapt, glowing intensity of the performance, thanks to Mark Elder's dedicated conducting of the Birmingham Orchestra, with radiant recording to match. Hamelin then makes light of the repetitiveness of figuration that can easily become tedious, while the evenness and clarity of the many scale-passages are breathtaking throughout, outshining all rivals. Above all, Hamelin and Elder (who earlier conducted in a live recording with Peter Donohoe) bring out the warmer, more colourful qualities behind the five massive movements, the leaping jollity of the second movement (*Pezzo giocoso*), the dedication of the long *Pezzo serioso*, beautifully sustained, and the Italian sparkle of the fourth movement *Tarantella*.

Music for 2 pianos: *Fantasia contrappuntistica; Duet concertino after the Rondo from Mozart's Piano concerto, K.459; Fantasia on Mozart's Fantasia for mechanical organ, K.608; Improvisation on Bach's Chorale Wie wohl ist mir, o Freund der Seele.*
(M) ** Warner/Fonit 3984 27599-2 [id.]. Michele Campanella, Laura de Fusco.

This disc comes from 1982 and collects all of Busoni's output for two pianos, arranging it in the order that the composer had drafted for a concert programme in 1922, probably intending to give it with his pupil, Egon Petri. The *Improvisation on Wie wohl ist mir, o Freund der Seele* is an impressive piece in every way and is splendidly played here. The two Mozart transcriptions are well played, as indeed is Busoni's strange and masterly *Fantasia contrappuntistica*. The sound in the Bach *Improvisation* is very good but elsewhere the pianists are too closely balanced with unpleasant results in the two Mozart transcriptions, and occasionally in the *Fantasia*.

SOLO PIANO MUSIC

7 Elegies; Indianisches Tagebuch.
(M) ** Warner/Fonit 3984 27597-2 [id.]. Michele Campanella.

Six *Elegies* were composed in 1907, and two years later Busoni added a seventh – the *Berceuse* – a piano version of the *Berceuse élégiaque* composed on the death of his mother. The *Elegies* draw on and rework material from various sources including the *Piano concerto*, and the operas *Turandot* and *Die Brautwahl*. The four pieces which make up the *Indianisches Tagebuch* based on Red Indian motifs are from 1915. Good performances by Michele Campanella recorded in 1980 but dry and shallow sound, which diminishes the value of this release.

4 Elegies; Sonatina seconda; Toccata. Arr. of Bach: Toccata & fugue in D min., BWV 565; Chorales: Ich ruf zu dir, Herr; Wachet auf.
*** MDG Dig. MDG 312 0436-2 [id.]. Claudius Tanski.

The German pianist Claudius Tanski is now in his early forties. A pupil of Brendel, he has made a strong impression for the seriousness and intelligence of his music-making. He proves a most persuasive Busoni interpreter, having the questing mind and sensitivity this repertoire calls for, not to mention the abundant technical prowess. There is a slight change of balance between the *Sonatina seconda* and the *Toccata* but this is of little moment. He plays four of the *Elegies*, Nos. 3–6. Both in Busoni's visionary pieces and the transcriptions of the Bach, he is more than equal to the technical and imaginative challenges this music presents. Artistically this is three-star playing and though the recording is not in the demonstration bracket it is vastly superior to Michele Campanella (see above).

24 Preludes, Op. 37.
** Divine Art Dig. 2-5011 [id.]. Trevor Barnard –
BLISS: *Piano sonata* **.

Trevor Barnard has spent much time in the USA and Australia where this recording was made. It is an intelligently planned disc, since neither the Bliss *Piano sonata* nor the Busoni *Preludes* are otherwise available. However the recording is a bit monochrome and shallow; the playing itself, though serviceable and conscientious, falls short of distinction.

Sonatina; Sonatina seconda; Sonata ad usum infantis; Sonatina in diem navitatis; Sonatina brevis; Sonatina super Carmen (Fantasia).
(M) ** Warner/Fonit 3984 27598-2 [id.]. Michele Campanella.

Michele Campanella's second disc collects all the Busoni sonatinas, from the purely virtuosic *Sonatina super Carmen* to the exploratory *Sonatina seconda* from 1912 (Busoni's most forward-looking and innovative score), which together with the *Nocturne symphonique* was his first study for his masterpiece, *Doktor Faust*. All come from the period 1910–20 and give a diverse picture of his personality, ranging from the questing *Sonatina in diem navitatis* to the *Sonata ad usum infantis*, which quotes from Colombina's minuet from the opera *Arlecchino*. Michele Campanella plays brilliantly enough, though he is not quite as well served by the recording, made in 1981, as is Claudius Tanski (see below). The acoustic is inclined to be a bit dry and the piano tone is at times unpleasingly shallow. This should not deter collectors attracted by the rarity and artistic value of this repertoire.

OPERA

Doktor Faust (complete).
**(*) Erato/Warner Dig. 3984 25501-2 (3) [id.].
Henschel, Begley, Hollop, Jenis, Kerl, Fischer-Dieskau, Lyon Opera Ch. & O, Kent Nagano.

Kent Nagano and his Lyon Opera forces fill an important gap in the catalogue with this first really complete recording of Busoni's masterpiece. It was recorded in conjunction with a stage production, using the score as completed after Busoni's death by his pupil Philipp Jarnach. The set seeks to get the best of both worlds by also offering the extended realization of the closing scenes prepared by Anthony Beaumont with the help of newly dis-covered extra sketches. It is neatly fitted on separate CD tracks that can be programmed as an alternative. With an excellent cast this supersedes the earlier DG recording, which though offering a superb ren-dering of the title role by Dietrich Fischer-Dieskau has a heavily cut text (427 413-2). Nagano pays tribute to that great singer by getting him to recite the opening and closing superscriptions, normally omitted in stage productions.

Dietrich Henschel may not be so searching or weighty an interpreter as Fischer-Dieskau or Sir Thomas Allen, who took the role of Faust in the English National Opera production, but the clarity and incisiveness of his singing are most impressive, leading to a noble account of the death scene, one of the passages expanded in the Beaumont version. He is well contrasted with the powerful Mephisto-pheles of Kim Begley, a tenor role Wagnerian in its demands. The rest of the cast is first rate, with voices well forward, but the impact of the performance is slightly blunted by the backward balance of the orchestra, distanced in a more spacious acoustic.

Butterworth, Arthur (born 1923)

Symphony No. 1, Op. 15.
*** Classico CLASSCD 274 [id.]. Munich SO, Douglas Bostock – GIPPS: *Symphony No. 2.*
***

How is it possible for a symphony of this quality to be so neglected by the British musical establish-ment? It is powerful, imaginative and atmospheric. Arthur Butterworth comes from Manchester and

played in the Hallé and Scottish National Orches-tras. His *First Symphony* is a large-scale 40-minute work which Sir John Barbirolli premièred in 1957. Sibelian in outlook (but none the worse for that) and with an innate feeling for the landscape of northern England and Scotland, it is powerfully argued and arresting – the product of a resourceful musical mind. It is possible to imagine a more finished performance than that by the Munich Orchestra under Douglas Bostock but readers are urged to investigate this issue. (This disc was in-cluded in our main volume, but we include it again in the hope that more collectors will seek it out.)

Buxtehude, Diderik (c. 1637–1707)

CHAMBER MUSIC

6 String sonatas (without Opus numbers): *in C min. D, BuxWV 266–7; in F, BuxWV 269; in G; in A min.; in B flat, BuxWV 271–3.*
*** Marco Polo DaCapo Dig. 8.224005 [id.]. John Holloway, Ursula Weiss, Jaap ter Linden, Mogens Rasmussen, Lars Ulrik Mortensen.
***Marco Polo DaCapo Dig. 8224121 (as above in a box with complete DaCapo Catalogue).

Diderik Buxtehude's name has survived through three centuries as that of the most important pre-Bach composer/performer of organ music, whom Johann Sebastian walked some 200 miles to hear and became so impressed by that he stayed far longer than he had planned. But Buxtehude also left us much chamber and instrumental music of high quality, which is only just being properly explored on CD.

These unpublished works come from an (un-dated) collection held in Uppsala, Sweden. They are scored for a more varied ensemble than the Op. 1 and Op. 2 sonatas and their other principal difference is that they contain considerably more solos than in the published collections. They are certainly not less inventive. The *D major Sonata*, BuxWV 267, scored for tenor and bass violas da gama (both given solos) plus violin, is darker in texture than usual, and the interchange at the opening of the lighter-timbred *F major*, BuxWV 269, which is for 2 violins and viola da gamba (all also given solos), is made doubly attractive by its organ continuo. Both the *G major*, BuxWV 271 (which opens the disc) and the *B flat major*, BuxWV 273 (which is a considerably expanded version of Op. 1/4) are particularly attractive, the latter in-cluding an *Allemande, Courant, Sarabande* and *Gigue* in quick succession, the former, with a series of violin solos, and a sprightly closing fugato, showing the composer at his most varied and light-hearted. BuxWV 266 (which closes the disc) is the most concentrated and complex of all. A dignified opening makes way for a dialogue for two violins, and the same thematic material is reused and varied throughout the work. There is a central, freely ruminative ('fantastic') violin solo, and the sonata culminates with a brief, sustained slow finale. The writer of the excellent accompanying notes, Nils Jensen, suggests that this (appropriately) C major work deserves the epithet of Buxtehude's 'Jupiter Sonata'. Performances throughout are excellent in every way and the recording well up to standard. As can be seen above, this CD comes both in a normal jewel-case, and also (subject to availability) in a box with a complete DaCapo Catalogue.

7 Trio sonatas, Op. 1, BuxWV 252–8.
*** Marco Polo DaCapo Dig. 8.224003 [id.]. John Holloway, Lars Ulrik Mortensen, Jaap ter Linden.

Buxtehude was nearly sixty when he published his *Sonatas*, Op. 1 and Op. 2. Each contains seven works and together they ambitiously explore all the major and minor keys, beginning with F major and omitting only F minor and B flat minor. For Buxtehude the number seven symbolized both the number of days in the week, and also the number of named planets in the heavens then known to astronomers. Their effigy confronted the composer every day on the facia of the great clock in St Mary's, Lübeck. What is immediately striking about both Op. 1 and Op. 2 is not just the variety of invention, but the way Buxtehude heightens the contrasting vitality of his allegros by introducing them with *Lentos* or *Adagios* of considerable expressive intensity. The works of Op. 1 seem to become steadily more assured. No. 3, in A minor, not only opens with an eloquent independent *Adagio*, but its finale is framed by equally touching slow sections. By contrast No. 4, in B flat major, is primarily lively and outgoing. It is in two movements, of which the first is a dancing set of variations of considerable complexity, based on a brief but catchy ostinato (a favourite device throughout the series). Then follows an *Adagio* and finally a jolly fugal treatment of the same idea. No. 5 is notable for the central solo violin arioso and No. 6 is the most innovative of all. In the so-called 'fantastic' style it continually alternates slow and fast sections, with unpredictable interludes marked *Con discretione*. It also includes an exhilarating recurring *Vivace* in saraband rhythm. No. 7 is more conventionally structured, but still brings stimulating changes of mood and tempo.

7 Trio sonatas, Op. 2, BuxWV 259–65.
*** Marco Polo DaCapo Dig. 8.224004 [id.]. John Holloway, Lars Ulrik Mortensen, Jaap ter Linden.

The sonatas of Opus 2 are on the whole less quirky, and seemingly more mature, than those of Op. 1. The very first, the *Sonata in B flat*, in five movements, brings an eloquent central *Grave* (a dialogue

between violin and cello) plus much to divert the listener throughout. The first movement of the *D major* (No. 2) characteristically frames its first movement *Allegro* between an *Adagio* and a *Largo*; then the central *Arietta* is fast, with nine busy variations. No. 3, in G minor, is the longest work of the set and characteristically diverse. No. 4, in C minor, begins with a touching *Poco adagio* and ends with a vigorous *Vivace*. No. 5, in A major, is another work in the 'fantastic' style, the freest, most fascinating of the seven. It opens with a bouncing, but brief *Allegro*; then comes a violin solo, marked *Concitato*, followed by a similarly improvisatory viola da gamba contribution. Nos. 6 and 7, both with noble opening slow sections, and very well balanced in their expressive and vigorous content, make a satisfying conclusion to a fine series. With John Holloway a very stylish leader, the performances here are expert, fresh and alive, using period instruments brightly without edginess or unattractive linear squeezing. The group is very well balanced and the recording immediate and real.

KEYBOARD MUSIC

Complete harpsichord music

Volume 1: *Aria in A min., BuxWV 249; Canzona in C, BuxWV 166; Canzonetta in A min., BuxWV 225; Chorale variations: Wie schöne leuchtet der Morgernstern, BuxWV 223; Fugue in B flat, BuxWV 176; Partita: Auf meinen lieben Gott, BuxWV 179; Suites: in C, BuxWV 226; in D, BuxWV 233; Toccata in G, BuxWV 165.*
*** DaCapo Dig. 8.224116 [id.]. Lars Ulrik Mortensen (harpsichord).

Volume 2: *Aria: More Palatino in C, BuxWV 247; 2 Canzonettas in G, BuxWV 171–2; Chorale: Nun lob, meine Seele, den Herren, BuxWV 215; Courante zimble in A min., BuxWV 245; Fugue in C, BuxWV 174; Suites: in E min., BuxWV 235; in G min., BuxWV 242.*
*** DaCapo Dig. 8.224117 [id.]. Lars Ulrik Mortensen (harpsichord).

Volume 3: *Aria: La Capricciosa in G, BuxWV 250; Canzonetta in D min., BuxWV 168; Prelude in G, BuxWV 162; Suites: in F, BuxWV 238; in A, BuxWV 243.*
*** DaCapo Dig. 8.224118 [id.]. Lars Ulrik Mortensen (harpsichord).

Buxtehude's keyboard and organ music is not clearly defined: much of it could be played on organ, harpsichord or clavichord, although the works requiring the pedal were obviously primarily intended for the organ. The modestly conceived, but very agreeable *Suites* (each a group of four dance movements – *Allemande, Courante, Sarabande* and *Gigue*) were obviously intended for the domestic keyboard. In his excellent survey Lars Ulrik

Mortensen has carefully chosen the works most suitable for the harpsichord, including chorales and other sets of variations (notably the *Arias*), which were Buxtehude's strongest suit, and in which he displays consistent ingenuity and musical skill, always holding the listener's interest. The selected Fugues are all jauntily appealing.

Mortensen uses a copy of a Ruckers harpsichord made by Thomas Mandrop-Poulsen, an excellent instrument on which he produces a remarkable range of colour (it includes also a muted effect). His performances are of the highest order, spontaneous and flexible and exciting in their sheer dexterity. Volume 1 opens with a brilliant *Toccata*, while the *Canzona* is another bravura piece and the delightful closing *Canzonetta* is treated as a feather-light scherzo. There are a characteristic pair of *Suites*, and the finale of the *C major*, BuxWV 226 is a sprightly, infectious *Gigue*. Of the variations, the *Aria in A minor* (a sarabande) is a modest example, with a somewhat melancholy theme, but this is genially elaborated with a swirl of virtuosity in the closing third variation. The *Partita* is essentially another suite, using a chorale as its basis.

The *Aria* that opens Volume 2 is much more expansive in its treatment than BuxWV 249, and the *Courant zimble* is another entertaining example of Buxtehude's elaboration of a simple dance theme. The *G major Canzonetta* is a lightweight, imitative moto perpetuo, played with great flair, the *Canzona in C* more thoughtful.

Volume 3 brings what is undoubtedly Buxtehude's keyboard masterpiece, *La Capricciosa*, a virtuoso showpiece nearly 30 minutes in length, consisting of 32 variations on an *Aria in G minor*, a bergamasca, which later is transformed variously into a gigue, sarabande and minuet. The composer's kaleidoscopic invention knows no bounds, and this work clearly anticipates Bach's *Goldberg variations*. It is less profound, but continually diverting and requires both imagination and brilliance from its performer. Superbly played here, it makes this third collection the obvious point for the collector to enter Buxtehude's very rewarding keyboard world.

ORGAN MUSIC

Canzona in D min., BuxWV 168; Choral fantasia on Gelobet seist du, Jesu Christ, BuxWV 188; Ciacona in E min., BuxWV 160; Fugue in C, BuxWV 174; Magnificat primi toni, BuxWV 203; Passacaglia in D min., BuxWV 161; Prelude in D min., BuxWV 140; Prelude in F sharp min. (transposed into G min.), *BuxWV 146; Toccatas: in D min., BuxWV 155; in F, BuxWV 157.*
(BB) *** Arte Nova Dig. 74321 63633-2 [id.].
Rainer Oster (Arp-Schnitger organ, St Jacobi, Hamburg).

Although the mid-priced two-disc collection from Marie-Claire Alain still remains the most compre-

hensive and desirable introduction to Buxtehude's organ music for the general collector (Erato 0630 12979-2), this super-bargain sampler by Rainer Oster is very attractive in its own right. Oster presents all this music spontaneously in vivid colours. The resplendent openings of the *Toccata in F* and the transposed *Prelude in G minor*, and the variety of registration in the ambitious *Choral fantasia*, are surely matched by the *Fugue in C*, delightfully registered on the flute stop and treated lightly and rhythmically. Oster closes with the compelling *Toccata in D minor* which shows so well the influence Buxtehude exerted over the young Bach, who walked so far to hear him play. The recording is first class.

Byrd, William (1543–1623)

The Byrd Complete Edition, Volume 3: Early Latin church music: Benigne fac Domine; Christus qui lux est; Circumspice Jerusalem; Domine ante te omne desiderium; Domine Deus omnipotens; Petrus beatus; Reges Tharsis et insulae; Sacris solemnis; Super flumina Babylonia; Te lucis; 4 Propers for Epiphany.
*** ASV Gaudeamus Dig. CDGAU 179 [id.].
Cardinall's Musick, Andrew Carwood (with Philippe DE MONTE: *Quomodo cantabimus ***).

In Volume 3 of their ongoing survey, Andrew Carwood and his specialist choir, Cardinall's Musick, here turn to rare music, mostly pieces which Byrd left unpublished. Many of these motets have had to be reconstructed, their inner parts restored with scholarly care. The *4 Propers for Epiphany* come from an incomplete set of Gradualia, published in 1607, yet this music shows Byrd at his most imaginative. Most moving of all is the culminating item, an eight-part setting of four verses from Psalm 136, reflecting the trials of a recusant Catholic in Elizabeth I's England, with the poignant message (in Latin), 'How shall we sing the Lord's song in a strange land?' Also included is a fine setting of Psalm 136 by the Flemish Philippe de Monte which prompted Byrd to write his response. Performances throughout are beautifully shaped, yet with great underlying intensity.

The Byrd Complete Edition, Volume 4: Cantiones sacrae, Book I (1575): complete.
*** ASV Gaudeamus Dig. CDGAU 197 [id.].
Cardinall's Musick, Andrew Carwood.

Byrd published the first of his three Books of *Cantiones sacrae* in conjunction with his teacher and mentor, Thomas Tallis, contributing seventeen motets to this initial collection. *Tribue Domine . . ., Te deprecor . . ., Gloria Patri* (here sung together as the penultimate number before *Libera me, Domine*) were given separate numbers to reach this total.

Although these ASV performances encounter considerable competition in the present catalogue, this is, at present, the only recommendable CD (74 minutes) offering the entire contents of Book I, and the performances are beautifully blended, while Andrew Carwood's tempi move the music on at what seems a natural pacing. David Skinner's edition seems to meet the various problems inherent in the setting, notably that of pitch, to suit the present group of voices. The recording is well up to the fine standard of this series.

Complete keyboard music.
(M)*** Hyperion Dig. CDA 665551/7 [id.]. Davitt
   Moroney (harpsichords, muselar virginal,
   organ, chamber organ, clavichord).

Davitt Moroney has previously recorded a two-disc set of Byrd's Pavans and Galliards for Harmonia Mundi (HMC 90 1241/2) including the sequence of nine Pavans and Galliards which Byrd composed in the 1570s and '80s which come from *My Ladye Nevell's Booke* (1591) and which are included here on Disc 6, plus the other items which are associated with this particular source. But of course this is only scratching the surface of an impressively comprehensive undertaking which includes also the organ music played on the highly suitable Ahrend organ of L'Eglise-Musée des Augustins, Toulouse, which Moroney often registers with ear-tickling skill as in the *Gloria tibi trinitas* or in the first version of the *Fancie for my Ladye Nevell*. To add maximum variety, he also uses a variety of keyboard instruments based on north European seventeenth-century models, including a clavichord by the estimable Thomas Goff, a chamber organ by Martin Goetz and Domenic Gwynn, and harpsichords by Hubert Bédard and Reinhard von Nagel.

The most fascinating of these instruments is the so-called muselar virginal (by John Philips of Berkeley after a 1650 Couchet), which has a remarkably rich timbre and also a beautiful painting on the lid (a colour photograph is printed on the back of the booklet of notes). Moroney tells us that for all its fullness of sound, the instrument fell out of favour because of its very characteristic drawback. The placing of the keyboard to the far right means that the strings are plucked right in the middle of their sounding length (instead of at one extremity as is usual). This requires particularly long keys and places the action for the left hand in the middle of a highly resonant keyboard. The inevitable result is 'amplified' clicks, especially in rapid left-hand scales. However, this instrument is heard at its finest and most spectacular (on Disc 7) in Byrd's description of *The Battel*, with its introductory *Marche* and a *Galliard for the Victorie*.

Quite as aurally fascinating are the five items with which Moroney closes his programme. Four different versions of *Praeludium to the Fancie* from Book 12 are given, each heard on a different instrument, and he concludes with the *Fantasia* from Book 13, one of the composer's most complex and original pieces, presented with considerable flair.

Throughout, the playing is committed, authoritative and nicely embellished, though at times a shade didactic. The recording is most realistic, though it is important not to set the volume level too high. The accompanying notes are as thorough as they are scholarly and comprehensive. Moroney has something to say, both intellectually and musically, about every one of these 138 pieces. The set is offered at a special price: seven discs for the cost of five.

Cage, John (born 1912)

Concerto for prepared piano and chamber orchestra (1950/51); *The Seasons* (ballet); *Seventy-four* (for orchestra), *Versions I & II; Suites for toy piano* (original and orchestral version, scored by Lou Harrison).
*** ECM Dig. ECM 1696; 465 140-2. (i)
   Margaret Leng Tang (prepared piano; toy
   piano); American Composers' Orchestra,
   Dennis Russell Davies.

The editor once attended what was certainly a superbly 'prepared' performance of John Cage's avant garde *Concerto* in the Library of Congress, and was as much perplexed by it as he is now. *Seventy-four*, hypnotic in atmosphere, is nevertheless remarkably static. *The Seasons* is in the composer's own words 'an attempt to express the traditional Indian view as quiescence (winter), creation (spring), preservation (summer), and destruction (fall)'. It is not easy to follow, but certainly has plenty of movement, and its textures are exotic. (Both Virgil Thomson and Lou Harrison helped with the orchestration.) The simplistic *Suite for toy piano* has also been ingeniously scored by Lou Harrison and most listeners will respond to the vividly contrasting sonorities of this instrumental version, which has instant appeal. The performances here are dedicated and of the highest calibre, and the recording excellent. In his *Gramophone* review of this collection, Peter Dickinson declared 'This is an enchanting CD, every item a sheer delight' – not a view which we wholly share, but the only way to discover your own reaction is to sample the disc for yourself.

Caldara, Antonio (1670–1736)

Sonata da camera in E min., Op. 1/5; Trio sonata in D, Op. 2/3; (i) Cantatas: *D'improvviso amore felice; Medea in Corinto; Soffri mio caro Alcino; Vicino a un rivoletto.*
(BB) **(*) Virgin Veritas/EMI 2 x 1 VBD5
   61588-2 (2). (i) Gérard Lesne, Il Seminario
   Musicale – STRADELLA: *Motets.* **(*)

Gérard Lesne is in his element in these fine cantatas. The most immediately striking is *Medea in Corinto*, based on the legend of the betrayal of Medea by Jason of Golden Fleece fame; it is both highly dramatic and expressively moving by turns. But the finest and most extended is the memorable *Vicino a un rivoletto*, where the voice shares a long, echoing interchange with a solo violin (splendidly played here) followed by a gravely noble arioso with cello obbligato. The two *Sonatas* are used as interludes, but they are fine works in their own right – the melancholy *Adagio* of the four-movement *Trio sonata*, Op. 1/5 is particularly affecting. These performances could hardly be more authentic or more communicative and they are naturally balanced and recorded. The Stradella couplings are equally distinguished, and this Virgin 2 x 1 Double is remarkably inexpensive. The one great snag is the absence of either translations or adequate notes about the music.

Missa Sanctorum Cosmae et Damiani; Gradual: *Benedicta et venerabilis es;* Motet: *Caro meo vere es cibus.*
*** Virgin Veritas/EMI VC5 45387-2. Monica Frimmer, Ralf Popken, Wilfried Jochens, Klaus Mertens, Westfalia Kantorei, Capella Agostino Steffani, Lajos, Rovatkay (with Franz TUMA: *Sonata a 4 in E min.; Sonata a 5 in E min.* ***).

Caldara's *Missa Sanctorum Cosmae et Damiani* is one of the finest of his thirty or so festive masses, a joyfully extrovert work, both lyrical and high spirited and fully scored with trumpets gleaming. The subdivisions of the *Gloria*, the heart of the work, with soloists and chorus alternating, are enhanced by instrumental obbligati: the alto's *Dominus Deus* features a trombone, the soprano's contribution to *Domine fili* is ornamented by a bravura trumpet. The four closing sections are all short but telling, the *Benedictus* is a touching soprano solo (beautifully sung), and the polyphonic closing *Dona nobis pacem* uses the full forces with satisfying finality. Two short, but attractive *String sonatas* by Caldara's Bohemian contemporary,Tuma are used as interludes between the Mass, the very touching motet, *Caro meo* (a soprano–alto duet), and the closing, more ambitious Marian gradual, *Benedicta et venerabilis es*. With more contrasts between soloists and chorus this is another freshly appealing work, which ends rather suddenly. Very well sung and excellently recorded, this collection will give much pleasure.

Campion, Thomas (1567–1620)

Lute songs: *Author of light; Beauty, since you so much desire; Come let us sound with melody; Come you pretty fals-ey'd wanton; Faire, if you expect admiring; Fire, fire, fire, fire!; Her rosie cheeks; I care not for these ladies; It fell on a sommers daie; Jacke and Jone they think no ill; Most sweet and pleasing are thy ways; Never weather-beaten saile; Shall I come, sweet love to thee?; Sweet exclude mee not; The Sypres curtain of the night; There is a garden in her face; There is none, O none but you; Though you are yong and I am olde; Thou joy'st, fond boy; To musicke bent; Tune thy musicke to thy hart; Turn all thy thoughts to eyes; What is it that all men possess?; When to her lut Corrina sings; Vaile, love mine eyes* (with ROSSETER: *My sweetest Lesbia; When then is love but mourning?;* ANON: *Miserere my maker*).
(BB) **(*) Naxos Dig. 8.553380 [id.]. Steven Rickards, Dorothy Linell.

It is good to have an inexpensive and representative selection of the lute songs of Thomas Campion, the only music of his to survive. Lawyer and doctor, poet as well as composer, he contributed to the entertainment at the court of King James I. His song output was second only to Dowland's and he shared that composer's ability to touch the listener with melancholy. *Author of light, The Sypres curtain of the night* and *Though you are yoong and I am olde* are outstanding examples, but there are many others here. *Never weather-beaten saile* is certainly memorable. Of course, there are lighter settings too. *I care not for these ladies* could hardly have naughtier implications in its repeated pay-off line: 'She never will say no'. Steven Rickards, a young American counter-tenor who studied at Aldeburgh with Pears and Robert Spencer, has a pleasing voice and delivery. At times one listens in vain for more variety of colour, but his presentation is appealingly simple, as are the lute accompaniments of Dorothy Linell who attempts no elaborations or embellishments. They are well recorded in a pleasing acoustic and, with full texts included, this is yet another enterprising Naxos disc well worth its modest cost.

Campra, André (1660–1744)

Idoménée (tragédie-lyrique): complete.
(B) *** HM Dig. HMX 2901396.98 (3) [id.]. Bernard Deletré, Sandrine Piau, Monique Zanetti, Jean-Paul Fouchécourt, Marie Boyer, Les Arts Florissants, William Christie.

In this first complete recording of any opera by Campra, Christie opts for the later revision of the piece which the composer made for the revival in 1731, eliminating two incidental characters and reworking several scenes. In the manner of the time, it relies on free cantilena rather than formal numbers, with set-pieces kept short and with the chorus often contributing to such brief arias as there are. Christie with his talented Les Arts Florissants team presents the whole work with a taut feeling for its dramatic qualities, though there is nothing here to compare with the big moments in Mozart's opera. The matching of voices to character is closer here than we would conventionally expect in Mozart, and in the breadth of its span and its frequent hints as to what Purcell might have achieved had he tackled a full-length opera, this is a fascinating work, vividly recorded. It is all the more attractive reissued in Harmonia Mundi's bargain opera series. An excellent booklet with full translation is included.

Canteloube, Marie-Joseph
(1879–1957)

Chants d'Auvergne: Baïlèro; 3 Bourrées; Brezairola; Lou Boussu; Lou coucut; Chut, chut; La Délaïssádo; Lo Fïolairé; Jou l'pount d'o Mirabel; Malurous qu'o uno fenno; Oï ayaï; Pastourelle; La pastrouletta; Postouro, sé tu m'aymo; Tè, l'co, tè; Uno jionto postouro.
(BB) *** Virgin Classics 2 x 1 Dig. VBD5 61742-2 [CDVB 61742]. Arleen Augér, ECO, Yan Pascal Tortelier – RAVEL: *Alborada; Shéhérazade,* etc. **(*)

Arleen Augér's lovely soprano is ravishing in the haunting, lyrical songs like the ever-popular *Baïlèro.* In the playful items she conveys plenty of fun, and in the more boisterous numbers the recording has vivid presence. Augér returns to sing Ravel's exotic song cycle *Shéhérazade* as part of a new coupling, which includes four of that composer's key orchestral works.

Caplet, André (1878–1925)

Epiphany (fresco for cello and orchestra after an Ethiopian Legend).
(B) *** EMI Début CZS5 73727-2 [id.]. Xavier Phillips, Bavarian Chamber PO, Emmanuel Plasson – FAURE: *Elégie;* LALO: *Cello concerto.* ***

The underrated André Caplet is a true original whose music ought to be much better known. 'Fresco' is a perfect description of this impressionistically etched evocation, which depicts the arrival in Bethlehem of Caspar, the black member of the three kings, the bringer of gold to 'honour the King of the World'. Caplet creates a fascinating opening texture of woodwind colour, which the cello first embroiders, then rhapsodically dominates. There is a long central cadenza placed against a steady drumbeat, then the work ends with an exotic dance when the King's young black retainers join in the celebration. Caplet's sound imagery is oriental and yet French (just as Ravel's can be), but the work demands, and receives here, enormous bravura from the cello soloist. The clear recording and the skill of the conductor ensure that, without loss of allure, every detail is in focus.

Cartellieri, Casimir (1772–1807)

Clarinet concertos Nos. 1 in B flat; 3 in E; Adagio pastorale (Concerto No. 2).
*** MDG Dig. MDG 301 0527-2 [id.]. Dieter Klöcker, Prague CO.

Highly attractive concertos by this gifted but little-known contemporary of Beethoven. He is listed neither in the Eric Blom/David Cummings *Everyman's Dictionary* nor in *Grove.* He was of Italian stock but brought up in Danzig, though he left home at thirteen to fend for himself when his parents' marriage broke down. He studied in Vienna with Salieri and Albrechtsberger, and was sufficiently well thought of to share the Vienna concert at which Beethoven played his *First Piano concerto.* Cartellieri was represented by the first part of his *Gioas, Re di Giuda (Jehoash, King of Judah)* and a symphony. He became Director of Music at the court of Prince Lobkowitz in 1796, in whose service he died at the age of thirty-four. The *Clarinet concertos* Nos. 1 and 3 recorded here together with the *Adagio pastorale* from No. 2 are really quite a find. They are inventive, fluent and full of imaginative touches. They are not profound but they are even more delightful and unpredictable than those of such contemporaries as Weber and Spohr. First-class performances and excellent recorded sound enhance the claims of this disc, which will well reward the curiosity of readers.

Double concerto for 2 clarinets in B flat; (i) Flute concerto in G; Movement for clarinet and orchestra in B flat.
*** MDG Dig. MDG 301 0960-2 [id.]. Dieter Klöcker, Sandra Arnold; (i) Kornelia Brandkamp; Prague CO.

The *Concerto for 2 clarinets* reaffirms the strong impression made by its companions above. It bubbles over with high spirits and has a strikingly original opening. Dieter Klöcker speaks of Cartellieri in his note as 'a committed individualist', and the reminders of his contemporaries are as much of composers to come as masters such as Haydn and Beethoven. Klöcker and his pupil, Sandra Arnold, give a masterly account of the piece, and Kornelia Brandkamp is hardly less expert in the diverting and delightful *Flute concerto.* As always with the Dabringhaus und Grimm label, the recordings are beautifully balanced and very natural. Not great music, perhaps, but very rewarding all the same.

Catoire, Georgy (1861–1926)

Piano music: *Caprice, Op. 3; Chants de crépuscule (4 Morceaux), Op. 24; Intermezzo, Op. 6/5; 3 Morceaux, Op. 2; 5 Morceaux, Op. 10; 4 Morceaux, Op. 12; Poème, Op. 34/2; Prélude, Op. 6/2; 4 Préludes, Op. 17; Prélude, Op. 34/3; Scherzo, Op. 6/3; Valse, Op. 36; Vision (Etude), Op. 8.*
*** Hyperion Dig CDA 67090 [id.]. Marc-André Hamelin.

Georgy Catoire was born in Moscow to parents of French extraction. His music has been all but forgotten, which makes this dazzling collection of his piano music especially welcome, prompting Hamelin to astonishing feats of virtuosity combined with poetry. Catoire was a pupil of the Austrian Karl Klindworth – who made the first piano arrangement of Wagner's *Ring* cycle. Though Catoire was mainly occupied as a teacher, he wrote a handful of major works, including a piano concerto – something, no doubt, for Hamelin to record in the Hyperion 'Romantic Concerto' series. He also left a big collection of piano miniatures, many not published at his death, of which this collection of twenty-eight is an attractive sample. They are played in order of opus number, giving an idea of Catoire's development from echoing Chopin, Liszt and Tchaikovsky to adventuring more towards the world of Wagner and of the French impressionists. If there is a Russian he echoes, it is Scriabin, and it is the fluency of his writing for the keyboard rather than memorability of material which strikes home, with Hamelin an ideal interpreter. He later studied in Berlin and on his final return to Russia in 1887 he was a pupil of Rimsky-Korsakov, which led to the first set of *Morceaux*, and Liadovv which produced the dazzling *Caprice*. Yet for all these influences, in many ways he is his own man, and his music, particularly the *Morceaux*, is often very seductive. One might sample the *Soirée de hiver* of Op. 2, the lovely *Rêverie* of Op. 10 and the disconsolate *Chant du soir*, or the *Nocturne*, of Op. 12 to discover how haunting is his melodic gift when he is writing simply. Marc-André Hamelin also shows how he can tickle the ear with a scherzando lightness as in the two engaging pieces from Op. 6. This is not a recital to play continuously, but drawn on it will give much refreshment and pleasure. Hamelin is given an outstandingly natural recording, bright, yet with full sonority and colouring.

Cerha, Friedrich (born 1926)

String quartets Nos. 1–3; (i) 8 movements after Hölderlin fragments for string sextet.
*** CPO Dig. CPO 999 646-2 [id.]. Arditti Qt; with (i)Thomas Kakuska, Valentin Erben.

Friedrich Cerha is best known as a champion of the second Viennese school and as the scholar-composer who completed the third Act of Alban Berg's *Lulu*. Born in Vienna, his studies were interrupted by his induction into the military but while on duty in Denmark he made contact with the resistance there. After working as a mountain guide in the Tyrol, he returned after the war to academic life, and was much involved with new music movements. The three quartets recorded here come from the period 1989–92: the *First Quartet* is subtitled *Maqam*, inspired by the Arab music with which he came in contact during a longish stay in Morocco. It makes liberal use of microtones, as does, though to a lesser extent, the minimalist *Second* inspired by his contact with the Papuan peoples at Sepik in New Guinea. The *Hölderlin fragments* (1995) are settings for string sextet without voice, though the poems which inspired them are reproduced in the excellent and detailed booklet. The Arditti Quartet play with great expertise and attention to detail, and are vividly recorded. Recommended for those with a special interest in contemporary Austrian music; but others may question whether Cerha possesses a distinctive enough musical personality to prompt one to return to this repertoire.

Chabrier, Emmanuel (1841–94)

España (rhapsody); Habanera; Joyeuse marche; Lamento; Prélude pastorale; Suite pastorale; Le Rroi malgré lui: Danse slave; Fête polonaise.
(BB) **(*) Naxos 8.554248 [id.]. Monte-Carlo PO, Hervé Niquet.

A very well-recorded programme, played with considerable idiomatic flair if without always the very last degree of finesse (*Sous-bois*, for instance, could be more delicate in the bass). But the rumbustious pieces have plenty of sparkle and *España* does not lack gusto. Enjoyable and good value for money.

Chadwick, George (1854–1931)

Symphonic sketches.
(M) **(*) Mercury [434 337-2].
  Eastman-Rochester O, Howard Hanson –
  MACDOWELL: *Suite* **(*); PETER: *Sinfonia.* **

George Whitfield Chadwick belongs to the same generation as Elgar and Janáček. He studied at (and subsequently became Director of) the New England Conservatory. The first two movements, *Jubilee* and *Noel,* come from 1895 and, written in the wake of Dvořák's American visit, rather endearingly recall that composer's music. The third and fourth movements were written later: indeed the charming third movement, *Hobgoblin,* did not see the light of day until 1904. The suite is very well played and brilliantly and glowingly recorded. Not great music perhaps, but amiably melodic and colourfully orchestrated.

Charpentier, Marc-Antoine
(1643–1704)

Ballet music: *La Descente d'Orphée aux Enfers; Médée; Les Plaisirs de Versailles.*
*** Erato/Warner Dig. 3984 26129-2 [id.]. Les Arts Florissants, William Christie – RAMEAU: *Les fêtes d'Hébe; Hippolyte et Aricie* ***.

This recording celebrated the twenty-fifth anniversary of William Christie and Les Arts Florissants by combining colourful, lightweight ballet sequences from major dramatic works by Charpentier with more extended ballets of Rameau. These shorter selections are characteristically colourful and played with great vivacity and colour.

(i) *Amor vince ogni cosa* (pastoraletta); (ii) *Les plaisirs de Versailles;* (iii) *3 Airs on stanzas from Le Cid.*
*** Erato/Warner Dig. 0630 14774-2 [id.]. (i) Patricia Petibon, Olivier Lallouette; (i; ii) Sophie Daneman, François Piolino, (ii) Katalin Károlyi, Steve Duardin, Jean-François Gardeil; (i; iii) Paul Agnew, Les Arts Florissants, William Christie.

This is one of the most attractive and entertaining Charpentier collections available and it would make a splendid entrée to this composer's world for any collector. *Les plaisirs de Versailles* is a 'mini-opera' in which the characters are Music, Conversation, Le Jeu, Comus and Un Plaisir. They engage in a vociferous dialogue which is in turns lyrical, dramatic, and bizarrely humorous, arguing at length about which is the most essential of the King's pleasures, with Comus mediating and suggesting fine wines, pastries, and sweetmeats. Finally the protagonists are reconciled and the piece ends with a happy chorus.

Amore vince ogni cosa is a charming pastoral conversation piece (with shepherds' chorus) about unrequited love. The three ardent airs from Corneille's *Le Cid* make a passionate central interlude. Throughout the solo singing is delightful and full of lively and charming characterization, while the Charpentier's orchestration is equally diverting. With William Christie and his Arts Florissants providing elegant, sparkling accompaniments, this splendidly recorded collection is treasure trove indeed.

Caecilia, virgo et martyr; Filius prodigus (oratorios); *Magnificat.*
(B) *** HM Musique d'abord Dig. HMA 190066 [id.]. Grenat, Benet, Laplenie, Reinhard, Studer, Les Arts Florissants, Christie.

The music's stature and nobility are fully conveyed here. The *Magnificat* is a short piece for three voices and has an almost Purcellian flavour. One thing that will immediately strike the listener is the delicacy and finesse of the scoring. All this music is beautifully recorded; the present issues can be recommended with enthusiasm, especially at Musique d'abord price.

9 Noëls; Christmas motets: *Canticum in nativitatem Domini, H.393; In nativitatem Domini canticum, H.314 In nativitatem Domini canticum: Chanson, H.416; In nativitatem Domini Nostri Jesus Christi, H.414.*
(BB) *** Naxos Dig. 8.554514 [id.]. Acadia Ensemble, Kevin Mallon.

Marc-Antoine Charpentier, blocked in his lifetime by his arch-rival, Lully, now emerges as much the more inspired composer. In this Christmas disc with a difference, the talented Canadian group, the Acadia Ensemble, warmly recorded, present the nine charming sets of simple variations Charpentier wrote on French Christmas carols, or Noëls. Standing out from the rest is the minor-key *Or nous dites Marie*, with chromatic writing like Purcell's. Those instrumental pieces are set alongside a sequence of lively vocal motets on a Christmas theme, culminating in a miniature Nativity oratorio.

OPERA

Médée (tragédie-lyrique): complete.
(M) *** HM HMX 2901139.41 (3) [id.]. Jill Feldman, Gilles Ragon, Agnès Mellon, Sophie Boulin, Jacques Bona, Philippe Cantor, Les Arts Florissants, William Christie.

Christie's highly communicative first recording of *Médée* in 1985 won both the International Record Critics' Award and the Early Music prize in *Gramophone*, so its credentials are impeccable. This was Charpentier's only *tragédie-lyrique*, and it richly extends our knowledge of the composer, Christie's account has excellent soloists and the performance has a vitality and sense of involvement which bring out the keen originality of Charpentier's writing, his implied emotional glosses on a formal subject. Les Arts Florissants in the stylishness of its playing on period instruments matches any group in the world and the recording is excellent. This reissue is admirably documented and includes a full libretto with translation and makes an excellent bargain.

However, Christie has since re-recorded the work for Erato with an even finer cast, Lorraine Hunt outstanding in the title role and Mark Padmore coping superbly with the role of Jason. The new interpretation easily surpasses the earlier one in extra brightness and vigour with the drama even more clearly established (⬤ 4509 96558-2 – see our main volume).

Chausson, Ernest (1855–99)

Mélodies: *Le colibri; Hébé; Nocturne;* (i) *La nuit. Printemps triste;* (i) *Réveil. Le temps des lilas.*
*(*) DG Dig. 459 682-2 [id.]. Christine Schäfer, Irwin Gage; (i) with Stella Doufexis – DEBUSSY: *Mélodies* *(*).

Chausson's song output is better represented now than it was some years ago; even so Christine Schäfer's recital would be more welcome were she more completely at ease in the style, and her French more idiomatic. Hers is a lovely voice, but even so this collection disappoints. Very good recorded sound.

Chávez, Carlos (1899–1978)

Symphonies Nos. (i) *1 (Sinfonia de Antigona);* (ii) *2 (Sinfonia india);* (i) *4 (Sinfonia romántica);* (iii) *Baile (symphonic painting); The daughter of Colchis (symphonic suite).*
** ASV Dig. CDDCA 1058 [id.]. (i) RPO; (ii) Mexico PO; (iii) Mexico State SO; Enrique Bátiz.

A useful compilation that offers three of the Chávez symphonies including the best known, *Sinfonia india,* in performances by one of his most dedicated interpreters. Now that Mata's set of all six is not in circulation, this serves as an admirable visiting card for this exuberant if noisy composer. Both the *First (Sinfonia de Antigona)* composed in 1933 and the *Fourth (Sinfonia romántica)* of twenty years later, were recorded in the mid 1980s and the remainder of the programme in the 1990s. It is mostly colourful stuff, though the *Sinfonia india,* once relatively familiar, does not wear well. It has two folksy themes which are repeated rather than developed. Enrique Bátiz produces good results from his various orchestras and the sound is more than acceptable.

Cherubini, Luigi (1760–1842)

Anacréon overture.
(***) BBC Legends BBCL mono 4016-2 (2) [id.] BBC SO, Toscanini – BEETHOVEN: *Missa solemnis; Symphony No. 7* (**(*)); MOZART: *Symphony No. 35 (Haffner).* (***)

Cherubini's fine *Anacréon Overture* enjoyed considerably more exposure in the 1930s and 1940s, for not only was it in Toscanini's repertoire but Furtwängler also recorded it, with the Vienna Philharmonic. (At the time of writing there is no modern recording at all!) Toscanini's account comes from 1935 and finds the BBC Symphony Orchestra at its most responsive and alert. For a 1930s broadcast the sound, though not the highest of fi, is really very good indeed.

(i) *Symphony in D; Médée overture;* (ii) *Requiem mass No. 2 in D min.*
(M) ** Supraphon SU 3429-2 011 [id.]. (i) Prague CO; (ii) Czech PO & Ch.; Markevitch.

The important thing here is the *D minor Requiem* for male voices and orchestra, conducted by Igor Markevitch. The performance is dignified and when required, as in the *Dies irae,* fiery. The sound is a little opaque but far from unpleasing. Recorded in 1962, when DG were collaborating with Supraphon, this is also available in a generally superior DG Originals transfer (457 744-2 – see our main volume). The *Symphony in D major,* which Cherubini composed for London (and subsequently transcribed as his *Second String quartet*) and the Overture to *Médée* are given well-drilled if rather stiff performances by the conductorless Prague Chamber Orchestra. As if to compensate for the absence of a conductor, their ensemble is just a bit too disciplined – almost strait-jacketed – and the playing lacks in real warmth.

String quartets Nos.1 in E flat; 2 in C.
*** BIS Dig. CD 1003 [id.]. David Qt.

String quartets Nos. 3 in D min.; 4 in E.
*** BIS Dig. CD 1004 [id.]. David Qt.

Cherubini's quartets are of very high quality and it is good to have outstanding new recordings of them. Listening to them makes one realize the justice of Beethoven's admiration for the composer, for Cherubini's art is informed by lofty ideals and often noble invention. His melodic inspiration is often distinguished and instinctive, there is always a fine musical intelligence at work and polished craftsmanship is always in evidence.

The *First quartet* (1814) apparently uses ideas borrowed from the operas of Méhul, but one would hardly guess that they were not the composer's own, with all four movements springing readily from the same basic material. The Theme and variations of the *Larghetto* are particularly fine, and the delightful rondo finale, played with great virtuosity here, has something of the dash of a scherzo of Mendelssohn. No. 2 is a reworking of the *Symphony in D,* though Cherubini composed a dramatic new slow movement. The Scherzo (Cherubini was very good at Scherzi) is light-hearted without being trivial and the finale combines high spirits with a neat central fugato.

The *Third* and *Fourth quartets* are if anything even finer. Both first movements are full of interest. The slow movement of the *D minor* brings a ravishing aria from the first violin; the Scherzo is a genially rhythmic three-part fugue, and produces a charmingly elegant trio; the finale is as robust as it is good humoured. The *Larghetto* of the *E major* is more searching, with dramatic, recurring bursts of energy, and again the so-called Scherzo, with its solemn chorale, later embroidered by the lead violin, is characteristically unpredictable. The finale bursts with energy, yet has a luscious second subject very like a Slavic folk-tune. Dvořák immediately springs to mind. Both works bring an exhilarating response from this excellent group, who are superb individual players yet tonally perfectly integrated. They are thoroughly at home in Cherubini's sound world. In short these modern-instrument performances could hardly be bettered, and the recording, as one expects from this label, is in every way first class.

Chopin, Frédéric (1810–49)

The Complete Chopin Edition

DG Complete Chopin Edition.
(B) **(*) DG Dig./Analogue 463 047-2 (17) [id.].

To commemorate the 150th anniversary of Chopin's death, DG have assembled, for the first time, the complete works of Chopin – even making several new recordings to fill in the gaps. Where this edition falls down in places is in the choice of performance. There are many outstanding Chopin recordings here – notably from Argerich, Pollini and Zimerman – but there are several where DG might have made a better choice, the *Waltzes* and *Mazurkas* for example. At a bargain price and with a lavishly illustrated booklet, it is still good value and one can always supplement this set with other recordings. The merits of each volume, which are available separately, are discussed below.

Volume 1: Works for piano and orchestra: (i; ii) *Piano concerto Nos. 1 in E min., Op. 11;* (i; iii) *2 in F min., Op. 21;* (i; iii) *Andante spianato et Grande polonaise brillante, Op. 22;* (iv) *Grande fantasia on Polish airs, Op. 13;* (v) *Krakowiak concert rondo, Op. 14;* (iv) *Variations on 'Là ci darem la mano' from Mozart's Don Giovanni, Op. 2.*
(M) *** DG 463 048-2 (2) [id.]. (i) Zimerman; (ii) Concg. O, Kondrashin; (iii) LAPO, Giulini; (iv) Arrau, LPO, Inbal; (v) Askenase, Hague Residente O, Otterloo.

Krystian Zimerman's Chopin concerto recordings have always been admired. They are fresh, poetic and individual accounts, always sparkling and beautifully characterized. DG have chosen for the *E minor Concerto* to use his 'live' 1979 performance at the Concertgebouw (recorded by Hilversum Radio), rather than the studio one with Giulini, perhaps as there is a touch more spontaneity in the former. If the piano is marginally too close in both concertos, the sound is acceptable, with surprisingly little difference between the studio and concert

sources. Claudio Arrau's contributions (originally Philips) are very fine too: the playing is immaculately aristocratic; but his use of rubato will not suit everyone. Askenase's *Krakowiak concert rondo* – dating from 1959, but still sounding good – is most enjoyable and the programme ends with a sparkling account of the *Andante spianato et Grande polonaise brillante* from Zimerman.

Volume 2: (i) *Ballades Nos. 1–4;* (ii) *Barcarolle, Op. 60; Berceuse, Op. 57; Etudes, Op. 10, 1–12; Op. 25, 1–12;* (iii) *3 Ecossaises, Op. 72/3; 3 Nouvelles études;* (i) *Fantasy in F min., Op. 49;* (iii) *Funeral march, Op. 72/2.*
(M) *** DG Dig./Analogue 463 051-2 (2) [id.]. (i) Krystian Zimerman; (ii) Maurizio Pollini; (iii) Anatol Ugorski.

Krystian Zimerman's impressive set of the *Ballades* and the *Fantasy* are touched by distinction throughout and have spontaneity as well as tremendous concentration to commend them. His *Ballades* are a first choice for many and the 1987 recordings of high DG quality. Maurizio Pollini's electrifying account of the *Etudes*, from 1972, remains as satisfying as ever with the remastering sounding fresh and full. The *Barcarolle* and *Berceuse* (1990) are hardly less impressive. This disc is completed by a series of mainly trifles recorded in 1999 (excepting the *Funeral march Op. 72/2*) and well played by Anatol Ugorski. This is an outstanding set.

Volume 3: (i) *Mazurkas 1–49.* Mazurkas without Opus numbers: (ii) *2 Mazurkas in A min.: (ami Emile Gaillard); (notre temps); Mazurka in A flat; 2 Mazurkas in B flat; Mazurka in C; D; & G.*
(M) *(*) DG Dig. 463 054-2 (2) [id.]. (i) Jean-Marc Luisada; (ii) Lilya Zilberstein.

The gifted Tunisian-born pianist Jean-Marc Luisada first came to attention when he gained a place in the finals of the 1985 Chopin Competition in Warsaw. He brings considerable elegance and finesse to the *Mazurkas* but alas, has difficulty in finding real simplicity of expression. There is the eloquence that submerges eloquence: he cannot let the composer speak for himself and Chopin's line is so often the victim of wilful rubato. There are some good things during the course of this survey, but they are too few and far between to permit anything other than the most qualified recommendation. For the *Mazurkas* without Opus numbers, DG have made new recordings with Lilya Zilberstein, which although they are better played and have novelty value, do not compensate for the poor set of the famous ones. Good recordings, but this is the least attractive set in the DG's Chopin Edition.

Volume 4: *Nocturnes Nos. 1–21.*
(M) *** DG Dig. 463 057-2 (2) [id.]. Daniel Barenboim.

Barenboim's playing is of considerable eloquence, the phrasing beautifully moulded, yet with undoubted spontaneous feeling. If compared with Rubinstein these performances lack a mercurial dimension, they have their own character, with moments of impetuosity preventing any suggestion of blandness. The 1981 recording is first class.

Volume 5: Polonaises and minor works: (i) *Andante spianato et Grande polonaise brillante, Op. 22;* (ii) *Polonaises Nos. 1–7;* (iii) *3 Polonaises, Op. 71; Polonaises* (without Opus numbers): *in A flat; B flat; B flat min.; G min.; G flat & G sharp min.; Album Leaf in E; 2 Bourrées; Cantabile in B flat; Fugue in A min.; Galop marquis in A flat; Largo in E flat.*
(M) *** DG Dig./Analogue 463 060-2 (2) [id.]. (i) Martha Argerich; (ii) Maurizio Pollini; (iii) Anatol Ugorski.

Pollini offers playing of outstanding mastery as well as subtle poetry and the DG engineers have made a decent job of the CD transfer. This is magisterial playing, in some ways more commanding than Rubinstein (and better recorded) though not more memorable. Argerich's *Andante spianato* (1974) is everything it should be: wonderfully relaxed to start with and extrovertly sparkling in the *Grande polonaise.* As in other sets in this Edition, Anatol Ugorski fills in the gaps with some of Chopin's early works: interesting to hear, sometimes entertaining, but containing only glimpses of the greatness that was to emerge. Excellent value.

Volume 6: Impromptus, Preludes, Rondos and Scherzos: (i) *Impromptus Nos. 1–3; 4 (Fantaisie-impromptu);* (ii) *24 Preludes, Op. 28; Prelude in C sharp min., Op. 45; Prelude in A flat, Op. Posth.;* (iii) *Rondo in C min., Op. 1; Rondo (La mazur) in F, Op. 5;* (iv) *Rondo in E flat, Op. 16;* (v) *Rondo for Two Pianos in C, Op. Posth. 73;* (vi) *4 Scherzos.*
(M) **(*) DG Dig./Analogue 463 063-2 (2) [id.]. (i) Stanislav Bunin; (ii) Martha Argerich; (iii) Lilya Zilberstein; (iv) Mikhail Pletnev; (v) Kurt Bauer and Heidi Bung; (vi) Maurizio Pollini.

A wide range of pianists in this set. The *Preludes* show Martha Argerich at her finest, spontaneous and inspirational, though her moments of impetuosity may not appeal to all tastes. But her instinct is sure, with many poetic and individual touches. Stanislav Bunin follows on with the *Impromptus* and here the result is not so impressive: he is technically brilliant, but can be self-aware and idiosyncratic at times. However, the *A flat Impromptu* is impressively individual and these performances were among the best on the original LP. There is no want of intellectual power or command of keyboard colour in Pollini's accounts of the *Scherzi.* This is eminently magisterial playing. Yet the powerfully

etched contours and hard surfaces may inspire more admiration than pleasure. Zilberstein's account of two of the *Rondos* is enjoyable enough, but not as imposing as the Pletnev *Rondo in E flat* which follows, nor as beautifully recorded. This set concludes with Bauer and Bung in the *Rondo for 2 Pianos:* here the recording, dating from 1958, is rather thin in sound with noticeable tape hiss, but the performance is acceptable. In all, another rather mixed bag.

Volume 7: Piano Sonatas and Variations: (i) *Piano sonatas Nos. 1 in C min., Op. 4;* (ii) *2 in B flat min., Op. 35; 3 in B min., Op. 58;* (iii) *Introduction and variations on a German national air, Op. Posth.;* (iv) *Introduction and variations on a theme of Moore for piano (four hands), Op. Posth.;* (i) *Variations in A major (Souvenir de Paganini);* (iii) *Variations brillantes in B flat major, Op. 12;* (v) *Variation No. 6 from the cycle 'Hexameron'.* Miscellaneous pieces: *Allegro de concert, Op. 46;* (vi) *Bolero, Op. 19; Tarantella, Op. 43.*
(M) **(*) DG Dig. 463 066-2 (2) [id.]. (i) Lilya Zilberstein; (ii) Maurizio Pollini; (iii) Tamás Vásáry; (iv) Vladimir and Vovka Ashkenazy; (v) Vladimir Ashkenazy; (vi) Anatol Ugorski.

This set opens with a newly recorded version of the *First Sonata,* well played by Lilya Zilberstein. Of course, having the two most famous *Sonatas* in equally famous performances following, puts it rather in the shade, but it is good to have all three together. Pollini's readings of the *Second* and *Third* are enormously commanding and his mastery of mood and structure gives these much-played works added stature. The slow movement of the Op. 35 has tremendous drama and atmosphere, so that the contrast of the magical central section is all the more telling. Both works are played with great distinction, but the balance is just a shade close. The second CD is of lighter fare taken from a variety of sources: Vásáry opens with an enjoyable set of the Op. 12 *Variations,* recorded in 1965 and sounding just a little thin. The Ashkenazys are borrowed from Decca and are in excellent form. Zilberstein's and Ugorski's contributions have been newly made and are (like the sound) good without being exceptional. On the whole a worthwhile set.

Volume 8: Chamber Music and Waltzes: (i) *Cello sonata in G min., Op. 65;* (ii) *Grand duo concertant for cello and piano in E;* (i) *Introduction and polonaise brillante for cello and piano in C, Op. 3;* (iii) *Piano trio in G min. Op. 8;* (iv) *Waltzes 1–17;* (v) *Waltzes in E flat (Sostenuto); in A min., Op. Posth.*
(M) **(*) DG Dig./Analogue 463 069-2 (2) [id.].
(i) Rostropovich and Argerich; (ii) Anner Bylsma and Lambert Orkis; (iii) Beaux Arts

Trio; (iv) Jean-Marc Luisada; (v) Lilya Zilberstein.

It seems a curious idea to combine the chamber music with the *Waltzes*, particularly as the recordings DG chose for the bulk of the latter are not inspired. Jean-Marc Luisada, although possessing a certain freshness in his playing and eminently musical, lacks a strong profile: he does not convey the authority needed to persuade the listener that this is the only way this music can be played. Compared to the best available, these accounts seem pale, even though the recorded sound (1990) is good. The chamber music on the second CD is far stronger in performance personality: the *Piano trio*, an early work, is not wholly characteristic of Chopin, but is certainly of interest. The Beaux Arts' performance could hardly be improved upon and the 1970 recording (originally Philips) is excellent. With such characterful artists as Rostropovich and Argerich challenging each other, a memorable account of the *Cello sonata*, Chopin's last published work, was guaranteed – music which clicks into focus in such a performance. The contrasts of character between expressive cello and brilliant piano are also richly caught in the *Introduction and polonaise* and the recording is warm and vivid. In between these two works is the *Grand duo concertant*, played by Anner Bylsma and Lambert Orkis. But the performance does not have the excellence of the Rostropovich/Argerich ones which flank it, nor as flattering a recording – there are plenty of grunts, sniffs and squeaks thrown in for free! A mixed bag then and the second, chamber music CD needs to be issued separately.

Volume 9: *17 Songs, Op. Posth. 74; Czary, Op. Posth.; Dumka, Op. Posth.*
(M) **(*) DG Dig. 463 072-2 [id.]. Elzbieta Szmytka, Malcolm Martineau.

Nothing establishes Chopin more clearly as a red-blooded Pole than these generally simple, unsophisticated settings with their plain folk melodies and sharp Slavonic rhythms. The Polish soprano Elzbieta Szmytka (newly recorded in 1999) has the full measure of these songs and is well supported by Malcolm Martineau. If these performances don't quite erase memories of the Söderström and Ashkenazy CD (a Decca issue that is currently withdrawn), they are well recorded and are much more than a stopgap. One is surprised how few recordings there have been of these songs, generally a neglected area of Chopin's output, for they are often surprisingly emotional and no lover of this composer or of song in general should be without them. The CD plays for under 47 minutes – Chopin disappointingly not having written enough songs to really fill up a CD!

'Chopin masterworks'
(BB) *(**) Arte Nova Dig. 74321 63638-2 (5)

[id.]. Ricardo Castro, Sinfonia Varsovia, Volker Schmidt-Gertenbach.

(i) *Piano concertos No. 1–2; Andante spianato & grande polonaise brillante, Op. 22; Ballades Nos. 1–4; Polonaises: in C sharp min., Op. 26/1; in A flat, Op. 53.*
(BB) **(*) Arte Nova Dig. 74321 59217-2 (2) [id.]. Ricardo Castro; (i) Sinfonia Varsovia, Volker Schmidt-Gertenbach.

Nocturnes Nos. 1–21.
(BB) *** Arte Nova Dig. 74321 30494-2 (Nos. 1–10); 74321 54451-2 (Nos. 11–21) [id.]. Ricardo Castro.

Piano sonatas Nos. 1–3: 3 Waltzes, Op. 64/1–3; Nocturne in E flat, Op. 9/2 with variations by Castro.
(BB) *(*) Arte Nova Dig. 74321 63676-2 [id.]. Ricardo Castro.

We have already given high praise in our main volume to Ricardo Castro's highly poetic set of *Nocturnes*, which like the other three discs here, are available separately as well as in a slipcase. By comparison the rest of Castro's Chopin survey brings a considerable element of disappointment. The *First concerto* opens rather meekly, but perks up later, and while there is much that is poetic in both concertos, they are not always convincing as overall interpretations.

A similar comment might be applied to the four *Ballades*, which have playing which is at times seductive and at others impulsively wayward, but which on the whole give pleasure. Of the three *Sonatas* the *Third* comes off best, especially the slow movement. Elsewhere there is some over-enthusiastic and sometimes imprecise bravura, and the interpretations do not always seem to be thought through. No complaints about the recording, except in the concertos, where the overall focus could be firmer. But collectors would do best to stay with the separate issue of the Nocturnes, and then look elsewhere (perhaps to Ashkenazy) for the other works.

Opus Chopin edition

Piano concerto No. 2 in F minor, Op. 21; Fantasy on Polish airs, Op. 13.
*** Opus 111 Dig. OPS 2008 [id.]. Janusz Olejniczak, Das Neue Orchester, Christoph Spering (with ELSNER: *Overture, Lezek Bialy*. KURPINSKI: *Overture, Zamek na Czorsztynie*. PAER: *La Biondina in gondoletta* (with Olga Pasiechnyk)).

Etudes, Op. 25; 24 Preludes, Op. 28; Piano sonata No. 2.
*** Opus 111 Dig. OPS 2009 [id.]. Grigory Sokolov.

'*Chopin's last concert in Paris*' (with music by Bellini, Donizetti, Mozart and Meyerbeer).
*** Opus 111 Dig. OPS 2012 [id.]. Janusz Olejniczak, Olga Pasiechnyk, etc.

The year 1999 marked the 150th anniversary of Chopin's death and brought a flurry of activity from various companies, none more original or imaginative than that of the Paris-based Opus 111 label. There are ten volumes in all (OPS 2006–15) handsomely produced and intelligently planned, two of which we list above. The first, '*Racines*' (*Roots*) (OPS 2006), produces the traditional folk music and dances that Chopin would have heard in his youth and that played such a formative role in his musical development. Not only do we get so much fascinating folk material – mazurkas, polkas and obereks – but we also hear instruments of the period including the suka, an eighteenth-century string instrument. This affords a most useful insight into the world that the boy Chopin must have encountered. A second two-CD set brings 9 *Polonaises* and 23 *Mazurkas* played by Janusz Olejniczak (OPS 2007). But it is the third set (detailed above) which should make the most convenient entry point into this series. It reproduces on period instruments the programme on which Chopin made his Warsaw début after his triumph in Vienna, with the *F minor Concerto* and the *Fantasy on Polish airs*. The programme also included overtures by his teacher, Jozef Elsner, and by Karol Kurpinski and soprano variations by Ferdinando Paër. Janusz Olejniczak strikes us as wonderfully idiomatic and is far more convincing than any other account we have heard on period instruments. He has fine poetic feeling and a refined sensitivity, and Das Neue Orchester under Christoph Spering give splendid support as well as spirited accounts of the overtures.

Grigory Sokolov's two-CD set of the *Etudes*, Op. 25, the *Preludes*, Op. 28 and the *Second Piano Sonata* is also something of a must, certainly well worth shortlisting, for he is an artist of real insight and vision. When Olejniczak 'sits down in front of an 1831 Pleyel piano', the notes tell us, 'Chopin's strength, tenderness, and virtuosity re-emerge as never before', and when one proceeds to his recital entitled '*Chopin privé*' (*Chopin at Home*) (OPS 2010), these extravagant claims are vindicated. He is a most imaginative player. Another disc, '*Chopin intime*' (OPS 2011), offers readings of his correspondence with Georges Sand together with appropriate music illustrations. The letters are beautifully read by Sonia Rykiel and Andrzej Seweryn of the Comédie-Française, and English and German translations are given in the accompanying booklet for those whose French is a little fractured.

One of the most absorbing issues (listed above) is a reconstruction of Chopin's last concert in Paris in February 1848. The Salle Pleyel had been fully subscribed by the privileged, so that posters and concert bills advertising the programme were never printed. We have to rely on contemporary accounts and letters for its actual content. Janusz Olejniczak shines in the Chopin pieces, and the Bellini, Donizetti, Meyerbeer and Mozart items are equally well served by the team that Opus 111 have assembled. Few records so successfully convey the atmosphere of this poignant occasion – and a sense of what concerts were like at that period. The remaining discs – jazz improvisations by the Andrzej Jagodzinski Trio (OPS 2013), and 'Chopin tomorrow' (OPS 2014), are not mandatory purchases, though they have their rewards, as does the last CD, which presents some of the writings about Chopin by such diverse thinkers and writers as Nietzsche, Heine, Proust, Gide, Hermann Hesse and Tolstoy. An enterprising and thought-provoking set which is well worth exploring, but two of the listed discs (OPS 2008 and 2012) are outstanding.

Other Chopin recordings

(i) *Piano concerto No. 1* (complete); (ii) *Romanze only. Berceuse in D flat, Op. 67; Chant polonaise* (arr. Liszt) *Etudes: in E, Op. 10/1; in G flat, Op 10/5* (2 versions); *Mazurkas: in B flat min., Op. 24/4; in C sharp min., Op. 63/3* (3 versions); *in G, Op. 67/1; Waltzes: in C sharp min., Op. 64/1; in E min., Op. posth.*
(***) Biddulph mono LHW 040 [id.]. Moriz Rosenthal; with (i) Berlin State Op. O, Frieder Weissmann; (ii) NBC SO, Black.

Listening to this painstaking transfer by Ward Marston, it is easy to understand why Moriz Rosenthal was held in such veneration. When he was a boy he studied with Karl Mikuli, a pupil of Chopin, whose legatissimo was legendary, and later on with Liszt. His own poetic feeling and extraordinary delicacy of touch come across in the smaller pieces. In the *E minor Concerto* his playing is of enormous elegance and refinement of tone, which can be discerned even in this primitive 1930 recording, originally issued on a mix of 10- and 12-inch 78-r.p.m. records. Frieder Weissmann makes even larger cuts in the introductory orchestral ritornello than those usual in the 1930s. The recordings all date from 1929–31 when this artist was in his late sixties to early seventies, save for the slow movement of the concerto, which survives in a live broadcast marking the pianist's seventy-fifth birthday. Some allowances must be made for the frail sound but the playing has unfailing beauty and finesse.

Piano concertos Nos. 1 in E min., Op. 11; 2 in F min., Op. 21.
(M) **(*) EMI CDM5 67232-2 [567261]. Samson François, Monte-Carlo Op. O, Louis Frémaux.
(B) ** Ph. Virtuoso 434 145-2 [id.]. Arrau, LPO, Inbal.

** DG Dig. 459 684-2 [id.]. Krystian Zimerman,
Polish Festival Orchestra.
(M) *(*) Decca 466 422-2 [id.]. Jorge Bolet,
Montreal SO, Charles Dutoit.

The French have a great admiration for Samson
François, so his coupling is an understandable
French EMI choice for the 'Great Recordings of the
Century' but one with which we would not wholly
identify, especially when one thinks of Pollini's
magical HMV record of the E minor work. However, these remain impressive performances. If
François's rather grand first entry in the *E minor* is
slightly mannered, there is much fine playing here,
and the solo contribution in the finales of the both
concertos often scintillates. Frémaux's accompaniments of outer movements are strong in vitality,
and certainly supportive in the beautiful *Larghettos*,
where again much of the solo playing is persuasive.
The remastering of the late 1960s recordings certainly gives both the forwardly placed soloist and
the orchestra a vivid presence, with sparkling piano
timbre.

As so often with Arrau's performances in the
recording studio, his accounts of the Chopin piano
concertos with Inbal are marred by rubato, which
at times seems mannered, with the performances as
a whole lacking convincing spontaneity. The early
1970s recording is average (with the piano too forward) and has a surprising amount of tape hiss. At
bargain price, Arrau fans may consider this CD
worth while, for his playing is certainly aristocratic
throughout, but there are many better recommendations for the general collector.

DG supplement their handsome Chopin Edition,
issued to mark the 150th anniversary of the
composer's death, with a newly recorded pairing of
the two concertos from that aristocrat of pianists,
Krystian Zimerman, and the Polish Festival
Orchestra. Alas, any sense of momentum or naturalness is submerged by uncharacteristically disruptive
rubato. Hardly a phrase comes to a natural close but
is lingered over and cosseted. For once Zimerman's
musical judgement fails him. After his mercurial and
impeccable Ravel concertos with Boulez, these self-
aware performances are puzzling. Both concertos are
the same – full of intrusive touches and pulled out of
shape. Far better to have his earlier set with Giulini
and the Los Angeles Orchestra, elegant, aristocratic
and sparkling (DG 415 970-2 – see our main
volume), which remains first choice for these works.

Jorge Bolet made his CD of the Chopin concertos
with the Montreal Orchestra in May 1989, the last
year of his life. As always with this artist there is
some fine pianism and refined tonal colouring, but
although both slow movements are appealingly
gentle, there is an element of lethargy elsewhere,
and the finales of both concertos need far more
sparkle and vivacity. The Decca sound is excellent
and Dutoit is admirably supportive but, given the

competition presently available, these accounts are
unlikely to win favour.

Piano concerto No. 2 in F min., Op. 21.
(B) *** Decca Penguin 460 653-2 [id.]. Vladimir
Ashkenazy, LSO, Maazel – TCHAIKOVSKY:
Piano concerto No. 1. ***

Ashkenazy's 1965 recording is a distinguished performance: conductor and orchestra are obviously
in full rapport with their soloist and the vintage
recording has remastered well. This performance is
also available in Decca's 'Classic Sound' series
(less ideally coupled with Bach and Mozart), but the
(cheaper) Penguin Classics disc, with its excellent
Tchaikovsky coupling, is the better deal. The author's note is by Angela Huth.

Les Sylphides (orchestrations by Leroy Anderson
and Peter Bodge).
(M) ** RCA 09026 63532-2 [id.]. Boston Pops O,
Fiedler – LISZT: *Les Préludes; Mazeppa* *;
PROKOFIEV: *The Love for 3 Oranges: suite.*
**(*)

Apart from a few distracting tempi, *Les Sylphides*
receives a generally good performance by Fiedler,
dating from 1960, and in lively 'Living Stereo'
sound. The souped-up orchestration has some nice
moments, but the familiar Roy Douglas version is
by far the most successful. Karajan's superb version
is available on either a single disc (● 429 163-2
– see our main volume) or in a sparkling Berlin
Philharmonic two-disc anthology of ballet music
praised in the Concerts section below.

SOLO PIANO MUSIC

Andante spianato et Grande polonaise, Op. 22
(***) BBC Legends mono 4031-2 [id.]. Sviatoslav
Richter, LSO, Kyrill Kondrashin – LISZT:
*Piano concertos Nos. 1–2; Hungarian
fantasia.* (***)

When Richter paid his celebrated 1961 visit to
London he also made his classic recording of the
two Liszt concertos for Philips. The concert performances of these (also with the LSO under Kondrashin) plus a stunning *Hungarian fantasia* are the
main items on this BBC Legends CD. One of the
other concerts included the Dvořák concerto and
Chopin's *Andante spianato et Grande Polonaise*,
Op. 22, and this latter piece makes a delightful
bonus. Both in the *Andante* and the *Polonaise,*
Richter is at his most magical, not just brilliant but
intensely poetic too, the more moving in a live
performance. The playing has great delicacy and
bravura. The BBC's mono recording balances him
much closer than the orchestra and at times his
pedalling is audible.

*Ballades Nos. 1–4; Fantasia in F min., Op. 49;
Prelude in C sharp min., Op. 45.*

**(*) DG Dig. 459 683-2 [id.]. Maurizio Pollini.

Although any new Pollini excites the highest expectations, this new CD is so modestly filled that however impressive the playing, it strikes us as poor value. Only 48 minutes of music at full price is a lot to ask – even if it is Pollini. The performances are commanding, masterly and well recorded even if Perahia goes closer to the heart of this music. His remain our preferred choice and his set of the *Ballades* received a ● in our main volume (Sony SK 64399).

Ballades Nos. 1–4; Scherzi Nos. 1–4; Prelude in C sharp min., Op. 45.
(M) *** Decca 466 499-2 [id.]. Vladimir Ashkenazy.

Ashkenazy's four *Ballades* date from 1964, the *Scherzi* from three years later. Those wanting the present coupling will find this reissue in Decca's Legends series equally satisfactory and the pianist's admirers will relish the photographs of the pianist as a young man and indeed the excellent notes by Bryce Morrison. The readings of the *Ballades* are thoughtfully poetic, with the bravura rising spontaneously out of the music. The openings of each show this quality well, with Ashkenazy's gentle intimacy immediately communicating with the listener. In the *Scherzi* the playing is chimerically dazzling, and the isolated Op. 45 *C sharp minor Prelude*, a pianistic tone poem in its own right, makes an ideal interlude before the *B minor Scherzo* bursts in on the listener. Very good recording, particularly impressive in the *Scherzi*, which have a fine depth of sonority.

Etudes, Op. 10/1–12; Op. 25/1–12; Fantaisie in F min., Op. 49; Piano sonatas Nos. 1–3.
(B) *** Decca Double 466 250-2 (2) [id.]. Vladimir Ashkenazy.

These recordings span a period of about five years, for Ashkenazy recorded his Chopin survey as far as possible in chronological order. The sets of *Etudes* from 1975 offer playing of total mastery and can safely be recommended alongside Pollini on DG and more recently Louis Lortie on Chandos (offering the finest recorded sound of all). The *C minor Sonata* (No. 1) is still a comparative rarity on disc, an early work (1827) and not deeply characteristic. Ashkenazy's account (1976) enjoys classic status alongside the more recent version of Andsnes. His 1980 performance of the *Funeral march Sonata* (No. 2) is no less dazzling than his earlier live recording of 1972 and in some respects surpasses it. It has wonderful panache. Indeed, the first movement in particular seems more concentrated in feeling and the finale is very exciting indeed. The *B minor Sonata*, recorded a year later, is also memorable and involving, although there is a shade less tenderness and vision in the slow movement than in some rival versions. An authoritative account of

the *F minor Fantasy* provides an excellent makeweight in very realistic sound. Indeed, the analogue recordings for the most part still sound first class, although the timbre in the first set of *Etudes*, Op. 10, is a bit dry and over-bright on top.

Nocturnes Nos. 1–21; Mazurkas Nos. 13 in A min., Op. 17/4; 32 in C sharp min., Op. 50/3; 35 in C min., Op. 56/3; Waltzes Nos. 3 in A min.; 8 in A flat, Op. 64/3; 9 in A flat; 10 in B min., Op. 69/1-2; 13 in D flat, Op. 70/3.
(B) **(*) EMI Double fforte CZS5 73830-2 (2). Alexis Weissenberg.

Alexis Weissenberg recorded the *Nocturnes* in the late 1960s but they soon disappeared from view, and they have been out of the catalogue until now. No doubt EMI have restored them after seeing that Weissenberg has joined the ranks of Philips's 'Great pianists' series. On the evidence of this reissue, he is a thoughtful, serious artist and a natural Chopin player with highly poetic feeling for rubato.

He opens the First *B flat minor Nocturne* very beautifully and the famous *E flat Nocturne, Op. 9/ 2* is played gently and exquisitely. But at times he gets impulsively carried away, and in the central section of the *B major* work, the playing accelerates too hastily. This also happens in the passionate climax of the *E minor* work, Op. 48/1, and occasionally elsewhere some of the elusive nocturnal quality is lost.

The *Mazurkas* too are very volatile, but here the strong rhythmic pointing is more appropriate, and the *Waltzes* sparkle more delicately. Overall one would not want to make too much of Weissenberg's passionate outbursts, for much of his playing is memorably gentle and affecting, helped by a natural piano sound, which has fine colour and sonority. This set certainly establishes his individuality.

Polonaises Nos. 1–6; 7 (Polonaise-fantaisie); Andante spianato & Grande polonaise brillante; Nocturnes Nos. 1, 2, 4, 5, 8, 9, 11, 13–19.
(BB) ** Royal Long Players DCL 705712 (2) Garrick Ohlsson.

Back in 1970, while still barely out of his teens, Garrick Ohlsson won the Chopin Contest in Warsaw, and a year or two later he recorded a comprehensive collection of the *Polonaises* (plus the *Andante spianato et Grande polonaise brillante*) for EMI. This reissue includes the seven best known, including the *Polonaise-fantaisie*, and supplements them with fourteen of the *Nocturnes*, recorded six years later, which are played poetically and with pleasing intimacy. In the *Polonaises*, Ohlsson demonstrates a weighty style and technique very much of the American school, but with it all he is thoughtful. When he uses a flexible beat it is only rarely that the result sounds wilful. The EMI recording is very good, but while this inexpensive reissue makes an excellent visiting card, it seems a pity that neither of his surveys was offered complete.

Polonaises Nos. 1–9; Waltzes Nos. 1–19.
(B) ** Ph. Duo 462 874-2 (2) [id.]. Adam Harasiewicz.

Adam Harasiewicz offers keenly musical performances of the complete *Waltzes* and is especially sympathetic in the posthumous ones. They are well recorded, but in the last resort the musical characterization is not so memorable as in other sets. The same can also be said of the *Polonaises*. He includes the *Polonaise-fantaisie*, in which he displays a thoughtful poetic feeling that is already apparent in the opening C sharp minor work, Op. 26/1. He is less commanding in the *Military polonaise*, but there is some glittering dexterity in No. 8, in D minor, and he is at his best both here and in the flexible account of No. 9, in B flat. The sound, dating from 1967–70, is bold and full and this Duo is fair value.

24 Preludes, Op. 28; Scherzos Nos. 1 in B min., Op. 20; 2 in B flat min., Op. 31; 4 in E, Op. 54.
*** Naim Dig. NAIMCD 028 [id.]. Håvard Gimse.

The Norwegian pianist Håvard Gimse has consistently impressed us with his natural and refined musicianship. He is a cultured player, whose talent is primarily lyrical. This is seen to great advantage in the *Preludes* and the three *Scherzos* for which there is room on this CD. He is at his best in the self-communing, poetic side of these wonderful pieces but there is no want of fire, though perhaps more could be made of the dramatic and dynamic contrasts in the *B minor Scherzo*. Gimse is a most sensitive and thoughtful player. The Sofienberg Church in Oslo offers an excellent acoustic and the recording is pleasingly natural.

24 Preludes, Op. 28; Piano sonata No. 2 in B flat minor, Op. 35; Polonaise in A flat, Op. 53.
** RCA Dig. 09026 63535-2 [id.]. Evgeny Kissin.

In a recent RCA film (available on video or DVD), *Evgeny Kissin: Gift of Music*, this wonderful pianist tells of his great feeling for Chopin. His new recital offers some masterly, indeed dazzling pianism, but we miss the fresh, spontaneous quality that has distinguished most of his earlier recitals. He makes pretty heavy weather of the *E minor Prelude (No. 9)* though the close RCA balance probably makes him sound heavier than he is.

There was a certain self-aware quality about his recent set of the *Ballades* which disappointed too. Give the RCA video a miss, for although it offers some valuable glimpses of his playing, they are mostly just bits and pieces (though some Prom encores are heard in full) and there is an unctuous and embarrassing commentary.

Piano sonatas Nos. 1–3; Ballades Nos. 1–4; Scherzos Nos. 1–4; Barcarolle in F sharp, Op. 60; Fantaisie in F min., Op. 49.

(B) *(*) Ph. Duo 464 025-2 (2) [id.]. Adam Harasiewicz.

These performances are quite good, but are not helped by generally indifferent sound. There are too many fine bargain Chopin records around to give this set a strong recommendation.

Piano sonata No. 3 in B minor, Op. 58; Polonaise No. 6 in A flat, Op. 53.
(B) **(*) EMI Début Dig. CDZ5 73500-2 [id.]. Alex Slobodyanik – SCHUMANN: *Kinderszenen, Op. 15; Papillons, Op. 2.* **

Alex Slobodyanik is now in his mid-twenties and on the brink of a promising career. He studied in Moscow and subsequently in Cleveland, where he won various awards. He has gone on to appear with major orchestras all over the world. His account of the *B minor Sonata* is sensitive and intelligent and, along with the Schumann couplings, serves as an admirable visiting card for this young artist. At the same time, it does not have quite the strong personality of such CD rivals as Kissin (DG), Howard Shelley (Hyperion), Andsnes (Virgin) or Pletnev, who has incredible pianism if marred by occasionally intrusive rubato. Excellent and natural recorded sound.

RECITAL COLLECTIONS

Ballade No. 1 in G min., Op. 23; Fantaisie in F min., Op. 49; Nocturnes: in F sharp, Op. 15/2; in D flat, Op. 27/2; in E min., Op. Posth. 72/1; Scherzo No. 2 in B flat min., Op. 31.
(B) *(*) EMI Dig. Double Fforte CZS5 73656-2 (2). [CDFB 73676] Youri Egorov – DEBUSSY: Recital. **(*)

Egorov, a sensitive, temperamental and elusive defector from the Soviet Union, gives here flashes of the artistry which has given him such a reputation, particularly in the United States. Alas, only in the *Nocturnes* does his vision bring consistently satisfying performances. Excellent piano sound, but the (unexpected) Debussy coupling fares better.

Barcarolle in F sharp min., Op. 60; Berceuse in D flat, Op. 57; Mazurkas Nos. 13 in A min., Op. 17/4; 23 in D, Op. 33/2; 33 in B, Op. 56/1; Nocturnes Nos. 1 in B flat min., Op. 9/1; 8 in D flat, Op. 27/2; 10 in A flat, Op. 32/2; 12 in G, Op. 37/2; 17 in B, Op. 62/1; Polonaises Nos. 3 in A, Op. 40/1; No. 6 in A flat (Héroïque); Scherzo No. 2 in B flat min., Op. 31 Waltzes: in C sharp min., Op. 64/2.
(M) (**(*)) EMI mono CDM5 67007-2 [id.]. Artur Rubinstein.

There are many who hold that Rubinstein made his very finest Chopin records for EMI in the 1930s. The present selection, carefully arranged to make a satisfactory ongoing recital, dates from between 1928 (the charismatic account of the *Barcarolle,* which sounds unbelievably good) and 1939 (the *B flat Mazurka*, Op. 56/1).

Certainly the younger Rubinstein (he was in his forties) has a wonderfully chimerical touch, especially when he has to play a sudden burst of dazzling filigree decoration, as in some of the *Nocturnes* and indeed the *Berceuse*, which he paces fairly briskly. He brings very special touch to the *Mazurkas* (strikingly so in the *A minor*, Op. 17/4), and his rubato throughout is as uniquely personal as it is convincing. The transfers are a shade dry, and at times a little lacking in sonority, but pretty faithful otherwise.

Fugue in A min., Op. Posth.; Lento con gran espressione in C sharp min., Op. Posth.; Nocturnes: in E flat, Op. 9/2; in C min., Op. Posth.; Polonaise in B flat min., Op. Posth.; Waltzes in A min., Op. 34/2; in A min. Op. Posth.; in E min.; in F sharp min., Op. Posth.
(*) Etcetera Dig. KTC 1231 [id.]. Helge Antoni – FIELD: *Largo; Nocturnes,* etc. *

This may at first appear to be an unenticing collection of early, often immature Chopin pieces, but its primary purpose is to make a direct comparison with similar works, written even earlier, by John Field, who invented the *Nocturne* in the year Chopin was born. The young Polish composer was well aware of Field's style – he played the latter's *Third Piano concerto* at the age of thirteen in Warsaw. Some of the similarities between the two young composers have already been documented (notably Field's *E flat major Romance* and Chopin's famous *Nocturne* in the same key from Opus 9). But other musical links are equally fascinating. Helge Antoni plays simply and poetically, not seeking quite the degree of rubato familiar in most Chopin performances today; but this serves to point up his comparisons. He is naturally recorded in a pleasing acoustic.

VOCAL MUSIC

Songs: *The bridegroom; Drinking song; Faded and vanished; Reverie (Dumka); Handsome lad; Hymn from the tomb; Lithuanian song; The maiden's wish; Melodia (Elegy; Lamento); The messenger; My darling; Out of my sight; The ring; Sad river; Spring; There where she loves; The two corpses; The warrior; Witchcraft.* Songs arr. Pauline Viardot from Chopin Mazurkas: *Berceuse* (from Op. 33/3); *Faible coeur* (from Op. 7/3); *La Danse* (from Op. 50/1); *La Fête* (from Op. 6/4); *Plainte d'amour* (from Op. 6/1).
*** Hyperion Dig. CDA 67125 [id.]. Urszula Kryger, Charles Spencer.

Chopin wrote these songs for relaxation, just to please himself, never publishing them, and that may explain why the Polish flavour is so strong. He was reflecting his own early background, and the results are charming. Mazurka rhythms abound, as in the

haunting *Handsome lad*, with the collection rounded off in the one song which goes deeper, *Melodia*, the heartfelt lament of an exile. The five arrangements of Chopin Mazurkas made for her own use by the leading singer, Pauline Viardot, are comparably charming, making the ideal fill-up. Urszula Kryger, with her vibrant Slavonic tone well controlled, makes the most sympathetic interpreter, sensitively accompanied by Charles Spencer.

Songs: *Hulanka; Melodya; Moja Piesczotka (My sweetheart); Narzeczony (The bridegroom); Niema czego Trzeba (There is no need); Spiew Grobowy (Hymn from the tomb); Wiosna (Spring).*
(BB) ** Belart 461 626-2 [id.]. Robert Tear, Philip Ledger – RACHMANINOV *Songs .***

Robert Tear and Philip Ledger couple songs by two composers and though generally it works better on record to concentrate on a single composer, the contrasts here are refreshing and illuminating. Both are Slavic composers, Chopin the simpler of the two as a songwriter is directly reflecting the folk music of Poland. Robert Tear commendably sings in Polish, but his style is often not direct enough to capture the full freshness. Even so this is rare repertoire and it is well recorded. The snag is the absence of adequate documentation with texts and translations. But this disc is very inexpensive and collectors may well be tempted by its modest cost.

Ciurlionis, Mikalojus Konstantinas (1875–1911)

Concord, VL255; Folksong transcriptions : *Did the winds blow, VL274; Oh, my mother, VL277; A willow on the hill, VL289; Fugue in B flat minor, VL345; Impromptu, VL181; Nocturne, VL178; Pater Noster, VL260; Preludes: VL169; VL182a; VL184; VL186; VL187; VL188; VL239; VL325; VL335; VL338; VL331; VL337a; VL310; 4 Variations on 'Run, you fields', VL279; 5 Variations on 'You, my forest', VL276; 6 Variations on 'Sefaa Esec', VL258.*
(M) **(*) EMI Dig. CDM5 66791-2 [id.].
Vytautas Landsbergis.

Ciurlionis was something of a polymath, for in addition to his achievements as the leading Lithuanian composer of his day, he was also a painter (and is exhibited in Kaunas). He studied in Warsaw and Leipzig, and developed a harmonically free style, as did his younger contemporary Szymanowski. Readers who recall the dying days of the Soviet Union will recognize the pianist's name: Vytautas Landsbergis became the first President of the new Lithuanian republic and is a musicologist by profession and the leading authority on Ciurlionis's music. Indeed, he is Ciurlionis's 'Köchel', for the VLs after the titles of the pieces are the Landsbergis numbers he has allocated to the works.

The piano pieces here are mostly miniatures, often poetic and lyrical; some are quite slight but others come near to the language of Szymanowski. Professor Landsbergis is a sensitive player but the instrument on which he plays is a bit hard and not in ideal condition and nor is the recording acoustic ideal. An interesting issue all the same. What little we have heard of his orchestral music suggests that Ciurlionis was a composer of some substance.

Clementi, Muzio (1752–1832)

Piano sonatas in G; B min.; D, Op. 40/1–3.
(BB) *** Naxos Dig. 8.553500 [id.]. Pietro De Maria.

After their earlier success in the Clementi sonatas with the Hungarian pianist Balázs Szokolay, Naxos have elected to continue with Pietro De Maria – and he, too, is hardly less captivating. A native of Venice, now in his early thirties, he has an impressive portfolio of prizes to his credit. His account of the three *Sonatas* of 1802 which make up Op. 40 is impeccable not only in terms of virtuosity (not for nothing was he awarded the *Premier Prix de Virtuosité* in Geneva) but in musicianship and artistry. His playing is meticulous, beautifully articulated, his command of dynamics and naturalness of phrasing admirable. He is accorded first-class sound, fresh and present, as one might expect from the acoustic of St George's, Brandon Hill, Bristol. Very good value for money.

Clérambault, Louis-Nicolas (1676–1749)

Cantatas: Apollon et Doris; L'Isle de Délos; Léandre et Héro; Pirame et Tisbé.
(M) *** Opus 111 Dig. 10-006 [id.]. Isabelle Poulenard, Gilles Ragon, Ens. Amalia.

A contemporary of Couperin and Rameau, Louis-Nicolas Clérambault was the son of a musician at the Court of Louis XIV and went on to become organist of the Eglise de Saint-Sulpice in Paris. Apart from his keyboard music he is perhaps best remembered for his chamber cantatas, and published five collections of them. Between 1710 and 1742 Clérambault produced some twenty-six cantatas for varying instrumental combinations. Both *Léandre et Héro* and *Pirame et Tisbé* come from 1713 and are redolent of tragedy, and exhibit a sensibility of great refinement. *L'Isle de Délos* comes from 1716 and evokes the pleasures of the island, while *Apollon et Doris* (1720) serves to reaffirm the feeling that as a master of the secular chamber cantata he was second to none. Affecting performances from Isabelle Poulenard and Gilles Ragon, well supported throughout by the Ensemble Amalia. The recording, a co-production with

WestDeutscher Rundfunk, Cologne, made at the Lebanese Church in Paris is first-rate.

Le Triomphe d'Iris (pastorale).
(BB) *** Naxos Dig. 8.554455 [id.]. Gaëlle Méchaly, Claire Geoffroy-Dechaume, Goubioud, Bona, Duthoit, Novelli, Lombard, Le Concert Spirituel, Hervé Niquet.

Clérambault also produced lively court entertainments like this delightful Pastorale. Though the date of 1706 is fixed, no one knows the event for which *Le Triomphe d'Iris* was written. Parallel to the *Grand opéra*, France had developed a less-imposing genre called the *Petit opéra* which comes close to the Masque in England. In a manner typical of that style and period the present work presents in three Acts or Entrées a story of two pairs of shepherd and shepherdess lovers, Daphnis and Sylvie, and Tircis and Philis, brought together at the end by the goddess, Iris, representing Love. There is relatively little recitative and the melodic invention is of variable quality. What matters most is the vitality of Clérambault's writing in a sequence of brief arias, choruses and dances, underlined in the rhythmic bite of this performance from the period instruments of Le Concert Spirituel. The refined, very French team of singers is well drilled and agile, untroubled by brisk speeds. Clear, refined recording to match.

Clifford, Hubert (1904–59)

Symphony.
*** Chandos Dig. CHAN 9757 [id.]. BBC PO, Vernon Handley – BAINTON: *Symphony No. 2*; GOUGH: *Serenade*. ***

Hubert Clifford began by exploring chemistry at the University of Melbourne, at the same time as music at the Conservatoire. He then came to England to study at the Royal College of Music in London with Vaughan Williams, though, judging from this work, Clifford's musical sympathies are with Walton and Bliss rather than the former. He never returned to Australia and after a spell of teaching joined the BBC as Empire Music Supervisor and then became head of Light Music Programmes. He subsequently became director of music for Alexander Korda, commissioning scores for such films as *The Winslow Boy*, *The Fallen Idol* and *Anna Karenina*. His four-movement *Symphony* occupied him from 1938 to 1940 and is an ambitious score which runs to forty-three minutes. It is compelling, expertly fashioned and vividly scored, even if no distinctive voice emerges. Its idiom at times comes close to the English film music of the 1940s and 1950s. It is well argued and it would be difficult to imagine a more persuasive and convincing account than it receives from the BBC Philharmonic and Vernon

Handley or better-recorded sound. An enterprising release.

Coleridge-Taylor, Samuel
(1875–1912)

4 Characteristic waltzes, Op. 22; Gipsy suite, Op. 20; Hiawatha overture, Op. 30; Othello suite, Op. 79; Petite suite de concert, Op. 77; Romance of the prairie lilies, Op. 39.
*** Marco Polo Dig. 8.223516 [id.]. Dublin RTE Concert O, Leaper.

It would be sad to think that Coleridge-Taylor is only remembered for his *Hiawatha* trilogy (of which the charmingly melodramatic overture is included here). He wrote much delightful orchestral music, the most famous being the charming *Petite suite de concert*. It opens robustly, before turning into a graceful waltz; the two central movements are reflectively pastoral, and the suite ends in a lively Tarantella.

The composer's feeling for the genre is also apparent in the *4 Characteristic waltzes*. Each is nicely coloured: there is a nostalgic *Valse Bohémienne*, a countrified *Valse rustique* (the oboe so easily conjuring up the countryside), a stately *Valse de la Reine*, and a lively *Valse Mauresque*.

The *Gipsy suite* is a piquantly coloured four-movement work of considerable appeal, whilst the *Othello suite*, beginning with a lively dance, has an engaging *Willow song* and ends with a stirring *Military march*. Performances and recording are excellent, and this is altogether a winning if essentially lightweight collection, perhaps more for aficionados than the general collector.

Copland, Aaron (1900–90)

(i) Appalachian spring; Billy the Kid (complete ballet); (ii) Dance symphony; (iii) Danzón Cubano; El salón México; (ii) Fanfare for the common man; The Red Pony (suite); (i) Rodeo (complete ballet).
(B) *** EMI Dig. Double Fforte CZS5 73653-2 (2) [CDFB 73676]. (i) St Louis SO, Slatkin; (ii) Mexico City PO, Bátiz; (iii) Dallas SO, Mata.

A first-class collection. Slatkin's was the first complete recording of *Billy the Kid*, which includes about ten minutes of extra music omitted from the usual suite – including two delightful waltzes. The complete ballet *Rodeo* consists essentially of the usual four colourful movements, though here a piano interlude is included (an old upright piano of 'doubtful' lineage was used for this recording, according to the original booklet). Both are given terrific performances under Slatkin, and the sound is superb. Bátiz's orchestra doesn't have the technical

excellence of Slatkin's, but he is a lively and persuasive interpreter of Copland. The *Dance symphony* is well done, though the ensemble is not as precise as it could be. *The Red Pony* suite – a colourful and nostalgic score for Lewis Milestone's film, is among the most endearing lighter scores Copland wrote and is very enjoyable. Mata's Dallas performances of *Danzón Cubano* and *El salón México* are as good as any – brilliant performances in demonstration sound. In every sense this set is a splendid bargain.

(i) Appalachian spring; Billy the Kid (suite); (ii) El salón México; (i) Rodeo: 4 dance episodes.
(M) *** RCA High Performance 09026 63467-2 [id.]. (i) Phd. O, Ormandy; (ii) Dallas SO, Mata.

An excellent Copland anthology, reissued on RCA's High Performance label. Under Ormandy the playing of the Philadelphia Orchestra is wonderfully rich and refined and of course totally idiomatic in this repertoire, even if his *Appalachian spring* does not surpass the composer's own on the same label. The 1969 recording lacks the impact of rival versions, but is fully acceptable. Mata's performances date from 1978 and there's nothing to grumble about sonically at all. Nor is there about the performances: they are lively and enjoyable and show just how good the Dallas Orchestra was at that time.

Appalachian spring (ballet suite: original chamber version); Billy the Kid (ballet suite); Fanfare for the common man; Music for the theatre.
(M) **(*) Classic fm Dig. 76505 570362 [id.]. Eos O, Jonathan Sheffer.

The Eos is a chamber-sized orchestra, made up of first-class players, resident in New York. They have already given us an outstanding Gershwin CD including the *Piano concerto* and *Rhapsody in blue* (with Michael Boriskin), which received a ◉ in our main volume (Classic fm 76505 57012-2). Here they are custom-built for the original score (thirteen instrumentalists) of *Appalachian spring*, which, truthfully recorded, is more striking for its rhythmic zest and vivid woodwind detail than the richer sweep of string tone which comes with a full orchestral version like Hickox's below. The same approach gives the sharpest focus to the popular rhythmic elements of *Music for the Theatre* and the *Billy the Kid* ballet suite, where the gentle nostalgia of *Prairie night* and *Billy's death* are more gently caught by the small string group. The *Celebration sequence* is very wittily pointed, while the final view of *The open prairie* certainly does not lack evocative power; but again some might prefer a more lavish patina of orchestral tone.

Appalachian spring (complete: original chamber score); Billy the Kid: excerpts: Waltz; Prairie

night; Celebration dance. Down a country lane; 3 Latin American dances; Music for the theatre; Quiet city; (i) *Old American songs* (sets 1–2); (ii) *8 Poems of Emily Dickinson.*
(B) *** Teldec/Warner Dig. 3984 28169-2 (2)
   [id.]. Saint Paul Chamber Orchestra, Hugh
   Wolff; with (i) Thomas Hampson; (ii) Dawn
   Upshaw.

All this is vintage Copland and this splendidly recorded Ultima anthology is very desirable indeed. Hugh Wolff and his fine Saint Paul Orchestra are completely at home here and it is good to have the original version of *Appalachian spring* played (and recorded) so beautifully. The composer's markings of the last two sections – 'like a prayer' and 'very calm' – are perfectly evoked. *Quiet city* brings some impressive solo playing from cor anglais (Thomas Tempel) and trumpet (Gary Bordner), but here the textural balance is less delicately atmospheric and less well integrated than in the famous Marriner version. It is good to have the composer's own scoring of his engaging *Down a country lane* (originally a piano piece). However, the highlights are the two superbly sung song cycles. We have previously had fine versions of the *Old American songs*, but Thomas Hampson is in a special class. His noble delivery of *At the river* followed by the deliciously lighthearted *Ching-a-ring* is unforgettable. So is Dawn Upshaw's eloquent set of the *Emily Dickinson poems*, now easily the finest on record, full of character, and with much beauty of tone and line. She relishes the words theatrically (*Going to heaven* is marvellously sung), yet like Hampson she can both ravish and tickle the ear by turns. The closing song, *The Chariot*, has a touching simplicity. It is a pity that only three excerpts were included from *Billy the Kid* (there was plenty of room on the disc for the whole ballet!), but they make an enjoyable postlude. Very highly recommended.

Appalachian spring (ballet suite); *Fanfare for the common man.*
(M) *** Penguin Classics Decca Dig. 460 656-2
   [id.]. Detroit SO, Dorati – BARBER: *Adagio for strings*; BERNSTEIN: *Candide overture; West Side story dances.* **(*)

Dorati's *Appalachian spring* (the suite, not the complete score) is among the finest and most brilliant versions on record, and the *Fanfare* makes a superb impact, both helped by the expansive Detroit ambience. However, the Baltimore performances which act as couplings are at a lower level of tension.

(i) *Appalachian spring* (ballet suite); (ii) *Fanfare for the common man;* (i; iii) *Quiet city;* (iv) *Piano sonata.*
(M) **(*) Virgin Classics VM5 61702-2 [id.]. (i) City of L. Sinf, Hickox; (ii) LPO, Carl Davis; (iii) with Crispian Steele-Perkins, Helen McQueen; (iv) Peter Lawson.

It is easy to enjoy Richard Hickox's warmly atmospheric account of Copland's greatest ballet score. The full orchestral version is made seductively opulent by the spacious recording, and the same comment applies to the rich textures of *Quiet city*, embroidered by first-class trumpet and cor anglais soloists who are perhaps a shade too forwardly balanced. Yet the principal attraction in this 'centenary tribute' is the inclusion of the rarely recorded *Piano sonata*. Peter Lawson's highly concentrated, yet essentially cool reading, is rhythmically strong but emotionally spare until the soliloquizing closing sequence when the music mellows into a trance-like nostalgia and the closing diminuendo is touchingly sustained.

(i) *Clarinet concerto. Music for the theatre; Music for movies;* (ii) *Quiet city.*
**(*) Music Masters Dig. 7005-2 [id.]. (i) William Blount; O of St Luke's, Dennis Russell Davies; (ii) with Chris Gekker, Stephen Taylor.

Four key Copland works, which make an admirably balanced programme. The more vibrant *Music for the theatre* with its brash *Prologue* and *Dance* and ironic *Burlesque* nicely offsetting the mellower New England evocations of *Music for movies*, although here *Sunday traffic* makes another lively contrast and the *Threshing machines* are very busy too. *Quiet city* is beautifully evoked and William Blount is a rich-toned soloist in the *Clarinet concerto*, with spacious, long-drawn phrasing in the opening movement, which some might find too languid, contrasting with the brilliant central cadenza and roisterously jazzy finale. This is a reissue of a 1988 CD, but the vivid projection and warmth of the sound suggest more modern provenance.

Film music: *The Heiress* (suite, reconstructed Arnold Freed); *Music for movies; Our Town; Prairie journey (Music for radio); The Red Pony* (suite).
*** RCA Dig. 09026 61699-2 [id.]. Saint Louis SO, Leonard Slatkin.

Copland's film score for *The Red Pony* opens with a harmonic/rhythmic sequence that is wholly characteristic. It is one of his most delightful works, with its series of charming folksy vignettes, all warmly characterized, following the film narrative. The music for *The Heiress* dates from the same year (1948) and is more emotionally plangent, distinctly Hollywoodian in its sweeps of string tone, but Copland also slips into the score a hint of Martini's *Plaisir d'amour* to represent the amorous suitor. The present continuous selection is neatly woven together by Arnold Freed. *Music for movies* (which draws primarily on the films *The City* and *Of Mice and Men*) is a series of pastoral evocations, some quite lively, set in the New England countryside, while the shorter piece derived from *Our Town* has a similar warm nostalgic feeling. All this music is appealingly melodic, and is orchestrated and harmonized in the now familiar manner which we associate with the early ballet music. Copland seldom used actual folk songs, but created ideas that fell naturally into their melodic and harmonic mould. The closing *Prairie journey* (1936), commissioned as 'Music for Radio' by CBS, is cast in a single vibrant movement built from nagging ostinatos, but with nostalgic interludes. In its balletic way it anticipates the scores of *Rodeo* and *Billy the Kid*. All this music is played with great affection and the most vivid colouring by the excellent Saint Louis Orchestra under the ever persuasive Leonard Slatkin, with the glowing ambience of Powell Symphony Hall adding much to the listener's pleasure.

PIANO MUSIC

Piano sonata; 4 Piano blues; Scherzo humoristique: The cat and the mouse.
*** Nimbus Dig. NI 5585 [id.]. Mark Anderson –
GERSHWIN: *3 Preludes; Arrangements of songs; An American in Paris.* ***

Mark Anderson gives an outstanding account of the *Piano sonata*, making it seem emotionally warmer and less texturally and harmonically spare than usual. His reading will surely make new friends for the work, it is 'freely expressive' (as the first movement is marked by the composer), and with the restless rhythmic mood of the central *Vivace* spontaneously caught, with even a brief jazz inflection. The closing *Andante sostenuto* is movingly tapered down and leaves the listener aware that this is a remarkably individual and original work. The *Four piano blues* are in Copland's easily accessible style and are also very well characterized, while the witty portrait of *Le chat et la souris* makes a brilliant encore for what is a live recital in Nimbus's own concert hall.

OPERA

The Tender Land (arr. Sidlin; complete).
**(*) Koch Dig. 3-7480-2 (2) [id.]. Suzan Hanson, Milagro Vargas, Robert MacNeil, Douglas Webster, Richard Zeller, Amy Hansen, Third Angle New Music Ens., Murry Sidlin.

When the conductor Murry Sidlin approached Aaron Copland suggesting that he should arrange this opera for an ensemble of thirteen instruments, 'achieving a Copland sound similar to *Appalachian Spring*', he received an immediate reply – 'What a good idea!' The aim was to carry out more effectively the composer's original plan to provide an all-American opera suitable for music academies and conservatories. That is the version recorded here, which in default of a current recording of the original is welcome for offering a fresh, sensitive

reading of a work which matches the simple plot with music in Copland's most open-air American mood. Sidlin has modified the score in other ways too – with the composer's approval – adapting the Introduction to the original Act III as a prelude to the whole work, and inserting arrangements of two of Copland's Old American folk-songs – *Zion's Walls* and *Long time ago* – in the party scene of Act II. In that, he follows Copland's own procedure in rejigging other Old American folk-songs in such numbers as the *Square Dance – Stomp your foot.*

Though it would be better still to have the original restored to the catalogue, this is an enjoyable, unpretentious reading of the revised score, with a cast of fresh young singers, well supported by the ensemble. This is a gentle rather than fiery opera, which is well suited to listening on disc. The intimate, relatively dry acoustic is apt for the work as arranged.

Corelli, Arcangelo (1653–1713)

Oboe concerto (arr. Barbirolli).
*** Dutton Lab./Barbirolli Soc. CDSJB 1016 [id.]. Evelyn Rothwell, Hallé O, Sir John Barbirolli – HAYDN; MARCELLO: *Oboe concertos.* *** (with Recital: C. P. E. BACH; LOEILLET; TELEMANN: *Sonatas* etc. ** – see Instrumental Recitals below).

Barbirolli's *concerto* is cunningly arranged from a trio sonata and in its present form it makes one of the most enchanting works in the oboe repertoire. The performance here is treasurable. The opening, with its beautiful Handelian theme, is shaped with perfect dignity, and the gracious, stately allegro that follows has a touch of gossamer from the soloist. The finale is no less delectable, and the clear, natural recording projects the music admirably.

Couperin, Armand-Louis (1725–1789)

Pièces de clavecin: L'Affligée; Allemande; L'Arlequine ou la Adam; La Blanchet; La de Boisgelou; La du Breüil; La Chéron; Courante la de Croissy; L'Enjouée; La Foucquet; Gavottes 1 & 2; La Grégoire; L'Intrépide; Menuets 1 & 2; La Turpin; La Seimillante ou la Joly; Les tendres sentimens; La Victoire.
**(*) CPO Dig. CPO 999 312-2 [id.]. Harald Hoeren (harpsichord).

Born during the reign of Louis XV, Armand-Louis Couperin died only a few months before the French revolution. His grandfather was the brother of Louis Couperin. His father, Nicolas, a cousin of Couperin-le-grand, was the organist at Saint-Gervais, to which position Armand-Louis succeeded on his death, ultimately rising to organist at the Royal Chapel at

Versailles. His *Pièces de clavecin* appeared in 1751 and some, such as the *Allemande* and *La Grégoire a* show a debt to Rameau but others such as *L'Affligée* and *La Chéron* are more forward-looking. Harald Hoeren, a pupil of Kenneth Gilbert and Gustav Leonhart, plays an instrument by Klaus Ahrend based on Flemish models of the 1750s. He is a persuasive artist, though he is not helped by the rather close recording balance. Satisfactory results can be obtained by a low-level setting of the volume control.

Pièces de clavecin: L'Affligée; La du Breüil; Les tendres sentimens.
**(*) BIS Dig. CD 982 [id.]. Asami Hirosawa (harpsichord) – François COUPERIN; Louis COUPERIN: *Pièces de clavecin.* **(*)

Another thunderous harpsichord so closely balanced that immediate action is called for to reduce the level setting. No quarrels however with Ms Hirosawa's playing, which has great expressive feeling. Her account of *L'Affligée* has greater poignancy than Harald Hoeren's and if the volume is turned down a satisfactory result can be secured.

Couperin, François (1668–1733)

Les Goûts-réunis: Nouveaux concerts: Concertos Nos. 5 in F; 6 in B flat; 7 in G min.; 8 in G; 9 in E; 10 in A min.; 11 in C min.; 12 in A; 13 in G; 14 in D min.
(B) **(*) DG Double 459 484-2 (2) [id.]. Brandis, Aurèle Nicolet, Sax, Holliger, Ulsamer, Strehl, Jaccottet.

Like the more famous *Concerts royaux*, the *Nouveaux concerts* comprise nearly all first-rate music, and this reissue does justice to their excellence. This present set, using modern instruments, has lively musicality to commend it and the recording is clearly focused and natural; indeed, it sounds highly realistic in its latest bargain format.

   If there are some reservations, it is because these artists do not seek to find the music's peculiarly French flavour. *Notes inégales* are not always observed and there are inconsistencies in matters of ornamentation. But the non-specialist listener will find that there is much to delight the ear, for the playing itself is sensitive and alert.

Pièces de clavecin, Book 3: Ordre 13.
**(*) BIS Dig. CD 982 [id.]. Asami Hirosawa (harpsichord) – Armand-Louis COUPERIN; Louis COUPERIN: *Pièces de clavecin.* **(*)

Asami Hirosawa studied with Masaaki Suzuki and other well-established figures such as Bob van Asperen and Lars Ulrik Mortensen. On this CD she couples the marvellous *Treizième Ordre* with two of Louis Couperin's *Suites* and three pieces by Armand-Louis. She is thoroughly inside the French

style and shows a natural feeling for its rhythmic flexibility. A very close microphone balance produces pretty deafening results but a drastic reduction of volume makes for more satisfactory listening.

VOCAL MUSIC

Leçons de ténèbres pour le Mercredi Saint; Magnificat; Motets: Laetentur coeli; Victoria! Christo resurgenti.
** O-L Dig. 466 776-2 [id.]. Les Talens Lyriques, Rousset.

Couperin's first two *Leçons de ténèbres pour le Mercredi Saint* were written for solo soprano, the third for two voices. One would have thought that the present performances would have been ideal, with two excellent soloists and the accompaniments directed by Christophe Rousset. Sandrine Piau and Véronique Gens take turns in the first two *Leçons* and match their voices convincingly in the third, and later in the *Magnificat* and motets. Yet the result is disappointingly cool and chaste and curiously unmoving. The most effective piece here is the fervent closing Easter motet, *Victoria! Christo resurgenti*, where the *Alléluias* have real emotional resonance.

Leçons de Ténèbres pour le Mercredi Saint Nos.1–3; Quatre Versets du Motet.
*** Erato/Warner Dig. 0630 17067-2 [id.]. Sophie Daneman, Patricia Petibon, Les Arts Florissants, William Christie.

The *Leçons de Ténèbres* are well represented on CD but this newcomer with Sophie Daneman, Patricia Petibon and Les Arts Florissants must probably rank as the best. They are among the most intense and inward-looking of Couperin's works and are heard to striking effect in these intimate and poignant performances. The first two *Leçons* are divided between the two sopranos, who join together for the last. As the *Trois Leçons de ténèbres* take less than forty minutes, the *Quatre Versets du Motet* (eight minutes) make an ungenerous fill-up. However, these are exquisite performances and are beautifully recorded.

Messe pour les couvents.
(BB) *** Arte Nova Dig. 74321 65413-2 [id.]. Ens. Canticum, Christoph Erkens; Helmut Deutsch (Koenig organ, St Avold, France) – MARCHAND: *Te Deum.* ***

Couperin's two organ masses, one for the parishes and the other for the monastery chapels, are both interspersed with chant. The *Messe pour les couvents* is well represented on CD but not at bargain price. Helmut Deutsch came to international attention after winning the First Prize at the 1993 Franz Liszt Competition in Budapest. He uses the Koenig organ at the former St Nabor Abbey in

St Avold, France, modelled on a 1776 instrument by Mercadier de Belesta. Very impressive and vivid recorded sound, and fine playing. Arte Nova give details of the registration of the organ but are not wholly scrupulous elsewhere. Although the presentation gives Couperin's date of death accurately, the label gives it as being between 1708 and 1712!

Couperin, Louis (c. 1626–61)

Pièces de clavecin: Suites in A min. & C.
**(*) BIS Dig. CD 982 [id.]. Asami Hirosawa (harpsichord) – Armand-Louis COUPERIN; François COUPERIN: *Pièces de clavecin.* **(*)

Asami Hirosawa couples two of Louis Couperin's suites with pieces by Armand-Louis, and the *Treizième Ordre* by Couperin-le-grand. She is an impressive advocate, admirably flexible in such pieces as the *Prélude à l'imitation de M. Froberger.* We occasionally felt the need for greater variety of colour, though in this respect she is not helped by a very close microphone balance.

Couperin, Marc Roger Normand (1663–1734)

Livre de tablature de clavecin (c. 1695): complete.
*** Hyperion Dig. CDA 67164 [id.]. Davitt Moroney (harpsichord).

An outstanding find, Marc Roger Normand's book contains fifty-seven pieces – many attributed to other composers including Chambonnières, Le Bègue and Lully (which he arranged from the music of stage works). His choice is unerringly perceptive. Virtually all these miniatures are very personable, especially those by Paul de la Pierre and members of his family. Normand was a first cousin of François Couperin and dropped his father's name in favour of that shared by his three more-famous uncles. He was clearly a first-rate musician and no doubt collected these pieces to play himself. Apart from his own works he includes an extended set of variants (twenty-seven couplets) on the famous *Folies d'Espagnes.* Moroney is a persuasive advocate. He plays with style and spontaneity and consistently entertains the listener. He uses a splendid Italian virginal dating from the seventeenth century, which is beautifully recorded. If you enjoy the harpsichord and the musical period this collection can be very highly recommended.

Creston, Paul (1906–85)

Symphonies Nos. 1, Op. 20; 2, Op. 35; 3 (Three Mysteries), Op. 48.
(BB) *** Naxos Dig. 8.559034 [id.]. Ukraine National SO, Theodore Kuchar.

Paul Creston was among the most approachable of American symphonists, as is illustrated by these first three of his four works in this genre. The *First,* dating from 1940, is exuberantly colourful and strongly rhythmic with clean-cut themes. The titles of the four compact movements – *With Majesty, With Humour, With Serenity* and *With Gaiety* – reflect the openness of the emotions. No. 2 (1944) is much darker, with each of its two substantial movements divided in two, each moving from darkness towards a lightened mood. No. 3 (1950) outlines the life of Christ in its three symphonic sections, with a peaceful opening, almost pastoral, representing the Nativity and leading to a joyful allegro. The second movement, representing the Crucifixion, is a heartfelt lament, avoiding bitterness and anger, before the Resurrection finale, where Creston is at his most specifically American, almost Copland-like, with jagged syncopations leading on to a triumphant close. The Ukraine Orchestra, very well rehearsed, plays with warmth and an idiomatic flair surprising from a non-American band, and is very well recorded.

Crusell, Bernhard (1775–1838)

Clarinet quartets Nos. 1 in E flat, Op. 2; 2 in C min., Op. 4; 3 in D, Op. 7.
(B) *** Hyperion Helios CDH 55031 [id.]. Thea King, Allegri Qt (members).

These are captivatingly sunny works, given superb performances, vivacious and warmly sympathetic, Thea King's tone is positively luscious and the sound is generally excellent. The CD transfer is highly successful and its migration to the bargain-price Helios label makes it even more attractive.

Divertimento in C, Op. 9.
(B) **(*) Hyperion Helios CDH 55015 [id.]. Sarah Francis, Allegri Qt – KREUTZER: *Grand quintet*; REICHA: *Quintet.* **(*)

Crusell has something of a light industry at Hyperion, who have recorded much of his output, including the delightful clarinet concertos. His music has charm and grace, and the *Divertimento,* Op. 9 is no exception. The performance here is nicely played and recorded, and the couplings are attractive; it is now offered at bargain-price, but the CD plays for under 50 minutes.

Dallapiccola, Luigi (1904–75)

Tartiniana for violin and orchestra.
(M) (***) Sony mono SMK 60725 [id.]. Ruth Posselt, Columbia SO, Bernstein – LOPATNIKOFF: *Concertino;* SHAPERO: *Symphony.* (***)

Dallapiccola's *Tartiniana* was composed at

Tanglewood and commissioned by Koussevitzky. The composer spoke of his stay at Tanglewood as being 'a particularly happy period in my life', and reworks themes from Tartini's sonatas in a refreshing neoclassical style. The language is neoclassic and diatonic. Good playing from Ruth Posselt and Bernstein's orchestra, and the 1953 mono recording comes up well in this well-transferred and intelligently planned compilation.

D'Astorga, Emanuele (c. 1680–1757)

Stabat Mater.
*** Hyperion Dig. CDA 67108 [id.]. Susan Gritton, Susan Bickley, Paul Agnew, Peter Harvey, King's Consort Ch., King's Consort, Robert King – BOCCHERINI: *Stabat Mater.* ***

Emanuele d'Astorga's *Stabat Mater* predates Boccherini's – with which it is coupled – by nearly a century and, unlike that work (and the Pergolesi setting on which it is based), is written like a miniature oratorio with soloists and chorus. The chorus opens and closes the work – the opening with touching melancholy, but the closing *Christe quam sit hinc exire* much more upbeat. In between, the various solos and duets are expressively quite intense, and overall this is a remarkable accomplished and rewarding piece, especially when sung as eloquently as it is here with excellent soloists and a fine choral contribution, all very well recorded.

Debussy, Claude (1862–1918)

6 Epigraphs antiques (orch. Ansermet); *Estampes: Pagodes* (orch. André Caplet); *Printemps* (suite symphonique; original 1887 choral version, reconstructed Emil de Cou); *Prélude: La puerta del vino* (orch. Henri Büsser); *Suite bergamasque* (orch. Gustave Cloez & André Caplet).
*** Arabesque Dig. Z 6734 [id.]. San Francisco Ballet O, Emil de Cou; (i) with soloists and Ch.

A fascinating disc, and most fascinating of all is the original choral version of *Printemps*, which sounds positively voluptuous in this superbly rich recording. When entering the work for the Prix de Rome, Debussy told the judging panel that he had orchestrated it in 1887, but that the score was lost in a publishing-house fire, and he submitted instead a format for piano and chorus. (It was turned down, with Saint-Saëns, who was one of the judges, commenting: 'One does not write for orchestra in six sharps.')
In 1913 Henri Büsser orchestrated the piece from the four-hand piano score, omitting the vocal material and 36 bars of music, including 12 bars of orchestral transition to the final choral entry (which

when reinstated, as here, reminds one of Ravel's *Daphnis et Chloé*). Emil de Cou has gone back to the full original manuscript and provided his own highly convincing re-scoring. The result will intrigue all Debussians and its seductive impact will surely thrill all listeners.
The orchestrated piano pieces are also very successful. In the *Suite bergamasque, Clair de lune* sounds lovely on strings, but both the *Minuet* and *Passepied* too are effective in orchestral dress. Ansermet himself recorded his fastidiously scored *Epigraphs antiques* (originally written for piano duet) and one would have liked rather more of the sharply-etched detail for which his version was famous.
But Emil de Cou goes for atmospheric evocation and certainly No. 2 (*Pour le tombeau sans nom*), with its instant reminder of *Images*, is very beguiling, and the whole set is made to sound lustrous in its impressionistic colouring. The San Francisco Ballet Orchestra plays very well indeed, and the spacious acoustic provides an impressively full and naturally balanced sound picture.

Images.
(M) **(*) DG 463 615-2 [id.]. Boston SO, Thomas – TCHAIKOVSKY: *Symphony No. 1 in G min.***(*).

Michael Tilson Thomas's set of the *Images* dates from the early 1970s. The approach is youthfully impulsive and enjoyable and conveys the atmosphere of *Gigues* and the languor of the middle movement of *Ibéria* better than many eminent rivals. It is not a top choice, but is still thoroughly recommendable.

Images: Ibéria. La Mer (with rehearsal); (i) *Nocturnes.*
(**) DG 453 194-2 (3 + 1) [id.]. Stuttgart SWR RO, Celibidache; (i) with SWR Female Ch. – RAVEL: *Alborada; Daphnis,* etc. **

As so often with Celibidache, attention focuses primarily on the conductor and the refinement of sonority he can command. And he does produce a beautiful sound from the Stuttgart Orchestra, who give a slow-motion account of the three *Nocturnes*, taking well over half-an-hour. *Fêtes* is beautifully controlled, but Celibidache dawdles over *Nuages*, taking some 11 minutes, and a spectacular 14 for *Sirènes*, about twice its usual length! His *Ibéria* is almost as ruinous and *Les parfums de la nuit* at almost 13 minutes is intolerable. However, it is not only a matter of the static tempi; the affected phrasing is even more unpleasing. The Ravel items are generally less offensive but for many the Debussy will be a travesty. It is only fair to add that Celibidache's admirers, who include many respected musicians and critics, respond positively. However, without disrespect to them, it is true to say that if we awarded *minus* stars and 🌑s, this would be in line for a generous helping. The recordings come from the 1970s and are not always as successfully balanced as is usual from Südwestfunk.

Jeux; La Mer; (i) *Nocturnes.*
** RCA Dig. 74321 64616-2 [id.]. VPO, Lorin Maazel; (i) with Schoenberg Ch.

Readers who heard Simon Rattle and the Vienna Philharmonic in the 1999 Proms will need no reminder that the orchestra is superb in French repertoire. They play magnificently for Lorin Maazel, though the readings are not so memorable as to displace Haitink in *Jeux* and the *Nocturnes*, or Karajan in *La Mer*, not forgetting the likes of Reiner and Münch. Nor, strangely enough, is the recording particularly outstanding, though it is very good. In short, there are no serious reservations but at the same time there is nothing special here.

La Mer; (i) *Nocturnes. Prélude à l'après-midi d'un faune.*
(M) *** Decca Penguin Classics 460 636-2 [id.]. O de Paris, Barenboim; (i) with Ch.

This is one of Barenboim's best records. His account of *La Mer* is highly individual in choice of tempo but has great atmosphere as well as electricity. The *Jeux de vagues* reaches a superb climax and the finale is no less exciting. The same comments apply to the *Nocturnes*: although they have not the subtlety of the finest versions, they make up for it in sheer fervour – *Sirènes* develops a feeling of soaring ecstasy and the closing pages with the chorus are very beautiful. If the *Prélude* is a bit too languorous, it is still very good indeed. The 1978, DG recordings are excellent (the *Prélude* is a digital recording from 1981), and the personal essay is by Marina Warner. A winner in the Penguin Classics series.

Nocturnes. (Nuages; Fêtes; (i) *Sirènes).*
(B)*** Decca Penguin Classics Dig. 460 649-2 [id.]. Montreal SO, Dutoit; (i) with female ch.
– RAVEL: *Le tombeau de Couperin; La Valse;* SATIE: *3 Gymnopédies.****

If the programme suits, this makes a recommendable alternative to the Penguin Classics disc above, conducted by Barenboim. Dutoit's *Nocturnes* have a persuasive ebb and flow of languorous rubato, while the glittering processional in *Fêtes* is sharply rhythmic. The atmospheric recording is well up to the expected high Montreal standard and the couplings are equally fine.

Prélude à l'après-midi d'un faune; La cathédrale engloutie (orch. Stokowski).
(M) (**(*)) Cala mono CACD 0526 [id.]. NBC SO, Stokowski – GOULD: *2 Marches for orchestra;* HOLST: *The Planets.* (***)

The *Prélude à l'après-midi d'un faune* derives from

a NBC broadcast dating from March 1943. Apart from a couple of blemishes (the opening has a fair amount of swish), the sound is acceptable, but the performance is more than that: it is individual and compelling, with the faune's reverie celebrated with some particularly lush string playing. The same comments apply to Stokowski's superb account of his transcription of *La cathédrale engloutie*, dating from a February 1944 broadcast, but sounding rather shrill. There are some technical faults: a sudden brief drop in level quite early on, some pitch fluctuation, etc., but the magnetism of the performance is never in doubt. Two attractive fill-ups for an individual account of *The Planets*.

Première rapsodie (for clarinet and orchestra).
*** EMI Dig. CDC5 56832-2 [id.]. Sabine Meyer, Berlin PO, Abbado – MOZART: *Clarinet concerto;* TAKEMITSU: *Fantasma/cantos.* ***

This evocative Debussy work reveals to the utmost Sabine Meyer's special gift for using the clarinet seductively, drawing on a ravishing tonal range and creating a dream-like world of sound. Not only is this a beautiful performance, it is a dramatic one too, with high contrasts underlined, helped by immaculate playing from the Berlin Philharmonic under Abbado. An unusual but magical coupling for the Mozart masterpiece.

CHAMBER MUSIC

(i; ii) *Danses sacrée et profane;* (iii; iv) *Cello sonata;* (i; v; vi) *Sonata for flute, viola and harp;* (vii) *String quartet;* (vi) *Syrinx;* (viii; iv) *Violin sonata.*
(M) **(*) Calliope Dig./Analogue CAL 3822.4 (3) [id.]. (i) Pierre; (ii) La Follia Ens.; (iii) Pernoo; (iv) Rigollet; (v) Xuereb; (vi) Beaumadier; (vii), (viii) Roussin – RAVEL: *Chamber music; Chansons madécasses.* **

The *String quartet in G minor* was recorded in 1972 and very good it is too. The three sonatas are digital and recent and, like the *Danses sacrée et profane* and *Syrinx*, come from 1997. They are very well played, though none would necessarily be a first choice when the likes of Grumiaux, Kyung-Wha Chung and Cho-Liang Lin are available playing the *Violin sonata,* or Rostropovich and Britten performing the *Cello sonata*. A serviceable recommendation all the same.

Piano trio in G (1880).
*** Hyperion Dig. CDA 67114 [id.]. Florestan Trio – FAURE; RAVEL: *Piano trios.* ***

Debussy's *Piano trio*, a product of his teenage years, may reveal few signs of his mature style but it makes a very apt and delightful coupling for the Ravel and Fauré works, representing different periods of each composer's career. The Scherzo brings fascinating echoes of Mendelssohn, while the surprising similarities with Puccini may reflect a common influence from Massenet rather than anything direct. With personnel drawn from the piano quartet group Domus, led by the pianist Susan Tomes, the Florestans follow up the success of their prizewinning Schumann disc for Hyperion in a strong and urgent reading, at once highly polished and flexibly expressive. Vivid sound.

String quartet in G min., Op. 10.
❀ (M) *** DG 463 082-2 [id.]. Melos Qt –
RAVEL: *String quartet.* *** ❀

This outstanding recording was made in 1979 and is in every way a great performance. The playing of the Melos Quartet is distinguished by perfect intonation and ensemble, scrupulous accuracy in the observance of dynamic markings, a natural sense of flow and great tonal beauty. It would be difficult to imagine a finer account of the Debussy than this and the sound in its latest Galleria format remains very impressive.

Syrinx; Bilitis (arr. Lenski). (i) *La plus que lente.*
*** EMI CDC5 56982-2 [id.]. Emmanuel Pahud;
(i) Stephen Kovacevich – PROKOFIEV:
Flute sonata, Op. 94; RAVEL: *Chansons Madécasses.* ***

Syrinx has rarely sounded more erotic yet other-worldly. The *Bilitis,* incidentally, is not the *Chansons de Bilitis* song-cycle of 1897 but a transcription by Karl Lenski of the *Six épigraphes antiques* for piano duet (1914). They derive from the incidental music Debussy composed in 1901 for two flutes, two harps and celeste, to accompany the recitation of the Pierre Louÿs poems. For the sixth movement Lenski returned directly to this original 1901 score. Emmanuel Pahud, first flute of the Berliner Philharmoniker, is sensitive both to every nuance and dynamic subtlety and to the spirit of this highly effective transcription. Stephen Kovacevich gives a beautifully characterized account of Debussy's satire of a salon waltz, *La plus que lente,* as good as any and better than most.

PIANO MUSIC

Ballade; Berceuse héroïque; Children's corner; Danse (Tarantelle styrienne); Elégie; Etudes, Books I & II; Etude retrouvée (reconstructed Roy Howatt); *Hommage à Haydn; Images I & II; Mazurka; Page d'album; Le petit nègre; La plus que lente; Suite bergamasque; Valse romantique.*
*** Decca Dig. 460 247-2 (2) [id.]. Jean-Yves Thibaudet.

This completes Jean-Yves Thibaudet's survey of Debussy's solo piano music (Volume 1 is on Decca 452 022-2) and Debussy-playing doesn't come any better than this. As before, these performances are full of evocative atmosphere (especially the

Images), and ever-imaginative in their infinite variety of colour and dynamic.

Even the early pieces, especially the gentle *Ballade*, have an added poetic dimension, and the more familiar works, *Children's corner* and *Suite bergamasque* sound wonderfully fresh. The quirky vignettes like *La petit nègre, Hommage à Haydn* and the charmingly brief *Page d'album* are delightfully done, and the sombre *Berceuse héroïque* is darkly memorable. But most impressive are the *Etudes*, unsurpassed on record in their strong characterization, flair and virtuosity – not even by Mitsuko Uchida's famous Philips set – and with Decca's recording so real and immediate, they project with vivid spontaneity as at a live recital. A clear first choice among modern digital recordings of this totally absorbing repertoire.

Estampes; Préludes, Books 1–2; Images: Reflets dans l'eau.
(B)**(*) EMI Dig. Double Fforte CZS5 73656-2
(2) [CDFB 73656]. Youri Egorov – CHOPIN:
Recital. *(*)

Egorov is much happier in the Debussy than in the Chopin on this CD. He gives performances of commanding keyboard technique, exquisite refinement, and atmosphere. The recording is good, a shade reverberant perhaps, but the Chopin coupling is a handicap.

Préludes, Books 1–2 (complete).
❀ (M) *** EMI mono CDM5 67233-2 [567262].
Walter Gieseking.

Gieseking's classic set of both Books of the Debussy *Préludes* now takes its rightful place as one of EMI's 'Great Recordings of the Century' and now has proper documentation. The current remastering again confirms the natural realism of the 1953/4 Abbey Road recording, with Book 1 produced by Geraint Jones and Book 2 by Walter Legge, although there is a touch of hardness on *forte* passages.

Préludes, Book 1; L'isle joyeuse.
*(*) DG Dig. 445 187-2 [id.]. Maurizio Pollini.

Maurizio Pollini may be Maurizio Pollini, but only 43 minutes is on the stingy side for a full-price disc. The *Danseuses de Delphes* is ponderous, *Les sons et les parfums tournent dans l'air du soir* could have more atmosphere, as indeed could *Les collines d'Anacapri,* whose climaxes are hard. *Ce qu'a vu le vent d'ouest* sounds as if he is attacking Rachmaninov or Prokofiev. There are good things too alongside and the pianism and control are masterly (as in *Des pas sur la neige*) but generally speaking one remains outside Debussy's world. The recording was made in Munich's Herkulesaal and has abundant clarity and presence. However, Walter Gieseking's mono recording is pretty impressive and he offers both Books of *Préludes* (see above) as does Martin Tirimo, whose playing is very fine indeed and who will probably be a first choice for those wanting a modern digital set (Carlton 30367 0079-2).

VOCAL MUSIC

Mélodies: *La Belle au bois dormant; Beau soir; 3 Chansons de Bilitis; Fêtes galantes I; Fleur des blés; Noël des enfants qui n'ont plus de maison; Nuit d'étoiles.*
*** Virgin/EMI Dig. VC5 45360-2 [id.].
  Véronique Gens, Roger Vignoles – FAURE;
  POULENC: *Mélodies.* ***

Véronique Gens gives an impressive and imaginative account of these songs, allowing Debussy's subtle art to register without any expressive exaggeration. She certainly makes a beautiful sound and has the benefit of Roger Vignoles' intelligent support, and excellent and natural recording.

Mélodies: *Dans la forêt du charme et de l'enchantement, Op. 36/2; Fêtes galantes: I; Nuits blanches; Proses lyriques; Quatre mélodies, Op. 13.*
*(*) DG Dig. 459 682-2 [id.]. Christine Schäfer, Irwin Gage; (i) with Stella Doufexis – CHAUSSON: *Mélodies* *(*).

Christine Schäfer is not really any more successful with Debussy than she is with Chausson. Non-French speakers may be less worried by some imperfect pronunciation, and her voice is one of striking beauty, but this is not the best recording this wonderful singer has given us nor among the best recitals.

De la Barre, Michel (*c*. 1675–1745)

Flute suites Nos. 2 in C min.; 4 in G min.; 6 in C; 8 in D; Sonata No. 1 in B flat.
**(*) ASV Gaudeamus Dig. CDGAU 181 [id.].
  Nancy Hadden, Elizabeth Walker, Lucy
  Carolan, Erin Headley, Lynd Sayce.

Michel de la Barre played the transverse flute in the Paris Opéra Orchestra and also played at the Court of Louis XIV with the status of Flûte de la Chambre. His suites are among the earliest pieces written for the remodelled instrument and they have a certain pale charm, balancing a pervading melancholy with brighter, more lively airs, gigues and chaconnes. The charming *Sonata* is for a pair of unaccompanied flutes, the *Suites* for solo flute with continuo, here harpsichord, viola da gamba and theorbo. These expert period instrument performances are stylishly refined and delicate, and certainly pleasing if taken a work at a time.

Delalande, Michel-Richard
(1657–1726)

Confitebor tibi Domine; Super flumina Babilonis; Te Deum.
(B) *** HM Musique d'abord Dig. HMA 1901351
  [id.]. Gens, Piau, Steyer, Fouchécourt, Piolino, Corréas, Les Arts Florissants, Christie.

Confitebor tibi Domine (1699) and *Super flumina Babilonis* (1687) have much expressive writing, and the performances under William Christie are light and airy but not wanting in expressive feeling. The more familiar *Te Deum* is given as good a performance as any that has appeared in recent years. The sound is airy and spacious, and the performances combine lightness and breadth. This is now a splendid bargain on Harmonia Mundi's Musique d'abord label.

De la Rue, Pierre (*c*. 1460–1518)

Missa de feria; Missa Sancta Dei gentrix; Motet: *Pater de celis Deus;* (i) Motets arr. for lute: *O Domine, Jesu Christe; Regina celi; Salve Regina.*
*** Hyperion Dig. CDA 67010 [id.]. Gothic Voices, Christopher Page; (i) Christopher Wilson and Shirley Rumsey (lutes).

Pierre de la Rue is still an unfamiliar name, yet he was prolific, and we now know something about his progress, moving from Brussels to Ghent, on to Cologne and ending his career in the Hapsburg-Burgundian Chapel. His music seems solemn, partly because he is fond of lower vocal ranges, but his ready use of intervals of the third and sixth gives it a harmonic lift and a special individuality. The *Missa de feria* is in five parts and is vocally richer than the more austerely concise *Missa Sancta Dei gentrix* in four; but they are distantly related by sharing an identical musical idea on the words '*Crucifixus*' and '*et resurrexit*'. The canonic imitation which is at the heart of Pierre's polyphony is heard even more strikingly in the superbly organized six-part motet *Pater de celis Deus*, where the mutually interdependent entries create an extraordinarily full and integrated texture, like a closely woven cloth. To provide interludes Christopher Wilson and his partner play three of his lute-duet intabulations, which he has arranged from other motets, a normal practice at the time, and their closing *Salve Regina* makes a quietly serene postlude. Christopher Page and his Gothic Voices are thoroughly immersed in this repertoire and period (as we know from their ongoing Hyperion series – see Vocal Recitals below), and these stimulating performances could hardly be more authentic. The recording too is well up to standard.

Delibes, Léo (1836–91)

Complete ballets: (i) *Coppélia;* (ii) *Sylvia;* (iii) *La Source.*
(B) *** Decca Analogue/Dig. 460 418-2 (4) [id.].
   (i) Nat. PO; (ii) New Philh.O; (iii) ROHCGO;
   Richard Bonynge.

Delibes's *Coppélia* (1870) marked a turning point in the history of ballet music and is his masterpiece. There is not a dull bar in it – it brims with vitality and melodic invention and perfectly conveys the quirky rustic quality of E. T. A. Hoffmann's engaging tale of the puppet-maker that thinks he can bring his 'daughter' to life. Bonynge's digital recording sparkles from start to finish. There is tremendous energy in the many vigorous numbers and a Mozartean elegance in the phrasing and colouring. The contribution of the woodwind is a continual delight and the balance between all the players is both realistic and striking. Indeed, the recording is of demonstration quality and this performance will not disappoint.

Although not so consistently inspired as *Coppélia*, *Sylvia* is immensely enjoyable. Rather more serious and symphonic in approach, there are many exciting set pieces, much piquant writing and colouring, and a haunting *leitmotif,* which runs throughout. The New Philharmonia play with tremendous energy and style and the 1972 recording is as brilliant as you could wish. *La Source* is the composer's first ballet, though he wrote only Acts II and III. Its elegantly lightweight style was a success and alerted the world to his talent for writing for the dance theatre. Although the personality of the composer is not fully developed, the music is tuneful and well crafted, with his felicitous use of the orchestral pallet readily discernible – clearly showing this as a forerunner for *Coppélia* and *Sylvia*. The complete ballet is given here, with Acts I and IV written by Minkus, whose contribution is rather more melancholy than Delibes's, but is well written and enjoyable. The ROHCGO plays with great style and the digital recording is warm and detailed – well up to the house standard. At bargain price, this set is exceptional value.

Delius, Frederick (1862–1934)

(i) *Cello sonata. Violin sonatas Nos.* (ii) *1–2;* (iii) *3.*
(B) *** EMI Dig. CZS5 73992-2 (2). (i) Moray
   Welsh; (ii) Janice Graham; (iii) Alexander
   Barantschick; (i–iii) Israela Margalit – ELGAR:
   Piano quintet, etc. **(*).

Those looking for modern digital recordings of these four works will find that these performances by members of the LSO are in every way satisfying. Moray Welsh provides warm tone and much depth

of feeling in the *Cello sonata* and Janice Graham's passionate advocacy in the earlier *Violin sonatas* matches that of Alexander Barantschick in the *Third.* Israela Margalit's pianism in all four works is full of personality, and the recording is resonant and forwardly balanced, and satisfyingly full. However the Elgar couplings are rather less memorable.

Docker, Robert (1918–1992)

(i) *3 Contrasts for oboe and strings;* (ii) *Legend; Pastiche variations* (both for piano and orchestra); *Air; Blue ribbons; Fair dance reel; Scènes de ballet; Scène du bal; The spirit of Cambria; Tabarinage.*
*** Marco Polo Dig. Dublin RTE Concert O,
   Barry Knight; with (i) David Presley; (ii)
   William Davies.

Robert Docker is probably best known as a composer of film music (including a contribution to *Chariots of Fire*). His *Legend,* which opens this collection, is a tuneful example of a miniature 'film-concerto' ranking alongside, but musically greatly preferable to, the similar works written by others for *Dream of Olwen* and *Cornish rhapsody.* The closing *Pastiche variations,* opening with a horn solo, is more expansive and romantic, but witty too. Based on *Frère Jacques* it has something in common with Dohnányi's *Nursery-theme variations.* The piano introduction of the theme, echoed by the clarinet, is most seductive, and what follows is attractively inventive, both melodically and in its orchestral colouring. William Davies proves a most persuasive soloist. In between comes an attractive lightweight suite of *Scènes de ballet,* three engaging *Contrasts for oboe and strings* (lovely playing from David Presley, especially in the central pastoral *Romance*), and a series of engaging short pieces. Perhaps the best known is the catchy *Tabarinage.* The delicate *Scène du bal* is a very English waltz in spite of its French title. There are also some spirited folksong arrangements. *Blue ribbons* is based on *Oh dear, what can the matter be*, and the Irish *Fairy dance reel* is appropriately introduced by the solo flute. *The Spirit of Cambria* (although the composer is a Londoner) was written for St David's Day in 1972 and effectively uses four different traditional Welsh melodies. All this music is played with polish and warmth by the Dublin Radio Orchestra under Barry Knight and pleasingly recorded.

Dodgson, Stephen (born 1924)

(i) *Guitar concerto* (for guitar and chamber orchestra). *Partita No. 1 for solo guitar.*
(B) **(*) Sony SBK 61716 [id.]. John Williams;
   (i) with ECO, Groves – RODRIGO: *Concierto de Aranjuez, etc.* **(*)

DOHNANYI 116

Stephen Dodgson is a civilized composer whose invention is matched by good taste and fine craftsmanship. John Williams proves an eloquent and authoritative exponent and the *Concerto* could hardly hope for a more persuasive performance. Much the same goes for the *Partita* and these make original and worthwhile couplings for the ubiquitous Rodrigo works. The recording is good, but not exceptional.

Piano sonatas Nos 1; 3 (Variations on a rhythm); 6.
*** Claudio Dig. CC 4941-2 [id.]. Bernard Roberts.

Piano sonatas Nos 2; 4; 5.
*** Claudio Dig. CC 4431-2 [id.]. Bernard Roberts.

The thoughtfulness and cogency of Stephen Dodgson's piano writing inspire Bernard Roberts to magnetic playing. Those who know Stephen Dodgson's guitar music may be initially disconcerted that the style here is grittier, more demanding and quirky at times, as in the multiple movements of the *Sonata No. 4*. In that work the note-writer, Professor Wilfrid Mellers, highlights an 'Alice-in-Wonderland' quality – apt from a composer distantly related to the Dodgson who was author of that fantasy, Lewis Carroll.

That comes on CC 4431-2, but the companion CD, CC 4941-2, gives a wider insight into the composer's development, from the *Sonata No. 1* of 1959, in which English echoes can still be detected, to the more freely expansive writing of the *Sonata No. 6* of 1994, inspired by Roberts's performances on the first disc. Most ingenious in its complex organization is the *Sonata No. 3* of 1983, subtitled *Variations on a rhythm*, with Dodgson at his most original. Excellent, well-balanced sound.

Dohnányi, Ernst von (1877–1960)

Suite in F sharp min., Op. 19; Variations on a nursery theme, Op. 25; The Veil of Pierrette: suite, Op. 18.
*** Chandos Dig. CHAN 9733. Howard Shelley, BBC PO, Matthias Bamert.

For all their popularity, Dohnányi's variations on 'Twinkle, twinkle, little star', with their witty parodies, have been meanly treated on disc. This brilliant version with Howard Shelley the sparkling soloist is especially welcome, when it offers two other examples of Dohnányi the charmer. The *Wedding waltz* from the mimed entertainment *The Veil of Pierrette* was once well known, dashingly Viennese, as are the other three movements, previously unrecorded, including a *Merry funeral march* which parodies Mahler. The *Suite* too is engagingly colourful. Brilliant performances, sumptuously recorded.

(i) *Konzertstücke for cello and orchestra, Op. 12;* (ii) *Cello sonata in B flat min., Op. 8; Ruralia Hungarica, Op. 32d; Adagio ma non troppo.*
(BB)*(*) Naxos Dig. 8.554468 [id.]. Maria Kliegel; with (i) Nicolaus Esterházy O, Halász; (ii) Jenö Jandó.

The *Konzertstücke* was in Starker's repertoire and he recorded it with Walter Susskind and the Philharmonia in the early days of stereo. Maria Kliegel proves hardly less persuasive a soloist, though the Nicolaus Esterházy Orchestra is distinctly subfusc. Ms Kliegel is no less successful in the *Cello sonata* where she is well supported by the ubiquitous Jenö Jandó. The recording, particularly in the cello version of the so-called *Gypsy Andante* from the *Ruralia Hungarica,* is poor. Recommendable only for the *Cello sonata.*

Variations on a nursery theme, Op. 25.
(B) *** Decca Double 458 361-2 (2) [id.]. Julius Katchen, LPO, Boult – LISZT: *Piano concertos 1–2,* etc. ***

Having made the best ever mono recording of the *Nursery variations,* Katchen and Boult returned to the Kingsway Hall to record it again in 1959 with comparable panache and the advantage of Decca's finest analogue stereo, which is still demonstration-worthy more than four decades later. The Wagnerian opening is a *tour de force* and the first appearance of the famous theme is most winning. The performance overall sparkles with wit.

Violin sonata in C sharp min., Op. 21; Andante rubato (Ruralia Hungarica).
**(*) Biddulph LAW 015 [id.]. Oscar Shumsky, Seymour Lipkin – WEINER: *Violin sonatas Nos. 1 & 2.* **(*)

The Biddulph label is associated in our minds with specialized historic records which are transcribed to high artistic standards. This record of three Hungarian sonatas – Dohnányi's *C sharp minor* (1912) and two by Leó Weiner – is an exception. Oscar Shumsky and Seymour Lipkin were recorded in New York in 1993 and they make out an excellent case for this neglected but fine piece. Shumsky's playing is not quite as polished or masterly as it was in the early 1980s but it is still supremely musical. A worthwhile addition to the catalogue.

PIANO MUSIC

6 Concert études, Op. 28; Pastorale; Ruralia Hungarica, Op. 32a; Variations on a Hungarian folk song, Op. 29.
❀(BB)*** Naxos Dig. 8.553332 [id.]. Markus Pawlik.

The *6 Concert études,* Op. 28, of 1916 are among the most technically demanding pieces in the repertoire, and though the last, the *Capriccio,* has been recorded by the likes of Rachmaninov, Horowitz,

Godowsky and so on, the remainder are not represented in the catalogue. Nor is the *Ruralia Hungarica* generously represented on disc: of the few that are to be found, this is the best. When he was sixteen, Markus Pawlik won the European Union Young Musician of the Year competition. and then went on to win several major competition prizes. He was still in his twenties when he recorded these pieces and his playing is remarkable for its dazzling virtuosity, sensitivity, finesse and good taste. His dexterity and wonderful clarity of articulation in the *D flat Etude* are remarkable. His is a formidable talent and we hope to hear much more of him. Decent recorded sound. Recommended with all enthusiasm.

Donizetti, Gaetano (1797–1848)

(i) *Clarinet concertino in B flat. Study No. 1 for solo clarinet.*
(BB) *** ASV Quicksilva Dig. CDQS 6242 [id.].
   Joy Farrall; (i) with Britten Sinfonia, Nicholas Daniel – MERCADANTE: *Clarinet concertos;* ROSSINI: *Variations in B flat & C.* ***

Donizetti's *Clarinet concertino* is also available in a recommendable anthology (see below) but Joy Farrall's performance is hardly less winning and she is most stylishly accompanied and beautifully recorded. She gets a chance to show her mettle first in the bravura of the solo *Study.* These performances are neatly framed by two sets of witty variations by Rossini and a pair of delightful concertos by Mercadante, and this generous collection is one of the highlights of the ASV Quicksilva bargain catalogue.

(i) *Clarinet concertino in B flat;* (ii) *Cor anglais concertino in G;* (iii) *Flute concertino in C min.;* (iv) *Oboe concertino in F;* (v) *Double concertino in D min. for violin & cello;* (vi) *Sinfonia a soli instrumenti di fiato in G min. Sinfonia in D min. per la Morte di Capuzzi.*
🌑 *** Marco Polo Subaru 8.223701 [id.]. (i) Béla Kovács; (ii) Agnes Girgás; (iii) Imre Kovács; (iv) Jószef Kiss; (v) Andás Kiss, Judiy Kiss Domonkos; (vi) Soloists, Budapest Camerata, László Kovács.

Various musicians have had a hand in orchestrating or reconstructing these very operatic works, and to all of them we must be grateful. We already know the *Concertino for cor anglais,* which is a galant set of variations of innocuous charm. It is played here with a delectable timbre and a nice feeling for light and shade. The *Clarinet concertino* brings a touch of melancholy to its opening cantilena, yet the finale chortles. The *Flute concertino* also opens with an eloquent aria, but the closing rondo is irrepressibly light-hearted, with an infectiously carefree Rossinian wit. The *Oboe concerinto* has a vigorous

hunting finale, played here with bouncing zest. The *Double concertino,* in three movements, is the most ambitious work, established by its fairly long introductory ritornello. The violin then leads in a truly operatic duet in the *Andante,* and the finale has a comparably charming interplay, with phrase by phrase imitation, the two soloists matching their timbres most adroitly. In short all these concertos are most winning, as elegant as they are inventive, and all of the expert soloists (several of whom seem to be interrelated) smilingly convey the music's Italian sunshine. The concertos are framed by two contrasting *Sinfonias.* The opening G minor work dates from the composer's student years and is in essence a sinfonia concertante with nine wind soloists. The closing *D minor Sinfonia,* which is much later, brings a momentary touch of gravitas, but Rossini wittily returns in its finale. It was written for the funeral of the leader of the Bergamo orchestra and string quartet with which the composer was associated. Both are played very persuasively, and throughout the collection László Kovács and his Budapest Chamber Orchestra provide supportive and stylish accompaniments. The recording could hardly be bettered, and the result is a collection which will give great and repeated pleasure.

Sinfonias in D; D min.; C.
*** Koch Dig. 3-6733-2 [id.]. Krakau State PO, Roland Bader – BELLINI: *Sinfonias.* ***

A real find. Collectors sampling the *D major Sinfonia,* in essence an operatic-style overture, will surely do an aural double-take, so like to Rossini is it, complete with jaunty second subject and crescendo. The secondary theme of the C major work is no less obviously patterned, so that it almost sounds like a crib. Both make delightfully infectious listening. The *D minor* is slightly less characteristic, but still most enjoyable. Fine, stylish performances too, very well recorded.

CHAMBER MUSIC

Introduzione for strings; String quartets Nos. 10 in G min.; 11 & 12 in C.
*** CPO Dig. CPO 999 279-2 [id.].
   Revolutionary Drawing Room.

This excellent CPO series reveals Donizetti as a considerable contributor to the string quartet medium, offering works that in their craftsmanship and quality of invention can stand comparison with all but the very finest of Haydn. These three and the following four, Nos. 13–16, all date from around 1821, when the composer was in his early twenties. They are very much Haydn-influenced (in the best sense), especially the witty downward scale which forms the diverting Minuet finale of No. 10 and the winning outer movements of No. 11. Unfortunately the performers have chosen a less than apt collective

DOWLAND   118

name: the style of their music-making is neither
revolutionary nor does it suggest the cosiness of a
drawing room. Instead these players are completely
at home on their period instruments: their execution
is fresh, vital and expressive, without any linear
eccentricities. The simple eloquence of the melancholy *Introduzione* which opens the disc, and which
reflects the composer's grief (in 1829) over his
stillborn child, is most affecting, while the Theme
and variations which forms the *Andante* of No. 12
is beautifully shaped. There is fine tonal matching
and a nicely elegant solo from the leader as its
centrepiece. First-rate recording too.

String quartets Nos. 13 in A; 14 in D; 15 in F.
**(*) CPO Dig. CPO 999 280 [id.]. Revolutionary
    Drawing Room.

The *A major* is the only quartet of the Donizetti
canon which is at all well known. It is nearer to
early Beethoven than to Haydn and has an endearing
first movement, a comparatively searching *Adagio*,
but is most famous for its Scherzo, echoing that
in Beethoven's *Eroica Symphony*. The pointedly
rhythmic finale is hardly less striking. No. 14 in D
is programmatic, and we hear the storm gathering
immediately at the opening: its full force is soon
sweeping through the music. The hushed *Adagio*
sadly contemplates the havoc left behind, but the
genial Minuet suggests that life goes on, with repairs
carried out in the Trio, while the hammering work-
men sing to themselves. The thoughtful opening
of the finale leads to a lively interchange, as the
whole community joins in and the quartet ends
peacefully.

The *F major* opens thoughtfully, but the genial
spirit of the first movement again recalls Haydn,
and that master's humanity is also reflected in the
Andante. After an unusual Minuet with a songful
trio, comes another solemn introduction for a finale
which maintains the music's lyrical good-nature.
All three quartets are played with spirit, warmth
and finesse, and the recording is vivid, though not
quite as smooth as the previous CD, revealing a
degree of edge on the timbre of the lead violin.

*String quartets Nos. 16 in B min.; 17 in D; 18 in
E min.*
*** CPO Dig. CPO 999 282-2 [id.].
    Revolutionary Drawing Room.

No. 16 is the last of the 1821 quartets and the jolly,
energetic triplets of its first movement are clearly
forward-looking, almost Schubertian. The *Largo* is
thoughtfully serene, even sombre. But the clouds
lift for the Minuet and the finale dances gracefully.
No. 17 was written four years later and is noticeably
more warmly romantic, with a lovely, simple
Larghetto, a popular Italianate minuet and trio, and
the main theme of the finale has moto perpetuo
vivacity. Finest of the whole series is the mature *E
minor Quartet* of a decade later, splendidly assured

in its light-hearted first movement, which the
composer used as a basis for his *Linda di Chamonix*
overture. The tranquil yet searching *Adagio* is very
touching and is followed by an irresistible, bouncing
Scherzo with a floating operatic melody for its trio.
The gypsy rondo of the *alla polacca* finale confirms
this as Donizetti's masterpiece in the form, and it
ought to be much better known. It is splendidly
played; indeed the performances throughout this
CD are among the finest in the series, and the
recording is first class too – that edge on the leader's
tone noticed above has disappeared and the balance
is excellent.

OPERA

The Elixir of love (complete in English).
(M) **(*) Chandos Dig. CHAN 3027 (2) [id.].
    Barry Banks, Mary Plazas, Ashley Holland,
    Andrew Shore, Helen Williams, Geoffrey
    Mitchell Ch., Philh. O, David Parry.

This lively account under David Parry in the Peter
Moores Foundation's series will delight anyone devoted to opera in English, bringing out the high
spirits of the piece, even if inevitably there are
resulting echoes of Gilbert and Sullivan. Central to
the performance's success is the vivacious Adina
of Mary Plazas, sparkling and sweet-toned, guaranteed to ensnare any man around.

Barry Banks gives a forthright performance as
the innocent hero, Nemorino, even if the tone is not
really Italianate enough for this music, whatever the
language. Ashley Holland as Sergeant Belcore and
Andrew Shore as Dr Dulcamara are lively and
characterful, agile in rapid patter, even if their
voices could be more sharply focused. The excellent
translation is by Arthur Jacobs. Vigorous singing
from the Geoffrey Mitchell Singers and excellent
playing from the Philharmonia, warmly recorded.

Dowland, John (1563–1626)

*Lute songs, Book I (1597): Awake sweet love; All
ye whom love or fortune hath betraid; Can she
excuse my wrongs with vertues cloak?; Come
again: sweet love doth now invite; Deare, if you
change, ile never chuse again; Goe crystal teares;
If my complaints could passions move; Sleep
wayward thoughts.* Book II (1600): *Come ye
heavie states of night; Fine knacks for ladies;
Flow my teares fall from your springs; If fluds of
teares could cleanse my follies past; I saw my lady
weepe; Shall I sue, shall I seek for grace?; Stay
sorow stay; Tymes eldest sonne, old age the heire
of ease . . . Then sit thee down and say thy 'Nunc
dimittis' . . . When others sings 'Venite
exultemus'.*
*** Metronome Dig METCD 1010 [id.]. Paul
    Agnew, Christopher Wilson.

Lute songs, Book III (1603): Behold a wonder here; Flow not so fast ye fountaines; I must complaine, yet do enjoy; Lend your eares to my sorrow good people; Say love if ever thou didst finde; Time stands still; Weepe you no more sad fountaines; What if I never speed; When Phoebus first did Daphne love. A Musicall Banquet (1610): In darkness let me dwwll; Lady if you so spight me. A Pilgrim's Solace (1612): If that a sinners sighes be angels foode; Love those beames that breede Shall I strive with wordes to move; Stay time while thy flying; Thou mightie God . . . When Davids life by Saul . . . When the poore criple.
*** Metronome Dig. METCD 1011 [id.]. Paul
   Agnew, Christopher Wilson.

Between them, these two discs span Dowland's musical life with some distinction. Paul Agnew's tenor voice has a certain darkness of colouring in the middle range that seems just right for the dolour of such songs as *Come ye Heavie states of night* and *Flow not so fast ye fountaines*, or the despondent *If that a sinners sighes be angels foode* (a lovely performance), yet he can lighten it attractively for lively numbers like *What if I never speede* or *Fine knacks for ladies.*

On the first disc, *Come again: sweet love doth now invite* has a passionate forward flow that is almost operatic. In the tripartite *Tymes eldest sonne* Dowland separates the three stanzas with excerpts from the actual liturgy, while *Thou mightie God* maintains its lamenting mood consistently throughout its three semi-narrative sections.

Christopher Wilson's intimate accompaniments could not be more gently supportive, and the recording balance is admirable within a pleasingly atmospheric acoustic. Each disc is handsomely presented with a beautifully printed booklet containing full texts and illustrations, all within a slipcase.

Four-part lute songs, Book I: Awake with these self-loving lads; If my complaints could passions move; Now! oh now I needs must part; Think'st thou then by thy feigning. Book II: Fine knacks for ladies. Book III: Me, me and none but me; Say love, if ever thou didst find; What if I never speed?; When Phoebus first did Daphné love. Book IV: In this trembling shadow; Stay, sweet awhile; Tell me true love; Wherever sin sore wounding. Solo: Tell me true love.
**(*) Lyrichord LEMS 8031 [id.]. Saltire Singers
   (Patricia Clark, Jean Allister, Edgar Fleet,
   Frederick Westcott), Desmond Dupré.

The Saltire Singers are a superb vocal group from the early 1960s. Patricia Clark and Edgar Fleet were both performers with Deller's Consort, and Desmond Dupré was Deller's lutenist. The vocal blend here is ravishing. Seldom have individual singers matched their voices more richly in this repertoire, with Patricia Clark leading with a sweet,

soaring soprano, her gentle touch of vibrato ideal for Dowland's melodic lines.

The choice of songs too is admirable, offering some of Dowland's very finest inspirations. The rocking *Now! oh now I needs must part* and *Me, me and none but me*, the charming pastoral *When phoebus first did Daphne love* and the lively closing *Fine knacks for ladies* are all captivating. The extended *Tell me true love* brings opportunities for lovely solo contributions from each member of the team, but most touching of all is the melancholy *Wherever sin sore wounding*, which shows Dowland at his most profound.

The recording of the voices could hardly be bettered, except that they tend at times to overwhelm the lute. The only other small caveat is the relatively short measure (44 minutes), but the quality of the singing more than compensates, and Lyrichord throw in a well-compiled (and tempting sampler-disc demonstrating the breadth of this enterprising specialist catalogue of early music. Full texts are provided.

Draeseke, Felix (1835–1913)

(i) *Piano concerto in E flat, Op. 36. Symphony No. 1 in G, Op. 12.*
** MDG Dig. 335 0929-2 [id.]. (i) Claudius
   Tanski; Wuppertal SO, George Hanson.

Felix Draeseke was best known as a critic and is scantily represented on CD. His *Third Symphony* was recorded in the days of mono LP and started off just like Brahms save only for its propensity to slide rather queasily into spiralling modulations. The *First*, composed in 1873, has touches of *Lohengrin* and there are even reminders of Berlioz as well as Schumann and Brahms. The *Piano concerto* (1885–6) is inevitably Lisztian, though much more conventional. Claudius Tanski makes out a good case for it and the American George Hanson pilots us through these raffish backwaters with some skill. A composer of considerable culture but insufficient individuality to hold centre stage. Decent sound but not a disc that excites enthusiasm.

Dreyschock, Alexander (1818–69)

Piano concerto in D min., Op. 137.
*** Hyperion Dig. CDA 67086 [id.]. Piers Lane,
   BBC Scottish SO, Niklas Willén – KULLAK:
   Piano concerto in C min. ***

This is one of the very finest of Hyperion's 'Romantic Piano Concerto' series, pairing two forgotten works that have plenty of attractive ideas, rewarding the soloist with the kind of bravura excitement that cannot but compel the listener. Piers Lane rises to the occasion with glittering dexterity and fine romantic flair, while the orchestra provides enthusiastic support, introducing the endearing main theme of the *Andante* with affectionate warmth. As in the coupled Kullak concerto there are echoes of Liszt and Chopin in the passage work, and the strong finale combines Weberian brilliance with Mendelssohnian sentiment in the charming secondary theme. The splendidly balanced recording presents the polished dialogue between solo piano and the often flamboyant orchestra in an ideal perspective.

Dukas, Paul (1865–1935)

L'apprenti sorcier; La péri (with *Fanfare*); *Symphony in C.*
**(*) Telarc Dig. CD 80515 [id.]. Cincinnati SO, Jésus López-Cobos.

After the richly resonant *Fanfare*, the diaphanous opening of *La péri* is beautifully played in Cincinnati and the climax has proper sensuous passion. The orchestra is equally committed in the *Symphony*, but Jésus López-Cobos does not manage to retain the same degree of grip on the structure of the first movement as Leonard Slatkin on RCA (09026 88022-2), who has the same couplings, or Yan Pascal Tortelier on Chandos, who offers the *Polyeucte overture* (CHAN 9225). The slow movement, however, is very successful on Telarc and the finale very spirited. *L'apprenti sorcier* is lively too, but without quite the wit and rhythmic buoyancy of the very finest accounts. The Telarc recording is impressively full-bodied and well-balanced, but the hall resonance does not provide quite enough transparency to reveal the fullest detail in the more complex climaxes.

Duncan, Trevor (born 1924)

Children in the park; Enchanted April; The girl from Corsica; High heels; Little Debbie; Little suite; Meadow mist; Maestro variations; Sixpenny ride; St Boniface down; La Torrida; 20th Century Express; Valse mignonette; The visionaries: grand march; Wine festival.
*** Marco Polo Dig. 8.223517 [id.]. Slovak RSO (Bratislava), Penny.

Trevor Duncan is perhaps best known for the signature tune of the TV series 'Dr Finlay's Casebook', the *March* from *Little suite*, which is offered here, along with the two other numbers which make up that suite. But more of his popular pieces are included: the *20th Century Express*, with its spirited 'going on holiday feel', the exotic *Girl from Corsica*, and the tunefully laid-back *Enchanted April*, which was also used on a television programme. The *Valse mignonette* is particularly piquant and memorable, while *Wine festival* and *La Torrida* find the composer in Mediterranean mode *à la Girl from*

Corsica. The bright and breezy *Children in the park* is most winning, as is *Meadow mist*, in a more reflective way. All the music here is nostalgically tuneful, with enough invention of melody and colour to sustain interest. Andrew Penny and the Bratislavan orchestra sound as though they have played it all for years, and recording is excellent. Full and helpful sleeve notes complete this attractive collection of good-quality light music.

Duruflé, Maurice (1902–86)

Requiem, Op. 9.
(M) *** Decca 466 418-2 [id.]. Robert King, Christopher Keyte, St John's College, Cambridge, Ch., Stephen Cleobury (organ), George Guest – FAURÉ: *Requiem.* ***

George Guest's St John's coupling of the Duruflé and Fauré *Requiems*, with its attractive use of boy trebles, has already been praised in our main volume, where it appears as part of a Decca Double (436 486-2) which includes much other fine choral music by both composers. The alternative organ accompaniment is used and the 1974 recording is vividly atmospheric.

Requiem, Op. 9; Messe Cum jubilo, Op. 11; 4 Motets sur les thèmes grégoriens, Op. 10; Notre Prère, Op. 14 (both for a capella choir).
*** EMI Dig. CDC5 56878-2. (i) Anne Sofie von Otter, Thomas Hampson, Marie-Claire Alain; Orfeon Donostiarra, O de Capitole Toulouse, Michel Plasson.
*** Nimbus Dig. NI 5599 [id.]. (i) Kathryn Turpin, William Clements, Peter Morton (treble); Iain Farrington, St John's College, Cambridge, Ch., Christopher Robinson.

Here are two outstanding but quite different new recordings of the glorious Duruflé *Requiem*, each similarly and ideally coupled, for those who already have the usual CD pairing with the Fauré *Requiem*. The most important difference is that the St John's performance under Christopher Robinson uses the highly effective organ-accompanied score. With a superb contribution from Ian Farrington this works admirably, especially in the *Libera me*, but it has to be admitted that the French orchestra makes a spectacular contribution to the *Gloria* (and elsewhere), and again later adds much colour to the lovely *Messe Cum jubilo*.

The choral sound too, makes a quite different impression in each version. Plasson's performance was recorded in the spaciously resonant acoustic of Toulouse's Notre Dame La Daurade and, as is immediately obvious in the opening *Kyrie*, the chorus is backwardly placed, floating in a misty atmosphere and although at climaxes the vocal sound expands thrillingly, at other times Plasson's comparatively relaxed pacing mean that the music-making has less tension.

Robinson's account was recorded at St John's and still has a warm ecclesiastical acoustic but the chorus is brighter and clearer; though the overall balance is natural the effect is undoubtedly fresher with little loss of evocative atmosphere.

Both recordings have first-rate soloists, although the warmer voice of Thomas Hampson has a special appeal; on the other hand while Sophie von Otter sings beautifully and eloquently, her vibrato brings a hint of the opera-house at the climax of the *Pie Jesu*. Kathryn Turnpin is hardly less fine, and she has a noticeable vibrato too (neither is like a choirboy), but her climax is that bit less histrionic.

In short, both performances of both masses (and the shorter work is hardly less appealing), are satisfying in different ways, for the calibre of the choral singing is splendid. In the St John's performance of the delightful a cappella Motets, a treble soloist sings the chant first before the choir enters, a very happy idea, and this is an instance where the extra clarity of the recording is advantageous.

Dvořák, Antonín (1841–1904)

(i) *American suite, Op. 98b;* (ii) *Czech suite, Op. 39; Nocturne for strings in B, Op. 40; Polka for Prague students in B flat, Op. 53a; Polonaise in E flat; Prague waltzes;* (i) *Slavonic dances Nos. 1–16, Op. 46/1–8, Op. 72/1–8;* (ii) *Slavonic rhapsody No. 3, Op. 45.*
(B) *** Decca Double Dig./Analogue 460 293-2 (2) [id.]. (i) RPO; (ii) Detroit SO; Antal Dorati.

Dvořák's *American suite*, which has clear influences from the New World, was written first in a piano version (1894), but turned into an orchestral piece the following year. It is slight but charming music. Dorati has its measure and the RPO are very responsive. The Kingsway Hall recording balance suits the scoring rather well, but the hall resonance seems to have offered more problems in the *Slavonic dances* recorded at the same time (1983) and the louder tuttis are not as sweet here in the upper range of the strings although otherwise the sound is full and pleasing. Dorati's performances have characteristic brio, the RPO response is warmly lyrical when necessary and the woodwind playing gives much pleasure. Sparkle is the keynote and there is no lack of spontaneity. The rest of the programme is made up of a collection of rarities, exhilaratingly performed in Detroit (in 1980) and given brilliant and warmly atmospheric recording of near-demonstration standard. The *Czech suite* can sometimes outstay its welcome, but certainly not here. The other items too have the brightness and freshness that mark out the *Slavonic dances*, especially the *Polka* and *Polonaise* with their attractive rhythmic spring. The most charming piece of all is

the set of *Waltzes*, written for balls in Prague – Viennese music with a Czech accent – while the lovely *Nocturne* with its subtle drone bass makes a winning interlude. The *Slavonic rhapsody*, with its opening suggesting a troubadour and his harp, makes a vivacious end to what the documentation rightly describes as 'two-and-a-half hours of Dvořák's most tuneful orchestral music'.

(i) *Cello concerto in B min., Op. 104; Scherzo capriccioso* (with rehearsal).
(BB) (**) Naxos mono 8.110819 [id.]. (i) Edmund Kurtz; NBC SO, Toscanini (with broadcast commentary by Ben Grauer).

With dry, clear transfers of the limited radio sound, this is one of the more successful of Naxos's Toscanini recordings. Edmund Kurtz is a strong enough soloist to persuade Toscanini to relax more than he often did, so that the big melodies are allowed a degree of expansion. So it is that though the slow movement opens in a matter-of-fact way, Kurtz quickly warms the atmosphere, bringing the conductor with him, and the meditation of the epilogue finds them both similarly relaxed. The *Scherzo capriccioso* also finds Toscanini at his warmest, relishing the lilting rhythms, even finding charm. Sadly, the rehearsal sequence, with Toscanini muttering in the distance, brings little or no illumination.

(i) *Cello concerto in B minor, Op. 104;* (ii) *Symphony No. 9 in E min. (From the New World), Op. 95.*
(BB) (***) Naxos mono 8.110901 [id.]. (i) Emanuel Feuermann; Berlin State Op. O, cond. (i) Michael Taube; (ii) Erich Kleiber.

This pioneering account of the *Cello concerto* was made in 1928–9 by Emanuel Feuermann whose luminous, voluptuous tone and sensational technical command sound astonishing, though the recording cannot be said to wear its years lightly. Anyone who recalls his set of Bloch's *Schelomo* with Stokowski will expect something rather special – and this, indeed, is what we get! As in the classic Casals version of almost ten years later, speeds are far faster than those we expect today. Feuermann, a passionate soloist, at times seems intent on showing just how fast he can play, with phenomenally clean articulation but with the occasional flaw of intonation. Well transferred by Mark Obert-Thorn from pre-EMI Parlophone pressings, the sound is limited but clear. Erich Kleiber's 1929 recording of the *New World Symphony* equally brings an electrifying performance, fast and furious in allegros and tenderly expressive in the slow movement. The surface noise is sometimes obtrusive, but hardly detracts from the impact of an at times inspirational reading.

Cello concerto in B min., Op. 104; Rondo for cello and orchestra, Op. 94; Silent woods, Op. 68/5.

(M) *** Sony Great Performances Dig. SMK 66788 [id.]. Yo-Yo Ma, BPO, Maazel.

Sony have restored the original coupling for their reissue of Ma's first recording of the Dvořák *Cello concerto,* with Maazel. Undoubtedly Ma's rapt concentration and refined control of colour bring an elegiac dimension to this reading. Maazel, having provided a spaciously powerful orchestral introduction (with superb BPO playing), accompanies with understanding and great sensitivity, fining down the orchestral textures so that he never masks his often gentle soloist, yet providing exuberant contrasts in orchestral fortissimos. The solo cello is most skilfully balanced, and this ensures that the pianissimo detail of the *Adagio* registers naturally. The twilight evocation of *Silent woods* is equally well caught. However, we are inclined to prefer Ma's later recording, with Masur, in many ways more commanding, more spontaneous – sounding than with Maazel (Sony SK 67173 – see our main volume). However, that is at full price.

Piano concerto in G min.
** Athene Dig. CD 21 [id.]. Andreas Boyde, Freiburg PO, Johannes Fritzsche – SCHOENFIELD: *Piano concerto.* **

This Athene disc serves as a showcase for the German pianist Andreas Boyde. His formidable gifts and keen virtuosity are heard to good effect here but he is not perhaps best served by his coupling. In the Dvořák *Concerto* he is competing against the likes of Firkušný (RD 60781) and Richter (CDM5 66895; [CDM5 66947]), both recorded with great orchestras. Not that he is in the least inadequate – far from it – or the orchestral response in any way lacklustre, but by their side he is not competitive. In any event the balance places him so far forward that the Freiburg Orchestra is often masked. The Schoenfield piece is a somewhat arbitrary choice as a companion.

Violin concerto in A min., Op. 53.
(BB) *** Royal Long Players DCL 705742 (2). Krebbers, Amsterdam PO, Kersjes – BRAHMS; SIBELIUS; TCHAIKOVSKY: *Violin concertos.* ***

Krebbers offers a characteristically fresh and incisive reading, bringing out the Czech overtones in the first movement and giving a simple and reposeful account of the slow movement and an infectiously lilting one of the finale. He receives good support from the Amsterdam Orchestra and the recording is extremely vivid, perhaps a bit too brightly lit, but not lacking support in the lower range. The CD transfer is excellent and this is part of an extraordinarily attractive super-bargain package, which is consistently enjoyable throughout.

Czech suite in D, Op. 39; Notturno for strings, Op. 40; Serenade for strings, Op. 22.

*** Arabesque Dig. Z 6697 [id.]. Padova CO, David Golub.

David Golub is best known for his trio partnership with Mark Kaplan and Colin Carr, which has produced unfailingly satisfying artistic results. He takes a more relaxed view than usual of the opening movement of the adorable *Czech Suite* (no harm in that) and presents the quicker movements with an unforced charm that it is captivating. The fourth movement, *Romance,* is really affecting, as for that matter is the eloquent *Notturno, Op. 40.* The Padua Chamber Orchestra respond to his sensitive direction with evident sympathy in the *Serenade,* though he tries to make a little too much of the contrasting idea of the first movement. Generally very well-judged tempi. Enjoyable and musical playing, enhanced by a natural recording.

Romance for violin and orchestra, Op. 11.
(M) ** RCA High Performance 09026 63591-2 [id.]. Perlman, Boston SO, Leinsdorf – SIBELIUS; TCHAIKOVSKY: *Violin concertos.*(*)

This is a lovely work (originally part of a quartet), full of melody and invention, and the most successful thing on this CD. Perlman plays well, but the orchestral sound and Leinsdorf's conducting are below par.

Serenade for strings in E, Op. 22.
(BB) *** Virgin Classics 2 x 1 Dig. VBD5 61763-2 (2) [CDVB 61763]. LCO, Christopher Warren-Green – ELGAR: *Introduction and allegro; Serenade;* SUK: *Serenade;* TCHAIKOVSKY: *Serenade;* VAUGHAN WILLIAMS: *Fantasia on Greensleeves; Fantasia on a theme of Tallis; Lark ascending.* ***

Christopher Warren-Green and the excellent London Chamber Orchestra bring their characteristically fresh, spontaneous approach to the Dvořák *Serenade.* If without the winning individuality of the outstanding COE version under Schneider, or the ripeness of Stokowski on EMI (CDM5 66760-2), it is still very enjoyable, and the amazingly generous couplings make this one of Virgin's most desirable 2x1 super-bargain collections.

(i) *Serenade for strings in E, Op. 22;* (ii) *Serenade for wind, Op. 44.*
(B) ** CfP Dig. 574 0042. (i) ECO, Mackerras; (ii) ECO Wind Ens. (without conductor).

The Classics for Pleasure reissue offers sound that is exceptionally clear in both works, although the strings in Op. 22 have a degree of early 'digital-edge', that some ears may find slightly aggressive. Mackerras is surprisingly direct in the *Serenade for strings* and his seemingly deliberate lack of charm is emphasised by the sound. The *Wind serenade* is played without a conductor and the result is agreeably crisp and sparkling, with vivid recording.

Serenade in D min. for wind, Op. 44
(**(*))Testament mono SBT 1180 [id.]. L. Bar.
Ens., Karl Haas – MOZART: *Serenades Nos.
11 in E flat, K. 375; 12 in C min., K.388*
(**(*)).

Karl Haas's preference for fast speeds and metrical rhythms is well illustrated in this reading of Dvořák's *Wind serenade*, in which the opening march has more of a military flavour than usual. As a generous supplement to Mozart's two great serenades for wind octet, this makes an ideal coupling of three of the greatest of all wind works, performed by an ensemble which included some of the finest British players of the post-war period, including Dennis Brain, Frederick Thurston and Terence Macdonagh. Vivid immediate sound, well transferred.

(i) *3 Slavonic rhapsodies, Op. 45;* (ii) *Rhapsody in A min., Op. 14.*
(BB) *** Naxos Dig. 8.550610 [id.]. Slovak PO, (i) Zdenék Košler; (ii) Libor Pešek.

Dvořák's three *Slavonic rhapsodies* of 1878 are surprisingly rarely heard either on record or in the concert hall. Although they are spirited in the way of the *Slavonic dances*, they are much more like symphonic poems without a programme, and while overflowing with characteristic ideas and colourful scoring, they are also loosely constructed and melodramatic.

The most often heard (and the best) is the *Third,* which opens with a bardic harp, very like Smetana's *Vyšehrad.* The strings then dance off with the theme gaily and here the spirit of the Slavonic dances takes over, with engaging woodwind writing, and yet another dance measure to follow. The music then becomes more rhapsodic in mood, with lyrical interludes before the coda whirls the listener away towards the surprisingly gentle closing section, capped with a simple fortissimo cadence. The performances are in every way first class, with the Slovak players in their element and the fully-bloodedly resonant recording just right for the music.

But it is the earlier *Rhapsody in A minor* which is the most ambitious work here. It was actually conceived as a symphonic poem, completed in 1874 (following the *Fourth Symphony*), but not published until 1912. It is essentially episodic, very nationalistic in feeling, and has plenty of attractive Slavic themes, some quite lilting. Pešek's performance is splendid, with a vigorous response from the orchestra,who even bring off the bombastic, patriotic coda. This is every bit as enjoyable as the Op. 45 *Rhapsodies,* although it is not as sophisticated as No. 3. This Naxos collection would be recommendable even if it cost far more.

Suite in A, Op. 98b.
(M) (***) Supraphon mono SU 1924-2 001 [id.].

Czech PO, Karel Sejna – MARTINU: *Concerto for double string orchestra; Symphony No. 3.* (***)

A lovely performance of the beautiful *A major Suite,* recorded in mono in 1956, but the real attraction on this disc are the Martinů pieces – especially the *Third Symphony* – which are very special.

Symphonies Nos. 1–9; Overture Carnaval; Scherzo capriccioso; The wood dove.
(B) *** DG 463 158-2 (6) [id.]. BPO, Kubelik.

Kubelik's set from the late 1960s and early 1970s has much to recommend it, first and foremost being the glorious playing of the Berlin Philharmonic and the natural idiomatic warmth Kubelik brings to his music-making. He seems less convinced by the earlier symphonies and in No. 3 there is an element of routine, something which does not happen with Kertész on Decca. In spite of some idiosyncratic touches, however, he achieves glowing performances of Nos. 6–9, and (especially) No. 7; also, in No. 8 he is more compelling than his Decca competitor. The remastered DG sound is impressively wide-ranging, and is especially fine in the last (and greatest) three symphonies. Many will also be glad to have his memorable account of *The wood dove.* The set now reappears at bargain price in DG's Collector's Edition with good documentation and is well worth considering as an alternative to Kertész on Decca (430 046-2), even if Nos. 4 and 5 are each split over two CDs.

Symphonies Nos. 1–3.
(B) *** Decca Double 466 739-2 (2) [id.]. LSO, Kertesz.
(B) ** Ph. Duo 446 527-2 (2). LSO, Witold Rowicki.

Kertész's vibrant accounts of the first three Dvořák symphonies sound as fresh today – in sound and in performance – as they did around thirty years ago. These early symphonies are by no means among his greatest works but it is fascinating to hear the development of the young composer. If there are some long-winded passages, there equally are some delightful ones, and by the *Third symphony,* the full exuberance of Dvořák's genius is clearly felt. This Double Decca is listed as Volume I: presumably the rest of the cycle will follow. However, the complete set is already available in a bargain box (◉ Decca 430 046-2 – see our main volume).

Rowicki's interpretative approach to the early Dvořák symphonies is to keep the music moving along fairly briskly. This has the advantage of freshness, but in the first movement of No. 1 there is nearly three minutes' difference, and Rowicki sounds too fast. In almost all respects, Kertész is to be preferred: he sounds as if he really believes in this music. The Philips sound (from the early 1970s) is smooth, bright and full, but the Decca is more dramatic in its incisiveness, with the orchestral colours showing rather more glow and sparkle. Clearly the Decca series is the one to go for.

Symphony No. 4 in D min., Op. 13; Czech suite, Op. 39; My home: overture, Op. 62a.
(BB) **(*) Virgin Classics 2 x 1 Dig. VBD5 61739-2 [CDVB 61739]. Czech PO, Pešek – SMETANA: *Má Vlast.* ***

The Czech Philharmonic always have something individual to say in Dvořák's music and their playing in the lyrically jubilant *My home overture* and the five, folk-influenced pastoral movements of the *Czech suite* is very appealing. In the *Fourth Symphony* it is the Scherzo which one remembers most, with its main theme given an infectious, lolloping rhythmic gait, while the finale, too, is as racy and vigorous as anyone could want. But Pešek's reading, although it is crisply rhythmic at the opening of the first movement, fails to develop sufficient thrust, nor does he attempt to disguise the Wagnerian influences, which can weigh heavily on the slow movement. The recording is good rather than outstanding, but this is generous measure, and the coupling is highly recommendable. First choice for the *D minor Symphony* rests with Järvi on Chandos (CHAN 8608, coupled with the *Biblical songs*).

Symphony No. 7 in D min., Op. 70.
** Sony SMK 60561 [id.]. NYPO, Bernstein – SMETANA: *Má Vlast: Vltava; Bartered Bride* (excerpts). **(*)

The unknowing listener to Bernstein's reading might be forgiven for thinking this was a German performance. The scoring is made to seem thick in texture and the symphony's affinities with Brahms are ever prevalent, particularly in the finale. It is a well played, reasonably satisfying performance and the transfer is good, but this CD does not show Bernstein at his magnetic best.

(i) *Symphony No. 8 in G, Op. 88; Nocturne for strings, Op. 40;* (ii) *Overtures: Carnival, Op. 92; In nature's realm overture, Op. 91.*
(M) *** Chandos Dig. CHAN 7123 [id.]. (i) LPO; (ii) Ulster O, Vernon Handley.

We have previously underrated Handley's admirable 1983 recording of Dvořák's delightful *Eighth Symphony*. True the conductor's manner is direct, with the opening relatively straight, not eased in. But that is the very virtue of the reading: it has an ongoing freshness, and its affectionate touches – as in the way Handley lilts the glorious string melody at the centre of the scherzo – are subtle not egocentric. Indeed with first-class playing from the LPO, the life and spontaneity of the performance are most winning. The *Nocturne* makes a most agreeable encore and is also beautifully played. The Ulster Orchestra takes over in the two overtures, linked by a recurring leitmotif, both most attractively done,

with *In nature's realm* glowing with evocative colour. The recording contributes, of course: it is of Chandos's usual high standard.

Symphony No. 9 in E min. (New World), Op. 95; Overture Carnaval, Op. 92; Slavonic dances, Op. 46: Nos. 1 in C; 3 in A flat.
(M) * Sony SMK 60563 [id.]. NYPO, Bernstein.

Symphony No. 9 in E min. (New World); Overture Othello, Op. 93.
**(*) DG Dig. 457 651-2 [id.]. BPO, Abbado.

Symphony No. 9 in E min. (From the New World); Polonaise in E flat; Rusalka: Polonaise.
(**) Biddulph mono WHL 048 [id.]. Czech PO, Vaclav Talich – SUK: *Fairy-tale suite.* (**)

Symphony No. 9 in E min. (New World); The Water goblin, Op. 107.
*** Teldec/Warner Dig. 3984 25254-2 [id.]. Cong. O, Harnoncourt.

Like Abbado's version, Harnoncourt's *New World* was recorded live and it is a good deal more successful than the DG account. Harnoncourt's first movement, with its bold, clipped rhythms and a nice relaxation for the lyrical second group generates plenty of excitement, with exposition repeat made part of the structure. The *Largo* by contrast is gentle, with the cor anglais solo very delicate, almost like an oboe, and with some superb pianissimo string playing to follow. The Scherzo lilts as it should, and the finale is well thought out so that it moves forward strongly, yet can look back to the composer's reprise of earlier themes with touching nostalgia.

This is not quite as compulsive a performance as Harnoncourt's companion disc of the Bruckner *Seventh*, but it is an account to be reckoned with and the CD is made the more attractive by the superbly atmospheric and magnetic account of one of Dvořák's most colourful symphonic poems. Indeed, there is no finer version on record: the tension Harnoncourt sustains in the magically quiet closing section is remarkable.

On Abbado's disc the opening *Othello overture* is superbly done, and combines warmly observed detail with an ongoing concentration that is more elusive in the symphony, the more surprisingly so, as these are live performances. In the *New World* the Berlin Philharmonic often play gloriously, but excitement is more sporadic – welling up at the end of the first movement, and emerging throughout a sparkling account of the Scherzo. But, although beautifully played, the *Largo* is very relaxed, and the forward sweep one needs in the finale is elusive, so this cannot be counted among the finest versions of this much-recorded work. The sound is first class, full and glowing, but 58' is short measure for a premium-priced CD.

Although Vaclav Talich's records of the *D minor*

and *G major Symphonies* were issued before the war, the present issue, made during the Nazi occupation in 1941 (and allotted HMV 'DB' numbers), did not appear in Britain for obvious reasons. Nor was it released here after the war. Talich's interpretation is well known from his subsequent recordings of the piece on Supraphon – one on 78s and the other made on LP. This version is something of a rarity but it is not perhaps quite as special or as personal as one had expected. The Suk coupling is much more special.

Bernstein's 1962 performance of the *New World* is a sad disappointment. It begins promisingly with a fresh, brilliant account of the first movement, followed by a beautifully played *Largo*. But then it's all down hill. The third movement does not relax enough nor beguile as it should, and the finale is plain dull. It is just played through, with no magic when the earlier themes are recalled, lacking the imaginative personal touch normally associated with this conductor. The fill-ups are enjoyable enough, but the recordings are glassy.

CHAMBER MUSIC

(i) *Piano quintet in A, Op. 81. String quartet No.10 in E flat, Op. 51.*
*** Decca Dig. 466 197-2 [id.]. (i) Andreas Haefliger; Takács Qt.

Competition is thick on the ground in this repertoire, especially for the great *A major Piano quintet*, Op. 81, but this newcomer by Andreas Haefliger and the Takács Quartet can hold its own with the best. Haefliger is as always a deeply musical player and his approach, like that of the Takács, is sober and dedicated without any oversweetness. Some may find the tempo of the first movement a little too measured. Both here and in the *E flat Quartet*, Op. 51 the Takács acquit themselves in exemplary fashion and the recorded sound is, in the best traditions of the house, bright and present.

(i) *Piano quintet in A, Op. 81. String quartet No. 12 in F (American).*
* Arabesque Dig. Z 6731 [id.]. (i) Peter Serkin; Orion Qt.

The Arabesque recording calls for some tolerance. The quiet opening of the *Piano quintet* is deceptive and does not prepare you for the unpleasant, harsh and constricted sound in climaxes. The upfront balance leaves the impression that the playing is aggressive – it is impassioned to the point of being overdriven. A totally different world from the Decca recording above.

Piano trios Nos. 1 in B flat, Op. 21; 2 in G min., Op. 26; 3 in F min., Op. 65; 4 in E min. (Dumky), Op. 90.
*** Arabesque Dig. Z 6726-2 (2) [id.]. David Golub, Mark Kaplan, Colin Carr.

A new set of the *Piano trios* that can be recommended without reservation. David Golub, Mark Kaplan and Colin Carr make an ideally balanced group; Golub produces a wide range of keyboard colour and combines subtlety with a vital yet flexible rhythmic grip. Kaplan plays with great artistry and we can't remember hearing cello-playing of greater eloquence in these trios than we get from Colin Carr. Splendidly characterized playing and totally idiomatic in style. Throughout there is feeling and freshness, yet nothing is overstated. The recording places one fairly near the artists but there is room for the music to expand in climaxes and the overall effect has plenty of presence. An altogether delightful set, which gives great pleasure and is now a first choice at full-price, although at medium-price the Solomon Trio (Carlton 30366 00247-2) and the Trio Fontenay on Teldec (9031 76458-2) more than hold their own – see our main volume.

Piano trios Nos. 1 in B flat, Op. 21; 4 in E min. (Dumky), Op. 90.
*** Nimbus Dig. NI 5472 [id.]. Vienna Piano Trio.

The Vienna Piano Trio show admirable musicianship and sensitivity in the *B flat Trio*, Op. 21 and in the famous *Dumky Trio*. In terms of musical characterization honours are almost evenly divided between them and the Golub–Kaplan–Carr Trio on Arabesque, but in the last resort the latter find the greater poignancy and depth of feeling. The Viennese ensemble, recorded in 1995 (but not submitted for review until now), have unfailing charm and keen musical intelligence to commend them and are very well recorded too, though again the Golub–Kaplan–Carr team score with more present and vivid sound.

4 Romantic Pieces, Op. 75; Slavonic dances, Op. 46/2; Op. 72/2 & 8 (arr. Kreisler).
*** Ph. Dig. 462 621-2 [id.]. Akiko Suwana, Boris Berezovsky – BRAHMS: *Sonata, Op. 120/ 2 etc.*; JANACEK: *Violin sonata.* ***

Akiko Suwana and Boris Berezovsky make out the strongest case for these charming pieces: their playing is wonderfully natural and unforced. The recording is quite remarkably alive and brings the artists into your living room. A recital of distinction.

String quartets Nos. 1–14; Cypresses, B.152; Fragment in F, B.120; 2 Waltzes, Op. 54, B.105.
(B) *** DG 463 165-2 (9) [id.]. Prague Qt.

Dvořák's *Quartets* span the whole of his creative life. The glories of the mature *Quartets* are well known, though it is only the so-called *American* which has achieved real popularity. The beauty of the present set, made in 1973–7, is that it offers more *Quartets* (not otherwise available) plus two *Quartet movements*, in *A minor* (1873) and *F major*

(1881), plus two *Waltzes* and *Cypresses* for good measure, all in eminently respectable performances and decent recordings. The present transfers are most satisfactorily managed, with a nice balance between warmth and presence. At bargain price, neatly packaged and with good documentation this is self-recommending.

String quartets Nos. 5 in F min., Op. 9; 7 in A min., Op. 16.
(BB) *** Naxos Dig. 8.553377 [id.]. Vlach Qt, Prague.

Although there is stiffer competition now that DG have reissued the Prague Quartet set of the Dvořák canon at bargain price, the Vlach is as good a way of exploring this repertoire as any. The *F minor Quartet* is from 1873 and its companion here from the following year – the period of the *E flat* and *D minor* (No. 4) symphonies. Warm, well-characterized performances in good sound and all for a modest outlay. (Nos. 8 and 11 are already issued on Naxos 8.553372; No. 9 and the *Terzetto* on 8.553373; and Nos. 10 and 14 on 8.553374 – see our main volume).

VOCAL MUSIC

Saint Ludmila (oratorio), *Op. 74.*
*** Orfeo Dig. C 513992H (2) [id.]. Liviá Aghová, Michelle Breedt, Piotr Beczala, Ludek Vele, Prague Chamber Ch., WDR Cologne Ch. & SO, Gerd Albrecht.

Although it enjoyed some success in its day, *Saint Ludmila* has fallen out of the repertoire. The oratorio was written for the 1886 Leeds Festival, but Dvořák defiantly ignored the request that the subject should be biblical and the length limited to 90 minutes, exceeding that by almost an hour. According to John Clapham it was composed under great pressure: 'the whole thing is very unpleasant and worries me greatly,' Dvořák wrote. Yet even if there are a few passages that make one understand the composer's doubts, overall the result, like the choral ballad *The spectre's bride*, is a winningly vigorous, dramatic work, reflecting the composer we know from the symphonies in its rhythmic strength and lyrical warmth. It is a piece full of white-hot inspiration, punctuated with lively choruses and arias, often feeling operatic. Not only is it a rarity in the concert hall, it is also neglected on CD. Gerd Albrecht's recording is only the third (Vaclav Smetáček recorded it in the 1960s and again twenty years later).

The oratorio tells how Ludmila, the daughter of a Serb prince, married the Prince of Bohemia and, by her conversion in 874, turned the whole nation to Christianity. As is to be expected, since it comes from the same period as the *Seventh Symphony*, there are many glorious pages. The opening is wonderfully fresh and the first section brings a sequence of choruses illustrating a heathen ceremony, before the Christian hermit, Ivan, angrily smashes the idol of the goddess. The second section finds Ludmila receiving Christian instruction, before she is joined by her husband. The final section depicts their baptism, and that of their people, leading to a triumphant choral finale which in places echoes that of Beethoven's *Ninth*.

This Orfeo issue, a co-production with West German Radio, offers a strong, colourful performance, which points the drama well, using four first-rate Czech-speaking soloists – not one a Slavonic wobbler – and with the Cologne Choir augmented by the Prague Chamber Choir. The result is both polished and idiomatic, helped by warm, full sound, even though the chorus is set behind the orchestra. A piece which, despite the length, well deserves to be in the repertory.

Stabat Mater, Op. 58.
*** Telarc Dig. 2CD 80506 (2) [id.]. Christine Goerke, Marietta Simpson, Stanford Olsen, Nathan Berg, Atlanta SO & Ch., Robert Shaw.

The *Stabat Mater* blazed the trail for Dvořák's cause during his lifetime but has now become something of a rarity in the concert hall. It seems to be gaining ground in the CD catalogues and inspires the late Robert Shaw to considerable heights. He brings great dedication and obvious feeling to this score and gets a fine response from the Atlanta Symphony Orchestra and Chorus and an admirable line-up of soloists. Its lyrical breadth and gentleness come over well in this new Telarc recording and the only possible grumble might be the lack of real front-to-back depth of perspective in the balance. There is too little space round the aural image. In that respect the Kubelik is preferable (DG Double 453 025-2 – see our main volume), and this earlier version is generously coupled with the *10 Legends*, Op. 59.

OPERA

Rusalka: highlights.
*** Decca Dig. 466 356-2 [id.] (from complete recording with Renée Fleming, Ben Heppner; Czech PO, Mackerras).

The splendid Decca recording of *Rusalka* justly received a ● in our main volume (460 568-2). As it runs to three CDs, there will be those collectors who will be satisfied with just highlights, and here the heroine's famous *Invocation to the moon* opens a well-chosen 74-minute selection. Texts and translations are included.

Elgar, Edward (1857–1934)

(i) *Cockaigne overture;* (ii; iii) *Cello concerto;* (iii) *Falstaff: interludes;* (iv) *Froissart overture;* (v) *In the south overture.*

(M) (***) EMI mono CDM5 67298-2 [id.]. (i)
Royal Albert Hall O; (ii) Beatrice Harrison;
(iii) New SO; (iv) LPO; (v) LSO; all cond.
Composer.

Symphony No. 1 in A flat, Op. 55; Falstaff.
(M) (***) EMI mono CDM5 67296-2 [id.]. LSO,
composer.

Symphony No. 2 in E flat, Op. 63 (including two
rehearsal sequences).
(M) (***) EMI mono CDM5 67297-2 [id.]. LSO,
composer.

The above CDs are taken from EMI's Elgar Edition,
which comprises three box sets of three CDs. These
single CDs retain the characteristics of the original
transfers and are ideal for those not wishing to
invest in the complete Edition. Readers should refer
to our comments under the Elgar Edition in our
main volume.

*Cockaigne overture, Op.40; Pomp and
circumstance marches, Op. 39/1–5;* (i) *Sea
pictures, Op. 37.*
(B) *** CfP 574 0032. LPO, Vernon Handley; (i)
with Bernadette Greevy.

Bernadette Greevy, in glorious voice, gives the performance of her recording career, in an inspired
partnership with Vernon Handley whose accompaniments are no less memorable, with the LPO
players finding a wonderful rapport with the voice.
The singer's magical illumination of the words is a
constant source of delight, and her tenderness both
in the *Sea slumber song* and the delightfully idyllic
In haven contrasts with the splendour of the big
central and final songs, where Handley revels in the
music's surging momentum. Here he uses a telling
ad lib organ part to underline the climaxes of each
final stanza. The recording balance is ideal, the
voice rich and clear against an orchestral background shimmering with atmospheric detail.

The coupled *Marches* are exhilaratingly brilliant,
and if Nos. 2 and (especially) 3 strike some ears
as too vigorously paced, comparison with the
composer's own tempi reveals an authentic precedent. Certainly the popular *First* and *Fourth* have
an attractive gutsy grandiloquence. *Cockaigne* is
given a performance that is expansive but never
hangs fire. The recording is excellent.

Cello concerto in E minor, Op. 85.
*** Virgin/EMI Dig. VC5 45356-2 [id.]. Truls
Mørk, CBSO, Sir Simon Rattle – BRITTEN:
Cello symphony. ***

Truls Mørk recorded the Elgar in Bergen in the late
1980s with Neeme Järvi but since then his view of
it has deepened. He has the requisite blend of fervour and dignity, yet there is a freshness and directness here which is affecting. Rattle and the
Birmingham Orchestra give excellent support and

the recording has excellent internal balance and
naturalness of perspective.

(i; ii) *Cello concerto in E min., Op. 85;* (iii) *Violin
concerto in B min., Op. 61;* (ii) *Dream children,
Op. 43.*
(M) (**) Pearl mono GEM 0050 [id.]. (i) W. H.
Squire; (ii) Hallé O, Harty; (iii) Albert
Sammons, New Queens Hall O, Sir Henry
Wood.

It is apt that the two Elgar concerto recordings on
the Columbia label, which in the early days defied
HMV's monopoly of recordings by Elgar himself,
should come as a neat coupling. The Albert Sammons performance of the *Violin concerto* with Sir
Henry Wood conducting has been issued repeatedly
on LP and CD, a thrustful performance at speeds
faster than those latterly adopted, which yet poignantly conveys deep spiritual intensity, often by
understatement. The fire of the finale has never
been surpassed, though the Pearl transfer, warm but
boomy in the bass, cannot quite match Anthony
Griffiths' original LP transfer for EMI, long unavailable. The noticeable surface hiss also exposes
some 78-r.p.m. side-joins, but with little harm done.
The W. H. Squire version of the *Cello concerto* is
far rarer, a noble reading which in the first three
movements can match almost any in its concentration, but which then in the finale finds Squire's
intonation less precise in what emerges as a rougher
performance. The cello is vividly caught, and
though the orchestra is relatively dim, one quickly
adjusts to the sound. The miniature, *Dream children*, also with Harty and the Hallé, is a charming
makeweight.

(i) *Cello concerto, Op. 85;* (ii) *Enigma variations,
Op. 36.*
(B) *** Australian Decca Eloquence 450 021-2. (i)
Harrell, Cleveland O, Maazel; (ii) LAPO,
Mehta.

Lynn Harrell's outstanding account of the *Cello
concerto* with the Cleveland orchestra remains
among the very finest versions. With eloquent support from Maazel and his fine orchestra (the woodwind play with appealing delicacy), this deeply felt
reading, balances a gentle nostalgia with extrovert
brilliance. The slow movement is tenderly spacious,
the scherzo bursts with exuberance, and after a
passionate opening, the finale is memorable for the
poignantly expressive reprise of the melody from
the slow movement – one of Elgar's greatest inspirations. The recording of the orchestra is brightly
lit but attractively so, and the cello image is rich
and full, a little larger than life perhaps, but convincingly focused.

In the *Enigma variations* Mehta proves a strong
and sensitive Elgarian, and this is a highly enjoyable
performance which has long been admired. If there
are no special revelations, the transition from the

nobly conceived and spacious climax of *Nimrod* to a delightfully graceful *Dorabella* is particularly felicitous. The vintage Decca recording, with the organ entering spectacularly in the finale, is outstanding in its CD transfer – a real demonstration disc, and this is one of Mehta's very finest records. Good for Australian Decca for making this coupling available at bargain price!

(i; ii) *Cello concerto in E min., Op. 85;* (iii) *Enigma variations, Op. 36; Pomp and circumstance marches Nos. 1 & 4.*
*** Sony SK 60789 [id.]. (i) Jacqueline du Pré; (ii) Phd. O; (iii) LPO; Barenboim.

Jacqueline du Pré's second recording of the Elgar *Cello concerto* was taken from live performances in Philadelphia in November 1970, and this is a superb picture of an artist in full flight, setting her sights on the moment in the Epilogue where the slow-movement theme returns, the work's innermost sanctuary of repose. Barenboim's most distinctive point in *Enigma* is in giving the delicate variations sparkle and emotional point, while the big variations have full weight, and the finale brings extra fierceness at a fast tempo. The recording has now been effectively remastered (the sound in the concerto is particularly impressive in its clarity of profile) and handsomely repackaged to include not only a fine colour portrait of Du Pré, but also a reproduction of the familiar old LP sleeve. The programme now opens with Barenboim's rumbustious accounts of the two favourite *Pomp and circumstance marches*.

Enigma variations; Elegy for strings (2 versions); *Introduction and allegro for strings* (2 versions); *Symphony No. 1 in A flat, Op. 55.*
(B) (*******) Dutton Double mono/stereo CDSJB 1017 (2) [id.]. Hallé O, Sir John Barbirolli.

Barbirolli recorded both the *Enigma variations* and the beautiful *Elegy* (for which he had a special affection) three times, and the *Introduction and allegro* six times! (the first for the National Gramophone Society). Here we are offered the third (1947) mono and fifth (1956) stereo versions of the latter. The interpretations are broadly the same, but they are both distinctly individual performances, the later obviously gaining from the greater richness of stereo. Yet in the earlier mono account the recapitulation of the big striding theme in the middle strings already has superb thrust and warmth.

The *Enigma* recording is the first (mono) also from 1947, and it sounds very well in the present transfer, though the later and very exciting Pye stereo version, and the 1962 HMV version (see below) are finer on both performance and sonic grounds. Which is not to say that this strikingly fresh earlier version is not worth having.

But what make the present collection special is the inclusion of the first 1956 (originally Pye) stereo account of the *First Symphony*. While the later (1962) HMV version has the advantage of more modern recording and the Philharmonia playing is more polished than the Hallé's, the tempo of the first movement, after the march introduction is much slower. The Hallé plays at a good spanking allegro, and the music surges along. In the slow movement too there is greater warmth, with really affectionate playing in the three glorious main themes – the last one reserved for the very end of the movement. The remaining movements have comparable intensity and in this new Dutton transfer the sound, though not as ripe as the later EMI version is a good deal more than acceptable.

Introduction and allegro for strings, Op. 47; Serenade for strings in E min., Op. 20.
(BB) ******* Virgin Classics 2 x 1 Dig. VBD5 61763-2 (2) [CDVB 61763]. LCO, Christopher Warren-Green – DVORAK: *Serenade for strings in E, Op. 22;* SUK: *Serenade;* TCHAIKOVSKY: *Serenade;* VAUGHAN WILLIAMS: *Fantasia on Greensleeves; Fantasia on a theme of Tallis; Lark ascending.* *******

(i; ii) *Introduction and allegro for strings, Op. 47;* (i) *Serenade for strings in E min., Op. 20;* (iii) *Elegy, Op. 58; Sospiri, Op. 70.*
✹ (M) ******* EMI CDM5 67240-2 [567264]. (i) Sinfonia of L.; (ii) Allegri Qt; (iii) New Philh. O; Barbirolli – VAUGHAN WILLIAMS: *Greensleeves & Tallis fantasias.* ******* ✹

Barbirolli's famous record of English string music (the *Elegy* and *Sospiri* were added later) might be considered the finest of all his records and it remained in the catalogue at full price for over three-and-a-half decades. Now it not only costs less, but rightly takes its place as one of EMI's 'Great Recordings of the Century', with the current remastering of an originally magnificent recording losing nothing, combining bite and excellent inner definition with the fullest sonority.

Christopher Warren-Green, directing and leading his London Chamber Orchestra, directs the *Introduction and allegro* with tremendous ardour. The whole work moves forward in a single sweep and the sense of a live performance, tingling with electricity and immediacy, is thrillingly tangible. It is very difficult to believe that the group contains only seventeen players (6-5-2-3-1), with the resonant but never clouding acoustics of All Saints' Church, Petersham,. helping to create an engulfingly rich body of tone. Appropriately, the *Serenade* is a more relaxed reading yet has plenty of affectionate warmth, with the beauty of the *Larghetto* expressively rich but not overstated. This now comes as part of one of the most desirable of Virgin's superbargain doubles.

Symphony No. 3 (from the composer's sketches, realized by Payne).
🌑 (BB) *** Naxos Dig. 8.554719 [id.].
Bournemouth SO, Paul Daniel.

As the original NMC recording of Anthony Payne's realization of Elgar's fragmentary sketches became a bestseller, it is not surprising that Naxos should want to issue a rival version at super-budget price. In every way, this performance by the Bournemouth Orchestra under Paul Daniel matches the earlier one from Andrew Davis. If on NMC the BBC Symphony sounds richer and more sumptuous, relating the work to earlier Elgar, the leaner sound of the Bournemouth Orchestra brings out the originality even more, with textures clear and transparent. The passages such as the opening exposition section which Elgar completed himself, again make it clear that he was pointing forward, developing his style. Paul Daniel is particularly successful too in drawing the threads together in the finale, the movement which was the most problematic for Anthony Payne. The slow epilogue is even more moving here than in the earlier performance, ending in mystery on a question mark. First-rate sound.

CHAMBER MUSIC

Piano quintet in A min., Op. 84; Harmony music No. 4: The Farmyard. Sospiri, Op. 70.
(B) **(*) EMI Dig. CZS5 73992-2 (2) [CDZB 573992]. Israela Margalit, with members of the LSO – DELIUS: *Violin sonatas*, etc. ***.

This is another instance where the apparently logical pairing of two different sets of performances into a two-disc set brings uneven results. Both the pianist Israela Margalit, and the cellist Moray Welsh are involved in the Delius couplings, and the latter makes an eloquent contribution here to the *Piano quintet's* slow movement. But overall, the performance, while musically sensitive, lacks the panache and sense of vigorous involvement generated by the competing versions from Piers Lane and the Vellinger Quartet (also on EMI, CD-EMX 2229), Ian Brown and the Nash Ensemble (Hyperion CDA 66645), or indeed the Naxos and Discover super-bargain alternatives (see our main volume). Both the touching *Sospiri* and the excerpt from Elgar's *Harmony music* for wind come off very successfully.

PIANO MUSIC

Piano duet

Serenade in E min. (composer's version for 2 pianos).
*** Olympia Dig. OCD 683 [id.]. Goldstone and Clement – HOLST: *The Planets* (original version), *Cotswolds Symphony: Elegy*;

BAINTON: *Miniature suite* *** (with BURY: *Prelude and fugue in E flat*.***).

As with Holst's *Planets,* it is a surprise to find just how well this sounds on two pianos (especially the *Larghetto*) when played so sensitively by this excellent duo, who are most faithfully recorded.

Adieu; Concert allegro, Op. 46; Dream children, Op. 43; Enigma variations, Op. 36 (arr. Elgar)*; Griffinesque; In Smyrna; Presto; Salut d'amour; Serenade; Skizze; Sonatina.*
*** ASV Dig. CDDCA 1065 [id.]. María Garzón.

The main work here is Elgar's own transcription of the *Enigma variations,* which precedes the orchestral version by three months. It is marvellously played but was, of course, made before the days when one could get to know the piece through the gramophone. However, if you are going to have this in its keyboard form, it could hardly be better played. The Spanish pianist María Garzón has sensitivity and fervour and plays it and the other Elgar pieces, such as the *Concert allegro*, the *Sonatina* and *In Smyrna* (which he composed after a Mediterranean cruise as a guest of the Royal Navy), as if she were born and bred in Worcester rather than Madrid.

Enescu, Georges (1881–1955)

Poème roumain (symphonic suite), *Op. 1;* (i) *Vox maris* (symphonic poem), *Op. 31. Voix de la nature (Nuages de l'automne sur le forêt).*
(BB) **(*) Arte Nova Dig. 74321 65425-2 [id.].
Georges Enescu Ens., Bucharest PO & Ch., Cristian Mandeal; (i) with Florin Diaconescu.

An inexpensive introduction to the Romanian composer for those who know him only through the *Roumanian rhapsody No. 1.* It couples his very first opus, the *Poème roumain (*a two-movement symphonic suite for voices and orchestra), with one of his most eloquent works – the symphonic poem, *Vox maris* (for tenor soloist, chorus and orchestra), on which he worked during 1929, and revised and finished towards the end of his life. It comes roughly between his masterpiece *Oedipe* and the *Third Orchestral suite.* There is a quasi-mystical feel to much of it, though it is a little overheated and amorphous. His *Voix de la nature* remained unfinished, but a fragment survives – its first movement, entitled *Nuages de l'automne sur le forêt.* It is scored for a small orchestra with an unusual group of solo strings, two each of violas and cellos and one double-bass. The recordings are a little coarse in climaxes and wanting in transparency and refinement.

Légende for trumpet and piano.
*** EMI Dig. CDC5 56760-2 [id.]. Håkon Hardenberger, Leif Ove Andsnes – BRITTEN:

Piano concerto, Op. 13; SHOSTAKOVICH: *Piano concerto No. 1 in C min., Op. 35.* ***

A fine makeweight to the Shostakovich concerto which provides an admirable opportunity for Håkon Hardenberger to display his incredible legato phrasing.

Violin sonata No. 3 (dans le caractère populaire roumaine), Op. 25.
**(*) Decca Dig. 455 488-2 [id.]. Ida Haendel, Vladimir Ashkenazy – BARTOK: *Rhapsody No. 1; Rumanian folkdances;* SZYMANOWSKI: *Mythes* ** ; with Recital: *'The Decca years, 1940–47'*(***).

There are more-inspired performances of the En-escu on disc, for although Haendel is in excellent form, Vladimir Ashkenazy is more perfunctory in matters of dynamic nuance and this matters here. All the same Haendel's musical personality is such that no readers should overlook this, particularly in view of the companion disc which brings some of the records she made for Decca during and just after the war, expertly restored in these transfers.

Englund, Einar (1916–99)

Symphonies Nos. 2 (Blackbird); 4 (Nostalgic); (i) Piano concerto No. 1.
(BB) *** Naxos Dig. 8.553758 [id.]. Turku PO, Jorma Panula (i) with Niklas Sivelöv.

The Finnish composer Einar Englund was old enough to serve in the Winter War and his *First (War) Symphony* caused quite a stir when it appeared in 1947. The *Second* (1948) is full of imaginative things, though its debt to Shostakovich is heavy (the second group of the first movement from 2:48 minutes onwards (track 1) is straight out of the *Fifth Symphony*). In the *First Piano concerto* (1955) with its touches of Prokofiev and strongly Gallic overtones, Niklas Sivelöv proves a most musical and accomplished soloist. The more we hear him the more we like his playing. The *Fourth Symphony* is much later (1976) and a tribute to Shostakovich, who died that year. Rather good performances and recording make this an admirable introduction to this gifted composer.

(i) Symphony No. 6 (Aphorisms) (ii) Cello Concerto.
*** Ondine ODE 951-2 [id.]. Tampere PO, Eri Klas; with (i) Jan-Erik Gustafsson, (ii) Tampere Philh Ch.

The *Cello concerto* (1954) precedes the *First piano concerto*, and is highly imaginative. Shostakovich is still a presence in Englund's musical make-up but his music is nevertheless quite haunting, and his writing both inventive and resourceful. There is always something happening and the music unfolds naturally.

The *Sixth Symphony* (1986) is a choral setting of Heraclitus, again inventive and direct in utterance. (It is far more rewarding, say, than the symphonies of Kokkonen or Pettersson.) Jan-Erik Gustafsson is the eloquent soloist in the *Cello concerto* and the orchestral support under Eri Klas first-class. It is in much finer shape than when it recorded the Merikanto concertos a year or so back. The recording has much greater body and richness of detail than the Naxos disc listed above.

Falla, Manuel de (1876–1946)

El amor brujo (ballet): complete.
(M) **(*) BBC Music BBCB 8012-2 [id.]. Anna Reynolds, ECO, Britten – TCHAIKOVSKY: *Francesca da Rimini; Romeo and Juliet.* **

In this BBC recording made at the Aldeburgh Festival in 1971, the last year when he was able to take an active part as a performer, Britten conducts a warmly evocative reading of the Falla ballet. Not only does he bring out the atmospheric beauty of the writing, he characteristically points rhythms in a seductively idiomatic way, as in his treatment of the haunting *Pantomime.* Anna Reynolds may not sound very Spanish, but she too is warmly responsive and characterful. However, the Tchaikovsky coupling ultimately lacks the kind of strong adrenalin flow so essential in this repertoire.

(i) El amor brujo (Love, the magician); (ii) The Three-cornered hat (ballet); La Vide breve: Interlude and Dance.
(M) *** Decca 446 991-2 [id.]. SRO, Ansermet, with (i) de Gabarain; (ii) Berganza.

Listening to Ansermet's early 1960s version of *The Three-cornered hat,* you understand why his recordings are cherished by audiophiles: the sound is glitteringly brilliant and full. The performance has lots of character and shows the conductor and his orchestra on top form. *El amor Brujo* is not quite so brilliant as a recording, or as a performance, but it is still very good, with plenty of nice touches here and there. It is always a pleasure to hear the *Interlude and Dance* from *La Vide breve,* the *Dance* of which – a most catchy tune – is especially vivid here. A very colourful and worthy addition to Decca's Legends label.

Nights in the gardens of Spain.
(M) *** DG 463 085-2 [id.]. Margrit Weber, Bav. RSO, Kubelik – MARTINU: *Fantasia concertante* ***; TCHEREPNIN: *10 Bagatelles* ***; WEBER: *Konzertstück.* **(*)

Kubelik brings out all the excitement of Falla's vivid score, if slightly at the expense of atmosphere, and Margrit Weber gives a brilliant account of the solo part, particularly in the later movements. The overall effect is sparkling and the 1965 recording is very good. Imaginative new couplings, too.

(i) *Nights in the gardens of Spain;* (ii) *The three-cornered hat* (ballet; complete).
*** Teldec/Warner Dig. 0630 17415 [id.].
    Chicago SO, with (i) Barenboim (piano), cond. Plácido Domingo; (ii) Jennifer Larmore, cond. Barenboim.

The catalogue is well served by luminous recordings of Manuel da Falla's *Nights*, in fragrantly evocative Spanish gardens. Rubinstein, Eduardo del Pueyo and Alicia da Larrocha have all served the composer well, and the latter's lambent Decca account has the same coupling as above (● 430 703-2). But a first-class new version is very welcome indeed, and Barenboim and Domingo make a outstanding partnership, catching the perfumes of the Spanish night and the shimmering background of flamenco dance rhythms. The gentle entry into the jasmin-scented *Generalife* in Granada is subtly managed by Domingo, and Barenboim's crystal-clear yet highly poetic response at first suggests the water flowing in those astonishing 400-year-old Moorish fountains. The great climax at the end brings a thrilling burst of passion. From the glittering central 'Danza lejana' we are lead into the final sequence with sparkling pianism, and the closing pages bring a richly languorous apotheosis.
    Barenboim moves from keyboard to rostrum for *The three-cornered hat* and opens briskly and vigorously. Jennifer Larmore is the vibrant if not especially individual mezzo soloist. Again the superb Chicago Orchestra revels not only in the vivid colouring and bold rhythms, but also in the gentler moments: the engaging entry of the Corregidor, the delicacy of the sequence called *The grapes* and the dancing violins heralding the *Neighbours' dance*. The Miller's *Farruca* brings a stoically gutsy pulse and the boisterous final *Jota* is vigorous and uninhibited. The live recording if not in the demonstration bracket is full-blooded and yet has plenty of transparency.

The three-cornered hat (ballet): 3 dances.
(B) *** Decca Penguin Classics Dig. 460 638-2
    [id.]. Montreal SO, Dutoit – RODRIGO:
    Concierto de Aranjuez; Fantasia para un gentilhombre. *** ●

These three dances, taken from Dutoit's excellent 1981 complete ballet, make a colourful interlude between two outstanding performances of Rodrigo. The personal essay is by Victoria Glendinning.

Fauré, Gabriel (1845–1924)

Elégie in C min., Op. 24.
(B) *** EMI Début CZS5 73727-2 [id.]. Xavier
    Phillips, Bavarian Chamber PO, Emmanuel

Plasson – CAPLET: *Epiphany;* LALO: *Cello concerto.* ***

From the impressive Xavier Phillips, a poetically songful and only marginally recessive performance, with orchestra and soloist at one in their response to Fauré's emotional and dynamic contrasts.

(i) *Pelléas et Mélisande (suite), Op. 80;* (ii) *Pavane, Op. 50.*
(B) **(*) Sony SBK 62644 [id.]. (i) New Philh. O,
    Andrew Davis; (ii) Philadelphia O, Ormandy –
    IBERT: *Divertissement; Escales* **(*);
    ROUSSEL: *Bacchus et Ariane.* ***

Andrew Davis turns in an attractive performance of the *Pelléas* music, though there have been more magical accounts. The 1975 sound is good, but not exceptional. The *Pavane* is also nicely done, but this bargain CD is mainly valuable for the *Escales* and *Bacchus et Ariane* couplings.

CHAMBER MUSIC

Cello sonatas Nos. 1, Op. 109; 2, Op. 117; Après un rêve (trans. Casals); *Elégie, Op. 24; Papillon, Op. 77; Romance, Op. 69; Sicilienne, Op. 78; Sérénade, Op. 98.*
*** Opus 111 Dig. OPS 30-242 [id.]. Peter Bruns,
    Roglit Ishay.

The two *Cello sonatas* are among Fauré's most substantial works and are well served here. But this is Fauré with a difference. Peter Bruns plays the Tonino cello that Casals once owned and Roglit Ishay plays an Erard. This has a more brittle timbre than the modern piano but Fauré himself much liked its lighter action. Those who want the sonatas in the sonorities the composer himself might have heard should investigate this, which in any case is probably a first choice for this repertoire. These two artists both play with appropriate eloquence and the miniatures come off well.

Piano quartets Nos. 1 in C min., Op. 15; 2 in G min., Op. 45.
(BB) **(*) ASV Quicksilva CDQS6237 [id.].
    Schubert Ens. of London.

A very serviceable coupling of both the Fauré *Piano quartets* which offers very good value. Very musical playing, attentive to the letter and the spirit of these scores without, perhaps, the last ounce of distinction that the Domus team brought to them on Hyperion (● CDA 66166). Very well recorded indeed. Well worth the modest asking price – and more!

Piano quartet No. 2 in G min., Op. 45; Piano quintet No. 2 in C min., Op. 115.
*** Decca Dig. 455 150-2 [id.]. Pascal Rogé,
    Ysaÿe Qt.

Decca have followed up their coupling of the *First Piano quartet,* in C minor and the much later *First Piano quintet,* recorded in the Salle Wagram (455

149-2) with their successors. This was recorded in St George's, Brandon Hill, Bristol. The playing of all concerned is excellent, alive and subtle with expert and sensitive contributions from the distinguished pianist. As in its predecessor the aural image is not in ideal focus, with Pascal Rogé very slightly too much to the fore and the quartet not as well defined. But such is the quality of the playing that it would be curmudgeonly to withhold a third star.

Piano trio in D min. Op. 120.
*** Hyperion Dig. CDA 67114 [id.]. Florestan
    Trio – DEBUSSY; RAVEL: *Piano trios.* ***

Following up the success of their *Gramophone* prizewinning disc of Schumann trios, also for Hyperion, the Florestans here offer this unique and very apt coupling of three sharply contrasted French works. Fauré is represented in mellow old age, Debussy as a teenager and Ravel in high maturity. With personnel drawn from the piano quartet group Domus, led by the pianist Susan Tomes, the Florestans give an exceptionally strong, unapologetic reading, at once highly polished and flexibly expressive, revealing what power Fauré retained to the end of his life. Vivid sound.

Violin sonatas Nos. 1 in A, Op. 13; 2 in E min., Op. 108.
(B) *** Hyperion Helios CDH 55030 [id.]. Krysia
    Osostowicz, Susan Tomes.

Krysia Osostowicz and Susan Tomes bring an appealingly natural, unforced quality to their playing and they are completely persuasive, particularly in the elusive *Second Sonata*. The acoustic is a shade resonant but, such is the eloquence of these artists, the ear quickly adjusts. At Helios price, this disc becomes highly recommendable.

PIANO MUSIC

Barcarolles Nos. 3 in G flat, Op. 42; 9 in A min., Op. 101; Impromptus Nos. 1 in E flat, Op. 25; 2 in F min., Op. 31; 3 in A flat, Op. 34; 4 in D flat, Op. 91; 5 in F sharp min., Op. 102; Nocturne No. 3 in A flat, Op. 33/3; 8 Pièces brèves, Op. 84; 9 Préludes, Op. 103; Valse-caprice No. 1 in A, Op. 30.
(**) VAI Audio VAIA 1165 [id.]. Grant
    Johannesen.

Older collectors will recall Grant Johannesen as a sensitive and subtle exponent of Fauré and this reissue of his 1961 recordings serves as a reminder of his artistry. This is lovely playing, reflective and intelligent, all but wrecked by the recording, made in a small, dry acoustic, which produces brittle, shallow piano tone.

Mazurka, Op. 32; Pavane, Op. 50; Pelléas et Mélisande – suite; Valses-caprices, Opp. 30, 38, 59 & 62.

(BB) * Naxos Dig. 8.553741 [id.]. Pierre-Alain
    Volondat.

The latest in Pierre-Alain Volondat's survey of the Fauré piano music is no more satisfying than his earlier release (see our *Penguin Bargain Guide*). He appreciates Fauré's gentleness of spirit and has a refined tonal sense. However, the music has almost no sense of pulse; he comes to an almost complete stop every few bars in the *Prélude* to *Pelléas et Mélisande,* and the *Mazurka,* Op. 32 is not allowed to speak for itself either. Good recorded sound.

VOCAL MUSIC

Mélodies: Après un rêve; Au bord de l'eau; Les berceaux; Clair de lune; Lydia; Mandoline; Le papillon et la fleur; Sylvie.
*** Virgin/EMI Dig. VC5 45360-2 [id.].
    Véronique Gens, Roger Vignoles – DEBUSSY;
    POULENC: *Mélodies.* ***

Véronique Gens is a highly accomplished artist and certainly makes a beautiful sound. She allows Fauré's art to speak for itself, although there are times when you feel stronger characterization would not come amiss. She is sensitively accompanied by Roger Vignoles and recorded with great naturalness.

3 Mélodies, Op. 23 (Les berceaux; Notre amour; Le secret); 5 Mélodies de Venise, Op. 58 (Mandoline; En sourdine; Green; A Clymene; C'est l'extase); Mélodies, Op. 39: 2, Fleur jetée; 4, Les roses d'Ispahan.
(BB) *** Belart 461 624-2 [id.]. Felicity Palmer,
    John Constable – RAVEL: *Chansons; Mélodies; Poèmes* **(*)

Felicity Palmer is in splendid form here. True there is still a hint of the beat, which is also noticeable in the Ravel couplings. But she has the measure of Fauré's subtle and elevated art, which she shows most impressively in the *Cinq mélodies de Venise,* while the closing *Fleur jetée* is sung with great passion. She has the advantage moreover of John Constable's imaginative accompanying and altogether first-class analogue recording from the mid 1970s. There is 74 minutes of music on this Belart reissue and though no texts or translations are included, it is still a remarkable bargain.

Requiem, Op. 48.
❀ **(*) BBC Legends BBCL 4026-2 [id.]. Janet
    Price, John Carol Case, BBC Ch., BBC SO,
    Nadia Boulanger – BOULANGER: *Psaumes 24
    & 130; Pie Jesu.* **(*) ❀
(M) *** Decca 466 418-2 [id.]. Jonathon Bond,
    Benjamin Luxon, St John's College,
    Cambridge, Ch., ASMF, Stephen Cleobury
    (organ), George Guest – DURUFLE:
    Requiem.***

In 1968, the year of the turbulence in Paris, Nadia Boulanger visited London to conduct some of her sister's work and direct this performance of the Fauré *Requiem*. Her teachers at the beginning of the last century included Fauré, which lends this performance special interest and authority. Fauré himself spoke of the piece as not expressing fear of death but rather 'an aspiration towards happiness above, rather than as a painful experience'. Nadia Boulanger's account, recorded at Croydon's Fairfield Hall with the BBC Chorus and Symphony Orchestra, has dignity and gravity. Tempi throughout are on the slow side but seem absolutely right. The Introitus has what John Warrack's excellent notes call 'an almost tragic severity'. There may be better sung and played accounts of the *Requiem* but this has a keenly devotional feeling throughout and a special radiance that is moving. A rather special musical document.

The St John's account of the Fauré *Requiem* has a magic that works from the opening bars onwards. Jonathon Bond and Benjamin Luxon are highly sympathetic soloists and the smaller scale of the performance is probably nearer to Fauré's original conception than some of the more ambitious competing versions. This coupling with Duruflé is highly praised in our main volume where it appears on a Decca Double with more rewarding choral music by both composers (436 486-2).

Field, John (1782–1837)

Piano concertos Nos. 2 in A flat; 3 in E flat.
**(*) Teldec/Warner Dig. 3984 21475-2 [id.].
Andreas Staier, Concerto Kölne, David Stern.

The performances here are certainly authentic, with Staier's nimble, twinkling (some would say tinkly) roulades contrasting with the robust orchestral tuttis. But, as with the music of Chopin, it is difficult to prefer the sound here to that of the modern piano, except perhaps in the innocent *Rondo* which closes No. 2, which is delightfully pointed by Staier's crisp keyboard articulation.

Complete Piano Music, Volume 1

Nocturnes Nos. 1–9; Piano sonatas Nos. 1 in E flat; 2 in A, Op. 1/1–2.
(BB) *** Naxos Dig. 8.550761 [id.]. Benjamin Frith.

Benjamin Frith's playing is delectably coaxing, and he makes these *Nocturnes* so often seem exquisitely like Chopin, yet still catches their naïve innocence, especially in the *A flat major* work. He hops, skips and jumps delightfully in the Irish Rondo finale of the *First sonata* and is hardly less beguiling in the rather more imposing opening movement of the *Second*. The Naxos recording is first class, and made in a very pleasing acoustic. If the following volumes

are as good as this first instalment, they will be hard to beat.

Largo in C min.; Nocturnes in B flat; C min.; E min.; Prelude in C min.; Romance in E flat; Waltzes in A; E (Sehnsucht).
*** Etcetera Dig. KTC 1231 [id.]. Helge Antoni – CHOPIN: Recital. **(*)

Under the title 'Crossfire' this fascinatingly devised recital readily demonstrates links and influences between the music of the Irish John Field (who invented the Nocturne) and Chopin, his young Polish successor. Contemporary opinion was divided on the comparative merits of their music. A German critic (Rellstab) suggested that 'Where Field smiles, Chopin makes a grinning grimace; where Field sighs, Chopin groans'. But Liszt more perceptively observed that 'Field in his Nocturnes with their wealth of melody and refinement of harmony, charged them with shy, serenely tender emotions. Chopin in his poetic Nocturnes, sang not only the harmonies which are the source of our most ineffable delights, but likewise the restless agitated bewilderment to which they often give rise. His flight is loftier, though his wing be more wounded.'

Helge Antoni is a notably sensitive advocate of Field's music and his simple style readily draws parallels with alternated pieces by Chopin. Field's *Nocturne in C minor* of 1812 is presented alongside Chopin's work in the same key, written twenty-five years later, and there are similar influences to be found in the *Waltzes*. A recital that is both stimulating and musically enjoyable too, as it is naturally recorded.

Finzi, Gerald (1901–56)

(i) *Clarinet concerto;* (ii) *Introit for violin and orchestra.*
(M) *** BBC Music BBCM 5015-2 [id.]. (i) Janet Hilton, BBC Northern SO, Bryden Thomson; (ii) Gerald Jarvis, LPO, Boult – LEIGH: *Harpsichord concertino* *** (with Concert: 'English music' ***).

Finzi's *Clarinet concerto*, recorded in the Milton Hall, Manchester in 1978, is played most nimbly by Janet Hilton, admirably supported by Bryden Thomson, especially in the lovely *Adagio,* which is memorably intense. The present transfer is strikingly fresh and natural. The virtually unknown *Introit for violin and orchestra* brings another memorable theme and is very much worth having; it originally formed the middle movement of a larger work, whose outer movements Finzi withdrew. It is a meditative, thoughtful piece, very well played by Gerald Jarvis and the LPO under Sir Adrian Boult in 1969 and, although the recording does not have the transparency or dynamic range one would expect from a commercial recording of this period, again the current transfer gives a very pleasing sound picture, warm and natural. This is part of a 77-minute concert of English music including the delicious *Harpsichord concertino* of Walter Leigh. This is considered under its composer entry; the rest of the music is discussed in our Concerts section below.

Fischer, Johann Caspar Ferdinand (c. 1670–1746)

Musical Parnassus, Volume 1: *Suites Nos. 1–6 (Clio; Calliope; Melpomène; Thalia; Erato; Euterpe).*
(BB) *** Naxos Dig. 8.554218 [id.]. Luc Beauséjour (harpsichord).

J. C. F. Fischer (not to be confused with Johann Christian Fischer), who used to feature prominently in the diet of piano students during the 1940s and '50s, is remembered for his *Ariadne musica* (1715), a series of twenty preludes and fugues, each in a different key, thus anticipating Bach's *Wohltemperierte Klavier.* His Opus 1 is the orchestral suite *Le journal du printems* (1695), dedicated to the Margrave Ludwig Wilhelm of Baden, with whose family Fischer remained for the rest of his life. The Court was strongly permeated by French culture and Fischer's role in music history was to fuse the style of the Lullian suite with the classical core of dance suite movements favoured by Froberger. He published his *Musicalischer Parnassus* in 1738, which comprises nine suites named after the Muses. The first six are included on this disc and are often fresh and inventive, rarely routine. The Canadian Luc Beauséjour plays them with some flair and is very vividly recorded.

Forqueray, Antoine (1671–1745)

Pieces for 3 viols in D min.; Suite for 3 viols in D.
*** Virgin Veritas/EMI Dig. VC5 45358-2.
Jérôme Hantaï, Kaori Uemura, Alix Verzier, Pierre Hantaï – MARAIS: *Pièces à violes.* ***

It is not absolutely sure that these works are by Forqueray, a contemporary of Marais, but they share the austere style we recognize in that composer's writing for viol consort. Whoever composed this six-movement *Suite,* it is music of considerable expressive depth, especially the eloquent *Sarabandes* and ends with a lively extended *Chaconne.* The performances here are sympathetically expert and very well recorded.

Foulds, John (1880–1939)

April, England; Egoistic; English tune with Burden, Op. 89; Essays in the modes, Op. 78;

Music-Pictures Groups VI (Gaelic melodies), Op. 81; VII (Landscapes), Op. 13; Variations and improvisations on an original theme, Op. 4.
*** BIS Dig. CD 933 [id.]. Kathryn Stott.

Kathryn Stott proves brilliant and persuasive in this repertoire. She also has the advantage of quite exceptionally truthful and vivid recording quality – indeed one of the most natural of recent piano recordings with a perfectly conditioned instrument. (Not surprising, as when you look up the recording details it was made in the wonderful acoustic of the Gothenburg Concert Hall.) The *Essays in the modes* (1928) which opens the disc is interesting stuff; one is reminded of *Petrushka* in the first and of Busoni elsewhere. Ms Stott characterizes these pieces and everything here with strong personality. Try *Prismic,* the last of the *Essays,* and the intelligence and wit of her playing will make a striking impression. Foulds wrote for the piano throughout his life, and if his music from the 1920s is obviously the more rewarding, even the youthful *Variations and improvisations on an original theme* shows a pleasing fluency. Not great music but played like this one is almost persuaded that it is.

Franck, César (1822–90)

Symphony in D min.
(B) ** Australian Decca Eloquence 460 505-2.
Cleveland O, Maazel – BIZET: *L'Arlésienne: Suites Nos. 1–2; Jeux d'enfants* ***.

Maazel's account of the somewhat elusive Franck *Symphony* is exciting and brilliantly played and recorded, but a lack of lyrical tenderness robs the work of some of its more appealing qualities. The rich melody of the second subject finds Maazel introducing tenutos, which in so clipped and precise a performance seem obtrusive. Maazel's earlier account with the Berlin Radio Orchestra on DG is in almost every way preferable and is now part of DG's Originals series, coupled with an equally fine account of Mendelssohn's *Fifth (Reformation) Symphony* (449 720-2).

Piano trios Nos. 2 in B flat (Trio de salon), Op. 1/ 2; 3 in B min., Op. 1/3; 4 in B min., Op. 2.
** Chandos Dig. CHAN 9742 [id.]. Bekova Sisters.

These early trios come from Franck's student years and are in no way representative of his mature personality. They emanate from the world of Weber and Mendelssohn and offer little of real substance, even the fugal Op. 2, which he dedicated to Liszt. Eleonora Bekova, the pianist, proves the dominant personality in the trio and some will find her just a bit too assertive. Neither the music nor the playing is really three star but the recording is realistic in the best tradition of the house.

Violin sonata in A.
*** EMI Dig. CDC5 56815-2 [id.]. Itzhak
   Perlman, Martha Argerich – BEETHOVEN:
   Violin sonata No. 9 in A (Kreutzer). ***

As in the Beethoven *Kreutzer Sonata*, Perlman and
Argerich challenge each other to thrilling effect in
this live recording, made in Saratoga in 1999. Here,
in a less formally structured sonata, their spontaneous interplay makes for an apt feeling of rhapsodic improvisation. The very opening finds
Argerich deeply reflective before Perlman launches
into the allegro at a far faster tempo. Some may
resist the expressive freedom, whether in phrasing,
rubato or in fluctuations of speed, but the magnetism
will for most be irresistible, even when the playing
is not immaculate, as in the second movement
allegro. As in the Beethoven coupling, audience
noises are intrusive at times.

PIANO MUSIC

*Eglogue (Hirtengedicht), Op. 3; Les plaintes
d'une poupée; Prélude, aria et final; Prélude,
choral et fugue; Premier Grand caprice, Op. 5.*
(BB) *** Naxos Dig. 8.554484 [id.]. Ashley Wass.

Ashley Wass hails from Lincolnshire and came to
international attention as first-prize winner of the
1997 World Piano Competition. One does not need
to know that to realize that he is an artist of quality
who has intelligence together with a wide and refined tonal palette to commend him. Franck's piano
music is decently represented in the catalogue but
there is little at bargain price, and although both the
Prélude, aria et final and the *Prélude, choral et
fugue* are readily available, the *Eglogue (Hirtengedicht)*, Op. 3 is not otherwise listed and the *Premier
Grand caprice*, Op. 5 is only to be found on Stephen
Hough's outstanding Hyperion disc. It is by this
exalted yardstick that any newcomer must be
judged, and it is a measure of his achievement that
Wass registers on the Hough scale.

   Both the *Eglogue*, meditative with a massive
central climax, and the *Grande caprice*, a flamboyant showpiece, were written when Franck was
in his early twenties, each dedicated to one of his
rich women pupils. What Wass brings out in those
and the major items is the technical brilliance of the
keyboard writing, very different from the heavyweight style Franck tended to adopt both in his
writing for the organ and for the orchestra. Wass
uses a ravishing range of tone, lightening the
Prélude, aria et final with a flowing speed in the
Prélude and a mysterious opening for the *Final*.
The two lyrical miniatures are charmingly done, but
most impressive is the finest of Franck's piano
works, the *Prelude and choral*, leading to a
powerful, clean-cut account of the *Fugue*, which
makes one want to hear Wass in Bach. Heavy fortissimos tend to clang – partly the eager pianist's fault
– but otherwise the sound is full and vivid.

ORGAN MUSIC

*3 Chorals (in E; B min.; A min.); 3 Pièces:
(Fantaisie in A; Cantabile; Pièce héroïque); 6
Pièces: (Fantaisie No. 1 in C, Op. 16; Grande
pièce symphonique, Op. 17; Prélude, fugue et
variation, Op. 18; Pastorale, Op. 19; Pière, Op.
20; Final, Op. 21.*
◉ *** Erato/Warner Dig. 0630 12706-2 (2) [id.].
   Marie-Claire Alain (Cavaillé-Coll organ of
   Saint-Etienne, Caen).

These two CDs include all of Franck's most important works for organ: the *6 Pièces*, written between
1860 and 1862, the *3 Pièces* of 1878 and the
3 Chorals of 1890, the last year of the composer's
life. Marie-Claire Alain recorded all these works on
LP for Erato on a Cavaillé-Col organ at Lyons.
Now she has returned to them, using an even finer
instrument at Caen. The Cavaillé-Coll organs are
as closely related to Franck's music as say, Peter
Pears' voice was to Britten's. These new performances are even finer than the earlier ones, full of
spontaneous feeling and the registration brings
some glorious sounds, notably in the Op. 16 *Fantaisie*, the *Third Choral*, where the detail is quite
remarkably clear, and the exultant closing *Final*.
The sympathy which this player brings to this music
and the authority of the results gives this survey a
special claim on the allegiance of collectors, and
the digital recording is superb, very much in the
demonstration bracket.

(i) *3 Chorals (in E; B min.; A min.); Prélude,
fugue et variation, Op. 18;* (ii) *3 Pièces:
Cantabile;* (iii) *Panis angelicus* (arr. Britton).
(BB) ** ASV Quicksilva Analogue/Dig. CDQS
   6175 [id.]. (i) Francis Grier (organ of Christ
   Church Cathedral, Oxford); (ii) James
   Lancelot (organ of Winchester Cathedral); (iii)
   Harold Grier (organ of Walsall Town Hall).

Francis Grier plays the comparatively new Rieger
organ at Christ Church Cathedral, Oxford. The
acoustic is dryish and the closely balanced
recording brings remarkably clarity, but is not
wholly convincing, especially in the *Third Choral*
where the climax is fierce. But Grier is a fine player,
of that there is no doubt and there is much to praise
here. The two extra items have been added on
for the reissue: they are well played and naturally
recorded. But heard alongside Alain's set above,
this Quicksilva CD seems less of a bargain than at
first sight.

Choral No. 2.
*** Chandos Dig. CHAN 9785 [id.]. Ian Tracey
   (organ of Liverpool Cathedral), BBC PO, Yan
   Pascal Tortelier – GUILMANT: *Symphony No. 2
   for organ and orchestra, Op. 91;* WIDOR:
   Symphony No. 3 for organ and orchestra.* ***

Franck's *Second Choral* is an expansive *Passaca-*

glia, which reaches a great climax and then gently fades away in the valedictory closing bars. Although the Liverpool organ is not entirely right for it (one needs better definition), Ian Tracey's performance can hardly be faulted, and the result is nothing if not spectacular, enough to make a suitable encore for the two concertante works.

Frost, Stephen (born 1959)

(i; ii) *Bassoon concerto;* (iii) *Oboe concerto;* (ii; iv) *The Lesson.*
**(*) Chandos Dig. CHAN 9763 [id.]. (i) Sigyn Birkeland; (ii) Bournemouth SO; (iii) Simon Elmes, Ens. 2000; (iv) Arve Bergset; cond. Tony Harrison.

The work for oboe is undoubtedly the finer of these two concertos, succinctly inventive, with a rhythmically quirky opening movement, and a meditative pastoral centrepiece, whose mood is to return to close the vivacious finale. The *Bassoon concerto* is perhaps somewhat over-extended when its genial opening toccata gives way to a long central soliloquy, decorated with percussion but also featuring a solo piano, which is to provide a link into the energetic finale.

Both soloists are excellent players (the work for bassoon was written for Sigyn Birkeland), and performances overall are of high quality. *The Lesson* is an original conception which will not perhaps be to all tastes – a floating vocal melisma using the poem by W. H. Auden. The speaker is placed within the orchestra and no attempt is made to focus the words sharply (and no text is included) so one assumes they are merely a starting point for a a piece which is above all evocative. Excellent recording.

Frühling, Carl (1868–1937)

Clarinet trio, Op. 114.
*** RCA Dig. 09026 63504-2 [id.]. Michael Collins, Steven Isserlis, Stephen Hough –
BRAHMS: *Clarinet trio;* SCHUMANN: *Märchenerzählungen; Träumerei.* ***

It was the cellist Steven Isserlis who unearthed this warmly seductive trio for clarinet, cello and piano, setting it against the masterpiece for the same instruments which crowns Brahms's sequence of chamber works. Frühling was a composer writing against fashion in a frankly Brahmsian idiom, which yet has strong purpose and individuality, built on memorable themes. The Schumann suite is a fine makeweight, with Isserlis tackling the viola part on the cello. Michael Collins and Stephen Hough, equally magnetic as recording artists, are ideal partners.

Frye, Walter (died 1475)

Missa Flos Regalis; Song: *Alas, alas.*
*** Signum Dig. SIGCD 015 [id.]. Clerk's Group
– Edward Wickham (with ANON: *Kyrie: Deus creator from Sarum Chant Pryncesse of youthe.* BEDYNGHAM: *Myn hertis lust; Fortune alas; Mi very joy; So ys emprentid ***) –
PLUMMER: *Missa Sine nomine.* ***

This enterprising and very rewarding Signum collection is entitled '*Brussels 5557*', as all the music is taken from a manuscript catalogued under that number, held in the Brussels Bibliothèque Royale. The presence of English music in an anthology which includes works by Du Fay confirms its importance and indeed the *Missa Flos Regalis* (which may have been composed for the wedding of Charles, Duke of Burgundy, and Margaret of York in 1468) is a remarkably individual setting. Often the polyphony is comparatively simple, but Frye's melismatic style is all his own, with the serene *Sanctus* followed by an even more beautiful *Agnus Dei*. We are then offered a group of memorable secular songs, including three by another virtually unknown composer, John Bedyngham, which are equally individual, especially the delightful *So ys emprentid*, although Frye's *Alas, alas* is perhaps finest of all. The performances, as one anticipates from this splendid group, are dedicated and impressively secure. The recording too could hardly be bettered, nicely set back in a warm ambience.

Furtwängler, Wilhelm (1886–1954)

Symphonic concerto: Adagio
(**) Testament SBT 1170 [id.]. Edwin Fischer, Berlin PO, Furtwängler – BRAHMS: *Piano concerto No. 2.* (**(*))

It makes a valuable bonus to the radio recording of the Brahms concerto to have a further, very personal example of these two great artists' rapport in working together, in a movement from one of the conductor's most ambitious works. Furtwängler was of a generation of German musicians who were not ashamed to be judged on their compositions. This may not be great music, but with its echoes of Bruckner leading to passionate climaxes it makes agreeable listening in this studio recording of 1939, even with limited sound.

Gabrieli, Andrea (c. 1510–1586)

Madrigali e Canzoni: *Angel del terzo ciel; Cantiam di Dio, Cantiamo; Canzona à 4; Come havrò pace in terra; Caro dolce ben mio; A le guacie i rose; Gratie che'l mio Signor; I'vo piangendo i miei passati tempi; Mentre la greggia errando; Mentr'io vi miro; Quanti, sepolti giù nel*

foco eterno; Hor che nel suo bel seno; O Dea;
Piangi pur, Musa; Ricercare Va 4; Rimanti,
Amor; O soave al mio cor dolce catena; Sento,
sent' un rumor; Tirsi, che fai cosi dolente a
l'ombra; Tirsi morir volea; Vaghi Augeletti; La
verginella è simile alla rosa; Vostro fui e sarò
mentre ch'io viva.
**(*) CPO Dig. 999 642-2 [id.].
    Weser-Renaissance Bremen, Manfred Cordes.

Andrea Gabrieli spent almost all his life in Venice, apart from a long visit to Frankfurt for the coronation of Emperor Maximilian II, and Munich where he came into contact with Lassus and other major figures of the day. On his return to Venice he rose to be second organist at San Marco after Merulo in the 1560s, becoming first organist in 1585; his nephew, Giovanni succeeded him as second. He composed prolifically in most genres and this collection of madrigals, performed here by singers and instrumentalists of the Weser-Renaissance, brings together pieces from several different publications. Neither his vocal nor instrumental music is as generously represented on CD as that of his illustrious nephew, though there is much that is of quality. Where the singers and instrumentalists are together, there is a tendency for nuances of word-colouring and dynamics to be ironed out. Although there are moments of dubious intonation (about 50 seconds into the fifth madrigal, *I'vo piangendo i miei passati tempi*), performances are generally dedicated, and the recording clean and well focused. A useful addition to the catalogue.

Gardner, John (born 1917)

Half-holiday overture, Op. 52; (i) Flute concerto,
Op. 220. Irish suite, Op. 231; Prelude for strings,
Op. 148a; Sinfonia piccola for strings, Op. 47;
Symphony No. 3 in E min., Op. 189.
(M) *** ASV Dig. CDWHL 2125 [id.]. Royal
    Ballet O, Gavin Sutherland; (i) with Jennifer
    Stinton.

John Gardner was born in Manchester. After service in the RAF he joined the staff at the Royal Opera House, and concurrently the Royal Academy of Music and then (following in famous footsteps) St Paul's Girls' School at Hammersmith. His first symphony was premièred at the Cheltenham Festival in 1951, and the opera, *The Moon and Sixpence* at Sadler's Wells in 1957. After that he suffered a degree of eclipse. But this programme shows an impressively wide-ranging talent.

    The catchy *Half-holiday* overture has an engaging pastoral secondary theme. Appropriately, it is half-length and doesn't go on a moment too long. The *Flute concerto*, written for Jennifer Stinton in 1995, has a relaxed conversational opening movement followed by a poignant *Nocturne*. The third movement is an elegant *Gavotte*, with lively

drone/musette interruptions, and the rondo finale gives the flute plenty of opportunities for sparkling virtuosity.

    The delicacy of orchestration of the *Third Symphony* does not reveal for a moment that it was scored for the same combination as Brahms's *Second Symphony* with which it shared the programme at its début. Its later motivation suggests influences from Shostakovich, which persist in the solemn threnodic *Adagio*. The finale restores the mood of genial humanity. The elegiac *Prelude for strings* derives from a string quartet.

    Most successful of all is the *Sinfonia piccola.* (How is that English composers write so perceptively for strings?) The *Andante* moves over a thoughtful pizzicato underlay and proves to be a searching passacaglia, always a source of stimulation in the hands of a fine composer. The finale has a touch of Britten's *Simple Symphony* about it. The *Irish suite* genially celebrated the composer's eightieth birthday. It includes four traditional tunes, but the fifth, the *Spring song,* is the composer's own. Fine performances and an excellent recording serve to recommend this collection well, and congratulations to ASV for issuing it at mid-price.

Gates, Philip (born 1963)

Airs and graces; Clarinet sonata; Flute sonata;
Danzas del Sud; Mood music; Rio bound.
**(*) Shellwood Productions Dig. SWCD 15 [id.].
    Janet Way, Thomas Kelly, Ian Clarke, Roy
    Willox, Composer.

Philip Gates, who studied the piano under Phyllis Sellick, is of a promising new generation of composers who are trying to communicate directly with the ordinary music-lover, and aren't ashamed of tunes and sonata form. He obviously has a special feeling for the flute and is clearly influenced by twentieth-century French writing for this instrument, including the jazzy inflections. The engagingly cool nostalgia of the central movement of his *Sonata* has a few unpredictable interruptions from the piano, for which Gates also writes very naturally. The finale's rhythmic influences are Latin-American. The six *Airs and graces* are lightweight vignettes, the most striking being *At Loch Leven* (with its Scottish snap in the melody) and the neatly syncopated *Rag-a-muffin*. The *Clarinet sonata* flows amiably, with a bluesy central *Cantabile*. But it is the snappy finale that stands out. *Rio bound* makes a good final encore. The *Mood music* pieces for alto-saxophone are less striking. The *March hare* gambles robustly, but *Sax-Blue* and *Soft-Shoe* are too predictable. The performances are excellent and so is the recording.

Geminiani, Francesco (1687–1762)

Concerti grossi, Op. 3/5–6; Op. 7/1–6.
(BB) *** Naxos Dig. 8.553020 [id.]. Capella
Istropolitana, Jaroslav Kreček.

This CD continues the Naxos series of Geminiani's
Concerti grossi, concluding Op. 3 and including the
whole of Op. 7. However the extra parts (in Nos. 2,
4 and 5 for flutes, and 6 for bassoon) are not used
here as they are in Iona Brown's outstanding set
with the ASMF, which remains a primary recommendation for Op. 7 (ASV CDDCA 724). Nevertheless the performances by the Capella Istropolitana
match those on their first disc (8.553019) in freshness and vitality, and they are very well recorded.
Bargain hunters need not hesitate.

Gerhard, Roberto (1896–1970)

Symphony No. 4 (New York); Pandora suite.
*** Chandos Dig. CHAN 9651 [id.]. BBC SO,
Matthias Bamert.

Written only two years before the composer's death,
when he knew his time was limited, Roberto Gerhard's *Fourth Symphony* can be seen as the culminating achievement of his extraordinary last period.
Throwing caution aside, he here indulges in his
exuberant love of wild and exotic orchestral sounds.
This half-hour, single-movement span is at once
uninhibited yet tautly conceived, with complex and
highly original textures that emerge with pin-point
clarity in this superb recording conducted by
Matthias Bamert. The *Pandora suite* from 1942,
written for the Kurt Jooss ballet in colourful tonal
writing, reveals Gerhard at his most approachable.

German, Edward (1862–1936)

*Berceuse; The Conqueror; Gipsy suite; Henry
VIII: 3 dances; Merrie England: suite; Nell Gwyn:
suite; Romeo and Juliet: suite; Tom Jones: Waltz.*
*** Marco Polo Dig. 8.223419 [id.].
Czecho-Slovak RSO (Bratislava), Leaper.

*Richard III overture; The Seasons; Theme and six
diversions.*
** Marco Polo Dig. 8.223695 [id.]. RTE Concert
O, Penny.

*Symphony No. 2 in A min. (Norwich); Valse
gracieuse; Welsh Rhapsody.*
*(*) Marco Polo Dig. 8.223726 [id.]. Nat. SO of
Ireland, Penny.

Of the three Edward German CDs listed above, the
first is definitely the one to go for. These suites
essentially consist of a string of piquant, rustic-type
dances of considerable charm. Most of the
composer's most famous numbers are here: the

items from *Merrie England* and *Henry VIII*, the
pseudo-exotic *Gipsy suite*, the memorable *Waltz*
from *Tom Jones*, plus a few rarities. All of it is
effectively presented by the ever-reliable Adrian
Leaper, and his Bratislava orchestra play as though
they were from the home counties. Definitely an
enticing collection in Marco Polo's valuable British
Light Music series, most of which shows this
composer at his best.

German's 'symphonic suite' *The Seasons* does
not match the melodic inspiration of Glazunov's
work of the same name, but it is certainly appealingly tuneful, colourfully orchestrated and enjoyable. The darker colours in *Autumn* provide a certain
gravitas (there's even an echo of Wagner if you
stretch your imagination a bit), whilst *Winter* has
plenty of scurrying strings and woodwind to paint
the scene. If the *Richard III overture* is no towering
masterpiece, it is not dull either, and has enough
ideas and a certain Romantic sweep to keep it going.
A robust theme in D minor on the brass opens the
Theme and 6 diversions, and the ensuing variations
are enjoyable and nicely varied – some highly vigorous, others olde English (including another
'*Gipsy dance*') and a waltz. The caveat is that although the music is well conducted and played with
enthusiasm, the orchestra is a bit scrawny in the
string department. Nor is the recording first class – it
lacks richness and bloom. But the music's character
does come through.

The *Second Symphony* was commissioned by the
Norwich Festival (hence its title '*Norwich*') in 1893.
It has a certain charm – the spirits of Mendelssohn
and Dvořák vaguely hover around in the background, but in the last resort, the writing fails to be
memorable. The charming *Valse gracieuse* and the
deservedly well-known *Welsh rhapsody* show the
composer on better form. The performances are
committed, but the sound is only average.

Gernsheim, Friedrich (1839–1916)

*Symphonies Nos. 1 in G min., Op. 32; 2 in E flat,
Op. 46; 3 in C min. (Miriam), Op. 54; 4 in B flat,
Op. 62.*
(BB) *** Arte Nova Dig. 74321 636352 [id.].
Rheinland-Pfalz State PO, Siegfried Köhler.

While revivals of long-forgotten composers can
too often prove disappointing, this is a set that
triumphantly demonstrates the joys of such an exercise in four richly inventive symphonies in
Brahmsian mould, beautifully orchestrated and here
presented in strong, sympathetic performances very
well recorded. Born into a prominent Jewish family
in Worms, Gernsheim studied at Leipzig with
Moscheles and Ferdinand David. He spent a further
five years in Paris where he met Rossini, Saint-
Saëns and Lalo. After a period at Saarbrücken and
then Cologne – where, incidentally, one of his

pupils was Humperdinck – he became director of music at Rotterdam (1874–90), after which he settled in Berlin. Gernsheim was a contemporary, close friend and great champion of Brahms, whom he had met in the late 1860s, and whose music was the dominant influence on him. Yet though the cut of his melodies may echo that master, the results are still distinctive and always strongly and individually argued. The *First Symphony* comes from 1875, just before Brahms's *First*, and the *Fourth* from 1895. The ripe, warm melody of the second subject in that first symphony establishes the pattern, and from then on the musical material in each movement and its treatment consistently establish the confident mastery of a composer who may not plumb any depths of feeling, but who in his open optimism leaves you satisfyingly comforted, rather as Mendelssohn or Dvořák do in their symphonies. Gernsheim was a teacher and academic most of his life, which may account for his unjustified neglect. What he offers, which so many minor composers do not, are memorable ideas persuasively presented, as in the *Tarantella* movement of the *Second Symphony* (or any of the Scherzos), the first movement of No. 3 (subtitled 'Miriam', having been inspired by a performance of Handel's *Israel in Egypt*), or the bold outer movements of No. 4. The performances by the Staatsphilharmonie Rheinland-Pfalz under Siegfried Köhler are dedicated. A happy discovery, the more welcome for being offered at super-budget price.

Gershwin, George (1898–1937)

An American in Paris; Cuban overture; Lullaby for strings; (i) Rhapsody in blue (version for 2 pianos).

(M) ** Decca Dig. 466 424-2. (i) Katia & Marielle Labèque; Cleveland O, Chailly.

Chailly's Decca programme has characteristically spectacular Cleveland recording, which gives vivid projection and colour to the dance rhythms of the *Cuban overture*, a warm glow to the strings in the *Lullaby* (a fine piece), and a brightly lit Parisian scene. The performance of *An American in Paris* is notable for its powerfully extrovert trumpet solo in the blues sequence, and Chailly's account is altogether invigorating. There seems no special reason for preferring the two-piano version of the *Rhapsody*, and the Labèque duo make their account more controversial by adding their own improvisatory element (more decorative than substantial) to the piano parts. Their playing does not lack sparkle and they certainly convey their enjoyment, but the performance is not entirely idiomatic.

Piano concerto in F; I got rhythm variations for piano and orchestra; Rhapsody in blue; Second Rhapsody.

⬤ (M) *** Virgin/EMI Dig. VM5 61478-2 [id.].
Wayne Marshall, Aalborg Symphony.

Wayne Marshall, virtuoso pianist and conductor, is one of those extraodinary multi-talented musicians that America, every so often, seems to produce almost at the drop of the hat. He is an artist of enormous charisma. The Editor heard him play the *Rhapsody* live at Preston and then conduct the Hallé Orchestra in an unforgettable account of Dvořák's *New World Symphony*, which was extraordinary for its freshness of insight. The slow movement in particular, was Elysian in its rapt concentration and gentle beauty, and Marshall found detail in the score which astonished ears that had heard this unforgettable masterpiece so many times, live and on record.

So it is with this dazzling Gershwin programme in which Marshall both acts as soloist and directs the orchestra. The performance of the *Rhapsody in blue* even outshines Bernstein's famous New York account in its glittering brilliance and excitement. Marshall manages spontaneously to coalesce both the symphonic and Jazz character of the piece, with a hell-for-leather 'bezaz' in the fast brass tuttis (the tuba comes through splendidly) contrasting with a rapturous account of the big tune, with saxophone timbre shining through the strings as it must. He also accentuates the melody's syncopated horn decoration and then proves its importance in the passage to follow.

The disc opens with a scintillating account of the *I got rhythm variations*, played wth comparable bravura and panache, full of affectionate and witty touches. He opens the *Concerto* much faster than usual and this too is a peppy transatlantic reading, but one that can relax wonderfully for the heart-touching trumpet blues theme of the slow movement, superbly played here, and by a Danish player and orchestra no less! The following passage is deliciously skittish.

The *Second rhapsody* is almost as dazzling as the first, with the closing pages winningly brought off. The recording (balanced by our own Mike Hatch) is superb: the violins have just the right degree of brightness and edge to add bite where necessary. Even if you already have a record of the *Rhapsody in blue*, this CD is an essential purchase.

PIANO MUSIC

3 Preludes; An American in Paris (arr. Daly); Songs (arr. Gershwin): *Fascinating rhythm; I got rhythm; I'll build a stairway to paradise; The man I love; Oh Lady be good; Liza; Somebody loves me; Sweet and low down; 'S wonderful; Who cares?*

**(*) Nimbus Dig. NI 5585 [id.]. Mark Anderson
– COPLAND: *Piano sonata*, etc. ***

Recorded at a live recital in Nimbus's own concert

hall this is an enjoyable enough collection of Gershwin favourites. Mark Anderson plays very well, if without those subtle rhythmic inflections that mark most American performances and especially Gershwin's own piano-roll recordings. But why transcribe *An American in Paris*? It sounds so much better in its full orchestral costume.

Girl crazy (musical).
(M) *** Elektra-Nonesuch/Warner Dig. 7559-79437-9. [id.]. Judy Blazer, Lorna Luft, David Carroll, Eddie Korbich, O, John Mauceri.

Girl crazy, despite its hit numbers – *Embraceable you, I got rhythm* and *Bidin' my time* – has always been counted a failure; but this lively recording, with an ensemble of distinguished New York musicians conducted by John Mauceri, gives the lie to that. It is an escapist piece, typical of the early 1930s, about a New Yorker, exiled by his rich father to the Wild West, who sets up a dude ranch in an outpost previously bereft of women. The story of love and misunderstanding is largely irrelevant, but the score has point and imagination from beginning to end, all the brighter here for having had the sugar-coating which Hollywood introduced in the much-mangled film version of 1943 removed. The casting is excellent. Judy Blazer takes the Ginger Rogers role of Kate, the post-girl, while Judy Garland's less well-known daughter, Lorna Luft, is delightful in the Ethel Merman part of the gambler's wife hired to sing in the saloon. David Carroll is the New Yorker hero, and Frank Gorshin takes the comic role of the cab driver, Gieber Goldfarb. The whole score, 73 minutes long, is squeezed onto a single disc, packaged with libretto and excellent notes, the first of a projected Gershwin series. The only serious reservation is that the recording is dry and brassy, aggressively so – but that could be counted typical of the period too. Undoubtedly a bargain at its new mid-price.

Gibbons, Orlando (1583–1625)

Consort music: (i) *Fantazia No. 1 for 2 treble viols; Fantazias Nos. 3 and 5 a 6; Fantazia No. 1 for great double bass* (for organ & 3 viols); *Galliard a 3; Galliard a 6; Go not from my window a 6; In nomine a 4; Pavane a 6*. (ii) Keyboard pieces: *Almain in F; The fairest nymph (mask) Lincoln's Inn mask; The Lord of Salisbury his pavane and galliard. Organ Preludium in G*. (Vocal): (i; iii) *Behold thou hast made my days; Glorious and powerful God* (both for 5 voices & 5 viols). Solo voice and viols: (i; iv) *Dainty fine bird; Fair is the rose; I feign not friendship where I hate; I see ambition never pleased; I tremble not at noise of war; I weigh not fortune's frown; The silver swan*.

(BB) *** Naxos Dig. 8.550603 [id.]. (i) Rose Consort of Viols; (ii) Timothy Roberts; with (iii) Red Byrd; (iv) Tessa Bonner.

This makes the perfect supplement to the excellent Naxos issue of Gibbons's church music, with twenty-two items that cover a wide range of songs as well as instrumental music. The players of the Rose consort, with agreeably tangy string tone, contribute most of the instrumental pieces, culminating in two magnificent *Fantazias* in six parts: No. 3 with ear-catching harmonic clashes, No. 5 with side-slipping chromatic writing, pointing forward to later centuries.

Timothy Roberts is the soloist in keyboard music on harpsichord, virginals and organ, while the soprano, Tessa Bonner, is the bright-toned soloist in a sequence of songs with consort accompaniment, notably four linked ones with words by Joshua Sylvester, and a solo setting of *The silver swan*, Gibbons's most celebrated piece. Standing out too are two fine anthems, one written for the funeral of a Dean of Windsor, with Red Byrd accompanied by the consort, five voices and five instruments. The highly informative notes by the leader of the consort, John Bryan, are a model of clarity.

Anthems: *Almighty and everlasting God; Hosanna to the son of David; O clap your hands; O God, the King of glory; O Lord, in thy wrath; O Lord of Lords; Lift up your heads; Out of the deep; See, see, the word is incarnate; Second Service: Magnificat; Nunc dimittis. Short Service: Nunc dimittis*. (Organ) *Fantazia of 4 parts; Preludes in D min.; G*.
(BB) *** Naxos 8.553130 [id.]. Oxford Camerata, Jeremy Summerly; Laurence Cummings.

Using his small professional choir, twelve singers at most, and often fewer, Jeremy Summerly directs fresh, finely focused readings of an outstanding collection of Gibbons's anthems. This may not have so much of the ecclesiastical aura of a traditional cathedral performance with boys' voices, but it amply makes up in clarity and incisiveness for any lack of weight and warmth. That is particularly so in the six magnificent unaccompanied full anthems which are included, where the astonishing harmonic clashes and progressions in the counterpoint come out with wonderful impact, generally with just a single voice per part.

In addition there are three fine verse anthems, drawing on the full complement of singers with organ accompaniment, plus Gibbons's two evening services, the short one much simpler than the second one. Three organ pieces are also included, though Laurence Cummings's account of the extended *Fantazia* in four parts is not as varied as it might be. Fine, clear, atmospheric sound.

Anthems and verse anthems: *Behold, thou hast made my days; Blessed are they that fear the*

Lord; Glorious and powerful God; Great King of Gods; Hosanna to the son of David; If ye be risen again with Christ; O clap your hands; O God, the King of glory; O Lord in thy wrath rebuke me not; Sing unto the Lord; This is the record of John; Thou God of wisdom; Second Evening Service: Magnificat; Nunc dimittis. Organ Fantasia in A min. (MB XX/12).
*** Hyperion Dig. CDA 67116 [id.]. Robin Blaze, Stephen Varcoe, Winchester Cathedral Ch., David Hill; Stephen Farr or Sarah Baldock.

Orlando Gibbons's *Hosanna to the son of David* is among the very finest anthems of the period, a glory of English music, and aptly that is the opening item for this excellent collection of Gibbons's church music, very well performed and recorded. Robin Blaze is an outstandingly sweet-toned countertenor soloist, well matched by Stephen Varcoe in the verse anthems. The only pity is that the collection concentrates on verse anthems, nine of them plus the *Second Evening Service*, as against only three full anthems with their excitingly elaborate counterpoint. The *Fantasia in A minor* for organ makes an apt supplement.

Gipps, Ruth (born 1921)

Symphony No. 2, Op. 30.
*** Classico CLASSCD 274 [id.]. Munich SO, Douglas Bostock – BUTTERWORTH: *Symphony No. 1.* ***

We apologize to Ruth Gipps for spelling her name wrongly in our main volume. But it is rectified now, and it gives us a second opportunity to recommend this stimulating coupling to those who might pass it by. Ms Gipps studied with Vaughan Williams and during the war years played the oboe in the City of Birmingham Symphony Orchestra. She became a tireless champion of neglected repertoire and an excellent teacher. Her *Second Symphony* comes from 1945, the immediate post-war years, and though indebted to Vaughan Williams, is well argued and inventive. It is decently played and recorded.

Glass, Philip (born 1937)

Violin concerto.
*** Telarc Dig. CD 80494 [id.]. Robert McDuffie, Houston SO, Christoph Eschenbach – ADAMS: *Violin concerto.* ***
*** DG Dig. 445 186-2 [id.]. Gidon Kremer, VPO, Dohnányi – BERNSTEIN: *Serenade after Plato's Symposium*; ROREM: *Violin concerto* ***.

Glass's *Violin concerto* with its hypnotic minimalist exploration of simple basic material is one of his best and most approachable works. The repeated four-note downward scale on which the soloist weaves his serene soliloquy in the slow movement is particularly haunting, the effect very like a chaconne, which links it readily to the coupled Adams concerto. However, some might feel the repeated ostinatos of the finale outlast their welcome and that the touching coda might have arrived a bit sooner.

Gidon Kremer's disc brings together recordings of three different vintages. His version of the Glass *concerto*, with the Vienna Philharmonic under Christoph von Dohnányi, dates from 1992, and proves a warmly expressive reading, which seeks to mould Glass's endless ostinatos persuasively, characterizing strongly over a wide expressive range, helped by vivid recording made in the Musikverein in Vienna with the soloist closely balanced. However Kremer's approach is in some ways less idiomatic than Robert McDuffie's reading of 1987 which is notable for the way that, partnered by Eschenbach, he gives a persuasively jazzy lift to the ostinato rhythms with their implied syncopations. His tone may not be as beautiful as Kremer's, but it is a warmly felt performance, which sustains its slower tempo for the long third movement convincingly. Very well recorded and more aptly coupled with the Adams concerto of 1993, this Telarc disc is in every way recommendable.

Violin concerto; Company; Akhnaten: Prelude and dance.
(BB) **(*) Naxos Dig. 8.554568 [id.]. Adele Anthony, Ulster O., Takuo Yuasa.

Adele Anthony is a talented violinist from Tasmania, winner of the Carl Nielsen competition in Copenhagen, who here gives a sweetly expressive reading of the Glass *Violin concerto*, despite a rather plodding account of the very opening. In the central movement she finds a rare tenderness, as well as on the high harmonics at the end of the whole work. The concerto makes an excellent centrepiece for a complete disc of Glass's music, with Yuasa and the Ulster Orchestra equally persuasive in the four brief movements of *Company* and in the two orchestral passages from the opera, *Akhnaten*.

Einstein on the Beach: highlights.
*** Teldec/Warner Dig. 7559 79435-9 [id.]. Soloists, Philip Glass Ens., Riesman.

This 75-minute highlights disc is ideal for those not wishing to submerge themselves in the full 190 minutes of this bizarre and relentless opera. As the surreal title implies, the work is more dream than drama and Glass's minimalist opera style is all his own. The vivid sound – with spoken voices given such presence as to startle the listener – is as though someone had burst into the room! The formidable group of vocalists and instrumentalists are brilliantly directed and it would be hard to imagine a better performance.

Glazunov, Alexander (1865–1936)

A la mémoire de Gogol, Op. 86; A la mémoire d'un héros, Op. 8; (i) *Chant du ménestrel for cello and orchestra, Op. 71; Concerto ballata for cello and orchestra, Op. 108; 2 pieces for cello and orchestra, Op. 20.*

(BB) *** Naxos Dig. 8.553932 [id.]. Moscow SO, Igor Golovschin (i) with Alexander Rudin.

Although Rostropovich has recorded both the *Concerto ballata* and the *Chant du ménestrel*, they remain rarities and are not otherwise available at bargain price. The second of the Op. 20 *Pieces* is not currently in the catalogue and, apart from a pre-electric recording by Casals, the first is only available in Julian Lloyd Webber's Philips recording. The *Concerto ballata* is a late work, written for Casals and dating from 1931. Although its fund of melody is neither as rich nor as fresh as, say, the *Violin concerto*, it deserves better than the neglect it seems to have inspired among cellists. The *Chant du ménestrel* is much earlier, and comes from 1900 between the *Sixth* and *Seventh* symphonies. It has an easy charm that delights the ear. Neither of the purely orchestral pieces is in the catalogue: *A la mémoire de Gogol* comes from 1909, the centenary of his birth, and is a dignified, well-shaped piece which belies (as does the *Concerto ballata*) Glazunov's reputation for scoring too thickly. We admired Alexander Rudin's recording of the Kabalevsky cello concertos (Naxos 8.553788 – see our main volume) and his playing here is no less eloquent. The Moscow Orchestra plays well for Igor Golovschin and the sound has pleasing warmth and clarity.

Carnaval overture, Op. 45.

(M) *** RCA High Performance 09026 63308-2 [id.]. Boston Pops O, Arthur Fiedler –
SHCHEDRIN: *Carmen* (ballet);
SHOSTAKOVICH: *Hamlet:* incidental music.
***

Glazunov's vivacious, spring-like overture is most attractive, with a lilting main theme; the surprise is the gentle organ interlude at the centre. Fiedler's performance could hardly be more persuasive and the Boston playing is superbly spirited. Excellent recording too, splendidly remastered.

Le chant du destin, Op. 84; 2 Préludes, Op. 85; Suite caractéristique in D, Op. 9.

(BB) **(*) Naxos Dig. 8.553857 [id.]. Moscow SO, Igor Golovschin.

Le chant du destin, written in 1907, is dominated by a sombre two-phrase theme which curiously reminds one of Gershwin's song *'S wonderful*, only the mood and colouring are utterly different. The music, which is eloquently presented, still has its longueurs. The eight-movement *Suite caractéris-* *tique*, from two decades earlier, is vintage Glazunov, an orchestral transcription of piano pieces. The central *Pastorale* (winningly scored) is particularly diverting and the following *Danse oriental* is at first piquant in a pseudo-oriental manner, but reaches an expansive climax. The *Elégie*, too, begins gently and then is passionately interrupted (in a surprisingly Tchaikovskian manner). The grand closing *Cortège* uses the theme of the Introduction but now resplendently transformed into the major. The two *Préludes* date from 1906 and 1908 respectively. One remembers, in a sombre valedictory mood, Vladimir Stassov (famous for naming Balakirev and his contemporary group of Russian composers 'the mighty handful'); the second (much more extended) opens surprisingly like Tchaikovsky's *Francesca da Rimini* and this curious leitmotif dominates the early part of the piece. It is inscribed '*à la mémoire de Rimsky-Korsakov*' and is well played, as indeed is the *Suite*. The recording is very good too. At Naxos price this is worth considering.

The Seasons.

(M) **(*) Decca 460 315-2 [id.]. SRO, Ansermet
– KHACHATURIAN: *Gayaneh*; *Spartacus*: excerpts. ***

Ansermet's recording dates from 1966 and is of vintage Decca quality. The performance takes a little while to warm up, but perhaps that is not inappropriate in the opening *Winter* sequence, where the conductor's meticulous ear for detail is a plus point, for the wind playing throughout is engagingly pointed. At the opening of *Summer* one might wish for a richer, more sumptuous sound from the Suisse Romande violins, but the zestful opening of *Autumn* is firm to the point of fierceness.

Symphony No. 1 in E (Slavyanskaya), Op. 5; (i) *Violin concerto, Op. 82.*

*** Chandos Dig. CHAN 9751 [id.]. Russian State SO, Polyansky; (i) with Julia Krasko.

Glazunov's *First Symphony* (1882) was the product of a precocious sixteen-year-old. It is an endearing work, well crafted in the received European symphonic tradition, but the graceful secondary material is immediately Russian in colour. The dancing Scherzo is peasant-like in rhythm and character: its trio (using a Polish folk tune) demonstrates the orchestral felicity that was to make this movement the highlight of the later Glazunov symphonies. The *Adagio* has a Russian amalgam of introspective melancholy and passionate outbursts, plus a gorgeous horn solo. It is very sympathetically played here. Polyansky's pacing keeps the music alive throughout, and the finale, delightfully scored and in effect a set of variations on a simple theme, is one of the most successful closing movements for any of the composer's symphonies. Polyansky

manages the tempi changes in an engagingly spontaneous way and the Chandos sound, full and with
glowing wind colouring, is flattering. The *Violin
concerto* is a late work of great charm. Julia Krasko
plays it warm-heartedly and with confidence and
ready bravura, and she receives fine support from
the Russian Orchestra. The Chandos sound is well
up to standard.

Symphonies Nos. 3 in D, Op. 33; 9 in D min.
(unfinished, orch. Gavril Yudin).
(BB) ** Naxos Dig. 8.554253 [id.]. Moscow SO,
   Alexander Anissimov.

Glazunov's *Third Symphony* is not easy to bring
off: its outer movements are over-long and can
easily outstay their welcome, as they tend to do
on this Naxos disc. Anissimov opens lightly, and
initially creates a Mendelssohnian atmosphere over
the throbbing woodwind. His is a lyrical reading,
with plenty of warmth, but as the movement proceeds, in spite of fine playing and some vigorous
brass passages, the underlying pulse is that bit too
relaxed to carry the music consistently forward; the
same problem recurs in the finale. The Scherzo has
charm and the slow movement brings ardour in
the strings. But this is a serviceable rather than a
remarkable account.

The main interest of this Naxos CD is the inclusion of the single movement of the composer's
incomplete final symphony which he left sketched
out in short score. It was orchestrated in 1947 by
Gavril Yudin. The movement is an elliptical structure, beginning and ending slowly, and indeed it is
the Russian melancholy of the coda that remains in
the memory. The main themes are drawn from the
slow introduction, but they are not memorable and
although here Anissimov and his orchestra play the
piece with passionate commitment they are unable
to convince us that it is worth resurrecting.

Symphony No. 6 in C min., Op. 58; The Forest
(tone poem), *Op. 19.*
(BB) **(*) Naxos Dig. 8. 554293 [id.]. Moscow
   SO, Alexander Anissimov.

Glazunov's *Sixth Symphony* (1896) has one of his
most successful first movements. The themes are
all drawn from the sombre, Slavic introduction,
almost a chorale, and their exciting sequential progress is in many ways Tchaikovskian. The second
movement shows the composer at his very finest: a
delightful set of variations which bring some of
Glazunov's most winsome woodwind writing. The
third movement is a graceful balletic *Intermezzo*.
The work's Russianness is confirmed by the maestoso rhythms of the finale, essentially in rondo style;
but fortunately Glazunov lightens his texture lyrically in the intervening episodes and so avoids
pompousness.

Anissimov handles the symphony admirably and
with the Moscow players responding persuasively,
the performance is a great success. *The Forest* is
an over-extended pantheistic tone poem, with an
ingenuous programme. The foreboding opening atmosphere evaporates with the coming of dawn, and
later nymphs appear in the glades. But they are
disturbed by a vigorous hunting party. Eventually
serenity returns and the evocative closing section,
with songful flute, oboe, clarinet solos, and piccolo
bird calls, confirm that the world of nature has taken
over. The performance is sympathetic, the recording
very good, but Anissimov fails to persuade us that
this piece is not too long for its material. Yet the
work is rarely if ever performed, and the fine
account of the symphony is worth its modest Naxos
price.

Glinka, Mikhail (1804–57)

*Capriccio brillante on the Jota aragonese
(Spanish overture No. 1); Kamarinskaya;
Souvenir of a summer night in Madrid (Spanish
overture No. 2); Valse-fantaisie; A Life for the
Tsar: Overture and suite (Polonaise; Krakowiak;
Waltz; Mazurka; Epilogue).*
*** ASV CDDCA 1075 [id.]. Armenian PO, Loris
   Tjeknavorian.

Glinka is rightly regarded as the father of Russian
music. Therefore it is proper that he should have a
really first-class disc devoted to his orchestral
pieces, for their colourful scoring provides the basis
on which both Tchaikovsky and the 'famous five'
Russian composers developed their own vivid
orchestral palette. The key work is *Kamarinskaya*,
a kaleidoscopic fantasy on two Russian folk songs.
Tchaikovsky said it contained 'the whole of Russian
music, just as the acorn holds within itself the oak
tree'. It was to be a model for much subsequent
repertoire, notably inspiring the remarkable finale
of Tchaikovsky's own *Little Russian Symphony*.
The two Spanish overtures created another genre,
the orchestral 'picture postcard' which Russian
composers brought home from their travels abroad,
of which Tchaikovsky's *Capriccio Italien* and
Rimsky-Korsakov's *Capriccio espagnol* are
famous examples. But Glinka's two pieces have a
glitter and atmospheric appeal all of their own,
especially the *Capriccio brillante*, featuring a 'jota
aragonese' also used by Liszt. But the seductive
scoring of *Summer night in Madrid* was in some
ways even more influential. The *Valse-fantaisie* is
a charmer, but the Overture and suite from *A Life
for the Tsar* are more conventional. The dance
movements were to be a model for Tchaikovsky in
his own operas and the *Krakowiak* was used later
by Khachaturian in his ballet scores. The whole
programme is played here with a natural vitality,
great charm and a delightful feeling for its Russianness by a first-class orchestra under a conductor
who is a composer himself. The bright recording,

full-bodied and glowing, is one of the finest we
have received from ASV.

PIANO MUSIC

*Andalusian dance, Las Mollares; Bolero;
Contredanse, La couventine; Contredanse in G;
Cotillon in B flat; A farewell waltz; French
quadrille; Galop; Grande valse in G; 6 Mazurkas;
Polka; Polonaise in E; The skylark* (trans.
Balakirev); *Tarantella; Valse-favorite; Valse
mélodique; Variations on a theme by Mozart;
Variations on the terzetto from the opera A life for
the Tsar* (trans. Alexandr Gourilyov).
** BIS Dig. CD 981 [id.]. Victor Ryabchikov.

Victor Ryabchikov's present survey of Glinka's
piano music here includes a supplement of three
alternative versions of the *Variations on a theme by
Mozart* which was included on the first CD, in its
1822 version for piano or harp, plus Balakirev's
transcription of *The skylark* made a few years after
Glinka's death, and the *Variations on the terzetto
from A life for the Tsar* transcribed by Alexandr
Gourilyov. No masterpieces are uncovered among
these salon pieces, though there are some attractive
numbers such as the *Bolero* and *A farewell waltz*.
These are the kind of dances that you might have
heard at any ball in Russia and Ryabchikov plays
them in the order you might have conceivably heard
them in at such a function. For the most part, they
are slight and vapid. Three-star playing and clear,
rather forward recording made in the Melodiya
Studios in Moscow but distinctly one-star music
and by no means as worthwhile as the companion
volumes.

Gluck, Christoph (1714–87)

*Arias: Orfeo ed Euridice: Che farò; Che puro ciel.
Telemaco: Se per entro.*
*** Virgin/EMI Dig. VC5 45365-2 [id.]. David
  Daniels, OAE, Harry Bicket – MOZART;
  HANDEL: *Arias*. ***

Even in a generation which has produced an extraordinary crop of fine counter-tenors, the American
David Daniels stands out for the clear beauty and
imagination of his singing. The best-known items
here – the two principal solos from Gluck's *Orfeo*
– are done with a tender expressiveness that matches
any performance by a mezzo, with Daniels's natural
timbre, at once pure and warm, completely avoiding
counter-tenor hoot. Not only that, his placing of the
voice is flawless, with the florid singing equally
impressive in its brilliance and precision.

Orfée et Euridice (complete).
(M)*** EMI Dig. CDC5 56885-2 [CDCB 56885]
  (2) [id.]. Hendricks, Von Otter, Fournier,
  Monteverdi Ch., Lyon Opera O, Gardiner.

EMI have reissued Gardiner's earlier, 1989
recording of the Berlioz edition of Gluck's opera
sung in French. It is now at mid-price and many
will be glad to have this set, which aimed at combining the best of both the Vienna and Paris versions, although he omits the celebratory ballet at
the end of the opera. Anne Sophie von Otter is a
superb Orfée, dramatically most convincing. The
masculine forthrightness of her singing matches the
urgency of Gardiner's direction; and both Barbara
Hendricks as Euridice and Brigitte Fournier as
Amour are also excellent. The chorus is Gardiner's
own Monteverdi Choir, superbly clean and stylish,
and the recording is full and well-balanced. However, his newest set, for Philips, is even finer (even
though once again he does not include the ballet
sequence). The tautness of the original Italian version is here given a bite and sense of drama, both
totally in period and deeply expressive (434 093-2
– see our main volume).

Godowsky, Leopold (1870–1938)

*53 Studies, based on the Etudes of Chopin, Op. 10
& Op. 25* (complete).
❀ *** Hyperion Dig. CDA 67411/2 [id.].
  Marc-André Hamelin.

Ian Hobson offers a selection of these legendary
pieces on the Arabesque label and Carlo Grante
has done them all in masterly fashion on Altarus,
but Marc-André Hamelin supersedes them both.
Godowsky's celebrated studies are of unbelievable
difficulty, and arouse both excitement and admiration and, in some places, horror that some of their
contortions should have been attempted at all.
Godowsky's *tour de force* is realized with supreme
virtuosity and – more to the point – artistry by
Marc-André Hamelin. It is quite stunning, an
extraordinary achievement even by Hamelin's own
standards. No one with an interest in the piano
should pass this by.

Goldmark, Karl (1830–1915)

String quartet in B flat, Op. 8. (i) *String quintet in
A min., Op. 9.*
**(*) ASV Dig. CDDCA 1071 [id]. Fourth
  Dimension String Qt; (i) with David Smith.

Goldmark's *String quartet in B flat* is a fluent,
beautifully fashioned piece, dating from 1860 and
very much in the Schumann and Mendelssohn tradition. The music is more civilized than individual,
though one is in no doubt that the musical argument
is guided by a sense of purpose. The *String quintet*
is an even stronger piece, sure in its feeling for
musical movement and with some good ideas. The
quintet is not otherwise available and the quartet,
though recorded, is hard to come by. The Fourth

Dimension String Quartet makes its début, with David Smith as the second cello in the quintet. Decent performances, though the tonal blend leaves something to be desired, and one would welcome greater richness of timbre.

Gottschalk, Louis (1829–69)

Complete solo piano music: 'An American composer, bon Dieu!'

Volume 1: *Le Bananier (Chanson nègre), Op. 5; Le Banjo; Chanson de Gitano; Columbia (Caprice américain), Op. 34; Danza, Op. 33; Le Mancenillier, Op. 11; Mazurka; Minuit à Seville, Op. 30; Romanze; Souvenir de la Havana (Grand caprice de concert), Op. 39; Souvenir de Porto Rico, marche des Gibaros, Op. 31; Les yeux créoles (Danse cubaine), Op. 37; Union (Paraphrase de concert), Op. 48.*
*** Hyperion CDA 66459 [id.]. Philip Martin.

'I was the first American pianist, not of stature, but in time,' Gottschalk said of himself and he invented the conception of the composer/recitalist in America, just as Liszt had in Europe. Gottschalk, born a Creole in New Orleans, was the progeny of a Jewish father and a French mother. He was a prodigiously gifted pianist and at twelve went to Paris to study. When he made his début four years later at the Salle Pleyel, his playing received the imprimatur of Chopin. As a touring virtuoso he had great audience appeal, and if his music is lightweight it is well crafted and tuneful, pay homage to both Liszt and Chopin. Its exotic folk-influences are drawn colloquially and naturally from the Deep South, with syncopated rhythms as the strongest feature.

Philip Martin's continuing complete survey on Hyperion is in every way distinguished. He is naturally sympathetic to the transatlantic idioms, yet he treats the music as part of the romantic mainstream, bringing out its various derivations. He plays with elegance, brilliance, style and above all spontaneity. He is very well recorded in an ideal acoustic.

In Volume 1 he finds all the charm of the *Sixième Ballade* and is equally persuasive in the composer's perky ostinato treatment of 'My old Kentucky home' (*Columbia*), followed by the glittering *Les yeux créoles* and the rhythmically characterful *Le Bananier*. He closes with the celebrated and grandiose *Union (Paraphrase de concert)* which Gottschalk, a dedicated abolitionist, played for President Lincoln and his First Lady in 1864.

Volume 2: *Ballade; Berceuse, Op. 47; Caprice polka; Grand scherzo, Op. 57; La jota aragonesa (Caprice espagnol), Op. 14; Manchega (Etude de concert), Op. 38; Marche de nuit, Op. 17; Miserere du Trovatore (Paraphrase de concert), Op. 52; Pasquinade (Caprice), Op. 59; Polkas in*

A flat; in B flat; La Savane (Ballade créole), Op. 3; Scherzo romantique; Souvenirs d'Andalousie (Caprice de concert), Op. 22; Souvenir de Lima (Mazurka), Op. 74; Suis-moi! (Caprice), Op. 45; Ynés.
*** Hyperion CDA 66697 [id.]. Philip Martin.

Volume 2 opens with nicely judged syncopation in the Caprice *Suis-moi!* making it seem quite lyrical, almost like a Chopin Mazurka. The *Paraphrase of Verdi's Miserere* all but upstages Liszt. It opens gently and first introduces Leonora's *D'amor sull' ali rosee* romantically, but becomes more dramatically sombre for its powerful climax. One can imagine how the composer's contemporary audiences would have loved its melodrama. The glittering but gentle bursts of decoration that are a feature of the *Berceuse* are intimately handled, while both the *Jota aragonesa* and the similar *Souvenis d'Andalousie* are a *tour de force* of extrovert dexterity, followed by the equally catchy *Manchega*. The *Caprice polka* is polished and sparkling and *Ynés* a most winning miniature, while the *Souvenir de Lima* returns to an engagingly Chopinesque idiom. Again, a very good recording.

Volume 3: *Bamboula (Danse des nègres), Op. 2; La chute des feulles (Nocturne), Op. 42; The dying poet (Meditation); Hercule (Grande étude de concert); Murmurs éoliens; O ma charmante, épargnes-moi (Caprice); Gottschalk's melody; Grand fantaisie triomphale sur l'hymne national Brésilien; The last hope; Symphony No. 1 (La nuit des tropiques): 1st movement: Andante (arr. Napoleão); Tournament galop.*
*** Hyperion Dig. CDA 66915 [id.]. Philip Martin.

Philip Martin plays the ingenuous *O ma charmante* with admirable simplicity, while *Gottschalk's own Melody* is brief but *très romantique*. *The dying poet* and *The last hope*, (which the composer described tongue in cheek as a 'succès de larmes' (tears)), are treated with a nice discretion. *Hercule* (given a striking march theme with simple decorative variants) is built to a fine rhetorical climax, as is the slow movement of the *Symphony No. 1* (in this not entirely advantageous transcription), and is followed by the engaging Nocturne *La chute des feuilles* ('Falling leaves'), which is as much Lisztian as Chopinesque. The closing, very orchestral *Tournament galop* is superbly thrown off. It has a Rossinian vivacity, but its roulades are very much Gottschalk's own.

Volume 4: *Apothéose (Grande marche solennelle), Op. 29; La Colombe (petite polka), Op. 49; Fantôme de bonheur (Illusions perdues), Op. 36; Forest glade polka (Les follets), Op. 25; La Gitana (Caprice caractéristique), Op. 35; La Moissonneuse (Mazurka caractéristique), Op. 8; Morte!! (Lamentation), Op. 55; Ossian (2*

Ballades), Op. 4/1–2; Pensée poétique; Polonia, Op. 35; Reflets du passé, Op. 28; La Scintilla (L'Etincelle: Mazurka sentimentale), Op. 20; Ricordati (Nocturne, méditation, romance), Op. 26; Le songe d'une nuit d'été (Caprice élégant), Op. 9; Souvenir de Cuba (Mazurka), Op. 75.
*** Hyperion Dig. CDA 67118 [id.]. Philip Martin.

If you decide to explore this enjoyable Hyperion survey, Volume 4 is a good place to start, for much of its content is little known and every piece is enjoyable. In Martin's hands the 'petite polka' La Colombe opens the programme with delectable delicacy and the following Mazurka, La Moissonneuse, glitters. The Lisztian Le songe d'une nuit d'été, the thoughtful Pensée poétique, La Scintilla (with its iridescence) all have great charm. Morte!! brings an elegaic contrast and has a distinctly sentimental ambience. Polonia is a jolly peasant dance, while the Forest glade polka curiously anticipates the music of Billy Mayerl. The second Ossian Ballade is quite haunting, and there is a flamboyant closing Apothéose, which takes a fair time to reach its zenith, but proceeds to do so with panache.

COLLECTIONS

Piano music for 4 hands: (i) Le Bananier (Chanson nègre), Op. 5; La Gallina (Danse cubaine), Op. 53; Grande tarantelle, Op. 67; La jota aragonesa (Caprice espagnol), Op. 14; Marche de nuit, Op. 17; Ojos criollos (Danse cubaine – Caprice brillante), Op. 37; Orfa (Grande polka), Op. 71; Printemps d'amour (Mazurka-caprice de concert), Op. 40; Réponds-moi (Danse cubaine), Op. 50; Radieuse (Grand valse de concert), Op. 72; La Scintilla (L'Etincelle – Mazurka sentimentale), Op. 21; Ses yeux (Célèbre polka de concert), Op. 66. Solo piano music: Le Banjo; Berceuse (cradle song); The dying poet (meditation); Grand scherzo; The last hope (religious meditation); Mazurka; Le Mancenillier (West Indian serenade); Pasquinade caprice; Scherzo romantique; Souvenirs d'Andalousie; Tournament galop; The Union: Concert paraphrase on national airs (The Star Spangled Banner; Yankee Doodle; Hail Columbia).
(B) ** Nimbus NI 7045/6 (2) [id.]. Alan Marks; (i) with Nerine Barrett.

Much of Gottschalk's music exists in alternative two- and four-handed arrangements and Alan Marks and Nerine Barrett make an effervescent Gottschalk partnership in the latter, playing the more dashing pieces to the manner born. The drawback is that this very personable piano duo are recorded – realistically enough – in an empty, resonant hall, and although one adjusts the effect is not advantageous.

The solo recital is still resonant, but not exaggeratedly so, and Alan Marks plays with considerable flair: the Souvenirs d'Andalousie glitters with bravura, his felicity of touch and crisp articulation bring much sparkle to the Grand scherzo and Scherzo romantique, while he sounds like a full orchestra in the Tournament galop. Most importantly he finds simplicity and charm in the delightful Berceuse and the serenade Le Mancenillier, while there is not a hint of sentimentality in The dying poet or The last hope, the composer's most famous piece, which was to find its way into the hymnbooks of many religious denominations. For those wanting an inexpensive survey of Gottschalk this Nimbus Double will serve well enough, but the Hyperion series is artistically and sonically preferable.

Gough, John (1903–51)

Serenade for small orchestra.
*** Chandos Dig. CHAN 9757 [id.]. BBC PO, Vernon Handley – BAINTON: Symphony No. 2 in D min.; CLIFFORD: Symphony. ***

John Gough worked for a time as a studio manager or balance engineer in the BBC and was later Pacific Service Music Organizer during the war years. After the war he became a features producer during the period when that BBC department was at the height of its fame. The short but charming Serenade for small orchestra reveals a genuine creative talent and was written in 1931 for Hubert Clifford's wedding. Exemplary playing and first-rate recorded sound.

Gould, Morton (born 1913)

2 Marches for orchestra.
(M) (***) Cala mono CACD 0526 [id.]. NBC SO, Stokowski – DEBUSSY: Prélude à l'après-midi d'un faune; La cathédrale engloutie (**(*)); HOLST: The Planets. (***)

These two stirring wartime marches were 'written in tribute to two of our gallant allies': the first is Chinese in character (complete with marching effects), the second colourfully employs two Red Army songs. An enjoyable end to a fascinating Stokowski disc and the sound, emanating from an NBC broadcast from March 1943, is fully acceptable.

Gounod, Charles (1818–93)

Roméo et Juliette: highlights.
(M) *** EMI Dig. CDM5 67299-2 [id.] (from complete recording with Roberto Alagna, Angela Gheorghiu, José van Dam, Toulouse Capitole Ch. & O, Plasson).

A well-chosen and very generous set of highlights (just short of 80 minutes) from a splendid set, highly recommended in our main volume. However, unlike Decca's mid-priced reissue series, EMI have not seen fit to offer a translation. But the cued synopsis serves well enough.

Grainger, Percy (1882–1961)

The Crew of the Long Serpent; Danish folk song suite; Kleine Variationen-Form; Stalt Vesselil (Proud Vesselil); To a Nordic princess; (i) (Vocal) *Dalvisa; Father and daughter (Fadit og Dóttir); The Merry wedding; The Rival brothers; Song of Värmland; Under un Bro (Bridge).*
*** Chandos Dig. CHAN 8721 [id.]. Danish Nat. RSO, Hickox; (i) with Pamela Helen Stephen, Johan Reuter, Danish Nat. R. Ch.

From his earliest years Grainger was drawn to Scandinavian and Icelandic literature. (At the age of nine he first read *Grettir's Saga.*) This stimulating and rewarding collection centres on music directly influenced by his immersion in those cultures, all little known, except perhaps the *Danish folk song suite*, with its highly exotic orchestration, winningly presented here. Among the other orchestral items the rollicking *Crew of the Long Serpent*, the colourful *Variations*, and the much more extended and lusciously scored *Tribute to a Nordic princess* stand out. In the complex opening choral piece, *Father and daughter*, a traditional Danish folk dance is mixed up with a theme of Grainger's own. The jolly, concerted *Merry wedding* is sung in English: it draws on a folk poem for its text, but is musically original. *Dalvisa* is a delightful vocalise, using the same melody Alfvén featured as the centrepiece in his *Midsummer rhapsody*. Splendid performances and top-class Chandos sound.

Granados, Enrique (1867–1916)

Allegro de concierto; El Pelele; Goyescas: El Fandango del Candil; Quejas a La Maja y el Ruiseñor.
(M) ** DG Dig. 459 430-2 (2) [id.]. José María Pinzolas – ALBENIZ: *Iberia* (complete). **(*)

José María Pinzolas is rather less impressive here than in the coupled music of Albéniz. The dashing *Allegro de concierto* certainly has glittering bravura, and *El Pelele* is characterful enough, but the two excerpts from *Goyescas* (and especially the lovely *Quejas o La Maja y el Ruiseñor*) are much more magnetic in the hands of Alicia de Larrocha (see our main volume).

Goyescas (complete).
(BB) * Naxos Dig. 8.554403 [id.]. Douglas Riva.

We are well served with fine recordings of *Goyescas*, and the gifted American pianist Douglas Riva does not really challenge existing recommendations – not least Alicia de Larrocha. These pieces must have been tossed off with ease and one needs a transcendental technique to achieve that illusion. The recording is too ill-ventilated and studio bound.

Grechaninov, Alexander Tikhonovich (1864–1956)

Vespers; 3 Motets.
*** Hyperion Dig. CDA 67080 [id.]. Holst Singers, Layton.

Three years before Rachmaninov wrote his *Vespers* or *All-night vigil*, Grechaninov in 1912 wrote this mellifluous setting of the same Russian Orthodox texts, not so tough or austere, but offering equally rapt and dedicated choral writing, close in spirit to the music of such modern composers as Tavener and Pärt. Two years ago on a collection called '*Ikon*', the Holst Singers under Stephen Layton gave us a flavour of Grechaninov's religious music, including his popular setting of the *Creed*. This is both more ambitious and more beautiful still, seductively performed and ravishingly recorded, supplemented by three beautiful motets.

All-night vigil (Vespers), Op. 59; Nunc dimittis (Lord now lettest Thou Thy servant), Op. 34/1; The Seven Days of the Passion; (i) *In Thy Kingdom, Op. 58/3. Now the Powers of Heaven, Op. 58/6.*
*** Hyperion Dig. CDA 67080 [id.]. (i) James Bowman; Holst Singers, Stephen Layton.

Grechaninov's vast output continues to amaze and his *All-night vigil* is a most welcome addition to his growing discography. It was composed in 1912, three years before Rachmaninov's celebrated setting. It is almost exclusively major in tonality, rarely straying into minor keys, and at about three-quarters of an hour is somewhat shorter than the Rachmaninov. It is a work of great beauty; radiance might be a better word, particularly as presented here by Stephen Layton and the Holst Singers. Marina Rakhmanova speaks of its grand ('essentially epic') scale, and its handling of choral texture is masterly. The singing is strikingly idiomatic and the Temple Church, London, provides an ideal acoustic. The recording balance could hardly be improved on; there is plenty of space round the sound and yet the choral focus is firm. There is an ideal balance, too, between choir and the chant intoned by James Bowman in *In Thy Kingdom*. Really something of a triumph.

Grieg, Edvard (1843–1907)

Piano concerto in A min., Op. 16.
(M) *** Decca 466 383-2 [id.]. Radu Lupu, LSO, Previn – SCHUMANN: *Piano concerto.* ***

Decca's remastering of Radu Lupu's fine 1973 coupling of the Grieg and Schumann concertos arrived just as we were going to press with our main volume and we fear it was undervalued. The brilliance of the original Kingsway Hall recording, one of Decca's very best of the period, suits the style of the performance, which is boldly compelling in the outer movements, but has warmth and poetry too, especially striking in the slow movement, where Previn's hushed opening is particularly telling. Indeed, the orchestral contribution is a strong one throughout, while Lupu's playing has moments of touching delicacy. Now that Ronan O'Hora's account of the Grieg on Tring is no longer available, this Decca performance must stand high on the list of mid- and bargain-priced recommendations.

(i) *Piano concerto in A min., Op. 16.* Solo piano music: *Agitato* (1865); *Album leaves, Op. 28/1 & 4; Lyric pieces, Opp. 43, 54 & 65; Piano sonata in E min., Op. 7; Poetic tone pictures, Op. 3/4–6.*
⦿ (BB) *** Virgin Classics 2 x 1 VBD5 61745-2 (2) [CDVB 61745]. Leif Ove Andsnes; (i) with Bergen PO, Kitaienko.

Virgin Classics have now put together Andsnes's distinctive account of the *Piano concerto* with his later piano recital, to which we gave a ⦿. As a 2 x 1 Double it makes a remarkable bargain. In the concerto Andsnes wears his brilliance lightly. There is no lack of bravura and display, but no ostentation either. Indeed, he has great poetic feeling and delicacy of colour, and Grieg's familiar warhorse comes up with great freshness. He is excellently balanced in relation to the orchestra. His solo recital rightly won golden opinions. Besides the *Sonata* and various other short pieces, he offers three sets of the *Lyric pieces,* including Op. 43, which opens with the famous *Butterfly.* Book VIII (Op. 65) is now included, with its touching *Melancholy* and lively *Wedding day at Troldhaugen,* which Grieg later orchestrated, as he did Op. 54. Andsnes's virtuosity is always at the service of the composer and he plays with real imagination and lightness of touch.

(i) *2 Elegiac melodies, Op. 34;* (ii) *Holberg suite, Op. 40;* (iii) *Lyric suite, Op. 54; Peer Gynt suites Nos. 1, Op. 46; 2, Op. 55;* (iv) *String quartet in G min., Op. 27;* (v) *Violin sonata No. 3, Op. 45;* (vi) *Lyric pieces: Wedding-day at Troldhaugen.*
(B) **(*) Finlandia/Warner Ultima Dig. 8573 81964-2 (2) [id.]. (i) Ostrobothnian Chamber O, Kangas; (ii) Helsinki Strings; (iii) Norwegian Radio O, Rasilainen; (iv) New Helsinki Qt; (v) Söderblom, Tateno; (vi) Lagerspetz.

A generally recommendable set – the highlight being the New Helsinki Quartet's account of the *String quartet*: a dramatic, well-shaped and vital performance, yet full of sensitivity and well recorded. In the *Peer Gynt* suites, the Norwegian Radio Orchestra is not in the same rank as the Oslo Philharmonic (the strings do not possess the tonal opulence or weight). But they are a good orchestra in their own right; under their Finnish conductor, Ari Rasilainen, their account is certainly enjoyable and the performances give pleasure, while the recording is good, but not outstanding. Similar comments apply to the lovely *Lyric suite* (with the same forces) which follows. The *Holberg suite* with the Helsinki strings comes off very well – lots of life in the vital outer movements matched by tenderness in the haunting *Andante religioso.* The *Sonata for violin and piano* receives a strong performance and is well recorded (the finale is especially captivating), and with two other attractive short fillers, this double Ultima CD is good value at bargain price, though there is virtually no information about the music in the documentation, only a short biography of the composer.

Symphony in C min.; In Autumn: Overture, Op. 11; Old Norwegian melody with variations, Op. 51; Funeral march in memory of Rikard Nordraak.
*** DG (IMS) 427 321-2 [id.]. Gothenburg SO, Järvi.

Symphony in C min.; Symphonic dances, Op. 64.
(BB) ** Virgin Classics 2 x 1 Dig. VBD5 61621-2 (2) [CDVB 61621]. Bergen PO, Kitaienko – Vocal music: *Bergliot; Olav Trygvason; Funeral march.****

Grieg's *Symphony in C minor* is an early student work, which the composer disowned after he had heard the first performance of the Svendsen *D major* Symphony. It is not particularly characteristic and, though Grieg may have been unduly self-critical in condemning it to total oblivion, it does not hold a candle to the Svendsen. Järvi's is the best recording to appear so far, both artistically and as a recording. Indeed, Järvi produces excellent, fresh accounts of all four works on his disc. Most natural and unaffected performances, beautifully balanced.

Kitaienko and the Bergen Philharmonic offer a well-prepared account of the *Symphony* and it is well recorded. But the performance is by no means as persuasive as the reading by Järvi. Nor does Kitaienko's account of the *Symphonic dances* displace Järvi's earlier account. The principal appeal of this Virgin 2 x 1 Double is its economy and the coupled vocal music, which is altogether more successful.

CHAMBER MUSIC

Violin sonata No. 3 in C min., Op. 45.
(B) *** EMI Début CZS5 72825-2 [id.]. Rafal
Zambrzycki-Payne, Carole Presland –
BRITTEN: *Suite for violin and piano, Op. 6*;
SZYMANOWSKI: *Violin sonata, Op. 9.* ***

Rafal Zambrzycki-Payne is the young Polish-born
player who was the 1996 'BBC Young Musician of
the Year'. He studied at the Menuhin School and
later in Manchester, and was nineteen when this
recording was made. In the *C minor Sonata*, he has
a youthful ardour that carries the listener with him.
There is a strong musical personality here and his
partner Carole Presland is hardly less impressive.
The Abbey Road recording is expertly balanced and
sounds very natural.

String quartets Nos. 1 in G minor, Op. 27; 2 in F
(unfinished).
*** Hyperion Dig. CDA 67117 [id.]. Chilingirian
Qt.

The days when Grieg's *G minor Quartet* was automatically coupled with the Sibelius *Voces intimae*
have gone. As a glance at our main volume shows,
no fewer than four versions offer it in harness with
the unfinished torso of the *Second,* which Grieg's
friend, the Dutch composer Julius Röntgen, put into
shape after Grieg's death in 1907. The *G minor
Quartet* is one of Grieg's most deeply felt pieces,
and gave him a lot of trouble (the first movement
completely changed direction). The *F major* gave
him even more. Two movements were completed
(and the second is first-rate) but inspiration deserted
him. Even in the last years, he spoke of his continuing struggles with it. The Raphael Quartet on
Olympia (OCD 432) give us Röntgen's conjectural
completion just where the Chilingirians leave off where
Grieg did, just as the Oslo Quartet do on Naxos
(8.550879). They have lavished much care on it and
their disc is expertly engineered by Arne Kaselborg
and Andrew Keener. Recommended alongside the
Naxos (which is also excellent in every way) and the
New Helsinki Quartet on Finlandia (3984 21445-2)
which offers Op. 27 coupled with Sibelius.

PIANO MUSIC

*Carnival scene, Op. 19/3; 7 Fugues, EG.184a–g.
Lyric pieces: Berceuse, Op. 38/1; Butterfly; To
Spring, Op. 43/1 & 6; Melody, Op. 47/3; March of
the Trolls; Scherzo; Bell-ringing, Op. 54/3, 5 & 6;
Brooklet, Op. 62/4; In Ballad Vein; Wedding day
at Troldhaugen, Op. 65/5 & 6; Grandmother's
Minuet, Op. 68/2. Piano sonata in E minor, Op. 7.*
❂ *** DG Dig. 459 671-2 [id.]. Mikhail Pletnev.

There are fewer *Lyric pieces* here than on Gilels's
classic DG recording, which has held sway for more
than a quarter of a century. But Pletnev finds room
for the *E minor Sonata,* the *Carnival scene,* and

seven early *Fugues.* (He recorded nineteen of the
Lyric pieces for Melodiya in the 1980s but the
present collection has the advantage of much better
recording.) The general approach is similar save
for *Bell-ringing* which is far brisker than before.
Pletnev brings great delicacy, control of keyboard
colour, and freshness to Grieg's youthful *Sonata,*
which can be recommended alongside Andsnes
(Virgin – see above). The *Fugues* are student exercises from Grieg's Leipzig years and although he
did not specifically forbid performances, as he did
with the *C minor Symphony,* it is hard to believe
that he would have wanted them played in public,
let alone recorded. All the same Pletnev succeeds
in making them sound like music. This CD is likely
to be to the next quarter of a century what Gilels
was to the last.

*Lyric pieces: Book I, Op. 12; Book II, Op. 38;
Book III, Op. 43; Book IV, Op. 47; Book V, Op.
54; Book VI, Op. 57; Book VII, Op. 62; Book VIII,
Op. 65; Book IX, Op. 68; Book X, Op. 71.*
(BB) **(*) Arte Nova Dig. 74321 63647-2 [id.].
Florian Henschel.

Florian Henschel is a young German pianist who
has enjoyed a successful concert career, first as a
double-bass player and more recently as an accompanist, chamber-musician and soloist. He is both
sensitive and intelligent and his survey is accorded
very well-balanced recorded sound. The accompanying notes are short – just as well, perhaps, as
they are the most ignorant we have seen (Grieg did
not go to study in Leipzig when he was twelve but
fifteen; Liszt was not a mentor of long standing,
and did not 'arrange' a scholarship for Grieg to go
to Rome, though he wrote a letter in his support;
nor (wildest of all) did Grainger give the première
of the *Piano concerto* or 'bring his piano music to
the attention of the music world', where it had been
very well established for the best part of thirty
years!)

VOCAL MUSIC

*(i) Bergliot, Op. 42; (ii) Den Bergtekne (The
mountain thrall), Op. 32; (iii & iv) Foran sydens
kloster (Before a southern convent); (ii & iii) 7
Songs with orchestra: Den første møde; Solveigs
sang; Solveigs vuggesang; Fra Monte Pincio; En
svane; Våren; Henrik Wegeland.*
(B) *** DG Classikon Dig. 469 026-2 [id.]. (i) Rut
Tellefsen, (ii) Håkan Hagegård; (iii & iv)
Barbara Bonney; (iii) Randi Stene;
Gothenburg SO, Neeme Järvi.

Before a southern convent is based on a Bjørnson
poem which tells how Ingigerd, the daughter of
a chieftain, has seen her father murdered by the
villainous brigand, Arnljot. He was on the verge of
raping her but relented and let her go; she seeks
expiation by entering a foreign convent, and the

piece ends with a chorus of nuns who admit her to their number. It's not great Grieg but it's well worth investigating, and is very naturally balanced. Generally speaking, the quality on all these DG recordings is excellent – which is not surprising, as they're made by the same Gothenburg team who have recorded for the BIS label. *Bergliot* is an orchestral melodrama with narration, and one is aurally gripped, even while not understanding a word! For the whole collection is reissued without either texts or translations. It is sad that a company like DG could do this. Surely better to charge mid-price, and offer proper documentation.

(i) *Bergliot, Op. 42;* (ii) *Olav Trygvason, Op. 50; Funeral march for Rikard Nordraak.*
(BB) *** Virgin Classics 2 x 1 Dig. VBD5 61621-2 (2) [CDVB 61621]. (i) Lise Fjeldstad; (ii) Solveig Kringelborn, Randi Stene, Per Vollestad, Trondheim Ch.; Trondheim SO, Ole Kristian Rudd – Orchestral music: *Symphony; Symphonic dances.* **

The three scenes from *Olav Trygvason* are all that survives of Grieg's only operatic project. They show no great dramatic sense and, when they reached London, were greeted with particular scorn by Bernard Shaw, who dismissed them as 'a tissue of puerilities'; indeed, they are more like a cantata than scenes from an opera. Neither *Olav Trygvason* nor *Bergliot*, for all their merits, is top-drawer Grieg, though the latter enjoyed great success in Grieg's lifetime and met with much acclaim at its première in Christiania (as Oslo was then known) in 1885. Strange though it may seem, *Bergliot* also enjoyed quite a vogue in France in the late 1880s. But the fashion for *mélodrame* (music as an accompaniment for declamation) has long passed and it is unlikely that *Bergliot* will return to the concert hall. These Norwegian performances have great freshness and spirit, though the DG accounts on Classikon have the greater polish and finesse. All the same, no one investing in these performances (offered most inexpensively) will have occasion to feel disappointed, even though the coupled orchestral works are less distinctive – see above.

Peer Gynt suites Nos. 1, Op. 46; 2, Op. 55; Lyric suite: March of the Trolls, Op. 54/3. Norwegian dance, Op. 35/2.
(M) ** Sony SMK 63156 [id.]. NYPO, Bernstein – SIBELIUS: *Finlandia; The Swan of Tuonela; Valse triste.* **

The slightly mannered performance of *Anitra's dance* and the touch of melodrama in the *Second suite* add individuality to Bernstein's performance of the *Peer Gynt* incidental music, of which the performances in general are good, though the 1967 recording is not especially distinguished. The two other Grieg pieces are attractive, but there are much better versions available of *Peer Gynt.*

Guilmant, Félix (1837–1911)

Symphony No. 2 for organ and orchestra, Op. 91.
*** Chandos Dig. CHAN 9785 [id.]. Ian Tracey (organ of Liverpool Cathedral), BBC PO, Yan Pascal Tortelier – FRANCK: *Choral No. 2;* WIDOR: *Symphony No. 3 for organ and orchestra.* ***

Guilmant's *Second Symphony* is a hugely effective transcription of his *Eighth Organ sonata*. It opens gently with an anticipatory fanfare-like figure on the violins, then after the grandiose organ entry with tutti, the allegro sets off with infectious vigour. The secondary theme is warmly lyrical, but it is the spectacle that one most remembers. The *Adagio con affetto* is romantic, but still reminds us we are in a cathedral, as does the shorter *Andante sostenuto*, which follows the rumbustious Scherzo. The finale opens evocatively with the horns floating over a deep sustained pedal note and then becomes instantly animated, working towards a splendidly grandiloquent ending. The performance has great gusto and if the wide resonance of Liverpool Cathedral prevents any chance of internal clarity, it certainly gives the music a superb impact. Full marks to the Chandos engineers.

Gyrowetz, Adalbert (1763–1850)

Symphonies: in E flat; F, Op. 6/2–3; in D, Op. 12/1.
*** Chandos Dig. CHAN 9791 [id.]. L. Mozart Players, Matthias Bamert.

The Bohemian composer Adalbert Gyrowetz, a talented contemporary of Haydn and Mozart, outlived both of them. He met Mozart in Vienna in 1785 and they became friends when Mozart included one of his symphonies in a subscription concert. Later he met his other idol, Haydn, in London and no doubt told him with respectful satisfaction that earlier in Paris another of the Gyrowetz symphonies had been played there and attributed to the greater master. This is not at all surprising, as they are delightful, full of characterfully individual invention, with Gyrowetz adding *galant* touches of his own. The engaging bravura horn solo in the Trio of the Minuet of Op. 6/2 is truly Bohemian, as is the genial opening movement of Op. 6/3, while the *Andante* soon produces a winning arioso for the oboe followed by a bouncing half Scherzo, half Ländler and a Haydnesque finale. There are catchy ideas too in the *Andante* of the later *D major Symphony* and again in the nicely scored finale. In short these are most enjoyable works and they are played (on modern instruments) with great elegance and sparkle and are beautifully recorded. Well worth seeking out.

Hahn, Reynaldo (1875–1947)

(i) Piano quintet in F min. String quartets Nos. 1 in A min.; 2 in F.
**(*) Audivis Valois Dig. V 4848 [id.]. (i) Tharaud; Quatuor Parisii.

Reynaldo Hahn is today remembered for his songs, but he also wrote a modest number of fine chamber works of which the *Piano quintet* of 1921, with its Franckian undertones, was understandably the most popular during the composer's lifetime. The first movement has striking themes and surges along with a flowing romantic impetus. The slow movement, opening with a cello solo, is comparatively pensive and well sustained, the finale also essentially lyrical. All in all, a thoroughly rewarding piece, which deserves to return to the repertoire. It is persuasively played here, particularly by the pianist, Alexandre Tharaud, who is well inside its sensibility, and it is a pity that the recording of the strings does not produce riper textures. Both string quartets date from 1939. The *Second Quartet,* ambitiously modelled on the Franck *Quartet,* was never published, but has a memorably atmospheric slow movement, the strings muted throughout. The *First Quartet* is a thoughtful, delicate evocation of considerable Gallic charm, with a yearning *Andantino* and a light-hearted finale. It is played most appealingly and here the recording is better balanced and more naturally integrated.

Songs: L'Air; A Chloris; L'Automne; 7 Chansons grises; La chère blessure; D'une prison; L'enamourée; Les étoiles; Fêtes galantes; Les fontaines; L'Incrédule; Infidélité; Offrande; Quand je fus pris au pavillon; Si mes vers avaient des ailes; Tyndaris.
(B) *** Hyperion Helios CDH 55040 [id.]. Martyn Hill, Graham Johnson.

If Hahn never quite matched the supreme inspiration of his most famous song, *Si mes vers avaient des ailes,* the delights here are many, the charm great. Martyn Hill, ideally accompanied by Graham Johnson, gives delicate and stylish performances, well recorded. The reissue on the Helios bargain label should tempt collectors to sample this attractive repertoire, particularly when full translations are included.

Halvorsen, Johan (1864–1935)

Askeladden: suite; Gurre (dramatic suite), Op. 17; The Merchant of Venice: suite.
*** Simax Dig. PSC 1198 [id.]. Latvian Nat. SO, Terje Mikkelsen.

Festival march; Kongen (The King): suite; Tordenskjold (suite); Vasantasena: suite.
*** Simax Dig. PSC 1199 [id.]. Latvian Nat. SO, Terje Mikkelsen.

In his youth, Halvorsen made a name for himself as a violinist, and during his student days in Helsinki led a string quartet whose second violin was the young Jean Sibelius. Halvorsen's three symphonies and the *Norwegian rhapsodies* have been recorded on LP but his main activity lay in the field of theatre music. He was in charge of the Theatre orchestras in Bergen and Christiania (as Oslo was then known) for well over three decades and composed extensively for the stage. The suite from *The Merchant of Venice* on the first CD is second-rate salon stuff, but that is the only disappointment. The music to Holger Drachmann's play *Gurre,* written shortly after Halvorsen took over in Christiania is not only expertly laid out for the orchestra but delightfully fresh. The idiom is indebted to Grieg but he obviously knew his Berlioz and Svendsen. *Sommernatsbryllup (Summer night's wedding)* has much charm and brilliance and so has the opening *Aftenlandskap (Evening scene),* an atmospheric and appealing piece. *Askeladden* is a play for children by Alfred Maurestad, a Hardanger fiddle-player, and the suite recorded here has abundant charm. The second disc brings music for Bjørnstjerne Bjørnson's play, *Kongen (The King),* whose delightful second movement, *Hyrdepigernes Dans (Dance of the shepherdesses)* is quite irresistible. It is difficult to get it out of your head. *Vasantasena* aspires to an oriental exoticism which, though pale by our standards, was not so in 1890s Norway. It is quite endearing and charming. The Latvian National Orchestra play splendidly for Terje Mikkelsen, and the recording is state of the art, with beautifully transparent strings and with plenty of space round the sound.

Handel, George Frideric (1685–1759)

Concerti grossi, Op. 3/1–6; Concerto grosso in C (Alexander's Feast); (i) Music for the Royal Fireworks; Water music (complete).
(BB) *(*) Virgin Classics 2 x 1 Dig. VBD5 61656-2 (2) [CDVB 61656] [id.]. Linde Consort; (i) with Cappella Coloniensis.

These are good, quite well-characterized performances, nicely recorded, but not much more than that. This repertoire is richly covered by excellent authentic and modern instrument versions, so we must relegate this Virgin Double – despite its bargain price – to the second division.

Concerti grossi, Op. 3/1–6; Op. 6/1–12; Concerto grosso in C (Alexander's Feast); 2 Concerti a due cori, Nos. 2–3, HWV 333–4; Music for the Royal Fireworks; Water music (both complete).
(B) **(*) DG Dig. 463 094–2 (6) [id.]. English Concert, Pinnock.

A generous bargain set of some of Handel's most famous orchestral music, which Pinnock's admirers will not want to miss. His accounts of the *Fireworks* and *Water music* have tremendous zest and are among the best of the available period-instrument performances. The six Op. 3 concertos with their sequences of brief jewels of movements also find Pinnock and his English Concert at their freshest and liveliest, with plenty of sparkle and little of the abrasiveness associated with the earlier examples of authentic music-making. The twelve Op. 6 concertos however are not quite so recommendable: these are performances to admire and sample, but not everyone will warm to them. If listened through, the sharp-edged sound eventually tends to tire the ear; there is comparatively little sense of grandeur and few hints of tonally expansive beauty. But Pinnock's English Concert are never unresponsive and they offer much fine solo playing helped by an attractively atmospheric acoustic. The ornamentation is often elaborate, but never at the expense of line and in spite of the above reservation, there is much to enjoy. The *Alexander's Feast concerto grosso* also has vitality and imagination to recommend it, as have the *Concerti a due cori*, and all are well recorded.

(i) Harpsichord concerto, Op. 4/6. Suite No. 15: Air and variations.
(**(*)) Biddulph mono LHW 032 [id.]. Wanda Landowska; with O, Eugène Bigot – BACH: *Concerto No. 1 in D min., BWV 1052* (**); HAYDN: *Concerto in D; Sonata No. 36 in C sharp min.: Minuet; German dance No. 5.* (***)

We more usually hear this concerto on the organ or harp, but Wanda Landowska makes a fairly good case for the harpsichord, although her predilection towards grandeur means that her presentation is on the heavy side. The *Air and variations* is played with much character and is made to be every bit as memorable as *The harmonious blacksmith*. The recording is vivid throughout and very well transferred.

KEYBOARD MUSIC

Harpsichord suites Nos. 1 in B flat min.; 2 in G; 3 in D min.; 4 in D min.; 5 in E min.; 6 in G min.
*** Chandos Dig. CHAN 0644 [id.]. Sophie Yates.

Vivacious and intelligent performances, competitively priced and very well recorded.

Harpsichord suites Nos. 3 in D min.; 8 in F min.; 11 in D min.; 13 in B flat; 14 in G; 15 in D min.
(M) *** Lyrichord LEMS 8034 (2) [id.]. Paul Wolfe (harpsichord).

The Texan harpsichordist Paul Wolfe was a pupil and protégé of Wanda Landowska. He made these recordings in 1958/9, when stereo was in its infancy in the USA. But the quality is extremely vivid, both real and present, and the chosen acoustic excellent. While the performances are of high calibre, there is as much interest here in the instrument itself as the music-making. Following the practice of his famous mentor, who favoured a large Pleyel instrument, Wolfe had a harpsichord specially built for him by Frank Rutkowski of Stoney Creek, Connecticut. It is a magnificent creature, dubbed by its maker '*The Queen Mary*' because of its length – nine feet! It has two manuals with a range of just over five octaves, and seven pedals to alter and mute the timbre and includes a buff (or lute) stop which creates a dry, pizzicato sound. The range of colour is aurally fascinating and Wolfe makes the very most of the tonal and dynamic contrasts possible in Handel's music, especially in the variations.

The playing itself is infectiously full of life; one's only comment is that Wolfe usually chooses to pace the *Allemandes* very slowly and grandly, even the *Sarabande variée* in the *11th Suite*, which is based on *La Follia*. The deep bass stop (also favoured by Landowska) can be heard to its fullest effect in the *Prelude* of the *F minor Suite* (No. 8), which provides a lively end to the second disc. The two-CD set, which has 85 minutes of music, is offered at a special price.

VOCAL MUSIC

Acis and Galatea (complete).
*** Erato/Warner Dig. 3984-25505-2 (2) [id.]. Sophie Daneman, Patricia Petibon, Paul Agnew, Joseph Cornwell, Alan Ewing, Andrew Sinclair, François Piolino, David Le Monnier, Les Arts Florissants, William Christie.

Gardiner and Marriner are strong contenders in this field, but William Christie's new account on Erato is if anything even better and probably now a first recommendation. He gives us a chamber performance with forces similar to those Handel used for the Cannons performances. Tempi are inclined to be brisk and rhythms crisp but he has marshalled expert singers; Alan Ewing's Polyphemus is particularly good, well characterized and spirited. Indeed, the whole performance is full of life and personality, and William Christie holds everything together with finesse and grace. The sound, too, is well balanced and natural.

Chandos Anthems: (i) As pants the hart; (ii; iii) I will magnify thee, O God; (iii) In the Lord put I my trust; (iv) Let God arise; (i) The Lord is my light; (iv, v) O praise the Lord with one consent.
(B) *** Decca 458 389-2 (2) [id.]. King's College, Cambridge, Ch., ASMF, Willcocks; with (i) April Cantelo, Ian Partridge; (ii) Caroline Friend; (iii) Philip Langridge; (iv) Elizabeth

Vaughan, Alexander Young; (v) Forbes Robinson.

Sir David Willcocks's well-known performances are self-recommending. Dating from 1965–1973, this (originally Argo) series was never completed. Yet it has stood the test of time and only extreme authenticists will fail to respond to the warmth and beauty of the playing and singing, as well as its robust vigour. The recordings are bright and full, and if the CD transfer sometimes gives the sound a bit of an edge, many will find that appropriate in our 'authentic' age. A bargain, especially as texts are included.

(i) *4 Coronation anthems* (for the coronation of King George II and Queen Caroline): *Zadok the Priest; The King shall rejoice; My Heart is inditing; Let thy hand be strengthened;* (ii) *Ode for the birthday of Queen Anne.*
(B) *** Australian Decca Eloquence 466 676-2. (i) King's College Ch., ECO, Willcocks; (ii) Kirkby, Nelson, Minty, Bowman, Hill, Thomas, Christ Church Cathedral Ch., Oxford, AAM, Preston.

Willcocks's famous 1961 recordings of these four anthems sound much better on CD than they ever did on LP, and are greatly enjoyable. They are coupled with a fine performance of the *Ode for the Birthday of Queen Anne*, recorded in the late 1970s, and sound very good indeed. An excellent bargain CD.

Coronation anthem: Zadok the Priest.
(M) *** Decca 458 623-2 [id.]. King's College, Cambridge, Ch., ASMF, Marriner – HAYDN: *Nelson mass;* VIVALDI: *Gloria, RV 589.* ***

Many collectors will be glad to have a separate recording of this fine King's performance of *Zadok the Priest* coupled with Vivaldi's most famous *Gloria* to say nothing of the favourite among Haydn's late masses. Moreover the current transfer has added to the impact of the choir, so that it soars out well over the orchestra.

The Messiah (complete).
(BB) (***) Belart mono 461 629-2 (3) [id.]. Jennifer Vyvyan, Norma Proctor, George Maran, Owen Brannigan, LPO Ch., LPO, Boult – *Arias.***(*)

Boult's *Messiah* dates from just before the arrival of stereo and was highly regarded in its day as a model of how to present the much-loved oratorio without the plush Victorian overlay favoured by Sargent. The mono recording was of high quality, admirably spacious, as it still is in this most realistic transfer. Of course, Boult's tempi are much slower than we would expect today – hence the third CD, and one has to readjust to the choral pacing. But this is easy to do when the singing is fresh and Boult's direction is persuasively warm and direct.

Julian Herbage's edition was used to ensure faithfulness to Handel's text and Thurston Dart provided a continuo, which comes through effectively and audibly. The four soloists are of one mind in the matter of ornaments (they have no use for them!). Of the four, Jennifer Vyvyan is outstanding for her accuracy, tonal beauty and agility, and George Maran for his musical phrasing (though the quality of the voice is at times a little on the light side). Owen Brannigan is one of the principal joys of the set: his singing is full of personality and he brings his usual touch of geniality to the runs. All in all, once you adjust to the tempi, this is greatly enjoyable, and Kenneth McKellar's recital of arias (see below) is a considerable plus point. The presentation is simple but appealing.

Ode for St Cecilia's day.
(M) (*) Sony SMK 60731 [id.]. Addison, McCollum, Rutgers University Ch., NYPO, Bernstein.

It is difficult to see why this performance was resurrected on CD, though it is always interesting to hear what Bernstein does in any music. A romantic approach in baroque and classical repertoire is valid even in our authentic climate, but this performance is leaden and unimaginative and neither the 1959 recording nor the vocal contributions do enough to redeem matters.

OPERA

Alcina (complete).
*** Erato/Warner Dig. 8573 80233-2 (3) [id.]. Renée Fleming, Susan Graham, Natalie Dessay, Kathleen Kuhlmann, Juanita Lascarro, Timothy Robinson, Laurent Naouri, Les Arts Florissants, Christie.

This fine Erato set was recorded live at a series of five performances at the Paris Opéra, with a cast of principals that would be hard to match. Though the auditorium of the Palais Garnier is dangerously large for such a Handel opera, the recording minimizes that problem, with arias well balanced, allowing the solo voices ample bloom without excessive reverberation. Only in recitatives do stage noises ever intrude, and the tensions of a live reading help to minimize the drawback of an opera containing only one ensemble number (the Act III terzetto) in addition to the traditional brief choral finale. Christie too is masterly at avoiding any monotony in the long sequence of da capo arias, with recitative superbly timed and reprises beautifully decorated. It is striking that the star singers here, each with an exclusive contract for another company – Fleming for Decca, Graham for Sony, and Dessay for EMI – are not just brilliant in tackling elaborate passage work and ornamentation, but are stylishly scrupulous in avoiding unwanted aspirates. Fleming is in glorious voice as Alcina, with

Susan Graham characterizing well in the trouser-role of Ruggiero. Natalie Dessay as Alcina's sister, Morgana, relishes the challenge of the brilliant *Tornami a vagheggiar* (appropriated by Joan Sutherland in the unauthentic Decca set), helped by Christie's relatively relaxed tempo. He also sets relaxed speeds in some of the great slow arias such as *Verdi prati*, encouraging an expressive approach which yet remains within the bounds of period style.

The EMI set (CDS7 49771-2) conducted by Richard Hickox, with Arleen Augér in the title role, remains a strong contender, starrily cast too, with Kathleen Kuhlmann, as here, characterful in the contralto role of Bradamante. If the live recording conveys dramatic tension more clearly, the contrast between voices is more marked in the earlier set, with the male singers exceptionally strong.

VOCAL COLLECTIONS

Arias: Acis and Galatea: Love in her eyes sits playing. Jephtha: Deeper and deeper still . . . Waft her, angels. Judas Maccabaeus: Thanks to my brethren . . . How vain is man; My arms against this gorgias will I go . . . Sound an alarm. Ptolemy: Silent worship (Did you not hear my lady?). Semele: Where'er you walk. Xerxes: Ombra mai fù.
(BB) **(*) Belart 461 629-2 (3) [id.]. Kenneth McKellar, LPO, Boult – *Messiah*. (***)

When this recital was first issued in 1960, a friendly Decca executive invited critics into his office and played the disc to them. Receiving a favourable response, he asked his listeners to name the singer and received some astonishing replies. Kenneth McKellar's voice was then at its freshest and he sings in good style, the words strikingly clear, notably so in the two splendid dramatic arias from *Judas Maccabaeus*. In the lyrical numbers, however, Handel's melisma needs perfectly managed breath control if it is to fall into its natural shape, and McKellar was not an experienced enough Handelian always to calculate the music's line perceptively. At times there is a suggestion, if not of strain, that the voice is being taxed to the limit at the end of a long phrase. However, one can make too much of this: his beautiful tone brings much to enjoy, and Boult's accompaniment is most sympathetic and, like the voice, most naturally recorded. A nice bonus for an inexpensive complete *Messiah*.

Opera arias: Agrippina: Bel piacere. Orlando: Fammi combattere. Partenope: Furibondo spira il vento. Rinaldo: Or la tromba; Cara sposa; Venti turbini; Cor ingrato; Lascia ch'io pianga mia cruda sorta. Serse: Frondi tenere; Ombra mai fù.
(M) *** Erato 0630 14069-2 [id.]. Marilyn Horne, I Solisti Veneti, Scimone – VIVALDI: *Orlando*: Arias. ***

Marilyn Horne (recorded at her peak in 1978) gives here virtuoso performances of a wide-ranging collection of Handel arias. The flexibility of her voice in scales and trills and ornaments of every kind remains formidable, and the power is extraordinary down to the tangy chest register. The voice is spot-lit against a reverberant acoustic. Purists may question some of the ornamentation, but most collectors will revel in the sheer confidence of this singing, and the reissue is made the more attractive by the apt inclusion of three key arias from Vivaldi's setting of one of the same operas, *Orlando*.

'The glories of Handel opera': Alcina: Dream music; (i) *Sta nell'ircana pietrosa tana.* (ii) *Tornami a vagheggiar.* (iii) *Atalanta: Care selve.* (iv) *Berenice: Si, trai ceppi.* (v) *Ezio: Se un bell'ardire. Giulio Cesare:* (vi) *Da tempesta il legno infranto;* (i) *Piangero la sorte mia.* (vii) *Orlando: Ah stigie larve; Gia latra cerbero; Vaghe pupille, non piangente, no.* (viii) *Riccardo Primo: Atterrato il muro cada.* (ix) *Rinaldo: Laschia ch'io pianga. Rodelinda:* (x) *Dove sei;* (vi) *Io t'abbraccio.* (x) *Semele: Iris, hence away.* (xi) *Xerxes: Ombra mai fù.*
(M) *** Decca Analogue/Dig. 458 249-2 [id.]. (i) Berganza; (ii) Kirkby; (iii) Pavarotti; (iv) Evans; (v) Robinson; (vi) Sutherland; (vii) Bowman; (viii) Mingardo; (ix) Greevy; (x) Horne; (xi) Tebaldi.

An ingenious anthology of Handel show-stoppers, drawing on a wide range of artists and recordings. Such a various programme makes stimulating listening, as much for the rarities as for the glittering showpieces. There recordings are nearly all bright and vivid, and full texts and translations are included as always in Decca's well-conceived Opera Gala series. Highly diverting.

Overtures and Arias (1704–1726) from Almira; Amadigi di Gaula; Giulio Cesare in Egitto; Rinaldo; Rodelinda; Rodrigo; Scipione (with March);*Silla; Tamerlano.*
*** Hyperion Dig. CDA 66860 [id.]. Emma Kirkby, Brandenburg Consort, Roy Goodman.

Overtures and Arias (1729–1741) from: Alcina; Ariana in Creta; Atalanta; Berenice, regina d'Egitto; Deidamia; Ezio; Lotario; Partenope; Sosarme, re di Media.
*** Hyperion Dig. CDA 67128 [id.]. Emma Kirkby, Brandenburg Consort, Roy Goodman.

It might be thought that a collection interspersing Handel arias and overtures would not be particularly stimulating, but Emma Kirkby (in glorious voice) and Roy Goodman directing invigorating playing by the Brandenburg Consort prove just how enjoyable such a concert, or pair of concerts, can be. The first disc covers the first half of Handel's operatic career. After opening with Handel's second overture to *Almira*, Kirkby clears her throat with the sprightly roulades of *Vedrai s'a tuo dispetto*, and then enchants us with the melancholy line of *Perché viva il caro sposo* from *Rodrigo*. The opening ritornella of the following vigorous *Vo' far Guerra*, from the same opera, includes a virtuoso harpsichord solo (Alistair Ross). *Desterò dall'ampia Dite*, from *Amadigi di Gaula*, then brings a superb trumpet (Robert Farley) and oboe (Katharina Arfken) obbligato duet, and the oboe is again prominent in the introduction to the famous *V'adoro pupille* (from *Giulio Cesare*) while the lovely *Ombre piante* brings an echoing flute. Both are ravishingly sung and the trumpet returns for the lively closing regal number from *Scipione*.

Volume 2 deals with Handel's later operas and opens with the virtually unknown overture to *Lotario* (1729). The lively allegro is built over a repeating ground bass just six notes long, the texture coloured with florid oboe writing, and the piece ends with an elegant gavotte. Queen Adelaide's feisty aria which follows, shows Emma Kirkby at her nimblest, although she is hardly less dazzling in *Dite pace* from *Sosarme*. Other highlights include the lovely *Caro padre* from *Ezio* and the anguished recitative *Ah! Ruggiero* from *Alcina*, with its dramatic pauses, and a lovely flowing aria, *Ombre pallide*, both of which show Kirkby at her very finest. Perhaps the most delightful item here is *Chi t'intende?* from *Berenice*, where Kirkby clearly enjoys her continuing duet with the solo oboe. The closing number, *M'hai resa infelice,* comes from Handel's very last opera, *Deidamia,* of 1741, which received only three performances. It opens with a touching lament and then its heroine curses Ulysses spectacularly for taking her lover Achilles away from her to the war against Troy.

Arias: Partenope: Sento amor; Ch'io parta?; Furibondo spira il vento. Tolomeo: Stille amare.
*** Virgin/EMI Dig. VC5 45365-2 [id.]. David Daniels, OAE, Harry Bicket – GLUCK, MOZART: *Arias.* ***

One of the *Partenope* arias provides the title for this exceptional disc of counter-tenor arias, ranging wide in its expressiveness, with Daniels using his extraordinarily beautiful voice, clear and pure with none of the usual counter-tenor hoot, with the keenest artistry. Whether in deeply expressive lyrical numbers or in brilliant florid passages, his technique is immaculate, with the voice perfectly placed.

Hartmann, Johan Peter Emilius
(1805–1900)

The Valkyrie, Op. 62.
** CPO Dig. 999 620-2 (2) [id.]. Frankfurt RSO, Michail Jurowski.

Written for Bournonville, Hartmann's ballet has a pretty lurid scenario, with plenty of blood and thunder. However, *The Valkyrie* remains curiously bland and tame, and its melodic ideas are obstinately unmemorable. Good playing and recording, and Bournonville fans will surely want it, but the music itself does not represent Hartmann at his best and we would hesitate to press its claims on non-specialists.

Hartmann, Karl Amadeus
(1905–63)

Symphonies Nos. (i) *1 (Versuch eines Requiem); 6; Miserae.*
*** Telarc Dig. CD 80528 [id.]. LPO, Leon Botstein; (i) with Jard van Nes.

For many, the symphonies of Karl Amadeus Hartmann are a hard nut to crack. Kubelik recorded three (Nos. 4, 6 and 8) at various times and Wergo included them in their survey of all eight, derived from broadcast and other sources. Ingo Metzmacher has also recorded a number for EMI (we discussed his account of the *Third* in our 1996 edition). They have inspired the dedication of many discerning musicians, including John McCabe and, to judge from this CD, Leon Botstein, who gives very committed accounts of the two recorded here. Jard van Nes is a distinct asset in the *First Symphony*. Those who want to investigate this challenging and respected composer (and who do not want to embark on the Metzmacher cycle) should find this a satisfying buy.

Harty, Hamilton (1879–1941)

Music for cello and piano: Butterflies; Romance and scherzo, Op. 8; Wood-stillness.
(M) *** Dutton Epoch Dig. CDLX 7102 [id.]. Andrew Fuller, Michael Dussek – HURLSTONE: *Cello sonata in D*; PARRY: *Cello sonata in A.* ***

Slight but quite pleasing pieces that are fill-ups for the two cello sonatas by Hurlstone and Parry. Effective and accomplished playing from Andrew Fuller and Michael Dussek – and very well recorded too.

Haug, Halvor (born 1952)

(i) Symphony No. 3 (The Inscrutable Life); Furuenes sang (Song of the Pines). (ii) Silence for strings; Insignia: symphonic vision.
*** Simax Dig. PSC 1113 [id.]. (i) Norrköping SO; (ii) ECO; Ole Kristian Ruud.

The Norwegian composer Halvor Haug is a composer of substance who made quite a stir with

his *First Symphony* in the 1980s. Born in Trondheim, he studied in Oslo, Helsinki, where he was a
pupil of Einar Englund and Erik Bergman, and
London, where Robert Simpson served as his
mentor. But it is immediately obvious that he is his
own man. His sensibility is strongly Nordic and at
one with the sounds and the landscape of those
latitudes. The *Third Symphony* (1991–3) is a large-
scale piece in two parts, lasting some 36 minutes.
Its subtitle incidentally alludes to the famous *Ines-
tinguibile* of Nielsen. The textures are transparent
and carefully placed but those who look for the vital
sense of momentum that you find in Holmboe and
Tubin will look in vain. This is meditative, concentrated in atmosphere and static. The ending uses a
nightingale as does Respighi in *The Pines of Rome*
but the effect will not convince all his admirers.
Stillhet or *'Silence'* (1977) is an evocation of
tranquillity (a better translation might have been
'stillness'); and *Song of the Pines* (1987), a threnody
on the desecration of the natural world, has real
eloquence. *Insignia* (1993) is a response to the
other-worldly landscape of the Lofoten islands. Ole
Kristian Ruud gets good results from the Norrköping Orchestra and the sound is excellent.

Haydn, Josef (1732–1809)

*Cello concertos Nos. 1 in C; 2 in D, Hob VIIb/
1–2.*
**(*) DG 463 180-2 [id.]. Jian Wang, Gulbenkian
O, Muhai Tang.
(M) **(*) EMI CDM5 67234-2 [567263].
Rostropovich, ASMF.

Born in 1969, the young Chinese cellist Jian Wang
was launched on his career outside China thanks
to the sponsorship of Isaac Stern. He is rapidly
establishing a formidable reputation. His trio
recordings with Augustin Dumay and Maria João
Pires have shown him to be a fine chamber-music
player and the present disc leaves no doubts as to
his calibre as a soloist. Here he gives authoritative,
warm, finely conceived and detailed readings of
both concertos. For many listeners the big test will
be in the slow movements, in which Wang adopts
very spacious speeds, sustaining them well with
rapt intensity, very much in the modern tradition,
with no concern for period practice. Speeds otherwise are generally well chosen, even if the finale of
the *C major* is hectically fast, challenging Wang
(like Rostropovich) to wonderfully clean articulation. Warm, full sound. Excellent recording, and
our only regret is that room was not found for
another work, as 52 minutes is rather short measure
these days for a premium-price disc.

Rostropovich's virtuosity is astonishing. True,
there are moments of breathless phrasing, and
Rostropovich's style has acquired a degree of self-
indulgence in the warmth of expressiveness and this

is reflected in the accompaniment from the ASMF,
which he also directed. Just the same, the solo
playing is very compelling for all its romantic emphasis and slow movements are certainly beautiful.
So while there have to be doubts about EMI's inclusion of this coupling as one of their 'Great
Recordings of the Century', admirers of the great
cellist will still relish his ardent response to this
music and the fine recording.

*(i) Harpsichord concerto in D, Hob XVIII/11.
Sonata No. 36 in C sharp min.; Minuet; German
dance No. 5 (Ballo tedesco).*
(***) Biddulph mono LHW 032 [id.]. Wanda
   Landowska; (i) with O, Eugène Bigot – BACH:
   *Harpsichord Concerto No. 1 in D min., BWV
   1052* (**). HANDEL: *Concerto, Op. 4/6; Suite
   No. 15: Air and variations.* (**(*))

With neatly scaled playing from Landowska, and a
crisp clean accompaniment from Bigot, the Haydn
concerto is much more attractive than its heavyweight Bach coupling and the encores too are very
pleasing, especially the sharply rhythmic *German
dance*. The recording is surprisingly good (a bit thin
on violin timbre, but not unpleasantly so) and this
is a most refreshing view of Haydn, dating back to
1937.

Oboe concerto in C, Hob VIIg/C1.
*** Dutton Lab./Barbirolli Soc. CDSJB 1016
   [id.]. Evelyn Rothwell, Hallé O, Sir John
   Barbirolli – CORELLI; MARCELLO: *Oboe
   concertos.* *** (with Instrumental Recital:
   C. P. E. BACH; LOEILLET; TELEMANN:
   Sonatas etc. **).

Haydn's *Oboe concerto* is of doubtful authenticity,
but in this account played by Evelyn Rothwell,
deftly accompanied by her husband, Haydn surely
would have welcomed the attribution. The orchestra
is given a very positive classicism by Barbirolli's
firmness, and in the opening movement his wife's
delicacy makes a delightful foil for the masculine
orchestral presentation. The slow movement is well
brought off and the delicacy of articulation returns
in the finale. The 1958 recording is resonant and
the skilful Dutton transfer almost entirely disguises
its age.

*Piano concertos in F; in G; in D, Hob XVIII 3, 4
& 11.*
*** EMI Dig. CDC5 56950-2 [id.]. Leif Ove
   Andsnes, Norwegian CO.

Leif Ove Andsnes gives inspired performances of
the three Haydn piano concertos that are fully auth-
enticated, not just the early *F major* and *G major*,
here made to sparkle brightly, but the best known
and finest of the series, *No. 11 in D*. Andsnes justifies his generally brisk speeds for outer movements
in subtle pointing of rhythm and phrase, articulating
crisply – always individual without being self-

conscious. His preference is for speeds on the slow side in middle movements, more measured than eighteenth-century manners might allow, but rapt and naturally expressive, notably in the lovely *Adagio* of the *D major*; in his hands and those of the Norwegian Chamber Orchestra, which he directs from the keyboard, these concertos blossom. These are fresh, poetic and brilliant performances, recorded with exemplary clarity. Good though Emanuel Ax and the Franz Liszt Chamber Orchestra were on Sony (see our main volume) these are now a clear first choice in the repertory, though we would not be without Pletnev's characterful account of the *D major* on Virgin (VC5 45196-2).

Violin concertos Nos. 1 in C, Hob VIIa/1; 4 in G, Hob VIIa/4; (i) *Sinfonia concertante in B flat for violin, cello, oboe and bassoon, Hob I/105;* (ii) *Symphonies Nos. 26 in D min. (Lamentatione); 52 in C min.; 53 in D (L'Imperiale).*
(BB) *** Virgin Classics 2 x 1 Dig. Double VBD5 61800-2 [CDVB 61800] (2). Elizabeth Wallfisch; OAE; (i) with Robson, Warnock, Watkin; (ii) La Petite Bande, Kuijken.

A thoroughly successful bargain pairing. On the first CD Elizabeth Wallfisch appears as the soloist and director in the two early violin concertos. She leads the Orchestra of the Age of Enlightenment from her bow and proves a highly sensitive soloist. Her serenely reflective account of the *Adagio molto* of the *C major* is memorable, and outer movements are jauntily rhythmic. In the *Sinfonia concertante* the smiling interplay of the various wind and string soloists has never been bettered on record and the use of period instruments brings a pleasing intimacy and plenty of spirit.

Kuijken and La Petite Bande take over for the symphonies, which include two of the most striking of Haydn's *Sturm und Drang* works, plus one of the celebratory symphonies which he wrote while emerging from that self-questioning period. Although the strings sound a little abrasive, the ear quickly adjusts. These fresh, vital, cleanly articulated readings wear their authenticity lightly, and are more expansive and affectionate in slow movements than some purists might allow, although the plangent quality of the *Adagio* of the *Lamentione* is fully conveyed. Again, excellent recording.

Sinfonia concertante in B flat for violin, cello, oboe, bassoon and orchestra.
(M) *** DG 463 078-2 [id.]. Zukerman, Leonhard, Winters, Breidenthal, LAPO, Barenboim – BEETHOVEN: *Violin concerto in D, Op. 61.* ***

Barenboim's enjoyably spontaneous performance comes from 1977 but we have not discussed it before. The four soloists work splendidly together as a team and the *Andante* is particularly successful. The recording is well balanced and well transferred.

Symphonies Nos. 6 in D (Le Matin); 45 in F sharp min. (Farewell); 48 in C (Maria Theresia); 82 in C (The Bear); 92 in G (Oxford); 94 in G (Surprise).
(B) *** Nimbus Dig. NI 7041/2 [id.].
Austro-Hungarian Haydn O, Adám Fischer.

Nimbus could hardly have made a better selection to demonstrate the excellence of their warmly stylish modern-instrument series of Haydn symphonies. The two *Sturm und Drang* works are particularly fine, with Fischer bringing out the originality of the *Adagio* of the *Farewell* and making the famous finale memorable by securing most elegant playing from the instrumentalists before they depart. The slow movement of the *Oxford* is also memorable, and the *Bear* is sheer delight. Perhaps it was a pity that No. 94 was included, as most collectors will already have it, but no one could fault the 'surprise' itself. The recording is of high quality, full bodied and resonant, but not blurred.

'Sturm und drang' symphonies: Symphonies Nos. 26 in G; 35 in B flat; 38 in C; 39 in G min.; 41 in C; 42 in D; 43 in E flat (Mercury); 44 in E min. (Trauer); 45 in F sharp min. (Farewell); 46 in B; 47 in G; 48 in C (Maria Theresia); 49 in F min. (La Passione); 50 in C; 51 in B flat; 52 in C min.; 58 in F; 59 in A (Fire), 65 in A.
(B) *** DG 463 731-2 (6) [id.]. English Concert, Trevor Pinnock.

Pinnock's forces are modest (with 6.5.2.2.1 strings), but the panache of the playing conveys any necessary grandeur. It is a new experience to have Haydn symphonies of this period recorded in relatively dry and close sound, with inner detail crystal clear (harpsichord never obscured) and made the more dramatic by the intimate sense of presence, yet with a fine bloom on the instruments. Some may find a certain lack of charm at times, and others may quarrel with the very brisk one-in-a-bar minuets and even find finales a little rushed. However, at bargain price, it is certainly value for money.

Symphonies Nos. 45 in F sharp min (Farewell); 55 in E flat (Schoolmaster).
(M) (**(*)) Decca mono 458 869-2. Aldeburgh Fest. O., Britten – MOZART: *Piano concerto No. 12 in A, K.414* (**(*)).

Like the Mozart *piano concerto* with which they are coupled, these two mid-period Haydn symphonies were recorded live at the 1956 Aldeburgh Festival, exceptional practice for Decca at the time. Recorded in the dry acoustic of Jubilee Hall, Aldeburgh, the sound is limited but close and immediate, bringing out the vigour and bite of Britten's approach to Haydn, using a small chamber band.

In the *Farewell* he brings out the *Sturm und Drang* drama of the piece, the implied tragedy of the minor-key writing, with dynamic contrasts underlined. His speeds in the last two movements are fresh and brisk – remarkably so for the period – relaxing for the *Adagio* epilogue. That is so beautifully timed over the departure of one player after another that the very end, with only two violins left, inspires laughter. The *Schoolmaster* is strongly characterized too, with brisk allegros and with high dynamic contrasts wittily pointed. The offbeat, mid-air ending of the finale is also delectably timed, and – as in the *Farewell* – the amusement of the audience is clearly audible.

Symphonies Nos. *82 in C (The Bear); 83 in G min (The Hen); 84 in E flat; 85 in B flat (The Queen); 86 in D; 87 in A (Paris).*
⊙ (BB) *** Virgin Classics 2 x 1 Dig. Double VBD5 61659 [CDVB 61659] (2). OAE, Kuijken.
*** Philips Dig. 462 111-2 (2) [id.]. O. of the 18th Century, Frans Brüggen.

The Sigiswald Kuijken's set of the *Paris Symphonies* – warmly and vividly recorded – is among the most enjoyable period-performance recordings of Haydn ever. Kuijken and his players wear their authenticity lightly and the slow movements are allowed to relax beautifully, while the one-in-a-bar treatment of the minuets produces a delightful Ländler-like swing. With dynamic contrasts underlined, the grandeur of Haydn's inspiration is fully brought out, along with the rigour; yet Kuijken gives all the necessary sharpness to the reminiscence of *Sturm und Drang* in the near-quotation of the *Farewell* in the first movement of No. 85, *La Reine*. The magnificence of that movement is underlined by the observance of the second-half repeat. Above all, he and his players convey the full joy of Haydn's inspiration in every movement and the reissue at bargain price is surely irresistible.

Franz Brüggen, continuing his excellent Haydn series with his talented Dutch period orchestra is here, as ever, an outstandingly characterful interpreter of Haydn, with rhythms beautifully sprung. These are strong, positive performances of the *Paris Symphonies*, helped by immediate sound giving a vivid sense of presence. There is no discrepancy in the quality for No. 86, recorded earlier than the rest. However, good as these performances are, they are upstaged by Kuijken, and not only just on price (the Philips set costs about three times as much as the Virgin Double!).

Symphonies Nos. *88 in G; 89 in F; (i) Sinfonia concertante in B flat for violin, cello, oboe, bassoon & orchestra.*
**(*) Philips Dig. 462 602-2 [id.]. O. of the 18th Century, Frans Brüggen; (i) with Lucy van Dael, Wouter Möller, Ku Ebbinge, Danny Bond.

This neatly fills in a gap between Brüggen's two-disc set of the six *Paris Symphonies* and the *London Symphonies*. No. 88, originally coupled with No. 86

from that set, was recorded much earlier than the rest, with no significant discrepancy of sound. Even so, one might detect an earlier vintage of performances in the relative heaviness of the lovely slow movement, although one would not want to make too much of this for it flows along warmly enough.

Otherwise, these are all winningly lively and virile performances, rhythmically resilient, in bright, full, immediate sound. The *Hungarian dance* of the finale of No. 89 is a delight. The *Sinfonia concertante*, with four excellent soloists from the orchestra – the oboist, Ku Ebbinge's reedy tone is most individual – makes a most enjoyable bonus, though the contrast in sound between solo and tutti is rather extreme.

Symphonies Nos. *93–104 (London Symphonies).*
(BB) **(*) Arte Nova Dig. 74321 72109-2 (4) [id.]. L. Fest. O, Ross Pople.

Ross Pople conducts his London Festival Orchestra in lively accounts of the twelve *London Symphonies*. They are neatly fitted, in numerical order, onto only four CDs thanks to the omission of the exposition repeat in No. 104. These are amiable rather than high-powered or highly polished readings, but with rhythms well lifted they are consistently enjoyable. The players are set in a relatively intimate acoustic, with horns braying out warmly, even if tuttis tend to grow a little cloudy. Well paced, they bring brisk Ländler-like Minuets, and fresh, alert outer movements. Excellent value and well worth considering at their modest cost. But they do not upstage the superb Colin Davis set on a pair of Philips Duos (⊙ 442 611-2 and 442 614-2) nor indeed do they have quite the character of Jeffrey Tate's underrated recordings of Nos. 94, 96 and 104 in the same budget price range – see below.

Symphonies Nos. *94 in G (Surprise); 96 in D (Miracle); 104 in D (London).*
(BB) *** Royal ROY 6443 [id.]. ECO, Jeffrey Tate.
(M) **(*) DG Dig. 463 083-2 [id.]. BPO, Karajan.

With first-class playing from the ECO, Jeffrey Tate's modern-instrument Haydn performances are as fine as any in the catalogue and can be recommended alongside those of Sir Colin Davis. The slow introductions to each of these three symphonies are particularly impressive, while his lightness of touch in second subjects brings out their full charm. There is a gracious elegance in slow movements, and the Minuets have plenty of rhythmic lift. Tempi are never forced, yet finales bring wonderfully deft string playing. The *Miracle Symphony* is particularly enjoyable in that respect, while the *London Symphony* has a culminating gravitas which is most satisfying. The recording is full, yet detail emerges clearly. A first-class bargain in all respects.

Karajan's *London Symphony* has impressive power and dignity with altogether splendid string playing from the Berlin Philharmonic, with none of the interpretative self-indulgence which sometimes marred this conductor's later performances. Similar comments also apply to the *Surprise* and *Miracle* symphonies: these are beautifully played works, weighty by modern standards, but not ponderous. Other conductors (Jochum and Davis, for example) bring more wit and sparkle to this repertoire, but with a playing time of 76 minutes, this is an excellent way to sample Karajan's plush approach to Haydn. Good recording.

CHAMBER MUSIC

String quartets Nos. 75 in G; 76 in D min. (Fifths); 77 in C (Emperor), Op. 76/1–3.
*** ASV Dig. CDDCA 1076 [id.]. Lindsay Qt.

The Lindsays crown their series of Haydn recordings with this superb disc of three of the supreme masterpieces from Opus 76, marvellously played and truthfully recorded, and looking set to sweep the board. In their hands these quartets are made to sound among the greatest ever written, which of course they are. The Lindsays have covered two of these works before, in live recordings, but this time not only is the sound more refined, the performances are too, while keeping the strength and warmth which characterizes all the Lindsays' playing. The first of the three may be less frequently performed than the others but after an exhilarating account of the chirpy first movement, where the delicacy of articulation and refinement of ensemble are most striking, the hushed, nobly restrained *Andante sostenuto* has in their hands a transcending Beethovenian depth and profundity. The purposeful first movement of the *Fifths* is taken briskly, but every detail tells, and here the lighter mood of the *Andante o più allegretto* is enchantingly caught. The famous slow movement of the *Emperor*, also, has unusual refinement as well as warmth, and this too is a performance as vital as it is polished. Very highly recommended.

String quartets Nos. 75 in G; 79 in D; 80 in E flat, Op. 76/1, 5 & 6 (Erdödy Quartets).
*** EMI Dig. CDC5 56826-2 [id.]. Alban Berg Qt.

This completes the Alban Berg Quartet's set of Op. 76 (Nos. 2–4 are on CDC5 561661-2). As before, this is peerless playing, with poised slow movements, simply and beautifully played, yet with every note perfectly in place. At times one might venture a suspicion that everything is too perfectly calculated, but such a judgment would be unfair, for Haydn's spirit hovers over this music-making. The balance between vigour and precision in the Minuet/Scherzo of Op. 76/1 is matched by the elegance of the *Allegretto* opening of Op. 76/5, and the finale of the

same work is wonderfully crisp and vital. The Trio of the Minuet of the last of the set, with its rising and falling scales, has a rather subtle smile, and the lightness of touch in the Minuet itself is impossible to resist. The rhythmically quirky finale based on the same material is equally sharp in focus. The recording is vividly real and clear.

KEYBOARD MUSIC

Piano sonatas Nos. 3 in C, Hob XVI/3; 13 in E flat, Hob XVI/45; 14 in D, Hob XVII/D1; 22 in D, Hob XVI/24; 29 in E, Hob XVI/31; 45 in E flat, Hob XVI/52.
(BB) **(*) Arte Nova Dig. 74321 59211-1.
    Carmen Piazzini.

Carmen Piazzini is an Argentine pianist of some quality who studied with such keyboard luminaries as Wilhelm Kempff and Hans Leygraf. This bargain-price disc offers six sonatas, played with fine musicianship and taste even if at times she is a little monochrome. She is very well recorded and, like John McCabe (Decca) and Jenö Jandó (Naxos), a sound guide for this repertoire in this price range. She is not the equal (nor are they) of Schiff or Andsnes.

Piano sonatas Nos. 10, Hob XVI/1; 12, Hob XVI/12; 14, Hob XVI/3; 15, Hob XVI/13; 28, Hob XVI/5; 34, Hob XVI/33; 6 Menuets de la redoute, Hob IX/15.
(BB) * Discover Dig. DICD 920502 [id.]. Walid Akl.

Piano sonatas Nos. 33, Hob XVI/20; 37, Hob XVI/22; 38, Hob XVI/23; 48 Hob XVI/35; Adagio and five variations in D, Hob XVII/7.
(BB) * Discover Dig. DICD 920501 [id.]. Walid Akl.

Walid Akl, a Lebanese pianist based in Paris who was a pupil of Yvonne Lefebure and Jacques Février, sadly died in his early fifties. Here his Haydn is highly sensitive, though he is not free from self-indulgence and frequently comes to a completely full stop at the end of a musical paragraph. He is fluent of finger but the price advantage of his disc is offset by an inferior recording acoustic. The piano tone is pale and anaemic with rather papery sonority. It sounds like a fortepiano rather than the modern Steinway given on the sleeve. The pianism almost warrants two stars but the disc falls short in terms of both style and quality of engineering.

Piano sonatas Nos. 48 in C, Hob XVI/35; 49 in C sharp min., Hob XVI/36; 50 in D, Hob XVI/37; 51 in E flat, Hob XVI/38; 52 in G, Hob XVI/39.
*** BIS Dig. CD 992 [id.]. Ronald Brautigam (fortepiano).

Piano sonatas Nos. 53 in E min., Hob XVI/34;

54 in G, Hob XVI/40; 55 in B flat, Hob XVI/41; 56 in D, Hob XVI/42; 57 in F, Hob XVI/47; 58 in C, Hob XVI/48.
*** BIS Dig. CD 993 [id.]. Ronald Brautigam (fortepiano).

Piano sonatas Nos. 59 in E flat, Hob XVI/49; 60 in C, Hob XVI/50; 61 in D, Hob XVI/51; 62 in E flat, Hob XVI/52.
*** BIS Dig. CD 994 [id.]. Ronald Brautigam (fortepiano).

Fresh from his remarkably impressive survey of the Mozart sonatas, Ronald Brautigam has now embarked on the Haydn for BIS. He plays a fortepiano by Paul McNulty in 1992, modelled on an instrument by Anton Gabriel Walter of *circa* 1795, and is recorded in the pleasing acoustic of Länna Church in Sweden. His first disc is given over to five of the so-called *Auenbrugger sonatas*, Nos. 48–52 or Hob XVI/35–39, which derive their name from the dedicatees, Katharina and Marianna Auenbrugger, two wealthy and talented sisters, and come from 1780. Ronald Brautigam is hardly less vital and imaginative here than in Mozart. Apart from his technical virtuosity, his playing has tremendous flair and sparkle. This is spirited and life-loving music-making and almost ideally recorded. The second disc (CD993) includes the *Bossler sonatas* (Nos. 54–6), so-called because they were published by the house of Bossler. Brautigam gives them with tremendous flair and, in the Presto of *G major* (No. 54, Hob. XVI/40), great wit. The *B flat Sonata* (No. 55, Hob. XVI/41) is played with conspicuous relish, and in fact the whole disc is a delight from beginning to end. The third (CD994) brings the *Genzinger sonata* (No.59), so named because of Marianne von Genzinger, its dedicatee, whose husband was the personal physician to Prince Esterházy, and three *London sonatas*, composed in 1794–5, when Haydn was in his early sixties. The *E flat Major* (No. 62, Hob XVI/52) is the biggest and most symphonic of all. Exhilarating playing which augurs well for the rest of the series, which we assume will be appearing during the lifetime of this volume.

VOCAL MUSIC

Masses Nos. 1 in F (Missa brevis), Hob XXII/1; 11 in D min. (Nelson), Hob XXII/11; Ave Regina in A, Hob XXIIIb/3.
*** Chandos Dig. CHAN 0640 [id.]. Susan Gritton, Pamela Helen Stephen, MarK Padmore, Stephen Varcoe, Collegium Musicum 90, Richard Hickox.

Masses Nos. 1a in G (Rorate coeli desuper), Hob XXII/3; (i) 13 in B flat (Schöpfungsmesse), Hob XXII/13 (with Haydn's alternative Gloria).
*** Chandos Dig. CHAN 0599 [id.]. (i) Gritton,

Stephen, Padmore, Varcoe; Collegium Musicum 90, Richard Hickox.

Masses Nos. 6 in G (Missa Sanctae Nicolai), Hob XXII/6; 9 in B flat (Missa Sancti Bernardi von Offida (Heiligmesse)), Hob. XXII/10.
*** Chandos Dig. CHAN 0645 [id.]. Lorna Anderson, Stephen, Padmore, Varcoe, Collegium Musicum 90, Richard Hickox.

Masses Nos. 7 in B flat: Missa brevis Sancti Joannis de Deo (Little organ mass); 12 in B flat (Theresienmesse).
*** Chandos Dig. CHAN 0592 [id.]. Watson, Stephen, Padmore, Varcoe, Collegium Musicum 90, Richard Hickox.

Mass No. 10 in C: Missa in tempore belli (Paukenmesse), Hob. XXII/9; Alfred, König de Angelsachsen (incidental music): Aria of the Guardian spirit; Chorus of the Danes. 2 Te Deums in C, Hob XXIIIc/1–2.
*** Chandos Dig. CHAN 0633 [id.]. Nancy Argenta, Catherine Denley, Padmore, Varcoe, Collegium Musicum 90, Hickox.

Mass No. 11 in D min. (Nelson): Missa in augustiis, Hob XXII/11.
(M) *** Decca 458 623-2 [id.]. Stahlman, Watts, Wilfred Brown, Krause, King's College, Cambridge, Ch., LSO, Willcocks – HANDEL: *Coronation anthem: Zadok the Priest*; VIVALDI: *Gloria, RV 589.* ***

Mass No. 14 in B flat (Harmoniemesse); Salve regina in E.
*** Chandos Dig. CHAN 0612 [id.]. Argenta, Stephen, Padmore, Varcoe, Collegium Musicum 90, Richard Hickox.

In his superb series of Haydn recordings for Chandos, Richard Hickox offers performances which consistently bring out the freshness and originality of the writing, with crisp, bright singing from his excellent chorus, and first-rate soloists. The Chandos recording is well-scaled too, with chorus and soloists set in a natural balance, not spotlit, and with the lively acoustic giving agreeable bloom to the voices as well as a sense of space, while conveying ample detail. Though some may prefer performances using boys' voices, the women singers of Collegium Musicum 90 are clear and youthful-sounding, allowing bitingly incisive attack in Haydn's many exuberant numbers, not least the settings of the final *Dona nobis pacem* in each mass, which so often joyfully reflect the motif which he had the habit of putting at the end of his scores, *Laudis Deo*, 'Praise to God'. Some of the earlier masses take a more conventional view, so that the *Missa brevis Sancti Joannis de Deo*, which comes as the coupling for the *Theresienmesse*, sets the

Dona nobis pacem as simply an extended gentle cadence.

It is a great merit of this series that early masses and shorter choral works are included as couplings for the late, great masses written for the namedays of the Princess Esterházy, not least Haydn's last major work of all, the *Harmoniemesse* of 1802. Those extra items include some masterly works, and it is fascinating to hear Haydn's very first Mass – the coupling for the *Nelson mass*, most popular of all – which he wrote in his teens, a wonderfully fresh, bright inspiration. It is good too as one of the couplings for the *Schöpfungsmesse* to have the alternative setting of the *Gloria*, with the quotation from Haydn's oratorio *The Creation* ('Schöpfung') removed in deference to an objection from the Austrian Empress.

It was Sir David Willcocks who made Argo's pioneering recording of the *Nelson mass* in 1962, a work that is clearly among Haydn's greatest music. The solo singing is uniformly good, Sylvia Stahlman negotiating her florid music with great skill, while Willcocks maintains quite remarkable tension throughout. The splendid recording is admirably remastered and the added Handel and Vivaldi bonuses for this reissue on Decca's Legends label make the reissue very competitive. It is characteristically well documented.

The Seasons (complete; in English).
🌑 (B) *** Ph. Duo 464 034-2 (2) [id.]. Heather Harper, Ryland Davies, John Shirley-Quirk, BBC Chorus and SO, Sir Colin Davis.

Davis directs a tinglingly fresh performance of Haydn's last oratorio, which ranks alongside his great Haydn symphony performances (also on Philips Duo). The soloists are excellent and Davis's direction can hardly be faulted, even in our age of authentic enlightenment. This set makes a strong case for an English translation, though that no doubt will militate against it in non-English-speaking countries. Still, their loss is our gain and although no libretto is provided, the English generally comes over with clarity. The 1968 recording is exceptionally vivid and full, and this is another great bargain in the Philips Duo series.

Heinichen, Johann David
(1683–1729)

Dresden wind concerti in A min., S 212; in E min., S 218; in E min., S 222; in D, S 225; in G min., S 237; in G min., S 238.
**(*) CPO Dig. 999 637-2 [id.]. Fiori Musicale, Thomas Albert.

Johann David Heinichen was an influential theorist in his day and a considerable composer. His representation in the current catalogues is largely centred on the Archive recordings by Reinhard

Goebel and the Musica Antiqua Köln, and it is fortunate that the present issue from Thomas Albert and his Bremen group involves no duplication. And so for those who have the Archive sets, this will be a welcome supplement, though it must be said that the playing is by no means as accomplished or elegant as that ofthe Cologne group. Not an essential purchase then, but one which will nonetheless give pleasure.

Henze, Hans Werner (born 1926)

Music for 2 guitars: Memorias se El Cimarrón; Minette (Canti e rimpianti ariosi); 3 Märchenbilder from the opera Pollicino.
*** MDG Dig. 304 0881-2 [id.]. Jürgen Ruck, Elena Càsoli.

Henze has produced some important music for the guitar; indeed, few other living composers of standing can match him in this respect. What fascinates him, as Jürgen Ruck says in his notes, is that the guitar has found its way into the simplest folk music as well as into music of the highest sophistication. Of the three pieces recorded here, *Memorias se El Cimarrón* (1995) is the most immediately striking. It retraces and paraphrases the course of his opera *El Cimarrón* and exploits an extraordinarily wide range of sonorities and expressive devices, which Jürgen Ruck and Elena Càsoli of the Ensemble Villa Musica bring vividly to life. Highly imaginative and resourceful writing, reproduced with exemplary subtlety and naturalness by the recording engineers. *Minette* (1997) returns to the theme of his opera *The English cat* and reworks, recreates and sometimes freshly composes its material. For the *Märchenbilder from Pollicino* Henze returns to the children's opera he composed for Montepulciano, 'a delightful self-immersion in simple music for the purpose of escorting the younger generation into the world of today's musical language', as the composer himself put it. The whole programme is played with effortless mastery and imagination.

Hérold, Ferdinand (1791–1833)

Overture: Zampa.
*** Chandos Dig. CHAN 9765 [id.]. (i) Royal Liverpool PO Ch., BBC PO, Yan Pascal Tortelier (with Concert: 'French bonbons' ***).

Hérold's famous bandstand overture is played here with fine panache and given first-class recording. The rest of the programme of 'French bonbons' is equally diverting – see Concerts section below.

Hess, Nigel (20th Century)

East coast pictures; Global variations; Thames journey; Scramble!; Stephenson's Rocket; (i) *To the stars!; The TV detectives; The winds of power.*
**(*) Chandos Dig. CHAN 9764 [id.]. L. Symphonic Wind O, Composer; (i) with children from Daubney Middle School, Bedford.

Nigel Hess has made his name primarily as a composer for television and theatre, contributing to twenty productions at the Royal Shakespeare Company. He knows how to score and he has a ready fund of melody. This is demonstrated in *The TV detectives,* which brings together five rather striking TV themes, including 'Dangerfield', 'Wycliffe' and 'Hetty Wainthrop Investigates'. Of the concert music here, easily the most impressive piece is the flamboyant *To the stars!,* which gets a real lift-off from the vocal energy of the children of Daubney Middle School. *Thames journey* opens with trickling woodwind at its source, like Smetana's *Vltava,* and then introduces a Wiltshire folk melody on the horn as its main theme, but overall it is little more than a well-crafted potpourri, with *Greensleeves* and later *The Lass of Richmond Hill* also introduced. The three *East coast pictures* evoke the Eastern seaboard of the USA, but are curiously without any strong American colouring. *Stephenson's Rocket* is rugged and vigorous, but not much of a train imitation. *The winds of power* is more evocative, but rather loosely laminated. *Scramble!* is more succinct and celebrates the Battle of Britain vividly enough. Indeed, all these works have plenty of vitality, even if they are not really distinctive. They are brilliantly played here under the composer and given excellent Chandos sound.

Hindemith, Paul (1895–1963)

Kleine Kammermusik for 5 wind instruments, Op. 24/2.
(BB) **(*) Naxos Dig. 8.553851-2 [id.]. Michael Thompson Wind Quintet – BARBER: *Summer music* **(*); JANACEK: *Mládí* **(*); LARSSON: *Quattro tempi.* **

The *Kleine kammermusik for wind quintet,* Op. 24/2 is abundantly available, albeit not at bargain price. The Michael Thompson Wind Quintet give an excellently spirited and alert performance with plenty of wit. The playing is wonderfully accomplished and sensitive but the close balance is a distinct handicap. If you think this would not worry you, it is worth the modest outlay.

(i) Kammermusik Nos. 2 (Piano concerto); (ii) 3 (Cello concerto), Op. 36/1–2; (iii) 6 (Viola d'amore concerto); (iv) 7 (Organ concerto), Op. 46/1–2.
*** EMI Dig. CDC5 56831-2 [id.]. (i) Lars Vogt; (ii) Georg Faust; (iii) Wolfram Christ; (iv) Wayne Marshall; BPO, Abbado.

This outstanding issue fills in the gaps left by Abbado's earlier EMI disc (CDC5 56160-2) of the compact, offbeat concertos which Hindemith labelled *Kammermusik.* The ones here are respectively for piano, cello, viola d'amore and organ, with Lars Vogt giving an electrifying account of the piano part in No. 2, making an exhilarating start. Wayne Marshall as the organ soloist in No. 7 copes well with thick textures, and Wolfram Christ, the orchestra's principal viola, finds beauty in the intractable writing for viola d'amore in No. 6, with his cellist colleague a strong and positive soloist in No. 3. Abbado's control of rhythm and texture is masterly, helped by glowing EMI sound. He finds special inspiration in the slow movements, which bear the main emotional weight in these works, totally rebutting any idea of dryness in Hindemith's writing.

(i) Kammermusik No. 4, Op. 36/3. Tuttifäntchen: orchestral suite; (i) Violin concerto.
**(*) CPO Dig. 999 527-2 [id.]. Queensland SO, Werner Andreas Albert; (i) Dene with Olding.

The main work here is the *Violin concerto* of 1939, in which Dene Olding acquits himself well. He is particularly impressive in the slow movement, which is thoughtful and inward-looking. There is a good, truthful balance between soloist and orchestra here, though on the *Kammermusik No. 4,* Op. 36/3 the balance is too close and claustrophobic, and the results unpleasing. Hindemith's music needs all the help it can get from a flattering acoustic. Of good broadcasting standard rather than a first choice in the commercial record field.

Kammermusik No. 5, Op. 36/4 (for viola and large chamber orchestra); Konzertmusik (for viola and large chamber orchestra), Op. 48; Der Schwanendreher (Viola concerto); Trauermusik (for viola and strings).
*** CPO Dig. CPO 999 492-2 [id.]. Brett Dean, Queensland SO, Werner Albert.

The viola was Hindemith's own instrument and he writes gratefully for it. The *Kammermusik No. 5* is generously represented on disc, whilst the *Konzertmusik,* Op. 48 (1929–30) (also with large chamber orchestra and with no violins or violas in the string selection, hence its rich sonorities in the bass-baritone end of the spectrum) is relatively neglected, and undeservedly so, for it has a particularly engaging first movement and an imaginative and deeply felt slow movement. It operates at a higher level of inspiration than the oft-recorded *Der Schwanendreher,* good though that is, and the *Trauermusik* that Hindemith composed at high speed on the death of George V. (As he put it in a letter to his publisher, 'I received a studio of my own, the copyists were slowly warmed up, and from eleven to five I did a lot of mourning'.) The Australian violist and composer Brett Dean gives masterly accounts of all four pieces and the Queensland Orchestra plays with excellent ensemble and precision for Werner Albert. Recommended with enthusiasm.

Nobilissima visione.
(M) *** RCA High Performance 09026 63315-2 [id.]. Chicago SO, Jean Martinon – BARTOK: *The Miraculous Mandarin: suite*; VARESE: *Arcana*. ***

Martinon delivers a splendid account of this finely conceived and often very beautiful score. *Nobilissima visione* is one of Hindemith's most approachable works and those who investigate it will be amply rewarded. The Chicago Orchestra play with tremendous attack and discipline and the recording, though it could be richer, has satisfactory sonority.

Nobilissima visione (suite).
(M)(**(*)) EMI CDM5 67337-2 [id.]. Philh. O, Klemperer – STRAVINSKY: *Symphony in three movements*; WEILL: *Kleine Dreigroschenmusik* *** (with KLEMPERER: *Merry waltz* **).

Klemperer recorded only the three-movement suite from *Nobilissima visione*, but three movements incorporate music from all five numbers of the ballet. The Philharmonia play gravely and nobly (especially in the final *Passacaglia*), and Klemperer's rather austere style suits the music. The 1954 Kingsway Hall recording is made available in stereo here for the first time. The sound remains two-dimensional, dry, but vivid, and this disc is a worthwhile addition to EMI's 'Klemperer Legacy'.

Sinfonia serena; Symphony (Die Harmonie der Welt).
*** Decca Dig. 458 899-2 [id.]. Leipzig Gewandhaus O, Blomstedt.

The *Sinfonia serena* and the *Symphony (Die Harmonie der Welt)* come from the immediate post-war years. The *Sinfonia serema* must be ranked among Hindemith's finest works and the symphony based on material from the opera *Die Harmonie der Welt* does not lag far behind. As his *Mathis der Maler* with the San Francisco Orchestra showed, Blomstedt has proved to be one of the most persuasive advocates of the composer and this newcomer confirms and enhances this impression. The clarity of his conception is well served by the lucidity of the Decca recording and the Leipzig Orchestra produces a finely cultured sound. Hindemith himself recorded both works, the former for Walter Legge's Columbia blue label, and the latter for Deutsche Grammophon and these are important documents. There is formidable competition is this coupling from Yan Pascal Tortelier and the BBC Philharonic on Chandos (CHAN 9217), to which we awarded a Rosette, but this newcomer can be recommended alongside it.

Hol, Richard (Rijk) (1825–1904)

Symphonies Nos. 1 in C min.; 3 in B flat, Op. 101.
*(**) Chandos Dig. CHAN 9796 [id.]. Hague Residentie O, Matthias Bamert.

Dutch music between Sweelinck and Diepenbrock is a closed book for all but a handful of specialists. The son of an Amsterdam milkman, Richard (or Rijk) Hol was an influential figure in the second half of the nineteenth century, both as a conductor and as a teacher. He introduced much new music of the day to Dutch audiences, including Berlioz, Liszt, Wagner and Brahms, though his own work was predominantly conservative in outlook and has brought about some difference of opinion between us as to its intrinsic value. Hol was prolific and like Brahms he wrote four symphonies, but they are nearer to Schumann in their musical ethos, although the scoring owes more to Brahms and Mendelssohn, who provided the inspiration for the engaging Scherzo which is the highlight of the later, B flat major work. The melodic invention is somewhat conventional, but is lyrical and pleasing throughout each symphony here. R. L. feels that whatever may be said of his originality or importance, Hol was a *real* symphonist who has total command over his material and has a sense of architecture and pace. For E. G. the orchestral writing is attractive, but the musical material hardly deserves such extended treatment, with too many passages depending on empty gestures, with trite repetitions and sequences, and melodies which turn back on themselves. One can appreciate the intentions, but Hol, sadly, is not the lost Dutch master one had hoped for. For R. L. Hol has a sense of both dignity and nobility, and this interesting repertoire engages his sympathy and attention from first to last. E. G.'s summation is that this is an undemanding disc of mid-romantic orchestral music, very well played and recorded: it can be recommended primarily to anyone searching for rarities. For I. M. this is not music he would wish to return to very often. However, we are all agreed that the performances, from a first-class orchestra who are naturally at home in the repertoire, are warmly sympathetic and the full-bodied Chandos sound presents the composer's orchestration persuasively.

Holbrooke, Joseph (1878–1958)

Piano concerto No. 1 (Song of Gwyn ap Nudd), Op. 52.

*** Hyperion Dig. CDA 67127 [id.]. Hamish Milne, BBC Scottish SO, Martyn Brabbins – Haydn WOOD: *Piano concerto.* ***

Once described as a cockney Wagner, Joseph Holbrooke had the misfortune to develop his high romantic style just when it was being superseded on almost every front. It has taken a long time for his star to rise again, but this ambitious piano concerto provides a fair sample of his writing, presenting both its strengths and its weaknesses. The grandeur of the manner is not often enough matched by memorable material and when a melody does emerge to catch in the mind – like the songful theme representing the heroine, Cordelia, of the poem illustrated in this concerto – it verges on the banal. The piano-writing too often suggests a popular idiom, making this an apt coupling for the fine concerto by a composer who did find his success in light music, Haydn Wood. What makes this recording of the concerto most enjoyable despite the weaknesses is not only the brilliance of the performance – with Hamish Milne masterly in finding poetry in the Chopinesque figuration – but also the presentation. As in the score, the twenty-two index-points are linked directly to the text of the poem which inspired the piece, telling the evocative story. Full, well-balanced recording.

Holmboe, Vagn (1909–96)

String quartets Nos. 13, Op. 124; 14, Op. 125; 15, Op. 135.

*** Dacapo Dig. 8.224127 [id.]. Kontra Qt.

In all, Holmboe composed some twenty string quartets, though there are about ten preceding the official No. 1, Op. 46 from 1948 and he was working on other quartets after the last, No. 20, Op. 160 (1985). Nos. 14 and 15 were issued in the days of LP by the Copenhagen Quartet ,who recorded Nos. 1–10 complete at a time when interest in Holmboe's work was at a relatively low ebb. Both the *Thirteenth* and *Fourteenth Quartet*s come from 1975 and No. 13 must be numbered among the most eloquent of his works. Indeed, both find him at the height of his intellectual powers. The *Fifteenth Quartet* (1977–8) preceded the *Eleventh Symphony*, arguably the most inspired of his later works. There is a certain severity and rigour about these pieces and the Kontras give them all with the concentration and dedication they require. The recordings made in 1997–8 are excellent without any of the hardness we detected in its immediate predecessor. Strongly recommended to admirers of this composer.

Holst, Gustav (1874–1934)

The Planets, Op. 32.

(M) (***) Cala mono CACD 0526 [id.]. NBC SO, Stokowski – DEBUSSY: *Prélude à l'après-midi d'un faune; La cathédrale engloutie* (**(*)); GOULD: *2 Marches.* (***)

There is no doubting that Stokowski is in charge here: his personality is stamped on every note of this individual and exciting reading of *The Planets*. What is so striking is the conviction of the NBC SO who were performing this work (taken from an NBC broadcast in February 1943) for the first time. (Toscanini at the time became alarmed at how his orchestra had been so quickly Stokowskized by the great magician!) The tempi, with the exception of a few exaggerated examples, are remarkably similar to Holst's own, though the performance is very individual. Each planet is vividly characterized, with plenty of atmosphere running through each of the seven movements. The sound calls for some tolerance: although basically full – the opening of *Mars* (which makes a thrilling impact) is particularly effective – there is a fair amount of distortion at the climaxes and the surface noise can at times make its presence felt. But not too much should be made of this as the performance tends to make one forget technical imperfections. As usual in Cala's Stokowski series, Edward Johnson provides a perceptively helpful essay.

The Planets (original version for 2 pianos); Cotswolds Symphony: Elegy: In memoriam William Morris (original version for 2 pianos).

*** Olympia Dig. OCD 683 [id.]. Goldstone and Clement – ELGAR: *String serenade;* BAINTON: *Miniature suite *** (with Bury: *Prelude and fugue in E flat ***).*

Holst's *Planets suite* was first heard in its two-piano version in the music hall of St Paul's Girls' School in Hammersmith at a Music Society concert in 1918, with Vaughan Williams in the audience. The first public performance of the orchestral version was not until two years later when Albert Coates conducted the LSO at its première in London's Queens Hall. When one thinks of the brilliance and colour of Holst's orchestration it comes as a surprise to find how effective the score sounds on two pianos, and one often thinks of Ravel (especially so in the closing, very watery *Neptune*) who wrote first for piano, and scored his music afterwards. *Mars*, grumbling ominously in the bass certainly does not lack menace or power at its climax, *Venus* has remarkable translucence, and if nimble pianism cannot match a delicate string tracery in *Mercury*, *Saturn* is highly evocative.

Jupiter is ebullient enough although the performers here choose to play the famous central tune quite slowly and almost elegiacally, and to good effect. *Uranus* opens baldly and strongly, then is made to dance along spiritedly. Altogether a great success, partly because of the spontaneity of playing by a fine duo who obviously are very familiar with the orchestral version. The *Elegy*, part of the neglected *Cotswolds Symphony* stands up well on its own, but is rather less effective in the composer's unpublished piano version, well played as it is.

Honegger, Arthur (1892–1955)

Cello concerto.
** MDG Dig. MDG 0321 0215-2 [id.]. Ulrich Schmid, NW German PO, Dominique Roggen – BLOCH: *Schelomo.* **

Honegger's delightful *Cello concerto* is not generously represented on CD, though it is included in Rostropovich's retrospective anthology. Ulrich Schmid and the Nordwestdeutsche Philharmonie under the Swiss conductor Dominique Roggen give a dedicated account of it. All the same, at only 42 minutes' playing-time, this would be distinctly uncompetitive even at bargain price let alone premium rate.

Le roi David (complete).
(M) *** Erato/Warner 2292 45800-2. Eda Pierre, Collard, Tappy, Petel, Valere, De Dailly, Philippe Caillard Ch., Instrumental Ens., Dutoit.
(BB) **(*) Naxos Dig. 8.553649 [id.]. Jacques Martin, Christine Fersen, Danielle Borst, Marie-Ange Todorovitch, Gilles Ragon, Clara Guedj, Ch. Régional Vittoria d'Ile de France, O de la Cité, Michel Piquemal.

Strangely enough, in these days of superabundance we have had no sumptuously recorded new version of Honegger's powerful oratorio *Le roi David* (1921). Both Dutoit's 1970 version and the Naxos set give us the original scoring for seventeen instruments, the double-bass being the only string instrument. In 1923, Honegger scored it in the familiar concert version adding the narration which Naxos use here. Michel Piquemal's performance is a good one and though there are certain weaknesses (the tenor's vibrato will not be to all tastes), there is a good feeling for the dramatic shape of the work. Piquemal keeps a firm grip on the proceedings and the instrumentalists play with real commitment, whilst the recording is very adequate. However, now that Erato have restored the Dutoit set to the catalogue, that takes pride of place. It is a very compelling performance of strong dramatic coherence, and no one could guess that the excellent recording is thirty years old.

Hovhaness, Alan (1911–2000)

(i) *Symphonies Nos. 1 (Exile), Op. 17/2*; (ii) *22 (City of Light), Op. 236*; (iii) *Bagatelles Nos. 1–4*; (i) *Fantasy on Japanese woodprints, Op. 211*; (iv) *The flowering peach, Op. 125*; (i) *Prayer of St. Gregory*; (v) *A rose tree blossoms, Op. 246/4*; (iii) *String quartet No. 4 (The ancient tree), Op. 208/2.*
(B) **(*) Delos Dig. Double DE 3700 (2) [id.]. Seattle SO, (i) Schwarz; (ii) Hovhaness; (iii) Shanghai String Qt.; (iv) Ohio State University Concert Band, Brion; (v) St. John's Episcopal Cathedral Ch., Pearson.

The music on this CD is all melodic and easy to come to terms with. The persecution of Armenians in Turkey in the 1930s was the inspiration of the *Symphony No. 1*: its modal, oriental tonalities setting the scene quite hauntingly, whilst the violent outbursts sound distinctly gothic. *City of light* is agreeable enough, if conventional, and the *Prayer of St. Gregory*, essentially a chorale, has a certain innocent appeal. *The flowering peach* was a serio-comic retelling of the Noah's Ark story, performed on Broadway in 1954, for which Hovhaness wrote the incidental music; it has some atmosphere, but is not very interesting or memorable.

A rose tree blossoms is a short but charmingly simple choral work, and the *Bagatelles* are unassuming, milk-and-water pieces. The *Fantasy on Japanese woodprints* produces lots of bizarre sounds (horror-film-type noises), but to little effect. The performances and recordings are more than adequate and the two-for-the-price-of-one format makes this good value for the composer's admirers.

Symphony No. 2 (Mysterious Mountain), Op. 132.
(M) *** RCA 09026 61957-2 [id.]. Chicago SO, Reiner – PROKOFIEV: *Lieutenant Kijé (suite)* **(*); STRAVINSKY: *Le baiser de la fée (Divertimento).* ***

The *Mysterious Mountain Symphony* is Hovhaness's most famous work and has a cult following: it begins with pastoral, modal writing, leading to a central fugal climax and returning to rich, expressive serenity. Fritz Reiner's performances is excellent in every way and the 1958 recording hardly sounds dated at all; this makes an ideal CD for those curious about this composer, for the couplings are superb.

(i) *Symphonies Nos. 2 (Mysterious Mountain); 50 (Mount St. Helens), Op. 360*; (ii) *53 (Star Dawn), Op. 377*; (i) *Alleluia and fugue; And God created great whales; Celestial fantasy; Meditation on Orpheus, Op. 155; Prelude and quadruple fugue*; (iii) *String quartet No. 3 (Reflections on my childhood), Op. 208/1; Suite from string quartet No. 2.*
(B) *** Delos Dig. DE 3711 (2) [id.]. (i) Seattle

SO, Schwarz; (ii) Ohio State University Concert Band, Brion; (iii) Shanghai String Qt.

The *Symphony No. 2* was championed by Fritz Reiner (see above). More action-packed is the extravagant *Mount St. Helens Symphony*, with an awe-inspiring volcano eruption in the finale (with some quite shattering orchestral effects), as well as the genuinely evocative *Spirit Lake* central movement. The *Star Dawn Symphony*, evoking travelling in space towards heaven, is quite effectively depicted, though after the allegro climax, the following slow movement lets the listener down.

The *String quartets* are attractive with some nice touches, without being really memorable. But the most sensational piece here is *And God created great whales*, which reaches a hugely spectacular climax and interpolates tapes of actual song of the humpbacked whale. The effect is very grandiose indeed and everyone rises to the occasion, including both the whales and the recording engineers. The performances are dedicated and very well presented so this is excellent value if the musical scenario appeals.

Jesus Christ is risen today; Jesus lover of my Soul; The Lord's prayer; Magnificat, Op. 157; O for a shout of sacred joy; O God our help in ages past; Out of the depths; Peace be multiplied; Psalm 23 (Cantata from Symphony No. 12); A rose tree blossoms.

(b) (*) Delos Dig. DE 3176 (2) [id.]. St. John's Cathedral Ch. and O, Pearson.

The opening of the *Magnificat* has some growling lower strings which sound rather ominous, but the following tune in the brass is banal, not helped by the third-rate quality of playing. There is nothing unpleasant about this work, but its endless modal melody becomes monotonous after a while. Though this type of 'mystical' minimalism is currently very fashionable, Hovhaness finds neither the imaginative resource nor the orchestral skill of a composer like John Adams. The shorter, less pretentious works which follow are more attractive and show him in a better light. However while one might tolerate such performances at a concert (the choir and orchestra are nothing if not dedicated and enthusiastic) the standard is not good enough for CD repetition. The recording is just about adequate.

Howells, Herbert (1892–1983)

Collegium regale: Office of Holy Communion; Requiem. St Paul's service: Magnificat; Nunc dimittis. Motets: Like as the hart; Long, long ago; Take him earth. Organ music: Paean; Rhapsody No. 3.

(bb) *** Naxos Dig. 8.554659 [id.]. St John's College Ch., Christopher Robinson; Iain Farrington.

No composer this century has surpassed Herbert Howells in the beauty and imagination of his Anglican church music. Naxos, in its prize-winning English music series, here offers a generous selection in seductive performances from the Choir of St John's College, Cambridge, that match and often surpass any previous versions. This will have King's Choir down the road looking to its laurels, helped by immaculate sound at once atmospheric and cleanly focused.

Hummel, Johann (1778–1837)

Piano trios Nos. 1 in E flat, Op. 12; 3 in G, Op. 35; 4 in G, Op. 65; 7 in E flat, Op. 96.

(b) *** Ph. Virtuoso 446 077-2 [id.]. Beaux Arts Trio.

These are characteristically cultivated and pleasing works. The Rondo finales of all four here are played with a witty verve and infectious sparkle. Slow movements have an appealing elegance and warmth.

The trios range across Hummel's life from the *First*, in E flat, Op. 12, published in 1803, through to the *Seventh*, Op. 96, which appeared about twenty years later. The music may plumb no great depths but these trios are fresh and inventive and their shallows sparkle with delight. The performances have all the vitality and finesse we expect from the Beaux Arts team, and the Philips recording is perfectly balanced and very real and present. The originals date from as recently as 1997 and this bargain reissue rather sweeps the board in this repertoire.

Hurlstone, William (1876–1906)

Cello sonata in D.

(m) *** Dutton Epoch Dig. CDLX 7102 [id.]. Andrew Fuller, Michael Dussek – HARTY: *Butterflies; Romance and scherzo, Op. 8; Wood-stillness;* PARRY: *Cello sonata in A.* ***

Hurlstone's *Cello sonata* is as well fashioned and musicianly as you would expect from this gifted composer. It receives excellent advocacy from Andrew Fuller, who also writes the intelligent notes, and his fine pianist. At the same time it is not easy to discern a distinctive voice here beneath the Brahmsian veneer. The recording is excellent, well balanced and present.

Ibert, Jacques (1890–1962)

Divertissement; Escales.

(b)**(*) Sony SBK 62644 [id.]. Philadelphia O, Ormandy – FAURE: *Pelléas et Mélisande,* etc. **(*); ROUSSEL: *Bacchus et Ariane* ***.

Ormandy's 1960 *Divertissement* is enjoyable if without quite the unbuttoned *joie de vivre* which Martinon (Decca) brought to it. In *Escales*, the Philadelphia strings produce a memorably sumptuous tone, and a noticeable intensity runs throughout the work. The sound is good considering its 1960 CBS provenance (it's a bit dry and up front), but this is music-making of quite a high order. The Roussel coupling is even more compelling, and this bargain CD is well worth its modest cost.

Sinfonia concertante for oboe and strings.
*** Koch Campanella Dig. C 130045 [id.].
Hansjörg Schellenberger, Franz Liszt CO, Budapest, Zoltán Peskó – LUTOSLAWSKI: *Double concerto for oboe and harp;* MARTIN: *3 Danses for oboe, harp, string quintet and string orchestra.* ***

Like the other two works on this outstanding CD, the Ibert *Sinfonia concertante* was given its première (in 1951) by Paul Sacher. It is a complex piece, scored in the spirit of a concerto grosso, with soloists from all the string groups joining the oboist. The writing in the outer movements has enormous vitality and impulse and demands great virtuosity from the orchestra, which is certainly forthcoming here. The extended central *Adagio* has a wan, expressive poignancy. Schellenberger is a first-class soloist and Peskó and the Budapest strings provide a spirited backing, presenting the fugato writing of the finale with great energy and sharply focused detail. The recording is excellent.

Complete chamber music

Vol. 1: *Aria for flute, violin & piano; Française* (for solo guitar); *Le jardinier de Samos* (for flute, clarinet, trumpet, violin, cello & percussion); *Jeux (Sonatine for flute & piano); 2 Movements for wind quartet; Paraboles for 2 guitars; Pastorale for 4 pipes; 3 Pièces brèves for wind quintet; 5 Pièces en trio for oboe, clarinet & bassoon; 6 Pièces for harp.*

Vol. 2: *Ariette* (for solo guitar); *Caprilena for solo violin; Carignane for bassoon & piano; Chevalier errant: L'âge d'or* (for alto sax & piano); *Entr'acte for flute & guitar; Etude-caprice pour un tombeau de Chopin; Ghirlarzana* (both for solo cello); *Impromptu for trumpet & piano; 2 Interludes for flute, violin & harpsichord; String quartet; Trio for violin, cello & harp.*
(B)*** Olympia Double Dig. OCD 707 A+B (2) [id.]. Pameijer, Oostenejk, Colbers, Gaesterland, Bornkamp, Jeurissen, Masseurs, Stoop, Franssen, de Rijke, Grotenhuis, van Delft, Marinissen, New Netherlands Qt, Hulsmann, Biesta, Oldeman, van Staalen.

This pair of Olympia discs (now attractively re-

issued as a 2 x 1 Double) offer music which is not only delightful but (for the most part) very little known, with the exception of the *Trois Pièces brèves,* which are justly familiar. Yet the *Trio for violin, cello and harp* is hardly less distinctive, while the *Cinq Pièces en trio* have a winning pastoral flavour. French composers were especially good at writing Spanish music (Chabrier and Ravel spring immediately to mind), so it is not surprising that Ibert's music featuring the guitar has such southern Mediterranean feeling. But then so do the *Deux Interludes* for flute, violin and harpsichord, another very winning trio and with something of a gypsy flamenco flavour. The two CDs, each lasting around 80 minutes, are arranged in order of composition, so the *Six Pièces* for solo harp come at the beginning to entice the listener with their smooth melodic flow. But there is not a dull or unimaginative item here, and these excellent Dutch players have the full measure of the witty, piquant Poulenc manner. They are very well recorded. This is music to cheer you up on a dull day.

Ireland, John (1879–1962)

(i) *The Holy Boy*; (ii) *Phantasie trio in A min.*; (iii) *Violin sonata No. 1 in D min.*; (iv) *Violin sonata No. 2 in A min.*
(M) (***) Dutton Epoch mono CDLX 7103 [id.]. Florence Hooton with (i) Lawrence Pratt (ii) Frederick Grinke, Kenneth Taylor. John Ireland with (iii) Frederick Grinke, (iv) Albert Sammons.

We have long treasured Frederick Grinke's 78 r.p.m. set of the *Violin sonata No. 1* with the composer at the piano, and can confirm that the Dutton transfer of this 1945 recording brings its sound to life with striking effect. It is possible that there have been better recordings but not a more vibrant or more authoritative performance. Unless we are much mistaken, it has never been transferred to LP or CD before. The *Violin sonata No. 2*, on the other hand, again with John Ireland at the piano but with its dedicatee, the legendary Albert Sammons, has never been issued at all before, for reasons which remain obscure. Recorded fifteen years earlier in 1930, it still sounds very well for its age, as does the *Phantasie trio*, in which Grinke is joined by Florence Hooton and Kenneth Taylor. An invaluable and self-recommending set which readers should cherish. Outstanding transfers.

PIANO MUSIC

Aubade; February's child; The Darkened valley; Decorations; April; Leaves from a child's sketchbook; Merry Andrew; 3 Pastels; Rhapsody; Sonatina; Summer evening; The Towing path.

(BB) *** Naxos Dig. 8.553889 [id.]. John
Lenehan.

Few British composers have matched John Ireland
in the point and individuality of his piano music,
with its offbeat melodies and tangy dissonances.
Making up for serious neglect, John Lenehan is
making a complete survey for Naxos and the first
collection is discussed in our main volume
(8.553700). This second programme offers a score
of miniatures including two of Ireland's most hauntingly atmospheric pieces, *The Towing path* and *The
Darkened valley*, a Blake inspiration. The longest
work here is the *Sonatina* in three short movements,
with the opening *Moderato* bringing echoes of Ireland's colourful *Piano concerto*, the second a dark
meditation leading to a galloping finale. Impeccable
performances vividly recorded.

VOCAL MUSIC

Songs: Disc 1: *Earth's call; Five songs to poems
by Thomas Hardy; Great things; Hope the
Hornblower; If there were dreams to sell; If we
must part; I have twelve oxen; Love is a sickness
full of woes; Santa Chiara; Songs sacred and
profane; Spleen; Spring sorrow; Two songs;
Three songs; Three songs to poems by Thomas
Hardy; Tryst; Tutto è sciolto; When I am old.*

Songs: Disc 2: *Bed in summer; The Bells of San
Marie; During music; Five XVIth Cent. poems;
The journey; Mother and child; The heart's
desire; Ladslove; Remember; The Sacred flame;
Sea Fever; Songs of a wayfarer; Three songs; The
vagabond; We'll to the woods no more; What art
thou thinking of?; When I am dead, my dearest;
When lights go rolling round the sky.*
**(*) Hyperion Dig. CDA 67261/2 (2) [id.]. Lisa
Milne, John Mark Ainsley, Christopher
Maltman, Graham Johnson.

John Ireland's settings of English verse are among
the most sensitive of the early twentieth century, as
this welcome collection of sixty-eight songs makes
plain. They include one of the best-known of all
songs of the period, his setting of John Masefield's
Sea fever, a haunting tune that completely transcends the genre of the drawing-room ballad.
Mostly, Ireland's songs are more sophisticated, and
his gift of writing distinctively for the piano is
consistently revealed in the accompaniments with
their ear-catching harmonies. Each song is beautifully crafted, heightening the impact of the words,
but what this collection brings out is that slow,
reflective songs greatly outnumber the vigorous
ones. This is a collection best heard in sections
rather than at a single session.

Graham Johnson relishes the felicity of the piano-
writing, but the singing is less consistently
satisfying. Lisa Milne uses her light, bright soprano
very sympathetically in the women's songs, while

John Mark Ainsley, if not in his sweetest voice, is
similarly sensitive in the tenor songs, just over a
dozen of them. But almost half of the selection
features Christopher Maltman, who (as caught here
by the microphones) sings with fluttery tone, often
undistracting, but regularly under pressure making
the sound gritty and unfocused, as in the late setting
of William Cornish's *A Thanksgiving*. That was
one of the last songs Ireland wrote, in 1938, almost
a quarter-century before he died. With so many
songs included it seems a pity that the loveliest of
all Ireland songs, *The Holy Boy*, adapted from a
piano-piece, has been omitted. Clear, well-balanced
recording. In the excellent documentation, the lively
commentary of Andrew Green adds greatly to the
value of the set.

Ives, Charles (1874–1954)

(i) *Symphonies Nos. 1 in D min.; No. 2;* (ii) *No. 3*
(iii; iv) *No. 4;* (iii) *Orchestral set No. 1;* (iii; iv)
Orchestral set No. 2; (iii) *Three places in New
England.*
(B) **(*) Decca Double Analogue/Dig. 466 745-2
(2) [id.]. (i) LAPO, Mehta; (ii) ASMF,
Marriner; (iii) Cleveland O, Dohnányi; (iv)
Cleveland Ch.

Mehta's Los Angeles recordings of the first two
symphonies are very well recorded indeed. The
First is a charming work, much influenced by
Dvořák and Tchaikovsky, but still with touches of
individuality. It is superbly played, but the drawback here is a substantial cut in the last movement.
The more uneven *Second symphony* is given an
equally committed performance, with the rich but
brilliant Decca sound revealing every detail, though
it is not over-lit or too analytical. Marriner's account
of the *Third symphony* is first-rate in every way,
just as successful as Bernstein's account, and much
better recorded. For the *Fourth Symphony, Orchestral set No. 2*, and the masterly *Three places in
New England*, we move into the digital era with
Dohnányi's Cleveland forces: these performances
are very fine, and the sound is superb. In short, if
you don't mind about the cut mentioned above, this
is an inexpensive way of making a representative
collection of Ives's major works at a modest outlay.

Symphonies Nos. 2; (i) *4.*
(M) **(*) RCA 09026 63316-2 [id.]. Philadelphia
O, Ormandy; (i) John Alldis Choir, LPO,
Serebrier.

Ives composed his *Second Symphony* between 1897
and 1901. As the composer told us 'it expresses the
musical feelings of the Connecticut country around
here (Redding and Danbury) in the 1890s, the music
of the country folk. It is full of tunes they sang and
played then.' Indeed, it is full of all sorts of things,
a mixture of nineteenth-century Romanticism and

hymns, folk tunes, patriotic songs, college ditties – Ives's eclecticism already emerging strongly. It is an uneven work, perhaps, but very approachable. Ormandy offers a reasonably good account (1973), but there are more exciting and better recorded versions available (Bernstein's pioneering account on Sony, for example). José Serebrier acted as subsidiary conductor for Stokowski when he conducted the world première of Ives's wild and complex *Fourth Symphony* in New York. In this English performance (recorded during the 1974 three-day week, mid-winter, with no heat and RCA having to supply its own electricity) he managed to find his way through multi-layered textures which have deliberately conflicting rhythms. The players respond loyally and the movement representing *Chaos* is particularly colourful and dramatic in its sharp contrasts of dynamic; it is brutal yet somehow poetic. *Order* is represented by a fugue, and the finale brings an apotheosis. A vivid, gripping work, if perhaps not such great music as some American commentators thought at the time. For the CD collector it at least provides a storehouse of fantastic orchestral sound, and the sound is certainly vivid, if unrefined at times. A reasonable bargain on the 'High Performance' label.

Jacquet de La Guerre, Elisabeth
(1665–1729)

Pièces de clavecin: Premier Livre (1687); Pièces de clavecin (1707): Suites: in D min.; G.
*** Metronome Dig. METCD 1026 [id.]. Carole Cerasi (harpsichord).

Elisabeth Jacquet de La Guerre was presented at the French Court at the age of five to entertain King Louis XIV with her harpsichord playing. At the age of twenty-two she published her first book of keyboard pieces, and in 1694 her opera, *Céphale et Procris,* was performed at the Académie Royale de Musique. The following year came a set of trio sonatas and in 1707 came two more *Harpsichord suites,* each of eleven movements, but without the *Préludes* that are so striking in the earlier set. This is remarkable music and, like Barbara Strozzi, more than half-a-century earlier, Elisabeth Jacquet de La Guerre emerges as a major musical talent of her time, composing music of very high quality which can compare with and match the output of her more famous contemporaries.

Carole Cerasi's recital includes all her solo keyboard works, and her CD won the *Gramophone's* 1999 Award for baroque instrumental music. It received the special accolade of Stanley Sadie who commented that Cerasi 'plays all this music with real command: she knows where in the passionate pieces to press forward and where to linger, how to let the rhythms flow in the dances, how to shape the

extended chaconnes and how to make the most of Jacquet's expressive harmony.'

To this we would add her skill in giving an improvisatory impression in her freedom of line in the remarkable *Préludes.* We would add one proviso, and it is an important one. Her ornamentation is profuse and continuing, and it certainly affects the line of the music: some listeners may have problems with this, so an element of caution must accompany our otherwise strong recommendation. She plays a characterful seventeenth-century Ruckers harpsichord, rebuilt in 1763, and is excellently if fairly resonantly recorded.

Janáček, Leoš (1854–1928)

Idyll; Suite for string orchestra.
✹ *** Chandos Dig. CHAN 9816 [id.].
Norwegian CO, Iona Brown – BARTOK:
Divertimento for strings *** ✹.

The *Idyll* and the *Suite for strings* are both from the late 1870s and are already available on Chandos in good performances by Gregory Rose and the Jupiter Orchestra, and of course, on Supraphon and Decca. However, the Norwegian Chamber Orchestra and Iona Brown sweep the board. Their playing is vibrant, full of enthusiasm and vitality, and yet finding also a touching nostalgia in the slow sections of the *Idyll* and an even more subtle and haunting espressivo in the two lovely *Adagios* of the *Suite.* The ebb and flow of the performances is seemingly spontaneous, yet the ensemble of this splendid orchestra is that of a first-class string quartet, and they play with comparable integration of feeling. The recorded sound is absolutely state-of-the-art and the Bartók coupling quite outstanding.

Mládí.
(BB) **(*) Naxos Dig. 8.553851-2 [id.]. Michael Thompson Wind Quintet – BARBER: *Summer music* **(*); HINDEMITH: *Kleine Kammermusik* **(*); LARSSON: *Quattro tempi.* **

Janáček's *Mládi* is superbly played by the Michael Thompson Wind Quintet, who are sensitive to every nuance of this glorious and haunting score. Wonderfully accomplished and sensitive though they are, they are let down by a close balance which robs the music of atmosphere.

String quartets Nos. 1 (Kreutzer Sonata); 2 (Intimate letters).
(B)**(*) HM Musique d'abord Dig. HMT 7901380 [id.]. Melos Qt.

These days the two Janáček *Quartets* alone do not really represent the good value for money they represented in the days of LP. The Melos Quartet offer nothing in addition to the two *Quartets,* but theirs are performances of considerable character and fire and, though the playing-time is ungenerous and the recording a bit fierce, they are worth consideration. The performances are very idiomatic and appealing, the recording far from inferior, and this record will give pleasure. At least they are now offered at bargain price.

Violin sonata.
*** Ph. Dig. 462 621-2 [id.] Akiko Suwana, Boris Berezovsky – BRAHMS: *Sonata, Op. 120/2,* etc.; DVORAK: *4 Romantic Pieces, Op. 75,* etc. ***

In the hands of this Philips partnership of Suwana and Berezovsky, the sonata receives a most distinguished performance, arguably the finest in the catalogue. Both artists are completely natural and unaffected, and the recording is well nigh perfect. However, the Virgin/EMI version by Christian Tetzlaff and Leif Ove Andsnes (Virgin VC5 45122-2) is also highly eloquent and they offer perhaps more appropriate couplings, the sonatas of Debussy, Nielsen (No. 2) and Ravel.

Glagolitic mass.
(B) *** Australian Decca Eloquence 466 902-2. Teresa Kubiak, Anne Collins, Robert Tear, Wolfgang Schöne, Brighton Festival Ch., RPO, Kempe – KODALY: *Laudes organi; Psalm 114* ***.

In its day, this was a highly regarded recording of the *Glagolitic mass,* although Kempe's interpretation and the singing of the Brighton Festival Chorus do not always have the snapping authenticity of Rattle's and Mackerras's versions. Instead Kempe stresses the lyrical elements of the score rather than going for outright fervour, but the orchestra and chorus are fully committed, and the solo singing is first-rate too, with Teresa Kubiak particularly impressive. Everything is helped by the most realistic recording which has transferred very well to CD. The unusual Kodály coupling is appropriate and adds to the interest of this reissue on Australian Decca's Eloquence label.

Jenkins, John (1592–1678)

Consort music: Divisions for 2 bass viols in D; Fantasies: a 4 in D; in F (2); a 5 in C min. (2); & D; a 6 in A min. & C min.; In nomines: a 6 in E min. & G min.; Pavan for 2 bass viols; Pavan a 6 in F; Pieces for lyra viol; Suites Nos. 4 in C for two trebles, bass and organ; 7 in D min., for treble, two basses & organ in D min.
*** Virgin Veritas EMI Dig. VC5 45230-2. Fretwork with Paul Nicholas.

Consort music: Ayres a 4 in D min. & G min. (Ayre; Almaine; Couranto); Divisions for 2 basses in C; Fantasia: in C min.; D; E min.; Fantasias in C min.(2); Fantasia in F (All in a garden green);

Fantasy-suite in A min.; In nomine in G min.; Newarke Seidge: (Pavan; Galliard); Pavan in F.
(B) *** Naxos Dig. 8.550687 [id.]. Rose Consort of Viols with Timothy Roberts.

John Jenkins spent his life in Norfolk and then lapsed into obscurity. Yet on the evidence of these two fine, complementary CDs his viol music is of high quality and well worth rediscovering. It does not seek great profundity, although the beautiful *Pavane in F major,* common to both discs, is memorable and all the *Fantasias* are well crafted – their invention appealingly immediate. Where there are several in the same key, each differs from the others, yet uses the same basic theme. In terms of colour, Jenkins's combination of viols with organ is quite ear-tickling.

Although they overlap, both collections are thoroughly recommendable with the difference between them accentuated by the difference in performance pitch, with Fretwork slightly higher, giving a brighter, fresher impression, whereas the Rose Consort have a somewhat warmer tonal blend, especially noticeable in that fine *Pavane.*

Kaiser-Lindemann, Wilhelm
(20th century)

Hommage à Nelson M., Op. 27.
(BB) * Naxos Dig. 8.554485 [id.]. Maria Kliegel (cello), Stephan Froleyks (percussion).

A difficult disc to evaluate. The cellist Maria Kliegel was so inspired – and rightly so – by reading Nelson Mandela's autobiography, *A Long Walk to Freedom,* that she commissioned a work from the composer Wilhelm Kaiser-Lindemann in his honour. (The notes, incidentally, are completely silent about the composer, not even his year or place of birth are given.) The scoring is for cello and percussion, and during its four movements both artists are required to vocalize wordlessly. The four movements cover episodes in Mandela's life, and the idiom ranges from Western classical music to elements of jazz and folk music. There is much virtuosity from both players, but listeners looking for the successful fusion of these disparate musical traditions will find little to satisfy them. The invention is limited and pallid: there is one passage vaguely reminiscent of the fisherman's song in *Le rossignol,* but little of real substance throughout its 40 minutes. It barely registers even on crossover terms. The proceeds go to the Nelson Mandela Children's Fund so that you can try it at least and make up your own mind, knowing that the proceeds are going to a good cause. You may find more in it than the present listener.

Kálmán, Emmerich (1882–1953)

Die Herzogin von Chicago (complete).
*** Decca Dig. 466 057-2 (2) [id.]. Monica
Groop, Deborah Riedel, Endrik Wottrich, Brett
Polgate, Pär Lindskog, Voler Horn,
Schoenberg Ch., Berlin RSO, Bonynge.

What happens when Viennese operetta is confronted by 1920s jazz? Kálmán provides the answer
in this frothy operetta, which somewhat improbably
comes in Decca's revelatory Entartete Musik series
of music condemned by the Nazis. Kálmán was in
good company in 1928, when the piece was first
given in Vienna. That première was just after
Krenek's jazz opera, Jonny spielt auf, had appeared
and just before Weill's Dreigroschenoper, but
Kálmán's aims were far less radical. Within the
conventional operetta frame he introduced foxtrots
and charlestons alongside his usual waltzes and
csárdás numbers, and the wonder is that his melodies are just as catchy on whichever side of the
fence he is working. The story is typically slight
and silly, with a hero-prince who hates American
jazz, but who falls in love with an American heiress.
What matters on the way to their union (on the
hit number, Ein kleiner Slowfox mit Mary) is the
carefree music, sparklingly directed by Richard
Bonynge with forces from Berlin Radio. Endrik
Wottrich as Prince Sándor may lack charm with his
throaty baritonal tenor, but the others are a delight,
notably Deborah Riedel, radiantly sweet as the
heroine, Mary Lloyd, and the rich-toned Monica
Groop as the poverty-stricken Princess Rosemarie.
Full, warm, atmospheric recording with the excellent chorus nicely balanced.

Khachaturian, Aram (1903–78)

Gayaneh (ballet): excerpts; Spartacus (ballet):
excerpts.
(M) *** Decca 460 315-2 [id.]. VPO,
Khachaturian – GLAZUNOV: The Seasons.
**(*)

Khachaturian came to Vienna in 1962 to record
these inspired performances of the most popular
numbers from his two ballets. He was to return
and re-record them fifteen years later, even more
sumptuously with the LSO, for EMI, including one
extra item from Gayaneh. But make no mistake,
this Decca record (reissued in Decca's Legends
series) is the one to go for. It is superbly remastered
to restore and even improve on the demonstration
quality of the original LP, recorded in the Sofiensaal. Like the sound, the performances are much
fresher. The disc opens with the famous Adagio
from Spartacus (made famous by the BBC's
'Onedin Line' TV series), wonderfully expansive,
while the famous Sabre dance from Gayaneh has

superb crispness and zest without being pressed too
hard. Gayaneh's own Adagio is gracefully refined
and delicate and the closing Gopak delightfully
witty. The Glazunov coupling, if not quite so fine,
is very well played and shows Ansermet at his best.
As usual in this series, good documentation and
photographs of both conductors.

Kodály, Zoltán (1882–1967)

(i) Dances of Galánta; Dances of Marosszék; (ii)
Háry János suite, instrumental excerpts &
Singspiel; (i) Gergëly-Járás; (ii) Táncnóa; Túrót
eszik a cigány.
*** Ph. Dig. 462 824-2 [id.]. Budapest Festival O,
Iván Fischer; with (i) Children's Ch.
Magnificat, Budapest; (ii) Children's Ch.
Miraculum, Kecskemét.

Iván Fischer's Kodály is no less successful than his
recent Bartók records. His set has the advantage of
totally idiomatic playing from a very fine orchestra
and superbly well-defined recording from the
Philips engineers. This is now the front runner in
the Kodály discography, and the point from which
lovers of this genial composer should set out. The
extra items are very enticing.

(i) Dances of Galánta; (ii) Dances of Marosszék;
Háry János suite; (i) Variations on a Hungarian
folksong (The Peacock).
**(*) BIS Dig. CD 875 [id.]. (i) Brno State PO (ii)
SWF SO, Baden-Baden; José Serebrier.

José Serebrier gets very good playing from the Brno
Orchestra in both the Dances of Galánta and the
Peacock variations, and the remaining two works
with the Südwestfunk Orchestra in Baden-Baden
are, if anything, even better and the recording
warmer. In a choice between the very good and the
outstanding, Iván Fischer remains a clear first but
no one investing in the well-filled BIS disc need
feel short-changed. There is plenty of character in
the orchestral playing of both ensembles and the
BIS recordings are up to house standard.

Variations on a Hungarian folksong 'Peacock'.
(M) ** RCA 09026 63309-2 [id.]. Boston SO,
Leinsdorf – BARTOK: Concerto for orchestra.
*(*)

Leinsdorf is more successful in this work than in
the Bartók coupling: this is a reading of genuine
feeling and conviction. Helpfully, each individual
variation has been separately cued. But it is a pity
that instead of the Bartók the original coupling of
the Háry János suite was not chosen. Good up-front
sound, but only a half-good disc.

Laudes organi (Fantasia on a 12th-century
sequence); Psalm 114 (from the Geneva Psalter).
(B) *** Australian Decca Eloquence 466 902-2.

Brighton Festival Ch., Heltay, Gillian Weir –
JANACEK: *Glagolitic Mass* ***.

These works were written towards the end of
Kodály's career; they are richly rewarding and show
that even when the composer took on dramatic
subjects, his was a relatively gentle art (in contrast
to his friend Bartók). Heltay directs persuasive performances, with Gillian Weir brilliant as the organ
soloist (the *Laudes organi* performance receives its
CD debut here). The recording is excellent, and
these works make a fine bonus for the Janáček
coupling.

Korngold, Erich (1897–1957)

*Baby serenade, Op. 24; Sursum corda (symphonic
overture), Op. 13; Der Schneemann: Prelude and
Serenade. Die tote Stadt: Prelude. Das Wunder
der Heliane: Interlude.*
*** ASV Dig. CDDCA 1074 [id.]. Linz Bruckner
  O, Caspar Richter.

This is a delightful disc, centring on a work new to
the catalogue, the *Baby serenade*. Korngold wrote
it in 1928 on the birth of his second son, George, a
follow-up to Strauss's *Domestic symphony* in providing a musical evocation of family life with a
baby. Unlike the Strauss, the five movements here
are miniatures, charmingly unpretentious. After a
jolly overture, the slow movement, picturing a good
baby, is built on a theme Korngold wrote at the age
of seven. That and the rest in many ways anticipate
the music Korngold was to write for films in Hollywood – warm and colourful. The *Overture, Sursum
corda* is like Respighi with a German accent, and
even the excerpts from *The Snowman*, an opera
written when Korngold was only eleven, are rich
and lush, though the orchestration is by Zemlinsky
– a point not mentioned in the booklet. The other
two operatic excerpts make up the warmly enjoyable programme, helped by excellent playing and
recording.

String quartet No. 2 in E flat, Op. 26.
*** Vanguard Dig. 99209 [id.]. Brodsky Quartet –
  KREISLER: *String quartet in A min.* ***

The Brodsky Quartet are masterly in their control
of expressive rubato in this richly post-romantic
music, playing with flawless unanimity and fine
balance. They capture nicely the hints of salon
music in writing which only finds full weight in the
third movement *Romanze*, but the finesse of the
writing throughout is a delight. A fascinating coupling with the Kreisler *Quartet*.

Krebs, Johann Ludwig (1713–80)

*Music for harpsichord: Preludes Nos. 2 in D
min.;3 in E min.; 5 in G; 6 in A min.; Suites in B
min.; in C min.; Organ chorales: Allein Gott in der
Höh' sei Ehr; Auf meinen lieben Gott (2 settings);
Christ lag in Todesbanden; Jesu meine Freude (2
settings); Jesus meine Zuversicht (2 settings); Sei
Lob und Ehr dem Höchsten Gut; Vater unser im
Himmelreich; Von Gott will ich nicht lassen;
Warum betrübst du dich, mein Herz?; Wass Gott
will ich nicht lassen; Wass Gott tut, das ist
wohlgetan (2 settings); Wer nur den lieben Gott
lässt walten (2 settings).*
*** Meridian CDE 84306 [id.]. Gerald Gifford
  (harpsichord or chamber organ).

The title of this collection, 'The best crayfish in the
brook', is a pun on the composer's name, often
attributed to his mentor. Krebs (which also covers
the fish) was a favourite pupil of Bach (which also
means brook). On the evidence of this highly attractive recital he was a very talented pupil too, who
obviously absorbed much of his master's contrapuntal style in his organ chorales, even if their
expressive and imaginative range is more limited.
But Krebs's clavier music has a strong personality
in its own right. His harpsichord dance *Suites* and
Preludes demonstrate a lively mixture of French
and Italianate manners, and their invention is consistently attractive. Gerald Gifford plays with a
vividly communicative yet scholarly style, alternating harpsichord and organ music to make a
stimulating and diverting programme. His harpsichord is a copy of a Hemsch, his organ a modern
copy of a small eighteenth-century instrument in
Nuremberg. Both are beautifully recorded. This is
a disc you might easily pass by. But don't. Professor
Gifford is a highly persuasive advocate and his two
instruments are perfectly recorded.

*Organ music: Chorales: Herr Gott, dich loben
alle wir; Herzlich lieb had ich dich, O Herr; Wir
glauben all an einen Gott; Zeuch ein zu deinen
Toren; Chorale fantasia sopra 'Wer nur den
lieben Gott lässt walten'; Fantasia a giusto
Italiano; Fugue in B flat on B-A-C-H; Preludes
and fugues in C; in D; Trios in E flat; D min.*
**(*) ASV Gaudeamus Dig. CDGAU 125 [id.].
  Graham Barber (organ of St Peter Mancroft,
  Norwich).

Graham Barber certainly catches the amiable
quality of the Krebs style, and if this collection
is perhaps less distinctive than Gerald Gifford's
programme it includes much to divert, not least the
opening *Fantasia a giusto Italiano*. Yet the chorale
Herr Gott, dich loben, with its powerful imitation
in the pedals, is imposing, and the closing *D major
Prelude and fugue* also shows Krebs in his best
Bach imitative style. Elsewhere the polyphony is

often distinctly lightweight as in the *C major Fugue* and the jolly finale of the *Trio in E flat*, while Barber's registration of the cantus firmus in the *Chorale fantasia* is agreeably quirky. Krebs was one of the first composers to write a fugue based on the notes of Bach's name and he spells it out unequivocally at the opening with the close impressively full-blooded. The Norwich organ brings a bright, cleanly focused palette, which suits the music.

Kreisler, Fritz (1875–1962)

String quartet in A min.
*** Vanguard Dig. 99209 [id.]. Brodsky Quartet – KORNGOLD: *String quartet No. 2.* ***

Kreisler, one of the supreme violinists of the twentieth century, is well known for his charming salon pieces but here he aims higher, and the result is not just skilled, but warmly imaginative and attractively varied. The quicksilver brilliance of the Scherzo, and the fantasy and sparkle of the finale, may reflect the salon-music composer we know, but there is a point and individuality which sets them apart, and that is even more strikingly so in the other two, more ambitious movements. In this second of two discs labelled 'Music from Vienna', the Brodsky Quartet give a strongly characterized and beautifully refined reading, subtler than the one on Kennedy's Kreisler album for EMI. Excellent, warm sound.

Kreutzer, Rodolphe (1766–1831)

Grand quintet in C.
(B) **(*) Hyperion Helios CDH 55015 [id.].
   Francis, Allegri Qt – CRUSELL: *Divertimento;*
   REICHA: *Quintet.* **(*)

This is the Kreutzer of the Beethoven sonata – not to be confused with Conradin Kreutzer (1780–1849). The *Grand quintet* is thought to date from the 1790s; it is rather bland but rather enjoyable when it is played as beautifully as it is here. This is part of an attractive triptych, now offered by Hyperion at bargain-price. However, the CD plays for under 50 minutes.

Krommer, Franz (Kramar, František) (1759–1831)

Partitas in E flat; in B flat Op. 45/1–2; in E flat with 2 horns, FVK 2d.
(BB) *** Naxos Dig. 8.553868 Michael Thompson
   Wind Ensemble.

Franz Krommer, born three years after Mozart and died four years after Beethoven, was the honoured Court music director in Vienna. He specialized in

music for wind instruments, of which these three miniature symphonies are splendid examples, obviously fun to play, and fun to hear. The two *Partitas*, Op. 45 were always among his most popular works, exploiting the conventional wind band (or Harmonie) of flutes, oboes, horns and bassoons in pairs, plus trumpet on occasion. Even more striking – and not published till this century – is the third *Partita* here, with the two horns given virtuoso solo roles, a concerto in all but name. Vividly recorded, this Naxos issue offers masterly performances from the ensemble of leading London performers previously led by Barry Tuckwell.

Kuhnau, Johann (1660–1722)

Magnificat in C.
*** BIS Dig. CD 1011 [id.]. Miah Persson, Akira
   Tachikawa, Gerd Türk, Chiyuki Urano, Bach
   Collegium, Japan, Masaaki Suzuki – BACH:
   Magnificat in D; ZELENKA: *Magnificats in C
   & D.* ***

A generation older than Bach, Johann Kuhnau is best remembered for his *Biblical sonatas*. He died the year before the Bach *Magnificat* came into being in its first – E flat – incarnation. Kuhnau's own setting is his most ambitious work and calls for large forces (a five-part chorus, three trumpets, timpani, two oboes, strings including two viola parts and continuo) and is thought to have been composed for a Christmas Service at Leipzig. It is not otherwise available on CD and any rival will have to be pretty stunning to match this version from Masaaki Suzuki and his largely Japanese forces. It is not as consistently inspired as the Zelenka (let alone the Bach) but it is well worth hearing. Apart from the excellence of his singers and instrumentalists, the recorded sound is quite exemplary.

Kullak, Theodor (1818–82)

Piano concerto in C min., Op. 55.
*** Hyperion Dig. CDA 67086 [id.]. Piers Lane,
   BBC Scottish SO, Niklas Willén –
   DREYSCHOCK: *Piano concerto in D min.* ***

Theodor Kullak was one of the foremost piano teachers of the latter half of the nineteenth century, and on the evidence of this most attractive concerto, written around 1850, he was a very gifted composer too, with melody coming easily to him. A strong march-like theme dominates the first movement and, when the piano enters, the glittering passage work lies somewhere between that in the Liszt and Chopin concertos, while the romantic secondary tune has a comparable heritage. The central movement is equally engaging, with bursts of energy, never languishing, and the glittering Weberian finale makes one smile with pleasure at the witty audacity of the main theme. The work is given a scintillating performance by Piers Lane, vigorously and sensitively supported by the BBC Scottish players under Niklas Willén. The recording is first class.

Lalo, Edouard (1823–92)

Cello concerto in D min.
(B) *** EMI Début CZS5 73727-2 [id.]. Xavier
Phillips, Bavarian Chamber O, Emmanuel
Plasson – CAPLET: *Epiphany;* FAURE: *Elégie.*
***
(M) *** DG 457 761-2 [id.]. Fournier, LOP,
Martinon – BLOCH: *Schelomo;* BRUCH: *Kol
Nidrei;* SAINT-SAENS: *Cello Concerto No. 1.*
***

Emmanuel Plasson and his Bavarian Chamber orchestra open Lalo's cello concerto with a bold dramatic flourish, and Xavier Phillips enters with a firm, full timbre, his line romantically strong. Yet he soon slips into gentle lyricism for Lalo's lovely secondary theme, and the first movement's turbulent dialogue continues with both soloist and the orchestra maintaining a perfectly balanced partnership, passionate and lyrical. In the *Intermezzo* the orchestral woodwind create an engaging delicacy of feeling, framing the soloist's ardent climax. It is he who soliloquizes magnetically before the finale sets off with a splendid burst of energy and encouraging fanfares from the horns. The unusually clear (yet not unflattering) acoustic means that Lalo's scoring never congeals, and the cello focus is clean and truthful. In short this version of a much recorded work matches any of its competitors and its imaginative Caplet coupling makes it especially enticing, when the disc is so inexpensive. A first-class début for both conductor and soloist.

Fournier's performance has dignity and character and he is well supported by Martinon, who secures spirited playing from the Lamoureux Orchestra. The recording, from 1960, has never sounded better than in this new DG Originals transfer. Excellent value.

(i) *Concerto russe; Violin concerto in F; Scherzo.
Le roi d'Ys overture.*
*** Chandos Dig. CHAN 9758 [id.]. (i) Olivier
Charlier; BBC PO, Yan Pascal Tortelier.

Tortelier opens with a marvellously rumbustious account of *Le roi d'Ys overture*, with its melodramatic brass and luscious cello solo, and include also an equally fine account of the orchestral *Scherzo*. But the main value of this disc is Olivier Charlier's seductive accounts of the two concertante works (both written for Sarasate). The *Violin concerto* is engagingly songful and ought to be better known, but the real find is the *Concerto russe*, in essence a sister work to the *Symphonie espagnole*, but with

Slavic rather than sultry Spanish inspiration. Lalo calls his slow movement *Chant Russe*, but its Russian melody demonstrates the universality of folk music, for it has distinct rhythmic snaps which surprisingly recall the Bruch *Scottish fantasy*. The *Intermezzo* has witty offbeat comments from the timpani and there is a sparkling finale introducing two more striking ideas. Charlier is obviously in his element throughout both works, relishing their lyricism, and often floating them (as with the haunting second subject of the first movement of the *Concerto russe*) with subtle delicacy. Tortelier – with the help of Lalo – provides a vivid orchestral backcloth and the opulent, well-balanced Chandos recording adds to the listener's pleasure.

Lambert, Constant (1905–51)

Concerto for piano and nine players, etc.

See under Richard Rodney Bennett in Instrumental Recitals.

(i) *Piano concerto* (1924). *Merchant seamen
(suite); Pomona; Prize fight.*
(M) *** ASV Dig. CD WHL 2122 [id.]. BBC
Concert O, Barry Wordsworth with (i) David
Owen Norris.

Prodigiously talented like his friend William Walton, Constant Lambert was already a mature composer in his teens, yet the manuscripts of many of his early works have long been inaccessible. The three examples here, all very characterful, are a revelation. The *Piano concerto* of 1924 is not to be confused with the later *Concerto for piano and seven wind instruments*. It was composed three years before *The Rio Grande* and survives only in short score; the present edition has been made by Giles Easterbrook and Michael Shipley. Lambert's preferred scoring was for two trumpets, strings and timpani. It is very characteristic, with something of the spirit of Milhaud, jazzy and entertaining. *Prize fight*, also from 1924, is Lambert's first ballet and his earliest surviving orchestral score. It is a rumbustious work for the same forces as the concerto and lasts a mere nine minutes. Lambert was a keen film-buff and actually wrote film criticism for a time. His score for the documentary *Merchant seamen* dates from 1940 and he drew on this for a five-movement suite two years later. It is very much of its period and not top-drawer Lambert. The most familiar of the pieces here is the ballet *Pomona*, which receives a most sympathetic performance at the hands of the excellent BBC Concert Orchestra and Barry Wordsworth. In fact, the playing throughout is very good indeed, and so is the ASV/ BBC recording.

Langgaard, Rued (1893–1952)

Sinfonia interna: Angelus; The dream; Sea and sun; Epilogue; The star in the east, BVN 180.
**(*) Dacapo Dig. 8.22413 [id.]. Dahl, Hansen, Jensen, Canzone Ch., Aarhus SO, Frans Rasmussen.

Langgaard started work on the *Sinfonia interna* in 1915 and the piece underwent many changes. He recycled its music in a number of other contexts. As always with Langgaard, one senses that he is content with the raw material of art and quite happy to pass it off as the finished article. All the same, there are some visionary moments in this amorphous but lush post-Wagnerian score, and Frans Rasmussen gets very good results from his singers and the Aarhus Orchestra. Good recorded sound.

Larsson, Lars-Erik (1908–86)

Quattro tempi (Divertimento for wind quintet).
(BB) ** Naxos Dig. 8.553851-2 [id.]. Michael Thompson Wind Quintet – BARBER: *Summer music* **(*); HINDEMITH: *Kleine Kammermusik* **(*); JANACEK: *Mládi.* **(*)

Lars-Erik Larsson's *Quattro tempi* are pleasing open-air pieces written in 1968 which have not made their way into the repertory. (There is only one alternative currently listed, by the Stockholm Wind Quintet.) The Michael Thompson Wind Quintet give a most expert and sensitive performance, but the close balance is even more disturbing than in its couplings and seriously detracts from the pleasure this music should give. Disappointing.

Leigh, Walter (1905–42)

Concertino for harpsichord and string orchestra.
(M) *** BBC Music BBCM 5015-2 [id.]. George Malcolm, ASMF, Marriner – FINZI: *Clarinet concerto; Introit *** (with Concert: *English music* ***).

Like George Butterworth, whose *Banks of Green Willow* is included on this disc, Walter Leigh was killed in action before his gifts could develop fully. His *Concertino for harpsichord and string orchestra*, with its heavenly slow movement, which dates from 1936, is an inventive and resourceful score, whose delights remain undimmed. It is currently unrepresented in the commercial catalogues and has surely never been played more winningly than it is here by George Malcolm. The balance with Marriner and his Academy is perfectly judged, so that the appearance of so lively a performance (from 1972), expertly engineered by the late James Burnett, usefully fills a gap. This is a highlight of a desirable bargain collection of English music, by Butterworth, Finzi, Vaughan Williams and Warlock – see our Concerts section, below.

Libert (or Liebert), Reginaldus (born c. 1425/35)

Missa de Beata Virgine. Kyrie à 4.
*** Lyrichord Dig. LEMS 8025 [id.]. Schola Discantus, Kevin Moll.

We know very little indeed about Reginaldus Libert (or Liebert, as the name is given on the Lyrichord documentation), except that he was probably one-time Director of the boy choristers at Cambrai Cathedral. His Marian mass has the distinction of being – like Dufay's *Missa Sancti Jacobi* – one of the earliest to survive that includes settings of both the Ordinary and Proper. Moreover the Mass is made cohesive by being based on a very striking, melismatic cantus firmus, which is always recognizable as it is usually appears in the upper voice, decorated with ornamental notes. The three-voiced counterpoint is comparatively simple, with the third voice subordinate to the upper parts, enriching the sonority. Even so, the Credo is powerful and ambitious, followed by a particularly fine *Sanctus*. In short this is an appealing and memorable work, and the performance here is an eloquent one, with well-judged pacing. With the addition of the separate four-part *Kyrie* this disc includes all the music positively attributed to Libert. The recording is first class, made in a spacious acoustic and the documentation very good, except that for the text and translation of the *Kyrie* and *Gloria* we are referred to another Lyrichord issue (LEMS 8010), a curious proposition, as we are not told any more about this CD. The presentation also associates Libert's mass with Jeanne d'Arc, and gives her biography, but although she was a contemporary of the composer and this music, there is no other connection.

Lindblad, Adolf Fredrik (1801–78)

Symphonies Nos. 1 in C, Op. 19; 2 in D.
*** Marco Polo Dig. 8.225105 [id.]. Uppsala CO, Gérard Korsten.

Lindblad is best known for his songs, of which there are some 250. Indeed, he is generally spoken of as 'the father of Swedish song'. After studies in Uppsala he became a pupil of Zelter in Berlin, where he formed a lifelong friendship with Mendelssohn. On his return to Sweden, Lindblad immersed himself in teaching and composition. It was in his opera *Frondörerna (The rebels)*, that the 15-year-old Jenny Lind made her début. The *First Symphony* (1832) and the overture to *Frondörerna* were recorded on a sumptuously illustrated Caprice LP some years ago with the Stockholm Philharmonic

Orchestra under Okko Kamu. This was sub-sequently transferred to CD with a different coupling, a generous group of his songs. Mendelssohn thought highly enough of the symphony to conduct it at Leipzig with the Gewandhaus Orchestra. Gérard Korsten and the Uppsala Chamber Orchestra give splendid accounts of both symphonies, ex-tremely vital and spirited with infectious high spirits in the first movement of the *C major Symphony*. And what delightful pieces these are, not strong on individuality perhaps but like the Weber sym-phonies highly attractive. Quite a find and very good sound, warm and well focused.

Liszt, Franz (1811–86)

Concerto pathétique
*** EMI Dig. CDC5 56816-2 [id.]. Martha
    Argerich, Nelson Freire – BARTOK: *Contrasts*;
    PROKOFIEV: *Quintet.* ***

This performance, like the companion pieces on this CD, comes from live concerts at the Saratoga Arts Festival in 1998. The *Concerto pathétique* is a reworking for two pianos of the *Grosses Konzert-solo* of 1850 with which Liszt wrestled for some years and which survives in a number of forms. It is marvellously played here and (although there is little opposition anyway) is unlikely to be superseded.

Piano concertos Nos. 1 in E flat; 2 in A;
Hungarian fantasia.
(***) BBC mono Legends 4031-2 [id.]. Sviatoslav
    Richter, LSO, Kondrashin – CHOPIN: *Andante
    spianato & Grande Polonaise, Op. 22.* (***)

Here is a memento of Richter's celebrated first major concert in London. That was in July 1961, when the marvel of Richter's virtuosity was first sweeping Britain, and the ecstatic response of the Albert Hall audience reflects that. After playing the two Liszt concertos, he took them into the studio for Philips. The newly remastered transfer of that made by the Mercury team who recorded the orig-inal for Philips has the finer sound, with a wider frequency range and of course a stereo picture (432 002-2 – see our main volume). Like them, the BBC engineers here place Richter very much in the fore-ground, and the mono recording is really rather good for its age, though orchestral detail has less transparency. Broadly the interpretations, spon-taneously poetic as well as powerful, reveal little difference between live and studio, with the impor-tant exception that the rush of adrenalin at the end of each finale brings speeds a fraction more urgent, with virtuosity even more daring. Perhaps too Richter has slightly more abandon in the first move-ment of the *E flat Concerto* here. But the disc is a must for the *Hungarian fantasia*. This is electrifying playing and even finer than the account he recorded

in Budapest shortly afterwards with János Ferencsik, with the music presented with power rather than wit. It makes a fine supplement, inspiring the audience to effusions well before the end and this CD fully captures a real sense of occasion. The Chopin, recorded at a concert two days earlier, provides a delightful bonus.

(i) *Piano concertos 1–2;* (ii; iii) *Fantasia on Hungarian folk tunes; Malédiction; Totentanz;* (ii; iv) Arr. of Schubert: *Wanderer fantasia* (all for piano and orchestra).
(B) *** Decca Double 458 361-2 (2) [id.]. (i)
    Julius Katchen, LSO, Argenta; (ii) Jorge Bolet;
    (iii) LSO, Iván Fischer; (iv) LPO, Solti –
    DOHNANYI: *Variations on a nursery tune, Op.
    25.* ***

This splendid Double combines sparkling pianism from two of Decca's most distinguished keyboard lions, both of whom died all too soon, while at the peak of their form. Katchen is superb in the *E flat Concerto*, only slightly less successful with the changes of mood of the *Second*. But by any standard these are commanding performances, and he found an erstwhile partner in Ataulfo Argenta, who also died sadly young. Bolet is no less masterful in the splendid triptych of shorter concertante works, which thrillingly bring out all his characteristic bra-vura. The digital recording remains in the demon-stration bracket. He and Solti also make out a fairly convincing case for Liszt's concertante arrange-ment of Schubert's *Wanderer fantasia*. With such a poetic response the central *Adagio* loses nothing on the solo version, and the scintillating pianism in the finale compensates for any moments of un-Schubertian hyperbole in the orchestration.

(i) *Dante symphony;* (ii; iii) *A Faust symphony,*
G.108; (ii; iv) *Les préludes; Prometheus.*
(B) **(*) Decca-Double Analogue/Dig. 466 751-2
    (2) [id.]. (i) Voltaire College Ch., SRO, López-
    Cobos; (ii) Solti; (iii) Jerusalem, Chicago Ch.
    & SO; (iv) LPO.

López-Cobos's account of the *Dante symphony* comes with Liszt's alternative conclusion, a sudden loud outburst of 'Hallelujahs' from the trebles after the usual *ppp* ending. It is most effective, crowning a performance which is more remarkable for its refinement of sound and balance than for its dra-matic thrust. It is not underpowered, however, and the early digital recording is rich and full, whilst the SRO is on better form than it was in Ansermet's day. Solti's Liszt is almost always successful. His performance of the *Faust symphony* is spacious, yet brilliant, with superb playing from his Chicago orchestra, though the bright recording underlines the fierce element in his reading and removes some of the warmth. The Mephisthophelean finale brings the most impressive playing of all, with Solti's fierceness chiming naturally with the movement's demonic quality. The two tone poems, recorded in the 1970s, are brilliantly played and recorded. Even with the reservations expressed this is excellent value.

(i) *Hunnenschlacht; Mazeppa; Orpheus;* (ii) *Les Preludes* (symphonic poems).
(B) *** Australian Decca Eloquence 466 706-2. (i) LAPO; (i) VPO; Mehta.

Zubin Mehta is in his element here. The performances are red-blooded and tremendously exciting. Liszt's vulgarity is played up in a swaggeringly extrovert way, but there is plenty of character too. The rich, vibrant recording is an audiophile's delight – the staggered entries throughout the strings in *Mazeppa* are thrilling. Equally praiseworthy is the pastoral atmosphere Mehta creates in *Orpheus* – with real sensitivity from the Los Angeles orchestra. His style of playing Liszt could not be more different from Haitink's more refined manner, and Masur is less at home in the melodrama, which Mehta does not shirk (see our main volume). Although Karajan's Berlin Philharmonic account of *Mazeppa* is in a class of its own, those who like Liszt with all the stops out will certainly enjoy this Australian bargain reissue, especially when the CD transfer is so vivid.

Mazeppa; Les Préludes.
(M) * RCA 09026 63532-2 [id.]. Boston Pops O, Fiedler – CHOPIN: *Les Sylphides* **; PROKOFIEV: *Love for 3 Oranges: suite.* **(*)

These performances are too literal and clipped to make a positive recommendation. Moreover the orchestral playing is sometimes sloppy (the opening of *Mazeppa* especially so) and the 1960 sound is coarse under pressure. Those wishing for these two works should go straight to Karajan's supreme readings on DG (453 130-2 – see our main volume) which are vastly superior in every way.

PIANO MUSIC

Années de pèlerinage: Au bord d'une source; Au lac de Wallenstadt; Les jeux d'eau à la Villa d'Este. Harmonies poétiques et religieuses: Bénédiction de Dieu dans la solitude. Liebesträume No. 3; Mephisto waltz No. 1; Hungarian rhapsody No. 12; Variations on B-A-C-H.
(BB) *** Virgin Classics 2 x 1 Dig. VBD5 61757-2 (2) [CDVB 61757] Kun Woo Paik – *Recital of French piano music.* ***

This fine 1990 Liszt recital has been out of the catalogue too long. Kun Woo Paik is an outstanding Lisztian. Whether in the delicacy of Liszt's watery evocations from the *Années de pèlerinage*, the devilish glitter of the upper tessitura of the *Mephisto waltz*, or the comparable flamboyance of the *Hungarian rhapsody*, this is playing of a high order.

The famous *Liebesträume* is presented more gently, less voluptuously than usual and the wide range of the *Bénédiction* is controlled very spontaneously; it is only at the climax of the *B-A-C-H variations* that perhaps a touch more restraint would have been effective. Fine recording and the coupled French repertoire is also very stimulating.

Ballade No. 2; Harmonies poétiques et religieuses: Bénédiction de Dieu dans la solitude. Mephisto waltz No.1; Sposalizio; En rêve; Schaflos!; Unstern!
(BB) *** Arte Nova Dig. 74321 67525-2 [id.]. Alfredo Perl.

The Chilean pianist Alfredo Perl has already made a powerful impact on disc with his superb complete cycle of the thirty-two Beethoven sonatas for the budget label Arte Nova. Here, in playing equally commanding, he tackles Liszt, making an imaginative choice of pieces, four of them substantial, three of them miniatures. In his rapt concentration Perl brings weight to Liszt's sequential arguments, underlining the link between the magnificent *Ballade* over its 15-minute span and Liszt's sonata in the same key. Even more expansive is the surgingly lyrical *Bénédiction*, with the first *Mephisto waltz* bringing virtuoso fireworks at the end. Excellent, well-balanced sound.

Concert paraphrases of Beethoven's Symphonies Nos. 2 & 5.
(BB) *** Naxos Dig. 8.550457 [id.]. Konstantin Scherbakov.

It is Scherbakov's achievement that he makes Liszt's piano transcriptions of these Beethoven symphonies sound so pianistic. With wonderfully crisp articulation and fluent passage work textures clarified, and the freshness and energy of the writing are strongly brought out both in the exuberantly youthful No. 2 and the darkly dramatic No. 5. This is as imaginative as Cyprien Katsaris's Teldec accounts from the days of LP, and no one with a taste for keyboard heroism should overlook them. He is vastly superior to Leslie Howard's pedestrian set on Hyperion. He is, so to speak, more of a Weingartner than a Toscanini (as was Katsaris) but his *Fifth* still has that barnstorming quality that arrests your attention. At super-bargain price, well worth investigating even by those who shy away from transcriptions. Excellent, clear piano sound.

Concert paraphrases of Beethoven's An die ferne Geliebte; Mignon; Schumann Lieder: Widmung; Frühlingsnacht.
*** Chandos Dig. CHAN 9793 [id.]. Louis Lortie – SCHUMANN: *Fantaisie in C, Op. 17.* ***

Louis Lortie is an outstanding pianist who is rather taken for granted in this country. His latest Chandos recital appears under the title 'To the Distant Beloved', after Beethoven's song cycle *An die ferne*

LISZT   178

Geliebte, which he plays in Liszt's transcription (together with a pair of Schumann Lieder) and very impressively too. But collectors will want this for the Schumann *Fantasy,* which is the centre-piece of the recital and is given an outstanding performance.

Concert paraphrases of Schubert Lieder: *Auf dem Wasser zu singen; Erlkönig; In der Ferne; Ständchen.*
⊛ *** Sony Dig. SK 66511 [id.]. Murray Perahia
 – BACH/BUSONI: *Chorales.* MENDELSSOHN: *Songs without words.* *** ⊛

Murray Perahia brings to these transcriptions a poetic finesse that is very much his own. Impeccable artistry and taste are blended with a wonderful naturalness.

Hexaméron (Grande bravura variations on the March from *I Puritani,* by Liszt, Thalberg, Pixis, Herz, Czerny and Chopin).
(M) *** RCA 09026 63310 2 [id.]. Raymond Lewenthal – ALKAN: *Barcarolle; 12 Studies in all the minor keys, Op. 39, Nos. 4, 5, 6 (Symphonie), 7, 12 (Le festin d'Esope),* etc. ***

Hexaméron was the brainchild of Princess Belgioioso whose idea it was to have the six most famous pianists of the day perform at one of her glittering social occasions. Although the event never took place, she managed, after months of hounding, to extract each composer's assignment, with Liszt acting as the binding force. This musical curiosity became a favourite vehicle of Liszt because of its fiendish difficulty, yet is contrasted enough to be musically satisfying. Raymond Lewenthal's performance is as brilliant as can be imagined, and makes an enjoyable bonus to his flamboyant Alkan recital.

Hungarian rhapsodies Nos. 1 in E; 2 in C sharp min.; 3 in B flat; 4 in E flat; 5 in E min.; 6 in D flat; 7 in D min.; 8 in F sharp min.; 9 in E flat (Carnaval de Pesth).
(BB) ** Naxos Dig. 8.554480 [id.]. Jenö Jandó.

Hungarian rhapsodies Nos. 10 in E; 11 in A min.; 12 in C sharp min.; 13 in A min.; 14 in F; 15 in A min. (Rákóczy March); 16 in A min.; 17 in D min.; 18 in F sharp min.; 19 in D min.
(BB) ** Naxos Dig. 8.554481 [id.]. Jenö Jandó.

This repertoire calls for virtuosity of the highest order and a musical personality of outsize stature – Arrau, Cziffra, Berman and the like. Jenö Jandó is not quite in that league but his performances are far from negligible. The price tag is attractive but Cziffra, who is also inexpensive (EMI CZS5 69003-2 – see our main volume), rivets the attention in a way that Jandó does not.

Complete piano music, Vol. 57: Hungarian rhapsodies Nos. 1–19.

*** Hyperion CDA 67418/2 [id.]. Leslie Howard.

This splendid set represents a high artistic peak within Leslie Howard's distinguished survey, offering as it does the final version of material much of which we have already heard in Volume 29. Clearly this is music which inspires the pianist and he plays every piece not only with great élan and virtuosity but also with an appealing sense of fantasy. His performances convey a spontaneity not always apparent in earlier volumes, and his readings are full of imagination. There is some quite magical playing in No. 5 (*Héroïde-élégiaque*) and his delectable filigree articulation in No. 8 in F sharp minor is equally engaging. The second disc opens dramatically with a superb account of No. 10 in E major and Howard's rubato in No. 12 in C sharp minor is most seductive. Similarly the marvellously crisp articulation in the following A minor work captivates the ear. The set concludes with one of the most impressive performances of all, No. 19, which is '*after the Csárdás nobles of Abrányi*'. The recording is first class. In this repertoire György Cziffra's set (EMI CZS5 69003-2) remains memorable for its dazzling bravura, a remarkable achievement; but Leslie Howard's technical command and control of colour are always equal to the occasion, and in his hands much of this writing is shown to have an unexpected depth of feeling.

VOCAL MUSIC

Lieder: *Du bist wie eine Blume; Die drei Zigeuner; Der du von dem Himmel bist; Es war ein König in Thule; Die Fischerstochter; Freudvoll und leidvoll; Im Rhein, im schönen Strome; Die Lorelei; S'il est un charmant gazon; Uber allen Gipfeln ist Ruh'; Die Vätergruft; Das Veilchen.*
(B) *** EMI Double fforte CZS5 73836-2 (2). Dame Janet Baker, Geoffrey Parsons – MENDELSSOHN: *Lieder;* SCHUMANN: *Liederkreis, Op. 39.* ***

Dame Janet Baker's selection of songs – starting with one of the most beautiful and the most ambitious, *Die Lorelei* – brings out the wide range of Liszt in this medium. His style is transformed when setting a French text, giving Parisian lightness in response to Hugo's words, while his setting of *King of Thule* from Goethe's *Faust* leaps away from reflectiveness in illustrating the verses. The glowing warmth of Dame Janet's singing is well matched by Geoffrey Parsons's keenly sensitive accompaniments. The recording is excellent, and the couplings admirably chosen, but there are no texts and translations.

Lloyd, George (1913-98)

Concerto for violin and strings; Concerto for violin and winds.
*** Albany Dig. TROY 316 [id.]. Cristina Anghelescu, Philh. O, David Parry.

George Lloyd's pair of *Violin concertos*, written seven years apart, are among his very finest works, darker, more introvert and certainly more intense in inner feeling than many of his symphonies. The two works could hardly be more different. The *Concerto for violin and strings* is very much in the great English tradition of writing for string orchestra, with or without a soloist. Its plaintive opening develops a plangent melancholy in the first movement, yet towards the end of the first movement, after a period of angst, the main theme suddenly turns into a life-enhancing chorale on the full strings. The rhythmically quirky Scherzo which follows is more cheerful, but the clouds do not lift entirely, even though the flowing secondary theme has plenty of confidence. The apparently serene *Largo* opens with a sense of deep nostalgia and remains troubled; its tensions are not entirely resolved at the close. It is left to the dancing finale to round off the work but the closing bars are curiously equivocal. The *Concerto with winds* is more robustly extrovert, neoclassical, acerbic, and brilliantly and originally scored. Its slow movement is bitter-sweet, very touching, but again producing an ambivalence of feeling, which strays into the initially light-hearted, dancing finale, which also has its abrasive moments in spite of its jaunty main theme, even becoming ruminative in the elaborate cadenza. In both works the Romanian soloist Cristina Anghelescu has just the right temperament for the music's quixotic changes of mood: her lyrical line is wholly persuasive while she revels in the spicy rhythms of the second work. She is obviously thoroughly immersed in the music and totally assured. Both concertos were recorded during the week that the composer died, and in his absence David Parry proved an inspiring substitute, directing, in partnership with his soloist, definitive recorded performances of which George would have been proud. The recording too is first class, and most realistically balanced.

Locatelli, Pietro (1695-1764)

12 Trio sonatas, Op. 2.
(M) **(*) Van. Dig. 99099 (2) [id.]. Jed Wentz, Musica ad Rhenum.

A reader has kindly drawn our attention to a mistake in our main volume where the above works were wrongly listed as concertos! We apologize for this editorial error, but it remains a desirable set, fluent and highly musical. The continuo group (including

organ in Nos. 2, 4, 6, 9, and 11) is very effective; and if Jed Wentz's period flute is a little pale, it is very well balanced and recorded. It is important to note that the cueing goes wrong for the final double sonata (in which, presumably, Wentz plays a duet with himself) which starts at track 19 (not 18), since the previous sonata has four sub-divisions, not the indicated three.

Locke, Matthew (1622-77)

The Tempest (incidental music)*; Canon on a plain song by Mr William Brode of Hereford.*
**(*) Teldec/Warner Dig. 3984 21464-2 [id.]. Il Giardino Armonico (with ZELENKA: *Fanfare;* ANON: *Tune for the woodlark;* ONOFRI: *Ricercare for viola da gamba & lute*) – BIBER: *Battaglia; Passacaglia; Partita VII for 2 viole d'amore and continuo; Violin sonata representativa.* **(*)

Matthew Locke wrote only the instrumental pieces for the 1674 London performance of *The Tempest*, which was a hybrid work, almost an opera, with contributions from various composers in addition to spoken dialogue. However, this collection of lively dances (often strikingly English in spirit) and more expressive and sometimes piquant Act Tunes works well as a suite. It is presented with great vitality by Il Giardino Armonico, although they tend to overdramatize music intended to divert and their aggressive rhythmic and bowing style will appeal mainly to those totally won over to period-instrument practice. The recording is vivid but close.

Lopatnikoff, Nikolai (1903-76)

Concertino for orchestra, Op. 30.
(M) (***) Sony mono SMK 60725 [id.]. Columbia SO, Bernstein – DALLAPICCOLA: *Tartiniana for violin and orchestra;* SHAPERO: *Symphony.* (***)

Nikolai Lopatnikoff left Russia after the Revolution, proceeding first to Finland and then Germany where he graduated in civil engineering and studied composition with Ernst Toch. He left Berlin in 1933 and spent some time in London before settling in America where he taught composition in Connecticut and Westchester, New York. He is otherwise not represented on CD. His work includes an opera based on Romain Rolland's *Danton* and four symphonies. Listening to the *Concertino for orchestra* (1944) whets the appetite. Lopatnikoff was championed by Koussevitzky (like Bernstein) and the *Concertino* was commissioned by him. The music is neoclassical in outlook without being in the least arid, and the invention is bright, imaginative and lively. A most enjoyable piece, and the

1953 mono recording comes up well in this well-transferred and intelligently planned compilation.

Lourié, Arthur (1892–1966)

(i) *Concerto da camera;* (ii) *A little chamber music*; (iii) *Little Gidding.*
*** DG Dig. 437 788-2 [id.]. (i & iii) Gidon
· Kremer;(ii) Thomas Klug; (iii) Kenneth
Riegel; Deutsche Kammerphilharmonie.

Arthur Lourié is known by repute rather than achievement. He began his career in St Petersburg as a 'futurist', an advocate of all things modern. After the Revolution, Anatoly Lunacharsky, the Soviet minister in charge of Cultural matters, appointed him as Commissar for Music. This DG record is an excellent introduction to his music. *A little chamber music* comes from 1924 and was started in Wiesbaden where this recording was made, and finished in Paris where he settled until 1941. It has a strongly Russian feel to it and quite a bit of Stravinsky. By this time, Lourié was being absorbed into the latter's circle and became his musical factotum for a time, though they subsequently became estranged. While still in Russia, Lourié became a Catholic convert and wrote a good deal of music inspired by Gregorian chant. As a Jew, he was in great danger but succeeded in escaping to the USA where he sank into neglect and obscurity. The two remaining works come from his American years: the *Concerto da camera* and the setting of *Little Gidding* from Eliot's *Four Quartets* for tenor, both from 1945. By then, he had come to sympathize with Eliot's aesthetic as well as his conservative and classical values. Neither work is a masterpiece and we doubt whether many readers would return to them very often, but both are of genuine musical interest and value. First-rate performances from Kremer and the Deutsche Philharmonie and, in the *Little Gidding* setting, Kenneth Riegel. The recording is excellent.

String quartets Nos. 1–3 (Suite); (i) *Duo for violin and viola.*
**(*) ASV Dig. CDDCA 1020 [id.]. Utrecht Qt;
(i) Eeva Koskinen, Daniel Raiskin.

The three quartets were composed in quick succession: the *First* comes from 1921 when, as Lunacharsky's 'Commissar for Music', the composer had left Russia for Berlin. It is a two-movement piece lasting half an hour, whose first movement (nearly 20 minutes) is very amorphous and wanting in concentration. The *Second Quartet* (1923) is a much shorter, one-movement work with a hint of Stravinskian neoclassicism and humour. But it is the economical and well-wrought *Duo for violin and viola* that is most Russian. The *Third Quartet* (1924), subtitled *Suite* (its movements are called *Prélude, Choral, Hymne* and *Marche funèbre*),

comes from Lourié's Paris years and save for the last movement, does not make as strong an impression as *A little chamber music* from the same year (see above). There is little sense of development and one has little feeling of concentration, or any evolving organic process. Nevertheless this is an interesting byway explored with great dedication by these players.

Lumbye, Hans Christian (1810–74)

The complete orchestral works

Volume 1: *Amélie waltz; Britta polka; Artist dreams fantasia; Cannon galop; Champagne gallop; Columbine polka-mazurka; Copenhagen Steam Railway gallop; Dagma polka; Deborah polka mazurka; King Christian IX's march-past; Otto Allin's drum polka; Queen Louise waltz; Saecilie waltz; Salute to August Bournonville galop; A summer night at the Mön Cliffs fantasia; (Berlin) Vauxhall polka.*
** Marco Polo Dig. 8.223743 [id.]. Tivoli SO, Bellincampi.

Volume 2: *Amanda waltz; Camilla polka; Crinoline polka-mazurka; The dream after the ball; Goodnight polka; King Carl XV's march-past; A little ditty for the party galop; Master Erik's polka; Military galop; Minerva polka; Regatta festival waltz; Rosa and Rosita waltz; Salute to Capri polka; Victoria Bundsen polka-mazurka; Victoria galop; Wally polka.*
** Marco Polo Dig. 8.223744 [id.]. Tivoli SO, Bellincampi.

Volume 3: *Amager polka, No. 2; Carnival joys; Pictures from a masquerade; Concert polka for two violins; Festival polonaise in A; The Guardsmen of Amager: finale-galop; New year greeting march; Ornithobolaia galop; Sounds from Kroll's Dance Hall; Tivolis concert salon galop; Tivoli Volière galop; Torchlight dance.*
** Marco Polo Dig. 8.225122 [id.]. Tivoli SO, Bellincampi.

Following on from their monumental Strauss Edition, Marco Polo now turn their attention to the 'Strauss of the North', Hans Christian Lumbye. The three volumes released at the time of writing are sympathetically and enjoyably played, but the recordings are not ideal: they are too reverberant and backwardly-balanced, taking away some of the warm intimacy, as well as the sparkle this music should ideally have. But collectors who wish to explore this composer's output in depth will find much to enjoy here. Like the Strausses, Lumbye's fund of melody is seemingly inexhaustible, and the various novelty pieces are often delightful. Much of the writing has a robust quality which is most infectious, and the orchestration is always colourful.

There are three really outstanding single CD Lumbye collections (on Unicorn DKPCD 9089 and 9143, and Chandos CHAN 9209) recommended in our main volume, but these Marco Polo discs, despite the too-resonant sound, will certainly give pleasure.

Lutoslawski, Witold (1916–94)

(i; ii; iii) Cello concerto; (i; ii; iv) Concerto for oboe, harp and chamber orchestra; (v) Concerto for orchestra; (ii; ix) Dance preludes; (i; vi; vii) Les espaces du sommeil; (v) Funeral music; (i; vii) Symphony No. 3; (viii) Variations on a theme by Paganini; (v) Venetian games.
(b) *** Philips Duo Analogue/Dig. 464 043-2 (2) [id.]. (i) Composer; (ii) Bav. RSO; (iii) Schiff; (iv) H. and U. Holliger; (v) Nat. SO of Warsaw, Rowicki; (vi) Fischer-Dieskau; (vii) BPO; (viii) Argerich, Freire; (ix) Brunner.

This is an excellent bargain-price introduction to Lutoslawski, which includes many of his most important works. The Third Symphony is an impressively argued 35-minute work, given an authoritative performance under the direction of the composer. It was originally released coupled to Les espaces du sommeil, performed by its dedicatee, Dietrich Fischer-Dieskau, and more definitive versions could hardly be imagined. The superb digital sound dates from 1985. Recorded around the same time in equally impressive performances was the Cello concerto with Heinrich Schiff, a fine work, with fascinating sonorities and certain aleatoric elements in the score. The Concerto for oboe, harp and chamber orchestra was written in 1980 for the Holligers, who perform it here; it mingles charm, irony and intelligence in equal measures. The Dance preludes date from 1953 and were later scored for clarinet and orchestra (1955) as recorded here, and then nine instruments (1959). They are more folklike in idiom and are attractively presented by Eduard Brunner (clarinet). The Paganini variations, a piano duo dating from 1941, is exhilarating and is played with great virtuosity by Martha Argerich and Nelson Freire. The Rowicki performances date from 1964. The Funeral music is an angular work, which makes some impression, but is rather empty. Venetian games contains more aleatoric interpolations and is music of wider appeal, whilst the famous Concerto for orchestra – a brilliant and highly attractive work – is thoroughly idiomatic. All the Rowicki performances are excellently recorded and have transferred very well to CD. A bargain set in every way.

Concerto for orchestra; Jeux vénitiens; Livre pour orchestre; Mi-parti; Musique funèbre; Symphonic variations; Symphonies Nos. 1–2.

(b) *** EMI Double fforte CZS5 73833-2 (2). Polish Nat. RSO, Composer.

This eminently recommendable pair of discs is a 'retrospective', drawing many of the key orchestral works from an even more comprehensive six-LP set dating from the late 1970s. Opening with the enticing early Symphonic variations, with their highly individual colouring and atmosphere (sparklingly recorded), the set includes not only the Concerto for orchestra, but both symphonies, dating from 1947 and 1966/8 respectively. These plus the Variations are also available separately (CDM5 65076-2), but most collectors will surely opt for the more extended coverage. Even today some of this music, notably Jeux vénitiens, Livre and Mi parti, still sounds very avant garde, but the latter piece is hauntingly atmospheric in the composer's hands. Indeed, with performances so obviously authoritative and of a high standard, and the recording exceptionally vivid, they show this composer's sound world to good advantage.

Double concerto for oboe, harp and chamber orchestra.
*** Koch Campanella Dig. C 130045 [id.]. Süss, Schellenberger, Franz Liszt CO, Budapest, Zoltán Peskó – IBERT: Sinfonia concertante; MARTIN: 3 Danses for oboe, harp, string quintet and string orchestra. ***

Like the other two concertante works on this CD, Lutoslawski's Double concerto was commissioned by Paul Sacher and composed (in 1970) for the oboist Heinz Holliger and the harpist Ursula Holliger. The work was premièred in 1980. Lutoslawski develops the widest range of aurally intriguing colouristic patterns. The first movement opens with the strings buzzing like a hive of bees, with oboe and harp soon offering their own alternative mêlée. The central Dolente shimmers with pizzicato and other glistening sounds, yet the oboe melisma dominates; the finale is a piquant Marciale e grotesco. The concerto has brief aleatory elements, but they are framed within a carefully controlled structure. This is remarkable music and the performance and recording are in every way worthy of Lutoslawski's unpredictable progress.

Maazel, Lorin (born 1930)

(i) Music for cello and orchestra; (ii) Music for flute and orchestra; (iii) Music for violin and orchestra.
*** RCA 09026 68789-2 [id.]. (i) Rostropovich; (ii) James Galway; (iii) composer; Bavarian RSO, Arthur Post.

The austere titles of these works of Lorin Maazel – products of his increased activity as a composer in the mid 1990s – belie the fact that Maazel is at root a late romantic, working to no formula but expressing what he feels, often lyrically, always with colour and fine feeling for orchestral timbres. This is not easy music, but his own descriptions of each work, given here as notes, bear out the emotional element, even if they dismiss the idea of underlying programmes behind his inspiration. The most outward-going of the three is the flute piece for James Galway, reflecting the dedicatee's flamboyant character as an artist. It ends with a big cadenza, accompanied by percussion, leading into a brilliant coda heightened by blatant brass. The cello piece written for Rostropovich is the most demanding of the three, an extended half-hour made up of eight contrasted sections, one developing from the other and ending as the work began with a darkly reflective coda. Maazel wrote the violin piece for himself to play, dedicating it to his wife, who inspired it. Again the music is largely reflective, ending on an epilogue marked 'tranquillo' which yet includes a pained climax. Excellent performances and recording.

McCabe, John (born 1939)

(i) *Flute concerto. Symphony No. 4 (Of Time and the River).*
*** Hyperion Dig. CDA 67089 [id.]. BBC SO, Vernon Handley; (i) with Emily Beynon.

Celebrating the composer's sixtieth birthday, this is the finest disc yet of the music of John McCabe. Completed in 1994, his *Fourth Symphony*, entitled *Of Time and the River* after Thomas Wolfe's novel, is a magnificent work in two substantial movements – fast to slow, then slow to fast. The idiom is warmer and more approachable than in McCabe's earlier music, echoing in its atmospheric orchestration and some of the melodic lines Britten on the one hand and Sibelius on the other, while remaining distinctive and new. Superb performances and vivid recording, not just of the *Symphony* but of the large-scale *Flute concerto* McCabe wrote for James Galway. Ideal notes as well.

Edward II (ballet; complete).
*** Hyperion Dig. CDA 67135/6 (2) [id.]. Royal Ballet Sinfonia, Barry Wordsworth.

This full-length ballet, in two acts of nearly an hour each, is not only John McCabe's most ambitious work, it is among the most powerful as well as the most approachable of all his music. Taking as his starting point the Marlowe play *Edward II*, McCabe (in a scenario devised in collaboration with the choreographer David Bintley) has also drawn on Brecht's rethinking of that play, as well as the satirical fourteenth-century *Le roman de Fauvel* (which was itself inspired by the story of the English king and his weaknesses). That last source has helped him to introduce a contrasting element of

humour. McCabe's score is at once colourfully atmospheric as well as symphonic in its thinking, vividly telling the story in mood and action, drawing on medieval sources for themes and for the 'tuckets and alarums' which add point to such a plot. Having abandoned the more severely serial stance of his earlier music, McCabe as in his superb *Third Symphony* (also issued on Hyperion) adopts a tonal idiom which is yet distinctively his, not at all derivative. The dramatic and emotional contrasts are strongly presented, with the dark ceremonial of the Court music set against music reflecting both the King's equivocal relationship with his wife Isabella, and his love for Gaveston. Act I ends with a powerful section illustrating the King's agonized reaction to the death of Gaveston, with Act II dealing with the troubled plotting which leads to the King's murder. There have been few full-length ballet scores impressive as this since Prokofiev and Britten, inspiring Barry Wordsworth and the Royal Ballet Sinfonia to a strong and colourful performance, vividly recorded.

MacDowell, Edward (1860–1908)

2 Fragments after the Song of Roland, Op. 30: The Saracens; The lovely Aldä. Hamlet/Ophelia, Op. 22; Lancelot and Elaine, Op. 25; Lamia, Op. 29.
*** Bridge Dig. BRIDGE 9089 [id.]. RPO, Karl Krueger.

For the seven years between 1884 and 1890, Mac-Dowell occupied himself with writing Lisztian symphonic poems. The two *Fragments from the Song of Roland* are the middle movements of what was intended as a programme-symphony, and *The lovely Aldä* is a gentle portrait which has something in common with MacDowell's 'Wild rose', if not as melodically memorable. The portraits of *Hamlet* and *Ophelia* are highly romantic and, like both the symphonic poems, the lyrical writing is very appealing. There is a distinct flavour of Tchaikovsky, and Lisztian hyperbole is absent from the more vigorous passages. *Lancelot and Elaine* (drawing on Tennyson's 'Idylls of the King') is particularly evocative with a poignant theme portraying the heroine's unrequited love for Lancelot, and fine writing for the horns. *Lamia* is based on a poem by Keats. She is an enchantress in the form of a serpent, but changes into a lovely maiden in order to win the love of Lycius. MacDowell's music resourcefully varies the theme representing Lamia to indicate her changes of form and the events of the narrative, which ends badly for both characters. The performances here are very persuasive. Karl Krueger is a splendid and dedicated advocate and the RPO playing is warmly seductive and beautifully recorded.

Suite for large orchestra, Op. 42.
(M) **(*) Mercury [434 337-2] [id.].
   Eastman-Rochester O, Howard Hanson –
   CHADWICK: *Symphonic sketches* **(*);
   PETER: *Sinfonia.***

MacDowell is best known for his miniature, *To a wild rose*. The suite – although it too has evocative titles – is more ambitious, but has amiable rather than memorable invention. The performance is of high quality, as one would expect from this source; the 1961 recording is well up to Mercury standard, though the upper violin timbre is a bit tight.

Machaut, Guillaume de (1300–77)

Ballades, rondeaux, virelais: *Amours me fait desirer; Blauté qu toutes autres pere; Dame a qui; Dame, a vous sana retollir; Dame, de qui toute ma joie vent; Dame je sui cliz/Fins cuers doulz; Dame mon coeur en vous remaint; Douce dame jolie; Foy porter; Je vivroie liement; Rose, liz, printemps, verdure; Tuit mi penser;* Motet: *Inviolata genitrix/Felix virgo/Ad te suspiramus.*
*** Hyperion Dig. CDA 66087 [id.]. Emma Kirkby, Gothic Voices, Christopher Page.

Although (until recently) primarily celebrated for his church music, Guillaume de Machaut, one-time secretary to the King of Bohemia, poet-composer, canon and lover (even in his sixties), led the fullest secular life. He was immensely successful on all levels, living in his later years in a large elegant house in Rheims, where he was friend and adviser to the nobility, including the future King Charles V. He finally assembled his own poetry and music and arranged to have it elaborately illustrated and copied into a permanent anthology. The ballades and virelais included here are written imploringly, and in elaborate admiration, to ladies of great beauty and of all other virtues, except apparently a willingness to respond, which in turn produces languishing distress in the unsuccessful admirer. The fluid part-writing of the ensemble pieces is unique, but the solo pieces are very appealing, especially when sung, as two of them are here, by an artist of the calibre of Emma Kirkby. One wishes she had played a larger part in the programme, but Rogers Covey-Crump, Colin Scott-Mason, Emily Van Evera and Margaret Philpot all make sympathetic individual contributions. As a group the Gothic Voices certainly know how to shape the melancholy melismas of the concerted items: they blend beautifully together, giving effective unexaggerated tweaks to the passing moments of dissonance. The closing four-part motet, a Triplum, celebrates the Virgin Mary and is perhaps the most beautiful work on the disc. Excellent recording.

Chansons: (Ballads, rondeaux, viralais): *Certes mon oueil; Comment puet on; De toutes flours; En*

amer a douce vie; En vipere; De Fortune; Hel dame de valour; Je ne cuit pas; Je puis trop bien; Liement me deport; Ma fin est mon commencement; Mors sui; Se quanque amours; Tant doucement.
**(*) DG Dig. 457 618-2 [id.]. Orlando Consort.

The explicit and amorous colour print which illuminates this Archiv CD illustrates what the lyrics confirm, that Machaut's chansons are about the longing and desire for physical love with a lady of beauty, 'who knows honour', the joy of consummation, and the pain of refusal. The opening and closing four-part melismas, *Tant doucement* ('So sweetly am I imprisoned') and *De toutes flours* ('If all the flowers'), are characteristic of Machaut's hypnotic flowing style. Moreover, the duet *Mors suis* ('I die if I do not see you') is a highlight, showing his writing at its most intensely melodic, while in *En amer a douce vie* ('In bitter love'), one of the composer's earliest four-part ballades, the twists of the melodic line and plangent touches in the part-writing have a remarkable emotional ambivalence.

The Orlando Consort blend beautifully together, led by Robert Harre-Jones whose richly coloured alto line is most appealing. But the snag here is the basic sameness of colour inevitable with two, three or four unaccompanied male voices, however expressively they sing, and however pleasingly recorded. In that respect the Hyperion disc above is much more appealing.

Madetoja, Leevi (1887–1947)

Symphonies Nos. 1 in F, Op. 29; 2 in E flat, Op. 35; 3 in A, Op. 55; Comedy overture, Op. 53; Okon Fuoko, Op. 58; Pohjolaisia suite, Op. 52.
(M) *** Chandos Dig. CHAN 7097 (2) [id.].
   Iceland SO, Petri Sakari.

Symphonies Nos. 1 in F, Op. 29; (i) *2 in E flat, Op. 35;* (ii) *3 in A, Op. 55;* (iii) *Comedy overture, Op. 53;* (iv) *Okon Fuoko, Op. 58; Pohjolaisia suite, Op. 52;* (i) *Kullervo, Op. 15.*
(B) **(*) Finlandia/Warner Ultima Double 8573 81971-2 (2) [id.]. Finnish Radio SO, Segerstam, (ii) Saraste, (i) Tampere PO, Rautio; (iii) Helsinki PO, Panula; (iv) Finnish Radio SO, Segerstam, Okko Kamu.

Apart from Sibelius himself, with whom Madetoja briefly studied, there are many influences to be discerned in the *First Symphony* (1915–26) – figures like Strauss, the Russian post-nationalists, Reger and above all the French, for whom Madetoja had a lifelong admiration. The *Second Symphony* (1917–18), composed at about the same time as Sibelius was working on the definitive version of his *Fifth*, is expertly fashioned and despite the obvious debts there is some individuality too. The *Third* was written in the mid 1920s while Madetoja was living in Houilles, just outside Paris. Gallic elements surface most strongly in this piece (he had hoped to study with Vincent d'Indy and as a conductor championed both d'Indy and Debussy, as well as such contemporaries as Szymanowski and Janáček). The French critic Henri-Claude Fantapié mentioned Madetoja's affinities with that 'little known but important branch of French music which evolved in the shadow of impressionism' and which was represented by Roussel, Magnard or Paul Le Flem. The *Comedy overture* (1923) is an absolute delight, and both the suite from the opera *Pohjolaisia* (*The Ostrobothnians*) and the ballet-pantomime *Okon Fuoko* show an exemplary feeling for colour and atmosphere. Now that the excellent Chandos set under Petri Sakari has been transferred to the Double format at mid-price, it deserves to carry our first recommendation. Both the performances and the spacious natural recordings are exemplary and Sakari gets imaginative and sensitive playing from his Reykjavik forces.

No real grumbles about the Finlandia performances which are well worth the money and will give pleasure, but the Icelandic set is the more distinguished of the two and worth the extra cost.

Magnard, Albéric (1865–1914)

Symphonies Nos. 1–4; Chant funèbre; Hymne à la justice; Ouverture.
(B) *** EMI CZS5 72364-2 (3). Capitole Toulouse O, Plasson.

Symphonies Nos. 1 in C min., Op. 4; 3 in B flat min., Op. 11.
**(*) BIS Dig. CD 927 [id.]. Malmö SO, Thomas Sanderling.

Symphonies Nos. 2 in E, Op. 6 ; 4 in C sharp min., Op. 21.
**(*) BIS Dig. CD 928 [id.]. Malmö SO, Thomas Sanderling.

Of the four so-called Franckist symphonists (Vincent d'Indy, Chausson, Dukas and Albéric Magnard), it is clear that Magnard is not the least rewarding of them. Although he was very occasionally broadcast on the Third Programme along with Guy Ropartz, with whom he was at one time twinned like Bruckner and Mahler (they were fellow students), it was Ansermet's 1968 LP of the *Third Symphony* (1896) that put him on the map. Plasson's version is in every way superior. The music has a sustained nobility that strikes one from the opening bars, and has the breadth and pulse of real symphonism. Magnard shared a birthday with Nielsen and so was an exact contemporary of Glazunov and Sibelius. Although he had a privileged background and his father was editor of *Le Figaro*, he nurtured great independence of spirit and determination.

The *First Symphony* (1889–90) was composed in the shadow of his friend and mentor Vincent d'Indy, and follows more strictly cyclical principles. Yet its ideas still show individuality of character, even though there is a strong post-Wagnerian aftertaste. There is a magical passage of almost Brucknerian mystery, about seven minutes into the first movement, which is really quite inspired. Despite the debt to Wagner and Franck, the last two symphonies have distinct personalities; they are separated by seventeen years. The *Fourth* comes from 1913, a year before its composer was shot by the invading Germans and his house burnt. The work has an impressive intellectual power, and is well crafted with no shortage of ideas. For all the appearance of academicism, there is a quiet and distinctive personality here, and dignity too. The *Chant funèbre* is an earlier work that has a vein of genuine eloquence. The Toulouse Capitole Orchestra under Michel Plasson play this music as if they believe every note, as indeed they should, and the recording is sonorous and well defined.

Generally speaking Thomas Sanderling opts for broad tempi: he takes 44:19 minutes over the *Third Symphony* as opposed to the 37:33 of Jean-Yves Ossonce (Hyperion) and 40:20 of Michel Plasson and the Toulouse Orchestra (EMI). Indeed, his leisurely tempi compel BIS to accommodate the *Second* and *Fourth Symphonies* on a separate CD, retailing them for the price of one. In the *Fourth* Sanderling is almost five minutes longer than his two rivals. He is the best recorded of the three but both Plasson and Ossonce get a more powerfully concentrated response from their players. Plasson spreads to three CDs but offers extra items and the EMI set is at bargain price and is excellent value. But in almost all respects the Hyperion set (using two full-priced discs, CDA 67030 and CDA 67040) takes pride of place, with warm, cleanly focused sound.

Mahler, Gustav (1860–1911)

Symphonies Nos. 1–9; 10 (Adagio).
(B) ** DG 463 738-2 (10) [id.]. Arroyo, Mathis, Morison, Spoorenberg, Hamari, Procter, Marjorie Thomas, Grobe, Fischer-Dieskau, Crass, Bav. R Ch., N German R Ch., W. German R Ch., Regensburger Domchor, Munich Motteten Ch. Bav. RSO, Kubelik.

Kubelik's is a fastidious and generally lyrical view of Mahler, most persuasive in the delightful performances of the least weighty symphonies, Nos. 1 and 4. In much of the rest these sensitive performances lack something in power and tension, tending to eliminate the neurotic in Mahler; but there is a fair case for preferring such an approach for relaxed listening. As can be seen he has excellent soloists and distinguished choral contributions in Nos. 2 and

8. Other sets more compellingly compass the full range of Mahler's symphonic achievement, but with good sound and in a bargain box, this is worth considering if Kubelik's less flamboyant view seems appealing.

Symphony No. 1 in D (Titan); (i) Lieder eines fahrenden Gesellen.
(B) **(*) Decca Penguin 460 654-2 [id.]. Bav. RSO, Kubelik (i) with Dietrich Fischer-Dieskau (baritone).

Kubelik gives an intensely poetic reading. He is here at his finest in Mahler and though, as in later symphonies, he is sometimes tempted to choose a tempo on the fast side, the result could hardly be more glowing. The rubato in the slow funeral march is most subtly handled. In its CD reissue (originally DG) the quality is a little dry in the bass and the violins have lost some of their warmth, but there is no lack of body. In the *Lieder eines fahrenden Gesellen* the sound is fuller, with more atmospheric bloom. No one quite rivals Fischer-Dieskau in these songs, and this is a very considerable bonus at Penguin Classics price. The essay is by Michael Dibdin.

Symphonies Nos. 1 in D (Titan); 3 in D min.
(B) ** RCA High Performance 09026 63469-2 (2) [id.]. BSO, Leinsdorf.

Neither of the Leinsdorf performances is completely recommendable. The *Titan* is hard driven, almost brutal, in no sense Viennese and lacking in atmosphere, yet one cannot deny that it is exciting at times. He is more successful in the *Third* where his straightforward approach makes for more convincing results. The recordings (from 1962 and 1966) are very up-front, brilliant in hi-fi terms, though not a genuine concert image. A CD mainly for audiophiles.

Symphonies Nos. 1 in D min.; No. 5 in C sharp min.
(B) **(*) DG Dig. Double 459 472-2 (2) [id.]. Philharmonia O, Sinopoli.

Sinopoli's account of the *First symphony* is warmly satisfying and passionately committed, with refined playing from the Philharmonia. He allows the fullest expressiveness with bold theatrical gestures thrust home purposefully. In the *Fifth* he draws a sharp distinction between the dark tragedy of the first two movements, and the relaxed *Wunderhorn* feeling of the rest. He seems intent in not overloading the big melodies with excessive emotion. This comes out more clearly in the central movements, where relaxation is the key-note, often with pastoral atmosphere. The celebrated *Adagietto* brings a tenderly wistful reading, songful and basically happy, not tragic. Warmly atmospheric recording throughout, though detail is not ideally clear in the *Fifth,* this is still a recommendable coupling.

Symphony No. 2 in C min. (Resurrection).
(M) *** EMI CDM5 57235-2 [567255].
Schwarzkopf, Rössl-Majdan, Philh. Ch. & O, Klemperer.
(M) *** Decca 446 992-2 [id.]. Cotrubas, Ludwig, V. State Op. Ch., VPO, Mehta.

Klemperer's performance – one of his most compelling on record – comes back to the catalogue on a single CD as one of EMI's 'Great Recordings of the Century' sounding better than ever. The remastering of the Kingsway Hall recording is impressively full and clear, with a real feeling of spectacle in the closing pages. The first movement, taken at a fairly fast tempo, is intense and earth shaking, though in the last movement (which incidentally is generously cued) some of Klemperer's speeds are designedly slow, he conveys supremely well the mood of transcendent, heavenly happiness in the culminating passage, with the Philharmonia Chorus and soloists themselves singing like angels.

Mehta's account of the *Second symphony*, if not quite in Klemperer's league, is far more impressive than one might have expected, and is indeed one of his most distinguished recording achievements. The refinement of the VPO playing, recorded with glorious richness and clarity, places it amongst the finest versions of this symphony available. At the very start, Mehta's fast tempi brings resilience, not aggressiveness, and the *espressivo* lyricism is equally persuasive, The second movement has *grazioso* delicacy, and though the third movement begins with the sharpest possible timpani strokes, there is no hint of brutality, and the *Wunderhorn* rhythms have a delightful lilt.

The enormous span of the finale (which has Christa Ludwig in superb form) brings clarity as well as magnificence, with fine placing of the soloists and chorus; there is glorious atmosphere in such moments as the evocation of birdsong over distant horns, as heavenly a moment as Mahler ever conceived. The performance has now been squeezed onto a single CD lasting just over 80 minutes, and while not a first choice, is surely a very worthy addition on the Decca's Legends label.

(i) *Symphony No. 3 in D min.; (ii) Kindertotenlieder; Des Knaben Wunderhorn: Das irdische Leben; 3 Rückert Lieder: Ich atmet' einen linden Duft; Ich bin der Welt abhanden gekommen; Um Mitternacht.*
(M) *** Sony SM2K 61831 [id.]. (i) Martha Lipton, Schola Cantorum Ch., Boys' Ch. of the Church of Transfiguration; (ii) Jennie Tourel; NYPO, Bernstein.

Bernstein's 1961 account of Mahler's *Third Symphony*, strong and passionate, has few of the stylistic exaggerations that sometimes overlaid his interpretations. Here his style in the slow movement is heavily expressive but many will respond to his extrovert involvement. The recording, made in New York's Manhattan Center, the venue of so many of the best of his early records, has added spaciousness and body in this very successful remastering for CD. The vocal contributions from Martha Lipton and the two choirs contribute to the success of this venture and the generous Lieder coupling is well worth having, and Jennie Tourel is in excellent voice.

Symphony No. 4 in G.
(M) *** RCA 09026 63533-2 [id.]. Lisa Della Casa, Chicago SO, Reiner.
(*) Decca Dig. 466 720-2 [id.]. Barbara Bonney, Concg. O, Chailly – BERG: *7 early songs* *.
(B) ** Ph. Virtuoso 442 394-2 [id.]. Elly Ameling, Concg. O, Haitink.
** DG Dig. 463 257-2 [id.]. Juliane Banse, Cleveland O, Boulez.

Symphony No. 4 in G; Four early songs.
*** RCA Dig. 75605 51345-2 [id.]. Ziesak, RPO, Daniele Gatti.

Daniele Gatti conducts a beautifully paced reading of the *Fourth* which is among the finest of recent digital versions, with the Royal Philharmonic playing superbly. It is a mark of Gatti's Mahlerian understanding that he can so perfectly time such a passage as the close of the first movement with its witty pay-off. That leads on to an account of the Scherzo which brings out its macabre humour, a dance of death. Gatti also paces the dedicated slow movement very impressively, with contrasts of tempo finely judged, and the finale too brings sharply defined contrasts, with Ruth Ziesak a sweetly girlish-sounding soloist. The *Four early songs* make an apt and generous coupling, also beautifully sung by Ziesak. Full, vivid sound.

This remarkable new transfer of Reiner's 1958 recording has astonished us. None of the Chicago Hall ambience, warmth and bloom has been sacrificed, indeed it seems enhanced. Yet the vividness of the detail is now so clear, and the bass response so naturally resonant, that one has a genuine illusion of sitting in the hall itself. The symphony's two big climaxes, in the first and third movements, expand spectacularly, even if the dynamic range is not quite so wide as on a modern digital recording. Reiner's performance with its affectionate waywardness is undoubtedly further enhanced with everything sounding spontaneous. The glorious slow movement combines warmth with striking intensity, with its rapt closing pages leading on gently to the finale in which Lisa Della Casa, in ravishing voice, matches Reiner's mood. This must now rank alongside Szell's outstanding Cleveland performance.

With rich immediate recording, Chailly draws brilliant playing from the Concertgebouw. The detail and clarity are extraordinary, with solos regularly highlighted, though at times too much so, as in the eerie *scordatura* violin solo of the Scherzo. Speeds are on the broad side both in the outer movements and the slow movement, with moulding of detail often meticulously underlined. Barbara Bonney is a delightfully girlish soloist in the *Wunderhorn* finale, both sweet and characterful, but she sounds even more appealing in the seven early Berg songs which come as a very generous coupling. Chailly, and the orchestra too, seem a degree more committed to Berg than in the Mahler.

Haitink's earlier, late-1960s Concertgebouw recording now returns to the catalogue on Philips's Virtuoso bargain label. It is predictably well played and the recording still sounds very good. The performance is sober, but has an attractive simplicity, and Elly Ameling matches Haitink's approach in her serene contribution to the finale.

Nothing could be further removed from the warmth of Fritz Reiner than Pierre Boulez's account of the *Fourth Symphony* with the Cleveland Orchestra and Juliane Banse as soloist in the finale. It is a generally brisk, rather understated performance that takes a cool, analytical view of Mahler. The playing is immaculate, the recording excellently judged, and the music's pace controlled with refined musical judgement, but the result lacks spontaneity except in the slow movement, where Boulez's simple dedication, far from sounding uninvolved, conveys a depth of feeling rather missing in the rest. Elsewhere the terrain is perfectly mapped but the inner landscape goes uncharted.

Symphony No. 5 in C sharp min.
(B) *** DG Classikon 439 429-2 [id.]. BPO, Karajan.

Karajan's 1973 version makes a very welcome reissue on DG's Classikon label. This is one of the most beautiful and intense versions available, starting with a highly compelling account of the first movement which brings biting funeral-march rhythms. Karajan's characteristic emphasis on polish and refinement goes with sharpness of focus. This is a performance of stature and, with excellent sound, a genuine bargain.

Symphony No. 7 in E min.
*** RCA Dig. 09026 63510-2 (2) [id.]. LSO, Michael Tilson Thomas.
**(*) Telarc Dig. 2CD 80514 (2) [id.]. Atlanta SO, Yoel Levi.
(**) BBC Legends mono BBCL 4034-2 (2) [id.]. Hallé O & BBC Northern O, Sir John Barbirolli – BRUCKNER: *Symphony No. 9* (**).

Michael Tilson Thomas conducts a strong, purposeful reading of the *Seventh*, no longer the Cinderella of the series, with polished and refined playing from the LSO and recording to match. His terracing of textures and dynamics is perfectly judged. The result may be less atmospheric and evocative than in some readings, but the relative coolness of the second *Nachtmusik*, for example, makes one appreciate the work the more keenly for its symphonic qualities. Although the fragmentary structure of the finale is in no way disguised, the pointedness of the playing holds it firmly together. A strong contender in a hotly competitive field.

Yoel Levi conducts a reading of the *Seventh* which gains in strength and purpose as it progresses. If the very slow tempo for the first movement makes it seem a degree subdued, the strong colouring of later movements, as in the nightmare quality he gives to the central Scherzo, makes an increasingly characterful impression, though the relatively fast tempo for the second *Nachtmusik* does not quite avoid a jog-trot. The sound is close and brilliant, overpowering in big tuttis, if not ideally clear on detail.

Sir John never recorded the *Seventh Symphony* commercially, and the recording presented here comes from 1960 and was part of the BBC's Centenary Mahler cycle. The performance received the accolade of Deryck Cooke no less, though his enthusiasm would probably not have extended to the somewhat primitive recorded quality. The playing of the combined BBC Northern and Hallé Orchestras was first class and already by this time Barbirolli was as fervent and committed a Mahlerian as he was Sibelian or Elgarian, and totally attuned to the composer's world. He is unhurried and expansive: indeed at 84 minutes, he is more leisurely than almost any other conductor, but paradoxically makes the overall performance seem more concentrated and convincing. Despite the poor sound this should be heard.

Symphony No. 8 in E flat (Symphony of a thousand).
(**) Orfeo mono C 519 992 B [id.]. Mimi Coertse, Hilde Zadek, Lucretia West, Ira Malaniuk, Giuseppe Zampieri, Hermann Prey, Otto Edelmann, Konzertvereinigung Wiener Staatsopernchor, Singverein der Gesellschaft der Musikfreunde, Wiener Sängerknaben, VPO, Dimitri Mitropoulos.

Dimitri Mitropoulos's acclaimed 1960 account of the *Eighth Symphony*, with a fine line-up of soloists, choirs and the Vienna Philharmonic, will doubtless be sought after by Mahlerians and Mitropoulos admirers alike. This great conductor possessed a selfless dedication to whatever work he was performing and this certainly shines through. Artistic considerations aside, the ORF (Austrian Radio) recording lets it down. One has only to compare the sound their engineers achieved with the vivid stereo that BBC engineers produced for Horenstein in 1959 to realize how inadequate is the present engineering.

Symphony No. 9 in D min.
(M) ** DG 463 609-2 (2) [id.]. Chicago SO,

Giulini – SCHUBERT: *Symphony No. 8 (Unfinished)* **.

Giulini's 1977 Chicago performance of the *Ninth Symphony* curiously lacks the very quality one expects from this conductor: dedication. It opens atmospherically, but the tempi are too measured for a sense of impetus to assert itself. The orchestral playing is of the highest standard, but the listener's interest is not consistently sustained, despite some fine moments. The sound is rather glamorized and this is a curious choice for DG's Originals label.

Symphony No. 10 in F sharp (revised performing edition by Deryck Cooke).
*** EMI Dig. CDC5 56972-2 [id.]. BPO, Rattle.

In 1980, at the beginning of his recording career, Simon Rattle recorded this inspired realization of Mahler's five-movement concept. With the Bournemouth Symphony Orchestra, that remains an electrifying account, weightily recorded, but his new version with the Berlin Philharmonic, recorded live, transcends it in almost every way.

It is not only the extra refinement of the Berliners but also the extra detail that Rattle brings out in almost every phrase, that goes with an even greater concentration. His interpretation remains broadly the same, though the slow outer movements are a shade more spacious than previously, with the finale and its brutal hammer blows – inspired by a funeral procession heard from afar – becoming a degree more consolatory than before, conveying hope after death.

The contrast of the middle movements with their *Wunderhorn* echoes is also more strongly characterized. With seamless phrasing from the magnificent Berlin strings, this performance consistently reflects the conductor's belief in this controversial realization as a valid expression of Mahler's intentions, a magnificent work fully worthy to be set alongside the earlier symphonies. Full, refined, spacious recording, transferred at a relatively low level.

LIEDER AND SONG CYCLES

Kindertotenlieder; Lieder eines fahrenden Gesellen; 5 Rückert Lieder.
(BB) (*) Naxos Dig. 8.554164 [id.]. Hidenori Komatsu, Hanover RPO, Cord Garben.

The Japanese baritone Hidenori Komatsu trained in Germany, and he is plainly fluent in the language, but he makes an anaemic, uncharacterful soloist in Mahler's three great orchestral song cycles. This is music that deserves far stronger treatment, and Cord Garben's accompaniments do not help in their square cautiousness.

Des Knaben Wunderhorn.
(M) *** EMI CDM5 67236-2 [567256].
Schwarzkopf, Fischer-Dieskau, LSO, Szell.

Szell's 1968 Kingsway Hall recording of *Des*

Knaben Wunderhorn was a primary recommendation for three decades at premium price. Now it rightly joins EMI's 'Great Recordings of the Century' and the careful remastering plus the lower price will surely extend its catalogue life for a considerable time to come. The superb singing of Schwarzkopf and Fischer-Dieskau is underpinned by wonderfully sensitive playing from the LSO under Szell, who matches and even surpasses his achievement with his own Cleveland Orchestra in the *Fourth Symphony*.

Lieder eines fahrenden Gesellen.
*** Orfeo C 522 991 B [id.]. Christa Ludwig, VPO, Karl Boehm – BEETHOVEN: *Symphony No. 4*; SCHUMANN: *Symphony No. 4*. ***

As the chosen soloist in an electrifying concert conducted by Karl Boehm in August 1969, Christa Ludwig excels herself in a deeply moving, strongly characterized reading of the 'Wayfaring Lad' songs. The spontaneity of the performance makes up for any incidental flaws of the moment, with the voice gloriously firm and rich. No texts or translations are given of the songs, but every word is clear in this helpfully balanced radio recording.

Das Lied von der Erde.
(M) *** BBC Classics BBCM 5012-2 [id.]. Dame Janet Baker, John Mitchinson, BBC Northern SO, Leppard.
**(*) BBC Legends BBCL 4042-2 [id.]. Alfreda Hodgson, John Mitchinson, BBC Northern SO, Horenstein.
** Sony SK 60646 [id.]. Plácido Domingo, Bo Skovhus, LAPO, Salonen.

Taken from a performance for radio in the Free Trade Hall, Manchester, the Leppard version offers Dame Janet Baker at her very peak in 1977, giving one of the most moving and richly varied readings of the contralto songs ever. The final *Abschied* has a depth and intensity, a poignancy and, at the end, a feeling of slipping into the unconscious, that set it above even Dame Janet's earlier recording with Haitink. John Mitchinson may not have the most beautiful tenor, but his voice focuses ever more securely through the work, with many cleanly ringing top notes. Raymond Leppard defies any idea that he is just a baroque specialist, finding wit as well as weight and gravity. He draws fine playing from the orchestra, now renamed the BBC Philharmonic, though the body of strings is thin for Mahler. Acceptable BBC sound, with the voices naturally placed, not spotlit: with any reservations, this remains an essential purchase for admirers of Dame Janet and Mahler.

It was sad that Jascha Horenstein as a great Mahlerian recorded so little of his music. That makes this 1972 radio recording of *Das Lied* especially cherishable, a dedicated and authoritative performance – he obviously loves the score – with outstanding contributions from the two British soloists. As ever, Horenstein favours spacious speeds, sustaining them magnetically, not just over the meditative songs of the alto – with Alfreda Hodgson bringing echoes of Kathleen Ferrier, subtle and moving in her tonal shading – but in the tenor's lighter songs, at once relaxed and crisply pointed. John Mitchinson is here at his finest, contrasting his firm heroic tone in the first song against delicate half-tones, using his head-voice. Though the strings could be fuller and sweeter, the BBC Manchester recording is well balanced even if it now sounds rather opaque. In a brief interview Horenstein talks of his experience of the work.

By contrast, Salonen choses speeds faster than usual, but gives a warmly sympathetic and sensitive reading which brings out the full emotion of the writing. There are good precedents on record for an all-male *Das Lied* (Murray Dickie, Dietrich Fischer-Dieskau and the Philharmonia Orchestra under Kletzki on HMV, and Bernstein with James King and Fischer-Dieskau again on Decca are among them). And whether or not you prefer the contrast of timbre a contralto brings, there is a lot to admire and enjoy here. Plácido Domingo in Heldentenor mode produces a gloriously firm and full tone, but the subtler shadings required in Lieder-singing, even with orchestra, rather elude him. Bo Skovhus, following Mahler's option of using a baritone in place of the mezzo, has rarely sounded so clear and true on disc, subtly shading his tone, singing with perfect diction. The recording places the soloists well forward, with the orchestra in soft focus behind so that the violins, though refined, lack body.

11 Lieder aus der Jugendzeit; Lieder eines fahrenden Gesellen; 4 Rückert Lieder.
(M) **(*) Sony SMK 61847 [id.]. Fischer-Dieskau, Bernstein (piano).

A fascinating CD, as much for Bernstein's accompaniment as for Fischer-Dieskau's supreme artistry. Both artists respond to each other in an almost impressionistic way, producing a consistently expressive style. The Four *Rückert Lieder* inspire Fischer-Dieskau to a velvety legato, while *Scheiden und Meiden*, one of the eleven 'Youth' songs, is given an exhilarating bounce; *Nicht wiedersehen* from the same set is taken at half the normal speed, and evokes a totally different, magical world. The 1968 sound is excellent. This is one of the more impressive reissues in Sony's Bernstein Century edition.

Manfredini, Francesco (1684–1762)

Concerti grossi, Op. 3/1–12.
✹ (BB) *** Naxos Dig. 8.553891 [id.]. Capella Istropolitana, Jaroslav Krček.

As far as we can trace, this is the first CD entirely devoted to the music of Francesco Manfredini and it cannot be too highly recommended. Not a great deal is known about the composer's life and career, but it has been established that this splendid set of twelve concertos, published in Bologna in 1718, was dedicated to Prince Antoine I of Monaco, with whose Court orchestra Manfredini was associated. The most famous of them is No. 12, a *Christmas concerto* in the style of Torelli and Corelli, opening with a delightful *Pastorale* in siciliano rhythm. And if there are other influences here too, of Vivaldi in particular, and even anticipations of Handel, the music has its own individuality and is endlessly inventive. Allegros are vital and buoyant, slow movements tenderly touching, often featuring one or two solo violins. The performances here are both fresh and penetrating, with bouncing outer movements and expressive *Adagios*. Moreover the playing is perfectly in style, demonstrating how using modern instruments can be just as authentic as period manners in baroque music, with textures clean and transparent, impeccable tuning, simplicity of phrasing, and enticing beauty of timbre. The recording is absolutely natural, very much in the demonstration bracket.

Marais, Marin (1656–1728)

Pièces à violes: Book I: Tombeau de M. Meliton for 2 viols; Book IV: Suite for 3 viols in D.
*** Virgin Veritas/EMI Dig. VC5 45358-2. Jérôme Hantaï, Kaori Uemura, Alix Verzier, Pierre Hantaï – FORQUERAY: *Pièces for 3 viols; Suite.* ***

These works were both part of a larger collection of solo viol pieces which Marais published in 1686. Their ethos is comparatively austere, yet the nine-movement *Suite* of dances has plenty of variety: the central *Sarabande* has a noble dignity followed by a lighter *Gigue* and an engaging *Petite paysanne*. The *Tombeau* for two bass viols – the composer's longest work in this form – sustains a mood of dark, profound melancholy and this fine performance holds the listener firmly in its spell. The recording is vividly real.

Pièces à voiles: Suites for viola da gamba and continuo: Book II: in E min; Book III: in D; Book IV: Suite d'un goût étranger: Le Labyrinthe; Book V: in A min.
*** HM Dig. HMC 905248 [id.]. Juan Manuel Quintana, Dolores Costoyas, Attilio Cremonesi.

Juan Manuel Quintana plays the viola da gamba with superb assurance and virtuosity and he is more than equal to all the technical challenges posed by these suites of dance movements (eight in the minor key works and ten in the D major). He bounces his way through the *Rondeau* of the *D major Suite*, but when he comes to the deeply expressive *Plainte*, the penultimate movement, a degree more of expressive freedom would have been welcome. Even so it remains very affecting. Quintana is heard at his finest in *Le Labyrinthe*, a continuing kaleidoscope of changing tempi describing the uncertainty of a man lost in a maze, but who eventually finds his way out, to the strains of a culminating chaconne. The final movement of the *E minor Suite* is a *Tombeau pour Monsieur de Sainte-Colombe* (Marais's revered teacher) and this is certainly eloquently and characterfully played. There is good, if rather discreet, continuo support, and this remains a highly recommendable collection.

Marcello, Alessandro (1669–1747)

Oboe concerto in C min. (arr. Rothwell).
*** Dutton Lab./Barbirolli Soc. CDSJB 1016 [id.]. Evelyn Rothwell, Hallé O, Sir John Barbirolli – CORELLI; HAYDN: *Oboe concertos* *** (with Recital: C. P. E. BACH; LOEILLET; TELEMANN: *Sonatas* etc. ** – see Instrumental Recitals below).

Sir John's subtlety in matters of light and shade within an orchestral phrase brings this music immediately alive, and at the same time prevents the rather jolly opening tune from sounding square. The exquisitely beautiful *Adagio* is followed by a gay finale, both showing the soloist at her finest, and the well-balanced 1969 recording and excellent transfer add to one's pleasure.

Marchand, Louis (1669–1732)

Te Deum.
(BB) *** Arte Nova 74321 65413-2 [id.]. Ens. Canticum, Christoph Erkens; Helmut Deutsch (Koenig organ, St Avold, France) – François COUPERIN: *Messe pour les couvents.* ***

Louis Marchand was a year younger than Couperin-le-grand and died a year before him. Born in Lyons, he was a child prodigy and became organist of Nevers Cathedral at fourteen and then Auxerre before settling in Paris. He was among the most brilliant improvisers and virtuosi of the day. Like the Couperin organ masses, his *Te Deum* is interspersed with chant. A fine piece, it ends with a particularly magnificent *Grand jeu*. Helmut Deutsch plays with magisterial authority on the Koenig organ at the former St Nabor Abbey in St Avold, France. Very good and lifelike recordings and impressive playing. A most worthwhile issue.

Markevitch, Igor (1912–83)

Rébus; Hymnes.
*** Marco Polo Dig. 8 223724 [id.]. Arnhem PO, Christopher Lyndon-Gee.

The bare facts of Markevitch's career are outlined in our main volume. *Rébus* was written in 1931 for Massine, though he never mounted or danced it. It is remarkable for a youth of nineteen – there is quite a lot of Stravinsky, Prokofiev and even Hindemith in the *Variations* movement (track 4). No less an authority than Henri Prunières hailed it as a work of genius: it is certainly an interesting piece of immense talent. Mengelberg invited Markevitch to conduct it in Amsterdam (he took lessons from Monteux), thus laying the foundation of his future career. *Hymnes* was completed in 1933, though the final section, *Hymne à la Mort,* was not added until 1936. There is also much Stravinsky in the very imaginative *Prélude* and *Pas d'acier* in the first section, *Hymne au Travail,* and a strong sense of atmosphere in *Hymne au printemps.* This CD gave us much pleasure and is well worth investigating. Very acceptable playing from the Arnhem Orchestra under Christopher Lyndon-Gee and good recorded sound too.

Lorenzo il Magnifico; Psaume.
*** Marco Polo 8.223882. Lucy Shelton, Arnhem PO, Christopher Lyndon-Gee.

What is striking about Markevitch's music is that there is a real sense of line. His vocal symphony *Lorenzo Il Magnifico* was composed in 1940 and sets poems by Lorenzo de' Medici. It is said to be his masterpiece, and it is not only highly imaginative but quite masterly in its variety of pace and feeling of growth. There is a real sense of mystery here; small wonder that he excited the admiration of Bartók and Milhaud. *Psaumes* comes from 1933 when Markevitch was twenty-one and enjoyed a *succès de scandale* at the time. It is powerful stuff, rather Milhaudesque at times, prophetic of the latter's *Moses.* There is again quite a bit of Stravinsky and Honegger but at the same time much evidence of a distinctive and original mind. Lucy Shelton sings the demanding solo-part well in both scores and the playing and recording are eminently serviceable (there is a slight drop in level between the two works). Those who have been dismissive of the hype surrounding Markevitch should hear these two pieces. He is a composer of substance and some distinction.

Martin, Frank (1890–1974)

3 Danses for oboe, harp, string quintet and string orchestra.
*** Koch Campanella Dig. C 130045 [id.]. Süss, Schellenberger, Franz Liszt CO, Budapest, Zoltán Peskó – IBERT: *Sinfonia concertante;* LUTOSLAWSKI: *Double concerto for oboe and harp.* ***

Like the other two concertante pieces on this enterprising Campanella CD the *Trois Danses* were commissioned by Paul Sacher, and composed (in 1970) for the oboist Heinz Holliger and the harpist Ursula Holliger. In Martin's triptych, a work with strong flamenco influences, the solo strings are not used concerto grosso style, but to provide haunting added textural colour against which the solo oboe, with his harpist partner, can weave his spell. The central movement opens with a melancholy oboe soliloquy and the harp enters mysteriously against a gauze of solo strings. The finale features a rumba rhythm, but the sound and rhythmic patterns soon become kaleidoscopic. It is a masterly piece, full of aural imagination, and it is superbly played, with equal virtuosity from soloists and orchestra. The vivid recording is admirably balanced.

Piano trio on Irish folktunes.
*** Simax Dig. PSC 1147 [id.]. Grieg Trio – BLOCH: *3 Nocturnes;* SHOSTAKOVICH: *Piano trios.* ***

At one time just after the Second World War, the *Piano trio on Irish folktunes* was frequently included in concert and broadcast programmes. It is now something of a rarity despite the resurgence of interest in Martin. Like the Bloch with which it is coupled, the *Trio* comes from 1924, and while not characteristic of Martin at his finest it is a vital and spirited piece. It is expertly played here and the interest of the couplings further enhances the value of this issue, arguably the best the Grieg Trio has given us. The Simax recording is first rate.

Martinů, Bohuslav (1890–1959)

Piano concerto No. 5 in B flat (Fantasia concertante).
(M) *** DG 463 085-2 [id.]. Margrit Weber, Bav. RSO, Kubelik – TCHEREPNIN: *10 Bagatelles* ***; WEBER: *Konzertstück* **(*); FALLA: *Nights in the gardens of Spain.* ***

Martinů's *Fantasia concertante* is a terse, cyclic work, aggressively brilliant in a twentieth-century manner, but with an underlying stream of lyricism. This is expressed mainly through the second theme, which the composer develops convincingly. The performance is ideal, brash and extrovert, the performers glorying in the music's strong personality and willingness to wear its heart on its sleeve. The 1965 sound is excellent.

(i) *Concerto for double string orchestra, piano and timpani, H.271*; *Symphony No. 3, H 299.*
(***) Supraphon mono/stereo SU 1924-2 001 [id.]. (i) Jan Panenka, Josef Hejduk; Czech PO, Karel Sejna – DVORAK: *Suite in A, Op. 98b.* (***)

Sejna's account of the *Third Symphony*, made in 1947, was a first recording and there is the vivid, intense quality about the performance which you often find in premières. (The 78s were particularly difficult to get hold of.) The frequency range is naturally limited and much effort has been made to brighten the sound. It is a wonderful performance. The *Double concerto* (recorded in 1958 and in stereo) is not the first recording (Kubelik recorded it with the Philharmonia in the late 1940s) but the dark events that inspired it were sufficiently close to be vivid in the minds of all Czechs. Both performances have a dimension that is not always completely realized in more recent and better recorded versions.

3 Frescos of Piero della Francesca.
(**) Orfeo mono C 521 991 B [id.]. VPO, Rafael Kubelik – TCHAIKOVSKY: *Symphony No. 6.* (**)

Martinů dedicated the *Three Frescos of Piero della Francesca*, one of his most inspired and colourful scores, to Rafael Kubelik. This performance recorded at the 1956 Salzburg Festival was its première (Kubelik recorded them commercially on a mono HMV LP not long afterwards but that did not survive very long in the catalogue). His reading of the first movement is fractionally more measured than we often get nowadays and gains in its breadth. The mono sound is not bad for its period but this, of course, is a score which benefits from good modern sound.

Cello sonatas Nos. 1, H 277; 2, H 286; 3, H 340; 7 Arabesques, H 201a; Arietta, H 188b.
(BB) **(*) Naxos Dig. 8.554502 [id.]. Sebastian Benda, Christian Benda.

Martinů's three *Cello Sonatas* span the period 1939–52 and are full of rewarding musical invention. Christian Benda was a Fournier protégé and his playing, like that of his partner, is commendably direct in utterance, though these versions do not match the subtlety of Isserlis and Evans (Hyperion CDA 66296). The shorter pieces come from the early 1930s and were originally for violin and piano. They are not top-drawer Martinů but the *Cello sonatas* are fine pieces. These are eminently acceptable rather than distinguished performances and were recorded in the Ernest Ansermet Studios in Geneva. Not state-of-the-art sound but perfectly serviceable, with a decent balance between the two instruments.

Worth the money, but the performances are not as involving as those of their more expensive rivals.

Music for violin and piano

7 Arabesques H 201A; Arietta H 188A; Czech rhapsody H 307; Intermezzo H 261; 5 Madrigal stanzas H 297; Rhythmic études H 202; Violin sonatas Nos. 2 H 308; 3 H303; Sonatina in G H 262.
(M) *** Supraphon Dig. SU 3412-2 (2) [id.]. Bohuslav Matoušek, Petr Adamec.

Concerto H 13; Elegy H 3; Impromptu H 166; 5 Short pieces H 184; Violin sonata No. 1 H 182; Sonatas in C H 120; D min. H.152.
(M) *** Supraphon Dig. SU 3410-2 (2) [id.]. Bohuslav Matoušek, Petr Adamec.

Enormously prolific in most genres and combinations, Martinů's output for violin and piano is fairly extensive – nineteen pieces in all. These two handsomely produced and well-recorded double-CD sets cover his whole output: from the age of nineteen when he composed the *Elegy*, and the *Concerto* from the following year, through to his mid-fifties and the *Sonata No. 3* (1944) and the *Czech rhapsody* written for Kreisler (1945). It is popular, relatively speaking, most of it having been recorded before in one form or another. The only exceptions are the *Elegy*, the *Concerto* and the *Five Short pieces* from 1928. At times, Martinů is given to self-imitation and there are occasions when his muse is on autopilot but, for the most part, they are few and far between. The *Third Sonata* in particular is very impressive. There are many rewards here, and Bohuslav Matoušek and Petr Adamec are completely inside the idiom, having played Martinů virtually from the cradle. The sleeve annotation is full of interest.

PIANO MUSIC

Bagatelle (Morceau facile), H 323; Dumka No. 3, H 285bis; Fantasia et toccata, H 281; The fifth day of the fifth moon, H 318; Eight preludes, H 181; Piano sonata, H 350.
** Chandos Dig. CHAN 9655 [id.]. Eleonora Bekova.

Martinů's piano music has been well served in the past and no one who has acquired the uniquely authoritative RCA disc by Rudolf Firkušný will need any other. At present the only rival of note is the three-CD Supraphon set by Emil Leichner, as the Firkušný is at present out of circulation. Eleonora Bekova's set fills a gap for those who do not want to invest in the Leichner. The playing is more than serviceable without being really distinguished and the recording is eminently truthful.

OPERA

Les larmes du couteau; The voice of the forest.
*** Supraphon Dig SU 3386-3 631 [id.]. Hana
Jonášová, Lenka Šmidová, Roman Janál,
Prague Philharmonia, Jiří Bělohlávek.

The two one-act operas recorded here are both short,
roughly half an hour each, and a welcome addition
to Martinů's representation on CD. *Les larmes du
couteau* (1928) was neither published nor performed in the composer's lifetime. *The voice of the
forest*, on the other hand, was commissioned by
Prague Radio in 1935, but unlike *Comedy on the
bridge*, written the same year, it has never caught
on. With the Dadaist *Les larmes du couteau* (or *The
knife's tear*) we are close to the world of *L'histoire
du soldat*, Les six and Kurt Weill. The jazz elements
serve as a reminder that *La revue de cuisine* comes
from the same period. It is entertaining if insubstantial, and diverts the listener. Good soloists and
recording, with the musical and speech elements
well balanced. *The voice of the forest* offers a more
familiar Martinů. It is far more individual in style
and like the ballet *Špalíček*, draws on Czech folklore
and melody. In it, Martinů's invention is unfailingly
fresh and although one can see why it has never
made waves it has much to offer. The set is packaged
as one disc in a box for two, so as to accommodate
the copious and handsomely produced documentation.

Marx, Joseph (1882–1964)

*Quartetto chromatico; Quartetto in modo
classico; Quartetto in modo antico.*
*** ASV Dig. CDDCA 1073 [id.]. Lyric Qt.

Joseph Marx, born in Graz, became Director of the
Vienna Music Academy in 1922, and that same year
his symphony was premièred by Weingartner. He
viewed serial music with disdain and in 1923, with
the help of Korngold, Zemlinsky and others, he
organized an 'alternative Salzburg Festival' representing the best of contemporary music, but music
which stopped short of serial techniques. Yet the
influence of early Schoenberg is strong in his music,
especially the luscious *Quartetto chromatico*
(written in 1936 but revised in 1948) which opens
very like *Verklärte Nacht*, and while not quite
reaching orgasm, sustains its chromatic sensuality
almost throughout. There is a sprightly Scherzo, but
the third movement is particularly intense, although
the passion is at least partly dispelled in the finale.

By contrast the *Quartetto in modo antico* (1937/
8) opens in spring-like pastoral mood, using the
Mixolydian mode for its harmonic language. Although the music's progress is restless it retains a
firm melodic appeal. The touching *Adagio* has a
lovely chorale-like theme in the Phrygian mode,
and after an elegant neoclassical Minuet, the finale

is light-heartedly fugal, with a song-like secondary
episode, yet overall retaining the restless mood of
the opening. The *Quartetto in modo classico* (1940/
1) sheds the expressively drenched intensity of the
First Quartet in favour of a fresher, late classical
Romantic feeling. The sweetness of the lyricism is
balanced by elegance, the Scherzo is light-hearted,
the elegiac and beautiful *Adagio*, still rich in its
harmonic palette, yet brings solo legato lines and is
delicately refined in atmosphere. The dancing 6/8
finale introduces another fugato, but the movement
closes expressively by recalling the work's opening.

Marx's music may be conservative for its time,
but it is rewardingly rich in lyrical feeling, and the
performances here from a very appropriately named
quartet, whose full tonal blending is ideal for the
music, are persuasively committed, and full of spontaneous feeling. The recording is warm, truthful and
clear. Highly recommended.

Mascagni, Pietro (1863–1945)

Cavalleria rusticana (complete).
(M) *** DG 457 764-2 [id.]. Cossotto, Bergonzi,
Allegri, Guelfi, Martino, Ch. & O of La Scala,
Milan, Karajan.

It is good to see that Karajan's outstanding
recording, hitherto linked to *Pagliacci*, is now available separately. Karajan pays Mascagni the tribute
of taking his markings literally, so that well-worn
melodies come out with new purity and freshness,
and the singers have been chosen to match that.
Cossotto quite as much as Bergonzi keeps a pure,
firm line that is all too rare in this much abused
music – not that there is any lack of bite (except
that the original recording could have made the
chorus better defined). However, it has never
sounded more vivid than on this Originals CD –
which manages to squeeze just under 81 minutes
on a single disc – and with texts and translations,
this is now a top recommendation alongside
Levine's fine RCA version with Scotto and Domingo (74321 39500-2 – see our main volume).

Massenet, Jules (1842–1912)

(i) *Mélodie: Elégie* (arr. Mouton); *Les erinnyes:
Tristesse du soir;* (ii) *Thaïs: Méditation. La
Vierge: Le dernier sommeil de la Vierge.*
*** Chandos Dig. CHAN 9765 [id.]. (i) Peter
Dixon; (ii) Yuri Torchinsky; Royal Liverpool
PO Ch.; BBC PO, Yan Pascal Tortelier (with
Concert: *French bonbons*.***).

This is Beechamesque material (especially *Le
dernier sommeil de la Vierge*) and beautifully
played and recorded too. It is part of a particularly
delectable collection of French music including a
number of familiar overtures – see Concerts below.

Werther (complete).
*** EMI Dig. CDS5 56820-2 (2) [CDCB 56820].
Roberto Alagna, Angela Gheorghiu, Thomas
Hampson, Patricia Petibon, Tiffin Children's
Ch., LSO, Pappano.
*** RCA Dig. 74321 58224-2 (2) [id.]. Ramón
Vargas, Vesselina Kasarova, Christopher
Schaldenbrand, Dawn Kotoski, Berlin
Knabenchor & Deutsche SO, Jurowski.

It makes a formidable line-up to have the starry
husband-and-wife team of Roberto Alagna and
Angela Gheorghiu joined by the ever-responsive
Antonio Pappano. Though Alagna with his French
background is an ideal choice for Werther himself,
Gheorghiu with her bright soprano is a less obvious
one for the role of the heroine, Charlotte, normally
given to a mezzo. But as a magnetic actress she
conveys an extra tenderness and vulnerability, with
no lack of weight in such a solo as '*Laisse couler
mes larmes*' in Act III.

Alagna makes a characterful Werther, using his
distinctive tone-colours most sensitively, with
Thomas Hampson outstanding as Albert and Patricia Petibon a sweet-toned Sophie. As in Puccini
Pappano is subtle as well as powerful, using rubato
idiomatically and with refinement to heighten the
drama and point the moments of climax. Good
warm sound.

The RCA set makes the perfect alternative to the
EMI version. Here is casting of the two principals
that in every way is centrally satisfying. With her
vibrant mezzo, Vesselina Kasarova is a natural
choice for Charlotte, full and intense at the big
moments, even if the vibrancy, as caught by the
microphone, turns into unevenness under pressure.

Ramon Vargas with his clear, precise tenor is the
perfect hero here. He may not be as distinctive as
Alagna, but he sings such a solo as '*Pourquoi me
reveiller*' with greater purity, shading the voice
down most sensitively. The other principals are not
so strongly cast, with Dawn Kotoski rather shrill as
Sophie, but Jurowski's conducting is warm and
dramatic, even if it lacks the distinctive subtleties
of Pappano and Mackerras on rival sets. The sound
is brilliant and clear.

Werther (complete; in English).
(M) *** Chandos CHAN 3033 (2) [id.]. John
Brecknock, Dame Janet Baker, Patrick
Wheatley, Harold Blackburn, Joy Roberts,
John Tomlinson, ENO Ch. & O, Mackerras.

Recorded live at the Coliseum in 1977 in vividly
atmospheric sound, full of presence, Sir Charles
Mackerras's version offers an exceptionally warm
reading in English which is strong in dramatic
thrust. It is magnetic from first to last, one of the
finest issues in the Peter Moores Foundation's
Opera in English series. The cast is exceptionally
strong, with John Brecknock clear, fresh and firm
in the title role. Yet it is the performance of Dame

Janet Baker as Charlotte which provides the
linchpin, rising to great heights in the tragedy of
Act IV. This is Dame Janet at her very finest, singing with heartfelt fervour, using the full tonal
range of her unique voice, always fresh and clear in
attack.

Joy Roberts is a bright, agile Sophie, and the other
male singers can hardly be faulted. Remarkably, this
was taken from a single performance, not edited
from a series. Voices are close enough for every
word of Norman Tucker's excellent translation to
be heard.

Maw, Nicholas (born 1935)

Violin concerto (1993).
*** Sony Dig. SK 62856 [id.]. Joshua Bell, LPO,
Norrington.

It is good to welcome a new violin concerto that so
boldly and strongly adopts full-blooded romantic
manners. Maw has long defied fashion in the warm
lyricism of his writing, regularly working on the
biggest scale, never cowed by caution. Yet here he
excels himself in a work specifically written for
Joshua Bell, who responds superbly with playing of
heartfelt warmth as well as brilliance. The opening
Moderato movement has something of the fervour
of the Walton *Violin concerto*, with Maw firmly
establishing his personal approach to tonality in
seamless lyricism, leading up to a grinding climax.
Coming second, the Scherzo is the longest movement, with Walton again brought to mind in the
spiky brilliance, set against a central section with a
ripe horn solo. The third movement, *Romanza*, is
then a calm interlude before the carefree surging
thrust of the finale, leading to a bravura conclusion,
not the slow fade so often favoured latterly by
concerto composers. Roger Norrington and the LPO
are strong and sympathetic partners, with warm,
full recording to match.

Mayer, Emilie (1812–1883)

String quartet in G min., Op. 14.
*** CPO Dig. CPO 999 679-2 [id.]. Basle Erato
Qt. – Fanny MENDELSSOHN: *String quartet;*
SIRMEN: *Quartets 2–3.* ***

We know comparatively little about Emilie Mayer,
except that she was born in Mecklenburg, took
composition lessons from Carl Loewe and later in
Berlin from Adolf Marx, where she was able to
promote a series of concerts, and also in 1860 pub-
lish her own compositions. Her Op. 14 was the only
string quartet included in her printed works and
it was evidently valued, and rightly so. It is an
ambitious, well-crafted work, romantic in feeling,
with appealing ideas – the extended first movement
opens with an engaging dialogue between violin

and cello. The fine slow movement touchingly introduces the chorale '*Wer nur den lieben Gott lässt walten*' over a pizzicato accompaniment, before the reprise of the serene main theme. The busy finale has a Mendelssohnian lightness of touch, but overall the music has genuine individuality. The performance here is highly persuasive and naturally recorded.

Medtner, Nikolai (1880–1951)

Piano concertos Nos. 1 in C min., Op. 33; 3 in E min. (Ballade), Op. 60.
(BB) *** Naxos Dig. 8.553359 [id.]. Konstantin Scherbakov, Moscow SO, Vladimir Ziva.

As we said in our review of Konstantin Scherbakov's account of the *Second concerto*, coupled with the *Piano quintet* (Naxos 8.553390 – see our main volume), Scherbakov is highly sympathetic and offers very musical playing. In the companion pieces, he strikes us as infinitely more imaginative and subtle in both his range of dynamics and diversity of colour than any of his rivals. True, Geoffrey Tozer (Chandos) has the finer recording, but taken all round Scherbakov's would make an eminently satisfactory first choice: artistically it is impeccable, as a recording it is very natural and well balanced and, not least, the price is right.

PIANO MUSIC

Forgotten melodies, Op. 39; Two Skazki, Op. 48; Etude in C minor; I loved thee, Op. 32/4; Sonata minacciosa, Op. 53/2.
(M) *** CRD Dig. CRD 3509 [id.]. Hamish Milne.

Hamish Milne was one of the pioneering champions of Medtner on LP. But these are new performances (unlike the LP transfers listed in our main volume) and such is the quality of Milne's playing that one is never tempted to think of this music as pale Rachmaninov. Hamish Milne has lived with Medtner for the best part of a lifetime and this tells. His playing has refinement and authority, and the transcription he has made of the Pushkin setting, *I loved thee*, is quite magical. In the *Sonata minacciosa*, though Milne's playing might be more mercurial and incandescent, he brings valuable insights of his own. Very good recording.

Mendelssohn, Fanny (1805–47)

String quartet in E flat.
*** CPO Dig. CPO 999 679-2 [id.]. Basle Erato Qt. – Emilie MAYER: *Quartet No. 14;* SIRMEN: *Quartets 2 & 3.* ***

Fanny Mendelssohn and her brother were affectionately close and often composed in tandem. Even

so, for whatever reason, he resisted the publication of his sister's music until the year before her death. Fanny's *String quartet*, written in 1834, was influenced – notably in its layout and key sequence – by her brother's Op. 12, but the delectable Scherzo is the only movement that might be mistakenly assumed to be Felix's work; otherwise the music is wholly her own. The pervasive melancholy, which permeates the opening movement and the *Romanze*, is strikingly personal, perhaps reflecting Fanny's unwilling resignation to the eclipse of her music by her brother's success. But most remarkable of all is the forward-looking *Molto vivace* finale, with its determined energy, which is so like the finale of Tchaikovsky's *Souvenir de Florence* in its passionate forward impulse. The performance here is first class in every way, as is the recording; the couplings are stimulating too.

Lieder: Abenbild; Bergeslust; Du bist die ruh; Bitte; Dämmrung senkte sich von oben; Dein ist mein herz; Die ersehnte; Erwin; Ferne; Die Frühen graber; Frühling; Gondellied; Ich wandelte unter den bäumen; Im herbste; Italien; Der maiabend; Maienlied; Die mainacht; Morgenständchen; Nach Süden; Nachtwanderer; Der rosenkranz; Die schiffended; Schwanenlied; Suleika; Traum; Vorwurf; Wanderlied; Warum sind denn rosen so blass.
*** Hyperion Dig. CDA 67110 [id.]. Susan Gritton, Eugene Asti.

Fanny Mendelssohn – too often bracketed to her disadvantage either with her brother, Felix, or with Clara Schumann – is here treated to an entire disc of her songs. In her response to German poets from Goethe to Heine she is at least the equal of her brother, at once memorably tuneful and subtle in her illumination of the texts, adding distinctively to the Lieder tradition. Her writing is not just poetic but often vigorous, with fine accompaniments to match. Susan Gritton, sweet if just a little unvaried in tone, and Eugene Asti are refreshing, consistently sympathetic interpreters. They provide their own perceptive notes: Fanny's caustic comments on the poet Heine bring the man vividly to life.

Mendelssohn, Felix (1809–47)

Double piano concerto in E.
*** Chandos Dig. CHAN 9711 [id.]. Güher and Süther Pekinel, Philh. O, Marriner – BRUCH: *Double piano concerto in A flat min.;* MOZART: *Double piano concerto in E flat, K.365.* ***

Mendelssohn wrote his *Double piano concerto* when he was only fourteen, yet it contains many ideas that are entirely characteristic of his mature style. Arguably it outstays its welcome – this is easily the longest of the three double concertos which make up this unique and attractive coupling. Yet in such a performance as this its freshness justifies the length, for unlike the rival version from the Labèque sisters on Philips – which has only the Bruch for coupling – this one brings an accompaniment from Marriner and the Academy, finely pointed, which does not inflate the piece. The Pekinel sisters as in the other two works give a fresh, alert performance with pin-point ensemble. Warm, full sound.

(i) *Violin concerto in E min., Op. 64. Symphony No. 4 in A (Italian), Op. 90; Athalie, Op. 74: War March of the Priests; The Hebrides overture, Op. 26.*
(M) ** Sony SMK 61843 [id.]. (i) Zukerman, NYPO, Bernstein.

Zukerman gives a sweet-toned but never cloying account of the *Violin concerto*. His playing is impeccable from a technical point of view and the support he receives from Bernstein and his orchestra is thoroughly sympathetic. An extremely fine performance, and one which would be a match for almost any, were it not for the 1969 recording, which is not as naturally balanced or as rich in tone as one would like. However, it is better than many of Bernstein's NYPO recordings and Sony have improved matters in this CD transfer. The snag with this release is the performance of the *Italian Symphony*: it is a glossy reading lacking in charm and with some distracting mannerisms too. *The Hebrides overture* lacks the distinction of its best rivals, and it was a pity that the *Concerto* couldn't have been better coupled.

(i) *Double concerto in D min. for violin, piano and strings. Violin concerto in D min.*
(BB) *** Naxos Dig. 8.553844 [id.]. Marat Bisengaliev, Northern Sinf., Andrew Penny; (i) with Benjamin Frith.

Two juvenilia: the *D minor Violin concerto* was written when Mendelssohn was thirteen and the *Concerto for violin, piano and strings* comes from 1823 when he was fourteen. They are dispatched with zest and freshness by these excellent musicians even if in the *D minor Violin concerto* Bisengaliev's finale is a bit headlong. Spirited playing from the Northern Sinfonia under Andrew Penny and a predictably stylish contribution from Benjamin Frith. At less than a fiver, this is well worth considering.

Symphonies Nos. 3 in A min. (Scottish), Op. 56; 4 in A (Italian), Op. 90.
(M) *** Virgin/Veritas EMI VM5 61735-2 [id.]. L. Classical Players, Norrington.
(B) *** Australia Decca Eloquence 458 176-2. LSO, Abbado.

As in his comparable Schumann coupling (see below), Norrington opts for unexaggerated speeds

in the outer movements, relatively brisk ones for the middle movements. The results are similarly exhilarating, particularly in the clipped and bouncy account of the first movement of the *Italian*. The *Scottish Symphony* is far lighter than usual, with no hint of excessive sweetness. The Scherzo has rarely sounded happier, and the finale closes in a fast gallop for the 6/8 coda with the horns whooping gloriously. Good, warm recording, only occasionally masking detail in tuttis.

It is good to have Abbado's outstanding 1968 coupling with the LSO back in the catalogue again on Australian Decca's Eloquence label. His *Scottish Symphony* is beautifully played and the LSO respond to his direction with the greatest delicacy of feeling, whilst the *Italian Symphony* has comparable lightness of touch, matched with lyrical warmth. The vintage Kingsway Hall recording is freshly detailed, yet full, with glowing wind colour, and is in some ways preferable in sound to his later digital account on DG. The only drawback is the absence of the first-movement exposition repeat in the *Scottish* (though not in the *Italian*).

Symphony No. 3 in A min. (Scottish), Op. 56; (i) A Midsummer night's dream: Overture and incidental music.
❀ (M) *** Decca 466 990-2 [id.]. LSO, Peter Maag, with (i) Vyvyan, Lowe, ROHCG female Ch.

Maag's classic account of the *Scottish Symphony* quite rightly finds itself on the Legends label, for it is indeed memorable, remarkable for its freshness and spontaneity. (At the time of the recording at the beginning of the 1960s, the LSO had not played the work for two decades and their pleasure in Mendelssohn's sympathetic writing can be felt in every bar.) The opening cantilena is poised and very gracious and this sets the mood for what is to follow. A pity that the exposition repeat is not included, and though the final *Maestoso* is measured, the effect remains most compelling, almost Klemperian in manner, with superb horn playing.

The *Midsummer Night's Dream* excerpts date from 1957 and sound equally fresh and the character of the playing is again superb: and whilst Maag's treatment of the *Overture's* forthright second subject strikes the ear as rhythmically mannered, the recording includes a strong contribution from a fruity bass wind instrument, which might possibly be Mendelssohn's ophicleide, but is probably a well-played tuba. The recording is warm and well projected, and this new Legends mastering includes the vocal and choral numbers on the original LP (at the expense of *Fingal's Cave*), but which were not included on the previous reissue. Strongly recommended. A wholly delightful disc.

Symphony No. 4 (Italian), Op. 90.
(B) *** Decca Penguin Classics Dig. 460 643-2

[id.]. San Francisco SO, Blomstedt –
SCHUBERT: *Symphony No. 8 (Unfinished)*. **
(***) Testament mono SBT 1173 [id.]. Philh. O,
Cantelli – BRAHMS: *Symphony No. 3*. (***)

Among the many splendid recorded accounts of the
Italian Symphony, Blomstedt's 1990 recording is
one of the very finest. Not only does he choose
ideal speeds – not too brisk in the exhilarating first
movement, nor sentimental in the slow one – he
conveys a feeling of spontaneity throughout,
springing the rhythms infectiously. The recording
is outstanding, but it is a pity that the original
coupling of an equally fine performance of the *Scottish Symphony* (still available at full price, 433
811-2 and worth it) was replaced with Schubert's
Unfinished, which is considerably less successful.
The personal commentary is by John Guare.

Guido Cantelli, tragically short-lived, recorded
Mendelssohn's *Italian Symphony* twice with the
Philharmonia. His later version of August 1955,
originally published by EMI and long-admired, is
already available on Testament (SBT 1034), but
this 1951 version, the very first recording Cantelli
made with the Philharmonia, was never issued, as
after a row with the orchestra the temperamental
conductor refused to approve it. In fact, as close
comparison reveals, it is even finer than the later
version, a degree more biting and urgent in the
first movement with more light and shade, more
spontaneously expressive in the middle movements,
and clearer and lighter in the *Presto* finale. In first-
rate mono sound it makes a very welcome coupling
for Cantelli's glowing account of the Brahms.

CHAMBER MUSIC

*String quartets: in E flat; Nos. 1 in E flat, Op. 12;
4 in E min., Op. 44/2.*
(BB) *** Naxos Dig. 8.550862 [id.]. Aurora Qt.

*String quartets Nos. 2 in A min., Op. 13; 5 in E
flat, Op. 44/3; Scherzo in A min., Op. 81/2; Theme
and variations in E, Op. 81/1.*
(BB) *** Naxos Dig. 8.550863 [id.]. Aurora Qt.

*String quartets Nos. 3 in D, Op. 44/1; 6 in F min.,
Op. 80; Capriccio in E min., Op. 81/3; Fugue in E
flat, Op. 81/4.*
(BB) *** Naxos Dig. 8.550861 [id.]. Aurora Qt.

At Naxos price, the new Aurora set of Mendelssohn's complete music for string quartet tends to
sweep the board. The performances have a natural
Mendelssohnian charm and elegance, but their
strength and passion acknowledge the fact that the
young composer in his teens wrote them under
the influence of the Beethoven quartets. Indeed, the
account of the *F minor* work, composed after his
sister Fanny's death, is perhaps the highlight of the
set. The allegros are full of passionate angst and the
Adagio expresses the composer's pain.

The engaging early *E flat Quartet* of 1823, with
its confident closing *Fuga*, written when the
composer was only fourteen is included, together
with the four varied pieces of Op. 81 – notably
the delightful *Scherzo in A minor*, here as light as
thistledown. The very opening of the *First quartet*,
Op. 12 is invitingly persuasive and the charming
'fairy' *Canzonetta* which follows is delightfully
crisp and pointed. Slow movements throughout are
beautifully shaped and played with warmth and
feeling, never sentimentalized; scherzi always
sparkle; allegros have vivacity and bite. The
recording is first class, and for those not seeking
period-instrument performance, this is an easy first
choice.

*String quintets Nos. 1 in A, Op. 18; 2 in B flat,
Op. 87.*
*** Sony SK 60766 [id.]. L'Archibudelli.

L'Archibudelli plays these two delightful works
with much elegance and grace, and their lightness
of touch and the transparency of texture characteristic of period instruments is revelatory, especially
in the Scherzo of Op. 87 and the engaging *Andante
scherzando* of Op. 87. The *Adagio e lento* of the
latter work is played with warm expressive feeling.
There are one or two passionate lunges, but these
are fully acceptable as part of the overall period style
and the recording is excellent. Those preferring
modern instruments can turn to the Laredo ensemble, also on Sony (MPK 45883), but these new
versions are undoubtedly very rewarding.

PIANO MUSIC

*Songs without words, Opp. 19/1, 3, 5; 30/2, 4, 6;
38/2, 3, 6; 53/4; 62/2; 67/1–2, 4; 103/5.*
⬤ *** Sony Dig. SK 66511 [id.]. Murray Perahia
  – BACH/BUSONI: *Chorales*. LISZT: *Concert
  paraphrases of Schubert Lieder*. *** ⬤

As his earlier records have so amply demonstrated,
Murray Perahia has a quite unique feeling for Mendelssohn. He invests these pieces with a depth of
poetic feeling that is quite special.

VOCAL MUSIC

Lieder: *Auf Flügeln des Gesanges; Der
Blumenkranz; Der Blumenstrauss; Es weiss und
rät es doch Keiner; Frage; Frühlingsglaube;
Herbstlied; Hexenlied; Ich hör ein Vöglein; Im
Grünen; Morgengruss; Nachlied; Neue Liebe;
Reiselied; Scheidend; Die Sterne scheu'n in stiller
Nacht.*
(B) *** EMI Double fforte CZS5 73836-2 (2).
  Dame Janet Baker, Geoffrey Parsons – LISZT:
  Lieder; SCHUMANN: *Liederkreis, Op. 39*. ***

Mendelssohn's songs, often dismissed as trivial
ballads, bring repeated revelations from Dame
Janet, with Geoffrey Parsons a comparably percep-

tive accompanist. Whether in the airy beauty of the most famous of the songs, *Auf Flügeln des Gesanges* ('On wings of song'), the golden happiness of *Morgengruss*, the darkness of *Reiselied* or the expressive narrative of *Hexenlied*, Dame Janet sings not only with rare intensity and acute sense of detail, but also with an unexpected heightening of expression in tone-colours, beautifully contrasted. Mendelssohn's songs, she tells us, are not just tuneful, they can communicate with the resonance of Schubert Lieder. Well-balanced recording and fair documentation but no texts or translations.

Motets: *Aus tiefer Noth schrei'ich zu dir; 2 Geistliche Choere: Beati mortui; Periti autem, Op. 115; Heilig; Mitten wir im Leben sind, Op. 23.* (i) *3 Motets, Op. 39. 6 Sprüche, Op. 79.*
**(*) Paraclete Press Dig. GDCG 107 [id.]. Gloria Dei Cantores, Elizabeth C. Patterson; (i) with James E. Jordan (org.) – BRAHMS: *Motets.*
**(*)

This excellent choir, based at Cape Cod, Massachusetts, is very much at home in Mendelssohn, and this rewarding repertoire is most persuasively presented and beautifully recorded in the ideal ambience of the Mechanics Hall in Worcester, Massachusetts. They open with a radiant account of the miniature, *Helig* ('Sanctus'), followed by the equally beautiful *Beati mortui* (excellently sung by a male quartet), and the stirring *Periti autem*. Then comes the highly dramatic eight-voiced *Mitten wir im Leben sind mit dem Tod umfangen* ('In the midst of life, we are surrounded by death'). The even more ambitious *Aus tiefer Noth schrei'ich zu dir*, with its beautifully harmonized dominating chorale, again shows the sonority and blend of this fine choir to moving effect. However, it is worth noting that the solo singing somewhat lets the side down, acceptable rather than distinguished, and in the three works for female voices with organ, Op. 39, the soloists (again from the choir) are insecure in *Surrexit pastor bonus*. But this is a relatively small blot on what remain eloquent performances and the six brief *Sprüche* ('Sayings') make a splendid closing group. Mendelssohn uses Lutheran texts and the set was completed in the year before his death, one each for the principal festivals of the church calendar, and sung here in that order. With the reservations noted this remains a most rewarding collection. Full texts and translations are included.

Hymne: Hor mein Bitten, Herr (Hymn of praise); Motets: *Ehre sei Gott in der Höhe; Herr, nun lässest du deinen Diener in Frieden fahren; Mein Gott, warum hast du mich verlassen; Mitten wir im Leben sind; Warum toben die Heiden; 6 Sprüche, Op. 79.*
(B) *** HM Musique d'abord HMA 1901142 [id.]. Paris Chapelle Royale, Collegium Vocale de Ghent, Herreweghe; Johan Huys.

Herreweghe's motet performances are splendidly fresh and vital, bringing out the composer's acknowledged debt to earlier models. *Mitten wir im Leben sind* features antiphonal alternation of male and female choirs and uses a chorale previously used by Bach. The part writing is made admirably clear. Comparison with the recording by Gloria Dei Cantores of the *6 Sprüche*, Op. 79 shows the American choir rather more warmly expressive, but the slight reserve of the Herreweghe performances is enjoyable in a different way. Their account (in German) of the famous *Hymn of praise* is very dramatic, shedding Anglican sentimental associations, with the excellent soloist, Greta de Reyghere, clear and true in the famous 'Oh for the wings of a dove'. The recording is excellent, cleanly focused within a non-blurring ecclesiastical ambience. The documentation is good, but the German texts and the English translations are not placed side by side.

Mercadante, Saverio (1795–1870)

Sinfonia caratteristica; Sinfonia fantastica; La Danza; (i) *Fantasia on Lucia di Lammermoor for cello and orchestra; Fantasia on themes from Rossini's Stabat Mater; Il lamento di Bardo.*
*(*) Warner Fonit Dig. Orchestra Philharmonia Mediterranea, Luigi De Filippi.

The *Sinfonia caratteristica* is delightful, very like a Rossini overture, and almost as tuneful and witty, even if Mercadante can't quite manage an authentic 'crescendo'. The episodic *Sinfonia fantasica* is less remarkable, and *Il lamento di Bardo* is melodramatic, if rather endearingly so. *La Danza* is not nearly as infectious and catchy as Rossini's famous piece, and is rather like second-class ballet music; the two *Fantasias* need bolder advocacy than they receive here: the solo cello in *Lucia di Lammermoor* is wan and low-profiled. The orchestra play well enough and are pleasingly recorded, but only in the first piece does Luigi De Filippi display the kind of flair the programme needs throughout.

Clarinet concertos in B flat; E flat.
(BB) *** ASV Quicksilva Dig. CDQS 6242 [id.]. Joy Farrall, Britten Sinfonia, Nicholas Daniel – DONIZETTI: *Clarinet concertino; Study;* ROSSINI: *Variations in B flat & C.* ***

The Neapolitan composer Saverio Mercadante writes in the galant style of Hummel and these two *Clarinet concertos* are full of pleasing ideas. Indeed, the opening theme of the better-known B flat work is immediately inviting: it is in two movements with an ingenuous Theme and variations forming the second part, providing the soloist plenty of opportunities for sparkling bravura. The three-movement *E flat Concerto* opens with classical formality but its secondary theme is most gracious. The *Andante* is a melancholy aria, and then the sunny finale lifts the spirits. Joy Farrall, with her lilting touch and luscious roulades, plays both works with infectious, light-hearted charm, and Nicholas Daniel and the Britten Sinfonia provide elegant, neatly pointed accompaniments. With first-class recording and equally diverting couplings, this disc is a winner all the way.

Merikanto, Aarre (1893–1958)

(i) Concerto for violin, clarinet, horn and string sextet; (ii) Nonet; (iii) Works for male choir.
**(*) Ondine ODE 703-2 [id.]. (i) Kagan, Brunner, Jolley, Erlich, Oramo, Hirvikangas, Mendelssohn, Sariola, Karttunen, Söderblom; (ii) Ens., Söderblom; (iii) Polytech Ch., Länsiö.

Both the Concerto for violin, clarinet, horn and string sextet and the Nonet come from the mid 1920s, when Merikanto was in his early thirties and in his radical period. The concerto, incidentally, won a competition in 1925, organized by the publisher Schott, and is sometimes known as the 'Schott Concerto'. Its atmosphere is quite heady, not unlike Schreker, Szymanowski or even Honegger, and there is little sense of it being Nordic in feeling.

The Nonet (1926) for flute, cor anglais, clarinet, piano, violins, viola, cello and double bass, inhabits a similar world, and is an evocative piece with occasional reminders of the Ravel of the Mallarmé songs or Aoua from the Chanson madécasses. Good performances, as might be expected from an ensemble including Oleg Kagan, Eduard Brunner and the young Sakari Oramo, but the recording is a trifle hard. The choral pieces are less adventurous in their harmonies except for To the last living being, but often quite haunting. Old Lemminkäinen is a striking piece. Despite less than distinguished recording, this is strongly recommended for the sake of some extraordinary music.

Messiaen, Olivier (1908–92)

(i) Et expecto resurrectionem mortuorum (for wind orchestra and metallic percussion); (ii) Quatuor pour la fin de temps (Quartet for the end of time).
(B) *** Ph. Virtuoso 446 578-2. (i) Concg. O, Haitink; (ii) Beths, Pieterson, Bijlsma, De Leeuw.

Messiaen's Et expecto resurrectionem mortuorum is surprisingly little recorded, but in Haitink's impressive performance with members of the Concertgebouw Orchestra (which we have not heard before) it certainly exerts a hypnotic grip over the listener for much of the time. Its curiously inert yet strongly atmospheric world – as so often with this composer – draws liberally on bird song as a source of inspiration, ranging from Brazil to New Zealand. It makes a generous coupling for a very fine performance of a greater work, Messiaen's visionary Quartet for the end of time, composed during the composer's days in a Silesian prison camp. As in the orchestral piece, the Dutch team are given the benefit of very good recording which has transferred well to CD; moreover their account has the merit of outstanding teamwork, and Reinbert de Leeuw has a keen sense of atmosphere, though he does not dominate the proceedings. There is also some superbly eloquent playing from George Pieterson (clarinet) and Anner Bijlsma (cello). A genuine bargain, with a playing time of 73 minutes.

Vingt régards sur l'Enfant-Jésus.
*** Teldec/Warner Dig 3984 26868-2 (2) [id.].
Pierre-Laurent Aimard (piano).

Pierre-Laurent Aimard has not only received the composer's praise for his 'magnifique technique, sonorité claire et timbrée, et interprétations d'un rare intelligence', but his live performance of the present work at the London Barbican at the time of making this recording also received a eulogy from Alfred Brendel for being 'among the truly exceptional piano recitals in my memory'. Aimard's performance on disc is technically remarkable (although the virtuosity is always at the service of the music) and atmospherically perceptive. Fascinatingly, he is very relaxed at the opening but evocation is in no doubt and the concentration steadily grows and with it the tension. The piano is very well recorded indeed and this can be strongly recommended alongside the classic account of Yvonne Loriod (Erato 4509 96222-2 – see our main volume) and the fine super-bargain version on Naxos by Haakon Austbø, who also has excellent credentials in this repertoire (8.550829/30).

Saint François d'Assise (complete).
*** DG Dig. 445 176-2 (4) [id.]. José van Dam, Dawn Upshaw, John Aler, Tom Krause, Arnold Schoenberg Ch., Hallé O, Kent Nagano.

It was a labour of love over a full eight years, writing this massive four-hour opera. Though the original 1983 production in Paris was recorded and issued on CD, this superb set completely supersedes that. The live recording made in the Felsenreitschule in Salzburg during the 1998 Festival is astonishingly vivid, with voices and orchestra clear and immediate but with ample bloom in the helpful acoustic. The discs actually improve on the live experience not only in the extra clarity, but in the audibility of words, with the libretto an extra help in following the measured progress of a work that tells the story of St Francis in eight tableaux that fight shy of conventional dramatic design, predominantly meditative at measured speeds.

In such a performance as this the result is magnetic, with Nagano (assistant to the composer and Seiji Ozawa for the original production) drawing inspired playing from the Hallé, with José van Dam masterly in the title role, outshining even his own earlier Paris performance, and Dawn Upshaw radiant in the role of the Angel. The rest of the cast is comparably strong. Messiaen himself regarded this as his greatest achievement, a synthesis of what he represented musically and a supreme expression of his Catholic faith. His characteristic use of birdsong here reaches its zenith – aptly so with such a subject – when in his hypnotic patterning he claims to have used every example he had ever notated. It is a work which demands patience from the listener, but this monumental set provides the ideal approach to a unique masterpiece.

Meyer, Edgar (born 1960)

Violin concerto.
*** Sony Dig. SK 89029 [id.]. Hilary Hahn, St Paul CO, Hugh Wolff – BARBER: *Violin concerto.* ***

Edgar Meyer, double-bass virtuoso as well as composer, wrote this *Violin concerto* specially for Hilary Hahn, providing an unusual but apt coupling for the Barber concerto, equally an example of American late romanticism. Unashamedly tonal and freely lyrical, it opens with a yearning folk-like melody that echoes Vaughan Williams, and there is also a folk-like pentatonic cut to some of the writing in both of the two substantial movements. The first is a free set of variations, leading to a virtuoso exercise in using a persistent pedal note, while avoiding monotony. The movement in clearly defined sections easily erupts at times into a rustic dance, and ends on a dazzling coda. Hahn plays with passionate commitment, amply justifying her choice of coupling.

Mielck, Ernst (1877–99)

Symphony in F minor, Op. 4; (i) *Concert piece in E minor for piano and orchestra, Op. 9.*
** Sterling CDS 1035-2 [id.]. (i) Liisa Pohjola; Turku PO, Hannu Lintu.

Ernst Mielck's *Symphony*, Op. 4, preceded Sibelius's *First* by two years and its success is said to have acted as a spur to that great composer to complete his own. Born in Viborg (or Viipuri) Mielck studied with Max Bruch in the mid 1890s but tragically succumbed to tuberculosis only two days short of his twenty-second birthday. Kajanus conducted the *Symphony*'s première in 1897, when the composer was still nineteen (Mielck played the Grieg *Concerto* in the same programme). It was subsequently given in both Dresden and Berlin

under Armas Järnefelt (and Nikisch expressed an interest in it) but Kajanus never took it into his permanent repertory. It is a four-movement work, some 40 minutes in length. Although it begins promisingly, neither of its main ideas can lay claim to any strong personality, though there is a genuine sense of form. The finale, too, has a sense of symphonic momentum, and there are some effective touches of orchestral colour. Probably the best movement is the lyrical and endearing slow movement. By and large it offers promise rather than fulfilment. The Turku Orchestra under Hannu Lintu plays decently. The *Concert piece*, Op. 9 is rather dreadful, though the central *Largo* has some poetic writing. A valuable release which will be of interest to Sibelians in deepening their historical perspective about his background, but Mielck is no Arriaga.

Monteverdi, Claudio (1567–1643)

Madrigals, Book 8: *Madrigali guerri et amorosi:* Volume I: *Sinfonia: Altri canti d'Amor; Lamento della Ninfa; Vago augelletto; Perchè t'en fuggi, o Fillide?; Altri canti di Marte; Due belli occhi fur l'ami; Ogni amante è guerrier; Hor che'l ciel e la terra; Gira il nemico, insidioso Amore; Dolcissimo usignolo; Ardo, ardo avvampo.*
*** Opus 111 Dig. OPS 30-187 [id.]. Concerto Italiano, Rinaldo Alessandri.

Rinaldo Alessandri and his Concerto Italiano here continue their superlative series of recordings of Monteverdi's madrigals with the first part of Book 8, *Madrigals of war and love*. As before, the singing combines Italianate fire and lyricism in ideal proportions and the instrumental accompaniments could hardly be finer. The present disc includes famous items like the three-part *Lamento della Ninfa* and the two-part *Hor che'l ciel e la terra*. The recording too is first class.

Madrigals, Book 8: Volume I: (i) *Il combattimento di Tancredi e Clorinda;* (ii) *Il ballo delle ingrate.*
*** Opus 111 Dig. OPS 30-196 [id.]. (i) Elisa Franzetti, Gianluca Ferrarini, Roberto Abbondanza; (ii) Francesca Ermolli, Rosa Dominguez, Daniele Carnovich, Elisa Franzetti, Concerto Italiano, Alessandrini.

There is no more commandingly dramatic account of *Il combattimento* on record than this dramatic Italianate version with superb singing from all three principals. Roberto Abbondanza is a splendidly histrionic narrator and in the death scene Elisa Franzetti, singing her farewell, is exquisitely moving.

Franzetti returns at the end of *Il ballo delle ingrate* to eloquently bid adieu on behalf of the ungrateful souls, condemned for rebelling against earthly love, to be echoed by Monteverdi's infinitely poignant closing chorus from her companions. The performance overall is cast from strength. Daniele

Carnovich is a true basso profundo (as we know from his contribution to the disc above) and makes a superb Pluto, but Francesca Ermolli and Rosa Dominguez are equally fine as Amor and Venus, respectively. The vivid recording is warmly atmospheric

Motets: (i) *Adoramus te, Christe; Cantate Domino; Domine, neinfurore tuo;* (ii; iii) *Exulta filia Sion;* (iv; i) *Exultent caeli;* (v; vi) *Laudate pueri Dominum I;* (ii; iii) *Laudate Dominum II;* (viii) *Laudate Dominum III;* (ix) *Magnificat* (1610); (x) *Messa da capella* (1640); *Messa da capella* (1650); (ii; iii) *Salve, o Regina;* (vii; iii) *Salve Regina; Sancta Maria;* (v; vi) *Ut queant laxis.*
(B) **(*) Decca Double 458 829-2 (2). (i) Monteverdi Ch., Gardiner; (ii) Nigel Rogers; (iii) AAM, Hogwood; (iv) John Messana, Martyn Hill, Philip Jones Brass Ens.; (v) Michael Turner, Benjamin Odom; (vi) ASMF Strings, Guest; (vii) Emma Kirkby, Judith Nelson; (viii) Simon Cooper, Stuart Leask, Magdalen College, Oxford, Ch., Rose; (ix) London Carmelite Priory Ch., Malcolm; (x) St John's College, Cambridge, Ch., Guest.

This is an ingeniously gathered Monteverdi miscellany rather than a planned collection. The chosen *Magnificat* is part of the 1610 *Vespers*, but is the less elaborate version for six voices and organ. The refreshing performance by George Malcolm's Carmelite Priory Choir is excellent in every way. The four-part *Mass* from 1640 is full of remarkable passages in which the metre undergoes sudden changes and the harmony becomes expressive in an almost secular style. In both this and the later work, which is less innovatory, the part-writing comes over with eminent clarity. The singing under George Guest is extremely good, though the trebles (Michael Turner and Benjamin Odom) have a 'fluting' quality that is heard more effectively in the first, string-accompanied *Laudate pueri Dominum* (for six voices) and the *Ut queant laxis* (a hymn for St John the Baptist). Nigel Rogers is strong in the solo *Laudate Dominum*, and another excellent pair of trebles (Simon Cooper and Stuart Leask) are suitably angelic in the third version, with contrasting sonorities from the Magdalen College Choir, plus sonorous brass. Following on agreeably, the combination of the voices of Emma Kirkby and Judith Nelson is a highlight in the Elysian *Salve Regina* and *Sancta Maria*.

Closing the collection, Gardiner's performances of the motets *Adoramus te, Christe, Cantate Domino* and *Domine, ne in furore tuo*, which also come from the *Selva morale et spirituale*, are also marked by excellent singing with firm tone and intonation. Dynamics and tempi are rather extreme, but there is no doubt that the music comes fully to life. In the *Exultent caeli* ('Let the heavens rejoice'),

which ends the concert, the gentle central verses, which are concerned with the Virgin Mary and the conception of Jesus, are effectively framed by a jubilant opening and conclusion, where the singers are joined by the Philip Jones Brass Ensemble. The recording throughout is admirable, full translations are included, and there are adequate notes.

'Pianato della Madonna': Motets for solo voice: *Confitebor tibi Domini (Missa a 4 voci e salmi,* 1650). *Currite populi; Ecce sacrum paratum; O quam pulchra es (Ghirlanda sacra,* 1645). *Exulta, Filia Sion (Sacri canti,* 1629); *Jubilet a voce sola in dialogo; Lamento dell'Arianna: Pianato della Madonna; Laudate Dominum* (all from *Selva Morale e Spirituale,* 1640). *Salve, O Regina (Sacre canti,* 1624); *Venite, videte* (1625).
❀ *** HM Dig. HMC 901680 [id.]. Maria Cristina Kiehr, Concerto Soava, Jean-Marc Aymes (with Bianco MARINI: 2 *Sinfonias* (from *Church sonatas*). Costanto ATEGNATI: *Ricercar.* Claudio MERULO: *Toccata con minute ***).

Maria Cristina Kiehr has already provided a cherishable collection of motets by Monteverdi's remarkably talented female contemporary, Barbara Strozzi, pupil of Cavalli, to which we gave a ❀ in our main volume (ED 13048). This new compilation of music by an even greater composer is more beautiful still, and once again the vocal items are contrasted with short instrumental ritornellos by other musicians from the same period. We cannot praise this recital too highly. Every work is glorious and is ravishingly sung.

At the very opening of *Confitebor tibi Domine,* Maria Cristina catches the listener in her spell, and its close brings an enchanting cadential turn, echoed by the accompanying violins. *Currite populi* introduces a lovely flowing *Alleluia; O quam pulchra es* ('How fair thou art, my love') is permeated with an exquisite melancholy, which returns in several later items, and especially the famous excerpt from the *Lamento dell'Arianna* which give the CD its title.

The fresh, spring-like *Jubilet* has a delightful echo effect, with a nice touch of added resonance, and *Exulta, Filia Sion* is another joyful song, with florid runs and a jubilant closing *Alleluia.* The closing *Laudate Dominum* makes a wonderful apotheosis, with alleluias and echoing phrases adding to its paean of praise. Superb music, superb singing and playing, and warmly atmospheric recording all here combine to bring the listener the very greatest musical rewards.

Vespro della Beata Vergine (Vespers); Selva morale e spirituale: Beatus vir; Confitebor tibi Domine; Dixit Dominus; Laudate pueri; Laudate Dominum; Salve Regina.
(BB) *** Virgin Veritas 2 x 1 Dig. VBD5 61662-2

(2) [CDVB 61662]. Kirkby, Rogers, Thomas, Taverner Ch., Cons. and Players, Parrott.

Although Parrott uses minimal forces, with generally one instrument and one voice per part, so putting the work on a chamber scale in a small church setting, its grandeur comes out superbly through its very intensity. Far more than usual with antiphons in Gregorian chant it becomes a liturgical celebration, so that the five non-liturgical compositions or concerti are added to the main Vespers setting as a rich glorification. They are brilliantly sung here by the virtuoso soloists, above all by Nigel Rogers, whose distinctive timbre may not suit every ear but who has an airy precision and flexibility to give expressive meaning to even the most taxing passages. With fine all round singing and playing, and a warm atmospheric recording which, despite an ecclesiastical ambience, allows ample detail through, this set is recommended. The other items, from the *Selva morale e spirituale,* are not quite so impressive – this singing is a bit bloodless – but are fully acceptable as a bonus. There are no texts or translations and minimal notes, but this is very inexpensive.

OPERA

L'Incoronazione di Poppea (complete).
(M) *** Virgin Veritas Dig. VCT5 61783-2 (3).
  Arleen Augér, Della Jones, Linda Hirst, James Bowman, City of L. Bar. Sinfonia, Hickox.

On Virgin, the tender expressiveness of Arleen Augér in the title role of Monteverdi's elusive masterpiece combines with a performance from Richard Hickox and the City of London Baroque Sinfonia which consistently reflects the fact that it was recorded in conjunction with a stage production in 1988. Hickox daringly uses a very spare accompaniment of continuo instruments, contrasting with the previous period performance on record by Nikolaus Harnoncourt and the Concentus Musicus of Vienna, who had a far wider, more abrasive range of instrumental sound.

Hickox overcomes the problems of that self-imposed limitation by choosing the widest possible range of speeds. So the exuberant Nero–Lucan duet after the death of Seneca is very fast and brilliant, while the heavenly final duet of the lovers – apparently not by Monteverdi at all – is extremely slow, rapt and gentle. The purity of Augér's soprano may make Poppea less of a scheming seducer than she should be, but it is Monteverdi's music for the heroine which makes her so sympathetic in this oddly slanted, equivocal picture of Roman history, and one that has seldom sounded subtler or more lovely on record than this.

Taking the castrato role of Nero, Della Jones sings very convincingly with full, rather boyish tone while Gregory Reinart is magnificent in the bass

role of Seneca. James Bowman is a fine Ottone, with smaller parts taken by such excellent singers as Catherine Denley, John Graham-Hall, Mark Tucker and Janice Watson. Linda Hirst sounds too raw of tone for Ottavia, making her a scold rather than a sympathetic suffering widow. Fitted onto three well-filled mid-priced CDs the opera comes with libretto and translation.

(i) *L'Incoronazione di Poppea* (abridged version, realized by Raymond Leppard); (ii) Madrigals: *Al lume delle stelle; A quest'olmo; Cor mio, mentre vi miro; Io mi son giovinetta; Lamento d'Arianna; Ohimé se tanto amaie; Volgendo il ciel* (ballo).
(B) **(*) EMI Double fforte CZS5 73842-2 (2). (i) Magda László, Frances Bible, Richard Lewis, Oralia Dominguez, Lydia Marimpietri, Carlo Cava, Walter Alberti, Hugues Cuénod, Glyndebourne Fest. Ch., RPO, Pritchard; (ii) April Cantelo, Eileen Poulter, Helen Watts, Gerald English, Robert Tear, Christopher Keyte, ECO, Leppard.

It was a bold move of Sir John Pritchard to introduce Monteverdi to Glyndebourne early in the 1960s, winning instant success. When it was first issued, Pritchard's abridged version of *L'Incoronazione di Poppea* was an important milestone in the history of Monteverdi on record. It was the first of his operas to be recorded in stereo (apart from a Vox set which could not measure up to it in standards of performance) and was also the first to show a real feeling for style as opposed to the more academic manifestations, including plentiful use of old and supposedly authentic instruments.

However, today Raymond Leppard's edition of this equivocal masterpiece will probably shock baroque purists with sounds that are sumptuous rather than spare, while he makes use of two harpsichords, two organs, two cellos, lute, guitar and harp for the continuo group – a most generous array of instruments which certainly serve to colour the score in the best baroque manner.

Even in this cut version, the honeyed warmth of the production comes over vividly with Magda László and Richard Lewis fresh and dramatic. The bass, Carlo Cava, is a weighty Seneca, fully conveying the character of the noble and revered philosopher and statesman whose tragic suicide in this edition rounds off Act I. Throughout, his excellent low register never loses its flexibility.

Nero's comic duet of rejoicing (with the unique Hugues Cuénod as Lewis's brilliant partner) could hardly be bettered as a musical picture of inebriation (hiccups and all), and this then sets the contrasted tone of Act II, leading to Nero and Poppea's ecstatic final duet. Frances Bible as Ottavia, and Walter Alberti as Ottone portray the cast-off wife and lover with admirable skill. Vocally superior to these are Lydia Marimpietri, whose Drusilla is a marvel of characterization, and Orelia Dominguez, who plays the difficult and exacting role of Poppea's nurse and confidante.

John Pritchard coaxes from the Royal Philharmonic Orchestra a truly Monteverdian sound, and the Glyndebourne Chorus makes brief but significant contributions, notably in the scene of Seneca's farewell. The stars of the piece, Richard Lewis and Magda László are on top of their form and their final love duet comes as a magnificent end to a great opera. The recording is remarkably opulent.

This timely bargain issue is well supplemented by a collection of madrigals, recorded three years later with an entirely different cast. The singers here are all fine artists in their own right, but the choice of a group of soloists for this repertoire proves not to be the best way of ensuring a good blend between the parts, with individual voices tending to stick out at times from the overall texture.

Fortunately the key item, the beautiful *Lament of Arianna* heard in its full ensemble version is successful and this comes as the final item. In general, it is the gentle music which comes off best; when the part writing is more complex the sound is less comfortable. However the performances certainly do not lack character and there are no complaints about the recording itself. In the opera no texts are given, but a detailed synopsis is related to the CD tracks, without however giving the Italian titles of each arias or excerpt, which are listed separately. There are no texts and translations for the madrigals.

Moscheles, Ignaz (1794–1870)

Piano concertos Nos. 2 in E flat, Op. 56; 4 in E, Op. 64.
*** Zephyr Dig. Z 116-99 [id.]. Ian Hobson, Sinfonia da Camera.

Vox introduced us to Moscheles on LP with his best-known *G minor Concerto* back in the 1970s. A friend and contemporary of Beethoven, he was born in Prague, but spent part of his later career in London. He was a well-liked man, and the character of his music comes over in both these concertos, with their debt to Hummel but with a clear anticipation of Chopin's concertos in the passage work. The *E flat Concerto* opens with the timpani setting the mood for an imposing march, with a Hummelian dotted rhythm, and they later set off the jolly *Polonaise* of the finale. (Moscheles at the time doubted the wisdom of this scoring, for apparently early nineteenth-century timpanists had problems getting the passage correctly tuned.) The E major work has a more expansively ambitious opening tutti, and its slow movement centres on a romantic horn solo. The horns then announce the closing set of bold variations on 'The British Grenadiers' which gives Ian Hobson plenty of opportunities for glittering bravura. He plays spiritedly throughout both works,

yet obviously relishes their galant lyricism, while effectively directing the accompaniments from the keyboard. The recording is truthful and well balanced, and altogether this is a most enjoyable coupling.

Mozart, Wolfgang Amadeus
(1756–91)

(i) *Bassoon concerto in B flat, K.191;* (ii) *Clarinet concerto in A, K.622;* (iii) *Flute concerto in G, K.313.*
(M) *** DG 457 719-2 [id.]. VPO, Karl Boehm; with (i) Dietmar Zeman; (ii) Alfred Prinz; (iii) Werner Tripp.

These are meltingly beautiful accounts. All three soloists perform with the utmost distinction under Boehm, who lets the music unfold in an unforced way: relaxed yet vital. Excellent mid 1970s sound makes this a highly recommendable DG Originals disc.

(i; ii) *Bassoon concerto in B flat, K.191;* (iii; iv) *Clarinet concerto in A, K.622;* (v) *Flute concerto No. 1 in G, K.313;* (vi; iv) *Horn concertos Nos. 1– 4, K.412, K.417, K.447 & K.495;* (vii; ii) *Oboe concerto in C, K.314.*
(B) *** Decca Double Dig./Analogue 466 247-2 (2) [id.]. (i) David McGill; (ii) Cleveland O, Dohnányi; (iii) Gervase de Peyer; (iv) LSO, Peter Maag; (v) William Bennett, ECO, Malcolm; (vi) Barry Tuckwell; (vii) John Mack.

These recordings readily demonstrate the ongoing excellence of the Decca coverage of the Mozart wind concertos over three decades. Peter Maag and the LSO provided elegant, very stylish accompaniments in 1959 and 1960 for the works for clarinet and horn. The orchestral crispness gives an attractive buoyancy to allegros, and the clean, leonine violin timbre, with a touch of thinness, fits in well with today's ideas of what an eighteenth-century string section would have sounded like. Gervase de Peyer is admirable in the *Clarinet concerto* and his account remains as fine as any available, fluent and lively, with masterly phrasing in the slow movement and a vivacious finale. Tuckwell at the time was proving a natural inheritor of the mantle of Dennis Brain. His easy technique, smooth, warm tone and obvious musicianship command allegiance and give immediate pleasure. William Bennett a decade later, but again in the Kingsway Hall, is hardly less impressive in the *G major Flute concerto*. Every phrase is shaped with both taste and affection and the playing of the ECO under George Malcolm is fresh and vital. Throughout, the recording is clean and well detailed, with enough resonance to add bloom to the sound. The CD transfers are immaculate.

For the *Bassoon* and *Oboe concertos* we turn to Cleveland and a digital recording made as recently as 1992. The oboist, John Mack, has an appealingly sweet (but not too sweet) timbre; he plays most stylishly and his sprightly closing Rondo is a delight. Then David McGill, in the work for bassoon, immediately establishes his keen individuality, matching the high polish of his colleague, and readily assuming the central role ahead of the conductor. He does not overdo the humour in the finale. Both performances are beautifully recorded and attractively balanced. All-in-all very enjoyable music-making by musicians from both sides of the Atlantic who are equally at one with Mozart.

Clarinet concerto in A, K.622
*** DG 457 652-2 [id.]. Michael Collins, Russian Nat. O, Pletnev – BEETHOVEN: *Clarinet (Violin) concerto in D, Op. 61* ***.
*** EMI Dig. CDC5 56832-2 [id.]. Sabine Meyer, Berlin PO, Abbado – DEBUSSY: *Première rapsodie*; TAKEMITSU: *Fantasma/cantos*. ***

Though Michael Collins, leading British clarinettist of his generation, delayed recording this supreme masterpiece of the genre, he has here provided the weightiest, most challenging, if controversial, coupling in Mikhail Pletnev's arrangement for clarinet of the Beethoven *Violin concerto*. The result is a masterly disc in which Collins offers one of the finest versions of the Mozart ever. Like his teacher, Thea King, Collins uses a basset clarinet in that masterpiece, relishing the extra downward range and richness of timbre.

Otherwise he provides a fascinating contrast with Thea King on her Hyperion disc. Collins's speeds in the outer movements are markedly faster than King's, wonderfully agile with the cleanest articulation and crisp rhythmic pointing as well as fine detail. It is a reading not just elegant but powerful too, as well as deeply poetic in the slow movement. There Collins comes closest to King, fining down his tone to the gentlest pianissimo on the reprise of the main theme. The playing of the Russian National Orchestra under Pletnev is refined and elegant to match.

Sabine Meyer here appears as soloist with the very orchestra which refused to accept her as Karajan's nominee for the post of first clarinet, and she proves a natural soloist rather than an orchestral player. This 1998 performance brings out how much her individual artistry has intensified even in the ten years between this and her first recording of this greatest of clarinet works, also for EMI (CDM5 66897-2, where she chose to use the basset clarinet – see our main volume). She again opts for speeds faster than usual, but finds time to point phrasing and shade dynamics in more detail and with sharper contrasts, always with keen imagination and a feeling of spontaneity. As before, where appropriate, she adds cadenza-like flourishes, as in the

honeyed lead-back to the reprise in the central *Largo*. Though this new version is preferable to the old, with lighter accompaniment and more transparent sound, not everyone will want the less apt coupling, even though Meyer is at her most magical both in Debussy and in Takemitsu.

(i) *Flute and harp concerto in C, K.299;* Symphony No. 27 in G, K.199; Divertimento No. 2 in D, K.131 (with Minuet from No. 15 in B flat). Overture: Die Zauberflöte.
(M) (***) Dutton Lab. mono CDLX 7037 [id.]. RPO, Sir Thomas Beecham; (i) with Le Roy, Lily Laskine.

Like other Dutton issues of Beecham, this one offers recordings from an interim period of his career which has been sadly neglected. It is astonishing that this recording of the early *Symphony No. 27*, the first ever, was only issued by RCA on 78 in the United States and never in Britain. It is a typically elegant performance, leading to a delightfully care-free account of the *Presto* finale. The *flute and harp concerto*, featuring two outstanding French soloists (the harpist, Lily Laskine, had earlier played in Piero Coppola's pioneering version of 1931), also brings uncontroversial tempi, with the slow movement warmly romantic but flowing more freely than many modern performances. Sadly, the recording of the orchestra is dimmer than in the other items here, though the two soloists are both well defined. The early *Divertimento*, deliciously pointed, brings a textual oddity. In place of one of the Minuets Beecham substitutes a Minuet from a later *Divertimento* in a different key.

Flute concerto No. 1 in G, K.331; Andante in C, K. 315; (i) *Flute and harp concerto in C, K.299.*
(B) *** Ph. Virtuoso 420 880-2 [id.]. Claude Monteux; (i) Osian Ellis; ASMF, Marriner.

First published in the early 1970s, these Philips performances with Claude Monteux as the principal soloist, have regularly popped in and out of the catalogue over the years. Now they reappear on the bargain Virtuoso label. Exquisite playing from all concerned. The solo instruments sound larger than life as balanced, but in every other respect this splendidly remastered disc is highly recommendable.

Flute concertos Nos. 1–2; Andante in C, K.315; Rondo in D, K.Anh184; (i) Flute and harp concerto, K.299.
(B) *(*) Sony SB2K 60381 (2) [id.]. Frans Vester, Amsterdam Mozart-Ens., Brüggen; (i) with Edward Witsenberg.

These 1971 recordings were among the first 'authentic performances' to be put on LP. They are musical accounts, with Frans Vester an understanding flute soloist, but the playing – especially of the orchestra – has neither the beauty of tone nor the refinement that is expected today. The two CDs play for just under 90 minutes, which surely must be one of the shortest playing times of any double CD.

(i; ii) *Flute concertos Nos. 1 in G; 2 in D, K.313–14; (i–iii) Flute and harp concerto in C, K. 29; (iv) Divertimento for strings No. 1 in D, K.136; 2 Marches, K.335; Serenades Nos. 6 in D (Serenata notturna), K.239; 9 in D (Posthorn), K.320; (v) Symphonies Nos. 35 (Haffner); 36 (Linz); 38 (Prague); 39 in E flat, K.543; 40 in G min., K.550; 41 in C (Jupiter).*

✿ (BB) *** Virgin Classics 5 x 1 Dig. VBD5 61678-2 (5). (i) Samuel Coles, (ii) ECO; (iii) Naoko Yoshino; (iv) Lausanne CO; (v) Sinfonia Varviso; Menuhin.

In many ways this is the outstanding Mozartean CD bargain of all time – five discs for the price of one. Moreover the set would be highly desirable if it cost several times as much. Both the flute concertos are stylishly and pleasingly played by Samuel Coles and when Naoko Yoshino joins him in the delectable *Flute and harp concerto* the interplay is fluently appealing. Menuhin directs the orchestra very precisely in the opening movement of this work; his is a firmly classical view of Mozart, but the *Andantino* is warm and flexible and the finale gay and sprightly. No complaints about the sound either and there is no doubting the character of these performances. The *Serenata notturna* and the *Divertimento* (the first and most winning of the so-called 'Salzburg Symphonies') are graceful and fresh, and so is the *Posthorn Serenade*. Menuhin's approach is above all elegantly light-hearted, and the central movements, especially the *Concertante*, bring some delightful wind playing, with the string phrasing just as persuasive in the *Andantino*. Crispian Steele-Perkins, too, has his brief moment of glory as the posthorn soloist in the Minuet.

Yet when we turn to the six last symphonies we encounter playing and interpretations of a very special order. The Sinfonia Varviso, consisting of players drawn from a range of Polish orchestras, responds warmly to Menuhin as the group's chosen President. Though modern instruments are used, the scale is intimate with textures beautifully clear, and the fresh, immediate sound highlights the refined purity of the string playing. In Nos. 35 and 36 there is elegance and charm as well as energy in outer movements and in the slow movements Menuhin moulds the phrasing with Beechamesque magic, yet never adopts excessively slow speeds or over-romantic manners.

It may then come as a surprise to find that (as in the *Flute and harp concerto*) he becomes a complete classicist in the remaining four symphonies. Speeds are on the fast side, yet he does not sound at all rushed. He treats the third-movement trio of No. 39 as a brisk Ländler, almost hurdy-gurdy like,

refusing – after consultation with the autograph – to allow a rallentando at the end. Otherwise his only other oddity is the omission of the exposition repeat in the first movement, when as a rule he is generous with repeats.

If anything the accounts of Nos. 40 and 41 are even more refreshing, with the *G minor* especially memorable – among the finest ever recorded. With speeds again on the fast side and playing of precision, clarity and bite, one constantly has the feeling of live music-making. Exposition repeats are observed in both first and last movements of the *Jupiter* and this performance, like its partner, takes its place alongside Bernstein's electrifying versions as a joint top recommendation for the two last symphonies, irrespective of cost. The five discs come in a pair of boxes (with accompanying booklet), in a slipcase, and are surely an essential purchase, even if some duplication is involved.

Horn concertos Nos. 1 in D, K.412 (including Rondo in D, K.514, completed Süssmayr); 2–4 in E flat, K.417, K.447 & K.495; Concert rondos in E flat, K.371; in D (alternative finale to K.412, completed John Humphries).
*** Hänssler Dig. 98.316 [id.]. Timothy Brown, ASMF, Iona Brown.

Horn concertos Nos. 1 in D, K.412; 2–4 in E flat, K.417, K.447 & K. 495; Concert rondo in E flat, K.371; Fragments: in E, KAnh.98a; in E flat, K.370b; in D, K.524 (all ed. Tuckwell).
(M) *** Decca Dig. 458 607-2 [id.]. Barry Tuckwell, ECO.

Timothy Brown has already recorded the four regular concertos and the *Concert rondo*, K.371, plus the incomplete *Fragment*, K.494a, on a hand-horn for Virgin Classics and very good they are too. The only snag is that they are now offered on a Virgin Double, not very appropriately coupled with some of Mozart's concert arias (VBD5 61573-2). This time Brown chooses a modern instrument, and the latest set is very beautiful indeed. His timbre, although rich in colour, is not too broad, and once again his persuasive lyrical line, imaginative phrasing and neat use of cadenzas shows him as a true Mozartean. Another of the memorable features of this fine Hänssler disc is the warmth and finesse of Iona Brown's stylish accompaniments, always light of touch, refined in dynamic contrast, and ever graceful. The recording too is most natural in balance and sound quality, and this CD stands high among modern versions of these ever-fresh concertos. However, there remains strong competition from Michael Thompson's splendid and inexpensive Naxos collection, which includes also the *Fragment*, K.370b, reconstructed by Humphries (8.553592), while the Oiseau-Lyre performances by Anthony Halstead, using an eighteenth-century hand-horn, are very special indeed (⊕ O-L 443 216-2 – see our main volume).

The Decca Ovation reissue offers Barry Tuckwell's third set of the four concertos in excellent digital sound, recorded in the Henry Wood Hall in 1983. He plays as well as ever and also directs the accompanying ECO, ensuring that the string phrasing echoes the horn in every detail. The orchestra provides crisp, polished and elegant accompaniments to make a perfectly scaled backcloth for full-timbred solo playing which again combines natural high spirits with a warmly expressive understanding of the Mozartean musical line. Unlike the earlier full-priced CD, this reissue now includes the rest of Mozart's concertante horn music. Added to the *Rondo, K.371* are three fragments which Tuckwell presents as Mozart left them, but edited for concert performance, and this disc is now better value than Tuckwell's later Collins CD, which contains less music (1153-2).

Piano concertos Nos. 5–6, 8–9, 11–27; (i)
Double piano concerto, K.365; (i; ii) *Triple piano concerto, K.242. Concert rondos Nos. 1–2.*
(B) *** DG Dig. 463 111-2 (9) [id.]. Malcolm
    Bilson (fortepiano), E. Bar. Soloists, Gardiner;
    with (i) Robert Levin; (ii) Melvyn Tan.

Malcolm Bilson's complete set of the piano concertos now appears in DG's Collector's Edition at bargain price, well documented. Bilson is an artist of excellent musical judgement and good taste and his survey is still the only one at present available on the fortepiano. The overall musical standard is very high, and the concentration and vitality of the music-making is very compelling – especially so in Nos. 20 in D minor and 21 in C (K.466–7) which received a ⊕ for their separate issue (see our main volume).

Piano concertos Nos. 5 in D, K.175; 6 in B flat, K.238; 8 in C, K.246.
***Teldec/Warner Dig. 3984 21483-2 [id.].
    Daniel Barenboim, BPO.

Barenboim continues his current Mozart cycle with the Berlin Philharmonic with these three early concertos. They sound very fresh and the orchestral sonority is pleasingly well nourished. The recording is full-blooded, a bit forward but not excessively so, and the whole disc radiates pleasure.

Piano concertos Nos. 5 in D, K.175/382 (1782 version); 14 in E flat, K.449; 16 in D, K.451.
*** O-L Dig. 458 285-2 [id.]. Levin, AAM,
    Hogwood.

In this seventh issue in an ongoing series, the unusual point is that Levin and Hogwood have preferred the final version of K.175 to the one usually recorded. In this, the *Rondo, K.382,* written some nine years after the first version appeared in 1773,

replaces the original finale. It is certainly a colourful, lively piece, but so is the original at half the length, which is stylistically more consistent. This version is different also in that Mozart reworked the wind parts of the first two movements. Compared with Malcolm Bilson's versions in his concerto cycle with John Eliot Gardiner and the English Baroque Soloists, the striking contrast is between the sound of the fortepianos in each. Where Bilson's instrument is unmistakably a piano, the tinkly top of Levin's evidently smaller fortepiano gives one constant reminders of the harpsichord. Maybe as a result Levin tends to favour speeds a fraction faster than Bilson's. Anyone following the Levin series will not be disappointed, and his own improvised cadenzas add to the freshness.

Piano concertos Nos. 9 in E flat, K.271; 12 in A, K.414; 21 in C, K.467; 27 in B flat, K.595.
(BB) **(*) Royal Long Players DCL 70572-2 (2).
    Christoph Eschenbach, LPO.

Christoph Eschenbach, directing Mozart from the keyboard, secures a good sense of movement and line, and the orchestral playing is taut and lively. Perhaps these readings lack the ultimate sparkle that Barenboim, Perahia, Kovacevich and Brendel have achieved over recent years; yet the *A major,* K.414 is particularly felicitous here, and in this lowest possible price range they are all still to be reckoned with. The recording is well balanced and natural and anyone wanting this particular group of concertos will surely not be disappointed. He plays Mozart's cadenzas except in K.467 where he uses his own.

Piano concerto No. 9 in E flat, K.271; 25 in C, K.503.
*** Nonesuch/Warner Dig. 7559 79454-2 [id.].
    Richard Goode, Orpheus CO.

Richard Goode, having given us an outstanding set of the Beethoven sonatas is now embarking on a Mozart concerto series, like Murray Perahia before him, working with a first-class, modern-instrument chamber orchestra. However in this instance, as the Orpheus group plays without a conductor, one assumes that the pianist is not directing the accompaniments from the keyboard. Whether or not this is so, they are consistently at one with him in matters of phrasing and style, and they immediately establish the boldly expansive character of the great *C major Concerto,* K.503. Similarly, their gentle but gravely intense opening of the slow movement of K.271 invites a response from the pianist which is refreshing in its directness and subtlety of dynamic nuance, followed by a delightful lightness of articulation in the brisk finale. These are performances of much character, beautifully recorded. Mozart's cadenzas are used in K.271 but Goode uses his own in K.503.

Piano concerto No.12 in A, K.414.
(M) (**(*)) Decca mono 458 869-2. Aldeburgh
   Fest. O., Britten – HAYDN: *Symphonies Nos 45
   (Farewell); 55 (Schoolmaster)* (**(*)).

Decca's 'Britten in Aldeburgh' series is generally
devoted to BBC radio recordings, but this one of
K.414, as well as the two Haydn symphonies with
which it is coupled, was a live recording made by
Decca at the Festival in 1956, exceptional at a
time when studio recordings were the rule. It is a
winningly spontaneous performance, with Britten
as a light, sparkling soloist leading his players on at
challengingly fast speeds in the outer movements,
pressing ahead of the beat. The central slow movement similarly reveals Britten's magnetism as a
pianist, warmly expressive at a slow tempo. Close,
dry mono recording gives violins an acid edge, but
the concentration of the performance makes one
forget the sound.

*Piano concertos No. 12 in A, K.414; 14 in E flat
K.449; Rondo in D, K.382.*
(BB) **(*) Arte Nova Dig. 74321 72117-2 [id.].
   Matthias Kirschnereit, Bamberg SO, Frank
   Bermann.

The Westphalian pianist Matthias Kirschnereit is a
new name to us but, having won various prizes, he
already has a considerable reputation in his homeland. He has close links with the Bamberg Symphony Orchestra with whom he is to record all
Mozart's concertos for Arte Nova.

   This first disc makes an auspicious start. It opens
with an engagingly fresh account of the well-known
D major Rondo and follows with a warm and cultivated account of K.414, to which Frank Bermann's
elegant and supportive accompaniment makes a
very considerable contribution. K.449 is characterful and enjoyable too, though it is less individual
than Barenboim's version. Mozart's cadenzas are
used throughout. The recording is very good, the
balance realistic, and this is excellent value.

*Piano concertos Nos. 14 in E flat, K.449; 15 in B
flat, K.450; 16 in D, K.451.*
✪ *** Teldec/Warner Dig. 0630 16827-2 [id.].
   Daniel Barenboim, BPO.

These three delightful concertos were all composed
within a few weeks of each other (beginning in
February 1784) and they show Barenboim in his
very finest Mozartean style, both at the keyboard
and in directing the Berlin Philharmonic. Their contribution in opening movements is imposing without
being too heavy, and they bring much grace to *Andantes*. Finales are no less engaging: witness the string
playing at the opening of the superb Rondo of K.449.
The *B flat concerto* is a live performance, but the
others are by no means studio-bound. Barenboim's
keyboard articulation is a constant joy, as is his pearly
tone, but it is the joyous spontaneity of the music-
making that makes this triptych so cherishable.

*Piano concertos Nos. 20 in D min., K.466; 24 in C
min., K.491.*
*** Ph. Dig. 462 622-2 [id.]. Alfred Brendel,
   SCO, Mackerras.

Brendel recorded this coupling with Neville Marriner in 1974 and now, more than a quarter of a
century later, gives accounts that are hardly less
thoughtful without being wanting in spontaneity.
Although his basic approach has not undergone any
profound change, his playing is if anything more
searching and articulate without being touched by
the self-consciousness that has affected some of his
solo Mozart records. Moreover in Mackerras he
here has a partner who is one of the most experienced of Mozarteans. This is a popular coupling: it
is recorded with great realism, and can be accommodated among top recommendations.

*Piano concertos Nos. 21 in C, K.467; 23 in A,
K.488; Rondos for piano and orchestra Nos. 1 in
D, K.382; 2 in A, K.386.*
(M) *** Sony Great Performances Dig./Analogue
   SMK 64128 [id.]. Murray Perahia, ECO.

For once, Sony's claim with this uneven mid-priced
reissue series is indisputable. These are certainly
great performances and both concertos capture Perahia's very special Mozartean sensibility, and are
beautifully recorded. The recording of the *C major
Concerto* dates from the mid 1970s. If the first
movement is given delicacy and charm, rather than
strength in the way of Brendel or Kovacevich, the
opposite is true of the exquisite slow movement
(with very beautiful orchestral playing), and lively
finale. The account of K.488 has enormous delicacy
and inner vitality, yet a serenity that puts it in a very
special class. The slow movement has an elevation
of spirit that reaffirms one's conviction that this is
one of the classics of the gramophone. There is
however a robust quality about the finale and a fresh
but controlled spontaneity. The digital recording is
particularly fresh and natural. This very generous
collection is completed with the two *Concert
rondos*, which when recorded in 1983 incorporated
for the first time on record the closing bars newly
rediscovered by Professor Alan Tyson.

(i) *Piano concerto No. 22 in E flat, K.482. Adagio
and fugue in C min., K.546;* (ii) *Sinfonia
concertante in E flat, K.364.*
(M)*** BBC Music stereo BBCB 8010-2 [id.]. (i)
   Sviatoslav Richter; (ii) Brainin (vn.), Schidlof
   (va.); ECO, Benjamin Britten.

Sviatoslav Richter was rarely so relaxed in his performances as at the Aldeburgh Festival. With
Britten as partner he gives an inspired reading of
the Mozart concerto, for which Britten specially
wrote new cadenzas, which are in use here. Though
the sound is not so cleanly focused as in a studio
recording, it is warmly atmospheric, as it is in the
other two works. In the *Sinfonia concertante* Britten

equally charms his two soloists from the Amadeus Quartet, making them relax in spontaneously expressive playing, with the lightness of the finale a special delight.

Piano concertos No. 23 in A, K.488; 24 in C min., K.491.
*** Nonesuch/Warner Dig. 7559 79489-2.
   Richard Goode, Orpheus CO.

From Goode and the Orpheus Chamber Orchestra comes an outstandingly fresh and satisfying account of Mozart's most lovable *A major concerto*, the slow movement serenely beautiful and the finale delightfully vivacious. The opening tutti of K.491 is formidably strong and forward-listing, but the movement unfolds with a natural Mozartean flexibility and Goode's playing in the *Larghetto*, as in the slow movement of K.488 has a ravishing simplicity. The jaunty finale is nicely paced, and gets attractively bolder as it proceeds.

   Throughout both works, the ear notices the sensitive contributions of the Orpheus woodwind as well as the elegant finish and warmth of the strings. Goode uses Mozart's cadenza in K.488, and enterprisingly, one by Paul Badura-Skoda in K.491. These recordings are being made at the Manhattan Center, and very good they are too, with a most attractive ambient bloom.

Piano concertos Nos. 24 in C min., K.491; 27 in B flat, K.595.
(B) *** DG Classikon 463 264-2 [id.]. Géza Anda, Camerata Academica of the Salzburg Mozarteum.

These were two of the very finest performances in Géza Anda's complete survey of the Mozart concertos made in the late 1960s. Anda's Mozart is as sparkling and polished as one could wish for, and yet there is no sense that the tragic or prophetic overtones in the *C minor* are lost sight of. His account of K.595 is equally fresh, his playing deft and lively.

   The recordings too are excellent for their time, with clear sound, no lack of orchestral warmth and a natural image of the piano. Only the upper strings suggest the recording's age, but there is a pleasing bloom on the woodwind. Most enjoyable: one wonders why this was not reissued as one of DG's Originals, instead of on their bargain Classikon label.

Piano concerto No. 25 in C, K.503.
**(*) EMI CDC5 56974-2 [id.]. Martha Argerich, Netherlands CO, Szymon Goldberg –
   BEETHOVEN: *Piano concerto No. 1 in C, Op. 15* **(*).

Martha Argerich is an inspirational pianist whose finest flights of imagination come in live performance. Like the Beethoven, recorded at the Concertgebouw fourteen years later, this 1978 live

recording offers a performance of the weighty *C major Concerto* magnetic in its spontaneity. There is nothing deferential about Argerich's way with Mozart, the opposite of the 'Dresden china' approach. This is muscular, positive playing, which sparkles in the outer movements, and finds a natural gravity in the central Andante. The recording is on the thin side, but never prevents one from enjoying a unique performance.

(i) *Piano concerto No. 25 in C, K.503. Symphony No. 38 (Prague);* (i; ii) Concert aria: *Ch'io mi scordi di te.*
*** MDG Dig. MDG 340 0967-2 [id.]. (i)
   Christian Zacharias (piano); Lausanne CO,
   Zacharias; (ii) with Bernarda Fink.

This is a delightful disc, offering a nicely balanced Mozart group of symphony, aria and concerto. Zacharias, in consistently refreshing performances, relishes his multiple roles not just conducting a fresh and lively account of the *Prague Symphony*, but also acting as piano soloist; in the concerto, he directs the weighty K.503 from the keyboard, and also provides a crisply pointed obbligato in the most taxing of Mozart's concert arias, *Ch'io mi scordi di te.* The sense of freedom and spontaneous enjoyment is enhanced by the clarity of the recording, made in the Metropole, Lausanne.

   Though tuttis are big and weighty, Zacharias finds rare transparency in lighter passages, with a vivid sense of presence. Zacharias's great merit as a Mozart pianist is the crispness of his articulation, playing with jewelled clarity and keen imagination even in the fastest, trickiest passagework. In many ways most striking of all is the concert aria. Bernarda Fink with her firm, creamy voice, officially a mezzo, is untroubled by the soprano tessitura, giving the most characterful interpretation, imaginatively pointing words and phrases. One of the most impressive of all versions of this notorious test-piece since Schwarzkopf, rounded off with a virtuoso display of coloratura.

Piano concerto No. 26 in D (Coronation), K.537.
*** BBC Legends BBCL 4020-2 [id.]. Clifford
   Curzon, BBC SO, Boulez – BEETHOVEN:
   Piano concerto No. 5 (Emperor). ***

As in the Beethoven coupling, recorded three years earlier, Curzon and Boulez in this 1974 Prom performance of the *Coronation concerto* make rewarding partners. The combination of introspection and intellectual rigour results in an inspired reading of one of the more problematic Mozart piano concertos, fresh, bright and resilient in the outer movements with pearly passage work, and thoughtfully unmannered in the slow movement. Full-bodied sound set in the warm acoustic of the Royal Albert Hall.

(i; iv) *Piano concerto No. 27 in B flat, K.595;* (i;

ii; iv) *Double piano concerto in E flat, K.365;* (i; iii) *Double piano sonata in D, K.448.*
(***) BBC Legends stereo/mono BBCL 4037-2 [id.]. (i) Clifford Curzon; (ii) Barenboim (piano); (iii) Benjamin Britten; (iv) ECO, Barenboim.

These radio recordings with Curzon date from two different periods. The two concertos, set in the warm Royal Albert Hall acoustic, come from a Prom concert in 1979, with Barenboim directing from the keyboard in the *Double concerto* and conducting in Mozart's last piano concerto, K.595, Curzon's favourite. This is Mozart at his most joyous, with Curzon losing any of the inhibitions that sometimes dogged him in the studio, warmly supported by his younger colleague in both roles. Speeds in outer movements are broad enough to allow the most elegant pointing, not least in the jaunty finales. Slow movements are warmly expressive at broad speeds, concentrated and sustained. The *Duo Sonata* finds Curzon in 1960 in a partnership with Britten at Jubilee Hall, Aldeburgh, and though the mono sound is far drier, it is firm and immediate, letting one appreciate another exuberant performance, this time with the outer movements challengingly fast, and the middle movement bringing delectable interplay between the players.

Double piano concerto in E flat, K.365.
*** Chandos Dig. CHAN 9711 [id.]. Güher and Süther Pekinel, Philh. O, Marriner – BRUCH: *Double piano concerto in A flat min.;* MENDELSSOHN: *Double piano concerto in E.* ***

This unique coupling of double piano concertos, devised by the Pekinel sisters, is an inspired one, even though the Mozart is the only masterpiece among the three works. It receives a fresh, alert reading, marked by superb ensemble from the two soloists, helped by vivid Chandos sound.

Double piano concerto in E flat, K.365; (i) *Triple piano concerto in F, K.242;* (ii) *Piano quartet in G min., K.478.*
(M)**(*) Sony SMK 60598 [id.]. Gold, Fizdale, NYPO, Bernstein; (i) with Bernstein also as pianist; (ii) Bernstein (piano), Juilliard Qt (members).

Bernstein's piano playing rarely fails to convey the enjoyment of someone having a day out – it is as though he feels more able to relax than when he is on the conductor's rostrum. His performance of the *Piano quartet* – recorded in 1965 and sounding excellent – may not be as poised in every detail as some rival versions, but its power of communication more than makes amends. As for the *Double* and *Triple concertos* – they are similarly relaxed and enjoyable accounts, romantic in approach, and if occasionally they miss that last ounce of sparkle, the quality of the music-making is never in doubt.

The recordings, from the early 1970s, are a bit too closely miked, but are acceptable.

Violin concertos Nos. 1–5; Serenade in D (Haffner): Andante, Minuet & Rondo, K.250.
(BB) **(*) Arte Nova Dig. 74321 72104-2 (2) [id.]. Pamela Frank, Zurich Tonhalle O, David Zinman.

The young American violinist Pamela Frank is a strong, imaginative artist, very well matched here by the Tonhalle Orchestra under David Zinman, who shows himself just as inspired an interpreter of Mozart as he is of Beethoven. Outer movements are fresh and bright at speeds on the urgent side, while slow movements are spaciously expressive without sentimentality. As a super-bargain purchase, the two discs can be warmly recommended, even if Frank's tone and the coloration she gives to the upper register are not ideally sweet and pure. First-rate sound. The three concertante movements from the *Haffner Serenade* provide an original and apt makeweight. However, in the bargain range first-choice for the five concertos rests with Simon Standage (with Hogwood) in a superb set of period-instrument performances on a Oiseau-Lyre Double (455 721-2), who offers also the concertante *Adagio*, K.261 and the two *Rondos*, K.269 and K.373. Those preferring a modern-instrument version can turn to Grumiaux on a Philips Duo (438 323-2). These performances are among the most beautifully played in the catalogue, and besides the *Adagio in E* and *Rondo*, K.269, this set offers also the sublime *Sinfonia concertante*, K.364, where Grumiaux is joined in a sensitive partnership by Arrigo Pellicia.

Notturno (Serenade) in D for 4 orchestras, K.236; Serenade No. 6 (Serenata notturna), K.289; Symphony No. 32 in G, K.318; Thamos, King of Egypt (incidental music): 4 Interludes (Nos. 2–5), K.345; 6 German dances, K.600/1, 2 & 5 (Der Kanarienvogel); K.602/3 (Der Leiermann); K.605/2 & 3 (Sleigh ride).
(M) *** Decca 466 500-2 [id.]. LSO, Peter Maag.

A splendid compilation, very highly recommended, for Peter Maag is an outstanding Mozartean. These performances are first class, stylish, full of vitality and grace, the *Serenata notturna* made the more elegantly attractive by a not too insistent contribution from the timpani. The *Notturno* is an ingenious Mozartean gimmick piece. It opens graciously (rather like Gluck) and is made interesting by a combination of left–right with forward–backward placements, to suggest the composer's four instrumental groups echoing each other. The rest of the programme is far finer music, with the *G major Symphony* given a fizzing performance with a quite lovely central *Andante*. The *Lucio Silla* overture and *Thamos incidental music* are delightful and again played with the crisply pointed style at which this conductor is so adept.

The *German dances* have been added for the present reissue. They are played with enormous vigour, some may feel that the uninhibited use of such a large orchestra is inappropriate for such simple material. (Our original review in the 1961 *Stereo Record Guide* spoke of 'an elephant's trappings on a simple mule', and suggested that with a third of the number of players the sound would have been just right.) However, after the gutsy opening horns the canary effect in K.600/5 is neatly done, and Maag similarly scales down for the gentle entry of the hurdy-gurdy in K.602/3. The *Sleigh ride* ('Schlittenfahrt' in German!) swings along realistically, urged on by a superb post-horn solo.

The transfers of these vintage 1959 recordings (made in Kingsway Hall or Walthamstow) are most adept: the sound is remarkably full and natural and undated. Excellent documentation and session photographs.

Serenades Nos. 6 in D (Serenata notturna), K.239; 7 in D (Haffner), K.250 (with March in D, K.249); 9 in D (Posthorn), K.320 (with March in D, K.335/1); 13 in G (Eine kleine Nachtmusik), K.525.

🌑 (B) *** Ph. Duo Dig./Analogue 464 022-2 (2) [id.]. ASMF, Marriner.

There are plenty of fine recordings of Mozart's four key orchestral *Serenades*, but none to surpass those on this Philips Duo which tends to sweep the board. Marriner's accounts of the *Haffner* and *Posthorn* are cultured, warm, spacious and marvellously played. The Academy string-tone is sweet and smooth, yet articulation is neat, with admirable rhythmic freshness in outer movements. Iona Brown makes a superb contribution in the concertante violin role of the *Haffner*, playing with sparkle as well as expressive grace. The posthorn which gives K.320 its sobriquet, takes only a minor (if rather engaging) role in the Trio of the second Minuet, and Michael Laird's contribution here is characterfully elegant. The work's kernel is central movements which – in the place of the usual miniature violin concerto – make a compelling case for modern instruments, as do the strings in the lovely *Andantino* which follows, where the mood darkens. The two marches are used as entrance and exit music. The performance of the *Serenata notturna*, too, is first class, crisply rhythmic in the first movement with the drums clearly focused. As for the most famous work of all, Sir Neville's polished and elegant account of *Eine kleine Nachtmusik* is clearly designed to caress the ears of traditional listeners wearied by period performance. The second-movement *Romanze* is even more honeyed than usual on muted strings. Throughout, the Philips engineers provide a natural sound balance, with rich, full textures. The fairly resonant recording (made either in St John's Smith Square or the Henry Wood Hall in the early 1980s) adds to the feeling of breadth without blurring detail.

Serenades Nos. 11 in E flat, K.375; 12 in C min., K.388.

(**(*))Testament mono SBT 1180 [id.]. L. Bar. Ens., Karl Haas – DVORAK: *Serenade* (**(*)).

This historic reissue of pioneering recordings from Karl Haas and the London Baroque Ensemble of three of the greatest of all wind works is valuable not only for performances that are ahead of their time in their brisk, no-nonsense manners, but also for the note written by Lionel Salter just before his death early in 2000. As the regular keyboard player for the Ensemble, he paints a delightful portrait of Karl Haas, the formidable musicologist who arrived in England as a refugee in 1939 and who 'with his impish sense of humour' adopted the word 'Baroque' in the group's title, recognizing that the term can also mean 'bizarre'.

George Martin, long before he discovered the Beatles, as Artists and Recording Manager of the Parlophone label was persuaded to make these and other recordings, just as short-playing 78 discs were giving way to LPs. Lionel Salter mentions the 'friendly arguments' at recording sessions about Haas's fast speeds, with the works often tackled impromptu. There is a brisk, military flavour in allegros, yet the mastery of individual players still defies the idea of over-rigid performances, with delectable interplay between the principals. Vivid and immediate transfers of recordings set in a dry acoustic.

Sinfonia concertante in E flat, for violin, viola and orchestra, K.364.

(M) *** RCA 09026 63531-2 [id.]. Heifetz, Primrose, RCA Victor SO, Izler Solomon – BACH: *Double violin concerto in D min.*; BRAHMS: *Double concerto for violin and cello.* ***

(***) BBC Legends BBCL 4019-2 [id.]. David & Igor Oistrakh, Moscow PO, Yehudi Menuhin – BEETHOVEN: *Violin concerto in D, Op. 61* (***).

Our comments did not do full justice to this fruitful 1956 Heifetz/Primrose partnership when it was discussed in our 1997/8 Yearbook as part of the 'Heifetz Edition' – most of which is no longer available in the UK. True, the recording is too closely balanced and, brisk pace of the finale may not suit all tastes, but the crisp interchange is fresh and joyful and in the slow movement the warmly responsive interchange between the two great soloists is genuinely moving, with the cadenza outstanding.

In 1963 the Moscow Philharmonic Orchestra and Kyrill Kondrashin visited London's Royal Albert Hall for a short season and on 28 September Menuhin played the Beethoven *Violin concerto* seraphically with David Oistrakh conducting. And in the second half they reversed roles when Oistrakh playing the viola and his son Igor the violin gave the Mozart *Sinfonia concertante* under Menuhin's baton. It is a most spontaneous and vivid performance and the BBC recording gives us truthful and natural sound. Self-recommending.

Sinfonia concertante in E flat for violin, viola and orchestra, K.364.
(**(*)) Testament mono SBT 1157 [id.]. Norman Brainin, Peter Schidlof, L. Mozart Players, Harry Blech – SCHUBERT: *String quintet in C.* (**)

Originally on EMI, this version of the Mozart *Sinfonia concertante*, was recorded at Abbey Road in 1953, just when Brainin and Schidlof were first establishing the high reputation of the Amadeus Quartet. The studio recording, cleanly transferred, focuses the soloists sharply, giving warmth and body to the tone – exceptionally rich from Peter Schidlof on the viola. If the slow movement is a degree broader and heavier with Blech than with Britten on the radio recording of 1967 (issued in the BBC Legends series), the finale is jollier at a marginally more relaxed tempo.

Symphonies 13–36; 38–41.
(B) *** EMI Dig. CZS 5 73631-2 [CDZI 73631] (5). ECO, Tate.

For those wishing to collect the majority of Mozart's symphonies without the very earliest ones, this set is ideal. The performances are full of vitality, engagingly light in texture, with some lovely playing from individual members of the orchestra. Throughout, Tate provides a winning combination of affectionate manners, clean articulation and keen attention to detail, making for fresh results. In the *Paris Symphony*, the alternative *Andante* slow movement is included as well as the usual one, so you can programme which ever you prefer. The later symphonies can stand competition with any: the *Jupiter* has an apt scale, which allows the grandeur of the work fully to come out. On the one hand it has the clarity of a chamber orchestra, whilst on the other, with trumpets and drums, its weight of expression never underplays the scale of argument which originally prompted the unauthorized nickname. In both Nos. 40 and 41, exposition repeats are observed in the outer movements, particularly important in the *Jupiter* finale. With excellent recording quality (1984–93) – detailed with a pleasant reverberation – this set makes a fine bargain, especially in such attractive space-saving slimline packaging.

Symphonies Nos. 13 in F, K.112; 14 in A, K.114; 20 in D, K.133.
*** Teldec/Warner Dig. 0630 17110-2 [id.]. VCM, Harnoncourt.

These three symphonies date from 1771/2, while Mozart was in his mid-teens, although the *D major* work, written in Milan, is by far the most ambitious.

By observing repeats, Harnoncourt widens the scale of all three. Indeed, the first movement of No. 20 is extended to 10'44", but with lusty period-horns it has great vitality in the outer movements, and the Andante does not lack charm.

Harnoncourt gives vigorous readings of all three, as ever with a bold element of gruffness, but this certainly adds to their character. The *A major Symphony* comes off particularly well, with the Minuet not pressed as hard as with Mackerras's Prague account on the same label. Excellent, resonant recording.

Symphonies Nos. 25 in G min., K.183; 29 in A, K.201; 31 in D (Paris), K.297; Adagio and fugue in C min., K.546; Overture: Così fan tutte.
(M) **(*) EMI CDM5 67331-2 [id.]. Philh. O, or New Philh. O; Klemperer.

Symphonies Nos. 33 in B flat, K.319; 34 in C, K.338; 40 in G min., K.550; Masonic funeral music, K.477.
(M) **(*) EMI CDM5 67332-2 [id.]. New Philh. O, or Philh. O; Klemperer.

Symphonies Nos. 35 in D (Haffner), K.385; 36 in C (Linz), K.425; 38 in D (Prague), K.504; Overture: Die Zauberflöte, K.620.
(M) **(*) EMI CDM5 67333-2 [id.]. Philh. O, or New Phil. O; Klemperer.

Symphonies Nos. 39 in E flat, K.543; 41 in C (Jupiter), K.551; Serenade No. 13 in G (Eine kleine Nachtmusik), K.525.
(M) **(*) EMI CDM5 67334-2 [id.]. Philh. O, or New Philh. O; Klemperer.

Klemperer's recordings of the key Mozart symphonies, plus the orchestral works listed above and a few more overtures, were originally collected in a six-LP box. Now for the 'Klemperer Legacy' they reappear on four separate mid-priced CDs. The recordings (of different vintage) were divided between Abbey Road and the Kingsway Hall and they have never sounded fresher than in the present remastering, with fullness too and warmth. Of course since they were made period-instrument practice has changed our view of symphonic Mozart, but not to the extent that these monumentally characterful readings cannot find and hold a place in the catalogue. Those who respond to Klemperer's brand of Mozart are likely to respond very deeply, and for them this is an essential set. If initially a Klemperer reading of, say, the first movement of the great *G minor Symphony*, No. 40, sounds heavy, rhythmic subtleties are there, so that the hidden power makes its impact. The account of No. 33 is strikingly fresh and No. 38 (the *Prague*) is among the greatest ever recorded. No. 39 has a strength and virility in the first movement that anticipates Beethoven, and Klemperer lifts the finale out of its usual Mendelssohnian rut and gives it a Beethovenian power without losing any of the instrumental charm. Almost all the allegros here are measured and meticulous, slow movements forthright rather than hushed, but power and purpose are never lacking. It is good that some of the shorter works are included, particularly the magnificent *Adagio and fugue* and *Funeral music*, while *Eine kleine Nachtmusik* is certainly not lacking in elegance, nor a lightness of touch in the finale.

Symphonies Nos. 29 in A, K. 201; 33 in B flat, K.319; 34 in C, K.338.
*** Ph. Dig. 462 906-2 [id.]. VPO, Muti.

Unlike earlier issues in Muti's Mozart series with the Vienna Philharmonic, this one is a total success, warmly recommendable to anyone who responds to Viennese Mozart. These earlier works find him and the orchestra at their most relaxed, with allegros which allow delicate pointing of rhythm and phrase, and with tenderly expressive slow movements. These are performances that follow tradition in full orchestral treatment, with few if any concessions to period practice, and none the worse for that. They are warmly recorded and the result is most enjoyable.

Symphonies Nos. 29 in A, K. 201; 35 in D (Haffner), K. 385; 38 in D (Prague), K. 504.
(***) BBC Legends mono BBCL 4027-2 [id.]. RPO, Sir Thomas Beecham.

As Beecham's post-war mono recordings of Mozart symphonies have long been consigned to limbo, it is good to have these broadcast performances from the 1950s, with the characterful bonus of Beecham's spoken introductions to No. 29 and the *Prague*. Interpretatively, it is fascinating to note the contrasts between these performances and those he recorded for EMI with the LPO – No. 29 in 1937, the *Haffner* in 1938/9 and the *Prague* in 1940. The extra elegance of these later RPO performances – with playing more lightly sprung and a degree more refined (the odd mishap apart), with speeds less extreme than before – is what comes out most clearly. That impression is enhanced, when the BBC sound is rather more spacious and airy than the pre-war EMI. In No. 29, the 1937 performance brings eccentrically slow speeds for the first three movements, where here they have completely lost any ponderousness.

Symphonies Nos. 35–36;38–41 – see also under *Flute concertos 1–2* (above).

Symphony No. 35 in D (Haffner), K.385.
(**) BBC Legends mono BBCL 4016-2 (2) [id.]. BBC SO, Toscanini – BEETHOVEN: *Missa solemnis; Symphony No. 7* (**(*)); CHERUBINI: *Anacréon overture.* ***

Mozart's *Haffner Symphony* was always a favourite with Toscanini, and this live performance, recorded in London, is warmer and more sympathetic than

either his early version with the New York Philharmonic or his later performance with the NBC Symphony. Though the recording is rather rougher than on the rest of the two-disc set, it makes a valuable bonus to the Beethoven items.

Symphonies Nos. 36 in C (Linz), K.425; 39 in E flat, K.543; Overtures: Così fan tutte; Le nozze di Figaro.
** Guild Dig. GMCD 7172 [id.]. Bournemouth Sinf., Terence Frazor.

These Bournemouth performances of a pair of favourite symphonies offer a model combination of warmth, elegance and finesse, though there is drama too, especially when the timpani open No. 39 so boldly. The recording is most naturally balanced. The overtures are neatly done, though they could have a shade more sparkle, especially *Così fan tutte*. But this is an enjoyable programme showing the conductor and orchestra as natural Mozarteans. However, this single disc is rather upstaged by the super-bargain reissue of Menuhin's performances of all the late Mozart symphonies (see above).

Symphonies Nos. 39 in E flat; 41 in C (Jupiter);
(i) *Concert arias: Si mostra la sorte, K.209; Per pieta, non ricercare, K.420.*
(M) (**(*)) Decca stereo/mono 466 820-2. (i) Peter Pears; ECO, Britten.

Though these radio recordings come in Decca's 'Britten at Aldeburgh' series, only one was made live at the Festival – the *Jupiter Symphony,* given in Blythburgh church in June 1966. It is a strong, direct reading, with brisk outer movements that bring out the power of the writing, even though the second-half repeat in the finale is omitted – regular practice in live performances. The slow movement by contrast is beautifully moulded at a spacious tempo, with the opening repeat observed.

The stereo sound in a helpful church acoustic is warmly atmospheric, where the BBC studio recordings in mono for the other three works are drier, if clear and well balanced. The bite of the cleanly focused timpani in the slow introduction to No. 39 makes an aptly dramatic opening gesture, then leads on to an easily relaxed view of the main Allegro at a lilting 3/4. The other three movements also bring infectiously sprung rhythms, with the finale not so fast as to imperil clear violin articulation or a sense of fun. The studio acoustic is not so helpful to Peter Pears, whose voice sounds dry, with vibrato exaggerated, though the poise and stylishness of the singing cannot be faulted.

CHAMBER MUSIC

Clarinet quintet in A, K.581.
*** DG Dig. 459 641-2 [id.]. David Shifrin,
Emerson Qt – BRAHMS: *Clarinet quintet.* ***

David Shifrin achieves a particularly fine partnership with the Emerson Quartet and the recording
balance is beautifully managed. The flowing
opening movement has an appealing simplicity and
the *Larghetto* is comparably songful and refined in
feeling. Perhaps finest of all are the variations of
the finale with the sunny solo-playing balanced with
pleasing delicacy from the strings. The thoughtful
central *Adagio* and return to the spirited opening
mood are particularly successful. If you want a
coupling with Brahms this can be strongly recommended.

*Clarinet quintet in A, K.581; Allegro in B flat for
Clarinet quintet, K.516c.*
**(*) ASV CDDCA 1079 [id.]. Emma Johnson,
Takacs-Nagy, Hirsch, Boulton, Shulman –
WEBER: *Clarinet quintet ***.

The coupling of Weber's and Mozart's *Clarinet
quintets* is surprisingly rare, with Emma Johnson
here offering a welcome, if brief, bonus in the fragment of a further quintet which Mozart wrote some
time after 1790 just before his death, and which
frustratingly breaks off just after the end of the
exposition. Emma Johnson gives characterful readings, warmly expressive in the first movement of
the main work, dashing in the last two movements.

The close balance of the clarinet means that the
slow movement is less poised than it can be, with
some tonal unevenness. Sensitive support from four
formidable chamber-players, but this is a less impressive account than the sparkling Weber coupling
where the soloist returns to her most spontaneous
form. Apart from the alternatives listed here, readers
are urged to consult our main volume before
choosing a CD of this much-recorded work.

*Clarinet quintet in A, K.581; Clarinet trio in E
flat, K.498.*
(B) **(*) HM Musique d'abord Dig. HMA
1901384 [id.]. Walter Boeykens & Ensemble.

It is surprising that the Mozart *Clarinet quintet* is
not more often coupled with the *Trio*, a less inspired
but still very enjoyable work. Both performances
here are of high quality and beautifully recorded.
Walter Boeykens's sensitive solo playing is well
matched by his colleagues. Perhaps the *Larghetto*
of the *Quintet* has been played even more imaginatively elsewhere, but here its gentle serenity is paramount. Excellent value.

(i) *Clarinet quintet in A, K.581;* (ii) *Horn quintet
in E flat, K.407;* (iii) *Oboe quartet in F, K.370.*
*** Nimbus Dig. NI 5487. (i) Karl Leister; (ii)
Gerd Seifert; (iii) Lothar Koch; Brandis Qt.

We have heard these fine soloists before, all ex-
principals of the Berlin Philharmonic. Karl Leister
provides an essentially light-hearted account of the
Clarinet quintet, with the slow movement tranquil
and beautifully poised. Gerd Seifert is just as lively
and sensitive in the work for horn, even if his tone
is a little plump. Koch is equally personable in the
Oboe quartet, although perhaps just a trifle studied
in sustaining the *Adagio* (so beautifully opened by
the Brandis Quartet). The recording, comparatively
forward, is vividly present.

(i) *Clarinet quintet in A, K.581. String quartet
No. 19 in C (Dissonance), K.465.*
**(*) Calliope Dig. CAL 6256 [id.]. (i) Philippe
Cuper; Talich Qt.

For their newest, digital recording of the *Clarinet
quintet* the Talich group have chosen Philippe
Cuper, a fine and sensitive soloist. Both works here
are immaculately played with many felicitous
touches (notably the gentle reprise of the slow
movement of the *Quintet*). But neither performance
has that extra dimension of spontaneous feeling that
makes for true memorability, although the
recording is natural, and the playing by no means
lacking concentration. Best to choose instead the
earlier Talich recording of the *Quintet* with
Bohuslav Zahradnik, which is exquisitely done.
That comes on Calliope's bargain Approche label
with a pair of violin sonatas (CAL 6628).

*Flute quartets Nos. 1 in D, K.285; 2 in G, K.285a;
3 in C, K.285b; 4 in A, K.298.*
*** EMI Dig. CDC5 56829-2 [id.]. Emmanuel
Pahud, Christoph Poppen, Hariolf Schlicht,
Jean-Guihen Queras.

The Swiss flautist Emmanuel Pahud, the young
principal flute of the Berlin Philharmonic, gives
inspired performances of the four Mozart *Flute
quartets*. These are all early works, generally lightweight, but with one movement of deep emotional
feeling, the B minor *Adagio* of the *First Quartet*,
K.285. In that songful piece Pahud finds new mystery through his subtly shaded phrasing. Otherwise
this is a fun disc, full of youthful high spirits,
charming and witty, with Pahud lighter and fresher
than such rivals as his Berlin predecessor, James
Galway. Galway may include an extra work on his
RCA/BMG disc (RCA 09026 60442-2), but Pahud
is more generous with repeats. Even more than his
earlier disc of Mozart concertos for EMI this signals
the arrival of a new master flautist. There are other
fine versions listed in our main volume (on period
as well as modern instruments) and some offer extra
items. But this is now probably first choice among
those discs just offering the four quartets.

*Piano concerto No. 12 in A, K.414 (version for
piano and string quartet); Piano quartet No. 2 in E
flat, K.493.*

*** EMI Dig. CDC5 56962-2 [id.]. Alfred Brendel, Alban Berg Quartet.

Breaking the bonds of his exclusive recording contract, Alfred Brendel joins the Alban Berg Quartet in live recordings made in the Konzerthaus in Vienna. Together they give electrifying performances, warm and immediate. Brendel is fresh and forward to match the quartet, while the four string players respond to his example in Mozart-playing more flexible than usual, warmly expressive. The rapt *Andante* slow movement of the concerto brings playing of Beethovenian gravity, intensified still further on the entry of the piano. The concerto works surprisingly well in this chamber version, in which Mozart makes no changes to the score, but simply points out that the wind parts can be omitted, and that those for strings can be played by four solo instruments. Brendel is here more relaxed than in his Philips recording of the full concerto, with delightful interplay between piano and quartet. The *Piano quartet* brings a performance equally illuminating with Brendel at his most sparkling in the finale, playing with sparklingly clear articulation. The recording is bright, immediate and well balanced to match.

Piano quartets in G min., K.478; E flat, K.493.
(BB) ** Naxos Dig. 8.554274 [id.]. Menuhin Festival Piano Quartet.

The Menuhin Festival Piano Quartet is an international ensemble with an excellent German pianist, Friedemann Rieger, an American violinist, Nora Chastain, the Scottish-born violist Paul Coletti and a French cellist, Francis Gouton. They give very spirited accounts of both quartets, observing not only the exposition but also second-time repeats in the first movements, though the brilliant pianist is a little monochrome. They are not as tonally subtle as our first recommendations, but the acoustic in which they are recorded is a bit dry and so does not flatter them.

String quartet No. 19 in C (Dissonance), K.465;
(i) *String quintet No. 6 in E flat, K.614.*
*** ASV Dig. CDCA 1069 [id.]. Lindsay Qt; (i) with Louise Williams.

The Lindsays continue their combined series of Mozart's string quartets and quintets with one of the finest discs in the series so far. The striking harmonic atmosphere at the opening of K.465 immediately registers why it was nicknamed 'Dissonance', yet the following allegro is sunny and the *Andante* has both serenity and depth of feeling to make a foil for the delightful Minuet and lighthearted finale. The *Quintet* is hardly less successful, with its witty finale brought off in a true Haydnesque spirit. The recording is real and immediate.

Violin sonatas Nos. 17–28; 32–4; Sonatina in F, K.547.

(B) *** DG Dig. 463 749-2 (4) [id.]. Perlman, Barenboim.

It is good to have the Perlman/Barenboim Mozart Violin sonatas in one nicely packaged bargain box. These artists form a distinguished team, with alert, vital playing, and a sense of spontaneous music-making which pervades these four CDs. There is much attention to detail (though never fussy sounding) which makes these come over as strikingly fresh accounts. Those who invest in this set will not be disappointed, and the recordings are vividly realistic.

(i) *Violin sonatas Nos. 18 in G, K.301; 21 in E min., K.304; 32 in B flat, K.454;* (ii) *Rondo in B flat for violin and orchestra, K.269.*
**(*) EMI Dig. CDC5 56872-2 [id.]. Maria-Elisabeth Lott; with (i) Sontraud Speidel (fortepiano); (ii) Salzburg Mozarteum O, Markus Tomasi.

EMI are surely looking to the future here, although this collection should have been issued on their Début bargain label rather than at premium price. However, there is a double interest in that Maria-Elisabeth Lott (eleven years old at the time these recordings were made) is not only immensely talented – her playing was praised by Menuhin – but she uses here the violin on which Mozart performed as a child, which is smaller than half size. Yet she creates a warm full timbre, remarkably so in the *Andante* of the B flat major Sonata, while in her spirited performances of fast movements her spick-and-span execution is ever stylish, although one would have liked a little more dynamic light and shade. Her older partner, Sontraud Speidel, gives her every support on a 1790 Viennese fortepiano which is a copy of one owned by Mozart – nicely matched to the violin and comparably pleasing in tone. Lott is astonishingly mature for her age. Her approach is very much in the modern tradition, with no concessions to period practice – despite the instruments used. The orchestral *Rondo* which opens the programme is full of charm. And so this disc gives pleasure, for the recording balance cannot be faulted, the effect warm and immediate.

PIANO DUET

Adagio and allegro in F min., K.594; Andante and 5 variations in G, K.501. Fantasia in F min., K.608; Sonatas in: C, K.19d; B flat, K.358; D, K.381; F, K.497; C, K.521; Sonata for two pianos in D, K.448.
(B) *** DG Double 459 475-2 (2) [id.]. Eschenbach, Frantz.

The Eschenbach/Frantz accounts of the Mozart Piano duets were made between 1972 and 1975. They play with exemplary ensemble and fine sensitivity, and although finer performances of individual pieces may have come one's way, the standard maintained by these artists remains high throughout. The recordings are clean and well balanced, if occasionally a shade dry, but this is without doubt an excellent DG bargain Double.

SOLO PIANO MUSIC

Piano sonatas Nos. 1–18; Sonatas in C, K.46d; in F, K.46e; Fantasia in C min., K.475.
(B) *** DG 463 137-2 (5) [id.]. Christoph Eschenbach.

Christoph Eschenbach gives consistently well-turned, cool and elegant performances without affectation or mannerism. Those looking for an unidiosyncratic, direct approach to Mozart should find this poised, immaculate pianism to their taste. The famous *Andante grazioso* variations which form the first movement of the *Sonata in A*, K.331 are entirely characteristic, played very simply and directly. Other pianists are gentler, more romantic, but Eschenbach's taste cannot be faulted. Reissued at bargain price in DG's Collector's Edition this is very competitive indeed, and the set is neatly packaged and well documented.

Piano sonatas Nos. 10 in C, K.330; 11 in A, K.331; 16 in B flat, K. 570; Rondo in A min., K.511.
*** Ph. Dig. 462 903-2 [id.]. Alfred Brendel.

Although for the most part recorded 'live', Brendel's performances here have an appealingly thoughtful intimacy, as if he were hardly conscious of the audience. Even the famous *Alla Turca Rondo* of K.331, though articulated with delectable crispness, is without any feeling of extrovert bravura. Yet one still has the sense of being in Brendel's presence, and the *Andante grazioso* with variations which opens the same sonata charms the ear with its delicacy. Interestingly the studio recording of the *C major Sonata*, K.330 seems very slightly less spontaneous in feeling than the rest of the programme.

But altogether this is playing of distinction, with the poised *Adagio* of K.570 showing Brendel at his finest, and with the following *Allegretto* most engagingly pointed. Audience noises are minimal (although applause is included), and the recording, although fairly closely observed, is very natural.

VOCAL MUSIC

Masses: Nos. 1 in G (Missa brevis), K.49; 2 in D min. (Missa brevis), K.65; 3 in C, (Domicus), K.66; 4 in C min. (Waisenhaus), K.139; 5 in G (Pastoral), K.140; 6 in F (Missa brevis), K.192; 7 in C (Missa in honorem Ssmae Trinitas); 9 in D (Missa brevis), K.194; 10 in C (Spatzenmesse), K.220; 11 in C (Credo), K.257; 12 in C (Spaur), K.258; 13 in C (Organ solo), K.259; 14 in C (Missa longa), K.262; 15 in B flat (Missa brevis),
K.275; 16 in C (Coronation mass), K.317; 17 in C (Missa solemnis), K.337; 18 in C min. (Great), K.427; 19 in D min. (Requiem), K.626. Alma Dei creatoris, K.72; Ave verum corpus, K.168; Benedictus sit Deus, K.117; Dixit et Magnificat, K.193; Ergo interest, an quis . . . Quaere superna, K.143; Exsultate, jubilate, K.165; Grabmusik, K.42; Hosanna, K.223; Inter natos mulierum, K.72; Kyries: K.33; K.89; K.90; K.322; K.323; K.341; Litaniae Lauretanae, K.195; Litaniae de venerabili altaris sacramento in B flat, K.125; Litaniae de venerabili altaris sacramento in E flat, K.243; Litaniae Lauretanae, K.109; Miserere in A min., K.85; Misericordias Domini, K.222; Quaerite primum regnum Dei, K.86; Regina coeli in C, K.108; Regina coeli in B flat, K.127; Regina coeli in C, K.276; Sancte Maria, mater, Dei, K.273; Scande coeli limina, K.34; Sub tuum praesidium, K.198; Tantum ergo in B flat, K.142; Tantum ergo in D, K.197; Te Deum laudamus, K.141; Veni Sancte Spiritus, K.47; Venite populi, K.260; Vesperae de Dominica, K.321; Vesperae solennes de confessor, K.339.
(M) *** Teldec/Warner Dig. 3984 21885-2 (13) [id.]. Barbara Bonney, Elisabeth von Magnus, Charlotte Margiono, Sylvia McNair, Eva Mei, Joan Rodgers, Krisztina Láki, Zsuzsanna Dénes, Angela Maria Blasi, Eva Mei, Rachel Yakar, Ortrud Wenkel, Kurt Equiluz, Håkon Hagegård, Thomas Hampson, Herbert Lippert, Christoph Prégardien, Josef Protschka, Uwe Heilmann, Gilles Cachemaille, Deon van der Welt, László Polgár, Robert Holl, V. State Op. Konzertvereinigung, Vienna State Op. Ch., Vienna Hofburgkapelle Choral Scholars, Arnold Schoenberg Ch., VCM, Harnoncourt.

Harnoncourt's consistently alive, and superbly sung and played survey of Mozart's complete sacred works is a remarkable achievement, and can be strongly recommended, with only the single reservation that the *Requiem*, which came first in 1981, is a disappointment and ought to have been re-recorded for this complete edition. The bite of the singing is all but negated by the washiness of the recording of the voices. The sound is very over-resonant and though it flatters the fine team of soloists, it is a curious anomaly to have an orchestra of period instruments, clearly focused, set against such a flabby choral sound. But most collectors will own another version of Mozart's final masterpiece, and the rest of the survey earns the highest marks.

As can be seen there is an extraordinarily distinguished team of soloists, led by the splendid Barbara Bonney, which never lets the side down, either individually or grouped. Harnoncourt is at his very best in his fresh, vibrant accounts of the early *Missae breves*, but in the later works the soloists also distinguish themselves, and the choral and instrumental contributions are no less stimulating.

There is not space here to detail individual accounts of this remarkable coverage; sufficient to say that Mozart's sacred music has a consistently high level of inspiration (with the lovely solo writing often reminding the listener of the opera house), and that Harnoncourt rises to the occasion. The recordings were made over a decade from 1986 to 1996 and are consistently of the highest quality, well balanced within an attractively resonant acoustic.

Masses: Nos. 2 in D min. (Missa brevis), K.65; 3 in C, (Dominicus), K.66; 4 in C min. (Waisenhaus), K.139; 7 in C (Missa in honorem Ssmae Trinitas); 10 in C (Spatzenmesse), K.220; 11 in C (Credo), K.257; 12 in C (Spaur), K.258; 13 in C (Organ solo), K.259; 16 in C (Coronation mass), K.317; 17 in C (Missa solemnis), K.337; 18 in C min. Great), K.427; 19 in D min. (Requiem), K.626; Ave verum corpus, K.618.
(BB) **(*) Virgin Classics Dig. VBD5 61769-2 (5). Monika Frimmer, Patrizia Kwella, Ann Monoyios, Diana Montague, Barbara Schlick, Elisabeth Graf, Ull Groenewold, Michael Chance, Oly Pfaff, Christoph Prégardien, Markus Schäfer, Klaus Mertens, Franz-Josef Selig, Cologne Chamber Ch., Collegium Cartusianum, Peter Neumann.

As can be seen from our comments about the Virgin Double below, Peter Neumann's performances are fresh, stylish, and warmly enjoyable and very well sung. Most importantly these artists give a very fine, dramatic account of the *Requiem* (not included below), and the recording here is excellent, clear and vivid. The soloists are all very good throughout, and the other masses, early and late, have plenty of character. The backward balance of the chorus is not enough of a problem to make this other than a worthwhile collection of some of Mozart's finest non-operatic vocal music for those not wanting to stretch to the complete Harnoncourt edition.

(i) *Masses Nos. 16 in C (Coronation), K.317; 17 in C (Missa solemnis), K.337;* (ii) *18 in C min. (Great), K.427; Kyrie in D min., K.341.*
(BB) **(*) Virgin Veritas 2 x 1 Dig. VBD5 61665-2 (2) [CDVB 61665]. Cologne Chamber Ch., Collegium Cartusianum, Neumann, with (i) Kwella, Groenwold, Prégardien, Selig; (ii) Schlick, Frimmer, Prégardien, Mertens.

Neumann directs an enjoyable account of the *Coronation Mass*, as well as the much rarer *Missa solemnis*, which is on a similar scale and is also very well sung. The singers, a well-blended team, are balanced somewhat backwardly within an ecclesiastical acoustic, which takes a little of the bite from the chorus too, but the effect remains vivid. The *C minor Mass* has much to commend it: fine soloists – with Barbara Schlick always fresh and captivating

in the *Laudamus te* – spacious choral singing (if, again, somewhat backwardly balanced) and excellent playing from an authentic-sized orchestra on original instruments. The only caveat is that the chorus lacks the bite to make the performance really gripping, though the recording is partly to blame. The rather solemn *Kyrie* has plenty of character, with the performance darkly lyrical rather than dramatic. A good bargain set (if without texts or translations) which has much to recommend it.

Requiem mass (No. 19) in D min., K.626 (new edition by H. C. Robbins Landon).
*** Sony Dig. SK 60764 [id.]. Marina Ulewicz, Barbara Hölzl, Jörg Hering, Harry van der Kamp, Tölz Boys' Ch., Tafelmusik, Bruno Weil.

Bruno Weil's splendid new period performance of Mozart's *Requiem* stands alone and distinctive in that it uses a completely new edition by H. C. Robbins Landon. In the accompanying notes he explains in detail how it was prepared, combining the work of Mozart's three pupils, Süssmayr, Eybler and Freystädler, which he suggests is 'nearer to the spirit of the torso than any twentieth-century reconstruction could be'.

Bruno Weil conducts a highly dramatic, powerfully committed performance with a fine team of soloists, incisively vital choral singing, given excellent orchestral support. It is very well recorded indeed, in a spacious acoustic and stands very high among current recorded performances, irrespective of the edition used. For many it could be first choice.

Requiem mass (No. 19) in D min., K.626; (i) *Grabmusik, K.42: Beatracht dies Herz; Vesperae solennes de confessore, K.339: Laudate Dominum.*
*** DG Dig. 463 181-2 [id.]. (i) Harnisch; Mattila, Mingardo, Schade, Terfel, Swedish R Ch., BPO, Abbado.

Recorded live in July 1999 in Salzburg Cathedral, Abbado's performance of the traditional score with the Berlin Philharmonic was given to commemorate the tenth anniversary of the death of Herbert von Karajan. The dedicated atmosphere of such an occasion is powerfully caught, with the DG engineers clarifying the sound to a remarkable degree, with fine detail as well as ample weight.

With the brilliant Swedish Radio Choir singing with exceptionally clear focus such choruses as the *Dies irae* are thrillingly intense, and the starry yet youthful line-up of soloists – none of whom Karajan would ever have heard – makes an outstanding team. In the two extra items, among Mozart's loveliest soprano solos, Rachel Harnisch sings with warmth and refinement. This can be recommended to those wanting a traditional, modern-instrument account of Mozart's choral masterpiece.

Concert aria: *Ch'io mi scordi di te?, K.505.*
(***) Testament SBT 1178 [id.]. Elisabeth
Schwarzkopf, Géza Anda, Philh. O,
Ackermann – BACH: *Cantatas 68: Aria; 199;
202; 208: Aria.* ***

As John Steane points out in his most illuminating
note, there is a fascinating contrast between this
account of *Ch'io mi scordi di te?* recorded in 1955
with Géza Anda playing the difficult piano obbligato, and Schwarzkopf's classic recording with
Alfred and George Szell of 1968. The voice may be
fuller in the later one, but this is uniquely fresh and
urgent, with Schwarzkopf's vehement side given
freer rein. A splendid and valuable supplement to
the Bach recordings which have also remained
unissued for far too long.

Concert aria: *Ombra felice, K.255;* Opera arias:
*Ascanio in Alba: Ah di si nobil alma; Mitridate:
Venga pur, Gia dagli occhi.*
*** Virgin/EMI Dig. VC5 45365-2 [id.]. David
Daniels, OAE, Harry Bicket – GLUCK;
HANDEL: *Arias.* ***

Under the title '*Sento amor*', David Daniels offers
one of the finest of counter-tenor recitals. In the
arias from early Mozart operas, the brilliance of his
singing is what stands out above all, giving beauty
and energy to the florid writing, as well as a deeper
expressiveness to the lyrical passages than one
might expect. At once pure and warm, completely
avoiding the usual counter-tenor hoot, placing his
voice flawlessly, Daniels is exceptional even in an
age which has produced many outstanding rivals.

OPERA

Don Giovanni (complete).
❀ (M) *** Decca 466 389-2 (3) [id.]. Della Casa,
Danco, Siepi, Corena, Dermota, V. State Op.
Ch., VPO, Krips.

Krips's version, recorded in 1955 for the Mozart
bicentenary, has remained at or near the top of
the list of recommendations ever since. Freshly
remastered, it sounds better than ever. Its intense,
dramatic account of the Don's disappearance into
Hell has rarely been equalled, and never surpassed
on CD, though there are many equally memorable
sequences: the finale to Act I is also electrifying.
As a bass Don, Siepi is marvellously convincing,
but there is hardly a weak link in the rest of the cast.
The early stereo recording is pretty age-defying,
full and warm, with a lovely Viennese glow which
is preferable to many modern recordings. It is good
to see this set lovingly packaged on Decca's
Legends label, and it ranks alongside the classic
Giulini version on EMI.

Don Giovanni (highlights).
(M) * Decca 458 245-2 [id.]. Price, Nilsson, Siepi,
Corena V. State Op. Ch., VPO, Leinsdorf.

This Decca set has an impressive cast and a collection of starry names but, alas, Leinsdorf's conducting is uninspired. In any case, Siepi and Corena
are heard to far better effect in Krips's classic account on the same label, and Nilsson and Price seem
mis-cast. The reissue is nicely packaged, and the
recording is vivid, but that's about it.

Idomeneo (complete).
(B) (***) EMI Double fforte mono CZS5 73848-2
(2). Richard Lewis, Léopold Simoneau, Sena
Jurinac, Lucille Udovick, James Milligan,
William McAlpine, Hervey Alan,
Glyndbourne Fest. Ch. & O, Pritchard.

The very first 'complete' recording of *Idomeneo*,
made in 1955 with Glyndebourne forces under John
Pritchard, makes a timely reappearance on EMI's
Double fforte label. Though it uses a severely cut
text and the orchestral sound is rather dry, it wears
its years well. The voices still sound splendid, notably Sena Jurinac as a ravishing Ilia, Richard Lewis
in the title role, and Léopold Simoneau so delicate
he almost reconciles one to the casting of Idamante
as a tenor (from Mozart's compromised Vienna
revision). The cuts mean that the whole opera is
fitted on to two discs instead of the usual three. A
cued synopsis is provided, but as usual in this
Double fforte series there is no aria or ensemble title
with each cue.

Le nozze di Figaro (complete).
❀ (B) *** EMI Double fforte CZS5 73845-2 (2).
Sciuti, Jurinac, Stevens, Bruscantini,
Calabrese, Cuénod, Wallace, Sinclair,
Glydebourne Ch. & Fest. O, Gui.

Gui's effervescent Glyndebourne set (see our main
volume) has been promoted from Classics for Pleasure to EMI's own bargain Double fforte label. It
costs a little more, but is worth every penny. It
remains a classic set with a cast that has seldom
been bettered, and the only regret is that there is a
(very minor) cut to fit the recording on to two discs.
There is no libretto, but the cued synopsis follows
the narrative in detail, yet not giving the Italian
titles of each item, only telling the listener what the
character or characters are singing about. A pity,
for this makes the set less easy to dip into.

COLLECTIONS

Arias from: *La clemenza di Tito; Così fan tutte;
Don Giovanni; Die Entführung aus dem Serail; Le
nozze di Figaro; Il re pastore; Zaïde; Die
Zauberflöte.*
(M) *** Analogue/Dig. Decca 458 233-2 [id.].
With Burrows, Evans, Horne, Te Kanawa,
Ramey, Popp, Prey, Siepi, Von Stade,
Sutherland.

A typically expert collection of Mozart arias on
Decca's well-planned Opera Gala series. Many

obvious items are here, some taken from complete sets: Solti's *Magic Flute* and *Marriage of Figaro*, Krips's *Don Giovanni*, etc., whilst others are from recital discs, including Sutherland's splendid *'Marten aller Arten'* from *Die Entführung*. What makes this particularly worthwhile is the inclusion of lesser-known arias from *La clemenza di Tito*, *Il re pastore* and *Zaïde*, and they have been arranged most judiciously. The recordings all are excellent, and with full texts and translations, this is as good a Mozart aria compilation as any available. It is far preferable to the Penguin Classics disc below, which only costs a little less.

Arias from: *La clemenza di Tito; Così fan tutte; Don Giovanni; Le nozze di Figaro; Il rè pastore; Zaïde; Die Zauberflöte.*
(M) ** Decca Penguin Classics 460 651-2 [id.].
  Bacquier, Berganza, Burrows, Deutekom, Ghiaurov, Krause, Lorengar, Krenn, Popp, Tomowa-Sintow (with various orchestras and conductors).

With the star-studded collection of singers contributing to this collection, there is little here to really disappoint. The performances range from good to excellent, and there are a couple of rarities thrown in as well. Some may find the collection a bit piecemeal, but for anyone wanting just over an hour of Mozart arias, this CD fits the bill. The personal note is by Antonia Fraser, but there are no texts or translations.

Mussorgsky, Modest (1839–81)

Night on the bare mountain (arr. Rimsky-Korsakov); *Pictures at an exhibition* (orch. Ravel).
(BB) ** Virgin Classics 2 x 1 Dig. VBD5 61751-2 (2) [CDVB 61751]. R Liverpool PO & Ch. O, Mackerras – BORODIN: *Prince Igor: Overture and Polovtsian dances* ***; RIMSKY-KORSAKOV: *Scheherazade* **(*); TCHAIKOVSKY: *The Tempest.* ***

Mackerras's characterization of Mussorgsky's picture gallery comes over at a lower voltage than expected. The opening *Promenade* is fairly brisk, but the first few pictures, although well played, are almost bland, and while *Bydlo* reaches a fairly massive climax, it is not until *Limoges* that the performance springs fully to life; then *The Hut on fowl's legs* is powerfully rhythmic, with an impressive tuba solo. *The Great Gate of Kiev* is not as consistently taut as some versions, but is properly expansive at the close, with the recording, always full-bodied, producing an impressive breadth of sound. *Night on the bare mountain*, although vivid enough, lacks Satanic bite and its closing pages fail to wrench the heartstrings.

Pictures at an exhibition (orch. Ravel).

(**(*)) BBC Legends mono BBCL 4023-2 [id.].
  Philh. O, Giulini – TCHAIKOVSKY: *Symphony No. 6 (Pathétique).* (**(*))

Though the initial impact of the dry mono sound of 1961 is disconcerting, made striking by the unhelpful acoustic of the Usher Hall, Edinburgh, there are ample compensations for losing the full beauty of Ravel's orchestration in this characterful reading. The bite and impact of a performance under Giulini at his most electrifying is intensified, so that in such a movement as the *Hut on fowl's legs*, one even begins to think of this as a precursor of the *Rite of spring*. The fast, light articulation of *Limoges* is very exciting, and the *Catacombs* brass fiercely sepulchral. Solo playing is immaculate too, despite the lack of bloom, and the closing *Great Gate of Kiev* makes a spectacularly spacious impact, with a fine contribution from the tam-tam. A generous coupling.

Nielsen, Carl (1865–1931)

Symphonies Nos. 2 (Four Temperaments), Op. 16; (i) 3 (Sinfonia expansiva), Op. 27.
*** Dacapo Dig. 8.224126 [id.]. Danish Nat. SO, Michael Schønwandt; (i) with Dam-Jensen, Elming.

Symphonies Nos. 2 (Four Temperaments), Op. 16; 5, Op. 50.
*** Classico Dig. CD296 [id.]. Royal Liverpool PO, Douglas Bostock.

Both Michael Schønwandt and Douglas Bostock use the new scholarly Complete Edition. In the *Second Symphony*, Nielsen made minor corrections in the orchestral parts after the first printing and these are restored. Michael Schønwandt gets very cultured playing from his fine orchestra, and judges tempi to excellent effect. There is breadth and nobility in *The Four Temperaments* and his account of the *Espansiva* is equally well paced. Its attractions are greatly enhanced by the fine singing of both soloists. This can hold its own with the best.

Douglas Bostock's account of *The Four Temperaments* has tremendous character. Indeed, such is its authenticity of feeling that one's thoughts turn to the pioneering set by Thomas Jensen. In the *Fifth*, he really inspires his players, who convey enthusiasm and freshness. Bostock has real identification with Nielsen and though the playing has some rough edges and does not match the finesse or bloom of Blomstedt's San Francisco orchestra, it more than compensates in fire and intensity.

However, the Blomstedt set on a pair of Decca Doubles remains a primary recommendation in this repertoire, with Nos. 1, 2, 3 and the *Aladdin suite* on 460 985-2 and 4, 5, and 6 plus the *Hymnus amoris* on 460 988-2.

NORMAN   218

Symphonies Nos. (i) *3 (Sinfonia expansiva), Op.*
27; 5, Op. 50; Saul and David – Prelude to Act II.
⦿ (M) (***) Dutton Lab. mono CDK 1207 [id.].
   (i) Inger Lis Hasing, Erik Sjøberg; Danish
   State Radio SO, Erik Tuxen.

These were among the first recordings that introduced Nielsen to British audiences after the war.
The *Sinfonia expansiva* was recorded as long ago
as 1946 for Decca on nine 78-r.p.m. sides and was
regarded as state-of-the-art at the time. It shows just
how advanced Decca engineering was. Amazingly
it has never been transferred to CD and although it
was issued in the early days of LP, it never enjoyed
a further incarnation on vinyl. It is a vibrant, beautifully judged performance, which casts a stronger
spell than many of its successors. The *Fifth Symphony* recorded in 1950 in the same year that the
Danish Orchestra visited the Edinburgh Festival
was another pioneering recording though it was
soon eclipsed by Thomas Jensen's LP. In many
respects it is its equal and brings us close to this
extraordinary score. It has been reissued by EMI
but the Dutton transfer has the greater detail and
presence.

(i) *Symphonies Nos. 4 (The Inextinguishable), Op.
29; 5, Op. 50;* (i; ii) *Clarinet concerto;* (iii) *Violin
concerto;* (v) *Aladdin: Oriental march;* (vi) *At the
bier of a young artist; Bohemian-Danish folk tune.*
(B) *** Finlandia/Warner Ultima Dig.
   8573-81966-2 (2) [id.]. (i) Finnish RSO,
   Saraste; (ii) Kojo; (iii) Hannisdal, Norwegian
   Radio O, Mikkelsen; (v) Royal Stockholm O,
   Andrew Davis; (vi) Ostrobothnian Chamber O,
   Kangas.

The glory of this Ultima set is Saraste's coupling of
the *Fourth* and *Fifth Symphonies* – both among the
best performances to have appeared in recent years.
Saraste and his Finnish orchestra capture the explosive character of the opening of No. 4 to perfection,
and although there are moments when one feels the
current could flow with a higher charge, for the
most part this performance is splendidly shaped
and impressively executed. The *Fifth* is hardly less
successful: the conception is spacious yet there is
no want of movement. The recorded sound has
clarity, though the acoustic is a shade dry. Henrik
Hannisdal's account of the *Violin concerto* is a good
one, though not the finest available. The Norwegian
orchestra do not match the excellence of the Oslo
Philharmonic, but under their conductor, Terje
Mikkelsen, they turn in an appealingly unaffected
account, and the recording is good. The *Clarinet
concerto*, with Kullervo Kojo, is a strong performance and thoroughly recommendable. With three
highly attractive, lighter fill-ups (two of which are
quite rare), this Ultima Double is good value.

CHAMBER MUSIC

Aladdin (for solo flute); *Børnene leger; Canto
serioso; Fantasistykke; 2 Fantasistykker, Op. 2;
Moderen (The mother); Serenata in vano; Taagen
letter; Tro og håb spiller; Wind quintet, Op. 43.*
Kontrapunkt Dig. 32288 [id.]. Selandia Ensemble.

This disc scores in collecting all Nielsen's music
for wind but the balance is quite impossible, with a
jumbo flute in *Taagen letter* and a huge harp. There
are about a dozen versions of the lovely *Wind
quintet* now available on disc, and this is the one *not*
to have. The acoustic is small and the instruments all
uncomfortably large and loud. Difficult to listen to
with any pleasure and impossible to accord any
stars.

*String quartets Nos. 1 in F min., Op. 5; 2 in G
min., Op. 13.*
(BB) *** Naxos Dig. 8.553908 [id.]. Oslo Qt.

This is every bit as good as the companion coupling
the *Third* and *Fourth quartets*, which appeared last
year (see our main volume). Although the first two
are not their equal, they are distinguished by a
characteristic freshness of invention and warmth.
Despite its later opus number, the *G minor, Op. 13*,
was actually composed in the same year as the *Little
Suite for strings, Op. 1* and indebted to Svendsen
and Brahms. Nielsen delayed its publication until
he had revised it in the late 1890s. The *F minor
Quartet* of 1890, which precedes the *First Symphony*, is the finer of the two. The Oslo Quartet play
with an invigorating ardour that is totally compelling. They are the best currently available irrespective of price – indeed the best since the Copenhagen
Quartet recorded them on LP in the 1960s.

Norman, Ludwig (1831–85)

*Symphonies Nos. 1 in F min., Op. 22; 3 in D min.,
Op. 58.*
*(*) Sterling CDS 1038-2 [id.]. Nat SO of South
Africa, Mika Eichenholz.

Ludwig Norman was best known during his lifetime
as a conductor and pianist, and he travelled widely
with his wife, the violinist Wilhelmina Nuruda, who
later married Sir Charles Hallé. Norman was an
interesting figure in Swedish musical life. A champion of Berwald, whose influence can be discerned
in the *First Symphony*, he was much drawn to the
world of Schumann and Mendelssohn. The former
remains the dominant influence not only here but
elsewhere in his output. Not a strongly individual
composer, perhaps, and not particularly well served
here. The orchestral playing is wanting in finish and
the strings are particularly scruffy. There is little
space in which the tutti can expand and the texture
lacks transparency.

Nystedt, Knut (born 1915)

Canticles of Praise: Kristnikvede. A song as in the night.
** Simax Classics Dig. PSC 1190 [id.]. Bergen
    Cathedral Ch. and O, Magnar Magnersnnes.

At eighty-five, Knut Nystedt is the doyen of Norwegian composers. The bulk of his large output is choral, not unsurprisingly since he founded and conducted the Norsk soloistkor (Norwegian Soloists' Choir). The *Kristnikvede* or *Canticles of Praise* was commissioned in 1995 to commemorate Olav Trygvason's arrival in Norway in AD 995 and its conversion to Christianity; *A song as in the night* was written for a Swedish choral society in the university city of Uppsala. Nystedt's musical language is very direct in utterance, diatonic and well written. He knows exactly what voices can do. There is a faint wisp of Stravinsky and Honegger too. Worthwhile music decently performed, though the choir is not in the first flight and neither is the orchestra. But Nystedt is a composer of substance and his representation on CD all too meagre.

Ockeghem, Johannes (*c.* 1410–97)

Missa L'homme armé; Missa sine nomine; Salve Regina (probably by Philippe Basiron).
*** ASV Gaudeamus Dig. CDGAU 204 [id.].
    Clerk's Group, Edward Wickham (with Robert
    Morton (attrib.): *Rondeau: Il sera pour vous
    (L'homme armé)* ***).

Ockeghem's striking *L'homme armé mass* is easy to follow as its cantus firmus is so characterful. Here it is quoted first in a rondeau, attributed to Ockeghem's contemporary, Robert Morton, where it is used mockingly and it is surprising that no translation is given, although it is provided for the other music. Just the *Missa sine nomine* and the *Salve Regina* are dubiously attributed to Ockeghem, but he would surely have been glad to acknowledge the rich polyphony of the latter.

The *Sine nomine mass* for three voices, however, is much less characteristic, although to our ears its flowing lines are very attractive. The performances here are well up to the standard of this excellent group, but readers are reminded of the splendid Naxos recording of the *Missa L'homme armé* by the Oxford Camerata which is even more attractively coupled (● 8.554297 – see our main volume).

Missa prolationum; Marian motets: Alma redemptoris mater; Ave Maria; Intemerata Dei mater; Salve Regina (2 settings).
**(*) Virgin/Veritas EMI Dig. VER5 61484-2.
    Hilliard Ens.

When this Hilliard collection first appeared (on EMI in 1989) its authenticity and the smoothness of execution were widely praised. The mass, famous for its polyphonic complexities, is sung with perfect vocal blend and immaculate ensemble, but the characteristic austerity of the Hilliard approach now sounds a little cool alongside the newer version by the Clerks' Group under Edward Wickham on ASV (CDGAU 143). However, the added attraction of the Hilliard programme is that it also includes similarly flowing accounts of all the known motets of Ockeghem, although the shorter of the two *Salve Regina* settings is now re-attributed to Philippe Basiron. Full texts and translations are provided, so this remains a valuable reissue.

Offenbach, Jacques (1819–80)

Gaîté parisienne (ballet: complete);
Offenbachiana (both arr. Rosenthal).
(BB) ** Naxos Dig. 8.554005 [id.]. Monte-Carlo
    PO, Manuel Rosenthal.

Naxos must have felt that it was quite a feather in their cap to get Manuel Rosenthal to record his own arrangements of these two Offenbach ballets. If *Offenbachiana* sounds a little pastel-shaded beside the vividly inspired scoring of *Gaîté parisienne*, it still gathers together many delightful melodies from *Barbe-bleue*, *La Grande Duchesse de Gérolstein*, *La Fille du tambour-major* and *La Vie parisienne*. But alas, as he proved with his previous recording also with the Monte Carlo Orchestra for EMI, Rosenthal is a less inspiring conductor than he is an arranger. He obviously chooses ballet dance tempi and while the orchestra responds with playing of elegance and polish, and the wind soloists are all very good, the absence of uninhibited zest is a great drawback, especially in the famous final *Can-can*. The recording is excellent but this disc is primarily of documentary value. Arthur Fiedler's superb recording of *Gaîté parisienne* with the Boston Pops is currently withdrawn, but no doubt that will soon resurface in RCA's High Performance series.

Gaîté parisienne (ballet: excerpts); *Orpheus in the Underworld: overture.*
(M) ** Sony SMK 61830 [id.]. NYPO, Bernstein –
    BIZET: *Symphony in C* **; SUPPE: *Beautiful
    Galathea:* overture. ***

This quite enjoyable performance of excerpts from *Gaîté parisienne* dates from 1969, and would be more recommendable if the ballet were recorded complete and the sound was less brash. The *Orpheus in the Underworld* overture comes off well, and the (1967) recording is richer here than in *Gaîté parisienne*.

Overture: La Belle Hélène (arr. Haensch); *Les Contes d'Hoffmann:* (i) *Entr'acte et Barcarolle.*
*** Chandos Dig. CHAN 9765 [id.]. (i) Royal
    Liverpool PO Ch.; BBC PO, Yan Pascal
    Tortelier (with Concert: *French bonbons.* ***)

Haensch's *Overture La Belle Hélène* is a far better piece than the more famous overture to *Orpheus in the Underworld*. A stylish pot-pourri, it includes two of the opera's best tunes, the disarmingly seductive waltz, and a delightfully songful siciliano given to the oboe; it then ends with a brief, infectious can-can. Tortelier has its full measure, shaping it with great style and affection, and reminding us of Martinon's justly famous LPO mono Decca version (which needs a Dutton Lab. reissue). The *Barcarolle*, too, is very seductive, and both are given state of the art recording. This is part of an unmissable concert of '*French bonbons*' – see below.

Orff, Carl (1895–1982)

Carmina Burana.
(B) ** Decca Penguin Classics 460 646-2 [id.]. Burrows, Devos, Shirley-Quirk, Brighton Festival Ch., RPO, Dorati.

Dorati's version was recorded in the Kingsway Hall in 1976 in Decca's Phase Four system. The result is a beefy, vibrant account with good singing and playing. Despite some eccentric speeds, Dorati shows a fine rhythmic sense, but the performance cannot match the best available. The remastered recording brings a bold impact in fortissimos, but the quieter, more atmospheric passages are less cleanly defined. Now reissued on the bargain Penguin Classic label with an essay by John Berendt, it hardly makes a primary choice.

Catulli Carmina.
(B) **(*) Sony SBK 61703 [id.]. Blegen, Kness, Temple University Ch., Phd. O, Ormandy – STRAVINSKY: *Symphony of Psalms* ***.

Orff's successor to *Carmina Burana* uses four pianists and percussion instead of an orchestra, but the result is vivid enough, and those who respond to the earlier work should not be disappointed here. The exotic colours and rhythmic ostinatos are well brought out by the Temple University Choir, and Ormandy's vigorous performance produces an altogether rougher experience than Jochum's version on DG (see our main volume), for all the virtuosity of the players and singers. But the bluff humour of the piece comes out boldly. The 1967 recording is generally good, a little thin by modern standards, particularly at the top-end, but nothing too serious. An undoubted CD bargain with the excellent Stravinsky coupling.

Paganini, Niccolò (1782–1840)

Violin concertos Nos. 1–6; 24 Caprices, Op. 1; Duo merveille; Introduction and variations on 'Di tanti palpiti' from Rossini's Tancredi; Introduction and variations on 'Nel cor più non

mi sento' from Paisiello's La Molinara; Maestoso sonata sentimentale; Perpetuela; La Primavera; Sonata with variations on a theme by Joseph Weigl; Sonata Napoleone; Le streghe (Variations on a theme by Süssmayr), Op. 8; Variations on 'God save the King'; Variations on Non più mesta from Rossini's La Cenerentola.
(B) *** DG 463 754-2 (6) [id.]. Accardo, LPO, Dutoit.

A self-recommending set. The Accardo/Dutoit Paganini cycle remains a secure first choice: the concertos are brilliantly and imaginatively played and well recorded accounts which do not fall down in any department. The individual discs are discussed in our main volume. They are now released in an excellently packaged DG bargain box.

Violin concertos Nos. (i; ii) 1 in D, Op. 6; (iii; iv) 2 in B min. Op. 7; (v) 3 in E; (i; ii) 4 in D min; (i; vi) Introduction and variations on 'Di tanti palpiti' (arr. Kreisler); Le streghe, Op. 8 (arr. Kreisler); (iii; vii) Caprices, Op. 1, Nos. 13 and 20 (arr. Kreisler), 24 (arr. Auer); (viii) Moto perpetuo, Op. 11.
(B) ** Ph. Duo 462 865-2 (2) [id.]. (i) Grumiaux; (ii) Monte Carlo Op. O, Bellugi; (iii) Gitlis; (iv) Warsaw Nat. Philharmonic SO, Wislocki; (v) Szeryng, LSO, Gibson; (vi) Castagnone (piano); (vii) Janopoulo (piano); (viii) ASMF, Marriner.

This set is a mixed success. The first CD contains Grumiaux's 1972 recordings of the *First* and *Fourth Concertos*, which are extremely good performances, full of bravura, yet highly musical. Grumiaux really comes into his own in the slow movements, and the outer movements tingle with excitement. The orchestra plays with passion, and the recording, albeit within the characteristic Monte Carlo acoustic, is warm and full. In the *Third Concerto*, Szeryng is not so well recorded, and Gibson's accompaniments, whilst fully acceptable, lack flair. The snag with this set is the *Second Concerto*: the performance is undistinguished and the sound thin. At bargain price, the set is worth considering for Grumiaux's readings alone, and the various fill-ups are a bonus.

(i) Violin concerto No. 1 in D, Op. 6; Introduction and variations on 'Nel cor più non mi sento' (from Paisiello's La molinara); (ii) Cantabile; La Campanella; Moses fantasia.
⊕ *** BIS Dig. CD 999 [id.]. Ilya Gringolts; with (i) Lahti SO, Osmo Vänskä; (ii) Irina Ryumina.

The seventeen-year-old Russian violinist Ilya Gringolts plays the Paganini *D major Concerto* and the remainder of this recital not only with quite astonishing virtuosity but also with impeccable taste. Like Salvatore Accardo in the 1970s, he brings a refinement and noblesse to this repertoire, and indeed manages to make some of these display pieces really sound like music. There is an ardent quality to the playing, and a natural finesse that silences criticism. In the *Violin concerto* and the *Introduction and variations on 'Nel cor più non mi sento'* (from Paisiello's *La molinara*), the Lahti Orchestra under Osmo Vänskä give excellent support, and the BIS recording is in the highest traditions of the house – natural and lifelike.

24 Caprices, Op. 1.
(M) *** EMI CDM 67237-2 [CDM5 67257].
    Itzhak Perlman.

Perlman's superbly played 1972 set now returns to the catalogue at mid-price as one EMI's 'Great Recordings of the Century'. The transfer is immaculate, the violin image very real and vivid, and this can now be recommended without reservation alongside Accardo on DG (429 714-2).

Palestrina, Giovanni Pierluigi da
(1525–94)

Missa Beata Mariae virginis II; Missa Descendit angelis Domini; Jubilate Deo (for double choir); Motets: *Ad te levavi oculos meos; Miserere nostri Domine; Sitivit anima mea; Super flumina Babylonis.*
** Paraclete Press Dig. GDCD 106 [id.]. Gloria Dei Cantores, Elizabeth C. Patterson; Chant conductor: Richard Pugsley.

This fine American choir has the advantage of singing and recording in the superb acoustics of the Mechanics' Hall in Worcester, Massachusetts (where Caruso once sang, Paderewski and Rubinstein have played, and Dvořák conducted). They sing and blend beautifully and those looking for an essentially serene approach to these two Palestrina masses will find much to enjoy. However, there is a distinct lack of Latin fervour, and the different sections, *Kyrie*, *Gloria* and *Credo*, are sung in much the same somewhat bland style. The motets fare better, for one can sense the underlying intensity in *Super flumina Babylonis* ('By the waters of Babylon we sat down and wept') and *Miserere nostri Domine*. The concert ends with *Jubilate Deo*, and this has more momentum, but even here the joy could be more unbuttoned. The recording is outstandingly fine.

Missa Ecce ego Johannes; Cantantibus organis; Laudate pueri; Magnificat quarti toni; Peccantem me quotidie; Tribulationes civitatum; Tu es Petrus.
*** Hyperion Dig. CDA 67099 [id.]. Westminster Cathedral Ch., James O'Donnell.

Even among the Westminster Cathedral Choir's superb records (and not forgetting their award-winning set of the Pizzetti and Frank Martin

Masses), this disc stands out. Perfect chording and ensemble, natural and musical phrasing, spot-on intonation and a glorious tonal blend, make this issue one to treasure. The recording serves the choir well and there are scholarly notes by Ivan Moody.

Officium defunctorum: Ad Dominum cum tribularer clamavi; Domine quando veneris; Heu mihi Domine; Libere me, Domine (with Plainchant taken from Graduale Romanum).
**(*) ECM Dig. ECM 1653: 457 851-2 [id.].
    David James, Rogers Covey-Crump, John Potter, Gordon Jones – VICTORIA:
    Responsories **(*).

This CD combines music by Palestrina and Victoria, for the Office and Matins for the Dead and the Burial service, including one text, *Libera me Domine*, set by both composers. These 'composed pieces' are surrounded by the appropriate plainchant, of which there is a great deal. But it could hardly be more convincingly or beautifully sung. Indeed the four singers blend their voices beautifully and sing with eloquence, and are beautifully recorded. However the pervasive mood of doom and gloom will not suit all tastes!

Palmgren, Selim (1878–1951)

'Meet the Composer': Piano concertos Nos. (i–ii) 1, Op. 13; (iii; ii) *2 (The River), Op. 33;* (iv; ii) *3 (Metamorphoses), Op. 41;* (iii; ii) *4 (April), Op. 85;* (v; ii) *5, Op. 99;* (ii) *Pictures from Finland, Op. 24;* (vi) *Piano sonata in D min., Op. 11;* Piano pieces: *Raindrops, Op. 54/1; Preludes Nos. 12 (The Sea); 24 (The War), Op. 17/12 & 24; Spring: Dragonfly; May night, Op. 27/3–4; Dusk, Op. 47/1.*
(B) *** Finlandia/Warner Ultima Double Dig. 3984 28171-2 (2) [id.]. (i) Eero Heinonen; (ii) Turku PO, Jacques Mercier; (iii) Juhani Lagerspetz; (iv) Matti Raekallio; (v) Raija Kerppo; (vi) Izumi Tateno.

Palmgren is familiar to piano students, particularly of the older generation, through pieces like *May night* and *Moonlight*. At one time in Finland itself he was even thought to threaten Sibelius's pre-eminence. During the First World War the public found it easier to assimilate Palmgren's *Second* and *Fourth Piano concertos* and his piano miniatures than the more severe and challenging *Fourth* and *Fifth Symphonies* of Sibelius. Palmgren was spoken of as 'the Chopin of the north', for he wrote more idiomatically for the piano than did his countryman; but his music is limited both in its emotional range and in its repertory of pianistic devices. He was a fine pianist and accompanied his wife, Maikki Järnefelt, who by her first marriage had been Sibelius's sister-in-law and a noted interpreter of his songs. Palmgren taught briefly in America at the

Eastman School of Music when Howard Hanson had become its first director.

This valuable Double in Finlandia's 'Meet the Composer' series collects the five *Piano concertos*, which range in the composer's career from 1903 to 1941, and some of his piano miniatures, as well as the early *Sonata in D minor*, Op. 11, of 1900. There is poetic feeling here, tinged at times by a certain gentility. Palmgren was influenced by impressionism, though his melancholic sensibility is undoubtedly Nordic. All the soloists are persuasive in the concertos and are well supported by the Turku orchestra under Jacques Mercier. The orchestra gives an eminently acceptable account of the *Pictures from Finland*, Op. 24, from 1908. In the *Sonata* and the solo miniatures the pianist is the Japanese-born Izumi Tateno, who has lived in Finland since his student days. He plays these pieces with great sympathy and is very well recorded. A useful survey of Palmgren's music, recorded in very decent sound.

Parry, Hubert (1848–1918)

Cello sonata in A.
(M) *** Dutton Epoch Dig. CDLX 7102. Andrew Fuller, Michael Dussek – HARTY: *Butterflies; Romance and scherzo, Op. 8; Wood-stillness;* HURLSTONE: *Cello sonata in D.* ***

Parry's *Cello sonata* is finely wrought, though it does not wear its debt to Brahms lightly – understandably, perhaps, since it is a fairly early piece dating from 1879. It is designed on an almost symphonic scale – particularly the sinewy *Allegro* first movement. A splendid performance and recording.

Pärt, Arvo (born 1935)

(i) *Fratres;* (ii) *Magnificat; 7 Magnificat antiphons.*
*** Sony Dig. SK 61753 [id.]. (i) Moray Welsh, Alaistair Blayden, Michael Stirling; Taverner Choir, Andrew Parrott – TAVENER: *Canticle; Ikon; Out of the night; Threnos* ***.

It may be considered an advantage or a disadvantage that in coupling the hypnotic and often static music of Pärt and Tavener, the ear is drawn to the similarity of the style of the two composers. *Fratres*, which exists in many versions, is heard here in its comparatively spare instrumental scoring to make a centrepiece in what is essentially a choral programme. The simplicity of the *Magnificat* setting is its prime virtue, but the *Antiphons* are more varied, although still very compelling when so beautifully sung and recorded.

Pergolesi, Giovanni (1710–36)

Stabat Mater.
(M) **(*) DG 459 454-2 (2) [id.]. Mirella Freni, Teresa Berganza, Soloists from the Scarlatti Orchestra of Naples – A. SCARLATTI: *Concerti grossi; Stabat Mater.* **(*)

Unlike the splendid coupling of the Pergolesi and Scarlatti settings of the *Stabat Mater* highly praised in our main volume (OPS 30-160), this DG reissue involves a pair of discs. In the vocal works there is fine, eloquent singing from both soloists, and they match their close vibratos skilfully. They are well accompanied and naturally recorded, and this performance is affecting, if not as moving as its competitor, which earned Gemma Bertagnolli, Sara Mingardo and Rinaldo Alessandrini accompanying the Concerto Italiano a ◐.

(i; ii) *Stabat Mater;* (ii) *Salve Regina in A min.;* (i) *Salve Regina in F min.*
*** Decca Dig. 466 134-2 [id.]. Andreas Scholl, Barbara Bonney, Les Talens Lyriques, Christophe Rousset.

The combination of Andreas Scholl's alto and Barbara Bonney's soprano makes a remarkably individual, well-matched and certainly individual tonal blend and they often sing exquisitely, both solo and in tandem. Their *Stabat Mater* has plenty of drama as well as a fine expressive intensity and the closing *Quando corpus* is movingly restrained and beautiful. Both settings of the *Salve Regina* are authentic: Andreas Scholl sings the *A minor*, Barbara Bonney the *F minor*. Throughout, Christophe Rousset's period-instrument accompaniments are outstanding fine and full of life, and the Decca recording is splendidly real. But this version of the *Stabat Mater* needs to be sampled before purchase: you may be captivated by it or not. Our vote still goes to the Bertagnolli/Mingardo account mentioned above.

(i; ii) *Stabat Mater;* (iii) *Salve Regina;* (i; iv) *Cantatas: Chi non ode e chi non vede; Dalsigre, abi, mia Dalsigre; Luce degli occhi mei; Nel chiuso centro (Orfeo).*
(B) **(*) Erato/Warner Ultima 3984 28172-2 (2) [id.]. (i) Luciana Ticinelli-Fattori; (ii) Maria Minetto; (iii) Basia Retchitzka; (i; ii) Societa Camerista di Lugano, Edwin Loehrer; (iii) Nuovo Concerto Italiano, Claudio Gallico.

The cantatas were (very well) recorded in the late 1960s, and the *Stabat Mater* and *Salve Regina* come from 1972. Erato have understandably reissued them, for although none of the soloists have familiar names, their singing is of a high standard and the modern-instrument accompaniments are pleasingly stylish and nicely scaled. In the famous *Stabat Mater*, Luciano Sgrizzi's harpsichord continuo comes through the strings clearly, and the two voices – both pleasing in tone and line – blend well; each singer makes a strong solo contribution, dramatically open-voiced and meditative by turns. The small, sweet-timbred Basia Retchitzka is genuinely touching in the *Salve Regina*. The four little-known cantatas are in many ways even more demanding and Ticinelli-Fattori, articulating lightly, but singing with rich espressivo, rises to the occasion, especially in the most ambitious of the four, *Nel chiuso centro*, a most beautiful work. Three out of the four have a string quartet to support the keyboard accompaniment and very effective it is. With truthful, well-balanced recording this would have received a stronger recommendation had the set included texts and translations. Even so it is worth exploring.

Peter, Johann (1746–1813)

Sinfonia.

(M) ** Mercury [434 337-2]. Eastman-Rochester O, Howard Hanson – CHADWICK: *Symphonic sketches;* MACDOWELL: *Suite for large orchestra, Op. 42.* **(*)

The Dutch composer Johann Peter copied and studied the scores of symphonies by Abel, J. S. Bach and others. But instead of writing symphonies himself, he gave us six string quintets, of which this is the *Third*, here presented by a chamber orchestra as a *Sinfonia*. The music is graceful and has something of the charm of Boccherini, but sounds more like pastiche. Agreeable enough, it is very neatly played, but not memorable enough to return to very often.

Pinto, George Frederick
(1785–1806)

Fantasia & Sonata in C min. (completed Joseph Woelfl); *Grand sonatas Nos. 1 in E flat; 2 in A, Op. 3/1–2; in C min.; Minuetto in A flat; Rondo in E flat; Rondo on an Irish air, 'Cory Owen'.*
*** Chandos Dig, CHAN 9798 [id.]. Míceál O'Rorke (piano).

This unmissable Chandos collection reveals another forgotten composer of distinction, who might have become a very considerable figure had he not died prematurely at the age of twenty-one. He was born in London within a musical family and began playing in public at the age of eleven. His first two *Grand sonatas* were published in 1801 when Pinto was sixteen and already a very accomplished composer indeed, with a distinct individuality, yet writing in a forward-looking lyrical style, that sometimes reminds us of the young Schubert. The *C minor Sonata*, however, is dedicated to John Field and delightfully identifies with that composer's

melodic simplicity. But most striking of all is the *Fantasia and Sonata in C minor*, left unfinished at the composer's death, the opening quite worthy of Mozart, with a following *Adagio – Fugato* which has all the serenity of Bach, followed by a Beethovenian finale, which yet still has a personality of its own. Míceál O'Rorke plays all this music very persuasively indeed and is beautifully recorded.

Pizzetti, Ildebrando (1880–1968)

(i) *Piano concerto. Preludio per Fedra;* (ii) *Sinfonia del fuoco* (for the film *Cabiria*).
** Marco Polo Dig. 8.225058 [id.]. Robert Schumann Phil. O, Oleg Caetani; with (i) Susanna Stefani; (ii) Boris Statsenko, Städtischer Opera Ch. Chemnitz.

It is good that interest in Pizzetti is increasing. No doubt Hyperion's prizewinning disc of the *Requiem* with the Westminster Cathedral Choir has helped fuel this. Of course, we still lack recordings of the *Concerto dell'estate*, which Toscanini premièred, and the *Symphony in A*. The present issue brings the eloquent Act I *Prelude* to the opera Pizzetti composed with Gabriele d'Annunzio, plus the *Sinfonia del fuoco*, drawn from the incidental music Pizzetti wrote in 1914 for an elaborate production of *Cabiria* (again with d'Annunzio) in which silent film was used. But the most substantial work is the *Piano concerto 'Song of the High Seasons'* of 1930. It is a little overripe perhaps, and at times even rather like Rachmaninov. The soloist Susanna Stefani is a pupil of Tatiana Nikolayeva and Alicia de Larrocha, and acquits herself well. The *Fedra* prelude is the finest thing here and the Robert Schumann Philharmonie of Chemnitz give decent, serviceable performances. However, at less than 50 minutes' playing time this CD is over-priced.

La Pisanella; 3 Preludii sinfonici (per L'Edipo Re); Preludio a un altro giorno; Rondò Veneziano.
**(*) Hyperion Dig. CDA 67084 [id.]. BBC Scottish SO, Osmo Vänskä.

This well-filled programme makes an excellent introduction to Pizzetti. The *Rondò Veneziano* of 1929 was first performed by Toscanini; the three preludes from the opera *L'Edipo Re* are full of interest and *La Pisanella* is a sunny and glorious work, which dates from 1913. That was the year of *Le Sacre du printemps*, from which Pizzetti's piece could not be further removed. Three movements of the suite were recorded after the war by Carlo Zecchi and the LPO on two Decca 78s (still treasured by R. L.) and again in the days of stereo LP by Lamberto Gardelli. This is only its third recording, though Osmo Vänskä does give rather more of the score than they. He plays all these pieces with appropriate feeling but the string sound lacks real body and richness, particularly at the bass end of the spectrum.

Pleyel, Ignaz (1757–1831)

Symphonies in D min. (Ben147); C, Op. 66 (Ben154); G, Op. 68 (Ben156).
*** Chandos Dig. CHAN 9525 [id.]. London Mozart Players, Matthias Bamert.

This is one of the excellent Chandos series exploring the contemporaries of Mozart. Pleyel, a pupil of Vaňhal and Haydn, became Kapellmeister to Count Erdödy in 1777 before moving to Salzburg. It was Pleyel who gave the rival series of London concerts to Haydn and Salomon in 1792. He settled in Paris, founding the celebrated Pleyel piano factory. The earliest of the three symphonies, the *D minor*, has hints of *Don Giovanni* and the *C major* has Rossinian overtones. The invention is a bit variable but the playing of the London Mozart Players under Matthias Bamert has charm and grace, and the recording is in the best traditions of the house.

Plummer, John (died c. 1487)

Missa Sine nomine.
*** Signum Dig. SIGCD 015 [id.]. Clerks' Group, Edward Wickham (with BEDYNGHAM: *Myn hertis lust; Fortune alas; Mi verry joy*; ANON: *Kyrie; Song; Pryncesse of youthe* ***) – FRYE: *Missa Flos Regalis, etc.* ***

We know very little about the English composer, John Plummer, whose mass only survives in a Brussels manuscript. His setting is rather bare and primitive in its part writing, less inspired than its coupling by Walter Frye, but it makes a fascinating aural glimpse into an unfamiliar period of English polyphony. The coupled songs by Bedyngham are delightful and this whole collection, beautifully sung and recorded, is treasurable.

Ponchielli, Amilcare (1834–86)

La Gioconda (complete).
(M) (***) Warner Fonit mono 3984 29355-2 (3) [id.]. Maria Callas, Fedora Barbieri, Maria Amadini, Giulio Neri, Gianni Poggi, Turin R. Ch. & O, Votto.

Like the companion Callas set of *La Traviata*, this was recorded (for Cetra in 1952) very early in the diva's career. She was to re-record the opera in 1959, again with Votto, but, as in the remake, the present set shows her dramatic powers at their peak and the voice fresher than ever. The famous *Suicidio* is sung with an intensity that has rarely if ever been equalled and the closing scenes of both Acts I and IV (with Maria Amadini and Paolo Silveri respectively) are memorable. Barbieri and Neri also make fine contributions and Poggi's contribution is suitably ardent. Votto conducts with understanding, maintaining a spontaneous dramatic flow and the remastering of the old mono recording is surprisingly good. The soloists are well caught, and although the chorus is sometimes backward, one soon adjusts: Callas admirers are accustomed to accepting sound which is far less agreeable. The Italian libretto is without a translation.

Popov, Gavriil (1904–72)

Symphony No. 5 in A, 'Pastoral', Op. 77; (i) *Symphonic suite No. 1.*
**(*) Olympia Dig. OCD 598 [id.]. USSR State SO, Gurgen Karapetian; (i) Glushkova, Polyakov, Moscow Radio & TV SO, Edvard Chivzhel.

You will find a more detailed account of this composer in our main volume. The *Symphonic suite No. 1* derives from the score he composed in 1933 for the film *Komsomol is the Chief of Electrification*, an early example of Socialist-Realist cinema! The *Suite* produced a telegram of congratulation from Eisenstein no less. The *Fifth Symphony*, on the other hand, is much later – composed in 1956, three years after Shostakovich's *Tenth*. In *A Guide to the Symphony* (OUP) David Fanning speaks of its individuality and points out that it is almost unique among Soviet symphonies in ending with a slow movement. It is certainly well structured, the first and last of the five movements are subtitled 'Pastorale' and the intervening three are inventive, with an excellent sense of orchestral colour. The performances are thoroughly committed even if the sound is a bit raw in climaxes.

Poulenc, Francis (1899–1963)

Complete chamber music: *Clarinet sonata; Sonata for 2 clarinets; Cello sonata; Sonata for clarinet and bassoon; Elégie for horn and piano (in memory of Dennis Brain); Flute sonata; Oboe sonata; Sarabande for guitar; Sextet for piano, flute, oboe, clarinet, bassoon and horn; Sonata for horn, trumpet & trombone; Trio for piano, oboe & bassoon; Villanelle for piccolo (pipe) and piano; Violin sonata.*
*** Hyperion Dig. CDA 67255/6 [id.]. Nash Ens. with Ian Brown.

Poulenc's delightful chamber music has done well in recent years: the set by various British artists on Cala has strong claims on the collector, and so has the Decca account with Patrick Gallois, Maurice Bourgue, Pascal Rogé and friends. Poulenc (or 'Poolonk', as he is called on BBC Radio 3 these days) is quintessential Nash territory and their Hyperion survey is of predictable excellence. Common to most of these works is the pianist Ian Brown, a stylist if ever there was one, whose playing lends such character to the proceedings. There are few performances that fail to delight and fewer that are surpassed elsewhere. Very good recorded sound makes this an excellent recommendation – in every way superior to the very uneven EMI compilation which appeared early in 1999, the centenary year, but which we did not include in our main volume.

Complete chamber music, Vol. 1: *Flute sonata; Oboe sonata; Sextet for piano, flute, oboe, clarinet, bassoon and horn; Trio for piano, oboe & bassoon; Villanelle for piccolo (pipe) and piano.*
(BB) * Naxos Dig. 8.553611 [id.]. Bernold, Tharaud, Doise, Van Spaendonck, Lefèvre, Joulain.

We normally welcome Naxos's enterprise, which brings repertoire within the range of those who might want to investigate it but can only afford a modest outlay to satisfy their curiosity. However, this will give little pleasure, for the acoustic of the Temple du Bon Secours, Paris, is unpleasing, reverberant and glassy, and the playing of these artists (most of whom come from the Opéra Orchestra) is curiously wanting in elegance and style. In Poulenc, charm and finesse are essential elements. The Cala set (CACD 1018 – see our main volume) is in every way superior and a remarkable bargain.

Complete piano music: Volume 1: *Bourrée au Pavilon d'Auvergne; Feuillets d'album; Intermezzi; Nocturnes; Pastourelle (L'Eventail de Jeanne); Promenades; Suite in C; Valse; Villageoises.*
(BB) (*) Naxos 8.553929 [id.]. Olivier Cazal.

The first volume in a projected survey on budget label of all Poulenc's piano music. Olivier Cazal hails from Toulouse and has an enviable number of prizes to his credit. However, his playing is strangely unidiomatic: Poulenc calls for charm, sophistication and lightness of touch as well as depth of feeling. These surface all too rarely here.

Volume 2: *Badinage; Cinq impromptus; Française; Humoresque; Les soirées de Nazelles; Mélancolie; Pièce brève sur le nom d'Albert Roussel; Presto in B flat; Suite française; Valses impromptus sur le nom de Bach; Trois mouvements perpétuels.*
(BB) (*) Naxos 8.553930 [id.]. Olivier Cazal.

A non-starter. Olivier Cazal brings little style and less subtlety to this glorious repertoire. He does not lack virtuosity but there is little delicacy here. No challenge (even allowing for its price advantage) to Pascal Rogé, whose boxed complete set is self-

recommending on three mid-priced Decca CDs (❁ 460 598-2 – see our main volume).

VOCAL AND CHORAL MUSIC

Ave verum corpus; Exsultate Deo; Figure humaine; Quatre petites prières de Saint François d'Assise; Un soir de neige; Quatre motets pour le temps de Noël; Salve Regina; Sept chansons.
** ASV Dig. CDDCA 1067 [id.]. Joyful Company of Singers, Peter Broadbent.

As a glance at our main volume will show, Poulenc's choral music is very well represented on disc. This newcomer from the Joyful Company of Singers and Peter Broadbent is not without merit, but in terms of ensemble, chording and tonal blend does not outclass the recommendations listed there.

Mélodies: Banalités; Les chemins de l'amour; 2 Mélodies de Guillaume Apollinaire.
*** Virgin/EMI Dig. VC5 45360-2 [id.].
Véronique Gens, Roger Vignoles – DEBUSSY; FAURE: *Mélodies.* ***

Véronique Gens possesses a delightful voice of much beauty, and is very much at home in Poulenc's world. As with the Debussy, she is both imaginative and characterful. She receives sensitive support from Roger Vignoles, and Virgin give her excellent and natural sound.

Prokofiev, Serge (1891–1953)

(i) *Violin concertos Nos. 1 in D, Op. 19; No. 2 in G min., Op. 63. Symphony No. 5 in B flat, Op. 100; Romeo and Juliet, Op. 64: suite (Nos. 1–10); Scythian suite, Op. 20.*
(M) **(*) Decca 466 996-2 (2) [id.]. (i) Ruggiero Ricci; SRO, Ansermet.

Ansermet's Prokofiev is always characterful, and if one accepts the less than ideally polished playing of the Swiss orchestra, there is much to enjoy here. The *Fifth Symphony* was one of Ansermet's finest performances, straight and unaffected, and the recording as brilliant as you could wish. The *Scythian suite* comes off very well too: it is a grossly underrated score because of its parallels with *The Rite of Spring.* The aggressive passages are particularly threatening, largely due to the brilliant recording (wonderful timpani and bass drums), though the performance as a whole is not quite forceful enough.

The *Romeo and Juliet suite* is also rather impressive, though it is the conductor's attention to detail, rather than orchestral virtuosity, which impresses. The *Violin concertos* are new to CD – and how good they sound. They are hardly top recommendations (intonation on the part of the soloist as well as the orchestra is not immaculate), but they have plenty of character and are not dull.

A collection which will be of particular interest to Ansermet admirers, particularly as the vintage sound has been so vividly transferred to CD.

Lieutenant Kijé (suite), Op. 60.
(M) **(*) RCA 09026 61957-2 [id.]. Chicago SO, Reiner – HOVHANESS: *Mysterious Mountain symphony*; STRAVINSKY: *Le baiser de la fée.*
***

Reiner's *Lieutenant Kijé* is very well played and sounds astonishing good for 1959, but is just a bit too straight-faced to bring out all the humour in the music. Still, all Reiner performances have authority, and this is no exception.

Lieutenant Kijé (suite); The Love for three oranges (suite), Op. 33; Symphony No. 1 in D (Classical), Op. 25.
(B) **(*) Ph. Virtuoso 426 640-2. LSO, Marriner.

This bargain Philips disc offers good playing and recording and there is nothing to disappoint. Individually these works are available in other versions that are as good as (or better than) this compilation, but these are lively performances, and the remastered sound is fresh and open.

The Love for 3 oranges: suite.
(M) **(*) RCA 09026 63532-2 [id.]. Boston Pops O, Fiedler – CHOPIN: *Les Sylphides* **; LISZT: *Les Préludes; Mazeppa.* *

This performance shows Fiedler on top form: it is full of life and character – the *Scène infernale* is especially effective, with some electrifying string playing. The 1961 recording is generally impressive too – brilliant in the 'Living Stereo' manner, with splendid definition set in the Boston Symphony Hall acoustic (the bass drum sounds particularly realistic). The only fault is some slight distortion, but that is soon forgotten in the vitality of the playing.

Peter and the wolf.
(M) Virgin/EMI VM5 61782-2 [id.]. Lenny Henry, Royal Liverpool PO, Libor Pešek – BRITTEN: *Young person's guide to the orchestra* **(*); SAINT-SAENS: *Carnival of the animals* (chamber version) ***.
(M) * Sony SMK 60175 [id.]. NYPO, Bernstein (conductor and narrator) – SAINT-SAENS: *Carnival of the animals* *; BRITTEN: *Young person's guide to the orchestra.* (*)

Lenny Henry's colloquial narration is enthusiastic, clear and communicative. Children will certainly respond to his individual 'voices' for the characters in the tale and also his additional vocalized effects. He manages a spectacular gulp when the poor duck is swallowed alive, while the wolf 'snaps' very angrily indeed, and is properly furious when he is finally caught. The orchestral accompaniment is lively, following the narrative closely and por-

traying the closing procession very grandly. But the record's appeal is reduced to virtually nil by the extraordinarily inept new instrumental characterization for each of the characters in the tale. The piece was specifically designed by Prokofiev to introduce young listeners to the orchestral palette, and the dumbing-down here robs his score of this primary purpose, plus almost all its elegance and wit. Peter stays with the strings; but instead of a flute, the bird is portrayed by a Chinese 'mouth organ', the duck is a squealing Catalan 'tiple'. Even more unfortunately, the wolf is represented by three very bland accordions; and worst of all the engagingly feline clarinet, with which Prokofiev identified the cat, is changed to an oboe d'amore in order to produce a semblance of a 'miaow'. The only really telling substitution is the use of a grumpy-sounding serpent to personify Grandfather. Within the narrative itself the composer's carefully balanced scoring is quite ruined by the various squawks from the intruders. Let us recommend instead Dame Edna Everage on Naxos, who is child-friendly in every sense of the word, yet her sharply detailed accompaniment, from the Melbourne Symphony Orchestra under John Lanchbery, retains all the sophisticated colour of the composer's original conception (8.554170).

Bernstein opens his narration with a kind of quiz on which instrument represents which character. The effect is mildly patronizing, as is his narration throughout. If you are a Bernstein *aficionado* you may well take to it. The playing is excellent, though the performance lacks charm. Vivid 1960 sound.

Symphonies Nos. 1–7; Lieutenant Kijé (suite).
(B) * DG Dig. 463 761-2 (4) [id.]. BPO, Ozawa.

Ozawa's BPO set of Prokofiev symphonies is a non-starter. The performances are well played, but are very routine: without looking at the documentation, it would be hard to recognize this celebrated orchestra, which here produces a general purpose sonority which Karajan would never have countenanced in his day. *Lieutenant Kijé* is sadly lacking in sparkle. Decca's rival bargain box with Walter Weller is infinitely preferable (430 782-2), and so is Järvi's digital set on Chandos (CHAN 8931/4), though that costs quite a bit more.

Symphonies Nos. 1–4; Hamlet, Op. 77 (incidental music).
(B) **(*) BMG/Melodia Twofer 74321 66979-2 (2) [id.]. USSR RTV Grand SO, Rozhdestvensky.

It is good to have authentically Russian performances of these sometimes intractable works. Rozhdestvensky's set begins with a brilliant performance of the *Classical Symphony* (one of the finest available in its day) with sparkling outer movements, while the slow movement and Minuet are admirably paced. The *Second Symphony*, with its unremittingly loud first movement (conceived with an eye to shock the Parisians in the mid 1920s), must be among the noisiest music Prokofiev ever wrote. However, the second movement, with its beautiful set of variations and some highly imaginative writing, occupies quite another world, and Rozhdestvensky and his orchestra adapt well to the conflicting demands of both. The *Third Symphony* receives a fiery performance, though the powerful atmosphere of the slow movement is not entirely realized. The *Fourth Symphony* receives a similarly committed performance and its overall success makes one wonder why its acceptance took so long in coming. All four were recorded in the 1960s, and though the sound is a little dated, and the Russian brass will not be to everyone's liking, Rozhdestvensky's total commitment makes up for any minor reservations. The *Hamlet* incidental music was recorded in 1988 and makes a rare and enjoyable fill-up. All in all this is excellent value.

Symphony No. 5 in B flat, Op. 100.
(M) *** DG 463 613-2 [id.]. BPO, Karajan –
    STRAVINSKY: *Rite of spring* **(*).

Karajan's reading of the *Fifth symphony* is outstanding in every way. It is a totally unaffected, beautifully played account, with the Berlin Philharmonic on top form, and the DG engineers at their best. The recording is a model of its kind, allowing all the subtleties of the orchestral colouring to register without any distortion of perspective. It has splendid range and fidelity and is wholly free from any artificial balance. It is now paired with his highly individual version of *The Rite of Spring* to make an intriguing coupling in DG's Originals series.

CHAMBER MUSIC

Music for cello and piano: Adagio (Cinderella), Op. 97; Ballade in C min., Op. 15; Cello sonata in C, Op. 119; Solo cello sonata, Op. 133; 5 Mélodies, Op. 35 bis (arr. Wallfisch); *The Love for three oranges: March, Op. 33; The Tale of the stone flower: Waltz, Op. 118.*
*** Black Box Music Dig. BBM 1027 [id.].
    Raphael Wallfisch, John York.

Adagio (Cinderella), Op. 97; Ballade in C min., Op. 15; Cello sonata, Op. 119.
*** Chant du Monde Dig. LDC 2781112 [id.].
    Gary Hoffman, Philippe Bianconi –
    SHOSTAKOVICH: *Cello sonata; Moderato.*
    **(*)

In addition to the *Cello sonata*, of which there are now over two dozen versions, Raphael Wallfisch and John York give us the early *Ballade*, Op. 15, as well as Wallfisch's own transcription of the enchanting *Cinq Mélodies*, Op. 35, more often heard in Prokofiev's own arrangement for violin and piano, and the solo sonata he began just before his

death whose first movement Vladimir Blok put into shape some years later. Wallfisch is recorded in the excellent acoustic of St George's, Brandon Hill, save for the *Cinq Mélodies* and the other arrangements by Piatigorsky and Prokofiev himself, but the engineers match the two acoustics most expertly. Wallfisch plays with superb and golden tone and with great expressive eloquence. John York is a sensitive and intelligent partner. Their sonata can rank with the best.

Gary Hoffman and Philippe Bianconi are hardly less fine than their distinguished rivals and are every bit as well recorded. Indeed, there is more air round the aural image in their recital. They opt for the more traditional Shostakovich coupling but do offer the early *Ballade*. Not too much to choose between the two newcomers, though their Shostakovich may not be to all tastes.

Flute sonata, Op. 94.
*** EMI CDC5 56982-2 [id.]. Emmanuel Pahud,
    Stephen Kovacevich – DEBUSSY: *Syrinx;
    Bilitis*, etc.; RAVEL: *Chansons madécasses.*
    ***

The *Flute sonata* of 1943 was subsequently arranged for violin at the request of David Oistrakh and is more frequently heard on that instrument. Played like this, it is quite captivating. Emmanuel Pahud and Stephen Kovacevich set ideal tempi in each movement and their characterization is perfect as a result. The familiar ideas sound completely fresh and novel. Easily a first recommendation. A perfectly balanced recording.

Quintet (for oboe, clarinet, violin, viola and cello), Op. 39.
*** EMI Dig. CDC5 56816-2 [id.]. Richard
    Woodhams, Michael Collins, Chantal Juillet,
    Isabelle van Keulen, Harold Robinson –
    BARTOK: *Contrasts*; LISZT: *Concerto
    pathétique.* ***

Quite the best version of the *Quintet* to have appeared since the Berlin Philharmonic recorded it on a Deutsche Grammophon LP. A pretty flawless account of a haunting and often poignant work, originally designed for the ballet. Impeccable playing by all concerned and good, well-balanced sound.

String quartets Nos. 1 in B min., Op. 50; 2 in F, Op. 92; (i) Overture on Hebrew themes, Op. 34.
(B) **(*) Helios Dig. CDH 55032 [id.]. Coull Qt
    (i) with Angela Malsbury, David Pettit.

Good, well-recorded performances whose attractions are enhanced by the competitive price. At the same time, they are not a first recommendation given the excellence of the American Quartet (Olympia OCD 340) and the Aurora (Naxos 8.553136).

Violin sonatas Nos. (i)*1 in F min., Op. 80;* (ii) *2 in D, Op. 94;* (iii) *Sonata for 2 violins, Op. 56.*
*** Finlandia Dig. 3984 23399-2 [id.]. Pekka Kuusisto; with (i) Ilkka Paananen; (ii) Raija Kerppo; (iii) Jaakko Kuusisto.

The young Finnish violinist Pekka Kuusisto enters a competitive field with the likes of Perlman, Oistrakh, Stern, Schlomo, Mintz and many other distinguished artists. He was the winner of the Sibelius Competition some years back, and his playing has a youthful ardour and vitality that is refreshing. Of course, Oistrakh has special claims on the allegiance of collectors since he premièred the *First Sonata* and commissioned the arrangement of the *Flute sonata* that became the *Second.* However, this newcomer is extremely good and ranks among the best, with excellent modern recording. No one investing in it is likely to be disappointed.

Puccini, Giacomo (1858–1924)

La Bohème (complete).
*** Decca Dig. 466 070-2 (2) [id.]. Angela Gheorghiu, Roberto Alagna, Elisabetta Scano, Simon Keenlyside, Ildebrando D'Arcangelo, La Scala, Milan, Verdi Ch., & O, Chailly.

The husband-and-wife partnership of Gheorghiu and Alagna is formidably demonstrated here, though with Chailly in taut control and speeds consistently on the fast side, this is a performance that misses some of the tenderness in the score, as well as some of the fun. Gheorghiu's glorious singing is powerfully matched by the heroic tones of Alagna, culminating in a deeply moving death scene. The ravishing portrayal of the heroine by Angela Gheorghiu stands out, with the creamy sound of her soprano never more sensuously caught on disc, so that she dominates the performance whenever she appears. Happily, Chailly allows for ample expansion in the big solo numbers, most notably for the ever-imaginative Gheorghiu. With voices well forward and with words exceptionally clear, in an acoustic more open than most Milan recordings, the brilliance of Chailly's reading is enhanced. Roberto Alagna as Rodolfo is more impulsive here than in EMI's Pappano recording, made four years earlier, responding no doubt to Chailly's fast speeds, but the manner is less affectionate. His is a heroic reading rather than a tender one, just as Gheorghiu's Mimì is a fully tragic heroine, not just a Puccinian 'little woman'. These are performances for a big opera-house, with shading less subtle than with Pappano (● CDC5 56120-2 – see our main volume). The notable casting among the rest is that of Simon Keenlyside, promoted to Marcello this time from Schaunard in the EMI set, again consistently responsive and alert. Elisabetta Scano is a light, bright Musetta, strongly contrasted with Gheorghiu, if a little shrill on top. Roberto di Candia

makes a positive Schaunard, but Ildebrando d'Arcangelo as Colline is not helped by the close vocal balance, with a flutter emerging in the Act IV Coat Song.

Manon Lescaut (complete).
**(*) DG Dig. 463 186-2 (2) [id.]. Maria Guleghina, José Cura, Lucio Gallo, Luigi Roni, La Scala, Milan, Ch. & O, Muti.

The problems of recording live at La Scala weigh heavily in the Muti recording for DG. The stage noises are often intrusive in crowd scenes and moments of action with occasionally odd balances; the orchestral sound lacks body, and choral ensemble is often poor. Muti too is encouraged to underline too heavily such big dramatic moments as the end of Act III. Though Maria Guleghina sings affectingly as the heroine, the lovely soprano tone tends to spread under pressure in the upper register. José Cura sings strenuously from his very first aria, *Tra voi belle*, onwards, though he too characterizes well, and is occasionally persuaded to modify his strong, heroic tone. Though DG's earlier set conducted by Sinopoli dates from 1983/4, it is preferable in almost every way (413 893-2), but first choice probably remains with Levine's Decca set, with Freni and Pavarotti (440 200-2 – see our main volume).

Tosca (complete).
(M) *** Decca 466 384-2 (2) [id.]. Leontyne Price, Giuseppe di Stefano, Giuseppe Taddei, V. State Op. Ch., VPO, Karajan.
(M) ** RCA 09026 63305-2 (2) [id.]. Zinka Milanov, Jussi Björling, Leonard Warren, Rome Op. Ch. & O, Leinsdorf.

Karajan's 1962 Vienna *Tosca* was produced by John Culshaw and is rightly now assigned its place in Decca's Legends series. It was previously available on a Decca Double and now costs more, but as it includes a libretto/translation is well worth its mid-price bracket. Karajan deserves equal credit with the principal singers for the vital, imaginative performance, recorded in Vienna. Taddei himself has a marvellously wide range of tone-colour, and though he cannot quite match the Gobbi snarl he has almost every other weapon in his armoury. Leontyne Price is at the peak of her form and Di Stefano sings most sensitively. The sound of the Vienna orchestra is enthralling – both more refined and richer than usual in a Puccini opera – and it sounds quite marvellous in its digitally remastered format, combining presence with atmosphere.

At mid-price Leinsdorf's version makes a fair bargain, despite dated 1950s recording and the conductor's heavy style. But the set will be of principal interest to admirers of the veteran singer in the cast. Jussi Björling was at the peak of his fame as Cavaradossi. Though Zinka Milanov was past her best and was sometimes stressed by the role, there is much beautiful singing here from a great soprano who recorded all too little. Leonard Warren was another characterful veteran, but the furry edge to the voice makes him a less-than-sinister Scarpia. However, those wanting a vintage version will surely turn back to the famous EMI De Sabata mono version, where Di Stefano is partnered with Callas at her finest and Tito Gobbi is an unforgettable Scarpia (CDM5 66444-2).

Tosca (complete in English).
(M) *** Chandos Dig. CHAN 3000 (2) [id.]. Jane Eaglen, Dennis O'Neill, Gregory Yurisich, Geoffrey Mitchell Ch., Peter Kay Children's Ch., Philh. O, David Parry.

David Parry, with Jane Eaglen in one of her finest performances on disc, directs a gripping account of Puccini's red-blooded drama, sung in English. With the help of opulent, atmospheric Chandos sound, the bite and energy of the Philharmonia bring out the expressive warmth of the score, not least in the love music, whether in the power of the big tuttis or in magical, whispered pianissimos.

What above all seals the success of the set is the power and command of Jane Eaglen as Tosca. The confident sureness with which she attacks every top note is a delight, so that in Act I she expresses her jealousy with the vehemence of a Wagnerian, while singing with warm, rounded tone. She is well matched by Dennis O'Neill as Cavaradossi, aptly Italianate, and Gregory Yurisich makes a powerful Scarpia, younger-sounding than most and therefore a plausible lover. The others are well cast too, notably Peter Rose as a fresh-voiced Angelotti. The Geoffrey Mitchell Choir and children's choir are superb in the crowd scenes of Act I.

COLLECTIONS

Arias: *La Bohème: Quando m'en vo' soletta. Gianni Schicchi: O mio babbino caro. Madama Butterfly: Un bel dì. Manon Lescaut: In quelle trine morbide. La Rondine: Chi il bel sogno di Doretta; Ore dolci e divine. Tosca: Vissi d'arte. Le Villi: Se come voi piccina.*
(M) *** Sony Great Performances SMK 60975 [id.]. Kiri Te Kanawa, LPO, Pritchard or LSO, Maazel – VERDI: Arias *** (with MOZART: *Don Giovanni: Ah! fuggi il traditor; In quali eccessi . . . Mi tradì;* HUMPERDINCK: *Der kleine Sandmann bin ich;* DURUFLE: *Requiem: Pie Jesu.* ***)

In a recital recorded in 1981 the creamy beauty of Kiri Te Kanawa's voice is ideally suited to these seven lyrical Puccini arias including the little waltz-like song from *Le Villi*. The other excerpt from this opera comes from the complete set made around the same time. Throughout, expressive sweetness is more remarkable than characterization, but in such music it is difficult to complain. Kiri was also in top form in her 1978 assumption of the role

of Elvira in Mozart's *Don Giovanni* (again with Maazel), and the delightful Sandman aria from *Hänsel und Gretel* and Duruflé's beautiful, serene *Pie Jesu* again show the voice at its most appealing.

Purcell, Henry (1659–95)

Chaconne in G min.; Overtures in D min.; G; and G min.; 3 Parts on a ground in D; 2 Pavans in A; Pavan in A min.; 2 Pavans in B flat; 2 Pavans in G min.; Sonatas Nos. 6 in G min.; 7 in E min.; 12 in D; Suite in G.
(B) **(*) HM Musique d'Abord Dig. HMT 7901 327 [id.]. London Baroque.

What a rich composer Purcell is, always full of surprise. Most of the music here was composed at the same time as his well-known four-part *Fantasias* of 1680, and shows the young composer exploring the various instrumental styles available to him. The *Three parts on a ground* has some quite unexpected harmonies, while the *Pavan à 4 in G minor* uses some haunting and forward-looking minor-keyed progressions. But all these overtures, suites and sonatas are rewardingly inventive. The London Baroque perform them well, though lacks a little in dynamic range. It may also have been better to have arranged the programme differently (with four pavans playing one after another), but one can reprogramme the order, and this bargain CD is certainly worth considering.

Anthems: Man that is born of woman; O God, thou has cast us out; Lord, how long wilt thou be angry?; O God, thou art my God; O Lord God of hosts; Remember not, Lord, our offences; Thou knowest, Lord, the secrets of our hearts. Verse anthems: *My beloved spake; My heart is inditing; O sing unto the Lord; Praise the Lord, O Jerusalem; They that go down to the sea in ships. Morning Service in B flat: Benedicte omnia opera; Cantate Domino; Deus miscreatur; Magnificat; Nunc dimittis. Evening service in G min.: Magnificat; Nunc dimittis. Latin Psalm: Jehovah, quam multi sunt hostes mei. Te Deum and Jubilate in D.*
(B) *** DG Double 459 487–2 (2) David Thomas, Christ Church Cathedral, Oxford Ch., E. Concert, Simon Preston.

Recorded in the Henry Wood Hall in 1980, this admirable collection of Purcell's church music is self-recommending. Apart from David Thomas's fine contribution (in the verse anthems) the soloists come from the choir, and very good they are too, especially the trebles. The performances are full of character, vigorous, yet with the widest range of colour and feeling, well projected in a recording which is both spacious and detailed. The sound is excellent in its current transfer, and as a DG Archiv Double this is even more attractive.

Songs and Duets: Here let my life; In vain the am'rous flute; Music for a while; Sweetness of nature.
**(*) Virgin Veritas/EMI Dig. VC5 45342-2.

Gérard Lesne, Steve Dugardin, La Canzona –
BLOW: *An ode on the death of Mr Henry Purcell; Fugue in G min.; Grounds in C min.; in D min.; Sonata in A; Suite in G.* **(*)

It makes an illuminating programme to have John Blow's moving tribute to his former pupil, Purcell, set alongside some of Purcell's songs and duets, even more striking in their ideas. Though the recorders of La Canzona are on the abrasive side, Gérard Lesne and his counter-tenor colleague are stylish singers, well attuned to this repertory. Though *Music for a while* is the best-known item here, such a duet as *In vain the am'rous flute* is just as memorable with its side-slipping chromatics over a ground bass. Close recording.

Rachmaninov, Sergei (1873–1943)

Piano concertos Nos. 1–3; Rhapsody on a theme of Paganini.
(BB) *** EMI Dig. CZS5 73765-2 (3). Mikhail Rudy, St Petersburg PO, Jansons –
TCHAIKOVSKY: *Piano concerto No. 1 ***.*

Mikhail Rudy and the St Petersburg Philharmonic under Mariss Jansons consistently demonstrate that extrovert bravura is not everything in Rachmaninov piano concertos, and that poetry and refinement can offer exceptionally rewarding results in works which emerge here as far more than conventional warhorses. These are cultured but yet strongly characterized performances with some beautiful orchestral playing and pianism of elegance and finesse. There is plenty to admire and relish. The results are fresh and unhackneyed from first to last, with Rudy's light, clean articulation adding sparkle. Not that he lacks weight, and the strong support of Jansons and the St Petersburg Philharmonic intensifies the idiomatic warmth, with mystery alongside passion in Rachmaninov's writing. This account of the *Fourth Concerto* is especially valuable in offering the original, uncut version of the finale, as well as the usual revised text. On their last appearance, we underestimated these versions, but now the three discs (each originally issued at full price), come repackaged at super-budget price to make an excellent recommendation, even if you already have a set of the concertos, for the Tchaikovsky coupling is similarly enticing.

(i) *Piano concerto No. 3 in D min., Op. 30. Elegy, Op. 3/1; Polichinelle; Preludes in C sharp min., Op. 3/2; in B flat; G min.; E flat, Op. 23/2, 5, & 6; in G; G sharp min., Op. 32/ 5 & 12.*
✿ *** Elan Dig. CD 82412 [id.]. Santiago

Rodriguez; (i) with Lake Forest LSO, Paul McRae.

A reader has drawn our attention to this pianist about whom we have also heard from American friends and colleagues. Judging from this CD their enthusiasm is well placed. Santiago Rodriguez is Cuban by birth but like Bolet has made his home in the United States, distinguishing himself in the 1981 Van Cliburn Competition. There is no doubt from the opening bars of the *Third Concerto* that he is a Rachmaninov interpreter of outstanding calibre, whose playing withstands the most exalted comparisons. Indeed, as one plays this disc, one's thoughts turn only to the greatest exponents of this repertoire – Horowitz, Rachmaninov himself and William Kapell. Rodriguez, too, has dazzling virtuosity at his command and also fine musicianship and a rare keyboard authority. He plays the first-movement cadenza (and how!) that Rachmaninov himself favoured rather than the alternative one that came into fashion with Vladimir Ashkenazy. The eight remaining pieces are of the same exalted standard. A most exciting issue.

(i) *Piano concerto No. 3 in D min., Op. 30. Variations on a theme of Chopin, Op. 22.*
(BB) *(*) Arte Nova Dig. 74321 69509-2 [id.].
Andrei Pisarev; (i) with Russian PO, Samuel Friedmann.

The prizewinning young Russian Andrei Pisarev offers fresh, direct readings of both the *Third Concerto* and the formidable *Chopin variations*. Brilliant as Pisarev's technique is, these performances lack a degree of refinement and detail – not helped by close recording which sabotages pianissimos. Yet they are always enjoyable, strong, generally thrustful readings at speeds a shade faster than usual. At super-budget price they might be considered, for the coupling is unusual, but this is hardly a prime recommendation for either work.

Piano concerto No. 4 in G min., Op. 40.
✿(M) *** EMI CDM5 67238-2 [CDM5 67258].
Michelangeli, Philh. O, Gracis – RAVEL: *Piano concerto in G.* ***✿

There are few records in the catalogue more worthy of being described as a 'Great Recording of the Century' than Michelangeli's superb coupling of Rachmaninov and Ravel. It has been with us for four decades and time has not diminished its unique appeal from the commanding opening onwards. The current remastering has been expertly managed and at mid-price it should be included in even the most modest collection.

Symphonic dances, Op. 45; (i) The Bells, Op. 35.
**(*) Chandos CHAN 9759 [id.]. (i) Olga Lutsiv-Ternovskaya, Leonid Bomstein, Vyacheslav Pochapsky, Russian State Cappella; Russian State SO, Valeri Polyansky.

There are currently some twenty versions of the *Symphonic dances* available, and a dozen of *The Bells*, two of them on the Chandos label (one from Neeme Järvi and the Royal Scottish National, and the other by Dmitri Kitaienko and Danish Radio forces). Valeri Polyansky is a bit self-indulgent in the *Symphonic dances* and lingers, particularly in the middle movement, while the *Lento assai* section of the finale nearly crawls to a stop. The playing of the Russian State Orchestra is very fine and the recording is little short of spectacular in its clarity, definition and warmth. Artistically this is not a first choice. However, *The Bells* comes off well and is much helped by good soloists and the glorious recorded sound.

Symphony No. 1, in D min., Op. 13; Caprice bohémien, Op. 12.
(BB) ** Naxos Dig. 8.55006 [id.]. Nat. SO of Ireland, Alexander Anissimov.

Taken on its own merits, the budget account from Alexander Anissimov and the National Symphony Orchestra of Ireland is more than adequate. Were none of the excellent alternatives available – like Ormandy and the Philadelphia Orchestra (part of a superb bargain two-disc set offering all three symphonies on Sony SB2K 63257) and, more recently, Mariss Jansons's highly committed account with the St Petersburg Orchestra on EMI (CDC5 56754-2) – this could be recommended. The latter is well worth the extra outlay involved and brings one of the finest versions of *Isle of the Dead* to have appeared since Reiner.

Symphony No. 2 in E min., Op. 27; Vocalise, Op. 34/14; Aleko: Intermezzo and Women's dance.
❀ (M) *** EMI CDM5 66982-2 [CDM 566997]. LSO, Previn.

Previn's 1973 recording of the *Second Symphony* dominated the catalogue for over a decade in the analogue era. Now it has been vibrantly and richly remastered for CD as one of EMI's 'Great Recordings of the Century'. Its passionate intensity combines freshness with the boldest romantic feeling, yet the music's underlying melancholy is not glossed over. With vividly committed playing from the LSO and a glorious response from the strings, this remains a classic account, not even surpassed by Sanderling's, now that the recording has such opulence and weight in the bass. The addition of the engaging *Aleko* excerpts, plus a fine lyrical account of the *Vocalise*, makes for a generous reissue playing for nearly 75 minutes.

(i) *Symphony No. 3 in A min., Op. 44;* (ii; iii) *Spring* (cantata), *Op. 20;* (iii) *3 Unaccompanied choruses.*
*** Chandos Dig. CHAN 9802 [id.]. (i) Russian State SO; (ii) Tigram Martyrosayan; (iii) Russian State Symphonic Capella, Valeri Polyanski.

A splendid, very Russian account of the *Third Symphony*, volatile but convincingly so, with some glorious playing from the strings, especially in the lovely, nostalgic secondary theme of the first movement which is so very Slavic in feeling. The choral works too are superbly done, with the widest range of dynamic in the masterly unaccompanied choruses, while Tigram Martyrosayan is a richly resonant bass soloist in the cantata. The singers are helped by the resonant acoustic which creates the richest vocal sonorities. For the symphony, competition is strong, with Stokowski and Previn vying for position at mid-price, but with state-of-the-art Chandos sound this new version is well worth considering.

PIANO MUSIC

Andante ma non troppo in D min.; Canon in E min.; Fragments (1917)*; Fughetta; Lento in D min. (Song without words)* (1866–7)*; Moments musical, Op. 16/2* (rev. version 1940)*; Morceau de fantaisie in G min.; Oriental sketch* (1917)*; Prelude in F* (1891)*; Variations on a theme of Chopin, Op. 22.*
(BB) (**) Naxos Dig. 8.554426 [id.]. Idil Biret.

The main work here on the Naxos disc is the Op. 22 set of *Variations on a theme of Chopin*, which is not generously represented on CD. The Turkish-born Idil Biret is no stranger to the Naxos catalogue. A pupil of Cortot, Kempff and at one time Nadia Boulanger, she has had a long and distinguished concert career. She is fleet of finger and possesses both technical address and good musical feeling.

Idil Biret's Rachmaninov recital here brings a powerful yet poetic reading of the *Chopin variations*, one of Rachmaninov's finest piano works, coupled with miniatures and rarities including many rare early pieces. Biret's reading of the *Variations*, a work seriously neglected, brings out the high dramatic contrasts, cleanly establishing the character of each section and setting the whole structure (overall almost sonata-like) in relief. The fill-ups include an unpretentious little piece, *Lento*, that Rachmaninov wrote at thirteen, and demonstrations of his prowess in writing counterpoint, untypical but crisply refreshing. Excellent sound to bring out the subtleties of Biret's tonal shading.

Morceaux de fantaisie, Op. 3; Sonata No. 2 in B flat minor, Op. 36 (revised, 1931 version)*; Variations on a theme of Corelli, Op. 42.*
*** Danacord Dig. DACOCD 525 [id.]. Oleg Marshev.

Oleg Marshev comes from Baku and studied in Moscow with Mikhail Voskrensky, a pupil of Lev Oborin. He went on to be the first-prize winner at the Pilar Bayona Festival in Spain, and collected the *Prima Premio Assoluto* in Rome in 1992. As befits an artist of this pedigree, he possesses the grand manner, and has won golden opinions for his Russian repertoire, including a Prokofiev sonata cycle on Danacord (not submitted for review). Listening to his Rachmaninov, one can see why, for, apart from flawless technical address and sensitivity, he has an innate feeling for this repertoire. His account of all three pieces belongs up there with the finest, though in the *Corelli variations* Pletnev is in a class of his own. Marshev has a strong musical personality and commands a wide range of keyboard colour and dynamics. Some allowance must be made for the recording made in the Concert Hall at Sønderborg in Denmark, which does not do him full justice in fortissimo passages. The dryish recording, if not ideal, is perfectly serviceable and should not deter readers from investigating some superbly idiomatic Rachmaninov playing.

Piano sonata No. 2, Op. 36 (original,1913 version)*; Etudes-tableaux, Op. 39;* (with Kreisler's *Liebesleid,* trans. Rachmaninov).
*** BIS CD-1042 [id.]. Freddy Kempf.

Rachmaninov-playing in the grand manner. Freddy Kempf has a real feeling for this composer, and the authority and technical prowess to go with it. He is also a narrative pianist – from the very beginning he has you in the palm of his hand. The *Second Sonata* in the original, 1913 version is as good as any now before the public, and the *Etudes-tableaux* come off equally well. Vivid, realistic piano sound.

VOCAL MUSIC

Songs (sung in Russian): *The answer; Believe it or not; Beloved let us fly; By the grave; The fountains; Let me rest here alone; The little island; The moon of life; The muse; Night is mournful; No prophet I; O never sing to me again; The Pied Piper; The pity I implore; The quest; To her; To the children.*
(BB) ** Belart 461 626-2 [id.]. Robert Tear, Philip Ledger – CHOPIN: *Songs.* **

Robert Tear is always sensitive and musical, shows a good understanding of the Russian poetry, and only occasionally seems to suffer strain on top notes. Ledger accompanying and the Decca (originally Argo) recording from the mid 1970s are of a good standard; the artists are not too closely balanced and there is a pleasing ambience. At super-bargain price this is a more than acceptable way of discovering some fine Rachmaninov songs. But there are no texts and translations.

Rameau, Jean-Philippe (1683–1764)

Ballet music: *Les fêtes d'Hébé; Hippolyte et Aricie.*
*** Erato/Warner Dig. 3984 26129-2 [id.]. Les

Arts Florissants, William Christie – Marc-Antoine CHARPENTIER: *La Descente d'Orphée aux Enfers; Médée; Les Plaisirs de Versailles ***.*

These extended selections from two of Rameau's ever-inventive and charmingly scored opera ballets were recorded to celebrate the twenty-fifth anniversary of William Christie and Les Arts Florissants. This is all delightfully fresh and inventive music and Rameau's scoring is ever-resourceful and as presented here constantly sparkling and ear-tickling. Most entertaining and beautifully recorded.

Rathaus, Karol (1895–1954)

Symphony No. 1, Op. 5; Der letzte Pierrot.
*** Decca Dig. 455 315-2 [id.]. Deutsches SO Berlin, Israel Yinon.

Karol Rathaus was born in Poland, and his music was taken up in Weimar Germany by the likes of Walter, Furtwängler, Horenstein and other conductors of the day. He left Germany just before the Nazis came to power, and worked in Paris and London before settling in America where he became professor of composition at Queen's University, New York. He studied with Schreker, whose influence is clearly discernible, though it is Honegger, Scriabin or Berg to whom one's thoughts also turn. His music's language is distinctly expressionist, albeit not atonal, and is expertly laid out for the orchestra.

The *First Symphony* unleashed a torrent of critical abuse at its première in 1926, and was not heard again in Rathaus's lifetime. Indeed, the composer thought of the score as lost, and a copy did not surface until 1993. In fact it is a striking and arresting score, which can be strongly recommended. The ballet *Der letzte Pierrot* which followed in 1927 is also rewarding, full of variety and interesting ideas. There are jazz elements and the motivic organization is skilful. It enjoyed some popularity in the late 1920s and deservedly so. The performances under Israel Yinon are very good indeed and the recording quite outstanding.

Rautavaara, Einojuhani (born 1928)

Piano concerto No. 3 (Gift of dreams); Autumn gardens.
*** Ondine Dig. 950-2 [id.]. Helsinki PO, Vladimir Ashkenazy.

The *Third Piano concerto* is a new work, written in 1998 for Vladimir Ashkenazy both to play and to conduct. It is predominantly meditative and unconcerned with conventional bravura. It gets its subtitle from a Baudelaire setting, *Le mort des pauvres,* which Rautavaara made in the late 1970s and in which the words '*le don des rêves*' appear. *Autumn gardens*, from 1999, also has a dreamlike feel to it. There is little of the Bartók and Prokofiev which influenced the *First Concerto*, though some of the harmonic language is redolent of Honegger. The performances are exemplary and the recording is in the demonstration class. The disc also includes a conversation between Einojuhani Rautavaara and Vladimir Ashkenazy.

Symphony No. 7 (Angel of Light); Cantus Arcticus (Concerto for birds and orchestra) Op. 61; (i) Dances with the winds (Concerto for flutes and orchestra).
*** BIS Dig. CD 1038. (i) Petri Alanko; Lahti SO, Osmo Vänskä.

The *Seventh Symphony* comes from 1994–5 and was almost immediately recorded by Leif Segerstam and the Helsinki Philharmonic on Ondine (see our main volume). The new version is every bit as good both artistically and as a recording. The sound is pretty state-of-the-art, though its rival has the deeper perspective. The *Seventh* is Rautavaara's strongest symphony so far, and the finest Finnish symphony of the last decade. Vänskä's performance has impressive power and atmosphere; he keeps the music moving and casts the stronger spell. Both shorter pieces, the familiar *Cantus Arcticus* and the *Dances with the winds*, a concerto in which the solo flautist plays four members of the flute family (though not at the same time), are from the 1970s, and these fine performances have appeared before in other couplings.

Etudes, Op. 42; Icons, Op. 6; Partita, Op. 34; Preludes, Op. 7; Piano sonatas Nos. 1 (Christus und die Fischer), Op. 50; 2 (The fire sermon), Op. 64.
(BB) *** Naxos Dig. 8.554292 [id.]. Laura Mikkola.

Rautavaara enjoys increasing exposure on CD but his piano music has received relatively little attention. The admirably lucid performances by Laura Mikkola fill an important gap. The *First sonata* (*Christus und die Fischer*) comes from 1969, the same year as the *First Piano concerto*, which this artist has also recorded with such success, and the *Second* (1970) is also most convincingly done. She is given first-class recorded sound. An excellent and economical way of filling in your picture of this fine composer.

Ave Maria; Magnificat; Canticum Mariae Virginis; Missa Duodecanonica.
*** Ondine Dig. ODE 935-2 [id.]. Finnish Radio Chamber Ch, Timo Nuoranne.

Rautavaara has written extensively for the voice and has a strong feeling for the medium. This disc includes music from most periods of his career. The *Ave Maria* (1957) for male voices and the *Missa*

Duodecanonica (1963) for female voices are both serialist, albeit in much the same way as was Frank Martin's at one time. The *Magnificat* of 1979, the first Finnish setting of the text, has dignity and eloquence. The singing of the Finnish Radio Chamber Choir under Timo Nuoranne has security of pitch, subtle colouring and purity of tone. Expert, well-balanced Ondine recording.

Ravel, Maurice (1875–1937)

(i) *Alborada del gracioso; Boléro;* (ii) *Daphnis et Chloé: suite No. 2; Rapsodie espagnole;* (i) *La valse.*
(M) **(*) Sony SMK 60565 [id.]. Bernstein, with (i) Orchestre Nat. de France; (ii) NYPO.

This is repertoire at which Bernstein excels: *La valse* has a genuinely intoxicating quality, *Alborada del gracioso* glitters as it should, and the *Boléro* is most effective. These French recordings were made in 1975 and are very good, though not in the demonstration class. The *Daphnis suite* dates from 1961, and is excellent too, with an immensely exciting finale (the recording is not quite so satisfactory though), and the 1973 *Rapsodie espagnole*, if a little indulgent here and there, has atmosphere and imagination. An enjoyable collection.

Alborada del gracioso; Daphnis et Chloé (suite no. 2); Rapsodie espagnole; Le tombeau de Couperin; La valse.
** DG 453 194-2 (3 + 1) [id.]. Stuttgart RSO, Celibidache – DEBUSSY: *Images: Ibéria. La Mer* (with rehearsal); *Nocturnes.* (**)

For Celibidache, refinement of sonority is the *sine qua non* of his music making. And he does produce a beautiful sound from the Stuttgart Orchestra, though the affected phrasing is tiresome. The Ravel pieces are far less offensive than the almost intolerable Debussy. Indeed, there are moments of beauty. The middle section of the *Alborada* has great mystery and atmosphere though it is still terribly slow. The recordings come from the 1970s and are not always as successfully balanced as is usual from Südwestfunk.

Alborada del gracioso; Pavane pour une infante défunte; La valse; (i) *Shéhérazade* (song cycle); *Vocalise en forme de habanera* (orch. Hoérée).
(BB) *** Virgin Classics 2 x 1 Dig. VBD5 61742-2 (2) [CDVB 61742]. (i) Arleen Augér; Philh. O, Pešek – CANTELOUBE: *Chants d'Auvergne.* ***

This is a particularly attractive programme, brilliantly recorded. The Philharmonia are in exuberant form. The *Alborada* glitters, the *Boléro* is built steadily to a splendid climax, and among the solos the flamboyant trombone is particularly memorable. The *Pavane* has a noble dignity and *La valse* liltingly generates plenty of adrenalin. Arleen Augér's lovely voice is ideally suited to a languorous account of *Shéhérazade*, which she makes entirely her own, opening *Asie* gently and seductively but expanding to a passionate climax, while *La flûte enchantée* is more intimate, with some delicately refined playing from the Philharmonia solo flute. If you also want the (excellent) coupling, this is a fine bargain.

(i) *Boléro; Daphnis et Chloé: suite No. 2; Ma mère l'Oye: suite;* (ii) *Rapsodie espagnole; La valse.*
(B) **(*) Australian Decca Eloquence 466 667-2.
   (i) LAPO, Mehta; (ii) LSO, Monteux.

Mehta's Ravel is very high powered, but the visceral excitement he produces is most compelling. *La valse* is full of tension, and the *Daphnis suite* builds up to a splendid climax. *Ma mère l'Oye* is brilliantly played too, although here the music's sense of gentle rapture is less fully realized. Not surprisingly, *Boléro* is a great success. Throughout, one marvels at the vivid Decca sound and the brilliance of the playing of the Los Angeles orchestra, and one feels that this period (late 1960s and 1970s) was Mehta's golden recording era. Monteux's LSO account of the *Rapsodie espagnole* is justly famous; it is a memorably glowing account, drenched in atmosphere and, despite some tape hiss, it still sparkles. A stimulating reissue on the Australian Eloquence label – especially as the Mehta recordings have not been available on CD before.

Piano concerto in G.
☼ (M) *** EMI CDM5 67238-2 [CDM5 67258].
   Michelangeli, Philh. O, Gracis –
   RACHMANINOV: *Piano concerto No. 4.* *** ☼

Ravel's masterpiece is well served on CD but this reissue in EMI's 'Great Recordings of the Century' is second to none. Michelangeli's slow movement is ravishing, and the sparkle of the outer movements is underpinned by a refined Ravelian sensitivity. The remastering of the early stereo master (1957) is wholly beneficial, the sound full yet remarkably transparent in revealing detail.

Ma mère l'Oye (suite); La valse.
** Chandos Dig. CHAN 9799 [id.]. Danish Nat RSO, Temirkanov – TCHAIKOVSKY: *The Nutcracker* (ballet), Act II: *suite* ** (with GADE: *Tango: Jalousie*).

It is difficult to know quite for whom this recording is designed. Recordings of the *Ma mère l'Oye* suite and *La valse* are hardly in short supply and most collectors will want a more logical coupling than bits of Act II of *Nutcracker.* Including the Gade items was a curious idea. No complaints about the sound.

Le tombeau de Couperin; La valse.
(M) *** Decca Penguin Classics Dig. 460 649-2

[id.]. Montreal SO, Dutoit – DEBUSSY: *Nocturnes;* SATIE: *3 Gymnopédies.* ***

Dutoit's account of Ravel's delightful *Tombeau de Couperin* is wonderfully sensitive and sympathetic, and the recording offers demonstration quality, transparent and refined, with the textures beautifully balanced and expertly placed. Jonathan Cope, who provides the author's note, should be very happy with this performance which will surely rekindle his nostalgic memories of that first heady discovery of this wonderful music. *La valse* too is a model of its kind, and again the playing of the Montreal Orchestra is absolutely first class, while the Decca recording has a clarity, range and depth of perspective that is equally satisfying. But what a pity room was not found for Dutoit's exquisite account of *Ma Mère l'Oye.*

CHAMBER MUSIC

(i; ii) *Introduction and allegro for harp, flute, clarinet and string quartet;* (ii; iii; iv) *Piano trio;* (v) *String quartet;* (ii; iii) *Violin sonata;* (vi) *Sonata for violin and cello;* (vii) *Chansons madécasses.*
(M) ** Calliope analogue CAL 3822.4 (3). (i) Jamais & Ens.; (ii) Barda; (iii) Carracilly; (iv) Heitz; (v) Talich Qt; (vi) Hanover String Duo; (vii) Jacques Herbillon, Larde, Degenne, Paraskivesco – DEBUSSY: *Chamber music* **(*).

The *String quartet* was recorded in 1972 and very good it is too. The remaining performances in the repertoire date from 1974 and are decent rather than distinguished. The recordings are all analogue – and none the worse for that! But this is serviceable rather than special.

Piano trio in A min.
*** Hyperion Dig. CDA 67114 [id.]. Florestan Trio – DEBUSSY; FAURE: *Piano trios.* ***

Led by the masterly pianist Susan Tomes, the Florestan Trio here give an outstanding account of the Ravel masterpiece. They generally adopt speeds on the fast side, but with no feeling of haste, thanks to playing at once highly polished and flexibly expressive. The couplings are unique and apt, with each composer represented at a different period of his career. Vivid sound.

String quartet in F.
(M) *** DG 463 082-2 [id.]. Melos Qt – DEBUSSY: *String quartet in G min.* *** ☼

The Melos account is one of the very finest this work has received on record. The playing is perfect in ensemble, has fine attack and great beauty of tone. The slow movement offers the most refined and integrated matching of timbre; in terms of internal balance and blend it would be difficult to surpass, and the reading has great poetry. In both the Scherzo and finale the Melos players evince the highest virtuosity, with complete identification with Ravel's sensibility. The (1979) sound remains excellent in its Galleria transfer, and this disc remains among the primary recommendations for this coupling.

VOCAL MUSIC

Chansons madécasses.
*** EMI CDC5 56982-2 [id.]. Katerina Karnéus, Emmanuel Pahud, Truls Mørk, Stephen Kovacevich – DEBUSSY: *Syrinx; Bilitis,* etc.; PROKOFIEV: *Flute sonata, Op. 94.* ***

The collector is spoilt for choice as far as the ever-topical *Chansons madécasses* is concerned. This new version is primarily a vehicle for the virtuosity – or rather artistry – of Emmanuel Pahud, for there is no egotism in his playing, the virtuosity is merely by the by. He and Stephen Kovacevich are joined by the young Swedish mezzo Katerina Karnéus and the Norwegian cellist Truls Mørk. Great sensitivity, powerful atmosphere, lucidity of diction and clarity of texture. This is an outstanding recital.

(i) *Chansons madécasses;* (ii) *5 Mélodies populaires grecques; Histoires naturelles;* (i) *3 Poèmes de Stéphane Mallarmé.*
(BB) **(*) Belart 461 624-2 [id.]. Felicity Palmer; with (i) Nash Ens., Rattle; (ii) John Constable – FAURE: *Mélodies.* **(*)

Felicity Palmer has revealed herself a sensitive performer of French songs, and so she is here, even if the microphone brings out a slight beat to her voice rather distractingly and the interpretations are less characterful than the finest currently available (see our main volume). Yet the atmospheric accompaniments from the Nash Ensemble under Simon Rattle and from the equally sensitive John Constable are a strong plus point. There is no comparable collection available in this budget price range and the grouping of these four evocative cycles with songs by Fauré is pleasingly apt. Outstanding mid-1970s (originally Argo) recording, but no texts or translations.

Shéhérazade (song cycle).
❀ (M) *** Decca Legends 460 973-2 [id.]. Régine Crespin, SRO, Ansermet – BERLIOZ: *Les nuits d'été* *** (with *Recital of French Songs***).

Crespin is right inside these songs and Ravel's magically sensuous music emerges with striking spontaneity. She is superbly supported by Ansermet who, aided by the Decca engineers, weaves a fine tonal web round the voice. Her style has distinct echoes of the opera house; but the richness of the singer's tone does not detract from the delicate languor of *The enchanted flute,* in which the slave-girl listens to the distant sound of her lover's flute playing while her master sleeps. The new transfer of the 1963 recording adds to the allure of the remarkably rich and translucent Decca sound.

OPERA

(i) *L'enfant et les sortilèges* (complete). *Ma Mère l'Oye* (complete ballet).
*** DG Dig. 457 589-2 [id.]. (i) Stephen, Owens, Lascarro, Johnson, Soloists New L. Children's Ch., LSO Ch.; LSO, André Previn.

With opulent recording heightening the sumptuousness of Ravel's orchestration, and with Previn infectiously pointing rhythms at generally spacious speeds, this evocative one-acter could not be more persuasive, with the atmospheric magic beautifully captured. Though a French-speaking cast might have sounded more idiomatic, characterizations here are exceptionally vivid, with Pamela Helen Stephen as the Child easily outshining her predecessor on Previn's EMI version, and the others making a strong team. The apt and substantial fill-up, the complete *Mother Goose* ballet, also beautifully done, makes a welcome bonus. While Ernest Bour's classic mono set on Testament should not be forgotten (❀ SBT 1044) this stands high among modern versions.

(i) *L'heure espagnole. Rapsodie espagnole.*
*** DG Dig. 457 590-2 [id.]. (i) Barber, Gautier, Ollman, Wilson Johnson, Ainsley; LSO, André Previn.

Just as in his companion recording of *L'enfant,* Previn, with his subtle pointing of rhythm at spacious speeds, heightens the atmospheric beauty, so in this charming farce he brings out the wit of the score, not least in Ravel's Spanish dance rhythms and parodies. Again the casting is strong and characterful, with commendably clear French from mainly non-French singers. Kimberly Baker is a seductive Concepcion and Kurt Ollman a fine forthright Ramiro. Warm, full sound. Again the coupling is very apt, if less generous. One must not forget Maazel's pairing of both operas as DG Originals at mid-price (449 769-2) and that also has attractive couplings – see our main volume.

Rawsthorne, Alan (1905–71)

Film music: *Burma Victory* (suite). *The Captive Heart* (suite) (both arr. Gerard Schurmann). *The Cruel Sea: Main titles and Nocturne. The Dancing Fleece: 3 Dances* (both scores arr. & orch. Philip Lane). *Lease of Life: Main titles and Emergency. Saraband for Dead Lovers: Saraband and Carnival* (both arr. Schurmann). *Uncle Silas: Main titles and opening scene; Valse caprice; End titles. West of Zanzibar: Main titles. Where no Vultures Fly: Introduction; Main titles and opening scene. Surveying the game* (all arr. and orch. Philip Lane).

*** Chandos Dig. CHAN 9749 [id.]. BBC PO,
Rumon Gamba.

Between 1937 and 1964 Rawsthorne wrote music
for twenty-seven British films. These scores have
the imprimatur of Hans Keller, who was unequivocal: 'they [are] magnificent music – all of
them, and however intricate and cogent their relation to the visual, they would lose absolutely
nothing if that relation were lost.'

The composer himself felt that 'music from the
films is rarely satisfactory on its own'. However,
Rawsthorne's own work contradicts that assertion.
He was not a ready melodist like Malcolm Arnold,
but he could write memorable paragraphs, imaginatively and powerfully scored, and Gerard Schurmann's two suites from *The Captive Heart* and the
fine documentary *Burma Victory* demonstrate his
remarkable ability to characterize situations in
music. Scenes in the former like 'Letters from
home' (nostalgic writing for oboe and strings), the
busy scherzando of 'Repatriation' and the exuberance of 'VE Day' are matched in the latter by the
vignettes describing 'Dropping supplies', 'Dawn',
'Building boats' and the final nobilmente anticipation of freeing 'Mandalay'.

He is very good at flamboyant, Hollywoodian
title music, yet the charming delicacy of the *Valse
caprice* from *Uncle Silas* shows the other side of
his musical nature and makes for a number well
worth preserving independently. The *Three dances*
from *The Dancing Fleece* are further examples of
Rawsthorne's wan lyricism. Gerard Schurmann had
worked with the composer in preparing the original
scores, and Philip Lane demonstrates his skills of
reconstruction using the original soundtracks when
the manuscripts are missing. The consistency of the
orchestration, often spectacular, sometimes lean,
always individual, is remarkable. The music is
splendidly played and given Chandos's top-quality
sound.

Reger, Max (1873–1916)

(i) *Ballet suite for orchestra, Op. 130; Variations
and fugue on a theme by Mozart, Op. 132;* (ii)
*Variations and fugue on a theme by Mozart, Op.
132.*
(B) ** Teldec/Warner Ultima Double stereo 3984
28175-2 (2) [id.]. (i) Hamburg Philharmonic
State O, Hiller; (ii) Bamberg SO, Keilberth.

These are straight transfers of a pair of LPs reviewed
in the first (1966) *Penguin Guide to Bargain
Records*. Reger had a genuine talent for the variations form and if his Mozart set immediately takes
the winsome theme (composed for the keyboard)
soaring into the voluptuous textures of Richard
Strauss and early Schoenberg, there is no denying
the attractive qualities of some of the later sections,

particularly the *Fifth* and *Sixth variations*. The
closing fugue is taken fairly sedately by Keilberth,
but on the whole these are impressive accounts,
very well played, especially the engaging *Ballet
suite*. In the Hiller set one notices Reger's debt to
Brahms, but this too is agreeably presented. The
recordings are of good quality, with plenty of ambience, but show their age in a certain fierceness in
the fortissimo upper strings.

*Serenade in G for orchestra, Op. 95; Suite im
alten Stil, Op. 93.*
*** Koch Schwann Dig. 3-1566-2 [id.]. Bamberg
SO, Horst Stein.

The neglect of Reger's beautiful *Serenade in G
major* is baffling. Here is one of the loveliest, most
lyrical scores of the twentieth century which should,
if there were any justice in this world, be as available
in as many duplications as any Mahler symphony.
It is never heard in the concert hall and a rarity both
in broadcast concerts and on CD. Carl Schuricht
gave a memorable account of it with the BBC Symphony Orchestra in the 1950–60s, but it has never
been taken up by the likes of Barenboim, Abbado
or even Sir Colin Davis, who is sympathetic to
Reger's cause. The *Serenade* has a wonderful
warmth and humanity, and Horst Stein's performance of it is full of eloquence. The pastiche *Suite in
the olden style*, originally a *Duo* for violin and
piano, which Reger scored later in life, has much
charm. But it is the *Serenade* which is essential
listening in this persuasive and well-recorded
account.

CHAMBER MUSIC

*Cello suites Nos. 1 in G; 2 in D min.; 3 in A min.,
Op. 131c.*
(BB) *** Arte Nova Dig. 74321 65428-2 [id.].
Guido Schiefen.

A pupil of Maurice Gendron and Siegfried Palm,
Guido Schiefen is now in his early thirties and
proves an authoritative and persuasive advocate of
the three Reger *Cello suites*, Op. 131c. These were
composed immediately before the *Variations and
fugue on a theme by Mozart* and were modelled on
Bach, whom they at times paraphrase. Not essential
listening perhaps, but played like this they are quite
impressive and they are well recorded too.

(i) *Clarinet quintet in A, Op. 146. String quartet in
E flat, Op. 109.*
*** Nimbus Dig. NI 5644 [id.]. () Karl Leister;
Vogler Qt.

The *String quartet in E flat* (1909) was the very first
of the Reger quartets to be recorded, way back in
the days of 78s. The mellifluous *Clarinet quintet*,
his very last work, has never found its rightful place
in the concert hall or the record catalogues. Karl

Leister has recorded it before and his artistry and eloquence are very persuasive, as indeed are those of the wonderful Vogler Quartet. Their naturalness of pace, range of tone and completely civilized approach are a refreshing change from some of the high-powered, gleaming ensembles now before the public. The Nimbus engineers place us rather too close to the artists and we would welcome rather more space round the sound, but there is no doubt that these are very distinguished performances that call for a strong recommendation.

PIANO MUSIC

5 Humoresken, Op. 20; Improvisationen, Op. 18; In der nacht; Träume am Kamin, Op. 143.
(BB) *** Naxos Dig. 8.553331 [id.]. Markus Pawlik.

Reger's greatest piano works are the Variations and fugue on a theme of Bach, Op. 81 and the Variations and fugue on a theme of Telemann, Op. 134, which Marc-André Hamelin has recorded for Hyperion and which should form the corner-stone of any collection (❂ CDA 66996 – see our main volume). This newcomer brings the Five Humoresques, Op. 20 which are also included on the Hamelin CD, but otherwise here there is no duplication. The Op. 18 Improvisations, composed in the same year, 1896, together with In der nacht (1902) and the twelve miniatures Träume am Kamin ('Fireside dreams') composed in the last year of the composer's life, make up a well-filled disc. Markus Pawlik, now in his early thirties, has an enviable reputation, having a number of major competition prizes to his credit. When he was sixteen he won the European Community Young Musician of the Year competition. In any event he is a most musical and sensitive player who captures the intimacy of the Träume am Kamin to perfection. They are predominantly poetic and gentle pieces, but elsewhere, in the Humoresques he shows formidable virtuosity. Very acceptable sound – and those with a taste for music off the beaten track will find this well rewards the modest outlay.

Reicha, Antonín (1770–1836)

Quintet in F, Op. 107.
(B) **(*) Hyperion Helios CDH 55015 [id.].
    Francis, Allegri Qt – CRUSELL: Divertimento;
    KREUTZER: Grand quintet. **(*)

Born in the same year as Beethoven, Antonín Reicha was an enormously productive composer, as well as a respected teacher whose pupils included Liszt and Berlioz. The F major Quintet, Op. 107, dates from the first half of the 1820s and is spectacularly unmemorable but always amiable.

The performance is of high quality and is well recorded, but the CD plays for under 50 minutes.

Respighi, Ottorino (1879–1936)

Feste romane; The Pines of Rome.
(M) *** Decca 466 993-2 [id.]. Cleveland O,
    Maazel – RIMSKY-KORSAKOV: Le coq d'or
    suite ***.

This CD represents Maazel's Decca Cleveland period at its finest. In its day (the mid 1970s) Feste romane was something of a revelation: the Decca recording is extremely sophisticated in its colour and detail, and Respighi's vividly evocative sound picture is brought glitteringly to life. The orchestral playing shows matching virtuosity, and the final scene (The night before Epiphany in the Piazza Navona), with its gaudy clamour of trumpets and snatches of melody from the local organ grinder, is given a kaleidoscopic imagery exactly as the composer intended. Elsewhere, the superbly stylish playing has an almost baroque colouring, so wittily is it pointed. The Pines of Rome is given a strong, direct characterization, undoubtedly memorable, though it does not efface memories of Karajan's classic account. But this whole CD has a breathtaking, demonstration vividness and makes a fine addition to Legends label. The fill-up is equally impressive.

The Fountains of Rome; The Pines of Rome; Metamorphosen (Modi XII): Theme and variations for orchestra.
*** Telarc Dig. CD 80505 [id.]. Cincinnati SO,
    Jésus López-Cobos.

We are used to the Pines and Fountains of Rome invariably being coupled with the third element of the triptych, the Feste romane. But above Maazel and Decca omit the Fountains and this equally impressive new Telarc disc springs a surprise in making a new pairing with the Theme and variations for orchestra. This suffers from the somewhat ungainly title of Metamorphosen Modi XII, but as those who know the earlier Chandos recording will testify, it is a marvellously inventive and resourceful score.

Like Stravinsky's Symphony of Psalms, Prokofiev's Fourth and Honegger's First Symphonies, it was commissioned by Koussevitzky for the fiftieth anniversary of the Boston Symphony Orchestra. The theme itself is rather severe, but as the variations proceed the richness of Respighi's invention impresses more and more. Expert and sympathetic playing by the excellent Cincinnati Orchestra under Jésus López-Cobos and (not unexpectedly from Telarc) altogether excellent recording which is spectacular, but also both natural in perspective and impressively detailed, with splendid range.

Riisager, Knudåge (1897–1974)

(i) *Concertino for trumpet and strings, Op. 29*;
*Darduse, Op. 32; Slaraffenland (Fools' paradise):
suites Nos. 1 & 2; Tolv med Posten, Op. 37.*
*** Marco Polo Dig. 8.224082 [id.]. (i) Håkan
Hardenberger; Hälsingborg SO, Thomas
Dausgaard.

Knudåge Riisager was born in Estonia but moved
to Denmark in his infancy and, apart from his
studies in Paris with Roussel and Paul Le Flem, he
spent the rest of his life in Frederiksberg. The bulk
of his working life was spent as a civil servant; he
was a departmental head at the Ministry of Finance.
He is best known for his neoclassic works from the
1930s, and all the music on this CD comes from
that decade: both the *Concertino for trumpet and
strings* and the ballet, *Slaraffenland (Fools' paradise)* represented him in the catalogue, the former
in the early days of LP and the latter on a much
treasured (by R. L.) set of Danish Parlophone 78s.

Fools' paradise has a fair amount of circus-like
music *à la manière de* Satie and Milhaud but the
touching lyricism of *Prinsesse Sukkergodt (Princess Sweets)*, is captivating. The whole work has
bags of charm and deserves the widest currency.
Håkan Hardenberger is in good form in the *Concertino*, though the orchestral support could have
greater lightness of touch and finesse. *April* from
Tolv med Posten, on the other hand, has much
elegance. Readers who investigate this CD will find
little depth, but much to entertain them. Generally
good performances under Thomas Dausgaard but
rather bass-light sound.

Rimsky-Korsakov, Nikolay
(1844–1908)

Le coq d'or: suite.
(M) ******* Decca 466 993-2 [id.]. Cleveland O,
Maazel – RESPIGHI: *Feste romane; Pines of
Rome* *******.

A sumptuously played and recorded account of
sumptuously exotic music: Maazel wallows in the
luxuriant aural magic of Rimsky-Korsakov's
scoring, but his warmth of affection strongly communicates, and he creates a superb climax with
*The Marriage feast and the lamentable end of King
Dodon*. The sound is as brilliant as could be
imagined on this fine Decca Legends CD.

Scheherazade (symphonic suite), Op. 35.
(M) ******* EMI CDM5 66983-2 [CDM 566998].
RPO, Beecham (with BORODIN: *Polovtsian
dances.* *******)
(BB) ****(*)** Virgin Classics 2 x 1 Dig. VBD5
61751-2 (2) [CDVB 61751]. LPO, Andrew
Litton – BORODIN: *Prince Igor: Overture and
Polovtsian dances* *******; MUSSORGSKY: *Night

on the bare mountain; *Pictures at an
exhibition* ******; TCHAIKOVSKY: *The Tempest.*
***
(M) ****(*)** DG 463 614-2 [id.]. BPO, Karajan –
TCHAIKOVSKY: *Capriccio italien; 1812
overture* ****(*)**.

Litton's first movement brings strong dramatic contrasts and the violin soloist, David Nolan, plays
seductively. The *Andantino* has a Beechamesque
languor and the freedom given to the woodwind
soloists also recalls the Beecham version, which is
also coupled with the Borodin *Polovtsian dances*
(we list it again here as the wrong catalogue number
for the UK issue is given in our main volume).
Litton's finale is less than overwhelming, indeed
less exciting than Beecham's, and although the
Virgin recording is opulent as well as brilliant,
the RPO performance brings a greater sense of
spontaneity, although Litton's version has more
modern sound and is certainly enjoyable in its
spaciousness.

In Karajan's account it is the brilliance and
prowess of the Berlin Philharmonic which is immediately apparent from the sensitive opening
violin solo from Michel Schwalbé onwards. The
recording is full-blooded and vivid, but is a little
light on bass – although in the present remastering
this is less obvious. The first movement is hard
driven but has plenty of excitement; the finale (a
resounding success) has even more, but the inner
movements do not glow as you would ideally expect
them to. A typically individual Karajan account
then, and if he is not quite on his best it is still
impressive. It now reappears on the Originals label
with some typically Karajanesque Tchaikovsky
which is certainly not less exciting, especially *1812*.
First choice at full price remains with Mackerras on
Telarc (● CD 80208) which is superbly played and
recorded.

*Scheherazade, Op. 35; Capriccio espagnol,
Op. 34.*
(B) ****(*)** Australian Decca Eloquence 466 907-2.
(i) LAPO; (ii) Israel PO; Mehta.
(M) ****** Sony SMK 60737 [id.]. NYPO,
Bernstein.

Mehta's *Scheherazade* was considered a demonstration disc in its day (mid-1970s) and still sounds
impressive. Though it is a high-powered performance, there is affection too, and despite the odd
mannerism, it is very enjoyable, and the orchestral
leader, Sydney Harth, offers a sinuously seductive
image for Scheherazade herself. The Israeli version
of *Capriccio espagnol* is not quite so successful in
terms of sound or performance, but still entertains,
and makes a fair bonus for the main work, which
is more exciting than many more recent digital
versions.

Bernstein's 1959 *Scheherazade* is too idiosyncratic to be fully recommendable: the first

movement is undramatic and tends to put one off from the start; however, the slow movement is warmly romantic, and the finale has brilliance and excitement. Similarly the *Capriccio espagnol* starts off rather coolly, but warms up and ends in a blaze of excitement. The recordings sound better than they have done in the past, but in such a crowded market, this CD is hardly a strong recommendation.

Scheherazade, Op. 35; Capriccio espagnol, Op. 34; Tsar Saltan: Flight of the bumble-bee.
** Teldec/Warner Dig. 0630 17125-2 [id.].
    NYPO, Masur.

Characteristically, Masur is cool and objective rather than passionate in these Russian showpieces. Though *Scheherazade* was recorded live, there is little or no rush of adrenalin. Ensemble is phenomenally precise, with the cleanest articulation, and Masur's control is so complete that even the rhapsodic solos, both from the solo violin and from the woodwind, have little feeling of freedom. Dynamic shading is similarly precise, with speeds steadier than usual. The approach is similar in the *Capriccio espagnol*, fast and fierce, missing jollity. Some may find the results of Masur's approach refreshing, and the *Flight of the bumble-bee* does bring a dazzling performance full of wit and fun, but there is a missing dimension here and most collectors will surely opt for Mackerras (❂ Telarc CD 80208) or, at mid-price, Kondrashin (Philips 442 643-2, which also includes the *Russian Easter festival overture*) or Beecham (see above). The Teldec disc offers clean, well-detailed sound, but lacks sumptuousness.

OPERA

Kashchey the Immortal (complete).
*** Ph. Dig. 446 704-2 [id.]. Konstantin
    Pluzhnikov, Marina Shaguch, Alexander
    Gergalov, Larissa Diadkova, Alexander
    Morozov, Kirov Op. Ch. & O, Gergiev.

With its prominent use of the exotic whole-tone scale and other devices, this one-act fairy-tale opera of 1901 puzzled and surprised early audiences, the most radical of Rimsky's operas up to that time. Gergiev with a strong, characterful cast from his Kirov company proves a persuasive interpreter of this rich, colourful piece.

The evil Kashchey of Russian legend is best known through Stravinsky's *Firebird ballet*, but here he is the central character throughout, dying only when his daughter, Kascheyevna, is stirred to pity and weeps – the signal for rejoicing in a final ensemble. The first of the three tableaux has Kashchey in dialogue with the Princess he has imprisoned, with Konstantin Pluzhnikov darkly incisive in the title-role and Marina Shaguch bright and clear if edgy as the Princess.

The oddity of the casting is that there is no tenor soloist, with Alexander Gergalov as Prince Ivan an aptly heroic-sounding baritone and Alexander Morozov equally well-focused as the Storm Knight, father of the Princess. Most characterful of all is the mezzo, Larissa Diadkova, as Kascheyevna, at once rich-toned and sinister. Recorded in concert at the Philharmonic Hall in St Petersburg, the sound is clear and generally well-balanced.

The Legend of the Invisible City of Kitezh (complete).
*** Ph. Dig. 462 225-2 (2) [id.]. Galina
    Gorchakova, Vladimir Galuzin, Nicolai
    Putilin, Nicolai Ohotnikov, Yuri Marusin,
    Bulat Minjilkiev, Vladimir Ognovienko, Kirov
    Opera Ch. & O, Gergiev.

Recorded live at the Mariinsky Theatre in St Petersburg, this long fairy-tale piece (lasting almost three hours) shows Rimsky in his penultimate opera following up the radical one-acter, *Kashchey the Immortal*, with another colourful, far more expansive score. Though this too has its radical qualities, it relies above all on the cadences of Russian folk-song. The plot is more direct than most.

Act I, set in a forest, is devoted entirely to the meeting of Prince Vsevolod, wounded in a bear hunt, and the beautiful Fevroniya, child of nature, with whom he promptly falls in love. As usual with Russian folk-tales the plot brings a curious mixture of jollity and bitterness. Though the Prince dies in battle in the middle of Act III – illustrated in an interlude – he is resurrected in Act IV, when the disappearing City of Kitezh is magically transformed into Paradise, with hero and heroine united in life after death.

What adds spice to the plot is the equivocal character of the drunkard, Grishka, comic only in part, who initially is prompted to attack Fevroniya, but who later is befriended by her. Galina Gorchakova sings powerfully as Fevroniya and Yuri Marusin is a strong, idiomatic Prince, whose distinctive tenor is well contrasted with that of Vladimir Galuzin as an incisive Grishka, characterizing splendidly. Despite moments of strain, the rest of the Kirov cast makes an excellent team. Live recording inevitably brings intrusive stage noises and odd balances, but this is another warmly recommendable set in Gergiev's excellent Philips series.

The Tsar's Bride (complete).
*** Ph. Dig. 462 618-2 (2) [id.]. Gennady
    Bezzuhenkov, Marina Shaguch, Dmitri
    Hvorostovsky, Sergei Alexashkin, Evgeny
    Akinov, Olga Borodina, Kirov Ch. & O,
    Gergiev.

Recorded in the Maryinsky Theatre, St Petersburg under studio conditions, this is among the finest of

Gergiev's many opera recordings with his Kirov Company. He firmly establishes *The Tsar's Bride* as a most richly enjoyable opera, full of outstanding set numbers, such as the banqueting song in the party scene of Act I, which uses the Tsar's Hymn in opulent counterpoint. The story itself, set at the time of Ivan the Terrible, is a curious mixture of darkness and light, of fairy-tale fantasy and melodramatic realism. Jealousy is the dominant emotion, when the sinister adventurer, Gryaznoy, and the scheming Lyubasha take priority over even the hero and heroine.

In the casting here that priority is a great source of strength, when Dmitri Hvorostovsky as Gryaznoy and Olga Borodina as Lyubasha give superb performances, not just singing with rich, firm tone but characterizing powerfully. Marina Shaguch is fresh and clear as Marfa the heroine, if edgy under pressure, and Evgeny Akimov with his typically Slavonic tenor sings idiomatically if with forced tone. In Act IV, with the plot turning sour, Rimsky is prompted to round the work off with a sequence of remarkable numbers, including a splendid quintet with chorus, when Gryaznoy stabs Lyubasha to death, and a mad-scene for Marfa. A rich offering, strongly recommended.

Rodrigo, Joaquín (1901–99)

Concierto de Aranjuez.
*** Guild Dig. GMCD 7176 [id.]. Rafael Jiménez, Bournemouth Sinf., Terence Frazor –
ANGULO: *Guitar concerto No. 2 (El Alevín);*
VILLA-LOBOS: *Guitar concerto.* ***

Rafael Jiménez and the Bournemouth Sinfonietta under Terence Frazor make a fine partnership in this much-recorded concerto. The slow movement brings an appealing, ruminative intimacy to contrast with its bold, passionate climax, and the finale also has a neat delicacy of touch from the soloist, with buoyant rhythmic pointing from the orchestra. The recording is very good too, although not quite as fine as the Virgin version below.

(i; ii) *Concierto de Aranjuez;* (i; iii) *Fantasia para un gentilhombre.*
❂ (B) *** Decca Penguin Classics 460 638-2 [id.]. Bonell, Montreal SO, Dutoit – FALLA: *The Three-cornered hat: 3 dances* ***.
(BB) *** Virgin Classics 2 x 1 Dig. VBD5 61627-2 (2)[CDVB 61627]. Sharon Isbin, Lausanne CO, Lawrence Foster –
SCHWANTER: *From afar* (fantasy) **; Recital: *'Latin romances'.* ***
(B) **(*) Sony SBK 61716 [id.]. (i) John Williams; (ii) Philadelphia O, Ormandy; (iii) ECO, Groves – DODGSON: *Concerto,* etc. **(*).

(i) *Concierto de Aranjuez; Fantasia para un gentilhombre.* Guitar pieces: *En los trigales; Fandango; Hommage à Falla.*
(M) *** Sony Dig./Analogue SMK 64129 [id.].
John Williams; (i) with Philharmonia O, Louis Frémaux.

The Bonell/Dutoit performances (1980) of these works still retain their place at the top of the list. They are warm yet sparkling accounts, ideally recorded, and in every way outstanding. Their latest incarnation is on the Penguin Classics label and graced by a personal essay by Victoria Glendinning. The Falla dances are also first class, but it is worth consulting our main volume as these ❂ Rodrigo performances are also available in two different alternative couplings.

Sharon Isbin's recordings of Rodrigo's two most popular works with the Lausanne Chamber Orchestra under Lawrence Foster received the imprimatur of the composer before he died, and justly so. They are both played with flair and the orchestral detail could not be more vivid, while the famous slow movement of the *Concierto* is most atmospherically done. The recording is in the demonstration bracket. The snag is that the Schwanter coupling is a good deal less tangible.

John Williams's third version (digital, 1983) of the *Concierto,* with Frémaux, is very successfully recorded: the soloist may be a little forward, the guitar image is admirably related to the orchestra, while the inner detail is impressively clear. The acoustic has agreeable warmth, yet climaxes have brilliance without overemphasis, and the performance is even finer than his previous analogue partnership with Barenboim. The slow movement is wonderfully atmospheric with the soloist's introspective yet inspirational mood anticipated and echoed by Frémaux, who secures most beautiful orchestral playing. The finale is light and sparkling with an element of fantasy and much delicacy of articulation in the accompaniment. The performance of the *Fantasia* is no less memorable, with much subtlety of detail and colour from both orchestra and conductor. This is altogether a winning coupling, and for its issue on Sony's 'Great Performances' label, three attractive solo guitar pieces have been added. An excellent CD in every way.

With Ormandy providing a rich orchestral tapestry Williams's earlier version is a distinctly romantic reading of the *Concierto.* If the later recording is maturer and has greater subtlety of detail, this performance, taken a little bit faster, remains fresh and enjoyable. The guitar is quite well balanced against the orchestra, but the orchestral sound from 1965 sounds just a little dated. Groves and the ECO take over for the *Fantasia,* and once again, the interpretation is a shade brisker than the later, digital version. Here, the analogue sound is more vivid and open than in the *Concierto*, and the orchestral response is crisp and fresh. This remains a genuine bargain, especially if the rare Dodgson works appeal.

Rorem, Ned (born 1923)

Violin concerto.
*** DG Dig. 445 186-2 [id.]. Gidon Kremer, Israel PO, Composer – BERNSTEIN: *Serenade after Plato's Symposium;* GLASS: *Violin concerto.* ***

Ned Rorem has been neglected on disc, a great character among American composers, whose eclecticism takes in an alarming range of styles. So the six brief movements in this concerto, beautifully played by Kremer with Bernstein conducting in the year before he died, start with a gritty first movement, but by the Romance of the third movement he has veered towards lyrical sweetness, following that with a longer, more thoughtful slow movement, *Midnight*. An interesting coupling for the other two American concertante works.

Songs: *Alleluia; Clouds; Do I love you more than a day?; Early in the morning; Little elegy; Far far away; Ferry me across the water; For Poulenc; For Susan; I am rose; I will always love you; I strolled across an open field; A journey; Jeannie with the light brown hair; Look down fair moon; The Lordly Hudson; Love; Now sleeps the crimson petal; Ode; O do not love too long; O you, whom I often and silently come; Orchids; Santa Fé, Op. 101/2, 4, 8 & 12; The serpent; The tulip tree; Sometimes with one I love; Stopping by woods on a snowy evening; To a young girl; That shadow, my likeness.*
*** Erato/Warner Dig. 8573 80222-2 [id.]. Susan Graham, Malcolm Martineau.

Although his *Third Symphony* and a handful of other works are on record, Rorem's important output for the voice remains neglected. Susan Graham, so much at home in the French repertoire, puts us in her debt with this recital. Ned Rorem spent many of his formative years in Paris during the 1950s, when he came to know Poulenc and Auric, but he never lost the American flavour that makes his style so distinctive. This recital, encompassing settings of English, American and French verse, gives a good idea of his melodic resource and feeling for words. His songs, such as the *Santa Fe* series and the setting of Tennyson's *Now sleeps the crimson petal*, bear witness to a rich imagination and a marvellous feel for both the voice and the piano. Susan Graham does them all proud, and Malcolm Martineau gives impeccable support.

Rosenberg, Hilding (1892–1985)

Piano concertos Nos. 1 & 2.
*** Daphne Dig. DR 1006 [id.]. Mats Widlund, Swedish Radio SO, Petter Sundkvist.

The *First Piano concerto* is a recent discovery. Composed in 1930, Rosenberg had passed the manuscript of the first two movements to the pianist Sven Brandel for his comments and had obviously forgotten about it. When the *Second* (1950) was premièred, Rosenberg hinted at the existence of an earlier concerto but until recently the *Second* was thought of as his only piano concerto. The two movements of the *First* were discovered among Brandel's papers together with sketches for the finale. One can understand Rosenberg's doubts: the orchestral writing occasionally swamps the texture, and the range of keyboard devices is very limited. The *Second Concerto* is the more rewarding and the keyboard writing more interesting and varied. There are occasional reminders of Bartók and some highly imaginative invention. There is some particularly atmospheric writing for strings and wind in the central *Andante tranquillo*. The score lacks concentration perhaps, and a sure sense of direction, but all the same it is rewarding and serves to fill in our picture of an underrated composer. Mats Widlund is the excellent soloist and Petter Sundkvist impresses with his sensitivity and musicianship. The recordings, made in the cold acoustic of Stockholm's Berwald Hall, have good definition and the balance between soloist and orchestra is very well judged. Not the equal of the *Third* or *Fourth Symphonies* but well worth investigating.

Improvisationer; Plastiska Scener; Små föredragsstudier; Sonatas Nos. 1 & 3.
** Daphne Dig. 1001 [id.]. Mats Widlund.

Sonatas Nos. 2 & 4; Sonatina; Suite; Tema con variazioni.
** Daphne Dig. 1003 [id.]. Mats Widlund.

Rosenberg's piano music comes mostly from the 1920s. Of the ten works recorded here, only the *Improvisations* (1939), *Tema con variazioni* and *Sonatina* (both 1949) are exceptions. The musical quality is variable: the cosmopolitan influences are obvious and Rosenberg is at his best in the smaller-scale miniatures such as the *Små föredragsstudier (Small performing studies)*, composed while he was teaching in the school at which he, like Stenhammar before him, had studied. He obviously knew his Ravel and Honegger, and in the *Largamente* from the *Plastiska Scener* there are hints of Schoenberg. The *Third Sonata* in particular is arid and its companions are not uniformly rewarding. But the smaller pieces are well worth having and like the sonatas are new to the catalogue. Mats Widlund is a dedicated advocate and the recordings are very natural.

Rosetti, Antonio (c. 1750–1792)

(i) *Clarinet concertos Nos. 1 in E flat, K.III:55; 2 in E flat, K.III:57;* (i) *Double horn concerto in F, K.III: 52.*
**(*) CPO Dig. CPO 999 621-2 [id.]. (i) Dieter Klöcker; (ii) Klaus Wallendorf, Sarah Willis; SW R SO, Baden-Baden & Freiburg, Holger Schröter-Seebeck.

Born in Northern Bohemia, Franz Anton Rössler changed his name to Rosetti when in 1773 he moved to Germany to take up a court appointment with the orchestra of Kraft Ernst, Prince of Oettingen-Wallerstein – first as a double-bass player and later as Kapellmeister. His two clarinet concertos are very Bohemian in flavour; both are melodically quite attractive, with the *Rondo* of the *First* and the *Romanze* and *Rondo scherzante* of the *Second* all equally striking. Dieter Klöcker certainly finds the lighthearted Bohemian spirit of this music and is a sympathetic soloist with a luscious tone. The *Double horn concerto* is less memorable musically, but demands considerable virtuosity in its solo interplay and certainly receives it here, especially in the buoyant finale. With sympathetic accompaniments and a pleasing recording this is all enjoyable, if not distinctive.

Sinfonias: in D, K.I:12; in C, K.I:21; in G, K.I:22; in A, K.I:24.
**(*) Chandos Dig. CHAN 9567 [id.]. L. Mozart Players, Matthias Bamert.

Sinfonias: in D (La Chasse), K.I:18; in C, K.I:21; in G, K.I:22 in D, K.I:30.
*** Teldec/Warner Dig. 0630 18301-2 [id.]. Concerto Köln.

Sinfonias: in E flat, K.I:23; in B flat, K.I:25; in G min., K.I:27; in E flat, K.I:32.
*** Teldec/Warner Dig. 4509 98420-2 [id.]. Concerto Köln.

As a court composer, first in South and later in North Germany, Rosetti composed a fair number of symphonies, and those recorded here come from the 1780s. In the hands of the London Mozart Players under Matthias Bamert they are amiable works, engagingly melodic and nicely scored for the normal classical orchestra. Haydn would have admired the minuets for they are the most striking movements and the minuet of the *G major work*, Kaul I:22 sounds very like '*We wish you a merry Christmas*'. The Chandos recording is well up to standard as is the playing of the London Mozart group, polished and nicely turned.

But when one turns to the period-instrument Concerto Köln, the music springs to life with far greater zest and vitality, and in the two symphonies common to both groups, Kaul I:21 and 22 there is no doubt that the Cologne performances give the music a much stronger profile, while the charm of the second movement *Romanze: Andante grazioso* of the *C major Symphony* comes over just as engagingly, if not more so. The first Teldec disc opens with the most striking symphony of all, *La Chasse*, ('eine starke Sinfonie' as the composer described it to his employer) written in 1782 after a visit to Paris and published there in 1786.

In the splendidly vigorous account from the Concerto Köln, the outer movements, with rasping horns and brilliant brass, certainly convey a picture of the hunt in full cry, and to bring contrast the central movements are a lyrical *Romance*, with pleasing writing for woodwind, and a maestoso Minuet. The recording is vivid to match and this is the disc to try first if you are tempted by late-eighteenth-century symphonies with a flavour of both Italy and Bohemia.

Rossi, Luigi (1597–1653)

Orfeo (opera; complete).
(B) **(*) HM Dig. HMX 2901358.60 (3) [id.]. Agnès Mellon, Monique Zanetti, Sandrine Piau, Dominique Favat, Jean-Paul Fouchécourt, Jean-Marc Salzmann, Jérôme Corréas, Bernard Deletré, Les Arts Florissants, William Christie.

Luigi Rossi's *Orfeo* has a much more complex classical story than the Monteverdi, yet in its artificial way it is less effectively dramatic. Even so, it offers such incidental delights as a slanging match between Venus (enemy of Orfeo, when he represents marital fidelity) and Juno. That hint of a classical send-up adds sparkle, contrasting with the tragic emotions conveyed both in Orfeo's deeply expressive solos and in magnificent Monteverdi-like choruses. William Christie draws characteristically lively and alert playing from Les Arts Florissants, but his cast is not as consistent as those he usually has in his Harmonia Mundi recordings. Too many of the singers sound fluttery or shallow, and even Agnès Mellon as Orfeo is less even and sweet of tone than usual. Nevertheless this remains a most welcome recording of an important rarity, and at bargain price, with full libretto and translation included, it is well worth considering.

Rossini, Gioachino (1792–1868)

Introduction, theme and variations in B flat;
Variations in C (for clarinet and orchestra).
(BB) *** ASV Quicksilva Dig. CDQS 6242 [id.].
Joy Farrall, Britten Sinfonia, Nicholas Daniel
– DONIZETTI: *Clarinet concertino; Study;*
MERCADANTE: *Clarinet concertos.* ***

Joy Farrall chortles her way through Rossini's
characteristically witty sets of variations, playing
with a smiling charm, and a lovely lyrical line and
winningly beautiful tone in the introductions (that
in B flat is for all the world like an operatic aria).
She is stylishly accompanied and most naturally
recorded. A highly recommendable disc that is more
than the sum of its parts.

String sonatas Nos. 1–6.
(BB) *** Arte Nova Dig. 74321 30480-2 [id.].
St Petersburg Soloists, Michail Gantvarg.

At last a really first-class super-bargain set of the
Rossini *String sonatas*, played with elegance, wit
and polish, and often fizzing virtuosity by a superb
Russian string group of fifteen players – an ideally
sized ensemble for this ever-fresh repertoire written
with precocious charm by the 12-year-old Rossini.
The ensemble may not be quite as immaculate as
that of the famous ASMF set under Marriner (see
our main volume), but the playing has finesse and
affection, yet sparkles with life. And the double-bass
contribution is pretty impressive too. Just sample
the baroque-like dynamic contrasts in the finale of
No. 2 in A. The recording, made in a warm acoustic,
is absolutely real and natural.

String sonatas Nos. 1 in G; 2 in A; 3 in C; 6 in D.
(M) **(*) DG 457 914-2 [id.]. BPO, Karajan –
BOCCHERINI: *Quintet: La Ritirada di Madrid*
***

Rossini's delightful string sonatas cannot fail to
entertain and nor do they here. Karajan's examples
are sumptuously played, but are too suave to bring
out all the wit and sparkle of Rossini's youthful
inspiration. The 1972 recording is as rich as can be
imagined.

The Barber of Seville (in English).
(M) **(*) Chandos Dig. CHAN 3025 (2) [id.].
Della Jones, Bruce Ford, Alan Opie, Peter
Rose, Andrew Shore, ENO Ch. & O, Gabriele
Bellini.

Boldly, with help from the Peter Moores Foundation, long devoted to this cause, Chandos here offers
at mid-price this *Barber* in English, using the bright
translation of Amanda and Anthony Holden.
Strongly cast, it is a genial performance, very well
played and recorded. The only reservation is over
the relaxed conducting of Gabriele Bellini which
lacks dramatic bite. Compensating for that, the principal singers not only characterize vividly but together form a lively ensemble. Alan Opie is a strong,
positive Figaro, while Della Jones as Rosina both
exploits her rich mezzo tones and brings sparkle to
the coloratura. It is good too to have so accomplished a Rossini tenor as Bruce Ford singing
Almaviva. Peter Rose as Basilio and Andrew Shore
as Dr Bartolo, both young-sounding for these roles,
are fresh and firm too. Excellent documentation
includes a full English libretto.

Il Barbiere di Siviglia: highlights.
(M) **(*) DG 463 086-2 [id.] (from complete
recording with Berganza, Prey, Alva,
Montarsolo, Ambrosian Ch., LSO, Abbado).

This is a generous 70-minute highlights CD which
reflects the merits of the complete performance:
Teresa Berganza's Rosina is agile and reliable, as
is the Figaro of Hermann Prey, and the rest of the
cast is generally excellent. The orchestra play well
for Abbado, whose direction is clean and satisfying,
but the performance as a whole lacks the last ounce
of sparkle. At mid-price, and with good (1971)
sound, it is good value, but the packaging, with no
texts and translations, is parsimonious compared
with Decca's Opera Gala series.

Otello (complete).
*** Opera Rara ORC 18 (3) [id.]. Bruce Ford,
Elizabeth Futral, William Matteuzzi,
Ildebrando d'Arcangelo, Juan José Lopera,
Philharmonia O, David Parry.

Justifiably overshadowed by Verdi's masterpiece,
this early opera of Rossini, written in 1816 for
Naples, is best approached by not thinking of Shakespeare. It is a piece very much of its time, with the
changes in Shakespeare's story making the drama
more conventional: a love-letter is substituted for
the fatal handkerchief, and Desdemona is stabbed
instead of being smothered, while she also acquires
a new father, Elmiro. Even so, Rossini is inspired
by a serious subject to produce a striking series of
arias and ensembles, which culminate in what was
then a revolutionary course in Italian opera, a tragic
ending. Significantly, later, in 1820 and pressured
by the authorities, Rossini provided a happy ending,
when Otello is finally convinced of Desdemona's
innocence. That alternative close is the first of three
important appendices included in this very well-
documented set. Where the previous Philips
recording, more starrily cast, provided a badly cut
text on two CDs merely, this one stretches to three
very well-filled discs.

It is a credit to Opera Rara that three formidable
Rossini tenors are here involved, not just Bruce
Ford in the title role, strong and stylish if a little
gritty as recorded, but also Juan José Lopera as
Iago, who is also impressive, and, singing even
more sweetly, William Matteuzzi as Rodrigo, here
given a relatively big role. Elizabeth Futral is a

strong, dramatic heroine, rising superbly to the challenge of the final Act, which, coming closer to Shakespeare, brings the most memorable music, including a lovely *Willow song*. Enkeljda Shkosa sings most beautifully as Emilia, as she does too in the alternative Malibran version of the Act II duet, in which she sings Otello, transformed into a breeches-role. David Parry excels himself in drawing powerful, sensitive playing from the Philharmonia, dramatically paced, with some outstanding solo work from the wind. Vivid, well-balanced sound.

Arias from: *Il barbiere di Siviglia; La cambiale di matrimonio; La cenerentola; Guglielmo Tell; L'Italiana in Algeri; Otello; Semiramide.*
(M) **(*) Decca Analogue/Dig. 458 247-2 [id.].
   With Nucci, Sutherland, Horne, Pavarotti, Berganza, Ghiaurov, Tebaldi.

A generally fine Rossini anthology: Sutherland glitters in her coloratura, whilst Horne's bravura is a marvel. Berganza is engaging in her numbers from *Cenerentola* and *L'Italiana*, whilst Pavarotti and Ghiaurov keep the men's side up. A good collection, but it does not quite maintain the very highest standards of Decca's always reliable Opera Gala series, which come with full texts and translations.

Rota, Nino (1911–79)

Piano concertos in C; E (Piccolo mondo antico).
*** EMI Dig. CDC5 56869-2 [id.]. Giorgia Tomassi, La Scala PO, Riccardo Muti.

The *First Piano concerto* (1959–60) was composed for Michelangeli, and the neo-romantic *E major (Piccolo mondo antico)* from 1978 was Rota's last composition. Even if they are too prolix, they are both inventive and expertly crafted works in the received tradition with reminders of Prokofiev and Rachmaninov. Giorgia Tomassi is a formidable soloist who skilfully negotiates the extreme difficulties of the keyboard role while Muti secures sumptuous tone from the fine La Scala Orchestra. Good recording too. Not great music, but worth investigating.

Piano concertos in C; E min.
**(*) CHAN 9681 [id.]. Palumbo, I Virtuosi Italiani, Boni.

Disconcertingly for the collector, the *C major Concerto* is also on the EMI disc above, but the *E minor Concerto* (1960) is new to the catalogue. It begins (*Allegro tranquillo*) in an attractively melancholy way, somewhere between film music and Rachmaninov, and goes on in a similar vein for some sixteen minutes, with occasional lively outbursts. It is all attractive, but goes on too long; it doesn't help that another melancholy movement follows, lacking the necessary contrast. The finale is lively enough

and brings the work to a jolly conclusion. Enjoyable, but not great music, and it would have benefited from a bit of pruning. The performances and recording are good, but not quite as polished or as vivid as the EMI disc above. Both discs will give pleasure to those interested in little-known romantic piano concertos, and they are worthwhile additions to the catalogue.

Concerto for strings; The Leopard: Dances; La Strada: ballet suite.
*** Sony Dig. SK 66279 [id.]. La Scala PO, Muti.

This music was written in the 1960s, during the composer's most mature period. The ballet *La Strada* (1960), inspired by Fellini's celebrated picture of the same name, was commissioned by La Scala and first performed there in 1966. It is a highly attractive score, drawing heavily from Rota's own film music, and is full of colour as well as atmosphere (it also has good tunes – rare for a new ballet at that time). The *Concerto for strings* was written in the mid 1960s and revised in 1977. It has a meltingly beautiful beginning, and a dream-like quality which is quite haunting. In the Scherzo, the atmosphere of dance forms is evoked – waltzes and minuets – which are divided by more vibrant passages. The following *Aria* is rather more serious in nature, and the finale is a lively quirky galop – a most enjoyable work. The *Dances* from the film *The Leopard* (1963) are actually arrangements of unpublished dance music by Verdi. They are exhilaratingly tuneful (very much like Verdi's own ballet music) and have been delightfully orchestrated by Rota. This is a most entertaining disc and, with such splendid playing and vivid sound, is strongly recommended.

Symphonies Nos. 1 in G; 2 in F (Tarantina – Anni di pellegrinaggio).
** BIS Dig. CD 970 [id.]. Norrköping SO, Ole Kristian Ruud.

Best known though he may be for his film scores for Fellini and Coppola, Nino Rota was a composer of some substance. These pieces come from the 1930s when he was in his twenties and had undergone studies in America. The *First Symphony* (1935–9) shows the imprint of Stravinsky, Copland, Hindemith and even Sibelius. It is well scored and often inventive. The *Second* (subtitled *Tarantina – Anni di pellegrinaggio*, alluding to the period he spent in Taranto, southern Italy, as a teacher) is even more indebted to Copland. They are thoroughly accessible pieces which engage the interest not only of the listener but also the Norrköping players and their Norwegian conductor. Good sound.

Rouse, Christopher (born 1949)

(i) *Flute concerto; Phaeton; Symphony No. 2.*
*** Telarc Dig. CD 80452 [id.]. (i) Carol
Wincenc; Houston SO, Eschenbach.

The remarkable five-movement *Flute concerto*, commissioned by the present soloist, followed two years after Rouse's *Trombone concerto* (see below). The beautiful first and last movements, with their serene, soaring solo line, are connected thematically, and share the Gaelic title *Anhran* ('Song'). They frame two faster, much more dissonant and rhythmically unpredictable movements, with the ebullient penultimate Scherzo, in the composer's words continually 'trying to become a jig'. The kernel of the work is the gripping central *Elegia*, written in response to the terrible murder of the two-year-old James Bulger by two ten-year-old schoolboys. Rouse introduces a rich, Bach-like chorale, which moves with a wake-like solemnity towards a central explosion of passionate despair. Throughout, the solo writing demands great bravura and intense emotional commitment from the flautist, which is certainly forthcoming here, and although Carol Wincenc's timbre, as recorded, is bright and metallic, it certainly fits the composer's quixotic rhythmic patterns and achieves a contrasting tranquillity.

Rouse conceived his first two symphonies together in 1984, but the *Second* was not finalized until ten years later. It is a three-part structure, with the outer movements again using identical material to frame the anguished central slow movement. In the composer's words that forms a 'prism' through which the mercurial opening material is 'refracted' to yield the angry, tempestuous finale. The influence of Shostakovich is clear, not only in the jaunty opening toccata/ostinato but also in the string cantilena which opens the desperately grieving *Adagio*, another threnody, but for a personal friend and colleague, Stephen Albert, killed in a car accident in 1992. *Phaeton* is a savage, explosive early work (1986), which could hardly be more different from the tone poem of Saint-Saëns. Helios's sun chariot, immediately out of his son's control, charges its way across the heavens with horns roistering, and is very quickly blown out of the sky by Zeus's thunderbolt. Performances here are excellent, very well played and recorded, and the *Flute concerto* is unforgettable.

(i) *Trombone concerto. Gorgon; Iscariot.*
⊙ *** RCA Dig. 09026 68410-2 [id.]. (i) Joseph
Alessi; Colorado SO, Marin Alsop.

Rouse's Pulitzer-prize winning *Trombone concerto*, dedicated to the memory of Leonard Bernstein, is a stunning piece and this, its dynamic recording première, is unlikely to be surpassed. Joseph Alessi's solo performance is breathtaking, and the sheer electricity Marin Alsop generates in the orchestra is equally astonishing. The listener is gripped from the very opening, when the soloist emerges from the profoundest depths, through the central eruptions to the sombre, elegiac finale, where the trombone returns to its lowest register after a valedictory intonation of the solemn *Kaddish* from Bernstein's *Third Symphony*. A masterly work, given a masterly performance.

Gorgon, written a decade earlier, pictures the hideous female creatures of Greek myth, producing ferocious music that in its continuing rhythmic ostinatos outguns the Stravinsky of the *Rite of spring*, with the percussive volume of Rock drumming, yet with slithery interludes to suggest snakes in the hair. Here it is unrelentingly powerful in impact, especially the third section depicting the death of Medusa.

The composer describes *Iscariot* (1989), dedicated to John Adams, as 'a symbol of betrayal'. It primarily depends on intense, concentrated string sonorities, taking its sound and ethos from Ives's *Unanswered question*, yet is much more complex and remains individual, closing with a brief but riveting quotation of Bach's chorale *Es ist genug* ('It is enough'). The continuing dynamism of Marin Alsop's performances of both works is matched by a virtuoso and intensely committed response from the Colorado players, and the spacious acoustic of Denver's Boettcher Hall provides sound of the most spectacular demonstration quality with the widest dynamic range.

Roussel, Albert (1869–1937)

Bacchus et Ariane: suite No. 2.
(B) *** Sony SBK 62644 [id.]. Philadelphia O,
Ormandy – FAURE: *Pelléas et Mélisande*, etc.
**(*); IBERT: *Divertissement; Escales* **(*).

This is among the very best available performances of the second suite: it has some splendidly characterful playing from all members of the orchestra – the opening is compellingly atmospheric (those wonderful Philadelphia strings), and much of the woodwind playing is quite electric. Ormandy maintains the tension throughout, and the finale is thrillingly exciting. Indeed, it must be regretted that he did not record the complete ballet. The 1960 Sony (CBS) recording is full and vivid, and the couplings (especially *Escales*) certainly worthwhile. A bargain.

Rubbra, Edmund (1901–86)

(i) *Violin sonatas Nos. 1, Op. 11; 2, Op. 31; 3, Op. 135; 4 Pieces, Op. 29. Variations on a Phrygian theme for solo violin, Op. 105.*

(M)*** Dutton Lab. Dig. CDLX 7101. Krysia Ososttowicz; (i) with Michael Dussek.

The *Second Violin sonata,* with Albert Sammons and Gerald Moore was the first Rubbra work to reach the gramophone, on two HMV plum-label 78s. Although Frederick Grinke and the composer himself recorded it for Decca in the early days of LP, there has been no decent modern recording. Krysia Ososttowicz and Michael Dussek are worth waiting for, since not only the recording but also, surprisingly, the performance eclipses both its distinguished predecessors. The *First Sonata,* Op. 11, from the 1920s (there was an earlier piece but this does not survive), is heavily indebted to Debussy and Rubbra's teacher, Gustav Holst. The *Third* is a sinewy work from 1963, formidably argued and finely laid out for the medium. The Op. 29 *Pieces* are really teaching material, as is the set of variations for violin alone.

Saint-Saëns, Camille (1835–1921)

Carnival of the animals.
(M) * Sony SMK 60175 [id.]. NYPO, Bernstein (conductor and narrator) – BRITTEN: *Young person's guide to the orchestra* (*); PROKOFIEV: *Peter and the wolf, Op. 67* *.

Bernstein not only provides the narration, but also tells us the derivations of Saint-Saëns's orchestral jokes. This might work well on a TV or radio programme, but it is not suitable for repeated listening. Young musicians play the solos within the orchestra (*The Swan* is played on a double bass) and are effusively introduced. The 1962 recording has transferred well onto CD, but this is not a performance to return to with any relish.

Cello concerto No. 1 in A min., Op. 33.
(M) *** DG 457 761-2 [id.]. Fournier, LOP, Martinon – BLOCH: *Schelomo;* BRUCH: *Kol Nidrei;* LALO: *Cello concerto.* ***

Fournier brings his customary nobility to the concerto, and is well supported by Martinon, who provides stylish support with the Lamoureux Orchestra. The recording from 1960 has never sounded better than on this new DG Originals transfer, and the collection is excellent in every way.

Violin concertos Nos. 1 in A, Op. 20; 2 in C, Op. 58; 3 in B min., Op. 61.
*** Hyperion Dig. CDA 67074 [id.]. Philippe Graffin, BBC Scottish SO, Martyn Brabbins.

Following up on the success of its 'Romantic Piano Concertos' series, Hyperion began its parallel series of 'Romantic Violin Concertos' with this issue, conveniently coupling all three of the Saint-Saëns works. Though his *Third Concerto* is relatively well known, with its charming central *Andantino* set between two bravura movements, and the *First*

Concerto, in a single movement, has not been neglected either, the delightful surprise here is the *Second Concerto.* Despite its numbering it is the earliest and longest, yet arguably the most memorable – full of the youthful exuberance of a 23-year-old. The French violinist Philippe Graffin, with a rich, firm tone, gives performances full of temperament, warmly supported by Martyn Brabbins and the BBC Scottish Symphony Orchestra, and the recording cannot be faulted.

Violin concerto No. 1 in A, Op. 20; Havanaise in E, Op. 83; Introduction and Rondo capriccioso, Op. 28; Morceau de concert, Op. 62; Romance in C, Op. 48; Sarabande, Op. 93/1.
*** BIS Dig. CD 860 [id.]. Tapiola Sinf., Jean-Jacques Kantorow.

Having much admired Kantorow's earlier record with the Tapiola Sinfonietta of the *Urbs Roma* symphony and the *Symphony No. 2 in A minor* (see our main volume), it is a pleasure to welcome this companion which brings the short and early *First Violin concerto* with such rightly popular display pieces as the *Introduction and Rondo capriccioso* and the *Havanaise.* Everything is expertly played and Kantorow has the right blend of panache and spontaneity. First-class sound as one expects from this source.

CHAMBER MUSIC

Carnival of the animals (chamber version).
(M) *** Virgin/EMI VM5 61782-2 [id.]. Nash Ens. – BRITTEN: *Young person's guide to the orchestra* **(*); PROKOFIEV: *Peter and the wolf.*

Saint-Saëns's original chamber version could hardly be more sparklingly presented than it is here by members of the Nash Ensemble, with Ian Hobson and Susan Tomes the solo pianists. At the opening the piano timbre seems a little hard, but overall the sound is very good. However, the present coupling of *Peter and the wolf* is a non-starter (see above) and readers are referred to our main volume where the *Carnival* is offered on a Virgin 2 x 1 bargain Double within an attractive collection of chamber music by Saint-Saëns and Dvořák (VBD5 61516-2).

Cello sonatas Nos. 1 in C min., Op. 32; 2 in F, Op. 123; Le cygne (from *Carnival of the animals,* trans. Godowski).
*** Hyperion Dig. CDA 67095 [id.]. Mats Lidström, Bengt Forsberg.

Mats Lidström and Bengt Forsberg have given us some impressive CDs of late, but none finer than this coupling of the two *Cello sonatas.* Written thirty years apart, they have an abundant and fluent invention, and are captivating when played with such fervour and polish. These artists radiate total conviction and a life-enhancing vitality and sensitivity.

Sallinen, Aulis (born 1935)

(i; ii) *Cello concerto, Op. 44;* (iii) *Chamber music I, Op. 38;* (i; iii) *Chamber music III, Op. 58;* (iii) *Some aspects of Peltoniemi Hintrik's funeral march;* (iv) *Sunrise serenade* (for 2 trumpets and chamber orchestra), *Op. 63;* (ii) *Shadows, Op. 52; Symphonies Nos. 4, Op. 49; 5 (Washington mosaics), Op. 57.*
(B) *** Finlandia/Warner Ultima Dig. 8573 81972-2 (2) [id.]. (i) Artos Noras; (ii) Helsinki PO, or (iii) Finland Sinfonietta, Kamu; (iv) Harjanne, Välimäki, Avanti CO.

This Ultima set brings an extensive survey of Sallinen's music, and provides an inexpensive entry into the composer's world. Apart from the symphonies, the *Cello concerto* of 1976 is the most commanding piece here. Sallinen's ideas resonate in the mind. Artos Noras has its measure and plays with masterly eloquence. *Shadows* is an effective short piece which reflects or 'shadows' the content of the opera *The King goes forth to France. Some aspects of Peltoniemi Hintrik's funeral march* is a transcription for full strings of the *Third Quartet* (1969), a one-movement work in five variations that never loses sight of its basic folk-inspired idea; not one of the composer's strongest works, but persuasively presented here. The middle movement of the *Fourth Symphony* is marked *Dona nobis pacem;* throughout the finale, bells colour the texture, as is often the case with Sallinen's orchestral writing. *Washington mosaics* is a five-movement work in which the outer movements form the framework for three less substantial but highly imaginative intermezzi. There are Stravinskian overtones in the first movement and the intermezzi cast a strong spell. The work has a feeling for nature and a keen sense of its power. The performances, under Okko Kamu, are very impressive and the recording quite exemplary. Overall, excellent value.

Sarasate, Pablo de (1844–1908)

Zigeunerweisen.
(B) **(*) EMI Début Dig. CDZ5 73501-2 [id.]. Ittai Shapira, ECO, Charles Hazlewood – BLOCH: *Baal Shem* ***; BRUCH: *Violin concerto No. 1 in G min., Op. 26* **; BUNCH: *Fantasy* **.

Ittai Shapira is a twenty-four-year-old Israeli violinist, whose début recording this is. The closing part of the *Zigeunerweisen* shows that EMI's confidence in him is not misplaced, as does the splendid *Baal Shem*. But the account of the Bruch concerto is not really quite as special as the expectations it aroused.

Satie, Erik (1866–1925)

Music for piano, 4 hands: (i) *La belle excentrique; 3 Morceaux en forme de poire.* Solo piano music: *Avant-dernières pensées; Embryons desséchés; 6 Gnossiennes; Croquis et agaceries d'un gros bonhomme en bois; 3 Gymnopédies; 5 Nocturnes; Sonatine bureaucratique; Véritables préludes flasques (pour un chien).*
(M) *** EMI Dig. CDM5 67239-2 [567260]. Aldo Ciccolini; (i) with Gabriel Tacchino.

Aldo Ciccolini offered these pieces on LP during the 1960s and recorded the present selection again during the 1980s and he is completely in sympathy with their style. He is totally inside this music and makes the most of its (not particularly wide) contrasts of mood and atmosphere. The recorded sound, harder in outline and not as rich as afforded to Pascal Rogé in his complete survey on Decca, is still very good. And some may feel that the slight edge given to the sharply articulated pieces (the *Embryons desséchés* and the *Sonatine bureaucratique* for instance) adds to their witty vitality. Gabriel Tacchino joins his colleague for the four-handed pieces. In many ways this is one of the most distinctive Satie collections in the catalogue.

3 Gymnopédies.
(B) *** Decca Penguin Classics Dig. 460 649-2 [id.]. Pascal Rogé – DEBUSSY: *Nocturnes;* RAVEL: *Le tombeau de Couperin; La valse* ***.

Those wanting just the three famous *Gymnopédies* will find that Pascal Rogé captures their bittersweet melancholy to perfection.

Gymnopédies; Ogives; Sarabandes.
(B) ** Ph. Virtuoso 420 472-2 [id.]. Reinbert de Leeuw.

Taken from his three-LP set, first released in 1980, this bargain disc comprises three representative works, including the most famous, the *Gymnopédies.* Reinbert de Leeuw is a sensitive pianist who is thoroughly attuned to Satie's personality; he takes the composer at his word by playing *très lent,* though at times one feels a little more movement would be an advantage. The recording is good, but not exceptional; the playing time of less than 50 minutes is ungenerous, but the reissue is at bargain price.

Scarlatti, Alessandro (1660–1725)

(i) *Concerti grossi Nos. 1–6;* (ii) *Stabat Mater.*
(M) **(*) DG 459 454-2 (2) [id.]. Mirella Freni, Teresa Berganza, Paul Kuenz CO, Mackerras

(ii) Solisti from Scarlatti Orchestra of Naples, Gracis – PERGOLESI: *Stabat Mater* **(*).

Ettore Gracis's recording of these six fine *Concerti grossi* was made in the 1960s. The first three act as a postlude to Scarlatti's memorably searching setting of the *Stabat Mater*; the remainder are used in a similar way for the coupled Pergolesi setting. In the vocal work, recorded a decade later, there is fine singing from both soloists, and the beauty of the writing is never in doubt, even if the balance unduly favours the voices, while the orchestral playing could be more resilient. The accounts of the *Concerti grossi* are alive and workmanlike, but not as fresh or accomplished as those by I Musici, which are praised in our main volume (Philips 434 160-2). Moreover, the competing coupling of the two *Stabat Mater* settings on Opus 111 (OPS 30-160) comes on a single disc and is artistically preferable.

(i) *Salve Regina;* (i; ii) *Stabat Mater;* (iii) Motet: *Quae est ista.*
**(*) Virgin Veritas/EMI Dig. VC5 45366-2. (i) Gérard Lesne; (ii) Sandrine Piau; (iii) Jean-François Novelli; Il Seminario Musicale.

All three works here are dedicated to the Virgin Mary. Gérard Lesne is heard at his finest in Scarlatti's eloquent A minor setting (one of five) of the *Salve Regina*, expressive and dramatic by turns. But when he joins with Sandrine Piau for the *Stabat Mater* the combination of voices is characterful in its contrast rather than a vocal symbiosis. Sandrine Piau's singing is pure, and tenderly touching, Lesne is more dramatic and brings a wider range of vocal colour, but his contribution is less moving. The two singers are successfully joined by the tenor Jean-François Novelli for the attractive closing motet, *Quae est ista*, which is widely varied in style; but again it is the soprano who stands out, not least for her remarkable bravura in *Hanc auroram conflagrans adore* ('Oh with what fiery love'). Il Seminario give pleasing authentic support and this is a stimulating collection, but collectors primarily interested in the *Stabat Mater* will find that the performance by Gemma Bertagnolli and Sara Mingardo with the Concerto Italiano remains unsurpassed (Opus 111 OPS 30-160).

Scarlatti, Domenico (1685–1757)

Keyboard sonatas, Kk.1, 27, 39, 87, 266, 298, 299, 366, 367, 374, 377, 379, 400, 417, 426, 484, 518, 519, 526, 545.
*** Sanctus Dig. SCS 016 [id.]. Nikolai Demidenko (piano).

Demidenko's are modern pianistic performances, fully coloured, neatly decorated, but with plentiful use of the pedal, judicious enough, but especially noticeable in K.367, where there is a degree of blurring. Yet the very opening *D major Sonata*,

K.298, with its crisp bursts of staccato repeated notes, is most engaging, as is the simpler *B flat major*, K.266, and the flightier K.1. Demidenko has not followed the often suggested grouping in pairs, but has chosen his own order and effectively so. Towards the end of the recital comes a particularly attractive group, with two *B minor Sonatas*, the first, K.87, played freely and touchingly, the second, K.27, a gentle *Allegro*, more simple and direct. They are framed by a pair of *D major* works, K.400 and K.484: the former is articulated with the lightest touch, yet in the latter the underlying bass part is brought out winningly. Then Demidenko closes purposefully with the fugal *D minor*, K.417. Excellent recording.

Keyboard sonatas, Kk.2, 35, 87, 132, 193, 322, 386, 427, 437, 515, 519.
(***) Ph./Westminster mono 464 018-2 [id.]. Clara Haskil.

This 38-minute 1947 recital comes as a bonus sampler disc with the final Volume 10 of the Philips 'Great Pianists of the Twentieth Century' series and is not available separately. It comes sealed in a cardboard sleeve, without documentation and is well transferred from a Westminster LP. The mono sound is a trifle confined, but fully acceptable. This repertoire suits the youthful Clara Haskil admirably and her simplicity of approach and keyboard dexterity give much pleasure. The *B minor Sonata*, K.87, for instance, is both gentle and searching and it is followed by a delightfully crisp account of the *C major* work, K.515.

Keyboard sonatas, Kk 12, 25, 27, 45, 118, 183, 187, 197, 201, 213, 233, 409, 239, 340, 517, 545.
Essercizi: 'Cats fugue' in G min., K.30.
**(*) Lyrichord Dig. LEMS 8043 [id.]. Elaine Comparone (harpsichord).

It was Clementi who nicknamed the last of Scarlatti's *Essercizi* the 'Cat's fugue', which gives this Lyrichord collection its sobriquet; and – with foreknowledge – on first encountering its striking seven-note ascending theme one can imagine a cat picking its way up the keyboard. Fortunately Elaine Comparone is not tempted to overdo such a pictorial suggestion and in her hands this becomes an engaging encore, placed halfway through her 74-minute recital.

She uses a modern Hubbard copy of a 1646 Ruckers harpsichord, enlarged in 1780 by Taskin, which she plays with bold, clear articulation and plenty of rhythmic lift. Her strong, direct style and crisp, clean decoration are stimulating, and these performances have much in their favour, for she provides a fair degree of light and shade. However we would have liked a little more relaxation at times in some of the minor key works, where she makes little attempt to seduce the ear with a more gentle approach. The recording is real and vividly present, but, as so often with harpsichord CDs, one has to turn the volume down quickly when the recital begins.

Schierbeck, Poul (1888–1949)

The Chinese flute, Op. 10; Queen Dagmar; The Tinder-box, Op. 61.
*** Dacapo Dig. 224104 [id.]. Dam-Jensen, Dolberg, Larsen, Van Hal, Dreyer, Odense SO, Giordano Bellincampi.

Keen cinéastes may possibly remember Poul Schierbeck's name appearing on the credits of Carl Dreyer's powerful film *Vredens dag* (*Day of Wrath*). His score was both memorable and affecting. Schierbeck belongs to the generation midway between Nielsen, with whom he studied, and Vagn Holmboe; his reputation rests primarily on his opera *Fête galante* and on his songs and cantatas. Until recently he was unrepresented in the catalogue, now no fewer than three versions of his charming songs *The Chinese flute*, to poems by Hans Bethge, which inspired many composers, not least Mahler in *Das Lied*, are available and the present issue also brings the cantata *Dronning Dagmar* (*Queen Dagmar*). Composed during the last four years of his life and finished only a few weeks before his death, it leaves no doubt as to his expertise in handling voices and his skills as an orchestrator. The melodrama *Fyrtøjet* (*The Tinder-box*), based on Hans Andersen, is both inventive and imaginative. This is an excellent introduction to a gifted minor master. Inger Dam-Jensen is excellent in the Bethge settings and the orchestral playing and recording are first class. Our only (minor) complaint is that the narrator in *The Tinder-box* sounds a little larger than life.

Studies; Sou'wester, sweater and shag, Op. 31; (v) The Chinese flute, Op. 10.
(*) Classico Dig. CLASSCD 290 [id.]. (i) Ens., Copenhagen, Morten Ryelund Sørensen; (ii) Copenhagen Younger Strings; (iii) Marianne Granvig; (iv) Rosalind Bevan; (v) Elsebeth Elmedal Johansen, Hanne Hokkerup.

The *Violin sonata* is very Brahmsian, the Op. 4 *Etudes* show the influence of Nielsen, and the *Capriccio*, a wind piece from the war years, is full of character and is decently played. The other performances are pretty ordinary and unimaginative and the soprano in *The Chinese flute* barely adequate. Readers who enjoyed the Dacapo should not go on to explore this.

The Chinese flute, Op. 10.
(**(*)) Bluebell mono ABCD 075 [id.]. Birgit Nilsson, Swedish Radio O, Tor Mann – BARTOK: *Bluebeard's Castle* (**(*)).

Nilsson's first recording was in 1946 of an aria from

Berwald's *Estrella di Soria*, and this comes from a Swedish Radio broadcast two years later. What a voice! It comes with a haunting but unaccountably cut *Bluebeard's Castle* under Fricsay.

Schoenberg, Arnold (1874–1951)

Chamber symphony, Op. 9 (arr. Webern); (i) *Ode to Napoleon. Verklaerte Nacht* (string sextet version), *Op. 4.*
(BB) **(*) Virgin Classics 2 x 1 VBD5 61760-2 (2) [CDVB 61760]. Nash Ens.; (i) with Thomas Allen – SHOSTAKOVICH: *Piano quintet; Piano trio No. 2; 4 Waltzes ***.*

The Nash Ensemble give us Webern's arrangement of the *Chamber symphony, Op. 9* reduced to the same group of five instruments used in the *Ode to Napoleon*. Contrapuntal detail is certainly clarified, but the Nash players ensure that the work's emotional content comes over expressively in spite of the less opulent textures. Thomas Allen provides a congenial, characterful narration for the strange *Ode* and although the close balance in *Verklaerte Nacht* is less than ideally alluring, throughout the Nash Ensemble play with easy virtuosity, intensity and fine blending. As so often with bargain reissues, no text is provided for the *Ode*, and the notes are sparse. An intriguing issue, just the same, for the Shostakovich couplings are first class.

Variations for orchestra, Op. 31.
(M) *** DG 457 760-2 [id.]. BPO, Karajan – BERG: *Lyric suite*, etc.; WEBERN: *Passacaglia.* ***

This, the most challenging of Schoenberg's orchestral works, receives a reading under Karajan which vividly conveys the ebb and flow of tension within the phrase and over the whole plan. The recording is superb and it is part of an equally impressive programme of twentieth-century music, reissued on DG's Originals label.

Verklaerte Nacht (string sextet version).
*** Nimbus Dig. NI 5614 [id.]. Brandis Quartet with Küssner, Schwalke – Richard STRAUSS: *Metamorphosen; Capriccio: Prelude. ***

The Brandis Quartet with two colleagues from the Berlin Philharmonic are in excellent form in *Verklaerte Nacht* in its original form for string sextet. They possess an unforced eloquence and expressive beauty that is impressive. The Nimbus recording is well balanced and very lifelike.

String quartets Nos. 1 in D min., Op. 7; (i) 2, Op. 10. 3, Op. 30; 4, Op. 37.
(B) ** Philips Duo 464 047-2 (2) [id.]. (i) Evelyn Lear; New Vienna Qt.

String quartet (1897); String quartet No. 1, Op. 7.
*** MDG Dig. MDG 307 0919-2 [id.]. Leipzig Qt.

String quartets Nos. (i) *2, Op. 10; 4, Op. 37.*
*** MDG Dig. MDG 307 0935-2 [id.]. (i)
Christiane Oelze; Leipzig Qt.

MDG and the Leipzig Quartet do go in for extravagant layout. (Their set of the Schubert string quartets
ran to no fewer than nine CDs as opposed to the six
of the Melos (DG) and Auryn (CPO) Quartets).
Their Schoenberg runs to three CDs – No. 3 is
coupled with *Verklaerte Nacht* on a third disc which
we have not heard. It is difficult to fault them in the
two early quartets or for that matter in the *Second,*
Op. 10, in which Christiane Oelze sings beautifully
of the *Luft von anderem planeten.* They phrase with
great naturalness, their ensemble is perfect and they
have great warmth, richness and tonal beauty,
though nothing is overstated or projected. If any
ensemble or recording could win doubting listeners
over to this repertoire, this is it. 'Why does Schoenberg always sound so ugly?' asked William Glock
on one occasion. Well, here he doesn't. The
recording balance is perfect.

The New Vienna recordings on Philips come
from 1969 and unless we are much mistaken did
not appear at the time in the UK. They are far from
negligible performances – indeed, they are more
than adequate – but by no means as persuasive as
the Leipzig Quartet. Of course, they enjoy a distinct
price advantage which may tempt some readers but
they don't give us the early *D major Quartet* of
1897. The Leipzig set is well worth the extra outlay.

*3 Piano pieces, Op. 11; 6 Little pieces, Op. 19;
5 Pieces, Op. 23; 2 Pieces, Op. 33a & b; Suite,
Op. 25.*
(BB) *** Naxos Dig. 8.553870 [id.]. Peter Hill –
BERG: *Piano sonata;* WEBERN: *Variations,
Op. 27.* ***

Peter Hill may not challenge Pollini's magisterial
survey of the Schoenberg canon but his is highly
intelligent, thoughtful playing, acutely sensitive to
dynamic and tonal shading. In some ways he is
more persuasive than Pollini in that one feels more
completely drawn into this musical world. In any
event, given the low price tag and the high quality
of the recorded sound, this is self-recommending.

VOCAL MUSIC

(i) *Gurrelieder* (complete); (ii) *Chamber
symphonies No. 1, Op. 9b; No. 2, Op. 38.*
(B) **(*) Ph. Duo 464 040-2 (2) [id.]. (i) James
McCracken, Jessye Norman, Tatiana
Troyanos, Werner Klemperer, Tanglewood
Festival Ch., Boston SO, Ozawa; (ii) Frankfurt
Radio SO, Inbal.

Ozawa directs a gloriously opulent reading of *Gurrelieder.* The playing of the Boston SO has both
warmth and polish and is set against a resonant
acoustic; among the soloists, Jessye Norman gives

a performance of radiant beauty, reminding one at
times of Flagstad in the burnished glory of her tone
colours. As the wood dove, Tatiana Troyanos sings
most sensitively, though the vibrato is at times
obtrusive; and James McCracken does better than
most tenors at coping with a heroic vocal line
without barking. The live 1979 recording is good,
though obviously not up to studio standards and the
absence of a libretto will be a drawback for some.
However, at bargain price, and with the inclusion
of the *Chamber symphonies* (two of the composer's
most accessible works), bracingly conducted by
Inbal, this Duo is good value.

Schoenfield, Paul (born 1947)

Piano concerto (Four parables).
** Athene Dig. CD 21 [id.]. Andreas Boyde,
Dresden SO, Jonathan Nott – DVORAK: *Piano
concerto* **.

The American composer Paul Schoenfield is now
in his early fifties and has made few inroads into the
concert hall outside the USA, the present recording
made at a live concert in Dresden being an exception. This CD is of the 1998 European première of
his *Piano concerto (Four parables)* which draws
on a variety of styles – popular music, vernacular
and folk traditions and 'the normal historical traditions of cultivated music often treated with sly
twists'. It has some degree of flair but from the
multiplicity of styles, no distinctive personality
emerges. Very brilliant playing from the talented
Andreas Boyde but this is not music which arouses
enthusiasm.

Schreker, Franz (1878–1934)

*Ekkehard (symphonic overture), Op. 12;
Fantastic overture, Op. 15; Interlude from Der
Schatzgräber; Nächtstuck (from Der ferne Klang);
Prelude to a drama; Valse lente.*
*** Chandos Dig. CHAN 9797 [id.]. BBC PO,
Vassily Sinaisky.

From his breakthrough in 1908 right through to the
early 1920s, Schreker was fêted as one of the
leading opera composers of the day in Germany,
but by the late 1920s a reaction had set in and the
emergence of the Nazis sealed his fate. The shock
of his dismissal as head of the Hochschule in Berlin
is said to have occasioned a stroke, which led to his
death in 1934. His reputation was slow to recover
after the war, when he suffered the venom of Adorno
– so, of course, did Sibelius. But to judge from the
present catalogue things are decidedly looking up,
and in this anthology by Vassily Sinaisky and the

BBC Philharmonic, he has found a committed champion.

Schreker reused material from his stage works to produce concert pieces such as the ones here, all demonstrating his gift for drawing sumptuous sounds from the orchestra. This sequence of six pieces presents a good cross-section of his output, demonstrating Schreker's development from the *Symphonic overture, Ekkehard*, and the charmingly unpretentious *Valse lente*, to the later works, which remain sumptuously late-romantic but which were regarded as daringly modern by early audiences. Both the *Nachtstück* from *Der ferne Klang* (1909) and the *Prelude to a drama* (1913) – the drama in question being the opera *Die Gezeichneten* – are powerfully imaginative. Perhaps the most seductive piece is the *Valse lente*. Schreker had a wonderful sense of fantasy, a feeling for colour, and impressive mastery of the orchestra. The textures are lush and overheated. Sinaisky draws seductively beautiful playing from the BBC Philharmonic, heightened by gloriously rich Chandos sound, and the whole disc serves to advance Schreker's cause.

Schubert, Franz (1797–1828)

(i) *Symphony No. 1 in D, D.82*; (ii) *Marche militaire, Op. 51/1*; (iii) Overtures: *Fierrabras, D.796; Des Teufels Lustschloss;* (iv) *4 Waltzes and 4 Ecossaises* (2 sets).

(B) ** Australian Decca Eloquence 466 908-2. (i) Israel PO, Mehta; (ii) VPO, Knappertsbusch; (iii) VPO, Kertész; (iv) Boskovsky Ens.

Mehta is no Beecham, but his account of the *First symphony* is a fresh, straightforward account which gives pleasure, even if it does not quite bubble as much as it should. The Israeli orchestra lacks something in polish and sophistication too, particularly in the strings. But there are no such problems for the ensuing Viennese recordings, which give this bargain disc its appeal. Knappertsbusch's noble and trusty account of the *Marche militaire*, and the little-known overtures under Kertész are always a joy to hear. *Des Teufels Lustschloss* is a juvenile work, and its bright-eyed freshness shows much in common with the music of the young Mendelssohn. *Fierrabras* is more melodramatic, but lively in invention. To cap an imaginative programme, Boskovsky gives delectable accounts of the charming dance pieces, and all are well recorded.

Symphony No. 5 in B flat, D.485.

(M) (***) Dutton Lab. mono CDK 1208 [id.].
  Concg. O, Eduard van Beinum (with
  BEETHOVEN: *Creatures of Prometheus:*
  Overture (LPO)) – BERLIOZ: *Symphonie*
  fantastique, Op. 14 (***).

**(*) DG 445 471–2 (4) [id.]. Stuttgart SW RSO, Celibidache – BRUCKNER: *Symphonies Nos. 7–9* *(**).

From Eduard van Beinum and the Concertgebouw Orchestra cultured playing and well-balanced sound. Not the equal of Beecham's version from pre-war days but very good indeed and better recorded. An enjoyable reminder of the fine results Eduard van Beinum achieved in Amsterdam.

Celibidache is surprisingly brisk in the opening movement, and his affectionately indulgent reading is at its most individual in the lovely *Andante*. Admirers of this conductor will want this alongside the Bruckner couplings, but for others there are more obvious recommendations. The recording is very good.

Symphonies Nos. 5 in B flat, D.485; 8 in B min. (Unfinished), D.759; Rosamunde: Overture; Entracte, No. 2; Ballet, No. 2.

(M) *(*) Mercury 462 954-2 [id.]. Minneapolis O, Skrowaczewski.

Skrowaczewski's Schubert is alert and well played, but unsmiling and not relaxed enough for this composer. The recording emphasizes aggression rather than charm, and this is a Mercury CD to pass by.

Symphonies Nos. 5 in B flat, D.485; 8 in B min. (completed by Brian Newbold); 9 in C (Great); Rosamunde (ballet music), D.797: No. 2 in G.

(B) *** Virgin Classics Dig. 2 x 1 Double VBD5 61806-2 (2) [id.]. OAE, Mackerras.

Mackerras was the first to use period instruments in Schubert's *Ninth* and with the Orchestra of the Age of Enlightenment produced this winning performance which will please both those who prefer conventional performance and devotees of authenticity. The characterful rasp on the period brass instruments and the crisp attack of timpani are much more striking than any thinness of string-tone. It is a performance of outstanding freshness and resilience.

The *Fifth* is not quite as magnetic as the *Ninth*, but still has comparable qualities. Tempi are only marginally brisker than conventional performances, and the slow movement has grace if not quite the degree of warmth that Boehm and Walter find. The special claim of this second disc is the inclusion of the *Unfinished Symphony* heard here as 'finished' by Brian Newbold. Mackerras opens in the mysterious depths with the darkest *pianopianissimo*, and the plangent period timbres bring a real sense of *Sturm und Drang*, with powerful contrasts and strong, forceful accents in the second movement. The recording is excellent throughout, and at bargain price, this stimulating set can certainly be recommended.

Symphony No. 8 (Unfinished), D.759.
(M) ** DG 463 609-2 (2) [id.]. Chicago SO,
  Giulini – MAHLER: *Symphony No. 9* **.
(B) ** Decca Penguin Classics Dig. 460 643-2
  [id.]. San Francisco SO, Blomstedt –
  MENDELSSOHN: *Symphony No. 4 in A
  (Italian).* ***

There are some very good things in Giulini's deeply
felt 1978 reading of the *Unfinished*, with much
carefully considered detail. But his glowing earlier
1962 Philharmonia account on EMI is much preferable. In any case, the Mahler coupling is not a prime
recommendation.

Blomstedt's account of the *Unfinished* is beautifully played, but only in the second movement
does the performance glow as it should – the first
movement is rather uneventful. The recording is
excellent, but the superb coupling over-shadows
this performance. The accompanying essay in the
Penguin Classics CD is by John Guare.

*Symphonies Nos. 8 in B min. (Unfinished), D.759;
9 in C (Great), D.944.*
(M) **(*) EMI CDM5 67338-2 [id.]. Philh. O,
  Klemperer.
(M) ** Sony SMK 61842 [id.]. NYPO, Bernstein.

Klemperer's approach to the *Unfinished* is utterly
individual. Gone is any attempt to charm: instead
the work is seen as a massive two-part symphonic
structure. And massive it is if one regards the two
movements in relation to the first halves of other
symphonies. But Klemperer's approach is anything
but stodgy, for his determination to play the score
straight has inspired his players to keen, alert
playing that never lets the attention flag. The quiet
opening is deliberately purposeful, but when the
second subject finally arrives there is no attempt to
beautify the melody and it acquires an unusual
purity. So it is at the opening of the second movement and through the whole performance. Some
listeners may resist, but it remains an outstanding
example of Klemperer's interpretative genius. The
Ninth Symphony too is nothing if not individual,
with a measured performance after a massive introduction. Again the reading is deliberately literal, but
also rather heavy, particularly in the first movement.
Yet once the speeds and severe approach are
accepted, the power of the performance is matched
by its fascination and there is some glorious playing
from the Philharmonia. The oboe solo at the beginning of the slow movement is deliciously pointed.
Once again the new CD transfer for this Legacy
reissue has enhanced the Kingsway Hall recording
from the early 1960s, which is rich and full and
most realistically balanced.

Bernstein gives a dramatic account of the *Unfinished*, with a great surge of energy in the first-
movement development. Yet there is lyrical warmth
too and at times a sense of mystery. The playing of
the NYPO is first class and the recording from 1963

is acceptable. The account of the *C major Symphony*
is less consistent. There is plenty of vitality, but it
lacks the unforced spontaneity which can make this
symphony so exhilarating. Every now and again
there is a clipped quality to the playing, the effect
exacerbated by the upfront 1967 recording. The
finale charges along like a runaway express train,
exciting and brilliant, yes, but a bit charmless too.
However, it is not dull, and Bernstein fans will
almost certainly want this coupling.

CHAMBER MUSIC

(i) *Fantasia in C for violin and piano, D.934.
Fantasia in C (Wanderer fantasia), D.760.*
**(*) ECM Dig. ECM 1699; 464 320-2 [id.].
  András Schiff; (i) with Yuuko Shiokawa.

As might be expected, András Schiff's account of
the *Wanderer fantasia* is finely paced and highly
sensitive, and entirely free from expressive exaggeration. He has the advantage of lifelike and full-
bodied recorded sound. The coupling is another *C
major Fantasy*, for violin and piano, with Yuuko
Shiokawa, his partner in previous recordings. However the piano is very dominant, and Shiokawa very
backwardly placed. At 50 minutes the disc is short
measure anyway. A pity since this is a distinguished
Wanderer.

Octet in F, D.803.
❂ (M) *** Decca 466 580-2 [id.]. Vienna Octet –
  SPOHR: *Octet in E* ***.

The Vienna Octet's 1958 recording of the Schubert
Octet has stood the test of time. It has a magical
glow with the group at its peak under the leadership
of Willi Boskovsky. The horn has a Viennese fruiti-
ness which helps to make the performance more
authentic, and these fine players never put a foot
wrong throughout. The remastered recording is
warm, full and modern sounding. The delightful and
unusual Spohr coupling makes this a fine addition to
Decca's Legends series.

(i) *Piano quintet in A (Trout), D.667;* (ii) *String
quartet No. 14 in D min. (Death and the Maiden),
D.810.*
(M) *** Decca Penguin Classics 460 650-2 [id.].
  (i) Clifford Curzon, Vienna Octet (members);
  (ii) VPO String Qt.

Curzon's *Trout* has been swimming for over forty
years, and still remains near the surface of the
stream. It is a memorable performance, with a distinguished account of the piano part, and splendidly
stylish support from the Vienna players. If the violin
tone – a bit thin sounding – betrays the age of
the recording (1958), the ear quickly adjusts. The
Vienna Philharmonic players treat the *Death and
the Maiden Quartet* with comparable affection, yet
bring out all the music's vitality. Indeed, the playing
is peerless: Boskovsky, the leader, shows his fine

musicianship throughout the work, and in the variations in particular. The 1963 sound is as fresh as paint, and the specialist essay is by Dan Jacobson. The *Trout* is also available with a different coupling on Decca's 'Classic Sound' label, but this Penguin Classics disc is a preferable choice, if both works are wanted.

Piano trio No. 2 in E flat, D.929; Notturno in E flat, D.897.
*(*) ECM Dig. 453 300-2 [id.]. Schneeberger, Thomas Demenga, Dähler.

These fine players do not help themselves by choosing an all too leisurely tempo in the first movement. They are just a shade ponderous and heavy-handed at times in both pieces, though the actual quality of the recorded sound is more than serviceable.

String quartets Nos. 1–15; Quartet movement in C min., D.103.
(B) **(*) DG 463 151-2 (6) [id.]. Melos Qt of Stuttgart.

The Melos Quartet give us an inexpensive survey of all the Schubert quartets. The early works have a disarming grace and innocence and some of their ideas are most touching (witness the *Adagio* introduction of No. 4 in C). The Melos Quartet give impressive, unmannered accounts of all these works, finding the drama as well as the music's inner tensions. They are let down by the recording which, although faithful, is rather too closely balanced. The remastering provides good presence, and conveys a wide dynamic range, but fortissimos can be a little fierce. Nevertheless this well-documented set is value for money and worth considering when the full-priced competition (from the New Leipzig Quartet on MDG, and the Auryn on CPO – see our main volume) costs twice as much.

String quartet No. 15 in G, D.887.
*** DG Dig. 457 615-2 [id.]. Hagen Qt –
BEETHOVEN: *String quartet No. 11 in F min., Op. 95* **(*).

The Hagen Quartet give a thoughtful and perceptive account of the great *G major Quartet*, D.887. They have dramatic intensity (indeed, they are a shade too intense at times) and an impressive virtuosity. Dynamic extremes are scrupulously projected but do not draw excessive attention to themselves, save perhaps in the opening of the slow movement. As quartet-playing it is masterly and, though not the equal of the Quartetto Italiano, it is thoroughly compelling. As with the Beethoven *F minor*, Op. 95, with which it is coupled, there is an aggressive feel in tutti at times, as in the impassioned outbursts in the slow movement. All the same the DG recording has exemplary warmth and clarity.

String quintet in C, D.956.
(**) Testament mono SBT 1157 [id.]. Amadeus

Qt, Pleeth – MOZART: *Sinfonia concertante, K.364* (**(*)).

EMI made this recording of the great *C major Quintet* just when the Amadeus Quartet was establishing its high reputation, before their long-term contract with DG. Comparison with their later versions of this same masterpiece brings out, first of all, the difference of recording balance, with EMI's close placing offering fuller-bodied string tone. If the first movement is a degree warmer and more purposeful than in the later versions, the slow movement at a more flowing speed lacks the inner intensity of the later recordings, partly a question of pianissimos not being registered so gently. Also the finale at a marginally broader speed lacks the exuberance of later recordings, but the youthful freshness and strength of the whole performance are most winning, helped by an excellent transfer. The Mozart coupling is both generous and illuminating. However, there are many finer versions of the Schubert, and the alternative Testament account by the augmented Hollywood Quartet was given a ✿ in our main volume (SBT 1031). The Lindsays stand high among modern recordings (ASV CDDCA 537).

PIANO MUSIC

Piano music for four hands

Allegro moderato & Andante, D.968; Divertissement on original French themes, D.823; 2 Ecossaises, from D.783; Fantaisie, D.48; Marche héroïque in C, D.602/2.
** Olympia Dig. OCD 677 [id.]. Anthony Goldstone, Caroline Clemmow (with Robert SCHUMANN: *Polonaises No. 7 in G min.; 8 in A flat **).

16 Deutscher Tänze from D.783; Fugue in E min., D.952; Grande marche et trio in B min., D.819/3; Marche héroïque in B min., D.602/1; Overture in G min., D.668; 2 Polonaises in D min., D.824/1 & D.599/1; Sonata in B flat, D.617; Variations on a theme from Hérold's opera Marie, D.908.
** Olympia Dig. OCD 676 [id.]. Anthony Goldstone, Caroline Clemmow (with Robert SCHUMANN: *Polonaise No. 6 in E **).

Deutscher Tanz in C, D.783/9; Fantaisie, D.9; Grande marche héroïque, D.885; 2 Marches caractéristiques, D.886; Duo in A min. (Lebensstürme), D.947; Polonaise in E, D.824/6; D.599/3; Variations on a French song, D.624.
** Olympia Dig. OCD 675 [id.]. Anthony Goldstone, Caroline Clemmow (with Robert SCHUMANN: *Polonaise No. 5 in B min. **).

Fantaisie, D.1; Grande marche funèbre in C min., D.859; Grande marche et trio in D, D.819/4; 2 Ländler in C min. and C, D.814/3 and D.814/4; March in G (Kindermarsch), D.928; Polonaise in

D, D.824/4; Variations on an original theme in A flat, D.813.
** Olympia Dig. OCD 674 [id.]. Anthony Goldstone, Caroline Clemmow (with Robert SCHUMANN: *Polonaise No. 4 in B flat **).

Deutscher Tanz in E flat, D.783/8; Divertissement à la hongroise, D.818; Grande marche et trio in G min., D.819/2; 2 Ländler in E flat and A flat, D.814/1 and D.814/2; 3 Marches militaires, D.733; Polonaises in A, D.824/5; B flat, D.618a, sketches (realized by Anthony Goldstone); *Rondo in A, D.951.*
** Olympia Dig. OCD 673 [id.]. Anthony Goldstone, Caroline Clemmow (with Robert SCHUMANN: *Polonaise No. 3 in F min. **).

Schubert's extensive output for piano four hands is decently represented on CD, and no one wrote more original music for the medium than he did. There are several superb sets now on offer, most notably the Duo Tal and Groethuysen (Sony), and Christoph Eschenbach and Justus Frantz (EMI). The Anthony Goldstone and Caroline Clemmow partnership are a husband-and-wife team who give eminently musical and shapely accounts with plenty of sensitive observation. They can be confidently recommended (save for the recorded sound which is not of uniform quality) but not in preference to Tal and Groethuysen or their EMI rivals which have the advantage of also being less expensive, while Anne Queffélec and Imogen Cooper on Erato should not be forgotten either (see our main volume). The Schumann *Polonaises* are rarer repertoire and make acceptable bonuses for each disc.

Fantasia in F min., D.940; Grand duo sonata in C, D.812; Variations in A flat, D.813.
(M) *** Decca 466 822-2 [id.]. Sviatoslav Richter, Benjamin Britten.

It was an inspired partnership, devised for the Aldeburgh Festival in 1964 and 1965, when Sviatoslav Richter joined Benjamin Britten in Schubert duets. As these electrically intense performances demonstrate – including what are arguably the two greatest piano duets ever written, the *Fantasia* and *Grand duo* – they favoured fast speeds, which yet allowed crisply sprung rhythms and warmly lyrical phrasing. Britten, playing secondo, explained years later what a problem it was achieving full expressiveness with his right hand, when Richter, unused to having another player at a single keyboard, so splayed out his left elbow, getting in the way. You would hardly know that from the results, with phenomenally crisp articulation from both players. The two major works were recorded in 1965 in Jubilee Hall, Aldeburgh, the *Variations* in the Parish Church a year earlier, both with clear, immediate stereo-sound balanced for radio by BBC engineers.

Solo piano music

(i) *Fantasy in F min., D.940;* (ii) *Impromptus 1–4, D.899; Piano sonatas Nos. 18 in G, D.894;* (iii) *20 in A, D.959.*
(B) **(*) Erato/Warner Ultima Analogue/Dig. 394 27004-2 (2) [id.]. Maria João Pires with (i) Huseyin Sermet; (ii) Anne Queffélec; (iii) Michel Dalberto.

At the modest asking price we have a more than serviceable Schubert piano anthology. Maria João Pires and Huseyin Sermet are perfectly attuned in the *F minor Fantasy* from the composer's last year and the recording from 1989 is very good. The four D.899 *Impromptus* are sensitively played by Anne Queffélec and the analogue recording wears very well. Maria João Pires lingers long and lovingly over the first movement of the *G major Sonata*, D.894 but it is a finely musical pout that may not appeal to all listeners. But the disc can be warmly recommended to her admirers.

Piano sonatas Nos. 1 in E, D.157; 2 in C, D.279; 3 in E, D.459; 4 in A min., D.537; 5 in A flat, D.557; 6 in E min., D.566; 7 in E flat, D.568; 9 in B, D.575; 11 in F min., D.625; 13 in A, D.664; 14 in A min., D.784; 15 in C, D.840 (Relique); 16 in A min., D.845; 17 in D, D.850; 18 in G, D.894; 19 in C min., D.958; 20 in A, D.959; 21 in B flat, D.960.
(B) *** DG 463 766-2 (7) [id.]. Wilhelm Kempff.

Wilhelm Kempff's cycle was recorded over a four-year period (1965–9) and has been much admired over the years. These are among the most consistently satisfying accounts of the sonatas, with a wisdom that puts them in a category of their own. Indeed their insights are very special indeed. The recording has a touch of shallowness, but is generally excellent. All seven CDs are now available in a convenient, inexpensive bargain box, and represent exceptional value.

Piano sonata No. 4 in A min., D.537.
(M) ** DG Analogue/Dig. 457 762-2 [id.]. Michelangeli – BEETHOVEN: *Piano sonata No. 4 in E flat, Op. 7 *; BRAHMS: *Ballades.*
***

Michelangeli rushes the opening theme of the *A minor Sonata* and rarely allows the simple ideas of the first movement to speak for themselves. Elsewhere his playing, though aristocratic and poised, is not free from artifice, and the natural eloquence of Schubert eludes him. Fine 1981 digital recording, but on this CD only the Brahms finds this artist at his best.

Wanderer fantasia, D.760.
● (M) *** Decca mono 466 498-2 [id.]. Clifford Curzon – SCHUMANN: *Fantasia in C, Op. 17; Kinderszenen, Op. 15.* *** ●

Curzon's famous account of the *Wanderer fantasia* dates from 1949 and the clear, dry recording emphasizes his dramatic approach to the outer movements, putting his infinitely touching account of the sadly yearning central *Adagio* into bold relief. It is this movement which expresses the message of the song on which the work is based: *Dort, wo du nicht bist, dort ist das Glück!* ('Happiness is where you are not!').

VOCAL MUSIC

The Graham Johnson Schubert Lieder Edition

Lieder, Vol. 33: (i) *Lebenstraum (Gesang in C min.); Lebenstraum; Pensa, che questo istante; Totengräberlied;* (ii) *Entra l'uomo allor che nasce (Aria di Abramo); L'incanto degli occhi; Misero pargoletto; O combats, o désordre extrême!; Ombre amene, amiche piante (La Serenata); Quelle' innocente figlio (Aria dell' Angelo); Rien de la nature; Son fra l'onde;* (iii) *Klaglied;* (iv) *Entra l'uomo allor che nasce (Aria di Abramo); Erinnerungen; Geisternähe;* (v) *Serbate o dei custodi;* (vi) *Die Befreier Europas in Paris;* (vii) *Der abend;* (viii) *Ammenlied; Die Nacht;* (ix) *Dithyrambe; Trinklied; Viel tausend Sterne prangen.*
*** Hyperion Dig. CDJ 33033 [id.]. Marie McLaughlin, Ann Murray, Catherine Wyn-Rogers, Philip Langridge, Daniel Norman, Adrian Thompson, Maarten Koningsberger, Stephen Varcoe and soloists, London Schubert Chorale, Stephen Layton; Graham Johnson.

Entitled 'The Young Schubert', this volume brings together a mixed bag of songs from the years of the composer's boyhood, 1810–14, which for various reasons have not been included in previous volumes. Thanks to Graham Johnson and his powers of coordination, the result is intensely compelling; it even offers what, through scholarly detective work, is now thought to be the very first Schubert song: probably written before 1810, an extended piece of 394 bars, previously described simply as 'Gesang in C minor', when the words were unknown. Now, as *Lebenstraum*, 'Life's dream', it has been persuasively fitted with words from a poem by Gabriele von Baumberg, which Schubert also used in another song on the disc. It is fascinating too to find the boy Schubert doing arrangements of arias by Gluck, and no fewer than ten of these early songs set Italian words. Standing out among the original songs is the tenderly beautiful *Klaglied* lament of 1812, magically sung by Marie McLaughlin. Though the recordings were made from a whole sequence of sessions between 1990 and 1999, Johnson and his chosen singers offer performances of consistent excellence, very well recorded.

Lieder, Vol. 34: (i) *Abend;* (ii) *Das Abendrot;* (iii) *Der Alpenjäger;* (iv) *Atys;* (v) *Kantate zum Geburtstag des Sängers Michael Vogl;* (vi) *Das Dörfchen;* (vii) *Die Einsiedelei;* (viii) *Frohsinn;* (ix) *Die gefangenen Sänger;* (x) *Die Gesellikeit (Lebenslust);* (xi) *Das Grab;* (xii) *Grenzen der Menschheit; Der Kampf;* (xiii) *Das Mädchen;* (vi) *La pastorella al prato;* (xiv) *Prometheus;* (xv) *Sing-Ubungen;* (xvi) *Uber allen Zauber Liebe;* (iii) *Wandrers Nachtlied II.*
*** Hyperion CDJ 33034 [id.]. Lorna Anderson, Lynne Dawson, Patricia Rozario, Marjana Lipovšek, Martyn Hill, Philip Langridge, Daniel Norman, Michael Schade, Gerald Finley, Matthias Gorne, Thomas Hampson, Simon Keenlyside, Stephan Loges, Christopher Maltman, Neal Davies (with Catherine Denley, John Mark Ainsley, Ian Bostridge, Jamie MacDougall, Michael George); Graham Johnson; L. Schubert Chorale, Stephen Layton.

It is one of the great merits of Graham Johnson's inspired method of presenting the collected Schubert songs that he gives such a clear perspective on Schubert's career over each year of his short working life. This thirty-fourth Volume brings together the songs that Schubert wrote between 1817 and 1821 not previously included in the Edition. As Johnson explains, the years 1815 and 1816 were the most productive for songs, leading to the present years when other commitments left him with fewer opportunities for songwriting. The nineteen items here, presented in chronological order, offer a wide range of pieces, including several vocal quartets, one of them the delectable *Die Gesellikeit,* 'Zest for life', and a ten-minute cantata written for the birthday of his singer-friend and advocate, Michael Vogl. Other jewels include some fine Goethe settings, notably the dramatic *Prometheus,* and the second version of the *Wandrers Nachtlied,* a miniature of just a few bars that delves astonishingly deep. Consistently fine performances from sessions recorded between 1991 and 1999.

Lieder, Vol. 35: (1822–25): *Bootgesang; Coronach; Dass sie hier gewesen!; Du bist die Ruh; Gebet (Du Urquell aller güte); Gondelfahrer; Gott in der Natur; Greisengesang; Lachen und Weinen; Lied des gefangenen Jägers; Lied eines Kriegers; Pilgerweise; Schwestergruss; Der Sieg; Der Tanz; Totengräbers Heimwehe; Die Wallfahrt; Der zürnende Barde.*
*** Hyperion Dig. CDJ 33035 [id.]. Lynne Dawson, Geraldine McGreevy, Philip Langridge, Thomas Hampson, Maarten Konigsberger, Christopher Maltman; Graham Johnson

Rounding off his magnificent project of recording all Schubert's songs, Graham Johnson gathers together what might have seemed loose ends, concentrating on songs from the years of the composer's late twenties. It was a period which, as Johnson explains in his ever-informative notes, brought more extreme highs and lows in the composer's life than ever before.

Central to the scheme are the five settings of poems by Rückert, four of them masterpieces including two of the best-known songs here, the playful *Lachen und weinen* (lightly touched by in by Geraldine McGreevy), and the glorious *Du bist die Ruh*, with Lynne Dawson rapt and dedicated in its soaring vocal line.

Also from the Rückert group the tenor song, *Dass sie hier gewesen*, winningly sung by Philip Langridge, and a fine sixteen-bar fragment only recently discovered. Another song to note is *Totengräbers Heimwehe*, a baritone song which in its marching tread seems to anticipate *Winterreise*, powerfully sung by Christopher Maltman if with gritty tone on sustained notes.

Rarities that prove a revelation include the poised *Schwestergruss* (McGreevy again), with four fine ensemble pieces framing the collection, starting with *Gott in der Natur*, written at the time of the *Unfinished Symphony*, and ending with the exuberant quartet, *Der Tanz*, 'the Dance'. Recordings from different periods are all beautifully balanced.

Goethe Lieder, Vol. 1: *An den Mond* (1st and 2nd versions); *An schwager Kronos; Bundeslied; Der Fischer; Ganymed; Geistes-Gruss; Gesang des Harfners* (1st, 2nd, and 3rd versions); *Der Gott und die Bajadere; Grenzen der Menschheit; Harfenspieler* (1st and 2nd versions); *Heidenröslein; Der König in Thule; Mahomets Gesang; Meeres Stille; Prometheus; Der Rattenfänger; Der Schatzgräber; Wandrers Nachtlied* (1st and 2nd versions).
(BB) *** Naxos 8.554665. Ulf Bästlein, Stefan Laux.

This fine Goethe collection is one of the first of a series of Schubert Lieder discs masterminded for Naxos by the pianists Stefan Laux and Ulrich Eisenlohr. They aim to choose only German-speaking singers from the younger generation, and Ulf Bästlein certainly qualifies. His is a firm, warm baritone which he uses most sensitively, shading tone and dynamic with fine feeling for words, as in his rapt account of *Meeres Stille*, 'Becalmed'. Though the selection includes the popular favourite *Heidenröslein*, and such masterly songs as *An den Mond* (both settings) and *Ganymed*, the choice is imaginative, and it is good to have such multiple settings of the same words, sensitively contrasted by singer and pianist. Unlike many bargain discs of Lieder, this offers full texts and translations.

Lieder: *Abendstern; An die Entfernte; Atys; Auflösung; Ganymed; Der Musensohn; Nähe des Geliebten.*

(M) (***) BBC Music BBCB 8015-2 [id.]. Peter Pears, Benjamin Britten – BRITTEN: *On this island;* WOLF: *7 Mörike Lieder ***;* (with ARNE: *Come away death; Under the greenwood tree.* QUILTER: *O mistress mine.* WARLOCK: *Take, o take those lips away.* TIPPETT: *Come unto these yellow sands* (***)).

Britten as accompanist in Lieder regularly conveyed a sense of spontaneity and here – in a shrewdly chosen group of songs, not all well known – he seems almost to be improvising. The lightness and agility of his accompaniment in the best-known songs, *Der Musensohn*, is a marvel. Fine, sensitive singing from Pears in these 1969 performances.

Lieder: (i) *An die Freunde; Auf der Donau; Aus Heliopolis; Fischerweise; Freiwilliges Versinken; Gruppe aus dem Tartarus;* (ii) *Der Hirt auf dem Felsen;* (i) *Prometheus; Der Strom; Der Wanderer; Der Wanderer an den Mond.*
(M)*** BBC Music BBCB 8011-2 [id.]. (i) Dietrich Fischer-Dieskau; (ii) Heather Harper, Thea King; Benjamin Britten – WOLF: *3 Christmas songs; 3 Michelangelo Lieder ***.*

Fischer-Dieskau has rarely if ever been more inspired in his recordings of Schubert than here, in live performances given with Britten at the Snape Maltings in 1972 – the last year Britten was able to take an active part in the Aldeburgh Festival. The great baritone, then at his peak, was plainly inspired by the inspirational quality of his accompanist's playing, and the selection of songs, well contrasted, brings together an attractive mixture of rare and well known. Similarly, in the *Shepherd on the rock*, with Thea King producing honeyed tone in the clarinet obbligato, the magnetism is irresistible. The Wolf songs from Pears and Shirley-Quirk make an attractive bonus.

Mass No.6 in E flat, D.950
*** BBC Legends BBCL 4029-2 (2) Scottish Festival Ch., New Philh. O, Giulini – VERDI: *Requiem ***.*

Schubert's last and most ambitious setting of the Mass makes a generous coupling for Giulini's inspired account of the Verdi *Requiem*. It was recorded at the Edinburgh Festival in 1968 with radio sound remarkably free and full for a performance in Usher Hall. As in the Verdi Giulini directs a dedicated performance, again with incandescent choral singing from the Scottish Festival Chorus.

Rosamunde: Overture (Die Zauberharfe, D.644); and incidental music (complete), *D.797.*
(B) *** Australian Decca Eloquence 466 677-2. Yachmi, Vienna State O Ch., VPO, Münchinger.

Münchinger's performance of the delightful *Rosamunde* music glows with an affectionate warmth and understanding which places this as one of his very best records. Its unavailability on CD until this Australian disc appeared is unaccountable: there is an unforced spontaneity as well as strength here, and the 1970s recording is rich and naturally balanced. The vocal numbers are superbly done and the VPO is at its magnificent best. A real bargain.

Song cycles

Schwanengesang (collection), *D.957*. Lieder: (i) *Auf dem Strom. Herbst; Lebensmut.*
(BB) ** Naxos Dig. 8.554663 [id.]. Michael Volle, Ulrich Eisenlohr; (i) with Sjön Scott.

In Naxos's enterprising Schubert Lieder Edition, Michael Volle adds three settings of poems by Ludwig Rellstab to the seven which come in the late collection of songs, *Schwanengesang*. It is an imaginative bonus, when they include the extended song with horn obbligato, *Auf dem Strom*, 'On the river'. Volle is as yet a rather cautious Lieder singer, not always avoiding the squareness that can overtake strophic songs, and he seems unable to convey a smile in his voice, with the tone growing plaintive at the top. Yet with his clear diction, this is still a disc worth hearing and, as in the rest of the series, full words and translations are provided.

Winterreise (song cycle), *D.911*.
(BB) ** Naxos 8.554471 [id.]. Roman Trekel, Ulrich Eisenlohr.

Roman Trekel's baritone is more remarkable for sensitive inflection than for beauty, and though the tone grows fluttery under pressure of emotion, as in the last two songs of this supreme song cycle, the concentration and intelligence of the performance are considerable compensation. This may not rival the finest available versions of this challenging work, but it is good to hear a German singer towards the beginning of his career giving a young man's view. Ulrich Eisenlohr, one of the two pianists who have masterminded the Naxos series, does not always help with accompaniments that are too square at times. Full texts and translation as in the rest of the series.

Schumann, Robert (1810–56)

(i) *Cello concerto;* (ii) *Piano concerto in A min.;* (iii) *Violin concerto in D min.;* (ii) *Introduction and Allegro appassionato;* (iv) *Konzertstück in F for four horns and orchestra, Op. 86.*
(B) **(*) EMI Rouge et Noir Analogue/Dig. CZS7 67521-2 (2). (i) Paul Tortelier, RPO, Yan Pascal Tortelier; (ii) Barenboim, LPO, Fischer-Dieskau; (iii) Kremer, Philh. O, Muti; (iv) Hauptmann, Klier, Kohler, Seifert, BPO, Tennstedt.

This is a useful collection of Schumann's con-

certante works and it is a pity that it is let down somewhat by Barenboim's rather too direct account of the works for piano. Tortelier's is a characteristically inspirational performance of the *Cello concerto*, at its most concentrated in the hushed rendering of the slow movement. The *Violin concerto* comes off pretty well in the hands of Gidon Kremer and he has good support from the Philharmonia under Riccardo Muti. The (digital) recording was made in the Kingsway Hall in 1982 and is vivid and convincingly balanced. What makes this two-disc set well worth considering in EMI's Rouge et Noir series (offering two CDs for the price of one) is the inclusion of the exuberant *Konzertstück* with its brilliant horn playing. The four soloists from the Berlin Philharmonic play with superbly ripe virtuosity and Tennstedt's direction is both urgent and expansive. The 1978 recording is admirably full-blooded.

Piano concerto in A min., Op. 54.
(M) *** Decca 466 383-2 [id.]. Radu Lupu, LSO, Previn – GRIEG: *Piano concerto ***.

As with the Grieg coupling, we regret that the Lupu/ Previn performance of Schumann's more elusive concerto was underrated in our main volume, as was the quality of the new transfer of the 1973 recording. This now seems to us to suit the music admirably, with the piano lucidly and truthfully caught against a natural orchestral backcloth. Lupu's clean boldness of approach in the outer movements is appealingly fresh, with the finale brilliant yet unforced, while the *Intermezzo* has both warmth and the necessary tender delicacy. This reissue in Decca's Legends series must move up to stand alongside other current mid-priced recommendations.

(i) *Piano concerto in A min., Op. 54;* (ii) *Piano quintet in E flat, Op. 44.*
*** DG Dig. 463 179-2 [id.]. Maria João Pires; (i) COE, Abbado; (ii) Dumay, Capuçon, Caussé, Wang.

It makes an excellent if unusual coupling to have the Schumann *Piano concerto* alongside the most heroic of his chamber works. In both Pires is inspired to give freely spontaneous performances, at once powerfully persuasive and poetic. In the *Quintet* the interplay between musicians is delightful, each distinguished individually but who plainly enjoy working together. The funeral march of the slow movement brings the keenest concentration, conveying mystery. Consistently Pires leads the team to play with natural, unselfconscious rubato in all four movements, with speeds perfectly chosen and the structure firmly held together.

In the *Concerto* Pires is also at her most persuasive. With the ever-responsive Chamber Orchestra of Europe, Abbado matches the volatile quality in Pires's performance with beautifully transparent accompaniment. The central *Intermezzo* is light and fresh at a flowing *Andantino grazioso*, with free rubato making it sound like an improvisation, leading to a sparkling account of the finale, which lightly brings out the scherzando quality of the writing. Two beautifully judged performances, both very well recorded.

Symphonies Nos. 1–4.
(M) *** RCA Dig. 74321 61820-2 (2) [id.]. NDR SO, Christoph Eschenbach.

John Eliot Gardiner's period-instrument recording of the Schumann symphonies has special insights to offer and received a Rosette in our main volume (DG 457 591-2). However, among recordings on modern instruments, Christoph Eschenbach's set with the North German Radio Symphony Orchestra is one of the finest to have appeared for many years. There is a consistent feeling for line and a firm yet flexible pulse. Tempi are sensible, phrases shaped with natural feeling and without any hint of the fussy intrusive touches that attract attention to the interpreter rather than the composer. Moreover Eschenbach is most responsive to the textures, so often written off as thick. He brings a warmth and above all clarity that almost dispels the traditional view of Schumann's orchestration as opaque. As one recalls from his performances as a pianist earlier in his career, he has a keen affinity with the Schumann sensibility. Good, clean recording too. This is the first modern set that can be recommended alongside the classic Sawallisch (EMI CMS7 64815-2) and above all Karajan (DG 429 672-2) recordings, and it offers probably the best sound of all.

Symphonies Nos. 1 in B flat (Spring), Op. 38; 2 in C, Op. 61; Genoveva overture, Op. 81.
(B) **(*) Australian DG Eloquence 463 200-2. BPO, Kubelik.

Symphonies Nos. 3 in E flat (Rhenish), Op. 97; 4 in D min., Op. 120; Manfred overture, Op. 115.
(B) **(*) Australian DG Eloquence 463 201-2. BPO, Kubelik.

Kubelik's accounts of the symphonies are beautifully played and well recorded. The readings have not the drive of Karajan, notably in No. 4 but they undoubtedly have both eloquence and warmth. They are straightforward and unmannered and recorded in a spacious acoustic with good CD transfers. Kubelik's ear for balance removes all suspicions of heaviness in the orchestration, and the recordings, dating from the mid-1960s, still sound good. Two enjoyable overtures are offered as a bonus.

(i) *Symphonies Nos. 1 in B flat (Spring), Op. 38;* (ii) *2 in C, Op. 61.*
(M) (**) Dutton Lab. mono CDK 1209 [id.]. (i)

National SO, Piero Coppola; (ii) LPO, Georges Enescu.

Piero Coppola's *Spring Symphony*, recorded in July 1946, is basically a vigorous reading, but with a great deal of ebb and flow in its pacing. The *Larghetto* is shaped with a considerable expressive impulse, and if here one notices that the National Symphony strings (Sydney Beer's famous pick-up orchestra) do not provide quite the body of tone one would expect in the Concertgebouw or Staatskapelle, they play with fair refinement of feeling. The Scherzo has rhythmic verve, and the finale sets off brightly. But then there is a Furtwängler-style pulling back to prepare for the horn entry. However, after the flute cadenza the momentum steadily increases for an exultant coda.

In the *C major Symphony*, dating from a year later, Enescu's approach is far more direct (at least until the finale), more thrusting in the first movement, and with a buoyant Scherzo. But the heart of his interpretation lies in the slow movement, opening nobly, spaciously paced, and with considerable concentration when the strings take over for the richly lyrical climax. The finale is comparatively easy-going, although towards the end the momentum begins to pick up, only to relax again before Enescu gathers the threads together for his strongly enunciated coda. I have to say that not all listeners will be convinced by this finale, but overall these are fascinating performances. Neither of these Kingsway Hall recordings were among Decca's *ffrr* demonstration 78s, but they have come up uncommonly well in these characteristically full and well-balanced Dutton transfers.

Symphonies Nos. 2 in C, Op. 61; 3 in E flat (Rhenish), Op. 97.
(B) **(*) DG Dig. 469 030-2. BPO, Levine.

Levine's 1988 DG recording is rich and full and allows the greatness of the Berlin orchestra to shine through. The readings are in general positive and full of energy, though at times a little too forced to allow the charm, as well as the greatness, of these works to emerge. But at bargain price, this is an inexpensive way to sample Levine's way with this composer.

Symphony No. 2 in C, Op. 61; 4 Pieces from Carnaval, Op. 9 (arr. Ravel); 6 Pieces from Kinderjahr, Op. 68 (arr. Adorno).
**(*) BIS Dig. CD 1055 [id.]. RPO, Dirk Joeres.

The Dutch pianist Dirk Joeres has turned to the baton in recent years and he offers an idiomatic and sensitive account of the *Second Symphony*. He has the advantage of excellent playing from the Royal Philharmonic and even if memories of Karajan are not banished in the *Adagio* – surely Schumann's most inspired slow movement – this is a performance of some quality. The extra items are undeniably enterprising: there are four fragments that survive from Ravel's orchestration of *Carnaval*, never before recorded, which only came to light in the 1970s; with *Kinderjahr*, there is a transcription by the philosopher and once-composer Theodor Wiesengrund Adorno (better known for his impenetrable and convoluted prose) of six of the Op. 68 *Album for the young*.

Symphonies Nos. 3 in E flat (Rhenish), Op. 97; 4 in D min., Op. 120.
(M) *** Virgin/Veritas EMI VM5 61734-2 [id.].
    L. Classical Players, Norrington.

With Schumann's orchestration usually accused of being too thick, there is much to be said for period performances like this. Norrington not only clarifies textures, with natural horns in particular standing out dramatically, but, at unexaggerated speeds for the outer movements – even a little too slow for the first movement of No. 3 – the results are often almost Mendelssohnian. Middle movements in both symphonies are unusually brisk, turning slow movements into lyrical interludes. Warm, atmospheric recording.

Symphony No. 3 in E flat (Rhenish), Op. 97; Overture, scherzo and finale; Overture: Genoveva.
*(*) DG Dig. 459 680-2 [id.]. Philh. O, Christian Thielemann.

Christian Thielemann disappointed us in his earlier recording for DG of the *Second Symphony* (453 480-2 – see our main volume). Once again here he draws glowing sounds from the Philharmonia in the *Rhenish Symphony*, helped by a weighty recording marked by opulent horn tone. Yet for all its power, the reading is too often self-conscious in moulding of phrases and changes of speed, while the *Cologne Cathedral* movement is taken surprisingly fast, making it a casual perambulation rather than a meditation.

Symphony No. 3 in E flat (Rhenish), Op. 97; (i) *Des Sängers Fluch, Op. 139.*
*** Chandos Dig. CHAN 9760 [id.]. Danish Nat. RSO, Michael Schonwandt; (i) with Fischer, Rorholm, Wagenführer, Henschel, Hansen, Danish Nat. R. Ch.

Schonwandt and the fine Danish orchestra give a fresh, spontaneous-sounding, well-paced reading of Schumann's warmest symphony. Schonwandt lifts rhythms infectiously in a performance full of light and shade, giving rapt intensity to the inner meditation of the *Cologne Cathedral* movement. The playing of the fine Copenhagen Orchestra is unfailingly cultured. A strongly competitive and compelling account, beautifully recorded by the Danish Radio engineers. The rare and generous coupling is most welcome, the 40-minute long choral ballad *The Minstrel's curse*. A late work, it comes from 1852 and is a setting of Ludwig Uhland's ballad,

which Schumann's collaborator Richard Pohl interspersed with other Uhland poems. No less a Schumann authority than Joan Chissell rates it well above the companion choral pieces of the period, and it has some delightful moments. It may lack the lyrical freshness of the symphony, but in this dedicated performance it impressively reveals Schumann's dramatic side, with foretastes even of Wagner. Not all the soloists are ideally steady, but the chorus is outstanding. First-rate sound.

Symphony No. 4 in D min., Op. 120.
*** Orfeo C 522 991 B [id.]. VPO, Karl Boehm –
    MAHLER: *Lieder eines fahrenden Gesellen;*
    BEETHOVEN: *Symphony No. 4.* ***
(M) *** EMI CDM5 67336-2 [id.]. Philh. O,
    Klemperer – TCHAIKOVSKY: *Symphony No. 6 (Pathétique).* **(*)

Boehm's thrilling account of Schumann's *Fourth*, incandescent from first to last, crowns what was a very special Salzburg Festival concert in August 1969. In his studio recordings Boehm was rarely so fiery as here, with biting attack and strong rhythmic emphasis from the Vienna Philharmonic in superb form. The second movement *Romanze* is set in sharp contrast: the deeply meditative opening theme gives way to lightness and transparency. The mystery of the slow introduction to the finale maintains the high voltage too, and though the close is something of a scramble with its successive accelerandos, the result could not be more exciting. Good radio sound, if with some edge on high violins.

Klemperer's is a masterly performance. His slow introduction has a weight and consequence that command attention, and the slow tempo for the allegro is equally weighty and compelling, even if initially one disagrees with it. The Scherzo with its striking main theme packs enormous punch and the brief slow movement is exquisitely played. For the finale Klemperer's speed is faster than many, and he makes the conclusion most exciting. Plainly the Philharmonia players were on their toes throughout the recording session: the intensity of Klemperer's conviction comes over in shaping of phrases that is often quite breathtaking. The 1961 Kingsway recording is full, rounded and fresh in EMI's best manner and the new coupling for the Klemperer Legacy is most generous.

CHAMBER MUSIC

Märchenerzählungen, Op. 132; Kinderszenen: Träumerei.
*** RCA Dig. 09026 63504-2 [id.]. Michael Collins, Steven Isserlis, Stephen Hough –
    BRAHMS; FRÜHLING: *Clarinet trios* ***.

It makes a delightful coupling on an outstandingly successful disc having Schumann's *Fairy-tale suite* – an association not explained in the booklet, which leaves you simply with the daunting German title –

with Steven Isserlis on the cello taking the original viola part. *Träumerei*, offered as an encore to the three main works on the disc, comes in an arrangement for the same forces by Stephen Hough.

Piano quartet in E flat, Op. 47; Piano quintet in E flat, Op. 44.
(M) **(*) Berlin Classics 0094032BC [id.]. Peter Rösel, Gewandhaus Qt.

These Leipzig performances were recorded in 1983 and are thus digitally remastered from an analogue source. They both sound very good, though a little more amplitude round the aural image would perhaps be welcome. The playing of Peter Rösel and the Gewandhaus Quartet is keenly alive and very musical. Tempi are fairly brisk but phrasing is affectionate and sensitive. Not necessarily a first choice, but a very good one. This is playing of quality and good value at mid-price. However, the Beaux Arts offer both works plus the three *Piano trios* on a Philips Duo and they remain the best value of all (456 323-2).

Piano trios Nos. 1 in D min., Op. 63; 2 in F, Op. 80.
(BB) *** Naxos 8.553836 [id.].Vienna Brahms Trio.

The Vienna Brahms Trio give eminently musical accounts of both scores and are satisfactorily recorded. The Beaux Arts Trio on Philips still remain the best bet and are every bit as competitive. There is a choice between the Duo mentioned above and their modern digital set at full price (Philips 432 165-2) which is even finer.

Violin sonata No. 1 in A min., Op. 105.
(***) Biddulph mono LAB 165 [id.]. Busch and Serkin – BRAHMS: *String quartets Nos. 1–2* (**(*)) (with REGER: *Violin sonata No. 5, Op. 84: Allegretto* (***)).

The Biddulph sleeve-note hails the 1937 Busch–Serkin account of the *A minor Sonata*, Op. 105, erroneously billed as No. 2 on both the label and sleeve, as 'never having been equalled for its intensity and romantic ardour'. This is absolutely right. If there has been a finer performance on or off record, we have never heard it. The disc throws in the only Reger that Busch recorded, the *Allegretto* from the *F sharp minor Sonata*, Op. 84. Amazingly (if you know the piece), the seventeen-year-old Busch played the mammoth *Violin concerto* to the composer from memory, and never lost his affection for Reger's music.

PIANO MUSIC

Allegro, Op. 8; Gesänge der Frühe, Op. 133; Novelletten, Op. 21; 3 Fantasiestücke, Op. 111.
**(*) Olympia Dig. OCD 436 [id.]. Ronald Brautigam.

As the opening *Allegro* shows, this is strong, spontaneously impulsive playing, though in the *Novelletten* some might wish for less passion and more poise. However, there is poetry too: the second and, especially, the third of the *Fantasiestücke* are very appealing. The *Gesänge der Frühe* ('Morning songs') brings the most responsive playing of all and is most touchingly done. Clear, bold piano recording.

Fantasia in C, Op. 17.
*** Chandos Dig. CHAN 9793 [id.]. Louis Lortie
– LISZT: *Concert paraphrases of Beethoven's An die ferne Geliebte; Mignon; Schumann Lieder.* ***

Lortie is an unfailingly thoughtful and thought-provoking artist of compelling utterance, who always has something new to say – and whose expressive eloquence is always at the service of the composer. This newcomer ranks alongside the finest and most satisfying versions of the *C major Fantasia* now around.

Fantasia in C, Op. 17; Kinderszenen, Op. 15.
✿ (M) *** Decca mono 466 498-2 [id.]. Clifford Curzon – SCHUBERT: *Wanderer fantasia* *** ✿.

Clifford Curzon made his mono recordings of these contrasting Schumann masterpieces in March 1954, and in many ways they have never since been surpassed. The *Fantasia* is a work indelibly associated with the composer's love for Clara and the spell that she cast over him. Curzon's extraordinarily chimerical and romantic reading of the first movement is matched by the depth of poetic feeling and passion he finds in the finale. Surely in this instance, to use his own metaphor, he perfectly succeeded in 'catching the butterfly on the wing' in a performance which is so 'live' and spontaneous in feeling, that it is difficult to believe it was made in the studio. The gentle *Kinderszenen* (also inspired by Clara) are equally magical, full of wistful imagery illuminated with flashes of bravura, but ending in peaceful serenity. The recording is dry but faithful.

Impromptus on a theme of Clara Wieck, Op. 5; Variations on a theme of Beethoven; Variations on an original theme (Geistervariationen); Variations on a theme of Schubert.
** Athene Minerva Dig. ATHCD 23 [id.]. Andreas Boyde – BRAHMS: *Variations on a theme of Schumann* **.

An intelligently planned recital, which brings repertoire little-known even to those who know their Schumann. The ten *Impromptus on a theme of Clara Wieck* of 1833 are well represented in the catalogue but the remainder are relatively neglected. The Beethoven variations of 1830 are based on the slow movement of the *Seventh Symphony*. The *Geistervariationen* was Schumann's very last work, and so-called because he believed it to have been dictated by the angels (he told the leader of the Düsseldorf Orchestra that the spirit of Schubert had appeared to him and delivered a ravishing melody). Andreas Boyde has reconstructed the *Variations on a theme of Schubert* which Schumann began in 1829 and to which he returned five years later. Accomplished but not highly sensitive playing, though this impression may in part be due to the close and two-dimensional recording.

Kinderszenen, Op. 15; Papillons, Op. 2.
(B) ** EMI Début Dig. CDZ5 73500-2 [id.]. Alex Slobodyanik – CHOPIN: *Piano sonata No. 3; Polonaise No. 6* **(*).

EMI's admirable Début series serves as a visiting card for young artists on the brink of their careers. Alex Slobodyanik, now twenty-five, studied in Moscow and subsequently in Cleveland where he won various awards. He has gone on to appear with major orchestras all over the world. His accounts of both *Papillons* and *Kinderszenen* are undoubtedly sensitive and distinguished by great beauty of touch. There are many imaginative touches but the performance is somewhat marred by moments of affectation, from which the Chopin is relatively free. The recorded sound is absolutely natural and first class.

VOCAL MUSIC

Hyperion Schumann Edition

Lieder, Vol. 4: 5 Lieder und Gesange, Op. 51; 6 Romanzen und Balladen, Op. 45 including *O weh des Scheidens, das er tat* by Clara SCHUMANN; *20 Poems from Liebesfrühling, Op. 37* (including 4 settings by Clara SCHUMANN).
**(*) Hyperion Dig. CDJ 33104. Stella Doufexis, Oliver Widmer, Graham Johnson.

In his fourth selection for the Hyperion Schumann Edition, Graham Johnson offers as centrepiece a sequence of twenty settings of poems from Rückert's *Liebesfrühling*, including four by Schumann's wife, Clara. Other Rückert settings are included too, as well as settings of Heine, Eichendorff and Goethe, all presented with the compelling scholarship with was associated with his monumental Schubert series. This time, instead of well-known singers, he has chosen to work with two sensitive artists relatively little known.

The German mezzo, Stella Doufexis, has a bright, girlish voice, which suits the songs for a woman's voice well, including those of Clara Schumann. The voice of the Swiss baritone, Oliver Widmer, is more problematic when, for all his feeling for word-meaning and musical sharping, the voice with a hint of flutter grows unpleasantly uneven under pressure, most notably in the first song of all, *Sehnsucht*, making an unpromising start. Otherwise, clear, well-balanced sound.

(i) Dichterliebe, Op. 48; (ii) Frauenliebe und Leben, Op. 42.
(B) ** DG Analogue/Dig. 439 417-2 [id.]. (i) Dietrich Fischer-Dieskau, Christoph Eschenbach; (ii) Brigitte Fassbaender, Irwin Gage.

Fischer-Dieskau's earlier DG *Dichterliebe* (recorded between 1973 and 1977) is not quite as emotionally plangent as his later, digital version on Philips, but the contrasts between expressive warmth and a darker irony are still apparent. Eschenbach is always imaginative and the recording has fine presence. Fassbaender's account of *Frauenliebe und Leben* is certainly strongly characterized, with a wide range of expression and fine detail, but she conveys little sense of vulnerability. If the underlying sentimentality of the poems is here concealed, so is much else. Irwin Gage is an excellent accompanist and the digital recording is very vivid.

Liederkreis, Op. 39.
(B) *** EMI Double fforte CZS5 73836-2 (2). Dame Janet Baker, Daniel Barenboim – LISZT; MENDELSSOHN: *Lieder.* ***

With Barenboim an endlessly imaginative if sometimes reticent accompanist, this song cycle is a classic example of Dame Janet Baker's art, the centrepiece in a superb recital which contrasts the high romantic and sometimes tragic world of Schumann with fine collections of hardly less fine settings of Liszt and Mendelssohn.

Liederkreis, Op.39; 4 Husarenlieder. Other Lieder: *Aus der hebräischen Gesängen; Auftrage; Die beiden Grenadiere; Dein Angesicht; Du bist wie eine Blume; Die fiendlichen Brüder; Geständnis; Der Kontrabandiste; Meine Wagen roller langsam; Melancholie; Der Nussbaum; Myrthen (Widmung); Der Schätzgräber; Talismane;* (i) *Tragödie. Venetianisches Lied I–II.*
**(*) DG 447 042-2 [id.]. Bryn Terfel, Malcolm Martineau; (i) with Lorna Anderson, Timothy Robinson.

For E.G. this is among the most characterful discs that even Bryn Terfel has yet recorded, with the great Welsh bass tackling no fewer than thirty-four songs with an electrifying spontaneity and a fearless range of expression. Some may feel that his emphasis on the dramatic element is too great, straying from Lieder to opera, and R.L. suggests that, while this is a glorious voice, not everyone will feel comfortable with Terfel's tendency to over-characterize and overproject in a way that can detract from, rather than enhance, the emotional impact of the songs.

But we are agreed that it is thrilling to hear singing of such spontaneous intensity, as though the singer himself, superbly aided by his pianist, was in the instant creating each song afresh. The range of expression in Terfel's account of the

Eichendorff *Liederkreis* is very wide indeed, so that he seems to relate the encounter with the Lorelei in *Waldesgesprach* directly to the very similar story in Schubert's *Erlking*.

Bitingly dramatic as most of the songs are, with the military songs standing out, including the best-known, *Die beiden Grenadiere*, Terfel's honeyed tone is gloriously caught in *Mondnacht*, hushed and tender, and in the best-known song of all, *Der Nussbaum*. In spite of any reservations this is an outstanding collection in every way. The two other singers appear only in a brief duet, which comes as the third item in *Tragödie*.

Schütz, Heinrich (1585–1672)

Christmas day Vespers 1664 (including: *Christmas story; Magnificat with Christmas interpolations; O bone Jesu, fili Mariae* (sacred concerto); *Warum toben die Heiden*).
*** DG Dig. 463 046-2 [id.]. (i) Charles Daniels, Boys Ch. & Congregational Ch. of Roskilde Cathedral, Gabrieli Consort and Players, Paul McCreesh.

As in his earlier hypothetical re-creation of Vespers, at St Mark's, Venice, Paul McCreesh here celebrates *Christmas Vespers* as it might have been heard at the Dresden Court in 1664. The result is an immensely varied vocal and instrumental tapestry, ranging from congregational hymns, to Schütz's glorious *Magnificat* setting including such familiar Christmas interpolations as the chorales *Lobt Gott, ihr Christen all zugleich* and *In dulci jubilo,* and ending with a burst of magnificence in the organ postlude, *Benedicamus Domino* by Samuel Scheidt. The centrepiece is a very fine performance of Schütz's *Christmas story* with Charles Daniels a lyrical rather than a dramatic Evangelist. Other soloists are drawn from the Gabrieli Consort and the instrumental group includes wind instruments, cornetts and sackbutts, strings and a widely varied palette of continuo. The cathedral ambience adds to the sense of occasion and the variety of the music here is matched by the colourful and dedicated response of the performers. A remarkable achievement.

(i) *Christmas story (Weihnachtshistorie);* (ii) *Easter oratorio (Historia der Auferstehung Jesu Christi); Cantiones sacrae: Quid commisisti* (cycle of five 4-part motets); (iii) *Deutsches Magnificat;* Motets for double choir: *Ach, Herr, straf mich nicht* (Psalm 6); *Cantate Domino* (Psalm 96); *Herr unser Herrscher* (Psalm 8); *Ich freu mich des* (Psalm 122)*; Unser Herr Jesus Christus.*
(B) **(*) Decca Double 452 188-2 (2) [id.].
Heinrich Schütz Ch.; with (i) Partridge, Palmer, Soloists, Instrumental Ens., Philip

Jones Brass Ens.; (ii) Pears, Tear, Langridge, Elizabethan Consort of Viols, London Cornett & Sackbutt Ens.; (iii) Symphoniae Sacrae Chamber Ens.; Norrington.

The *Christmas story* offers some extremely fine singing from Ian Partridge as the Evangelist, while Peter Pears shows impressive authority and insight as well as singing beautifully in the same role for its companion work. The Heinrich Schütz Choir phrases with great feeling and subtlety; indeed, some may feel that their singing is a little too self-consciously beautiful for music that is so pure in style. The *Deutsches Magnificat* is given with admirable authority and is one of the best things in this very generous collection. Indeed, this set offers much to admire, and the vintage recordings, made between 1969 and 1975, have fine sonority, with the ambitious double motets given a proper sense of spectacle.

Schwanter, Joseph (born 1943)

From afar . . . (fantasy for guitar and orchestra).
(BB) ** Virgin Classics 2 x 1 Dig. VBD5 61627-2 (2) [CDVB 61627]. Sharon Isbin, Saint Paul CO, Hugh Wolf – RODRIGO: *Concierto de Aranjuez; Fantasia para un gentilhombre ***;* Recital: *'Latin romances' ***.*

Sharon Isbin commissioned Schwanter's *From afar* . . . and the insert note describes it as 'an intense fantasy which unfolds in a combination of brilliant passages and lyrical episodes'. So it does, but well played as they are, they are neither remarkably cohesive nor memorable, and the best part of the work by far is the cadenza, which the soloist sustains with brilliant playing and personal magnetism.

Scriabin, Alexander (1872–1915)

Piano concerto in F sharp minor, Op. 20; Fantasy (arr. Rozhdestvensky)*; (i) Prometheus.*
**(*) Chandos Dig. CHAN 9728 [id.]. Victoria Postnikova; Residentie O, Rozhdestvensky, (i) Hague Ch.

(i) *Piano concerto in F sharp minor, Op. 20. Le Poème de l'extase, Op. 54;* (i–ii) *Prometheus.*
** DG Dig. 459 647-2 [id.]. (i) Anatole Ugorski; (ii) Chicago S Chorus; Chicago SO, Pierre Boulez.

This is Boulez's second recording of *Le Poème de l'extase*. It is short on ecstasy and not too strong on poetry either. Though beautifully proportioned and revealing of every strand in the complex texture, ultimately it is analytical and detached. Boulez does restrain Anatole Ugorski's propensity to pull things out of shape, and both the *Piano concerto* and *Prometheus* receive straightforward and at times elegant performances with excellent recorded sound. All the same this is not a first choice for any of these pieces: the concerto is far better served by Konstantin Scherbakov (see below).

Victoria Postnikova and her husband, Gennadi Rozhdestvensky, replace *Le Poème de l'extase* with a transcription of the early *Fantasy*, otherwise offering the same coupling as Boulez and the Chicago Orchestra. The Chandos sound is exemplary and the performance of the *Piano concerto* both sensitive and poetic. A good account of *Prometheus* even if it does not displace Ashkenazy (Decca 417 252-2) and other existing recommendations.

(i) *Piano concerto in F sharp minor, Op. 20. Le Poème de l'extase, Op. 54. Symphonies Nos. 2 in C min., Op. 29; 3 (Le divin poème), Op. 43.*
**(*) BMG/Melodiya Twofer Analogue/Dig. 74321 66980 (2) [id.]. (i) Alexander Nasedkin; USSR SO, Yevgeni Svetlanov.

On BMG/Melodiya, the *Second* and *Third Symphonies* are full-blooded and idiomatic performances recorded way back in the 1960s. They have conviction and authority and are unlikely to disappoint, with the Russian sound, whilst not ideally sumptuous, coming up very well for the period. *Le Poème de l'extase* is later (taken from a live concert in 1977) and we much admired it on its first appearance. It receives the passionate direction needed to sustain such a work, although with no want of atmosphere. Only the *Piano concerto in F sharp minor* is digital, coming from 1990, but here the sound is rather vague compared with the earlier recordings. A good, well-shaped account, though Alexander Nasedkin is by no means as sensitive a player as Konstantin Scherbakov on Naxos. That remains a first choice for the concerto as Pletnev is for the *Third Symphony* and *Le Poème de l'extase* (see below). But this twofer is value for money.

(i) *Piano concerto in F sharp minor, Op. 20; (i; ii) Prometheus, Op. 60; (i) Preludes, Op. 11/6, 10, 15, & 17; Fragilité, Op. 51/1; Sonata No. 1, Op. 6: Marche funèbre* (orch. Vasili Rogal-Levitsky).
(BB) *** Naxos Dig. 8.550818 [id.]. (i) Konstantin Scherbakov; (ii) Russian State TV and R. Ch.; Moscow SO, Igor Golovschin.

On Naxos Konstantin Scherbakov gives a most poetic account of the Chopinesque *F sharp minor Concerto*, which is as good as any in any price range. The improvisatory musings of the slow movement come over beautifully, and *Prometheus* is no less characterful. Of course, the Moscow Symphony are not in the same league as, say, the Russian National Orchestra but they play with ardour, and the sound is very natural without being in the demonstration category.

Le Poème de l'extase, Op. 54.
*** BBC Legends BBCL 4018-2 [id.]. New Philh.

O, Stokowski (and conversation with Deryck Cooke) – BERLIOZ: *Symphonie fantastique* **(*).

Stokowski conducted the American première of *Le Poème de l'extase* in 1917 and it is difficult to imagine a performance of greater luminosity and energy from an octogenarian over half a century later. This account comes from a 1968 Festival Hall concert with the New Philharmonia Orchestra. Orgiastic, no holds barred, totally abandoned and wonderfully dedicated playing. Both of Boulez's recordings sound tame and prosaic alongside this, which is still rather special even if the BBC sound is less than ideally transparent in its handling of detail.

Symphonies Nos. 1 in E, Op. 26; 2 in C min., Op. 29; 3 in C min. (Le divin poème), Op. 43; Le Poème de l'extase, Op. 54.
(B) **(*) Ph. Duo 454 271-2 (2) [id.]. Frankfurt RSO, Eliahu Inbal.

For those wanting a modest-priced set of the three Scriabin symphonies plus the *Poème de l'extase*, the Inbal/Frankfurt set, recorded in 1978–9, has the field to itself. This same orchestra went on later to re-record the symphonies under Kitaienko, but that set stretches to three (bargain) discs, to include also *Prometheus* and the early, Chopinesque *F sharp minor Piano concerto* (RCA 74321 20297-2). Moreover, Kitaienko does not shrink from adding to the percussion at will. Not content with that, he goes even further and adds a chorus at the closing section of the *Poème de l'extase*! The Philips Frankfurt recordings are full, smooth and clear and the orchestral playing is refined and committed, albeit less intoxicatingly vivid than in Muti's full-priced EMI set, which is distinctly superior. The *Poème de l'extase* is beautifully played and has plenty of atmosphere and, if it is not as passionately voluptuous as in Muti's hands, it makes a considerable impression and is pleasingly lacking in vulgarity. Overall, this Philips Duo remains a valuable and recommendable alternative investment for those with limited budgets.

(i; ii) *Symphonies Nos. 1 in E, Op. 26; (i) 2 in C min., Op. 29; (iii) 3 (Le divin poème), Op. 43; Le Poème de l'extase, Op. 54.*
(B) **(*) Decca Double Dig. 460 299-2 (2) [id.]. (i) Berlin Deutsche SO; Ashkenazy; (ii) Brigitte Balleys, Sergei Larin, Berlin R. Ch.; (iii) Berlin RSO.

Decca have now put together Ashkenazy's Berlin performances of the three Scriabin symphonies, plus *Le Poème de l'extase*, and by breaking the *Second* halfway they have managed to get all three on a pair of discs, making a pretty formidable bargain Double. If recording were the sole criterion, these performances would be a first choice. The sound is sumptuous, extraordinarily well detailed in the *First Symphony*, with both allure and presence, and only slightly less well defined in the *Second*. But in the *First Symphony* one misses that wild-eyed demonic fire that is so strong an ingredient in Scriabin's makeup. The *Second Symphony* is more impetuously volatile and has a good deal more vigour and sense of internal combustion, especially in the second movement and the *Tempestuo* fourth. There is an atmosphere of simmering passion in the *Andante*, which often wells ardently to the surface, enriched by the voluptuous sound quality. The *Third* brings an even more highly charged feeling from the Berlin forces, which carries through into *Le Poème de l'extase*. Again the Decca engineers rise to the occasion and the recording is very impressive. Overall there is much to relish and certainly there is no suspicion of routine, yet overall the performances do not have the sheer grip of Muti's Philadelphia accounts (EMI CDS7 54251-2 – see our main volume).

Symphony No. 3 (Le divin poème), Op. 43; Le Poème de l'extase, Op. 54.
*** DG 459 681-2 [id.]. Russian Nat. O, Mikhail Pletnev.

It is a long time since we have had so persuasive an account of *Le divin poème*. This is the last of Scriabin's orchestral works to be called a symphony, though *Le Poème de l'extase* and *Prometheus* are sometimes included in the canon. Mikhail Pletnev's account of the *Third Symphony* is gripping and commanding, and its architecture every bit as well held together as in Muti's 1988 Philadelphia account (EMI). Everything is always beautifully shaped and there is an expressive freedom. The playing has ardour but the lushness and delicacy of the orchestral textures are finely conveyed. Pletnev is as profoundly inside these symphonies as he is in the piano music. In *Le Poème de l'extase* he has masterly control of pace and secures sumptuous orchestral sound. The brass are particularly impressive and have real nobility. Excellent sound and now a first recommendation in both scores.

PIANO MUSIC

Etudes (complete): Etude in C sharp min., Op. 2/1; 12 Etudes, Op. 8; 8 Etudes, Op. 42 (1903); Etude in E flat, Op. 49/1; Op. 56/4 (1908); 3 Etudes, Op. 65.
**(*) Hyperion Dig. CDA 66607 [id.]. Piers Lane.

Piers Lane makes light of the various technical problems in which these pieces abound and he plays with an admirable sense of style. Yet he does not give us the whole picture. He has sensibility and produces a good sonority, aided in no small measure by an excellently balanced recording; but one misses the nervous intensity, the imaginative flair and the feverish emotional temperature that the later pieces call for.

Piano sonatas Nos. 2 in G sharp min., Op. 19; 5 in F sharp, Op. 53; 6 in G, Op. 63; 7 in F sharp (White Mass), Op. 64; 9 in F (Black Mass), Op. 68; Fantaisie in B min., Op. 28.
(BB) ** Naxos Dig. 8.553158 [id.]. Bernd Glemser.

This is announced as being the first volume of the complete Scriabin *Sonatas* and for those who want merely to get to know the notes, as it were, this would make an eminently serviceable choice at its modest asking price. Bernd Glemser is a young German pianist of obvious talent who shows a natural sympathy for this repertoire. He commands a keen imagination, a wide range of keyboard colour and he possesses an impressive technical address. No one buying these sonatas will feel short-changed – but of course they will not feel as satisfied as they would by Hamelin, Szidon or Ashkenazy (see our main volume).

Piano sonatas Nos. 4, Op. 30; 5, Op. 53; 9 (Black Mass), Op. 68; 10, Op. 70; Etude in C sharp min., Op. 2/1; 8 Etudes, Op. 42.
**(*) ASV Dig. CDDCA 776 [id.]. Gordon Fergus-Thompson.

Fergus-Thompson is thoroughly inside this idiom. At the same time it must be conceded that his performances are not as manic or high-voltage as those of Richter and Horowitz and in the cruelly competitive world of recorded music would not be a first choice. Nevertheless there is much musical nourishment here to satisfy the collector.

Segerstam, Leif (born 1944)

(i) *Symphonies Nos. 21 (September; Visions at Korpijärvi); (ii) 23 (Afterthoughts, questioning questionings).*
**(*) Ondine ODE 928-2 [id.]. (i) Finnish Radio SO; (ii) Tampere PO (both without conductor).

There are some refined and sensitive touches in the course of these shapeless and sprawling pieces. They seem more like the improvisational sketches a composer makes prior to composition than the finished work of art. There is no feeling of a distinctive musical personality. The heavily scored and seemingly interminable tutti subdue and overpower the listener but the overall impact is underwhelming. Very good performances and excellent recording. If you try these pieces, you may like them more than we do.

Serebrier, José (20th century)

(i) *Partita (Symphony No. 2); Fantasia; Winterreise; (ii) Sonata for solo violin.*
*** Reference Dig. RR 90 CD [id.]. LPO, composer; (ii) Gonzalo Acosta.

Stokowski (understandably) admired the funeral-march slow movement of the *Partita* (or *Symphony No. 2*) and played it separately as the *Poema elegiaca*. But the whole work is attractive and its exuberant finale sparkles with Latin-American dance rhythms. The *Fantasia for strings* convincingly combines energy with lyricism, while *Winterreise* titillates the listener's memory by ingeniously quoting, not from Schubert, but from seasonal inspirations of Haydn, Glazunov and Tchaikovsky's *Winter Daydreams Symphony*, using all three snippets together, plus the *Dies irae* at the climax. The *Solo Violin sonata* is unashamedly romantic and very well played, as are the orchestral works under the composer. Clearly the LPO enjoy themselves and so do we. An enterprising and worthwhile issue to show that not all conductors write eclectic assimilations of the music they best interpret.

Séverac, Déodat de (1872–1921)

Piano, 4 hands: *L'Album pour les enfants petits et grands: Le Soldat de plomb (Histoire vraie en trois récits).* Solo piano: *Baigneuses au soleil (Souvenir de Banyuls-sur-mer); Cerdaña (5 Etudes pittoresques); Le Chant de la terre (poème géorgique); En Languedoc (suite); En vacances (petites pièces romantiques); Les Naïades et le faune indiscret; Pipperment-get (Valse brillante de concert); Premier Recueil (Au château et dans le parc); Deuxième Recueil (inachevé); Sous les lauriers roses ou Soir de Carnaval sur la Côte Catalane; Stances à Madame de Pompadour; Valse romantique.*
(B) **(*) EMI CMS5 72372-2 (3). Aldo Ciccolini.

Déodat de Séverac came from the Pays d'Oc and always retained his roots in the region. He first studied law at Toulouse before deciding on music and becoming a pupil of Magnard and then d'Indy. He was a friend of Ravel, to whom his musical language is much indebted. All the music on these CDs is civilized and has great charm. The recordings were made between 1968 and 1977 and are serviceable rather than distinguished. But the set will give much pleasure.

Shankar, Ravi (born 1920)

Sitar concertos Nos. (i) *1;* (ii) *2 (A garland of ragas). Morning love (based on the Raga Nata Bhairav); Raga Purlya Kalyan;* (iii) *Prahhati (based on the Raga Gunkali); Raga Piloo. Swara-Kākall.*
(B) **(*) EMI Double Fforte Analogue/Dig. CZS5 76255-2 (2) [(M) id. import]. Ravi Shankar; with (i) LSO, Previn; (ii) LPO, Mehta; (iii) Lord Menuhin.

This record is an oddity. It would be easy to dismiss this pair of concertos, particularly as they are in four movements each and seem very long (the first runs for 40 minutes, the second for nearly 52 minutes!) and, except for *aficionados*, will undoubtedly outstay their welcome. Fairly evidently they are neither very good Western music nor good Indian music. The idiom is sweet – arguably too sweet and unproblematic – but at least they represent a 'crossover' in the real sense – a painless tour over the geographical layout of the raga. It also prompts brilliant and atmospheric music-making both from Previn and the LSO and from Mehta (himself Indian-born) and the LPO. Not to mention the composer himself, who launches into solos which he makes sound spontaneous in the authentic manner, however prepared they may actually be. He opens the first CD with a very Westernized raga, which he calls *Morning love*; and in the ragas *Piloo* and *Prabhati*, when he is joined by Menuhin (who is on very good form), the latter's contribution draws an obvious parallel with Eastern European folk music.

Shapero, Harold (born 1920)

Symphony for classical orchestra.
(M) (***) Sony mono SMK 60725 [id.]. Columbia SO, Bernstein – DALLAPICCOLA: *Tartiniana for violin and orchestra;* LOPATNIKOFF: *Concertino.* (***)

Harold Shapero is of distinguished lineage or, should we say, pupillage – studying with Nicolas Slonimsky, Walter Piston, Hindemith, Stravinsky and Nadia Boulanger. Stravinsky and Copland are the major influences on his exhilarating and masterly *Symphony for classical orchestra.* Copland spoke of his 'wonderfully spontaneous musical gift' and the listener is held throughout by his powerful sense of momentum. Although he is perhaps almost too much in thrall to Stravinsky, this is a gripping and inspiriting score, which benefits greatly from Bernstein's advocacy. The performance is greatly superior to its only rival so far by Previn and the Los Angeles Orchestra, which is less well held together. The 1953 mono recording comes up well in this well-transferred and intelligently planned compilation.

Shchedrin, Rodion (born 1932)

Carmen (ballet, arr. from Bizet; complete).
(M) *** RCA High Performance 09026 63308-2 [id.]. Boston Pops O, Arthur Fiedler –
GLAZUNOV: *Carnival overture;*
SHOSTAKOVICH: *Hamlet: incidental music.*
***

Rodion Shchedrin's free adaptation of Bizet's

Carmen music uses Bizet's tunes, complete with harmony, and reworks them into a new tapestry using only strings and percussion, including tubular bells and vibraphone. The whole thing is brilliantly done. Arthur Fiedler offers the complete score and the result is dazzling, with superb playing from the Boston strings, especially in the tender and passionate *Adagio* (Don José's *Flower song*) and the equally vibrant sequence called *The Fortune teller* which quotes from Carmen's passionate music in the Card scene. The finale whimsically opens in the manner of Saint-Saëns with a sparkling xylophone solo, then after various reprises, the ballet ends gently. With extremely vivid remastering of the excellent 1969 recording this is one of Fiedler's finest records, for the couplings are equally successful.

Concerto cantabile.
*** EMI Dig. CDC5 56966-2 [id.]. Maxim Vengerov, LSO, Rostropovich – STRAVINSKY: *Violin concerto*; TCHAIKOVSKY: *Sérénade mélancolique.* ***

Those who only known Rodion Shchedrin by his *Carmen* ballet score will be brought up short by this concerto. The composer has said that he understands the term *cantabile* to express 'firstly a certain tension in the "soul" of the notes, and also the manner in which they are produced. The term also refers to the juxtaposition, interweaving, conflict and resolution of the soloist's singing lines against the orchestra'. The serene opening is deceptive, for the composer's arch-like structure forms a complex and at times dissonant work, even if 'in the finale the sound of the solo violin should come to resemble that of a shepherd's pipe'. With the vibrant support of Rostropovich, Maxim Vengerov's performance combines a powerful lyricism with the composer's required 'tonal variety'. The dancing centrepiece brings splendid bite of bow on strings, combined with a genuine sense of fantasy, and the finale produces a burst of radiance in the orchestral strings which the soloist follows with a ruminative soliloquy. An unexpected and imaginative choice for Vengerov's first CD under his new exclusive contract with EMI. The Abbey Road recording is first class.

Shostakovich, Dmitri (1906–75)

The Age of gold (suite), Op. 22.
(M) **(*) EMI (SIS) CDM5 65922-2 [id.]. Philh. O, Irving (with BARTOK: *Miraculous Mandarin:* suite; KABALEVSKY: *The Comedians* (suite); KHACHATURIAN: *Gayaneh; Masquerade:* suites. **(*))

The Age of gold is early Shostakovich, 1929 vintage, and the idiom is very much a cynical Russian pastiche of smart 1920s music from the West. Irving

and the Philharmonia give a strongly characterful account of the suite and the 1960 Kingsway Hall recording is remarkably full and clear.

The Age of gold (suite), Op. 22; Ballet suites Nos. 1–3; Pirogov, Op. 76a (suite from the film); *Zoya, Op. 64* (suite from the film).
(B) *** BMG/Melodiya Twofer 74321 66981-2 (2) [id.]. Bolshoi Theatre Ch. and O, Maxim Shostakovich.

This is an enjoyable collection: the *Ballet suites* show Shostakovich at his most entertaining and tuneful – tempered with irony – and full of imaginative orchestral colours. The music from *The Bolt* is more bitingly ironic and some of the best music from the complete ballet is recorded here. The audaciously witty *Age of gold* suite is well known, but the music from the films *Zoya* and *Pirogov* is rare: these suites are a degree more serious but are no less enjoyable – they contain several attractive tunes wrapped in consistently imaginative orchestration, and though not great music are well worth having. The performances (under the direction of the composer's son) of the Bolshoi Orchestra and chorus could hardly sound more authentic, and the 1966 recording is good for the period. With the rare fill-ups, this set is well worth exploring at bargain price. However, Järvi's mid-priced recording of all five *Ballet suites* (plus other music) on Chandos offers spectacularly wide-ranging modern recording and remains in a class of its own (CHAN 7000/1).

Ballet suites Nos. 1 & 3; Jazz suites Nos. 1 & 2.
*(*) RCA Dig. 09026 68304-2 [id.]. Frankfurt RSO, Kitaenko.

This music shows Shostakovich at his wittiest best – full of good tunes and colourful orchestration, but although these performances are quite well played and recorded, they are lacking in character and enthusiasm. Järvi's account of the *Ballet suites* (Chandos) and Chailly's of the *Jazz suites* (Decca) have far more personality and energy than these, and bring out the flavour more fully. They are better recorded too.

(i) *Cello concerto No. 2, Op. 126. Symphony No. 12 (The Year 1917), Op. 112.*
** Chandos Dig. CHAN 9585 [id.]. (i) Frans Helmerson; Russian State SO, Valery Polyansky.

This fine Swedish cellist plays with eloquence and authority in the *Second Cello concerto* but the orchestral response is a little disappointing. Moreover, the *Twelfth Symphony* calls for the advocacy of an outsize personality if it is to make a really positive impression.

Piano concerto No. 1 in C min., Op. 35.
*** EMI Dig. CDC5 56760-2 [id.]. Leif Ove Andsnes, Hardenberger, CBSO, Järvi –

BRITTEN: *Piano concerto*; ENESCU: *Légende for trumpet and piano.* ***

This is the finest account of the *Concerto for piano, trumpet and strings* to have appeared for many years. Recorded at a live concert, it has well-judged tempi and offers sensitive, incisive pianism from Andsnes and great sensitivity and elegance from Håkan Hardenberger. Very good sound. This is now a first choice in this repertoire.

(i) *Piano concerto No. 1 for piano, trumpet and strings, Op. 35;* (ii) *Symphony No. 5 in D min., Op. 47.*
(B) **(*) Australian Decca Eloquence 466 664-2.
    (i) John Ogdon, Wilbraham, ASMF, Marriner;
    (ii) SRO, Istvan Kertész.

John Ogdon's clean, stylish performance of the *First Piano Concerto* – which encompasses both the humour and romanticism of the score – was one of his best records. He keeps a little more detached than Marriner in the tender slow movement, but the trumpet playing of John Wilbraham is masterly in the finale. Though the balance gives the performance a chamber quality, the sound is full and vivid.
    Making its CD debut, Kertész's early Swiss version of the *Fifth Symphony* was recorded in the early 1960s, though you would hardly guess it (despite some tape hiss). It is a thoroughly musical reading but somewhat circumspect, not the most dramatic or intense available, but not uncommitted. Kertész is especially good at the close of movements, and both the first and third end in a mood of radiant simplicity, although others find much more tension and colour in the climax of the *Largo*. The finale is taken steadily, but there is a splendid outburst of controlled exuberance for the coda, and the excellent recording – with some impressive timpani – projects the reading effectively. An enterprising coupling.

Hamlet (1932 production): incidental music (*suite*).
(M) *** RCA High Performance 09026 63308-2 [id.]. Boston Pops O, Arthur Fiedler –
    GLAZUNOV: *Carnival overture;* SHCHEDRIN: *Carmen* (ballet). ***

Fiedler chooses a baker's dozen of items from Shostakovich's vivacious, inventive score and the music suits the Boston Pops' vibrant style admirably. If *Ophelia's song* is piquantly light-hearted, the following *Lullaby* is most tenderly and delicately played by the Boston violins, while the *Requiem* quotes the *Dies irae*, first dolefully and then with more passion. But most of the music is irreverently high spirited and is presented here with appropriately infectious gusto. The vivid 1968 recording is brilliantly remastered.

Symphonies Nos. 5 in D min. Op. 47; 9 in E flat, Op. 70.

(M) **(*) Sony SMK 47615-2. NYPO, Bernstein.

This was Bernstein's first recording of the *Fifth*, made in 1959; he re-recorded it later digitally. His view of the work was admired by the composer, perhaps because the finale opens so ferociously. Bernstein revels in the high spirits of the *Ninth*, and he also manages the alternation of moods very successfully. The sound has been greatly improved in both symphonies.

Symphony No. 7 in C (Leningrad), Op. 60.
** RCA Dig. 09026 62548-2 [id.]. St Petersburg PO, Yuri Temirkanov.

Yuri Temirkanov and the St Petersburg orchestra have good playing and recording to commend them but the interpretation is not gripping and intense as one might expect. Temirkanov is not averse to intrusive highlighting – early on he holds back in the first bars for expressive emphasis, and although there are good things here and there, this is far from a first recommendation.

Symphonies Nos. 7 in C (Leningrad), Op. 60; 11 in G min. (1905), Op. 103.
(B) **(*) EMI Double fforte CZS5 73839-2 (2). Bournemouth SO, Berglund.

Berglund directs a strong, powerful performance of the *Seventh*, a symphony of Shostakovich that is too often underestimated. Though Berglund is not always sensitive to finer points of expressiveness, it is still a reading that holds together convincingly, especially when the sound is so full as well as vivid. In the *Eleventh* too, Berglund lets the music speak for itself, keeping the long opening *Adagio* at a very steady, slow tread, made compelling by the high concentration of the Bournemouth playing. Indeed, he is at his finest here, again helped by exceptionally vivid, full-bodied recording.

Symphony No. 8 in C min., Op. 65.
(B) ** DG Dig. 463 262-2 [id.]. LSO, Previn.

Previn's (second) 1992 recording of this symphony for DG was a disappointment. He gets some very fine playing from the orchestra, especially the pianissimo strings, and the DG recording is resonantly spectacular. But the reading lacks the concentration and thrust of his earlier HMV analogue version, the scherzo movements lack bite and the *Largo* has not the intensity of that EMI version which awaits reissue.

Symphony No. 9 in E flat, Op. 70.
**(*) Athene Dig. ATH CD16 [id.]. Freiburg PO, Johannes Fritzsch – TCHAIKOVSKY: *Piano concerto No. 2* **.

A very serviceable account, though not in the front rank.

Symphony No. 14 in G min., Op. 135.
(M) **(*) BBC music BBCB 8013-2 [id.]. Galina

Vishnevskaya, Mark Rezhetin, ECO, Britten –
BRITTEN: *Nocturne* **(*).

This was the symphony which Shostakovich dedicated to Britten, and this Snape Maltings performance of 1970 with the ECO conducted by Britten
was the very first outside Russia. Galina Vishnevskaya's sharply distinctive soprano has rarely
sounded so rich or firmly focused on disc, and the
bass, Mark Rezhetin, firm and dark, sings gloriously
too. The tensions of a live performance add to the
drama of a piece on the theme of death, poignantly
so, when both Britten and Shostakovich were facing
terminal illness. Sadly this mid-priced issue gives
none of the important texts.

Symphony No. 15 in A, Op. 141; (i) *Cello concerto
No. 1 in E flat, Op. 107.*
*(*) Chandos Dig. CHAN 9550 [id.]. (i) Frans
Helmerson; Russian State SO, Valery
Polyansky.

Valery Polyansky and the Russian State Symphony
give a straightforward but ultimately rather undistinguished account of the *Fifteenth Symphony*. The
slow movement in particular is lacking in atmosphere. In the *First Cello concerto*, the distinguished
Swedish soloist plays well but ensemble is not impeccable.

*Symphony No. 15, Op. 141; October, Op. 131;
Overture on Russian and Kirghiz folk themes, Op.
115.*
(B) **(*) DG Dig. 469 029-2 [id.]. Gothenburg
SO, Järvi.

Neeme Järvi has a good feeling for this composer
and his account is competitive: it has personality
and is played characterfully by the Gothenburg
orchestra. *October* is a powerful work, written for
the fiftieth anniversary of the Revolution in 1967,
while the *Overture*, written in 1963 to mark the
centenary of Kirghiz's 'incorporation' into Tsarist
Russia, begins rather severely, but builds up to a
lively, tuneful conclusion. Good sound, and if there
are greater accounts of the symphony, the excellent
couplings and bargain price make this CD a good
bargain choice.

Symphony No. 15 in A, Op. 141; (i) *Piano sonata
No. 2 in B min., Op. 61.*
✿ (M) *** RCA 09026 63587-2 [id.]. Phd. O,
Eugene Ormandy; (i) Emil Gilels.

Ormandy gave the American première of the *Fifteenth Symphony* as well as a number of other Shostakovich works, including the *Fourth, Thirteenth*
and *Fourteenth Symphonies* and the *First Cello
concerto* with Rostropovich. He was not so much
underrated as taken for granted during the early
1970s when this recording was made, but there is
no doubt as to his authority and mastery. The
playing could hardly be surpassed and the recording
originally appeared in RCA's brand of Quadra-

phony, when it sounded pretty spectacular. Even
now it sounds superb and stands up well against
subsequent versions – and its coupling, Gilels's
incomparable account of the wartime *Second
Sonata*, recorded at Carnegie Hall in January 1965,
is one of the classics of the gramophone. An indispensable reissue.

CHAMBER MUSIC

*Cello sonata in D min., Op. 40; Moderato in A
min.*
**(*) Chant du Monde Dig. LDC 2781112 [id.].
Gary Hoffman, Philippe Bianconi –
PROKOFIEV: *Adagio; Ballade; Cello sonata,
Op. 119*, etc. ***

Expert and elegantly fashioned playing from Gary
Hoffman and Philippe Bianconi. There are some
exaggerations (they pull the second group of the
first movement around a little) and some listeners
may find the inward, withdrawn tone of the cellist
in the third movement a bit affected. Still, the
playing has enormous finesse and accomplishment
and gives great pleasure. The *Moderato* is a slight
piece composed in the same year, disinterred only
after the composer's death.

Cello sonata in D min., Op. 40; (i) *Piano trio
No. 2 in E min., Op. 67.*
**(*) Sony Dig. MK 44664 [id.]. Yo-Yo Ma,
Emanuel Ax; (i) with Isaac Stern.

The *Trio* receives a deeply felt performance, one
which can hold its own with any issue, past or
present. The *Sonata* is another matter; the playing
is as beautiful as one would expect, but here Ma's
self-communing propensity for reducing his tone is
becoming a tiresome affectation. Ax plays splendidly and the CBS recording is very truthful.

*Piano quintet in G min., Op. 57; Piano trio
No. 2 in E min., Op. 67; 4 Waltzes for flute,
clarinet and piano.*
(BB) *** Virgin Classics 2 x 1 VBD5 61760-2 (2)
[CDVB 61760]. Nash Ens. – SCHOENBERG:
Chamber symphony, Op. 9, etc. **(*).

The Nash Ensemble on Virgin offer the ideal coupling – plus an interesting makeweight – of two of
Shostakovich's key chamber works, written before
his quartet series developed, when he had completed
only the first, relatively trivial work. The *Piano
trio* is a particularly painful and anguished work,
dedicated to the memory of a close friend, Ivan
Sollertinsky, who died in the year of its composition. The Nash players bring out the dedicated
intensity in this very personal writing, with refined
readings which can be warmly recommended, even
if they are not quite as characterfully individual as
the very finest, and the new pairing with Schoenberg
makes for a highly intriguing collection, well worth
its modest cost.

Piano trios Nos. 1 in C min., Op. 8; 2 in E min.,
Op. 67.
*** Simax Dig. PSC 1147 [id.]. Grieg Trio –
BLOCH: *3 Nocturnes;* MARTIN: *Piano trio on*
Irish folktunes ***.

Three of the works on this disc come from the
period 1924–5: the Bloch *Nocturnes,* the Martin
Trio on Irish folktunes and the first of the Shostakovich *Piano trios.* This last remained in the obscurity
of manuscript, until one of Shostakovich's students,
the composer Boris Tischenko, put it into perform-
able shape (twenty bars had gone missing). The
Grieg Trio play it with vital feeling and sensitivity;
its dreamy opening, a kind of impressionistic Schumann, sounds exceptionally convincing in their
hands. Moreover they give as fine an account of the
wartime *Piano trio in E minor* as any now before
the public. The couplings further enhance the value
of this issue.

String quartets Nos. 1–15; Adagio (Elegy after
Katerina's aria from Scene 3 of Lady Macbeth of
the Mtsensk District); Allegretto (after Polka from
The Age of Gold ballet, Op. 22).
** DG Dig. 463 284-2 (5) [id.]. Emerson Qt.

If sheer brilliance and virtuosity were all that mat-
tered, the Emerson Quartet would lead the field.
They offer us all fifteen quartets in chronological
order on five CDs, plus two attractive encores, thus
scoring over their main rivals who all take six. (Of
course both the Borodins and the Fitzwilliam enjoy
a price advantage). In terms of recorded sound the
Emersons are wonderfully realistic, if a trifle too
closely balanced. Their playing is immaculate
technically, with spot-on intonation, accuracy and
unanimity of ensemble. But they bring an unrelieved intensity to everything they touch and offer
little real repose, when that is called for.
    Gleaming and dazzling then, but they don't get
very far under the surface here. There is infinitely
more of Shostakovich's inner spirit to be found in
the Borodin (RCA 74321 40711-2) or Fitzwilliam
(Decca 433 078-2) sets, not to mention the old
Beethoven Quartet, who premièred nearly all these
works. The CD transfers of the latter (see our main
volume) may not be ideal (the sound is a bit shrill
and strident and has to be tamed), but the performances are. If it is an exaggeration to say that the
Emersons see the cycle as a vehicle for their own
virtuosity, they certainly set great store by superb
execution. These are public rather than private com-
munications and one is not left feeling close to the
anguish of most of this music.

String quartets Nos. 2 in A, Op. 68; 3 in F, Op. 73.
**(*) Hyperion Dig. CDA 67153 [id.].
St Petersburg Qt.

The St Petersburg Quartet have won golden
opinions wherever they have appeared and have
now embarked on a complete cycle of the Shostako-

vich quartets. These performances display appropriate intensity and enthusiasm even if *piano* and
pianissimo markings are at times a little exaggerated. The leader plays with evident feeling in the
Recitative and Romance movement of the wartime
Second Quartet, though intonation is not always
impeccable. Some will find the first movement a
little rushed. A promising start but the playing in
tutti can be rough and the recording lends a certain
hardness and glassiness to the leader's tone. There
are plenty of fine alternatives listed in our main
volume, and those collectors who want these two
quartets together should be well satisfied with the
Borodin Quartet on a Virgin Double which also
includes Nos. 7, 8 and 12 for less than the cost of
this Hyperion CD (VBD5 61630-2).

String quartets Nos. 4 in D, Op. 83; 6 in G, Op.
101; 8 in C min., Op. 110.
** Hyperion CDA 67154. St Petersburg Qt.

The *Fourth Quartet* (1949) is one of the most poignant of the cycle, and the St Petersburg have obviously given it much thought. All the same they
would not be a first choice. The leader's rapid
rubato will not be to all tastes and the performance
throughout is far too self-conscious: the last few
pages are not allowed to speak for themselves.
Pianissimos are underlined and tutti overheated.
These Russian players give a good account of the
Sixth (1956), but the *Eighth* is too full of emotion
and vehemence: the greater reticence of the Borodins is the more telling. The St Petersburg group
are decently recorded, though they reproduce more
comfortably on less critical speakers; there is just a
touch of wiriness above the stave. Allegiance to
existing recommendations remains unchanged –
and, indeed, unchallenged.

Viola sonata, Op. 147.
*(*) Olympia Dig. OCD 625 [id.]. Yuri Bashmet,
Sviatoslav Richter – BRITTEN: *Lachrymae;*
HINDEMITH: *Viola sonata, Op. 11/4.* *(*)

A partnership that excites the highest expectations
in this repertoire proves disappointing. Recorded
live in Germany in 1985, the forward balance and
unpleasant acoustic robs this record of much of its
value. The sound is too close and hard.

PIANO MUSIC

24 Preludes, Op. 34; Prelude and fugue in D min.,
Op. 87/24; Piano sonatas Nos. 1, Op. 12; 2 in B
min., Op. 61.
*** Athene Dig. ATH CD18 [id.]. Raymond
    Clarke.

Readers of our main volume will know that we
found Raymond Clarke's accounts of the three
Szymanowski *Piano sonatas* most impressive (as
indeed we did his Hyperion survey of Robert
Simpson's piano music). The positive impression

they made is confirmed in this exemplary Shostako-vich set, which generously couples the two sonatas with the aphoristic and witty *Preludes*, Op. 34, and these new performances are a viable first-choice for anyone coming to this repertoire afresh.

Sibelius, Jean (1865–1957)

Academic march; Finlandia (arr. composer); *Har du mod?, Op. 31/2; March of the Finnish Jaeger Battalion, Op. 91/1;* (i) *The origin of fire, Op. 32; Sandels, Op. 28; Song of the Athenians, Op. 31/3.*
** BIS CD 314 [id.]. (i) Sauli Tilikainen, Laulun Ystävät Male Ch.; Gothenburg SO, Järvi.

The origin of fire is by far the most important work on this record. Sauli Tilikainen is very impressive indeed, and the playing of the Gothenburg Sym-phony Orchestra under Neeme Järvi has plenty of feeling and atmosphere. None of the other pieces is essential Sibelius. The singing of the Laulun Ystävät is good rather than outstanding, and the Gothenburg orchestra play with enthusiasm. Fine recording in the best BIS traditions.

Violin concerto in D min., Op. 47.
(BB) *** Royal Long Players Dig. DCL 705742 (2). Emma Verhey, Netherlands Radio PO, Hans Vonk – BRAHMS; DVORAK; TCHAIKOVSKY: *Violin concertos.* ***
(M) *(*) RCA High Performance 09026 63591-2 [id.]. Perlman, Boston SO, Leinsdorf – DVORAK: *Romance* **; TCHAIKOVSKY: *Violin concerto.* *(*)

Emma Verhey's unforgettably full-blooded account of the Sibelius concerto comes from Netherlands EMI and has not previously been issued on CD. The force of personality of the solo playing is matched by its ardour and technical security. Al-though the orchestra is well back within a spacious acoustic, and the soloist placed forwardly, tuttis have impact, even if detail is not always ideally clear. With any reservations it is impossible not to respond to a performance of such eloquence.

The fault of Perlman's RCA disc – a fault which runs throughout this CD – is the orchestral sound and Leinsdorf's conducting, both of which are below par. Perlman's artistry is never in doubt, of course, but this is hardly a competitive reissue in view of the strong competition.

(i) *Violin concerto. Karelia suite; Belshazzar's feast (suite), Op. 51.*
**(*) Ondine Dig. ODE 8782 [id.]. (i) Pekka Suusisto; Helsinki PO, Leif Segerstam.

Helped by a close balance and a full, rich and immediate recording, the Finnish violinist Pekka Suusisto, barely twenty, gives a strong and passionate reading, very outward-going, lacking some of the meditative, inner qualities that others

find but compensating in his volatile imagination. His speeds are on the broad side, but the urgency and concentration are never in doubt. With a Finnish conductor and orchestra too, the result is both powerful and idiomatic. The playing is equally positive in the two suites. The exotic colours of *Belshazzar's feast* are vividly caught.

(i) *Violin concerto in D min., Op. 47;* (ii) *Symphony No. 7 in C, Op. 105; Tapiola, Op. 112.*
(***) Ondine mono ODE 809-2 [id.]. (i) David Oistrakh, Finnish RSO, Nils-Eric Fougstedt; (ii) Helsinki PO, Beecham.

David Oistrakh's account of the *Violin concerto* has a marvellous strength and nobility, as well as an effortless virtuosity that carries all before it. His artistry inspires a warm response from the Finnish Radio Orchestra under Nils-Eric Fougstedt, who give magnificent support. There was always a special sense of occasion, too, at any Beecham concert and the opening of the *Seventh Symphony* is more highly charged than his EMI commercial recording with the RPO. *Tapiola* also has great intensity, though the orchestral playing does not have the finesse, magic and tonal subtlety of the RPO recording. Subfusc recording, but a coupling well worth investigating all the same.

Finlandia, Op. 26; Karelia suite, Op. 11; Kuolema: Valse triste, Op. 44/1; Legend: The Swan of Tuonela, Op. 22/2; Scènes historiques: Festivo, Op. 25/3; Tapiola, Op. 112.
(M) (***) DG mono 447 453-2 [id.]. BPO, Rosbaud.

Karajan was not the only champion of Sibelius's music in post-war Germany: Hans Rosbaud, the high priest of the Second Viennese School and the 1950s avant-garde, also included it in his repertory and indeed insisted on conducting the *Fourth Symphony* when he came to the BBC Symphony Orchestra some months before his death in 1962. These recordings come from the mid-1950s and, although some allowance must be made for the mono sound, the performances themselves have the ring of conviction. The *Tapiola* is something special, among the most terrifying evocations of that dark Nordic forest, and worthy to keep com-pany with those of Beecham, Koussevitzky and Karajan. The *Swan of Tuonela* is a little brisk, but it is not wanting in atmosphere. The *Alla marcia* of the *Karelia suite* is a bit sedate, heavy-footed even, but Sibelians will want this disc for Rosbaud's intensely cold *Tapiola*.

Finlandia, Op. 26; Legends: The Swan of Tuonela; Kuolema: Valse triste.
(M) ** Sony SMK 63156 [id.]. NYPO, Bernstein – GRIEG: *Peer Gynt: suites Nos. 1 & 2; Norwegian dance; March of the Trolls.* **

Bernstein's account of *Finlandia* is quite exciting,

but the recording is rather harsh. *The Swan of Tuonela* is beautifully played, with finesse and a sense of brooding atmosphere, and there is some lovely relaxed string playing in *Valse triste*. The sound is acceptable but not exceptional.

Finlandia, Op. 26; Legends: The Swan of Tuonela, Op. 22/2; The Oceanides, Op. 73; Pohjola's daughter, Op. 49; Tapiola, Op. 112.
(M) **(*) Chandos CHAN 6508 [id.]. RSNO, Gibson.

The Oceanides is particularly successful and, if Karajan finds even greater intensity in *Tapiola*, Gibson's account certainly captures the icy desolation of the northern forests. He is at his most persuasive in an elusive piece like *The Dryad*, although *En Saga* is also evocative, showing an impressive overall grasp. The RSNO are on peak form.

4 Legends, Op. 22 (with 1896 versions of Nos. 1 & 4 and alternative 1897 ending of No. 4).
*** BIS CD 1015 [id.]. Lahti SO, Osmo Vänskä.

Everyone knows that Sibelius was hard to satisfy: he revised both *En Saga* and the *Violin concerto*, whilst the *Fifth Symphony* alone went through two major overhauls lasting the best part of seven years. The *Four Legends* (1895–6) were revised twice, first in 1897 and then again in 1900 – and in the case of *Lemminkäinen and the Maidens of the Island* and *Lemminkäinen in Tuonela* there were further revisions before Sibelius agreed to their publication. Osmo Vänskä brings us not only the familiar final version but also the 1896 versions of the first Legend and of *Lemminkäinen's homeward journey*. (Lemminkäinen is on his way and has not yet arrived, so *Lemminkäinen's return* is not the correct title!) He is very nearly twice as long on this first journey and comparison of the two shows Sibelius's growing powers of concentration. We are also given the alternative 1897 ending and a bit of *Lemminkäinen in Tuonela* which Sibelius cut from the finished score. Authoritative performances by Osmo Vänskä and the Lahti Orchestra and a natural, wide-ranging and lifelike recording. The *Swan of Tuonela* is a particularly evocative performance. A fascinating issue.

4 Legends, Op. 22; Karelia suite; Op. 11. Finlandia, Op. 26.
(BB) **(*) Naxos 8.554265 [id.]. Iceland SO, Petri Sakari.

Petri Sakari's account of the *Legends* with the Iceland Orchestra has a lot going for it and is very decently recorded. Why he reverses the order of the middle two is something of a mystery. After Sibelius made the 1939 revisions to the first, he expressly placed the *Swan of Tuonela* second instead of third, as it had been originally. The *Karelia suite* and *Finlandia* are well played and most CD machines can reprogramme the order of the

Legends. On the whole, good value for money but not a first choice; that lies with Segerstam, although he too perversely reverses the playing order (ODE 852-2).

4 Legends, Op. 22; Night ride and sunrise, Op. 55.
**(*) Finlandia/Warner Dig. 3984 27890-2 [id.]. Toronto SO, Jukka-Pekka Saraste.

It is only six years since Saraste recorded the *Four Legends* with the Finnish Radio Symphony Orchestra for RCA, and it is reasonable to wonder whether we need his views on this wonderful score again so soon – or at all! His 1992 recording was very good, but it must be admitted that this Canadian account is better, both in the quality of the orchestral playing and the recorded sound. Like Sakari on Naxos, Saraste reverses the order of the two central *Legends*, and those who wish to follow Sibelius's wishes have to programme their machines accordingly (1, 3, 2, 4). No lack of atmosphere all the same, particularly in *Lemminkäinen in Tuonela*, and no want of passion.

Yet Saraste does not match the urgent momentum and level of excitement in *Lemminkäinen's homeward journey* that Beecham, Segerstam or Vänskä achieve, and in the *Night ride* Saraste sounds pedestrian by the side of Sir Colin Davis or Jochum. This remains recommendable, but not in preference to Vänskä or Segerstam. EMI have deleted their classic account of the *Legends* by Ormandy and the Philadelphia Orchestra. Perhaps it is still available in the USA: if so, it is cordially recommended to American readers, but let us hope it will soon return to the UK.

4 Legends, Op. 22; Night ride and Sunrise, Op. 55; Pohjola's daughter, Op. 49.
**(*) DG Dig. 453 426-2 [id.]. Gothenburg SO, Neeme Järvi.

Järvi's DG recording again has the advantage of the glorious acoustics of the Gothenburg Concert Hall and the expertise of the same recording team. The DG version has slightly greater transparency and smoothness, though the BIS version has marginally more presence. In any event this new account is, technically speaking, among the very best *Legends*. The orchestral playing is first class but this time round Neeme Järvi is inclined to be inattentive to atmosphere – so important in this music. He knocks about six minutes off his earlier tempo and seems too intent on keeping things moving. Yet though his *Lemminkäinen's return* is faster than in 1985, it has lower voltage and less excitement. *Pohjola's daughter* and *Night ride and Sunrise* are far more successful. The recording is three star but the performances are not.

SYMPHONIES

Symphonies Nos. 1–7.
(M) (**) Finlandia mono 3984-22713-2 (3) [id.].
Stockholm PO, Sixten Ehrling.
*(*) Finlandia Dig. 3984-23389-2 (3) [id.]. COE,
Paavo Berglund.

Ask most Sibelians which conductor first recorded all the Sibelius symphonies, and they will answer Anthony Collins with the LSO on Decca. Wrong – but understandably so! The very first survey comes from 1952–3, conducted by Sixten Ehrling and issued together with the Violin concerto with Camilla Wicks and the Lemminkäinen Legends. The Legends were issued over here on the Capitol label, though the symphonies never came out in Britain but appeared on Metronome in Sweden and Mercury in America. Their handsome sleeves are reproduced here. Neither the Stockholm Philharmonic nor the Swedish Radio Orchestra were anywhere near their present quality in the mid 1950s. (Incidentally, the original LPs speak of the 'Stockholm Radio Symphony Orchestra': perhaps these sessions drew on both bands.) Sibelius himself is said to have heard and liked them.

Ehrling is an admirably sound interpreter. In the first two symphonies the playing has more temperament than polish. In the Third, Ehrling – giving the symphony its first recording since the pioneering Kajanus set – is more measured than Collins, who set very brisk tempi in both the first and second movements. The Fourth is impressively dark and in the Fifth the transition between the body of the first movement and its scherzo section is well negotiated. Not a real challenge to Collins, but though it lacks finesse and has some vulnerable wind intonation, it provides an interesting insight into how these symphonies sounded at the time.

Berglund's survey is available not only as a complete set but also broken down into separate formats. Nos. 1–3 are offered together on 3984-23388-2; Nos. 4 and 6 on 0630 14951-2; and Nos. 5 and 7 on 0630 17278-2. They are the product of an enthusiastic collaboration with the Chamber Orchestra of Europe. Berglund knows this music as intimately as any one alive, and has made a detailed study of the autographs of many of them. He is totally devoid of the posturing that disfigures many maestros and offers the scores plain and unadorned. There are good things – namely, a sober and vigorous Third and a finely paced and sensitively moulded Sixth – as well as one or two ugly details such as the ungainly stress he gives to the rhetorical string passage in the first movement of the Second (1 hour 35 minutes, five bars before letter B). One has to decide whether these performances, good though they are, convey enough new insights to justify displacing his earlier cycles with the Bournemouth and Helsinki Orchestras. Those earlier sets, though they have solid merits, fall short of the ideal in

terms of poetic imagination. But the same goes for this new set. In some ways Berglund's very first, 1969 recording of the Fourth Symphony, issued in 1973, remains the freshest and most keenly felt of his Sibelius recordings!

Symphonies Nos. 1–7; Finlandia, Op. 26; Karelia suite, Op. 11; Kuolema: Valse triste. Legends, Op. 22: The Swan of Tuonela; Lemminkäinen's return; Pelléas et Mélisande: suite, Op. 46; Pohjola's daughter, Op. 49; Rakastava, Op. 14; Romance for strings in C, Op. 42; Scènes historiques: All'overtura; The hunt; Scena.
(M) **(*) CMS5 67299-2 (5) [id.]. Hallé O,
Barbirolli.

It is good to have Barbirolli's characteristically vibrant Sibelius oeuvre (recorded between 1966 and 1970) now for the first time gathered together in a box. Barbirolli liked to talk about what he and the Hallé Orchestra had learned in playing the seven symphonies chronologically (which he did more than once in Manchester): 'No. 2, like the first is very rhetorical. No. 3 I call the transition symphony. The technique and spirit are changing. With the last four symphonies we come to a new Sibelius. Stylistically you have to change. You have to revise your method of bowing. You have to produce entirely different sounds. By doing from No.1 through to No. 7 you get in the way of this.'

Barbirolli favoured spacious tempi, but almost always held the listener in his spell. This certainly applies to the present account of the First Symphony which has a freshness and ardour that are very appealing. It is undoubtedly gripping, even if, compared with his enthusiastic account of the Second, it is just a little lacking in panache. All seven symphonies were recorded in the Kingsway Hall. The first two date from 1966, but in No. 1 in the present remastering string fortissimos are made fierce. No. 2 is in every way more successful. The Hallé play particularly well and give a warm-hearted account, romantic in approach, Barbirolli's reading stressing the Slav ancestry and Italianate warmth of the work. The recording is splendidly full blooded.

In No. 3, tempi are well judged, but the inner tension is less well maintained than in No. 2. Even so, there is some very fine wind-playing in the Andante and the transition to the finale is very convincingly managed.

Barbirolli's account of No. 4 has great authenticity of feeling. Here the Hallé strings produce an admirably chilling quality, far removed from the well-nourished string sound in Karajan's Berlin Philharmonic versions. Unfortunately things come adrift in the development of the first movement where the wind and strings are out of step for quite a few bars. However, at this stage in time one is willing to accept such a blemish when the rest of the performance is so deeply idiomatic, and so sonorously recorded.

The *Fifth*, like the *Second*, is one of the finest of the series and has great breadth and nobility. Sir John draws playing of high quality from the orchestra, who are on top form throughout. He takes a characteristically unhurried view of the first movement, but as with the *Fourth* the sparer, less opulent string tone has a more Nordic sound to commend that and his *Fifth*. The *Seventh* is also powerful. The finale is admirably broad and extremely imposing. The *Seventh* makes a fine culmination for the cycle, bringing a feeling of power and a sense of inevitability which increases as the work progresses. The build-up to its climax is well paced. The recording is very fine.

Barbirolli included the *Sixth Symphony* in the last concert he conducted in Manchester on 3 May 1970, and he recorded it three weeks later, only two months before he died. Though ensemble is not perfect, and the orchestral playing is not quite up to the standards of the rest of the cycle, it is easy to sense an elegiac feeling in the performance, which remains most compelling, especially in the beautiful closing passage for the strings, given the benefit of radiant sound.

The shorter orchestral works were recorded at Abbey Road during the same period and the charismatic 1966 collection including *Finlandia*, the *Karelia suite*, *Valse triste*, *Lemminkäinen's return* and *Pohjola's daughter* was for some years one of Barbirolli's most successful discs. The suite from *Pelléas et Mélisande* is powerfully atmospheric, as is *The Swan of Tuonela*, but here Sir John's rather endearing vocalizations are clearly audible. *Pohjola's daughter* is very strongly characterized, as are the *Scènes historiques*. *Rakastava*, and especially the touching *Romance for strings*, are much rarer, originally having a short catalogue life. They are very well played and recorded. Barbirolli had a special feeling for Sibelius's world and this shows through. The 1960s were a good period as far as EMI sound is concerned, and Barbirolli was a great-hearted conductor; at its best his Sibelius has a vibrant feel to it. All in all this is a cherishable box, attractively illustrated with some of the original LP sleeve pictures.

Symphonies Nos. 1–4.
(B) *** EMI Double Fforte Dig. CZS5 68643-2 (2). Helsinki PO, Berglund.

This is a very impressive set and first-class value as an EMI Double Fforte. Berglund's rugged, sober but powerful readings bring a good feeling for the architecture of the music and no want of atmosphere. Both the playing and the interpretation of the *First* are involving in their breadth and concentration (even if in the first movement the climactic timpani echo of the main theme does not come through). In the *Second*, Berglund is scrupulously faithful to the letter of the score as well as to its spirit, although the Scherzo and finale are of a lower

voltage than in the finest versions. The Helsinki Philharmonic respond with no mean virtuosity and panache, but the last degree of intensity eludes them. In the *Third*, Berglund adopts sensible tempi throughout and shapes all three movements well; he evokes a haunting feeling of tranquillity in the withdrawn middle section of the slow movement, a passage where Sibelius seems to be listening to quiet voices from another planet. This was Berglund's third account of the *Fourth* and it is a performance of considerable stature: it has a stark grandeur that resonates in the mind. There is not a great deal of *vivace* in the second movement but Berglund's finale is superb, even if some may find the closing bars not sufficiently cold and bleak. The digital recording throughout the set is excellent.

Symphony No. 1 in E min.; The Oceanides.
(M) **(*) EMI Dig. CDM7 64119-2 [id.]. CBSO, Simon Rattle.

If Simon Rattle's account of the whole symphony were as fine as that of the first movement, this would carry a strong recommendation. Rattle has a powerful grasp of both its structure and character. The slow movement is for the most part superb, but he makes too much of the commas at the end of the movement, which are so exaggerated as to be disruptive. The Scherzo has splendid character but is a good deal slower than the marking. *The Oceanides* has an atmosphere that is altogether ethereal. Simon Rattle has its measure and conveys all its mystery and poetry.

(i) *Symphony No. 2 in D, Op. 43; En Saga, Op. 9; Finlandia, Op. 26;* (ii) *Andante festivo for strings; Kuolema: Valse triste, Op. 44/1; Pelléas et Mélisande: suite, Op. 46; Rakastava, Op. 14; Suite champêtre, Op. 98b; Suite mignonne, Op. 98a.*
(B) *(*) Nimbus Dig. Double NI 7716/7 (2) [id.].
(i) RPO; (ii) (Augmented) E. String O; William Boughton.

These performances are well played and expansively recorded but the collection, although inexpensive, generally does not rise much above the ordinary.

Symphony No. 2 in D; Finlandia, Op. 26; Pohjola's daughter, Op. 49; The Swan of Tuonela, Op. 22/2.
(M) (**(*)) RCA mono GD 60294 [09026 60294]. NBC SO, Toscanini.

Three recordings of the *Second Symphony* survive from Toscanini's baton: one from his BBC season in 1938, a second from 1939 and the present issue from 1940. All offer some superb playing but are a shade hard-driven. The account of *Pohjola's daughter* is arguably the most powerful and exciting ever committed to disc and in its elemental power even surpasses Kajanus and Koussevitzky.

Symphony No. 2 in D, Op. 43; (i) *Luonnotar, Op. 70. Pohjola's daughter, Op. 49.*
(M) ** Sony SMK 61848 [id.]. NYPO, Bernstein; with (i) Phyllis Curtin.

There is no lack of spirit or warmth in Bernstein's version of the *Second Symphony*, which offers some exciting and committed playing from the NYPO. There are some mannered touches in the slow movement and finale, but on the whole this performance has a spontaneity and virtuosity that are impressive. *Luonnotar* is not as successful: it is rather insensitively played and sung and lacks mystery, though *Pohjola's daughter* finds the conductor back on form in this strong, well-proportioned reading. The recordings, dating from the mid-1960s, are acceptable, but there are many more positive recommendations.

Symphonies Nos. 2 in D, Op. 43; 6 in D min., Op. 104.
*(*) Sony Dig. SK 53268 [id.]. Pittsburgh SO, Maazel.

Lorin Maazel comes into direct competition with the Davis/LSO coupling, and comparison is not to his advantage. The *Second Symphony* is overblown and inflated in the manner of his earlier Pittsburgh recordings of Nos. 1 and 7. In the slow movement he adds two minutes to his earlier timing with the Vienna Philharmonic, made for Decca in the 1960s, and nearly as much to the first movement. Not that statistics count for anything – one just longs for a sense of real momentum. The *Sixth Symphony* fares much better. It was the least admired of his earlier cycle. This is very much closer to the spirit of the score and there is relatively little point-making. The tempi are well judged and the wind players of the Pittsburgh orchestra distinguish themselves. All the same, this is by no means a first choice.

Symphonies Nos. 3 in C, Op. 52; 6 in D min., Op. 104.
**(*) Decca Dig. 448 817-2 [id.]. San Francisco SO, Herbert Blomstedt.

Blomstedt is very impressive in this coupling, and so is the Decca recording. They are both performances of integrity and musicianship. All the same, Sir Colin Davis on RCA is ultimately finer and is to be preferred, although his couplings are different (see our main volume). He has deeper and more poetic insights than Blomstedt.

Symphonies Nos. 4 in A min., Op. 63; 5 in E flat, Op. 82.
(BB) *** Naxos Dig. 8.554377 [id.]. Iceland SO, Petri Sakari.

Earlier issues in Petri Sakari's Sibelius cycle have made a strong impression and so does this. Had one heard either of these performances in the concert hall, one would have left feeling very satisfied. Both grip the listener. They are straightforward and

unaffected, dedicated and selfless, and free from interpretative point-making. Tempi are for the most part uncommonly well judged, and you feel that Sakari really sees the works as a whole, rather than as a sequence of wonderful episodes. The first movement of the *Fourth* is perhaps just a little wanting in concentration and tautness but everything else comes off well. The finale is particularly imposing, well built up and with a good feel for its changing moods and powerful currents. The closing paragraph with the descending oboe figure, which Sibelius told his son-in-law, Jussi Jalas, represented Peter's thrice denial of Christ, is moving and atmospheric. The first movement of the *Fifth* has splendid breadth, and the transition into the scherzo section is expertly handled. The Iceland Orchestra may not be in the luxury league but their responses are keen and alert, and the performances have much greater inner life than, say, Paavo Berglund's set on EMI. Moreover the sound is truthfully balanced and well detailed. Of course, the field is so keenly competitive, with outstanding mid-price accounts from Ashkenazy, Sir Colin Davis, Rattle and Karajan, that Sakari is unlikely to be your first choice. All the same, no one investing in this disc is likely to feel short-changed.

Symphonies Nos. 4 in A min., Op. 63; No. 7 in C, Op. 105; Tapiola, Op. 112.
❀ (M) *** Decca 466 995-2 [id.]. VPO, Maazel.

Maazel's accounts of the *Fourth* and *Seventh symphonies* were undoubtedly the finest of his 1960s Decca cycle. He brings great concentration and power to this music: the first movement of the *Fourth* is as cold and unremitting as you could wish, and throughout the work Maazel comes as close to the atmosphere and mystery of this music as almost anyone since Beecham.

The *Seventh* has a rugged epic power which is truly thrilling – it ranks alongside Koussevitzky's famous account, and no praise could be higher. *Tapiola* is a most impressive performance and grows in power and impact as it proceeds. He takes the famous storm section very slowly, and it gains immeasurably from this. The recording throughout this CD is quite superlative, and these accounts are fully worthy of the Decca Legends label.

Symphonies Nos. 4 in A min., Op. 63; 7 in C, Op. 105; Pelléas et Mélisande: suite, Op. 46; Swanwhite, Op. 54; Tapiola, Op. 112; The Tempest (incidental music)*: Dance of the nymphs.*
(M) (***) BBC Legends mono BBCL 4041-2 (2) [id.]. RPO, Sir Thomas Beecham (with British and Finnish National anthems, and speeches by Sir Thomas Beecham including Beecham on Sibelius).

This concert commemorated Sibelius's ninetieth birthday on 8 December 1955, when the BBC made special arrangements with their Finnish colleagues to relay the programme so that the composer himself could hear it in his home. Beecham never re-recorded the *Fourth Symphony* commercially after his 1938 recording but, judging from this perform-ance, his basic approach remained little changed. He also never recorded the *Swanwhite* suite. Here he omits only *The prince alone*. He did make stereo versions of the *Pelléas et Mélisande* music (without the brief *By the seashore* movement) and *Tapiola* a few days on either side of the birthday concert. He also recorded the *Seventh* commercially at the same time but this performance comes from a Royal Albert Hall concert of the previous year and is slightly higher in voltage than his Abbey Road recording. There is a tremendous sense of occasion here, which is supplemented by his famous talk describing his long friendship with Sibelius and recounting his hilarious visit to his home the pre-vious year. An invaluable issue and, considering the date, perfectly acceptable sound.

Symphonies Nos. 5 in E flat, Op. 82; 6 in D min., Op. 104; 7 in C, Op. 105; Finlandia, Op. 26; The Oceanides, Op. 73; Tapiola, Op. 112.
(B) **(*) EMI Double Fforte Dig. CZS5 68646-2 (2). Helsinki PO, Berglund.

This forte double completes Berglund's Sibelius cycle, which is now among the least expensive recommendable sets of the symphonies in the cata-logue. Nos. 1–4 are on a companion reissue (see above). Sober, straightforward, powerful readings which maintain the high standards of performance and recording that have consistently distinguished Berglund's EMI Sibelius records. There is a good feeling for the architecture of this music and no want of atmosphere. In the *Fifth Symphony*, the development section of the first movement has a mystery that eluded Berglund first time around, and there is splendid power in the closing pages of the finale. The *Sixth* is particularly fine, though the Scherzo may strike some listeners as too measured. The *Seventh* is arguably one of the finest now before the public: it has real nobility and breadth, and Berglund has the full measure of all the shifting changes of mood and colour. Moreover the Helsinki orchestra play magnificently and seem to have a total rapport with him. Berglund's account of *The Oceanides* is splendidly atmospheric and can be put alongside Rattle's, which is praise indeed! The recording is well detailed and truthful, and the per-spective natural. *Tapiola* is given its impact by a spacious ruggedness, and the very close of the work has a moving intensity. All the same, despite the very good recorded sound and the economical price and packaging, these cannot be recommended in preference to or even alongside the earlier Colin Davis set with the Boston Symphony, which is similarly priced and packaged on a pair of Philips Duos (446 157-2 and 446 160-2). That is the one to go for.

Symphony No. 5 in E flat, Op. 82; En Saga; Finlandia; Kuolema: Valse triste. Pohjola's daughter, Op. 49.
(M) ** Sony Great Performances SMK 66234 [id.]. Philh. O, Swedish RO, or LAPO, Salonen.

Salonen's is an exceptionally spacious account of the *Fifth Symphony* and although there is much beauty of detail, even grandeur, the tension needs to be held in a tighter grip if such a broad ap-proach is to succeed. In spite of fine playing from the Philharmonia Orchestra, the transition to the Scherzo section is not very deftly managed. On the other hand, the breadth of the reading works really well in the finale, which has genuine nobility. The account of *Pohjola's daughter* certainly does not lack excitement, and the other items (added for this reissue) are well enough done too. But overall, in spite of the fine recording, this cannot be placed among the most commanding versions of the sym-phony on CD, and certainly it is hardly an apt choice for reissue in Sony's Great Performances series.

CHAMBER MUSIC

Music for violin and piano: Andante grazioso in D major (1884–5); 5 Pieces (1886–7); Violin sonata in A minor (1884); Sonata movement (1885); Sonata fragment in B minor (1887); Suite in D minor (1887–8); Various short movements and fragments.
*** BIS Dig. CD 1022 [id.]. Jaakko Kuusisto, Folke Gräsbeck.

This disc collects some of Sibelius's youthful output for violin and piano, and covers the years 1884–8, from his school years through to his time at Hel-sinki. Another disc is promised. Apart from John Rosas's study of the unpublished chamber music (and the first volume of *Tawaststjerna*), most of Sibelius's juvenilia remain unknown. The violin was his chosen instrument and his writing for it is totally idiomatic with a natural fluency. None of the music has been heard before. The *A minor Sonata* of 1884, from his school years, is redolent of the early Beethoven sonatas: it is highly accomplished but totally derivative. There are a number of short movements, some mere fragments, and not all of them are worth committing to disc. The *Suite in D minor* (1887–8) is another matter and shows just how good his writing for the instrument was; Sibelius himself thought well enough of it to show it to his first biographer, Erik Furuhjelm. Very good playing from Jaakko Kuusisto and Folke Gräsbeck, as well as good and scholarly sleeve notes from the latter. Excellent sound.

PIANO MUSIC

Bagatelles, Op. 34; Barcarole, Op. 24/10; Esquisses, Op. 114; Kyllikki, Op. 41; 5 Pieces,

Op. 75; Piano transcriptions: *Finlandia, Op. 26; Valse triste, Op. 44/1.*
(***) Ondine Dig. ODE 847-2 [id.]. Ralf Gothoni.

This is how Sibelius's piano music should be played – with the highest musical intelligence and imagination. Gothoni makes the most of every expressive gesture and every gradation of keyboard colour, without indulging in any exaggeration. These performances make out a stronger case for Sibelius's piano music than almost any other. Unfortunately they are badly let down by the recording, which is reverberant and clangorous; the piano itself hardly sounds in ideal shape. The repertoire differs from Marita Viitasalo's choice (see below) but, where they overlap, comparison is to Gothoni's advantage. A pity about the sound.

6 Impromptus, Op. 5.; Sonata in F, Op. 12; 10 Pieces, Op. 24.
(BB) *** Naxos Dig. 8.553899 [id.]. Håvard Gimse.

Sibelius never thought naturally in terms of the piano but, as Glenn Gould put it in the sleeve notes to his own recording of the *Sonatinas,* he never writes against the grain of the instrument. The *Sonata* and *Impromptus* are early and come from the year in which the first version of *En Saga* was composed. The *Sonata* has a genuine sense of forward movement and some of its ideas are appealing. The Op. 24 *Pieces* were written at various times between 1894 and 1903. The Norwegian pianist Håvard Gimse has consistent tonal beauty and unfailing musicianship. He is imaginative and has that kind of natural eloquence which allows the music to speak for itself yet still makes it sound fresh and unsentimental. This is distinguished playing and a first recommendation at any price level.

Kyllikki, Op. 41; 2 Rondinos, Op. 68; 3 Sonatinas, Op. 67; Sonata in F, Op. 12; Piano transcription: *Finlandia.*
**(*) Finlandia/Warner Dig. 4509-98984-2 [id.]. Marita Viitasalo.

Good performances of *Kyllikki* and the Op. 67 *Sonatinas,* by general consent the finest of Sibelius's piano compositions. Marita Viitasalo is an idiomatic interpreter of this repertoire, and though the rival survey by Servadei is marginally better recorded, there is not much to choose between them, and readers can invest in the Finlandia anthology with reasonable confidence.

CHORAL MUSIC

Academic march (1919); *Andante festivo* (1922); (i) *Cantata for the Conferment ceremony of 1894;* (ii) *Coronation cantata* (1896); *Finlandia, Op. 26/7.*
**(*) Ondine ODE936-2 [id]. (ii) Soile Isokoski,

Jaakko Kortekangas; (i & ii) Finnish Ph. Ch.; Helsinki PO, Leif Segerstam.

These two early cantatas are completely new to the repertoire. Only two sections of the *Academic cantata* or *Cantata for the Conferment ceremony of 1894* survive. It is hardly top-drawer Sibelius though there are occasional flickers of individuality in the orchestral writing. It is not to be compared to *The Wood nymph.* The *Coronation cantata,* written for the accession of Tsar Nicholas II, has not been heard since 1896 and its inspiration is thin and commonplace, hardly worthy of the composer of the contemporaneous *Lemminkäinen Legends.* Good solo singing from Soile Isokoski and Jaakko Kortekangas and decent performances from all concerned. Segerstam's *Finlandia* was recorded in 1994, five years before the rest of the programme. It is a particularly striking account and the whole programme is very well recorded.

Finlandia (version for orchestra and mixed chorus), *Op. 26; Homeland (Oma maa), Op. 92; Impromptu, Op. 19;* (i) *Snöfrid, Op. 29. Song to the earth (Maan virsi), Op. 95; Song to Lemminkäinen, Op. 31; Väinö's song, Op. 110.*
** Ondine Dig. ODE 754-2 [id.]. (i) Stina Rautelin (reciter); Finnish Nat. Op. Ch. & O, Eri Klas.

While most of Sibelius's songs are to Swedish texts, the choral music is predominantly Finnish. *Oma maa* ('Homeland') is a dignified and euphonious work and includes a magical evocation of the wintry nights with aurora borealis and the white nights of midsummer. *Väinö's song* is an appealing piece which bears an opus number between those for *The Tempest* and *Tapiola* – though it is not really fit to keep them company. The performances and the recording are decent rather than distinguished.

Kullervo Symphony, Op. 7.
**(*) Chandos Dig. CHAN 9393 [id.]. Isokoski, Laukka, Danish Nat. RSO, Segerstam.
**(*) Virgin Dig. VC5 45292-2 [id.]. Stene, Mattei, Nat. Male Voice Ch., Royal Stockholm PO, Paavo Järvi.

Segerstam completes his Sibelius cycle with Sibelius's early symphony-cum-symphonic-poem, *Kullervo,* and gives what is for him an uncharacteristically straightforward account of this remarkable work. There are none of the idiosyncrasies that have proved so disruptive elsewhere. His soloists are good and both the playing of the Danish Radio Orchestra and the skill of their engineers are admirable. But this is not a first choice.

There is a lot right about Paavo Järvi's fine reading with the Royal Stockholm Philharmonic and his Swedish choir. The first two movements are admirably paced and in the central movement the Norwegian mezzo-soprano Randi Stene and the Swedish baritone Peter Mattei make admirable soloists. No reservations about the Scherzo, *Kullervo goes to war*, or the excellent EMI/Virgin recording. The big snag is the finale, *Kullervo's death*, which Järvi *fils* drags out to almost fifteen minutes while most others get through it in about ten. The result is to make it sound bombastic and overblown.

The Tempest (incidental music), *Op. 109* (complete).
**(*) Ondine Dig. ODE 813-2 [id.]. Groop, Viljakainen, Hynninen, Silvasti, Tiilikainen, Op. Festival Ch., Finnish RSO, Saraste.

If clarity and definition are a first priority, the Ondine version under Saraste is the one to go for. There is good singing here, too, from Monica Groop, Jorma Hynninen and the rest of the cast. The performance is given in Danish (as it would have been in the 1926 version, rather than the Finnish text used by BIS). However, Saraste is nowhere near as sensitive as Vänskä and does not have his sense of mystery or atmosphere. His *Prospero* is too fast, almost routine by comparison with Vänskä, who draws the listener more completely into Sibelius's and Shakespeare's world. Both accounts are recommendable and either is to be acquired rather than none. But the BIS makes a clear first choice (see our main volume).

Simpson, Robert (1921-97)

(i) *Clarinet quintet*; *String quartet No. 13*; (ii) *String quintet No. 2.*
*** Hyperion Dig. CDA 66905 [id.]. (i) Thea King; (ii) Christopher van Kampen; Delmé Qt.

The *Clarinet quintet* of 1968 was recorded by Bernard Walton in the early 1970s but that is not currently available, so Thea King's new version with the Delmé Quartet is all the more welcome. It is a strong piece in one continuous movement which falls into five sections. It is arguably the most searching example of the genre to have appeared since the war and not just in this country. From the opening, with the model of Beethoven's *C sharp minor Quartet*, Op.131, not far from view, right to the ending, this is a subtle, concentrated and profoundly original – and profound – work. It is one of those pieces which is more than the sum of its parts and which resonates long in the memory. The *Thirteenth Quartet* (1990) is a powerfully concentrated piece and the Delmé are ideal exponents. The *String Quintet No. 2* occupied the composer between 1991 and 1994 during the first period of the stroke which afflicted his last years and left him in continuous pain. It is a powerful and severe work, whose bleak and unconsoling closing paragraphs resonate in the memory. A powerful though not always comfortable musical experience.

String quartets Nos. 14 & 15; (i) *Quintet for clarinet, bass clarinet and strings.*
*** Hyperion Dig. CDA 66626 [id.]. (i) Joy Farrall, Fiona Cross; Vanbrugh Qt.

The *Fourteenth Quartet* comes from 1990, and the *Fifteenth*, written when Simpson was seventy (in 1991), was his last. This is surely the greatest quartet cycle produced in the last half of the twentieth century and in terms of contrapuntal ingenuity and musical depth belongs with Bartók, Shostakovich and Holmboe. The *Clarinet quintet* is not to be confused with the 1968 work listed above; it is an arrangement for clarinet, bass clarinet and string trio of a 1983 quintet intriguingly scored for clarinet, bass clarinet and three double basses. These are powerful Beethovenian scores whose stature and musical processes are easier to recognize than describe. Dedicated performances, superbly recorded.

Sirmen, Maddelena Lombardini (1735-99)

String quartets Nos. 2 in B flat; 3 in G min.
*** CPO Dig. CPO 999 679-2 [id.]. Basle Erato Qt – Emilie MAYER: *Quartet No. 14;* Fanny MENDELSSOHN: *String quartet.* ***

We already have two fine recordings of all six of the *String quartets* of Maddelena Lombardini (her married name was Sirmen) – see our main volume. But many collectors will be satisfied with just two, particularly as the couplings here are so enterprising. They are two-movement works and fit rather well together: the catchy finale of the *B flat major* nicely complements the elegant opening *Tempo giusto* of the *G minor*. The performances here are excellent and so is the recording.

Smetana, Bedřich (1824-84)

Má Vlast (complete).
(BB) **(*) Virgin Classics 2 x 1 Dig. VBD5 61739-2 [CDVB 61739]. Czech PO, Pešek – DVORAK: *Symphony No. 4; Czech suite; My Home: overture* **(*).

Pešek's reading does not miss the music's epic patriotic feeling, yet never becomes bombastic. There is plenty of evocation, from the richly romantic opening of *Vyšehrad* to the more mysterious scene-setting in *Tábor*, while the climax of *Sárka*, with its potent anticipatory horn-call, is a gripping piece of melodrama. The two main sections of the work, *Vltava* and *From Bohemia's woods and fields*, are especially enjoyable for their vivid characterization, while at the very end of *Blaník* Pešek draws together the two key themes – the *Vyšehrad* motif and the Hussite chorale – very satisfyingly. This now comes coupled with a somewhat less recommendable Dvořák programme, but is very competitively priced.

Má Vlast (complete); The Bartered bride: Overture; 2 dances.
(B) ** Teldec/Warner Dig. Ultima 3984 28174-2 (2) [id.]. Frankfurt RSO, Inbal.

The Teldec digital recording is strikingly fine and this is music where the vividly coloured and well-balanced, clear sound can be especially telling. The orchestral playing is first class too, and Inbal's reading is dramatic. The progress of the Vltava river is vividly detailed and From Bohemia's woods and fields has plenty of strong contrasts. Sárka is certainly exciting and if, here and in the last two pieces, the patriotic fervour brings powerful accenting and bold brass, the balancing pastoral folk idiom of Blank is well caught. However, the overall playing-time of the performance, at around 78 minutes, means that it would have fitted on to a single CD, and the Bartered bride bonus is hardly generous. Kubelik's superb Czech version (Supraphon 11 1208-2) costs no more, and is a far preferable choice, while Antoni Wit's splendid Naxos account with the Polish National Radio Orchestra is an obvious bargain alternative (8.550931).

Má Vlast: Vltava. The Bartered bride: Overture and Dances.
(M) **(*) Sony SMK 60561 [id.]. NYPO, Bernstein – DVORAK: Symphony No. 7 **.

Bernstein's Bartered Bride excerpts are vivaciously entertaining, with much attractive pointing of detail. His Vltava is similarly enjoyable, and the mid 1960s recordings are full and detailed. A pity that the coupling is not so recommendable, which reduces the attractions of this reissue.

Má Vlast: Vltava. The Bartered bride: Overture; Polka; Furiant; Dance of the Comedians. The Kiss: Overture. Libuše: Overture. The Two Widows: Overture & Polka.
**(*) Decca (IMS) Dig. 444 867-2 [id.]. Cleveland O, Dohnányi.

A good Smetana anthology from the Cleveland Orchestra under Christoph von Dohnányi in excellent Decca sound. Charm may not be Dohnányi's strong suit, but this music induces enchantment all by itself. The Cleveland Orchestra play with great brio and virtuosity and, even though there is not too much in the way of spontaneous joy, this anthology will still give pleasure. At 57 minutes and premium price, it is, however, perhaps short measure these days.

Piano trio in G min., Op. 15; (i) Fantasy on a Bohemian Song; From my homeland.
(M) ** Supraphon SU 3449-2 131. (i) Ivan Klánsky, (i) Ceněk Pavlík, Marek Jerie.

Idiomatic performances of the G minor Piano trio

and of the Fantasy on a Bohemian Song and From my homeland, both for violin and piano. Decent recording, too, but at only 47 minutes' playing time, it is hardly good value, even at mid-price.

String quartets Nos. 1 in E min.; 2 in D min.
(M) **(*) Supraphon SU 3450-2 131. Panocha Qt.

The two string quartets from the Panocha Quartet are short measure at 45 minutes! These are well-played and intelligently shaped performances but there are finer, more spirited versions in the catalogue, notably those from the Medici (Koch 3-6436-2), Artis (Sony SK 53282) and Takács (Decca 452 239-2) Quartets, all differently coupled (see our main volume).

Memories of Bohemia in the form of polkas, Op. 12; Op. 13; 3 Poetic polkas, Op. 8; Polkas in F min.; A; E; G min.; 3 Salon polkas, Op. 7.
** Teldec/Warner Dig. 3984 21261-2 [id.]. András Schiff.

This issue serves as a reminder of the excellence and freshness of Smetana's keyboard music. Two-thirds of his output is for the piano. András Schiff is as sympathetic an interpreter as one could wish for, but the attractions of the disc are somewhat diminished by the claustrophobic acoustic, which lends a brittle tone to the instrument.

Spohr, Ludwig (1784–1859)

Octet in E, Op. 32.
(M) *** Decca 466 580-2 [id.]. Vienna Octet – SCHUBERT: Octet in F, D.803 *** ❂.

It is very good news that the Vienna Octet's vintage recording of Spohr's Octet is now back in the catalogue: it is a charming work, and the variations on Handel's Harmonious Blacksmith, which forms one of the central movements, offer that kind of naïveté which, when so stylishly done as here, makes for delicious listening. The playing is expert throughout, with the five strings blending perfectly with the two horns and clarinet, and altogether this is a winning performance. The 1960 recording is fresh and open and leaves little to be desired. A very welcome addition to Decca's Legends label, and it is coupled to the same group's equally fine account of the Schubert Octet.

Stainer, John (1840–1901)

The Crucifixion.
(B) *** CFP CD-CFP 4519. David Hughes, John Lawrenson, Guildford Cathedral Ch., Barry Rose; Gavin Williams.

(i) The Crucifixion. Come thou long-expected Jesus (hymn); I saw the Lord (anthem).
(B) *** Decca 436 146-2 [id.]. (i) Richard Lewis,

Owen Brannigan; St John's College, Cambridge, Ch., Guest.

All five hymns in which the congregation is invited to join are included on the Decca (originally Argo) record. Owen Brannigan is splendidly dramatic and his voice makes a good foil for Richard Lewis in the duets. The choral singing is first class and the 1961 recording is of Argo's best vintage, even finer than its CfP competitor. Moreover the Decca disc includes two bonuses: a hymn set to the words of Charles Wesley and a fine eight-part anthem, *I saw the Lord*, both of which are equally well sung.

The Classics for Pleasure version (from the late 1960s) is of high quality and, although one of the congregational hymns is omitted, in every other respect this can be recommended. John Lawrenson makes a movingly eloquent solo contribution and the choral singing is excellent. The remastered recording sounds first class, but the Decca version is finer still.

Steinberg, Maximilian (1883–1946)

Symphony No. 1 in D, Op. 3; Prélude symphonique, Op. 7; Fantaisie dramatique, Op. 9.
*** DG Dig. 457 607-2 [id.]. Gothenburg SO, Neeme Järvi.

These days, Maximilian Steinberg is best remembered as the teacher of Shostakovich. Born in the Lithuanian capital, Vilnius, he went to St Petersburg as a student where he studied with Liadov, Glazunov and Rimsky-Korsakov, whose son-in-law he was to become. The *First Symphony* (1905–6) is very much influenced by Glazunov and is in no way inferior: indeed, Steinberg's scoring is more transparent and less congested. The melodic invention is perhaps less distinguished but, without making excessive claims, the music is well worth reviving. The *Prélude symphonique* dates from 1908 and is dedicated to the memory of Rimsky-Korsakov who had died that year. The *Fantaisie dramatique* (1910) is inspired by Ibsen's *Brand* and like its companions on this enterprising disc bears witness to Steinberg's continuing debt to his mentors. Although no strikingly individual personality emerges, his is a real talent and his feeling for the orchestra little short of remarkable. Neeme Järvi proves an invigorating and refreshing guide in these genial and sympathetic pieces, and the fine Gothenburg Orchestra respond to his enthusiasm. The recording is the product of the Gothenburg partnership of Lennart Dehn and Michael Bergek and is absolutely state-of-the-art, beautifully defined and present, yet transparent in detail.

Stenhammar, Wilhelm (1871–1927)

2 Sentimental romances, Op. 28.
(BB) **(*) Naxos Dig. 8.554287 [id.]. Tobias Ringborg, Swedish CO, Niklas Willén – AULIN; BERWALD: *Violin concertos* **(*).

These two charming Stenhammar pieces, first performed by Tor Aulin, are seldom heard these days and are played to excellent effect in Tobias Ringborg's hands. Decent and well-balanced recorded sound.

Serenade for orchestra, Op. 31.
✪ *** Finlandia 3984-25327-2 [id.]. Royal Stockholm PO, Sir Andrew Davis – BRAHMS: *Serenade No. 1 in D, Op. 11* ***.

The *Serenade for orchestra* is Stenhammar's masterpiece, its richness of invention, effortless contrapuntal ingenuity and subtlety of harmony giving constant delight and refreshment. The scoring and colours are full of fantasy and imagination. Its *Notturno* perfectly encapsulates the magic of the late Swedish summer nights. Sir Andrew Davis has a natural sympathy with and much feeling for the score, and is meticulous in his care for dynamic shadings and refinement of texture. Neeme Järvi on BIS includes the *Reverenza* movement that Stenhammar eventually discarded – and rightly so – when he transposed the outer movements from E major to F. Davis's is a wonderfully convincing account, very well recorded too.

Symphony No. 2 in G min., Op. 34; Excelsior! overture, Op. 13; Serenade in F, Op. 31: Reverenza; (i) 2 Songs, Op. 4.
** Virgin/EMI Dig. VC5 45244-2. Royal Stockholm PO, Paavo Järvi; (i) with Anne Sofie von Otter.

Paavo Järvi gives a finely shaped and sensitive account of both the symphony and the *Excelsior! overture*, its usual coupling. Virgin too have added the *Reverenza* movement, which originally formed part of the *Serenade for orchestra* but which Stenhammar subsequently excised, feeling it made the work too long. It is a charming piece and is beautifully played by the Stockholm Orchestra, as for that matter is the symphony. The two Runeberg settings, Op. 4, date from 1892 and so Stenhammar's setting of *Flickan kom ifrån sin älsklings nöte* ('The girl returned from meeting her lover') precedes Sibelius's by almost a decade – and in some ways is the more refined of the two. The orchestration, which has never been recorded before, is masterly. Anne Sofie von Otter sings both to the manner born. The recording is acceptable, but wanting in real transparency and is two-dimensional, not having enough front-to-back perspective; there is also a slight coarseness on some climaxes. Not serious enough to inhibit a recommendation on artistic grounds, maybe, but a little disappointing all the same.

VOCAL MUSIC

7 Songs from Thoughts of Solitude, Op. 7; 5 Songs to texts of Runeberg, Op. 8; 5 Swedish songs, Op. 16; 5 Songs of Bo Bergman, Op. 20; Songs and Moods, Op. 26; Late Harvest.
**(*) BIS Dig. CD 654 [id.]. Mattei, Lundin.

Only two of the three-dozen Stenhammar songs on this disc last longer than four minutes: *Jungfru Blond och Jungfru Brunett* ('Miss Blonde and Miss Brunette') and *Prins Aladin av Lampan* ('Prince Aladdin of the Lamp'), both of which are to be found on the set of thirty songs recorded by Anne Sofie von Otter and Håkan Hagegård (Caprice MSCD 623 – see our main volume). As a song composer Stenhammar was often inspired, and never routine in his responses to his poets (he shared Sibelius's taste for Fröding and Runeberg); his craftsmanship is always fastidious and in the post-humously published *Efterskörd* ('Late Harvest') and the *Thoughts of Solitude*, Op. 7, he brings to light some songs of great eloquence and beauty that are not readily available outside Sweden. Peter Mattei is an intelligent singer, well endowed vocally; the voice is beautiful, but he has a tendency to colour the voice on the flat side of the note, and on occasion (in *Prins Aladin*, for example) is flat. Bengt-Ake Lundin deserves special mention for the sensitivity and responsiveness of his accompanying, and the recording is excellent.

Tirfing (opera): excerpts.
*** Sterling Dig. CDO 1033-2 [id.]. Tobiasson, Morling, Taube, Stockholm Royal Op. O, Leif Segerstam.

Tirfing (1898) was Stenhammar's second opera; his first, *Gillet på Solhaug* based on the Ibsen play, enjoyed some success in Germany, but *Tirfing*, his most extended score (790 pages in all), all but disappeared after its first performances. Its failure plunged the composer into a fit of depression, and though he toyed in the 1920s with a Shakespearean opera, *Twelfth Night*, he never returned to the genre. *Tirfing* is a 'mystical saga-poem', based on the Hervarar Saga, and tells of the warrior Angantyr, his valkyrie daughter Hervor and Tirfing, a sword with the magical power to destroy everything. It is all terribly Wagnerian, but even so, the music has the power and sweep of Stenhammar. There are characteristic modulations (one is reminded of *Excelsior!* among other things). Above all, even at its most Wagnerian, the music grips the listener from start to finish. Leif Segerstam gets first-rate results from the Royal Opera Orchestra and the same from the three soloists, in particular Ingrid Tobiasson as Hervor. Good wide-ranging recording. The growing band of Stenhammar's admirers will want this.

Stradella, Alessandro (1644–82)

Motets: (i) *Benedictus Dominus Deo; Chare Jesu suavissime. Crocifissione e morte di N. S. Giesù Christo; Lamentatione per il Mercoledì Santo; O vos omnes qui transitis.*
(BB) **(*) Virgin Veritas/EMI 2 x 1 VBD5 61588-2 (2). Gérard Lesne, Il Seminario Musicale; (i) with Sandrine Piau – CALDARA: *Sonatas; Cantatas* **(*).

Throughout his life, Alessandro Stradella was associated with scandals, both financial and sexual, and he was finally murdered, although the reasons for this are obscure. He wrote church music which combined drama with remarkable serenity and expressive beauty. *Benedictus Dominus Deo* is a particularly beautiful duet cantata in which God is thanked for sending his son to earth to redeem mankind. *O vos omnes*, a solo cantata, is shorter but no less potent. The text first expresses a languishing adoration of Jesus, with sensuous use of descending chromatics, and the work ends with lively *Alleluias*. Lesne is a master of this repertoire, and in the former cantata he is radiantly joined by Sandrine Piau, who then goes on to dominate the joyously lyrical *Chare Jesu suavissime*, sweetly praising Saint Philip Neri. These works are framed by the more austere *Crocifissione e morte di N. S. Giesù Christo* (which has a memorably eloquent instrumental introduction, after which the solo line is both grave and plaintive) and the closing *Lamentatione for Ash Wednesday*, which is also restrained but touchingly beautiful. The accompaniments, by a small, authentic-instrument group, are very sensitive indeed. This is perhaps specialist repertoire, but Gérard Lesne has made it his own and his artistry is unsurpassed. Now reissued very inexpensively indeed, aptly coupled to dramatic cantatas and sonatas of Caldara, this is very recommendable – with the very important proviso that now no texts are included.

The Strauss family

Strauss, Johann Sr (1804–49)
Strauss, Johann Jr (1825–99)
Strauss, Josef (1827–70) Strauss, Eduard (1835–1916)

(all music listed is by Johann Strauss Jr unless otherwise stated)

'2000 New Year concert': Csárdás from *Ritter Pasman;* March: *Persischer.* Polkas: *Albion; Eljen a Magyar; Hellenen; Process; Vom Donaustrande.* Waltzes: *An der schönen blauen Donau; Lagunen; Liebeslieder; Wein Weib und Gesang.* Eduard STRAUSS: Polkas: *Mit Extrapost;*

Gruss an Prag. Josef STRAUSS: Polkas: *Die Libelle; Künstler-Gruss;* Waltz: *Marien-Klänge.* Johann STRAUSS Snr.: *Radetzky march.*
(M) *** EMI Dig. CDC5 67323-2 (2) [id.]. VPO, Riccardo Muti (with SUPPE: *Overture: Morning, noon and night in Vienna*).

It is amazing how a conductor's musical personality is affected by the New Year's Day concert in Vienna. Like Lorin Maazel before him, Riccardo Muti loses any prickly qualities, concentrating on charm rather than bite, as is obvious from the very opening number in the 2000 Concert. The *Lagunen waltz* of Johann Strauss II makes the gentlest possible start, leading to a couple of sparkling novelties, never heard at these concerts before, the brisk *Hellenen polka* and the feather-light *Albion polka*, dedicated to Prince Albert. That sets the pattern for the whole programme. For all the brilliance of the playing, it is the subtlety of the Viennese lilt (as in Josef Strauss's *Marien-Klänge*, another novelty) that one remembers, or the breathtaking delicacy of the pianissimo which opens the first of the encores, the *Blue Danube*, perfectly caught by the EMI engineers. For its Millennium concert the Vienna Philharmonic could not be more seductive. The two-disc format at mid-price – with the first half shorter than the second – allows the whole programme to be included without cuts.

Overtures: *Die Fledermaus; Waldmeister. Perpetuum mobile.* Polkas: *Eljen a Magyar!; Pizzicato* (with Josef); *Tritsch-Tratsch; Unter Donner und Blitz; Vergnügungszug.* Waltzes: *Accelerationen; An der schönen, blauen Donau; G'schichten aus dem Wienerwald; Kaiser; Morgenblätter; Rosen aus dem Süden.* Josef STRAUSS: Polkas: *Frauenherz; Die Libelle; Ohne Sorgen; Die tanzende Muse.* Waltzes: *Aquarellen; Delirien; Sphärenklänge; Transaktionen.* Johann STRAUSS, Sr: *Radetzky march.*
(B) **(*) DG Double Dig. 453 052-2 (2) [id.]. VPO, Maazel.

The presence of a New Year's Day audience is most tangible in the *Pizzicato polka*, where one can sense the intercommunication as Maazel manipulates the rubato with obvious flair. He also gives a splendid account of *Transaktionen*, which has striking freshness and charm. The *Waldmeister overture* is a delightful piece and readily shows the conductor's affectionate response in its detail, while the opening of the *Aquarellen waltz* brings an even greater delicacy of approach and the orchestra responds with telling pianissimo playing. For the rest, these are well-played performances of no great memorability. The digital sound is brilliant and clear, somewhat lacking in resonant warmth.

Egyptischer march; Perpetuum mobile. Polkas: *Auf der Jagd; Pizzicato.* Waltzes: *An der schönen, blauen Donau; Frühlingsstimmen; Geschichten*

aus dem Wienerwald; Rosen aus dem Süden; 1001 Nacht; Wiener Blut.
(M) *** Decca Penguin 460 648-2 [id.]. VPO, Willi Boskovsky.

These performances, which include six favourite waltzes, have the magical Viennese glow that marked all of Boskovsky's Strauss Decca recordings right through from 1958 to 1979, with sound ranging from good to excellent. It makes an admirable collection for those thinking the Decca/ Boskovsky 6-CD box (455 254-2 – see our main volume) too much of a good thing. These works could not sound more authentic if Johann Strauss himself were conducting. The specialist essay is by Allan Massie.

Banditen-Galopp; Quadrille nach Motiven der Operette. Marches: *Egyptischer; Kaiser Franz Josef.* Polkas: *Annen-Polka; Auf der Jagd; Eljen a Magyar; Fata Morgana; Furioso-Polka quasi Galopp; Tritsch-Tratsch; Unter Donner und Blitz.* Waltzes: *An der schönen, blauen Donau; Morgenblätter; Rosen aus dem Süden; 1001 Nacht; Wiener Blut; Wiener Bonbons.* Eduard STRAUSS: *Weyprecht-Payer* (march); *Saat und Ernte* (polka). Waltzes: *Leuchtkäferlin; Schleir und Krone.* Josef STRAUSS: Polkas: *Die Libelle; Farewell!; Moulinet; Ohne Sorgen.* Waltzes: *Aquarellen; Perlen der Liebe.* J. STRAUSS Snr: *Cachucha-Galopp.*
(M) **(*) Chan. CHAN 7129 (2) [id.]. Johann Strauss O, Jack Rothstein.

These are relaxed, enjoyable performances which are hard to fault. If they lack the Viennese distinction of Boskovsky or the individuality of Karajan, the varied programme with plenty of novelties, makes up for it. There are several agreeable surprise items in this 2-CD set and the sound is very good.

'The Strauss family in London': J. STRAUSS Snr: *Almack's Quadrille; March of the Royal Horse Guards* (orch. Georgiadis); *Huldigung der Königen Victoria Grossbritannien* (waltz). Polkas: *Alice; Exeter-Polka; Fredrika.* Eduard STRAUSS: *Greeting Waltz, on English airs; Old England for ever* (polka, orch. Georgiadis). J. STRAUSS II: *Erinnerung an Covent-Garden* (waltz); *Potpourri-Quadrille* (orch. Peak). J. STRAUSS III: *Krönungs-Walzer.*
(M) *** Chan. CHAN 7128 [id.]. LSO, John Georgiadis.

A waltz which starts with *Rule, Britannia* and ends with *God save the Queen* may seem unlikely, but that's exactly how *Huldigung der Königen Victoria Grossbritannien* goes. The music here is the result of visits made to England by the Strausses, the first one instigated by one of their greatest admirers: Queen Victoria. Like Jack Rothstein's companion set this disc is full of delightful surprises and with idiomatic playing from the LSO, fine Chandos sound, and excellent sleeve notes by Peter Kemp, it is surely an essential purchase for all Straussians. The most striking novelty is the inclusion of a waltz by the now virtually forgotten Johann Strauss III.

Die Fledermaus (complete).
(B) *** Ph. Duo Dig. 464 031-2 (2) [id.]. Kiri Te Kanawa, Gruberová, Leech, Wolfgang Brendel, Bär, Fassbaender, Göttling, Krause, Wendler, Schenk, V. State Op. Ch., VPO, Previn.
(B) *** EMI Double fforte CZS5 73851-2 [CDFB 73851] (2). Scheyrer, Lipp, Dermota, Berry, Ludwig, Terkal, Waechter, Kunz, Philh. Ch. & O, Ackermann.
(M) *(*) DG 457 765-2 (2) [id.]. Julia Varady, Lucia Popp, Hermann Prey, Kollo, Weikl, Rebroff, Kusche, Bav. State Op. Ch. & O, Carlos Kleiber.

André Previn here produces an enjoyably idiomatic account of Strauss's masterpiece, one which consistently conveys the work's exuberant high spirits. Dame Kiri Te Kanawa's portrait of Rosalinde brings not only gloriously firm, golden sound but also vocal acting with star quality. Brigitte Fassbaender is the most dominant Prince Orlofsky on disc. Singing with a tangy richness and firmness, she emerges as the genuine focus of the party scene. Edita Gruberová is a sparkling, characterful and full-voiced Adèle; Wolfgang Brendel as Eisenstein and Olaf Bär as Dr Falke both sing very well indeed, though their voices sound too alike. Richard Leech as Alfred provides heady tone and a hint of parody. Tom Krause makes a splendid Frank, the more characterful for no longer sounding young. Anton Wendler as Dr Blind and Otto Schenk as Frosch the jailer give vintage Viennese performances, with Frosch's cavortings well tailored and not too extended. This now goes to the top of the list of latterday *Fledermaus* recordings, though with one serious reservation: the Philips production in Act II adds a layer of crowd noise as background throughout the Party scene, even during Orlofsky's solos. Strauss's gentler moments are then seriously undermined by the sludge of distant chatter and laughter, as in the lovely chorus *Bruderlein und Schwesterlein*, yearningly done. Otherwise the recorded sound is superb, with brilliance and bite alongside warmth and bloom, both immediate and well balanced. Like Kleiber on DG, Previn opts for the *Thunder and lightning polka* instead of the ballet. Its reissue at bargain price is welcome and retains all the qualities of the original (except texts and translations).

Like Gui's Glyndebourne *Nozze di Figaro*, Ackermann's vintage *Die Fledermaus* (see our main volume) has been promoted from Classics for Pleasure to EMI's own Double fforte bargain label. It remains splendid value, for the singing sparkles,

and the opera has an infectious sense of Viennese style. The recording is excellent.

The glory of the Kleiber set is the singing of the two principal women – Julia Varady and Lucia Popp, magnificently characterful and stylish as mistress and servant – but much of the set is controversial, to say the least. Kleiber is certainly exciting at times and rejects many older conventions in performing style, which some will find refreshing, but he is not at all easy going. Other conductors allow the music's intrinsic charm to bubble to the surface like champagne; with Kleiber, one feels the charm, if one can call it that, being rammed down one's throat. But that is nothing compared to the falsetto of Ivan Rebroff, which has to be heard to be believed – it sounds grotesque and is likely to put most listeners off this recording. As in many of Kleiber's recordings, the performance may well have a cult following, and those wishing to brave his style will be pleased to know of its attractive packaging, with full texts and translations, on DG's Originals label. The performances are certainly not dull!

Die Fledermaus: highlights.
(B) *** [EMI Red Line Dig. CDR5 69839]. Popp, Baltsa, Lind, Domingo, Bav. R. Ch., Munich RSO, Domingo.
(M) *** EMI CDM7 69598-2 (with Rothenberger, Holm, Gedda; cond. Boskovsky).

It was not originally intended that Plácido Domingo should sing the role of Alfred as well as conducting EMI's newest digital recording of *Fledermaus*, but the tenor who had originally been engaged cancelled at the last minute, and Domingo agreed to do the double job, singing over accompaniments that had already been recorded. The happiness of the occasion is reflected in a strong and amiable, rather than an idiomatically Viennese, performance. Lucia Popp makes a delectable and provocative Rosalinde and Seiffert a strong tenor Eisenstein, with Baltsa a superb, characterful Orlofsky. With ensembles vigorous and urgent, this is a consistently warm and sympathetic selection.

Most should be happy with the excerpts from the mid-priced Boskovsky set, which is well cast; but the complete Ackermann version on Double Fforte costs little more and is obviously a better proposition.

Der Zigeunerbaron: highlights.
**(*) Teldec/Warner Dig. 4509 98821-2 [id.] (from complete set, with Coburn, Lippert, Schasching, Hamari, Holzmair, Oelze, Von Magnus, Lazar, Arnold Schönberg Ch., VSO, Harnoncourt).

Though the Harnoncourt *Zigeunerbaron* brings uneven casting, his conducting is sparklingly fresh and there is much to enjoy in this generous (71 minutes) set of highlights, which also has the great advantage, not shared by the complete set from which it derives, of not being overladen with German dialogue. However, unusually for this Telarc series, no translations are provided.

Strauss, Richard (1864–1949)

An Alpine symphony, Op. 64.

(B) *** Australian Decca Eloquence 466 670-2. LAPO, Mehta.

Mehta's version of *An Alpine Symphony* is perhaps the best of his Decca Strauss recordings. It is a virtuoso performance and he is supported by a superb recording which is wide in range and rich in detail. It is not overlit, yet the Decca engineers allow every strand of the texture to 'tell' without ever losing sight of the overall perspective, and it has transferred strikingly well to CD.

An Alpine Symphony; Don Juan; Salome: Salome's dance of the 7 veils.

(B) **(*) Decca Eclipse Dig. 448 714-2 [id.]. Cleveland O, Ashkenazy.

The Cleveland Orchestra commands as rich a sonority and as much virtuosity as any of its illustrious rivals. Ashkenazy's well-controlled and intelligently shaped reading of the *Alpine Symphony* has much to recommend it, but is not quite as strong in personality as the very finest versions. That applies also to *Don Juan*, which brings comparable virtuosity from the Clevelanders. However, with recording of Decca's top quality, this is good value at bargain price.

An Alpine Symphony, Op. 64; Feierlicher Einzug der Ritter des Johanniterordens; Vienna Philharmonic fanfare.
** Ph. Dig. 454 448-2 [id.]. VPO, Seiji Ozawa.

Ozawa's performance of the *Alpine Symphony* comes over as a mountain stroll, rather than generating any great tension, although the closing section is evocative enough. The orchestral playing is admirable but the recording, while vivid, is not as overwhelmingly sumptuous as the finest versions. The piece is framed by two fanfares, the one written for the VPO in 1924 and a slightly longer but hardly more memorable *Solemn entry of the Knights of St John* dating from fifteen years earlier.

An Alpine Symphony, Op. 64; Don Juan, Op. 20; Suite for 13 wind instruments, Op. 4; Symphonia domestica, Op. 53; Till Eulenspiegel, Op. 28.
(BB) **(*) Virgin Classics Double Dig. VBD5 61460-2 (2) [CDVB 61460]. Minnesota O, Edo de Waart.

An excellent and inexpensive anthology, very well played and recorded, over which there are only minor reservations. There is no lack of spectacle in the *Alpine Symphony*, which ends with an impressive storm and a rich-hued sunset: only the echoing horns on the way up seem rather too far away; but nothing is inflated needlessly. Similarly, anyone who feels that Strauss's domestic revelations need tempering with a little discretion will enjoy this performance, which is also very well played by the excellent Minnesota Orchestra. The *Suite in B flat* is beautifully blended and comparably refined. In *Don Juan* the orchestra may not succeed in producing quite the same sophisticated opulence of texture as is achieved by such Straussians as Reiner in Chicago or Karajan in Berlin, but they still play very well indeed; and throughout, the sound has both depth and clarity. Good value.

(i) *Also sprach Zarathustra, Op. 30;* (ii) *An Alpine Symphony; Death and transfiguration, Op. 24. Don Juan, Op. 20; Ein Heldenleben, Op. 40;* (i) *Festliches Praeludium, Op. 61; Der Rosenkavalier: waltzes from Act III;* (i) *Salome: Dance of the seven veils; Till Eulenspiegel, Op. 28.*
(B) *(**) DG mono/stereo 463 190-2 (3) [id.]. (i) BPO; (ii) Dresden State O; Boehm.

Boehm's Strauss is impressive and this bargain box, comprising some mono but mainly stereo recordings, is a fine tribute to his natural affinity with this composer. *An Alpine Symphony, Don Juan* and *Ein Heldenleben* are mono, but are excellent performances: it is Boehm's attention to detail which one most enjoys, though there is excitement too, even if this music ideally requires stereo to make its full impact. The rest of the performances are stereo. *Also sprach Zarathustra* dates from 1958 and the sound is good if a little thin; it is a spacious and satisfying account, with splendid playing to support the conductor's conception. The rustic portrayal of *Till*, and the *Waltzes* from *Der Rosenkavalier*, are both effective, as is the highly sensuous account of *Salome's Dance*. The *Prelude*, written in 1913 for the opening of the Konzerthaus in Vienna, is a fascinating bonus: it is a somewhat inflated work, for organ and a huge orchestra, where the composer piles sequence upon sequence to produce a climax of shattering sonority. Boehm manages to give the work a dignity not really inherent in the music. All these were recorded a few years after *Also sprach Zarathustra* and have fuller sound. For *Death and transfiguration*, Boehm's 1972 live Salzburg Festival recording was used; it is a performance of excitement and strong tensions (despite a couple of irritating coughs at the beginning), even if the recording is slightly overweighted at the top. At bargain price, this set is worth considering, and an essential purchase for admirers of this distinguished conductor.

(i) *Also sprach Zarathustra, Op. 30;* (ii) *Symphonia domestica, Op. 53.*
(M) **(*) Carlton Dig. 30366 00932. Nat. Youth

O of Great Britain; (i) Skrowaczewski; (ii) Christopher Seaman.

Absolutely no apologies need be made for the playing of the National Youth Orchestra in these bravura Strauss scores. The strings may not be as opulent or as finely polished as those of the Berlin Philharmonic, but they still sound pretty good, and both performances glow with life and feeling. For some reason the very opening of Skrowaczewski's *Also sprach Zarathustra* (recorded in Symphony Hall, Birmingham, in 1997) is not quite as sumptuous as usual, with the underpinning organ pedal recessed and almost self-effacing when it acts briefly as a pendant at the end of the sequence. But the strings take up the music of 'great longing' with ardour, as do the thrusting horns in their eloquent 'expression of joys and pleasures'. The violins' upper tessitura is not found wanting later, and the work's final climax generates great intensity. If anything, the *Symphonia domestica*, recorded four years earlier under Christopher Seaman, is even finer. Not surprisingly, these young players respond readily to the orgasmic passion of the 'Love scene', but the wind soloists also revel in the charming detail of the opening movement. The joyous apotheosis is splendidly managed, and overall Seaman holds the structure together with admirable cohesion. The recording, made in Watford Town Hall, approaches the demonstration bracket.

Le bourgeois gentilhomme (incidental music): *Suite Op. 60; Intermezzo: 4 symphonic interludes, Op. 72.*
(BB) *(*) Naxos Dig. 8.553379 [id.]. Melbourne SO, Michael Halász.

Recordings of *Le bourgeois gentilhomme* are legion but the four *Symphonic interludes* from the opera *Intermezzo* are not. Unfortunately the playing is pretty scrappy and when in *Le bourgeois gentilhomme*, Beecham, Reiner or Kempe are available at budget- or mid-price, this is uncompetitive. The *Intermezzo* interludes are not available at less than full-price but even so the performances under Michael Halász are distinctly wanting in finesse.

(i) *Horn concerto No 1 in E flat, Op. 11; Don Juan, Op. 20*; (ii) *Don Quixote, Op. 35.*
*** Sony MHK 63123 [id.]. Cleveland O, Szell, with (i) Myron Bloom; (ii) Pierre Fournier.

A superb CD in every way: Szell's *Don Juan* is one of the finest on disc – it has great thrust and is passionately lyrical, impetuous yet never rushed; in short, a great performance, founded on the supreme virtuosity of the Cleveland orchestra. *Don Quixote* is no less impressive: this was one of Pierre Fournier's showpieces and he does not disappoint. Perhaps surprisingly with Szell, it is the warmth and human frailty of the Don that is brought out most memorably here, though the characterization throughout is strong. A splendidly played version

of the *First Horn concerto*, with Myron Bloom on top form, completes a stimulating programme, with the early 1960s recordings excellent throughout. It is handsomely packaged in the Sony's Masterworks Heritage series, which means the CD costs rather more than mid-price.

(i; ii) *Oboe concerto in D;* (ii) *Metamorphosen for 23 solo strings;* (iv) *Violin sonata in E flat;* (ii; iii) Orchestral Lieder: *Befreit; Freundliche Vision; Die Heiligen drei Könige aus Morgenland; Meinem Kinde; Morgen!; Ruhe, meine Seele; Waldseligkeit; Wiegenlied; Winterweihe.*
(BB) **(*) Virgin Classics 2 x 1 Dig. VBD5 61766-2 (2) [CDVB 61766]. (i) Ray Still; (ii) Academy of L., Richard Stamp; (iii) Gundula Janowitz; (iv) Dimitry Sitkovetsky, Pavel Gililov.

Ray Still, the principal oboe of the Chicago Symphony Orchestra, is fully equal to the technical and lyrical demands of Strauss's florid concerto. His accompaniment is warmly supportive, but Richard Stamp could be subtler in controlling the work's complex detail. However, the Academy play the *Metamorphosen* confidently, and with refinement and ardour, reaching a passionate climax, yet ensuring every textural line makes its fullest effect. They also provide a rich backcloth for Gundula Janowitz's creamily sensuous performances of nine of Strauss's most beautiful Lieder. She captures the listener immediately with her opening *Ruhe, meine Seele*, and is even more ravishing in *Waldseligkeit*, and utterly charming in *Wiegenlied*. There is a certain uniformity about her approach to all these songs, but she certainly feels the words, and her rich timbre and flowing lines are so beautiful that criticism is disarmed. Dimitry Sitkovetsky also makes a comparably ardent lyrical response to the *Violin sonata*. He is a passionate and characterful player and gives a powerful account of this early work. Pavel Gililov too is a perceptive artist, but his playing is not quite the equal of Krystian Zimerman's who has made an outstanding recording of this work with Kyung Wha Chung for DG (457 907-2). Nevertheless the Virgin sound balance is praiseworthy throughout this disc and this anthology is excellent value at its modest asking price.

Violin concerto in D minor, Op. 8; (ii) *Violin sonata in E flat, Op. 18.*
*** EMI Dig. CDC5 56870-2 [id.]. Sarah Chang; with (i) Bavarian RSO, Sawallisch; (ii) Sawallisch (piano).

Composed when he was a mere seventeen, the *Violin concerto* is the Cinderella among the Strauss concertos and is currently represented by a mere handful of recordings in the current catalogue. Sarah Chang enjoys the support of that most authoritative of Straussians, Wolfgang Sawallisch, and a great Strauss orchestra. She brings out a youthful freshness in the writing, both in the *Concerto* and in the *Sonata* of five years later. The Bavarian Radio engineers give Ms Chang a lifelike balance without any of the larger-than-life focus that spoils so many new concerto recordings. Having these two works together helpfully underlines the way that Strauss was developing when, instead of echoing composers from Mendelssohn to Brahms, he suddenly emerged as a radical new voice. In both works, Chang and Sawallisch are at their most memorable in the slow movements, which in their hushed intensity sound winningly spontaneous. The *Sonata in E flat* was written in 1887 just after Strauss had finished *Aus Italien* (and a few months later than the César Franck *Sonata* and at the same time as the Brahms *D minor Sonata*). Sawallisch is just as impressive at the keyboard as he is conducting, always matching Chang's characterful playing. The sound is warm and full, and brings out the violinist's subtlety of tonal shading. It is a sign of the times that no details of the producer, recording venue or date are given, though the sleeve does credit the stylist, make-up stylist and even hair stylist (Ariel from the 'Frankpaul salon') of the soloist's photos! Strongly recommended, just the same.

Don Juan, Op. 20; Ein Heldenleben, Op. 40.
(B) (***) Dutton Lab. mono CDEA 5125 [id.].
    Concg. O, Willem Mengelberg.

(i) *Don Juan, Op. 20; Ein Heldenleben, Op. 40;*
(ii) *Till Eulenspiegel, Op. 28.*
(M) (**) Telefunken 3984-28409-2 [id.]. (i)
    Concg. O, Mengelberg; (ii) VPO, Clemens
    Krauss.

Willem Mengelberg and the Concertgebouw Orchestra were jointly the dedicatees of Richard Strauss's most ambitious orchestral work, *Ein Heldenleben*. Even in 1941, under the stress of the Nazi occupation of Holland, they give a heartfelt performance, freely spontaneous and expansive, with old-fashioned string portamento intensifying the warmth. The splendid Dutton transfer is clear on detail with plenty of body and fair bloom on top. The *Don Juan* recording of 1938 is even more cleanly focused.

Telefunken's own transfer is full and beefy but not nearly so cleanly focused as the splendid Dutton transfer. The *Don Juan* recording of 1938 brings an even sharper contrast in favour of Dutton. Though the Telefunken disc has a bonus in Krauss's *Till Eulenspiegel*, the price is higher.

(i) *Ein Heldenleben*; (ii) *Der Rosenkavalier: Waltz sequence No. 1.*
(B) ** Australian Decca Eloquence 466 669-2.
    LAPO; (ii) VPO; Mehta.

Mehta's is a hi-fi performance of *Ein Heldenleben* to impress the Straussian weaned on the opening bars of *Also sprach Zarathustra*. It is very exciting,

but misses some of the subtler qualities of a richly varied score. The *Der Rosenkavalier* coupling is similarly high-powered and brilliant, in sound as well as performance.

Symphony in F min., Op. 12; (i) *6 Lieder, Op. 68.*
**(*) Chandos Dig. CHAN 9166 [id.]. (i) Eileen
    Hulse; RSNO, Järvi.

The *F minor* is neither a good symphony nor good Strauss, though Järvi makes out a better case for it than any previous recording. The work is cunningly crafted and the young master puts his ideas through their paces with skill and proficiency. But the ideas themselves are not really very distinguished – or indeed characteristic. Järvi paces the score with real mastery and gets very good playing from the Royal Scottish National Orchestra. The glorious Brentano *Lieder*, Op. 68 date from 1918 and Strauss transcribed them for orchestra in 1941. Eileen Hulse produces some beautiful tone and is sensitively supported throughout. Not core repertory this, but a disc for Straussians.

(i) *Metamorphosen* (arr. for string septet).
Capriccio: Prelude.
*** Nimbus Dig. NI 5614 [id.]. Brandis Quartet,
    with Küssner, Schwalke – SCHOENBERG:
    *Verklaerte Nacht ***.*

The first ideas for *Metamorphosen* came to Strauss as a string septet, and it was only when he received a commission from Paul Sacher for a work for his Basle Chamber Orchestra that the familiar score for twenty-three solo strings began its life. In 1990, Strauss's pencil sketch came to light and, with the aid of that and the definitive score, Rudolf Leopold has carefully reconstructed the original. The Brandis Quartet and three Berlin colleagues play with magnificent artistry and eloquence, both here and in the opening sextet from *Capriccio*. The sleeve note dwells gratuitously on Strauss and the Nazis, and even speaks of *Capriccio* as an embodiment of Nazi aesthetics. (Webern, who was perversely blind to the Nazis' criminality, seems to escape this armchair moralizing.) The Nimbus sound is first class.

Enoch Arden, Op. 38 (Melodrama for narrator and piano).
**(*) VAI Audio VAIA 1179-2 (2) [id.]. Jon
    Vickers, Marc-André Hamelin.

Enoch Arden is an oddity. Strauss wrote it in 1896/7 for himself to perform accompanying a friend – the Munich director, Ernst von Possart. Tennyson's poem was highly popular at the time in a variety of German translations, and the note for this VAI issue even suggests that the piece brought more fame to the composer at the time than his symphonic poems. Jon Vickers, the narrator here recommends (in English) how so 'soul-satisfying' a piece gives a powerful reminder of 'the timeless truths of Love,

Patience, Fidelity and Steadfastness'. In his powerful declamation he makes a persuasive case for the piece, but even Marc-André Hamelin, equally persuasive, cannot mask the fact that the piano-writing in its illustrative naivety has much in common with the accompaniments for silent films, which soon after became so popular. From the idiom it is hard to identify the composer at any time, a point that is brought home the more forcibly on disc. The live recording (with much applause beforehand) is aptly atmospheric.

Four Last songs; Orchestral Lieder: Cäcilie; Freundliche Vision; Frühlingsfeier; Gesang der Apollopriesterin; Verführung; Waldseligkeit.
*** DG Dig. 445 182-2 [id.]. Karita Mattila, BPO, Claudio Abbado.

With Abbado and the Berlin Philharmonic providing sensuously beautiful support, Karita Mattila gives one of the most moving of all the many recordings of Strauss's Four Last songs. She is at once youthfully ardent, yet poised and controlled, floating her loveliest, creamy tone in breathtaking pianissimos, as at the start of the final song, Im Abendrot. She touches the deeper emotions behind these valedictory pieces, using a wide tonal and dynamic range. Consistently she brings out their mystery, in singing the more intense for being recorded live. The fill-up offers very short measure (50 minutes in all), but the orchestral songs, recorded under studio conditions, bring performances just as commanding. Warm, full sound to match.

OPERA

Complete operas: Arabella; Ariadne auf Naxos; Elektra; Die Frau ohne Schatten; Der Rosenkavalier; Salome.
(M) **(*) Decca Analogue/Dig. 458 700-2 (14) [id.]. Various artists, VPO (or, in Ariadne, LPO); Solti.

Solti's accomplishment in the operas of Richard Strauss almost matches his achievement in Wagner. Certainly Elektra, Die Frau ohne Schatten (especially), and Salome hold their own with any other versions recorded since, and the quality of singing and orchestral playing is matched by the Decca engineers. All six operas have been vividly remastered, taking advantage of modern technology, and one must single out the new transfer of Der Rosenkavalier as being a very marked improvement on the previous CD incarnation. All the operas are available separately at premium price (collectors will note that the individual sets of both Arabella and Ariadne now cost more than they did), but the present handsome boxed set, which offers each work separately packaged, is reasonably priced.

Vienna State Opera: Volume 5 (1933–43): (i) Die Aegyptische Helena: excerpts; (ii) Daphne:

excerpts; (iii) Die Frau ohne Schatten: excerpts.
(M) (***) Koch Schwann mono 3-1455-2 (2) [id.]. V. State Op. O; with (i) Viorica Ursuleac, Franz Völker, Margit Bokor, Alfred Jerger, Helge Roswaenge, cond. Clemens Krauss; (ii) Maria Reining, Alf Rauch, Anton Dermota, cond. Rudolf Moralt; (iii) Torsten Ralf, Hilde Konetzni, Elisabeth Höngen, Josef Herrmann, Else Schulz, Herbert Alsen, Emmy Loose, Wenko Wenkoff; cond. Karl Boehm.

These excerpts from Die Aegyptische Helena from 1933 are conducted by Clemens Krauss, with Franz Völker superb but with Viorica Ursuleac rather raw in the title-role. The Daphne excerpts under Rudolf Moralt date from 1942, with Maria Reining below her best but with two excellent tenors, Alf Rauch as Apollo and the lyrical Anton Dermota as Leukippos. Central to this volume is the selection from Die Frau ohne Schatten under Karl Boehm, almost an hour and a half of excerpts with Torsten Ralf as the Emperor and Hilde Konetzni as the Empress, though Boehm went on to make two complete recordings of this opera with infinitely better sound. A fascinating pair of discs, just the same, in spite of the very primitive sound.

'Vienna State Opera Live': Volume 15: (i) Arabella: excerpts; (ii) Friedenstag: complete; (iii) Ariadne auf Naxos: excerpts.
(M) (**) Koch Schwann mono 3-1465-2 (2) [id.]. (i) Viorica Ursuleac, Margit Bokor, Alfred Jerger, Adele Kern, Gertrude Rünger, Richard Mayr; (ii) Hans Hotter, Ursuleac, Herbert Alsen, Josef Wit, Hermann Wiederman, Mela Bugarinovic; V. State Op. O; both cond. Clemens Krauss; (iii) Anny Konetzni, Sev Svanholm, Kern, Else Schulz, Jerger, Alexander Pichler, Alfred Muzzarelli; V. State Op. O, Rudolf Moralt.

Strauss's one-Act opera Friedenstag was first heard in 1938, barely a year before the outbreak of the Second World War. It ends in a triumphalist final ensemble which plainly roused the audience, and could well do the same in a modern performance. This is one of only two complete operas in the May Archive of Vienna State Opera recordings, and in one brief patch of 30 seconds the sound is totally submerged beneath the background noise, which remains heavy throughout. Happily, the voices generally come over well. Clemens Krauss, to whom the opera was dedicated, is a warmly responsive interpreter, drawing out the rich lyricism of this score, not least when his wife, the principal soprano, Viorica Ursuleac, is singing. Her monologues, as well as the duets with the heroine's husband, the Commandant of a besieged fortress, are the high points of the score.

It is also fascinating to have, on the first disc, four extracts from the first Vienna production of

Arabella, given only four months after the Dresden première, with the same principals and conductor, Krauss again. In 1933 Ursuleac is even warmer and firmer than in 1938, though the sound is even more seriously obscured by background noise. The *Ariadne* excerpts, recorded in 1941, are also valuable but even more frustrating, with the extracts fading in and out of big numbers at awkward moments. The casting too is flawed, with Anny Konetzni a fruity and none too steady Ariadne, Else Schulz shrill on top as the Composer, while the brilliant contribution of the Zerbinetta, Adele Kern, is undermined by suddenly distant recording.

Ariadne auf Naxos (complete).
(M) (*(**)) DG (IMS) 445 332-2 (2) [id.]. Della Casa, Gueden, Seefried, Schock, Schöffler, VPO, Boehm.

Boehm's affection for this elegant, touching score glows through the whole performance. Lisa della Casa is a poised, tender Ariadne, totally rapt in the final duet with Bacchus. Even though her later studio recordings of the *Lament* are more assured than this, the passion of the climax of that key solo is most involving. As in Karajan's studio recording, Irmgard Seefried as the Composer and Rudolf Schock as Bacchus have few equals; but what crowns the whole performance is the charming Zerbinetta of Hilde Gueden, not just warmly characterful but fuller-toned than almost any. The snag is the recording, fizzy in the orchestral sound, even the voices rather thinly recorded.

Capriccio (complete).
(M) **(*) DG 445 347-2 (2) [id.]. Janowitz, Troyanos, Schreier, Fischer-Dieskau, Prey, Ridderbusch, Bav. RSO, Karl Boehm.
**(*) Orfeo C 518 992 1 (2) [id.].
Tomowa-Sintow, Schöne, Büchner, Grundheber, Jungwirth, Schmidt, Ridder, Scarabelli, Ballo, Minth, VPO, Horst Stein.

In this elusive opera it is impossible to avoid comparison with Sawallisch's classic mono version with Schwarzkopf and Fischer-Dieskau. On DG, Gundula Janowitz is not as characterful and pointful a Countess as one really needs (and no match for Schwarzkopf), but Boehm lovingly directs a most beautiful performance of a radiant score, very consistently cast, beautifully sung and very well recorded for its period (1971). There is full documentation, including translation.

The Austrian Radio recording from Orfeo offers a warm, rich performance in satisfyingly full sound, made the more compelling for being taken live at a Salzburg Festival performance in August 1985. That was only three months before Tomowa-Sintow went on to record the closing scene from the opera with Herbert von Karajan and the Berlin Philharmonic. Though the live account may not be quite so flawless, Tomowa-Sintow sings with poise and

tenderness. As the culmination of this loveliest of Strauss operas, far more than just a conversation piece, it is if anything even more moving, with the rest of the cast making a strong team. Outstanding is Trudeliese Schmidt as the flamboyant actress Clairon, and Horst Stein is inspired by the beauty of the score to conduct with more passion than in studio recordings. Though the jewel-case promises German and English texts, no libretto is provided, only a detailed synopsis, a serious shortcoming in this of all operas with its complex interchanges.

Die Frau ohne Schatten.
(M) (**(*)) DG mono 457 678-2 (3). Leonie Rysanek, Grace Hoffman, Christa Ludwig, Jess Thomas, Walter Berry, Lucia Popp, Fritz Wunderlich, V. State Op. Ch. & O, Karajan.

In 1964, when he was still music director of the Vienna State Opera, Karajan presented a centenary tribute to Richard Strauss in a production of his most ambitious opera, and the composer's own favourite, *Die Frau ohne Schatten*. This recording from Austrian Radio captures the intensity of the occasion, with ecstatic applause for each of the Acts. With orchestral sound in mono thin and limited (a serious shortcoming in Strauss) the voices are paramount, with words made the clearer by the closeness. The cast is an outstanding one, with Leonie Rysanek powerful as the Empress and Jess Thomas exploiting his cleanly focused Heldentenor as the Emperor. The young Walter Berry is firmly commanding as Barak, the Dyer; and best of all is Christa Ludwig as the Dyer's Wife, here early in her career singing with a freshness and intensity that she retained in her later studio recording with Solti for Decca. The mono sound is limited, but with voices well caught. A good set at mid-price, though the usual stage-cuts are made in this epic score.

Friedenstag (complete).
*** EMI Dig. CDC5 56850-2 [id.]. Weikl, Hass, Rhyhänen, Moll, Bavarian State Op. Ch. & RSO, Sawallisch.

Friedenstag is one of the rarities in the Strauss discography and this is only its second modern recording. Long neglected but full of the ripest inspiration, *Friedenstag*, dating from 1936, is the odd-one-out among Strauss operas in having no love interest. What matters is the fervour of the writing, leading from the darkness of the opening to a final optimistic ensemble which aims at echoing the end of Beethoven's *Fidelio*. A first-rate version has long been needed, and this perfectly fills the bill. On a single disc, EMI offers a live recording of a superb performance conducted by Sawallisch in 1988. The opera is set in a besieged city on the last day of the Thirty Years War in 1648. Originally it was to be called *Friedensvertrag* or *Der westfälische Friede* and its anti-war sentiment is obvious! It was first given with Hans Hotter as the Commandant and Viorica Ursuleac as his wife Maria in 1938, and their partnership under Clemens Krauss survives from a recording made the following year – in Volume 15 of the Vienna State Opera Live Recordings (see above). This new EMI recording derives from a broadcast taken from the Staatsoper, Munich, with one of the greatest living Strauss conductors at the helm and a magnificent cast. The central character is the Commandant, whose dedication to war is total and unflinching, however futile the cause and whatever the cost. Bernd Weikl, singing nobly, is a superbly authoritative Commandant and Sabine Hass, in radiant voice, sings powerfully as Maria, whose attempts to dissuade her husband from his inflexibility and dedication to duty are affectingly portrayed. She tackles the role's cruel demands with apparently effortless ease. Kurt Moll, the Hollsteiner, Commander of the besieging army, has impressive dignity and eloquence. *Friedenstag* is half-oratorio, half-opera, whose dramatic action is of the simplest. The chorus is in impressive form and Sawallisch gets a first-class response from the fine Munich orchestra.

Der Rosenkavalier (complete).
**(*) DG Dig. 423 850-2 (3) [id.].
  Tomowa-Sintow, Baltsa, Moll, Perry, Hornik, VPO Ch. & O, Karajan.

Karajan's digital set brings few positive advantages, not even in recorded sound: for all the extra range of the modern recording, the focus is surprisingly vague, with the orchestra balanced too far behind the soloists. For the principal role Karajan chose Anna Tomowa-Sintow; the refinement and detail in her performance present an intimate view of the Marschallin, often very beautiful indeed, but both the darker and more sensuous sides of the character are muted. The Baron Ochs of Kurt Moll, firm, dark and incisive, is outstanding, and Agnes Baltsa as Octavian makes the lad tough and determined, if not always sympathetic. Janet Perry's Sophie, charming and pretty on stage, is too white and twittery of tone to give much pleasure.

Der Rosenkavalier (complete; remastered under direction of Schwarzkopf).
(M) (**(*)) EMI mono CMS5 56113-2 (3).
  Schwarzkopf, Ludwig, Stich-Randall, Edelmann, Philh. Ch. & O, Karajan.

It was at the urgent request of Schwarzkopf herself that this original mono version of Karajan's classic set of *Rosenkavalier* was transferred to CD in a remastering she herself approved. The main contrast with the stereo version – itself subject to several remasterings over the years – is that the voices are more sharply focused and, as it seems, more forwardly placed. One can understand Schwarzkopf's preference, but the orchestral sound in the stereo version is warmer, fuller and richer, and will certainly be preferred by the majority of collectors. But that is at premium price (CDS5 56242-2).

Salome (complete).
(M) *** RCA CD 86644 (2) [6644-2-RG].
  Caballé, Richard Lewis, Resnik, Milnes, LSO, Leinsdorf.
(M) **(*) DG (IMS) 445 319-2 (2) [id.]. Gwyneth Jones, Fischer-Dieskau, Dunn, Cassilly, Hamburg State Op. O, Boehm.

Montserrat Caballé's formidable account of the role of Salome was recorded in 1968, utterly different from that of Birgit Nilsson on Decca and much closer to the personification of Behrens on the Karajan set on EMI (both at full price). For some listeners Caballé might seem too gentle, but in fact the range of her emotions is even wider than that of Nilsson. There are even one or two moments of fantasy, where for an instant one has the girlish skittishness of Salome revealed like an evil inverted picture of Sophie. As for the vocalization, it is superb, with a glorious golden tone up to the highest register and never the slightest hesitation in attack. Lewis, Resnik and Milnes make a supporting team that matches the achievement of the Decca rivals, while Leinsdorf is inspired to some of his warmest and most sympathetic conducting on record.

In this violent opera Boehm conducts a powerful, purposeful performance which in its rhythmic drive and spontaneity is most compelling, not least in *Salome's dance*, which seems a necessary component rather than an inserted showpiece. Gwyneth Jones, though squally at times, is here at her most incisive, and her account of the final scene is chilling, above all when she drains her voice for the moment of pianissimo triumph, having kissed the dead lips of Jokanaan. Fischer-Dieskau characteristically gives a searchingly detailed, totally authoritative performance as John the Baptist: one believes in him as a prophet possessed. With Richard Cassilly as a powerful Herod, the rest of the cast is strong, making this a fair contender among live recordings.

Die schweigsame Frau (complete).
**(*) Orfeo stereo C 516 992 (2) [id.]. Böhme, Mödl, McDaniel, Kusche, Grobe, Grist, Schädle, Loulis, Peter, Proebstl, Bellgardt, Strauch, Horn, Schreiber, Bavarian State Ch. and O, Wolfgang Sawallisch.

Recorded live at the Bavarian State opera in July 1971, this performance consistently demonstrates the mastery of Sawallisch as a Strauss interpreter. The orchestral sound is atmospheric if rather thin, and stage noises are often intrusive, but one can still readily appreciate how perfectly Sawallisch paces this adaptation of Ben Jonson's *The Silent Woman* to bring out not just the humour and vigour but the beauty of the score. Reri Grist is a charming heroine, with the edge on her bright soprano making her the more compelling as a scold. Kurt Böhme right at the end of his long career sings most characterfully as the old man, Sir Morosus, with the supporting team consistently strong. An enjoyable alternative to Karl Boehm on DG and Marek Janowski on EMI, though only the latter (on three discs, not two) offers the score without cuts. Disappointingly, despite the promise of German, English and French texts, no libretto is provided, only a synopsis.

COLLECTIONS

'Strauss's heroines': Arabella, Act I: Duet. Capriccio: Moonlight music and closing scene. Der Rosenkavalier, Act I: closing scene, Act III, Trio and finale.
*** Decca Dig. 466 314-2 [id.]. Renée Fleming, Barbara Bonney, Susan Graham, Vienna PO, Eschenbach.

Under the title 'Strauss's heroines', this ravishing disc offers a generous collection of the most seductive scenes in the Strauss operas. In the end of Act I of Rosenkavalier, Renée Fleming and Susan Graham come near to matching the example of Elisabeth Schwarzkopf and Christa Ludwig as the Marschallin and Octavian. Then, sadly, the Act III Trio has Christoph Eschenbach opting for an absurdly sluggish speed, but the singing is superb, and so it is in the lovely duet between the sisters in Arabella and the magical closing scene of Capriccio, where Fleming is at her most moving. Opulent sound to match.

Stravinsky, Igor (1882–1971)

Agon (ballet; complete); Petrushka (ballet; 1911 score; complete); Fireworks.
(BB) **(*) Virgin Classics 2 x 1 Dig. VBD5 61754-2 (2) [id.]. Melbourne SO, Iwaki – BARTOK: Concerto for orchestra; Miraculous Mandarin (complete) **(*).

Readers searching our main volume will be surprised not to find a recording of Agon listed, apart from the composer's own version in Sony's Stravinsky Edition (SM3K 46292). It was written in the mid 1950s when Stravinsky was beginning to turn his attention to what had been anathema to him, serialism. There are already signs here of the developments in idiom which were to mark his last period. But, although on first hearing it is not easily cogent listening, it is worth persevering, for in every bar the bright focus of the argument with its distinctive orchestral colourings is immediately identifiable as the work of Stravinsky. We hope that Decca have plans to reissue David Atherton's sharp-edged performance with the London Sinfonietta. Meanwhile, as part of a two-for-one Virgin Double, this Melbourne performance is a very acceptable

stopgap, atmospheric and very well played and recorded. As with the coupled Bartók, the reading lacks bite and dash, though remains aurally fascinating. Petrushka is crisply colourful, vividly dramatic and spontaneously enjoyable. Both ballets are generously cued and Fireworks acts as an effervescent encore.

Le baiser de la fée (Divertimento).
(M) *** RCA 09026 61957-2 [id.]. Chicago SO, Reiner – HOVHANESS: Mysterious Mountain symphony ***; PROKOFIEV: Lieutenant Kijé (suite) ***.

A delightful performance of Le baiser de la fée from Reiner: the playing has character and life, as well as charm, and the Pas de deux is beautifully done. The overall performance has great atmosphere, with distinguished woodwind and brass contributions, helped by the astonishingly realistic 1958 Chicago recording (accepting a bit of tape hiss).

(i) Le baiser de la fée (Divertimento); Danses concertantes; (ii) Dumbarton Oaks concerto in E flat for chamber orchestra; (ii) Scherzo à la russe; (iii) 2 Etudes for piano, Op. 7/2 & 4.
(*(*)) Pearl mono GEMCD 0065 [id.]. (i) RCA Victor SO, (ii) Dumbarton Oaks Fest. O, Igor Stravinsky; (iii) Soulima Stravinsky.

These recordings were all made in 1947 (although Soulima Stravinsky also recorded the two Etudes in Paris a year earlier). They never appeared in Britain at the time and they do not wear their years lightly, for the sound is very thin and wanting in body. The Dumbarton Oaks concerto is splendidly played, the orchestral personnel include the likes of Alexander Schneider and Bernard Greenhouse, and the performance of the Danses concertantes has lots of personality. A valuable document, but given the dry, top-heavy sound, of specialist rather than general interest.

Le baiser de la fée (Divertimento); Jeu de cartes.
(BB) * Arte Nova Dig. 74321 63643-2 [id.]. Giuseppe Verdi SO of Milan, Alun Francis.

This is a curate's egg of a disc, with a deeply disappointing account of the three movements of Jeu de cartes – totally lacking the bite and rhythmic spring needed for Stravinsky's neoclassical ballet score – coupled to an amiable reading of Le baiser de la fée. Although the playing is still not as incisive as it might be, there is much feeling here for Stravinsky's echoing of Tchaikovsky melodies, despite rather thin violin sound. Otherwise the recording, set in a relatively intimate acoustic, is warm and immediate.

Le chant du rossignol; Feux d'artifice; Petrushka (original version).
*** RCA Dig. 74321 57127-2 [id.]. VPO, Maazel.

It was the orchestral brilliance of *Feux d'artifice* (1908) that alerted Diaghilev to the presence of a young Russian composer of great originality and talent. The result was commissions for the Ballets Russes of *Petrushka* (1911) and *Le chant du rossignol* (1920), the latter arranged from Stravinsky's opera, *Le Rossignol*. Maazel first recorded *Le chant*, with the Berlin Radio Orchestra, at the beginning of his career in 1958. Its rich palette glows even more vividly in the Musikverein, with the players of the Vienna Philharmonic sounding unexpectedly at home in its exotic chinoiserie. The closing scene portraying the illness and death of the Emperor is marvellously evoked and very affecting. The VPO playing is hardly less brilliant in the other works, with *Petrushka* vividly dramatic yet affectionately detailed by Maazel. Once again it is the closing tableau which is the most memorable, taken fairly briskly and arrestingly involving at the appearance of Petrushka's ghost. The recording has a touch of fierceness in fortissimos (not out of place in Stravinsky), but otherwise is often of demonstration standard, especially in *Le chant*, where the atmospheric three-dimensional sound picture creates an uncanny ambient depth and definition. This is one of Maazel's finest records for some time and his brilliant account of *Feux d'artifice* brings a prophetic anticipation of the composer's later works.

Violin concerto.
*** EMI Dig. CDC5 56966-2 [id.]. Maxim Vengerov, LSO, Rostropovich – SHCHEDRIN: *Concerto cantabile*; TCHAIKOVSKY: *Sérénade mélancolique.* ***

A brilliant, biting account of Stravinsky's concerto from the symbiotic Russian partnership of Vengerov and Rostropovich, which admirably catches the work's wide range of mood, rhythm and colour, with its genial opening *Toccata* giving way to touchingly spare Stravinskian lyricism in the central *Arias*, and the superbly spiky *Capriccio* capping a reading of remarkable imaginative range. The brightness of the recording gives plenty of edge to the solo projection, yet the balance ensures that the orchestral detail makes the strongest impression. A *tour de force*.

(i) *Concerto for piano and wind. Danses concertantes;* (ii) *Pulcinella* (ballet; complete); (iii) *3 Pieces for clarinet solo; Pour Pablo Picasso.*
*** Koch Dig. 3 7470-2. (i) Misha Dichter, 20th Century Classics Ens.; (ii) Diana Montague, Robin Leggate, Mark Beesley, Philh. O; (i; ii) Robert Craft; (iii) Charles Neidich.

This delightful collection of Stravinsky works written between 1917 and 1942 completely gives the lie to the idea that Robert Craft, the composer's amanuensis, is a chilly interpreter. This is a delectably pointed and witty account of the complete *Pulcinella ballet*, beautifully played by the Philharmonia. Excellent solo singing, though Robin Leggate's tenor is too dry. The other items were recorded in America, with sound less immediate, though the rhythmic spring of the *Danses concertantes* and of the *Concerto*, with Dichter a fine soloist, is comparably infectious. The unaccompanied clarinet works include a 23-second fragment never recorded before, written over dinner with Picasso, when the composer was drunk.

The Firebird; The Rite of spring (complete ballets).
(B) *** Decca Penguin Classics 460 644-2 [id.]. Detroit SO, Dorati.

Dorati's Detroit version of *The Firebird* has the benefit of spectacular digital recording. The clarity and definition of dark, hushed passages are amazing, with the contra-bassoon finely focused, never sounding woolly or obscure, while string tremolos down to the merest whisper are uncannily precise. There is plenty of space round woodwind solos, and only the concertmaster's violin is spotlit. The performance is very precise, too; though Dorati's reading has changed little from his previous versions with London orchestras, there is just a little more caution. Individual solos are not so characterful and *Katschei's dance* lacks just a degree in excitement; but overall this is a strong and beautiful reading, even if the Mercury LP account, an electrifying example of 1960s analogue engineering, is not entirely superseded.

Similarly, in terms of recorded sound, Dorati's *Rite* with the Detroit orchestra scores over almost all its rivals. This has stunning clarity and presence, exceptionally lifelike and vivid sound, and the denser textures emerge more cleanly than ever before. It is a very good performance too, almost but not quite in the same league as those of Karajan and Muti, generating plenty of excitement. The only let-down is the final *Sacrificial dance*, which needs greater abandon and higher voltage. Nor are the Detroit strings as sumptuous as those of the Berlin orchestra, sounding distinctly undernourished in places. Yet too much should not be made of this. Although Dorati does not match the atmosphere of his finest rivals, the performance is so vivid that it belongs among the very best. Its release on Penguin Classics makes it an undoubted bargain. The personal essay is by Philip Hensher.

'Stravinsky in Moscow 1962': Orpheus (ballet suite); *Petrushka* (ballet suite); *Fireworks; Ode* (elegiac chant); *Song of the Volga boatmen* (arr. for wind and percussion).
(M) ** BMG/Melodiya 74321 33220-2 [id.]. Moscow PO or USSR SO, composer (with speech of thanks).

An issue of special historic interest in that it recorded Stravinsky's return to his native country in his eightieth year for the first time after the Revolution. The performances have a sense of occasion. The *Petrushka* starts just before the *Russian dance*, omits the whole of the Third Tableau and abruptly cuts short the Fourth, with the concert ending; it lasts eighteen and a half minutes. Stravinsky takes brisk (some might say headlong) tempi, and the impression is of the orchestra taking plenty of risks and playing to the very limits of their ability. The Moscow Philharmonic are pretty rough-and-ready and there is some coarse brass-tone. Nor is the *Orpheus* with the USSR Symphony Orchestra among the most idiomatic of performances. The 1917 arrangement of the *Song of the Volga boatmen* for wind and percussion is more effective. There is a short word of thanks from Stravinsky, and all devotees of the composer will want to have this memento of a historic occasion.

(i) *Petrushka* (1947 score); (ii) *Pulcinella* (suite)
**(*) Testament SBT 1156 [id.]. (i) New Philh O;
    (ii) Philh. O; Klemperer

Following a concert performance in 1967, Klemperer insisted on recording *Petrushka*. Though it was outside his usual repertory at that time, he had kept an admiration for Stravinsky's score from his adventurous days in Berlin in the 1920s. After three days of recording sessions EMI initially edited together a finished copy that was rejected. What Stewart Brown of Testament has done is to investigate the original tapes, and put together a recording drawn from the first day's sessions instead of the third – sharper and more intense. The result is a fascinating version, strong and symphonic rather than atmospheric, and magnetic from first to last. Vivid recording, full of presence. The *Pulcinella suite* of four years earlier has already appeared on CD, an attractively fresh performance, not quite as biting as that of *Petrushka*.

Petrushka (ballet; complete 1947 version); *The Rite of spring. Circus polka.*
(B) ** Australian Decca Eloquence 460 509-2.
    LAPO, Mehta.

Mehta's Los Angeles *Rite of spring*, despite extreme tempi, some very fast, others slow, is an interesting and individual reading, very well recorded. *Petrushka* is superbly played, but lacks the character of the finest versions. What makes it compelling, in its way, is the astonishingly brilliant recording, which startlingly brings the Los Angeles orchestra into your sitting room. The *Circus polka* makes a sparkling bonus, but this CD is primarily recommendable to audiophiles.

The Rite of spring (complete)
(M) **(*) DG 463 613-2 [id.]. BPO, Karajan –
    PROKOFIEV: *Symphony No. 5* ***.
(M) (**) Dutton Lab. mono CDK 1206 [id.].
    Concg. O, Eduard van Beinum – BARTOK:
    Concerto for orchestra (***) ❀.

Karajan's approach may have excitement but, next to other more extrovert accounts, it sounds a bit too smooth and civilized. His attention to detail is striking, but at the expense of sheer elemental strength, though it is interesting to hear such a sophisticated reading of this score. The recording is technically outstanding, with its vivid projection counteracting the high degree of reverberation. Not a top recommendation, but an interesting performance with integrity, which will not disappoint Karajan admirers, and those coming new to it will certainly see the work in a different light. The Prokofiev coupling is outstanding in every way.

This Decca version conducted by Eduard van Beinum was the first *Rite of Spring* to appear in Europe after the war, when Stravinsky's own set on five 78s, and Stokowski's on four, still held sway. The sound is pretty remarkable for its period and shows how far ahead the Decca engineers were in 1946. The performance was never reissued on LP as by then Ansermet's first version had superseded it. In terms of orchestral virtuosity the Concertgebouw was vastly superior but the overall impression is not as exciting as the astonishing Bartók with which it is coupled.

The Rite of spring; (i) *The Firebird* (suite; 1919 score).
(M) **(*) Sony SMK 60694 [id.]. LSO (i) NYPO;
    Bernstein.

Bernstein's *Rite* (1972) was recorded with quadraphonic 'surround sound' in mind, and E.G. well remembers the complex arrangement of the orchestral players situated at all points of the compass. The sessions were not particularly easy, but at the eleventh hour Bernstein decided just to play the whole work through, and the result – more or less the performance released – sounded far more spontaneous than the takes they had spent three days working on. Although it does not have the pinpoint precision of some other versions, the electric intensity is never in doubt. Bernstein is more consciously romantic in expressiveness than is common, but conveys the illusion of a live performance – it was this recording which convinced him of the advantages of recording live from then on. It still makes an impact on CD, but is not in the demonstration bracket. The *Firebird suite* (1957) is in most ways better recorded: more open, better defined and with rather greater depth. It is an exciting performance but lacks atmosphere.

Symphony in 3 movements.
(M) *** EMI CDM5 67337-2 [id.]. Philh. O,
    Klemperer – HINDEMITH: *Nobilissima visione;*
    WEILL: *Kleine Dreigroschenmusik* *** (with
    KLEMPERER: *Merry waltz* **).

Klemperer is not thought of as an advocate of twentieth-century music, but he greatly admired Stravinsky and he gave Berlin premieres of many of that composer's works, including *Apollo, Les Noces*, the *Capriccio* (with the composer as soloist) and the *Symphony of Psalms*. It was Stravinsky himself who conducted the first performance of the *Symphony in three movements* in New York in 1946, but Klemperer introduced the work to Los Angeles a year later.

With superb playing from the Philharmonia and a strong rhythmic pulse in the outer movements, this is a highly stimulating performance, which does not miss the work's balletic associations, while the Stravinskian subtleties of mood, colour and balance in the central movement are astutely caught. The recording has fine bloom and excellent detail.

Symphony in 3 movements; Symphonies of wind instruments; (i) *Symphony of psalms.*
**(*) DG Dig. 457 616-2 [id.]. BPO, Pierre Boulez; (i) with Berlin R. Ch.

It may seem an odd conjunction having the incisively intellectual Pierre Boulez recording Stravinsky with the orchestra over which the composer had serious doubts as an interpreter of his music (as he wittily put it, 'not out of their depth but in my shallows'). The results are refined rather than biting, at least in the *Symphony of psalms* and *Wind symphonies*, where Boulez's restraint combined with beautifully moulded ensemble gives way to dramatic power only at key climaxes. The poignancy of the *Wind symphonies* is reinforced, and the beauty of the *Symphony of Psalms* culminates in a glowing account of the final apotheosis, one of Stravinsky's most sublime inspirations. The chorus sounds relatively recessed until the climaxes, where there is no lack of power. The *Symphony in three movements* brings a more violent approach, with the Berliners relishing the jazzy outbursts of the outer movements and the warmth of the central slow movement. An unexpected but revelatory disc. Refined recording to match.

CHAMBER MUSIC

Ballad; Chanson russe; Danse russe; Divertimento; Duo concertante; Pastorale; Suite italienne.
*** Chandos Dig. CHAN 9756 [id.]. Lydia Mordkovitch, Julian Milford.

Lydia Mordkovich, truly Russian, defies the idea of Stravinsky as a cold composer, finding radiant intensity even in the neoclassical *Duo concertante*, notably in the lovely final *Dithyrambe*. This was a work Stravinsky wrote for himself to play with the violinist Samuel Dushkin, and the other pieces, all lighter, are arrangements he also made for their recitals, based on some of his most approachable works. So the ballets *Pulcinella* and *The Fairy's kiss* prompted respectively the *Suite italienne* and the *Divertimento*, while the other shorter pieces

culminate here in a fizzing account of the *Danse russe* from *Petrushka*.

VOCAL MUSIC

Symphony of Psalms (1948 version).
(B) *** Sony SBK 61703 [id.]. English Bath Festival Ch., LSO, Bernstein – ORFF: *Catulli Carmina* **(*).

Bernstein's *Symphony of Psalms* ranks among the finest ever recorded, though his view of the work is not as austere and ascetic as the composer's own. Yet there is grandeur and a powerful sense of atmosphere as well as first-class singing and playing from the chorus and orchestra. The recording is distinguished by clarity and range, and with few recommendable alternatives available this is an essential purchase for all Stravinskians.

OPERA

The Rake's progress (complete).
**(*) Decca Dig. 411 644-2 (2) [id.]. Langridge, Pope, Walker, Ramey, Dean, Dobson, L. Sinf. Ch. & O, Chailly.

Riccardo Chailly draws from the London Sinfonietta playing of a clarity and brightness to set the piece aptly on a chamber scale without reducing the power of this elaborately neo-classical work. Philip Langridge is excellent as the Rake himself, very moving when Tom is afflicted with madness. Samuel Ramey as Nick, Stafford Dean as Trulove and Sarah Walker as Baba the Turk are all first rate, but Cathryn Pope's soprano as recorded is too soft-grained for Anne. Charming as the idea is of getting the veteran Astrid Varnay to sing Mother Goose, the result is out of style. The recording is exceptionally full and vivid but the balances are sometimes odd: the orchestra recedes behind the singers and the chorus sounds congested, with little air round the sound.

(i) *Le Rossignol* (complete); (ii) *Renard* (histoire burlesque).
*** EMI Dig. CDC5 56874-2 [id.]. Paris Nat. Opéra Ch. & O, Conlon; (i) Natalie Dessay, Marie McLaughlin, Violeta Urmana, Albert Schagidullin; (i; ii) Vsevolod Grivnov, Laurent Naouri, Maxime Mikhailov; (ii) Ian Caley. Naouri, Maxime Mikhailov.

Stravinsky's early opera, *Le Rossignol*, in three compact acts, is a problematic work, and Conlon here provides a near-ideal reading, one which defies the contradiction between the first act, written before *The Firebird*, in a style like Debussy with a Russian accent, and the other two acts, written after *The Rite of spring*, when Stravinsky's style had entered a new world. Evocative and atmospheric in Act 1, the work is then transformed into something far more tautly dramatic, even while its Russian roots are still clear. Natalie Dessay with her bright soprano is very well suited to the role of the Nightingale, with the tenor Vsevolod Grivnov producing honeyed tones as the Fisherman who acts as commentator. Warm playing and singing from the whole company. The relatively brief burlesque *Renard* brings a performance just as committed, though it lacks the rustic bite and bluff humour that ideally are needed. Warm sound to match.

Suk, Josef (1874–1935)

Asrael Symphony, Op. 27.
(***) Sup. mono 11 1902-2 (2) [id.]. Czech PO,
     Talich (with DVORAK: *Stabat Mater* (*)).

Václav Talich's pioneering mono account from the early 1950s has great intensity of utterance and poignancy and provides a link with the composer himself. Talich knew him well and conducted many Suk premières. The sound is very acceptable for the period, and it is a pity that it comes harnessed to a less successful Dvořák *Stabat Mater*.

(i) *Epilogue, Op. 37; A Fairy tale, Op. 16.*
*** Virgin Classics Dig. VC5 45245-2 [id.]. (i)
     Luba Orgonasova, Iván Kusnjer, Peter
     Mikulás; Royal Liverpool PO & (i) Ch., Libor
     Pešek.

The *Epilogue,* for soprano, baritone, bass, large and small mixed choruses and orchestra, occupied Suk for the bulk of the 1920s. It is a big piece, taking some 40 minutes. Suk spoke of it as the last part of a cycle, beginning with *Asrael* and 'going through the whole of human life, into reflection on death and the dread of it', before the appearance of the song of earthly love – all this leading up to the 'exhilarating song of liberated mankind'. It is a powerful and eloquent summation of his work, and Pešek gets very fine results from his Liverpool forces. There is a fine account of *A Fairy tale* as a generous makeweight. Excellent recording and very good notes from John Tyrrell.

Fairy-tale suite.
(**) Biddulph mono WHL 048 [id.]. Czech PO,
     Václav Talich – DVORAK: *Symphony No. 9
     (New World); Polonaises* (**).

The four movements of the *Fairy-tale suite* were recorded in 1940, only five years after the composer's death. Talich was a friend of Suk, and conveys its character with great poignancy and warmth. The sound is very acceptable given its period, and the disc is worth having for this piece alone.

Serenade for strings in E flat, Op. 6.
(BB) *** Virgin Classics 2 x 1 Dig. VBD5
     61763-2 (2) [CDVB 61763]. LCO, Christopher
     Warren-Green – DVORAK: *Serenade for
     strings in E, Op. 22*; ELGAR: *Introduction and*

allegro; Serenade; TCHAIKOVSKY: *Serenade*;
VAUGHAN WILLIAMS: *Fantasia on
Greensleeves; Fantasia on a theme of Tallis;
Lark ascending.* ***

Warren-Green and his LCO give a wonderfully persuasive account of Suk's *Serenade*, making obvious that its inspiration is every bit as vivid as in the comparable work of Dvořák. The recording, made in All Saints', Petersham, is fresh, full and natural without blurring from the ecclesiastical acoustic. This now comes as part of an incredibly generous Virgin Double, one of the most desirable bargain collections of string music in the catalogue.

A Summer tale, Op. 29; A Winter's tale, Op. 9.
(BB) **(*) Naxos Dig. 8.553703 [id.]. Slovak
     RSO, Andrew Mogrelia.

Good, very musical performances with fine sound to boot. The Slovak Orchestra are not the equal of the Czech Philharmonic but they produce eminently decent results. This is lovely music and the performances are enjoyable and well worth the modest outlay.

Sullivan, Arthur (1842–1900)

*Symphony in E (Irish); Imperial march; Overture
in C (In Memoriam); Victoria and Merrie England
suite.*
** CPO Dig. CPO 999 171-2 [id.]. BBC Concert
     O, Owain Arwel Hughes.

Sullivan's *Irish Symphony* is a pleasing work, lyrical, with echoes of Schumann as much as the more predictable Mendelssohn and Schubert. The jaunty *Allegretto* of the third movement with its 'Irish' tune on the oboe is nothing less than haunting. On CPO, the first movement obstinately refuses to take off and, as Hughes observes the exposition repeat, its 16 minutes' length seems like a lifetime. The other movements are rather more successful, but in almost every way this performance is inferior to the excellent EMI/Groves version (currently withdrawn). The other items here pass muster, with the ballet suite easily the most enjoyable item, especially the finale, *May Day festivities*, which might well have been an undiscovered interlude from *The Yeomen of the Guard.*

Cox and Box (original full-length 1866 version).
*** Divine Arts 2-4104 [id.]. Leon Berger, Ian
     Kennedy, Donald Francke, Kenneth Barclay.

Cox and Box was Sullivan's first operetta – without Gilbert – using a libretto by F. C. Burnand, which he adapted from his own play with its title 'Box and Cox' reversed. This lively and enjoyable performance re-creates the original version of *Cox and Box*, first heard at a private gathering at Burnand's own house in May 1866, with Sullivan himself improvising the accompaniment at the piano. The

orchestration came a year later for the work's prè-
miere at the Adelphi Theatre, and the Overture and
the duet *Stay Bouncer stay* were also subsequently
added. The piece moved to another venue and was to
enjoy a successful extended run, opening in March
1869 and continuing for nearly 300 performances.

The present account (based on a professional
production for London Chamber Opera) is spirited
and polished, and will be an essential purchase
for all Savoyards, although its considerable length
(over an hour) serves to demonstrate the reasons for
Sullivan's own shortened version in 1894. It was
further truncated in 1921 by Harry Norris and J. M.
Gordon (Musical and Stage Directors of the D'Oyly
Carte Company at that time) to produce the excellent concise version which remained in the D'Oyly
Carte Company's repertoire until the late 1970s.
This can be heard (in harness with *Ruddigore*)
splendidly sung and acted by Alan Styler, Joseph
Riordan, with Donald Adams an irrepressible
Bouncer, on Decca 417 355-2 (see our main
volume).

However, the performance on the present disc is
most enjoyable and does not outstay its welcome.
Donald Francke is a splendidly rumbustious
Bouncer – his first *Rataplan* with its vigorous laugh
raises an immediate smile. Also included is the
charming original compound-time version of the
Bacon lullaby, considerably different from the song
known in the revised score. *Stay Bouncer stay* is
added in for good measure. Of course, one misses
the orchestra, but the piano accompaniment, using
a suitable period instrument, is well managed. The
dialogue is recorded in a drier acoustic than the
music, but one soon adjusts to this, and (although a
full text is provided) words are admirably clear, a
consideration which would surely have been just as
important to Burnand as to Gilbert. It is good to see
that the production is dedicated to the memory of
the late Arthur Jacobs, biographer of Sullivan, at
whose insistence this recording (sponsored by the
Sullivan Society) was issued commercially.

Cox and Box; (i) *Trial by Jury.*
Polygram Video 632 5203. Soloists, Ambrosian
  Op. Ch., LSO, Alexander Faris; (i) with
  Frankie Howard.

The principal interest of this video is the casting of
Frankie Howard, hamming it up as the Judge in
Trial by Jury. Although his delivery of the musical
numbers leaves much to be desired, aficionados
may enjoy his contribution, for the rest of the cast
is good, and the Ambrosian Chorus excellent. *Cox
and Box*, however, is a non starter. Apart from a lack
of pace, the stage producer has brought superfluous
extraneous characters into the action, so that a
chorus can be included at the end, which Sullivan
did not write. The video also features background
information about the making of the video, which
few would wish to see more than once (if that)!

HMS Pinafore.
⬤ *** Telarc Dig. CD 80774 [id.]. Suart, Allen,
  Evans, Schade, Palmer, Adams, Ch. & O of
  Welsh Nat. Opera, Mackerras.

The Mikado.
⬤ *** Telarc Dig. CD 80284 [id.]. Adams, Rolfe
  Johnson, Suart, McLaughlin, Palmer, Van
  Allan, Folwell, Ch. & O of Welsh Nat. Opera,
  Mackerras.

The Pirates of Penzance.
*** Telarc Dig. CD80353 [id.]. Mark Ainsley,
  Evans, Suart, Van Allan, Adams, Knight, Ch.
  & O of Welsh Nat. Opera, Mackerras.

(i) *The Yeomen of the Guard;* (ii) *Trial by Jury.*
*** Telarc Dig. 2CD 809404 (2) [id.]. (i) Mellor,
  Archer, Palmer; (i; ii) Suart, Adams, Maxwell;
  (ii) Evans, Banks, Savidge; Ch. & O of Welsh
  Nat. Opera, Mackerras.

*HMS Pinafore; The Mikado; The Pirates of
Penzance; Trial by Jury; The Yeomen of the
Guard.*
⬤ (M)*** Telarc Dig. CD 80500 (5) [id.]. Above
  five complete recordings cond. Mackerras.

Although it was issued in 1993, we have not previously discussed the Mackerras version of *The
Pirates of Penzance*. It is characteristic of the rest
of this splendid Telarc series that by cutting the
overture and little else (as with the other key
operas), the whole opera, without dialogue, has
been fitted onto a single CD. Mackerras's exuberant
direction often brings fast tempi (as in *How beautifully blue the sky*) but the underlying lyricism is as
ardently conveyed as ever, especially by John Mark
Ainsley, who is a really passionate Frederic.
Rebecca Evans makes him a good partner and sings
with great charm as Mabel. Their duet, *O leave me
not to pine alone*, is a highlight. Needless to say
Richard Suart is a memorable Major General (his
patter song is thrown off at great speed) and Donald
Adams has not lost his touch. His vintage portrayal
of the Pirate King is well matched by Gillian
Knight's Ruth in their engaging 'Paradox' duet of
Act II. While memories of Owen Brannigan are far
from banished, Richard van Allan is a suitably
bumptious Sergeant of the Police, and the Welsh
Opera Chorus are splendidly fervent in *Hail poetry!*
The recording has fine depth and realism; the overall
effect is less brilliant than the Decca D'Oyly Carte
series. The Decca set (which also features Donald
Adams, plus Valerie Masterson as a gracefully winsome Mabel) remains treasurable (425 196-2), for
it also includes the dialogue. But as a single-disc
modern digital version this will be hard to beat.

As can be seen, the five Telarc operas also now
come together in a slip-case, with the five CDs
offered for the cost of three – in every way a superb
bargain.

(i) *HMS Pinafore;* (ii) *The Pirates of Penzance* (both complete, without dialogue).
(***) Romophone mono 89002-2 (2) [id.]. (i) Henry Lytton, George Baker, Charles Goulding, Elsie Griffin, Bertha Lewis, Darrell Fancourt, Ch. & LSO; (ii) Peter Dawson, George Baker, Derek Oldham, Elsie Griffin, Leo Sheffield, Dorothy Gill, Ch. & Light Op. O; Dr Malcolm Sargent.

These were the first electrical recordings of the *Pirates* and *Pinafore*, recorded in 1929 and 1930 respectively. They are clearly and cleanly remastered and expertly transferred to CD by Mark Olbert-Thorn, with a minimum of background noise, and give considerable pleasure, for the words are very clear. But what is astonishing is the slackness of ensemble, not only with the pick-up chorus (immediately noticeable in *We sail the ocean blue* at the opening of *Pinafore*) but more remarkably in the concerted numbers from the principals. Obviously in that early part of his career, Dr Sargent was not the stickler for polish that he was later to become.

The cast lists here include principals who were not established D'Oyly Carte singers, notably Peter Dawson as a stirring Pirate King, and George Baker, an excellent Major-General, who was later to participate in the HMV stereo recordings, yet never became a member of the company. Derek Oldham, who did, portrays Frederic with rather dated, slightly 'posh vowels', yet makes the climax of *Pirates*, with its Gilbertian paradox, more dramatically like grand opera than usual, and in this Elsie Griffin's touching Mabel gives him fine support. (*O leave me not to pine alone* is most delicately done.) Leo Sheffield, another company stalwart, gives a curiously low-key portrayal of the Sergeant of the Police, even adding embellishments to his famous solo.

HMS Pinafore is dominated by a vintage performance from Sir Henry Lytton (who was knighted while this recording was being made). Vocally acidulous, his gaunt portrayal of a sparsely timbred Sir Joseph Porter is very much that of an old man, less humorously sympathetic than usual. This makes the resolution of the plot the more telling, especially as Charles Goulding as Ralph, and Elsie Griffin as Josephine, make a highly sympathetic pair of lovers. George Baker is again on form as the Captain, and that greatest of Savoyards, Darrell Fancourt, makes his sinister mark as Dick Deadeye. Bertha Lewis is a particularly pleasing Buttercup, singing freshly with *mezzo* colouring: no wonder the Captain thought of her so affectionately as 'a plump and pleasing person'. (The cast list, incidentally, reveals the name of the character as a widowed Mrs Cripps.) While it is a pity that it was never HMV policy to use all D'Oyly Carte principals in the recording studio, one still has a sense of history

when enjoying these spirited performances, for all their continued lapses when voices fail to stay together, or (as in the case of the Major-General's patter-song) with the orchestra.

(i) *The Merchant of Venice (Masquerade); Henry VIII* (incidental music): suite. *Overture: The Sapphire necklace; Overture in C (In Memoriam).*
** Marco Polo Dig. 8.223461 [id.]. RTE Concert O, Dublin, Andrew Penny; (i) with Emmanuel Lawler.

We have had both the rather inflated but at times quite engaging *In Memoriam overture* and excerpts from Sullivan's incidental music for *The Merchant of Venice* before. But here is a more extended suite *Merchant of Venice* which includes a solo tenor *Barcarolle* with a strong flavour of *The Gondoliers*. There are plenty of good ideas here, and nice orchestral touches, and a grand G&S-style finale to round things off spiritedly. The *Henry VIII* incidental music opens with regal trumpet fanfares and the scoring is well laced with brass (which made it popular on the bandstand) but it is also notable for a pleasing tenor contribution, *King Henry's song* (well sung here by Emmanuel Lawler). The *Sapphire necklace overture* is a re-arrangement of the military band score. The piece is well constructed and has a rumbustious ending, but it would have been more effective had it been shorter. It is much more redolent of the Savoy Theatre than of Covent Garden. Andrew Penny secures lively, well-played performances throughout; but in the last resort this is a disc for curious Sullivan fans rather than for the general collector.

COLLECTIONS

'The best of Gilbert and Sullivan': highlights from *The Gondoliers; HMS Pinafore; Iolanthe; The Mikado; Patience; The Pirates of Penzance; Ruddigore; Trial by Jury; The Yeomen of the Guard.*
(B) *** EMI CZS5 73869-2 (3) [id.]. Elsie Morison, Monica Sinclair, Marjorie Thomas, George Baker, Richard Lewis, Owen Brannigan, Alexander Young, Ian Wallace, John Cameron, Sir Geraint Evans, James Milligan, Glyndebourne Festival Ch., Pro Arte O, Sargent.

This three-disc EMI set makes a good supplement for the comparable Double Decca collection called appropriately *'The very best of Gilbert and Sullivan'* (❀ 460 010-2), to which we give the highest praise in our main volume. The Sargent recordings are generally more grandly operatic in style and at times they are rather less fun. But, as might expect from the starry cast list, there is some outstandingly fine solo and concerted singing from the principals in the lyrical numbers.

Obviously with the film *Topsy-Turvy* in mind, the

major selection is from *The Mikado* (some twenty items), and Sargent's expansive manner has much in common with Carl David's approach (especially in the Finale). With Owen Brannigan as The Mikado, Monica Sinclair as Katisha, Richard Lewis as Nanki-Poo, Elsie Morison as Yum-Yum and Ian Wallace as Pooh Bah, the results will surely please those who enjoyed the movie.

Princess Ida and *The Sorcerer* are not represented, but the other key operas (apart from the single Learned Judge's number from *Trial by Jury*) have from between five to eight items each, including the substantial and treasurable finales from *Iolanthe* and (to conclude the programme) *The Yeomen of the Guard*. Besides taking the role of the Judge in *Trial*, George Baker is a stalwart of the series, skilfully portraying the Lord Chancellor (*Iolanthe*), Sir Joseph Porter, KCB (*Pinafore*), Major General Stanley (*Pirates*), and Bunthorne (*Patience*), and he delivers the famous patter songs with aplomb.

No less than Sir Geraint Evans takes his place as the Duke of Plaza-Toro (*Gondoliers*), and Jack Point (*Yeomen*). Owen Brannigan is an unforgettable Sergeant of Police (*Pirates*), and is hardly less memorable as Private Willis (*Iolanthe*), and Sir Despard (*Ruddigore*). The choral contribution is first class, and Sir Malcolm Sargent conducts freshly throughout, although not always with the sparkle that Godfrey commanded, as is instanced by his curiously measured *Cachucha* in *The Gondoliers*. But the selections from *Patience* and *Ruddigore* show him and this talented company (Elsie Morison especially) at their very finest.

'The best of Gilbert and Sullivan': excerpts from: *The Gondoliers; HMS Pinafore; Iolanthe; The Mikado; Patience; The Pirates of Penzance; The Yeomen of the Guard.*
(M) **(*) Sony Dig. SMK 89248 [id.]. Soloists, D'Oyly Carte Opera Company Ch. & O, John Owen Edwards or John Pryce-Jones.

Intended as a companion selection to *Topsy-Turvy* below, these present-day D'Oyly Carte recordings have plenty of life and vigour. Indeed, both conductors favour very brisk tempi, and often there is a sense that the music is being driven very hard, with the *Tripping thither* chorus in *Iolanthe* rhythmically almost over-pointed. Simon Butteriss's *Am I alone and unobserved* is very dramatic indeed, but this certainly gives the number a fresh impetus. There is plenty of good singing, and among the other principals Richard Suart does not disappoint in the Lord Chancellor's patter songs in *Iolanthe* and in *From the sunny Spanish shore* from the *Gondoliers*. Eric Robertson takes over effectively as the Major-General, and Eric Rogers is an engaging Ko-Ko for *Tit-willow* in *The Mikado*. Marilyn Hill-Smith's *Poor wandr'ing one* is pleasingly fresh and Donald Maxwell provides a military zest for his two

numbers in *Patience*. The disc is generously full, but each selection is rather meagre. *The Yeomen of the Guard* only has two items, and the second, *Here's a man of jollity*, cuts off rather suddenly. Better to have omitted the two overtures (beautifully played as they are) and perhaps to have concentrated on fewer operas and offered more music from each. Still this is all enjoyable enough and vividly recorded.

'Topsy-Turvy' (music from the film soundtrack, with interludes arr. Carl Davis): includes excerpts from: *The Grand Duke* (orchestral only); *The Mikado; Princess Ida; The Sorcerer; The Yeomen of the Guard; The Lost chord; The Long day closes* (arr. Davis).
**(*) Sony Dig. SK 61834 [id.]. Soloists Ch. & O, Carl Davis.

Mike Leigh's film *Topsy-Turvy* was a personal indulgence. He grew up with his childhood regularly enlivened by theatrical visits to hear the touring D'Oyly Carte Company, and his stated aim was 'more to evoke the spirit and atmosphere of Gilbert and Sullivan's world than simply to document their story'. The result has its longueurs, but to compensate there is remarkable Victorian detail. The choice of music is also personal and arbitrary, and not all of it works especially effectively in the cinema. But the film centres on the conception, writing and première of *The Mikado*. The excerpts from this masterpiece are as splendidly sung as they are extravagantly costumed, although, considering its importance as the emotional climax of the plot, it is surprising that the Mikado's famous Act II solo is not heard complete. Carl Davis's arrangements used as interludes are pleasing if not charismatic, but for many the principal weakness of this collection will be Davis's often over-deliberate tempi. Yet the quality of the singing triumphs over this drawback, with Timothy Spall and Louise Gold splendid as the Mikado and Katisha respectively, while Martin Savage is in his element in the patter songs. But why, oh why, was *Tit-willow* omitted? The recording is outstanding, often approaching demonstration quality, and the accompanying booklet is handsomely colour-illustrated and includes full texts.

Suppé, Franz von (1819–95)

Complete overtures

Volume 1: Overtures: *Carnival; Die Frau Meisterin; Die Irrfahrt um's Glück (Fortune's Labyrinth); The Jolly Robbers (Banditenstreiche); Pique Dame; Poet and Peasant; Des Wanderers Ziel (The Goal of the Wanderers). Boccaccio: Minuet & Tarantella. Donna Juanita: Juanita march.*

** Marco Polo Dig. 8.223647 [id.]. Slovak State PO (Košice), Alfred Walter.

Volume 2: Overtures: *Beautiful Galatea (Die schöne Galatea); Boccaccio; Donna Juanita; Isabella; Der Krämer und sein Kommis (The Shopkeeper and his Assistant); Das Modell (The Model); Paragraph 3; Tantalusqualen. Fatinitza march.*
** Marco Polo Dig. 8.223648 [id.]. Slovak State PO (Košice), Alfred Walter.

Volume 3: Overtures: *Fatinitza; Franz Schubert; Die Heimkehr von der Hochzeit (Homecoming from the wedding); Light Cavalry; Trioche and Cacolet; Triumph. Boccaccio: March. Herzenseintracht polka; Humorous variations on 'Was kommt dort von der Höh'?'; Titania waltz.*
** Marco Polo Dig. 8.223683 [id.]. Slovak State PO (Košice), Alfred Walter.

Franz von Suppé had a Belgian father and grandfather – though his mother was Viennese-born. In 1840 he made his début as an 'honorary' conductor in the Josefstadt Theatre; his first successful stage work dates from a year later. But it was not until 1860 that he began writing his inconsequential Viennese operettas, and most of his famous overtures (all that have survived of this output outside Vienna) date from the 1860s. *Poet and Peasant* (of which countless arrangements were made) predates the others and was written well before 1846, when the comedy with songs, to which it was finally appended, first appeared.

Walter's performances here are unsubtle, but they have a rumbustious vigour that is endearing and, with enthusiastic playing from the Slovak Orchestra who are obviously enjoying themselves, the effect is never less than spirited. Many of the finest of the lesser-known pieces are already available in more imaginative versions from Marriner (see our main volume). But Walter has uncovered some attractive novelties, as well as some pleasing if inconsequential interludes and dances. On Volume 1 *Carnival* (nothing like Dvořák's piece), opens rather solemnly, then introduces a string of ideas, including a polka, a waltz and a galop. *Die Frau Meisterin* also produces an engaging little waltz. *Des Wanderers Ziel* begins very energetically and, after brief harp roulades, produces a rather solemn cello solo and brass choir; later there is an attractive lyrical melody, but there are plenty of histrionics too, and the dancing ending brings distinctly Rossinian influences.

In Volume 2 *Isabella* is introduced as a sprightly Spanish lady, but Viennese influences still keep popping up, while *Paragraph 3* summons the listener with a brief horn-call and then has another striking lyrical theme, before gaiety takes over. *Das Krämer und sein Kommis* proves to be an early version (the ear notices a slight difference at the

dramatic opening) of an old friend, *Morning, noon and night in Vienna. Donna Juanita* brings a violin solo of some temperament; then, after some agreeably chattering woodwind, comes a grand march.

On the third CD, *Trioche and Cacolet* immediately introduces a skipping tune of great charm and, after another of Suppé's appealing lyrical themes, ends with much rhythmic vigour. The biographical operetta about *Schubert* opens with an atmospheric, half-sinister reference to the *Erlkönig* and follows with further quotations, prettily scored; however, the writing coarsens somewhat vulgarly at the end. But the prize item here is a set of extremely ingenious variations on a local folksong, which translates as *What comes there from on high?* It seems like a cross between 'A hunting we will go' and 'The Grand old Duke of York'.

Beautiful Galatea: overture.
(M) *** Sony SMK 61830 [id.]. NYPO, Bernstein
    – BIZET: *Symphony in C.* OFFENBACH: *Gaîté parisienne,* etc. **.

An excellent performance of the *Beautiful Galatea overture* from Bernstein: frothy in the fast sections, but sensitive in the quiet passages – especially in the strings. The 1967 recording is warm and vivid, though the couplings are not quite so recommendable.

Overtures: *Beautiful Galatea; Fatinitza; Flotte Bursche; Jolly robbers; Light Cavalry; Morning, noon and night in Vienna; Pique dame; Poet and peasant. March: O du mein Osterreich.*
(BB) **(*) LaserLight Dig. 15 611 [id.].
    Hungarian State Op. O, János Sándor.

Sándor's LaserLight collection is very generous and the Hungarian State Opera Orchestra know just how to play this repertoire: the *zigeuner* section in the middle of *Light Cavalry* is most winning, while the cello solo in *Morning, noon and night* has an attractive, romantic simplicity. Sándor offers two extra novelties in *Flotte Bursche* (which brings an amiable quotation of *Gaudeamus igitur*) and a vivid Viennese-style march. The digital recording is basically full-bodied but has brilliance too, and this is a real bargain.

Szymanowski, Karol (1882–1937)

Mythes, Op. 30.
**(*) Decca Dig. 455 488-2 [id.]. Ida Haendel, Vladimir Ashkenazy – BARTOK: *Rhapsody No. 1; Rumanian folkdances.* ENESCU: *Violin sonata No. 3* **(*); (with Recital: 'The Decca years, 1940–1947'(***)).

The Szymanowski *Mythes* call for piano playing of the utmost refinement which – uncharacteristically – Ashkenazy denies us. He is inattentive to matters of finesse and dynamic nuance, although Ida

Haendel's contribution is far finer. However her earlier recordings from 1940–47 are of much interest and are almost worth the price of this issue alone.

Violin sonata in D min., Op. 9.
(B) *** EMI Début CZS5 72825-2 [id.]. Rafal Zambrzycki-Payne, Carole Presland – BRITTEN: *Suite for violin and piano, Op. 6*; GRIEG: *Violin sonata No. 3.* ***

Rafal Zambrzycki-Payne is Polish-born. He was nineteen when this recording was made. It is appropriate that he should play a neglected Polish work along with another from the country in which he spent his formative years, as well as a classic of the repertoire – the Grieg *C minor Sonata*. Szymanowski's *D minor Sonata*, Op. 9 is generously represented on CD with fine accounts from Oistrakh, Lydia Mordkovitch and others, but Zambrzycki-Payne more than earns a place in the Szymanowski discography. He has a strong musical personality and intelligence, and gets splendid support from his pianist, Carole Presland. The Abbey Road recording is expertly balanced and sounds very natural.

(i) *King Roger* (complete); (ii) *Symphony No. 4 (Sinfonia concertante for piano and orchestra), Op. 6).*
❀ *** EMI Dig. CDC5 56823-2 (2) [id.]. (i) Thomas Hampson, Elzbieta Szmytka, Ryszard Minkiewicz; CBSO Ch. & Youth Ch.; (i; ii) CBSO, Sir Simon Rattle; (ii) Leif Ove Andsnes.

King Roger stands on the borderline between opera and music drama (as Zofia Helman says in her preface to the full score), a hybrid, with elements of oratorio and mystery play. The opening in Palermo Cathedral is of awesome opulence, and given such sounds one hardly needs a stage representation. All the singers are first-rate: Thomas Hampson has what one can only call magisterial presence, and the Roksana is quite ethereal. Only Ryszard Minkiewicz's Shepherd is, perhaps, wanting in tonal bloom. Of course, the glorious orchestral tapestry is the centre-piece of attention: the opening of the Hellenic Third Act is inspired and atmospheric. Already in his early records Rattle had shown great feeling for Szymanowski, and he does not disappoint us here. He is accorded excellent recording, though there are times when Hampson looms too large in the aural picture. There have been three earlier recordings, all Polish: Mierzejewski's set from the 1960s has long disappeared, Robert Satanowski's 1988 Warsaw version (Koch) and Karol Stryja's 1990 Katowice account (Marco Polo) were recently reissued on Naxos. But this sweeps the board and has much more refined sound. Incidentally, there is a bonus, for, at the end of the first CD, Roksana's famous aria is given with its concert ending. An even more important bonus comes in

the shape of the *Fourth Symphony*, the *Sinfonia concertante for piano and orchestra*. This has greater lucidity of textures than any of its previous rivals and brings magical playing from the soloist.

Takemitsu, Toru (1930–96)

Fantasma/cantos.
*** EMI Dig. CDC5 56832-2 [id.]. Sabine Meyer, Berlin PO, Abbado – DEBUSSY: *Première rapsodie*; MOZART: *Clarinet concerto.* ***

In this sequence of works designed to bring out the full artistry of Sabine Meyer, the hypnotic 16-minute span of this Takemitsu work seems to develop out of the evocative Debussy piece, similarly inhabiting a dream-like world of sound, with ravishing clarinet tones over the widest range. An unusual but revealing coupling.

Tallis, Thomas (c. 1505–85)

Complete music, Volume 4: Music for the Divine Office: *Dum transisset sabbatum; In pace in idipsum; Jam Christus astra ascenderat; Jesu salvator saeculi; Hodie nobis caelorum; Loquebantur variis linguis; Magnificat; Quod chorus vatum; Salvator mundi; Sermone blando; Videte miraculum.*
*** Signum Dig. SIGCD 010 [id.]. Chapelle du Roi, Alistair Dixon.

Volume 4 in this ever-rewarding series is the first to concentrate on music for the cycle of eight services, Matins, Lauds, Prime, Terce, Sext, None, Vespers, and Compline, sung daily in Latin Christendom. The riches of the polyphony here are unending. *Dum transisset sabbatum* and the six-part *Videte miraculum* are particularly fine, while the seven-part *Loquebantur variis linguis* with its recurring *Alleluias*, spins an even more complex contrapuntal web. Even the simplest of the settings here, *Quod chorus vatum* is moving by its comparative austerity. The earlier four-part version of the *Magnificat* ends the programme, considered not to be one of the composer's most felicitous settings, but it still makes a resounding closing piece. Splendid singing, as ever from this group, and recording which could hardly be bettered in its clarity and vocal bloom.

Ave Dei patris; Ave rosa sine spinis; Missa Salve intemerata; Salve intemerata.
** Metronome Dig. METCD 1014. Canterbury Cathedral Choir, David Flood.

A disappointing collection. The recording was made in the Cathedral nave, and the radiantly resonant sound of eighteen trebles, four male altos, five tenors and four basses cannot fail to impress the ear, soaring heavenwards. But neither in refinement nor the positive control of the line of the music (which here at times seems to float without a great deal of purpose) can these performances match those by the Alistair Dixon's smaller group, Chapelle du Roi, or indeed the Tallis Scholars (see our main volume).

God grant we grace; Hear the voice and prayer; If ye love me; Spem in alium; In ieiunio et fletu; Lamentations, Parts I–II; Mihi autem nimis; O Lord give thy Holy Spirit; O nata lux de lumine; O sacrum convivium; Salvator mundi; Te lucis ante terminum.
(M) **(*) Carlton Classics 30366 00952 [id.]. Pro Cantione Antiqua, Mark Brown.

This well-planned and rewarding programme opens with a simple Psalm setting (more familiar as a hymn), *God grant we grace*, which is sung most beautifully. All the music is in four or (more often) five parts, intimately presented, with one voice to a part. The great 40-part motet *Spem in alium*, which comes second, is the exception, and here the full 14-voice group is augmented. It brings a spectacular contrast, but though the music reaches a rich climax Mark Brown's control of tension is uneven. The highlight of the concert is the pair of *Lamentations*, which are movingly sung; and the group's refined, expressive style is heard at its best in the Latin hymns and motets, particularly the last three items, *Salvator mundi*, *O nata lux de lumine* and *Te lucis ante terminum*. The recording is natural and not too forwardly balanced.

Taneyev, Sergei (1856–1915)

Symphonies Nos. (i) *2 in B flat* (ed. Blok); (ii) *4 in C min., Op. 12*.
** Russian Disc RD CD11008. (i) USSR R. & TV Grand SO, Fedoseyev; (ii) Novosibirsk PO, Katz.

In the *Fourth Symphony* Arnold Katz and the Novosibirsk orchestra give a spirited, characterful reading, which can hold its own against Neeme Järvi's excellent account on Chandos. The recording is very good, though not quite in the three-star bracket. This version of the *Second Symphony in B flat* seems to be identical with Fedoseyev's 1969 LP; climaxes are a bit raw and raucous. The performance itself is satisfactory, and there is at present no alternative.

Tartini, Giuseppe (1692–1770)

Violin sonata in G min. (Devil's trill), arr. Zandonai for violin and strings.
(*) DG Dig. 463 259-2 [id.]. Anne-Sophie Mutter; Trondheim Soloists – VIVALDI: *The Four Seasons* *.

Mutter, as in her previous recording of the sonata – one of the items on a virtuoso showpiece disc (*Carmen Fantasy*) – uses Zandonai's string arrangement, this time with harpsichord and cello rather than piano continuo. As in the Vivaldi, Mutter again takes an unashamedly romantic view of the piece, providing an unauthentic but interesting make-weight to a version of *The Four Seasons* which, whatever its controversial points, is magnetic from first to last.

Tavener, John (born 1944)

(i; ii) *Canticle of the Mother of God;* (i; ii) *Ikon of the Nativity;* (iii) *Out of the night (Alleluia);* (iv) *Threnos*.
*** Sony Dig. SK 61753 [id.].(i) Taverner Choir, Andrew Parrott; (ii) Claron McFadden; (iii) Jane Atkins, Leigh Nixon; (iv) Moray Walsh – PART: *Fratres; Magnificat; 7 Magnificat antiphons* ***.

Tavener's music is here effectively juxtaposed with works by his Estonian contemporary, Arvo Pärt, with the sustained but brief *Out of the night* (for tenor voice and viola) acting as an evocative repeated refrain as it is heard (and performed) four times throughout this programme. The *Canticle of the Mother of God*, with its strange soprano melisma and choral dissonance, is ecstatically powerful and contrasts with the ruminative cello solo of *Threnos*, while the *Ikon of the Nativity* (which ends the concert ardently) is a set of three variations heard within a long melodic arch. The performances are undoubtedly compelling, the resonant sound just right for the music.

Fall and Resurrection.
*** Chandos Dig. CHAN 9800 [id.]. Patricia Rozario, Michael Chance, Martyn Hill, Stephen Richardson, Adrian Peacock, BBC Singers, St Paul's Cathedral Ch., City of L. Sinf., Hickox.

Fall and Resurrection is the hour-long work which Tavener wrote for the Millennium celebrations in January 2000. Heard first in the echoing expanses of St Paul's Cathedral, it was simultaneously televised, and here comes in a sound recording of that première which in important ways brings advantages. Not only is there greater clarity, with clean directional stereo effects heightening the impact of the writing in massive blocks of sound, with chords endlessly sustained, but the inclusion of a full text in the booklet lets one follow the slow progress of the piece more closely.

Tavener's ambitious aim is to 'encompass in brief glimpses the events which have taken place since the beginning of time and before time'. Using broad brush-strokes in illustrative effects, both choral and instrumental, this becomes a physical experience rather than a musical argument, an example of Taverner's spiritual minimalism at its most extreme. Though traditionalists may object that this is thin music, not designed for close analysis, there is no doubting its primal impact in the context for which it was written. So, after the slow emergence of the prelude out of silence, darkness and the representation of Chaos (with massive banks of timpani), the voice of Adam is heard against a chill flute solo, a simple dedicated vision.

The first of the three parts is then devoted to the fall of Adam and Eve, with the Serpent illustrated by a whining saxophone. The second section, representing prediction, leads from the fall to a quotation from Psalm 121, *I lift my eyes to the hills*, movingly sung by the countertenor, Michael Chance. The final part, *The Incarnation of the Logos*, in telegraphic brevity encompasses the birth of Jesus, the Crucifixion and finally the Resurrection in a Cosmic dance, when 'all is transfigured'. The final sustained chord fades away to reveal the sound of the bells of the cathedral outside, ringing out to the world, a theatrical coup. The concept is so bold that many may object that the building blocks are too simple, not worthy of such a supreme vision, but the sincerity of the composer is never for a moment in doubt, underpinned by a heartfelt performance here under Richard Hickox with a superb team of choirs and soloists.

Taverner, John (c. 1495–1545)

Missa Corona spinea; Motets: *Gaude plurium; In pace.*
🌑 (B) *** Hyperion Helios Dig. CDH 55051 [id.]. The Sixteen, Harry Christophers.

Missa Corona spinea; Motet: *O Wilhelme, pastor bone.*
**(*) ASV Gaudeamus CDGAU 115 [id.]. Christ Church Cathedral Ch., Francis Grier.

As with the *Missa Mater Christi sanctissima* below, we are offered a choice of performance style for the inspired *Missa Corona spinea*, perhaps the most thrilling of all the Taverner mass settings. The Christ Church performance would appear to have the balance of advantage, for Taverner himself was in charge of the music there rather more than four centuries ago, and the choir format has not changed much, only the singers! But Francis Grier has transposed the music up, and his choir, although always eloquent, have to try very hard to cope with the highest tessitura. The Sixteen, using professional singers (and secure female trebles), have no such problems and they sing gloriously throughout. Taverner's inspiration is consistent and his flowing melismas are radiantly realized, with fine support from the lower voices; indeed, the balance and blend are nigh perfect. The two motets are no less

beautifully sung, and the recording, made in St Jude's Church, Hampstead, is outstanding both in clarity and in its perfectly judged ambience. A superb disc and an astonishing bargain.

Missa gloria tibi Trinatas; Audivi vocem (responsory); ANON.: *Gloria tibi Trinitas.*
(B) *** Hyperion Helios CDH 55052 [id.]. The Sixteen, Harry Christophers.

This six-voice setting of the mass is richly varied in its invention (not least in rhythm) and expressive in a deeply personal way very rare for its period. Harry Christophers and The Sixteen underline the beauty with an exceptionally pure and clear account, superbly recorded and made the more brilliant by having the pitch a minor third higher than modern concert pitch. The reissue of this fine CD on Hyperion's bargain Helios label, together with its companions above and below, is especially welcome.

Missa Mater Christi sanctissima; Hodie nobis coelorum rex; Magnificat a 4: Nesciene mater. Mater Christi sanctissima; (ii) *In nomine a 4; Quemadmodum a 6.*
(B) *** Hyperion Helios CDH 55053 [id.]. (i) The Sixteen, Harry Christophers; (ii) Fretwork.

Continuing their outstanding Taverner survey The Sixteen here offer the *Missa Mater Christi sanctissima* plus the votive anthem on which it is based. Unlike the excellent Nimbus CD from Christ Church Cathedral (NI 5218 – see our main volume) Christophers presents the mass as it stands, and he uses female sopranos rather than trebles, while the music itself is all sung a tone up, which certainly makes it sound brighter. His pacing however is rather more restrained than Darlington's, and that adds a touch of breadth. Both performances are valid in their different ways, and certainly both are very rewarding for the listener. But the Helios disc is not only less expensive, it includes also extra music, including the Christmas responsory *Hodie nobis*, a fine four-part *Magnificat* and, a surprise – two rather grave pieces for viols from Fretwork to frame the mass itself. The recording is outstandingly fine, spacious yet clear.

Mass, O Michael; Dum transisset Sabbatum; Kyrie a 4 (Leroy).
(B) *** Hyperion Helios CDH 55054 [id.]. The Sixteen, Harry Christophers.

The *Missa O Michael* is an ambitious six-part mass lasting nearly 40 minutes which derives its name from the respond *Archangeli Michaelis interventione*, which prefaces the performance. The chant on which the mass is built appears no fewer than seven times during its course. The so-called *Leroy Kyrie* (the name thought to be a reference to *le roi* Henry) fittingly precedes it: the *Missa O Michael* has no *Kyrie*. The Easter motet *Dum transisset Sabbatum* completes an impressive disc.

Missa Sancti Wilhelmi; Dum transisset Sabbatum;
Ex eius tumba; O Wilhelme, pastor bone.
(B) *** Hyperion Helios CDH 55055 [id.]. The
    Sixteen, Harry Christophers.

The *Missa Sancti Wilhelmi* (known as 'Small Devotion' in two sources and possibly a corruption
of *S. Will devotio*) is prefaced by the antiphon *O
Wilhelme, pastor bone*, written in a largely syllabic,
note-against-note texture, and the second of Tavener's two five-part settings of the Easter respond
Dum transisset Sabbatum, and washed down, as
it were, by the Matins respond for the Feast of
St Nicholas, *Ex eius tumba*, believed to be the only
sixteenth-century setting of this text. The singing of
The Sixteen under Harry Christophers is expressive
and ethereal, and the recording impressively
truthful. Recommended with confidence.

*Mass: The Western Wind; Alleluia, Veni, electa
mea; O splendor gloria; Te Deum.*
(B) *** Hyperion Helios Dig. CDH 55056 [id.].
    The Sixteen, Harry Christophers.

Taverner's *Western Wynde mass* is based on a soaring melody, which constantly recurs throughout,
varied and decorated, yet which is always recognizable. Hence this work has rightly become one of
the most popular mass settings of its period. It is
beautifully sung and recorded by Harry Christophers' Sixteen in what must be regarded as an
ideally paced and proportioned performance. But
what makes this inexpensive Helios reissue doubly
attractive is the collection of other works included.
O splendor gloria carries the exulted mood inherent
in its title (referring to Christ and the Trinity) and
the *Alleluia* is equally jubilant.

   Most remarkable and individual of all is the masterly five-part *Te Deum*, a profoundly poignant setting, harmonically and polyphonically, even richer
than the mass, and using those momentary shafts of
dissonance that can make music of this period sound
so forward-looking. The recording is superb and
this CD is obviously the place to start for those
wanting to explore the Hyperion series of music by
this great sixteenth-century English musician, who
also served Cromwell in preparing for the dissol-
ution of the smaller monasteries and friaries, yet
who carried out this unenviable task with reputedly
great concern for the welfare of the monks and friars
themselves.

Tchaikovsky, Peter (1840–93)

*Andante cantabile, Op. 11; Chant d'automne, Op.
37/10; Nocturne, Op. 19/4 (all arr. for cello &
orchestra); Pezzo capriccioso, for cello &
orchestra, Op. 62; Sérénade mélancolique, Op.
26; Valse sentimentale, Op. 51/6 (both arr. for
cello & orchestra); Variations on a rococo theme*

*for cello & orchestra, Op. 33; Eugene Onegin:
Lensky's aria (arr. for cello & orchestra).*
**(*) RCA Dig. RD 60758 [09026 60758-2]. Ofra
    Harnoy, LPO, Mackerras.

Ofra Harnoy plays with much lightness and grace
in this Tchaikovsky programme, bringing together
almost every item which might be transcribed for
cello and orchestra. The most successful performance here is *Lensky's aria* from *Eugene Onegin*,
which Harnoy plays with gentle lamenting ardour.
In the *Variations on a rococo theme* Harnoy at times
fines the melodic line down seductively to just a
thread of tone, but at others she could be more
robust. In the rest of the programme this delicacy
and refinement work well enough. Mackerras
accompanies sensitively, while the recording balance is ideal, within a pleasingly warm ambience.

Capriccio italien; (i) 1812 overture.
(M) **(*) 463 614-2 [id.]. BPO, Karajan; (i) with
    Don Cossack Ch. – RIMSKY-KORSAKOV:
    Scheherazade **(*).

Karajan's *1812* is very well presented and very
exciting with fine orchestral playing, and the Russian chorus used to open the piece certainly adds an
extra dimension, sonorously recorded. If the closing
pages have the cannon added in a calculated fashion
rather than showing a touch of engineering flair, the
result is still impressive. Although Karajan takes a
while to get going, the *Capriccio italien* is also
impressive, with the Berlin brass particularly
telling. The combination of sophistication and panache (without any special affection conveyed) again
makes for a very professional kind of excitement;
the recording is bright and vividly resonant, but
there are more genuinely idiomatic accounts
available.

*Capriccio italien, Op. 45; 1812 Overture, Op. 49;
Marche slave, Op. 31; Swan Lake (ballet): suite.*
**(*) Teldec/Warner Dig. 4509 90201-2 [id.].
    Israel PO, Mehta.

This is a quite generously conceived popular Tchaikovsky collection, very well played and given full-
bodied, resonant sound, much more flattering than
we are used to from the Mann Auditorium in Tel
Aviv. With the Israel brass sonorously robust, the
concert opens with a lively and warmly conceived
Capriccio italien, a Slavonically solemn yet exciting *Marche slave* and an exuberant *1812* with a
spectacular fusillade at the end. The highlight is
the suite from *Swan Lake*, played with style and
affection and with good contributions from woodwind, violin and cello soloists.

(i) *Capriccio italien, Op. 45; 1812, Op. 49; (ii)
Fatum, Op. 77; Francesca da Rimini, Op. 32;
Hamlet, Op. 67; (i) Marche slave; (ii) Romeo and
Juliet (fantasy overture); The Tempest, Op. 18;
The Voyevoda, Op. 78.*

(B) **(*) Decca Double 443 003-2 (2) [id.]. (i)
National SO of Washington, DC; (ii) Detroit
SO; Antal Dorati.

Dorati made his recordings of the symphonic poems
in Washington in the early 1970s, while the triptych
of *Capriccio italien*, *1812* and *Marche slave* marked
the return of the Detroit orchestra to the recording
scene at the beginning of 1979. The recording has
the benefit of the splendid Detroit acoustics, although *1812*, rather endearingly, has a spectacular
laminated eruption of American Civil War cannon
and bells – including Philadelphia's Liberty Bell –
at the end. The spectacular results were aimed at
the hi-fi demonstration market of the time. The
performance of the *Capriccio* is not without elegance, but *Marche slave* seems too sombre until
the brisk coda. The symphonic poems are vividly
done. *Fatum* is quite successful, but Dorati's accounts of *Francesca da Rimini* and *Hamlet* are
rather underpowered compared with Stokowski,
but they are spacious, individual readings. *Romeo
and Juliet* after a cool start works up persuasively,
and *The Tempest* is vividly done. *The Voyevoda*
is not one of the composer's more inspired pieces,
but Dorati makes the most of its melancholy
and dark wind colouring, matching sombre lower
strings.

*Capriccio italien; 1812 Overture; Marche slave;
Nutcracker suite.*
(M) ** Decca Dig. 466 419-2 [id.]. Montreal SO,
Dutoit.

Dutoit's performances are individually characterized and by no means conventional in approach.
The *Capriccio italien* is particularly successful, far
from superficial, with high spirits and elegance
nicely balanced. In the *Nutcracker suite* there is an
almost chamber music refinement, not only in the
Miniature overture but in the characteristic dances,
which have both a piquant sense of colour and
delicacy of articulation. However, the *Waltz of the
flowers*, while pleasing, is rather restrained. *Marche
slave* is sombre and dignified, while *1812*, complete
with bells and cannon (provided by a Quebec regiment), is exciting, but not enough to generate a
physical thrill, as does the famous Dorati Mercury
version. The sound is full and luminous and now
seems to have more weight and impact than in the
original issue.

*Piano concertos Nos. (i) 1 in B flat min.; (ii) 2 in
G; (iii) 3 in E flat; (iv) Violin concerto in D; (v)
Variations on a rococo theme for cello and
orchestra.*
(B) **(*) EMI Rouge et Noir Analogue/Dig. CZS5
69695-2 (2) [CDZB 69695]. (i) Georges
Cziffra, Philh. O, Vandernoot; (ii) Sylvia
Kersenbaum, Fr. R. O, Martinon; (iii) Peter
Donohoe, Bournemouth SO, Barshai; (iv)
Leonid Kogan, Paris Conservatoire O,

Silvestri; (v) Pierre Fournier, Philh. O,
Sargent.

The outstanding Rouge et Noir compilation from
French EMI is one of a series in which different
groups of artists play the music of a single
composer. Although Cziffra's *B flat minor Piano
concerto* is disappointingly idiosyncratic, everything else is very valuable indeed, notably Kogan's
splendid account of the *Violin concerto* and Fournier's distinctive and stylish *Rococo variations*.
After Cziffra, brilliant but wilful in the *B flat minor
Concerto*, Sylvia Kersenbaum's 1972 account of
the *Second Piano concerto* with Martinon is a
different matter, absolutely complete in its text. The
tempo for the opening movement is perfect, and
Martinon's opening has a sweep to compare with
that of the *B flat minor Concerto*. The violin and
cello soloists in the slow movement play most sensitively, as does the pianist, and she is splendidly
ebullient in the finale. One's only slight reservation
concerns the recording, full but very resonant. Peter
Donohoe provides a totally satisfying account of
the *Third Concerto*, in an excellent, modern, digital
recording. The compilation is crowned by Kogan's
warm and spontaneous-sounding 1959 version of
the *Violin concerto*, and Fournier's aristocratic and
elegant account of the *Rococo variations*, dating
from 1956, with sound still full and brilliant.

Piano concerto No. 1 in B flat min., Op. 23.
(BB) *** EMI Dig. CZS5 73765-2 (3). Mikhail
Rudy, St Petersburg PO, Jansons –
RACHMANINOV: *Piano concertos Nos. 1–3;
Rhapsody on a theme of Paganini ***.*
(B) *** Decca Penguin Classics 460 653-2 [id.].
Vladimir Ashkenazy, LSO, Maazel – CHOPIN:
*Piano concerto No. 2 ***.*

Like the Rachmaninov collection with which it is
coupled, Mikhail Rudy's account of the Tchaikovsky *Concerto* treats it less as a warhorse than as
a fresh, unhackneyed masterpiece, with poetry and
refinement set alongside bravura display. As
always, Rudy exhibits much artistry and taste in
this eloquent St Petersburg account, partnered by
Mariss Jansons. His playing is not short on virtuosity and command, but never at the expense of
poetic feeling; the warmly idiomatic orchestral
playing under Mariss Jansons has great character
and personality. The recording balance too does
justice to both soloist and orchestra. Altogether it
makes a refreshing alternative version, here offered
in a bargain package with equally illuminating accounts of the Rachmaninov concertos. Excellent
sound, full and vivid.

Ashkenazy too refuses to be stampeded by Tchaikovsky's rhetoric, and the biggest climaxes of the
first movement are made to grow naturally out of
the music. In the *Andantino*, too, Ashkenazy refuses
to play flashily. The finale is very fast and brilliant,
yet the big tune is broadened at the end in the

most convincing way. The remastering is highly successful: the piano sounds splendidly bold and clear while the orchestral balance is realistic. A bargain in its Penguin Classics incarnation, and the specialist essay is by Angela Huth.

(i) *Piano concerto No. 1 in B flat min., Op. 23.*
Nutcracker (ballet): excerpts.
(M) **(*) RCA 09026 68530-2 [id.]. (i) Emil Gilels; Chicago SO, Reiner.

Gilels's early (1955) RCA recording is over-reverberant, with the sound less refined than usual from this source. The *Nutcracker* ballet music, very well played if without much charm, is also rather inflated. The performance of the concerto, however, is very exciting and full-blooded, with Gilels giving a beautifully gentle account of the outer sections of the slow movement.

Piano concerto No. 2 in G, Op. 44.
** Athene Dig. ATH CD16 [id.]. Andreas Boyde, Freiburg PO, Johannes Fritzsch –
SHOSTAKOVICH: *Symphony No. 9* **(*).

These Athene recordings come from public performances given in Freiburg. Andreas Boyde is blessed with much brilliance and excellent technical command but he is brash and does not find the poetic depths that Gilels and Pletnev uncover here. Mind you, the piano tone is shallow and the recording is not always as clearly detailed as in rival versions.

Piano concertos Nos. 2 in G, Op. 44; 3 in E flat, Op. 75.
(BB) *(*) Arte Nova Dig. 74321 65429-2 [id.]. Arkady Sevidov, Russian PO, Samuel Friedman.

Alas, this coupling is a non-starter. Sevidov is a sensitive-enough soloist, but he is ill-served by his conductor, who sets far too slow a pace for the opening movement: its timing is over 25 minutes! Lethargy sets in and when the pianist begins what should be a thrilling cadenza, it is more like Chopin than Tchaikovsky. The slow movement goes well enough with pleasing contibutions from Michail Shestakov (violin) and Andrei Demin (cello), but the finale sounds skittish rather than sparkling: one needs more freely running adrenalin than this. The *Third concerto*, too is given a low profile by the conductor. No complaints about the recording itself.

Violin concerto in D, Op. 35.
(BB) *** Royal Long Players Dig. DCL 705742 (2). Vladimir Spivakov, Philh. O, Ozawa –
BRAHMS; DVORAK; SIBELIUS: *Violin concertos.* ***
(M) ** Sony Great Performances Dig. SMK 64127 [id.]. Isaac Stern, National SO of Washington, Rostropovich (with BEETHOVEN: *Romance No. 1 in G, Op. 40* *; MENDELSSOHN: *Violin concerto* **).

(M) (**) DG mono 463 175-2 (2) [id.]. Yehudi Menuhin, Berlin RIAS SO, Fricsay –
BEETHOVEN: *Violin sonatas Nos. 5, 7 & 9; Rondo in G* ***.
(M) *(*) RCA High Performance 09026 63591-2 [id.]. Perlman, Boston SO, Leinsdorf –
SIBELIUS: *Violin concerto* *(*); DVORAK: *Romance* **.

Spivakov's reading, rich and warm, may be extrovert, but is easy to enjoy, helped by exceptionally full digital recording and a close balance of the violin. At the same time, with Ozawa directing a most persuasive accompaniment from the Philharmonia, this is also a reading which brings out the almost Mozartean elegance of much of the writing, not missing the gentle Russian melancholy of the central *Canzonetta*, but emphasizing the overall happiness of Tchaikovsky's inspiration. Coupled with three other outstanding performances, this two-disc set is an outstanding bargain.

Stern was on peak form when he made his first stereo recording with Ormandy (SMK 66829 – see our main volume). This later 1977 version with Rostropovich is a good deal more impressive than its Mendelssohn coupling but whether it is a 'great performance' is open to question. Stern's technique is still impeccable and this too is a distinguished and often sensitive account. The orchestral response is more than adequate and often responsive, though Rostropovich is not free from the charge of over-emphatic accentuation in one or two places. The balance somewhat favours the soloist but is not as exaggeratedly forward as in the earlier, analogue version and in general the sound is satisfactory.

Menuhin's 1949 account of the Tchaikovsky *Violin concerto* is his only recording of the piece. It first appeared in 1994 as part of the ten-CD set devoted to Ferenc Fricsay when it was coupled with the *Pathétique Symphony*. There is no doubt that it is deeply felt and touches a vein of raw emotion, though there are one or two moments of dubious intonation to offset the undoubted insights Menuhin brings, and the great violinist is probably best remembered by other things.

There is no doubting Perlman's artistry, but this is not a recommendable CD: neither the sound, nor Leinsdorf's manner is especially ingratiating and with so many fine versions of this work available, this is uncompetitive.

(i) *Violin concerto;* (ii) *Variations on a rococo theme, Op. 33.*
**(*) EMI Dig. CDC7 54890-2 [id.]. (i) Kennedy, LPO, Kamu; (ii) Paul Tortelier, N. Sinfonia, Yan Pascal Tortelier.

Nigel Kennedy gives a warmly romantic and very measured reading of the *Concerto*, full of temperament. For all his many *tenutos* and *rallentandos*, however, Kennedy is not sentimental, and his range of tone is exceptionally rich and wide, so that the big moments are powerfully sensual. Okku Kamu and the LPO do not always match their soloist, sometimes sounding a little stiff in tuttis. This per-formance is available coupled to an outstanding version of the Sibelius *Concerto* with Sir Simon Rattle (EMI CDC7 54559-2) as well as in this pairing with Paul Tortelier's finely wrought account of the *Rococo variations*, with excellent analogue recording.

(i) *Violin concerto in D, Op. 35;* (ii) *Symphony No. 5 in E min., Op. 64;* (iii) *Capriccio italien; 1812 overture; Eugene Onegin: Polonaise and Waltz; Marche slave; Romeo and Juliet (fantasy overture).*
(B) **(*) Sony SB2K 63281 (2). (i) Francescatti, NYPO, Schippers; (ii) Cleveland O, Szell; (iii) Philadelphia O, Ormandy.

Francescatti's 1965 account of the *Violin concerto* does not disappoint: it has brilliance and flair, with sterling support from Schippers and his New York orchestra, and a particularly exciting finale. Szell's 1959 version of the *Fifth symphony* is also superb – almost matching his classic, thrilling account of the *Fourth* on Decca. Its sense of romantic urgency is finely judged, with a splendid surging momentum in the outer movements. The style of the horn soloist in the *Andante* may not suit every taste, but in all other respects, the orchestral playing is first rate. The Ormandy performances of the popular orches-tral works all offer polish and characteristic Phila-delphia panache; the sound is good throughout the set, though the Philadelphia recordings are a touch glossy at times.

1812 Overture; Francesca da Rimini; Marche slave; Romeo and Juliet (fantasy overture).
(M) *** EMI Eminence Dig. CD-EMX 2152. RLPO, Sian Edwards.

The control of the emotional ebb and flow of *Francesca da Rimini* shows Sian Edwards as an instinctive Tchaikovskian. Francesca's clarinet entry is melting and the work's middle section has a Beechamesque sense of colour. *1812* is also very enjoyable indeed, full of vigour and flair, it has a majestic final sequence with superbly resounding cannon. In *Romeo and Juliet*, the love theme is ushered in very naturally and blossoms with the fullest ardour, while the feud music combined with the Friar Laurence theme reaches a very dramatic climax. *Marche slave*, resplendently high-spirited and exhilarating, makes a perfect foil. The full-bodied recording is well balanced and thrilling.

1812 overture, Op. 49; Marche slave, Op. 31; Romeo and Juliet (fantasy overture); *The Tempest, Op. 18.*
**(*) DG Dig. 453 496-2 [id.]. BPO, Abbado.

Abbado's *1812* is both exciting and satisfyingly

held together, with some superbly placed 'cannon shots' during the spectacular closing section, which all but dwarf the orchestra. The *Slavonic march* opens rather slowly, but the very Russian melody evokes a profound sense of melancholy; the pacing then gathers momentum and excitement and the coda is thrilling. The performance of *The Tempest* is unsurpassed. After the evocative opening, with its flowing horn theme depicting Prospero's enchanted island and the sea, the storm sequence is vigorously exciting. The ecstatic lover's theme is introduced with touching delicacy of feeling and its climactic reappearance near the close explodes with passion. But Abbado's expansive approach to *Romeo and Juliet* is rather less successful. Here the introduction of the love theme is touchingly refined, but as the veiled moonlight sequence creeps in Abbado with-draws to a pianissimo, and the tension slips a little. The development is really exciting, capped by the thrilling return of the Friar Laurence theme on the trumpets and a passionate romantic apotheosis; but overall this is not an entirely convincing reading, in spite of the marvellous Berlin Philharmonic playing and brilliant, full-blooded recording.

(i) *1812 Overture;* (ii) *Romeo and Juliet* (fantasy overture); (iii) *Serenade for strings in C, Op. 48.*
(B) **(*) DG Classikon Dig. 439 468-2 [id.]. (i) Gothenburg SO, Järvi; (ii) Philh. O, Sinopoli; (iii) Orpheus CO.

Järvi's *1812* is exciting – and not just for the added Gothenburg brass and artillery or for the fervour of the orchestra at the opening. He clearly knows how to structure the piece, and he obviously enjoys the histrionics, and so do we. Sinopoli's reading of *Romeo and Juliet* is not so spontaneous-sounding, with a hint of self-consciousness at the first entry of the big love theme, but there is plenty of uninhibited passion later. In the *Serenade for strings* no one could accuse the Orpheus Chamber Orchestra of lack of energy in the outer movements. Overall it is an impressive performance, even if the problems of rubato without a conductor are not always easily solved. The sound is first class.

(i) *1812 Overture* (arr. Buketoff). *Sleeping Beauty* (ballet), *Op. 66:* excerpts; *The Voyevoda* (symphonic ballad), *Op. 78;* (i; ii) *Moscow* (coronation cantata).
**(*) Delos Dig. DE 3196 [id.]. Dallas SO, (i) and Ch.; (ii) with Svetlana Furdui and Vassily Gerello; Andrew Litton.

Tchaikovsky's *Voyevoda* was underrated – even by the composer, who, soon after he had written it, destroyed the score. Fortunately the orchestral parts survived. Taken from Pushkin, it has a rather similar plotline to *Francesca da Rimini*. Its Tchaikovskian melancholy is most persuasively brought out by the excellent Dallas Symphony under Andrew Litton. He is equally impressive in a rather arbitrary set of excerpts from the *Sleeping Beauty* ballet. The programme opens with a choral *1812* in Ivor Buketoff's arrangement, which returns to the words of the original folksongs on which the music is based. At the close the Dallas chorus sings with an expansiveness that almost overwhelms cannon and carillon. Tchaikovsky's cantata *Moscow* was an 1883 commission for the coronation of Alexander III, a lyrical work, sung here with feeling by the chorus and two ardently Slavonic soloists. The recording is rich and spacious.

(i) *Fatum* (symphonic poem), *Op. 77;* (ii; iii) *Francesca da Rimini* (fantasy after Dante), *Op. 32;* (ii; iii) *Hamlet* (fantasy overture), *Op. 67a;* (iv; v) *Romeo and Juliet* (fantasy overture); (i) *The Storm, Op. 76; The Tempest, Op. 18; The Voyevoda, Op. 78* (symphonic poems); (iv; iii) *1812 overture, Op. 49.*

(B) **(*) Ph. Duo 442 586-2 (2) [id.]. (i) Frankfurt RSO, Eliahu Inbal; (ii) New Philh. O; (iii) Igor Markevitch; (iv) Concg. O; (v) Bernard Haitink.

On this two-for-the-price-of-one Duo set come strongly committed performances of four of Tchaikovsky's little-known symphonic poems in excellent recordings from the mid-1970s. The most remarkable piece (which is superbly performed by Inbal and the Frankfurt orchestra) is *The Storm* of 1864, well-argued in sonata form, Tchaikovsky's first fully fledged orchestral composition. *The Voyevoda* is a very late work which is unconnected with the opera of the same name, but *Fatum*, written four years after *The Storm*, is less successful. *The Tempest* is here passionately performed and Markevitch's accounts of *Francesca da Rimini* and *Hamlet* have characteristic intensity and drive. Haitink's *Romeo and Juliet* is full of atmosphere and spaciously conceived. *1812*, distinctively paced, makes a lively bonus. The four novelties are what make this set worthwhile.

Francesca da Rimini; Romeo and Juliet (fantasy overture).

(M) ** BBC Music BBCB 8012-2 [id.]. ECO, Britten – FALLA: *El amor brujo* **(*).

Britten's love of the music of Tchaikovsky may seem strange when he was so vitriolic about other high romantics like Puccini. He conducted these live performances at the Aldeburgh Festival – *Romeo* in 1968 and *Francesca* in 1971. Although the lack of weight in the ECO strings (not helped by recording balances) and the overall lack of brilliance tells against these pieces being as dramatic as they might be, the warmth of feeling in spontaneous expressiveness is never in doubt. But this is for Britten's admirers rather than Tchaikovskians.

(i) *The Nutcracker, Op. 71* (complete ballet); *The Sleeping Beauty: suite, Op. 66a;* (ii) *Romeo and Juliet (fantasy overture).*

(B) ** DG Analogue/Dig. Double 459 478-2 (2) [id.]. (i) Boston SO; (ii) San Francisco SO, Ozawa.

Ozawa's digital *Nutcracker* dates from 1990. It is a beautifully played and recorded version, but other versions have more individuality and drama: the *Divertissement* is rather bland, and the big moments don't thrill as they should. The same comments apply to the *Sleeping Beauty* suite, though the quality of the Boston orchestral playing in both ballets is never in doubt. The *Romeo and Juliet* recording dates from 1972, but Ozawa's reading lacks the gripping sense of drama which this work should have from the very first bar.

Nutcracker suite, Op. 71a; Romeo and Juliet (fantasy overture).

**(*) DG Dig. Gold 439 021-2 [id.]. BPO, Karajan.

Originally designed to accompany a picture biography of Karajan, this not very generous Tchaikovsky coupling brings superbly played performances. The suite is delicate and detailed, yet perhaps lacks a little in charm, notably the *Arab dance* which, taken fairly briskly, loses something of its gentle sentience. The performance of *Romeo and Juliet* is both polished and dramatic, but Karajan draws out the climax of the love theme with spacious moulding, and there is marginally less spontaneity here than in his earlier recordings.

The Nutcracker (ballet): Act II: *suite*.

** Chandos Dig. CHAN 9799 [id.]. Danish Nat. RSO, Temirkanov – RAVEL: *Ma Mère l'Oye (suite); La valse* ** (with GADE: *Tango Jalousie*).

This CD offers only some of the *Nutcracker* and the Ravel coupling is hardly a rarity. The fine Danish Radio Orchestra plays excellently but Temirkanov is, as so often, all too idiosyncratic. No complaints about the sound.

The Nutcracker, Op. 71; The Sleeping Beauty, Op. 66; Swan Lake, Op. 20 (complete ballets).

(B) **(*) Decca 460 411-2 (6) [id.]. Nat. PO, Bonynge.

(B) **(*) EMI CZS5 73624-2 (6). LSO, Previn.

Bonynge's Tchaikovsky performances are all recommendable. *Swan Lake* receives a red-blooded performance where the forward impulse of the music making is immediately striking. The 1975 recording is vivid and bright, though a little dry, producing a leonine string-tone sound rather than a feeling of sumptuousness. But the sound in general is excellent, and the brass in the 'fairy castle' fanfares have the atmosphere of a medieval tournament. If the full romantic essence of this masterly score is not totally conveyed (partly as a result of the recording), the commitment of the orchestral playing is never in doubt. There is a consistent freshness here and many of the spectacular moments are thrilling. *The Sleeping Beauty* was recorded a year later with similarly vivid sound. Bonynge secures brilliant and often elegant playing from the National Philharmonic, and his rhythmic pointing is always characterful. He is especially good at the close of Act II when, after the magical *Panorama*, the Princess is awakened – there is a frisson of tension here and the atmosphere is most evocative. If the Pletnev DG version (● 457 634-2) has a unique, sparkling brilliance, Bonynge's has more the feel of a genuine ballet performance in progress. After a rather literal opening, Bonynge's *Nutcracker* really comes to life at the beginning of the magic, as the Christmas tree expands, and the *Transformation scene* is finely done. In the latter part of the ballet Bonynge is at his best, with fine passion in the Act II *Pas de deux* and plenty of colour in the characteristic dances. The recording from 1974 is rich and brilliant. All are packed in Decca's excellent 'Collector Boxes' and this set is undoubtedly a bargain.

Honours between the Previn and Bonynge sets are fairly evenly divided: both were recorded in the 1970s and offer fine performances in different ways. Previn (recorded during his great period with the LSO) is more warmly expansive than Bonynge, with EMI engineering a more sumptuous sound than Decca, who opt for a more vivid, upfront picture. Previn's 1972 *Nutcracker* is superbly played by the LSO – it is a wonderfully warm account which gets more involving as it goes along. If *The Sleeping Beauty* is not as vital as it could be (though never slack), it makes up for it with the superb playing of the orchestra: the *Panorama* is beautifully done. The recording (1974) could sparkle a little more though. *Swan Lake* (1976) is given a similarly warm performance, though the overall effect is at times just that bit too 'cosy' for such dramatic writing. The music never drags though, and the excellence of the orchestral playing does much to enhance one's pleasure. The choice between these two bargain boxes is a matter of personal taste: Bonynge offers the more vivid performances (thanks also to the sound), while Previn has more opulence. Both are equally enjoyable and well packaged.

The Nutcracker: suite; The Sleeping Beauty (excerpts)*; Swan Lake* (excerpts).
(B) ** Decca Penguin Classics 460 639-2 [id.]. SRO, Ansermet.

Ansermet's Tchaikovsky is always characterful: indeed, were his magical complete *Nutcracker* reissued, it would still be one of the top recommendations. What we have here is a pretty meagre selection of excerpts (60 minutes – similar to the previous LP) which fails to convey the full effect Ansermet achieved in the complete sets from which these are taken. The late 1950s recordings, despite some tape hiss, are excellent (especially in *The Nutcracker* and *The Sleeping Beauty*). The contributory essay is by Sir Roy Strong.

(i) *Romeo and Juliet* (fantasy overture)*; Sleeping Beauty: Waltz;* (ii; iii) *Serenade for strings in C;* (iii; iv) *Symphony No. 5 in E min., Op. 64;* (iv; iii) *Symphony No. 6 in B min. (Pathétique), Op. 74.*
(BB) **(*) Royal Long Players DCL 70570-2 (2) [id.]. (i) RPO, Sargent; (ii) LSO; (iii) Barbirolli; (iv) Hallé O; (v) Horenstein.

This is a bit of a mixed bag, but it is so inexpensive that it remains well worth its bargain basement cost. The main snag is Horenstein's *Pathétique*, one of those recording sessions that just didn't come off. There are moments of excitement, mostly generated by the playing rather than the interpretation. Horenstein displays little real feeling for the music and his straightforwardness, although it makes the main points of the outer movements (with a sober restraint in the finale), finds absolutely no charm in the second. Also, he manages a curious broadening at the reprise of the big tune in the Scherzo, like a railway train putting its brakes on. The recording is brilliant but dry. There are no such complaints about Barbirolli's romantically passionate account of the *Fifth*, while his gorgeous performance of the *Serenade* with a sumptuously large string group, is the highlight of the set. Sargent's *Romeo and Juliet* is very professional, but the love music is held back by the conductor in what can only be described as an English effort not to be vulgar. The music's inherent passion is still implicit, but there are more exciting versions available, even if the early stereo makes an impressive impact.

Sérénade mélancolique (for violin and orchestra), *Op. 26.*
*** EMI Dig. CDC5 56966-2 [id.]. Maxim Vengerov, LSO, Rostropovich – SHCHEDRIN: *Concerto cantabile;* STRAVINSKY: *Violin concerto.* ***

The disarmingly simple lyricism of Tchaikovsky's gentle, yet ardent *Serenade* is well caught by Vengerov and Rostropovich in a refined reading that catches the composer's Russian melancholy to perfection. It makes a perfect encore for Vengerov's superb account of the spikier Stravinsky concerto.

Serenade for strings in C, Op. 48.
(BB) *** Virgin Classics 2 x 1 Dig. VBD5 61763-2 (2) [CDVB 61763]. LCO, Christopher Warren-Green – DVORAK: *Serenade for strings in E, Op. 22*; ELGAR: *Introduction and allegro; Serenade;* SUK: *Serenade;* VAUGHAN WILLIAMS: *Fantasia on Greensleeves; Fantasia on a theme of Tallis; Lark ascending.* ***

Not surprisingly, Christopher Warren-Green's reading of Tchaikovsky's *Serenade* with the excellent London Chamber Orchestra is full of individuality. The first movement's secondary idea has an appealing feathery lightness, and when the striding opening theme reappears at the end of the movement it brings a spontaneous-sounding burst of expressive intensity characteristic of this group. The *Waltz* lilts gently, with the tenutos nicely managed, the *Elégie* has delicacy as well as fervour, and the finale develops plenty of energy. Very well recorded, it is a performance to give pleasure for its freshness and natural impetus, and the couplings are amazingly generous and equally stimulating.

The Sleeping Beauty (ballet), *Op. 66* (complete).
(M) **(*) EMI (SIS) CMS7 64840-2 (2) [CDQB 54814]. LSO, Previn.

In Previn's 1974 complete set the analogue EMI recording is less brilliant than some, the balance slightly recessed so that the sound is sumptuous with a richly resonant bass. With warm, polished orchestral playing, Previn conveys his affection throughout, but too often – in the famous *Waltz*, for instance – there is a lack of vitality. On the other hand, the *Panorama* shows Previn and his orchestra at their very best, the tune floating over its rocking bass in the most magical way. With Previn's tempi sometimes indulgently relaxed, it has been impossible to get the complete recording onto a pair of CDs, and the *Pas berrichon* and *Sarabande* included in the original (three-disc) LP issue have been cut.

Swan Lake (ballet), *Op. 20* (complete).
(B) **(*) DG Double 453 055-2 (2) [id.]. Boston SO, Ozawa.
**(*) EMI (SIS) Dig. CDS5 55277-2 (2). Phd. O, Sawallisch.
(M) (**(*)) Mercury mono 462 950-2 [id.]. Minneapolis SO, Dorati.
(B) ** BMG/Melodiya Twofer 74321 66978-2 (2) [id.]. USSR R. & TV Grand SO, Rozhdestvensky.

Ozawa's version omits the Act III *Pas de deux* but otherwise plays the complete original score. His performance is alive and vigorous (as at the opening *Allegro giusto*), but it has not quite the verve of Lanchbery's CfP version; Ozawa's approach is more serious, less flexible. Yet with polished, sympathetic playing from the Boston orchestra there are many impressive and enjoyable things here, with wind (and violin) solos always giving pleasure. The end result is a little faceless, in spite of a spectacular, wide-ranging analogue recording, as vivid as it is powerful.

Sawallisch approaches Tchaikovsky's greatest ballet score with appealing freshness, as if it had been written yesterday, and the Philadelphia Orchestra play superbly. But, as so often, they are let down by the recording, with its unnaturally close microphone placing. There is no lack of atmos-

phere, as the very opening demonstrates, yet fortissimos are unrefined, with fierce cymbals, grainy violins. But there is also much to enjoy, and splendid vigour. The first and most famous *Waltz* (gorgeously played) lilts attractively, and the thrilling final climax (with gorgeously full horn-tone at the restatement of the famous *idée fixe*) makes an overwhelming apotheosis, even with shrill violins.

Dorati's 1954 mono *Swan Lake* has long held cult status amongst record collectors: it is a very exciting performance, with a character and forward thrust which is very compelling. The Mercury recording is characteristically vivid, with the bass drum thundering through the speakers with almost alarming effect, but some ears will find the brightness on top and lack of sumptuousness characteristic of recordings from this source a drawback. So this set is not for the faint-hearted, but it should find new friends in its excellent new transfer. The sleeve note documentation is copious and the slim-line packaging attractive.

Rozhdestvensky's is a sympathetic and idiomatic performance that does not disappoint. The caveat is the 1969 recording, which does not offer the richness and depth this colourful music ideally demands. At bargain price, it might be worth considering, especially if you like the distinctive Russian brass, but bargain hunters will find that John Lanchbery's 1982 Philharmonia set on Classics for Pleasure is preferable on almost all counts (CD-CFPD 4727).

Symphonies Nos 1–6; (i) *Piano concerto No. 1 in B flat minor, Op. 23;* (ii) *Violin concerto in D, Op. 35; Capriccio italien; Eugene Onegin: Polonaise and waltz; Marche slave; The Nutcracker suite; 1812 Overture; Romeo and Juliet (Fantasy overture); Sleeping Beauty: suite; String serenade; Swan Lake: suite;* (iii) *Variations on a rococo theme.*
(B) *(**) DG 463 774-2 (8) [id.]. (i) Richter, Vienna SO; (ii) Ferras; (iii) Rostropovich; BPO, all cond. Karajan.

Having recorded the last three Tchaikovsky symphonies three times over in little more than a decade, Karajan then turned to the early symphonies, and brought to them the same superlative qualities. These Berlin performances are fine in every way; perhaps a bit of over-refinement creeps in from time to time, but by any standards they are a magnificent achievement.

The *Violin concerto* is superbly shaped by Karajan, though some will find Ferras's tone lacking charm – his close vibrato in lyrical passages tends to emphasize schmaltz on the G string. Richter and Karajan are controversial to say the least in the *Piano concerto*: the element of struggle for which his work is famous is only too clear here. Each chooses different tempi for the second subject in the finale and maintains it in spite of the other. However, in both the dramatic opening and closing pages of the work they are agreed in a hugely mannered, bland stylization which is not easy to enjoy. Elsewhere in the first movement, both artists play havoc with any sense of forward tempo (though there are occasional bursts of real excitement), and Richter's excessive rubato in the lyrical second subject sounds unspontaneous. Clearly two major artists at work, but the result is none too convincing.

The *Rococo variations* with Rostropovich is a breath of fresh air after all that – lovely glowing accounts – and the orchestral music is generally fine, but not outstanding, and a hint of glossiness creeps in from time to time (though the *Sleeping Beauty* and *Swan Lake suites* are quite superb). The sound throughout the set is of a generally high standard.

Symphony No. 1 in G min. (Winter daydreams).
(M) **(*) DG 463 615-2 [id.]. Boston SO, Thomas
– DEBUSSY: *Images* **(*).

Michael Tilson Thomas's is a good, affectionate account which captures well the spirit of the music. The slow movement is hauntingly atmospheric, with the Russian melancholy brought out to great effect. It is a pity that the recording is a bit over-reverberant: it tends to dull the conductor's pointing in the first movement and, especially, in the scherzo. The finale too, although splendidly played, loses its full bite and impact. But this performance is easy to enjoy, and has never sounded better than on this remastered DG Originals CD.

Symphonies Nos. 1 in G min. (Winter daydreams), Op. 13; 2 in C min. (Little Russian), Op. 17.
(BB) **(*) Belart 461 322-2. VPO, Lorin Maazel.

Having restored Maazel's Sibelius symphonies to the catalogue, Polygram's super-bargain Belart label here sets about reissuing his equally successful Tchaikovsky cycle, also made with the VPO in the 1960s. In the first two symphonies Maazel's performances clearly look forward to the emotional tautness of the mature symphonies from the *Fourth* onwards, rather than seeking to bring out the charm of the young composer's earliest essays in symphonic form. The resonant analogue recording, as transferred, has a degree of harshness and tends to prevent the music from smiling. Excellent value just the same: a disc that is well worth trying.

Symphony No. 4 in F min., Op. 36; Capriccio italien, Op. 45.
(M) * Sony SMK 61556 [id.]. NYPO, Bernstein.

This is music in which one expects Bernstein to excel, but instead he is too self-indulgent in the *Symphony* – the first movement is expansive and mannered, and generates little excitement. In fact, the performance as a whole is eccentric, and it is

small compensation that the 1959 recording sounds better than many of Bernstein's other NYPO discs. Performances such as Szell's electrifying Decca account show just why this one is a non-starter in today's market, though the *Capriccio italien* fill-up is enjoyable enough.

Symphony No. 4; Capriccio italien; Romeo and Juliet (fantasy overture).
*** Lodia Dig. LO-CD 791 [id.]. Moscow New Russian O, Carlos Païta.

Païta offers a highly compelling, at times interpretatively eccentric, Tchaikovsky collection, played with great ardour and conviction, if with not always precise ensemble by the Moscow New Russian Orchestra. The recording, made in the Great Hall of the Moscow Conservatoire in 1994, has all the necessary richness and amplitude, and plenty of brilliance; although orchestral textures are at times a little thick, the overall effect is full-bloodedly spectacular. *Romeo and Juliet*, which opens the concert, begins rather sombrely, but there is a riveting climax at the trumpet entry with the Friar Laurence theme and no lack of passion. Païta's *Capriccio italien* makes a superb encore after the symphony. It is exhilaratingly uninhibited, the opening fanfare matched by a sensational climax which almost defeats the engineers by its amplitude.

(i) *Symphony No. 4 in F min., Op. 36;* (ii) *Nutcracker suite, Op. 71a.*
(*) Gramophono mono AB 78 836 [id.]. (i) NBC SO; (ii) Phd. O, Stokowski.

Stokowski's 1941 recording of the *Fourth Symphony* is an extraordinary performance. It moves forward at an incredible speed throughout, as if the conductor had a train to catch. There are various idiosyncrasies, but far less than in his exasperating later stereo version with the American Symphony Orchestra, and only a small cut in the finale. But the constant feeling of rush sounds as if Stokowski were trying to ape Toscanini in pressing the music on ruthlessly (even in the middle section of the *Andantino*). In the finale the orchestral virtuosity is breathtaking, and no one can deny the excitement in the coda.

No explanation is given in the accompanying inadequate documentation, and one is left to wonder if he had to fit the performance into a tight broadcasting schedule: the overall timing is 39 minutes. But this reissue will do no service to the conductor's reputation, particularly as the recording is distant, dry and lustreless. It is even more insecure and poorly focused in the *Nutcracker suite*. In the *Miniature overture* the violins sound shrill and raw. Even so some of the Stokowskian magic is there, and images of *Fantasia* well up in the *Dance of the Sugar plum fairy*, with its seductive tenuto on the bass clarinet solo, and the *Arab* and *Chinese dances*.

(i) *Symphony No. 4 in F min., Op. 36;* (ii) *Romeo and Juliet* (fantasy overture).
🌑 (M) *** Decca Penguin Classics 460 655-2 [id.]. (i) LSO, Szell; (ii) VPO, Karajan.

This is one of the finest Tchaikovsky CDs in the catalogue with both performances unsurpassed. The *Fourth Symphony* even upstages Abbado's splendid version, helped by the more expansive Decca recording. All four movements show how Szell has rethought every detail of the score. The Scherzo has seldom sounded more kaleidoscopic in its colour contrasts, and the characterization of the slow movement is equally strong. The reading has great emotional power and a surging spontaneity underpinned by finely rehearsed orchestral playing and Szell's consistency. The finale is breathtaking and thereby hangs a tale. John Culshaw, so the story goes, felt that during the recording sessions Szell might be spurred on to even greater heights. So he played back the master tape of the finale to the conductor at a comparatively low level, cutting back the upper range to make the result sound duller than it really was. With that, Szell marched back to the rostrum and unleashed his full titanic power on the orchestra, and inspired the searingly white-hot culmination recorded here. The actual sound is something of a marvel too: full-blooded, detailed, warm and clear, and only in the loudest climaxes does one feel it wasn't recorded yesterday (it was recorded in 1962). Karajan's even earlier *Romeo and Juliet* is hardly less distinguished, far finer than his later DG version. The VPO bring a chilling beauty to the opening, subtly setting the scene for the ensuing drama. The great love theme has real passion, yet the delicate 'moonlight' sequence is played with ethereal beauty. The recording is rich and full (the timpani make a wonderful impact). This is a Penguin bargain not to be missed on any account. The specialist essay is by David Leavitt.

Symphony No. 5; The Tempest, Op. 18.
(M) **(*) Virgin/EMI Ultraviolet Dig. CUV5 61325 [CDC 59598]. Bournemouth SO, Andrew Litton.

Litton is surprisingly slow and steady in the first movement of the *Fifth*. The other three movements are first rate. The slow movement brings a beautiful horn solo, with the sound exquisitely distanced and with Litton sustaining his slow *Andante* well. Atmospherically recorded with slightly distanced sound in the Virgin manner, and transferred at a lower level than the rival issues, this version certainly has its attractions, when it has so rare and generous a fill-up. *The Tempest* makes an outstanding coupling.

Symphony No. 6 in B min. (Pathétique), Op. 74.
(M) **(*) EMI CDM5 67336-2 [id.]. Philh. O, Klemperer – SCHUMANN: *Symphony No. 4.*
***

(**(*)) BBC Legends mono BBCL 4023-2 [id.]. Philh. O, Giulini – MUSSORGSKY: *Pictures at an exhibition* (**(*).
(**) Orfeo mono C 521 991 B [id.]. VPO, Rafael Kubelik – MARTINU: *Three Frescos of Piero della Francesca* (**).

Klemperer's *Pathétique* was recorded in the Kingsway Hall in 1960 and in the present remastering it sounds splendid, far fuller than it ever did on LP and yet with no lack of brilliance. Nobility rather than agonized intensity is the keynote, and the climax of the first movement carries that hallmark (with a superb contribution from the Philharmonia trombones). The Scherzo/March is much more of a march than a scherzo but the neatly articulated playing prevents heaviness, and the finale is given a spacious dignity, even if the emotional thrust sounds consciously under control. But with such an impressive response from the Philharmonia strings the closing pages have great poignancy.

Giulini conducted this live performance at the 1961 Edinburgh Festival soon after recording the same work with the Philharmonia for EMI. The live reading is not so noticeably different. As in the studio, Giulini preserves a degree of restraint, finding nobility in Tchaikovsky's great melodies. But here the adrenalin of a live occasion brings a slightly more passionate treatment, although with the reprise of the second subject at the end of the first movement Giulini makes a spurt of accelerando which is not entirely convincing. However, the big melody of the slow finale is more flexible than before. Although this is not the most overwhelming of recorded *Pathétiques* it still represents Giulini at his most impressive, but the snag, almost as much as in the coupled Mussorgsky is the dryness of the mono sound, recorded in the unhelpful acoustic of the Usher Hall, Edinburgh. Alas the audience is never quite silent, and the beginnings of movements are especially prone to various noises, although there are no really disastrous bronchial afflictions and this remains a generous coupling, well worth hearing.

Kubelik's *Pathétique* formed the second part of a concert at the 1956 Salzburg Festival comprising the Dvořák *Violin concerto* and, to start with, the première of Martinů's *Three Frescos of Piero della Francesca*, of which Kubelik was the dedicatee. As with his performance of the *Fourth*, reissued on Royal Classics, Kubelik's account of the *Sixth* has a much going for it even if it lacks the demonic power and taut grip of a Mravinsky or a Karajan. Tempi are well judged and the performance has undoubted feeling, but the rather opaque mono sound will deter many collectors.

Symphony No. 6 in B min. (Pathétique); Romeo and Juliet (fantasy overture).
**(*) Ph. Dig. 456 580-2 [id.]. Kirov O, Valery Gergiev.

Valery Gergiev's performance of the *Sixth Symphony* with the Kirov Orchestra was recorded in Mikkeli, Finland, in 1995. His 1998 Salzburg Festival account of the *Fifth* with the Vienna Philharmonic was one of the highlights of 1999, and the *Pathétique* has much of the intensity and dramatic power of his *Fifth* but less of its pathos. Some may find it hard driven at times. There is no want of excitement or firmness of grip, though Gergiev is by no means as subtle, certainly in matters of dynamic nuance, as Pletnev (◉ VBD5 61636-2, with *The Seasons* – see comment below), though his Scherzo is nearly as headlong. The recording has impressive depth and impact, and must be ranked along with the best. The performance will be a little more controversial and will not appeal to everyone.

(i) *Symphony No. 6 (Pathétique);* (ii) *Swan Lake* (ballet): *suite.*
(BB) **(*) ASV Quicksilva Dig. CDQS 6091 [id.].
(i) LPO; (ii) RPO; Bátiz.
** Ph. Dig. 446 725-2. Saito Kinen O, Ozawa.

Bátiz's (1982) reading of the *Pathétique* is attractively fresh and direct, with the great second-subject melody the more telling for being understated and with transitions a little perfunctory. The brass are set rather forward, but this makes for very exciting climaxes. Otherwise the balance is good and the sound excellent. It is even better in the *Swan Lake* suite, recorded five years later. The RPO playing is polished, warm and alert, with Barry Griffiths and Françoise Rive sensitive string soloists in the *Danse des cygnes.* An excellent super-bargain coupling.

Characteristically, Seiji Ozawa brings out the balletic overtones in Tchaikovsky's symphonic masterpiece – a point emphasized by having the *Swan Lake* coupling. With him the start of the symphony is deceptively light, not ominous, and the sweet beauty of the Saito Kinen string playing adds to the feeling of poise and control. With exceptionally clean ensemble, even the central development section has no hint of hysteria. Taken very fast, the third movement march is so light it might almost be fairy music, opening out brilliantly as the march develops. The ballet suite, by contrast, comes in an understated performance, less alert than that of the symphony. The Japanese recording enhances the refinement and transparency of the playing.

The Tempest, Op. 18.
(BB) *** Virgin Classics 2 x 1 Dig. VBD5 61751-2 (2) [CDVB 61751]. Bournemouth SO, Andrew Litton – BORODIN: *Prince Igor: Overture and Polovtsian dances*; MUSSORGSKY: *Night on the bare mountain*; *Pictures at an exhibition* **; RIMSKY-KORSAKOV: *Scheherazade* **(*).

The Shakespearean symphonic fantasy *The Tempest* – not to be confused with the much less ambitious

overture of the same name, written for Ostrovsky's play – is given a glowing performance under Litton, passionately committed, yet refined, to suggest a forgotten masterpiece. It is a pity that the rest of the performances here do not measure up to this standard, although all are very well played and recorded.

CHAMBER MUSIC

Piano trio in A min., Op. 50.
(B) *(**) EMI Double Fforte CZS5 73650-2 (2) [CDFB 73650]. Zukerman, Barenboim, Du Pré – BEETHOVEN: *Violin sonatas.* **(*)

The Zukerman, Barenboim, Du Pré performance was taped at a concert given in 1972 at the Mann Auditorium, Tel Aviv, made by the Israel Broadcasting Authority and digitally remastered by EMI. This performance has great ardour and all the immediacy of a live concert, and that more than compensates for the odd inelegance that might have been corrected in the recording studio, or the occasional moment of impetuosity from the pianist in the formidable piano part. There is nothing routine about Barenboim's playing: he takes plenty of risks and is unfailingly imaginative; it is a pity that the instrument itself is not worthy of him, for it sounds less than fresh. Zukerman also sustains a high level of intensity and at times is close to schmaltz. However, this is without doubt a high-voltage performance, though the sound quality is very average. Incidentally, the traditional cut sanctioned by the composer is observed here. An exciting bonus for a recommendable set of the Beethoven *Violin sonatas.*

PIANO MUSIC

Album for the young, Op. 39: (i) original piano version; (ii) trans. for string quartet by Dubinsky.
*** Chandos CHAN 8365 [id.]. (i) Luba Edlina;
(ii) augmented Borodin Trio.

These 24 pieces are all miniatures, but they have great charm; their invention is often memorable, with quotations from Russian folksongs and one French, plus a brief reminder of *Swan Lake*. Here they are presented twice, in their original piano versions, sympathetically played by Luba Edlina, and in effective string quartet transcriptions arranged by her husband, Rostislav Dubinsky. The Borodin group play them with both affection and finesse. The CD has plenty of presence.

The Seasons, Op. 37b; Aveu passioné; Berceuse, Op. 72/2; Méditation, Op. 72/5; Polka peu dansante, Op. 51/2; Tendres reproches, Op. 72/3.
*** Decca Dig. 466 562-2 [id.]. Vladimir Ashkenazy.

It is good to see more attention being paid to Tchaikovsky's piano music. Vladimir Ashkenazy gives a poised and finely prepared account of *The Seasons* which is very well recorded. At the same time it does not match Pletnev in terms of poetic insight or tenderness. The charming numbers from the *Eighteen Pieces*, Op. 72 are beautifully done too. But Pletnev's superb account of *The Seasons* is on a Virgin 2 x 1 Double and also includes his performance of the *Pathétique Symphony* (● VBD5 61636-2 – see our main volume).

Piano sonata No. 2 in G (Grand), *Op. 37a; Capriccio in G flat, Op. 8; Children's album, Op. 39; 12 Pieces, Op. 40; Romance in F min., Op. 5.*
(B) *** BMG/Melodiya Twofer 74321 66975-2 (2) [id.]. Mikhail Pletnev.

Although Pletnev's outstanding set of *The Seasons* (● Virgin VBD5 61636-2) and Sviatoslav Richter's miscellaneous recital on Olympia (OCD 334) should not be forgotten (see our main volume), this Melodiya Twofer is now the most important and most desirable single selection of Tchaikovsky's piano music currently available. These performances all come from 1986–7 when Pletnev was in his late twenties and, though some appeared briefly on specialist labels, the majority of the repertoire enjoyed limited or no exposure. It includes a wholly convincing account of the *G major 'Grand' Sonata*, with its long and somewhat intractable first movement splendidly handled. Pletnev's virtuosity is dazzling, and the delicacy and range of keyboard colour together with his depth of feeling, is ever in evidence. Much poetry is found in the *Andante*, with a brilliant display of bravura reserved for the vivace finale. The twenty-three miniatures which make up the delightful *Children's album* and the *12 Pieces, Op.* 40 'of average difficulty' consistently show the composer's melodic gift at its most engaging, and Pletnev's playing is wonderfully sympathetic. The strong characterization of the children's pieces (many descriptive, like the charming *Dolly* triptych ending with *Dolly's funeral*) gives them a much stronger melodic profile than usual, while Pletnev finds a Chopinesque influence in the two charming *Waltzes* of Op. 40. Yet always the Russian colouring brings a special flavour of its own; and this applies particularly to the *Romance in F minor*. The Melodiya digital recording is of unexpectedly good quality. There is a touch of hardness in the more forceful playing in the *Sonata*, where the sound is shallow and does not do full justice to his tone, but the calibre of his playing still shines through. Elsewhere, the piano timbre is for the most part quite full, and at lower dynamic levels warmly coloured. Most enjoyable – music to return to for sheer pleasure. Pletnev recorded the *Eighteen Pieces*, Op. 72 with exceptional brilliance at about the same time, and we must hope that BMG/Melodiya will also issue this over here.

VOCAL MUSIC

The Snow Maiden, Op. 12 (complete incidental music).
(M) *** Chant du Monde Dig. RUS 788090. Natalia Erasova, Alexander Arkipov, Nikolai Vassiliev, Sveshnikov Russian State Ch., Bolshoi Theatre O, Andrey Chistiakov.
(BB) **(*) Naxos Dig. 8.553856 [id.]. Elena Okolysheva, Arkady Mishenkin, Moscow Capella, Moscow SO, Golovschin.

Ostrovsky's play *The Snow Maiden*, based on a Russian folk-tale, prompted Tchaikovsky to compose incidental music, no fewer than 19 numbers, lasting 80 minutes, a cherishable rarity. Much of it is vintage material, very delightful, bringing reminders of *Eugene Onegin* in the peasant choruses and some of the folk-based songs, and of the later Tchaikovskian world of *The Nutcracker* in some of the dances. He himself thought so well of the music that he wanted to develop it into an opera, but was frustrated when Rimsky-Korsakov wrote one first.

Chistiakov's fine 1994 performance, now reissued on Chant du Monde's mid-priced Russian label, is in every way recommendable at mid-price. The three excellent soloists are characterfully Slavonic, rather too forwardly balanced but well caught by the recording, and the fine singing of the chorus is given both sonority and plenty of bite. The orchestral playing is highly persuasive in a pleasingly atmospheric acoustic.

Tchaikovsky's engaging score also inspires Golovschin and his Moscow forces to a warmly idiomatic performance on Naxos, richly and colourfully recorded, if without quite the same degree of vividness. This may not match the Chant du Monde version in vitality, which at generally faster speeds sparkles more and offers crisper ensemble, but it is similarly persuasive. The conductor's affection is obvious. There are only two soloists to share the vocal music, but they are convincingly Slavonic and they are balanced slightly less forwardly. This Naxos disc is well worth its more modest cost. Both recordings offer full translations. However, Jarvi's Chandos version is even finer (CHAN9324) – see our main volume.

OPERA

Eugene Onegin (complete).
**(*) Ph. Dig. 438 235-2 (2) [id.]. Hvorostovsky, Focile, Shicoff, Borodina, Anisimov, St Petersburg Chamber Ch., O de Paris, Bychkov.

Dmitri Hvorostovsky makes a strong, heroic Onegin in the Philips set, though Bychkov's conducting does not always encourage him to be as animated as one wants, and the voice at times comes near to straining. Nuccia Focile also emerges at her most convincing only in the final scene of confrontation with Onegin. Earlier, her voice is too fluttery to convey the full pathos of the young Tatiana in the *Letter scene*, edgy at the top. Neil Shicoff as Lensky also suffers, though he sings with passionate commitment, conveying the neurotic element in the poet's character. As Gremin, Alexander Anisimov also has a grainy voice. Olga Borodina sings impressively as Olga, but on balance the other characters are better cast in Solti's Decca set.

Tcherepnin, Alexander (1899–1977)

10 Bagatelles for piano and orchestra, Op. 5.
(M) *** DG 463 085-2 [id.]. Margrit Weber, RSO, Berlin, Fricsay – MARTINU: *Fantasia concertante* ***; WEBER: *Konzertstück* **(*); FALLA: *Nights in the gardens of Spain* ***.

Tcherepnin's *Ten bagatelles*, originally piano pieces, are full of imaginative touches. Essentially light in spirit, they are not without some haunting melancholy passages too. The performances are ideal, and the 1960 recording is full and vivid.

(i) *Piano concerto No. 5, Op. 96. Symphonies Nos. 1 in E, Op. 42; 2 in E flat, Op. 77.*
*** BIS Dig. CD 1017 [id.]. Singapore SO, Lan Shui (i) with Noriko Ogawa.

(i) *Piano concerto No. 6, Op. 99. Symphonies Nos. 3 in F sharp, Op. 83; 4 in E , Op. 91.*
*** BIS Dig. CD 1017 [id.]. Singapore SO, Lan Shui (i) with Noriko Ogawa.

Alexander Tcherepnin was the son of the composer Nikolai, who conducted when the Diaghilev Ballet made its Paris début. After the Revolution he went to Tiflis, where Georgian folk music made a strong impression on him. In 1921 he settled in Paris, becoming one of the group of composers known as *l'école de Paris* whose members included Tansman and Martinů. He spent some time in China during his thirties, where he taught at the Shanghai Conservatoire, so it is appropriate that a Chinese conductor should champion him. The rest of his life was divided between concert and teaching commitments in Paris, Chicago, New York and London. The *First Symphony* of 1927 caused a stir, not so much on account of its radical musical language as the fact that its Scherzo was written for percussion only. It is inventive and stimulating, and full of personality. The *Second Symphony* did not follow until the end of the 1939–45 war, and two successors followed in the 1950s: the *Third* in 1952, and the *Fourth*, commissioned by Charles Münch and the Boston Orchestra, in 1958–59.

It is with the *Fourth* that the newcomer to Tcherepnin's music should start. Its invention is wonderfully alert and fresh, and the control of pace masterly. Ideas are introduced at what one feels

is exactly the right time and never outstay their welcome. It is neoclassical in feeling with a great sense of wit and style. This well-recorded account displaces the Slovak Orchestra's version on Marco Polo, discussed in our main volume where it was inadvertently listed under Nikolai Tcherepnin's entry. The two piano concertos are from the 1960s and are elegantly played by Noriko Ogawa. The Singapore Orchestra has greatly improved since its early Marco Polo records under Choo Hoey and the Chinese conductor Lan Shui gets generally good results from them.

Telemann, Georg Philipp
(1681–1767)

Flute concertos in B min.; C; D (2); E; E min.
*** VAI Audio VAIA 1166 [id.]. Robert Stallman, Phd. Concerto Soloists CO.

This is one of the most delightful Telemann collections in the catalogue. Every one of these fine concertos, galant and Italianate by turns, shows the composer's invention at its most fertile and imaginative. All but one is in four movements. The *E minor*, which is in five, is perhaps finest of all. It has three vigorous *Prestos* framing two central *Adagios*, the first of which the flute shares with a solo violin against a pizzicato accompaniment, and the second, a languorous intermezzo, introduces the dancing finale. The Vivaldian *Dolce e staccato* opening movement of the *E major* is particularly striking. The *D major*'s finale is a bouncing Minuet, with delicious bird trills in the Trio, while in the extended first movement of the B minor work Telemann heralds the return of the final tutti with a repeated 'posthorn' call from the soloist emerging distinctly from his running roulades. Robert Stallman is a stylish and elegant player and he is given crisply sympathetic modern instrument accompaniments from the Philadelphia Chamber Orchestra. Excellent recording too and detailed notes from Arbie Orenstein, which tell us that these scores (held in Darmstadt Library) have not yet been given TWV numbers, which is a pity as two of them are in D major.

Concerto for flute, oboe d'amore and viola d'amore in E; Concerto polonois; Double concerto for recorder and flute in E min.; Triple trumpet concerto in D; Quadro in B flat.
*** O-L Dig. (IMS) 411 949-2 [id.]. AAM with soloists, Hogwood.

'An attentive observer could gather from these folk musicians enough ideas in eight days to last a lifetime,' wrote Telemann after spending a summer in Pless in Upper Silesia. Polish ideas are to be found in three of the concertos recorded here – indeed, one of the pieces is called *Concerto polonois*. As always, Telemann has a refined ear for sonority, and the musical discourse with which he diverts us is unfailingly intelligent and delightful. The performances are excellent and readers will not find cause for disappointment in either the recording or presentation.

(i) *Concerto for 2 flutes, 2 oboes and strings in B flat;* (ii) *Triple concerto for flute, oboe d'amore, violin and strings in E; Oboe d'amore concerto in D; Trumpet concerto in D;* (iii) *Concerto for trumpet and 2 oboes in D;* (ii) *Double viola concerto in G;* (i) *Concerto for 3 trumpets, 2 oboes, timpani and strings in D;* (iv) *Double concerto for violin, trumpet and strings in D;* (i) *Suite in G (La Putain); Tafelmusik, Part I: Conclusion in E min. for 2 flutes and strings.*
(M) *** Van. 08.9138.72 (2) [id.]. (i) Soloists, Esterházy O, David Blum; (ii) Soloists, I Solisti di Zagreb, Antonio Janigro; (iii) Peter Masseurs, Amsterdam Bach Soloists; (iv) Mincho Minchev, Nikolai Chochev, Sofia Soloists, Vasil Kazandiev.

The interest of the repertoire here outweighs any minor reservations about the recording, which comes from the 1960s, for the sound is warm and full and the performances are expert. The diversity of Telemann's inexhaustible invention is well demonstrated. In the *Concerto for two violas* the soloists interweave with the orchestral texture, a device borrowed from Vivaldi, who named it 'violette all'inglese'. The solo *Oboe d'amore concerto* and *Trumpet concerto* are both fine, four-movement works, but it is the collective concertos that offer the greatest interest. The *Concerto for two flutes, two oboes and strings* begins elegantly with richly mellifluous blending; then, after a busy *Presto*, the two oboes open the *Cantabile* unaccompanied in a gravely Handelian melody. The *Triple concerto for flute, oboe d'amore and violin in E major* opens with an imposingly spacious *Andante*, very like an introduction to an aria or a chorus from an oratorio; then, after a lively allegro, comes a particularly fine *Siciliano*. The *Concerto for three trumpets, two oboes and timpani* brings a sprightly Handelian fugue, including trumpets and oboes within the part-writing. The oboes gently dominate the gravely expressive *Largo* arietta, followed by a rollicking finale. The result is irresistible. The suite *La Putain* ('The Prostitute') contains an invitation by way of a folksong (*Ich bin so lang nicht bei dir g'west*) to 'Come up and see me sometime'. The suite of strongly characterized dances which follows reminds one of the incidental music of Lully and Rameau in its feeling for colour. The *Concerto for trumpet and two oboes in D* is added on to the end of the first CD, and the performance by the Amsterdam Bach Soloists (with Peter Masseurs a splendid trumpet soloist) appears to use original instruments. The second CD closes the programme with a brief contribution from Sofia, the *Concerto for violin, trumpet and strings in D*, vividly played but rather thinly recorded. But overall this highly stimulating set must receive the warmest possible welcome.

Concerto in D for trumpet, strings and continuo; Concerto in D for trumpet, 2 oboes and continuo; Concerto in D for trumpet, 2 oboes, strings and continuo; Double trumpet concerto in E flat; Concerto in D for 3 trumpets, timpani, 2 oboes, strings and continuo; Overture in D for 4 trumpets (originally 2), timpani, strings and continuo; Sinfonia for trumpet, 3 trombones, recorder, viola da gamba (cello), oboe, strings and continuo; Suite in D for trumpet, strings and continuo.
*** Nimbus Dig. NI 5189 [id.]. John Wallace and soloists, E. String O, William Boughton.

It might be thought that so many trumpet works placed together might be too much of a good thing, but while we would not suggest that this is a CD to play all at one go, these concertos are amazingly diverse in colour and texture. The familiar D major solo concerto is a very fine work and so is the eight-movement *Suite* for trumpet and strings. But the concertante pieces which mix oboes and other instruments into the cooking-pot show the amazing variety of colour Telemann could command, and his inexhaustible supply of melody is expressive and vivacious. The programme opens with the *Overture*, where four trumpets are regally substituted for two: the effect is spectacular. Superb solo playing throughout, from John Wallace in particular, and all his colleagues, excellent accompaniments from the English String Orchestra under Boughton, and warmly resonant recording, made in a favourite Nimbus venue, the Great Hall of Birmingham University. The only real criticism here, and it is a very real one, is the lack of proper identification of each work, except the *Double concerto in E flat* which comes from the *Tafelmusik*.

Oboe concertos in C min.; D; D min.; E min.; F min.
*** Ph. Dig. (IMS) 412 879-2 [id.]. Holliger, ASMF, Iona Brown.

The *C minor Concerto* with its astringent opening dissonance is the most familiar of the concertos on Holliger's record. Telemann was himself proficient on the oboe and wrote with particular imagination and poignancy for this instrument. The performances are all vital and sensitively shaped and a valuable addition to the Telemann discography. Well worth investigation.

Recorder concertos in C; in F; Suite in A min. for recorder and string; (i) *Sinfonia in F.*
**(*) Hyperion Dig. CDA 66413 [id.]. Peter

Holtslag, Parley of Instruments, Peter Holman or (i) Roy Goodman.

The three solo concertos here are a delight. Peter Holtslag's piping treble recorder is truthfully balanced, in proper scale with the authentic accompaniments, which are neat, polished, sympathetic and animated. The *Sinfonia* is curiously scored, for recorder, oboe, solo bass viol, strings, cornett, three trombones and an organ, with doubling of wind and string parts. Even with Roy Goodman balancing everything expertly the effect is slightly bizarre. About the great *Suite in A minor* there are some reservations: it is played with much nimble bravura and sympathy on the part of the soloist, but the orchestral texture sounds rather thin.

Darmstadt Overtures (Suites): for 3 oboes, bassoon, and strings: in C, TWV 55/C6; in D, TWV 55/D15; in G min., TWV 55/G4.
(BB) *** Naxos Dig. 8.554244 [id.]. Cologne CO, Helmut Müller-Brühl.

These three overtures or suites originate from Telemann's period in Frankfurt, and were almost certainly composed for the Darmstadt Court. They are in either seven or eight movements, for the most part dances, such as Loures and Gigues, but also include free instrumental diversions with titles such as *Harlequinade, Irrésoluts, Espagnole, Sommeille, Bourée en trompette* and *Réjouissance*, and it is here that the composer lets his hair down a little, with piquant instrumental effects. But the scoring throughout brings much variety of colour and plenty of tuneful invention. These modern-instrument performances are delightfully vivacious and elegant. This is a first-class chamber orchestra and Müller-Brühl's light rhythmic touch keeps the dance movements sparkling. The recording is excellent. A most entertaining collection.

Suites: in B flat, TW 55/B 10; in C, TWV 55/C6; in D, TWV 55/D 19.
(B) *** DG Classikon Dig. 463 260-2 [id.]. E. Concert, Trevor Pinnock.

There is some marvellous music here, and each suite has its own lollipops, the Hornpipe and charming Plainte in the *B flat major Suite*, the sensuous Someille in the *C major* work (although one can imagine this would sound even creamier on modern wind instruments) while the *D major* work has a most fetching Bourrée, fully worthy of Handel. It brings a feather-light moto perpetuo for strings at its centre, and the Ecossaise with its witty Scottish snap has a similar contrast, bringing the neatest possible articulation from the English Concert players. There is lots of vitality here and crisp, clean rhythms. Just occasionally one feels the need for more of a smile and greater textural warmth – the rasping, integrated hunting horns don't add a great deal to the *D major Suite* – but this is still a very worthwhile and generous collection (76 minutes), realistically recorded.

Reissued on DG's Classikon label it is a very real bargain.

Tafelmusik: Productions 1–4 (complete).
(B) **(*) Naxos Dig. 8.553724/5 & 8.553731 [id.]. Orchestra of the Golden Age.
**(*) MDG Dig. MDG 311 0580-2 (3) [id.]. Camerata of the 18th Century, Konrad Hünteler.

The Orchestra of the Golden Age is a new chamber group based in Manchester, playing with a good sense of style, plenty of life and a convincing linear manner in expressive music. They represent one of Naxos's first excusions into period-instrument music-making and are very well recorded. While Brüggen and the Concerto Amsterdam (Teldec 4509 95519-2) and Reinhard Goebel's Cologne Musiqua Antiqua (DG 427 619-2) have something special to offer in this music, this Naxos set is excellent value and will give considerable satisfaction.

The Camerata of the 18th Century are based in Amsterdam. They too give expert performances of this repertoire which show an appealing affectionate warmth. But they are recorded in a fairly resonant church acoustic and while this gives a pleasing added warmth, and makes the overall effect more orchestral, with less chamber intimacy, inner detail is less readily revealed. But the solo playing is felicitous and many will enjoy the fuller string textures here.

Thomas, Ambroise (1811–96)

Mignon: Overture and Gavotte.
*** Chandos Dig. CHAN 9765 [id.]. BBC PO, Yan Pascal Tortelier (with Concert: 'French bonbons' ***).

Thomas's opera *Mignon* has one of the most delectable of all French overtures, with its opening woodwind and harp solos followed by a romantic horn tune. It is beautifully played and recorded in this first-rate concert of French lollipops – see Concerts below.

Tiomkin, Dimitri (1894–1979)

Film music: The Fall of the Roman Empire: Overture; Pax Romana. The Guns of Navarone: Prologue-Prelude; Epilogue. A President's country. Rhapsody of steel. Wild is the wind.
(M) **(*) Unicorn UKCD 2079 [id.]. Royal College of Music O, Willcocks; D. King (organ).

Dimitri Tiomkin contributed scores to some of the most famous movies of all time, for Hitchcock and Frank Capra among others. But it was Carl Foreman's *High noon* that produced his most memorable idea, and he quotes its famous theme, among others, in *A President's country*, a well-crafted medley used as background music for a documentary about President Johnson's Texas. *Wild is the wind* is another familiar melody; Christopher Palmer's arrangement makes a tastefully scored showcase. The latter has arranged and orchestrated all the music here except *Rhapsody of steel*, a complex pseudo-symphonic score written for another documentary, which lasts some 22 minutes. The music of *Pax Romana* has the robust character of a typical Hollywood epic costume spectacular, featuring a bold contribution from the organ. All the music is played with obvious enjoyment by the Orchestra of the Royal College of Music; no apologies need be made for their technique, which is fully professional. Sir David Willcocks conducts with understanding of the idiom and great personal conviction. The recording is very impressive too, if with brass and percussion rather too prominent.

Tippett, Michael (1905–98)

A Child of our time (oratorio).
(M) **(*) Carlton Dig. 30367 0205-2 [id.].
   Armstrong, Palmer, Langridge, Shirley-Quirk, Brighton Festival Ch., RPO, Previn.

Previn's is a colourful and winning performance, warmer and more expressive than Davis's, helped by the conductor's natural understanding of jazz rhythms. This is a reading which leaves you in no doubt as to the depth of emotion felt by the composer; but ensemble is not always ideally crisp, the chorus is set rather backwardly and the characterful soloists have uneven moments. The digital recording is unobtrusively natural, if slightly recessed.

Tomlinson, Ernest (born 1924)

Aladdin: 3 dances (Birdcage dance; Cushion dance; Belly dance); Comedy overture; Cumberland Square; English folk-dance suite No. 1; Light music suite; Passepied; (i) Rhapsody and rondo for horn and orchestra. Brigadoon; Shenandoah (arrangement).
*** Marco Polo Dig. 8.223513 [id.]. (i) Richard Watkins; Slovak RSO (Bratislava), composer.

This second collection of the light music of Ernest Tomlinson is every bit as enjoyable as the first. The opening *Comedy overture* is racily vivacious, and there are many charming vignettes here, delectably tuneful and neatly scored, and the pastiche dance movements are nicely elegant. The *Pizzicato humoresque* (from the *Light music suite*) is every bit as winning as other, more famous pizzicato movements, and in the *Rhapsody and rondo* for

horn Tomlinson quotes wittily from both Mozart and Britten. The composer finally lets his hair down in the rather vulgar *Belly dance*, but the concert ends well with the charming *Georgian miniature*. The playing is elegant and polished, its scale perfectly judged, and the recording is first class.

An English overture; 3 Gaelic sketches: Gaelic lullaby. Kielder Water; Little serenade; Lyrical suite: Nocturne. Nautical interlude; 3 Pastoral dances: Hornpipe. Silverthorne suite; 2nd Suite of English folk dances; Sweet and dainty; arr. of Coates: *The fairy coach; Cinderella waltz.*
*** Marco Polo Dig. 8.223413 [id.]. Slovak RSO (Bratislava), the composer.

Ernest Tomlinson's orchestral pieces charm by the frothy lightness of the scoring. The winningly delicate *Little serenade*, which opens the disc, is the most famous, but the gentle, evocative *Kielder Water*, the captivating *Canzonet* from the *Silverthorne suite* and the *Nocturne* are hardly less appealing. *Love-in-a-mist* is as intangible as it sounds, with the most fragile of oboe solos, and it is not surprising that *Sweet and dainty* has been used for a TV commercial. There is robust writing too, in the *Folk song suite* – but not too robust, although the jolly *English overture* begins with *Here's a health unto His Majesty* and certainly does not lack vitality. The music is played with much grace and the lightest possible touch by the remarkably versatile Slovak Radio Orchestra under the composer, and the vivid recording has delightfully transparent textures, so vital in this repertoire.

Torch, Sidney (1908–1990)

All strings and fancy free; Barbecue; Bicycle Belles; Comic cuts; Concerto incognito; Cresta run; Duel for drummers; Going for a ride; London Transport suite; Mexican fiesta; On a Spring note; Petite valse; Samba sud; Shooting star; Shortcake walk; Slavonic rhapsody; Trapeze waltz.
*** Marco Polo Dig. 8.223443 [id.]. BBC Concert O, Wordsworth.

Sydney Torch was one of the most talented and prolific writers of British light classical music of the last century, though interestingly he was of Russian-Jewish origin. He worked frequently with the BBC Concert Orchestra – the orchestra on this CD – and for many he is remembered for his weekly broadcasts: 'Friday Night is Music Night'. The *London Transport suite* was commissioned by the BBC for their Light Music festival of 1957, and was inspired by the withdrawal of 'The Brighton Belle' on the London to Brighton railway service. Each of its three movements represents a mode of transport: *The Hansom cab, Rosie, the red omnibus* and *The 5:52 from Waterloo.*

It is an engagingly witty piece, full of appropriate noises – whips, horse and steam-train noises – even a back-firing car – and of course some endearing tunes, all delightfully presented. In fact, all the music here is tuneful, sometimes wistful and nostalgic, at others bright and breezy – *All strings and fancy free* is both. *Barbecue* sounds like a Scottish snap, whilst the *Trapeze waltz* is reminiscent of the circus music of Satie. The *Concerto incognito* is very much in the *Warsaw concerto* mould, and the *Petite waltz* (also with piano), is more robust than its title suggests.

The *Mexican fiesta* and *Samba Sud* produce some fine local colour and are very jolly, whilst the *Slavonic rhapsody* (with two pianos) is a fun work drawing on the music of Rimsky-Korsakov, Tchaikovsky, Knipper, Borodin and Khachaturian, to form an entertaining if outrageous pastiche. The longest work is the *Duel for drummers* which, as its title suggests, is a *tour de force* for the percussion department; it has some ideas which are reminiscent of Eric Coates and a few surprises, including a cockerel crowing, and a desert-island storm in the central movement. It ends with a lively galop. Barry Wordsworth conducts with flair and the recording is excellent.

Torke, Michael (born 1961)

(i) *Book of Proverbs;* (ii) *4 Proverbs.*
**(*) Decca Dig. 466 721-2 [id.]. (i) Valdine Anderson, Kurt Ollman, Netherlands R. Ch. & PO, Edo de Waart; (ii) Catherine Bott, Argo Band, composer.

Taking cryptic fragments from the Book of Proverbs in the Old Testament, Michael Torke uses the words to create musical patterns, both in the eight orchestral songs of *Book of Proverbs* and in the four chamber-scale settings of the second work. This is all warmly approachable music, often sounding suspiciously like Aaron Copland in full American mode, with syncopated rhythms and colourful instrumentation. Only two of the orchestral set involve soloists – both excellent – with the choir warmly expressive as the main protagonist, even if the backward balance is hardly a help. Catherine Bott, best known as an early music specialist, proves an outstanding soloist in the chamber-scale songs, singing with sensuous tone, though Torke as a conductor is less incisive than de Waart in the Dutch performances.

Tower, Joan (born 1939)

Concerto for orchestra; Duets for orchestra; Fanfares for the uncommon woman Nos. 1–5.
*** Koch Dig. 3-7469-2 [id.]. Colorado SO, Marin Alsop.

Joan Tower studied and began composing as a serialist, but hearing Messiaen's *Quartet for the end of time* was 'bowled over by the emotional directness of the music . . . I felt like an acrobat . . . it [serial music] was a sport, it wasn't like being a musician. So I pulled out'. Although the *First* makes an opening nod towards Copland, the style of the *Five Fanfares* is nearer to John Adams, although there are influences from Stravinsky too. The writing is complex and florid, rhythmically vibrant and vivid: each is different in instrumentation and texture. (Incidentally, the detailed notes in the booklet, giving the scoring of each, are confusing, suggesting that the order of performance probably exchanges Nos. 2 and 5.) In the ambitious *Concerto for orchestra*, Bartók (not surprisingly) can be discerned too, but it is the atmospheric use of colour and the yearningly lyrical kernel of the work that one remembers, for all the dynamism and orchestral brilliance, and that applies equally to the *Duets*. This is emotional, communicative writing, but Joan Tower needs to draw again from John Adams and focus her melodic lines more positively. Marin Alsop presents all this music with a Bernstein-like intensity and dedication, and the Colorado Symphony produce playing of great bravura and obvious depth of response, with an eloquent tuba among the lyrical solos at the centre of the *Concerto*. The recording in the spacious acoustic of Denver's Boettcher Concert Hall could hardly be bettered.

Trimble, Joan (born 1915)

(i) *Phantasy trio.* (ii; iii) Music for 2 pianos: *The Baird of Lisgoole; Buttermilk point; The green bough; The humours of Carrick (Hop-jig); Pastorale: Homage à Poulenc; Puck Fair; Sonatina.* 3 Traditional songs: *The cows are a-milking; Gartan Mother's lullaby; The heather glen.* (iv; iii) County Mayo song cycle: *The County Mayo; Peggy Mitchell; Inis Fail; In the poppy field.* (v; iii) 3 Songs: *Girl's song; Green rain; My grief on the sea.*
**(*) Marco Polo Dig. 8.225059 [id.]. (i) Dublin Piano Trio; (ii) Una Hunt; (iii) Roy Holmes; (iv) Joe Corbett; (v) Patricia Bardon.

In the 1930s, at the suggestion of Arthur Benjamin, Joan and Valerie Trimble established a celebrated piano duo, and in turn he wrote for them the *Jamaican rumba*, which they made world famous. But Joan proved a talented composer in her own right, drawing on the rich vein of Irish folk song and composing her own pieces in a similar style. Their simplicity and freshness of inspiration give much pleasure, as does the deft keyboard writing. There are other influences too, from the French school in the *Sonatina* and the *Pastorale* and from Vaughan Williams, who suggested the composition of the passionate, yearning *Piano trio* (*Phantasy*), which is very English in feeling. But it is for the winning Irish keyboard duo pieces that Joan Trimble will be remembered and they are played here with just the right lightness of touch. The songs are certainly worth preserving on disc, although their performances are less so. Joe Corbett is a sympathetic 'Irish' interpreter of the *County Mayo cycle*, but his presentation is only really distinctive in the lively final song, *In the poppy field*, with the *Buttermilk reel* piano duo making a sparkling postlude. The soprano songs, although eloquently sung, are let down by Patricia Bardon's intrusively wide vibrato.

Ustvolskaya, Galina (born 1919)

(i) *Piano concerto* (for piano, string orchestra and timpani); (ii; iii) *Grand duet* (for cello and piano); (iv) *Octet* (for 2 oboes, 4 violins, timpani and piano); (iii) *Piano sonata No. 3.*
(M) ** BMG Melodiya 74321 49956-2 [id.]. (i) Pavel Serebryakov, Leningrad State Philharmonic Soc. CO; (ii) Oleg Stolpner; (iii) Oleg Malov; (iv) Kosoyan, Chinakov & Ens.

Galina Ustvolskaya was first a pupil of Shostakovich at the Leningrad Conservatoire and then became his assistant until the Zhdanov decree resulted in their dismissal along with Shebalin and others. Despite Shostakovich's support, her music remained in the shadows during the Soviet years, and it was only in the 1990s that she came into her own. The *Piano concerto* comes from 1946, the period of her studies with Shostakovich, whose imprint it bears; and this 1970 performance by Pavel Serebryakov and the Leningrad Chamber Orchestra was its première. The *Octet*, a strong piece with some of the heiratic feeling of Stravinsky, was composed in 1949–50 but again not premièred until the 1970s. There are six piano sonatas, composed between 1947 and 1988, and the *Third*, from 1952, has a spare, uncompromising angularity that is extraordinarily radical for the early 1950s, astonishingly so for the Soviet Union. In its rather arid writing there is a lack of rhythmic variety and it asserts and repeats its ideas rather than developing them. The *Cello duet* was composed in the 1960s for Rostropovich. For many it will be a tough nut to crack, but there is no doubt that, like so much of the music of this reclusive figure, it springs from a genuine vision. An interesting and worthwhile issue, though (with the exception of the *Cello duet*) the recordings come from the 1970s and are not top-drawer.

Vainberg, Moishei (1919–96)

Piano sonatas Nos. 1, Op. 5; 2, Op. 8; 3, Op. 31; 17 Easy pieces, Op. 34.

** Olympia Dig. OCD 595 [id.]. Murray McLachlan.

Piano sonatas Nos. 4, Op. 56; 5, Op. 58; 6, Op. 73.
** Olympia Dig. OCD 596 [id.]. Murray McLachlan.

Vainberg's output was extensive (twenty-two symphonies and some seventeen string quartets) but he wrote very little for the piano. He was a good pianist himself and a duet partner of Shostakovich on occasion. The first two sonatas come from the early 1940s and are close in idiom to Prokofiev and Shostakovich. The *Third Sonata* and the *17 Easy pieces* are both post-war (1946). The impressive *Fourth Sonata* (1955) enjoyed the advocacy of Gilels, who recorded it two years after its composition (he had also given the earlier sonatas in recital programmes). Its two successors are strong, well-wrought pieces, and the *Fifth* has an imposing well-argued *Passacaglia*, but after the *Sixth* (1960), Vainberg seems to have abandoned the medium. The enterprising Murray McLachlan has already put us in his debt with his recordings of the nine Miaskovsky sonatas and his commitment to and belief in the present repertoire is never in doubt. He is recorded in Gothenburg (not in the Concert Hall unfortunately but the university's hall) and although the sound is satisfactory it is not as open or fresh. All the same, those whose appetite has been aroused by the *Fourth Symphony* or the late *Chamber symphonies* will want to explore these for themselves. The notes by Per Skans are very informative.

Vaňhal, Jan (1739–1813)

Symphonies in A, Bryan: A9; in C, Bryan: C3; in C, Bryan: C11; in D, Bryan: D17.
(BB) *** Naxos Dig. 8.554341 [id.]. Nicolaus Esterházy Sinfonia, Uwe Grodd.

Even amongst the many new discs of forgotten music by Mozart's contemporaries this Naxos issue stands out. Born in Bohemia in 1739 of peasant stock, Johann Baptist (Jan) Vaňhal was one of the most successful composers in Vienna, producing over 1,300 compositions in many genres. These four compact symphonies, representing different periods of his career, are all winningly colourful and inventive, often bringing surprises that defy the conventions of the time. The Esterházy Sinfonia under Uwe Grodd give attractively lively performances with some stylish solo work, vividly recorded.

Symphonies in A min.; C (Sinfonia comista); D min.; E min.; G min.
**(*) Teldec/Warner Dig. 0630 13141-2 [id.]. Concerto Köln.

Vaňhal (or Wanhal, as he himself signed his name) was born in Bohemia but spent the bulk of his life in Vienna, where these works were composed during the 1760s and 1770s. This was the period of the so-called *Sturm und Drang* symphonies in a minor key with a keen, driving intensity, of which Haydn's *La Passione* is a good example. These are works of vivid and lively invention which also embrace a wide diversity of approach. The *C major* (*Sinfonia comista*), one of his later symphonies, differs from its companions in its richness of scoring and programmatic inspiration. The Concerto Köln play with spirit, enthusiasm and style, but the recording is too forwardly balanced so that the tuttis are at times a little rough.

Varèse, Edgar (1883–1965)

Amériques; Arcana; Density 21.5; Intégrales; Ionisation; Octandre; Offrandes.

(M) *** Sony Analogue/Dig. SK 45844 [id.].
Yakar, NYPO, Ens. InterContemporain, Boulez.

In the inter-war period Varèse was regarded as a wild man of the avant-garde in writing a work like *Ionisation* for percussion alone and abandoning conventional argument in favour of presenting blocks of sound. Yet performances like these show what a genius he had – not for assaulting but for tickling the ear with novelty. Boulez brings out the purposefulness of his writing, not least in the two big works for full orchestra, the early *Amériques* and *Arcana*, written for an enormous orchestra in the late 1920s. Those two works, here played by the New York Philharmonic, are not digitally recorded. The selection recorded more recently in digital sound covers his smaller but equally striking works for chamber ensembles of various kinds, with Rachel Yakar the excellent soprano soloist in *Offrandes*.

Arcana.

(M) *** RCA High Performance 09026 63315-2 [id]. Chicago SO, Jean Martinon – BARTOK: *The Miraculous Mandarin* (ballet): *suite*; HINDEMITH: *Nobilissima visione*. ***

Varèse is one of the major avant-garde figures of the 1920s, with a rugged integrity combined with a Dadaist exuberance. *Arcana* is a splendidly high-spirited work; it requires an enormous orchestra and is a good introduction to this composer who was admired by such contrasting figures as Debussy and Stravinsky. Excellent recording – not quite as stunning as some recent versions – but this High Performance CD is well worth considering, especially as Martinon conducts with such dash and virtuosity.

Vaughan Williams, Ralph
(1872–1958)

(i) *Concerto accademico. Fantasia on Greensleeves; Five variants of Dives and Lazarus; 2 Hymn tune preludes*; (i) *The Lark ascending.* (ii) *Oboe concerto. Old King Cole (ballet); The Poisoned Kiss: overture; Prelude: 49th Parallel; Prelude on an old carol tune; 2 Preludes on Welsh hymn tunes; The Running set; Sea songs: Quick march; Serenade to music (orchestral version)*; (iii) *5 Mystical songs.*

(B) *** EMI Dig. CZS5 73986-2 (2). (i) Bradley Creswick; (ii) Roger Winfield; (iii) Stephen Roberts; N. Sinfonia of England, Hickox.

This disc comprises the bulk of three LPs Hickox made in the mid-1980s. It includes some rarities and occasional pieces written for particular events or projects, such as the *Prelude* to the film *49th Parallel*. The ballet music for *Old King Cole* is lively and full of charm, as is the tuneful overture to the sadly neglected opera, *The Poisoned Kiss*. Bradley Creswick's account of the *Concerto accademico* is one of the finest available, with the complex mood of the *Adagio*, both ethereal and ecstatic, caught on the wing, and he seems equally at home in *The Lark ascending*.

Roger Wingfield is hardly less engaging in the *Oboe concerto*, his timbre full of pastoral colour, whilst he displays a deliciously light touch in the finale. *Greensleeves* is taken spaciously, but Hickox brings out the breath as well as the lyrical beauty of the melody. *Dives and Lazarus*, rich in sonority, and the two *Hymn tune preludes* have their elegiac mood judged perfectly. The *Five mystical songs* are sensitively done, though Stephen Roberts displays a rather gritty vibrato. All in all, an excellent bargain collection, very well recorded. The *Serenade to music*, however, loses a dimension in its orchestral version.

(i) *Oboe concerto. English folksongs suite; Fantasia on Greensleeves; Fantasia on a theme by Thomas Tallis; Partita for double string orchestra.*

(B) **(*) EMI Eminence Dig. CD-EMX 2179 [(M) id.]. (i) Jonathan Small; RLPO, Vernon Handley.

The charmingly lyrical *Oboe concerto* is given a delectable performance here by Jonathan Small, the flowing pastoralism of its first movement perfectly caught and the more demanding finale impressively handled by conductor and soloist alike. The rarer *Partita for double string orchestra* is also very well played and sonorously recorded. It is chiefly remembered for the *Intermezzo* headed 'Homage to Henry Hall', a unique tribute to the 1940s' leader of a dance-band. Handley gives a rhapsodic account of the *Tallis fantasia*, relaxing in its central section and introducing an accelerando in the climax. Ideally the recording needs a little more resonance, although it is rich-textured and truthful.

(i) *Oboe concerto. Fantasia on Greensleeves; Fantasia on a theme of Thomas Tallis; Five variants of Dives and Lazarus;* (ii) *The Lark ascending. The Wasps: Overture.*
(M) *** Nimbus Dig. NI 7013 [id.]. (i) Maurice Bourgue; (ii) Michael Bochmann; English String O or SO, William Boughton.

Opening with an exuberant account of *The Wasps overture*, this is a very attractive and generous 70-minute collection of favourite Vaughan Williams orchestral pieces, most sympathetically played under William Boughton and presented atmospherically. The spacious acoustic of the Great Hall of Birmingham University ensures that the lyrical string-tune in the overture is properly expansive without robbing the piece of bite, and that both the deeply felt *Tallis fantasia*, with its passionate climax, and *Dives and Lazarus* have a rich amplitude of string-sound. Michael Bochmann, the sympathetic soloist in *The Lark ascending*, playing simply yet with persuasive lyrical freedom, is nicely integrated with the warm orchestral backing. More questionable is the *Oboe concerto*, with the superb French soloist Maurice Bourgue balanced too close. Bourgue's playing, sharply rhythmical and with a rich, pastoral timbre, is ideally suited to the piece.

(i) *Double piano concerto in C;* (ii) *Job (A masque for dancing).*
(M) *** EMI CDM5 67220-2 [id.].(i) Vronsky, Babin, LPO; (ii) LSO, Boult.

Sir Adrian Boult is the dedicatee of *Job*, and this 1970 LSO performance was his fourth and probably most successful recording of the score. The LSO plays superbly throughout and the recording has exceptional range and truthfulness, which is the more impressive on CD. The *Double concerto* was created when Vaughan Williams decided that his solo concerto would be more effective with two pianos, and this new arrangement was first performed in 1946. It remains one of VW's less tractable works with its characteristic first movement *Toccata*, but Vronsky and Babin are very persuasive with the authoritative help of Boult and the LPO. The 1969 recording is very good, with the thick textures well handled by the engineers.

Fantasia on Greensleeves; (i) *Fantasia on a theme of Thomas Tallis.*
🌓 (M) *** EMI CDM5 67240-2 [567264].
Sinfonia of L.; (i) with Allegri Qt; Barbirolli –
ELGAR: *Introduction and allegro for strings, Op. 47; Serenade for strings,* etc. *** 🌓.

Barbirolli's inspirational performance of the *Tallis fantasia* now rightly takes its place among EMI's 'Great Recordings of the Century'. His ardour combined with the magically quiet playing of the second orchestra is unforgettable. The recording has magnificent definition and sonority, achieving dramatic contrasts between the main orchestra and the distanced solo group, which sounds wonderfully ethereal.

Fantasia on Greensleeves; Fantasia on a theme of Tallis; (i) *The Lark ascending.*
(BB) *** Virgin Classics 2 x 1 Dig. VBD5 61763-2 (2) [CDVB 61763]. LCO, Christopher Warren-Green; (i) with Warren Green (vn) –
DVORAK: *Serenade for strings in E, Op. 22;*
ELGAR: *Introduction and allegro; Serenade;*
SUK: *Serenade;* TCHAIKOVSKY: *Serenade.* ***

Christopher Warren-Green and his London Chamber Orchestra give a radiant account of *The Lark ascending*, in which Warren-Green makes a charismatic solo contribution, very free and soaring in its flight and with beautifully sustained true pianissimo playing at the opening and close. For the *Tallis fantasia*, the second orchestra (2.2.2.2.1) contrasts with the main group (5.4.2.2.1) and here, though the effect is beautifully serene, Warren-Green does not quite match the ethereal, otherworldly pianissimo that made Barbirolli's reading unforgettable. The performance overall has great ardour and breadth, almost to match the coupled *Introduction and allegro* of Elgar in its intensity. The recording, made at All Saints' Church, Petersham has resonant warmth and atmosphere yet sharp definition. This now comes as part of one of the most desirable of all the Virgin 2 x 1 Doubles, offering a remarkably generous programme of string music, all very well played and recorded.

Fantasia on Greensleeves; Fantasia on a theme of Thomas Tallis; Five variants of Dives and Lazarus; (i) *Flos Campi.*
(M) *** Van. 08.4053.71 [OVC 4071]. (i) Sally Peck, Utah University Ch.; Utah SO, Maurice Abravanel.

On Vanguard *Greensleeves* is slow and gracious, and there are more passionate versions of the *Tallis fantasia* available, but the important point is the way Abravanel catches the inner feeling of the music. Both here and in *Dives and Lazarus* the full strings create a gloriously rich sonority. Sally Peck, the violist, is placed with her colleagues rather than as a soloist in *Flos Campi* (following the composer's expressed intention), yet her personality still emerges well. Abravanel, always a warm, energetic conductor, displays keen understanding, allowing the music to relax as it should in this evocation of the Song of Solomon, but never letting it drag either. The CD transfer is excellent, retaining the naturalness of the original recording.

(i) *Fantasia on Greensleeves;* (ii) *Fantasia on a theme by Thomas Tallis; Five variants on Dives*

and Lazarus; In the Fen country; (i; iii) *The Lark ascending;* (ii) *Norfolk rhapsody No. 1.*
*** Chandos Dig. CHAN 9775 [id.]. (i) LSO; (ii) LPO; Bryden Thomson; (iii) with Michael Davis.

It is good to have *In the Fen country* and the *First Norfolk rhapsody* in such beautiful modern digital sound and played so sympathetically. Indeed, Bryden Thomson is a most persuasive guide in all this repertoire, although in the *Tallis fantasia* he is rather more concerned with sonority, beauty and contrasts of texture than with subtlety. Michael Davis makes a rich-toned soloist in *The Lark ascending,* presenting it as more than a gentle pastoral invocation. Although these recordings are now nearly a decade old, the generous measure (79 minutes) almost compensates for the continued premium price.

Fantasia on a theme by Thomas Tallis; Five variants of Dives and Lazarus; In the Fen country; Norfolk Rhapsody No. 1 in E min.; Variations for orchestra (orch. Jacob); *The Wasps: Overture.*
**(*) Ph. Dig. 442 427-2 [id.]. ASMF, Marriner.

Opening with a bright and brisk account of *The Wasps overture,* this collection is valuable in including the rare *Variations,* written as a brass band test-piece in 1957 and skilfully orchestrated by Gordon Jacob. Not a masterpiece, but worth having on disc. The other works are very well played; but *Tallis,* though beautiful, lacks the last degree of ethereal intensity. Marriner makes up with the climax of *Dives and Lazarus* which is richly expansive, and he and the ASMF are at their finest in the gentle, evocative opening and closing sections of the *First Norfolk rhapsody. In the Fen country* brings more fine playing and overall this is an enjoyable programme, if not showing these artists at their very finest. The recording too, though spacious, is good rather than outstanding.

Symphonies Nos. 4 in F min.; 5 in D.
** Teldec/Warner Dig. 4509 90844-2 [id.]. BBC SO, Andrew Davis.

Though Andrew Davis draws beautiful, refined playing from the BBC orchestra in both symphonies, there is a lack of dramatic tension, which – particularly in the violent No. 4 – prevents the performance from catching fire. One can pick out many passages which, with the help of superb recorded sound, are as beautiful as any ever recorded, but the parts do not add up to a satisfying whole.

Symphony No. 4; Fantasia on Greensleeves; Fantasia on a theme by Thomas Tallis; (i) *Serenade to music.*
(m) **(*) Sony SMK 47638 [id.]. NYPO, Bernstein, with (i) vocal soloists.

Bernstein's account of the *Fourth Symphony* is strangely impressive. His first movement is slower than usual but very well controlled; he captures the flavour and intensity of the score as well as the brooding quality of the slow movement. The New York Orchestra plays extremely well and the 1965 recording is full and vivid. The *Serenade to music* is less successful: the solo singers are too forwardly balanced and the sound in general is unimpressive, though the performance itself is not without interest. The two *Fantasias* are expansively done (American performances of *Greensleeves* are always slow), and the *Tallis* certainly has plenty of tension.

Symphony No. 6 in E min.; In the Fen country. (i) *On Wenlock Edge.*
**(*) EMI Dig. CDC5 56762-2 [id.]. LPO, Bernard Haitink; (i) with Ian Bostridge.

As in his other recordings of Vaughan Williams symphonies, Bernard Haitink takes a direct, literal view of No. 6, bringing out the power and thrust of the argument at steady speeds. It may miss some of the mystery of the piece, as in the contrapuntal writing of the hushed epilogue, but the purposefulness is tellingly conveyed with superb playing from the LPO and firm, refined sound. With Ian Bostridge the sensitive, honey-toned soloist, the Housman song-cycle makes a welcome fill-up. However for the symphony readers are referred to the versions by Boult (Belart mono 461 117-2), Handley (Eminence CD-EMX 2230) and Andrew Davis (Teldec 9031 73127-2), all discussed in our main volume

VOCAL MUSIC

Fantasia on Christmas carols; Hodie.
**(*) EMI Dig. CDC7 54128-2 [id.]. Gale, Tear, Roberts, London Symphony Ch., LSO, Hickox.

Though the three soloists cannot match the original trio in Sir David Willcocks's pioneering version (on EMI, now withdrawn), Hickox directs a more urgent and more freely expressive reading of the big Christmas cantata, *Hodie,* helped by refined and incisive choral singing. As on the earlier disc, the *Christmas carol fantasia* proves an ideal coupling, also warmly done.

(i; ii) *An Oxford elegy;* (i; iii) *Flos campi;* (iv) *Sancta civitas;* (i) *Whitsunday Hymn.*
(m) *** EMI CDM5 67221-2 [id.]. King's College, Cambridge Ch., Willcocks, with (i) Jacques O; (ii) John Westbrook (speaker); (iii) Cecil Aronowitz; (iv) Partridge, Shirley-Quirk, Bach Choir, LSO.

An Oxford elegy, written in 1949, is an example of a work that rises well above its original commission – its richly flowing inspiration characteristic of the composer's ripe Indian summer. The spoken quotations from Matthew Arnold are effectively presented by John Westbrook, whilst the Cambridge choir is admirable in its words of tribute to Oxford. *Flos campi*, with its inspiration in the Song of Solomon, is one of the composer's most sensuously beautiful works, with its deeply expressive solo for the viola – here beautifully played by Cecil Aronowitz. It needs a persuasive interpretation and that it certainly receives.

Sancta civitas ('The holy city') is a product of the composer's visionary years in the early twenties. A masterpiece, elusive in its apparent meandering, but in fact as sharply focused as his *Pastoral Symphony* of the same period. The words are mostly from the Book of Revelation and are set to sublime, shifting choral textures (with the main chorus set against a semi-chorus and an off-stage boys' chorus) and the whole effect is evocatively captured on this CD.

The *Whitsunday hymn* is a short, but beautiful piece composed for the Leith Hill Festival at Dorking in 1929, yet it somehow remained unpublished at the time; this performance provides its CD début and, like the rest of the programme, is a tribute to the conductor in his eightieth birthday year. A valuable and stimulating release.

Songs of travel; The House of Life (6 sonnets); *4 Poems by Fredegond Shove; 4 Last songs: No. 2, Tired;* Songs: *In the spring; Linden Lea.*
**(*) Chandos Dig. CHAN 8475 [id.]. Benjamin Luxon, David Williams.

Though Benjamin Luxon's vibrato is distractingly wide, the warmth and clarity of the recording help to make his well-chosen collection of Vaughan Williams songs very attractive, including as it does not only the well-known Stevenson travel cycle but the Rossetti cycle, *The House of Life* (including *The Water mill*), as well as the most famous song of all, *Linden Lea*.

Velasquez, Glauco (1884–1914)

Album-leaves Nos. 1–2; Brutto Sogno; Canzone Strana; Danse de silphes; Devaneio; Divertimento No. 2; Impromptu; Melancolia; Minuetto e Gavotte Moderni; Petite Suite; Prelúdios Nos. 1–2; Prelúdio e Scherzo; Rêverie; Valsa lenta; Valsa romântica.
*** Marco Polo Dig. 8.223556 [id.]. Clara Sverner.

Glauco Velasquez was an illegitimate child, born in Naples to a Brazilian mother and fathered by a Portuguese singer. When their relationship collapsed, his mother took the boy to Brazil, where he was brought up in ignorance of his father's identity. He soon showed musical aptitude, and by his mid-twenties he had attracted some attention in musical circles with his piano miniatures, recorded here.

Their heady melancholy, often in Scriabinesque chromatic writing, is most beguiling. Clara Sverner brings out the personality and charm, and they are very well recorded.

Verdi, Giuseppe (1813–1901)

Complete Preludes, Overtures and Ballet music.

Volume 1: Overtures and Preludes: *Alzira* (Overture); *Attila* (Prelude); *La battaglia di Legnano* (Overture); *Il Corsaro; I due Foscari; Ernani* (Preludes); *Un giorno di regno (Il finto Stanislao); Giovanna d'Arco* (Overtures); *Macbeth* (Prelude with ballet music); *I Masnadieri* (Prelude); *Nabucco; Oberto* (Overtures).
*** Chandos Dig. CHAN 9510 [id.]. BBC PO, Edward Downes.

Volume 2: *Jérusalem* (Overture and ballet music); *Luisa Miller* (Overture); *Rigoletto* (Prelude); *Il Trovatore* (ballet music).
*** Chandos Dig. CHAN 9594 [id.]. BBC PO, Edward Downes.

Volume 3: *Un ballo in maschera* (Prelude); *Simon Boccanegra* (Prelude: 1st version, 1857); *La Traviata* (Preludes to Acts I & III); *Les Vêpres siciliennes: Ballet of the Four Seasons.*
*** Chandos Dig. CHAN 9696 [id.]. BBC PO, Edward Downes.

Volume 4: *Aida* (Prelude for Cairo première, 1871; Overture for Italian première, 1872; 2 Dances & Act II ballet music); *Don Carlos* (Prelude to Act III and ballet music: *La peregrina); La forza del destino* (Prelude, 1862); *Otello* (ballet music, Act III).
*** Chandos Dig. CHAN 9788 [id.]. BBC PO, Edward Downes.

Preludes, Overtures and Ballet music (as above).
*** Chandos Dig. CHAN 9787 (4) [id.]. BBC PO, Edward Downes.

Since we went to print with our main volume, Edward Downes's Verdi survey has been extended to cover virtually all the overtures, preludes and ballet music, the latter full of charm when so elegantly played and beautifully recorded. Original versions are chosen where available, so we get the first 1857 score of the Prelude to *Simon Boccanegra* and the brief 1862 Overture to *La forza del destino*, rather than the familiar expanded 1869 version. (It is most successful here in its more succinct format, although one misses the tune made famous by the film *Manon des sources*.) The outstanding novelty is Verdi's extended 1872 overture written for the Italian première of *Aida*. The composer rehearsed it secretly, and then wisely decided that first thoughts were best, and the shorter Prelude heard at the opera's Cairo première was substituted at the last moment. The 1872 piece was never heard of again. The ballet music was of course an essential requirement if a work was to be performed at the Paris Opéra. (Legend has it that wealthy patrons insisted on its inclusion in order to choose their newest mistresses, after watching the dancers.) To fit the ballet into Act III of *Otello* the stage entry of the Venetian ambassador was announced and the dancers entertained him for a brief six minutes before the narrative continued. Verdi often rises to the occasion and produces charming, tuneful music, felicitously scored. In the suite from *Il Trovatore* (an unlikely subject for a balletic diversion), the delightful third section, *La bohémienne,* is worthy of Delibes in its use of the graceful violins and piquant woodwind. Not surprisingly Edward Downes has the full measure of this music. The finer overtures are played with bold characterization and dramatic fire, *Nabucco,* with its dignified sonority, and *Giovanna d'Arco* both show the BBC Philharmonic brass at their finest in quite different ways, and *Luisa Miller* is another very strong performance. The strings play most beautifully in the *Traviata Preludes.* With such richly expansive recording, showing Chandos engineering at its most spectacular, the effect is less bitingly leonine than in Karajan's electrifying two-disc survey, which makes a splendid bargain as a DG Double (453 058-2). But even if not all of this music is top-class Verdi, the Chandos set offers much to enjoy, and the spontaneity and elegance of the music-making are never in doubt.

Overtures and Preludes: *Aida: Prelude. Alzira: Sinfonia. Aroldo: Sinfonia. Attila: Prelude. Un ballo in maschera: Prelude. Il Corsaro: Prelude. Luisa Miller: Sinfonia. Oberto, Conte di San Bonifacio: Sinfonia. La Traviata: Preludes to Acts I & III. I vespri siciliani: Sinfonia.*
(BB) **(*) Naxos Dig. 8.553018 [id.]. Hungarian State Op. O, Pier Giorgio Morandi.

Overtures and Preludes: *La battaglia di Legnano: Sinfonia. Don Carlos: Prelude to Act III. I due Foscari: Prelude. Ernani: Prelude. La forza del destino: Sinfonia. Un giorno di regno: Sinfonia. Giovanna d'Arco: Sinfonia. Macbeth: Sinfonia. I Masnadieri: Prelude. Nabucco: Overture. Rigoletto: Prelude.*
(BB) **(*) Naxos Dig. 8.553089 [id.]. Hungarian State Op. O, Pier Giorgio Morandi.

Morandi has served his time conducting at La Scala and he gives ripely robust accounts of these colourful overtures and sinfonias, with excellent playing from his Hungarian musicians, notably from the strings in the *Traviata* and *Aida Preludes* and from the brass in *Nabucco. La forza del destino* ends the second disc strongly. Full-bloodedly resonant sound (with the second collection at times marginally sharper in definition) makes this an ex-

cellent bargain, even if the readings are not as individual as those of Chailly and Karajan.

Overtures and Preludes: *Aida* (Prelude); *Attila* (Overture); *Un ballo in maschera* (Prelude); *La battaglia di Legnano; La forza del destino; Giovanna d'Arco; Luisa Miller* (Overtures); *I Masnadieri* (Prelude); *Nabucco* (Overture); *La Traviata* (Preludes to Acts I & III); *I vespri siciliani* (Overture).
**(*) Sony Dig. SK 68468 [id.]. La Scala PO, Riccardo Muti.

As he demonstrates in the opening *Forza del destino overture,* where the arching string-melody is elegantly and sensuously shaped, Muti offers warmly romantic performances, full of colourful detail. The result is very attractive, with more languorous string-playing in the *Traviata Preludes* and much delicacy in the *Prelude* to Act I of *Aida.* The woodwind make a glowing contribution to *Giovanna d'Arco,* and the brass come into their own in *Nabucco* and *La battaglia di Legnano.* Spaciously natural sound.

Requiem Mass.
*** BBC Legends BBCL 4029-2 (2) [id.]. (i) Amy Shuard, Anna Reynolds, Richard Lewis, David Ward, Philh. Ch. and O., Giulini (with *Overture La forza del destino* ***) – SCHUBERT: *Mass in E flat.* ***
(M) (**(*)) EMI (SIS) mono CMS5 65506-2 (2). Schwarzkopf, Dominguez, Di Stefano, Siepi, La Scala, Milan, Ch. & O, De Sabata (with VERDI: *La Traviata: Preludes to Acts I & III; I vespri siciliani: Overture;* WOLF-FERRARI: *Susanna's secret: Overture and Intermezzo*; RESPIGHI: *The Fountains of Rome*; ROSSINI: *William Tell overture* **(*)).
(M) **(*) RCA 09026 61403-2 (2) [id.]. L. Price, J. Baker, V. Luchetti, Van Dam, Chicago Symphony Ch. & SO, Solti.
**(*) DG (IMS) Dig. Gold 439 033-2 (2) [id.]. Tomowa-Sintow, Baltsa, Carreras, Van Dam, V. State Op. Konzertvereingung, VPO, Karajan.
(M) **(*) Sony SM2K 47639 (2) [id.]. Arroyo, Veasey, Domingo, Raimondi, L. Symphony Ch., LSO, Bernstein.

(i) *Requiem Mass;* (ii) *4 Sacred pieces.*
(B) **(*) Decca Double 444 833-2 (2) [id.]. (i) L. Price, Elias, Björling, Tozzi, V. Musikverein, VPO, Reiner; (ii) Minton, Los Angeles Master Ch., LAPO, Mehta.

Giulini's performances of the Verdi *Requiem* in the early 1960s have become legendary, electrifying occasions that led to a benchmark studio recording of 1964, still unsurpassed. Here the BBC Legends series puts an important gloss on that in offering a Prom recording of 1963, even more dramatically involving for the extra spontaneity of a live performance. The stereo sound is first-rate, and though the British soloists may not be such stars as their studio counterparts, they sing beautifully, with firm, clear tone. The Schubert *Mass*, recorded at the Edinburgh Festival 1968, makes a welcome and generous coupling.

Victor de Sabata's legendary 1954 recording unashamedly adopts the most spacious speeds and a deeply devotional manner, helped by a starry quartet of soloists. When it came out, it was not well received by many, who found the slow speeds self-indulgent, the very opposite of those adopted by Tullio Serafin, whose early recording made an obvious comparison, lasting a full 22 minutes less. Also, this de Sabata version, master-minded by Walter Legge, was due to be superseded ten years later by Giulini's stereo version. It never reappeared on LP, making this CD transfer very welcome, limited in sound but with fine dynamic contrasts. Dedication is the keynote in a performance of extremes, totally concentrated but very personal in its new look. The four superb soloists respond with total commitment, Schwarzkopf most of all, in radiant voice. Oralia Dominguez excels herself, as cleanly focused as Schwarzkopf, with her rapid flicker-vibrato adding character to the firm mezzo timbre. Giuseppe di Stefano sings with headily fresh tone, while Siepi is splendid too. The chorus sing lustily but not always with discipline. The fill-ups are just as characterful: the *Traviata Preludes*, rapt and finely shaded, the Respighi sensuously atmospheric, the *William Tell overture* given surprising refinement. Best of all are the two little Wolf-Ferrari items, witty and sparkling. A revelatory set.

Reiner's opening of the *Requiem* is very slow and atmospheric. He takes the music at something like half the speed of Toscanini and shapes everything very carefully. Yet as the work proceeds the performance soon sparks into life, and there is some superb and memorable singing from a distinguished team of soloists. The recording has a spectacularly wide dynamic range, enhanced by the CD format, and, with the chorus singing fervently, the *Dies irae* is overwhelming. Mehta's performance of the *Sacred pieces* is enhanced by brilliant, sharply focused recording.

On RCA, Solti's 1977 Chicago version, with an unusually sensitive and pure-toned quartet of soloists – Luchetti perhaps not as characterful as the others, Leontyne Price occasionally showing strain – and with superb choral singing and orchestral playing, has all the ingredients for success. The set is well worth having for Janet Baker's deeply sensitive singing, but the remastered recording – not well balanced – tends to be fierce on climaxes, and, in other ways too, Solti's earlier, Decca/Vienna set is preferable.

Though Karajan's smooth style altered relatively little after his earlier version, the overall impression in his later DG set is fresher, though as transferred the recording is inconsistent. Even with 'original image bit reprocessing' improving the focus and impact, the sound is not impressive. Though Tomowa-Sintow's un-Italian soprano sometimes brings a hint of flutter, she sings most beautifully in the final rapt account of *Libera me*.

Bernstein's 1970 *Requiem* was recorded in the Royal Albert Hall. By rights, the daring of that decision should have paid off; but with close balancing of microphones the result is not as full and free as one would have expected. Bernstein's interpretation remains most persuasive, with the drama exaggerated at times, red-blooded in a way that is hard to resist. The quartet of soloists is particularly strong, notably the young Plácido Domingo.

OPERA

Aida: highlights.
(B) **(*) DG Classikon Dig. 439 482-2 [(M) id. import] (from complete recording, with Ricciarelli, Obraztsova, Domingo, Nucci, Ghiaurov, La Scala, Milan, Ch. & O, cond. Abbado).
(B) **(*) [EMI Red Seal CDR5 72562]. Caballé, Domingo, Cossotto, Ghiaurov, ROHCG Ch., New Philh. O, Muti.
(M) (***) EMI mono CDM5 66668-2 [id.]. Callas, Tucker, Barbieri, Gobbi, La Scala, Milan, Ch. & O, Serafin.

In Abbado's 1981 La Scala *Aida*, it was the men who stood out, Domingo a superb Radames, Ghiaurov as Ramphis, Nucci a dramatic Amonasro, and Raimondi as the King. Ricciarelli is an appealing Aida, but her legato line is at times impure above the stave, and Elena Obraztsova produces too much curdled tone as Amneris. The recording is bright and fresh, but not ideally expansive in the ceremonial scenes. As is usual with DG's bargain Classikon series, the documentation is good, though without translations. The selection offers 64 minutes of music.

On Muti's set of highlights, Caballé's portrait of the heroine is superb, full of detailed insight into the character and with plenty of examples of superlative singing, while Cossotto makes a fine Amneris. Domingo produces a glorious sound, but this is not one of his most imaginative recordings. The sound is relatively small-scale, underlining the fierceness of Muti's reading.

The set of highlights from the Callas *Aida* includes the Nile scene and is slightly more generous, at 58 minutes, than many other reissues in this series. It certainly conveys the overall strength of the cast.

Un ballo in maschera (complete).

(M) *** EMI (SIS) CMS5 66510-2 (2) [Angel
CDMB 66510]. Arroyo, Domingo,
Cappuccilli, Grist, Cossotto, Howell, ROHCG
Ch., New Philh. O, Muti.

The quintet of principals here is unusually strong,
but it is the conductor who takes first honours in a
warmly dramatic reading. Muti's rhythmic resilience and consideration for the singers go with keen
concentration, holding each Act together in a way
he did not quite achieve in his earlier recording for
EMI of *Aida*. Arroyo, rich of voice, is not always
imaginative in her big solos, and Domingo rarely
produces a half-tone, though the recording balance
may be partly to blame. The sound is full and vivid,
and for the present reissue a new booklet has been
provided with full translation.

Don Carlos (complete).
**(*) Sony Dig. S3K 52500 (3) [id.]. Furlanetto,
Millo, Zajick, Sylvester, Chernov, Ramey,
Battle, NY Met. Ch. & O, James Levine.
**(*) DG Dig. 415 316-2 (4) [id.]. Ricciarelli,
Domingo, Valentini Terrani, Nucci, Raimondi,
Ghiaurov, La Scala, Milan, Ch. & O, Abbado.

While Levine's heavy-handedness as a Verdian is
exaggerated by the full, forward sound, the performance has a thrust and bite that reflect opera-house
experience. In the title-role the American tenor
Michael Sylvester produces a fine, clear, heroic
tone, and he is not afraid to shade his voice down
to a pianissimo. Aprile Millo's ripe soprano is apt
for the role of Elisabetta, though her vibrato tends
to become obtrusive. As Eboli, Dolora Zajick's
fruity mezzo is not well caught by the close-up
recording, again with unevenness exaggerated, but
this is a rich characterization. As King Philip, Fer-
ruccio Furlanetto is not as firm as he usually is,
while Vladimir Chernov as Rodrigo is not flattered
either, with fluttery timbre exaggerated in a charac-
terless reading, leaving a disappointing blank where
one wants the keenest intensity.

Abbado's set was the first recording to use the
language which Verdi originally set, French, in the
full five-Act text. The first disappointment lies in
the variable quality of the sound, with odd balances,
yet the cast is a strong one. Domingo easily outshines his earlier recording with Giulini (in Italian),
while Katia Ricciarelli as the Queen gives a tenderly
moving performance, if not quite commanding
enough in the Act V aria. Ruggero Raimondi is
a finely focused Philip II, nicely contrasted with
Nicolai Ghiaurov as the Grand Inquisitor in the
other black-toned bass role. Lucia Valentini Terrani
as Eboli is warm-toned if not very characterful, and
Leo Nucci makes a noble Posa.

Ernani (complete).
(M) **(*) Ph. Dig. 446 669 [id.]. Lamberti, Sass,
Kovats, Miller, Takacs, Hungarian State Op.
Ch. & O, Gardelli.

Originally issued on Hungaraton, this early digital
set returns to the catalogue on Philips at mid-price
with full libretto and translation. Gardelli's conducting is most sympathetic and idiomatic in the
Hungarian version and, like Muti's, it is strong on
ensembles. Sylvia Sass is a sharply characterful
Elvira, Callas-like in places, and Lamberti a bold
Ernani, though both are vocally flawed. Capable
rather than inspired or idiomatic singing from the
rest. The digital recording is bright and well balanced, although the CD transfer brings out the
resonant acoustic.

Falstaff (complete).
(M) **(*) DG Dig. 447 686-2 (2). Giuseppe
Taddei, Raina Kabaivanska, Janet Perry,
Christa Ludwig, Rolando Panerai, Francisco
Araiza, Piero de Palma, Heinz Zednik, V. State
Op. Ch., VPO, Karajan.

Karajan's second (1980) recording of Verdi's last
opera, made over twenty years after his classic EMI
Philharmonia version with Gobbi and Schwarzkopf
(CMS5 67083-2), is far less precise in a relaxed and
genial way. With the exception of Kabaivanska,
whose voice is not steady enough for the role of
Alice, it is a good cast, with Ludwig fascinating as
Mistress Quickly. Most astonishing of all is
Taddei's performance as Falstaff himself, full,
characterful and vocally astonishing from a man in
his sixties. The digital sound is faithful and wide-
ranging, and the CD transfer vividly captures the
bloom of the original reverberant recording.

La forza del destino: highlights.
(B) *** DG Classikon Dig. 463 261-2 (from
complete set with Rosalind Plowright, José
Carreras, Renato Bruson, Agnes Baltsa, Amb.
Op.Ch., Philh. O, cond. Sinopoli).

A self-recommending set of highlights from a first-
class complete set (see our main volume). With a
65-minute selection and a cued synopsis this is
excellent value.

Luisa Miller (complete).
(B) *** DG Double 459 481-2 (2) [id.].
Ricciarelli, Obraztsova, Domingo, Bruson,
Howell, ROHCG Ch. & O, Maazel.

Maazel's 1979 Covent Garden set returns to the
catalogue as a DG Double and would have been very
competitive indeed had it included a full libretto and
translation instead of just a synopsis. Though taut
in his control, Maazel uses his stage experience of
working with these soloists to draw them out to their
finest, most sympathetic form. Ricciarelli gives one
of her tenderest and most beautiful performances
on record, Domingo is in glorious voice and Bruson
as Luisa's father sings with a velvet tone. Gwynne
Howell is impressive as the Conte di Walter and
Wladimiro Ganzarolli's vocal roughness is apt for

the character of Wurm. The snag is the abrasive Countess Federica of Elena Obraztsova.

Otello (complete).
(M) *** EMI (SIS) CMS7 69308-2 (2) [Ang. CDMB 69308]. Vickers, Freni, Glossop, Ch. of German Op., Berlin, BPO, Karajan.

Karajan directs a big, bold and brilliant account, for the most part splendidly sung and with all the dramatic contrasts strongly underlined. There are several tiny, but irritating, statutory cuts, but otherwise on two mid-price CDs this is well worth considering. Freni's Desdemona is delightful, delicate and beautiful, while Vickers and Glossop are both positive and characterful, only occasionally forcing their tone and losing focus. The recording is clarified on CD.

Rigoletto (complete).
(M) **(*) DG 457 753-2 (2) [id.]. Cappuccilli, Cotrubas, Domingo, Obraztsova, Ghiaurov, Moll, Schwarz, V. State Op. Ch., VPO, Giulini.

Unlike Solti, Giulini, ever thoughtful for detail, seems determined to get away from any conception of *Rigoletto* as melodrama; however, in doing that he misses the red-blooded theatricality of Verdi's concept, the basic essential. Although it may be consistent with Giulini's view, the dramatic impact is further reduced by the fact that Cappuccilli (with his unsinister voice) makes the hunchback a noble figure from first to last, while Domingo, ever intelligent, makes a reflective rather than an extrovert Duke. Cotrubas is a touching Gilda, but the close balance of her voice is not helpful, and the topmost register is not always comfortable. The recording, made in the Musikverein in Vienna, has the voices well to the fore, with much reverberation on the instruments behind, an effect emphasized by the CD transfer. This is hardly a suitable candidate for DG's 'Legendary Originals'.

Rigoletto (highlights).
(M) *** Decca 458 243-2 [id.]. Sutherland, Pavarotti, Milnes, Tourangeau, Ambrosian Op. Ch., LSO, Bonynge.

Bonynge's *Rigoletto* has kept its place as one of the successful recordings since its first release in 1974. There is barely a weak link in it, and the sound is full and vivid. This new highlights selection includes more music (70 minutes) than before, and Decca provide full texts and translations for their handsome Opera Gala reissue.

Rigoletto (complete in English).
(M) *** Chandos Dig. CHAN 3030 (2) [id.]. John Rawnsley, Helen Field, Arthur Davies, John Tomlinson, ENO Ch. & O, Mark Elder.

The flair of the original English National Opera production, setting *Rigoletto* in the Little Italy area

of New York in the 1950s and making the Mafia boss the 'Duke', is superbly carried through to this originally EMI studio recording. The intensity and fine pacing of the stage performances are splendidly caught, thanks to Mark Elder's keenly rhythmic conducting, making this one of the most successful of the ENO's Verdi sets. Outstanding vocally is the heady-toned Duke of Arthur Davies, and though neither John Rawnsley as Rigoletto nor Helen Field as Gilda has a voice so naturally beautiful, they too sing both powerfully and stylishly. Excellent recording, clean and full, and the production of the opening scene includes an effective crowd ambience of the kind pioneered by Decca.

La Traviata (complete).
(B) **(*) EMI Double Fforte CZS5 73824-2 (2). De los Angeles, Del Monte, Sereni, Rome Op. Ch. & O, Serafin.
(M) (**(*)) Warner/Fonit mono 3984 29354-2 (2) [id.]. Maria Callas, Francesco Albanese, Ugo Savarese, Turin R. Ch. & O, Santini.
(B) **(*) Decca Double 443 002-2 (2) [id.]. Lorengar, Aragall, Fischer-Dieskau, Ch. & O of German Op., Berlin, Maazel.
**(*) Ph. Dig. 438 238-2 (2) [id.]. Te Kanawa, Kraus, Hvorostovsky, Maggio Musicale (Florence) Ch. & O, Mehta.
(M) **(*) RCA 09026 68885-2 (2) [id.]. Anna Moffo, Richard Tucker, Robert Merrill, Rome Op. Ch. & O, Previtali.

Even when Victoria de los Angeles made this EMI recording in the late 1950s, the role of Violetta lay rather high for her voice. Nevertheless it drew from her much beautiful singing, not least in the coloratura display at the end of Act I which, though it may lack easily ringing top notes, has delightful sparkle and flexibility. As to the characterization, De los Angeles is a most sympathetically tender heroine. Though neither the tenor nor the baritone can match her in artistry, their performances are both sympathetic and feeling, thanks in part to the masterly conducting of Serafin. All the traditional cuts are made, not just the second stanzas. The CD transfer is vivid and clear and at bargain price a fair recommendation, though only a synopsis is provided.

Like the companion Cetra set of *La Gioconda*, this was made by Callas very early in her career (in 1952). She was to record it again three years later with Giulini and Di Stefano, and that is still available (EMI CDM5 66450-2) showing her at her very peak, but the sound of the transfer deteriorates towards the end. The 1952 recording is more consistent, noticeably fierce at the opening (affecting both the orchestral strings and the vocal fortissimos), but it seems to settle down (with occasional peakiness) and in the present transfer the overall effect is quite open. Callas's characterization of Violetta had not fully reached maturity, but the fresh youthfulness of the voice more than compensates. All the singing is very characteristic (including an odd mistake in the vocal flurries before *Sempre libera* – otherwise an excitingly brilliant account). Francesco Albanese is a sympathetic Alfredo, especially in the closing Act, but Ugo Savarese as Germont *père* is no more distinguished than Bastianini in the later La Scala set. However, Callas admirers will surely find this well-managed reissue worth having alone for Callas's very moving closing scene. The Italian libretto, though, is without a translation.

With the 1968 Maazel set, much will depend on the listener's reaction to Lorengar's voice. Her interpretation is most affecting, deeply felt and expressive, but the vibrato is often intrusive. That will not worry all ears, and with Fischer-Dieskau a searchingly intense Germont (if hardly an elderly-sounding one) and Aragall making a ringingly impressive Alfredo, this is a strong cast. Maazel's conducting is characteristically forceful. The recording quality is excellent and the fine CD transfer belies the age of the recording.

Though both Alfredo Kraus as Alfredo and Dmitri Hvorostovsky as Germont sing well on Philips, they offer an unconvincing partnership. Kraus's musical imagination is masked by a dry tone and strain on top, with a very gusty entry for example in the duet *Parigi o cara*. Equally the rich-toned Hvorostovsky hardly sounds fatherly, though he does his best in a firm, spacious account of the aria *Di Provenza*. Dame Kiri Te Kanawa is tenderly beautiful as Violetta, finely poised in *Ah fors'è lui* and the Farewell, as well as in a hushed, intense account of the Act II duet with Germont.

Anna Moffo makes a most beautiful Violetta in a performance that is never less than sympathetic. She is not as assured as she might be in the coloratura of Act I, but everywhere else her unaffected manner and care for phrasing and tonal nuances make for a performance to match almost any in the catalogue at whatever price. Richard Tucker too sings powerfully as Alfredo and, though Robert Merrill is not as understanding a Germont here as he was in the earlier Sutherland set, it makes a strong, consistent cast. The conducting of Previtali could be more colourful, and the performing cuts which were usual at that time are made, but the recording still sounds well.

La Traviata: highlights.
**(*) Decca Dig. 458 274-2 [id.]. Gheorghiu, Lopardo, Nucci, ROHCG Ch. & O, Solti.
(M) *** EMI CDM5 65573-2. Scotto, Kraus, Bruson, Amb. Op. Ch., Philh. O, Muti.
(B) **(*) DG Classikon 439 421-2; *439 421-4* [(M) id. import]. Cotrubas, Domingo, Milnes, Bav. State Op. Ch. & State O, Carlos Kleiber.

The Decca set of highlights (74 minutes) from the Gheorghiu/Solti set would seem to be highly recommendable, but it is a premium-priced disc and offers only a synopsis and no texts and translations. Musically and technically there are no grumbles. Curiously the *Prelude* to Act I is included, but not the *Prelude* to Act III.

Muti's complete set is hardly a first choice at full price, so many will be glad to have this 61-minute, mid-price disc of highlights, including both the Act I and Act III *Preludes* and a well-balanced selection from each of the three Acts, with most of the key numbers included.

For many, Cotrubas makes an ideal star in *Traviata*, but unfortunately the microphone-placing in Carlos Kleiber's complete set (DG 415 132-2) over-emphasises technical flaws and the vibrato is exaggerated. With singing of magical intensity, her characterization combines strength with vulnerability, while Kleiber's direction is equally controversial with more than a hint of Toscanini-like rigidity in the party music. The strong contributions of Domingo and Milnes make this bargain-priced Classikon highlights CD highly recommendable, with 71 minutes of music, including the two *Preludes*. The documentation is well thought out, except that it omits a track-by-track synopsis of the narrative.

Il Trovatore (complete).
(M) **(*) EMI (SIS) CMS7 69311-2 (2) [CDMB 69311]. Price, Bonisolli, Cappuccilli, Obraztsova, Raimondi, German Op. Ch., Berlin, BPO, Karajan.
(BB) ** Arte Nova 74321 72110-2 (2) [id.]. Anda-Louise Bogza, Boiko Svetanov, Graciela Alperyn, Igor Morosow, Bratislava Nat. Op. Ch, Bratislava Slovak RSO, Ivan Anguelov.
(B) *(*) Decca Double 460 735-2 (2) [id.]. Sutherland, Pavarotti, Wixell, Horne, Ghiaurov, L. Op. Ch., Nat. PO, Bonynge.

The later Karajan set with Leontyne Price promised much but proves disappointing, largely because of the thickness and strange balances of the recording, the product of multi-channel techniques exploited over-enthusiastically. So the introduction to Manrico's aria *Di quella pira* provides full-blooded orchestral sound, but then the orchestra fades down for the entry of the tenor, Bonisolli, who is in coarse voice. In other places he sings more sensitively, but at no point does this version match that of Mehta on RCA (✪ 74321 39504-2). CD clarifies the sound but makes the flaws in the original recording all the more evident.

The Arte Nova version, an enjoyable super-bargain issue, stems from a live concert performance, well-recorded, with a good team of young soloists and fresh, vigorous playing and singing from the Bratislava choir and orchestra under the conductor Ivan Anguelov. This may not be a subtle performance, but the dramatic bite of a live occasion, well-rehearsed, comes over very well.

Anda-Louise Bogza makes a strong, vehement Leonora with plenty of temperament, and Boiko Svetanov as Manrico sings with clear, firm tone if explosively from time to time. Shining out even from the others is Graciela Alperyn as Azucena with a firm, strong mezzo and a splendid chest register, well-controlled, attacking notes fearlessly. As the Conte di Luna, Igor Morosow is strong and clear except under strain on top. A full libretto in Italian is provided but no translation.

Bonynge in most of his opera sets has been unfailingly urgent and rhythmic, but his account of *Il Trovatore* is at an altogether lower level of intensity, with elegance the dominant quality, rather than dramatic power. Nor does the role of Leonora prove very apt for Sutherland late in her career; the coloratura passages are splendid, but a hint of unsteadiness is present in too much of the rest. Pavarotti for the most part sings superbly, but he falls short in, for example, the semiquaver groups of *Di quella pira* and, like Sutherland, Marilyn Horne as Azucena does not produce a consistently firm tone. Wixell as the Count sings intelligently, but a richer tone is needed. The CD transfer cannot be faulted – atmospheric, with voices naturally balanced against an open acoustic, but even at Decca Double price this can hardly be counted a strong contender.

COLLECTIONS

Arias and excerpts from: *Aida; Un ballo in maschera; Don Carlo; La forza del destino; Luisa Miller; Otello; Simon Boccanegra; La Traviata; Rigoletto; Il Trovatore; I vespri siciliani.*
(M) *** RCA 09026 68446-2 [id.]. Placido Domingo (with various orchestras & conductors).

A fine Verdian survey showing the amazing consistency of Domingo's voice throughout his recording career. While the opening *Ah! sì, ben mio* and *Di quella pira* come from Mehta's famous complete set, the four excerpts from *Otello* derive from three different sources. *Già nella notte* (with Katia Ricciarelli) is a highlight as are *Sì, pel ciel mamoreo giuro!* and the famous *Don Carlo* duet, both with Sherrill Milnes.

Sento avvampa nell'anima from *Simon Boccanegra* is comparably memorable, but every item comes up freshly and vibrantly and the differently sourced recordings, with accompaniments from ten different combinations of orchestra and conductor, are skilfully transferred to make an effective ongoing recital. Full texts and translations are included but, curiously, recording dates are omitted.

Arias, Volume I: *Don Carlos: Tu che le vanità. Ernani: Surta è la notte . . . Ernani! Ernani, involami. Macbeth: Nel dì della vittoria . . . Vieni!, t'affretta; La luce langue; Una machia è qui tuttora! (Sleepwalking scene). Nabucco: Ben io t'invenni . . . Anch'io dischiuso un giorno.*
(M) *** EMI CDM5 66460-2 [id.]. Maria Callas, Philh. O, Nicola Rescigno.

Originally issued under the title 'Verdi heroines', this recital marked Callas's only visit to record at Abbey Road, in September 1958. Much of it shows the great diva at her very finest. Despite the top-note wobbles, the performances are enthralling in the vividness of characterization and the musical imagination, not least as Lady Macbeth in her Act I aria and the Sleepwalking scene, and as Elisabetta in *Don Carlos*, which are magnetic. Abigaille, Elvira and Elisabetta all come out as real figures, sharply individual. Finely balanced recording, with the CD transfer well up to the high standard of the Callas Edition. This is the disc to choose from these three collections of Verdi arias.

Arias, Volume II: *Aroldo: Ciel ch'io respir!. . . Salvami, salvami tu gran Dio! O Cielo! Dove son io. Don Carlos: Non pianger, mia compagna; O don fatale. Otello: Mia madre aveva una povera ancella . . . Piangea cantando . . . Ave Maria piena di grazia.*
(M) **(*) EMI CDM5 66461-2 [id.]. Maria Callas, Paris Conservatoire O, Nicola Rescigno.

Arias, Volume III: *Aida: Ritorna vincitor. Attila: Liberamente or piangi!. . . Oh! ne! fuggente nuvolo. Un ballo in maschera: Ecco l'orrido campo; Morrò, ma prima in grazia. Il Corsaro: Egli non riede ancor . . . Non so le tetre immagini; Né sulla terra . . . Vola talor dal carcere . . . Verrò . . . Ah conforto è sol la speme. Il Trovatore: Tacea la notte placida . . . Di tale amor. I vespri siciliani: Arrigo! ah parli a un core.*
(M) **(*) CDM5 66462-2 [id.]. Maria Callas, Paris Conservatoire O or Paris Opéra O, Rescigno.

For her second and third collections of Verdi arias, Callas went to Paris in December 1963 and February 1964 (Volume II); and then she began a third compilation in April 1964, returning in 1965 and 1969. She approved some of the tracks for release in 1972, and the rest first appeared in 1978. In the second volume, the Shakespearean challenge of the Desdemona sequence from *Otello* is commandingly taken, very distinctive, and all the singing is dramatic. Allowances have to be made, but there is much here to cherish. The third is much more uneven, with the later items coming from a period when the voice had detrioated, particularly in the items recorded as late as 1969. There are exceptions: Aida's *Ritorna vincitor*, vehemently done, is magnificent, and the two arias from *Il Corsaro*, although among her last recordings, show the vocal technique at its most assured (particularly in the legato phrasing) and the artistry at its most commanding. This third disc is essential for Callas devotees only.

Arias: *Don Carlos: Tu che la vanità. La Traviata: Ah fors è lui. Il Trovatore: Timor di me . . . D'amor sull'ali rosee.*

(M) *** Sony Great Performances SMK 60975 [id.]. Kiri Te Kanawa, LPO, Pritchard or LSO, Maazel – PUCCINI: Arias *** (with MOZART: *Don Giovanni: Ah! Fuggi il traditor; In quali eccessi . . . Mi tradì;* HUMPERDINCK: *Der kleine Sandmann bin ich;* DURUFLE: *Requiem: Pie Jesu ***).*

These three substantial Verdi arias are less obviously apt for the singer, but in each case the singing is felt as well as beautiful. The coloratura of the *Traviata* and *Trovatore* items is admirably clean, and it is a special joy to hear Elisabetta's big aria from *Don Carlos* sung with such truth and precision. The additional items are discussed under the Puccini couplings, but they are of fine quality.

Choruses from: (i) *Aida: Gloria all'Egitto (Triumphal march and ballet music). Attila: Urli rapine. La Battaglia di Legnano: Giuriam d'Italia.* (ii) *La Forza del destino: Compagni, sostiamo.* (i) *I Lombardi: O Signore, del tetto natio.* (iii) *Macbeth: Chi osò mandarvi a noi?; Patria oppressa!; Di destarlo per tempo . . . schiudi, inferno.* (i) *Nabucco: Gli arredi festivi; Va, pensiero (Chorus of the Hebrew slaves).* (iv) *Otello: Una vela!; Esultate!; Fuoco di gioia!* (ii) *La Traviata: Avrem lieta ...* (i) *Il Trovatore: Vedi, le fosche (Anvil chorus); Squilli echeggi.*

(M) **(*) Decca 458 237-2 [id.]. Ch. and Orch. of the St Cecilia Academy, Rome, with (i) Franci; (ii) Molinari-Pradelli; (iii) Schippers; (iv) Erede.

Carlo Franci's performances, recorded in the mid-1960s, were notable for their brilliance in sound and in performance, rather than for any special refinement. The chorus and orchestra has plenty of bite, and displays a willingness to sing softly and with a degree of refinement which is unusual for an Italian chorus. All the less well-known items sound fresh, and the *Aida* Triumphal scene gets the full stereo treatment. Schippers's performances of the *Macbeth* choruses a very brilliant indeed, and it is only the Molinari-Pradelli and Erede performances (recorded in the mid 1950s) which sound a little dated. A most enjoyable programme, with full texts and translations included in this Opera Gala release.

Choruses: *Aida: Gloria all'Egitto. Don Carlos: Spuntato ecco il dì. I Lombardi: Gerusalem!; O Signore, dal tetto natio. Macbeth: Patria oppressa! Nabucco: Va pensiero; Gli arredi festivi. Otello: Fuoco di gioia! Il Trovatore: Vedi! le fosche; Or co' dadi . . . Squilli, echeggi.*

(M) **(*) Ph. 462 064-2. Dresden State Op. Ch. & O, Varviso.

Varviso's collection of choruses brings polished and full-bodied but at times soft-grained perform-

ances, beautifully supported by the magnificent Dresden orchestra. The gentler choruses are excellent, but the dramatic ones lack something in bite. One of the highlights is the *Fire chorus* from *Otello*, in which the choral and woodwind detail suggests the flickering flames of bonfires burning in Otello's honour. The recording is warmly atmospheric and natural, but the selection is short measure at barely 46 minutes.

'The world of Verdi': (i) *Aida: Celeste Aida;* (ii) *Grand march and ballet.* (iii) *La forza del destino: Pace, pace, mio Dio.* (iv) *Luisa Miller: O! Fede negar potessi . . . Quando le sere al placido.* (v) *Nabucco: Va pensiero.* (vi) *Otello: Credo. Rigoletto:* (vii) *Caro nome;* (viii) *La donna è mobile;* (vii; viii; ix) Quartet: *Bella figlia dell'amore.* (x) *La Traviata: Prelude, Act I;* (vii; xi) *Brindisi: Libiamo ne'lieti calici. Il Trovatore:* (xii) *Anvil chorus;* (xiii) *Strida la vampa;* (viii) *Di quella pira. I vespri siciliani:* (xiv) *Mercè, diletti amiche.*

(M) *** Decca 433 221-1. (i) Vickers; (ii) Rome Op. Ch. & O, Solti; (iii) G. Jones; (iv) Bergonzi; (v) Amb. S., LSO, Abbado; (vi) Evans; (vii) Sutherland; (viii) Pavarotti; (ix) Tourangeau, Milnes; (x) Maggio Musicale O, Fiorentino, Pritchard; (xi) Bergonzi; (xii) L. Op. Ch., Bonynge; (xiii) Horne; (xiv) Chiara.

Opening with the *Chorus of the Hebrew Slaves* from *Nabucco* and closing with Pavarotti's *Di quella pira* from *Il Trovatore*, this quite outstandingly red-blooded Verdi compilation should surely tempt any novice to explore further into Verdi's world, yet at the same time it provides a superbly arranged 74-minute concert in its own right. The choice of items and performances demonstrates a shrewd knowledge of both popular Verdi and the Decca catalogue, for not a single performance disappoints. Joan Sutherland's melting 1971 *Caro nome* with its exquisite trills is the first of three splendid excerpts from *Rigoletto*, ending with the famous *Quartet*, and other highlights include Dame Gwyneth Jones's glorious *Pace, pace, mio Dio* from *La forza del destino*, Sir Geraint Evans's superb account of Iago's evil *Credo* from *Otello* and Marilyn Horne's dark-timbred *Strida la vampa* from *Trovatore*. Solti, too, is at his most electric in the great March scene from *Aida*. The stereo throughout is splendidly vivid.

Veress, Sándor (1907–92)

(i; ii) *Concerto for piano, strings and percussion;* (i; ii; iii) *Hommage à Paul Klee;* (i) *6 Csárdás.*
*** Teldec/Warner Dig. 0630-19992-2 [id.]. (i) András Schiff; (ii) Budapest Fest. O, Heinz Holliger; (iii) Dénes Várjon.

Sándor Veress studied with Bartók and Kodály and

became assistant to László Lajtha at the Budapest Ethnological Museum. He taught at the Franz Liszt Academy for a time, where his pupils included Ligeti and Kurtág. In 1949 he left his native Hungary to settle in Switzerland where he first saw some of Klee's work. The *Hommage à Paul Klee* (1951) takes the form of seven fantasias for two pianos and strings (the pictures that inspired them are reproduced in the informative booklet). They are all inventive and diverting; the second, *Fire wind*, in particular, is dazzling as is the last, *Little Blue Devil*, which Gunther Schuller was later to include in his *Klee Studies*. The *Concerto for piano, strings and percussion* (1952) was commissioned by Paul Sacher and is an appealing and finely fashioned score – which springs from the world of Bartók and perhaps Hindemith but, as you come to know it, inhabits an individual place of its own. The exuberant Bartókian quasi-serial finale comes off brilliantly. András Schiff is the expert and authoritative soloist and he dispatches the *Six Csárdás* (1939) for solo piano with great spirit. They are dance paraphrases that conceal studies in strict counterpoint. Heinz Holliger, who studied with Veress at the Berne Conservatory, directs with great sympathy, and the engineers produce excellent sound. It would be good to have the *Quattro danze transilvane* and the *Violin concerto* on CD.

Victoria, Tomás Luis de

(*c.* 1548–1611)

Missa Gaudeamus; Missa Pro Victoria; Motets: *Cum beatis Ignatius; Descendit Angelus Domini; Doctor bonus, amicus Dei Andreas; Ecce sacerdos magnus; Estote fortes in bello; Hic vir despiciens mundum; O decus apostolicum; Tu es Petrus; Vieni sponsa Christis.*
⚫ *** ASV Gaudeamus Dig. CDGAU 198 [id.].
Cardinall's Musick, Andrew Carwood.

This is one of the most rewarding CDs yet to come from the splendid Cardinall's Musick, and one of the very finest and most generous (78 minutes) representations of the composer in the catalogue. Happily the name of the opening *Missa Gaudeamus* for six voices, celebrates the label on which it is issued. It is a relatively serene 'backward-looking' work, yet with the closing *Sanctus* and *Agnus Dei* richly memorable. The shorter *Missa Pro Victoria* is even finer, indeed one of Victoria's most powerful expressive utterances.

Published in Madrid in 1600, it is the composer's only work for nine voices (contrasting writing for five-part and four-part choirs) and is unique in being based on a secular chanson, *La guerre, escoutez tous gentilz* by Janequin. Andrew Carwood's performance moves forward with true Latin passion and grips the listener from first to last. The *Gloria* is very arresting, while the beautiful *Sanctus*, opening

with echoing trebles, is followed by a radiant *Agnus Dei*. Among the nine very varied additional motets *Tu es Petrus* and *O decus apostolicum* and the remarkable *Descendit Angelus Dominum* stand out. The recording is of the very highest quality.

Officium decorum (1592): *Libera me Domine; Peccantem me quotidie. Officium decorum* (1605): *Taedet animam meam. Libera me Domine* (with Plainchant taken from Graduale Romanum).
**(*) ECM Dig. ECM 1653: 457 851-2 [id.].
David James, Rogers Covey-Crump, John Potter, Gordon Jones – PALESTRINA: *Responsories* **(*).

This CD combines music by Palestrina and Victoria for the Office and Matins for the Dead and the Burial service, including one text, *Libera me Domine* set by both composers. The four singers blend their voices persuasively and are beautifully recorded, but the prevailing mood is of unremitting deep melancholy.

'*Música española*': (i) *Officium defunctorum (Requiem);* (ii) Mass and Motet: *O quam gloriosum;* (iii) *Responsories for Tenebrae;* (i) Motets: *Ascendens Christus in altum; Ave Maria; Gaudent in coelis; Litaniae de Beata Virgine; Magnificat primi toni; O Magnum mysterium.*
(B) **(*) Decca Double Analogue/Dig. 433 914-2 (2) [id.]. (i) St John's College, Cambridge, Ch., Guest; (ii) King's College, Cambridge, Ch., Cleobury; (iii) Westminster Cathedral Ch., Malcolm.

The motets included here must be counted among the finest Victoria gave us and the *Requiem* is masterly too. On the whole the St John's performances are admirably done. The snag in the *Requiem* is the choirboys' lack of robustness in the plainchant and the men, too, sing with a big vibrato. But one has to accept that English choirs usually lack the harsh lines drawn by the firmer-toned Spanish bodies. The King's College Choir under Cleobury offer eloquent but slightly reserved accounts of the Mass and Motet *O quam gloriosum*, although the voices are finely blended to produce an impressive range of sonority. However, they sound very different from the Westminster Cathedral Choir. Their recording of the *Tenebrae responsories* dates from 1960, a period when the choir was at its peak under George Malcolm. The performance has great vigour and ardour, and the recording is excellent. On the whole this '*Música española*' Double would make a good, inexpensive starting point for a collector who wants to sample this composer or period.

Vieuxtemps, Henry (1820–81)

(i) *Violin concertos Nos. 1 in E, Op. 10;* (ii) *4 in D min., Op. 31.*
(BB) *** Naxos Dig. 8.554506 [id.]. Misha Keylin

(i) Janáček PO, Dennis Burkh; (ii) Arnhem PO, Takuo Yuasa.

Misha Keylin has already given us first-rate accounts of the *Second* and *Third Concertos* (Naxos 8.554114 – see our main volume). Now he turns to the equally unfamiliar *First* and pairs it with the much better-known *D minor Concerto*, which we are told he plays on a famous Stradivarius violin. Certainly its *Andante religioso* brings a generous-toned romanticism. But the solo timbre in the E major work is sweet and full, and he plays the dazzling lightweight finale with charm as well as sparkle. This is an excellent coupling, very well recorded and both accompanying groups, Czech and Dutch respectively, are very supportive indeed.

Villa-Lobos, Heitor (1887–1959)

Bachianas brasileiras Nos. 1–9; Chôros Nos. 2 (for flute & orchestra); 5 (for piano, Alma Brasileira); 10 (for chorus & orchestra); (i) 11 (for piano & orchestra). 2 Chôros (bis) (for violin & cello); (i) Piano concerto No. 5. Descobrimento do Brasil; Invocação em defesa da Patria; (i) Mômoprecóce (fantasy for piano & orchestra). Symphony No. 4. Qu'est-ce qu'un Chôros? (Villa-Lobos speaking).
(M) (**(*)) EMI (SIS) mono CZS7 67229-2 (6). De los Angeles, Kareska, Basrentzen, Braune, Tagliaferro, Du Frene, Plessier, Cliquennois, Bronschwak, Neilz, Benedetti; (i) Blumental; Chorale des Jeunesses Musicales de France, Fr. Nat. R. & TV Ch. & O, composer.

This six-CD box is a colourful, warm-hearted collection, not helped by dull mono recordings and ill-disciplined performances, but full of a passionate intensity that plainly reflects the personality of a composer of obvious charisma, if of limited ability as a conductor. Endearingly, there is a 10-minute track spoken in French by Villa-Lobos himself. All nine of the *Bachianas brasileiras* are recorded here, including the celebrated No. 5 for soprano and eight cellos, with Victoria de los Angeles a radiant soloist. That recording is already well known, but most of the others have had very limited circulation. Despite the dull sound, the warmth of the writing never fails to come over.

Bachianas brasileiras Nos. 2 (The little train of the Caipira); 4; (i) 5 for soprano and 8 cellos; (ii) Chôros No. 10: Rasga o Coração; (iii) Miniaturas Nos. 2 (Viola); 3, Cantilena; (iv) Mômoprecóce (fantasy for piano and orchestra).
(***) EMI stereo/mono CDC5 55224-2 [id.]. (i) French Nat. RO, composer; (i) with Victoria de los Angeles; (ii) Ch. des Jeunesses Musicales de France; (iii) Fredrick Fuller; (iv) Magda Tagliaferro.

No one has been more persuasive than the composer in *The little train of the Caipira*, and the recording certainly has plenty of local colour with its exotic percussive effects. Victoria de los Angeles' golden voice sounds ravishing in the famous *Bachianas brasileiras No. 5*, even if the recording is not entirely flattering; and the other, rarer works, notably the *Fantasy for piano and orchestra*, are welcome in this reissue in EMI's Composer in Person series, which now takes the two most familiar items into the premium-price bracket.

Guitar concerto.
*** Guild Dig. GMCD 7176 [id.]. Rafael Jiménez, Bournemouth Sinf., Terence Frazor –
ANGULO: *Guitar concerto No. 2 (El Alevín);*
RODRIGO: *Concierto de Aranjuez.* ***

Rafael Jiménez proves a natural soloist for Villa-Lobos's intimate concerto and Terence Frazor and the Bournemouth Sinfonietta make the very most of the orchestral colouring, which sounds more vivid than usual. Yet the balance integrates the soloist appealingly within the orchestral texture.

CHAMBER MUSIC

String quartets Nos. 2 (1915); 7 (1941).
** Marco Polo Dig. 8.223394 [id.]. Danubius Qt.

The *Seventh Quartet* comes from 1941 – a good vintage for Villa-Lobos – and is conceived on an ambitious scale, not far short of 40 minutes. Unlike Villa-Lobos's music from the 1930s, this is less exotic in feel, and his discovery of Bach in the *Bachianas brasileiras* also makes itself felt here. There is an abundance of melodic invention and contrapuntal vitality, even if his musical thinking remains essentially rhapsodic. The Danubius Quartet give a straightforward if rather languid account of the piece. The *Second Quartet* of 1915 is much shorter and of less interest.

Vivaldi, Antonio (1678–1741)

La Stravaganza (12 Concertos), Op. 4 (complete).
(BB) **(*) Naxos 8.55323 (Nos.1–6); 8.55324 (Nos. 7–12) [id.]. Andrew Watkinson, CLS, Nicholas Kraemer.

Nicholas Kraemer has fully absorbed period-instrument manners, and these athletic performances, full of vitality, on modern instruments, certainly have an authentic feel and sound. However Andrew Watkinson's solo personality is not strong in individuality and while this set, which is very well recorded, is excellent value, those looking for the very best in an inexpensive format should turn to Christopher Hogwood's sparkling version with the Academy of Ancient Music (and four different soloists), on a Decca Double (458 078-2), which also throws in for good measure Simon Preston's period performances of the six *Flute concertos*, Op. 10.

The Trial between harmony and invention (12 Concertos), Op. 8.
(M) **(*) Teldec/Warner 0630 13572-2 (2) [id.].
Alice Harnoncourt, Jürg Schaeftlein, VCM, Harnoncourt.

The Teldec complete set is original in approach and full of character; there is, however, an element of eccentricity in Nikolaus Harnoncourt's control of dynamics and tempi, with allegros often aggressively fast and sharp changes of mood not always convincing. Alice Harnoncourt's timbre with a baroque instrument is leonine and her tone production rather astringent. The dramatic style of the solo playing is certainly at one with the vivid pictorialism of Vivaldi's imagery. The shepherd's dog in *Spring* barks vociferously, and the dance rhythms at the finale of the same concerto are extremely invigorating. The interpretative approach throughout emphasizes this element of contrast. The sound is bright, vivid and clean, if dry-textured and sometimes fierce in the Telefunken manner. The two discs, originally issued separately, are now in a box together.

The Trial between harmony and invention (12 concertos), Op. 8; (i) *Double concertos: for violin, cello and strings in A, RV 546; for two violins in G, RV 516.*
(BB) *** Virgin Veritas 2 x 1 Dig. VBD5 61668-2 [CDVB 61668] (2). Monica Huggett, Raglan Bar. Players, Nicholas Kraemer; (i) with Elizabeth Wallfisch and Timothy Mason (cello).

Kraemer's complete Op. 8 concertos with Monica Huggett make a fine recommendation in its new Virgin 2 x 1 format. In the *Four Seasons*, a lovely spontaneous feeling emerges: the light textures and dancing tempo of the finale of *Spring* are matched by the sense of fantasy in the central movement of *Summer*, while the rumbustious energy of the latter's last movement is gloriously invigorating. The adagio of *Autumn* has a delicate, sensuous somnambulance, and only the opening of *Winter* is relatively conventional, though certainly not lacking character. The rest of the concertos are hardly less imaginative, with no exaggeration of phrasing, which used to haunt early-music performances, and the recording is excellent. With two other enjoyable concertos thrown in for good measure, this is highly recommendable.

The Trial between harmony and invention, Op. 8: Concertos Nos. 5–12.
(B) *** Sony SBK 53513 [id.]. Pinchas Zukerman, Neil Black, ECO, Philip Ledger.

Zukerman's solo playing is distinguished throughout, and the ECO provide unfailingly alert

and resilient accompaniments. In *Concerto No. 9 in D min.* oboist Neil Black takes the solo position and provides a welcome contrast of timbre – Vivaldi designed this concerto as optionally for violin or oboe, but it probably sounds more effective on the wind instrument. The full recording is lively, with a close balance for the soloists. This 77-minute CD encapsulates all the concertos from Op. 8 except the first four and includes such favourites as *La tempesta di mare* (RV 253), *Il piacere* (RV 108) and *La Caccia* (RV 362).

The Four Seasons, Op. 8/1–4.
*** DG 463 259-2 [id.]. Anne-Sophie Mutter, Trondheim Soloists – TARTINI: *Devil's trill sonata **(*).
**(*) DG Dig. 400 045-2 [id.]. Simon Standage, E. Concert, Pinnock.
**(*) BIS Dig. CD 275 [id.]. Nils-Erik Sparf, Drottningholm Bar. Ens.
(M) **(*) Carlton Classics Dig. PCD 2000 [id.]. Jaime Laredo, SCO.
**(*) EMI Dig. CDC7 49557-2 [id.]. Kennedy, ECO.

The Four Seasons, Op. 8/1–4 (with sonnets in Italian and English).
(B) *** Helios/Hyperion CDH 88012; [id.]. Bruni, Edwards (readers), Adelina Oprean, European Community CO, Faerber.

(i) *The Four Seasons, Op. 8/1–4;* (ii) *Bassoon concerto in A min., RV 498;* (iii) *Double concerto for 2 oboes in D min., RV 535;* (iv) *Piccolo concerto in C, RV 443.*
(M) *** Decca 466 232-2 [id.]. (i) Alan Loveday; (ii) Martin Gatt; (iv) Neil Black, Celia Nicklin; (iii) William Bennett; ASMF, Marriner.

(i) *The Four Seasons;* (ii) *Oboe concertos in C, RV 447; in F, RV 457.*
(B) **(*) Sony Seon SBK 60711 [id.]. (i) Sigiswald Kuijken, La Petite Bande; (ii) Bruce Haynes, O of 18th Century, Brüggen.

The Four Seasons; (i) *L'Estro armonico: Quadruple violin concerto in B min., RV 580, Op. 3/10.*
(B) *** Discover Dig. DICD 920202 [id.]. Oldřich Vlček; (i) with Hessová, Kaudersová, Nováková; Virtuosi di Praga.

(i) *The Four Seasons; Concerto for strings in G (Alla rustica), RV 151;* (ii) *Violin concerto in E (L'amoroso), RV 271; Sinfonia in B min. (Al Santo Sepolcro), RV 169.*
(B) *** DG Classikon 439 422-2. (i) Michel Schwalbé; (ii) Thomas Brandis; BPO, Karajan.

As we said in our main volume, Marriner's 1970 Academy of St Martin-in-the-Fields version of the *Seasons* still remains at the top of the list and now (as we predicted) it returns again on the Legends label, with a bonus of three of Vivaldi's most popular wind concertos, just as stylishly played.

Mutter's is a highly personal reading of Vivaldi's much-recorded set of concertos, even more so in many ways than Kennedy's much-publicized version on EMI with its gimmicky glissando passages. Mutter is above all deeply reflective, reacting emotionally to each movement, allowing herself a free expansiveness at generally broad speeds. Not surprisingly, this is a far more intimate reading than her previous version with Karajan and the Vienna Philharmonic, with sound bright and immediate so that dynamic contrasts are dramatically underlined, with Mutter less spotlit than most violin virtuosos tackling this work. With the Norwegian players consistently reacting as chamber-music partners, the result is a performance which repeatedly brings out mystery in these atmospheric sound-pictures. She takes a similarly romantic view of the Tartini, using Zandonai's string arrangement, as she did in her previous recording.

Karajan's 1972 recording of *The Four Seasons* was a popular success and remains very enjoyable. Its tonal beauty is not achieved at the expense of vitality and, although the harpsichord hardly ever comes through, the overall scale is acceptable. Michel Schwalbé is a memorable soloist; his playing is neat, precise and imaginative, with a touch of Italian sunshine in the tone. The remastering for DG's bargain label, Classikon, has restored the body and breadth of the original, and in the additional works (recorded in the St Moritz Französische Kirche in Switzerland two years earlier) the string-sound is glorious. The charismatic BPO playing, notably in the expressive *Sinfonia al Santo Sepolcro*, is difficult to resist, and the *Concerto alla rustica* sounds sumptuous.

An excellent bargain version comes from the Virtuosi di Praga, fresh, bright and clean, with a strong, highly responsive soloist in Oldřich Vlček. *Spring* is immediately vivacious and the viola produces a nice little rasp for the shepherd's dog. *Autumn* is delicately somnambulant, and the opening of *Winter* is well below zero and is decorated with a clink from the continuo. The *Concerto for four violins* makes for a popular encore. Excellent sound and very good value.

The Archiv version by Simon Standage with the English Concert, directed from the harpsichord by Trevor Pinnock, creates a relatively intimate sound, though their approach is certainly dramatic with the solo contribution having impressive flair and bravura. The effect is refined, treating the pictorial imagery with subtlety, finding a natural balance between vivid projection and atmospheric feeling. The digital recording is first class.

The BIS recording by Nils-Erik Sparf and the Drottningholm Baroque Ensemble has astonishing clarity and presence, and the playing is remarkable in its imaginative vitality. These Swedish players make the most of all the pictorial characterizations without ever overdoing them: they achieve the feat of making one hear this eminently familiar repertoire as if for the very first time.

The novelty of the Helios issue is the inclusion of the sonnets which Vivaldi placed on his score to give his listeners a guide to the illustrative detail suggested by the music. Before each of the four concertos, the appropriate poem is read, first in a romantically effusive Italian manner and then in BBC English (the contrast very striking). On CD one can conveniently programme out these introductions. The performances are first class. Adelina Oprean is an excellent soloist, her reading full of youthful energy and expressive freshness; her timbre is clean and pure, her technique assured. Faerber matches her vitality, and the score's pictorial effects are boldly characterized in a vividly projected sound-picture.

On Seon, La Petite Bande, with Kuijken as soloist and director, offers an authentic version of considerable appeal. Although the accompanying group can generate plenty of energy when Vivaldi's winds are blowing, this is essentially a small-scale reading, notable for its delicacy, and the result is refreshing. The new coupling is a pair of *Oboe concertos* played on a characterfully squawky and not entirely tractable period instrument by Bruce Haynes. If the end result is less refined than the main work, the duck-like noises occasionally bring a smile.

Jaime Laredo's performance has great spontaneity and vitality, emphasized by the forward balance, which is nevertheless truthful, with a bright upper range balanced by a firm, resonant bass. Laredo plays with bravura and directs polished, strongly characterized accompaniments. Pacing tends to be on the fast side; but although the reading is extrovert the lyrical music – played responsively – is made to offer a series of interludes to the vigour of the allegros. There is no extra item.

Kennedy's account is among the more spectacular in conveying the music's imagery, with *Autumn* involving controversially weird special effects, including glissando harmonics in the slow movement and percussive applications of the wooden part of the bow to add rhythmic pungency to the hunting finale. There is plenty of vivid detail elsewhere. The ECO's playing is always responsive, to match the often very exciting bravura of its soloist, and allegros have an agreeable vitality. However, at 41 minutes, with no fillers, this is not generous and it would not be our first choice for repeated listening.

6 Flute concertos, Op. 10.
(M) **(*) RCA 09026 61351-2. James Galway, New Irish CO.

James Galway most effectively directs the New Irish Chamber Orchestra from the flute. The playing is predictably brilliant and the goldfinch imitations in *Il Gardellino* (which comes first on the disc) are charming. Slow movements demonstrate Galway's beauty of timbre and sense of line to consistently good effect, although some may find the sweet vibrato excessive for baroque repertoire. First-rate recording quality.

Guitar concertos: in C, RV 425; for 2 guitars in G, RV 532; for 4 guitars in D, RV 93; in B min., RV 580 (from L'Estro armonico, Op. 3/10); for guitar, violin, viola & cello in A, RV 82.
(B) *** Ph. 426 076-2; 426 076-4. Los Romeros, San Antonio SO, Alessandro.

Though their composer did not conceive these works with guitars in mind, they sound quite effective in their present formats. Vivaldi's concertos of this kind are often more enjoyable when grouped in a miscellaneous collection with varying solo timbres. However, guitar and mandolin enthusiasts should find this satisfactory, for the recording is truthful, if a little studio-ish in feeling.

Concertos for strings, Volume 1: Paris concertos: Nos. 1 in G min., (with woodwind), RV 157; 2 in E min., RV 133; 3 in C min., RV 119; 4 in F, RV 136; 5 in C (with woodwind), RV 114; 6 in G min., RV 154; 7 in A, RV 160; 8 in D min., RV 127; 9 in B flat, RV 164; 10 in D, RV 121; 11 in G (with woodwind), RV 150; 12 in A, RV 159.
*** Chandos Dig. CHAN 0547 [id.]. Collegium Musicum 90, Simon Standage.

Vivaldi wrote over forty *concerti a quattro* for strings alone, without a soloist, and the present group were gathered together in a single manuscript, written in the hand of Vivaldi's father, and have been preserved in the Paris Conservatoire Library ever since. They are each in three movements, with the central slow movement, quite brief and acting as an expressive interlude linking the two vivacious framing allegros. The exception is RV 114, which is in two movements, the first moving from a sharply dotted allegro to adagio, with a jolly *Chaconne* to round things off. RV 133 has a striking *Rondeau* finale, and it is thought that these two works may have been composed separately from the others. They are all freshly inventive and played here with springing rhythms and plenty of vitality. In three concertos, though not specified by the composer, woodwind have been added to give extra colour. The touch of abrasiveness on the string sound is aurally bracing, and slow movements have a nicely ruminative improvisatory feel. The recording is first class.

Miscellaneous concerto collections

Bassoon concertos in A min., RV 497; in B flat (La notte), RV 501; Double mandolin concerto in G, RV 532; Piccolo concerto in C, RV 443; Viola d'amore concerto in D min., RV 394; Double

violin concerto for violin and violin per eco lontano in A, RV 552.
(M) *** Pierre Vernay Dig. PV 730052. Soloists, Paul Kuentz CO, Kuentz.

Although described as 'six rare concertos', this most enjoyable, 71-minute collection is made up entirely of favourites, all played with much character. The two mandolinists, Takashi and Sylvia Ochi, are as personable as the sprightly bassoonist, Fernand Corbillon, with his woody French timbre, while the *Echo violin concerto* (the echoes feature in the ripieno as well as the solo writing) comes off to great effect. Fine accompaniments from Kuentz and first-rate digital sound, naturally balanced.

Bassoon concerto in A min., RV 498; Flute concerto in C min., RV 441; Oboe concerto in F, RV 456; Concerto for 2 oboes in D min., RV 535; Concerto for 2 oboes, bassoon, 2 horns and violin in F, RV 574; Piccolo concerto in C, RV 444.
(B) *** Decca Penguin Classics 460 745-2 [id.]. ASMF, Marriner.

The playing here is splendidly alive and characterful, with crisp, clean articulation and well-pointed phrasing, free from overemphasis. The *A minor Bassoon concerto* has a delightful sense of humour. Altogether the musical substance may not be very weighty, but Vivaldi was rarely more engaging than when, as here, he was writing for wind instruments, particularly if he had more than one in his team of soloists. Well-balanced and vivid recording; this is highly recommendable for all those who do not insist on original instruments in this repertoire. The recordings were made in 1976/7 and have been transferred to CD with pleasing freshness; their bargain release on Penguin Classics (with contributory essay by Vikram Seth) makes this an excellent modern-instrument choice.

Concerti con molti instrumenti: Concerto funèbre in B flat for oboe, chalumeau, violin, 3 viole all'inglese, RV 579; Concerto in C for 2 recorders, oboe, chalumeau, violin, 2 viole all'inglese; 2 violins 'in tromba marina', 2 harpsichords, RV 555; Concerto in D min. for 2 oboes, bassoon, 2 violins, RV 566; Double trumpet concerto in D, RV 781; Concerto in F for viola d'amore, two horns, two oboes and bassoon, RV 97; Concerto in F for violin, 2 oboes, bassoon, two horns, RV 574; Concerto in D for violin, 2 oboes, 2 horns, RV 562.
*** Hyperion Dig. CDA 67073 [id.]. Soloists, King's Consort, Robert King.

This is one of the most attractive of all the CD groupings of Vivaldi's often extraordinarily scored multiple concertos, in which the period-instrument playing is not only expert, but constantly tweaks the ear. The braying horns often dominate, especially in the pair of concertos, RV 562 and RV 574, either rasping buoyantly or boldly sustaining long notes. The oboes are used to decorate the *Grave* of the latter, and elegantly open the finale of the former, before a bravura violin sends sparks flying. The horns again return spectacularly for the outer movements of RV 97, but the central *Largo* brings a delightful interplay between the languishing viola d'amore, and the oboes.

The *Concerto funèbre*, not surprisingly, opens with a *Largo* and combines the remarkable solo combination of muted oboe, tenor chalumeau, a trio of viole all'inglese accompanied by muted strings. After that the *Double trumpet concerto* seems almost conventional, yet it is given an infectiously spirited performance. Then (in RV 555) comes the most remarkable array of all. Vivaldi even throws in a pair of harpsichords for good measure, and they are given some most attractive solo passages and used to provide a gentle rocking background for a most engaging violin soliloquy in the central *Largo*.

The chirruping recorders charmingly introduce both first and second movements of the *D minor concerto* RV 566, but Vivaldi uses his full colour palette constantly. Throughout the solo playing is wonderfully stylish and appealing, and Robert King maintains a fine vigour in allegros and an often gentle espressivo in slow movements. The recording is first class. Very highly recommended.

Concertos with titles: *Double cello concerto in G min., RV 531; Concerto for flute, oboe, bassoon & violin in F (La tempesta di mare), RV 570; Concerto funèbre in B flat for violin, oboe, salmoe & 3 viole all'inglese, RV 579; Flute concerto in G min. (La notte), RV 439; Violin concertos: in D (L'inquietudine), RV 234; in E (Il riposo – per il Natale), RV 270; in A (Per eco in lontano), RV 552.*
*** Virgin Veritas/EMI VC5 45424-2 [id.].
Europa Galante, Fabio Biondi.

This collection of some of Vivaldi's most imaginative concertos, played on period instruments, is just as attractive as it looks. All the special effects, from the ghost and sleep evocations in *La notte* to the echoing second violin in RV 552, are neatly managed, and the atmosphere of the *Concerto funèbre* is well sustained. This concerto features a theme taken from *Tito Manlio* where it was used as part of a procession to execution, and the scoring is very telling (see above). Fabio Biondi leads an excellent team of soloists and directs sparkling accompaniments, with a touch of vintage dryness to the bouquet of string timbre. Excellent recording.

CHAMBER MUSIC

12 Sonatas for Violin and continuo, Op. 2.
**(*) Signum Dig. SIGCD 014 (2) [id.]. Cordaria (Walter Reiter, Shalev Ad-El, Katherine Sharman or Lyda Sayce).

Vivaldi's Op. 2 was first published in 1709 in Venice and dedicated at short notice to the King of Denmark who opportunely passed by at the time. In 1712 the sonatas were republished, more elegantly printed in Amsterdam, so they must have been a success. They are early rather than mature Vivaldi, but pleasingly inventive all the same, with the bass line fairly free, sometimes detaching itself from the continuo and engaging in dialogue with the violin. The performances here are lively and musical, not distinctive, but Walter Reiter is certainly up to the bravura demanded of him in some fizzing *Presto* finales. Good, clear recording.

VOCAL MUSIC

(i–v) *Beatus vir in G, RV 597;* (vi) *Introduction to Gloria, RV 639;* (i; iv; vi; vii) *Gloria in D, RV 588;* (I; ii; viii) *Gloria in D, RV 589;* (i; iii; vi; vii; ix) *Magnificat in G min., RV 611;* (x) *Nulla in mundo pax sincera, RV 630;* (xi) *Stabat Mater, RV 621.*
(B) *** Ph. Duo 462 170-2 (2) [id.]. (i) Margaret Marshall; (ii) Ann Murray; (iii) Anne Collins; (iv) Anthony Rolfe Johnson; (v) Robert Holl; (vi) Linda Finnie; (vii) Felicity Lott; (viii) Birgit Finnilä; (ix) Sally Burgess; (x) Elly Ameling; (xi) Jochen Kowalski; John Alldis Ch., ECO, Negri.

This Philips Duo offers a splendid selection of Vivaldi's choral works. It includes the two *Glorias* and the double-choir version of the *Magnificat*, while the *Beatus vir*, also for two choirs, is a similarly stirring piece. The collection opens with striking vocal bravura from Linda Finnie, who sings the *Introduction* to *Gloria*, RV 639 with spectacular virtuosity; later there is a comparable display from Elly Ameling in *Nulla in mundo pax sincera*, with the brilliant upper tessitura of the closing *Alleluia* testing her to the limit of her powers. Jochen Kowalski is the fine soloist in the touching *Stabat Mater*. The other soloists are also splendid, while the choir, vividly recorded, captures the dark, Bach-like intensity of many passages, contrasted with more typical Vivaldian brilliance. The analogue recordings are transferred to CD most impressively. A splendid introduction to Vivaldi's inspired writing for voices.

Beatus vir, RV 597; Canta in Prato; Credo in E min., RV 591; Gloria in D, RV 589; In furore; Kyrie in G min., RV 587; Lauda Jerusalem, RV 609; Magnificat in G min., RV 610; Nulla in mundo pax sincera, RV 630.
(B) **(*) Erato/Ultima 0630 18969-2 (2) [(M) id. import]. Jennifer Smith, Wally Staempfli, Verena Schweizer, Uta Spreckelsen, Nicole Rossier, Hanna Schaer, Jean-Pierre Maurer, Philippe Huttenlocher, Lausanne Vocal Ens. & CO, Corboz.

About the time Negri was making his Vivaldi recordings for Philips, Michel Corboz, an equally fine choral conductor, was working in Lausanne. Modern instruments are used to produce a warm, well-focused sound; the acoustic is spacious and the performances vital and musical. The professional singers of the Lausanne Choir are admirable, and the soloists are sweet-toned. The programme opens with a lively performance of the more famous *Gloria*, and the first CD closes with the *Magnificat* given in its simpler first version on a relatively small scale, with the chorus singing the alto solo *Fecit potentiam*. The *Kyrie in G minor* with its double chorus, double string orchestra, plus four soloists makes a fine contrast in its magnificence. The *Beatus vir* is another stirring piece, used to open the second disc. Warmly recommendable, even if the Negri survey is stylistically the more satisfying.

Gloria, RV 589.
(M) *** Decca 458 623-2 [id.]. Elizabeth
   Vaughan, Dame Janet Baker, Ian Partridge,
   Christopher Keyte, King's College,
   Cambridge, Ch., ASMF, Marriner – HANDEL:
   Coronation anthem: Zadok the Priest; HAYDN:
   Nelson mass. ***

Marriner's version authentically uses comparatively small forces, and has an excellent team of soloists. It is very stylish and very well recorded. Some might feel that consonants are too exaggerated but, in consequence, words are admirably clear.

OPERA

Opera Arias and scenas: *Bajazet (Il Tamerlano): Anch'il mar par che sommerga. Dorilla in Tempe: Dorilla'aura al sussurrar. Farnace: Gelido in ogni vena. La fida ninfa: Alma opressa; Dite, oimè. Griselda: Dopo un'orrida procella. Giustino; Sorte, che m'invitasti . . . Ho nel petto un cor sì forte. L'Olympiade: Tra le follie . . . Siam navi all'onde algenti. L'Orlando finto pazzo: Qual favellar? . . . Anderò volerò griderò. Teuzzone: Di trombe guerrier.* Arias with unidentified sources: *Di due rai languir costante; Zeffiretti, che sussurrate.*
*** Decca Dig. 466 569-2 [id.]. Cecilia Bartoli, Il
   Giardino Armonico (with Arnold Schoenberg
   Ch.).

This remarkable collection is as much valuable for its exploration of unknown Vivaldi operas (what Cecilia Bartoli herself describes as 'a fascinating voyage of discovery') as it is for coloratura singing of extraordinary bravura and technical security – a recital to compare with Marilyn's Horne famous collection of Rossini arias, although if anything even more astonishing.

It is a pity that the programme (understandably) opens with the excerpt from *Dorilla in Tempe* with its echoes of *Spring* from *The Four Seasons*, as

the chorus, although enthusiatic in praising those seasonal joys, is less than sharply focused. But the following aria from *Griselda*, with its stormy horns and fiendish leaps and runs, shows just how expertly Cecilia Bartoli can deliver the kind of thrilling virtuosity expected by Vivaldi's audiences of their famous castrato soloists. Farnace's tragic aria, *Gelido in ogni vena* (based on the *Winter* concerto) shows the other side of the coin with some exquisite lyrical singing of lovely descending chromatics.

Similarly, while *Alma opressa* (from *La fida ninfa*) brings a remarkable display of melismatic runs with its almost unbroken line of semiquavers, the following *Dite, oimè*, very movingly sung, has an almost desperate melancholy. Vivaldi's imaginative accompaniments, too, have their own delights. *Di due rai languir costante* is delectably decorated by a pair of flageolets (miniature recorders), to express the exquisite torments of love, heard against muted violins and pizzicato violas and cellos; and in the closing number from *Teuzzone*, written for one of Vivaldi's favourite sopranos, Margherita Gualandi, the trumpets and drums add to the martial evocation.

In short, this is dazzling singing of remarkable music, most stylishly and vividly accompanied. Indeed the Storm aria from *Bajazet* brings a delivery of such speed and sharpness of articulation that the rapid fire of a musical machine-gun springs instantly to mind. Moreover, Decca have done their star mezzo proud with fine documentation, full translations and a presentation more like a handsomely bound hardback book than a CD.

Orlando furioso: Arias: Act I: *Nel profondo;* Act II: *Sorge l'irato nembo;* Act III: *Fonti di pianto.*
(M) *** Erato Dig. 0630 14069-2 [id.]. Marilyn
   Horne, I Solisti Veneti, Scimone – HANDEL:
   Arias ***.

These three key arias, the second fiery, the third very touching, come from Scimone's complete recording of Vivaldi's opera and show Horne in superb form. They make an apt bonus for a remarkable collection of Handel arias, recorded five years earlier and including an excerpt from Handel's own setting of the same narrative.

Vives, Amadeo (1871–1932)

Doña Francisquita.
**(*) Sony Dig. S2K 66563 (2) [id.]. Domingo,
   Arteta, Mirabel, Del Portal, Cordoba Theatre
   Ch., Sevilla SO, Roa.

Even among the hundred and more zarzuelas written by this composer, *Doña Francisquita*, a light-hearted love story, is by far the most popular: no fewer than 5,000 performances were given in Spain over the twenty years after its first performance in 1923. It is full of charming ideas, skilfully presented. This version stands out from previous complete recordings through the strength of Plácido Domingo in the role of the hero, Fernando. Domingo's love of the genre shines out in every note he sings, with his diction immaculately clear. Even if vocally he is hardly matched by Ainhoa Arteta in the title-role, her light, bright, agile soprano is well suited to the part of an *ingénue*. Linda Mirabel, a warm-toned mezzo, sings Aurora the actress, but the second tenor, Enrique del Portal, as the hero's friend, Cardona, is very thin-toned. At least there is no confusion with Domingo. Miguel Roa, who earlier conducted an electrifying account of Penella's *El gato montes* for DG, also with Domingo as the hero, understands the idiom perfectly, but here with an indifferent orchestra and the sound a little backward the impact of the performance is less, for all the brightness and energy.

Voormolen, Alexander (1895–1980)

Baron Hop suites 1–2; (i) *Double oboe concerto; Eline (Nocturne for orchestra).*
*** Chandos Dig. CHAN 9815 [id.]. Hague Residentie O, Mathias Bamert; (i) with Pauline Oostenrijk; Hans Roerade.

Apart from Diepenbrock, late-nineteenth- and early-twentieth-century Dutch orchestral music still remains a virtually unexplored area. All the more reason to welcome this highly entertaining collection. Alexander Voormolen was born in Rotterdam, but his musical life centred on The Hague. His maternal grandmother was a Rameau (a descendant of Jean-Philippe's brother), which accounts for the French influences in his musical genes, which were to attract the attention of Ravel, who became his sponsor, and whose personal recommendation ensured that the music was published.

Voormolen sought to create a truly Dutch style in his writing, but his genes thwarted him, and its charming eccentricity and unpredictability gives a very un-Dutch impression. Indeed, one might think of him as a Netherlands equivalent of Lord Berners. His orchestral skill and witty humour is ideally suited to his musical evocations of the world of Baron Hop, a genial larger-than-life eighteenth-century Dutch diplomat and *bon viveur*, who so loved coffee that he had a famous sweetmeat made of it called 'Haagsche Hopjes'.

The two *Baron Hop suites* (1924 and 1931) draw on material from an aborted *opéra comique*, and their spirited neo-classicism is well nourished by a richly coloured orchestral palette, and sprightly rhythms. There are Dutch popular tunes, and others too. In the first suite the witty opening overture (it has a false ending) quotes a snatch of the *Marseillaise*, and the closing *March of the Hereditary Prince-Stadtholder* even includes *The British Grenadiers*. In between come a slightly sensuous *Sarabande* and an engaging *Polka*.

The *Concerto for two oboes* is quaintly colourful with a unique 'quacking' closing Rondo. *Eline* (originally a piano work) is languorous and faintly Delian, but has other influences too. All this music is played very persuasively indeed by the composer's home orchestra, directed with complete understanding, the nicest touches of rubato and neat rhythmic pointing by Bamert. The Chandos recording is glowingly full and vivid. A real find.

Wagner, Richard (1813–83)

Siegfried idyll; A Faust overture; Die Meistersinger: Prelude to Act I; Tannhäuser: Overture; Tristan und Isolde: Prelude and Liebestod.
(M) *(*) Sony SMK 64108 [id.]. NYPO, Boulez.

There is little or no mystery in Boulez's view of Wagner. The most successful item here is the *Meistersinger Prelude*, spacious and well pointed, and the *Faust overture*, after a matter-of-fact introduction, brings out the dark, biting quality in Boulez's conducting; but *Tannhäuser* sounds more like Meyerbeer, and *Tristan* lacks tension. The sound, dating from 1970 is acceptable, but there are far better Wagner collections available.

Siegfried idyll. Der fliegende Holländer: Overture. Götterdämmerung: Siegfried's funeral march. Lohengrin: Prelude to Act 1. Die Meistersinger: Prelude to Act 1; Hymn. Parsifal: Prelude to Act 1. Rienzi: Overture. Tannhäuser: Overture and Bacchanale. Tristan und Isolde: Prelude to Act 1.
(B) *** Decca Double Analogue/Dig. 440 606-2 (2) [id.]. VPO, Solti.

Solti's way with Wagner is certainly exciting: some may find the early 1960s performances of the *Rienzi* and *The Flying Dutchman* overtures a little hard-driven. But the *Siegfried idyll*, played in its chamber version by members of the VPO, is most beautifully done, and the *Lohengrin Prelude* is similarly relaxed until its climax – two welcome moments of repose amid such drama.

Elsewhere one is easily caught up in the sheer force of Solti's music-making, and in the later recordings in the 1970s Solti has mellowed a little, and the *Meistersinger overture* has genuine grandeur and nobility. The VPO play splendidly, of course, and Decca has supplied brilliant sound to match. An inexpensive way to explore Solti's special charisma in orchestral Wagner.

(i; ii) *Siegfried idyll.* (iii; iv) *Overture: Der fliegende Holländer.* (i; v) *Götterdämmerung: Siegfried's Rhine journey. Lohengrin:* (i; ii) *Prelude to Act I;* (vi; iv) *Prelude to Act III. Die Meistersinger:* (vi; iv) *Overture;* (vii; viii) *Prelude to Act III.* (ix; viii) *Parsifal: Prelude & Good Friday music. Overtures:* (vi; iv) *Rienzi;* (vii; x) *Tannhäuser. Tristan und Isolde:* (iii; iv) *Preludes*

to *Acts I & III;* (vi; iv) *Death of Isolde.* (i; v) *Die Walküre: Ride of the Valkyries.*
(B) *** DG Double 439 687-2 (2) [id.]. (i) BPO; (ii) Kubelik; (iii) Bayreuth Festival O; (iv) Karl Boehm; (v) Karajan; (vi) VPO; (vii) German Op., Berlin, O; (viii) Jochum; (ix) Bav. RSO; (x) Otto Gerdes.

The *Siegfried idyll* is beautifully shaped by Kubelik and equally beautifully played by the Berlin Philharmonic. He also conducts an impressive *Lohengrin* Act I *Prelude,* again with the BPO. Boehm not only provides a richly sustained opening for *Rienzi* but is exciting in *Der fliegende Holländer* and at his finest in the *Tristan Preludes* – taken from his 1966 Bayreuth complete set – which glow with intensity. Karajan contributes only two items, but both surge with adrenalin. The highlight of the set comes last, Jochum's electrifying performance of the *Prelude* and *Good Friday* music from *Parsifal.* Recorded in the Munich Herculessaal, it is not only a demonstration record from the earliest days of stereo, but the playing has a spiritual intensity that has never been surpassed. The recordings, dating from the late 1950s to the early 1980s, have all been transferred vividly, mostly with fuller and more refined sound. The documentation is sadly inadequate.

Siegfried idyll; Der fliegende Holländer: Overture; Götterdämmerung: Dawn and Siegfried's Rhine journey; Die Meistersinger: suite; Rienzi: Overture; Tristan und Isolde: Prelude to Act III; Die Walküre: Wotan's farewell and Magic fire music.
(M) ** Mercury 434 383-2 [id.]. Detroit SO, Paray.

Paray made many excellent recordings for Mercury in the 1950s and 60s, particularly of French music, but his style in Germanic repertoire is controversial. Many will regard these performances as too fast and too clipped, and the vivid upfront Mercury recording (from 1956–60) – though astonishingly vivid – is tiring after a while. But one cannot doubt the excitement of music-making here – spurting off with a highly charged *Flying Dutchman overture* – though the *Siegfried idyll* is far too high-powered to make its full effect. In short, this is not a disc for all tastes, but it is in a way unique, and is the type of recording which is not likely to be made today.

(i) *Der fliegende Holländer: Overture.* (ii) *Lohengrin: Prelude to Act I. Die Meistersinger: Overture.* (iii) *Parsifal: Prelude and Good Friday music.* (iv) *Tannhäuser: Overture.*
(B) **(*) DG Classikon 439 445-2. (i) Bayreuth (1971) Festival O, Boehm; (ii) BPO, Kubelik; (iii) Bav. RSO, Jochum; (iv) German Op. O, Berlin, Otto Gerdes.

Most of these performances are duplicated in a most attractive DG Double set of Wagner's orchestral

excerpts, mentioned above, but this shorter, Classikon bargain collection includes Jochum's superb account of the *Parsifal* excerpts and is also well worthwhile.

(i) *Der fliegende Holländer: Overture;* (ii) *Lohengrin: Prelude to Act I; Die Meistersinger: Overture;* (i) *Rienzi: Overture;* (ii) *Tannhäuser: Overture;* (i) *Tristan und Isolde: Prelude;* (ii) *Die Walküre: Ride of the Valkyries.*
(M) **(*) Decca 458 214-2 [id.]. (i) VPO; (ii) Chicago SO; Solti.

Recorded between 1960 (*Rienzi*) and 1986 (the *Lohengrin Prelude*) these performances were newly made in the studio, not taken from complete opera sets. So this is the self-contained *Tannhäuser overture* from the Dresden version, and very exciting it is, with brilliant sound. The following *Meistersinger Prelude* is fuller and more expansive, but all the music-making here demonstrates Solti's characteristic Wagnerian flair and brings a high degree of tension. In *Der fliegende Holländer* the VPO are driven too hard and the effect is fierce, but *Rienzi* is mellower, with the big tune at the opening obviously relished. The CD transfers are vivid, if not always refined.

Götterdämmerung: Dawn and Siegfried's Rhine journey; Siegfried's death and funeral music. Die Meistersinger: Prelude. Das Rheingold: Entrance of the gods into Valhalla. Siegfried: Forest murmurs. Die Walküre: The Ride of the Valkyries.
(M) *(**) Decca Phase Four (IMS) 443 901-2 [id.]. LSO, Stokowski.

This collection of *Ring* excerpts was first issued in 1966 and was not one of Decca's most successful Phase Four recordings. There is a shrill, superficial brilliance, and patches of roughness in the highly modulated recording – but no matter when this is vintage Stokowski. He is at his most electrifying in *Siegfried's Rhine journey*, while the gods enter Valhalla like a procession of Roman juggernauts. The opening *Ride of the Valkyries* is especially affected by the top-heavy balance, but *Forest murmurs* with its chirruping birds has never sounded more atmospherically potent. The *Mastersingers Prelude* was recorded 'live' at the London Festival Hall in 1972 and, if the orchestra is too close, the overall balance is better and the sound more refined. The performance is full of adrenalin but has warmth and grandeur too, with some glorious playing from the LSO strings.

Lohengrin: Preludes to Acts I & II. Die Meistersinger: Prelude to Act I. Parsifal: Prelude to Act I; Good Friday music. Tristan und Isolde: Prelude to Act I.
** DG Dig. 453 485-2 [id.]. Phd. O, Christian Thielemann.

This is an impressively recorded and beautifully

played Wagner programme, but it is not really distinctive. At the radiant opening pianissimo the great *Lohengrin* Act I *Prelude* lacks the kind of concentration that distinguished Furtwängler's famous account. Yet the climax is well prepared and the diminuendo handled very musically. The *Parsifal* Act I *Prelude* is one of the finest performances on the disc, beautifully shaped, and the opening of the *Tristan Liebestod* also brings real tension, and if this not quite consistently maintained, the climax expands grippingly (even if the Philadelphia violins are not entirely flattered by the hall acoustics in Collingswood, New Jersey). The *Meistersinger Prelude* is expansive in the German tradition.

Die Meistersinger: Prelude to Act III.
Tannhäuser: Overture and Venusberg music.
Tristan und Isolde: Prelude and Liebestod.
**(*) DG (IMS) Dig. Gold 439 022-2 [id.]. BPO, Karajan.

In Karajan's digital concert the orchestral playing is superlative. But, in spite of the reprocessing, the upper strings lack space, and climaxes should be freer. The overall effect is rather clinical in its detail, instead of offering a resonant panoply of sound, but the playing is eloquent and powerful. The measure is not very generous for a reissued premium-price CD.

OPERA

Der fliegende Holländer (complete).
(M) **(*) EMI (SIS) Dig. CMS7 64650-2 (2) [Ang. CDMB 64650]. Van Dam, Vejzovic, Moll, Hofmann, Moser, Borris, V. State Op. Ch., BPO, Karajan.
**(*) Decca (IMS) 414 551-2 (3) [id.]. Bailey, Martin, Talvela, Kollo, Krenn, Isola Jones, Chicago S & O Ch. O, Solti.
(B) **(*) Decca (IMS) Double 460 738-2 (2) [id.]. London, Rysanek, Tozzi, ROHCG Ch. & O, Dorati.

The extreme range of dynamics in EMI's recording for Karajan, not ideally clear but rich, matches the larger-than-life quality of the conductor's reading. He firmly and convincingly relates this early work to later Wagner, *Tristan* above all. His choice of José van Dam as the Dutchman, thoughtful, finely detailed and lyrical, strong but not at all blustering, goes well with this. Van Dam is superbly matched and contrasted with the finest Daland on record, Kurt Moll, gloriously biting and dark in tone, yet detailed in his characterization. Neither the Erik of Peter Hofmann, nor – more seriously – the Senta of Dunja Vejzovic matches this standard; nevertheless, for all her variability, Vejzovic is wonderfully intense in *Senta's Ballad* and she matches even Van Dam's fine legato in the Act II duet. The CD transfer underlines the heavyweight quality of the recording, with the *Sailors' chorus* made massive, but effectively so, when Karajan conducts it with such fine spring.

What will disappoint some who admire Solti's earlier Wagner sets is that this most atmospheric of the Wagner operas is presented as a concert performance with no Culshaw-style production whatever. Characters halloo to one another when evidently standing elbow to elbow, and even the Dutchman's ghostly chorus sounds close and earthbound. But with Norman Bailey a deeply impressive Dutchman, Janis Martin a generally sweet-toned Senta, Martti Talvela a splendid Daland, and Kollo, for all his occasional coarseness, an illuminating Erik, it remains well worth hearing.

Dorati, with rhythms well sprung, draws strong and alert playing and singing from his Covent Garden forces in a consistently purposeful performance, helped by apt sound-effects. The well-spread recording is full and atmospheric and, like the EMI set, the reissue is offered on two mid-price CDs. George London's Dutchman brings one of his most powerful performances on disc, occasionally rough-toned but positive. Leonie Rysanek may sound too mature for Senta, but as a great Wagnerian she brings a commanding presence and the most persuasive sense of line. There is no weak link in the rest of the cast, well set up at the start by the characterful Richard Lewis as the Steersman, and at its Decca Double reissue price this is well worth its modest cost. There is a cued synopsis and Decca's usual 'listening guide'.

Der fliegende Holländer: highlights.
(M) **(*) Ph. (IMS) Dig. 446 618-2 [id.]. Estes, Balslev, Salminen, Schunk, Bayreuth Festival (1985) Ch. & O, Nelsson.
**(*) Sony Dig. SK 61969 [id.]. Morris, Voigt, Heppner, Rootering, Svendén, Groves, Met. Op. Ch. & O, James Levine.
(M) **(*) EMI (SIS) Dig. CDM5 66052-2 . Van Dam, Vejzovic, Moll, Hofmann, Moser, Borris, V. State Op. Ch., BPO, Karajan.

A generous (76 minutes) and well-chosen selection from the outstanding Philips set is let down by the absence of any documentation, save a list of the twelve excerpts.

The highlights Sony CD is generously selected (76 minutes) and includes the Overture. But again there is no translation and the synopsis is not cued.

This EMI highlights disc is only slightly more generous than most of the rest of the series (67 minutes) but will be useful for those wanting to sample Karajan's 1983 recording, particularly as José Van Dam as the Dutchman and Kurt Moll as Daland are both so impressive, and *Senta's Ballad* (Dunja Vejzovic) is very movingly sung. The synopsis relates each excerpt to the narrative.

Götterdämmerung (complete).
(M) *** Ph. 434 424-2 (4) [id.]. G. Jones, Jung,

Hübner, Becht, Mazura, Altmeyer, Killebrew,
(1979) Bayreuth Festival Ch. & O, Boulez.
(M) (***) Testament mono SBT 4175 (4) [id.].
Varnay, Aldenhoff, Uhde, Mödl, Weber,
Bayreuth Fest. Ch. & O, Knappertsbusch.

Boulez's 1979 analogue recording is warm and urgent. The passion of the performance is established in the Dawn music before the second scene of the Prologue and, with a strong if not ideal cast, it has a clear place as a first-rate mid-price recommendation. Manfred Jung as Siegfried gives a fresh, clean-cut performance. Jeannine Altmeyer sings Gutrune, sweet but not always ideally clean of attack; Fritz Hübner is a weighty Hagen, Franz Mazura a powerful Gunther and Gwendoline Killebrew a rich, firm Waltraute. Dame Gwyneth Jones as Brünnhilde, always very variable, has some splendid moments, notably at the close of the Immolation scene. The sound is aptly atmospheric but lacks something in weight in the brass, though there is no lack of excitement at the end of Act II.

The legendary recording made in 1951 during the first Bayreuth Festival after the war has, for almost half a century, been buried in the Decca archive for copyright reasons. By sheer persistence Stewart Brown has sorted out contractual problems and, with the original tapes finally edited, has produced for his Testament label a set astonishing in its vividness. This live recording was supervised by the Decca producer John Culshaw (later to mastermind Solti's complete *Ring* cycle) and the mono sound is even fuller and weightier than on the recording of *Parsifal* he also made at Bayreuth in 1951. Both operas were conducted by Hans Knappertsbusch, who in *Götterdämmerung* is even more electrifying than in *Parsifal*, defying his reputation as a relaxed, expansive Wagnerian. Vocally the star is Astrid Varnay, shiningly firm and incisive as Brünnhilde, rising magnificently to the final challenge of the Immolation scene. Siegfried is sung by the short-lived Bernd Aldenhoff, strained at times like most Heldentenoren, but generally lyrical and boyish. Hermann Uhde as Gunther and Ludwig Weber as Hagen are both outstanding too, with the immediacy and sense of presence carrying one on from first to last.

Götterdämmerung: highlights.
(M) **(*) Ph. (IMS) 446 616-2 [id.] (from above
complete (1979) Bayreuth set, with Jones,
Jung, etc.; cond. Boulez).

Many collectors will want to sample the Boulez set, and this CD offering 78 minutes of highlights should serve admirably, except for the lack of either translation or synopsis – or, indeed, any kind of documentation at all except for detailing the sixteen excerpts. They include *Siegfried's Rhine journey* and *Funeral march* and the final *Immolation scene.*

Lohengrin (complete).
(M) **(*) EMI CMS5 66519-2 (3) [CDMD
693142]. René Kollo, Anna Tomowa-Sintow,
Dunja Vejzovic, Siegmund Nimsgern, Karl
Ridderbusch, German Op. Ch., Berlin, BPO,
Karajan.
(M) **(*) Ph. 446 337-2 (3) [id.]. Jess Thomas,
Silja, Vinay, Varnay, Crass, Krause, Bayreuth
Festival Ch. & O, Sawallisch.

Karajan, whose DG recording of *Parsifal* is so naturally intense, fails in this earlier but related opera to capture comparable spiritual depth. So some of the big melodies sound a degree over-inflected and the result, though warm and expressive and dramatically powerful, with wide-ranging recording, misses an important dimension. Nor is much of the singing as pure-toned as it might be, with René Kollo too often straining and Tomowa-Sintow not always able to scale down to the necessary purity her big, dramatic voice. Even so, with strong and beautiful playing from the Berlin Philharmonic, it remains a powerful performance, and it makes a fair mid-priced version on three CDs.

The Sawallisch recording was of a live performance at Bayreuth in 1962 and has a propulsive thrust over Wagner's expansive paragraphs, encouraged by the presence of an audience. For this dramatic tension one naturally has to pay in stage-noises, occasional slips and odd balances, but the recording captures the unique flavour of the Festspielhaus splendidly. What above all will dictate a listener's response is their reaction to the voices of Anja Silja as Elsa and of Astrid Varnay as Ortrud. Though Silja has been far less steady on record in other sets, this is often not a pretty sound, and Varnay was firmer in her earlier Bayreuth recording for Decca in mono. Jess Thomas is here not as reliable as he has been in other performances; but Sawallisch's direction is superb, fresh and direct, never intrusive. On CD the sound is marvellously refined as well as atmospheric. The opera fits neatly on three discs, with each Act complete and unbroken.

Die Meistersinger von Nürnberg (complete).
**(*) Decca (IMS) 417 497-2 (4) [id.]. Bailey,
Bode, Moll, Weikl, Kollo, Dallapozza,
Hamari, Gumpoldskirchner Spatzen, V. State
Op. Ch., VPO, Solti.
(M) (***) EMI (SIS) mono CMS7 64154-2
[CDMD 641542]. Ferdinand Frantz, Rudolf
Schock, Elisabeth Grümmer, Gottlob Frick,
Benno Kusche, Gerhard Unger, Marga
Höffgen, St Hedwig's Cathedral Ch., German
Op., Berlin, Ch., BPO, Kempe.

The great glory of Solti's earlier set is the mature and involving portrayal of Sachs by Norman Bailey. Kurt Moll as Pogner, Bernd Weikl as Beckmesser and Julia Hamari as Magdalene are all excellent, but the shortcomings are comparably serious. Both Hannelore Bode and René Kollo fall short of their far-from-perfect contributions to earlier sets, and Solti for all his energy gives a surprisingly square reading of this most appealing of Wagner scores, pointing his expressive lines too heavily and failing to convey spontaneity. It remains an impressive achievement for Bailey's marvellous Sachs, and the Decca sound comes up vividly on CD.

Though Kempe's classic EMI set is in mono only, one misses stereo surprisingly little when, with closely balanced voices, there is such clarity and sharpness of focus. The orchestra to a degree loses out, sounding relatively thin; but with such an incandescent performance – not quite as intense as Karajan's live Bayreuth version of 1951 but consistently inspired – one quickly adjusts. The cast has no weak link. Elisabeth Grümmer is a meltingly beautiful Eva, pure and girlish, not least in the great Act III Quintet, and Rudolf Schock gives the finest of all his recorded performances as Walther, with his distinctive timbre between lyric and heroic well suited to the role. Ferdinand Frantz is a weighty, dark-toned Sachs, Gottlob Frick a commanding Pogner, Benno Kusche a clear-toned Beckmesser and Gerhard Unger an aptly light David.

Die Meistersinger: highlights.
(M) *** DG 445 470-2 (from complete set, with Fischer-Dieskau, Domingo, Ligendza, Lagger, Hermann, Laubenthal, Ludwig, German Op. Ch. & O, Berlin, Jochum).
(B) (***) CfP CD-CFP 6086 [(M) id. import]. Frantz, Schock, Grümmer, Frick, Kusche, Unger, Höffgen, St Hedwig's Cathedral Ch., German Op., Berlin, Ch., Berlin State Op. Ch., BPO, Kempe.
(M) **(*) EMI CDM7 63455-2 (from complete set, with Adam, Evans, Kelemen, Ridderbusch, Kollo, Schreier, Donath, Hess, Leipzig R. Ch., Dresden State Op. Ch. & State O, Karajan).

Jochum's DG excerpts are especially valuable for giving fair samples of the two most individual performances: Fischer-Dieskau as a sharply incisive Sachs, his every nuance of mood clearly interpreted, and Domingo a golden-toned if hardly idiomatic Walther. The 76-minute selection, opening with the *Overture*, includes the Act III Quintet, and also the opera's closing scene. The recording, made in March 1976 in the Berlin Jesus-Christus Kirche with the voices placed rather closely, matches the fine quality of the complete set.

The 72-minute selection from Kempe's classic EMI mono set provides generous samples of Ferdinand Frantz's comparatively weighty, dark-toned Sachs. Rudolf Schock, with his distinctive timbre between lyrical and heroic, is ideally suited to the role of Walther, and Elisabeth Grümmer is a meltingly beautiful Eva, particularly so in the great Act III Quintet. Voices are closely balanced and there is striking clarity of focus so that, although the

orchestra sounds relatively thin, one soon adjusts when the singing is so fine and there is good ambience.

Many will prefer to have a sampler rather than investing in the complete Karajan stereo set, which is let down by the casting of Theo Adam as Sachs. The selection runs to nearly 68 minutes.

Parsifal (complete).
**(*) Koch-Schwann 3-1348-2 (4) [id.]. Kollo, Adam, Cold, Schröter, Bunger, Teschler, Leipzig and Berlin R. Choirs, Thomanenchor Leipzig, Leipzig RSO, Kegel.
**(*) DG Dig. 437 501-2 (4) [id.]. Domingo, Norman, Moll, Morris, Wlaschiha, Rootering, Met. Op. Ch. & O, James Levine.
(M) **(*) DG 435 718-2 (3) [id.]. James King, Gwyneth Jones, Stewart, Ridderbusch, McIntyre, Crass, (1970) Bayreuth Festival Ch. & O, Boulez.
**(*) Ph. 416 390-2 (4) [id.]. Jess Thomas, Dalis, London, Talvela, Neidlinger, Hotter, (1962) Bayreuth Festival Ch. & O, Knappertsbusch.
(M) (***) Teldec/Warner mono 9031 76047-2 (4). Windgassen, Mödl, Weber, London, Uhde, Van Mill, (1951) Bayreuth Festival Ch. & O, Knappertsbusch

Recorded live at a concert performance in East Berlin in 1975, the Kegel version presents a refreshing alternative to most latterday interpretations, brisk and electric, bringing out the dramatic thrust of the piece far more than usual at speeds that flow fluently and easily. Kegel, best known as the creator of the Leipzig Radio Choir, is a more passionate Wagnerian than Pierre Boulez, similarly brisk in this opera. Kegel draws incandescent singing from his massed choirs, with the spacious recording capturing the bloom on the vocal sound atmospherically, with choral antiphonies most beautiful. René Kollo as Parsifal and Theo Adam as Amfortas were then still in their prime and sing magnetically. The others, less celebrated, still comprise a fresh-sounding team, clean of attack, notably Ulric Cold as Gurnemanz. Gisela Schröter, lighter of tone than usual for Kundry and with a tight vibrato, also sings beautifully. Reid Bunger is a youngish-sounding Klingsor with a villainous snarl. The layout on four discs is not only inconvenient (with breaks in each Act) but extravagant, when it could easily have been accommodated on three.

James Levine's speeds outstrip almost anyone in slowness, with the New York studio performance at times hanging fire – as in the Transformation scene of Act I. Many will find it a small price to pay for a performance, vividly recorded, involving a cast as starry as any that could be assembled. Jessye Norman as Kundry and Plácido Domingo in the title-role give performances that in every way live up to their reputations, not just exploiting beauty of sound but backing it with keen characterization and concern for word-meaning. Kurt Moll as Gurnemanz and Ekkehard Wlaschiha as Klingsor are both magnificent, firm and characterful, while James Morris as Amfortas gives a powerful performance, with a slightly gritty tone adding to the character's sense of pain. Jan-Henrik Rootering's bass as Titurel is atmospherically enhanced by an echo-chamber, pointing the relative lack of reverberation in the main, firmly focused recording, one of the most vivid yet made in the Manhattan Center. Levine's slow speeds will prevent this from being a first choice with most Wagnerians, but it is most compelling.

Boulez's speeds are so consistently fast that in the age of CD it has brought an obvious benefit in being fitted – easily – on three discs instead of four, yet Boulez's approach, with the line beautifully controlled, conveys a dramatic urgency rarely found in this opera, and never sounds breathless, with textures clarified in a way characteristic of Boulez. Even the flower-maidens sing like young apprentices in *Meistersinger* rather than seductive beauties. James King is a firm, strong, rather baritonal hero, Thomas Stewart a fine, tense Amfortas, and Gwyneth Jones as Kundry is in strong voice, only occasionally shrill, but Franz Crass is disappointingly unsteady as Gurnemanz. The live Bayreuth recording is impressively transferred to CD.

Knappertsbusch's expansive and dedicated 1962 reading is caught superbly in the Philips set, one of the finest live recordings ever made in the Festspielhaus at Bayreuth, with outstanding singing from Jess Thomas as Parsifal and Hans Hotter as Gurnemanz. Though Knappertsbusch chooses consistently slow tempi, there is no sense of excessive squareness or length, so intense is the concentration of the performance, its spiritual quality; and the sound has been further enhanced in the remastering for CD. The snag is that the stage noises and coughs are also emphasized, particularly disturbing in the *Prelude*.

Knappertsbusch was the inspired choice of conductor made by Wagner's grandsons for the first revivals of *Parsifal* after the war. The Teldec historic reissue is taken from the first season in 1951 and makes a striking contrast with the later Knappertsbusch recording, made in stereo for Philips eleven years later. The 1951 performance is no less than twenty minutes longer overall, with Knappertsbusch, always expansive, even more dedicated than in his later reading. The cast is even finer, with Wolfgang Windgassen making most other Heldentenors seem rough by comparison, singing with warmth as well as power. Ludwig Weber is magnificently dark-toned as Gurnemanz, much more an understanding human being than his successor, Hans Hotter, less of a conventionally noble figure. Martha Mödl is both wild and abrasive in her first scenes and sensuously seductive in the long Act II duet with Parsifal, and Hermann Uhde is bitingly

firm as Klingsor. Though the limited mono sound is not nearly as immediate or atmospheric as the later stereo, with much thinner orchestral texture, the voices come over well, and the chorus is well caught.

Das Rheingold (complete).
(M) *** Ph. 434 421-2 (2) [id.]. McIntyre, Schwarz, Zednik, Pampuch, Becht, (1980) Bayreuth Festival O, Boulez.
(M) **(*) Ph. 412 475-2 (2) [id.]. Adam, Nienstedt, Windgassen, Neidlinger, Talvela, Böhme, Silja, Soukupová, (1967) Bayreuth Festival Ch. & O, Boehm.

Like the Boehm set, also recorded live by Philips at Bayreuth, the Boulez version, taken from the 1980 Festival, comes on two discs at medium price. The early digital sound has plenty of air round it, giving a fine impression of a performance in the Festspielhaus with all its excitement, though voices are not caught as immediately as on the Boehm set. Sir Donald McIntyre here gives a memorable, noble performance as Wotan, far firmer than his rival for Boehm, Theo Adam. Heinz Zednik is splendid as Loge and Hanna Schwarz is a powerful Fricka, while Siegfried Jerusalem brings beauty of tone as well as distinction to the small role of Froh. Hermann Becht is a weighty rather than incisive Alberich, and the only weak link is Martin Egel's unsteady Donner. Though not as bitingly intense as Boehm, Boulez, with speeds almost as fast, shatters the old idea of him as a chilly conductor.

Boehm's preference for fast speeds means that the *Vorabend* is easily fitted on two CDs. The pity is that the performance is marred by the casting of Theo Adam as Wotan, keenly intelligent but rarely agreeable on the ear, at times here far too wobbly. On the other hand, Gustav Neidlinger as Alberich is superb, even more involving here than he is for Solti, with the curse made spine-chilling. It is also good to have Wolfgang Windgassen as Loge; among the others, Anja Silja makes an attractively urgent Freia.

'The best of The Ring': excerpts from *Das Rheingold; Die Walküre; Siegfried; Götterdämmerung*.
(B) *** Ph. Duo 454 020-2 (2) (from (1967) Bayreuth Festival recordings; cond. Karl Boehm).

The Ring: 'Great scenes': *Das Rheingold: Prelude & Scene 1; Entry of the Gods into Valhalla. Die Walküre: Winterstürme; Ride of the Valkyries; Wotan's farewell and Magic fire music. Siegfried: Forging scene; Forest murmurs. Götterdämmerung: Siegfried's Rhine journey; Siegfried's funeral march; Brünnhilde's immolation scene.*
(B) *** Decca Double 448 933-2 (2) [id.].

Nilsson, Windgassen, Kotter, Stolz, King, Crespin, VPO, Solti.

Although the Solti and Karajan single-disc selections have their appeal – and there are more extended highlights available from each opera – as potted 'Rings' go, the Philips Duo is probably the best buy. Taken from Boehm's outstanding complete recording, it can be warmly enjoyed as a summary of Wagner's intentions, with most of the key scenes included. The only snag is that Bernard Jacobson's very brief synopsis of the narrative fails to relate each track to the story.

With 144 minutes of music included on this Decca Double, the excerpts from Solti's *Ring* are quite extended. *Das Rheingold* begins with the Prelude and the sequence continues for 24 minutes, the *Entry of the Gods into Valhalla* opens spectacularly and offers some 10 minutes of music, while the excerpts from *Die Walküre* include the Sieglinde/Siegmund *Winterstürme* duet (15 minutes) and the whole of *Wotan's farewell and Magic fire music*. *Götterdämmerung* leads with *Siegfried's Rhine journey* and closes with the *Immolation scene* – some 20 minutes for each excerpt, with the tailoring expertly done in between. The only snag is the absence of any narrative cues within the sparse documentation; but the music itself is thrillingly projected.

The Ring: highlights: *Das Rheingold: Lugt, Schwestern! Die Wenken lacht in den Grund; Zur Burg führt die Brücke. Die Walküre: Der Männer Sippe sass hier im Saal; Ride of the Valkyries; Wotan's farewell and Magic fire music. Siegfried: Forest murmurs; Aber, wie sah meine Mutter wohl aus?; Nun sing! Ich lausche dem Gesang; Heil dir, Sonne! Heil dir, Licht!. Götterdämmerung: Funeral music; Fliegt heim, ihr Raben!*
(B) *** DG Classikon 439 423-2 [(M) id. import] (from complete recording; cond. Karajan).

The task of selecting highlights to fit on a single disc, taken from the whole of the *Ring* cycle, is daunting. But the DG producer of this Classikon super-bargain issue has extended the previous selection to 77 minutes and managed to assemble many key items, either very well tailored or ending satisfactorily. The whole of Wotan's great *Farewell* scene with the *Magic fire music* is included, and much else besides. Moreover the *Funeral music* from *Götterdämmerung* (where the previous CD ended) is now followed by *Brünnhilde's Immolation* and continues to the end of the opera. The transfers are extremely brilliant, making this a most attractive bargain reissue.

Siegfried (complete).
(M) *** Ph. Dig. 434 423-2 (3). Jung, G. Jones, McIntyre, Zednik, Becht, Wenkel, Hübner, Sharp, (1980) Bayreuth Festival O, Boulez.

Like the first two music-dramas in his Bayreuth

Ring cycle, Boulez's version takes a disc less than usual and comes at mid-price in the Philips Bayreuth series. Here the advantage is even greater when each Act is complete on a single disc. It was recorded in 1980. If anything, Boulez is even more warmly expressive than in *Rheingold* or *Walküre*, directing a most poetic account of the *Forest murmurs* episode and leading in each Act to thrillingly intense conclusions. Manfred Jung is an underrated Siegfried, forthright and, by latterday standards, unusually clean-focused, and Heinz Zednik is a characterful Mime. As in the rest of the cycle, Sir Donald McIntyre is a noble Wotan, though Hermann Becht's weighty Alberich is not as strongly contrasted as it might be. Norma Sharp as the Woodbird enunciates her words with exceptional clarity and, though Gwyneth Jones as Brünnhilde has a few squally moments, she sings with honeyed beauty when the Idyll theme emerges, towards the end of the love duet. The digital sound is full and atmospheric, though it is a pity that the brass is not caught more weightily.

Tannhäuser (Paris version; complete).
(M) (**(*)) DG mono 457 682-2 (3) [id.]. Hans Beirer, Eberhard Wächter, Gottlob Frick, Gré Brouwenstijn, Waldemar Kmentt, Christa Ludwig, Gundula Janowitz, V. State Op. Ch. & O, Karajan.

Tannhäuser was the one Wagner opera in the central canon which Karajan did not record for a regular record company, failing in that to match his rival, Sir Georg Solti. That makes this Austrian Radio recording in mono the more valuable, dry and limited in sound as it is, with voices well forward and with little bloom on either voices or instruments. Using the revised and expanded Paris version of the score, the recording dates from January 1963, revealing how Karajan varied his approach to each Act. With a hectic account of the *Venusberg music* he is urgent and passionate in Act I, but that leads to a more measured manner in Act II, and an unusually spacious one in the tragedy of Act III. In the title-role the Heldentenor Hans Beirer is variable, with no bark in his powerful voice but with some juddery unevenness to spoil the focus, more happily cast in Acts II and III than in Act I. As in her later recording for Solti, Christa Ludwig is a magnificent Venus, and the Dutch soprano Gré Brouwenstijn, too little recorded, an impressive Elisabeth. Gottlob Frick is a powerful, dark-toned Hermann, and Eberhard Wächter a lyrical Wolfram, with fine legato in *O star of Eve*.

Tannhäuser (Dresden version; complete).
(M) **(*) EMI CMS7 63214-2 (3). Hans Hopf, Elisabeth Grümmer, Dietrich Fischer-Dieskau, Marianne Schech, Gottlob Frick, German State Op., Berlin, Ch. & O, Konwitschny.

The Konwitschny set is a fine one, marred by one

serious flaw: the coarse singing of Hans Hopf in the title role; he fails to convey the joyous lyricism of the part, straining much of the time and with plenty of intrusive aitches. The opening scene with Venus is particularly daunting since Marianne Schech is the other disappointing member of the cast and, when they wobble together, the result is not far from comic. Happily things improve rapidly. Elisabeth Grümmer, Fischer-Dieskau and Gottlob Frick are all magnificent, and Konwitschny draws enthusiastic playing and singing from everyone. The chorus, important in this opera, is especially good, and the atmospheric recording adds to the warmth of the performance.

Tannhäuser (Dresden version): highlights.
(M) *(**) Ph. (IMS) 446 620-2 [id.] (from complete set, with Windgassen, Silja, Waechter, Bumbry, (1962) Bayreuth Festival Ch. & O, Sawallisch).

With a generally good cast, and with Bumbry's sensuous Venus getting the opera off to an impressive start, many collectors will be glad to have these extensive (78 minutes) excerpts from Sawallisch's dedicated performance of the Dresden version of *Tannhäuser*; the major drawback is the lack of a cued synopsis.

Tristan und Isolde (complete).
(M) *** Decca 443 682-2 (4) [id.]. Mitchinson, Gray, Howell, Joll, Wilkens, Folwell, Welsh Nat. Op. Ch. & O, Goodall.

Based on the much-praised production of the Welsh National Opera company, Goodall's recording of *Tristan* was made in 1980/81, not on stage but at Brangwyn Hall, Swansea, just when the cast was prepared for stage performances. Typically from Goodall, it is measured and steady, but the speeds are not all exceptionally slow and, with rhythms sharply defined and textures made transparent, he keeps the momentum going. The WNO orchestra is not sumptuous, but the playing is well-tuned and responsive. Neither Linda Esther Gray nor John Mitchinson is as sweet on the ear as the finest rivals, for the microphone exaggerates vibrato in both. But Mitchinson never barks, Heldentenor-style, and Gray provides a formidable combination of qualities: feminine vulnerability alongside commanding power. Gwynne Howell is outstandingly fine as King Mark, making his monologue at the end of Act II, so often an anti-climax, into one of the noblest passages of all. This may not have the smoothness of the best international sets but, with its vivid digital sound, it is certainly compelling, and a libretto in three languages is an additional bonus.

Tristan und Isolde (slightly abridged).
(B) (**) Naxos mono 8.110008/10 [id.].
Melchior, Traubel, Thorborg, Huehn, Kipnis, Gurney, NY Met. Op. Ch. & O, Erich Leinsdorf.

Recorded live at the Met. in New York in February 1943, the historic Naxos set offers a performance which vividly conveys the atmosphere of a big occasion on stage despite very limited and variable sound. Act I fares best, with the voices forward and well focused, working up to a thrilling, almost frenzied climax at the end of the Act. Lauritz Melchior gives a performance very similar to that in the EMI recording from Covent Garden in the 1930s (conducted partly by Beecham, partly by Reiner), establishing him as arguably the finest exponent of the role this century. Helen Traubel may not have the total security of Kirsten Flagstad, whether in that earlier historic recording or in Furtwängler's studio set, and in the love duet she misses out the difficult top C's, but it is a rich, warmly expressive performance. Sadly, the glowing account of the *Liebestod* at the end is marred by some of the worst recording in the whole set. Acts II and III (both slightly cut, following the custom of the time) bring crumbly orchestral sound, and as a rule the voices are not as clear and fresh as in Act I, yet one can readily sense the stage atmosphere. The rest of the cast make a strong team, with Alexander Kipnis outstanding as King Mark, making his monologue into a magnetic experience.

Die Walküre (complete).
**(*) EMI (SIS) Dig. CDS7 49534-2 (4) [Ang. CDCD 49534]. Marton, Studer, Morris, Goldberg, Salminen, Meier, Bav. RSO, Haitink.
(M) **(*) Ph. 434 422-2 (3) [id.]. Hofmann, Altmeyer, G. Jones, McIntyre, Schwarz, Salminen, (1980) Bayreuth Festival O, Boulez.
** Decca Dig. 440 371-2 (4) [id.]. Poul Elming, Alessandra Marc, Gabriele Schnaut, Robert Hale, Alfred Muff, Anja Silja, Karin Goltz, Cleveland O, Christoph von Dohnányi.

Haitink's is a broad view, strong and thoughtful yet conveying monumental power. That goes with searching concentration and a consistent feeling for the detailed beauty of Wagner's writing, glowingly brought out in the warm and spacious recording, made in the Herkulessaal in Munich. The outstanding contribution comes from Cheryl Studer as Sieglinde, very convincingly cast, giving a tenderly affecting performance to bring out the character's vulnerability in a very human way. At *Du bist der Lenz* her radiant singing brings an eagerly personal revelation, the response of a lover. Despite some strained moments, Rainer Goldberg makes a heroic Siegmund, and Eva Marton is a noble, powerful Brünnhilde, less uneven of production than she has often been on record. Waltraud Meier makes a convincingly waspish and biting Fricka and Matti Salminen a resonant Hunding. James Morris is a fine, perceptive Wotan, and the voice, not an easy one to record, is well focused here.

The major advantage of the Boulez Bayreuth version of 1980 is that it comes at mid-price on only three discs, with atmospheric digital sound and a strong, if flawed, cast. Jeannine Altmeyer is a generally reliable Sieglinde, but Peter Hofmann's tenor had already grown rather gritty for Siegmund. Donald McIntyre makes a commanding Wotan, Hanna Schwarz a firm, biting Fricka and Gwyneth Jones is at her least abrasive, producing a beautiful, gentle tone in lyrical passages. Boulez's fervour will surprise many, even if he does not match Boehm's passionate urgency in this second instalment of the tetralogy.

The glory of Dohnányi's version of *Die Walküre* is the recorded sound, full and opulent in Decca's best Cleveland manner, but as in the *Rheingold* set with the same forces there is a smoothness in the performance, a lack of dramatic bite in the long exchanges, which makes it too comfortable, not fully involving, rather like a concert performance. Act I fares best, with Poul Elming a fine, incisive Siegmund (as he is for Barenboim on Teldec) and Alessandra Marc a warm, understanding Sieglinde. The gruff, poorly focused Hunding of Alfred Muff then lets the performance down. In the remaining two acts Robert Hale is a reliable Wotan, but as in *Rheingold* he is rather bland, while Gabriele Schnaut's main claim as Brünnhilde is the power of her voice, certainly not its beauty, shrill, sour and unsteady as it often is. Anja Silja characterizes superbly as Fricka, but as so often the microphone brings out the heavy beat in her voice.

Die Walküre: Act I (complete).
(M) *** Ph. (IMS) 442 640-2 [id.]. Leonie Rysanek, James King, Gerd Nienstedt, (1967) Bayreuth Festival O, Boehm.
(M) (***) EMI (SIS) mono CDH7 61020-2 [id.]. Lehmann, Melchior, List, VPO, Bruno Walter.
**(*) Teldec 3984-23294-2 [id.]. Plácido Domingo, Deborah Polaski, John Tomlinson, Berlin Staatskapelle, Barenboim.

Having Act I of *Die Walküre* offered alone on disc works well. The sequence of events between Siegmund, Sieglinde and Hunding makes a miniature drama in itself. This well-transferred Boehm CD makes a good sampler of the highly involving performance from 1967.

One is consistently gripped by the continuity and sustained lines of Walter's reading, and by the intensity and beauty of the playing of the Vienna Philharmonic. Lotte Lehmann's portrait of Sieglinde, arguably her finest role, has a depth and beauty never surpassed since, and Lauritz Melchior's heroic Siegmund brings singing of a scale and variety – not to mention beauty – that no Heldentenor today can match. Emanuel List as Hunding is less distinguished but reliable.

Barenboim's live recording of Act I is memorable for Plácido Domingo's magnificent portrayal of Siegmund, warm, heroic and unstrained, and he is well matched by John Tomlinson as a dark and incisive Hunding. Deborah Polaski is at her warmest in the opening scenes, but as the performance progresses the voice acquires an unwelcome shrillness on top. Conversely, the Berlin Staatskapelle sounds a little underpowered at the start, but grows ever more incisive up to the excitement of the closing duet, *Siegmund bin ich.* The sound is full and rich, and the relatively close balance of the voices gives extra immediacy to the drama.

(i) *Die Walküre:* Act 1 (complete).
Götterdämmerung: Siegfried's funeral march.
(B) **(*) Australian Decca Eloquence 466 678-2. VPO, Knappertsbusch; (i) with Svanholm, Flagstad, van Mill.

It was Kirsten Flagstad's wish that she should be able to record Sieglinde in Act I of Walküre, and she also wanted to work with the great Wagner conductor, Hans Knappertsbusch. Thanks to Decca's John Culshaw, this recording was made possible, and he was also able to experiment with stereo technology, in preparation for his complete Ring Cycle with Solti (Solti was rather irritated that he didn't conduct this disc himself).

If Flagstad is a bit too matronly for the role, it hardly matters, for there is an electric tension in this performance which makes it compellingly moving. The 1958 recording, though a bit tubby, is amazingly detailed, rich and full, and allows the inimitable Vienna glow to come through. With Siegfried's funeral march thrown in too, this Australian bargain CD is well worth seeking out.

Die Walküre: Act III (complete).
(M) (***) EMI (SIS) mono CDH7 64704-2 [id.]. Varnay, Rysanek, Bjoerling, (1951) Bayreuth Festival O, Karajan.

Recorded in 1951, the first season after the war, Karajan's Bayreuth version of Act III shows the still-young conductor working at white heat. Speeds are far faster than in his DG studio recording, and very close to those in his live recording made at the Met. in 1969 (Nuova Era). Ensemble inevitably is not as taut as it was in the studio performance, but the electricity is far keener, and his cast is a characterful one. Astrid Varnay is an abrasive Brünnhilde, presenting the Valkyrie as a forceful figure, even in penitence prepared to stand up against her father. Leonie Rysanek is a warm Sieglinde, powerful rather than pure, with a rather obtrusive vibrato even at that date. Sigurd Bjoerling by contrast, the least-known of the principals, proves a magnificently virile Wotan, steady as a rock in the *Farewell*, but colouring the voice with a near-shout at the command, '*Loge, hier!*' The mono sound is transferred with bright immediacy, with some harshness on top but plenty of weight in the bass. This makes a splendid supplement to Karajan's superb Bayreuth *Meistersinger*, also recorded live in 1951.

Die Walküre: highlights.
(M) *** Ph. (IMS) 446 614-2 [id.] (from above (1980) Bayreuth Festival recording, with Hofmann, Altmeyer, McIntyre, G. Jones, etc.; cond. Boulez).

As with the others in this otherwise excellent Philips series of Wagnerian highlights, the documentation is totally inadequate, with the excerpts listed baldly and with no synopsis provided to relate each to the narrative. But as this is by no means a first choice among recordings of this opera, many collectors will be interested in such a generous sampler (78 minutes) rather than the complete recording.

VOCAL COLLECTIONS

Operatic scenes: *Götterdämmerung: Immolation scene. Tristan und Isolde: Prelude and Liebestod. Die Walküre: Hojotoho!*
**(*) Sony Dig. SK 62032 [id.]. Jane Eaglen, ROHCG O, Elder – BELLINI: Scenes from *Bianca e Fernando* etc. **(*)

Jane Eaglen with her rich, powerful voice copes splendidly with three of the most formidable passages which Wagner ever wrote for soprano: Isolde's *Liebestod* (preceded by the *Tristan Prelude*), Brünnhilde's *Immolation scene* and her cries of Hojotoho! in *Walküre*. The bright clarity of her top notes, fearlessly attacked with pinging precision, is thrilling, and she rounds off both the *Tristan* and *Götterdämmerung* solos with tenderness and great beauty, but with speeds so relentlessly steady that there is a static feeling, so that the music rather fails to carry you on, lacking the necessary thrust – partly the fault of Elder's conducting. Yet, in this coupling with Bellini scenes, this is an impressive demonstration of a young singer's potential.

Walton, William (1902–83)

(i) *Capriccio burlesco;* (ii) *Music for children; Portsmouth Point overture;* (i) *The Quest* (ballet suite); *Scapino overture;* (ii) *Siesta;* (i; iii) *Sinfonia concertante.*
*** Lyrita SRCD 224 [id.]. (i) LSO; (ii) LPO; composer; (iii) with Peter Katin.

When Walton made these recordings, he was in his late sixties, and his speeds had grown a degree slower and safer. *Portsmouth Point* loses some of its fizz at so moderate a speed. By contrast *Scapino* suffers hardly at all from the slower speed, rather the opposite, with the opening if anything even jauntier and the big cello melody drawn out more expressively. *Siesta* too brings out the piece's ro-

mantically lyrical side, rather than making it a relatively cool intermezzo. The *Capriccio burlesco* and the ten little pieces of the *Music for children* are delightful too, with the subtleties of the instrumentation beautifully brought out. Much the biggest work here is the *Sinfonia concertante,* and in the outer movements the performance lacks the thrust that Walton himself gave it in his very first wartime recording, in which Phyllis Sellick was a scintillating soloist (see below). Yet Peter Katin is a very responsive soloist too, and the central slow movement is much warmer and more passionate than on Conifer, with orchestral detail rather clearer. It is good too to have the first stereo recording of the suite from Walton's wartime ballet based on Spenser's 'Faerie Queene', *The Quest,* only a fraction of the whole but bright and colourful.

(i) *Cello concerto;* (ii) *Violin concerto in B min.*
(BB) *** Naxos Dig. 8.554325 [id.]. (i) Tim Hugh; (ii) Dong-Suk Kang; English Northern Philh. O, Paul Daniel.

In an apt and surprisingly rare coupling of the two largest string concertos, Naxos's excellent Walton series here offers an outstanding version of the *Cello concerto* coupled with a very fine one of the *Violin concerto.* In many ways Tim Hugh's reading of the *Cello concerto* is the most searching yet. He finds an intense thoughtfulness, a sense of mystery, of inner meditation in the great lyrical ideas of all three movements, daring to play with a more extreme pianissimo than any rival. The bravura writing finds him equally concentrated, always sounding strong and spontaneous in face of any technical challenge. As in their previous Walton recordings, Paul Daniel and the English Northern Philharmonia equally play with flair and sympathy, so that the all-important syncopations always sound idiomatic, even if the strings lack a little in weight. In the *Violin concerto* Dong-Suk Kang here follows up the success of his Naxos recording of the Elgar *Violin concerto,* playing immaculately with a fresh, clean-cut tone, pure and true above the stave. If this is a degree more objective than more overtly romantic readings, Kang makes a virtue of opting for speeds rather faster than usual, evidently aware of the example of the dedicatee, Jascha Heifetz.

(i–iii) *Cello concerto;* (iv; ii; iii) *Violin concerto;* (v) *Overtures: Portsmouth Point; Scapino. Symphonies Nos.* (vi) *1 in B flat min.;* (v) *2.*
(B) ** EMI Analogue/Dig. Double fforte CZS5 73371-2 (2). (i) Paul Tortelier; (ii) Bournemouth SO; (iii) Berglund; (iv) Ida Haendel; (v) LSO, Previn; (vi) Philh. O, Haitink.

Tortelier's account of the *Cello concerto* is characteristically passionate. After the haunting melancholy of the first movement, the central Scherzo emerges as a far weightier piece than most such movements, while the final variations have seldom on record developed with such a sense of compulsion. Ida Haendel's version of the *Violin concerto* is warmly appealing. Previn is at his finest in the *Second Symphony*, sparkling in the outer movements, warmly romantic in the central slow movement, while in the two overtures he finds more light and shade than usual. However, Haitink's reading of the *First Symphony* is more controversial. The malevolent demon which inhabits the first two movements is somewhat tamed, and in the opening movement some will feel that the lack of the relentless forward thrust demonstrated in the finest versions (including Previn's RCA reading) underplays the music's character. However, Haitink's directness leads to spacious and noble accounts of the slow movement and finale. The bright, digital recording is a little lacking in bass and not as impressive as the fine analogue sound that EMI provide for Previn in No. 1.

(i) *Viola concerto;* (ii) *Violin concerto;* (iii) *Partita for orchestra.*
(M) **(*) EMI CDM5 65005-2 [id.]. (i) Menuhin, LSO; (ii) Menuhin, New Philh. O; (iii) Philh. O; composer.

This disc couples Menuhin's late 1960s recordings of the two concertos with the 1959 one of the *Partita.* This transfer of the latter is fuller than in its pre-1994 incarnations, and reveals what fun the composer himself finds in his bouncing of the rhythms. Though Menuhin's account of the *Viola concerto* is a little effortful, not always flowing as it should, his viola sound is gloriously rich and true, and when it comes to the *Violin concerto,* this is a vintage Menuhin performance, marked by his very distinctive tone and poignantly tender phrasing.

(i) *Viola concerto in A min.;* (ii) *Violin concerto in B min.;* (iii) *Sinfonia concertante.*
(M) (**(*)) Avid mono AMSC 604 [id.]. (i) William Primrose; (ii) Jascha Heifetz; Cincinnati SO, Eugene Goosens; (iii) Phyllis Sellick, CBSO, Composer.

It makes an ideal coupling having Walton's three pre-war concertante works together – two of them in première recordings. In many ways, Heifetz's pioneering wartime version of the *Violin concerto,* recorded in Cincinati in 1941 at speeds far faster than we are used to now, has never been surpassed – even finer than his later remake with Walton and the Philharmonia, more fiery, with even more flair and spontaneity. This account of the *Viola concerto* was the first of two which Primrose recorded, markedly cooler than the première recording on Decca, with the young Frederick Riddle accompanied by Walton and the LSO. The central Scherzo is taken at an astonishingly fast speed, on the verge of sounding breathless. By contrast, the première recording of the *Sinfonia concertante* with Phyllis

Sellick is exceptionally warm and expressive, an interpretation never quite matched since. Despite the rough Avid transfers, such historic performances offered in a coupling on a bargain disc are self-recommending.

(i) *Violin concerto. Capriccio burlesco; Henry V: Suite; Spitfire prelude & fugue.*
**(*) HM Dig. HMU 907070 [id.]. (i) Aaron Rosand; Florida PO, Judd.

Judd draws warmly idiomatic playing from the Florida Philharmonic Orchestra in the colourful pieces based on wartime film music for *The First of the Few* and *Henry V,* with the oboe solo in the *Bailero* theme after the Agincourt music achingly beautiful, and with the brass consistently ripe and resonant. The *Capriccio burlesco* is aptly witty and spiky. It is good to have Aaron Rosand returning to the recording studio, and in this formidable concerto he shows that his virtuosity is as impressive as ever. The snag is that the recording balances the soloist so close that orchestral detail is dim, and tuttis lack the bite and thrust they need. Despite the dryness of sound in the concerto and a lightness in bass, Rosand's performance is most refreshing, while the *Henry V* and *Spitfire music* are treated with great warmth.

Capriccio burlesco; Coronation marches: Crown imperial; Orb and sceptre. Hamlet: Funeral march; Johannesburg festival overture; Richard III: Prelude and suite; Scapino (comedy overture); Spitfire prelude and fugue.
(M) **(*) EMI CDM5 67222-2 [id.]. RLPO, Groves.

The 1969 collection of Walton's shorter orchestral pieces was made in Studio 2 (EMI's hi-fi-conscious equivalent of Decca's Phase 4) and now seems slightly over-bright with its digital remastering. The sound tends to polarize, with a lack of opulence in the middle range, so necessary in the nobilmente of the big tunes of the stirring *Spitfire prelude and fugue* and *Crown imperial.* The Shakespearean film music was recorded much later (1984) and the quality is fuller, more warmly atmospheric. Although the two *Coronation marches* could do with a little more exuberance, Groves is otherwise a highly sympathetic interpreter of this repertoire, and the playing of the Liverpool orchestra is excellent.

Coronation marches: Crown imperial; Orb and sceptre; Façade suites Nos. 1 & 2; (i; ii) *Gloria;* (ii) *Coronation Te Deum.*
(M) *** EMI CDM7 64201-2 [id.]. (i) Robothom, Rolfe Johnson, Rayner Cook, CBSO Ch.; (ii) Choristers of Worcester Cathedral; CBSO, Frémaux.

The three Walton works inspired by coronations are here splendidly coupled with the grand setting of the *Gloria.* Frémaux directs a highly enjoyable performance of this but it rather pales before the *Coronation Te Deum*, which may use some of the same formulas but has Walton electrically inspired, exploiting every tonal and atmospheric effect imaginable between double choirs and semi-choruses. The two splendid marches are marvellously done too. The rich, resonant recording is apt for the music, spacious and with excellent perspectives, and it has transferred splendidly to CD, with the brass both sonorous and biting and the choral sound fresh as well as with plenty of weight. The *Façade suites* have been added for the CD and here the remastering is even more telling, adding point to playing which is already affectionately witty. Frémaux's rhythmic control gives a fresh, new look to familiar music: his jaunty jazz inflexions in *Old Sir Faulk* are deliciously whimsical.

Façade (complete, including *Façade 2*).
**(*) ASV Dig. CDDCA 679 [id.]. Prunella Scales, Timothy West, L. Mozart Players (members), Jane Glover.
**(*) Chandos Dig. CHAN 8869 [id.]. Lady Susana Walton, Richard Baker, City of L. Sinfonia (members), Richard Hickox.

Scales and West as a husband-and-wife team are inventive in their shared roles, and generally it works well. *Scotch rhapsody* is hilariously done as a duet, with West intervening at appropriate moments, and with sharply precise Scots accents. Regional accents may defy Edith Sitwell's original prescription – and her own example – but here, with one exception, they add an appropriate flavour. The exception is *Popular song*, where Prunella Scales's cockney accent is quite alien to the allusive words, with their 'cupolas, gables in the lakes, Georgian stables'. For fill-up the reciters have recorded more Sitwell poems, but unaccompanied.

Susana Walton, widow of the composer, makes a bitingly characterful reciter, matching with her distinctive accent – she was born in Argentina – the exoticry of many numbers. Richard Baker, phenomenally precise and agile in enunciating the Sitwell poems, makes the perfect foil, and Hickox secures colourful and lively playing from members of the City of London Sinfonia, who relish in particular the jazzy inflexions. *Façade 2* consists of a number of Sitwell settings beyond the definitive series of twenty-one. All of them are fun and make an apt if not very generous coupling for the regular sequence. Warm sound, a little too reverberant for so intimate a work.

Film music

Scenes from Shakespeare (compiled Christopher Palmer): *As You Like It; Hamlet; Henry V; Richard III*.
(M) **(*) Chandos Dig. CHAN 7041 [id.]. Sir John Gielgud, Christopher Plummer, ASMF, Marriner.

This makes an apt and attractive compilation, putting together well-chosen selections from the recordings of Walton's Shakespeare film music, first issued in the complete Chandos edition, not just for the three masterly films directed by Laurence Olivier, but also for the pre-war *As You Like It*. Roughly two-thirds of the *Henry V* music is included here, and about half of each of the other three. However, many collectors will opt to have more music and will prefer to hear the Shakespearean text in the theatre or cinema.

Henry V: suite (arr. Mathieson) *and* (i) *scenes from the film; Richard III: Prelude and Suite; Spitfire prelude and fugue*.
(M) *** EMI stereo/mono CDM5 65007-2 [id.].
   (i) Sir Laurence Olivier (speaker); Philh. O, composer.

This 'Walton Edition' reissue contains some of the composer's finest film music. It includes the 1963 recordings of the *Henry V suite, Richard III prelude and suite*, and the *Spitfire prelude and fugue*. The performances are vital and exciting, and with the sound vivid and full the result is hugely enjoyable. Also included is the complete 1946 *Henry V* sequence with Laurence Olivier, as recorded on four 78s, and originally issued on LP by RCA with seven minutes of cuts. This is the restored complete version, and it has been excellently transferred, though the mono sound lacks body. The recording has great atmosphere though, with Olivier at his magnificent best, and the orchestra responding with tremendous energy: the sound of the arrows at the climax of the Agincourt sequence has never seemed more chilling. A wonderful CD.

Macbeth: Fanfare & march; Major Barbara (suite); Richard III (Shakespeare scenario).
*** Chandos Dig. CHAN 8841 [id.]. Sir John Gielgud (nar.), ASMF, Marriner.

Disappointingly, Sir John Gielgud underplays Richard III's great 'Now is the winter of our discontent' speech, but working to the underlying music – much of it eliminated in the film – may have cramped his style. The performance generally has all the panache one could wish for, leading up to the return of the grand Henry Tudor theme at the end. The six-minute piece based on Walton's music for Gielgud's wartime production of *Macbeth* is much rarer and very valuable too, anticipating in its Elizabethan dance-music the *Henry V* film-score. *Major Barbara* also brings vintage Walton material. Marriner and the Academy give performances just as ripely committed as in their previous discs in the series, helped by sonorous Chandos sound.

Symphony No. 1; (i) *Belshazzar's Feast*.
(M) (***) EMI mono/stereo CDM5 65004-2 [id.].
   (i) Donald Bell; Philh. Ch. & O, composer.

The *First Symphony* (mono) was recorded in 1951

and always suffered from a poor transfer in its LP days. Its promotion to CD in 1994 was something of a revelation: the sound now has far more body and bite than its long-deleted LP incarnation, and reveals just what an exciting performance it really was. Walton treats the persistent syncopated rhythms with a jazzy freedom, while the passion behind the performance is intense, most of all in the slow movement, which gains from some superb playing from the Philharmonia soloists. Comparing Walton's 1959 stereo version of *Belshazzar* here with his earlier, 1943 account is fascinating, with speeds consistently more spacious, but with tensions just as keen, and ensemble crisper, though with less mystery conveyed. The one snag is the soloist, Donald Bell, clean of attack but uncharacterful. Never mind, this is a superb CD, and makes a generous 78-minute coupling of some wonderful music-making.

Symphony No. 1; Portsmouth Point overture.
(M) **(*) Virgin/EMI Dig. CUV5 61146-2 [id.].
LPO, Slatkin.

The brilliance, bite and clarity of sound in Slatkin's version of the *First Symphony* reinforce the tautness of the performance, nagging the mind with repetitive rhythms and tension piled on tension. Slatkin does not have quite the rhythmic mastery in giving a jazzy lift to syncopations or in moulding Waltonian melody that you find in both Previn versions, and the Scherzo is almost breathlessly fast. But the finale is magnificent, bringing thrust and power, and culminating superbly in the uninhibited triple timpani passage near the end. Slatkin takes an equally electric view of the *Portsmouth Point overture*, again played brilliantly by the LPO.

CHAMBER MUSIC

Piano quartet (1921); *String quartet in A min.* (1947).
(BB) *** Naxos Dig. 8.554646 [id.]. (i) Peter Donohoe; Maggini Qt.

This superb disc of Walton chamber music makes a splendid follow-up to the fine orchestral recordings already included in Naxos's Walton series. The young players of the Maggini Quartet – who earlier recorded Elgar for Naxos – give performances both refined and powerful of both works.

The opening of the 1947 *String quartet* is presented in hushed intimacy, making the contrast all the greater when Walton's richly lyrical writing emerges in full power. There is a tender, wistful quality here, which culminates in a rapt, intense account of the slow movement, with the world of late Beethoven much closer than most interpreters have appreciated. The poignancy of those two longer movements is then set against the clean bite of the second movement Scherzo and the

brief hectic finale, with textures clear and transparent.

With Peter Donohoe a powerful, incisive pianist, the early *Piano quartet*, an astonishing achievement for a teenage composer, is also given a performance of high contrasts. The echoes of Stravinsky's *Petrushka* are colourfully brought out in the finale, a movement that looks forward more clearly than the rest to the mature Walton, even though the pentatonic writing in the earlier movements is here most persuasively presented. First-rate recording, even if the piano is a shade too forwardly balanced. This supersedes the earlier Meridian CD of this coupling by John McCabe and the English Quartet (CDE 84139)

(i; ii) *Piano quartet*; (i; iii) *Violin sonata*; (iv) *5 Bagatelles (for guitar).*
(B) *** EMI Dig. CZS5 573989-2 (2) [ZDZB 573989]. (i) Graham; (ii) Silverthorne, Welsh, Margalit; (iii) Alley; (iv) Kerstens – BRITTEN: *Cello sonata, etc.* ***.

The two major works here are also coupled in Chandos's 'Walton Edition', but here you get a worthwhile bonus in the *Bagatelles* for guitar, with Tom Kerstens even lighter and more volatile than Julian Bream, for whom they were written. With Israela Margalit injecting fire, the performance of the *Piano quartet* is also lighter and more volatile than in the Chandos edition, though the extra weight of that rival adds up increasingly in the last two movements. Janice Graham is the soloist in the *Violin sonata*, again fanciful and light, whilst bringing warmth and purposefulness to a work that can easily seem wayward. Though the three pieces were recorded in different venues, the sound is consistent, excellent in each. An excellent bargain set.

CHORAL MUSIC

All this time; Antiphon; Chichester service: Magnificat; Nunc dimittis. Jubilate Deo; King Herod and the cock; A Litany (Drop, drop, slow tears); Make we now joy in this fest; Missa brevis; Set me as a seal upon thine heart; The Twelve; What cheer?; Where does the uttered music go?
**(*) Nimbus Dig. NI 5364 [id.]. Christ Church Cathedral Ch., Oxford, Stephen Darlington.

There are special reasons for welcoming performances from Christ Church Cathedral Choir. It was this choir which Walton joined as a boy of ten, and he was still a member when at the age of fifteen he wrote the beautiful *a cappella* setting of Phineas Fletcher's *A Litany*, the first item on this disc. Later he wrote both the powerful setting of the *Jubilate* and the longest piece here, *The Twelve*, setting words specially written by another Christ Church man, W. H. Auden. The clear distinction between the Christ Church performances and those of other choirs, giving a strikingly different timbre as well as a different scale, is that you have boy trebles singing instead of sopranos. The trebles on their own even manage the tricky opening of the *Kyrie* of the *Missa brevis* with confidence at a flowing speed, and in the *Missa brevis* Christ Church observes the Roman order of the Mass, with the *Gloria* after the *Kyrie*. That reordering makes nonsense of Walton's intended musical scheme, which is that after the three *a cappella* sections the organ should enter dramatically for the *Gloria*, following traditional Church of England practice from the Prayer-book. What works superbly is the Christ Church performance of *Where does the uttered music go?*, the setting of John Masefield written as a memorial tribute to Sir Henry Wood. At a much faster speed than usual, it has new freshness and a winning flexibility, bringing out the word-meaning. The snag about the Nimbus version is that it omits a major item included by both rivals, the *Cantico del sole* of 1974, setting words of St Francis of Assisi in the original Italian.

Weber, Carl Maria von (1786–1826)

(i) *Clarinet concertos Nos. 1 in F min.; 2 in E flat;* (ii) *Konzertstück in F min. for piano and orchestra;* (iii) *Invitation to the dance* (orch. BERLIOZ), *Op. 65; Overtures: Abu Hassan;* (iv) *Euryanthe; Der Freischütz; Oberon;* (v) *Symphony No. 1 in C., Op. 19;* (vi) *Clarinet quintet.*
(B) ** Ph. Duo 462 868-2 (2) [id.]. (i) Michallik, Dresden State O, Sanderling; (ii) Magaloff, LSO, Sir Colin Davis; (iii) LSO, Mackerras; (iv) Concg. O, Dorati; (v) New Philh. O, Boettcher; (vi) Stahr, Berlin Philharmonic Octet (members).

This Philips Duo, described over-ambitiously as 'The best of Weber', is a bit of a mixed bag. The two *Clarinet concertos* are well played by Oskar Michallik, with good support from Sanderling and the fine Dresden Orchestra. But, as in Herbert Stahr's Berlin account of the *Quintet*, these artists are at their best in slow movements. Elsewhere, though thoroughly musical, the playing could do with more dash. However, Magaloff's poised and well-characterized account of the *Konzertstück* is most satisfying, well recorded and altogether one of the best versions on the market. The two performances under Mackerras are also a delight: *Abu Hassan* light and sparkling, and an elegant *Invitation to the dance*. But in the other three overtures, the Concertgebouw string sound as recorded is brilliant to the point of fierceness and the effect is to emphasize Dorati's concentration on drama rather than atmosphere (though there is some beautiful

horn playing). However the engaging *First Symphony* is well served both by the New Philharmonia and Boettcher, who favours a weighty approach but does not lack a lighter touch when needed. Overall this is fair value

Konzertstück.
(M) **(*) DG 463 085-2 [id.]. Margrit Weber, RSO, Berlin, Fricsay – MARTINU: *Fantasia concertante;* FALLA: *Nights in the gardens of Spain;* TCHEREPNIN: *10 Bagatelles.* ***

An excellent performance of the *Konzertstück*, let down a little by the 1960 sound, which while quite full and vivid is rather dry. But this should not deter anyone from trying this imaginatively programmed Galleria CD.

Clarinet quintet in B flat, Op. 34
*** ASV Dig. CDDCA 1079 [id.]. Emma Johnson, Takacs-Nagy, Hirsch, Boulton, Shulman – MOZART: *Clarinet quintet; Allegro in B flat, K.516c* **(*).

Emma Johnson, always a characterful player with her distinctive reedy tone, gives a scintillating account of the Weber with brilliant support from her team of experienced chamber players. In this less well-known work she is more spontaneous-sounding than in the Mozart, full of sparkle and fun in the outer movements as well as the Scherzo, finding a rare depth of expression in the hushed writing of the second movement Fantasia, marked Adagio. The clarinet is forwardly balanced, but less obtrusively so than in the Mozart.

OPERA

Der Freischütz (complete).
(M) **(*) EMI CMS5 65757-2 (2) [CDMB 65757]. Nilsson, Köth, Gedda, Berry, Ch. & O of Bav. State Op., Heger.

Heger's EMI set, recorded in Munich in 1969, cannot match Keilberth's earlier EMI version (CMS7 69342-2) of 1958 in atmospheric intensity, with the Wolf's Glen scene markedly less chilling in its dramatic impact. Yet otherwise, with warm, open sound, there is a nice feeling for a stage performance, with an excellent team of soloists from the Bavarian State Opera. Nicolai Gedda as Max is stylish, even if he tends to bluster, while Birgit Nilsson masterfully scales her massive Wagnerian voice down, to produce a pure, sweet tone and smooth legato in Agathe's two sublime arias. Erika Köth is a light, bright, agile Aennchen, and the chorus sing splendidly. An enjoyable set, if not the finest version at mid-price. Helpfully, the dialogue is put on separate tracks.

Webern, Anton (1883–1945)

Collected works:

Disc 1: (i) *Im Sommerwind; 5 Movements for string quartet* (orchestral version), *Op. 5; Passacaglia, Op. 1; 6 Pieces for large orchestra, Op. 6.* Arrangements of: BACH: *Musical offering: Fugue;* SCHUBERT: *German dances, D.820.*

Disc 2: (i) *5 Pieces for orchestra* (1913); *Symphony, Op. 21; Variations for orchestra, Op. 30;* (iii; iv; v) *Das Augenlicht, Op. 26; Cantatas Nos. 1, Op. 29; 2, Op. 31; 3 Orchesterlieder* (1913–24).

Disc 3: (ii; vi) *Concerto for 9 instruments, Op. 24;* (ii) *5 Pieces for Orchestra, Op. 10;* (ii; vi) *Piano quintet; Quartet, Op. 22* (for piano, violin, clarinet & saxophone); (ii; iii; v; vii) *5 Canons on Latin texts, Op. 15; Entflieht auf Leichten Kähnen, Op. 2; 2 Lieder, Op. 8; 4 Lieder, Op. 13; 6 Lieder, Op. 14; 5 Geistliche Lieder, Op. 15; 3 Lieder, Op. 18; 2 Lieder, Op. 19; 3 Volkstexte, Op. 17.*

Disc 4: (iii; viii) *3 Gedichte* (1899–1903); *8 frühe Lieder* (1901–4); *3 Avenarius Lieder* (1903–4); *5 Dehmel Lieder* (1906–8); *5 St George Lieder; 5, Op. 4; 4 St George Lieder* (1908–9); *4 Lieder, Op. 12; 3 Jone Gesänge, Op. 23; 3 Jone Lieder, Op. 25.*

Disc 5: (ix; x) *6 Bagatelles for string quartet, Op. 5; (Langsamer) Slow movement for string quartet* (1905); *5 Movements for string quartet, Op. 5; 3 Pieces for string quartet* (1913); *Rondo for string quartet* (1906); *String quartet* (1905); *String quartet, Op. 28; String trio, Op. 20; Movement for string trio, Op. posth.* (1925).

Disc 6: (xi; xii) *Cello sonata* (1914); *2 Pieces for cello and piano* (1899); *3 Small pieces for cello and piano, Op. 11;* (xiii; xiv) *4 Pieces for violin and piano, Op. 7;* (xv) Piano: *Kinderstück* (1924 & 1925); *Piece* (1906); *Sonata movement (Rondo)* (1906); (xiv) *Variations, Op. 27.*

(M) *** DG 457 637-2 (6) [id.]. (i) Berlin PO, or (ii) Ens. Intercontemporain, Boulez; (iii) Christiane Oelz; (iv) Gerald Finley; (v) BBC Singers; (vi) Pierre-Laurent Aimard; (vii) Françoise Pollet; (viii) Eric Schneider; (ix) Emerson Qt; (x) Mary Ann McCormick; (xi) Clemens Hagen, (xii) Oleg Maisenberg; (xiii) Gidon Kremer; (xiv) Krystian Zimerman; (xv) Gianluca Cascioli.

It is over thirty years since Pierre Boulez masterminded a revelatory set of Webern's complete works with opus number, but one of his main concerns in signing his exclusive contract with DG in 1989 was to supervise this monumental set, which goes far farther in its illumination of Webern as one of the great musical pioneers of the twentieth

century. The first point is that where the earlier set limited itself to the numbered works, this one covers so much more (on six discs instead of three) with a far fuller portrait presented not only in the early works but also in such offerings as the incidental chamber works and his arrangements of Bach (the *Ricercar* from the *Musical offering*) and Schubert (a collection of waltzes). Boulez's interpretations of the numbered works have developed too, with the Berlin Philharmonic exceptionally responsive, bringing out often unsuspected warmth and beauty. The point and purposefulness of these performances is particularly helpful in making such thorny late inspirations as the two *Cantatas* so much more readily approachable. The vocal soloists have been ideally chosen, with the fresh-toned Christiane Oelze taking on the majority of songs, but with Françoise Pollet and Gerald Finley equally assured. The starry list of instrumental contributors could not be bettered either, including as it does such luminaries of DG as the Emerson Quartet and Krystian Zimerman, and the recordings made over a period of years are uniformly excellent.

Passacaglia for orchestra, Op. 1.
(M) *** DG 457 760-2 [id.]. BPO, Karajan –
  BERG: *Lyric suite*, etc.; SCHOENBERG: *Variations*. ***

This is a beautifully played and recorded version of Webern's *Passacaglia*, which will disappoint no one. It sounds especially haunting – even magical – in Karajan's hands, and has been superbly transferred on this DG Originals CD. It is part of a desirable programme of twentieth-century music and is highly recommended.

Variations for piano, Op. 27.
(BB) *** Naxos Dig. 8.553870 [id.]. Peter Hill –
  BERG: *Piano sonata;* SCHOENBERG: *Piano pieces; Suite*. ***

The *Variations*, Op. 27, Webern's only mature piano piece, dates from the mid 1930s and calls for the most eloquent playing if it is to persuade the listener. Webern himself stressed that the music's structural intricacies must give rise to a 'profound expressiveness'. They have been recorded by Pollini, Glenn Gould and other celebrated pianists. Peter Hill can hold his own against any of the competition.

Weill, Kurt (1900–1950)

Kleine Dreigroschenmusik.
(M) EMI CDM5 67337-2 [id.]. Philh. O, Klemperer – HINDEMITH: *Nobilissima visione;* STRAVINSKY: *Symphony in three movements;* *** (with KLEMPERER: *Merry waltz* **).

Klemperer is thoroughly at home in the Kurt Weill suite, evoking perfectly the mood and style of the first performance in 1929 by the Prussian State Military Band and his stately and ironically Prussian version of *Mack the Knife* has a character all its own. Klemperer's own waltz is pleasant, modestly tuneful, chromatic, and with a strong flavour of Richard Strauss, although this disappears in the middle section which is more like a march.

Die Bürgschaft (complete).
** EMI Dig. CDS5 56976-2 (2) [CDCB 56976].
   Margaret Thompson, Frederick Burchinal,
   Dale Travis, Joel Sorenson, Ann Panagulias,
   Westminster Ch., Spoleto Festival USA O,
   Julius Rudel.

Die Bürgschaft, 'The Surety', is Kurt Weill's most ambitious theatre-piece, a full-scale opera in three acts first seen in Berlin in 1932. Lasting with intervals almost four hours, it was rapturously received as marking a breakthrough in modern opera, one critic even likening it to Wagner's *Ring* cycle. Weill made substantial cuts when it was taken up by other opera-houses but the following year – like the rest of Weill's music – it was promptly banned by the Nazis, though it was not just them but others who deplored the heavy left-wing moralizing in a tale telling of how life in the ideal state of Urb is corrupted by greed. The disappointment of this première recording, taken from the first American production in 1998, is that the piece lacks the satirical bite of Weill's popular theatre-pieces of his German period. There are many characteristic sharp and colourful ideas, but too much is prettified Weill and even in its cut form, outstays its welcome. The performance, crisp and well-rehearsed, is well cast with fresh young voices, but the lack of bite in the orchestral sound – damped down in relation to the singers – seriously undermines any feeling of energy, with Julius Rudel less incisive than usual. None the less, devotees of Weill will find this an essential set.

(i; ii) *Die sieben Todsünden (The Seven deadly sins); (i) Songs: Berlin im Licht; Complainte de la Seine; Es regnet; Youkali; Nannas Lied (Meine Herren, mit Siebzehn); Wie lange noch?*
**(*) HM Dig. HMC 90 1420 [id.]. (i)
   Fassbaender; (ii) Brandt, Sojer, Komatsu,
   Urbas; Hanover R. PO, Garben.

This Harmonia Mundi version of *The Seven deadly sins* stars Brigitte Fassbaender who, using the original pitch, brings a Lieder-singer's feeling for word-detail and a comparable sense of style. Her account is obviously less street-wise than Lemper's (Decca 430 075-2) which remains first choice, but there is a plangent feeling that is highly appropriate. The songs are equally impressive, mostly connected in some way or another with the main piece but, especially alongside Rattle, the conductor, Cord Garben, at times seems on the leisurely side in his choice of tempi. Excellent, vivid recording.

Der Silbersee (complete).
*** RCA Dig. 09026 63447 (2) [id.]. Kruse,
   Gruber, Lascarro, Clark, Dernesch, Zednik,
   Wyn-Davies, Karnéus, Whelan, Saks, Alder,
   Weale, London Sinf. Ch. and O, Markus
   Stenz.

Weill wrote *Der Silbersee*, 'The Silver Lake', subtitled *A Winter's tale*, in 1932 for a production in Leipzig in February 1933 – an ill-starred date as Hitler and the Nazis had just come to power. The complete play with music, as written and devised by Georg Kaiser, lasts about four hours, of which some 85 minutes involve Weill's music. This excellent recording, recorded in the studio after a highly successful concert performance at a Prom in London, offers the complete musical score, including the passages of melodrama, speech over music, from Acts I and III.

It is an angry piece, which inspired Weill to write strong, biting and positive music, here splendidly performed with the London Sinfonietta under Markus Stenz. The casting is exceptionally strong, including in small roles such leading singers as the veterans Helga Dernesch and Heinz Zednik, tenor Graham Clark and rising star Katarina Karnéus. Both Heinz Kruse as the principal character, Severin, and H. K. Gruber as Olim, the policeman, are brightly idiomatic in German cabaret style, while Juanita Lascarro as the heroine, Fennimore, with her bright clear soprano provides the necessary contrast.

The Threepenny Opera (complete).
*** RCA Dig. 74321 66133-2 (2) [id.]. Raabe,
   Gruber, Hagen, Macdonald, Hellman, Böwe,
   Brauer, Holtz, Ens. Modern, H. K. Gruber.
** Decca 430 075-2 [id.]. Kollo, Adorf, Dernesch,
   Lemper, Milva, Berlin RIAS Chamber Ch. &
   Sinfonietta, Mauceri.

Using the new Kurt Weill Edition, which includes extra stage music, H. K. Gruber conducts a bitingly dramatic, well-paced account of *The Threepenny Opera*, brightly recorded in full, immediate sound. Gruber himself sings the role of Peachum with flair, and he is matched by a strong cast, both characterful and stylish, with vocal qualities paramount, even if Nina Hagen as Mrs Peachum comes near to screaming. The performance reflects throughout the experience of live performance, with Sona Macdonald at once idiomatic, firm and often beautiful in vocal production. Max Raabe as Macheath makes a believably youthful rogue, also firm and clear. Though the recording stretches to a second disc, it offers a more complete text than single-disc rivals, with reprises included.

The Decca version on a single disc may offer a temptingly starry cast, but all apart from Helga Dernesch as a rich, fruity Mrs Peachum are disappointing. René Kollo sounds far too old as Macheath, his voice a mere shadow of what it was, severely strained on top, while even Ute Lemper is disappointing, brilliantly characterful in fast music, but with the voice fluttery and unsteady in sustained lines. Mario Adorf as Peachum sings unsteadily, and none of the principals or the orchestra are helped by the slightly distanced recording balance, so that John Mauceri, normally an inspired conductor in this repertory, too often fails to make the music bite, often adopting relatively broad speeds. The RCA set is far preferable.

Weiner, Léo (1885–1960)

Violin sonatas Nos. 1 in D, Op. 9; 2 in F sharp min. Op. 11
(*) Biddulph LAW 015 [id.]. Oscar Shumsky, Seymour Lipkin – DOHNANYI: *Violin sonata in C sharp min., Op. 21; Andante *(*).

The two violin sonatas of Léo Weiner were composed in 1911 and 1919 respectively, and they are heard here in good performances by Oscar Shumsky and Seymour Lipkin. They were recorded in New York in 1993 and if Shumsky's playing does not have the effortless mastery it possessed in the early 1980s, he still performs a service in restoring these enjoyable works to the wider musical public. A most worthwhile issue.

Weyse, Christoph Ernst Friedrich (1774–1842)

Symphonies Nos. 1 in G min., DF117; 2 in C, DF118; 3 in D, DF119.
** Marco Polo/Da Capo 8.224012 [id.]. Royal Danish O, Schønwandt.

The example of Haydn affected Weyse strongly, and the minor-key symphonies in particular are reminiscent of Haydn's *Sturm und Drang* symphonies. Michael Schønwandt gives vital yet sensitive accounts of all three symphonies and is well served by the engineers. This lively music is worth investigating.

Widor, Charles-Marie (1844–1937)

Symphony No. 3 for organ and orchestra, Op. 69.
*** Chandos Dig. CHAN 9785 [id.]. Ian Tracey (organ of Liverpool Cathedral), BBC PO, Yan Pascal Tortelier – GUILMANT: *Symphony No. 2 for organ and orchestra, Op. 91*; FRANCK: *Choral No. 2*. ***

Widor's *Third Symphony* for organ and orchestra was commissioned by Sir Daniel Barton, English Consul General in Geneva, intended (in 1894) to show off the acoustics of the newly built Victoria Hall. Although in two sections, the work moves in a series of episodes: *Adagio – Andante* (introducing

a luscious string tune) – *Allegro* (end of first movement); *Vivace – Tranquillamente – Allegro* (which with its horn calls and galloping energy brings a curious reminder of Franck's *Chasseur maudit*); finally comes an overwhelmingly majestic *Largo* with the chorale melody shared by organ and orchestra, bursting at the seams in sheer amplitude. The decibels of the coda are worthy of the finest speakers. Ian Tracey makes the most of his opportunities, as does Tortelier. Certainly the huge Liverpool organ and the resonant cathedral acoustics seem custom made for such spectacle and the Chandos engineers capture it all with aplomb.

Organ Symphonies No. 2 in D, Op. 13/2; 8 in B, Op. 42/4.
*** BIS Dig. BIS-CD-1007 [id.]. Hans Fagius.

A demonstration disc for audio enthusiasts. The Swedish organist Hans Fagius plays two Widor symphonies, the *Second in D major* and the *Eighth in B major*, on a new instrument made by the Swedish makers Åkerman and Lund, in Kallio Church in Helsinki. The *Second Symphony* is one of four published in 1872 and the *Eighth* comes from a second set of four, published fifteen years later in 1887. The instrument itself is five years old and is modelled on the symphonic organs of Cavaillé-Coll tradition with which César Franck and Widor were so closely associated. Its disposition was the work of Kurt Lueders of Paris. Hans Fagius serves the music well and the engineers produce particularly impressive results. The opening *Allegro* of the *Eighth Symphony* gives a good idea of the impressive range this disc covers.

Wieniawski, Henryk (1835–80)

Violin concertos Nos. 1 in F sharp min., Op. 14; 2 in D min., Op. 22; Fantaisie brillante on themes from Gounod's Faust, Op. 20.
(BB) *** Naxos Dig. 8.553517 [id.]. Marat Bisengaliev, Polish Nat. RSO, Antoni Wit.

Antoni Wit handles the long opening ritornello of the *F sharp minor concerto* most impressively, and Marat Bisengaliev proves a natural, understanding soloist in both concertos, playing slow movements with warmly romantic feeling and sparkling with brilliance in the display passages and especially in the finales. The *Faust variations* make a substantial (19-minute) and attractively tuneful bonus. Marat Bisengaliev has a fairly small, but sweet and beautifully focused tone; he is balanced naturally in relation to the orchestra, and both are very well recorded in the Polish Radio Concert Hall, which has an attractively warm acoustic.

Capriccio-waltz, Op. 7; Gigue in E min., Op. 27; Kujawiak in A min.; Légende, Op. 17; Mazurka in G min., Op. 12/2; 2 Mazurkas, Op. 19; Polonaise No. 1 in D, Op. 4; Russian carnival, Op. 11;

Saltarello (arr. Lenehan); *Scherzo-tarantelle in G min., Op. 16; Souvenir de Moscou, Op. 6; Variations on an original theme, Op. 15.*
(BB) **(*) Naxos Dig. 8.550744 [id.]. Marat Bisengaliev, John Lenehan.

All the dazzling violin fireworks are ready to bow here, from left-hand pizzicatos in the *Russian carnival* to multiple stopping (and some lovely, warm lyricism) in the *Variations on an original theme*, plus all the dash you could ask for in the closing *Scherzo-tarantelle*, while the beautiful *Légende* (which Wieniawski dedicated to his wife as a nuptial gift) is both touchingly gentle and passionately brilliant. Marat Bisengaliev is without the larger-than-life personality of a Perlman, but he is a remarkably fine player and a stylist. John Lenehan provides his partner with admirable support throughout. The snag is the very reverberant acoustic of the Rosslyn Hill Chapel, Hampstead – so obviously empty; otherwise the sound and balance are natural enough.

Wolf, Hugo (1860–1903)

Goethe Lieder: *Anakreons Grab; 3 Harfenspieler Lieder.*
*** Decca Dig. 458 189-2 [id.]. Matthias Goerne, Concg. O, Chailly – BRUCKNER: *Symphony No. 6 in A ***.*

The three *Harfenspieler* songs, setting verses from the novel, *Wilhelm Meister*, as well as *Anakreons Grab* make a valuable and generous fill-up for Chailly's superb, refined reading of the Bruckner symphony. Matthias Goerne with his headily lyrical baritone makes an ideal, thoughtful interpreter, well balanced in the warmly atmospheric recording.

Mörike Lieder: *An eine Aeolsharfe; Bei einer Trauung; Denk' es, o Seele!; Heimweh; Im Frühling; Jägerlied; Lied eines Verliebten.*
(M) *** BBC Music BBCB 8015-2 [id.]. Peter Pears, Benjamin Britten – BRITTEN: *On this island*, etc.; SCHUBERT: *7 Lieder *** (with ARNE: *Come away death; Under the greenwood tree;* QUILTER: *O mistress mine;* WARLOCK: *Take, o take those lips away;* TIPPETT: *Come unto these yellow sands ***).*

In the BBC's sensitive performances of seven of Wolf's Mörike settings – recorded at the Snape Maltings in 1972, not long before Britten was stricken by terminal illness – these unfailingly convey a sense of spontaneity, capturing the inspiration of the moment in a way that is rare on disc, thanks above all to Britten's accompaniments. Excellent radio sound.

Mörike Lieder: *An den Schlaf; Auf ein altes Bild; Auf einer Wanderung; Begegnung; Bei einer Trauung; Denk' es, o Seele!; Der Feuerreiter; Fussreise; Der Gärtner; Gebet; Gesang Weylas; Im Frühling; In der Frühe; Jägerlied; Der Knabe und das Immlein; Lebe wohl; Nimmersatte Liebe; Peregrina 1 & 2; Schlafendes Jesuskind; Selbstgeständnis; Storchenbotschaft; Das verlassene Mägdlein; Verborgenheit; Zum neuen Jahr.*
*** Decca Dig. (IMS) 440 208-2 [id.]. Brigitte Fassbaender, Thibaudet.

Here is a dangerous, even violent singer who, with light in the eye, heightens the character of each song, bringing out the good humour in such a song as *Fussreise*, rambling, drawing out the beauty of line in *Verborgenheit*, but often positively taking an individual approach. So there is passionate intensity as much as rapt concentration behind *Schlafendes Jesuskind*, and the loss of a lover in *Das verlassene Mägdlein* is treated not as tragedy but as something to be shrugged off by the servant-girl. Characteristically, Fassbaender concludes with a shattering account of the most violent of Wolf songs, normally reserved for men, *Der Feuerreiter* ('The fire-rider').

(i) 3 Christmas songs: *Auf ein altes Bild; Nun wandre, Maria; Schlafendes Jesuskind;* (ii) 3 Michelangelo Lieder: *Alles endet, was entstehet; Fühlt meine Seele; Wohl denk' ich oft.*
(M)*** BBC Music BBCB 8011-2 [id.]. (i) Peter Pears; (ii) John Shirley-Quirk, Britten – SCHUBERT: *11 Lieder ***.*

John Shirley-Quirk in his singing of three of Wolf's Michelangelo settings at the 1971 Aldeburgh Festival has never been more mellifluous on disc, just as sensitive in his treatment of Lieder as the others, and the whole programme is delightfully rounded off by Pears's charming performances of the three Wolf Christmas songs. Excellent sound.

Wolpe, Stefan (1902–72)

(i) *Symphony No. 1;* (ii) *Chamber pieces Nos. 1–2;* (iii) *Yigdal cantata.*
(BB) *** Arte Nova Dig. 74321 46508-2. (i) NDR SO, Johannes Kalitzke; (ii) Instrumental Ens.; (iii) NDR Ch., H. Neumann.

Stefan Wolpe was one of Webern's most distinguished pupils. The *Yigdal cantata* sets Hebrew texts in a way which brilliantly reconciles a serial technique with traditional Jewish music, warm and expressive. The purely instrumental works are far tougher, with the *Symphony* crisp and purposeful. The two *Chamber pieces*, each for fourteen instruments, very much in the manner of Webern, are among Wolpe's last works, even more compressed, with each seeming to reflect his frustration and defiance over suffering from Parkinson's disease. At Arte Nova price, well worth investigating by the adventurous.

Wood, Haydn (1882–1959)

Volume I: *Apollo overture; A Brown bird singing* (paraphrase for orchestra); *London cameos* (suite) *Miniature overture: The City; St James's Park in the spring; A State ball at Buckingham Palace. Mannin Veen* (Manx tone-poem); *Moods* (suite): *Joyousness* (concert waltz). *Mylecharane* (rhapsody); *The Seafarer (A nautical rhapsody); Serenade to youth; Sketch of a Dandy.*
*** Marco Polo Dig. 8.22340-2. Slovak RSO (Bratislava), Adrian Leaper.

Haydn Wood, an almost exact contemporary of Eric Coates and nearly as talented, spent his childhood on the Isle of Man, and much of his best music is permeated with Manx folk-themes (original or simulated). *Mannin Veen* ('Dear Isle of Man') is a splendid piece, based on four such folksongs. The companion rhapsody, *Mylecharane*, also uses folk material, if less memorably, and *The Seafarer* is a wittily scored selection of famous shanties, neatly stitched together. The only failure here is *Apollo*, which uses less interesting material and is over-ambitious and inflated. But the English waltzes are enchanting confections and *Sketch of a Dandy* is frothy and elegant. Adrian Leaper is clearly much in sympathy with this repertoire and knows just how to pace it; his Czech players obviously relish the easy tunefulness and the sheer craft of the writing. With excellent recording in what is surely an ideal acoustic, this is very highly recommendable.

Volume II: *A day in fairyland suite: Dance of a whimsical elf; An evening song; Frescoes suite; London landmarks: Horse guards march; A Manx rhapsody; May-Day overture; Paris suite; Roses of Picardy; Soliloquy; Variations on a once popular humorous song.*
*** Marco Polo Dig. 8.223605 [id.].
Czech-Slovak RSO (Bratislava), Tomlinson.

The second CD opens with the charming *May-Day overture*, with its dreamy sound-picture of dawn, giving way to the day's festivities. The *Variations* are effective, and the composer's *Paris suite* introduces a distinct Gallic flavour: the *Montmartre march* is especially enjoyable. Wood's beloved Isle of Man inspired the *Manx rhapsody*, which finds the composer again in his attractive folksy-mode, and the composer's most famous piece, *Roses of Picardy*, is a slightly dated highlight of this volume. The rest of the programme is equally enjoyable, and the performances, this time with Ernest Tomlinson, are excellent. The recording is a bit richer than in the Volume I.

Piano concerto in D min.
*** Hyperion Dig. CDA 67127 [id.]. Hamish

Milne, BBC Scottish SO, Martyn Brabbins –
HOLBROOKE: *Piano concerto No. 1 ****.

It is ironic that while the Holbrooke concerto coupling brings many hints of light music, even echoing the style of Ivor Novello, Haydn Wood – who had great success as a composer of light music – sustains a serious manner more consistently. He writes fluently and attractively throughout both for the piano and the orchestra, demonstrating why he was a favourite pupil of Stanford. The piece was completed in 1909, well before Wood switched his main concern to light music, and in its echoes of Grieg and Rachmaninov. with an English accent, it establishes itself as one of the more striking British piano concertos of the period. The orchestral introduction provides a grand fanfare for the entry of the piano with a strong main theme and, even when melodies enter which might have developed into drawing-room ballads, Wood ensures that they avoid banality. The slow movement is a tenderly beautiful interlude with muted strings, and the finale, built on a bold motif, leads to two grandiloquent climaxes based on the one theme which skirts banality. The result is exciting nonetheless, suggesting that, unlike some works resurrected in the Hyperion 'Romantic Piano Concerto' series, this could become a viable repertory piece. Brilliant playing from Hamish Milne and warm, well-balanced recording.

Ysaÿe, Eugène (1858–1931)

6 Sonatas for solo violin, Op. 27.
*** BIS Dig. CD 1046 [id.]. Leonid Kavakos.
(BB) *** Arte Nova Dig. 74321 67511-2 [id.].
Benjamin Schmid.

The technical and artistic challenges of the Ysaÿe *Solo violin sonatas* naturally fascinate violinists – more so than they do the wider musical public. Were they always played with as much character and artistry as they are by Leonid Kavakos, things might be different. This Greek violinist came to notice when he recorded the first version of the Sibelius concerto for BIS, and he impresses every bit as much here. Each sonata reflects the personality of the great violinists such as Szigeti, Thibaud, Kreisler and Enescu to whom they are dedicated. A very impressive recording, which displaces the two versions listed in our main guide.

While not displacing Kavakos on BIS artistically, for they both bring different insights to these fine sonatas, Benjamin Schmid is in every way an impressive player and very well recorded. No one investing in his recording (and the outlay is modest) will be disappointed, for these performances are full of imagination and this is satisfying in its own right. However, Kavakos makes one see these pieces in a fresher light.

Zelenka, Jan Dismas (1679–1745)

Magnificats in C and D, ZWV 107–8.
*** BIS Dig. CD 1011 [id.]. Miah Persson, Yukari Nonoshita, Akira Tachikawa, Gerd Türk, Chiyuki Urano, Bach Collegium, Japan, Masaaki Suzuki – BACH: *Magnificat in D;* KUHNAU: *Magnificat in C.* ***

Zelenka came out of the shadows in the late 1970s and early 1980s, thanks to the efforts of Supraphon and DG Archiv. He studied in Prague and later in Vienna and Venice; he then served in Dresden for many years where he became *Kirchenkomponist,* not *Kapellmeister* as he had desired. These two *Magnificats* are quite delightful, very fresh and inventive. They are not otherwise available on CD. Masaaki Suzuki and his fine team of singers and players serve them with enthusiasm and affection, and the recorded sound is absolutely first class.

(i) *Missa in D: Missa gratias agimus tibi. 5 Responsoria pro Hebdomada Sancta; Antiphon: Su tuum praesidium.*
*** Supraphon/Koch Dig. 11 0816-2 [id.]. (i) Jonášová, Mrázová, Doležal, Mikuláš, Czech PO, (i; ii) Czech Philharmonic Ch., Bělohlávek.

This *Mass* (1730) is a splendid work; the *Responsoria* (for Maundy Thursday and Good Friday), were composed seven years earlier. The programme is completed with a movingly simple Marian antiphon, written after the Mass. These works could hardly be more authentically or persuasively presented than in these very fine Supraphon recordings from 1984. Remarkably individual music, distinctively performed and very well recorded.

Zemlinsky, Alexander von (1871–1942)

Der Geburtstag der Infantin (opera; abridged first version).
*** Schwann Dig. CD 11626 [id]. Nielsen, Riegel, Haldas, Weller, Berlin RSO, Albrecht.

The Birthday of the Infanta tells of a hideous dwarf caught in the forest and given to the Infanta as a birthday present. Even after recognizing his own hideousness, he declares his love to the princess and is casually rejected. He dies of a broken heart, with the Infanta untroubled: 'Oh dear, my present already broken.' Zemlinsky, dwarfish himself, gave his heart to the piece, reproducing his own rejection at the hands of Alma Mahler. Kenneth Riegel gives a heart-rendingly passionate performance as the dwarf declaring his love. His genuine passion is intensified by being set against lightweight, courtly music to represent the Infanta and her attendants. With the conductor and others in the cast also experienced in the stage production, the result is a deeply involving performance, beautifully recorded.

Ziehrer, Carl Michael (1843–1922)

Auersperg-marsch; Landstreicher-Quadrille. Polkas: *Burgerlich und romantisch; Pfiffig; Die Tänzerin; Loslassen!* Waltzes: *Clubgeister; Diesen Kuss der ganzen Welt; Libesrezepte; Osterreich in Tönen; Wiener Bürger.*
**(*) Marco Polo Dig. 8.223814 [id.]. Razumovsky Sinfonia, Alfred Walter.

Fächer-polonaise; Mein feld ist die welt-marsch. Polkas: *Endlich allein! Im Fluge; Lieber Bismarck, schaukle nicht; Matrosen.* Waltzes: *Heimatsgefühle; Herreinspaziert!; Sei brav; In der Sommerfrische; Tolles Mädel.*
**(*) Marco Polo Dig. 8.223815 [id.]. Razumovsky Sinfonia, Dittrich.

Collectors of Viennese dance music will welcome the news that Marco Polo have started this survey of music by Ziehrer: they label the CDs as Vol. 1 & 2 of 'selected dances and marches', so presumably, it will not be a complete edition, but it will include the cream of his output (including première recordings) which is all even specialists will want. Ziehrer's style is very much in the Johann Strauss tradition but, unlike many of Strauss's rivals, Ziehrer's music has a distinctive, robust quality, probably attributable to his career as a military band leader for many years.

Throughout his life, his fortunes were mixed – he had his successes for sure, but he died penniless. His music overflows with tunes, is thoroughly entertaining, and will disappoint no one who responds to the Viennese tradition.

Volume I opens with his most famous piece, *Wiener Bürger,* a delightful waltz that rivals the best of J. Strauss. The *Die Tänzerin* polka uses themes from the opera of the same name as its basis – to invigorating effect; the *Landstreicher-Quadrille* is composed in the same way, and contains some particularly jaunty numbers. Not surprisingly, Ziehrer was adept at writing marches, and the *Auersperg-Marsch* is one of his best – it had to be repeated several times at its première. The almost forgotten *Osterreich in Tönen waltz (Melodies of Austria)* is another highlight: all its melodies are in fact original, but it has an agreeably localized ethnic flavour.

Volume II offers more of the same: it begins with the fine *Herreinspaziert* waltz which soon lunges into a richly contoured theme to rival *Wiener Bürger*. The *Fächer* ('Fan') polonaise is memorable, and is still used to introduce the prestigious annual Philharmonic Ball in Vienna. The polkas are wittily crafted, and none of the waltzes here is without at least one memorable theme. The *Tolles Mädel* ('Crazy girl') waltz even begins to look forward to the American musical and is a winner in every way, as is the *Sei brav* ('Be good') waltz – a lively confection of music from Ziehrer's operetta *Fesche Geister* ('Lively spirits').

The performances from both conductors are lively and sympathetic, the recordings bright and vivid (the second disc a little less so), and the sleeve notes helpful and informative. If this music-making is not quite of the calibre of Boskovsky's Decca VPO series, it is still quite polished and attractively idiomatic.

CORNUCOPIA OF CONCERTS, INSTRUMENTAL AND VOCAL RECITALS

CONCERTS OF ORCHESTRAL AND CONCERTANTE MUSIC

Art of conducting

'The Art of conducting': Video: 'Great conductors of the past' (Barbirolli, Beecham, Bernstein, Busch, Furtwängler, Karajan, Klemperer, Koussevitzky, Nikisch, Reiner, Stokowski, Richard Strauss, Szell, Toscanini, Walter, Weingartner): BRUCKNER: Symphony No. 7 (rehearsal) (Hallé O, Barbirolli). GOUNOD: Faust: ballet music (with rehearsal) (RPO, Beecham). Silent film (BPO, Nikisch). Richard STRAUSS: Till Eulenspiegel (VPO, Richard Strauss). WEBER: Der Freischütz overture (Paris SO, Felix Weingartner). WAGNER: Tannhäuser overture (Dresden State O, Fritz Busch). MOZART: Symphony No. 40 (BPO, Bruno Walter). BRAHMS: Symphony No. 2 (rehearsal) (Vancouver Festival O, Bruno Walter). BEETHOVEN: Egmont overture; Symphony No. 9 (Philh. O, Klemperer). WAGNER: Die Meistersinger overture. SCHUBERT: Symphony No. 8 (Unfinished). BRAHMS: Symphony No. 4 (both rehearsals) (BPO, Furtwängler). VERDI: La forza del destino overture; La Traviata: Coro di zingarelle. RESPIGHI: The Pines of Rome (NBC SO, Toscanini). PURCELL (arr. Stokowski): Dido and Aeneas: Dido's lament. RESPIGHI: The Pines of Rome (BBC SO). TCHAIKOVSKY: Symphony No. 5 (NYPO) (both cond. Stokowski). BEETHOVEN: Egmont overture (Boston SO, Koussevitzky). TCHAIKOVSKY: Violin concerto (Heifetz, NYPO, Reiner). BEETHOVEN: Symphony No. 7 (Chicago SO, Reiner). BRAHMS: Academic festival overture. BEETHOVEN: Symphony No. 5 (Cleveland O, Szell). BEETHOVEN: Symphony No. 5. DEBUSSY: La Mer (BPO, Karajan). SHOSTAKOVICH: Symphony No. 5 (rehearsal and performance) (LSO). MAHLER: Symphony No. 4 (VPO) (both cond. Bernstein). BEETHOVEN: Symphony No. 9 (Philh. O, Klemperer).

(Commentary by John Eliot Gardiner, Isaac Stern, Jack Brymer, Beecham, Menuhin, Oliver Knussen, Suvi Raj Grubb, Szell, Walter, Klemperer, Hugh Bean, Werner Thärichen, Richard Mohr, Stokowski, Julius Baker, Karajan).
✲ *** Teldec/Warner VHS 4509 95038-3 [id.].

This extraordinary video offers a series of electrifying performances by the great conductors of our century, all seen and heard at their very finest. Enormous care has been taken over the sound, even in the earliest recordings, for it is remarkably full-bodied and believable. But most of all it is to watch conductors weaving their magic spell over the orchestra which is so fascinating. And sometimes they do it imperceptibly, like Richard Strauss conducting Till Eulenspiegel with apparent nonchalance, yet making music with the utmost aural vividness; Fritz Busch creating great tension in Wagner; Bruno Walter wonderfully mellow in Brahms; Klemperer in Beethoven hardly moving his baton and yet completely in control; Furtwängler rehearsing the finale of Brahms's Fourth Symphony with a tremendous flow of adrenalin; Toscanini the martinet in Verdi; Stokowski moulding gloriously beautiful sound with flowing movements of his hands and arms; and, most riveting of all, Bernstein creating enormous passion with the LSO in Shostakovich's Fifth Symphony.

Of the many commentaries from other artists and various musicians, the experience of Werner Thärichen stands out. He was participating in a Berlin performance when he suddenly realized that the sound around him had changed: it had become uncannily more beautiful. Not understanding why, he looked to the back of the hall ... and saw that Furtwängler had just walked in. The great Nikisch is seen conducting (on silent film) but not heard – and no one knows what the music was!

OTHER CONCERTS

Academy of Ancient Music, Christopher Hogwood

PACHELBEL: *Canon & Gigue.* HANDEL: *Water music: Air. Berenice: Overture*; *Minuet*; *Gigue.* VIVALDI: *Flute concerto in G min. (La notte), Op. 10/2.* BACH: *Christmas oratorio, BWV 248: Sinfonia. Quadruple harpsichord concerto in A min., BWV 1065.* CORELLI: *Concerto grosso (Christmas concerto), Op. 6/8.* A. MARCELLO: *Oboe concerto in D min.*

(M) **(*) O-L Analogue/Dig. 443 201-2.

It seems a curious idea to play popular baroque repertoire in a severe manner; Pachelbel's *Canon* here sounds rather abrasive and lacking in charm. But those who combine a taste for these pieces with a desire for authenticity should be satisfied. The selection for this reissue has been expanded and altered. Handel's *Queen of Sheba* no longer arrives – and she is not missed (for she was much more seductive in Beecham's hands) – and the highlight of the original, full-priced compilation (a pair of Gluck dances) is no longer present! Instead, we get several new items taken from another Academy of Ancient Music compilation of baroque music associated with Christmas, notably Corelli's splendid Op. 6/8, in which the playing has a suitably light touch, and Vivaldi's engaging *La notte Flute concerto*, while Bach's *Quadruple harpsichord concerto* substitutes for the famous Vivaldi work for four violins (Op. 3/10). On the whole an enjoyable mix. The new playing time is 67 minutes.

Academy of St Martin-in-the-Fields, Sir Neville Marriner

'Portrait of Sir Neville Marriner': HANDEL: *Water music: suite No. 2. Solomon: Arrival of the Queen of Sheba.* MOZART: *Le nozze di Figaro overture.* TCHAIKOVSKY: *Andante cantabile for strings, from Op. 11.* FAURE: *Pavane, Op. 50.* BOCCHERINI: *String quintet in E, Op. 13/5: Minuet.* CHERUBINI: *Overtures: Les Abencérages ou L'Etendard de Grenade*; *Médée.* WAGNER: *Siegfried idyll.* GRIEG: *Peer Gynt suite No. 1* (with Ambrosian Singers). ALBINONI arr. GIAZOTTO: *Adagio* (with Iona Brown). BACH: *Cantata 147: Jesu joy of man's desiring* (with King's College, Cambridge, Choir). SHOSTAKOVICH: *The Gadfly: Romance.* PONCHIELLI: *La Gioconda: Dance of the hours.* VIVALDI: *Double trumpet concerto in C, RV 537* (with Maurice André and Bernard Soustrot). NICOLAI: *Overture: The Merry Wives of Windsor.* RESPIGHI: *The Birds.*

❀ (BB) *** Royal Long Players Dig./Analogue DCL 70597-2 (2).

This is the first and easily the finest of an attractive 2-disc series of conductors' portraits, all using recordings derived from the EMI back catalogue, issued at bargain-basement price – lower even than Naxos. We list it under the Academy, as this wonderful orchestra was synonymous with Marriner's name through more than three decades, from the late 1950s onwards. Moreover Marriner was the most successful conductor of the stereo LP era: he made more highly praised records than even Karajan.

The present selection may be lightweight, but it includes many cherishable items like the radiant account of the *Siegfried idyll* in which solo strings are used for the gentler passages, a fuller ensemble for the ardent climaxes. The *Peer Gynt* suite all but upstages Beecham: the *Death of Aase* is wonderfully delicate and tender, while the Ambrosian Trolls enter the Mountain King's hall very lustily indeed. It is good, too, that Iona Brown is featured as soloist in the pleasantly refined account of the Albinoni/Giazotto *Adagio* and also, probably – for she is uncredited – in Shostakovich's passionate *Romance* from *The Gadfly*. She was Marriner's remarkably talented protégée, and is currently enjoying a distinguished independent career as musical director of the Norwegian Chamber Orchestra.

The Handel items are also treasurable and here the *Queen of Sheba* trots in more briskly than in her first Academy appearance on Decca/Argo. By contrast *Jesu joy of man's desiring* is warm and leisurely. The delicacy and sparkle of the *Dance of the hours* is matched by the one novelty here, Cherubini's delightfully scored *Les Abencérages*, while the opening of Nicolai's more familiar *Merry Wives overture* is magically atmospheric. Maurice André and Bernard Soustrot are spectacular soloists in the *Double trumpet concerto*, which reminds us that Marriner was also a distinguished Vivaldi pioneer.

Finally comes Respighi's engaging aviary, showing the elegance and wittily picaresque detail of the ASMF ensemble at its most endearingly sophisticated. Almost all the recordings are digital and from the 1980s; the Respighi is earlier and analogue, but most beautifully transferred to CD.

Even if some duplication is involved this is a selection not to be missed: it makes a marvellous ongoing entertainment.

'Fantasia on Greensleeves': VAUGHAN WILLIAMS: *Fantasia on Greensleeves*; *The Lark ascending* (with Iona Brown); *English folksongs suite*. WARLOCK: *Serenade*; *Capriol suite*. GEORGE BUTTERWORTH: *A Shropshire lad*; *Two English idylls*; *The Banks of green willow*. DELIUS: *A Village Romeo and Juliet: The walk to the Paradise Garden. Hassan: Intermezzo and serenade. A song before sunrise*; *On hearing the first cuckoo in spring)*; *Summer night on the river*; *La Calinda*. ELGAR: *Serenade for strings, Op. 20*; *Sospiri for strings, harp and organ*; *Elegy for strings, Op. 58*; *The Spanish Lady (suite)*; *Introduction and allegro, Op. 47*.
(B) *** Decca Double 452 707-2 (2) [(M) id. import].

This exceptionally generous programme, mainly of English pastoral evocations but including Iona Brown's Elysian account of *The Lark ascending* and Elgar's two string masterpieces in not wholly idiomatic but very characterful performances, is self-recommending, for the Academy are thoroughly at home here and play with consistent warmth and finesse, while the vintage Decca sound never disappoints. Marvellous value for money.

'English Classics': VAUGHAN WILLIAMS: *Fantasia on Greensleeves*; *English folk song suite* (trans. Gordon Jacob). ELGAR: *Serenade for strings, Op. 20*. BUTTERWORTH: *The Banks of green willow*. WARLOCK: *Capriol suite*. DELIUS: *On hearing the first cuckoo in Spring*; *The walk to the Paradise Garden*.
(B) *** Decca Penguin Classics Analogue/Dig. 460 637 [id.]. ASMF, Marriner.

These recordings are rarely out of the catalogue, and rightly so. They are lovely performances and show the Academy on vintage form; there is much subtlety of detail here as well as striking commitment and depth of feeling, and although the recordings range from 1967–81, they are all rich and full. Reissued on the Penguin Classics label, they come with a personal appraisal by Jim Crace. However the fuller selection on the Decca Double above is an even more attractive proposition.

German Operetta overtures: HEUBERGER: *Der Opernball*. HUMPERDINCK: *Hänsel und Gretel*. LORTZING: *Zar und Zimmermann*. MARSCHNER: *Hans Heiling*. NICOLAI: *The Merry Wives of Windsor*. REZNICEK: *Donna Diana*. Johann STRAUSS Jr: *Die Fledermaus*. SUPPE: *Poet and peasant*. WEBER: *Euryanthe*.
*** Ph. Dig. 456 576-2 [id.].

Operetta here includes opera, as the typography of the title indicates, bringing together a sequence of overtures full of warmth and colour. With a winning formula, Marriner and the Academy are inspired to the most brilliant playing, flawless in ensemble and ripely recorded. Such warhorses as *Poet and peasant* emerge fresh-minted, and it is good to find the Heuberger *overture* including a quotation from the most popular aria in *The Opera Ball, Im chambre separée*. Best of all is the fizzing overture to Reznicek's *Donna Diana*, with Marriner even matching the exuberance of Karajan in his classic mono recording. A delightful cocktail of a disc.

Adler, Larry (harmonica)

'The genius of Larry Adler' (with arrangements by, & Orchestra cond. by, Douglas Gamley): MASSENET: *Thaïs: Meditation*. DEBUSSY: *Clair de lune*. ADLER: *Genevieve waltz*; *Screw's blues*. DINICU: (arr. HEIFETZ/ADLER): *Hora staccato*. KHACHATURIAN: *Gayaneh: Sabre dance*. FALLA: *El amor brujo: Ritual fire dance*. ALFVEN: *Swedish rhapsody* (abridged). VILLA-LOBOS: *Bachianas brasileiras No. 5*. DVORAK: *Symphony No. 9 (New World): Largo* (abridged). RAVEL: *Boléro* (abridged; with BBC Concert O, Dunk). GERSHWIN: *Rhapsody in blue* (arr. composer for Adler; accompanied by Gershwin on player piano); *Porgy and Bess: Summertime*. JOPLIN: *The entertainer*. RODRIGO: *Concierto de Aranjuez: Adagio* (abridged).
*** Decca Dig 466 133-2 [id.].

Recorded as he approached his 85th birthday, Adler spins his magic in this stream of imperishable melodies, played with enormous style, great affection and wit. He almost upstages Heifetz in the dazzling *Hora staccato*, and makes the haunting Villa-Lobos melody sound completely his own. About the special arrangement of *Rhapsody in blue*, Gershwin said 'The Goddam thing sounds as if I wrote it for him' and Adler uses the composer's own piano-roll recording as an accompaniment as he plays the great bluesy melody in the middle, and much else besides. Very properly, Adler's own very fetching *Genevieve waltz* is included, written for a 1953 film that is still cherished. Douglas Gamley's arrangements cannot be faulted, the recording is near perfect and this is very entertaining indeed.

American masterpieces

'American masterpieces' (with (i) Cleveland O, Louis Lane; (ii) Phd. O, Eugene Ormandy; (iii) NYPO, André Kostelanetz): (i) BERNSTEIN: *Candide overture*. (ii) IVES: *Variations on 'America'*. (iii) William SCHUMAN: *New England triptych*. (ii) BARBER: *Adagio for strings*. GOULD: *American salute*. (iii) GRIFFES: *The pleasure dome of Kubla Khan*. (ii) MACDOWELL: *Woodland*

sketches: To a wild rose. (iii) GERSHWIN:
Promenade. (ii) GOTTSCHALK: *Cakewalk: Grand walkaround* (arr. Hershy Kay). (i) BENJAMIN:
Jamaican rumba. RODGERS: *On Your Toes: Slaughter on 10th Avenue.* Virgil THOMSON:
Louisiana story (film score): *Arcadian songs and dances.*
(B) **(*) Sony SBK 63034 [id.].

Not everything here is a masterpiece, and Arthur Benjamin, who makes the wittiest contribution, was an Australian! But there are some obvious favourites included and one or two novelties, among them the attractively folksy *Arcadian songs and dances* of Virgil Thomson, affectionately directed in Cleveland by Louis Lane. He is well recorded, and so, on the whole, is Ormandy, who presents the Ives *Variations* with charm as well as panache, while the Philadelphia strings are powerfully eloquent in Barber's *Adagio* and warmly persuasive in MacDowell's engaging *To a wild rose.* Kostelanetz conducts with plenty of personality and zest and is at his best in the Gershwin *Promenade* and the touching central movement of Schuman's *New England triptych.* But here the up-front recording of the NYPO is overlit and the climaxes of the otherwise atmospheric *Kubla Khan* sound aggressive. A stimulating programme, just the same.

Amsterdam Loeki Stardust Quartet, Academy of Ancient Music, Christopher Hogwood

'Concerti di flauti': HEINICHEN: *Concerto a 8 in C.* SCHICKHARDT: *Concerto No. 2 in D min. for 4 recorders & continuo*; *Concerto No. 3 in G for 4 recorders & continuo.* TELEMANN: *Concertos for 2 recorders & strings: in A min.; in B flat.*
MARCELLO: *Concerti di flauti in G.* VIVALDI:
Concerto in A in due cori, con flauti obbligati, RV 585.
*** O-L (IMS) Dig. 436 905-2 [id.].

The Heinichen *Concerto a 8* (which doesn't mean there are eight soloists!) is a charmer, with a barely scored drone effect in the *Pastorel* followed by a graceful minute-long *Adagio* to counter the chortling in the outer movements. The Schickhardt D minor work opens equally invitingly (with the effect of a carol) and is elegantly tuneful throughout. In its companion in G major, the solo style is very chordal, with moments almost like a piquant harmonium. Both the Telemann works are predictably inventive and enjoyable; perhaps the first, in A minor, wins by a short head, while in the happy Marcello piece one can feel the Italian sunshine.

But the most masterly concerto here is the splendid Vivaldi antiphonal *Concerto in A major* which uses violin soloists as well as the recorders

(used sparingly as an obbligato) and even brings in a brief solo organ contribution. The slow movement is dominated by the violin duo. Needless to say, the whole programme is expertly and authentically presented. The recording, made in London's Henry Wood Hall, has a nice ambience, though the balance is a trifle close (particularly in the Vivaldi). A very stimulating concert just the same.

Anderson, John (oboe), Philharmonia Orchestra, Simon Wright

'Venetian oboe concertos': ALBINONI: *Concertos in B flat, Op. 7/3; in D, Op. 7/6.* MARCELLO:
Concerto in D min. VIVALDI: *Concertos in D, RV 453; in F, RV 455; in A min., RV 461.* CIMAROSA/
BENJAMIN: *Concerto in C min.*
(M) **(*) Nimbus Dig. NI 7027 [id.].

John Anderson is principal oboist of the Philharmonia and he plays these concertos with warmth, elegance and grace. The one slight drawback is the rather plushy tuttis from the resonantly recorded Philharmonia Orchestra. Although they give delicate support in the Marcello *Adagio*, the orchestral touch is heavier in the *Larghetto* of the Vivaldi *A minor*, RV 461. The concerto arranged by Arthur Benjamin from the music of Cimarosa is a highlight, the *Introduction* delicately tender and the second movement deliciously pointed.

André, Maurice (trumpet)

Trumpet concertos (with BPO, Karajan):
HUMMEL: *Concerto in E flat.* Leopold MOZART:
Concerto in D. TELEMANN: *Concerto in D.*
VIVALDI: *Concerto in A flat* (ed. Thilde).
(M) **(*) EMI CDM5 66909-2 [CDM 66961].

A key collection of trumpet concertos, brilliantly played by André. His security in the upper register in the work by Leopold Mozart and the fine Telemann concerto is impressive, with Karajan and the BPO wonderfully serene and gracious in the opening *Adagio* and the *Grave* slow movement of the latter. The jaunty quality of the Hummel is not missed, and the finale of this work, taken at breakneck pace, is certainly exhilarating, while the cantilena of the *Andante* is nobly contoured.

The Vivaldi work is arranged from the *Sonata in F major for violin and continuo, RV 20*, and makes a very effective display piece. The 1974 recording has generally been well transferred to CD. Although the trumpet timbre is very bright and the violins are not absolutely clean in focus, there is plenty of ambience. However, this reissue has a playing time of only 47 minutes and hardly seems an apt choice for EMI's 'Great Recordings of the Century' series.

Trumpet concertos (with ASMF, Marriner): STOLZEL: *Concerto in D.* TELEMANN: *Concerto in C min; Concerto in D for trumpet, 2 oboes and strings* (with Nicklin and Miller). VIVALDI: *Double trumpet concerto in C, RV 537* (with Soustrot); *Double concerto in B flat for trumpet and violin, RV 548* (with I. Brown).
(B) *** EMI Red Line Dig. [CDR 569874].

Maurice André is peerless in this kind of repertoire and the accompaniments under Marriner are attractively alert and stylish. The Academy provides expert soloists to match André on the concertante works by Telemann (in D) and Vivaldi (RV 548) which come together towards the end and offer much the most interesting invention. The concerto by Stölzel is conventional, but has a fine slow movement. Throughout, André's smooth, rich timbre and highly musical phrasing give pleasure. The recording is first class, with the CD adding extra definition and presence. Now reissued on Angel's bargain Red Line label this collection is currently withdrawn in the UK.

Music for trumpet and organ (with Jane Parker-Smith or Alfred Mitterhofer): CHARPENTIER: *Te Deum: Fanfare.* ALBINONI: *Adagio* (arr. Giazotto). BACH: *Violin Partita in E: Gavotte & Rondeau. Orchestral suite No. 3: Air. Cello suite No. 4: Bourrée. Cantata No. 147: Chorale: Jesu joy of man's desiring.* CLARKE: *Trumpet voluntary.* SENAILLE: *Allegro spiritoso.* STANLEY: *Trumpet tune.* BACH/GOUNOD: *Ave Maria.* MOZART: *Exsultate jubilate: Alleluja.* PURCELL: *The Queen's dolour* (aria). Music for trumpet and orchestra: HANDEL: *Concerto in D min.* (arr. Thilde from *Flute sonata in B min.*). ALBINONI: *Concertos: in B flat and D, Op. 7/3 & 6* (arr. of *Oboe concertos*). TELEMANN: *Concerto in D for trumpet and oboe* (all with ECO, Mackerras). HERTEL: *Concerto in E flat.* HAYDN: *Concerto in E flat.* TELEMANN: *Concerto in F min.* (arr. of *Oboe concerto*). ALBINONI: *Concerto in D min.* (arr. of *Chamber sonata for violin and continuo, Op. 6/4*). Alessandro MARCELLO: *Concerto in C* (originally for oboe) (all with LPO, Jesús López-Cobos).
(B) *** EMI Double fforte CZS5 73374-2 (2) [id.].

Both these discs open with a series of famous tunes arranged for trumpet and organ, which for baroque repertoire works well enough. Played with rich tone, cultured phrasing, and when needed, dazzling bravura, they are sumptuously presented, if you don't mind an excess of resonance. The programme opens with a larger-than-life account of the famous Charpentier *Te Deum*, and includes Clarke's famous *Voluntary* and the comparable trumpet piece by Stanley.

But otherwise the repertoire ranges wide, encompassing music originally written for other, very different instruments. These include pieces by Bach for solo violin and cello, by Albinoni and others for oboe, a famous bassoon encore by Senaillé and even (in the case of Mozart) a display-piece for the soprano voice. But André's presentation is so assured that one could be forgiven at times for thinking that they were actually conceived for the trumpet. Indeed the Bach *Gavotte and Rondeau* are most attractive on the trumpet.

Much the same applies to the concertos. The first group, vivaciously conducted by Mackerras, includes an ingenious Handel concoction, which even brings a brief reminder of the *Water music*, and the Telemann multiple concerto is also very diverting. Then André negotiates the Hertel concerto, with its high tessitura, with breathtaking ease.

The second group, also given lively accompaniments, by the LPO under López-Cobos, are particularly successful, with the famous Haydn concerto most elegantly played, and in the transcriptions of works by Albinoni and Marcello slow movements are warmly phrased and André's stylishness and easy execution ensure the listener's enjoyment. Throughout, the analogue recording from the mid to late 1970s is of high quality and very well transferred to CD. It is a pity that room was not found for the Hummel concerto, but this is undoubtedly excellent value.

Argerich, Martha (piano) with other artists

Martha Argerich Collection.
(M) **(*) DG Analogue/Dig. 453 566-2 (11) [id.].

Volume I: *Concertos:* BEETHOVEN: *Piano concertos Nos. 1 in C, Op. 15; 2 in B flat, Op. 19* (with Philh. O, Sinopoli). CHOPIN: *Piano concertos Nos. 1 in E min., Op. 11* (with LSO, Abbado); *2 in F min., Op. 21.* SCHUMANN: *Piano concerto in A min., Op. 54* (both with Nat. SO, Rostropovich). TCHAIKOVSKY: *Piano concerto No. 1 in B flat min., Op. 23* (with RPO, Dutoit). LISZT: *Piano concerto No. 1 in E flat* (with LSO). PROKOFIEV: *Piano concerto No. 3 in C, Op. 26.* RAVEL: *Piano concerto in G* (with BPO) (both cond. Abbado).
(M) **(*) DG Analogue/Dig. 453 567-2 (4) [id.].

The chimerical volatility of Martha Argerich's musical personality comes out again and again in this impressive survey of her recorded repertory. Her ability in concertos to strike sparks in a musical partnership with the right conductor (Giuseppe Sinopoli in Beethoven and Abbado in Chopin's *First Concerto*) brings characteristically spontaneous music-making, bursting with inner life.

If Chopin's *F minor Concerto*, recorded ten years later in 1978, is rather less successful, she is back on form again in Tchaikovsky (with Dutoit), to produce a performance which has a genuine sense of scale and which balances poetry with excitement. Her temperament takes less readily to the Schumann *Concerto* (here with Rostropovich), a performance which has dynamism, vigour and colour, and delicacy in the slow movement, but which does not quite capture the work's more refined romantic feeling in the outer movements.

Yet her Liszt *E flat Concerto* is surprisingly restrained, gripping without any barnstorming. She is perhaps at her very finest in Prokofiev's *Third Concerto* and hardly less impressive in the Ravel *G major*, a performance full of subtlety, but vigorous and outgoing too. Abbado was again her partner in the three last-mentioned works and together they found a rare musical symbiosis. DG have generally given Argerich's concertos excellent recording, and there is nothing here which will not provide stimulating repeated listening. All these performances (except the Chopin *Second Concerto*) are discussed in greater depth under their composer entries in our main Volume.

Volume II: Chopin and Bach: CHOPIN: *Piano sonatas Nos. 2 in B flat min., Op. 35; 3 in B min., Op. 58; Barcarolle in F sharp, Op. 60; Scherzos Nos. 2 in B flat min., Op. 31; 3 in C sharp min., Op. 39; 24 Preludes, Op. 28; Preludes in C sharp min., Op. 45; in A flat, Op. posth.; Andante spianato & Grande polonaise brillante, Op. 22; Polonaise No. 6 in A flat, Op. 53; Polonaise-Fantaisie in A flat, Op. 61; 3 Mazurkas, Op. 59.* BACH: *Toccata in C min., BWV 911; Partita No. 2 in C min., BWV 826; English suite No. 2 in A min., BWV 807.*

(M) **(*) DG 453 572-2 (3) [id.].

Argerich's accounts of the two Chopin *Sonatas* are fiery, impetuous and brilliant, with no want of poetic vision to discommend them. Both, however, have a highly strung quality that will not be to all tastes. The *Preludes* show Argerich at her finest, full of individual insights. The *Scherzo No. 3* and *Barcarolle* are taken from her remarkable début LP recital of 1961 and are very impetuous indeed, and are also less easy to live with. She seems not to want to provide a firm musical control, but is carried away on a breath of wind. Many of the other pieces are played splendidly, with the *Scherzo No. 2* impressively demonstrating her technical command. Her Bach, too, is lively but well conceived. The digital remastering gives the piano-image striking presence, and the recording is resonant and full in timbre, although at fortissimo levels the timbre becomes hard.

Volume III: Music for piano solo and duo: SCHUMANN: *Kinderszenen, Op. 15; Kreisleriana, Op. 16; Piano sonata No. 2 in G min., Op. 22.* LISZT: *Piano sonata in B min.; Hungarian rhapsody No. 6.* BRAHMS: *Rhapsodies, Op. 79/1–2.* PROKOFIEV: *Toccata, Op. 11.* RAVEL: *Gaspard*

de la nuit; Jeux d'eau; Sonatine; Valses nobles et sentimentales. Ma Mère l'Oye; Rapsodie espagnole (arr. 2 pianos & percussion). BARTOK: *Sonata for 2 pianos & percussion* (with Freire, Sadlo, Guggeis). TCHAIKOVSKY: *Nutcracker suite, Op. 71a* (arr. 2 pianos). RACHMANINOV: *Symphonic dances for 2 pianos, Op. 45* (with Economou).

(M) **(*) DG Analogue/Dig. 453 576-2 (4) [id.].

The third box contains much of interest. There is no doubting the instinctive flair or her intuitive feeling for Schumann. However, she is let down by an unpleasingly close recording of *Kinderszenen* and *Kreisleriana*. Her Ravel again shows her playing at its most subtle and perceptive, yet with a vivid palette, even if at times a little more poise would be welcome. Taken from her début recital of 1961, the Brahms *First Rhapsody* is explosively fast; then suddenly she puts the brakes on and provides most poetic playing in the central section. Such a barnstorming approach is more readily at home in the Prokofiev *Toccata*, and she goes over the top in the Liszt *Hungarian rhapsody* with a certain panache.

In the Liszt *Sonata*, although the playing demonstrates an impressively responsive temperament, the work's lyrical feeling is all but submerged by the brilliantly impulsive virtuosity. The Ravel arrangements (with percussion!) are done with eminently good taste, restraint and musical imagination but, all the same, is there a need for them at all? They are more interesting to hear once or twice than to repeat.

The Bartók, though, has tremendous fire and intensity. The aural image is very good and discreetly balanced. The Tchaikovsky *Nutcracker* arrangement of Nicolas Economou works well. The playing is of a very high order. The Rachmaninov *Dances* are played with great temperament, and everything is marvellously alive and well thought out. There is much sensitivity and a lively sense of enjoyment in evidence, as well as great virtuosity. The recording is good.

'*Duo Piano Extravaganza*': MOZART: *Andante with 5 variations, K.501.* DEBUSSY: *En blanc et noir* (both with Stephen Kovacevich). BARTOK: *Sonata for 2 pianos and percussion* (with Kovacevich, Goudswaard, De Roo). RACHMANINOV: *Suite No. 2 for 2 pianos, Op. 17.* LUTOSLAWSKI: *Variations on a theme of Paganini.* RAVEL: *La valse* (all with Nelson Freire). BARTOK: *Concerto for 2 pianos and percussion* (with Freire, Labordus, Pustjens, Concg. O, Zinman). SAINT-SAENS: *Carnival of the animals* (with Freire, Kremer, Van Keulen, T. Zimmermann, Maisky, Hörtnagel, Grafenauer, Brunner, Steckeler & Salmen-Weber).

(B) *** Ph. (IMS) Duo Dig./Analogue 446 557-2 (2) [(M) id. import].

Mozart's charming *Andante and variations* is here taken at a rather brisker tempo than usual, but the playing of Argerich and Kovacevich is unfailingly sensitive and vital, and they are equally imaginative in Debussy's *En blanc et noir*, which comes from the last years of his life and is full of unexpected touches. Then, joined by Willy Goudswaard and Michel de Roo, they give a strongly atmospheric and finely characterized performance of Bartók's *Sonata for two pianos and percussion*.

At that point Argerich changes keyboard partners and, with Nelson Freire, two more percussionists and the Concertgebouw Orchestra under Zinman, offers us the *Concerto* which Bartók drew from his sonata. Comparing the two, one might wonder why a full orchestra was necessary, to add relatively little. Argerich and Freire continue with a dazzling virtuoso account of Rachmaninov's *Second Suite*, rushing the waltzes off their feet (the movement is marked presto, but they play it *prestissimo*).

Their virtuosity is further tested by Lutoslawski's *Variations* for piano duo (based wittily on that famous Paganini tune), dating from 1941, and they are not found wanting: the result is exhilarating. Their contribution concludes charismatically with Ravel's own transcription of *La valse*. The recital ends with an affectionate but distinctly eccentric account of Saint-Saëns' *Carnaval des animaux* presented in the composer's own original chamber version.

From the very beginning, pacing is deliberately slow, the approach essentially refined (but with the instrumentalists adding a few jocular individual comments), and the *Tortoises* nearly grind to a halt. The *Kangaroos*, however, are very light on their feet, the Aquarium ethereally transparent, the *Cuckoo in the woods* mistily atmospheric, and the *Birds* flit about daintily. The self-consciously clumsy *Pianists* bring us back to the human world, and after the *Fossils* have had their witty gamble the *Swan* glides in very gently and gracefully on Mischa Maisky's elegant cello. The finale springs to life with sparkling rhythmic pointing and dashing roulades from the piano duo. This is perhaps not a *Carnaval* for all seasons, but it is refreshingly different and, like the rest of this superb collection, it is very well recorded.

'Ballet gala', Sir Georg Solti

'Ballet gala' (with (i) ROHCG O; (ii) BPO; (iii) L. Symphony Ch., LSO; (iv) Israel PO): (i) PONCHIELLI: *La Gioconda: Dance of the hours*. GOUNOD: *Faust: ballet music*. OFFENBACH (arr. Rosenthal): *Gaîté parisienne ballet music*. GLUCK: *Orfeo ed Euridice: Dance of the Furies; Dance of the Blessed Spirits*. (ii) MUSSORGSKY: *Khovanshchina: Dance of the Persian slaves*. (iii) BORODIN: *Prince Igor: Polovtsian dances* (both

ed. Rimsky-Korsakov). (iv) ROSSINI–RESPIGHI: *La Boutique fantasque* (complete ballet).
(B) **(*) Decca Double 448 942-2 (2) [(M) id. import].

Scintillating performances of high polish and prodigious vitality, recorded with great brilliance, mostly in the late 1950s. At times one might feel that the strings are overlit, although there is glowing woodwind colour and plenty of ambience, even if the Israel recording of *La Boutique fantasque* is drier than the rest. Yet they play very well, the strings are on very good form indeed, there are moments of affectionate charm, and this is easy to enjoy.

The bright, intense Solti style suits the *Faust ballet music* less well (compared, say, with Beecham's affectionate coaxing) but the sparkle is in no doubt. Solti drives Offenbach's *Gaîté parisienne ballet music* hard, with strongly accented rhythms. But the Covent Garden Orchestra respond vivaciously (as they do in Ponchielli's *Dance of the hours*) and give a virtuoso performance: their bravura is certainly infectious, if sometimes a little breathless.

Solti seldom recorded with the Berlin Philharmonic, and this great orchestra seems to have had a slight softening effect on his vibrant musical nature: the sensuously sinuous playing in the Mussorgsky/Rimsky-Korsakov *Dance of the Persian slaves* is certainly seductive. This derives from a 1959 Berlin Philharmonic concert which is no longer available. The characterful Gluck dances come from the complete set of a decade later. Overall this programme is highly stimulating – Solti couldn't be dull even if he tried.

Baltimore Symphony Orchestra, David Zinman

'Russian sketches': GLINKA: *Overture: Ruslan and Ludmilla*. IPPOLITOV-IVANOV: *Caucasian sketches*. RIMSKY-KORSAKOV: *Russian Easter Festival overture*. TCHAIKOVSKY: *Francesca da Rimini, Op. 32. Eugene Onegin: Polonaise*.
**(*) Telarc Dig. CD 80378 [id.].

Opening with a fizzingly zestful performance of Glinka's *Ruslan and Ludmilla overture*, with impressively clean articulation from the violins, this remarkably well-recorded concert of Russian music readily demonstrates the excellence of the Baltimore Symphony in every department.

The *Caucasian sketches* are a disappointment, but only because Zinman's conception of the evocative first three movements (*In the Mountain Pass*, *In the Village* and *In the Mosque*) is too refined, not Russian enough in feeling; but the famous *Procession of the Sardar* has plenty of piquant colour and impetus. *Francesca da Rimini* brings the most brilliant playing and the middle section, with its rich, Tchaikovskian woodwind palette, is glowingly beautiful.

However, the impact of the closing pages here depends more on the spectacular Telarc engineering than on the conductor, who does not generate the necessary degree of passionate despair in the work's great climax. Rimsky-Korsakov's *Russian Easter Festival overture* is a different matter, generating considerable excitement. It is superbly done, with lustrous colours from every section of the orchestra and a memorable solo contribution from the trombones (who are also very impressive in *Francesca*). The recording here is very much in the demonstration bracket and shows Telarc engineering at its most realistic, thrilling in its breadth and body of orchestral tone, with excellent detail and a convincing presence in a natural concert-hall acoustic.

Bamberg Symphony Orchestra, Rudolf Kempe

'In memoriam': BRAHMS: *Symphony No. 2 in D, Op. 73*; *Variations on a theme of Haydn, Op. 56a*. SCHUBERT: *Symphony No. 8 (Unfinished)*. SMETANA: *Má Vlast: From Bohemia's woods and fields*. MOZART: *Serenade No. 13 (Eine kleine Nachtmusik), K.525*. BIZET: *L'Arlésienne: suites 1–2*.

(B) *** RCA 74321 32771-2 (2) [(M) id. import].

A first-class tribute to a fine conductor, with the single proviso that the Bamberg violins in this 1963 recording are made to seem a bit emaciated above the stave; otherwise the sound is full and nicely resonant. The Brahms *Second* is a splendidly alive reading with a strong lyrical impetus, and the *Variations* are comparably successful. But it is the electrifying account of Schubert's *Unfinished* that resonates in the memory, immensely dramatic, yet with the opening and close of the second movement radiantly beautiful in its contrasting repose. The shorter works all go well, the Bizet the least individual, but still played with affection and style.

Barbirolli, Sir John (cello) and conducting various orchestras

'Glorious John': Barbirolli centenary collection (1911–69): Disc 1: (1911–47): VAN BIENE: *The broken melody* (Barbirolli, cello). MOZART: *String quartet in E flat, K.428: Minuet* (with Kutcher Qt). MASCAGNI: *Cavalleria rusticana: Santuzza's aria* (with Lilian Stiles-Allen). VERDI: *Otello: Niun me tema* (with Renato Zanelli). PUCCINI: *Tosca: Tre sbirri, una carozza* (with Giovanni Inghilleri). Johann STRAUSS Jr: *Die Fledermaus: Brother dear and sister dear*. SAINT-SAENS: *Valse-caprice, Op. 76* (with Yvonne Arnaud,

piano). BALFE: *The Bohemian girl overture* (with Symphony Orchestra). COLLINS: *Overture*. WEINBERGER: *Christmas* (with New York Philharmonic Orchestra). WEBER: *Euryanthe overture*. DELIUS: *Walk to the Paradise Garden* (with Vienna Philharmonic Orchestra).

Disc 2: (1948–64) (all with Hallé Orchestra): STRAVINSKY: *Concerto in D*. MOZART: *Cassation in G, K.63: Andante*; *Divertimento No. 11 in D, K.251: Minuet*. GRIEG, arr. Barbirolli: *Secret*. VILLA-LOBOS: *Bachianas brasileiras No. 4*. FALLA: *Seguidilla murciana* (with Marina de Gabarain). LEHAR: *Gold and silver waltz*. BACH, arr. Barbirolli: *Sheep may safely graze*. BERLIOZ: *Damnation of Faust*: rehearsal sequence. Interview: Barbirolli and R. Kinloch Anderson.

(B) (***) Dutton mono/stereo CDSJB 1999 (2) [id.].

It was Vaughan Williams who referred to Barbirolli as 'Glorious John', hence the title of this budget-priced compilation to celebrate the great conductor's centenary: twenty historic items, five of them previously unpublished, plus a rehearsal sequence and an interview full of reminiscences. From 1911 you have the eleven-year-old Giovanni Barbirolli playing the cello, swoopy but perfect in intonation.

As a budding conductor he accompanies star soloists, including Yvonne Arnaud in Saint-Saëns's charming *Valse-caprice*, while items from his underprized New York period include a delightful Weinberger piece, otherwise unavailable, *Christmas*. Also unexpected is Barbirolli's pioneering account with the Hallé of Stravinsky's *Concerto in D*, recorded in 1948, two years after the work first appeared. And how revealing to have the Vienna Philharmonic heartfelt in Delius's *Walk to the Paradise Garden!*

The rehearsal of the *Dance of the Sylphs* dates from 1957, and in many ways most endearing of all is the 1964 conversation between the gravel-voiced Barbirolli and his recording producer Roland Kinloch Anderson, covering such subjects as Mahler, the Berlin Philharmonic and Elgar – a splendid portrait.

'Portrait': DEBUSSY: *La mer* (with Orchestre de Paris). BRAHMS: *Variations on a theme of Haydn, Op. 56a* (with Vienna Philharmonic Orchestra). MAHLER: *Lieder eines fahrenden Gesellen* (with Dame Janet Baker). TCHAIKOVSKY: *Romeo and Juliet (fantasy overture)*. DVORAK: *Serenade for wind in D min., Op. 44*. BRAHMS: *Double concerto for violin, cello and orchestra, Op. 102*: 1st movt only (with Campoli & Navarra). BERLIOZ: *Symphonie fantastique: Scène aux champs* (all with Hallé Orchestra).

(BB) ** Royal Long Players DCL 705902 (2).

This 'Portrait' may not always show Barbirolli at

his finest, but is worth considering if only for the *Variations on a theme of Haydn* (the finest of the Brahms recordings he made with the VPO in the late 1960s) and his understandingly spontaneous partnership with Dame Janet Baker in the Mahler song cycle (dating from the same period). His *La Mer* suggests a southern climate, and shows a strong feeling for atmosphere, but there is some lack of inner tension in the playing of the Orchestre de Paris. However, the Hallé are ardent enough in the Tchaikovsky and the wind players are in good form in the Dvořák *Serenade*, which has plenty of charm. The documentation does not make it clear that only the first movement is included of the Brahms *Double concerto*. However, we understand that later copies of this set will include the complete work, so do check before purchase.

Barenboim, Daniel (conductor and pianist)

'*Portrait*': FAURE: *Requiem, Op. 48*; *Pavane, Op. 50* (with Sheila Armstrong, Dietrich Fischer-Dieskau, Edinburgh Fest. Ch.). BIZET: *L'Arlésienne suite No. 1* (both with Orchestre de Paris). DVORAK: *Serenade for strings, Op. 22.* MOZART: *Symphony No. 41 in C (Jupiter), K.551* (both with ECO). BEETHOVEN: *Piano sonata No. 14 (Moonlight), Op. 27/2.*

(BB) *** Royal Long Players DCL 705942 (2).

A well-rounded 'Portrait' of a fine artist, heard as both conductor and pianist at the peak of his career in the late 1960s and early 1970s. The performances of the Fauré *Requiem* and a warmly luminous account of the *Pavane* with chorus, underline the music's expressive beauty, yet with flowing tempi both sound admirably spontaneous. The first *L'Arlesiénne suite*, also with the Orchestre de Paris, is similarly vivid and affectionate, although here the sound is over-resonant, yet, as with the Fauré, it is of EMI's best analogue quality.

In the Dvořák *Serenade* the eloquence of the ECO playing is in no doubt, though one or two details are underlined with rather more expressive emphasis than necessary. The recording is open and fresh. In Mozart's last and greatest symphony Barenboim rightly focuses attention on the finale, observing the second-half repeat as well as the first, to give Mozart's complex fugal design a majesty comparable only with Beethoven, and that at a brisk, swashbuckling tempo. The rest of the symphony is interpreted with similar flair. Turning to the keyboard, Barenboim shows equal compulsion in the most famous of Beethoven's named sonatas, sustaining a natural intensity that holds the listener throughout. Once again he is most truthfully recorded.

Baroque music

'*Music of the Baroque*' (played by: (i) Orpheus CO; (ii) Simon Standage; (iii) David Reichenberg; (iv) Trevor Pinnock (harpsichord); (v) English Concert Ch.; (vi) English Concert, Trevor Pinnock; (vii) Söllscher (guitar), Camerata Bern, Füri; (viii) Hannes, Wolfgang & Bernhard Läubin, Simon Preston, Norbert Schmitt): (i) HANDEL: *Solomon: Arrival of the Queen of Sheba.* (vi) *Water music: Allegro – Andante*; *Air*; *Bourrée*; *Hornpipe.* (i) *Xerxes: Largo.* (v, vi) *Messiah: Hallelujah chorus.* (vi) *Music for the royal fireworks: La Réjouissance.* (iii; iv; vi) *Oboe concerto No. 1 (Adagio*; *Allegro).* (vi) *Concerto grosso, Op. 6/12 in B min. (Aria*; *Larghetto e piano).* (i) PACHELBEL: *Canon in D.* (viii) MOURET: *Rondeau.* J. S. BACH: (i) *Jesu, joy of man's desiring.* (vi) *Brandenburg concerto No. 3 in G (Allegro).* PURCELL: *Sound the trumpet, sound.* (ii; vi) VIVALDI: *The Four seasons: Winter (Largo).* (vii) *Lute concerto in D (Largo).* (i) ALBINONI: (arr. GIAZOTTO): *Adagio in G min.* CORELLI: *Christmas concerto, Op. 6/8 (Allegro*; *Pastorale*; *Largo).* (iv) DAQUIN: *Le Coucou.*

(B) *** DG Classikon Dig. 449 842-2 [(M) id. import].

This 75-minute concert draws on various digital recordings made during the 1980s to make a most agreeable entertainment. The various items have all been issued previously, and their performance pedigrees, on either modern or original instruments, cannot be gainsaid. The opening *Arrival of the Queen of Sheba* and the elegantly played Pachelbel *Canon* feature the Orpheus Chamber Orchestra, but Pinnock's suite from the Handel *Water music* is equally persuasive in demonstrating the advantages of period instruments in baroque repertoire. Such contrasts are aurally stimulating and, with plenty of favourite items included, this makes a very successful bargain sampler, when all the music is consistently well played and recorded. However, the lack of proper documentation is a drawback: the two excellent vocal soloists in Purcell's *Sound the trumpet* are unnamed.

BBC Concert Orchestra, Vernon Handley

'*The essential British light music*': GOODWIN: *633 Squadron* (film theme). ELLIS: *Coronation Scot.* FARNON: *Westminster waltz*; *Jumping bean.* COATES: *London suite: Knightsbridge march*; *Covent Garden. By the sleepy lagoon. Dam Busters march.* ANCLIFFE: *Nights of gladness* (waltz). HOPE: *Mexican hat dance.* BINGE: *Sailing by*; *Elizabethan serenade.* Haydn WOOD: *The*

Horse Guards, Whitehall. DUNCAN: *Little suite: March.* BENJAMIN: *Jamaican rumba.* TOMLINSON: *Concert jig.* WHITE: *Puffin' Billy.* COLLINS: *Vanity Fair.* BUCALOSSI: *Grasshopper's dance.* Arthur WOOD: *Barwick Green.*

(M) *** Classic fM Dig. 76505 57003-2 [id.].

There are now many nostalgic CD collections of these delightfully tuneful musical lollipops, many associated with radio or TV programmes as signature tunes, but none better than this. Ernest Bucalossi's *Grasshopper's dance,* for instance, a novelty number from a bygone age, now unexpectedly conjures up dancing milk-bottles in a TV commercial. Vernon Handley conducts everything with zest. Indeed, some might feel that his pacing of Ron Goodwin's *633 Squadron* title-sequence (perhaps the most memorable horn-theme since Richard Strauss) is a fraction too fast; yet it is thrilling when played with such panache.

However, Robert Farnon's *Westminster waltz* brings a relaxed charm, and Peter Hope's *Mexican hat dance* has an oboe interlude as its centrepiece, played most delectably here. Handley presents Ronald Binge's *Sailing by* with seductive languor, while the *Elizabethan serenade* has winning delicacy, as has Anthony Collins's *Vanity Fair.* Arthur Wood's *Barwick Green,* indelibly associated with 'The Archers', begins with an introductory fanfare and is re-scored for woodwind. The middle section is omitted, and not all will respond to this new arrangement. The Eric Coates marches are perhaps most famous of all. Handley's alert vigour (particularly in the *Dam Busters*) is infectious, yet his vivacity doesn't prevent him from a grand broadening for the final presentation of the big tune at the close.

BBC Philharmonic Orchestra, Matthias Bamert

'Stokowski encores': HANDEL: *Overture in D min.* GABRIELI: *Sonata piano e forte.* CLARKE: *Trumpet Prelude.* MATTHESON: *Air.* MOZART: *Rondo alla turca.* BEETHOVEN: *Adagio from Moonlight sonata.* SCHUBERT: *Serenade.* FRANCK: *Panis Angelicus.* CHOPIN: *Funeral march.* DEBUSSY: *The Girl with the flaxen hair.* IPPOLITOV-IVANOV: *In the manger.* SHOSTAKOVICH: *United Nations march.* TCHAIKOVSKY: *Andante cantabile.* ALBENIZ: *Festival in Seville.* SOUSA: *The Stars and Stripes forever.* (all arr. Leopold Stokowski).
*** Chandos Dig. CHAN 9349 [id.].

However outrageous it may seem to take a tiny harpsichord piece by a contemporary of Bach and Handel, Johann Mattheson, and inflate it on full strings, the result caresses the ear, and the Chandos engineers come up with recording to match. Amazingly, Mozart's *Rondo alla turca* becomes a sparkling moto perpetuo, Paganini-like, with Stokowski following Mozart himself in using 'Turkish' percussion, *Entführung*-style.

The opening *Adagio* of Beethoven's *Moonlight sonata* with lush orchestration then echoes Rachmaninov's *Isle of the Dead,* with menace in the music. Stokowski's arrangement of the Handel *Overture in D minor* (taken from the *Chandos anthem No. 2*) is quite different from Elgar's transcription of the same piece, opulent in a different way, with timbres antiphonally contrasted.

If Bamert cannot match the panache of Stokowski in the final Sousa march, *The Stars and Stripes forever,* that is in part due to the recording balance, which fails to bring out the percussion, including xylophone. The least attractive item is Schubert's *Serenade,* given full Hollywood treatment not just with soupy strings but with quadruple woodwind trilling above. Hollywood treatment of a different kind comes in the *United Nations march* of Shostakovich, in 1942 used as the victory finale of an MGM wartime musical, *Thousands Cheer.* Stokowski promptly cashed in with his own, non-vocal arrangement. A disc for anyone who likes to wallow in opulent sound.

BBC Philharmonic Orchestra, Yan Pascal Tortelier

'French bonbons': Overtures: ADAM: *Si j'étais roi.* AUBER: *Le cheval de bronze* (The bronze horse). HEROLD: *Zampa.* MAILLART: *Les dragons de Villars.* THOMAS: *Mignon: Gavotte.* OFFENBACH: *La Belle Hélène* (arr. Haensch); *Contes d'Hoffmann: Entr'acte & Barcarolle.* CHABRIER: *Habanera; Joyeuse marche.* GOUNOD: *Marche funèbre d'une marionette.* MASSENET: *Thaïs: Méditation* (with Yuri Torchinsky, violin; both with Royal Liverpool PO Choir). *Mélodie: Elégie* (with Peter Dixon, cello); *Les erinnes: Tristesse du soir. La Vierge: Le dernier sommeil de la Vierge.*
✹ *** Chandos Dig. CHAN 9765 [id.].

As Sir Thomas Beecham well knew there is something special about French orchestral lollipops and this is a superb collection, beautifully played and given demonstration standard recording – just sample the brass evocation of Maillart's Dragoons, and in *La Belle Hélène,* which is played with much warmth and style. Gounod's whimsical *Funeral march of a marionette,* which Hitchcock has made famous, is delightfully done, and the other bandstand overtures have plenty of sparkle and zest, yet are not driven too hard – the galop which climaxes *The bronze horse* is exhilaratingly jaunty. Highly recommended.

BBC Symphony Orchestra, Sir Adrian Boult

'Boult's BBC years': BEETHOVEN: *Symphony No. 8 in F, Op. 93.* HUMPERDINCK: *Overture Hansel and Gretel.* TCHAIKOVSKY: *Capriccio italien, Op. 45; Serenade for strings, Op. 48.*
(***) Beulah mono 1PD12 [id.].

These recordings return to the catalogue for the first time since the days of shellac and will almost certainly be new to the majority of younger collectors. The Beethoven is a strong, sturdy performance which gives a good idea of the excellence of the BBC Symphony Orchestra in the early days of its existence. It comes from 1932 and the strings produce an opulent, weighty sound without having the opaque quality they developed in the post-war years. The recording is not at all bad for the period, and the transfer does it justice. The Tchaikovsky *Serenade* was recorded five years later in the same Abbey Road studio but with the acoustic sounding much drier. A patrician account with no nonsense about it that may since have been surpassed by many other great partnerships but which will give pleasure to those old enough to remember Sir Adrian's pre-war and wartime broadcasts. The Colston Hall, Bristol, in which the orchestra recorded the *Capriccio italien* in 1940, has the richer acoustic, and the performance combines dignity and freshness.

Belgian Radio & TV Philharmonic Orchestra, Brussels, Alexander Rahbari

Romantic symphonic music from Antwerp: MORTELMANS: *Spring idyll.* ALPAERTS: *Pallieter: Wedding feast.* VAN HOOF: *1st Symphonic suite.* BLOCKX: *Milenka: Flemish Fair.* STERNFIELD: *Song and dance at the court of Mary from Burgundy.*
(BB) ** Koch/Discover Dig. DICD 920100 [id.].

Flemish rhapsodies: BRUSSELMANS: *Flemish rhapsody.* SCHOEMAKER: *Flemish rhapsody.* DE JONG: *Flemish rhapsody.* ABSILL: *Flemish rhapsody.* ROUSSEL: *Flemish rhapsody.* DE BOECK: *Flemish rhapsody.*
(BB) **(*) Koch/Discover DICD 920101 [id.].

This is all unknown repertoire – easy-going late nineteenth- or twentieth-century music from Belgium. On the first CD, Mortelmans' *Spring idyll* is lyrically appealing but perhaps a shade extended for its thematic content, the Jef Van Hoof and Jan Blockx *suites* agreeably inventive but innocuous. By far the most attractive music comes in the suite of *Song and dance from Burgundy*, nicely scored

and piquantly harmonized dances by Susato and his sixteenth-century contemporaries, somewhat comparable with Respighi's *Ancient airs and dances.*

The *Flemish rhapsodies* all use folk material very effectively, although Brusselmans employs themes of his own invention, written in folk style. All these works are colourfully orchestrated and make agreeable listening, using jolly tunes which in flavour are often like Christmas carols. By far the most striking is the work by the Frenchman Albert Roussel, which has a characteristic touch of harmonic astringency to tickle the ear. The playing of the Brussels orchestra under Rahbari is enthusiastic yet does not lack finesse, and the recording has an attractive concert-hall ambience and balance. It is not always too sharply defined in some of the more elaborately scored climaxes of the rhapsodies, but the effect is natural. The documentation is excellent.

Berlin Philharmonic Orchestra, Herbert von Karajan

'Meditation' (Overtures and Intermezzi): J. STRAUSS Jr: *Der Zigeunerbaron overture.* MASSENET: *Thaïs: Méditation* (with Anne-Sophie Mutter). CHERUBINI: *Anacréon overture.* WEBER: *Der Freischütz overture.* SCHMIDT: *Notre Dame: Intermezzo.* PUCCINI: *Intermezzi: Suor Angelica; Manon Lescaut.* MASCAGNI: *L'amico Fritz: Intermezzo.* HUMPERDINCK: *Hansel and Gretel overture.* MENDELSSOHN: *Hebrides overture (Fingal's Cave), Op. 26.*
(M) *(*) EMI Dig./Analogue CDM7 64629-2.

A curiously planned if generous (78 minutes) programme, deriving from three different sources. It opens with a rather weighty analogue account of Strauss's *Zigeunerbaron overture*, then moves on to the digital items, first the *Méditation* from *Thaïs* (with Anne-Sophie Mutter a gently restrained soloist), immediately followed by the *Anacréon overture*, with textures reminiscent of plum pudding. The Weber and Humperdinck overtures, too, are disappointing, the first lacking electricity, the second charm. The *Intermezzi* are much more successful, played very passionately and sumptuously, with the ample recording providing somewhat overnourished string-textures with a touch of grit in the treble. The best piece by far is the closing *Hebrides overture*, recorded much earlier (in 1960) and beautifully managed.

CHOPIN: *Les Sylphides* (orch. Roy Douglas). DELIBES: *Coppélia: ballet suite.* GOUNOD: *Faust: ballet music and Waltz.* OFFENBACH: *Gaîté parisienne* (ballet, arr. ROSENTHAL): extended excerpts. TCHAIKOVSKY: *Sleeping Beauty: suite.* PONCHIELLI: *La Gioconda: Dance of the hours.*
🅑 *** DG 459 445-2 (2) [id.].

This scintillating collection of ballet music is superbly played, and every item shows Karajan and his great orchestra at their finest. The very beautiful performance of Roy Douglas's exquisite arrangement of *Les Sylphides* – with its ravishing string playing, and glowingly delicate woodwind solos – has never been matched on record. It is also available on a single bargain disc together with the exhilaratingly racy *Gaîté parisienne* selection (which includes most of the ballet), and the *Coppélia suite*; but the latter is cut.

The missing movements are restored here and sound marvellous, as does the vivacious *Faust ballet music* and *Waltz*, the latter played with irresistible panache. Another riveting moment comes in the thrilling crescendo at the climax of the *Introduction* to the *Sleeping Beauty ballet suite*, yet there is much elegance and delicacy of colour to follow. The closing *Dance of the hours* – so affectionately phrased – also sparkles as do few other recorded performances, and throughout, these excellent CD transfers demonstrate DG's finest analogue quality from the 1960s and 1970s.

Boskovsky Ensemble, Willi Boskovsky

'Viennese bonbons': J. STRAUSS Sr: *Chinese galop; Kettenbrücke Waltz; Eisele und Beisele Sprünge; Cachucha galop.* J. STRAUSS Jr: *Weine Gemüths waltz; Champagne galop; Salon polka.* LANNER: *Styrian dances; Die Werber & Marien waltzes; Bruder halt galop.* MOZART: *3 Contredanses, K.462; 4 German dances, K.600/1 & 3; K.605/1; K.611.* SCHUBERT: *8 Waltzes & Ländler.*

(M) *** Van. 8.8015.71 [OVC 8015].

This is a captivating selection of the most delightful musical confectionery imaginable. The ensemble is a small chamber group, similar to that led by the Strausses, and the playing has an appropriately intimate Viennese atmosphere. The transfer is impeccable and the recording from the early 1960s, made in the Baumgarten Hall, Vienna, is fresh, smooth and clear, with a nice bloom on sound which is never too inflated.

Boston Pops Orchestra, Arthur Fiedler

'Fiedler encores': SIBELIUS: *Finlandia.* GRIEG: *Peer Gynt suite No. 1; Suite No. 2: Solveig's song.* DVORAK: *Slavonic dance, Op. 46/1.* SMETANA: *Má Vlast: Vltava.* VAUGHAN WILLIAMS: *English folksongs suite.* IVES: *Variations on 'America'.*

(M) **(*) Decca Phase Four 448 952-2 [id.].

These recordings derive from a pair of LPs originally published in 1975 and 1978. The 1975 performance of the *Peer Gynt* excerpts is direct, alive and spontaneous. It is recorded with exceptional life and vividness and is very enjoyable indeed. There are more tender accounts of *Solveig's song* available, but that is the only reservation.

The other items make a characteristically lively concert. Fiedler always keeps the pot boiling, even if his balance of the various ingredients lacks subtlety at times. The outer movements of the *English folksongs suite* come off with robust vigour, and he gives a splendidly rumbustious account of Ives's *Variations on 'America'*. The overall balance is forward, which precludes wide dynamic contrasts but ensures good projection and detail if not the last degree of refinement.

GADE: *Jalousie.* KETELBEY: *In a Persian market.* FALLA: *Ritual fire dance.* SOUSA: *The stars and stripes forever.* WALDTEUFEL: *The Skaters' waltz.* MENDELSSOHN: *Midsummer's night dream: Scherzo. Athelie: War march of the priests.* LISZT: *Liebestraum* (orch. V. HERBERT). CHABRIER: *España.* SIBELIUS: *Karelia suite: Alla marcia.* TCHAIKOVSKY: *Eugene Onegin: Polonaise.* RIMSKY-KORSAKOV: *Flight of the bumble bee.* WAGNER: *Ride of the Valkyries.*

(M) ** RCA 09026 63304-2 [id.].

Fiedler's Boston Pops recording of Gade's *Jealousy*, was a huge hit when it first appeared (making Koussevitzky jealous of his second-in-command's great commercial success). Here it begins a selection of famous showpieces, all played with vigour, if not always perfection in execution (the strings in the opening of the *Skaters' waltz* have the odd glitch). The 1958 recording is good for the period: the programme is all enjoyable, but not electrifying.

'Slaughter on 10th Avenue': RODGERS: *On Your Toes: Slaughter on 10th Avenue.* GOULD: *Interplay (Gavotte; Blues).* BERNSTEIN: *Fancy free (Galop; Waltz; Danzon).* FALLA: *Three-cornered hat: 3 Dances.* SHOSTAKOVICH: *Age of Gold: Polka.* COPLAND: *Rodeo: Hoe-down.* GINASTERA: *Estancia: Malambo.* KHACHATURIAN: *Gayaneh: Sabre dance.*

(M) **(*) RCA 09026 68550-2 [id.].

Fiedler and his players give a superb account of Rodgers's miniature ballet *Slaughter on 10th Avenue*, which, with its sound effects (pistol-shots and police whistle), is integrated into the plot of the musical from which it is derived. Within its brief compass it has a trio of good tunes, and Fiedler makes a splendid climax out of the bouncing syncopated theme which is the most memorable of the three. The rest of the programme is well devised and the performances are equally lively, particularly the colourful dances from Falla's *The Three-cornered hat*, although some might find that Ginastera's *Malambo* repeats its slender musical idea once too often. The bright-eyed recording, with its backing Symphony Hall ambience, comes up well in the new 'Living Stereo' transfer.

Boston Symphony Orchestra, Serge Koussevitzky

COPLAND: *El salón México*. FOOTE: *Suite in E min., Op. 63*. HARRIS: *Symphony (1933)*; *Symphony No. 3*. MCDONALD: *San Juan Capistrano – Two Evening Pictures*.
(M) (***) Pearl mono GEMMCD 9492.

Koussevitzky's performance of the Roy Harris *Third Symphony* has never been equalled in intensity and fire – even by Toscanini or Bernstein – and Copland himself never produced as exhilarating an *El salón México*. The Arthur Foote *Suite* is unpretentious and has great charm. Sonic limitations are soon forgotten, for these performances have exceptional power and should not be missed.

Boston Symphony Orchestra, Charles Munch

'The French touch': DUKAS: *L'apprenti sorcier*. SAINT-SAENS: *Omphale's spinning wheel, Op. 31*. RAVEL: *Ma Mère l'Oye: suite*. FRANCK: *Le chasseur maudit*.
(M) ** RCA 09026 68978-2 [id.].

This 'Living Stereo' reissue invites a certain nostalgia as (originally offered without the César Franck symphonic poem) it was discussed by us in our very first 1960 hardback *Stereo Record Guide*. The rather fetching LP sleeve design is effectively reused for the front of the CD. We quote our original review: 'There is both beautiful and brilliant, even virtuoso playing from the orchestra, yet in much of the music the conductor's approach seems insensitive and tired. *The Sorcerer's apprentice* is played with élan, yet somehow it does not quite catch fire. *Omphale's spinning wheel* is begun brashly; again the actual orchestral playing has a sureness of touch, and only in the central section does the conductor communicate any enjoyment of his own.

Mother Goose comes off best. The translucent quality of the recording gives such a pure and lovely sound to the orchestral texture that Ravel's beautiful music cannot fail to make an effect.' We thought also that Munch seemed caught up in its shimmering radiance and praised the exquisite tone of the muted strings here (and in *Omphale*). The recording from the late 1950s, which catches the Boston Hall acoustic impressively enough, also adds a touch of harshness to fortissimos, noticeable also in the exciting *Le chasseur maudit*. This was recorded later (1962). Munch seems in his element here and this makes an advantageous bonus.

Boult, Sir Adrian

'Portrait' (with LPO or New Philharmonia Orchestra): WAGNER: *Overtures: Die Meistersinger; Der fliegende Holländer. Götterdämmerung: Siegfried's funeral march. Die Walküre: Ride of the Valkyries.* BACH: *Brandenburg concertos Nos. 3 & 4. BWV 1048–9.* BRAHMS: *Tragic overture, Op. 81.* ELGAR: *Serenade for strings, Op. 20.* MOZART: *Piano concerto No. 24 in C min., K.491* (with André Previn and LSO). VAUGHAN WILLIAMS: *Fantasia on a theme by Thomas Tallis*.
(BB) **(*) Royal Long Players DCL 705952 (2).

Sir Adrian's 'Portrait' is especially valuable in reminding us of his range, when present-day catalogue listings concentrate on his recordings of English music. Of course in this repertoire he is uniquely idiomatic, as the present LPO performances of the Elgar *Serenade* (warmly nostalgic) and the Vaughan Williams *Tallis fantasia* (refined in its contrasts and yet richly passionate in a very English way) readily demonstrate.

But Boult was a distinguished Brahmsian too – witness the powerful account of the *Tragic overture*, and his distinctive Bach *Brandenburgs* use a full orchestra yet draw simultaneously on both older and more authentic styles. The *Third* is endearingly richly upholstered. As an accompanist he was perhaps more variable: in this recording of Mozart's great *C minor Concerto* he seems to discipline the performance a degree too much. One suspects that Previn alone would have produced more sparkle. But this is still fine Mozart playing, if a little cool. His Wagner too is uneven. The *Valkyries* ride in with real spirit, but *Siegfried's funeral march* has not the breadth and power that some conductors find. The two overtures are more successful, especially the nobly spacious account of *Die Meistersinger*.

Bournemouth Sinfonietta, Richard Studt

English string music: BRITTEN: *Variations on a theme of Frank Bridge, Op. 10*. HOLST: *St Paul's suite, Op. 29/1*. DELIUS: *2 Aquarelles*. VAUGHAN WILLIAMS: *5 Variants of Dives and Lazarus*. WARLOCK: *Capriol suite*.
(BB) *** Naxos Dig. 8.550823 [id.].

This is the finest of the concerts of string music recorded for Naxos by Richard Studt and the excellent Bournemouth Sinfonietta. The Britten *Frank Bridge variations* is particularly memorable, showing easy virtuosity yet often achieving the lightest touch, so that the Vienna waltz movement sparkles in its delicacy. The *Funeral march* may not be so desperately intense as Karajan's famous mono version with the Philharmonia, but it is still very touching; and the following *Chant* is ethereal in its bleakly refined atmosphere.

The sprightly Holst *St Paul's suite* and Warlock's *Capriol*, agreeably robust, could hardly be better played, while Vaughan Williams's *Dives and Lazarus* is especially fresh and conveys the famous biblical story of the rich man and the beggar most evocatively, especially in the very beautiful closing section, when Lazarus finds himself in heaven. The recording, made in St Peter's Church, Parkstone, is full-bodied, immediate and real – very much in the demonstration bracket.

20th-century string music: BARTOK: *Divertimento*. BRITTEN: *Simple Symphony, Op. 4*. WALTON: *2 Pieces from Henry V: Death of Falstaff (Passacaglia); Touch her soft lips and part*. STRAVINSKY: *Concerto in D*.
(BB) ** Naxos Dig. 8.550979 [id.].

This is the least successful of the three concerts of string music recorded by Naxos in Bournemouth. The Sinfonietta players do not sound completely at ease in the shifting moods of the Bartók *Divertimento* and their ensemble could be crisper in the Stravinsky *Concerto*. The *Simple Symphony* comes off brightly, with a gently nostalgic *Sentimental sarabande* and a brisk, alert finale, but the *Playful pizzicato* could be more exuberant, especially in its famous trio which the composer wrote so joyously. The two Walton pieces are warmly atmospheric, and there are no complaints about the sound.

Scandinavian string music: GRIEG: *Holberg suite*. Dag WIREN: *Serenade, Op. 11*. SVENDSEN: *2 Icelandic melodies; Norwegian folksong; 2 Swedish folksongs, Op. 27*. NIELSEN: *Little suite in A min., Op. 1*.
(BB) *** Naxos Dig. 8.553106 [id.].

The liltingly spontaneous account of the Dag Wirén *Serenade* ensures a welcome for this enjoyable collection of Scandinavian music. The performance of Grieg's perennially fresh *Holberg* suite is hardly less successful in its combination of energy and polish, folksy charm and touching serenity in the famous *Air*. Nielsen's *Little suite* also has plenty of style and impetus, the changing moods of the finale neatly encompassed. The Svendsen folksong arrangements belong to the 1870s. The two *Icelandic melodies* are melodically robust but the *Norwegian folksong* is gentler and quite lovely. Yet it is the second of the two *Swedish folksongs* that most reminds the listener of Grieg. All are played with a natural expressive feeling, and the recording, made in the Winter Gardens, Bournemouth, has a fine, full sonority to balance its natural brilliance.

Bournemouth Symphony Orchestra, Constantin Silvestri

TCHAIKOVSKY: *1812 overture* (with Band of Royal Marines); *Capriccio italien, Op. 45*; *Eugene Onegin: Polonaise*. SIBELIUS: *Finlandia, Op. 26*. SAINT-SAENS: *Danse macabre*. DUKAS: *L'apprenti sorcier*. RAVEL: *Pavane pour une infante défunte*. RIMSKY-KORSAKOV: *Scheherazade, Op. 35*. MUSSORGSKY (arr. Rimsky-Korsakov): *Night on the bare mountain*. BORODIN: *In the Steppes of Central Asia*.
(BB) **(*) Royal Long Players DCL 705882 (2).

Just as Marriner's name is synonymous with the Academy of St-Martin-in-the-Fields and Previn's key 1970 recordings are indelibly associated with the LSO, so Silvestri's name is usually coupled with that of the Bournemouth Symphony, which in the mid to late 1960s he turned into one of England's crack orchestras. The EMI programme takes this well into account, for most of the programme (including the Tchaikovsky items) is made up of show-pieces which – brilliantly played – were recorded in the hi-fi conscious Studio Two system, where the treble response was highlighted. The result is sometimes to rob the music-making of some of its warmth and refinement. Ravel's *Pavane* is a case in point. But *Night on the bare mountain* is very successful, and *Scheherazade* is a pretty formidable performance, which does not sound in the least like a provincial orchestra. There is excitement in plenty and the first movement has bite without losing its romantic sweep. The bright recording is very clearly detailed, yet the sound balance plays down the colouristic magic and there is no real glow to the textures, with the strings made to sound wiry rather than gutsy. *The Sorcerer's apprentice* has plenty of sparkle, if not the geniality that makes Previn's version so endearing, but both *Danse macabre*, exciting as well as atmospheric, and (unexpectedly) *In the Steppes of Central Asia* are vividly evocative.

Brain, Dennis (horn)

BEETHOVEN: *Horn sonata in F, Op. 17* (with Denis Matthews). MOZART: *Horn concertos Nos. 2 in E flat, K.417* (with Philharmonia Orchestra, Susskind); *4 in E flat, K.495* (with Hallé Orchestra); *Horn quintet in E flat, K.407* (with Griller Quartet). Richard STRAUSS: *Horn concerto No. 1 in E flat, Op. 11* (with Philharmonia Orchestra, Galliera).
(M)(**(*)) Pearl mono GEM 0026 [id.].

Dennis Brain recorded the Beethoven *Sonata* with Denis Matthews in February 1944 on a simple, valved Boosey and Hawkes French horn (which legend has it cost £12). Because of its valve system, this was a more flexible instrument than the Viennese hand-horns used in Mozart's own time, but also a more imperfect one, with a few insecure upper harmonics. Brain's timbre is unique, his articulation is endearingly musical, his technique phenomenal, but never showy; even so there is the occasional slightly insecure note. Yet the passagework in both Beethoven and Mozart is full of imaginative touches. In the Beethoven *Sonata* Denis Matthews provides an elegant Mozartean-styled partnership, his lightness of touch balances nicely with Brain's elegance. How beautifully they exchange the question and answer of the briefly melancholy *Andante* and then launch into the robust finale so spiritedly!

The programme opens with the lovely Mozart *Quintet* (recorded eight months later). The Grillers play very sweetly and adroitly for the dominating horn, and the finale sparkles, but remains elegant. The two Mozart concertos followed. K.495 came first in 1943 (with the Hallé Orchestra – the strings in rather indifferent form, conducted by their leader, Laurence Turner), K.417 (with the Philharmonia under Susskind) in 1946. In both Brain's phrasing, of the lovely slow movement melodies is Elysian and the jaunty finale of K.417 remains unforgettable. When he came to re-record the Mozart *Horn concertos* with Karajan in 1953 (reissued in EMI's 'Great Recordings of the Century' series – CDM5 66898-2) he had adopted the wide-bore German double horn, which has a fatter, more spreading sound, not a timbre Mozart would have recognized. So there is a case for preferring Brain's earlier performances because Mozart simply sounds better on the narrower bore instrument, and that is not to disparage the marvellous playing on the Karajan disc.

It is not certain which instrument Brain used for the present 1947 recording of the Richard Strauss, but the playing is wonderfully ebullient and crisply articulated, all difficulties swept aside: it sounds like a French rather than a German horn. The effect is to echo the work's Mozartean inspiration and in the great soaring romantic theme at the centre of the slow movement – here, unfortunately affected by intrusive, uneven scratchy surface noise – the lyrical surge is thrilling, but not inflated, and this is one of his very finest solo performances on record. The Pearl transfers are faithful and agreeable (there is no edginess on the strings). But it surely ought to have been possible to diminish the background surface noise.

Brass Partout

'*Playgrounds for angels*': GRIEG: *Sorgemarsj over Rikard Nordraak*. NYSTEDT: *Pia Memoria*. RAUTAVAARA: *A Requiem in our time*; *Playgrounds for angels*. SIBELIUS: *Overture in F*

minor; *Allegro*; *Andantino and Menuett*; *Förspel (Preludium)*; *Tiera*.
*** BIS Dig. CD 1054 [id.].

Brass Partout (or rather brass partout, all fashionably lower case), is a virtuoso group of brass and percussion players, drawn from the Berlin Philharmonic, and other major German orchestras. The disc takes its title from the ingenious piece the Finnish composer Einojuhani Rautavaara composed for the Philip Jones Brass Ensemble. The *Requiem in our time* put Rautavaara on the map in 1953, and is only available in one other version.

All the Sibelius rarities are from 1889, before *Kullervo*, except only *Tiera* (1899).They fill in our picture of his growth during those formative years, though none is a masterpiece. The splendid *Pia Memoria*, a requiem for nine brass instruments, by the Norwegian, Knut Nystedt, has nobility and dignity. So, too, does Grieg's *Sorgemarsj over Rikard Nordraak* to whose strains the composer himself was buried. The playing is pretty stunning and so, too, is the superb BIS recording.

Brendel, Alfred (piano)

'The Art of Alfred Brendel' (complete)
(B) *** Ph. Analogue/Dig. 446 920-2 (25) [id.]
    (includes bonus CD).

'The Art of Alfred Brendel', Volume 1: HAYDN: *Andante con variazione in F min., Hob. XVII/6*; *Piano sonatas in E flat, Hob. XVI/49*; *in C, Hob. XVI/50*; *Sonata in E flat, Hob. XVI/52*. MOZART: *Piano concertos Nos. 14 in E flat, K.449*; *15 in B flat, K.450*; *19 in F, K.459*; *21 in C, K.467*; *26 in D (Coronation), K.537*; *27 in B flat, K.595*; *Double piano concerto in E flat, K.365* (with ASMF, Marriner; *K.365* with Imogen Cooper). *Adagio in B min., K.540*; *Piano sonatas Nos. 8 in A min., K.310*; *11 in A, K.331*; *13 in B flat, K.333*; *14 in C min., K.457*; *Fantasia in C min., K.475*; *Rondo in A min., K.511*.
(M) *** Ph. Analogue/Dig. 446 921-2 (5) [id.].

Volume 2: BEETHOVEN: *Piano concertos Nos. 4 in G, Op. 58*; *5 in E flat (Emperor), Op. 73* (with Chicago SO, Levine). *Andante in F (Andante favori), WoO 57*; *Bagatelle in A min. (Für Elise), WoO 59*; *6 Bagatelles, Op. 126*; *6 Ecossaises, WoO 83*; *Piano sonatas Nos. 3 in C, Op. 2/3*; *11 in B flat, Op. 22*; *18 in E flat, Op. 31/3*; *23 in F min. (Appassionata), Op. 57*; *24 in F sharp, Op. 78*; *29 in B flat (Hammerklavier), Op. 106*; *30 in E, Op. 109*; *5 Variations on 'Rule, Britannia', WoO 79*; *6 Variations in F, Op. 34*; *15 Variations and fugue on a theme of Prometheus (Eroica), Op. 35*; *33 Variations on a waltz by Diabelli, Op. 120*.
(M) **(*) Ph. Dig./Analogue 446 922-2 (5).

Volume 3: SCHUBERT: *Sonatas Nos. 4 in A min., D.537*; *13 in A, D.664*; *14 in A min., D.784*; *15 in*

C (Relique), D.840; 16 in A min., D.845; 19 in C min., D.958; 20 in A, D.959; 21 in B flat, D.960; Allegretto in C min., D.915; 11 Ecossaises, D.781; Fantasy in C (Wanderer), D.760; 12 German dances, D.790; 16 German dances, D.783; Hungarian melody in B min., D.817; 6 Moments musicaux, D.780.

(M) *** Ph. (IMS) Analogue/Dig. 446 923-2 (5).

Volume 4: LISZT: Piano concertos Nos. 1–2; Totentanz (paraphrase on the Dies irae) (with LPO, Haitink); Années de pèlerinage: Book 1: 1st year: Italy; Book 2: 2nd & 3rd years: Italy; Sonata in B min. Concert paraphrase: WAGNER: Tristan: Isoldes Liebestod. Csárdás macabre; En rêve (Nocturne); Harmonies poétiques et religieuses: Invocations; Bénédiction de Dieu dans la solitude; Pensée des morts; Funérailles. Klavierstück in F sharp; Légendes; La lugubre gondola Nos. 1–2; Mosonyis Grabgeleit; RW (Venezia); Schlaflos! Frage und Antwort; Trübe Wolken (Nuages gris); Unstern: Sinistre; Valse oubliée No. 1; Vexilla regis prodeunt; Weihnachtsbaum (Christmas tree/Arbre de Noël) suite (excerpts); Weinen, Klagen, Sorgen Zagen.

(M) *** Ph. (IMS) Analogue/Dig. 446 924-2 (5).

Volume 5: BRAHMS: Piano concertos Nos. 1–2 (with BPO, Abbado). 4 Ballades, Op. 10; Theme and variations in D min. (from String sextet, Op. 18). SCHUMANN: Piano concerto in A min., Op. 54 (with LSO, Abbado). Abendlied, Op. 85/12; Adagio and Allegro in A flat, Op. 70; Fantasiestücke, Op. 73; 3 Romances, Op. 94; 5 Stücke im Volkston, Op. 102 (all with Heinz Holliger). Etudes symphoniques, Op. 13; Fantasia in C, Op. 17; Fantasiestücke, Op. 12; Kinderszenen, Op. 15; Kreisleriana, Op. 16.

(M) *** Ph. (IMS) Analogue/Dig. 446 925-2 (5).

Weihnachtsbaum (A Christmas tree) (suite).

(***) Ph. mono 454 140-2 [id.] (bonus disc).

'The Art of Alfred Brendel' subdivides into five boxes, each of five CDs, and we have surveyed them in some depth under their composer entries in our main volume. Brendel aficionados will have to decide whether to invest in the complete set (with the five individual boxes in a slip-case), which offers some saving in cost, or to pick and choose.

Brendel's overall achievement in a wide breadth of repertoire is quite remarkable, as indeed is the consistency of the Philips engineering: few (if any) artists have enjoyed such reliably truthful recording. However, while the Haydn/Mozart, the Liszt and the Schubert boxes can be recommended almost without serious reservation, the Beethoven collection is slightly marred by the inclusion of Brendel's digital recordings of the Fourth and Emperor Piano concertos, which are considerably inferior on almost all counts to his earlier, analogue versions.

The problem with the Brahms collection is again

the inclusion of Brendel's recent digital versions of both concertos, but here for the opposite reason, since they are outstandingly fine and thus will probably have already found their way into the collections of most of his admirers! The choice for Volume 4 of his most recent, 1991 recording of the Liszt Sonata is also difficult to fathom when, by general consensus, both his earlier versions are superior in almost all respects. But the rest of the Liszt package is very impressive indeed, as is the Schubert box, which offers many of his analogue recordings not otherwise available.

With the complete set comes a bonus disc of Liszt's Christmas tree suite, a mono recording from 1951–2. While it is unique, its appeal is limited by its poor technical quality: a blurred focus at higher dynamic levels, and moments of distortion. The music itself, written by Liszt for his granddaughter to play, is of relatively limited interest. Only the complete set is available in the USA.

British light music

'British light music' (with (i) Light Music Society O, Sir Vivian Dunn; (ii) Pro Arte O, George Weldon; (iii) Studio Two Concert O, Reginald Kilbey; (iv) Eric Coates and his O): (i) DUNCAN: Little suite: March. CURZON: The Boulevardier. BINGE: The Watermill. DOCKER: Tabarinage. HOPE: The Ring of Kerry suite: The jaunting car. (ii) COATES: Springtime suite: Dance in the twilight. COLLINS: Vanity Fair. CURZON: Punchinello: miniature overture. TOMLINSON: Little serenade. BINGE: Miss Melanie. Alan LANGFORD: Waltz. BAYCO: Elizabethan masque. DEXTER: Siciliano. Haydn WOOD: Moods suite: Joyousness. (iii) Paris suite: Montmartre. BINGE: Elizabethan serenade. VINTER: Portuguese party. OSBORNE: Lullaby for Penelope. FARNON: Portrait of a flirt. HARTLEY: Rouge et noir. (iv) COATES: Impression of a Princess; Wood nymphs; The Dam Busters march.

(M) *** EMI CDM5 66537-2.

Obviously inspired by the great success of the three programmes of British light music recorded (at premium price) by Ronald Corp for Hyperion, EMI have delved into their archives and brought out this equally attractive selection, drawing on four different sources, all of the highest quality. Moreover this EMI CD is offered at mid-price and includes 76 minutes of ear-catching melody. The obvious favourites are here, from Ronald Binge's famous Elizabethan serenade to his delectable vignette evoking The Watermill, Anthony Collins's Vanity Fair (the popularity of which he valued above his fame as a conductor) and Robert Farnon's witty Portrait of a flirt.

But also included are many more novelties of equal charm: Bayco's winning pastiche, Eliza-

bethan masque, Binge's wistful portrait of *Miss Melanie,* Alan Langford's pastel-shaded *Waltz,* Harry Dexter's lilting *Siciliano,* Leslie Osborne's gently touching *Lullaby for Penelope,* and the delicious Irish whimsy of Peter Hope's *Jaunting car.* To bring lively contrast come Robert Docker's roisterous *Tabarinage* and Gilbert Vinter's equally vivacious *Portuguese party.* The stereo recordings, made at Abbey Road between 1963 and 1970, are excellent and very pleasingly transferred. Appropriately, the programme opens and closes with the music of Eric Coates, and the last three items are conducted by the composer, ending with a vigorous account of *The Dam Busters march.* These are mono recordings, but of high quality.

'British light music' (played by the Slovak or Czecho-Slovak Radio Symphony Orchestra, Andrew Penny, Adrian Leaper (with male chorus), Ludovit Raijter or Ernest Tomlinson; BBC Concert Orchestra, Kenneth Alwyn; Dublin RTE Concert Orchestra, Ernest Tomlinson or Proinnsias O Duinn):

Volume 1: COATES: *By the sleepy lagoon.* QUILTER: *Children's overture.* ADDINSELL: Film music: *Tom Brown's Schooldays.* CURZON: *Robin Hood suite.* Haydn WOOD: *Sketch of a dandy.* DUNCAN: *Little suite.* COLLINS: *Vanity Fair.* KETELBEY: *Suite romantique.* (8.554709).

Volume 2: KETELBEY: *In a monastery garden.* FARNON: *Colditz march.* GERMAN: *Gypsy suite.* Haydn WOOD: *Roses of Picardy; Serenade to youth.* DUNCAN: *Enchanted April.* CURZON: *La Pienneta.* QUILTER: *Rosmé waltz.* ELLIS: *Coronation Scot.* (8.554710).

Volume 3: ADDINSELL: Film music: *Goodbye Mr Chips.* GERMAN: *Romeo and Juliet* (incidental music): *suite.* DUNCAN: *20th-century express.* Haydn WOOD: *The Seafarer.* FARNON: *Pictures in the fire.* COATES: *The selfish giant.* QUILTER: *As you like it: suite.* BENJAMIN: *Jamaican rumba.* KETELBEY: *Bells across the meadow.* (8.554711).

Volume 4: ADDINSELL (arr. Roy Douglas): *Warsaw concerto.* BATH: *Cornish rhapsody.* Richard Rodney BENNETT: *Murder on the Orient Express: Theme and waltz.* Charles WILLIAMS: *Dream of Olwen* (with Philip Fowke). FARNON: *Lake in the woods; Westminster waltz.* DUNCAN: *Girl from Corsica; Visionaries' grand march.* CURZON: *Bravada: Paso doble.* Haydn WOOD: *Evening song.* TOMLINSON: *Little serenade.* (8.554712).

Volume 5: COATES: *Dam Busters march.* ADDINSELL: Film music: *Fire over England.* GERMAN: *Nell Gwynn: 3 dances; Tom Jones: Waltz.* KETELBEY: *In the moonlight.* BINGE: *Elizabethan serenade.* FARNON: *Peanut polka.* QUILTER: *3 English dances.* Haydn WOOD:

May-Day overture. MAYERL: *Marigold.* KETELBEY: *In a Persian market.* (8.554713). (BB) *** Naxos Dig.8.505147 (5) [id.].

Unlike the set of 'British orchestral masterpieces' below, in which five existing CDs are offered in a slipcase, *'The Best of British light music'* has been specially compiled, with items selected from a number of Naxos CDs. It offers a wide selection, well over five hours of music, so is less selective than the full-priced Hyperion CDs of the New London Orchestra under Ronald Corp. The NLO are also rather more characterful and even better recorded (see below) but the Naxos set remains excellent value. Although Kenneth Alwyn directs most of the film music, much of the rest is played, surprisingly idiomatically, by the Slovak Radio Symphony Orchestra, usually conducted by the erstwhile Adrian Leaper, although Ernest Tomlinson directs his own music (including his delicate lollipop, *Little serenade*). The highlights include Roger Quilter's lovely *Children's overture,* Anthony Collins's *Vanity Fair* (which he greatly prized), Binge's *Elizabethan serenade and Sailing by,* Benjamin's *Jamaican rumba* and mostly familiar items by Eric Coates. Robert Farnon is well represented by *Colditz,* his charming *Westminster waltz* and the catchy *Peanut polka,* as well as two rather effective tone pictures, *Lake in the woods* and *Pictures in the fire,* and there are other obvious hits like Vivian Ellis's *Coronation Scot* and of course the 'film concertos'. Not everything else is quite so memorable, but Edward German, Haydn Wood and Ketèlbey are all well represented and everything is brightly played and well recorded. The five records come for the price of four, and all are quite well documented.

'British orchestral masterpieces'

'British orchestral masterpieces' (played by (i) RSNO; (ii) E. Northern Philh. O; (iii) David Lloyd-Jones; (iv) Paul Daniel; (v) with Tim Hugh (cello)): (i; iii) BAX: *Symphony No. 1; The garden of Fand; In the faery hills.* (ii; iii) BLISS: (v) *Cello concerto. Music for strings, Op. 54; 2 Studies, Op. 16.* ELGAR: *Falstaff, Op. 68; Elegy, Op. 58; The Sanguine fan* (ballet), *Op. 81.* (i; iii) HOLST: *Beni Mora; Egdon Heath; Fugal overture; Hammersmith;* (v) *Invocation for cello and orchestra. Somerset rhapsody.* (ii; iv) WALTON: *Symphony No. 1; Partita.* (BB) *** Naxos Dig. 8.505154 (5) [id.].

With the five CDs offered for the price of four, this is an exceptionally successful anthology and a self-recommending bargain of the highest order. All these discs are fully reviewed in our main volume, except the Bliss collection, which is discussed in our 1998 *Bargain Guide.* This is the only disc about which there are any reservations and these are minor, mostly concerning the recording, which is not as full and forward as usual from this source, with the solo cello rather backwardly balanced in the *Concerto*. Hugh's reading is reflective to match. Poetry rather than power is the keynote, centring on the *Larghetto* slow movement. In the Bax, David Lloyd-Jones draws warmly sympathetic performances from the RSNO, most impressively recorded, and the RSNO play extremely well for him. Tim Hugh is again a most responsive soloist in the rare Holst *Invocation*, with the rest of the Holst items hardly less distinguished. Lloyd-Jones's account of *Falstaff* brings tinglingly brisk tempi tempered with a highly idiomatic ebb and flow of rubato and *The Sanguine fan* is equally persuasive, alongside a touching account of the Elgarian *Elegy*. To cap the set comes Paul Daniel's outstanding version of the Walton *Symphony*, as bitingly intense as any in the catalogue, with the joyful *Partita* hardly less stimulating.

Brymer, Jack; David Glazer; Joza Ostrack (clarinet)

'Clarinet concertos': KROMMER: *Concerto in E flat*. WAGNER (Baermann): *Adagio for clarinet and strings*. DEBUSSY: *Première rapsodie*. (Jack Brymer, Vienna State Opera Orchestra, Felix Prohaska). WEBER: *Clarinet concerto No. 1 in F min.*; *Clarinet concertino, Op. 26*. STAMITZ: *Concerto No. 3* (David Glazer, Württemberg CO, Faerber). MOZART: *Clarinet concerto in A, K.622* (Joza Ostrack, Mozart Festival Orchestra, Lizzio). (M) *** Vanguard 08.9176.72 (2).

Jack Brymer's performance of the Krommer *Concerto* with its melting *Adagio* and delightful, chortling finale is a joy, while the Baermann *Adagio* (once attributed to Wagner) and the Debussy *Rapsodie* are also superbly poised. David Glazer's Weber (the *First Concerto* and the engaging *Concertino*) is most elegant, with the slow movement of the concerto beautifully phrased and both finales winningly jocular – the close of the *Concertino* chirrups just as it should. The Stamitz is plainer but still very agreeable. Joza Ostrack's performance of the greatest work of all, by Mozart, agreeably combines warmth and finesse; so altogether this makes a worthwhile anthology. Accompaniments are well managed and the recordings are all fully acceptable, if not absolutely refined; but the interest of the repertoire – so conveniently gathered together – more than compensates. No recording dates are given.

Camden, Anthony (oboe)

'The art of the oboe' (with (i) London Virtuosi, John Georgiadis; (ii) City of L. Sinfonia, Nicholas Ward): (i) ALBINONI: *Oboe concertos in C, Op. 7/ 12*; *in D min., Op. 9/2*; *in C, Op. 9/5*. (ii) HANDEL: *Concerto No. 3 in G min.*; *Rondo in G*; *Rigaudon*. RIGHINI: *Idomeneus concerto*. CORELLI: *Concerto*. CIMAROSA: *Concerto in C min*. BELLINI: *Concerto in E flat*. (BB) *** Naxos Dig. 8.553991 [id.].

This collection has something in common with Evelyn Rothwell, Lady Barbirolli's collection of oboe concertos with her husband directing, but has the advantage of modern digital sound of high quality. Anthony Camden is a first-class soloist and these are vividly played performances, stylishly accompanied by both groups. Camden's tempi are not always quite so apt as his predecessor, but slow movements are always sensitive and finales sparkle. Most enjoyable.

Camden, Anthony (oboe), City of London Sinfonia, Nicholas Ward

Italian oboe concertos: CIMAROSA, arr. Arthur BENJAMIN: *Concerto in C*. BELLINI: *Concerto in E flat*. RIGHINI: *Concerto in C*. FIORILLO: *Sinfonia concertante in F* (with Julia Girdwood). CORELLI, arr. BARBIROLLI: *Concerto in A*. PERGOLESI/BARBIROLLI: *Concerto in C min*. (BB) **(*) Naxos Dig. 8.553433 [id.].

This collection again recalls the series of outstanding recordings made by Evelyn Rothwell for Pye/PRT with her husband, Sir John Barbirolli, conducting. He specially arranged the highly engaging pastiche works of Corelli and Pergolesi for her to play and put his signature firmly on the *Sarabanda* of the Corelli *Concerto*, which he scored as a duet for oboe and cello, his own instrument. Lady Barbirolli's recordings have just been restored to the catalogue but at full price.

Meanwhile these sympathetic and stylishly played performances from Anthony Camden will suffice admirably, particularly at Naxos price. He has a most attractive timbre, and Nicholas Ward's accompaniments are impeccable. There are two very small reservations. The Fiorillo *Sinfonia concertante*, which features a pair of oboes (the second part is neatly managed by Julia Girdwood), although nicely written for the two soloists, is very conventional in its material and the first movement is a shade too long. The other point concerns the delightful five-note opening phrase of Arthur Benjamin's delicious Cimarosa confection, which Camden plays curiously lethargically, echoed by

Ward. It is a small point, but Lady Barbirolli's account still lingers in the memory. The Naxos recording is excellently balanced and truthful.

Capella Istropolitana, Adrian Leaper

'English string festival': DOWLAND: *Galliard a 5.* ELGAR: *Elegy, Op. 58; Introduction and allegro, Op. 47; Serenade, Op. 20.* BRIDGE: *Lament.* PARRY: *An English suite; Lady Radnor's suite.* (BB) **(*) Naxos Dig. 8.550331 [id.].

It is fascinating and rewarding to hear these excellent Slovak players turn their attention to essentially English repertoire, and with a considerable degree of success. The brief Dowland *Galliard* makes a strong introduction, and the attractive pair of neo-Baroque Parry suites of dance movements, played with warmth, finesse and spirit, are given bright and lively sound. In the Elgar *Introduction and allegro* the violins above the stave have their upper partials over-brilliantly lit by the digital recording, the focus not quite sharp; but otherwise the sound is full, with plenty of resonant ambience. The playing is strongly felt, but the fugue is a bit too measured, and the great striding theme, played in unison on the G string, could also do with more pace, especially when it returns. Otherwise this is persuasive, and the *Serenade* is presented simply, combining warmth and finish. At super-bargain price, this is worth exploring.

Casals , Pablo (conductor & cello)

Casals Edition (orchestral and concertante recordings)

BACH (with Prades Festival O): *Brandenburg concerto No. 5 in D, BWV 1050* (with Eugene Istomin, Joseph Szigeti, John Wummer); *Piano concerto in F min., BWV 1056* (with Clara Haskil); *Violin concerto in A min., BWV 1041* (with Isaac Stern); *Violin and oboe concerto in C min., BWV 1061* (with Isaac Stern, Marcel Tabuteau).
(M) (**(*)) Sony mono SMK 58982 [id.].

All these recordings come from the early 1950s, when Casals directed festivals at Prades and Perpignan and assembled some of the greatest artists of the day for these summer nights of music-making. This Bach disc comes from Prades and all the performances date from the first festival, in 1950. The *Brandenburg concerto No. 5* with Istomin as pianist, Szigeti and the flautist John Wummer is a rarity – and, if Sony's publicity is to be believed, has not appeared before. It is let down by Szigeti's (at times) scrawny tone, and the orchestral playing is a bit heavy-footed.

Clara Haskil's playing in the *F minor Concerto*, BWV 1056 is as eloquent and sensitive as one would expect, and Isaac Stern's account of the *A minor Violin concerto* is hardly less impressive. Perhaps the most moving thing on the disc is the slow movement of the *C minor Violin and oboe concerto*, where the oboist is the legendary Marcel Tabuteau. Music-making from another age.

MOZART (with Perpignan Festival O): *Violin concerto No. 5 in A (Turkish), K.219* (with Erica Morini); *Sinfonia concertante in E flat, K.364* (with Isaac Stern, William Primrose).
(M) (**(*)) Sony mono SMK 58983 [id.].

The Mozart performances come from Perpignan and July 1951. The *A major Violin concerto*, K.219 is played superbly by Erica Morini. Her Mozart playing is classically lithe and free from any striving after effect. The *Sinfonia concertante* (with Stern and Primrose) is also fine but is rather measured, and really needs to be a little lighter in touch.

MOZART (with Perpignan Festival O): *Piano concertos Nos. 14 in E flat, K.449* (with Eugene Istomin); *27 in B flat, K.595* (with Mieczyslaw Horszowski); *Concert aria: Ch'io mi scordi di te?* (with Jennie Tourel).
(M) (**) Sony mono SMK 58984 [id.].

Horszowski's playing in the *B flat Concerto, K.595*, is a model of style and elegance, though Casals gives him robust rather than discreet support. But neither the Istomin account of the *E flat, K.449* nor the Mozart *Ch'io mi scordi* with Jennie Tourel is well served by the engineers – though nor, for that matter, is Horszowski.

SCHUBERT (with Prades Festival O): *Symphony No. 5 in B flat. String quintet in C, Op. 163, D.956* (with Isaac Stern, Alexander Schneider, Milton Katims, Paul Tortelier).
(M) (***) Sony mono SMK 58992 [id.].

The Schubert *Fifth Symphony*, recorded in 1953, omits the first-movement exposition repeat but, as with everything this great musician does, is full of musical interest. It has not been issued in the UK before, eclipsed by the later (and perhaps even finer) performance by the 1970 Marlboro Orchestra in stereo. However, this earlier account boasts a particularly eloquent reading of the slow movement. The Casals account of the sublime Schubert *C major String quintet* has rarely been absent from the catalogue: it first appeared on Philips and then CBS, and is too familiar to require detailed comment. Recorded in 1952, it sounds as marvellous as ever. This coupling is surely a must for all Casals admirers.

SCHUMANN (with Prades Festival O, Ormandy): *Cello concerto in A min., Op. 129. Piano trio in D min., Op. 63* (with Mieczyslaw Horszowski,

Alexander Schneider). *5 Stücke im Volkston* (with Leopold Mannes).

(M) (**(*)) Sony mono SMK 58993 [id.].

The Schumann *Cello concerto* was recorded in Prades in 1953 with Ormandy conducting the Prades Festival Orchestra, while the Op. 63 Trio and the *Fünf Stücke im Volkston* date from the previous year. Although one leading magazine claimed that the *Trio* had not appeared in the UK before, it was in fact released in a CBS commemorative box. The sound naturally calls for tolerance but that should be enthusiastically extended. Casals once said that 'In Schumann . . . every note is so much from the heart.' Casals plays it for all it is worth, and some might wish for slightly more subdued and restrained emotions. Casals recorded the *D minor Trio* for HMV with Thibaud and Cortot in 1928, and this 1952 Prades performance with Schneider and Horszowski is, if anything, even finer. A performance of stature, with less of the heart-on-sleeve approach which distinguishes the *Concerto*, this was again listed in one source as 'new to the UK', but it has appeared both on LP and on CD. The sensitive and imaginative phrasing is a model of its kind. Whatever reservations one might have, these are all performances to be reckoned with.

Chicago Symphony Orchestra

Historic telecasts, Volume 1 (1954): **Fritz Reiner**

BEETHOVEN: *Symphony No. 7 in A, Op. 92*; *Egmont overture, Op. 84.* HANDEL: *Solomon: Arrival of the Queen of Sheba.*

(***) VAI Video VAI 69601 [id.].

Historic telecasts, Volume 2 (1961): **George Szell**

MUSSORGSKY: *Prelude to Khovanshchina.* BEETHOVEN: *Symphony No. 5 in C min., Op. 67.* BERLIOZ: *Le carnaval romain overture, Op. 9.*

(***) VAI Video VAI 69602 [id.].

Historic telecasts, Volume 3 (1962): **Leopold Stokowski**

BACH, arr. STOKOWSKI: *Toccata and fugue in D min.* BRAHMS: *Variations on a theme of Haydn* (St Anthony chorale). RIMSKY-KORSAKOV: *Capriccio espagnol, Op. 34.*

(***) VAI Video VAI 60603 [id.].

Historic telecasts, Volume 4 (1961): **Pierre Monteux.**

BEETHOVEN: *Symphony No. 8 in F, Op. 93.* WAGNER: *Die Meistersinger: Prelude to Act III.* BERLIOZ: *Le carnaval romain overture, Op. 9.*

(***) VAI Video VAI 60604 [id.].

The above four videos are even more valuable than the wider but more piecemeal coverage of the *'Art of conducting'* above. They offer us four great conductors at the height of their powers directing a great

orchestra, and every performance is memorable. We even have a chance to compare Szell's and Monteux's interpretations of Berlioz's supreme orchestral masterpiece, *Le carnaval romain*, Szell the more electrifying, Monteux the more colourful.

These telecasts are part of a series inaugurated in Chicago in 1951 (under Kubelik). But when Reiner took over the orchestra in 1953 the programmes were extended to 45 minutes, broadcast first on Sunday afternoons, and subsequently (in 1959) at 8 p.m. on Sunday evenings, with Deems Taylor as initial host. The list of guest conductors who joined the series is wide-reaching, including Barbirolli, Beecham, Copland, Hindemith, Martinon, Munch and Previn. Announcements and commentaries are omitted from the published videos and the music is presented without introductions.

It was right that Reiner should carry on the series, at a live concert in Symphony Hall in 1954. With the bold swathe of his strong, clear up-and-down beat, a serious mien, and frowning gaze, he establishes total control of the orchestra. Although the early recording quality brings the usual sound-track discolouration of woodwind upper partials, with moments of distortion in the wide amplitude of string sound, the warmth of the playing projects readily, as does its spontaneous feeling (after the single hour-long run-through rehearsal, which was standard for the series).

It is a pity that no Richard Strauss was included, but the Beethoven performances generate enormous electricity. The camera work is fairly primitive, and it is interesting that the producer misses the dominating role of the horns in the thrilling furioso close of the outer movements of the *Seventh Symphony* and focuses instead on the woodwind, whereas in *Egmont* the horn section is portrayed at the key moments. Reiner, stiff and unrelenting in manner throughout, permits himself a half smile to acknowledge the applause, and even gives the oboes a bow – after the Queen of Sheba has arrived and departed rather fiercely.

Szell's clear beat is hardly less concentrated, achieving extraordinary precision and powerful clipped rhythms in Beethoven's *Fifth*; but he uses his left hand much more subtly than Reiner. It is a great performance, creating and gathering intensity in a formidable progress to its gripping finale. The first movement repeat is observed (as it is later by Monteux in the *Eighth*) and the strings flowingly decorate the main theme of the slow movement with appealing warmth. Before that has come the evocatively detailed Mussorgsky *Khovanshchina Prelude*, with the delectable Rimsky-Korsakov orchestration glowing in the coda, and the following Berlioz overture is quite riveting in its orchestral bravura, almost upstaging the symphony in sheer adrenalin.

Reiner, Monteux and Szell conduct from memory, but Stokowski uses scores throughout, even in his famous Bach arrangement. Here the remarkably imaginative orchestration is made to seem the more vivid by camera close-ups which even feature the glockenspiel and show the great horn entry at the climax of the fugue, before the thrilling upward rushes of strings. Where his colleagues favour batons, Stokowski uses his eversupple hands to shape the music. This means slightly less precision of ensemble in the Bach (where he is concerned with the range of sonority and colour), but not the Brahms, a richly idiomatic account, in no way idiosyncratic, although the lyrical warmth of the string writing is brought out in the closing variations. Rimsky's *Capriccio* is then played with enormous virtuosity (especially at the close) and the camera relishes the opportunity to portray each of the orchestral soloists in turn. As with the Szell concert, this is a studio recording, with a much drier acoustic, but the middle strings still glow as Stokowski coaxes their phrasing affectionately.

For the Monteux concert we return to Symphony Hall, with an audience, and this tape offers the best sound of the four – warm and well-detailed. Monteux's dapper, genial manner is deceptive, yet it brings the most relaxed atmosphere of all and at one endearing moment the camera catches one of the violin players on the back desks turning to his companion and smiling. The performance of Beethoven's *Eighth* is superb, polished, wonderfully detailed, and with a perfectly judged forward flow. When Monteux wants to be forceful he clenches his left fist, and the result catches the music's full intensity without fierceness. The glorious horn playing (on which the camera dwells indulgently) gives great warmth and nobility to the following Wagner *Prelude*, and the Berlioz overture ends the programme with a fizzing burst of energy at its very close.

Historic telecasts, Volume 5 (1963): **Charles Munch**

RAMEAU/D'INDY: *Dardanus suite*. BERLIOZ: *Les Troyens: Royal hunt and storm*. RAVEL: *Valses nobes et sentimentales; La valse*.
(***) VAI Video VAI 69605 [id.].

Historic telecasts, Volume 6 (1963): **Paul Hindemith**

HINDEMITH: *Concert music for strings and brass*. BRUCKNER: *Symphony No. 7: first movement* (only). BRAHMS: *Academic festival overture*.
✿ (***) VAI Video VAI 69606 [id.].

Historic telecasts, Volume 7 (1961): **George Szell**

MOZART: *Overture: Le nozze di Figaro; Violin concerto No. 5 in A (Turkish), K.219* (with Erica Morini). BEETHOVEN: *Overture: Leonora No. 3*.
(***) VAI Video VAI 60607 [id.].

This second batch of videos arrived just as we were going to print and includes the most valuable of all,

a video of Paul Hindemith conducting 'live' in Chicago's Orchestra Hall, where understandably the priviledged audience give him an hero's welcome. With his lips pursed seriously throughout, and using a clear, purposeful stick technique, he directs an electrifying account of his own *Concert music for strings and brass*, with the Chicago strings and brass responding with the most glorious sounds. One might even use the adjective voluptuous in relation to the strings, except that rich though the textures are, Hindemith's lyricism remains sinewy – for that is its strength. The fugato (nicely observed by the camera) also has splendid bite. He also conducts a superbly paced account of the first movement of Bruckner's *Seventh*, full of humanity. This follows a brief filmed interview when he is suitably articulate on the music's universality to a not very imaginative TV interviewer. The closing Overture, spacious and exciting, is richly Brahmsian. The sound really is remarkably good.

By the side of this, Munch's concert is just a shade disappointing. The Rameau/D'Indy suite is elegant enough, but lacking the incandescence of a Beecham touch, sounds anachronistic, and the *Royal hunt and storm*, beautifully played as it is, takes a little while to warm up. However, the climax when it comes does not disappoint (with the camerawork among the brass adding a great deal to the visual effect), and the closing horn solo is poetically atmospheric. The Ravel performances are warmly idiomatic, but here the sound lacks enough transparency to bring out the lustrous detail.

Szell, after a brilliant, if ungenial *Nozze di Figaro* overture, has the advantage of a very stylish soloist, Erica Morini, in Mozart's most popular *Violin concerto*. She plays with beautiful tone, splendid assurance, and a disarming simplicity of line, and only the three cadenzas (rather too much of a good thing) give any cause for criticism. *Leonora No. 3* makes a meticulously detailed but exciting finale. Good sound, with the solo violin well caught, although balanced very forwardly.

Chicago SO; LPO; LSO; Royal Opera House, Covent Garden Orchestra; VPO; Sir Georg Solti

Overtures: SUPPÉ: *Light cavalry; Pique Dame; Morning, noon and night in Vienna; Poet and peasant.* GLINKA: *Ruslan and Ludmilla.* VERDI: *La Traviata: Prelude to Act I.* WAGNER: *Die Meistersinger von Nürnberg: Prelude to Act I; Der fliegende Holländer.* BERLIOZ: *Les Francs-juges.* MOZART: *Le nozze di Figaro.* BEETHOVEN: *Egmont; Leonora overture No. 3.* WEBER: *Oberon.* BRAHMS: *Academic festival overture.* ROSSINI: *Il barbiere di Siviglia.* GLAZUNOV: *Prince Igor.* BIZET: *Carmen:*

Prelude to Act I. HUMPERDINCK: *Hänsel und Gretel.* MUSSORGSKY: *Khovanshchina: Prelude.*
(B) **(*) Decca Double Analogue/Dig. 460 982-2 (2) [id.].

It was appropriate that this collection should include the four favourite Suppé overtures, as it was this repertoire in earlier mono versions with which Solti made his Decca orchestral début, and the virtuosity he generated with the LPO impressed Toscanini. These later (1960) VPO stereo versions are equally brilliant, but here Culshaw's recording balance was miscalculated, having an exceptionally wide dynamic range, too wide for the cello solos in *Morning, noon and night* and *Poet and peasant,* where the instrument is backward and sounds not unlike a viola. The rest of the collection ranges across Solti's recording career, through the 1960s and 1970s, including such highlights as his famous, fizzing LSO account of Glinka's *Ruslan and Ludmilla,* his electrifying *Les Francs-juges* and with several opera recordings derived from his complete opera recordings, most recently the Act I *Prelude* from his outstanding 1995 version of Verdi's *La Traviata.* For the most part, vintage Decca recording of high quality.

Chicago Symphony Orchestra, Fritz Reiner

'*Russian showpieces':* MUSSORGSKY: *Pictures at an exhibition* (orch. Ravel); *Night on the bare mountain* (arr. RIMSKY-KORSAKOV). TCHAIKOVSKY: *Marche slave*; *Suite No. 1: Marche miniature.* BORODIN: *Polovtsian march.* KABALEVSKY: *Colas Breugnon overture.* GLINKA: *Ruslan and Ludmilla overture.*
(M) *** BMG/RCA 09026 61958-2 [id.].

Reiner's famous (1957) recording of the *Pictures* is linked with a powerful *Night on the bare mountain* within a 1959 concert of shorter Russian pieces, all brilliantly played and spectacularly recorded. Reiner's account of the *Ruslan and Ludmilla overture* is not quite as taut as Solti's famous LSO version, but its racy geniality is very attractive. *Colas Breugnon* with its syncopated cross-rhythms has plenty of gusto; the *Polovtsian march* is robustly rhythmic and Tchaikovsky's *Marche slave* suitably sombre, yet with an exciting coda.

Chicago Symphony Orchestra, Frederick Stock

WAGNER: *Die Meistersinger overture.* BRAHMS: *Hungarian dances Nos. 17–21.* GOLDMARK: *In*

the springtime overture. SUK: *Fairy tales: Folkdance* (polka). GLAZUNOV: *Les ruses d'amour: Introduction and waltz.* TCHAIKOVSKY: *Symphony No. 5 in E min.* PAGANINI: *Moto perpetuo, Op. 11* (orch. Stock). WALTON: *Scapino: comedy overture.* DOHNANYI: *Suite for orchestra, Op. 19.* R. STRAUSS: *Also sprach Zarathustra.* STOCK: *Symphonic waltz. Op. 8.*
✪ (M) (***) Biddulph mono WHL 021/22 [id.].

Frederick Stock, born in Germany in 1872, studied composition and violin at the Cologne Conservatoire; among his teachers was Humperdinck, and Mengelberg was a fellow student. He began his career as an orchestral violinist, and in 1895 he emigrated to America to join the ranks of the Chicago Symphony as a viola player. The orchestra was then four years old. In 1905 he was hired on a temporary basis as its musical director; but he stayed on for nearly forty years until he died in October 1942.

He built the orchestra into the splendid ensemble which Fritz Reiner was eventually to inherit and established its world reputation, especially for its brass playing, although (on the evidence of these recordings) the strings were equally impressive. Like Reiner, he had the advantage of the marvellous acoustics of Chicago's Symphony Hall in which to make his records, which, alongside Stokowski's Philadelphia recordings, are technically among the finest to come out of America in the late 1920s. Indeed, the sound in Tchaikovsky's *Fifth* (1927) is so warm and full-bodied that in no time at all one forgets one is listening to an old recording and simply revels in the rich string patina and fine woodwind colours (heard at their finest in the elegantly played waltz movement). The brass come fully into their own in the finale.

Stock's interpretation is endearingly wilful, very like Mengelberg's more famous reading, which was made only six months later. Stock pulls back at the entry of the secondary group in the first movement. The effect is emphasized because of a side change but is consistent in the recapitulation. The slow movement is very much *con alcuna licenza* (Tchaikovsky's marking) and the horn soloist must have needed great nerve to sustain his great solo at the chosen spacious tempo. But Stock has that supreme gift of being able to create the feeling of a live performance while making a recording, and this *Fifth,* for all its eccentricities, is very enjoyable. The finale has the traditional cut which was so often observed at that time, but the effect is seamless and the final brass peroration has only ever been topped by Stokowski's 78-r.p.m. Philadelphia set.

The programme opens with a thrillingly sonorous account of *Die Meistersinger overture* (1926), with the tension held right to the end, in spite of the big rallentando at the majestic reprise of the introductory 'fanfare'. The Brahms dances, played with virtuosity and considerable panache, were recorded in 1925 but never issued, and both the Suk *Polka* (1926) and the charming Glazunov *Waltz* (1929) show the colourful palette of Stock's Chicago woodwind section, while Goldmark's *In the springtime overture* sounds uncommonly fresh in this early (1925) performance. The Dohnányi suite too (1928) is stylishly and pleasingly done, with nice touches of wit and plenty of lilt in the waltz featured in the closing movement, where Stock handles the tempo changes with affectionate sophistication. But here for some reason the recording is very closely miked and dry; was it actually recorded in Symphony Hall, one wonders, for there is little ambient effect?

Stock's most famous record is of Walton's *Scapino overture*, which he commissioned for the orchestra's fiftieth anniversary celebrations. It is played here with fizzing virtuosity and much élan and is particularly valuable in being the only existing recording of Walton's original score before the composer made his revisions. This and an equally brilliant account of Paganini's *Moto perpetuo*, deftly played in unison by the orchestral violins, were recorded in 1941, the sound brightly lit (the violins are closely miked in the Paganini) but retaining underlying warmth.

The set ends appropriately with a work indelibly associated with Chicago because of Reiner's superb, later, stereo version: Strauss's *Also sprach Zarathustra*. But Stock's account certainly does not come under its shadow. The spectacular opening is remarkably well caught and the passion of the violins is thrilling. This was made in 1940, and here the Columbia engineers made a compromise between brilliance and richness of timbre, with the hall ambience adding a natural breadth.

The range of dynamic is striking, and Stock's reading must be placed among the finest, for it is seemingly completely spontaneous, yet splendidly controlled and shaped. The orchestral concentration is held at the highest level throughout, and particularly so during the darkly dormant section of the score on the lower strings associated with *'Science'* and the later passage on the high violins; Stock then follows with an exciting accelerando to reach the spectacular climax in *'The Convalescent'*. He maintains this thrust through to the closing pages, with the tolling bell coming through plangently, and the coda very touching. Then for an encore the conductor provides a charmingly tuneful *Symphonic waltz* of his own composition, endearingly inflated but not boring when presented with such zest, and sumptuously recorded in 1930. Yet there is nothing 'historic' about live music-making of this calibre, and this fascinating set is very highly recommended. It certainly does Stock's reputation full justice.

(i) Chicago Symphony Orchestra, Frederick Stock; (ii) Cincinnati SO, Eugene Goossens

English music: (i) BENJAMIN: *Overture to an Italian comedy.* ELGAR: *Pomp and circumstance march No. 1.* (ii) VAUGHAN WILLIAMS: *A London Symphony (No. 2;* original version*);* WALTON: *Violin concerto* (with Jascha Heifetz (violin)) (***) Biddulph mono WHL 016 [id.].

This superbly transferred Biddulph issue celebrates the fact that some of the very finest recordings of British music have come from America. Heifetz's historic first recording of the Walton *Violin concerto* is imaginatively coupled with the only recording ever made (also by Goossens and the Cincinnati Orchestra, immediately following the Walton sessions in 1941) of the 1920 version of Vaughan Williams's *London Symphony*. As welcome fill-ups come Elgar's *Pomp and circumstance No. 1* and Arthur Benjamin's *Overture to an Italian comedy*, brilliantly played by the Chicago orchestra under Frederick Stock.

Chung, Kyung Wha (violin)

Kyung Wha Chung Edition (complete).
(M) **(*) Decca Analogue/Dig. 460 016-2 (10).

PROKOFIEV: *Violin concertos Nos. 1 in D, Op. 19; 2 in G min., Op. 63;* STRAVINSKY: *Violin concerto* (with LSO, André Previn) (425 003-2 [id.]).

BARTOK: *Violin concertos Nos. 1, Op. posth.* (with Chicago SO); *2 in B min.* (with LPO) (both cond. Sir Georg Solti) (425 015-2 [id.]).

SIBELIUS: *Violin concerto in D min, Op. 47;* TCHAIKOVSKY: *Violin concerto in D, Op. 35* (with LSO, André Previn) (425 080-2 [id.]).

BRUCH: *Violin concerto No. 1 in G min., Op. 26; Scottish fantasia for violin and orchestra* (with RPO, Rudolf Kempe) (448 597-2 [id.]).

BERG: *Violin concerto* (with Chicago SO, Sir Georg Solti). BACH: (Unaccompanied) *Violin partita No. 2 in D min.; Sonata No. 3 in C* (460 005-2 [id.]).

FRANCK: *Violin sonata in A.* DEBUSSY: *Violin sonata in G min.* (both with Radu Lupu). CHAUSSON: *Poème for violin and orchestra, Op. 25* (with RPO, Charles Dutoit) (460 006-2 [id.]).

LALO: *Symphonie espagnole, Op. 21* (with Montreal SO, Dutoit). VIEUXTEMPS: *Violin concerto No. 5 in A, Op. 37* (with LSO, Lawrence Foster). RAVEL: *Tzigane* (with RPO, Dutoit) (460 007-2 [id.]).

SAINT-SAENS: *Violin concertos Nos. 1 in A, Op. 20* (with Montreal SO, Charles Dutoit); *3 in B min., Op. 61* (with LSO, Lawrence Foster);

Havanaise, Op. 83; Introduction and Rondo capriccioso (with Montreal SO, Dutoit) (460 008-2 [id.]).

BEETHOVEN: *Violin concerto in D, Op. 61* (with VPO, Kirill Kondrashin). WALTON: *Violin concerto* (with LSO, André Previn) (460 014-2 [id.]).

ELGAR: *Violin concerto in B min., Op. 61* (with LPO, Sir Georg Solti). MENDELSSOHN: *Violin concerto in E min., Op. 64* (with Montreal SO, Charles Dutoit) (460 015-2 [id.]).

This mid-priced set celebrates Kyung Wha Chung's remarkable achievement during her highly successful recording period with Decca between 1970 and 1983. The great majority of her Decca records were inspirational and all were given the benefit of first-class sound – first analogue, then digital. The exceptions are the disappointing partnership with Kondrashin in the Beethoven *Concerto*, and her over-romantic approach to Bach's works for unaccompanied violin – here rather inappropriately coupled with Berg. The ten CDs are offered for the price of nine in a slipcase, but most collectors will prefer to pick from the separate issues – all discussed under their composer entries.

'The great violin concertos': MENDELSSOHN: *Concerto in E min., Op. 64* (with Montreal SO, Dutoit). BEETHOVEN: *Concerto in D, Op. 61* (with VPO, Kondrashin). TCHAIKOVSKY: *Concerto in D, Op. 35.* SIBELIUS: *Concerto in D min., Op. 47* (both with LSO, Previn).

(B) **(*) Decca Double Analogue/Dig. 452 325-2 (2) [(M) id. import].

This Decca Double begs comparison with Grumiaux's Philips Duo called, more sensibly, *'Favourite violin concertos'* (see below). Grumiaux offers Brahms instead of Sibelius and concentrates on repertoire in which his refined, poetic style produces satisfying results in all four works. Chung only scores three out of four. Her collection is let down by the 1979 account of the Beethoven which, measured and thoughtful, lacks the compulsion one would have predicted, due largely to the often prosaic conducting of Kondrashin. There is poetry in individual movements – the minor-key episode of the finale, for example, which alone justifies the unusually slow tempo – but, with too little of the soloist's natural electricity conveyed and none of her volatile imagination, it must be counted a disappointment, despite the first-class digital sound.

The Mendelssohn, made two years later, could not be more different. Chung favours speeds faster than usual in all three movements and the result is sparkling and happy, with the lovely slow movement fresh and songful, not at all sentimental. With warmly sympathetic accompaniment from Dutoit and the Montreal orchestra, amply recorded, the result was one of her happiest recordings.

The Sibelius/Tchaikovsky pairing (from 1970) is highly praised in our main volume. She brings an equally sympathetic and idiomatic response to both concertos, and Previn's accompaniments are of the highest order. The latter is a much better investment than the latest format, unless the Mendelssohn is essential.

Cincinnati Pops Orchestra, Erich Kunzel

'Favourite overtures': SUPPE: *Light cavalry*; *Poet and peasant.* AUBER: *Fra Diavolo.* HEROLD: *Zampa.* REZNICEK: *Donna Diana.* OFFENBACH: *Orpheus in the Underworld.* ROSSINI: *William Tell.*

*** Telarc Dig. CD 80116 [id.].

In this spectacularly recorded (1985) collection of favourite bandstand overtures the playing has fine exuberance and gusto (only the galop from *William Tell* could perhaps have had greater impetus) and the resonant ambience of Cincinnati's Music Hall lends itself to Telarc's wide-ranging engineering, with the bass drum nicely caught. Perhaps the opening of *Fra Diavolo* would have benefited from a more transparent sound, but for the most part the opulence suits the vigorous style of the music-making, with *Zampa* and the Suppé overtures particularly successful.

'Pomp and Pizazz': J. WILLIAMS: *Olympic fanfare.* SUK: *Towards a new life.* ELGAR: *Pomp and circumstance march No. 1.* IRELAND: *Epic march.* TCHAIKOVSKY: *Coronation march.* BERLIOZ: *Damnation de Faust: Hungarian march.* J. F. WAGNER: *Under the Double Eagle.* FUCIK: *Entry of the gladiators.* SOUSA: *The Stars and Stripes forever.* HAYMAN: *March medley.*

*** Telarc Dig. CD 80122 [id.].

As enjoyable a march collection as any available, with characteristically spectacular and naturally balanced Telarc recording, with its crisp transients and wide amplitude. The performances have comparable flair and sparkle. The inclusion of John Ireland's comparatively restrained *Epic march* and the Tchaikovsky *Coronation march*, with its piquant trio and characteristic references to the Tsarist national anthem, makes for attractive contrast, while the Hayman medley (including *Strike up the band, 76 Trombones, South Rampart Street Parade* and *When the Saints go marching in*) makes an exuberant, peppy closing section. By comparison the Berlioz *Rákóczy march* is quite dignified. The sound is in the demonstration class. Most entertaining.

'Symphonic spectacular': SHOSTAKOVICH: *Festival overture, Op. 96.* WAGNER: *Die Walküre: Ride of the Valkyries.* FALLA: *El amor brujo:*

Ritual fire dance. BIZET: *L'Arlésienne:*
Farandole. JARNEFELT: *Praeludium.* CHABRIER:
España. TCHAIKOVSKY: *Marche slave, Op. 31.*
HALVORSEN: *Entry of the Boyars.* ENESCU:
Rumanian rhapsody No. 1, Op. 11.
KHACHATURIAN: *Gayaneh: Sabre dance.*
*** Telarc Dig. CD 80170 [id.].

With spectacular recording, well up to Telarc's best standards, this is a highly attractive collection of orchestral lollipops. Everything is played with the special flair which this orchestra and conductor have made their own in this kind of repertoire. Most entertaining, and technically of demonstration standard.

'*The Fantastic Leopold Stokowski*' (transcriptions for orchestra): BACH: *Toccata & fugue in D min., BWV 565;* Little fugue in G min., BWV 578.
BOCCHERINI: *Quintet in E flat: Minuet.*
BEETHOVEN: *Moonlight sonata: adagio sostenuto.*
BRAHMS: *Hungarian dance No. 6.* DEBUSSY: *Suite bergamasque: Clair de lune. Prélude: La cathédrale engloutie.* ALBENIZ: *Fête-Dieu à Seville.* RACHMANINOV: *Prelude in C sharp min., Op. 3/2.* MUSSORGSKY: *Night on the bare mountain; Pictures at an exhibition: The Great Gate of Kiev.*
✹ *** Telarc Dig. CD-80338 [id.].

Stokowski began his conducting career in Cincinnati in 1909, moving on to Philadelphia three years later; so a collection of his orchestral transcriptions from his first orchestra is appropriate, particularly when the playing is so committed and polished and the recording so sumptuous. Indeed, none of Stokowski's own recordings can match this Telarc disc in sheer glamour of sound. The arrangement of *La cathédrale engloutie* is very free and melodramatically telling. Most interesting is *Night on the bare mountain*, which has a grandiloquent brass chorale added as a coda. Any admirer of Stokowski should regard this superbly engineered CD as an essential purchase. It is now reissued with two extra items added, the Brahms *Hungarian dance No. 6* and Stokowski's extraordinary transcription of *The Great Gate of Kiev from Mussorgsky's Pictures at an exhibition.* Kunzel has the advantage of Telarc's bass-drum recording, and at the very close there is a highly imaginative added touch as the old magician introduces an evocation of Moscow cathedral bells.

City of Prague Philharmonic Orchestra, Gavin Sutherland

Music from the 'Carry On' films: *Carry on Camping; Carry on Suite* (music from *Carry on Sergeant, Teacher* and *Nurse*); *Carry on Cabby; Carry on Cleo; Carry on Jack; Carry on Behind;*

Raising the Wind; Carry on at your Convenience; Carry on up the Khyber; Carry on Doctor again.
(M) *** ASV Dig. CD WHL 2119 [id.].

Some readers may raise a quizzical eyebrow at the inclusion of this collection, for the famous 'Carry On' series of films is the epitome of British vulgarity. Yet their incidental music shows the British light music tradition at its best. The early scores were written by Bruce Montgomery (*Carry on Teacher, Nurse, Cabby,* etc) where a flavour of the late 1950s is evoked: the main '*Carry On*' theme is unashamedly jazzy, yet has a central counter-theme which is delightfully nostalgic and totally British. For the later films, Eric Rogers took over – he peppered the films with quotes from famous classical pieces, whilst his own melodies are distinctly appealing, reflecting the 'swinging sixties'. The *Carry on Camping* and *Carry on Doctor* suites are perhaps the best, not just for their vivaciousness, but also for the remarkably piquant and deft orchestration throughout. *Carry on at your Convenience* evokes the production line of a toilet-bowl factory, and the Prague orchestra respond with enthusiasm (the timpani are especially impressive); then there is an unexpectedly charming romantic passage which is quite touching, before the riotous ending. The imperial opening music of *Carry on up the Khyber* (perhaps the wittiest of the series), is strongly characterized, and the *Carry on Cleo* suite, with a Hollywood-style opening march *à la* Rozsa, is also effective. Altogether the invention is surprisingly varied. The orchestra perform as though they have played it all their lives, no doubt a tribute to the conductor Gavin Sutherland, and the producer, Philip Lane. The recording is also superb. Thoroughly recommended for those on the 'Carry On' wavelength, and for other lovers of this musical genre who are simply curious.

Cleveland Symphonic Winds, Fennell

'*Stars and stripes*': ARNAUD: *3 Fanfares.* BARBER: *Commando march.* LEEMANS: *Belgian Paratroopers.* FUCIK: *Florentine march, Op. 214.* KING: *Barnum and Bailey's favourite.* ZIMMERMAN: *Anchors aweigh.* J. STRAUSS Sr: *Radetzky march.* VAUGHAN WILLIAMS: *Sea songs; Folksongs suite.* SOUSA: *The Stars and Stripes forever.* GRAINGER: *Lincolnshire posy.*
*** Telarc Dig. CD 80099 [id.].

This vintage collection from Frederick Fennell and his superb Cleveland wind and brass group is one of the finest of its kind ever made. Severance Hall, Cleveland, has ideal acoustics for this programme and the playing has wonderful virtuosity and panache. Add to all this digital engineering of Telarc's highest calibre, and you have a very special issue.

Columbia Symphony Orchestra or New York Philharmonic Orchestra, Bruno Walter

Bruno Walter Edition, Volume 1 (complete)
(M) **(*) Sony stereo/mono SX10K 66246 (10).

MAHLER: *Symphonies Nos. 1 (Titan)* (with Columbia SO); *2 (Resurrection)* (with Emilia Cundari, Maureen Forrester, Westminster Ch., NYPO); *Lieder eines fahrenden Gesellen* (with Mildred Miller, Columbia SO) (SMK 64447) (2) [id.].

MAHLER: *Symphony No. 4* (with Desi Halban, NYPO); (ii) *Lieder und Gesänge: Frühlingsmorgen; Erinnerung; Hans und Grethe; Ich ging mit Lust durch einen grünen Wald; Starke Einbildungskraft; Ablösung im Sommer; Scheiden und Meiden; Nicht wiedersehen* (Halban & Walter, piano) (mono SMK 64450) [id.].

MAHLER: *Symphony No. 5* (with NYPO) (mono SMK 64451) [id.].

MAHLER: *Symphony No. 9* (with rehearsal & conversation between Bruno Walter and Arnold Michaelis) (with Columbia SO) (SMK 64452) (2) [id.].

MAHLER: *Das Lied von der Erde* (with Mildred Miller, Ernst Haefliger, NYPO) (SMK 64455) [id.].

WAGNER: *Siegfried idyll* (with rehearsal); *Der fliegende Holländer: Overture; Die Meistersinger: Prelude to Act I; Lohengrin: Prelude to Act I; Parsifal: Prelude to Act I; Tannhäuser: Overture and Venusberg music* (with Columbia SO) (SMK 64456) (2) [id.].

BEETHOVEN: *Violin concerto* (with Joseph Szigeti, NYPO). MENDELSSOHN: *Violin concerto* (with Nathan Milstein, NYPO) (mono SMK 64459) [id.].

The first volume of Sony's Bruno Walter Edition understandably concentrates on Mahler, with the recordings of the *First, Second* and *Ninth Symphonies* and, to a lesser extent, *Das Lied von der Erde*, an indispensable part of the catalogue. Nos. 4 and 5 are mono, but Walter aficionados will want these too, although, for all the conductor's magnetism, the orchestral playing in New York is less refined.

In the first movement of the *Fifth*, Walter's seamless and seemingly spontaneous control of the Funeral march is memorable, as of course is the glowing *Adagietto*. The Lieder recital, which is a makeweight to the glorious mono version of the *Fourth Symphony*, is made special by his piano accompaniments for Desi Halban, reticent as they are. Walter's Wagner orchestral recordings also show him at his finest, and here the ear notices the greater amplitude and weight with which the Sony engineers have enhanced the sound.

Szigeti's account of Beethoven's *Violin concerto* comes from New York in 1947. His classical purity of line is still evident, but the loss of bloom on his timbre and the moments of disturbing vibrato which troubled the great violinist in the last decade of his career had already begun to surface. Milstein's patrician account of the Mendelssohn *Concerto* was recorded two years earlier and is undoubtedly distinguished, although he re-recorded the work in stereo with Abbado for DG with equal success. All these recordings are available separately, and the stereo CDs are discussed in greater detail in our main volume under the appropriate composer listing. The rehearsal recordings add to the value and interest of these important reissues.

Columbia Symphony Orchestra, Bruno Walter

Bruno Walter Edition, Volume 2 (complete)
(M) **(*) Sony stereo/mono SX10K 66247 (10).

BEETHOVEN: *Symphonies Nos. 1 in C, Op. 21; 2 in D, Op. 36; Coriolan overture* (SMK 64460).

BEETHOVEN: *Symphonies Nos. 3 in E flat (Eroica), Op. 55; 8 in F* (SMK 64461).

BEETHOVEN: *Symphonies Nos. 4 in B flat, Op. 60; 6 in F (Pastoral), Op. 68* (SMK 64462).

BEETHOVEN: *Symphonies Nos. 5 in C min., Op. 67; 7 in A, Op. 92* (SMK 64463).

BEETHOVEN: *Symphony No. 9 in D min., Op. 125* (with Cundari, Rankin, Da Costa, Wilderman, Westminster Ch.) (SMK 64464).

BEETHOVEN: *Symphonies Nos. 4, 5, 7 & 9* (rehearsals) (SMK 64465).

BARBER: *Symphony No. 1, Op. 9.* Richard STRAUSS: *Don Juan; Death and transfiguration.* DVORAK: *Slavonic dance, Op. 46/1* ((mono) SMK 64466).

Johann STRAUSS Jr: *Waltzes: An der schönen blauen Donau; Geschichten aus dem Wiener Wald; Kaiser; Weiner Blut; Overtures: Die Fledermaus; Der Zigeunerbaron.* BRAHMS: *Hungarian dances Nos. 1, 3, 10 & 17.* SMETANA: *Vltava* (both with NYPO) ((mono) SMK 64467).

MOZART: (i) *Violin concertos Nos. 3 in G, K.216; 4 in D, K.218. Serenade No. 13 (Eine kleine Nachtmusik), K.525* ((i) with Zino Francescatti) (SMK 64468).

BRAHMS: (i) *German Requiem*; (ii) *Alto rhapsody, Op. 53* (with (i) Seefried, London, Westminster Ch., NYPO; (ii) Mildred Miller, Occidental College Concert Ch., Columbia SO) ((mono/ stereo) SMK 64469).

Although he enjoyed a position of pre-eminence in the 1930s, Bruno Walter was never invited to record a Beethoven cycle. Duplication was less frequent then than it is now, and Weingartner and Toscanini dominated the field. (Walter's glorious pre-war records of the *Pastoral Symphony* with the Vienna Philharmonic give some idea of how good it might have been.) After he settled in the United States he recorded all nine symphonies with the New York Philharmonic and Philadelphia orchestras, but the set offered here is with the Columbia Symphony, made in California in 1958/9, not long before he died, and by general consent the finer of the two by a considerable margin.

These performances embody the humane, songful approach which characterized his finest work, their warmth standing out in contrast against the gaunt, often matter-of-fact approach of Klemperer. Tempi are not exaggerated and, although Walter may not have had the electricity and fiery qualities that distinguish Toscanini's NBC Beethoven, there is no lack of either rhythmic vitality or lyrical intensity.

There is also a rehearsal disc (available as part of the set) which shows his courteous, gentle, yet firm approach to music-making in the slow movement of the *Fourth*, the first movements of the *Fifth* and *Seventh* and the Scherzo of the *Ninth*. All these recordings are discussed more fully under their individual entries in our main volume, as they are all available separately. Of particular interest in the present set is the 1945 version of Barber's *First Symphony*, which makes its first appearance since the two blue-label 78-r.p.m. discs were withdrawn in the early 1950s. Not only is this the only American symphony, it is the only contemporary symphony, Walter recorded: his repertoire never embraced much modern music (though he did conduct Wellesz's *Prospero's spell*). Like the two Strauss tone-poems with which it is coupled, it is a mono disc and, though the resulting transfer produces cleaner and better-focused sound than the originals, it still calls for some tolerance. Walter's Mozart was particularly notable for its humane qualities, and he gives admirable support to Francescatti, his soloist in the two best-known violin concertos, who is at times over-tense – what the French would call *nerveux*.

The Brahms *Requiem* with the youthful Irmgard Seefried and George London comes from 1954 and is also in mono. Its companion, the *Alto rhapsody*, with Mildred Miller, comes from 1962, the year of his death, and is less successful. However, this is a collection which serious collectors will want to have.

Columbia Symphony Orchestra or New York Philharmonic Orchestra, Bruno Walter

Bruno Walter Edition, Volume 3 (complete)
(M) **(*) Sony stereo/mono SX10K 66248 (10).

BRAHMS: *Symphony No. 1 in C min., Op. 68; Variations on a theme of Haydn, Op. 56a; Academic festival overture.*
(M) *** Sony SMK 64470 [id.]. Columbia SO Walter.

BRAHMS: *Symphonies Nos. 2 in D, Op. 73; 3 in F, Op. 90.*
(M) *** Sony SMK 64471 [id.]. Columbia SO Walter.

BRAHMS: *Symphony No. 4 in E min.; Tragic overture; (i) Song of destiny (Schicksalslied), Op. 54.*
(M) *** Sony SMK 64472 [id.]. Columbia SO Walter; (i) with Occidental College Concert Ch.

MOZART: (i) *Symphonies Nos. 25 in G min., K.183; 28 in C, K.200; 29 in A, K.201; (ii) 35 in D (Haffner), K.385.*
(M) (***) Sony mono SMK 64473 [id.]. (i) Columbia SO; (ii) NYPO, Walter.

MOZART: *'The birth of a performance'* (recorded rehearsals of *Symphony No. 36*); (i) *Symphonies Nos. 36 in C (Linz), K.425; (ii) 38 in D (Prague), K.504.*
(M) *** Sony mono SM2K 64474 (2) [S2K 64474]. (i) Columbia SO; (ii) NYPO, Walter.

MOZART: *Symphonies Nos. 39 in E flat, K.543; 40 in G min., K.550; 41 in C (Jupiter), K.551.*
(M) (**) Sony mono SMK 64477 [id.]. NYPO Walter.

SCHUBERT: *Symphony No. 9 in C (Great); Rosamunde: Overture; Ballet music; Entr'acte No. 3.*
(M) **(*) Sony SMK 64478 [id.]. Columbia SO Walter.

(i) BEETHOVEN: *Triple concerto for piano, violin and cello in C, Op. 56.* (ii) BRAHMS: *Double concerto for violin, cello and orchestra in C, Op. 102.*
(M) *(**) Sony mono/stereo SMK 64479 [id.]. (i) Walter Hendl, John Corigliano, Leonard Rose, NYPO; (ii) Francescatti, Fournier, Columbia SO, Walter.

(i) BRUCKNER: *Te Deum.* (ii) MOZART: *Requiem mass in D min., K.626.*
(M) ** Sony mono 64480 [id.]. (i) Yeend, Lipton, Lloyd, Harrel; (ii) Seefried, Tourel, Simoneau, Warfield; Westminster Ch., NYPO, Walter.

Walter's set of the Brahms symphonies is self-recommending, still standing high on the list of recommendations. The present remastering has improved detail, with a very slight loss of bloom on the violins. His Schubert *Ninth* is also endearing, and the mono Mozart recordings from the 1950s also bring much refreshment – although, surprisingly, the last three symphonies are less successful than the earlier ones.

The rehearsal sequence for the *Linz Symphony* remains as fascinating as ever. All these recordings are discussed fully under their composer entries in our main volume. The relative disappointments are the Beethoven *Triple concerto*, which is unattractively balanced, and the two choral works. Both are spaciously dramatic performances (and the Mozart *Requiem* has a splendid solo team), but the choral singing, although ardent, is not as polished as we would expect today.

Bruno Walter Edition, Volume 4 (complete).
(B) **(*) Sony stereo/mono SX9K 66249 (9).

BRUCKNER: *Symphony No. 4 in E flat (Romantic)* (SMK 64481) [id.].

BRUCKNER: *Symphony No. 7 in E* (SMK 64482) [id.].

BRUCKNER: *Symphony No. 9 in D min.* (✹ SMK 64483) [id.].

DVORAK: *Symphonies Nos. 8 in G; 9 in E min. (New World)* (SMK 64484) [id.].

(all above with Columbia SO)

HAYDN: *Symphonies Nos. 88 in G; 100 in G (Military)* (with Columbia SO); *102 in B flat* (with NYPO) (stereo/mono SMK 64485) [id.].

HAYDN: *Symphony No. 96 in D (Miracle)* (with NYPO). MOZART: *3 German dances, K.605/1–3; Masonic funeral music, K.477; Minuets, K.568 & 599; Overtures: Così fan tutte; The Impresario; Le nozze di Figaro; Die Zauberflöte* (with Columbia SO) (mono/stereo SMK 64486) [id.].

SCHUBERT: *Symphonies Nos. 5 in B flat, D.485; 8 in B min. (Unfinished).* BEETHOVEN: *Overture: Leonora No. 3* (with Columbia SO or NYPO) (stereo/mono SMK 64487) [id.].

SCHUMANN: *Symphony No. 3 in E flat (Rhenish)* (with NYPO). BEETHOVEN: *Overtures: Egmont; Leonora No. 2* (with Columbia SO) (mono/stereo SMK 64488) [id.].

BEETHOVEN: *Piano concerto No. 5 (Emperor)* (with Serkin, NYPO). SCHUMANN: *Piano concerto in A min.* (with Eugene Istomin, Columbia SO) (mono/stereo SMK 64489) [id.].

The highlights of this set are Bruckner's *Fourth* and (especially) *Ninth Symphony*; by their side the *Seventh* is comparatively disappointing. The coupling of Dvořák's *Eighth* and *New World Symphonies* is also very special, and Walter's way with Schubert has an endearing grace and warmth. The Haydn

symphonies are of more mixed appeal. Only Nos. 88 and 100 are stereo (made in 1961) and the glorious slow movement of the former drags, while similarly slow tempi in the *Military Symphony* also bring heaviness. The finales of both works are the most successful movements; overall, the effect is more of a rehearsal than live performances.

The Mozart programme is much more characteristic. Walter's tempi in the overtures are unerringly apt, but readers should note that these are not Walter's more recent, stereo recordings but his earlier, mono versions made in 1954. The account of the *Masonic funeral music* is particularly fine. Good sound, too. The performance of Schumann's *Rhenish Symphony* is impressive, although this is mono; of the Beethoven overtures, *Leonora No. 2* is really outstanding. This is stereo; the other two are mono. However, neither of the concertos could be placed among the more remarkable versions of these works in the current catalogue, although Serkin's mono *Emperor* is more memorable than Istomin's Schumann (which is early stereo).

Concerto Copenhagen, Andrew Manze (with soloists)

'Swedish rococo concertos': AGRELL: *Flute concerto in B minor* (with Maria Bania); *Oboe concerto in B flat* (with Lars Henriksson). Heinrich Philip JOHNSEN: *Double bassoon concerto in F* (with Mats Klingfors & Christian Beuse). Ferdinand ZELLBELL: *Bassoon Concerto in A minor: Allegro.* (with Mats Klingfors). (v) *Cello Concerto in D* (with Åse Åkerberg).
*** Musica Sveciae Dig. MSCD 411[id.].

These composers inhabit the outer fringes of the catalogue. None is represented by more than one work. Heinrich Philip Johnsen (1717–79) was born in Northern Germany and came to Stockholm with his princely employer, Adolf Frederik of Holstein-Gottorp, who was elected to the Swedish throne. Johan Agrell (1701–65) was born in Sweden but spent the bulk of his life in Germany, and of the three only Ferdinand Zellbell (1719–80) was born, bred and died in Sweden.

With the exception of the Handelian *Oboe concerto* of Agrell, all these pieces are in manuscript. The *F major Concerto for two bassoons* by Heinrich Philip Johnsen is rather delightful. It is fresh and entertaining, and played with polish and elegance. (Johnsen enjoys the distinction of having written an opera, *The Bartered Bride.*)

Zellbell was a pupil of Roman and went to Hamburg where he studied with Telemann, and to Hanover, where in 1741 he composed this *Cello concerto*. He spent the bulk of his life in Stockholm where he succeeded to his father's position as organist of the Storkyrkan (cathedral) but he was unpaid for many years and died heavily in debt. The movement from his *A minor concerto* is a witty piece, and the *Cello concerto* is inventive and at times touching. Andrew Manze and the Concerto Copenhagen give first-class support to the talented soloists and the aural perspective is eminently truthful. Impeccable scholarly notes by Martin Tegén.

Curzon, Clifford (piano)

BRAHMS: *Piano concerto No. 2 in B flat, Op. 83* (with VPO, Knappertsbusch). GRIEG: *Piano concerto in A min., Op. 16* (with LSO, Fjeldstad). RACHMANINOV: *Piano concerto No. 2 in C min., Op. 18* (with LPO, Boult). TCHAIKOVSKY: *Piano concerto No. 1 in B flat min., Op. 23* (with VPO, Solti).
(B) *(**) Decca stereo/mono Double 460 994-2 (2) [id.].

Any student of fine piano playing would surely want to experience Curzon's performances, and here we have four great concertos at bargain price, with the Grieg a classic. Recorded in 1959, it has remained at or near the top of the list ever since, notable as much for its freshness and power as for its lyrical tenderness. It is available with different couplings on Decca's 'Classic Sound' and 'Legends' labels. The partnership between Solti and Curzon in the Tchaikovsky may seem unlikely, but works well.

If, like the recording, it is not quite in the same league as the Grieg, it is still very exciting. Curzon's 1957 Rachmaninov would be better known had it been recorded in stereo as this technical advance rather eclipsed it – as it did Katchen's more extrovert Decca recordings at that time. However, Curzon's comparatively classical approach is both individual and telling and the recording is very good for its time. In the 1955 Brahms No. 2, Knappertsbusch is inclined to linger over much, but with these two imposing artists, a certain integrity comes over. The mono recording is a bit dry and close, but tolerable. All in all, this is a thoroughly worthwhile set.

Czech Philharmonic Orchestra, Gerd Albrecht

HAAS: *Studies for string orchestra*. SCHULHOF: *Symphony No. 2*. ULLMANN: *Symphony No. 2*. KLEIN: *Partita for strings*.
*** Orfeo Dig. C 337941 A [id.].

Like the issues in Decca's *Entartete Musik* series, this Orfeo disc features music dismissed by the Nazis as decadent, all here by Jewish composers from Czechoslovakia slaughtered in the Holocaust.

Pavel Haas, often counted as Janáček's most important pupil, wrote his *Studies* in Theresienstadt, the prison camp where the Nazis assembled Jewish intellectuals, later to be killed in death camps. Tautly argued in four sections lasting eight minutes, it was given its first performance in the camp under one of the then inmates who happily managed to survive, Karel Ančerl, later the conductor of the Czech Philharmonic. Albrecht and today's Czech Philharmonic bring out the vitality of the writing, with no hint in it of self-indulgence or self-pity. This is a composer writing in sight of death simply because he has to, relishing a last opportunity.

The *Symphony No. 2* of Erwin Schulhof was written in 1932, long before the Germans invaded Czechoslovakia, a work very much of its period with a charming *Scherzo alla Jazz* influenced by Stravinsky's *Soldier's tale*. The *Symphony No. 2* of Viktor Ullmann, also in four crisp movements, was one of no fewer than twenty-five works that he wrote in Theresienstadt, including the opera *The Emperor of Atlantis*, also on disc. Though he was a pupil of Schoenberg, he here returned to tonality, communicating directly.

The youngest of the four, Gideon Klein from Moravia, more specifically drew inspiration from folk roots, very much in the way that Bartók did in Hungary. His *Partita for strings*, like the Pavel Haas *Studies*, has darkness in it, notably in the central variation movement, but here too the piece culminates in a mood of energetic optimism, a heartwarming expression of defiance. Very well played and recorded, the four works are the more moving for giving only momentary hints of what the composers were going through. First-rate sound.

Daniel, Nicholas (oboe), Peterborough String Orchestra

Italian oboe concertos: VIVALDI: *Concerto in C, RV 44*. ALBINONI: *Concerto in D min., Op. 9/2*. BELLINI: *Concertino in E flat*. MARCELLO: *Concerto in D min*. CIMAROSA: *Concerto in C* (arr. Arthur BENJAMIN).
(B) **(*) Hyperion Helios CDH 55034 [id.].

All the music here is tunefully undemanding, with the minor-key concertos adding a touch of expressive gravitas. Arthur Benjamin's arrangement of the delightful Cimarosa concerto is always a delight, and the lovely Bellini *Concertino* sounds like one of his operatic arias arranged for oboe – complete with cabaletta finale. Nicholas Daniel is closely miked, but he is a stylish performer and draws lively support from the Peterborough orchestra. The disc plays for just under 55 minutes, but is offered at bargain-price.

Damiens, Alain (clarinet), Ensemble Intercontemporain, David Robertson

'American clarinet': Elliott CARTER: *Concerto*; *Gra for solo clarinet*. Steve REICH: *New York counterpoint for clarinet and tape*. Howard SANDCROFT: *Tephillah for clarinet and electronics*. ADAMS: *Gnarly buttons for clarinet and small orchestra* (with André Troutlet, clarinet).
*** Virgin Classics Dig. VC5 45351-2 [id.].

Elliott Carter's *Concerto* is written in six sections, for different instrumental groups (percussion, strings, woodwind and so on). In a live performance the soloist moves among them. The music is characteristically complex and unpredictable, yet has a strong lyrical core. The solo *Gra* is more fragmented. Reich's *New York counterpoint* is written in eleven clarinet parts, only one of which is live. The soloist plays with his own recordings which are held in endless ostinato loops. There are three movements, and the last has syncopated jazz inflections. The composer demands a performance 'without charm', but the end result is very diverting. Sandcroft's *Tephillah* is based on Hebrew chant, although its fragmentation means that you might not guess it! The soloist is 'electronically' shadowed. By the side of these works John Adams's *Gnarly buttons* is positively traditional, readily communicative, with a central *Hoe down*, and the lyrical finale melodically haunting, with the soloist providing a burst of virtuosity to dominate a surge of energy near the close. The vivid performances throughout this anthology certainly illustrate the pluralism of twentieth-century American music.

Desperados Steel Orchestra, Trevor 'Inch High' Valentine

'Classical transcriptions': OFFENBACH: *Overture Orpheus in the Underworld*. PONCHIELLI: *La Gioconda: Dance of the hours* (abridged). SIBELIUS: *Finlandia*. MASCAGNI: *Cavalleria rusticana: Intermezzo*. PADILLA/GARCIA/CATELVI: *El Relicario*. BIZET: *Symphony in C: Finale*. BACH: *Suite No. 3 in D: Air*. TRAD: *Amazing grace*. JOPLIN: *The entertainer*. HANDEL: *Messiah: Hallelujah chorus*.
(B) ** EMI Début CDZ5 73502-2 [id.].

The Desperados Steel Orchestra make an unexpected début, on an EMI label usually reserved for soloists, instrumental and chamber groups. West Indian steel bands came about when local youths discovered in the 1940s that oil drums (called pans) could be 'tuned' and used to cover the full range of a normal band or orchestra of normal instruments. The Desperados are one of the oldest steel bands in Trinidad and Tobago. The performing musicians play by ear, learning the music note by note. But that does not inhibit performances of exhilarating virtuosity, and the arrangements are often remarkably effective. The items that come off best are the Offenbach overture, the Mascagni intermezzo, Scott Joplin and, most surprisingly, the *Hallelujah chorus*. The band is very brightly recorded and this is music which perhaps sounds best in the open air, but as a novelty disc this is certainly very successful.

Detroit Symphony Orchestra, Neeme Järvi

'Encore!': CHABRIER: *Fête polonaise*. GLINKA: *Kamarinskaya*; *Valse fantaisie*. SIBELIUS: *Andante festivo for strings*. BOLZONI: *Minuet*. DVORAK: *Humoresque*. DARZINS: *Valse mélancolique*. ELLINGTON: *Solitude* (trans. for strings). SHOSTAKOVICH: *The Gadfly: Romance*. MUSSORGSKY: *Gopak*. DEBUSSY: *Suite bergamasque: Clair de lune*. SCHUMANN: *Abendlied, Op. 107/6*. MEDINS: *Aria*. GERSHWIN: *Promenade: walking the dog*. SOUSA: *The Stars and Stripes forever*.
**(*) Chandos Dig. CHAN 9227 [id.].

The acoustics of Detroit's Orchestra Hall, made famous by the Mercury engineers at the end of the 1950s, remain impressive and the Detroit orchestra is flattered here by opulently glowing sound, which especially suits the Glinka pieces and the lovely Sibelius *Andante festivo*. The rest of the programme is rather slight, consisting entirely of lollipops, some well-known, plus a few engaging novelties. All are presented with Järvi's customary flair and are very well played. If you enjoy this kind of concert, there is no need to hesitate, for the programme is generous: 73 minutes.

Detroit Symphony Orchestra, Paul Paray

'French opera highlights': HEROLD: *Overture: Zampa*. AUBER: *Overture: The Crown diamonds*. GOUNOD: *Faust: ballet suite*; *Waltz* (from Act II). SAINT-SAENS: *Samson et Dalila: Bacchanale*. BIZET: *Carmen: Danse bohème*. BERLIOZ: *Les Troyens: Royal hunt and storm*. *Phèdre overture*. THOMAS: *Mignon: Gavotte*.
(M) *** [Mercury 432 014-2].

Paul Paray's reign at Detroit tempted the Mercury producers to record a good deal of French music under his baton, and here is a good example of the Gallic verve and sparkle that were achieved. The only disappointment is the unslurred horn phrasing at the magical opening and close of the *Royal hunt and storm*. This is not now available in the UK.

'Marches and overtures à la française':
MEYERBEER: *Le Prophète: Coronation march*.
GOUNOD: *Funeral march for a marionette*.
SAINT-SAENS: *Marche militaire française*;
Marche héroïque. DE LISLE: *La Marseillaise*.
Overtures: ADAM: *Si j'étais roi*. BOIELDIEU: *La Dame blanche*. ROSSINI: *William Tell*.
OFFENBACH: *La belle Hélène*; *Orpheus in the Underworld*. *Contes d'Hoffmann: Barcarolle etc*.
(M) **(*) Mercury (IMS) 434 332-2 [id.].

A generous and flavourful Gallic concert, recorded in three different Detroit venues, with acoustics not entirely flattering to the orchestra, who nevertheless always play splendidly. The Adam and Boieldieu overtures need the glow of Kingsway Hall: here the resonance of Cass Technical High School slightly clouds detail. The marches and the Offenbach items were recorded in 1959 in Old Orchestral Hall, and the sound is more expansive. The most memorable pieces are the wittily engaging Gounod (always to be remembered as Alfred Hitchcock's TV signature-tune) and the spirited *Belle Hélène* overture, not put together by the composer, but none the worse for that. Throughout, the élan of the playing always brings enjoyment, and the virtuosity of the fiddles in the *William Tell* galop is exhilarating.

Dichter, Misha (piano),
Philharmonia Orchestra, Sir Neville Marriner

Concertante works: ADDINSELL: *Warsaw concerto*. GERSHWIN: *Rhapsody in blue*. LITOLFF: *Concerto symphonique, Op. 102: Scherzo*.
CHOPIN: *Fantasia on Polish airs, Op. 13*. LISZT: *Polonaise brillante* (arr. of WEBER: *Polacca brillante, Op. 72*).
(B) *** Ph. Virtuoso Dig. 411 123-2 [(M) id. import].

Never before has the orchestral detail of Addinsell's indelible pastiche emerged so beguilingly on record as it does here under Marriner; he and Misha Dichter combine to give the music genuine romantic memorability, within a warmly sympathetic acoustic. Gershwin's famous *Rhapsody* is hardly less successful, the performance spirited yet glowing. To make a foil, the Litolff *Scherzo* is taken at a sparkingly brisk tempo and projected with great flair. The Chopin *Fantasia* has a lower voltage, but the closing Liszt arrangement of Weber glitters admirably. The sound is first rate and is very believable in its CD format.

Driessche, André van (horn),
Belgian Radio & TV Orchestra, Rahbari

'Flemish romantic horn concertos' by
MEULEMANS; DE JONG. HERBERIGS: *Cyrano de Bergerac*. EECHAUTE: *Night poem*.
(BB) *** Discover Dig. DICD 920299 [id.].

Four Flemish composers, very little known outside Belgium, here offer a series of richly enjoyable works, very well recorded, all with solo horn brilliantly played by André van Driessche. The most striking is the Straussian symphonic poem, *Cyrano de Bergerac*, by Robert Herberigs, inspired by Rostand's play, with heroic outer sections and love music in the middle. The *Horn concertos* of Arthur Meulemans and Marinus de Jong, each in three compact movements, also have ripe Straussian echoes, as well as anticipations of Hollywood film music, while Prosper van Eechaute's *Night poem* brings the most sensuous music of all. At superbargain price, this is well worth investigating.

Du Pré, Jacqueline (cello)

'The Art of Jacqueline du Pré' (with (i) LSO, Sir John Barbirolli; (ii) RPO, Sir Malcolm Sargent; (iii) New Philh. O; (iv) Chicago SO; (v) ECO; (vi) Daniel Barenboim; (vii) Valda Aveling; (viii) Gerald Moore; (ix) Ernest Lush; (x) Steven Bishop): (i) ELGAR: *Cello concerto in E min., Op. 85*. (ii) DELIUS: *Cello concerto*. (iii; vi) SAINT-SAENS: *Cello concerto No. 1 in A min., Op. 33*. (iv; vi) DVORAK: *Cello concerto in B min., Op. 104*; *Waldesruhe, Op. 68*. (iii; vi) SCHUMANN: *Cello concerto in A min., Op. 129*. (i; vii) MONN: *Cello concerto in G min*. HAYDN: *Cello concertos in* (i) *C and* (v; vi) *D, Hob VIIb/1–2*. (vi) CHOPIN: *Cello sonata in G min., Op. 65*. (vi) FRANCK: *Cello sonata in A*. (viii) FAURE: *Elégie in C min., Op. 24*. (viii) BRUCH: *Kol Nidrei, Op. 47*. BACH: *(Unaccompanied) Cello suites Nos. 1–2, BWV 1007/8*. (ix) HANDEL: *Cello sonata in G min*.
BEETHOVEN: (vi) *Variations in G min. on Judas Maccabaeus: See the conqu'ring hero comes, WoO 45*; (x) *Cello sonatas Nos. 3, in A, Op. 69*; *5 in D, Op. 102/2*. (vi) *Variations on themes from 'The Magic Flute': 7 variations in D, WoO 46 (Bei Männern, welche Liebe fühlen); 12 variations in F, 66 (Ein Mädchen oder Weibchen)*.
(B) *** EMI CZS5 68132-2 (8) [(M) id. import].

Admirers of this remarkably gifted artist, whose career ended so tragically, will welcome this survey of her major recordings, made over the incredibly brief period of a single decade. Her first recordings (1961) have a BBC source and her last (the Chopin and Franck *Sonatas*) were made at Abbey Road in

1971. But of course she made her real breakthrough in 1965 with the justly famous Kingsway Hall recording of the Elgar *Concerto* with Barbirolli. Some items included here are not otherwise currently available and, with excellent transfers, this set is an admirable and economical way of exploring her art. There are good if brief notes and some heart-rending photographs showing this young prodigy playing with characteristic concentration and joyously in conversation with her equally young husband, Daniel Barenboim.

Cello concertos: BOCCHERINI: *Concerto in B flat* (arr. GRUTZMACHER). HAYDN: *Concertos in C & D, Hob VIIb/1–2* (with ECO, Barenboim or LSO, Barbirolli). SCHUMANN: *Concerto in A min., Op. 129*. SAINT-SAENS: *Concerto No. 1 in A min., Op. 33* (with New Philh. O., Barenboim). DVORAK: *Concerto in B min., Op. 104; Silent woods, Op. 68/5* (with Chicago SO, Barenboim). DELIUS: *Concerto* (with RPO, Sargent). MONN: *Concerto in G min.* ELGAR: *Cello concerto in E min., Op. 85* (both with LSO, Barbirolli). Richard STRAUSS: *Don Quixote, Op. 35* (with New Philh. O, Boult).
(B) *** EMI CZS5 67341-2 (6) [id.].

Those not wanting the chamber music on the above eight-disc coverage of the 'Art of Jacqueline du Pre', will find that this six-disc set is no less desirable, adding as it does the Boccherini/Grützmacher *Concerto*, most endearingly played, plus the recently remastered 1968 *Don Quixote* (with Boult), which is particularly fine. Fine transfers and excellent value.

'A Lasting inspiration' (with Daniel Barenboim, cond. or piano): BOCCHERINI: *Cello concerto in B flat* (arr. GRUTZMACHER). DVORAK: *Cello concerto (Adagio); Silent woods, Op. 68/5*. HAYDN: *Cello concerto in C*. BEETHOVEN: *Piano trio No. 5 in D (Ghost), Op. 70/1; 7 Variations on 'Bei Männern'* (both with Pinchas Zukerman). BRAHMS: *Cello sonata No. 1 in E min., Op. 38*. FRANCK: *Sonata in A* (arr. DELSART) *(Allegro ben moderato)*.
(M) **(*) EMI CMS5 66350-2 (2) [(M) id. import].

A medium-priced anthology that is self-recommending if the more comprehensive programme is of appeal. The chamber-music performances have the same qualities of spontaneity and inspiration that have made Du Pré's account with Barbirolli of Elgar's *Cello concerto* come to be treasured above all others. Any tendency to self-indulgence, plus a certain leaning towards romantic expressiveness, is counterbalanced by the urgency and intensity of the playing. In the Brahms *Sonata* it is hard to accept the blatant change of tempo between first and second subjects, but here too there is warmth and flair. If some find Du Pré's approach to Haydn too romantic, it is nevertheless difficult to resist in its ready warmth. The Beethoven *Ghost Trio* is comparably individual and inspirational. The sound-quality is fairly consistent, for all the remastered transfers are successful.

Eastman-Rochester Orchestra, Howard Hanson

American orchestral music: BARBER: *Capricorn concerto, Op. 21* (with Joseph Mariano (flute), Robert Sprenkle (oboe), Sidney Mear (trumpet)). PISTON: *The Incredible flutist* (ballet suite). GRIFFES: *Poem for flute and orchestra*. KENNAN: *3 Pieces*. MCCAULEY: *5 Miniatures for flute and strings* (all with Joseph Mariano (flute)). BERGSMA: *Gold and the Señor Commandante* (ballet suite).
(M) *** Mercury [434 307-2].

A first-rate concert of pioneering recordings, made between 1957 and 1963. The collection is worth having for Barber's *Capricorn concerto* alone, a less characteristic work than, say, any of the *Essays for orchestra*, or the solo concertos. Walter Piston's ballet *The Incredible flutist* comes from 1938 and the suite is one of the most refreshing and imaginative of all American scores.

Griffes' *Poem* with its gentle, shimmering textures is French in feeling but is thoroughly worthwhile in its own right. Joseph Mariano is an excellent soloist as he is in the more simplistic but engaging *Miniatures* of the Canadian William McCauley (born 1917). Kent Kennan's *Three Pieces* are clearly influenced by the ballet music of Stravinsky. Bergsma's ballet is rather noisy at times, and fails to be memorable, though brightly scored. Excellent performances throughout and typically vivid Eastman-Rochester sound.

American orchestral music II: MCPHEE: *Tabuh-Tabuhan (Toccata for orchestra)*. SESSIONS: *The Black maskers (suite)*. Virgil THOMSON: *Symphony on a hymn tune; The Feast of love* (with David Clatworthy).
(M) *** Mercury [434 310-2].

McPhee's *Tabuh-Tabuhan*, written in 1936, uses Balinese music for its main colouring and rhythmic background. Roger Sessions' *Black maskers suite* was written as incidental music for a play by Andreyev about devil worship and the Black Mass, but it is not in the same class as, say, Prokofiev's *Scythian suite*. This is no fault of the performance or recording. The Virgil Thomson *Symphony*, although based on hymn-like material, is attractively quirky (reflecting the composer's Parisian years, the influence of Les Six, and Satie in particular). The cantata *The Feast of love* could hardly be more contrasted in its warmly flowing lyricism, a heady setting of an anonymous Latin love poem. The poet revels in the erotic joys of love, and the composer and his excellent soloist are obviously delighted by the voluptuous feeling of the words. As always the vintage Mercury sound is vivid with colour.

American music: MOORE: *Pageant of P. T. Barnum.* CARPENTER: *Adventures in a perambulator.* Bernard ROGERS: *Once upon a time (5 Fairy tales).* Burrill PHILLIPS: *Selection from McGuffey's Reader.*
(M) *** Mercury [434 319-2].

John Alden Carpenter's suite was a favourite of American audiences before the Second World War and is diverting and often charming. The idiom is amiably innocuous but surprisingly seductive, not least the closing number, *Dreams.* Douglas Moore's *Pageant of P. T. Barnum* is hardly less accessible, with its engaging portraits of *Jenny Lind, General and Mrs Tom Thumb* and *Joice Heth,* a negress who was supposedly 160 years old!

Bernard Rogers's set of *Five Fairy tales* is scored with whimsical charm. William Holmes McGuffey's *Readers* formed the staple textbook diet of schoolchildren in mid-nineteenth-century America. The gently nostalgic second movement of Burrill Phillips's *Selection* pictures *John Alden and Priscilla* (who sailed on the *Mayflower*), and the noisy finale depicts *Paul Revere's midnight ride.* If this is perhaps the least memorable of the four works included here, its composer sums up rather succinctly the ethos of the whole programme. The performances are affectionate and committed throughout and the early stereo (1956–8) remarkably truthful. The above three CDs and the two below are now withdrawn in the UK.

Eastman-Rochester Orchestra or Philharmonia, Howard Hanson

'*Music for quiet listening*': John LA MONTAINE: *Birds of paradise, Op. 34* (with the Composer, piano). GRIEG: *Elegiac melody: The last spring.* LIADOV: *The enchanted lake*; *Kikimora.* Charles Martin LOEFFLER: *2 Rhapsodies: L'Etang (The pool)*; *La Cornemuse (The bagpipe)* (with Robert Sprenkle, oboe; Francis Tursi, viola, Armand Basile, piano). HANSON: *Fantasy variations on a theme of youth* (with David Burge, piano).
(M) *** Mercury [434 390-2].

Under a rather deceptive title, Wilma Cozart-Fine, the Mercury producer, has gathered together an exceptionally imaginative compilation which is considerably more than the sum of its individual musical components. John La Montaine's *Birds of paradise* is eclectic but ear-tickling, and it is recorded with that glittering sharpness of focus and bold colouring for which the Mercury engineers

were justly famous. With the composer at the (concertante) piano, its opening evokes Messiaen and its close Debussy. Prefaced by a quotation from Wilfred Owen, it is artfully crafted and imaginatively scored, and not too long.

A particularly eloquent account of Grieg's most beautiful *Elegiac melody* is then followed by vividly atmospheric accounts of two of Liadov's most memorable orchestral miniatures. The orchestra then stays silent while Robert Sprenkle (a piquant-timbred oboist), Francis Tursi and Armand Basile present Charles Martin Loeffler's engaging – indeed haunting – pair of rhapsodic miniatures.

Loeffler was concertmaster of the Boston Symphony but resigned from his first desk in 1903 to devote himself to composition. (He was born in Alsace and before his Boston appointment had played as a member of the court orchestra of a Russian nobleman, wintering in Nice and spending the summers at Lake Lugano!) His elegantly fastidious style is undoubtedly Gallic, and these two pieces are more subtly written and offer a far wider range of invention than their titles suggest.

The programme ends with a set of variations for piano and orchestra by Howard Hanson, full of lyrical warmth and imbued with that strongly personal, nostalgically Nordic melodic imprint which makes this splendid composer's music so striking. It is gloriously played and richly recorded.

(i) Eastman-Rochester Pops Orchestra, or (ii) London Pops Orchestra, Frederick Fennell

'*Popovers II*': (i) RACHMANINOV: *Prelude in G min.* GLIERE: *Russian Sailors' dance.* WEINBERGER: *Schwanda: Polka and Fugue.* (ii) RODGERS: *Carousel waltz.* MASSENET: *Le Cid: Aubade; Aragonaise.* BOLZONI: *Minuet.* GERMAN: *Henry VIII: Dances.* BENJAMIN: *Cotillon Suite.* ROSSINI: *William Tell: Passo a sei.* RIMSKY-KORSAKOV: *Dance of the Tumblers*; *Procession of the Nobles.*
(M) ** Mercury [434 356-2].

A good collection of sweetmeats, made all the more enjoyable by the inclusion of rarities: Arthur Benjamin's *Cotillon suite* is a collection of eighteenth-century airs and ballads in modern orchestral dress, and is charmingly rustic. German's once-popular *Henry VIII dances* conjure up a similarly rural scene, whilst Bolzoni's *Minuet* is neatly elegant. Fennell's direction is vivacious throughout (though not always producing perfection in ensemble, especially in the Eastman-Rochester recordings), especially in the spectacular numbers of Rimsky-Korsakov, Glière, and Weinberger.

The two excerpts from the *Le Cid* ballet music leave one hankering after the complete suite. The one great snag to this disc is the quality of the recording – it is vivid and bright in the Mercury manner, but doesn't allow for any real pianissimos, with the upper strings inclining to shrillness in high registers, especially in the earlier 1959 American recordings (the London ones date from 1965). An enjoyable collection all the same. But like many of the Eastman discs above, this has been withdrawn in the UK.

(i) Eastman-Rochester Pops Orchestra, or (ii) Eastman Wind Ensemble, Frederick Fennell

'Fabulous marches': WALTON: Orb and sceptre. BEETHOVEN: The ruins of Athens: Turkish march. SIBELIUS: Karelia suite: Alla marcia. BORODIN: Prince Igor: March. SCHUBERT: Marche militaire. GRIEG: Siguard Jorsalfar: Homage march. WAGNER: Tannhäuser: Grand march; (ii) Rienzi: overture. Parsifal: Good Friday music.
(M) *** Mercury 434 394-2 [id.].

An invigoratingly robust collection. It begins with a stirring account of Walton's Orb and sceptre, made all the more exciting by the brilliant Mercury sound, and the piquant little Beethoven march which follows is toe-tappingly catchy. If the Karelia suite march takes a little while to warm up, the following Borodin piece grips from the word go (it sounds a bit sinister too) with well-pointed vibrant strings.

Schubert's Marche militaire is briskly done, and the Grieg and Wagner marches are most enjoyable. Two Wagner pieces, very effectively arranged for wind band, have been added to the original LP collection, and make an excellently played and unusual bonus. The 1959/60 recording is spectacular in the Mercury manner, closely miked, a bit dry, a bit of tape hiss, but remarkable even by modern standards. If the programme appeals, go ahead.

Eastman Wind Ensemble, Frederick Fennell

American wind band music: Morton GOULD: West Point (Symphony for band). GIANNINI: Symphony No. 3. HOVHANESS: Symphony No. 4, Op. 165 (cond. A. Clyde Roller).
(M) ** Mercury [434 320-2].

Fine playing, but the music here is often too inflated to give pleasure on repetition. Gould's West Point Symphony is in two movements, Epitaphs (which at 11 minutes 55 seconds is far too long) and Marches. The Symphony No. 3 of Vittorio Giannini improves as it proceeds: the Scherzo and finale are the most interesting movements and the most

attractively scored. Best by far is the Hovhaness Symphony No. 4 (admirably directed by A. Clyde Roller) with its bold, rich, brass sonorities in the slower outer movements contrasting with marimba, vibraphone and other tuned percussion instruments in the central Allegro. Splendid sound, too.

Music from ballet and opera: SULLIVAN/ MACKERRAS: Pineapple Poll: suite (arr. DUTHOIT). ROSSINI/RESPIGHI: La boutique fantasque: suite (arr. Dan GODFREY). GOUNOD: Faust: ballet suite (arr. WINTERBOTTOM). WAGNER: Lohengrin: Prelude to Act III; Bridal chorus (arr. WINTERBOTTOM); Elsa's procession (arr. CAILLET). Das Rheingold (arr. Dan GODFREY).
(M) ** Mercury 434 322-2 [id.].

Although played with characteristic Eastman verve, this is essentially a programme for admirers of wind band transcriptions – here mostly traditional scorings by prominent British military band arrangers. Little of this music gains from its loss of string textures, and the famous Rossini/Respighi Boutique fantasque lacks sumptuousness. All this would be entertaining on the bandstand, but at home the ear craves the full orchestra.

'Hands across the sea – Marches from around the world': SOUSA: Hands across the sea; The US Field Artillery; The Thunderer; Washington Post; King Cotton; El Capitan; The Stars and Stripes forever. GANNE: Father of victory (Père de la victoire). Mariano SAN MIGUEL: The golden ear. TIEKE: Old comrades. PROKOFIEV: March, Op. 99. HANSSEN: Valdres march. Davide DELLE CESE: Inglesina. COATES: Knightsbridge. MEACHAM: American patrol. GOLDMAN: On the Mall. MCCOY: Lights out. KING: Barnum and Bailey's favourite. ALFORD: Colonel Bogey. KLOHR: The Billboard.
(M) *** Mercury (IMS) 434 334-2 [id.].

March records don't come any better than this, and nor does military/concert-band recording. The sparkling transients at the opening of Hands across the sea and the peppy spirit of the playing (as with all the Sousa items, and especially The Stars and Stripes forever) give the listener a real lift, while the French Father of victory and German Old comrades are just as full of character. The Prokofiev is as witty as you like, and Fennell shows he understands the more relaxed swagger of the British way in Colonel Bogey. First rate – but, with a 65-minute programme, this needs to be taken a march or two at a time, unless you want to fall out with the neighbours – this is not a CD to reproduce gently!

'Spirit of '76': Music for fifes and drums based upon the field music of the U.S. Army: Drum solo (2 versions); The camp duty; Marching tunes (6 versions); Service calls; Traditional fife and drum

duets. 'Ruffles and Flourishes': Music for field trumpets and drums based upon the field music of the U.S. Armed Forces: *Music for rendering honours* (3 versions); *Marching tunes and inspection pieces* (15 versions); *Drum solo*; *Bugle Calls for the U.S. Army* (excerpts).
(M) *** Mercury 434 386-2 [id.].

The sound quality of this CD is remarkably vivid, often startling, as though the cavalry is just about to burst into your sitting room; it was recorded in 1956 and it a wonderful tribute to the engineering of Mercury at that time. The sixty-six tracks cover American military music from the time of the Revolutionary War to the Civil War; the first half is fife and drum music, and the second group is for trumpets and drums. This is certainly not a disc to be played all in one go, with its lack of instrumental variety and brevity of duration (one piece lasts eight seconds!).

Some collectors might feel that it is not a disc to play at all! It is, none the less, a fascinating project. Frederick Fennell takes you through the music in a detailed booklet essay and generates plenty of electricity throughout the programme with his battery of percussion instruments. An eccentrically enjoyable disc then, but for whatever reason you buy it, it is hoped that you have tolerant neighbours. As most American readers will probably know, a similar 2CD collection called *'The Civil War'* is also available in the USA [Mercury 432 591-2], which is just as startling, and has one of the most detailed booklets in the history of the Compact Disc. If the above disc appeals, then so will that.

Elizabethan serenade

'Elizabethan serenade' (played by (i) Slovak RSO, Andrew Penny; (ii) Czecho-Slovak RSO, Adrian Leaper; (iii) RTE Concert O or Czecho-Slovak or Slovak RSO, Ernest Tomlinson; (iv) Slovak RSO, Gary Carpenter): (i) COATES: *By the sleepy lagoon*; (ii) *London suite: Knightsbridge march. Dam Busters march.* CURZON: *Robin Hood suite: March of the bowmen.* KETELBEY: *Bells across the meadows*; *In a monastery garden*; *In a Persian market* (both with chorus). (iii) ELLIS: *Coronation Scot.* (ii) Haydn WOOD: *Sketch of a dandy*; (iii) *Roses of Picardy.* (ii) FARNON: *Westminster waltz.* (i) DUNCAN: *Little suite: March.* (iii) BINGE: *Sailing by*; *Elizabethan serenade.* BENJAMIN: *Jamaican rumba.* TOMLINSON: *Little serenade.* WHITE: *Puffin' Billy.* (ii) GERMAN: *Tom Jones: Waltz.* (iii) COLLINS: *Vanity Fair.* (iv) MAYERL: *Marigold.*
(BB) *** Naxos Dig. 8.553515 [id.].

This Naxos collection is in effect a super-bargain sampler for a worthwhile (full-priced) Marco Polo Light Music composer series, and it inexpensively duplicates a great deal of the repertoire included on other, similar programmes by various orchestras (see above and below). Our allegiance to their excellence remains, but the strong appeal of the present collection is obvious. The performances are a little more variable but are always very good, and those conducted by Ernest Tomlinson, who includes his own delightful *Little serenade*, are excellent, notably Edward White's *Puffin' Billy*, Arthur Benjamin's *Jamaican rumba* and the morceau by Anthony Collins. There are no complaints about the recording either. Excellent value.

English Chamber Orchestra, Daniel Barenboim

English music (with (i) Neil Black; (ii) Pinchas Zukerman): DELIUS: *On hearing the first cuckoo in spring*; *Summer night on the river*; *2 Aquarelles*; *Fennimore and Gerda: Intermezzo.* VAUGHAN WILLIAMS: *Fantasia on Greensleeves*; (i) *Oboe concerto*; (ii) *The Lark ascending.* WALTON: *Henry V* (film incidental music): *Passacaglia*; *The death of Falstaff*; *Touch her soft lips and part.*
(M) *** DG 439 529-2 [id.].

We have always had a soft spot for Barenboim's warmly evocative ECO collection of atmospheric English music. Even if the effect is not always totally idiomatic, the recordings have a warmth and allure that are wholly seductive.

English Chamber Orchestra, Richard Bonynge

'Handel overtures and Overtures of the 18th century': HANDEL (ed. Bonynge): *Solomon: Overture and Arrival of the Queen of Sheba. Overtures: Berenice*; *Teseo*; *Ariodante*; *Jephtha (Sinfonia)*; *Esther*; *Rinaldo* (with *March and Battle*); *Sosarme*; *Faramondo*; *Judas Maccabaeus*; *Radamisto*; *Arminio*; *Deidamia*; *Scipio*; *Belshazzar (Sinfonia)*; *Julius Caesar* (with Act I *Minuet*); *Semele: Sinfonia* (Act II). 18th-century overtures: J. M. KRAUS: *Olympia.* Florian GASSMANN: *L'amore artigiano.* BOIELDIEU: *Zoraime et Zulnar.* Ferdinando PAER: *Sargino.* GRETRY: *Le Magnifique.* SACCHINI: *La Contadina in Corte* (Sinfonia). HAYDN: *Orlando Paladino.* SALIERI: *La fiera di Venezie.*
(B) *** Australian Decca Double 466 434-2 (2).

This remarkably generous Double (150 minutes) comes to us courtesy of Australian Decca who are exploring areas of the back catalogue hitherto not yet reissued on CD by their parent company, here covering the contents of three LPs from 1968–71. The Handel collection may include the *Arrival of* the Queen of Sheba, but much of the rest has been left unheard, and all credit to Bonynge for resurrecting it with such vigour. Handel's cosmopolitan qualities give such music the benefit of all the traditions of the time – French finesse, Italian elaboration, English plainspokenness. Bonynge uses his scholarship to produce results that are the very opposite of the dry-as-dust approach which can affect hard-line authenticists.

He may use double-dotting, notes inégales and added appoggiaturas beyond what other scholars would allow, but the baroque elaboration is justified in the exuberance of the end result. The rarities included here are all delightful and if the English Chamber Orchestra fields a larger body of strings than we expect today, the playing is splendidly alert, and the recording is exceptionally vivid.

The overtures by lesser names are much less inspired, but they undoubtedly have an aural fascination. Olympia is like Gluck without the inspiration, and L'amore artigiano is conventional, if with an attractive middle section. Zoraime et Zulnar, an early work of Boieldieu, shows something of the wit and melodic flair of the better-known overtures. But Sargino is altogether more striking, offering more in the way of memorable tunes, and a distinct flavour of Rossini.

Grétry's Le Magnifique, if somewhat optimistically titled, is also quite memorable. Unexpectedly opening with a side-drum like Auber's Fra Diavolo, it gradually builds up to its middle section, a hauntingly serene and rather beautiful minor-keyed passage, before concluding as it began in military style. The Salieri piece, too, is pleasingly fresh, helped like the rest by first-class advocacy from conductor, orchestra and recording engineers alike. The CD transfers are excellent.

English Chamber Orchestra, Sir Benjamin Britten

'Britten at the Aldeburgh festival': BEETHOVEN: Coriolan overture. DEBUSSY: Prélude à l'après-midi d'un faune. HAYDN: Symphony No. 95 in C min. MENDELSSOHN: Overture Fingal's Cave. MOZART: Symphony No. 35 in D (Haffner).
(M) **(*) BBC Music BBCB 8008-2 [id.].

Though this is a strange mixture, Britten as conductor brings to each item a striking freshness, giving a vivid idea of the electricity he conveyed in his performances at the Aldeburgh Festival. Mendelssohn's Hebrides overture – the item which opens the sequence – is urgent and vigorous, giving a storm-tossed view of the Hebrides, while bringing out the strength of the musical structure. That and the Beethoven overture, given a similarly alert and dramatic reading in a 1966 performance at

Blythburgh church, are especially valuable, as Britten otherwise made no commercial recordings of either composer's music.

The Debussy too is wonderfully fresh, with Richard Adeney's mistily cool flute solo at the start, presenting the whole score with a rare transparency, leading to a passionate climax. The recording, also made at Blythburgh, is a degree more immediate, less atmospheric than those from the Maltings, but the extra impact is an advantage – as it is in Britten's account of the Haydn symphony, which in its C minor angularity at the start has the biting toughness of Sturm und Drang. Mozart's Haffner Symphony, recorded in the Maltings in 1972, brings sound rather less focused than on the rest of the disc, but it is an amiable performance, energetic in the outer movements, warmly affectionate in the slow movement.

'English music for strings': PURCELL (ed. Britten): Chacony in G min. ELGAR: Introduction and allegro, Op. 47. BRITTEN: Prelude and fugue for strings, Op. 47; Simple Symphony, Op. 4. DELIUS: 2 Aquarelles. BRIDGE: Sir Roger de Coverley for string orchestra.
✹ (M) *** Decca 448 569-2 [id.].

This rich-toned recording, still sounding extraordinarily real and vivid, was surely a prime candidate for reissue in Decca's 'Classic Sound' series. It was one of the first made at The Maltings, Snape, in 1968 (although the Prelude and fugue, which has been added to fill out the CD, dates from three years later). The warm acoustic gives the strings of the English Chamber Orchestra far greater weight than you would expect from their numbers. Britten drew comparably red-blooded playing from his band, whether in his own Simple Symphony (a performance unsurpassed on disc), the engaging Bridge dance or the magnificent Purcell Chacony, which has never sounded more imposing.

It is good to find him treating his own music so expressively. In the Delius the delicacy of evocation is delightful, while the Elgar is in some ways the most interesting performance of all, moving in its ardour yet with the structure of the piece brought out far more clearly than is common. An indispensable reissue to set alongside Barbirolli's coupling of the string music of Elgar and Vaughan Williams.

English Chamber Orchestra, Raymond Leppard

'Music of the Baroque': Marc-Antoine CHARPENTIER: Te Deum in D: Introduction. ALBINONI (arr. GIAZOTTO): Adagio in G min. (played by La Grand Ecurie et la Chambre du Roy, Jean-Claude Malgoire). PACHELBEL: Canon and Gigue in D. HANDEL: Solomon: Arrival of the Queen of Sheba. Berenice: Minuet. GLUCK: Orfeo

ed Euridice: Dance of the Blessed Spirits. BACH: *Orchestral suites: No. 2 in B min., BWV 1067: Badinerie*; *No. 3 in D, BWV 1068: Air. Cantata No. 78: Wir eilen mit schwachen* (duet; arr. Leppard). MARCELLO: *Oboe concerto in D min.: Adagio*. VIVALDI: *L'Estro armonico: Violin concerto in D, Op. 3/9: Larghetto* (with José-Luis Garcia). PURCELL: *Abdelazar: orchestral suite. The Old Bachelor: suite*.
(M) *** Sony Theta SMK 60161.

Although it contains a number of favourite baroque lollipops which are presented by the ECO with characteristic elegance and finish, the major items here are two suites of Purcell's theatre music. The writing is consistently inventive, and *Abdelazar* includes the tune (a Rondeau) – taken briskly here – which Britten made famous in his variations. Leppard ensures that rhythms are keenly resilient and the expressive playing is nicely judged.

The elaborately decorated account of Pachelbel's *Canon* is also very attractive, opening and closing gently but with a fine central climax, while Leppard's arrangement of the jolly *Duetto* from Bach's cantata, *Jesu der du meine Seele*, is equally winning. William Bennett is the highly musical flute soloist in Gluck's *Dance of the Blessed Spirits*.

The forward balance and resonant acoustic produce agreeably warm sound-quality, but this may seem too well upholstered to ears used to the Academy of Ancient Music, with the harpsichord artificially balanced and only just audible in the quieter lyrical music. However, the bright violin timbre more than compensates. The programme opens with Charpentier's fanfare *Introduction* for his *Te Deum* which is instantly familiar as the signature tune of European television. La Grand Ecurie et la Chambre du Roy, directed by Jean-Claude Malgoire, ends the 74-minute concert with a memorably fresh version of the Albinoni/Giazotto *Adagio*. Altogether this is a superior collection of its kind.

English music

English music ((i) LPO; (ii) New Philh. O; (iii) Sir Adrian Boult; (iv) ASMF, Marriner; (v) Hirsch Chamber Players, Leonard Hirsch; (vi) BBC Northern SO, Bryden Thomson): (i; iii) George BUTTERWORTH: *The Banks of green willow*. (ii; iii) VAUGHAN WILLIAMS: *Fantasia on a theme of Thomas Tallis*. (iv) LEIGH: *Harpsichord concertino* (with George Malcolm). (v) WARLOCK: *Capriol suite*. FINZI: (vi) *Clarinet concerto* (with Janet Hilton); (i; iii) *Introit for violin and orchestra* (with Gerald Jarvis).
(M) *** BBC Music BBCM 5015-2 [id.].

This mixed bag of BBC recordings from various sources offers a delightful collection. The charming

Walter Leigh *Concertino* in three compact movements – including a heavenly central *Andante* – has never been recorded so ravishingly as by George Malcolm. It is also good to have a Finzi novelty in the beautiful *Introit* (with another memorable main theme). Finzi's *Clarinet concerto* is also very successful, especially the beautiful slow movement. Both these works are discussed under their composer entries. Boult as ever is most persuasive in all he conducts. His *Tallis Fantasia* is completely different from Barbirolli's famous version, but certainly does not lack passion. It is good to have a vintage artist like Leonard Hirsch conducting his own orchestra in Warlock, a mellow performance with a sprightly finale. The sound is good throughout and this 77-minute concert is well worth its cost.

English Northern Philharmonia, David Lloyd-Jones

'Victorian concert overtures': MACFARREN: *Chevy Chase*. PIERSON: *Romeo and Juliet, Op. 86*. SULLIVAN: *Macbeth*. CORDER: *Prospero*. ELGAR: *Froissart, Op. 19*. PARRY: *Overture to an unwritten tragedy*. MACKENZIE: *Britannia, a nautical overture, Op. 52*.
*** Hyperion Dig. CDA 66515 [id.].

Sir George (Alexander) Macfarren (1813–87) was an English composer of Scottish descent who taught at and eventually became Principal of the Royal Academy of Music. His music was very successful in its day; he was a distinguished early editor of Purcell's *Dido and Aeneas* and of major stage works of Handel; many of his own operas were produced in London, including one based on the story of Robin Hood.

A CD showing us a wider range of his music is overdue; meanwhile he makes a strong contribution to this collection of Victorian concert overtures with *Chevy Chase*, a spirited, tuneful piece that was admired by Mendelssohn. Pierson's *Romeo and Juliet* hardly explores its theme with any substance but Frederick Corder's *Prospero* has a certain flamboyant gravitas. Mackenzie's *Britannia* is a pot-boiler featuring a borrowed tune now famous at the Proms. Against all this and more, Elgar's *Froissart* stands out as the early masterpiece it was. The whole concert is persuasively performed by the excellent Northern Philharmonia under the versatile David Lloyd-Jones.

English Sinfonia, Sir Charles Groves

'Entente cordiale': FAURE: *Masques et bergamasques, Op. 112*; *Pavane, Op. 50*. ELGAR:

Chanson de nuit; *Chanson de matin, Op. 15/1–2*.
DELIUS: *On hearing the first cuckoo in spring*.
RAVEL: *Pavane pour une infante défunte*.
WARLOCK: *Capriol suite*. George BUTTERWORTH:
The Banks of green willow. SATIE: *Gymnopédies
Nos. 1 & 3* (orch. Debussy).
(B) *** Carlton Dig. PCD 2017 [(M) id.].

Having given us some attractive Haydn and Schubert recordings with the English Sinfonia, Sir
Charles Groves then offered a happy juxtaposition
of French and British music. He opens with a performance of Fauré's *Masques et bergamasques*
which is sheer delight in its airy grace, and later he
finds passion as well as delicacy in the Butterworth
rhapsody, very effectively followed by Debussy's
languorous orchestrations of the Satie *Gymnopédies*. Groves's approach to Warlock's *Capriol
dances* is essentially genial (Marriner's version has
more zest); but all this music-making is easy to
enjoy. The playing is polished and spontaneous and
the recording, made at Abbey Road, quite splendid.

English String Orchestra or English Symphony Orchestra, William Boughton

'*The spirit of England*': ELGAR: *Overture
Cockaigne*; *Introduction and allegro, Op. 47*;
Sospiri, Op. 70. DELIUS: *Summer evening*. George
BUTTERWORTH: *The Banks of green willow*; *A
Shropshire lad*. FINZI: *Suite from Love's Labour's
Lost*; *Clarinet concerto* (with Alan Hacker).
VAUGHAN WILLIAMS: *The Lark ascending* (with
Michael Bochmann); *Oboe concerto* (with
Maurice Bourgue); *Fantasia on a theme of
Thomas Tallis*; *Fantasia on Greensleeves*. PARRY:
Lady Radnor's suite. BRIDGE: *Suite for string
orchestra*. HOLST: *St Paul's suite*. WARLOCK:
Capriol suite. BRITTEN: *Variations on a theme of
Frank Bridge, Op. 10*.
⊙ (BB) *** Nimbus Dig. NI 5210/3 (4) [id.].

The Birmingham-based English String and Symphony Orchestras under William Boughton are
completely at home in this repertoire. One has only
to sample the excitingly animated account of
Holst's *St Paul's suite* (which also has much delicacy of feeling), the ideally paced Warlock *Capriol
suite*, or the vibrant account of Britten's *Frank
Bridge variations*, to discover the calibre of this
music-making. The recordings were made in the
Great Hall of Birmingham University which, with
its warm reverberation, gives the strings a gloriously
rich body of tone, supported by sumptuous cello
and bass sonorities.

The Elgar *Introduction and allegro* expands wonderfully at its climax (yet the fugue is not blurred)
and in Vaughan Williams's *Lark ascending*, where

the violin solo is exquisitely played with wonderful
purity of tone by Michael Bochmann, the closing
pianissimo seems to float in the still air.

The work most suited to such an expansive
acoustic is Vaughan Williams's *Tallis fantasia*, a
deeply expressive performance which gives the
listener the impression of sitting in a cathedral, with
the solo string group, perfectly matched and blended
in timbre, evoking a distant, ethereal organ. The
lovely Butterworth pieces are tenderly sympathetic,
and Alan Hacker's rhapsodically improvisatory account of Finzi's *Clarinet concerto* is full of colour
and warmth. Perhaps Maurice Bourgue's oboe is
balanced a little too closely in Vaughan Williams's
Oboe concerto but the ear adjusts. On the other
hand, the flutes melt magically into the strings in
the famous *Greensleeves fantasia*. Delius's *Summer
evening*, an early work, is quite memorable, and
the suites of Parry and Finzi are full of colourful
invention. The Bridge *Suite for strings* brings a
lively response, with sumptuous textures. Only the
opening *Cockaigne overture* of Elgar is a little
lacking in profile and drama – and even here
Boughton's relaxed, lyrical approach is enjoyable,
for he broadens the final climax very satisfyingly.
Very inexpensively priced indeed, this box makes
an outstanding bargain.

English Symphony Orchestra; English String Orchestra; Philharmonia Orchestra; William Boughton

'*The spirit of England*', Volume II: HOLST: *The
Planets, Op. 32*; *The Perfect Fool* (ballet music),
Op. 39. ELGAR: *Enigma variations, Op. 36*; *The
Wand of Youth suite No. 2, Op. 1b*. PARRY: *An
English suite*. FINZI: *Eclogue* (with Martin Jones,
piano). BRIDGE: *There is a willow grows aslant a
brook*. DELIUS: *Florida suite*. VAUGHAN
WILLIAMS: *The Wasps: Overture*. IRELAND:
Downland suite: Minuet. BERKELEY: *Serenade for
strings*. BRITTEN: *Peter Grimes: 4 Sea interludes*.
Young person's guide to the orchestra.
(B) **(*) Nimbus Dig. NI 5450/3 (4) [id.].

An enjoyable enough bargain collection, warmly
and often vividly played and given characteristically spacious and resonant sound which is always
pleasing to the ear. However, it is much too richly
upholstered for Elgar's *Wand of Youth* (and why
offer the second suite and not the first?), although it
suits Boughton's enjoyably expansive account of
Enigma, even if *Nimrod*, paced very slowly, lacks
something in ultimate tension. *The Planets* is well
played by the Philharmonia Orchestra, but *Mars*
fails the malignancy test and Boughton's reading
overall is somewhat undercharacterized (except in

the strikingly poignant *Saturn*); the use of the Royal Albert Hall for this recording has meant close microphones, which have produced a surprisingly small-scale effect for such a spectacular venue.

The Finzi *Eclogue* (with Martin Jones the sympathetic soloist), the Delius *Florida suite*, Parry's *English suite* and the Berkeley *String serenade* are very successful, as are the shorter pieces, by Bridge, Ireland and Vaughan Williams; but the Britten performances, though evocative (notably the first *Sea interlude*), are lacking something in dramatic profile and bite, and the *Young person's guide to the orchestra* ideally needs a sharper definition.

European Community Chamber Orchestra, Eivind Aadland

HINDEMITH: *5 Pieces for strings, Op. 11.* BARBER: *Adagio, Op. 11.* BRITTEN: *Simple Symphony, Op. 4.* WARLOCK: *Capriol suite.* BARTOK: *Romanian folk dances.*

(B) ** Carlton IMP Dig. PCD 2044 [(M) id.].

Excellent playing from this fine group of European musicians. However, they cannot make Hindemith's rather austere set of string pieces (written for student performance) sound much more than utility music, and they miss the final degree of passion at the climax of Barber's *Adagio*, which is otherwise eloquently played. Some of the tempi in the *Capriol suite* seem slightly eccentric, but the Bartók dances are vibrant and, apart from a lack of a nursery-rhyme exuberance in the *Playful pizzicato*, the account of the Britten *Simple Symphony* has comparable liveliness and crispness of ensemble.

'Concertos for the Kingdom of the Two Sicilies': A. SCARLATTI: *Concerto No. 6 in E* (for strings). *Sinfonia di concerto grosso No. 12 in C min.* PERGOLESI: *Flute concerto in G* (both with Giulio Viscardi). PORPORA: *Cello concerto in G* (with Giovanni Sollima). DURANTE: *Concerto per quartetto No. 1 in F min.*

(B) *** Hyperion Helios Dig. CDH 55005 [id.].

This most engaging and beautifully recorded collection is centred on Naples, the musical focus of the so-called 'Two Sicilies', which once embraced Southern Italy. The programme is lightweight but played – on modern instruments – with an airy lightness. Whereas Scarlatti's E major work is a concerto grosso, the *Sinfonia di concerto* features a solo flute and matches the concerto attributed to Pergolesi in charm, when the flute playing is so nimble. In Porpora's *Cello concerto* (again with an impressive soloist) exuberantly vivacious *Allegros* frame an eloquent central *Largo*. Durante's splendid little concerto grosso has a sombre introduction and is comparatively serious in mood; even the *Amoroso* third movement, using the solo

quartet, is touching rather than romantic, but the tension lifts in the gay, rhythmically pointed finale.

European Union Chamber Orchestra, Dmitri Demetriades

'The concerto in Europe': PAISIELLO: *Harp concerto in D.* GRETRY: *Flute concerto in C.* GARTH: *Cello concerto No. 2 in B flat.* STAMITZ: *Viola concerto in D, Op. 1.*

(B) **(*) Hyperion Helios CDH 55035 [id.].

A collection of quietly attractive and tuneful, rarely heard concertos. The Paisiello *Harp concerto*, originally a keyboard work, is graceful and elegant, with a touching central movement and a jolly, if brief, finale. Grétry's operatic leaning is felt at the opening of his *Flute concerto*, and at intervals throughout; the central movement flirts with minor keys, but it is generally a sunny work. The English are represented by a cello concerto by John Garth: it is an interesting piece with some robust cello writing, stylistically a bit earlier than the other concertos (more baroque in flavour) but no less enjoyable for that. Stamitz's *Viola concerto* is the most substantial work with some nice ideas, especially in the slow movement, and has secured a place in the viola concerto repertoire. The performances and recordings are good, though at times a hint of blandness creeps in. The CD, which plays for just under an hour, is worth considering if the programme appeals.

Fernández, Eduardo (guitar), English Chamber Orchestra

Guitar concertos: RODRIGO: *Concierto de Aranjuez.* CASTELNUOVO-TEDESCO: *Concerto No. 1 in D, Op. 99* (both cond. Miguel Gómez Martinez). GIULIANI: *Concerto in A, Op. 30.* VIVALDI: *Concerto in D, RV 93* (both cond. George Malcolm). PONCE: *Concierto del sur.* VILLA-LOBOS: *Concerto* (both cond. Enrique Garcia Asensio). ARNOLD: *Concerto.*

(B) **(*) Decca Double Dig. 455 364-2 (2) [(M) id. import].

There are few guitar concertos to match the effectiveness of the jazz-inflected piece by Malcolm Arnold. Fernández is in his element in this work, making the haunting melody of the first movement's second subject warm and not sentimental, echoed by the glowing ECO strings, while the full depth of the blues-inspired slow movement is also movingly conveyed. Yet outer movements are fizzingly vital, the playing spikily incisive in bringing out the jazz overtones.

As we have said elsewhere, Fernández is a musician's guitarist whose playing is consistently refined and sensitive, and he is again at his most inspired in the concertos by Ponce and Villa-Lobos, creating magical evocation in the atmospheric slow movements, where Enrique Garcia Asensio is a persuasive partner.

The Giuliani and Castelnuovo-Tedesco concertos are presented with warm, refined elegance; the *Andantino* of the latter is made to sound charmingly ingenuous, and the Vivaldi too brings refinement rather than extrovert brilliance. It is in the most famous concerto of all, the Rodrigo *Concierto de Aranjuez*, that some listeners may feel Fernández falls short in his total unwillingness to treat the music as a vehicle for extrovert display. The beautiful *Adagio* is unusually ruminative, but the outer movements, too, are comparatively laid back, delicate in feeling, yet by no means lacking in vitality. We found all the music-making here most refreshing, and certainly the Decca digital recording is consistently well balanced and of the highest quality.

Fleisher, Leon (piano), Boston Symphony Orchestra, Seiji Ozawa

Left-hand Piano concertos: BRITTEN: *Diversions for piano and orchestra*. PROKOFIEV: *Piano concerto No. 4*. RAVEL: *Piano concerto in D for the left hand*.
*** Sony Dig. SK 47188 [id.].

These superb concertante works, originally written for the one-armed Austrian pianist Paul Wittgenstein, but rejected by him, make the perfect vehicle for one of the finest of all American pianists, Leon Fleisher. Unable to play with his right hand any longer, Fleisher here shows that his power and artistry are undiminished from the days when he was the favourite recording pianist of Georg Szell with the vintage Cleveland orchestra. Though the Ravel and Prokofiev concertos have been recorded many times, these accounts are a match for any of them, while Britten's highly original set of variations is a rarity on disc, very welcome indeed in Fleisher's masterly performance.

Flute concertos

MOZART: *Flute concertos Nos. 1 in G, K.313; 2 in D, K.314* (with William Bennett, ECO, Malcolm).
VIVALDI: *Flute concerto in C min., RV 441*; J. S. BACH: *Flute concerto in G min, from BWV 1056* (with William Bennett). attrib. GRETRY: *Flute concerto in C* (with Claude Monteux) (both with ASMF, Marriner). CIMAROSA: *Concerto in G for 2 flutes* (with Aurèle & Christiane Nicolet); C. P. E. BACH: *Flute concerto in D min., Wq. 22*

(with Aurèle Nicolet) (both with Stuttgart CO, Münchinger). SALIERI: *Concerto for flute and oboe in C* (with Richard Adeney, James Brown, ECO, Bonynge).
(B) *** Decca Double 460 302-2 (2) [id.].

William Bennett's recordings of the two Mozart concertos are second to none, and the recordings which Marriner accompanies so stylishly (Vivaldi, Bach and Grétry) are equally enjoyable. The double concertos, by Cimarosa and Salieri, bring a fair amount of elegant chatter, but there is nothing here which fails to please, and the recording is consistently of Decca's vintage analogue standard.

(i) French Radio Orchestra, (ii) Philharmonia Orchestra, Igor Markevitch

PROKOFIEV: (i) *Love for 3 Oranges (suite), Op. 33*; (ii) *Le pas d'acier (suite), Op. 41*; (i) *Scythian suite, Op. 20*. STRAVINSKY: (i) *Le baiser de la fée (Divertimento)*; (ii) *Petrushka: suite*; (i) *Pulcinella (suite)*; (ii) *The Rite of spring*.
(B) (**(*)) EMI Rouge et Noir mono/stereo CZS5 69674-2 (2).

Igor Markevitch was the last and most unusual of Diaghilev's protégés and married the daughter of his first, Nijinsky. Markevitch's career initally took off as a composer and pianist. However, after the end of the Second World War, during which he served in the Italian resistance, he gave up composition to concentrate on conducting full time. He was an excellent ballet conductor whose cool elegance can be readily observed in these recordings. His mono (1952) account of *Le Sacre* with the Philharmonia Orchestra caused quite a stir in its day, but this 1959 stereo re-make, undertaken at very short notice when Klemperer was taken ill, has much to recommend it, even if the former has perhaps the greater atmosphere.

Markevitch gets good results from the Philharmonia Orchestra throughout and a very professional response from the French Radio Orchestra, which was in better shape than the Conservatoire Orchestra at this period. *Le pas d'acier* is a rarity these days and is hardly ever encountered in the concert hall; it sounds to excellent effect here. The Paris recordings come from 1954–5 and the Philharmonia *Petrushka* and *Pas d'acier* from 1954. Only the 1959 *Le Sacre* is in stereo.

Fröst, Martin (clarinet), Malmö Symphony Orchestra, Lan Shui

Clarinet concertos: ARNOLD: *Concerto No. 2, Op. 112*. COPLAND: *Concerto for clarinet and string*

orchestra, with harp and piano. HINDEMITH: *Concerto.*
*** BIS Dig. CD 893 [id.].

Three first-class performances of three outstanding twentieth-century concertos, all originally written for Benny Goodman. Fröst is an eloquently spontaneous soloist, stealing in gently against a magical orchestral pianopianissimo at the opening of the Copland; and he is equally at home in Hindemith's more sinewy lyricism. Both he and the persuasive conductor, Lan Shui, obviously relish the verve and energy of the Malcolm Arnold concerto and they play the slow movement very seductively, before romping away into the rooty-tooty finale, with its audacious orchestral whoops, the kind of music to bring the house down at a Promenade concert. The recording is splendid in every way and this can receive the strongest recommendation.

Gallois, Patrick (flute)

'Une flûte à l'opéra' (with L. Festival O, Ross Pople): Opera arias for flute and orchestra from VERDI: *La Traviata* (arr. GENIN; orch. GUIOT); *Un ballo in maschera* (arr. GENIN; orch. PIERRE). ROSSINI: *William Tell* (arr. DEMERSSEMAN/ BERTHELEMY; orch. GALLOIS). GODARD: *Berceuse de Jocelyn.* MASSE: *Les noces de Jeanette: Air du rossignol* (both arr. & orch. PIERRE). MASSENET: *Thaïs: Méditation* (arr. PREZMAN). BIZET: *Carmen fantasia* (arr. BORNE; orch. PIERRE).
*** DG (IMS) Dig. 445 822-2 [id.].

Patrick Gallois is clearly a new international star in the flautists' firmament. His tone is uniquely recognizable and beautiful, his playing naturally stylish, his musicianship impeccable and, as this light-hearted and entertaining collection demonstrates, his technique is dazzling. He plays a modern wooden flute which he suggests is particularly suitable for the present repertoire as it has 'more colour and juster intonation than a traditional wooden flute . . . and its timbre is closer to that of the human voice than a metal instrument'. He certainly makes it tell in the scintillating coloratura with which he surrounds the selection from Verdi's *La Traviata* and the excerpts from *William Tell*, which feature a brief but witty morsel of the famous Galop with the most engaging additional embroidery.

Ross Pople opens the famous *Berceuse de Jocelyn* with lovely, gentle playing from the orchestral strings, and the charm of the flute solo here is very seductive, while in the equally popular *Méditation* from *Thaïs* the melodic line is richly expressive without any feeling of sentimentality. Finally we are offered all those hits from *Carmen* which Sarasate arranged so effectively for the violin. Gallois' claim as to the vocal possibilities of his

instrument is readily apparent here in the quite beautiful performance of the *Flower song*; he is hardly less bewitching in the 'Habanera' and then decorates it with great panache, finally frolicking nimbly through the *Danse bohème* and genially introducing the *Toreador song* as a surprise just before a breathtaking final burst of bravura.

'Flute concertos from Sans-Souci' (with C. P. E. Bach CO, Peter Schreier): C. P. E. BACH: *Concerto in G, Wq. 169.* BENDA: *Concerto in E min.* FREDERICK THE GREAT: *Concerto No. 3 in C.* QUANTZ: *Concerto in G.*
*** DG (IMS) Dig. 439 895-2 [id.].

C. P. E. Bach (fairly briefly), Benda and Quantz were all musicians in the employ of Frederick the Great, whose own *Flute concerto* included here is rather impressive, notably its *Grave* slow movement. The Bach concerto is well known and the chamber orchestra carrying his name makes the very most of its sprightly outer movements while Gallois' contribution throughout the programme is impeccably stylish and elegant and his decoration always imaginative.

The *Adagio un poco Andante* of the Benda *Concerto* shows his luminous line, as does the rather lovely *Arioso* which is the centrepoint of the Quantz work; it is played most delectably, followed by a lively moto perpetuo finale of equal charm. Here the neat string articulation and the soloist's finesse mirror each other equitably, as they do in the catchy last movement of the Benda work. Fresh, clean recording and a bright string-sound demonstrate that modern instruments can present this repertoire with the same lightness and transparency as original instruments. There are few collections of baroque flute concertos in this bracket and none more generous (77 minutes) – but this is not a concert to be played all at once.

Galway, James (flute)

'Pachelbel's Canon and other Baroque favourites' (with various orchestras & conductors): VIVALDI: *Concerto in D (Il Gardellino), Op. 10/3:* 1st & 2nd movts. *Four Seasons: Spring* (arr. GALWAY). TELEMANN: *Suite for strings in A min.: Réjouissance; Polonaise.* PACHELBEL: *Canon.* HANDEL: *Sonatas in A min., Op. 1/4:* 4th movt; *in F, Op. 1/11: Siciliana; Allegro* (both with Sarah Cunningham, Philip Moll). *Solomon: Arrival of the Queen of Sheba* (arr. GERHARDT). *Messiah: Pifa (Pastoral Symphony). Xerxes: Largo.* BACH: *Suites Nos. 2 in B min., BWV 1067: Minuet & Badinerie; 3 in D, BWV 1068: Air. Trio sonata No. 2 in G, BWV 1039:* 4th movt (with Kyung Wha Chung, Moll, Welsh); *Flute sonatas Nos. 2 in E flat, BWV 1031: Siciliano* (with Maria Graf, harp); *4 in C, BWV 1033:* 2nd movt (arr.

GERHARDT for flute & O). *Concerto in E min.,
BWV 1059/35* (ed. Radeke): 3rd movt. ALBINONI:
Adagio. QUANTZ: *Concerto in C: Finale.* MARAIS:
Le Basque (arr. GALWAYGERHARDT).
*** BMG/RCA Dig./Analogue 09026 61928-2
[id.].

If the famous Bach *Air* from BWV 1068 is spun
out somewhat romantically and the *Siciliano* from
BWV 1031 (with harp accompaniment) is too
solemn, Handel's famous *Largo* is gloriously managed, completely vocal in feeling. Galway certainly
dominates Pachelbel's *Canon* in a way not intended
by the composer, but his elegant line and simple
divisions on the lovely theme are very agreeable.

Any of the composers included here would surely
have been amazed at the beauty of his tone and the
amazing technical facility, always turned to musical
effect. He is a wonderful goldfinch in Vivaldi's Op.
10/3, while Gerhardt's arrangement of Handel's
Arrival of the Queen of Sheba, which exchanges
oboes for flutes, is ear-tickling. The engaging
Quantz concerto movement is as sprightly in the
strings (of the Württemberg Chamber Orchestra) as
it is in the felicitously decorated solo part. The Bach
and Handel sonata excerpts are refreshing and the
(Handel) Siciliana from Op. 1/11 is matched in
pastoral charm by the beautiful account of the *Pifa*
from *Messiah*, but is not more engaging than the
lollipop of the whole concert: the delicious *Le
Basque* of Marais, one of Galway's most endearing
arrangements. The recording naturally balances the
soloist forward, but the sound is first class
throughout. This is a full-price record but it includes
68 minutes of entertainment, perfect for a fine
summer evening.

'Dances for flute' (with Nat. PO, Gerhardt or
Mancini; I Solisti di Zagreb, Scimone; The
Chieftains; RPO, Myung-Whun Chung; and other
artists): GODARD: *Waltz.* CHOPIN: *Minute waltz in
D flat, Op. 64/1.* DEBUSSY: *La plus que lente;
Petite suite: Ballet.* J. S. BACH: *Suite No. 2, BWV
1067: Polonaise; Menuet; Badinerie.* TRAD.:
*Crowley's reel; Brian Boru's march; Belfast
hornpipe.* KHACHATURIAN: *Waltz; Sabre dance.*
MERCADANTE: *Concerto in D: Polacca.* MANCINI:
Pie in the face polka; Pennywhistle jig. RODRIGO:
Fantasia para un gentilhombre: Canario.
BENJAMIN: *Jamaican rhumba.* MOZART:
Divertimento in D, K.334: Menuetto. VIVALDI:
Concerto in D (Il Gardellino): Cantabile. DINICU:
Hora staccato. GOSSEC: *Tambourin.* KREISLER:
Schön Rosmarin.
*** BMG/RCA 09026 60917-2 [id.].

Galway can certainly make his flute dance – often
in scintillating fashion. This collection is essentially
for the sweet-toothed, but its consummate artistry
is remarkable: just sample the delicious opening
Godard *Waltz.* The traditional pieces are especially
enjoyable, and two real lollipops are the Mercadante

Polacca (from a virtually forgotten concerto) and
the (Beechamesque) Gossec *Tambourin.* We also
have a soft spot for Mancini's *Pennywhistle jig.*
Good sound and 64 minutes of music.

Gilels, Emil (piano)

'Gilels Edition'

(M) (**) BMG/Melodiya 74321 40116-2 (5) [id.].
BEETHOVEN: *Piano sonatas Nos. 8 (Pathétique),
Op. 13; 14 (Moonlight), Op. 27/2.* SCHUBERT:
Impromptu, D.935/1. RAVEL: *Pavane pour une
infante défunte; Jeux d'eau.* MEDTNER:
Sonata-reminiscenza, Op. 38/1. CHOPIN: *Etude,
Op. 25/2.* PROKOFIEV: *The Love for 3 Oranges:
Scherzo; March* (74321 40117-2).

CHOPIN: *Piano concerto No. 1.   :
Concert champêtre in D* (with Moscow PO,
Kondrashin) (74321 40118-2).

MOZART: *Piano sonatas, K.281 & K.310;.
Fantasia, K.397; 6 Variations, K.398; 10
Variations, K.455* (74321 40119-2).

SCHUBERT: *Moments musicaux, D.780.*
SHOSTAKOVICH: *Sonata No. 2, Op. 64.*
SCHUMANN: *Arabeske.* CHOPIN: *Ballade No. 1*
(74321 40120-2).

SCRIABIN: *Piano sonata No. 3; 5 Preludes, Op.
74.* BEETHOVEN: *Sonata No. 29 (Hammerklavier),
Op. 106* (74321 40121-2).

These five CDs are available as a boxed set, but no
longer separately. Nothing by Gilels is less than
distinguished. As one American critic wrote at
about the time of these recitals, 'With the very first
notes anyone with half an ear must realize he is in
the presence of one of the greatest of pianists.'
But the quality of sound of these recordings is so
variable as to justify detailed comment and grading.

The first disc (74321 40117-2) comes from a
recital Gilels gave in the Grand Hall of the Moscow
Conservatoire just before Christmas 1968, in front
of a very attentive audience. The programme is
close to a Carnegie recital which HMV recorded in
February 1969, including the *Moonlight sonata* and
an incomparable performance of the Medtner
Sonata-reminiscenza. The present recital includes
some particularly beautiful Ravel and a no less
eloquent account of the Medtner sonata. The short
Prokofiev excerpts from *Love for Three Oranges*
are much to be relished. The recording calls for
tolerance: it is shallow and in no way does justice
to the sheer beauty of sound one recalls Gilels
making in the flesh. Three stars for the playing, one
for the sound.

The next CD (74321 40118-2) couples the
Chopin *Piano concerto No. 1* with the Poulenc
Concert champêtre, played on the piano, not the
harpsichord, with Kondrashin and the Moscow

Philharmonic. Here the recordings, which are from 1962, present more serious problems. The Chopin is pretty rough and climaxes are distinctly coarse. Gilels makes the *Concert champêtre* sound convincing enough, such is the extraordinary range of colour he commanded.

The Mozart disc (74321 40119-2) comes from a live recital given in January 1970 in the Grand Hall of the Moscow Conservatoire. According to BMG/Melodiya's documentation, none of the performances has been available before. From the early *B flat sonata*, K.281, whose finale is delivered with such wit, through to the marvellously characterized *A minor*, K.310, this finds Gilels at his most individual and sublime, exquisite in every detail, without the slightest trace of preciosity. The sound is not as distinguished as the playing but is perfectly acceptable. The performances are certainly three-star and Rosette-worthy, but the sound rates two stars.

The Schubert *Moments musicaux*, D.780 and Shostakovich *Sonata No. 2* (74321 40120-2) together with the Schumann and Chopin pieces come from a recital given in March 1965. Gilels recorded the Schubert and the Shostakovich for HMV and RCA respectively in the West not long afterwards, both in marginally better sound. The present performances are every bit as fine, and the recording is perfectly acceptable. Gilels's account of the Shostakovich *Sonata* has never been surpassed on disc.

The Scriabin *Sonata No. 3* and the *Preludes*, Op. 74, and Beethoven's *Hammerklavier sonata* (74321 40121-2), are the highlights of the set. Recorded at a 1984 recital, only a fortnight before he gave much the same programme at London's Festival Hall, they offer eminently satisfactory sound – though again it does not do full justice to the range of colour or delicacy of touch Gilels commanded in real life. But then, nor does his DG *Hammerklavier* (410 527-2), which has great presence and clarity but is marred by a certain glare. This live recording comes closer to capturing what those who attended his London recital will recall. One of the most impressive *Hammerklaviers* now available.

Glennie, Evelyn (percussion)

'Light in darkness': Music by GLENNIE; ABE; MCLEOD; EDWARDS; MIKI; TANAKA.
**(*) RCA Dig. RD 60557.

'Dancin'' (with Nat. PO, Barry Wordsworth): Music by RODGERS; HEROLD; SAINT-SAENS; J. STRAUSS Jr; arr. by Gordon LANGFORD.
*** RCA Dig. RD 60870.

Evelyn Glennie's remarkable artistic skills have caught the fancy of the wider public, fascinated with the idea of her apparently insuperable affliction

– for a musician. But she tells us that, such is the ingenuity of nature, she can sense everything directly, through her body. Included on the first collection is her own imaginative piece, *Light in darkness*, using tuned percussion instruments and highlighting the exotic marimba. Here she explores music from a wide geographical range for which the percussion condiment is essential.

However, for most listeners the more obviously popular alternative collection called *Dancin'* will be an easy first choice. Here she receives splendid back-up from Barry Wordsworth and the National Philharmonic in the widest range of music for the dance, which surely does make one's feet tap, whether it be a clever arrangement by Gordon Langford, pieces by Johann Strauss, a ballet by Richard Rodgers, a medley associated with the Broadway team of Ginger and Fred, or the irresistible *Clog dance* from *La fille mal gardée*. The recording is first rate and makes one recall the title of an early RCA stereo demonstration LP dominated by percussion, called *'Music for Band, Brrroom and harp'* (which RCA should dig out of their vaults and reissue).

'Rebounds' (with Scottish CO, Paul Daniel): MILHAUD: *Concerto pour batterie et petite orchestre*. Richard Rodney BENNETT: *Concerto for solo percussion and chamber orchestra*. ROSAURO: *Concierto para marimba e orquestra de cordas*. MIYOSHI: *Concerto for marimba and strings*.
*** BMG/RCA Dig. 09026 61277-2; 09026 61277-4 [id.].

Here is a chance for Glennie to show what she can do with more ambitious concert music – although, of course, there are popular influences and jazz rhythms in the works by both Richard Rodney Bennett and Rosauro. Bennett even offers an aleatory element for the percussionist. But his concerto is imaginatively thought out and has plenty of atmosphere and colour. The Milhaud concerto (its title sounds so much more inviting in French) is a most spontaneous piece, without fireworks but very effectively written.

Other than that, the most enjoyable work here is the tuneful four-movement concerto by the Brazilian Ney Rosauro, with a haunting *Lament* for the slow movement, an engaging *Dança*, followed by an imaginative finale. The Miyoshi *Marimba concerto* is in a kaleidoscopic single movement. All these works are brilliantly played and the collection is much more diverse and entertaining than one might expect. The recording engineers have a field day yet they do not try to create exaggerated effects.

Gould, Glenn (piano)

Glenn Gould Edition

BACH: *Harpsichord concertos Nos. 1–5; 7, BWV 1052–6 & BWV 1058* (with Columbia SO, Bernstein (No. 1) or Golschmann).
(M) (**) Sony mono (No. 1)/stereo SM2K 52591 (2) [S2K 52591].

BACH: *Fugues, BWV 953 & BWV 961; Fughettas, BWV 961 & BWV 902; 6 Little Preludes, BWV 933–8; 6 Partitas, BWV 825–30; Preludes, BWV 902 & 902/1a; Prelude and fugue, BWV 895; 2 Preludes & fughettas, BWV 899–900.*
(M) (**) Sony SM2K 52597 (2) [S2K 52597].

BACH: *Goldberg variations, BWV 988; Three-part Inventions, BWV 788–801.*
(M) (**) Sony SMK 52685 [id.] (live recordings from Salzburg and Moscow).

BACH: *Goldberg variations, BWV 988; Well-tempered Clavier: Fugues in E, BWV 878; F sharp min., BWV 883.*
(M) (**(*)) Sony mono SMK 52594 [id.] (1955 recording).
(M) (**) Sony Dig. SMK 52619 [id. (Variations only)].

BACH: *15 Two-part Inventions; 15 Three-part Inventions, BWV 772–801.*
(M) (**) Sony SMK 52596 [id.].

BACH: *Well-tempered Clavier, Book I, Preludes and fugues Nos. 1–24, BWV 846–69.*
(M) (**) Sony SM2K 52600 (2) [S2K 52600].

BACH: *Well-tempered Clavier, Book II, Preludes and Fugues Nos. 25–48, BWV 870–93.*
(M) (**) Sony SM2K 52603 (2) [S2K 52603].

BACH: *Well-tempered Clavier: Preludes and fugues in E, BWV 878; in F sharp min., BWV 883.* HANDEL: *Harpsichord suites Nos. 1–4, HWV 426–9.*
(M) (**) Sony mono/stereo SMK 52590 [id.].

BACH: *Sonata for violin and harpsichord No. 4 in C min., BWV 1017.* BEETHOVEN: *Violin sonata No. 10 in G, Op. 96.* SCHOENBERG: *Phantasy for violin and piano, Op. 47* (all with Yehudi Menuhin).
(M) (**) Sony mono SMK 52688 [id.].

BEETHOVEN: *Piano concertos Nos. 1–5* (with Columbia SO, Golschmann (No.1); Columbia SO, Bernstein (Nos. 2–3); NYPO, Bernstein (No. 4); America SO, Stokowski (No. 5)).
(M) (***) Sony SM3K 52632 (3) [S3K 52632].

BEETHOVEN: *7 Bagatelles, Op. 33; 6 Bagatelles, Op. 126; 6 Variations in F, Op. 34; 15 Variations with fugue in E flat (Eroica), Op. 35; 32 Variations on an original theme in C min., WoO 80.*
(M) (**) Sony SM2K 52646 (2) [S2K 52646].

BEETHOVEN: *Piano sonatas Nos. 24 in F sharp, Op. 78; 29 in B flat (Hammerklavier).*
(M) (**) Sony SMK 52645 [id.].

BIZET: *Nocturne No. 1 in F; Variations chromatiques.* GRIEG: *Piano sonata in E min., Op. 7.* SIBELIUS: *Kyllikki (3 Lyric pieces), Op. 41; Sonatinas Nos. 1–3, Op. 67/1–3.*
(M) (**(*)) Sony SM2K 52654 (2) [S2K 52654].

BRAHMS: (i) *Piano quintet in F min., Op. 34.* SCHUMANN: (ii) *Piano quartet in E flat, Op. 47* (with (i) Montreal Qt; (ii) Juilliard Qt (members)).
(M) (**) Sony SMK 52684 [id.].

BRAHMS: *4 Ballades, Op. 10; Intermezzi, Op. 76/6–7; Op. 116/4; Op. 117/1–3; Op. 118/1, 2 & 6; Op. 119/1; 2 Rhapsodies, Op. 79.*
(M) (**) Sony Analogue/Dig. SM2K 52651 (2) [S2K 52651].

HAYDN: *Piano sonata in E flat, Hob XVI:49.* MOZART: *Piano concerto No. 24 in C min., K.491* (with CBC SO, Walter Susskind); *Fantasia (Prelude) and fugue in C, K.394; Sonata in C, K.330.*
(M) (**) Sony SMK 52626 [id.].

HINDEMITH: (i) *Alto horn sonata in E flat;* (ii) *Bass tuba sonata;* (i) *Horn sonata;* (iii) *Trombone sonata;* (iv) *Trumpet sonata* (with (i) Mason Jones; (ii) Abe Torchinsky; (iii) Henry Charles Smith; (iv) Gilbert Johnson).
(M) (**) Sony SM2K 52671 (2) [S2K 52671].

HINDEMITH: *Piano sonatas Nos. 1–3.*
(M) (**(*)) Sony SMK 52670 [id.].

LISZT: *Concert paraphrases of Beethoven's Symphonies Nos. 5 in C min.; 6 in F (Pastoral): 1st movt.*
(M) (**) Sony SMK 52636 [id.].

LISZT: *Concert paraphrase of Beethoven's Symphony No. 6 in F (Pastoral).*
(M) (*) Sony SMK 52637 [id.].

Richard STRAUSS: *Piano sonata in B min., Op. 5; Enoch Arden, Op. 38; 5 Pieces, Op. 3;* (i) *Ophelia Lieder, Op. 67* ((i) with Elisabeth Schwarzkopf).
(M) (**(*)) Sony Dig./Analogue SM2K 52657 (2) [S2K 52657].

Contemporary music: MORAWETZ: *Fantasy in D min.* ANHALT: *Fantasia.* HETU: *Variations, Op. 8.* PENTLAND: *Ombres.* VALEN: *Piano sonata No. 2.*
(M) (**) Sony SMK 52677 [id.].

Consort music: BYRD: *1st Pavane & Galliard.* GIBBONS: *Fantasy in C min.; Allemande; Lord Salisbury's pavane & galliard.* BYRD: *Hugh Ashton's ground; 6th Pavane & galliard; A Voluntary; Selliger's round.* SWEELINCK: *Fantasia in D (Fantasia cromatica).*
(M) (**) Sony stereo/mono SMK 52589 [id.].

GOULD: *Lieberson madrigal; So you want to write a fugue* (McFadden, Keller, Fouchécourt, Van Kamp, Naoumoff, Ens., Rivvenq); *String quartet*

No. 1 (Monsaingeon, Apap, Caussé, Meunier);
2 Pieces for piano; Piano sonata (unfinished)
(Naoumoff); *Sonata for bassoon and piano*
(Marchese, Naoumoff).
(M) (**) Sony Dig. SMK 47814 [id.].

Glenn Gould is an artist who excites such strong
passions that guidance is almost superfluous. For his
host of admirers these discs are self-recommending;
those who do not respond to his pianism will not be
greatly interested in this edition. For long he enjoyed cult status, enhanced rather than diminished
by his absence from the concert hall. There is too
much that is wilful and eccentric in these performances for any of them to rank as a sole first recommendation. Yet if for his devotees virtually all his
recordings are indispensable, for the unconverted a
judicious approach is called for.

Generally speaking, his earlier recordings are to
be recommended to those who are sceptical as to
his gifts. There is nothing eccentric about the early
recordings. His 1957 performances of the Beethoven *Second Piano* concerto with Ladislav Slovák
in Leningrad and Bernstein in New York are first
rate in every respect. He leaves everything to his
fingers rather than his head, and his performance is
eminently sensitive. We have commented on these
individually and on the set of Beethoven concertos,
made with Golschmann, Bernstein and Stokowski.
(The *C major Concerto*, with Vladimir Golschmann, is particularly exhilarating, and both this and
the C minor with Bernstein command admiration.)
There is no questioning Gould's keyboard wizardry
or his miraculous control of part-writing in Bach,
for which he had much intuitive feeling. The majority of his Bach discs evidence strong personality
and commitment throughout, even though the tiresome vocalise (which became an increasing source
of frustration, particularly later in his recording
career) is a strain. The famous 1955 38-minute
repeatless mono recording of the *Goldberg* sounds
more of a curiosity nowadays, but it is nothing if
not a remarkable feat of digital prestidigitation.

Gould possessed a fine and inquiring mind and
both a sharp and an original intellect, as readers of
the strongly recommended collection of his writings
on music, *The Glenn Gould Reader*, will know.
(Judging from the sampler Sony CD, widely available also on videocassette and laserdisc and containing *So you want to write a fugue* and some of
his CBC television appearances, his sense of
humour was less sophisticated, in fact pretty cringe-
making.) His enterprise and intellectual curiosity,
however, inspire respect. Everything he does is the
result of artistic conviction, whether it is cham-
pioning Bizet's *Nocturne* and *Variations chromatiques* ('a giddy mix of Chopin and Chabrier') or
Schoenberg. He had great feeling for Hindemith
and championed this composer at a time when he
had become comparatively unfashionable, and likewise *Kyllikki* and the three *Sonatinas* of Sibelius. In

fact his tastes are always unpredictable: Strauss's
Enoch Arden, Grieg's early *Sonata*, and the *Second
Piano sonata* of the Norwegian 12-note master,
Fartein Valen. And who, nowadays, would dare to
play Byrd and Gibbons on the piano?

Sony deserve congratulations on this formidable
enterprise, and collectors will note that the sound-
quality of the originals has in the main been much
improved – as indeed it needed to be. However,
the sound generally has insufficient freshness and
bloom, and the eccentricity (some might say
egocentricity) of some of Gould's readings and the
accompanying vocalise are often quite insup-
portable.

Grumiaux, Arthur (violin)

'Favourite violin concertos' (with (i) Concg. O;
(ii) New Philh. O; (iii) Sir Colin Davis; (iv)
Bernard Haitink; (v) Jan Krenz): BEETHOVEN: (i;
iii) *Concerto in D*; (i; iv) *Romance No. 2 in F*. (ii;
iii) BRAHMS: *Concerto in D*. (ii; v)
MENDELSSOHN: *Concerto in E min*.
TCHAIKOVSKY: *Concerto in D*.
✹ (B) *** Ph. Duo 442 287-2 (2) [(M) id. import].

Another extraordinary Duo bargain set from
Philips, containing some of the great Belgian violinist's very finest performances. He recorded the
Beethoven twice for Philips, and this is the later
account from the mid-1970s with Sir Colin Davis.
Grumiaux imbues this glorious concerto with a
spirit of classical serenity and receives outstanding
support from Davis. If we remember correctly, the
earlier account with Galliera had slightly more of a
sense of repose and spontaneous magic in the slow
movement, but the balance of advantage between
the two versions is very difficult to resolve as the
Concertgebouw recording is fuller and richer and
(even if there is not absolute orchestral clarity) there
is less background noise.

The performance of the Brahms, it goes without
saying, is full of insight and lyrical eloquence, and
again Sir Colin Davis lends his soloist the most
sympathetic support. The (1973) account of the
Mendelssohn is characteristically polished and
refined, and Grumiaux, even if he does not wear his
heart on his sleeve, plays very beautifully
throughout: the pure poetry of the playing not only
lights up the *Andante* but is heard at its most magical
in the key moment of the downward arpeggio which
introduces the second subject of the first movement.

Similarly in the Tchaikovsky his playing – if
less overtly emotional than some – has the usual
aristocratic refinement and purity of tone to recommend it. His reading is beautifully paced and has
a particularly fine slow movement; both here and in
the brilliant finale he shows superb aplomb and
taste. With excellent accompaniments in both works
from Krenz, this adds to the attractions of the set,

for the 1970s recording has a wide range and is firmly focused in its CD format.

Concert (with Lamoureux Orchestra of Paris, Manuel Rosenthal): LALO: *Symphonie espagnole, Op. 21.* SAINT-SAENS: *Introduction et rondo capriccioso, Op. 28; Havanaise, Op. 83.* CHAUSSON: *Poème, Op. 25.* RAVEL: *Tzigane.* (BB) **(*) Australian Ph. Eloquence 462 579-2.

A worthwhile collection of French music. Grumiaux's playing is always individual, not showy or extrovert, but with plenty of colour and relaxed bravura. The orchestral support is lively and sympathetic, and lets the soloist dominate in the right way. The Lamoureux Orchestra is not the most refined of instruments, but is reasonably stylish, with a French timbre which is nice to hear in these conformist times. The recording is a little thin sounding (it dates from the mid 1960s), but is acceptable and well balanced.

Gutman, Michael (violin), Royal Philharmonic Orchestra, José Serebrier

'Four seasons': MILHAUD: *Spring concertino.* RODRIGO: *Concierto d'estio (Summer concerto).* CHAMINADE (orch. Paul Ut): *Autumn.* SEREBRIER: *Winter concerto.*
**(*) ASV Dig. CDDCA 855 [id.].

This is a well-conceived anthology that went a bit awry. Milhaud's *Spring concertino* is a fresh one-movement piece with a whiff of jazz *à la française*, and Rodrigo's *Concierto de estio*, conceived in the manner of Vivaldi, was the composer's own favourite among his many concertos; the central movement is an engaging *Sicilienne* with variations. Chaminade's *Autumn* is the composer's arrangement for violin and piano of her most successful lollipop, which another hand has subsequently orchestrated. The snag is that the conductor here, José Serebrier, has produced an undistinguished and rather wild concerto for *Winter*, even quoting themes associated with that season from Haydn, Glazunov and Tchaikovsky: the result is a bit of a hotch-potch. Performances and recording do not let the side down, but ASV need to reissue this with a further winter appendix – there is plenty of room, for the CD plays for only around 54 minutes.

Hallé Orchestra, Sir John Barbirolli

'Barbirolli at the opera': Richard STRAUSS: *Die Liebe der Danae* (symphonic fragments; arr. Clemens Krauss); *Der Rosenkavalier: suite.* WEBER: *Der Freischütz; Euryanthe: overtures.*

VERDI: *La Traviata: Preludes to Acts I & III.* MOZART: *Le nozze di Figaro overture.* WAGNER: *Lohengrin: Preludes to Acts I & III.*
(***) Dutton Lab. mono CDSJB 1004 [id.].

Hearing these glowing performances, full of Barbirollian expressiveness and panache, brings it home how sad it is that he recorded so few complete operas in the studio. It is tantalizing to realize what a great interpreter of *Rosenkavalier* he would have been, when his account of the much-maligned suite is so warm and persuasive, a première recording of 1946. Every item demonstrates the quality of the Hallé as trained by Barbirolli in the immediate post-war period, notably the strings. The Dutton transfers are first rate, though the original recordings used here were obviously more limited than those on some earlier Barbirolli Society issues, and this collection is too highly priced.

'Hallé favourites – 2': SUPPE: *Overture The Beautiful Galatea.* TURINA: *Danzas fantásticas.* CHABRIER: *España.* LEHAR: *Gold and silver waltz.* SIBELIUS: *Valse triste.* WALDTEUFEL: *The Skaters' waltz.* GRIEG: *Two Elegiac melodies; Peer Gynt suite No. 1.*
(***) Dutton Lab. mono/stereo CDSJB 1013 [id.].

Some of the recordings here have an EMI mono source from the 1950s; the rest, including the Sibelius and Grieg items (which are particularly warmly played), were early stereo with a Pye source. All the transfers are up to Dutton standard and Chabrier's *España* and the two waltzes have plenty of lilt and sparkle. It is a pity that – as it is sponsored by the Barbirolli Society – this disc is comparatively expensive.

Hallé Orchestra, Vernon Handley

'Russian spectacular': GLINKA: *Ruslan and Ludmilla overture.* MUSSORGSKY: *Night on the bare mountain* (arr. Rimsky-Korsakov). RIMSKY-KORSAKOV: *Capriccio espagnol, Op. 34; Russian Easter Festival overture, Op. 36.* BORODIN: *In the Steppes of Central Asia; Prince Igor overture.*
(B) ** CfP 574 0062.

The finest performance here is the *Capriccio espagnol*, with the Hallé players relishing the warmth and colour of Rimsky's orchestration. The rest of the programme is well played and often romantically expansive (as in the richly coloured secondary theme of the *Prince Igor overture*). There is no lack of energy, but at times – as in *Night on the bare mountain* – one feels Handley's approach is a shade too easygoing. The recording, made in Manchester's Free Trade Hall, is often spectacular and always vivid, but this is not the most exciting collection of Russian music available and readers are referred instead to Solti's *'Romantic Russia'* with the LSO below.

Hälsingborg Symphony Orchestra, Okko Kamu

'Swedish orchestral favourites': SODERMAN: *Swedish festival music.* STENHAMMAR: *The Song* (cantata): *Interlude.* LARSSON: *Pastoral suite; A Winter's Tale: Epilogue.* PETERSON-BERGER: *Frösöblomster: 4 Pieces.* ALFVEN: *Roslagspolka; Midsummer vigil; Gustavus Adolphus II suite.* WIREN: *Serenade for strings: Marcia.*
(BB) *** Naxos Dig. 8.553115 [id.].

A useful anthology of popular favourites from the Swedish repertory, nicely played by the Hälsingborg orchestra and Okko Kamu, which should have wide appeal, not only in but outside Sweden. The playing is lively, the performances of the Alfvén and Lars-Erik Larsson pieces are as good as any in the catalogue, the recording is excellent and the price is right.

Hardenberger, Håkan (trumpet)

'Famous classical trumpet concertos': HUMMEL: *Concerto in E.* HERTEL: *Concerto No. 1 in E flat.* STAMITZ: *Concerto in D.* HAYDN: *Concerto in E flat* (all with ASMF, Marriner). RICHTER: *Concerto in D.* Leopold MOZART: *Concerto in D.* MOLTER: *Concerto No. 1 in D.* Michael HAYDN: *Concerto No. 2 in C* (all with LPO, Howarth). CORELLI: *Sonata for trumpet, 2 violins and continuo.* ALBINONI: *Concerto in B flat, Op. 7/3* (with I Musici). ALBINONI/GIAZOTTO: *Adagio in G min.* CLARKE: *Trumpet Tune* (attr. PURCELL). BACH: *3 Chorale preludes.* BACH/GOUNOD: *Ave Maria* (all with Simon Preston, organ).
✿ (B) *** Ph. Dig. Duo 464 028-2 (2) [id.].

This is simply the finest collection of concertante music for trumpet in the catalogue. Hardenberger's playing in the famous Haydn concerto, with his noble line in the *Andante*, no less telling than his sparkling bravura in the finale, is matched by his account of the Hummel which he plays in E, rather than the expected key of E flat, which makes it sound brighter than usual. Neither he nor Marriner miss the galant lilt inherent in the dotted rhythm of the first movement, while the slow movement cantilena soars beautifully over its jogging pizzicato accompaniment, and the finale captivates the ear with its high spirits and easy virtuosity. The Stamitz concerto is a comparatively recent discovery. The writing lies consistently up in the instrument's stratosphere and includes some awkward leaps. It is inventive, however, notably in the exhilarating finale. There is no lack of panache here or in the lesser concerto by Hertel, and throughout Marriner's accompaniments are consistently elegant and polished. Apart from these obvious highlights there is much to enjoy in the lesser works too. The wealth of melody is apparent, and if not all the music here is in the masterpiece league, it is played as if it were. Hardenberger is as brilliant in the fast movements as he is sensitive in the slow ones, and his phrasing and tone are superb in both. In the two attractive baroque concertos by Albinoni and Marcello he plays with similar flair and gleaming tone, and he is a dab hand at embellishment, without overdoing thingas. The recordings and accompaniments are comparably fine, and it is difficult to imagine a better programme of this kind at any price.

Harle, John (saxophone), Academy of St Martin-in-the-Fields, Sir Neville Marriner

DEBUSSY: *Rapsodie for alto saxophone and orchestra.* IBERT: *Concertino da camera.* GLAZUNOV: *Concerto.* Richard Rodney BENNETT: Concerto. HEATH: *Out of the cool.* VILLA-LOBOS: Fantasia.
(B) *** [EMI Red Line CDR5 72109].

A first-class disc in every way. These are all attractive and well written for their instrument, and John Harle is its master. The Debussy, Ibert and Glazunov are all works well worth getting to know. The recording is excellent. This is not available in the UK.

Harnoy, Ofra (cello)

'Triology' (Cello concertos): BOCCHERINI: *Concerto in B flat* (arr. Grützmacher). Josef MYSLIVECEK: *Concerto in C.* VIOTTI: *Concerto in C.*
*** RCA Dig. 09026 61228-2 [id.].

Ofra Harnoy's account of the first movement of Grüzmacher's arrangement of Boccherini is romantically free, but she plays exquisitely in the confected Adagio, and gives an engagingly sprightly account of the finale. She is at her finest in the other two works, and very well accompanied by I Soloisti Veneti under Scimone. They are strongly characterized and both slow movements are touchingly expressive, outer movement crisply vital and búoyant. The orchestral recording is rather resonant, but the balance with the cello is wholly natural.

'Portrait': DVORAK: *Silent woods; Cello concerto in B min., Op. 104: Finale* (with Prague SO, Mackerras). SAINT-SAENS: *The Swan.* ELGAR:

Salut d'amour. FOSS: *Capriccio.* FAURE: *Après un rêve.* DEBUSSY: *La fille aux cheveux de lin* (with Michael Dussek, piano). VIVALDI: *Double concerto for violin and cello in F, RV 544* (with Igor Oistrakh); *Cello concerto in B min., RV 424.* HAYDN: *Cello concerto in C: Allegro molto* (all with Toronto CO, Paul Robinson). TCHAIKOVSKY: *Variations on a rococo theme, Op. 33; Andante cantabile.* BRUCH: *Kol Nidrei* (with LPO, Mackerras). LALO: *Cello concerto in D min.: Intermezzo.* OFFENBACH: *Andante for cello and orchestra* (both with Bournemouth SO, Antonio de Almeida). BOCCHERINI: *Cello concerto in B flat:* Allegro moderato. RIMSKY-KORSAKOV: *Flight of the bumblebee.* FALLA: *El amor brujo: Ritual fire dance.* GERSHWIN: *Summertime* (with Catherine Wilson, piano). SARASATE: *Zapateado* (with Helena Bowkun, piano). FRANCK: *Cello sonata* (arr. from *Violin sonata*): *Allegro poco mosso* (with Cyprien Katsaris, piano).
(B) *** RCA Twofer Dig. 74321 46574-2 (2) [id.].

This programme is very well planned to show the talents of a cellist who has too often been underrated because her CDs have usually been adorned by glamorous portraits. But she plays beautifully too! Although the collection contains a few individual movements from complete works, they all stand up well on their own, notably Lalo's delightful *Intermezzo*, the highlight of the concerto from which it is drawn, and the Dvořák finale ends the concert spiritedly.

Ofra Harnoy sustains this collection from beginning to end with playing which is unfailingly stylish, beautifully phrased and warm in tone. She can produce sparkling fireworks too, as in the Foss *Capriccio* and the fizzing Sarasate *Zapateado*, but for the most part she ravishes the ear with her delicacy of timbre and feeling, notably so in the Bruch *Kol Nidrei*, the Tchaikovsky *Rococo variations*, the lollipop *Andante for cello and orchestra* of Offenbach and Debussy's delicate evocation of *The maid with the flaxen hair*.

She is consistently well accompanied and always flatteringly recorded in a warm acoustic, yet she puts on an equally persuasive baroque mantle for her lively and cultured accounts of the two Vivaldi concertos, both of which have memorable slow movements. Highly recommended for late evening listening.

Harp concertos

Harp concertos (played by: (i) Marisa Robles; (ii) ASMF, Iona Brown; (iii) Osian Ellis, LSO, Bonynge; (iv) Werner Tripp, Hubert Jellinek, VPO, Münchinger; (v) Philh. O, Dutoit): (i; ii) BOIELDIEU: *Harp concerto in C.* DITTERSDORF:

Harp concerto in A (arr. PILLEY). (iii) GLIERE: *Harp concerto, Op. 74.* (i; ii) HANDEL: *Harp concerto, Op. 4/6.* (iv) MOZART: *Flute and harp concerto in C, K.299.* (i; v) RODRIGO: *Concierto de Aranjuez.*
(B) *** Decca Double 452 585-2 (2) [(M) id. import].

Boieldieu's *Harp concerto* has been recorded elsewhere but never more attractively. The (originally Argo) recording is still in the demonstration class and very sweet on the ear. Dittersdorf's *Harp concerto* is a transcription of an unfinished keyboard concerto with additional wind parts. It is an elegant piece, thematically not quite as memorable as Boieldieu's, but captivating when played with such style. Glière's is an unpretentious and tuneful work, with Osian Ellis performing brilliantly. Excellent (1968) Kingsway Hall recording. Handel's Op. 4/6 is well known in both organ and harp versions.

Marisa Robles and Iona Brown make an unforgettable case for the latter by creating the most delightful textures while never letting the work sound insubstantial. The ASMF accompaniment, so stylish and beautifully balanced, is a treat in itself, and the recording is well-nigh perfect. The much earlier, Vienna recording of Mozart's *Flute and harp concerto* is played stylishly and has stood the test of time, the recording smooth, full, nicely reverberant and with good detail. Refinement and beauty of tone and phrase are a hallmark throughout, and Münchinger provides most sensitive accompaniments.

The glowing acoustic of St Barnabas's Church, London, creates an attractively romantic aura for Marisa Robles's magnetic and highly atmospheric account of the composer's own arrangement for harp of his *Concierto de Aranjuez.* Robles is so convincing an advocate that for the moment the guitar original is all but forgotten, particularly when, with inspirational freedom, she makes the beautiful slow movement sound like a rhapsodic improvisation. It is a haunting performance, and the digital sound is first rate. Altogether an excellent anthology; however, the Boieldieu, Dittersdorf and Handel concertos on the first disc are also available separately at mid-price, and we gave a Rosette to this disc in our main volume (Decca 425 723-2).

Haskil, Clara (piano)

Clara Haskil: The Legacy:
(Volume 2: Concertos)

(for Volumes 1 & 3, see below under Instrumental Recitals)

BEETHOVEN: *Piano concerto No. 3 in C min., Op. 37.* CHOPIN: *Piano concerto No. 2 in F min., Op. 21.* FALLA: *Nights in the gardens of Spain* (all with LOP, Markevitch). MOZART: *Piano*

concertos Nos. 9 in E flat (Jeunehomme), K.271; 23 in A, K.488; Concert rondo in A, K.386 (with VSO, Sacher or Paumgartner); Piano concertos Nos. 20 in D min., K.466 (two versions, with VSO, Paumgartner or LOP, Markevitch); 24 in C min., K.491 (with LOP, Markevitch). SCHUMANN: Piano concerto in A min., Op. 54 (with Hague PO, van Otterloo).
(M) **(*) Ph. (IMS) mono/stereo 442 631-2 (4) [id.].

This second box of recordings, issued in the Philips 12-disc 'Clara Haskil Legacy', is of concertante works. The earliest of Haskil's concerto records is the Schumann (1951) and is not quite as poetic as that of her compatriot, Lipatti (Haskil was born in Bucharest), though there are some wonderful things, such as the reposeful development section of the first movement and the slow movement. The Hague orchestra's oboe has a surprisingly wide vibrato. Haskil's refinement and grace are to be heard at their best in the Mozart concertos (K.466 and K.491 were recorded in the month before her death), and her fire and temperament, albeit beautifully controlled, in the Falla Nights in the gardens of Spain. Her family had originally come from Spain. One snag about the set is that the Beethoven is split over two CDs.

Hauk, Franz (Klais organ in Liebfrauenmünster Ingolstadt), Ingolstadt Philharmonic, Alfredo Ibarra

Music for organ and orchestra: WIDOR: Symphony No. 3 for organ and grand orchestra, Op. 42. JONGEN: Alleluja, Op. 112; Hymne, Op. 78 (both for organ and orchestra). Horatio PARKER: Organ concerto in E flat, Op. 55.
**(*) Guild Dig. GMCD 7182 [id.].

In terms of sheer hyperbole Widor does this better than almost anyone. His G minor concertante Symphony is made up from two solo organ symphonies: the spectacular outer movements, including the brilliant closing Toccata, well laced with brass, are drawn from the Sixth, Op. 42/2, and the central Andante from the Second, Op. 13/2, composed ten years earlier.

The Jongen works are both lyrically colourful. The nobilmente Alleluja was composed to inaugurate a new organ in the concert hall of Belgian Radio in 1940, and with its closing fanfares sounds rather like wartime film music. The Hymne (for organ and strings) is a threnody of some character, well sustained and making a welcome contrast with the surrounding flamboyance.

The American Horace Parker earned the contempt of his pupil, Charles Ives, for 'imposing second-hand German romanticism on the patriots

of New England'. But his readily tuneful if at times overblown edifice is endearing for its somewhat sentimental romantic feeling, symbolised by the violin and horn solos in the Andante. The work was modelled on a concerto of Rheinberger, and its third movement Allegretto is also lightly scored and has charm. The finale includes a fugato, a vigorous pedal cadenza, a bit like a recitative, and a resounding close to bring the house down. Here the finale cadence echoes away in the long reverberation period of the Liebfrauenmünster. The organ itself is a maginficent beast and is played with great bravura and expressive flair by Franz Hauk; the orchestra accompany with spirit and enthusiasm even if at times they are all but drowned in the resonant wash of sound. The recording copes remarkably well, although it is hardly refined.

'Triumphal music for organ and orchestra': GOUNOD: Fantaisie on the Russian national hymne; Suite concertante. DUBOIS: Fantaisie triomphale. GUILMANT: Adoration. GIGOUT: Grand choeur dialogue.
*** Guild Dig. GMCD 7185 [id.].

Gounod's Fantaisie on the Tsarist anthem is imposing enough, if a bit repetitive; the Dubois Fantaisie is also suitably grand and pontifical, to be followed by Guilmant's very romantic Adoration, a rather beautiful soliloquy for organ and strings. After more pomp from Gigout, we return to Gounod, and an amiably attractive four-movement suite, with hunting horns setting off the jolly scherzo, followed by a songful Andante (nicely registered here). But, not surprisingly, it is the catchy vivace finale that steals the show: a bouncy tune that could become a hit if it got more exposure. It is most winningly played and completes an attractive concertante programme that does not rely on decibels for its main appeal. The performances are excellent and here the very reverberant acoustic seems for the most part under control

Heifetz, Jascha (violin)

'Heifetz the supreme': BACH: (Unaccompanied) Violin Partita No. 2, BWV 1004: Chaconne. BRAHMS: Violin concerto in D, Op. 77. TCHAIKOVSKY: Violin concerto in D, Op. 35 (with Chicago SO, Fritz Reiner). BRUCH: Scottish fantasy, Op. 46 (with New SO of London, Sir Malcolm Sargent). SIBELIUS: Violin concerto, Op. 47 (with Chicago SO, Walter Hendl). GLAZUNOV: Violin concerto, Op. 82 (with RCA Victor SO, Walter Hendl). GERSHWIN (transcribed Heifetz): 3 Preludes (with Brooks Smith, piano).
(M) *** RCA 74321 63470-2 (2) [id.].

For once the hyperbole of a record company's title is not exaggerated: truly Heifetz is the supreme virtuoso among violinists, and this generously compiled two-disc set shows him at his very finest. The performance of the great Bach *Chaconne* is not only technically phenomenal, it has an extraordinary range of feeling and dynamic, while Heifetz exerts a compelling grip over the structure. The performances of the five concertante works (discussed more fully in our main volume) are not only inspired and full of insights, they show how well Heifetz chose his accompanists, notably Fritz Reiner in Brahms and Tchaikovsky. Sargent too gives most sensitive support in the Bruch *Scottish fantasy* – the atmospheric opening is most evocative. Finally come the dazzling and touching Gershwin showpieces, showing that quicksilver bow arm at its most chimerical, even if here the recording is much too closely observed.

(i) **Hilversum Radio PO** or (ii)
**London Symphony Orchestra,
Leopold Stokowski**

(i) FRANCK: *Symphony in D min.* RAVEL: *L'eventail de Jeanne.* (ii) CHOPIN: *Mazurka in A min., Op. 17/4* (orch. Stokowski). MESSIAEN: *L'Ascension.* DUPARC: *Extase* (orch. Stokowski). (M) ** Cala CACD 0526 [id.].

These recordings were made in the early 1970s in Decca's hi-fi conscious Phase-Four system, and the exaggerated sound goes with the flamboyance of Stokowski's interpretations. The Franck *Symphony* is the most controversial reading on this disc. The conviction with which Stokowski moulds a romantic symphony like this is always striking. But here, by underlining the vulgarities in this score which most conductors seek to conceal, the overall balance of the work is disturbed, and the reading is less than satisfying. Of course, it has its moments, but Stokowski too often ventures perilously close to the cliff edge. The Hilversum orchestra does not have the virtuosity of the LSO in the companion pieces, but plays with energy as well as warmth. The rest of the programme is much more successful. After the Ravel *Fanfare* which is startling in its vividness, the following Chopin and Duparc pieces are richly atmospheric and show Stokowski at his most magical. Messiaen's *L'Ascension* is an early work, written first for organ but then orchestrated in 1935 with a different third movement. Stokowski is characteristically persuasive in developing the smooth flow of the music, though some will object to the opulence of the sound he and the engineers favour in the sweet meditation for strings alone, *Prayer of Christ ascending to the Father*.

Hofmann, Josef (piano)

'The Complete Josef Hofmann', Vol. 2 (with Curtis Institute Student O, cond. Reiner or Hilsberg): BRAHMS: *Academic festival overture.* RUBINSTEIN: *Piano concerto No. 4 in D min.* CHOPIN: *Ballade No. 1 in G min., Op. 23; Nocturne in E flat, Op. 9/2; Waltz in A flat, Op. 42; Andante spianato et Grande polonaise brillante in E flat, Op. 22* (2 versions); *Nocturne in F sharp, Op. 15/2; Waltz in D flat, Op. 64/1; Etude in G flat, Op. 25/9; Berceuse in B flat, Op. 57; Nocturne in C min., Op. 48/1; Mazurka in C, Op. 33/3; Waltz in A flat, Op. 34/1.* HOFMANN: *Chromaticon for piano & orchestra* (2 versions). MENDELSSOHN: *Spinning song in C, Op. 67/4.* RACHMANINOV: *Prelude in G min., Op. 23/5.* BEETHOVEN–RUBINSTEIN: *Turkish march.* MOSZKOWSKI: *Caprice espagnole, Op. 37.* ❀ (***) VAI Audio mono VAIA/IPA 1020 (2) [id.].

Josef Hofmann's amazing 1937 performance of Rubinstein's *Fourth Piano concerto* has long been a much-sought-after item in its LP format, and those who possess it have treasured it. The performance was attended by practically every pianist around, including Rachmaninov and Godowsky. (It was the latter who once said to a youngster who had mentioned a fingerslip in one of Hofmann's recitals, 'Why look for the spots on the sun!') In no other pianist's hands has this music made such sense: Hofmann plays his master's best-known concerto with a delicacy and poetic imagination that are altogether peerless.

Olin Downes spoke of his 'power and delicacy, lightning virtuosity and the capacity to make the keyboard sing, the richness of tone colouring and incorruptible taste'. The 1937 concert included the Brahms overture, a speech by Walter Damrosch, the incomparable performance of the Rubinstein concerto and, after the interval, a Chopin group. One is tempted to say that the *G minor Ballade* has never been surpassed. The second CD includes four later items, recorded in 1945. Once again – and it can't be said too often – the Rubinstein is phenomenal.

**Hungarian State Orchestra,
Mátyás Antal**

'Hungarian festival': KODALY: *Háry János: suite.* LISZT: *Hungarian rhapsodies for orchestra Nos. 1, 2 & 6* (arr. DOEPPLER). HUBAY: *Hejre Kati* (with Ferenc Balogh). BERLIOZ: *Damnation de Faust: Rákóczy march.* (BB) *** Naxos Dig. 8.550142; 4550142 [id.].

The Hungarian State Orchestra are in their element

in this programme of colourful music for which they have a natural affinity. There are few more characterful versions of the *Háry János suite* and Hubay's concertante violin piece, with its gypsy flair, is similarly successful, even if the violin soloist is not a particularly strong personality. The special interest of the Liszt *Hungarian rhapsodies* lies in the use of the Doeppler orchestrations, which are comparatively earthy, with greater use of brass solos than the more sophisticated scoring most often used in the West. The performances are suitably robust and certainly have plenty of charisma. The brilliant digital recording is strong on primary colours but has atmosphere too, and produces plenty of spectacle in the Berlioz *Rákóczy march*.

Indianapolis Symphony Orchestra, Raymond Leppard

'American dreams': CHADWICK: *Symphonic sketches: Noël.* BARBER: *Adagio for strings, Op. 11.* FOOTE: *Suite for strings, Op. 63: Pizzicato and Adagietto.* CARPENTER: *Sea drift.* CANNING: *Fantasy on a hymn tune by Justin Morgan for string quartet and orchestra.* GERSHWIN: *Lullaby.* CARMICHAEL: *Johnny Appleseed suite: Prayer and Cathedral vision.*
*** Decca Dig. 458 157-2 [id.].

'American nostalgia' would have been a better title for this collection of music, which totally ignores Charles Ives's heritage of stark originality, instead inhabiting a more easygoing orchestral world and following an essentially European tradition. The music of Chadwick, Foote and Carpenter is readily enjoyable when played and recorded as well as this, and though Foote's *Pizzicato* recalls Britten's 'playful' example in the *Simple Symphony*, and Canning's *Fantasy* equally obviously owes a considerable debt to Vaughan Williams and Tallis, that does not imply that they are not highly effective. The Hoagy Carmichael pieces too are engagingly folksy. But the Barber *Adagio* (played with great intensity) is, in a sense, out of place here because of its sheer originality and because it is a work of the highest calibre, while the slinky Gershwin *Lullaby* belongs to an altogether different arena of popular music.

Järvi, Neeme, with various orchestras

'The early Melodiya recordings'

BRAHMS: *Symphonies Nos. 2 in D, Op. 73; 3 in F, Op. 90* (with Moscow PO).
(M) *(*) BMG/Melodiya 74321 40719-2.

PAGANINI: *Violin concerto No. 1 in D, Op. 6;*

TCHAIKOVSKY: *Violin concerto in D, Op. 35* (with Viktor Tretyakov, Moscow PO).
(M) ** BMG/Melodiya 74321 40720-2.

SAINT-SAENS: *Piano concerto No. 2 in G min., Op. 22;* TCHAIKOVSKY: *Piano concerto No. 1 in B flat min., Op. 23* (with Grigory Sokolov, USSR SO).
(M) **(*) BMG/Melodiya 74321 40721-2.

BEETHOVEN: *Piano concerto No. 4 in G, Op. 58* (with Maria Grinberg, USSR SO). Richard STRAUSS: *Don Juan; Till Eulenspiegel* (with USSR TV and R. Large SO).
🌑 (M) ** BMG/Melodiya 74321 40722-2.

HAYDN: *Cello concerto No. 2 in D, Hob. VIIb/2* (with Danill Shafran, USSR SO). TCHAIKOVSKY: *Variations on a rococo theme, Op. 33; Pezzo capriccioso in B min., Op. 62; Andante cantabile, Op. 11; Nocturne in D min., Op. 19/4* (with Valentin Feighin, Estonian State SO).
(M) **(*) BMG/Melodiya 74321 40724-2.

These issues of some of his first Melodiya recordings, made mostly in the 1960s, were published to mark Neeme Järvi's sixtieth birthday and have been chosen by him. They are available separately. Technically they are variable, though the age of the recordings is by no means an indication of quality. Danill Shafran's marvellous Haydn concerto from 1962 is superior to the coarse and unpleasing sound the engineers produce in the brilliant performances of the Strauss tone-poems recorded in 1974. The Brahms symphonies, recorded with the Moscow Philharmonic in 1966, do not rise much above the routine; but there are some outstanding things that make the set well worth having. Dazzling accounts of the Paganini *D major* and Tchaikovsky *Violin concertos* from the nineteen-year-old Viktor Tretyakov and a hardly less impressive Tchaikovsky *B flat minor Concerto* from the sixteen-year-old Grigory Sokolov. But perhaps the greatest finds are Maria Grinberg's seraphic Beethoven *G major Concerto* and Danill Shafran's Haydn.

Johnson, Emma (clarinet)

Disc 1: *Concertos* (with the ECO): MOZART: *Concerto in A, K.488* (cond. Raymond Leppard). CRUSELL: *Concerto No. 2 in F min., Op. 5.* BAERMANN (attrib. WAGNER): *Adagio in D* (both cond. Sir Charles Groves). Malcolm ARNOLD: *Concerto No. 2, Op. 115* (cond. Ivor Bolton).

Disc 2: *Recital*: READE: *The Victorian kitchen garden (suite)* (with Skaila Kanga, harp). RIMSKY-KORSAKOV: *Flight of the bumblebee.* RACHMANINOV: *Vocalise, Op. 34/12.* MILHAUD: *Scaramouche.* SATIE; *Gymnopédie no. 1.* GERSHWIN (arr. COHN): *3 Preludes.* MACDOWELL (arr. ISAAC): *To a Wild Rose.* BLAKE: *The Snowman: Walking in the air.* BENJAMIN:

Jamaican rumba. (all with Julian Drake, piano). SCHUMANN: *Fantasiestücke, Op. 73.* DEBUSSY: *La fille aux cheveux de lin.* RAVEL: *Pavane pour une infante défunte* (with Gordon Black, piano). finzi: *5 Bagatelles, Op. 23* (with Malcolm Martineau, piano).
(M) *** ASV Dig. CDDCS 238 (2) [id.].

Emma Johnson's recording of Bernhard Crusell's *Second Concerto* made her a star and earned a Rosette for the original disc (ASV CDDCA 559) coupled with Baermann's rather beautiful *Adagio* (once attributed to Wagner) and music of Rossini and Weber. In return she put Crusell's engagingly lightweight piece firmly on the map, and later went on to record its two companion works (ASV CDDCA 784 – see our main volume). Here it comes coupled with Malcolm Arnold and her magnetic performance of the greatest clarinet concerto of all, by Mozart.

The solo pieces on the second CD derive from several compilations recorded over the last decade, two of which are listed below under Instrumental Recitals. But many will find the present collection works well as an ongoing recital, as it covers such a wide range. Highlights include her heartfelt account of the Schumann *Fantasy pieces*, and the 5 *Bagatelles* of Gerald Finzi. The charming – almost Ravelian – douceur of Paul Reade's *Victorian kitchen garden suite* is matched by the simplicity of MacDowell's *To a wild rose* and the famous *Snowman* theme is hauntingly presented. There is plenty of virtuosity too – *Scaramouche* is uninhibitedly scatty – the rhythmic sparkle here and in the *Jamaica rumba* is delightful, and Rimsky's *Bumblebee* is almost jet-propelled. The various pianists all accompany helpfully and the recording is excellent.

(Philip) Jones Brass Ensemble

'La Battaglia': SCHEIDT: *Battle suite.* SUSATO: *Susato suite.* BYRD: *The battle.* BANCHIERI: *Listen, here are the trumpets.* KUHNAU: *Biblical sonata No. 1 (The battle between David and Goliath).* JENKINS: *Newark Siege fantasia.* HANDEL: *Royal Fireworks music: La Réjouissance.*
(M) *** Decca 448 183-2 [id.].

If Frederick Fennell's Mercury recordings of Military music concentrated on functional military pieces, this CD offers music intended to entertain – and it certainly does that. Most of it was written in the heyday of *Battaglia* – military music for domestic playing, usually written for the keyboard, which was in vogue from 1500–1650. Here it has been brilliantly arranged for brass ensemble, which obviously brings out the martial elements even more forcibly. Whilst much of the writing is brilliantly

virtuosic, some of it is quite reflectively haunting. Kuhnau's *The trembling of the Israelites* is an early example of programme music, taken from one of of his descriptive compositions, and sounds rather modern.

As one would expect, drums are prominent throughout this disc, but always their use is varied and imaginative. One of the highlights must be Byrd's *The battle*, in essence a suite of dances and marches, often rather piquant in effect and thoroughly entertaining. But it does seem a bit tactless to place a Morris dance right after *The burying of the dead*! The sound is of demonstration class.

Juillet, Chantal (violin), Montreal SO, Charles Dutoit

'Rêverie and Caprice': YSAYE: *Poème élégiaque, Op. 12.* RAVEL: *Tzigane.* FAURE: *Berceuse, Op. 16; Romance, Op. 28.* LALO: *Fantaisie-ballet from Namouna; Guitare, Op. 28.* BERLIOZ: *Rêverie et caprice, Op. 8.* CHAUSSON: *Poème, Op. 25.*
**(*) Decca Dig. 458 143-2 [id.].

This is a most welcome collection of concertante pieces too readily neglected in the age of the CD, including not only staple items like *Tzigane* and Chausson's *Poème*, but a sequence of charming rarities, atmospherically recorded, but with the soloist balanced backwardly. That goes with a reticence in the solo playing, which prevents such a piece as the *Poème élégiaque* from having the brilliant impact it needs. Significantly, in Ravel's *Tzigane* the long unaccompanied solo at the start has far more impact than the rest.

Karajan, Herbert von

'Portrait': BRAHMS: *German Requiem, Op. 45* (with Anna Tomowa-Sintow, José van Dam, Vienna Singverein). SMETANA: *Má Vlast: Vltava.* MENDELSSOHN: *Hebrides overture, Op. 26.* SIBELIUS: *Finlandia, Op. 26* (all with Berlin Philharmonic Orchestra). OFFENBACH: *Contes d'Hoffmann: Barcarolle.* CHABRIER: *España.* TCHAIKOVSKY: *Overture 1812* (all with Philharmonia Orchestra).
(BB) **(*) Royal Long Players DCL 705872 (2).

Karajan's 1977 EMI version of the *German Requiem* is in almost every way preferable to his earlier DG set. The choral sound is altogether warmer, bigger and closer, with sharper dramatic contrasts. The soloists are both excellent, Tomowa-Sintow sings with a rich, creamy tone-colour, while José van Dam is equally impressive, with a smooth, firm tone. Moreover the CD transfer has improved definition and added immediacy. The rest of the programme is more uneven. But if *Eine kleine*

Nachtmusik lacks charm, the Berlin Philharmonic provides atmospheric, beautifully played accounts of Smetana's *Vltava* and Mendelssohn's *Fingal's Cave*, plus a powerfully robust *Finlandia*. The Philharmonia, on top form, contribute a sparkling Chabrier *España* and a warmly romantic Offenbach *Barcarolle*. In the closing Tchaikovsky *1812* Karajan takes the lyrical string melody indulgently, but there is a very bold climax, with impressive pealing bells and precise cannon fire.

Karajan Edition (EMI)

The Berlin years, Vol. 1

BEETHOVEN: *Piano concertos Nos. 1 in C, Op. 15; 2 in B flat, Op. 19.*
Alexis Weissenberg BPO (CDM5 66090-2).

BEETHOVEN: *Piano concertos Nos. 3 in C min., Op. 37; 5 in E flat (Emperor), Op. 73.*
Alexis Weissenberg BPO (CDM5 66091-2).

BEETHOVEN: (i) *Piano concerto No. 4 in G, Op. 58;* (ii) *Triple concerto in C, Op. 56.* (i) Alexis Weissenberg; (ii) David Oistrakh, Rostropovich, Richter; BPO (CDM5 66092-2).

BRAHMS: *Variations on a theme of Haydn, Op. 56a;* (i) *Piano concerto No. 2 in B flat, Op. 83.*
BPO; (i) with Hans Richter-Haaser (CDM5 66093-2).

BRUCKNER: *Symphony No. 4 in E flat (Romantic).*
BPO (CDM5 66094-2).

BRUCKNER: *Symphony No. 7 in E.*
BPO (CDM5 66095-2).

HAYDN: *Symphonies Nos. 83 in G min. (The Hen); 101 in D (Clock); 104 in D (London).*
BPO (CDM5 66097-2).

MOZART: *Symphonies Nos. 29; 35 (Haffner); 36 (Linz); 38 (Prague); 39; 40; 41 (Jupiter). Rehearsal extracts.*
BPO available separately: *Nos. 29, 35 & 36* (CDM5 66098-2); *Nos. 38 & 39* (with rehearsal extracts) (CDM5 66099-2); *Nos. 40 & 41* (with rehearsal extracts) (CDM5 66100-2).

MOZART: (i) *Sinfonia concertante in E flat, K.297b.* BRAHMS: (ii) *Violin concerto in D, Op. 77.*
(i) Steins, Stähr, Hauptmann, Braun; (ii) Kremer; BPO (CDM5 66101-2) (all BPO).

SCHUBERT: *Symphonies Nos. 1–2* (with WEBER: *Der Freischütz: overture*) (CDMS5 66102-2); *Nos. 3–4* (with *Rosamunde ballet music, D.797*) (CDMS5 66103-2); *Nos. 5–6* (with *Rosamunde overture (Die Zauberharfe), D.644*) (CDMS5 66104-2); *Nos. 8–9* (CDM5 66105-2).

R. STRAUSS: *Don Quixote, Op. 35.* WAGNER:

Tannhäuser: (i) *Overture and Venusberg music. Die Meistersinger: Overture.*
BPO; (i) with German Op. Ch. (CDM5 66106-2).

R. STRAUSS: *Symphonia domestica, Op. 53.*
WAGNER: *Tristan und Isolde: Prelude & Liebestod. Lohengrin: Preludes to Acts I & III.*
BPO (CDM5 66107-2).

R. STRAUSS: *Ein Heldenleben, Op. 40.* WAGNER: *Der fliegende Holländer: Overture. Parsifal: Preludes to Acts I & III.*
BPO (CDM5 66108-2).

BRAHMS: *Tragic overture, Op. 81.* HINDEMITH: *Mathis der Maler* (symphony). BRUCKNER: *Symphony No. 8 in C min.*
BPO (CMS5 66109-2 (2)).

Karajan's period with EMI, after he had left Decca, was less consistently successful than his later, DG era, when he probably reached the peak of his recording career. Some collectors will resist the sumptuous orchestral sound he was given in the works of Haydn and Mozart and also perhaps in Schubert too, where we are now accustomed to more transparent textures. In the Beethoven concertos he was not well partnered by Weissenberg, but in the Brahms *B flat Concerto* it was surely Karajan, rather than his soloist, Hans Richter-Haaser, who was responsible for the waywardness of the interpretation. Not surprisingly, he is heard at his finest in the music of Bruckner, Richard Strauss, Wagner and Hindemith. All these recordings are separate issues.

King, Thea (clarinet)

'The clarinet in concert': BRUCH: *Double concerto in E min. for clarinet, viola and orchestra, Op. 88* (with Nobuko Imai).
MENDELSSOHN: *2 Concert pieces for clarinet and basset horn in F min., Op. 113; in D min., Op. 114* (with Georgina Dobrée). CRUSELL: *Introduction and variations on a Swedish air, Op. 12* (all 4 works with LSO, Alun Francis). SPOHR: *Variations in B flat for clarinet and orchestra in a theme from Alruna.* RIETZ: *Clarinet concerto in G min., Op. 29.* SOLERE: *Sinfonie concertante in F for 2 clarinets* (with Georgina Dobrée). HEINZE: *Konzertstück in F* (all with ECO, James Judd or Andrew Litton).
(B) *** Hyperion Dyad Dig. CDD 22017 (2) [id.].

A thoroughly engaging programme of forgotten music (the Bruch is not even listed in the *New Grove*), all played with skill and real charm, and excellently recorded. The Bruch *Double concerto* is particularly individual, but the two attractive Mendelssohn concert pieces (each in three brief movements) and the quixotic Crusell *Variations* are by no means insubstantial. They are discussed more fully under their composer entries in our main volume. The novelties on the second disc are slighter but no less entertaining: the jaunty Spohr *Variations* followed by the galant concerto by Julius Rietz (1812–77) with its engaging lyrical flow. In Etienne Solère's *Sinfonie concertante*, one cannot help but smile at the garrulous chatter between the two solo instruments, which evokes the clinking of tea-cups, while Gustav Heinze's warmly tuneful *Konzertstück* has a jocular, Hummelian finale to match the bouncing closing Rondeau of the Solère. The playing brings many chortling roulades and a seductive timbre from the ever-stylish Thea King, and Georgina Dobrée is a nimble partner in the *Sinfonie concertante*. The accompaniments are excellent too, while the recording has fine range and presence.

Koussevitzky, Serge (double-bass and conductor)

(see also under Boston Symphony Orchestra)

Collection (with (i) Pierre Luboshutz; (ii) Boston SO; (iii) Bernard Zighera, Pierre Luboshutz): BEETHOVEN: (i) *Minuet in G* (arr. Koussevitzky) (ii) *Symphony No. 6 in F (Pastoral)*. (iii) ECCLES: *Largo*. (i) LASKA: *Wiegenlied*. (ii) KOUSSEVITZKY: *Concerto, Op. 3: Andante; Valse miniature*. Johann STRAUSS: *Wiener Blut; Frühlingsstimmen*.
(M) (***) Biddulph mono WHL 019 [id.].

In his youth and before he was established as a conductor of international celebrity, Koussevitzky was regarded as the greatest double-bass virtuoso of the age. In 1928–9, in his mid-fifties, he was enticed into the New York Studios to record the above with the pianist Bernard Zighera, but he then re-recorded everything with Pierre Luboshutz the following year. These performances confirm that he brought to the double-bass the same lyrical intensity and feeling for line and sonority that distinguished his conducting.

Judging from the two concerto movements included here, he was no great composer, but the 1928 recording of the *Pastoral Symphony* with the Boston Symphony Orchestra is little short of a revelation. As an interpretation it feels just right; generally speaking, it is brisk but totally unhurried, each phrase wonderfully shaped. Given the fact that he never lingers, the paradox is that this performance seems strangely spacious. One young and knowledgeable collector to whom we played this thought it quite simply 'among the best *Pastorals* ever'; moreover the recorded sound is remarkable for its age and comes up very freshly. This disc, though comparatively expensive, is worth it.

Kraggerud, Henning (violin), Razumovsky Symphony Orchestra, Bjarte Engeset

'Norwegian violin favourites': Ole BULL: *The herd-girl's Sunday; La Mélancholie* (arr. Kraggerud);*Concerto in E min.: Adagio.* SINDING: *Suite im alten Stil, Op. 10.* SVENSEN: *Romance in G, Op. 26.* HALVORSEN: *Norwegian dances 1–2; Maiden's song; The old Fisherman's song; Wedding march; Andante religioso.* GRIEG: *I love thee* (arr. Kraggerud); *Elegiac melody: The last spring*.
(BB) *** Naxos Dig. 8.554497 [id.].

Ole Bull, born in Bergen in 1810, was a virtuoso of the traditional Norwegian 'Hardanger' fiddle, which he took to Europe, where he achieved a considerable success in Paris. He was one of the first gatherers of Norwegian folk tunes, which he used in his own music. The opening piece here, *The herd-girl's Sunday*, with its charming melancholy, is characteristic, but the touching *Adagio* from his *Violin concerto* shows that he also used his folk material more ambitiously and his influence remained. The best-known piece here, Svensen's disarmingly memorable *Romance*, although more sophisticated in construction is in a similar melodic vein. Johan Halvorsen continued this tradition and his miniatures are equally attractive, as is the Sinding *Suite*. Henning Kraggerud plays a modern violin, and invests all these pieces with a simplicity of style and a beauty of tone that gives great pleasure, ending with two Grieg favourites including a transcription of his most famous song. With excellent accompaniments and a most natural sound balance this collection gives much pleasure.

Lawson, Colin (clarinet, basset horn), Parley of Instruments, Peter Holman

'English classical clarinet concertos': John MAHON: *Concerto No. 2 in F; Duets Nos. 1 & 4 in B flat for 2 basset horns* (with Michael Harris). J. C. BACH: *Concerted Symphony in E flat.* James HOOK: *Concerto in E flat*.
** Hyperion Dig. CDA 66869 [id.].

The clarinet (invented around 1700) did not achieve a strong solo profile until well into the eighteenth century, and even then it was not favoured by amateurs. Mozart remains the only composer of that period to have written really great music for it. Thus, even more than in his companion disc of violin concertos (listed under Wallfisch), Peter Holman has had to scrape the barrel a bit and even include a *Concerted symphony* by J. C. Bach, which in the event is the most enterprising work here, but features (besides a pair of clarinets) two oboes, a bassoon and two horns. It has a very striking first movement and a touching *Larghetto*, which opens with a bassoon solo; the flute then takes over, and the clarinets enter much later. The most unusual scoring is in the closing Minuet, where in the Trio the woodwind take over entirely.

John Mahon's *Duos* for basset horns are agreeable but sub-Mozart. His *Concerto*, however, goes even further than the contemporary violin concertos (see below), by using a complete Scottish folksong for his ingenious *Andante* and another popular tune (*The wanton God*) for the Rondo finale. James Hook's *Concerto* has little that is individual to say in its conventional and rather long opening movement, yet it includes the prettiest roulades for the clarinet soloist. However, the composer reserves the real fireworks for the final Rondo, especially in the spectacular closing episode, introduced by the horns, where the clarinet ripples hectically up and down its register in a quite abandoned manner. Colin Lawson is fully equal to such bravura and he plays with fine style throughout. Holman provides excellent accompaniments, but it is a pity that the music itself is so uneven.

Leningrad Philharmonic Orchestra, Yevgeni Mravinsky

The Mravinsky Edition: Volumes 1–10

(M) **(*) RCA 74321 25189-2 (10) [id.].

Volume 1: BRAHMS: *Symphony No. 2 in D, Op. 73.* SCHUBERT: *Symphony No. 8 in B min. (Unfinished), D.759.* WEBER: *Oberon: Overture.*
(M) **(*) RCA 74321 25190-2 [id.].

Volume 2: MOZART: *Overture: The Marriage of Figaro; Symphony No. 39 in E flat, K.543.* MUSSORGSKY: *Khovanshchina: Prelude to Act I.* SIBELIUS: *Legend: The Swan of Tuonela, Op. 22/2; Symphony No. 7 in C, Op. 105.*
(M) **(*) RCA 74321 25191-2 [id.].

Volume 3: STRAVINSKY: *Agon* (complete). SHOSTAKOVICH: *Symphony No. 15 in A, Op. 141.*
(M) **(*) RCA 74321 25192-2 [id.].

Volume 4: BRUCKNER: *Symphony No. 9 in D min.*
(M) ** RCA 74321 25193-2 [id.].

Volume 5: TCHAIKOVSKY: *The Nutcracker:* excerpts. PROKOFIEV: *Romeo and Juliet: suite No. 2.*
(M) *** RCA 74321 25194-2 [id.].

Volume 6: HINDEMITH: *Symphony, Die Harmonie der Welt.* HONEGGER: *Symphony No. 3 (Symphonie liturgique).*
(M) *** RCA 74321 25195-2 [id.].

Volume 7: BEETHOVEN: *Symphony No. 4 in B flat,*

Op. 60. TCHAIKOVSKY: *Symphony No. 5 in E min.*
(M) **(*) RCA 74321 25196-2 [id.].

Volume 8: BARTOK: *Music for strings, percussion and celeste.* DEBUSSY: *Prélude à l'après-midi d'un faune.* STRAVINSKY: *Apollo* (ballet; complete).
(M) **(*) RCA 74321 25197-2 [id.].

Volume 9: SHOSTAKOVICH: *Symphonies Nos. 6 in B min., Op. 54; 10 in E min., Op. 93.*
( ) **(*) RCA 74321 25198-2 [id.].

Volume 10: WAGNER: *Götterdämmerung: Siegfried's Funeral march. Lohengrin: Preludes to Acts I & III. Die Meistersinger: Overture. Tannhäuser: Overture. Tristan und Isolde: Prelude & Liebestod. Die Walküre: Ride of the Valkyries.*
(M) **(*) RCA 74321 25199-2 [id.].

Yevgeni Mravinsky's stature has gained increasing recognition among the wider musical public outside his native country since his death in 1988. Mravinsky did not make many commercial records: the derisory terms offered to the Leningrad orchestra during the days of the Soviet Union were not conducive to recording. Moreover Mravinsky did not like recording under studio conditions, and so the bulk of his legacy derives from the concert hall. These discs are now only available as a ten-CD set.

(Volume 1: 74321 25190-2) Mravinsky's accounts of the Brahms *Second Symphony* and the Schubert *Unfinished Symphony*, together with the Weber *Oberon overture*, come from concerts given at the end of April 1978. They should not be confused with the performances he gave at the Vienna Festwochen later that summer (for which they were obviously preparation) and which appeared briefly on a four-LP EMI/Melodiya set in the early 1980s, including also the *Fifth Symphonies* of Tchaikovsky and Shostakovich. (Then the Vienna *Oberon*, at under 9 minutes, occupied a whole LP side!) Generally speaking these performances are, if anything, finer, with a moving *Unfinished* and a lyrical but vital Brahms.

(Volume 2: 74321 25191-2) The Mozart pieces, the *Figaro overture* and the *Symphony No. 39 in E flat*, come from the same 1965 concert as the two Sibelius works, *The Swan of Tuonela* and the *Seventh Symphony*. The Mussorgsky *Dawn on the Moscow river*, the evocative *Prelude* to the first Act of *Khovanshchina*, was given two days earlier. The *Seventh* is a performance of stature. Even if Mravinsky rushes the very opening ascent in the cellos and the trombone does have a wide vibrato, it has that intensity this score must have. Although the characterful account of the *Figaro overture* has been available before on Olympia, the Mozart symphony has not; it is a performance of the old school, with great power and again much lyrical intensity. There is a slight drop in pitch at 5 minutes 15 seconds into the slow movement.

(Volume 3: 74321 25192-2) That same intensity is to be found in the 1965 performance of Stravinsky's *Agon*, even if it is evident that the players are not completely inside this particular score; some of the jewelled, hard-edged sound-world Stravinsky evokes is missing. The sound is perfectly acceptable without being in the first flight. Shostakovich's *Fifteenth Symphony* comes from May 1976. Authenticity of feeling and dramatic power compensate for imperfections of execution – and generally rough recording – and the darkness and intensity of the slow movement come over superbly in Mravinsky's hands. There is no doubting the special insights he brings to the work. The new transfer has perhaps a fractionally sharper image.

(Volume 4: 74321 25193-2) Bruckner's *Ninth Symphony* comes from a public performance in 1980, though, for all the skill of the RCA team, the sound still remains fairly coarse and rough-grained. The performance has tremendous grip and strong personality, though Mravinsky moves things on sometimes where greater breadth might be better, there are some idiosyncratic touches (excessive slowness at letter R in the Novak Edition, track 1, 15 minutes 50 seconds), and sonic limitations do inhibit a strong recommendation.

(Volume 5: 74321 25194-2) The excerpts from Tchaikovsky's *Nutcracker* and the *Second Suite* from Prokofiev's *Romeo and Juliet* are identical with the performances that previously appeared on Philips in 1988. The Tchaikovsky is quite magical, possessing all the warmth and enchantment one could wish for, and the sound is every bit as good as the Philips transfer. The Prokofiev, too, is musicmaking of real stature. As we said first time round, 'phrases breathe and textures glow; detail stands in the proper relation to the whole. There is drama and poetry, and wonderfully rapt *pianissimi*.' However, the fourth movement, the *Dance* in the printed score, is omitted from this recording.

(Volume 6: 74321 25195-2) Both the Hindemith *Symphony*, *Die Harmonie der Welt*, and Honegger's masterly *Symphonie liturgique* come from 1965. Both are performances of stature and few allowances need to be made for the sonic limitations of either work. Sonically this is infinitely superior to the 1980 Bruckner *Ninth* or the 1976 Shostakovich *Tenth*. In fact the CD is among the most desirable of the present set. Mravinsky maintains a tremendous grip on the Hindemith and his *Liturgique* is a very distinguished and imaginative performance.

(Volume 7: 74321 25196-2) The Beethoven *Fourth Symphony* dates from 29 April 1973. It is a performance that calls only the most exalted comparisons to mind – Weingartner, Toscanini's prewar BBC performances. The Tchaikovsky *Fifth Symphony* comes from the same concert – and what a concert it must have been! The performance is even more electrifying than either of the earlier DG versions, though climaxes are somewhat

rough. RCA's advanced technology has managed to tame them a little, and this account can certainly be recommended alongside the DG versions – and the coupling certainly makes it highly recommendable.

(Volume 8: 74321 25197-2) The performance of Bartók's *Music for strings, percussion and celeste*, the Debussy *Prélude à l'après-midi d'un faune* and Stravinsky's *Apollo* all come from 1965, which would seem to be a good vintage for Leningrad recordings and, in the Bartók at least, an unbronchial time for audiences. Even the pianissimo introduction to the Bartók is relatively (though not completely) undisturbed. The Stravinsky, which is new to UK catalogues, finds the Leningrad strings in splendid form, although Mravinsky rather favours a more heavily accented articulation and less seductive tone-quality than we find in Markevitch's 1963 LSO recording. The balance is closer than in the Bartók. There are some extraneous audience noises here, too, which will irritate some listeners.

(Volume 9: 74321 25198-2) Mravinsky's account of the Shostakovich *Sixth* comes from 1972. Though its first movement is not in fact slower than his 1965 account, it is not quite as intense in feeling. The *Tenth Symphony* was among the symphonies Mravinsky conducted in 1976 to mark what would have been the composer's seventieth birthday. The opening bars suffer from an intrusively restive audience (and the microphones do not capture the very first note). The performance (31 March 1976) is tremendously intense and of great documentary interest. The recording is, it would seem, mono (though this is not stated on the disc, it certainly sounds as if it is). Generally speaking, the recording is not as good as its 1972 companion.

(Volume 10: 74321 25199-2) Mravinsky's Wagner has stature and breadth. The anthology of pieces collected here ranges from 1965 to 1982, the year of his retirement. Variable quality but invariably fine playing from the Leningrad orchestra, and decent transfers. Incidentally, the complete set comes in a very flimsy cardboard slipcase – ours came unstuck within the first few minutes' use!

The Mravinsky Edition: Volumes 13–20

BRUCKNER: *Symphony No. 8 in C min.*
(M) (**) BMG/Melodiya mono 74321 29402-2 [id.].

Richard STRAUSS: *An Alpine Symphony;* (i) *Horn concerto No. 1 in E flat, Op. 11.*
(M) (**) BMG/Melodiya mono/stereo 74321 29403-2 [id.]. (i) with Vitaly Buyanovsky.

OVSYANIKO-KUILIKOVSKY: *Symphony No. 21 in G min.* SHOSTAKOVICH: *Symphony No. 5 in D min., Op. 74.*
(M) (**) BMG/Melodiya mono 74321 29404-2 [id.].

SHOSTAKOVICH: *Symphony No. 7 in C (Leningrad), Op. 60.*
(M) (**) BMG/Melodiya mono 74321 29405-2 [id.].

SHOSTAKOVICH: *Symphony No. 8 in C min., Op. 65.*
(M) (**) BMG/Melodiya mono 74321 29406-2 [id.].

TCHAIKOVSKY: *Symphony No. 4 in F min., Op. 36.* GLAZUNOV: *Symphony No. 4 in E flat, Op. 48.*
(M) (*(*)) BMG/Melodiya mono 74321 29407-2 [id.].

TCHAIKOVSKY: *Symphony No. 6 in B min. (Pathétique).* RIMSKY-KORSAKOV: *Tale of the invisible city of Kitezh.*
(M) (*(*)) BMG/Melodiya mono 74321 29408-2 [id.].

TCHAIKOVSKY: *Capriccio italien, Op. 45; Francesca da Rimini, Op. 32; Serenade for strings, Op. 48.*
(M) (*) BMG/Melodiya mono 74321 29409-2 [id.].

Unlike the earlier edition (discussed above), only eight out of the ten CDs originally issued are available individually at mid-price. Inevitably they are variable in quality. Mravinsky's account of Bruckner's *Eighth Symphony* comes from 1959, and Melodiya copies were briefly available in specialist outlets in the late 1960s. It is a noble performance, much tauter than, say, Furtwängler – whose Testament issue runs to nearly 79 minutes as opposed to Mravinsky's 73 minutes 42 seconds. There is breadth and dignity, and the slow movement is very spacious and beautiful.

The 1962 performance of Strauss's *Alpine Symphony* was first discussed in our 1989 *Yearbook*, when it appeared on the Olympia label along with *Siegfried's funeral music* from *Götterdämmerung*. We wrote then that it is 'marvellously concentrated in feeling and spacious in conception; if only the recording were rich enough to do it full justice, it would be a strong recommendation . . . it is obviously a performance of grandeur and almost transcends the limitations of the recording'. The superb orchestral response still remains a source of wonder and Mravinsky's control is pretty awesome. It is difficult to discern any significant improvement in the mono sound. Their excellent notes tell us that Mravinsky conducted the *Alpine Symphony* five times, as many times as he did *Till Eulenspiegel*. These and the *First Horn concerto* constituted his entire Strauss repertory. Vitaly Buyanovsky was first horn in the Leningrad orchestra, and Shostakovich must have had his virtuosity in mind when writing his *First Cello concerto, with its important solo horn part*. His vibrato will be a little too wide for many tastes, but he is a wonderfully musical player all the same. Again, the recording, made in 1964, though in stereo, calls for tolerance.

The name of the Ukraine composer Nikolai Ovsyaniko-Kuilikovsky (1768–1848) will not be found in *Grove* or in any other dictionary. His *Twenty-first Symphony* was said to have been written for the opening of the Odessa Theatre in 1809. The work was published by the State Opera House in 1951 but is in fact by Mikhail Goldstein and belongs with the hoaxes of Kreisler, Henri Casadesus, Klenovsky and others. This elegant four-movement pastiche, to which Mravinsky and the Leningrad orchestra lent their names, is engaging and is played with great delicacy and lightness of touch. Like the Shostakovich *Fifth Symphony*, with which it is coupled, it was recorded at a concert in April 1954.

Mravinsky's association with the Shostakovich symphonies was closer than almost any other maestro's. He conducted the first performances of the *Fifth, Sixth, Seventh, Eleventh* and *Twelfth Symphonies*, and went on to conduct the *Fifth* more than 100 times: there are four other Mravinsky performances in the catalogue – all, of course, with the Leningrad orchestra – from 1965 (Russian Disc, coupled with No. 6 – at full price), 1966 (again Russian Disc, with Salmanov's *Symphony No. 2*), 1967 (Praga, with No. 9), an LP from the Vienna Festwochen of 1978 and 1984 (Erato – no coupling). The present version is the earliest, and fewer allowances need be made for the (mono) sound than one might expect. Mravinsky's authority is everywhere in evidence and the slow movement is particularly intense.

Mravinsky's account of the *Leningrad Symphony* (74321 29405-2) is the 1953 recording, at various times available on Melodiya LP, but the *Eighth Symphony* (74321 29406-2) is a newcomer. There are several accounts in circulation, including his 1960 performance at the Festival Hall (which appeared on Melodiya LPs) and his 1982 account on Philips (which was more accurately transferred on Russian Disc). The present version is in some ways the most intense of all. It comes from 1947, when the scars of wartime suffering and privations were fresh in every Russian mind. This Moscow performance was given just before the Leningrad orchestra set out on their visit to Prague where the *Eighth Symphony* made so deep an impression, conquering an initially hostile audience. Its intensity is extreme and almost painful. The listener is gripped as in a vice, and in its expressive power and anguish the symphony makes an overwhelming effect. Those who fear that the actual sound will resemble the soundtrack of wartime Russian films, with masses of distortion, can be reassured. Given the fact that it is over fifty years old, the sound is remarkably good. The upper strings are uncomfortably hard, but such is the quality of this great performance that such things are soon forgotten.

Those who have Mravinsky's 1960 Tchaikovsky *Fourth Symphony* (in the DG stereo set – the 1956 mono *Fourth* was with Sanderling) will probably opt to skip this Melodiya performance, taut and dramatic though it is, in favour of the finer DG sound. It is coupled with a superb, highly persuasive account of Glazunov's *Fourth Symphony*. The BMG/Melodiya engineers have enormous skill, but the 1947 sound resists even their expertise. Similar qualifications apply to the suite from Rimsky-Korsakov's *Tale of the invisible city of Kitezh* and the Tchaikovsky *Sixth Symphony*, both of which come from the spring of 1949. Pretty fabulous playing, of course, and there are superb things in the *Pathétique*; but for the non-specialist collector Mravinsky's 1956 or 1960 DG recordings will – and, indeed, should – take priority.

The other Tchaikovsky recordings (74321 29409-2) come from 1948–1950, and BMG have done a good job on the transfers. The earliest of them, *Francesca da Rimini*, has an electrifying opening and tremendous dramatic intensity. The upper strings, however, sound a little wanting in opulence at the top end of the spectrum (no doubt the microphone placement was in some measure to blame), and there is some execrable brass intonation (at about 12 minutes in). The playing in the *Serenade for strings* has an impressive eloquence, but the majority of collectors may find the quality of sound here and in the *Capriccio italien* an inhibiting factor.

Leonhardt, Gustav ((i) harpsichord; (ii) cond.) Orchestra of the Age of Enlightenment

'Portrait': BACH: (i) *English suite No. 3, BWV 808; Partita No. 1, BWV 825;* (ii) *Double harpsichord concerto No. 2 in C, BWV 1061* (with Bob van Asperen, Melante Amsterdam). C. P. E. BACH: *Hamburg Sinfonia, Wq. 183/2.* PURCELL: *Ode for Queen Mary: Love's goddess sure was blind* (with Julia Gooding, James Bowman, Christopher Robson, David Wilson-Johnson and OAE Chorus).

(M) **(*) Virgin/Veritas EMI Dig. VM5 61400-2 [id.].

Leonhardt opens ebulliently with the *G minor English suite* and he is also at his thoughtful best in the *B flat Partita*. The *Double harpsichord concerto* is lively too, although here the resonant acoustic means that the overall sound-picture is less than ideally clear in focus. The other highlight is the lively C. P. E. Bach *Sinfonia*, with its remarkably colourful, though brief, central *Adagio*. The single vocal item, the Purcell *Ode*, brings distinguished solo singing and refined detail, but could ideally be more robust in feeling. Readers wanting to sample Leonhardt's special contribution to the world of baroque music would do better to choose from his own Teldec Edition below, under Instrumental Recitals.

Lindberg, Christian (trombone), BBC National Orchestra of Wales, Grant Llewellyn

American trombone concertos: CHAVEZ: *Concerto.* ROUSE: *Concerto in memory of Leonard Bernstein.* Augusta Read THOMAS: *Meditation.*

(***) BIS Dig. CD 788 [id.].

By the time he started writing his concerto, Chavez was already in the terminal stages of cancer and his wife had just died. The work opens with an extended morose soliloquy in which the orchestra provides dissonantly pungent support; at times the pacing quickens, but the disconsolate atmosphere remains and, though some percussive intrusions towards the end provide more lively contrast, this music undoubtedly brings longueurs and is essentially depressing.

The *Meditation* by Augusta Read Thomas opens much more positively, with the soloist proceeding over a series of lively orchestral interjections. Bell effects (echoed by the strings) and a percussive spicing add variety, and there is a final eruption of energy. But the meagre musical invention is unenticing.

Easily the finest work here is the concerto by Rouse, which, though darkly atmospheric, readily holds the listener most compellingly. The music climbs up from the lower depths (the opening evocation rather like that at the beginning of the Ravel *Left-hand Piano concerto*). After an exciting climax the soloist has a ruminative cadenza before dashing off in a dazzling Scherzo (superb bravura from Lindberg), with the orchestra just about managing to keep up, yet doing so with some panache. There is a series of hair-raising orchestral explosions, followed by a mêlée of urgently volatile brass figurations which then die away slowly, leading to the touching finale, marked *Elegiaco, lugubre*.

This is designated by Rouse as a memorial to Leonard Bernstein and quotes what is described as the 'Credo' theme from Bernstein's *Third (Kaddish) Symphony*. The movement has an unrelenting thrust and the central orchestral declamation of grief makes a powerful statement, before the soloist steals in with his own gentle and moving valedictory lament. Then, Orpheus-like, he returns into the depths. Superb solo playing throughout this disc, and very fine recording. But the Rouse is the only piece here of real memorability, and it badly needs new couplings. It is also available on RCA in a collection of Rouse's other music, conducted in Colorado by Marin Alsop (see Composer index above).

Lipatti, Dinu (piano)

'*The Legacy of Dina Lipati*' with Nadia
Boulanger; Philh. O, Zürich Tonhalle O, Lucerne
Festival O; Galliera, Ackermann, Karajan): BACH:
Chorale, Jesu, joy of man's desiring (arr. HESS,
from BWV 147); *Chorale preludes, BWV 599 &
639* (both arr. BUSONI); *Partita No. 1, BWV 825;
Siciliana* (arr. KEMPFF, from BWV 1031). D.
SCARLATTI: *Sonatas, Kk. 9 & 380.* MOZART:
*Piano concerto No. 21 in C, K.467; Piano sonata
No. 8 in A min., K.310.* SCHUBERT: *Impromptus
Nos. 2–3, D.899/2 & 3.* SCHUMANN: *Piano
concerto in A min., Op. 54.* GRIEG: *Piano
concerto in A min., Op. 16.* CHOPIN: *Piano
concerto No. 1 in E min., Op. 11; Barcarolle, Op.
60; Etudes, Op. 10/5 & 25/5; Mazurka No. 32,
Op. 50/3; Nocturne No. 8, Op. 27/2; Piano sonata
No. 3 in B min., Op. 58; Waltzes Nos. 1–14.*
LISZT: *Années de pèlerinage, 2nd Year: Sonetto
104 del Petrarca.* RAVEL: *Alborada del gracioso.*
BRAHMS: *Waltzes* (4 hands), *Op. 39/1–2, 5–6, 10,
14–15.* ENESCU: *Piano sonata No. 3 in D, Op. 25.*
🌑 (M) (***) EMI CZS7 67163-2 (5) [partly
    included in CDH 630382, CDH 698002].

This set represents Lipatti's major recording
achievements. Whether in Bach (*Jesu, joy of man's
desiring* is unforgettable) or Chopin – his *Waltzes*
seem to have grown in wisdom and subtlety over
the years – Scarlatti or Mozart, these performances
are very special indeed. The remastering is done
well, and this is a must for anyone with an interest
in the piano.

Lloyd Webber, Julian (cello)

'*English idyll*' (with ASMF, Neville Marriner):
VAUGHAN WILLIAMS: *Romanza.* ELGAR:
Romance in D min., Op. 62; Une idylle, Op. 4/1.
DELIUS: *2 Pieces for cello and chamber
orchestra.* GRAINGER: *Youthful rapture; Brigg
Fair* (arrangement). DYSON: *Fantasy.* IRELAND:
The holy boy. WALFORD DAVIES: *Solemn melody.*
HOLST: *Invocation, Op. 19/2.* Cyril SCOTT:
Pastoral and reel.
**(*) Ph. 442 530-2 [id.].

The highlights of Julian Lloyd Webber's programme of English concertante miniatures are the
Holst *Invocation*, with its nocturnal mood sensitively caught, and George Dyson's *Fantasy*, where
the playing readily captures Christopher Palmer's
description: 'exquisitely summery and sunny – its
chattering moto perpetuo evokes images of bees
and butterflies'. Grainger's passionate *Youthful rapture* is given just the right degree of ardent espressivo, as are Delius's warmly flowing *Caprice* and
Elegy, written (during the composer's last Fenby
period) for Beatrice Harrison.

The two transcriptions, Vaughan Williams's
Romanza (originally part of the *Tuba concerto*) and
the Elgar *Romance*, conceived with the bassoon in
mind, were both arranged for the cello by their
respective composers and are effective enough in
their string formats, although by no means super-
seding the originals. However, Lloyd Webber gives
the full romantic treatment both to John Ireland's
simple tone-picture, *The holy boy*, and to Grainger's
arrangement of *Brigg Fair*, to which not all will
respond. For the closing Cyril Scott *Pastoral and
reel* (with its telling drone effect) he returns to a
more direct style, with pleasing results. Sympathetic
accompaniments and warm, atmospheric recording.

'*The Julian Lloyd Webber collection*' (with ECO
or RPO, (i) Barry Wordsworth,(ii) Nicholas
Cleobury): Andrew LLOYD WEBBER: *Theme and
Variations 1–4.* (i) *Aspects of Love: Love changes
everything. Phantom of the Opera: Music of the
night.* (ii) SAINT-SAENS: *The Swan.* MOZART:
Rondo alla Turca. DEBUSSY: *Clair de lune.*
BACHGOUNOD: *Ave Maria.* VANGELIS: *Un
après-midi* (with Vangelis & synthesizers).
LENNON/MCCARTNEY: *When I'm sixty-four.*
TRAD.: *Skye boat song; Londonderry air.*
ALBINONI: *Adagio* (arr. GIAZOTTO). BERNSTEIN:
West Side Story: Somewhere. BACH: *Jesu, joy of
man's desiring.* LEHAR: *You are my heart's
delight.* RIMSKY-KORSAKOV: *Flight of the
bumblebee.* Johann & Josef STRAUSS: *Pizzicato
polka.* SCHUMANN: *Träumerei.* ELGAR: *Cello
concerto:* 1st movt (cond. Y. Menuhin).
** Ph. Dig. 446 050-2 [id.].

Seventy-five minutes of cello lollipops may be too
much of a good thing for some tastes. Julian Lloyd
Webber describes the content as being 'drawn –
with one important exception – from [his] less
"serious" recordings', and the programme establishes its popular credentials by opening with the
Andrew Lloyd Webber *Paganini variations*, used
as the signature tune for ITV's 'South Bank Show'.

There are many good tunes here, but mostly
romantic ones; a few more bumblebees would have
been advantageous. However, this fine British
cellist knows how to shape a good tune: Schumann's *Träumerei*, for instance, is presented very
persuasively. The 'exception' ends the programme:
the first movement of Elgar's *Cello concerto*,
tempting enough, but ending rather abruptly: the
slow movement would surely have been a better
choice. Pleasant recording.

'*Favourite cello concertos*': DVORAK: *Concerto in
B min., Op. 104* (with Czech PO, Neumann).
TCHAIKOVSKY: *Variations on a rococo theme*
(original version), *Op. 33* (with RPO, Cleobury).
FAURE: *Elégie, Op. 24.* SAINT-SAENS: *Concerto
No. 1 in A min., Op. 33; Allegro appassionato,
Op. 43* (with ECO, Yan Pascal Tortelier).

Carnaval des animaux: Le cygne (with ECO,
Cleobury). ELGAR: *Concerto in E min., Op. 68*
(with RPO, Lord Menuhin); *Romance in D min.,
Op. 62* (with ASMF, Marriner); *Idylle, Op. 4/1*
(arr. for cello and organ). ALBINONI: *Adagio* (arr.
GIAZOTTO). SCHUMANN: *Kinderszenen:
Träumerei* (arr. PARKER). BACH: *Cantata No.147:
Jesu, joy of man's desiring.* RIMSKY-KORSAKOV:
Flight of the Bumblebee. BACH/GOUNOD: *Ave
Maria* (all with ECO, or RPO, Cleobury). Julian
LLOYD WEBBER: *Jackie's song.*
(M) *** Ph. 462 505-2 (2) [id.].

Lloyd Webber is at his finest in the Elgar concerto.
Nor is there any lack of intensity in the Dvořák, a
strong and warmly sympathetic reading. He has
the advantage of Menuhin to direct the RPO most
idiomatically in the former, and the Dvořák
specialist, Neumann, with the Czech Philharmonic
to accompany him in the latter. The Czech orchestral attack has fine bite and the clipped style of
articulation brings out the folk element. The horn
soloist plays the great second subject melody
with a degree of vibrato but he is a fine artist, and
Lloyd Webber's playing is marked by a ripe, rich
tone. Intonation is excellent, but the soloist's occasional easing of tempi may not appeal to some
listeners.

Both Saint-Saëns works are played with considerable virtuosity and again there is the advantage
of a first-class accompaniment, from Yan-Pascal
Tortelier and the ECO. Tchaikovsky's original
score is used for the *Rococo variations*, which is
presented affectionately and elegantly. All in all, if
the various encores also appeal, this is an attractive
enough package, very well recorded in Philips's
most natural manner. *Jackie's song*, Lloyd
Webber's catchy little tribute to Jacqueline du Pré,
is added as an ardent postscript.

'Cello moods' (with Royal Philharmonic
Orchestra, James Judd): FRANCK: *Panis angelicus.*
ELGAR: *Chanson de matin; Salut d'amour.* Julian
LLOYD WEBBER: *Jackie's song.* DEBUSSY:
Rêverie. BACH: *Suite No 3: Air.* MASSENET: *Thaïs:
Méditation.* CACCINI: *Ave Maria.* BORODIN:
Nocturne. GLAZUNOV: *Mélodie, Op. 20/1.*
CHOPIN: *Nocturne, Op. 9/2.* BOCCHERINI: *Cello
concerto: Adagio.* RHEINBERGER: *Cantilena.*
BRUCH: *Kol Nidrei.*
*** Ph. Dig. 462 588-2 [id.].

Decorated with extraordinary artwork by Jane
Powell, which shows an unclothed cellist, covered
only with shadowy music staves (the cello hiding
any suggestion of immodesty), this collection of
lollipops is obviously aimed at the cross-over
market. The playing is of high quality, with none of
these famous tunes sentimentalized. Franck's *Panis
angelicus* and Massenet's *Méditation* here sound
almost noble on the cello. The other highlights are
the charming Glazunov *Mélodie*, the Rheinberger

Cantilena, and the very eloquent Max Bruch *Kol
Nidrei.* If you enjoy this kind of programme it
couldn't be better played or recorded.

London Gabrieli Brass Ensemble

'The splendour of baroque brass': SUSATO: *La
Danserye: suite.* G. GABRIELI: *Canzona per
sonare a 4: La Spiritata.* SCHEIDT: *Suite.* PEZEL:
Ceremonial brass music. BACH: *The Art of fugue:
Contrapunctus IX.* CHARPENTIER: *Te Deum:
Prelude in D.* arr. JAMES: *An Elizabethan suite.*
CLARKE: *The Prince of Denmark's march.*
HOLBORNE: *5 Dances.* STANLEY: *Trumpet tune.*
LOCKE: *Music for His Majesty's sackbutts and
cornetts.* PURCELL: *Trumpet tune and ayre. Music
for the funeral of Queen Mary* (with Chorus).
⦿ (BB) *** ASV Quicksilva CDQS 6013 [(M)
id.].

This is one of the really outstanding brass anthologies, and the digitally remastered analogue
recording is very realistic. The brass group is comparatively small: two trumpets, two trombones,
horn and tuba; and that brings internal clarity, while
the ambience adds fine sonority. The opening Susato *Danserye* is splendid music, and the Scheidt
Suite is similarly inventive. Pezel's *Ceremonial
brass music* is also in effect a suite – it includes a
particularly memorable *Sarabande*; while Matthew
Locke's *Music for His Majesty's sackbutts and cornetts* opens with a very striking *Air* and offers six
diverse movements overall.

With the Gabrieli *Canzona*, Purcell's *Trumpet
tune and ayre* and the Jeremiah Clarke *Prince of
Denmark's march* (better known as the *Trumpet
voluntary*) all familiar, this makes a superb entertainment to be dipped into at will. The closing *Music
for the funeral of Queen Mary* brings an eloquent
choral contribution. Introduced by solemn drum-
beats, it is one of Purcell's finest short works and
the performance here is very moving. The arrangements throughout the concert (usually made by
Crispian Steele-Perkins, who leads the group both
sensitively and resplendently) are felicitous and the
documentation is excellent. This is a very real
bargain.

London Gabrieli Brass Ensemble, Christopher Larkin

Original 19th-century music for brass:
BEETHOVEN: *3 Equales for 4 trombones.*
CHERUBINI: *Trois pas redoublés et la première
marche; Trois pas redoublés et la seconde
marche.* DAVID: *Nonetto in C min.* DVORAK:
Fanfare. LACHNER: *Nonet in F.*

RIMSKY-KORSAKOV: *Notturno for 4 horns.*
SIBELIUS: *Overture in F min.: Allegro;*
Andantino; Menuetto; Praeludium.
*** Hyperion Dig. CDA 66470 [id.].

'From the steeples and the mountains': IVES:
From the steeples and the mountains; Let there be
light. BARBER: *Mutations from Bach.* HARRIS:
Chorale for organ and brass. Virgil THOMSON:
Family portrait. COWELL: *Grinnell fanfare; Tall*
tale; Hymn and fuguing tune No. 12; Rondo.
GLASS: *Brass sextet.* RUGGLES: *Angels.* CARTER:
A Fantasy upon Purcell's Fantasia about one
note.
(B) *** Hyperion Helios Dig. CDH 55018 [id.].

It is difficult to decide which of these two programmes is the more enterprising and the more
rewarding. If you are responsive to brass sonorities
and you acquire one of them, you will surely want
its companion. Beethoven's *Equales* were used at
the composer's funeral. They are brief, but noble
and dignified. The Sibelius suite is folksy, uncharac-
teristic writing, but has genuine charm.

The second concert opens and closes with the
always stimulating music of Charles Ives. *From the*
steeples and the mountains is scored for four sets
of bells, trumpet and trombones, and its effect is
clangorously wild! Elliott Carter's Purcell arrangement also has tolling bells, and is quite haunting.
Of the other pieces the most striking is the Barber
Mutations, which draws on the chorale *Christe du*
Lamm Gottes with highly individual effect. Most
passionate of all is Ruggles's pungently compressed, muted brass *Angels*, yet the piece is marked
'Serene'! The brass playing throughout the two
discs is as communicative as it is expert and the
recording is splendidly realistic and present.

London Philharmonic
Orchestra, Sir Thomas Beecham

'Beecham favourites': BIZET: *L'Arlésienne: suite*
No. 1: Prélude; Minuet; Adagietto; suite No. 2:
Minuet (from *The Fair Maid of Perth*); *Farandole.*
GRIEG: *Peer Gynt: suite No. 1, Op. 46.*
TCHAIKOVSKY: *Francesca da Rimini, Op. 32.*
GRETRY: *Zémire et Azor: Air de ballet.*
CHABRIER: *España (rhapsody).*
🌑 (B) (***) Dutton Lab. mono CDEA 5017 [(M)
id.].

Beecham re-recorded both the *L'Arlésienne* and
Peer Gynt suites with the RPO in stereo, but he
did not surpass these earlier, LPO performances,
recorded for the Columbia label in the late 1930s.
The sound was remarkably good for its time, but in
these fine Dutton transfers it is better than ever,
glowing and warm yet with plenty of brightness for
the violins, so that the earthily rumbustious *In the*
Hall of the Mountain King unleashes a thrilling

climax. But (even if the upper woodwind harmonics
are not absolutely clean) it is perhaps the gentler
evocations which remain most firmly in the memory
and it is the oboist, Leon Goossens, who makes
Morning from *Peer Gynt* unforgettable and who
points the delicate rhythm of the famous Grétry *Air*
de ballet so exquisitely.

The Bizet and Grieg suites were recorded at
Abbey Road, except for the *Death of Aese*, for
which Beecham chose Kingsway Hall, with warmly
ravishing results, especially at the moving closing
section; and Anitra has never danced with more
alluring delicacy. Kingsway Hall was also used for
Francesca da Rimini and *España*. In *Francesca*,
Bernard Walton's clarinet solo which introduces the
heroine in the middle section is delectably seductive
and (in the words of Neville Cardus) Beecham's
baton seems 'to bring the hell-fire outer sections of
the work visually before us'. The closing pages
have great ferocity, with a superb final burst from
the timpani which all but drowns the tam-tam.

España was perhaps the most famous of all
Beecham's 78s and was cherished by all three of
the authors of this book. It always sounded marvellous, and so it does here. Beecham's combination
of swagger and *joie de vivre* is balanced by Gallic
elegance. He recorded the two 78 sides at two
separate sessions, three weeks apart, but one would
never guess that this sparkling performance was not
played continuously. This CD offers one Beecham
anthology that no admirer of this greatest of English
conductors should miss. It has splendid notes by
Lyndon Jenkins, and it is ridiculously inexpensive.

HANDEL, arr. Beecham: *The Great elopement*
(ballet). HAYDN: *Symphony No. 97 in C.* MOZART:
Serenade (Eine kleine Nachtmusik); La clemenza
di Tito: Overture.
(**) Biddulph mono WHL 041 [id.].

BEETHOVEN: *Symphony No. 4 in B flat, Op. 60.*
MOZART: *Die Entführung aus dem Serail:*
Overture. SCHUBERT: *Symphony No. 6 in C,*
D.589.
(**) Biddulph mono WHL 042 [id.].

BERLIOZ: *Les Troyens: Royal hunt and storm;*
Trojan march. BORODIN: *Prince Igor: Overture.*
MENDELSSOHN: *Symphony No. 5 in D min.*
(Reformation), Op. 107. RIMSKY-KORSAKOV:
May night: Overture. TCHAIKOVSKY: *Eugene*
Onegin: Waltz; Polonaise.
(**) Biddulph mono WHL 043 [id.].

These three discs are most welcome for filling in
the least-known period of Beecham's recording
activities, towards the end of the Second World
War, working with the newly self-governing LPO,
before he founded the RPO. These recordings had
a sadly brief period in the catalogue, and unlike
Beecham's pre-war recordings have remained in
limbo ever since.

The second of the three discs, coupling Mozart,

Beethoven and Schubert, is the most substantial Beecham's account of Beethoven's *Fourth Symphony* – a work he never returned to on record – has great flair and vitality, with fierceness set alongside elegance. The *Entführung overture* here is very similar to the one in his classic recording of the complete opera, but with a concert ending.

This 1944 version of Schubert's *Sixth* was a first recording, differing from his RPO remake in that the outer movements are faster, and the middle two broader, notably the *Andante*. On the first disc, the finale of *Eine kleine Nachtmusik* in this 1945 version is more an *Allegretto* than an *Allegro*, idiosyncratically slow but deliciously sprung. In the *Clemenza overture*, originally issued by Victor not HMV, Beecham takes a lightweight view, as though this is early Mozart, but the Haydn *97th Symphony* comes in a typically alert reading, with fierceness and elegance set in contrast, rather as in the Beethoven. The Biddulph transfers here lack sufficient body to sustain the top emphasis. That is very evident when one compares this transfer of the Handel–Beecham *Great Elopement* recording with the Dutton version.

On the third disc the sound for the Beecham lollipops – delectably done – is still thin, but the 1945 version of Mendelssohn's *Reformation Symphony* is generally better, with the brass full, bright and well separated, and with gentle string pianissimos (as in the '*Dresden Amen*') beautifully caught. A valuable trio of discs, which should be considered by Beecham devotees despite the reservations over the transfers and the fact that they are not inexpensive.

London Philharmonic Orchestra in sparkling and sensitive form and are given vintage Decca recording of very high quality.

Butterworth's two beautiful evocations of the English countryside have wonderful delicacy of texture and feeling, while Bax's *Tintagel* is both evocative and passionately full-blooded at its climax. Holst's *Perfect fool* ballet suite sounds remarkably fresh and vivid, and Vaughan Williams's *Old King Cole* (taken from another ballet, of 1923) is both jolly and boisterous, as befits the image of that famous nursery-rhyme monarch. Elgar's paired miniatures of morning and night have characteristically affectionate warmth, and here the full ambience of the recording might almost be mistaken for stereo.

The second disc includes more amiable Elgar and Walton's ballet based on the music of Bach where, without loss of character, Boult merges the spirit of the two musical eras with great success. Of the two Walton overtures, *Portsmouth Point* is vigorous enough but has not quite the rhythmic bite of Boult's earlier, HMV recording (first issued on a ten-inch 78-r.p.m. disc); *Scapino*, however, effervesces brilliantly. Finest of all is Boult's pioneering set of Malcolm Arnold's *English dances*, never surpassed in subtlety of characterization or indeed vividness. The exquisite fragility of the first dance (*Andantino*) and the haunting nostalgia of the third (*Mesto*) are set in bold relief by the ebullience of the *Vivace* which comes in between. Here the Decca Kingsway Hall recording remains in the demonstration bracket it occupied from the day the music first appeared, on a Decca medium-play 10-inch LP.

London Philharmonic Orchestra, Sir Adrian Boult

'The Boult historic collection'

George BUTTERWORTH: *A Shropshire lad* (rhapsody); *The Banks of green willow* (idyll). BAX: *Tintagel* (tone-poem). HOLST: *The perfect fool* (ballet suite). VAUGHAN WILLIAMS: *Old King Cole* (ballet). ELGAR: *Chanson de nuit; Chanson de matin, Op. 15/1–2.*

(BB) (***) Belart mono 461 354-2.

ARNOLD: *English dances Nos. 1–8, Sets 1 (Op. 27) & 2 (Op. 33).* WALTON–BACH: *The Wise virgins* (ballet). WALTON: *Siesta; Overtures: Portsmouth Point; Scapino.* ELGAR: *3 Bavarian dances, Op. 27.*

(BB) (***) Belart mono 461 359-2.

Apart from his major Elgar recordings for EMI, Boult's special skills as an interpreter of English music have never been heard to better effect on record than in this pair of Belart collections, deriving from the Decca mono catalogue of the 1950s. Both programmes are played superbly by the

London Philharmonic Orchestra, Zubin Mehta, Mstislav Rostropovich

'Sir Georg Solti: A Celebration':

BEETHOVEN: *Egmont overture.* MOZART: Arias from *Mass in C min.; Le nozze di Figaro* (with Anne Sofie von Otter). TCHAIKOVSKY: *Violin concerto* (with Maxim Vengerov). Arias from VERDI: *La forza del destino;* PUCCINI: *Gianni Schicchi* (with Angela Gheorghiu). WAGNER: *Götterdämmerung: Dawn and Siegfried's Rhine journey; Closing scene.*

**(*) Decca Dig. 466 000-2 [id.].

Inevitably a mixed bag, this is a live recording of the Gala concert in October 1998 at the Royal Albert Hall in London celebrating the life and music of Sir Georg Solti. Mehta in Beethoven and Wagner may pale before the example of Solti himself, but the soloists are all most impressive, von Otter an immaculate Mozartean, Gheorghiu formidable in Verdi, *Pace pace, mio Dio!* from *Forza*, a little heavy in *O mio babbino caro* from Puccini's *Gianni Schicchi*. Best of all is the electrifying performance of Vengerov in the Tchaikovsky concerto – with Rostropovich conducting – not just brilliant but deeply dedicated in moments of repose, even finer than his studio recording for Teldec. Warm, well-balanced sound.

London Symphony Orchestra; National Philharmonic Orchestra, Richard Bonynge

'Bonynge Ballet festival':

Volume 1: WEBER (orch. Berlioz): *Invitation to the dance.* CHOPIN (arr. Douglas): *Les Sylphides.* J. STRAUSS jnr. (arr. Gamley): *Bal de Vienne.* LUIGINI: *Ballet égyptien* (complete).

Volume 2: TRAD.(arr. O'Turner): *Bolero 1830.* PUGNI: *Pas de quatre.* MINKUS: *La Bayadère* (excerpts). DRIGO: *Pas de trois.* ADAM: *Giselle* (excerpts). lovenskjold: *La Sylphide* (excerpts).

Volume 3: *'Homage to Pavlova'*: SAINT-SAENS: *The Swan.* TCHAIKOVSKY: *Melody; Noël.* RUBINSTEIN: *Danses des fiancées de Cachemir.* CZIBULKA: *Love's dream after the ball.* KREISLER: *The Dragonfly (Schön Rosmarin).* ASSAFIEFF: *Papillons.* LINCKE: *Gavotte Pavlova (Glow worm idyll).* DELIBES: *Naïla: Intermezzo.* CATALANI: *Danza delle Ondine.* KRUPINSKI: *Mazurka (Polish Wedding).*

Volume 4. *'Pas de deux'*: AUBER: *Pas classique.* MINKUS: *Don Quixote: Pas de deux. Paquita: Pas de deux.* TCHAIKOVSKY: *The Nutcracker: Pas de deux. Sleeping beauty: Pas de deux.* DRIGO: *Le Corsaire: Pas de deux. La Esmeralda. Pas de deux.* HELSTED: *Flower festival at Genzano.*

Volume 5: *'Ballet music from opera'*: ROSSINI: *William Tell.* DONIZETTI: *La Favorita.* GOUNOD: *Faust; La Reine de Saba (waltz).* MASSENET: *Ariane; Le Roi de Lahore.* BERLIOZ: *Les Troyens.* (B) *** Australian Decca 452 767-2 (5).

A valuable set of Richard Bonynge's ballet recordings which includes much music not otherwise available. Volume 1 has two rarities: *Bal de Vienne* – a particularly felicitous arrangement of Johann Strauss's lesser-known works, with an exhilarating finale, and (surprisingly) the only complete recording of Luigini's delightful *Ballet Egyptien* (Fistoulari only recorded the four-movement suite).

Volume 2 draws from Bonynge's *'The art of the Prima Ballerina'* set: each of the rarities by Minkus, Drigo and Pugni has at least one striking melody, and all are vivacious and colourfully orchestrated; the *Bolero 1830* is short but piquant.

Volume 3, *'Homage to Pavlova'* is more reflectively nostalgic and has delightful rarities: many are just salon pieces, but show their worth when played so beautifully on a full orchestra.

Volume 4's collection of *Pas de deux* is both elegantly and robustly enjoyable, with the Auber, Minkus and Drigo numbers especially lively and memorable.

Volume 5 comprises generally better known ballet music from operas. It includes the lovely Massenet ballet music from *Le Roi de Lahore*, which starts off ominously in a minor key, before a theme, magically introduced on the saxophone, builds up into a magnificent full orchestral waltz swirling around the whole orchestra. The *Dance of the Gypsy* from Saint-Saëns's *Henry VIII* is another gem: it begins sinuously, but ends in a jolly *valse macabre*.

This is music in which Bonynge excels: he has exactly the right feel for it and produces an infectious lift throughout. The recordings are in Decca's best analogue tradition – vivid, warm and full (though a few are from equally fine digital sources), and all sound pristinely fresh in these transfers. With full sleeve-notes included, this is a splendid bargain collection of highly entertaining music well worth seeking out.

London Symphony Orchestra, Albert Coates

'Russian favourites': GLINKA: *Ruslan and Ludmilla: Overture; Kamarinskaya.* BORODIN: *In the Steppes of Central Asia; Prince Igor: Polovtsian march.* LIADOV: *8 Russian folksongs, Op. 58.* MUSSORGSKY: *Sorochintsy Fair: Gopak.* TCHAIKOVSKY: *Marche slave.* RIMSKY-KORSAKOV: *May night overture; Dubinushka; Maid of Pskov: Storm music; Mlada: Procession of the Nobles; Snow Maiden: Danse des bouffons.* STRAVINSKY: *The Firebird: The princesses' game; Infernal dance.* (***) Koch mono 37700-2 [id.].

On the Koch Historic label comes a collection of Coates's recordings with the LSO of Russian lollipops, vividly transferred by H. Ward Marston. Made between 1928 and 1930, they sound astonishingly fresh, with brass bright and forward. The *Procession of the Nobles* from Rimsky-Korsakov's *Mlada* has never been recorded with such flair and excitement, and consistently these performances reflect the natural understanding of a musician of British parentage born in Russia. As well as four other Rimsky items, the disc also has nine favourite pieces by Glinka, Borodin (a famous version of *In the Steppes of Central Asia*), Liadov, Mussorgsky, Tchaikovsky and Stravinsky.

London Symphony Orchestra, Antal Dorati

ENESCU: *Romanian rhapsody No. 2*. BRAHMS: *Hungarian dances Nos. 1–7; 10–12; 15; 17–21; Variations on a theme of Haydn, Op. 56a.*
(M) ** Mercury (IMS) 434 326-2 [id.].

Dorati is completely at home in the Enescu *Second Rhapsody* (played passionately – but, as music, not nearly as memorable as No. 1) and the Brahms *Hungarian dances*, where he captures a true Hungarian spirit. When he takes a piece faster than expected, one does not feel he is being wilful or intent on showing off, but simply that he and his players are enjoying themselves. If the delicious rubato in No. 7 does not spell enjoyment, one would be very surprised. The recording, made at either Watford or Wembley, sounds firmer and cleaner than on LP. The *Variations* are enjoyable but not distinctive.

London Symphony Orchestra, Roderick Dunk

'That's entertainment': SCHWARTZ–DIETZ: *That's entertainment*. GERSHWIN: *Girl Crazy overture*. LOEWE: *My Fair Lady: symphonic suite*. LLOYD WEBBER: *Evita interlude*. STYNE–MERRILL: *Funny Girl: Don't rain on my parade*. BOCK: *Fiddler on the roof overture*. Noel GAY: *Me and my girl*: selection. KERN: *Showboat*: selection. HERMAN: *Mack and Mabel overture*. SONDHEIM–STYNE: *Gypsy: Everything's coming up roses*.
(B) *** Carlton LSO Double Dig. 30368 01257 (2) [(M) id.] – GERSHWIN: *An American in Paris; Piano concerto; Rhapsody in blue*. ***

This group of selections from famous musicals is brightly and warmly played and very well recorded. It is perhaps not distinctive music-making, but it is very professionally presented and easy to enjoy. However, tuneful as it all is (particularly the suite from *My Fair Lady*), it is not a CD that most collectors would want to replay too often, while the splendid Gershwin coupling certainly is.

London Symphony Orchestra, Skitch Henderson

'Children's Classics' PROKOFIEV: *Peter and the wolf, Op. 67* (narrative revised). SAINT-SAENS: *Carnival of the animals* (with verses by Ogden Nash, and animals from the London Zoo; both with Beatrice Lillie). TRAD. (arr. Sharples) *'Uncle Ken's Nursery Rhymes'* (with Kenneth McKellar,

and orchestral accompaniment directed by Robert Sharples).
(B) **(*) Australian Decca Eloquence 466 673-2. Beatrice Lillie (narrator), LSO, Henderson.

This collection includes a fascinating early LP version of *Peter and the Wolf* involving a 'cabaret act' by Beatrice Lillie to words by 'Bidrum Vabish' (a pseudonym for John Culshaw), full of asides and additions like 'the cat climbed up the tree *before you could say Prokofiev*'. The original LP was most notable for the correspondence it provoked (after the record's review in *The Gramophone*), between Mr Culshaw Vabish and Vetrov Hayver (Guess who?). Curious older readers are referred to the issues of November and December 1960.

The orchestral part of the performance is rather less than distinguished, but the conductor adopts a determined and unflagging pace, and after all it is Miss Lillie's record. Its enjoyment depends on whether or not you take to her rather arch contribution and the new text which she undoubtedly points up in lively fashion, as she does with the words (by Ogden Nash) which are a superfluous addition to Saint-Saëns's witty menagerie.

The grafted-on animal noises which set the scene for the *Carnival* were recorded at London Zoo: the lion's roar at the beginning is startling to say the least!. What also makes this disc of interest is that Julius Katchen and Gary Graffman, no less, are the pianists, and the Decca sound from the early 1960s, which is remarkably vivid. The fill up is a charming medley of the A-Z of nursery rhymes, inimitably sung by Kenneth McKellar, with nicely detailed orchestral accompaniments by Robert Sharples – it will appeal to children of all ages. A collector's item.

(i) London Symphony Orchestra, or (ii) Vienna Philharmonic Orchestra, André Previn.

'Portrait of André Previn': (i) BERLIOZ: *Le carnaval romain overture, Op. 9*. TCHAIKOVSKY: *Romeo and Juliet (fantasy overture); Swan Lake: suite* (with Ida Haendel, violin). RAVEL: *La valse*. DEBUSSY: *Prélude à l'après-midi d'un faune*. RODRIGO: *Concierto de Aranjuez* (with Angel Romero, guitar). GERSHWIN: *Rhapsody in blue* (with Previn, piano/conductor). BARBER: *Adagio for strings, Op. 11*. DUKAS: *L'apprenti sorcier*. (ii) Richard STRAUSS: *Don Juan, Op. 20*.
(BB) *** Royal Classics Long Players DCL 707912 (2) [id.].

Alongside the 'Portrait' of Marriner and his ASMF this is easily the most desirable of the Royal Classics series. It is marvellous value, and worth getting, even if some duplication is involved. The admirably varied collection covers the 1970s, when, as the exuberant and inspirational conductor-in-chief of the LSO, Previn was at the peak of his career, also endearing himself to the public at large with his deadpan appearance as 'André Preview' on the 'Morecambe and Wise' TV show.

Opening with a fizzing account of *Le carnaval romain*, the Tchaikovsky items follow with comparable panache, superbly played, and with Ida Haendel making a rich-toned contribution to the latter. The Rodrigo *Concierto* is also very successful, with an understanding and responsive soloist, yet with Previn dominating and revelling in the colourful orchestral detail. Especially fine performances too of Barber's *Adagio* and the Debussy *Prélude* (with memorably beautiful flute playing from William Bennett).

In many ways most memorable of all is *L'apprenti sorcier*, showing Previn and his orchestra thoroughly enjoying themselves in Dukas's masterpiece, with the bounce of the opening bassoon solo matched by the spectacle of the climax. Previn is also very much at home at the keyboard, directing a sparkling account of Gershwin's *Rhapsody in blue*. The performance of *Don Juan* shows that at the end of the 1970s he also established a special rapport with the players of the Vienna Philharmonic, whose response is equally wholehearted. Indeed, his strength of personality means that this is not a Viennese-type performance, but relatively direct, strong and urgent, refreshing rather than idiomatic. The sound throughout is of EMI's best analogue quality, brilliant yet with fine warmth and ambience.

London Symphony Orchestra, Sir Georg Solti

'Romantic Russia': GLINKA: *Ruslan and Ludmilla overture.* MUSSORGSKY: *Khovanshchina: Prelude; Night on the bare mountain* (arr. RIMSKY-KORSAKOV). BORODIN: *Prnce Igor: Overture and Polovtsian dances* (with LSO Chorus). TCHAIKOVSKY: *Symphony No. 2 (Little Russian), Op. 17* (with Paris Conservatoire Orchestra).

🔘 (M) *** Decca Legends 460 977-2 [id.].

This was a demonstration record in its day and the analogue recording remains of Decca's vintage quality with marvellous detail and a warm ambience. The account of the *Ruslan and Ludmilla overture* is justly famous for its sheer brio, and Solti's *Polovtsian dances* are as exciting as any in the catalogue with a splendid contribution from the LSO Chorus. The *Prince Igor overture* is warmly romantic, yet has plenty of fire and spontaneity, and a lovely horn solo. *Night on the bare mountain*

makes a forceful impact, but brings a tender closing section.

Solti also recorded the evocative *Khovanshchina Prelude* with the Berlin Philharmonic Orchestra around the same time, and that had marginally more lustre, but the LSO create plenty of atmospheric tension. The performance of Tchaikovsky's *Little Russian Symphony* has been added for this reissue. It dates from the late 1950s and the recording is noticeably less opulent. After a commanding opening, there is no lack of vitality, and the delightful slow movement is affectionately shaped. The Scherzo lacks something in elegance and charm, partly the fault of the French orchestral playing, but the finale certainly does not lack adrenalin. Overall this is surprisingly memorable and makes a splendid addition to Decca's 'Legends' series.

London Symphony Orchestra, Leopold Stokowski

Orchestral transcriptions: BYRD: *The Earl of Salisbury and Galliard pavan.* CLARKE: *Trumpet voluntary.* SCHUBERT: *Moment musical No. 3 in F min.* CHOPIN: *Mazurka in A min., Op. 17/4.* TCHAIKOVSKY: *Chant sans paroles.* DUPARC: *Extase.* RACHMANINOV: *Prelude in C sharp min., Op. 3/2* (with Czech PO: BACH arrangements: *Chorale prelude: Wir glauben all' an einen Gott ('Giant fugue'), BWV 680; Easter cantata, BWV 4: Chorale; Geistliches Lied No. 51: Mein Jesu, BWV 487; Passacaglia and fugue in C min., BWV 582; Toccata and fugue in D min., BWV 565; Well-tempered Clavier, Book 1: Prelude No. 8 in E flat min., BWV 853*).

(M) *** Decca Phase Four (IMS) 448 946-2 [id.].

Sumptuously recorded, with the LSO on top form in 1974, these lollipops are often flagrantly far removed from their composers' original conceptions, becoming virtually newly composed in their vivid, Stokowskian orchestral flamboyance. The *Trumpet voluntary* is surely a collectors' item, with its sweetly anachronistic violins in the middle section, and the Chopin *Mazurka* is hardly less extraordinary in its transformation, opening mysteriously with *sul ponticello* strings, and turning into a dreamy rhapsody with its indulgent flute solo. The Byrd *Pavan* is treated as romantically and seductively as the *Song without words* of Tchaikovsky, yet the Schubert *Moment musical* has a bouncing charm.

There are plenty of bold histrionics in the scoring of Rachmaninov's most famous *Prelude*, but imaginative touches too, and the LSO respond passionately. With its collection of Bach transcriptions, recorded two years earlier in Czechoslovakia, this is a treasurably unique stereo sampler of Stokowski's orchestral magic – his persistent search for the warmest espressivo and sonorously rich beauty of texture, irrespective of any other considerations. The CD transfers are highly successful.

its scoring. The recording is excellent, spacious and well detailed. The CD is available from the orchestra direct, whose website is www.lbso.org

(i) London Symphony Orchestra; (ii) Royal Philharmonic Orchestra; (iii) Anatole Fistourlari; (iv) Gaston Poulet

'French favourites': (i; iii) POULENC: Les Biches (ballet suite). (ii–iii) Aubade (choreographic concerto for piano and 18 instruments). DEBUSSY: Fantaisie for piano and orchestra (both with Fabienne Jacquinot, piano). (i; iv) RAVEL: Alborada del gracioso; Une barque sur l'océan. (B) *** Dutton Lab. mono CDEA 5501 [(M) id.].

Here are some more splendidly fresh performances from the early-1950s Parlophone label. Expert and attractive accounts of Alborada del gracioso and Une barque sur l'océan from the LSO under Gaston Poulet are coupled with two Poulenc works: a sparkling and vivacious Les Biches from Fistoulari and the same orchestra, and a captivating Aubade with Fabienne Jacquinot. She is hardly less persuasive in Debussy's neglected Fantaisie, both with the RPO (billed on the LP at the time, as older collectors will remember, as the Westminster Symphony Orchestra for contractual reasons). In any event, these are thoroughly delightful performances and few allowances need be made, for the recorded sound is little short of amazing.

Long Beach Symphony Orchestra, JoAnn Falletta

'Impressions of the sea': MENDELSSOHN: The Hebrides overture (Fingal's Cave). DEBUSSY: La Mer. LIADOV: The enchanted lake. BRIDGE: The Sea (suite). DEBUSSY: Prélude: La cathédral engloutie (arr. BUSSER).
*** LBSO Dig. 6698-1 [id.].

It is good to find an orchestra of this calibre, under the excellent JoAnn Falletta, producing playing of such high quality, especially in an often thrilling and certainly evocative account of La Mer where the body of orchestral tone is most impressive. Liadov's Enchanted lake is also atmospherically evoked, but best of all is Frank Bridge's Suite with the opening Seascape and penultimate Moonlight scenes pictured with memorable vividness of colour. Finally comes Henri Büsser's orchestration of Debussy's La cathédral engloutie, not as outrageously original as the celebrated Stokowski version, but still imaginative, and richly sonorous in

Los Angeles Philharmonic Orchestra, Zubin Mehta

'Spectacular orchestral showpieces': HOLST: The Planets. Richard STRAUSS: Also sprach Zarathustra. John WILLIAMS: Film scores: Close Encounters of the Third Kind (suite); Star Wars (suite).
(B) **(*) Decca Double 452 910-2 (2) [(M) id. import].

Zubin Mehta's set of Planets ranks high in stellar splendour and has been a demonstration record since it was first issued on LP in 1971. The performance is strongly characterized and splendidly played. It is discussed more fully under its composer entry in our companion volume, where it is paired with Holst's Perfect fool suite. However, hi-fi buffs will surely think this Double Decca set well worth considering with such appropriate couplings. In the never-to-be-forgotten opening of Also sprach Zarathustra Mehta has the distinction of stretching those famous first pages longer than any rival. From the start, this 1969 recording was also plainly intended for demonstration with its extrovert sonic brilliance, and as such it succeeds well; but other versions are more interesting interpretatively.

Mehta is a good, even a passionate Straussian, but he is a forceful rather than an affectionate one. The two John Williams film scores were recorded later, in 1977, and again offer a spectacular soundstage. However eclectic the inspiration, both scores are undeniably attractive and each draws considerable appeal from the imaginative orchestration. The music from Star Wars forms a definite suite of six movements; the shorter piece from Close Encounters is continuous and essentially atmospheric. Both are very well played in Los Angeles and, if Mehta's approach has an element of hyperbole, in Star Wars the Hollywoodian theme picturing Princess Leia includes a horn solo which is played quite gorgeously, while the closing section has an appropriate swagger.

Los Angeles Philharmonic Orchestra or Chamber Orchestra, Zubin Mehta

'Concertos in contrast' (with soloists): HAYDN: Trumpet concerto in E flat. VIVALDI: Piccolo concerto in A min., P.83. WEBER: Concertino for clarinet and orchestra, Op. 26. WIENIAWSKI: Polonaise de concert, Op. 4; Scherzo-Tarentelle,

Op. 16. BLOCH: *Schelomo* (with Janos Starker (cello), Israel Philharmonic Orchestra).
(B) **(*) Australian Decca Eloquence 466 683-2.

Contrasting concertos indeed – but the programme works. All are played with polish and sparkle, with the soloists (except in *Schelomo*) principals of the Los Angeles orchestra. The Wieniawski show-pieces are brilliant rarities, and the delightful Weber piece has all the melodic freshness of his better-known concertos. The famous Haydn and Vivaldi concertos receive beefy performances, but not at all heavy, and it is a pleasure to hear them in such a rich sound. The recordings throughout are particularly full, though the Israeli strings in *Schelomo* cannot quite match those of the American orchestra. But the performance with Starker is very fine indeed.

Lympany, Moura (piano)

'The Decca recordings': KHACHATURIAN: *Piano concerto* (with LSO, Fistoulari). BALAKIREV: *Islamey.* POULENC: *Novelette No. 1.* DOHNANYI: *Capriccio in F min.* MENDELSSOHN: *Capriccio brillant in B min., Op. 22* (with Nat. SO, Boyd Neel); *Rondo brillante in E flat, Op. 29* (with LSO, Royalton Kisch).
(M) (***) Dutton Lab. CDEA 5506 [id.].

Moura Lympany 1945 *ffrr* recording of the Khachaturian concerto, a work she had premièred, has a dash and sparkle which have never been matched on record since, while Khachaturian's Armenian melodies are given their full character under Fistoulari's baton. The Dutton transfer is well up to standard. Lympany cannot quite match Katchen in *Islamey*, although it is still brilliant playing, and there is plenty of charm and character in the Mendelssohn concertante pieces and the other solo items. But it is for the Khachaturian that this reissue will primarily be valued.

Ma, Yo-Yo (cello)

'Great cello concertos': HAYDN: *Concerto in D, Hob VIIb/2* (with ECO, Garcia). SAINT-SAENS: *Concerto No. 1, Op. 33* (with O Nat. de France, Maazel). SCHUMANN: *Concerto in A min., Op. 129* (with Bav. RSO, Colin Davis). DVORAK: *Concerto in B min., Op. 104* (with BPO, Maazel). ELGAR: *Concerto in E min., Op. 85* (with LSO, Previn).
(M) *** Sony Dig./Analogue M2K 44562 (2) [id.].

An enticing mid-priced package, offering at least two of the greatest of all cello concertos, in Yo-Yo Ma's characteristic and imaginatively refined manner. Only the performance of the Haydn gives cause for reservations and these are slight; many will enjoy Ma's elegance here. He is also lucky in his accompanists, and the CBS sound gives no reasons for complaint.

Maazel, Lorin

'Portrait': TCHAIKOVSKY: *Piano concerto No. 1 in B flat min., Op. 23* (with Gilels). RAVEL: *Alborada del gracioso; Boléro; Pavane pour une infante défunte* (all with New Philharmonia Orchestra). DVORAK: *Slavonic dances, Op. 46/1– 8* (with Berlin Philharmonic Orchestra). MUSSORGSKY (orch. Ravel): *Pictures at an exhibition.* Richard STRAUSS: *Till Eulenspiegel, Op. 28* (both with Philharmonia Orchestra).
(BB) **(*) Royal Long Players DCL 705922 (2).

This is a true 'portrait' and demonstrates how Maazel could be relied on to achieve the most brilliant orchestral playing, whichever ensemble he chose to conduct. It was excellent planning to include Gilels's exhilarating 1972 account of the Tchaikovsky *B flat minor Concerto,* as the conductor contributes to the excitement, and although the piano is placed forward, he keeps the orchestra well in the picture.

The extrovert Ravel performances too, spectacularly recorded, have characteristic flair and intensity, and if *Boléro* is rhythmically mannered at the climax, the *Pavane* is played very beautifully. With the Philharmonia on top form it is not surprising that Mussorgsky's *Pictures* are so vividly characterized, with a spaciously gripping closing *Great Gate of Kiev,* while *Till Eulenspiegel* is racily portrayed. The one comparative disappointment here is the high-powered set of Dvořák *Slavonic dances,* boldly rhythmic, where the adrenalin certainly runs free and the orchestral bravura is in no doubt, but one ideally wants more relaxed affection and charm.

Marches

'40 Famous marches' (played by various ensembles, including the Philip Jones Brass, Vienna Philharmonic Orchestra, Boskovsky and Knappertsbusch, Carlo Curley, organ): ALFORD: *Colonel Bogey.* C. P. E. BACH: *March.* BEETHOVEN: *Turkish march.* BERLIOZ: *Damnation de Faust: Hungarian march.* BIZET: *Carmen: Marche des contrebandiers.* BLISS: *Things to come: March.* CHABRIER: *Marche joyeuse.* CLARKE: *Trumpet voluntary.* COATES: *The Dambusters march.* ELGAR: *Pomp and Circumstance marches Nos 1 and 4 in D.* FUCIK: *Entry of the gladiators.* GOUNOD: *Funeral march of a marionette.* HANDEL: *Occasional Oratorio: March. Rinaldo: March. Saul: Dead march.* KARG-ELERT: *Marche triomphale.* MENDELSSOHN: *Athalie: War march of the priests. Midsummer night's dream: Wedding*

march. MEYERBEER: *Coronation march.* NIELSEN: *Oriental festive march.* PROKOFIEV: *The Love for 3 Oranges: March.* PURCELL: *Funeral march.* RIMSKY-KORSAKOV: *The procession of the nobles; The Tale of Tsar Saltan: March.* SCHUBERT: *Marche militaire.* SIBELIUS: *Karelia Suite: All marcia.* SOUSA: *Stars and stripes forever; Washington Post.* J. STRAUSS Jnr: *Egyptian march; Jubel march; Napoleon march; Persian march; Russian march; Spanish march.* J. STRAUSS Snr: *Radetzky march.* TCHAIKOVSKY: *The Nutcracker: Marche miniature.* VERDI: *Aida: Grand march.* wagner: *Tannhäuser: Grand march.* WALTON: *Crown Imperial (Coronation march).*

(B) *** Decca Double 466 241-2 (2) [id.].

Most of the obvious marches are here, but this splendid collection is made all more interesting by a shrewd choice of imaginative repertoire and performance, often in unexpected arrangements – the Philip Jones Brass Ensemble in the *Aida* and *Tannhäuser* marches (played with considerable brilliance), Carlo Curley's organ arrangement of Beethoven's *Turkish march,* and so on. Highlights include a string of J. Strauss's most exotic marches (*Egyptian, Persian, Russian* and *Spanish*) under Boskovsky, a crisply executed example from Rimsky's *The Tale of Tsar Saltan* by Martinon. Ansermet's demonstration version of Chabrier's *Marche joyeuse,* a simple but striking march by C. P. E Bach, arranged by the late Philip Jones, and many others. The Nielsen march is another unexpected choice, and no Decca collection of marches would be complete without Knappertsbusch's noble account of the *Marche militaire.* This is one of the best collections of its kind, and with recordings ranging from good to spectacular, it will not fail to lift the spirits.

Marsalis, Wynton (trumpet), ECO, Leppard

'The London concert': HAYDN: *Concerto in E flat.* L. MOZART: *Concerto in D.* FASCH: *Concerto in D.* HUMMEL: *Concerto in E.*

*** Sony Dig. SK 57497 [id.].

The title of this collection suggests a live occasion, but in fact these four concertos were recorded over a period of a week in 1993, at St Giles's Church, Cripplegate. The playing is as expert and stylish as we have come to expect from this remarkable American player. His approach, as we have noticed before, is just a little cool but none the worse for that, for there is also admirable poise, and in the finale of the Hummel he lets himself go with the most infectious bravura. Incidentally there is no improvising in cadenzas: 'I don't feel comfortable enough to improvise in music of this period,'

Marsalis tells us candidly in the notes. The recording gives him a striking but not exaggerated presence in relation to the orchestra.

Menuhin, Yehudi (Lord) (violin and conductor)

'Portrait': (as conductor): BACH: *Orchestral suite No. 3 in D, BWV 1068* (as violinist & conductor): *Double violin concerto in D, BWV 1043* (with Christian Ferras, violin; both with Bath Festival Orchestra): (as violinist): VIVALDI: *The Four Seasons* (with Camerata Lysy Gstaad, Alberto Lysy). DELIBES: *Coppélia & Sylvia: Ballet Suites* – in *Pas de Deux* only (with Philharmonia Orchestra, Robert Irving). BRAHMS: *Violin concerto in D, Op. 77* (with Berlin Philharmonic Orchestra, Kempe); *String sextet No. 1, Op. 18* (with Robert Masters, Cecil Aronowitz, Ernst Wallfisch, Maurice Gendron, Derek Simpson). SCHUBERT: *Piano trio No. 2, D.929: Andante con moto* only (with Maurice Gendron, cello). BEETHOVEN: *Violin sonata No. 5 (Spring): Rondo* only (both with Hephzibah Menuhin, piano).

(BB) ** Royal Classics Long Player DCL 705892 (2) [id.].

No one can say that this is not a rounded portrait of Menuhin, with the various recordings made over the years from 1958 to 1980 – even if does not always flatter his solo playing. The digital version of *The Four Seasons* is a case in point. Here the violin timbre sounds rather shrill, and Menuhin's rhythmic control is not always stable (notably in the opening movement of *Autumn*). While this is a characteristically communicative account, it is robust and exuberant rather than refined. It is well enough accompanied by the youthful Camerata Lysy.

However, Menuhin is at his finest in his glorious early stereo recording of the Brahms *Concerto,* with Kempe; but that is available, more attractively coupled, in another Royal Classics Long Player (see under the composer above). The Bach *Double concerto,* made soon afterwards, with Christian Ferras matching his style beautifully to that of Menuhin, is also an unqualified success, as is the direction of the Bach *Third suite,* where the phrasing of the famous *Air* has the nobility one would expect. His minor contributions (just the *Pas de deux* in each case) to the paired Delibes *ballet suites* are also pleasingly elegant, but these excellent performances are also available on an alternative Royal 'Portrait' – of the conductor, Robert Irving – see below. The inclusion of the three odd movements from chamber works was not a happy idea: it would have been better to have chosen one, and presented it complete.

Meyer, Sabine or Wolfgang Meyer (clarinet)

'A Tribute to Benny Goodman' (with Bamberg SO or Bamberg SO Big Band, Ingo Metzmacher): ARNOLD: *Clarinet concerto No. 2*. COPLAND: *Clarinet concerto*. STRAVINSKY: *Ebony concerto*. BERNSTEIN: *Prelude, Fugue and Riffs*. PAGANINI: *Caprice*, etc.
*** EMI Dig. CDC5 56652-2 [id.].

Starting with a dazzling account of Sir Malcolm Arnold's *Second Concerto*, the one written for Benny Goodman, this is not just a tribute to the great polymath among clarinettists but a most attractive collection of music which is middle-of-the-road in the best sense, echoing the achievement of Goodman himself in crossing barriers. Only one of the longer works, the *Ebony Concerto*, and one of the shorter ones, the Paganini *Caprice* in jazzed-up form, feature Sabine Meyer, though four of the Big Band arrangements feature them both in duet.

It is not hard to deduce that the brother is the prime mover behind this whole programme, when in his flamboyant way he plays with an extra freedom and panache compared with his sister. Where he revels in the extrovert show of such a movement as the pre-Goodman *Rag* which closes the Arnold *Concerto*, Sabine Meyer is more reticent. Crisp accompaniment from the Bamberg Orchestra, though the Big Band conveys the fun behind this music even more winningly in the jazz arrangements. First-rate recording.

Meyer, Sabine (clarinet), Zurich Opera Orchestra, Franz Welser-Möst

'A night at the opera': VERDI: *Fantasia de concerto on themes from Rigoletto* (arr. HERRLINGERGIAMPIERI). MOZART: *Die Zauberflöte: Dies Bildnis*. DANZI: *Konzertstück: Variations on 'La ci darem la mano' from Mozart's Don Giovanni*. WEBER: *Der Freischütz: Leise, leise; Theme and variations concertante in B flat, Op. 33*. ROSSINI: *Il barbiere di Siviglia: Una voce poco fa* (arr. SCHOTTSTADT); *Introduction, theme and variations in E flat*.
** EMI Dig. CDC5 56137-2 [id.].

Sabine Meyer is a clarinettist of luscious tone and impeccable technique, but she is inclined to languish too much in this operatic programme, most strikingly so in Agathe's *Leise, leise* from *Der Freischütz*, and the long selection from *Rigoletto* tends to outstay its welcome. She is at her best in the cabaletta of *Una voce poco fa*, where there is even a touch of wit, and she manages the jocular final

variation of Weber's *Variations* (which is very like the *Clarinet concertino*) very winningly. Not surprisingly she is at her finest in Rossini's spectacular display piece, which closes the concert with an infectious combination of flair and technical brilliance. Welser-Möst accompanies attentively, and the recording is agreeable if a bit resonant.

Minneapolis Symphony Orchestra, Antal Dorati

Concert: GERSHWIN: *An American in Paris*. COPLAND: *Rodeo (4 Dance episodes)*. SCHULLER: *7 Studies on themes of Paul Klee*. BLOCH: *Sinfonia breve*.
(M) ** Mercury [434 329-2].

This is a disappointing collection, a rare occurrence for this label. Dorati's *Rodeo* lacks the incandescent vitality of Bernstein's electrifying New York version, and Gershwin's *American in Paris* doesn't suit the Hungarian conductor too well either (try the big blues tune at its trumpet entry). The almost over-detailed recording does not help, either here or in Bloch's rather dry *Sinfonia breve*, which needs richer string textures. It is highly suitable for Schuller's sharply etched *Seven studies on themes of Paul Klee* but, brilliantly though this is played, the music itself does not live up to the promise of titles like *The twittering machine* and *Little blue devil*.

ALBENIZ: *Iberia* (suite, orch. Arbós). FALLA: *La Vida breve: Interlude and dance*. MUSSORGSKY: *Khovanshchina: Prelude; Dance of the Persian slaves*. SMETANA: *The Bartered Bride: Overture and 3 Dances*.
(M) ** Mercury 434 388-2 [id.].

The Northrop Auditorium in Minnesota never proved an ideal venue acoustically for the Mercury recording team. Although the sound is not without warmth and the woodwind have bloom, there is an underlying acoustic dryness. Using the favoured M56 Telefunken microphones, closely placed, this produced an unattractive glare, even a fierceness in fortissimos, an artificial brilliance likely to appeal only to hi-fi buffs. Of course, the somewhat brash Arbós scoring in *Iberia* does not help, and certainly Dorati catches the sinuous Spanishry of this music. He is equally vital in the rest of the programme, which is all brilliantly played; but easily the highlight here is Mussorgsky's highly atmospheric *Khovanshchina Prelude*. With its orchestration expertly touched in by Rimsky-Korsakov, it magically pictures the sun rising over the Kremlin. Although the timbre of the orchestra's principal oboe is not opulent, this is one of the most evocative accounts in the CD catalogue, and here the recording cannot be faulted.

Minnesota Orchestra, Eije Oue

'Orchestral fireworks': KABALEVSKY: *Overture Colas Breugnon.* Deems TAYLOR: *Through the Looking glass: Looking glass insects.* RIMSKY-KORSAKOV: *Tsar Sultan: Flight of the bumblebee.* LISZT: *Les Préludes.* brahms: *Hungarian dance No. 3 in F.* DINICU: *Hora staccato.* DVORAK: *Slavonic dance, Op. 71/2.* JARNEFELT: *Praeludium.* BERLIOZ: *Damnation de Faust: Danse des sylphes.* klemperer: *Merry waltz.* CHABRIER: *Habanera.* RAVEL: *Boléro.*
*** Reference Dig. RR-92 CD [id.].

From the evidence of this enjoyable concert the Minneapolis Orchestra is in excellent shape under its new conductor, Eije Oue, and they play with refinement as well as virtuosity. *Les Préludes*, for instance, is a particularly impressive performance, entirely without vulgarity, with a dignified opening, yet the closing pages generate much excitement and the final peroration is really powerful. The slightly bass-heavy recording adds to the weight of the piece. And how warmly and elegantly does the orchestra play the Brahms and Dvořak dances, while the slinky Chabrier *Habanera* is very seductive. A attractive novelty here is the Deems Taylor scherzo, reminiscent of early Stravinsky, but very colourful in its own right.

Hora staccato, and Rimsky's *Bumblebee* are both played with the lightest touch, the orchestral virtuosity sparkling throughout, while it is good to welcome the charming Jarnefelt *Praeludium*. But the surprise is the Klemperer *Waltz*, turned into a real lollipop, and more persuasive here than the conductor/composer's own version (see above). *Boléro* is very well played indeed (the opening woodwind solos especially so), but it is also very relaxed until a sudden burst of adrenalin at the close. The recording is spacious and full, with warm, pleasing string quality, but the bass is at times a trifle boomy.

Musica da Camera, Robert King

Baroque chamber works: BACH: *Cantata No. 42: Sinfonia.* CORELLI: *Concerto grosso in G min. (Christmas), Op. 6/8.* PACHELBEL: *Canon and Gigue.* HANDEL: *Concerto grosso in B flat, Op. 3/ 2.* VIVALDI: *L'Estro armonico: Concerto in D min., Op. 3/11.* ALBINONI, arr. GIAZOTTO: *Adagio for organ and strings.*
*** Linn Dig. CKD 012 [id.].

An exceptionally successful concert of baroque music, with a very well-chosen programme, presented on an authentic scale, with what appears to be one instrument to a part. Phrasing is thoroughly musical and the intimacy and transparency of sound are achieved without loss of sonority or disagreeable squeezing of phrases. The familiar *Largo* of

the Corelli *Christmas concerto* is particularly fresh, and the opening of the famous Pachelbel *Canon* on a sombre solo bass-line is very telling. The colour of the lively Bach and Handel works (using wind as well as strings) is attractively realized. Excellent, realistic recording.

'Música española'

'Música española': Spanish music by foreign composers: GLINKA: *Jota aragonesa.* RAVEL: *Rapsodie espagnole; Pavane pour une infante défunte; Alborada del gracioso; Boléro* (SRO, Ansermet). LALO: *Symphonie espagnole* (with Ricci). RIMSKY-KORSAKOV: *Capriccio espagnol.* MOSZKOWSKI: *Danzas españolas: Book 1.* CHABRIER: *España* (LSO, Argenta). DEBUSSY: *Images: Iberia* (SRO, Argenta).
(B) **(*) Decca Double 433 911-2 (2) [id.].

These are all vintage performances from Decca's early stereo catalogue. Argenta's *Capriccio espagnol, España* and the Moszkowski *Spanish dances* are splendidly played by the LSO, and Ansermet's classic Ravel performances have real magnetism, re-emerging with remarkable freshness, even if the SRO playing is not always ideally polished. Of course, they are helped by the remarkable Decca recording from the late 1950s and early 1960s. *Boléro* remains in the demonstration class, its climax superbly graduated.

I Musici

ALBINONI: *Adagio in G min.* (arr. GIAZOTTO). BEETHOVEN: *Minuet in G, WoO 10/2.* BOCCHERINI: *Quintet in E, Op. 11/5: Minuet.* HAYDN (attrib.): *Quartet, Op. 3/5; Serenade.* MOZART: *Serenade No. 13 in G* (*Eine kleine Nachtmusik*), *K.525.* PACHELBEL: *Canon.*
*** Ph. (IMS) Dig. 410 606-2 [id.].

A very enjoyable concert, recorded with remarkable naturalness and realism. The effect is very believable indeed. The playing combines warmth and freshness, and the oft-played Mozart *Night music* has no suggestion whatsoever of routine: it combines elegance, warmth and sparkle. The Boccherini *Minuet* and (especially) the Hoffstetter (attrib. Haydn) *Serenade* have an engaging lightness of touch.

'Neapolitan Serenade': GIORDANI: *Harpsichord concerto in G.* LEO: *Cello concertos in D and F min.* PAISIELLO: *Harpsichord concerto in G.*
*** Ph Dig. 454 476-2 [id.].

This is a charming disc. None of the music is great or profound, but it is all tuneful and entertaining. The harpsichord concertos are fairly unfamiliar: each has sparkling *allegros*, and the finale of the

Paisiello – a highlight – has a cheekily simple tune which lodges itself in the mind, as well as a delightfully piquant pizzicato passage. The *Larghettos* are often quite touching.

The cello concertos provide a bit more gravitas – especially Leonardo Leo's *F minor concerto* – but nothing approaching *Sturm und Drang*. It is all excellently played by I Musici (Maria Teresa Garatti, the harpsichordist, deserves a special mention) in warmly recorded sound, and is ideal for those wishing for an hour or so of undemanding listening.

'Evergreens for strings': ALBINONI/GIAZOTTO: *Adagio in G min.* BACH: *The Art of Fugue, BWV 1080: Contrapunctus 1; Suite No. 3 in D: Air.* DVORAK: *Waltzes in A and D, Op. 54/1 & 4.* RESPIGHI: *Ancient airs and dances, Suite No. 3: Siciliana.* BARBER: *Adagio for strings, Op. 11.* PACHELBEL: *Canon and Gigue.* HOFFSTETTER (attrib. HAYDN): *String quartet No. 17 in F (Serenade): Andante cantabile.* MOZART: *Divertimento in D, K.136: Andante.* TCHAIKOVSKY: *Elegy in G.* BRITTEN: *Simple Symphony, Op. 4: Playful pizzicato.*
** Ph Dig. 462 598-2 [id.].

A pleasant enough collection of mainly quiet string music, ideal for late-night listening or undemanding background music. If Barber's *Adagio* doesn't have the emotional fervour of some other recordings, it is, like the rest of the programme, well played. Not surprisingly, the baroque items are the most successful. The recording is excellent.

Mutter, Anne-Sophie (violin)

MOZART: *Violin concertos Nos. 2 in D, K.211; 4 in D, K.218* (with Philharmonia O, Muti). BACH: *Concertos Nos. 1 in A min., BWV 1041; 2 in E, BWV 1042; Double violin concerto in D min., BWV 1043* (with ECO, Accardo). LALO: *Symphonie espagnole, Op. 21.* SARASATE: *Zigeunerweisen, Op. 20* (with O Nat. de France, Ozawa).
(M) *** EMI Dig. CMS5 65538-2 (3) [id.].

Anne-Sophie Mutter followed up her celebrated early coupling of Mozart's *G major*, K.216 and *A major*, K.219 *Violin concertos* (now reissued as a DG Original – see under the Composer entry in our main volume) with the two *D major Concertos* on HMV, and a different orchestra and conductor. The results are hardly less successful. Her variety of timbre as well as the imagination of her playing is extremely compelling, and while the degree of romantic warmth she adopts in her Bach playing is at odds with today's 'authentic school', her performance of the slow movement of the *E major Concerto* is finer than almost any other version

except Grumiaux's, with marvellous shading within a range of hushed tone.

Accardo's accompaniment here (as throughout the collection) is splendidly stylish and alert. In principle the slow movement of the *Double concerto* – where Accardo takes up his bow to become a solo partner, scaling down his timbre – is too slow, but the result could hardly be more beautiful, helped by EMI recording which gives body to the small ECO string band. The account of Lalo's Spanish show-piece makes an excellent foil, with its dazzling display of bravura offset by Mutter's delicacy of phrasing, although there is no lack of passionate eloquence in the central movements. Here the balance is a shade too forward, and the digital recording brings a touch of digital edge to the sound. The Sarasate offers more violinistic fireworks, but some may find that Mutter's playing of the famous principal lyrical melody a little chaste. Overall, however, this makes a fine showcase for a splendid artist.

'Modern': STRAVINSKY: *Violin concerto in D* (with Philh. O, Sacher). LUTOSLAWSKI: *Partita for Anne-Sophie Mutter* (with Philip Moll, piano); *Chain II* (with BBC SO, composer). BARTOK: *Violin concerto No. 2.* MORET: *En rêve* (with Boston SO, Ozawa). BERG: *Violin concerto.* RIHM: *Time chant* (with Chicago SO, Levine).
(M) *** DG Dig. 445 487-2 (3).

Here is an unexpected portrait of an outstanding young artist linked with the attractions of inexpensively cutting one's teeth on twentieth-century violin repertoire, offered in brilliant, modern, digital recordings. The Stravinsky *Concerto* makes a splendid opener: there is no more recommendable version, with wit and feeling nicely balanced, and excellent, sharply defined sound. The Berg is hardly less successful. Mutter opens with the most delicate pianissimo and her reading is intensely passionate.

Her Bartók is more controversial, played with stunning virtuosity and brilliance but at times over-characterized, even glossy in its brilliance, and in the scherzando section of the second movement she is much faster than the metronome marking; indeed, the performance tends to sensationalize the concerto, although the playing is not unfelt and the bravura is astonishing. The Lutoslawski pieces are among the best of his recent compositions and evoke a powerful response from their dedicatee. The Moret is a slight but enticing piece with plenty of shimmering sonorities and a dazzling solo part. The finale erupts suddenly but the introspective musing of the earlier writing returns with sporadic bursts of energy from the soloist which bring the piece to a lively conclusion. The Rihm concerto is a rhapsodical, meditative piece, its effect heightened by the orchestral backing. It is played with superb concentration.

Mutter, Anne-Sophie (violin), Vienna Philharmonic Orchestra, James Levine

'Carmen-fantasie': SARASATE: Zigeunerweisen; Carmen fantasy. WIENIAWSKI: Légende. TARTINI: Sonata in G min. (Devil's trill). RAVEL: Tzigane. MASSENET: Thaïs: Méditation. FAURE: Berceuse.
*** DG Dig. 437 544-2 [id.].

This is an unashamedly fun record, with Mutter playing with freedom and warmth and obviously enjoying herself. Comparing the Carmen fantasy of Sarasate with Perlman shows Mutter as equally sharp in characterization, yet Perlman's easy style is in the end the more beguiling. But Mutter's Ravel Tzigane is made stunningly Hungarian in its fiery accelerando at the end, while Tartini's famous Devil's trill sonata is played as a virtuoso piece, rather than placed back in the eighteenth century – no harm in that in the present context. The recording is vividly close.

Nakariakov, Sergei (trumpet)

Concertos (with Lausanne Chamber Orchestra, López-Cobos): JOLIVET: Concertino for trumpet, piano and strings (with Alexander Markovich, piano). HUMMEL: Concerto in E flat. HAYDN: Concerto in E flat. TOMASI: Concerto in D.
*** Teldec/Warner Dig. 4509 90846-2 [id.].

The very gifted teenage Russian trumpeter makes a brilliant contribution to the Jolivet Double concerto. His partner, the pianist Alexander Markovich, plays very well too, but the balance is less than ideal. Yet, at under ten minutes, the work does not outstay its welcome and it has a catchy, angular main theme. The Tomasi solo concerto is more kaleidoscopic, with lyrical and rhythmic elements alternating and a whiff of jazz in the melodic style.

In the Haydn and Hummel Concertos Nakariakov does not quite match the famous Hardenberger performances, and the orchestral playing in Lausanne is serviceable rather than outstanding. Nakariakov plays the Hummel in the key of E flat, rather than the brighter E major favoured by Hardenberger, but both this and the Haydn bring a superb solo contribution from the young Russian virtuoso, and the lovely Andante of the latter work is memorably warm and graceful before a sparkling finale which matches that of the Hummel in high spirits.

'No limit' (playing trumpet and flugel horn, with Philharmonia Orchestra, Vladimir Ashkenazy; arrangements by Mikhail Nakariakov & Timothy Dokshitser) of: SAINT-SAENS: Trumpet: Introduction and rondo capriccio. GERSHWIN: Rhapsody in blue. Flugel-horn: TCHAIKOVSKY: Andante cantabile; Variations on a rococo theme. BRUCH: Canzone. MASSENET: Thaïs: Méditation.
(***) Teldec/Warner Dig. 8573 80651-2 [id.].

Sergei Nakariakov's tone is so beautiful, his phrasing so naturally musical, his virtuosity so effortless and dazzling, that he almost reconciles one to these arrangements. Certainly the Saint-Saëns display-piece is presented with great flair – and Nakariakov's breathtakingly fast tonguing at the close is extraordinary.

But Tchaikovsky's Andante cantabile, on the flugel horn instead of the cello, just will not do. For all the warmth of line and tasteful vibrato, the atmosphere of the bandstand remains. The Rococo variations works rather better, played very stylishly, with the melodic line here often lying higher up. But again it sounds far better on a cella.

Max Bruch's Canzona and Massenet's 'Méditation' are effective enough, and undoubtedly Nakariakov is a natural in Gershwin, where he returns to the trumpet. It is a brilliant performance, with a strong jazzy inflection. The instrument's middle and lower range is used to good effect, and there is a touch of humour when the bassoon makes a solo entry. The big tune is introduced delicately and played with a cup mute; but in the following string climax the saxes fail to come through (if they are there). Throughout Ashkenazy provides good support, although the balance makes his contribution no more than an accompaniment. But that Gershwin opening should have been left to the clarinet.

National Symphony Orchestra

'This is full frequency range recording' (cond. (i) Sydney Beer; (ii) Anatole Fistoulari; (iii) Boyd Neel; (iv) Victor Olof): (i) BIZET: L'Arlésienne: suite No. 1. (ii) BERLIOZ: Damnation de Faust: Hungarian march. GLIERE: The Red Poppy: Russian sailors' dance. TCHAIKOVSKY: Marche slave; The Oprichnik: Overture. (i) WAGNER: Götterdämmerung: Siegfried's Rhine journey. (iii) SAINT-SAENS: Danse macabre. WOLF-FERRARI: The Jewels of the Madonna: Intermezzos, Acts I and II. (i) DELIUS: Irmelin prelude. (iv) CHABRIER: España.
(M) (***) Dutton mono CDK 1200 [id. full price].

Made by the National Symphony Orchestra between June and November 1944, these recordings represented the full emergence of Decca's newly developed recording process with an extended range. The founder of the orchestra, using his wealth benevolently, was Sidney Beer, who persuaded many star players to join him. Particularly impressive are his readings of the Bizet suite and the Wagner, with wind and brass superbly caught.

Boyd Neel steps away from his usual image as a chamber conductor in a crisp, flamboyant account of *Danse macabre* with Leonard Hirsch, the NSO leader, a prominent and firm soloist. The Wolf-Ferrari interludes are less successful, with higher hiss and violins less sweet. Fistoulari's bright, rhythmically alert contributions inspire recordings of such vividness one can hardly believe they are over fifty years old; the rare *Oprichnik overture* is especially welcome.

Most spectacular of all is the final item, Chabrier's *España*, with Victor Olof, best known as recording producer for both EMI and Decca, here whizzing the players thrillingly through this show-piece. The occasion prompted his engineering colleague, Arthur Haddy, to produce sound that is so vivid, with a remarkably wide dynamic range, one could almost swear it is in stereo. Malcolm Walker provides a model note, not just outlining the background of *ffrr* but giving an impressively detailed history of the Decca company from 1929 onwards.

NBC Symphony Orchestra, Arturo Toscanini

'Great symphonies': MOZART: *Symphony No. 40 in G min., K.550*. HAYDN: *Symphony No. 94 in G (Surprise)*. CHERUBINI: *Symphony in D*. SCHUMANN: *Symphony No. 3 in E flat (Rhenish), Op. 97*. DVORAK: *Symphony No. 9 (New World), Op. 95*.
(B) (**(*)) RCA mono Twofer 74321 59481 (2) [id.].

This may be a mixed bag of symphonies, classical and romantic, but each one demonstrates the electrical intensity of Toscanini's conducting. Even in the new transfers the Haydn and Mozart sound rather thin as well as harsh, and the Cherubini, one of his most celebrated records, is only a little better. The two romantic symphonies on the other hand benefit greatly, with a sense of space and full-bodied sound, notably in the 1949 recording of Schumann, the earliest here.

Baroque music (with Mischa Mischkoff, Edwin Bachmann, Frank Miller, Yella Pessl): BACH: *Suite No. 3 in D; Passacaglia and fugue in C min.* (arr. RESPIGHI); HANDEL: *Concerto grosso in B min. Op. 6 No. 12;* VIVALDI: *Violin concerto in B flat, RV 370*.
(BB) (**(*)) Naxos mono 8.110835 [id.].

Toscanini demonstrates his devotion to this baroque repertory at the very start of this programme of 1947, when he sings along enthusiastically with the orchestra in the opening of the Bach *D major Suite*. Speeds are fast and rhythms crisply articulated, while the celebrated *Air* at a flowing speed avoids all sentimentality. This may be very different from period style, but it is also very different from the

ponderousness of most Bach performances at that time.

The Handel is freshly done too, with the slow movement given a noble performance, set against hectic *Allegros*. The Vivaldi also, one of the rarer violin concertos, is chiefly remarkable for the lovely central slow movement. The Respighi arrangement finds Toscanini back on home ground, with high dynamic contrasts brought out, prompting wild applause at the end. A refreshingly different slant on Toscanini. The transfers give the dry sound more body than most from this source, though scratchiness develops on high violins after the Bach suite.

New London Consort, Philip Pickett

'The Feast of Fools': *1st Vespers; Music from the Office; The drinking bout in the cathedral porch; Mass of the asses, drunkards and gamblers; 2nd Vespers; Ceremony of the Baculus; The banquet; Processional.*
*** O-L Dig. 433 194-2 [id.].

Philip Pickett and the New London Consort, inspired in their treatment of early music, present an invigorating, ear-catching sequence drawn from the roistering parodies of church practice that in medieval times were celebrated between Christmas and Epiphany. In modern terms the jokes may be heavy-handed, whether involving vestry humour, drunken cavortings or animal-imitations (as in the *Kyrie* of the *Asses*, 'Hinhan Eleison'), but the wildness of much of the music is infectious, performed here with uninhibited joy. Carl Orff's *Carmina Burana* (inspired from similar Latin sources) hardly outshines these originals.

New London Orchestra, Ronald Corp

'American light music classics'; SOUSA: *Washington Post.* Kerry MILLS: *Whistling Rufus.* GOULD: *American Symphonette No. 3: Pavane.* Felix ARNDT: *Nola (A silhouette).* PRYOR: *The whistler and his dog.* Leroy ANDERSON: *Belle of the ball; Plink, plank, plunk.* TRAD.: *The Arkansas traveller (The old fiddler's breakdown).* BRATTON: *Teddy bears' picnic.* MACDOWELL: *Woodland sketches: To a wild rose.* HOLZMANN: *Blaze away!* FRIML: *In love (Chanson).* Raymond SCOTT: *The toy trumpet.* GERSHWIN: *Promenade.* HERBERT: *Babes in Toyland: March of the toys.* ROSE: *Holiday for strings.* NEVIN: *Water scenes: Narcissus.* Don GILLIS: *Symphony No. 5 1/2 (A Symphony for fun).* RODGERS: *Carousel waltz.*
*** Hyperion Dig. CDA 67067 [id.].

The surprise here is instantly to recognize so many

catchy tunes, and then find they come from the other side of the Atlantic. After the familiar Sousa march (played with spirit and a touch of panache, rather than Yankee bezaz), Kerry Mills's *Whistling Rufus*, with its cakewalk rhythm, is unmistakably American. Abe Holzmann's *Blaze away!*, complete with piccolo solo, is equally identifiable. So is the engaging Gould *Pavane* and the two witty Leroy Anderson encore pieces, while the New Yorker Edward MacDowell's tender little portrait of a wild rose, delightfully played here, remains his most famous piece. But *Nola, The whistler and his dog* (complete with 'barking' coda), *Narcissus* and David Rose's winning pizzicato *Holiday for strings* all seem so familiar that they feel more like local items.

The *Teddy Bears' picnic* was an American instrumental piece, but became a British song, and a huge hit in England. Rudolf Friml's *Chanson (In Love)* also became famous when words were added to it – for its appearance in the Hollywood film *The Firefly*, and it was renamed the *Donkey serenade*. I. M. has a treasured childhood memory of seeing another 1930s film, *Babes in Toyland*, where Laurel and Hardy helped to defeat the evil Bogeymen to the strains of Victor Herbert's famous *March*. In that instance the toy soldiers were six feet tall, as Stanley, who had ordered them for Father Christmas, fortunately got the measurements wrong! The music sounds as piquant as ever. Don Gillis's *Symphony for fun* doesn't seem as audacious as it once did, but still enjoyably bears out its descriptive title. As in the rest of this splendid Hyperion series, performances are as polished as they are spontaneous, and the recording is first class.

'British light music classics': Vol. 1: COATES: *Calling all workers*. TOYE: *The haunted ballroom*. COLLINS: *Vanity Fair*. FARNON: *Jumping bean*. BAYNES: *Destiny*. CURZON: *The Boulevardier*. LUTZ: *Pas de quatre*. BINGE: *The Watermill; Elizabethan serenade*. WILLIAMS: *The Devil's galop*. GIBBS: *Dusk*. WHITE: *Puffin' Billy*. KETELBEY: *Bells across the meadows*. Charles WILLIAMS: *The old clockmaker*. JOYCE: *Dreaming*. ELLIS: *Coronation Scot*. ANCLIFFE: *Nights of gladness*.
*** Hyperion Dig. CDA 66868 [id.].

Almost as soon as it was issued, Ronald Corp's stylish and beautifully played collection of inconsequential but engaging English miniatures rose up and held its place in the bestseller lists. This was the kind of music that used to be heard on seaside piers and which was played by spa orchestras in the years between the two World Wars – orchestras that have long since disappeared.

The robust *Nights of gladness* (1912) was composed by Charles Ancliffe on return from service as a bandmaster in India, while Sydney Baynes's *Destiny waltz*, from the same year, has a

cello solo which, years later, was played by Sir John Barbirolli at Hallé balls; Archibald Joyce's *Dreaming* dates from the previous year, while two other hauntingly atmospheric pieces, *Dusk* by Armstrong Gibbs and Geoffrey Toye's *Haunted ballroom*, were both written in 1935. Vivian Ellis's *Coronation Scot*, a catchy sound-picture of a steam locomotive, dates from 1939 and became famous when it was used as the signature tune for BBC radio's 'Paul Temple' detective series. More recently, Ronald Binge has added his engaging *Elizabethan serenade* (1951) and a delicate portrait of *The Watermill* (1958). It was the famous Sibelius conductor, Anthony Collins, who wrote the delectable morsel, *Vanity Fair*, and he once said in a radio interview that he valued its composition above all his other achievements 'because it will keep my name alive long after my records have been forgotten'. The affectionate, polished performances here will certainly help to do that: they give much pleasure, and Tony Faulkner's recording balance is beautifully judged.

'British light music classics', Vol. 2: COATES: *London suite: Knightsbridge*. FLETCHER: *Bal masqué*. BUCALOSSI: *Grasshopper's dance*. Arthur WOOD: *'The Archers' theme'*: Barwick Green. HARTLEY: *Rouge et Noir*. FARNON: *Peanut polka; Westminster waltz*. FRANKEL: *Carriage and pair*. Haydn WOOD: *The Horse Guards, Whitehall (Down your Way* theme). DUNCAN: *Little suite: March (Dr Finlay's Casebook* theme). BINGE: *Sailing by*. VINTER: *Portuguese party*. RICHARDSON: *Beachcomber*. FINCK: *In the shadows*. DOCKER: *Tabarinage*. KETELBEY: *Sanctuary of the heart*. ELGAR: *Carissima*. Charles WILLIAMS: *Girls in grey*. WHITE: *The runaway rocking horse*. CURZON: *Robin Hood suite: March of the bowmen*.
*** Hyperion Dig. CDA 66968 [id.].

Ronald Corp's second collection of popular evergreens is just as delightful as the first, for the supply of catchy and popular numbers shows no sign of drying up. Radio and television signature-tunes provide the cornerstones, with *Barwick Green (The Archers)* by Arthur Wood pointing the way, a piece inspired not by the West Country or the fictional world of Ambridge, but by a village near Leeds. From Eric Coates's *Knightsbridge march* onwards, chosen in the early 1930s to introduce the pioneering radio magazine programme *In Town Tonight*, here is a rich source of nostalgia, including Haydn Wood's *Horse Guards march (Down your Way)*, Ronald Binge's *Sailing by* (Radio 4 signing off) and Trevor Duncan's catchy *March (Dr Finlay's Casebook)*, which reminds one a little of the *Marcia* of Dag Wirén and is here played most delicately.

What comes out from every one of these twenty pieces is not just their catchy memorability and tunefulness, but the brilliance and subtlety of the instrumentations. They are full of the sort of effects that only a really practical musician, close to players, could think up; and they are here made the more enjoyable by the warmth and clarity of the sound. It is welcome that Elgar is this time included with one of his lesser-known pieces, *Carissima*, not to mention Ben Frankel with the jaunty *Carriage and pair*, with its clip-clopping rhythm vividly evoking the period Parisian atmosphere of the film *So Long at the Fair*. A must for anyone at all given to nostalgia.

'British light music classics', Vol. 3: Haydn WOOD: *Montmartre*. Clive RICHARDSON: *Melody on the move*. Trevor DUNCAN: *The girl from Corsica*. Lionel MONCKTON: *Soldiers in the park*. Felix GODIN: *Valse Septembre*. BINGE: *Miss Melanie*. Ivan CARYLL: *Pink Lady waltz*. FARNON: *Portrait of a flirt*. DEXTER: *Siciliano*. KETELBEY: *In a Persian market* (with chorus). Jack STRACHEY: *Theatreland*. Archibald JOYCE: *Songe d'automne*. Vivian ELLIS: *Alpine pastures*. TOMLINSON: *Little serenade*. MELACHRINO: *Woodland revel*. Tolchard EVANS: *Lady of Spain*. ANCLIFFE: *Smiles, then kisses*. TORCH: *On a spring note*. COATES: *Rediffusion march: Music everywhere*.
*** Hyperion Dig. CDA 67148 [id.].

Volume 3 is well up to the standard of its attractive predecessors, warmly and sparklingly played, with the orchestra clearly enjoying the melodic profusion. Haydn Wood's opening *Montmartre* would cheer anyone up, and the following *Melody on the move* and *In the party mood* maintain the spirited forward momentum. Many of the later items are justly famous. No collection of British light music would be complete without Ketèlbey, and the New London Light Opera Chorus makes a lusty contribution in the *Persian market*.

Farnon's *Portrait of a flirt*, Harry Dexter's delectably fragile *Siciliano* and Tomlinson's equally charming *Little serenade* are all winningly personable, while Melachrino's *Woodland revel* begins wittily with a simple interplay on a melodic fragment, which then flowers romantically, generating a rumbustious climax. The Ancliffe waltz is delightfully English in rhythmic inflection, and after Sidney Torch's catchy reminder of spring, Eric Coates provides a rousing conclusion. The recording is crisp and clear within a pleasingly warm ambience. Most refreshing.

'European light music classics': JESSEL: *Parade of the tin soldiers*. LEHAR: *Gold and silver* (waltz). PIERNE: *Album pour mes petits amis: Marche des petits soldats de plomb*. Johann STRAUSS Jr: *Tritsch-Tratsch polka*. LINCKE: *Glow worm idyll*. ALFVEN: *Swedish polka*. GOUNOD: *Funeral march of a marionette*. WALDTEUFEL: *The Skaters waltz*. HEYKENS: *Serenade*. PADILLA: *El relicaro*.

BECUCCI: *Tesoro mio!* HELLMESBERGER: *Ball scene*. WEINBERGER: *Schwanda the Bagpiper: Polka*. FETRAS: *Moonlight on the Alster*. HALVORSEN: *Entry of the Boyars*.
**(*) Hyperion Dig. CDA 66998 [id.].

Although there is much to enjoy here, this is a less enterprising collection than usual in this series. The highlights are what one might call the Palm Court trifles, the two evocations of miniature soldiers (Pierné's unmistakably French), Lincke's exquisite *Glow worm idyll*, the Heykens *Serenade* and the *Entry of the Boyars*, which is most winningly played. *Moonlight on the Alster*, too, is a famous waltz by an unfamous composer and Waldteufel's *Skaters* are always welcome. But why choose the *Tritsch-Tratsch polka* and *Gold and silver* which are readily available elsewhere; the latter is one of Barbirolli's specials? Performances and recordings are pretty well up to standard.

New Philharmonia Orchestra, Raymond Leppard

'18th-century overtures': J. C. BACH: *Catone in Utica*. RAMEAU: *Les Paladins; Zaïs; Pygmalion*. BOYCE: *Cambridge Installation Ode*. Alessandro SCARLATTI: *Il giardino di rose*. CIMAROSA: *I traci amanti*. PERGOLESI: *L'Olimpiade*. HANDEL: *Il pastor fido*. GRETRY: *Le jugement de Midas*. BONONCINI: *Polifemo*. SACCHINI: *Oedipe à Colone*. MEHUL: *La chasse du jeune Henri*.
(M) *** Ph. (IMS) 446 569-2.

This is a winning collection if ever there was one, with half as many items again as in the original LP collection, all extremely interesting and tuneful music – much of it little known – and full of surprises. Rameau's *Les Paladins* and *Pygmalion* are a delight, while *Zaïs* is remarkably dramatic with its unusual timpani contributions. Boyce's *Cambridge Installation Ode*, a considerable piece, opens with proper dignity but later offers some neat contrapuntal writing.

Scarlatti's *Il giardino di rose* opens delicately, then introduces a lively allegro featuring duetting trumpets. Cimarosa's *I traci amanti* has the strings dancing gaily; Sacchini's *Oedipe à Colone* is another charmer, and the rest of the programme is hardly less diverting. Best of all is Méhul's *La chasse du jeune Henri* with its splendid echoing horn-calls, justly a favourite of Sir Thomas Beecham's; and the artistry and lightness of touch that distinguish Raymond Leppard's direction of the New Philharmonic are at times worthy of Sir Thomas. The late-1960s recording is full and lifelike; textures are less transparent than we would expect today, but many will respond to the lithe beauty of the modern string-sound.

(i) **New Philharmonia Orchestra,**
(ii) **London Symphony**
Orchestra, Richard Bonynge
'Overtures and ballet music of the nineteenth century':

Disc 1: (i) Overtures: AUBER: *Marco Spada; Lestocq.* ADAM: *Giralda; La poupée de Nuremburg.* LECOCQ: *La fille de Madame Angot.* THOMAS: *Mignon.* PLANQUETTE: *Les cloches de Corneville.* BOIELDIEU: *Le calife de Bagdad; La dame blanche.* MEYERBEER: *Le Prophète: Coronation march.* MASSENET: *La Navarraise: Nocturne.* GOUNOD: *La Reine de Saba, Act II:* Waltz. BIZET: *Don Procopio, Act II: Entr'acte.*

Disc 2: (ii) Overtures: DONIZETTI: *Roberto Devereux.* ROSSINI: *Torvaldo e Dorliska.* MAILLART: *Les Dragons de Villars.* OFFENBACH: *La fille du tambour-major.* VERDI: *Giovanna d'Arco.* HEROLD: *Zampa.* WALLACE: *Maritana.* AUBER: *La Neige.* MASSENET: *Cherubin, Act III: Entr'acte. Don César de Bazan: Entr'acte Sevillana. Les Erinnyes: Invocation.* GOUNOD: *Le tribut de Zamora, Act III: Danse grecque.* SAINT-SAENS: *Henry VIII, Act II: Danse de la gypsy.* DELIBES: *Le roi l'a dit, Act II: Entr'acte.*

(B) *** Australian Decca Double 466 431-2 (2) [id.].

By delving further into the back catalogue, Australian Decca have come up with an even more delectable collection of overtures and orchestral sweetmeats than in the companion eighteenth-century compilation above. The programme is again based on three Bonynge LPs, two from the LSO and one from the New Philharmonia Orchestra, again from the late 1960s and early 1970s. The format of the nineteenth-century overture is a pretty standard one, usually a potpourri, but sometimes more sophisticated in layout, as with Thomas's *Mignon*, and to a lesser extent, Hérold's *Zampa*. But it is the tunes that count.

Of the three Auber overtures *Marco Spada* has a wonderfully evocative opening, suggesting a sunrise, before bursting champagne-like into one of his typical galloping allegros; *Lestocq* contains a memorably wistful tune for the oboe, while *La Neige*, more subtle than usual, shows the composer's gift for writing catchy tunes quite early in his career. Adam's *Giralda* and *La poupée de Nuremburg* display all the delicacy and skill we know from his ballet scores, the former features glittering castanets, the latter an unexpected passage for string quartet. Boieldieu's charming *La dame blanche* is as light as thistledown and *The calife of Bagdad* has never sounded more resplendent. Lecocq's *La fille de Madame Angot* is quite delicious.

Among the LSO performances, *Maritana* stands out. Bonynge does this gorgeously, the melodramatic opening arresting, and the shaping of the hit tune *'Scenes that are brightest'* lusciously presented. Rossini's *Torvaldo e Dorliska* is interesting in including the second subject of the *Cenerentola* overture, while Donizetti's *Roberto Devereux* flagrantly draws on *'God save the King'*. Offenbach's winning *La fille du tambour-major*, piquantly scored, ends with an exuberant can-can played with superb gusto.

We also turn to the LSO for the ballet music. Besides a brilliant account of Meyerbeer's *Coronation march*, there is a series of delightful *bon bouches* including a famous Massenet cello solo (the *Invocation* from *Les Erinnyes*) and the *Nocturne* from *La Navarraise*. Gounod's *Grande valse* from *La Reine de Saba* sounds as though it has been left over from the *Faust* ballet music, while Saint-Saëns's *Gypsy dance* from *Henry VIII*, with its ominous timpani strokes, turns into a tuneful valse-macabre. The programme ends with a charming pastiche *Minuet* from Delibes's *Le roi l'a dit*. Bonynge is a complete master of this repertoire, which he clearly loves, and all this music is so chic and poised in his hands and so brilliantly played and recorded, that enjoyment is assured. We are glad to say that Decca are to issue this fine set in the UK towards the end of 2000.

New York Philharmonic Orchestra or Columbia Chamber Orchestra, Leonard Bernstein

'French Masterpieces': (i) DUKAS: *L'apprenti sorcier.* HONEGGER: *Rugby; Pastorale d'été; Pacific 231.* DEBUSSY: *Rhapsody for saxophone and orchestra* (all with NYPO). MILHAUD: *La création du monde, Op. 81.* RAVEL: *Shéhérazade* (with Colombia Chamber Orchestra & Jennie Tourel).

(M) ** Sony SMK 60695 [id.].

Bernstein's *L'apprenti sorcier* is a lively account in good, but not outstanding, sound and the three works of Honegger make an acceptable triptych, with the *Pastorale d'été* as a peaceful centrepiece to offset the athletic stridency of the other two, literally descriptive evocations. The performances certainly have character, but the early 1960s sound emphasizes clarity at the expense of atmosphere. Bernstein misses some of the underlying lyricism of *Pacific 231*, though the train journey is exciting enough. Debussy's *Rhapsody* receives a well-played, sensitive reading, with a lovely atmospheric opening. *La création du monde*, however, is a mono recording dating from 1951: the sound is vivid enough, but a bit too dry and upfront, even if the performance is sympathetic and lively. *Shéhérazade* was recorded in 1950, and once again the sound is too dry for a song cycle which relies so much on atmosphere. Although she sings sympathetically, Jennie Tourel's tone (probably due to the recording) is not as seductive as it might be.

Noras, Arto (cello); **Finnish Radio Symphony Orchestra, Oramo or Saraste; Norwegian Radio SO, Rasilainen**

DVORAK: *Cello concerto* (with Finnish Radio Symphony Orchestra, Oramo). DUTILLEUX: *Cello concerto (Tout un monde lointain).* ELGAR: *Cello concerto.* LALO: *Cello concerto in D min.* SAINT-SAENS: *Cello concerto No. 1.* BARTOK: *Rhapsody No. 1* (originally for violin and orch.) (all with Finnish RSO, Saraste). SHOSTAKOVICH: *Cello concertos Nos 1 & 2.* Richard STRAUSS: *Romanze in D* (1883) (with Norwegian Radio Symphony Orchestra, Ari Rasilainen).
(B) *** Finlandia/Warner Dig 3984 26836-2 (3) [id.].

This fine collection of cello concertos comes in just one of the many bargain-boxes issued to celebrate the twentieth anniversary of the Finlandia label. The Finnish cellist Arto Noras makes an outstanding soloist in this wide range of works, with his impressive technique, flawless intonation and firm, full tone. In generous couplings the Elgar concerto, dedicatedly done, is just one of eight full concertos, all excellently done in fresh, clear interpretations, as well as shorter works by Bartók and Strauss. Brilliant, full sound.

Northern Ballet Theatre Orchestra, Pryce-Jones

Twentieth-century English ballets: FEENEY: *Cinderella.* MULDOWNEY: *The Brontës.* Carl DAVIS: *A Christmas carol.*
(BB) *** Naxos 8.553495 [id.].

This enterprising disc is of music taken from full-length ballet scores commissioned by the Northern Ballet Theatre. The most instantly appealing work is Carl Davis's *A Christmas carol*, delightfully nostalgic with its mixture of sentimental and vigorous numbers – these include a lively, rustic-sounding dance as some poorly clad Londoners try to keep themselves warm. It is an appealing score, with much piquant orchestration and a neat use of the harpsichord. Davis introduces well-known Christmas carols to present the story of Scrooge in a fresh way.

Philip Feeney's *Cinderella* is more severe, reflecting the story as told by the Brothers Grimm, rather than the more romanticised version by Perrault. Feeney uses a battery of percussion instruments to tell the tale, and the result lacks really memorable tunes. But it is not at all dull and has plenty of rhythm and colour. The *Courtly dances* begin with an array of bells, percussion instruments and a gong, then the composer switches to the harpsichord halfway through to striking effect. *The Red Ball*, where the prince introduces himself, is quirky in a haunting way, and the finale is an up-beat conclusion.

The Brontës, with music by Dominic Muldowney, is a series of vignettes portraying the Brontë family, as seen through the eyes of the father, Rev. Patrick Brontë, who outlived all his six children. The opening *Toy soldiers' fantasy* is charming, with its trumpet fanfares set against a robust marching tune; *The Moors* and *Wuthering Heights* numbers are appropriately broody, whilst *Charlotte in Brussels* is a jaunty little waltz, with witty writing throughout the orchestra. It is thoroughly entertaining. The performances and recording are outstanding, and this bargain CD is recommendable to any true lover of ballet music.

Northern Philharmonia Orchestra of England, Leeds Festival Chorus, Paul Daniel

'Rule, Britannia – The last night of the Proms':
WALTON: *Coronation marches: Crown imperial; Orb and sceptre.* PARRY: *Jerusalem.* ELGAR: *Enigma variations: Nimrod. Pomp and circumstance march No. 1.* WOOD: *Fantasia on British sea songs* (including *Rule, Britannia*). ARNOLD: *Overture Tam O'Shanter.* PARRY: *I was glad.*
(BB) **(*) Naxos Dig. 8.553981 [id.].

If it seems a little perverse to record such a programme without the contribution of the Prommers and the heady last-night atmosphere, it has to be said that this is a very good concert in its own right and the Leeds Chorus makes an impressive contribution in *Rule, Britannia* and especially in the reprise of the great *Pomp and circumstance* melody (which is the more effective at Paul Daniel's spacious tempo). The two Walton marches have panache and Arnold's *Tam O'Shanter* is splendidly done. Here the recording is of a spectacular demonstration quality. Excellent value.

Oistrakh, David (violin)

'The Originals' (with (i) VSO; (ii) Igor Oistrakh; (iii) RPO, Goossens; (iv) Dresden State O,

Konwitschny): BACH: (i) *Violin concertos Nos. 1 in E; 2 in A min;* (ii–iii) *Double violin concerto in D min., BWV 1041–3.* (iii) BEETHOVEN: *Romances Nos. 1 in G, 2 in F, Opp. 40 & 50.* (iv) BRAHMS: *Violin concerto, Op. 77.* TCHAIKOVSKY: *Violin concerto, Op. 35.*
(M) (***) DG stereo/mono 447 427-2 (2) [id.].

In 'The Originals' series at mid-price, DG here offers reissues of classic Oistrakh recordings unavailable for years in any format. Rarest are the 1954 mono recordings of the Brahms and Tchaikovsky *Concertos*, more relaxed, more volatile readings than those Oistrakh recorded later in stereo. Oistrakh moves effortlessly from dashing bravura to the sweetest lyricism, the complete master. The Bach and Beethoven offerings are hardly less welcome.

Allowing for the practice of the time, these Bach performances are all strong and resilient, consistently bringing out the sweetness and purity of Oistrakh's playing, not least in the rapt accounts of the slow movements. Directing the Vienna Symphoniker from the violin, Oistrakh may make the tuttis in the two Bach solo concertos rather heavy, but he then transforms everything the moment he starts playing. The Bach *Double concerto* with Oistrakh father and son, accompanied by Goossens and the RPO, is more magnetic still, and they accompany him no less sympathetically in the warm, poised readings of the two Beethoven *Romances*.

Concertante works and Duos (with Igor Oistrakh): VIVALDI: *Concerto grosso in A min., Op. 3/8* (with RPO). SARASATE: *Navarra, Op. 33* (with Leizig Gewandhaus Orchestra, Franz Konwitschny). BACH: *Sonata for 2 violins and harpsichord in C, BWV 1037* (with Hans Pischner, harpsichord). HANDEL: *Sonata for 2 violins and harpsichord in G min., Op. 2/7.* BENDA: *Trio sonata in E* (both with Wladimir Yampolsky, piano). WIENIAWSKI: *3 Etudes-caprices for 2 violins, Op. 18.*
(M) (***) DG mono/stereo 463 616-2 [id.].

The second Oistrakh reissue in DG's Original series, again joining father and son, gathers together an oddly assorted programme of recordings made in 1957/8 and 1960, with (surprisingly) only the Vivaldi item in stereo, although the sound throughout is very good indeed. The Bach hardly needs recommendation, the Handel sonata is a gem, and even the Benda – a slight but pleasing work – has its moments.

'The essential David Oistrakh' (with Moscow Philharmonic Orchestra): MOZART: *Violin concerto No. 1 in B flat, K.207.* BRAHMS: *Violin concerto in D, Op. 77* (both cond. Kiril Kondrashin). BEETHOVEN: *Romances Nos. 1-2, Opp. 40 & 50.* (cond. Gennady Rozhdestvensky).

SHOSTAKOVICH: *Violin concertos: Nos. 1 in A min., Op. 99* (with Leningrad Philharmonic Orchestra, Yevgeny Mravinsky); *2 in C sharp min., Op. 129* (with Moscow PO, Kondrashin).
(M) **(*) RCA stereo/mono 74321 71914-2 (2) [id.].

The pair of DG Originals above are here supplemented by RCA's excellently remastered Melodiya recordings, of which the Mozart, Brahms, and Beethoven works (from 1963 and 1968) have not appeared before. The sound is just a little papery on top, but the stereo ambience provides warmth and the audience ensures the spontaneity and concentration of a live occasion. There are a few muted coughs, but these are all memorable performances, the Mozart wonderfully stylish, the Brahms warm and passionate, and the second of the two Beethoven *Romances* particularly fine.

Apart from a couple of minor horn fluffs in the slow movement of the Brahms – a richly lyrical account – the orchestral support is excellent. The Shostakovich performances are special: the *First concerto* is mono and dates from 1956: it has all the electricity of a premiere. It once appeared on an Artia LP but sounds very much better here. This *Second concerto* is stereo and was made a decade later. A self-recommending set on all counts.

Opera ballets: 'Dance of the hours'

PONCHIELLI: *La Gioconda: Dance of the hours* (National PO, Bartoletti). SAINT-SAENS: *Henry VIII: Dance of the gypsy* (LSO, Bonynge); *Samson et Dalila: Bacchanale.* GOUNOD: *Faust: ballet music* (both Montreal SO, Dutoit); *La Reine de Saba: waltz.* ROSSINI: *William Tell: ballet music* (both LSO Bonynge). SMETANA: *The Bartered bride: Polka; Furiant* (Israel PO, Kertész). MUSSORGSKY: *Khovanshchina: Dance of the Persian slaves* (SRO, Ansermet). VERDI: *Aida: Grande march and ballet; Otello: ballet music* (Bologna Teatro Comunale O, Chailly).
(M) **(*) Decca Analogue/Dig. 458 229-2 [id.].

Most of the operatic ballet music here is well known and it is all unfailingly entertaining. Rarities include the delightful *Dance of the gypsy* from Saint-Saëns's *Henry VIII*, which has a sinuously evocative beginning, then bursts into a *valse macabre*, and Gounod's *La Reine de Saba* waltz, which sounds as though it belongs to the *Faust* ballet music (which is itself elegantly played, if not sparkling). Kertész's vividly exciting *Bartered bride* dances pack a punch, and as always, Verdi's ballet music makes one hanker for more. A good, nicely packaged CD, but not one to match Karajan's Berlin Philharmonic set, which includes a scintillating *Dance of the hours*.

Orchestra of St John's, Smith Square, John Lubbock

'On hearing the first cuckoo in spring': VAUGHAN WILLIAMS: *Fantasia on Greensleeves; Rhosymedre*. GRIEG: *Peer Gynt: Morning*. RAVEL: *Pavane*. DELIUS: *On hearing the first cuckoo in spring*. faure: *Masques et bergamasques: Overture. Berceuse, Op. 56*. SCHUBERT: *Rosamunde: Entr'acte No. 2; Ballet music No. 2*. MOZART: *Divertimento in D, K.136: Presto*.
(BB) **(*) ASV Quicksilva Dig. CDQS 6007 [(M) id.].

An enjoyable bargain collection of essentially atmospheric music for late evening. Fine playing throughout: tempi are very relaxed, notably in the Grieg, Fauré and Schubert items, but the evocation is persuasive. The digital recording is first class, full and clear, yet not too clinical in its detail. Some might feel that the music-making here verges on the somnolent in its consistently easy-going manner – the Delius piece is indicative of the conductor's style – but the closing Mozart *Presto* ends the concert with a sparkle.

Orchestre National de France, Charles Munch

'Hommage à Charles Munch'.

BEETHOVEN: *Symphonies Nos. 4 in B flat; 7 in A Overture: Consecration of the house* (*(*) V 4825).

BERLIOZ: *Symphonie fantastique, Op. 14; Overtures: Le Corsaire, Op. 21; Benvenuto Cellini, Op. 23* (* V 4826).

BRAHMS: *Symphony No. 2 in D, Op. 73*. SCHUMANN: *Symphony No. 4 in D min., Op. 120* (** V 4827).

DEBUSSY: *Images: Iberia; La Mer; Fantaisie for piano and orchestra* (with Nicole Henriot) (** V 4828).

FRANCK: *Symphony in D min*. FAURE: *Pelléas et Mélisande: suite* (** V 4829).

HONEGGER: *Symphony No. 1*. DUTILLEUX: *Symphony No. 2* (**(*) V 4830).

HONEGGER: *Symphonies Nos. 2* (for strings and trumpet obbligato); *5 (Di tre re); Le chant de Nigamon; Pastorale d'été* (** V 4831).

ROUSSEL: *Symphonies Nos. 3 in G min., Op. 42; 4 in A, Op. 53; Bacchus et Ariane: suite No. 2* (** V 4832).

'Hommage à Charles Munch' (complete).
(BB) ** Audivis Valois V 4822 (8) [id.] (with the complete set: SIBELIUS: *Legends: The swan of Tuonela; Lemminkäinen's return*).

An eight-CD set called *Hommage à Charles Munch* commemorates his work with the Orchestre National after his return from Boston. If you buy the whole set – and it is very inexpensive – you get a 1964 recording of two of the *Four Legends* made while the orchestra was on tour in Finland. The discs are available separately and bring some outstanding performances, albeit in variable sound.

The Beethoven *Fourth* (V 4825) was recorded in Stockholm on the same Scandinavian tour and the *Seventh* and, appropriately enough, *The Consecration of the house* come from the inaugural concert in the *Maison de la Radio* in Paris in 1963. Not first-class but acceptable sound, as is the Berlioz (V 4826). The *Symphonie fantastique*, recorded in a rather dry acoustic in Lisbon in 1963, is a bit hard-driven, as was his Boston account. *Un bal* is horribly rushed.

Good though his Franck, Brahms and Schumann may be, it was for his Honegger and Roussel that Munch is best remembered. Always a champion of good contemporary music, he conducted the Honegger and Dutilleux (V 4830) in 1962. Both works are closely associated with Boston. Koussevitzky commissioned the Honegger *First Symphony* (along with the Roussel *Third*) for the 50th anniversary of the founding of the Boston Symphony and Munch conducted the première of the Dutilleux *Symphony* during his Boston years. The Honegger recording is not absolutely first class – a bit strident and narrower in frequency range than some of its companions – but the Dutilleux is very good – and what a performance!

Two other Honegger symphonies, Nos. 2 and 5 (V 4831), come from performances taken from the orchestra's 1964 European tour, the *Symphony for strings* in San Sebastien in Spain and the *Fifth* from Helsinki. The early *Le chant de Nigamon*, an amazingly original piece, was recorded at the Théâtre des Champs-Elysées two years earlier and though not first-class sound is perfectly acceptable (it briefly captures the conductor's vocalise!). Neither of the symphonies is superior to his Boston performances from the 1950s and the rather shrill-sounding *Symphony for strings* is nowhere near as impressive as his 1969 EMI recording with the Orchestre de Paris. The Helsinki recording of the *Fifth* sounds better.

The Roussel *Third* (V 4832) has plenty of drive, too, but the recording balance is poor. It comes from the 1964 Edinburgh Festival and the string melody at the opening has to struggle to make itself heard against the percussive accompaniment. The *Fourth Symphony*, recorded two years later at the Théâtre des Champs-Elysées, is better, though the *Bacchus et Ariane* suite, whose provenance is not given, is more transparent and present than either. Munch was closely identified with Roussel all his life and though this disc is better than nothing, if you can get hold of his commercial recording of the symphonies on Erato they are better served in terms of sound. All the same, despite its sonic limitations this is a set to have. Munch was a conductor of stature and his work with the Orchestre National is well worth commemorating.

Ormandy, Eugene (conductor and violinist)

'The art of Eugene Ormandy': Ormandy as violinist: RIMSKY-KORSAKOV: *Le Coq d'Or: Hymn to the sun. Sadko: Song of India.* Victor HERBERT: *Mlle.Modiste: Kiss me again.* DRDLA: *Souvenir.* DVORAK: *Humoresque.* Ormandy and his Salon Orchestra: BRAHMS: *Hungarian Dance No. 2 in D minor.* HOSMER: *Southern Rhapsody.* With Dorsey Brothers' Concert Orchestra: COSLOW-SPIER-BRITT: *Was it a dream?.* With Minneapolis Symphony Orchestra: ZEMACHSON: *Chorale and fugue in D min., Op. 4.* ZADOR: *Hungarian dance.* GRIFFES: *The Pleasure dome of Kubla Khan, Op. 8.* HARRIS: *When Johnny comes marching home.* With Philadelphia Orchestra: BARBER: *Essay No. 1, Op. 12.* MENOTTI: *Amelia goes to the ball overture.* MIASKOVSKY: *Symphony No. 21 in F sharp Min., Op. 51.* Richard STRAUSS: *Sinfonia domestica, Op. 53.* With Yeend, Beech, Coray, Kullman, Harrell, London, Los Angeles Chorus, Hollywood Bowl Symphony Orchestra: (vi) MAHLER: *Symphony No. 8:* 1st movement only.
(***) Biddulph mono WHL 064/5 [id.].

This two-disc set gives a fascinating profile of Ormandy's early career. He arrived in America seeking a position as a violinist and in the first five tracks we hear him as a good deal more than capable in that role. These recordings, dating from the 1920s, have a warm nostalgic glow and the sound is generally good.

His next progression was conducting light classical and salon music for radio, of which there are three examples from the late 1920s, including a characteristic 1920s account (with vocals) of *Was it a dream?*

Ormandy's great turning point came when he stood in for Toscanini, who sudddenly pulled out of a Philadelphia Orchestral engagement, and Ormandy took over. His concerts were a triumph and, thanks to a talent scout, resulted in a series of recordings with the Minneapolis SO, of which four (from the mid 1930s) are included here. The repertoire is comparatively rare today, which makes their inclusion valuable, especially as they are so enjoyable.

But it is the Philadelphia recordings which are the glories of this set: Barber's *Essay No. 1* has rarely been equalled in performance, whilst the Menotti overture is as brilliant as it could be. The Miaskovsky is magnetic in concentration and at-

mosphere, and one just has to hear the sumptuous string tone to appreciate why the Philadelphia sound is legendary. The *Sinfonia domestica* is also perceptively characterized, and again, there is something quite magnetic about the performance.

The first movement of Mahler's *Eighth Symphony* is an interesting reminder of Ormandy's pioneering importance in this repertoire, but the recorded sound, from a live broadcast in 1948, leaves something to be desired. A fascinating collection just the same, with helpful sleeve notes and convenient slim-line packaging.

Osipov State Russian Folk Orchestra, Vitaly Gnutov

'Balalaika favourites': BUDASHIN: *Fantasy on two folk songs.* arr. GORODOVSKAYA: *At sunrise.* KULIKOV: *The Linden tree.* OSIPOV: *Kamarinskaya.* MIKHAILOVSHALAYEV: *Fantasy on Volga melodies.* ANDREYEV: *In the moonlight; Under the apple tree; Waltz of the faun.* SOLOVIEV/SEDOY: *Midnight in Moscow.* TCHAIKOVSKY: *Dance of the comedians.* SHISHAKOV: *The living room.* arr. MOSSOLOV: *Evening bells.* arr. POPONOV: *My dear friend, please visit me.* RIMSKY-KORSAKOV: *Flight of the bumblebee.*
⊙ (M) *** Mercury 432 000-2 [id.].

The Mercury recording team visited Moscow in 1962 in order to make the first recordings produced in the Soviet Union by Western engineers since the Revolution. The spirit of that unique occasion is captured wonderfully here – analogue atmosphere at its best. The rippling waves of balalaika sound, the accordion solos, the exhilarating accelerandos and crescendos that mark the style of this music-making: all are recorded with wonderful immediacy. Whether in the shimmering web of sound of *The Linden tree* or *Evening bells*, the sparkle of the folksongs or the sheer bravura of items like *In the moonlight*, which gets steadily faster and louder, or in Rimsky's famous piece (sounding like a hive full of bumblebees), this is irresistible, and the recording is superbly real in its CD format.

Perlman, Itzhak (violin)

'A la carte' (with Abbey Road Ens., Lawrence Foster): MASSENET: *Thaïs: Méditation.* GLAZUNOV: *Mazurka-Obéreque; Méditation, Op. 32.* RACHMANINOV: *Vocalise, Op. 34/14.* SARASATE: *Zigeunerweisen, Op. 20; Introduction and Tarantelle, Op. 43.* RIMSKY-KORSAKOV: *Russian fantasy* (arr. KREISLER). TCHAIKOVSKY: *Scherzo, Op. 42/2* (orch. Glazunov). WIENIAWSKI: *Légende, Op. 17.* KREISLER: *The old refrain; Schön Rosmarin.*

**(*) EMI Dig. CDC5 55475-2 [id.].
Perlman is in his element in this luscious concert of
mostly Russian lollipops – although, as it happens,
the most delectable playing of all comes in the
Sarasate *Zigeunerweisen*. But the pieces by Glazunov, Tchaikovsky's sparkling *Scherzo* and the
Rimsky-Korsakov *Fantasy* also show the extraordinary range of colour and sheer charisma of this
fiddling. Alas, as always, the violin is too closely
balanced, and this is most disadvantageous in the
Wieniawski *Légende*, which loses much of its romantic atmosphere. Perlman's closing solo encore,
Kreisler's *Schön Rosmarin*, ends the programme
with extraordinary panache. Otherwise Lawrence
Foster accompanies discreetly.

'Concertos from my childhood' (with Juilliard
Orchestra, Lawrence Foster): RIEDING: *Violin
concerto in B min., Op. 25.* SEITZ:
Schuler-Konzert No. 2, Op. 13 (orch. ADOLPHE).
ACCOLAY: *Violin concerto No. 1 in A min.*
BERIOT: *Scenes de ballet, Op. 100.* VIOTTI: *Violin
concerto No. 22 in A min.*
*** EMI Dig. CDC5 56750-2 [id.].
Itzhak Perlman here returns in nostalgia to the concertos which, from the age of six onwards, helped
to shape his phenomenal technique. None of this is
great music, not even the longest and best-known
piece, the Viotti *Violin concerto No. 22.* But playing
with obvious love, Perlman brings out freshness
and sparkle in each of them. He turns even passing
banalities into moments of joy. Oscar Rieding and
Friedrich Seitz are so obscure that even their dates
seem to be unknown, yet their miniature concertos
here are totally charming, with Perlman springing
rhythms infectiously. The student orchestra plays
brilliantly too.

'The Art of Itzhak Perlman' (with Israel PO,
Mehta; Pittsburgh SO, Previn; LPO, Ozawa; RPO,
Foster; also Ashkenazy, Bruno Canino, Samuel
Sanders, Previn (piano) and other artists): BACH:
Concerto, BWV 1056; Partita No. 3, BWV 1006.
VIVALDI: *Concerto, RV 199.* MOZART: *Oboe
quartet, K.370.* BRAHMS: *Sonata No. 3;
Hungarian dances 1–2, 7 & 9.* SINDING: *Suite,
Op. 10.* WIENIAWSKI: *Concerto No. 1.* SIBELIUS:
Concerto. KHACHATURIAN: *Concerto.*
KORNGOLD: *Concerto.* STRAVINSKY: *Suite
italienne.* ANON.: *Doyna.* YELLENPOLLACK: *My
Yiddishe Momma.* FOSTER arr. HEIFETZ): *The Old
folks at home.* PONCE arr. HEIFETZ): *Estrellita.*
JOPLIN: *The Rag-time dance; Pineapple rag.*
SMETANA: *Zdomoviny.* KREISLER: *Liebesfreud;
Liebesleid.* RACHMANINOV (arr. PRESSGINGOLD):
Vocalise. GRAINGER: *Molly on the shore.* PREVIN:
Look at him; Bowing and scraping. TRAD. (arr.
KREISLER): *Londonderry air.* SARASATE: *Carmen
fantasy.*
(M) *** EMI Analogue/Dig. CMS7 64617-2 (4)
    [ZDMD 64617].

This box contains a feast of this great violinist's
recordings. He made the choice himself and, while
the concertos, particularly the Wieniawski,
Sibelius, Khachaturian and Korngold (and not forgetting the dazzling concertante *Carmen fantasy* of
Sarasate or the *Suite* of Sinding), are all indispensable, the shorter pieces on the last disc just as
readily display the Perlman magic. They include
the delectable jazz collaboration with Previn, the
beautifully played Kreisler encores, and many
popular items which are readily turned into lollipops. The stylish account of the Stravinsky *Suite
italienne* which ends disc three is also one of the
highlights of the set. For the most part the recordings
have the violin very forwardly balanced, but that
was Perlman's own choice; the sound is otherwise
generally excellent.

'Great romantic violin concertos' (with (i)
Chicago SO or (ii) Philh. O, Giulini; (iii) Concg.
O, Haitink; (iv) RPO, Lawrence Foster; (v) Phd.
O, Ormandy): (i) BRAHMS: *Concerto in D, Op. 77.*
(iii) BRUCH: *Concerto No. 1 in G min., Op. 26.* (ii)
BEETHOVEN: *Concerto in D, Op. 61.* (iv)
PAGANINI: *Concerto No. 1 in D, Op. 6.* (iii)
MENDELSSOHN: *Concerto in E min., Op. 64.* (v)
TCHAIKOVSKY: *Concerto in D, Op. 35.*
(M) **(*) EMI Analogue/Dig. CMS7 64922-2 (3)
    [ZDMC 64922].
These major Perlman recordings include his earlier
(1980) studio recording of the Beethoven *Concerto*;
it is among the most commanding of his readings
and the element of slight understatement, the refusal
to adopt too romantically expressive a style, makes
for a compelling strength, perfectly matched by
Giulini's thoughtful, direct accompaniment. The
(1976) Brahms is also a distinguished performance,
again finely supported by Giulini, this time with the
Chicago Orchestra, a reading of darker hue than is
customary, with a thoughtful and searching slow
movement rather than the autumnal rhapsody which
it so often becomes. The (1983) Bruch *G minor
Concerto* must be counted a disappointment, however, not helped by the harsh, early digital recording
which gives an edge to the solo timbre. The performance is heavily expressive and, like the Mendelssohn (recorded at the same time), is not nearly
as spontaneous as Perlman's earlier, analogue
recording with Previn. The Paganini (1971) is one
of Perlman's very finest records and, although the
traditional cuts are observed, the performance has
irresistible panache and has been transferred to CD
very well. In the Tchaikovsky (1978) the soloist
is placed less aggressively forward than is usual.
Perlman's expressive warmth goes with a very bold
orchestral texture from Ormandy and the Philadelphia Orchestra. However, admirers of these artists
are unlikely to be disappointed.

'Cinema serenade': Film themes (with Pittsburg
SO, John Williams): TEMPERTON/ROSENBAUM:

The Colour Purple. GARDEL: *Scent of a Woman (Tango).* Elmer BERNSTEIN: *The Age of Innocence.* John WILLIAMS: *Far and Away; Sabrina; Schindler's List.* LEGRAND: *The Umbrellas of Cherbourg.* PREVIN: *The Four Horsemen of the Apocalypse.* John BARRY: *Out of Africa.* BONFA: *Black Orpheus.*
*** Sony Dig. SK 63005 [id.].

Over the centuries all the great violin virtuosi have indulged themselves with the popular tunes of the day, and in our time quite a few of the best of them come from film scores. Perlman relishes their melodiousness, playing them with an easy sophistication and an unashamed tonal succulence. He is immediately beguiling in the title theme from *The Colour Purple* and then dances to the tango rhythms of *Pur una cabeza* from *Scent of a Woman.*

Most of these concertante arrangements have been skilfully managed by John Williams, and in his own score for *Far and Away,* he has created a sparkling scherzando to offset the lyrical melody. *Il Postero* and *Sabrina* bring a more delicate charm, but Elmer Bernstein's music for *The Age of Innocence* and John Barry's score for *Out of Africa* develop a Hollywoodian orchestral opulence. The engaging tune Michel Legrand was inspired to write for *The Umbrellas of Cherbourg* seems custom-made for Perlman's stylish languor, and for contrast *Black Orpheus* brings a more intimate duet for violin and guitar.

But our own favourite is the charmingly romantic music Andrea Morricone wrote for *Cinema Paradiso,* a nostalgic score for one of the more memorable films of the last decade. But there is too little of it, and there would have been room for more. Throughout, the easy bravura and panache of the solo playing recall Heifetz, and Williams and the excellent Pittsburg Orchestra provide spectacular accompaniments. The recording is spacious with Perlman (as usual), upfront in a spotlight; the orchestra is full and warm, but could be better focused.

Petri, Michaela (recorder)

'English concertos' (with Academy of St Martin-in-the-Fields, directed K. Sillito): BABEL: *Concerto in C for descant recorder, Op. 3/1.* HANDEL: *Concerto in B flat for treble recorder and bassoon, Op. 4/6* (with G. Sheene). BASTON: *Concerto No. 2 for descant recorder in D.* JACOB: *Suite for treble recorder and strings.*
✿ *** Ph. (IMS) Dig. 411 056-2 [id.].

The *Concerto* by William Babel (c. 1690–1723) is a delight, with Petri's sparkling performance of the outer movements full of good humour and high spirits, matched by Kenneth Sillito's alert accompaniments. The Handel is yet another arrangement of Op. 4/6, with the organ part felicitously re-scored

for recorder and bassoon. The two instruments are nicely balanced and thus a familiar work is given an attractive new look. John Baston's *Concerto* has individuality and charm, and the finale is quirkily infectious. Gordon Jacob's *Suite* of seven movements balances a gentle bitter-sweet melancholy in the lyrical writing with a rumbustious, extrovert quality in the dances. Altogether a highly rewarding concert, beautifully played and recorded.

'The ultimate recorder collection': VIVALDI: *The Four Seasons: Spring* (with Guildhall String Ens., George Malcolm). *Concerto in D (Il gardellino), Op. 10/3: Finale. Concerto in G min. (La Notte), Op. 10/2, RV 439.* SAMMARTINI: *Recorder concerto in F* (all with Moscow Virtuosi, Vladimir Spivakov). SATIE: *Gymnopédie No. 1.* GLUCK: *Orfeo: Melody & Dance of the Blessed Spirits.* BACH: *Suite in D, BWV 1067: Air.* SCHEINDIENST: *Variations.* TARTINI: *Sonata in G min. (Devil's trill).* KOPPEL: *Nele's dances Nos. 15–18.* JACOB: *An encore for Michaela* (all with Lars Hannibal, arr. for recorder and guitar). GRIEG: *Peer Gynt: Solveig's song; Anitra's dance. Lyric pieces: Butterfly; Little bird, Op. 43/1 & 4; March of the Trolls, Op. 54/3; Once upon a time, Op. 71/1; 2 Norwegian dances, Op. 35/1–2* (all arr. Langford). KOPPEL: *Moonchild's dream: conclusion.* ARNOLD: *Recorder concerto, Op. 133: Lento.* CHRISTIANSEN: *Dance suite, Op. 29: Molto vivace* (all with ECO, Okko Kamu). HANDEL: *Sonata in G min., Op. 1/2.* BACH: *Sonata in E flat* (transposed G), *BWV 1031* (with Keith Jarrett, harpsichord). TELEMANN: *Trio sonata No. 3 in F min.* (with Hanne Petri, harpsichord, David Petri, cello). *Sonata No. 5 in D min. for 2 recorders* (with Elisabeth Selin). CORELLI: *Concerto grosso, Op. 6/8 (Christmas): Finale* including *Pastorale* (with Nat. PO, Martin Neary). BACH: *Cantata No. 140: Chorale: Wachet auf* (with Westminster Abbey Ch., Alistair Ross, organ; cond. Neary).
(B) ** RCA Twofer 74321 59112-2 (2); *74321 48020-4* [id.].

This is a collection that will best appeal to amateur recorder players, and might make a good birthday present for a young beginner, who will surely be impressed by Michaela Petri's easy virtuosity and will respond to a string of such famous melodies. Not all of them transcribe too well, and many are far more effective on the instruments for which they were written. Vivaldi's *Spring* from *The Four Seasons* is indestructible, but Bach's famous *Air* sounds puny, while Grieg's *Second Norwegian dance* is much better suited to the oboe. However, there is quite a lot of genuine recorder repertoire here, stylishly presented, which hopefully should tempt any budding young soloist to explore further. The recording balance is generally well managed and the effect is truthful and not overblown.

'Scandinavian moods' (with LPO, James Judd & (i) Bo Skovhus): GRIEG: *Peer Gynt (Morning).* *Elegiac melody: The last spring.* ALFVEN: *Theme from Midsummer Vigil.* LOVLAND: *Nocturne.* TRAD.: *Oh Värmland, so beautiful; A crow perched high up in a tree; Per Spelman; Paul lets his hen flutter in the garden;* (i) *In the deep calm of the forest.* NIELSEN: *Spinning top; The fog is lifting.* HENRIQUES: *Lullaby; Dance of the mosquitos.* NEUMANN: *Love waltz.* PETERSON-BERGER: *Summersong.* Finn ZIEGLER: *Waltz for you.* TAUBE: *Nocturne.* (i) BELLMAN: *I see the winged butterfly in the garden.* BULL: *The herdgirl's Sunday.* RIEDEL: *I make the flowers bloom.*
*** RCA Dig. 74321 67950-2. [id.].

Michaela Petri here turns to the world of Scandinavian folksong, both arranged and 'composed', and almost all the orchestrations show a good deal of imagination. The only two pieces here that fail to come off really seductively on the recorder are by Grieg, but the famous Alfvén theme (more popularly known as the *Swedish rhapsody*) is a delight, as is Ole Bull's *Herdgirl's Sunday.*

There are many lovely lyrical melodies here which readily respond to Petri's artistry, and the warmly affectionate accompaniments from Judd and and the LPO, not least the haunting *Nocturne* of Rolf Lövland and the similar but more romantic piece of Evert Taube. Nielsen's charming *The fog is lifting* is as atmospheric as the title suggests, and he is also responsible for one of the engaging scherzando pieces, *The spinning top,* which is played with light, tasteful bravura. Two of the items are sung, simply and directly by Bo Skovus.

The traditional *Oh Värmland, so beautiful* turns out to be the source of the famous melody which dominates Smetana's *Vltava.* This is presented in a more extended semi-jazz improvisatory style, with pizzicato double-bass embroidery, and *Paul lets his hen flutter in the garden* responds well to similar treatment. What strikes the ear so often here is how international is the musical vocabulary of folksong. Many of these tunes could have equally well come from Celtic or other geographical sources. But all of them are memorable when so pleasingly played and recorded.

Philadelphia Orchestra, Eugene Ormandy

SAINT-SAENS: *Danse macabre; Samson et Dalila: Bacchanale.* DUKAS: *The Sorcerer's apprentice.* CHABRIER: *España.* MUSSORGSKY (arr. Rimsky-Korsakov): *Night on the bare mountain.* SMETANA: *Bartered Bride: Dance of the comedians.* PONCHIELLI: *La Gioconda: Dance of the hours.* BRAHMS: *Hungarian dance No. 5.*

GLIERE: *Russian sailors' dance.* FALLA: *El amor brujo: Ritual fire dance.* KABALEVSKY: *The Comedians: Galop.*
(M) * RCA High Performance 09026 63313-2 [id.].

It is strange that these low performance recordings should be chosen for RCA's High Performance label. The opening *Danse macabre* never really gets off the ground, though the following *Sorcerer's apprentice* is better, and the *Night on the bare mountain* is quite impressive. Of course, there are nice touches here and there, but a feeling of lassitude pervades. The soupy recording doesn't help either.

Philadelphia Orchestra, Wolfgang Sawallisch

Stokowski orchestral transcriptions: BACH: Chorales from cantatas: *Sheep may safely graze; Wachet auf; Ein 'feste Burg ist unser Gott. Toccata and fugue in D min., BWV 565.* BOCCHERINI: *Minuet, Op. 13/5.* BEETHOVEN: *Piano sonata No. 14 (Moonlight): 1st movt.* CHOPIN: *Prelude in E min., Op. 28/4.* FRANCK: *Panis angelicus.* TCHAIKOVSKY: *Andante cantabile, Op. 11; At the ball* (with Marjana Lipovšek). DEBUSSY: *Suite bergamasque: Clair de lune. Prélude: La cathédrale engloutie.* RACHMANINOV: *Prelude in C sharp min., Op. 3/2.*
**(*) EMI Dig. CDC5 55592-2 [id.].

Though Stokowski's own recordings, even those he made in extreme old age, generally have a degree more flair and dramatic bite than any of these from the latterday Philadelphia Orchestra, this makes a fine tribute from the great orchestra he created. The selection of items is an attractive one, not least the Tchaikovsky song orchestration, with Marjana Lipovšek an aptly Slavonic-sounding soloist, though balanced too close.

Sawallisch brings out the evocative magic of Stokowski's impressionistic view of the *Moonlight sonata* movement, and *Clair de lune* is similarly free in its expressiveness. With warm, resonant sound, firmer in the bass than usual from this source, this makes a sumptuous collection, even if some will prefer the brighter, sharper focus of rival Stokowski collections such as Kunzel's on Telarc or Bamert's on Chandos. It is worth noting that Bamert's even more generous selection of fifteen encore pieces overlaps in only three items, and it includes more fun pieces.

Philadelphia Orchestra, Leopold Stokowski

(see also under **Stokowski RCA Edition**)

'Fantasia': BACH, orch. Stokowski: *Toccata and Fugue in D min.* DUKAS: *L'apprenti sorcier.* MUSSORGSKY, arr. Stokowski: *Night on the bare mountain.* STRAVINSKY: *The Rite of spring.* TCHAIKOVSKY: *Nutcracker suite.*

(M) (***) Pearl mono GEMMCD 4988.

A self-recommending disc. *The Rite of spring* comes from 1929–30 and the *Nutcracker* from as early as 1926, though one would never believe it. Everything Stokowski did at this period was full of character, and the engineers obviously performed miracles. The latest recording is Stokowski's amazing arrangement of *Night on the bare mountain*, which dates from 1940. Such is the colour and richness of sonority Stokowski evokes from the fabulous Philadelphians that surface noise and other limitations are completely forgotten. The transfers are very good.

'Philadelphia rarities' (1928–1937): arr. STOKOWSKI: *2 Ancient liturgical melodies: Veni, Creator Spiritus; Veni, Emmanuel.* FALLA: *La vida breve: Spanish dance.* TURINA: *Gypsy dance, Op. 55/5.* DUBENSKY: *Edgar Allan Poe's 'The Raven'* (narr. Benjamin DE LOACHE). arr. KONOYE: *Etenraku: Ceremonial Japanese prelude.* MCDONALD: *The legend of the Arkansas traveller; The Festival of the workers (suite): Dance of the workers. Double piano concerto* (with Jeanne Behrend & Alexander Kelberine). EICHHEIM: *Oriental impressions: Japanese nocturne. Symphonic variations: Bali.* SOUSA: *Manhattan Beach; El Capitan.*

(M) (***) Cala mono CACD 0501 [id.].

All these recordings show what splendid recorded sound Stokowski was achieving in Philadelphia as early as 1929. The opening Stokowski liturgical arrangements show how that master of orchestral sonority could make liturgical chants his very own, with a discreet tolling bell to indicate their source. Falla's *Spanish dance* shows him at his most sparklingly chimerical. Dubensky's music does not add a great deal to Edgar Allan Poe, but the narrator, Benjamin de Loache, certainly does, presenting the narrative with the essentially genial, melodramatic lubricity of Vincent Price.

Hidemaro Konoye and Stokowski and his players conspire between them to provide an extraordinarily authentic Japanese sound in *Etenraku*, and then in *The legend of the Arkansas traveller* we have a complete change of local colour for Alexander Hilsberg's folksy, sub-country-and-western violin solo. Henry Eichheim's Japanese and Balinese impressions are suitably exotic, but not music one would wish to return to. As for Harl McDonald's

Double piano concerto, the piano writing is splashy and the finale is spectacularly based on the *Juarezca*, a jazzy Mexican dance.

The two soloists provide convincing, extrovert dash, and Stokowski obviously revels in what Noël Coward might have described as 'potent cheap music' if with nothing like the melodic appeal of Coward's own work. The two Sousa marches have both poise and élan, but here the sound is barely adequate – not the fault of the CD transfer. The programme lasts for 78 minutes and Stokowksi *aficionados* need not hesitate.

Philharmonia Orchestra, Robert Irving

'Great ballet music': ADAM: *Giselle: highlights.* CHOPIN: *Les Sylphides* (arr. Roy Douglas). DELIBES: *Sylvia (suite); Coppélia (suite)* (both with Yehudi Menuhin). SCHUMANN: *Carnaval, Op. 9.*

(BB) *** Royal Long Players DCL 70577-2 (2).

These recordings date from 1959/61 when Robert Irving, one of very finest English ballet conductors, was Music Director at Sadler's Wells (later Royal) Ballet. He went on to the New York City Ballet. He chose some 40 minutes from the older European score of *Giselle* and with first-class playing from the Philharmonia his approach is strikingly fresh and graceful. He is more indulgently languorous in Roy Douglas's miraculous orchestration of *Les Sylphides*, but again the playing is warmly seductive, and he is at his most imaginative in the two Delibes suites (music which Tchaikovsky so much admired), where Menuhin provides elegant solos in the two *Pas de deux*.

The scoring of *Carnaval* is by many hands, including Arensky, Rimsky-Korsakov and Liadov; if it is less effective than *Sylphides*, it is still worth having on CD. Altogether this is an outstanding set, beautifully recorded in an attractive ambience, with sound that is not in the least dated, indeed is more natural than many modern digital recordings. A real bargain at this low asking price.

Philharmonia or New Philharmonia Orchestra, Otto Klemperer

'Portrait of Klemperer': BACH: *Brandenburg concerto No. 2, BWV 1047.* MOZART: *Symphony No. 36 in C (Linz), K.425.* BEETHOVEN: *Choral fantasia, Op. 80* (with Daniel Barenboim & New Philharmonia Chorus); *Symphony No. 6 (Pastoral): Finale (Shepherds' hymn).* BRAHMS: *Academic festival overture.* MENDELSSOHN:

Symphony No. 4 (Italian). SCHUBERT: *Symphony No. 8 (Unfinished).*

(BB) *** Royal Long Players DCL 705932 (2).

Klemperer's account of the *Second Brandenburg* brings strangely slack discipline, and the slow speeds tend to plod. Not everyone will respond either to his account of the *Linz Symphony*, which although well played ideally needs a lighter touch: the slow movement lacks the kind of gracious quality that Beecham can bring to it when using a full modern orchestra. But the rest of the programme is well worth having. The *Choral fantasia* and *Academic festival overture* are splendidly alive, while both the exhilarating *Italian Symphony* (marvellously played, yet never rushed off its feet) and the Schubert are among his finest recordings. Klemperer's approach to the *Unfinished* is utterly individual. It is seen as a powerfully romantic symphonic structure, and he inspires his players to keen, alert playing that never lets the music sag and reveals Schubert's score as a supreme masterpiece. The *Shepherd's hymn* from the *Pastoral Symphony* makes a glowingly exultant coda.

Philharmonia Orchestra, Nicolai Malko

BORODIN: *Prince Igor: Overture; Polovtsian dances; Polovtsian march. Symphony No. 2 in A min.* RIMSKY-KORSAKOV: *Maid of Pskov (Ivan the Terrible): Overture.* LIADOV: *8 Russian folksongs.* GLAZUNOV (with Sokolov and Liadov): *Les vendredis: Polka.*

(**) Testament mono/stereo SBT1062 [id.].

Nicolai Malko, from 1926 the chief conductor of the Leningrad Philharmonic and the first interpreter of Shostakovich's *First Symphony*, made all too few recordings; though some of these with the Philharmonia lack tautness, his feeling for the Slavonic idiom is unerring. This reading of the *Prince Igor* overture is light and transparent (in newly unearthed stereo) but lacks dramatic bite, and so do the *Polovtsian dances*, polished but not involving. The *Polovtsian march* is quite different: a tense, swaggering performance which reveals the true Malko. Then after an amiable, low-key account of the first movement of the Borodin symphony, the Scherzo second movement brings a virtuoso performance. Best of all is the Rimsky-Korsakov overture, in full-bodied stereo. After a relaxed, colourful account of the Liadov *Folksongs*, the corporately written *Polka* makes a charming encore, an Elgar-like salon piece.

Philharmonia Orchestra, Igor Markevitch

'Orchestral portrait': BARTOK: *Dance suite.* RAVEL: *La valse.* SATIE: *Parade.* BUSONI: *Tänzwalzer.* LIADOV: *Kikimora.* CHABRIER: *Le roi malgré lui: Fête polonaise.* LISZT: *Mephisto waltz.*

(***) Testament (mono) SBT 1060 [id.].

The seven varied items here make an illuminating portrait of a conductor who at the time seemed destined to be more central in the world of recording than he became. With immaculate transfers the 1950s mono recordings have astonishing vividness and presence. In the effervescent account of Satie's *Parade* (sadly cut in the last movement) the brass and percussion (including the celebrated typewriter) have wonderful bite, and so have the joyful brass fanfares at the start of the Chabrier *Polonaise*, done in Viennese style. Perhaps most vivid of all is the virtuoso performance of the *Mephisto waltz*.

Pierlot, Pierre (oboe)

'The magic of the oboe' (with Sol. Ven., Scimone; or Paillard CO, Jean-François Paillard): VIVALDI: *Concertos in C, RV 452; F, RV 455.* ALBINONI: *Concerto a cinque in D min., Op. 9/2.* CIMAROSA: *Concerto* (arr. BENJAMIN). ZIPOLI: *Adagio for oboe, cello, organ and strings* (arr. GIOVANNINI). MARCELLO: *Concerto in C min.* BELLINI: *Concerto.*

(M) *** Erato/Warner 4509 92130-2.

For once, a record company's sobriquet for a collection does not disappoint: this is indeed a magical and very generous (74 minutes) collection, well recorded. One might say the cream of baroque oboe concertos are included here, and Benjamin's arrangement of movements by Cimarosa with its delightful central *Siciliano* and spiccato finale as engaging as any. The Albinoni and Marcello concertos have memorable slow movements, too, and the Bellini a catchy Polacca finale. The novelty is Zipoli's *Adagio*, sumptuously arranged by Francesco Giovannini after the manner of Giazotto's 'Albinoni *Adagio*'. It doesn't quite come off, but it is a very near miss. Throughout, Pierlot's sweet, finely focused timbre and graceful phrasing are a constant pleasure.

Piffaro (The Renaissance Band), Joan Kimball and Robert Wiemken

'A Flemish feast': Anonymous Flemish melodies from the late 15th and early 16th centuries and

music by: Pierre DE LA RUE; OBRECHT; AGRICOLA; LAPICIDA; SUSATO; GHISELIN; Clemens NON PAPA; TYLING; PULLOIS; BRASSART.
**(*) DG Dig. 457 609-2 [id.].

No one could accuse Piffaro of a lack of instrumental resources or imagination in conjecturally recreating this early music, using bagpipes, recorders, crumhorns, shawms, sackbuts, dulcian, hurdy-gurdy, lute and harp. The music itself is both piquant and sonorous, gay and expressive. But some intervening vocal items are sorely needed to make this a more varied entertainment, and Joan Kimball and Robert Wiemken do not compensate the listener (as David Munrow could and did) by creating bizarre combinations of sounds to add a touch of humour to the aural palette.

Radio Television Eireann Concert Orchestra, Dublin, Ernest Tomlinson

'British light music – Miniatures': Anthony COLLINS: Vanity Fair. Mark LUBBOCK: Polka dots. Armstrong GIBBS: Dusk. Benjamin FRANKEL: Carriage and pair. Vivian ELLIS: Coronation Scot. Arthur BENJAMIN: Jamaican song; Jamaican rumba. Robert DOCKER: Tabarinage. ELGAR: Beau Brummel. Harry DEXTER: Siciliano. Ken WARNER: Scrub, brothers scrub! Gordon JACOB: Cradle song. Thomas ARNE, arr. TOMLINSON: Georgian suite: Gavotte. Gilbert VINTER: Portuguese party. Geoffrey TOYE: The Haunted ballroom (concert waltz). Edward WHITE: Puffin' Billy. George MELACHRINO: Starlight Roof waltz. Clive RICHARDSON: Beachcomber.
**(*) Marco Polo Dig. 8.223522 [id.].

Anthony Collins was right to be proud of his delightful vignette 'Vanity Fair', for its theme is indelible, and it comes up very freshly here in a programme of unassuming orchestral lollipops, including many items with almost equally catchy musical ideas, even a Gavotte by Thomas Arne, arranged by the conductor to sound just a little like a caricature. The tunes are usually pithy and short, like Harry Dexter's daintily wispy Siciliano, but sometimes the writing is gently evocative, like the two romantic waltzes, Dusk by Armstrong Gibbs, and Geoffrey Toye's Haunted ballroom, and Gordon Jacob's delicate Cradle song.

Novelties like Benjamin Frankel's clip-clopping Carriage and pair, Edward White's Puffin' Billy, and Ken Warner's moto perpetuo, Scrub, brothers scrub! readily evoke the world of Leroy Anderson, while Clive Richardson's quirky Beachcomber makes one want to smile. The conductor, Ernest

Tomlinson, understands that their very slightness is part of the charm of nearly all these pieces, and he presents them with a simplicity that is wholly endearing. The only relative disappointment is Vivian Ellis's wittily evoked Coronation Scot, which needs much more verve than it receives here. Good playing and good recording, although the acoustic effect noticeably becomes more brash for the second item, Mark Lubbock's breezy Polka dots.

Rahbari, Sohre (saxophone), Belgian Radio and TV Orchestra, Brussels, Alexander Rahbari

Music for saxophone and orchestra: MILHAUD: Scaramouche (suite). GLAZUNOV: Concerto in E flat, Op. 109. DEBUSSY: Rapsodie. IBERT: Concertino da camera. MUSSORGSKY: Pictures at an exhibition: The old castle. Sohre RAHBARI: Japanese improvisation for solo saxophones (BB) ** Naxos 8.554784 [id.].

The Ibert is the most successful piece here and the concertante version of Scaramouche works well too, with its lively quotation of 'Ten green bottles', but the Glazunov rather outstays its welcome. Sohre Rahbari is a fine player and responds to Debussy's exoticism with an attractive freedom of line. Alexander Rahbari is at his best and the Belgian Orchestra gives quite persuasive support, although their playing could be more refined. The recording is good, but rather resonant. Value for money, but not distinctive.

Rampal, Jean-Pierre (flute)

'20th-century flute masterpieces' (with (i) LOP, Froment; (ii) O de L'ORTF, Martinon; (iii) LOP, Jolivet; (iv) Robert Veyron-Lacroix): (i) IBERT: Concerto. (ii) KHACHATURIAN: Concerto (arr. from Violin concerto). (iii) JOLIVET: Concerto. (iv) MARTINU: Sonata. HINDEMITH: Sonata. PROKOFIEV: Sonata in D. POULENC: Sonata. (M) **(*) Erato/Warner 2292 45839-2 (2) [id.].

The concertos on the first CD have less than perfectly focused orchestral strings, and the Khachaturian arrangement is dispensable. But the Ibert Concerto is winning and the more plangent Jolivet not inconsiderable. The highlights of the collection are all on the second disc, three out of the four of them inspired works delightfully written for the instrument and marvellously played. Only the first movement of the Hindemith is a bit below par in its utilitarian austerity; the cool slow movement and more vigorous finale have something approaching charm. The Prokofiev Sonata (also heard in a version for violin – but the flute is the original) is a masterpiece, and Rampal makes the very most of it. Then comes the delightful Poulenc piece with its disarmingly easy-flowing opening, delicious central cantilena and scintillating finale with hints of *Les Biches*. The recording of the sonatas, made in 1978, is vividly firm and realistic. If this set is reissued later on a Bonsai Duo, it will be well worth seeking out.

Reilly, Tommy (harmonica)

'Harmonica concertos' (with (i) Munich RSO, Gerhardt; (ii) Basel RSO, Dumont; (iii) SW German RO, Smola; (iv) Munich RSO, Farnon; (v) Farnon O, Farnon): (i) SPIVAKOVSKY: *Harmonica concerto*. (ii) ARNOLD: *Harmonica concerto, Op. 46*. (iii) VILLA-LOBOS: *Harmonica concerto*. (iv) MOODY: *Toledo (Spanish fantasy)*. (v) FARNON: *Prelude and dance*.
*** Chandos Dig. CHAN 9248 [id.].

This is most attractive. The Spivakovsky is a particularly winning piece, with a catchy tune in the first movement, rather like a Leroy Anderson encore, a popular, romantic central interlude, marked *Dolce*, and a delicious moto perpetuo finale. Not surprisingly, the Malcolm Arnold is very appealing too, one of this composer's best miniature concertos, written in 1954 for the BBC Proms. The Villa-Lobos, written in 1955, should be much better known. Scored for a small orchestra of strings, single wind, harp, celesta and percussion, it has a neo-classical character. It produces a quite lovely melody for the *Andante*; only the finale, which moves along at a genial pace, has piquant hints of the composer's usual Brazilian preoccupation. James Moody's *Spanish fantasy* might be described as good cheap music, and it offers the soloist a glittering chance to demonstrate his bravura with infectious panache. Farnon's hauntingly nostalgic *Prelude and dance* (a charmingly inconsequential little waltz) brings a felicitous interleaving of both themes. The recording balance is surely as near perfect as one could wish.

Rostropovich, Mstislav (cello)

'The Rostropovich Edition': Cello concertos: DVORAK: *Concerto in B min., Op. 104* (with LPO, Giulini). BRAHMS: *Double concerto for violin and cello in A min., Op. 102* (with David Oistrakh, Cleveland O, Szell). HAYDN: *Cello concertos in C & D, Hob VIIb/1–2* (with ASMF, Marriner). BLOCH: *Schelomo* (with O Nat. de France, Bernstein). Richard STRAUSS: *Don Quixote, Op. 35* (with BPO, Karajan). MIASKOVSKY: *Cello concerto in C min., Op. 66* (with Philh. O, Sargent).

(M) **(*) EMI (SIS) CMS5 65701-2 (3) [ZDMC 65701].

Rostropovich recorded the Dvořák *Concerto* three times before this version (with Talich, Boult and Karajan), and this 1977 EMI performance is his least successful on record. He makes heavy weather of most of the concerto, and his unrelieved emotional intensity is matched by Giulini, who focuses attention on beauty of detail rather than structural cohesion. Even so, there are many incidental beauties that compel admiration, and the engineering is impressive.

The Brahms *Double concerto* (recorded eight years earlier in Cleveland with David Oistrakh and Szell) is a different matter altogether and can be counted among the most powerful and eloquent performances on record (in the same league as Heifetz/Feuermann and Thibaud/Casals). In Bloch's *Hebraic rhapsody* the collaboration of Rostropovich and Bernstein is a triumph. The ripe expressiveness of both artists blends superbly, so that the rhapsodic flow conveys total concentration, from the deeply meditative opening phrases (*con somma espressione*) onwards. The recording is ripe to match, but spotlights the soloist.

The two solo Haydn *Concertos*, which date from 1975, are more controversial. Rostropovich's earlier recording of the *C major Concerto* with Britten was brilliant enough but, at even faster speeds in the outer movements, his virtuosity in the EMI performance is astonishing. However, apart from the extra haste (which brings its moments of breathless phrasing), both here and in the more familiar *D major Concerto*, there is a degree of self-indulgence in the warmth of expressiveness.

However, the Karajan/Rostropovich *Don Quixote*, which came a year later, rights the balance. It is predictably fine and its only failing is a tendency for Rostropovich to dominate the aural picture. He dominates artistically too. His Don is superbly characterized and the expressiveness and richness of tone he commands are a joy in themselves. There are moments when one wonders whether the intensity of his response does not lead to an over-emphatic tone, but in general both the cello and viola soloists and the Berlin orchestra under Karajan silence criticism. In many ways the Miaskovsky *Concerto*, the earliest recording here (1956), is the most valuable item of all, and Rostropovich's recording with Sir Malcolm Sargent remains unsurpassed.

'The Russian years'

BEETHOVEN: *Triple concerto in C, Op. 56* (with David Oistrakh, Sviatoslav Richter, Moscow PO, Kondrashin). SCHUMANN: *Cello concerto, Op. 129*. TCHAIKOVSKY: *Variations on a rococo theme, Op. 33* (both with USSR State O, Rozhdestvensky). STRAVINSKY: *Mavra: Russian song. Baiser de la fée: Pas de deux*. MILHAUD:

Saudades do Brasil: Tijuca. FALLA: *El amor brujo: Ritual fire dance.* SINDING: *Suite im alten Stil, Op. 10: Presto.* FAURE: *Après un rêve.* DEBUSSY: *Clair de lune; Nocturne & Scherzo.* POPPER: *Dance of the Elves.* SCHUBERT: *Impromptu in G flat, D.899/3* (trans. HEIFETZ/ROSTROPOVICH). HANDEL: *Sonata in D, HWV 371: Larghetto.* PROKOFIEV: *Cinderella: Adagio* (all with Alexander Dedyukhin, piano). *Waltz-Coda. Love for 3 Oranges: March* (with Alexei Zybtsev, piano). SCRIABIN: *Etude in B flat min., Op. 8/11.* DVORAK: *Silent woods.* R. STRAUSS: *An einsamer Quelle.* SHAPORIN: *Romance: I see you; Elegy* (with Vladimir Yampolsky, piano); *Scherzo, Op. 25/5* (with Aza Amintayeva, piano).
(M) (**(*)) EMI mono CZS5 72294-2 (2) [id.].
SHOSTAKOVICH: *Cello concertos Nos. 1 in E flat, Op. 107* (with Moscow PO, Rozhdestvensky); *2 in G, Op. 126* (with USSR State SO, Svetlanov). *Cello sonata in D min., Op. 40* (with composer, piano). KABALEVSKY: *Cello sonata in B flat, Op. 71* (with composer, piano). Karen KHACHATURIAN: *Cello sonata* (with composer, piano).
(M) (**(*)) EMI mono CZS5 72295-2 (2) [id.].
PROKOFIEV: *Cello sonata in C, Op. 119* (with Sviatoslav Richter, piano); *Symphony-concerto for cello and orchestra in E min., Op. 125* (with Israel Gusman & Rozhdestvensky); *Cello concertino, Op. 132* (orch. Kabalevsky) (with Moscow R & TV O, Rozhdestvensky). TANEIEV: *Canzona* (with Alexander Dedyukhin, piano). MIASKOVSKY: *Cello concerto in C min., Op. 66.* GLAZUNOV: *Concerto ballata, Op. 108* (both with USSR State SO, Svetlanov).
(M) (**(*)) EMI mono CZS5 72296-2 (2) [id.].
BRITTEN: *Suites Nos. 1–2 for solo cello, Op. 72 & Op. 80. Symphony for cello and orchestra* (with Moscow PO, composer). VILLA-LOBOS: *Bachianas brasileiras No. 1: Prelúdio for 8 cellos* (Rostropovich, cello/director). RESPIGHI: *Adagio con variazioni.* R. STRAUSS: *Don Quixote, Op. 35* (both with Moscow PO, Kondrashin). HONEGGER: *Cello concerto* (with USSR State SO, Dubrovsky).
(M) (***) EMI mono CZS5 72297-2 (2) [id.].
LOPES-GRACA: *Concerto da càmera* (with Moscow PO, Kondrashin). KNIPPER: *Concerto-monologue for cello, 7 brass instruments and two kettledrums.* VAINBERG: *Cello concerto, Op. 43* (with USSR State SO, Rozhdestvensky). TISHCHENKO: *Concerto for cello, seventeen wind instruments, percussion & organ, Op. 23* (with Leningrad PO, Blazhkov). KHACHATURIAN: *Concert-rhapsody* (with Aza Amintayeva, piano). TOYAMA: *Cello concerto* (with Moscow R & TV O, composer).
(M) (**(*)) EMI mono CZS5 72298-2 (2) [id.].
In 1997 EMI marked the 70th birthday of Mstislav

Rostropovich with an ambitious, celebratory survey called 'The Russian Recordings – 1950–74', which consisted of thirteen discs (EMI CZS5 72016-2) from which the present five two-CD sets are drawn. Rostropovich chose them himself from archival recordings in Russia. They range from such relatively familiar records as the 1964 Moscow première of Benjamin Britten's *Symphony for cello and orchestra*, which is available in other transfers, to more rare material like Moshei (now Mieczyslaw) Vainberg's *Cello concerto* and Tishchenko's *Concerto*, both dedicated to the great Russian cellist – as are many other pieces on these discs. All the performances are three star but the sound does not always do justice to his glorious tone.

CZS5 72294-2 brings commanding performances of the Beethoven *Triple concerto* with Oistrakh and Richter – made in 1970 just before the famous Karajan version – and the Schumann *A minor Concerto* and Tchaikovsky *Rococo variations*, both with Rozhdestvensky from 1960. These come with shorter pieces mainly recorded in the 1960s. Incomparable playing but variable recorded sound.

CZS5 72295-2 concentrates on Shostakovich and includes a 1961 concert performance of the *First Cello concerto* and the very first performance of the *Second*, in 1966, given under Svetlanov and in the presence of the composer, who was celebrating his 61st birthday. The accompanying sonatas were all recorded with their respective composers, though no date is given for the Shostakovich. Rostropovich recalls that some tempi are on the brisk side: 'it was a beautiful day and Shostakovich was anxious to visit friends in the country'. The performance sounds identical to the one issued in the USA in 1958 on the Monitor label (MC 2021), though the sound has been rebalanced.

CZS5 72296-2 is mainly given over to Prokofiev. The *Symphony-concerto,* or as it is usually called, *Sinfonia concertante*, Op. 125, is a compilation, the first movement coming from a 1972 performance and the rest from 1964, both in the same hall. This set also includes the 1950 account of the *Cello sonata* with Richter made in Prokofiev's presence (which also appeared on MC 2021). The 1964 record of the Miaskovsky *Concerto* with Svetlanov conducting (the Glazunov comes from the same concert) is very fine, though not as well recorded as his early EMI recording with Sargent.

CZS5 72297-2 is self-recommending in bringing together the première of Benjamin Britten's *Cello Symphony* and two of the solo cello suites. Honegger's delightful 1929 concerto, and the Respighi *Adagio con variazione* are not to be missed either. The Honegger concerto comes off beautifully, and this is the set to go for if you want just one of these reissues, though it is a pity that space could not have been found for Sauguet's charming concerto (*Mélodie concertante*). EMI once coupled this with the Tishchenko *Concerto for cello, seventeen wind instruments, percussion and organ*, which is included on the last set.

CZS5 72298-2 offers a number of Russian works from the Soviet era. The finest piece on the last pair of discs is the Vainberg concerto rather than the somewhat unrewarding Tishchenko and Khachaturian concertos.

If you see copies of the thirteen-CD set still in circulation, it should be given priority. It includes Miaskovksy's *Second Cello sonata* with that superb pianist Alexander Dedyukhin, as well as the Chopin *Sonata*. (R. L. recalls hearing this partnership in a BBC Home Service Thursday Concert in the early 1960s, when their Chopin playing was as distinguished as any he had ever heard.) It also includes three other works dedicated to Rostropovich, Schnittke's *Second Sonata* of 1994, Galina Ustvolskaya's *Grand Duet* and *Le Grand Tango* by Astor Piazzolla.

'*Masterpieces for cello*' (with various orchestras and conductors): BERNSTEIN: *3 Meditations for cello and orchestra* (from *Mass*). BOCCHERINI: *Cello concerto No. 2*. GLAZUNOV: *Chant du Ménestrel*. SHOSTAKOVICH: *Cello concerto No. 2*. TARTINI: *Cello concerto*. TCHAIKOVSKY: *Andante cantabile; Variations on a rococo theme*. VIVALDI: *Cello concertos, RV 398 and RV 413*. (B) *** DG Double 437 952-2 (2) [id.].

A self-recommending set, with two CDs for the price of one. Each of the works included is discussed under its Composer entry in our main volume. The only drawback is the inadequate documentation.

Rousseau, Eugene (saxophone), Paul Kuentz Chamber Orchestra, Kuentz

Saxophone concertos: IBERT: *Concertino da camera for alto saxophone and 11 instruments*. GLAZUNOV: *Alto saxophone concerto in E, Op. 109*. VILLA-LOBOS: *Fantasia for soprano saxophone, 3 horns and string orchestra*. DUBOIS: *Concerto for alto saxophone and string orchestra*. (M) *** DG 453 991-2 [id.].

An enterprising anthology. The Glazunov is a late work and the best known and most often recorded of the pieces here. However, both the Villa-Lobos *Fantasia* and the Ibert *Concertino da camera* are as appealing and exotic, and there is much to give pleasure. The longest work is the *Concerto for alto sax* by Max-Pierre Dubois, a pupil of Milhaud: fluent, well crafted and civilized. Eugene Rousseau is an expert and persuasive soloist and the recording, which dates from the early 1970s, is first class.

Royal Ballet Orchestra, David Lloyd-Jones

'*English string miniatures*': RUTTER: *Suite*. Charles ORR: *Cotswold hill tune*. MELACHRINO: *Les jeux*. Peter DODD: *Irish idyll*. Armstrong GIBBS: *Miniature dance suite*. Frank CORDELL: *King Charles's galliard*. David LYON: *Short suite*. Roy DOUGLAS: *Cantilena*. Philip LANE: *Pantomime*. (BB) *** Naxos Dig. 8.554186 [id.].

A delightful collection. John Rutter shows how artfully he can write for strings, using traditional tunes the invigorating '*A-Roving*', the gentle '*I have a bonnet trimmed with blue*', the touchingly simple *O, Waly, Waly* and the fizzing energy of *Dashing away with the smoothing iron*. Much of the other music is permeated with influences from British folksong. Orr's *Cotswold hill tune* and Dodd's flimsy *Irish idyll* have much melodically in common, while George Melachrino's *Les jeux* makes an engaging contrast, a gossamer dance tapestry, alternating with a semi-luscious lyrical tune.

Frank Cordell's melancholy *Galliard*, of noble contour, and the *Miniature dance suite* of Armstrong Gibbs both have a hint of the pastiche flavour of Warlock's *Capriol suite*. The serene *Aria*, the penultimate movement of the equally attractive *Short suite* of David Lyon, shares an evocative link with the longer, gentle *Cantilena* of Roy Douglas. Philip Lane's *Pantomime* is another three-movement miniature suite of dainty charm and energy: its bouncing closing *Vivace* ends the concert winningly. Performances are persuasively polished and vivacious and the Naxos recording is excellent: this disc is rewarding value for money.

Royal Ballet Orchestra, Andrew Penny

'*Welsh classical favourites*': Grace WILLIAMS: *Fantasia on Welsh nursery rhymes*. Walford DAVIES: *Solemn melody*. Gareth WALTERS: *Overture Primavera; A Gwent suite*. Trevor ROBERTS: *Pastorale*. HODDINOTT: *Folksong suite*. Mervyn BURTCH: *Aladdin: overture*. MATHIAS: *Serenade*. Ian PARROTT: *Fanfare overture (for a Somerset festival)*. (BB) *** Naxos Dig. 8.225048 [id.].

The Welsh have a long and enduring vocal and choral heritage. But only in the twentieth century has there been an orchestral tradition, and so Welsh folk melodies had not received the concert-hall exposure of comparable English tunes. Then, in 1940, Grace Williams completed her *Fantasia*, using eight very attractive ideas, arranging them into a kind of pot-pourri, winningly scored. Walford

Davies had preceded her in the 1930s and he left us the famous hymn-like *Solemn melody*. Trevor Roberts's delicate *Pastorale* readily evokes the Pembrokeshire countryside, with a lovely oboe solo and an expressive string climax, somewhat in the manner of George Butterworth.

Alun Hoddinott's *Folksong suite* is similarly felicitously scored. Mervyn Burtch's *Aladdin* concert overture has a syncopated main theme of considerable character, and Gareth Walters's vigorous spring-inspired overture is hardly less spontaneously inventive. The colourful orchestration of the latter's sets of dances is matched in the extrovert finale of Mathias's *Serenade*, where the main theme is presented in constantly changing colours, and in the exuberant opening and closing movements of the Walters *Gwent suite*. All this music is vividly played by Penny and his Royal Ballet Orchestra and given excellent recording, with a flattering ambience. The disc is generously full and good value. Worth exploring.

Royal Ballet Sinfonia, Gavin Sutherland

'Brian Kay's British light music discoveries': ARNOLD: *The Roots of Heaven overture*. ALWYN: *Suite of Scottish dances*. SARGENT: *An impression on a windy day*. PARKER: *Overture: The Glass Slipper*. LANGLEY: *The coloured counties*. JACOB: *Overture: The Barber of Seville goes to town*. JOHNSTONE: *Tarn Hows (Cumbrian rhapsody)*. LANGFORD: *Two worlds (overture)*. R. R. BENNETT: *Little suite*. DYON: *Joie de vivre*.
(M) *** ASV Dig. CDWHL 2113 [id.].

Brian Kay (of BBC Radio 3) has certainly made some felicitous discoveries here: this is a most entertaining programme, summed up perfectly by Ernest Tomlinson's quoted definition of light music as 'where the melody matters more than what you do to it'. There are plenty of melodies here and the opening rumbustious Malcolm Arnold *Overture* (a concert work based on film music) has a characteristic share. William Alwyn's *Scottish dances* are charmingly scored, with *Colonel Thornton's* elegant *Strathspey* a highlight. Sir Malcolm Sargent's breezy scherzo *An impression on a windy day* follows, and after the frothy *Glass slipper overture*, James Langley's *Coloured counties* (which describes the spectacularly English view from Bredon Hill) brings an engaging oboe solo. Gordon Jacob's pastiche is agreeable enough and the whimsy of Langford's *Two worlds overture* leads neatly into Sir Richard Rodney Bennett's *Little suite* with its charming bird-imagery and delicate *Ladybird waltz*. The only disappointment is Maurice Johnstone's *Tarn Hows*, a pleasantly evocative pastoral idyll, but unworthy of that man-made gem, up in the hills

above Hawkshead, perhaps the most beautiful tarn in the whole English Lake District.

British light music: Malcolm ARNOLD: *Little suite No. 4, Op. 80a* (orch. LANE). BLEZARD: *The River*. CRUFT: *Hornpipe suite*. FENBY: *Overture:Rossini on Ilkla Moor*. WARREN: *Wexford Bells – suite on old Irish tunes*. Arthur BUTTERWORTH: *The Path across the moors*. HEDGES: *An Ayrshire serenade, Op. 42*. LEWIS: *An English overture*. LANE: *Suite of Cotswold folkdances*.
(M) *** ASV Dig. CD WHL 2126 [id.].

An excellent collection of British light music, all imbued with a strong rustic flavour, and valuable for rarities. Adrian Cruft's *Hornpipe suite* is nautically enjoyable, with each dance nicely contrasted; Raymond Warren's *Wexford Bells suite* draws on traditional melodies, yet with modest orchestral forces, each movement nicely atmospheric.

Arthur Butterworth's *The Path across the moors* is highly enjoyable – its title perfectly describing its content – and Fenby's witty *Rossini on Ilkla Moor* gives us an idea of what Rossini might have sounded like had he been a Yorkshireman! Robustly enjoyable is *An English overture* by Paul Lewis, written in 1971 for the opening of Westward TV in the west of England; it uses folk songs from that area.

William Blezard's *The River* is a beautiful, haunting, slightly melancholy piece, whilst Anthony Hedges's three-movement *Ayrshire Serenade*, with its breezy outer-movements and nostalgic centrepiece is a good find. Philip Lane's superb arrangements and re-constructions of film music are greatly valued, and it is good to hear some of his own music: his suite of *Cotswold folkdances* is piquantly orchestrated, as is his arrangement of Arnold's *Little suite*. Gavin Sutherland understands exactly how this music should go, and the recording is excellent.

Royal Ballet Sinfonia, John Wilson

'Scottish light music': DAVIE: *Royal Mile*. DODS: *Highland fancy*. HAMILTON: *Scottish dances*. MACCUNN: *The Land of the mountain and flood (overture); Highland memories*. MATHIESON: *From the Grampians (suite)*. ORR: *Fanfare and Processional; Celtic suite*. ROBERTON: *All in the April evening*.
(M) *** ASV Dig. CDWHL 2123 [id.].

What a good idea to assemble a disc of comparatively rare light Scottish music, which with its characteristic folksy influences, proves most entertaining. The most famous piece here, MacCunn's *The land of mountain and flood overture*, begins the programme robustly, while the same composer's *Highland memories* (1897) for strings offers contrast: two rather nostalgic movements followed by a more lively *Harvest dance* (which is curiously reminiscent of the second movement of Schubert's *Ninth symphony*). Muir Mathieson is widely known for his work in countless films and the opening of the *Grampians suite* (1961) could well begin some Scottish swashbuckler; the rest of the *Suite* is thoroughly diverting too.

Buxton Orr's *Fanfare and Processional* (1968) is more angular than its companion pieces, while in his *Celtic suite* (1968), a four-movement work using dance rhythms as a basis, he pays tribute to his Celtic origins (the last movement, *Port-a-Beul*, means 'mouth music'). Cedric Thorpe Davie's robustly enjoyable *Royal Mile* (recorded complete for the first time) is subtitled 'a coronation march' and was written in 1952 for one of a series of concerts leading up to that celebrated event. Iain Hamilton's *Scottish dances* were, like Sir Malcolm Arnold's, composed for the BBC Light Music Festival and premièred on St Andrew's Day, 1956. They are comparably enjoyable. Marcus Dods's amusing *Highland fancy* and Sir Hugh Roberton's touching *All in the April evening* complete the programme. Full marks for an original collection, committed performances, a vibrant recording – and all at mid-price.

Royal Philharmonic Orchestra, Sir Thomas Beecham

'The RPO legacy,' Vol. 1: BERLIOZ: *Le Corsaire(overture)*. SIBELIUS: *Tapiola, Op. 112*. MUSSORGSKY: *Khovanshchina: Dance of the Persian slaves*. DEBUSSY: *Printemps*. BACH: *Christmas oratorio: Sinfonia*. SMETANA: *The Bartered Bride: Overture; Polka; Dance of the Comedians*. CHABRIER: *Marche joyeuse*.
(M) (***) Dutton mono CDLX 7027 [id.].

With astonishingly full mono sound, this first disc in the 'RPO Legacy' series vividly captures the tense excitement of the months following Beecham's founding of the orchestra in 1946. It starts with the thrilling recording of the Berlioz *Corsaire overture*, which was the very first from the RPO to be published. *Tapiola*, recorded a few weeks later in November 1946, has a rugged intensity as well as polish, with the terracing of texture and dynamic beautifully brought out even in mono.

Finest of all in the collection is the Debussy *Printemps*, a work which Beecham conducted as early as 1913, but which he never recorded again. Bach, not a composer generally associated with Beecham, inspires him to a performance which suggests French rather than German music, sweet and elegant, and the Smetana and Chabrier are

electrifying, not least the horn trills in the Chabrier. The Dutton transfers have a vivid sense of presence.

'The RPO Legacy, Volume 5': MENDELSSOHN: *The Fair Melusina overture; Octet, Op. 20: Scherzo*. SAINT-SAENS: *Le Rouet d'Omphale*. DELIUS: *Summer evening*. DVORAK: *The Golden spinning wheel*. MASSENET: *La Vierge: Le dernier sommeil de la Vierge*. MEHUL: *Overture: Les deux aveugles de Tolède*. HAYDN: *Symphonies Nos. 40 in F; 102 in B flat*. BERLIOZ: *King Lear overture*. LISZT: *Orpheus*. PAISIELLO: *Overture: Nina, o la pazza d'amore*. HANDEL–BEECHAM: *The Great Elopement (Love in Bath): suite*.
✿ (M) (***) Dutton mono 2CDEA 5025 (2) [id.].

An indispensable set. This double CD comprises 95 per cent new material, and is in every way a success. It contains charming overtures by Méhul and Paisiello – two Beecham favourites – much sought after by collectors in their original formats: just hear how wittily he points the strings. The superb evocation in Dvořák's *Golden spinning wheel* paints the scene as vividly as a Brueghel painting; *Le Rouet d'Omphale* is exquisitely done – the playing has a gossamer-like texture at the opening, and a better performance has yet to emerge. Haydn is represented by stylish readings of *Symphony 102*, and Beecham's only recording of *Symphony 40*, with some superb horn playing in the Minuet and trio, with Dennis Brain at the head. The suite from the charming ballet *The Great Elopement* was published in 1951, in between Beecham's later complete recording and the 1945 version of the suite. Another highlight is *Orpheus*, Liszt's most beautiful symphonic poem, and Beecham's account is hauntingly atmospheric. The rest of the programme – the Mendelssohn, Delius, Massenet and Berlioz – shows the conductor on top form, and Dutton has produced his usual superb transfers from the original shellac pressings of recordings, made between 1947 and 1951. This is a 'must-have' reissue in the Beecham catalogue.

Royal Philharmonic Orchestra, Per Dreier

'Norwegian rhapsody': GRIEG: *Peer Gynt suite No. 1. Elegiac melody: The last spring. Norwegian dance No. 2.* SVENDSEN: *Polonaise; Variations on a Norwegian folk tune; Norwegian artists' carnival.* KJERULF: *The Wedding in Hardanger.* BULL: *Solitude.* NORDRAAK: *Maria Stuart: Purpose; Valse caprice. Olav Trygvason; National anthem.* HALVORSEN: *Entry of the Boyars; Danse visionnaire.*
(M) *** Carlton Dig. 30367 0083-2 [id.].

A cheap and cheerful CD of popular Scandinavian repertoire, presented with character and charm by the late Per Dreier and the RPO. The novelties by Kjerulf and Nordraak are just as appealing as the better-known items. Thoroughly recommendable performances, and good recording.

Royal Philharmonic Orchestra, Sir Charles Groves

'An English celebration': ELGAR: Serenade for strings, Op. 20. BRITTEN: Variations on a theme of Frank Bridge, Op. 10. VAUGHAN WILLIAMS: Fantasia on a theme by Thomas Tallis. TIPPETT: Fantasia concertante on a theme of Corelli.
❂ (B) *** Carlton Dig. 30367 0068-2 [(M) id.].

With gloriously full and real recording, providing the most beautiful string textures, this is one of Sir Charles Groves's very finest records and it makes a worthy memorial to the achievement of the closing decade of his long career. The RPO players give deeply felt, vibrant accounts of four great masterpieces of English string music.

Royal Philharmonic Orchestra, Adrian Leaper

'Orchestral spectacular': CHABRIER: España. RIMSKY-KORSAKOV: Capriccio espagnol. MUSSORGSKY: Night on the bare mountain (arr. Rimsky-Korsakov). BORODIN: Prince Igor: Polovtsian dances. RAVEL: Boléro.
(BB) *** Naxos Dig. 8.550501 [id.].

Recorded in Watford Town Hall by Brian Culverhouse, this concert would be highly recommendable even if it cost far more. All these performances spring to life, and the brilliant, full-bodied sound certainly earns the record its title. The brass in the Mussorgsky/Rimsky-Korsakov Night on the bare mountain has splendid sonority and bite, and in the Polovtsian dances the orchestra 'sings' the lyrical melodies with such warmth of colour that the chorus is hardly missed. Leaper allows the Capriccio espagnol to relax in the colourful central variations, but the performance gathers pace towards the close. Chabrier's España has an attractive rhythmic lilt, and in Ravel's ubiquitous Boléro there is a strong impetus towards the climax, with much impressive playing on the way (the trombone solo, with a French-style vibrato, is particularly strong).

(i) Royal Philharmonic Orchestra or (ii) Philharmonia Orchestra, Vladimir Ashkenazy

'Russian delights': (i) TCHAIKOVSKY: Capriccio italien, Op. 45; Francesca da Rimini, Op. 32. (ii) RIMSKY-KORSAKOV: The Tale of Tsar Saltan: suite, Op. 57; Flight of the bumblebee. BORODIN: Prince Igor: Polovtsian dances (with Matthew Best, L. Opera Ch.).
(B) *** Decca Eclipse Dig. 448 989-2 [(M) id. import].

This Ashkenazy compilation is first class in every respect, and the recordings (made between 1983 and 1988) are of Decca's finest vintage. Capriccio italien is superb, spectacular, elegant and possessed of exhilarating impetus. Francesca da Rimini is very exciting too, with much fine wind-playing from the RPO in the lyrical central section. Ashkenazy is also in his element in the dazzlingly scored Tsar Saltan suite, and the Philharmonia players obviously relish the good tunes, sonorous brass writing and glittering effects. In the Polovtsian dances the singing of the London Opera Chorus has striking fervour, with solo interjections from Matthew Best (normally not included) to bring an added edge of excitement, although it is a pity that the percussion-led opening dance is omitted.

Royal Philharmonic Society Orchestra, Sir Thomas Beecham

ATTERBERG: Symphony No. 6 in C. DELIUS: Walk to the Paradise Garden. GRIEG: The Nightingale's secret; The Emigrant (with Dora Labbette). MOZART: Symphony No. 34 in C; Die Zauberflöte: Overture (with LSO).
(M) *** Dutton mono CDLX 7026 [id.].

Here is buried treasure from the store of the recordings Beecham made in the 1920s, well before he founded his own LPO. This valuable Dutton disc, vividly transferred, starts with the recording of Mozart's Magic Flute overture that he made with the LSO, at his very first recording session using the electrical process, on 30 March 1926. The sound is astonishingly clear and vivid with plenty of body, better than the rather misty recording of the Delius interlude made in December 1927, which the composer himself loved to hear. In that same month Beecham recorded with Dora Labbette the two Grieg songs, originally issued with no mention of the conductor.

This version of Mozart's 34th Symphony, made in October 1928, is clearer and more buoyant than his 1940 version with the LPO, and he responds winningly to the lyricism of the Atterberg Sixth

Symphony. This was the winner of the Schubert centenary competition organized by Columbia in 1928, and Beecham's recording sold 25,000 copies, a phenomenal figure at that time. In Beecham's hands it surges warmly, helped by the full-bodied transfer. The word 'Society' is included in the title of the orchestra – a pick-up band assembled for the Society's concerts – to distinguish it from Beecham's last orchestra.

St Paul Chamber Orchestra, Bobby McFerrin

'Paper music': MOZART: *Le nozze di Figaro overture; Serenade No. 13 in G (Eine kleine Nachtmusik).* BOCCHERINI: *String quintet in E: Minuet.* FAURE: *Pavane.* STRAVINSKY: *Pulcinella: Minuet and Finale.* VIVALDI: *Double cello concerto in G min., RV 531* (with Peter Howard). MENDELSSOHN: *A Midsummer Night's Dream: Scherzo.* BACH: *Violin concerto in A min., BWV 1041: 1st movt.* TCHAIKOVSKY: *Andante cantabile, Op. 11.*
**(*) Sony Dig. SK 63600 [id.].

Bobby McFerrin began his musical career in the world of pop music, and in 1988 had a hit single which reached No. 1. His background, however, included a father who was the first black singer at the Met. and a mother who was both a singer and a teacher. So it was not surprising that he found himself being drawn back to the classical sound-world. He made his début with the San Francisco Symphony in 1990 and went on to conduct most of America's top orchestras. Now he is director of the Saint Paul Chamber Orchestra and spends much of his time as a musical evangelist in schools. He is already a famous figure in the USA.

'Paper music' is an American jazz musician's term for music that is written down rather than improvised. If one hears McFerrin play this kind of popular repertoire at a concert, the effect of his personality is highly communicative; but here, although the music-making is alive, elegantly turned and aptly paced (especially *Eine kleine Nachtmusik*), there is nothing especially individual about it until he introduces his wordless vocal melismas in a voice a little like that of a counter-tenor. His feeling for dynamic nuance is remarkable, as is his range.

In the present concert he sweetly vocalizes the Boccherini *Minuet* and Fauré's *Pavane* in this way, then he replaces the solo violin line in the Bach concerto and follows up by taking over the second cello part in Vivaldi's *Double concerto*. He does this with such skill that one is almost convinced that it is a viable approach, especially if for the musical novice the result is often both magnetic and appealing. The highlight of his vocalizing here is

Tchaikovsky's *Andante cantabile*, which he intones while conducting a refined accompaniment. This is obviously not a CD for general recommendation, but it speaks well for McFerrin's musicianship; if he can bring a new audience into the concert hall, then he has our full support.

Sakonov, Josef (violin), London Festival Orchestra

'Violin encores': HUBAY: *Hejre Kati.* GODARD: *Berceuse de Jocelyn.* TCHAIKOVSKY: *Valse sentimentale; None but the lonely heart.* STERNHOLD: *Fêtes tziganes.* MASSENET: *Thaïs: Méditation.* HEUBERGER: *Opernball: Im chambre séparée.* KORNGOLD: *Garden scene.* MONTI: *Czárdás*
(M) *** Decca Phase Four 444 786-2 [id.] (with miscellaneous works by KETELBEY ***).

This collection makes an admirable coupling for Decca's Ketèlbey collection. Josef Sakonov is a specialist in Hungarian fireworks and Zigeuner melodies. He plays on one of a pair of Guarnerius violins dating from 1735 and he certainly produces a sumptuous tone, helped by the very forward balance of the Phase Four recording. Heuberger's *Im chambre séparée* is used to show off the luscious effects possible on the lower strings of this superb instrument, while there are some dazzling fireworks in the bravura items (Sternhold's *Fêtes tziganes* is a real highlight). There is taste as well as flamboyance here, and the opening melody and Tchaikovsky's *Valse* are very nicely done. With vivid sound, this disc is most enjoyable when presented with such flair.

Sargent, Sir Malcolm

'Portrait': BEETHOVEN: *Symphony No. 3 (Eroica), Op. 55.* TCHAIKOVSKY: *Romeo and Juliet (fantasy overture)* (both with Royal Philharmonic orchestra). ELGAR: *Enigma variations, Op. 36; Serenade for strings, Op. 20.* VAUGHAN WILLIAMS: *Fantasia on a theme by Thomas Tallis* (both with Philharmonia Orchestra); *Fantasia on Greensleeves* (with LSO); *Serenade to music* (with Elsie Morison, Marjorie Thomas, Duncan Robertson, Trevor Anthony, LSO Chorus & LSO).
(BB) *** Royal Long Players DCL 705962 [id.].

A truly cherishable 'Portrait' of a highly accomplished musician who (like André Previn in the 1970s) was a favourite with the wider musical public, and who during the last war became a public celebrity when he joined the broadcasting team of the BBC's 'Brains Trust'. Sargent was less liked by orchestral players, who called him, unaffectionately, 'Flash Harry', and with whom he was frequently high-handed and very rude. But he secured fine playing just the same, and not only in English music.

His *Eroica* is always alive and interesting and certainly does not lack tension, even if speeds are comparatively relaxed. The slow movement is lyrical rather than dramatic, but its elegiac quality is genuinely moving. In Tchaikovsky's *Romeo and Juliet* the inherent passion is implicit, not worn on the sleeve. And, as with the Beethoven, the early stereo is very impressive. So it is too in the *Enigma variations*, warm and full in sonority, and the closing pages, replete with organ foundation, are very exciting. The reading is a traditional one, and makes much of the nobilmente of the score. The *Serenade* is elegant and polished, with a touch of nostalgia.

Again it is the rich string tone in the *Tallis fantasia*, with the Philharmonia playing gloriously, that carries the day in an account that misses much of the deep ethereality inherent in the writing for the second group. Finest of all is the beautifully played and sung account of the *Serenade to music*, in every way sympathetic, with a splendid group of soloists, and even though the 1957 stereo is atmospheric most of the words are clear.

'*Sir Malcolm Sargent conducts British music*' (with (i) LPO; (ii) LSO; (iii) Mary Lewis, Tudor Davies & O; (iv) Royal Choral Soc.; (v) New SO): (i) HOLST: *Perfect fool: suite.* (ii) BRITTEN: *Young person's guide to the orchestra.* (iii) VAUGHAN WILLIAMS: *Hugh the Drover: Love duet.* ELGAR: (iv) *I sing the birth;* (ii) *Pomp & circumstance marches Nos. 1 & 4.* (v) COLERIDGE TAYLOR: *Othello: suite.* (ii) BAX: *Coronation march.* (***) Beulah mono 1PD13 [id.].

Sargent was at his finest in this repertory, and it is very welcome to have his personal electricity so vividly conveyed throughout the disc, and most of all in the recording, taken from the sound-track of the original COI film, of Britten's *Young person's guide*. The optical transfer by Martin Sawyer produces far more vivid and satisfyingly weighty results than one would ever expect. The *Love duet* from *Hugh the Drover* was recorded in 1924 in limited pre-electric sound, but the Elgar part-song, recorded live at the Royal Albert Hall in 1928, also soon after the first performance, is vividly atmospheric. The *Othello suite* of Coleridge Taylor, another première recording, is a sequence of brief genre pieces, with recording more than lively and colourful enough to make one forget the high surface-hiss. The three marches at the end were recorded for the Queen's coronation in 1953, with Sargent taking an uninhibitedly broad view of the great tunes in both the Elgar favourites, and with Bax doing a fair imitation of Walton.

Savall, Jordi (viola da gamba and conductor)

Jordi Savall Edition: Orchestral recordings

Jordi Savall is a distinguished advocate and player of the bass viol or viola da gamba, an instrument which has come back into favour for the performance of early music after being superseded by the cello, and regarded for a considerable period as obsolete. As musical director of various vocal and instrumental ensembles, including La Capella Reial, Le Concert des Nations, and Hespèrion XX, Savall has achieved a further reputation in larger-scale instrumental and vocal music.

His scholarship is matched by a vivid imagination and a feeling for the sonorities of period performance, and all his music-making is characterized by great expressive vitality. To celebrate his current achievement, Harmonia Mundi's sister label, Astrée, has reissued twenty of his key CDs at mid-price, handsomely packaged in a special Edition. All are available separately and are discussed in three groups, the first immediately below, the other two under Instrumental and Vocal Recitals respectively.

Eustache DU CAURROY: *Fantaisies* (1610) *in 3, 4, 5 and 6 parts* with Hespèrion XX.
(M) *** Audivis Astrée Dig. ES 9931 [id.].

Eustache du Caurroy, born in 1549, was, at the time of his death in 1609, 'Superintendent of the Music to King Henry IV of France' and his *42 Fantaisies* were published the following year. About half of them are offered here. The music is strikingly rich in both melody and consonant harmonic feeling, combining melancholy with appealing human warmth. Each is based on a clear cantus firmus, and the texts with which they are associated (secular chansons, hymns or antiphons, sometimes psalms) give an indication of their mood and character. They were intended to be played by an instrumental ensemble (an early precursor of the chamber orchestra), although no actual instrumentation is suggested.

Savall makes his usual imaginative choices, moving from viols for the touching opening *29th Fantaisie* based on *Une jeune fillette*, to lutes and harps, cornets and sackbuts, and renaissance flutes, all finely blended, beautifully played and sonorously recorded. This is one of the most rewarding finds of the Jordi Savall Edition.

HANDEL: *Water music: suites 1, 2; Music for the Royal Fireworks* (with Le Concert des Nations). (M) *** Audivis Astrée Dig. ES 9920 [id.].

Jordi Savall's period-instrument set of Handel's complete *Water* and *Fireworks music* is wonderfully fresh and sprightly – the dance movements are delightfully nimble, yet the big moments are as

OTHER CONCERTS

spectacular as one could wish. The *Overture* for the *Fireworks music* is splendidly grandiloquent, yet the following allegro has a thrusting momentum with crisp dotting of rhythms. Throughout, the interplay of colour and sonority is matched by the musicians' vigour, and the closing Minuets, taken fast, are exhilarating. The recording is splendid.

HAYDN: *The Seven Last Words of Christ on the Cross* (original orchestral version) (with Le Concert des Nations).

(M) *** Audivis Astrée Dig. ES 9935 [id.].

The original, orchestral score of *Seven Last Words of Christ on the Cross* was a work of Haydn's maturity, written in 1786/7. It was commissioned for first performance at Easter in a darkened Cadiz Cathedral illuminated by a single lamp, with the Bishop pronouncing the seven texts one at a time, each followed by one of Haydn's *Adagios*. Haydn acknowledged the difficulty of his commission, but the result proved so moving and successful that he later made arrangements for other groups, and the version for string quartet, published in 1788, has come to be far more familiar than the original. There is no doubt that the orchestral score – scored fully, but sombre in colour – is very telling, especially in this very fine performance, which has genuine gravitas and is never boring. Each of the movements is introduced with the appropriate reading (in Latin, and separately cued) by Rafael Taibo. Finally comes the spectacular 'earthquake' which, according to Christian teaching, followed the death of Christ. The resonant acoustic is aptly chosen, and the documentation is excellent.

PURCELL: *Suites: The Fairy Queen; The Prophetess* (with Le Concert des Nations).

(M) *** Audivis Astrée Dig. ES 9934 [id.].

Collectors wanting this vigorously inventive and colourful masque music in orchestral form, brilliantly played on period instruments without voices, will find Savall's extended selections as authentic, stylish and vivacious as any in the catalogue. There is a good deal of bright work for the trumpets, but there is much too for strings and wind that is gentler and more piquant. The *Chair dance* in the comparatively short suite from *The Prophetess,* and the following *Soft music* which introduces the *Dance of the Furies,* are both memorable, while the Second and Third Act suites from *The Fairy Queen* titillate the ear with items like *A bird's prelude, Echo, Fairies' dance,* and the *Dances for the Followers of Night, Green men* and *Haymakers.* The Fourth Act has a fine extended introductory *Symphony* and the Fifth Act produces a very English *Monkey's dance* and a totally unoriental chaconne for the *Dance of the Chinese man and woman.* Most entertaining, with first-rate sound.

La Scala Philharmonic Orchestra, Riccardo Muti

CATALANI: *Contemplazione; Scherzo.* PONCHIELLI: *Elegia.* PUCCINI: *Preludio sinfonico; Capriccio sinfonico; Le Villi: La tregenda.*
**(*) Sony Dig. SK 63025 [id.].

It makes an apt coupling having long-buried pieces by Ponchielli (Puccini's teacher) and Catalani (Puccini's contemporary from the same city, Lucca) alongside the three most impressive examples of Puccini's early orchestral writing. This easily lyrical music has been resurrected by the Italian musicologist Pietro Spada. The Ponchielli *Elegia* anticipates film music, and the Catalani pieces were both orchestrated from piano works, but the Puccini pieces are markedly more memorable. The *Capriccio sinfonico,* later to provide the opening theme of *La Bohème,* was written as a graduation exercise, very well orchestrated, with structure well controlled. Muti brings out the emotional warmth in all these works, with Sony sound atmospheric rather than detailed.

Scottish Chamber Orchestra, Laredo

'*String masterpieces*': ALBINONI: *Adagio in G min.* (arr. GIAZOTTO). HANDEL: *Berenice: Overture. Solomon: Arrival of the Queen of Sheba.* BACH: *Suite No. 3, BWV 1068: Air. Violin concerto No. 1 in A min., BWV 1041: Finale.* PACHELBEL: *Canon.* PURCELL: *Abdelazar: Rondo. Chacony in G min.*
(B) *** Carlton Dig. PCD 2001 [(M) id. import].

An excellent issue. The playing is alive, alert, stylish and committed without being overly expressive. The Bach *Air* has warmth and Pachelbel's *Canon* is fresh and unconventional in approach. The Purcell *Rondo* is the tune made familiar by Britten's orchestral guide; the *Chaconne* is played with telling simplicity. The sound is first class, especially spacious and convincing on CD, well detailed without any clinical feeling.

Segovia, Andrés (guitar)

'*Escenas españolas*': RODRIGO: *Fantasia para un gentilhombre.* PONCE: *Concierto del sur* (both with Symphony of the Air, Enrique Jorda). TORROBA: *Cantillos de españa; Romanza de los pinos.* MILAN: *6 Pavanas.* NARVAEZ: *Canción del Emperador. Variations on 'Guárdame las vacas'.* SANZ: *Gallardas; Españoleta.* SOR: *Minuets in E, Op. 11/10; in G. Op. 32; Variations on a theme by*

Mozart. GRANADOS: *Danza española No. 5.*
ESPLA: *Antano.* CASSADO: *Preámbulo y Sardana.*
MOMPOU: *Suite compostelana.* DE VALERA: *Nana;*
Intermezzo.
(M) *** Millennium stereo/mono UMD 80467 (2)
[id.].

Here is a rare, indeed indispensable, two-disc
Segovia collection, excellently recorded between
1952 and 1969, with very little background noise.
All but three of the tracks are stereo, including the
Rodrigo *Fantasia para un gentilhombre* and the
engagingly intimate *Concierto del sur* of Manuel
Ponce (both with sympathetically idiomatic accompaniments from Jorda). These, together with
Tórroba's *Cantillos de españa* and Mompou's
whimsical *Suite compostelana*, are the highlights of
a wide-ranging programme consistently demonstrating the subtlety of Segovia's articulation and
colouring. He is curiously imperturbable, even detached, in the early music – the *Pavanas* of Luis de
Milán, pieces by Luys de Narváez, Sanz and the
Sor *Minuets*; he is very indulgent with rubato in
the famous *Spanish dance No. 5* of Granados.
Bream is much more magical in this piece. But
generally this is playing of the very highest calibre.
There is a minor pitch change with the (mono) Sor
Variations on a theme by Mozart but otherwise the
transfers are first class.

'Serenade'

'Serenade': TCHAIKOVSKY: *Serenade for strings
in C, Op. 48.* DVORAK: *Serenade for strings in E,
Op. 22.* wiren: *Serenade, Op. 11* (all with ASMF,
Marriner). BRAHMS: *Serenade No. 2 in A, Op. 16.*
DVORAK: *Wind serenade in D min., Op. 44* (both
LSO, Kertész). SUK: *Serenade for strings in E flat,
Op. 6* (Los Angeles Chamber Orchestra,
Marriner).
(B) *** Decca Double 466 459-2 (2) [id.].

A most enjoyable programme: it begins with
Marriner's first-class 1969 performance of the
Tchaikovsky *Serenade*, with its glowing sense of
joy combined with the finest pointing and precision
of ensemble. He is equally at home in the perennially fresh Wirén *Serenade*, recorded in 1977 and
sounding rich and full. It is impossible to choose
which of the two Brahms *Serenades* is the more
enjoyable. Here we have the *Second* in Kertész's
fine LSO account from 1967 – wonderfully fresh
playing and very good sound to match – and the
Dvořák *Wind serenade* with the same forces is
hardly less compelling. Suk's *Serenade* ought to be
better known; it is a work of considerable charm,
but has an underlying power and eloquence, as this
fine account from Marriner demonstrates. The Los
Angeles performance is more brightly lit than the
ASMF recordings we are more used to, but the

recording is of high quality and naturally balanced.
Excellent value.

Serenades: 'Favourite serenades'

'Favourite serenades' (played by (i) Netherlands
CO, Zinman; (ii) ECO, Leppard; (iii) I Musici;
(iv) ASMF, Marriner; (v) Accardo, Leipzig GO,
Masur; (vi) Netherlands Wind Ens., Edo de Waart;
(vii) Catherine Michel, Monte Carlo Op. O,
Almeida): (i) TCHAIKOVSKY: *String serenade,
Op. 48.* (ii) DVORAK: *Serenade for strings, Op. 22.*
(iii) MOZART: *Eine kleine Nachtmusik.* (iv)
HOFFSTETTER/HAYDN: *Serenade from String
quartet in F, Op. 3/5.* (v) BRUCH: *Serenade for
violin and orchestra, Op. 75.* (iii) WOLF: *Italian
serenade in G.* (vi) R. STRAUSS: *Serenade for
wind, Op. 7.* (vii) RODRIGO: *Concierto serenade
for harp and orchestra.*
(B) **(*) Ph. (IMS) 438 748-2 (2) [(M) id. import].

A generous 156-minute anthology about which
there are few reservations. Zinman's account of the
Tchaikovsky *Serenade* has not the very strongest
profile, but it is polished and warmly recorded. I
Musici play Wolf's infectiously gay little masterpiece extremely well, even if perhaps they do not
do full justice to its effervescent spirit and sheer *joie
de vivre*. Everything else here will certainly give
pleasure, especially the rare Max Bruch concertante
serenade, so enticingly tuneful with Accardo in
ravishing form. Catherine Michel's account of
Rodrigo's *Serenade concerto* for harp is not quite
as enticing as Zabaleta's famous DG version, but
the spicy harmonies are made to catch the ear with
piquant abrasiveness. Excellent sound (mostly from
the 1970s) and smooth remastering ensure aural
pleasure throughout.

Slovak Philharmonic Orchestra

'Russian fireworks' (cond. (i) Richard Hayman;
(ii) Kenneth Jean; (iii) Stephen Gunzenhauser; (iv)
Michael Halász): (i) IPPOLITOV-IVANOV:
Caucasian sketches: Procession of the Sardar. (ii)
LIADOV: *8 Russian folksongs.* KABALEVSKY:
Comedians' galop. MUSSORGSKY: *Sorochintsy
Fair: Gopak. Khovanshchina: Dance of the
Persian slaves.* (iii) LIADOV: *Baba Yaga; The
enchanted lake; Kikimora.* (iv) RUBINSTEIN:
*Feramor: Dance of the Bayaderes; Bridal
procession. The Demon: Lesginka.* (ii)
HALVORSEN: *Entry of the Boyars.*
(BB) *** Naxos Dig. 8.550328 [id.].

A vividly sparkling concert with spectacular digital
sound, more than making up in vigour and spontaneity for any lack of finesse. The Liadov tone-poems

are especially attractive and, besides the very familiar pieces by Ippolitov-Ivanov, Halvorsen and Mussorgsky, it is good to have the Rubinstein items, especially the *Lesginka*, which has a rather attractive tune.

Slovak State Philharmonic Orchestra (Košice), Mika Eichenholz

'Locomotive music (A musical train ride)', Vol. 1: LANNER: *Ankunfts waltz.* Johann STRAUSS Sr: *Reise galop; Souvenir de Carneval 1847 (quadrille); Eisenbahn-Lust (waltz).* HOYER: *Jernban galop.* Johann STRAUSS Jr: *Reiseabenteuer waltz.* MEYER: *Jernvägs-Galop.* Eduard STRAUSS: *Glockensignale waltz; Mit Dampf polka; Lustfahrten waltz; Tour und Retour polka.* Josef STRAUSS: *Gruss an München polka.* GRAHL: *Sveas helsning till Nore waltz.* LUMBYE: *Copenhagen Steam Railway galop.*
**(*) Marco Polo Dig. 8.223470 [id.].

'Locomotive music', Vol. 2: LANNER: *Dampf waltz.* FAHRBACH: *Locomotiv-Galop.* Johann STRAUSS Jr: *Wilde Rosen waltz; Vergnügungszug polka; Spiralen waltz; Accelerationen waltz.* GUNGL: *Eisenbahn-Dampf galop.* Eduard STRAUSS: *Polkas: Reiselust; Ohne Aufenthalt; Treuliebchen; Ohne Bremse; Von Land zu Land; Bahn frei; Feuerfunken waltz.* ZIEHRER: *Nachtschwalbe polka.*
**(*) Marco Polo Dig. 8.223471 [id.].

This seems a happy idea on which to base a two-CD collection of Viennese-style dance music, but in the event the only piece which celebrates the effect of a train journey really successfully is the *Copenhagen Steam Railway galop.* The Slovak performance has rather a good whistle but seems more concerned with rhythm than with charm and cannot compare with the account included in the splendid Unicorn collection of Lumbye's dance music so beautifully played by the Odense Symphony Orchestra under Peter Guth (DKPCD 9089 – see our main volume). The first Marco Polo disc opens with Lanner's *Ankunfts* ('Arrival') *waltz,* which ironically dates from before the railway had even arrived in Vienna. It is enjoyable for itself; the other highlights are more descriptive. Frans Hoyer's *Jernban galop* makes a fair shot of a train starting up and has a rather engaging main theme, while Jean Meyer's *Jernvägs-Galop* follows Lumbye's pattern of an elegant opening and a whistle start, with the side-drum snares giving a modest railway simulation. This too is attractive melodically, but the coda is too abrupt. Eduard Strauss's *Mit Dampf polka* has a rather half-hearted whistle but plenty of energy, and his *Lustfahrten waltz* is lyrically appealing.

The second disc opens with Lanner again, but the *Dampf* refers to the steam of a coffee house! It is followed by Fahrbach's jolly *Locomotiv-Galop,* where the effects are minimal and primitive. However, Joseph Gungl does better, with an opening whistle which returns on a regular basis against supporting bass-drum beats. Johann Strauss's *Vergnügungszug polka* concentrates on the exhilaration of a day out on an excursion train, but Eduard Strauss's *Bahn frei,* comparably zestful, manages a cleverly brief introductory train imitation, and *Ohne Aufenthalt* has a gentle bell to set off. If most of this repertoire is unadventurous in terms of evocation, it is all tuneful and brightly presented; the playing is not without finesse and has plenty of zest, and the orchestra is very well recorded – and not in a train shed either. But these are full-priced CDs and one is plainly not travelling in a first-class carriage with the VPO.

Steele-Perkins, Crispian (trumpet)

Six Trumpet concertos (with ECO, Anthony Halstead): J. HAYDN: *Concerto in E flat.* TORELLI: *Concerto in D.* M. HAYDN: *Concerto No. 2 in C.* TELEMANN: *Concerto for trumpet, two oboes and strings.* NERUDA: *Concerto in E flat.* HUMPHRIES: *Concerto in D, Op. 10/12.*
(M) *** Carlton 30366 0066-2 [id.].

Collectors who have relished Håkan Hardenberger's famous collection of trumpet concertos might well go on to this equally admirable concert, which duplicates only the Michael Haydn and Joseph Haydn – and in performances hardly less distinguished. Crispian Steele-Perkins has a bright, gleaming, beautifully focused timbre and crisp articulation, with easy command of the high tessitura of the Michael Haydn work and all the bravura necessary for the sprightly finales of all these concertos. His phrasing in the slow movement of Joseph Haydn's shapely *Andante* is matched by his playing of the *Largo* of the Neruda and the *Adagio–Presto–Adagio* of the Torelli, another fine work. Anthony Halstead with the ECO gives him warmly sympathetic support. The recording balance gives the soloist plenty of presence, but the orchestra is recorded rather reverberantly, an effect similar to that on the Hardenberger record.

Steele-Perkins, Crispian (trumpet), Tafelmusik, Jeanne Lamon

STRADELLA: *Sonata for 8 strings and trumpet.* BIBER: *Sonatas Nos. 1 & 4 for trumpet, strings & continuo; Trumpet duets Nos. 1, 5, 11 & 13.* VIVALDI: *Concerto for 2 trumpets.* ALBINONI: *Trumpet concerto.* TELEMANN: *Trumpet concerto.* HANDEL: Arias from: *Serse: Caro voi siete*

all'alma; Admeto: Se L'arco avessi. Marches from: Scipone; Judas Maccabaeus; Atalanta (overture).'
*** Sony Dig. SK 53365 [id.].

The Stradella and Biber Sonatas are in essence trumpet-led miniature suites, interspersing slow and fast movements appealingly; while Biber's four brief duets are also full of character. The Vivaldi Double concerto is comparatively well known, and the Albinoni work which combines solo trumpet with three oboes is divertingly colourful, especially with baroque oboes. The Telemann Concerto is a splendid piece, and in the Aria Steele-Perkins plays with an exquisitely fined-down tone against the equally subtle continuo. He is a superb soloist and uses a natural baroque trumpet with almost unbelievable refinement, yet is appropriately robust when the music calls for it. In the works involving two instruments he has a fine partner in John Thiessen. What makes this collection special is the beauty of the accompaniments from the superb Tafelmusik, playing their original instruments under the direction of Jeanne Lamon – although in the Stradella and Biber Sonatas the partnership between trumpet and ripieno is more equal. The recording is of the highest quality.

Stern, Isaac (violin)

'A Life in music': Boxes I–II (for Boxes III–IV, see under Instrumental Recitals)

'A Life in music': Box I.
(M) *** Sony Analogue/Dig. SX11K 67193 (11) [SXK 67193].

Volume 1: VIVALDI: The Four Seasons, Op. 8/1–4 (with Jerusalem Music Centre CO); Concertos for 2 violins, RV 516, 524 (arr. RAMPAL) (with Jean-Pierre Rampal (flute), Franz Liszt CO); Concerto for 3 violins, RV 551 (with Pinchas Zukerman, Itzhak Perlman, NYPO, Mehta); L'estro armonico: Double concerto in A min., Op. 3/8 (arr. FRANKO); Concertos for 2 violins, RV 514, 517, 509, 512 (with David Oistrakh, Phd. O, Ormandy). Carl STAMITZ: Sinfonia concertante in D (with Pinchas Zukerman (viola), ECO, Barenboim) (SM2K 66472 (2)) [S2K 66472].

Volume 2: BACH: Violin concertos 1–2, BWV 1041–2 (with ECO, Schneider); Concerto for 2 violins, BWV 1043 (with Itzhak Perlman, NYPO, Mehta); Concerto for oboe & violin in C min., BWV 1060 (with Harold Gomberg, NYPO, Bernstein) (SMK 66471) [id.].

Volume 3: MOZART: (i) Violin concertos No. 1, K.207; (ii) No. 2, K.211; (iii) No. 3, K.216; (ii) No. 4, K.218; (i) No. 5, K.219; (ii) Adagio in E, K.261; Rondo in C, K.373; (iv) Concertone for 2 violins in C, K.190; (v) Sinfonia concertante for

violin & viola, K.364 ((i) Columbia SO, Szell; (ii) ECO, Schneider; (iii) Cleveland O (members), Szell; (iv; v) Pinchas Zukerman, ECO; (iv) Schneider; (v) Barenboim) (SM3K 66475 (3)) [S3K 66475].

Volume 4: BEETHOVEN: Violin concerto in D, Op. 61 (with NYPO, Barenboim); Triple concerto in C, Op. 56 (with Eugene Istomin (piano)). BRAHMS: Double concerto in A min., Op. 102 (both with Leonard Rose (cello), Phd. O, Ormandy); Violin concerto in D, Op. 77 (with NYPO, Mehta) (SM2K 66941 (2)) [S2K 66941].

Volume 5: MENDELSSOHN: Violin concerto in E min., Op. 64. DVORAK: Violin concerto in A min., Op. 53; Romance in F min., Op. 11 (with Phd. O, Ormandy) (SMK 66827) [id.].

Volume 6: TCHAIKOVSKY: Violin concerto in D, Op. 35. SIBELIUS: Violin concerto in D min., Op. 47 (with Phd. O, Ormandy) (SMK 66829) [id.].

Volume 7: WIENIAWSKI: Violin concerto No. 2 in D min., Op. 22. BRUCH: Violin concerto No. 1 in G min., Op. 26 (with Phd. O, Ormandy). TCHAIKOVSKY: Méditation, Op. 42/1 (orch. Glazunov) (with Nat. SO, Rostropovich); Sérénade mélancolique, Op. 26 (with Columbia SO, Brieff) (SMK 66830) [id.].

There is a feast of superb playing here. It is a pity that the choice of the Beethoven and Brahms Concertos features Stern's recent versions instead of his more inspired, earlier accounts (with Bernstein and Ormandy respectively) and the Dvořák Concerto, too, is something of a disappointment. But the Bruch, Mendelssohn, Sibelius and Tchaikovsky are glorious, and both the Bach Double concerto and Mozart Sinfonia concertante bring comparably inspirational music-making. The solo Mozart Concertos also give much pleasure, while in the Vivaldi collection, where Stern's partner is David Oistrakh, there are some more marvellous performances of baroque double concertos, and the results are very compelling indeed. Although too often recordings are balanced very forwardly, the remastered sound is a very great and consistent improvement on the old LPs.

'A Life in music': Box II.
(M) **(*) Sony stereo/mono SX9K 67194 (9) [SXK 67194].

Volume 9: BARTOK: Violin concertos Nos. (i) 1; (ii) 2 ((i) with Phd. O, Ormandy; (ii) with NYPO, Bernstein) (SMK 64502) [id.].

Volume 10: PROKOFIEV: Violin concertos Nos. 1–2 (with NYPO, Mehta). BARTOK: 2 Rhapsodies for violin and orchestra (with NYPO, Bernstein) (SMK 64503) [id.].

Volume 11: BERG: Violin concerto (with NYPO, Bernstein); Chamber concerto for piano, violin &

13 wind (with Peter Serkin, LSO (members),
Abbado) (SMK 64504) [id.].

Volume 12: STRAVINSKY: *Violin concerto in D*
(with Columbia SO, composer). ROCHBERG:
Violin concerto (with Pittsburgh SO, Previn)
(SMK 64505) [id.].

Volume 13: BARBER: *Violin concerto, Op. 14*
(with NYPO, Bernstein). MAXWELL DAVIES:
Violin concerto (with RPO, Previn) (SMK 64506)
[id.].

Volume 14: HINDEMITH: *Violin concerto* (with
NYPO, Bernstein). PENDERECKI: *Violin concerto*
(with Minnesota O, Skrowaczewski) (SMK
64507) [id.].

Volume 15: BERNSTEIN: *Serenade for violin,
strings, harp and percussion, after Plato's
Symposium* (with Symphony of the Air,
composer). DUTILLEUX: *Violin concerto 'L'Arbre
des songes'* (with O Nat. de France, Maazel)
(SMK 64508) [id.].

Although there are a few more reservations here
than with Box I, there are some unforgettable performances too. The Barber *Concerto* remains unsurpassed and unsurpassable, as does the Stravinsky,
recorded in mono with the composer, while the
Dutilleux and Hindemith works are almost as fine.
In the Stravinsky, no apology need be made for
the sound and the performance is electrifying. The
two-disc set which includes music of Lalo, Saint-
Saëns, Chausson and others is particularly enticing
and makes a good sample of the sheer calibre and
remarkable charisma of Stern's playing; unfortunately Sony have withdrawn it.

Stern, Isaac (violin), Franz Liszt CO, János Rolla

BEETHOVEN: *Romances Nos. 1 & 2, Op. 40 & 50.*
HAYDN: *Violin concerto in G.* MOZART: *Serenata
notturna; Adagio in E, K.261; Rondo in C, K.273.*
**(*) Sony Dig. SK 62693 [id.].

Balanced naturally, without the spotlighting that
used to mark his concerto recordings, Isaac Stern
gives fresh and stylish readings of this attractive
collection of short concertante pieces, immaculately
tuned, a tribute to his mastery even in his late
seventies. True, these are not works which call for
virtuoso flair, but in the little cadenza at the end of
Mozart's *Rondo in C* you do have that sense of
joyful freedom which has always marked Stern's
playing. The speeds for both *Romances* are nicely
flowing, not as slow as in most traditional performances. Sympathetic accompaniment from Rolla and
the excellent Hungarian chamber orchestra, well
recorded, though the timpani at the start of the
Serenata notturna are disconcertingly boomy.

Stockholm Sinfonietta, Esa-Pekka Salonen

'A Swedish serenade': WIREN: *Serenade for
strings, Op. 11.* LARSSON: *Little serenade for
strings, Op. 12.* SODERLUNDH: *Oboe concertino*
(with A. Nilsson). LIDHOLM: *Music for strings.*
**(*) BIS Dig. CD 285 [id.].

The most familiar piece here is the Dag Wirén
Serenade for strings. Söderlundh's *Concertino for
oboe and orchestra* has a lovely *Andante* whose
melancholy is winning and with a distinctly Gallic
feel to it. It is certainly played with splendid artistry
by Alf Nilsson and the Stockholm Sinfonietta. The
Lidholm *Music for strings* is somewhat grey and
anonymous, though it is expertly wrought. Esa-
Pekka Salonen gets good results from this ensemble
and the recording lives up to the high standards of
the BIS label. It is forwardly balanced but has
splendid body and realism.

Stockholm Sinfonietta, Jan-Olav Wedin

'Swedish pastorale': ALFVEN: *The Mountain
King, Op. 37: Dance of the cow-girl.* ATTERBERG:
Suite No. 3 for violin, viola and string orchestra.
BLOMDAHL: *Theatre music: Adagio.* LARSSON:
*Pastoral suite, Op. 19; The Winter's Tale: Four
vignettes.* ROMAN: *Concerto in D for oboe
d'amore, string orchestra and harpsichord, BeRI
53.* ROSENBERG: *Small piece for cello and string
orchestra.*
*** BIS Dig. CD 165 [id.].

In addition to affectionate accounts of the *Pastoral
suite* and the charming vignettes for *The Winter's
Tale,* the Stockholm Sinfonietta include Atterberg's
Suite No. 3, which has something of the modal
dignity of the Vaughan Williams *Tallis fantasia.* It
has real eloquence and an attractive melancholy, to
which the two soloists, Nils-Erik Sparf and Jouko
Mansnerus, do ample justice. The Blomdahl and
Roman works are also given alert and sensitive
performances; they make one think how charming
they are. Hilding Rosenberg's piece is very short
but is rather beautiful. A delightful anthology and
excellent (if a trifle closely balanced) recording.
Confidently recommended.

Stokowski, Leopold

'Stokowski Stereo Collection'.
(M) *** [RCA 09026 68443-2] (14).

Disc 1: (i) BACH: *Transcriptions.* (ii) HANDEL:
Music for the Royal Fireworks – with (i) LSO; (ii)
RCA Victor SO (09026 62605-2).

Disc 2: (i) BEETHOVEN: *Symphony No. 3 in E flat (Eroica), Op. 55; Overture Coriolan.* (ii) BRAHMS: *Academic festival overture* – with (i) LSO; (ii) New Philh. O (09026 62514-2).

Disc 3: CANTELOUBE: *Songs of the Auvergne.* VILLA-LOBOS: *Bachianas brasileiras No. 5.* RACHMANINOV: *Vocalise* – all with Anna Moffo, American SO (09026 62600-2).

Disc 4: (i) DVORAK: *Symphony No. 9 in E min. (From the New World), Op. 95.* (ii) SMETANA: *Vltava; Overture: The Bartered bride* – with (i) New Philh. O; (ii) RCA Victor SO (09026 62601-2).

Disc 5: (i) MAHLER: *Symphony No. 2 in C min. (Resurrection).* (ii) BRAHMS: *Symphony No. 4 in E min., Op. 98* – with (i) Brigitte Fassbaender, Margaret Price, LSO and Ch.; (ii) New Philh. O (09026 62606-2 (2)).

Disc 6: RIMSKY-KORSAKOV: (i) *Scheherazade;* (ii) *Russian Easter Festival overture* – with (i) RPO; (ii) Chicago SO (09026 62604-2).

Disc 7: SHOSTAKOVICH: *Symphony No. 6 in B min., Op. 54; The Age of Gold: suite.* KHACHATURIAN: *Symphony No. 3 (Symphonic poem)* – all with Chicago SO (09026 62516-2).

Disc 8: PROKOFIEV: *Romeo and Juliet* (excerpts). MENOTTI: *Sebastian: suite* – both with members of NBC SO (09026 62517-2).

Disc 9: (i) TCHAIKOVSKY: *Symphony No. 6 in B min. (Pathétique), Op. 74.* (ii) ENESCU: *Roumanian rhapsody No. 1.* LISZT: *Hungarian rhapsody No. 2* – with (i) LSO; (ii) RCA Victor SO (09026 62602-2).

Disc 10: WAGNER: Volume 1: excerpts from: *Das Rheingold; Die Walküre; Rienzi; Tannhaüser; Tristan und Isolde* – with soloists, Symphony of the Air; RPO (09026 62597-2).

Disc 11: WAGNER: Volume 2: orchestral excerpts from: *Tristan und Isolde; Die Meistersinger; Götterdämmerung* – with RPO, LSO (09026 62598-2).

Disc 12: *'Inspiration':* BACH, BEETHOVEN, HANDEL, GLUCK, TCHAIKOVSKY, WAGNER, RACHMANINOV, etc., with Norman Luboff Ch., N. SO of L., RCA SO (09026 62599-2).

Disc 13: *'The Final Bach Toccata and fugue; rehearsals and sessions':* BACH, BEETHOVEN, MAHLER, WAGNER, LSO, RPO, NBC SO (members) (09026 62560-2).

RCA's Stokowski Collection is discussed together below, rather than in the composer index. However, the discs are all available separately.

The first disc contains characteristic Bach transcriptions (from 1974), richly played and warmly expressive at slow tempi. The opening *Chaconne* from the *Violin partita No. 3 in E major* (which in

turn is based on Busoni's piano transcription) is very spacious indeed, running to nearly 18 minutes, which must be a record. But the LSO make a glorious string-sound, helped by the ample acoustics of St Giles, Cripplegate. Bach's famous *Air* and the chorale *Ein' feste Burg* have never sounded more opulent, yet (except for purists) the effect can still be moving, for the playing is obviously deeply felt. In the *Royal Fireworks music* (dating from 1961) Stokowski uses a very large group of wind (to follow Handel's original scoring) plus strings. Tempi are again very grand and measured, and at the end (reasonably enough, but only Stokowski would dare do it) the sounds of real fireworks and enthusiastic crowd-noises are introduced momentarily, laminated to the closing tutti.

Stokowski's *Eroica* comes from 1974. He was 93, but this didn't inhibit his energy. Indeed, he is electrifying in the outer movements, strong and superbly controlled with a sense of forward movement that never loses its grip. The *Funeral march* is spontaneously lyrical rather than hushed and intense, not a weighty reading, to match the rest. The Scherzo is superbly resilient at high speed. The Walthamstow recording is full and well balanced. This disc also includes the conductor's brief but touchingly sincere 'thank you' to the orchestra: 'You make the music sound profound,' he tells them, 'and that's not easy.'

The warmly sensuous triptych of Canteloube's *Chants d'Auvergne* and the *Bachianas brasileiras No. 5* of Villa-Lobos (with Anna Moffo singing creamily and seductively) was completed by the *Vocalise* of Rachmaninov with Moffo's wordless melisma quite seamless, and this has been one of the conductor's enduring successes. It has stayed fairly permanently in the catalogue and is still there now.

Above all, Stokowski's 1960 *New World Symphony* reveals the maestro's genius for moulding phrases and tempi, for pointing the drama of such music as this. There are one or two Stokowskian idiosyncrasies – trumpet-trills at the end of the first movement, for example – and almost every repeat is omitted; but as a document of a great musician at a vintage period it provides a warming experience. Sharp stereo separation and particularly vivid reproduction of timpani and brass.

In 1974 Stokowski recorded a Mahler symphony for the first time, presenting a youthful and surprisingly direct view. The crisp attack and relatively fast tempi of the first three movements, with dotted rhythms sharply pointed, are the hallmark of a youthful approach. Though his mezzo soloist Brigitte Fassbaender's singing in *Urlicht* is less hushed than it should be (partly a question of balance), the massive finale erupts superbly, with the final passage with its vision of heaven very telling indeed. That same year the veteran Brahmsian recorded a wonderfully vigorous account of his

Fourth Symphony, its urgency tempered with a glowingly warm lyricism, so effective within the spacious Walthamstow ambience. This was the last performance Stokowski was to give of this work, and the CD provides a fitting Brahmsian swan-song. The glorious slow movement is at the heart of a superbly controlled reading that, with its surging *Passacaglia* finale, is very satisfying indeed.

Stokowski recorded *Scheherazade* more than once, but his 1975 version is characteristic of his warmly sensuous approach. The RPO make some alluringly beautiful orchestral sounds, recorded in a warmly resonant acoustic (achieved at Abbey Road), which at the climax of the last movement could be more sharply defined (and here the bass drum adds to the weight). With Erich Gruenberg in the title-role providing a sweet-toned commentary, the first and second movements are almost linked. Stokowski is at his most charismatic in the slow movement, and his nudgings of rubato are not always spontaneous, despite the rich sheen of tone he creates. Although there is no lack of drama, in the last analysis this reading does not show him at his most vital, although the coupled *Russian Easter Festival overture* (another Rimsky piece he made very much his own) is as vivid and colourful as one could wish.

Khachaturian's *Third Symphony* might almost have been designed to demonstrate how not to write symphonically. The composer's chronic tendency to repeat a phrase *ad nauseam*, his refusal to appreciate that enough is enough – there is a truly terrible organ passage in mad triplets early in this symphony – are the antithesis of true development. Even so, Stokowski's richly expressive direction and the virtuoso playing of the Chicago Symphony Orchestra in 1968 almost make the results tolerable, particularly when the recording is so spectacular. He recorded the Shostakovich *Sixth* at the same time, a wholly different approach to symphonic writing. Though Stokowski's is essentially a romantic view, finding little bitterness, the underlying poignancy of feeling is not lost when expressed in a more optimistic way. His expressive moulding of the composer's long-breathed melodic lines is naturally spontaneous, and the powerful first movement makes a memorable impression. The control of tempo throughout is wholly convincing – flexible without being over-indulgent – and the finale has a fine rhythmic point and sparkle. The characterization of the *Age of Gold suite* is no less vivid, the *Adagio* richly expansive to contrast with the famous *Polka*, which has never sounded wittier. Excellent recording, atmospheric and with a wide dynamic range.

The curious pairing in 1954 of Prokofiev and Menotti was among Stokowski's first stereo recordings for RCA (although he had already recorded in stereo for the soundtrack of Walt Disney's *Fan-*

tasia). The selection from *Romeo and Juliet* (still comparatively little known at that time) concentrated on the score's lyrical and passionate movements and endowed them with ardent romantic feeling. The coupling is colourful and surprisingly tuneful music from Menotti's ballet *Sebastian*; indeed, the *Barcarolle* and *Sebastian's dance* (a delicate, pastel-shaded waltz) are equally charming, helped by Stokowski's affectionate warmth.

Stokowski's *Pathétique*, however, is for *aficionados* only: it is very wayward. Impressively played and recorded, at Walthamstow in 1973, the performance shows too much evidence of Stokowski's desire to regard his interpretation as a personal document, and to impose his own personality on the music. The two famous rhapsodies by enescu and Liszt (and Stokowski was always closely associated with the *Second Hungarian rhapsody*) are played with characteristic charisma and zest.

The pair of Wagner CDs bring a truly Stokowskian approach. In the highly dramatic *Ring* sequences the voices are very noticeably absent; but when he does use singers, as in his programme with the Symphony of the Air, they are kept totally subservient to the conductor's luxuriantly rich orchestral conception. That is the only possible description of the string playing in the *Tristan Prelude*. This kind of approach – dedicated to sensuous beauty of sound alone – misses the inner quality of the music, and the closing pages of the *Venusberg music*, wonderfully rich though they are, have little feeling of spirituality. But with exciting performances of both the *Tannhäuser overture* (with vivid detail in the middle section) and the *Ride of the Valkyries*, this is still recommendable for Stokowski's unique treatment of Wagner.

The penultimate CD offers Stokowski's inflated orchestration of his own selected suite from Handel's *Water music*, plus a series of choral lollipops, beautifully sung by the Norman Luboff Choir, ranging from Bach's *Jesu, joy of man's desiring* and *Sheep may safely graze* to Wagner's *Pilgrims' chorus* from *Tannhäuser* and the spiritual, *Deep river*. The concert opens with a surprisingly successful choral arrangement of a Beethoven song called 'The heav'ns are telling' and closes with Gluck's *Dance of the Blessed Spirits*, which is treated similarly.

The final disc includes Stokowski's last recording of his most celebrated Bach transcription, plus excerpts from Wagner's *Rienzi overture* (including rehearsal sequences) and the Mahler *Second*. A brief but vivid 7-minute extract from the finale of Beethoven's *Pastoral Symphony*, played by members of the NBC Symphony Orchestra and taken from a very early stereo session, comes as a bonus. The standard of transfers throughout the series can reflect only credit on the current RCA engineering team. The notes by the well-known

Stokowskian expert Edward Johnson are brief but always interestingly informative.

J. S. BACH: *Suite 3, BWV 1068: Air; Chorale: Wachet auf,* from *BWV 140* (both arr. Stokowski). BEETHOVEN: *Coriolan overture* (all with the LSO). BRAHMS: *Academic festival overture* (with the New Philharmonia Orchestra. enesco: *Roumanian rhapsody No. 1.* LISZT: *Hungarian rhapsody No. 2.* SMETANA: *Má Vlast: Vltava* (all with RCA Victor SO). PROKOFIEV: *Romeo and Juliet* (scenes) (with NBC SO (members)). RACHMANINOV: *Vocalise.* VILLA-LOBOS: *Bachianas brasileiras No. 5* (both with Anna Moffo and American SO). RIMSKY-KORSAKOV: *Russian Easter Festival overture.* SHOSTAKOVICH: *Age of Gold (suite)* (both with Chicago SO). WAGNER: *Die Walküre: Magic fire music* (with RPO).

(B) *** RCA 74321 70931-2 (2) [id.].

One extraordinary thing about Stokowski is his ability to imbue every orchestra (especially the strings) with his very own Stokowskian magic. This collection gives a fair representation of both his overwhelming influence and his eccentricities, yet it is his ability to create fizzing excitement at the flick of the wrist which one most remembers. The recordings, mainly from the 1960s, are larger than life too – the drama of the opening of Liszt's *Hungarian rhapsody* is startling. All work well (even if they are a bit unrefined at times) within Stokowski's musical parameters. The sleeve notes contain nothing about the music (only a biography), but at bargain price this set makes a characteristic – if at times emotionally exhausting – collection of colourful music in magnetic performances.

Stolzman, Richard (clarinet), Berlin Deutsche Symphony Orchestra, Lukas Foss

Clarinet concertos: William Thomas MACKINLEY: *Concerto No. 2.* Einar ENGLUND: *Concerto.* Lukas FOSS: *Concerto.*
*** RCA Dig. 09026 61902-2 [id.].

Three major twentieth-century clarinet concertos (two American, one Swedish), superbly played by a master-clarinettist, splendidly conducted by one of the three featured composers, admirably recorded in Berlin, makes for an obviously strong recommendation. The work by Thomas McKinley opens uninhibitedly. Its scherzando first movement is marked *Allegro dramatico e tempestoso,* but the underlying lyricism is immediately obvious. The *Andantino* introduces what is essentially a 17-bar jazz blues (delectably inflected by the soloist), and the finale is a wild waltz (a touch Ravelian).

The atmospheric geography immediately

changes to a north-European clime for Englund's concerto, a haunting work with its at times darkly evocative central '*Serenata*' followed by a perky, unpredictable finale, here full of brio. The Lukas Foss Concerto is in four movements, the opening *Lento* concentrated and atmospherically compelling, followed by a jokey scherzo. The *Più lento* has controlled aleatory elements, followed an engagingly quirky grazioso close.

All in all, a stimulating triptych, which readily opens up for the listener with familiarity. The recording, made in Berlin's famous Jesus-Christus Kirche, is excellent.

Stuttgart Chamber Orchestra, Münchinger

'*Baroque concert*': PACHELBEL: *Canon.* GLUCK: *Orfeo: Dance of the Blessed Spirits.* HANDEL: *Water music: Suite No. 3; Organ concerto in F (Cuckoo and the nightingale)* (with M. Haselböck); *Oboe concerto No. 3 in G min.* (with L. Koch). L. MOZART: *Toy Symphony.* ALBINONI: *Adagio in G min.* (arr. GIAZOTTO). BACH: *Suite No. 3, BMV 1068: Air.* BOCCHERINI: *Minuet* (from *String quintet in E, Op. 13/5*).
(B) **(*) Decca Eclipse Dig. 448 239-2 [(M) id. import].

Beautifully recorded – this is an attractive concert with a very well-played suite from Handel's *Water music,* and the engaging *Cuckoo and the nightingale Organ concerto* (with Martin Haselböck an excellent soloist) to give a little ballast. The performance of Pachelbel's *Canon* is a little heavy-handed, but the strongly expressive account of Albinoni's *Adagio* is convincing. The *Toy Symphony* has some piquant special effects, and the shorter lollipops are played quite elegantly. The overall mood is a trifle serious, but that is Münchinger's way. For the Eclipse reissue, an elegant performance of a Handel *Oboe concerto* has been added.

SWR Stuttgart Radio Symphony Orchestra, Celibidache

MUSSORGSKY: *Pictures at an exhibition.* STRAVINSKY: *Le Baiser de la fée; The Firebird: suite.* RIMSKY-KORSAKOV: *Scheherazade.* PROKOFIEV: *Romeo and Juliet: excerpts; Scythian suite; Symphony No. 5.*
(*) DG 445 139-2 (3) [id.].

One hardly knows where to begin with this set! The opening *Promenade* of *Pictures at an Exhibition* begins lethargically – but that is nothing compared to the ludicrous tempo distortions of the following

Gnomus (marked *vivo*), which almost grinds to a halt at one point. Other eccentricities abound, and the result veers between the irritating and the boring: the finale is elongated beyond belief. Similar agogic distortions occur in the usually indestructible *Scheherazade*: the second movement, for example, begins rather beautifully, before rhythmic distortions utterly spoil the forward flow: the bassoon's lovely melody, 39 seconds in, is quite ruined. The *Firebird suite* opens with a certain amount of atmosphere, but very soon one has the urge to push the music forward; by 1 minute 50 seconds, the woodwind, in imitation, sound as though they are stuck in a groove. Reactions to the Prokofiev are more mixed. The *Scythian suite* is pretty feeble, the *Fifth symphony* is perhaps the best thing on this disc, but by no means overwhelming, and the *Romeo and Juliet* excerpts (three numbers on a free bonus CD) have a cool beauty, but again lack impetus. Every now and again, there are genuinely imaginative touches with Celibidache, but they are negated by his perverse eccentricity. The sound (these are all live recordings) is very average. This set is for total devotees of Celibidache only.

Symphonies: 'Great Symphonies'

BEETHOVEN: *Symphony No. 5 in C min., Op. 67* (Philharmonia Orchestra, Ashkenazy). BRAHMS: *Symphony No. 3 in F, Op. 90*; DVORAK: *Symphony No. 9 in E min. (From the New World), Op. 95.* (Vienna Philharmonic Orchestra, Kertész). HAYDN: *Symphony No. 94 in G (Surprise)* (Philharmonia Hungarica, Dorati). MENDELSSOHN: *Symphony No. 3 in A min. (Scottish), Op. 56* (LSO, Abbado). MOZART: *Symphony No. 40 in G min., KV.550* (VPO, Karajan). SAINT-SAENS: *Symphony No. 3 in C min. (Organ), Op. 78* (Los Angeles PO, Mehta). SCHUBERT: *Symphony No. 9 in C (Great), D.944* (Israel PO, Mehta). SIBELIUS: *Symphony No. 7 in C, Op. 105* (VPO, Maazel). TCHAIKOVSKY: *Symphony No. 4 in F min., Op. 36* (LSO, Szell).
(B) *** Australian Decca Analogue/Dig. 466 444-2 (5).

This set contains two really outstanding recordings: Szell's Tchaikovsky *Four*, and Maazel's Sibelius *Seventh*, with the Kertész *New World* not far behind. There is nothing substandard about anything else in this set either – most of the performances are well worth hearing, not least Ashkenazy's superbly recorded Beethoven *Fifth*, Dorati's Haydn *Surprise* and Mehta's vintage Decca version of the Saint-Saëns *Organ symphony*. He is less successful in Schubert's *Ninth*, but the low cost of this set – which includes excellent sleeve-notes – renders any quibbles of less importance.

Thames Chamber Orchestra, Michael Dobson

'The baroque concerto in England' (with Black, Bennett): ANON. (probably HANDEL): *Concerto grosso in F.* BOYCE: *Concerti grossi in E min. for strings; in B min. for 2 solo violins, cello and strings.* WOODCOCK: *Oboe concerto in E flat; Flute concerto in D.*
(M)*** CRD CRD 3331 [id.].

A wholly desirable collection, beautifully played and recorded. Indeed, the recording has splendid life and presence and often offers demonstration quality – try the opening of the Woodcock *Flute concerto*, for instance. The music is all highly rewarding. The opening concerto was included in Walsh's first edition of Handel's Op. 3 (as No. 4) but was subsequently replaced by another work. Whether or not it is by Handel, it is an uncommonly good piece, and it is given a superbly alert and sympathetic performance here. Neil Black and William Bennett are soloists of the highest calibre, and it is sufficient to say that they are on top form throughout this most enjoyable concert.

Toulouse Capitole Orchestra, Michel Plasson

French symphonic poems: DUKAS: *L'apprenti sorcier*. DUPARC: *Lénore; Aux étoiles*. FRANCK: *Le chasseur maudit*. LAZZARI: *Effet de nuit*. SAINT-SAENS: *Danse macabre*.
*** EMI Dig. CDC5 55385-2 [id.].

An interesting and (on the whole) successful programme, let down by the brilliant but unbeguiling account of *The Sorcerer's apprentice*. There is more fun in this piece than Plasson finds. Similarly, the humour of *Danse macabre* is not within Plasson's perceptions, although he gives an excitingly dramatic account of the piece and there is a seductive violin solo from Malcolm Stewart. There is plenty of gusto in *Le chasseur maudit*, where the opening horn-call is arresting, the chase is properly demonic and the malignant middle section masterful, when Christian stalwarts are sinisterly warned of the Satanic welcome waiting for those choosing the hunt rather than the church for their Sunday morning occupation.

Hardly less telling is Duparc's *Lénore*, an equally melodramatic scenario (also espoused by Liszt, with narrative included). This concerns a ghoulish midnight embrace with a skeleton after the eager heroine has been carried off on horseback by her dead lover. But the two most memorable pieces here are the radiantly serene *Aux étoiles* ('The astral light of dawn'), also by Duparc, and – most haunting of all – Sylvio Lazzari's impressionistic *Effet de nuit*, with its bleakly sinuous evocation on the bass clarinet of the scaffold silhouetted in the rain against the darkening evening sky. Its climax depicts 'three ghastly prisoners marching dejectedly' in the pitiless downpour, urged on by 225 halberdiers. The recording is excellent: spacious, yet vivid; it is a shame about *L'apprenti sorcier*.

Trumpet: 'The sound of the trumpet'

'The sound of the trumpet': CLARKE: *Trumpet voluntary*. M.-A. CHARPENTIER: *Te Deum: Prelude* (arr. Hazel). PURCELL: *Trumpet tune and air* (arr. Hurford) (all with Peter Hurford, organ, Michael Laird Brass Ens.). HAYDN: *Trumpet concerto in E flat* (Alan Stringer, trumpet, ASMF, Marriner). BACH: *Christmas oratorio: Nun seid ihr wohl gerochen* (arr. Reeve). SCHEIDT: *Galliard battaglia*. HANDEL: *Occasional oratorio: March* (arr. Hazel); *Royal Fireworks music: Overture* (arr. & cond. Howarth) (all with Philip Jones Brass Ens.); *Messiah: The trumpet shall sound* (with Gwynne Howell, bass). VIVALDI: *Double trumpet concerto in C, RV 537* (with John Wilbraham, Philip Jones, trumpets). HUMMEL: *Trumpet concerto in E* (with John Wilbraham, trumpet) (all three with ASMF, Marriner). STANLEY: *Trumpet tune in D* (arr. Pearson; with Leslie Pearson, organ). ARBAN: *Carnival of Venice* (arr. & cond. Camarata; L. Festival O) (both with John Wilbraham, trumpet).
⊙ (M) *** Decca Analogue/Dig. 458 194-2 [id.].

The Decca production team are particularly adept at compiling an anthology like this, and there is simply no better single-disc recommendation for those who enjoy the sound of trumpets – regal and exciting – on the lips of true virtuosi. Such indeed are John Wilbraham and the individual players of the Michael Laird and Philip Jones Ensembles (especially in Elgar Howarth's highly effective brass arrangement of the *Overture* from Handel's *Royal Fireworks music*). The popular favourites by Jeremiah Clarke, once attributed to Purcell, and Purcell himself, his *Trumpet tune and air*, are equally appealing.

Wilbraham's account of the Hummel *Concerto* is among the finest ever recorded, elegant in the slow movement and with the finale sparkling irresistibly. Marriner and the ASMF, during their vintage period, accompany with comparable polish, as they do Alan Stringer, who plays the Haydn *Concerto* excellently, with a bolder and more forthright open timbre which is undoubtedly authentic. Peter Hurford, when he participates, is similarly stylish.

Almost every item here is a winner, and the stereo interplay in Scheidt's *Galliard battaglia* is indicative of the demonstration standard of many of the recordings included. The programme ends with a dazzling display from John Wilbraham in Camarata's lollipop arrangement of the most famous of all cornet solos, Arban's variations on the *Carnival of Venice*. The CD has good documentation and a particularly enticing frontispiece, with the title of the anthology embossed in gold lettering on the jewel-case – truly worthy of our Rosette.

Tuckwell, Barry (horn), Academy of St Martin-in-the-Fields, Sir Neville Marriner or (i) with English Chamber Orchestra

Horn concertos: TELEMANN: *Concerto in D*. CHERUBINI: *Sonata No. 2 in F for horn and strings*. Christoph FORSTER: *Concerto in E flat*. WEBER: *Concertino in E min., Op. 45*. Leopold MOZART: *Concerto in D*. Giovanni PUNTO: *Concertos Nos. 5 in F; 6 in E flat; 10 in F; 11 in E*. (i) Michael HAYDN: *Concertino in D* (arr. SHERMAN). (i) Joseph HAYDN: *Concerto No. 1 in D*.
⊙ (B) *** EMI Double Fforte CZS5 69395-2 (2) [CDFB 69395].

Barry Tuckwell readily inherited Dennis Brain's mantle and held his place as Britain's pre-eminent horn player for several decades before finally retiring in 1997. This EMI Double Fforte set celebrates his supreme achievement in nearly a dozen of the finest concertos for his instrument; the Tuckwell recordings of the key works by Wolfgang Amadeus and Richard Strauss are of course available elsewhere. His supreme mastery and ease of execution, his natural musicality and warm lyricism of line – to say nothing of his consistent beauty of tone – make every performance here memorable, and he has the advantage of polished, graceful accompaniments from the ASMF under Marriner, except in the works by Michael and Joseph Haydn, in which he directs the ECO himself with comparable elegance.

The concerto of Telemann opens with a catchy *moto perpetuo*, despatched with aplomb; then comes a fine *Adagio* which often moves to the very top of the horn's upper range before the tension is released in the buoyant finale. The Cherubini *Sonata* opens with a melancholy *Largo*, then erupts into joyous high spirits, while the racing opening arpeggios of the concerto by Leopold Mozart and the tight trills in the finale (with harpsichord echoes) are managed with comparable exuberance. The Weber is an attractively diverse and extensive (17 minutes) set of variations and includes a good example of horn 'chords', where the soloist plays one note and hums another; it also has an exceptionally joyful finale.

One of the novelties is a delightful concerto by the virtually unknown Christoph Forster (1693–1745) with its amiably jogging first movement marked *Con discrezione* and its brief, disconsolate *Adagio* followed by a closing Rondo in which, though the clouds clear away, the lyrical feeling remains. In some ways most striking of all is the collection of four concertos by the Bohemian virtuoso Giovanni Punto, a successful and highly cultivated composer whose music is enjoyably distinctive, a mixture of Mozartean influences and Hummelian *galanterie*. The individual CD of these four works was issued to celebrate Barry Tuckwell's fiftieth birthday, and the performances show him at his best. The recording throughout is of EMI's finest analogue quality, and the remastering retains the warmth and beauty of the originals.

Turner, John (recorder), Royal Ballet Sinfonia, Gavin Sutherland or Edward Gregson

English recorder music for recorder and strings: LANE: *Suite ancienne.* ARNOLD: *Concertino, Op. 41a.* PITFIELD: *Concerto for recorder, string orchestra and percussion; 3 Nautical sketches.* GREGSON: *3 Matisse impressions.* LYON: *Concertino.* PARROTT: *Prelude and Waltz.* BULLARD: *Recipes.*
*** Olympia Dig. OCD 657 [id.].

Who could have guessed that eight concertante works for recorder and strings would have been so entertainingly diverse? Philip Lane's *Suite* in the olden style is unrepentant pastiche with an irresistibly exuberant finale (*Beau Brummel's bath night*). Arnold's *Concertino* is even more quirky, with a haunting central *Chaconne*. Thomas Pitfield was a distinguished Professor of Composition at the Royal Manchester College and subsequently the Royal Northern College of Music, and his *Concerto*, which uses both treble and descant recorders, moves easily from English pastoralism to a *Tarantella* dance finale.

The *Nautical sketches* draw on sea-shanties with equally light touch. Edward Gregson cleverly catches the mood of three Matisse paintings: the evocative style is predictably French but also individual. David Lyon's *Concertino* is the most recent work (1999) and its wry opening movement nicely offsets the delicacy of the haunting central waltz. Parrott's *Prelude* opens more abrasively, bringing a welcome astringency, then he relents into another delectably embroidered waltz. Bullard's very entertaining *Recipes* certainly titillates the palette, with a *Barbecue blues* wittily followed by a *Prawn* habanera, and, after a Chinese *Special chop suey*, ends

with a circus galop enthusiastically celebrating *Fish and chips*.

The invention of all these works is consistently diverting and with a masterly soloist in John Turner, excellent accompaniments from the Royal Ballet Sinfonia under Gavin Sutherland (or Gregson, who conducts his own work) this is very enjoyable throughout and highly recommendable.

Udagawa, Hideko (violin)

Concertante works (with LPO, Klein): GLAZUNOV: *Violin concerto in A min., Op. 82.* TCHAIKOVSKY: *Souvenir d'un lieu cher, Op. 42.* CHAUSSON: *Poème, Op. 25.* SARASATE: *Romanze andaluza, Op. 22/1.* SAINT-SAENS: *Caprice, Op. 52.*
(B) *** Carlton Dig. 30367 0031-2 [(M) id.].

With the violin balanced forward, the Glazunov receives a heartfelt performance which rivals almost any, even if the finale does not offer quite such bravura fireworks as Itzhak Perlman (at full price). It is valuable to have all three of the haunting pieces which Tchaikovsky called *Souvenirs d'un lieu cher* – the *Méditation* and *Mélodie* much better known than the central *Scherzo*. They are here done in Glazunov's orchestral arrangements. The Chausson *Poème* is warmly convincing if a little heavy-handed, the Sarasate Andalusian *Romanze* dances delightfully, and only in the final Saint-Saëns *Caprice* does Udagawa's playing sound a little effortful in its virtuosity. Warm, full recording to match.

Ulsamer Collegium, Josef Ulsamer, with Konrad Ragossnig (lute) and Eduard Melkus Ensemble

'Dance music through the ages'

I: *Renaissance dance music:* ANON.: *Lamento di Tristano; Trotto; Istampita Ghaetta; Istampita Cominciamento di gioia; Saltarello; Bassa danza à 2; Bassa danza à 3.* GULIELMUS: *Bassa danza à 2.* DE LA TORRE: *Alta danza à 3.* ATTAIGNANT: *Basse danses: La brosse – Tripla – Tourdion; La gatta; La Magdelena.* DALZA: *Calata ala Spagnola.* NEUSIEDLER: *Der Judentanz; Welscher Tanz.* MILAN: *Pavana I/II.* MUDARRA: *Romanesca guarda me las vacas.* PHALESE: *Passamezzo – Saltarello; Passamezzo d'Italye – Reprise – Gallarde.* LE ROY: *Branle de Bourgogne.* B. SCHMIDT: *Englischer Tanz; Tanz: Du hast mich wollen nemmen.* PAIX: *Schiarazula Marazula; Ungaresca – Saltarello.* SUSATO: *Ronde.* GERVAISE: *Branle de Bourgogne; Branle de Champagne.*

II: *Early baroque dance music:* MAINERIO:

Schiarazula Marazula; Tedesca – Saltarella; Ungaresca – Saltarella. BESARDO: *Branle – Branle gay.* MOLINARO: *Saltarello; Ballo detto Il Conte Orlando: Saltarello.* GESUALDO: *Gagliarda del Principe di Venosa.* CAROSO: *Barriera (Balletto in lode della Serenissima D. Verginia Medici d'Este, Duchessa di Modena); Celeste Giglio (Balletto in lode delli Serenissimi Signori Don Ranuccio Farnese, e Donna Margarita Aldobrandina Duca, e Duchessa di Parma e di Piacenza etc.).* CAROUBEL: *Pavana de Spaigne; 2 Courantes; 2 Voltes.* HOLBORNE: *Pavane: The Funerals; Noel's galliard; Coranto: Heigh ho holiday.* ANON.: *Kempe's jig.* DOWLAND: *Queen Elizabeth her galliard; Mrs Winter's jump.* SIMPSON: *Alman.* GIBBONS: *Galliard.* PRAETORIUS: *Galliarde de la guerre; Reprise.* HAUSSMANN: *Tanz; Paduan; Galliard; Catkanei.*

III: *High baroque dance music:* ANON.: *Country dances: Running footman; Greensleeves and Pudding eyes; Cobler's jigg; How can I keep my maiden head.* SANZ: *Canarios.* CORRETTE: *Menuet I/II.* HOTTETERRE: *Bourrée.* BOUIN: *La Montauban.* SANZ: *Pasacalle de la Cavalleria de Napoles; Españoletas; Gallarda y Villano.* CHEDEVILLE: *Musette.* REUSNER: *Suite Paduan (Allemande; Courantel Sarabande; Gavotte; Gigue).* POGLIETTI: *Balletto (Allemande; Amener; Gavotte; Sarabande; Gavotte).* DESMARETS: *Menuet; Passe-pied.* FISCHER: *Bourrée; Gigue.* anon.: *Gavotte.* LOEILLET IL DE GANT: *Corente; Sarabande; Gigue.* LULLY: *L'Amour malade* (opéra ballet): *Conclusion; Une Noce de Village* (dance suite).

IV: *Rococo dance music* (Eduard Melkus Ensemble): C. P. E. BACH: *5 Polonaises, Wq.190; 2 Menuets with 3 Trios, Wq.189.* RAMEAU: *Zoroastre: Dances (Air tendre en Rondeau; Loure; Tambourin en Rondeau; Sarabande; Gavotte gaye avec Trio; Premier Rigaudon; Air en Chaconne).* STARZER: *Contredanse; Gavotte mit Trio; Pas de deux; Menuet; Gavotte mit Trio; Moderato; Gavotte; Menuet mit Trio; Gavotte mit Trio; Passe-pied mit Trio.*

V: *Viennese classical dance music:* EYBLER: *Polonaise.* HAYDN: *2 Menuets, Hob IX/11:4 & IX/16:12.* GLUCK: *Orfeo ed Euridice: Ballet; Don Juan (Allegretto).* MOZART: *6 Landerische, K.606; 5 Kontretänze, K.609.* ZEHN: *Deutsche.* BEETHOVEN: *4 Kontretänze, WoO 14/4, 5, 7 & 12.* SALIERI: *Menuetto.* WRANITZKY: *Quodlibet.*

VI: *Viennese dance music from the Biedermeier period (1815–48):* PALMER: *Waltz in E.* BEETHOVEN: *Mödlinger Tänze Nos. 1–8, WoO 17.* MOSCHELES: *German dances with trios and coda.* SCHUBERT: *5 Minuets with Trios, D.89; 4 komische Ländler, D.354.* ANON.: *Linzer Tanz; Vienna polka.* LANNER: *Hungarian galop in F.*

❂ (B) *** DG 439 964-2 (4) [(M) id. import].

This collection, on four well-filled CDs (recorded between 1972 and 1974), explores the history of European dance music from the beginning of the fifteenth century right through to the first three decades of the nineteenth century, just about the time when Johann Strauss Senior was making his début. The members of the Ulsamer Collegium play an extraordinary range of authentic period instruments. Keyboards, strings, wind and plucked vihuela, as well as guitar, lute and hurdy-gurdy, are used with the greatest imagination, always to seduce the ear with variety of colour. There is not a whiff of pedantry or of abrasiveness of the kind that too often accompanies 'authentic' performances, yet the documentation is characteristically and fascinatingly thorough. The consistent tunefulness of the music is a continued source of pleasure and surprise.

Among the composers of early baroque dance music, Pierre Francisque Caroubel and Mario Fabrizio Caroso stand out: the suite of dances by the former, played variously on gambas and recorder consort, is most diverting. On the second CD, the keyboard, gamba and lute pieces from the English Elizabethan school hardly need advocacy, but they are beautifully played (the lute and guitar solos of Konrad Ragossnig are most distinguished throughout the set) as is the jolly suite of dances by Valentin Haussmann – another unfamiliar name to turn up trumps.

Among the high baroque composers Esaias Reusner (1636–79) provides another diverting dance suite which, like the ballet music of Alessandro Poglietti, proves as elegant and finished as the ballet suite of Lully. In the rococo era, Carl Philipp Emanuel Bach contributes five spirited *Polonaises*, and after a gracious interlude from Rameau there is a set of more robust and extrovert dances from Josef Starzer (1726–87). We enter the Viennese classical period with a clash of cymbals enlivening a *Polonaise* by Joseph Eybler (1764–1846), who sounds ahead of his time; but the two *Minuets* of Haydn stay well in period. At this stage of the proceedings the excellent Eduard Melkus Ensemble take over.

The first of the Mozart *Contredanses*, K.609, which opens the fifth CD makes reference to a famous tune from *Figaro*, and Paul Wranitzky quotes from the same opera in his *Quodlibet*. Beethoven produced irresistible music. Moscheles and Schubert follow his example, the latter providing some deliciously flimsy *Ländler*, while the delicate *E major Waltz* of Michael Palmer (1782–1827), the two anonymous dances from Linz and Vienna and the *Hungarian galop* of Joseph Lanner (which ends the programme) point onwards to the heyday of Viennese dance music, when Johann Strauss Junior was to reign supreme. Overall, this is a most stimulating and rewarding survey.

USSR Symphony Orchestra, Evgeny Svetlanov

'Waltzes and Polonaises by Russian composers':
LIADOV: *Polonaise in C, Op. 49.* ARENSKY: *Suite No. 3, Op. 33: Polonaise in D; Waltz.*
NAPRAVNIK: *Dubrovsky: Polonaise.* GLINKA: *A Life for the Tsar: Waltz and Polonaise.*
TCHAIKOVSKY: *Swan Lake: Polonaise and Waltz. Sleeping Beauty: Polonaise and Waltz. The Nutcracker: Waltz of the flowers. Eugene Onegin: Polonaise and Waltz. Cherevicki: Polonaise.*
LYAPUNOV: *Polonaise in D min., Op. 16.*
GLAZUNOV: *Raymonda: Grand waltz. Les ruses d'amour: Waltz. Scènes de ballet: Waltz and Polonaise.* RUBINSTEIN: *Valse caprice, Op. 86.*
RIMSKY-KORSAKOV: *Christmas Eve: Polonaise. Pan Voyevoda: Polonaise.* MUSSORGSKY: *Boris Godunov: Introduction and Polonaise.*
(B) ** BMG/Melodiya Twofer 74321 53456-2 (2) [(M) id. import].

Although the polonaise is a Polish dance-form, Russian composers have virtually adopted the style for themselves. Tchaikovsky wrote the best of them, but Rimsky too brought the polacca rhythm to life with brilliant orchestral colouring, and Mussorgsky's *Polonaise* in *Boris Godunov* is predictably individual. Those by Liadov which open the collection are a bit pompous here but have pleasingly lyrical middle sections; the piece by Napravnik sparkles more. When it comes to waltzes, Tchaikovsky again leads the field, but Glazunov could charm the ear too, as the three ballet waltzes on the second disc demonstrate. Rubinstein's *Valse caprice* is rather cheap. The performances are warm, lively and polished, but at times the recording, generally very good, is a bit over-brilliant on top, with fierce percussion.

Vienna Philharmonic Orchestra, Sir John Eliot Gardiner

'Vienna soirée: SUPPE: *Overture Morning, noon and night in Vienna.* ZIEHRER: *Wiener Bürger waltz; Fächer-Polonaise; Schönfeld march.*
LEHAR: *Waltzes: Ballsirenen; Gold and Silver.*
LANNER: *Die Schönbrunner waltz; Tourbillon galopp.* HEUBERGER: *Der Opernball Overture.*
*** DG Dig. 463 185-2 [id.].

Sir John Eliot Gardiner here shows how the Viennese tradition might prosper even without a Strauss contribution. The Vienna Philharmonic is in scintillating form in this delightful collection of overtures, waltzes and shorter pieces, some of them rare, with one item not otherwise available, Lanner's dashing *Tourbillon-Galopp.* Gardiner's account of the Suppé overture is at once high-powered, highly

polished and deliciously sprung, setting the pattern for the rest. This is playing of pin-point precision, gloriously resonant, and Gardiner, as in his Vienna recording of Lehár's *Merry Widow*, enters fully into the Viennese spirit. That same composer's *Ballsirenen waltz* is in fact a fantasy on themes from the operetta, refined and tender as well as ebullient. The other Lehár item too, the *Gold and silver waltz*, brings magical pianissimos. Most winning of all are the rarer, shorter items, with Ziehrer's *Fächer-Polonaise* and *Schönfeld march* played uninhibitedly with irresistible zest and bounce. The DG recording, made in the Vienna Musikverein, has ideal freshness and clarity.

Vienna Philharmonic Orchestra, Herbert von Karajan

'The great Decca recordings': BRAHMS: *Symphonies Nos. 1 in C min., Op. 68; 3 in F, Op. 90; Tragic overture, Op. 81.* HAYDN: *Symphonies Nos. 103 in E flat (Drumroll); 104 in D (London).* MOZART: *Symphonies Nos. 40 in G min., K.550; 41 in C (Jupiter), K.551.* TCHAIKOVSKY: *Romeo and Juliet (fantasy overture); Nutcracker suite; Swan Lake (ballet): suite; Sleeping Beauty (ballet): suite.* ADAM: *Giselle (ballet; abridged).* BEETHOVEN: *Symphony No. 7 in A, Op. 92.* DVORAK: *Symphony No. 8 in G, Op. 88.* GRIEG: *Peer Gynt (incidental music): suite No. 1; suite No. 2: Ingrid's lament; Solveig's song.* HOLST: *The Planets (suite), Op. 31.* Johann STRAUSS Jr: *Die Fledermaus: Overture and ballet music. Der Zigeunerbaron: Overture.* Polkas: *Annen; Auf der Jagd.* Waltz: *Geschichten aus dem Wiener Wald.* Josef STRAUSS: *Delirien waltz.* Richard STRAUSS: *Till Eulenspiegel; Salome: Dance of the 7 veils. Don Juan, Op. 20; Also sprach Zarathustra, Op. 30.*
(B) **(*) Decca 448 042 (9) [(M) id. import].

Following directly on after his EMI Philharmonia recordings with Walter Legge, Karajan's five-year Decca period with the Vienna Philharmonic – master-minded by producers John Culshaw and Erik Smith – lasted from 1959 until 1964. Though the epithet 'great' can be applied to only a handful of the recordings in this box, almost all of them have far more character and musical appeal than many of the more anonymous records flooding the present-day CD market. Certainly Karajan's 1960 *Romeo and Juliet* stands the test of time, not only for its passion but also for its delicacy of feeling in the 'moonlight' music, and his virtually complete (1961) recording of Adam's *Giselle* (with sumptuous sound still approaching demonstration standard) shows what a fine ballet conductor he was, the playing combining affectionate warmth, elegance and drama.

OTHER CONCERTS 466

The suites from the three Tchaikovsky ballets have comparable panache and generate considerable excitement; apart from the rather plangent timbre of the VPO's principal oboe, they have plenty of glowing colour, with the *Panorama* from *Sleeping Beauty* endearingly suave and the final climax from *Swan Lake* riveting in its histrionic power. The *Nutcracker suite* has more vivid characterization than the later, Berlin Philharmonic account, with the *Waltz of the flowers* lilting agreeably. The remastering scores over the analogue DG versions in its greater ambient depth.

The excerpts from *Peer Gynt* bring the freshest response from the VPO, with gutsy Trolls galloping into the *Hall of the Mountain King*, and *Solveig's song* radiantly beautiful. Again, the 1961 Decca recording stands up well alongside the later DG analogue version (which we count as marginally the most alluring of his three stereo accounts) and in many ways is superior in body and naturalness. As for *The Planets*, dating from that same vintage year, this is certainly a great performance, with *Mars* among the most thrilling ever put on disc. With whining Wagnerian tubas it makes a terrifying impact; then *Venus* follows, transmuted into sensuous balm – the *Venus* of gentle ardour rather than mysticism. *Jupiter* is bucolic and breezy, the Vienna strings bringing their own characteristic tone-colour to the big central tune. *Saturn* with its slow, sad march and *Uranus* with superb VPO brass are no less outstanding, and the wordless chorus at the end of *Neptune* is more atmospheric than in almost any other version. The analogue recording is so stunningly vivid that it could have been made yesterday.

Karajan never surpassed his 1960 VPO collection of overtures, polkas and waltzes by Johann and Josef Strauss until he came to make his wonderful (DG) 1987 New Year concert with the same orchestra. His later, BPO records sound glossy by comparison, yet here his rhythmic touch is unerring in the two overtures, while the polkas have all the flair you could ask for. However, the highlight is the highly seductive account of *Tales from the Vienna woods*, played most beautifully, an account which may have been equalled, but has never been surpassed.

The superlative performances of the Richard Strauss tone-poems are hardly less remarkable, and they sound wonderfully fresh. In this repertoire no one can quite match Karajan in the panache and point of his conducting. This programme is available separately in Decca's Legends series and is discussed above under its Composer entry.

In the symphonic repertoire the results are less even. Of the two Haydn symphonies, No. 103 is more urbane than No. 104, though both offer enjoyably polished VPO playing: there is plenty of robust vigour in the latter and both slow movements are beautifully shaped. The same comments might apply to Mozart's *Fortieth* and *Jupiter Symphonies*. In the *G minor* every detail remains beautifully in place, each phrase nicely contoured and in perspective. Beautifully articulate, this performance has genuine dramatic power, even though one feels that it all moves within carefully regulated limits. The reading of the *Jupiter* is strong and direct and has breadth as well as warmth. Exposition repeats are observed in the first movements of each symphony, but not in the finale of the *Jupiter*.

Of the two Brahms symphonies, No. 1 gives the impression of being over-rehearsed. Its pacing does not always seem spontaneous, with an overall lack of tension; though towards the end of the finale Karajan cannot help creating genuine excitement, this is dissipated in a very slow chorale reference in the coda. The *Third* is much more successful. Here is another case in which the Vienna performance rivals the quality of the later, DG Berlin version. In both, Karajan takes the opening expansively; in both, he omits the exposition repeat. The third movement, too, is very slow, but the overall reading has plenty of grip and tension, and the Decca recording has a fuller and more resonant bass than the DG, and this well suits Brahms.

The recording of Beethoven's *Seventh* is also full-bodied, though not as fine as that for the Dvořák *Eighth*. 1961 was certainly a vintage year for the Decca engineers. The Beethoven performance is massive rather than incandescent and refuses to catch fire or grip the listener emotionally. The Dvořák is another matter, a most winning performance with superb orchestral playing. There are moments of slight self-indulgence in the Trio of the Scherzo, but the result is delectable when the Vienna strings are at their creamiest; overall, this account blends polish and spontaneity in almost equal measure. The orchestra are clearly enjoying themselves and so do we.

Vienna Philharmonic Orchestra, Rudolf Kempe

'The Vienna Philharmonic on holiday':
MASCAGNI: *Cavalleria rusticana:Intermezzo.*
PONCHIELLI: *La Gioconda: Dance of the hours.*
SCHMIDT: *Notre Dame: Intermezzo.* GOUNOD: *Faust: Waltz.* BAYER: *Die Puppenfee: suite.*
OFFENBACH: *Orpheus in the Underworld: Overture.* GOTOVAC: *Ero the joker (dance).*
SCHUBERT: *Rosamunde: Overture (Die Zauberharfe); Entr'acte in B flat; Ballet in G.*
GLUCK: *Orfeo et Euridice: Dance of the Blessed Spirits.*
*** Testament SBT 1127 [id.].

It is good to be reminded so vividly of an aspect of Rudolf Kempe's mastery too easily forgotten – his Beechamesque charm in light music. Waltz rhythms are given a delicious lilt not just in Viennese items like the delightful Josef Bayer suite, *Die Puppenfee*, but in Gounod too, with Kempe bringing out the delicacy as well as the vigour. Kempe's use of rubato is often extreme – arguably too much so in the Schubert *Rosamunde* music – but it never fails to be winning in a very Viennese way, as in the rare Franz Schmidt *Intermezzo*. The Ponchielli, once so popular, now neglected, sparkles with uninhibited joy, as does the Offenbach, and it is good to have such a rarity as the *Kolo* by the Zagreb conductor and composer Jakob Gotovac, rhythmic and colourful. The recordings were all made in the Musikvereinsaal in Vienna in December 1961, with the glowing EMI recording well caught in Testament transfers which bring out both warmth and depth of focus.

Vienna Philharmonic Orchestra, Carlos Kleiber

'1992 New Year Concert': J. STRAUSS Jr: Overture: *Der Zigeunerbaron*. Polkas: *Neue pizzicato; Stadt und Land; Tritsch-Tratsch; Unter Donner und Blitz; Vergnügungszug*. Waltzes: *An der schönen, blauen Donau; Tausend und eine Nacht. Persischer march*. J. STRAUSS Sr: *Radetsky march*. Josef STRAUSS: Waltzes: *Dorfschwalben aus Osterreich; Sphärenklänge*. NICOLAI: Overture: *The Merry Wives of Windsor*.
*** Sony Dig. SK 48376 [id.].

When Carlos Kleiber conducted the 1989 event, he seemed at times a little stiff. But here he manages precision alongside lilt, discipline as well as verve. There is plenty of elegance and warmth too, in a programme entirely without novelties but where the waltzes nearly always go as spontaneously as the polkas, though the *Blue Danube* is no match for Karajan's version of two years earlier. The recording is well up to standard, vivid yet spacious and full.

Vienna Philharmonic Orchestra, Hans Knappertsbusch

'Orchestral favourites': J. STRAUSS Sr: *Radetzky march*. KAREL KOMZAK: Waltz: *Bad'ner Mad'ln*. J. STRAUSS Jr: Polkas: *Annen polka; Tritsch-Tratsch polka; Leichtes Blut*. Waltzes: *Accelerationen. G'schichten aus dem Wienerwald*. ZIEHRER: Waltz: *Wiener Bürger*. WEBER/BERLIOZ: *Invitation to the dance*. NICOLAI: Overture: *The Merry Wives of Windsor*. TCHAIKOVSKY: *Nutcracker suite*. BRAHMS: *Variations on a theme of Haydn; Academic festival overture*. SCHUBERT: *Marche militaire, Op. 51/1*.

(B) ** Decca Double 440 624-2 (2) [(M) id. import].

Hans Knappertsbusch has earned a gramophone reputation for rather slow and sometimes lethargic tempi, but the Strauss performances are lively enough, if without real magic. However, the *Nutcracker suite* is given rather a po-faced account. The Weber/Berlioz *Invitation to the dance*, although a little stiff, has something of a swing, and the Nicolai overture goes quite well. The recordings are fair for their day: the Strauss items (1957) sound a bit dated, but the later part of the programme (1960) is quite vividly focused. However, this set does not show the conductor in his very best light.

Vienna Philharmonic or Royal Philharmonic Orchestra, Rafael Kubelik

'Portrait of Kubelik': MOZART: Serenade: *Eine kleine Nachtmusik, K.525; Symphony No. 36 in C (Linz), K.425*. TCHAIKOVSKY: *Symphony No. 4 in F min., Op. 36*. SCHUBERT: *Symphony No. 9 in C (Great)*.
(BB) ** Royal Long Players DCL 705892 (2).

These performances are all well played and recorded, but neither provide a rounded portrait of Kubelik, nor show him at his best. The Mozart readings are fresh enough (the *Linz* is preferable to Klemperer's) but not in any way distinctive, and the *Great C major Symphony* of Schubert fails to take off until the finale. It is not so much that Kubelik makes positive errors of judgment, but that the whole does not add up to the sum of its parts in the way that Josef Krips's early Decca version does. His reading of the Tchaikovsky *Fourth* is more consistent. It has real qualities of understanding and its freedom from idiosyncrasies is a plus point too, for it is very well played and warmly and brightly recorded. But in the last resort the lack of free running adrenalin counts against it and placed alongside Szell, (see above under the composer) it is comparatively half-hearted.

Vienna Philharmonic Orchestra, Riccardo Muti

'1993 New Year Concert': J. STRAUSS Sr: *Sperl-Galopp; Radetzsky march*. J. STRAUSS Jr: *Klipp Klapp galop; Egyptische-Marsch; Overture Indigo und die Vierzig Räuber; Perpetuum mobile*; Polkas: *Auf der Jagd; Diplomaten; Pizzicato polka; Veilchen*; Waltzes: *Die Publicisten; An der schönen blauen Donau*. Josef STRAUSS: *Transaktionen*. LANNER: *Steyrische-Tänz; Hans-Jörgel*.

*** Ph. (IMS) Dig. 438 493-2 [id.].

Riccardo Muti seems an unlikely candidate for sweet-toothed Vienna *bon-bons*, but the atmosphere of this celebrated occasion has its usual effect and he clearly lets his hair down after a while. Once again there are novelties and they sparkle readily when Muti can produce such unselfconscious Straussian manners. Lanner's *Steyrische-Tänz* provides the surprise of the CD by unexpectedly turning out to be the source of the barrel-organ waltz in Stravinsky's *Petrushka*. The tension is not quite consistent throughout the concert, with the second half (beginning with the overture) setting an even more compelling atmosphere; but overall this is such a happy occasion that one cannot but enjoy the experience. Applause is nicely edited and is not too much of a problem. The documentation reveals the history of the event, fascinating in itself. Excellent recording.

Virtuosi di Praga, Oldřich Vlček

Music for strings: GRIEG: *Holberg suite.*
RESPIGHI: *Ancient airs and dances: Suite No. 3.*
ELGAR: *Serenade in E min., Op. 20.* ROUSSEL:
Sinfonietta, Op. 52.
(BB) **(*) Discover Dig. DICD 920236 [id.].

The Prague Virtuosi are an expert body of soloists who command an impressive sonority in spite of their modest size (here eleven players). Some ears might feel that the Elgar *Serenade* lacks ripeness of Elgarian feeling, yet the *Larghetto* is tenderly affecting. Equally, the Respighi suite of *Ancient airs* sounds fresher, less anachronistically voluptuous than usual. The chamber scale suits the *Holberg suite* admirably, with plenty of energy and bite. But undoubtedly the most effective performance here is the Roussel *Sinfonietta*, bracingly astringent and grippingly vital.

Wallfisch, Elizabeth (violin), Parley of Instruments, Peter Holman

'English classical violin concertos': James
BROOKS: *Concerto No. 1 in D.* Thomas LINLEY Jr:
Concerto in F. Thomas SHAW: *Concerto in G.*
Samuel WESLEY: *Concerto No. 2 in D.*
**(*) Hyperion Dig. CDA 66865 [id.].

Peter Holman and his Parley of Instruments expend much energy and Elizabeth Wallfisch considerable musical sensibility to bring these concertos from the late eighteenth century fully to life. They succeed admirably in that, working hard over music which is usually felicitous and always well crafted but too often predictable. In first movements one keeps getting the impression of second-rate Haydn. However, the opening movement of the James Brooks

Concerto is amiably pleasing in its melodic contours and offers the soloist plenty of lively bravura. Its brief *Largo affettuoso* is agreeable too, and the dancing finale sparkles on the Wallfisch bow, and she produces a neat cadenza.

Thomas Linley offers a *galant* Moderato first movement, another all-too-brief but graceful slow movement with a nice rhythmic snap; the finale is a charming gavotte. But Thomas Shaw goes one better in his *Adagio*, creating the best tune on the disc, for his slow movement, again with a Scottish snap, is most winning, very like a folksong. The finale bounces and the horns hunt boisterously. Wesley's first movement is vigorous and assured, if too long; and in the slow movement a pair of the orchestral violins join the soloist in a trio. The finale is very jolly and buoyant. The recording is excellent and, dipped into, this collection will give pleasure, providing you do not expect too much.

Williams, John (guitar)

Guitar concertos (with ECO, (i) Sir Charles Groves; (ii) Daniel Barenboim): (i) GIULIANI: *Concerto No. 1 in A, Op. 30.* VIVALDI: *Concertos in A and D.* RODRIGO: *Fantasia para un gentilhombre;* (ii) *Concierto de Aranjuez.*
VILLA-LOBOS: *Concerto.* (i)
CASTELNUOVO-TEDESCO: *Concerto No. 1 in D, Op. 99.*
(M) *** Sony M2YK 45610 (2) [id.].

This bouquet of seven concertante works for guitar from John Williams could hardly be better chosen, and the performances are most appealing. Moreover the transfers are very well managed and, if the guitar is very forward and larger than life, the playing is so expert and spontaneous that one hardly objects. All these performances are among the finest ever recorded, and Groves and Barenboim provide admirably polished accompaniments, matching the eager spontaneity of their soloist.

'The Seville concert' ((i) with Orquesta Sinfónica de Sevilla, José Buenagu): ALBENIZ: *Suite españolas: Sevilla; Asturias.* BACH: *Lute suite No. 4, BWV 1006a: Prelude.* D. SCARLATTI: *Keyboard sonata in D min., Kk 13* (arr. WILLIAMS). (i) VIVALDI: *Concerto in D, RV 93.* YOCUH: *Sakura variations.* KOSHKIN: *Usher waltz, Op. 29.* BARRIOS: *Sueño en la Floresta.* (i) RODRIGO: *Concierto de Aranjuez: Adagio.*
*** Sony Dig. SK 53359 [id.].

With so much reappearing from the Julian Bream archive, it is good to have a first-rate, modern recital from the estimable John Williams. It was recorded in Spain (in the Royal Alcázar Palace) as part of a TV programme, which accounts for its hour-long duration and the inclusion of the ubiquitous Rodrigo *Adagio* as the closing item. The recording is very realistic and present, yet the balance is natural and the effect not jumbo-sized. John Williams's intellectual concentration is as formidable as his extraordinary technique.

This playing comes as much from the head as from the heart. He is first rate in the Bach and brings a sense of keyboard articulation to the engaging *D minor Sonata* of Scarlatti (who was Bach's almost exact contemporary). His strength is felt in the flamenco accents of Albéniz's *Asturias*, a sense of the darkly dramatic is powerfully conveyed in Koshkin's *Usher waltz* (after Edgar Allan Poe). Yet his playing can be charmingly poetic, as in the delicate account of the *Largo* of the Vivaldi concerto; touchingly gentle, as in Yocuh's charming pentatonic evocation of cherry blossoms; or thoughtfully improvisational, as in the Barrios *Sueño en la Floresta*.

Zabaleta, Nicanor (harp)

'Great concertante works for harp': MOZART: *Flute and harp concerto, K.299* (with Karlheinz Zöller, BPO). BOIELDIEU: *Harp concerto.* RODRIGO: *Concierto serenata* (with Berlin RSO, Märzendorfer). HANDEL: *Harp concerto, Op. 4/6.* ALBRECHTSBERGER: *Harp concerto in C.* DITTERSDORF: *Harp concerto in A.* DEBUSSY: *Danse sacrée et danse profane.* RAVEL: *Introduction and allegro for harp, string quartet, flute and clarinet* (all with members of Paul Kuentz CO).
(B) *** DG Double (IMS) 439 693-2 (2) [(M) id. import].

Zabaleta was an absolute master of his instrument and all these performances are touched with distinction. Johann Albrechtsberger taught Hummel and Beethoven, and his lightweight concerto is very pleasing when played with such flair and delicacy. The same might be said of the charming Boieldieu and Dittersdorf works, both of which display invention of some character, while the Handel and Mozart concertos are acknowledged masterpieces. In the latter, Karlheinz Zöller makes a distinguished partner.

When it was first issued on LP, we gave Zabaleta's version of Rodrigo's delectable *Concierto*

serenata a Rosette. In the outer movements especially, the delicate yet colourful orchestration tickles the ear in contrast to the beautifully focused harp timbre. Zabaleta is marvellous too in Ravel's *Introduction and allegro*, with sensitive support from members of the Paul Kuentz Chamber Orchestra, and warmly atmospheric sound. The Mozart, Boieldieu and Rodrigo works come from the early 1960s; the others are later and, with excellent transfers, this 145 minutes of concertante harp music will surely offer much refreshment, though these are obviously not CDs to be played all at once.

Harp concertos: (i) BOIELDIEU: *Harp concerto in 3 tempi in* C (with Berlin RSO, Märzendorfer). SAINT-SAENS: *Morceau de concert in G, Op. 154.* TAILLEFERRE: *Concertino for harp and orchestra* (with ORTF, Martinon). RAVEL: *Introduction and allegro for harp, flute, clarinet and string quartet* (with members of the Kuentz CO).
(M) **(*) DG 463 084-2 [id.].

Two rarities – the Tailleferre and Saint-Saëns – make this collection interesting. Germaine Tailleferre's *Concertino* dates from 1927 and contains influences of Ravel, Poulenc and even Stravinsky peeping over the composer's shoulder. It is elegantly written and not without its own degree of urbanity, even if the lyrical element is comparatively diffuse. The three movements have an attractive impetus, with the jolly finale developing real exuberance. Saint-Saëns's *Morceau de concert* was written when he was 83 years old. Its four miniature movements – the dainty Scherzo only runs for 1' 54'' – have a structure which has much in common with that of the *Second Piano concerto*. But the work's charm rests on its delicacy of texture and the skill with which the accompaniment is tailored, so that it supports but never overwhelms the soloist. Yet the invention has characteristic facility. Both performances are superb, with Martinon providing stylish accompaniments in good 1969 DG sound. The Ravel and Boieldieu performances are both stylish, but neither is quite the finest available, and the sound is not ideally full either. A pity that the Ginastera *Concerto*, originally on the Martinon disc, was dropped, for this disc plays for under 65 minutes.

INSTRUMENTAL RECITALS

The Art of the Piano

'The Art of the Piano': Great pianists of the 20th Century: (Paderewski; Hofmann; Rachmaninov; Moiseiwitsch; Horowitz; Cziffra; Myra Hess; Rubinstein; Planté; Cortot; Backhaus; Edwin Fischer; Gilels; Richter; Michelangeli; Gould; Arrau).
**(*) Warner/NVC Arts Video 3984 29199-3 [id.].

This fascinating video is in the line of 'The Art of Conducting'. Unfortunately it is musically flawed because so many of the most interesting visual images are taken from old films and cinema soundtracks which, with their inherent unsteadiness and fluctuations of timbre and pitch, have in the past been notoriously unkind to the piano. Most of the examples here offer marbled tone and harmonic distortion to varying degrees. However the video's introduction still brings a spectacular display of technical wizardry. We see and hear a kaleidoscope of stormy performances of Beethoven's Appassionata Sonata edited together in a rapid ongoing sequence, with Solomon first (in 1956), swiftly followed by Arrau (1983), then Dame Myra Hess (1945), Sviatoslav Richter (1992), and finally the aristocratic Artur Rubinstein (1975). Even with such short snippets, the different pianistic personalities of the five players emerge vividly.

We next focus on Paderewski, Prime Minister as well as a somewhat eccentric musician, but an artist whose personal magnetism projected strongly. Like Liszt, whose music he plays, he was irresistible to women. Hence his success in a 1936 Hollywood movie, Moonlight Serenade. Josef Hofmann, a legend among fellow pianists, is much more patrician: his approach to the ubiquitous Rachmaninov C sharp minor Prelude has no nonsense about it. Rachmaninov follows on playing his own music with natural authority, and then we meet one of his greatest contemporary interpreters, Moiseiwitsch. A pity there is not more of the Second Piano concerto (conducted by Constant Lambert) as the plum-label HMV records of this work were considered by some collectors even finer than the composer's own set with Stokowski.

The extraordinary dash of Horowitz (filmed in the Carnegie hall in 1968) in Scriabin and Bizet, his hands (to quote Támás Vásáry) 'like race horses!' virtually matched by those of the underrated Cziffra in Liszt.

Dame Myra Hess always felt intimidated by the recording studio, but here her performance of the first movement of Beethoven's Appassionata Sonata (of which we have previously heard a brief excerpt) demonstrates the full power and concentration of her live performances. Rubinstein follows magisterially with Chopin's A flat Polonaise (in 1953), then creates magic in the closing pages of the first movement of Beethoven's Fourth concerto, with Antal Dorati fifteen years later; and here the recording is faithful enough to make a real highlight.

But perhaps it is Cortot who provides the most intriguing cameo in the first part of the video. We see and hear him playing The poet speaks from Kinderszenen to a 1953 master class, commenting throughout Schumann's intimate reverie, and suggesting that the performer's aim should be 'to dream the piece rather than play it'.

Backhaus (filmed during his Decca recording sessions) now plays the slow movement of his favourite concerto, Beethoven's Fourth. He quotes Hans Richter who called it the 'Greek' concerto. In this central movement, Backhaus tells us 'Orpheus pleads to set Eurydice free; he meets with fierce resistance before his entreaties are answered'.

We move on to Edwin Fischer's pioneering Bach with its 'luminous' sound quality and intellectual spontaneity and then meet a very young Gilels in a Soviet wartime propaganda film playing Rachmaninov to a carefully staged group of Russian service personnel. Cut to his electrifying and extraordinarily imaginative 1959 performance of the cadenza from the first movement of Tchaikovsky's B flat minor Piano concerto (conducted by André Cluytens). This is followed immediately by Sviatoslav Richter, with his 'overwhelming presence' and extraordinary visceral bravura in the finale of the same work, and a comparable 'transcendental virtuosity' in a performance of Chopin's Revolutionary study.

After that Michelangeli's narcissistically self-aware keyboard personality makes a strange contrast, but his immaculate performance of a Scarlatti sonata is blurred by poor sound. Glenn Gould makes his entry playing Bach eccentrically, with intrusive vocalise, but is then heard at his most magnetically inspirational in partnership with Bernstein in the closing part of the first movement of the D minor Clavier concerto, where he is totally absorbed in creating an extraordinary diminuendo. But it is Claudio Arrau who has the last word, and is just as articulate talking about music-making as he is at the keyboard, where his closing except from Beethoven's last, *C minor Piano sonata* is played with a beauty and concentration to transcend the recorded sound.

'*The Art of the piano*' (CD supplement):

LISZT: *Hungarian rhapsody No. 2 in C sharp min.* (Paderewski). RACHMANINOV: *Prelude in C sharp min., Op. 3/2* (Josef Hofmann); *Moment musical No. 2 in E flat min., Op. 16* (Rachmaninov); *Prelude in B min., Op. 32/10* (Moiseiwitsch). CHOPIN: *Etude in F, Op. 10/8.* BIZET/HOROWITZ: *Variations on a theme from Carmen.* LISZT: *Grand galop chromatique* (Cziffra). BEETHOVEN: *Sonata No. 23 in F min., (Appassionata), Op. 57*: 1st movement only (Dame Myra Hess). CHOPIN: *Polonaises: in A flat, Op. 53; in A, Op. 40/1* (Rubinstein); *Etude in C, Op. 10/7* (Francis Planté). SCHUMANN: Kinderszenen, Op. 15 (Cortot). BEETHOVEN: Piano concerto No. 4 in G, Op. 58 (Backhaus, VPO, Schmidt-Isserstedt).

BACH: *Well-tempered Clavier: Prelude and fugue in C, BWV 846; Prelude in E flat min.; Fugue in D sharp min., BWV 853* (Edwin Fischer). BEETHOVEN: *Sonata No. 23 in F min. (Appassionata), Op. 57* (Gilels).

(M) (***) Ph. mono/stereo 464 381-2 (3) [id.].

This three-disc set is surely an essential supplement to the video as most of the recordings, even the early ones, sound quite respectable and many of them, mono or stereo are very good. Highlights include Cortot's complete performances of *Kinderszenen* (EMI, 1935), Edwin Fischer's Bach (EMI,1933), and Gilels's breathtaking *Appassionata Sonata* (DG, 1973). Sviatoslav Richter's 1959 recording of the entire Tchaikovsky *B flat minor concerto* is pretty riveting, and far preferable to his DG recording with Karajan, but Arrau's Philips reading of Beethoven's *Op. 111* fails to catch the spontaneous magic of the excerpt on the video.

'Great Pianists of the Twentieth Century'

Tom Deacon's celebration of the hundred greatest pianists of the twentieth century is a laudable enterprise – to some extent inhibited by the availability of recordings. Of course, not everyone will agree with all his choices of artists for inclusion (or omission!), but certainly most of the CDs in this series are of great interest and many of the performances are of very high quality. No one could quarrel with the attractive presentation, which moves away from the ubiquitous jewel-case. Documentation is satisfactory, and the generous presentation in each volume of two discs for the price of one reminds us that it was Philips who conceived the idea of a Duo format for reissued material. The only snag is that while for newcomers to CDs this could prove a treasure trove, piano buffs who already have extensive collections will find that the duplication of recordings which are already available may consistently present a problem.

Just over half of the hundred volumes were covered in our main volume. The others are discussed below, although five (recordings by Fischer, Haebler, Byron Janis, Kissin and Richter) were unfortunately given wrong catalogue numbers so have been relisted below. All are available separately.

Anda, Géza

Volume 1: BARTOK: *Piano concerto Nos. 1; 2; 3* (all with RSO Berlin, Ferenc Fricsay). MOZART: *Piano concerto No. 21 in C, K.467* (with Camerata Academica des Salzburger Mozarteums, Géza Anda); CHOPIN: *Waltzes in E flat (Grande valse brillante), Op. 18; A flat (Valse brillante), Op. 34/ 1; A min., Op. 34/2; F (Valse brillante), Op. 34/3; A flat (Grande valse), Op. 42; D flat (Minute), Op. 64/1; C sharp min., Op. 64/2; A flat, Op. 64/3; A flat (Farewell), Op. 69/1; B min., Op. 69/2; G flat, Op. 70/1; F min./A flat, Op. 70/2; D flat, Op. 70/3.*
(B) **(*) Ph. 456 772-2(2) [id.].

The three Bartók concertos have scarcely been out of circulation since their first appearance in 1960–61; their most recent reincarnation was in DG's handsomely produced 'The Originals'. (It would have been good to have Anda's lovely recording of Bartók's *For Children* too, though that is now available on the Testament label.) Similarly, the Mozart *C major concerto, K.467*, recorded at the same period, has enjoyed a high profile in the catalogues (it was this particular recording that the Swedish director, Bo Widerberg, used in his film

Elvira Madigan in the mid-1960s). Less familiar are the thirteen Chopin *Waltzes* made for RCA in 1975, a year before Anda's death, which have not enjoyed similar currency. Most serious collectors will have the concertos, but those who don't may find this a useful package.

Argerich, Martha

Volume 3: CHOPIN: *Mazurkas in A min., Op. 59/ 1; A flat, Op. 59/2; F sharp min., Op. 59/3; Polonaise in A flat, Op. 53 (Heroic); Polonaise-Fantaisie in A flat, Op. 61; 24 Preludes, Op. 28; Prelude in C sharp min., Op. 45; Scherzos Nos. 2 in B flat min., Op. 31; 3 in C sharp min., Op. 39; Piano sonatas No. 3 in B min., Op. 58.* SCHUMANN: *Piano sonata No. 2 in G min., Op. 22.* LISZT: *Hungarian rhapsody No. 6 in D flat; Piano sonata in B min.*
(B) *** Ph. 456 703-2(2) [id.].

Although Argerich's stature is not in question, to allocate three Volumes to her – as opposed to one only for Perahia, Ashkenazy, Solomon and Pletnev and none at all to such great artists as Simon Barere and Rudolf Firkušný – seems a bit unbalanced. Again, as with earlier issues in this series, the majority of these performances will be familiar and our admiration for Argerich's Liszt *Sonata* and the Schumann *Sonata in G minor, Op. 22* (both recorded in 1970) remains as undimmed as ever. It is good to have some recordings made before she sprang to world fame in 1965 at the Warsaw Competition. Both the *Hungarian Rhapsody* and the Chopin *C sharp minor Scherzo* come from 1960, three years after her successes at the Bolzano and Geneva Competitions at the age of sixteen. Her other recordings have been enthusiastically annotated over the years and anyone who wants this particular compilation need not hesitate.

Arrau, Claudio

Volume 6: CHOPIN: *Nocturnes Nos. 1 in C sharp min., 2 in F sharp min., Op. 48/1–2; 24 Preludes, Op. 28; Preludes in C sharp min., Op. 45; A flat, Op. posth.* GRANADOS: *Goyescas: Quejas ó la maja y el ruiseñor.* VERDI/LISZT: *Aida: Danza sacra e duetto final.* LISZT: *Années de pèlerinage: 1st Year (Switzerland); Vallée d'Obermann.* SCHUBERT: *Moments musicaux Nos. 1–6, D.780.* DEBUSSY: *Images, Book 2: Cloches à travers les feuilles; Et la lune descend sur le temple qui fut; Poissons d'or.* MOZART: *Fantasia in C min., K.475.*

(B) *** Ph. mono/stereo 456 712-2(2) [id.].

Familiar Arrau repertory here, except for the Granados recorded in 1951, which is full of poetry. The Liszt *Vallée d'Obermann* and the *Aida* transcription, recorded in 1969 and 1971, are pretty stunning. Arrau's Debussy was always superlative (particularly his mono recordings from the late 1940s–early 1950s which are not included here) and the Second Book of the *Images* from 1979 has extraordinary finesse and atmosphere. The Chopin *Nocturnes* and *Preludes* come from the 1970s and, though masterly and distinguished by great tonal refinement and subtlety, are somewhat idiosyncratic. The *Moments musicaux* come from the last year of Arrau's life when something of his individual colour and sonority had begun to desert him.

Barenboim, Daniel

Volume 9: MOZART: *Piano concerto No. 25 in C, K.503.* BEETHOVEN: *Piano concerto No. 1 in C, Op. 15* (with New Philh. O, Klemperer) LISZT: *Années de pèlerinage, 2nd Year (Italy): Sonette 47, 104 & 123 del Petrarca. Concert paraphrase of Tristan (Isoldens Liebestod (Wagner).* BRAHMS: *Piano concerto No. 1 in D min., Op. 15* (with Philh.O, Barbirolli).

(B) *** Ph. 456 721-2 (2) [id.].

Two magisterial accounts of the Mozart K.503 and Beethoven C major concertos by Barenboim, though the former is not as spontaneous as his ECO account, and his imposing Brahms *D minor concerto* with Sir John Barbirolli has great warmth and power. Those who do not have them in other incarnations can invest in these with confidence.

Bolet, Jorge

Volume 10: BACH–BUSONI: *Violin partita 2 in D min.: Chaconne. Violin partita 3 in E: Prelude.* BIZET: *L'Arlésienne suite 1: Minuet.* CHOPIN: *Preludes, Op. 28.* LISZT; *Concert paraphrases: Reminiscences of Lucia di Lammermoor; on Wagner's Tannhäuser overture.* KREISLER: *Liebesleid; Liebesfreud.* MENDELSSOHN: *A Midsummer night's dream: Scherzo.* MOSZKOWSKI: *La Jongleuse.* MUSSORGSKY: *Hopak.* RACHMANINOV: *Polka de W. R.;* RIMSKY-KORSAKOV: *Tsar Sultan: Flight of the bumble bee.* RUBINSTEIN: *Etude in E (Staccato), Op. 23/2.* Johann STRAUSS Jnr, arr. SCHULZ-ELVER: *Arabesques on An die schönen blauen Donau.* Johann STRAUSS Jnr/TAUSIG: *Man lebt nur einmal Nachfalter.* TCHAIKOVSKY: *Lullaby.*

(B) *** Ph. 456 724-2 (2) [id.].

Jorge Bolet's 1974 Carnegie Hall recital was a dazzling affair and presents an altogether different picture of him than the more circumspect studio recordings he made in the late 1970s and 1980s after Decca signed him up. Here he played without any of the reserve that tinged his later recordings, and with an abandon and bravura that are truly thrilling. The studio recordings that make up the remainder of the two-CD package are from the same period (made at the RCA New York Studios) and are also high voltage. This is one of the 'Great Pianists' recordings that really is worth having, for the Carnegie Hall performances are not readily available elsewhere.

Volume 11: LISZT: *Années de pèlerinage: 2nd Year (Italy): Sonetto del Petrarca; Supplement: Venezia e Napoli: Gondoliera; Canzone; Tarantella. Années de pèlerinage: 1st Year (Switzerland). Consolation No. 3 in D flat; Deux études de concert: Gnomenreigen. Etudes d'exécution transcendante: Harmonies du soir; Ricordanza. Etudes d'exécution transcendante d'après Paganini: No. 3 (La campanella). Harmonies poétiques et religieuses: Funérailles. Hungarian rhapsody No. 12 in C sharp min.; Liebestraum No. 3 in A flat; Mephisto waltz, No. 1. Trois études de concert: La leggierezza.* BELLINI/LISZT: *Réminiscences de 'Norma'.* VERDI/LISZT: *Rigoletto paraphrase.* MOZART/LISZT: *Réminiscences de 'Don Juan'.*

(B) *** Ph. Dig 456 814-2(2) [id.].

The bulk of these Liszt performances emanate from the recordings Bolet made in the Decca Studios in the late 1970s and 1980s. They exhibit qualities of clarity and lucidity; they are, for the most part, performances of refinement and culture that are missing the sheer abandon that marked the finest of his concert performances. Eminently satisfying, though readers who have collected the originals will not need to consider the present compilation.

Brendel, Alfred

Volume 14: MENDELSSOHN: *Variations sérieuses, Op. 54.* WEBER: *Konzertstücke in F min., Op. 79* (with LSO, Abbado). BRAHMS: *Piano concerto No. 1 in D min., Op. 15* (with Berlin Philharmonic Orchestra, Abbado). CHOPIN: *Polonaise in F sharp min., Op. 44.* LISZT: *Années de pèlerinage, 1st Year (Switzerland): Vallée d'Oberman; Orage; 2nd Year (Italy): Sposalizio. Totentanz* (with LPO, Haitink). *Bagatelle without tonality. Hungarian rhapsody No. 15 in A min. (Rákoczy march); La lugubre gondola.* BUSONI: *Toccata.*

(B) *** Ph. Analogue/Dig. 446 733-2 (2) [id.].

The *Totentanz* recorded with the LPO and Haitink in the late 1970s, along with the Liszt concertos, was one of Brendel's most electrifying performances, and his Weber *Konzertstücke* with Abbado as well as the Brahms *D minor Concerto* have much to recommend them. Brendel's Liszt has always been among the finest on record and those who haven't acquired this repertoire before, will find much to satisfy and nourish them.

Casadesus, Robert

Volume 16: RAMEAU: *Pièces de clavecin: Gavotte; Le rappel es oiseaux; Les sauvages; Les niais de Sologne.* BACH: *French suite No. 6 in E, BWV 817.* Domenico SCARLATTI: *Sonatas, Kk. 14, 23, 27, 380, 430, 533.* BEETHOVEN: *Sonata No. 2 in A, Op. 2/2.* DEBUSSY: (2 pianos): *En blanc et noit.* FAURE: (4 hands): *Dolly, Op. 56* (both with Gaby Casadesus). *Préludes: in D flat; G min.; D min., Op. 103/1, 3 & 5. Nocturne No. 7 in C sharp min., Op. 74. Barcarolle No. 5 in F sharp min., Op. 66; Impromptu No. 5 in F sharp min., Op. 102.* RAVEL: *Piano Concerto for the Left Hand* (with Philadelphia Orchestra, Ormandy).
(B) *** Ph. mono/stereo 456 739-2 [id.].

Nowadays Robert Casadesus is relatively little known among younger collectors; perhaps the fact that his discography was less extensive than many of his contemporaries is partly responsible for this, yet he belongs among the 'Greats'. The veneration accorded by the French critics and public to Samson François would be better directed to this great artist. His Scarlatti is of the finest delicacy and precision (it was included in the now deleted EMI compilation issued in 1997 and discussed in our 1998 *Bargain Guide*), and his account of the early Beethoven *A major Sonata, Op. 2, No. 2* has wonderful elegance. Contractual reasons may have been responsible for the omission of one of his superb Mozart concertos with Szell or the Fauré *Ballade* with Bernstein, but the Ravel *Left-hand concerto* with Ormandy recorded in mono in 1947 makes this a most desirable compilation. The Fauré *Nocturnes* come from 1951 as does the Bach *E major suite. En blanc et noir* and the *Dolly* suite which he recorded with his wife Gaby are more familiar (they were last reviewed in our 1998 *Bargain Guide*) and have been in and out of the catalogue since they first appeared in the early 1960s. A good introduction to Casadesus's art.

Cherkassky, Shura

Volume 18: TCHAIKOVSKY: *Piano concertos Nos. 1 in B flat min., Op. 23* (with Berlin Philharmonic Orchestra, Ludwig); *2 in G* (arr.Siloti), *Op. 44* (with Berlin Philharmonic Orchestra, Richard Kraus). LITOLFF: *Scherzo from Concerto symphonique, Op. 102* (with LPO, Sir Adrian Boult). SCHUMANN *Symphonic studies, Op. 13;*

Kreisleriana, Op. 16. Johann STRAUSS jnr. arr. SCHULT-EVLER: *Arabesques on An der schönen blauen Donau.* Johann STRAUSS jnr arr. GODOWSKY: *Wein Weib und Gesang.*
(B) *** Ph. mono/stereo 456 745-2 (2) [id.].

This compilation does sum up the personality of the artist and present him at his most mercurial and characteristic. His mono Tchaikovsky *B flat minor concerto,* with a rather staid Leopold Ludwig, is full of those capricious flights of fantasy and spontaneity that made him such a delight in the concert hall. For a time during the 1950s his *Second* was the sole LP version to be had. The sound is more transparent than in the B flat minor. DG chose the Siloti version of the score with its truncated slow movement but Cherkassky's playing has warmth and in the finale dazzling high spirits. Cherkassky was more at ease in front of an audience than in the studio and that shows in the Schumann *Symphonic studies* and *Kreisleriana,* which come from a 1975 recital at the Queen Elizabeth Hall, London previously issued on the Oiseau Lyre label. An eminently satisfying set, if you do not mind the sluggish tempo for the first movement of Tchaikovsky's *Second concerto.*

Eschenbach, Christoph

Volume 24: SCHUMANN: *Abegg Variations, Op. 1; 6 Intermezzi, Op. 4.* SCHUBERT: *Sonata No. 20 in A, D.959.* HAYDN: *Sonatas: in E min., HobXVI:34; in D HobXVI:37.* MOZART: *12 Variations on 'Ah vous dirai-je Maman', K.265.* BEETHOVEN: *Concerto No. 1 in C, Op. 15* (with Berlin Philharmonic Orchestra, Karajan).
(B) **(*) Ph. 456 763-2 (2) [id.].

We have always admired Eschenbach's record of the Beethoven *C major concerto* with Karajan and the Berlin Philharmonic. He was a fine Beethoven player and his *Hammerklavier* ranked among the finest of its time. It would have been good had it had been included here but there may be contractual constraints that inhibit this. His Schubert is impressive on all counts but the Haydn and Mozart, though admirable in many respects, are not outstanding. Worth having if you haven't got his Beethoven or the Schumann.

Fischer, Edwin

Volume 25: BACH: *Well-Tempered Clavier, Books I & II: excerpts; Clavier concertos Nos. 1 in D min., BWV 1052; 4 in A, BWV 1055; 5 in F min., BWV 1056* (with Edwin Fischer Chamber Orchestra); *Chromatic fantasia and fugue, BWV 903; Fantasia in A min., BWV 992; Fantasia and fugue in A min., BWV 904.* BACH/BUSONI: *Chorale: Ich ruf zu dir Herr Jesu Christ.*

(B) (***) Ph. mono 456 766-2 (2) [id.].

The first CD of this very distinguished set offers eight *Preludes and Fugues* from Book I and five from Book II of Edwin Fischer's pioneering complete set of the '*48*', made in the 1930s. The second disc carries the three concertos and the remaining keyboard pieces. A useful sampler for those who do not already have, or cannot find these famous recordings elsewhere. We regret that this set appeared in our main volume with an incorrect catalogue number.

Volume 26: MOZART: *Concerto No. 20 in D min., K.466* (with LPO); *Fantasia in C min., K.475.* BEETHOVEN: *Concerto No. 5 (Emperor)* (with Philharmonia Orchestra, Furtwängler). *Piano sonatas: No. 23 (Appassionata), Op. 57; 31 in A flat, Op. 110.* SCHUBERT: *Impromptus, D. 899/1–4.*

(B) *** Ph. 456 769-2 (2) [id.].

Edwin Fischer's account of the *Emperor Concerto* with Furtwängler and the Philharmonia Orchestra is one of the all-time greats. It enjoyed classic status in the 1950s and there are few later versions to surpass it. His Mozart *D minor Concerto* with the LPO, which he conducted from the keyboard in 1933, long dominated the catalogue and set standards by which successors were judged. The *Appassionata* and *Op. 110* are also from the 1930s and have special insights. Not to be missed.

François, Samson

Volume 28: BACH–BUSONI: *Toccata, adagio and fugue in C.* CHOPIN: *4 Impromptus, Opp. 29, 36, 51; Etude No. 6. Sonata No. 2 in B flat min., Op. 35; Waltzes Nos. 1, Op. 18; 7, Op. 64/2; 11, Op. 70/1; 13, Op. 70/3; 4 Ballades, Opp. 23, 38, 47 & 52.* DEBUSSY: *Suite bergamasque: Clair de lune. L'isle joyeuse; Pour le piano.* FAURE: *Impromptu No. 2 in F min., Op. 31; Nocturne No. 2 in G, Op. 33/2.* MOZART: *Variations on 'Ah, vous dirai-je, Maman', K.265.* PROKOFIEV: *Toccata in D min., Op. 11.* RAVEL: *Gaspard de la nuit: Scherzo.* SCHUMANN: *Toccata In C, Op. 7.*

(B) *(*) Ph. 456 778-2 (2) [id.].

Samson François enjoys a legendary reputation in France – one which must be puzzling to outsiders. He has none of the aristocratic sensibility of Jean Philippe Collard or tonal refinement of Pascal Rogé, neither represented in this collection, and his inclusion must be in deference to Gallic sentiment and the fierce allegiance he commands in his own country. His formidable fingers are heard to good advantage in the Schumann and Prokofiev *Toccatas* but dynamic gradations and tonal subtlety are not conspicuous features of his artistic armoury. In the Debussy he can wilfully disregard *pianopianissimo* markings and there are times where he sounds

almost brutal. The recordings are mainly from the 1960s and are more than acceptable but this volume can be recommended only to his committed admirers.

Freire, Nelson

Volume 29: SCHUMANN: *Fantasy in C, Op. 17.* CHOPIN: *Impromptu No. 2 in F sharp, Op. 36; Mazurkas in C sharp min., Op. 41/1; B flat min., Op. 24/4; Piano sonata No. 3 in B min., Op. 58; Scherzo No. 4 in E, Op. 54.;* MOZART: *Sonata No. 12 in F, K.332.* BRAHMS: *Sonata No. 3 in F min., Op. 5.* Johann STRAUSS/GODOWSKI: *Fledermaus paraphrase.* Richard STRAUSS/ GODOWSKI: *Ständchen.* LISZT: *Hungarian rhapsody No. 10 in E. Totentanz* (with Munich PO, Rudolf Kempe).

(B) *** Ph. Analogue/Dig. Duo 456 781-2 (2) [id.].

Nelson Freire has some fine recordings to his credit and is undoubtedly an artist of the front rank. But whether his inclusion in the present pantheon is warranted is another matter. These are fine and sometimes superb rather than great performances: they are thoroughly recommendable and well worth having, for Freire's current representation in the catalogue is really rather meagre.

Gavrilov, Andrei

Volume 31: BACH: *French suite No. 5 in G, BWV 516.* HANDEL: *Suite in D min., HWV 447.* MOZART: *Fantasia in D min., K. 397.* SCHUMANN: *Papillons, Op. 2.* CHOPIN: *Ballade No. 2 in F, Op. 38.* RACHMANINOV: *Moments musicaux, Op. 16/ 3-6.* GRIEG: *Lyric piece: Norwegian march, Op. 54/2.* PROKOFIEV: *Piano concerto No. 1 in D flat, Op. 10* (with LSO, Simon Rattle); *10 Pieces from Romeo and Juliet, Op. 75.* SCRIABIN: *Sonata No. 4 in F sharp, Op; 30.* TCHAIKOVSKY: *Variations on an original theme, Op. 19/6.* BALAKIREV: *Islamey.*

(B) *** Ph. Analogue/Dig. Duo 456 787-2 (2) [id.].

There are some marvellous things here, including first and foremost Gavrilov's brilliant 1978 account of Prokofiev's *First Piano Concerto* with Simon Rattle and the LSO. In fact, most of his Russian repertoire is of special quality and in particular the Scriabin *Fourth Sonata*, the Rachmaninov *Moments musicaux* and, the display piece of display pieces, Balakirev's *Islamey*. All these come from his EMI recordings while the Bach, expertly judged in every way and distinguished by an innate sense of style, together with the Prokofiev *Romeo and Juliet* pieces are from the early 1990s when he was with DG. Generally excellent recorded sound.

Gieseking, Walter

Volume 33: MOZART: *Piano sonata in C min.,*
K.457. BEETHOVEN: *Piano sonatas in C*
(Waldstein), Op. 53; F min. (Appassionata), Op.
57. RAVEL: *Gaspard de la nuit.* DEBUSSY:
Estampes. Préludes, Books 1–2.
(B) (***) Ph. 456 790-2 [id.].

Those who have acquired Gieseking's Debussy
either in the four-CD box or the recent EMI set
should not be deterred from investigating this.
Those all emanate from the period 1951–5 and were
produced by Walter Legge and Geraint Jones. The
present set of the *Préludes* were legendary in their
day, and were made in London in 1937-38, as was
Ravel's *Gaspard de la nuit.* An invaluable insight
into Gieseking's art before the war, and further
proof, if that were needed, of the special authority
he brought to French repertoire.

Gilels, Emil

Volume 36: BRAHMS: *Piano concerto No. 2 in B*
flat, Op. 83 (with BPO, Eugen Jochum). GRIEG:
Lyric pieces: Melody, Op. 47/3; Brooklet, Op. 62/
4; Solitary traveller, Op. 43/2; Butterfly, Op. 43/1.
SCHUBERT: *Fantasy in F min. for piano duet*
D.940 (with Elena Gilels). CLEMENTI: *Piano*
sonata in C, Op. 34/1. SCHUMANN: *Arabeske in C,*
Op. 18. CHOPIN: *Etude in F min., Op. 25/2; Piano*
sonatas Nos. 2 in B flat min. (Funeral march), Op.
35; 3 in B min., Op. 58.
(B) *** Ph. 456 799-2(2) [id.].

Again, most readers will probably have acquired
the Brahms *B flat Concerto* that Gilels recorded
with Jochum in the late 1970s, which has been a
front-running recommendation over the years – as
indeed have been the wonderful Grieg *Lyric pieces*
which are represented here. The Schubert *F minor*
Fantasy, recorded with his daughter Elena, and the
Chopin *B flat minor* and *B minor sonatas* are equally
familiar. Those who have missed out on these in
Deutsche Grammophon's 'The Originals' series,
should not miss them here. All the same, preference
should be given to the latter as all the Grieg are
mandatory purchases and so is the Brahms package
with the *D minor Concerto* and the *Fantasias, Op.*
116. The Clementi, recorded in 1960, is a relative
rarity and done with characteristic elegance.

Ginsburg, Grigory

Volume 37: LISZT: *Hungarian rhapsodies Nos. 2,*
6, 10, 13, 17 & 18. BEETHOVEN: *Ruins of Athens:*
Turkish march; Rondo a capriccio, Op. 129.
LISZT: *Grand Etude after Paganini: La*
Chasse.Concert paraphrase of Schubert's

Ständchen. Concert paraphrase of Polonaise from
Tchaikovsky's Eugene Onegin. PABST: *Eugene*
Onegin paraphrase. ALIABIEV/LISZT: *The*
nightingale. TCHAIKOVSKY: *Sonata in G, Op. 37.*
prokofiev: *Sonata No. 3 in A, Op. 28.* MEDTNER:
Sonata reminiscenza in A min., Op. 38/1; Prelude
in B flat min., Op. 58.
(B) (***) Ph. mono 456 802-2 (2) [id.].

Grigory Ginsburg (1904–61) never made much of
an impression outside the Soviet Union, for his
recordings never gained more than limited currency
in the West. A pupil of Alexander Goldenweiser
who also taught Tatiana Nikolayeva, he was particularly celebrated as a Liszt interpreter (we awarded
the stunning recital included in BMG/Melodiya's
Russian Piano School II a ❂ – see below). The
present CDs are a useful addition to his meagre
representation in the catalogue but they should not
be acquired in preference to the Melodiya disc.
There are marvellous things here: Medtner's *Sonata*
reminiscenza is as searching and inward-looking as
the famous Carnegie Hall Gilels account from the
1960s. The Liszt transcription of Aliabiev's *The*
nightingale has a wonderful eloquence and melancholy. The Tchaikovsky *G major Sonata* is pretty
impressive, though not the equal of Richter or
Pletnev, and the 1947 recording calls for great tolerance. All the same there is some memorable pianism
and fine music-making here.

Haebler, Ingrid

Volume 42: BACH: *French suite No. 6 in E, BWV*
817. HAYDN: *Piano concerto in D, Hob XVIII:11;*
Variations in F min., Hob. XVII: 6. MOZART:
Piano concerto No. 18 in B flat, K.456 (with LSO,
Sir Colin Davis). *9 Variations on a minuet by*
Duport, K.573. SCHUBERT: *Sonata No. 14 in*
A min., D.784. SCHUMANN: *Kinderszenen, Op. 15.*
CHOPIN: *Waltz in E flat, Op. 18.*
(B) **(*) Ph. 456 824-2 (2) [id.].

There is some musical playing here, but whether it
can be described as great is a moot point! Ingrid
Haebler has elegance and nimble fingers but many
(including her admirers) would hesitate before
placing her alongside such exalted company as Perahia, Richter and Horowitz. Having said that, this
pair of CDs will undoubtedly give pleasure – particularly the *B flat concerto,* K.456 – but that is
another matter. We regret that this set appeared
in our main volume with an incorrect catalogue
number.

Hess, Myra

Volume 45: Domenico SCARLATTI: *Sonatas, K.11*
& K.14. SCHUMANN: *Carnaval, Op. 9; Symphonic*
studies. GRANADOS: *Goyescas: Quejas ó la maya*

y el ruiseñor. MENDELSSOHN: *Song without words, Op. 102/5.* BRAHMS: *Waltz in A flat, Op. 39/15; Intermezzo in C, Op. 119/3.* SCHUMANN: *Concerto in A min., Op. 54* (with Philharmonia Orchestra, Rudolf Schwarz). BEETHOVEN: *Sonatas Nos. 30 in E, Op. 109; 31 in A flat, Op. 110.* BACH, arr. HESS: *Jesu, joy of man's desiring.*
(B) (***) Ph. mono 456 832-2 [id.].

As the recent account of the *Emperor Concerto* on BBC Legends shows, there was more to Myra Hess than the rather cosy *Jesu, joy of man's desiring* halo that she came to acquire. Not only was she thoughtful and poetic but she commanded considerable intellectual strength. The two late Beethoven sonatas are unfailingly beautiful and have great tonal refinement and subtlety. The only disappointment, perhaps, is the Schumann *A minor concerto* with Rudolf Schwarz conducting, which has less freshness and poetic spirit than her pre-war account with Walter Goehr. She was closely associated with this piece, making her Concertgebouw debut with it in 1912 under Mengelberg, and playing it in her first Queen's Hall appearance with Beecham four years later. As was customary in her day, she plays the *Symphonic studies* without the five posthumous variations that Brahms published, and the 1938 account of *Carnaval*, of which she herself thought highly, was long (and rightly) regarded as a benchmark by which newcomers were judged.

Hofmann, Josef

Volume 46: SCHUBERT, Arr. TAUSIG: *Marche militaire No. 1.* LISZT: *Concert paraphrases: of Schubert's Erlkönig; of Chopin's Chants polonais: The maiden's wish; My darling. Liebestraume No. 3; Années de pèlerinage (supplement: Venezia e Napoli): Tarantella . Hungarian rhapsody No. 2 in C sharp min.; Concert study No. 1: Waldesrauchen.* MENDELSSOHN: *Songs without words: Hunting song, from Op. 19; Spring song, from Op. 62; Bee's wedding (from Op. 67); Rondo capriccioso, Op. 14* (abridged). CHOPIN: *Polonaise No. 3 in A, Op. 40/1* (2 versions); *Waltzes: in A flat, Op. 34/1; in C sharp min., Op. 64/2; in E min., Op. posth.; Fantaisie-impromptu, Op. 66; Berceuse, Op. 57; Nocturne in F sharp min., Op. 15/2; Scherzo in B min., Op. 20* (abridged). RUBINSTEIN: *Valse caprice; Melody in F, Op. 3/1.* SCHUMANN: *Fantaisistücke, Op. 12: Warum?;* STERNBERG: *Etude No. 3 in C min., Op. 120.* Josef HOFMANN: *The sanctuary; Mignonettes: Nocturne.* GRIEG: *Lyric piece: Butterfly, from Op. 43.* MOSZKOWSKI: *Capriccio espagnol* (abridged). *La jongleuse, Op. 52/4.* PADEREWSKI: *Minuet in G, Op. 14/1.* PARKER: *Valse gracile.* DILLON: *Birds at dawn, Op. 20/2.* GLUCK (arr. BRAHMS) *Pardie ed Elena: Gavotte in A.* Domenico SCARLATTI, arr. TAUSIG:

Pastorale e Capriccio. RACHMANINOV: *Preludes: in C sharp min., Op. 3/2; in G min., Op. 23/5.* WAGNER arr. Brassin: *Die Walküre: Magic fire music.* BEETHOVEN: *The Ruins of Athens: Turkish march* (Arr. Rubinstein).
(B) (***) Ph. mono 456 836-2 (2) [id.].

It was to Josef Hofmann that Rachmaninov dedicated the *Third Piano Concerto* and it was he who gave its New York première with Mahler conducting. His peers spoke of him as the greatest pianist of their days, and many pianists today regard him as the greatest of the last century. His technique was incredible, his command of colour limitless and his memory prodigious (he once heard Godowsky playing his arrangement of melodies from *Fledermaus* and returned the following week and played the complete transcription from memory). His 1937 account of Rubinstein's *Fourth Concerto*, unfortunately not included here, leaves no doubt as to his stature and his magical delicacy of touch. Nor is his magical Chopin *G minor Ballade* here, but the collection is valuable in offering a wide range of his relatively few records from 1912–23, and his pioneering 1903 discs. Not exactly hi-fi but not to be missed.

Horowitz, Vladimir

Volume 47: SCHUMANN: *Toccata in C, Op. 7; Arabesque, Op. 18; Fantasiestücke: Traumeswirren, Op. 12/7. Sonata No. 2: Presto passionato* (original ending). *Kreisleriana, Op. 16; Humoresque, Op. 20; Concerto without orchestra, Op. 14; Novelette in F, Op. 21/1; 3 Fantasiestücke, Op. 111; Kinderszenen, Op. 15.*
(B) (***) Ph. 456 838-2 (2) [id.].

Most people associate Horowitz with Chopin, Liszt and Rachmaninov rather than Schumann, though his dedication to that master is not in doubt. *Kreisleriana* and *Kinderszenen* are both taken from the 1980s, the latter from a recital in Vienna. There are some delights from the 1930s: the *Toccata*, wonderfully played and the *Presto passionato*, originally intended for the *G minor Sonata* and pretty breathtaking it is too. Not all the RCA recordings from the late 1970s are ideal, such as the *Concerto, Op. 14*, but they are a great improvement on the sound CBS was giving him in the 1960s.

Volume 49: CHOPIN: *Barcarolle in F sharp, Op. 60. Mazurkas: in F min., Op. 7/3 (2 versions); in B flat min., Op. 24/4; in B min.; in D flat; in C sharp min. (2 versions), Op. 30/2, 3 & 4; in C sharp min.; in E min., Op. 41/1–22; in C sharp min., Op. 50/3 (2 versions); in F sharp min., Op. 59/3; In F min.; in C sharp min., Op. 63/2–3. Etudes: in E; C sharp min. (2 versions); in G flat (2 versions); in F, Op. 10/ 3, 4, 5, & 8; in F, Op. 25/3. Polonaise in A flat, Op. 52.* BEETHOVEN:

Piano concerto No. 5 in E flat (Emperor), Op. 73.
RACHMANINOV: *Piano concerto No. 3 in D min.,*
Op. 30 (both with RCA Victor SO, Fritz Reiner).
(B) *** Ph. mono 456 841-2 (2) [id.].

The Rachmaninov *Third Piano Concerto* and the *Emperor* were both recorded with Reiner in 1951 and 1952 respectively. The former bears witness to his magisterial virtuosity and the latter is testimony to the nobility and seriousness that lay behind the virtuoso surface. They were available in the RCA Horowitz Edition and individually, but both are now deleted in the UK, and those attracted to the present compilation will be rewarded by playing of patrician elegance. The Chopin recordings come from the 1930s and '40s and make a welcome reappearance. They alone are well worth the price of this compilation.

Janis, Byron

Volume 50: BACH: *Prelude and fugue in A min.,*
BWV 543. BEETHOVEN: *Piano sonata No. 17 in D*
min. (Tempest), Op. 31/2. SCHUBERT: *Impromptu*
in E flat, D.899/2. BRAHMS: *Waltzes Op. 39 Nos.*
1 in B, 2 in E, 6 in C sharp, 15 in A flat. Johann
STRAUSS/SCHULZ-EVLER: *Arabesques on An der*
schönen, blauen Donau. LISZT: *Consolation*
No. 5 in E, (Andantino); Hungarian rhapsody
No. 6 in D flat; Liebesträum No. 3 in A flat;
Rigoletto concert paraphrase; Années de
pèlerinage: Sonetto 104 Petrarca. CHOPIN:
Ballade No. 1 in G min., Op. 23; Etudes in E
(Tristesse), Op. 10/3; G flat, (Black keys), Op. 10/
5; F, Op. 10/8; F, Op. 25/3; Impromptu No. 1 in A
flat, Op. 29; Mazurka in A min., Op. 67/4; Scherzo
No. 3 in C sharp min., Op. 39; Sonata No. 2 in B
flat min., (Funeral march), Op. 35; Waltzes in E
min., Op. post.; A min., Op. 34/2.
(B) (***) Ph. mono/stereo 456 848-2 (2) [id.].

Byron Janis was a protégé of Horowitz and possessed an altogether outstanding virtuosity. This issue justifies its inclusion in this series in a way that many others don't. It presents us with material that has not been in circulation for many years and some recordings appear for the first time. A pupil of Josef and Rosina Lhévinne, Janis attracted Horowitz's attention in 1944 when he was sixteen and was hailed by Olin Downes in ecstatic terms. His career was cut short in the 1973 by psoriatic arthritis. The present survey includes recordings from the late 1940s and early '50s of Chopin, Liszt and Beethoven which are both remarkable and new to CD. We regret that this set appeared in our main volume with an incorrect catalogue number.

Volume 51: LISZT: *Piano concerto No. 1 in E flat.*
RACHMANINOV: *Piano concerto No. 1 in F sharp*
min., Op. 1 (both with Moscow PO, Kiril
Kondrashin); *Piano concerto No. 2 in C min., Op.*

18 (with Minneapolis SO, Antal Dorati).
PROKOFIEV: *Piano concerto No. 3 in C, Op. 26*
(with Moscow PO, Kiril Kondrashin).
SCHUMANN: *Variations on a theme by Clara*
Wieck (Piano sonata No. 3 in F min, Op. 14); 3
Romanzen, Op. 28: No. 2 in F sharp.
TCHAIKOVSKY: *Piano concerto No. 1 in B flat*
min., Op. 23 (with LSO, Herbert Menges).
(B) *** Ph. 456 850-2(2) [id.].

All these concerto recordings find Byron Janis at the height of his powers and were made in 1960–62. He enjoyed the acclaim of Horowitz, whose pupil he became, and of Gilels who heard his Moscow appearance in which he played three concertos (Rachmaninov's *First*, the Schumann and Prokofiev's *Third*). The playing is distinguished by great fervour and virtuosity. The *Wieck variations* were recorded in 1964, a decade before the onset of psoriatic arthritis brought his concert career to an end.

Kapell, William

Volume 52: RACHMANINOV: *Piano concerto*
No. 2 in C min., Op. 18 (with Robin Hood Dell
Orchestra, William Steinberg); *Rhapsody on a*
theme by Paganini, Op. 43. PROKOFIEV: *Piano*
concerto No. 3 in C, Op. 26 (with Dallas SO,
Antal Dorati). BACH: *Partita No. 4 in D, BWV*
828. CHOPIN: *Piano sonata No. 3 in B min., Op.*
58. ALBENIZ: *Iberia,* Book I: *Evocación.* LISZT:
Années de pèlerinages: Sonetto 104 del Petrarca.
Hungarian rhapsody No. 11; Mephisto waltz
No. 1.
⊕ (B) *** Ph. mono 456 853-2 (2) [id.].

William Kapell achieved fame as a 20-year-old with his sensational performance of the Khachaturian concerto. (Indeed he became so identified with this piece during the war years that he was known briefly as 'Khachaturian Kapell'.) He had little more than a decade left before his death in 1953 at the age of thirty-one. This gives an invaluable insight into his art. There may have been a more electrifying, higher-voltage account of the Prokofiev *Third Concerto* but we have yet to encounter it. Kapell's is of quite staggering brilliance and power, and his version of the Rachmaninov *Paganini variations* must be ranked alongside the composer's own. It would be tedious to shower superlatives on everything else in this collection but impossible not to. This is altogether a *must* for all collectors and performances where sonic limitations are of no account given such astonishingly vivid playing.

Kissin, Evgeny

Volume 58: LISZT: *Etudes d'exécution*
transcendante Nos. 10 in F min.; 11, Harmonies

du soir; 12, Chasse-neige; Hungarian rhapsody No. 12; Liebesträum No. 3 in A flat; Spanish rhapsody. SCHUBERT/LISZT: *Concert paraphrases: Auf dem Wasser zu singen; Die forelle; Gretchen am spinnrade.* LISZT (after SCHUBERT): *Valse-caprice no.* SCHUBERT/ TAUSIG: *Marche militaire.* PROKOFIEV: (i) *Piano concerto No. 3 in C, Op. 26* (with BPO, Claudio Abbado); *Etude in C min., Op. 2/3; Overture on Hebrew themes, Op. 34; Piano sonata No. 6 in A, Op. 82; Visions fugitives, Op. 22 Nos. 10 (Ridicolosamente); 11 (Con vivacitá); 16 (Dolente); 17 (Poetico).*
(B) *** Ph. Dig. 456 772-2 (2) [id.].

This remarkable pianist is not yet thirty and most of the performances collected here were made when he was not out of his teens; the Prokofiev *Visions fugitives* when he was in his fourteenth year. Of the two versions he has recorded of the Prokofiev *Sixth Sonata*, the producer has rightly chosen the RCA Carnegie Hall account made when he was nineteen in preference to the even wilder (but less accurate) version he put on disc four years earlier in Tokyo for Sony. The Liszt is pretty breathtaking, but in the Prokofiev concerto with Abbado a little more abandon would have been appropriate in the outer movements. No doubts here about the wisdom of Tom Deacon's choice. We regret that this set appeared in our main volume with an incorrect catalogue number.

Larrocha, Alicia de

Volume 63: BACH: *Italian concerto in F, BWV 971; Chorales: Liebster Jesu, BWV 731; Ertöt uns durch deine Güte* (from *BWV 22*); *French suite No. 6 in E, BWV 817.* Domenico SCARLATTI: *Sonatas, Kk.6, Kk.9, Kk.11, Kk.13 & Kk.28.* HANDEL: *Suite No. 5 in E, HWV 430: The harmonious blacksmith.* HAYDN: *Andante with variations in F min., Hob XVII:6.* MOZART: *Rondo in D, K.485; Piano sonatas: 8 in A min., K.310; 10 in C, K.330; 11 in A, K.331; 18 in D, K.576.*
(B) *** Ph. Analogue/Dig. 456 886-2 (2) [id.].

Larrocha's celebrity as one of the greatest (if not *the* greatest) living exponent of Spanish music has overshadowed her prowess in a wider repertoire. This useful compilation redresses the balance and serves as a reminder of how wide-ranging is her artistry and how well-developed are her classical instincts. Most of these recordings were made for Decca in the 1970s and have both clarity and warmth. Only the Handel comes from the 1980s and the digital era.

Magaloff, Nikita

Volume 67: HAYDN: *Piano sonata No. 58 in C, Hob XVI:48.* CHOPIN: *Nocturnes: in B flat min.; in E flat; in B, Op. 9/1–3. Boléro in C, Op. 19; Sonata No. 1 in C min., Op. 4. Tarantelle in A flat, Op 43; Mazurkas: in B flat, E min., A flat, A min., Op. 17/1-5; Rondo à la mazur in F, Op. 5; Variations brillantes, Op. 12; Allegro de concert in A, Op. 46; Ecossaises Nos. 1–3, Op. 72/3–5.* LISZT: *6 Grandes Etudes après Paganini.* SCHUMANN: *Carnaval, Op. 9.*
(B) ** Ph. 456 898-2 (2) [id.].

Nikita Magaloff was a fine pianist, a musician of much culture and an influential teacher, but his claims to a place among the great pianists of the twentieth century alongside Gilels, Perahia and Richter (and when the likes of Firkušný and Simon Barere are unrepresented), must be respectfully questioned. All these are eminently serviceable performances but not special.

Michelangeli, Arturo Benedetti

Volume 69: BEETHOVEN: *Piano sonata No. 4 in E flat, Op. 7.* SCHUMANN: *Album für die Jugend, Op. 68: 3 Pieces. Carnaval, Op. 9.* BRAHMS: *Variations on a theme by Paganini, Op. 35; 4 Ballades, Op. 10.* CHOPIN: *Mazurkas: in B min., Op. 30/2; in C, in G sharp min.; in B min., Op. 33/1 & 4; in C, Op. 56/2; in G min.; in A min., Op. 67/2 & 4; in C ; in A min., Op. 68/1–2.* MOMPOU: *Canción y danza No. 1.*
(B) *** Ph. 456 904-2 (2) [id.].

The Beethoven *Sonata in E flat, Op. 7,* emanates from a 1971 DG LP and finds the great pianist completely on auto-pilot and totally uninvolved. The Brahms *Paganini variations* and the Mompou *Canción y danza* were made in the 1940s and listening to them again, one realizes that this is playing of supreme artistry. The Chopin *Mazurkas* come from 1972 and have a certain detachment but much style, and much the same can be said of the Brahms *Op. 10 Ballades* which have a crystalline icy quality. All the same, a mandatory acquisition.

Ogdon, John

Volume 73: BALAKIREV: *Islamey.* LISZT: *Mephisto waltz No. 1; Réminiscences de Don Juan (Mozart); Réminiscences de Simon Boccanegra (Verdi); Liebesträum No. 3; La Campanella (arr. Busoni). Funéraillles; Après une lecture de Dante.* RACHMANINOV: *Preludes: in C sharp min., Op.3/ 2; in G min., Op. 23/5; in G, Op. 32/5; in G sharp min., Op. 32/12; 8 Etudes-tableaux, Op. 33; 9 Etudes-tableaux, Op. 39.*

(B) *** Ph. 456 928-2 (2) [id.].

John Ogdon's dedication to exploring unfamiliar repertoire is best seen in his companion Volume (No. 72) in our main guide. But he is heard at his very finest here in his Liszt, wonderfully concentrated and effortlessly virtuosic.

Pires, Maria João

Volume 76: BACH: *French suite No. 2 in C min., BWV 813.* SCHUMANN: *Arabeske.* SCHUBERT: *Moment musical in A flat, D.780/6.* CHOPIN: *Nocturnes: in C min.; in F sharp min., Op. 48/1–2; in E, Op. 62/2.* MOZART: *Piano concerto No. 14 in E flat, K. 449* (with Vienna Philharmonic Orchestra, Abbado). *Piano sonatas Nos. 4 in E flat, K.282; 11 in A, K.331; 13 in B flat, K.333; 16 in C, K.545.*
(B) *** Ph. 456 928-2 (2) [id.].

An artist of strong personality and impeccable taste, Maria João Pires gives admirable accounts of all these pieces. Whether or not she belongs among the pantheon or not, she is a very distinguished pianist and this compilation will give great satisfaction to those who want an introduction to this artist.

Pollini, Maurizio

Volume 79: CHOPIN: *Sonata No. 2 in B flat min., Op. 35; Nocturnes: in F; in F sharp, Op. 15/1–2; in C sharp min.; in D flat, Op. 27/1–2; Polonaise in F sharp min., Op. 44; Polonaise in A flat (Heroic), Op. 53; Polonaise-fantaisie in A flat, Op. 61. Etudes, Op. 10/1–12; Berceuse, Op. 57; Barcarolle, Op. 60. Piano concerto No. 1 in E min., Op. 11* (with Philharmonia Orchestra, Paul Kletzki).
(B) *** Ph. 456 940-2 (2) [id.].

The Chopin *E minor concerto* which he recorded with Kletzki and the Philharmonia in 1960 serves as a reminder of Pollini's youthful ardour and freshness. The other Chopin pieces recorded at various times between 1968–90 have much the same perfection, though generally speaking they evince less spontaneity. Remarkable pianism and well worth acquiring.

Richter, Sviatoslav

Volume 82: MUSSORGSKY: *Pictures at an exhibition.* SCHUBERT: *Impromptus in E flat, D.899/2; A flat, D.899/4; Moment musical in C, D.780/1.* CHOPIN: *Etude in E, Op. 10/3.* LISZT: *Etudes d'exécution transcendante Nos. 5, Feux follets; 11, Harmonies du soir. Valses oubliées Nos. 1 in F sharp; 2 in A flat.* RACHMANINOV: *Prelude in G sharp min., Op. 32/12.* PROKOFIEV:

Piano sonatas Nos. 6 in A, Op. 82; 7 in B flat, Op. 83; 8 in B flat, Op. 84.
(B) (***) Ph. 456 946-2 (2) [id.].

Pictures at an exhibition is very special to Richter; even Horowitz does not quite match his interpretative detail and power. The present writer has heard him play it live – an unforgettable experience. The performance here is also live, and totally compelling, wonderfully imaginative in detail. The closing *Great Gate of Kiev* is electrifying, triumphing over the indifferent, resonant, and slightly blurred piano focus, and the asthmatic problems of the Sofia audience. The Schubert, Chopin, Liszt and Rachmaninov items also come from this same 1958 recital, and bring more dazzling playing: here the sound is for the most part, firmer. The uniquely authoritative performances of the three Prokofiev Sonatas have an arresting dynamism and electricity, to say nothing of poetic feeling (No. 7 is the BMG/Melodiya recording). Here the sound is clear and well focused, quite satisfactory. This is a set that no serious collector can ignore. We regret that this set appeared in our main volume with an incorrect catalogue number.

Volume 84: RACHMANINOV: *Piano concerto No. 2 in C min., Op. 18* (with Warsaw PO, Stanislaw Wislocki); *Preludes in B flat, D, G min., C min., Op. 23/2; 4; 5; & 7; in C, B flat min., Op. 32/1 & 2.* SCRIABIN: *Etudes: in C sharp min. Op. 2/1; in E; B flat min.; Op. 8/5 & 11; in F sharp min., F sharp, F sharp, C sharp min., D flat, E flat, Op. 42/2; 3; 4; 5; 6; 8; in B flat, C sharp, G, Op. 65/1–3.* SCHUMANN: *Fantasie in C, Op. 17; Fantasiestücke, Op. 12/1 Des abends; 2 Aufschwung; 3 Warum; 5 In der nacht; 7 Traumes wirren; 8 Ende vom Lied; Toccata in C, Op. 7; Waldszenen, Op. 82.*
(B) *** Ph. mono/stereo 456 952-2 [id.].

The merits of Richter's account of the Rachmaninov *C minor Concerto* of which the public rightly never tires, have been often detailed in these pages. Apart from this, we are offered some wonderfully idiomatic Scriabin, dating from 1952 and his classic Abbey Road recording of the Schumann *Fantasy* of 1961. It was with the *Toccata* and *Waldszenen* that Richter made his DG debut in the 1950s, and their inclusion here is mandatory. A most welcome issue.

Rubinstein, Artur

Volume 86: CHOPIN: *Piano concerto No. 2 in F min., Op. 21* (with Symphony of the Air, Wallenstein). GRIEG: *Piano concerto in A min., Op. 16* (with RCA Victor SO, Wallenstein) SAINT-SAENS: *Piano concerto No. 2 in G min., Op. 22* (with RCA Victor SO, Wallenstein). SCHUMANN: *Piano concerto in A min., Op. 54* (with RCA Victor SO, Josef Krips).

TCHAIKOVSKY: *Piano concerto No. 1 in B flat min., Op. 23* (with Boston SO, Leinsdorf). (B) *** Ph. 456 958-2 (2) [id.].

All these classic accounts come from the late 1950s–early 1960s, when Rubinstein was in top form. The Saint-Saëns is particularly delightful and so is the Grieg, even if the earlier wartime set he made in San Francisco was arguably fresher. In any event Rubinstein admirers who do not have these performances should acquire them now (although they are also included in the Rubinstein Edition).

Schiff, András

Volume 88: BACH: *2 & 3 Part Inventions, BWV 772–801; Chromatic fantasia and fugue, BWV 903; English suite No. 2 in A min., BWV 807.* MOZART: *Piano sonatas: in C, K.545; in D, K.576.* SCHUBERT: *6 Moments musicaux, D. 780; 3 Klavierstücke, D.946.* (B) *** Ph. 456 925-2 (2) [id.].

All these recordings come from 1980–90 and their merits are well detailed. Those who have not invested in them separately and who are attracted by this particular compilation will find much delight here, and very good recorded sound.

Solomon

Volume 92: BACH: *Prelude and fugue in A min., BWV 543.* MOZART: *Sonata No. 13 in B flat, K.333.* BEETHOVEN: *Sonata No. 29 in B flat (Hammerklavier), Op. 106.* CHOPIN: *Berceuse, Op. 57; Ballade No. 4 in F min., Op. 52; Fantaisie in F min., Op. 49; Polonaise in A (Heroic),*

Op. 53. LISZT: *Etude de concert: La leggierezza. Années de pèlerinage: Au bord d'un source. Hungarian rhapsody No. 15 in A min. (Rákóczy march).* BRAHMS: *Variations and fugue on a theme by Handel, Op. 24; Intermezzo in B flat min., Op. 117/2.* (B) *** Ph. mono 456 973-2 (2) [id.].

Magisterial though his *Hammerklavier* is, Solomon would have been better represented by his *Op. 111* or either of the Brahms concertos he made in the post-war years. However the Brahms *Variations and fugue on a theme by Handel* is an ideal choice and mandatory listening, as is the remainder of the collection. It is strange though, that Solomon's representation is confined to one disc while others such as Gulda, Larrocha and Ogdon run to two.

Tureck, Rosalyn

Volume: 94: BACH: *French overture (Partita) in B min., BWV 831; Goldberg variations, BWV 988. Italian concerto in F, BWV 971; Four duets Nos. 1 in E min., BWV 802; 2 in F, BWV 803; 3 in G, BWV 804; 4 in A min., BWV 805.* (B) *** Ph. mono 456 979-2 [id.].

The high priestess of Bach recorded these at the height of her celebrity in the late 1950s and they remain outstanding examples of Bach playing. They have long been out of circulation and their return here is as long overdue as it is welcome. The clarity of the keyboard articulation, the delineation of the part-writing and the sheer inner vitality of the playing are a source of wonder and the mono HMV recordings serve her admirably. A mandatory purchase for all lovers of Bach and of the piano.

Other Instrumental Recitals

Alain, Marie-Claire (organ)

'A Celebration'.
(M) *** Erato/Warner Analogue/Dig. 0630
15343-2 (6) [id.].

CD 1: *J. S. Bach and his predecessors:* LEBEGUE:
*Magnificat du premier ton; Noël: Où s'en vont ces
gais bergers; Pour l'amour de Marie.* TUNDER:
*Choral-fantasia: Jesu Christus, wahr' Gottes
Sohn.* BRUHNS: *Prelude and fugue in E min.*
BUXTEHUDE: *Chorales: In dulci jubilo, BuxWV
197; Der Tag, der ist so freudenreich, BuxWV
182; Magnificat primi toni, BuxWV 203.* BOHM:
Chorale: Gelobet seist du, Jesu Christ. BACH:
*Fuga sopra il Magnificat, BWV 733; Canonic
variations on Vom Himmel hoch, BWV 769;
Prelude and fugue in C, BWV 547.*

CD 2: *The late baroque:* BACH: *Toccata and fugue
in D min., BWV 565; Trio sonata in C, BWV 529;
Fugue in G min., BWV 578; Trio (Adagio) (after
BWV 1027); (Allegro) BWV 1027a; Concerto in D
min. (after Vivaldi), BWV 596.* HANDEL: *Concerto
in B flat, Op. 4/6.* C. P. E. BACH: *Concerto in E
flat, Wq. 35* (both with Paillard CO).

CD 3: *The 19th century:* BOELY: *Fantasia and
fugue in B flat, Op. 18.* MENDELSSOHN: *Prelude
and fugue in C min.* LISZT: *Prelude and fugue on
B-A-C-H.* BOELLMAN: *Gothic suite, Op. 25.*
WIDOR: *Symphony No. 5: Allegro cantabile;
Toccata.* FRANCK: *Prélude, fugue et variation,
Op. 18.* GUILMANT: *Sonata in D min. (Allegro
assai).*

CD 4: *The 20th century:* VIERNE: *Suite No. 2, Op.
53: Toccata in B flat.* A. ALAIN: *Scherzo in E min.;
Toccata on l'Antienne 'Cantemus Domino'.* J.
ALAIN: *2 Danses à Agni Yavishta; Intermezzo;
Litanies; Aria.* POULENC: *Concerto in G min. for
organ, strings and timpani* (with ORTF,
Martinon). MESSIAEN: *La Nativité du Seigneur:
Les bergers; Dieu parmi nous.*

CD 5: *Rare recordings: from Pachelbel to
Mozart:* BACH: *Cantata No. 35: Sinfonia No. 2*
(with Paillard CO); *14 Canons on the Goldberg
bass* (with O. Alain). PACHELBEL: *Toccata in C;
Prelude in D min.; Chorals: Vom Himmel hoch;
Chaconne in F min.* BACH: *10 Canons from The
Musical offering, BWV 1079.* VIVALDI: *Concerto
in D min. for violin, organ and strings, RV 541*
(with Toso, Sol. Ven., Scimone). MOZART:
*Fantasia for mechanical organ in F min., K.608;
Sonata in C, K.336 (Allegro).*

Bonus disc: BACH: *Prelude and fugue in G, BWV
541; Chorale, BWV 721; Aria, BWV 587;
Canzona, BWV 588.* C. P. E. BACH: *Sonata
No. 6 in G min., Wq.70/6.*

Marie-Claire Alain's recording career is justly celebrated here by Erato, for she has been making
recordings for this label since 1953. The sixth
(bonus) CD offered here includes four works which
were on that first Bach LP, plus a sampler of her
latest recording of organ sonatas by Bach's son,
Carl Philipp Emanuel, made in 1996. The other five
discs survey her achievement over the intervening
forty or so years. There is very little here that is not
of high calibre and the range is remarkable, always
using organs suitable for the repertoire.

The five recitals are arranged in historical order,
beginning with Johann Sebastian and his predecessors, followed by a second disc of Bach but with
concertos by Carl Philipp Emanuel and Handel.
Then comes the nineteenth century, ranging from
Boëly, Mendelssohn and Liszt to the French School
– Boëllman, Widor, Franck and Guilmant. Compact
disc 4 moves on to the twentieth century but stays
in France, and all of it is real music, by Vierne,
Poulenc, Alain and – of course – Messiaen.

The fifth CD purports to be 'rare recordings', but
they are not really so very rare, including Bach
Canons and a Vivaldi *Concerto for violin, organ
and strings* which is not one of the plums. But
overall this set is well worth considering, especially
by those who want some basic organ repertoire for
a modest-sized collection. The reproduction is of a
high standard.

Amato, Donna (piano)

'A piano portrait': LISZT: *Hungarian rhapsody
No. 2 (cadenza by Rachmaninov); Consolation
No. 3; Liebestraum No. 3.* DEBUSSY: *Arabesque
No. 1; Suite bergamasque: Clair de lune.
Préludes: La fille aux cheveux de lin; La
cathédrale engloutie.* RAVEL: *Pavane pour une
infante défunte.* GERSHWIN: *3 Preludes; Rhapsody
in blue* (solo piano version). Song transcriptions:
*The man I love; Swanee; Oh, lady be good; I'll
build a stairway to paradise; 'S wonderful; I got
rhythm.*
*** Olympia OCD 352 [id.].

The young American pianist Donna Amato here
proves her mettle in standard repertoire and, more
importantly, confirms her ability to create "live"

performances in the recording studio. None of the readings is routine or conventional: the Liszt *Consolation* has an attractive simplicity and the famous *Liebestraum*, while not lacking romantic impulse, has an agreeable lack of gush. Her Debussy is particularly impressive: the *Arabesque* has a lightly chimerical variety of touch and colour and the two most famous pieces are made to seem refreshingly unhackneyed. The highlight, however, is *La cathédrale engloutie*, an unforgettably powerful evocation, played quite superbly. She is, not surprisingly, completely at home with Gershwin. The song transcriptions are splendidly stylish and sparkling and her solo account of the *Rhapsody in blue* is highly idiomatic. In its strong, natural impulse and rhythmic freedom it can be spoken of in the same breath as Bernstein's version, although it has completely its own character. Donna Amato's style is not that of a Horowitz, and so it was perhaps a pity she chose to open with the Liszt *Hungarian rhapsody*, which would have been better placed later on in the programme, while the Ravel *Pavane* is a little too sober; but as a whole this 76-minute recital, recorded very realistically indeed in Salen Church Hall, Ski, Norway, is most enjoyable.

Anderson, John (oboe), Gordon Back (piano)

'*Capriccio*': PONCHIELLI: *Capriccio*. HUE: *Petite pièce*. PALADILHE: *Solo*. KALLIWODA: *Morceau de salon, Op. 228*. PASCULLI: *Concerto sopra motivi dell'opera 'La Favorita' di Donizetti*. FAURE: *Pièce*. DONIZETTI: *Solo*. SCHUMANN: *3 Romances, Op. 94*. FRANCK: *Pièce No. 5*. SINIGAGLIA: *Variations on a theme of Schubert, Op. 19*.
(M) **(*) ASV Dig. CDWHL 2100 [id.].

The three *Romances* by Schumann are the highlight of the programme: they have more substance than the rest and are beautifully played, while Sinigaglia's ingenious variations on one of Schubert's most charming melodies make for an engaging finale. The decoratively florid *Capriccio* of Ponchielli which opens the recital receives the most stylish bravura from the soloist; but it is completely inconsequential. The *Petite pièce* of Georges Hue is more distinctive and Paladilhe's *Solo* (in fact a duo with piano) is amiable too, as is the Kalliwoda *Morceau*, although it is rather longer than a morceau.

When we come to Pasculli's cleverly contrived fantasia on Donizetti's *La Favorita*, the tunes are more indelible, and the resulting virtuosity is impressive. Donizetti's own *Solo* is another attractive miniature, as is the lilting Franck *Pièce*. John Anderson is a first-rate oboist and he is persuasively supported throughout by Gordon Back. The recording is very real and immediate. But this light-weight 75-minute concert needs to be dipped into rather than taken all at once.

Andreasen, Henri Wenzel (flute), Anna Oland (piano)

Flute music of the Danish Golden Age:
HARTMANN: *Sonata in B flat, Op. 1; Prelude in G min.* FROLICH: *Sonata in A min.* WEYSE: *Rondeau in D min.* KUHLAU: *Duo brillant, Op. 110/1*.
(BB) *** Naxos Dig. 8.553333 [id.].

The Danish Golden Age is, roughly speaking, the period of the artists C. W. Eckersberg and Christen Købke (the first half of the nineteenth century) and it was then that the present repertoire was composed. It is best summarized as slight but pleasing music, and the performances are alert and fresh with good, bright – but not overbright – sound.

Andsnes, Leif Ove (piano)

'*The Long, long winter night*': GRIEG: *Norwegian folksongs, Op. 66; Peasant dances, Op. 72*. Geirr TVEITT: *Fifty folktunes from Hardanger, Op. 150*. David Monrad JOHANSEN: *Pictures from Nordland: Suite No. 1, Op. 5*. Fartein VALEN: *Variations for piano, Op. 23*. SVERUD: *Tunes and dances from Siljustøl, Opp. 22, 24, 25; Peer Gynt: Hymn against the Boyg, Op. 28*.
🌑 *** EMI Dig. CDC5 56541-2.

A recital of unusual excellence and distinction from Leif Ove Andsnes devoted to his fellow countrymen. The disc takes its title, 'The Long, long winter night', from one of the *Hardanger folktunes* by Geirr Tveitt. His programme ranges widely from some of the late and extraordinarily characterful *Slåtter* or *Peasant dances* of Grieg to the *Variations* by Fartein Valen, the pre-war Norwegian apostle of dodecaphony. Grieg's biographer David Monrad Johansen (best-known perhaps for his tone-poem, *Pan*) is represented by two early piano pieces that are of more than passing interest. He also includes seven of the Op. 150 set of *Hardanger folktunes*, which could be as popular here as they are in Norway if they were given the chance.

Although his symphonies are now gaining ground on CD, Harald Sverud was arguably at his best as a miniaturist, and Andsnes gives us a handful of his distinctive, original *Slåtter og stev fra Siljustøl*, which have such winning titles as 'The cotton grass plays on a moonbeam fiddle' (variously translated as 'The windflowers twiddle the moonbeam fiddle'). He also includes *Kjmpeviseslåtten* ('The Ballad of revolt') that came to symbolize Norwegian resistance to the Nazis during the occupation. A well-planned and imaginative recital, and an exhibition of masterly pianism. Very good recording indeed.

Argerich, Martha (piano)

CHOPIN: *Scherzo No. 3 in C sharp min., Op. 39; Barcarolle in F sharp min., Op. 60.* BRAHMS: *2 Rhapsodies, Op. 79.* PROKOFIEV: *Toccata, Op. 11.* RAVEL: *Jeux d'eau.* LISZT: *Hungarian rhapsody No. 6; Piano sonata in B min.*
(M) (**) DG 447 430-2 [id.].

This particular 'Legendary Recording' in DG's series of 'Originals' presents Argerich's remarkable début LP recital, recorded for DG in 1961. The phenomenal technique (she was twenty-one at the time) is as astonishing as the performances are musically exasperating. This artist's charismatic impulsiveness is well known, but in presenting Chopin and Brahms she is too impetuous by half, although *Jeux d'eau* brings a certain Ravelian magic. The Liszt *Sonata* has been added on; it dates from a decade later and yet again, although the bravura is breathtaking and there is no lack of spontaneity, the work's architecture and indeed its breadth are to some extent sacrificed to the insistent forward impulse of the playing. Good but not exceptional recording, a bit hard in the Liszt, though that may well reflect faithfully the percussive attack of Argerich's powerful hands.

Barere, Simon (piano)

'The complete HMV recordings, 1934–6': LISZT: *Etude de concert (La leggierezza), G.144/2. Années de pèlerinage, 2nd Year (Italy): Sonetto 104 del Petrarca, G.161/5. Gnomenreigen, G.145/2; Réminiscences de Don Juan, G.418* (2 versions); *Rapsodie espagnole, G.254; Valse oubliée No. 1, G.215.* CHOPIN: *Scherzo No. 3 in C sharp min., Op. 39; Mazurka No. 38 in F sharp min., Op. 59/3; Waltz No. 5 in A flat, Op. 42.* BALAKIREV: *Islamey* (2 versions). BLUMENFELD: *Etude for the left hand.* GLAZUNOV: *Etude in C, Op. 31/1.* SCRIABIN: *Etudes in C sharp min., Op. 2/1; in D sharp min., Op. 8/12* (2 versions). LULLY/GODOWSKI: *Gigue in E.* RAMEAU/GODOWSKI: *Tambourin in E min.* SCHUMANN: *Toccata in C, Op. 7* (2 versions).
❂ (***) Appian mono CDAPR 7001 (2) [id.].

This two-CD set offers all of Barere's HMV recordings, made in the mid-1930s, including the alternative takes he made in the studio. What can one say of his playing without exhausting one's stock of superlatives? His fingerwork is quite astonishing and his virtuosity almost in a class of its own. The set contains an absolutely stunning account of the *Réminiscences de Don Juan*, and his *Islamey* knocks spots off any successor's in sheer virtuosity and

excitement; it is altogether breathtaking, and much the same might be said of his *Rapsodie espagnole*. Nor is there any want of poetry – witness the delicacy of the Scriabin *C sharp minor Etude* or Liszt's *La leggierezza*. Readers wanting to investigate this legendary artist should start here. One of the most important functions of the gramophone is to chart performance traditions that would otherwise disappear from view, and this set is one to celebrate.

Barrueco, Manuel (guitar)

'Cuba!': LECUONA: *La Comparsa; Dana Lecami; A la Antiga.* BROUWER: *Preludio; Rito de los Orisbas.* FARINAS: *Cancón triste; Preludio.* UBIETA: *New York rush (Theme from El Super).* ANGULO: *Cantos Yoraba de Cuba.* ARDEVOL: *Sonata.*
**(*) EMI Dig. CDC5 56757-2 [id.].

Manuel Barrueco, Cuban by birth, is clearly at home in this late-evening programme of mostly gentle music. The three opening Lecuona pieces are totally seductive, as is Brouwer's lovely *Preludio* and the haunting *Theme from El Super*, which is built on a rhythmic bass ostinato of Caribbean extraction. Even the series of nine brief vignettes which make up Angulo's *Cantos Yoraba*, and which are based directly on folk melodies, are primarily evocative (No. 4, *Borotití*, is like a berceuse). And it is only in Ardévol's *Sonata* with its central variations and vibrant closing *Danza* that the music becomes really animated.

This is maintained in the closing group of five Dances and Evocacións from Brouwer's *Rito de los Orisbas*, which bring plenty of chances for rhythmic bravura. (They should have been individually cued, however.) Barrueco plays with a spontaneous, ruminative style, and he is most naturally recorded (at Abbey Road).

VILLA-LOBOS: *Preludes Nos. 1–5; Chôros No. 1 in E min.* BROUWER: *Danza caracteristica; Canticum; Canción de cuna (Berceuse); Elogio de la danza; Ojos brujos; Guajira criolla.* Julián ORBON: *Preludio y danza.*
(M) *** EMI Dig. CDM5 66576-2 [id.].

The Cuban guitarist Manuel Barrueco is the latest star in the line of great guitarists which began with Segovia and includes, of course, both John Williams and Julian Bream. His breadth of repertoire is remarkable and his playing is often electrifying, yet showing the most subtly imaginative touches in the control of rhythm, colour and dynamics. Barrueco is naturally at home in the music of his compatriots Leo Brouwer and the young Julián Orbon. The latter was a pupil of Aaron Copland, but his *Preludio y danza* comes nearer to the world of Villa-Lobos, with which Barrueco also has a ready affinity.

The Brouwer pieces, including the *Canticum*

(dazzlingly vibrant and evocative by turns), the deliciously seductive *Canción de cuna*, the haunting *Elogio de la danza* and the *Guajira criolla* with its enticing opening pizzzicatos (violin style), are all marvellously done. Barrueco is perhaps not quite as winningly flexible as Bream in the famous *Third Prelude* of Villa-Lobos, but he makes No. 4 totally his own with a magical vibrato on the repeated tenutos. The *Chôros* is played with engaging intimacy, and the recording cannot be faulted.

FALLA: *The Three-cornered hat: Night; Miller's dance; Dance of the Corregidor; Dance of the Miller's wife. Omaggio per chitarra (Scritto per le tombeau de Debussy).* PONCE: *Sonatina meridional.* RODRIGO: *Invocación y danza (Homenaje a Manuel de Falla); 3 Piezas españolas.*
(M) *** EMI Dig. CDM5 66577-2 [id.].

What comes over here is not just the (often unostentatious) dazzling bravura and the evocative feeling, but the appealingly warm intimacy with which Barrueco communicates so directly to the listener. He finds all the colour and flamenco rhythms in Falla's *Three-cornered hat* ballet music without ever going over the top; but he is at his very finest in the delicate nocturnal evocation of Rodrigo's very personal tribute to Falla. Falla's own *Homenaje for Debussy* flashes vibrantly, as does the *Zapateado* finale of the Rodrigo *Spanish pieces*; but, for all the astonishing technical mastery of this playing, one always feels that Barrueco is looking beneath the music's surface and seeking to find added depth and atmosphere. If you enjoy Spanish guitar music, this recital is unmissable.

Bate, Jennifer (organ)

Eighteenth-century organ music on period instruments from Adlington Hall, the Dolmetsch Collection, St Michael's Mount, Kenwood House, Killerton House, Everingham chapel.

Vol. 1: John READING: *Airs for French horns & flutes.* STANLEY: *Voluntaries, Op. 5/7 & 10; Op. 6/5; Op. 7/3.* HANDEL: *Fugue in B flat.* ROSEINGRAVE: *Voluntary in G min.* TRAVERS: *Voluntary in D min. & major.* WALOND: *Voluntary in A min.* RUSSELL: *Voluntary in E min.* Samuel WESLEY: *Short pieces Nos. 7 & 12; Voluntary, Op. 6/1.*
*** Unicorn Dig. DKPCD 9096 [id.].

Vol. 2: GREENE: *Voluntary in C min.* STANLEY: *Voluntaries, Op. 5/6 & 9; Op. 6/7; Op. 7/2.* HANDEL: *Fugue in A min.* LONG: *Voluntary in D min.* WALOND: *Voluntary in B min.* NARES: *Introduction and fugue in F.* RUSSELL: *Voluntary in A min.* Samuel WESLEY: *Short piece No. 9; Voluntary, Op. 6/3.*
**(*) Unicorn Dig. DKPCD 9099 [id.].

Vol. 3: GREENE: *Voluntary in B min.* STANLEY: *Voluntaries, Op. 6/1 & 10; Op. 7/1 & 6.* WALOND: *Voluntary in G.* HANDEL: *Fugue in B min.; Voluntary in C.* BURNEY: *Cornet piece in E min.* RUSSELL: *Voluntary in A.* Samuel WESLEY: *Short pieces Nos. 6 & 8; Voluntary, Op. 6/6.*
*** Unicorn Dig. DKPCD 9101 [id.].

Vol. 4: GREENE: *Voluntary in E flat.* STANLEY: *Voluntaries, Op. 5/8; Op. 6/6, 8 & 9; Op. 7/7.* HANDEL: *Voluntary in C; Fugue in G min.* ROSEINGRAVE: *Fugue No. 13.* DUPUIS: *Voluntary in B flat.* Samuel WESLEY: *Voluntary, Op. 6/9.*
**(*) Unicorn Dig. DKPCD 9104 [id.].

Jennifer Bate is making a survey of eighteenth-century English organ music, using five different English organs from stately homes to secure maximum variety of presentation. But these instruments are all relatively light-textured and sound bright and sweet. The four programmes are all made up in much the same way: mostly opening with an agreeable *Voluntary* of Maurice Greene, then offering a clutch of *Voluntaries* by John Stanley, followed in most cases by music by Walond and Handel among others, and usually ending with *Short pieces* by Samuel Wesley.

None of these are great composers, save Handel of course, and his chosen examples are relatively minor works. Jennifer Bate plays all this music in impeccable style and she is beautifully recorded; so the particular attractions of each disc depend on the items included. Easily the most engaging are the works which use cornet or trumpet stops, which are colourful and jolly, while the Vox humana stop, as in the finale of Stanley's Op. 6/5 on the first disc, is also ear-tickling.

Indeed, the first volume is a good place to start, with Op. 5/7 by the same composer also quite engaging. The voluntaries are usually in two sections, but William Russell's E minor piece is in three with an imposing opening and the fugue used as a centrepiece. Samuel Wesley's *Short piece No. 12* is a contrapuntal moto perpetuo. The second disc offers more examples of Stanley's ready facility, notably Op. 7/2 and Op. 5/6, but on the whole this is a less interesting programme than Volume 3, which again shows Stanley at his more inventive in Op. 7/1; Op. 6/1 begins with a pleasing *Siciliano.* Handel's *Voluntary in C* brings some attractive interplay of parts in its second movement and it is followed by Burney's *Cornet piece*, which has a whiff of the *Hallelujah chorus.*

In Volume 4 Jennifer Bate registers Stanley's Op. 5/8 with piquant skill (this is a three-part work), while the trumpet theme in Op. 6/6 might almost have been written by Purcell. Volume 1, however, is the disc to try first, then, if you enjoy this, go on to Volume 3. But only the real enthusiast will want all four CDs, for much of the writing here is fairly conventional.

British organ music: ELGAR: *Sonata No. 1 in G, Op. 28* (Royal Albert Hall organ). Samuel Sebastian WESLEY: *Air with variations (composed for Holsworthy church bells); Introduction and fugue in C sharp min.* STANFORD: *Prelude and postlude on a theme of Orlando Gibbons, Op. 105/ 2; 2 Short preludes and postludes, Op. 101/2 & 4.* PARRY: *Fantasia and fugue in G min.* (organ of St James's Church, Muswell Hill). WALFORD DAVIES: *Solemn melody.* VAUGHAN WILLIAMS: *Prelude on a Welsh hymn tune No. 2: Rhosymedre.* ELGAR: *Imperial march, Op. 32* (arr. martin) (organ of St Andrew's Church, Plymouth). (BB) **(*) ASV Dig./Analogue CDQS 6160 [id.].

As can be seen from the organs used, this 75-minute recital draws on three different sources. The Elgar *Sonata* features the Royal Albert Hall organ, used impressively and flamboyantly, although quieter passages recede. The recordings made at Muswell Hill draw on a recital originally published on the Hyperion label which we greeted enthusiastically with the comment that the offered programme could stand alongside many, more fashionable French compilations for quality and variety of invention.

Samuel Sebastian Wesley's rather gentle *Variations on Holsworthy church bells* have charm, and his *Introduction and fugue* is strongly argued and well structured, but less flamboyant than the comparable piece by Parry. Other items in the original programme (by Wesley's father, Samuel, and by Russell, Stanley and Charles Wood) have been replaced by three more obviously popular pieces, by Walford Davies, Vaughan Williams and Elgar, whose *Imperial march* could use more uninhibited panache than is offered here. However, generally speaking Jennifer Bate's choice of tempi and registration is admirable, and the organs seem well chosen for the repertoire.

'Stanford and his contemporaries' (British organ music played on the organs of Brangwyn Hall, Swansea; St James's Church, Muswell Hill, London and St Andrew's Parish Church, Plymouth): STANFORD: *Fantasia and toccata in D min., Op. 57; Preludes: in the form of a minuet; in the form of a chaconne; in the form of a toccata, Op. 88/1–3.* Percy WHITLOCK: *Extemporisations Nos. 1 (Carol); 2 (Divertimento).* Harvey GRACE: *Psalm tune on 'Martyrs'.* PARRY: *Toccata and fugue in G (Wanderer).* Charles WOOD: *Prelude on 'St Mary's'.* JACOB: *Festal flourish.* William HARRIS: *A Fancy; Reverie.* BAIRSTOW: *Prelude in C; Evening song.* COCKER: *Tuba tune.* (BB) *** ASV Quicksilva CDQS 6222 [id.].

Cocker's *Tuba tune* is one of the most brightly colourful of today's organ favourites, and alongside Gordon Jacob's *Festal flourish* it enlivens this collection of English organ music, framed by Stanford, and including three attractive genre pieces from his Op. 88 plus a number of other impressive and enjoyable items which suit the characteristically warm, full-bodied sound of British organs. Parry's *Toccata and fugue* pictures an ocean voyage and Charles Wood's *'St Mary's'* prelude builds a solemn Elgarian march theme to a big climax. The *Psalm tune Postlude* of Harvey Grace is also quite memorable. Very well recorded, Jennifer Bate is thoroughly at home in the repertoire and she brings her comparatively lightweight programme fully to life.

Belgian Wind Quintet

'Summer music': BEETHOVEN: *Wind quintet in E flat.* HOLST: *Wind quintet in A flat, Op. 14.* BARBER: *Summer music, Op. 31.* ARRIEU: *Quintet in C.* (BB) *** Koch Discovers Dig. DICD 920322 [id.].

A delightful collection, well worth its modest price. The many felicities of the Barber *Summer music* are matched by those of the much less familiar work of Holst, contemporary with the *Military band suites.* Claude Arrieu (born 1903) also writes very engagingly: his *Quintet* is both elegant and witty. The playing of the Belgian group is polished and spontaneous, and they are very well recorded.

Bennett, Richard Rodney (piano)

'British piano music of the '20s & '30s': MAYERL: *Marigold; Punch; Ace of Hearts; Antiquary; Shallow Waters; Printer's Devil; Sleepy Piano; Railroad Rhythm.* BLISS: *The Rout Trot.* Gerrard WILLIAMS: *Déjeuner dansant: Valsette brute; Raguette extra-sec.* GOOSSENS: *Folk-tune.* WALTON (arr. Rodney BENNETT): *Façade: Old Sir Faulk.* LAMBERT: *Elegiac blues; Elegy. Concerto for piano and nine players* (with members of the English Sinfonia, Dilkes). (M) **(*) EMI CDM 5 65596-2 [id.].

Constant Lambert's *Concerto for piano and nine players* presents a clever marriage between neo-classical and jazz manners. In a poor performance, the work can seem very dry indeed, but here (in 1974) Richard Rodney Bennett makes the music sparkle with wit, pointing the rhythms with subtle nuances that bring it to life. The sleight of hand pay-off endings to each movement are delectably done. The couplings could hardly be more apt: a collection of short pieces by Lambert and others with direct debts to jazz. The main addition to the original LP is eight characteristic pieces by Billy Mayerl – including his most famous, *Marigold.* Their carefree jazz style is neatly brought out by the pianist, even though here, the piano is too backwardly balanced. Lambert's *Elegiac blues* is rather leisurely, but very expressive, whilst the *Elegy*, which is more ambitious in scale, is less sharply inspired. The two miniatures by Gerrard Williams are slight but attractive. But every item here has a point: Bliss's piece is like a cross between Scott Joplin and Grainger's *Country gardens*, while Walton's *Old Sir Faulk* shines out as the finest example of all in this tiny but delightful genre. A most enjoyable collection which fully conjures up the spirit of the 1920s and 30s, and the sound, with the caveat about the (1975) Mayerl pieces already mentioned, is remarkably good.

Bergen Wind Quintet

BARBER: *Summer music, Op. 31.* SVERUD: *Tunes and dances from Siljustøl, Op. 21a.* JOLIVET: *Serenade for wind quintet with principal oboe.* HINDEMITH: *Kleine Kammermusik, Op. 24/2.* *** BIS CD 291 [id.].

Barber's *Summer music* is a glorious piece dating from the mid-1950s; it is in a single movement. Sverud's *Tunes and dances from Siljustøl* derive from piano pieces of great charm and sound refreshing in their transcribed format. Jolivet's *Serenade* is hardly less engaging, while Hindemith's *Kleine Kammermusik*, when played with such character and finesse, is no less welcome. Throughout, the fine blend and vivacious ensemble give consistent pleasure.

Berman, Lazar (piano)

Live recital – 27 June 1992: SCHUBERT: *Piano sonata No. 21 in B flat, D.960.* LISZT: *Concert paraphrases of Schubert Lieder: Der Leiermann; Täuschung; Gretchen am Spinnrade; Die junge Nonne; Ave Maria; Erlkönig. Mephisto waltz; Années de pèlerinage, 1st Year: Chapelle de Guillaume Tell.* BEETHOVEN/RACHMANINOV: *Extract from The Ruins of Athens.* (BB) ** Koch Discover DICD 920164/5 (2) [id.].

Berman's 1992 recital is uncommonly well recorded for a live occasion and the presence of the artist is in no doubt; indeed, we have to wait a full half-minute for him to start after the introductory applause. His account of Schubert's last and greatest sonata is obviously both felt and considered. It is certainly dramatic but also wayward, and not all will respond to Berman's agogic distortions of the flow, particularly in the first movement. The Liszt items provide repertoire for which he is famous and the *Mephisto waltz* shows him at his most commanding. Some of the Schubert song transcriptions may be felt to be over-dramatized, though no one could complain about the *Erl-King*. The Beethoven/Rachmaninov encore is properly piquant.

Bok, Henri (bass clarinet), Rainer Klaas (piano)

20th-century music for bass clarinet and piano: HINDEMITH: *Sonata.* SCHOECK: *Sonata, Op. 41.* Lubos SLUKA: *Sonata.* Václav REHAK: *Sonnet III.* Stefan HEUCKE: *Sonata, Op. 23.* Burkhardt SOLL: *Lumen.* *** Clarinet Classics Dig. CC 026 [id.].

A remarkably stimulating collection with a group of four diverse sonatas which between them explore every lyrical and virtuosic possibility of the bass clarinet's colour spectrum and virtuosic range. From Hindemith comes an unexpectedly enticing mixture of wit and wan pastoralism, while Rehak's *Sonnet III* is a darkly atmospheric interlude before the most ambitious piece here, by Stefan Heucke. It is in three sections, a *Ballade*, an extraordinary set of central *Variations* full of original and unexpected rhythms and sounds, followed by a plangent closing *Elegie*. Soll's *Lumen* then acts as a lighter, entertaining encore. The performances throughout are in every way superb and the recording excellent.

Bowyer, Kevin (organ)

'A feast of organ exuberance' (Blackburn Cathedral organ): WOLF–G. LEIDEL: *Toccata Delectatione, Op. 5/35.* SWAYNE: *Riff-Raff.* BERVEILLER: *Suite; Cadence.* (M) *** Priory Dig. 001.

The spectacular sound made by the magnificent 1969 Walker organ in Blackburn Cathedral is well demonstrated by this first-rate recital. Leidel is from the former East Germany, and his acknowledged influences from Messiaen and Scriabin are well absorbed into his own style. The *Toccata for pleasure* is titillating in its colouring and certainly exuberant in its extravagant treatment of its basic idea, which goes far beyond the minimalism achieved by many of his contemporaries. Giles Swayne is Liverpool-born and his quirky *Riff-Raff*, in the words of the performer, suggests 'isolated flashes of light of varying intensity'. Berveiller comes from the traditional French school of Dupré. His *Suite* is eminently approachable music, with a whimsical second-movement *Intermezzo* to remain in the memory, and a smoothly rich *Adagio*, before the Widorian finale. His *Cadence* provides a lightweight but by no means trivial encore. What one remembers most of all from this concert is the magnificent sonority of the organ, beautifully captured within its natural ambience, and that in itself shows how well composers and performer have combined their talents.

Bream, Julian (guitar or lute)

⊙ *'The Julian Bream Edition'* (BMG/RCA).

The Julian Bream Edition runs to some thirty CDs (available as a boxed set in the USA: RCA 09026 61583-2), representing three decades of a remarkably distinguished recording career. Bream has now moved over to EMI, so this edition is essentially retrospective. A few of the miscellaneous recitals are considered below, although most of the individual volumes have now been withdrawn. The concertante collections are listed as Composer entries in our main volume, and the Elizabethan lute songs are listed under Peter Pears among Vocal Recitals.

Bream, Julian (lute)

Volume 1. *'The golden age of English lute music'*: Robert JOHNSON: *2 Almaines; Carman's whistle.* John JOHNSON: *Fantasia.* CUTTING: *Walsingham; Almaine; Greensleeves.* DOWLAND: *Mignarda; Galliard upon a galliard of Daniel Bachelar; Batell galliard; Captain Piper's galliard; Queen Elizabeth's galliard; Sir John Langton's pavan; Tarleton's resurrection; Lady Clifton's spirit.* ROSSETER: *Galliard.* MORLEY: *Pavan.* BULMAN: *Pavan.* BACHELAR: *Monsieur's almaine.* HOLBORNE: *Pavan; Galliard.* BYRD: *Pavana Bray; Galliard; Pavan; My Lord Willoughby's welcome home.*
(M) *** BMG/RCA 09026 61584-2 [id.].

Bream is a natural lutenist and a marvellously sensitive artist in this repertoire, and here he conjures up a wide range of colour, matched by expressive feeling. Here Dowland is shown in more extrovert mood than in many of his lute songs, and overall the programme has plenty of variety. The CD combines two recitals, the first fifteen items recorded by Decca in London in September 1963, and the rest of the programme in New York City two years later. The recording is exemplary and hiss is minimal.

Bream, Julian (guitar)

Volume 8. *'Popular classics for the Spanish guitar'*: VILLA-LOBOS: *Chôros No. 1; Etudes in E min. & C sharp min.; Prelude in E min.; Suite popolar brasileira: Schottische-chôro.* TORROBA: *Madraños.* FALLA: *Homenaje pour le tombeau de Debussy. Three-cornered hat: Miller's dance* (arr. BREAM). TURINA: *Fandanguillo.* arr. LLOBET: *El testament d'Amelia.* SANZ: *Canarios.* M. albeniz: *Sonata* (arr. pujol). RODRIGO: *En los trigales.* MOZART: *Larghetto and Allegro, K.229.* GIULIANI: *Sonata in C, Op. 15: Allegro. Rossiniana No. 1, Op. 119* (both ed. Bream).

(M) *** BMG/RCA Analogue/Dig. 09026 61591-2 [id.].

This collection in itself admirably scans Bream's RCA recording career, opening with material from an outstanding early recital made at Kenwood House in 1962, to which other items have been judiciously added from as early as 1959, and from 1965–8 and 1971, plus the two digital Falla pieces which are as late as 1983. Not surprisingly, the tension is a little variable, though the recital makes a very satisfactory whole. The highest voltage comes in the Villa-Lobos pieces which, though often thoughtful and ruminative, sound wonderfully spontaneous, and the Turina *Fandanguillo* is also very fine. The Mozart and Giuliani excerpts are appropriately mellow. Very real recording, with the various acoustics always well managed.

Volume 9. *'Baroque guitar'*: SANZ: *Pavanas; Galliardas; Passacalles; Canarios.* GUERAU: *Villano; Canario.* J. S. BACH: *Prelude in D min., BWV 999; Fugue in A min., BWV 1000.* WEISS: *Passacaille; Fantaisie; Tombeau sur la mort de M. Comte de Logy.* VISEE: *Suite in D min.* FRESCOBALDI: *Aria con variazione detta la Frescobalda* (arr. segovia). D. SCARLATTI: *Sonata in E min., K.11* (arr. BREAM); *Sonata in E min., K.87* (arr. SEGOVIA). CIMAROSA: *Sonata in C sharp min.; Sonata in A* (both arr. BREAM).
(M) *** BMG/RCA 09026 61592-2.

The four Sanz pieces are strong in colour and atmosphere, and Sylvius Weiss also emerges with an individual voice. The eight-movement *Suite* by Robert Visée, a French court lutenist who lived from about 1650 until 1725, has the most attractive invention. The famous 'La Folia' emerges seductively as the *Sarabande* (it is beautifully played); and the *Gavotte*, two *Minuets*, *Bourrée* and *Gigue* which follow are all loosely based on its melodic contour. Frescobaldi's *Aria con variazione* is another memorable work. Scarlatti's keyboard sonatas transcribe well enough for guitar and the two sonatas of Cimarosa, though not strictly baroque music, are very personable.

Volume 26. *'La guitarra romántica'* (Music of Spain): TARREGA: *Mazurka in G; Etude in A; Marieta; Capricho árabe; Prelude in A min.; Recuerdos de la Alhambra.* MALATS: *Serenata.* PUJOL: *Tango espagñol; Guajira.* llobet: *Canciones populares catalanas.* TURINA: *Fandanguillo, Op. 36; Sevillana, Op. 29; Homenaje a Tárrega.*
(M) *** BMG/RCA Dig./Analogue 09026 61609-2.

A mainly digital recital of Spanish music opens with an attractive, lightweight Tárrega group including the *Capricho árabe* and his most famous evocation, the *Recuerdos de la Alhambra*, which in Bream's hands is curiously muted and withdrawn.

Then after works by Malats and Pujol (his *Guajira* has some fine special effects) there follows the delightful Llobet suite of nine *Canciones populares catalanas*. The programme ends with the vibrant flamenco-inspired music of Turina, including the composer's last (two-part) guitar work, the *Homenaje a Tárrega*. Bream's dynamism in these performances makes one almost believe he was Spanish-born. The final work (consisting of a *Garrotín* and *Solearas*) was recorded at Kenwood House in 1962 and is exceptional in that here the resonance inflates the guitar image; for the rest of the recital the recording is ideal in all respects.

Volume 27. *'Guitarra'* (Music of Spain): MUDARRA: *Fantasias X & XIV.* Luis DE MILAN: *Fantasia XXII.* Luis DE NARVAEZ: *La canción del Emperador; Conde claros.* Santiago DE MURCIA: *Prelude & Allegro.* BOCCHERINI: *Guitar quintet in D, G.448* (arr. for 2 guitars): *Fandango.* SOR: *Gran solo, Op. 14; Variations on a theme of Mozart, Op. 9; Fantasie, Op. 7; Sonata, Op. 25: Minuet.* AGUADO: *Rondo in A min., Op. 2/3.* TARREGA: *Study in A; Prelude in A min.; Recuerdos de la Alhambra.*
(M) *** BMG/RCA Dig./Analogue 09026 61610-2.

An admirable survey covering 400 years and featuring several different instruments, all especially built by José Ramanillos and including a Renaissance guitar and a modern classical guitar. Bream's natural dexterity is matched by a remarkable control of colour and unerring sense of style. Many of the earlier pieces are quite simple but have considerable magnetism. The basic recital was recorded digitally in 1983 at Bream's favourite venue, Wardour Chapel, Windsor, and is laid out chronologically. Two additional Sor items, the *Fantasie*, Op. 7 and the *Minuet* from Op. 25, were made eighteen years earlier in New York and, as they are analogue, have sensibly been added at the end.

Other collections

'Popular classics for Spanish guitar':
VILLA-LOBOS: *Chôros No. 1; Etude in E min.* TORROBA: *Madroños.* TURINA: *Homenaje a Tárrega, Op. 69: Garrotín; Solearas. Fandanguillo.* ALBENIZ: *Suite española, Op. 47: Granada; Leyenda (Asturias).* FALLA: *Homenaje pour le tombeau de Debussy.* TRAD., arr. LLOBET: *Canciones populares catalanas: El testament d'Amelia.*
(M) **(*) RCA 09026 68814-2 [id.].

This outstanding early recital, recorded at Kenwood House in 1962, was one of Bream's very finest LP collections. The electricity of the music-making is consistently communicated, and all Bream's resources of colour and technical bravura are brought into play. The Villa-Lobos pieces are particularly

fine, as is the Turina *Fandanguillo* (which comes at the end), and the Albéniz *Leyenda* is a *tour de force* and makes an almost orchestral effect. The recording (originally produced by James Burnett, with Bob Auger the engineer) has been splendidly remastered for RCA's 'Living Stereo' series (the equivalent of Decca's 'Classic Sound') and Bream is given a remarkable presence, with the analogue background noise all but vanquished. However, the playing time is only 42 minutes, and while Volume 8 of 'The Julian Bream Edition' (BMG/RCA 09026 61591-2) remains available (see above), this must take second place. That earlier reissue includes most of the present items, plus a great deal more music.

'Baroque guitar': SANZ: *Pavanos; Canarios.* J. S. BACH: *Prelude in D min., BWV 999; Fugue in A min., BWV 1000; Lute suite in E min., BWV 996.* SOR: *Fantasy and Minuet.* WEISS: *Passacaille; Fantaisie; Tombeau sur la mort de M. Comte de Logy.* VISEE: *Suite in D min.*
(BB) *** RCA Navigator 74321 24195-2.

This is a shorter version of the baroque recital which forms Volume 9 of the 'Julian Bream Edition'. It still includes well over an hour of music as Bream's superb account of Bach's *E minor Lute suite* has been added. The recording is very natural, and this makes a fine recital in its own right, realistically recorded. A very real bargain in RCA's bargain-basement Navigator series.

Bream, Julian (guitar and lute)

'The ultimate guitar collection' ((i) with Monteverdi O, Gardiner): (i) VIVALDI: *Lute concerto in D, RV 93* (ed. Bream). Lute PIECES: CUTTING: *Packington's round; Greensleeves.* DOWLAND: *A Fancy (Fantasia).* Guitar pieces: SANZ: *Canarios.* Mateo ALBENIZ: *Sonata in D* (arr. PUJOL). Isaac ALBENIZ: *Suite española, Op. 47: Cataluña; Granada; Sevilla; Cádiz; Leyenda (Asturias). Mallorca, Op. 202. Cantos de España: Córdoba, Op. 232/4.* FALLA: *Three-cornered hat: Miller's dance.* TARREGA: *Recuerdos de la Alhambra.* VILLA-LOBOS: *Chôros No. 1; Preludes Nos. 1 in E min.; 2 in D.* RODRIGO: *En los trigales;* (i) *Concierto de Aranjuez. Tres piezas españolas.* granados: *Cuentos para la juventud: Dedicatoria. Tonadilla: La Maja de Goya. Danzas españolas Nos. 4 (Villanesca); 5 (Valses poéticos).*
🟢 (B) *** RCA Dig./Analogue 74321 33705-2 (2).

The extraordinary achievement of RCA's 'Julian Bream Edition' is admirably summed up by this inexpensive pair of CDs which include two and a half hours of the most popular repertoire for guitar, plus a small group of lute pieces for good measure. There is not a single item here that is not strong in musical personality, and every performance springs vividly and spontaneously to life. John Eliot Gardiner provides highly distinguished accompaniments for the two justly famous concertos by Vivaldi (for lute) and Rodrigo (for guitar).

The first of the two CDs provides a well-planned historical survey, opening with Elizabethan lute music and progressing through to include three magnetic pieces by Villa-Lobos. Highlights include an electrifying performance of Falla's *Miller's dance* from *The Three-cornered hat* and, of course, the most famous guitar piece of all, the *Recuerdos de la Alhambra* of Tárrega.

The second collection, which is entirely digital (from 1982–3), concentrates mainly on Isaac Albéniz and Granados (not forgetting the superb accounts of the *Córdoba* by the former and the *Danza española No. 5* by the latter, which are highly praised in our Composer section). It ends appropriately with Rodrigo's *Tres piezas españolas*, with its remarkable central *Passacaglia*. The recordings are of the highest quality and are excellently transferred to CD.

Bream, Julian and John Williams

(guitar duo)

'*Together*': Disc 1: CARULLI: *Serenade in A, Op. 96.* GRANADOS: *Danzas españolas: Rodella aragonesa; Zambra, Op. 37/6 & 11.* ALBENIZ: *Cantos de España: Bajo la palmera, Op. 232/3. Ibéria: Evocación.* GIULIANI: *Variazioni concertanti, Op. 130.* JOHNSON: *Pavan & Galliard* (arr. BREAM). TELEMANN: *Partie polonaise.* DEBUSSY: *Rêverie; Children's corner: Golliwog's cakewalk. Suite bergamasque: Clair de lune.*

Disc 2: LAWES: *Suite for 2 guitars* (arr. BREAM). CARULLI: *Duo in G, Op. 34.* SOR: *L'encouragement, Op. 34.* ALBENIZ: *Cantos de España: Córdoba, Op. 232/4; Suite española: Castilla (Seguidillas).* GRANADOS: *Goyescas: Intermezzo* (arr. pujol). *Danzas españolas: Oriental, Op. 37/2.* FALLA: *La vida breve: Spanish dance No. 1.* RAVEL: *Pavane pour une infante défunte.* FAURE: *Dolly (suite), Op. 56* (both arr. BREAM).

(B) *** RCA 74321 20134-2 (2).

The rare combination of Julian Bream and John Williams was achieved by RCA in the studio on two separate occasions, in 1971 and 1973, providing the basic contents of these two recitals. Further recordings were made live in Boston and New York in 1978, during a North American concert tour.

Curiously, it is the studio programmes which seem the more spontaneous, and Fauré's *Dolly suite*, which sounds a little cosy, is the only disappointment (it also brings some audience noises).

Highlights are the music of Albéniz and Granados (notably the former's haunting *Evocación* from *Iberia*, and *Córdoba*, which Bream also included on a very successful solo recital). The transcription of the *Goyescas intermezzo* is also very successful, as is Debussy's *Golliwog's cakewalk*, in a quite different way. Giuliani's *Variazioni concertanti*, actually written for guitar duo, brings some intimately gentle playing, as does the Theme and variations which forms the second movement of Sor's *L'encouragement*, while the *Cantabile* which begins this triptych is delightful in its simple lyricism.

The Carulli *Serenade* opens the first recital very strikingly, while on the second disc the performance of Ravel's *Pavane*, very slow and stately, is memorable. The Elizabethan lute music by Johnson and Lawes and the Telemann *Partie polonaise* (written for a pair of lutes) bring a refreshing change of style in what is predominantly a programme of Spanish music. The concert ends with Albéniz's *Seguidillas*, and an appropriately enthusiatic response from the audience. With the overall timing at a very generous 149 minutes, the pair of discs comes for the cost of a single premium-priced CD and can be recommended very strongly indeed. This is music-making of the very highest order, and the CD transfers bring fine presence and a natural balance.

Brendel, Alfred (piano)

Vanguard 'Alfred Brendel Collection'

Volume 1: MOZART: *Piano concertos Nos. 9 in E flat, K.271; 14 in E flat, K.449* (with I Solisti di Zagreb, Janigro); *Piano sonata No. 8 in A min., K.310; Fantasia in C min., K.396; Rondo in A min., K.511; 9 Variations on a Minuet by Duport, K.573.*
(M) *** Van. 08 9161 71 (2).

Volume 2: CHOPIN: *Andante spianato et Grande polonaise brillante, Op. 22; Polonaises Nos. 4 in C min., Op. 40/2; 5 in F sharp min., Op. 44; 6 in A flat, Op. 53; 7 (Polonaise-fantaisie), Op. 61.* LISZT: *Hungarian rhapsodies Nos. 2–3, 8, 13, 15 (Rákóczy march); Csárdás obstinée.*
(M) **(*) Van. 08 9163 72 (2) .

Volume 3: SCHUBERT: *Piano sonatas Nos. 15 in C (Unfinished), D.840; 19 in C min., D.958; 16 German dances, D.783.* SCHUMANN: *Etudes symphoniques; Fantasia in C.*
(M) *** Van. 08 9165 72 (2).

Vanguard have now produced their own 'Alfred Brendel Collection' from recordings made in the 1960s. Each set of two CDs is offered in a slip-case but with no price saving. The separate discs are discussed in our main volume, under their Composer headings.

Britton, Harold (organ)

'Organ spectacular' (organ of Royal Albert Hall): SUPPE: *Light Cavalry overture.* LEMARE: *Andantino in D flat.* VERDI: *Aida: Grand march.* ALBINONI: *Adagio* (arr. giazotto). WAGNER: *Ride of the Valkyries.* BACH: *Toccata and fugue in D min., BWV 565.* TCHAIKOVSKY: *None but the lonely heart.* ELGAR: *Pomp and circumstance march No. 1.* SOUSA: *Liberty Bell.* WIDOR: *Symphony No. 5: Toccata.*

(BB) *** ASV Quicksilva CDQS 6028 [(M) id. import].

If one is to have a collection mainly of arrangements of orchestral lollipops on an organ, the instrument at the Royal Albert Hall is surely an ideal choice: it offers the widest dynamic range, including an effective recession of quieter passages readily at the player's command – used to good purpose in *Light Cavalry* – but can also produce truly spectacular fortissimos, with a wide amplitude and a blaze of colour from its multitude of stops. Harold Britton is obviously fully at home on the instrument and plays in an aptly extrovert style for such a recital, obviously enjoying himself. The CD is in the demonstration class – there are few problems of muddying from reverberation.

Brodsky Quartet

'Music from Vienna', Volume l: SCHOENBERG: *String quartet in D.* WEBERN: *Langsamer Satz (Slow movement).* ZEMLINSKY: *String quartet No. 1 in A.*

(M) *** Vanguard Dig. 99208 [id.].

In the first of two discs titled 'Music from Vienna', the Brodsky Quartet have devised a fascinating grouping of early works by musical pioneers which give little idea of radical developments to come. The Schoenberg offers a surprising range of Dvořákian echoes from the opening onwards, and Dvořák is one of the influences too in the early Zemlinsky quartet, again with Brahms part of the mixture. The Webern (dated 1905, the same year as his earliest atonal works) is even more ripely romantic, with echoes of Schoenberg's *Verklärte Nacht* and little astringency. The Brodsky Quartet give flawless performances, at once stirring and subtle with superbly polished ensemble in deeply expressive music. For Volume 2, see in our main volume under composers Korngold and Kreisler.

Brüggen, Frans (recorder)

'The Frans Brüggen Edition' (complete)

(M) *** Teldec/Warner 4509 97475-2 (12) [id.].

Volume 1: TELEMANN (with Anner Bylsma, Gustav Leonhardt): *Essercizii musici: Sonatas in C, TWV 41:c5; in D min., TWV 41:D4. Fantasias in C, TWV 40:2; in D min., TWV 40:4; in F, TWV 40:8; in G min., TWV 40:9; in A min., TWV 40:11; in B flat, TWV 40:12. Der Getreu Musik-Meister: Canonic sonata in B flat, TWV 41:b3; Sonatas in C, TWV 41:c2; in F, TWV 41:f2; in F min., TWV 41:F1* (4509 93688-2).

Volume 2: *Italian recorder sonatas* (with Anner Bylsma, Gustav Leonhardt): CORELLI: *Sonatas: in F, Op. 5/4; La Follia (Variations in G min.), Op. 5/12.* BARSANTI: *Sonata in C.* VERACINI: *Sonatas in G; in A min.* (1716). bigaglia: *Sonata in A min.* CHEDEVILLE: *Sonata in G min., Op. 13/6.* MARCELLO: *Sonata in D min., Op. 2/11* (4509 93669-2).

Volume 3: *English ensemble music* (with Kees Boeke, Walter van Hauwe, Anner Bylsma, Gustav Leonhardt, Brüggen Consort): HOLBORNE: *Dances and airs.* TAVERNER: *In nomine.* TYE: *In nomine (Crye).* BYRD: *In nomine; The leaves be green.* Thomas SIMPSON: *Bonny sweet Robin.* MORLEY: *La Girandola; Il Lamento; La Caccia.* JEFFREYS: *Fantasia.* PARCHAM: *Solo in G.* Robert CARR: *Divisions upon an Italian ground.* William BABELL: *Concerto in D.* PEPUSCH: *Sonata in F.* PURCELL: *Chaconne in F* (4509 97465-2).

Volume 4: *Early baroque recorder music* (with Kees Boeke, Walter van Hauwe, Anner Bylsma, Wouter Möller, Bob van Asperen, Gustav Leonhardt): Jacob VAN EYCK: *Batali; Doen Daphne d'over schoonne Maeght; Pavane Lachryme; Engels Nachtegaeltje.* FRESCOBALDI: *Canzon: La Bernadina.* Giovanni Paolo CIMA: *Sonatas in D & G.* Giovanni Battista RICCIO: *Canzon in A; Canzon in A (La Rosignola).* SCHEIDT: *Paduan a 4 in D.* anon.: *Sonata in G* (4509 97466-2).

Volume 5: *Late baroque recorder music* (with Jeanette van Wingerden, Kees Boeke, Walter van Hauwe, Frans Vester, Joost Tromp, Brian Pollard, Anner Bylsma, Wouter Möller, Gustav Leonhardt, Bob van Asperen): TELEMANN: *Quartet in D min., TWV 43:D1.* FASCH: *Quartet in G.* LOEILLET: *Quintet in B min.* QUANTZ: *Trio sonata in C.* Alessandro SCARLATTI: *Sonata in F.* Johann MATTHESON: *Sonata No. 4 in G min.* (4509 97467-2).

Volume 6: *French recorder suites* (with Kees Boeke, Nikolaus Harnoncourt, Anner Bylsma, Gustav Leonhardt): Charles DIEUPART: *Suites in G min. & A.* HOTTETERRE: *Suite No. 1* (4509 97468-2).

Volume 7: *French recorder sonatas* (with Kees Boeke, Walter van Hauwe, Anner Bylsma, Gustav Leonhardt): Philibert DE LAVIGNE: *Sonata in C (La Barssan).* BOISMORTIER: *Sonata in F.* PHILIDOR: *Sonata in D min.* Louis-Antoine

DORNEL: *Sonata (a 3 Dessus) in B flat*. François
COUPERIN: *Le rossignol-en-amour* (4509
97469-2).

Volume 8: VIVALDI: *Chamber concertos* (with
Jürg Schaefleit, Otto Fleischmann, Alice
Harnoncourt, Walter Pfeiffer, Nikolaus
Harnoncourt, Gustav Leonhardt): *in C, RV 87; in
D, RV 92 & RV 94; in G min., RV 105; in A min.,
RV 108; in C min., RV 441; in F, RV 442* (4509
97470-2).

Volume 9: HANDEL: *Recorder sonatas* (with Alice
Harnoncourt, Anner Bylsma, Nikolaus
Harnoncourt, Gustav Leonhardt, Herbert Tachezi):
*in G min., HWV 360; in A min., HWV 362; in C,
HWV 365; in F, HWV 369, Op. 1/2, 4, 7 & 11; in
F, HWV 389, Op. 2/4. Fitzwilliam sonatas Nos.
1 in B flat, HWV 377; 3 in D min., HWV 367a*
(4509 97471-2).

Volume 10: TELEMANN: *Concertos and orchestral
music* (with VCM, Harnoncourt): *Concertos in C;
à 6 in F; Suite (Overture) in A min., TWV 55:A2*
(4509 97472-2).

Volume 11: J. S. BACH: *Chamber and orchestral
music* (with Jeanette van Wingerden, Leopold
Stastny, Marie Leonhardt, Nikolaus Harnoncourt,
Gustav Leonhardt, Herbert Tachezi): *Concertos in
A min., BWV 1044; in F, BWV 1057; Sonata
concerto from Cantata No. 182; Sonatina from
Cantata No. 106; Trio sonata in G, BWV 1039*
(4509 97473-2).

Volume 12: *Recorder sonatas and concertos* (with
Frans Vester, Alice Harnoncourt, Nikolaus
Harnoncourt, Anner Bylsma, Gustav Leonhardt,
Herbert Tachezi, VCM; Amsterdam CO):
LOEILLET: *Sonata in C min.; Sonata in G*.
SAMMARTINI: *Concerto in F*. HANDEL: *Trio
sonata in B min*. NAUDOT: *Concerto in G*.
TELEMANN: *Double concerto in E min.* (4509
97474-2).

Frans Brüggen is perhaps the greatest master of the
recorder of the post-war era. In his hands phrases
are turned with the utmost sophistication, intonation
is unbelievably accurate and matters of style exact.
There is spontaneity too and, with such superb
musicianship and the high standard of recording we
have come to expect from the Teldec Das Alte Werk
series, these reissues in Brüggen's own special edition can almost all be recommended without reservation. He is equally at home in early or late baroque
music. Throughout the collection, Frans Brüggen
and his estimable colleagues demonstrate various
period instruments; Anner Bylsma, Gustav Leonhardt and Bob van Asperen are present to provide a
distinguished continuo, while Harnoncourt and the
Vienna Concentus Musicus and Schröder's
Amsterdam Chamber Orchestra are available for
authentic concerto accompaniments.

Volume 1 is a single-disc anthology of Tele-

mann's chamber music. Brüggen plays with his
usual mastery and, as one would expect from Gustav
Leonhardt's ensemble, the performances have
polish and authority, and they are excellently
recorded.

Volume 2 with its collection of Italian recorder
sonatas is surely a perfect sampler for the whole
edition, for it gives the opportunity for this king of
recorder players to demonstrate his expertise and
musicianship to maximum effect, admirably partnered by Anner Bylsma and Gustav Leonhardt.
Corelli puts the famous 'Follia' melody through all
possible hoops and Brüggen obliges with nimble
virtuosity. The Veracini works are also primarily
for violin, though the recorder is an optional alternative for the *G major Sonata*. All this music is played
with exemplary skill, and no recorder enthusiast
will want to be without this splendid example of
Brüggen's art.

The collection of English ensemble music which
constitutes Volume 3 is particularly diverting,
opening with Holborne's *Suite of dances and airs*
which alternates recorder and viols. The several
In nomines are all differently scored and are very
different in character too, while the folksong
arrangements by Byrd and Simpson are touching.
The *Solo* (Suite) by Andrew Parcham, the *Divisions*
of Robert Carr and Pepusch's *Sonata* are all engaging and are played with characteristic skill and
musicianship so that only occasionally does the ear
detect the limitations of early instruments.

Volume 4 introduces works by Jacob Van Eyck,
which are unaccompanied but are aurally titillating,
particularly the primitive *Batali* with its 'bugle'
calls, while the florid upper tessitura of *Engels
Nachtegaeltje* really takes wing. The Frescobaldi
Canzon and the works by Cima and Riccio use an
organ and cello continuo, and the delightful *La
Rosignola* is for recorder trio with cello and harpsichord.

Late baroque chamber music is represented on
Volume 5, with works by Alessandro Scarlatti, Telemann and Johann Mattheson standing out, while
Volume 6 brings entertainingly elegant and tuneful
Suites by Dieupart (a French-born musician who
taught in London around 1700 and whose harpsichord music influenced Bach) and Hotteterre
(known as Le Romain). These suites are very much
cast in the style favoured by Telemann, with an
Overture and a collection of dances.

Volume 7 concentrates on French recorder sonatas and brings another vivid nightingale evocation
– *Le rossignol-en-amour*, by François Couperin.

Volumes 8–10 are composer collections of music
by Vivaldi, Handel and more Telemann, all discussed in detail under their Composer entries, in
our main volume. Volume 11, offering a Bach collection, is the only relative disappointment. Two of
the major works here are transcribed, and BWV
1044 comes off more effectively than BWV 1057.

Best is the *Trio sonata in G*, BWV 1039, although the two cantata excerpts are pleasing.

A final excellent sampler is provided by the collection of *Recorder sonatas* and *concertos* which makes up Volume 12, featuring a chamber ensemble and both the Amsterdam Chamber Orchestra and the Vienna Concentus Musicus. The Telemann *Double concerto in E minor for recorder and flute* is a particularly fine one, and the dulcet duet in the slow movement begins rather like Handel's *Where'er you walk*. The Sammartini *Concerto* has an unexpectedly solemn *Siciliano* for its slow movement. The Handel *Trio sonata* is a splendid work, and the two Loeillet *Sonatas* are light and airy and full of charm, while even the less striking Naudot piece emerges as music of character. All these performances are outstandingly successful.

The recordings were nearly all made during the 1960s, with a few dating from the following decade, and they are of the highest quality, as are the vivid CD transfers. Documentation is very good. As we go to press, the individual issues are still available separately.

Campoli, Alfredo (violin)

'Homage to Kreisler': (with Eric Gritton; or Norihko Wada, piano): KREISLER: *Praeludium and allegro; Liebesleid; Liebesfreud; Polichinelle-serenade; Schön Rosmarin; Caprice viennois; Tamborin chinois; Rondo on a theme by Beethoven; La Chasse; La Gitana.* Arrangements: PADEREWSKI: *Minuet in G.* WIENIAWSKI: *Caprices in E flat; A min.* GRANADOS: *Dance Espagnole.* TARTINI: *Variations on a theme of Corelli.* ALBENIZ: *Tango.* BRAHMS: *Waltz in A flat.* YAMADA: *Akatonbo; Jogashima no ame.* BACH: *Arioso.* SCHUBERT: *Ave Maria.* MOZART: *Divertimento No. 17: Rondo.*

(B) (***) Australian Decca Eloquence mono/ stereo 466 666-2.

This disc not only pays 'Homage to Kreisler', but also to Alfredo Campoli. None of the music here is deeply profound, but it is all very entertaining – whether it be breathtakingly showy, or charmingly sentimental. Many of Kreisler's encore hits are included and Campoli's performances are full of flair, while the Decca recordings, both mono and stereo, are all characterstically vivid, though the stereo brings greater depth and richness.

Cann, Claire and Antoinette
(piano duo)

'Romantic favourites on 2 pianos': SAINT-SAENS: *Danse macabre.* DEBUSSY: *Petite suite.* TCHAIKOVSKY (arr. CANN): *Nutcracker suite: excerpts.* BRAHMS: *Variations on a theme of Haydn (St Anthony chorale), Op. 56b; Waltzes, Op. 39/1–2, 5–6, 9–11 & 15.* MACDOWELL (arr. NIEMANN): *Hexentanz.* LISZT (arr. BRENDEL): *Hungarian rhapsody No. 2.*

🌑 (M) *** Apollo Recordings Dig. ARCD 961.

We are glad to welcome the début recital of the Cann duo back to the catalogue. With the demise of the Pianissimo label it was unavailable for some time but it now returns on the Apollo label, distributed in the UK by Canterbury Classics. It is difficult to imagine a more scintillating piano duet record than this. Saint-Saëns's skeletons – summoned by an evocative midnight bell – dance as vigorously as do MacDowell's witches in the brilliant *Hexentanz*, while Debussy's delightful *Petite suite* – played here very effectively on two pianos, rather than with four hands on one – is full of charm. The Cann sisters then produce a rich-textured fullness of tone for the Brahms *Haydn variations*, which are every bit as enjoyable here as in their orchestral dress. Most remarkable of all are the excerpts from the *Nutcracker suite*, conceived entirely pianistically and glittering with colour. Indeed, the *Sugar plum fairy* has a much stronger profile than usual and the *Chinese dance* an irresistible oriental glitter. The *Hungarian dances* bring beguiling variety of mood and texture and display an easy bravura, ending with a lovely performance of the famous *Cradle song (No. 15 in A flat)*, while the dazzling Liszt *Hungarian rhapsody* ends the recital with great exuberance and much digital panache. The recording, made in Rosslyn Hill Chapel, is exceptionally real and vivid and is ideally balanced.

Casadesus, Robert and Gaby
(piano)

'Two pianos and piano four hands': DEBUSSY: *Petite suite; En blanc et noir.* FAURE: *Dolly.* CASADESUS: *3 Danses Méditerranéennes.* SATIE: *3 Morceaux en forme de poire.*

(M) **(*) Sony stereo/mono MPK 52527 [id.].

These accounts come from 1959, save for Robert Casadesus's *Trois Danses Méditerranéennes*, which were recorded in 1950 and are in mono, and *En blanc et noir*, which is from 1963. Although the recording is not in the top bracket (the sound is a bit synthetic and hardens in fortissimo passages), the playing of Robert and Gaby Casadesus has such style and panache that technical limitations should not deter anyone with a taste for this repertoire. They have perfect unanimity and control, as well as wonderfully articulated rhythm. Casadesus's own *Danses Méditerranéennes* are inventive and attractive, distinctly Gallic though not highly personal, and the recording, though shallow, is perfectly acceptable. Fauré's *Dolly suite* is given with charm, and the Satie *Trois Morceaux en forme de poire* are also a delight. Some of the octave unisons in *En blanc et noir* are out of tune, but it is a fine performance for all that.

Casals, Pablo (cello)

Casals Edition (instrumental and chamber music)

BEETHOVEN: *Cello sonatas Nos. 1–5, Op. 5/1–2; Op. 69; Op. 102/1–2; 7 Variations on 'Bei Männern' (from Mozart's 'Die Zauberflöte'), WoO 46; 12 Variations on 'Ein Mädchen' (from Mozart's 'Die Zauberflöte'), WoO 66* (with Rudolf Serkin).
(M) (**) Sony mono SM2K 58985 (2) [id.].

These Casals accounts of the Beethoven *Cello sonatas* come from 1953 and 1958 and exhibit strong personality but less finish, understandably so when one considers that by the latter date Casals was approaching eighty. In spite of the keyboard expertise of Serkin, these performances do not match his performances with Horszowski, made between 1931 and 1938 and now reissued on EMI, coupled with the Brahms *Second Cello sonata*, in which the pianist is Otto Schulhof, an altogether excellent set ((M) (***) CHS5 65185-2).

BEETHOVEN: *Piano trio No. 1 in E flat, Op. 1/1* (with Eugene Istomin, Joseph Fuchs). SCHUBERT: *Piano trio No. 2 in E flat, D.929* (with Mieczyslaw Horszowski, Alexander Schneider).
(M) (***) Sony mono SMK 58988 [id.].

The *E flat Piano trio*, Op. 1, No. 1 with the much and rightly admired Joseph Fuchs and Eugene Istomin is first class, and the Schubert *E flat Trio* with Horszowski and Schneider is a commanding account that is well worth considering.

BEETHOVEN: *Piano trio No. 2 in G, Op. 1/2.* SCHUBERT: *Piano trio No. 1 in B flat, D.898* (with Eugene Istomin, Alexander Schneider).
(M) (**) Sony mono SMK 58989 [id.].

BEETHOVEN: *Piano trios Nos. 4 in B flat, Op. 11; 7 in B flat (Archduke), Op. 97* (with Eugene Istomin, Alexander Schneider).
(M) (**) Sony mono SMK 58990 [id.].

The Schubert *B flat Trio* on SMK 58989 has its impressive insights, but the *Archduke* on the companion disc does not extinguish memories of the famous pre-war set with Thibaud and Cortot; but there is, as one might expect, perceptive and felicitous and touching phrasing. It comes with the *B flat Trio*, Op. 11, the transcription of the *Clarinet trio*.

BEETHOVEN: *Piano trios Nos. 5 in D (Ghost), Op. 70/1* (with Eugene Istomin, Joseph Fuchs); *6 in E flat, Op. 70/2* (with Eugene Istomin, Alexander Schneider); *12 Variations on a theme from*

Handel's 'Judas Maccabaeus', WoO 45 (with Rudolf Serkin).
(M) (***) Sony mono SMK 58991 [id.].

The two Op. 70 *Trios*, the '*Ghost*' with Fuchs and Istomin and the *E flat* with Istomin and Schneider, are given with great spirit and are arguably superior to Casals's later (1958) versions with Végh and Engel.

BRAHMS: *Piano trio No. 1 in B, Op. 8* (with Dame Myra Hess, Isaac Stern); *String sextet No. 1 in B flat, Op. 18* (with Isaac Stern, Alexander Schneider, Milton Katims, Milton Thomas, Madeline Foley).
(M) (***) Sony mono SMK 58994 [id.].

The Brahms performances, the *B major Trio*, Op. 8 and the *B flat Sextet*, Op. 18 are hardly less celebrated. The *Trio* with Isaac Stern and Myra Hess is a noble and beautifully phrased performance. The majestic and passionate account of the *Sextet* enjoyed cult status in France and elsewhere when it was used in Louis Malle's 1958 film *Les amants*; and it remains a classic of the gramophone – one of the artistic peaks of the Casals Edition.

Chung, Kyung Wha (violin), Philip Moll (piano)

'*Con amore*': KREISLER: *La Gitana; Liebeslied; Praeludium and allegro in the style of Pugnani; Liebesfreud.* POLDINI: *Dancing doll.* WIENIAWSKI: *Scherzo-Tarantelle; Caprice in A min.* ELGAR: *Salut d'amour, Op. 12; La Capricieuse, Op. 17.* TCHAIKOVSKY: *Valse sentimentale.* NOVCEK: *Moto perpetuo.* DEBUSSY: *Beau soir.* CHOPIN: *Nocturne in C sharp min.* GOSSEC: *Gavotte.* CHAMINADE: *Sérénade espagnole.* SAINT-SAENS: *Caprice (after a study in the form of a waltz), Op. 52/6.* BRAHMS: *Hungarian dance No. 1.*
*** Decca (IMS) Dig. 417 289-2 [id.].

Kyung Wha Chung's collection 'Con amore' reflects that title in a delightfully varied choice of items, sweet as well as brilliant. When she claims in all seriousness that she does not think of herself as a virtuoso violinist, she really means that technical brilliance is only an incidental for her, and the poise and flair of all these items show her at her most winningly characterful, helped by Philip Moll's very sympathetic accompaniment, and well-balanced recording, which has fine presence on CD and sounds pretty good on chrome cassette, too.

Clarion Ensemble

'*Trumpet collection*': FANTINI: *Sonata; Brando; Balletteo; Corrente.* MONTEVERDI: *Et e pur dunque vero.* FRESCOBALDI: *Canzona a canto*

solo. PURCELL: *To arms, heroic prince.* A.
SCARLATTI: *Si suoni la tromba.* BISHOP: *Arietta
and Waltz; Thine forever.* DONIZETTI: *Lo L'udia.*
KOENIG: *Posthorn galop.* arban: *Fantasia on
Verdi's Rigoletto.* CLARKE: *Cousins.* ENESCU:
Legende.
✹ *** Amon Ra CD-SAR 30 [id.].

The simple title 'Trumpet collection' covers a fascinating recital of music for trumpet written over
three centuries and played with great skill and musicianship by Jonathan Impett, using a variety of
original instruments, from a keyed bugle and
clapper shake-key cornopean to an English slide
trumpet and a posthorn. Impett is a complete master
of all these instruments, never producing a throttled
tone; indeed, in the Purcell and Scarlatti arias he
matches the soaring soprano line of Deborah
Roberts with uncanny mirror-image precision.
Accompaniments are provided by other members
of the Clarion Ensemble. The Frescobaldi *Canzona*
brings a duet for trumpet and trombone, with a
background harpsichord filigree, which is most
effective. With demonstration-worthy recording, this
is as enjoyable as it is interesting, with the
Posthorn galop and Arban's *Rigoletto variations*
producing exhilarating bravura.

Cohler, Jonathan (clarinet)

'Cohler on clarinet' (with Judith Gordon, piano):
BRAHMS: *Sonata No. 1 in F min., Op. 120/1.*
WEBER: *Grand duo concertante, Op. 48.*
BAERMANN: *Quintet No. 3, Op. 23: Adagio* (arr.
for clarinet & piano). SARGON: *Deep Ellum nights
(3 Sketches).*
*** Ongaku Dig. 024-101 [id.].

This fine collection marks the recording début of an
outstanding, Boston-born, American clarinettist. He
has a splendid technique and a lovely tone, and he
is already master of an extraordinarily wide range
of repertoire. The opening Brahms *F minor Sonata*
is a supreme test, and he passes with distinction.
The Weber *Grand duo concertante* is suitably good-
natured, with a songful central cantilena and plenty
of wit in the finale.

The Baermann *Adagio* shows how ravishingly
Cohler can shape a melting legato line with a breath-
catching pianissimo at its peak. He then throws his
hat in the air in the three exuberant *Sketches* of
Simon Sargon, where sultry melodic lines are interrupted by all kinds of jazzy glissandos and uninhibited syncopations, notably an explosive burst of
energy intruding into the *Quiet and easy* central
section. The finale is like a flashy cakewalk. The
recording is truthful, but the piano is placed behind
in a too resonant acoustic (the empty Paine Concert
Hall at Harvard University), which is a tiresome
misjudgement. Even so, Judith Gordon provides

sympathetic support and the playing more than
compensates.

'More Cohler on clarinet' (with Randall
Hodgkinson, piano): BRAHMS: *Sonata No. 2 in E
flat, Op. 120/2.* POULENC: *Sonata.* SCHUMANN:
Fantasiestücke, Op. 73. MILHAUD: *Sonatina, Op.
100.* STRAVINSKY: *3 Pieces* (for solo clarinet).
*** Ongaku Dig. 024-102 [id.].

Cohler's second disc is much more satisfactorily
balanced. His excellent partner, Randall Hodgkinson, is fully in the picture. The opening of the
Brahms *E flat Sonata* is agreeably warm and relaxed, and the Theme and variations finale brings a
pleasing interplay between the two artists. Poulenc's *Sonata* is beautifully done, the lovely
Romanza (*Très calme*) is cool in the way only a
player who knows about jazz can manage, while
the fizzing finale also brings a hint of rapture in
its contrasting lyrical theme. The warmth of the
Schumann pieces, for which Cohler imaginatively
modifies his timbre, contrasts with the outrageous
Milhaud sonatina, with both outer movements
marked *Très rude* but the *Lent* centrepiece quite
magical. The three dry Stravinsky fragments make
a perfect close to a disc which is outstanding in
every way.

Crabb, James and Geir Draugsvoll (accordions)

Début recital: STRAVINSKY: *Petrushka* (ballet;
complete). MUSSORGSKY: *Pictures at an
exhibition* (both arr. CRABB/DRAUGSVOLL).
(B) **(*) EMI Début CDZ5 69705-2 [(M) id.].

It seems impossible to believe that Stravinsky's
brilliantly scored ballet, played on a pair of piano
accordions, could sound remarkably like the orchestral version; but this phenomenal transcription
brings all the colours of the Stravinskian palette
vividly before the listener. Only the bold sound of
unison horns and the bite of massed strings eludes
these virtuosi, and they bring the ballet's drama and
pathos fully to life. This is an extraordinary listening
experience. Mussorgsky's *Pictures at an exhibition*
is equally ingenious but is far less consistently
effective, for one's ear is used to bold brass sonorities and spectacle. *Catacombs* and the big finale do
not really come off, although the grotesque *Baba-
Yaga* certainly does, played with proper rhythmic
venom; otherwise the most effective pictures are
those in which we normally expect woodwind
chattering: *Tuileries, Limoges* and the cheeping
chicks. Nevertheless it's a good try, and the playing
itself has astonishing bravura. Well worth sampling
on EMI's bargain Début label. The recording cannot
be faulted.

Curley, Carlo (organ)

'*Toccata: Organ favourites*' (organ of Girard College Chapel, Philadelphia): BACH: *Toccata and fugue in D min., BWV 565; Cantata No. 22: Subdue us by thy kindness; Suite No. 3 in D: Air. Cantata No. 147: Jesu joy of man's desiring. Cantata No. 140: Wachet auf. Cantata No. 29: Sinfonia in D.* ALBINONI, arr. GIAZOTTO/ CURLEY: *Adagio.* GUILMANT: *March on a theme by Handel, Op. 15.* SOLERBIGGS: *Emperor's fanfare.* SCHUBERT, arr. CURLEY: *Ave Maria.* KARG-ELERT: *Chorale improvisation: Now thank we all our God (Trauung, Taufe, Emtefest).* LIDON: *Sonata on the first tone.* SAINT-SAENS: *Carnival of the animals: The Swan.* dussek, arr. THALBEN-BALL: *Andante in F.* MOZART: *Fantasia in F min., K. 608.* WIDOR: *Organ Symphony No. 5: Toccata.* STANLEY: *Suite in D: Introduction & Trumpet tune, Op. 6/6.* MULET: *Tu es Petrus.* VIERNE: *Carillon de Westminster.* BEETHOVEN, arr. CURLEY: *Ruins of Athens: Turkish march.* SCHUBERT: *Moment musical in F min.* HANDEL: *Concerto in F, Op. 4/5: Allegro* (both arr. CURLEY). RACHMANINOV, arr. BIRD: *Vocalise.* BOELLMANN: *Suite gothique, Op. 25.* HOLST: *The Planets: Jupiter* (theme, arr. curley). SOUSA, arr. CURLEY: *Washington Post.*
(B) *** Decca Double Dig. 458 364-2 (2) [id.].

On the original issue which contained the *Emperor's fanfare* (an anachronistic but irresistible arrangement of Soler's music by E. Power Biggs, which provides an opportunity for great splashes of throaty timbre and uses the powerful *Tuba mirabilis* stop) the flamboyant Carlo Curley described with engaging enthusiasm the organ he plays here: 'Nearly one hundred feet from the [Girard] Chapel's marble floor and above the vast, coffered ceiling, entirely covered incidentally with real gold leaf, the organ, all thirty-five metric tonnes, and with 6,587 handmade pipes, is miraculously suspended. In a chapel so cavernous, and with such remarkable reverberation, it is well nigh impossible to identify the source of the sound.'

Yet the Decca (Argo) engineers manage to provide an excellent focus and capture the extremely wide range of Curley's playing with precision at both ends of the spectrum. The performances are full of drama and temperament, unashamedly romantic, yet very compelling. A great deal of this music is not ideally suited to the organ but Curley's panache almost convinces one that it is, and this collection cannot fail to entertain any organ fancier when the recording is so spectacularly vivid.

Daniel, Nicholas (oboe), Julius Drake (piano) – see below under Snowden, Jonathan (flute)

Claude Debussy Wind Quintet

'*The new interpreters*': LIGETI: *6 Bagatelles; 10 Pieces.* JANACEK: *Mládi; Concertino* (with Philippe Cassard, piano, Bruno Martinez & members of Parish Qt).
(B) *** HM Dig. HMN 911624 [id.].

Anyone who thinks of Ligeti as a 'difficult' composer should sample this infectious performance of the *Six Bagatelles*, especially the riotous élan of the opening *Allegro con spirito* and the more wry wit of the finale. There is unexpected melodic charm too in the *Allegro grazioso* (No. 3), and the sombre tribute to Bartók is darkly memorable. The *Ten Pieces* are thornier, but still stimulating. The penultimate number is marked *Sostenuto stridente* and the finale *Presto bizzare*, but the music remains ear-catching. The two better-known Janáček works are also played with keen rhythmic feeling and, although this is in essence a sampler, it makes a highly enjoyable concert; the recording gives these excellent players a very tangible presence within a nicely judged acoustic.

Demidenko, Nikolai (piano)

'*Live at Wigmore Hall*': VORISEK: *Fantasia in C, Op. 12.* HAYDN: *Variations in F min., Hob XVII/6.* D. SCARLATTI: *Sonatas Kk. 11, 377.* SCHUMANN: *Variations on a theme of Clara Wieck.* MENDELSSOHN: *Fantasy in F sharp min., Op. 28.* KALKEBRENNER: *Nocturne in A flat, Op. 129.* LISZT: *Concert paraphrase of Beethoven's An die ferne Geliebte.* BERG: *Sonata in B min., Op. 1.* BUXTEHUDE/PROKOFIEV: *Prelude & fugue in D min., BuxWV 140.* GUBAIDULINA: *Ciacona.* LISZT: *Funérailles.* SCHUBERT: *Impromptu, D.899/4.*
(M) **(*) Hyperion Dyad Dig. CDD 22024 (2) [id.].

With the advantage of the superb Wigmore Hall acoustics, Nikolai Demidenko, recorded live at a series of concerts between January and June 1993, comes over charismatically, and the programme is certainly diverse. Mendelssohn's *Fantasy* could hardly be played more brilliantly and this set, which has received an enthusiastic press, is a must for the pianist's admirers, even if perhaps the general collector would not be drawn to hearing some of this music very often. The Liszt/Beethoven song-cycle transcription, for instance, has not too much to offer compared with a vocal version. The Gubaidulina

Ciacona is a stunning, indeed overwhelming, example of extrovert bravura and (like the spectacular Liszt *Funérailles*) receives a deserved ovation. But it leaves the listener somewhat battered! One welcomes the simpler appeal of the Schubert *Impromptu* with which the recital closes.

Duchable, François-René (piano)

Recital: CHOPIN: *Scherzi Nos. 1–4; Fantaisie in F min., Op. 49.* LISZT: *Etudes d'exécution transcendante Nos. 5, Feux follets; 10, Appassionata. Années de Pèlerinage, 2nd Year (Italy): Petrarch Sonnet No. 104. Grand Etude de Paganini: La Campanella. Nocturne No. 3 (Rêve d'amour). Polonaise No. 2 in E. Mephisto waltz. Consolation No. 3. Harmonies poétiques et religieuses: Funérailles. Concert paraphrase of Berlioz: Symphonie fantastique* (revised Duchable). DUKAS: *Sonata in B flat min.* SAINT-SAENS: *Etude en forme de valse, Op. 52/6; 6 Etudes, Op. 111; Allegro appassionato; Mazurka, Op. 66.*

(B) *** EMI CZS5 72356-2 (3).

François-René Duchable's three-CD set is worth having, not so much for the Liszt – though that is brilliant enough – but for his commanding account of the Saint-Saëns rarities and, above all, for his magisterial Dukas *Sonata*. A pity that the French planners did not include *La plainte au loin du faune* and the *Prélude élégiaque sur le thème proposé Haydn*, which was on the original Dukas LP. Judged by modern standards, the 1978 sound is a bit synthetic. There is much more to admire here, including an impressive *Symphonie fantastique*.

Duo Reine Elisabeth (Wolfgang Manz and Rolf Plagge)

Russian music for two pianos: STRAVINSKY: *Petrushka.* SCRIABIN: *Romance in A min.* SHOSTAKOVICH: *Concertino, Op. 94.* RACHMANINOV: *6 Morceaux, Op. 11.*

(BB) *** Discover Dig. DICD 920150 [id.].

Petrushka has plenty of colour and a surprising degree of charm; the finale swings along infectiously. The melodically lavish, early Scriabin *Romance* then contrasts aptly with the wittily audacious Shostakovich *Concertino*, which has the temerity to open with an echo of the slow movement of Beethoven's *G major Piano concerto*. The six Rachmaninov *Morceaux* are strongly and colourfully characterized, and their diversity gives much pleasure. In short, Wolfgang Manz and Rolf Plagge create an impressive artistic symbiosis, playing with spontaneity as well as commanding impressive

technical resource. Very good recording too – not too reverberant. A bargain.

Du Pré, Jacqueline (cello)

Recital (with (i) Gerald Moore (piano); (ii) Roy Jesson (organ); (iii) Osian Ellis (harp); (iv) John Williams (guitar)): (i) PARADIS: *Sicilienne.* SCHUMANN: *3 Fantasy pieces, Op. 73.* MENDELSSOHN: *Song without words in D, Op. 109.* FAURE: *Elégie in C min., Op. 24.* BRUCH: *Kol Nidrei, Op. 47.* (ii) BACH: *Adagio from BWV 564.* (iii) SAINT-SAENS: *The Swan.* (iv) FALLA: *Suite populaire espagnole: Jota.*

*** EMI CDC5 55529-2 [id.] (with DELIUS: *Cello concerto ***).

This heart-warming recital collects together more recordings Jacqueline du Pré made in her teens for EMI, plus the beautiful performance of Fauré's *Elégie* she recorded in 1969 with Gerald Moore for his seventieth-birthday record. There have been few performances of *The Swan* to match this in natural, unforced expressiveness (beautifully accompanied on the harp by Osian Ellis), and the other items all have one marvelling afresh at the maturity of so young a virtuoso. Excellent transfers.

BACH: *Cello suites Nos. 1 in G; 2 in D min., BWV 1007–8.* BRITTEN: *Cello sonata in C, Op. 65 (Scherzo and Marcia)* (with Stephen Kovacevich). FALLA: *Suite populaire espagnole.* BRAHMS: *Cello sonata No. 2 in F, Op. 99.* HANDEL: *Sonata in G min.* (all with Ernest Lush). F. COUPERIN: *Treizième concert (Les goûts-réunis)* (with William Pleeth).

(B) *** EMI Double fforte mono CZS5 73377-2 (2).

Here are some of the radio performances which Jacqueline du Pré gave in her inspired teens. Her 1962 recordings of the first two Bach *Cello suites* may not be immaculate, but her impulsive vitality makes phrase after phrase at once totally individual and seemingly inevitable. In two movements from Britten's *Cello sonata in C*, with Stephen Kovacevich as her partner, the sheer wit is deliciously infectious, fruit of youthful exuberance in both players. The first of the two discs is completed by Falla's *Suite populaire espagnole*, with the cello matching any singer in expressive range and rhythmic flair. The second has fascinating Couperin duets played with her teacher, William Pleeth; the Handel *Sonata* is equally warm and giving. Best of all is the Brahms *Cello sonata No. 2*, recorded at the 1962 Edinburgh Festival.

Fanning, Diana (piano)

'Musical treasures': JANACEK: *On an overgrown path* (1911). DEBUSSY: *L'isle joyeuse.* CHOPIN: *Piano sonata No. 3 in B min., Op. 58.* ***

The American pianist Diana Fanning is a member of the music faculty at Middlebury College in Vermont and also a well-known soloist and chamber music performer in her native state. She has that special gift of being able to bring music spontaneously to life in the recording studio. The highlight of this recital is a splendidly alive and romantically compelling account of the Chopin *B minor Sonata*, which exerts more magnetism than many accounts by more famous artists. Her account of *L'isle joyeuse* is compellingly exciting too, and yet *On an overgrown path* has a pleasingly poetic intimacy. The recording is real and vivid, the ambience attractive, although a shade over-resonant for the fullest detail to emerge in the Debussy piece. The CD appears to have no catalogue number, but is available direct from Franck Publications, PO Box 96, Middlebury, Vermont 05753, USA.

Fergus-Thompson, Gordon (piano)

'Reverie': DEBUSSY: *Rêverie; Arabesque No. 1; Suite bergamasque: Clair de lune.* SCRIABIN: *Etude, Op. 42/4.* BACH: *Chorales: Wachet auf* (trans. Busoni); *Jesu, joy of man's desiring* (trans. Hess). GLINKA: *The Lark* (trans. Balakirev). GODOWSKY: *Alt Wien.* SAINT-SAENS: *The Swan* (arr. GODOWSKY). SCHUMANN: *Arabeske in C, Op. 18; Kinderszenen: Träumerei.* BRAHMS: *Intermezzo in A, Op. 118.* GRIEG: *Lyric pieces: Butterfly, Op. 43/1; Nocturne, Op. 54/4.* RAVEL: *Le tombeau de Couperin: Forlane. Pavane pour une infante défunte.*
(M) *** ASV Dig. CDWHL 2066 [id.].

This 76-minute recital fills a real need for a high-quality recital of piano music for the late evening, where the mood of reverie is sustained without blandness. Gordon Fergus-Thompson's performances are of high sensibility throughout, from the atmospheric opening Debussy items to the closing Ravel *Pavane*. Perhaps his Bach is a little studied but the rest is admirably paced, and the two favourite Grieg *Lyric pieces* are particularly fresh. Excellent recording.

Fernández, Eduardo (guitar)

'The World of the Spanish guitar': ALBENIZ: *Sevilla; Tango; Asturias.* LLOBET: *6 Catalan folksongs.* GRANADOS: *Andaluza; Danza triste.* TARREGA: *Estudio brillante; 5 Preludes; Minuetto; 3 Mazurkas; Recuerdos de la*

Alhambra. SEGOVIA: *Estudio sin luz; Neblina; Estudio.* TURINA: *Fandanguillo; Ráfaga.*
(M) *** Decca Dig 433 820-2.

Fernández is most naturally recorded in the Henry Wood Hall. His programme is essentially an intimate one and centres on the highly rewarding music of Tárrega, although opening colourfully with items from Albéniz's *Suite española*. The Llobet group of *Folksongs*, and Segovia's hauntingly atmospheric *Neblina* ('Mist'), make further highlights. Later there is bravura from Turina, notably the spectacular *Ráfaga* ('Gust of wind') but even here, though the playing is vibrant, there is no flashiness. With an hour of music and digital sound, this well-chosen programme is excellent value.

Fierens, Guillermo (guitar)

'Spanish guitar music': VILLA-LOBOS: *Preludes Nos. 1–3.* PONCE: *Preludio, Balletto & Giga.* CASTELNUOVO-TEDESCO: *Capriccio diabolico; Sonata.* ALBENIZ: *Asturias.* TURINA: *Fandanguillo.* SOR: *Introduction and allegro (Gran solo), Op. 14.*
(B) *** ASV Quicksilva Dig. CDQS 6190 [(M) id.].

Argentinian-born Guillermo Fierens studied under Segovia and has won several international prizes, including a First at Rio de Janeiro's Villa-Lobos competition. He is thoroughly sympathetic to that composer's music, and he presents this whole programme brightly and sympathetically, with plenty of personality and character. His technique is commandingly immaculate, his rubato nicely judged. He is very personable in the lively Ponce triptych (pastiche pieces of some charm) and the attractively spontaneous *Sonata* by Castelnuovo-Tedesco, particularly the two engaging central movements, and he finds plenty of bravura for the same composer's *Capriccio diabolico.* (Although it hardly matches Paganini in diabolism, it still makes a strong impression.) The *Gran solo* of Sor is equally appealing, but the highlight of a well-balanced programme is a magically evocative account of the famous *Asturias* of Albéniz. The recording has a vivid presence without being on top of the listener. Excellent value on all counts.

Fischer, Annie (piano)

'Les Introuvables d'Annie Fischer': BEETHOVEN: *Piano sonatas Nos. 8 in C min. (Pathétique), Op. 13; 14 in C sharp min. (Moonlight), Op. 27/2; 18 in E flat, Op. 31/3; 24 in F sharp, Op. 78; 21 in C (Waldstein), Op. 53; 30 in E, Op. 109; 32 in C min., Op. 111.* SCHUBERT: *Impromptus in A flat, Op. 111. SCHUBERT: Impromptus in A flat, D. 935/2 & 4; Piano sonata in B flat, D.960.* SCHUMANN: *Fantaisie in C, Op. 17; Carnaval,*

Op. 9; Kinderszenen, Op. 15; Kreisleriana, Op. 16.
(B) **(*) EMI stereo/mono CZS5 69217-2 (4).

Annie Fischer's Schumann is special, remarkably fine. *Kreisleriana*, recorded in Vienna in 1965 in a smallish studio, is magnificent, impassioned and full of fire, though one wishes that the sound had room in which to expand. Her Beethoven is perhaps less impressive and commanding – particularly the *Pathétique*, which, despite much sensitivity, suffers from a certain want of depth and sweep. Nevertheless whatever she does is distinguished by unfailing musicality.

Fretwork

'In nomine': 16th-century English music for viols: TALLIS: *In nomine a 4, Nos. 1 & 2; Solfaing song a 5; Fantasia a 5; Libera nos, salva nos a 5.* TYE: *In nomine a 5 (Crye); In nomine a 5 (Trust).* CORNYSH: *Fa la sol a 3.* BALDWIN: *In nomine a 4.* BULL: *In nomine a 5.* BYRD: *In nomine a 4, No. 2. Fantasia a 3, No. 3.* TAVERNER: *In nomine; In nomine a 4.* PRESTON: *O lux beata Trinitas a 3.* JOHNSON: *In nomine a 4.* PARSONS: *In nomine a 5; Ut re mi fa sol la a 4.* FERRABOSCO: *In nomine a 5; Lute fantasia No. 5; Fantasia a 4.*
*** Amon Ra CD-SAR 29 [id.].

This was Fretwork's début CD. The collection is not so obviously of strong popular appeal as the later collections for Virgin but is nevertheless very rewarding and distinguished, and it includes the complete consort music of Thomas Tallis. The sound is naturally pleasing in a fairly rich acoustic and readers can be assured that there is no vinegar in the string-timbre here; indeed, the sound itself is quite lovely in its gentle, austere atmosphere.

'Heart's ease': HOLBORNE: *The Honiesuckle; Countess of Pembroke's paradise; The Fairie round.* BYRD: *Fantasia a 5 (Two in one); Fancy in C.* DOWLAND: *Mr Bucton, his galliard; Captaine Digorie Piper, his galliard; Lachrimae antiquae pavan; Mr Nicholas Gryffith, his galliard.* BULL: *Fantasia a 4.* FERRABOSCO: *In nomine a 5.* GIBBONS: *In nomine a 5; Fantasia a 4 for the great dooble base.* LAWES: *Airs for 2 division viols in C: Pavan of Alfonso; Almain of Alfonso. Consort sett a 5 in C: Fantasia; Pavan; Almain.*
*** Virgin Dig. VC7 59667-2.

An outstanding collection of viol consort music from the late Tudor and early Stuart periods; the playing is both stylish and vivacious, with a fine sense of the most suitable tempo for each piece. The more lyrical music is equally sensitive. This is a tuneful entertainment, not just for the specialist collector, and Fretwork convey their pleasure in all this music. The William Byrd *Fancy* (from *My Ladye Nevells Booke*) is played exuberantly on the

organ by Paul Nicholson, to bring some contrast before the closing Lawes *Consort sett*. The recording is agreeably warm, yet transparent too.

'Portrait: Music for viols' ((i) with Michael Chance (counter-tenor), Christopher Wilson (lute), Paul Nicholson (organ)): BYRD: *Pavan a 6; Galliard a 6;* (i) *Come to me, grief for ever; Ye sacred muses.* BEVIN: *Browning a 3.* GIBBONS: *Go from my window a 6; Fantasy a 6; In nomine a 5.* DOWLAND: *Lachrimae antiquae; Lachrimae Coacte; Mr John Langtons Pavan; The Earl of Essex galliard; Mr Henry Noell his galliard.* (i) *Lasso vita mia.* LAWES: *Pavan a 5 in C min.; Fantasy a 6 in F; Aire a 6 in F min.* HOLBORNE: *The Honie-suckle; The Fairie-round.*
(M) *** Virgin/Veritas EMI VM5 61402-2.

A quite outstanding concert, with the consort music nicely leavened by three vocal solos. Much of the atmosphere is melancholic, but with the arrival of the two dances by Holborne the mood (and timbre) changes completely, while the following Dowland *Galliards*, if less upbeat, bring yet another change of character. The two vocal highlights are by Byrd, *Come to me, grief for ever*, in which he outflanks Dowland in dolour, and the beautiful *Ye sacred muses*, both sung ravishingly by Michael Chance. Lawes's *Pavan a 5 in C minor* which follows embroiders a particularly memorable theme and features the use of the chamber organ subtly to fill out the sonority, as it does the touching Gibbons *In nomine a 5*, while in the Lawes *Fantasy a 6* the organ has a delicate contrapuntal role. Excellent – if close – recording.

Fromentin, Lawrence and Domenique Plancade (piano duo)

Début: 'French piano duets': POULENC: *Sonata.* DEBUSSY: *Petite suite.* RAVEL: *Ma Mère l'Oye suite.* FAURE: *Dolly (suite), Op. 56.* BIZET: *Jeux d'enfants* (complete).
(B) *** EMI Début CDZ5 72526-2 [id.].

Lawrence Fromentin and Domenique Plancade, both Gold Medal winners at the Paris Conservatoire and pupils of Pascal Devoyon, decided to join together as a duo in 1992, and this is their recording début. The results are very impressive indeed. They encompass the wide stylistic contrasts of their programme with sympathy and panache, from the brittle wit of Poulenc and its underlying innocence, to the exquisitely delicate Ravelian atmosphere of *Ma Mère l'Oye* and the gentle charm of Fauré's *Dolly*. Debussy's *Petite suite* is winningly spontaneous, while the perceptively characterized *Jeux d'enfants* of Bizet is the more valuable for being complete, including all twelve movements, not just those familiar in the orchestral suite. The recording is excellent. A genuine bargain in every sense.

Galimir Quartet

BERG: *Lyric suite.* MILHAUD: *String quartet No. 7 in B flat.* RAVEL: *String quartet in F.*
(**) Rockport Dig. RR 5007 [id.].

Like the Hagens, the Galimir was a family quartet, founded in 1929 by Felix Galimir with his three sisters. They recorded the Milhaud and Ravel quartets in 1934 in the presence of their respective composers, and the *Lyric suite* in 1935 just before Berg's death. Felix Galimir emigrated to the United States just before the outbreak of the Second World War and taught at the Juilliard School until his death earlier this year. The performances naturally carry authority, though the somewhat dry acoustic of the Berg calls for tolerance. The present transfer of the latter is much better than the Continuum version coupled with Louis Krasne's broadcast of the violin concerto, with Webern conducting.

Galway, James (flute)

'The French recital' (with Christopher Riley, piano): FAURE: *Sonata, Op. 13.* WIDOR: *Suite for flute and piano, Op. 34.* DEBUSSY, arr. GALWAY: *Prélude à l'après-midi d'un faune; La plus que lente; Prélude: La fille aux cheveux de lin. Petite suite: En bateau.*
**(*) RCA Dig. 09026 68351-2 [id.].

Galway's silvery timbre is well suited to Fauré. He does not miss the work's simplicity of line, and he makes his own special colouring tell in the soaring *Andante*, while the Scherzo is deliciously vivacious, although here the resonant recording refuses to separate flute and piano completely. Fortunately Galway is sympathetically partnered by Christopher Riley, and they are very well balanced. Both play the tripping theme of the finale with an engaging insouciance. The surprise here is the Widor *Suite*, a wonderful quiz item – for who would guess that this was the composer of the Famous Organ *Toccata*? The delightful, flowing opening movement has much in common with Fauré (although it was written twenty-three years earlier), and the skippity-jig Scherzo is most winning. Then comes a lovely, innocuous, slightly sentimental (and very French) 'Romance' with a swirling cadenza before the winning reprise. The finale sets off gaily, then produces yet another pleasing lyrical idea, before giving the soloist plenty of opportunity for bravura roulades in its scintillating closing section. Most enjoyable and a real find.

But why, instead of offering another of the countless French flute sonatas readily available, did Galway choose to offer transcriptions? It can only be said that to offer the *Prélude à l'après-midi d'un faune* as a flute solo is almost unbelievably self-regarding. How can this artist think that after the introduction, which is his by rights, the sensuous allure of the glowing middle section for strings can sound anything but inadequate on flute and piano? The two-piano transcriptions are rather more effective and perfectly acceptable, but the lovely *En bateau* also needs to rock gently on orchestral waters.

Gilels, Emil (piano)

'The giant': MOZART: *Fantasia in D min., K. 397; Sonata No. 8 in A min., K. 310.* BEETHOVEN: *Sonatas Nos. 8 in C min. (Pathétique), Op. 13; 14 in C sharp min. (Moonlight), Op. 27/2; 32 Variations on an original theme in C min., WoO 80.* SCHUBERT: *Moments musicaux, D. 780/1-6.* SCHUMANN: *Arabeske in C, Op. 18.* LISZT: *Rhapsodie espagnole.* RAVEL: *Pavane pour une infante défunte; Jeux d'eau.* SCRIABIN: *Sonata No. 3 in F sharp min., Op. 23.*
(M) *** RCA 74321 75523-2 (2) [id.].

The chosen descriptive adjective here for once is not in the least exaggerated. This perceptively chosen collection is drawn from Gilels's live recitals recorded by Melodiya between 1965 and 1970, and (the Scriabin) in 1984. Well recorded too: there are no complaints about the piano sound, which has good focus and sonority. Inevitably there are some bronchial afflictions in the audience, occasionally ill-timed, but they are generally muted. The opening Mozart *Fantasia* is Elysian, and the following Sonata hardly less beautiful. The two Beethoven Sonatas are superbly strong and authoritative, yet the *Adagio cantabile* of the *Pathétique* and the mysterious veiled opening of the *Moonlight* are ravishingly gentle, while in finales Gilels's bravura never plays to the gallery. The *C minor Variations* are most diverting.

On the second disc the Schubert *Impromptus* bring countless individual insights: *No. 2 in A flat* is exquisitely played, and the familiar following *F minor* sheer delight, while No. 5 is arrestingly stormy. Schumann's *Arabeske* then casts a subtle Romantic spell over the listener. The Liszt *Rhapsodie* glitters; the *Pavane* has a touching melancholy; and in *Jeux d'eau* the trickling water twinkles in the sunlight but later becomes something of a waterfall. The closing Scriabin Sonata brings a melting performance of the slow movement and rumbustious bravura in the prolix finale. The overall playing time is 154 minutes: what more could you ask for?

Green, Gareth (organ)

English organ music (organ of Chesterfield Parish Church): LANG: *Tuba tune, Op. 15.* HOWELLS: *3 Psalm preludes, Op. 32.* ELGAR: *Sonata No. 1, Op. 28.* VAUGHAN WILLIAMS: *Rhosymedre (Hymn prelude).* WHITLOCK: *Hymn Preludes: on Darwell's 148th; on Song 13.* COCKER: *Tuba tune.* (BB) *(*) Naxos Dig. 8.550582 [id.].

The organ as recorded here has no clarity of profile, and even the two characterful *Tuba tunes* fail to make their full effect. The sound in the *Hymn* and *Psalm Preludes* is washy and indistinct. Gareth Green plays the early Elgar *Sonata* very well but it makes an impact only in its more powerful moments, and it is difficult to find a volume level which reveals the unfocused, quieter detail while not having the climaxes too loud.

Grumiaux, Arthur (violin), István Hajdu (piano)

'Favourite violin encores': PARADIS: *Sicilienne.* MOZART: *Rondo, K.250; Divertimento in D, K.334: Minuet.* GLUCK: *Mélodie.* GRANADOS: *Danza española No. 5.* KREISLER: *Schön Rosmarin; Liebesleid; Liebesfreud; Rondino on a theme of Beethoven; Andantino in the style of Padre Martini.* VERACINI: *Allegro; Largo* (arr. CORTI). VIVALDI: *Siciliano* (arr. from *Op. 3/11*). LECLAIR: *Tambourin.* BEETHOVEN: *Minuet in G.* SCHUBERT: *Ave Maria; Ständchen.* DVORAK: *Humoresque in G flat, Op. 101/7; Songs my mother taught me, Op. 55/4; Sonatine in G, Op. 100: Larghetto.* MASSENET: *Thaïs: Méditation.* TCHAIKOVSKY: *Valse sentimentale, Op. 51/6.* ELGAR: *La Capricieuse.* FAURE: *Après un rêve, Op. 7/1; Les berceaux, Op. 23/1.* ALBENIZ: *Tango, Op. 165/2.* PONCE: *Estrellita.* SIBELIUS: *Nocturne, Op. 51/3.* PERGOLESI: *Andantino.* SCHUMANN: *Kinderszenen: Träumerei.* BACH/ GOUNOD: *Ave Maria.* PAGANINI: *Sonata No. 12 in E min., Op. 3/6.* WIENIAWSKI: *Souvenir de Moscou, Op. 6.* RAVEL: *Pièce en forme de habanera; Tzigane.* SARASATE: *Zigeunerweisen, Op. 20/1.* FIOCCO: *Allegro.* BLOCH: *Baal Shem: Nigun.* KODALY: *Adagio.*
(B) *** Ph. Duo 446 560-2 (2) [(M) id. import].

Marvellous fiddler as he is, Grumiaux is not an extrovert in the manner of a Perlman who likes to dazzle and be right on top of the microphones; instead, these are essentially intimate performances. Yet when fire is needed it is certainly forthcoming, as in the superb account of Ravel's *Tzigane.* But Grumiaux is completely at home in what are mostly elegant *morceaux de concert,* and especially the Kreisler encores. He brings a particularly nice touch

of rubato to *Schön Rosmarin* and produces a ravishingly stylish *Liebesleid,* while the *Andantino in the style of Martini* is engagingly ingenuous. Schumann's *Träumerei* is made to sound as if originally conceived as a violin solo. The *Méditation* from *Thaïs* is delectably romantic without being oversweet, and the following *Valse sentimentale* of Tchaikovsky has just the right degree of restraint.

But Grumiaux's simplicity of style is heard at its most appealing in Wieniawski's *Souvenir de Moscou,* with its warm melody elegantly decorated and then let loose in a burst of Paganinian fireworks. István Hajdu accompanies with comparable taste, notably in Bach's unwitting contribution to Gounod's *Ave Maria,* while his simple introduction to Elgar's *La Capricieuse* is a model of how to set the scene for a salon piece of this kind. He is equally helpful in echoing Grumiaux in Schubert's lovely *Serenade* and in his discreet backing for Ponce's gently voluptuous *Estrellita.* The recording is most natural, without any edginess on the violin-tone, and the piano is pleasingly balanced within a warm acoustic.

Haendel, Ida (violin)

'The Decca years, 1940–47': BEETHOVEN: *Violin sonata in G, Op. 30/3.* ALBENIZ: *Malagueña, Op. 71/6.* (with Noel Mewton-Wood). SCHUBERT: *Sonatina in G min., D.408.* BRAHMS: *Waltz, Op. 39/15.* KREISLER: *Tambourin chinois, Op. 3; Schön Rosmarin.* SARASATE: *Zapateado, Op. 23/ 2.* WIENIAWSKI: *Scherzo tarantelle, Op. 16.* FALLA: *La vida breve: Danza no. 1.* SZYMANOWSKI: *Notturn e Tarantella, Op. 28; Roxana's song* from *King Roger.* (all with Adela Kotowska). ACHRON: *Hebrew melody* (with Alice Haendel). BARTOK: *Rumanian folk dances* (with Ivor Newton).
(***) Decca mono 455 488-2 [id.] – BARTOK: *Rhapsody* etc. ENESCU: *Sonata 3;* SZYMANOWSKI: *Mythes* **(*).

This outstanding recital (which is given as a bonus with the CD including new recordings of Bartók, Enescu and Szymanowski) shows Ida Haendel's extraordinary talent and musicianship as a young artist when she made her first recordings for Decca (which include the Tchaikovsky *Violin concerto* given a Rosette in our main volume). The freshness of this playing is remarkable, and the transfers are of excellent quality.

Hamelin, Marc-André (piano)

'Live at Wigmore Hall': BEETHOVEN (arr. ALKAN): *Piano concerto No. 3:* first movt. CHOPIN (arr. BALAKIREV): *Piano concerto No. 1: Romanza.* ALKAN: *Trois grandes études.* BUSONI:

Sonatina No. 6 (Chamber fantasy on Carmen).
MEDTNER: *Danza festiva, Op. 38, No. 3.*
⬥ *** Hyperion Dig. CDA 66765.

This is among the most spectacular piano issues of the decade. It captures live one of the programmes given in June 1994 at Wigmore Hall by the French-Canadian pianist Marc-André Hamelin, in a series called 'Virtuoso Romantics'. Bizarre as the mixture is, it works magnificently, thanks not only to Hamelin's breathtaking virtuosity, finger-perfect, but to his magnetism. As well as the *Trois grandes études* of Alkan, he plays Alkan's arrangement of the first movement of Beethoven's *Third Piano concerto*. Thanks to his sharp clarity, one marvels afresh at the purposefulness of the writing, and he revels in Alkan's manic six-minute cadenza, which in dotty inspiration even quotes the finale of Beethoven's *Fifth Symphony*. Balakirev's arrangement of the *Romanza* from Chopin's *First Piano concerto* then offers yearning poetry, with two flamboyant display-pieces as encores: Busoni's *Carmen fantasy* and Medtner's *Danza festiva*.

Hardenberger, Håkan (trumpet)

'The virtuoso trumpet' (with Roland Pöntinen):
ARBAN: *Variations on themes from Bellini's 'Norma'.* FRANCAIX: *Sonatine.* TISNE: *Héraldiques.* HONEGGER: *Intrada.* MAXWELL DAVIES: *Sonata.* RABE: *Shazam!.* HARTMANN: *Fantasia brillante on the air Rule, Britannia.*
*** BIS CID 287 [id.].

This collection includes much rare and adventurous repertoire, not otherwise available and very unlikely to offer frequent access in live performance. Moreover, Hardenberger plays with electrifying bravura in the Maxwell Davies *Sonata* and the virtuoso miniatures. Antoine Tisné's five *Héraldiques* are eclectic but highly effective on the lips of such an assured player; *Scandé* and the following *Elégiaque* are notably characterful. But easily the most memorable item is the Françaix *Sonatine* (originally for violin and piano) in which two delicious brief outer movements frame a pleasing central *Sarabande*. Honegger's improvisatory *Intrada* is an effective encore piece. The recording is eminently realistic, with the CD giving superb presence.

Haskil, Clara (piano)

Clara Haskil: The Legacy:
Volume 1: Chamber music (with Arthur Grumiaux): BEETHOVEN: *Violin sonatas Nos. 1–10.* MOZART: *Violin sonatas Nos. 18; 21; 24; 26; 32; 34.*
(M) (***) Ph. (IMS) mono 442 625-2 (5).
Volume 3: Solo piano music: BEETHOVEN:

Sonatas Nos. 17 in D min. (Tempest), Op. 31/2; 18 in E flat, Op. 31/3 (two versions). MOZART: *Sonata in C, K.330; 9 Variations on a Minuet by Jean-Pierre Duport, K.573.* RAVEL: *Sonatine.* Domenico SCARLATTI: *Sonatas in E flat, Kk. 193; B min., Kk. 87; F min., Kk. 386.* SCHUBERT: *Sonata No. 21 in B flat, D.960.* SCHUMANN: *Abegg variations, Op. 1; Bunte Blätter, Op. 99; Kinderszenen, Op. 15; Waldszenen, Op. 82.*
(M) **(*) Ph. (IMS) mono/stereo 442 635-2 (3).

Clara Haskil is a much-venerated pianist, as the very appearance of this 'Legacy' set shows. Each of the three volumes is available separately but single discs from the collection are not. The first volume (five CDs) is devoted to the Beethoven and Mozart sonatas with her long-standing partner, Arthur Grumiaux; the second (see concerts above), of four CDs, is devoted to her various concerto recordings, including two of the Mozart *D minor*, K.466, one with the Wiener Symfoniker and Paul Sacher in mono (1954), the second with the Lamoureux Orchestra and Markevitch (1960); the third volume (three CDs) collects her solo repertoire, including two different accounts of the Beethoven sonatas (1955 and 1960).

The earliest recordings, the three Scarlatti sonatas, Ravel's *Sonatine* and the Schumann *Abegg* variations and *Piano concerto in A minor* (with Willem van Otterloo conducting the Hague Orchestra) come from 1951, and the last, the Mozart *Piano concertos in D minor*, K.466 and *C minor*, K.491, and the Beethoven *C minor Concerto*, from 1960, the year of her death. Although it is doubtless a truism, her playing is more private than public; hers is a reflective, inward-looking sensibility with nothing of the virtuoso or showman. Her musical dedication is total. Her Schumann is particularly searching and penetrating. And there is an innocence about her Mozart which makes it wonderfully fresh and immediate.

Perhaps part of the success of her partnership with Arthur Grumiaux in the cycle of Beethoven and Mozart sonatas may spring from the understanding she gained of the violin as well as the experience of her earlier partnerships with Enescu, Szigeti and Francescatti. Philips are reticent in disclosing whether they are mono or stereo: they are in fact mono. Notwithstanding, the sound is very pleasing indeed and the playing is beautifully natural yet innately aristocratic.

The solo recordings are equally self-recommending and her Schumann in particular is of exceptional insight. The set is accompanied by very perceptive notes by Max Harrison.

Headington, Christopher (piano)

British piano music of the twentieth century:
BRITTEN: *Holiday diary.* DELIUS: *3 Preludes.*

ELGAR: *Adieu; In Smyrna; Serenade.*
HEADINGTON: *Ballade-image; Cinquanta.*
IRELAND: *The island spell.* MOERAN: *Summer valley.* PATTERSON: *A Tunnel of time, Op. 66.*
*** Kingdom Dig. KCLD 2017 [id.].

The novelties here are fascinating. The Delius *Preludes* (1923) have much of the luminous atmosphere of the orchestral music, while Britten's *Holiday diary* (what a happy idea for a suite!), written when he was just twenty, is most winning. The Elgar pieces are well worth having, and Headington again reveals himself as an appealing composer. Both his pieces were written for fiftieth-birthday celebrations and the *Ballade-image* expressly seeks to conjure up an atmosphere combining the influences of Chopin and Debussy. It is most engaging. John Ireland's *Island spell* is beautifully played. A 69-minute recital which is skilfully planned to be listened to in sequence. Good, if not outstanding, recording.

Heifetz, Jascha (violin)

'*The Legendary Heifetz*' (with Emanuel Bay or Arpad Sandor piano): BAZZINI: *La ronde des lutins, Op. 25.* WIENIAWSKI: *Scherzo-tarantelle in G min., Op. 16.* DEBUSSY: *L'enfant prodigue; Prélude.* ALBENIZ: *Suite española: Sevillañas.* ELGAR: *La Capricieuse, Op. 17.* MOSZKOWSKI: *Guitarre, Op. 45/2.* FALLA: *Danza española No. 1.* Cyril SCOTT: *Tallahassee suite: Bygone memories.* DOHNANYI: *Ruralia hungarica, Op. 32a: Gypsy Andante.* CASTELNUOVO-TEDESCO: *Valse.* POULENC: *Mouvements perpétuelles No. 1.* VIVALDI: *Sonata in A, Op. 2/2.* PAGANINI: *Caprice, Op. 1/13.* BACH: *English suite No. 3 in G min., BWV 808: Gavottes Nos. 1 & 2 (Musette).* FRANCK: *Sonata in A:* First movement *Mosso* (with Artur Rubinstein).
(M) (**) EMI mono CDM5 67005-2 [id.].

Although the playing here offers the sophistication of bow-arm technique, and fabulous assurance, for which Heifetz is famous, the recorded sound detracts very considerably from the listener's pleasure. All these recordings were made at Abbey Road (for the most part in 1934, and a few in 1937) but they are a credit neither to the original EMI engineers nor to the current EMI remastering process. The acoustic is dry, the violin uncomfortably close to the microphone, minimizing the breadth of tone, making it sound top-heavy and peaky. It is surely possible to do better than this! As it is, the extraordinary virtuosity of *La ronde des lutins*, Wieniawski's *Scherzo-tarantelle* and famous *Hora staccato*, the veiled beauty of tone in the Debussy *Prélude* to *L'enfant prodigue* and the evocation of Cyril Scott, are all but lost. The Vivaldi sonata, superbly stylish, and the excerpt from the Franck

Sonata (with Rubinstein) seem almost to triumph over the sound but even so, one needs to replay this disc with the aural equivalent of top-quality dark-glasses to enjoy the music-making.

Hill–Wiltschinsky Guitar Duo

Recital: D. SCARLATTI: *Sonata, Kk. 141.* SOR: *Fantaisie, Op. 54.* ANON.: *Jota.* HILL: *Rondo for 2 guitars; Canzone. The lark in the morning.* MENDELSSOHN: *Song without words, Op. 19/1.* DOWLAND: *2 Elizabethan lute duets: Le rossignol; My Lord Chamberlaine, his galliard.* WILTSCHINSKY: *Nocturne.* PETIT: *Toccata.* KOMPTER: *Milan suite.* CASTELNUOVO-TEDESCO: *Prelude and fugue in F sharp min.* GIULIANI: *Variazioni concertanti, Op. 130.* FAMPAS: *Fantasie.* FALLA: *Three-cornered hat: Ritual fire dance.*
(M) *** Carlton IMP Dig. 30367 00612 [id.].

Here is an attractively intimate, late-evening recital of music for guitar duo that could too easily be passed by. The only item which does not suit the laid-back evening mood of this well-matched pair (Robin Hill and Peter Wiltschinsky) is the vibrant *Ritual fire dance* of Manuel de Falla, which is far more electrifying in Bream's solo performance. But this still leaves an enticing hour-long programme in which every number has a distinct appeal.

The Sor 'Introduction, theme and variations' which make up his *Fantaisie, Op. 54* (wrongly attributed here to Scarlatti) and the equally agreeable Giuliani *Variazioni concertanti* are well matched by Hill's own *Rondo*, and his *Canzone* is charming, as is his colleague's *Nocturne*. The Mendelssohn *Song without words* flows winningly and the novelties by Petit and Fampas are very striking. Then the amateur Jan Marten Kompter (the managing director of a Dutch chemical firm) provides four beguiling pastiches which look backward in time. The playing is spontaneously immaculate, and the duo is beautifully recorded.

Hilton, Janet (clarinet), Keith Swallow (piano)

'*Rhapsodie*': POULENC: *Clarinet sonata.* RAVEL: *Pièce en forme d'habanera.* DEBUSSY: *Première rhapsodie.* SAINT-SAENS: *Clarinet sonata, Op. 167.* ROUSSEL: *Aria.* MILHAUD: *Duet concertante, Op. 351.*
(M) ** Chandos Dig. CHAN 6589 [id.].

There are some highly beguiling sounds here, and the languorous style adopted throughout is emphasized by the reverberant acoustic, which is less than ideal, creating the feeling of an empty hall. The Ravel and Debussy are given an evocative sentience and the Poulenc comes off very well too; overall, however, there is a feeling that a little more vitality and a more sharply focused sound-picture would have been advantageous.

Horowitz, Vladimir (piano)

'The Horowitz Edition': CHOPIN: Sonata No. 2; Etudes, Opp. 10/12; 25/7; Scherzo No. 1. RACHMANINOV: Etudes-tableaux, Opp. 33/2; 39/ 5. SCHUMANN: Arabesque, Op. 18; Kinderszenen, Op. 15; Toccata, Op. 7. LISZT: Hungarian rhapsody No. 19 (trans. Horowitz).
D. SCARLATTI: Sonatas, Kk. 322, 455, 531. BEETHOVEN: Sonata No. 8. SCHUBERT: Impromptu No. 3. DEBUSSY: 3 Préludes, Book II. SCRIABIN: Poème, Op. 32/1; Etudes, Opp. 2/1; 8/ 12 (S2K 53457 (2)). D. SCARLATTI: Sonatas, Kk. 25, 33, 39, 52, 54, 96, 146, 162, 197, 198, 201, 303, 466, 474, 481, 491, 525, 547 (SK 53460). BACH/BUSONI: Toccata, Adagio & Fugue, BWV 564. SCHUMANN: Fantaisie, Op. 17; Träumerei, Op. 15/7; Blumenstück, Op. 19. SCRIABIN: Sonatas Nos. 9–10; Poème, Op. 32/1; Etude in C sharp min., Op. 2/1. CHOPIN: Mazurkas, Opp. 30/ 4; 33/4; Etude, Op. 10/8; Ballade No. 1; Polonaise-fantaisie, Op. 61; Nocturne, Op. 72/1. DEBUSSY: Serenade for the doll; L'Isle joyeuse. MOSZKOWSKI: Etude in A flat, Op. 72/11. MOZART: Sonata No. 11, K.331. HAYDN: Sonata, Hob XVI/23. LISZT: Vallée d'Obermann. (S3K 53461 (3)). CHOPIN: Ballade No. 1; Nocturne, Op. 55/1; Polonaise, Op. 44. D. SCARLATTI: Sonatas, Kk. 55; 380. SCHUMANN: Arabeske, Op. 18; Traümerei. SCRIABIN: Etude, Op. 8/12. HOROWITZ: Variations on a theme from Carmen (SK 53465). CLEMENTI: Excerpts from: Sonatas, Opp. 12/2; 25/3; 50/1. Adagio sostenuto in F, from Gradus ad Parnassum, Book I/14. J. S. BACH: Chorale prelude: 'Ich ruf zu dir, Herr Jesu Christ'. D. SCARLATTI: Sonatas, Kk. 260; 319. HAYDN: Sonata, Hob XVI/48. BEETHOVEN: Sonata No. 28, Op. 101 (SK 53466). BEETHOVEN: Sonatas Nos. 14, Op. 27/2 (Moonlight); 21, Op. 53 (Waldstein); 23, Op. 57 (Appassionata) (SK 53467). CHOPIN: Mazurkas, Opp. 7/3; 17/4; 30/3; 33/2; 41/2; 50/3; 59/3; Etudes, Op. 10/3–6, 12; 3 Nouvelles études: No. 2. Introduction & rondo, Op. 16; Waltzes, Op. 34/2; 64/2; Polonaises, Opp. 40/1; 53; Préludes, Op. 28/6, 15. SCHUMANN: Variations on a theme by Clara Wieck; Kreisleriana, Op. 16 (S2K 53468 (2)). SCHUBERT: Impromptus, D.899/2, 4; D.935/1–2. LISZT: Consolation No. 2; Scherzo & Marsch. DEBUSSY: Pour les arpèges composées; La terrasse des audiences du clair de lune. MENDELSSOHN: Etude, Op. 104b/3 (SK 53471). SCRIABIN: Feuillets d'album Opp. 45/1; 58; Etudes, Opp. 8/ 2, 8, 10–11; 42, 3–5; 65/3; 2 Poèmes, Op. 69;

Vers la flamme. MEDTNER: Fairy tale, Op. 51/3. RACHMANINOV: Sonata No. 2; Prélude, Op. 32/ 12; Moment musical, Op. 16/3; Etudes-tableaux, Opp. 33/2, 5; 39/9.
(M) (***) Sony mono SX13K 53456 (13) [id.].

The strength of this Sony box which runs to thirteen CDs and includes all Horowitz's recordings from 1962 to 1973 resides in the fact that nearly all these discs are essential repertory for Horowitz collectors but in any case are not now obtainable separately in the UK. Hardly any of these performances can be passed over, whether it be the Scarlatti sonatas or the stunning accounts of Scriabin's Ninth and Tenth. There is almost nothing that does not show him in top form – and the sound, though not ideal, is greatly improved.

Recital: BACH/BUSONI: Chorale prelude: Nun komm, der Heiden Heiland. MOZART: Piano sonata No. 10 in C, K.330. CHOPIN: Mazurka in A min., Op. 17/4; Scherzo No. 1 in B min., Op. 20; Polonaise No. 6 in A flat, Op. 53. LISZT: Consolation No. 3 in D flat. SCHUBERT: Impromptu in A flat, D.899/4. SCHUMANN: Novellette in F, Op. 21/1. RACHMANINOV: Prelude in G sharp min., Op. 32/12. SCRIABIN: Etude in C sharp min., Op. 2/1. MOSZKOWSKI: Etude in F, Op. 72/6 (recording of performances featured in the film Vladimir Horowitz – The Last Romantic).
*** DG (IMS) Dig. 419 045-2 [id.].

Recorded when he was over eighty, this playing betrays remarkably little sign of frailty. The Mozart is beautifully elegant and the Chopin A minor Mazurka, Op. 17, No. 4, could hardly be more delicate. The only sign of age comes in the B minor Scherzo, which does not have the leonine fire and tremendous body of his famous 1950 recording. However, it is pretty astonishing for all that.

'The studio recordings': SCHUMANN: Kreisleriana, Op. 16. D. SCARLATTI: Sonatas in B min., Kk. 87; in E, Kk. 135. LISZT: Impromptu (Nocturne) in F sharp; Valse oubliée No. 1. SCRIABIN: Etude in D sharp min., Op. 8/12. SCHUBERT: Impromptu in B flat, D.935/3. SCHUBERT/TAUSIG: Marche militaire, D.733/1.
● *** DG (IMS) 419 217-2 [id.].

The subtle range of colour and articulation in the Schumann is matched in his Schubert Impromptu, and the Liszt Valse oubliée offers the most delicious, twinkling rubato. Hearing Scarlatti's E major Sonata played with such crispness, delicacy and grace must surely convert even the most dedicated authenticist to the view that this repertoire can be totally valid in terms of the modern instrument. The Schubert–Tausig Marche militaire makes a superb encore, played with the kind of panache that would be remarkable in a pianist half Horowitz's age. With the passionate Scriabin Etude as the central romantic pivot, this recital is uncommonly well balanced to show Horowitz's special range of sympathies.

'In Moscow': D. SCARLATTI: *Sonata in E, Kk. 380.* MOZART: *Sonata No. 10 in C, K.330.* RACHMANINOV: *Preludes in G, Op. 32/5; in G sharp min., Op. 32/12.* SCRIABIN: *Etudes in C sharp min., Op. 2/1; in D sharp min., Op. 8/12.* LISZT/SCHUBERT: *Soirées de Vienne; Petrarch Sonnet 104.* CHOPIN: *Mazurkas, Op. 30/4; Op. 7/ 3.* SCHUMANN: *Kinderszenen: Träumerei.*
*** DG (IMS) Dig. 419 499-2 [id.].

This is familiar Horowitz repertoire, played with characteristic musical discernment and spontaneity. Technically the pianism may not quite match his finest records of the analogue era, but it is still both melting and dazzling. The sound too is really excellent, much better than he ever received from his American engineers in earlier days.

'Discovered treasures (1962–1972)': BACH/ BUSONI: *Chorale prelude: Ich ruf zu dir, Herr Jesu Christ.* CHOPIN: *Nouvelle étude No. 1 in A flat; Etude in E flat min., Op. 10/6; Prelude in D flat (Raindrop), Op. 28/15.* CLEMENTI: *Piano sonata in E flat, Op. 12/2: Rondo. Gradus ad Parnassum, Book I, No. 14: Adagio sostenuto in F; Piano sonata in B flat, Op. 25/3: Rondo. Piano sonata in A, Op. 50/1: Adagio.* LISZT: *Consolation in E.* MEDTNER: *Fairy tale in A, Op. 51/3.* D. SCARLATTI: *Sonatas in G, Kk. 547; B min., Kk. 197; F sharp min., Kk. 25; D min., Kk. 52; G, Kk. 201; C min., Kk. 303.* SCRIABIN: *Feuillet d'album, Op. 58; Etude, Op. 65/3.*
*** Sony SK 48093-2 [id.].

The earliest of these recordings, the Liszt *Consolation,* comes from 1962, and the last, the Scriabin *Feuillet d'album* and *Etude,* Op. 65, No. 3, from 1972. All were made in the studio and were approved by Horowitz himself but were never included on records, purely for planning reasons. Horowitz was fastidious in seeing that each of the LPs he released made a logical programme, and hence there was in the Archives quite a lot of unused studio material.

'At the Met': Domenico SCARLATTI: *Sonatas in A flat, Kk.127; F min., Kk.466; F min., Kk.184; A, Kk.101; B min., Kk.87; E, Kk.135.* CHOPIN: *Ballade No. 4 in F min., Op. 52; Waltz in A flat, Op. 69/1 'L'adieu'.* LISZT: *Ballade No. 2 in B min.* RACHMANINOV: *Prelude in G minor, Op. 23, No. 5.*
(M) *** RCA High Performance 09026 63314-2 [id].

The sound Horowitz makes has rarely been captured on recordings with such consistent truthfulness as in this live 1981 recording: this is extraordinary playing and fully demonstrates the highly distinctive tone-quality he commands. This disc is an essential purchase for all admirers of this artist, and of great piano playing in general. It sounds excellent in this new transfer and was an excellent choice for RCA's High Performance label. A worthwhile investment, even if the playing time is just under 50 minutes. Quality, not quantity.

'The indispensable Horowitz': CHOPIN: *Polonaise-fantaisie in A flat, Op. 61; Scherzi Nos. 1 in B min., Op. 20; 2 in B flat, Op. 31; Etudes in C sharp min., Op. 10/4; in C sharp min., Op. 25/7; Nocturnes in B, Op. 9/3; in C sharp min., Op. 27/ 1; in E min., Op. 72/1; Barcarolle, Op. 60; Polonaise in A flat, Op. 53; Ballade No. 1 in G min., Op. 23.* Domenico SCARLATTI: *Keyboard sonatas, Kk. 87, 127, & 135.* RACHMANINOV: *Humoresque, Op. 10/5; Preludes in G min., Op. 23/5; in G, Op. 32/5; Barcarolle, Op. 10/3.* MOSZKOWSKI: *Etincelle, Op. 36/6; Etude in F, Op. 72/6.* LISZT: *Hungarian rhapsodies Nos. 2 & 15 (Rákóczy march)* (both arr. HOROWITZ); *Mephisto waltz No. 1.* BIZET/HOROWITZ: *Variations on a theme from Carmen.* SCRIABIN: *Etudes in C sharp min., Op. 2/1; in B flat min., Op. 8/7; in D sharp min., Op. 8/12; in C sharp min., Op. 42/5.* SOUSA/HOROWITZ: *The Stars and Stripes forever.*
⦿ (B) *** RCA stereo/mono, Dig./Analogue 74321 63471-2 (2) [id.].

The notes with this remarkably generous collection include a quote from Neville Cardus, who once described Horowitz as 'the greatest pianist alive or dead'. Later he added that this comment 'perhaps was not positive enough about pianists still unborn'. His eulogy still holds true at the time of writing and the programme here demonstrates why. If you look for astonishing, barnstorming virtuosity you will find it in Horowitz's own *Carmen variations,* the Liszt *Hungarian rhapsody* 'arrangements' or the closing *Stars and Stripes;* but if you seek bravura delicacy, the Moszkowski *F major Etude* is a supreme example, while his Scarlatti is unforgettable. Romantic poetry constantly illuminates his Chopin (the *Barcarolle* and *G minor Ballade* are especially memorable) and his Rachmaninov (the *G major Prelude* is exquisite), while throughout this is playing of unique distinction which offers infinite rewards.

Scriabin, another of Horowitz's special composers, is generously represented, not only by Horowitz's favourite, *D sharp minor Etude* (taken from a 1982 live recital), but also by the more prolix *C sharp minor,* recorded three decades earlier. What is surprising is the fairly consistent quality of the sound: one of the earliest mono recordings (from 1950), of Scriabin's Op. 2/1, is remarkably warmly coloured. Of course, the later stereo recordings are ever finer, as the commanding opening *Polonaise-*

fantaisie of Chopin (1982) readily shows. But on sonic grounds there is little to criticize; artistically this pair of discs are in a class of their own.

Hough, Stephen (piano)

'Piano album':

Disc 1: MACDOWELL: *Hexentanz, Op. 12.* CHOPIN: *Chant polonaise No. 1.* QUILTER: *The crimson petal; The fuchsia tree.* DOHNANYI: *Capriccio in F min., Op. 28/8.* PADEREWSKI: *Minuet in G, Op. 14/1; Nocturne in B flat, Op. 16/ 4.* SCHLOZER: *Etude in A flat, Op. 1/2.* GABRILOVICH: *Mélodie in E; Caprice-burlesque.* RODGERS: *My favourite things.* WOODFORDE-FINDEN: *Kashmiri song.* FRIEDMAN: *Music box.* SAINT-SAENS: *Carnival of the animals: The Swan* (arr. GODOWSKY). ROSENTHAL: *Papillons.* GODOWSKY: *The Gardens of Buitenzorg.* LEVITZKI: *Waltz in A, Op. 2.* PALMGREN: *En route, Op. 9.* MOSZKOWSKI: *Siciliano, Op. 42/2; Caprice espagnol, Op. 37.*

Disc 2: CZERNY: *Variations brillantes, Op. 14.* LEVITZKI: *The Enchanted nymph.* SCHUMANN: *Der Kontrebandiste.* RUBINSTEIN: *Melody in F.* LIEBERMANN: *Gargoyles, Op. 29.* REBIKOV: *The Musical snuffbox.* RAVINA: *Etude de style (Agilité), Op. 40/1.* WOODFORDE-FINDEN: *Till I wake.* QUILTER: *Weep you no more.* RODGERS: *March of the Siamese children.* MOSZKOWSKI: *Valse mignonne; Serenata, Op. 15/1.* BACH: *Violin sonata No. 2: Bourrée.* GODOWSKY: *Erinnerungen.* BIZET: *L'Arlésienne: Adagietto.* TAUSIG: *Ungarische Zigeunerweisen.*

(BB) *** Virgin Classics Dig. Double VBD5 61498-2 (2) [CDVB 61498].

There are few young pianists who can match Stephen Hough in communicating on record with the immediacy and vividness of live performance; this dazzling two-disc recital of frothy show-pieces presents the perfect illustration. Indeed, this Virgin Classics bargain Double captures more nearly than almost any other recent record – even those of Horowitz – the charm, sparkle and flair of legendary piano virtuosos from the golden age of Rosenthal, Godowsky and Lhévinne.

So many of the items are frivolous that it may be surprising that any serious pianist can stomach them; yet on the first disc the very opening item, MacDowell's *Hexentanz (Witches' dance)*, launches the listener into pure pianistic magic, and the second, with Czerny's fizzing *Variations brill-antes*, similarly offers totally uninhibited playing, with articulation and timing that are the musical equivalent of being tickled up and down the spine.

One would hardly expect Hough's own arrange-ments of sentimental little songs by Roger Quilter or Amy Woodforde-Finden to be memorable – yet,

in their tender expressiveness, they are most affecting. In the grand tradition, Hough does a Valse-caprice arrangement he himself has made of *My favourite things* from *The Sound of Music,* as well as an equally attractive but simpler arrange-ment of Rodgers's *March of the Siamese children.* Firework pieces by Rosenthal and Moszkowski, among others, go along with old-fashioned favour-ites like Paderewski's *Minuet in G,* Rubinstein's *Melody in F* (here sounding fresh and unfaded) and Godowsky's arrangement of the Saint-Saëns *Swan.*

Not all of Lowell Liebermann's *Gargoyles* are menacing (there is a charming *Adagio semplice*) but the *Feroce* marking for the closing number is pungently realized. Then follow two different miniature portrayals of a *Musical snuffbox,* the first, by Vladimir Rebikov, not a whit less delightful than the more famous version by Liadov. The pro-gramme ends with an arresting account of Tausig's *Ungarische Zigeunerweisen.* Altogether it is a feast for piano lovers, very well recorded, the first disc in 1986 (in London and New York), the second in 1991 using the BBC's Manchester studio.

'New piano album':

LISZT: *Concert paraphrase of Schubert: Soirées de Vienne.* SCHUBERT (arr. GODOWSKY): *Moment musical in D min., D.780/3; Die schöne Müllerin: Morgengrüss.* GODOWSKI: *Alt Wien.* MOSZKOWSKI: *Etincelle Op. 36/6.* PADEREWSKI: *Mélodie in G flat,Op. 16/2.* CHAMINADE: *Pierrette (Air de ballet), Op. 41; Autrefois, Op. 87/4.* KALMAN (arr. HOUGH): *Was weiss ein nie geküsster Rosenmunde.* HOUGH: *Musical jewellery box; Etude de concert.* RODGERS (arr. HOUGH): *Hello young lovers; Carousel waltz.* TRAD. (arr. HOUGH): *Londonderry air.* RACHMANINOV: *Humoresque, Op. 10/5; Mélodie, Op. 3/3* (revised 1940 version). TCHAIKOVSKY: *Humoresque, Op. 10/2.* TCHAIKOVSKY, arr. WILD: *Swan Lake: Pas de quatre.* TCHAIKOVSKY/ PABST(arr. HOUGH): *Sleeping Beauty paraphrase.* *** Hyperion Dig. CDA 67043 [id.].

In his latest collection, Stephen Hough demon-strates yet again the flair with which he tackles trivial party pieces like the twenty varied items here. Such encore material has in his hands a sparkle and point that magick the ear whether in the virtuoso display of pieces by Godowsky, Moszkowski and Rachmaninov or in the loving lyricism of pieces by Chaminade, Kalman and others. As well as offering two witty showpieces of his own, Hough also plays his arrangements of two Richard Rodgers numbers and the *Londonderry air.* Among the four Tchai-kovsky items, it is good to have the haunting little *Humoresque,* best known through Stravinsky's ballet *The Fairy's kiss.* Vivid sound.

Hurford, Peter (organ)

'*Great Romantic organ works*' (played on organs at Ratzeburg Cathedral, the Royal Festival Hall, or in the Basilica of Saint-Sermin, Toulouse): WIDOR: *Symphony No. 5: Toccata; Symphony No. 6, Op. 42: Allegro.* FRANCK: *Chorals Nos. 1–3; Pièce héroïque.* MENDELSSOHN: *Preludes and fugues: in C min., Op. 37/1 and D min., Op. 37/3; Sonata in A, Op. 65/3.* GIGOUT: *10 piéces: Scherzo.* KARG-ELERT: *Marche triomphale: on Nun danket alle Gott.* VIERNE: *24 pièces en style libre: Berceuse; Symphony No. 1, Op. 14: Final.* BRAHMS: *Choral preludes: Es ist ein Ros entsprungen; Herzlich tut mich verlangen; Schmücke dich.* LISZT: *Prelude and fugue on B-A-C-H.* SCHUMANN: *Four sketches, Op. 58/4: Allegretto.* REGER: *Introduction and passacaglia in D min.* BOELLMAN: *Suite gothique, Op. 25.*
(B) *** Decca Double Dig. 466 742-2 (2) [id.].

A self-recommending set of organ favourites at bargain price in splendid digital sound, for the most part played on the magnificent organ at Ratzeburg Cathedral. Not many collections of Romantic organ music match this in colour, breadth of repertoire, and brilliance of performance. Hurford's playing defies all considerations of Victorian heaviness, and the programme includes many key repertoire works. You cannot go wrong here.

'*Organ favourites*': Sydney Opera House organ: BACH: *Toccata and fugue in D min., BWV 565; Jesu, joy of man's desiring.* ALBINONI: *Adagio* (arr. GIAZOTTO). PURCELL: *Trumpet tune in D.* MENDELSSOHN: *A Midsummer Night's Dream: Wedding march.* FRANCK: *Chorale No. 2 in B min.* MURRILL: *Carillon.* WALFORD DAVIES: *Solemn melody.* WIDOR: *Organ Symphony No. 5: Toccata.* Royal Festival Hall organ: FRANCK: *Pièce héroïque.* Ratzeburg Cathedral organ: BOELLMANN: *Suite gothique.*
(B) **(*) Decca Eclipse Dig. 452 166-2 [(M) id. import].

Superb sound here, wonderfully free and never oppressive, even in the most spectacular moments. The Widor is spiritedly genial when played within the somewhat mellower registration of the magnificent Sydney instrument (as contrasted with the Ratzeburg Cathedral organ), and the pedals have great sonority and power. The Murrill *Carillon* is equally engaging alongside the Purcell *Trumpet tune*, while Mendelssohn's wedding music has never sounded more resplendent. The Bach is less memorable, and the Albinoni *Adagio*, without the strings, is not an asset to the collection either. The *Pièce héroïque* and the *Suite gothique* have been added for the Eclipse reissue.

Isbin, Sharon (guitar)

'*Latin romances*': de la MAZA: *Zapateado.* RODRIGO: *Invocación y Danza.* BARRIOS: *La Catedral.* ABREU: *Quejas (Lament).* JOBIM: *Estrada do Sol.* TARREGA: *Capricho árabe.* BROUWER: *El Decameron negro.* VILLA-LOBOS: *Sentimental melody; Etude No. 8.* ALBENIZ: *Mallorca; Asturias.*
(BB) *** Virgin Classics 2 x 1 Dig. VBD5 61627-2 (2) [CDVB 61627] (with RODRIGO: *Concierto de Aranjuez; Fantasia para un gentilhombre ***. SCHWANTNER: *From afar . . . (fantasy) **).

Sharon Isbin is a masterly guitarist and has inherited Segovia's gift of achieving natural spontaneity in the recording studio, so that this solo recital is consistently fresh and communicative, the playing brilliant and evocative by turns. Rodrigo's *Invocación y Danza* and Tárrega's *Capricho árabe* are only two of the familiar pieces which project magnetically, as does the Albéniz *Asturias* which ends the recital so vibrantly. The novelty is *The Black Decameron* of Leo Brouwer, a programmatic triptych which is sharply characterized and atmospherically realized. Isbin is given great presence by the recording, and he plays the key Rodrigo concertante works with no less distinction. The Schwantner piece is less recommendable, but this two-disc set remains a bargain.

Isoir, André (organ)

French Renaissance organ music (Koenig organ at Bon Pasteur, Angers): *Bransles, Galliards and other dances* by GERVAIS; FRANCISQUE; ATTAIGNANT. JANEQUIN: *Allez my fault.* SANDRIN: *Quand ien congneu.* Eustache du CAURROY: *Fantaisie sur une jeune fillette.* ATTAIGNANT: *3 Versets du Te Deum; Prélude aux treize motets; Kyrie cunctipotens. Fantaisies* by GUILLET; LE JEUNE; RACQUET. RICHARD: *Prélude in D min.* THOMELIN: *Duo.* LA BARRE: *Sarabande.* Henri du MONT: *Prélude No. 10 in D min.; Pavane in D min.* ANON.: *Fantaisie; Ave Maris Stella.* ROBERDAY: *Fugue et caprice No. 3 in C; Fugues Nos. 10 in G min.; 12 in D.*
(M) *** Cal. CAL 6901 [id.].

The Angers organ has a spicy régale stop which is used tellingly in several of the dance movements included in the programme, notably Gervaise's *Bransle de Bourgogne* and a *Basse dance, Bransle* and *Gaillarde* of Attaignant and also in Sandrin's *Quand ien congneu.* A warmer palette is found for Eustache du Caurroy's agreeable *Fantaisie sur une jeune fillette.* This is a French equivalent to the divisions found in Elizabethan music, whereas the piquant *Fantaisie sur orgue ou espinette* of Guillaume Costeley is very succinct. Attaignant's *Kyrie cunctipotens* and the *Third Fantaisie* of Charles Guillet are essentially chorale preludes, as is the more elaborate *Fantaisie* of Charles Racquet, but the *Second Fantaisie* of Claude Le Jeune, a remarkable piece, anticipates the chorale variations of Bach, but using two different fugal subjects. Joseph Thomelin's (two-part) *Duo* is a winning miniature and Joseph de la Barre's *Sarabande* also has a gentle charm, while the three *Fugues* of François Roberday show impressive craftsmanship. No. 12, which ends the recital resplendently, is a good example of Isoir's imaginative registrations, which find ear-tickling contrasts between the plangent and mellow timbres that this organ offers, while the music is kept very much alive. A generous (76 minutes) and stimulating recital, although not to be played all at one sitting.

Isserlis, Steven (cello)

'Cello world' (with Thomas Adès, Maggie Cole, Michael Tilson Thomas, Dudley Moore): BEETHOVEN: *Andante and Variations.* SCHUMANN: *Violin sonata: Intermezzo.* FAURE: *Morceau de concours.* LEONARD: *L'âne et l'ânier.* DVORAK: *Romantic piece.* SEIBER: *Dance suite* (all arr. Isserlis). DEBUSSY: *Nocturne et Scherzo.* BERLIOZ: *La captive.* TAVENER: *The child lives* (both with Felicity Lott). SAINT-SAENS: *Le Cygne.* VILLA-LOBOS: *O canto do cisne negro.* MARTINU: *Duo.* RACHMANINOV: *Lied.* SCRIABIN: *Romance.* POPPER: *Dance of the elves.* ISSERLIS: *Souvenir russe.* TSINTSADZE: *Chonguri.* VINE: *Inner world.* *** RCA Dig. 09026 68928-2 [id.].

This is a cello recital with a difference, attractive in an off-beat way. The last and longest item, *Inner world*, by the Australian Carl Vine, is for amplified cello with electronic support, a cult piece, modern but not difficult. Otherwise, there are only two regular cello show-pieces, Saint-Saëns's *Swan*, exquisitely portrayed, and Popper's *Dance of the elves*, with Isserlis flamboyant. The Beethoven *Variations*, with harpsichord accompaniment, were transcribed from a *Sonatina for mandolin and piano* (1796), but most of the transcriptions are from violin originals, including the comic Leonard piece, full of ever more exaggerated hee-haws, set against the carter's song in the middle. In most items, Thomas Adès is the inspired accompanist and inspired too is the accompaniment by Maggie Cole, relishing the witty 1920s parodies in Matyas Seiber's *Dance suite*. The two items with Felicity Lott bring extra freshness and beauty, not just in the Berlioz song but also in the Tavener piece with accompaniment for cello alone. First-rate sound.

(i) Jackson, Francis
(organ of York Minster);

(ii) Michael Austin
(organ of Birmingham Town Hall)

'Pipes of splendour': (i) COCKER: *Tuba tune.* PURCELL: *Trumpet tune and almand.* JACKSON: *Division on 'Nun Danket'.* LEIGHTON: *Paean.* DUBOIS: *Toccata in G.* GUILMANT: *Allegretto in B min., Op. 19.* GIGOUT: *Scherzo in E.* MULET: *Carillon-Sortie.* (ii) REGER: *Toccata and fugue in D min./major, Op. 59/5–6.* DUPRE: *Prelude and fugue in B, Op. 7.* FRANCK: *Final in B flat.* (M) *** Chandos CHAN 6602 [id.].

It was Francis Jackson who made Cocker's *Tuba tune* (with its boisterous, brassy, principal tune) justly famous, and it makes a splendid opener. But the entire programme shows that it is possible to play and record an English organ without the result sounding flabby. The *Toccata* of Dubois is very winning and, in its quieter central section, the detail is beautifully clear, as it is in the charming Guilmant *Allegretto* and the lightly articulated Gigout *Scherzo.* Mulet's *Carillon-Sortie* rings out gloriously and Leighton's *Paean* brings a blaze of tone. The items played in Birmingham by Michael Austin are no less stimulating, especially the two French pieces, which have a fine piquant bite, while the Reger isn't in the least dull. Superb transfers of demonstration-standard analogue recording from the early 1970s.

John, Keith (organ)

'Great European organs No. 10': Tonhalle, Zurich: MUSSORGSKY (trans. John): *Pictures at an exhibition.* ALAIN: *3 Danses (Joies; Deuils; Luttes).* *** Priory Dig. PRCD 262 [id.].

Keith John has made his own transcription of Mussorgsky's *Pictures* – and pretty remarkable it sounds. Only the pieces like *Tuileries* that require pointed articulation come off less well than on orchestra or piano, but *Gnomus* and *Bydlo* and, especially, the picture of the two Polish Jews are all remarkably powerful, while the closing sequence of *Catacombs, The Hut on fowl's legs* and *The Great Gate of Kiev* are superb. The three Alain pieces make a substantial encore. This is as much a demonstration CD as an orchestral version of the Mussorgsky.

'Great European organs No. 26': Gloucester Cathedral: STANFORD: *Fantasia and toccata in D min., Op. 57.* REGER: *Prelude and fugue in E, Op. 56/1.* SHOSTAKOVICH: *Lady Macbeth of Mtsensk: Passacaglia.* SCHMIDT: *Chaconne in C min.* RAVANELLO: *Theme and variations in B min.* *** Priory Dig. PRCD 370 [id.].

Keith John, having shown what he can do with Mussorgsky, turns his attention here to little-known nineteenth- and twentieth-century organ pieces. The programme is imaginatively chosen and splendidly played – indeed, the bravura is often thrilling – and most realistically recorded on the superb Gloucester organ. Both the Schmidt *Chaconne* and Ravanello *Theme and variations* are fine works, and the Shostakovich *Passacaglia*, an opera entr'acte, was originally conceived as a work for organ.

'Toccata!' (organ of St Mary's, Woodford): BACH/BUSONI: *Partita No. 2 in D min., BWV 1004: Chaconne* (trans. K. John). BACH/RACHMANINOV: *Partita No. 3 in E, BWV 1006: suite* (trans. K. John). GUILLOU: *Sinfonietta.* HEILLER: *Tanz-Toccata.*
(M) *** Priory Dig. PRCD 002 [id.].

It was a most imaginative idea to use Busoni's arrangement of Bach's famous *D minor Partita for unaccompanied violin* as a basis for an organ transcription, and the result is like nothing you have ever heard before – especially when Keith John gets cracking on the pedals. The three excerpts from the *E major Partita* (as originally transcribed by Rachmaninov) are hardly less successful: how well the opening *Prelude* sounds on the organ, and one can forgive Keith John's affectionately mannered touch on the famous *Gavotte*. We then have a dramatic, almost bizarre change of mood and colour with Jean Guillou's 'neoclassical' (more 'neo' than 'classical') *Sinfonietta*. Even though it opens with a Bachian flourish, its colouring and atmosphere are highly exotic, the austere central *Allegretto* leading to a somewhat jazzy but naggingly insistent, partly contrapuntal and plangent, *Gigue*. Heiller's *Tanz-Toccata*, with its complex rhythms and chimerical changes of time-signature, finally brings a positive link with Stravinsky's *Rite of spring* during the insistent motoric final pages. After his remarkable Bach performances, Keith John's kaleidoscopic registration here shows how adaptable and versatile is the modern (1972) organ at St Mary's, Woodford.

Johnson, Emma (clarinet)

'A clarinet celebration' (with Gordon Back, piano): WEBER: *Grand duo concertante; Variations concertantes.* BURGMULLER: *Duo.* GIAMPIERI: *Carnival of Venice.* SCHUMANN: *Fantasy pieces, Op. 73.* LOVREGLIO: *Fantasia de concerto, La Traviata.*
*** ASV Dig. CDDCA 732 [id.].

ASV have reissued and repackaged Emma Johnson's outstanding 72-minute collection, dating from 1990. It is still at full price but is worth it. These are party pieces rather than encores, all of them drawing electric sparks of inspiration from

this winning young soloist. Even in such virtuoso nonsense as the Giampieri *Carnival of Venice* and the Lovreglio *Fantasia* Johnson draws out musical magic, while the expressiveness of Weber and Schumann brings heartfelt playing, with phrasing creatively individual. Gordon Back accompanies brilliantly, and the sound is first rate.

'British clarinet music' (with Malcolm Martineau (piano); (i) Judith Howard (soprano)): IRELAND: *Fantasy sonata in E flat.* VAUGHAN WILLIAMS: *6 Studies in English folksong;* (i) *3 Vocalises for soprano voice and clarinet.* BAX: *Clarinet sonata.* BLISS: *Pastoral;* (i) *2 Nursery rhymes.* STANFORD: *Clarinet sonata.*
*** ASV Dig. CDDCA 891 [id.].

Stanford's *Sonata* has the usual Brahmsian flavour but uses an Irish lament for the expressive central *Adagio*; then the finale has the best of both worlds by combining both influences. Vaughan Williams's *Six Studies in English folksong* (1927) are beguilingly evocative, while the *Vocalises* for soprano voice and clarinet are brief but rather touching; they were written in the last year of the composer's life. Both the Bax two-movement *Sonata* and the Ireland *Fantasy sonata* are fine works, and Bliss's *Pastoral* is wartime nostalgia, written while the composer was in France during the First World War. Needless to say, Emma Johnson plays everything with her usual spontaneity and musicianship, and she has a fine partner in Malcolm Martineau, while Judith Howard's contribution is pleasingly melismatic. Excellent, atmospheric recording, made in the London Henry Wood Hall.

Juilliard String Quartet

'50 Years', Volume 1: BARTOK: *String quartets Nos. 3–4; 6.*
(M) *** Sony mono/stereo SMK 62705 [id.].

This CD collects three Bartók performances, one from each of the Juilliards' cycles, in 1949, 1963 and 1981. It is discussed in our main volume under the composer.

'50 Years', Volume 2: BACH: *The Art of fugue: Contrapuncti 1–4.* BEETHOVEN: *String quartets Nos. 9 in C (Rasumovsky), Op. 59/3; 16 in F, Op. 135.* HAYDN: *String quartet in D, Op. 76/5: Largo* (only).
(M) ** Sony mono/stereo SMK 62706 [id.].

The first four *Contrapuncti* of *The Art of fugue* come from the impressive set the Juilliards made in 1987, to which we awarded three stars. The two Beethoven *Quartets* are drawn from different cycles: the *C major Rasumovsky*, Op. 59, No. 3 comes from 1964 and its companion, the *F major*, Op. 135, from 1982. Both are played with the formidable technical address the Juilliards command, but the acoustic in neither the CBS Studios nor the Coolidge Auditorium of the Library of Congress is ideal. One thinks longingly of the transparency and warmth of the old Quartetto Italiano set on Philips.

'50 Years', Volume 3: MOZART: *String quartet No. 19 in C (Dissonance), K.465.* SCHUBERT: *String quartet No. 15 in G, D.887.*
(M) ** Sony SMK 62707 [id.].

The Mozart was recorded in the CBS Studios in New York in 1977 and the Schubert two years later. Perhaps owing to the group's generous vibrato, the opening of the Mozart is not as mysterious as it could be, though the playing is of the highest order of accomplishment. Tempi are well judged and the first-movement exposition repeat is observed. The Schubert is high-powered and at times sounds too well-upholstered in tone, perhaps the fault of the closer balance; but there are many sympathetic and imaginative moments and much to admire. However, there are deeper and more penetrating accounts on disc.

'50 Years', 'The Scherzo through time': Minuets and Scherzi by HAYDN; BEETHOVEN; SCHUBERT; MENDELSSOHN; BRAHMS; FRANCK; RAVEL; SIBELIUS; BARTOK; SCHOENBERG; BERG; CARTER.
(M) * Sony SMK 62712 [id.].

There is some splendid playing here, but it is difficult to imagine any but a few collectors wanting isolated Scherzos from great string quartets, however superbly they are played.

'50 Years', Volume 4: DEBUSSY: *String quartet in G min.* HAYDN: *String quartet in D (Frog), Op. 50/6.* VERDI: *String quartet in E min.*
(M) ** Sony SMK 62708 [id.].

Sony have chosen the 1970 performance of the Debussy rather than the 1989. It is immaculate technically but a trifle overblown; the upfront recording renders the aural image oversized rather than intimate. However, the slow movement is wonderful and manages to shake off the impression of 'public' music-making rather than music played in the home. The Haydn quartet is new to the catalogue and was recorded in 1985, again in a rather resonant acoustic; a very enjoyable performance, though again it is almost symphonic and some will want a greater lightness of touch. The Verdi, recorded in 1989 (and previously coupled with the Sibelius *Voces intimae*), is impeccable in technical address – perhaps less winning in terms of charm. All the same, those wanting this particular coupling will find much to reward them.

'50 Years', Volume 5: DVORAK: *Piano quintet in A, Op. 81* (with Rudolf Firkušný, piano). BARBER: *Dover Beach, Op. 3* (with Dietrich Fischer-Dieskau). SCHOENBERG: *Verklärte Nacht* (with Walter Trampler, viola). SCHUMANN: *Piano quintet in E flat, Op. 44* (with Leonard Bernstein, piano). COPLAND: *Sextet for clarinet, piano and string quartet* (with Harold Wright, clarinet, and the composer, piano). FRANCK: *Piano quintet in F min.* (with Jorge Bolet, piano).
(M) ** Sony SM2K 62709 (2) [S2K 62709].

Apart from the Bartók, this is probably the most desirable of the Juilliard's fiftieth anniversary set. The Dvořák *Piano quintet* is marvellously played by Rudolf Firkušný (recorded in 1975), and so, too, is the magnificent Franck *Piano quintet* with Jorge Bolet (recorded in 1978), which this fine pianist plays with a restrained ardour that is impressive, though at times the Juilliard emote rather too much for comfort. The Copland *Sextet* with the composer himself (1966) and Samuel Barber's absurdly neglected and noble setting of *Dover Beach* with Fischer-Dieskau (1967) are valuable additions to the current catalogue and sound considerably better than on LP. The 1991 *Verklärte Nacht* is a little too over-heated to be ideal, with rather too much vibrato, but it still gives pleasure, while the 1964 version of the Schumann *Quintet* with Bernstein as pianist is coarsely recorded.

Kang, Dong-Suk (violin), Pascal Devoyon (piano)

French violin sonatas: DEBUSSY: *Sonata in G min.* ravel: *Sonata in G.* POULENC: *Violin sonata.* SAINT-SAENS: *Sonata No. 1 in D min.*
(BB) *** Naxos Dig. 8.550276 [id.].

One of the jewels of the Naxos catalogue, this collection of four of the finest violin sonatas in the French repertoire is self-recommending. The stylistic range of this partnership is evident throughout: they seem equally attuned to all four composers. This is warm, freshly spontaneous playing, given vivid and realistic digital recording in a spacious acoustic. A very real bargain.

Katchen, Julius (piano)

The art of Julius Katchen

Volume 7: BEETHOVEN: *Piano sonatas Nos. 23 in F min. (Appassionata), Op. 57; 32 in C min., Op. 111.* MOZART: *Piano sonatas Nos. 13 in B flat, K.388; 16 in C, K.545. 33 Variations on a waltz by Diabelli, Op. 129; 6 Bagatelles, Op. 126; Polonaise in C, Op.89.*
(B) *** Australian Decca Double mono/stereo 466 714-2 (2) [id.].

Katchen recorded his impressive (mono) *Appassionata* in 1956 and his sparkling account of the *Diabelli variations* (a work that proved ideal for his pianistic talents) in 1961, but Opus 111 dates from the year before his death. Already the cancer which would kill him was taking its toll, for the playing, although still prodigious, is no longer immaculate. But the performance has great power, total spontaneity, and a profound searching inner quality in the *Adagio*. The Mozart sonatas, also from 1956 and mono, are sheer delight, wonderfully crisp and stylish, yet with just the right degree of underlying expressive feeling. All the recordings have come up well and Katchen is given a very real presence.

Volume 8: SCHUBERT: *Fantasy in C (Wanderer), D.760.* SCHUMANN: *Carnaval, Op. 9; Toccata in C, Op. 7; Arabeske in C, Op. 18.* DEBUSSY: *Suite bergamasque: Clair de lune.* FALLA: *El amor brujo: Ritual fire dance.* CHOPIN: *Piano sonatas Nos. 2 in B flat min. (Funeral march), Op. 36; 3 in B min., Op. 58; Fantaisie-impromptu, Op. 66; Polonaise No. 6 in A flat (Heroic), Op. 53.* MENDELSSOHN: *Rondo capriccioso, Op. 14.* LISZT: *Concert paraphrase of Mendelssohn's On wings of song.* BACH, arr. HESS: *Jesu, joy of man's desiring.*
(B) *** Australian Decca Double mono/stereo 466 717-2 (2) [id.]

Another Double to show the remarkable range of a great pianist who died sadly young at the age of 42. The performance of *Carnaval* stands out for its skittishness as well as its infinite variety of mood and colour, while the *Arabeske* has a delightful sense of fantasy. The *Wanderer fantasia* also shows both Katchen's imaginative range, and his feeling for Schubert. But what stands out here is the Chopin, powerful, yet with a natural lyrical feeling. His virtuosity comes into play too, in the dazzling account of the *Fantasie-inpromptu*, while the finale of the *B flat minor Sonata* is quite breathtaking in its evenness and clarity, and the Scherzo of the *B minor* just as remarkable in its clean articulation. Yet both slow movements are deeply felt. The famous *A flat Polonaise* is arresting and the two Mendelssohn pieces which follow show in turns sparkling dexterity and an unsentimentally bold romantic impulse, while Debussy's *Clair de lune* has an exquisite simplicity. The sound throughout is excellent.

Kayath, Marcelo (guitar)

'*Guitar classics from Latin America*': PONCE: *Valse.* PIAZZOLA: *La muerte del angel.* BARRIOS: *Vals, Op. 8/3; Choro de saudade; Julia florida.* LAURO: *Vals venezolanos No. 2; El negrito; El marabino.* BROUWER: *Canción de cuna; Ojos brujos.* PERNAMBUCO: *Sons de carrilhões; Interrogando; Sono de maghia.* REIS: *Si ela perguntar.* villa-lobos: *5 Preludes.*
(B) *** Carlton Dig. PCD 2012 [(M) id.].

Marcelo Kayath's inspirational accounts of the Villa-Lobos *Preludes* can stand comparison with

the finest performances on record. He plays everything here with consummate technical ease and the most appealing spontaneity. His rubato in the Barrios *Vals* is particularly effective, and he is a fine advocate too of the engaging Lauro pieces and the picaresque writing of João Pernambuco, a friend of Villa-Lobos. The recording, made in a warm but not too resonant acoustic, is first class.

'*Guitar classics from Spain*': TARREGA: *Prelude in A min.; Capricho árabe; Recuerdos de la Alhambra.* GRANADOS: *La Maja de Goya.* ALBENIZ: *Granada; Zambra Granadina; Sevilla; Mallorca.* TORROBA: *Prelude in E; Sonatina; Nocturno.* RODRIGO: *Zapateado.* TRAD.: *El Noy de la mare.*
(B) *** Carlton IMP Dig. PCD 2037 [(M) id.].

Following the success of his first, Latin-American recital, Marcelo Kayath gives us an equally enjoyable Spanish collection, full of colour and spontaneity. By grouping music by several major composers, he provides a particularly revealing mix. The two opening Tárrega pieces are predominantly lyrical, to bring an effective contrast with the famous fluttering *Recuerdos de la Alhambra*, played strongly. Then after the Granados come four of Albéniz's most colourful and tuneful geographical evocations, while the Tórroba group includes the *Sonatina*, a splendid piece. After Rodrigo he closes with the hauntingly memorable *El Noy de la mare*. There is over an hour of music and the recording has a most realistic presence; but take care not to set the volume level too high.

Kazakevich, Mikhail (piano)

'*More piano moods*': RACHMANINOV: *Preludes in E flat min.* (1887)*; F* (1891)*; in C sharp min., Op. 3/2; in D min.; C sharp min.; G flat, Op. 23/3, 7 & 10; in B min.; G sharp min., Op. 32/10 & 12.* Domenico SCARLATTI: *Sonatas, Kk. 73; in D, Kk. 96; in C, Kk. 513.* CHOPIN: *Nocturne in E min., Op. 72/1; Polonaise in C sharp min., Op. 26/1; Sonata No. 3 in B min., Op. 58: Largo.* LISZT: *Concert paraphrase of Schubert's 'Gretchen am Spinnrade'.* BACH: *Italian concerto, BWV 971: Andante.* MAHLER (arr. KAZAKEVICH): *Antonius von Padua.* SCHUMANN: *Kinderszenen (excerpts): Träumerei; Fast zu ernst; Kind im Einschlummern. Blumenstücke in D flat, Op. 19. Etudes symphoniques, Op. 13: Variations V & VII.* BRAHMS: *Intermezzi in A min.; E, Op. 116/2 & 4; in A; E flat min., Op. 118/2 & 6.* SCHUBERT: *Sonata No. 13 in A, D.664: Finale: Allegro. Moment musical in A flat, D.780; Sonata No. 21 in B flat, D.960: Andante.*
(B) *** BMG/Conifer Dig. 75605 51310-2 (2) [(M) id.].

Although we are not usually enamoured of a 'mood

music' collection which features odd movements rather than complete works, this recital works very well because of the distinctive and spontaneous quality of Mikhail Kazakevich's playing, which is remakably 'live' and communicative. While much of the programme is reflective, this is far from a continuing reverie of romantic lollipops. Indeed, the programme is well planned to give constant variety of mood and style.

There is a good deal of Brahms and Rachmaninov (although each piece is usually followed by another from a different composer), and Kazakevich proves equally at home in their quite different sound-worlds, as he does with Scarlatti and Schumann. The first disc ends with the finale from Schubert's *A major Sonata*, D.664, played with the lightest touch, but the recital closes with Rachmaninov's extended *Prelude in B minor* and so ends comparatively sombrely, yet leaves the listener wanting more. Most enjoyable for the late evening, and well recorded too.

Kennedy, Nigel (violin), Lynn Harrell (cello)

Duos for violin and cello: RAVEL: *Sonata.* HANDEL: *Harpsichord suite No. 7 in G min.: Passacaglia* (arr. Halvorsen/Press). KODALY: *Duo.* BACH: *2-Part Invention No. 6 in E.*
⚜ *** EMI Dig. CDC5 56963-2 [id.].

An extraordinarily successful collaboration between the extrovert Kennedy and the more reticent Harrell, in which the listener has the constant impression of inspirational live intercommunication, and no suggestion whatsoever of the recording studio. The Ravel *Sonata* opens with disarming simplicity and immediately takes off, producing an enormous intensity of feeling – whether in the sheer gutsy energy and fireworks of the *Très vif* Scherzo, or the veiled delicacy of the slow movement, begun very gently by Harrell.

The playing in the first movement of the masterly Kodály *Duo* is so closely and powerfully intertwined, so completely integrated in its ebb and flow of phrasing, dynamic and tension, that it is as if violin and cello were the flip-sides of the same coin. The superb Handel *Passacaglia* is played with confident and captivating bravura and the programme ends coolly and satisfyingly with simple Bach polyphony, the interchange quite perfectly balanced. The recording is forward and gives the illusion of an extremely vivid presence, within an open acoustic.

King, Thea (clarinet), Clifford Benson (piano)

English clarinet music: STANFORD: *Sonata, Op. 29.* FERGUSON: *4 Short pieces, Op. 6.* FINZI: *5 Bagatelles, Op. 23.* HURLSTONE: *4 Characteristic pieces.* HOWELLS: *Sonata.* BLISS: *Pastoral.* REIZENSTEIN: *Arabesques.* COOKE: *Sonata in B flat.*
(B) *** Hyperion Dyad CDD 22027 (2) [id.].

This Hyperion Dyad aptly combines two separate recitals, now offered for the price of one. They were recorded at the beginning of the 1980s and are in many ways complementary. Stanford's *Clarinet sonata* is clearly influenced by Brahms but has plenty of character of its own. The other works on the first disc are all appealingly communicative, lighter in texture and content, but well crafted.

The second CD opens with the Howells *Sonata*, among the finest written since Brahms, a warmly lyrical piece in two extended movements that bring out the instrument's varied colourings. Bliss's early *Pastoral* follows, thoughtful and unassuming, improvisatory in feeling. Reizenstein's short piece then acts as an interlude before the Cooke *Sonata*, strong but undemanding, with a darkly nostalgic *Adagio* and a chirpy finale. Thea King's warm, naturally expressive playing makes her an ideal advocate, not only for the music, but for her instrument; and her partner, Clifford Benson, is no less eloquent. Smooth, natural, analogue recording.

Kipnis, Igor (harpsichord)

'First solo recordings (1962)': BACH: *French suite No. 6 in E, BWV 817; Fantasia in G min., BWV 917; Prelude, fugue and allegro in E flat, BWV 998. Toccata in E min., BWV 914.* HANDEL: *Suite No. 5 in E (HWV 430).* SOLER (attrib.): *Fandango in D min.* DUSSEK: *The sufferings of the Queen of France.*
*** VAI Audio VAIA 1185 [id.].

With a photo of the young Kipnis as the frontispiece, this superb recital demonstrates a prodigious keyboard talent, and playing that is thoughtful, scholarly yet alive. His Bach is of a high calibre, and equally impressive is the Handel suite (which includes a breathtaking account of the *Harmonious blacksmith*). Soler's extended *Fandango* is equally brilliant and diverting, and he ends with his own edition of Dussek's vividly pictorial programmatic fantasia, describing the suffering, imprisonment and execution of Marie Antoinette – played with great imaginative flair, and bravura. The harpsichord is not named, but it is a most attractive instrument, with a wide range of colour and is most naturally recorded.

Kissin, Evgeni (piano)

'Carnegie Hall début' (30 September 1990), Highlights: LISZT: Etude d'exécution transcendante No. 10; Liebestraum No. 3; Rhapsodie espagnole. SCHUMANN: Abegg variations, Op. 1; Etudes symphoniques, Op. 13; Widmung (arr. LISZT).
*** BMG/RCA Dig. 09026 61202-2 [61202].

Evgeni Kissin has phenomenal pianistic powers; this is a tour de force not only in terms of technical prowess but also in sheer artistry. Both sets of Schumann Variations are remarkable. The Liszt Rhapsodie espagnole is played with superb bravura. Kissin's range of colour and keyboard command throughout are dazzling. The Carnegie Hall was packed and the recording balance, while a bit close, is perfectly acceptable. The excitement of the occasion is conveyed vividly.

BEETHOVEN: Piano sonata No. 14 in C sharp min. (Moonlight), Op. 27/2. BRAHMS: Variations on a theme of Paganini, Op. 35. FRANCK: Prélude, chorale et fugue.
*** RCA Dig. 09026 68910-2 [id.].

Strongly projected playing from this outstanding (and still young) artist. There is impressive concentration in the Beethoven, an effortless virtuosity in the Brahms, and great poetic feeling in the Franck. Everything here bears witness to a powerful musical mind allied to consummate pianistic mastery. Excellent recorded sound.

'In Tokyo' (12 May 1987): CHOPIN: Nocturne in A flat, Op. 32/2; Polonaise in F sharp min., Op. 44. LISZT: Concert studies Nos. 1 in D flat (Waldesrauschen); 2 in F min. (La Leggierezza). PROKOFIEV: Sonata No. 6 in A, Op. 82. RACHMANINOV: Etudes tableaux, Op. 39/1 & 5; Lilacs. SCRIABIN: Etude in C sharp min., Op. 42/ 5; Mazurka in E min., Op. 25/3.
*** Sony Dig. SK 45931 [id.].

Kissin was only fifteen at the time of his Tokyo début, but he sounds fully mature throughout this recital. He plays Prokofiev's Sixth Sonata for all it is worth with no holds barred, and the effect is altogether electrifying – one finds oneself on the edge of one's chair. He is no less at home in the Rachmaninov Etudes tableaux and the Liszt La Leggierezza, which he delivers with marvellous assurance and poetic feeling. His Scriabin, too, is pretty impressive. The microphone placing is too close – but no matter, this is breathtaking piano playing.

Kynaston, Nicholas (organ)

'Great organ music' (played on the organ of (i) Clifton Cathedral; (ii) Royal Albert Hall): (i) J. S.

BACH: Fantasia and fugue in G min., BWV 542; Fugue in G (Alla gigue), BWV 577; Prelude and fugue in B min, BWV 544; Toccata and fugue in F, BWV 540; Concerto No. 2 in A min., BWV 593 (after Vivaldi); (ii) Toccata and fugue in D min., BWV 565. SCHUMANN: Canon in B min., Op. 56/ 5. MENDELSSOHN (arr. BEST): Athalie: War march of the priests. SAINT-SAENS: Fantaisie in E flat; Fantaisie II in D flat, Op. 101. GIGOUT: Grand choeur dialogue; Toccata in B min. WIDOR: Symphonies Nos. 1 in C min., Op. 13/1: Marche pontificale; 4 in F min., Op. 13/4: Andante cantabile; 5 in F min., Op. 42/1: Toccata; 6 in C min, Op. 42/2: Allegro; 9 in C min. (Gothique), Op. 70: Andante sostenuto. BONNET: Etude de concert. MULET: Carillon-Sortie.
(BB) **(*) CfP Silver Double CDCFPSD 4760 (2) [(B) id.].

Nicholas Kynaston's recital (drawing on three LPs, recorded between 1970 and 1975) uses two organs. The opening Toccata and fugue in D minor is played on the Royal Albert Hall organ, with its resonant sonority and wide dynamic range effectively demonstrated but not exaggerated. The change of timbre with the second Bach piece, the Fantasia and fugue in G minor, is disconcerting, for this, like the rest of the Bach items, is played on the organ of Clifton Cathedral, beautifully recorded with clean, brilliant treble and a clear yet ample bass response sounding very like a baroque organ. Kynaston's performance is buoyant, as is the lively Fugue à la gigue (which may not be authentic but is most enjoyable when registered so piquantly).

The other works are more considered and didactic, while in the attractively registered Vivaldi transcription (derived from the eighth concerto in L'Estro armonico) the central Adagio is rather subdued. Using the Royal Albert Hall organ for the French repertoire is perhaps more controversial but the two Gigout pieces are very colourful and effective, and the movements from the Widor symphonies come off well too, with the grandiose opening of the Allegro of the Sixth Symphony matched by the climaxes of the Marche pontificale of the First, while the swirling figurations of the famous Toccata from the Fifth are balanced by the massive effects from the pedals. In the Saint-Saëns and Liszt pieces, the exaggeratedly wide dynamic contrasts characteristic of this instrument are at the very heart of Kynaston's interpretations, and some might find the gentler music seems too recessed. But overall this is an impressive achievement.

Labèque, Katia and Marielle (piano duo)

'Encore!': Adolfo BERIO: Polka; Maria Isabella (Waltz); La Primavera (Mazurka). BACH: Jesu, joy of man's desiring (arr. HESS). GERSHWIN:

Preludes Nos. 1–3; Promenade (Walking the dog). STRAVINSKY: *Tango; Waltz.* Luciano BERIO: *Wasserklavier.* BRAHMS: *Waltz in A flat.* TCHAIKOVSKY: *The Seasons: June.* BERNSTEIN: *West Side story: Jet song; America.* JOPLIN: *Bethena (Ragtime waltz); The Entertainer.* JAELL: *Valse.* BARTOK: *New Hungarian folksong.* SCHUMANN: *Abendlied.*
*** Sony Dig. SK 48381 [id.].

The Labèque sisters have never made a better record than this; the playing scintillates, especially the Bernstein and Stravinsky items, while the Labèques' Scott Joplin is admirably cool and the account of Myra Hess's arrangement of the famous Bach chorale is gentle and quite beautiful. Luciano Berio's evocative *Wasserklavier* is a real lollipop, but the surprise is the selection of four catchy and often boisterous pieces by his grandfather, Adolfo, a church organist 'of doubtful faith' (according to his grandson); Luciano gives his imprimatur to the lively Labèque performances, even while he feels that their 'modern and uninhibited pianism' might not have suited his more conventional grandfather.

Landowska, Wanda (harpsichord)

'Portrait': F. COUPERIN: *La favorite; Les moissonneurs; Les Langueurs-Tendres; Le gazouillement; La commère; Le moucheron; Les bergeries; Les tambourins; Les fastes de la grande ménestrandise; Le dodo, ou l'amour au berceau; Musette de Taverny; Les folies françaises ou les Dominos; Les calotins et les calotines; Les vergers fleuris; Soeur Monique.* RAMEAU: *Suite in G min.* BACH: *Goldberg variations, BWV 988.* HANDEL: *Suites Nos. 2 in F, HWV 427; 5 in E, HWV 430; 7 in G min., HWV 432.*
(M) (***) Grammofono 2000 mono AB 78715/6 [id.].

It is good to have a representative collection of the art of Wanda Landowska, who put the harpsichord back on the musical map in the twentieth century. She was not the first to try to do so; Violet Gordon Woodhouse actually made earlier acoustic recordings of some distinction, but it was Landowska's larger-than-life personality that soon made her a star. She gave her first performances on this instrument in 1903, and she toured Europe over the next two decades, visiting the United States from 1923 onwards. She persuaded Falla and Poulenc to write concertos (in 1926 and 1927 respectively) and had Pleyel build a large, modern instrument especially for her concerts.

Yet, as is readily apparent here, in the music of Couperin and Rameau she could articulate with the greatest delicacy (*La Poule* is delightful) and she kept her big guns in reserve for appropriate moments. Her *Goldberg variations* was rightly cele-

brated, the playing robust when required but suitably restrained at other times. Her overall timing is surprisingly close to Leonhardt's but her approach, without any loss of seriousness of purpose, is freer and more imaginative, and her reprise of the *Aria* reminds one of Rosalyn Tureck in its delicacy of feeling.

The recordings of French music were made in 1934, the *Goldberg* in 1933, and the quality is excellent, although in the French *pièces de clavecin* there are pitch differences between some items. The Handel *Suites* are a little more variable in sound, but still impressive, and in No. 5 *The harmonious blacksmith* (1935) strikes his anvil at first robustly but later with varying degrees of delicacy: there is no more spontaneous account in the catalogue. In the *Overture* which opens Handel's *Seventh Suite*, Landowska flamboyantly sounds like a full orchestra, and she plays the closing *Passacaglia* with similar satisfying weight, but in between there is a wider range of dynamic. Above all, this great artist communicated her joy in everything she played, and these excellent transfers ensure that we fully share it.

Larrocha, Alicia de (piano)

'Música española': Piano music, Volume IV: FALLA: *The Three-cornered hat: 3 Danzas. El amor brujo: suite.* TURINA: *Sacro Monte; Zapateado.* HALFFTER: *Danza de la pastora; Danza de la gitana.* MONTSALVATGE: *Sonatina para Yvette; Divertimento No. 2 'Habanera'.* NIN-CULMELL: *6 Tonadas.* SURINACH: *3 Canciones y danzas españolas.* MOMPOU: *Impresiones intimas; Preludio a Alicia de Larrocha; Música callada, IV; Canciones y danzas.*
✹ (B) *** Decca Double 433 929-2 (2) [id.].

Alicia de Larrocha is ideally cast here. Much of the music is delightful and all of it interesting. Joaquín Nin-Culmell's *6 Tonadas* are flashingly characterful in their folk feeling: the closing *Muñeira (Galicia)* brings spectacular flamenco fireworks. Xavier Montsalvatge's *Sonatina* in its finale quotes 'Twinkle twinkle little star', yet its audaciously quirky satire has more in common with Poulenc and Satie than Debussy's *Children's corner*. Alicia de Larrocha plays the whole sonata with breathtaking virtuosity. The coupled Mompou pieces, which are superbly played, have much charm and an atmosphere all their own – they are discussed in more detail under their Composer entry. They are digitally recorded; the rest of the recital is analogue, but hardly less real.

LaSalle Quartet

Chamber music of the Second Viennese School:
BERG: *Lyric suite; String quartet, Op. 3.*
SCHOENBERG: *String quartets: in D; No. 1 in D
min., Op. 7; No. 2 in F sharp min., Op. 10/3* (with
Margaret Price); *No. 3, Op. 30; No. 4, Op. 37.*
WEBERN: *5 Movements, Op. 5; String quartet*
(1905); *6 Bagatelles, Op. 9; String quartet, Op.
28.*
(M) *** DG (IMS) 419 994-2 (4) [id.].

DG have compressed their 1971 five-LP set onto
four CDs, offering them at a reduced and competitive price. They have also retained the invaluable
and excellent documentary study edited by Ursula
Rauchhaupt – which runs to 340 pages! It is almost
worth having this set for the documentation alone.
The LaSalle Quartet give splendidly expert performances, even if at times their playing seems a
little cool; and they are very well recorded. An
invaluable issue for all who care about twentieth-
century music.

Lawson, Peter, and Alan MacLean (piano duet)

English music for piano duet: BERNERS: *Valses
bourgeoises; Fantasie espagnole; 3 Morceaux.*
Constant LAMBERT: *Overture* (ed. Lane); *3 Pièces
nègres pour les touches blanches.* RAWSTHORNE:
The Creel. WALTON: *Duets for children.* Philip
LANE: *Badinages.*
*** Troy Dig. TROY 142 [id.].

This collection centres on Lord Berners, who had a
recurring twinkle in the eye and loved to parody;
moreover his inspiration regularly casts a glance in
the direction of Satie and Poulenc, as the *Trois
Morceaux* readily demonstrate. Both Walton and
Constant Lambert were his friends, admired his
individuality and came under his influence. Lambert's *Trois Pièces nègres* have a Satiesque title,
yet they are all the composer's own work: the *Siesta*
is quite haunting and the catchy *Nocturne* brings
sparkling Latin-American rhythmic connotations,
far removed from Chopin.

The four engaging Rawsthorne miniatures, inspired by Izaak Walton's *Compleat Angler*, fit
equally well into the programme. The Walton *Duets
for children* have a disarming simplicity and often
a nursery rhyme bounce, *Hop scotch* is particularly
delightful, and vignettes like *The silent lake* and
Ghosts will surely communicate very directly to
young performers. Walton's final *Galop* was
arranged by Philip Lane, who also provides four of
his own pieces to close the concert with a strongly
Gallic atmosphere. The performances by Peter
Lawson and Alan MacLean are strong on style

yet also convey affection. Excellent recording in a
nicely resonant but not muddy acoustic.

Leach, Joanna (piano)

'Four square': SOLER: *Sonata No. 90 in F sharp.*
HAYDN: *Sonata in C, Hob XVI/1.* J. S. BACH:
*Partita No. 1 in B flat: Prelude; Minuets I & II;
Gigue.* MOZART: *Fantasia in D min., K.397;
Sonata No. 11 in A, K.331.* SCHUBERT:
Impromptu in A flat, D.899/4. MENDELSSOHN:
Songs without words, Op. 19/1.
*** Athene Dig. CD 3 [id.].

There is no more convincing fortepiano recital than
this. Joanna Leach uses an 1823 Stodart with its
effectively dark lower register for the Soler *Sonata*,
then plays the same instrument later to show its
attractive upper range in an almost romantic performance of Mozart's *Fantasia in D minor*; she
ends the recital with the *A major Sonata*, K.331,
with the introductory variations particularly inviting. For the Haydn, she chooses a 1789 Broad-
wood, a more brittle sound, and for the Bach a very
effective 1787 instrument made by Longman &
Broderip. In the Schubert and Mendelssohn pieces
an 1835 D'Almaine brings us that bit nearer a
modern piano. Fine performances throughout, and
excellent recording. A fascinating way of discovering what the modern piano's ancestors could
do best.

Leonhardt Consort, Gustav Leonhardt (director, and playing: harpsichord, organ, virginal, viol)

Leonhardt Edition

(B) **(*) Teldec/Warner 3984 21349-2 (21) [(M)
id.].

Gustav Leonhardt has made an exceptionally distinguished contribution to period-instrument performances of baroque music. During the 1960s he
directed and performed in many first recordings for
Das Alte Werk label, and it is appropriate that
Teldec should have celebrated the fortieth anniversary of that label with a twenty-one-disc Leonhardt
Edition. The excellent Ensemble which bears his
name always sought to make a sound which, although transparent, also had body, as well as being
in believable period style. Similarly for his own
many keyboard recordings, he chose instruments
which would colour the music pleasingly as well as
authentically.

Leonhardt's scholarship, his understanding of the
finer points of baroque performance detail, not least
ornamentation, showed a remarkable combination
of musicality and scholarship. If his readings sometimes erred on the side of literal directness and

sobriety, he could never be accused of self-regarding eccentricity, and it is apt that these reissued records should carry with their documentation printed tributes from such current experts in the period-instrument field as Bob van Asperen and Ton Koopman. Although we have reservations about recommending the set as a whole, certain of these CDs are very desirable indeed, for the technical standard of the recordings is remarkably high. All these discs are available separately.

BACH: Harpsichord concertos (with (i) Frans Brüggen (flute), Marie Leonhardt (violin); (ii) Eduard Müller; (iii) Anneke Uittenbosch; (iv) Alan Curtis; (v) Janny van Wering). *Concertos:* (i) *in A min., for flute, violin and harpsichord, BWV 1044; Nos. 2 in E; 3 in D; 4 in A; 5 in F min., for solo harpsichord, BWV 1053–6; 6 for harpsichord and 2 recorders in F, BWV 1057; 7 in G min.; 8 in D min., for solo harpsichord, BWV 1058–9; Double harpsichord concertos Nos.* (ii) *1 in C min., BWV 1060;* (iii) *2 in C, BWV 1061;* (ii) *3 in C min., BWV 1062;* (iii–iv) *Triple harpsichord concertos Nos. 1 in D min.; 2 in C, BWV 1063–4;* (ii–iii; v) *Quadruple harpsichord concerto in A min., BWV 1065*
((M) *(*) Teldec/Warner 3984 21350-2 (3)).

The one clear drawback to this Edition as a complete set (apart from the curious omission of the *First Concerto*, BWV 1052) is Leonhardt's set of harpsichord concertos; this has many fine qualities, including Brüggen's contribution (immediately apparent in the *A minor Concerto*, BWV 1044), but it is surprisingly lacking in imagination and spontaneity. The recording is warm and resonant (comparable with the sound we usually expect from the Collegium Aureum) and reproduces smoothly, but inner clarity leaves much to be desired and the keyboard reproduction in the multiple concertos is much too opaque. In the solo works Leonhardt's steady – at times seemingly unrelenting – progress in allegros wearies the ear and, although he can be sensitive enough in slow movements (witness the famous *Largo* of the *F minor Concerto*), this is very disappointing, all things considered.

BACH: *Goldberg variations, BWV 988*
((M) ** Teldec/Warner 3984 21351-2).

There are no complaints about the recording of the *Goldberg variations* (from 1965, using Leonhardt's favourite copy of a Dulcken harpsichord), which sounds fresh and vivid in its present incarnation. The reading is clear and direct, if not producing any especially individual resonances. Leonhardt was to re-record the work later for Deutsche Harmonia Mundi, and that version has a more spontaneous feeling; but it is not currently available.

BACH: Works for harpsichord: *Chromatic fantasia and fugue in D min., BWV 903; Sonata in D min.,*

BWV 964; Sonata in G, BWV 1005; Suite in E min., BWV 996; Toccata in G, BWV 916
((M) ** Teldec/Warner 3984 21352-2).

It has to be said that Bach's music does not always show Leonhardt at his very best. This miscellaneous recital is played on a modern harpsichord, but one which is a reproduction of a mid-eighteenth-century Dulcken. The sounds are authentic and attractive; unquestionably Leonhardt's playing reflects what would have been possible in Bach's time and, with judicious ornamentation of repeated sections, the scholarship behind the playing is impeccable. The opening *Chromatic fantasia and fugue* brings exciting dexterity, and so does the *Allegro assai* finale of the *Sonata in G*, which is an arrangement of the work for unaccompanied violin in C, BWV 1005. In between, however, a good deal of the playing is rather metronomic, and the *Suite in E minor* (which Bach probably intended for the now obsolete lute-harpsichord) could do with a lighter touch. The recording is rather close, but the CD transfer cannot be faulted.

BACH: *Violin sonatas* (for violin and harpsichord) *Nos. 1–6, BWV 1014–19* (with Lars Frydén)
((M) **(*) Teldec/Warner 3984 21353-2 (2)).

The six *Sonatas for violin and harpsichord* are far less well known than the works for unaccompanied violin or cello, and their relative obscurity is quite undeserved. They contain music of great character and beauty: who could forget the beautiful *Siciliana* which opens the *C minor* (No. 4) (played most persuasively here by Lars Frydén) or the more solemn dignity of the first movement of the *B minor Sonata* (No. 1), which Leonhardt opens very simply and which glows with life at the violin entry.

Frydén proves to be a most stylish and sympathetic exponent. He uses a baroque violin, made in London in 1767, and lets it sing and dance, just as Bach intended. Although he is balanced fairly closely, if not at the expense of his partner, his timbre is full and cleanly formed and never sounds scratchy – witness his *Dolce* opening of the *A major Sonata* (No. 2). Throughout these works the polyphony of the allegros is always engagingly fresh, and the continuo offers plenty of opportunities to the imaginative harpsichordist.

Alas, Leonhardt does not always take them, for the most part being content to provide ongoing background support. When he is on his own (as again at the opening of the *F minor*, No. 5) he proceeds uneventfully onwards until the warm entry of the solo violin transforms the music. In a flowing *Andante*, as in the A major work, he is content to provide a straightforward accompaniment and let his partner soar above him. However, better this than eccentric rubato, and in the jolly second movement of the *E major* (No. 3), the players work well together, while the finale sparkles with energy. An excellent transfer to CD, but don't play the disc at too high a volume.

BACH: *Quodlibet*, canons, chorales, songs and keyboard works (with Anner Bylsma (cello), Agnes Giebel, Marie Luise Gilles, Bert van t'Hoff, Peter Christoph Runge): *Canons in 2 parts, BWV 1075; in 7 (8) parts, BWV 1078; in 4 parts, BWV 1073; in 4 (5) parts, BWV 1077;* (Keyboard) *Capriccio in B flat (sopra la lontananza del suo fratello dilettissimo), BWV 992; Preludes in F, BWV 927; in E, BWV 937; in G min., BWV 929; in D, BWV 925; in C, BWV 939; Fugue in C, BWV 952; Prelude and Fugue in A min., BWV 895; Prelude and Fughetta in D min., BWV 899; Suite in F min., BWV 823. Quodlibet, BWV 524.* Arias: *Erbauliche Gedanken eines Tobackrauchers, BWV 515a; Gieb dich zufrieden und sie stille, BWV 511; Vergiss mein nicht, mein allerliebster Gott! BWV 505.* Chorales: *O Herzensangst, o Bangigkeit und Zagen! BWV 400; Nicht so traurig, nicht so sehr, BWV 384; Dir, dir Jehova, will ich singen, BWV 452; Was betrübst du dich, mein Herze, BWV 423; Wer nur den lieben Gott lässt walten* (3 versions), *BWV 691 BWV 434* (M) *** Teldec/Warner 3984 21354-2.

Much of this material comes from Anna Magdalena's *Klavierbüchlein*, intended for use by Bach's sons: keyboard pieces, together with simple chorales and songs for domestic entertainment rather than public performance. They show another side of Bach, as a genial but painstaking family man, and the music brings out the best in Leonhardt, who plays the brief keyboard pieces in an appropriately light-hearted manner.

He gives a colourful account of the designedly programmatic *Capriccio in B flat* ('On the departure of a beloved brother'), personally announcing the title of each section in German. The brief *Canon in 2 parts* wittily introduces a recorder, while the *Canon in 7 (8) parts* fills out quickly and ends in mid-air.

The arias and chorales are agreeably outgoing. In *So oft ich meine Tobacks-Pfeife* (subtitled 'The edifying thoughts of a tobacco-smoker') Bert van t'Hoff (or Peter Runge – it is not quite clear which) genially reflects on Bach's 'contented puffing on my small pipe', while the serene *Gieb dich zufrieden und sie stille* ('Be of good cheer and hold your peace') is sung delightfully by Agnes Giebel. The chorale *Was betrübst du dich, mein Herz* ('Why are you sad, my heart?') touchingly appears to reflect on a family crisis.

But the highlight of the concert is the *Quodlibet* ('As you wish') for vocal quartet, which by definition is an informal, light-hearted piece, but here is a true musical joke, originally intended for performance at a wedding. The manuscript is incomplete (both the beginning and the end are missing) but what there is (about 10 minutes) is set to out-

rageous words which flit from image to image, not unlike Gilbert's famous Nightmare song, and ending with the observation, 'Oh what a delightful fugue this is!' The whole piece is captivating, especially when sung so freshly. To end the collection, Leonhardt returns to his more didactic Bach keyboard style for BWV 823, BWV 895 and BWV 899, but the closing *Fughetta* of the latter work is pleasingly jaunty. The recording throughout is excellent, and altogether this is a most entertaining concert.

English consort and keyboard music: DOWLAND: *Pavan in C.* LAWES: *Suites Nos. 1 in C min.; 2 in F; Sonata No. 7 in D min.; Suite No. 3 in B flat: In nomine.* COPRARIO: *Fantasia; Suite.* BYRD: *Pavan; Galliard; Fantasia No. 3.* Thomas SIMPSON: *Ricercar: Bonny sweet robin.* Thomas LUPO: *Fantasia.* BYRD: *Pavan; Galliard; Miserere.* MORLEY: *Nancie; Fantasia.* John BULL: *Hexachord fantasia; The Duchesse of Brunswick's toye.* William RANDALL: *Dowland's Lachrymae; Galliard: Can't she excuse my wrongs.* TOMKINS: *Pavan; Galliard; A sad pavan for these distracted times.* GIBBONS: *Pavan.* FARNABY: *Fantasia; Spagnioletta.* William TISDALE: *Mrs Katherin Tregians pavan.* ANON.: *A toye* ((M) *** Teldec/Warner 3984 21760-2 (2)).

This two-CD compilation draws on three Das Alte Werk LPs from 1965–6 and 1970, and the result is an unusually comprehensive survey which gives an excellent overall picture of the various composers writing music in Elizabethan and Jacobean England. The programme opens appropriately with Byrd, a consort *Pavane*, and later we are to have a harpsichord *Pavane and Galliard* and two consort *Fantasias*. In between come the highly individual *Suites* of William Lawes, who was a member of the Chapel Royal and a very considerable contributor to early seventeenth-century consort music. His *In nomine* (taken from the *Third Suite*) is particularly eloquent. But the surprise is perhaps the music of William Coprario (Cooper), whose *Fantasia* (for two violins, viola, viol and cello) is very striking indeed, to be followed by a tuneful and light-hearted *Suite in three parts* and the equally engaging *Ricercar on Bonny sweet Robin* by Thomas Simpson.

The first CD ends with Lupo's *Fantasia*, another piece of real quality. There could perhaps be more ornamentation in these performances, but on the whole they are in excellent taste and style. There is nothing anaemic about the string textures, nor are they edgy, while the playing itself has plenty of life and spirit. The recording is impeccable.

The music of Byrd again opens the second disc with a consort pavane and galliard to introduce his beautiful *Miserere*, which is most touchingly played by Leonhardt on a chamber organ. He continues with a series of keyboard pieces, alternating harpsichord (choosing between two different instruments) and virginal. All come from the Fitzwilliam Virginal Book, except for the Gibbons *Pavane* and the two pieces by Randall. Predictably fine are the Bull *Fantasia* and the three pieces by Thomas Tomkins: here Leonhardt changes instruments for the third, *A sad pavane for these distracted times*. Farnaby's jolly *Spagnioletta* makes a spirited contrast and the programme ends with an encore – a brief, anonymous *Toye*.

Consort music: BIBER: *Harmonia artificiosa-ariosa: diversi mode accordata: Partita No. 3 in A; Mensa sonora: Part 3; Fidicinium sacro-profanum: Sonatas 3–6.* MUFFAT: *Armonico tributo: Sonata No. 2 in G min.* ROSENMULLER: *Sonata No. 7 a 4.* SCHEIDT: *Paduan a 4.* SCHMELZER: *Sacro-profanus concentus musicus: Sonatas Nos. 7, 9* (M) *** Teldec/Warner 3984 21761-2.

It was Leonhardt who introduced us (in the late 1960s) to much of Biber's instrumental music, the excellence of which is only now being fully explored. The best-known set is the *Harmonia artificiosa-ariosa*, a collection of seven *Partitas* or suites for strings (published posthumously), and here we are offered the *Third* with its remarkable finale, an elaborately decorated *Chaconne/Canon*.

The *Mensa sonora* sonatas (from 1680) are – as the title suggests – essentially homophonic, more concerned with richness of texture and harmony than with contrapuntal ingenuity. Again we are offered Partita III, in five movements, written for a modest chamber ensemble and continuo. The music is warmly expressive: even the fourth-movement *Chaconne* is mellow.

Four of the twelve *Fidicinium sacro-profanum* sonatas follow. They were published three years later and are scored for 2 violins, 2 violas, 2 cellos and continuo. As their title suggests, contrast is the order of the day, with the expressive movements quite dolorous, while allegros are lively and lighthearted. The *Sixth Sonata* (the last here) opens quite solemnly, and Leonhardt fills out the texture with an organ continuo.

The following Muffat *Sonata* opens even more sombrely, but it becomes an inventive series of linked movements alternating Grave slow sections with buoyant allegros. The two Schmelzer *Sonatas* (1662) for two violins, viola and continuo seek contrast in the same way as Biber's music and are similarly entitled *Sacro-profanus concentus musicus*. They are of high quality, as is the briefer work by Johann Rosenmüller and the stately *Paduan* (Pavane) of Samuel Scheidt. As can be seen, all this music, much of which is well off the beaten track, comes from the same fertile period, and Leonhardt and his players (six in all) are persuasive advocates. They use period instruments which are tuned to seventeenth-century pitch, but the sounds they make are full-timbred, and expressive phrasing is not eccentric but warmly musical.

FROBERGER: Organ and harpsichord works: Organ: *Capriccio II; Fantasia III; Toccata XI alla levazione; Ricercar II; Canzona II.* Harpsichord: *Toccata IX; Suite XVIII; Toccata XVIII; Suite XII* ((M) *** Teldec/Warner 3984 21762-2).

Froberger was a pupil of Frescobaldi and one of the most exploratory and inward-looking composers of the seventeenth century. Leonhardt, who is an authoritative guide, offers here two groups of pieces, the first five played on the now familiar eighteenth-century organ (at the Waalse Kerk, Amsterdam), and the second group on a modern harpsichord, copied from an Italian instrument from the same period. The opening organ *Capriccio* is joyously buoyant, but the *Chorale fantasia* is more thoughtful and in its steady progress anticipates Bach. The *Toccata alla levazione* has much of Frescobaldi's improvisatory feeling, while the *Ricercar II* brings a remarkably solemn profundity. The *Harpsichord suites*, skilfully decorated, are more lively and outgoing and readily show the composer's resourceful melodic and harmonic flare. Most striking is the opening movement of the *Twelfth Suite*, which laments the death of King Ferdinand IV in 1654. The closing *Sarabande* has comparable regal dignity. Excellent recording of both instruments.

KUHNAU: *Musikalische Vorstellung einiger biblischer Historien: Sonatas 1–6 (1: The combat between David and Goliath; 2: Saul healed by David with the help of music; 3: Jacob's marriage; 4, Hezekiah is mortally ill and restored to health; 5: Gideon, the saviour of Israel; 6: The death and burial of Jacob)* (M) *(*) Teldec/Warner 3984 21763-2 (2).

Johann Kuhnau was Bach's predecessor at St Thomas's, Leipzig, and this is his fourth and last keyboard work. The *Musical depiction of some biblical stories* (in six *Sonatas*) dates from 1700. Each programmatically illustrates a story from the Old Testament, which is filled out by a narrative – an introduction at the beginning of each work, plus titles for each section, the latter usually spoken over the music. Here these introductions, recounting each biblical story in full, given in German – and, fortunately, separately banded on the CDs – are written and spoken by Leonhardt himself, and they are very subjective.

Alas, Kuhnau's musical resources are not equal to the pictorial task he has set himself: they are most striking for their naïvety and seldom show much descriptive skill: *The combat between David and Goliath* is depicted with singular lack of imagination. However, when Gideon leads the Israelites into battle, the 'blast of trombones and trumpets' is more tellingly depicted, and the scalic flight of pursued enemy forces, both here and earlier in the David/Goliath narrative, is effective enough.

Kuhnau is also rather better at portraying melancholy, as in Saul's rather extended bout of it, before David's not very believable musical cure, and again during Hezekiah's mournful sickness before God relents and restores him to health. In the most intriguing story of all, *Jacob's marriage*, the devious Laban, using the cover of darkness, places his elder, ugly daughter, Leah, in the bridal bed instead of the younger, the beautiful Rachel (whom Jacob is expecting). Such duplicity is represented with melodramatically florid flourishes. Then, in a section lasting two minutes, Jacob's relishing of the wedding night consummation is depicted with an amiable little theme, until 'his heart tells him something is amiss'. But in the dim light his misgivings cannot be confirmed and he 'finally falls asleep' – to a single chord. The next morning he discovers his mistake and is none too pleased about it. However, he agrees to keep Leah after the promise that in seven years he can have Rachel too; so the piece ends with a second wedding and repeated celebrations!

The organ is used for *Sonatas Nos. 1*, 2 and 4, the harpsichord for the remainder. Generally it is the latter instrument which works best in the primitive narrative detail, as Leonhardt brings a certain improvisational feeling to the disconsolate music. But to claim this as a 'great work', as Lothar Hoffmann-Erbrecht does in his accompanying note, is singularly misguided. It has historical interest, to be sure, but little else, although one wonders whether a more extrovert account would bring it more fully to life. The documentation is good, if a little unwieldy, with full narrative translations, and the titles given for each section.

MONDONVILLE: (with Lars Frydén) *Violin sonatas Op. 3, Nos. 1 in G min.; 2 in F; 3 in B; 4 in C; 5 in G; 6 in A*
(M) **(*) Teldec/Warner 3984 21765-2.

Mondonville's *Violin sonatas* are important in that they helped the development away from the violin-plus-continuo style to the form as we know it today. Thus both instruments are given proper 'solo' parts to play, and they are often very florid parts. One might be forgiven for occasionally thinking that the composer had forgotten himself and allotted two accompaniment parts instead! But generally the music is inventive enough, and the disc has real historical interest in demonstrating the duet sonata when ideas concerning the marriage of two instruments were very much in the melting pot. Opus 3 dates from about 1734 and predates by fourteen years the fascinating Opus 5 set, which also includes the human voice and which is listed and discussed in our main volume. The recording here, made in 1966, is good but is rather more forward than the earlier (1963) recording by these same artists of the

Bach *Violin and harpsichord sonatas*. This means that the full timbre of Lars Frydén's baroque violin is less flattered, although he can still be serenely expressive in the *Arias* which form the slow movements – witness the fine flowing melody of No. 4 in C major – and Leonhardt's harpsichord (a Kirckman, made in London in 1766) is a little sharp-toned. But the two instruments are generally well balanced – and the players seem pretty sure of themselves. Tempi are often brisk and very lively (try the infectious *Giga* finale of that same *C major Sonata*).

Organ and harpsichord music: F. COUPERIN: *Messe à l'usage ordinaire des Paroisses: Offertoire sur les grands jeux. L'Art de toucher le clavecin: 8 Préludes.* Alessandro POGLIETTI: *Ricercar primi toni.* Nicolas de GRIGNY: *Cromorne en taille à deux parties.* RAMEAU: *Pièces de clavecin.* ANON.: *Daphne; Resonet in laudibus*
(M) **(*) Teldec/Warner 3984 21766-2.

This collection creates a stimulating variety of timbres and textures from the various keyboard instruments which Leonhardt chooses. He first seeks a French association rather than a specific French accent in presenting the Couperin *Offertoire* rather grandly on the Müller organ at the Waalse Kerk (or French church) in Amsterdam, which dates originally from 1680. The instrument has clarity and all the necessary bite in the reeds. He then plays eight *Préludes* from *L'Art de toucher le clavecin* very stylishly and pleasingly on a copy of a Rück harpsichord by an eighteenth-century Dresden maker, C. A. Gräbner, which works equally well.

The solemn *Ricercar* by Alessandro Poglietti, an influential Italian who became organist at the Viennese Imperial Chapel, follows on yet another organ, which it suits admirably. Leonhardt then returns to Amsterdam to find an engaging registration for Nicolas de Grigny's gentle *Cromorne en taille*.

According to the documentation, the same Rück/Gräbner harpsichord is used for the six *Pièces de clavecin* of Rameau as for the Couperin *Préludes*, but the recordings were made two years apart and the Rameau (from 1962) is mono, and is less easy on the ear: brighter, harsher and at times even clattery. But one soon adjusts, and the effect is certainly lively and characterful. The anonymous portrait of *Daphne* has a gentle melancholy, and for this Leonhardt uses a noticeably mellower 1648 Ruckers, a stereo recording of five years later, closing with the divisions on *Resonet in laudibus* played on the deliciously reedy Arp Schnitger organ at Noordbroek, Gronningen. Most entertaining.

RAMEAU: *Pièces de clavecin en concerts: Premier concert; Deuxième concert; Troisième concert;*

Quatrième concert; Cinquième concert (with Frans Brüggen, Wieland and Sigiswald Kuijken) (M) *** Teldec/Warner 3984 21767-2.

These ensemble versions of the *Pièces de clavecin en concerts*, published in 1741, were not pioneered by Leonhardt on LP: there were two previous recordings by Rampal, one on Nonesuch with Robert Veyron-Lacroix and the other on Fontana with Ruggiero Gerlin. But the present (1971) performance trumped its predecessors: it has a surer sense of style and a deeper understanding of the niceties of the period. It is a period-instrument performance, but a thoroughly stimulating and enjoyable one, beautifully recorded.

PURCELL: Anthems, instrumental music and songs (with Leonhardt Consort): Anthems (with James Bowman, Nigel Rogers, Max van Egmond, King's College, Cambridge, Choir, Willcocks): *Rejoice in the Lord alway; Blow up the trumpet in Sion; O God, thou art my God; O God, thou hast cast us out; My heart is inditing; Remember not, Lord, our offences.* Consort music: *Chacony in G min.; Overture in D min.; Pavan in B flat; Overture (with Suite) in G; Pavan in A min.; Fantasia (Chaconne): 3 Parts on a ground in D; Overture in G min.; Pavan of 4 parts in G min.; Sonata in A min.; Ground in D min.* Harpsichord music: *Suite in D; Sefauchi's farewell in D min.; A new ground in E min.* Songs: *Fly swift, ye hours; The Father brave; Return, revolting rebels* (with Max van Egmond, Leonhardt Consort). Consort music: *Fantasia a 4 No. 7* (Brüggen Consort)
❀ (M) *** Teldec/Warner 3984 21768-2 (2).

This Purcell collection is the pick of the bunch and should not be missed. The anthems are all very well sung indeed, with the King's College Choir's penchant for tonal breadth and beauty. Not all of them have instrumental accompaniments, but those that do enjoy a distinctive sound, with period instruments used in such a way that the performances overall happily blend scholarship and vigour, warmth and spontaneity. The recordings were not made at King's College, but in Holland, in 1969, and the acoustic is ideal, not too resonant, so that the effect is uncommonly fresh and clear. The delightful *Blow up the trumpet in Sion* has splendid antiphonal effects which remind one of Purcell's famous directional chorus in *King Arthur*. But the highlight must be *My heart is inditing*, an extended work, also for double chorus, in which the polyphony is a thing of wonder. It is superbly integrated and the choir conclude with a very beautiful performance of the unaccompanied *Remember not, Lord, our offences.*

Leonhardt's excellent Dutch ensemble experiences no difficulty in getting right inside the spirit of Purcell's instrumental music, which they perform with admirable taste and finesse of style. The *Fantasia on a ground*, a brilliant work exploiting the special sound of three violins above a repeated bass

motive, is one of the best recorded versions of this piece, as is that of the famous *Chacony in G minor.* The two *Overtures* are less familiar; while they may not rank, like the *Pavans* and *Sonatas* here, among Purcell's best music, it is good to have them in such neat and sparkling performances, and Leonhardt's intepretations of the harpsichord solos leaves little to be desired. The stereo sound from the late 1960s is warm and lively, and very successfully transferred.

Organ and harpsichord music: Organ: REINCKEN: *An den Wasserflüssen Babylon.* Heinrich SCHEIDEMANN: *Praeambulum in D.* BACH: *Prelude and fugue in D min., BWV 539.* Harpsichord: BOEHM: *Suites Nos. 6 in E flat; 8–9 in F min.* HANDEL: *Suite No. 8 in F min.* J. C. BACH: *Sonata in D, Op. 5/2*
(M) *** Teldec/Warner 3984 21769-2.

Johann Adam Reincken was a famed improviser, and Bach travelled to Hamburg to hear him play. Not surprisingly, his *Chorale fantasia* on *An den Wasserflüssen* is an ingeniously crafted work that projects readily in Leonhardt's fine performance. The following *D minor Prelude and fugue* of Bach might have been moved on a little more swiftly, yet Leonhardt certainly holds the listener's attention at his chosen pace.

He then turns to the harpsichord for the three attractive suites of Georg Böhm (French in form and layout, but German in sensibility) and the splendid work of Handel, and he closes with a remarkably modern-sounding *D major Sonata* of J. C. Bach, with its pair of *Allegro di molto* movements (played with great flair), followed by a closing minuet. Leonhardt uses two different organs and (more importantly) three different harpsichords: two copies and, for the J. C. Bach work, an original instrument made in London in 1775. The basic sound of each is quite different (the Boehm and Handel suites appear to be very good mono recordings), and Leonhardt makes the most of his colouristic opportunities. The balance is close but otherwise the CD transfer produces first-class results. Very stimulating.

Harpsichord and consort music: FRESCOBALDI: *Toccata settima; Toccata undecima in C; Canzona terza; Toccata in G; Fantasia sesta sopra doi soggetti; 5 Galliards.* Francesco TURINI: *Sonata in A.* CACCINI: *Amarilli mia bella.* Biagio MARINI: *Balletto secondo a tre & a quattro.* D. SCARLATTI: *Sonatas in A min., Kk. 3: Presto; in D min., Kk. 52: Andante moderato; in E, Kk. 215: Andante; in E, Kk. 216: Allegro*
(M) *** Teldec/Warner 3984 21770-2.

Another very enjoyable recital, in which Leonhardt uses four different early harpsichords. Frescobaldi's music suits him admirably, for he obviously relishes its improvisational freedom of style and its ability to take the listener by surprise. Alternating an Italian instrument and a sonorous London Kirkman, he plays the *Toccatas* with an entirely appropriate freedom and is equally appealing in the *Canzona*; it is only in the *Fantasia* that he progresses somewhat deliberately. But he finds an appropriately buoyant rhythmic touch for the five brief *Galliards*. Turini's *Trio sonata*, alternately expressive and vigorous, makes a strong contrast, played with elegance and spirit, while the following *Amarilli mia bella* of Caccini has a certain lovelorn air when played so responsively on a fine Ruckers.

The Ensemble returns for Marini's ballet suite, which has a surprisingly grave concluding *Pretirata*. The programme ends with nicely turned performances of four choice keyboard sonatas of Scarlatti, using a characterful instrument made by R. Schütz of Heidelberg. These appear to be more mono recordings (from 1962) but of high quality. The closing work in *E major, Kk. 216*, with its swirling bravura scales, is particularly engaging.

Lipatti, Dinu (piano)

CHOPIN: *Sonata No. 3 in B min., Op. 58.* LISZT: *Années de pèlerinage: Sonetto del Petrarca, No. 104.* RAVEL: *Miroirs: Alborada del gracioso.* BRAHMS: *Waltzes, Op. 39/1, 2, 5, 6, 10, 14 & 15* (with Nadia Boulanger). ENESCU: *Sonata No. 3 in D, Op. 25.*

(M) (***) EMI mono CDH7 63038-2 [id.].

The Chopin is one of the classics of the gramophone, and it is good to have it on CD in this excellent-sounding transfer. The Brahms *Waltzes* are played deliciously with tremendous sparkle and tenderness; they sound every bit as realistic as the post-war records. The Enescu *Sonata* is an accessible piece, with an exuberant first movement and a rather atmospheric *Andantino*, but the sound is not as fresh as the rest of the music on this valuable CD. A must for all with an interest in the piano.

Recital: BACH: *Partita No. 1 in B flat, BWV 825. Chorale preludes: Nun komm, der Heiden Heiland; Ich ruf zu dir, Herr Jesu Christ; Jesu, joy of man's desiring. Flute sonata No. 2 in E flat, BWV 1031: Siciliana* (arr. KEMPFF). D. SCARLATTI: *Sonatas, Kk. 9 & 380.* MOZART: *Sonata No. 8 in A min., K. 310.* SCHUBERT: *Impromptus in E flat; G flat, D.899/2–3.*

(M) (***) EMI mono CDM5 66988-2 [CDM 67003].

No collector should overlook this Lipatti CD. Most of the performances derive from the pianist's last recital in Besançon and have scarcely been out of circulation since their first appearance in the 1950s: the haunting account of the Mozart *A minor Sonata* and the Bach *B flat Partita* have both had more than one incarnation on LP and CD. The Schubert

Impromptus are equally treasurable, and the Scarlatti sonatas have been added for the present reissue in EMI's 'Great Recordings of the Century' series. The remastering is well done; and one notices that, among his other subtleties, Lipatti creates a different timbre for the music of each composer.

Little, Tasmin (violin), Piers Lane (piano)

'Virtuoso violin': KREISLER: *Prelude and allegro in the style of Pugnani; Caprice viennois.* BRAHMS: *Hungarian dances Nos. 1 & 5.* SHOSTAKOVICH: *The Gadfly: Romance.* DRIGO: *Valse bluette.* FIBICH: *Poème.* FALLA: *La vida breve: Spanish dance.* WIENIAWSKI: *Légende, Op. 17.* SARASATE: *Introduction and Tarantelle, Op. 43.* BLOCH: *Baal Shem: Nigun.* DEBUSSY: *Beau soir.* RIMSKY-KORSAKOV: *Flight of the bumblebee* (both arr. heifetz). DELIUS: *Hassan: Serenade* (arr. TERTIS). KROLL: *Banjo and fiddle.* RAVEL: *Tzigane.*

(B) *** CfP Dig. 573 1162 [(M) id. import].

A pretty dazzling display of violin fireworks from a brilliant young fiddler who conveys her delight in her own easy virtuosity The opening Kreisler pastiche, *Prelude and allegro*, is presented with real style, and later the *Caprice viennois* has comparable panache and relaxed charm. The schmaltzy daintiness of Drigo's *Valse bluette* is followed by an unexaggerated but full-timbred warmth in Fibich's *Poème*. The gypsy temperament of the Falla and the ready sparkle of Sarasate's *Tarantelle* and Kroll's *Banjo and fiddle* are offset by the lyrical appeal of the more atmospheric pieces. The violin is very present – perhaps the microphones are a fraction too close, but the balance with the piano is satisfactory and there is not the exaggerated spotlight here which virtually ruins Perlman's comparable 1994 collection with Samuel Sanders called 'Bits and Pieces' (EMI CDC7 54882-2), where immediately in the opening Corelli Op. 5 *La Folia* chaconne, as arranged by Kreisler, the violin-timbre is made to sound aggressive, even harsh.

Lloyd Webber, Julian (cello)

'British cello music' ((i) with John McCabe, piano): (i) RAWSTHORNE: *Sonata for cello and piano.* ARNOLD: *Fantasy for cello.* (i) IRELAND: *The holy boy.* WALTON: *Passacaglia.* BRITTEN: *Tema (Sacher); Cello suite No. 3.*
*** ASV Dig. CDDCA 592 [id.].

A splendid recital and a most valuable one. Julian Lloyd Webber has championed such rarities as the Bridge *Oration* at a time when it was unrecorded and now devotes this present issue to English music that needs strong advocacy; there is no alternative version of the Rawsthorne *Sonata*, in which he is most ably partnered by John McCabe. He gives this piece – and, for that matter, the remainder of the programme – with full-blooded commitment. Good recording.

'British cello music', Vol. 2 (with John McCabe, piano): STANFORD: *Sonata No. 2, Op. 39.* BRIDGE: *Elegy; Scherzetto.* IRELAND: *Sonata in G min.*
⚫ *** ASV CDDCA 807 [id.].

The Stanford *Second Cello sonata* (1893 – written between the *Fourth* and *Fifth Symphonies*) is revealed here as an inspired work whose opening theme flowers into great lyrical warmth on Lloyd Webber's ardent bow. The focus of the recording is a little diffuse, but that serves to add to the atmosphere. Ireland's *Sonata*, too, is among his most richly inspired works, a broad-spanning piece in which ambitious, darkly intense outer movements frame a most beautiful *Poco largamente*. Again Lloyd Webber, who has long been a passionate advocate of the work, conveys its full expressive power. The Bridge *Elegy* (written as early as 1911) is another darkly poignant evocation which points forward to the sparer, more austere style of the later Bridge, and the *Scherzetto* (even earlier, 1902) makes a winning encore: it should ideally have been placed at the end of the recital. John McCabe is a sympathetic partner – in spite of the balance – but this collection offers what are among Lloyd Webber's finest performances on disc.

London Wind Trio

'20th-century miniatures': IBERT: *5 Pièces en trio.* MILHAUD: *Pastorale; Suite d'après Corrette, Op. 161b.* TOMASI: *Concert champêtre.* POULENC: *Sonata for clarinet and bassoon.* VILLA-LOBOS: *Trio.*
*** Somm Dig. SOMMCD 013 [id.].

The personnel of the London Wind Trio consist of Neil Black, Keith Puddy and Roger Birnstingl, who are as adroit individually as they are perfectly matched as a team. They give attractively deft and fresh performances of these finely crafted French works, conveying their enjoyment of the music's melodic felicity. The wit, charm and nostalgia of Ibert's *Cinq Pièces* contrast with Milhaud's *Pastorale* which is more brazenly prolix, yet his *Suite d'après Corrette* has an ingenuous simplicity, while offering a neat condiment of dissonance in its *Menuet*, before the chirping of 'Le coucou'.

No less diverting is the cheeky Poulenc duo *Sonata* with its rueful central 'Nocturne' (*très doux*). Tomasi's rustic *Concert champêtre* is hardly less engaging, with its droll *Nocturne* temporarily interrupting the good humour before the folksy closing 'Vif'. The Villa-Lobos *Trio* is the most

ambitious piece, fascinatingly intricate in its rhythmic and harmonic texture, evoking the exotic, vividly colourful sounds of the Brazilian jungle, with the central *Languissamente* a darker, but still restless, tropical nocturnal. It is played with great character and unforced virtuosity. The well-balanced, natural recording gives these artists a fine presence and altogether this is a most diverting and rewarding recital.

Ma, Yo-Yo (cello), Lynn Chang, Ronan Lefkowitz (violins), Jeffrey Kahane, Gilbert Kalish (pianos)

IVES: *Trio for violin, clarinet and piano.* BERNSTEIN: *Clarinet sonata* (arr. MA). KIRCHNER: *Triptych.* GERSHWIN: *3 Preludes* (arr. HEIFETZ/MA).
*** Sony Dig. SK 53126 [id.].

An unexpectedly rewarding and beguiling mix which is more than the sum of its parts. The whole 65-minute recital is just the thing for late-evening stimulation. The early Bernstein sonata transcription is full of that ready melodic and rhythmic appeal which makes the composer's concert music so individual, and the Gershwin encore, equally felicitously transcribed, is hardly less appealing. The meat of the programme is in the Kirchner *Triptych*, while the jokesy Ives provides a *Trio* (quoting corny 'folk' tunes with relish), bringing the usual audacious 'remembering', this time picturing 'Sunday evening on the campus', thus concluding the entertainment with much spirit and aplomb.

McLachlan, Murray (piano)

Piano music from Scotland: SCOTT: *8 Songs* (trans. Stevenson): *Since all thy vows, false maid; Wha is that at my bower-door?; O were my love yon lilac fare; Wee Willie Gray; Milkwort and bog-cotton; Crowdieknowe; Ay waukin, O; There's news, lasses, news.* CENTER: *Piano sonata; 6 Bagatelles, Op. 3.; Children at play.* STEVENSON: *Beltane bonfire. 2 Scottish ballads: The Dowie Dens O Yarrow; Newhaven fishwife's cry.*
⚫ *** Olympia Dig. OCD 264 [id.].

Francis George Scott (1880–1958) was a prolific and striking composer of songs and Ronald Stevenson's very free transcriptions, somewhat after the fashion of Liszt's concert paraphrases, are imaginatively creative in their own right. Ronald Center's *Piano sonata* is restless and mercurial, lacking much in the way of repose, but the joyous syncopations of the first movement are infectious and the work is a major contribution to the repertory and not in the least difficult to approach. The *Six*

Bagatelles are even more strikingly diverse in mood. *Children at play* is an enchanting piece, with a musical-box miniaturism of texture at times, yet the writing is by no means inconsequential. All this music is played with commitment and considerable bravura by Murray McLachlan, who is clearly a sympathetic exponent, and the recording is extremely vivid and real. Our Rosette is awarded not just for enterprise, but equally from admiration and pleasure.

Malcolm, George (harpsichord)

'The world of the harpsichord': BACH: *Italian concerto, BWV 971; Chromatic fantasia and fugue in D min., BWV 903; French suite No. 5 in G, BWV 816; Toccata in D, BWV 912.* PARADIES: *Toccata.* DAQUIN: *The cuckoo.* RIMSKY-KORSAKOV: *Flight of the bumblebee* (arr. MALCOLM). RAMEAU: *Pièces de clavecin: La Poule; Le rappel des oiseaux; Tambourin.* François COUPERIN: *Pièces de clavecin: Le rossignol-en-amour; Le carillon de Cithère.* TEMPLETON: *Bach goes to town.* MALCOLM: *Bach before the mast.*
✺ (M) *** Decca 444 390-2.

This is a delectable collection, a CD of harpsichord music that should be in even the smallest collection, spanning as it does the full range of the late George Malcolm's wide repertory. His Bach performances are very considerable indeed: the *Chromatic fantasia* has an appropriate improvisatory element, the *Italian concerto* is full of vitality, and the best known of the *French suites* has a genial, lyrical intimacy to offset the buoyant *Toccata in D*. The comparative gravitas of Bach goes well with the charm of Rameau and Couperin, with their descriptive pieces realized with flair, notably *Le rappel des oiseaux* and *Le carillon de Cithère*.

The two witty Bach imitations make a tempting *hors d'oeuvre* and the Rimsky-Korsakov is similarly a fun piece, played with great bravura; but no one should dismiss the mixture, for there is plenty of real substance here and playing of great distinction. The 1960s recording of the harpsichord (unnamed, but almost certainly a modern copy of a fine baroque instrument) is in the demonstration class, beautifully balanced – not too close – and natural within an airy but not over-resonant acoustic.

Marsalis, Wynton (trumpet), Judith Lynn Stillman (piano)

'On the 20th century': RAVEL: *Pièce en forme de Habanera.* HONEGGER: *Intrada.* TOMASI: *Triptyque.* STEVENS: *Sonata.* POULENC: *Eiffel Tower polka* (trans. Stewart). ENESCU: *Légende.*

BERNSTEIN: *Rondo for Lifey.* BOZZA: *Rustiques.* HINDEMITH: *Sonata.*
*** Sony Dig. SK 47193 [id.].

What a wonderful player Wynton Marsalis is! His instrumental profile is so strong and stylish, his basic timbre unforgettably full of character, as at the very opening with the quiet, stately presentation of Ravel's *Pièce en forme de Habanera*. The Enescu *Légende* is hardly less distinctive, while the melodic line of Bozza's *Rustiques*, though not in the Ravel class, yet sounds remarkably special, and the jolly roulades of the finale bring the easy manner of true virtuosity. Yet for fizzing bravura turn to the witty Poulenc polka – like a silent movie speeded up (*Discours du général* from *Les mariés de la Tour Eiffel* – transcribed by Don Stewart for two trumpets in which Wynton takes both parts, with a little electronic help). The Halsey Stevens *Sonata* is a first-class piece, and Marsalis makes the Hindemith, which has an effectively dry slow movement and a *Trauermusik* finale, sound almost like a masterpiece, helped by the fine piano contribution of Judith Stillman. The recording has an uncanny presence and realism: it is as if this superb artist were just out beyond the speakers.

Mayer, Albrecht (oboe), Markus Becker (piano)

Leland COSSART: *Liebesgedicht, Op. 23/4.* Giovanni DAELLI: *Fantasy on themes from Verdi's Rigoletto.* KOECHLIN: *Le repos de tityre – Monodie, Op. 216/10.* NIELSEN: *2 Fantasy pieces, Op. 2.* SCHUMANN: *Abendlied, Op. 107/6; Ihre Stimme, Op. 96/3; Romanzen, Op. 94; Stille tränen, Op. 35/10.* Carlo YVON: *Sonata in F.*
✺ (B) *** EMI Début Dig. CDZ5 73167-2 [id.].

Albrecht Mayer is an artist of exceptional quality and his partnership with Markus Becker the meeting of true minds. Their playing on this EMI Début recital gives enormous pleasure for its subtlety, refinement and musicianship. Their choice of repertoire is unfailingly enterprising and the Schumann and Nielsen are as well played as we have ever heard. Mayer is principal oboe of the Berlin Philharmonic and will obviously be one of the great players of the next decade or so. Excellent recording.

Melos Ensemble

18th- and 19th-century chamber music: MOZART: *Piano and wind quintet in E flat, K.452.* BEETHOVEN: *Piano and wind quintet in E flat, Op. 16; Sextet in E flat for 2 horns, 2 violins, viola & cello, Op. 81b; March for wind sextet in B flat, WoO 29; Rondino in E flat, WoO 25; Duo No. 1 for clarinet and bassoon, WoO 27.* SCHUMANN:

*Fantasiestücke for clarinet and piano, Op. 73.
Märchenerzählungen, Op. 132.* BRAHMS: *Clarinet
quintet in B min., Op. 115.* REGER: *Clarinet
quintet in A:* 2nd movement: *Vivace.*
(B) *** EMI Double fforte CZS5 72643-2 (2) [(M)
id. import].

This collection, like its companion below, dates
from the late 1960s when the Melos Ensemble gathered together some of London's finest orchestral
musicians to make a series of recordings for EMI.
There is plenty of individual personality in the
music-making here, but how beautifully these fine
musicians blend together as a group! The polished
elegance and charm of their playing cannot be heard
to better effect than in the Mozart *Piano and wind
quintet*, dominated by the splendid musicianship of
the pianist, Lamar Crowson, and with some particularly felicitous oboe playing from Peter Graeme. Its
Beethoven successor follows on naturally, played
with a lighter touch than usual to emphasize the
Mozartean influences.

The *Sextet* brings some splendid bravura from
the two horn players, Neil Sanders and James Buck,
while the *March* (for wind alone) is very jolly. The
Duo for clarinet and bassoon is now thought not to
be by Beethoven but is very agreeable nevertheless.
Schumann's rarely heard *Märchenerzählungen*
('Fairy-tales') is late (1853) and is almost unique in
being scored for the same combination as Mozart's
Trio for clarinet, viola (here Gervase de Peyer and
Cecil Aronowitz) and piano. The *Fantasiestücke*,
for clarinet and piano, was written four years earlier.
Both performances are persuasively warm and
mellow, although Lamar Crowson again achieves a
strong backing profile.

For all their lyricism, these artists don't miss
Schumann's marking, '*mit Feuer*', in the finale of
Op. 73, and the second movement of Op. 132 is
strongly accented to make a bold contrast with the
flowingly romantic third, before the similarly bold
finale. Gervase de Peyer then relaxes completely to
present an essentially lyrical view of the Brahms
Clarinet quintet. It is a lovely performance,
achieving a wistful nostalgia in the slow movement,
but it is perhaps in the rippling execution of the
arpeggios of the finale that his playing is particularly
individual. The Reger lollipop Scherzo, which acts
as an encore, may be as light as thistledown, but its
central trio has a beguiling richness of style in
the post-Brahms tradition. All the recordings were
made at Abbey Road, and the sound is excellent
throughout; only in the Beethoven *Sextet* is there a
hint of thinness in the violins. Overall this will give
much refreshment and pleasure.

20th-century chamber music: RAVEL: *Introduction
and allegro for flute, clarinet, harp and string
quartet.* POULENC: *Trio for oboe, bassoon and
piano; Sonata for clarinet and bassoon.*
FRANCAIX: *Divertissement for oboe, clarinet and*
*bassoon; Divertissement for bassoon and string
quintet.* MILHAUD: *Suite for violin, clarinet and
piano.* BARTOK: *Contrasts for violin, clarinet and
piano.* SKALKOTTAS: *Octet; 8 Variations on a
Greek tune.* KHACHATURIAN: *Trio for clarinet,
violin and piano.* PROKOFIEV: *Overture on
Hebrew themes.*
(B) *** EMI Double fforte CZS5 72646-2 (2) [(M)
id. import].

If anything, the Melos survey of twentieth-century
music is even more enjoyable than their classical
programme. It opens with Ravel's sublime *Septet*
(with Richard Adeney, Gervase de Peyer and Osian
Ellis in the lead). The performance is very fine
indeed, and the 1967 Abbey Road recording is that
bit warmer and smoother than their earlier version
for Oiseau-Lyre/Decca, even if that might have a
degree more subtlety (Decca 452 891–2). Both
the Poulenc pieces are delightful, particularly the
delicious *Trio for oboe, bassoon and piano*, which
has an admirably dry wit and unfailing inven-
tiveness; the playing is above reproach. The two
Divertissements of the always elegant Jean Français
have much inconsequential charm, and the *Ouverture* and *Finale* of the irrepressible Milhaud *Suite*
sparkle lustrously, while the inner movements produce an engaging, gentle melancholy. The other
masterpiece here is the Bartók *Contrasts*, for the
same combination as the Milhaud but of altogether
stronger fibre. Both are played superbly. The works
by the neglected Greek composer Nikolaos Skalkottas (a Schoenberg pupil who died not long after
the Second World War) show a fairly strong personality, the *Octet* abrasively neo-classical, and both
pieces revelling in a mordant harmonic dissonance.
The surprise is Khachaturian's remarkably cultivated *Trio*, laced with attractively sinuous
Armenian ideas. Finally comes Prokofiev's *Overture on Hebrew themes*, another highly spontaneous
piece, presented with real style. The recording is
excellent throughout.

Menuhin, Yehudi and Stéphane Grapelli (violins)

'Menuhin and Grapelli play' (with rhythm group;
Alan Clare Trio; Orchestral Ensemble; cond.
Nelson Riddle and Max Harris): GERSHWIN:
*Fascinatin' rhythm; Soon; Summertime; Nice
work if you can get it; Embraceable you; Liza; A
foggy day; 'S wonderful; The man I love; I got
rhythm; He loves and she loves; They can't take
that away from me; They all laughed; Funny face;
Our love is here to stay; Lady be good.*
STRACHEY: *These foolish things.* RASKIN: *Laura.*
HARBURG & DUKE: *April in Paris.* KOSMA,
PREVERT & MERCER: *Autumn leaves.* DUKE:
Autumn in New York. BERLIN: *Cheek to cheek;*

Isn't this a lovely day; Change partners; Top hat, white tie and tails; I've got my love to keep me warm; Heat wave. KERN: *The way you look tonight; Pick yourself up; A fine romance; All the things you are; Why do I love you?* PORTER: *I get a kick out of you; Night and day; Looking at you; Just one of those things.* RODGERS & HART: *My funny Valentine; Thou swell; The lady is a tramp; Blue room.* GADE: *Jealousy.* carmichael: *Skylark.*
(B) *** EMI Double fforte Analogue/Dig. CZS5 73380-2 (2) [id.].

The partnership of Menuhin and Grapelli started in the television studio, many years before Menuhin was ennobled. Their brief duets (tagged on to interviews) were so successful that the idea developed of recording a whole recital (and then several), with each maestro striking sparks off the other in style, but matching the other remarkably closely in matters of tone and balance. One of the secrets of success of this partnership lies in the choice of material. All these items started as first-rate songs, with striking melodies which live in whatever guise, and here with ingenious arrangements (mostly made by Max Harris, but some by Nelson Riddle) which spark off the individual genius of each violinist, acting as a challenge, and inviting the players' obvious enjoyment. The result is delightful, particularly in numbers such as *Pick yourself up* where the arrangement directly tips a wink towards Bachian figuration. The CD transfers are immaculate and the high spirits of the collaboration are caught beautifully.

Miolin, Anders (ten-stringed guitar)

'The Lion and the Lute': WALTON: *5 Bagatelles.* RAWSTHORNE: *Elegy.* Lennox BERKELEY: *Sonatina, Op. 51; Theme and variations, Op. 77.* TIPPETT: *The Blue guitar.* BRITTEN: *Nocturnal, Op. 70.*
*** BIS Dig. CD 926 [id.].

Anders Miolin, born in Stockholm, designs his own guitars, allowing a greater compass and creating a richer palette. That is well borne out here by this unsurpassed collection of British twentieth-century guitar music; indeed, the colour inherent in the five Walton *Bagatelles* has never glowed so brightly, and this comment might also be applied to the whole programme, so attractively recorded in an open acoustic. The Rawsthorne *Elegy* is darkly expressive and both the Tippett and Britten works are highly charged and atmospheric. The Tippett was inspired indirectly by a Picasso painting, which stimulated Wallace Stevens to write a poem called 'The man with the blue guitar'. The Britten night music is a set of seven variations and a passacaglia on Dowland's song *Come heavy sleep.* Both make considerable imaginative as well as technical de-

mands on the player, and they could hardly be more persuasively presented or recorded. If you enjoy guitar music, this is not to be missed.

Moiseiwitsch, Benno (piano)

1938-1950 recordings: MUSSORGSKY: *Pictures at an exhibition.* BEETHOVEN: *Andanti favori, WoO 57; Rondo in C, Op. 51/1.* WEBER: *Sonata No. 1: Presto; Invitation to the dance* (arr. tausig). MENDELSSOHN: *Scherzo in E min., Op. 16.* SCHUMANN: *Romanzen: No. 2, Op. 28/2.* CHOPIN: *Nocturne in E flat, Op. 9/2; Polonaise in B flat, Op. 71/2; Barcarolle, Op. 60.* LISZT: *Liebestraum No. 3; Etude de concert: La leggierezza. Hungarian rhapsody No. 2 in C sharp min. Concert paraphrase of Wagner's Tannhäuser overture.* DEBUSSY: *Pour le piano: Toccata. Suite bergamasque: Clair de lune. Estampes: Jardins sous la pluie.* RAVEL: *Le tombeau de Couperin: Toccata.*
(**(*)) APR mono CDAPR 7005 (2) [id.].

Moiseiwitsch never enjoyed quite the exposure on records to which his gifts entitled him, though in the earlier part of his career he made a great many. Later, in the electrical era, he was a 'plum-label' artist and was not issued on the more prestigious and expensive 'red label'. In this he was in pretty good company, for Solomon and Myra Hess were similarly relegated. This anthology gives a good picture of the great pianist in a wide variety of repertory: his *Pictures at an exhibition*, made in 1945, was for some time the only piano version; and those who identify him solely with the Russians will find his Chopin *Barcarolle* and Debussy *Jardins sous la pluie* totally idiomatic. The transfers are variable – all are made from commercial copies, some in better condition than others.

'Música española' for guitar

'Música española' for guitar, Volume I (played by: William Gómez, Timothy Walker, John Williams, Eduardo Fernández, Carlos Bonell): ANON.: *Romance.* MUDARRA: *Fantasía X.* SOR: *Minuets Nos. 9, 25; Introduction and variations on a theme by Mozart; Gran solo; Sonatas in C min., Op. 15/2; in C, Op. 25; Estudios, Op. 35/16, 17; Op. 6/4, 6, 8; Op. 29/23; Les Adieux, Op. 21; Fantasía elegíaca.* TARREGA: *Recuerdos de la Alhambra; Estudio brillante; 5 Preludes; Minuet; 3 Mazurkas; Lágrima (Andante); La alborada; Introduction and fantasia on themes from La Traviata.* CHAPI: *Serenata morisca.* GRANADOS: *Goyescas: La Maja de Goya; Danzas españolas Nos. 5 (Andaluza); 10 (Melancólica).*
(B) *** Decca Double Dig./Analogue 433 932-2 (2) [id.].

This generous collection centres on a pair of outstanding digital recitals from the highly musical Eduardo Fernández of the music of Sor and Tárrega. Sor gets the lion's share including the two *Sonatas*, Op. 15/2 and Op. 25, 6 *Estudios*, and the *Fantasía elegíaca* (with its remarkable 14-minute *Marcha fúnebre*), which Fernández plays with a characteristic, restrained eloquence. Much of Sor's writing has a melancholy trait. The one-movement *Sonata in C* is thoroughly classical, but the *C minor Sonata* opens darkly and has an appealingly lyrical *Theme and variations* for its finale. The Tárrega pieces include, of course, the famous fluttering *Recuerdos de la Alhambra*, and the diverting *Introducción y fantasia sobre temas de La Traviata*, while John Williams plays Sor's famous *Variations on a theme of Mozart*. The other players who contribute include William Gómez, who opens the programme with the Anonymous but indelible *Jeux interdits*, Carlos Bonell in Granados, and Timothy Walker (who seems to be recorded at a fractionally lower pitch than his colleagues).

'*Música española*' for guitar, Volume II (played by Eduardo Fernández, John Williams, Carlos Bonell, William Gómez, Sergio and Eduardo Abreu, Timothy Walker): ALBENIZ: *Sevilla; Tango; Asturias; Cádiz. Torre bermeja.* VALVERDE: *Clavelitos.* LLOBET: *Scherzo-vals; 6 Canciones catalanas.* FALLA: *Homenaje a Debussy.* TURINA: *Homenaje a Tárrega; Fandanguillo; Ráfaga.* DE LA MAZA: *Habanera.* SEGOVIA: *Oración; Estudio; Neblina; Estudio sinz luz; Divertimento.* TORROBA: *Madroños; Fandanguillo; La danza; Canción y danza No. 1.* RODRIGO: *3 Piezas españolas. Concierto de Aranjuez; Fantasia para un gentilhombre* (both with Montreal SO, Charles Dutoit).
(B) **(*) Decca Double Analogue/Dig. 433 935-2 (2) [id.].

Fernández shares the limelight here with Carlos Bonell, and the other players listed make more modest contributions to what is certainly a well-varied programme (149 minutes). Fernández opens with Albéniz and continues with Llobet's *6 Canciones catalanas*. Bonell makes a vivid entry with Valverde's *Clavelitos* and then after Fernández has returned to play Tórroba's *Sonatina* and Rodrigo's *3 Piezas españolas*, Bonell is joined by Charles Dutoit and the Montreal Orchestra for Rodrigo's two most popular concertante works, splendidly played and recorded; but these are works which many collectors will have already.

Nakariakov, Sergei (trumpet), Alexander Markovich (piano)

'*Trumpet works*': GERSHWIN: *Rhapsody in blue* (arr. DOKSHITSER). ARENSKY: *Concert waltz.*

ARBAN: *Carnival of Venice.* RAVEL: *Pavane pour une infante défunte.* BERNSTEIN: *Rondo for Lifey.* GLAZUNOV: *Albumblatt.* STOLTE: *Burleske.* HARTMANN: *Arbucklenian polka.* FIBICH: *Poème.* RIMSKY-KORSAKOV: *Flight of the bumblebee.* DINICU: *Hora staccato.* GLIÈre: *Valse.* RUEFF: *Sonatina.*
*** Teldec/Warner Dig. 9031 77705-2 [id.].

An astonishing CD début by a brilliant Russian schoolboy virtuoso, barely fifteen at the time. Nakariakov's supreme command of the instrument is matched by instinctive musicality and taste. He manages to sound suitably transatlantic in an incredible full-length arrangement of Gershwin's *Rhapsody in blue*, and is even better in Bernstein's entertainingly ebullient *Rondo for Lifey*. Lovely tone and simplicity of line make Fibich's *Poème* sound appealingly restrained, and in the bandstand variations by Arban and Hartmann the playing is stylishly infectious. Highlights are Stolte's witty *Burleske* and the very considerable *Sonatina* by Jeanine Rueff in which trumpeter and pianist, as elsewhere, make a genuine partnership. But for ear-tickling bravura try Dinicu's *Hora staccato*, which surely would have impressed Heifetz. Excellently balanced and realistic recording.

ARBAN: *Variations on a theme from Bellini's 'Norma'; Variations on a Tyrolean song.* BIZET, arr. WAXMAN: *Carmen fantasy.* BRANDT: *Concert piece No. 2.* FALLA: *Spanish dance.* FAURE: *Le réveil.* PAGANINI: *Caprice, Op. 1/17; Moto perpetuo, Op. 11.* SARASATE: *Zigeunerweisen, Op. 20/1.* SAINT-SAENS: *Le cygne.*
**(*) Teldec/Warner Dig. 4509 94554-2 [id.].

Sergei Nakariakov exhibits some stunning technique in his second Teldec recital, coupling various trifles including Franz Waxman's *Carmen fantasy* and Paganini's *Moto perpetuo*, as well as the remainder of his programme. He was only seventeen when this recording was made and, although not many will want to hear more than a few of these pieces at a time, there is much to enjoy. He is a veritable Russian Håkan Hardenberger, save for the fact that, on the evidence of this disc, he does not always command the latter's extraordinary variety of tonal colour or his impeccable taste.

Navarra, André (cello), Erika Kilcher (piano)

Recital: Sonatas by: LOCATELLI; VALENTINI; BOCCHERINI: *in A & G.* GRANADOS: *Goyescas: Intermezzo.* FALLA: *Suite populaire espagnole* (arr. Maurice MARECHAL). NIN: *Chants d'Espagne: Saeta; Andalousie.*
(M) *** Cal. CAL 6673 [id.].

Navarra's recital dates from 1981 and shows this

fine cellist in top form. He is splendidly partnered by Erika Kilcher, who, although she is backwardly balanced in relation to the up-front cello (recorded somewhat dryly), makes a highly artistic contribution with her sympathetic accompaniments. This is immediately noticeable in the splendid opening sonata of Locatelli.

But it is the four-movement work by Giuseppe Valentini which is the highlight of the Italian repertoire, a most engaging piece with an elegant *Gavotte* and an aria-like *Largo*, framed by two energetic outer movements in which Navarra's spiccato-like articulation of moto perpetuo allegros is most infectious. He is equally at home in the Spanish half of the programme, and Kilcher joins him in providing colourful characterization of the five miniatures which make up the Falla suite. In the second of the two Nin pieces, *Andalousie*, Navarra's cello sounds like a larger-than-life Spanish guitar. However, it is a pity that the documentation does not identify the Italian sonatas more positively.

Nettle and Markham (two-piano duo)

'In England': CARMICHAEL: *Puppet overture.* GRAINGER: *Country gardens; Lisbon; The brisk young sailor; The lost lady found; Handel in the Strand; English waltz.* VAUGHAN WILLIAMS: *Fantasia on Greensleeves.* WALTON: *Façade: Popular song; Tango pasodoble; Old Sir Faulk; Swiss yodelling song; Polka.* NICHOLAS: *Quiet peace No. 1.* DRING: *Fantastic variations on Lilliburlero.* BRIDGE: *Sally in our alley.* COATES: *By the sleepy lagoon.* BLAKE: *Slow ragtime; Folk ballad.* GAY: *Lambeth Walk.* SCOTT: *Lotus Land.* LAMBERT: *3 Pièces nègres: Siesta.* WARLOCK: *Capriol suite: Pavane.* BRITTEN: *Mazurka elegiaca, Op. 23/2.* HOLST: *The Planets: Jupiter.*
(M) *** Carlton 30367 0017-2 [id.].

A recital of mostly brief lollipops lasting nearly 78 minutes might seem too much of a good thing, but Nettle and Markham play with such spirit that the result is almost always diverting. Perhaps they languish a bit in some of the slower pieces, the *Greensleeves fantasia* and Warlock's *Pavane*, for instance; but for the most part the effect is highly spontaneous, and especially so in the Grainger items, which are nicely sprinkled around the programme. *Lisbon, The brisk young sailor* and *The lost lady found*, however, all come together, following neatly after Cyril Scott's *Lotus Land*, to make a winning triptych. The recording is excellent.

New Century Saxophone Quartet

'Main Street USA': GOULD: *Pavane. Main Street waltz; Main Street march.* GERSHWIN:

Promenade; Three quartet blues; Merry Andrew. Porgy and Bess: Clara, Clara; Oh, I got plenty o' nuttin'; Bess, you is my woman now; Oh, I can't sit down; It ain't necessarily so; Summertime; There's a boat dat's leavin' for New York; Oh Lawd, I'm on my way. BERNSTEIN: *West Side story: I feel pretty; Balcony scene; Tonight; Cha-cha/Meeting scene; Jump; One hand, one heart; Gee, officer Krupke; Scherzo; Somewhere.*
*** Channel Classics Dig. CCS 9896 [id.].

Uncommonly fine playing, with superbly blended timbres and a subtly appealing melodic lead from Michael Stephenson on the soprano saxophone, means that this collection of famous show melodies is very appealing. Gould's delightful *Pavane* is presented with a neat degree of whimsy and the three Gershwin instrumental numbers have a pleasing sophistication. Stephenson's line in the songs is quite remarkably vocal in feeling. 'It ain't necessarily so' recalls Fats Waller, and the Balcony scene from *West Side story* is really touching. Steven Kirkman gives admirably restrained support on percussion, when needed, and the balance and recording could hardly be bettered.

Nishizaki, Takako (violin)

'Romantic violin favourites': trans. Fritz Kreisler (with Wolf Harden, piano): SCHUBERT: *Rosamunde: Ballet music.* BIZET: *L'Arlésienne: Adagietto.* RIMSKY-KORSAKOV: *Le coq d'or: Hymn to the sun. Sadko: Hindu song. Scheherazade: Oriental dance.* DVORAK: *Songs my mother taught me.* GLUCK: *Orfeo ed Eurydice: Dance of the Blessed Spirits.* HAYDN: *Piano trio in G: Hungarian rondo. Austrian imperial hymn.* MOZART: *Haffner serenade: Rondo.* SCHUMANN: *Romance, Op. 94.* GRIEG: *Lyric piece: To the spring.* RAMEAU: *Tambourin.* GRAINGER: *Molly on the shore.* TRAD.: *Song of the Volga boatmen; Londonderry air.*
(BB) **(*) Naxos Dig. 8.550125 [id.].

'Violin miniatures' (with Jenö Jandó, piano): KREISLER: *Schön Rosmarin; Rondino; Liebesleid; Liebesfreud; Caprice viennois.* RACHMANINOV: *Rhapsody on a theme by Paganini: Variation No. 18.* FIBICH: *Poème.* ELGAR: *Salut d'amour.* GRANADOS: *Spanish dance: Andaluza, Op. 37/5.* BRAHMS: *Hungarian dance No. 1.* SCHUBERT: *Moment musical in F min.* DVORAK: *Humoresque, Op. 101/7; Slavonic dance No. 1 in G min.* (all trans. Kreisler). BOCCHERINI: *Minuet.* DEBUSSY: *Clair de lune.* MASSENET: *Thaïs: Méditation.* TCHAIKOVSKY: *Chant sans paroles, Op. 2/3; Chanson triste, Op. 40/2.*
(BB) **(*) Naxos Dig. 8.550306 [id.].

Takako Nishizaki is a highly accomplished player who has recorded prolifically on the Marco Polo and Naxos labels. She has recorded Mozart sonatas with Jenö Jandó and a host of rare works, from Respighi's *Concerto gregoriano* to César Cui's *Suite concertante*. She delivers these miniatures with considerable charm and aplomb. Good recording – no one investing in these CDs is likely to be disappointed and, were there not even more virtuosic and authoritative versions in the catalogue, they would warrant an unqualified three stars.

O'Dette, Paul (lute)

'Alla Venetiana': DALZA: *Pavana alla veneziana; Saltarello; Piva I; Piva II; Piva III Ricercar; Calata ala spagnola ditto terzetti; Tastar de corde – Recercar dietro; Pavana alla ferrarese; Saltarello.* ANON. arr. DALZA: *Laudate Dio.* CAPIROLA: *Recercar primo; Recercar secondo; Recercar quinto; Non ti spiaqua l'ascoltar; La vilanela; Padoana belissima; Spagna seconda; Tientalora (Balletto da ballare).* VAN GHIZEGHEM: *De tous bien playne; De tous bien playne nel ton del primo recercar.* CARA: *O mia ciecha, e dura sorte.* PESENTI: *Che farala.* SPINACINO: *Recercare I; Recercare II.* MARTINI: *Malor me bat.* JOSQUIN DESPREZ: *Adieu mes amours; Qui tolis pechata mondi.*
*** HM Dig. HMU 907215 [id.].

The expert lutenist Paul O'Dette seldom disappoints. He draws here mainly on the very first Venetian books of solo lute music to be published, by Francesco Spinacino (1507) and Joan (Zuan) Ambrosio Dalza (1508). Lively dance pieces by the latter, who has a comparatively strong musical personality, are used to frame this varied 73-minute programme. The early repertory comes in three main categories, the improvisatory ricercare, and arrangements of vocal music and dances. O'Dette shows himself a master of the ruminative improvisatory style, but adding some splendid bravura flourishes, as in the first of Spinacino's *Recercare*; and his virtuosity is just as striking in the *Spagna seconda* of Capirola and Dalza's sparkling *Calata ala spagnola* (which must have been a hit in its day).

One of the most touching pieces is Martini's melancholy *Malor me bat*, which is followed by a most extrovert *Piva* by Dalza, and the darker mood then returns with the reflective Anonymous *Laudate Dio*. Capirola's haunting *La vilanela* is matched by the two reflective vocal transcriptions from Josquin Desprez.

This discerningly selected recital is beautifully played and recorded, and admirably documented. A sample page (in colour) from Capirola's richly illuminated Lute Book is upstaged by the frontispiece (taken from a miniature by Philippe de Mazerolles) elegantly picturing a Venetian brothel. A colourfully garbed lutenist is accompanying the less

venial pleasures: the naked men are clearly enjoying themselves, the young ladies are hardly more modest in their apparel, but look more circumspect.

Ogden, Craig (guitar), Alison Stephens (mandolin)

'Music from the novels of Louis de Bernières': VIVALDI: *Concerto in C, RV 425* (arr. BEHREND). HUMMEL: *Mandolin concerto in G: Andante with variations.* GIULIANI: *Grand duo concertante.* PERSICHINI: *Polcha variata.* CALACE: *Amor si culla, Op. 133.* PALUMBO: *Petite bolero.* SAGRERAS: *El Colibri (The humming bird).* LAURO: *4 Venezuelan waltzes.* BARRIOS: *Choro de Saudade; Las Abejas.* LLOBET: *El noi de la mare; El testament d'Amelia; El mestre.* ANON.: *Mis dolencias.* Celedonio ROMERO: *Suite andaluza: Soleares.* TURINA: *Homenaje a Tárrega: Soleares.*
*** Chandos Dig. CHAN 9780 [id.].

Not many gimmicky discs work as well as this. It makes a delightful mixture having the metallic 'plink plonk' of the mandolin set against the rich twanging of the guitar. The author of *Captain Corelli's Mandolin* has helped the two talented young performers here, Craig Ogden and Alison Stephens, in making a wide selection of music from Vivaldi to Villa-Lobos, mainly of works specifically mentioned in de Bernieres' novels – not just *Captain Corelli's Mandolin* but also the Latin trilogy – as well as of related pieces. Starting with Vivaldi's *Mandolin concerto* with the string accompaniment arranged for solo guitar, each of the twenty-three items is a charmer, not least those from unknown composers like Persichini, Calace and Sagreras.

Ogdon, John and Brenda Lucas (pianos)

RACHMANINOV: *Suites for 2 pianos Nos. 1 (Fantasy), Op. 5; 2 in C, Op. 17; Six pieces for piano duet, Op. 11; Polka italienne.* ARENSKY: *Suite for 2 pianos, Op. 15.* KHACHATURIAN: *Sabre dance.* SHOSTAKOVICH: *Concertino, Op. 94.* DEBUSSY: *Petite suite; Fêtes.* BIZET: *Jeux d'enfants.*
(B) **(*) EMI Double fforte CZS5 69386-2 (2).

John Ogdon and Brenda Lucas's readings of the two Rachmaninov *Suites*, not ideally imaginative but enjoyable nevertheless, are aptly coupled with other duet recordings made by them, including the delightful Arensky *Suite* which includes the famous waltz. It is good too to have the long-neglected *Concertino* of Shostakovich and the anything-but-neglected *Sabre dance*, which is rather heavy-going here. However, the Debussy *Petite suite* is very engaging, and most valuable of all is the complete recording of Bizet's *Jeux d'enfants* – all twelve movements. Only the five included by the composer in his orchestral suite are at all well known, and many of the others are equally charming, not least the opening *Rêverie* (*L'Escarpolette*), the Scherzo (*Les chevaux de bois*) and the *Nocturne* (*Colin-Mainard* – 'Blind man's buff'). Fine ensemble and sparkling fingerwork, but just occasionally a touch of rhythmic inflexibility. Good, mid-1970s recording.

Oslo Wind Ensemble

Scandinavian wind quintets: FERNSTROM: *Wind quintet, Op. 59.* KVANDAL: *Wind quintet, Op. 34; 3 Sacred folktunes.* NIELSEN: *Wind quintet, Op. 43.*

(BB) ** Naxos Dig. 8.553050 [id.].

A super-bargain account of the Nielsen *Quintet*, more relaxed in its tempi and measured in approach than the account by the Scandinavian Quintet on Marco Polo. Very decently recorded, too. The Swedish musician John Fernström was a prolific composer whose output runs to twelve symphonies and much else besides. He was for years solely represented in the catalogue by a *Concertino for flute, women's choir and small orchestra*. This *Wind quintet* is not quite so charming, but is well worth hearing – as, for that matter, is the *Wind quintet* by the Norwegian Johan Kvandal, a thoughtful figure who is a composer of imagination and substance.

Paik, Kun Woo (piano)

Recital: LISZT: *Années de pèlerinage: Au bord d'une source; Au lac de Wallenstadt; Les jeux d'eau à la Villa d'Este. Harmonies poétiques et religieuses: Bénédiction de Dieu dans la solitude. Liebestraum No. 3; Mephisto waltz No. 1; Hungarian rhapsody No. 12; Variations on B-A-C-H. French music:* POULENC: *Nocturnes Nos. 1, 5 & 6; Presto; Improvisations Nos. 10, 12 & 15; Intermezzo No. 2; Mouvements perpétuels Nos. 1–3.* DEBUSSY: *Pour le piano; Suite bergamasque: Clair de lune.* SATIE: *Gnossiennes Nos. 4 & 5; Ogives Nos. 1–2; Descriptions automatique: Sur un vaisseaux; Sur un casque. Chapitre tourné en tous sens: Celui qui parle trop. Croquis et agaceries d'un gros bonhomme en bois: Españaña. Embryons desséchés: D'Edriophtalma; De Podophtalma. Gymnopédies Nos. 1–3.*

(BB) *** Virgin Classics 2 x 1 Dig. VBD5 61757-2 (2) [CDVB 61257].

This Virgin 2 x 1 reissue pairs two outstanding individual recitals, a distinguished Liszt collection discussed under the composer, and the present

grouping of French repertoire, which is slightly more idiosyncratic, even including individual movements from suites of miniatures meant to be played as a group. However, the mixture works well when the playing is consistently magnetic. There is much to relish, notably Poulenc's *Mouvements perpétuels* and indeed other pieces by this composer. Kun Woo Paik's withdrawn performance of *Clair de lune* is a little indulgent and the *Gnossiennes* also find him a shade mannered, while the *Gymnopédies* are very languorous. But the outer movements of Debussy's *Pour le piano* bring some electrifying bravura and his imagination is given full rein in the quirkier Satie miniatures. There is 154 minutes of music here, and even if the back-up documentation is fairly sparse, the value is obvious, for the recording is excellent.

Parker-Smith, Jane (organ)

'Popular French romantics' (organ of Coventry Cathedral): WIDOR: *Symphony No. 1: Marche pontificale. Symphony No. 9 (Gothique), Op. 70: Andante sostenuto.* GUILMANT: *Sonata No. 5 in C min., Op. 80: Scherzo.* GIGOUT: *Toccata in B min.* BONNET: *Elfes, Op. 7.* LEFEBURE-WELY: *Sortie in B flat.* VIERNE: *Pièces de fantaisie: Clair de lune, Op. 53/5; Carillon de Westminster, Op. 54/6.*

*** ASV Dig. CDDCA 539 [id.].

The modern organ in Coventry Cathedral adds a nice bite to Jane Parker-Smith's very pontifical performance of the opening Widor *March* and creates a blaze of splendour at the close of the famous Vierne *Carillon de Westminster*, the finest performance on record. The detail of the fast, nimble articulation in the engagingly Mendelssohnian *Elfes* of Joseph Bonnet is not clouded; yet here, as in the splendid Guilmant *Scherzo* with its wider dynamic range, there is also a nice atmospheric effect. Overall, a most entertaining recital.

'Popular French Romantics', Vol. 2 (organ of Beauvais Cathedral): FRANCK: *Prélude, fugue et variation, Op. 18.* GUILMANT: *Grand choeur in D* (after Handel). MULET: *Carillon-Sortie.* RENAUD: *Toccata in D min.* SAINT-SAENS: *Prelude and fugue.* VIERNE: *Symphony No. 1: Finale. Stèle pour un enfant défunt.* WIDOR: *Symphony No. 4: Andante and Scherzo.*

*** ASV Dig. CDDCA 610 [id.].

With his *Prelude and fugue*, Saint-Saëns is in more serious mood than usual but showing characteristic facility in fugal construction; Widor is first mellow and then quixotic – his *Scherzo* demands the lightest articulation and receives it. High drama and great bravura are provided by the Vierne *Finale* and later by Albert Renaud's *Toccata* and Henri Mulet's *Carillon-Sortie*, while Franck's *Prélude, fugue et variation* and the poignant Vierne *Stèle pour un enfant défunt* bring attractive lyrical contrast: here Jane Parker-Smith's registration shows particular subtlety. The organ is splendidly recorded.

Perahia, Murray (piano)

25th Anniversary Edition: Domenico SCARLATTI: *Sonatas in B min., Kk. 27; A, Kk. 212.* MOZART: *6 German dances, K.509; Adagio, K.540. Piano concerto No. 27 in B flat, K.595* (with coe). SCHUBERT: *Impromptu in A flat, D.899/4.* SCHUMANN: *Papillons, Op. 2.* CHOPIN: *Ballade No. 1 in G min., Op. 23. Piano concerto No. 2 in F min., Op. 21* (with Israel PO, Zubin Mehta). LISZT: *Gnomenreigen.* RACHMANINOV: *Etudes-tableaux: Nos. 5 in E flat; 6 in A min., Op. 39/5–6.* BARTOK: *Suite, Op. 14; Improvisations on Hungarian peasant songs, Op. 20; Out of doors suite.* BERG: *Sonata, Op. 1.* TIPPETT: *Sonata No. 1.* BEETHOVEN: *Piano and wind quintet in E flat, Op. 16* (with members of ECO). SCHUMANN: *5 Lieder, Op. 40.* BRAHMS: *Piano quartet No. 1 in G min., Op. 25* (with members of Amadeus Qt).
(M) *** Sony Dig./Analogue SX4K 63380 (4) [id.].

This 1997 anthology effectively celebrates Murray Perahia's fiftieth birthday and his 25-year recording association with CBS/Sony. Opening delightfully with two Scarlatti sonatas, the variety of music here readily confirms Perahia's pianistic and artistic mastery over the widest musical range, with the Berg *Sonata* (attractively lyrical) and the Tippett (with its haunting *Andante tranquillo*) new to the catalogue. The recordings are technically a little variable but always good, often excellent, notably those made at the Maltings: the Mozart solo works, Liszt and Rachmaninov and the Beethoven *Piano and wind quintet*. The inclusion of the latter makes one wish that its Mozartean predecessor had also been featured, for that omission highlights the problem for many collectors: that, attractive as this mid-priced compilation is, it cuts across other issues which admirers of this great pianist may already possess.

Petri, Michala (recorder or flute)

'Recorder favourites' (with Hanne Petri, harpsichord, David Petri, cello): ANON.: *Greensleeves to a grounde; Divisions on an Italian ground.* Jacob VAN EYCK: *Prins Robberts Masco; Philis Schoon Herderinne; Wat Zal Men op den Avond Doen; Engels Nachtegaeltje.* CORELLI: *Sonata, Op. 15/5: La Follia.* HANDEL: *Andante.* LECLAIR: *Tambourin.* F. COUPERIN: *Le rossignol vainqueur; Le rossignol en amour.* J. S. BACH: *Siciliano.* TELEMANN: *Rondino.* GOSSEC: *Tambourin.* PAGANINI: *Moto perpetuo, Op. 11.*

BRUGGEN: *2 Studies.* CHRISTIANSEN: *Satie auf hoher See.* HENRIQUES: *Dance of the midges.* SCHUBERT: *The Bee.* MONTI: *Czárdás.* HERBERLE: *Rondo presto.* RIMSKY-KORSAKOV: *Flight of the bumblebee.*
(B) *** Ph. Virtuoso Dig. 420 897-2 [id.].

Marvellously nimble playing from Michala Petri, and 71 minutes, digitally recorded at bargain price, so one can afford to pick and choose. Some of the music opening the recital is less than distinctive, but the Couperin transcriptions are a delight and Paganini's *Moto perpetuo* vies with Henriques' *Dance of the midges* for sparkling bravura. There are some attractively familiar melodies by Bach and Handel, among others, to provide contrast, and Henning Christiansen's *Satie auf hoher See* is an unexpected treat. Monti's *Czárdás* ends the programme infectiously.

Petri, Michala (recorder), George Malcolm (harpsichord)

'Recorder sonatas': VIVALDI: *Il Pastor fido: Sonata No. 6 in G min., RV 58.* CORELLI: *Sonata in C, Op. 5/9.* D. BIGAGLIA: *Sonata in A min.* BONONCINI: *Divertimento da camera No. 6 in C min.* SAMMARTINI: *Sonata in G, Op. 13/4.* B. MARCELLO: *Sonata in F, Op. 2/1.*
*** Ph. (IMS) Dig. 412 632-2 [id.].

Six recorder sonatas in a row might seem too much of a good thing, but the playing is so felicitous and the music has such charm that the collection is immensely enjoyable even taken complete, and if sensibly dipped into is a source of much delight. There are many individual highlights. The Corelli *Sonata* has a memorable *Tempo di gavotta* as its finale which reminds one a little of Handel's *Harmonious blacksmith*; the work in A minor by the composer with the unlikely name of Diogenio Bigaglia (c. 1676–c. 1745) is a winner, with a nimble Minuet and sparkling finale.

Bononcini's *Divertimento da camera* alternates slow and fast sections, and in the third-movement *Largo* George Malcolm makes the delicate accompaniment sound like a harp. Sammartini's *Sonata* is enchanting, with its opening *Andante* in siciliano form and three more delectable movements to follow. Throughout, Michala Petri's playing is wonderfully fresh: she has made many records for Philips, but none more enticing than this. George Malcolm proves an equally imaginative partner, and both artists embellish with admirable flair and taste, never overdoing it. The Philips recording is quite perfectly balanced and wonderfully tangible.

Peyer, Gervase de (clarinet), Gwenneth Pryor (piano)

French music for clarinet and piano:
SAINT-SAENS: *Sonata, Op. 167.* DEBUSSY: *Première rhapsodie; Arabesque No. 2; Prélude: La fille aux cheveux de lin.* POULENC: *Sonata.* SCHMIDT: *Andantino, Op. 30/1.* RAVEL: *Pièce en forme de habanera.* PIERNE: *Canzonetta, Op. 19.*
🌑 *** Chandos Dig. CHAN 8526.

A gorgeous record. The Saint-Saëns *Sonata* is an attractively crafted piece, full of engaging invention. Poulenc's *Sonata* is characteristically witty, with contrast in its lovely central *Romanza* (*très calme*); and the other short pieces wind down the closing mood of the recital, with De Peyer's luscious timbre drawing a charming portrait of *The girl with the flaxen hair* before the nimbly tripping closing encore of Pierné. This is a quite perfect record of its kind, the programme like that of a live recital and played with comparable spontaneity. The recording is absolutely realistic; the balance could hardly be improved on.

Pinnock, Trevor (harpsichord or virginals)

'At the Victoria and Albert Museum': ANON.: *My Lady Wynkfylds rownde.* BYRD: *The Queens alman; The Bells.* HANDEL: *Harpsichord suite No. 5 in E.* CROFT: *Suite No. 3 in C min.* ARNE: *Sonata No. 3 in G.* J. C. BACH: *Sonata in C min., Op. 5/6.*
(M) *** CRD CRD 3307 [id.].

Trevor Pinnock recorded for CRD before he moved over to the DG Archiv label and this was his first solo recital, made at the Victoria and Albert Museum using virginals and other period harpsichords. He opens with three very colourful pieces played on an instrument originally belonging to Queen Elizabeth I, who was an accomplished virginal player. It is in splendid condition and has a most attractive sound. Pinnock plays it with enthusiasm and his performance of Byrd's extraordinarily descriptive *The Bells* is a *tour de force*. For the rest of the recital he uses two different harpsichords. His style in the works of Handel, Croft, Arne and J. C. Bach is less flamboyant, more circumspect, but the music is strongly characterized and boldly recorded. The Handel suite is the one which has the *Harmonious blacksmith* as its finale, which is played with considerable flair.

Pletnev, Mikhail (playing Rachmaninov's piano)

'Hommage à Rachmaninov': RACHMANINOV: *Variations on a theme of Corelli, Op. 42; 4 Etudes-tableaux, Op. 39/5; Opp. 44/6, 8–9.* BEETHOVEN: *Piano sonata No. 26 (Les Adieux), Op. 81a.* MENDELSSOHN: *Andante cantabile & Presto agitato; Andante & Rondo capriccioso, Op. 14.* CHOPIN: *Andante spianato et Grande polonaise brillant, Op. 22.*
🌑 *** DG Dig. 459 634-2 [id.].

Way back in 1982, when Pletnev was in his early twenties, Dr Mark Zilberquist (in *Russia's Great Modern Pianists*, New York) noted the young pianist's affinities with his aristocratic and patrician compatriot, Rachmaninov: 'discreet, reserved, outwardly restrained in showing emotion'. Pletnev certainly has something of the same commanding keyboard authority, the extraordinary range of colour and clarity of articulation of Rachmaninov. This recital is recorded at Rachmaninov's own summer home, the Villa Senar on the Vierwaldstätter See, near Lake Lucerne, using the composer's newly restored American Steinway. The playing is breathtaking, worthy of the composer at his best, and dazzling but never ostentatious. The delicacy of the Mendelssohn and the introductory *Andante cantabile* to the Chopin is magical. A quite exceptional recital even by the standards of this exceptional pianist.

Pollini, Maurizio (piano)

STRAVINSKY: *3 movements from Petrushka.* PROKOFIEV: *Piano sonata No. 7 in B flat, Op. 83.* WEBERN: *Variations for piano, Op. 27.* BOULEZ: *Piano sonata No. 2.*
(M) *** DG 447 431-2 [id.].

The Prokofiev is a great performance, one of the finest ever committed to disc; and the Stravinsky *Petrushka* is electrifying. Not all those responding to this music will do so quite so readily to the Boulez, fine though the playing is; but the Webern also makes a very strong impression. This is the equivalent of two LPs and is outstanding value. It is a natural candidate for reissue in DG's set of 'Originals' of legendary performances.

Preston, Simon (organ)

'The world of the organ' (organ of Westminster Abbey): WIDOR: *Symphony No. 5: Toccata.* BACH: *Chorale prelude, Wachet auf, BWV 645.* MOZART: *Fantasia in F min., K.608.* WALTON: *Crown imperial* (arr. MURRILL). CLARKE: *Prince of Denmark's march* (arr. PRESTON). HANDEL: *Saul:*

Dead march. PURCELL: *Trumpet tune* (arr. TREVOR). elgar: *Imperial march* (arr. MARTIN). VIERNE: *Symphony No. 1: Finale.* WAGNER: *Tannhäuser: Pilgrims' chorus.* GUILMANT: *March on a theme of Handel.* SCHUMANN: *Study No. 5* (arr. WEST). KARG-ELERT: *Marche triomphale (Now thank we all our God).*
(M) *** Decca 430 091-2.

A splendid compilation from the Argo catalogue of the early to mid-1960s, spectacularly recorded, which offers 69 minutes of music and is in every sense a resounding success. Simon Preston's account of the Widor *Toccata* is second to none, and both the Vierne *Finale* and the Karg-Elert *Marche triomphale* lend themselves admirably to Preston's unashamed flamboyance and the tonal splendour afforded by the Westminster acoustics. Walton's *Crown imperial,* too, brings a panoply of sound which compares very favourably with an orchestral recording. The organ has a splendid trumpet stop which makes both the Purcell piece and Clarke's *Prince of Denmark's march,* better known as the 'Trumpet voluntary', sound crisply regal.

Prometheus Ensemble

'French impressions': RAVEL: *Introduction & allegro for harp, flute, clarinet and string quartet.* DEBUSSY: *Danses sacrée et profane; Sonata for flute, viola and harp.* ROUSSEL: *Serenade.*
*** ASV Dig. CDDCA 664 [id.].

This young group gives eminently well-prepared and thoughtful accounts of all these pieces. The *Danses sacrée et profane* sound particularly atmospheric and the Debussy *Sonata* is played with great feeling and sounds appropriately ethereal. The Roussel, too, is done with great style and, even if the *Introduction and allegro* does not supersede the celebrated Melos account (Decca 452 891–2), the Prometheus do it well.

Purcell Quartet, Purcell Band, with Robert Woolley (harpsichord)

'La Folia (variations on a theme)': CORELLI: *Violin sonata in D min., Op. 5/12.* MARAIS: *Les folies d'Espagne.* VIVALDI: *Trio sonata in D min. (Variations on La Folia), Op. 1/12 (RV 63)* (Purcell Quartet). GEMINIANI: *Concerto grosso (La Folia) (after Corelli)* (Purcell Quartet & Purcell Band). Alessandro SCARLATTI: *Toccata No. 7 (Primo tono): Folia.* C. P. E. BACH: *12 Variations on Folies d'Espagne, Wq.118/9 (H.263)* (Robert Wooley).
*** Hyperion Dig. CDA 67035 [id.].

Just as the chanson *L'homme armé* was popular among composers as a basis for mass settings in the

fifteenth and early sixteenth centuries, so at the very end of the seventeenth and throughout the eighteenth, *La Folia* was in constant use for instrumental variations. The word '*folia*' is Portuguese in origin and means 'empty-headed', but also refers to a dance in triple time, which originated around the same time as that famous chanson. It changed its rhythmic accents over the years and the special character of the format we now recognize seems to have first come into use by Lully for an oboe tune around 1672.

Corelli probably appropriated it from Lully in 1700, resourcefully turning the piece into a chaconne, but Marais probably beat him to it: even though his *Folies d'Espagne* was not published until 1701, it was probably written some years earlier. Thereafter composers seemed to almost fall over each other to put it to good use in their instrumental music. The above six listings are excellent examples, among which Vivaldi's highly entertaining *Trio sonata* stands out alongside Carl Philipp Emanuel Bach's superb set of variations for the keyboard, which ought to be much better known. But all the versions here are stimulating, and played with fine, expressive vitality. The recording too is excellent. This is not a recital to play continuously, but dipped into a version at a time it will give much pleasure.

Puyana, Rafael (harpsichord)

'The Golden Age of harpsichord music': ANON.: *My Lady Carey's Dompe.* BULL: *Les Buffons; The King's hunt.* PEERSON: *The Primerose; The fall of the leafe.* BYRD: *La Volta.* PHILIPS: *Pavana dolorosa; Galliard dolorosa.* BESARD: *Branle gay.* Louis COUPERIN: *Tombeau de M. de Blancrocher; Pavane.* Antoine FRANCISQUE: *Branle de Montiradé.* BACH: *Keyboard concerto in D min., after Marcello.* FREIXANET: *Sonata in A.* Mateo ALBENIZ: *Sonata in D.* CHAMBONNIERES: *Le Moutier* (after Louis Couperin). RAMEAU: *Gavotte et Doubles.* DIEUPART: *Passepied.* François COUPERIN: *La Pantomime.*
⊛ (M) *** [Mercury 434 364-2].

If you think you don't enjoy listening to the harpsichord, Rafael Puyana, who was a pupil of Landowska, will surely persuade you otherwise in this remarkably diverse, 75-minute recital, for he is a supreme master of his instrument. He plays a large, modern, double-keyboard Pleyel harpsichord (replicating one of Landowska's own instruments). In his bravura hands it produces an astonishingly wide range of dynamic, colour and sonority, no better demonstrated than in the *Gavotte et Doubles* of Rameau, which is a continuously inventive set of variations, running on for about ten minutes. Puyana effectively uses every possible device to divert his listeners, to say nothing of demonstrating his own dexterity, which he does again more simply in the engagingly brief *Passepied* of Charles Dieupart (who died in 1740). Martin Peerson's modest variations on a popular song of the period, *The Primerose*, and his more dolorous evocation of *The fall of the leafe* both feature the highly effective dynamic contrasts which this instrument can provide.

The programme opens with the piquant *My Lady Carey's Dompe*, a lollipop if ever there was one, presented with great panache. John Bull's divisions on *Les Buffons* and *The King's hunt* have never sounded more vital, while Puyana's account of the charming *La Volta* of William Byrd makes one appreciate why it was reputedly a favourite dance of Queen Elizabeth I. Perhaps Puyana goes over the top a bit in his robust presentation of the pieces by Peter Philips, and he plays Bach's *Concerto in D minor* (supposedly after Alessandro Marcello, but sounding more like Vivaldi) in such a robust manner that it is almost if he were sitting at the keyboard of an organ. But the crisply articulated *Sonata* of Freixanet is very effective indeed, and the *Sonata* of Mateo Albéniz is a *tour de force*.

The instrument's resonant lower octave is really made to tell in Louis Couperin's *Tombeau*; while the elegant *Le Moutier* of Jacques Champion de Chambonnières brings a nice sonic contrast on three different levels, within a time period of just over two minutes. The Mercury recording is real and vivid, but please don't set the volume level too high. This is one of two harpsichord compilations that deserve a place in every collection: the other is George Malcolm's Decca anthology 'The world of the harpsichord', utterly different but equally rewarding – see above. Alas, the Puyana disc has now been withdrawn in the UK.

Rév, Lívia (piano)

'For children': BACH: *Preludes in E, BWV 939; in G min., BWV 930.* DAQUIN: *Le coucou.* MOZART: *Variations on Ah vous dirai-je maman, K.265.* BEETHOVEN: *Für Elise.* SCHUMANN: *Album for the young, Op. 63:* excerpts, CHOPIN: *Nocturne in C min., Op. posth.* LISZT: *Etudes, G. 136/1 & 2.* BIZET: *Jeux d'enfants: La Toupie.* FAURE: *Dolly: Berceuse.* TCHAIKOVSKY: *Album for the young, Op. 39: Maman; Waltz.* VILLA-LOBOS: *Prole do bebê:* excerpts. JOLIVET: *Chansons naïve 1 & 2.* PROKOFIEV: *Waltz, Op. 65.* BARTOK: *Evening in the country; For Children:* excerpts. DEBUSSY: *Children's corner:* EXCERPTS MAGIN: *3 Pieces.* MATACIC: *Miniature variations.*
*** Hyperion CDA 66185.

A wholly delectable recital, and not just for children either. The whole is more than the sum of its many parts, and the layout provides excellent variety, with the programme stimulating in mixing familiar with

unfamiliar. The recording is first class. Highly recommended for late-evening listening.

Reykjavik Wind Quintet

Jean-Michel DAMASE: *17 Variations.* DEBUSSY (arr. bozza): *Le petit nègre.* FAURE (arr. WILLIAMS): *Dolly suite: Berceuse, Op. 56/1.* FRANCAIX: *Quintet No. 1.* IBERT: *3 Pièces brèves.* MILHAUD: *La Cheminée du Roi René, Op. 205.* PIERNE: *Pastorale, Op. 14/1.* POULENC (arr. EMERSON): *Novelette No. 1.*
*** Chandos Dig. CHAN 9362 [id.].

A delightful recital for late-night listening. Elegant, crisp playing from this accomplished Icelandic ensemble. The Damase *Variations* are delightful, as indeed are the Françaix and Milhaud pieces, and the Chandos recording is in the best traditions of the house.

Ricci, Ruggiero (violin), Louis Persinger or Ernest Lush (piano)

PAGANINI: *Witches dance, Op. 8; Fantasia on the G string after Rossini's Mosè in Egitto; Moto perpetuo in C; Variations on 'Nel cor più mi sento' from Paisiello's La Molinara; Variations on God Save the Queen; La Campanella (from Violin concerto No. 2); Sonata No. 12 in E min, Op. 3/6; I Palpiti: Variations after Rossini's Tancredi* (arr. KREISLER). WIENIAWSKI: *Scherzo-Tarentelle in G min.* ELGAR: *La capricieuse.* VECSEY: *Caprice No. 1 (Le vent).* KROLL: *Banjo and fiddle.* CHOPIN: *Nocturne No. 20 in C sharp min.* (arr Milstein). SMETANA: *Má Vlast: Andantino.* SARASATE: *8 Spanish dances; Caprice basque; Introduction et Tarentelle; Zigeunerweisen; Jóta Aragonesa.* SUK: *Burleska.* ACHRON: *Hebrew Melody.* HUBAY: *The Zephyr.* MOSZKOWSKI: *Guitarre.* BAZZINI: *La Ronde des lutins: scherzo fantastique.*
(B) *** Australian Decca Double Mono/Stereo 458 191-2 (2).

Ricci gives us a dazzling display of violin pyrotechnics in all these pieces much prized by violinists, from Heifetz downwards – music to show off the virtuoso possibilities (and improbabilities) of the instrument, and this they surely do. Ricci uses every trick in the book to make one gasp at the sheer technical brilliance – try the final Bazzini number first, and then the music of Sarasate in which he was a specialist. The mono sound is naturally a little thin, but has transferred very well to CD, and half the programme is in excellent stereo. As much of this repertoire is rare in the concert hall these days, this collection is especially valuable, and this is the first time, thanks to Australian Decca, that it has appeared on CD, and it is shortly to appear as a Decca Double in the UK. Thoroughly recommended.

Richter, Sviatoslav (piano)

BEETHOVEN: *Piano sonatas Nos. 3 in C, Op. 2/3; 4 in E flat, Op. 7; 27 in E min., Op. 90.*
**(*) Olympia OCD 336 [id.].

SCHUBERT: *Piano sonatas Nos. 19 in C min., D.958; 21 in B flat, D.960.*
**(*) Olympia Dig. OCD 335 [id.].

RACHMANINOV: *Etudes-tableaux, Opp. 33 & 39; 6 Preludes, Op. 23/1–2, 4–5, 7–8; 7 Preludes, Op. 32/1–2, 6–7, 9–10, 12.*
**(*) Olympia Dig./Analogue OCD 337 [id.].

Sonically these recordings leave a good deal to be desired: in most instances the balance is fairly close and the acoustic on the dry side, without being unacceptably so. They call for tolerance, but this is well worth extending for the sake of this music-making. The early Beethoven sonatas are from 1975 and the *E minor*, Op. 90 comes from 1971. The *C major Sonata*, Op. 2, No. 3 is far more powerful than one is used to encountering, particularly in the intensity of the slow movement; Richter's view of the *E flat*, Op. 7, familiar from an earlier recording Philips issued in the 1960s, is further deepened. There is a marvellously inward feeling and a sense of profound euphony in the *E minor*, Op. 90.

The Schubert sonatas were recorded in the early 1970s; the *C minor Sonata*, D.958 in 1973, the *B flat*, D.960 in the previous year; neither has been in currency in the UK. Richter's way with Schubert is well known. Some listeners have difficulty in coming to terms with the sheer scale of his first movement: it seems almost timeless, just as the almost static inwardness of the slow movement is not for those in a hurry.

Some of the Rachmaninov *Etudes-tableaux* have been available before, but again most are new to this country. The majority of the pieces were recorded in 1971 but others are later. The playing is of a rare order of mastery and leaves strong and powerful resonances. Richter's conception goes far beyond the abundant virtuosity this music calls for, and the characterization of the music is strong and searching. If you invest in no other of these Olympia CDs, this is the one that is unique – which makes the poor sound-quality particularly regrettable.

'The Philips Richter Authorized Edition'

BACH: *Concerto in the Italian style, BWV 971; 4 Duets, BWV 802–5; English suites Nos. 3 in G min., BWV 808; 4 in F, BWV 809; 6 in D min., BWV 811; Fantasy in C min., BWV 906; French suites Nos. 2 in C min., BWV 813; 4 in E flat,*

BWV 815a; 6 in E, BWV 817; Overture (Partita) in the French style, BWV 831; Toccatas in D min., BWV 913; in G, BWV 916.
**(*) Ph. (IMS) 438 613-2 (3) [id.].

BEETHOVEN: *Piano sonatas Nos. 19 in G min.; 20 in G, Op. 49/1–2; 22 in F, Op. 54; 23 in F min. (Appassionata), Op. 57; 30 in E, Op. 109; 31 in A flat, Op. 110; 32 in C min., Op. 111.*
**(*) Ph. (IMS) Dig. 438 486-2 (2) [id.].

BEETHOVEN (with (i) Moraguès Qt; (ii) members of the Borodin Qt): (i) *Piano quintet in E flat, Op. 16;* (ii) *Piano trio in B flat, Op. 97. Rondos in C; in G, Op. 51/1–2; Piano sonatas Nos. 18 in E flat, Op. 31/3; 28 in A, Op. 101.*
**(*) Ph. (IMS) Dig. 438 624-2 (2) [id.].

BRAHMS: *Ballade in G min., Op. 118/3; Capriccio in C, Op. 76/8; Intermezzo in E min., Op. 116/5; Rhapsody in E flat, Op. 119/4; Piano sonatas Nos. 1 in C, Op. 1; 2 in F sharp min., Op. 2; Variations on a theme by Paganini, Op. 35.* SCHUMANN: *Blumenstück, Op. 19; 3 Concert Etudes on Caprices by Paganini, Op. 10/4–6; Fantasy in C, Op. 17; March in G min., Op. 76/2; 4 Nachtstücke, Op. 23; Novelette in F, Op. 21/1.*
**(*) Ph. (IMS) Dig. 438 477-2 (3) [id.].

SCHUBERT: *Piano sonatas Nos. 9 in B, D.575; 15 in C (Relique), D.840; 18 in G, D.894.*
*** Ph. (IMS) 438 483-2 (2) [id.].

CHOPIN: *Barcarolle in F sharp, Op. 60; Etudes, Op. 10/1–5, 10–12; Etudes, Op. 25/5–8, 11–12; Nocturne in F, Op. 15/1; Polonaises in C sharp min., Op. 26/1; in C min., Op. 40/2; Polonaise-fantaisie in A flat, Op. 61; Preludes, Op. 28/6–11, 17, 19, 23–24.* LISZT: *Consolation No. 6; Etudes d'exécution transcendante, Nos. 1– 3, 5, 7–8, 10–11; Etudes de concert: 'Un sospiro'; 'Gnomenreigen'; Hungarian rhapsody No. 17; Klavierstück in F sharp; Mephisto-Polka; Polonaise No. 2 in E; Piano sonata in B min.; Scherzo in G min.; Trübe Wolken.*
**(*) Ph. (IMS) Dig. 438 620-2 (3) [id.].

SCRIABIN: *2 Dances: 'Guirlandes'; 'Flammes sombres', Op. 73; Fantaisie in B min., Op. 28; Poème-Nocturne; Vers la flamme, Op. 72.*

PROKOFIEV: *Cinderella: excerpts, Op. 87; Danza and waltz, Op. 32/1 & 4; Légende, Op. 26/6; Piano sonatas Nos. 4 in C min., Op. 29; 6 in A, Op. 82; Visions fugitives, Op. 22/3–6, 8–9, 11, 14–15; 18.* SHOSTAKOVICH: *Preludes and fugues, Op. 87/4, 12, 14–15, 17, 23.*
*** Ph. (IMS) 438 627-2 (2) [id.].

Unusually for Philips, the documentation concerning the date and provenance of these records is meagre or non-existent. So, although many of the recordings appear to be digital, the quality of the sound is extremely variable. But, generally speaking, these are self-recommending performances which admirers of this pianist will want to have anyway. In Beethoven, Richter's voice is uniquely authoritative, in Schubert his profoundly spacious readings, recorded live, have extraordinary concentration.

The indispensable compilation of Prokofiev, Scriabin and Shostakovich is a combination of studio recordings and live recitals. The Liszt playing is little short of inspired, especially the *Sonata*, but the recordings are again confined. The Schumann performances, too, inhabit an area of repertoire in which Richter has something very special to say, and the playing triumphs over any sonic limitations; the Brahms sonatas, on the other hand, are made to sound hard at higher dynamic levels. All the Bach performances, aristocratic and masterly, were recorded live, and these superbly controlled interpretations, unashamedly pianistic, are often surprisingly generous with repeats.

'Sviatoslav Richter in the 1950s', Volume 1:
PROKOFIEV: *Cinderella: 5 Pieces; Visions fugitives, Op. 22:* excerpts; *Piano sonata No. 7 in B flat, Op. 83.* SCHUMANN: *Toccata in C, Op. 7.* DEBUSSY: *Images, Book II: Cloches à travers les feuilles* (2 performances); *Op. 10/1 & 3.* RACHMANINOV: *Preludes in F sharp min., Op. 23/ 1; in B flat, Op. 23/2; in D, Op. 23/4; in G min., Op. 23/5; in C min., Op. 23/7; in A flat, Op. 23/8; in A, Op. 31/9; in C, Op. 32/1; in B flat min., Op. 32/2; in F, Op. 32/7; in B min., Op 32/10; in G sharp min., Op. 32/12; in G sharp min., Op. 32/ 15.* TCHAIKOVSKY: *Piano sonata in G, Op. 37.* LISZT: *Valse oubliée No. 1.*
(M) (***) Parnassus mono PACD 96–001/2 (2) [id.].

We owe this double-pack of Richter to the dedication of some enthusiasts who have tracked down a considerable number of live performances from the 1950s, before his star had risen in the West, recordings which have never been issued before. The unsigned liner-note claims that Richter was at this time 'perhaps even more of a virtuoso than the more mature artist' and that 'he was more willing to dazzle audiences with his facility'. Another claim the producer makes, and one that must be upheld, is that 'the recorded sound while not the ultimate in fidelity is superior to what we might have expected from early Russian tapes'.

The first CD brings some dazzling Prokofiev, recorded in Moscow in April 1958. The transcriptions from *Cinderella*, the excerpts from *Visions fugitives* and the *Seventh Sonata* are little short of amazing. (The sonata was recorded two months before the BMG/Melodiya version made at a recital in the Great Hall of the Moscow Conservatoire, and is every bit as electrifying, though the BMG is better recorded.) The producer's claim that Richter took more risks in this concert performance of the Schumann *Toccata* than in the safer but still stunning DG studio recording later the same year is also on target.

The Tchaikovsky *G major Sonata*, Op. 37 comes from another Moscow recital, in December 1954, two years before the BMG account, as do two other pieces also played at that later recital, the *Cloches à travers les feuilles* and the Chopin *E major Study*, Op. 10, No. 3. Richter also recorded the Tchaikovsky sonata in the studio in the mid-1950s (it was issued in the UK on Parlophone). We would not wish to choose between the two presently before the public; what is undeniable is that both are pretty sensational. (There are some barely discernible bumps in the slow movement but the transfers are otherwise excellent.) So, for that matter, are the thirteen Rachmaninov *Preludes* in this recital. What pianisim!

'Sviatoslav Richter in the 1950s', Volume 2:
MUSSORGSKY: *Pictures at an exhibition.* SCHUMANN: *Abegg variations, Op. 1; 3 Fantasiestücke, Op. 12; Humoreske in B flat, Op. 20.* SCRIABIN: *12 Preludes, Op. 11; Sonatas Nos. 2 in G sharp min., Op. 19; 6, Op. 62.* TCHAIKOVSKY: *Piano concerto No. 1 in B flat min., Op. 23* (with USSR State SO, Nathan Rachlin).
(M) (**(*)) Parnassus mono PACD 96–003/4 (2) [id.].

The earliest performances here are the Mussorgsky *Pictures* and the Scriabin *Sixth Sonata*, which come from a 1952 Moscow recital. The BMG/Melodiya account comes from 1958, the same year as the famous Sofia recital, while their recording of the Scriabin comes three years later, in 1955. The other Scriabin repertoire, along with the Schumann pieces, come from June 1955 and the Tchaikovsky concerto with Nathan Rachlin from 1957. Though the playing is again dazzling, the orchestral recording is coarse and climaxes discolour, and in the climaxes the engineers can be heard reducing the level to avoid overloading. Apart from this, Richter is in a class of his own, and *aficionados* will surely want this.

DEBUSSY: *Estampes; Préludes, Book I: Voiles; Le vent dans la plaine; Les collines d'Anacapri.* PROKOFIEV: *Visions fugitives, Op. 22, Nos. 3, 6 & 9; Sonata No. 8 in B flat, Op. 84.* SCRIABIN: *Sonata No. 5 in F sharp, Op. 53.*
(M) *** DG 423 573-2.

The Debussy *Préludes* and the Prokofiev *Sonata* were recorded at concerts during an Italian tour in 1962, while the remainder were made the previous year in Wembley Town Hall. The former sound more open than the rather confined studio acoustic – but what playing! The Scriabin is demonic and the Debussy could not be more atmospheric. The performance of the Prokofiev *Sonata* is, like the legendary Gilels account, a classic of the gramophone. But these performances and much more are now available on the DG Double below.

Recital: BACH: *Well-tempered Clavier: Preludes and fugues Nos. 1–6, BWV 846–53.* HAYDN: *Piano sonata in G min.* SCHUBERT: *Allegretto in C min., D.915; Ländler in A, D.366.* CHOPIN: *Polonaise-fantaisie, Op. 61; Etudes in C; C min. (Revolutionary), Op. 10/7 & 12.* SCHUMANN: *Abegg variations, Op. 1.* DEBUSSY: *Estampes; Préludes: Voiles; Le vent dans la plaine; Les collines d'Anacapri.* SCRIABIN: *Sonata No. 5 in F sharp min., Op. 53.* RACHMANINOV: *Prelude in G sharp min., Op. 32/12.* PROKOFIEV: *Visions fugitives, Op. 22/3, 6 & 9; Sonata No. 8 in B flat, Op. 84.*

⚫ (B) *** DG Double 447 355-2 (2) [id.].

This remarkable Richter treasury collects many of the stereo recordings he made for DG (or which were licensed to DG) between 1962 and 1965, including those on the single disc listed above. They are all of good quality and often the sound is excellent, if a little dry. The recordings, taken from live recitals during his Italian tour, bring a cough or two. The opening Bach *Preludes and fugues* immediately bring rapt concentration.

The Chopin selection opens with a wonderfully poetic account of the *Polonaise-fantaisie*, and the *Revolutionary study* is almost overwhelming in its excitement. The audience noises may be found intrusive both here and in the superb Debussy performances, yet *Jardins sous la pluie* is quite magical, as is the gentle exoticism of *Pagodes* (both from *Estampes*). Richter's Schumann is no less special, and in the delicious account of the Schubert *Ländler* one can sense the smile in his eyes. In both the Scriabin and Prokofiev *Sonatas* it is the powerful dynamism of Richter's technique that projects the music so vividly, but of course there is much poetic feeling too. As an inexpensive cross-section of his art, this could hardly be bettered.

'In Memoriam – Legendary recordings (1959–1962)': BACH: *Well-tempered Clavier, Book I: Preludes and fugues Nos. 1, 4–6 & 8, BWV 846, 849–51 & 853.* HAYDN: *Sonata in G min., Hob XVI/44.* CHOPIN: *Ballades Nos. 3 in A flat, Op. 47; 4 in F min., Op. 52; Polonaise-fantaisie in A flat, Op. 61; Etudes in C; C min. (Revolutionary), Op. 10/1 & 12.* SCHUBERT: *Allegretto in C min., D.915. Ländler, D.366/1, 3 & 4–5.* SCHUMANN: *Abegg variations, Op. 1.* DEBUSSY: *Estampes; Préludes, Book I: Voiles; Le vent dans la plaine; Les collines d'Anacapri.* RACHMANINOV: *Preludes Nos. 3 in B flat; 5 in D; 6 in G min.; 8 in C min., Op. 23/2, 4–5 & 7; 12 in C; 13 in B flat; 23 in G sharp min., Op. 32/1–2 & 12.* PROKOFIEV: *Visions fugitives, Op. 22/3, 6 & 9.*

(B) *** DG Double 457 667-2 (2) [id.].

Over the years DG have made a number of different collections from the recordings Richter made at live recitals while on tour in Europe between 1959 and 1962. The present programme extends the Chopin coverage to include two *Ballades*, volatile, highly individual performances; the number of Rachmaninov *Preludes* is also increased to cover virtually all the favourites. The remastered recordings – the quality varies somewhat between items – are for the most part very good, though audience noises inevitably intrude at times.

The compelling accounts of the Scriabin and Prokofiev *Sonatas* previously included are here omitted. Each disc is generously full and the set is highly recommendable. The discography details are as follows: Rachmaninov *Preludes* (except Op. 32/12): Warsaw, 1959; Haydn *Sonata*, Chopin Op. 47, Debussy *Préludes*: Wembley Town Hall, 1961; Bach, Prokofiev, Chopin (except Op. 47), Debussy *Estampes*, Rachmaninov Op. 32/12, Schubert, Schumann: Italian tour, 1962.

Melodiya Richter Edition (complete)

(M) (*(**)) RCA mono 74321 29460-2 (10) [id.].

Volume 1: BACH: *English suite No. 3 in G min., BWV 808. Piano concerto in D min., BWV 1052* (with USSR SO, Kurt Sanderling). *Double piano concerto in C, BWV 1061* (with Anatoly Vedernikov, Moscow CO, Barshai).

(M) (**) RCA mono 74321 29461-2 [id.].

Volume 2: BEETHOVEN: *Piano sonatas Nos. 8 in C min. (Pathétique); 23 in F min. (Appassionata), Op. 57; Bagatelles, Op. 33/3 & 5; Op. 119/ 2, 7 & 9; Op. 126/1, 4 & 6.*

(M) (**(*)) RCA mono 74321 29462-2 [id.].

Volume 3: SCHUBERT: *Piano sonatas Nos. 16 in A min., D.845; 17 in D, D.850.*

(M) (***) RCA mono 74321 29463-2 [id.].

Volume 4: SCHUMANN: *Fantasiestücke, Op. 12; Humoreske in B flat, Op. 20; Novelleten, Op. 21.*

(M) (***) RCA mono 74321 29464-2 [id.].

Volume 5: SCHUBERT: *Moments musicaux, D.780/1, 3 & 6.* CHOPIN: *Etudes in E, Op. 10/3; in E min., Op. 25/5. Polonaise No. 1 in C sharp min., Op. 26/1.* FRANCK: *Prélude, choral et fugue.* BARTOK: *15 Hungarian peasant songs.*

(M) (**(*)) RCA mono 74321 29465-2 [id.].

Volume 6: CHOPIN: *Piano concerto No. 2 in F min., Op. 21* (with USSR SO, Svetlanov). SAINT-SAENS: *Piano concerto No. 5 in F, Op. 103.* FRANCK: *Les Djinns* (both with Moscow Youth O, Kondrashin).

(M) (*(**)) RCA mono 74321 29466-2 [id.].

Volume 7: RACHMANINOV: *Piano concertos Nos. 1 in F sharp min., Op. 1; 2 in C min., Op. 18* (with USSR R. & TV Large SO or Leningrad PO, both cond. Kurt Sanderling).

(M) (***) RCA mono 74321 29467-2 [id.].

Volume 8: RIMSKY-KORSAKOV: *Piano concerto in C sharp min., Op. 30.* GLAZUNOV: *Piano concerto No. 1 in F min., Op. 92.* PROKOFIEV:

Piano concerto No. 1 in D flat, Op. 10 (all with Moscow Youth O, Kondrashin).
(M) ((***)) RCA mono 74321 29468-2 [id.].

Volume 9: TCHAIKOVSKY: *Piano sonata in G, Op. 37.* MUSSORGSKY: *Pictures at an exhibition.*
(M) (**(*)) RCA mono 74321 29469-2 [id.].

Volume 10: SCRIABIN: *12 Etudes: Op. 2/1; Op. 8/5 & 11; Op. 42/2–6 & 8; Op. 65/1–3; Piano sonata No. 6, Op. 62.* MIASKOVSKY: *Piano sonata No. 3 in C min., Op. 19.* PROKOFIEV: *Piano sonata No. 7 in B flat, Op. 83.*
(M) ((***)) RCA mono 74321 29470-2 [id.].

All these discs which Richter made for the Melodiya label are available separately; the only gain in acquiring them all is a sturdy slipcase. Each disc is annotated separately, and the annotations are all authoritative and full of interest. Most of these recordings will be familiar to collectors of the older generation, but not all of them were issued on Western labels. The oldest of the recordings is of the *G minor English Suite*, which comes from 1948 when Richter would have been in his early thirties and, for all its sonic limitations, it is wonderfully alive. The Bach *D minor Concerto*, made in 1955 with Kurt Sanderling, originally appeared in the UK in a Parlophone series called 'Music from the USSR' not long after Richter's breakthrough Schumann recital on DG. At that time it was coupled with his Rachmaninov *First* from the same year – a dazzling performance, which here appears more logically coupled in the seventh volume of the set with the *Second*, made in 1959, not as well recorded as his DG set with Stanislaw Wislocki and the Warsaw Philharmonic the following year, but some feel the 1959 version to be a stronger performance, and certainly the orchestral support is impressive.

The Beethoven performances are of early provenance and call for some tolerance as far as the actual sound is concerned, though they are a great improvement on such original Melodiya LPs as we have. The *Pathétique* and the *Bagatelles* come from 1948 and 1955, and the recordings are shallow and a bit clangorous at climaxes. The *Appassionata* was recorded at a public concert in 1960 and was Richter's own preferred version. (He was not satisfied with the studio performance he made with RCA in America.) These are all performances of stature. The *Choral Fantasy*, sung in Russian, comes from 1952 and, although the sound calls for some tolerance, the performance is tremendously compelling.

The Schubert *Sonata in A minor*, D.845 had a disc to itself (with an *Impromptu* as fill-up) when it appeared on blue-label Melodiya LPs, complete with wow, swish and fairly heavy background noise, and it is good to renew its acquaintance in more acceptable sound. (These LPs were never officially issued here but were obtainable in an austere, sleeveless presentation for a derisory sum.) Although Richter made later Schubert recordings

for EMI, this *A minor* is in a class of its own for sheer depth of feeling. The two Schubert sonatas were recorded in mono in 1957–8.

Like Perahia, Richter has a special feeling for Schumann. The *Humoreske* in this set is the 1956 account mentioned above, and the *Fantasiestücke* come from roughly the same period as the famous DG LP, which was also recorded in 1956 while Richter was in Prague. If you have the DG disc, there is no need to add the present issue to your library except for the sake of the magisterial *Humoreske*.

The Schubert and Chopin on the next disc are of early provenance (1952), and again the recording is wanting in freshness and bloom – but not the playing! The Franck was made four years later and the Bartók comes from 1972. Like so much in this collection, it is self-recommending.

The Chopin *Concerto No. 2 in F minor* and the Saint-Saëns *Fifth Concerto*, the so-called *Egyptian*, are much less well known, and the dated sound-quality of the Saint-Saëns and Franck couplings, which come from 1952–3, may perhaps have limited their wider dissemination, though the RCA engineers have freshened them up considerably – and many will tolerate the shallowness and distortion of the climaxes for the sake of the performance. The *F minor Concerto* is of much later provenance (1966) and, though the sound is hardly the 'highest of fi', it is serviceable.

The Russian concertos on Volume 8 have all been available at one time or another in the 1950s and '60s, though the recordings sounded execrable. The Glazunov, recorded way back in 1952, has never been better played, and the same probably holds for the Rimsky-Korsakov, which Richter made with Kondrashin in 1950. The Prokofiev from 1952 is simply dazzling and is perhaps even more remarkable than the later (and better-recorded) version he made in Prague with Karel Ančerl. However, while the RCA engineers have improved the sound, there are limits to what even they can do with the shrill, hollow orchestral climaxes which suffer from distortion.

The famous 1956 account of the Tchaikovsky *Sonata in G major* shared a Parlophone disc with the Schumann *Humoreske* and is a (if not *the*) classic account of the piece on disc. The 1958 *Pictures at an exhibition* is not to be confused with the live performance Richter gave in Sofia, which was released on Philips. The Melodiya recording might at best be described as 'so-so'. (The notes remind us that Richter was an accomplished painter himself.)

The Scriabin *Etudes* come from 1952, and the *Sixth Sonata* was recorded three years later; he penetrates this music as few artists do. The Miaskovsky *Third Sonata*, recorded in 1953, is an interesting work and it is difficult to envisage more sympathetic advocacy. Much the same must be said of the stunning, demonic account Richter gives of the Prokofiev *Seventh Sonata* which makes most other pianists sound quite tame. Richter had given the first Moscow performance of this sonata in 1943 and this 1958 account finds him at the height of his powers. This extraordinary performance comes over in spite of all the distortion.

To sum up: despite the skill and dedication of those concerned with this project, considerable allowances have to be made for shallow sound-quality, and sometimes distortion too, while the occasional cough can disturb the listener in the live performances. However, allowances are worth making, as most of these performances find Richter in his youthful prime. For those who do not want the whole box, prime recommendations lie with the Schubert sonatas (Volume 3), the Rachmaninov concertos (7), the Tchaikovsky *G major Sonata* and the *Pictures* (9), and the stunning Prokofiev *Seventh Sonata* (10).

Robles, Marisa (harp)

'*The world of the harp*': FALLA: *Three-cornered hat: Danza del corregidor*. ALBENIZ: *Rumores de la Caleta; Torre Bermeja*. BIDAOLA: *Viejo zortzico*. EBERL (attrib. Mozart): *Theme, variations and rondo pastorale*. BEETHOVEN: *Variations on a Swiss song*. BRITTEN: *Ceremony of carols: Interlude*. FAURE: *Impromptu, Op. 86*. PIERNE: *Impromptu-caprice, Op. 9*. SALZEDO: *Chanson de la nuit*. BRAHMS: *Lullaby*. BACH: *Well-tempered Clavier: Prelude No. 1*. CHOPIN: *Mazurka, Op. 7/1; Prelude, Op. 28/15 (Raindrop)*. HASSELMANS: *La source*.
(M) *** Decca 433 869-2 [436 293-2].

The artistry of Marisa Robles ensures that this is a highly attractive anthology and the programme is as well chosen as it is beautifully played. As ex-Professor of the harp at the Madrid Conservatory, Miss Robles has a natural affinity for the Spanish music that opens her programme, and other highlights include a magnetic account of the Britten *Interlude* and the Salzedo *Chanson de la nuit* with its bell-like evocations. The Eberl *Variations* are highly engaging. The excellent recordings derive from the Argo catalogue of the 1960s and '70s, except for the Chopin, Brahms, Bach and Hasselmans pieces, which have been added to fill out the present reissue (75 minutes). The delicious Hasselmans roulades are the epitome of nineteenth-century harp writing. The CD has a most realistic presence.

'*Música española*': NARVAEZ: *Variaciones populares sobre 'Guárdame las vacas'*. CABEZON: *Pavana y variaciones*. SANZ: *La serenissima*. M. ALBENIZ: *Sonata in G*. I. albeniz: *Torre Bermeja*. FALLA: *The Three-cornered hat: Danza del corregidor*. GURIDI: *Viejo zortzico; Nere*

Maitea; Aritz Adarean; Ator, Ator Mutil; Agura Zarkilun; Garizuma Luzerik; Zorabitatua Naiz. GOMBAU: *Apunte bético*. ALFONSO: *Cadenza*. FRANCO: *Canción y danza*.
(B) *** Decca Double Analogue/Dig. 433 938-2 (2) [id.]. – RODRIGO: *Concierto de Aranjuez* (trans. for harp) (with Philh. O, Dutoit).
SARASATE: Music for violin and piano. ***

The harp is without the vibrant quality of the guitar in Spanish music, but in the hands of a master (or perhaps one should say a mistress) its swirling liquidity can have a magic of its own. Certainly Marisa Robles shows herself an artist of uncommon stamp in her subtlety in matters of colour. Her Spanish world is a personal one, its atmosphere contrasting vivid splashes of colour with the most delicate nuances of half-lighting, and her intimate musical feeling ensures the listener's continued fascination and pleasure. The music-making is entirely spontaneous and whether in the familiar writing of Falla or the piquant world of Basque folk music, this makes entirely delightful listening. She is beautifully recorded and the inclusion of Rodrigo's own arrangement for harp of his *Concierto de Aranjuez* is another plus point for this set, which also offers Campoli and Ricci at their finest in the violin and piano music of Sarasate.

Romero, Pepe (guitar)

Spanish music ((i) with Celín Romero): ANON.: *Jeux interdits*. ALBENIZ: *Suite española, Op. 47: Sevilla; Granada. Recuerdos de viaje, Op. 71: Rumores de la caleta. Mallorca* (barcarolle), *Op. 202. España (6 hojas de álbum), Op. 165: Asturias;* (i) *Tango*. GRANADOS: (i) *Danzas españolas, Op. 37: Andaluza*. (i) *Goyescas: Intermezzo*. Celedonio ROMERO: *Malagueña; Romantico*. TARREGA: *Capricho árabe; Pavana*. SOR: *Introduction & variations on a theme by Mozart, Op. 9*.
(M) **(*) Ph. (IMS) Dig. 434 727-2.

A thoroughly professional and immaculately played collection of favourites. The effect is intimate, pleasing rather than electrifying – the virtuoso showing his paces in familiar pieces. The flamenco-based pieces by the performer's father, Celedonio, bring a sudden hint of fire. For the reissue Celín Romero joins his brother for three duets, and this brings added spontaneity, although the intimate mood remains – witness the Granados *Spanish dance* which does not have the electricity of Julian Bream's solo version. The recording is very natural, but no information is provided about the music (except titles).

Los Romeros

Spanish guitar favourites (with Pepe Romero, Celín Romero, Celedonio Romero, Celino Romero): GIMONEZ: *La boda de Luis Alonso: Malagueña–Zapateado. El baile de Luis Alonso: Intermedio.* BOCCHERINI: *Guitar quintet No. 4 in D, G.448: Grave–Fandango.* Celedonio ROMERO: *Fantasia Cubana; Malagueñas.* FALLA: *El amor brujo: Ritual fire dance.* SOR: *L'encouragement, Op. 34.* PRAETORIUS: *Bransle de la torche; Ballet; Volta.* TARREGA: *Capricho árabe.* TURINA: *La oración del torero.* TORROBA: *Estampas.*
🌑 *** Ph. Dig. 442 781-2 [id.].

Opening with a compelling *Malagueña–Zapateado* of Jerénimo Gimónez and closing with an engaging and lighter *Intermedio* encore by the same composer, both from zarzuelas, this 74-minute collection of mainly Spanish music grips and entertains the listener as at a live concert. Celedonio contributes two pieces of his own, a charming solo lightweight *Fantasia Cubana*, and the others join him for his glittering flamenco *Malagueñas*, which has an improvisatory central section before the dashing coda with castanets.

Among the more famous pieces arranged for the four players are the very effective Falla *Ritual fire dance* and Turina's *La oración del torero* (full of evocation), while Sor's *L'encouragement*, with its ingenuous lilting *Cantabile*, a simple but artful Theme and variations and elegant closing *Valse*, is played as a duet by Pepe and Celino. Tárrega's haunting *Capricho árabe* is exquisitely phrased by Celino. The arrangement of the three Praetorius dances, with an added condiment of percussion, is colourfully in period. Tórroba's *Estampas* brings a highly imaginative response from the group, making this a highlight of the concert. The recording gives the guitars splendid presence against the attractively warm ambience, which in no way blurs the sharpness or focus of the players' attack.

Rosenthal, Moritz (piano)

CHOPIN: *Piano concerto No. 1 in E min., Op. 11* (with Berlin State Opera Orchestra, Frieder Weissmann); *Romanze* only (with NBC SO, Frank Black). *Berceuse, Op. 57; Chants polonais* (arr. LISZT); *Etudes, Op. 10/1; 10/5* (twice); *Mazurkas, Opp. 63/3* (three versions); *67/1; Waltz in C sharp min., E min. Op. posth.*
(***) Biddulph mono LHW 040 [id.].

Rosenthal was a pupil of Karl Mikuli, who was himself a Chopin pupil, and his Chopin is quite out of the ordinary. The *E minor Concerto* was made in 1930 and the ritornello is cut, but what pianism! (The alternative slow movement was recorded in New York on Rosenthal's 75th birthday.) Rosenthal's effortless virtuosity, lightness of touch, legatissimo and tonal subtlety are altogether remarkable. Playing of great culture from a distant age and beautifully transferred by Ward Marston.

Rossetti-Bonell, Dario (guitar)

'Début': BARRIOS: *2 Valses, Op. 8/3–4; Mazurka appassionata; Aconquija.* VIVALDI: *Mandolin concerto in C, RV 425* (transcribed for solo guitar by Rossetti-Bonell). VILLA-LOBOS: *Preludes Nos. 1–5.* GRANADOS: *Valses poéticos.*
(B) **(*) EMI CDZ5 73499-2 [id.].

Dario, son of Carlos Bonell, proves to be a masterly guitarist, and by no means in the shadow of his father. His technique is consummate and he knows just how to seduce the ear with subtle rubato, as in the Barrios *Mazurka appassionata*, or with a magnetically gentle melodic ebb and flow, as in the *A minor* or *E major* Villa-Lobos *Preludes*, and how to hold the listener with dramatic use of light and shade as in No. 4 in E minor. The engaging closing Granados *Valses poéticos* are presented with charm and much expertise in the matter of colour. However, the inclusion of the Vivaldi *Mandolin concerto*, arranged for guitar without orchestra, was a curious indulgence. It is very well played of course, but fails to make a case for a guitar taking over the orchestral as well as solo mandolin roles. The recording, made in Forde Abbey, Somerset, is wholly natural with a most pleasing acoustic.

Rothwell, Evelyn (oboe)

Recital: C. P. E. BACH: *Sonata in G min.* TELEMANN: *Sonata in E flat.* Michael HEAD: *Siciliana* (all with Valda Aveling, harpsichord, Dennis Nesbitt, viola da gamba). LOEILLET: *Sonata in C* (arr. ROTHWELL). HANDEL: *Air & Rondo* (arr. & ed. ROTHWELL). Nicholas MORGAN: *Melody* (all with Wilfred Parry, piano).
** Dutton Lab./Barbirolli Soc. CDSJB 1016 [id.].
(with CORELLI; HAYDN; MARCELLO: *Oboe concertos ***).

Evelyn Rothwell, as always, plays expressively with charm and poise. But the recording of Valda Aveling's harpsichord seems unnecessarily recessed and insubstantial. Even so the Telemann *Sonata* is enjoyable enough, and the Michael Head *Siciliana* brings a more positive effect. The items accompanied on the piano by Wilfred Parry are more successful. He is still rather backwardly placed but emerges with a stronger personality and the delightful Handel titbits and the Nicholas Morgan *Melody* are the highlights of the recital.

Rubinstein, Artur (piano)

'*The Rubinstein Collection*'

Volume 1: BRAHMS: *Concerto No. 2 in B flat. Op. 83* (with LSO, Albert Coates). TCHAIKOVSKY: *Concerto No. 1 in B flat Min., Op. 23* (with LSO, Sir John Barbirolli). (RCA mono 09026 63001-2.)

Volume 2: CHOPIN: *Waltzes, Op. 34/1; Op. 64/2; Mazurkas, Op. 33/2; Op. 56/3; Op. 63/1.* LISZT: *Consolation No. 3; Hungarian rhapsody No. 10; Liebesträume No. 3.* RACHMANINOV: *Prelude, Op 3/2.* DEBUSSY: *Le tombeau de Couperin: Forlane.* GRANADOS: *Goyescas: The Maiden and the nightingale.* FALLA: *El amor brulo: Dance of terror; Ritual fire dance.* VILLA-LOBOS: *Prole do bebê: 2, Moreninha; 6, A pobrezinha; 7, O Polichinelo.* (RCA mono 09026 63002-2.)

Volume 8: BACH/BUSONI: *Toccata, BWV 564.* SCHUBERT: *Impromptu; Sonata No. 18 in G, D.894: Minuetto.* SCHUMANN: *Romance No. 2 in F sharp, Op. 28; Arabesque; Träumerei; Widmung.* BRAHMS: *Capriccio in B min., Op. 79/ 2; Rhapsody in G min., Op. 79/2; Wiegenlied* (arr. Rubinstein). Anton RUBINSTEIN: *Valse caprice.* (RCA mono 09026 63008-2.)

Volume 13: GRIEG: *Concerto in A min., Op. 16* (with Philadelphia. Orchestra, Ormandy). *Ballade in G min., Op. 24; Album leaf, Op. 28/4; Lyric pieces: Cradle song; Spring song; Berceuse; Folk song; Papillon; Folk song (2); Spring dance; Shepherd boy; Little bird; Elfin dance; March of the dwarfs.* (RCA mono 09026 63013-2.)

Volume 16: CHOPIN: *24 Preludes, Op. 28; Berceuse in D flat, Op. 57; Barcarolle in F sharp, Op. 60; Sonata No. 2 in B flat min., Op. 60; Impromptu No. 3 in G flat, Op. 51.* (RCA mono 09026 63016-2.)

Volume 18: GRANADOS: *Danza española No. 5; The maiden and the nightingale.* FALLA: *Three-cornered Hat: Miller's dance. Andaluza; El amor brujo: Dance of terror; Ritual fire dance.. Nights in the gardens of Spain* (with Saint Louis SO, Vladimir Golschmann). ALBENIZ: *Córdoba; Iberia: Evocation; Navarra* (arr. Rubinstein); *Sevillanas.* MOMPOU: *Cançon i danza Nos 1; 6.* (RCA mono 09026 63018-2.)

Volume 24: MENDELSSOHN: *Piano trio in D min., Op. 49;* (with Jascha Heifetz and Emanuel Piatigorsky). BRAHMS: *Piano trio in B, Op. 8* (with Heifetz and Emanuel Feuermann). (RCA mono 09026 63024-2.)

Volume 30: FRANCK: *Prelude, chorale and fugue.* DEBUSSY: *La plus que lente; Homage à Rameau; Poissons d'or; Préludes, Book 1: La filleaux cheveux de lin; La catédral engloutie; Minstrels; Book 2: La terasse des audiences du clair du lune; Ondine; Masques.* GRANADOS: *Goyescas: The*

Maiden and the nightingale. LISZT: *Liebesträum in A flat, No. 3.* SCHUBERT: *Impromptus D.899/ 3 in G flat; 4 in A flat.* MENDELSSOHN: *Songs without words: Spinning song.* (RCA mono 09026 63030-2.)

Volume 34: BRAHMS: *Concerto No. 1 in D min., Op.15* (with Chicago SO, Reiner). *Capriccio in B min., Op. 76/2; Intermezzo in E flat min., Op. 118/ 6; Rhapsody in B min., Op. 79/1.* (RCA 09026 63034-2.)

Volume 35: RACHMANINOV: *Concerto No. 2 in C min., Op. 18; Rhapsody on a theme of Paganini, Op. 43* (with Chicago SO, Reiner); *Prelude in C sharp min., Op. 3/2.* (RCA mono/stereo 09026 63035-2.)

Volume 40: BEETHOVEN: *Violin sonatas Nos. 5 in F (Spring), Op. 24; 8 in G, Op. 30/3; 9 in A (Kreutzer), Op. 47* (with Henryk Szeryng). (RCA mono 09026 63040-2.)

Volume 41: BRAHMS: *Violin sonatas Nos. 1 in G, Op. 78; 2 in A, Op. 100; 3 in D min., Op. 108* (with Henryk Szeryng). (RCA 09026 63041-2.)

Volume 43: RAVEL: *Valses nobles et sentimentales; Le tombeau de Couperin: III Forlane; La vallée des cloches.* POULENC: *3 Mouvements perpétuels; Intermezzo in A flat; Intermezzo No. 2 in D flat.* FAURE: *Nocturne in A flat, Op. 33/3.* CHABRIER: *Scherzo-valse.* DEBUSSY: *Estampes: La soirée dans Grenade; Jardins sous la pluie; Images, set 1: Homage à Rameau; Réflets dans l'eau; La plus que lente; Images, set 2: Poissons d'or.* (RCA mono/stereo 09026 63043-2.)

Volume 44: CHOPIN: *Concertos Nos. 1 in E min., Op. 11* (with New SO of London, Stanislaw Skrowaczewski); *2 in F min., Op.21* (with Symphony of the Air, Alfred Wallenstein); *Trois nouvelles études, op. posth.* (RCA 09026 63044-2.)

Volume 47: CHOPIN: *Waltzes, Nos. 1–14; Impromptus Nos 1–4; Bolero, Op. 19.* (RCA 09026 63047-2.)

Volume 49: CHOPIN: *Nocturnes 1–19.* (RCA 09026 63049-2 (2).)

Volume 52: SCHUMANN: *Kreisleriana, Op. 16; Fantasie in C, Op. 17.* (RCA 09026 63052-2.)

Volume 53: SCHUMANN: *Concerto in A min., Op. 54* (with Chicago SO, Giulini). LISZT: *Concerto No. 1 in E flat* (with RCA Victor SO, Wallenstein). SAINT-SAENS: *Concerto No. 2 in G min., Op. 22* (with Symphony of the Air, Wallenstein). (RCA 09026 63053-2.)

Volume 54: SCHUBERT: *Sonata No 21 in B flat, D.960; Fantasia in C (Wanderer), D.760; Impromptus Nos. 3 in G flat; 4 in A flat, D.899.* (RCA 09026 63054-2.)

Volume 56: BEETHOVEN: *Sonatas Nos. 8 in C min. (Pathétique), Op. 13; 14 in C sharp min. (Moonlight), Op. 27/2; 23 in F min. (Appassionata), Op. 57; 26 in E flat (Les Adieux), Op. 81a.* (RCA 09026 63056-2.)

Volume 58: BEETHOVEN: *Concertos Nos. 4 in G, Op. 58; 3 in C min., Op. 73* (with Boston SO, Eric Leinsdorf). (RCA 09026 63058-2.)

Volume 61: MOZART: *Concertos Nos. 17 in G, K.453; 20 in D min., K.466; 21 in C (Elvira Madigan), K.467; 23 in A, K. 488;* (with RCA Victor SO, Alfred Wallenstein). *Concerto No. 24 in C minor, K.491* (with Joseph Krips). (RCA 09026 63061-2 (2).)

Volume 62: CHOPIN: *Polonaise Nos. 5–6; Impromptu No. 3; Nocturne No. 8; Sonata No. 2 in B flat min.; Barcarolle No. 60; Etudes Nos. 4–5; 13; 17; Waltzes Nos. 2–3.* SCHUMANN: *Fantasiestücke: Des abends, No. 1.* DEBUSSY: *Prélude: Ondine.* VILLA-LOBOS: *Prole do bebê: Polichinelle.* (RCA 09026 63062-2 (2)).

Volume 63: BRAHMS: *Sonata in F min., Op. 5; Ballades Nos. 1–4.* (RCA 09026 63063-2).

Volume 70: SAINT-SAENS: *Concerto No. 2 in G min., Op. 22.* FALLA: *Nights in the gardens of Spain* (with the Philadelphia Orchestra, Eugene Ormondy). *El amor brujo: Ritual fire dance.* FRANCK: *Symphonic variations* (with Symphony of the Air, Alfred Wallenstein). PROKOFIEV: *The Love of three oranges: March.* (RCA 09026 63070-2.)

Volume 71: BRAHMS: *Concerto no. 2 in B flat, Op. 83* (with Philadelphia. Orchestra, Ormandy). SCHUMANN: *Fantasiestüke, Op. 12.* (RCA 09026 63071-2.)

Volume 77: BEETHOVEN: *Concertos Nos. 1 in C, Op. 15; 2 in B flat, Op. 19* (with LSO, Barenboim). (RCA 09026 63077-2.)

Volume 78: BEETHOVEN: *Concertos Nos. 3 in C min., Op. 37; 4 in G, Op. 58.* (with LSO, Barenboim). (RCA 09026 63078-2.)

Volume 79: BEETHOVEN: *Concerto No. 5 in E flat, Op. 73* (with LSO, Barenboim). *Sonata No. 18 in E flat, Op. 31.* (RCA 09026 63079-2.)

RCA's Rubinstein Collection covers this great pianist's entire recording career and, as he was hugely prolific, runs to eighty-two Volumes, some consisting of a pair of CDs. The first twenty-nine are being issued just as we go to press and will be in the shops by the time we are in print. We have only been able to sample one or two of them, but the transfers are excellent and they are attractively packaged and generally well documented.

Volume 1 includes Brahms and Chopin concertos from 1929 and 1932, recorded in the Kingsway Hall and Abbey Road respectively; Volumes 2 and 8 cover solo recordings from the 1920s and 1930s (and a few from 1947), still mostly made at Abbey Road, but with a few items using a studio at the Small Queen's Hall. Volume 13 has the 1942 Philadelphia recording of the Grieg concerto, plus solo works recorded at the RCA studios in Hollywood in 1953.

The first Chopin recital, in Volume 16, including the *24 Preludes* was made in RCA's New York studio in 1946. The collection of Spanish music in Volume 18 is gathered together from various sessions between 1949 and 1955, mostly in Hollywood, except of course for the 1949 Saint Louis recording of *Nights in the gardens of Spain* with Golschmann. The Brahms and Mendelssohn Piano trios (Volume 24) date from 1941 and 1950 respectively, and the miscellaneous collection including French repertoire (Volume 30) includes more Hollywood recordings, primarily from the 1950s.

Volumes 34 and 35 bring us into the stereo era with the Brahms *D minor Concerto*, recorded in Chicago in 1954, and some solo pieces recorded in Italy in 1970, and the two key Rachmaninov works (again with Fritz Reiner) date from 1956. Volumes 40 and 41 (Beethoven and Brahms *Violin sonatas*, with Szerying), followed on between 1958 and 1961. The first major collection of French music in stereo (Volume 43) dates from 1963, but *Estampes* and *Images* are older mono recordings from 1945. The two Chopin concertos are coupled in Volume 44: the first, recorded in London with Skrowaczewski, dates from 1961, the second was made three years earlier in Carnegie Hall.

We now come to a pair of supreme highlights of the legacy. Chopin's *Waltzes* on Volume 47 (1963) sparkle like newly cut diamonds and join his unsurpassed complete set of the *Nocturnes* (1965 and 1967) on Volume 49, which are among Rubinstein's most poetic achievements in the recording studio. Here the remastered sound is very fine and this unmissable pair of discs appears now for the first time at mid-price.

Rubinstein's Schumann coupling on Volume 52 (*Kreisleriana* and the *Fantasy in C, Op. 17*) is another of his most succesful records, *Kreisleriana* recorded in Carnegie Hall in 1964, and the wonderfully subtle account of the *Fantasy* a year later in RCA's Italian studio. Volume 53 is especially generous in offering his 1967 account of the Schumann concerto (recorded in Chicago with Giulini) in a curious triptych with the New York recordings of Liszt's No. 1 in E flat, and Rubinstein's beloved Saint-Saëns No. 2 both from a decade earlier.

Volume 54 brings Schubert's last and greatest sonata plus the *Wanderer Fantasia* (from 1965), and a pair of *Impromptus*, while Volume 56 offers the four favourite named sonatas of Beethoven (from 1962/3). These are two more essential CDs showing the great pianist at his most illuminating.

Rubinstein's 1963/4 Boston recordings of the Beethoven concertos with Leinsdorf (Volume 58) proved a lot less stimulating than his later Kingsway Hall set with Barenboim (Volumes 77, 78 and 79), but we shall need to assess these again later. His Mozart concertos on Volume 61 are a different matter, and this is another of the most cherishable of these reissues, while the 1964 Moscow Recital (Volume 62) has the usual virtues of live recordings.

Volume 63 is a little more controversial, as here Rubinstein's impulsiveness in the Brahms *F minor Sonata* (1959) seems less penetrating than usual, and his (1972) recording of the *Second piano concerto* with Ormandy on Volume 71 did not match his much earlier recording with Krips, notable for its lyrical freshness. Similarly on Volume 70, his aristocratic 1969 recording of Falla's *Nights in the gardens of Spain* (again with Ormandy) did not quite measure up to his account with Jorda, made a decade earlier. However, his chimerical account of Franck's *Symphonic variations* show him on top form, as do two of his favourite encores, which act as a bonus.

'The last recital for Israel': BEETHOVEN: *Piano sonata No. 23 (Appassionata), Op. 57.* SCHUMANN: *Fantasiestücke, Op. 12.* DEBUSSY: *La plus que lente; Pour le piano: Prélude.* CHOPIN: *Etudes, Op. 25/5; Op. 10/4. Nocturne, Op. 15/2; Polonaise, Op. 53.*
** RCA 09026 61160-2 [id.].

When this disc first appeared, four years ago, it was to great acclaim. One of our finest judges of piano playing and recording called the *Appassionata* 'sensational'. It is amazing in its way, given the fact that the great pianist was eighty-eight when he gave this recital. But to be perfectly honest, this enthusiasm is difficult to share. Indeed, the *Appassionata* left R. L. comparatively uninvolved. Perhaps the poor sound-quality contributes to the monochrome impression; the keyboard colour and dynamic range are not as wide as we are used to from this artist, though the sound is better on the CD than on the video-tape (RCA 09026 61160-3). Of course, there are some good things during the programme, but on the whole it proves a disappointment.

Russian Baroque Ensemble

'Chamber music from the court of St Petersburg': STARTZER: *Divertimento in A min.* TITZ: *String quartet in G; Violin sonata in F sharp min.* BAILLOT: *Russian air.* MADONIS: *12 Diverse symphonies.* BEREZOVSKY: *Violin sonata in C.* STEIBELT: *Variations on 2 Russian folksongs.*
(BB) **(*) Arte Nova Dig. 74321 51626-2 (2) [id.].

All but one of these still obscure composers came from outside the Russian empire but gravitated to the court in St Petersburg, writing attractive and

civilized, if hardly original, music like this. The exception, Maxim Berezovsky, represented here by a fresh, lively *Violin sonata*, came from the Ukraine. In this two-disc collection, much the longest and most impressive work is the *Quartet in G* by the German, Anton Titz (1742–1810), with an extraordinarily ambitious first movement which alone lasts 20 minutes. He is also represented by a fine *Violin sonata in F sharp minor*. The only signs of ethnic Russian influence come in three sets of variations on Russian themes, and they are just as completely translated to the Viennese tradition as those in Beethoven's *Rasumovsky Quartets*. The performances on period instruments are lusty and heartfelt rather than subtle, given close recording to match. A fascinating, unusual offering.

Russian Piano School

Russian Piano School: *'The great pianists'* Volumes 1–10.
(M) (**(*)) BMG/Melodiya mono/stereo 74321 25172-2 (11) [id.].

RCA/Melodiya are currently offering eleven CDs that survey the Russian piano tradition from the generation of Goldenweiser and Neuhaus, whose pianistic pedigree goes back to the nineteenth-century masters, through to such younger virtuosi as Pletnev and Kissin. All of them have been digitally remastered with great care with 20-bit technology and NoNoise processing and, though the results are inevitably variable (particularly in the earlier recordings), the series affords an invaluable opportunity to steep oneself in the Russian pianistic tradition. The set is now only available in a slipcase. The only discs available separately at mid-price are Volumes 1 (Goldenweiser) and 10 (Kissin).

Goldenweiser, Alexander Borisovich

Volume 1: ARENSKY: *Forgotten rhythms: Sari, Op. 28/4.* BORODIN: *Petite suite: Mazurka.* goldenweiser: *Song and dance.* MEDTNER: *Novella in C min., Op. 17/2.* RACHMANINOV: *Morceaux de salon: Barcarolle in G min., Op. 10/3. Suite No. 2, Op. 17* (with Grigori Ginsburg). TCHAIKOVSKY: *Dialogue in B, Op. 72/8; Méditation, Op. 72/5; Romance in F, Op. 51/5; Valse sentimentale in F min., Op. 51/6.*
(M) (***) BMG/Melodiya mono 74321 25173-2 [id.].

Alexander Goldenweiser (1875–1961) was a pupil of Siloti, who was Rachmaninov's cousin and himself a pupil of Liszt, and Goldenweiser's classmates at the Moscow Conservatoire included Scriabin, Rachmaninov and Medtner. His composition studies were with Arensky, Ippolitov-Ivanov and Taneyev, all pupils of Tchaikovsky. He lived to be eighty-six and recorded these pieces between

1946 and 1955, when he would have been in his seventies. His own pupils included Tatiana Nikolayeva, Lazar Berman, Dmitri Bashkirov and the composer Kabalevsky. Of particular interest is his powerful 1948 recording of the Rachmaninov *Second Suite* (with Grigori Ginsburg as the second pianist), since the composer dedicated the piece to him. He wears his virtuosity lightly and, like all the greatest pianists, his lightness of touch leaves one unaware of hammers. The Tchaikovsky pieces of Op. 72 have a particularly touching quality. The recordings come up surprisingly well, given their age.

Neuhaus, Heinrich

Volume 2: MOZART: *Rondo in A min., K.511; Sonata in D for two pianos, K.448* (with Stanislav Neuhaus). DEBUSSY: *Préludes, Books I & II: Danseuses de Delphes; La sérénade interrompue; La puerta del vino; Des pas sur la neige; Les sons et les parfums tournent dans l'air du soir; Les collines d'Anacapri; Bruyères; Minstrels.* PROKOFIEV: *Visions fugitives, Op. 22.*
(M) (***) BMG/Melodiya mono 74321 25174-2 [id.].

Heinrich Neuhaus (1888–1964) is one of the most legendary figures among Russian pianists, the teacher of Richter and Gilels among others, a cousin of Szymanowski, much spoken of but scarcely glimpsed on a record label. He studied with Tausig and Godowsky before going on to become an influential teacher, as was his son, Stanislav (1927–80), with whom he recorded the Mozart *Sonata in D major*, K.448, in 1950. The eight Debussy *Préludes*, recorded in 1946 and 1948, have a powerful atmosphere and a refined sense of colour. Acceptable sound, though with not a great deal of top. It is difficult to imagine Prokofiev's *Visions fugitives*, recorded in 1956 when Neuhaus was in his late sixties, being played with greater character.

Feinberg, Samuil

Volume 3: BACH, trans. Feinberg: *Sonata No. 5 in C, BWV 529: Largo. Chorale preludes: Allein Gott in der Höh' sei Ehr, BWV 711; Allein Gott in der Höh' sei Ehr, BWV 662* (two versions); *Wer nur den lieben Gott lässt walten, BWV 647; Allein Gott in der Höh' sei Ehr, BWV 663.* MOZART: *Piano sonatas Nos. 4 in E flat, K.282; 18 in D, K.576; Fantasia and fugue in C, K.394; 12 Variations on an allegretto in B flat, K.500.*
(M) (***) BMG/Melodiya mono/stereo 74321 25175-2 [id.].

Samuil Yevgenyevich Feinberg (1890–1972) was a pupil of Goldenweiser and will be one of the discoveries of this collection for many non-specialist collectors. So wide a range of colour and sonority does he command that one is at times

tempted to believe that there is more than one pianist playing. His style has a melting lyricism, a limpid tone-quality and a miraculous pianissimo; his sonority is of exceptional richness and finesse. He is the opposite of the modern jet-setting virtuoso, and the transcriptions of the Bach organ works and the Mozart are of altogether exceptional beauty. The recordings date from 1951 to 1953, with the exception of four of his Bach transcriptions, which date from 1962. The recordings are very acceptable indeed: playing of this artistry deserves the widest dissemination.

Yudina, Maria

Volume 4: BARTOK: *Mikrokosmos, Books 5 & 6:* excerpts. BERG: *Sonata, Op. 1.* HINDEMITH: *Sonata No. 3.* KRENEK: *Sonata No. 2, Op. 59.* STRAVINSKY: *Serenade in A.*
(M) (***) BMG/Melodiya mono/stereo 74321 25176-2 [id.].

Maria Yudina (1899–1970) studied at first with the legendary Essipova, herself a Leschetizky pupil, and, after her death, was a fellow-student at Leningrad with Sofronitsky; Glazunov appointed her to a teaching post on the spot during her graduation recital. Her openness to modern developments in the West is well illustrated by the recordings assembled here. She carried on a long correspondence with Stravinsky, with whom she is pictured (in the sleeve-note) on his visit to Russia in 1962. These are impressive records: she makes Hindemith's *Sonata No. 3* sound more compelling than almost any other artist who has recorded it, and she succeeds in making Krenek's *Second Sonata* sound like music – no mean achievement! The recordings date from 1960–64 and are of eminently acceptable quality.

Sofronitsky, Vladimir

Volume 5: CHOPIN: *Nocturnes in F & F sharp, Op. 15/1–2; Scherzo No. 1 in B min., Op. 20.* MOZART: *Fantasia in C min., K.475.* PROKOFIEV: *Grandmother's Tales, Op. 31; Pieces for piano, Op. 12/2, 3 & 6–9; Sarcasm, Op. 17/3; Vision fugitive, Op. 22/7.* RACHMANINOV: *Moments musicaux, Op. 16/2 & 5.* SCHUBERT: *Impromptus, D.899/3 & 4.* SCHUMANN: *Sonata No. 1 in F sharp min., Op. 11.* SCRIABIN: *Sonata No. 4 in F sharp, Op. 30; Poème tragique, Op. 34; Valse in A flat, Op. 38; Etude in B flat min., Op. 8/11.*
(M) (**(*)) BMG/Melodiya mono 74321 25177-2 (2) [id.].

Vladimir Sofronitsky (1901–61) is best remembered as a Scriabin interpreter (he married the composer's daughter and was hailed by Tatiana Schloezer, Scriabin's widow, as the finest interpreter of her husband's music). He studied in Warsaw and had attracted the attention of Glazunov, who sent him to study with Alexander Michalowski. In the late 1920s he spent some time in Warsaw and Paris, where he earned the admiration of Prokofiev, whose friendship he enjoyed after Prokofiev's return to the Soviet Union. Sofronitsky was never cultivated by the Soviet regime and rarely appeared in the West, eventually succumbing to drink and drugs. All except the Prokofiev pieces come from a recital at the Small Hall of the Tchaikovsky Conservatoire in the year before his death. The Prokofiev Op. 31 comes from 1946 and the remainder of the group from 1953, recorded in the Scriabin Museum. In the fullness of time RCA will doubtless get round to reissuing all his Scriabin. In the meantime the *Fourth Sonata* gives a good idea why he is so much admired in this composer.

Richter, Sviatoslav

Volume 6: BACH: *Concerto in F in the Italian style, BWV 971.* BEETHOVEN: *Sonata No. 12 in A flat, Op. 26.* CHOPIN: *Ballades Nos. 1 in G min., Op. 23; 2 in F, Op. 38.* HAYDN: *Sonata No. 50 in C, Hob. XVI/50.*
(M) (*(*)) BMG/Melodiya mono 74321 25178-2 [id.].

The Bach *Italian-style concerto* was recorded in 1948, though it is difficult to credit it, given the excellence of its sound and the relative indifference (to put it mildly) of the later recordings offered here. It is much superior to the 1960 Haydn or Beethoven. Like most of the repertoire on this disc, it is given a performance of much distinction. The Haydn, Beethoven and Chopin items were recorded at recitals in 1960–63, but if the sound is shallow and poor in quality the playing is not. Richter recorded these pieces in the West, and older readers will doubtless recall the various CBS, RCA and EMI LP issues. Perhaps the first movement of the Haydn is too fast for comfort – but still, what playing! The Beethoven sounds very papery in tone and, though the playing is magisterial, the unpleasing sound makes its claims less pressing than many of the other discs in this collection.

Gilels, Emil

Volume 7: BACH: *Prelude and fugue in D, BWV 532.* BEETHOVEN: *32 Variations on an original theme, WoO 80.* LISZT: *Rhapsodie espagnole.* PROKOFIEV: *Visions fugitives, Op. 22/1, 3, 5 & 11.* WEBER: *Sonata No. 2 in A flat, Op. 39.*
(M) (**(*)) BMG/Melodiya mono 74321 25179-2 [id.].

Gilels is represented by a recital given in the Grand Hall of the Philharmonic in Leningrad in January 1968. Such is the quality of his pianism that the (very much less than state-of-the-art) recording does not make this anything other than a highly recommendable issue. There are some smudges (as

was often the case with Gilels in the concert hall) but they are of little account, given the musical insights and the beauty of sound he produced. The Liszt *Rhapsodie espagnole* is pretty breathtaking and the Weber *Sonata No. 2 in A flat* is played with elegance and finesse. Despite the fact that it was January in Leningrad, the audience is very quiet, warmed no doubt by the white-hot, risk-taking pianism which confronted them.

Berman, Lazar

Volume 8: LISZT: *Etudes d'exécution transcendante; Hungarian rhapsody No. 9 in E flat.*
(M) (**(*)) BMG/Melodiya mono 74321 25180-2 [id.].

The recordings of the *Etudes d'exécution transcendante* were made in the early part of 1959 and the *Hungarian rhapsody* (*Pesther Carneval*) two years later – and they leave something to be desired in terms of presence. However, the sound is vastly superior to the Richter CD reviewed above. As with the latter, no quarrels with the playing, which is absolutely stunning. Effortlessly virtuosic and brilliant, yet poetic and tender when required, and obviously with an immense dynamic range, only partly captured by the engineers. Pianistically this is without question a three-star recommendation.

Pletnev, Mikhail

Volume 9: MOZART: *Sonata No. 16 in B flat, K.570.* PROKOFIEV: *Sonata No. 7 in B flat, Op. 83.* SHCHEDRIN, arr. PLETNEV: *Prologue and Horse-racing from Anna Karenina.* tchaikovsky, arr. Pletnev: *Nutcracker suite.*
✿ (M) *** BMG/Melodiya Analogue/Dig. 74321 25181-2 [id.].

We have long been urging the reissue of Mikhail Pletnev's astonishing transcription of the *Nutcracker suite* which he recorded when he was twenty-one. (EMI originally issued this, but they never promoted it with vigour and, as a result, it disappeared within a couple of years.) Pletnev produces a wider range of colour from the keyboard than most orchestras command, and in the Shchedrin *Anna Karenina* an extraordinarily wide dynamic range. Small wonder that he has become so effective a conductor. Like the Prokofiev *Seventh Sonata*, these were all recorded after he won the Tchaikovsky Competition in 1978. The Mozart is later (1984) and completes a recital which is pre-eminent even in this remarkable series.

Kissin, Yevgeni

Volume 10: PROKOFIEV: *Visions fugitives, Op. 22/10, 11, 16 & 17; Dance in F sharp min., Op. 32/1.* RACHMANINOV: *Etudes-tableaux, Op. 39/1–6, 9;*

Preludes in G flat, Op. 23/10; A min., Op. 32/8. Lilacs, Op. 21/5 (trans. Kissin). SCRIABIN: *Preludes, Opp. 27/1–2; 37/1–4; Etude in C sharp min., Op. 42/5; 4 Pieces, Op. 51.* KISSIN: *2 Inventions.*
(M) *** BMG/Melodiya 74321 25182-2 [id.].

These recordings were made at recitals given at the Grand Hall of the Moscow Conservatoire in 1984 and 1986 when Kissin was twelve and fourteen respectively. (He had, after all, played both the Chopin *Concertos* when he was thirteen!) What is there left to say about this remarkable youngster, save that the playing has extraordinary assurance, dazzling technical address and splendid taste. This listener was left spellbound by the sheer passion and brilliance of the playing. The acoustic is a bit reverberant but, given this youth's poetic insight and artistry, technical reservations are of minimal importance.

Russian Piano School: 'The great pianists', Volumes 12, 14–20.

We have already covered the first ten CDs of the *Russian Piano School.* RCA followed it up with another set of ten but two of them have already been deleted. The artists represented in this second set are less well known (some of them are barely even names outside Russia), but the same astonishing standards of pianistic wizardry and poetic insight prevail. There are little-known but not less distinguished pianists to be discovered here, notably Edvard Syomin and, the youngest artist on the present roster, Yekaterina Ervy-Novitskaya. Readers will observe that we have given Grigory Ginsburg's remarkable collection of Liszt's *Concert paraphrases* a Rosette (BMG/Melodiya mono 64321 33210-2 – see below).

Ginsburg, Grigory

Volume 12: LISZT: Concert paraphrases: *Fantasia on two themes from Mozart's Nozze di Figaro'* (completed Busoni); *Reminiscences from: Mozart's 'Don Giovanni'; Bellini's 'Norma'; Verdi's 'Rigoletto'; Gounod's 'Faust'.* GINSBURG: *Transcription of 'Largo al factotum' from Rossini's 'Barbiere di Siviglia'.*
🟢 (M) (***) BMG/Melodiya mono 64321 33210-2 [id.].

Grigory Ginsburg featured in the earlier ten-volume collection in partnership with his teacher, Alexander Goldenweiser, but his solo recordings are quite dazzling. He was a celebrated Liszt performer and this disc is one of the highlights of a set that is itself all highlights! The *Fantasia on two themes from Mozart's 'Nozze di Figaro'* completed by Busoni beggars description for its lightness of touch and sheer virtuosity. Ginsburg's own transcription of the *Largo al factotum* from Rossini's *Barbiere*

di Siviglia has enormous sparkle and humour – not to mention virtuosity. Ginsburg died in 1961 and these recordings, which are of varying quality, come from 1948–58 (the earliest are by no means the most frail). In any event, such is the magnetism of the playing that any sonic limitations are forgotten.

Grinberg, Maria

Volume 14: SEIXAS: *Minuet in F min.; Toccata in F min.* SOLER: *Sonatas Nos. 2 in C sharp min.; 11 in G min.; 12 in F sharp min.* Domenico SCARLATTI: *Sonatas, Kk. 11, 22, 69 & 113.* MOZART: *Fantasia in C min., K.396* (completed Stadler). SCHUMANN: *Bunte Blätter, Op. 99,* excerpts: *Nos. 1–8; 10 & 13.* BRAHMS: *Variations on a theme of Schumann in F sharp min., Op. 11; Waltzes, Op. 39/1, 3, 6–7, 15–16.*
(M) **(*) BMG/Melodiya stereo/mono 74321 33212-2 [id.].

Maria Grinberg was born in Odessa in 1908 (the birthplace of so many Russian musicians, from Horowitz to Oistrakh) and made some appearances outside the then Soviet Union, including Holland, but did not make a lasting impression. She is obviously an artist of remarkable quality and the pieces by Seixas, Soler and Domenico Scarlatti, recorded in 1967, show an astonishing elegance and style. These are marvellous and subtle performances, alone worth the price of the disc. The Schumann *Bunte Blätter,* Op. 99 are played superbly but the 1947 recording is clangorous and messy. The Brahms *Variations on a theme of Schumann,* recorded in 1964 in decent sound, are quite masterly – among the best accounts of the piece to have been put on record.

Nikolayeva, Tatiana Petrovna

Volume 15: SCHUMANN: *3 Romances, Op. 28; Variations on an original theme in E flat.* PROKOFIEV: *Sonata No. 8 in B flat, Op. 84; Peter and the wolf, Op. 69* (music only; freely transcribed Nikolayeva).
(M) **(*) BMG/Melodiya 74321 33213-2 [id.].

Tatiana Nikolayeva has enjoyed celebrity in the West, thanks to her recordings of the Shostakovich *Preludes and fugues,* which were dedicated to her. The Schumann was recorded in 1983 (the sound is airless and close), the Prokofiev in the early 1960s. She certainly makes the Prokofiev *Eighth Sonata* very much her own and holds the listener in thrall in much the same ways as did Gilels and Richter. Her own transcription of *Peter and the wolf* is as imaginative as its execution. Performances of stature.

Zhukov, Igor

Volume 16: BACH: *Passacaglia in C min., BWV 582* (arr. ZHUKOV). SCHUMANN: *Waldszenen, Op. 82.* TCHAIKOVSKY: *Souvenir de Hapsal, Op. 2.* RACHMANINOV: *Barcarolle in G min., Op. 10/3.* PROKOFIEV: *Children's music (12 easy pieces), Op. 65.*
(M) ** BMG/Melodiya stereo/mono 74321 33214 [id.].

Ashkenazy, Vladimir

Volume 17: CHOPIN: *24 Etudes, Op. 10/1–12; Op. 25/1–12.* LISZT: *Mephisto waltz No. 1.*
(M) (***) BMG/Melodiya mono 74321 33215 [id.].

The two pianists featured in the pair of CDs listed above are familiar in the West, though Igor Zhukov less so than Vladimir Ashkenazy. Zhukov has recorded concertos by, among others, Medtner (No. 1), Rimsky-Korsakov and Balakirev, which have been in and out of the catalogue here. In them his virtuosity is pretty electrifying. By the exalted standards of this set as a whole, however, he is, relatively speaking, average – but that is no mean compliment in this context! If you are collecting individual discs rather than the whole box, this is not one to which you need give the highest priority. The Schumann *Waldszenen* and the Tchaikovsky and Rachmaninov items come off well, and the Prokofiev *Children's music*, Op. 65 is a rarity. The Ashkenazy recital is the familiar set of the *Etudes*, Opp. 10 and 25, from 1959–60, once available on Chant du Monde, and is one of the classics of the piano discography; the *Mephisto waltz No. 1* makes an admirable bonus. The sound is quite respectable.

Virsaladze, Eliso

Volume 18: CHOPIN: *Sonata No. 3 in B min., Op. 58; Ballade No. 3 in A flat, Op. 47; Mazurkas Nos. 21 in C sharp min., Op. 30/4; 23 in D, Op. 33/2; Waltzes Nos. 2 in A flat, Op. 34/1; 9 in A flat, Op. 69/1; Nocturne No. 8 in D flat, Op. 27/2; Polonaises Nos. 6 in A flat (Heroic), Op. 53; 7 (Polonaise-fantaisie), Op. 61.*
(M) ** BMG/Melodiya 74321 33216-2 [id.].

Syomin, Edvard

Volume 19: GODOWSKY: *Renaissance* (free arrangements after Rameau), *Nos. 1, 3 & 6.* CHOPIN: *Souvenir de Paganini; Berceuse in D flat, Op. 57.* STANCHINSKY: *3 Preludes* (1907); *5 Preludes* (1907–12). MEDTNER: *Fairy-tales, Op. 20.* EIGES: *Sonata-Toccata No. 4, Op. 15.* ALBENIZ: *Navarra; Tango in D, Op. 165/2.* BUSONI: *Chamber fantasia on Bizet's opera 'Carmen'.* GODOWSKY: *Künsterleben (symphonic metamorphoses on Johann Strauss's waltz).*
(M) *** BMG/Melodiya stereo/mono 74321 33217-2 [id.].

Eliso Virsaladze's Chopin is admirable but not special, certainly not as extraordinary as Edvard Syomin's recital. Nikolayeva spoke of Syomin's 'profound musical culture, virtuosity and freedom of self-expression'. Born in Moscow in 1945, he remains virtually unknown outside his native country, and the development of his career was, so Christoph Rueger's notes tell us, handicapped by a family tragedy and hindered by the Soviet regime. Fortunately he enjoyed the patronage of Melodiya and the Soviet Radio, and it is from their archives that the present recordings come. The recordings range from 1969 through to 1985 and are of variable quality, but the playing in the Busoni *Carmen fantasy* is astonishing. The *Preludes* by Alexei Stanchinsky (1888–1914) are quite touching and, apart from Daniel Blumenthal's record of the *Piano sonatas* for Marco Polo, his only current representation in the catalogue.

Ervy-Novitskaya, Yekaterina

Volume 20: PROKOFIEV: *Sarcasms, Op. 17; Visions fugitives, Op. 22; Romeo and Juliet: 10 Pieces, Op. 75.*
(M) *** BMG/Melodiya 74321 33218-2 [id.].

The youngest of the pianists in this collection is Yekaterina Ervy-Novitskaya, who was born in 1951. She received much encouragement from Lev Oborin, whose post-graduate assistant she became. When she was seventeen she won the first prize at the Concours Musicale Reine Elisabeth in Brussels. But the acclaim of such keyboard luminaries as Neuhaus and Rubinstein did not prevent her from retiring from the platform to settle in Brussels and devote herself to bringing up a family and to teaching. She made a comeback in Moscow in 1995; but these recordings come from 1969, when she was eighteen, save for the *Romeo and Juliet Pieces*, Op. 75, recorded in 1975. In any event she obviously has great affinity for the composer, and her accounts both of the *Fifth Sonata* (in its post-war, revised version) and of the *Visions fugitives* are impressively characterized.

Salomon Quartet

'The string quartet in 18th-century England':
ABEL: *Quartet in A, Op. 8/5.* SHIELD: *Quartet in C min., Op. 3/6.* MARSH: *Quartet in B flat.* WEBBE: *Variations in A on 'Adeste fidelis'.* Samuel WESLEY: *Quartet in E flat.*
** Hyperion Dig. CDA 66780 [id.].

A good idea, let down by the indifferent invention of much of the music itself. The amateur, John Marsh, stands up very well alongside his professional companions, and his five-movement

Quartet in B flat (modelled on Haydn's Op. 1/1 and almost as pleasing) is the first piece to catch the listener's attention, for Abel is a very dull dog indeed. Samuel Webbe's *Variations on 'O come all ye faithful'* do little but repeat the melody with decorations. Samuel Wesley begins conventionally and agreeably, then produces a real lollipop as the Trio of the Minuet and a similarly winning finale. No complaints about the performances: the Salomon Quartet play everything freshly and with total commitment, using original instruments stylishly and in the sweetest possible manner. They are very realistically recorded, too. Three stars for the performers but not the programme.

Satoh, Toyohiko (lute)

'Gaultier and the French lute school': Ennemond GAULTIER: *Tombeau de Mezangeau; Courante; Carillon; Rossignol; Testament de Mezangeau; Canarie.* Denis GAULTIER: *Tombeau de Mademoiselle Gaultier; Cleopâtre amante (Double).* Jacques GALLOT: *Prélude; Le bout de l'An de M. Gaultier; Courante la cigogne; Sarabande la pièce de huit heures; Volte la Brugeoise.* DUFAUT: *Prélude; Tombeau de M. Blanrocher; Dourante; Sarabande (Double); Gigue.* MOUTON: *Prélude. Tombeau de Gogo (Allemande); La belle homicide/Courante de M. Gaultier (Double de la belle homicide); Gavotte; La Princesse sarabande; Canarie.* Robert de VISEE: *Tombeau de M. Mouton (Allemande).*
*** Channel Classics Dig. CCS 8795 [id.].

Toyohiko Satoh has already given us a collection of the music of Robert de Visée (CCS 7795), whose *Tombeau de M. Mouton* provides one of the most affecting pieces here, to close a recital which is in essence a survey of French lute music of the seventeenth century. Satoh is clearly an expert in this field, and he plays an original lute made by Laurentius Grieff of Ingolstadt in 1613, which was modified into an eleven-course French baroque instrument around 1670.

It took four years for the Dutch lute-maker Van der Waals to restore it to playing condition, and its gut strings create a pleasingly warm sonority. Satoh's playing is robust yet thoughtful and it has an improvisatory freedom which extends even to the dance movements. (Dufaut's *Gigue*, for instance, is jolly enough but would be difficult to dance to.) This is apparently possible because, around 1630, a new French tuning was developed within the lute school centring round Le vieux Gaultier (Ennemond Gaultier of Lyon, 1575–1651). This allowed more freedom for the fingers of the left hand, enabling lutenists to write their music in a *style brisé* (broken style), which was later to spread across Europe.

Gaultier and his cousin Denis (Gaultier le jeune) were important innovators in their time and they also introduced the idea of the dignified 'tombeau' mementos, as well as vignettes with sobriquets like *Le rossignol* and *Carillon*, yet which are in no way imitative. The two versions of the *Canarie* (by Ennemond Gaultier and Mouton respectively) are based on the same melody and dance form, with a dotted rhythm, and both are among the more striking items here, alongside the expressive *Sarabande* of Dufaut and Mouton's *La Princesse*, which features the famous *La Folia*. Rather unexpectedly, the same composer's *La belle homicide* is a cheerful piece.

Savall, Jordi (viola da gamba and conductor)

Jordi Savall Edition: Instrumental recordings

Much of this is specialist repertoire, but we have tried to indicate its degree of appeal to the collector wishing to expand his or her musical boundaries under Savall's stimulating guidance.

John COPRARIO: *Fantasies for treble, tenor and bass viols* (with Christophe Coin, Sergi Casademunt).
(M) *** Audivis Astrée Dig. ES 9923 [id.].

Coprario, who became composer to King Charles I in 1625, gave his name (Cowper or Cooper) an Italianate form at a time when Italian music was becoming increasingly popular in England. His *Fantasias* are inventive and expressive, and certainly have the unpredictable element of an individual musical mind, even if they are not quite as memorable as those by Purcell. They are interspersed here by agreeable lighter rhythmic pieces in dance forms (*Corantos* and *Almaines*) but these too are stylized instrumental pieces and not intended for dancing. The playing and recording cannot be faulted, but this is perhaps not a record for the general collector.

François COUPERIN: *Pièces de violes* (1728): *Suites Nos. 1 in E min., 2 in A* (with Ton Koopman, Ariane Maurette).
(M) *** Audivis Astrée ES 9930 [id.].

Couperin's two *Suites for viols* are mature works (1728), written only five years before he died. They are scored – following the composer's practice in the 12th and 13th *Concerts* of *Les Goûts-réunis* – for a pair of viols, with the first very dominant, and the second viol part to be filled out (ad lib.) with a figured bass realized by the harpsichord. The *First Suite in E minor* appears to be the more ambitious, with five dance movements (the *Gavotte* is a *galanterie* traditionally inserted between the *Sarabande* and *Gigue*) framed by a solemn *Prélude* and a jaunty closing *Passacaglia ou Chaconne*.

But although the *Second Suite* has only four movements, it is the more remarkable work of the two, with its opening *Prélude* characterized by a noble serenity. Although this serious mood then lifts in the following *Fuguette*, there follows a melancholic *Pompe funèbre*, very like an undedicated *tombeau*. The music's character changes yet again in the pirouetting finale called *La chemise blanche* ('The white shirt'), a bravura *moto perpetuo* written lightly in the gamba's upper register. Savall, very much the soloist, throws it off in great style, and indeed the performances here are first rate and the recording most natural.

Tobias HUME (for solo bass viol): *Musicall Humors 1605: Captaine Humes Pavin; A Souldiers Galliard; The Duke of Holstones Almaine; My hope is decayed; Loves farewell; Harke, harke; Good againe; Death; Life; Touch me lightly; Beccus an Hungarian Lord his delight; A Souldiers resolution; A Pavin.*
(M) **(*) Audivis Astrée Dig. ES 9919 [id.].

Captain Tobias Hume (c. 1569–1645) was a professional soldier, composer and viol player of limited means. He deliberately ended his life in the Charterhouse Almshouse. His music for the solo bass viol has genuine vitality and feeling and a wide range of mood. The meditation on *Death* is particularly striking, as is *A Souldiers resolution* and the dolorous closing *Pavin*. The performances are strong and firm, although Savall's squeezing of phrases may not please all tastes.

LOCKE: *Consort of Fower Parts: suites Nos. 1 in D min.; 2 in D min./maj.; 3 & 4 in F; 5 in G min.; 6 in G* (with Hespèrion XX).
(M) *** Audivis Astrée Dig. ES 9921 [id.].

The Hespèrion playing here is more penetrating than that on the rival Virgin Veritas recording with Fretwork (see our main volume). Both sets of performances are highly musical, scholarly and well recorded, but in the dance movements there is an extra rhythmic vigour and buoyancy with Hespèrion, and in the *Ayres* of the *First* and *Second Suites*, for instance, there is extra expressive warmth. The remarkably ethereal *Fantazie* opening the *Fifth Suite*, magnetically presented here, can be measured against comparable music by Purcell. In the continuo, used sparingly, a double harp is preferred to the lute.

MARAIS: *Pièces de viole, Quatrième Livre* (1717): *Suite d'un goût étranger* (with Ton Koopman, Hopkinson Smith).
(M) *** Audivis Astrée Dig. ES 9932 [id.].

The association of Marin Marais with his mentor Sainte-Colombe was fascinatingly (if somewhat romantically) documented in Alain Corneau's atmospheric French film *Tous les matins du monde*. Marais absorbed much, not only from Sainte-Colombe but also from Lully, and, as a supreme virtuoso of the viol, became the greatest French

composer for this instrument at the turn of the seventeenth to eighteenth century.

Marais brought out the first printed music for the solo viol in France, and between 1686 and 1725 he published five Books of *Pièces* for one, two, or three viols with continuo. Book IV was sub-divided into three sections, with Part II described as *Suite d'un goût étranger* (for foreign tastes). In giving some of these pieces a pictorial quality, with sobriquets, Marais anticipated Rameau.

While the opening boldly rhythmic *Marche tartare* and the lively *Fétes champestres* speak for themselves, *Le Torbillon* ('Whirlwind') gives an opportunity for extraordinary bravura, excitingly taken here; *L'Arabesque* is a rondeau with a quixotically varied refrain, and the closing *Badinage* is intimate and graceful. But the most remarkable piece is the extended (12-minute) *Le Labyrinthe*, in essence a set of six variations with the pervasive feeling of improvisation, ending with a chaconne. Savall and his colleagues rise to the challenge and this proves a most stimulating collection.

Luis de MILAN: *El Maestro: Fantasies, pavanes and galliards* (with Andrew Lawrence-King, Sergi Casademunt, Eunice Brandão, Lorenz Duftschmid).
(M) **(*) Audivis Astrée Dig. ES 9927 [id.].

Luis Milán's set of vihuela pieces, *El Maestro* (1536), was written for the royal court in Valencia. Here they are arranged for renaissance harp, viols, and psaltérion, often with added simple percussion. The opening *Pavane* is very striking, and all these pieces are sensitively played and recorded. Some of the *Fantasias for viols* are very fine, especially the closing item, while the penultimate *Tiento* (for harp) is ruminatively beautiful. But the prevailing effect is of intimacy, and at times one would have liked some really robust items to bring a greater variety of mood.

PURCELL: *Fantasia upon one note; 3 Fantasias for 3 viols; 9 Fantasias for 4 viols; In nomine for 6 viols; In nomine for 7 viols* (with Hespèrion XX).
(M) *** Audivis Astrée Dig. ES 9922 [id.].

Purcell's remarkable *Fantasia upon one note* is so called because the fourth of the five parts maintains a sustained C throughout while the other voices weave their magic spell, alternating melancholy with vitality within a piece of just three minutes. The other *Fantasias* are searching and profound in feeling, and they are played with sombre nobility and powerful atmosphere by this fine group. Once again they come into competition with Fretwork on Virgin and are not found wanting. Moreover the recording is finely balanced and this Audivis disc now has a price advantage.

SAINTE-COLOMBE: *Concerts à deux violes: Nos. 3, Le tendre; 8, La conférence; 42, Dalain; 51,*

La Rougeville; 67, Le figuré (with Wieland Kuijken).
(M) *** Audivis Astrée Dig.
    ES 9933 [id.].

This is one of a pair of discs reviewed jointly in our main volume. We know very little about the reclusive Sainte-Colombe except that before Marais came on the scene he was France's most outstanding bass viol virtuoso, and a prolific composer. His music is gravely severe, and with its spartan emotional atmosphere may prove to be an acquired taste. Yet Savall and Kuijken are surely ideal advocates, and Savall's contribution to the sound-track of the biographical film mentioned above under Marais has undoubtedly attracted many new followers to Sainte-Colombe's cause.

Savall, Jordi (viola da gamba: lyra viol and bass viol)

'Les voix humaines': ABEL: *Prelude.* BACH: *Allemande* (from *BWV 1011*); *Minuets I & II; Gigue* (from *BWV 1007*); *Sarabande-Double* (from *BWV 1002*); *Bourrée* (from *BWV 1010*). SCHENCK: *Aria burlesca.* PLAYFORD: *Saraband in F (La Cloche).* MACHY: *Prelude in D min.* MARAIS: *Les voix humaines; Sarabande a l'Espagnole.* FORQUERAY: *La Du Vancel.* TELEMANN: *Vivace.* HUME: *Harke, harke; Good againe.* D'HERVELOIS: *Plainte.* SAINTE-COLOMBE: *Prelude in E min.; Fantaisie en Rondeau.* ANON.: *Lancashire pipes.*
**(*) Alia Vox Dig. AV 9803 [id.].

In its day, the viola da gamba was regarded as the instrument closest to the human voice, and Marais wrote a piece confirming this in its title. Although there are one or two livelier pieces here, like Playford's *Saraband (La Cloche)*, most of this music is melancholic. D'Hervelois's *Plainte* is quite memorable, but much of the music by Sainte-Colombe and Marais is even more gloomy. Jordi Savall is an eloquent exponent, and he is finely recorded, but the austerity of the writing and the pervading atmosphere of woe means that such a recital has a more specialist appeal than the *Folia* collection below. Savall is truthfully but closely recorded, so that we can also hear his effortful grunts.

'La Folia' (with Chamber ensemble): ANON.: *Improvisation after a Villancico from the Cancionero Musical de Palacio.* Music based on *La Folia* by: ORTIZ: *Recercada quarta.* CABEZON: *Para quien crié cabellos.* ENZINA: *Hoy comamos y bèbamos.* Antonio MARTIN Y COL: *Diferencias.* CORELLI: *Follias.* MARAIS: *Couplets.*
*** Alia Vox Dig. AV 9805 [id.].

One of the most famous of all dance songs of the Middle Ages, the *Folia* originated in Portugal (the Iberian Peninsula) but because of its catchy memor-

ability soon found its way all over Europe. Jordi Savall introduces it as an exotic medieval dance, winningly accompanied by organ, harp, guitar, and a percussive group including castanets and tambour. Four comparatively brief sixteenth-century pieces follow, all in improvisatory style, but each quite different in character, before the extended *Diferencias* of Antonio Martín y Col (again featuring a backing of harp, guitar and castanets) bring us into the eighteenth century. The following *Follias* of Corelli further develops a powerfully expressive variation format which is to reach its peak in the most extended piece of all, for bass viol and continuo, by Marin Marais, once more underlining the theme's melancholy character. The playing here is superbly spontaneous and Jordi Savall's timbre has never before been more richly caught on disc. Highly recommended.

Scandinavian Wind Quintet

Danish concert: NIELSEN: *Wind quintet, Op. 43.* HOLMBOE: *Notturno, Op. 19.* NORGARD: *Whirl's world.* ABRAHAMSEN: *Walden.*
*** Marco Polo Dacapo Dig. 8.224001 [id.].

The Scandinavian Wind Quintet give an eminently acceptable account of the Nielsen which can stand up to most of the competition. The Holmboe *Notturno* is a beautiful piece from 1940 whose language blends the freshness of Nielsen with the neoclassicism of Hindemith yet remains totally distinctive. The Nørgård is less substantial but is not otherwise available; Hans Abrahamsen's *Walden* is thin but atmospheric. Very present and lifelike recording.

Schiff, András and Peter Serkin (piano duo)

Music for 2 pianos: MOZART: *Fugue in C min., K. 426; Sonata in D, K.448.* REGER: *Variations and fugue on a theme of Beethoven, Op. 86.* BUSONI: *Fantasia contrappuntistica.*
*** ECM Dig. 465 062-2 or ECM 1676/77 (2) [id.].

András Schiff and Peter Serkin join here in a symbiotic partnership to give a quite superb and certainly gripping account of Busoni's formidable *Fantasia contrappuntistica* in which they find as wide a range of mood and colour as in Max Reger's *Variations* (on a Beethoven *Bagatelle* from Op. 119). The theme is presented with a disarming simplicity, but Reger soon introduces characteristically florid textures, yet returning to simplicity in the *Andante* and *Sostenuto* variations. These alternate with *Agitato* and *Vivace* sections leading to the spirited closing *Fugue.* The pair of early twentieth-century works are framed by two-piano music of

Mozart. Here the opening *Fugue in C minor* is strong and positive, and the first movement of the *D major Sonata*, too, is taken very seriously, not emphasizing what Alfred Einstein called its 'gallant character' until the arrival of the second subject, and then only momentarily. However, the mood lightens in the central *Andante*, in which the two players exchange phrases very beguilingly, and the finale is rhythmically most winning. Excellent, well-focused and not too resonant recording.

Schiller, Allan (piano)

'*Für Elise*': *Popular piano pieces:* BEETHOVEN: *Für Elise.* FIELD: *Nocturne in E (Noontide).* CHOPIN: *Mazurka in B flat, Op. 7/1; Waltz in A, Op. 34/2. 3 Ecossaisen, Op. 72/3; Fantaisie-impromptu, Op. 66.* MENDELSSOHN: *Songs without words: Venetian gondola song, Op. 19; Bees' wedding, Op. 67.* LISZT: *Consolation No. 3 in D flat.* DE SEVERAC: *The music box.* DEBUSSY: *Suite bergamasque: Clair de lune. Arabesques Nos. 1 and 2. Prélude: The girl with the flaxen hair.* GRIEG: *Wedding day at Troldhaugen; March of the dwarfs.* ALBENIZ: *Granada; Tango; Asturias.*

(BB) *** ASV Quicksilva CDQS 6032 [(M) id.].

A particularly attractive recital, diverse in mood, spontaneous in feeling and very well recorded. The acoustic is resonant, but the effect is highly realistic. There are many favourites here, with Allan Schiller at his most personable in the engaging Field *Nocturne*, De Severac's piquant *Music box* and the closing *Asturias* of Albéniz, played with fine bravura. The Chopin group, too, is most successful, with the Scottish rhythmic snap of the *Ecossaisen* neatly articulated and the famous *B flat Mazurka* presented most persuasively.

Scott Whiteley, John (organ)

'*Great romantic organ music*' (organ of York Minster): TOURNEMIRE: *Improvisation on the Te Deum.* JONGEN: *Minuet-Scherzo, Op. 53.* MULET: *Tu es Petra.* DUPRE: *Prelude and fugue in G min., Op. 3/7.* R. STRAUSS: *Wedding prelude.* KARG-ELERT: *Pastel in B, Op. 92/1.* BRAHMS: *Chorale prelude: O Gott, du frommer Gott, Op. 122/7.* LISZT: *Prelude and fugue on bach, G.260.*
*** York CD 101.

A superb organ recital, with the huge dynamic range of the York Minster organ spectacularly captured on CD and pianissimo detail registering naturally. John Scott Whiteley's playing is full of flair: the attractively complex and sparklingly florid *Prelude and fugue* of Marcel Dupré is exhilarating and reaches a high climax, while the grand Liszt piece is hardly less overwhelming. The opening Tournemire

Improvisation is very arresting indeed, while Jongen's *Minuet-Scherzo* displays Scott Whiteley's splendidly clear articulation.

Segovia, Andrés (guitar)

'*The Legendary Segovia':* BACH: *Cello suite in G, BWV 1007: Prelude* (arr. PONCE); (Unaccompanied) *Violin Partita No. 3 in E, BWV 1006: Gavotte & Rondo; Prelude in C min. for lute, BWV 999* (both arr. SEGOVIA). SOR: *Thème varié, Op. 9.* Robert de VISEE: *Minuet.* FROBERGER: *Gigue.* CASTELNUOVO-TEDESCO: *Hommage à Boccherini: Vivo e energico.* MENDELSSOHN: *String quartet No. 1 in E flat, Op. 12: Canzonetta* (arr. Segovia). MALATS: *Serenata.* ALBENIZ: *Suite española: Granada; Sevilla.* GRANADOS: *Danza española No. 10 in G, Op. 37.* TURINA: *Fandanguillo.* TORROBA: *Suite castellana: Fandanguillo. Sonatina in A: Allegretto. Preludio; Notturno.* PONCE: *Petite valse; Suite in A.* TARREGA: *Recuerdos de la Alhambra.*

(M) (***) EMI mono CDM5 67009-2 [id.].

It was Segovia's pioneering recitals in the 1930s that re-established the guitar in the public mind as a serious solo instrument. This collection consists of his early recordings, made over a span of twelve years from 1927 to 1939 either at Abbey Road or the Small Queen's Hall in London. There are quite a few transcriptions, including several Bach items, where the style of the playing is romantic (though never showing lapses of taste). However, the second part of the programme includes a high proportion of Spanish repertoire either written for or naturally suited to the guitar. What is so striking throughout this collection is the way all the music, slight or serious, springs vividly to life. Segovia had the gift of natural spontaneity in all he played, and he was in his prime at this period, so that technically this is wonderfully assured. His performance of Tárrega's famous *Recuerdos* is quite individual, with the underlying melodic line shaped like a song, rather than treated seamlessly. Guitar fans will find this generous 74-minute recital an essential purchase; others will be surprised to discover that no apologies need be made for the sound, which is natural in timbre and gives the instrument a ready projection.

Shifrin, David (clarinet), Lincoln Center Chamber Music Society

Five American clarinet quintets: CORIGLIANO: *Soliloquy for clarinet and string quartet.* Ellen ZWILICH: *Clarinet quintet.* Joan TOWER: *Turning points.* Bright SHENG: *Concertino for clarinet and string quartet.* Bruce ADOLPHE: *At the still point there the dance is.*

*** Delos Dig. DE 3183 (2) [id.].

A remarkable group of five surprisingly lyrical works, often searching and all readily approachable. John Corigliano's *Soliloquy*, adapted from the second movement of his *Concerto*, is essentially a haunting interplay between solo clarinet and violin. It was written in memory of his father, who was concertmaster of the New York Philharmonic, and is passionately elegiac. While sustaining its mood of desolation throughout, it leaves the listener uplifted rather than depressed.

Zwilich's *Quintet* opens with stabbing aggression from the strings and a continuing restlessness from the soloist, with moments of wildness carried through into the pungent second movement. Finally relative calm is reached in the third, but its language becomes increasingly plangent, until relative serenity returns towards the close. The brief Scherzo is ironically jocular, followed by an atmospheric epilogue.

Joan Tower's *Turning points* immediately features the device of a long slow crescendo for the soloist: its style is at first rhapsodic, with a central cadenza-like virtuoso display for the soloist and increasing agitation towards the end. The remaining two works are primarily atmospheric. Bright Sheng's attractively lyrical *Concertino* brings an exotic influence from Chinese folk music. It opens and closes reflectively, but its serenity does not run an even course, with energetic bursts from the clarinet. The Chinese influence is most strongly felt in the repeated scherzando ostinatos of the second movement.

Bruce Adolphe's *At the still point* is also ruminative, the first two movements, *Aria* and *Meditation*, move hauntingly towards the 'still point', though not without interruption, and then are released into the dance, which swirls, but in a relatively gentle minimalist manner. It is a work of immediate appeal. David Shifrin's performances are masterly and the recording is excellent. A most stimulating collection.

(i) **Snowden, Jonathan** (flute),
Andrew Litton (piano); (ii) **Nicholas Daniel** (oboe), **Julius Drake** (piano)

'French music for flute and oboe': (i) WIDOR: *Suite for flute and piano, Op. 34.* FAURE: *Fantaisie, Op. 79; Morceau de concours.* DEBUSSY: *Syrinx.* HONEGGER: *Danse de la chèvre.* ROUSSEL: *Jouers de flûte, Op. 27.* MESSIAEN: *Le Merle noir.* POULENC: *Flute sonata.* (ii) SAINT-SAENS: *Oboe sonata.* DUTILLEUX: *Oboe sonata.* KOECHLIN: *Oboe sonata, Op 28.* POULENC: *Oboe sonata.*
(BB) *** Virgin Classics VBD5 61495-2 (2) [CDVB 61495].

This Virgin Double aptly and inexpensively pairs two outstanding recitals of French instrumental music, originally issued separately, but which in this format complement each other admirably. Jonathan Snowden, deftly accompanied by Andrew Litton, a formidable pianist, first gathers a vintage collection of French works for flute. The Poulenc *Sonata* is dazzlingly done, and so are the other virtuoso pieces, all strongly characterized. The surprise is the opening item, by Widor, delicate and pointed, charmingly lyrical, a suite by a composer now remembered for his heavyweight organ works.

On the second disc Nicholas Daniel and Julius Drake concentrate equally persuasively on four major French oboe sonatas. Once again the Poulenc proves highly diverting, its outer movements, *Elégie paisiblement* and *Déploration: très calme*, proving as unpredictable as ever. The opening piece, by Saint-Saëns, is captivating but by no means trivial, with its central *Allegretto* framed by two sections giving the soloist a great deal of freedom.

Dutilleux's *Sonata* typically combines subtlety of colour and expressive depth with ingenuity. However, the most ambitious work is by Koechlin, its four movements running for 28 minutes. It opens in pastoral evocation, but afterwards the writing often becomes very prolix, the range of mood remarkably wide. The Daniel/Drake duo play it expertly and sympathetically, but they do not entirely erase one's suspicion that it would have been a stronger piece if more concise. Yet overall these paired recitals, well balanced and truthfully recorded, give much pleasure.

Staier, Andreas (harpsichord)

'Variaciones del fandango español': SOLER: *Fandango.* ALBERO: *Recercata, fuga y sonata in G; Recercata, fuga y sonata in D.* GALLES: *Sonatas Nos. 9 in C min.; 16 in F min.; 17 in C min.* LOPEZ: *Variaciones del fandango español.* FERRER: *Adagio in G min.; Sonata, Andantino in G min.* BOCCHERINI: *Fandango, Grave assai* (with Christine Schornheim, harpsichord & Adela Gonzáles Cámpa, castanets).
*** Teldec/Warner Dig. 3984 21468-2 [id.].

Framed by two great *Fandangos* by Soler and Boccherini, and with a sparkling further set of *Fandango variations* by Félix López as centrepiece, this is a fascinatingly conceived recital, superbly played on an ideal harpsichord – a modern French copy of an early eighteenth-century German instrument (associated with Silbermann). The rest of the programme includes a pair of inventive triptychs by Sebastián de Albero (1722–56) – 'polyphony used in a very Mediterranean way' (to quote Staier) – and three delightful miniature sonatas by Joseph Gallés: No. 16 in F minor (a single movement) is particularly winning, as are the two short pieces by José Ferrer.

Staier plays with fine sensibility and great virtuosity, always retaining the listener's interest. For the spectacular finale (which he has freely arranged from the finale of Boccherini's *D major Guitar quintet*, G.448) Staier is joined by an excellent second player, with a third artist to decorate the thrilling climax with castanets. The result is a semi-improvisational *tour de force*. The only small snag is that the recording is somewhat over-resonant – thus, setting a modest volume level is important, though not, of course, in the *Fandangos*.

Steele-Perkins, Crispian (trumpet), Stephen Cleobury (organ)

'The King's trumpeter': MATHIAS: *Processional*. L. MOZART: *Concerto in E flat*. BOYCE: *Voluntaries in D*. ANON.: *3 16th-century dances*. TELEMANN: *Concerto da caccia in D*. GOUNOD: *Méditation: Ave Maria*. STEELE: *6 Pieces, Op. 33*. **(*) Priory Dig. PRCD 189 [id.].

Crispian Steele-Perkins is here given a chance to show his paces on a modern trumpet. The programme opens with Mathias's distinctly catchy *Processional* and covers a fairly wide range of repertoire, ending with the six characterful pieces by Christopher Steele. The disc is relatively short measure (53 minutes), but the playing is first class and the balance most convincing.

Stern, Isaac (violin)

'A Life in Music': Boxes III–IV (for Boxes I–II, see under Orchestral and Concertante Music)

'A Life in music': Box III
(M) **(*) Sony Analogue/Dig. SX12K 67195 (12) [S12K 67195].

Volume 16: (i) BACH: *Trio sonatas in G, BWV 1038; in C min., BWV 1079*. W. F. BACH: *Trio sonata in A min*. (ii) J. C. BACH: *Trio sonata in C;* (iii) *Sonata in C*. (ii) TELEMANN: *Quartet (Trio sonata) in E min*. (with (i; ii; iii) Jean-Pierre Rampal (flute); (i) Leslie Parnas (cello); (ii) Mstislav Rostropovich (cello); (i; iii) John Steele Ritter ((i) harpsichord; (iii) fortepiano); (ii) Matthias Spaeter (lute)) (Dig. SMK 64509) [id.].

Volume 17: BEETHOVEN: *Piano trios Nos. 1–3, Op. 1/1–3; 8, WoO 38; 10 (Variations in E flat), Op. 44* (with Leonard Rose (cello), Eugene Istomin (piano)) (SM2K 64510 (2)) [S2K 64510].

Volume 18: BEETHOVEN: *Piano trios Nos. 4 in B flat, Op. 11; 5 in D (Ghost), Op. 70/1; 6 in E flat, Op. 70/2; 7 in B flat (Archduke), Op. 97; 9 in B flat, WoO 39; 11 (Variations on 'Ich bin der*

Schneider Kakadu'), *Op. 121a* (with Leonard Rose (cello), Eugene Istomin (piano)) (SM2K 64513 (2)) [S2K 64513].

Volume 19: (i) SCHUBERT: *Piano trios Nos. 1–2, Opp. 99, 100*. (ii) MOZART: *Piano quartet No. 2 in E flat, K.493*. (i) HAYDN: *Piano trio in E flat, Hob XV/10* ((i) with Leonard Rose (cello); (ii) with Milton Katims (viola), Mischa Schneider (cello); (i; ii) with Eugene Istomin (piano)) (SM2K 64516 (2)) [S2K 64516].

Volume 20: MENDELSSOHN: *Piano trios Nos. 1 in D min., Op. 49; 2 in C min., Op. 66* (with Leonard Rose (cello), Eugene Istomin (piano)) (SMK 64519) [id.].

Volume 21: BRAHMS: *Piano trios Nos. 1 in B, Op. 8; 2 in C, Op. 87; 3 in C min., Op. 101* (with Leonard Rose (cello), Eugene Istomin (piano)); *Piano quartets Nos. 1 in G min., Op. 25; 2 in A, Op. 26; 3 in C min., Op. 60* (with Jaime Laredo (viola), Yo-Yo Ma (cello), Emanuel Ax (piano)) (SM3K 64520 (3)) [S3K 64520].

Volume 22: (i) ANON.: *Greensleeves*. FOSTER: *I dream of Jeannie with the light brown hair*. KREISLER: *Liebesleid*. SCHUBERT: *Ave Maria*. (ii) MENDELSSOHN: *On wings of song*. (i) BRAHMS: *Hungarian dance No. 5*. DVORAK: *Humoresque*. RIMSKY-KORSAKOV: *Flight of the bumblebee*. (ii) RACHMANINOV: *Vocalise*. (i) TCHAIKOVSKY: *None but the lonely heart*. (ii) BORODIN: *Nocturne*. (i) BENJAMIN: *Jamaican rumba*. (ii) SATIE: *Gymnopédie No. 3*. (i) GERSHWIN: *Bess, you is my woman now*. COPLAND: *Hoedown* (with (i, ii) Columbia SO; (i) Milton Katims; (ii) Frank Brieff) (SMK 64537) [id.].

With Box III it is perhaps better to pick and choose rather than to go for the complete box. The *Trio sonatas* by Bach and his sons plus an attractive work of Telemann offer some very distinguished playing (especially in the performances featuring Rostropovich) and one can adjust to the up-front balance. The Beethoven and Brahms *Piano trios* and *Quartets* are indispensable, but the Schubert and Mendelssohn are not. Many will enjoy the final selection of lollipops, sumptuously recorded, although the effect is a bit schmaltzy and they are best taken in small doses. Superb playing, of course, as throughout all three Boxes. All the records (or smaller compilations) are available separately and most are discussed in detail under their Composer entries. Overall this is a remarkable achievement.

'A Life in music': Box IV: Chamber and instrumental music
(M) **(*) Sony Analogue/Dig. SX12K 67196 (12) [S12K 67196].

Box IV completes Sony's Isaac Stern Edition and in many ways it is one of the most attractive collections in the survey. Each issue is available separately.

Volume 23: C. P. E. BACH or J. S. BACH: *Sonata in G min., BWV 1020.* J. S. BACH: *Violin sonata* (for violin and harpsichord) *No. 3, BWV 1016; Sonata for violin and continuo, BWV 1023.* HANDEL: *Sonata in D, Op. 1/3.* TARTINI: *Sonata in G min. (Dido Abbandonata), Op. 1/10* (all with Alexander Zakin) (mono SMK 68361) [id.].

These recordings come from 1952–3 and, although the violin is balanced rather forwardly, in all other respects the mono recording is first class. Stern shows himself thoroughly at home in baroque repertoire; even though he uses a minimum of embellishments, the style is impeccable. The *Adagio* of the *G minor Sonata*, now thought to be by C. P. E. Bach, is glorious. Alexander Zakin is a splendid partner, playing simply and directly and making one feel for the moment that these works were intended to be heard in a violin/piano partnership, even the continuo sonata, BWV 1023.

Similarly in Handel, Stern plays the noble line of the *D major Sonata* with natural sympathy and unexaggerated warmth. The (originally three-movement) Tartini *Sonata* is heard in an arrangement by Leopold Auer, who added a *Largo* taken from the fifth sonata of the same opus, which makes a suitably dramatic interlude to lead into the lively finale. The connection of the work with Metastasio's libretto about Dido (set to music by at least four composers) is obscure, but it served to keep the sonata in the repertoire.

Volume 24: BEETHOVEN: *Violin sonatas Nos. 1–10* (with Eugene Istomin) (Dig./Analogue SM3K 64524 (3)) [S3K 64524].

Stern and Istomin make an inspirational partnership, obviously striking sparks off each other in performances that are brimming with zest and vitality. The performances have striking rhythmic strengths as well as lyrical appeal and are discussed more fully under their Composer entry.

Volume 25: SCHUBERT: *Violin sonatinas Nos. 1–3; Rondo in B min. (Rondeau brillant), D.895; Duo in A (Grand duo), D.574; Fantaisie in C, D.934* (with Daniel Barenboim). HAYDN: *Violin concerto in C, Hob VIIa/1* (with Columbia CO) (Dig./Analogue (mono) SM2K 64528 (2)) [S2K 64528].

Stern and Barenboim find an ideal partnership: the performances have a natural warmth and plenty of character, yet there is an unaffected simplicity and directness of style which especially suits the three early *Sonatinas*. The Haydn *Concerto*, excellently recorded in mono in 1947, is a very acceptable bonus.

Volume 26: BRAHMS: *Violin sonatas Nos. 1–3* (with Alexander Zakin) (SMK 64531) [id.].

Stern and Zakin give splendidly vital and charac-

terful performances of the Brahms *Sonatas*. They have genuine power and conviction, but the 1960 recording brings the usual CBS problem of that period: Stern was far too close to the microphones. The original LP produced a far from comfortable tone-quality, but the improvement in the CD remastering is very striking; his tone now emerges, closely scrutinized but unscathed, and despite the balance Alexander Zakin's contribution is not submerged. Admirers of these artists will still consider this disc worth its cost.

Volume 27: FRANCK: *Violin sonata in A.* DEBUSSY: *Violin sonata.* ENESCU: *Violin sonata No. 3 in A min., Op. 25* (all with Alexander Zakin) (SMK 64532) [id.].

Stern recorded the Franck *Sonata* in 1959. It is a work which suits him especially well and he gives a performance of heartfelt, extrovert feeling, especially in the slow movement, although some might not care for the portamento in its closing bars. Throughout there is much subtlety of detail too. As ever in that period, he was too closely recorded, but the projection suits the intensity of the finale. In some way the Debussy *Sonata* suits him less well; but this is still a commanding performance, impossible not to enjoy, even if it is one which rather wears its heart on its sleeve.

The Enescu *Third Sonata* (1926) is a remarkable work of great vitality and interest, strongly influenced by Romanian folklore, but through its harmonic flavours and rhythmic influences and styles rather than by quoting folksong. The exotic *Andante sostenuto e misterio* even suggests oriental influences from further east and has an improvisatory quality which Stern captures superbly, while the dashing finale throws off sparks of every kind. Its upper tessitura harmonics and histrionics are flawlessly managed, the glissando lyrical spurts given a gypsy passion. In this instance the very close microphones add to the bite, even though, at those times when Stern is pressing hard on the strings, the sound is not quite comfortable.

Volume 28: HINDEMITH: *Violin sonata.* BLOCH: *Violin sonata; Baal Shem, Three pictures of Chassidic life* (all with Alexander Zakin). COPLAND: *Violin sonata* (with composer) (mono/stereo SMK 64533) [id.].

The Hindemith *Sonata* (1939) is neither intimidating nor dull. It begins with a friendly if busy melodic flow, and there is a touching melody for the opening and close of the central movement. Stern obviously relishes its engaging moto perpetuo central section, and his dainty, light, bravura articulation is spellbinding as the introductory material is reintroduced. The fugal finale again opens simply and, even if its harmonic progressions seem devious at first hearing, their Hindemithian logic soon falls into place.

The mono recording, from 1946, is just a little confined but is otherwise very good.

Bloch has to be presented with whole-hearted conviction if his music is to make any contact at all, and this performance has just that quality. Stern's playing could hardly be more committed or full of passion and, despite a somewhat forward balance, we would recommend these most persuasive performances of both works, which have never been surpassed.

The Copland recording, which is new to us, is the highlight of the disc. It was made in 1967, with the composer at the piano, and is clearly definitive, for although Stern is still very forward the piano is very much in the picture. The lively central section of the first movement is framed by an *Andante semplice* in which the piano coolly repeats a chordal duplet whose harmonic flavour is instantly identifiable by anyone who has heard the famous Copland ballets.

The haunting central *Lento* has a comparable simplicity, and Stern's G-string re-statement of the main theme near the close is particularly telling. The sharply rhythmic finale with its dancing syncopations introduces material we have heard before, notably the coda (which recalls the opening), yet, with the piano chords transformed, the effect is much more upbeat. A marvellously compelling performance, and if Stern is again too near the microphones – as Klemperer once said about something entirely different – 'You will get used to it!'

Volume 29: PROKOFIEV: *Violin sonatas Nos. 1–2* (with Alexander Zakin) (SMK 64534) [id.].

Stern's performances with Zakin are of high quality, the *Andante* of the *F minor* (No. 1) memorably atmospheric, especially after the extrovert bravura of the *Allegro brusco*. But here, more than in most of these reissues, the close balance makes Stern's fortissimo timbre sound unnecessarily acerbic.

Volume 30: BARTOK: *Violin sonatas Nos. 1–2* (with Alexander Zakin). WEBERN: *4 Pieces for violin and piano, Op. 7* (with Charles Rosen) (SMK 64535) [id.].

Stern and Zakin are completely involved in the Bartók *Sonatas*, and the cantabile melisma which opens the *Adagio* of the *First Sonata* can never have sounded more lyrically beautiful on record, while the gutsy bravura of the finale is equally compelling. The rapt opening of the *Second Sonata* is comparably concentrated. The four brief, sharply focused Webern *Pieces* are presented with comparable intensity and authority. Once again one must complain about the too-close balance of the recordings, made in 1967 and 1971 respectively, but the effect is not destructive.

Volume 31: *'Encores with piano'*: SARASATE: *Caprice basque*. PUGNANI: *Sonata in D: Largo*

espressivo. NOVACEK: *Perpetuum mobile.* BLOCH: *Baal Shem: Nigun (Improvisation).* LECLAIR: *Sarabande et tambourin.* MOZART: *Haffner Serenade: Rondo allegro.* GLUCK: *Orpheus and Eurydice: Mélodie.* TCHAIKOVSKY: *Valse sentimentale.* SCHUMANN: *Waldszenen: Bird as prophet.* KREISLER: *Schön Rosmarin.* DVORAK: *Slavonic dance, Op. 46/2.* szymanowski: *Chant de Roxane; La Fontaine d'Arethuse.* stravinsky: *Firebird: Berceuse.* DINICU: *Hora staccato.* MILHAUD: *Saudades do Brasil: Tijuca.* PROKOFIEV: *Romeo and Juliet: Danse des jeunes filles des Antilles; Masques.* FALLA: *Suite after 7 Spanish popular songs* (all with Alexander Zakin) (mono SMK 64536) [id.].

Marvellous playing from Stern throughout: he is quite dazzling in the arrangement of the Rondo from Mozart's *Haffner Serenade*, while the Kreisler transcription of Gluck's most famous *Mélodie* from *Orfeo etd Euridice* is played with ravishing delicacy. Tchaikovsky's *Valse sentimentale* and Schumann's *Prophet bird* (from *Waldszenen*), arranged by Leopold Auer, are presented with comparably exquisite grace. If elegant flair is what you are looking for, try Kreisler's *Schön Rosmarin*, while Szymanowski's *Chant de Roxane* and *La Fontaine d'Arethuse* are ethereally sensuous, helped by Zakin's atmospheric backing.

The *Berceuse* from Stravinsky's *Firebird* is infinitely gentle and touching, while for sparkling, easy bravura the Dinicu *Hora staccato* takes some beating. The two excerpts from Prokofiev's *Romeo and Juliet* are indelibly characterized, and are no less seductive than the exotic closing Falla suite. The recordings are all mono, made in either 1947 or 1952, but the effect is faithful, if a little dry: the opening Sarasate *Caprice basque* ideally needs a more flatteringly sumptuous acoustic.

Stringer, Alan (trumpet), Noel Rawsthorne (organ)

'Trumpet and organ' (organ of Liverpool Cathedral): M.-A. CHARPENTIER: *Te Deum: Prelude.* STANLEY: *Voluntary No. 5 in D.* PURCELL: *Sonata in C; Two Trumpet tunes and Air.* BOYCE: *Voluntary in D.* CLARKE: *Trumpet voluntary.* BALDASSARE: *Sonata No. 1 in F.* ROMAN: *Keyboard suite in D: Non troppo allegro; Presto (Gigue).* FIOCCO: *Harpsichord suite No. 1: Andante.* BACH: *Cantata No. 147: Jesu, joy of man's desiring.* attrib. GREENE: *Introduction and trumpet tune.* VIVIANI: *Sonata No. 1 in C.* (M) **(*) CRD CRD 3308 [id.].

This collection is extremely well recorded. The reverberation of Liverpool Cathedral is under full control and both trumpet and organ are cleanly focused, while the trumpet has natural timbre and bloom. Alan Stringer is at his best in the classical pieces, the *Voluntary* of Boyce, the *Trumpet tunes* and *Sonata* of Purcell and the stylishly played *Sonata* of Viviani, a most attractive little work. He also gives a suitably robust performance of the famous *Trumpet voluntary*. Elsewhere he is sometimes a little square: the Bach chorale is rather too stiff and direct. But admirers of this repertoire will find much to enjoy, and the *Andante* of Fiocco has something in common with the more famous *Adagio* attributed to Albinoni in Giazotto's famous arrangement. The CD transfer improves definition satisfactorily.

Swiss Wind Quintet

20th-century wind quintets: JANACEK: *Mládi.* NIELSEN: *Wind quintet, Op. 43.* HINDEMITH: *Kleine Kammermusik, Op. 24/2.* LIGETI: *6 Bagatelles.*
(BB) *** Koch Discover Dig. DICD 920395 [id.].

Mládi isn't, strictly speaking, a quintet, as it has an additional bass clarinet part. But it is uncommonly well played by this excellent Swiss group, and they give an equally sympathetic account of the Nielsen *Quintet*, most winning in the *Minuet* as well as in the third-movement Theme and variations. The Hindemith *Kleine Kammermusik* is hardly less successful, notably the dolorous *Waltz* which hints at Walton's *Façade*, and the pensive nostalgia of the third movement, although there is plenty of sparkling vitality elsewhere. The riotously witty opening movement of Ligeti's *Six Bagatelles* is splendidly done. There is little to choose between this performance of an unexpectedly entertaining work and that by the competing Claude Debussy Quintet on Harmonia Mundi (see above). In some ways the programme on this excellently recorded Discover disc is the more tempting, but both CDs are equally recommendable.

Tal, Yaara and Andreas Groethuysen (piano duo)

DVORAK: *From the Bohemian forest, Op. 68.* RUBINSTEIN: *6 Characteristic pictures, Op. 50.* RACHMANINOV: *6 Pieces, Op. 11.*
*** Sony Dig. SK47199 [id.].

Anything that this remarkably musical and sensitive partnership has recorded is special, and this programme – and in particular the Rachmaninov Op. 11 pieces – proves no exception. They make every phrase breathe naturally and freshly.

Thurston Clarinet Quartet

'Clarinet masquerade': FARKAS: *Ancient Hungarian dances from the 17th century.* MOZART (arr. WHEWELL): *Divertimento No. 2.* TOMASI: *3 Divertissements.* GARNER (arr. BLAND): *Misty.* JOBIM (arr. BLAND): *The Girl from Ipanema.* DESPORTES: *French suite.* ALBINONI (arr. THILDE): *Sonata in G min.* STARK: *Serenade.* GERSHWIN (arr. BLAND): *Rhapsody: Summertime.* PHILLIPS (arr. HARVEY): *Cadenza;* (arr. FERNANDEZ): *Muskrat Sousa.*
(M) *** ASV Dig. CDWHL 2076 [id.].

A light-hearted concert, but an entertaining one which will especially appeal to those who like the clarinet's sonority, reedier than the flute's and with more character. The opening suite of Hungarian folk dances (with the chirps and cheeps in the finale very engaging) leads on to a Mozart *Divertimento* for basset horns. The other pieces, the insouciant Tomasi and the Desportes suite (full of Ravelian elegance) are all amiable, and the arrangement of Gershwin's *Summertime* has the famous opening swerve of *Rhapsody in blue* as its introduction. Finally there is the exuberant *Muskrat Sousa* which features a combination of *12th Street Rag* and *South Rampart Street Parade*. The recording is immaculately vivid.

Troussov, Kirill (violin), Alexandra Troussova (piano)

BEETHOVEN: *Violin sonata No. 5 in C min., Op. 30/2.* BRAHMS: *Violin sonata No. 3 in D min., Op. 108.* WIENIAWSKI: *Fantaisie brillante on themes from Gounod's 'Faust'.* ZIMBALIST: *Fantasy on Rimsky-Korsakov's 'The Golden Cockerel'.*
(B) *** EMI Début Dig. CDZ5 73212-2 [id.].

One of the best of the valuable EMI Début series. Kirill Troussov and Alexandra Troussova are a brother-and-sister team of remarkable skill. They are Russian and were both in their teens when this outstanding recital was recorded. Vibrant and committed playing from both artists and excellent recordings.

Tureck, Rosalyn (piano)

'Live at the Teatro Colón': BACH: *Adagio in G, BWV 968; Chromatic fantasia and fugue, BWV 903; Partita No. 1, BWV 825: Gigue. Goldberg variation No. 29, BWV 988; Klavierbüchlein for Anna Magdalena Bach: Musette in D.* MENDELSSOHN: *Songs without words, Op. 19/1.* SCHUBERT: *Moments musicaux Nos. 2 in A flat; 3 in F min.* BACH/BUSONI: *Chaconne (from BWV*

1004). BRAHMS: *Variations and fugue on a theme by Handel, Op. 24.*
**(*) VAI Audio Dig. VIAI 1024-2 (2) [id.].

Rosalyn Tureck has lost none of her magic, as this Buenos Aires (1992) live recital demonstrates, and it is good to find her so sympathetic in Schubert and Mendelssohn, as well as in Bach. Her articulation in the Brahms *Handel variations* suggests she is thinking as much of Handel as of Brahms, but that is a comment, not a criticism. The Bach/Busoni *Chaconne* is splendid. Excellent recording, but there are two snags: the almost hysterical applause which bursts in as soon as a piece has ended and the fact that this recital would almost have fitted on one CD. These two play for just 83 minutes 31 seconds.

Vieaux, Jason (guitar)

Recital: MERLIN: *Suite del recuerdo.* PUJOL: *Preludios Nos. 2, 3 , & 5.* ORBON (de SOTO): *Preludio y Danza.* KROUSE: *Variations on a Moldavian hora.* BARRIOS: *Valses, Op. 8/3 & 4; Julia Florida: Barcarola.* MOREL: *Chôro; Danza Brasileira; Danza in E min.* BUSTAMENTE: *Misionera.*
⚫ (BB) *** Naxos Dig. 8.553449 [id.].

This is the finest début guitar recital we have heard for some years. Jason Vieaux is a young American musician, already a prize-winner – and no wonder. This Latin-American repertoire is unfailingly diverting in his hands: there are no familiar names here except that of Barrios, yet almost every item is either memorably evocative or it makes the pulse quicken. Vieaux's completely natural rubato at the opening *Evocación* of José Luis Merlin's *Suite del recuerdo* is quite masterly and the slow crescendos in the final *Carnavalito* are thrilling; then there is a complete change of mood and the *Evocación* makes a haunting return before the final *Joropo*. The *Preludios* of Pujol are quite magical; Vieaux then lets his hair down for the *Candombe*. The two *Valses* of Barrios are deliciously fragile, with the central *Barcarola* hardly less subtle, while the more robust Brazilian dances of Jorge Morel have real panache. The Naxos recording has good ambience and is present yet not too closely balanced. Unforgettable.

Wagler, Dietrich (organ)

'Great European organs No. 24': Freiberg Dom, Silbermann organ: SCHEIDT: *Magnificat Noni toni.* CLERAMBAULT: *Suite de premier ton.* BUXTEHUDE: *Prelude and fugue in D min.* KREBS: *Choral preludes: Mein Gott, das Herze bring ich dir; Herr Jesus Christ, dich zu uns wend; Herzlich tut mich verlangen; O Ewigkeit, du Donnerwort.*

J. S. BACH: *Fantasie in G; Prelude and fugue in C.*
**(*) Priory Dig. PRCD 332 [id.].

The organ, rather than the player, is the star of this record; the latter's performances are sound but very much in the traditional German style. But he knows his instrument and the opening *Magnificat Noni toni* of Scheidt sounds resplendent, with the following Clérambault *Suite* also very effectively registered. A well-balanced programme, lacking only the last degree of flair in presentation.

Weir, Gillian (organ)

'King of instruments: The art of Dame Gillian Weir (A Feast of organ music from the 16th to 20th centuries')

Volume I: BACH: *Toccata, adagio and fugue in C, BWB 564; Fantasia in G, BWV 572; Trio sonata No. 1 in E flat, BWV 525; Passacaglia in C min., BWV 582* (Organ of St Lawrence, Rotterdam). Louis MARCHAND: *Pièces d'Orgue*, Premier Livre: *Dialogue sur les grands jeux; Récit de tierce en taille; Basse et dessus de trompette et de cornet; Récit de voix humaine;* Cinquième Livre: *Bass de coumorne ou de trompette; Duo; Récit; Plein-jeu; Fugue; Basse de trompette ou de cromorne; Récit de tierce en taille* (Organ of St Maximin, Thionville, France). BULL: *Dr Bull's my selfe; Dr Bull's jewell* (Organ of Hexham Abbey).

Volume II: CLERAMBAULT: *Suite de premier ton; Suite de deuxième ton* (Organ of St Leonard Kirche, Basel, Switzerland). BRUHNS: *Praeludium Nos. 1–3; Chorale: Nun komm, der Heiden Heiland* (Organ of Clare College, Cambridge).

Volume III: François ROBERDAY: *Fuges et caprices pour orgue Nos. 1–12* (Organ of St Leonhardkirche, Basel, Switzerland). LANGLAIS: *Dialogue sur les mixtures* (Organ of Hexham Abbey). SCHEIDT: *Passamezzo (Variations 1–12)* (Organ of Clare College, Cambridge).

Volume IV: DANDRIEU: *Premier Livre de Pièces d'Orgue: Pièces en A, Mi, La. Magnificat* (Organ of St Leonard, Basel, Switzerland); *Pièces en G, Ré, Sol minuer; Magnificat II.* Louis MARCHAND: *Pièces d'Orgue,* Troisième Livre: *Dialogue sur les grands jeux;* Quatrième Livre: *Duo; Fugue; Trio; Récit; Duo; Basse et trompette; Récit de tierce en taille* (Organ of St Maximin, Thionville, France). Nicolas DE GRIGNY: *Tierce en taille.* MULET: *Toccata Tu es Petrus* (Organ of Hexham Abbey).

Volume V: Charles CAMILLERI: *Missa Mundi* (Organ of Royal Festival Hall). WIDOR: *Symphony No. 6: Allegro.* VIERNE: *Impromptu.* DAQUIN: *Noël suisse.* DUPRE: *La Fileuse.* Thomas

TOMKINS: *Worcester braules.* SWEELINCK: *Chorale: Mein junges Leben hat ein End.* DUBOIS: *Toccata* (Organ of Hexham Abbey).

(B) *** Australian Argo/Decca 460 185-2 (5) [id.].

Gillian Weir made her début at the 1965 season of Proms, and soon established a formidable reputation over the widest range of organ repertoire, but especially in music of the French school. Over a period of five years in the latter half of the 1970s, she made a series of major recordings for Decca's Argo label and it is good that this logo has been retained for the present superbly remastered five-disc survey.

Her Bach, recorded on an ideal Dutch organ in Rotterdam, is cool and poised. The bravura in the deliciously registered *Fantasia in G* cannot escape the listener, yet there is no sense of the virtuosity being flaunted. The *Trio sonata* is equally colourful, but the remorseless tread of the *Passacaglia in C minor*, taken very steadily, is undoubtedly compelling, and the *Toccata, adagio and fugue* is hardly less telling in its sense of controlled power.

Louis Marchand (1669–1732) was Bach's French contemporary: his suites are not learned but meant to divert, which they certainly do here and especially the delectably registered *Basse et dessus de trompette et de cornet* from the first book and the comparable pieces in the second, again played on a highly suitable organ in France. The brief encores by John Bull are equally tangy and spirited.

Clérambault's *Livres d'orgue* date from 1710 and follow the same layout as those of Marchand: the music has slightly more formality, yet the influences of French dance music remain, and once again Weir's sparkling registration tickles the ear. The Swiss organ also features an authentic 'tremblant fort' stop, used in the piece called *Flûtes*, with a suprisingly modern effect, followed by the charming dialogue of the *Récit de Nazard* and a powerful closing *Caprice*.

Nikolaus Bruhns (1665–97) died young and left only five organ works, of which four are recorded here. His individuality is striking, and so is the quirky originality of his musical style, which freely interchanges fugal passages and sections of the most florid bravura. The *First Praeludium in G major* has the kind of immediate appeal which could make it famous if regularly heard; its memorable fugal subject is even more jaunty than Bach's *Fugue à la gigue*. Gillian Weir has the full measure of this music, finding a perfect balance between the fantasy and the structural needs of each piece. She dazzles the ear not only with her vigour and virtuosity but also with some quite scrumptious registration on an organ at Clare College, Cambridge that seems exactly right for the music. The recording is marvellous, a demonstration of clarity and sonority admirably combined.

François Roberday (1624–80) will be little more than a name – if that – to most readers. He is a *petite* *maître* who occasionally figures in recitals, but has until now not made a very striking presence in the CD catalogue. This recording of his twelve *Fugues et caprices* (over an hour of music) is made on a modern instrument in Basel which produces very authentic-sounding timbres. As usual Gillian Weir plays with enormous style and aplomb, but it would be idle to maintain that this is music of more than passing interest, except to the specialist collector. Once again the Argo recording has splendid range and presence.

On the other hand, Samuel Scheidt's *Passamezzo Variations*, taken from the first Volume of his *Tablatura nova* has a more general appeal, readily demonstrating the composer's mastery of variation technique, with imaginative invention throughout. Gillian Weir helps a great deal, not only by playing the music splendidly but by again choosing registrations with great flair and a marvellous sense of colour. The piquancy of several of her combinations is unforgettably apt and she is superbly recorded. This music was originally coupled with the Bruhns *Preludes* above but now it is joined with Roberday, with Langlais's rhythymically quirky *Dialogue for the mixtures* used as a colourful intermezzo.

Dandrieu was a younger contemporary of Couperin le Grand and, like him, came from a musical family. He spent most of his life as organist at Saint-Barthélemy in Paris and at the Royal Chapel. The First Book of organ pieces, published in 1739 a year after his death, contains a number of suites; two are recorded here, consisting of an offertory, several other short movements, and a series of couplets which comprise the organ's contribution to a pair of settings of the *Magnificat*.

The music is more than just historically interesting; the invention is full of individual character and resource. Gillian plays each *Suite* and *Magnificat* on a different instrument, both of them recorded in a lively acoustic and her interpretations are marked by a vivid palette, authority and taste. There follows a further selection of *Pièces* by Louis Marchand and a move forward in time for Nicolas de Grigny's serene *Tierce en Taille* (effectively decorated). The programme of this most stimulating disc ends with a famously brilliant twentieth-century Toccata, *Tu es petrus*, by Henri Mulet.

The composer who dominates the final disc, Charles Camilleri, is Maltese, but his background influence comes as much from the East as the West. The (45-minute) *Missa Mundi* is a highly mystical work, inspired by a meditative prose-poem by Teilhard de Chardin, *La Messe sur le Monde*, written in the middle of the Ordos Desert area of China in 1923. The music follows the five sections of the meditation: *The offering; Fire over earth; Fire in the earth; Communion; Prayer*. The poem introduces an astonishing range of organ technique and sonority from the frenzied *Fire in the earth* to the simplistic closing *Prayer*. Weir gives a thrillingly dedicated performance which immediately grabs the listener.

Certainly this playing offers both a personal identification with the music and great bravura in equal measure; at times it is as overwhelming as the composer envisaged, at others its simple statements show an eloquence that is notable for its gentleness. The recording is superb. It is as clear and clean as a whistle, immensely wide in dynamic range, and there is not a ripple of distortion of any kind. The rest of the programme is made up of a skilfully chosen selection of genre pieces, among which Vierne's rippling *Impromptu*, Daquin's charming fanfare-like *Noël suisse* and Dupré's delicate evocation of *La Fileuse* stand out. The jolly closing *Toccata* of Theodor Dubois (which has a whiff of Widor) makes an exhilarating finale.

Almost all this repertoire is most rewarding and can be cordially recommended even to those who normally fight shy of early organ composers. It could hardly be played more masterfully and the engineers provide first-class sound throughout. Readers interested in this repertory (and even those who are not) should investigate this thoroughly satisfying survey.

Williams, John (guitar)

'Spanish guitar music': I. ALBENIZ: *Asturias; Tango; Córdoba; Sevilla.* SANZ: *Canarios.* TORROBA: *Nocturno; Madroños.* SAGRERAS: *El Colibri.* M. ALBENIZ: *Sonata in D.* FALLA: *Homenaje; Three-cornered hat: Corregidor's dance; Miller's dance. El amor brujo: Fisherman's song.* CATALAN FOLKSONGS: *La Nit de Nadal; El noy de la mare; El testamen de Amelia.* GRANADOS: *La Maja de Goya. Spanish dance No. 5.* TARREGA: *Recuerdos de la Alhambra.* villa-lobos: *Prelude No. 4 in E min.* MUDARRA: *Fantasia.* TURINA: *Fandanguillo, Op. 36.*

(B) *** Sony SBK 46347 [id.].

John Williams can show strong Latin feeling, as in the vibrant *Farruca* of the *Miller's dance* from Falla's *Three-cornered hat*, or create a magically atmospheric mood, as in the hauntingly registered transcription of the *Fisherman's song* from *El amor brujo*. He can play with thoughtful improvisatory freedom, as in the Villa-Lobos *Prelude*, with its pianissimo evocation, or be dramatically spontaneous, as in the memorable performance of Turina's *Fandanguillo*, which ends the recital magnetically. The instinctive control of atmosphere and dynamic is constantly rewarding throughout a varied programme, and the technique is phenomenal, yet never flashy, always at the service of the music. The remastering brings a clean and truthful, if very immediate, image. Background is minimal and never intrusive.

Recital: THEODORAKIS: *3 Epitatios.* DOMENICONI: *Koyyunbaba, Parts 1–4.* ANON.: *Lamento di Tristan; Ductia; Saltarello.* HOUGHTON: *Stélé.* SATIE: *Gnossiennes Nos. 1–2. Gymnopédie No. 3* (arr. for guitar and small orchestra). WILLIAMS: *Aeolian suite* (for guitar and small orchestra) (both with orchestra cond. William Goodchild).
**(*) Sony Dig. SK 60585 [id.].

An insubstantial recital perhaps, but quite an attractive one, with every piece showing John Williams's supreme and easy mastery, and his ability to make music in front of studio microphones with concert-hall-like spontaneity. The three vivid miniatures by Theodorakis are followed by what is essentially an atmospheric set of variations by an Italian composer, Carlo Domeniconi, who lived in Istanbul. The result sounds curiously Andalusian. The three medieval dances then make a good foil (the *Ductia* is like a nursery rhyme) and lead naturally to John Williams's own *Aeolian suite*, a colourful pastiche, mixing original and borrowed ideas to good effect. With its simple orchestration it sounds rather like film music. Phillip Houghton's four evocations called *Stélé* (which translates as 'headstone') have Grecian influences and are slightly more plangent. It cannot be said that the orchestra adds much to the famous Satie *Gymnopédie*, pleasing as it is, and the two *Gnossiennes* which close the programme are played ruminatively in solo arrangements. The recording is remarkably real and present.

Wilson, Christopher (lute)

'La Magdalena' (Lute music in Renaissance France): BLONDEAU (publ. ATTAIGNANT): *La brosse (Recoupe et Tourdion); La Magdalena (Recoupe et Tourdion).* ANON. (publ. ATTAIGNANT): *Bransle de Poictou; Tant que vivray; Pavane; Gaillarde; Prelude; Une bergerotte.* FRANCESCO DE PARIGI: *2 Recercars.* BERLIN: *Fantaisie No. 3; Trio No. 2.* PALADIN: *Anchor che col partir; Fantaisie.* MORLAYE: *Bransle d'Ecosse No. 1; Bransle gay; Fantaisie; Sans liberté; Pavane; Gaillarde piemontoise.* ALBERT DE RIPPE: *Pleurés mes yeux; 2 Fantaisies; Galliarde.* Adrian LE ROY: *Passemeze; La souris.* BAKFARK: *Si grand è la pietà.*
*** Virgin Veritas/EMI Dig. VC5 45140-2.

An agreeable, unassertive, hour-long programme for the late evening, although perhaps a few more lively dances would have made the recital even more attractive. Certain items stand out, like the anonymous portrayal of *Une bergerotte*, the title-piece and the two works of Jean Paul Paladin (although *Anchor che col partir* is a transcription of a famous madrigal of the period – by Cipriano da Rore). Valentin Bakfark's *Si grand è la pietà* brings yet another madrigal arrangement (by Jacques Arcadelt). Most of this music has a character of gentle melancholy, so the exceptions, like the *Bransle gay* and the *Gaillarde piemontoise* (both by Morlaye), make a welcome diversion. The two pieces by Adrian Le Roy are also rather more extrovert, but the pervading atmosphere is doleful. Christopher Wilson plays with much sensitivity and he is beautifully recorded, provided one accepts the rather misty, ecclesiastical acoustic.

Yates, Sophie (virginals)

English virginals music: BYRD: *Praeludium – Fantasia; The barley breake; The Tennthe pavan (Sir William Petre); Galliard to the Tennthe pavan; The woods so wild; Hugh Aston's ground; The Bells.* DOWLAND: *Lachrymae pavan* (arr. byrd). James HARDING: *Galliard* (arr. BYRD). GIBBONS: *Fantasia.* ANON.: *My Lady Careys dompe.* TOMKINS: *Barafostus's dreame.* Hugh ASTON: *Hornepype.* BULL: *In nomine.*
** Chandos Dig. CHAN 0574 [id.].

Sophie Yates is a thoughtful and accomplished player and she uses a modern copy by Peter Bavington of an Italian instrument made at the very beginning of the seventeenth century. Her programme is well thought out and, even though it is dominated by the music of Byrd, it is musically well balanced. The snag is the resonant recording, which gives a larger-than-life impression of the instrument which even the lowering of the volume control does not entirely diminish.

Yepes, Narciso (guitar)

'The art of the guitar': SANZ: *Suite española: Españoletas; Canarios.* PISADOR: *Pavana muy llana para tañer.* MUDARRA: *Fantasia que contrahaza la harpa en la manera de Ludovico.* NARVAEZ: *La canción del emperador: Mille regretz* (Josquin Desprez). *Diferencias sobre Guádame las vacas.* ANON.: *Irish march* (11th century); *Saltarello* (both arr. YEPES). DOWLAND: *The King of Denmark his galliard.* SOR: *Studies in A; in C, Op. 6/6 & 8; in B flat; in G, Op. 29/1 & 11.* TARREGA: *Lágrima; Recuerdos de la Alhambra; Adelita.* GRANADOS: *Danza española No. 5.* TURINA: *Fandanguillo, Op. 36.* ALBENIZ: *Suite española: Asturias.*
*** DG CD PlusScore Analogue/Dig. 459 613-2 [id.].

Many of these recordings have appeared before and some already exist on bargain labels. But this recital has been carefully planned, expertly remastered, and affords great naturalness and presence. More-

over the special logo indicates that the CD can also be played via a CD-ROM drive on a PC, enabling the listener to follow the musical scores simultaneously on the screen while listening to the performances. The programme has been selected in an approximately historical sequence to show the great guitarist at his finest, whether in the delightful Sanz *Canarios*, the noble *Pavana* of Pisador, the two melancholy miniatures of Tárrega, which are perhaps less familiar than the famous *Recuerdos*. The *Diferencias* of Narváez (written for the vihuela) is one of the earliest Spanish examples of variation form; Mudarra's *Fantasia* is more complex; but later the Dowland *Galliard* (where Yepes simulates a bolder keyboard image) admirably demonstrates Elizabethan divisions. The kernel of the recital is provided by the four diverse Sor *Studies*, which are marvellously played, but then so is Turina's *Fandanguillo*, which follows the Granados *Spanish dance*, the latter more robust than Julian Bream's famous recording, offering a refreshingly different interpretation.

'Spanish guitar music': ALBENIZ: *Malagueña; Asturias (Leyenda).* SOR: *Tema con variaciones, Op. 9; Studies, Op. 35/14, 16, 22 & 21.* TARREGA: *Recuerdos de la Alhambra.* SANZ: *Suite española.* MUDARRA: *Fantasia que contrahaza la harpa en la manera de Ludovico.* SOLER: *Sonata in E.* FALLA: *El sombrero de tres picos: Danza del molinero/Farruca.*
(BB) *** Belart 461 276-2 [(M) id. import].

Narciso Yepes was not only an outstanding exponent of this repertoire, he also had that rare gift of constantly creating electricity in the recording studio, and all this music springs vividly to life. In popular favourites like the Tárrega *Recuerdos de la Alhambra*, the exciting transcription of Falla's *Miller's dance*, the earlier baroque repertoire (the Sanz *Suite* is particularly appealing), Yepes's assured, vibrant and always stylish advocacy brings consistent pleasure. He is recorded extremely vividly, and this disc can be recommended to anyone wanting an inexpensive and representative programme of Spanish guitar music.

Zabaleta, Nicanor (harp)

'Arpa española': ALBENIZ: *Malagueña, Op. 165/ 3; Suite española: Granada (Serenata); Zaragoza (Capricho); Asturias (Leyenda). Mallorca, Op. 202; Tango español.* FALLA: *Serenata andaluza.* TURINA: *Ciclo pianistico No. 1: Tocata y fuga.* GOMBAU: *Apunte bético.* GRANADOS: *Danza española No. 5.* HALFFTER: *Sonatina* (ballet): *Danza de la pastora.* LOPEZ-CHAVARRI: *El viejo castillo moro.*
✿ (M) *** DG (IMS) 435 847-2 [id.].

A good deal of the music here belongs to the guitar

(or piano) rather than the harp, but Nicanor Zabaleta, with his superb artistry and sense of atmosphere, makes it all his own. Throughout this delightful programme, Zabaleta gives each piece strong individuality of character. In the Granados *Spanish dance No. 5* he matches the magnetism of Julian Bream's famous recording, and Manuel de Falla's *Serenata andaluza* is hardly less captivating. DG's sound balance is near perfection, as is the choice of acoustic, and the magic distilled by Zabaleta's concentration, often at the gentlest levels of dynamic, is unforgettable.

VOCAL RECITALS AND CHORAL COLLECTIONS

Art of singing

'The Art of singing': Video: 'Golden voices of the century' (Björling, Callas, Caruso, Chaliapin, Christoff, Corelli, De los Angeles, De Luca, Di Stefano, Flagstad, Gigli, Martinelli, Melchior, Olivero, Pinza, Ponselle, Leontyne Price, Schipa, Stevens, Supervia, Sutherland, Tauber, Tebaldi, Tetrazzini, Tibbett, Vickers, Wunderlich): Excerpts from: PUCCINI: La Bohème. SAINT-SAENS: Samson et Dalila. VERDI: Rigoletto. LEONCAVALLO: I Pagliacci (all silent film excerpts with Caruso). DONIZETTI: Lucia di Lammermoor: sextet with Caruso, mimed. DE CURTIS: song Torna a Surriento (Giovanni Martinelli). HANDEL: Xerxes: Ombra mai fù (Beniamino Gigli). FLOTOW: Martha: M'appari (Tito Schipa). ROSSINI: Il barbiere di Siviglia: Largo al factotum (Giuseppe de Luca). flotow: Martha: M'appari (Luisa Tetrazzini). PUCCINI: La Bohème: Quando me'n vo (Conchita Supervia). BIZET: Carmen: Chanson Bohème; Habanera (Rosa Ponselle). SCHUBERT: Ständchen (Richard Tauber). RIMSKY-KORSAKOV: The Maid of Pskov. IBERT: Chanson du duc (both with Fyodor Chaliapin). WAGNER: Die Walküre: Hojotoho! (Kirsten Flagstad). BIZET: Carmen: Chanson du toréador (Lawrence Tibbett). SAINT-SAENS: Samson et Dalila: Mon coeur s'ouvre (Risë Stevens). WAGNER: Die Walküre: Winterstürme (Lauritz Melchior). MUSSORGSKY: Boris Godunov: Coronation scene (Ezio Pinza). PUCCINI: La Bohème: Che gelida manina; Mi chiamano Mimì; O soave fanciulla (Jussi Björling, Renata Tebaldi). FALLA: La vida breve: Vivan los que ríen (Victoria de los Angeles). MEYERBEER: Les Huguenots: O beau pays (Joan Sutherland). VERDI: Aida: O patria mia (Leontyne Price). MUSSORGSKY: Boris Godunov: Death scene (Boris Christoff). PUCCINI: Tosca: Vissi d'arte; (i) Act III duet (Magda Olivero, (i) with Alvinio Misciano). MOZART: Die Zauberflöte: Dies Bildnis ist bezaubernd schön (Fritz Wunderlich). BEETHOVEN: Fidelio: In des Lebens (Jon Vickers). PUCCINI: Turandot: Non Piangere, Liù (Franco Corelli). LEONCAVALLO: I Pagliacci: Vesti la giubba (Giuseppe di Stefano). (i) VERDI: La Traviata: Parigi, o cara. (ii) PUCCINI: Tosca: Duet and Vissi d'arte (both Maria Callas, with (i) Alfredo Kraus, (ii) Tito Gobbi). (Commentary by Magda Olivero, Thomas Hampson, Schuyler Chapin, Kirk Browning, Nicola Rescigno.)

*** Teldec/Warner VHS 0630 15893-3 [id.].

This is Teldec's vocal equivalent of 'The Art of Conducting'. While almost all the film excerpts included here are fascinating, this comparable vocal survey proves less uniformly compulsive than its orchestral equivalent. Moreover, while almost all the comments on the earlier video concerning the conductors themselves and their various idiosyncrasies proved very perceptive, the commentaries here, especially the contributions by the singers themselves, seem much less illuminating. Thomas Hampson's definition of the meaning of legato, a term which almost explains itself, is perversely over-complicated. But now to the singing.

Two performances stand out above the rest in magnetism. A live telecast, with good sound, from the Met. in 1956 brought Renata Tebaldi and Jussi Björling together in virtually the whole of the great Act I love scene in La Bohème, from Che gelida manina to their final exit, with their glorious voices ending the Act from offstage. They are dressed in a curiously formal way – one might even say overdressed – and Tebaldi is not shown to be the greatest actress in the world, but their voices match superbly. The other scene is even more electrifying – a live telecast made in December of the same year for which obviously no expense was spared, and the set and production were fully worthy. Boris Christoff's Death scene from Boris Godunov is deeply moving; Nicola Moscona is a hardly less resonant Pimen, and an unnamed boy is very touching as Boris's young son. Hardly less impressive is the great Kirsten Flagstad (at her vocal peak), introduced by Bob Hope, who manages to keep a straight face, in a Paramount movie, The Big Broadcast of 1938. She sings Hojotoho! thrillingly from Die Walküre, waving her spear with remarkable conviction.

Risë Stevens, Lauritz Melchior, Victoria de los Angeles in Falla and Joan Sutherland in Meyerbeer coloratura add to the vocal pleasures, and Leontyne Price's gloriously full-voiced O patria mia from Aida is engulfing. What a stage presence she has! Another highlight is Magda Olivero's charismatically seductive Vissi d'arte from Tosca. The great Callas ends the programme by singing the same aria (in 1964) but, although her presence is commanding, the actual singing, with its wobbling vibrato, is no match for Olivero.

The early recordings are interesting, but the sound is such that they are usually less than overwhelming vocally, with Gigli and Tito Schipa possible exceptions. A hilarious interlude is provided by a 1908 silent film with professional actors hopelessly overacting and miming the words of the Sextet (*Chi mi frena*) from *Lucia di Lammermoor*, designed to accompany the famous 1911 RCA recording by Caruso, Daddi, Journet, Scotti, Sembrich and Severina. Another smile comes when

Rosa Ponselle is shown singing *Carmen* for an MGM screen test in 1936 and her fan gets in the way of the camera! All in all, this is a considerable entertainment, but one hoped, unrealistically perhaps, for more items like *Boris* and *Bohème*.

Historical vocal recitals

EMI

The EMI Record of Singing'

Volume 3 (1926–1939): Part 1: The German school: Arias and excerpts from WAGNER: *Tannhäuser* (Lauritz Melchior; Göta Ljungberg with Walter Widdop); *Die Walküre* (Max Lorenz; Kirsten Flagstad); *Lohengrin* (Franz Völker); *Die Meistersinger* (Rudolf Bockelmann; Delia Reinhardt); *Das Rheingold* (Hans Hermann Nissen); *Der fliegende Holländer* (Elizabeth Ohms); *Siegfried* (Nanny Larsen-Todsen). WILLIE: *Königsballade* (Helge Rosvaenge). D'ALBERT: *Tiefland* (Torsten Ralf). Johann STRAUSS Jnr.: *Die Fledermaus* (Richard Tauber with Vera Schwarz). KIENZL: *Der Evangeligmann* (Marcel Wittrisch with Children's chorus). Richard STRAUSS: *Der Rosenkavalier* (Herbert Ernst Groh; Lotte Lehmann); *Arabella* (Alfred Jerger with Viorica Ursuleac; Tiana Lemnitz); *Daphne* (Margarete Teschemacher); *Die ägyptische Helena* (Rose Pauly). KORNGOLD: *Die tote Stadt* (Joseph Schmidt; Karl Hammes). MOZART: *Die Entführung aus dem Serail* (Julius Patzak). HUMPERDINCK: *Hänsel und Gretel* (Gerard Hüsch). KREUTZER: *Das Nachtlager in Granada* (Willi Domgraf-Fassbaender). MENDELSSOHN: *Elijah* (Friedrich Schorr); *Saint Paul* (Jo Vincent). LORTZING: *Zar und Zimmermann* (Heinrich Schlusnus; Leo Schützendorf); *Der Wildschütz* (Alexander Kipnis). NICOLAI: *Die lustigen Weiber von Windsor* (Wilhelm Strienz). VERDI: *Macbeth* (Ivar Andresen); *Un ballo in maschera* (Adele Kern). MEYERBEER: *Le Prophète* (Sigrid Onegin); *L'Africaine* (Elisabeth Rethberg). PONCHIELLI: *La Gioconda* (Karin Branzell). SAINT-SAENS: *Samson et Dalila* (Kerstin Thorborg). MOZART: *La clemenza di Tito* (Rosette Anday). FLOTOW: *Alesandro Stradella* (Fritz Jold). RIMSKY-KORSAKOV: *The Tsar's bride* (Miliza Korjus; Meta Seinemeyer). ADAM: *Le Postillon de Longumeau* (Felicie Hüni Mihacsek). PUCCINI: *Turandot* (Luise Helletsgruber); *La Bohème* (Maria Cebotari). GOLDMARK: *Die Königen von Saba* (Maria Nemeth). Lieder: BEETHOVEN: *Der Wachtelschlag* (Karl Erb). SCHUMANN: *Liederkreis: Mondnacht* (Leo Slezak); *Die Lotusblume* (Ursula van Diemen). WOLF: *Vers hwiegene Liebe* (Heinrich Schlusnus). SCHUBERT: *Die Stadt* (Herbert Jannsen); *Aufenthal* (Maria Olczewska); *Die Allnacht* (Marta Fuchs). BRAHMS: *Nicht mehr zu dir zu gehen* (Margarete Klose); *Feldeinsamkeit* (Elena Gerhardt); Volkslieder: *Schwesterlein* (Lulu Mysz-Gmeiner). SCHOECK: *Mit einem gemalten Bande* (Ria Ginster); *Nachtlied* (Margherita Perras). MARX: *Marienlied* (Elisabeth Schumann). ROSSINI: *Soirrées musicales; L'invito.* (Lotte Schöne). OBOUSSIER: *Weine du nicht* (Erna Berger). LISZT: *Es muss ein Wunderbares sein* (Emmy Bettendorf). REGER: *Waldeinsamkeit; Zum Schlafen* (Maria Müller). WAGNER: *Wesendonck Lieder: Schmerzen* (Frida Leider).

Part 2: The Italian school: Arias and excerpts from: PAISIELLO: *I zingari infiera* (Conchita Supervia). BIZET: *Carmen* (Giannina Pederzini). VERDI: Requiem (Irene Minghini-Catteneo; Ezio Pinza); *I Lombardi* (Giannina Aranji-Lombardi); *La forza del destino* (Dusolina Giannini); *Ernani* (Iva Pacetti). *Otello* (Hina Spani; Renato Zanelli); *Rigoletto* (Lina Pagliughi); *Falstaff* (Mariano Stabile). SAINT-SAENS: *Samson et Dalila* (Ebe Stignani). DONIZETTI: *La Favorita* (Florica Cristoforeanu); *Don Pasquale* (Afro Poli with Ernesto Badini). BOITO: *Mefistofele* (Pia Tassinari; Nazzareno de Angelis). CATALANI: *Loreley* (Bianca Scacciati). GIORDANO: *Siberia* (Maria Caniglia); *Andrea Chénier* (Lina Bruna Rasa; Cesare Formichi; Benvenuto Franci; Antonio Cortis); *Il Re* (Mercedes Capsir). PUCCINI: *La fanciulla del West* (Gina Cigna); *Madama Butterfly* (Margaret Sheridan); *Turandot* (Maria Zamboni; Magda Oliviero; Alessandro Ziliani); *Manon Lescaut* (Licia Albanese; Francesco Merli; Giacomo Lauri-Volpi); *La Bohème* (Tancredi Pasero); *Tosca* (Giovanni Inghilleri). PIETRI: *Maristella* (Rosetta Pampanini). MASCAGNI: *Iris* (Maria Farneti); *Lodeletta* (Malfada Favero; Galliano Masini); *Guglielmo Ratcliffe* (Carlo Galeffi). GOMES: *Il Guarany* (Bidù Sayão). CILEA: *Adriana Lecouvreur* (Adelaide Saraceni; Aurelio Pertile). RICCI: *Crispino e la comare* (Salvatore Baccaloni). PONCHIELLI: *Il figliuol prodigo* (Mario Basiola). LEONCAVALLO: *Zazà* (Apollo Granforte). BELLINI: *La sonnnambula* (Dino Borgioli with Maria Gentile, Ida Mannarini, Gina Pedroni; also Enzo de Muro Lomanto). MASSENET: *Werther* (Tito Schipa). GUERRERO: *Los Gavilanes* (Tino Folgar). VITTADINI: *Anima allegra* (Luigi Fort). OFFENBACH: *La Belle Hélène* (Jussi Bjoerling). Songs: TRAD: *Have you*

seen but a whyte lilie grow? (Conchita Supervia);
BUZZI-PECCIA: *Colombetta* (Claudia Muzio).
GRANADOS: *Tonadillas: El majo discreto; El majo timido* (Conchita Badia). JAMES: *Maori lullaby* (Toti da Monte). TIRINDELLI: *Mistica* (Carlo Tagliabue). TOSTI: *Ideale* (Riccardo Stracciari); *Aprile* (Beniamino Gigli).: *Do not go, my love* (Dino Borgioli). HAGEMAN LONGAS: *En effeuillant la marguerite* (Tito Schipa).

Part 3: The French school: Arias from: RAMEAU: *Hippolyte et Aricie* (Leila Ben Sedira).
OFFENBACH: *Les Brigands* (Emma Luart); *Contes d'Hoffmann* (André Pernet); *La Grande Duchesse de Gérolstein* (Yvonne Printemps); *Le Boulangère a des écus* (Reynaldo Hahn). DELIBES: *Lakmé* (Germaine Feraldy). ROSSINI: *Guillaume Tell* (Eidé Norena). MASSENET: *Marie-Magdeleine* (Germaine Martinelli); *Hérodiade* (René Maison). GOUNOD: *Sapho* (Suzanne Cesbron-Viseur; Germain Cernay); *Polyucte* (José Luccioni); *Mireille* (Gaston Micheletti). DUKAS: *Ariane et Barbe-Bleu* (Suzanne Balguerie). WAGNER: *Lohengrin* (Germaine Lubin). GLUCK: *Orphée* (Alice Raveau). REYER: *Sigurd* (Georges Thill; César Vezzani). HALEVY: *La Juive* (René Verdière). LAPARRA: *L'illustre Fregona* (Miguel Villabella). BAZIN: *Maître Pathelin* (André d'Arkor). VERDI: *Luisa Miller* (Giusppe Lugo). LALO: Le Roi d'Ys (Joseph Rogatchewsky). BERLIOZ: *L'enfance du Christ* (Jean Planel); *La Damnation de Faust* (Charles Panzéra). MAGNARD: *Guercoeur* (Arthur Endrèze). PALADILHE: *Patrie!* (Robert Couzinou). BERTHOMIEU: *Robert Macaire* (André Balbon). FLOTOW: *L'Ombre* (Lucien Fugère). Songs: SAINT-SAENS: *Le rossignol et la rose* (Lily Pons). FAURE: *Les berceux* (Ninon Vallin); *Aurore* (Pierre Bernac); *Lydia* (Roger Bourdin). TORELLI: *Tu lo sai* (Povla Frijsh). DEBUSSY: *Chansons de Bilitis: Le chevelure* (Jane Bathori). RAVEL: *Chants hébraïques: Kaddisch* (Madeleine Grey); *Don Quichotte à Dulcinée: Chanson épique* (Martial Singher). DE BREVILLE: *Une jeune fille parle* (Claire Croiza). HAHN: *D'un prison* (Charles Panzéra). MARTINI: *Plaisir d'amore* (Jean-Emil Vanni-Marcoux).

Part 4: The Anglo-American school: Arias and excerpts from: VERDI: *Falstaff* (Lawrence Tibett). THOMAS: *Hamlet* (John Charles Thomas; John Brownlee). ROSSINI: *Il barbiere di Siviglia* (Dennis Noble); *Stabat Mater* (Florence Austral). Songs: COWAN: *Onaway, awake, beloved* (Harold Williams). HANDEL: *Messiah* (Peter Dawson). OFFENBACH: *Contes d'Hoffmann* (Charles Kullman). BIZET: *La jolie fille de Perth* (Heddle Nash); *Carmen* (Marguerite D'Alvarez). Goring THOMAS: *Esmeralda* (Thomas Burke). PUCCINI: *Tosca* (Richard Crooks); *La Bohème* (Grace Moore; Ina Souez); *Madama Butterfly* (Joan

Cross); *Turandot* (Eva Turner). HANDEL: *Acis and Galatea* (Walter Widdop). PURCELL: *The Tempest* (Norman Allin). MENDELSSOHN: *St Paul* (Muriel Brunskill). HANDEL: *Theodora* (Isobel Baillie). DELIUS: *Irmelin* (Dora Labbette). SPONTINI: *La Vestale* (Rosa Ponselle). REYER: *Sigurd* (Marjorie Lawrence). Songs: DUNN: *The bitterness of love* (John McCormack). MONTEVERDI: *Maladetto sia l'aspetto* (Roland Hayes). MARTINI: *Minuet* (Mme Charles Cahier). SULLIVAN: *The lost chord* (Dame Clara Butt). SCHUBERT: *Der Tod und das Mädchen* (Marian Anderson). FAURE: *Le secret* (Susan Metcalfe-Casals). CANTELOUBE: *Baïlero* (Gladys Swarthout). PALADILHE: *Psyché* (Maggie Teyte). HAYDN: *My mother bids me bind my hair* (Florence Easton).

Part 5: The East European/Slavic school: Arias and excerpts from: DVORAK: *Rusalka* (Jarmila Novotná; Ada Nordenova). RIMSKY-KORSAKOV: *The Tsar's bride* (Nathalie Vechor). GOMES: *Salvator Rosa* (Mark Reisen). KODALY: *Háry János* (Imry Palló). Songs: GRETCHANINOV: *The wounded birch; Snowflakes* (Maria Kurenko with Composer, piano); *Lullaby* (Oda Slobodskaya). RIMSKY-KORSAKOV: *The rose and the nightingale* (Xenia Belmas). KARLOWICZ: *I remember golden days* (Ada Sari). DVORAK: *Leave me alone* (Maria Krasová). arr. BARTOK: *2 Hungarian folk songs* (Maria Basildes). DARGOMIJSKY: *Bolero* (Feodor Chaliapin). CUI: *Hunger* (Vladimir Rosing). KASHEVAROV: *Tranquility*(Sergei Lemeshev).
✿ (M) (***) Testament mono SBT 0132 (10) [id.].

The importance of EMI's monumental series, 'The Record of singing', cannot be exaggerated, and it is sad that although the fourth volume was issued on CD, covering the period from the start of electrical recording up to the end of the 78 era, the others have been allowed to languish. That fact makes it all the more creditable that Stewart Brown of Testament has boldly issued this beautifully produced CD reissue of the third volume, the work of Keith Hardwick, both in the selection of items, often unexpected but always keenly perceptive, and in the actual transfers, which set standards in clarity and accuracy too rarely matched by others. Inevitably in a very compact format, the background material is not quite so lavish as in the original LP issue, with separate booklets included covering details of recording and biographies of the 200 or so singers covered. Even so, essential details are all here, and the methodical covering of so many singers from so many different schools, divided mainly by nationality, could not be more illuminating. In a note written especially for this CD reissue Hardwick confesses that though initially he had misgivings over following up the earlier two volumes of golden age material with recordings from a period generally regarded as one of decline, he has more and more come to revise that opinion. Certainly, thanks to his brilliant choice of items, one has much to admire in every school represented, with reservations not so much over quality of singing as of performance style, where inevitably modern taste differs greatly, notably on such composers as Mozart. A magnificent achievement. One hopes that Testament may have the courage to bring out CD versions of the first two volumes of this indispensable series.

OTHER EMI REISSUES

Angeles, Victoria de los (soprano)

Opera arias from: VERDI: *Ernani; Otello*. PUCCINI: *La Bohème*. BOITO: *Mefistofele*. ROSSINI: *La Cenerentola*. MASCAGNI: *Cavalleria Rusticana*. CATALANI: *La Wally*. ç: *Le nozze di Figaro*. WAGNER: *Tannhäuser; Lohengrin*. MASSENET: *Manon*. GOUNOD: *Faust*.
(M) (***) EMI mono CDH7 63495-2 [id.].

Most of the items here are taken from an early LP recital by de los Angeles that has rarely been matched in its glowing beauty and range of expression. The *Willow song* and *Ave Maria* from *Otello* have never been sung with more aching intensity than here, and the same goes for the Mascagni and Catalani arias. The final cabaletta from *Cenerentola* sparkles deliciously with de los Angeles, as so often, conveying the purest of smiles in the voice. The CD reissue is augmented by the valuable Mozart, Massenet, Gounod and Wagner items, all recorded in the days of 78s.

Bjoerling, Jussi (tenor)

Bjoerling Edition: (Studio recordings 1930–59; with O, Nils Grevillius): Disc 1 (1936–41): Arias from VERDI: *Aida; Rigoletto; Requiem; La Traviata; Il Trovatore*. PUCCINI: *La Bohème; Tosca; La fanciulla del West*. PONCHIELLI: *La Gioconda*. MEYERBEER: *L'Africaine*. MASSENET: *Manon*. BIZET: *Carmen*. GOUNOD: *Faust*. FLOTOW: *Martha*. ROSSINI: *Stabat Mater*. FRIML: *The Vagabond King*. Songs by TOSTI; DI CAPUA; GEEHL. Disc 2 (1941–50): Arias from: PUCCINI: *La Bohème; Turandot; Manon Lescaut; Tosca*. VERDI: *Rigoletto; Un ballo in maschera*. GIORDANO: *Andrea Chénier; Fedora*. MASCAGNI: *Cavalleria rusticana*. LEONCAVALLO: *Pagliacci* (also song: *Mattinata*). DONIZETTI: *L'elisir d'amore*. BIZET: *Les Pêcheurs de perles*. GOUNOD: *Roméo et Juliette*. MASSENET: *Manon*. CILEA: *L'arlesiana*. GODARD: *Jocelyn (Berceuse)*. Song: TOSTI: *L'alba separa*. Disc 3: Arias (sung in Swedish) from: GOUNOD: *Roméo et Juliette*. VERDI: *Rigoletto; Il Trovatore*. LAPARRA: *L'illustre Fregona*. BORODIN: *Prince Igor*.

PUCCINI: *Tosca; La fanciulla del West*. LEONCAVALLO: *Pagliacci*. MASCAGNI: *Cavalleria rusticana*. ATTERBERG: *Fanal*. rimsky-korsakov: *Sadko*. OFFENBACH: *La belle Hélène*. Johann STRAUSS Jr: *Der Zigeunerbaron*. MILLOCKER: *Der Bettelstudent*. Traditional songs (in Swedish) and by PETERSON-BERGER; SJOBERG; SCHRADER; STENHAMMAR; ALTHEN; WIDE. Disc 4: Lieder and songs (1939–59): BEETHOVEN: *Adelaide*. R. STRAUSS: *Morgen; Cäcile*. RACHMANINOV: *In the silence of the night; Lilacs*. FOSTER: *Jeannie with the light brown hair*. D'HARDELOT: *Because*. SPEAKS: *Sylvia*. CAMPBELL-TIPTON: *A spirit flower*. BEACH: *Ah, love but a day*. SJOBERG: *I bless ev'ry hour*. SIBELIUS: *The diamond in the March snow*. ADAM: *O holy night*. Songs by NORDQVIST; SALEN; PETERSON-BERGER; SODERMAN; ALFVEN.
(M) (***) EMI mono/stereo CMS5 66306-2 (4) [ZDMD 666306].

All admirers of the great Swedish tenor should consider this comprehensive compilation, eighty-nine items chosen by Harald Henrysson from EMI's Swedish archives and admirably remastered at Abbey Road. The voice is caught freshly and truthfully. Bjoerling's wife, Anna-Lisa, also participates in duets from *La Bohème* and *Roméo et Juliette*, towards the end of the second disc. The selection of arias is almost entirely predictable (and none the worse for that); a number of the key items are offered twice, and sometimes again in Swedish (where they sound surprisingly effective, even an excerpt from Offenbach's *La belle Hélène*). All the songs have a direct popular appeal. Bjoerling opens Disc 4 with a winning account of Beethoven's *Adelaide*, and many will welcome the lighter songs, and particularly the English ballads. However, the closing group of eight Scandinavian songs is memorable: romantic and dramatic by turns, and closing with a bold final contrast, *The diamond in the March snow* of Sibelius, which is capped by Bjoerling's ardent version of Adam's *Cantique de Noël* in Swedish. Excellent documentation, with photographs and full translations.

Opera arias from: DONIZETTI: *L'Elisir d'amore*. VERDI: *Il Trovatore; Un Ballo in maschera; Aida*. LEONCAVALLO: *I Pagliacci*. PUCCINI: *La Bohème; Tosca; La Fanciulla del West; Turandot*. GIORDANO: *Fedora*. CILEA: *L'Arlesiana*. MEYERBEER: *L'Africana*. GOUNOD: *Faust*. MASSENET: *Manon*. FLOTOW: *Martha*. ROSSINI: *Stabat Mater*.
(M) (***) EMI mono CDH7 61053-2.

The EMI collection on the Références label brings excellent transfers of material recorded between 1936 and 1947 on the tenor's home-ground in Stockholm. The voice was then at its very peak, well caught in those final years of 78 r.p.m. discs, with artistry totally assured over this wide range of repertory.

Arias and excerpts from: VERDI: *Rigoletto* (with Hjördis Schymberg); *Requiem*. BIZET: *Les pêcheurs de perles; Carmen*. OFFENBACH: *La belle Hélène*. GOUNOD: *Roméo et Juliette*. MASSENET: *Manon*. PONCHIELLI: *La Gioconda*. MASCAGNI: *Cavalleria rusticana*. BORODIN: *Prince Igor*. PUCCINI: *Manon Lescaut; La Bohème* (with Anna-Lisa Bjoerling). GIORDANO: *Andrea Chénier*. Songs: RACHMANINOV: *In the silence of the night; Lilacs*. LEONCAVALLO: *Mattinata*. TOSTI: *Ideale*. BEETHOVEN: *Adelaide*. R. STRAUSS: *Morgen*.

(M) (**(*)) EMI mono CDH7 64707-2 [id.].

The second Références collection – particularly generous, with a 77-minute programme – is if anything even more attractive than the first, offering recordings over the full range of the great tenor's 78-r.p.m. recording career with EMI, from 1933 (*Vladimir's Cavatina* from *Prince Igor*) to 1949 (*O soave fanciulla* from *La Bohème*, with Anna-Lisa Bjoerling). Again the voice is in peak form, ringing out with that penetrating yet glowing vocal production that was the hallmark of Bjoerling's timbre, while the singing itself has that innate sense of style which made him such a satisfying artist.

It is a pity that the CD transfers are so very bright and edgy, affecting the orchestra as well as the voice. This is particularly annoying in the delicate *Manon* excerpt (*Instant charmant . . . En fermant les yeux*) from 1938, where the violins are particularly tiresome; but the overall tendency to shrillness tends to tire the ear before the recital is halfway through. One wonders why this effect cannot be mitigated – the voice does not lack either vividness or presence without artificial enhancement.

Caruso, Enrico (tenor)

'*The Legendary Caruso*': Opera arias and songs: Arias from: MASCAGNI: *Cavalleria Rusticana; Iris*. PONCHIELLI: *La Gioconda*. LEONCAVALLO: *I Pagliacci*; and song: *Mattinata*. BOITO: *Mefistofele*. PUCCINI: *Tosca*. GIORDANO: *Fedora*. CILEA: *Adriana Lecouvreur*. VERDI: *Rigoletto; Aida*. BIZET: *Les pêcheurs de perles*. MASSENET: *Manon*. DONIZETTI: *L'Elisir d'amore*. MEYERBEER: *Les Huguenots*. Songs: TOSTI: *La mia canzone*. DENZA: *Non t'amo più*; and by ZARDO & TRIMARCHI.

(M) (***) EMI mono CDM5 67006-2 [id.].

The EMI collection was originally on the Références label and has now been again remastered. It brings together Caruso's earliest recordings, made in 1902, 1903 and 1904 in Milan with at times misty piano accompaniment. The very first pieces were done impromptu in Caruso's hotel, and the rough-

ness of presentation reflects that; but the voice is glorious in its youth, amazingly well caught for that period and now remarkably fresh and free from horn resonances, even if the background noise, not always regular, is still obvious. But it was the vocal quality of these very recordings which, more than anything else, first convinced a wide public that the gramophone was more than a toy.

Chaliapin, Feodor (bass)

Russian opera arias: MUSSORGSKY: *Boris Godunov: Coronation scene; Clock scene; Farewell and Death of Boris*. GLINKA: *Life for the Tsar: They guess the truth. Ruslan and Ludmilla: Farlaf's Rondo; Field O field*. DARGOMINSKY: *Russalka: You young girls are all alike; Mad scene and death of the miller*. RUBINSTEIN: *The Demon; Do not weep, child*. BORODIN: *Prince Igor: Khan Konchak's aria*. RIMSKY-KORSAKOV: *Sadko: Song of the Viking guest*. RACHMANINOV: *Aleko: The moon is high*.

(M) (***) EMI mono CDH7 61009-2 [id.].

Not only the glory of the voice, amazingly rich and consistent as recorded here between 1908 (aged 35) and 1931, but also the electrifying personality is vividly caught in this superb Références CD. The range of expression is astonishing. If posterity tends to think of this megastar among basses in the role of Mussorgsky's *Boris* (represented here in versions previously unissued), he is just as memorable in such an astonishing item as *Farlaf's Rondo* from *Ruslan and Ludmilla*, with its tongue-twisting chatter made thrilling at such speed and with such power. The presence of the singer is unwaveringly vivid in model transfers, whether the original recording was acoustic or electric.

Christoff, Boris (bass)

'*The early recordings (1949–52)*': excerpts from: MUSSORGSKY: *Boris Godunov; Khovanshchina*. BORODIN: *Prince Igor*. RIMSKY-KORSAKOV: *Sadko; The Legend of the invisible city of Kitezh*. TCHAIKOVSKY: *Eugene Onegin*. MUSSORGSKY: *Songs. Russian folksongs*.

(M) (***) EMI mono CDH7 64252-2 [id.].

The magnetic quality of Christoff's singing is never in doubt here, and the compulsion of the singer's artistry as well as the vivid individuality of his bass timbres make this a real portrait, not just a collection of items. These were his first recordings of the *Boris Godunov* excerpts (in which he assumes three different characters), and in musical terms he probably never surpassed them. But his characterization here is just as impressive as the singing itself, full of variety. The EMI transfers are bold and brightly focused, less mellow than the effect Nimbus usually achieve, but with the most vivid projection.

'*Russian songs*' (with LOP, Tzipine; Paris Conservatoire O, Cluytens; Alexandre Labinsky, Alexandre Tcherepnine, Janine Reiss, Serge Zapolsky, or Nadia Gedda-Nova (piano); Gaston Marchesini, Maud-Martin Tortelier (cello)): GLINKA: *The Midnight review; Cradle song; What, young beauty; Where is our rose?; The Lark; Ah, you darling, lovely girl; Doubt; Grandpa, the girls once told me; How sweet to be with thee; Do not say the heart is sick; Hebrew song; Elegy; I remember the wonderful moment.* BORODIN: *Those folk; Song of the dark forest; From my tears; The Sea princess; The Pretty girl no longer loves me; The Magic garden; Arabian melody; The false note; The fishermaiden; Listen to my song, little friend; The Sleeping princess; Pride; For the shores of thy far native land; The sea; Why art thou so early, dawn?; My songs are poisoned.* CUI: *Songs, Op. 44: Le Hun; Berceuse; Le ciel est transi; Les songeants. Ici-bas; The tomb and the rose; The Love of a departed one; A Recent dream; Pardon!; Desire; Conspiracy; Song of Mary; The Imprisoned knight; Album leaf; The Prophet; The Statue of Tsarskoïe; In Memory of V. S. Stassov.* BALAKIREV: *Prologue; Song of Selim; Song: The Yellow leaf trembles; The Pine tree; Nocturne; Starless midnight, coldly breathed; The Putting-right; November the 7th; Dawn; Hebrew melody; The Wilderness; The Knight; The Dream; Look, my friend.* RIMSKY-KORSAKOV: *The Pine and the palm; On the hills of Georgia; The Messenger; Quietly evening falls; Hebrew song; Zuleika's song; Across the midnight sky; I waited for thee in the grotto at the appointed hour; The sea is tossing; The Upas tree; The Prophet; Quiet is the blue sea; Slowly drag my days; Withered flower; The rainy day has waned.* TCHAIKOVSKY: *Don Juan's serenade; The Mild stars shone for us; Child's song; Cradle song; Night; Do not ask; As they kept on saying, 'Fool'; To sleep; Disappointment; the canary; None but the weary heart; Again, as before, alone; A Legend.* RACHMANINOV: *Fate; How fair is this spot; When yesterday we met; All once I gladly owned; Morning; All things depart; Thy pity I implore; Christ is risen; Loneliness; O never sing to me again; The dream; The soldier's wife; The Harvest of sorrow; Oh stay, my love; The world would see thee smile; Night is mournful.* Folksongs: arr. SEROV: *The Evil power.* TRAD.: *Doubinouchka: Song of the Volga; The Bandore; Down Peterskaya Street; Going down the Volga; Notchenka* (Folksongs with Russian Ch., Potorjinsky).
(B) *** EMI mono/stereo CZS7 67496-2 (5) [CDZE 67496].

This survey covers recordings by the great Bul-

garian bass made between 1954 and 1969. The great majority come from the 1960s, the earliest are the Russian folksongs recorded in 1954 and the Rachmaninov and Rimsky-Korsakov (1959). But throughout this remarkably extensive programme, the magnificent voice is in perfect shape and the recordings are faithfully transferred. Some might think a big voice like Christoff's would be unsuitable for art songs, but his sensitivity is never in question and, whenever necessary, he scales it down, especially (for instance) in several of the Glinka songs where he has a cello obbligato. This repertoire is enormously rich in melody and, just as in the opera house, Christoff's art demonstrates the widest emotional range. Characterization is always strong and his feeling for words is just as striking here as in his performances of the stage repertory. Most of the songs are piano accompanied (with a whole range of excellent accompanists) but occasionally orchestral versions are used, as in Rimsky-Korsakov's *The Prophet* or Balakirev's *Prologue*, when the orchestra is vividly balanced. The collection ends with an exhilarating half-dozen traditional Russian folksongs in which Christoff is joined by an enthusiastic (if backwardly balanced) Russian chorus and balalaika ensemble. The result is irresistible, with melancholy and joy side by side in a wonderfully Slavonic way. These five well-filled discs not only demonstrate some of the riches hitherto hidden in EMI's international vaults; they also give us unique performances of repertoire most of which is otherwise totally inaccessible. The snag lies in the documentation. As this derives from EMI's French stable, even the song-titles are given in French. (It was a major task identifying and translating them!) No texts are provided, simply a two-page biographical note.

Gigli, Beniamino (tenor)

Opera arias from: GOUNOD: *Faust.* BIZET: *Carmen; Les Pêcheurs de perles.* MASSENET: *Manon.* HANDEL: *Serse.* DONIZETTI: *Lucia di Lammermoor; L'Elisir d'amore.* VERDI: *Rigoletto; Aida.* LEONCAVALLO: *I Pagliacci.* MASCAGNI: *Cavalleria Rusticana.* PUCCINI: *La Bohème; Tosca.* GIORDANO: *Andrea Chénier.* PIETRI: *Maristella.*
(M) (***) EMI mono CDH7 61051-2 [id.].

No Italian tenor has sung with more honeyed beauty than Beniamino Gigli. His status in the inter-war period as a singing superstar at a time when the media were less keenly organized is vividly reflected in this Références collection of eighteen items, the cream of his recordings made between 1927 and 1937. It is especially welcome to have two historic ensemble recordings, made in New York in 1927 and originally coupled on a short-playing 78-r.p.m. disc – the *Quartet* from *Rigoletto* and the *Sextet* from *Lucia di Lammermoor*. In an astonishing line-up Gigli is joined by Galli-Curci, Pinza, De Luca and Louise Homer. Excellent transfers.

Arias from: VERDI: *Aida; La forza del destino; Un ballo in maschera; Rigoletto; Requiem*. DONIZETTI: *L'elisir d'amore*. PUCCINI: *La Bohème; Tosca*. CILEA: *L'Arlesiana*. GIORDANO: *Andrea Chénier*. BIZET: *Carmen*. LEONCAVALLO: *Pagliacci*. MASCAGNI: *Cavalleria rusticana; Isabeau*. ROSSINI: *Stabat Mater*. HANDEL: *Serse; Atalanta*. Songs: SCHUBERT: *Ave Maria*. BIZET: *Agnus Dei*. GIORDANO: *Caro mio ben*. DE CURTIS: *Torna a Surriento*. TOSTI: *L'untima canzone; La serenata; Aprile*. CARDILLO: *Core'ngrato*. DENZA: *Funiculi, funicula*. FRANCK: *Panis angelicus*. BACHGOUNOD: *Ave Maria*. CACCINI: *Amarilli*. MARTINI: *Plaisir d'amore*. DI CAPUA: *O sole mio*. ROSSINI: *La danza*. LEONCAVALLO: *Mattinata*.
(BB) (***) Royal Classics Vocal Double mono DCL 706652 [id.].

This very inexpensive Royal Classics Double involves some duplication with the Références disc above but not enough to matter, and the present collection extends to include recordings pulished in the late 1930s and early 1940s, when the voice was still sounding warm and fresh: the 1941 *E la solita storia del pastor* from Cilea's *L'Arlesiana* is particularly affecting. It is good too, to have the songs, richly lyrical performances like Schubert's *Ave Maria*, and the glorious *Caro mio ben* (published in 1947), while Gigli shows he can let himself go splendidly in the Neapolitan favourites, especially *O sole mio*. The transfers are first class, but there is no documentation beyond a list of titles, accompaniment details, and publishing dates.

Jurinac, Sena (soprano)

Opera arias from: MOZART: *Così fan tutte; Idomeneo*. SMETANA: *The Bartered Bride; The Kiss*. TCHAIKOVSKY: *Joan of Arc; Queen of Spades*. R. STRAUSS: *Four Last Songs (Vier letzte Lieder)*.
(M) (***) EMI mono CDH7 63199-2 [id.].

This EMI Références issue, very well transferred, celebrates a magical, under-recorded singer. It brings together all of Jurinac's recordings for EMI outside the complete operas, and adds a live radio recording from Sweden – with Fritz Busch conducting the Stockholm Philharmonic Orchestra – of Strauss's *Four Last songs*, most beautifully done, if with rather generalized expression. Busch was also the conductor for the Glyndebourne recordings of excerpts from *Così fan tutte* and *Idomeneo*.

McCormack, John (tenor)

'*Songs of my heart'*: Trad.: *The garden where the praties grow; Terence's farewell to Kathleen; Believe me if all those endearing young charms; The star of the County Down; Oft in the stilly night; The meeting of the waters; The Bard of Armagh; Down by the Salley Gardens; She moved thro' the fair; The green bushes*. BALFE: *The harp that once through Tara's halls*. ROECKEL: *The green isle of Erin*. SCHNEIDER: *O Mary dear*. LAMBERT: *She is far from the land*. HAYNES: *Off to Philadelphia*. MOLLOY: *The Kerry dance; Bantry Bay*. MARSHALL: *I hear you calling me*. E. PURCELL: *Passing by*. WOODFORD-FINDEN: *Kashmiri song*. CLUTSAM: *I know of two bright eyes*. FOSTER: *Jeannie with the light brown hair; Sweetly she sleeps, my Alice fair*.
⊛ (M) (***) EMI mono CDM7 64654-2 [id.].

In Irish repertoire like *The star of the County Down* McCormack is irresistible, but in lighter concert songs he could also spin the utmost magic. *Down by the Salley Gardens* and Stephen Foster's *Jeannie with the light brown hair* are superb examples, while in a ballad like *I hear you calling me* (an early pre-electric recording from 1908) the golden bloom of the vocal timbre combining with an artless line brings a ravishing frisson on the closing pianissimo. Many of the accompaniments are by Gerald Moore, who proves a splendid partner. Occasionally there is a hint of unsteadiness in the sustained *piano* tone, but otherwise no apology need be made for the recorded sound which is first class, while the lack of 78-r.p.m. background noise is remarkable.

Schmidt, Joseph (tenor)

Complete EMI recordings: Arias (sung in German) from: MEYERBEER: *L'africaine*. FLOTOW: *Martha; Alessandro Stradella*. KIENZL: *Der Evangelimann*. KORNGOLD: *Die tote Stadt*. adam: *Der Postillon von Longjumeau*. MASSENET: *Manon; Der Cid*. TCHAIKOVSKY: *Eugene Onegin*. MORY: *La Vallière*. GOTZE: *Der Page des Königs*. Johann STRAUSS Jr: *1001 Nacht; Der Zigeunerbaron; Simplicus*. LEHAR: *Zigeunerliebe*. TAUBER: *Der Singende Traume*. DONIZETTI: *Der Liebestrank (L'elisir d'amore)*. VERDI: *Rigoletto; Der Troubadour (Il trovatore)*. LEONCAVALLO: *Der Bajazzo (Pagliacci)*. PUCCINI: *La Bohème; Tosca; Das Mädchen aus dem Goldenen Westen (Fanciulla del West); Turandot*. SERRANO: *El Trust de Los Tenorios*. SPOLIANSKY: *Das Lied einer Nacht* (film). Lieder & Songs: SCHUBERT: *Ständchen; Ungeduld*. BENATZKY: *Wenn du treulos bist*. NIEDERBERGER: *Buona notte, schöne Signorina*. LEONCAVALLO: *Morgenständchen*. LABRIOLA: *Serenata*. Biscardi: *L'ariatella*.

DENZA: *Funiculi, funicula*. BUZZI-PECCIA: *Lolita*. Di capua: *O sole mio*.
(M) (***) EMI mono CHS7 64676-2 (2) [id.].

Joseph Schmidt, born in 1904 in what is now Romania, studied in Berlin, and developed what by any standards is one of the most beautiful German tenor voices ever recorded, less distinctive than that of Richard Tauber, but even more consistently honeyed and velvety in the upper registers, exceptionally free on top, so that the stratospheric top notes in *Le Postillon de Longjumeau* have never sounded so beautiful and unstrained. This is the ideal lyric tenor voice, not just for the German repertory, including operetta, but for the Italian; it was tragic that, standing less than five foot high, he was precluded from having an operatic career. Nevertheless, he was most successful in his concert work as well as in his recording career, as this glowing collection demonstrates. He even had a brilliantly successful American tour in 1937; but sadly, as a Jew, he got caught up in Europe during the Second World War, and died from a chest complaint in a Swiss refugee camp in 1942. The records – with informative notes – make a superb memorial, here at last given full prominence in excellent transfers.

Tauber, Richard (tenor)

'*Opera arias and duos*' (with (i) Elisabeth Rethberg; (ii) Lotte Lehmann) from: MOZART: *Don Giovanni*. MEHUL: *Joseph*. OFFENBACH: *Contes d'Hoffmann*. THOMAS: *Mignon*. TCHAIKOVSKY: *Eugene Onegin*. SMETANA: (i) *The Bartered Bride*. WAGNER: *Die Meistersinger*. PUCCINI: *Turandot;* (i) *Madama Butterfly*. KORNGOLD: (ii) *Die tote Stadt*.
(M) (***) EMI mono CDH7 64029-2.

Starting as early as 1922 with Mozart's *Dalla sua pace* from *Don Giovanni*, then immediately following with the 1939 *Il mio tesoro*, this recital charts Tauber's recording career as far as 1945 with the Méhul *Champs paternels* from *Joseph*. Elisabeth Rethberg joins him now and then, notably in the *Butterfly* excerpt, sung in German. The voice is well caught by the transfers, but there are occasionally some noises off. Yet the standard of singing here is so consistently high that one can readily make allowances. For a sampler, try the glorious *Hoffmann* excerpts (1929) or *Lensky's aria* from *Eugene Onegin* (1923).

MOZART: *Don Giovanni: Il mio tesoro. Die Zauberflöte: Dies Bildnis*. Arias from: PUCCINI: *La Bohème; Madama Butterfly; Tosca; Turandot*. LEONCAVALLO: *Pagliacci*. VERDI: *Il Trovatore*. MEHUL: *Joseph in Aegypten*. OFFENBACH: *Contes d'Hoffmann*. THOMAS: *Mignon*. TCHAIKOVSKY: *Eugene Onegin*. SMETANA: *Bartered bride* (all sung in German). WEBER: *Der Freischütz*. LORTZING: *Undine*. KIENZL: *Der Evangelimann*. WAGNER: *Die Meistersinger*. R. STRAUSS: *Der Rosenkavlier*. KORNGOLD: *Die tote Stadt*. LEHAR: *Die lustige Witwe (Lippen schweigen; Vilja-Lied); Paganini; Friederike (O Mädchen, mein Mädchen); Das Land des Lächelns* (4 excerpts, including *Dein ist mein ganzes Herz*); *Giuditta; Die Zarewitsch*. KALMAN: *Die Zirkusprinzessin; Gräfin Mariza*. HEUBERGER: *Der Opernball (Im chambre séparée)*. STOLZ: *Adieu, mein kleiner Gardeoffizier; Im Prater blühn wieder die Bäume*. SIECZYNSKI: *Wien, du Stadt meiner Träume*. Johann STRAUSS Jr: *Geschichten aus dem Wienerwald; Rosen aus dem Süden*. ZELLER: *Der Vogelhändler*. DOELLE: *Wenn der weisse Flieder wider blüht*. ERWIN: *Ich küsse Ihre Hand, Madame*. Lieder: SCHUBERT: *Ständchen; Der Lindenbaum*.
(M) (*(**)) EMI mono CMS5 66692-2 (2) [id.].

If one begins with the second of these two CDs, it becomes immediately obvious why Tauber established his reputation with the wider public largely in the field of operetta. The uniquely honeyed voice makes simple melodies like *Lippen schweigen* from *The Merry Widow*, with its magical final cadence, or the *Vilja-Lied* utterly seductive, and that despite often inadequate transfers, with thin, whistly orchestral sound and plenty of distortion, even on the voice itself. One wonders why Tauber, more than most singers of his generation, so regularly suffers from this problem. It isn't that the basic recordings are bad, except for the thin orchestra (though there are frequent moments of blasting); usually the magic and power of the voice are well conveyed; yet the original sources too often seem prone to distortion. The first disc concentrates on opera and opens with a glowingly lyrical 1939 *Il mio tesoro*, but again there is distortion. *Dies Bildnis* (from *Die Zauberflöte*) is acoustic (1922) and rather better, and Tauber then makes *Your tiny hand is frozen* sound beguiling even in German! – the chosen language for most of his records. – There are many remarkable performances here, from the lilting *Legend of Kleinsach* (1928) to a stirring *Di quella pira* (1926) with a comic wind band accompaniment; there are also equally moving versions of Lenski's aria from *Eugene Onegin* (1923), when the band is less clumsy, and the ardent *On with the motley* (recorded in London in 1936 and sung in English). It is a pity the recordings are technically so inadequate, but the voice still enthrals the listener.

Thill, Georges (tenor)

French opera arias (with orchestras conducted by Bigot; Heurteur; Gaubert; Szyfer; Frigara): BERLIOZ: *La Damnation de Faust: Nature*

immense, impénétrable et fière. Les Troyens à Carthage: Inutiles regrets. BIZET: Carmen: La fleur que tu m'avais jetée. GLUCK: Alceste: Bannis la crainte et les alarmes. GOUNOD: Faust: Quel trouble inconnu me pénètre. Roméo et Juliette: L'amour, l'amour (with Germaine Feraldy). MASSENET: Le Cid: O noble lame étincelante; O souverain! O Juge! O père. Werther: Invocation à la nature; Un autre est son époux!. ROSSINI: Guillaume Tell: Asile héréditaire. SAINT-SAENS: Samson et Dalila: Air de la meule.
(M) (***) EMI mono CDM7 69548-2.

Georges Thill left an enormous discography, and this selection of 78 r.p.m. discs made between 1927 and 1936 will come as a revelation to younger collectors unacquainted with his work. He made his début at the Paris Opéra in 1924 and soon established himself as the greatest French tenor of his day. The tone is splendidly full and round and the phrasing masterly. In an age when one is lucky to make out what language is being sung, let alone the actual words, his diction is an object lesson. Every word resonates, and yet it is the musical line which remains paramount. At 74 minutes, this is a generous sampling of his recorded legacy, very well transferred and absolutely indispensable to anyone who cares about singing.

THE ROMOPHONE SERIES

The Romophone series is favoured by many vocal collectors, for the transfers are straightforwardly done, seeking as clear as possible a focus for the voice, aiming to match closely the original recording quality, and in so doing accepting a fairly high degree of background noise. But as always with transfer technology, it is the ear of the transfer engineer that is paramount and in many cases the vocal impression here is impressively vivid. Comparison with the Nimbus achievement (see below) is always fascinating, and preference for one or the other will inevitably be subjective. However, the Romophone collection is in the premium-price range, so in that respect the Nimbus series has a clear advantage.

Ancona, Mario (baritone)

'The Complete Victor recordings (1907–08)': Arias and duets from: LEONCAVALLO: I Pagliacci. GOUNOD: Faust. VERDI: La traviata; Ernani; Un ballo in maschera; Era la notte; Rigoletto (with Bessie Abbot); Il trovatore. BELLINI: I Puritani (with Journet). BIZET: I pescatore di perle (with Caruso). DONIZETTI: La Favorita. MEYERBEER: Dinorah. GIORDANO: Andrea Chenier. Songs by:

TOSTI: Mattinata; Invano. ROTOLI: Mia sposa sarà la mia bandiera. TCHAIKOVSKY: Sérénade de Don Juan.
(***) Romophone mono 82013-2 [id.].

Born in 1860 Mario Ancona came to prominence as the first Silvio in the premiere of I Pagliacci in 1892, and had a distinguished career for another twenty-five years. His was a firm clear baritone, marked by flawless control and clean attack. He was more concerned with fine singing than strong characterization, so that Iago's Era la notte is hardly sinister. A fascinating supplement offers three Pathé recordings of 1906 including stirring accounts of Rigoletto's solos, but which fail to convey any anger. Good transfers by Ward Marston with the voice clearly caught, and with surface noise that one quickly forgets.

Battistini, Mattia (baritone)

'The Complete recordings (1902–11)': Arias, duets and scenes from: MOZART: Don Giovanni (with Emilia Corsi). WAGNER: Tannhäuser. TCHAIKOVSKY: Eugene Onegin. RUBINSTEIN: The Demon. ROSSINI: Il barbiere di Siviglia. GOUNOD: Faust. DONIZETTI: La favorita; Don Sebastiani; Maria di Rohan. COCCHI: Per la patria. VERDI: Ernani (with Emilia Corsi, Aristodemo Sillich, Luigi Colazza); Un ballo in maschera. FLOTOW: Martha. BERLIOZ: La damnation de Faust. HEROLD: Zampa. LEONCAVALLO: I Pagliacci. massenet: Werther; Thaïs (with Ebe Boccolini, Attilia Janni). BELLINI: I puritani. THOMAS: Hamlet. PUCCINI: Tosca. Songs by: ALVAREZ: Lamantilla. DENZA: Occhi di fata. TOSTI: Ancora; Amour, amour. GOUNOD: Le soir.
(***) Romophone mono 82008-2 (2) [id.].

As Michael Scott's note points out in this magnificent collection of Battistini's early recordings, he is the oldest great singer (he was born in 1856) to have made records whilst still at the peak of his powers. Not that the first disc represents him at all fairly, characterful as it is, for it consists of a double rendering of Don Giovanni's 'champagne' aria astonishingly fast, so that even he with his dark, agile voice has to slide sketchily over many of the notes. The magnetism and projection make one share his obvious joy in the new medium, a fun occasion, and almost all the rest are a delight, for this was one of the finest baritone voices ever put on disc. Those sessions took place in Warsaw in 1902, then under the control of Imperial Russia, and that may account for the Tchaikosvky and Rubinstein items. Here was a singer who did not limit himself to the central nineteenth-century Italian repertory, for it was not until his next set of sessions in 1906 that he began to record Verdi, and even then not obvious arias, for six of them are from Ernani and two from Ballo, with *Eri tu* gloriously resonant and finely shaded, if again hardly conveying anger. As on Nimbus, the rare aria from Herold's *Zampa* is included, and it is good too to have among these 1902 recordings so poised an account of Wolfram's *O star of eve* from *Tannhäuser*, sung in Italian. Ward Marston's transfers give a vivid idea of the commanding voice, though he has not been able to eliminate the heavy surface noise on some of the rarer items.

Bori, Lucrezia (soprano)

'*The Victor Recordings (1914–25)*': Arias, duets and scenes from: LEONCAVALLO: *I Pagliacci*. VERDI: *La traviata* (with John McCormack); *Rigoletto* (with John McCormack, Josephine Jacoby and Richard Werrenrath). PUCCINI: *La bohème* (with John McCormack and with Tito Schipa). VALVERDE: *Nina Pancha*. MASCAGNI: *Iris; L'amico Fritz* (with Miguel Fleta). OFFENBACH: *Les contes d'Hoffmann*. CHAPI: *La revoltosa; El puñao de rosas* (both with Andrea Perello de Segurolla). MOZART: *Le nozze di Figaro; Don Giovanni; Così fan tutte*. WOLF-FERRARI: *Il segreto di Susanna*. DONIZETTI: *Don Pasquale*. RIMSKY-KORSAKOV: *The Snow Maiden*. GOUNOD: *Roméo et Juliette* (with Beniamino Gigli). MASSENET: *Manon*. DELIBES: *Lakmé*. BIZET: *Carmen* (with Miguel Fleta). VARNEY: *L'amour Mouillée*. Songs by: ROSSINI: *La danza*. PAGANS: *Malagueña*. YRADIER: *La paloma*. MARSHALL: *I hear you calling me*. VALVERDE: *Clavelitos*. SIBELLA: *Villanella*. MOORE: *When love is kind*. ARDITI: *Il bacio*. GRANADOS: *El majo discreto*. PESTALOZZI: *Ciribiribin*. DELFINO: *Milonguita*. NOVELLO: *The Little Damozel*. (***) Romophone mono 81016 [id.].

'*The Victor Recordings (1925–37)*': Arias and duets from: CHARPENTIER: *Louise*. PUCCINI: *La bohème; Madama Butterfly; La rondine*. OFFENBACH: *Les contes d'Hoffmann*. VARNEY: *Amour mouilée*. VERDI: *La traviata*. THOMAS: *Mignon*. MOZART: *Don Giovanni; Le nozze di Figaro*. MASSENET: *Manon*. DE FALLA: *La vida breve*. WOLF-FERRARI: *Il segreto di Susanna*. LITERES (arr. NIN): *Acis y Galatea*. LASERNA: *Amantes chasqueaos*. OBRADORS: *Don Quixote de la Mancha*. Songs by: GLAZUNOV: *La primavera d'or*. STRAUSS: *Tales from the Vienna Woods* (three versions). VALVERDE: *Cruz de majo; Clavelitos*. JOVES: *Patoteres sentimental*. RUMBOLD: *Simonetta*. SCHUMANN: *Into the woods* (with John McCormack). GORING-THOMAS: *Night hymn at sea* (two versions with McCormack). ARDITI: *Il bacio* (two versions). PESTALOZZA: *Ciribiribin*. PAGANS: *Malagueña*. GOETZ-PADILLA: *La violetera*. RIEMANN (arr.): *Seguidilla*. DE FALLA: *Jota;*

Seguidilla murciana. NIN: *Malagueña; Jota tortosina; Copias de curro dulce; Canto andaluz*. (***) Romophone mono 81017-2 (2) [id.].

Lucrezia Bori, a favourite at the Met in New York from her début in 1912 through to the 1930s, was a sparkling characterful singer, whose agility in coloratura went with clear, fresh projection, belying the size of voice. That quality is beautifully caught here in excellent Ward Marston transfers which characteristically prefer to keep the voice vivid rather than eliminating surface hiss. The first of the two double-disc boxes covers all Bori's pre-electric recordings – including some fine duets with McCormack, as well as her first four electric recordings of 1925. The second double-disc box containing the rest, demonstrates her later development, when with the voice as pure and sweet as ever she brought an extra emotional intensity into such numbers as 'Mimi's farewell', taken slower in 1926 than in 1914, singing with extra poise in Louise's *Depuis le jour*. Her gift of characterization comes out vividly in the contrast of the two solos from Thomas's *Mignon*, the one tender, the other sparkling. As usual with Romophone issues, it is fascinating to compare different versions of various numbers, many unpublished.

Destinn, Emmy (soprano)

'*The Complete Victor Recordings (1914–21)*': Arias and duets from: THOMAS: *Mignon*. PUCCINI: *Madama Butterfly; Tosca*. VERDI: *Aida; Il trovatore*. PONCHIELLI: *La gioconda*. WAGNER: *Allmächt'ge Jungfrau*. GOMES: *Il guarany* (with Caruso). MOZART: *Die Zauberflute*. DVORAK: *Rusalka*. KOVAROVICH: *Nazarene*. TCHAIKOVSKY: *The Queen of spades*. SCHUBERT: *Wiegenlied*. BACH–GOUNOD: *Ave Maria*. MOZART: *Wiegenlied*. Czech folk songs (all with Dinh Gilly). Songs by: TOSTI; GOUNOD; STANGE; LISZT; JINDRICH; DESTINN; HESS; STEPAN; SMETANA; VERDI; DVORAK. (M) (***) Romophone mono 81002-2 (2) [id.].

Emmy Destinn was the leading dramatic soprano of her day, the choice of Strauss for the role of Salome and of Puccini for Minnie, the Girl of the Golden West. Yet as this wide-ranging collection makes clear, the poise of her singing with its perfect control, was at least as remarkable as the power.

The finest examples here, all of them flawlessly controlled, include Aida's *O patria mia* and Tosca's *Vissi d'arte*. Pamina's *Ach ich fühl's* is similarly poised, with a superb trill at the end. The thirty-seven items offer Destinn's complete Victor recordings made between 1914 and 1921, but the choice of the opening item is unfortunate, when the aria from Thomas's *Mignon* (in German, not French) has Destinn singing with an ugly yodelling tone, using excessive portamento. As a Czech, she includes a number of Czech folksongs, but then sings the *Rusalka* aria in German, not Czech. The transfers capture the voice vividly, but surface hiss tends to be high.

Eames, Emma (soprano)

'*The Complete Victor Recordings (1905–11)*':
Arias and duets from: GOUNOD: *Faust; Roméo et Juliette*. PUCCINI: *Tosca*. MOZART: *Don Giovanni; Il flauto magico* (both with Emilio de Gogorza). VERDI: *Otello; Il trovatore* (with Gogorza). BIZET: *Carmen*. MASCAGNI: *Cavalleria rusticana; Le nozze di Figaro* (with Marcella Sembrich and with Gogorza). MASSENET: *Chérubin*. DELIBES: *Lakmé*. WAGNER: *Lohengrin*. MESSAGER: *Véronique*. BOHM: *Still wie die nacht* (two versions). BACH–GOUNOD: *Ave Maria*. FAURE: *Crucifix* (three versions with Gogorza). Songs by: HAHN; TOSTI; MASSENET; SCHUBERT; ARNOLD; EMMETT; HOLLMAN; PARKER; NEVIN; KOECHLIN; HENSCHEL; BEACH; BEMBERG. (Includes extracts of Calvé commenting on her records.)
(**(*)) Romophone mono 81001-2 (2) [id.].

Most of these recordings of the American soprano Emma Eames date from 1905 and 1906, the earlier ones involving piano accompaniment, even in operatic items. The voice in these transfers is variably caught, sometimes rather faint, behind heavy surface-hiss. Yet the flexibility of the voice, as well as its purity and projection, come out splendidly in such items as the two versions of the *Jewel song* from *Faust* and duplicate versions of the *Ave Maria* from Verdi's *Otello*, as well as a rapt account of Tosca's *Vissi d'arte*. Some of the most attractive excerpts are the duets with the superb baritone, Emilio de Gogorza.

Flagstad, Kirsten (soprano)

'*Grieg's Haugtussa and the complete 1937 Victor Recordings*': Arias from: BEETHOVEN: *Fidelio*. WEBER: *Oberon*. WAGNER: *Lohengrin; Die Walküre; Gotterdämmerung*. Songs by: GRIEG: *Haugtussa*. BEETHOVEN: *Ah, Perfido!*.
(***) Romophone mono 81023-2 [id.].

Kirsten Flagstad with her dramatic soprano on a heroic scale may not have been a natural Lieder singer, but Grieg's warmly characterful cycle, *Haugtussa*, plainly brings out her natural warmth, and with Edwin McArthur as her sympathetic accompanist she gives a magnetic performance. The recording favours the voice, which is placed rather close, but the Romophone transfer brings out bloom and warmth, and the Philadelphia recordings of 1937, also transferred on the Nimbus disc of Flagstad, are on balance preferable here, with the orchestra far fuller. Where on the Nimbus issue Flagstad's 1939 San Francisco recording of Brünnhilde's Immolation scene has been preferred, this earlier one of 1937, never issued at the time, is equally commanding, with the voice fresh and full throughout.

Galli-Curci, Amelita (soprano)

'*The Complete acoustic recordings (1916–20)*':
Arias, duets and scenes from: VERDI: *Rigoletto* (with Caruso, Flora Perini, Giuseppi De Luca, Marcel Journet and Angelo Bada); *La traviata* (with De Luca). DONIZETTI: *Lucia di Lammermoor* (with Caruso, Minnie Egener, etc.); *Don Pasquale*. GOUNOD: *Roméo et Juliette*. AUBER: *Manon Lescaut*. GRIEG: *Peer Gynt*. DELIBES: *Lakmé*. ROSSINI: *Il barbiere di Siviglia*. MEYERBEER: *Dinorah*. BELLINI: *La sonnambula*. FLOTOW: *Martha*. MOZART: *Le nozze di Figaro*. DAVID: *La perle du Brésil*. BELLINI: *I puritani*. THOMAS: *Mignon*. Songs by: ALVAREZ; BISHOP; BUZZI-PECCIA; GIORDANI; SEPPILLI; PROCH; MASSENET; BENEDICT; CHOPIN; SAMUELS; DELIBES; DELL'ACQUA; VALVERDE.
(***) Romophone mono 81003-2 (2) [id.].

'*The Complete acoustic recordings (1920–24)*':
Arias and duets from: BELLINI: *I puritani*; *La sonnambula* (with Tito Schipa). RIMSKY-KORSAKOV: *Le coq d'or; Sadko*. ADAM: *Le toréador*. BIZET: *Les pêcheurs de perles*. FLOTOW: *Martha*. PUCCINI: *Madama Butterfly*. MEYERBEER: *L'étoile du nord; Le pardon de Ploérmel (Dinorah)*. DONIZETTI: *Lucia di Lammermoor; Don pasquale* (both with Schipa); *Linda di Chamounix*. VERDI: *Rigoletto; La traviata* (both with Schipa); *Il trovatore*. HERBERT: *Orange blossoms; Mlle Modiste*. MASSENET: *Don César de Bazan; Manon*. ROSSINI: *Semiramide*. Songs by: COOKE; BISHOP; FOSTER; MOLLOY; DYKES; DANKS; PIERNE; STRICKLAND; RUSSELL; BISHOP; TRADITIONAL: arr. GUERVOS; DELIBES; CONRAD; PONCE.
(***) Romophone mono 81004-2 (2) [id.].

'*The Complete Victor Recordings (1925–28)*':
Arias and duets and scenes from: MEYERBEER: *Dinorah*. THOMAS: *Amleto (Hamlet)*. VERDI: *Il trovatore; Rigoletto* (with Giuseppi de Luca, Louise Horner and Beniamino Gigli, and with Tito Schipa); *La traviata* (with de Luca and with Schipa). CHAPI: *Las hijas del Zebedeo*. GRETRY: *Zémire et Azor*. ROSSINI: *Il barbiere di Siviglia*. DONIZETTI: *Lucia di Lammermoor* (with Gigli, Horner, de Luca, Ezio Pinza and Angelo Bada); *Don Pasquale* (With Schipa). THOMAS: *Mignon*. Songs by: MONK: arr. SAMUELS; DYKES; STRICKLAND; TOSTI; BENEDICT; ARDITI; PROCH;

ALABIEV; YRADIER; GREIG; BISHOP; MOLLOY; BAILY; MOORE; SCARLATTI: arr. Ary VAN LEEUWEN; VALVERDE; PONCE; FOSTER.
(***) Romophone mono 81020-2 (2) [id.].

'The Victor recordings (1930)': Arias and duets from: RIMSKY-KORSAKOV: *Sadko*. GOUNOD: *Philémon et Baucis; Roméo et Juliette*. VERDI: *Rigoletto; Il trovatore*. MEYERBEER: *L'étoile du nord*. DONIZETTI: *Lucia di Lammermoor* (with Tito Schipa). Songs by: ROSSINI; DELIBES; FOSTER; BISHOP; MOORE; GREVER and TRADITIONAL. (Includes excerpt of Galli-Curci radio interview.)
(***) Romophone mono 81021-2 [id.].

Amelita Galli-Curci was among the most vivacious singers of her time. It was not just the beauty and brilliance of her coloratura that captivated audiences, but also the caressing way she had with phrasing conveying a poignancy in cantilena, which made her flights of coloratura brilliance sound all the more carefree and charming by contrast. She was naturally characterful, and projected well, even if it was a relatively small voice. All those qualities come over impressively in this comprehensive collection of her recordings for Victor, seven discs in all. The pre-electric recordings, less well-known than the popular electrical issues from the late 1920s contained on the third of the four issues here, are just as impressive; both in the showpiece arias and in the many trivial items which were at the core of Galli-Curci's popular success, not least those in which she exploited the purity and sweetness of her topmost register in imitation birdsong. The last, single disc of her 1930 recordings contains, as a delightful supplement, a radio interview recorded in 1963, the year she died, confirming in her spoken words everything about her character that her singing suggests.

Garden, Mary (soprano)

'The Complete Victor recordings (1926–29)': Arias and duets from: CHARPENTIER: *Louise*. ALFANO: *Résurrection*. BIZET: *Carmen*. Songs by: CADMAN; HAHN; ROGERS; TATE; HUME; HARRISON; DEBUSSY; SZULE; GRETCHANINOV and TRADITIONAL.
(***) Romophone mono 81008 [id.].

The Scottish soprano Mary Garden, Debussy's first and favourite Mélisande, made sadly few recordings, but those here reveal a fresh, bright voice in performances marked by clean, fearless attack. If those are not quite the mysterious qualities one expects of the ideal Mélisande, these items effectively dispatch the idea, sometimes suggested, that the voice was undistinguished, and that she relied for her impact on her acting. Though she was a lyric soprano, it is striking how strong and characterful

her reading is of Carmen's 'Card scene' solo. It is fascinating too to compare the three contrasted versions of Louise's *Depuis le jour*, only one of them previously published. Fine Ward Marston transfers.

Gigli, Beniamino (tenor)

'The Complete Victor recordings (1921–25)': Arias and duets from: BOITO: *Mefistofle*. PUCCINI: *Tosca*. PONCHIELLI: *La gioconda*. DONIZETTI: *La favorita; L'elisir d'amore; Lucia di Lammermoor*. GOUNOD: *Faust; Roméo et Juliette* (with Lucrezia Bori). MASCAGNI: *Iris*. DRIGO: *I millioni d'Arlecchino*. LALO: *Le roi d'Ys*. LEONCAVALLO: *I Pagliacci*. GIORDANO: *Andrea Chénier*. PUCCINI: *Tosca*. MEYERBEER: *L'africana*. CATALANI: *Loreley*. FLOTOW: *Martha*. Songs by: DE CURTIS; MARIO; TOSELLI; SAINT-SAENS; BUZZI-PECCIA; CARNEVALI; TAGLIAFERRI; DE CRESCENZO; DI CAPUA.
(***) Romophone mono 82003-2 (2) [id.].

'The Complete Victor recordings (1926–28)': Arias, duets and scenes from: VERDI: *La forza del destino*. PUCCINI: *La bohème*. PONCHIELLI: *La gioconda* (all three with Titta Ruffa and with Giuseppe de Luca). PUCCINI: *Tosca; Manon Lescaut*. BOITO: *Mefistofele*. DRIGO: *I millioni d'Arlecchino*. BIZET: *I pescatori di perle*. DONIZETTI: *Lucia di Lammermoor* (with Ezio Pinza and with Amelita Galli-Curci, Louise Homer, Angela Bada, Pinza and de Luca). VERDI: *Rigoletto* (with Galli-Curci, Homer, and de Luca); *La traviata*. MASCAGNI: *Cavalleria rusticana*. THOMAS: *Mignon*. MEYERBEER: *L'africana*. Songs by: TOSELLI; BUZZI-PECCIA; MASCAGNI; MARIO; DE CRESCENZO; COTTRAU; DONNAUDY; DE CURTIS.
(***) Romophone mono 82004-2 (2) [id.].

'The Complete Victor recordings (1929–32)': Arias and scenes from: FLOTOW: *Martha*; PONCHIELLI: *La gioconda*; BIZET: *Pearlfishers*; DONIZETTI: *L'elisir d'amore*; VERDI: *I Lombardi & Attila* (both with Rethberg & Pinza); RIMSKY-KORSAKOV: *Sadko*. Songs by DEDA; DENZA; GASTALDON; DE CURTIS; KREISLER; NUTILE; SIMONS; ALBENIZ; SANDOVAL' DE CRESCENZO.
(***) Romophone mono 82005-2 (2) [id.].

'The Complete HMV recordings (1918–32)': Arias and duets from: BOITO: *Mefistofele* (with Carlo Scattola and with Gemma Bosini). PUCCINI: *Tosca; La bohème* (with Maria Zamboni). PONCHIELLI: *La Gioconda* (with Dario Zani and with Elvira Casazza). DONIZETTI: *La Favorita* (with Casazza). MASCAGNI: *Lodoletta; Iris; L'amico Fritz* (with Naldira Baldisseri); *Cavalleria rusticana* (with Dusolina Giannini and

with Zamboni). GOUNOD: *Faust* (with Zamboni).
BIZET: *Les pêcheurs des perles* (with Adolfo
Pacini). GIORDANO: *Fedora*. MASSENET: *Manon*.
ROSSINI: *Stabat Mater*. Songs by: CANNIO;
TOSTI; SULLIVAN; SCHUBERT; NIEDERMEYER; DE
CURTIS.
(***) Romophone mono 82011-2 (2) [id.].

'*The complete HMV recordings (1933-35)*':
LEONCAVALLO: *I Pagliacci* (complete) (with Iva
Pacetti, Mario Basiola and Giuseppe Nessi). Arias
and duets from: GIORDANO: *Andrea Chénier*.
MASCAGNI: *Cavalleria rusticana*. HANDEL: *Serse*.
LEONCAVALLO: *I Pagliacci*. DONIZETTI: *L'elisir
d'amore*. PUCCINI: *Tosca*. VERDI: *Rigoletto*.
BIZET: *Carmen*. GLUCK: *Paride ed Elena*. Songs
by: COTTRAU; DI CAPUA; DE CURTIS; BIXIO;
LEONCAVALLO; MARTINI; MASSENET;
SCHUBERT; MELICHAR.
(***) Romophone mono 82017-2 (2) [id.].

These five sets, nine discs in all, magnificently
cover the recording activity up to the mid 1930s of
Beniamino Gigli, both in Europe and America;
more than any tenor, he was the successor to Caruso.
It is striking throughout that Gigli with his honeyed,
golden-toned voice was one who unlike so many
other Italian tenors positively thrived on not singing
at a consistent *fortissimo*. He is hardly a stylist, or
the connoisseur's favourite, but no Italian tenor of
his generation quite compared with Gigli in the
magic quality he could give to a song or aria, both
in his colouring of tone and in the warm-hearted
magnetism which marked all his singing. It follows
that his forte lies in Puccini and Neapolitan song,
with 'Arie antiche' or Mozart revealing his stylistic
weaknesses, thanks to heavily aspirated divisions
and the occasional sob. His headily beautiful soft
singing can also turn into a near-croon. Whatever
those shortcomings, the results are consistently
magical, so that *M'appari tutt'amor* from *Martha*
may be aspirated, but its golden beauty has you
charmed. As usual in Romophone issues alternative
takes, usually unpublished, are included, often with
fascinating results, as with the two versions of the
Pearl fishers' aria on the 1929-32 Victor set. In
that same issue it is good too to have side-by-side
versions of the *Lombardi* and *Attila* trios with
Rethberg and Pinza. Italian is the preferred language
but the *Chanson hindoue* from Sadko comes in
French. Excellent transfers by Mark Obert-Thorn.

Lehmann, Lotte (soprano)

'*The Complete RCA Victor recordings (1947–
49)*': SCHUBERT: *Ständchen: Leise flehen meine
Lieder; An den Mond; An die Musik;Der Jüngling
an der Quelle; An die Nachtigall; Der Männer
sind méchant; Nacht und Träume; Der Erlkönig.*
BRAHMS: *Ziegeunerlieder* (excerpts);

Feldeinsamkeit; Der Kranz; Wiegenlied.
TRADITIONAL: *Adeste fideles*. GRUBER: *Stille
Nacht, heilige Nacht*. BERLIN: *God bless America*.
MOLLOY: *The Kerry dance*. SCHUMANN:
Träumerei. DUPARC: *La vie antérieure*.
PALADILHE: *Psyché*. STRAUSS: *Die Zeitlose;
Wozu noch, Mädchen; Du meines Herzens
Krönelein*.
(***)Romophone mono 81033-2

Most of these post-war Victor recordings by Lotte
Lehmann date from 1947, mostly of lieder with
Paul Ulanowski accompanying her. Though the
acoustic is uncomfortably dry, allowing little bloom
on the voice, the singing is still magnetic, while
the items with orchestra include such an oddity as
Irving Berlin's *God bless America*, with Lehmann
appropriately fervent. The Lieder and French mélodies from 1949 are better balanced, with the voice
more persuasively caught. Transfers by Mark
Obert-Thorn, which accurately convey the original
recording quality.

'*The Victor recordings (1935–40)*': Lieder and
songs: MOZART: *An Chloë; Die Verschweigung*.
SCHUBERT: *Ungeduld; Im Abendrot; Gretchen am
Spinnerade; Schlafe, schlafe; Die Nebensonnen;
Die Post; Der Stürmische Morgen; Der
Lindenbaum; Der Wegweiser; Die Krähe; Das
Wirtshaus; Täuschung; Mut!; Im Dorfe;
Rückblick*. SCHUMANN: *Die Kartenlegerin;
Waldgespräch; Du bist wie eine Blume;
Frühlingsnacht; Alte Laute; Er und sie; So wahr
die Sonne scheinet; Unterm Fenster;
Familien-Gemälde; Ich denke dein*. BRAHMS: *Der
Tod das ist die kühle Nacht; Therese; Meine Liebe
ist grün; Botschaft; Das Mädchen spricht; Mein
Mädchen hat einen Rosenmund*. WOLF: *Anakreons
Grab; In der Schatten meiner Locken;
Storchenbotschaft; Der Gärtner; Du denkst mich
zu fangen; Gebert; Früling übers Jahr; Auf ein
altes Bild; In der Frühe; Auch kleine Dinge;
Willst du Deinen Liebsten sehen; Peregrini I; Der
Knabe und das Immlein; Heimweh*. BALOGH: *Do
not chide*. GRETCHANINOFF: *My native land*.
WORTH: *Summer*. SODERO: *Fa la Nanna, Bambin*.
CIMARA: *Canto di primavera*. BEETHOVEN: *Ich
liebe dich*. HAHN: *D'une prison*. GOUNOD: *Vierge
d'Athènes*. PFITZNER: *Gretel*. MARX: *Selige
Nacht*. FRANZ: *Für Musik; Gute Nacht*. JENSEN:
Lehn' deine Wang' an meine Wang'. SJOBERG:
Visions. CALCOTT: *Drink to me only*.
TRADITIONAL: *Schlafe, mein süsses Kind*.
(***) Romophone mono 81013-2 (2) [id.].

These Victor recordings of Lehmann in Lieder present the voice at its freshest, superbly controlled,
and the recordings, less dry than the 1947 sessions
are far more sympathetic. The singer's enjoyment
as well as her understanding consistently come out
both there and in the recordings she went on to
make in 1937, 1939 and finally 1940, when she

essayed what only Elena Gerhardt had attempted before her, a woman's interpretation of Schubert's *Winterreise*, and it is sad that she covered only eleven of the songs. Though the voices are recorded close with thin orchestral accompaniments, the five Schumann duets with Melchior make a vividly characterful supplement to the Lieder, with operatic manners charmingly emerging.

Martinelli, Giovanni (tenor)

'*The Complete acoustic recordings (1912–1924)*': Arias, duets and scenes from: PUCCINI: *La bohème; Madama Butterfly* (both with Frances Alda); *Manon Lescaut; Tosca.* PONCHIELLI: *La Gioconda.* VERDI: *Rigoletto; Aida* (with Rosa Poncelle); *Un ballo in maschera; Il trovatore* (with Emmy Destinn); *Ernani; La traviata.* LEONCAVALLO: *I Pagliacci; Zazà.* MASCAGNI: *Cavalleria rusticana; Iris.* MEYERBEER: *L'africana.* DONIZETTI: *Lucia di Lammermoor; Don Pasquale.* FLOTOW: *Marta.* ROSSINI: *Guglielmo Tell* (with Marcel Journet and with Giuseppe de Luca and José Mardones). GOUNOD: *Faust.* MASSENET: *Werther.* HALEVY: *La Juive.* Songs by: TOSTI; MASCAGNI; BIZET; LEONCAVALLO; ROXAS; GASTELDO. (Includes extended excerpts from BIZET: *Carmen* with Geraldine Farrar.)
(***) Romophone mono 82012-2 (3) [id.].

Giovanni Martinelli, often described as Toscanini's favourite tenor, is more renowned for his electric recordings, but this comprehensive collection of his pre-electrics is most revealing in the way it shows how he developed into such a commanding singer. The voice was heroic and distinctive from the start, but the opening item, *Recondita armonia*, from Puccini's *Tosca*, recorded in 1912, finds him disconcertingly effortful, while Cavaradossi's Act III aria, *E lucevan le stelle*, is slow and heavy. His remakes of those arias only two years later show how quickly he learnt from his recordings, making them both more flowing and more characterful. As usual on Romophone these alternative takes are included, and it is good to have the five items from Bizet's *Carmen*, recorded in 1915 with Farrar singing the title role.

McCormack, John (tenor)

'*The Acoustic Victor and HMV recordings*' *(1910–11):* Arias, duets and scenes from: DONIZETTI: *Lucia di Lammermoor; L'elisir d'amore; La fille du régiment.* BIZET: *Carmen.* DELIBES: *Lakmé.* VERDI: *La traviata; Rigoletto* (with Nellie Melba, Edna Thornton and Mario Sammarco). PUCCINI: *La bohème.* BIZET: *Les Pêcheurs de perles.* ROSSINI: *Il barbiere di*

Siviglia. PONCHIELLI: *La gioconda.* GOUNOD: *Faust* (with Melba and all five with Sammarco). Songs by: BALFE; BARNARD; ANNE; LADY JOHN SCOTT; MARSHALL; CHERRY; BARKER; CROUCH; OLCOTT and BALL; HERBERT; MACMURROUGH; BLUMENTHAL; PARELLI; ROSSINI and TRADITIONAL.
(***) Romophone mono 82006-2 (2) [id.].
'*The Acoustic Victor and HMV recordings*' *(1912–14):* Arias from: HERBERT: *Natoma.* WOLF-FERRARI: *I gioielli della Madonna.* BOITO: *Mefistofele.* BIZET: *Les pêcheurs de perles; Carmen.* WALLACE: *Maritana.* massenet: *Manon.* VERDI: *Rigoletto.* GODARD: *Jocelyn.* Irish traditional songs including: *Eileen Aroon; The wearing of the Green; The harp that once through Tara's halls; Mollie Brannigan.* Songs and Ballads by: STERNDALE BENNETT; MARSHALL; TROTERE; LIDDLE;. CLUTSAM; DANKS; TOSTI; TUCKER; SCOTT; MARSHALL; FOX; BIMBONI; KENNEDY; SILESU; THOMAS; HATTON; PARKYNS; LEROUX; NEVIN: *The Rosary.* DANKS: *Silver threads among the gold.* CADMAN: *At dawning.* ADAMS: *Nirvana; Nearer my God to thee.* CLAY: *I'll sing thee songs of Araby.* TOURS: *Mother o'mine.* RONALD: *Down in the forest.* BRAGA: *Angel's serenade* (with Kreisler,violin). SCHUBERT: *Ave Maria.* BACH/GOUNOD: *Ave Maria.*
(***) Romophone mono 82007-2 (2) [id.].

Born in 1884, John McCormack developed early, belonging more to the age of Caruso than of Gigli. He used his heady, ringing Irish tenor, always distinctive, to produce singing of wonderful purity and evenness, whether in a Mozart aria or in the many popular ballads which were the staple of his repertory. His main achievement lay more in recital than on the opera stage, so that his accounts of popular arias, though always stylish tend to be emotionally restrained, even in Rodolfo's *Che gelida manina*. Unlike Gigli he would produce the smoothest legato line for *Una furtiva lagrima* with no hint of an aspirate. The first of the two Romophone sets of his acoustic recordings is the one which has the more substantial items, where the second two-disc box includes only nine operatic arias among the forty-nine items, among them rare arias by such composers as Victor Herbert and Wolf-Ferrari. First-rate transfers by Ward Marston.

Schumann, Elisabeth (soprano)

Lieder: MENDELSSOHN: *Auf Flügeln des Gesanges.* SCHUMANN: *Schneeglöckchen; Der Nussbaum; Er ist's; Aufträge; Mondnacht; Ständchen; O ihr Herren; Röselein, Röselein.* BRAHMS: *Wiegenlied; Vergebliches Ständchen; Nachtigall; Der Jäger; Sandmännchen; Der Tod*

das ist die kühle Nacht; Immer leiser wird mein Schlummer; Das mädchen spricht; Der Mond steht über dem Berge; Die schone Magelone: Ruhe, Süssliebchen; An eine Aolsharfe; Bitteres zu sagen denkst du; Blinde Kuh; Erlaube mir, fein's Mädchen; Wie komm' ich denn zur Tür herein?; In stiller Nacht; Mein Mädel hat einen Rosenmund; Schwesterlein; Och Moder, ich well en Ding han!
(***) Romophone mono 81018-2 [id.].

Over two-thirds of the songs here are by Brahms – delectable performances, intimate and engaging – with Schumann charming the listener with her individual pointing of words and phrase. Two of the most popular songs, *Wiegenlied* and *Immer leiser*, are with orchestra but the rest have the original piano accompaniment. The one Mendelssohn item, *On wings of song* (in the original German), also has orchestral accompaniment but the remaining nine songs, all by Schumann, have piano. Recorded between 1930 and 1938, this has the singer at her peak, with the voice angelically pure but with nuances of tone and phrase that are totally individual.

Arias from: MOZART: *Il re pastore; Le nozze di figaro; Don Giovanni*. Johann STRAUSS Jnr: *Die Fledermaus*. ZELLER: *Der Vogelhändler; Der Obersteiger*. ZIEHRER: *Der Landstreicher; Der Fremdenführer*. SCHUBERT: *Das Dreimäderlhaus*. HEUBERGER: *Der Opernball*. KREISLER: *Sissy*. BENATZKY: *Ich muss wieder einmal in Grinzing sein*. SIECZNSI: *Wein du Stadt meiner Träume*. Joseph STRAUSS: *Sphärenklänge waltz*.
(**(*)) Romophone mono 81019-2 [id.].

No German singer exuded quite such charm as Elisabeth Schumann, with her sweet, silvery soprano and sparkling manner. Nowhere does this come over more vividly than in this magical collection of Viennese operetta arias, deliciously idiomatic in their pointing. In such a favourite as *Sei nicht bös* from *Der Obersteiger* by Zeller, the element of naughtiness is beautifully caught, with a sparkle in the eye as well as the voice, and Adèle's arias from *Die Fledermaus* have never been so delectably characterized as here. Those thirteen numbers are preceded by eight of Mozart, recorded not in Vienna like most of the operetta items but in London. In contrast with her pre-electric versions, the original Italian is used, and though the portamento is still obtrusive, the point and control are keener. The only reservation is that the transfer brings out an extra brightness in the voice not quite true to life.

'*The Complete Edison and Polydor recordings (1915–23)*': Arias from: BEETHOVEN: *Fidelio*. WEBER: *Der Freischütz*. THOMAS: *Mignon*. MOZART: *Le nozze di Figaro; Don Giovanni; Die Entführung auf dem Serail; Die Zauberflöte;*

Exsultate jubilate. LORTZING: *Der Wildschütz*. GOUNOD: *Faust*. AUBER: *Fra Diavolo*. HUMPERDINCK: *Hansel und Gretel*. R. STRAUSS: *Die heiligen drei Könige aus Morgenland.*
(***) Romophone mono 81028-2 [id.].

This collection of rarities brings together Elisabeth Schumann's pre-electric recordings for the Edison and Polydor labels before she turned to HMV. Maybe because copies are so rare, surfaces are very intrusive, particularly on the four Pathés, recorded in 1915. Yet behind the heavy hiss you can hear the unmistakable magic voice in different repertory from her usual – Marzelline's aria from *Fidelio* and Aennchen's from *Der Freischütz*, more than just a soubrette. Also Mignon's *Connais-tu le pays*, translated back (awkwardly for the music) as 'Kennst du das Land'. Most of the Polydor recordings are of Mozart, all in German, as is the *Jewel song* from *Faust* and *Quel bonheur* from Auber's *Fra Diavolo*. The Mozart is charming, as one would expect, but like many singers of that period she had not yet learnt to limit the swoop of portamentos.

Schumann-Heink, Ernestine
(contralto)

The Complete recordings (1900–09)': Arias from: MEYERBEER: *Le prophète*. DONIZETTI: *Lucrezia Borgia*. SAINT-SAENS: *Samson und Dalila*. J. EDWARDS: *Love's lottery*. MENDELSSOHN: *Saint Paul*. HANDEL: *Rinaldo*. thomas: *Mignon*. GLUCK: *Orpheus und Euridike*. WAGNER: *Das Rheingold* (with Herbert Witherspoon); *Rienzi*. GOUNOD: *Sapho*. MOZART: *La clemenza di Tito*. Songs by: ARDITI; SCHUBERT; BRAHMS; TCHAIKOVSKY;. R. BECKER; NEVIN; BOND; MENDELSSOHN; LANG; Folk songs: GRUBER; CHADWICK; MILLOCKER; SCHUMANN; REGER; WEINGARTNER; HERMANN.
(***) Romophone mono 81029-2 (2) [id.].

Ernestine Schumann-Heink was the outstanding operatic contralto of her time, and the recordings here vividly explain why. Hers was a voice of extraordinary range, firm and clear in every register; on the one hand weighty and powerful, on the other extraordinarily agile, as is demonstrated in the four versions of the 'Drinking song' from Donizetti's *Lucrezia Borgia*, the first two from 1903 with piano, the last of 1909 brighter, clearer and freer and even more characterful. It is fascinating too to compare the five versions of Delilah's *Softly awakes my heart* (all in German), with the singer learning to reduce the swooping portamentos of the first of 1903. Not only was Schumann-Heink's voice a unique instrument, she was vividly characterful in everything she sang, projecting magnetically her involvement. The first Zonophone item from 1900 brings dim sound, and the Columbia recordings of 1906 (with piano) are restricted too, but the voice comes over splendidly, and the rest are treated to excellent Ward Marston transfers.

Sembrich, Marcella (soprano)

'*The Victor recordings (1904–08)*': Arias from: VERDI: *La traviata; Rigoletto; Ernani.* BELLINI: *La sonnambula; Norma; I puritani.* GOUNOD: *Faust.* MOZART: *Don Giovanni; Le nozze di Figaro* (with Emma Eames). DONIZETTI: *Lucia di Lammermoor; Don Pasquale.* HANDEL; *Alessandro.* FLOTOW: *Martha.* ROSSINI: *Il barbiere di Siviglia.* MONIUSZKO: *Halka.* THOMAS: *Hamlet* (with Emilio de Gogorza); *Mignon.* LEHAR: *Die lustige Witwe.* Songs by: Johann STRAUSS Jnr; Richard STRAUSS; SCHUMANN; CHOPIN; ARDITI; BISHOP; ARNE; ALABIEV; HAHN; SCHUBERT.
(**(*)) Romophone mono 81026-2 (2) [id.].

'*The Victor recordings (1908–19)*': With appendix of cylinder and grand opera recordings (c. 1900–03). Arias, duets and scenes from: VERDI: *Rigoletto* (with Mario Sammarco); *I vespri siciliani; Ernani; La traviata.* DONIZETTI: *Lucia di Lammermoor* (with Enrico Caruso, Gina Severina, Francesco Daddi, Antonio Scotti and Marcel Journet); *Linda di Chamounix; La fille du régiment.* ROSSINI: *Semeramide.* LEHAR: *Die lustige Witwe.* BARBIERI: *Barbarillo de lavapies.* FALL: *Dollar princess.* Oscar STRAUS: *Waltz dream.* MOZART: *Il flauto magico.* Songs by: Johann STRAUSS Jnr; LILLEJEBJORN; HEINE-RUBENSTEIN; MANNEY; Sara TEASDALE-WILLIAM; ARMS FISHER; STEBBINS; RUBINSTEIN; MASSENET; LA FORGE; PADEREWSKI; ARDITI and TRADITIONAL.
(***) Romophone mono 81027-2 (2) [id.].

Marcella Sembrich is a singer whose reputation – as the supreme coloratura soprano of her day – is hardly borne out by her recordings. There are many fine qualities here, but her undoubted daring in tackling coloratura results in some astonishingly sketchy passages with the notes skated over, whether in the early recordings of 1904–8 or the later recordings made up to her retirement after the First World War. She was not as ready as some other singers to learn from her earliest recordings that swooping protamentos needed to be avoided, but there are many impressive points to note, such as the tight, clean trills. The second of the pair of two-disc boxes has a higher proportion of trivial items, but offers a charming appendix in a series of Mapleson cylinder recordings of live performances, dim in sound but very revealing, as well as six rare recordings of 1903 from the Columbia Grand Opera series. The later recordings offer fine transfers with the voice bright and clear, with the voice in sharp focus, but with higher hiss than on the comparable Nimbus disc.

Tetrazzini, Luisa (soprano)

'*The Complete Zonophone (1904) and Victor recordings (1911–20)*': Arias from: VERDI: *Un ballo in maschera; La traviata; Rigoletto* (with Enrico Caruso, Josephine Jacoby and Pasquale Amato); *Il trovatore; La forza del destino; I vespri siciliani.* BELLINI: *La sonnambula.* BENEDICT: *Il carnavale di Venezia.* DONIZETTI: *Lucia di Lammermoor* (with Caruso, Jacoby, Amato, Marcel Journet and Angelo Bada); *Linda di Chamounix.* ROSSINI: *Il barbiere di Siviglia.* DAVID: *La perle du Brésil.* THOMAS: *Mignon.* CHAPI: *Las hijas del Zebedeo.* DELIBES: *Lakmé.* MEYERBEER: *Dinorah.* VERACINI: *Rosalinda.* BIZET: *Carmen.* MOZART: *Il flauto magico.* GOUNOD: *Romeo e Guilietta.* Songs by: MOORE; ECKERT; PROCH; COWAN; DE KOVEN; BRAHMS; VENZANO; GILBERT; CIAMPI; GRIEG.
(***) Romophone mono 81025-2 (2) [id.].

If Marcella Sembrich brings a fair measure of disappointment in her recordings, Luisa Tetrazzini is the coloratura, bright, clear and characterful, who consistently bewitches one not only with her dazzling technique but with her sparkle, charm, vivacity and vivid projection. Her singing is individual in every phrase, so that one readily forgives the stylistic flaws. The range was wide, so that the chest notes of Rosina's *Una voce poco fa* were rich and firm, and the recordings confirm as far as anything can that the size of the voice was greater than one would expect: it was sometimes described as a dramatic soprano with agility. Tetrazzini in *Ah non giunge* from Bellini's *Sonnambula* remains unsurpassed, and her portrayal of Violetta in her 1910 version of *Ah forse 'è lui* brings out the degree of pathos she could convey, no mere canary-bird. First-rate Ward Marston transfers with the surface hiss kept under fair control.

NIMBUS 'PRIMA VOCE' SERIES

The Nimbus company have taken a radical view of transferring historic 78-r.p.m. vocal recordings to CD. The best possible copies of shellac originals have been played on an acoustic machine with an enormous horn, one of the hand-made Rolls-Royces among non-electric gramophones of the 1930s, with Thorn needles reducing still further the need to filter the sound.

'The Golden age of Singing' (50 years of Great voices on Record)

'*The golden age of singing*', Volume I (1900-10): TCHAIKOVSKY: *Queen of Spades: Forgive me,*

Heavenly being; (Nicolay Figner). FLOTOW: *Marta: Chi mi dirà;* (Edouard de Reszke). BELLINI: *La sonnambula: Vi ravviso, o luoghio ameni;* (Pol Plançon); *Ah, non credea mirarti;* (Adelina Patti). VERDI: *Otello: Niun mi tema;* (Francesco Tamagno); *Era la notte;* (Victor Maurel); *Credo in un Dio crudel;* (Eugenio Giraldoni). *Aida: Fuggiam gli ardori inospiti;* (Celestina Boninsegna). *Ernani: O sommo Carlo;* (Mattia Battistini). *Luisa Miller: Quando le sere al placido;* (Alessandro Bonci). *Rigoletto: Caro nome;* (Nellie Melba). *Simon Boccanegra: Il lecerato spirito;* (Francesco Navarrini). *Falstaff: Quand' ero paggio;* (Antonio Scotti). DONIZETTI: *L'elisir d'amore: Una furtiva lagrima;* (Enrico Caruso). *Chiedi all'aura lusinghiera;* (Maria Galvany; Aristodemo Giorgini). *Don Pasquale: So anch'io la virtu magica;* (Rosina Storchio); *Sogno soave e casto;* (Giuseppe Anselmi). *La favorita: A tanto amor;* (Mario Ancona). *Lucrezia Borgia: Di pescatore ignobil;* (Francesco Marconi); *Il segreto per esser felice;* (Clara Butt). WAGNER: *Lohengrin: Elsa's dream;* (Félia Litvinne). *Rienzi: Gerechter Gott!;* (Ernestine Schumann-Heink). *Götterdämmerung: Fliegt heim ihr Raben;* (Gadski). GOUNOD: *Roméo et Juliette: Je veux vivre dans ce rêve;* (Emma Eames). MOZART: *Die Zauberflöte: O Isis und Osiris;* (Wilhelm Hesch). *Le nozze di Figaro: Heil'ge Quelle;* (Lilli Lehmann). GLINKA: *A Life for the Tsar: They guess the truth;* (Vladimir Kastorsky). MASSENET: *Le roi de Lahore: Promesse de mon avenir;* (Maurice Renaud). *Manon: Il sogno (en fermant les yeux);* (Fernando de Lucia). *Le Cid: O souverain! ô juge! o père!;* (Vilhelm Herold). MEYERBEER: *Le prophète: Sopra Berta l'amor mio;* (Francesco Vignas). *Les Huguenots: A ce mot;* (Olimpia Boronat); *O beau pays de la Touraine;* (Antonina Nezhdanova). PONCHIELLI: *La Gioconda: Ebbrezza! Delirio!;* (Eugenia Burzio and Giuseppe de Luca). BIZET: *Carmen: Habanera;* (Emma Calvé). ERKEL: *Hunyadi László: Ah rebéges;* (Lillian Nordica). THOMAS: *Hamlet: O vin, discaccia la tristezza;* (Titta Ruffo). PUCCINI: *Madama Butterfly: Con onor muore;* (Emmy Destinn). ROSSINI: *Il barbiere di Siviglia: La calunnia è un venticello;* (Adamo Didur). *Semiramide: Bel raggio Lusinghier;* (Marcella Sembrich). GOLDMARK: *Die Königin von Saba: Magische Töne;* (Leo Slezak). BOITO: *Mefistofele: Giunto sul passo estremo;* (Dmitri Smirnov). RIMSKY-KORSAKOV: *May night: Sleep, my beauty;* (Leonid Sobinov). HATTON: *Simon the cellarer;* (Sir Charles Santley).

(B) (***) Nimbus Double mono NI 7050/1 (2).

For the ordinary collector without a specialist interest in historical vocal repertoire this bargain Double should prove an ideal way of making an initial exploration. There are some forty-four widely varied items sung by as many outstanding singers. Some of the names will be unfamiliar – it is not always the most famous that make the greatest initial impression, although Tamagno's *Otello* aria (from 1902) is immediately commanding, Caruso is very winning in Donizetti, Battistini is joined by other singers, and the La Scala Chorus in a splendid 1906 scene from Verdi's *Ernani*. But it is the second disc that is particularly well planned, with a whole stream of superb performances that project vividly from Melba's *Caro nome* and Tito Ruffo's *Hamlet*, to Emmy Destinn's thrilling acount of Butterfly's final aria. Amor Didur's solemn *La culunnia*, Vilhelm Herold in Massenet are both memorable, and with Gadski in *Götterdämmerung*, the orchestra may sound puny, but not the glorious flow of vocal tone. One of the surprises is the lightly pointed coloratura of Clara Butt in Donizetti, the big voice fined down, yet the lower register still ringing out. Scotti's Falstaff, Leo Slezak in *Die Königen von Saba* are both highlights, and the programme ends in light-hearted vein with Sir Charles Santley' clear yet resonant *Simon the cellarer*. The transfers almost all show the Nimbus process at its best; only occasionally is the surface noise slightly intrusive.

Battistini, Mattia (baritone)

Arias from: TCHAIKOVSKY: *Eugene Onegin*. VERDI: *Un ballo in maschera; Ernani; La Traviata; Macbeth; Don Carlos*. FLOTOW: *Marta*. DONIZETTI: *La Favorita; Don Sebastiano; Linda di Chamounix*. HEROLD: *Zampa*. berlioz: *La Damnation de Faust*. MASSENET: *Werther*. THOMAS: *Hamlet*. NOUGUES: *Quo Vadis?*.
(M) (***) Nimbus mono NI 7831 [id.].

As with other Nimbus issues, the transfers are remarkably kind to the voice and are probably nearer to how Battistini sounded 'live'. It is a remarkable voice, with a fine, clear upper range. The programme is well chosen and the recordings date from between 1902 and 1922. While obviously the Verdi excerpts are essential to show the calibre of any baritone, it is good to have the rare *Pourquoi tremblez-vous?* from *Zampa*.

Björling, Jussi (tenor)

'*The first ten years*': Arias from: VERDI: *Il Trovatore; Rigoletto; Aida; Requiem*. PUCCINI: *Tosca; Fanciulla del West; La Bohème*. BORODIN: *Prince Igor*. LEONCAVALLO: *Pagliacci*. MASCAGNI: *Cavalleria rusticana*. RIMSKY-KORSAKOV: *Sadko*. MEYERBEER: *L'Africana*. PONCHIELLI: *La Gioconda*. MASSENET: *Manon*. ROSSINI: *Stabat Mater*. Song: FANAL: *I maünner oüver lag och raütt*.

(M) (***) Nimbus mono NI 7835; [id.].

Volume 2, 1911–1960: Arias from: PUCCINI: *Tosca; La Fanciulla del West; La Bohème.* VERDI: *Rigoletto.* FLOTOW: *Martha.* GOUNOD: *Faust.* BIZET: *Carmen.* OFFENBACH: *La Belle Hélène.* J. STRAUSS Jnr.: *Der Zigeunerbaron.* MILLOCKER: *Der Bettelstudent.* Songs: BEETHOVEN: *Adelaide.* SCHUBERT: *Ave Maria; Ständchen; An die Leier.* R. STRAUSS: *Cäcile.* SIBELIUS: *Svarta rosor; Säv, säv, susa.* ALFVEN: *Skogen sover.* EKLOF: *Morgon.* SJOBERG: *Tornerna.* TOSTI: *Ideale.* (M) (***) Nimbus mono NI 7842 [id.].

'Bjoerling in song': LEONCAVALLO: *Mattinata.* TOSELLI: *Serenata.* DI CAPUA: *O sole mio.* Songs by: ENDERS; CHRISTGAU; PETERSON-BERGER; ARTHUR; ELGAR; DE CURTIS; BALL; RAY; DAHL; SCHRADER; PEREZ-FREIRE; STENHAMMAR; ALTHEN; CARUSO; WIDESTEDT; TRAD.: *Tantis serenade.* Arias from LEHAR: *Das Land des Lächelns.* KALMAN: *Das Veilchen von Montmartre.* (M) (***) Nimbus mono NI 7879 [id.].

'Jussi Bjoerling in opera and song'. (M) (***) Nimbus NI 1776 (3) (NI 7835; 7842 & 7879) [id.].

The three Bjoerling discs above are brought together in a box, giving a comprehensive view of his early years, when from the age of nineteen (in 1930) he recorded regularly for the Swedish branch of HMV. That means that most of the items, including the early recordings of opera and all the operetta, are done in Swedish. Not that lovers of vocal art will worry overmuch, when even in 1930 the headily golden voice is both distinctive and rich, fully developed even then. Volume 2 covers recordings that Bjoerling made between 1936 and 1940, not just in Sweden but in 1939–40 in New York, when Victor recorded him in Lieder, not just Schubert, Strauss and Beethoven but Swedish song, in which he sounds even more at home. All but one of the items in the song disc are Swedish domestic recordings, but they lead in 1937 to his first red-label recording of song, sung in Italian, di Capura's *O sole mio.* The Nimbus process gives a vivid idea of the voice with ample bloom on it, but the surfaces are marked by a very noticeable but even swish, rather than a hiss.

Bjoerling, Jussi, Enrico Caruso, Beniamino Gigli (tenors)

'Three legendary tenors in opera and song'

Caruso: Arias from: BIZET: *Carmen.* MASSENET: *Manon.* VERDI: *Otello; La forza del destino; Aida.* GIORDANO: *Andrea Chénier.* PUCCINI: *Tosca.*

Gigli: Arias from: LEONCAVALLO: *I Pagliacci* (also Song: *Mattinata*). BIZET: *Les pêcheurs de perles* (also Duet: *Del tempo al limitar;* with Giuseppe de Luca). VERDI: *La Traviata.* PUCCINI: *Tosca.* Song: DI CAPUA: *O sole mio.*

Bjoerling: Arias from VERDI: *Rigoletto.* PUCCINI: *La Bohème; Turandot.* RIMSKY-KORSAKOV: *Sadko.* MEYERBEER: *L'Africana.* MASSENET: *Manon.* Song: TOSTI: *Ideale.* (M) (***) Nimbus mono NI 1434 [id.].

Nimbus caught on to the idea of promoting a selection from three legendary tenors from their archives and they decided that a single disc (75 minutes) would be the best proposition. Their system of playing-back 78-r.p.m. originals through a big fibre horn and re-recording them works very well here with the three voices naturally caught, but the orchestral backing more variable. The documentation is poor and no recording dates are given, but the excerpts are obviously hand-picked and recorded over a fairly wide time-span. Items which obviously stand out are: Caruso's *Un dì, all'azzurro spazio* from *Andrea Chénier* and of course *Celeste Aida* (with a remarkably believable brass fanfare); Gigli's honeyed *E lucevan le stelle* from *Tosca* and his thrilling *O sole mio*; and Bjoerling's *Che gelida manina* from *Bohème,* the seductive *Sadko* 'Song of India' and his glorious *Nessun dorma.* The collection ends splendidly with Caruso and De Luca matching their voices sensationally in the frisson-creating *Pearl fishers* duet.

Caruso, Enrico (tenor)

Caruso in opera, Volume I: Arias from: DONIZETTI: *L'Elisir d'amore; Don Sebastiano; Il duca d'Alba.* GOLDMARK: *La regina di Saba.* GOMEZ: *Lo schiavo.* HALEVY: *La juive.* LEONCAVALLO: *I Pagliacci.* MASSENET: *Manon.* MEYERBEER: *L'Africana.* PUCCINI: *Tosca; Manon Lescaut; Aida; Un ballo in maschera; La forza del destino; Rigoletto; Il Trovatore.* (M) (***) Nimbus mono NI 7803 [id.].

The Nimbus method of transfer to CD, reproducing ancient 78s on a big acoustic horn gramophone of the 1930s, tends to work best with acoustic recordings, when the accompaniments then emerge as more consistent with the voice. There is an inevitable loss of part of the recording range at both ends of the spectrum, but the ear can often be convinced. This Caruso collection, very well-chosen to show the development of his voice, ranges from early (1904) recordings of Massenet, Puccini and Donizetti with piano accompaniment to the recording that the great tenor made in 1920, not long before he died, of his very last role, as Eleazar in Halévy's *La juive,* wonderfully characterized.

Chaliapin, Feodor (bass)

Excerpts from: MUSSORGSKY: *Boris Godunov.*
RUBINSTEIN: *The Demon.* VERDI: *Don Carlos.*
RIMSKY-KORSAKOV: *Sadko.* BORODIN: *Prince
Igor.* GOUNOD:*Faust.* MOZART: *Don Giovanni.*
GLINKA: *A Life for the Tsar; Ruslan and
Ludmilla.* PUCCINI: *La Bohème.* BOITO:
Mefistofele. MASSENET: *Don Quichotte.*
RACHMANINOV: *Aleko.* DARGOMYZHSKY:
Rusalka.
(M) (**(*)) Nimbus mono NI 7823/4 (2) [id.].

As recorded by the Nimbus process Chaliapin's
unique bass sounds sepulchral – partly due, no
doubt, to the resonating effect of the horn gramophone on which the 78s are played. The EMI issues
of many of the same items as here on his disc
of Russian arias (CDH7 61009-2), including his
recordings of Boris, are much fuller and more immediate (as transferred by Keith Hardwick). However, this two-disc collection includes valuable
items outside the Russian repertory, including
Leporello's catalogue aria from *Don Giovanni*
(taken very fast, with detail only sketched though
very characterful) and Beethoven's song, *In questa
tomba*, not helped by a heavy surface-noise, but
bringing a thrilling expansion. In every item, one is
aware that this is not just one of the great voices
of the twentieth century but also one of the most
characterful singers; compassing not just the darkness and tragedy of Boris, but the sparkle and
humour of such an item as Farlaf's *Rondo* from
Glinka's *Russlan and Ludmila* with its dauntingly
rapid patter.

Divas

'Divas', Volume I 1906–35: (Tetrazzini; Melba;
Patti; Hempel; Galli-Curci; Ponselle; Lehmann;
Turner; Koshetz; Norena; Nemeth; Muzio): Arias
from: VERDI: *Un ballo in maschera; Rigoletto;
Aida; Il Trovatore.* THOMAS: *Mignon.* MOZART:
Die Zauberflöte. ROSSINI: *Il Barbiere di Siviglia.*
MASSENET: *Manon.* PUCCINI: *Madama Butterfly.*
BEETHOVEN: *Fidelio.* RIMSKY-KORSAKOV: *Sadko.*
BORODIN: *Prince Igor.* GOUNOD: *Roméo et
Juliette.* BOITO: *Mefistofele.* Songs: YRADIER: *La
Calesera.* DENAUDY: *O del mio amato ben.*
(M) (***) Nimbus mono NI 7802 [id.].

The six supreme prima donnas on this compilation
are all very well represented. The soprano voice
benefits more than most from the Nimbus process,
so that with extra bloom Tetrazzini's vocal 'gear-
change' down to the chest register is no longer
obtrusive. She is represented by three recordings of
1911, including Gilda's *Caro nome* from *Rigoletto*;
and Galli-Curci has three items too, including Rosina's *Una voce poco fa* from *Il Barbiere di Siviglia.*

The tragically short-lived Claudia Muzio and the
Russian, Nina Koshetz, have two each, while the
others are each represented by a single, well-chosen
item. They include Melba in *Mimi's farewell*, the
60-year-old Patti irresistibly vivacious in a Spanish
folksong, *La calesera*, and Frieda Hempel in what
is probably the most dazzling of all recordings of the
Queen of the Night's second aria from *Zauberflöte.*

'Divas' Volume 2, 1909–40: (Hempel,
Galli-Curci, Farrar, Kurz, Garrison, Gluck,
Ivogün, Onegin, Schoene, Norena, Ponselle,
Leider, Vallin, Teyte, Koshetz, Flagstad, Favero):
Arias from: BELLINI: *I Puritani.* MOZART: *Le
nozze di Figaro; Die Entführung aus dem Serail.*
PUCCINI: *Tosca.* VERDI: *Rigoletto; La forza del
destino.* OFFENBACH: *Les contes d'Hoffmann; La
Périchole.* GODARD: *Jocelyn.* BIZET: *Carmen*; J.
STRAUSS Jnr: *Die Fledermaus.* THOMAS: *Hamlet.*
WAGNER: *Tristan und Isolde; Die Walküre.*
MASSENET: *Werther.* PONCE: *Estrellita.*
MASCAGNI: *Lodoletta.*
(M) (***) Nimbus mono NI 7818 [id.].

As in the first *Divas* volume, the choice of items
will delight any lover of fine singing, a most dis-
criminating choice. Maria Ivogün, the teacher of
Schwarzkopf, contributes a wonderfully pure and
incisive *Martern aller Arten* (*Entführung*) dating
from 1923, and Lotte Schoene is unusually and
characterfully represented by Adele's *Mein Herr
Marquis* from *Fledermaus*. Frida Leider's *Liebestod* is nobly sung but is surprisingly fast by
latterday standards. Maggie Teyte sings delectably
in an aria from *La Périchole*; and though some of
the pre-electric items in Nimbus's resonant transfers
suggest an echo chamber, the voices are warm and
full.

Farrar, Geraldine (soprano)

Arias from: MOZART: *Le nozze di Figaro; Don
Giovanni.* WOLF-FERRARI: *Le donne curiose; Il
segreto di Susanna.* PUCCINI: *La bohème* (with
Enrico Caruso, Antonio Scotti and Gina Viafora);
Tosca; Madama Butterfly (with Josephine Jacoby,
Caruso and Scotti).
(M) (***) Nimbus mono NI 7857 [id.].

Geraldine Farrar, born in 1882, was in almost every
way an ideal recording soprano. Though she retired
from the stage before the arrival of electrical
recording, these acoustic recordings give a
wonderful idea of the glorious voice. Almost three-
dimensional in the way they convey the warmth and
firmness combined with power, it is a delight to
register the clarity of attack on even the most exposed notes. The Mozart and Wolf-Ferrari items
provide a charming introduction to the range of
Puccini recordings here, recorded between 1908
and 1912 when she was at the peak of her powers.

Most valuable of all are the items from *Madama Butterfly*, with two duets for Caruso and Scotti interspersed with those of Farrar, making it clear why this was one of her two most celebrated roles, at once tenderly expressive, yet powerfully dramatic.

French opera: Arias from: MASSENET: *Manon; Thaïs*. THOMAS: *Mignon*. GOUNOD: *Roméo et Juliette* (with Edmond Clément). OFFENBACH: *Contes d'Hoffmann* (with Antonio Scotto). BIZET: *Carmen* (extended excerpts with Giovanni Martinelli, Pasquale Amato).
(M) (***) Nimbus mono NI 7872 [id.].

This fine selection of Farrar's recordings of French opera concentrates on her most celebrated role as Carmen. Though nowadays it is almost always sung by a mezzo, Farrar demonstrates, by the dramatic intensity of her singing, with fine detail and flawless control, what benefits there are from having a full soprano in role. The fourteen items from that opera include not only Carmen's principal solos and ensembles but Micaela's aria, and - setting the rest in context - the Toreador's song, José's 'Flower song' and the 'Prelude to Act IV', in a rare acoustic recording conducted by Toscanini. The voice, bright, sweet and full, comes over vividly in these Nimbus transfers.

Flagstad, Kirsten (soprano)

Arias from: WAGNER: *Die Walküre; Tannhäuser; Lohengrin; Tristan und Isolde; Götterdämmerung*. WEBER: *Oberon*. BEETHOVEN: *Fidelio*. Concert aria: BEETHOVEN.
(M) (***) Nimbus mono NI 7847 [id.].

The eleven items here are drawn from the recordings that Flagstad made between 1935 and 1939. Five of them, dating from 1937, are with Eugene Ormandy and the Philadelphia orchestra, including commanding accounts of the 'Abscheulicher' from Beethoven's *Fidelio* and his concert aria, *Ah! perfido*. Four more items, including Isolde's *Liebestod* were recorded in 1935 with Hans Lange conducting, but the most substantial item is the fine, clean-cut account of Brünnhilde's 'Immolation' scene from Wagner's *Götterdämmerung* with Edwin McArthur (her regular piano accompanist) and the San Francisco Orchestra. The Nimbus transfers superbly convey the bloom and heroic power of the unique voice in its prime, full and even throughout its range, but the orchestral accompaniments are unpleasantly thin.

Galli-Curci, Amelita (soprano)

Arias from: AUBER: *Manon Lescaut*. BELLINI: *I Puritani; La Sonnambula*. DONIZETTI: *Don Pasquale; Linda di Chamounix; Lucia di*

Lammermoor. GOUNOD: *Roméo et Juliette*. MEYERBEER: *Dinorah*. ROSSINI: *Il Barbiere di Siviglia*. THOMAS: *Mignon*. VERDI: *Rigoletto; La Traviata*.
(M) (***) Nimbus mono NI 7806 [id.].

'Like a nightingale half-asleep,' said Philip Hope-Wallace in a memorable description of Galli-Curci's voice, but this vivid Nimbus transfer makes it much more like a nightingale very wide-awake. More than in most of these transfers made via an acoustic horn gramophone, the resonance of the horn itself can be detected, and the results are full and forward. Galli-Curci's perfection in these pre-electric recordings, made between 1917 and 1924, is a thing of wonder, almost too accurate for comfort; but tenderness is there too, as in the Act II duet from *La Traviata* (with Giuseppe de Luca) and the *Addio del passato*, complete with introductory recitative, but with only a single stanza. Yet brilliant coloratura is what lies at the root of Galli-Curci's magic, and that comes in abundance.

Volume II: Arias from: DELIBES: *Lakmé*. DONIZETTI: *Lucia di Lammermoor*. VERDI: *Rigoletto; Il Trovatore; La Traviata*. DAVID: *La perle du Brésil*. BIZET: *Les Pêcheurs de perles*. RIMSKY-KORSAKOV: *Le coq d'or; Sadko*. GOUNOD: *Philémon et Baucis*. THOMAS: *Hamlet*. PROCH: *Air and variations*.
(M) (***) Nimbus mono NI 7852 [id.].

This second Galli-Curci selection from Nimbus offers recordings from the pre-electric era between 1917 and 1924, as well as six electrical recordings from 1925–30, four of them in ensembles, the celebrated ones of the Lucia Sextet and Rigoletto quartet with Gigli, as well as the magical *Traviata* duets with Tito Schipa. The reproduction of the voice in both pre-electric and electric recordings is astonishingly vivid. Compared with the Romophone transfers, these give the voice more bloom, recorded from 78 discs in a helpful acoustic, but the surface-hiss has a swishy quality, easily forgotten, which not everyone will like.

Gigli, Beniamino (tenor)

Volume 1, 1918–24: Arias from: BOITO: *Mefistofele*. CATALANI: *Loreley*. DONIZETTI: *La Favorita*. FLOTOW: *Martha*. GIORDANO: *Andrea Chénier*. GOUNOD: *Faust*. LALO: *Le roi d'Ys*. LEONCAVALLO: *Pagliacci*. MASCAGNI: *Iris*. MEYERBEER: *L'Africana*. PONCHIELLI: *La Gioconda*. PUCCINI: *Tosca*. Songs.
(M) (***) Nimbus mono NI 7807 [id.].

Gigli's career went on so long, right through the electrical 78-r.p.m. era, that his pre-electric recordings have tended to get forgotten. This collection of twenty-two items recorded between 1918 and 1924 shows the voice at its most honeyed, even lighter and more lyrical than it became later, with the singer indulging in fewer of the mannerisms that came to decorate his ever-mellifluous singing. In aria after aria he spins a flawless legato line. Few tenor voices have ever matched Gigli's in its rounded, golden beauty, and the Nimbus transfers capture its bloom in a way that makes one forget pre-electric limitations. In the one item sung in French, by Lalo, he sounds less at home, a little too heavy; but the ease of manner in even the most taxing arias elsewhere is remarkable, and such a number as the *Serenade* from Mascagni's *Iris* is irresistible in its sparkle, as are the Neapolitan songs, notably the galloping *Povero Pulcinella* by Buzzi-Peccia. One oddity is a tenor arrangement of Saint-Saëns's *The Swan*.

Volume 2, 1925–40: Arias from: DONIZETTI: *L'elisir d'amore; Lucia di Lammermoor.* PUCCINI: *Manon Lescaut; La Bohème; Tosca.* VERDI: *La forza del destino; La Traviata; Rigoletto.* THOMAS: *Mignon.* BIZET: *I pescatori di perle.* PONCHIELLI: *La Gioconda.* MASSENET: *Manon.* GOUNOD: *Faust.* RIMSKY-KORSAKOV: *Sadko.* GLUCK: *Paride ed Elena.* CILEA: *L'Arlesiana.* CACCINI: Song: *Amarilli.* (M) (***) Nimbus mono NI 7817 [id.].

Issued to celebrate the Gigli centenary in 1990, the Nimbus selection concentrates on recordings he made in the very early years of electrical recording up to 1931, when his voice was at its very peak, the most golden instrument, ideally suited to recording. The items are very well chosen and are by no means the obvious choices, though it is good to have such favourites as the *Pearlfishers duet* with de Luca and the 1931 version of Rodolfo's *Che gelida manina.* The Nimbus transfers are at their best, with relatively little reverberation.

Great Singers

'Great singers', 1909–38: (Tetrazzini; Caruso; Schumann-Heink; McCormack; Galli-Curci; Stracciari; Ponselle; Lauri-Volpi; Turner; Tibbett; Supervia; Gigli; Anderson; Schipa; Muzio; Tauber): Arias from: BELLINI: *La Sonnambula; I Puritani; Norma.* LEONCAVALLO: *Pagliacci.* MOZART: *Don Giovanni; Die Zauberflöte.* ROSSINI: *Il Barbiere di Siviglia.* PUCCINI: *Turandot.* VERDI: *Un ballo in maschera.* BIZET: *Carmen.* PUCCINI: *La Bohème.* SAINT-SAENS: *Samson et Dalila.* MASCAGNI: *L'amico Fritz.* Song: REFICE: *Ombra di Nube.* (M) (***) Nimbus mono NI 7801 [id.].

The Tetrazzini item with which the selection opens – *Ah non giunge* from Bellini's *La Sonnambula* – is one of the supreme demonstrations of coloratura on record; the programme goes on to a magnificent Caruso of 1910 and an unforgettable performance of the coloratura drinking-song from Donizetti's

Lucrezia Borgia by the most formidable of contraltos, Ernestine Schumann-Heink. Then follows John McCormack's famous account of *Il mio tesoro* from Mozart's *Don Giovanni*, with the central passage-work amazingly done in a single breath. Other vintage items include Galli-Curci's dazzling account of *Son vergin vezzosa* from Bellini's *I Puritani*, Eva Turner in her incomparable 1928 account of Turandot's aria, Gigli amiably golden-toned in *Che gelida manina* from *La Bohème*, and a delectable performance of the *Cherry duet* from Mascagni's *L'amico Fritz* by Tito Schipa and Mafalda Favero – riches indeed!

'Great Singers' Vol. 2: 1903–1939 (Tamagno; Clavé'; Plançon; Farrar; Ruffo; Gluck; De Luca; Garden; Martinelli; Onegin; Pinza; Ivogu'n; Chaliapine; Rethberg; Melchior; Flagstad; Bjoerling; Favero): Arias from: VERDI: *Otello; Ernani.* FLOTOW: *Marta.* PUCCINI: *Madama Butterfly; Manon Lescaut.* MEYERBEER: *L'Africana; Les Huguenots.* HANDEL: *Atalanta.* BELLINI: *I Puritani.* alfano: *Resurrection.* R. STRAUSS: *Ariadne aux Naxos.* J. STRAUSS Jnr.: *Die Fledermaus.* WAGNER: *Rienzi; Lohengrin.* Songs by: MARIO; MASSENET; BEETHOVEN & TRAD. (M) (***) Nimbus NI 7812 [id.].

This was one of the first of Nimbus's series of archive recordings, taking a radical new view of the problem of transferring ancient 78-r.p.m. vocal recordings to CD. The best possible copies of shellac originals have been played on an acoustic machine with an enormous horn, one of the handmade Rolls-Royces among non-electric gramophones of the 1930s, with thorn needles reducing still further the need to filter the sound electronically. The results have been recorded in a small hall, and the sound reproduced removes any feeling of boxy closeness. Those who have resisted the bottled or tinny sound of many historic recordings will find the Nimbus transfers more friendly and sympathetic, even if technically there is an inevitable loss of recorded information at both ends of the spectrum because of the absolute limitations of the possible frequency range on this kind of reproducer.

Frieda Hempel (soprano)

Arias from: VERDI: *Rigoletto; La traviata; Ernani; Un ballo in maschera.* DONIZETTI: *Lucia di Lammermoor.* ROSSINI: *Il barbiere di Siviglia.* MOZART: *Le nozze di Figaro; Die Zauberflöte.* MEYERBEER: *Les Huguenots; Robert le Diable.* GOUNOD: *Mireille.* OFFENBACH: *Les contes d'Hoffmann.* LORTZING: *Der Wildschütz.* Song: MANGOLD: *Zweigesang.* ✪ (M) (***) Nimbus mono NI 7849 [id.].

This is one of the very finest of all the Nimbus 'Prima voce' series. The 78-r.p.m. sources are immaculate, background noise is steady and no problem. The recordings are nearly all early, mostly made between 1910 and 1913, the rest in the following four years, except for the final song which was much later (1935). It is an extraordinary voice, with an almost unbelievably free upper tessitura. The divisions in the Adam *Variations* (on 'Twinkle, twinkle little star') make you want to laugh, they are so outrageous, taking off into the vocal stratosphere like a series of shooting stars. *Caro nome*, too, which opens the programme arrestingly, is wonderfully free and open, and the final cadence is taken up. Even more than the *Lucia* Mad scene, Rossini's *Una voce poco fa*, with its added decorations, shows how a soprano voice can sparkle when the intonation is spot-on. Both are sung in German.

Frieda Hempel's Mozart is less stylish; the famous *Der Hölle Rache* almost runs away before the end. But the ravishing vocal line in *Ah fors' è lui*, with a deliberate tenuto on the cadence, is followed by a wonderfully frivolous cabaletta. The recording quality is astonishingly consistent and the vocal richness comes across with uncanny realism, while the decorations in Strauss's *Wine, women and song* make one's hair stand on end. Not to be missed!

Maria Ivogün (soprano)

Arias from: HANDEL: *L'allegro, il penseroso ed il moderato*. DONIZETTI: *Don Pasquale; Lucia di Lammermoor*. ROSSINI: *Il barbiere di Siviglia*. VERDI: *La Traviata*. MEYERBEER: *Les Huguenots*. NICOLAI: *Die lustigen Weiber von Windsor*. J. STRAUSS: *Die Fledermaus;* also Waltzes: *An der schönen blauen Donau, Geschichten aus dem Wienerwald* and *Frühlingsstimmen*. Songs: SCHUBERT: *Horch, horch, die Lerche; Winterreise: Die Post;* KREISLER: *Liebesfreud;* CHOPIN: *Nocturne in E flat, Op. 9/2*. 2 Folksongs arr. Gund: *O du liabs ängeli; Z'Lauterbach hab' i'mein Strumpf velor'n*.

(M) (***) Nimbus mono NI 7832 [id.].

Maria Ivogün is a less familiar name today than in the 1920s when she took Covent Garden by storm. Hers was a small voice but enchantingly focused; in that, she has much in common with a more familiar recent name, Rita Streich. Ivogün sang with both charm and sparkle, and the present Nimbus transfers show just what a delightful artist she was. Whether in Donizetti or Meyerbeer or, indeed, in the Strauss waltzes (*Frühlingsstimmen, G'schichten aus dem Wiener Wald* and the *Blue Danube*), this is singing to give great refreshment. The recordings were for the most part made between 1917 and 1925, and these respond especially well

to the Nimbus transferring system, but the folksongs were electrical, and her very last records, made in 1932.

Luca, Giuseppe de (baritone)

Arias from: VERDI: *Don Carlos, Ernani, Il Trovatore, La Traviata, Rigoletto*. ROSSINI: *Il Barbiere di Siviglia*. DONIZETTI: *L'elisir d'amore*. BELLINI: *I Puritani*. DIAZ: *Benvenuto Cellini*. PUCCINI: *La Bohème*. PONCHIELLI: *La Gioconda*. WOLF-FERRARI: *I gioielli della madonna*. Songs: DE LEVA: *Pastorale*. ROMILLI: *Marietta*.

(M) (***) Nimbus mono NI 7815 [id.].

There has never been a more involving account on record of the Act IV Marcello–Rodolfo duet than the one here with de Luca and Gigli, a model of characterization and vocal art. The baritone's mastery emerges vividly in item after item, whether in the power and wit of his pre-electric version of *Largo al factotum* (1917) or the five superb items (including the *Bohème* duet and the *Rigoletto* numbers, flawlessly controlled) which were recorded in the vintage year of 1927. Warm Nimbus transfers.

Giovanni Martinelli (tenor)

Volume I, Arias from: GIORDANO: *Andrea Chénier; Fedora*. LEONCAVALLO: *Pagliacci*. MASCAGNI: *Cavalleria Rusticana; Iris*. TCHAIKOVSKY: *Eugene Onegin*. VERDI: *Aida; Ernani; La forza del destino; La Traviata*.

(M) (***) Nimbus mono NI 7804 [id.].

This collection of seventeen fine examples of Martinelli's very distinctive and characterful singing covers his vintage period from 1915 to 1928, with one 1927 recording from Verdi's *La forza del destino* so clear that you can hear a dog barking outside the studio. The other two items from *Forza* are just as memorable, with Martinelli joined by Giuseppe de Luca in the Act IV duet, and by Rosa Ponselle and the bass, Ezio Pinza, for the final duet, with the voices astonishingly vivid and immediate.

Volume 2, Arias from: PUCCINI: *La Bohème; Tosca; Madama Butterfly* (with Frances Alda). PONCHIELLI: *La Gioconda*. VERDI: *Aida; Un ballo in maschera; Rigoletto; Don Carlos; Il Trovatore*. LEONCAVALLO: *Pagliacci*. MEYERBEER: *L'Africana*. BIZET: *Carmen*. ROSSINI: *Guillaume Tell*. MASSENET: *Werther*.

(M) (***) Nimbus mono NI 7826 [id.].

Martinelli's second collection is hardly less distinctive than the first, and admirers of this great tenor should not be disappointed with the transfers, which are well up to the convincingly natural standard now being achieved by the Nimbus process.

McCormack, John (tenor)

Arias and excerpts from: DONIZETTI: *Lucia di Lammermoor; L'elisir d'amore; La figlia del reggimento.* VERDI: *La Traviata; Rigoletto.* PUCCINI: *La Bohème.* BIZET. *Carmen; I pescatore di perle.* DELIBES: *Lakmé.* GOUNOD: *Faust.* PONCHIELLI: *La gioconda.* BOITO: *Mefistofele.* MASSENET: *Manon.* MOZART: *Don Giovanni.* WAGNER: *Die Meistersinger.* herbert: *Natomah.* HANDEL: *Semele; Atalanta.*
(M) (***) Nimbus mono NI 7820 [id.].

With the operas represented ranging from Handel's *Atalanta* and *Semele* to *Natomah*, by Victor Herbert, the heady beauty of McCormack's voice, his ease of production and perfect control are amply illustrated in these twenty-one items. His now legendary 1916 account of *Il mio tesoro* from *Don Giovanni*, with its astonishing breath control, is an essential item; but there are many others less celebrated which help to explain his special niche, even in a generation that included Caruso and Schipa. Characteristic Nimbus transfers.

McCormack, John and Fritz Kreisler (violin)

'*McCormack and Kreisler in recital*': Arias from: GODARD: *Jocelyn.* BENEDICT: *Lily of Killarney.* Songs: RACHMANINOV: *O, cease thy singing, maiden fair; When night descends.* Richard STRAUSS: *Morgen.* TOSTI: *Goodbye.* KREISLER: *Liebesfreud; Caprice viennoise* and *Cradle song* arr. from *Caprice viennoise.* SCHUBERT: *Rosamunde: Ballet music No.2.* BRAHMS: *Hungarian dance No. 5.* BRAGA: *Angel's serenade.* Songs by: COTTENET; PARKYNS; LEROUX; BALOGH; MOSZKOWSKI; LARCHET AND TRADITIONAL.
(M) (***) Nimbus mono NI 7868 [id.].

This is a delightful disc of two great artists enjoying themselves in undemanding repertory. On one occasion, when McCormack and Kreisler were both recording in the Victor studios in Camden, New Jersey, the tenor asked the violinist's advice on the tempo for a Rachmaninov song. Whereupon Kreisler provided an impromptu obbligato while McCormack sang. Happily the engineer had switched on his machine, and this recording is included here. Roughly half the items are of McCormack and Kreisler together. Others include McCormack's solo recordings of Kreisler pieces, including a Cradle song arranged from *Caprice viennois*. There are also solo recordings of Kreisler

playing favourite pieces of his, including arrangements. Recordings, all acoustic, date from between 1914–1924 when both artists were at their peak.

Melba, Nellie (soprano)

Arias from: MOZART: *Le nozze di Figaro.* HANDEL: *L'allegro, il pensero ed il moderato.* CHARPENTIER: *Louise.* MASSENET: *Don César de Bazan.* GOUNOD: *Faust.* THOMAS: *Hamlet.* LOTTI: *Armino.* VERDI: *Otello.* PUCCINI: *La bohème; Tosca.* BEMBERG: *Elaine.* Songs: BISHOP: *Lo here the gentle lark.* BEMBERG: *Sur le lac.* DEBUSSY: *Romance; Mandoline.* CHAUSSON: *Poème de l'amour et de la mer: Le temps des Lilas.* HAHN: *D'une prison.* TRAD: *Swing low sweet chariot.*
(M) (***) Nimbus mono NI 7890 [id.].

Though Melba among golden age sopranos is the one who even today is most regularly bracketed with Caruso as a legendary singer, her discs can seem disappointing, with a hardness regularly developing in the bright, clear voice. It says much for the Nimbus transfer process that this varied selection of songs as well as arias converys a fullness, even a sweetness, alongside consistent purity and precision, with the voice less edgy than in most transfers. It is thrilling to hear her riding easily over the voices of McCormack and Sammarco in the final trio from *Faust* and in some ways most revealing of all is a brief collection of distance tests, recorded in 1910, with Melba repeating a couple of phrases from Ophelia's aria in Thomas's *Hamlet* at different distances. As John Steane's illuminating note points out, one can then appreciate the star-like splendour of the voice. It is also good to have Melba's very last recording, made in 1928 at the age of 65, of the spiritual, *Swing low, sweet chariot*, with amazingly full tone.

Melchior, Lauritz (tenor)

Arias from: WAGNER: *Siegfried; Tannhäuser; Tristan und Isolde; Die Walküre; Die Meistersinger; Götterdämmerung.* LEONCAVALLO: *Pagliacci.* MEYERBEER: *L'Africana.* VERDI: *Otello.*
(M) (***) Nimbus mono NI 7816 [id.].

The Nimbus disc of Melchior, issued to celebrate his centenary in 1990, demonstrates above all the total consistency of the voice between the pre-electric recordings of *Siegfried* and *Tannhäuser*, made for Polydor in 1924, and the *Meistersinger* and *Götterdämmerung* extracts, recorded in 1939. Of those, the Siegfried–Brünnhilde duet from the *Prologue* of *Götterdämmerung* is particularly valuable. It is fascinating too to hear the four recordings that Melchior made with Barbirolli and the LSO in 1930–31: arias by Verdi, Leoncavallo and Meyerbeer translated into German. As a character, Otello is made to sound far more prickly. Characteristic Nimbus transfers.

Muzio, Claudia (soprano)

Arias from: MASCAGNI: *Cavalleria rusticana*. VERDI: *La forza del destino; Otello; Il Trovatore; La Traviata*. PUCCINI: *Tosca; La Bohème*. GIORDANO: *Andrea Chénier*. BOITO: *Mefistofele*. CILEA: *Adriana Lecouvreur; L'Arlesiana*. BELLINI: *La Sonnambula*. Songs by BUZZI-PECCIA; PERGOLESI; REGER; DELIBES; REFICE.

(M) (**(*)) Nimbus mono NI 7814 [id.].

This Nimbus collection of recordings by the sadly short-lived Claudia Muzio duplicates much that is contained on the EMI Références CD of her. The main addition here is the Act III duet from *Otello* with Francesco Merli, but some cherishable items are omitted. The Nimbus acoustic transfer process sets the voice more distantly as well as more reverberantly than the EMI, with its distinctive tang less-sharply conveyed.

Patti, Adelina (soprano) and other singers

'The Era of Adelina Patti' ((i) Adelina Patti, (ii) Victor Maurel; (iii) Pol Plançon; (iv) Mattia Battistini; (v) Mario Ancona; (vi) Lucien Fugère; (vii) Francisco Vignas; (viii) Emma Calvé; (ix) Maurice Renaud; (x) Fernando de Lucia; (xi) Francesco Tamagno; (xii) Nellie Melba; (xiii) Félia Litvinne; (xiv) Wilhelm Hesch; (xv) Lillian Nordica; (xvi) Mario Ancona; (xvii) Edouard de Reszke; (xviii) Marcella Sembrich; (xix) Francesco Marconi; (xx) Mattia Battistini; (xxi) Lilli Lehmann; (xxii) Sir Charles Santley): Arias from: VERDI: (ii) *Falstaff;* (i, iii) *Don Carlos;* (iv, xx) *Ernani;* (v, xiv) *Otello*. ADAM: (iii) *Le Chalet*. GLUCK: (vi) *Les Pèlerins de la Mecque*. MOZART: (i, ii, xx) *Don Giovanni;* (i, vii, xxi) *Le nozze di Figaro*. MEYERBEER: (vii) *Le Prophète*. BIZET: (viii) *Carmen*. MASSENET: (ix, xi) *Hérodiade;* (x) *Manon*. THOMAS: (xii) *Hamlet*. WAGNER: (xiii) *Lohengrin;* (xiv) *Die Meistersinger von Nürnberg*. ERKEL: (xv) *Hunyadi László*. DONIZETTI: (xvi) *La favorita;* (xix) *Lucrezia Borgia;* (xii) *Lucia*. BELLINI: (i) *La Sonnambula;* (xviii) *I Puritani*. FLOTOW: (xvii) *Martha*. ROSSINI: (x) *Il barbiere di Siviglia*. GOMES: (xx) *Il Guarany*. Songs by TOSTI; (vi) RAMEAU; (i, vi) YRADIER; (i) HOOK; (i) BISHOP; (ix) GOUNOD; (xv) R. STRAUSS; (xxii) HATTON.

(M) (***) Nimbus mono NI 7840/41 [id.].

The very first item on this wide-ranging collection

of historic recordings has one sitting-up at once. The voice ringing out from the loudspeakers prompts cheering from the singer's little audience. The clear-toned baritone is singing *Quand'ero paggio* from Verdi's *Falstaff* and, encouraged, he repeats it. Then, more cheering and a third performance, this time in French, to cap the occasion. The singer is Victor Maurel, the baritone whom Verdi chose as his first Falstaff in 1893 and, before that, his first Iago in *Otello*. The recording dates from 1907, and many lovers of historic vocal issues will remember it well. Yet hearing it on the Nimbus transfer to CD brings a sense of presence as never before.

That company's controversial technique of playing an ancient 78 disc with a thorn needle on the best possible acoustic horn gramophone is at its most effective here, with exceptionally vivid results on these acoustic recordings. They not only convey astonishing presence but also a sense of how beautiful the voices were, getting behind the tinny and squawky sounds often heard on old 78s. This is an ideal set for anyone not already committed to historic vocals who simply wants to investigate how great singing could be ninety years ago, providing such an unexpected mix of well-known items and rarities, to delight specialists and newcomers alike.

The first of the two discs offers recordings that Nimbus regards as technically the finest of their day, including Patti in 1906, not just singing but shouting enthusiastically in a Spanish folksong, *La Calesera*, '*Vivan los españoles!*' Recorded much later in 1928 comes the French baritone, Lucien Fugère, eighty at the time but singing with a firm focus that you might not find today in a baritone in his twenties.

The second of the two discs has just as fascinating a mixture, but the recordings 'have not survived the decades so well'. Even so, it is thrilling to hear Sir Charles Santley, born in 1834, the year after Brahms, singing *Simon the Cellarer* with tremendous flair at the age of seventy-nine, and the coloratura, Marcella Sembrich, sounding even sweeter in Bellini than on previous transfers.

Pinza, Ezio (bass)

Arias duets and scenes from: VERDI: *Il trovatore; I vespri Siciliani; Don Carlo; Aida* (with Grace Anthony and Giovanni Martinelli); *Attila*. DONIZETTI: *Lucia di Lammermoor*. HALEVY: *La juive*. BELLINI: *I puritani; Norma*. GOUNOD: *Faust* (with Aristodemo Giorgini). PUCCINI: *La Bohème*. MOZART: *Die Zauberflöte; Don Giovanni*. MEYERBEER: *Robert le diable*. THOMAS: *Mignon; Le caïc*.

(M) (***) Nimbus mono NI 7875 [id.].

This very well chosen selection of Pinza recordings concentrates on those he made early in his career, starting in 1933 when, at the age of 31, he demonstrates the already extraordinary richness and clarity of focus which made him pre-eminent among operatic basses of the inter-war period. Fine as his later recordings are, notably those with Toscanini, or even his characterful contribution to the musical, *South Pacific*, these early discs have an extra freshness. The subtlety with which Pinza shades his phrases using rich, firm tone and flawless legato is a constant delight. Philip II's aria from Verdi's *Don Carlos* has rarely been so nobly sung as here, and it is a mark of Pinza's sense of style that he is comparably commanding in the Mozart, Bellini, and Donizetti arias. As well as the six acoustically recorded items you have fourteen electrical recordings made between 1927 and 1930, all presenting the voice vividly in warm Nimbus transfers.

Ponselle, Rosa (soprano)

Arias from: BELLINI: *Norma*. PONCHIELLI: *La Gioconda*. SPONTINI: *La vestale*. VERDI: *Aida; Ernani; La forza del destino; Otello*. Songs by: ARENSKY; RIMSKY-KORSAKOV; DE CURTIS; DI CAPUA, JACOBS-BOND.

(M) (***) Nimbus mono NI 7805.

One of the most exciting American sopranos ever, Rosa Ponselle tantalizingly cut short her career when she was still at her peak. Only the Arensky and Rimsky songs represent her after her official retirement, and the rest make a superb collection, including her classic accounts of *Casta diva* from Bellini's *Norma* and the duet, *Mira o Norma*, with Marion Telva. The six Verdi items include her earlier version of *Ernani involami*, not quite so commanding as her classic 1928 recording, but fascinating for its rarity. Equally cherishable is her duet from *La forza del destino* with Ezio Pinza.

Vol. 2: Arias from: PUCCINI: *Madama Butterfly; Tosca; Manon Lescaut*. VERDI: *Il trovatore; Aida*. MASCAGNI: *Cavalleria rusticana*. HERBERT: *Mademoiselle Modiste*. RIMSKY-KORSAKOV: *Sadko*. HALEVY: *La Juive*. Songs by: TOSTI; MASSENET; BACHGOUNOD; CHARLES.

(M) (***) Nimbus mono NI 7846 [id.].

This second volume of Nimbus's Ponselle collection is mainly devoted to her early acoustic recordings, made for Columbia between 1918 and 1924 when she was still in her early twenties. Hers is a flawless voice, which takes very well to the Nimbus process, when just as in her later electrical recordings the pure creamy quality comes over vividly with ample bloom, set in a lively acoustic. With not a hint of strain she subtly shades her tone in such an aria as Tosca's *Vissi d'arte*, underlining the emotion. The poise and flawless legato of Leonora's *La vergine degli angeli* from *Forza del destino*, the earliest recording here, explains why from the start this taxing role was one for which she was specially

renowned; at the other extreme she gives a sparkling account of the Victor Herbert number, *Kiss me again*. The electrical recordings then include her early recordings of Aida, notably the whole of the death scene with Martinelli, a classic recording. The discs ends with a touchingly apt song, recorded in 1939 after her retirement at the age of forty, 'When I have sung my songs to you, I'll sing no more'.

Volume 3: Arias from: VERDI: *Aida; Ernani; Il trovatore; La forza del destino*. ROSSINI: *William Tell*. MEYERBEER: *L'africana*. PUCCINI: *La bohème*. LEONCAVALLO: *I Pagliacci*. Songs: DI CAPUA: *Maria, Mari!*. TOSTI: *Serenade; 'A Vucchella; Luna d'estate; Si tu le voulais;* and by: BLAND; FOSTER.

(M) (***) Nimbus mono NI 7878 [id.].

In this third Ponselle volume from Nimbus, the only electrical recordings are of ballads by Tosti, Stephen Foster and James Bland, which Ponselle magically transforms, giving distinction to trivial material. The acoustic recordings of arias include Aida's *Ritorna vincitor*, sung even more commandingly in 1923 than in her electrical recording of 1928 in Volume 2. The poise and flawless control in each are as remarkable as in the two earlier discs, and the nine operatic items plus two ballads include four recorded for Victor in 1923–5 but never released.

Rethberg, Elisabeth (soprano)

Arias from: VERDI: *Aida; Otello; Un ballo in maschera*. GIORDANO: *Andrea Chénier*. PUCCINI: *La bohème; Madama Butterfly*. WAGNER: *Tannhäuser; Lohengrin*. MOZART: *Le nozze di Figaro; Die Zauberflöte*. Johann STRAUSS Jnr: *Der Zigeunerbaron*. BIZET: *Carmen*.

(M) (***) Nimbus mono 7903 [id.].

Elisabeth Rethberg, counted by Toscanini as his favourite soprano, was once voted 'the most perfect singer in the world'. This excellent selection of her recordings, drawn from the years 1924–1930, helps to explain why. Consistently she was flawless in controlling her full, firm, finely projected voice both in phrase and dynamic over the widest expressive rang. No recording of *Aida's O patria mia* can quite match the subtlety of this pre-electric version, recorded for Brunswick in 1924 – one of the few where the culminating top C is sung *dolce*, as marked. Her characterisations of each role may not be the most individual, but few singers have matched her in these arias, whether in Verdi, Puccini, Mozart, or the Wagner of *Tannhäuser* and *Lohengrin*. The Nimbus transfers give a vivid idea of the voice, if not of the instrumental accompaniment, with six pre-electric items, twelve electrically recorded.

Royal Opera House, Covent Garden

Royal Opera House Covent Garden (An early history on record). Singers included are: Melba, Caruso, Tetrazzini, McCormack, Destin, Gadski, Schorr, Turner, Zanelli, Lehmann, Schumann, Olczewska, Chaliapin, Gigli, Supervia, Tibbett, Tauber, Flagstad, Melchior. Arias from: GOUNOD: *Faust.* VERDI: *Rigoletto; Otello.* DONIZETTI: *Lucia di Lammermoor.* VERDI: *La Traviata.* PUCCINI: *Madama Butterfly; Tosca.* WAGNER: *Götterdämmerung; Die Meistersinger; Tristan und Isolde.* R. STRAUSS: *Der Rosenkavalier.* MUSSORGSKY: *Boris Godunov.* GIORDANO: *Andrea Chénier.* BIZET: *Carmen.* MOZART: *Don Giovanni.*
(M) (***) Nimbus mono NI 7819 [id.].

Nimbus's survey of great singers at Covent Garden ranges from Caruso's 1904 recording of *Questa o quella* from *Rigoletto* to the recording of the second half of the *Tristan* love duet, which Kirsten Flagstad and Lauritz Melchior made in San Francisco in November 1939, a magnificent recording, never issued in Britain and little known, which repeated the partnership initiated during the 1937 Coronation season at Covent Garden. The Vienna recording of the *Rosenkavalier* Trio with Lehmann, Schumann and Olczewska similarly reproduces a classic partnership at Covent Garden, while Chaliapin's 1928 recording of the *Prayer* and *Death of Boris* was actually recorded live at Covent Garden, with the transfer giving an amazingly vivid sense of presence. Those who like Nimbus's acoustic method of transfer will enjoy the whole disc, though the reverberation round some of the early offerings – like the very first, Melba's *Jewel song* from *Faust* – is cavernous. Particularly interesting is the 1909 recording of part of Brünnhilde's Immolation scene, with Johanna Gadski commandingly strong.

Schipa, Tito (tenor)

Arias from: MASCAGNI: *Cavalleria rusticana. L'amico Fritz.* VERDI: *Rigoletto; Luisa Miller.* DONIZETTI: *Lucia di Lammermoor; Don Pasquale; L'elisir d'amore.* LEONCAVALLO: *Pagliacci.* MASSENET: *Manon; Werther.* ROSSINI: *Il barbiere di Siviglia.* THOMAS: *Mignon.* FLOTOW: *Martha.* CILEA: *L'Arlesiana.*
(M) (***) Nimbus mono NI 7813 [id.].

The first nine items on this well-chosen selection of Schipa's recordings date from the pre-electric era. The voice is totally consistent, heady and light and perfectly controlled, between the *Siciliana* from Mascagni's *Cavalleria*, recorded with piano in 1913, to the incomparable account of more Mas-

cagni, the *Cherry duet* from *L'amico Fritz*, made with Mafalda Favero in 1937. It says much for his art that Schipa's career continued at full strength for decades after that. The Nimbus transfers put the voice at a slight distance, with the electrical recordings made to sound the more natural.

Schumann-Heink, Ernestine (contralto)

Arias from: DONIZETTI: *Lucrezia Borgia.* MEYERBEER: *Le Prophète.* WAGNER: *Das Rheingold; Rienzi; Götterdämmerung.* HANDEL: *Rinaldo.* Songs by: ARDITTI; BECKER; SCHUBERT; WAGNER; REIMANN; MOLLOY; BRAHMS; BOEHM; TRAD.
M) (***) Nimbus mono NI 7811 [id.].

Ernestine Schumann-Heink was a formidable personality in the musical life of her time, notably in New York, as well as a great singer. 'I am looking for my successor,' she is reported as saying well-before she retired, adding, 'She must be *the* contralto.' Schumann-Heink combines to an astonishing degree a full contralto weight and richness with the most delicate flexibility, as in the *Brindisi* from Donizetti's *Lucrezia Borgia*. This wideranging collection, resonantly transferred by the Nimbus acoustic method, presents a vivid portrait of a very great singer.

Sembrich, Marcella (soprano)

Arias from: DONIZETTI: *Don Pasquale; Lucia di Lammermoor.* MUNIUSZKO: *Halka.* ROSSINI: *Semiramide; Il barbiere di Siviglia.* VERDI: *La traviata; Ernani; Rigoletto.* BELLINI: *Norma.* THOMAS: *Hamlet.* VERDI: *I vespri siciliani.* FLOTOW: *Martha.* BELLINI: *La sonnambula.* Songs: Johann STRAUSS Jnr; ARNE; ARDITI; BISHOP; HAHN; SCHUBERT; CHOPIN AND TRADITIONAL.
(M) (***) Nimbus mono NI 7901 [id.].

As an alternative to the four discs of the complete Romophone edition of Sembrich, this Nimbus issue is very welcome. Her reputation as the supreme coloratura of her day may be undermined, but the choice of twenty-one items is first-rate, with only three recordings from before 1907. The Nimbus transfer method, with 78 discs played in front of a modern stereo recording machine, presents the voice in a flattering three-dimensional setting, but with focus less sharp than on Romophone.

Supervia, Conchita (mezzo-soprano)

'In opera and song': BIZET: *Carmen*: excerpts (with Gaston Micheletti, Andrée Vavon, Andrée

Bernadet). Arias from: ROSSINI: *L'Italiana in Algeri; Il barbiere di Siviglia; La Cenerentola.* GOUNOD: *Faust.* THOMAS: *Mignon.* SAINT-SAENS: *Samson et Dalila.* SERRANO: *La Alegría del Batallón; El mal de amores.* Songs: FALLA: *7 Canciones populares españolas.* BALDOMIR: *Meus amores.* YRADIER: *La Paloma.* VALVERDE: *Clavelitos.*
(M) (***) Nimbus mono NI 7836/7 (2) [id.].

Readers who remember the 78s of Conchita Supervia, especially in Rossini – and in particular her dark, brittle mezzo with its wide vibrato ('like the rattle of shaken dice', as one critic described it) sparkling in the divisions of *Una voce poco fa* – may be astonished to discover the degree of vocal charm in other roles. Her reputation for dazzling the ear in Rossini was surely deserved (and she helped to restore *La Cenerentola* and *L'Italiana in Algeri* to the repertoire). Her Carmen, too, is unforgettable, as is her Delilah – but, more unexpectedly, her Mignon is also a highlight here, as is the brief Delibes item. As usual, the Nimbus transfers are kind to the voice (there is no suggestion of the 'death rattle' of one unkind description) and almost certainly more truthful than the edgier, brighter quality we have had from some other sources. The recordings date from between 1927 and 1935.

Tauber, Richard (tenor)

Arias from: R. STRAUSS: *Der Rosenkavalier.* WAGNER: *Die Walküre; Die Meistersinger.* KIENZL: *Der Evangelimann.* PUCCINI: *Tosca; La Bohème; Madama Butterfly; Turandot.* VERDI: *Il Trovatore.* MOZART: *Don Giovanni; Die Zauberflöte.* TCHAIKOVSKY: *Eugene Onegin.* BIZET: *Carmen.* KORNGOLD: *Die tote Stadt.* LORTZING: *Undine.* OFFENBACH: *Les contes d'Hoffmann.*
(M) (***) Nimbus mono NI 7830 [id.].

The Nimbus transfers come from the same decade as the EMI Référence disc above, between 1919 and 1929, and although there is some duplication of repertoire, Tauber admirers will probably want both CDs. The effect of Nimbus transfers is always most impressive in the pre-electric recordings, which predominate here, but the voice is always naturally focused, even in the 1929 excerpt from Offenbach's *Tales of Hoffmann.* The effect is mellower, more rounded than in the EMI transfers.

Richard Tauber (tenor) and Lotte Schöne (soprano)

Operetta arias from LEHAR: *Paganini; Zigeunerliebe; Der Land des Lächelns; Die lustige Witwe.* SUPPE: *Die schöne Galatea.*

SCHUBERT/BERTE: *Das Dreimäderlhaus (Lilac time).* J. STRAUSS Jr: *Die Fledermaus; Der lustige Krieg; Indigo und die vierzig Räuber; Cagliosto in Wien.* KALMAN: *Gräfin Mariza. Die Zirkusprinzessin.* MILLOCKER: *Der arme Jonathan.* ZELLER: *Der Vogelhändler; Der Obersteiger.* NESSLER: *Der Trompeter von Säckingen.*
(M) (***) Nimbus mono NI 7833 [id.].

These imaginatively chosen operetta excerpts, recorded over the same period (1919–29) as the operatic collections above, explain Tauber's phenomenal popularity over so many years. The collection is the more tempting for its inclusion of the contributions of Lotte Schöne, a delightful artist. Moreover there is much here that is very rare, and it is a pity that no duets were available – these are all solo items. The transfers are most successful.

Tetrazzini, Luisa (soprano)

Arias from: BELLINI: *La Sonnambula.* DONIZETTI: *Lucia di Lammermoor.* ROSSINI: *Il Barbiere di Siviglia.* THOMAS: *Mignon.* VERACINI: *Rosalinda.* VERDI: *Un ballo in maschera; Rigoletto; La Traviata; Il Trovatore; I vespri siciliani.*
(M) (***) Nimbus mono NI 7808 [id.].

Tetrazzini was astonishing among coloratura sopranos not just for her phenomenal agility but for the golden warmth that went with tonal purity. The Nimbus transfers add a bloom to the sound, with the singer slightly distanced. Though some EMI transfers make her voice more vividly immediate, one quickly adjusts. Such display arias as *Ah non giunge* from *La Sonnambula* or the *Bolero* from *I vespri siciliani* are incomparably dazzling, but it is worth noting too what tenderness is conveyed through Tetrazzini's simple phrasing and pure tone in such a tragic aria as Violetta's *Addio del passato*, with both verses included. Lieder devotees may gasp in horror, but one of the delightful oddities here is Tetrazzini's bright-eyed performance, with ragged orchestral accompaniment, of what is described as *La serenata inutile* by Brahms – in fact *Vergebliches Ständchen*, sung with a triumphant if highly inauthentic top A at the end, implying no closure of the lady's window!

Volume II: Arias from: BELLINI: *I Puritani; La Sonnambula.* DAVID: *Le Perle du Brésil.* DONIZETTI: *Linda di Chamounix.* ROSSINI: *Semiramide; Il barbiere di Siviglia.* GOUNOD: *Roméo et Juliette.* BIZET: *Carmen.* MEYERBEER: *Dinorah; Les Huguenots.* VERDI: *Il Trovatore; La Traviata.* Songs: TOSTI: *Aprile.* GRIEG: *Peer Gynt: Solveig's song.* BRAGA: *La Serenata.* BENEDICT: *Carnevale di Venezia.*
(M) (***) Nimbus mono NI 7891 [id.].

Tetrazzini's bright clear soprano with its characteristic touch of gold is ideally suited to the Nimbus
process, and with ample bloom on the sound these
early acoustic recordings, made between 1910 and
1914, give one a vivid idea not only of the beauty
and brilliance but of the scale of the voice. Not that
they disguise the technical shortcomings, such as
her tendency to attack the exposed start of florid
runs fearlessly with a little squawk, endearing as it
may be, or the way that some of the coloratura here
is on the sketchy side, as in the Queen's aria from
Meyerbeer's *Les Huguenots*. The disc ends with
three Zonophone recordings made in 1904 with
piano accompaniment, including an early version
of her party-piece, *Ah non giunge*, from Sonnambula and the first half only of Rosina's *Una voce
poco fa* from *Il barbiere di Siviglia*.

Tibbett, Lawrence (baritone)

'Tibbett in opera': excerpts from: LEONCAVALLO:
Pagliacci. BIZET: *Carmen.* PUCCINI: *Tosca.*
VERDI: *Un ballo in maschera; Simon Boccanegra;*
Rigoletto; Otello. ROSSINI: *Il barbiere di Siviglia.*
GOUNOD: *Faust.* WAGNER: *Tannhäuser; Die
Walküre.*
(M) (***) Nimbus mono NI 7825 [id.].

The scale and resonance of Lawrence Tibbett's
voice come over vividly in this fine selection of
his recordings made between 1926 and 1939. The
Nimbus process allows the rapid vibrato in his voice
to emerge naturally, giving the sound a thrilling
richness in all these varied items. Particularly interesting is the longest, the whole of *Wotan's farewell*,
with Stokowski conducting the Philadelphia
Orchestra in 1934. It is an over-the-top performance
that carries total conviction, even if the sheer
volume produces some clangorous resonances in
the Nimbus transfer. Also memorable is the celebrated *Boccanegra* Council chamber sequence,
recorded in 1939 with Martinelli and Rose Bampton
in the ensemble.

Other Vocal Recitals and Choral Collections

Alagna, Roberto (tenor)

'Sanctus': Sacred songs (with Toulouse Ch. and O, Plasson): BACH/GOUNOD: Ave Maria. GOUNOD: Repentance (O divine Redeemer); St Cecilia Mass: Sanctus; Angelic greeting (Ave Maria). FRANCK: Panis angelicus; The Procession. ADAM: Midnight, Christians. FAURE: O salutaris hostia; Crucifix. BERLIOZ: Requiem: Sanctus. SAINT-SAENS: Panis angelicus. BIZET: Agnus dei. CAPLET: Panis angelicus. L. BOULANGER: Piè Jesu.
* EMI Dig. CDC5 56206-2 [id.].

This sumptuously over-produced record has already been a big hit in France. After the opening Ave Maria, however, Alagna's singing gets buried in an over-resonantly unclear chorus until the Caplet Panis angelicus near the end. The Gounod items are unbelievably mushy.

American Boychoir, Atlantic Brass Quintet, James Litton

'Trumpets sound, voices ring: A joyous Christmas': arr. WILLCOCKS: O come all ye faithful; Once in Royal David's city. RUTTER: Angel tidings; Star carol; The Lord bless you and keep you. BRAHMS: Regina coeli. ELGAR: The snow. GAWTHROP: Mary speaks. MENDELSSOHN, arr. WILLCOCKS: Hark! the herald angels sing. VAUGHAN WILLIAMS: Hodie; Lullaby. FRASER: This Christmastide (Jessye's carol). CORELLI: Concerto grosso in G min. (Christmas), Op. 6/8. MANZ: E'en so, Lord Jesus, quickly come. TELEMANN: Lobet den Herrn, alle Heiden; Meine Seele, erhebt den Herrn. CASALS: Nigra sum. Spiritual: Go tell it on the mountain.
*** MusicMasters Dig. 01612 67076-2 [id.].

Gleaming brass fanfares introduce this lively and attractively diverse American collection featuring a gleaming treble line against full brass sonorities. The Americans follow the English King's College tradition at the opening of Once in Royal David's city but cap its climax resplendently. The three Rutter carols are ideal for boy trebles and the infectious Star carol brings an engagingly light rhythmic touch. Elgar's much less well-known portrayal of The snow is very touching, while Jessye's carol has one of those gentle but haunting melodies that persist in the memory: its descant is particularly

apt, and it builds to an expansive climax. Both Mary speaks and Paul Manz's E'en so, Lord Jesus are modern carols with an appealing simplicity, matched by Pablo Casals's better-known Nigra sum. The two Telemann items featuring famous chorales are both floridly testing of the boys' resources, and here the faster passages are not always completely secure. But they provide a nice baroque contrast, and it was a happy idea to include a brass transcription of Corelli's famous Christmas concerto grosso which, if sounding comparatively robust, is still highly effective when played so well. The choral singing is generally of a high calibre and the recording has a natural, warm ambience and is admirably clear.

Ampleforth Schola Cantorum, Ian Little

'Carols from Ampleforth': arr. WILLCOCKS: O come all ye faithful; Once in Royal David's city; Unto us a son is born; Sussex carol; God rest you merry, gentlemen. arr. HOLST: Personent Hodie. arr. JACQUES: Good King Wenceslas. arr. STAINER/WILLCOCKS: The first Nowell. PRAETORIUS: A great and mighty wonder. arr. RUTTER: Angel tidings. STEWART: On this day earth shall ring. WARLOCK: Adam lay ybounden. MATHIAS: Sir Christèmas. arr. WOOD: Past three o'clock; Ding, dong! merrily on high. arr. SULLIVAN: It came upon the midnight clear. arr. LEDGER: Still, still, still. arr. LITTLE: Come with torches. arr. PETTMAN: The infant king. GRUBER, arr. LITTLE: Silent night. MENDELSSOHN, arr. WILLCOCKS: Hark! the herald angels sing.
*** Ampleforth Abbey Records Dig. AARCD 1 [id.].

A splendidly robust selection of favourites, with the expansive Abbey acoustic and the superb organ adding much to the listener's pleasure. The sound itself is often thrilling with men and boys both singing ardently; there are a few minor blemishes of ensemble, but nothing to worry about when the projection is so vigorously communicative. Perhaps the rhythm of Mathias's Sir Christèmas is a bit heavy, but On this day earth shall ring makes a magnificent effect, with the organ adding a final blaze of sound at the close. There are gentler carols too, of course, though not all will like Ian Willson's added harmonies at the end of Silent night.

Angeles, Victoria de los (soprano)

'The fabulous Victoria de Los Angeles'

Disc 1: RAVEL: *Shéhérazade; 5 Mélodies populaires grecques; 2 Mélodies hébraïques.* DUPARC: *L'invitation au voyage; Phidylé.* DEBUSSY: *L'Enfant prodigue: L'année en vain chasse l'année.* CHAUSSON: *Poème de l'amour et de la mer.*

Disc 2: MONTSALVATGE: *5 canciones negras.* GRANADOS: *Colección se canciones amatorias; Llorad corazón; Iban al pinar.* RODRIGO: *4 madrigales amatorios; Triptic de Mossèn Cinto.* ESPLA: *5 canciones playeras españolas.* TOLDRA: *4 cançons.* TRAD.: *La Dama d'Aragó; El cant dels ocells; Canço de Sega.* MOMPOU: *El Combat del Somni.*

Disc 3: DEBUSSY: *Chansons de Bilitis; Fêtes galantes; Noël des enfants qui n'ont plus de maisons.* RAVEL: *Chants populaires.* HAHN: *3 jours de vendage; Le rossignol de lilas.* FAURE: *Tristesse; Au bord de l'eau; Les Roses d'Ispahan; Toujours.* FALLA: *7 canciones populares españolas. Psyché; Soneto a Córdoba.* TOLDRA: *12 canciones gallegas: As floriñas dos toxos.* TURINA: *Farruca.* RODRIGO: *Villancicos: Pastorcito santo.*

Disc 4: SACRATI: *Prosperina: E dove t'aggiri.* A. SCARLATTI: *Le violette.* HANDEL: *Joshua: Oh! had I Jubal's lyre.* SCHUBERT: *Der Tod und das Mädchen. Die schöne Müllerin: Wohin?; An die Musik; Mignon und der Harfner.* BRAHMS: *Dein blaue Auge; Vergebliches Ständchen; Sapphische Ode.* FAURE: *Chansons d'amour; Clair de lune; Pleurs d'or.* PURCELL: *Let us wander; Lost is my quiet.* HAYDN: *Schlaf in deiner engen Kammer.* J. C. BACH: *Ah! lamenta, oh bella Irene.* BEETHOVEN: *Irish songs: Oh! would I were but that sweet linnet; He promised me at parting; They bid me slight my Dermot dear. Welsh song: The dream.* BERLIOZ: *Les fleurs des landes: Le Trébuchet.* DVORAK: *Möglichkeit; Der Apfel.* TCHAIKOVSKY: *Scottish ballad.* SAINT-SAENS: *Pastorale.* MOZART: *La Pertenza.*

(M) *** EMI CMS5 65061-2 (4) [ZDMD 65061].

A seventy-fifth-birthday celebration, this well-documented set subdivides into a pair of CDs of French and Spanish repertoire with orchestra, and two more with piano. While the French classics give special delight, it is good that room was made for the two separate Rodrigo song selections, as this composer prized his vocal music above all else and it is too little known. Apart from the mélodies, the third disc includes some especially delightful folk-inspired repertoire from both countries, where de los Angeles was in her element; on the fourth, a wide-ranging programme (in which she has the estimable support of Gerald Moore) shows her remarkable versatility. The recordings were made in the 1960s when the voice was at its freshest. If you are an admirer of this lovely voice, snap the set up quickly, for it is unlikely to be around for very long.

'Diva': Arias from ROSSINI: *Il barbiere di Siviglia.* GOUNOD: *Faust.* VERDI: *La Traviata; Otello.* PUCCINI: *La Bohème; Madama Butterfly; Suor Angelica; Gianni Schicchi.* MASCAGNI: *Cavalleria rusticana.* LEONCAVALLO: *Pagliacci.* CATALANI: *La Wally.* MASSENET: *Manon.* BIZET: *Carmen.* GIMENEZ: *La Tempranica.* CABALLERO: *Gigantes y Cabezudos.* BARBIERI: *Il barberillo de Lavaplés.*

(M) *** EMI mono/stereo CDM5 65579-2 [id.].

This splendid compilation brings it home how many of the classic sets of the 1950s and 1960s have Victoria de los Angeles as a golden-toned heroine, responding with heartfelt expressiveness. These include the two incomparable Beecham sets of Puccini's *La Bohème* and Bizet's *Carmen*, Gui's Glyndebourne-based set of Rossini's *Barbiere*, Monteux's magical set of Massenet's *Manon*, Cluytens's recording of *Faust*, Serafin's of Puccini's *Il Trittico*, not to mention the RCA New York recording in 1953 of *I Pagliacci*, in which de los Angeles sings charmingly as Nedda communing with the birds – not the role one expects from her. These are well supplemented by two items from her superb (1954) opera recital, including a tenderly beautiful *Ave Maria* from *Otello* and three final numbers from Spanish zarzuelas, making a winning collection overall.

Songs of Spain: Disc 1: *Traditional songs* (arr. Graciano Tarragó; with Renata Tarragó & Graciano Tarragó, guitars); *Medieval songs* (early 14th century); *Renaissance and Baroque songs* (15th–18th centuries; with Ens., José María Lamaña).

Disc 2: *Medieval and Renaissance songs of Andalusia; Renaissance songs* (with Ars Musicae de Barcelona, Enrique Gisbert & José María Lamaña).

Disc 3: *19th- and 20th-century arrangements and art songs: Canciones Sefardies* (arr. Manuel Valls; with Jean-Claude Gérard, flute & Oscar Ghighia, guitar); *Canciones populares españoles* (arr. Lorca; with Miguel Zanetti, piano). Songs by MOMPOU; TOLDRA; MONTSALVATGE; RODRIGO (all with Gonzalo Soriano, piano); GRANADOS; GURIDU; HALFFTER; TURINA; NIN; VALVERDE (all with GERALD MOORE, piano); BARRERA & CALLEJA (arr. Los Angeles, guitar); MONTSALVATGE: *Madrigal* (with Barcelona City Orchestra, Garcia Navarro).

Disc 4: *Songs and opera arias*: GRANADOS: *Colección de tonadillas; Tres majas dolorosa* (with Gonzalo Soriano, piano); *Goyescas: La Maja y el ruiseñor*. FALLA: *La vida breve*: excerpts (with New Philharmonia Orchestra or Paris Conservatoire Orchestra, Rafael Frühbeck de Burgos. 1971 New York Recital (with Alicia de Larrocha, piano): Songs by LITERES; DE LASERNA; GIMENEZ. GRANADOS: *Canciones amatorias*. FALLA: *7 Canciones populares españolas*.

(M)*** EMI Analogue/Dig. mono/stereo CMS5 66937-2 (4) [id.].

Issued to celebrate the singer's seventy-fifth birthday in November 1998, this four-disc compilation of de los Angeles in her native Spanish repertory is a delight. Two of the four discs are devoted to traditional, medieval and renaissance songs, accompanied by the guitarist Renata Tarragó, as well as by her mentor in early music, José María Lamaña, with his own Ars Musicae of Barcelona and a British group. Recorded over two decades between 1950 and 1971, the set also includes de los Angeles's contribution to the closing ceremony of the 1992 Barcelona Olympic Games (the folk/madrigal *El cant dels ocells* of Montsalvatge), the voice carefully husbanded but still golden.

Overall, this lavish survey represents a cross-section of the varied types of art song which were current in the rich period of Spanish music between the thirteenth and sixthteenth centuries, and then moves on to include key nineteenth and twentieth-century repertoire. Earliest are monodic cantigas associated with the Virgin Mary, but most of the rest are secular, including a group of songs of the Sephardic Jewish tradition, also romances and villancicos (brief ballads), songs with vihuela accompaniments and madrigals – one might quibble about their presentation by a solo voice – of a later period. The first disc opens with eighteen traditional songs arranged by Graciano Tarregó, with guitar accompaniments, and the result has a captivating simplicity; moreover the mono recordings (from 1950–52) give a most natural presence for the voice.

Since the early days of her career, de los Angeles has been associated with the Ars Musicae ensemble of Barcelona. They play here on authentic instruments – fidulas, recorders, lute, vihuela de mano, viols and lira da braccio, and if the more complex later songs from the Courts of Charles V and Philip II hardly match the finest of our own Elizabethan songs, they are exquisitely done by de los Angeles and her friends. The Spanish folksongs arranged by the poet Lorca are mainly dance-songs, while the main Sephardic collection, arranged by Valls, gives an admirable sample of the music which was developing among Spanish Jews in the late Middle Ages, exotic and individual. The later Granados and Falla items are better known and no less winning. De los Angeles made her recording début with the two Falla arias years ago; these later versions come

from 1962. The collection ends with her live New York recital of 1971, where she forms a symbiotic partnership with her Catalan contemporary, Alicia de Larrocha, as accompanist, including the best loved of her encore numbers, Valverde's *Clavelitos* and *Adios Granada,* and ending with a riotous *Zapateado*. The voice is as fresh as ever. What matters most is that this is all music which inspires the singer to her fullest, most captivating artistry. The documentation could be more extensive, but full texts and translations are included.

Arias from: FAURE: *Requiem.* HANDEL: *Acis and Galatea.* ROSSINI: *Il barbiere di Siviglia.* PUCCINI: *La Bohème; Madama Butterfly; Suor Angelica; Gianni Schicchi.* LEONCAVALLO: *Pagliacci.* MASSENET: *Manon; Werther.* PURCELL: *Dido and Aeneas.* OFFENBACH: *Les contes d'Hoffmann.* VERDI: *La Traviata; Simon Boccanegra.* BIZET: *Carmen.* GOUNOD: *Faust.* Lieder and songs: MENDELSSOHN: *Auf Flügeln des Gesanges.* GRIEG: *Ich liebe dich.* BRAHMS: *Wiegenlied.* DVORAK: *Als die alte Mutter.* MARTINI: *Plaisir d'amour.* DELIBES: *Les filles de Cadiz.* YRADIER: *La Paloma.* CHUE/ CAVALVERDE: *Tango de la menegilda.* LORENTE: *Canción de la gitana.* FALLA: *El amor brujo:* excerpts; *Siete canciones populares españolas.* CANTELOUBE: *3 Chants d'Auvergne.* MOZART: *Exsultate jubilate, K.165.*

(BB)*** Royal Classics Vocal Double DCL 703972 (2).

The Royal Classics series of Vocal Doubles is just as enticing with its portraits of star singers as it is in the comparable coverage of conductors listed above, and there is surely no better place to start than with the golden-voiced Victoria de los Angeles. The well-chosen and remarkably comprehensive selection above takes a broad swath through her wide-ranging repertoire, from opera to Lieder, not forgetting Spanish song, happily framed by famous ecclesiastical items by Fauré and Mozart. As expected in this fine series, the EMI transfers are of the highest quality, there is charm in plenty, and this makes for a generous, treasurable and inexpensive collection, even if the documentation is limited to titles and publication dates.

Anonymous 4

'*The Lily and the lamb*' (Chant and polyphony from medieval England): *Conducti, Hymns, Motets, Sequences; Antiphon: Ave regina coelorum.*
*** HM Dig. HMU 907125 [id.].

The Anonymous Four (Ruth Cunningham, Marsha Genensky, Susan Hellauer and Johanna Rose) are an American vocal quartet whose voices merge into a particularly pleasing blend. They came together in 1986, bringing with them a variety of musical skills, including instrumental proficiency and a musicological background. The group focuses on medieval music, mainly sacred, spanning 500 years, from the eleventh to the fourteenth century. It is perhaps appropriate that this first collection should be devoted to hymns, sequences and motets dedicated to the Virgin Mary.

Women in medieval times identified with Mary and in particular her suffering as she saw her son dying on the cross. The second item in this programme, a monodic hymn, begins with the words 'The gentle lamb spread on the cross, hung all bathed with blood'. For women of those times, death was an everyday event, especially since only a small proportion of their many children survived into adulthood and they saw their young loved ones succumb to disease and other causes. The singers here blend their voices into one, whether singing monody or in simple polyphony, as in the sequence *Stillat in stelam radium*, or the beautiful motet *Veni mater gracie*. The voices are heard floating in an ecclesiastic acoustic and the effect is mesmeric.

'*An English Ladymass*' (13th- and 14th-century chant and polyphony in honour of the Virgin Mary): *Alleluias, Gradual, Hymn, Introit, Kyrie, Motets, Offertory, Rondellus, Sequences, Songs.*
**(*) HM Dig. HMU 907080 [id.]

In medieval times most large churches and cathedrals had a lady chapel, where a Ladymass could be sung regularly to the Virgin Mary. And these still exist today in larger Catholic cathedrals, like Chartres in France. They usually have an extraordinary atmosphere and one watches with respect as young mothers not only attend alone but also bring their children to present to the statue of the Virgin. Here the Anonymous Four have arranged their own Mass sequence with the Propers interspersed with appropriate motets, hymns, a Gradual and Alleluia, finally concluding with the hymn *Ave Maris stella*. In doing so they make their own homage to the Virgin Mother which is well planned. The music is beautifully sung, although this is perhaps not one of their most potent collections.

'*Miracles of Sant'Iago*' (Medieval chant and polyphony for St James from the Codex Calixtinus): *Agnus dei trope, Benedicamus tropes, Kyrie trope, Antiphon, Conducti, Hymns, Invitatory, Offertory, Prosae, Responsories.*
*** HM Dig. HMU 907156 [id.].

The Cathedral of Santiago in Compostela is the home of a manuscript of five books called collectively *Jacobus*, and its music was designed to be sung by groups of young French boy-trebles. It proves ideal material for the Anonymous Four and its musical interest is immediately demonstrated by the brilliantly decorated Benedicamus trope *Vox nostra resonet*. Much of the music is plainchant,

but the early examples of two-part polyphony are very striking. Again the singing here is magnetic and the warm resonance of the recording very flattering.

'*Love's illusion*' (French motets on courtly love texts from the 13th-century Montpellier Codex): *Plus bele que flor / Quant revient / L'autrier joer; Puisque bele dame m'eime; Amours mi font souffrir / En mai; Ne sai, que je die; Si je chante / Bien doi amer; Or ne sai je que devenir / puisque d'amer; Hé Dieus, de si haut si bas / Maubatus; Celui en qui / La bele estoile / La bele, en qui; Qui d'amours se plaint; Amours, dont je sui / L'autrier, au douz mois / Chose Tassin; Au cuer ai un mal / Ja ne m'en repentirai / Jolietement; Quant voi la fleur; Quant se depart / Onques ne sai amer; Joliement / Quant voi la florete / Je sui joliete; Amor potest conqueri / Adamorem sequitur; Ce que je tieng / Certes mout / Bone compaignie; J'ai si bien mon cuer assiz / Aucun m'ont; Ne m'oubliez mie; J'ai mis toute ma pensee / Je n'en puis; Blanchete / Quant je pens; Dame, que je n'os noumer / Amis donc est / Lonc tans a; Li savours de mon desir / Li grant desir / Non veul mari; Entre Copin / Je me cuidoie / Bele Ysabelos; S'on me regarde / Prennés i garde / Hé, mi enfant; Quant yver la bise ameine; Ne m'a pas oublié; On doit fin[e] Amor / La biauté; Ja n'amerai autre que cele; Quant je parti de m'amie.*
*** HM Dig. HMU 907109 [id.].

For this programme the Anonymous Four have moved away from liturgical music and chosen twenty-nine thirteenth-century motets from the Montpellier Codex, setting courtly love texts with simple and affecting polyphony. It is remarkable how the atmosphere of this music brings a more secular, plaintive quality. The means are the same but the expressive result is different, for the words are about the joys and regrets and the feelings of love. Many of these songs are dolorous but *Ne sai, que je die* (about pride, hypocrisy and avarice) and *Qui l'amours se plaint* are both dance songs. This is one of the most attractive of this fine group's collections. They are obviously moved, as women, by the words they sing, and they find remarkable variety of expressive feeling here. Occasionally a drone is added under the melodic line to telling effect, and one never misses an instrumental backing. The recording is well up to standard. A splendid disc.

'*On Yoolis night*' (Medieval carols and motets): *Antiphons, Carols, Hymns, Motets, Responsory, Rondella, Songs.*
*** HM Dig. HMU 907099 [id.].

This is a delightful collection. The carol *Alleluia, A new work* and the anonymous setting of *Ave Maria* are both enchanting discoveries, and many of these items have that curious, Christmassy colouring. The dance song *Gabriel from heaven-king* and the lovely *Lullay: I saw a sweet seemly sight* are matched by *As I lay on Yoolis night*, while the closing *Nowel* is wonderfully joyful. The simple medieval implied harmonies in no way inhibit the character but increase the special colour of these carols, which are sung tenderly or with great spirit by this excellent group. Here is a record to lay in store for next Christmas, but to play at other times too.

'*A Star in the East*' (Medieval Hungarian Christmas music): *Alleluias, Antiphons, Communion, Evangelium, Gradual, Hymns, Introit, Lectio, Motet, Offertory, Sanctus, Songs, Te Deum.*
*** HM Dig. HMU 907139 [id.].

The repertoire here is comparatively unsophisticated but full of charm, and the singing has the right kind of innocence. The programme came about by accident. While one of the group was researching the music of Hildegard of Bingen at Columbia University Library, a book of Hungarian Christmas music fell off the shelf at the researcher's feet, inviting its performance. There is not a great deal of polyphony here, but that is not a feature of many of our own favourite Christmas carols either. There is no lack of melody. Excellent recording and splendid documentation.

'*A Portrait*': excerpts from '*Miracles of Sant'Iago*'; '*The Lily and the lamb*'; '*A Star in the East*'; '*Love's illusion*'; '*An English Ladymass*'; '*On Yoolis night*'.
(B) *** HM Dig. HMX 2907210 [id.].

Here is a carefully chosen selection of highlights from the six CDs listed above. It's well worth sampling to find out whether the pure yet richly expressive vocal style of this remarkable female group will tempt you to explore further in one direction or another.

Ars Nova, Bo Holten

Portuguese polyphony: CARDOSO: *Lamentatio; Magnificat secundi toni.* LOBO: *Audivi vocem de caelo; Pater peccavi.* MAGALHAES: *Vidi aquam; Missa O Soberana luz; Commissa mea pavesco.* Manuel da FONSECA: *Beata viscera.* Bartolomeo TROSYLHO: *Circumdederunt.* Pedro de ESCOBAR: *Clamabat autem mulier.*
(BB) *** Naxos Dig. 8.553310 [id.].

In every respect this is an outstanding anthology. Apart from the major items from the Portuguese 'famous three' contemporaries, Cardoso, Lôbo and (the least-known) Filippe de Magalhães, which are discussed above under their respective Composer entries in our main volume, the motets by the earlier figures, Pedro de Escobar (*c.* 1465–1535), Bartolomeo Trosylho (*c.* 1500–*c.* 1567) and Manuel da Fonseca (*maestre da capela* at Braga Cathedral in the mid-sixteenth century), are all touchingly, serenely beautiful, if perhaps less individual. The singing of this Danish Choir is superb and so is the Naxos recording. Texts and translations are provided, although for some reason they are printed separately. A unique bargain of the highest quality.

Augér, Arleen (soprano)

'*Love songs*' (with Dalton Baldwin, piano): COPLAND: *Pastorale; Heart, we will forget him.* OBRADORS: *Del Cabello más sutil.* OVALLE: *Azulao.* R. STRAUSS: *Ständchen; Das Rosenband.* MARX: *Selige Nacht.* POULENC: *Fleurs.* CIMARA: *Stornello.* QUILTER: *Music, when soft voices die; Love's philosophy.* O. STRAUS: *Je t'aime.* SCHUMANN: *Widmung; Du bist wie eine Blume.* MAHLER: *Liebst du um Schönheit.* TURINA: *Cantares.* LIPPE: *How do I love thee?* COWARD: *Conversation piece: I'll follow my secret heart.* GOUNOD: *Serenade.* SCHUBERT: *Liebe schwärmt auf allen Wegen.* BRIDGE: *Love went a-riding.* FOSTER: *Why, no one to love.* DONAUDY: *O del mio amato ben.* BRITTEN (arr.): *The Salley Gardens.* LOEWE: *Camelot: Before I gaze at you again.*
✿ *** Delos Dig. D/CD 3029 [id.].

This extraordinarily wide-ranging recital is a delight from the first song to the last. Arleen Augér opens with Copland and closes with *Camelot*, and she is equally at home in the music by Roger Quilter (*Love's philosophy* is superbly done), Noël Coward and the *Rückert* song of Mahler. Britten's arrangement of *The Salley Gardens*, ravishingly slow, is another highlight. The layout of the recital could hardly have been managed better: each song creates its new atmosphere readily, but seems to be enhanced by coming after the previous choice. Dalton Baldwin's accompaniments are very much a partnership with the singing, while the playing itself is spontaneously perceptive throughout. With a good balance and a very realistic recording, this projects vividly like a live recital.

(i) Bach Choir, Sir David Willcocks; (ii) Philip Jones Brass Ensemble, Philip Jones

'*In dulci jubilo – A Festival of Christmas*': (i; ii) arr. WILLCOCKS: *Fanfare – O come all ye faithful; Gabriel's message; Angelus ad Virginem; Ding dong! merrily on high; God rest you merry, gentlemen; Unto us a son is born; Once in Royal David's city; Hush my dear, lie still and remember; Away in a manger; Sussex carol.*

TRAD.: *A virgin most pure; In dulci jubilo.*
RUTTER: *Shepherd's pipe carol; Star carol.*
GRUBER: *Stille Nacht.* MENDELSSOHN: *Hark the herald angels sing.* (ii) BACH: *Christmas oratorio: chorales: Nun seid Ihr wohl gerochen; Ach, mein herzliebes Jesulein.* TRAD.: *Lord Jesus hath a garden; Come all ye shepherds; Il est né.* arr. IVESON: *We three kings; Jingle bells – Deck the hall; The holly and the ivy.* arr. RUTTER: *Wassail song; We wish you a merry Christmas.*
(B) **(*) Decca Eclipse Dig. 448 980-2 [(M) id. import].

The titling and documentation of this otherwise admirable Eclipse collection is misleading. It is basically an early (1980) digital concert by the Bach Choir, colourfully accompanied by the Philip Jones Brass Ensemble, conducted by Sir David Willcocks. Fresh simplicity is the keynote: the brass fanfares bring a touch of splendour, but the accompaniments are not over-scored. *Silent night* has never sounded more serene, and the other carols bring a wide variety of mood, while the two engaging Rutter pieces make a further refreshing contrast. However, as a central interlude there is a selection of ten items taken from a separate collection of Christmas music by Philip Jones and his Brass Ensemble without the choir, recorded two years later, also in the Kingsway Hall. Once again sound and playing are of very high quality. Appropriately framed by two chorales from Bach's *Christmas oratorio*, these arrangements are again effectively varied, with *Jingle bells* and *We wish you a merry Christmas* making a sparkling contrast with the gentler and more solemn music. But it must be said that carols are meant to include the words!

Baillie, Dame Isobel (soprano)

'The unforgettable Isobel Baillie': HANDEL: *Samson: Let the bright Seraphim. Rodelinda: Art thou troubled. Messiah: I know that my Redeemer liveth; If God be with us. Theodora: Angels ever bright and fair. Joshua: Oh! Had I Jubal's lyre.* BACH: *Cantata No. 68: My heart ever faithful; Cantata No. 201: Ah yes, just so* (arr. MOTTL). MOZART: *La finta giardiniera: A maiden's is an evil plight. The Marriage of Figaro: O come, do not delay.* HAYDN: *The Creation: With verdure clad.* MENDELSSOHN: *Elijah: Hear ye, Israel.* OFFENBACH: *Tales of Hoffmann: Doll's song.* SCHUBERT: *The Shepherd on the rock* (with Charles Draper, clarinet); *To music.* ARNE: *Where the bee sucks.*
🌑 (M) (***) Dutton Lab. mono CDLX 7013 [id. full price].

It must be unique for a soprano's recording career to span over half a century, yet over all that time Isobel Baillie rarely if ever let down her maxim

which provided the title of her autobiography, 'Never sing louder than lovely'. Handel's *I know that my Redeemer liveth* was certainly her most popular record during the war years. Alan Blyth describes this famous 1941 performance in the accompanying insert leaflet: 'Notes are hit fully and truly in the middle, and they are joined together in a seamless line. At the same time Baillie was able to swell and diminish her tone with total ease.' Like the rest of the programme, it is flawlessly transferred by the miraculous Dutton/CEDAR process, and one can enjoy Leslie Heward's warm Hallé accompaniment alongside the voice.

In her duet with the trumpet (Arthur Lockwood) which opens the disc, *Let the bright Seraphim*, her bright, gleaming tone wins out every time, and elsewhere there are dazzling displays of agility (as in the 1930 *Doll's song* and the delightful Arne *Where the bee sucks* from 1943) as well as purity and loveliness (as in the 1941 *Art thou troubled* or Susanna's aria from *The Marriage of Figaro*, recorded in 1927). Her simplicity of style was just right for Schubert, and her account of *The Shepherd on the rock*, recorded a year later, shows the bright, fresh timbre, which was uniquely hers, under perfect control. The timbre of Charles Draper, the distinguished clarinettist who plays the obbligato, by comparison seems dry and lustreless. A record to treasure on all counts.

Baker, Dame Janet (mezzo-soprano)

'Janet Baker sings' (with Gerald Moore, piano): FAURE: *Automne; Prison; Soir; Fleur jetée; En sourdine; Notre amour; Mai; Chanson du pêcheur; Clair de lune.* STANFORD: *La belle dame sans merci.* PARRY: *Proud Masie; O mistress mine.* William BUSCH: *Rest.* WARLOCK: *Pretty ringtime.* VAUGHAN WILLIAMS: *Linden Lea.* GURNEY: *Fields are full.* BRITTEN: *Corpus Christi carol.* IRELAND: *Sally Gardens.* QUILTER: *Love's philosophy.* SCHUBERT: *Am Grabe; Anselmos; Abendstern; Die Vögel; Strophe aus Die Götte; Griechenlands; Gondelfahrer; Auflösung.* Richard STRAUSS: *Morgen!; Befreit.*
🌑 (M) *** EMI CDM5 65009-2.

Just after he had officially retired, in the late 1960s, Gerald Moore returned to the recording studio to accompany Janet Baker, an artist whom he counted high among the many great singers he had accompanied in his career. This recital brings together a sequence of magical perfomances of songs especially dear to Dame Janet, with the voice consistently golden in tone. The Fauré group brings out her intense love of singing in French, and her devotion to the German Lied shines out equally in Schubert and Strauss. The group of ten English songs demonstrates that this neglected genre has comparable claims in beauty and intensity, with such favourite items as Vaughan Williams's *Linden Lea* and Quilter's *Love's philosophy* given heartfelt performances. Even this singer rarely sang with more beauty than here.

RAVEL: *Shéhérazade* (with New Philh. O, Barbirolli). CHAUSSON: *Poème de l'amour et de la mer*. DUPARC: *Phidylé; La vie antérieure; Le manoir de Rosamonde; Au pays où se fait la guerre; L'invitation au voyage* (all with LSO, Previn). SCHUMANN: *Frauenliebe und Leben* (with Barenboim). BRAHMS: *Vier ernste Gesänge, Op. 121* (with Previn); *2 Lieder, with viola, Op. 91* (with Aronowitz, Previn); *4 Duets, Op. 28* (with Fischer-Dieskau, Barenboim).
(B) *** EMI Double Fforte CZS5 68667-2 (2) [CDFB 68667].

Dame Janet Baker was always at her finest in French music, and with her 1967 performance of *Shéhérazade* she inspired Barbirolli to one of his most glowing performances in this atmospherically scored music; her range of tone and her natural sympathy for the French language make for heartwarming singing which has a natural intensity. The account of Chausson's *Poème de l'amour et de la mer* is comparably glorious and heartfelt, both radiant and searching, so that this picture of love in two aspects, first emergent, then past, has a sharpness of focus often denied it; in this she is superbly supported by Previn and the LSO. Their partnership is hardly less persuasive in the five Duparc *mélodies* which the composer orchestrated himself – each a jewelled miniature of breathtaking beauty, with the extra richness and colour of the orchestral accompaniment adding to the depth and intensity of the exceptionally sensitive word-settings, especially in the greatest of them all, *Phidylé*.

It was Schumann's *Frauenliebe und Leben* that helped to establish Baker's early reputation, and she returned to this favourite cycle in early maturity with renewed freshness in the light of deeper experience. Where on her Saga record (now deleted) she transposed most of the earlier songs down a full tone, the later version keeps them in the original keys. Then by contrast it is the later songs which she transposes, reserving her warmer tones for those expressions of motherhood. The wonder, the inwardness, are even more intense, while the final song in some ways brings the most remarkable performance of all ('Now you have hurt me'), not at all a conventional expression of mourning. With Barenboim an endlessly imaginative – if sometimes reticent – accompanist, this is another classic example of Baker's art.

The Brahms Lieder were the last to be recorded, in 1977, and the gravity and nobility of her singing in the *Four Serious Songs* underline the weight of the biblical words while presenting them with a far wider and more beautiful range of tone-colour than is common. André Previn's piano is placed rather backwardly, but his rhythmic control provides fine support, and in the two viola songs, which are ravishingly sung and played, these artists are partnered by the late Cecil Aronowitz, making his last appearance on record.

To cap the recital come the four varied duets of Op. 28, in which Baker is joined by Dietrich Fischer-Dieskau, recorded at a live recital at London's Queen Elizabeth Hall in 1969. The vivacious closing *Der Jäger und sein Liebchen* makes a spiritedly vivacious coda to a collection which could hardly be bettered. Even if the presentation here omits texts and translations, this set still makes an amazing bargain.

'Italian love songs' (with ASMF, Marriner, James Tyler, lute, Nicholas Kraemer, harpsichord): GIORDANI: *Caro mio ben*. CACCINI: *Amarilli mia bella*. STRADELLA: *Ragion sempre addita*. SARRI: *Sen corre l'agnelletta*. CESTI: *Intorno all'idol mio*. LOTTI: *Pur dicesti, o bocca bella*. A. SCARLATTI: *Già il sole dal Gange; Sento ne core*. BONONCINI: *Deh più a me non v'ascondete*. DURANTE: *Danza fanciulla gentile*. CALDARA: *Sebben crudele me fai languir; Selve amiche*. PERGOLESI: *Ogni pena più spietata*. MARTINI: *Plaisir d'amore*. piccini: *O notte o dea del mistero*. PAISIELLO: *Nel cor più non mi sento*.
(B) **(*) Ph. Virtuoso 434 173-2.

A delightful collection of Italian classical arias (the original title of the CD was *'Arie amorose'*), marred only by the absence of libretti and translations. The documention is a marginal improvement on the original LP, but still inadequate when, apart from *Caro mio ben* and *Plaisir d'amore*, most of these pieces are better known to singers than the wider musical public. However, the programme is cleverly arranged to contrast expressive with sprightly music, and Baker's wide range of tonal gradation and beautiful phrasing are matched by an artless lightness of touch in the slighter numbers. The accompaniments are intimate and tasteful: there is no more fetching example than Pergolesi's *Ogni pena più spietata* with its deft bassoon obbligato (Graham Sheen) or the short closing song with harpsichord – Paisiello's *Nel cor più non mi sento*. The recording has a warm acoustic and the resonance is kind to the voice without loss of orchestral detail.

'Grandi voci': RAVEL: *3 Poèmes de Stéphane Mallarmé; Chansons madécasses*. CHAUSSON: *Chanson perpétuelle, Op. 37*. DELAGE: *4 Poèmes hindous* (all with the Melos Ensemble). Arias from: PURCELL: *Dido and Aeneas*. RAMEAU: *Hippolyte et Aricie* (both with ECO, Lewis). BACH: *Cantata, BWV 170* (with ASMF, Marriner). CAVALLI: *La Calisto* (with LPO, Leppard).
🌑 (M) *** Decca 440 413-2.

The performances of French *mélodies* included on

this record are very beautiful indeed. Chausson's extended cantilena about a deserted lover has a direct communication which Dame Janet contrasts with the subtler beauties of the Ravel songs. She shows great depth of feeling for the poetry here and an equally evocative sensitivity to the songs about India, written in 1912 by Ravel's pupil, Maurice Delage, which are by no means inferior to the songs by his more famous contemporaries. With superb, atmospheric playing by the Melos group and an outstanding 1966 (originally Oiseau-Lyre) recording, this ravishing collection must be placed among Dame Janet's most outstanding recordings. For the current reissue, more remarkable examples of her art have been generously added, not least the lovely Bach aria *Vergnügte Ruh'*, the dramatic excerpt from Cavalli's *La Calisto* in Raymond Leppard's imaginative realization, and, of course, her heartrending account of Dido's lament, *When I am laid in earth*.

'*The Legendary Dame Janet Baker*' (with various orchestras and conductors): HANDEL: *Joshua: O had I Jubal's lyre. Atalanta: Care selve. Serse: Ombra mai fù. Judas Maccabaeus: Father of Heav'n. Ariodante: Dopo notte. Rodelinda: Dove sei, amato bene?* ELGAR: *Sea pictures: Where corals lie.* GLUCK: *Orfeo ed Euridice: Che faro senza Euridice; Che puro ciel.* MARTINI: *Plaisir d'amore.* MOZART: *Così fan tutte: E amore un ladroncello; Ah, scostati! Smanie implacabili; La clemenza di Tito: Non più di fiori.* CACCINI: *Amarilli mia bella.* PURCELL: *Dido and Aeneas: When I am laid in earth.* GIORDANO: *Caro mio ben.*
*** Ph. 465 253-2 [id.].

There are a number of outstanding Baker recitals included here, at least two of which have earned Rosettes. Most of them are better documented than this, which although offered at premium price offers nothing but titles and performance details. But it cannot be said that the present 74-minute collection is not well compiled, with all the items except two dating from between 1972 and 1978 when the voice was warm and fresh and Dame Janet's interpretations had the maturity of experience. The two earlier exceptions are even more desirable, her very moving account of Purcell's *Dido's lament* from 1962, and the memorable *Where corals lie* from *Sea pictures*, recorded with Barbirolli in 1965, kindly contributed by EMI. As for the rest, the Handel arias are all gloriously sung, and the two excerpts from *Orfeo ed Euridice* are superb. It hardly needs saying that Dame Janet is a fine Mozartean, and the Italian songs are delightful, especially Giordano's *Caro mio ben.*

DUPARC: *L'invitation au voyage; Philydé.*
SCHUBERT: *Die Forelle; Ave Maria; An die Musik; An Sylvia.* R. STRAUSS: *Befreit; Morgen!*

HAYDN: *O can ye sew cushions.* BEETHOVEN: *The sweetest lad was Jamie.* DEBUSSY: *Chansons de Bilitis.* FAURE: *Notre amour; Clair de lune.* Excerpts and arias from: ELGAR: *Sea pictures; The Dream of Gerontius.* MAHLER: *Rückert Lieder.* HANDEL: *Messiah.* BERLIOZ: *La damnation de Faust; Nuits d'été.* RAVEL: *Shéhérazade.* MENDELSSOHN: *Elijah.* BACH: *Christmas oratorio; Cantata No. 161.* WAGNER: *Wesendonck Lieder.* MONTEVERDI: *L'incoronazione di Poppea.*
(BB) *** Royal Classics Vocal Double DCL 703942 (2).

Although many collectors will already have some of these items in the complete recordings from which they are taken (Elgar's *Sea pictures* with Barbirolli, for instance), this is hard to surpass as a summary of Dame Janet's achievement over a wide range of repertoire. For whether it is in French *mélodie*, Schubert and Mahler Lieder, or the glorious *He was despised* from Handel's *Messiah*, the touching *Wo unto them who forsake Him* from Mendelssohn's *Elijah*, or the sensuous delicacy and passion of Ravel's *La flûte enchantée*, the vocal richness and artistry emerge as individually as ever. The programme ends rapturously with the Angel's farewell and the closing pages of Elgar's *Gerontius*. The selection is generous and inexpensive, the transfers excellent, but no back-up documentation or texts and translations are included.

Bär, Olaf (baritone), Helmut Deutsch (piano)

'*Christmas Lieder'*: CORNELIUS: *6 Weihnachtslieder, Op. 8. Simeon; Christus der Kinderfreud; Christkind.* HUMPERDINCK: *Der Stern von Bethlehem; Altdeutsches Weihnachtslied; Das Licht der Welt; Christkindleins Wiegenlied; Weihnachten.* Richard TRUNK: *7 Christmas Lieder, Op. 71.* Joseph HAAS: *Krippen-lieder (6 Songs of the Crib), Op. 49.* REGER: *Morgengesang; Uns ist geboren ein Kindelein; Christkindleins Wiegenlied; Maria am Rosenstrauch; Ehre sei Gott in der Höhe!*
✿ *** EMI Dig. CDC5 56204-2 [id.].

Olaf Bär has never made a finer or more rewarding record than this superb collection of German Christmas songs, introducing two unfamiliar composers among the more famous names. Peter Cornelius was born on Christmas Eve so perhaps it is not surprising that his set of *Weihnachtslieder* so readily captures the seasonal mood with such spontaneity, while Humperdinck's Christmas settings have all the character and charm one would expect from the composer of *Hänsel und Gretel*.

The delightful contribution from Richard Trunk is one of the two surprises here. Trunk's remarkable feeling for words and easy melodic lyricism are very much in the mainstream of German Lieder and, even if the style of the music is more eclectic, its invention is engagingly individual. The highlight is the masterly *Idyll*, picturing Mary beneath a lime tree rocking her son to sleep with four angels on guard overhead. The setting is magically evocative and should be far better known. The other unfamiliar name is that of Joseph Haas. His strophic songs bring a romantic melodic style which also features a strong folk element, and Haas winningly favours a repeated refrain at the end of each verse of all six examples included here.

Max Reger's contribution sustains a more serious mood, but it is lightened by the easy spontaneity of Olaf Bär's singing and his consistent variety of colour and dynamic. Indeed, throughout he gives inspired performances, relishing the countless subtleties in the marriage of text and vocal line, while Helmut Deutsch's accompaniments are equally imaginative. This is by no means just a seasonal collection, but one to be enjoyed throughout the year. The Abbey Road recording is completely natural – very much in the demonstration bracket.

achingly vulnerable portrayal of the betrayed Dido is predictable, but her account of Diana's *Ardo, sospiro e piango* from Cavalli's *La Calisto* is hardly less moving. On a lighter note comes Teresa Berganza's deliciously coquettish *Stizzoso, mio stizzoso* from Pergolesi's *La serva padrona*. Richard Bonynge introduces the Handelian sequence with the *March and Battle* from *Rinaldo* which is more familiar as 'Let us take the road' in *The Beggar's Opera*, and then Bernadette Greevy richly reminds us that Almirena's *Lascia ch'io pianga* is as noble a melody as Handel ever wrote (undecorated, but none the worse for that).

She is followed by Marilyn Horne's astounding demonstration of vocal bravura as she leaps from one register to another and back again in *Vivi, tiranno* from *Rodelinda*. The art of Joan Sutherland is well represented (with all the recordings coming from the early 1960s, when the voice was at its sweetest) and it is she who ends the programme with sparkling virtuosity in *Tornami a vagheggiar*. The recording throughout is brilliant and atmospheric in Decca's best manner; the disc is handsomely packaged and full translations are included. Not to be missed!

Baroque opera: 'Treasures of baroque opera'

'Treasures of baroque opera': MONTEVERDI: *L'Orfeo: Toccata* (New London Consort, Pickett); *Prologo: Ritornello . . . Dal mio Permesso amato* (Catherine Bott). ARNE: *Rosamond: Rise, glory, rise* (Emma Kirkby). *Artaxerxes: The soldier tir'd.* PICCINI: *La buona figliuola: Furia di donna.* HANDEL: *Alcina: Tornami a vagheggiar* (Dame Joan Sutherland). *Rinaldo: March and Battle* (ECO, Bonynge); *Armida dispietatat! . . . Lascia ch'io pianga* (Bernadette Greevy). *Rodelinda: Vivi, tiranno* (Marilyn Horne). *Atalanta: Care selve* (Luciano Pavarotti). PURCELL: *Dido and Aeneas: Dido's lament.* CAVALLI: *La Calisto: Ardo, sospiro e piango* (Dame Janet Baker). RAMEAU: *Hippolyte et Aricie: Puisque Pluton est inflexible* (John Shirley-Quirk). *Le Temple de la gloire: Overture* (ECO, Raymond Leppard). *Les indes galantes: Soleil on a détruit tes superbes asiles* (Gérard Souzay). PERGOLESI: *La serva padrona: stizzoso, mio stizzoso* (Teresa Berganza). ✪ (M) *** Decca Analogue/Dig. 458 217-2 [id.].

This is truly a treasure-chest – one of the finest collections of baroque arias ever assembled on disc, and certainly the most generous, with sixteen excerpts, all performed superbly. The overall standard is astonishingly high, with almost every item a plum. After Philip Pickett's dramatic opening *Toccata*, Catherine Bott is in glorious voice as La Musica in *Orfeo* and Emma Kirkby's Arne is equally fresh. The inclusion of Dame Janet Baker's

Bartoli, Cecilia (mezzo-soprano)

Italian songs (with András Schiff): BEETHOVEN: *Ecco quel fiero istante!; Che fa il mio bene?* (2 versions); *T'intendo, si, mio cor; Dimmi, ben mio; In questa tomba oscura.* MOZART: *Ridente la calma.* HAYDN: *Arianna a Naxos.* SCHUBERT: *Vedi quanto adoro ancora ingrato!; Io vuo'cantar di Cadmo; La pastorella; Non t'accostar all'urna; Guarda, che bianca luna; Se dall'Etra; Da quel sembiante appresi; Mio ben ricordati; Pensa, che questo istante; Mi batte 'l cor!*
*** Decca Dig. 440 297-2 [id.].

Bartoli and Schiff make a magical partnership, each challenging the other in imagination. These seventeen Italian songs and one cantata by the great Viennese masters make a fascinating collection, not just Haydn and Mozart but Beethoven and Schubert as well. Beethoven's darkly intense *In questa tomba oscura* is well enough known but, as sung by Bartoli, with András Schiff adding sparkle, the lighter songs are just as magnetic, with Beethoven showing his versatility in two astonishingly contrasted settings of the same love-poem.

'A Portrait': Arias from: MOZART: *La clemenza di Tito; Così fan tutte; Le nozze di Figaro; Don Giovanni.* Concert aria: *Ch'io mi scordi di te?* ROSSINI: *Semiramide; Maometto II; La Cenerentola.* Songs: *Bella crudèle.* PARISOTTI: *Se tu m'ami.* GIORDANO: *Caro mio ben.* CACCINI: *Amarilli.* SCHUBERT: *La pastorella; Metastasio: Vedi quanto adoro ancora ingrato!*

*** Decca Dig. 448 300-2 [id.].

Cecilia Bartoli's portrait, covering a recording period from 1991 to 1995, could hardly be more enticing. Every lyrical aria displays her truly lovely voice with astonishing consistency. The very opening *Parto, parto, ma tu ben mio* from *La clemenza di Tito* could hardly be more inviting, with its engaging basset clarinet obbligato from Lesley Schatzberger, and *Come scoglio* shows her dramatic and vocal range to powerful and moving effect.

There is a delicious combination of charm and sparkle in Despina's *In uomini, in soldate* (wonderfully crisp trills echoing the orchestral violins), while Cherubino's *Voi che sapete* brings delightful innocence, and Susanna's *Deh vieni* the sunny joy of loving anticipation which ravishes the ear, especially at the leisurely close. The simpler classical songs bring contrast, with the silken line of *Caro mio ben* followed by the very touching and gloriously sung *Amarilli* of Caccini.

Finally Rossini, where Bartoli is unsurpassed among the present generation of mezzos (and measures up impressively to famous names from the past). After the beautifully spun line of the aria from *Maometto II* (with choral support) she captivates with a fizzing, crisply articulated and joyfully humorous *Non più mesta*. Top-class Decca recording throughout ensures the listener's pleasure and this hugely enjoyable collection would have earned a Rosette but for the totally inadequate documentation, with no translations – unacceptable in a premium-priced record.

'*Chant d'amour*' (with Myung-Whun Chung, piano): BIZET: Mélodies: *Adieux de l'hôtesse arabe; Chant d'amour; La coccinelle; Ouvre ton coeur; Tarantelle.* BERLIOZ: *La Mort d'Ophélie; Zaïde.* DELIBES: *Les filles de Cadiz.* VIARDOT: *Les filles de Cadiz; Hai luli!; Havanaise.* RAVEL: *4 Chansons populaires; 2 Mélodies Hébraïques; Tripatos; Vocalise-etude en forme de Habanera.*
*** Decca Dig. 452 667-2 [id.].

This is a delectable disc, a winning collection of French songs, many of them unexpected, which inspire Bartoli to the most seductive singing. One would have predicted that Delibes's sparkling setting of Musset's poem *Les filles de Cadiz* would draw out Carmen-like fire from her, but here that charming song is set alongside the setting of the same poem made by the great prima donna Pauline Viardot, giving a refreshingly different view. The other Viardot items too come as a delightful surprise, as do the Bizet songs, including *La coccinelle*, 'The Ladybird', a sparkling waltz, superbly characterized here. The better-known Berlioz and Ravel songs are beautifully done too, with Myung-Whun Chung revealing himself just as inspired in the role of pianist as of conductor. Excellent sound.

'*Live from Italy*' (with Jean-Yves Thibaudet

(piano), Sonatori de la gioiosa marca): BELLINI: *Malinconia ninfa gentile; Ma rendi pur contento.* BERLIOZ: *Zaïde.* BIZET: *Carmen: Près des ramparts de Séville.* CACCINI: *Al fonte al prato; Tu ch'hai le penne; Amarilli mia bella.* DONIZETTI: *La conocchia; Me voglio fa'na casa.* GIORDANI: *Caro mio ben.* HANDEL: *Il Trionfo del Tempo e del Disinganno: Lascia la spina.* MONTSALVATGE: *Canto negro.* MOZART: *Le nozze di Figaro: Voi che sapete. Concert aria: Oiseaux, si tous les ans.* ROSSINI: *Mi Lagnerò tacendo, Book I/2, 3 & 4. L'orpheline du Tyrol. Zelmira: Riedi al soglio. Canzonetta spagnuola.* SCHUBERT: *La pastorella al Prato.* VIARDOT: *Havanaise; Hai luli!* VIVALDI: *Griselda: Agitata da due venti.*
*** Decca Dig. 455 981-2 [id.].

Recorded live at the Teatro Olimpico in Vicenza, this recital vividly conveys the high-powered magnetism of Cecilia Bartoli. Encouraged by the rapturous audience, Bartoli may in some items go over the top in her individual characterization, but magic is there from first to last. The opening group of baroque items comes with string accompaniment, but then Thibaudet at the piano takes over as the most sympathetic partner, whether in the characterful little Schubert song, *La pastorella*, the tango-like *Havanaise* of Pauline Viardot or Berlioz's *Zaïde*, with Bartoli herself playing castanets. It is fascinating to have three widely contrasted settings by Rossini of the same Metastasio text, and crowning the whole recital – before a sparkling sequence of encores – is the longest item, a spectacular aria from Rossini's *Zelmira* with a breathtaking display of coloratura at the end. A fun disc, atmospherically recorded.

Bartoli, Cecilia (mezzo-soprano), Bryn Terfel (baritone)

'*Cecilia and Bryn*': Duets (with Santa Cecilia National Academy Orchestra, Myung-Whun Chung) from: MOZART: *Le nozze di Figaro; Così fan tutte; Don Giovanni; Die Zauberflöte.* ROSSINI: *Il barbiere di Siviglia; L'Italiana in Algeri.* DONIZETTI: *L'elisir d'amore.*
*** Decca Dig. 458 928-2 [id.].

The friendly title, '*Cecilia and Bryn*', though suggesting a crossover disc, is well justified when in each of these operatic duets these two charismatic singers are so characterful in their performances, both musically and dramatically. At times they come near to overacting but, with brilliant support from Chung and the orchestra, that goes with the virtuoso flair. Warm, full sound, though Bartoli is made to sound breathy.

Battle, Kathleen (soprano), Plácido Domingo (tenor)

'Battle and Domingo live' (with Metropolitan Opera O, Levine): Arias & duets from: VERDI: *La Traviata.* DONIZETTI: *Don Pasquale; Lucia di Lammermoor; L'elisir d'amore.* GOUNOD: *Roméo et Juliette.* MOZART: *Don Giovanni.* LEHAR: *Die lustige Witwe.* Overtures to: VERDI: *La forza del destino.* ROSSINI: *L'Italiana in Algeri.*
(M) *** DG (IMS) Dig. 445 552-2 [id.].

These gala occasions can often be very stimulating for the audience, but only very occasionally do they produce an outstanding record. The present recital is surely the exception that proves the rule. From Levine's vibrant *La forza del destino overture* onwards, the 'live' communication of these performances comes across readily. The *La Traviata* duet has great charm, with Domingo obviously matching his voice to the smaller but lovely sound which Battle naturally commands. The lesser-known duet from *Romeo and Juliet* is hardly less delightful, and *Là ci darem la mano* is engagingly relaxed and elegant: who wouldn't be seduced by this Don? No complaints about the solo arias either, but the unforgettable charmer is the final ravishing Waltz duet from *The Merry widow* which is (quite rightly) sung in English. The ringing final cadence is breathtaking. Few hours of operatic excerpts are as magical as this one, and the recording is splendid.

Berganza, Teresa (mezzo-soprano)

'Canciones españolas' (with Narciso Yepes, guitar, Félix Lavilla, piano): SABIO: *Rosa das rosas; Santa Maria.* FUENLLANA: *Pérdida de Antequera.* ANON.: *Dindirindin; Nuaves te traygo, carillo; Los hombres con gran plazer.* MUDARRA: *Triste estava el rey David; Si me llaman a mí; Claros y frescos rios; Ysabel, perdiste la tu faxa.* TORRE: *Dime, triste corazón; Pámpano verde.* VALDERRABANO: *De dónde venis, amore?* MILAN: *Toda mi vida os amé; Aquel caballero, madre.* TRIANA: *Dinos, madre del donsel.* ENCINA: *Romerico.* VAZQUEZ: *Vos me matastes; En la fuente del rosel.* NARVAEZ: *Con qué la lavaré?* ANCHIETA: *Con amores, la mi madre.* ESTEVE: *Alma sintamos.* GRANADOS: *La maja dolorosa: Oh, muerte cruel!; Ay, majo de mi vida!; De aquel majo amante. El majo discreto; El tra la lá y el punteado; El majo timido.* GURIDI: *Canciones castellanas: Llámale con el pañuelo; No quiero tus avellanas; Cómo quieres que adivine!* FALLA: *7 Canciones populares españolas.* LORCA: *13 Canciones españolas antiguas.* TURINA: *Saeta en forma de Salve a la Virgen de la Esperanza; Canto a Sevilla: El fantasma. Poema en forma de canciones: Cantares.* MONTSALVATGE: *5 Canciones negras.*
(M) *** DG (IMS) 435 848-2 (2).

This collection dates from the mid-1970s when Berganza was at her peak, the voice fresh, her artistry mature. In essence she provides here a history of Spanish song, opening with two pieces taken from the *Cantigas de Santa Maria*, dating from the thirteenth century, and moving on through Renaissance repertory and, with only one song from the eighteenth century, to the nineteenth and twentieth, traditional settings by Lorca, Falla's *7 Spanish popular songs* and the engaging *Canciones negras* of Montsalvatge. The collaboration with Narciso Yepes seems ideal, for he is an inspirational artist, while her husband, Félix Lavilla, provides the later piano accompaniments. This is not a specialist recital: the music communicates readily in the most direct way, and excellent notes and translations are provided. The balance is very natural and the CD transfers are immaculately managed. This is repertoire one first associates with Victoria de los Angeles, but Berganza makes it her own and there are not many more attractive Spanish song-recitals than this.

Bergonzi, Carlo (tenor)

Italian songs (with John Wustman, piano): BELLINI: *Vaga luna che inargenti.* VERDI: *Stornello.* DENZA: *Se . . .; Occhi fi fata.* DONIZETTI: *Me voglio fa 'na casa.* DONAUDY: *O del mio amato ben; Vaghissima sembianza.* TITIRINDELLI: *O primavera!* ROSSINI: *La Promessa; La danza.* MASCAGNI; *Serenata.* TOSTI: *Tormento!; L'lba sepera dalla luce l'ombra; Ideale.* BUZZI-PECCIA: *Lolita.* DE CURTIS: *Non ti scordar di me.* PUCCINI: *Edgar: Orgia, chimera dall'occhio vitreo* (with NY Opera Orchestra, Eve Queler).
(M) *(*) Sony SMK 60785 [id.].

This is repertoire with which the golden-voiced Gigli could continually ravish the ear and make one think every number a gem. Bergonzi was still in good voice when he made these recordings in 1977 (and he has a splendid accompanist in John Wustman), but as the opening Bellini song demonstrates, his phrasing is unmagical. He is better in the lighter, livelier songs like Verdi's *Stornello*, or the more ardent popular songs by De Curtis and Denza, and he does very well by Tosti, with whom he readily identifies. But when he begins the closing aria from Puccini's *Edgar*, he is on home ground and the singing really takes hold of the listener.

'Grandi voci': Arias from: VERDI: *Aida; Luisa Miller; La forza del destino; Il Trovatore; Un ballo in maschera; Don Carlos; La Traviata.* MEYERBEER: *L'Africana.* GIORDANO: *Andrea*

Chénier. CILEA: *Adriana Lecouvreur.* PUCCINI: *Tosca; Manon Lescaut; La Bohème.* PONCHIELLI: *La Gioconda.*

(M) **(*) Decca 440 417-2 [id.].

This recital, consisting mainly of Bergonzi's early stereo recordings, a dozen arias recorded with the Orchestra of the Santa Cecilia Academy, Rome, under Gavaazeni in 1957, shows him on consistently peak form. He does not attempt the rare pianissimo at the end of *Celeste Aida*; but here among Italian tenors is a thinking musical artist who never resorts to vulgarity. The lovely account of *Che gelida manina* (with Serafin) comes from two years later. The early stereo has transferred well and retains a bloom on the voice. The other recordings also derive from sets: *La Traviata* (1962), *Un ballo* (1960–61), *Don Carlos* (1965), all with Solti, while the stirring *Cielo e mar* from *La Gioconda* (1967) shows that Bergonzi's tone retained its quality. These added items help to make up a generous playing time of 71 minutes, besides adding variety to what was originally essentially a collection of favourites. Everything sounds fresh.

Bernac, Pierre (baritone)

'The essential Pierre Bernac' (with Francis Poulenc, Gerald Moore, Graham Johnson, piano): GOUNOD: *Sérénade; Ce que je suis sans toi; Au rossignol. 6 Mélodies* (cycle). DUPARC: *Soupir; L'invitation au voyage.* CHABRIER: *L'île heureuse.* CHAUSSON: *Le Colibri.* ROUSSEL: *Le Jardin Mouillé; Coeur en Péril.* SCHUMANN: *Dein Angesicht. Dichterliebe* (cycle), *Op. 48.* LISZT: *Freudvoll und Leidvoll; Es muss ein Wunderbares; Nimm einen Strahl der Sonne.* MILHAUD: *La Tourterelle.* VELLONES: *A mon fils.* BEYDTS: *La lyre et les amours* (cycle). FAURE: *Après un rêve; Le secret; Aurore; Prison; Soir; Jardin nocturne.* DEBUSSY: *3 Chansons de France. Fêtes galantes: Colloque sentimental. 3 Ballades de François Villon.* SATIE: *Mélodies Nos. 1 & 3.* RAVEL: *Don Quichotte à Dulcinée* (cycle). POULENC: *2 Chansons gailliards; Métamorphoses; Le bestiaire* (cycles). *2 Mélodies de Guillaume Apollinaire: Montparnasse. 2 Poèmes de Guillaume Apollinaire: Dans le jardin d'Anna. 2 Poèmes de Louis Aragon* (with O, Louis Beydts); *Telle jour telle nuit* (cycle). *Le Travail du peintre* (cycle). *L'Histoire de Babar, le petite éléphant.*

(***) Testament mono SBT 3161 (3) [id.].

When the duo of Pierre Bernac and Francis Poulenc provided a French equivalent of Pears and Britten, it is especially valuable to have this distinctive and often magical collection of recordings, made between 1936 and 1958. Most were recorded for EMI, notably those made in London just after the

end of the Second World War. But the core of the collection, the late recordings made in 1957–8, come from BBC sources, recorded from broadcast concerts.

The distinctive voice, with its flicker of vibrato, was not quite so evenly produced as earlier, but the artistry remains magical. As a supplement comes a broadcast interview, with Bernac questioned by Graham Johnson, and finally comes a performance of Poulenc's *Babar the elephant* with Johnson at the piano and Bernac a magnetic narrator. On the first disc as a sample of Bernac's Lieder-singing comes an EMI recording with Gerald Moore of Schumann's *Dichterliebe*, while as the perfect introduction there is Bernac's uniquely charming account with Poulenc of Gounod's *Sérénade*. Most moving of all are their readings of such deeper Poulenc songs as the first of the two *Poèmes de Louis Aragon*, 'C', inspired by the Nazi occupation of France.

Björling, Jussi (tenor)

'Great opera arias' (with RCA Victor Orchestra, Robert Shaw Chorale, Cellini or Rome Opera Orchestra, Perlea or Leinsdorf or (i) Frederick Schauwecker (piano)): MEYERBEER: *L'Africana: O paradiso.* VERDI: *Aida:* excerpts. *Il Trovatore:* excerpts (with Zinka Milanov, Fedora Barbieri, Leonard Warren). *Rigoletto:* excerpts (with Roberta Peters, Robert Merrill, Anna Maria Rota). PUCCINI: *La Bohème: Che gelida manina. Tosca: E lucevan le stelle; Amaro sol per te* (with Milanov). *Manon Lescaut: Ah! Manon mi tradisce* (with Licia Albanese); *No! no! pazzo son!* (with Enrico Campo). MASCAGNI: *Cavalleria rusticana:* excerpts (with Milanov). (i) BIZET: *Carmen: Flower song.* (i) MOZART: *Don Giovanni: Il mio tesoro.* (i) MASSENET: *Manon: Instant charmant; En fermant les yeux.* (i) GIORDANO: *Fedora: Amor ti vieta.* (i) PUCCINI: *Turandot: Nessun dorma.*

(M) *** RCA Gold Seal mono/stereo 09026 68429-2 [id.].

If you want a single disc to represent Jussi Björling, this is the one to have. The recordings date from between 1951 and 1959, the last decade of his life, when the voice was still astonishingly fresh. Most of the excerpts come from distinguished complete recordings, when the great tenor was partnered by artists of the calibre of Zinka Milanov and Licia Albanese (the duets from *Tosca* and *Manon Lescaut* are electrifying and the excerpts from *Aida, Il Trovatore* and *Cavalleria rusticana* are hardly less thrilling). The recordings, splendidly transferred, are all of high quality and show the great tenor in the very best light: even the 1958 live recital, with just a piano accompaniment, is treasurable for its famous arias from *Carmen* and *Manon*, and the closing, passionate *Nessun dorma*.

Operatic recital: Arias from: PONCHIELLI: *La Gioconda.* PUCCINI: *La Fanciulla del West; Manon Lescaut.* GIORDANO: *Fedora.* CILEA: *L'Arlesiana.* VERDI: *Un ballo in maschera; Requiem.* MASCAGNI: *Cavalleria rusticana* (with Tebaldi). LEHAR: *Das Land des Lächelns.* (M) *** Decca 443 930-2.

Jussi Björling provides here a flow of headily beautiful, finely focused tenor tone. These may not be the most characterful renderings of each aria, but they are all among the most compellingly musical. The recordings are excellent for their period (1959–60). The Lehár was the last solo recording he made before he died in 1960. The transfers to CD are admirably lively and present.

Bocelli, Andrea (tenor)

Operatic arias (with Maggio Musicale Fiorentino O, Gianandrea Noseda): PUCCINI: *La Bohème, Tosca, Madam Butterfly.* LEONCAVALLO: *La Bohème.* CILEA: *Andriana Lecouvreur.* BELLINI: *I puritani.* R. STRAUSS: *Der Rosenkavalier,* Etc. **(*) Ph. Dig. 462 033-2.

'Viaggio Italiano' (with Academy of Choir Art, Moscow RSO, Vladimir Fedoseyev): Arias from: PUCCINI: *Turandot.* CILEA: *L'Arlesiana.* VERDI: *Macbeth; Rigoletto.* DONIZETTI: *L'elisir d'amore.* Songs: FRANCK: *Panis angelicus.* SCHUBERT: *Ave Maria.* DI CAPUA: *O sole mio; L' te vurria vasà.* CARDILLO: *Core n'grato.* MARIO: *Santa Lucia luntana.* DE CURTIS: *Tu'ca nun chiagne!* GAMBARDELLA: *Marinarello.* TAGLIAFERRI: *Piscatore'e pusilleco.* TRAD.: *Adeste fidelis.* Spoken message. **(*) Ph. Dig. 462 196-2 [id.].

Trumpeted as one of today's greatest tenors, having emerged from a pop background, Andrea Bocelli on the first disc here shows his paces in a formidable collection of arias including even the tenor's aria from *Der Rosenkavalier*. Bocelli's great natural gift is a tenor of very distinctive timbre, not conventionally rounded in a Pavarotti-like way but above all virile with a baritonal tinge, used over a wide tonal range with not a suspicion of strain. He soars readily to a top C or even a C sharp, as in *A te o cara* from Bellini's *I Puritani*.

There is fair evidence too of lessons well learnt. Werther's *Pourquoi me reveiller* – among the most testing of French arias – inspires Bocelli to produce very refined mezza voce, beautifully sustained, and the *Flower song* from *Carmen* too is subtler than most. Yet there is a sequence of Puccini arias – the two from *Tosca*, one from *Butterfly* – which are disappointingly slow and heavy, though *Che gelida manina* is nicely detailed. And though in the nine

top Cs of Tonio's *Pour ton âme* from *La fille du régiment* – the final rip-roaring item here – he cannot quite match the flamboyance of Pavarotti, there are all too few recording tenors who could do it so confidently, or even at all.

The second disc was recorded in Moscow in 1994, and offers no vocal disappointments, with the darker timbre particularly striking in the arias from *Macbeth* and notably *Una furtiva lagrima* from *L'elisir d'amore*, which is strikingly different from a honeyed Gigli-like account. Franck's *Panis angelicus* and Schubert's *Ave Maria* are not sentimentalized. But not everyone will welcome the fact that half the recital is taken up with Neapolitan popular songs which are all rather similar in their ardent declarations. Bocelli sings them persuasively and the recital ends with a passionate 'live' recording of *Adeste fidelis*, where the choral contribution is made very spectacular by the resonance.

Bonney, Barbara (soprano)

'Diamonds in the snow' (with Antonio Pappano, piano): GRIEG: *Spring; I love you; With a water-lily; The princess; A swan; From Monte Pincio; 6 Lieder, Op. 48; Peer Gynt: Solveig's song.* SIBELIUS: *The diamond in the snow; Lost in the forest; Sigh, rushes, sigh; Was it a dream?; The girl came home from meeting her lover.* STENHAMMAR: *The girl came home from meeting her lover; Adagio; Sweden; Guiding spirit; In the forest.* ALFVEN: *Take my heart; The forest sleeps.* SJOBERG: *Music.* *** Decca Dig. 466 762-2 [id.].

Barbara Bonney, with her warm understanding of Scandinavia and its music, offers the most seductive choice of songs in this inspired collection. The Grieg group includes most of the well-known favourites, but with Antonio Pappano proving just as understanding a piano accompanist as he is a conductor, they all emerge fresh and new, animated and strongly characterized. There is a sensuousness and passion behind the love songs in particular, with free rubato sounding spontaneous, never studied. The Sibelius set brings ravishing tonal contrasts too, and it is fascinating to hear the settings of the same Swedish poem, first by Sibelius, then more simply but with warm feeling by Stenhammar. More than anything the disc disproves the idea of coldness in the Nordic make-up. Warm, full sound with Bonney's lovely voice glowingly caught.

Bostridge, Ian (tenor), Julian Drake (piano)

'The English Songbook': STANFORD: *La belle dame sans merci.* GURNEY: *Sleep; I will go with my father a-ploughing.* DUNHILL: *The cloths of*

heaven. William Denis BROWN: *To Gratiana dancing and singing.* SOMERVELL: *To Lucasta, on going to the wars.* DELIUS: *Twilight fancies.* GERMAN: *Orpheus with his lute.* WARLOCK: *Jillian of Berry; Cradle song.* FINZI: *The dance continued (Regret not me); Since we loved.* VAUGHAN WILLIAMS: *Linden Lea; Silent noon.* Irish air, arr. STANFORD: *My love's an arbutus.* Irish tune, arr. BRITTEN: *The Salley Gardens.* TRAD./ANON.: *The death of Queen Jane; The little turtle dove.* PARRY: *No longer mourne for me.* WARLOCK: *Rest, sweet nymphs.* QUILTER: *Come away death; Now sleeps the crimson petal.* grainger: *Bold William Taylor; Brigg Fair.*
*** EMI Dig. CDC5 56830-2 [id.].

Ian Bostridge with his clear, honeyed tone is in his element in this collection of twenty-four English songs, almost all of them neglected. He and his keenly responsive accompanist, Julius Drake, have made an imaginative, far from predictable choice of items, with only the two Vaughan Williams songs, *Linden Lea* and *Silent noon,* qualifying as popular favourites. It is good to find the collection delving as far back as Parry and Stanford (the first and most ambitious of the songs, memorably setting Keats's *La belle dame sans merci*), and including composers like Edward German, generally celebrated for his light music. It is a reflection on the singer's personality too that there is a high proportion of thoughtful, introspective songs, most sensitively matched by Drake in his accompaniments. One hopes that EMI's inclusion of French and German translations alongside the English texts will encourage new discovery outside Britain of a genre seriously underappreciated, one which directly reflects the magic of English lyric poetry.

Bott, Catherine (soprano), New London Consort, Philip Pickett

'Music from the time of Columbus': VERARDI: *Viva El Gran Re Don Fernando.* ANON.: *A los Maytines era; Propinan de Melyor; Como no le andare yo; Nina y viña; Calabaza, no sé, buen amor; Perdi la mi rueca; Al alva venid buen amigo; Dale si la das.* URREDA: *Muy triste.* J. PONCE: *Como esta sola mi vida.* ANCHIETA: *Con amores mi madre.* ENCINA: *Triste españa; Mortal tristura; Mas vale trocar; Ay triste que vengo; Quedate carillo.* MEDINA: *No ay plazer en esta vida.* DE LA TORRE: *Danza alta.* DE MONDEJAR: *Un solo fin des mis males.*
*** Linn Dig. CKD 007 [id.].

The songs offered here are broadly divided into two groups, the romantic ballads, usually of a melancholy disposition (the word 'triste' occurs frequently), and the usually jollier *villancio* form, which brings a repeated refrain. Catherine Bott is

the most delightful soloist, singing freshly and simply, often with a ravishing tone, and there is much to give pleasure. In the anonymous songs it is fascinating to discover just how international medieval folk music was, for more than once the listener is reminded of the Auvergne songs collected later in France by Canteloube. The two most delightful items are saved until the end, first a truly beautiful love song, *Al alva venid buen amigo* ('Come at dawn my friend'), in which a young woman reflects on her lover's visits, and then lets her thoughts change to consider the birth from the Virgin Mary of 'him who made the world'. In complete contrast is the robust and charmingly naughty villancio, *Dale si la das* ('Come on, wench of Carasa'). The recording is first class, naturally balanced in a pleasing acoustic, and full documentation is provided.

Bowman, James (counter-tenor)

'The James Bowman collection' (with The King's Consort, Robert King): BACH: *Erbarme dich; Stirb in mir.* HANDEL: *Almighty power; Crueltà nè lontananza; Impious mortal; Tune your harps; Welcome as the dawn of day; Thou shalt bring them in; Or la tromba; Eternal source of light.* PURCELL: *Britain, thou now art great; O solitude; By beauteous softness mixed; An Evening hymn; On the brow of Richmond Hill; Vouchsafe, O Lord.* ANON.: *Come tread the paths.* GABRIELI: *O magnum mysterium.* FORD: *Since I saw your face.* F COUPERIN: *Jerusalem, convertere.*
(B) *** Hyperion Dig. KING 3 [(M) id.].

Apart from the opening Bach item, which has not previously been published and which is not entirely flattering, this admirable 78-minute sampler will delight fans of James Bowman as it shows his art and fine vocal control over a wide range of repertoire at which he excelled. Robert King and his Consort provide admirable support.

Caballé, Montserrat (soprano)

'Diva': Arias from: PUCCINI: *Madama Butterfly; Tosca; Manon Lescaut; La Bohème; Turandot; La Rondine.* ROSSINI: *William Tell.* BELLINI: *Il Pirata; I Puritani.* VERDI: *Giovanna d'Arco; Macbeth; Don Carlos; Aida.* BOITO: *Mefistofele.* MASCAGNI: *Cavalleria rusticana.*
(M) *** EMI CDM5 65575-2 [id.].

This fine compilation is framed by items from Caballé's 1970 Puccini recital in which she impersonates Mimì, Tosca and Butterfly, singing more impressively than she characterizes. Otherwise these are items from complete sets made between 1970 (Giulini's *Don Carlos*) and 1980 (Muti's *I Puritani*). The items are not always the obvious choices from each opera but from first to last they demonstrate the consistent beauty of her singing at that period, responding to a wide range of conductors.

Arias from: PUCCINI: *La Bohème; Madama Butterfly; Tosca; Gianni Schicchi; Le Villi.* BELLINI: *Il Pirata; I Puritani.* VERDI: *Aida; La forza del destino; Giovanna d'Arco; Macbeth.* BOITO: *Mefistofele.* ROSSINI: *Guillaume Tell.* MEYERBEER: *Les Huguenots* (with MONTSALVATGE: *Canción.* R. STRAUSS: *Zueignung; Ruhe, meine Seele*).
(BB) *** Royal Classics Vocal Double DCL 703962 (2).

This two-disc collection expands the programme offered in Caballé's single-disc EMI recital above, including as it does her glorious Puccini recordings, made when the voice was at its freshest. The cost is rather less and a pair of highly desirable Strauss songs are thrown in for good measure. There are no texts, but the transfers are excellent and at its very low cost this remains a prime choice among the various Caballé recitals on offer.

'Great voice': Excerpts from: GOUNOD: *Faust; Roméo et Juliette.* MEYERBEER: *Les Huguenots.* CHARPENTIER: *Louise.* BIZET: *Carmen.* PUCCINI: *Manon Lescaut* (with Domingo). R. STRAUSS: *Salome* (closing scene).
(B) ** DG 431 103-2 [(M) id. import].

Most of the content of Caballé's contribution to DG's 'Grosse Stimmen' series is drawn from a 1971 recital of French arias. Although the quality of the voice is in no doubt, this was not in fact one of this artist's more distinctive recitals. The vocal line is sometimes not perfectly judged (her earlier, RCA recording of Charpentier's *Depuis le jour* was finer; here the aria's key moments are managed confidently but the performance as a whole is simply less beautiful). In the Gounod numbers the style is not fined down enough: the voice seems a trifle unwieldy. The Meyerbeer item is the most convincing. DG's recording is warm, with a resonant acoustic, kind to both the voice and the superb orchestral playing from the New Philharmonia under Reynald Giovaninetti. The duet from *Manon Lescaut* with Domingo (*Tu, tu amore?*) is vibrantly exciting, but the recording, made at a live performance, is somewhat less flattering. The highlight here is the final scene from *Salome*, recorded with Leonard Bernstein in 1978, although the orchestral sound could ideally be more sumptuous. But the performance is imaginatively full of contrasts, the sweet innocent girl still observable next to the bloodthirsty fiend. The disc is poorly presented, with nothing about music or artist, only titles and recording dates.

'Opera arias and duets' (with Luciano Pavarotti) from: VERDI: *Luisa Miller.* BELLINI: *Norma.*

BOITO: *Mefistofele.* PUCCINI: *Turandot.* GIORDANO: *Andrea Chénier.* PONCHIELLI: *La Gioconda.*
(M) *** Decca Dig./Analogue 458 231-2 [id.].

Although this disc centres on Caballé there are plenty of duets here and ensembles too. All the excerpts come from highly recommendable complete sets, and Pavarotti figures often and strongly. In Bellini, Giordano or Boito, and especially as Liù in *Turandot*, Caballé is often vocally ravishing, and she finds plenty of drama and power for Verdi and Ponchielli. There are at least two and sometimes three and four items from each opera, admirably chosen to make consistently involving entertainment. The presentation on this Opera Gala reissue is admirable, with full translations included.

'The ultimate collection' (with chorus and various orchestras and conductors): Arias and excerpts from: PUCCINI: *La Bohème; Suor Angelica; Tosca.* BELLINI: *Norma; La Sonnambula; Adelson e salvini.* ROSSINI: *L'assedio di Corinto; Semiramide* (with Shirley Verrett); *Armida; Stabat Mater.* GOUNOD: *Sapho.* VERDI: *Otello; Rigoletto; La Traviata* (with Carlo Bergonzi); *Il Corsaro; Il Trovatore; I vespri siciliani.* MASSENET: *Hérodiade.* DONIZETTI: *Lucrezia Borgia; Roberto Devereux; Anna Bolena.* LEONCAVALLO: *Pagliacci.* CILEA: *Adriana Lecouvreur.*
(M) *** RCA 74321 37714-2 (2) [id.].

An impressive survey recorded over three decades between 1964 and 1994 and including items from complete sets as well as solo recitals. The first disc opens with *Sì, mi chiamano Mimì*, a ravishing performance, taken from her *Bohème* with Domingo, conducted by Solti in 1974. There is fine singing too in the Act I *La Traviata* scene with Bergonzi, recorded a decade earlier, although here there is less emotional depth. The earliest recordings here were made in Barcelona, early in Caballé's career and already her commanding artistry was apparent, her ability to mould phrases imaginatively, her delight in caressing the ear with subtleties of half-tone. Desdemona's *Ave Maria* is exquisitely sung, as is Tosca's *Vissi d'arte*, but the longest item, with preliminary recitative, is the *Anna Bolena* aria *Al dolce guidami*. The two excerpts from Verdi's *Il Corsaro* (recorded in 1967) show her at her dramatic best, but the Rossini duet, with Shirley Verrett, is one of the few relative disappointments, not as sparkling as it might be. Yet taken as a whole this is a representative and rewarding portrait of a fine artist with a glorious voice.

Callas, Maria (soprano)

'La Divina I': Arias from: PUCCINI: *Madama Butterfly; La Bohème; Gianni Schicchi; Turandot; Tosca.* BIZET: *Carmen.* CATALANI: *La Wally.*

ROSSINI: *Il barbiere di Siviglia.* BELLINI: *Norma.*
SAINT-SAENS: *Samson et Dalila.* VERDI:
Rigoletto; La Traviata. GOUNOD: *Roméo et
Juliette.* MOZART: *Don Giovanni.* MASCAGNI:
Cavalleria rusticana. PONCHIELLI: *La Gioconda.*
**(*) EMI stereo/mono CDC7 54702-2 [id.].

'La Divina II': Arias from: GLUCK: *Alceste;
Orphée et Eurydice.* BIZET: *Carmen.* VERDI:
*Ernani; Aida; I vespri siciliani; La Traviata; Don
Carlos.* PUCCINI: *Manon Lescaut; La Bohème.*
CHARPENTIER: *Louise.* THOMAS: *Mignon.*
SAINT-SAENS: *Samson et Dalila.* BELLINI: *La
Sonnambula.* CILEA: *Adriana Lecouvreur.*
DONIZETTI: *Lucia di Lammermoor.*
*(*) EMI stereo/mono CDC5 55016-2 [id.].

'La Divina III': Arias and duets from: GIORDANO:
Andrea Chénier. SPONTINI: *La vestale.*
MASSENET: *Manon.* PUCCINI: *Manon Lescaut; La
Bohème* (with Giuseppe di Stefano*); Madama
Butterfly* (with Nicolai Gedda); *Turandot.* BIZET:
Carmen (with Nicolai Gedda). ROSSINI: *Il
barbiere di Siviglia* (with Tito Gobbi). DELIBES:
Lakmé. VERDI: *Aida; Il Trovatore.*
LEONCAVALLO: *Pagliacci.* MEYERBEER: *Dinorah.*
*** EMI stereo/mono CDC5 55216-2 [id.].

These three recital discs (with nearly four hours
of music) cover Callas's recording career pretty
thoroughly, although the first two are inadequately
documented, giving only the date each recording
was *published.* 'Divina III', however, provides both
the actual dates and venues of the recordings and
details of the other artists involved. Throughout the
three programmes, results are inevitably uneven
and if at times the rawness of exposed top-notes
mars the lyrical beauty of her singing, equally often
her dramatic magnetism is such that many phrases
stay indelibly in the memory.

Each disc has its share of highlights, with the
earlier recordings usually the more memorable.
What is perhaps surprising are the omissions:
nothing, for instance, from the collection of 'Mad
scenes' she recorded with Rescigno. However,
many of the choices are apt. 'La Divina I', for
instance, includes her sharply characterful, early
1954 recording of *Una voce poco fa* from Rossini's
Barbiere, and 'La Divina III' draws on the later,
complete set for the duet *Dunque io son,* with Tito
Gobbi. 'La Divina II' consistently shows her at her
finest or near it. The recordings cover a decade from
1954 to 1964 and include much that is arrestingly
dramatic (Gluck and Verdi) and ravishing (Puccini
and Cilea), while everything shows that special
degree of imagination which Callas brought to
almost everything she did. The *Mignon Polonaise*
is not ideally elegant but it has a distinctive character
and charm, and it is almost irrelevant to criticize
Callas on detail when her sense of presence is so
powerful. The excerpt from *La Traviata* was
recorded live in Lisbon in 1958 and even the audi-

ence noises cannot detract from its magnetism. All
three recital discs are available separately at full
price, with the third certainly the place to start, as it
centres on early recordings, including the excerpt
from *La vestale,* and opens with the movingly intense *La mamma morta* from *Andrea Chénier.* However, it is astonishing that, having provided so much
information about the singer, EMI chose not to
include any translations, resting content with a brief
synopsis of each aria.

Callas Edition

'Callas at La Scala' (with La Scala, Milan, O,
Tullio Serafin): CHERUBINI: *Medea: Dei tuoi figli.*
SPONTINI: *La Vestale: Tu che invoco; O nume
tutelar; Caro oggetto.* BELLINI: *La Sonnambula:
Compagne, teneri amici . . . Come per me sereno;
Oh! se una volta solo . . . Ah! non credea mirati.*
(M) (***) EMI mono CDM5 66457-2 [id.].

These recordings were made at La Scala in June
1955 and feature extracts from three operas which
at the time Callas had made all her own. However,
for some unexplained reason, the diva refused to
sanction publication of the *Sonnambula* items, so
the original LP was released in 1958 with substituted performances, taken from her complete set,
made the previous year. Yet, with Callas in her
prime, if anything more relaxed than in those later
versions, the remarkable quality is the total consistency: most details are identical in both performances. *Aficionados* will surely be delighted that the
original performances have been restored alongside
the Cherubini and Spontini arias. Throughout,
Callas is heard at her most magnetic. As usual in
this series, the CD transfers are very impressive.

'Lyric and coloratura arias' (with Philh. O, Tullio
Serafin): CILEA: *Adriana Lecouvreur: Ecco,
respiro appena . . . Io son l'umile; Poveri fiori.*
GIORDANO: *Andrea Chénier: La mamma morta.*
CATALANI: *La Wally: Ebben? Ne andrò lontana.*
BOITO: *Mefistofele: L'altra notte.* ROSSINI: *Il
barbiere di Siviglia: Una voce poco fa.*
MEYERBEER: *Dinorah: Shadow song.* DELIBES:
Lakmé: Bell song. VERDI: *I vespri siciliani:
Bolero: Mercè, dilette amiche.*
(M) (***) EMI mono CDM5 66458-2 [id.].

Recorded at the same group of sessions in September 1954 as her very first (Puccini) recital for
EMI, this is another of the classic early Callas
records, ranging extraordinarily widely in its repertory and revealing in every item the uniquely intense
musical imagination that set musicians of every
kind listening and learning. Coloratura flexibility
here goes with dramatic weight. Not all the items
are equally successful: the *Shadow song* from *Dinorah,* for example, reveals some strain and lacks
charm, but these are all unforgettable performances.
Callas's portrait of Rosina in *Una voce poco fa*

was never more viperish than here, and she never surpassed the heartfelt intensity of such numbers as *La mamma morta* and *Poveri fiori*. This mono re-issue is well balanced and cleanly transferred with the voice vividly projected against a convincing orchestral backdrop.

'Mad scenes' (with Philh. Ch. & O, Nicola Rescigno): DONIZETTI: *Anna Bolena: Piangete voi?... Al dolce guidami castel natio.* THOMAS: *Hamlet: A vos jeux ... Partagez-vous mes fleurs ... Et maintenant écoutez ma chanson.* BELLINI: *Il Pirata: Oh! s'io potessi ... Cor sorriso d'innocenza.*
(M) *** EMI CDM5 66459-2 [id.].

Recorded in the Kingsway Hall in September 1958, this is the record which, Desmond Shawe-Taylor suggested, more than any other summed up the essence of Callas's genius. If the rawness of ex-posed top notes mars the sheer beauty of the singing, few recital records ever made can match – let alone outshine – this collection of 'Mad scenes' in vocal and dramatic imagination.

Recital (with Paris Conservatoire O, Nicola Rescigno): BEETHOVEN: *Ah! perfido* (scena and aria), *Op. 65.* WEBER: *Oberon: Ocean! thou mighty monster.* MOZART: *Le nozze di Figaro: Porgi amor. Don Giovanni: Or sai chi l'onore; Crudele? ... Non mi dir; In quali eccessi, O numi! ... Mi tradi quell'alma ingrate.*
(M) ** EMI CDM5 66465-2 [id.].

The 1963–4 recording sessions in Paris which pro-duced these Beethoven, Mozart and Weber arias also included arias by Verdi which were not to appear until a decade later. They were to be among Callas's very last recordings, and the Beethoven scena immediately exposes the flaws that sadly emerged in the great voice towards the end of her career. Yet her fire-eating manner remains irre-sistible.

'Callas à Paris', Volume I (with Fr. Nat. R. O, Georges Prêtre): GLUCK: *Orphée et Euridice: J'ai perdu mon Euridice. Alceste: Divinités du Styx.* BIZET: *Carmen: Habanera; Seguidilla.* SAINT-SAENS: *Samson et Dalila: Printemps qui commence; Amour! viens aider ma faiblesse! Mon coeur s'ouvre à ta voix.* GOUNOD: *Roméo et Juliette: Ah! je veux vivre dans ce rêve.* THOMAS: *Mignon: Ah, pour ce soir ... Je suis Titania.* MASSENET: *Le Cid: De cet affreux combat ... pleurez.* CHARPENTIER: *Louise: Depuis le jour.*
(M) *** EMI CDM5 66466-2 [id.].

'Callas à Paris', Volume II (with Paris Conservatoire O, Georges Prêtre): GLUCK: *Iphigénie en Tauride: O malheureuse Iphigénie.* BERLIOZ: *Damnation de Faust: D'amour l'ardente flamme.* BIZET: *Les Pêcheurs de perles: Me voilà seule ... Comme autrefois.* MASSENET:

Manon: Je ne suis que faiblesse ... Adieu notre petite table. Suis-je gentille ainsi? ... Je marche sur tous les chemins. Werther: Werther! Qui m'aurait dit ... Des cris joyeuse (Air des lettres). GOUNOD: *Faust: Il était un Roi de Thulé ... O Dieu! que de bijoux ... Ah! je ris.*
(M) ** EMI CDM5 66467-2 [id.].

The first LP collection, *Callas à Paris*, dating from 1961, has the singer at her most commanding and characterful. The sequel disc was recorded two years later when the voice was in decline. The vocal contrast is clear enough, and the need at the time to patch and re-patch the takes in the later sessions makes the results sound less spontaneous and natural. But the earlier portraits of Carmen, Alceste, Dalila and Juliette find Callas still supreme, and her mastery of the French repertoire provides a fascinating slant on her artistry.

'Romantic arias': PUCCINI: *Gianni Schicchi: O mio babbino caro. Manon Lescaut: In quelle trine morbide. La Bohème: Donde lieta uscì. Madama Butterfly: Un bel dì vedremo.* VERDI: *Rigoletto: Caro nome. Il Trovatore: D'amor sull'ali rosee. Otello: Ave Maria.* BELLINI: *La Sonnambula: Come per me sereno.* MEYERBEER: *Dinorah: Ombra leggiera (Shadow song).* DELIBES: *Lakmé: Bell song.* MOZART: *Le nozze di Figaro: Porgi amor.* DONIZETTI: *L'elisir d'amore: Prendi, per me sei libro. Lucia di Lammermoor: Spargi d'amaro piano* (excerpt from *Mad scene*).
(B) *** EMI Eminence CD-EMX 2243.

A comparatively recent bargain assembly of Callas arias, attractively designed to show her lyrical gifts. The Puccini, Verdi and Meyerbeer recordings date from the 1950s, except for the *Ave Maria* from *Otello* which, like the *Nozze di Figaro* and *L'elisir d'amore* arias, comes from a decade later. The brief excerpt from the *Lucia* Mad scene is drawn from the 1960 complete set, and the Bellini *La Sonnambula* excerpt, although originally recorded in 1955, was not passed for publication by Callas until near her death.

Cambridge Singers, John Rutter

'There is sweet music' (English choral songs): STANFORD: *The blue bird.* DELIUS: *To be sung of a summer night on the water I & II.* ELGAR: *There is sweet music; My love dwelt in a Northern land.* VAUGHAN WILLIAMS: *3 Shakespearean songs: Full fathom five; The cloud-capp'd towers; Over hill, over dale.* BRITTEN: *5 Flower songs, Op. 47.* Folksongs: arr. MOERAN: *The sailor and young Nancy.* arr. GRAINGER: *Brigg Fair: Londonderry air.* arr. CHAPMAN: *Three ravens.* arr. HOLST: *My sweetheart's like Venus.* arr. BAIRSTOW: *The oak and the ash.* arr. STANFORD: *Quick! We have but a second.*

❀ *** Coll. Dig. COLCD 104 [id.].

Opening with an enchanting performance of Stanford's *The blue bird* followed by equally expressive accounts of Delius's two wordless summer evocations, this most attractive recital ranges from Elgar and Vaughan Williams, both offering splendid performances, to various arrangements of folksongs, less fashionable today than they once were, but giving much pleasure here. The recording, made in the Great Hall of University College, London, has an almost ideal ambience: words are clear, yet the vocal timbre is full and natural. A highly recommendable anthology.

'Flora gave me fairest flowers' (English madrigals): MORLEY: *My bonny lass she smileth; Fyer, fyer!; Now is the month of Maying.* EAST: *Quick, quick, away dispatch!* GIBBONS: *Dainty fine bird; Silver swan.* BYRD: *Though Amaryllis dance in green; This sweet and merry month of May; Lullaby.* WEELKES: *Hark, all ye lovely saints.* WILBYE: *Weep, weep, mine eyes; Flora gave me; Draw on sweet night; Adieu sweet Amaryllis.* TOMKINS: *Too much I once lamented; Adieu ye city-prisoning towers.* FARMER: *Little pretty bonny lass.* BENNETT: *Round about.* WEELKES: *Ha ha! this world doth pass; Death hath deprived me.* RAMSEY: *Sleep, fleshly birth.*
*** Coll. Dig. COLCD 105 [id.].

John Rutter's Cambridge Singers bring consistent unanimity of ensemble and a natural expressive feeling to this very attractive programme of madrigals. Perhaps the first group, devoted to love and marriage, may be thought rather too consistently mellifluous; but the second, 'Madrigals of times and season', is nicely contrasted, with the clean articulation of Morley's *Now is the month of Maying* made the more telling by the lightness of the vocal production. John Wilbye's lovely *Draw on sweet night*, which follows, makes a perfect contrast. After two items about 'Fairies, spirits and conceits', the concert closes in a mood of moving Elizabethan melancholy with a group devoted to mourning and farewell. Superb recording in a most flattering acoustic makes this collection the more enjoyable, though one to be dipped into rather than heard all at once.

'Faire is the Heaven' (Music of the English Church): PARSONS: *Ave Maria.* TALLIS: *Loquebantur variis linguis; If ye love me.* BYRD: *Misere mei; Haec dies; Ave verum corpus; Bow thine ear.* FARRANT: *Hide not thou thy face; Lord, not thou thy face; Lord for thy tender mercy's sake.* GIBBONS: *O clap your hands; Hosanna to the Son of David.* PURCELL: *Lord, how long wilt thou be angry; Thou knowest, Lord; Hear my prayer, O Lord.* STANFORD: *Beati quorum via.* arr. WOOD: *This joyful Eastertide.* HOWELLS: *Sing lullaby; A spotless rose.* WALTON: *What cheer?*

VAUGHAN WILLIAMS: *O taste and see.* BRITTEN: *Hymn to the Virgin.* POSTON: *Jesus Christ the apple tree.* HARRIS: *Faire is the Heaven.*
*** Coll. COLCD 107 [id.].

These recordings were made in the Lady Chapel of Ely Cathedral, and the ambience adds beauty to the sound without in any way impairing clarity of focus. The music ranges from examples of the Roman Catholic Rite as set by Tallis, Byrd and Robert Parsons (with a touch of almost Latin eloquence in the presentation), through widely varied Reformation music, to the Restoration, represented by three Purcell anthems, and on to the Anglican revival and the twentieth century. The Reformation group is particularly successful, with the opening Tallis and closing Gibbons works rich in polyphony and Byrd's *Bow thine ear* wonderfully serene. Of the modern items, the Howells pieces are quite lovely and Walton's *What cheer?*, with its engaging imitation, is attractively genial. The Britten and Poston items, both well known, are hardly less engaging; and the concert ends with the ambitious title-number, William Harris's *Faire is the Heaven*, sung with great feeling and considerable power. There is no more successful survey of English church music in the current catalogue and certainly not one presented with more conviction.

'The lark in the clear air' (Traditional songs; with members of the London Sinfonia): *I know where I'm going; She moved through the fair; The lark in the clear air; Down by the Salley Gardens; Dashing away with the smoothing iron; The sprig of thyme; The bold grenadier; The British Grenadiers; The keel row; The girl I left behind me; The cuckoo; O waly waly; Willow song; The willow tree; The Miller of Dee; O can ye sew cushions.* arr. VAUGHAN WILLIAMS: *The spring time of the year; The dark-eyed sailor; Just as the tide was flowing; The lover's ghost; Wassail song.*
**(*) Collegium Dig. COLCD 120 [id.].

Most of these songs are arranged by Rutter himself, often with simple and characteristic instrumental backings – the opening *I know where I'm going* has an oboe introduction, *Down by the Saley Gardens* a clarinet, and *The Miller of Dee* a genial bassoon. *The cuckoo* brings a harp, and in *The keel row* the woodwind interjections are delightful, while the evocative introduction to *Afton water* is particularly beautiful. Even so, several more memorable items, *O waly waly* for instance, are unaccompanied. The five arrangements by Vaughan Williams bring welcome contrast. The choir sings beautifully, but most of the programme is flowing and mellifluous and one would have welcomed more robust items like *Dashing away with the smoothing iron* and *The British Grenadiers*. The recording is richly atmospheric.

'Christmas day in the morning' (with City of

London Sinfonia; (i) Stephen Varcoe): TRAD., arr. RUTTER: *I saw three ships; Sans day carol; Un flambeau, Jeannette, Isabelle; Wexford carol; Quittes pasteurs; Go tell it on the mountain; Deck the hall; We wish you a merry Christmas;* (i) *Riu, riu, chiu.* RUTTER: *Mary's lullaby; Star carol; Jesus child; Donkey carol; Wild wood carol; The very best time of year; Shepherd's pipe carol; Christmas lullaby.* WILLAN: *What is this lovely fragrance?* WARLOCK: *Balulalow; I saw a fair maiden.* TAVENER: *The Lamb.* VAUGHAN WILLIAMS: (i) *Fantasia on Christmas carols.* TRAD., arr. WILLCOCKS: *Blessed be that maid Mary.*
**(*) Collegium Dig. COLCD 121 [id.].

Admirers of Rutter's own carols will certainly be drawn to his latest Christmas collection, for alongside the favourites there are several new ventures in his inimitably lively rhythmic style. The *Donkey carol*, too, becomes more passionate than in previous accounts. But in general, although the whole programme is enjoyable, beautifully sung and smoothly recorded, the feeling of spontaneous freshness, so enticing on his earliest Decca collection (currently withdrawn), made with the choir from Clare College, is less apparent here, and at times there is a hint of blandness (noticeable with the ritardando at the close of Tavener's *The Lamb*). *Go tell it on the mountain* does not sound entirely idiomatic, and while *We wish you a merry Christmas* ends the concert spiritedly, the Vaughan Williams *Fantasia*, even though it has a fine climax, does not quite match the King's College version (see below) in robust, earthy vigour.

'*A Banquet of voices*' (Music for multiple choirs): GUERRERO: *Duo seraphim.* ALLEGRI: *Miserere.* CALDARA: *Crucifixus.* SCHEIDT: *Surrexit pastor bonus.* TALLIS: *Spem in alium* (40-part motet). PHILIPS: *Ave Regina caelorum.* BRAHMS: *3 Fest- und Gedenksprüche.* MENDELSSOHN: *Mitten wir im Leben sind; Heilig.* BACH: Motet: *Singet dem Herrn, BWV 225.*
** Collegium Dig. COLCD 123 [id.].

The resonant acoustic of the Great Hall of University College, London, does not really suit the complex early polyphonic music here, often clouding the detail of writing for double or triple choir and producing a poorly focused climax in the spectacular Tallis *Spem in alium*. The singing too could be more robust in the Scheidt motet. The choir, seem much more at home in Brahms and Mendelssohn and the closing section of the Bach motet, *Singet den Herrn*, is vigorously joyful.

'*Portrait*': BYRD: *Sing joyfully; Non vos relinquam.* FAURE: *Cantique de Jean Racine; Requiem: Sanctus.* RUTTER: *O be joyful in the Lord; All things bright and beautiful; Shepherd's pipe carol; Open thou mine eyes; Requiem: Out of*

the deep. PURCELL: *Hear my prayer, O Lord.* STANFORD: *Beati quorum via; The blue bird.* TRAD.: *This joyful Eastertide; In dulci jubilo.* HANDEL: *Messiah: For unto us a child is born.* FARMER: *A pretty bonny lass.* MORLEY: *Now is the month of maying.* DELIUS: *To be sung of a summer night on the water I & II.* VICTORIA: *O magnum mysterium.* TERRY: *Myn lyking.*
(M) *** Coll. Dig./Analogue CSCD 500 [id.].

John Rutter has arranged the items here with great skill so that serene music always makes a contrast with the many exuberant expressions of joy, his own engaging hymn-settings among them. Thus the bright-eyed hey-nonny songs of John Farmer and Thomas Morley are aptly followed by the lovely wordless *To be sung of a summer night on the water* of Delius, and Stanford's beautiful evocation of *The blue bird* (one of Rutter's own special favourites). The sound, vivid and atmospheric, suits the colour and mood of the music quite admirably. Not to be missed!

'*The Cambridge Singers Collection*' (with Wayne Marshall, City of L. Sinf.): DEBUSSY: *3 Chansons d'Orléans.* Folksongs (arr. RUTTER): *The keel row; The willow tree.* Gregorian chant: *Regina caeli laetare.* BRUCKNER: *Ave Maria.* VERDI: *Laudi alla Vergine Maria.* STANFORD: *Magnificat in D; Te Deum in C.* PURCELL: *Remember not, Lord, our offences.* TAVERNER: *Christe Jesu, pastor bone.* PHILIPS: *O Beatum et sacrosanctum diem.* PEARSALL: *Lay a garland.* RUTTER: *Riddle song; Waltz; Magnificat* (1st movement); *The Wind in the Willows* (excerpt, with The King's Singers, Richard Baker, Richard Hickox). TRAD. (arr. RUTTER): *Sing a song of sixpence.*
(M) **(*) Coll. Dig. CSCD 501 [id.].

Here is an attractively chosen, 64-minute sampler, including a wide range of tempting repertoire from arrangements of folksongs to Stanford and Verdi. The Taverner and Philips items are particularly welcome. Rutter includes a fair proportion of his own music, but the opening (only) from his setting of *The Wind in the Willows* will not be something one would want to return to very often.

Carewe, Mary (soprano)

'*Tell me the truth about love*' (with Blue Noise, Philip Mayers, piano): GERSHWIN: *Blah, blah, blah; Embraceable you; They all laughed; Summertime; Love is here to stay; By Strauss.* WAXMAN: *Alone in a big city.* HOLLAENDER: *Chuck out the men.* SPOLIANSKY: *The smart set.* WEILL: *Speak low; The saga of Jenny; It never was you.* MULDOWNEY: *In Paris with you.* BRITTEN: *Tell me the truth about love; Funeral blues; Johnny; Calypso; When you're feeling like expressing your affection.*

(M) *** ASV Dig. CDWHL 2124 [id.].

In her brilliantly chosen collection of cabaret songs, Mary Carewe hits an ideal balance between cabaret style – with a touch of the old-fashioned 'belter' – and art-song style – with clean, firm vocal attack. Too often, Britten's five settings of Auden poems emerge as too refined Carewe's full-blooded approach brings them to life in a new way, not just as anaemic pastiche. The first and longest of them is what gives the collection its title, but the six Gershwin numbers which frame the programme at beginning and end are just as stylish, though Philip Mayers' sophisticatedly smoochy arrangement of *Summertime* from *Porgy and Bess* makes it almost unrecognizable. In some ways the most moving item is one of the three Kurt Weill songs, *It never was you*, and it is good to have Dominic Muldowney represented in nicely turned pastiche, the more impressive when set against numbers by such exiles in Hollywood as Waxman, Hollaender and Spoliansky. The only snag is the overblown recording, which emphasizes the pop style in aggressive closeness for voice and instruments.

Carreras, José (tenor)

Arias and excerpts from: MASCAGNI: *Cavalleria rusticana* (with Julia Hamari, Astrid Varnay). BIZET: *Carmen*. PUCCINI: *Turandot* (with Mirella Freni). GOUNOD: *Faust; Roméo et Juliette; Polyeucte*. LALO: *Le Roi d'Ys*. HALEVY: *La Juive*. OFFENBACH: *La Périchole* (with Teresa Berganza). VERDI: *Macbeth; Don Carlos* (with Piero Capuccilli); *Aida* (with Mirella Freni). LEONCAVALLO: *Pagliacci*. MASSENET: *Sapho; Le Cid; Hérodiade*. MEYERBEER: *L'Africaine*. (BB) *** Royal Classics Vocal Double DCL 704792 (2).

José Carreras has a less flamboyant personality than Pavarotti and has rather less vocal presence than Domingo, but he is a very pleasing and musical singer and can be a passionate one too, as in the opening excerpts from *Cavalleria rusticana*, where his style is entirely without vulgarity. Just occasionally there is a hint of strain, but among the *Turandot* items his vibrant *Nessun dorma* will disappoint no one.

He is less idiomatic in the French repertoire, but in the rarer arias from *Le Roi d'Ys*, *La Juive*, *Hérodiade* and *Sapho*, the more familiar scena from *L'Africaine* (all taken from a 1985 recital), and equally in the winning excerpts from the complete recording of *La Périchole*, the fine voice and savoir faire are much in evidence. His strong characterization of Macduff in *Macbeth* and the title role of *Don Carlos* (the Act I duet with Rodrigo is included) is balanced by his fresh, sensitive portrayal of Radames in *Celeste Aida* and the finely spun *O terra addio*, with Mirella Freni. All-in-all this 'Portrait' shows that Carreras is by no means least among the famous contemporary grouping of 'three tenors'. There are no texts or translations.

Catley, Gwen (soprano)

'Favourite coloratura arias and songs' (with various orchestras and conductors): FILES: *Lullaby*. HAYDN: *My mother bids me bind my hair*. ARNE: *The lass with the delicate air*. BISHOP: *Pretty mocking bird; Lo, here the gentle lark*. ROSSINI: *La pastorella*. SAINT-SAENS: *The nightingale and the rose*. REGER: *Virgin's slumber song*. Arias (sung in English) from MOZART: *Il Seraglio*. ROSSINI: *The Barber of Seville*. VERDI: *La Traviata*. THOMAS: *Mignon*. BIZET: *The fair maid of Perth*. MEYERBEER: *Dinorah*. OFFENBACH: *Tales of Hoffmann*. Johann STRAUSS Jr: *Die Fledermaus*. Waltzes: *Voices of spring*. ⊛(M) *** Dutton Lab. mono CDLX 7022 [id.].

Gwen Catley was surely born to sing *The lass with the delicate air*, for the description fitted her perfectly. The meltingly soft, sweet timbre of her voice was matched by astonishingly agile, flexible and accurate coloratura. She was a diminutive figure, but held the stage with the magnetism of her personality. Every one of these famous display arias shows her charm, and *The nightingale and the rose* can be readily compared with Rita Streich's famous version.

Catley's voice recorded perfectly, and so real is the present transfer that one cannot believe that these recordings come from 78s and date from between 1941 and 1952. She sang naturally in her native tongue and made every word clear without in any way sacrificing her bel canto line.

Her stage career really began with the role of Gilda in the Carl Rosa Opera Company's *Rigoletto*, and I. M. (who played in the Carl Rosa Orchestra in the early 1950s) remembers her coming out of retirement to sing that same role at a special gala performance in Belfast. At the end of *Caro nome* she walked slowly off the stage and back on again singing a high cadential trill (not written by Verdi) and brought the house down. In that same performance the famous *Quartet* had to be encored – the first time in nineteen years that Arthur Hammond, the company's Musical Director, had allowed an encore! This is a treasurable disc fully worthy of a much loved and versatile artist, whom Beecham chose for a famous broadcast of Bizet's *Fair maid of Perth* and who also took the role of Anne Trulove in the British radio première of Stravinsky's *Rake's progress*.

Cerquetti, Anita (soprano)

'Grandi voci': Arias from: VERDI: *Aida; I vespri siciliani; Nabucco; Ernani; La forza del destino*. BELLINI: *Norma*. SPONTINI: *Agnes von Hohenstaufen*. PUCCINI: *Tosca*. PONCHIELLI: *La Gioconda* (with Giulietta Simionato, Mario del Monaco, Ettore Bastianini, Florence Festival Ch. & O, Gianandrea Gavazzeni).
(M) ** Decca 440 411-2.

This recital sports a really fearsome portrait of Madame Cerquetti with raspberry lips pouting furiously – a *Casta diva* indeed! In the aria of that name, Cerquetti's entrance is rather marred by an unforgivably flat flute obbligato. Cerquetti's halftone at the beginning of the aria is most ingratiating (if not entirely free of squelching in toothpaste bursts), but the voice hardens when pressed. With such a big voice the degree of flexibility is credible, but ideally Bellini requires even greater sense of style.

The rare aria, *O re dei cieli*, from Spontini's *Agnes von Hohenstaufen* also brings shrill fortissimo attack, but the *Nabucco* excerpt shows up Cerquetti's voice more impressively, with a fine sense of attack in the dramatic recitative, and her richly spun *Vissi d'arte* suggests she was a formidable Tosca. The most impressive items here come from her 1957 complete set of *La Gioconda*; they are rather fine and certainly powerful. The recording is spacious and free without being markedly brilliant. In 1961 Cerquetti withdrew from the operatic stage (temporarily, as she thought) but her attempts to return were thwarted by the pre-eminence of Callas and Tebaldi.

Chadwell, Tracey (soprano), Pamela Lidiard (piano), John Turner (recorders)

'Songbook': MACONCHY: *Sun, moon and stars*; *Three songs*. LEFANU: *I am bread; A penny for a song*. WHITEHEAD: *Awa Herea*. CRESSWELL: *Words for music*. LUMSDAINE: *Norfolk songbook* (with John Turner, recorders). LILBURN: *3 Songs*. FARQUHAR: *6 Songs of women*. JOUBERT: *The turning wheel*. Rodney BENNETT: *A Garland for Marjory Fleming*.
*** British Music Society BMS 420/1 (2) [id.].

Tracey Chadwell, whose career was tragically cut short by leukaemia when she was still in her mid-thirties, was an exceptional singer, as this generous two-disc collection of songs makes plain. Hers was a light, bright soprano of extraordinary flexibility and sweetness. She might have become an operatic coloratura, but her special love was for new music. She had an extraordinary gift for making the most

impossibly craggy vocal lines sound grateful and expressive, as she does in many of the challengingly difficult songs here. Three of the song-cycles in the collection, by Elizabeth Maconchy, David Lumsdaine and the New Zealand composer, Gillian Whitehead, were specially written for her, as well as one of the separate songs, and one can understand the enthusiasm of composers to write for a singer so responsive. Not only did she sing with keen musical imagination, she projected her sparkling personality with a zest that matched the sparkle in her voice.

The recordings, drawn from BBC sources, are all first-rate, with Pamela Lidiard as her understanding piano accompanist, and with the recorder-player, John Turner, as her partner in the Lumsdaine cycle. The collection comes to a charming conclusion with Richard Rodney Bennett's settings of poems by an early-nineteenth-century child-poet, *A Garland for Marjory Fleming*. An illuminating collection of modern songs as well as a fitting memorial.

Chanticleer

'Sing we Christmas': PRAETORIUS: *Es ist ein Ros' entsprungen*. VICTORIA: *O magnum mysterium*. TRAD.: *In dulci jubilo* (with verse 2 arr. M. PRAETORIUS; verse 3 arr. H. PRAETORIUS; verse 4 arr. BACH). *O Jesuslein süss, O Jesuslein mild* (verse 1 arr. SCHEIDT; verse 2 arr. BACH). JOSQUIN DES PRES: *O virgo virginum*. HANDEL: *Hodie Christus natus est; Mirabile mysterium*. ANON.: *Verbo caro factum est: Y la Virgen le dezia*. GUERRERO: *A un niño llorando*. HOWELLS: *Here is the little door*. SAMETZ: *Noel canon*. arr. WILLCOCKS: *Quelle est cette odeur agréable*. arr. RIBO: *El Noi de la mare*. IVES: *A Christmas carol*. BILLINGS: *A virgin unspotted*. HOLST: *In the bleak midwinter*. arr. JENNINGS: *Glory to the newborn king* (fantasia on four spirituals). GRUBER: *Stille Nacht*.
**(*) Teldec/Warner Dig. 4509 94563-2 [id.].

The rich sonority of the very familiar opening Praetorius carol immediately demonstrates the body and homogeneity of the singing of this fine choral group of a dozen perfectly matched male voices; but while the choir's dynamic contrasts are not in question, the close balance prevents an absolute pianissimo, and the resonance brings a degree of clouding when lines interweave swiftly, as in Jacob Händl's *Hodie Christus natus est*. The lush blend of the slowly flowing *Mirabile mysterium*, with its haunting momentary stabs of dissonance, shows the choir at its finest, as does Victoria's contemplatively gentle setting (*O magnum mysterium*) and the rapt, interweaving polyphony of Josquin's *O virgo virginum*, where the depth of sonority is extraordinary.

If Herbert Howells's *Here is the little door* and Holst's *In the bleak midwinter* are made to seem too static, the Ives *Christmas carol* suits the sustained style, while Sametz's ingenious *Noel canon* is admirably vigorous, as is William Billings's *A virgin unspotted*. The extended sequence of four traditional gospel songs, arranged by Joseph Jennings, is perhaps the highlight of the concert, sung colloquially with some fine solo contributions, especially from the bass; and the closing *Stille Nacht* brings an unforgettably expansive resonance, with the voices blending like a brass chorale.

Christ Church Cathedral Choir, Oxford, Stephen Darlington

'English choral music 1514–1682'.
(BB) *** Nimbus Dig. NI 1762 (8) [(B) id.].

This is a superb set, offered at a ridiculously low price. The only disc about which there can be reservations is the collection of anthems, in itself an essential component in any comprehensive survey of early English cathedral choral music. Unfortunately the choice in this instance has been less than ideally representative, and the solo singing is uneven. But this is only one disc out of eight, and it is certainly not to be dismissed. Preparation, and the scholarship behind all these performances, cannot be faulted, nor can the high standard of both the choral singing and the recordings, made (between 1989 and 1995) not in Christ Church Cathedral, but at Dorchester Abbey, also in Oxfordshire, which proves to be an ideal choice acoustically.

John TAVERNER (c. 1490–1545): *Audivi vocem sabbatum de caeli; Kyrie le Roy; Alleluya V. Veni electa mea; Magnificat a 5; Ave Dei Patris filia. Ex eius tumba: sospitati dedit aegros; Dum transisset sabbatum* (2 versions) (Nimbus Dig. NI 5360).

John Taverner was himself Director of the choristers at Christ Church Cathedral. Appointed in 1526, he was there for only four years before moving on to a lesser post at Boston, Lincolnshire. Most of his music was composed during the 1520s, and its rich tapestries of sound reflect great spiritual confidence. The first work here, *Ex eius tumba*, is gloriously full-textured and surges forward splendidly; the *Magnificat* setting, too, is particularly fine – but then so is the *Ave Dei Patris filia*, an early work which opens radiantly, with the trebles soaring. *Dum transisset sabbatum* is heard in two different settings, both equally impressive. For *Audivi vocem sabbatum de caeli* the choral polyphony from the trebles is distanced, while the men sing the plainsong nearer at hand, a ravishing and indeed mystical effect. The recording, full and spacious, is of very high quality.

John TAVERNER: *Missa Mater Christi;* Antiphons:

O Wilhelme, pastor bone; Mater Christi sanctissima (Nimbus Dig. NI 5218).

This is a liturgical reconstruction by Andrew Carwood for the Feast of the Annunciation of Our Lady, at Eastertide, which intersperses Taverner's *Missa Mater Christi* with the appropriate chant. The disc also includes the motet, *Mater Christi*, on which the Mass itself is built, and the antiphon *O Wilhelme, pastor bone*. The singing under Stephen Darlington is first class, and the recording is difficult to fault: it is well focused and excellently balanced, with a firm image.

John SHEPPARD (c. 1515–59): *The Lord's Prayer; The Second service: Magnificat & Nunc dimittis. Gaude, gaude, gaude Maria; Filiae Ierusalem; Reges Tharsis et insulae; Spiritus sanctus procedens; Laudem dicite Deo nostro; Haec dies; Impetum fecerunt unanimes; Libera nos, salva nos* (Nimbus Dig. NI 5480).

This fine collection duplicates much that is already offered on the pair of Hyperion Dyads of Sheppard's music from Harry Christophers and The Sixteen, discussed in our companion volume. But that means that Stephen Darlington has chosen a great deal of the composer's finest music, and the effect here, from a traditional cathedral men's and boys' choir, gives a different and equally inspiring slant on the music. Moreover Darlington has chosen to open his programme with Sheppard's setting of *The Lord's Prayer*, followed by the *Magnificat* and *Nunc dimittis* from the *Second service*, also sung in English. Both these works were almost certainly written within a week or two of the composer's death and, while their climbing phrases readily identify the composer, their relatively simple harmonic style contrasts with the much more complex and daring polyphony of *Gaude, gaude, gaude Maria*, one of the composer's masterpieces, here including some impressive solo treble contributions.

Filiae Ierusalem which follows also has a wonderfully rich forward flow, with a memorable rocking melisma and again those momentary touches of dissonance which make this composer's music so individual. *Reges Tharsis et insulae* features a constant soaring of the treble line which is thrilling. Two responds bring contrast in being for men's voices alone. *Laudem dicite Deo nostro* is comparatively sombre, while *Impetum fecerunt unanimes* is more lofty in feeling. Splendidly recorded, this expansively ardent singing, with its striking unanimity of ensemble, does full justice to a still under-appreciated composer.

William BYRD (1543–1623): *Mass for 5 voices: Mass Propers for All Saints' Day: Gaudeamus omnes; Timete Dominum; Justorum animae; Beati mundo corde*. Motets: *Laudibus in sanctis; Laudate pueri Dominum; Laudate Dominum* (Nimbus Dig. NI 5237).

BYRD: *Mass for 4 voices: Mass Propers for the Feast of Corpus Christi: Cibavit eos; Oculi omnium; Lauda Sion salvatorem; Sacerdotes Domini; Quotiescunque manducabitis*. Motets: *Pange lingua gloriosi; Ave verum corpus; O salutaris hostia* (Nimbus Dig. NI 5287).

BYRD: *Mass for 3 voices: Mass Propers for the Nativity: Puer natus est nobis; Viderunt omnes fines terrae; Dies sanctificatus; Tui sunt coeli; Viderunt omnes fines terrae*. Motets: *Hodie Christus natus est; Christe redemptor omnium; O admirabile Commertium; A solis ortus cardine; O magnum mysterium* (Nimbus Dig. NI 5302).

These recordings have followed the approach pioneered by Harry Christophers and The Sixteen, in that each of the three Masses is interspersed with Mass Propers from the *Gradualia* and the performance placed at a key point in the Church year. The other motets or Psalm settings included on each disc reflect that choice, so that the *Mass for three voices*, for instance, includes suitable Christmas music. The performances are in the traditional English cathedral manner but are of high quality, the music's flowing lines bringing poise and serenity, but they are in no way dramatic: the choir is set back and the cathedral ambience is very telling.

Thomas WEELKES (c. 1576–1623): *Alleluja, I heard a voice; Give ear O Lord; Evening service for 5 voices: Magnificat; Nunc dimittis; Hosanna to the Son of David; When David heard; O Lord, grant the King a long life; Give the King Thy judgements; Gloria in excelsis Deo; Ninth service: Magnificat; Nunc dimittis* (Nimbus Dig. NI 5125).

Thomas Weelkes was the odd man out among his contemporaries. He was what Colin Wilson would, centuries later, define as an 'outsider'. He fell out with his ecclesiastical superiors and then the religious authorities in general, and he ended his career in disgrace, notorious as a drunkard and for his unholy language. Yet he wrote some of the most original and inspired music in Christendom, music that is constantly stimulating for its wayward, even wild part-writing, with extraordinary passing dissonances which sound so modern to today's ears. He was wonderfully good at endings, and especially at elaborately decorated '*Amens*'. Here the opening *Alleluja*, although gloriously impassioned, is relatively straightforward, but *Give ear O Lord* brings a fine example of one of those beautiful extended '*Amens*'. Even so, it is capped by the '*Amen*' which closes the *Magnificat* from the *Evening service for five voices*.

The Christ Church choristers are obviously continually caught up in this passionate polyphony, and they sing *Hosanna to the Son of David* and the moving setting of *When David heard*, with the greatest commitment and fervour. But most extraordinary of all is the closing *Magnificat* and *Nunc*

dimittis from the *Ninth service*. Weelkes surpasses himself with his plangent harmonic progressions towards the end of the *Magnificat* (from 'Glory be to the Father' onwards) and then in the *Nunc dimittis*, after opening with deceptive calm, he moves forward with constantly repeated overlapping phrases and audacious clashes which are momentarily almost bizarre. In many ways his writing here anticipates a twentieth-century work in the minimalistic style. In the event, this is the most thrilling collection in this whole anthology.

Chapel Royal anthems: BLOW: *The Lord even the most mighty; O Lord, thou hast searched me.* PURCELL: *I will love Thee; O Lord our Governor; Blessed is he whose righteousness; Who hath believed; Out of the deep; Hear me O Lord.* LOCKE: *How doth the city.* HUMFREY: *Hear, O Heav'ns* (Nimbus Dig. NI 5454).

On the face of it, this collection of anthems seems well chosen and quite representative, but the overall effect is curiously doleful, and a few more robust items would certainly have been welcome. The Purcell anthems are touchingly expressive and bring the best of the solo ensemble singing, but there is too little variety in the music itself; when one turns to the marvellous King's College collection within the Harnoncourt Edition, one discovers a vitality that is less obvious here. The opening Blow anthems make virtuoso demands on the bass soloists (Robert MacDonald and William Clements), and they fail to rise – or, rather, lower themselves – to the occasion: the descent to a bottom C and a low trill are negotiated cautiously. There are good things here, of course, not least the choral singing, which is fresh enough; if one takes each anthem individually, the fairly consistent use of the minor mode is less noticeable.

Christ Church Cathedral Choir, Oxford, Francis Grier

'*Carols from Christchurch*' (with Harry Bicket, organ): GARDNER: *Tomorrow shall be my dancing day.* TRAD.: *O thou man; In dulci jubilo.* HADLEY: *I sing of a maiden.* HOWELLS: *Sing lullaby; Here is the little door; A spotless rose.* WARLOCK: *Bethlehem Down.* MATHIAS: *Sir Christèmas.* arr. BACH: *O little one sweet.* TCHAIKOVSKY: *The crown of roses.* WISHART: *Alleluya, a new work is come on hand.* BRITTEN: *A ceremony of carols* (with Frances Kelly, harp); *Shepherd's carol; A Boy was born: Jesu, as Thou art our Saviour.* (M) *** ASV CDWHL 2097 [id.].

This is among the most attractive of mid-priced reissues of carol collections, the more particularly as it includes not only a first-class account of Britten's *Ceremony of carols*, plus *Jesu, as Thou art our*

Saviour, with its piercing momentary dissonances, but also the dialogue *Shepherd's carol*, so effectively featuring four soloists. The dozen other carols also bring some radiantly expressive singing, particularly in the three inspired Howells works; the Hadley carol, too, is delightful. They are framed by the admirably lively items by Gardner and Wishart, with Mathias's buoyant *Sir Christèmas* as a centrepiece. Generally good, analogue sound from the early 1980s.

Christofellis, Aris (sopraniste)

'Farinelli et son temps' (with Ensemble Seicentonovecento, Flavio Colusso): Arias from: DUNI: *Demofoonte*. GIACOMELLI: *Merope*. METASTASIO: *La Partenza*. HANDEL: *Ariodante; Serse*. BROSCHI: *Artaserse*. HASSE: *Artaserse; Orfeo*. ARIOSTI: *Artaserse*. PERGOLESI: *Adriano in Siria*.
*** EMI Dig. CDC5 55250-2 [id.].

What did operatic castratos sound like in the eighteenth century? The only recording of a genuine castrato, made at the turn of the last century, is a travesty, merely the squawking of an old man. By any reckoning, here is a much closer answer, a finely trained high falsettist who, in the beauty and evenness of the sound, with a minimum of ugly hooting, suggests that this may well approximate to the sound of a castrato.

A recording may exaggerate the size of Christofellis's voice – by report the singing of the great castratos was exceptionally powerful – but he is artist enough, with a formidable technique, to make a splendid show in this dazzling series of arias originally written for the great castrato Farinelli. Some of his cadenzas are breathtaking. One brief song is by Farinelli's greatest friend, the librettist Metastasio, and Farinelli's own setting of the same words is also included. The items from Handel's *Ariodante* and *Serse*, better known than the rest, come in performances which stand up well against those we have had from female singers, and Christofellis in his note pays tribute to the pioneering work of Marilyn Horne. The performances are all lively and alert, and the recording of the voice is full and vivid, though the instrumental accompaniment is backwardly placed.

Codex

Codex: 'Treasures from the DG Archiv Catalogue'.
(M) **(*) DG mono/stereo 453 161-2 (10).

The word 'Codex' originally described a quire of manuscript pages held together by stitching – the earliest format of a book; it went on to mean a collection of rare and valuable documents. So the term is used here, appropriately enough, to encapsulate what DG suggest are 'rare documents in sound from 50 years of pioneering recording, ranging from the serene counterpoint of a Machaut, the intensely spiritual polyphony of a Victoria to the imposing state music of a Handel'. The majority of these recordings have never before appeared on CD, and the only snag from the collector's point of view is that authentic styles of performance have changed greatly during the last half-century, as scholarship has re-researched its sources and re-determined the stylistic parameters. The highlight of the collection is Emilio De'Cavalieri's *Rappresentatione di Anima, et di Corpo*, which is well worth seeking out independently. Most of the discs are currently available separately (in the UK only).

Disc 1 (with Brussels Pro Musica Antiqua, Safford Cape): LEONIN: *Judaea et Jerusalem*. PEROTINUS: *Sederunt principes*. MACHAUT: *Messe de Nostre Dame*. DU FAY: *Vergine bella; Vexilla Regis; Flos florum. Veni creator spiritus; Alma redemptoris mater* (DG (IMS) mono 453 162-2).

The first disc here opens with an organum duplum, *Judaea et Jerusalem*, of Léonin, and an organum quadruplum, *Sederunt principes* of Pérotinus. The singers of Safford Cape's Pro Musica Antiqua are expertly matched and balanced, and their austere style, slow and deliberate, is not inappropriate. But one would have expected rather more vitality conveyed in Machaut's *Messe de Nostre Dame* (the first known complete polyphonic setting of the Ordinary of the Mass); here the approach is very pure and literal, and the accompaniment (for recorder, fiddles and lute) highly conjectural. All three alternative performances, listed in our main volume under the composer, are more stimulating. When one moves on to the selection of hymns, motets and antiphons by Du Fay, the singing suddenly springs to expressive life. The opening accompanied alto solo, *Vergine bella* (a setting of the first verse of an Italian canzona by Petrarch), is justly famous; *Flos florum*, for mixed voices and fiddles, is both complex and beautiful, as is the account of the (unaccompanied) three-voiced setting of the ninth-century Pentecostal hymn *Veni creator spiritus*; while the glorious *Alma redemptoris mater* (for accompanied alto, tenor and bass), which paraphrases an eleventh-century Marian antiphon, caps the collection eloquently.

Disc 2 (with Schola Cantorum, Francesco Coradini, Fosco Corti; (i) with Arnoldo Foà): ANON.: Marian Antiphons: *Alma redemptoris mater; Ave regina caelorum; Regina caeli laetare; Salve regina*. Francesco CORTECCIA: (i) *Passione secondo Giovanni (St John Passion)* (453 163-2).

The Florentine composer Francesco Corteccia (1502–71) took holy orders in 1526 and became organist at the Church of San Lorenzo in 1531;

he ended his career as chapel master at Florence Cathedral and he also supervised the music at the Medici Court. His *St John Passion* dates from 1527. The choral writing is simple and touchingly serene. The snag here is that the commentary of the Evangelist is not sung but spoken, and the cueing does not separate the spoken part of the performance, which will be frustrating for non-Italian-speaking listeners, seeking to hear the music without the narrative.

Nevertheless the various uninterrupted set-pieces for the choir, including *Tristis est anima mea usque ad mortem*, the exquisite *Tenebrae factae sunt* and notably *Caligaverunt oculi mei* (which we hear again, below, in Victoria's setting), are very moving, none more so than the desolate closing Evangelicum: *Post haec autem rogavit Pilatum Joseph ab Arimathea*, which is sung here very gently, with a superbly sustained closing pianissimo dying away in the closing fall. Arnoldo Foà speaks the part of the Evangelist with admirable simplicity, and the singing and recording could hardly be bettered. The disc opens with four Marian antiphons, which are also beautifully presented.

Disc 3: Tomás Luis de VICTORIA (with Regensburger Domchor, Hans Schrems): *Missa Vidi speciosam*. Motets and Responsories: *Vidi speciosam; Tamquam ad latronen; O Domine Jesu Christe; Amicus meus; Unus ex discipulis meis; Caligaverunt oculi mei; Dum complerentur; Surrexit Pastor Bonus. Lamentations of Jeremiah: Aleph. Ego vir didens paupertam meam* (453 164-2).

Victoria's *Missa Vidi speciosam* is a parody Mass based on a *Canticum canticorum* motet, also included here, whose words have a distinctly pantheistic character ('I have seen what was like a beautiful dove, rising above the rivers of water, whose fragrance was beyond value in its vestments; and, like spring days, flowers of roses and lilies of the valley surrounded it'). The perfumed symbolism of these words invaded the Mass and, although Victoria modified his musical style somewhat for his ecclesiastical setting, it gives the work an expressive richness which makes it suitable for performance by the mixed voices of the Regensburg Choir, even though their expressive manner and their use of vibrato are somewhat anachronistic.

The recording brings a limited dynamic range and the plangent Latin ardour of Victoria's writing is elusive, although the closing *Agnus Dei* is heartfelt. The choir are happier in the motets and responsories: the motet on which the Mass is based is beautifully sung, as is the deeply expressive *Caligaverunt occuli mei* ('My eyes have been stitched shut from my weeping'), and the excerpt from the *Lamentations of Jeremiah* is appealingly serene. The choir blends well, but the resonance prevents the clearest focus of inner detail and occasionally

intonation is slightly suspect. This CD is not available separately.

Disc 4: Emilio DE'CAVALIERI: *Rappresentatione di Anima, et di Corpo* (with Tatiana Troyanos, Hermann Prey, Kurt Equiluz, Herbert Lackner, Theo Adam, Teresa Zylis-Gara, Edda Moser, V. Chamber Ch., V. Capella Academica, Ens. Wolfgang von Karajan, Mackerras) (453 165-2).

We have not previously encountered this fine (1970) recording of Cavalieri's *The Dialogue of Soul and Body*, not an opera, but much more theatrical than an oratorio. It was not produced for Lent but, more appropriately, at carnival time in February 1600. Cavalieri was in charge of music at the Court of Grand Duke Ferdinand I of Tuscany, and he developed a novel kind of pastoral play in which dialogue, songs and choruses were all sung. The libretto philosophizes on the conflicting demands of hedonistic pleasures and the necessity of spiritual preparation for life's inevitable end.

Act I opens with the prudent consideration that time flies, and Time (the excellent Theo Adam) suggests that the audience had better make every moment count, before the sounding of the Last Trump. Good Counsel (the dry-voiced Herbert Lackner) opens Act II with the warning that 'Life is nothing but a battle', and at its close Earthly Life is disrobed and found to be death in disguise; Act III counts the blessings of Heaven and offers a dramatically explicit warning of Hell. At its close, all take the righteous path and glorify the Lord and virtue's victory.

With fine, animated choral singing as a backcloth – their first entry, *Questa vita mortale, per fuggir presto ha l'ale* ('This mortal life has wings to fly so fast'), is delightful – the principals bring the piece vividly to life. Tatiana Troyanos is in splendid voice as Anima, Soul: 'I did not fashion myself,' she sings 'And how can I calm these desires of mine'; and Hermann Prey is appropriately dark-voiced and commanding, even gruff, as Corpo (Body). In the small parts, Paul Esswood represents Pleasure, and Kurt Equiluz proves an ardently light-hearted Intellect when he points out in scene iii that 'Every heart loves happiness' (*Ogni cor ama il bene*), while in Act II Teresa Zylis-Gara is a fine Guardian Angel. Anima has an engaging echo dialogue with Heaven when she asks if the world should shun all pleasures, and receives an unequivocal reply. Later, the same echo device is used even more effectively when the four-part chorus are echoed in reply by a two-part chorus as they seek to confirm mankind's ultimate destiny in Heaven. All in all, this is a most attractive entertainment, with the most uplifting moral purpose to set against its hedonistic celebrations of human enjoyment. Mackerras was just the man for it: the performance swings along vivaciously, and it is excellently recorded. A real find.

Disc 5: Orlando GIBBONS: *Fantasias for viols Nos. I & II a 3; II a 4; In nomine a 5; O Lord I lift my heart to Thee; Thus Angels sung; Almighty and everlasting God; O my love, how comely now; O Lord, increase my faith; This is the record of John; What is our life?; The silver swan; The Cries of London: God give you good morrow; A good sausage* (with Alfred Deller, Deller Consort, Consort of Viols of Schola Cantorum Basiliensis, Wenzinger). MORLEY: *Good love, then fly thou to her; Farewell disdainful; Hark, jolly shepherds, hark; Now is the gentle season; My lovely wanton pearl; Sweet nymph, come to thy lover; Stay heart, run not so fast; O grief, even on the bud* (with Ambrosian Singers, Denis Stevens) (mono/stereo) (IMS) 453 166-2).

The Gibbons programme (from the mid-1950s) provides variety by effectively interspersing the vocal numbers with *Fantasias* for viols, which are played impeccably by Wenzinger and his Schola Cantorum Basiliensis. Deller leads his well-matched vocal group in a series of anthems and hymns that are expressively sung but, with consistently leisured tempi and a limited dynamic range, lack variety. The highlight is the fine verse anthem *This is the record of John*. The *Cries of London* are more lively, but they come off even more effectively when the style is more vernacular. The mono recording is full but closely balanced.

The Denis Stevens collection of songs and madrigals of Thomas Morley dates from a decade later and is sung by small groups of soloists with great charm and impeccable style. *Farewell disdainful* and *O grief, even on the bud* are particularly touching. The original collection from which these items are drawn had added variety from the inclusion of harpsichord pieces, admirably played by Valda Aveling. Unaccountably, they are here omitted and are a great loss, especially when there was plenty of room for them, for the overall playing time here is 63 minutes.

Disc 6: HANDEL: *Utrecht Te Deum and Jubilate; Coronation anthem: Zadok the Priest* (with Ilse Wolf, Helen Watts, Wilfred Brown, Edgar Fleet, Thomas Hemsley, Geraint Jones Singers & O, Jones) ((IMS) 453 167-2).

Handel's *Utrecht Te Deum and Jubilate*, first performed in 1713, shows how rapidly he absorbed the style of English cathedral music, improving on it, yet suggesting by his use of soloists and chorus the verse anthem style that goes back to Purcell and Gibbons. As a writer of occasional music Handel had few equals, and these works show him at his best and most brilliant.

Nobody now, apart from the historians, cares about the Peace of Utrecht, but the music Handel wrote for the happy year is still vividly before us in this lively performance by Geraint Jones. Ilse Wolf,

Edgar Fleet and Thomas Hemsley sing with excellent tone and style; Helen Watts brings her artistry to bear on what is really music for a counter-tenor. Wilfred Brown is a little below his usual high standard. There is adequate depth, even though small resources are used and, though the most famous coronation anthem is not as overwhelming as some like it to be, the 1959 sound remains very impressive and hardly dated.

Disc 7: Carl Philipp Emanuel BACH: *Keyboard fantasias in C, Wq. 61/6; in C min. (Probestücke), Wq. 63/6* (with Colin Tilney); Lieder: *Über die Finsternis kurz vor dem Tod, Jesu; Der Frühling; Prüfung am Abend; Morgengesang; Bitten; Trost der Erlösung; Passionslied; Die Güte Gottes; Abendlied; Wider den Übermut; Demut; Weihnachtslied; Jesus in Gethsemane; Der Tag des Weltgerichts. Psalms 19, 130 & 148* (with Dietrich Fischer-Dieskau, Joerg Demus) (453 168-2).

On the evidence of this collection, Carl Philipp Emanuel was not a true songsmith. Fischer-Dieskau makes the very most of these mainly brief items, but few are melodically memorable. The most attractive are *Trost der Erlösung* and *Die Güte Gottes*, although *Abendlied* and *Wider den Übermut* are quite pleasing. The Psalms are altogether more striking, all three quite memorable, No. 19 surprisingly lively, and the minuscule No. 148 most engagingly light-hearted. The Christmas Lied is also very attractive. Fischer-Dieskau's voice was at its warmest and freshest at the beginning of the 1970s, and Demus accompanies him sensitively, if rather distantly on a Tangentenflügel (a somewhat advanced fortepiano). The two rhythmically quirky *Fantasias* are attributed to Colin Tilney's clavichord, but it is recorded much too closely and the result is ugly: indeed, the instrument is difficult to recognize.

Disc 8: Michel-Richard DELALANDE: *Simphonies pour les souper du roi: Quatrième suite; Sixième suite – Premier Caprice*. Jean-Joseph MOURET: *Fanfares: Première suite. Simphonies: Seconde suite*. PHILIDOR: *Marche à quatre timbales*. LULLY: *Airs de trompettes, timbales et hautbois*. Marc-Antoine CHARPENTIER: *Te Deum: Prélude* (with Soloists, Paul Kuentz CO, Kuentz) (453 169-2).

The composer Lalande (or Delalande, all in one word, like Debussy) provided table music of considerable charm for the formal dinners of two French monarchs, Louis XIV and Louis XV, and in 1745 a definitive edition appeared in Paris. It is this score that Paul Kuentz uses as a basis for the two suites recorded here. Mouret, a contemporary of Delalande, captivated the Parisian public for many years with his stage and symphonic music, but his last years were clouded by insanity, due largely to a rapid loss of reputation which coincided with the ascendancy of Rameau.

As a musical servant of the French court and nobility, Mouret earned his title of '*le musicien des graces*', and the urbane charm of his symphonies evokes the spirit of the age in an inimitable and even forceful manner. His two attractive suites, the first featuring a solo trumpet and the second a pair of horns, both give their soloists attractive music to play while providing plenty of interest in the overall texture. The Lully set of *Airs* is consistently heavily scored and becomes a bit wearing to the ear, while Philidor uses drums alone; the Charpentier *Prélude* to the celebrated *Te Deum* makes a brief coda, playing for only a minute and a half. Paul Kuentz and his chamber orchestra, topped by the clear, high roulades of Adolf Scherbaum's trumpet, strive manfully to reproduce the spacious ambience at Versailles. If they fall short of their mark, it is due to acoustical rather than musical deficiences, for a Paris studio was used for the sessions and as a result the sound is a little tight and unresponsive. Nevertheless there is much to enjoy here, and the one vocal item in Delalande's *Fourth suite*, 'Quitte ici tes ailes', is well sung by Edith Selig.

Disc 9: TARTINI: *Violin concertos in D; in G.* NARDINI: *Violin concerto in E flat* (with Eduard Melkus, violin, Vienna Capella Academica, Wenzinger); *Violin sonata in G* (with Eduard Melkus, violin, Lionel Salter, harpsichord) (453 170-2).

Perhaps surprisingly, the DG Archivists have been unable to identify these two Tartini concertos very clearly, and the notes merely tell us that the *G major* dates from the middle period of the composer's creative career and may have been first heard in Prague in 1724, while the *D major* is most probably a late work. Like the Nardini with which they are coupled, both concertos are typical of their composer; because Tartini was a more individual musical personality, they come alive fully as individual works. With their Italianate melodic warmth, in some ways this pair of concertos looks forward to the nineteenth century, but if the florid virtuoso writing in the outer movements holds a balance between the classical style and the grander manner of the future, the slow movements are embroidered with an ornamentation that is essentially baroque in implication.

Both concertos are played with sensitivity and musical confidence, and in every respect the music-making here (solo and orchestral) has both warmth and charm. But to come off in the spirit in which they were written, they need more of the Heifetz and less of the scholar. They were primarily meant to entertain and perhaps astonish, and to do this they need to be thrown off like quicksilver. Nardini's concerto is more conventional, with long cadenza-like interpolations like those in Locatelli's *Art of*

the Violin. Eduard Melkus plays the fireworks confidently. Yet somehow, as with Tartini, the result fails to convey the excitement – the *raison d'être* of the music – which was obviously generated for listeners of 200 years ago. The *Sonata*, an agreeable little three-movement duo, is again devised to display the soloist, and here the backwardly balanced Lionel Salter makes the most of an indifferent supporting keyboard part. Excellent recording throughout. However, this CD is not available separately.

Disc 10: SOLER: *Concertos for 2 keyboard instruments Nos. 1–6* (with Kenneth Gilbert and Trevor Pinnock (harpsichords or fortepianos)) ((IMS) 453 171-2).

These Soler concertos are described in the surviving autograph as intended for two organs, but Kenneth Gilbert and Trevor Pinnock use either two harpsichords (copies of Florentine instruments after Vincenzio Sodi, 1782) or two fortepianos (copies by Adlam Burnett of Heilmann, c. 1785) – and very attractive they sound too. The music itself is not very substantial and does not possess the character of some of Soler's solo harpsichord music. Most of the concertos are in two movements, the second being minuets plus variations. These are highly skilful performances, well recorded; if the music is not of outsize personality, it is far from unpleasing.

'Coloratura spectacular'

'*Coloratura spectacular*' (with (i) Joan Sutherland; (ii) Sumi Jo (sopranos); (iii) Marilyn Horne (mezzo)): (i) OFFENBACH: *Contes d'Hoffmann: Doll song.* (ii) *Un mari à la porte: Valse tyrolienne.* (iii) PERGOLESI/LAMPUGNANI: *Meraspe o l'Olimpiade: Superbo di me stesso.* (i) VERDI: *Attila: Santo di patria . . . Allor che i forti corrono.* (ii) AUBER: *Le Domino noir: La belle Inès fait florès; Flamme vengeresse.* (i; iii) ROSSINI: *Semiramide: Serbami ognor si fido il cor.* (ii) MASSE: *La Reine Topaze: Ninette est jeune et belle.* (iii) ARDITI: *Bolero: Leggero, invisibile qual aura sui fiori.* (i) GLIERE: *Concerto for coloratura soprano, Op. 82;* (iii) DONIZETTI: *Lucrezia Borgia: Il segreto per esse felici.* (ii) MOZART: *Die Zauberflöte: Der Hölle Rache.* (M) *** Decca Analogue/ Dig. 458 240-2 [id.].

'Coloratura spectacular' is a dazzling display of vocal feux d'artifice from Decca's three top female vocal virtuosi, opening appropriately with Sutherland's sparklingly precise *Doll song*, followed by Sumi Jo's glittering and no less charming displays in Offenbach and Auber, plus an amazing *Carnaval de Venise*, where the flexibility of her upper tessitura has to be heard to be believed. Vibrant drama comes from Sutherland in Verdi's *Attila,* and Marilyn Horne shows her vocal range and fire-eating strength in a thrilling pastiche Pergolesi aria, Arditi's *Bolero* and *Il segreto per esse felici* from Donizetti's *Lucrezia Borgia*. The two divas then join together for a famous duet from Rossini's *Semiramide*, while Glière's two-movement *Concerto for coloratura soprano* again shows Sutherland at her most nimble and personable. Overall this is a remarkable demonstration to confirm that the present-day coloraturas can hold their own with the best from the so-called Golden Age. Full translations are included.

Columbus Consort

'Christmas in early America' (18th-century carols and anthems): BELCHER: *How beauteous are their feet.* HOLYOKE: *How beauteous are their feet; Th'Almighty spake and Gabriel sped; Comfort ye my people.* CARR: *Anthem for Christmas.* STEPHENSON: *If angels sung a Saviour's birth.* HUSBAND: *Hark! The glad sound.* HEIGHINGTON: *While shepherds watched their flocks by night.* FRENCH: *While shepherds watched their flocks by night.* BILLINGS: *While shepherds watched their flocks by night.* PETER: *Unto us a child is born.* ANTES: *Prince of Peace, Immanuel.* MICHAEL: *Hail Infant newborn.* HERBST: *To us a Child is born.* SCHULZ: *Thou Child divine.* DENCKE: *Meine Seele erhebet den Herrn.* GREGOR: *Hosanna! Blessed he that comes in the name of the Lord.* Charles PACHELBEL: *Magnificat anima mea Dominum.*
*** Channel Classics Dig. CC 5693 [id.].

A fascinating look back to the celebration of Christmas in the New World in the late eighteenth century, both by the British colonial settlers in New England and by their Moravian counterparts in Pennsylvania and North Carolina, where the inheritance was essentially in the European tradition. The English style is usually fairly simple and hymn-like, but with overlapping part-writing and occasional solo dialogues (as in the rhythmically interesting *Th'Almighty spake*).

Samuel Holyoke shows himself to be a strikingly fresh melodist; while, of the three settings of *While shepherds watched* to different tunes, William Billings's emerges as the most striking and imaginative. Benjamin Carr's *Anthem for Christmas* is a musical pastiche (indeed, a kind of 'musical switch' with brief quotations from Corelli's *Christmas concerto* and Handel's *Messiah* among other works). The Moravian/German music is usually more elaborate. Johann Peter's delightful motet-like carol, *Unto us a Child is born*, has characteristically resourceful accompanimental string-writing and those who follow him – David Moritz Michael, Johannes Herbst, J. A. P. Schulz and Jeremiah Dencke – all write in a tradition descended from the great German composers, capped by Charles

Pachelbel (son of the Johann Pachelbel of *Canon* fame). He played the organ in Boston, New York and Charleston in the 1730s and 1740s, and his *Magnificat* for double chorus celebrates a much more florid style, utterly different from the music which opens this programme.

The surprise is that this concert is performed not by American singers but by a Dutch group of expert vocal soloists, with a choral and string ensemble who sing and play with convincing authenticity and an agreeably stylish spontaneity. The recording is realistic and clear and made within a perfectly judged acoustic.

Corelli, Franco (tenor)

Arias from: VERDI: *Il Trovatore; Aida.* MASCAGNI: *Cavalleria rusticana.* PUCCINI: *Turandot; Manon Lescaut; Tosca.* GOUNOD: *Roméo et Juliette.* LEONCAVALLO: *Pagliacci.* GIORDANO: *Andrea Chénier.* BELLINI: *Norma.* DONIZETTI: *La Favorita.* PONCHIELLI: *La Gioconda.* CILEA: *Adriana Lecouvreur.* MEYERBEER: *Les Huguenots.* HANDEL: *Serse* (with SCHUBERT; BACH/GOUNOD: *Ave Maria.* ROSSINI: *Petite messe solennelle: Domine Deus.* FRANCK: *Panis angelicus.* DE LARA: *Granada.* CARDILLO: *Core 'ngrato.* DE CURTIS: *Torna a Surriento).*
(BB) **(*) Royal Classics Vocal Double DCL 704812 (2).

At his powerful best, Corelli was a really heroic if not a subtle tenor, as the opening *Di quella pira* and the following *Celeste Aida* lustily demonstrate. He is in equally good form as Turiddù in *Cavalleria rusticana*, and even finer as Canio in *Pagliacci*. Throughout this recital the glorious flow of tone and a natural feeling for the Italianate phrase (as in *Come un bel dì di maggio* from *Andrea Chénier* or the equally stirring *Cielo e mar* from *La Gioconda*) compensate for any lack of imagination. This together with the Donizetti, Puccini, and Meyerbeer items come from a 1962 recital, when Corelli was in excellent voice. The religious numbers (from the same period) are sung in a similar declamatory style, but Corelli's sense of line prevents vulgarization and he is in his element in the Neapolitan songs which close the programme. Accompaniments are sympathetic throughout, and the transfers project the voice vividly. There are no texts or translations.

Cotrubas, Ileana (soprano)

'Famous opera arias and duets' (with (i) Philharmonia Orchestra or (ii) Royal Opera House, Covent Garden, Orchestra, Sir John Pritchard): (i) Arias from DONIZETTI: *Don Pasquale.* MOZART: *Le nozze di Figaro; Die*

Zauberflöte; Die Entführung aus dem Serail.
PUCCINI: *Turandot; La Rondine; La Bohème.*
Gianni Schicchi (with LSO, Maazel). VERDI:
Rigoletto; La forza del destino. CHARPENTIER:
Louise (cond. George Prêtre). Arias & duets from
DONIZETTI: *L'elisir d'amore* (with Plácido
Domingo or Sir Geraint Evans).
(M) *** Sony SMK 60783 [id.].

Ileana Cotrubas recorded this basic recital in
1976, when she was at her prime. She was performing all the roles in the opera house at the
time (except Leonora in *Forza del destino*) and the
performances are beautifully sung (often ravishingly so, as in *Deh vieni, Caro nome* and the excerpt
from *La Rondine*) and almost always dramatically
convincing. The original LP collection is there supplemented with excerpts from her complete recordings, and Cotrubas makes a seductive Louise, and
a delightfully vivacious Adina in *L'elisir d'amore*,
well partnered by Domingo and Sir Geraint Evans.
It was sensible that such an extended selection was
included from this latter set, in which she was at
her very best. It is perhaps a pity that the final bonus
item, *O mio babbino caro* from Maazel's *Gianni
Schicchi*, shows a flutter in the voice, but this is a
tiny blemish, and there are few singers whose talents
have been more comprehensively covered on a
single CD. The accompaniments are very supportive, and the voice beautifully caught by the
recording team, led by the late Bob Auger.

Crespin, Régine (mezzo-soprano)

'*French songs*': BERLIOZ: *Les nuits d'été.* RAVEL:
Shéhérazade (with Suisse Romande Orchestra,
Ansermet). DEBUSSY: *3 Chansons de Bilitis.*
POULENC: *Banalités: Chanson d'Orkenise; Hôtel.
La Courte Paille: Le Carafon; La Reine de coeur.
Chansons villageoises: Les gars qui vont à la fête.
2 Poèmes de Louis Aragon: C; Fêtes galantes*
(with John Wustman, piano).
❀ (M) *** Decca Legends 460 973-2 [id.].

Régine Crespin's recordings with Ansermet of the
Berlioz and (especially) Ravel song cycles are
classics of the gramophone and sound marvellous
in these new Decca transfers. The other songs were
originally part of a 1967 song cycle recorded in
the Kingsway Hall with John Wustman. Crespin
cleverly chose repertoire to suit her voice and all
come over vividly, particularly the Debussy *Chansons de Bilitis* and the charming Poulenc song about
Le Carafon – 'The little water jug' – who wants
(like the giraffe at the zoo) to have a baby water
jug and, with the magical assistance of Merlin,
succeeds, much to the astonishment of the lady of
the house.

Cura, José (tenor)

'*Anhelo*': Argentinian songs (with Ernesto Bitetti,
guitar; Eduardo Delgado, piano; and orchestra).
**(*) Erato/Warner Dig. 3984-23138-2 [id.].

In his disc of Argentinian songs José Cura not only
sings but directs the performances – seven of them
involving a small orchestra – and arranges some of
the pieces, two of them his own compositions. It
makes a crossover disc that is not just 'middle-of-
the-road' but 'easy listening', evidently designed to
provide a sweet and unobtrusive background. The
bright little Ginastera song is one of the few which,
with its tango rhythm, has a Hispanic flavour. Most
of the rest are yearningly melancholy, with *La cam-
panilla*, the fifth of eight songs by Carlos Guastavino, a charming exception. In face of the general
mood, the title, *Anhelo*, 'Vehement desire', taken
from the last of the Guastavino songs, seems hardly
appropriate. Though the recording acoustic and
close balance do not allow the full bloom of Cura's
fine tenor to come out, these are warmly expressive
performances, not just from him but from his associates too.

Daniels, David (counter-tenor), Orchestra of the Age of Enlightenment, Harry Bicket

'*Sento amor*': Operatic arias from: MOZART:
Mitridate; Ascanio in Alba (also Concert aria:
Ombra felice . . . Io ti lascio, K.255). GLUCK:
Telemaco; Orfeo ed Euridice. HANDEL: *Tolomeo;
Partenope.*
*** Virgin Veritas/EMI Dig. VC5 45365-2 [id.].

There are few discs of counter-tenor arias to match
this. The American David Daniels uses his exceptionally beautiful and even voice with flawless
artistry and imagination, whether in Handel, Gluck
or Mozart. Even such a well-known aria as *Che faro*
from Gluck's *Orfeo* emerges with fresh individuality, and the coloratura is breath-taking in its precision and fluency throughout, not just a brilliant
technical exercise but a musical delight. One can
imagine singing like this from castratos of the time
delighting eighteenth-century audiences. Even
those who usually resist the falsetto voice will find
Daniels on this disc an exception in his naturalness
and freshness. Excellent sound.

Danish National Radio Choir, Stefan Parkman

'*Scandinavian contemporary a cappella*':
TORMIS: *Raua needmine.* NORGARD: *And time
shall be no more.* RAUTAVAARA: *Suite de Lorca,*

Op. 72. SANDSTROM: *A cradle song.* JERSILD: *3 Romantike korsange.*
*** Chandos Dig. CHAN 9264 [id.].

Tormis is an honorary Scandinavian: he hails from Estonia. Jørgen Jersild and Per Nørgård are both Danish, Sven-David Sandström Swedish (and mightily overrated in his homeland), and Einoju-hani Rautavaara comes from Finland. Stefan Parkman has brought the Danish National Radio Choir to considerable heights and now it almost (but not quite) rivals the Swedish Radio Choir in its heyday under Eric Ericsson. None of the music is quite good enough to enter the permanent repertory in the way that the sublime motets of Holmboe's *Liber canticorum* should and doubtless will. By their side, this is all pretty small beer, but the Jersild and Rautavaara are worth investigating.

Robert DeCormier Singers and Ensemble, Robert DeCormier

'Children go where I send thee' (A Christmas celebration around the world) (with soloists from the Choir): Traditional songs and carols from: Sweden (arr. DECORMIER): *Ritsch, ratsch, filibon.* Italy: *Dormi, dormi, O bel bambin.* Austria: *Da Droben vom Berge.* Nigeria: *Betelehemu.* Spain: *A la nanita, nanita;* (Catalonia): *El noi de la mare.* USA: *Children go where I send thee; Poor little Jesus;* (Appalachian): *In the valley.* Puerto Rico: *La Trulla.* Germany: *Es ist ein' Ros' entsprungen.* France: *Ecoutons donc les aubades.* India: *Lína avatárá.* Canada: *Huron carol.* Syria: *Miladuka.* Argentina: *La peregrinacion.* West Indies: *The Virgin Mary had a baby boy.*
*** Arabesque Dig. Z 6684 [id.].

The excellent Robert DeCormier Singers have already recorded a number of fine collections, including a John Dowland anthology ('Awake sweet love': Z 6622) and two previous Christmas collections ('A Victorian Christmas': Z 6525 and 'The first nowell': Z 6526), but none has been more attractive than this geographically wide-ranging programme of Christmas songs with children in mind. The arrangements are simple, for every number has great character and needs no embellishment.

The programme opens enticingly with a tick-tock (*Ritsch, ratsch*) Swedish carol which is immediately captivating; it is followed with an exquisite Italian lullaby. The oldest item is a Syrian Christmas hymn, *Miladuka* ('The Nativity'), which, based on plainchant, is thought to be more than 1,000 years old. It is presented here in harmonized form and is quite haunting, as is the example from Northern India, *Lína avatárá* ('He chose to be among us'), which is introduced softly on flute and chiming percussion. When the voices enter, the harmonies

are bare, whereas the Nigerian song about Bethlehem has rich upper intervals above the sonorous repeated bass and soon becomes exultant. The Argentinian carol, *The Pilgrimage*, is lusciously Latin, while the Spanish examples are simpler but lilting. The only really familiar carol is from Germany and it is beautifully and serenely presented. The concert ends swingingly with the more familiar West Indian *The Virgin Mary had a baby boy*, which is given the lightest, most infectious rhythmic touch. Altogether this splendidly recorded anthology, with its nicely judged instrumental accompaniments, will give great pleasure – to grown-ups as well as to children.

Deller, Alfred (counter-tenor)

Alfred Deller Edition

'Western wind and other English folksongs and ballads' (with Desmond Dupré, lute & guitar, John Southcott, recorder): *Western wind; Early one morning; Black is the colour; All the pretty little horses; Lowlands; The Sally gardens; Bendemeer's Stream; Annie Laurie; The Miller of the Dee; Cockles and mussels; Drink to me only; The foggy, foggy dew; The frog went a-courtin'; The turtle dove; Pretty Polly Oliver; The carrion crow; The wife of Usher's Well; Henry Martin; I am a poor wayfaring stranger; Cold blows the wind; Skye boat song; Every night the sun goes down; Song of a wedding.*
(M) *** Vanguard 08.5032.71 [id.].

A ravishing collection of folksongs, recorded in 1958 when the great counter-tenor was at the very peak of his form. The early stereo gives a lovely bloom to his voice, and here, as throughout this fine series, the CD transfers are of a high calibre. The opening *Western wind* is justly another of Deller's 'hits', but *Lowlands* is hardly less beautiful, and many other items here show the magic of his tonal nuancing and his natural, spontaneous musicianship. *Annie Laurie* is wonderfully fresh and brings a frisson as he soars up to the top of his range, while the irrepressible *Miller of Dee*, the petite *Pretty Polly Oliver*, and jaunty *Foggy, foggy dew* show him well able to lighten his presentation in the most sparkling manner. *Every night when the sun goes down* brings an almost Gershwinesque, bluesy feeling. In the charming *All the pretty little horses*, *The Frog went a-courtin'* and the *Skye boat song*, John Southcott touches in discreet obbligati on the recorder, and throughout Desmond Dupré provides persuasive lute accompaniments. The last four songs listed appear on record for the very first time in any format.

'The Silver swan and other Elizabethan and Jacobean madrigals' (with the Deller Consort): GIBBONS: *The Silver swan; What is our life?; Ah!*

Dear heart; Dainty fine bird. Francis
PILKINGTON: *Rest, sweet nymphs; Diaphenia like
the daffdowndilly; Have I found her; O softly
singing lute; Amyntas with his Phyllis fair.* BYRD:
*Though Amaryllis dance; This sweet and merry
month.* WARD: *Retrie, my troubled soul; Upon a
bank with roses; Out from the vale.*
(M) **(*) Vanguard 08.5038.71 [id.].

This collection comes from 1962 when the Deller
Consort included April Cantelo, Eileen Mc-
Loughlin, Wilfred Brown and Maurice Bevan. The
opening Gibbons title-number (in five parts) with its
gentle passing dissonances is particularly beautiful,
with the lullaby of Francis Pilkington, *Rest, sweet
nymphs*, following on naturally; the same
composer's lively portrait of the fair *Diaphenia*
brings a lively contrast. Yet later *O softly singing
lute* is ravishingly expressive, and an even deeper
note is struck with Orlando Gibbons's questioning
What is our life? (with the poem, surprisingly, by
Sir Walter Raleigh), sung with considerable intensity, as is *Ah! dear heart.* This composer's madrigals
bring out the best in the Deller Consort. Byrd's
Sweet and merry month of May might have had
more sparkle, and the programme overall could
have included more jolly numbers with advantage.
The group's intonation is true and the vocal
blending cannot be faulted, but the close recording
means a comparatively restricted dynamic range,
and the playing time is only 43 minutes. Full texts
are included.

'Catches, glees and other divers entertainments':
Tavern songs (with the Deller Consort): PURCELL:
*Man is for woman made; Sir Walter; To thee and
to the maid; Chiding catch; Once, twice, thrice;
When the cock begins to crow; Epitaph, Under
this stone; An ape, a lion, a fox, and an ass; True
Englishmen; Young Collin; If all be true.* Earl of
MORNINGTON: *'Twas you, sir.* SAVILE: *Had she
not care enough.* TURNER: *Young Anthony.* TRAD.:
Amo amas, I love a lass. CORNYSHE: *Ah, Robin;
Hoyda, jolly Rutherkin.* LAWES: *Bess Black; Sing
fair Clorinda; The captive lover.* ANON.: *I am
athirst; Troll the bowl; We be soldiers three; He
that will an alehouse keep; Inigo Jones; Summer
is icumen in.* ECCLES: *Wine does wonders.*
TRAVERS: *Fair and ugly, false and true.* BENNET:
Lure, falconers, lure. ROGERS: *In the merry month
of May.* SPOFFORTH: *L'ape e la serpe.* HILTON:
Call George again. ATTERBURY: *As t'other day.*
ARNE: *The street intrigue; Which is the properest
way to drink.* BLOW: *Bartholomew Fair; The self
banished; Galloping Joan.* BOYCE: *John Cooper.*
BARNABY: *Sweet and low.*
(M) **(*) Vanguard 08.5039.71 [id.].

In this extraordinarily generous 78-minute collection from 1956, forty items in all, the Deller Consort
consisted of Gerald English, Wilfred Brown,
Maurice Bevan, Edgar Fleet and Owen Grundy,

and they sing, unaccompanied, various catches and
glees, part-songs, rounds (of which *Summer is
icumen in* is a prime example) and semi-madrigals
from both Elizabethan and Restoration England,
right up to the pre-Victorian period. The opening
'Choice collection of the most diverting catches',
attributed to Purcell, are mainly bawdy, explicitly
about the joys of love-making in an age of frank-
ness. The Elizabethan romantic lute-songs had an
essential finesse and delicacy of feeling, so the more
robust dialogue pieces acted as a healthy counter-
balance. The popular ballads could also be restrained, and this opening group ends with a
touching glee, *Under this stone*, about the late-
lamented Gabriel John. There are many other part-
songs intended to charm with their vivacity, and
Young Anthony peeping through the keyhole, by
William Turner (1651–1740), becomes more complex as its hero eagerly joins the two ladies he has
overheard discussing their probity. *Ah, Robin*, a
lovely glee by William Cornyshe, is better known
today, slightly altered in rhythm, as *Sing we Nowell*,
while the music for the glee/madrigal *Amo, amas, I
love a lass*, with its naughty Latin parody text, could
have come straight out of *HMS Pinafore*. Purcell's
'patter' trio, *True Englishmen*, also shows how
much Sullivan borrowed from this fertile source.
We be soldiers three even quotes doggerel French
in the way of British soldiers who, in this instance,
have returned from the Flemish wars, while *L'ape e
la serpe*, a late-eighteenth-century glee by Reginald
Spofforth, is sung in Italian. The performances are
suitably direct, never prissy, and this especially
applies to the robust drinking songs, although
occasionally one would have welcomed a more
spontaneously earthy bite. The recording is clear
and immediate, the ambience dry but pleasing.

'The Connoisseur's Handel': excerpts from opera
and oratorio (with Eileen Poulter, Wilfred Brown,
Maurice Bevan, Handel Festival O, Anthony
Lewis): HANDEL: *Jephtha: 'Tis Heav'n's all
ruling power; O spare your daughter; Laud her
all ye virgins. Serse: Ombra mai fù. Orlando: Ah!
stigie larve; Cielo! se tu il consenti. L'Allegro: Let
me wander. Rinaldo: Lascia ch'io pianga.
Theodora: Kind Heaven; Wide spread his name;
Sweet rose and lily; To thee thou glorious son of
worth.*
(M) **(*) Vanguard 08.5043.71 [id.].

The highlight here is Deller's remarkable account
of one of opera's first great mad scenes, Orlando's
Ah! stigie larve, which is sung both dramatically
and with passages of touching lyrical beauty. He
also gives us the later florid *Cielo! se tu il consenti*
from the same opera, the opening *'Tis heav'n's all
ruling power* from *Jephtha* and, even more memorably, *Kind Heaven* and *Sweet rose and lily* from
Theodora. The concert ends with a duet from the
same oratorio, *To thee thou glorious son of worth*,

shared with the radiant-voiced Eileen Poulter, who has previously given an equally beautiful account of the touching *Lascia ch'io pianga* from *Rinaldo*. But unexpectedly it is Wilfred Brown who sings *Ombra mai fù*, and the other solos are well shared with Maurice Bevan. There is less ornamentation than we would expect today, although Deller never puts a note wrong in this respect. Not surprisingly, Anthony Lewis provides stylish and pleasing accompaniments with the excellent strings of the 1960 Handel Festival Orchestra. Full texts and translations (where needed).

HANDEL (with Oriana Concert Ch. & O, Honor Sheppard, Mary Thomas, Mark Deller, Maurice Bevan): *Ode for the birthday of Queen Anne. Coronation anthems: The King shall rejoice; Let thy hand be strengthened; Zadok the Priest.*
(M) ** Vanguard 08.5045.71 [id.].

In the *Ode* the highlight is Alfred Deller's opening solo, *Eternal source of light divine*, with his dueting melisma with the solo trumpet (the splendid Harold Lester). Otherwise the performance is only made distinctive by Deller's contributions: apart from the excellent Honor Sheppard, he is partnered by good, rather than outstanding, soloists, so the performance is enjoyable but not memorable. The *Coronation anthems* could do with more vitality in the accompaniments, especially the opening of *Zadok the Priest*, which has little anticipatory tension.

Italian songs (with Desmond Dupré, lute and viola da gamba; George Malcolm, harpsichord): CACCINI: *Pien d'amoroso affetto; Amarilli.* SARACINI: *Pallidetto qual viola; Da te parto.* DA GAGLIANO: *Valli profonde.* A. SCARLATTI: *Difesa non ha; O, cessate di piagarmi; Bellezza che s'ama; O dolcissima speranza; La speranza mi tradisce.* BERTI: *Da grave incendio.* DONATO: *Dolce mio ben.* WERT: *Dunque basciar* (with harpsichord pieces by PARADISI and Michelangelo ROSSI).
(M) *** Vanguard 08.5056.71 [id.].

This is another early collection from 1957. Deller is in freshest voice and top lyrical form here, and this repertoire suits him admirably. His phrasing is a model of melancholy elegance, as two Caccini songs immediately demonstrate, especially the lovely *Amarilli*, and as the poignant closing *Dunque basciar* (by Giaches Wert) readily shows. It is by no means a predictable programme, and there are two attractive harpsichord interludes from George Malcolm. Both he and Desmond Dupré provide admirable accompaniments. Full texts and translations are included, and the only criticism (apart from a curious drop in pitch at the opening of Berti's ambitiously sorrowful *Da grave incendio*) is Deller's repeated use of a very familiar (and authentic) cadential decoration. Recommended.

'*Deller's choice'* (with Gustav Leonhardt, organ or harpsichord; Marie Leonhardt, violin; Robert Scheiwein, cello): VIADANA: *Exaudi me Domine.* SCHUTZ: *In te Domine speravi.* PURCELL: *The Queen's Epicedium.* humfrey: *A Hymn to God the Father.* DE RORE: *Ancor che c'ol partire.* BLOW: *The Self-banished.* WELDON: *The Wakeful nightingale.* HANDEL: *Rodelinda: Dove sei.* bach (attrib.): *Bist du bei mir.* LOCKE: *Voluntaries in G and F.* FRESCOBALDI: *Toccata terza.* FROBERGER: *Toccata in D min.*
(M) *** Vanguard 08.5059.71 [id.].

Another quite outstanding solo recital from 1960, with a most imaginative programme interspersed with organ and harpsichord pieces, all very well played indeed. The effect is highly spontaneous and there are some remarkable examples of Deller's art here, including a superb account of Purcell's beautiful *Elegy on the death of Queen Mary* and – no less memorable – Cipriano de Rore's *Ancor che c'ol partire*, with ornaments by Bovicelli. Blow's *The Self-banished* is also very touching, then Weldon's *Wakeful nightingale* provides a charming interlude before Handel's famous aria *Dove sei*, simply and gloriously sung, while the closing *Bist du bei mir* is hardly less eloquent. The accompaniments are very distinguished indeed, and the recording balance could hardly be bettered. Excellent notes and full translations.

PURCELL (with the Deller Consort, (i) Oriana Concert Choir & O, (ii) L. Kalmar O, Walter Bermann, harpsichord): (i) *Come ye sons of art (Ode on Queen Mary's birthday, 1694); Rejoice in the Lord alway (Bell anthem);* (ii) *My beloved spake; Welcome to all pleasures (Ode on St Cecilia's Day, 1683).*
(M) **(*) Van. [08.5060.71].

These Purcell performances convey much joy in the music-making, even if for some ears the warmly upholstered (and tonally beautiful) overtures may sound slightly anachronistic. It is good to hear Deller in the famous solos, notably *Strike the viol* (in *Come ye sons of art*), with its intertwining flute obbligato, and *Here the Deities approve* (in *Welcome to all pleasures)*, while in the former he is joined by his son, Mark – who sounds more like a treble – for the 'counter-tenor' duet *Sound the trumpet*. The Deller Consort almost turns *My beloved spake* into a series of madrigals. Pleasingly full sound from 1962. This disc has been withdrawn in the UK.

'*Madrigal masterpieces*', Vol 1: *The Renaissance in France, Italy and England* (with Eileen Poulter, Mary Thomas, Wilfred Brown, Gerald English, Maurice Bevan, Geoffrey Coleby, Deller Consort): JANEQUIN: *Ce moys de may; La bataille de Marignan; Au joly boys.* LASSUS: *Mon coeur se recommande à vous; Matona mia cara.*

MARENZIO: *Scaldava il sol.* MONTEVERDI: *Baci, soavi, e cari; Ecco mormorar l'onde; A'un giro sol bell'occhi; Non piu guerra!; Sfogava con le stelle.* BYRD: *My sweet little baby* (lullaby). MORLEY: *Now is the month of maying.* GESUALDO: *Ecco moriro dunque/Hai gia mi disco loro.* TOMKINS: *When David heard that Absolom was slain.*
(M) ** Vanguard 08.5061.71 [id.].

We have moved on in the style of performance of Italian madrigals since this collection was (excellently, if closely) recorded in 1959. The Deller Consort are entirely happy in the English repertoire. Morley's *Now is the month of maying* almost explodes with spring-like vitality, and the Byrd and Tomkins items are beautiful. The Lassus *Mon coeur se recommande à vous* is touchingly serene in the same way, and *Matona mia cara* is freshly presented, but the Janequin and Monteverdi items are less successful, although *Baci, soavi, e cari* has an appealing simplicity.

'Madrigal masterpieces', Vol. 2 (with the Deller Consort): COSTELEY: *Allons, gay bergères; Mignonne, allons voir si la rose.* PASSEREAU: *Il est bel et bon.* MONTEVERDI: *Lagrime d'amante al sepolcro dell'amata; Incenerite spoglie; Ditelo voi; Dara la notte il sol; Ma te raccoglie; Ochioma d'or; Dunque amate reliquie; Zefiro torna e'l bel tempo rimena.* MARENZIO: *Solo e pensoso; Leggiadre Ninfe.* DE RORE: *Ancor che c'ol partire.* GESUALDO: *Morro lasso al mio duolo.* ARCADELT: *Il bianco e dolce cigno.* Robert JONES: *Fair Oriana seeming to wink at folly.*
(M) **(*) Vanguard 08.5057.71 [id.].

For this 1963 collection the Deller Consort consisted of Mary Thomas, Honor Sheppard, Deller himself, Robert Tear, Max Wortley and Maurice Bevan, and once again the ear is struck by how well these highly individual artists can blend their voices together. The opening three chansons are charmingly sung as is the penultimate madrigal, Arcadelt's *Il bianco e dolce cigno*, yet one would have welcomed a more robust approach at times, especially to Passereau's delicious *Il est bel et bon* (with its hens cackling while the wife takes her pleasure with her cousin, and the play on the word 'coquette') after the more extrovert manner of David Munrow. However, the Monteverdi items are most expressively done and Gesualdo's *Morro lasso* is quite profound in its despair. Not unusually with this group they respond best to the melancholy numbers, not least the glorious rise and fall of the closing madrigal by Robert Jones, *Fair Oriana, seeming to wink at folly*. Excellent documentation as usual.

'Madrigal masterpieces', Vol. 3 (with the Deller Consort): MONTEVERDI: *Lamento d'Arianna; Ohimè il bel viso.* MARENZIO: *Cedan l'antiche tue chiare vittorie.* GESUALDO: *Belta poi che t'assenti.* JANEQUIN: *Le chant des oiseaux; Le chant de l'Alouette.* JOSQUIN DES PRES: *La déploration de Jehan Ockeghem; Parfons regretz.* LASSUS: *La nuit froide et sombre.*
(M) *** Vanguard 08.5092.71.

Volume 3, from 1965, is the finest of these three discs of 'Madrigal masterpieces' and brings a further regrouping of the singers in the Consort, with Honor Sheppard joined by Sally le Sage, and Max Worthley and Maurice Bevan by Philip Todd, all in their finest form. This repertoire clearly suits them admirably, for they sing with vitality – comparatively robustly where needed, and always with deep feeling. While including earlier music by Josquin, the programme concentrates on Flemish and Italian madrigals from the 'golden age' of the late sixteenth century. But the famous opening work dates from 1614: Monteverdi's four-part cycle *Lamento d'Arianna* originated as the heroine's key arioso in the opera of the same name written six years earlier. The complex writing, alternating drama and espressivo brings out the very best from the group and Deller directs the work with a natural spontaneity.

Marenzio's glorious *Cedan l'antiche* is hardly less successful and Gesualdo's remarkable *Belta poi che t'assenti*, with its plangent harmonic dissonances is also very finely sung. The delightful Janequin *Chant des oiseaux* ('Wake up sleepy hearts') with its ingenious polyphonic bird calls, makes a perfect interlude before Josquin's profound lament for his older contemporary, Ockeghem. The dolorous mood is then sustained with most beautiful singing and perfect tonal matching in *Parfons regretz* and the sombre *Le nuit froide* of Lassus, which evokes the darkness just before sunrise. Again Janequin lifts our spirits with more charming bird imitations and the programme ends with another of Monteverdi's finest madrigals, *Ohimè ilo bel viso*, like the *Lamento* coming from Book VI.

Beautifully recorded, this is one of the very finest of all the collections from Deller's Consort, and his direction shows supreme understanding and musicianship. As usual with this series, full texts are included.

TALLIS (with Wilfred Brown, Gerald English, Eileen McLoughlin, Maurice Bevan, Deller Consort): *Lamentations of Jeremiah the Prophet.* 5 hymns alternating plainchant and polyphony: *Deus tuorum militum; Jam Christus astra ascenderat; Jesu Salvator Saeculi; O nata lux de lumine; Salvator mundi Domine.*
(M) ** Vanguard 08.5062.71 [id.].

Alfred Deller pioneered so much repertoire on LP, and even today Tallis's settings of the *Lamentations of Jeremiah* are not generously represented on disc. They are given poised, expressive performances and the motets are presented with their alternating plainsong, but the close recording robs the music-making of atmosphere and the dynamic range is very limited.

MONTEVERDI: *Il ballo delle Ingrate* (with Eileen McLoughlin, David Ward, April Cantelo, Amb. S., L. Chamber Players, Denis Stevens); *Lamento d'Arianna* (with Honor Sheppard, Sally le Sage, Max Worthley, Philip Todd, Maurice Bevan, Deller Consort).
(M)**(*) Vanguard 08.5063.71 [id.].

Deller's pioneering 1956 stereo recording of Monteverdi's *Il ballo delle Ingrate* would not, perhaps, be a first choice today, but at the time he had the advantage of Denis Stevens's scholarly assistance, and the performance has remarkable authenticity as well as considerable dramatic life. The famous *Lamento d'Arianna* is slightly less successful.

'The three ravens': Elizabethan folk and minstrel songs (with Desmond Dupré, guitar & lute): *The three ravens; Cuckoo; How should I your true love know; Sweet nightingale; I will give my love an apple; The oak and the ash;* (Lute) *Go from my window; King Henry; Coventry carol; Barbara Allen; Heigh ho, the wind and the rain; Waly, waly; Down in yon forest; Matthew, Mark, Luke and John;* (Lute) *A Toye; The Tailor and the mouse; Greensleeves; The Wraggle Taggle Gipsies; Lord Rendall; Sweet Jane; The frog and the mouse; The seeds of love; Near London town; Who's going to shoe your pretty little foot?; Blow away the morning dew; Searching for lambs; Sweet England; Dabbling in the dew; Just as the tide was flowing.*
(M) **(*) Vanguard 08.5064.71 [id.].

Opening charismatically with *The three ravens*, this very early (1956) recital contains some outstanding performances, notably of *Barbara Allen*, the delightful *Tailor and the mouse*, *The frog and the mouse*, and the captivating *Who's going to shoe your pretty little foot?*. *Searching for lambs* brings another favourite melody, and Deller's inimitable *Greensleeves* is certainly memorable. As before, Desmond Dupré provides highly sympathetic accompaniments, and here he also has a couple of solo opportunities in which to shine. But although the recording is admirably truthful, this collection is not quite so spontaneously appealing as the *'Western Wind'* recital listed above, even if it is comparably generous (73 minutes).

'The holly and the ivy': Christmas carols of old England (with April Cantelo, Gerald English, Maurice Bevan, Deller Consort, Stanley Taylor, recorder, Desmond Dupré, lute): *Patapan; We three kings of orient are; I saw three ships; The Coventry carol; It came upon the midnight clear;*

Good King Wenceslas; Once in Royal David's city; Rocking; The first nowell; God rest you merry gentlemen; Wither's Rocking hymn; Silent night; Wassail song; Dormi Jesus; Boar's head carol; Past three o'clock; Lullay my liking; Adam lay ybounden; Herrick's carol; Angelus ad Virginem; The holly and the ivy; O little one sweet; Song of the Nuns of Chester; Winter-Rose; In dulci jubilo.
(M) **(*) Vanguard [08.5065.71].

Opening vivaciously with *Patapan*, this Christmas collection, simulating a visit from a village group of waits, often has a pleasing simplicity, although at times its madrigalesque style may strike some ears as lacking robustness. The Consort is heard at its best in *I saw three ships*, *Good King Wenceslas* and *The holly and the ivy*. But the highlights are all from Deller himself, and he is in magical form in the *Angelus ad Virginem*, *Winter-Rose* (with a delicate recorder obbligato from Stanley Taylor) and *O little one sweet*, more robust in *Adam lay ybounden*, but again displaying his unique nuancing of colour and dynamic. His serene account of the *Coventry carol* is heard here on disc for the first time. This CD is no longer available in the UK.

François COUPERIN: *Leçons de ténèbres I–III* (excerpts) (with Wilfred Brown, Desmond Dupré, viola da gamba, Harry Gabb, organ).
(M) *(*) Vanguard 08.5066.71 [id.].

Although there is some remarkable singing here, Deller cannot compare with Gérard Lesne in this repertoire – his manner is curiously histrionic and self-aware, unusually so for this artist. Harry Gabb's discreet organ accompaniment is to be commended, but Dupré's viola da gamba is too backwardly balanced.

'Duets for counter-tenors' (with Mark Deller & Bar. Ens.): MORLEY: *Sweet nymph, come to thy lover; Miraculous love's wounding; I go before my darling.* PURCELL: *Sweetness of nature.* SCHUTZ: *Erhöre mich wenn ich; Der Herr ist gross.* JONES: *Sweet Kate.* ANON.: *Ah, my dear son.* MONTEVERDI: *Currite populi; Angelus ad pastores ait; Fugge, fugge, anima mea; Salve Regina.* BLOW: *If my Celia could persuade; Ah, heaven, what is't I hear.* DEERING: *O bone Jesu; In coelis.*
(M) *(*) Vanguard 08.5067.71 [id.].

Deller's style needs no advocacy, and he has trained his son well to follow faithfully in his footsteps. But although Mark has a fine (treble rather than alto) voice, he does not have his father's subtle instinct for light and shade. So in this case a succession of duets for counter-tenors proves far from ideal planning for a whole recital. Moreover the voices are placed very forwardly, somewhat edgily recorded, and robbed of a convincing dynamic range; there are no possibilities for pianissimo singing here.

'Byrd and his age' (with Wenzinger Consort of Viols of Schola Cantorum Basiliensis, August Wenzinger). William BYRD: *My sweet little darling; Lullaby, my sweet little baby* (both arr. FELLOWES); *Fantasia for viols in G min.; Ye sacred muses (Elegy on the death of Thomas Tallis); Come pretty babe* (arr. Peter LE HURAY & Thurston DART). ANON.: *Guishardo; Ah, silly poor Joas; O Death, rock me asleep.* WHYTHORNE: *Buy new brooms.* Richard NICHOLSON: *In a merry May morn.* Robert PARSONS: *Pandolpho* (all six arr. Peter WARLOCK). William CORKINE: *What booteth love?* (arr. Thurston DART). FERRABOSCO: *Fantasias for viols in F & G.*
(M) ** Vanguard 08.5068.71 [id.].

The advantage of accompaniments from the excellent Schola Cantorum Basiliensis under Wenzinger is reduced by the rather forward balance of the voice in relation to the string group, and when the viols play alone the effect is rather dry. It is on the whole a melancholy programme, although *Buy new brooms* comes centrally as a bright diversion. But it is *Ah, silly poor Joas*, the Byrd *Lullaby*, and especially the very touching *Pandolpho* that are memorable, while the closing *O Death, rock me asleep* shows Deller at his most moving.

BACH: *Cantata No. 170: Vergnügte Ruh', beliebte Seelenlust* (with Leonhardt Bar. Ens.); *Cantata No. 54: Widerstehe doch: Aria: Widerstehe doch; Recitative: Die Art verruchter Sünden; Aria: Wer Sünde tut, der ust vom Teufel. Mass in B min.: Agnus Dei.* HANDEL: Arias: *Orlando: Ah! stigie larve* (Mad scene). *Jephtha: Tis heav'n's all ruling power. Theodora: Kind Heaven; Sweet rose and lily.*
(M) ** Vanguard 08.5069.71 [id.].

These are among Deller's earliest recordings for Vanguard, dating from 1954. In the Bach cantatas Leonhardt provides dull, plodding accompaniments, and his ensemble of original instruments is uninspiringly meagre. The interest of this collection then centres on Deller himself, and he rises to the occasion, especially in the *Agnus Dei* from the *Mass in B minor*, which is most beautifully sung. The Handel accompaniments are more robust and it is good to hear Deller in these operatic excerpts, especially in Orlando's mad scene, but he is also at his finest in both the excerpts from *Theodora*.

DOWLAND (with the Deller Consort and Desmond Dupré, lute): Airs and partsongs: *Wilt thou, unkind, thus reave me?; Awake, sweet love; In darkness let me dwell; Me, me, and none but me!; Go, nightly cares; If my complaints could passions move; Sleep, wayward thoughts; Flow not so fast,*

ye fountains; Come again! Sweet love doth now invite; Sorrow, stay; If that a sinner's sighs; Fine knacks for ladies; Flow, my tears; Can she excuse my wrongs; (Lute) *Queen Elizabeth's galliard*
(M) **(*)Vanguard 08.5071.71.

For this 1965 collection, Honor Sheppard, Deller and Maurice Bevan are joined by Philip Todd. The performances are stylish enough but perhaps just a little cosy. *Go, nightly cares*, which is sung by Honor Sheppard as a solo with continuo, is most touching. Deller's solo contributions, *If my complaints could passions move*, *Flow not so fast, ye fountains*, *Sorrow, stay*, *If that a sinner's sighs*, and *Flow, my tears*, are the memorable items here, although *Fine knacks for ladies* and *Can she excuse my wrongs* are engagingly presented by the full group.

'The Cries of London and English ballads and folksongs': The Cries of London (with April Cantelo, Wilfred Brown, Amb. S., Deller Consort, L. Chamber Players): John COBB: *These are the cries of London.* RAVENSCROFT: *New oysters; Bellman's song; The painter's song; Brooms for old shoes.* DERING: *The cries of London* (all ed. Stevens); *Country cries* (ed. Revell). ANON.: *A quart a penny; I can mend your tubs and pails.* NELHAM: *Have you any work for the tinker?* (all ed. Stevens). WEELKES: *The cries of London* (ed. Noble). English ballads and folksongs (with Deller Consort; Desmond Dupré, lute): *When cockleshells turn silver bells; An Eriskay love lilt; Peggy Ramsay* (arr. Gerard WILLIAMS); *Bushes and briars; Brigg Fair; The cruel mother; A sweet country life* (arr. Imogen HOLST); *The bitter withy; Lang a-growing; The lover's ghost; Lovely Joan; She moved through the fair; A brisk young lad he courted me* (arr. Norman STONE); *Geordie.*
(M) **(*) Vanguard 08.5072.71 [id.].

Richard Dering's *Fantasia* is sophisticated and creates a continuous ten-minute musical kaleidoscope, ingeniously linking the airs in a seemingly natural sequence, ending with a melodious apotheosis on the words 'and so good night'. Weelkes's selection is little more than half as long, using one soloist, here the fresh-voiced April Cantelo. Even so, she gets through a great many lyrical exhortations to buy, ending with a gentle *Alleluia*.

The second half of the recital brings Deller back (in 1959) to the world of ballads and folksongs, opening with a bewitchingly gentle account of *When cockleshells turn silver bells*. Both *The lover's ghost* and the *Eriskay love lilt* take him soaringly upwards, rapturously comparable with *Annie Laurie* on an earlier recital. He is effectively joined by the Consort in *Peggy Ramsay* and they bring variety to the collection with characteristic accounts of *A sweet country life* and *A brisk young lad*. Dupré and his lute set the scene for the lovely *Bushes and briars*. *The cruel mother*, which tells a dreadful story of infanticide, also shows him imaginatively stretched, while *Lang a-growing* with its neat Scottish snap is most effectively done.

VAUGHAN WILLIAMS: Arrangements of folksongs (with Deller Consort, Desmond Dupré, lute): *An acre of land; Bushes and briars; Ca' the yowes; The cuckoo and the nightingale; The dark-eyed sailor; Down by the riverside; A farmer's son so sweet; Greensleeves; John Dory; Just as the tide was flowing; The jolly ploughboy; Loch Lomond; The lover's ghost; My boy Billy; The painful plough; The spring time of the year; The turtle dove; Ward the Pirate; Wassail song.*
(M) ** Vanguard 08.5073.71 [id.].

These highly artistic folksong settings can be effectively performed either by choir or by soloists, and here Deller often alternates his own estimable solo contributions with choral versions. The recording is a little dry, but the stereo adds to the sense of atmosphere. An enjoyable collection, but not one of the finest of the series.

'A Musical portrait of Shakespeare's England': (with the Deller Consort, Desmond Dupré, lute, Taylor Recorder Consort, Ambrosian Singers, Wenzinger Consort of Viols): ANON.: *We be soldiers three; The Wind and the rain; Munday's Joy* and *Watkins ale; Have you seen but a whyte lillie grow; Frog galliard, Coranto and borey, 'Mr Tollett'* (arr. DOLMETSCH); *Greensleeves; The Boar's head carol; The Agincourt song; O Death, rock me asleep* (arr. WARLOCK); *He who will an alehouse keep; Lord Rendall.* DOWLAND: *My Lady Hunsdon's Puffe.* WILBYE: *Ye that do live in pleasures.* RAVENSCROFT: *New oysters.* TALLIS: *O nata lux de lumine.* JOHNSON: *Alman.* BENNET: *Lure, falconers, lure.* MORLEY: *Sweet nymph.* FERRABOSCO: *Fantasia in G.* BYRD: *Non nobis Domine.*
(M) **(*) Vanguard 08.5075.71.

Another fairly early (1959) collection – which is particularly well planned – immediately invites the criticism that the opening *We soldiers three*, though admittedly sung in West-country accents, needs to be more earthily robust; a comment which applies equally to *He who will an alehouse keep*. However, Deller's own contributions with Dupré, *The wind and the rain*, the lovely *Have you seen but a whyte lillie grow* and *Lord Rendall*, are all of the utmost distinction. In *O Death, rock me asleep* he is joined by Wenzinger's Viol Consort, who also play a solo *Fantasia* of Ferrabosco. April Cantelo and Eileen McLoughlin join to sing Morley's *Sweet nymph*, and there are diverting instrumental interludes from an accomplished recorder consort and also from Gustav Leonhardt. The full Deller Consort contribute impressively in darker music of Tallis and Byrd.

WILBYE: Madrigals (with the Deller Consort): *Thus saith my Cloris bright; Happy, O happy he, who not affecting; Ye that do live in pleasures plenty; Ah, cannot sighs, nor tears, nor aught else move thee; Stay, Corydon, thou swain; Draw on, sweet Night, best friend unto those cares; Lady, your words do spite me; As fair as morn, as fresh as May; Weep, weep, mine eyes, my heart can take no rest; I always beg, yet never am relieved; Thus Love commands that I in vain complain me; Oft have I vowed how dearly I did love thee; Come, shepherd swains, that wont to hear me sing; The Lady Oriana.*
(M) **(*) Vanguard 08.5080.71.

This pioneering collection from 1957 is especially welcome, as even now Wilbye is not generously represented in the catalogue and the quality of his madrigals is consistently high. Gerald English here joins the other regulars and the vocal matching remains smoothly integrated. As ever it is the deeply expressive settings that are the most memorable, with *Ah, cannot sighs, nor tears, Draw on, sweet Night* and *Weep, weep mine eyes* all particularly beautiful. But the singing is always fresh and well captures the changing character of each item, revealing a composer who, if not as prolific as some of his contemporaries, was their equal in all other respects.

Elizabethan and Jacobean music (with Desmond Dupré, lute; Consort of Viols; Gustav Leonhardt, harpsichord; Nikolaus Harnoncourt, bass viol): DOWLAND: *Can she forgive my wrongs?; If my complaints could passions move. My Lady Hunsdon's puffe* (lute). *From silent night.* MORLEY: *Air for 3 viols.* BARTLETT: *Of all the birds that I do know.* JOHNSON: *Alman for harpsichord.* JENKINS: *Pavan* and *Fantasia in C, for 4 viols.* CAMPION: *I care not for these ladies.* PARSONS: *Pandolpho.* FARNABY: *Variations for harpsichord on Up tails all.*
(M) *** Vanguard 08.5094.71.

One of the earliest recorded of the series (1954), though the recording is remarkably natural, this collection is in every way outstanding. Deller is in superb voice and the whole programme is glowingly fresh. There are novelties too. Parsons's air, *Pandolpho* (taken from a stage play), brings just as touching a melancholy as Dowland's *If my complaints could passions move*, and Bartlett's air, *Of all the birds that I do know*, and Campion's *I care not for these ladies* are delightfully light-hearted. The programme is attractively interspersed with music for viols (both bright and sombre) and a couple of lively harpsichord pieces. One small point: the vocal programme ends with a most moving account of Dowland's *From silent night* from *The Pilgrim's Solace*, but then the closing harpsichord *Variations* brings a disconcerting slight change of pitch.

English lute songs and In nomines (with Desmond
Dupré, lute, and the In Nomine Players): Francis
PILKINGTON: *Rest, sweet nymphs.* DOWLAND:
*What if I never speed?; Shall I sue?; Come again!
Sweet love doth now invite; Me, me and none but
me; Wilt thou unkind.* CAMPION: *Care-charming
sleep; Shall I come sweet love to thee?* ANON.:
Have you seen but a whyte lillie grow. ROSSETER:
When Laura smiles. John DANYEL: *Chromatic
tunes.* MORLEY: *Will ye buy a fine dog? (In
nomines* by John BULL; TOMKINS; WHITE; TYE;
TAVERNER).
(M) *** Vanguard 08.5095.71.

This outstandingly well-balanced programme dates
from 1958 and again finds Deller in exquisite voice
in (among other items) his performances of Dowland's *Shall I sue?* and the traditional *Have you
seen but a whyte lillie grow* (most subtly decorated),
which is immediately followed by Rosseter's happy
When Laura smiles. Morley's *Will ye buy a fine
dog?* has an even lighter touch, but perhaps the
most remarkable (and rarest) work here is John
Danyel's *Chromatic tunes*, a highly expressive fan-
tasia-like melisma in three sections for solo voice
and lute, showing Deller and Dupré in total symbiosis.

The six *In nomines* are used as interludes and are
varied in mood and colour. The two by Christopher
Tye (*Trust* and *Crye*), both in five parts, are particularly engaging, but the most profound, which
ends the concert, is by John Taverner. The
instrumental playing is worthy of Deller's supreme
vocal art and with excellent documentation this
is another of the great counter-tenor's very finest
discs.

*Music of Purcell, John Jenkins and Matthew
Locke* (with Leonhardt Baroque Ensemble;
Consort of Viols; Gustav Leonhardt, harpsichord;
Nikolaus Harnoncourt, bass viol): PURCELL: *The
Fairy Queen: Secrecie's song; Mystery song; The
plaint. Fantasia for 4 viols. If ever I more riches
did desire* (cantata): *Here let my life. Welcome to
all pleasures: Here the Deities approve. History of
Dioclesian: Since from my dear Astrea's sight.*
Keyboard: *Prelude, air and hornpipe; Suite in D
min.* LOCKE: *Consort of 4 parts for viols.*
JENKINS: *Pavane for 4 viols.*
(M) *** Vanguard 08.5104.71 [id.].

Deller did so much to revive interest in Purcell's
stage works (as well as his songs and instrumental
music) that it is meet and right that the last disc of
the Vanguard series – although one of the first to be
recorded, in 1954 – should be devoted to the music
of England's greatest composer. Of the three items
from *The Fairy Queen*, the opening *Secrecie's song*
(with its accompanying pair of recorders) is delightful, but it is *The plaint* that stands out, one of
the most masterly of all Purcell's songs. It is here
superbly sung over a firm chromatic ground bass

(Nikolaus Harnoncourt) and with a delicate violin
obbligato. *Since from my dear Astrea's sight* is also
memorable and *Here let my life* has a melancholy
worthy of Dowland. The inclusion of music by
Locke and Jenkins means that the songs can be
interleaved with impressively performed instrumental pieces.

Other recordings

'O ravishing delight' (with David Munrow,
Richard Lee, Desmond Dupré, Robert Elliott):
ANON.: *Miserere my Maker.* DOWLAND: *Shall I
sue?; Come heavy sleep; I saw my lady weep; Wilt
thou unkind; Fine knacks for ladies; Flow my
tears.* CAMPION: *I care not for these ladies; The
Cypress curtain.* BARTLETT: *Of all the birds.*
ROSSETER: *What then is love; What then is love
but mourning.* Francis PILKINGTON: *Rest, sweet
nymphs.* BLOW: *The fair lover and his black
mistress; The Self-banished.* CLARKE: *The glory of
the Arcadian groves; In her brave offspring.*
ECCLES: *Oh! the mighty pow'r of love.* CROFT: *My
time, o ye Muses.* Daniel PURCELL: *O ravishing
delight.* HUMFREY: *A Hymne to God the Father.*
(B) **(*) HM Musique d'abord HMA 190215
[id.].

Deller's recording contract with Vanguard lasted
from 1954 to 1965 and he made more than sixty
LPs for this label. Then he had a second, shorter
recording period with Harmonia Mundi. The present collection dates from 1969 and one can hear
him husbanding his voice, using it lightly where
possible.

Many of the songs here are available in earlier
performances above, but they still sound pleasingly
fresh, and as can be heard in the very lovely opening
Miserere my Maker, he has not lost his magic touch.
Dowland's *Come heavy sleep* and *I saw my lady
weep* and Campion's *Cypress curtain of the night*
certainly bring the 'ravishing delight' of the title. It
is good to have also a pair of songs from Jeremiah
Clarke (of *Trumpet voluntary* fame), and *The glory
of the Arcadian groves* features a charming recorder
obbligato. The programme closes with a beautifully
refined performance of Dowland's famous *Flow my
tears.* Throughout, the accompaniments are of the
highest quality, as is the recording, and as texts
are included, this makes a fine bargain sampler of
Deller's later achievement.

Domingo, Plácido (tenor)

'Domingo favourites' Arias from: DONIZETTI:
L'elisir d'amore. VERDI: *Ernani; Il Trovatore;
Aida; Nabucco; Don Carlos.* HALEVY: *La Juive.*
MEYERBEER: *L'Africaine.* BIZET: *Les Pêcheurs de
perles; Carmen.* PUCCINI: *Tosca; Manon Lescaut.*
(M) *** DG Dig. 445 525-2.

The greater part of this collection is taken from a 1980 digital recital, recorded in connection with yet another gala in San Francisco. The result is as noble and resplendent a tenor recital as you will find. Domingo improves in detail even on the fine versions of some of these arias he had recorded earlier, and the finesse of the whole gains greatly from the sensitive direction of Giulini. Though the orchestra is a little backward, the honeyed beauty of the voice is given the greatest immediacy. The other items are taken from Domingo's complete sets of *Don Carlos* (with Abbado), *Nabucco*, *Manon Lescaut* and *Tosca* (with Sinopoli), and are well up to the high standards this great tenor consistently sets for himself.

'Domingo sings Caruso': Arias from LEONCAVALLO: *La Bohème; Pagliacci.* DONIZETTI: *L'elisir d'amore.* MASSENET: *Manon; Le Cid.* CILEA: *L'Arlesiana.* FLOTOW: *Martha.* puccini: *La Fanciulla del West; La Bohème.* VERDI: *Rigoletto; Aida.* MEYERBEER: *L'Africana.* GOUNOD: *Faust.* HALEVY: *La Juive.* MASCAGNI: *Cavalleria rusticana.*
(M) **(*) BMG/RCA 09026 61356-2 [id.].

Domingo's heroic stage presence comes over well, the ringing tone able to impress in a lyrical phrase, even though more fining down of the tone and a willingness to sing really softly more often would enhance the listener's pleasure. But in the theatre this is obviously a voice to thrill, and the engineers have captured it directly and realistically, from the sobbing verismo of *Pagliacci* to the crisp aristocracy in *Rigoletto*. The selection is an interesting one – the opening aria, from Leoncavallo's *Bohème*, suggests that this opera is worth reviving.

Domingo, Plácido (tenor), Sherrill Milnes (baritone) and Katia Ricciarelli (soprano)

Arias and duets (with LSO, Guadagno, or Santa Cecilia Academy Orchestra, Gavazzeni): VERDI: *La forza del destino; I vespri siciliani; Otello.* BIZET: *Les Pêcheurs de perles.* PUCCINI: *La Bohème; Madama Butterfly.* ZANDONAI: *Francesca da Rimini.* PONCHIELLI: *La Gioconda.*
*** BMG/RCA 09026 62595-2 [id.].

This is a self-recommending disc. It includes the complete 1970 duet collection with Sherrill Milnes, plus two arias from a later duet disc with Ricciarelli. It would be easy to claim that Domingo and Milnes lack the sheer characterization of Caruso and Scotti, or Gigli and De Luca, for example. But by any standards, these are fine performances of show-stopping duets, and these singers even surpass their illustrious predecessors in care and detail. If it seems a little unreasonable that this reissue is offered at full-price, at least there are full texts and translations. Good sound.

'Duets of love and passion'

Duets from: PUCCINI: *La bohème; Madama Butterfly; Manon Lescaut; Turandot.* VERDI: *Otello.* GOUNOD: *Faust.* SAINT-SAENS: *Samson et Dalila.*
(M) **(*) Decca 458 241-2 [id.].

This collection starts well with Butterfly's duet with Pinkerton, from Serafin's classic 1958 account with Tebaldi and Bergonzi, but the *Otello* duet, with Margaret Price and Cossutta (Solti, 1977) is not quite so successful: Price is in lovely voice, but Cossutta does not quite match her in character. The 1972 Tebaldi/Corelli duet from *Manon Lescaut* is certainly passionate, but Tebaldi is a little past her prime here. The *Faust* excerpt is taken from Bonynge's lively 1966 set, and if one forgets the questionable French, it is most enjoyable – how could it fail with Sutherland, Corelli and Ghiaurov? It was imaginative of Decca to use the Josephine Barstow recording (1989) for the *Turandot* number: this was the first recording of Alfano's completion of the opera in its original full form, and is much longer than the version we are used to. The *Samson and Delila* excerpt is strongly performed with Sandra Warfield and McCracken (1966), and the programme ends with another classic Tebaldi/Bergonzi duet from *Bohème* (1959). Full texts and translations are included in this mid-price Opera Gala collection.

Early Music Consort of London, David Munrow

Music of the Gothic era: LEONIN: *Viderunt omnes; Alleluya Pascha nostrum; Gaude Maria Virgo; Locus iste.* PEROTIN: *Viderunt omnes; Sederunt principes.* ANON.: *Alle, psallite cum luya; Amor potest; S'on me regarde; In mari miserie; On parole de batre; En mai, quant rosier sont flouri; Dominator Domine; El mois de mai; O mitissima; Hoquetus I–VII; La mesnie fauveline; Quant je le voi; Zelus familie; Quasi non ministerium; Clap, clap, par un matin; Lés l'ormel a la turelle; O Philippe, Franci qui generis; Febus mundo oriens; Degentis vita; Inter densas deserti meditans.* Petrus DE CRUCE: *Aucun ont trouvé.* Adam DE LA HALLE: *De ma dame vient; J'os bien a m'amie parler.* Philippe DE VITRY: *Impudenter circumivi; Cum statua.* Bernard DE CLUNY: *Pantheon abluitur.* Henri GILLES DE PUSIEUX: *Rachel plorat filios.* MACHAUT: *Lasse! comment oublieray; Qui es promesses; Hoquetus David; Christe, qui lux es.* ROYLLART: *Rex Karole, Johannis genite.*

(M) *** DG 453 185-2 (2) [id.].

In the 1970s David Munrow was pioneering reper-toire by composers who are now much more readily accessible. But Munrow's gift of bringing early music consistently to life for the non-specialist listener and finding ear-catching ways in presenting the instrumental pieces is as valid today as it was then. 'Music of the Gothic era', is particularly valu-able in providing a remarkably lively survey of medieval music during the two centuries when it was developing at a comparatively swift rate from early organa to the thirteenth-century motet, 'from the monumental to the miniature', as David Munrow says in his notes. So the choice of music moves from Léonin's organum to the *Rex Karole* of Philippe Royllart, dating from the second half of the fourteenth century. The set was originally on three LPs (now reduced to a pair of CDs), so the music comes in three groupings: I, Notre Dame period; II, Ars Antiqua Motetti; and III, Ars Nova Motetti, although there are instrumental items in-cluded among the vocal works. Munrow projects this music with characteristically buoyant rhythms and expressive liveliness. Its presentation is essen-tially conjectural, but to bring the music back to life is the most important thing, and Munrow certainly does that, and most entertainingly too. The recording is excellent.

'Music of the Gothic era' (excerpts): Notre Dame period: LEONIN: *Organum Viderunt omnes.* PEROTIN: *Organum Viderunt omnes.* Ars Antiqua: *Motets from the Bamberg and Montpellier Codices* by Petrus DE CRUCE, Adam DE LA HALLE and ANON. Ars Nova: *Motets from the Roman de Fauvel. Chantilly/Ivrea Codices* by MACHAUT: DE VITRY.

(B) *** DG 469 027-2 [id.].

This issue draws on the two-CD set above and will make a good sampler for those not wanting to stretch to the more comprehensive collection. David Munrow had exceptional powers, both as scholar-performer and as a communicator. These perform-ances are wonderfully alive and vital and the digital remastering is as expert as one would expect.

'The Art of the Netherlands': Secular songs (vocal and instrumental versions): JOSQUIN DESPREZ: *Scaramella va alla guerra; Allegez moy, doulce plaisant brunette; El grillo è buon cantore; Adieu mes amours.* ISAAC: *Donna di dentro della tua casa.* VAN GHIZEGHEM: *De tous biens plaine.* BRUMEL: *Du tout plongiet – Fors seulement l'attente.* OCKEGHEM: *Prenez sur moi vostre exemple amoureux; Ma bouche rit.* BUSNOIS: *Fortuna desperata* (with others by GHISELIN; ANON.). Sacred music: TINCTORIS: *Missa sine nomine: Kyrie.* BRUMEL: *Missa Et ecce terrae motus: Gloria.* JOSQUIN desprez: *Credo super De tous biens; De profundis; Benedicta es caelorum*

regina. DE LA RUE: *Missa Ave sanctissima Maria: Sanctus.* ISAAC: *Missa La bassadanza: Agnus Dei.* OBRECHT: *Haec Deum caeli; Laudemus nunc Dominum.* MOUTON: *Nesciens mater virgo virum.* OCKEGHEM: *Intemerata Dei mater* (with ANON.).

(M) *** Virgin/Veritas EMI VED5 61334-2 (2).

The coverage here concentrates on the latter half of the fifteenth century, and the first disc is devoted to secular songs and instrumental arrangements. Josquin immediately makes his presence felt with an ear-catching opening item, *Scaramella is off to war,* for vocal quartet with recorders, bass viol, guitar, harp and tambourine, and later he is to return with the unaccompanied *El grillo,* where the vocal interchanges are equally lively. As most of these vocal numbers are short, what follows is a kaleido-scope of concerted and solo items, alongside instru-mental arrangements (for lute duet, recorder consort, broken consorts or keyboard), providing plenty of contrast. Heinrich Isaac's jubilant quod-libet feaures nine singers, while Hayne van Ghiz-eghem's touching chanson, *De tous biens plaine,* is first sung as an accompanied counter-tenor solo, and then heard in three different instrumental arrangements. Many of the songs are richly ex-pressive, Ockeghem's canon *Prenez sur moi vostre exemple amoureux* and Brumel's *Du tout plongiet* are memorably poignant examples. Busnois's *Fortuna desperata* is first presented in a three-part vocal presentation, then in six parts (three singers with a trio of viols), and finally on a combination of tenor dulcian, recorder, rebec and two lutes.

The second section, a group of Mass movements, immediately brings a greater degree of gravitas with Johannes Tinctoris's *Kyrie,* solemnly presented by four low male voices, yet Brumel's robust *Gloria* is memorably gutsy. Pacing never drags; indeed, Isaac's six-part *Agnus Dei* flows forward strongly. The motets in the third section, many of them Marian, are more consistently expressively solemn, but all are strikingly beautiful, with Josquin's *De profundis,* with its firm bass line, particularly elo-quent. Full texts and translations are included and this seems an excellent way to explore this reper-toire as a prelude to acquiring CDs concentrating on a single composer. The standard of singing and playing is high, and the recording is as vivid as you could wish.

'The Art of courtly love' (with James Bowman, Charles Brett, Martyn Hill, Geoffrey Shaw): I: 'Guillaume de Machaut and his age': Jehan de LESCUREL: *A vous douce debonaire* (chanson). MACHAUT: *Amours me fait desirer; Dame se vous m'estés lointeinne; De Bon Espoir – Puis que la douce rousee; De toutes flours; Douce dame jolie; Hareu! hareu! le feu; Ma fin est mon commencement; Mes esperis se combat; Phyton le mervilleus serpent; Quant j'ay l'espart; Quant je*

suis mis au retour; Quant Theseus – Ne quier veoir; Se ma dame m'a guerpy; Se je souspir; Trop plus est belle – Biauté paree – Je ne sui mie certeins. P. des MOLINS: *Amis tout dous vis.* ANON.: *La Septime estampie real.* F. ANDRIEU: *Armes amours – O flour des flours.*
II: 'Late 14th century avant-garde': GRIMACE: *A l'arme a l'arme.* FRANCISCUS: *Phiton Phiton.* BORLET: *2 Variants on the tenor 'Roussignoulet du bois'; Ma tedol rosignol.* SOLAGE: *Fumeux fume; Helas! je voy mon cuer.* Johannes de MERUCO: *De home vray.* ANON.: *Istampitta Tre fontane; Tribum quem; Contre le temps; Restoés restoés.* HASPROIS: *Ma douce amour.* VAILLANT: *Trés doulz amis – Ma dame – Cent mille fois.* PYKINI: *Plasanche or tost.* Anthonello de CASERTA: *Amour m'a le cuer mis.* Matteo da PERUGIA: *Andray soulet; Le greygnour bien.*
III: 'The Court of Burgundy': DU FAY: *Ce moys de may; La belle se siet; Navré ju sui d'un dart penetratif; Lamention Sanctae Matris Ecclesiae Constantinopolitaine (O tres piteulx – Omnes amici); Par droit je puis bien complaindre; Donnés l'assault; Helas mon dueil; Vergine bella.* BINCHOIS: *Je ne fai tousjours que penser; Files a marier; Amoreux suy et me vient toute joye; Je loe Amours et ma dame mercye; Vostre trés doulx regart; Bien puist.* ANON.: *La Spagna* (basse danse) *Variants I & II.*
(M) *** Virgin Veritas/EMI VED5 61284-2 (2) [ZDMB 61284].
David Munrow's two-disc set 'The Art of courtly love' spans the period 1300–1475 in some depth. The survey is divided into three sections: 'Guillaume de Machaut and his age', 'Late fourteenth-century avant-garde' and 'The Court of Burgundy'. The first section is introduced arrestingly by two cornetts and an alto shawm, who accompany a striking chanson of Jehan de Lescurel (died 1304) which must have had 'hit' status in its time (*A vous douce debonaire*). The bare harmonies give a real tang to the tune. Then comes the first of many numbers by the justly famous Guillaume de Machaut, *Hareu! hareu! le feu . . . le feu d'ardant desir* which one hardly needs to translate, and it is certainly ardent!
   But it is the expressive romantic chansons of Machaut that make one appreciate how readily the composer came to dominate the combination of lyric poetry and music in fourteenth-century France and to epitomize the title, 'The Art of courtly love'. The virelais *Se ma dame m'a guerpy* ('If my lady has left me') and *Quant je suis mis au retour*, for solo tenor and chorus, with its sad introductory bass rebec solo, surely anticipate the melancholy eloquence of Dowland, while Machaut could also be attractively lighthearted as in *Se je souspir* ('If I sigh'), or robustly jolly and spiritedly extrovert (*Douce dame jolie*).
   The second CD opens with a particularly lovely

vocal trio by Jehan Vaillant (?1360–90) which anticipates *The first nowell* in its vocal line, and a following ballade, *Amour m'a la cuer mis*, by Anthonello de Caserta (whose career spanned the turn of the century) demonstrates how forward-looking were other composers of 'the late fourteenth-century avant-garde', while Solage is no less enterprising (flourished 1370–90) in providing lugubrious humour with his baritone solo *Fumeux fume* ('He who fumes and lets off steam provokes hot air') with its unlikely melodic line. (Not surprisingly, Munrow gives this rondeau an appropriately bizarre instrumental backing.) 'A man's true worth' (*De home vray*), a ballade by the late-fourteenth-century Johannes de Meruco, also brings lively melodic twists and turns.
Gilles Binchois (c. 1400–60) was another leading figure of the time, well represented here, and, like Machaut, he had a wide range. But it is the lovely rondeau duet *Amoreux suy et me vient toute joye* ('Filled with love, I am overjoyed, hoping that your kindness might bring sweet comfort') that one especially remembers. With its expressive pleading so direct in its appeal, it is one of the set's highlights and is ravishingly sung here. With the music from 'The Court of Burgundy' we also meet the remarkable Guillaume Du Fay, with his exhilarating rondeau *Ce moys de may*, so different in mood from his Masses, followed by an engagingly melancholy echoing duet for two counter-tenors, *La belle se siet au piet de la tour* ('The maiden sits . . . weeping, sighing and venting her grief'), while the virelai *Helas mon dueil*, a rejected lover's lament, is infinitely touching.
However, the collection ends in lively fashion with the anonymous basse danse *La Spagna*, and here (as in the other instrumental items) Munrow's choice of colour brings an extra dimension to what is basically a very simple dance. All the soloists are distinguished and at their finest. Incidentally, although the translations are not affected, the documentation for this set has the list of titles for the second disc mixed up, starting with bands 12–15, then following with 1–11, but they are all there.

'*Monteverdi's contemporaries*' (with James Bowman, Martyn Hill and Paul Elliott):
MAINERIO: *Il primo libro di balli: 10 Dances.* GUAMI: *Canzoni per sonar: Canzona a 8.* LAPPI: *Canzoni per sonar: La negrona.* PRIULI: *Sacrorum Concentuum: Canzona prima a 12.* PORTA: *Sacro convito musicale: Corda Deo dabimus.* BUSATTI: *Compago ecclesiastico: Surrexit Pastor bonus.* DONATI: *Concerti ecclesiastici, Op. 4: In te Domine speravi.* D'INDIA: *Novi concentus ecclesiastici; Isti sunt duae olivae.* GRANDI: *Motetti con sinfonie, Libro I: O vos omnes; Libro : O beate Benedicte.*
● (M) *** Virgin Veritas/EMI VER5 61288-2 [CDM 61288].

Munrow's art is shown to even greater advantage in his collection of music by Monteverdi's contemporaries, which has a comparatively short time-span (1535–1644). Opening with five dances from Giorgio Mainerio's *Il primo libro di balli*, vividly scored, mainly for wind and brass, but unexpectedly bringing a xylophone solo in the *Ballo francese*, the programme continues with other impressive instrumental pieces by Gioseffo Guami, Pietro Lappi and Giovanni Priuli. Then come five more of the Mainerio dances, two of which are solos for the cittern, notably the brilliant and catchy *Schiarazula marazula*, which is as intricately titillating as its title suggests.

But this all serves to act as a prelude to a superb collection of vocal music, nearly all of which is entirely unknown. Ercole Porta's sonorous setting of *Corda Deo dabimus* has the counter-tenor (James Bowman) and tenor (Martyn Hill) sonorously underpinned by sackbuts; Cherubino Busatti's *Surrexit Pastor bonus* which follows (James Bowman at his most inspired) is unforgettable. The setting of this short but deeply poignant motet dramatically alternates moods: bright and lighthearted for 'The good shepherd is risen – Alleluia' and then (with a sudden change) movingly eloquent in telling of the crucifixion, with a despairing downward scale for the word '*mori*' (die) which is infinitely touching. Ignazio Donati's tenor duet *In te Domine speravi* (Martyn Hill and Paul Elliott) is almost equally eloquent.

There is a fine motet from Sigismondo d'India, then comes the other highlight, Alessando Grandi's tragically beautiful *O vos omnes*, gloriously sung by Bowman. This too is unforgettable. The concert ends happily in celebration with Grandi's *O beate Benedicte*, with counter-tenor and tenor duetting happily, sometimes in harmony, at others in felicitous imitation, with the accompaniment for cornett, tenor sackbut, organ and bass violin adding to the simple polyphony. Here as elsewhere Munrow's instrumentation has an imaginative flair matched by no other exponent of this repertoire. The recording is superb and this collection, including several out-and-out masterpieces among much else that is rewarding, is on no account to be missed

(i) Early Music Consort of London, David Munrow; (ii) Musica Reservata, John Beckett

'Early music festival': (i) *Florentine music of the fourteenth century* (with James Bowman, counter-tenor, Nigel Rogers and Martyn Hill, tenors): LANDINI: *Ecco la primavera; Giunta vaga biltà; Questa fanciull' amor; De! dinmi tu; Cara mie donna; La bionda treçça; Donna 'l tuo partimento.* ANON.: *Lamento di Tristano; Trotto;*

Due saltarelli; Quan ye voy le duç; La Manfredini; Istampita Ghaetta; Biance flour. PIERO: *Con dolce brama.* TERAMO: *Rosetta.* Lorenzo di FIRENZE: *Chon brachi assai; Dà, dà, a chi avaregia.* Jacobo de BOLOGNA: *Fenice fu' e vissi.* (ii) *Florentine music of the sixteenth century* (with Jantina Noorman, mezzo-soprano, Grayston Burgess, counter-tenor, Nigel Rogers, tenor, John Frost, bass baritone): MONTEVERDI: *Orfeo: Toccata.* Music for Ferdinando de' Medici (incidental music for the play *La Pellegrina*): MARENZIO: *Second Intermedio.* MALVEZZI & CAVALIERI: *Sesto Intermedio.* FESTA: *Quando ritova.* ANON.: *Allemana-ripresa; Pavana: La cornetta; Gagliarda Giorgio; Ahimè sospiri; Pavana: Forze d'Ercole; Orsù, orsù, car'Signori; Pavana: El colognese.* Dance songs (vocal and keyboard settings): *Era di Maggio; El marchese di Salluzzo; In questo ballo; Non ci vogliam' partire; Bussa la porta; La pastorella; E su quel monte; Maggio valente; Sorella mi piacente.* TROMBONCINO: *Frottola: Io son l'occello.* NOLA: *Tri ciechi siamo.* CARA: *Frottola: Io non compro.* (B) *** Decca Double 452 967-2 (2) [id.].

This Decca Double happily combines two collections of Florentine music from two different authentic groups recording for the Argo label in the late 1960s and early 1970s. The repertoire may be a century apart, but this means that the contrast is the more striking. The fourteenth-century collection has a wide general appeal. Its key figure, Francesco Landini, has an immediate approachability, and this extends to much else here, especially when the variety of presentation, both vocal and instrumental, is so stimulating.

No one knows exactly how or on what instruments accompaniments would have been performed, but David Munrow and his Early Music Consort solve the problems with their usual combination of scholarship and imagination. The singers include artists of the distinction of James Bowman, and the players are first rate. David Munrow's recorder playing is virtuosic, and Andrea Zachara da Teramo's *Rosetta*, played on a chamber organ, is most piquant. Attractive music, expertly transcribed and beautifully recorded.

The sixteenth-century collection from Musica Reservata opens with a *Toccata* from Monteverdi's *Orfeo*, vigorously played on a colourful combination of baroque trumpet, sackbuts and percussion, which shows how much more elaborate musical presentation had become in the intervening century. The earthy style of Musica Reservata may be typified by the throaty roaring of the unforgettable Jantina Noorman, but the opening vocal number from Luca Marenzio's *Second Intermedio* (incidental music for the play *La Pellegrina*) is charmingly presented by three boy trebles, accompanied by lyra, viol and harp, and later the choruses (sometimes for double or triple choirs) are both expansive and beautiful.

The collection ranges wide in mood among vigorous dances, popular songs and ceremonial music, all of it refreshing to the modern ear. Full translations are included and both programmes can be highly recommended to anyone who wants to explore painlessly and with delight a rich period of musical history. Again the recording is excellent, and the only possible criticism about this straight reissue of a pair of highly recommended LPs is to mention that other explorations were made by Argo at that time; with 51 minutes' playing time on the first disc and 53 on the second, there would have been room to include more music, from the intervening period. But each concert here is self-sufficient in itself, and this Double is still worth its cost.

Emmanuel College, Cambridge, Chapel Choir, Timothy Prosser

'Carols from Cambridge': TRAD.: Veni, veni Emmanuel; The Angel Gabriel; In dulci jubilo. RUTTER: What sweeter music. GAUNTLETT: Once in Royal David's city. arr. WILLCOCKS: Ding dong! merrily on high; O come all ye faithful. BRITTEN: A Hymn to the virgin; Friday afternoons, Op. 7: New Year carol. arr. JACKSON: Noël nouvelet. arr. VAUGHAN WILLIAMS: This is the truth sent from above; Wither's rocking hymn. MATHIAS: Sir Christèmas. WARLOCK: Bethlehem Down; Benedicamus Domino. arr. HAMMOND: Swete was the song the Virgin Soong. GARDNER: Tomorrow shall be my dancing day. BERLIOZ: L'enfance du Christ: Shepherds' farewell. LEIGHTON: Lully, lulla, thou tiny Child. RAVENSCROFT: Remember, O thou man. HOPKINS: We three kings. ORD: Adam lay y-bounden. GRUBER: Stille Nacht. arr. RUTTER: Wexford carol.
(M) *** ASV Dig. CDWHL 2104 [id.].

Opening with the famous melodic chant Veni, veni Emmanuel, which turns out to be medieval in origin and not a Victorian hymn, this is a particularly appealing mid-priced collection, beautifully recorded. Although it includes (as the third item) Once in Royal David's city, sung in crescendo in the Willcocks arrangement, a strongly expressed O come all ye faithful, and Mathias's jovial Sir Christèmas, as outgoing and vigorous as one could wish, the style of performance, as befits a smaller chapel choir, is for the most part a pleasingly intimate one.

Unlike King's College, Emmanuel uses women's voices, but they are as sweet and pure as any boy trebles', the overall blending and ensemble are nigh perfect and the effect is disarmingly simple, notably

so in the lovely Shepherds' farewell from Berlioz's L'enfance du Christ. Anna Dennis is a pleasingly fragile soloist in Vaughan Williams's setting of Wither's rocking hymn; Rutter's What sweeter music and Warlock's Bethlehem Down are especially touching.

Enterprisingly, the famous Stille Nacht is presented in its charming original version for two solo voices (Julia Caddick and Sarah Fisher) and guitar. Grüber hastily scored it in this fashion when the organ broke down just before its first performance on Christmas Eve 1818 – in the appropriately named Church of St Nicholas (Oberndorf, Austria). Not all the choices are obvious, and Britten's New Year carol, taken from Friday afternoons, is an engaging novelty. Prosser and his splendid singers are equally impressive in the livelier carols: the rhythmic syncopations of Gardner's Tomorrow shall be my dancing day are as sparkling as the bounce of We three kings, and the choir's lightness of touch is equally appealing in Warlock's Benedicamus Domino, which ends the concert joyfully.

English opera: 'Stars of English opera'

'Stars of English opera' Arias and excerpts from: HANDEL: Alessandro (Isobel Baillie). VERDI: Simon Boccanegra (Joyce Gartside; James Johnston; Arnold Matters; Frederick Sharp; Howell Glynne); Un ballo in maschera (Jean Watson). GOUNOD: Faust (Joan Hammond; Owen Brannigan; Heddle Nash); La reine de Saba (Norman Allin). PUCCINI: La Bohème (Lisa Perli (Dora Labbette); Gerald Davies). MOZART: Le nozze di Figaro (Miriam Licette). TCHAIKOVSKY: The Maid of Orleans (Maggie Teyte). GLUCK: Orfeo ed Euridice (Kathleen Ferrier). CILEA: L'Arlesiana. MASSENET: Werther (Tano Ferendinos). donizetti: L'elisir d'amore (Heddle Nash).
(M) (***) Dutton mono CDLX 7024 [id. full price].

The sixteen tracks here – including three devoted to a rare 1948 recording, celebrating the first British production of Verdi's Simon Boccanegra, at Sadler's Wells – demonstrate what outstanding singers, almost all of them technically immaculate, were active in the years immediately after the Second World War. It is striking what clarity of focus marks almost all the singing, with hardly a wobble throughout and with words exceptionally clear, usually but not always involving an English text.

Isobel Baillie was never strictly an opera-singer, but it is good to hear her in an aria from Handel's Alessandro. The Ferrier recording of Orfeo's great aria, What is life?, from Gluck's opera was from a test disc she made with Gerald Moore at the piano, anticipating her Decca recordings, and the *Boccanegra* excerpts feature an excellent team of singers whose careers centred on Sadler's Wells: Joyce Gartside, James Johnston, Arnold Matters and Frederick Sharp, with Michael Mudie conducting, as in the theatre. Another fine ensemble recording of 1948 has Joan Hammond, Heddle Nash and Owen Brannigan in the garden scene from Gounod's *Faust*, and two tracks celebrate the superb voice of the long-neglected Greek-Welsh tenor Tano Ferendinos. Perhaps most striking of all is the pure, bright singing of Lisa Perli (pseudonym of Dora Labbette), with Beecham conducting, in *Mimi's Farewell* from Puccini's *La Bohème*. Transfers are vivid, full and immediate.

Estampie, John Bryan

'Under the greenwood tree' (with Deborah Catterall, Graham Derrick): Walther von VOGELWEIDE: *Palästinalied*. Richard COEUR DE LION: *Ja nuis homs pris*. BLONDEL DE NESLE: *A l'entrant d'este*. Raimbault DE VAQUERIAS: *Kalenda Maya*. CORNYSHE: *Ah! Robin*. STONINGES: *Browning my dear* (on the theme *The leaves be green*). GERVAISE: *4th Livre de Danceries: La Venissienne. 6th Livre de Danceries: Gailliarde*. PLAYFORD: *The Dancing Master: Greenwood; Nottingham Castle; Green Goose Fair; The green man*. SIMPSON: *Ricercar on Bonny sweet Robin*. WEELKES: *When Kempe did dance alone, or Robin Hood, Maid Marian and Little John are gone*. ANON.: *Novus miles sequitur; Estampie; Clap, clap un matin s'en aloit Robin; Robin Hood; The Wedding of Robin Hood; Under the greenwood tree; Sellenger's round; Greensleeves* (lute and vocal versions); *Robin Hood and the Curtal Friar; Robin Hood and the Tanner; Robin Hood and Maid Marian; Sweet angel of England* (to the tune *Bonny sweet Robin*); *O lusty May*.
(BB) ** Naxos Dig. 8.553442 [id.].

With John Bryan as music director and Graham Derrick as arranger and main performer, the early-music group Estampie here offer a well-devised group of dances and instrumental pieces, interspersed with songs, broadly inspired by the legend of Robin Hood and the ballad *Robin is to the greenwood gone* in its various forms. That in turn leads to celebrations in song and dance of Maytime and the annual revival of the Green Man. Items range from a song attributed to King Richard the Lionheart in the twelfth century to four items drawn (in arrangements by Graham Derrick) from John Playford's collection *The Dancing Master*, in the seventeenth.

The sequence is most illuminating, but the performances, always tasteful, rather lack the bite and earthiness which can make medieval music so invigorating. The final item, a Scottish song, *O lusty May*, is anything but that, though there and in the other songs the mezzo, Deborah Catterall, sings with a fresh, clear tone. Aptly intimate recorded sound.

Evans, Sir Geraint (baritone)

'Arias and sacred songs' (with (i) SRO, Balkwill; (ii) Shelley Singers, Lyrian Singers, Glendower Singers, BBC Welsh SO, Mansel Thomas). (i) HANDEL: *Berenice: Si trai ceppi. Semele: Leave me radiant light*. MOZART: *Le nozze di Figaro: Non più andrai. Don Giovanni: Madamina, il catalogo. L'oca del Cairo: Ogni momento. Die Zauberflöte: Der Vogelfänger*. BEETHOVEN: *Fidelio: Ha! welch'ein Augenblick!* LEONCAVALLO: *Pagliacci: Prologue*. DONIZETTI: *Don Pasquale: Un fuoco insolito*. VERDI: *Otello: Credo. Falstaff: Ehi! Paggio . . . l'onore! Ladri*. BRITTEN: *A Midsummer Night's Dream: Bottom's dream*. MUSSORGSKY: *Boris Godunov: Tchelkalov's aria*. (ii) MENDELSSOHN: *Elijah: Lord God of Abraham; Is not His word like a fire?* HANDEL: *Judas Maccabaeus: Arm, arm ye brave. Messiah: The Trumpet shall sound*. rossini: *Requiem: Pro peccatis*.
(BB) *** Belart 461 492-2 [(M) id. import].

This is a marvellous display of wide-ranging virtuosity, of artistic bravura such as we know from almost any performance that this ebullient and lovable singer gave. Part of Evans's mastery lay in the way he could convey the purest comedy, even drawing laughs without ever endangering the musical line through excessive buffoonery. His Mozart characters are almost unmatchable – Figaro, Leporello, Papageno – while it is good to be reminded that here is a singer who could be a formidable Iago as well as the most complete Falstaff of his day. Good accompaniment and recording, with a richly atmospheric orchestral backing, of one of Britain's greatest singers at the peak of his form.

Evans, Rebecca (soprano), Michael Pollock (piano)

'Début': BELLINI: *6 Ariette da camera*. VERDI: *Stornella*. RESPIGHI: *Notturno; Storia breve; Tanto bella; Lagrime; L'ultima ebbrezza; Luce*. ROSSINI: *Serate musicale, Vol. 1: L'invito; La pastorella delle Alpi; La promessa*. DONIZETTI: *Ah! rammenta, o bella Irene; A mezzanotte; La ninn-nanna*. WOLF-FERRARI: *4 Rispetti, Op. 11*.
(B) **(*) EMI Dig. CDZ5 69706-2 [id.].

The young Welsh soprano, Rebecca Evans makes an excellent choice of artist for the EMI Début series. This programme, devised by the excellent accompanist, Michael Pollock, a specialist in this area, consists almost entirely of miniatures, chips off the workbenches of great opera-composers, which consistently flaunt the Italian love of lyricism. It is striking how, after the opening Bellini group, Verdi immediately has one listening with new attention, when his two lively songs make the singer sparkle. The three Rossini items too – from the *Serate musicale* – bring extra vigour and striking tunes. Two of the Donizetti songs are longer and much closer to operatic models, but the Wolf-Ferrari group brings a charming conclusion, ending with a tiny squib of a tarantella. The recording is bright and forward, even if it does not quite catch the full beauty of Rebecca Evans's voice.

Ferrier, Kathleen (contralto)

Lieder, arias, songs and duets: MAHLER: *Kindertotenlieder* (with Vienna Philharmonic Orchestra, Bruno Walter). HANDEL: *Ottone: Spring is coming; Come to me.* Maurice GREENE: *O praise the Lord; I will lay me down in peace.* PURCELL: *Ode for Queen Mary: Sound the trumpet. The Indian Queen: Let us not wander. King Arthur: Shepherd, shepherd cease decoying.* MENDELSSOHN: *I would that my love; Greeting* (all with Gerald Moore, piano; Purcell & Mendelssohn duets with Isobel Baillie). GLUCK: *Orfeo ed Euridice:* excerpts including *Che farò* and *Che puro ciel.* (with Netherlands Opera Ch. & O, Charles Bruck).
(M) (***) EMI mono CDM5 66911-2 [CDM 566963].

It was especially tragic that Kathleen Ferrier made so few recordings in which the technical quality matched her magical artistry. This collection, rightly reissued as one of EMI's 'Great Recordings of the Century', includes many of her mono records from this source, which generally sound better than the Decca repertoire listed below. The Gluck *Orfeo* excerpts (deriving from an indifferent recording of a broadcast) have undoubtedly been enhanced for this reissue, although the choral entry in *Deh! placetevi con me* is still very fierce, and the Maurice Greene items are ill-focused. However, fortunately the 1949 *Kindertotenlieder* comes over very well. Particularly worth having are the duets with Isobel Baillie, as these artists obviously worked especially well together. The new transfers are vivid and show an enhancement of their early LP incarnations.

'The world of Kathleen Ferrier', Volume 1: TRAD.: *Blow the wind southerly; The Keel row; Ma bonny lad; Kitty my love.* arr. BRITTEN: *Come you not from Newcastle.* HANDEL: *Rodelinda: Art thou troubled? Serse: Ombra mai fù.* GLUCK: *Orfeo ed Euridice: What is life?* MENDELSSOHN:

Elijah: Woe unto them; O rest in the Lord. BACH: *St Matthew Passion: Have mercy, Lord, on me.* SCHUBERT: *An die Musik; Gretchen am Spinnrade; Die junge Nonne; Der Musensohn.* BRAHMS: *Sapphische Ode; Botschaft.* MAHLER: *Rückert Lieder: Um Mitternacht.*
✪ (M) (***) Decca mono 430 096-2.

This selection, revised and expanded from the original LP issue, admirably displays Kathleen Ferrier's range, from the delightfully fresh folksongs to Mahler's *Um Mitternacht* in her celebrated recording with Bruno Walter and the VPO. The noble account of *O rest in the Lord* is one of the essential items now added, together with an expansion of the Schubert items (*Die junge Nonne* and *An die Musik* are especially moving). The CD transfers are remarkably trouble-free and the opening unaccompanied *Blow the wind southerly* has uncanny presence. The recital plays for 65 minutes and fortunately there are few if any technical reservations to be made here about the sound quality.

'The world of Kathleen Ferrier', Volume 2: TRAD.: *Ye banks and braes; Drink to me only* (both arr. QUILTER); *I have a bonnet trimmed with blue; Down by the Salley Gardens; The stuttering lovers* (all arr. Hughes). PURCELL: *The Fairy Queen: Hark! the echoing air.* HANDEL: *Atalanta: Like the love-lorn turtle.* GLUCK: *Orfeo ed Euridice: Che puro ciel.* MAHLER: *Rückert Lieder: Ich bin der Welt abhanden gekommen.* SCHUMANN: *Frauenliebe und Leben: Er, der Herrlichste von allen.* BRAHMS: *Geistliches Wiegenlied; Von ewiger Liebe.* SCHUBERT: *Du bist die Ruh'; Rosamunde: Romance.* BACH: *Mass in B min.: Agnus Dei.* HANDEL: *Messiah: He was despised.*
(M) (***) Decca mono 448 055-2.

Volume 2 offers a comparable mixture, opening with more delightful folksongs, notably the charming *Stuttering lovers*, although it is *Ye banks and braes* and *Drink to me only* that show the full richness of this glorious voice. *Che puro ciel* stands out among the opera arias for its simple eloquence, and the Brahms *Geistliches Wiegenlied*, with its somewhat wan viola obbligato, is gently ravishing. The passionate *Du bist die Ruh'*, the *Rosamunde Romance* and *Von ewiger Liebe* come from a BBC acetate disc of her 1949 Edinburgh Festival recital with Bruno Walter at the piano, and here there is some uneven background noise and the quality deteriorates in the Brahms song. But the CD closes with one of her very last recordings, her unforgettably poignant *He was despised*, with those words given an uncanny presence.

Fischer-Dieskau, Dietrich (baritone)

'Fischer-Dieskau Lieder Edition' (complete).
✪ (BB) *** DG 447 500-2 (44) [(M) id. import].

SCHUBERT: Lieder (with Gerald Moore, piano): Volume I (1811–17); Volume II (1817–28); Volume III: Song cycles: *Die schöne Müllerin; Schwanengesang; Winterreise.*

(B) *** DG 437 214-2 (21) [(M) id. import].

Lieder, Volume I (1811–17): *Ein Leichenfantasie; Der Vatermörder* (1811); *Der Jüngling am Bache* (1812); *Totengräberlied; Die Schatten; Sehnsucht; Verklärung; Pensa, che questo istante* (1813); *Der Taucher* (1813–15); *Andenken; Geisternähe; Erinnerung; Trost, An Elisa; Die Betende; Lied aus der Ferne; Der Abend; Lied der Liebe; Erinnerungen; Adelaide; An Emma; Romanze: Ein Fräulein klagt' im finstern Turm; An Laura, als sie Klopstocks Auferstehungslied sang; Der Geistertanz; Das Mädchen aus der Fremde; Nachtgesang; Trost in Tränen; Schäfers Klagelied; Sehnsucht; Am See* (1814); *Auf einen Kirchhof; Als ich sie erröten sah; Das Bild; Der Mondabend* (1815); *Lodas Gespenst* (1816); *Der Sänger* (1815); *Die Erwartung* (1816); *Am Flusse; An Mignon; Nähe des Geliebten; Sängers Morgenlied; Amphiaraos; Das war ich; Die Sterne; Vergebliche Liebe; Liebesrausch; Sehnsucht der Liebe; Die erste Liebe; Trinklied; Stimme der Liebe; Naturgenuss; An die Freude; Der Jüngling am Bache; An den Mond; Die Mainacht; An die Nachtigall; An die Apfelbäume; Seufzer; Liebeständelei; Der Liebende; Der Traum; Die Laube; Meeres Stille; Grablied; Das Finden; Wandrers Nachtlied; Der Fischer; Erster Verlust; Die Erscheinung; Die Täuschung; Der Abend; Geist der Liebe; Tischlied; Der Liedler; Ballade; Abends unter der Linde; Die Mondnacht; Huldigung; Alles um Liebe; Das Geheimnis; An den Frühling; Die Bürgschaft; Der Rattenfänger; Der Schatzgräber; Heidenröslein; Bundeslied; An den Mond; Wonne der Wehmut; Wer kauft Liebesgötter?* (1815); *Der Goldschmiedsgesell* (1817); *Der Morgenkuss; Abendständchen: An Lina; Morgenlied: Willkommen, rotes Morgenlicht; Der Weiberfreund; An die Sonne; Tischlerlied; Totenkranz für ein Kind; Abendlied; Die Fröhlichkeit; Lob des Tokayers; Furcht der Geliebten; Das Rosenband; An Sie; Die Sommernacht; Die frühen Gräber; Dem Unendlichen; Ossians Lied nach dem Falle Nathos; Das Mädchen von Inistore; Labetrank der Liebe; An die Geliebte; Mein Gruss an den Mai; Skolie – Lasst im Morgenstrahl des Mai'n; Die Sternenwelten; Die Macht der Liebe; Das gestörte Glück; Die Sterne; Nachtgesang; An Rosa I: Warum bist du nicht hier?; An Rosa II: Rosa, denkst du an mich?; Schwanengesang; Der Zufriedene; Liane; Augenlied; Geistes-Gruss; Hoffnung; An den Mond; Rastlose Liebe; Erlkönig* (1815); *Der Schmetterling; Die Berge* (1819); *Genügsamkeit; An die Natur* (1815); *Klage; Morgenlied; Abendlied; Der Flüchtling; Laura am*

Klavier; Entzückung an Laura; Die vier Weltalter; Pflügerlied; Die Einsiedelei; An die Harmonie; Die Herbstnacht; Lied: Ins stille Land; Der Herbstabend; Der Entfernten; Fischerlied; Sprache der Liebe; Abschied von der Harfe; Stimme der Liebe; Entzückung; Geist der Liebe; Klage: Der Sonne steigt; Julius an Theone; Klage: Dein Silber schien durch Eichengrün; Frühlingslied; Auf den Tod einer Nachtigall; Die Knabenzeit; Winterlied; Minnelied; Die frühe Liebe; Blumenlied; Der Leidende; Seligkeit; Erntelied; Das grosse Halleluja; Die Gestirne; Die Liebesgötter; An den Schlaf; Gott im Frühling; Der gute Hirt; Die Nacht; Fragment aus dem Aeschylus (1816); *An die untergehende Sonne* (1816/17); *An mein Klavier; Freude der Kinderjahre; Das Heimweh; An den Mond; An Chloen; Hochzeitlied; In der Mitternacht; Trauer der Liebe; Die Perle; Liedesend; Orpheus; Abschied; Rückweg; Alte Liebe rostet nie; Gesänge des Harfners aus Goethes Wilhelm Meister: Harfenspieler I: Wer sich der Einsamkeit ergibt; Harfenspieler II: An die Türen will ich schleichen; Harfenspieler III: Wer nie sein Brot mit Tränen ass. Der König in Thule; Jägers Abendlied; An Schwager Kronos; Der Sänger am Felsen; Lied: Ferne von der grossen Stadt; Der Wanderer; Der Hirt; Lied eines Schiffers an die Dioskuren; Geheimnis; Zum Punsche; Am Bach im Frühling* (1816); *An eine Quelle* (1817); *Bei dem Grabe, meines Vaters; Am Grabe Anselmos; Abendlied; Zufriedenheit; Herbstlied; Skolie: Mädchen entsiegelten; Lebenslied; Lieden der Trennung* (1816); *Alinde; An die Laute* (1827); *Frohsinn; Die Liebe; Trost; Der Schäfer und der Reiter* (1817); *Lob der Tränen* (1821); *Der Alpenjäger; Wie Ulfru fischt; Fahrt zum Hades; Schlaflied; Die Blumensprache; Die abgeblühte Linde; Der Flug der Zeit; Der Tod und das Mädchen; Das Lied vom Reifen; Täglich zu singen; Am Strome; Philoktet; Memnon; Auf dem See; Ganymed; Der Jüngling und der Tod; Trost im Liede* (1817).

(B) *** DG 437 215-2 (9) [(M) id. import].

Lieder, Volume II (1817–28): *An die Musik; Pax vobiscum; Hänflings Liebeswerbung; Auf der Donau; Der Schiffer; Nach einem Gewitter; Fischerlied; Das Grab; Der Strom; An den Tod; Abschied; Die Forelle; Gruppe aus dem Tartarus; Elysium; Atys; Erlafsee; Der Alpenjäger; Der Kampf; Der Knabe in der Wiege* (1817); *Auf der Riesenkoppe; An den Mond in einer Herbstnacht; Grablied für die Mutter; Einsamkeit; Der Blumenbrief; Das Marienbild* (1818); *Litanei auf das Fest Allerseelen* (1816); *Blondel zu Marien; Das Abendrot; Sonett I: Apollo, lebet noch dein Hold verlangen; Sonett II: Allein, nachdenken wie gelähmt vom Krampfe; Sonett III: Nunmehr, da Himmel, Erde schweigt; Vom Mitleiden Mariä*

(1818); *Die Gebüsche; Der Wanderer; Abendbilder; Himmelsfunken; An die Freunde; Sehnsucht; Hoffnung; Der Jüngling am Bache; Hymne I: Wenige wissen das Geheimnis der Liebe; Hymne II: Wenn ich ihn nur hab; Hymne III: Wenn alle untreu werden; Hymne IV: Ich sag es jedem; Marie; Beim Winde; Die Sternennächte; Trost; Nachtstück; Prometheus; Strophe aus Die Götter Griechenlands* (1819); *Nachthymne; Die Vögel; Der Knabe; Der Fluss; Abendröte; Der Schiffer; Die Sterne; Morgenlied* (1820); *Frühlingsglaube* (1822); *Des Fräuleins Liebeslauschen* (1820); *Orest auf Tauris* (1817); *Der entsühnte Orest; Freiwilliges Versinken; Der Jüngling auf dem Hügel* (1820); *Sehnsucht* (1817); *Der zürnenden Diana; Im Walde* (1820); *Die gefangenen Sänger; Der Unglückliche; Versunken; Geheimes; Grenzen der Menschheit* (1821); *Der Jüngling an der Quelle* (1815); *Der Blumen Schmerz* (1821); *Sei mir gegrüsst; Herr Josef Spaun, Assessor in Linz; Der Wachtelschlag Ihr Grab; Nachtviolen; Heliopolis I: Im kalten, rauhen Norden; Heliopolis II: Fels auf Felsen hingewälzet; Selige Welt; Schwanengesang: Wie klage'ich's aus; Du liebst mich nicht; Die Liebe hat gelogen; Todesmusik; Schatzgräbers Begehr; An die Leier; Im Haine; Der Musensohn; An die Entfernte; Am Flusse; Willkommen und Abschied* (1822); *Wandrers Nachtlied: Ein Gleiches; Der zürnende Barde* (1823); *Am See* (1822/3); *Viola; Drang in die Ferne; Der Zwerg; Wehmut; Lied; Die Mutter Erde; Auf dem Wasser zu singen; Pilgerweise; Das Geheimnis; Der Pilgrim; Dass sie hier gewesen; Du bist die Ruh'; Lachen und Weinen; Greisengesang* (1823); *Dithyrambe; Der Sieg; Abendstern; Auflösung; Gondelfahrer* (1824); *Glaube, Hoffnung und Liebe* (1828); *Im Abendrot; Der Einsame* (1824); *Des Sängers Habe; Totengräbers Heimwehe; Der blinde Knabe; Nacht und Träume; Normans Gesang; Lied des gefangenen Jägers; Im Walde; Auf der Bruck; Das Heimweh; Die Allmacht; Fülle der Liebe; Wiedersehn; Abendlied für die Entfernte; Szene I aus dem Schauspiel Lacrimas; Am mein Herz; Der liebliche Stern* (1825); *Im Jänner 1817 (Tiefes Leid); Am Fenster; Sehnsucht; Im Freien; Fischerweise; Totengräberweise; Im Frühling; Lebensmut; Um Mitternacht; Uber Wildemann* (1826); *Romanze des Richard Löwenherz* (1827); *Trinklied; Ständchen; Hippolits Lied; Gesang (An Silvia); Der Wanderer an den Mond; Das Zügenglöcklein; Bei dir allein; Irdisches Glück; Wiegenlied* (1826); *Der Vater mit dem Kind; Jägers Liebeslied; Schiffers Scheidelied; L'incanto degli occhi; Il traditor deluso; Il modo di prender moglie; Das Lied im Grünen; Das Weinen; Vor meiner Wiege; Der Wallensteiner Lanznecht beim Trunk; Der Kreuzzug; Das Fischers Liebesglück* (1827); *Der Winterabend;*

Die Sterne; Herbst; Widerschein (1828); *Abschied von der Erde* (1825/6).
(B) *** DG 437 225-2 (9) [(M) id. import].

Lieder, Volume III: Song cycles: *Die schöne Müllerin; Schwanengesang; Winterreise.*
(M) *** DG 437 235-2 (3).

SCHUMANN: Lieder (with Christoph Eschenbach, piano): *Myrthen, Op. 25/1–3; 5–8; 13; 15–19; 21–2; 25–6. Lieder und Gesänge, Op. 27/1–5; Op. 51/4; Op. 77/1 & 5; Op. 96/1–3; Op. 98/2, 4, 6 & 8; Op. 127/2–3. Gedichte, Op. 30/1–3; Op. 119/2. Gesänge, Op. 31/1 & 3; Op. 83/1 & 3; Op. 89/1–5; Op. 95/2; Op. 107/3 & 6; Op. 142/1, 2 & 4; Schön Hedwig, Op. 106. 6 Gedichte aus dem Liederbuch eines Malers, Op. 36. 12 Gedichte aus Rückerts Liebesfrühling, Op. 37. Liederkreis, Op. 39. 5 Lieder, Op. 40. Romanzen und Balladen, Op. 45/1–3; Op. 49/1–2; Op. 53/1–3; Op. 64/3; Belsatzar, Op. 57. Liederkreis, Op. 24. 12 Gedichte, Op. 35. Dichterliebe, Op. 48. Spanisches Liederspiel, Op. 74/6, 7 & 10. Liederalbum für die Jugend, Op. 79; Der Handschuh, Op. 87. 6 Gedichte von Nikolaus Lenau und Requiem (Anhang, No. 7), Op. 90. Minnespiel, Op. 101. 4 Husarenlieder, Op. 117. Heitere Gesänge, Op. 125/1–3. Spanische Liebeslieder, Op. 138/2, 3, 5 & 7. Balladen, Op. 122/1–2. Sechs frühe Lieder, Op. posth. (WoO 21).*
(B) *** DG 445 660-2 (6) [(M) id. import].

BRAHMS: Lieder (with Daniel Barenboim, piano): *Gesänge, Op. 3/2–6; Op. 6/2–6; Mondnacht, Op. 7/1–4 & 6; Op. 43/1–4; Op. 46/1–4; Op. 70/1–4; Op. 71/1–5; Op. 72/2–5. Lieder und Romanzen, Op. 14/1–8; Gedichte, Op. 19/1–2, 3 & 5; Lieder und Gesänge, Op. 32/1–9; Op. 57/2–8; Op. 58/1–8; Op. 59/1–4, 6–7; Op. 63/1–9; Romanzen, Op. 33/1–15; Lieder, Op. 47/1–4; Op. 48/1, 2, 5–7; Op. 49/1–5; Op. 85/1–2, 4–6; Op. 86/2–5; Op. 94/1–3 & 5; Op. 95/2, 3 & 7; Op. 96/1–4; Op. 97/ 1–3, 5–6; Op. 105/4–5; Op. 106/1–5; Op. 107/ 1–2 & 4. Neuen Gesänge, Op. 69/3, 5 & 7. Vier ernste Gesänge, Op. 121.*
(B) *** DG 447 501-2 (6) [(M) id. import].

LISZT: Lieder (with Daniel Barenboim, piano): *Der Alpenjäger; Anfangs wollt' ich fast verzagen; Angiolin dal biondo crin; Blume und Duft; Comment, disaient-ils; Die drei Zigeuner; Du bist wie eine Blume; Der du von dem Himmel bist; Enfant, si j'étais roi; Eine Fichtenbaum steht einsam; Es muss ein Wunderbares sein; Es rauschen die Winde; Der Fischerknabe; Gastibelza; Gestorben war ich; Der Hirt; Hohe Liebe; Ich möchte hingehn; Ihr Glocken von Marling; Im Rhein, im schönen Strome; In Liebeslust; J'ai perdu ma force et ma vie; Klinge leise, mein Lied; Lasst mich ruhen; Die Lorelei; Morgens steh' ich auf und frage; Oh! quand je*

*dors; O Lieb, so lang du lieben kannst; Petrarch
Sonnets Nos. 1–3; Schwebe, schwebe blaues
Auge; S'il est un charmant gazon; Die stille
Wasserrose; Des Tages laute Stimmen schweigen;
La tombe et la rose; Der traurige Mönch; Uber
allen Gipfeln ist Ruh; Die Vätergruft; Vergiftet
sind meine Lieder; Le vieux vagabond; Wer nie
sein Brot mit Tränen ass; Wieder möcht' ich dir
Begegnen; Wie singt die Lerche schön.*
(M) *** DG (IMS) 447 508-2 (3).

Richard STRAUSS: Lieder (with Wolfgang
Sawallisch, piano): *5 kleine Lieder, Op. 69;
Lieder, Op. 10/2–7; Op. 15/2 & 5; Op. 17/2; Op.
19/1–6; Op. 26/1–2; Op. 27/1, 3 & 4; Op. 29/1 &
3; Op. 31/4; Op. 32/1–5; Op. 36/1 & 4; Op. 37/1–
2, 5–6; Op. 49/6; Op. 56/1 & 3; Op. 67/6.
Schlichte Weisen, Op. 21; Vier Gesänge, Op. 87.*
(M) *** DG (IMS) 447 512-2 (2).

WOLF: Lieder (with Daniel Barenboim, piano): *23
Eichendorff Lieder; 42 Goethe Lieder; 7 Heine
Lieder; 4 Lenau Lieder; 3 Gedichte von
Michelangelo; Mörike Lieder* (complete); *6
Reinick Lieder; 4 Gedichte von Robert Reinick. 3
Gedichte nach Shakespeare und Lord Byron.*
Miscellaneous Lieder by Peitl; Von Matthisson;
Körner; Herlossohn; Hebbel; Von Fallersleben;
Sturm; Von Scheffel.
(B) *** DG 447 515-2 (6) [(M) id. import].

To celebrate the seventieth birthday of the great
German baritone, DG had already published a justifiably extravagant Lieder Edition, summing up the
astonishing achievement of the greatest male Lieder
singer of our time. The set is offered at budget
price, with two discs thrown in for good measure
(forty-four CDs for the price of forty-two).

Each individual composer grouping is also available separately, still very competitively priced.
With consistent artistry from all concerned and
with first-class transfers, these CDs are self-
recommending. We have discussed the Schubert in
previous volumes, and much else, too, in individual
issues. Fischer-Dieskau's mastery never ceases to
amaze. Sample this set at almost any point and the
same virtues emerge: characteristic beauty of vocal
tone and an extraordinarily vivid power of characterization and vocal colouring. No less remarkable
are his accompanists, including the incomparable
Gerald Moore and Daniel Barenboim, whose sensitivity and command of keyboard colour make for
consistently memorable results. The Liszt collection is especially valuable. As in a number of other
fields, Liszt has been severely under-appreciated
as a song composer. This collection of forty-three
songs plus an accompanied declamation should do
much to right the balance. The sheer originality of
thought and the ease of the lyricism are a regular
delight. Fischer-Dieskau's concentration and inspiration never seem to falter, especially in the most
famous of the songs, the *Petrarch Sonnets*, and

Barenboim's accompaniments could hardly be
more understanding.

Fischer-Dieskau Edition

✪ (B) *** Mono/Stereo 463 500-2 (21) [id.].

This self-recommending set was a follow-up to the
Lieder Edition above and was released to celebrate Fischer-Dieskau's 75th birthday. The further
Rosette is surely obligatory for the sheer scope of
this achievement, not only for the great baritone's
consistent supreme artistry and astonishingly varied
repertoire, but also in appreciation to DG for re-
leasing over 300 works on CD for the first time –
with a recording of *Die schöne Müllerin* which had
never before been released. One of the other joys of
this Fischer-Dieskau Edition is that it has included a
great deal of music, much of it little known, either
side of his core nineteenth-century repertoire.

Of course, it will be a personal choice of which
of the various recordings of individual works one
prefers, but there is nothing remotely sub-standard
here. DG are also to be congratulated for their
superb transfers, many of which seem to defy time,
and also in providing full texts and translations. The
twenty CDs are available as a boxed set at bargain
price (with a Volume 21 offered as a bonus CD), or
individually at mid-price.

Volume 1: SCHUBERT: *Winterreise, D.911.*
(M) *** DG 463 501-2 [id.]. with Daniel
    Barenboim.

This is Fischer-Dieskau's fifth recording of Schubert's greatest cycle (1979), with the voice still in
superb condition. It is perhaps the most inspirational, prompted by Barenboim's spontaneous-
sounding, almost improvisatory accompaniment. In
expression, this is freer than the earlier versions, and
though some idiosyncratic details will not please
everyone, the sense of concentrated development is
irresistible. The recording is excellent.

Volume 2: SCHUBERT: *Die schöne Müllerin,
D.795.* Lieder: *Du bist die Ruh; Erlkönig; Nacht
und Träume; Ständchen.*
(M) *** DG 463 502-2 [id.]. with Jörg Demus.

This fascinating disc makes available Fischer-
Dieskau's 1968 recording of *Die schöne Müllerin*
with one of his favourite pianists, Jörg Demus, for
the first time. The reason for its previous non-
apperance were not artistic: Dieskau regards it as
one of his most successful interpretations of this
cycle, and edited and approved the disc for release.
It seems that DG, understandably, wanted to concentrated on the Gerald Moore recordings which
were then being undertaken, and with whom he
recorded the same cycle just three years later. The
result was this version was never issued. Comparisons with the 1971 Moore version are fascinating:
the earlier version has a greater feeling of risk, with

the dynamics noticeably more pointed, and as Alan Newcombe says in the sleeve note 'the result is starker, more elemental, less comfortable, and conceived on a larger scale'. Whereas the later version offers the more rounded polish – from both artists – and for many will be the safer recommendation, this 'new' version is just as compelling. The recording is excellent, and the four extra songs included on this disc are supremely done.

Volume 3: SCHUBERT: *Schwanengesang, D.957.* Lieder: *Im Abendrot; An die Musik; An Sylvia; Die Erde; Die Forelle; Heidenröslein; Der Musensohn; Der Tod und das Mädchen; Vollendung.*
(M) *** DG 463 503-2 [id.] with Gerald Moore.

Fischer-Dieskau's and Gerald Moore's 1972 performance of *Schwanengesang* – a work not conceived as a cycle by Schubert but grouped together by his publisher – is masterly. The singer may occasionally over-emphasize individual words, but the magnetism, poetry and insight – matched by Moore's playing – has one consistently marvelling. The remaining songs are superbly done, and both *Vollendung* and *Die Erde*, also recorded in 1972, receive their first release here. Excellent recording.

Volume 4: SCHUBERT: Lieder: *An die Leier; Aus Heliopolis I; Der entsühnte Orest; Fahrt zum Hades; Fragment aus dem Aeschylus; Freiwilliges Versinken; Frühlingslied; Jägers Liebeslied; Der Kreuzzug; Lied des Orpheus, als er in die Hölle ging; Lied eines Schiffers an die Dioskuren; Memnon; Orest auf Tauris; Philoktet; Schiffers Scheidelied; Vor meiner Wiege; Das Weinen; Der zürnenden Diana.*
(M) *** DG 463 504-2 [id.] with Jörg Demus.

Fischer-Dieskau was most adept at compiling recital discs, and this one comprises songs which conjure up evocations of antiquity. These recordings, dating from 1961 and 1965, receive their CD debut here, and have transferred very well. Both artists are on top form and there is nothing to quibble about artistically. This is a highly stimulating CD, and although the thread of antiquity gives the programme a slightly dark quality, this disc cannot fail to reward the listener.

Volume 5: SCHUMANN: (i) *Dichterliebe, Op. 48;* (ii) *12 Gedichte, Op. 35.* Lieder: *Freisinn; Schneeglöckchen; Des Sennen Abschied; Ständchen; Talismane; Venezianisches Lied I & II.*
(M) *** DG stereo/mono 463 505-2 [id.] with (i) Jörg Demus; (ii) Günter Weissenborn.

The beautifully intense and expressive performance of *Dichterliebe* – perhaps the most concentrated of all song cycles – was taped in 1965. Here, Fischer-Dieskau surpassed his famous mono version, with the voice sounding if anything in better condition

here, and with an even more tragic account of *Iche grolle nicht.* The other Lieder (mono) are no less attractive, and they all make their debut on CD here.

Volume 6: SCHUMANN: *Liederkreis, Op. 24; Myrten, Op. 25* (selection). Lieder: *Abends am Strand; Die beiden Grenadiere; Die feindlichen Brüder; Geständnis; Der Hidalgo; Der Kontrabandiste; Mein schöner Stern; Mein Wagen; Melancholie; O wie lieblich ist das Mädchen; Romanze; Sehnsucht; Tief im Herzen trag ich Pein; Weh, wie zornig ist das Mädchen; Zigeunerliedchen I & II.*
(M) *** DG 463 506-2 [id.] with Jörg Demus.

In *Liederkreis*, Fischer-Dieskau vividly conveys the range of emotion from the anguish of the spurned lover to the delight of the traveller. The rest of the programme is a typically judicious collection, dating from the early to the mid-sixties, and sounding rich and full on this, its first release on CD.

Volume 7: BEETHOVEN: *An die ferne Geliebte, Op. 98; Drei Gesänge, Op. 83.* Lieder: *Adelaide; Abendlied unterm gestirnten Himmel; Adelaide; L'amante impaziente (Nos 3 & 4); Andenken; An die Hoffnung; Ariette (Der Kuss); Aus Goethes Faust; Die Ehre Gottes aus der Natur; Ich liebe dich, so wie du mich; In questa tomba oscura; Der Jüngling in der Fremde; Der Liebende; Lied aus der Ferne; Maigesang; Marmotte; Seufzer eines Ungeliebten – Gegenliebe; Der Wachtelschlag.*
(M) **(*) DG 463 507-2 [id.] with Jörg Demus.

This Beethoven collection was recorded in 1966, finding Fischer-Dieskau at his vocal peak, especially in the song cycle which he made his very own. Though Demus's accompaniments are not quite so imaginative as the singer has received on other versions of these songs, Fischer-Dieskau's individuality is as positive as ever, with detail touched in as with few other singers. Excellent recording.

Volume 8: LISZT: (i) *Der Alpenjäger; Blume und Duft; Die drei Zigeuner; Es muss ein Wunderbares sein, S.314; Ihr Glocken von Marling; Oh, quand je dors; 3 sonetti di Petrarca, S270 Tristesse; Die Vätergruft; Vergiftet sind meine Lieder.* (ii) *Ein Fichtenbaum steht einsam; Hohe Liebe; Im Rhein, in schönen Strome; Morgens steh ich auf und frage; O lieb, so lang du lieben kannst; Der traurige Mönch.*
(M) *** DG 463 508-2 [id.] with (i) Jörg Demus; (ii) Daniel Barenboim.

This collection comprises Fischer-Dieskau's 1961 Liszt recital (with Demus), making its first appearance on CD here, with others he made with Barenboim in 1979 and 1981. One is struck at the consistent freshness of the singer, in performance and in sound, throughout this disc. The later performances if anything have even more richness and expressiveness, even if the voice obviously has not quite the youthful ardour of the earlier ones. The DG recording is impressive throughout, with the 1961 recording defying its age. A superb collection.

Volume 9: BRAHMS: *Vier ernste Gesänge, Op. 121.* Lieder: *Abenddämmerung; Alte Liebe; Auf dem Kirchhofe; Auf dem See; Es liebt sich so lieblich im Lenze; Es schauen die Blumen; Feldeinsamkeit; Frühlingslied; Heimweh II; Herbstgefühl; Kein Haus, keine Heimat; Meerfahrt; Mein Herz ist schwer; Mit vierzig Jahren; Mondenschein; Nachklang; Regenlied; Steig auf, geliebter Schatten; Sommerabend; Der Tod, das ist die kühle Nacht; Verzagen.*
(M) *** DG mono/stereo DG 463 509-2 [id.] with Jörg Demus.

At the opening of this recital, with the *Four serious songs*, the commanding eloquence of Fischer-Dieskau's singing is gripping, and this level of concentration is maintained throughout, with Dieskau exploiting his range of tone colour in interpreting the fullest meaning of the words. The recordings were made from 1957 to 1960, and are strikingly full and vivid – both in stereo and mono.

Volume 10: WOLF: *Mörike Lieder: Abschied; An die Geliebte; Auf einer Wanderung; Begegnung; Bei einer Trauung; Der Feuerreiter; Fußreise; Der Genesene an die Hoffnung; Im Frühling; In der Frühe; Der Jäger; Jägerlied; Lebewohl; Neue Liebe; Peregrina I and II; Storchenbotschaft; Verborgenheit.*
(M) **(*) DG 463 510-2 [id.] with Sviatoslav Richter.

The combination of Fischer-Dieskau and Richter is fascinating – this fifty-five-minute recital was recorded live in 1973, but the sound is good, there are few distractions from the audience, and no clapping. Although the performances have that spontaneity which one expects in live recordings, the surprising thing is that the actual expression is so consistent. Richter proves a lyrical magician, bringing out hidden inner lines of melody – a remarkable CD indeed – though it does not eclipse the singer's other versions of these songs, not least those with Barenboim.

Volume 11: Richard STRAUSS: (i) *Krämerspiegel, Op. 66.* Lieder: *Der Arbeitsmann; Blindenklage; Einerlei; Gefunden; Heimkehr; Das Rosenband; Stiller Gang; Winterweihe;* (ii) *Drei Lieder aus den Büchern des Unmuts des Rendsch Nameh, Op. 67.*
(M) *** DG 463 511-2 [id.] with (i) Jörg Demus; (ii) Karl Engel.

Fischer-Dieskau's Straussian credentials are well known: he has recorded much of the composer's repertoire over the years, but this collection is quite rare, and is released on CD for the first time. The

bulk of it was recorded in 1964, with the *Op. 67* taped in 1959. They are superb performances of these marvellously varied songs, and the transfers are excellent.

Volume 12: REGER: (i) *Aeolsharfe; Im April; Das Blatt im Buche; Ein Drängen; Einsamkeit; Flieder; Glückes genug; Gottes Segen; Grablied; Heimat; Der Himmel hat eine Träne geweint; Ihr, ihr Herrlichen!;Minnelied; Nelken; Schlecht Wetter; Das sterbende Kind; Traum durch die Dämmerung; Trost; Waldeinsamkeit; Winterahnung; Der zerrissne Grabkranz.*
PFITZNER: (ii) *An die Mark; Eingelegte Ruder; Hussens Kerker; In Danzig; Säerspruch; Sie haben heut Abend Gesellschaft; Tragische Geschichte; Zorn; Zum Abschied meiner Tochter;* (iii) *Sonett nach Petrarca.*
(M) *** DG 463 512-2 [id.] with (i) Günther Weissenborn; (ii) Karl Engel; (iii) Jörg Demus.

Another collection which makes its debut on CD. Reger was one of the most prolific of all masters and his songs are in particular need of advocacy. Some of them are little masterpieces and there is an original and memorable quality which runs through all those here. The 1966 recording has emerged stronger on CD than it was on LP, though the piano still sounds just a bit too much in the background. The Pfitzner songs were recorded, with the exception of the *Sonett nach Petrarca,* in 1959, though one would never guess the early date from the recorded sound. They are memorable works – more approachable for the non-German listener than you might think – and if they are not in the masterpiece class, they are well worth exploring. It would be hard to imagine a more persuasive advocate than Fischer-Dieskau, and this is altogether a valuable addition to the CD catalogue.

Volume 13: SCHOECK: (i) *Ach, wie schön ist Nacht und Dämmerschein; Auf ein Kind; Dämmrung senkte sich von oben; Das Ende des Festes; Ein Tagewerk I and II; Frühgesicht; Höre den Rat; Jetzt rede du! Jugendgedenken; Nachklang; Nachruf; Peregrina II; Reisephantasie; Venezianisches Epigramm;* (ii) *Liederzyklus, Op. 44.* Lieder: *Auskunft; Aus zwei Tälern; Im Kreuzgang von Santo Stefano; Keine Rast; Kennst du das auch?; Kindheit; Ravenna I; Das Ziel.*
(M) *** DG 463 513-2 [id.] with (i) Margrit Weber; (ii) Karl Engel.

Though Schoeck's songs haven't yet attained the universal popularity of, say, Schubert or Wolf, they certainly follow that lieder tradition in its fullest sense, with nicety of expression and aptness of music to word. It is arguable that Schoeck is the finest German song composer after Wolf, and those who know these examples will testify to their rare qualities. They provide a wonderful vehicle for

Fischer-Dieskau's art. *Liederzyklus* was recorded in 1977, and the rest of the programme in 1958, though the sound in both is excellent, and this is the first time they have been made available on CD.

Volume 14: DEBUSSY: (i) *Trois Ballades de François Villon*. IVES: (ii) *Abide with me; Ann Street; At the river; Autumn; The children's hour; A Christmas carol; Disclosure; Elégie; A farewell to land; Feldeinsamkeit; From 'The Swimmers'; Ich grolle nicht; In Flanders fields; Tom sails away; Two little flowers (and dedicated to them); Weil' auf mir; West London; Where the eagle; The white gulls*. RAVEL: (i; iii) *Chansons madécasses;* (i) *Cinq Mélodies populaires grecques; Don Quichotte à Dulcinée.*
(M) *** DG 463 514-2 [id.] with (i) Karl Engel
    (ii) Michael Ponti; (iii) Aurèle Nicolet;
    Irmgard Poppen.

A fascinating disc, offering some unexpected repertoire. Anyone who has fought shy of sampling the work of Ives should hear this delightful and often moving collection of his songs. Some of them are typically rumbustious, but equally memorable and ultimately more telling still are the reflective, poetic ones like *Feldeinsamkeit* or *Elégie*, or the very simple ones like *A Christmas carol*. They were recorded in 1975 and sound as fresh as paint. The French *Mélodies* have plenty of atmosphere and great colour; they were recorded in 1959 and the sound is astonishingly modern. The performances throughout this disc once again show Fischer-Diskau's supreme artistry in both the dramatic and reflective writing, and if his French doesn't always sound totally idiomatic, that becomes a secondary consideration in music making of this standard. The disc plays for just under 81 minutes.

Volume 15: Adolf BUSCH: (i) *Aus den Himmelsaugen droben; Nun die schatten dunkeln; Wonne der Wehmut*. Adolf BUSONI: (i) *Lied des Mephistopheles; Lied des Unmuts; Schlechter Trost; Zigeunerlied*. KEMPFF: (ii) *Alle; Der Gesang des Meeres; In einer Sturmnacht (Nikodemus); Liederseelen*. MAHLER: (iii) *Des Knaben Wunderhorn* (selection); *Phantasie aus Don Juan*. MINARDI: (i) *Con una fronda di mirto; Uomo del mio tempo*. REZNICEK: (iv) *Vier Bet- und Bussgesänge*. Bruno WALTER: (i) *Der junge Ehemann; Musikantengruss; Der Soldat*.
(M) *** DG 463 515-2 [id.] with (i) Jörg Demus;
    (ii) Wilhelm Kempff; (iii) Karl Engel; (iv)
    Günter Weissenborn.

This collection comprises the music of artist-composers and was recorded between 1960 and 1964. With the exception of the Kempff items, this is all new to CD, and is a doubly important release for including so many interesting rarities – there is nothing here which is not worth having. How fascinating to hear some of Bruno Walter's songs –

Musikantengruss ('*Musicians' greeting*') is quite magical, whilst the Kempff items are most animated and full of imagination. This is definitely a CD to sample, and the performances and recordings are first-rate.

Volume 16: MAHLER: (i) *Kindertotenlieder*; (ii) *Lieder eines fahrenden Gesellen*; (i) *Rückert Lieder: Blicke mir nicht in die Lieder; Ich atmet' einen linden Duft; Ich bin der Welt abhanden gekommen; Um Mitternacht.*
(M) *** DG 463 516-2 [id.] with (i) BPO, Böehm;
    (ii) Bavarian Radio SO, Kubelik.

Mahler was another composer in which Fischer-Dieskau excelled. Few can rival him in his range and beauty of tone in conveying the heartache of the young traveller the *Lieder eines fahrenden Gesellen*. Kubelik is a most persuasive Mahlerian too, and the 1968 sounds quite excellent. The *Kindertotenlieder* receives a superb performance too, and was recorded in 1963, with Boehm providing imaginative accompaniment. The 4 *Rückert Lieder* complete a totally successful collection.

Volume 17: BACH: (i) *Ich habe genug, BWV 82; Ich will den Kreuzstab gerne Tragen, BWV 56.* buxtehude: (ii) *Ich bin eine Blume zu Saron, BuxWV 45; Ich suchte des nachts, BuxWV 50.*
(M) (***) DG mono/stereo DG 463 517-2 [id.]
    with (i) Munich Bach Orchestra, Karl Richter;
    (ii) Helmut Krens, Berlin Bach Orchestra, Carl
    Gorvin.

The Buxtehude items were recorded in 1957 (mono) and make their CD debut here, with the singer emerging most vividly, and only a slight thinness in the orchestra betraying their age. This is ravishing singing, with the music imbued with a radiantly relaxed quality which is totally unaffected. The Bach performances were recorded in the late sixties and are rich and full in sound. If the orchestra here sounds a little earthbound at times, it is all most beautiful, with Fischer-Dieskau's usual colour and imagination ensuring the constant pleasure of the listener. Well worth considering.

Volume 18: Arias from: BACH: Cantatas: *Christ lag in Todesbanden, BWV 4; Meine Seufzer, meine Tränen, BWV 13; Wachet auf, ruft uns die Stimme, BWV 140. Mass in B minor; St Matthew Passion.*
(ii) BRAHMS: *A German Requiem*. (iii) HANDEL: *Belshazzar*. (iv) HAYDN: *(The Creation) Die Schöpfung*. (v) STOLZEL: Cantata: *Aus der Tiefe rufe ich.*
(M) *** DG 463 518-2 [id.]. with (i) Munich Bach
    Orchestra, Karl Richter; (ii) Edinburgh
    Festival Ch., LPO, Barenboim; (iii) Munich
    Chamber O, Stadlmair; (iv) Janowitz, BPO,
    Karajan; (v) Lucerne Festival Strings,
    Baumgartner.

This disc, titled 'Sacred arias', offers further examples of Fischer-Dieskau's sublimely beautiful and characterful way with baroque repertoire. The Bach excerpts are all most persuasively done, as is the rare Stölzel item, which is new to CD. The recordings are up to DG's high analogue standard, and the CD plays for just under 80 minutes.

Volume 19: Arias from: BEETHOVEN: *Fidelio.* CIMAROSA: *Il matrimonio segreto.* GLUCK: *Orfeo ed Euridice.* HANDEL: *Apollo e Dafne; Giulio Cesare; Serse.* MOZART: *Don Giovanni; Le nozze di Figaro; Die Zauberflöte.* WAGNER: *Die Meistersinger; Das Rheingold; Tannhäuser.* (M) *** DG mono/stereo 463 519-2 [id.] (with various orchestras and conductors).

Heard live on the operatic stage, Fischer-Dieskau's vocal image was sometimes too intimate for the bigger dramatic roles, but with the help of the recording microphone, these problems disappear, and one can do nothing but take pleasure in the singer's feeling for the words and dramatic situations. In Mozart, of course, Fischer-Dieskau has few peers, and the selection here includes his delightful Papageno arias from the *Magic flute,* as well as a beautifully turned performance of *Don Giovanni's Serenade.* The Wagner selection shows his warmly illuminating approach to this repertoire, with Wolfram's lovely solo from *Tannhäuser* quite magical, and the sharply individual Hans Sachs arias from *Die Meistersinger* equally unforgettable (if in some ways controversial). The bubbly Cimarosa aria is a joy and all the baroque arias are quite superb. The recordings, though, are excellent.

Volume 20: Arias from: BIZET: *Carmen; Les Pêcheurs de perles.* GIORDANO: *Andrea Chénier.* GOUNOD: *Faust.* LEONCAVALLO: *Pagliacci.* PUCCINI: *La Bohème.* ROSSINI: *Guglielmo Tell.* VERDI: *Falstaff; La forza del destino; Rigoletto; La Traviata.* (M) *** DG mono/stereo 463 520-2 [id.] (mainly with Berlin RIAS Chamber Ch.& RSO, Fricsay).

This second volume of arias concentrates on the French and Italian opera, and although he may not be totally idiomatic in all this repertoire, Fischer-Dieskau's unique artistry tends to disarm criticism, and one wonders if in fact there has ever been a more versatile artist. Just how good a Verdian he is can be heard in *Di Provenza il mar* from *La Traviata,* in which the lyrical phrasing is most beautiful. The vigorous characterization in the lively numbers is equally illuminating, and even though one might expect a darker voice in Gérard's monologue from *Andrea Chénier,* Dieskau's unique feeling for characterization enables him to carry it off with total success. Most of the items are from a 1961 recital disc conducted by Fricsay, whilst others are drawn from complete opera recordings. The Quartet from *La Bohème* (with Tröschel, Fehenberger, Streich,

conducted by Schmitz fascinatingly) dates from 1949, and sounds very good for its period. It marked Fischer-Dieskau's debut as an opera singer on record. All the items here are presented on CD for the first time.

Bonus CD

Volume 21: BEETHOVEN: Folksongs: (i) *Da brava, Catina; Horch auf, mein Liebchen; Kommt, schließt mir einen frohen; Kreis; O köstliche Zeit; Der treue Johnie; Trinklied;* (ii) *Could this ill world; Oh, had my fate; Once more I hail thee; The pulse of an Irishman; The return to Ulster; Sunset; Put round the bright wine.* HAYDN: Scottish songs: *Dort, wo durchs Ried; Fliess leise, mein Bächlein; Heimkehr; Maggy Lauder; Schläfst oder wachst du?* WEBER: (iii; iv) Scottish songs: *Bewunderung; Ein beglückter Liebender; Ein entmutigter Liebender; Glühende Liebe; Trinklied;* (iii) *Weine, weine, weine nur nicht.* (M) *** DG 463 521-2 [id.]. (i) Helmet Heller (violin), Irmgard Poppen (cello); (ii) Andreas Röhn (violin), Georg Donderer (cello); (iii) Karl Engel; (iv) Aurèle Nicolet (flute).

The bonus CD, offered free to those who buy the complete Fischer-Dieskau Edition, is a sheer delight. These folk-like songs are completely unpretentious, utterly enchanting pieces, full of lovely ideas and fresh melody. Their relative neglect is unaccountable, and this recital makes a hugely enjoyable hour of engaging music. The recordings date from 1961 and 1970 and all sound first class in this, their first CD incarnation.

Arias from: VERDI: *Otello; Il Trovatore; Rigoletto; Don Carlos; Un ballo in maschera; Falstaff.* WAGNER: *Der Fliegende Hollander; Die Walküre.* HANDEL: *Rinaldo.* BACH: *Christmas oratorio.* MAHLER: *Das Lied von der Erde: Von der Schönheit.* Lieder: SCHUBERT: *Das Lied im Grünen; Der Tod und das Mädchen; Du bist die Ruh'; Heidenröslein; Ständchen; Die Forelle.* BRAHMS: *Von ewige Liebe; Die Mainacht; Wiegenlied.* R. STRAUSS: *Morgen!; Freundlich Vision; Mit deinen blauen Augen.* (BB) *** Royal Classics Vocal Double DCL 706672 (2).

Even among the plethora of Fischer-Dieskau reissues currently reappearing, this inexpensive Double is not to be missed. Opening with Iago's two key scenes from Barbirolli's superb complete *Otello,* the selection continues with a number of arias taken from an early (1960) Verdi recital. Here Fischer-Dieskau is giving the most stylish and convincing performances and only the attention to detail betrays him as non-Italian. It is not, of course, the conventional baritone voice, but in *Il balen,* for example, there is a natural feel for the waltz rhythm as it picks up; throughout, the range of characterization is astonishing on any count. Then follow thrilling performances of the Dutchman's *Die frist ist um* and Wotan's tender farewell from *Die Walküre*, both excitingly supported by Kubelik and the Bavarian Radio Orchestra.

The second disc ranges wide, from stylish Bach and Handel to the excerpt from Kletzki's engagingly imaginative *Das Lied von der Erde*, six favourite Schubert Lieder (from 1965) and three of Strauss (1970), with Gerald Moore playing the introduction to *Morgen!* with the utmost magic, and three of Brahms (1974), including the *Wiegenlied* (with Sawallisch). The programme then ends with a brilliant account of *Ehi Paggio!* from *Falstaff*. Excellent, vivid transfers, but no texts.

Flagstad, Kirsten (soprano)

'*The Flagstad Legacy*', Volume 1: Opera arias from: BEETHOVEN: *Fidelio*. WAGNER: *Götterdämmerung; Lohengrin; Parsifal; Tannhäuser; Tristan und Isolde; Die Walküre*. WEBER: *Oberon*. Songs and arias by ALNS; BEETHOVEN; BISHOP; BRAHMS; BULL; FRANZ; GRIEG; GRONDAHL; HURUM; LIE; NORDRAAK; PALENZ; ROSENFELDT; SCHUBERT; SINDING; R. STRAUSS; THOMMESEN; THRANE.
(***) Simax mono PSC 1821 (3).

These three Simax CDs make up the first of five sets, running to thirteen CDs in all, which promise the most comprehensive overview of this great singer's legacy on records. It comes with a substantial article by Arne Dørumsgaard, himself a composer and translator. The contents range from the period of the First World War through to 1941, though the 1940 *Haugtussa* is not included. There is a thrilling *Dich, teure Halle* from *Tannhäuser*, recorded in New York in 1935 (hardly surprising that Flagstad took America by storm) and a *Liebestod* from the same year, as well as the 1936 Copenhagen recordings of Grieg and other Norwegian songs.

There are some Philadelphia and San Francisco Opera recordings under Ormandy with Melchior, and many feature her lifelong accompanist, Edwin McArthur. In Norwegian song, Grieg is not the whole story even if he is most of it. Flagstad included a number of her other and less familiar countrymen in her discography. These include Ole Bull, the violinist-composer who encouraged Grieg's family to send the boy to Leipzig, and whose *Sterjentens Søndag* ('The Herd Girl's Sunday') would have been mandatory at the time. Eyvind Alns's song *Lykkan mellem To Mennseskor* ('Happiness between two people') was also a favourite of hers.

Dørumsgaard tells of the 'disarming simplicity' of her 1929 version, the finest of her early electrics, released 'before fame struck'. It is indeed quite amazing and fresher than the 1936 record, which also suffers from the rather dry acoustic of the Copenhagen studio. The Simax will be indispensable to the serious collector, both for its comprehensiveness and for the generally high standard of its transfers.

Fleming, Renée (soprano)

Great opera scenes (with LSO, Solti) from: MOZART: *Le nozze di Figaro*. TCHAIKOVSKY: *Eugene Onegin*. DVORAK: *Rusalka*. VERDI: *Otello*. BRITTEN: *Peter Grimes*. Richard STRAUSS: *Daphne*.
✹ *** Decca Dig. 455 760-2 [id.].

Solti, in one of his very last recordings, here pays tribute to a soprano he especially admired and the wide choice of repertory movingly reflects an inspired collaboration. Far more than most operatic recitals, this presents fully rounded characterizations in extended scenes, from the Countess in *Figaro* through two Slavonic roles Tatiana and Rusalka (Fleming's favourite) to a tenderly girlish portrait of Verdi's Desdemona, wonderfully poised. Most moving of all is the final item – in effect a valediction – a ravishing, sensuous account of the heroine's final transformation into a tree in Strauss's late opera, *Daphne*.

'*I want magic!*': American opera arias (with Met. Op. O, James Levine) from: HERRMANN: *Wuthering Heights*. MOORE: *The Ballad of Baby Doe*. MENOTTI: *The Medium*. GERSHWIN: *Porgy and Bess*. BERNSTEIN: *Candide*. FLOYD: *Susannah*. STRAVINSKY: *The Rake's progress*. BARBER: *Vanessa*. PREVIN: *A Streetcar named Desire*.
*** Decca Dig. 460 567-2 [id.].

The title, 'I want magic!', is from André Previn's opera based on Tennessee Williams's *Streetcar named Desire*. Blanche Dubois's climactic aria – recorded even before the world première of the opera in 1998 – makes a moving conclusion to a varied and characterful collection. The beauty and power of Fleming's singing transforms arias from such operas as Bernard Herrmann's *Wuthering Heights*, Douglas Moore's *Ballad of Baby Doe* and Carlisle Floyd's *Susannah*, bringing out their lyricism. In arias from *Porgy and Bess* she is totally in style, and has both weight and brilliance in the big show-piece arias from Stravinsky's *Rake's progress*, Barber's *Vanessa* and Bernstein's *Candide*.

Freni, Mirella (soprano)

Arias from: DONIZETTI: *Don Pasquale; L'elisir d'amore*. PUCCINI: *Tosca; Madama Butterfly; Gianni Schicchi; Manon Lescaut; La Rondine; Suor Angelica; Turandot*. BIZET: *Carmen; Les*

Pêcheurs de perles. MASSENET: *Manon.* GOUNOD: *Faust; Roméo et Juliette.* BELLINI: *I Puritani.* VERDI: *La Traviata.* MASCAGNI: *Lodoletta; L'amico Fritz.* CILEA: *Adriana Lecouvreur.*

(BB) *** Royal Classics Vocal Double DCL 706492 (2).

Mirella Freni has the most engaging vocal personality and her voice has retained its quality and bloom over a long career. Most of the recordings here come from the mid to late 1960s when the voice was at its freshest, although the *Don Pasquale* excerpt is taken from the complete set of two decades later, when she still proved a naturally lyrical Norina. She sings Micaela's aria from *Carmen* exquisitely and is hardly less impressive in the very similar aria from *The Pearl fishers*. Indeed, all her French repertoire fully displays the lyrical charm for which she is famous.

The lesser-known Mascagni arias are ravishingly sung, as are the closing excerpts from *Adriana Lecouvreur*, while in the famous Act I scena from *La Traviata* the easy coloratura is a vocal delight. The Puccini items all come from a 1968 recital. It is not easy for any soprano to project herself into all Puccini's 'little women' roles, one after another, and she does very much better than most. The singing is charming, pointed and stylish, passionate in *Madama Butterfly*, with the excerpt from *La Rondine* especially welcome. The recordings all catch the voice naturally, and the transfers are excellent, but as usual with this series there is an absolute minimum of documentation.

'Grandi voci': Arias from: PUCCINI: *La Bohème; Tosca; Madama Butterfly.* ROSSINI: *Guglielmo Tell.* VERDI: *Falstaff.* LEONCAVALLO: *Pagliacci.* BOITO: *Mefistofele.* BELLINI: *Bianca e Fernando.* Folksongs, arr. BALILA PRATELLA: *Ninnananna di Modigliana; Ninnananna romagnola.*

(M) *** Decca (IMS) Analogue/Dig. 440 412-2 [id.].

Since making most of these recordings – many of them taken from complete Decca sets made between 1963 and 1980, including her superb Mimi and Butterfly with Karajan – Freni has expanded to even more dramatic roles, but her purity, clarity and sweetness in these mainly lyric roles are a constant delight, nicely varied. The recital ends with two delightful lullabies, essentially folksongs, arranged by Francesco Balila Pratella. The sound is consistently fresh.

'Songs my mother taught me' (with Ch. & O of Teatro Comounale di Bolgna, Leone Magiera): HANDEL: *Serse: Ombra mai fù.* Attrib. MOZART: *Nina Nanna.* SCHUBERT: *Ave Maria; Wiegenlied.* REGER/BOELITZ: *Maria Wiegenlied, Op. 76/52.* BRAHMS: *Nina Nanna.* BACH–GOUNOD: *Ave Maria.* DVORAK: *Songs my mother taught me.* ROSSINI: *La Caritá.* arr. BALILA PRATELLA:

Ninnananna di Modigliana; Ninnananna romagnola.

(BB) **(*) Belart 461 627-2 [id.].

Recorded at the very end of the 1970s, Mirella Freni's voice is at its warmest and freshest, although curiously a beat develops part way through the recital and is especially noticeable in the familiar Dvořák song which gives the recital its title. But for the most part simplicity is the keynote and Handel's most famous aria and the Schubert songs are beautifully sung, as is the delightful Reger arrangement of a famous German Christmas carol. The Rossini item is accompanied by an unlisted pianist. The two folksong arrangements with chorus, which perhaps come from the singer's hometown area in Italy, make a rather low-key ending. The absence of adequate documentation and the ungenerous playing time (forty-four minutes) are further minus points, but the recital is very well recorded and inexpensive.

Freni, Mirella (soprano), Luciano Pavarotti (tenor)

Arias and duets from: PUCCINI: *Tosca; La Bohème.* ROSSINI: *Guglielmo Tell.* BOITO: *Mefistofele.*

(M) *** Decca 458 221-2 [id.].

Both artists come from the same small town in Italy, Modena, where they were born in 1935; less surprisingly, they studied under the same singing teacher. Their artistic partnership on record has always been a happy one, and perhaps reached its zenith in their 1972 *Bohème* with Karajan (unexpectedly, recorded in the Jesus-Christus Kirche, Berlin).

Their great introductory love-duet as Mimì and Rodolfo, perhaps the most ravishing in all opera (from *Che gelida manina*, through *Sì, mi chiamano Mimì* to the soaring *O soave fanciulla*) is an obvious highlight here, but the much less familiar *Lontano, lontano* from *Mefistofele* shows no less memorably that the voices were made for each other. It was a very good idea to include a substantial selection from their 1978–9 *Tosca* (recorded in the Kingsway Hall), not a first choice as a complete set, but with some marvellous singing in Act III, of which some 17 minutes is offered (including *E lucevan le stelle* and the dramatic finale of the opera).

The recital opens very spontaneously with 13 minutes from Act I (*Mario! Mario!*), the engagingly temperamental interplay between the lovers, in the Church of Sant'Andrea della Valle. The only slight disappointment is Freni's *Vissi d'arte*; otherwise this is 70 minutes of vintage material, given Decca's top-drawer sound. Full translations are included.

Fretwork

'The English viol' (with Catherine Bott, soprano, Jeremy Budd, treble, Michael Chance, counter-tenor and (i) Red Byrd): ANON.: *The dark is my delight; Allemande and Galliard* (from *Lumley Books*); *In paradise.* FERRABOSCO I: *In Nomine a 5.* HOLBORNE: *Pavan and Galliard.* BYRD: *Christe redemptor a 4; In nomine a 5 No. 4; Ah silly soul.* DOWLAND: *Lachrimae gementes; Semper Dowland, semper dolens; M. Bucton his Galiard.* ferrabosco II: *Pavan and Alman.* GIBBONS: *Fantasia a 6 No. 2; Fantasia a 3 for the 'Great dooble bass'; The silver swan; Fantasia a 2.* (i) *The cry of London, Part II.* LAWES: *Fantasy a 5' on the playnesong' in G min.; Gather ye rosebuds; Aire a 6 in G min.* LOCKE: *Consort of 4 parts in F.* PURCELL: *Fantasia a 4 in B flat No. 5; In nomine a 6.* ✹ (M) *** Virgin Veritas/EMI Dig. VER5 61173-2.

Fretwork was one of the really outstanding groups of artists which Virgin Records promoted from their inception and they offer viol playing which is in a class of its own. This superb seventy-seven-minute anthology draws on recordings made between 1988 and 1994: the excellence is unvarying: these players catch perfectly the spirit of the late-Tudor and early-Stuart periods. The playing itself has immaculate ensemble and intonation, restrained feeling and great freshness. Much of the music is relatively austere but the effect on the listener is hypnotic.

The special character of Elizabethan romantic melancholy is well caught by Dowland (especially in his autobiographical *Semper Dowland, semper dolens*), but there is lively part-writing too, notably from Lawes and Locke. Lawes's *Fantasy a 5 'on the playnesong'* is touchingly expressive, the music's sonority coloured subtly by an (uncredited) chamber organ continuo, while the two pieces by Purcell are also quietly moving. The instrumental music is sprinkled with brief, cheerful, vocal items, delightfully sung, and the selection includes an excerpt from *The cry of London*, where the vocal group, Red Byrd, offer every conceivable commodity for sale, from a pair of oars and a good sausage to bread and meat 'for the prisoners of the Marshalsea'. Altogether an ideal introduction to a period in English history which was musically very productive. The recording could hardly be bettered.

Gabrieli Consort & Players, Paul McCreesh

'A Venetian coronation (1595)': Giovanni GABRIELI: *Canzonas Nos. XIII a 12; IX a 10; XVI a 15; Deus qui beatum Marcum a 10 Intonazione ottavo toni; Intonazione terzo e quarto toni;*

Intonazioni quinto tono alla quarta bassa; Omnes gentes a 16; Sonata No. VI a 8 pian e forte. Andrea GABRIELI: *Intonazione primo tono; Intonazione settino tono;* Mass excerpts: *Kyrie a 5–12; Gloria a 16; Sanctus a 12; Benedictus a 12; O sacrum convivium a 5; Benedictus dominus Deus sabbaoth.* BENDINELLI: *Sonata CCCXXXIII; Sarasinetta.* THOMSEN: *Toccata No. 1.* *** Virgin/EMI Dig. VC7 59006-2.

This recording and its DG successor below won *Gramophone* Early Music Awards in two consecutive years. '*A Venetian coronation*' is a highly imaginative if conjectural reconstruction of the Mass and its accompanying music as performed at St Mark's for the ceremonial installation of Doge Marino Grimaldi in 1595. The evocation begins with sounding bells (Betjeman would have approved) and the choice of music is extraordinarily rich, using processional effects to simulate the actual scene, like a great Renaissance painting. The climax comes with the Mass itself; and the sounds here, choral and instrumental, are quite glorious. The spontaneity of the whole affair is remarkable and the recording superb.

'Venetian Vespers', including: MONTEVERDI: *Laudate pueri; Laudate dominum; Deus qui mundum; Laetatus sum.* Giovanni GABRIELI: *Intonazione* (for organ). RIGATTI: *Dixit dominus; Nisi dominus; Magnificat; Salve regina.* GRANDI: *O intemerata; O quam tu pulchra es.* FASALO: *Intonazione* (for organ). BANCHIERI: *Suonata prima; Dialogo secondo* (for organ). FINETTI: *O Maria, quae rapis corda hominum.* CAVALLI: *Lauda Jerusalem.* MARINI: *Sonata con tre violini in eco.* ANON.: *Praeambulum.* (M) *** DG Dig. 459 457-2 (2) [id.].

Sequels can sometimes fall flat (as Hollywood so often demonstrates), but this one certainly doesn't, for the musical intensity of the performance is no less vivid here, and the spatial effects and polychoral interplay are equally impressive in this hypothetical re-creation of a Vespers at St Mark's. Grandiose effects alternate with more intimate sonorities, but the feeling of drama which was part and parcel of the Venetian Renaissance tradition is fully conveyed. Once again all the participants are on their toes, and playing and singing (soloists as well as chorus) are transcendent with detail in the accompaniment always effective and stylish. The recording is splendidly opulent, yet never loses its definition. This fine set is the more welcome, reissued at mid-price.

Galway, James (flute) with chorus and orchestra

'The James Galway Christmas collection'
(M) *** RCA Dig./Analogue 74321 41197-2 (2)
[id.].

Disc 1: 'James Galway's Christmas carol' (with BBC Singers, King's School, Canterbury, Choristers, RPO, cond. Galway): GRUBER: Silent night. RUTTER: Shepherd's pipe carol. BACH: Suite No. 3: Air. Christmas oratorio: Sinfonia and Chorale. Sheep may safely graze. OVERTON: Fantasia on 'I saw three ships'. TRAD.: Greensleeves; Zither carol; Patapan; Past three o'clock; I wonder as I wander. IRELAND: The holy boy. BACH/GOUNOD: Ave Maria. POSTON: Jesus Christ the apple tree. RYAN: We wish you a merry Christmas (09026 61233-2).

Disc 2: 'In dulci jubilo' (with Regensburger Domspätzen, Munich R. O, John Georgiadis): OVERTON: Fantasia on 'In dulci jubilo'. TRAD.: Il est né le divin enfant; Kling Glöckchen Klingeling; O Jesulein süss; Ein Kindlein in der Wiegen; O Tannenbaum; Adeste fidelis; O du Fröliche. arr. PRAETORIUS: Es ist ein Ros' entsprungen. BRAHMS: Prelude on 'Es ist ein Ros' entsprungen'. HANDEL: Messiah: Pastoral Symphony. ALBINONI: Adagio (arr. Giazotto/ Galway). FISCHER: Prelude on 'O Jesulein süss'. MENDELSSOHN: 6 Weihnachtsstücke (Christmas pieces). BACH/GOUNOD: Ave Maria. arr. LEHRNDORFER: Bethlehem geboren; In dulci jubilo. BACH: Prelude on 'In dulci jubilo'; Cantata No. 147: Jesu, joy of man's desiring. Arr. BIEBL: Still, still, still. PACHELBEL, arr. GALWAY: Canon. GRUBER, arr. Miesner: Silent night (RCA RD 60736).

In the first of these paired collections James Galway's silvery timbre introduces Grüber's Silent night unaccompanied before the choir joins in and he later adds an obbligato descant. These are all effectively simple arrangements in which Galway both directs chorus and orchestra and makes regular and attractive solo contributions. John Rutter's engaging Shepherd's pipe carol was an obvious choice in a programme that has a happy freshness about its presentation throughout. The interspersed orchestral numbers bring an effective degree of contrast. With clear yet full recorded sound, the ambience mellow but not too ecclesiastical, this is a Christmas compilation that will give a great deal of pleasure. Neither disc is now available separately.

The second collection, recorded in Munich in 1991, is even more winning. It opens with a charming concertante fantasia on In dulci jubilo in which another famous chorale is introduced to lend variety. Galway displays his lightest touch, and the nicely scored variants do not outstay their welcome.

The choral items from the Regensburg and Munich choirs have a pleasing simplicity of presentation, and the German traditional carols are particularly welcome, the orchestrations both atmospheric and tasteful. Some items (notably the lovely O Tannebaum) are unaccompanied, as is the first verse of Adeste fidelis. But here James Galway later adds his own descant, as he does for the closing Silent night. The Pastoral Symphony from Messiah sounds a little like Gluck when flute-dominated, but Galway's florid decoration of Pachelbel's Canon is remarkably inventive. The Bach/Gounod Ave Maria is presented as a flute solo with a delicate harp accompaniment, while the six brief concertante Christmas pieces of Mendelssohn are deliciously scored, like a box of Christmas bonbons. Warmly atmospheric recording, with the flute nicely balanced, adds to the appeal of this second highly enjoyable programme. Packaged in a slip-case, these two compilations work well together.

Gedda, Nicolai (tenor)

FAURE: Nell; Aprés un rêve; Fleur jetée. POULENC: A sa guitare; Hôtel. DEBUSSY: Mandoline. HAHN: L'heure exquise. RACHMANINOV: Spring waters; How fair this spot. BEETHOVEN: Adelaïde. R. STRAUSS: Ständchen; Befreit. TCHAIKOVSKY: Sérénade de Don Juan. GRIEG: Ich liebe dich. Arias from: MUSSORGSKY: Boris Godunov. R. STRAUSS: Capriccio. GOUNOD: Mireille. BERLIOZ: La damnation de Faust. BIZET: Carmen; Les Pêcheurs de perles. CORNELIUS: Der Barbier von Bagdad. PUCCINI: La Bohème. WEBER: Der Freischütz. ROSSINI: Il barbiere di Siviglia. DONIZETTI: L'elisir d'amore. MOZART: Idomeneo. OFFENBACH: La Belle Hélène. ADAM: Le postillon de Longjumeau. LEHAR: Giuditta; Der Graf von Luxemburg; Das Land des Lächelns. LORTZING: Undine. AUBER: Fra Diavolo. FLOTOW: Martha.
(BB) *(**) Royal Classics Vocal Double DCL 704802 (2).

In many ways Nicolai Gedda is every producer's ideal of a recording tenor. The present survey covers a period of three decades from 1955 (the Mireille excerpt, transferred very fiercely here) to 1985 (Lehár's Giuditta). During his career, Gedda covered an astonishingly wide range of repertoire. Some recordings bring hints of strain which latterly marred the upper register, but whether in opera of many schools, in operetta or song, this most polyglot of tenors had a seemingly innate sense of idiomatic style.

However, the opening group of French songs are not very flatteringly transferred and Ciccolini, though characterful, proves a less than subtle accompanist. Rachmaninov fares better, as does Berlioz, and once we reach the *Flower song* from *Carmen* with Beecham (1969) the quality improves, and Donizetti's *Una furtiva lagrima* is agreeably caught. But the fierceness returns in the *Der Freischütz* excerpt. The second disc opens with honeyed performances of songs by Beethoven and Strauss, but the peakiness then returns in Tchaikovsky, and ruins Grieg's *Ich liebe dich*. Among the operetta items which follow one admires Gedda's freedom on top in the Adam aria from *Le postillon de Longjumeau* and after the attractive Lehár selection the arias from Auber's *Fra Diavolo* and Flotow's *Martha* are particularly fresh. It is a great pity that the transfers are of such uneven quality.

Gens, Véronique (soprano)

'Nuit d'étoiles' (with Roger Vignoles): Songs: DEBUSSY: *3 Chansons de Bilitis etc.* FAURE: *Aprés un rêve, etc.* POULENC: *Banalités etc.*
*** Virgin VC5 45360-2.

This is one of the very finest of all discs of French mélodies, an inspired choice of well-known and rare songs sung with exceptional imagination and feeling for the idiom. Best known for her brilliant performances of baroque music, Gens here sings with a tone at once firmly focused and sensuously beautiful. In her distinctive and idiomatic characterization of each composer she is greatly helped by Roger Vignoles, by the brilliant accompaniment adding to the element of fantasy that runs through the whole sequence. The point and wit found in such a popular song as Fauré's *Mandoline* are exceptional, making one appreciate it afresh, and the waltz numbers from the Poulenc group, *Voyage à Paris* and *Les chemins de l'amour*, are equally seductive in their idiomatic lilt. The poise of Gens in the more serious songs is also exemplary, with the voice flawlessly placed. A magical disc.

Gheorghiu, Angela (soprano)

Arias (with Ch. & O of Teatro Regio, Turin, John Mauceri) from: VERDI: *Falstaff.* MASSENET: *Hérodiade; Chérubin.* CATALANI: *La Wally.* BELLINI: *I Capuleti e i Montecchi.* PUCCINI: *La Bohème.* BOITO: *Mefistofele.* GOUNOD: *Faust.* DONIZETTI: *Don Pasquale.* GRIGORIU: *Valurile Dunarii.*
**(*) Decca Dig. 452 417-2 [id.].

The star of Decca's *La Traviata* here makes her solo début in a recital which offers much lovely singing – the very opening excerpt from Verdi's *Falstaff* brings a ravishing line (and some fine orchestral playing, too) and the Massenet aria is quite melting and full of charm. But there is too little difference of characterization between the different

heroines, not enough fiery passion or, indeed, displays of temperament, which means that the *Jewel song* from *Faust* fails to sparkle as it should. Nevertheless the sample of Mimì in *La Bohème* promises well. The back-up here, from John Mauceri and the Turin chorus and orchestra, is impressive, and so is the glowing Decca recording.

Gheorghiu, Angela (soprano),
Roberto Alagna (tenor)

Opera arias and duets from: MASCAGNI: *L'amico Fritz.* MASSENET: *Manon.* DONIZETTI: *Anna Bolena; Don Pasquale.* OFFENBACH: *La belle Hélène.* BERNSTEIN: *West Side story.* GOUNOD: *Faust.* G. CHARPENTIER: *Louise.* BERLIOZ: *Les Troyens.* PUCCINI: *La Bohème.*
*** EMI Dig. CDC5 56117-2 [id.].

If Angela Gheorghiu's solo début is a little disappointing, this record of duets with her husband, Roberto Alagna, is not. Clearly they are a natural couple as artists as well as human beings. There is much here to delight, not least the opening Cherry duet from *L'amico Fritz*, in which the voices blend delightfully. *Manon* brings a comparable symbiosis, and the Donizetti items are as winning as the unexpected excerpt from *Les Troyens*. Solo arias also come off well here, notably Gheorghiu's aria from *Anna Bolena*, which suits her exactly; Alagna turns in a stylishly heady account of the delicious Waltz song from *La belle Hélène*. The excerpt from *West Side story* is tenderly touching but, as nearly always, the voices sound too mature for these starcrossed young lovers. Again the promise of that future complete *Bohème* comes in the closing alltoo-short *O soave fanciulla*. First-rate accompaniments under Richard Armstrong and superb sound contribute to the great success of this immensely pleasurable operatic hour.

Ghiaurov, Nicolai (bass)

'Russian songs' (with (i) Zlatina Ghiaurov (piano), or (ii) Kaval Ch. & O): (i) TCHAIKOVSKY: *None but the lonely heart; Not a word, O my love; Don Juan's serenade; It was in the early spring; Mid the noisy stir of the ball; I bless you, woods.* BORODIN: *For the shores of your far-off native land.* GLINKA: *Midnight review.* RUBINSTEIN: *Melody.* DARGOMIZHSKY: *The worm; Nocturnal breeze; The old corporal.* (ii) Folksongs: *The cliff; The Volga boatmen; The little oak cudgel; Bandura; Stenka Razin; Along Petersburg Street; In the dark forest; Dark eyes; Dear little night; The Twelve brigands; Farewell, joy.*
(B) *** Decca Double (IMS) 443 024-2 (2) [id.].

One of the problems of producing a record of

Russian songs is the inherent danger of monotony of dark colouring and Slavic melancholy. This difficulty is not entirely avoided in Ghiaurov's 1971 recital, as the Tchaikovsky songs have (understandably) been grouped together and have a recognizably similar idiom. Even so, there is some splendid music, and *It was in the early spring* and *I bless you, woods* are particularly memorable for their characteristically yearning melodic lines. With the appearance of Glinka's colourful *Midnight review* the mood lightens (even though this is a descriptive piece about old soldiers rising from their graves for a ghostly parade). The three Dargomizhsky songs are notably fine.

For the reissue, the solo recital has been paired with a vibrantly authentic collection of folksongs with the Kaval Chorus and Orchestra – plentifully spiced with balalaikas. Favourite items like the *Volga boatmen, Dubinushka* ('The little oak cudgel') and *Dark eyes* ('Ochi chorni') cannot fail when sung so vividly and presented so atmospherically.

'Grandi voci': Russian and Italian arias (with LSO Ch., LSO, Edward Downes) from: RIMSKY-KORSAKOV: *Sadko.* MUSSORGSKY: *Boris Godunov.* TCHAIKOVSKY: *Eugene Onegin; Iolanta.* RACHMANINOV: *Aleko.* GLINKA: *A Life for the Tsar.* RUBINSTEIN: *The Demon.* BORODIN: *Prince Igor.* BIZET: *Carmen.* VERDI: *Don Carlos; Nabucco; I vespri siciliani* (the latter cond. Abbado).

(M)'**(*) Decca 448 248-2 [id.].

Nicolai Ghiaurov's 76-minute recital in Decca's *Grandi voci* series is in the main compiled from two previous collections, recorded in 1962 and 1964, although it has now been extended to include Procida's aria from Verdi's *I vespri siciliani*, taken from a Verdi collection of 'Great scenes', admirably directed by Claudio Abbado. In the Russian repertoire Ghiaurov has to yield to his fellow Bulgarian, Boris Christoff, in sheer artistry, particularly on detail. He is best in the comparatively straightforward arias but the vocal quality is what matters, and this is all magnificent singing. The recording too is of Decca's most vivid and flatters Ghiaurov's lyrical line.

Gloriae Dei Cantores, Elizabeth Patterson

'By the rivers of Babylon (American Psalmody II)' (with James E. Jordan, organ): LOEFFLER: *By the rivers of Babylon, Op. 3* (with P. Clark, E. Ingwersen (flutes), M. Buddington (harp), H. Vacarro (cello)). Virgil THOMSON: *3 Antiphonal Psalms (Nos. 123, 133 & 136); De profundis.* SCHOENBERG: *De profundis.* TAYLOR: *Sing to the Lord a new song.* BERGER: *The eyes of*

all wait upon Thee. NEWBURY: *Psalm 150.* NEAR: *My song shall be alway of the loving-kindness of the Lord.* ADLER: *Psalm triology (Nos. 42, 84 & 113).* NESWICK: *Hallelujah! Sing to the Lord a new song.* WHITE: *Cantate Domino* (with brass Ens.).

**(*) Paraclete Press Gloriae Dei Cantores Dig. GDCD 027 [id.].

This collection of twentieth-century psalm settings includes music by 'those who are native Americans by birth or citizenship', which covers both Charles Loeffler, a late nineteeth-century émigré, and Schoenberg, who became an American citizen in 1941. The latter's atonal setting of the original Hebrew text of Psalm 120 (commissioned by Koussevitzky), with its dramatic spoken acclamations adding to the music's emotional impact, is the one really avant-garde piece here. It comes immediately after Virgil Thomson's admirably fresh but much simpler setting in English.

Loeffler's sensuously lush *By the rivers of Babylon*, which introduces the programme and gives the disc its title, is the most ambitious piece, very Gallic in feeling. It is richly sung and has a beautiful postlude for two flutes and cello, let down by imperfect intonation from the solo cellist. This closing section should have been re-recorded, for it all but spoils a superb performance. The rest of the music is traditional, but individually so, especially the very striking *Psalm triology* by Samuel Adler and the pieces by Clifford Taylor, Jean Berger (gently touching) and Bruce Neswick, his joyous *Hallelujah!*.

The choral singing is very fine and deeply committed throughout, and the choir has the advantage of the ideal acoustics of the Methuen Music Hall in Massachusetts, while James Jordan's organ accompaniments (when required) give admirable support, using the superb organ now located there. Even with the reservation about the Loeffler postlude, this splendid collection is well worth having. (Volume I, which we have not received for review, is available on GDCD 025.)

Glyndebourne Opera: London Philharmonic Orchestra with (i) Sir Andrew Davis, (ii) Franz Welser-Möst

'The EMI Centenary Gala at Glyndebourne': Arias from: BERNSTEIN: (i) *Candide* (overture). LEHAR: (ii) *Die lustige Witwe* (Gedda). MESSAGER: (ii) *L'amour masqué* (Lott). MOZART: (ii) *Die Zauberflöte* (Bostridge). HANDEL: (ii) *Alcina* (Ann Murray). MOZART: (ii) *Die Zauberflöte* (Bär). DVORAK: (ii) *Rusalka* (Roocroft). KERN: (ii) *Showboat* (Willard White).

NICOLAI: (ii) *Die lustigen Weiber von Windsor* (overture). VERDI: (i) *Falstaff* (Hampson). VERDI: (i) *Falstaff* (Hagley). HANDEL: (i) *Semele* (Ainsley). LEHAR: (i) *Giuditta* (Hendricks). BERNSTEIN: (i) *Candide* (Dessay). MASSENET: (i) *Manon* (Alagna and Gheorghiu).
**(*) EMI Dig. CDC5 56465-2 [id.].

Impossible as it is to devise a gala concert to represent the achievement of EMI over a hundred years, even just the vocal side, this one, highly enjoyable, boldly using young singers, yet misses the mark. Only at the very end does the undemanding programme capture the champagne atmosphere required, when Natalie Dessay gives a hilarious, uninhibited performance of *Glitter and be gay* from Bernstein's *Candide*, and Angela Gheorghiu and Roberto Alagna share a sensuously beautiful account of the Love duet from Massenet's *Manon*.

Among other items to cherish, Alison Hagley produces the loveliest sounds of all, with a ravishing silvery tone, in Nannetta's *Fairy song* from Verdi's *Falstaff*. That is preceded by the other *Falstaff* item, Ford's aria, sung with biting vehemence by Thomas Hampson, another high spot in the programme. Dame Felicity Lott is charmingly provocative in the Messager aria originally recorded for EMI by Yvonne Printemps, while other items to single out are the two arias from *Zauberflöte*: Ian Bostridge singing with a heady tone in *Dies Bildnis*, and Olaf Bär buoyant as Papageno in *Der Vogelfänger*. And Willard White, rounding off the first half of the programme, could not be more powerful in *Ol' man river* from *Showboat*. Otherwise, there are too many disappointments, and the recording tends to exaggerated vibratos and other unevenness in the voices.

Gobbi, Tito (baritone)

'*Heroes*': Arias and excerpts from: ROSSINI: *Il barbiere di Siviglia*. DONIZETTI: *Lucia di Lammermoor*. VERDI: *Rigoletto; La Traviata; Simon Boccanegra; Un ballo in maschera; Don Carlos; Otello; Falstaff*. LEONCAVALLO: *Pagliacci*. PUCCINI: *Tosca* (with Callas).
(M) (***) EMI CDM5 66810-2.

Tito Gobbi is not usually a hero figure in opera, although his portrayal of Rodrigo in Verdi's *Don Carlos* (sombre and powerful) undoubtedly has a heroic ring to it, and his uniquely charismatic portrayal of Verdi's *Falstaff* (the closing item) is heroic in its way, good-humouredly so. No other version of Rossini's *Largo al factotum* on record effervesces with such wit, yet has such subtle vocal inflection. Gobbi's portrayal of Rigoletto has a moving resonance, his Germont père in *La Traviata* and Tonio in *Pagliacci* are hardly less eloquent and his *Eri tu* in *Simon Boccanegra* is most soberly powerful of all.

But the roles for which he is most celebrated on disc are darker (Scarpia in de Sabata's 1953 *Tosca*) and cruel (Iago in Verdi's *Otello*) and these are superb examples of his supreme mastery.

Arias from: LEONCAVALLO: *Pagliacci*. ROSSINI: *Il barbiere di Siviglia; Guglielmo Tell*. DONIZETTI: *L'elisir d'amore*. CILEA: *Adriana Lecouvreur*. GIORDANO: *Fedora; Andrea Chénier*. VERDI: *Macbeth; Otello; Nabucco; Simon Boccanegra*. PUCCINI: *Tosca; La fanciulla del West*. WOLF-FERRARI: *I gioielli della Madonna*. CAVALLI: *Serse*. VIVALDI: *Cantata: Piango, gemo*. PAISIELLO: *L'amor contrastato (La molinara)*. A. SCARLATTI: *Il Pompeo*. MONTEVERDI: *Orfeo*. BERLIOZ: *La damnation de Faust*. Songs by COTTRAU; LAMA; PIGARELLI; TAGLIAFERRI; D'ANZI; SADERO; TOSTI; CARISSIMI; DURANTE; GIORDANI; GASTALDON; RESPIGHI; TRAD.; ANON.
(BB) *** Royal Classics Vocal Double DCL 706662 (2).

This remarkably varied compilation has many treasures, mostly on the operatic side (recorded between 1958 and 1965), showing the range of Gobbi's expression based on a unique range of such diverse characters as Boccanegra, Iago, Scarpia, Jack Ranch in *Fanciulla del West* and the swaggering Belcore in *L'elisir d'amore*. The excerpt from *The Jewels of the Madonna* is a welcome bonus. The songs are of lesser interest, although all are compellingly sung, especially those of Tosti. However, the *arie antiche* bring some exquisite performances, and any unstylishness can be forgiven when the singing itself is so fine, and the accompaniments often very well managed. The programme closes with an engaging version of Berlioz's *Song of the Flea* and *Tre sbirri* from Gobbi's later stereo *Tosca*. Transfers are good, but documentation sadly lacking. Even so this is an indispensable reissue.

Gomez, Jill (soprano), John Constable (piano)

'*Cabaret classics*' (with John Constable, piano): WEILL: *Marie Galante: 4 Songs. Lady in the Dark: My ship. Street scene: Lonely house. Knickerbocker holiday: It never was you*. ZEMLINSKY: *3 Songs from Op. 27*. SCHOENBERG: *4 Brettl Lieder*. SATIE: *3 Café-concert songs: La Diva de l'Empire; Allons-y, Chochotte; Je te veux*.
❀ *** Unicorn Dig. DKPCD 9055 [id.].

Jill Gomez's delicious Schoenberg performances make clear that writing these innocently diatonic numbers can have been no chore to the future ogre of the avant-garde. The same is true of the two Kurt Weill groups, strikingly contrasted at the beginning and end of the recital. The French-text songs from

Marie Galante use material adapted from *Happy End*. Weill's mastery is even more strikingly illustrated in the three Broadway songs, ravishing numbers all three: *My ship*, *Lonely house* and *It never was you*.

It is worth getting the record just for Gomez's ecstatic pianissimo top A at the end of that last item. The other groups, as delightful as they are revealing, are from Alexander von Zemlinsky (not quite so light-handed), and the Parisian joker, Satie, in three café-concert songs, including the famous celebration of English music-hall, *La Diva de l'Empire*. John Constable is the idiomatic accompanist. Gomez's sensuously lovely soprano is caught beautifully.

Gothic Voices, Christopher Page

'The Guardian of Zephirus' (Courtly songs of the 15th century, with Imogen Barford, medieval harp): DU FAY: *J'atendray tant qu'il vous playra; Adieu ces bons vins de Lannoys; Mon cuer me fait tous dis penser*. BRIQUET: *Ma seul amour et ma belle maistresse*. DE CASERTA: *Amour ma' le cuer mis*. LANDINI: *Nessun ponga speranza; Giunta vaga bilta*. REYNEAU: *Va t'en mon cuer, avent mes yeux*. MATHEUS DE SANCTO JOHANNE: *Fortune, faulce, parverse*. DE INSULA: *Amours n'ont cure le tristesse*. BROLLO: *Qui le sien vuelt bien maintenir*. ANON.: *N'a pas long temps que trouvay Zephirus; Je la remire, la belle*.
*** Hyperion CDA 66144 [id.].

In 1986 the Gothic Voices began what was to become a large-scale survey of medieval music, secular and sacred – for the two are inevitably intermingled. From the beginning, the project was an adventure in exploration, as much for the artists as for the listener, for comparatively little is known about how this music sounded on voices of the time.

The songs of the troubadours or trouvères – outside the church – sometimes drew on ecclesiastical chant, but other such chansons had a modal character of their own. They were essentially monophonic, i.e. a single line of music, perhaps with an instrumental accompaniment, but the rhythmic patterns were unrecorded and, like much else in this repertoire, are inevitably conjectural in modern re-creative performance.

Much of the repertoire on this first disc (and indeed elsewhere) is unfamiliar, with Du Fay the only famous name; but everything here is of interest, and the listener inexperienced in medieval music will be surprised at the strength of its character. The performances are naturally eloquent and, although the range of colour is limited compared with later writing, it still has immediacy of appeal, especially if taken in short bursts. The recording balance is faultless and the sound first rate. With complete security of intonation and a chamber-music vocal

blend, the presentation is wholly admirable. There is full back-up documentation.

'The Castle of Fair Welcome' (Courtly songs of the late 15th century, with Christopher Wilson, lute): ANON.: *Las je ne puis; En amours n'a si non bien; Mi ut re ut*. MORTON: *Le souvenir de vous me tue; Que pourroit plus; Plus j'ay le monde regardé*. REGIS: *Puisque ma dame*. BEDYNGHAM: *Myn hertis lust*. BINCHOIS: *Deuil angoisseux*. VINCENET: *La pena sin ser sabida*. FRYE: *So ys emprinted*. ENRIQUE: *Pues servicio vos desplaze*. CHARLES THE BOLD: *Ma dame, trop vous mesprenés*. DU FAY: *Ne je ne dors*.
*** Hyperion Dig. CDA 66194 [id.].

Christopher Page has by now established a basic procedure for his presentation of this early vocal repertoire: he has decided that it will be unaccompanied and usually performed by a modest-sized vocal group. So, in the present collection, further variety is provided with four instrumental pieces (played on harp and lute). Not surprisingly, the two most striking works here are by Du Fay (remarkably compelling) and Binchois; but the programme overall has been carefully chosen and it is given a boldly spontaneous presentation which cannot but intrigue the ear. As always, the recording is first class.

'The Service of Venus and Mars': DE VITRY: *Gratissima virginis; Vos quie admiramini; Gaude gloriosa; Contratenor*. DES MOLINS: *De ce que fol pense*. PYCARD: *Gloria*. POWER: *Sanctus*. LEBERTOUL: *Las, que me demanderoye*. PYRAMOUR: *Quam pulchra es*. DUNSTABLE: *Speciosa facta es*. SOURSBY: *Sanctus*. LOQUEVILLE: *Je vous pri que j'aye un baysier*. ANON.: *Singularis laudis digna; De ce fol, pense; Lullay, lullay; There is no rose; Le gay playsir; Le grant pleyser; Agincourt carol*.
*** Hyperion Dig. CDA 66283 [id.].

The subtitle of this collection is 'Music for the Knights of the Garter, 1340–1440'; few readers will recognize many of the names in the list of composers above. But the music itself is fascinating and the performances bring it to life with extraordinary projection and vitality. The recording too is first class, and this imaginatively chosen programme deservedly won the 1988 *Gramophone* award for Early Music. Readers interested in trying medieval repertoire could hardly do better than to start here.

'A song for Francesca': ANDREAS DE FLORENTINA: *Astio non mori mai. Per la ver'onesta*. JOHANNES DE FLORENTINA: *Quando la stella*. LANDINI: *Ochi dolenti mie. Per seguir la speranca*. ANON.: *Quando i oselli canta; Constantia; Amor mi fa cantar a la Francesca; Non na el so amante*. DU FAY: *Quel fronte*

signorille in paradiso. RICHARD DE LOQUEVILLE: *Puisquie je suy amoureux; Pour mesdisans ne pour leur faulx parler; Qui ne veroit que vos deulx yeulx.* HUGO DE LATINS: *Plaindre m'estuet.* HAUCOURT: *Je demande ma bienvenue.* GROSSIN: *Va t'ent souspir.* ANON.: *O regina seculi; Reparatrix Maria; Confort d'amours.* *** Hyperion Dig. CDA 66286 [id.].

The title, 'A Song for Francesca', refers not only to the fourteenth-century French items here, but to the fact that the Italians too tended to be influenced by French style. More specifically, the collection is a well-deserved tribute to Francesca MacManus, selfless worker on behalf of many musicians, not least as manager of Gothic Voices. The variety of expression and mood in these songs, ballatas and madrigals is astonishing, some of them amazingly complex. The Hyperion recording is a model of its kind, presenting this long-neglected music most seductively in a warm but clear setting.

'Music for the Lion-hearted King' (Music to mark the 800th anniversary of the coronation of Richard I): ANON.: *Mundus vergens; Noves miles sequitur; Anglia planctus itera; In occasu sideris.* BRULE: *A la douçour de la bele saison; Etas auri reditu; Pange melos lacrimosum; Vetus abit littera; Hac in anni ianua.* LI CHASTELAIN DE COUCI: *Li nouviauz tanz; Soi sub nube latuit.* BLONDEL DE NESLE: *L'amours dont sui espris; Ma joie me semont; Purgator criminum; Ver pacis apperit; Latex silice.* *** Hyperion Dig. CDA 66336 [id.].

Partly because of the intensity, partly because of the imaginative variety of the choral response, all this twelfth-century music communicates readily, even though its comparatively primitive style could easily lead to boredom. The performances are polished but vital, and there is excellent documentation to lead the listener on. This may be a specialist record, but it could hardly be better presented.

'The marriage of Heaven & Hell' (Anonymous motets, songs and polyphony from 13th-century France). Also: BLONDEL DE NESLE: *En tous tans que vente bise.* MUSET: *Trop volontiers chanteroie.* BERNART DE VENTADORN: *Can vei la lauzeta mover.* GAUTIER DE DARGIES: *Autre que je laureta mover.* *** Hyperion Dig. CDA 66423 [id.].

The title of this collection dramatically overstates the problem of the medieval Church with its conflicting secular influences. Music was universal and the repertoire of the trouvère had a considerable melodic influence on the polyphonic motets used by the Church, though actual quotation was very rare. Nevertheless, on occasion, vulgar associations in a vocal line could ensue and the clergy tore their hair. It all eventually led to the Council of Trent

when, the story goes, the purity of Palestrina's contrapuntal serenity saved the day. Certainly medieval church music was robust and full of character, but here one is also struck by its complexity and intensity. The performances have a remarkable feeling of authenticity, and the background is admirably documented.

'The Medieval romantics' (French songs and motets, 1340–1440): ANON.: *Quiconques veut; Je languis d'amere mort; Quant voi le douz tanz; Plus bele que flors; Degentis vita; Mais qu'il vous viegne.* SOLAGE: *Joieux de cuer.* de porta: *Alma polis religio.* MACHAUT: *C'est force; Tant doucement; Comment qu'a moy lonteinne.* TENORISTA: *Sofrir m'estuet.* SENLECHES: *En ce gracieux temps.* du fay: *Je requier a tous; Las, que feray.* VELUT: *Je voel servir.* LYMBURGIA: *Tota pulchra es.* *** Hyperion Dig. CDA 66463 [id.].

Machaut (fourteenth century) and Du Fay (fifteenth) are names which have now become individually established. Du Fay was master of the secular song-form called the 'virelai' (opening with a refrain, which then followed each verse) and Machaut was one of the first (if not *the* first) composers to set the Ordinary of the Mass; he too wrote chansons and virelais. But of course there is also much music here by other (unknown) composers and our old friend, Anon. The virelais are sung unaccompanied. Sometimes there are vocal melismas (extra parts without words) set against the textual line. So this collection represents the medieval blossoming of songs and part-songs alongside the motets, for secular and sacred never really grew apart. As usual, the Gothic Voices perform this repertoire with skill and confidence and lots of character, and the splendid documentation puts the listener fully in the historical picture.

'Lancaster and Valois' (French and English music, 1350–1420): MACHAUT: *Donnez, signeurs; Quand je ne voy; Riches d'amour; Pas de tor en thies pais.* SOLAGE: *Tres gentil cuer.* PYCARD: *Credo.* STURGEON: *Salve mater domini.* FONTEYNS: *Regail ex progenie.* CESARIS: *Mon seul voloir; Se vous scaviez, ma tres douce maistresse.* BAUDE CORDIER: *Ce jour de l'an.* ANON.: *Sanctus; Soit tart, tempre, main ou soir; Je vueil vivre au plaisir d'amours; Puis qu'autrement ne puis avoir; Le ior; Avrai je ja de ma dame confort?* *** Hyperion Dig. CDA 66588 [id.].

This stimulating series has always been essentially experimental, for we do not know just how unaccompanied medieval voices were balanced or how many were used. In the documentation with this record, Christopher Page suggests that on this disc he feels he has the internal balance just about right, and the vocal mix varies, sometimes led by a female voice, sometimes by a male. More Machaut here, some slightly later French settings, and the usual balance between sacred and secular. Everything sounds vital and alive.

'The study of love' (French songs and motets of the 14th century): ANON.: *Pour vous servir; Puis que l'aloe ne fine; Jour a jour la vie; Combien que j'aye; Marticius qui fu; Renouveler me feist; Fist on dame; Il me convient guerpir; Le ior; En la maison Dedalus; Combien que j'aye; Le grant biauté; En esperant; Ay las! quant je pans.* MACHAUT: *Dame, je suis cilz – Fin cuers; Trop plus – Biauté paree – Je ne suis; Tres bonne et belle; Se mesdisans; Dame, je vueil endurer.* SOLAGE: *Le basile.* PYCARD: *Gloria.*
*** Hyperion Dig. CDA 66619 [id.].

The Gothic Voices' exploration is moving sideways rather than forward, for Machaut is still with us. The present collection of settings demonstrates the medieval literary and poetic understanding of 'love' – romantic and spiritual. The Anonymous examples are often as stimulating as any of the songs and motets here by named composers, and the Pycard *Gloria* is obviously included to remind us again that church music is about the love of God. This and the previous three CDs should be approached with some caution, starting perhaps with 'The Medieval romantics'.

'The voice in the garden' (Spanish songs and motets, 1480–1530): JUAN DEL ENCINA: *Mi libertad; Los sospiros no sosiegan; Triste España sin ventura.* LUIS DE NARVAEZ: *Fantasias;* (after) *Paseávase el rey Moro.* FRANCISCO DE PENALOSA: *Precor te, Domine; Ne reminiscaris, Domine; Por las sierras de Madrid; Sancta Maria.* JULIUS DE MODENA: *Tiento.* PALERO:* (after) *Paseávase el Rey Moro.* ENRIQUE: *Mi querer tanto vos quiere.* LUIS MILAN: *Fantasias Nos. 10; 12; 18.* GABRIEL: *La Bella Malmaridada; Yo creo que n'os dió Dios.* ANON.: *Dentro en el vergel; Harto de tanta porfia; Entra Mayo y sale Abril; Dindirin; Ave, Virgo, gratia plena; A la villa voy; Pasa el agoa.*
*** Hyperion Dig. CDA 66653 [id.].

Here the Gothic Voices travel to Spain and take with them Christopher Wilson (vihuela) and Andrew-Lawrence King (harp). Their earlier concerts have included instrumental items, kept separate from the vocal music, and here the same policy is followed, but the mix of sacred, secular and instrumental is more exotic than usual. As throughout this series, the recording is of the highest quality.

'The Spirits of England and France' (Music of the Middle Ages for court and church, with Pavlo Beznosiuk, medieval fiddle): ANON.: *La uitime estampie real; La quarte estampie real; La septime estampie real; Credo; Virelais; Songs; Conducti; Conductus motets.* Matteo Da PERUGIA: *Belle sans per.* MACHAUT: *Ay mi! dame de valour.* PYKINI: *Plaissance, or tost.* PEROTINUS(?): *Presul nostri temporis.* ANON.: *Ave Maria.*
*** Hyperion Dig. CDA 66739 [id.].

This is the first of a series of CDs covering French and English music between the twelfth and fifteenth centuries. The first half of the present collection explores the sonorities of three- and four-part writing during the last decades of the fourteenth century and the first decades of the fifteenth. The second group goes back in time to anonymous settings from the twelfth and thirteenth centuries, although including one memorable piece possibly written by Perotinus. Although the items by Machaut (monodic) and Pykini (in four parts) are particularly striking, 'Anonymous' does not mean that the music is not full of character and individuality and the closing *Ave Maria*, with its series of triads, is as beautiful as many later settings. Pavlo Beznosiuk provides three instrumental interludes, a series of *Estampie*, winningly played on a medieval fiddle. The recording is excellent.

'The Spirits of England and France' (Songs of the trouvères, with Emma Kirkby, Margaret Philpot, Roger Covey-Crump, Leigh Nixon, Henry Wickham, Instrumental Ensemble): RICHART DE SEMILLI: *Je chevauchai.* BRULE: *Desconfortez plais de dolor; Quant define feuille et flor; De bien amer grant joie atent; Cil qui d'amours;* ANON.: *Estampie 1–3; Donna pos vos ay chausida; Quant voi la fleur nouvelle; Amors m'art con fuoc am flama.* GONTIER DE SOIGNES: *Dolerousement commence.* KAUKESEL: *Un chant novel; Fins cuers enamourés.* GAUTIER DE DARGIES: *La doce pensee.* ADAM DE LA HALLE: *Assénes chi, Grievilier.* ERNOUS LI VIELLE: *Por conforter mon corage.* AUDEFROI: *Au novel tens pascor.*
*** Hyperion Dig. CDA 66773 [id.].

The songs of the troubadours were inevitably monophonic, usually offering an expressive and touching melisma, lightly ornamented. To quote Christopher Page's excellent notes: 'their supreme genre was the *grand chant*, a protracted meditation upon the fortunes of loving'. One of the key composers in this style was Gace Brulé, and examples such as *Desconfortez plais de dolor*, *Quant define feuille et flor* and *De bien amer grant joie atent* convey an almost desperate melancholy. However, not all is despair: the opening *Je chevauchai* ('I rode out the other morning'), with its repeated refrain, is as spirited as it is optimistic – and rightly so, for the amorous singer has his way with the shepherdess he encounters by chance in the wood.

Ernous Li Vielle's *Por conforter mon corage* has a similar theme, only this time the seduction is more forceful. In contrast Wibers Kaukesel's *Fins cuers enamourés* ennobles the theme of love and being loved, while finally Audefroi tells of a husband who, after his wife Argentine, has borne him six sons, tires of her and takes a concubine, banishing her when she objects. The ingenuous moral of the tale is repeated after each verse: 'Whoever is wed to a bad husband often has a sad heart'. The singing and presentation here are admirable, and there are instrumental *Estampie* to provide interludes. A fascinating collection.

'The Spirits of England and France' (Binchois and his contemporaries, with Shirley Rumsey, Christopher Wilson, Christopher Page, lute): BINCHOIS: *Qui veut mesdire; Amoreux suy; Adieu mon amoreuse joye; Ay! doloureux; Magnificat secundi toni; Se la belle.* CARDOT: *Pour une fois.* VELUT: *Un petit oyselet; Laissiés ester.* ANON.: *Abide, I hope; Exultavit cor in Domino.* LE GRANT: *Se liesse.* DE LYMBURGIA: *Descendi in ortum meum.* POWER: *Gloria.* DUNSTABLE: *Beata Dei genitrix.* FONTAINE: *J'ayme bien celui.* MACHAUT: *Il m'est avis.* BITTERING: *En Katerina solennia.*
*** Hyperion Dig. CDA 66783 [id.].

Christopher Page and his group have been exploring early English and French repertoire in a number of earlier Hyperion anthologies. Here they turn to the early decades of the fifteenth century and to the music of Binchois (who died in 1460) and his contemporaries. Binchois is represented by a series of medieval love songs, all in three parts, very word-sensitive, even poignant in feeling, climaxed by the remarkably expressive *Ay! doloureux*, the most expansive and the most memorable. Then we turn to religious music and, besides a fine Binchois *Magnificat*, there is also Power's eloquent *Gloria* in five voices and fine examples of the music of Dunstable and even of Machaut. It is a heady mix, and it is the contrast here that makes this finely sung and recorded collection so stimulating.

'The Spirits of England and France' (with Shirley Rumsey, Christopher Wilson, Christopher Page, lute): ANON.: *The Missa Caput:* an English Mass setting from c. 1440 interspersed with the story of the *Salve Regina*. Carols: *Jesu for thy mercy; Jesu fili Dei; Make us merry; Nowell, nowell, nowell; Clangat tuba; Alma redemptoris mater; Agnus Dei* (Old Hall Manuscript).
*** Hyperion Dig. CDA 66857 [id.].

The inclusion here of the anonymous English *Missa Caput* gives a special interest to this collection. Composed around 1440, it survived in seven different manuscripts, and it is credited with having had a strong influence on the Masses of Ockeghem. The quality of the music is sure – it has long been attributed to Du Fay. Indeed, it is a remarkable and powerful setting, well worth discovering, and it is given added impact by the urgency of Christopher Page's direction.

The performance intersperses the Mass Propers with verses from a recently discovered Latin song narrating the origins of the Marian antiphon *Salve Regina*, with a view to alternating monody and polyphony, and this works remarkably well. The rest of the concert, a collection of early carols, makes an attractively lightweight pendant to the major work. The Gothic Voices sing with great eloquence throughout this sixty-six-minute programme and this is one of their most attractively conceived collections. The recording, as ever with this series, is first class.

'The Spirits of England and France': ANON.: *Missa Veterum hominem; Jesu, fili Virginis; Doleo super te; Gaude Maria virgo; Deus creator omnium; Jesu salvator; A solis ortuas; Salvator mundi; Christe, Qui lux es; To many a well; Sancta Maria virgo; Mater ora filium; Ave maris stella; Pange lingua.* DUNSTABLE: *Beata mater.*
*** Hyperion Dig. CDA 66919 [id.].

The *Missa Veterum hominem* might be considered as complementary to the *Missa Caput*, offered on the previous CD from the Gothic Voices, and the present compilation is equally successful. Both Masses were composed at about the same time, in the late 1440s; both were written for four voices. Once again, in performing this work (with comparable urgency) Christopher Page seeks to vary the vocal texture by opening with an early, three-part carol, *Jesu, fili Virginis*, and alternating the Mass polyphony with monodic plainchant hymns. There are three of these, the last of which, *Deus creator omnium*, uses the same liturgical text as is employed in the *Kyrie* of the Mass.

'Jerusalem: the vision of piece': ANON.: *Luto carens et latere; Jerusalem! grant damage me fais; Te Deum; O levis aurula!; Hac in die Gedeonis; In Salvatoris; Veri vitis germine.* GUIOT DE DIJON: *Chanterau pour mon corage.* Easter Day Mass in Church of Holy Sepulchre, Jerusalem (c. 1130): *Gradual; Alleluia; Gospel.* HUON DE ST QUENTIN: *Jerusalem se plaint et li pais; Luget Rachel iterum; Incocantes Dominum/ Psalm: Deus, qui venerunt; Congaudet hodie celestis curia.* HILDEGARD OF BINGEN: *O Jerusalem.*
*** Hyperion Dig. CDA 67039 [id.].

'Jerusalem: the vision of peace' was the underlying ideal which motivated the Crusades, as medieval pilgrims believed that such an armed expedition, with papal blessing – killing Saracens on the way – would lead to universal peace and harmony! Anti-Semitism was another factor in the crusading spirit, expressing Christian anger and contempt for the Jews' denial of Christ. *Veri vitis germine* calls strongly on Judaea to return to the Cross.

On a personal level was the tragedy of separation for women whose lovers and husbands had departed for the Holy Land, perhaps never to return. All these elements are reflected in the present diverse anthology, from the opening three-part song of confidence in the power of God, to Hildegard's rhapsodic closing monody, an ecstatic eulogy of longing for Jerusalem and all it represented. The melancholy of a deserted woman's loss is lamented in *Jerusalem! grant damage me fais*, while the *Te Deum*, heard against tolling bells, and the excerpts from the Easter Day Mass represent the liturgy of the period. Harmony, where it occurs, is organum and has great character, and certainly all the music here has great vitality, and is splendidly sung.

'Master of the Rolls' (Music by English composers of the 14th century, with Catherine King, Steven Harrold, Julian Podger, Leigh Nixon, Charles Daniels, Steven Charlesworth): ANON.: *Ab ora summa nuncius; Inter usitata/Inter tot et tales; Vexilla regni prodeunt; Singularis laudis digna; Dulcia [dona redemptoris]; Summum regen honoremus; Omnis terra/Habenti dabitur; Copiose caritatis; Missa Gabriel de celis; Pura, placens/ Parfundement plure; Letetur celi cura; Salve Regina; Jesu fili Virginis* (Plainsong); *Jesu fili/Jesu lumen; Jesu fili Virginis; Sospitati dat egrotos; Exultemus et letemur; Stella maris illustrans omnia; Veni dilectus meus; Pange lingua; O sponsa dei electa; Generosa Jesse plantula; Musicorum collegio/ In templo dei.*
*** Hyperion Dig. CDA 67098 [id.].

Very few English composers of the fourteenth century are remembered by name. The word used to describe accomplished musicians of the period was magister (master): hence the title of this collection. Only six items here are monodic and what is remarkable is how individual are some of these compositions. *Singularis laudis digna*, for instance, with its whirls of parallel writing, or the simple but touching harmonization of the Marian *Dulcia [dona redemptoris]* and the lovely, lilting *Missa Gabriel de celis*, while *Jesus fili* (a trio) has some engaging rhythmic triplets. Perhaps the most remarkable, original and forward-looking of all is *Stella maris illustrans omnia*, where a highly unusual text is matched by a comparably unpredictable use of chromatics.

'Gramophone Greats'

'20 Gramophone All-time Greats' (original mono recordings from 1907–1935): LEONCAVALLO: *Pagliacci: Vesti la giubba* (Caruso); *Mattinata* (Gigli). BISHOP: *Lo here the gentle lark* (Galli-Curci with flute obbligato by Manuel Beringuer). PURCELL: *Nymphs and shepherds* (Manchester Schools Children's Choir (Choir Mistress: Gertrude Riall), Hallé O, Harty). MENDELSSOHN: *Hear my prayer – O for the wings*

of a dove (Ernest Lough, Temple Church Ch., Thalben Ball). MARSHALL: *I hear you calling me* (John McCormack). ELGAR: *Salut d'amour* (New SO, composer). J. STRAUSS: *Casanova: Nuns' Chorus* (Ch. & O of Grossen Schauspielhauses, Berlin, Ernst Hauke). RACHMANINOV: *Prelude in C sharp min., Op. 3/2* (composer). TRAD.: *Song of the Volga boatmen* (Chaliapin). KREISLER: *Liebesfreud* (composer, Carl Lamson). MOSS: *The floral dance* (Peter Dawson, Gerald Moore). BACH: *Chorale: Jesu, joy of man's desiring* (arr. & played Dame Myra Hess). HANDEL: *Messiah: Come unto Him* (Dora Labette, O, Beecham). SAINT-SAENS: *Samson and Delilah: Softly awakes my heart* (Marian Anderson). BIZET: *Fair Maid of Perth: Serenade* (Heddle Nash). CHOPIN: *Waltz in C sharp min., Op. 64/2* (Cortot). LEHAR: *Land of Smiles: You are my heart's delight* (Richard Tauber). KERN: *Showboat: Ol' man river* (Paul Robeson). SULLIVAN: *The lost chord* (Dame Clara Butt).
(M) (***) ASV mono CDAJA 5112 [id.].

It seems strange and somewhat sad that this marvellous collection of classical 78-r.p.m. hit records, covering a period of three decades, should be coming from ASV rather than HMV (EMI), who are responsible for so many of the actual recordings. Their amazing technical excellence means that they can be enjoyed today as they were then, with only occasional clicks and generally not too intrusive a background 'surface' noise to create the right ambience.

Caruso still projects vividly from a 1907 acoustic master and Amelita Galli-Curci's soprano is as clear and sweet as the day the recording was made (1919). Other highlights (for us) include the Manchester Schools Children's Choir of 250 voices, electrically recorded in Manchester's Free Trade Hall in 1929. The story goes that, just before the record was made, Sir Hamilton Harty bought cream buns and pop for every child, and that accounts for the warm smile in the singing. Master Ernest Lough's *O for the wings of a dove* is another miracle of perfection from a young boy treble, and Peter Dawson's exuberant *Floral dance* has astonishing diction – you can hear every word – and here Gerald Moore's bravura accompaniment is a key part of the sheer pleasure this performance still gives.

Finally, Dame Clara Butt with her deep masculine contralto, clanging like a bell in its lowest register, delivers the sacred piece so beloved of Victorians, Sullivan's *Lost chord*. The transfers are all good (except perhaps for Dame Myra Hess's *Jesu, joy of man's desiring*, where the background noise surely could have been cut back a bit more).

Gueden, Hilde (soprano)

'Operetta favourites' (with Vienna State Opera Chorus and Orchestra, Max Schönherr or New Promenade Orchestra, Hans May): Excerpts from Johann STRAUSS Jr.: *Wiener Blut* (arr. Schönherr); *Die Fledermaus (Entr'acte); Die Tänzerin Fanny Elssler* (arr. Stalla). KREISLER: *Sissy.* LEHAR: *Die lustige Witwe; Zigeunerliebe. Der Zarewitsch; Schöne ist die Welt; Paganini.* KALMAN: *Gräfin Mariza.* Oscar STRAUS: *Der Tapfere Soldat (Chocolate soldier); Ein Walzertraum.* FALL: *Madame Pompadour; Die Dollarprinzessin.* ASCHER: *Hoheit Tanzi Walzer.* ZIEHRER: *Der Schätzmeister.* STOLZ: *Der Favorite.* DOSTAL: *Clivia; Die Flucht ins Glück.* GROTHE: *Die Schmedische Nachtigall.*

(BB) (***) Belart mono 461 623-2 [id.].

Hilde Gueden's many delightful gramophone contributions to operetta tended latterly to rest in the shadow of Elisabeth Schwarzkopf, who brought a Lieder-like skill with words even to relatively banal lyrics. Gueden's approach was more direct, but she had this repertoire in her very being, a lilting feel for a Viennese melodic line and a natural stage presence, which comes over on recordings too. Her lovely voice is heard here at its freshest in an early Decca mono recital from the beginning of the 1950s, when the full vocal bloom was winningly apparent. The chorus sounds well too, but the orchestra brings whistly violins, characteristic of Decca records of this period. Nevertheless this is an enchanting recital, with many delights in the key numbers from *Wiener Blut, Gräfin Mariza* and *The Chocolate Soldier,* and of course the greatest melody of all, *Lippen Schweigen,* the Merry Widow's Waltz song. Lehár, Fall and Kálmán are well represented, but there are also rarer items which are little known outside Vienna, by composers like Ascher, Dostal and Grothe. Alas the documentation is hopeless, listing twenty-six titles when there are only ten tracks; so you will have to find your way about in spite of this. But with such enchanting singing it's well worth it!

Gunn, Nathan (baritone), Kevin Murphy (piano)

'American anthem: From ragtime to art song': TRAD.: *Shenandoah.* GORNEY: *Brother can you spare a dime.* ROREM: *Early in the morning; The Lordly Hudson.* SCHEER: *At Howard Hawks' house; Holding each other; Lean away; American anthem.* NILES: *The lass from the low countree; I wonder as I wander.* MUSTO: *Recuerdo.* BARBER: *Nocturne; Sure on this shining night.* BOLCOM: *Fur (Murray the Furrier); Over the piano; Black Max (As told by the De Kooning Boys).* IVES:

Slugging a vampire; Two little flowers (and dedicated to them); General William Booth enters into heaven. HOIBY: *The Lamb.* arr. COPLAND: *At the river; Long time ago.*

(B) *** EMI Début Dig. CDZ5 73160-2 [id.].

The subtitle, 'From ragtime to art song', sums up the breadth of this delightful collection, the imaginative choice of Nathan Gunn – as he describes it himself, 'a beautiful forest of songs'. Gunn is one of the most promising of young American singers, possessor of a glorious baritone of a velvety beauty, consistent throughout its range. If anyone is disconcerted to have *Brother can you spare a dime* early on the list, it leads brilliantly to the most eclectic sequence, a reflection of Gunn's keen perception as well as of his musicianship. How welcome to have the work of such composers as Gene Scheer and William Bolcom well represented, alongside such predictable names as Charles Ives, Aaron Copland and Samuel Barber. The title, 'American anthem', comes from the last song on the CD, a surging expression of patriotism worthy of an American 'Last Night of the Proms'. Sensitive accompaniment and well-balanced recording.

Hagegård, Håkan (baritone), Warren Jones (piano)

BRAHMS: *5 Songs, Op. 105; Vier ernste Gesänge, Op. 121.* SIBELIUS: *Black roses (Svarta rosor), Op. 36/1; The dream (Drömmen), Op. 13/5; The first kiss (Den första kyssen), Op. 37/1; Sigh, sedges, sigh (Säv, säv, susa), Op. 36/4; The diamond in the March snow (Diamanten på marssnön), Op. 36/6; Was it a dream? Op. 37/4.* STENHAMMAR: *Adagio, Op. 20/5; Florez and Whiteflower (Florez och Blanzeflor), Op. 3; Prince Aladdin of the Lamp (Prins Aladin av lampen), Op. 26/10; Starry eye (Stjärnöga), Op. 20/1.*

**(*) RCA Dig. 09026 68097-2 [id.].

The distinguished Swedish baritone is on home territory in Stenhammar's and Sibelius's Swedish settings, and his sense of style and phrasing are unerring, both here and in the wonderful Brahms *Vier ernste Gesänge.* The voice has inevitably lost something of the youthful bloom that made his singing so radiant but the musical intelligence and artistry are unimpaired. He is well partnered by Warren Jones and excellently recorded.

Hagegård, Håkan (baritone), Thomas Schuback (piano)

'Dedication': BRAHMS: *An die Nachtigall; An ein Veilchen; An die Mond.* FOERSTER: *An die Laute.* GOUNOD: *A toi mon coeur.* HAHN: *A Chloris.*

MOZART: *An Chloë, K.524; Ich würd' auf meinem Pfad (An die Hoffnung), K.390.* SCHUBERT: *An Mignon; An den Tod; An den Mond; An den Leier; An die Musik; Am mein Herz.* R. STRAUSS: *Zueignung.* WOLF: *An eine Aeolsharfe.*
**(*) BIS CD 54 [id.].

This recital is called 'Dedication' and it begins with the Strauss song of that name. The collection first appeared in LP form in 1976 but was in circulation only intermittently in this country. The record was made at the outset of the distinguished Swedish baritone's career when he was in his mid-twenties and in wonderfully fresh voice. He sounds very much like a youthful Fischer-Dieskau but is at times a trace too studied, colouring the voice rather too expressively and adopting rather self-consciously deliberate tempi. There are times when one longs for him to be a little more unbuttoned. However, there is far more to admire and relish than to criticize, in particular the gloriously fresh vocal tone, and the sensitive playing of Thomas Schuback. Admirers of Hagegård will probably have this on LP; others need not hesitate.

know? MENKEN: *Beauty and the Beast: If I can't love he.*
*** EMI Dig. CDC5 55249-2 [id.].

Starting with a classic number by Jerome Kern, *All the things you are*, Hampson's Broadway selection ranges on up to *The Phantom of the Opera* and *Les Misérables*, where atmosphere and evocation seem to weigh more heavily than good tunes. The *Soliloquy* from *Carousel* – one of the few numbers from that great musical without a big tune – here can be seen to point forward, but one number (among the most recent here, dating from 1991) unashamedly returns to older standards of tunefulness, *How could I ever know?* from *The Secret Garden* by Marsha Norman and Lucy Simon. Hampson with his rich, dark voice seems totally at home in each number, finding no problems in adapting to this idiom, switching easily and aptly to half-speech in such a patter-number as the title-song from *Gigi*. Paul Gemignani conducts what is called the American Theater Orchestra, though you have to look through the small print to learn that information. Full, immediate recording.

Hampson, Thomas (baritone)

'German opera arias' from: KORNGOLD: *Die tote Stadt.* LORTZING: *Zar und Zimmermann; Der Wildschütz.* MARSCHNER: *Hans Heiling; Der Vampyr.* WEBER: *Euryanthe.* SPOHR: *Faust.* KREUTZER: *Das Nachtlager in Granada.* SCHREKER: *Der ferne Klang.* HUMPERDINCK: *Königskinder.* WAGNER: *Tannhäuser; Die Walküre.*
*** EMI Dig. CDC5 55233-2 [id.].

Hampson here presents a fascinating collection of rarities, many of them otherwise unavailable on disc, making one wonder, while listening to his red-blooded performances, why most of these items are so neglected. Anyone wanting to investigate the byways of German opera in the nineteenth and early twentieth centuries will find much treasure here, starting with a charming Korngold waltz song from *Die tote Stadt.* Returning to familiar repertory, giving perspective, he rounds the recital off with two Wagner items, *O star of Eve* from *Tannhäuser* and then – invading what is officially the Heldentenor repertory – Siegmund's 'Spring greeting' from *Walküre.* A recital to treasure, beautifully recorded.

'Leading man (Best of Broadway)': KERN: *All the things you are.* KRETZMER: *Les Misérables: Bring him home.* LLOYD WEBBER: *Phantom of the Opera: Music of the night.* RODGERS: *Carousel: Soliloquy.* LOEWE: *Gigi. Camelot: If ever I would leave you.* ADLER: *The Pajama Game: Hey there.* SONDHEIM: *Unusual way; Not a day goes by.* NORMAN: *The Secret Garden: How could I ever*

Hendricks, Barbara (soprano)

Operetta arias (with Philh. O, Lawrence Foster): LEHAR: *Giuditta: Meine Lippen sie küssen so heiss. Die lustige Witwe: Vilja. Friederike: Warum hast du mich wach geküsst?* STOLZ: *Der Favorite: Du sollst der Kaiser meiner Seele sein.* ZELLER: *Der Vogelhändler: Schenkt man sich Rosen in Tyrol.* J. STRAUSS Jr: *Die Fledermaus: Klänge der Heimat.* MESSAGER: *Madame Chrysanthème: Le jour sous le soleil béni. L'amour masqué: J'ai deux amants.* OFFENBACH: *La vie parisienne: Autrefois plus d'un amant. Le voyage dans la lune: Monde charmant que l'on ignore.* SULLIVAN: *The Pirates of Penzance: Poor wand'ring one. The Mikado: The sun whose rays are all ablaze.* ROMBERG: *New Moon: One kiss; Lover come back to me.* HERBERT: *Naughty Marietta: Ah! sweet mystery of life; Italian street song: Ah! my heart is back in Napoli.*
** EMI Dig. CDC7 54626-2 [id.].

This is a valuable collection, for so many operettas are remembered by a single number, and some of those are here. The selection is generous (71 minutes), and the documentation is adequate, although, extraordinarily, the lyrics are offered in French and German only, except where the original language is English, and then the German versions are omitted! But there are musical snags, too. Although Barbara Hendricks makes some gloriously rich sounds, the recording, made at EMI's Studio No. 1 at Abbey Road, is given too much resonance, and the brightness, so essential in this repertory, is blunted. The style of the singing, too, is essentially languorous, which especially suits the lovely *Le jour sous le soleil béni.*

Messager's *Madame Chrysanthème* is the French equivalent of Puccini's *Madama Butterfly*, and this romantic aria ravishingly expresses the Japanese heroine's heartbreak when her French lieutenant returns to his ship. But the earlier numbers by Lehár, Stolz and Zeller fail to effervesce, although again there is an exception with *Warum hast du mich wach geküsst?* ('Why have you kissed my heart awake?') from *Friederike*, where Hendricks' warmly sensuous, melancholy style is appropriate in a lament from another abandoned lover.

But Offenbach's *La vie parisienne* needs more of an uninhibited feeling of champagne corks popping and, although the waltz song for *Le voyage dans la lune* has charm, Lawrence Foster's rubato here (as elsewhere) is unconvincingly mannered, and one feels that he was not the right choice of accompanist for this programme. More surprisingly, the coloratura in *Poor wand'ring one* from *The Pirates of Penzance* lacks sparkle.

Yum-yum's lyrical aria from *The Mikado* brings a rich timbre and an eloquent line, and it is good to hear the Philharmonia Orchestra glowing in the charmingly scored accompaniments, both here and in *I could have danced all night* from *My Fair Lady* (delicious sounds from the woodwind), which has an agreeable lyrical flow. The playing is even more memorable in the comparatively restrained *Lover come back to me*, with its nostalgic orchestral introduction sounding quite gorgeous.

Then at the very close of the recital, after a delectable *Ah! sweet mystery of life* is built to a fine climax, the music-making suddenly sparks into vivacity in the *Italian street song*, from the same Victor Herbert operetta (*Naughty Marietta*) – a delicious performance, complete with chorus, to bring the house down. If only everything had had this kind of exuberance, the recital would have been a winner.

Spirituals (with Dimitri Alexeev, piano): *Deep river; Ev'ry time I feel the spirit; Fix me, Jesus; Git on boa'd little child'n; His name is so sweet; Hold on!; Joshua fit de battle of Jericho; Nobody knows de trouble I've seen; Oh what a beautiful city!; Plenty good room; Roun' about de mountain; Sometimes I feel like a motherless child; Swing low, sweet chariot; Talk about a child that do love Jesus; Were you there?; When I lay my burden down.*
*** EMI Dig. CDC7 47026-2 [id.].

So often spirituals can be made to seem too ingenuous, their deep reserve of feeling degraded into sentimentality. Not so here: Barbara Hendricks' vibrant identification with the words is thrilling, the jazz inflexions adding natural sophistication, yet not robbing the music of its directness of communication. Her lyrical singing is radiant, operatic in its

eloquence of line, yet retaining the ecstasy of spirit, while the extrovert numbers – *Joshua fit de battle of Jericho* a superb example – are full of joy in their gutsy exuberance. Dmitri Alexeev accompanies superbly and the very well-balanced recording has remarkable presence.

Hespèrion XX

'Llibre Vermell de Montserrat' (A fourteenth-century pilgrimage): *O Virgo splendens; Stella splendens in monte; Laudemus Virginem Mater est; Los set goyts recomptarem; Splendens ceptigera; Polorum regina omnium nostra; Cincti simus concanentes: Ave Maria; Mariam Matrem Virginem; Imperayritz de la ciutat joyosa; Ad mortem festinamus; O Virgo splendens hic in monte celso.*
(M) *** Virgin Veritas/EMI VER5 61174-2.

In the Middle Ages the Spanish monastery of Montserrat was an important place of pilgrimage and, although a great deal of the music held in the library there was lost in a fire at the beginning of the nineteenth century, one early manuscript, the Llibre Vermell (Red Book), has survived to remind us of the music of that period. It dates from 1400 and is especially fascinating in including ten anonymous choral songs for the use of the pilgrims 'while holding night vigil' who may 'sometimes desire to sing and dance in the Church Square (where only respectable and pious songs may be sung)'.

The music is extraordinarily jolly and robust, often written in the style of the French virelais (featuring alternating musical lines, with the first framing a central repeated tune). Canonic devices are also used and the effect is often quite sophisticated. There is no better example of this spirited music than *Los set goyts*, an infectious round dance complete with refrain. Various instrumental groupings add lively colour and support to the vocal line; the performances are full of joy, though at times emotionally respectful too. The analogue recording was made in France, but the resonant acoustic seems perfectly judged. This is a life-enhancing collection to cheer one up, and it shows that life in the Middle Ages was not always grim.

Hespèrion XX, La Capella Reial de Catalunya, Le Concert des Nations, Jordi Savall

'Ars Musicae':

I (1220–1670): Music by: ALFONSO X; ENZINA; ORTIZ; MORALES; DE ARRAUXO; VICTORIA; SCHEIDT; DE CASTRO; MONTEVERDI; CEREROLS.

II (1680–1820): Music by: CHARPENTIER; DUMANOIR; PURCELL; François COUPERIN;

BACH; HANDEL; HAYDN; MOZART; ARRIAGA; BEETHOVEN.

(M) *** Audivis Fontalis Dig. ES 9910 (2) [id.].

This consistently enjoyable and infinitely varied mid-priced set makes a highly stimulating survey of the development of instrumental and vocal music across seven centuries, beginning with Alfonso X and ending with excerpts from Bach's *Art of fugue*, Handel's *Royal Fireworks music* (with resplendent brass), Mozart's *Requiem*, and to herald the nineteenth century a very dramatic and thrusting account of Beethoven's *Coriolan overture*. With fine soloists led by Montserrat Figueras (soprano), and excellent choral and vocal groups, singing richly, and with Savall himself to lead the pieces featuring bass viol, whether by Ortiz, Marais, Couperin or Purcell, every one of these pieces springs to vivid life and the recording is consistently of the highest quality. The only snag is the almost total absence of back-up documentation, excepting for titles.

Hilliard Ensemble

English and Italian Madrigals:

English madrigals: MORLEY: *O griefe even on the bud; When loe, by breake of morning; Aprill is in my mistris face; Sweet nimphe, come to thy lover; Miraculous love's wounding; Fyer and lightning in nets of goulden wyers.* WEELKES: *Thule, the period of cosmographie; O care thou wilt dispatch mee; Since Robin Hood; Strike it up tabor.* WILBYE: *Sweet hony sucking bees; Adew sweet Amarillis; Draw in sweet night.* J. BENNET: *Weepe O mine eyes.* GIBBONS: *The silver swanne.* TOMKINS: *See, see the shepherd's queene.* WARD: *Come sable night.* VAUTOR: *Sweet Suffolk owle.*

Italian madrigals: GASTOLDI: *Cantiam lieti cantiamo.* CAPRIOLI: *E d'un bel matin d'amore; Quella bella e biancha mano; Una leggiadra nimpha.* COMPERE: *Venite amanti insieme.* VERDALOT: *Divini occhi sereni; Con l'angelico riso; Madonna, il tuo bel viso; Fuggi, fuggi, cor mio; Si liet'e grata morte.* ARCADELT: *Se la dura durezza; Ahimé, dové, bel viso; Madonna, s'io v'offendo; Il bianco e dolce cigno.* PATAVINO: *Donne, venete al ballo.* CASUALANA: *Morir non pué il mio cuore.* MARENZIO: *Se la mia vita.* RORE: *Mia benigna fortuna; Ancor che col partire; O sonno.* NOLA: *Chi la gagliarda; Medici noi siamo; Tre ciechi siamo.* WILLAERT: *Madonna mia fa.* BELL'HAVER: *Quando saré mai quel zorno.* LASSUS: *Matona, mia cara.*

(BB) *** Virgin Veritas 2 x 1 Dig. VBD5 616710-2 [CDVB 616710] (2).

The first of these two discs is of English madrigals and was recorded in 1987. It is an enchanting disc; and, as might be guessed from the above spelling, Tudor pronunciation is used which adds extra bite

to the vocal timbre. Intonation and ensemble are flawless, and some of the songs are in five or six parts. If one feels that they could be a shade more unbuttoned at times, and they do not always reflect the lighter moments with quite enough sparkle, there is so much here to beguile the ear that few will grumble. The Italian madrigals were recorded in 1991, and are hardly less enjoyable. Indeed, this second collection is is perhaps even more beautiful, and the programme is as rich and varied as in the English collection. A pity that there are no texts or translations and little about the music, but at super-bargain price one only expects such extras from Naxos.

'A Hilliard Songbook': New music for voices: GUY: *Un coup de dès.* FELDMAN: *Only.* MOODY: *Endechas y Canciones; Canticum Canticorum I.* HELLAWELL: *True Beautie* (cycle of 8 songs). ROBINSON: *Incantation.* TORMIS: *Kullervo's message.* ANON.: *Adoro te devote.* MACMILLAN: *. . . here in hiding . . .* PART: *And one of the Pharisees . . .; Summa.* LIDDLE: *Whale rant.* METCALF: *Music for The Star of the Sea.* FINNISSY: *Stabant autem iuxta cruceme.* CASKEN: *Sharp Thorne.*

*** ECM Dig. 453 259-2 (2) [id.].

The Hilliard Ensemble are best known for exploring the world of early music. In this CD, however, they survey modern trends and at times they find a surprising affinity with the repertoire with which they are more familiar. The opening number here is avant-garde with a vengeance. Extraordinary instrumental noises (contrived from an amplified double-bass) act as a prelude to *Un coup de dès*, and the performance appears to turn into a fight among the participants, with animal noises thrown in.

Then we turn to real music, Morty Feldman's touching, unaccompanied solo soliloquy *Only*, about flight (Rogers Covey-Crump). Ivan Moody's set of four *Endechas y Canciones* chime with the current trend towards medievalism, very bare in their part-writing but spiced with dissonances. Piers Hellawell's melodic lines are unpredictable, but his eight vignettes are all very brief and concentrated: the music fits the Elizabethan texts, which are about colours. The set is held together effectively by four different settings of *True Beautie*, which are quite haunting, and it is made the more effective by alternating baritone, tenor and counter-tenor soloists. The closing concerted number, *By falsehood*, is genuinely poignant.

Paul Robinson's *Incantation* (the text is Byron's) is an ambitious (15-minute) dialogue between lead singer (a bit like a cantor) and the main group, usually moving chordally using a spiced modal harmony. *Kullervo's message* is a lively ballad, setting an English translation from *The Kalevala*.

The second disc opens with Gregorian chant, then shocks the listener with the pungent fortissimo dissonance at the opening of James MacMillan's ingeniously woven motet. After the more familiar style of Arvo Pärt we move on to Elizabeth Liddle's mournful *Whale rant,* in which two texts are presented in bravura juxtaposition, one set to a famous hymn with the harmony touched up, the other a plangent soliloquy. The result is something of a *tour de force.* John Casken's *Sharp Thorne* brings exuberant bursts of sound, and we finally return to Ivan Moody setting texts from *The Song of Songs* which emphasize the link modern composers have found with the past. The whole programme is sung with great eloquence and is beautifully recorded, and no one could accuse any of the composers here of writing in a routine manner.

Holst Singers, Stephen Layton

'Ikon' (with (i) James Bowman, counter-tenor): SVIRIDOV: *Three choruses from Tsar Feodor Ioannovich; Four choruses from Songs of Troubled Times.* GRETCHANINOV: *The cherubic hymn;* (i) *The Creed. Our Father.* KALINNIKOV: *Radiant light.* TCHAIKOVSKY: *We hymn Thee; The cherubic hymn; Blessed are they.* PART: *Magnificat.* GORECKI: *Totus Tuus.* NYSTEDT: *Immortal Bach.*
*** Hyperion Dig. CDA 66928 [id.].

The Orthodox tradition has regularly inspired Russian composers to write with a rare fervour for unaccompanied chorus. This hauntingly beautiful disc was inspired by live performances given by the Holst Singers, beginning with pieces of extraordinary, dark intensity by Gyorgy Sviridov. Born in 1915, he defied all Soviet bans on religious music, echoing Tchaikovsky in his exotic harmonies and dramatic contrasts but with a twentieth-century flavour. A sequence of interlinked items by Tchaikovsky and Gretchaninov brings fascinating contrasts, leading to a fine *Magnificat* by Arvo Pärt and a long piece by Gorecki in the Polish Catholic tradition, touchingly simple in harmony. Radiant performances and recording, with James Bowman soaring away as counter-tenor soloist.

Huddersfield Choral Society, Brian Kay; Phillip McCann; Simon Lindley

'A Christmas celebration' (with Sellers Engineering Band): TRAD.: *Ding dong merrily on high; Kwmbaya; Joys seven; Away in a manger; Deck the hall; O Christmas tree (Tannenbaum); Coventry carol.* JAMES: *An Australian Christmas.* GRUBER: *Silent night.* BACH: *Cantata No. 140: Zion hears the watchmen's voices.* GARDNER: *The holly and the ivy.* arr. RICHARDS: *A merry little*

Christmas. HOLST: *In the bleak mid-winter.* arr. WILLCOCKS: *Tomorrow shall be my dancing day.* BRAHMS: *Lullaby.* arr. SMITH: *Santa Claus-Trophobia.* MATHIAS: *Sir Christèmas.* LANGFORD: *A Christmas fantasy.*
(M) *** Chandos Dig. CHAN 4530 [id.].

Sumptuously recorded in the generous acoustic of Huddersfield Town Hall, opening with a spectacular arrangement of *Ding dong merrily* and closing with Gordon Langford's colourful pot-pourri *Fantasy,* this CD offers rich choral tone, well laced with opulent brass. There are simple choral arrangements too, beautifully sung by the Huddersfield choir, like Stephen Cleobury's *Joys seven,* Langford's *Deck the hall* and David Willcocks's slightly more elaborate *Tomorrow shall be my dancing day,* while Grüber's *Silent night* remains the loveliest of all serene carols.

In other favourites the brass is nicely intertwined, as in *Away in a manger* and the *Coventry carol,* or it provides a sonorous introduction, as in Holst's *In the bleak mid-winter.* Mathias's rhythmically energetic *Sir Christèmas* provides a little spice. The brass are given their head in a solo spot, an effective novelty number, *Santa Claus-Trophobia,* arranged by Sandy Smith, which brings an impressive contribution from the solo tuba. Undoubtedly the brass contribution adds much to the entertainment value of this superbly recorded and well-presented 70-minute concert.

Hvorostovsky, Dmitri (bass)

'Songs and dances of death' (Russian songs and arias, with Kirov O, St Petersburg, Gergiev): MUSSORGSKY: *Songs and dances of death.* Arias from: RIMSKY-KORSAKOV: *Sadko; Kashei the Immortal; The Snow Maiden; The Tsar's Bride.* BORODIN: *Prince Igor.* RUBINSTEIN: *The Demon; Nero.* RACHMANINOV: *Aleko.*
*** Ph. (IMS) Dig. 438 872-2 [id.].

This magnificent collection, which displays the dark, tangy baritone of Hvorostovsky superbly, takes its title from the culminating items, Mussorgsky's *Songs and dances of death,* here given in their orchestral form. Only occasionally is the firm projection of the beautiful voice marred by a roughening under pressure. Otherwise this is among the finest recital discs of its kind, with fascinating rarities like the Demon's arias from Rubinstein's opera *The Demon,* and arias from four Rimsky-Korsakov operas, as well as the Prince's magnificent aria from Borodin's *Prince Igor.* Excellent sound and warm, intense accompaniments.

Jo, Sumi (soprano)

'Les bijoux': Arias from: GOUNOD: Roméo et Juliette; Faust. THOMAS: Mignon; Hamlet; Mireille. MEYERBEER: L'Etoile du nord; Les Huguenots. G. CHARPENTIER: Louise. MASSENET: Manon. BIZET: Les Pêcheurs de perles. MASSENET: Manon. OFFENBACH: Robinson Crusoë.
*** Erato/Warner Dig. 3984 23140-2 [id.].

For all the delights of French operetta and opéra-comique, it is good to hear the breadth of Sumi Jo's artistry when taking mature operatic roles. The famous Polonaise from Mignon sparkles iridescently, Gounod's waltz songs have both grace and charm, and in Meyerbeer's L'Etoile du nord the vocal/flute duet is as captivating as ever. But Louise's Depuis le jour brings an additional dimension in its warmly sympathetic phrasing, and Jo's portrait of Manon is equally touching, as is Leila's Cavatina from Les Pêcheurs de perles, with its characteristic Bizet horn writing. But perhaps the highlight is the Mad scene from Thomas's Hamlet, far more than a coloratura display. Here Jo is given fine support by the conductor, Giuliano Carella, with the opening beautifully prepared. The recital finishes on an upbeat with a charming Offenbach waltz song made famous by Joan Sutherland. As with the Decca disc below, this is a voice that takes naturally to recording, especially when the acoustic is pleasingly warm.

Virtuoso arias (with Monte Carlo PO, Olmi) from: ROSSINI: Il barbiere di Siviglia. BELLINI: La Sonnambula. DONIZETTI: Lucia di Lammermoor. DELIBES: Lakmé. R. STRAUSS: Ariadne auf Naxos. VERDI: Rigoletto. MEYERBEER: Dinorah. BERNSTEIN: Candide. MOZART: Die Zauberflöte (with O de Paris Ens., Jordan). YOUNG-HA HOON: Song: Boribat.
*** Erato/Warner Dig. 4509 97239-2 [id.].

This is among the most brilliant and commanding recitals of coloratura arias made in the 1990s. Though the recording brings out a slight flutter in Sumi Jo's lovely voice, the sweetness and tenderness of her singing, so different from the hardness of many coloratura sopranos, are formidably established over the widest range of arias. Sumi Jo's clarity, with no hint of stridency, coupled with a dreamy quality in the delivery, reminds one of the remark of an opera critic many years ago, that Galli-Curci sounded like 'a nightingale half-asleep'.

Not that there is anything sleepy in Sumi Jo's singing, which is beautifully controlled. That is so both in firework arias like Rosina's Una voce poco fa from Rossini's Barber and over the sustained spans of the big aria in Bellini's La Sonnambula (full recitative leading to Ah non credea mirarti and Ah! non giunge) and the Mad scene from Donizetti's Lucia di Lammermoor. Though Glitter and be gay from Bernstein's Candide lacks a little in fun, Delibes' Bell song from Lakmé is aptly sensuous and Zerbinetta's aria from Ariadne auf Naxos aptly extrovert, while the reading of the Queen of the Night's second aria from Mozart's Zauberflöte is lighter and even faster than with Solti in his Decca set. With tenderness and poise regular ingredients, alongside brilliance, not least in the honeyed sounds of the final, Korean song, all ten arias are to be cherished. The voice is well caught, though the orchestral accompaniment has less presence.

'Carnaval!' (with ECO, Richard Bonynge): French coloratura arias from: OFFENBACH: Un mari à la porte. MASSENET: Don César de Bazan. Félicien DAVID: La Perle du Brésil. GRETRY: L'Amant jaloux. BALFE: Le puits d'amour. MESSAGER: Madame Chrysanthème. THOMAS: Le songe d'une nuit d'été. ADAM: Les pantins de Violette; Si j'étais roi. HEROLD: Le pré aux clercs. DELIBES: Le roi l'a dit. BOIELDIEU: La fête du village voisin. MASSE: La Reine Topaze: Carnaval de Venise.
❀ *** Decca (IMS) Dig. 440 679-2 [id.].

If anything, this singing is even more astonishing than Sumi Jo's Erato recital, above. The music may be more frivolous, but what delectable freshness and vocal sparkle there is in every number! And this repertoire is far rarer. After the frothy Offenbach introduction, the nightingale lightness and precision in Massenet's Sevillana from Don César de Bazan are matched by the vocal poise in the Couplets du Mysoli from David's La Perle du Brésil, with William Bennett playing the flute solo. Equally, Jo trills along seductively in Adam's Chanson du canari, in which the song's pensive quality is also nicely caught.

This is Galli-Curci territory, and Sumi Jo doesn't come off second best; moreover her voice is fuller and warmer. The softness and delicious ease of her pianissimo top notes also recall Rita Streich at her finest, in both Adam and Thomas, and in the Grétry Je romps la chaîne qui m'engage. Her ravishingly easy legato in Balfe's Rêves d'amour is a joy, while Hérold's Jours de mon enfance brings a duet with a solo violin (the excellent Anthony Marwood), and here one is reminded of the young Sutherland. Delibes' Waltz song from Le roi l'a dit is bewitching, and the recital ends with a sparkling Boléro of Boieldieu and an unforgettable interpolation of the Carnival of Venice into an aria by Victor Massé, with astonishingly free divisions. Throughout, Bonynge provides stylish and beautifully pointed accompaniments, as he has done for Sutherland in the past, and the Decca recording could hardly be bettered.

'The Art of Sumi Jo' (with English Chamber Orchestra, Welsh National Opera Orchestra,

Richard Bonynge): Arias from AUBER: *Le Domino noir.* GRETRY: *L'Amant jaloux.* MOZART: *Die Zauberflöte.* OFFENBACH: *Le mari à la porte.* ADAM: *Le Toréador.* MASSENET: *Don César de Bazan.* DAVID: *La Perle du Brésil.* BOIELDIEU: *La fête du village voisin.* MASSE: *La Reine Topaz: Carnaval de Venise.*
*** Decca Dig. 458 927-2 [id.].

This is another of the most astonishing displays of light-voiced soprano coloratura ever put on record: even Galli-Curci is outshone. Sumi Jo's voice is not only wonderfully agile and pretty, it can deepen and become tender. Even in the middle of the unbelievable fireworks of David's *Couplets du Mysoli* (where the solo flute is quite upstaged in the many vocal interchanges), Jo can suddenly touch the listener with her gentleness. Five of the key items here are understandably also included in Decca's '*Coloratura spectacular*' (see above), including a thrilling *Der Hölle Rache* from *Die Zauberflöte,* the delicious Offenbach *Valse tyrolienne* and the closing *Carnaval de Venise,* which has to be heard to be believed. But there are many other delights, including exquisite singing in *Je romps la chaîne qui m'engage* from Grétry's *L'Amant jaloux,* and the excerpts from the recent complete recording of Adam's *Le Toréador,* where *Flamme vengeresse* is utterly winning, and the ensemble *Ah! vous dirai-je maman* is unforgettable for its light-hearted sparkle. Richard Bonynge, ever affectionate, displays the lightest touch in the accompaniments and the Decca recording projects the voice warmly without the slightest suspicion of edge or hardness.

Joyful Company of Singers, Peter Broadbent

'*A Garland for Linda*' (with: Phillippa Davies, flute; Robert Cohen, cello: TAVENER: *Prayer for the healing of the sick.* Judith BINGHAM: *Water lilies.* John RUTTER: *Musica Dei donum.* David MATTHEWS: *The doorway of the dawn.* MCCARTNEY: *Nova.* Roxana PANUFNIK: *I dream'd.* Michael BERKELEY: *Farewell.* Giles SWAYNE: *The flight of the swan.* Rodney BENNETT: *A Good-night.*
*** EMI Dig. CDC5 56961-2 [id.]

The tragic death of Linda McCartney led to this remarkable commemorative collection of music, notable for its serenity and lyrical beauty, with Paul McCartney's own piece, *Nova,* standing out alongside Michael Berkeley's moving *Farewell* and Richard Rodney Bennett's touchingly simple *Good-night.* The programme opens with Vaughan Williams's lovely *Silence and music,* for which his wife, Ursula, appropriately wrote the words. John Rutter's offering characteristically has a flute introduction, as does Giles Swayne's quite different,

haunting evocation of *The flight of the Swan,* but every piece here is moving and, beautifully sung and recorded; they will not only serve as a remembrance, but also give much pleasure to a great many listeners.

Kanawa, Dame Kiri Te (soprano)

'*Greatest hits*': Arias from: PUCCINI: *Suor Angelica; Turandot.* CILEA: *Adriana Lecouvreur.* BOITO: *Mefistofele.* GIORDANO: *Andrea Chénier* (with LSO, Myung-Whun Chung). G. CHARPENTIER: *Louise.* BIZET: *Les Pêcheurs de perles* (with Royal Opera House, Covent Garden, Orchestra, Jeffrey Tate). KORNGOLD: *Die tote Stadt* (with Philharmonia Orchestra, Julius Rudel). Songs: MOORE: *The last rose of summer.* TRAD.: *Greensleeves; Annie Laurie* (with Nat. PO, Gamley). KERN: *All the things you are; Smoke gets in your eyes.* BERLIN: *Always* (with Orchestra, Jonathan Tunick).
**(*) EMI Dig. CDC5 56722-2 [id.].

This collection certainly gives a rounded picture of the glorious voice and vocal art of Dame Kiri. But while the lovely aria from Korngold's *Die tote Stadt* is especially welcome, some ears will find the silky phrasing and voluptuous tone not quite idiomatic in the popular ballads of Jerome Kern and Irving Berlin, and certainly the traditional items like *Greensleeves* and *Annie Laurie* call for a more artless approach, even though all these songs bring a ravishing beauty of line. Four of the Italian and French arias are included on the mid-priced 'Diva' collection below, and this would seem an even more recommendable disc.

'*Classics*': Arias from: MOZART: *Die Entführung aus dem Serail; Idomeneo; Don Giovanni; Vesperae solennes de Confessore; Die Zauberflöte; Exsultate, jubilate.* HANDEL: *Samson.* GOUNOD: *Messe solennelle de Saint Cécile; Faust.* SCHUBERT: *Ave Maria.* J. STRAUSS Jr: *Die Fledermaus.*
(M) *** Ph. Dig. 434 725-2.

Admirers of Dame Kiri will find this a pretty good sampler of her diverse talents, including as it does Mozart's *Exsultate, jubilate* with its famous *Alleluia* and the similarly beautiful *Laudate dominum* from the *Solemn Vespers,* plus Handel's brilliant *Let the bright seraphim.* An excellent 74-minute selection from recordings made over two decades from the early 1970s onwards. The notes, however, concentrate on the singer rather than the music.

'*Diva*': Arias from: G. CHARPENTIER: *Louise.* MASSENET: *Manon; Hérodiade.* BERLIOZ: *La Damnation de Faust.* GLUCK: *Iphigénie en Tauride.* PUCCINI: *Suor Angelica.* LEONCAVALLO: *Pagliacci.* GIORDANO: *Andrea Chénier.* CILEA:

Adriana Lecouvreur. Richard STRAUSS: *Der Rosenkavalier.* TCHAIKOVSKY: *Eugene Onegin.* (M) *** EMI Dig. CDM 65578-2 [id.].

Like others in EMI's 'Diva' series of compilations, this selection has been shrewdly drawn from the limited number of recordings Dame Kiri has made for that company, principally a recital of French opera arias recorded in 1988 and an Italian opera recital made in 1989. These provide a fruitful source for the first nine items, but they are crowned by excerpts from two complete opera sets, the Marschallin's monologue and final solo from Act I of *Der Rosenkavalier* and (in English) *Tatiana's Letter scene* from *Eugene Onegin*, a recording made with Welsh National Opera forces. The beauty of the voice is beautifully caught.

Kansas City Chorale, Charles Bruffy

'American Christmas carols': SUSA: *3 Mystical carols: The shepherds sing; This endless night; Let us gather hand in hand.* John CARTER: *In time of softest snow.* ROREM: *Shout the glad tidings.* arr. Mark JOHNSON: *Silent night.* BELMONT: *Nativitas* (cycle of 8 carols). SOWERBY: *Love came down at Christmas.* IVES: *A Christmas carol.* FREED: *3 Shepherd carols: Shepherds! Shake off your drowsy sleep; O come to Bethlehem; Angels we have heard on high.* Dello JOIO: *The Holy Infant's lullaby.* MARTINSON: *There is no rose.* arr. FISSINGER: *I saw three ships.* COWELL: *Sweet was the song the Virgin sang.* arr. OLDHAM: *3 Carols, Op. 20: Silent night.* *** Nimbus Dig. NI 5413 [id.].

Very little here is familiar, and the ear is constantly being tweaked by the freshness of the harmonic progressions, with the choral writing of John Taverner occasionally springing to mind. Indeed, the affinity between the bare intervals of the earliest harmonized church music and the poignant dissonance so effectively used by these twentieth-century American composers is often very striking, notably so in the works which give the collection its title. *Nativitas* is a cycle of eight choral carols by Jean Belmont, born in California but now living in Kansas City. In setting two early chants, and other texts from the fifteenth, sixteenth and seventeenth centuries, she creates a flowing series of mystical and haunting evocations celebrating the Virgin Mary and the pastoral circumstances of the birth of her son, ending with a celebratory '*Noe, psallite, noe*'. The Pennsylvanian Conrad Susa's *Three Mystical carols,* which open the programme, are no less individual, the first picturing the joyous shepherds with a certain pungency, the second (*This endless night*) offering a comparatively restrained dialogue between solo soprano and tenor and the fuller

chorus, and the last in energetic medieval dance style. The triptych of Arnold Freed (of New York City) also features two lively, joyful carols to frame a dream-like picture of the sleeping child. John Carter's gentle *In time of softest snow* is more romantic but no less touching, while the burst of choral energy in Ned Rorem's *Shout the glad tidings* expends itself like a shooting star in 47 seconds.

The contribution from Charles Ives is surprisingly traditional, a richly glowing pastoral siciliano, while Henry Cowell's *Sweet was the song* is comparably ear-catching in its sensuous simplicity. Dello Joio's *Holy Infant's lullaby* has a delicate 'shepherd's pipe' organ introduction, and Joel Martinson's beautiful *There is no rose* is easily lyrical, with a hauntingly delicate refrain at the end of each verse. Both the so-called 'arrangements' of *Silent night* are re-composed variants. In the first, by Mark Johnson, the full carol finally emerges out of the mists, but austerely harmonized; in the second, ravishingly sung by Pamela Williamson in duet with solo flute (with harp), the original tune emerges only on the closing '*Alleluia*'. Edward Fissinger's *I saw three ships* keeps close to the original, though his delightful dancing rhythm is most infectious. A stimulating and unusually rewarding collection, superbly sung and recorded.

Karnéus, Katarina (mezzo-soprano), Roger Vignoles (piano)

Lieder: R. STRAUSS: *Die Nacht; Meinem Kinde; Begegnung; Nachtgang; Ruhe, meine Seele! Allerseelen; Mein Herz ist stumm; Morgen!; Wie sollten wir geheim sie halten.* MAHLER: *Frühlingsmorgen; Erinnerung; Hans und Grethe; Des Knaben Wunderhorn: Ich ging mit Lust durch einen grünen Wals; Ablösung in Sommer; Scheiden und Meiden. 4 Rückert Lieder.* MARX: *Und gestern hat er mir Rosen gebracht; Malenblüten; Hat dich die Liebe berührt; Wofür; Venetianisches Wiegenlied.* (B) *** EMI Début Dig. CDZ5 73168-2 [id.].

Winner of the Cardiff Singer of the World competition in 1995, Katerina Karnéus was born in Stockholm, but completed her singing studies in London. Hers is a beautifully warm and even mezzo which she uses with great imagination and fine attention to detail, in both words and music. This is a formidable Lieder collection in EMI's Début series, with the golden beauty of Strauss songs leading to a wide-ranging selection of Mahler songs, with charming early songs leading to four of the five *Rückertlieder* (*Um Mitternacht* the one left out). The Joseph Marx songs, simpler in style, provide an apt and attractive tailpiece. Roger Vignoles is the most sensitive partner. Well-balanced sound.

Kiehr, Maria Cristina (soprano)

'Cantala la Maddalena' (with Concerto Soave, Jean-Marc Aymes): Arias and scenas by: AGNELETTI; Luigi ROSSI; FRESCOBALDI; GRATIANI; MAZZOCCI; BEMABEL; FERRARI. Lute pieces by: FRESCOBALDI; Michelangelo ROSSI; KAPSBERGER.
**(*) HM Dig. HMC 901698 [id.].

After her two superb recitals of the music of Strozzi (in our main volume) and Monteverdi (above), this is a disappointment. The performances are altogether plainer, Kiehr's voice less honeyed. The repertoire is concerned with the subject of the many *Stabat Mater* settings – Mary in despair, grieving at the foot of the cross, and is of considerable interest, but the music itself is expressively sung rather than greatly moving the listener.

King's College, Cambridge, Choir, Stephen Cleobury

'Ikos': *Alma Redemptoris mater* (Marian antiphon). GORECKI: *Totus tuus; Amen. Ave Maria* (Offertory antiphon); *Regina coeli laetare* (Marian antiphon); *Alleluia – Venite ad me*. PART: *Magnificat; The Beatitudes. Beati mondo corde* (Communion antiphon). TAVERNER: *Magnificat and Nunc dimittis (Collegium Regale); Funeral Ikos. Requiem aeternam* (Introit antiphon with verse); *Ego sum resurrectio et vita; In paradisum – Chorus angelorum* (Funeral antiphons).
(M) *** EMI CDC5 55096-2 [id.].

In the notes for this admirable collection of modern liturgical settings, John Milsom suggests that their connecting link is 'ritual detachment'. He continues: 'Everything inclines to modesty, to mystery, to meditation, to musical refinement – and to the model of the past.' And that final comment is surely the key to this remarkably communicative *a cappella* music of our time which, for all its modernity, constantly seeks to identify with a medieval atmosphere of unquestioning faith.

Each of the composers here occupies ecclesiastical space with floating threnodies. Pärt's comparatively static *Magnificat* relies on intensity of sonority rather than movement; his better-known *Beatitudes*, gentle and rippling, is regularly pierced by dissonance, with the organ entering briefly and unexpectedly at the close to add a florid postlude and then disappear into infinity. Górecki's *Amen* is vocally much more dramatic and, although only having one word of text, continually explores its emotional potential, moving from serenity to sudden bursts of passion.

Taverner's undulating *Magnificat* is given its special character by flitting references to Byzantine chant. His simple and beautiful *Funeral Ikos* brings a haunting mixture of monody and chordal progressions on the word 'Alleluia', just occasionally touched with dissonance, and recalling his famous carol *The Lamb*. Górecki's masterly *Totus tuus* opens stirringly and is a superbly concentrated example of his minimalist choral progression. The music constantly redefines the intensity of the repetitions of the text, ending with a haunting diminuendo on *Mater mundi . . . Totus sum Maria!*, then with the constantly recurring name 'Maria' fading gently into silence.

The conductor, Stephen Cleobury, directs glorious, deeply felt performances of all this music and emphasizes the medieval associations by placing Latin chants before and after each piece, ending with two touching *Funeral antiphons*, the first sung by the men alone, the second, *In paradisum*, soaring radiantly with the trebles. The recording is superb: the famous King's acoustic adds much to the music.

'The King's Collection' (with James Vivian or Robert Quinney, organ): PARRY: *I was glad.* MOZART: *Ave verum corpus.* ALLEGRI: *Miserere* (ed. Guest). MENDELSSOHN: *Hear my prayer: O for the wings of a dove* (both with Alastair Hussain, treble). HANDEL: *Coronation anthem: Zadok the Priest.* BACH: *Cantata 147: Jesu, joy of man's desiring.* FAURE: *Cantique de Jean Racine.* FRANCK: *Panis angelicus.* WALTON: *Jubilate Deo* (with Edward Saklatvala, treble). BRITTEN: *Hymn to the virgin.* WALFORD DAVIES: *God be in my head.* BURGON: *Nunc dimittis* (with Thomas Hopkinson, treble). TAVERNER: *Song for Athene.* WIDOR: *Organ Symphony No. 5: Toccata* (Stephen Cleobury, organ).
**(*) Decca Dig. 460 021-2 [id.].

Magnificently recorded, with the choral tone sumptuous and clear, and resplendent sound from the organ, this unashamedly popular collection of choral favourites is bound to be a success. Certainly Handel's *Zadok the Priest* comes off exultantly, even if one misses the orchestral strings. Parry's *I was glad* is robustly presented, and so is the Mozart *Ave verum corpus*, which is just a shade stolid. However, Alastair Hussain is a true and pure treble soloist in the famous Allegri and Mendelssohn works, even if he is not quite so magical as Roy Goodman in the former, and Master Lough in the latter; and Thomas Hopkinson is genuinely touching in Burgon's equally famous *Nunc dimittis*.

The Walton and Britten pieces suit the King's style and acoustic particularly well, as does the lovely Taverner *Song for Athene*. This is well sustained, and its climax is powerful, but the last degree of spontaneity is missing. However, Walford Davies's simple setting of *God be in my head* is another highlight, and Franck's *Panis angelicus* is a surprising success. As a central interlude Cleobury gives a rousing, bravura account of Widor's famous *Toccata*.

King's College, Cambridge, Choir, Sir David Willcocks

'A Festival of Lessons and Carols' (recorded live in the Chapel, Christmas Eve 1958, with Simon Preston, organ): *Once in Royal David's city*. BACH: *Christmas Oratorio: Invitatory*. Lesson I. *Adam lay ybounden*. Lesson II. *I saw three ships*. Lesson III. *Gabriel's message; God rest you merry, gentlemen; Sussex carol*. Lesson IV. *In dulci jubilo*. Lesson V. *Away in a manger; While shepherds watched*. Lesson. VI. *O come, all ye faithful*. Lesson VII. *Hark! the herald angels sing*. (B) *** Decca 436 646-2 [(M) id. import].

It was the early mono recording of the King's Christmas Eve service of lessons and carols which – together with the BBC recording of Dylan Thomas's *Under Milk Wood* – brought initial success to the Argo label before it became part of the Decca group. With the coming of stereo the Festival was re-recorded to provide what only stereo can provide: an imaginary seat in the Chapel. The present CD offers that early stereo venture and shows the remarkable success with which the Argo engineers captured the magic of the chapel acoustic – the opening processional remains demonstration-worthy today. Seven of the nine lessons are interspersed with the favourite carols to remind us indelibly what Christmas is really about.

'Noël': Disc 1: MENDELSSOHN: *Hark the herald angels sing*. TRAD.: *The first nowell; While shepherds watched; I saw three ships; Ding dong! merrily on high; King Jesus hath a garden; Unto us a son is born; O come all ye faithful; Away in a manger; The holly and the ivy; God rest ye merry, gentlemen; See amid the winter's snow; Past three o'clock*. arr. BACH: *In dulci jubilo*. arr. VAUGHAN WILLIAMS: *O little town of Bethlehem*.
Disc 2: TRAD.: *Once in Royal David's city; Sussex carol; Rocking; Rejoice and be merry; Joseph was an old man; As with gladness men of old; The infant King; Christ was born on Christmas day; Blessed be that maid Mary; Lute-book lullaby; Personent hodie; In the bleak midwinter; Coventry carol; Shepherds, in the field abiding*. CORNELIUS: *The three kings; A great and mighty wonder*. WARLOCK: *Balulalow*. TCHAIKOVSKY: *The crown of roses*. TERRY: *Myn lyking*. JOUBERT: *Torches*. VAUGHAN WILLIAMS: *Fantasia on Christmas carols* (with Hervey Alan & LSO).
(B) **(*) Decca Double 444 848-2 (2) [id.].

This Decca Double is essentially a combined reissue of a pair of bargain-priced LP collections, made over a span of eight years at the end of the 1950s

and the beginning of the 1960s. They were counted excellent value when they first appeared in Decca's 'World of' series. The 50-minute programme on the first disc concentrates on established King's favourites; the second is not only more generous (66 minutes), but also includes novelties which are designed to get the listener inquiring further, such as Warlock's *Balulalow*, the engaging *Lute-book lullaby* and Joubert's *Torches*.

This collection opens with the famous processional version of *Once in Royal David's city* and closes with a superbly joyful performance of Vaughan Williams's *Fantasia on Christmas carols*, very well recorded, with Hervey Alan the excellent soloist. The sound is always pleasingly full and atmospheric, but with some of the earlier recordings from the late 1950s not quite as clean in focus as those made in the mid-1960s.

'Great choral classics': ALLEGRI: *Miserere* (with Roy Goodman, treble). PALESTRINA: *Stabat Mater*. TALLIS: *Spem in alium* (40-part motet; with Cambridge University Musical Society); *Sancte Deus*. BYRD: *Ave verum corpus*. VIVALDI: *Gloria in D, RV 589* (with Elizabeth Vaughan, Dame Janet Baker, Roger Lord, ASMF). GIBBONS: *This is the record of John* (with unnamed soloist and Jacobean Consort of Viols). BACH: *Jesu, priceless treasure (Jesu meine Freude), BWV 227*. HANDEL: *4 Coronation anthems: Zadok the Priest; My heart is inditing; Let thy hand be strengthened; The King shall rejoice* (with ECO).
(B) *** Decca Double 452 949-2 (2) [id.].

An admirably chosen group of choral masterpieces spanning the riches of the sixteenth and seventeenth centuries and the first half of the eighteenth, opening with Allegri's *Miserere* with its soaring treble solo, so confidently sung here by the same Roy Goodman who was later to make his mark as a conductor. Palestrina's *Stabat Mater* which follows is no less arresting in its bold contrasts, and the richness of texture of Tallis's *Spem in alium* is little short of astonishing. The resonant King's acoustic prevents sharp linear clarity, but it underlines the work's spiritual power and extraordinarily expansive sonority.

Byrd's beautiful *Ave verum corpus* then brings a serene simplicity, with Vivaldi's exuberant *Gloria* rounding off the first CD. The second programme opens with music by Orlando Gibbons, himself a chorister at King's, a delightfully intimate viol-accompanied solo motet with brief choral echoes. Bach's most famous motet follows, sung in English (none too clearly, because of the reverberation), and the concert closes resplendently with Handel's four *Coronation anthems*, including the most famous, *Zadok the Priest*. Here the sound is quite excellent.

King's College, Cambridge, Choir, Willcocks or Philip Ledger

'Favourite carols from King's': GAUNTLETT: *Once in Royal David's city.* TRAD., arr. VAUGHAN WILLIAMS: *O little town of Bethlehem.* TRAD., arr. STAINER: *The first nowell.* TRAD., arr. LEDGER: *I saw three ships.* TRAD. German, arr. HOLST: *Personent hodie.* TERRY: *Myn Lyking.* HOWELLS: *A spotless rose.* KIRKPATRICK: *Away in a manger.* HADLEY: *I sing of a maiden.* TRAD., French, arr. WILLCOCKS: *O come, o come Emmanuel.* TRAD., arr. WILLCOCKS: *While shepherds watched; On Christmas night.* arr. WOODWARD: *Up! Good Christian folk and listen.* DARKE: *In the bleak midwinter.* GRUBER: *Silent night.* TRAD., arr. WALFORD DAVIES: *The holly and the ivy.* TRAD., arr. SULLIVAN: *It came upon the midnight clear.* CORNELIUS: *Three kings.* SCHEIDT: *A Child is born in Bethlehem.* TRAD. German, arr. PEARSALL: *In dulci jubilo.* WADE: *O come, all ye faithful.* MENDELSSOHN: *Hark! the herald angels sing.*
(M) *** EMI CDM5 66241-2.

With 71 minutes of music and twenty-two carols included, this collection, covering the regimes of both Sir David Willcocks and Philip Ledger, could hardly be bettered as a representative sampler of the King's tradition. Opening with the famous processional of *Once in Royal David's city*, to which Willcocks contributes a descant (as he also does in *While shepherds watched*), the programme is wide-ranging in its historical sources, from the fourteenth century to the present day, while the arrangements feature many famous musicians. The recordings were made between 1969 and 1976, and the CD transfers are first class. The two closing carols, featuring the Philip Jones Brass Ensemble, are made particularly resplendent.

'A Festival of Lessons and Carols from King's' (1979) includes: TRAD.: *Once in Royal David's city; Sussex carol; Joseph and Mary; A maiden most gentle; Chester carol; Angels, from the realms of glory.* HANDEL: *Resonet in laudibus.* ORD: *Adam lay ybounden.* GRUBER: *Stille Nacht.* MATHIAS: *A babe is born.* WADE: *O come all ye faithful.* MENDELSSOHN: *Hark! the herald angels sing.*
(M) *** EMI CDM5 66242-2 [CDM 63180].

This 1979 version of the annual King's College ceremony has the benefit of fine analogue stereo, even more atmospheric than before. Under Philip Ledger the famous choir keeps its beauty of tone and incisive attack. The opening processional, *Once in Royal David's city*, is even more effective heard

against the background quiet of CD, and this remains a unique blend of liturgy and music.

'Procession with carols on Advent Sunday' includes: PALESTRINA (arr. from): *I look from afar; Judah and Jerusalem, fear not.* PRAETORIUS: *Come, thou Redeemer of the earth.* TRAD.: *O come, o come, Emmanuel!; Up, awake and away!; 'Twas in the year; Cherry tree carol; King Jesus hath a garden; On Jordan's bank the Baptist's cry; Gabriel's message; I wonder as I wander; My dancing day; Lo! he comes with clouds descending.* BYRT: *All and some.* P. NICOLAI, arr. BACH: *Wake, o wake! with tidings thrilling.* BACH: *Nun komm' der Heiden Heiland.*
(M) *** EMI CDM5 66243-2.

This makes an attractive variant to the specifically Christmas-based service, though the carols themselves are not quite so memorable. Beautiful singing and richly atmospheric recording; the wide dynamic range is demonstrated equally effectively by the atmospheric opening and processional and the sumptuous closing hymn.

'Christmas music from King's' (with Andrew Davis, organ, D. Whittaker, flute, Christopher van Kampen, cello, and Robert Spencer, lute): SWEELINCK: *Hodie Christus natus est.* PALESTRINA: *Hodie Christus natus est.* VICTORIA: *O magnum mysterium; Senex puerum portabat.* BYRD: *Senex puerum portabat; Hodie beata virgo.* GIBBONS: *Hosanna to the Son of David.* WEELKES: *Hosanna to the Son of David; Gloria in excelsis Deo.* ECCARD: *When to the temple Mary went.* MACONCHY: *Nowell! Nowell!.* arr. BRITTEN: *The holly and the ivy.* PHILIP (The Chancellor): *Angelus ad virginem.* arr. POSTON: *Angelus ad virginem; My dancing day.* POSTON: *Jesus Christ the apple tree.* BERKELEY: *I sing of a maiden.* TAYLOR: *Watts's cradle song.* campion: *Sing a song of joy.* PEERSON: *Most glorious Lord of life.* Imogen HOLST: *That Lord that lay in Assë stall.* WARLOCK: *Where riches is everlastingly.*
(M) *** EMI CDM5 66244-2.

A happily chosen survey of music (63 minutes), inspired by the Nativity, from the fifteenth century to the present day. As might be expected, the King's choir confidently encompasses the wide variety of styles from the spiritual serenity of the music of Victoria to the attractive arrangements of traditional carols by modern composers, in which an instrumental accompaniment is added. These items are quite delightful and they are beautifully recorded (in 1965). The motets, from a year earlier, were among the first recording sessions made by the EMI engineers in King's College Chapel, and at the time they had not solved all the problems associated with the long reverberation period, so the focus is less than sharp. Even so, this group demonstrates the unique virtuosity of the Cambridge choir, exploiting its subtlety of tone and flexibility of phrase.

'*Choral favourites from King's*': HANDEL: *Messiah: Hallelujah chorus*. BACH: *Cantata 147: Jesu, joy of man's desiring*. HAYDN: *The Creation: The heavens are telling*. PURCELL: *Rejoice in the Lord alway*. BRITTEN: *Saint Nicholas: The birth of Nicholas* (all three excerpts with soloists). FAURÉ: *Requiem: Sanctus* (all seven excerpts with ASMF). SCHUBERT: *Psalm 23: Gott ist mein Hirt* (with Philip Ledger, piano). ELGAR: *Coronation ode: Land of hope and glory* (with soloists, Band of Royal Military School of Music, Cambridge University Musical Society). DELIUS: *To be sung of a summer night on the water I of II* (with Robert Tear). BRITTEN: *Ceremony of carols: There is no rose* (with Osian Ellis, harp). William HARRIS: *Faire is the heaven*. Charles WOOD: *Hail, gladdening light*. John DYKES: *Holy, holy, holy* (with Philip Jones Brass Ens.; Ian Hare, organ).

(M) *** EMI CDM5 72812-2.

Even though it is a budget sampler, this King's collection makes a satisfying concert in its own right, besides tempting the listener to explore further. Opening with a joyful version of the *Hallelujah chorus*, with the radiant treble contribution very striking, the coverage is wide-ranging. Schubert's delightful setting of the Psalm 23 (with Philip Ledger's piano accompaniment) makes an ideal foil for the preceding Purcell anthem and the following excerpt from the Fauré *Requiem*. Similarly the introduction of *Land of hope and glory* into Elgar's *Coronation ode* begins a delightful sequence of music by Delius and Britten. The concert then closes with three fine examples of the continuing Anglican choral tradition from William Harris, Charles Wood and, ending more conventionally, John Dykes, with his familiar hymn *Holy, holy, holy*, but in Willcocks's imaginative arrangement with a descant. The warmly atmospheric King's ambience adds much to the music throughout; only in *The heavens are telling* from *The Creation* might one have liked a bit more choral bite.

King's College, Cambridge, Choir, (i) Stephen Cleobury with David Briggs (organ); (ii) Sir David Willcocks; (iii) Anthony Way (treble), St Paul's Cathedral Ch. and CO, John Scott

'*The ultimate carol collection*': (i) GAUNTLETT, arr. Ledger: *Once in Royal David's city*. arr. WILLCOCKS: *O come all ye faithful; The first*

nowell; (ii) *Unto us is born a son*; (i) *God rest ye merry, gentlemen; I saw three ships*; (ii) *See amid the winter's snow; Rocking*; (i) *The infant King*. (i) MENDELSSOHN, arr. Ledger: *Hark! the herald angels sing*. DARKE: *In the bleak midwinter*. arr. VAUGHAN WILLIAMS: *O little town of Bethlehem*. (ii) arr. PEARSAL: *In dulci jubilo*. praetorius: *A great and mighty wonder*. (i) arr. LEDGER: *Sussex carol*. (ii) TATE: *While shepherds watched*. (i) arr. CLEOBURY: *Away in a manger*. arr. WOOD: *Ding dong! Merrily on high*; (ii) *King Jesus hath a garden; Shepherds in the field abiding*. arr. WALFORD DAVIES: *The holly and the ivy*. arr. WOODWARD: *Up, good Christian folk*. (ii) arr. SHAW: *Coventry carol*. (i) GRUBER, arr. Cleobury: *Silent night*. (iii) SHANE, arr. Alexander: *Do you hear what I hear?*

(M) **(*) Decca Analogue/Dig. 458 863-2.

Decca's 'Ultimate' carol collection (issued in 1997) is hardly that, but it will suit those looking for an essentially atmospheric concert of tested favourites for Christmas Day. It centres on a 1984 compilation directed by Stephen Cleobury with *Once in Royal David's city* presented not as a processional but as an interplay between treble soloist (Robin Barter) and full choir. The choir is backwardly placed and the atmosphere overall is slightly subdued. However, the organ contribution from David Briggs (uncredited in the documentation) always makes its presence felt and is strongly featured in Willcocks's dramatic arrangement of *Unto us is born a son* and the powerful close of *God rest ye merry, gentlemen*. Philip Ledger's version of *Hark! the herald angels sing* also has a spectacular climax.

However, in general the recording does not seek to clarify textures but concentrates on capturing the ambient atmosphere. Thus the older recordings conducted by Willcocks, which are interspersed, match up well to the later collection. The modern carol *Do you hear what I hear?*, featuring the eloquent Anthony Way and opulently presented with orchestral accompaniment, while it may be a highlight for some listeners, fits rather uneasily in the middle of the programme (following after the *Sussex carol*), and not everyone will respond to Cleobury's elaboration of the closing *Silent night*, which takes an original turn after the opening verse.

Kirkby, Emma (soprano)

'*Madrigals and wedding songs for Diana*' (with David Thomas, bass, Consort of Musicke, Rooley): BENNET: *All creatures now are merry-minded*. CAMPION: *Now hath Flora robbed her bowers; Move now measured sound; Woo her and win her*. LUPO: *Shows and nightly revels; Time that leads the fatal round*. GILES: *Triumph now with joy and mirth*. CAVENDISH: *Come, gentle swains*. DOWLAND: *Welcome, black night*

. . . Cease these false sports. WEELKES: *Hark! all
ye lovely saints; As Vesta was.* WILBYE: *Lady
Oriana.* EAST: *Hence stars! too dim of light; You
meaner beauties.* LANIER: *Bring away this sacred
tree; The Marigold; Mark how the blushful morn.*
COPERARIO: *Go, happy man; While dancing rests;
Come ashore, merry mates.* E. GIBBONS: *Long live
fair Oriana.*
*** Hyperion CDA 66019 [id.].

This wholly delightful anthology celebrates early
royal occasions and aristocratic weddings, and in its
choice of Elizabethan madrigals skilfully balances
praise of the Virgin Queen with a less ambivalent
attitude to nuptial delights. Emma Kirkby is at her
freshest and most captivating, and David Thomas,
if not quite her match, makes an admirable contribution. Accompaniments are stylish and well balanced, and the recording is altogether first rate.

'O tuneful voice' (with Rufus Müller, Timothy
Roberts (fortepiano or harpsichord), Frances
Kelley (harp)): HAYDN: *O tuneful voice; She never
told her love; Sailor's song.* Samuel ARNOLD:
Elegy. PINTO: *Invocation to Nature; A Shepherd
lov'd a nymph so fair; From thee, Eliza, I must
go; Eloisa to Abelard; Minuet in A.* STORACE: *The
curfew.* LINLEY THE ELDER: *The lark sings high
in the cornfield; Think not, my love.* JACKSON: *The
day that saw thy beauty rise; Time has not thinn'd
my flowing hair.* SHIELD: *Ye balmy breezes, gently
blow; Hope and love; 'Tis only no harm to know
it, you know.* CARDON: *Variations on 'Ah vous
dirai-je, maman'.* HOOK: *The emigrant.*
SALOMON: *Go, lovely rose; Why still before these
streaming eyes; O tuneful voice.*
*** Hyperion Dig. CDA 66497.

This programme is centred in eighteenth-century
England, although Haydn could be included because of his London visits. Indeed, Salomon, his
impresario, is featured here as a composer, and a
very able one, too; but it is Haydn's comparatively
rare song which gives the CD its title and shows
Emma Kirkby on top form, just as charming but
with greater depth of expression than in her companion Hyperion and Oiseau-Lyre collections, the
latter having the same geographical basis but
offering repertoire from an earlier period. Kirkby
sings like a lark in the cornfield, and Rufus Müller
joins her in some duets by William Jackson and
also shares the solo numbers. There are innocently
rustic songs from William Shield in which each
artist participates, and much else besides: this 74-
minute programme has a wide range of mood and
style.

'A Portrait' (with AAM, Hogwood): HANDEL:
*Disseratevi, o porte d'Averno; Gentle Morpheus,
son of night.* PURCELL: *Bess of Bedlam; From
rosie bow'rs.* ARNE: *Where the bee sucks there
lurk I; Rise, glory, rise.* DOWLAND: *I saw the lady*

weepe. D'INDIA: *Odi quel rosignuolo.*
TROMBONCINO: *Se ben hor non scopro il foco.*
VIVALDI: *Passo di pena in pena.* J. S. BACH: *Ei!
wie schmeckt der Coffee süsse.* HAYDN: *With
verdure clad.* MOZART: *Laudate Dominum;
Exsultate, jubilate, K.165.*
⊛ (M) *** O-L Dig. 443 200-2 [id.].

Admirers of Emma Kirkby's style in early and
baroque music will delight in this well-chosen 76-
minute sampler of her work. L'Oiseau-Lyre have
altered and expanded the original issue and the
excerpt from Handel's *Messiah* has been replaced
by the remarkable Angel's aria, *Disseratevi, o porte
d'Averno*, from Part I of *La Resurrezione* (calling
on the gates of the Underworld to be unbarred, to
yield to God's glory). It opens with joyous baroque
trumpets and oboes, and Emma Kirkby shows with
her florid vocal line that anything they can do, she
can do better.

This is rather effectively followed by Purcell's
melancholy Mad song, *Bess of Bedlam*, and the
equally touching *From rosie bow'rs*. Music by Arne
lightens the mood and later there are excerpts from
Bach's *Coffee cantata* and popular solos by Haydn
and Mozart. This recital is as well planned as it is
enjoyable, and Hogwood ensures that accompaniments are consistently fresh and stylish. First-class
sound.

Arias (with AAM, Hogwood): HANDEL:
Alessandro Severo: Overture. Arias from: *Alcina;
Alexander's Feast; L'Allegro, il penseroso ed il
moderato; Saul; March in D; Hornpipe.* LAMPE:
*Britannia: Welcome Mars. Dione: Pretty
warblers.* ARNE: *Comus. Rosamond: Rise, glory,
rise. By the rusty-fringed bank; Brightest lady.
The Tempest: Where the bee sucks.* HAYDN: *The
Creation: With verdure clad; On mighty pens.*
MOZART: Concert arias: *Voi, avete un cor fedele;
Nehmt meinen Dank, ihr holden Gönner! Ch'io mi
scordi di te?* Arias from: *Il rè pastore; Zaïde.*
(B) *** Decca Double Dig. 458 084-2 (2) [id.].

Two of the Arne arias and one of Haydn's are
included in the 'Portrait' (see previous entry), and
Arne's *Rise, glory, rise* (showing the singer at her
very finest) also rightly appears in Decca's 'Treasures of baroque opera' (see above). The rest is
new. Of the novelties Lampe's charming *Pretty
warblers*, like Handel's *Sweet bird* from *L'Allegro,
il penseroso ed il moderato*, brings an illustrative
aviary from the solo flute, with Kirkby then adding
her own exquisite roulades. *Credete al mio dolore*
from *Alcina* has an important cello obbligato.
Kirkby's smooth sweet line and easy coloratura
give consistent pleasure, and the two famous arias
from Haydn's *Creation* are gloriously sung.

The extended Mozart programme, recorded in
1988/9, is discussed under its Composer entry.
Throughout, Hogwood's accompaniments are light
and stylish and give the singer every support, and

one's only criticism is that the Handel and Mozart selections would have benefited from more instrumental music in between the arias to add variety. But individually every item here is treasurable and the recording is first class, giving plenty of space and a fine bloom to the voice.

'The sweet voice of Emma Kirkby' (with AAM, Hogwood/Preston; or Consort of Musicke, Rooley): Arias from: HANDEL: *Alcina; Alceste; Esther.* ARNE: *Rosamond.* PERGOLESI: *Stabat Mater:* excerpt (with James Bowman). MOZART: *Le nozze di Dorina.* Also Concert aria: *Nehmt meinen Dank, K.383.* BACH: Excerpts from: *Cantata, BWV 202; Wedding cantata, BWV 509.* VIVALDI: *Gloria: Laudamus te* (with Judith Nelson). TROMBONCINO: *Vergine bella.* MONTEVERDI: *O come sei gentile.* PURCELL: *If music be the food of love; Pausanias: Sweeter than roses.* WILBYE: *Draw on sweet night.* **(*) Decca Dig. 466 322-2 [id.].

The voice is certainly as sweet as ever, the singing full of vitality and character. The accompaniments are just as sparkling as the singing, the recording is first class, and there is again not too much duplication here. Whether in the spectacular and charming little-known Mozart aria from *Le nozze di Dorina*, the flamboyant Handel and Arne arias with trumpets and, in the case of *Praise the Lord* from *Esther* (where Kirkby herself opens like a trumpet), a harp too, the lovely Bach cantata excerpts, including the famous *Bist du bei mir* (now attributed to G. H. Stölzel), or the duets by Pergolesi, Vivaldi and Tromboncino, the ear is constantly ravished, as it is again in the closing group of songs by Purcell and Wilbye. However, there seems no reason for paying full price for a sampler which is inadequately documented and contains no texts or translations. Indeed, the brief note is biographical only, and tells the collector nothing whatsoever about the music beyond a list of titles.

Kraus, Alfredo (tenor)

Arias and excerpts from: VERDI: *Rigoletto; La Traviata.* DONIZETTI: *Don Pasquale; Lucia di Lammermoor.* PUCCINI: *La Bohème.* BELLINI: *I Puritani.* MOZART: *Così fan tutte: Un'aura amorosa.*
(BB) ** Royal Classics Vocal Double DCL 706642 (2).

Alfredo Kraus, a light tenor and a stylish one, always gives pleasure, if at times one misses the thrill of a really big voice. These five sets of excerpts come from complete recordings in which he participated in the late 1970s and early 1980s, in partnership with Beverly Sills, Renata Scotto and others. He is heard at his stylish best in *Rigoletto*, is a tender Rodolfo in *Bohème* and is equally touching

in *Traviata*, although here the voice sounds thinner. He is also impressive alongside Edita Gruberová in *Lucia di Lammermoor.* Most of these recordings are far from first choices, so his admirers will be glad to have his contributions available separately.

Larin, Sergej (tenor), Eleonora, Bekova (piano)

'Songs by the Mighty Handful':
RIMSKY-KORSAKOV: *It was not the wind blowing from above; The octave; The nymph; Clearer than the singing of the lark; The scurrying bank of clouds disperses; On the hills of Georgia; Of what in the silence of the night; Captivated by the rose, the nightingale; Silence descends on the yellow cornfields; A pressed flower.* CUI: *A statue at Tsarskoye Selo; The burnt letter.* BORODIN: *The fair maid has stopped loving me; For the shores of the distant homeland.* BALAKIREV: *You are full of captivating bliss; Barcarolle; Look, my friend.* MUSSORGSKY: *Songs and dances of Death.*
*** Chandos Dig. CHAN 9547 [id.].

Sergej Larin with his outstandingly beautiful and expressive tenor presents vivid portraits of the five Russian composers grouped as 'The Mighty Handful', all but Mussorgsky here represented in miniatures. The ten Rimsky-Korsakov songs are totally unpretentious, simple ballads that he wrote in joyful relaxation, a mood which is reflected in the music. The two Cui songs are far more intense, as are the two by Borodin, one of them, *The fair maid has stopped loving me*, with cello obbligato played by Alfia Bekova. The three Balakirev songs are tiny chips from the workbench, beautifully crafted. Only Mussorgsky is presented at full stretch with the greatest and best-known of the items here, the *Songs and dances of Death*. Larin, having for the earlier songs used his most honeyed tones and velvety, seamless production, including a wonderful head-voice on top, here darkens his tone thrillingly, ending with a searing account of *The Field Marshal Death*. A superb disc, revealing a great artist.

Laudibus, Michael Brewer

'All in the April evening': ROBERTON: *All in the April evening.* arr. ROBERTON: *The banks o'Doon; An Eriskay love lilt; Dream Angus; All through the night; The wee Copper o'Fife; Drink to me only with thine eyes.* arr. VAUGHAN WILLIAMS: *Ca' the yowes; The turtle dove.* VAUGHAN WILLIAMS: *3 Shakespeare songs: Full fathom five; The cloud-capp'd towers; Over hill, over dale.* arr. BANTOCK: *O can ye sew cushions?.* Arr. MANSFIELD: *Wi' a hundred pipers.* MORLEY: *Fyer! fyer!* BENNET: *All creatures now are*

merry-minded. BYRD: *Ave verum corpus.* GRANT: *Crimond.* PARRY: *Never weather-beaten sail.* ELGAR: *My love dwelt in a northern land; As torrents in summer.* arr. WARLOCK: *Corpus Christi.* STANFORD: *The blue bird.* SULLIVAN: *The long day closes.*
*** Hyperion Dig. CDA 67076 [id.].

The twenty-two members of Laudibus are all recruited from the National Youth Choir. Their tuning is impeccable and they blend together with the natural flexibility which established the international reputation of Sir Hugh Roberton's Glasgow Orpheus Choir. The programme here is based on repertoire made famous by that now disbanded group, opening appropriately with the title piece, one of the simplest and loveliest examples of four-part writing in the English language. The programme is for the most part composed of similarly serene and evocative music, but every so often there is a lively item like *Wi' a hundred pipers,* Morley's *Fyer! fyer!,* or Bennet's *All creatures now are merry-minded,* to interrupt the reverie momentarily. The various soloists are drawn from the choir and very good they are too (sample the treble solo in Stanford's *Blue bird*). Beautifully recorded, this is a choral record for the late evening, and its consistency of mood is one of its virtues. The playing time is a generous 72 minutes.

Legge, Walter (producer)

'Les introuvables de Walter Legge': Disc 1: *Lieder:* WOLF: *Eichendorff Lieder: Der Freund; Der Musikant* (Herbert Janssen with Gerald Moore; 1937). *Mörike Lieder: In der Frühe; Mausfallen-Sprüchlein. Spanisches Liederbuch: In dem Schatten meiner Locken. Italienisches Liederbuch: Auch kleine Dinge; Und willst du deinen Liebsten. Wie glänzt der helle Mond.* HAYDN: *Canzonetta: She never told her love; Sailor's song.* MOZART: *Das Veichen* (Elisabeth Schumann with Gerald Moore; 1945/6). SCHUBERT: *Der Musensohn.* Yryö KILPINEN: *6 Lieder um den Tod, Op. 62* (Gerhard Hüsch with Hanns Udo Müller or Margaret Kilpinen; 1934/5). BRAHMS: *2 Lieder with viola, Op. 91* (Kirsten Flagstad with Herbert Downes and Gerald Moore; 1949). WOLF: *Goethe Lieder: Mignon II: Nur wer die Sehnsucht kennt.* SCHUMANN: *Die Kartenlegerin* (Elisabeth Höngen with Hans Zipper; 1946). SCHUBERT: *Der Wanderer* (Hans Hotter with Hermann von Nordberg; 1947). BRAHMS: *Feldeinsamkeit* (Tiana Lemnitz with Herta Klust; 1948). R. STRAUSS: *Cäcile* (Hilde Konetzni with Hermann von Nordberg; 1948).

Disc 2: *Voices:* O'CONNOR: *The old house.* THAYER: *A child's prayer* (John McCormack with Gerald Moore; 1939). Adrian BEECHAM: *The willow song; O mistress mine* (Nancy Evans, Sir Thomas Beecham; 1940). PURCELL: *The Blessed Virgin's expostulation* (Isobel Baillie with Arnold Goldsbrough, organ; 1941). GLUCK: *Orpheus and Eurydice: What is life to me without thee?* BRAHMS: *Liebestreu; Deutsche Volkslieder: Feinsliebchen* (sung in English). ELGAR: *The Dream of Gerontius: My work is done . . . It is because then thou didst fear.* Maurice GREENE: *I will lay me down in peace; O praise the Lord* (Kathleen Ferrier with Gerald Moore; 1944). GOUNOD: *Au rossignol* (Pierre Bernac with Francis Poulenc; 1945). R. STRAUSS: *Ariadne aux Naxos: Es gibt ein Reich . . . In den Schönen Feierkleidern* (Maria Cebotari, VPO, Karajan; 1948). *Salome:* Final scene, excerpt: *Sie ist ein Ungeheuer* (Ljuba Welitsch, Gertrud Schuster, Josef Witt, VPO, Karajan; 1948). WAGNER: *Tristan und Isolde: Tod denn Alles!* (Ludwig Weber, Elisabeth Schwarzkopf, Philh. O, Schüchter; 1951); *Die Meistersinger: Fliedermonologue* (Hans Hotter, VPO, Karajan; 1948). BOITO: *Mefistofele: L'altra notte* (Renata Scotto, Philh. O, Manno Wolf-Ferrari; 1958). MOZART: *Il rè pastore: L'amerò, sarò costante* (Anna Moffo, Philh. O, Galliera; 1958).

Disc 3: *Instruments:* BACH: *Toccata and fugue in D min., BWV 565* (Albert Schweitzer, organ of All Hallows by the Tower, Barking, Essex; 1935). MENDELSSOHN, arr. RACHMANINOV: *A Midsummer Night's Dream: Scherzo* (Moiseiwitch; 1939). SARASATE: *Danzas españolas: Playera; Zapateado* (Josef Hassid with Gerald Moore; 1940). SHOSTAKOVICH: *Prelude No. 24, Op. 34/24* (Harriet Cohen; 1942). SCHUBERT: *String quartet No. 14 (Death and the Maiden): Andante* (Philharmonia Qt; 1942). SZYMANOWSKI: *Notturno e Tarantella, Op. 28: Tarantella* (Arthur Grumiaux, Gerald Moore; 1945). WEBER: *Invitation to the dance.* BACH: *Chromatic fantasia and fugue, BWV 903* (Artur Schnabel; 1947/8). Domenico SCARLATTI: *Sonata in F, Kk. 7.* BACHBUSONI: *Cantata No. 140: Chorale: Wachet auf* (Solomon; 1948). Domenico SCARLATTI: *Sonatas in D min., Kk. 9; in D, KK. 33.* HANDEL: *Suite No. 5: The Harmonious blacksmith* (Walter Gieseking; 1951).

Disc 4: *Orchestral:* BEETHOVEN: *Overture: The Ruins of Athens* (LSO, Weingartner; 1940). LISZT: *Fantasia on a theme from Beethoven's 'Ruins of Athens'* (Egon Petri, LPO, Leslie Heward; 1938). WALTON: *Henry V* (film score): *Passacaglia: The death of Falstaff; Touch her soft lips and part* (Philh. O strings, composer; 1945). BLISS: *March: The Phoenix* (Philh. O, Constant Lambert; 1946). DVORAK: *Carnaval overture, Op. 9* (Czech PO, Kubelik; 1946). MOZART: *Serenade No. 7 (Haffner): Rondo* (Willi Boskovsky, VPO, Karl Boehm; 1947). BORODIN: *Overture: Prince Igor*

(Philh. O, Issay Dobrowen; 1949). PROKOFIEV: *Symphony No. 1 in D (Classical), Op. 25* (BPO, Sergiu Celibidache; 1948).

(B) (***) EMI mono CZS5 69743-2 (4) [(M) id. import].

Many of the items here may be so offbeat as to seem perverse in celebration of the work of the greatest of recording producers. The key word is '*introuvables*', recordings so rare that hardly anyone knows of them. It is surprising for example to have Legge's second wife, Elisabeth Schwarzkopf – she as much an inspiration to him as he always was to her – celebrated with an odd fragment from Wagner's *Tristan*. In the passage leading up to the final *Liebestod*, she acts as foil for the bass, Ludwig Weber, in the brief, poignant duet, *Tod denn Alles!*, between King Mark and Brangäne, a touching performance. It is good to have Legge's first wife also remembered, a lovely singer far less celebrated but much loved, Nancy Evans, who, accompanied at the piano by Sir Thomas Beecham, sings two Shakespeare settings by Beecham's son, Adrian.

Each of the four CDs is devoted to a different category: Lieder, Voices, Instruments and Orchestral. Rightly, the first disc begins with some of the Hugo Wolf recordings, part of the Hugo Wolf Society Edition – the project which first made Legge's reputation – with Herbert Janssen and Elisabeth Schumann the singers chosen here. One might have expected some songs from Elena Gerhardt, but maybe her recordings were counted too '*trouvable*'. A fascinating rarity follows, reminding us that, along with the most prominent Society editions promoted by Legge, covering Beethoven, Bach, Mozart, Sibelius, Delius and others, there was a celebration of a most sensitive Finnish composer, still largely unappreciated by the Yrjö Kilpinen Society edition, with his songs recorded by the great Lieder-singer Gerhard Hüsch, the central figure in Legge's Lieder projects in the 1930s.

The Voices disc ranges from John McCormack to Anna Moffo (enchanting in Mozart's *Il rè pastore*) by way of Ferrier, Cebotari and many others; and the Instruments disc goes from Albert Schweitzer in Bach to Walter Gieseking in Handel, by way of such neglected artists as the violinist Josef Hassid. The Orchestral disc then ranges from Weingartner in Beethoven's *Ruins of Athens* and Egon Petri's recording of Liszt's *Variations* on a theme from that work to Celibidache doing Prokofiev's *Classical Symphony* in a typically idiosyncratic way. Karajan, one supposes, was also too '*trouvable*' to be included – though, as he always resisted being anthologized next to others on disc, maybe that rule still applies. In the booklet Alan Sanders writes a searching and informative (if brief) essay on Legge, and there are some delightful photos, though no texts of vocal items. An offbeat, very enjoyable tribute, though no such compilation could adequately convey a full portrait of such a figure.

Lemper, Ute, Matrix Ensemble, Robert Ziegler

'*Berlin cabaret songs*' (sung in German) by SPOLIANSKY; HOLLAENDER; GOLDSCHMIDT; BILLING; NELSON.
*** Decca Dig. 452 601-2 [id.].

The tangy, sexy voice of Ute Lemper is here caught at its most provocative in a colourful sequence of cabaret songs reflecting the sleazy, decadent atmosphere of Berlin under the Weimar Republic, as observed in the popular cabarets of the city. With Lemper characterizing delectably, with German consonants adding extra bite, often 'over the top' as in the delightful *Ich bin ein Vamp*, the authentic flavour is here presented in music with new vividness.

The conductor, Robert Ziegler, has restored the original orchestrations as closely as he can (no scores survive, only piano reductions), and the result is a valuable addition to the 'Entartete Musik' series. Not only is the music fascinating and characterful, so are the words, including even a gay anthem, with oompah bass, *Das lila Lied*, written by Mischa Spoliansky under a pseudonym. It is good too to have included a song by Berthold Goldschmidt which he wrote for his wife in 1930.

'*Berlin cabaret songs*' (sung in English): SPOLIANSKY: *It's all a swindle; The smart set; When the special girlfriend; I am a vamp; L'heure bleue; Maskulinum.* HOLLAENDER: *Sex appeal; Take it off Petronella!; Chuck out the men!; Oh just suppose; I don't know who I belong to; A little yearning; Oh, how we wish that we were kids again; Munchausen.* NELSON: *Peter, Peter; A little Attila.* GOLDSCHMIDT: *The washed-up lover.* BILLING: *The Lavender song.*
*** Decca Dig. 452 849-2 [id.].

This offers the same programme as the disc above, but in English translation. Inevitably some of the bite is lost with softer English consonants, but it is amazing how much of the original tang and snarl Lemper manages to inject, and there is much to be said for having the words instantly identifiable to the English speaker, with diction crystal clear.

(i) Leonard, Sarah (soprano), (ii) Paul Leonard (baritone); Malcolm Martineau (piano)

'*A Century of English song*', Volume II: (i) PARRY: *My heart is like a singing bird; From a city window; The maiden; Armida's garden; My* *true love hath my heart; Goodnight; Crabbed age and youth.* Sir Arthur SOMERVELL: (ii) *A Shopshire lad* (cycle); (i) *Young love lies sleeping; Shepherd's cradle song; Come to me in my dreams.* STANFORD: (ii) *The fair; To the soul; The calico dress:* (i) *An Irish idyll* (cycle). **(*) Somm Dig. SOMMCD 214.

Sarah Leonard with her fresh, bright soprano and her brother Paul with his cleanly focused baritone are persuasive advocates in these largely neglected songs, helped by the imaginative accompaniments of Malcolm Martineau. All three composers rise above the limitations of the drawing-room ballad thanks to musical finesse and sensitive response to words, though Somervell's *Shropshire lad* cycle, open in its lyricism, completely misses the darkness implied behind seemingly innocent verses. Parry owes most to the example of Brahms, while Stanford, with Irish as well as English overtones, finds a personal magic in such songs as *The fairy lough*, the second song in the *Irish idyll*. Well-balanced recording, but with edge on the top of the soprano's voice.

London Symphony Chorus and Orchestra, Richard Hickox

'Great opera choruses': BIZET: *Carmen: Toreador chorus.* VERDI: *Il Trovatore: Anvil chorus. Nabucco: Gli arredi festivi; Va pensiero. Macbeth: Che faceste?. Aida: Grand march.* GOUNOD: *Faust: Soldiers' chorus.* BORODIN: *Prince Igor: Polovtsian dances.*
(BB) *** Carlton LSO Double Dig. 30368 01167 (2) [(B) id.] (with BIZET: *L'Arlésienne* and *Carmen suites* **(*)).

Most collections of opera choruses are taken from sets, but this is a freshly minted, digital collection of favourites, sung with fine fervour and discipline. The opening *Toreador chorus* from *Carmen* is zestfully infectious, and the *Soldiers' chorus* from *Faust* is equally buoyant. The noble line of Verdi's *Va pensiero* is shaped beautifully by Hickox, with the balance between voices and orchestra particularly good.

In *Gli arredi festivi* from *Nabucco* and the famous Triumphal scene from *Aida* the orchestral brass sound resonantly sonorous, even if the fanfare trumpets could have been more widely separated in the latter piece. The concert ends with Borodin's *Polovtsian dances,* most excitingly done. The recording, made at the EMI Abbey Road studio, has the atmosphere of an idealized opera house, and the result is in the demonstration bracket, with a projection and presence fully worthy of this polished but uninhibited singing. This is now reissued as an LSO Double, with colourful orchestral music by Bizet, also very well recorded.

Lorengar, Pilar (soprano)

'Grandi voci': Arias from: PUCCINI: *La Bohème; La Rondine; Madama Butterfly; Turandot; Gianni Schicchi.* DVORAK: *Rusalka.* G. CHARPENTIER: *Louise.* BIZET: *Carmen; Les Pêcheurs de perles.* MASSENET: *Manon* (with St Cecilia Ac. O, Patanè). MOZART: *Le nozze di Figaro.* BEETHOVEN: *Fidelio.* WEBER: *Der Freischütz.* WAGNER: *Tannhäuser.* KORNGOLD: *Die tote Stadt* (with Vienna Op. O, Walter Weller).
(M) *(*) Decca 443 931-2.

It was a mistake for Pilar Lorengar to open this collection – compiled from two separate, earlier recitals, recorded in 1966 and 1970 – with *They call me Mimi.* Hers is a vocal personality of strong character and temperament, but the style of her singing fails to convince here, and a surer legato is needed in this aria. She is much better as Butterfly and is impressive in Liù's aria. In the German repertoire her vibrato is troublesome in almost every item, with the trills in *Dove sono* barely distinguishable from sustained notes and the throat occasionally constricting to produce something not far from a yodel. The highlight of the collection is the famous *Invocation to the moon* from Dvořák's *Rusalka.*

Lott, Felicity (soprano), Graham Johnson (piano)

Mélodies on Victor Hugo poems: GOUNOD: *Sérénade.* BIZET: *Feuilles d'album: Guitare. Adieux de l'hôtesse arabe.* LALO: *Guitare.* DELIBES: *Eclogue.* FRANCK: *S'il est un charmant gazon.* FAURE: *L'absent; Le papillon et la fleur; Puisqu'ici-bas.* WAGNER: *L'attente.* LISZT: *O quand je dors; Comment, disaient-ils.* SAINT-SAENS: *Soirée en mer; La fiancée du timbalier.* M. V. WHITE: *Chantez, chantez jeune inspirée.* HAHN: *Si mes vers avaient des ailes; Rêverie.*
(B) *** HM Musique d'Abord HMA 901138 [(M) id. import].

Felicity Lott's collection of Hugo settings relies mainly on sweet and charming songs, freshly and unsentimentally done, with Graham Johnson an ideally sympathetic accompanist. The recital is then given welcome stiffening with fine songs by Wagner and Liszt, as well as two by Saint-Saëns that have a bite worthy of Berlioz. It makes a headily enjoyable cocktail. Now reissued in the Musique d'Abord series, this is a bargain not to be missed.

Ludwig, Christa (mezzo-soprano)

'The Art of Christa Ludwig' (with Gerald Moore or Geoffrey Parsons (piano) & (i) Herbert Downes

(viola); (ii) with Philh. O, Klemperer; (iii) with Berlin SO, Stein or Forster): BRAHMS: *Sapphische Ode; Liebestreu; Der Schmied; Die Mainacht. 8 Zigeunerlieder. 4 Deutsche Volkslieder: Och mod'r ich well en Ding han!; We kumm ich dann de Pooz erenn?; In stiller Nacht; Schwesterlein.* Lieder: *Dein blaues Auge; Von ewiger Liebe; Das Mädchen spricht; O wüsst ich doch; Wie Melodien zieht es mir; Mädchenlied; Vergebliches Ständchen; Der Tod, das ist die kühle Nacht; Auf dem See; Waldeinsamkeit; Immer leiser wird mein Schlummer; Ständchen; Gestillte Sehnsucht;* (i) *Geistliches Wiegenlied.* MAHLER: *Hans und Grete; Frühlingsmorgen. Des Knaben Wunderhorn: Ich ging mit Lust durch einen grünen Wald; Wo die schönen Trompeten blasen; Der Schildwache Nachtlied; Um schlimme Kinder; Das irdische Leben; Wer hat dies Liedlein erdacht; Lob des hohen Verstandes; Des Antonius von Padua Fischpredigt; Rheinlegendchen.* Rückert Lieder: *Ich atmet' einen linden Duft; Liebst du um Schönheit; Um Mitternacht; Ich bin der Welt abhanden gekommen.* SCHUMANN: *Frauenliebe und -Leben, Op. 42.* REGER: *Der Brief; Waldeinsamkeit.* SCHUBERT: *Die Allmacht; Fischerweise; An die Musik; Der Musensohn; Ganymed; Auf dem Wasser zu singen; Ave Maria; Die Forelle; Gretchen am Spinnrade; Frühlingsglaube; Der Tod und das Mädchen; Lachen und Weinen; Litanei auf das Fest Aller Seelen; Erlkönig; Der Hirt auf dem Felsen.* WOLF: *Gesang Weylas; Auf einer Wanderung.* R. STRAUSS: *Die Nacht; Allerseelen; Schlechtes Wetter.* ravel: *3 Chansons madécasses.* SAINT-SAENS: *Une flûte invisible.* RACHMANINOV: *Chanson géorgienne; Moisson de tristesse.* ROSSINI: *La regata veneziana* (3 canzonettas). (ii) WAGNER: *Wesendonck Lieder.* (iii) HANDEL: *Giulio Cesare: Cleopatra's aria.* BACH: *St John Passion:* Aria: *Es ist vollbracht!.* (ii) WAGNER: *Tristan und Isolde: Mild und leise.*
(M) *** EMI CMS7 64074-2 (4) [ZDMD 64074].

Christa Ludwig is an extraordinarily versatile artist with a ravishing voice, readily matched by fine intelligence and natural musical sensitivity which place her among the special singers of our time, including De los Angeles and Schwarzkopf (to name two from the same EMI stable). She was as impressive in Schubert as she was in Strauss and Brahms, and her Mahler is very special indeed. This compensates for the below-par Schumann song cycle. Her voice took naturally to the microphone, so this four-disc set is another source of infinite musical pleasure to be snapped up quickly before it disappears. The recordings come from the 1950s and 1960s and are very well transferred indeed.

'70th-birthday tribute' (with Deutsche Oper O, Hollreiser): Excerpts from R. STRAUSS: *Elektra; Ariadne; Die Frau ohne Schatten.* GLUCK:

Iphigenie in Aulis. ROSSINI: *The Barber of Seville.* WAGNER: *Götterdämmerung.*
(M) *** RCA 09026 68951-2 [id.].

For this 70th-birthday tribute RCA has delved into a long-buried archive to bring out this magnificent collection of Christa Ludwig's recordings made when she was at her supreme peak in 1964. Here in concert she tackles a range of operatic roles she would never have considered performing on stage. As Rosina she proves immaculate in Rossini (in German) and her portrayals in Strauss are heartfelt – Elektra's recognition scene and the big duet for the Dyer's Wife in *Die Frau ohne Schatten* (both with her then-husband, Walter Berry) as well as *Ariadne's Lament.* Crowning the collection comes her glorious account of Brünnhilde's Immolation scene.

McKellar, Kenneth (tenor)

'The Decca Years 1955–1975': TRAD., arr. KENNEDY-FRASER: *Kishmul's galley; An island sheiling song; The Christ-child's lullaby; The peat fire flame; To people who have gardens; Skye fisher's song; Sleeps the noon in the clear blue sky; An Eriskay love lilt.* TRAD., arr. SHARPLES: *An island sheiling song; Wi' a hundred pipers; The De'ils awa' wi' the exciseman; There was a lad was born in Kyle; Mary Morison; Ye banks and braes; Ca the Ewes.* TRAD., arr. KNIGHT: *Think on me; Ae fond kiss* (with Patricia Cahill); *Kalinka.* TRAD., arr. ROBERTON: *Dream Angus; Lewis bridal song.* TRAD., arr STANFORD: *Trottin' to the fair.* TRAD.. arr. BRITTEN; *Down by the Sally Gardens.* TRAD., arr. HUGHES: *She moved thro' the fair.* TRAD., arr. LAWSON: *Skye boat song.* FARNON: *Country girl.* DI CAPUA: *O sole mio.* HANDEL: *Xerxes: Ombra mai fù. Acis and Galatea: Love in her eyes sits playing.* MASSENET: *Manon: En fermant les yeux (Dream song).* BIZET: *The Fair maid of Perth: Serenade.* ELLIS: *This is my lovely day* (with Patricia Cahill). anka: *The longest day.* HOPPER: *By the short cut to the Rosses.* DONIZETTI: *L'elisir d'amore: Una furtiva lagrima.* MENDELSSOHN: *On wings of song.* BOUGHTON: *The Immortal hour: Faery song.* MURRAY: *I'll walk beside you.* SPEAKS: *On the road to Mandalay.* HARTY: *My lagen love.* BOCK: *Sunrise, sunset.* BERNSTEIN: *West Side story: Maria.* LAUDER: *Roamin' in the gloamin'.* GOULAY: *Song of the Clyde.* BANNERMAN, arr. ROBERTON: *Uist tramping song.* MURDOCH: *Hame o'mine.* OGILVIE: *Hail Caledonia.* SCHUBERT: *Great is Jehova.* TRAD., arr. MCPHEE: *I to the hills.* arr. WALFORD DAVIES: *God be in my head* (all three with Paisley Abbey Choir, George McPhee). LEMON: *My ain folk.* TRAD., arr. KNIGHT: *Will ye no come back again.*
(M) *** Decca 466 415-2 (2).

Both artistically and vocally, Kenneth McKellar's lovely singing of Scottish folksongs can be ranked alongside Count John McCormack's instinctive response to similar Irish melodies. Like McCormack, he had a natural feeling for their simplicity of line, and his artless phrasing and ravishingly beautiful upper range, together with splendid diction, and a spirited sense of fun, made him a uniquely gifted exponent, whether the song be lyrical or rhythmically catchy in its ready tunefulness. The sparkling *Lewis bridal song* was a BBC radio hit at one time, although the voice reproduces curiously here in this particular number. But McKellar's range was far wider than that.

Early in his career he played the Count in Rossini's *Barber of Seville* with the touring Carl Rosa Opera Company and, as Donizetti's *Una furtiva lagrima* shows, he could certainly spin an Italian lyric melody. But even finer is the delightful *Faery song* from *The Immortal hour*, and the *Dream song* from *Manon* brings a comparable delicacy of feeling and lovely tone. He could sing a sentimental ballad like *I'll walk beside you* with real style, and every word is clear in *The Road to Mandalay*. The duets with the charming soubrette Patricia Cahill show him in even lighter vein, while *God be in my head* (recorded in Paisley Abbey) has a touching combination of warmth and sincerity.

He was pretty good too at an Irish inflection. *Trottin' to the fair*, *By the short cut to the Rosses'*, the memorable *My lagen love* and (especially) the touching, unaccompanied *She moved thro' the fair* are splendid examples of his art. But it is the Scottish repertoire for which he will be uniquely remembered, and in which he had no peer, and this extremely generous concert ends very appropriately with *Will ye no come back again*. Accompaniments (often by Bob Sharples) are very well managed, the CD transfers are good and the set has an interesting extended reminiscence by McKellar's producer, Raymond Herricks.

'Kenneth McKellar's Scotland – Sleeps the noon in the clear blue sky' (with accompaniments directed by Robert Sharples): Disc 1: *'Songs of the Hebrides'* (arr. KENNEDY-FRASER): *Sleeps the noon in the clear blue sky; The peat fire flame; Land of heart's desire; The reiving ship; Aignish of the Machair; A fairy's love song; Skye fisher's song; A Clyde-side love lilt; Heart of fire love; Sea longing; To the people who have gardens; The Bens of Jura; The Birlinn of the White shoulders; Isle of my heart; Kirsteen; Ye Highlands and ye Lowlands.* *'Roamin' in the gloamin':* arr. KENNEDY-FRASER: *The road to the isles: An Eriskay love lilt; The cockle gatherer.* TRAD.: *Bonnie Mary of Argyle.* THOMSON: *The star o' Robbie Burns.* HANLEY: *Scotland the brave.* FOX: *Bonnie wee thing.* ROBERTON: *Westering home.* HUME: *Afton Water.* GOULAY: *Song of the Clyde.*

LAUDER: *Roamin' in the gloamin'; Keep right on to the end of the road.*

Disc 2: *'The Tartan':* TRAD.: *The March of the Cameron Men; Kishmul's Galley; The flowers of the forest; Lochnagar; Wi' a hundred pipers; Air Falalolo; An island sheiling song; Scots wha ha'e wi' Wallace bled.* SMITH: *Jessie, the flower of Dunblane.* SCOTT: *Annie Laurie.* MCKELLAR: *The Tartan; The Royal mile.* Folksongs (arr. SHARPLES): *McGregor's gathering; The Laird o'Cockpen; The bonnie Earl of Moray; O Gin I were a baron's heir; Turn ye to me; Hey, Johnny Cope; Ho-ro, my nut-brown maiden; Bonnie Strathyle; The wee Cooper o'Fife; Isle of Mull; A pair of nicky tams; The proud peaks of Scotland; Auld Lang Syne.*

✿ (M *** Australian Decca 844 840-2 (2).

Concurrently with the wider coverage above, Australian Decca have issued a second two-CD collection, entirely devoted to the finest of Kenneth McKellar's Scottish repertory. It is compiled from his most beautiful LP, 'Songs of the Hebrides', plus three others, 'Folk songs from Scotland's heritage' with much of the programme dealing with Scotland's colourful history, 'The Tartan', which is essentially a collection of Scottish popular genre songs, with elaborately arranged accompaniments, and 'Roamin' in the gloamin', McKellar's first stereo recital. This was recorded early in his career, when the voice was at its peak, with a marvellous freshness and bloom.

His simple presentation has a natural, spontaneous warmth and ardour, and the jaunty songs are most engagingly infectious, especially the wittily descriptive *Song of the Clyde*, with every word as clear as a bell. *Scotland the brave* and *Westering home* swing along splendidly, and the slightly sentimental Burns setting *Bonnie wee thing* could not be more charming. McKellar also includes the two most famous songs of his illustrious predecessor, Sir Harry Lauder, ending with a bold account of *Keep right on to the end of the road* of which that famous Scotsman would have surely approved. The orchestral arrangements here are nicely judged and show none of the inflation that marks the 'Tartan' collection, which is still very enjoyable for a' that.

But it is the ravishingly lovely collection of Hebridean songs which earns the set its Rosette. It opens with the sound of surf on sand, and this evocation returns between the items, many of which McKellar introduces himself, warmly and intimately. The lovely opening title song is followed by *The Peat fire flame*, sung with the lightest rhythmic touch, and then comes the most beautiful song of all, *Land of heart's desire* which is alone worth the rosette! Here the voice is slightly backwardly balanced, and McKellar's gently curving upward line is utterly melting. The melancholy *Aignish of the Machair* is another highlight and *The Fairy lover* (charmingly introduced) brings a delightful, lilting melody. Throughout, the accompaniments are delicately scored, often using pipes, and the voice itself is most naturally caught. But all these CD transfers are superb, the quality enhanced over the original LPs. Like the other Australian Decca issues, this set can be obtained to special order from the address given in the Introduction.

Mera, Yoshikazu (counter-tenor), Bach Collegium Japan, Masaaki Suzuki

Baroque arias: J. S. BACH: *Cantatas Nos. 12: Wir müssen durch viel Trübsal; Krenz und krone; 54: Widerstehe doch der Sünde; Die art verruchter Sünde; Wer Sünde tut; 132: Ich will, mein Gott; Christi Glieder, ach bedenket; 161: Komm, du süsse Todesstunde; Mein Jesus, lass mich nicht; In meinem Gott.* HANDEL: *Messiah: But who may abide; He was despised; Thou art gone up on high; Behold, a virgin; O Thou that tellest.* AHLE: *Prima pars; Secunda pars.* SCHUTZ: *Geistliche chormusik, Op. 11: Auf dem Gebirge hat man ein geschrei gehört.*
*** BIS Dig. CD 919 [id.].

The Japanese counter-tenor Yoshikazu Mera is one of the most impressive soloists on Suzuki's excellent recordings of choral works for BIS. This compilation drawn from various sources consistently displays his exceptionally sweet and even tone, even though his performances are not very sharply characterized. The voice is set against a helpfully reverberant acoustic.

Metropolitan Opera (artists from)

'Metropolitan Opera Gala': Arias from: BIZET: *Les Pêcheurs de perles* (Roberto Alagna; Bryn Terfel). G. CHARPENTIER: *Louise* (Renée Fleming). GOUNOD: *Faust* (Samuel Ramey; Plácido Domingo); *Roméo et Juliette* (Ruth Ann Swenson). LEHAR: *Giuditta* (Ileana Cotrubas). VERDI: *Don Carlos* (Dolora Zajick). MOZART: *Don Giovanni* (Fleming, Terfel, Jerry Hadley, Kiri Te Kanawa, Hei-Kyung Hong, Julien Robbins). Johann STRAUSS Jr: *Die Fledermaus* (Håkan Hagegård; Karita Mattila). MASSENET: *Werther* (Alfredo Kraus). SAINT-SAENS: *Samson et Dalila* (Grace Bumbry). WAGNER: *Tannhäuser* (Deborah Voight). OFFENBACH: *La Périchole* (Frederica von Stade). R. STRAUSS: *Der Rosenkavalier* (Fleming, Anne Sofie Von Otter, Heidi Grant Murphy). Tribute to James Levine (Birgit Nilsson).
**(*) DG Dig. 449 177-2; Video VHS 072 451-3 [id.].

Recorded live at James Levine's twenty-fifth anniversary gala in April 1996, this offers an extraordinary galaxy of stars, often teamed up in unexpected ways – as, for example, Alagna and Terfel in the first item, the *Pearl fishers* duet. The singers represented a range from such relative newcomers as those rising stars to veterans like Alfredo Kraus and Grace Bumbry. Few of the voices are heard at their very finest, not helped by a rather hard acoustic, but the variety of party pieces here is enough of a delight. The video re-creates the occasion the more satisfactorily, but it is worth hearing the disc for the end of Birgit Nilsson's speech, involving a shattering cry of '*Hojotoho!*'.

Miles, Alastair (bass)

Opera arias and scenes in English (with Clive Bayley (bass), Geoffrey Mitchell Choir) from VERDI: *Nabucco; The Lombards; Luisa Miller; Sicilian Vespers;* BELLINI: *Norma; The puritans;* ROSSINI: *Mahomet II; Moses in Egypt; Zelmira;* GOMES: *Salvator rosa.*
(M) *** Chandos Dig. CHAN 3032 [id.].

When so little of this repertory has ever been recorded in English before, it is welcome, thanks to the Peter Moores Foundation, to have a fine disc of bass arias, beautifully sung by Alastair Miles. With his firm, clear voice he is ideally suited to recording, boldly contrasting the lyrical and dramatic with a keen sense of style, even if he aspirates some of the elaborate passage-work. Many of the arias are presented in their setting with the Geoffrey Mitchell Choir contributing choruses, not least the famous *Chorus of Hebrew slaves* from *Nabucco.* The bass, Clive Bayley, sings strongly too as the principal supporting soloist.

Minstrelsy

'Songs and dances of the Renaissance and Baroque' (Carole Hofsted-Lee (soprano), Nancy Froseth, David Hays, David Livingstone (viola da gamba, baroque violin, recorders), Philip Rukavina (lute, archlute): SIMPSON: *Ballet.* ANON.: *2 Ballets; Mascarada; Volta.* arr. MCLACHLAN *When she cam ben, she bobbat.* PRAETORIUS: *Dances from Terpsichore* (suite). PACHELBEL: *Partita in C.* SALAVERDE: *Canzon a 2.* LAWES: *Suite in G min.* Songs: ROSSETER: *When Laura smiles.* DOWLAND: *I saw my lady weep; Shall I sue.* ARNE: *Under the greenwood tree.* CAMPION: *It fell upon a summer's day.*
*** Lyrichord Dig. LEMS 8018 [id.].

A most entertaining, lightweight consort, full of life and charm, although one wonders if Renaissance and Baroque musicians could have achieved such sophistry of intonation, blending and playing! The period instruments here are made to integrate smoothly and without any rough edges. The singing of Carole Hofsted-Lee too is pure in tone and line. She is naturally at home in the simplicity of Arne, and her lovely voice caresses the songs of Dowland and Campion with considerable feeling, even if her range of vocal colour is less intense than that of, say, Alfred Deller. There is much to delight in the instrumental music.

Some half-a-dozen of the ensemble pieces come from the *Taffel-Consort*, published by Thomas Simpson in 1621, a collection which has much in common with Praetorius's *Terpsichore*. John McLachlan's *When she cam ben, she bobbat* is very Scottish, a treble to a ground, with sparkling divisions. But perhaps the highlight is Pachelbel's *Partita*, which is not unlike his more famous *Canon* in making use of an ostinato bass, but is a more elaborate chaconne, with a dozen variations. The recording is beautifully balanced to match this sprightly and elegant music-making.

'Música española'

'Música española': Canciones: GRANADOS: *Goyescas: La maja y el ruiseñor.* FALLA: *La vida breve: Vivan los que rien; Allí está, riyendo.* TURINA: *Canto a Sevilla* (Pilar Lorengar, SRO, López Cobos). granados: *9 Tonadillas; 3 Majas dolorosas; 6 Canciones amatorias* (with Alicia de Larrocha). OBRADORS: *5 Canciones clásicas españolas* (Kiri Te Kanawa, Roger Vignoles). FALLA: *7 Spanish popular songs.* NIN: *4 Villancicos españoles* (Marilyn Horne, Martin Katz). GURIDI: *Cómo quieres que adivine; Mañanita de San Juan.* LAVILLA: *4 Canciones vascas.* TURINA: *Saeta en forma de salve; Farruca* (Teresa Berganza, Félix Lavilla).
(B) ** Decca Double Analogue/Dig. 433 917-2 (2) [id.].

With a celebrated Spanish soprano, accompanied in Granados by the most vividly characterful of Spanish pianists or, alternatively, by the highly sympathetic López-Cobos, and the Suisse Romande Orchestra providing a vivid orchestral backcloth in Falla and Turina, the casting might seem ideal. But Pilar Lorengar's tone, seldom perfectly steady, has grown slacker with the years and her vibrato more intrusive. Thanks to de Larrocha, Spanish fire is rarely lacking, but the partnership is unequal.

Granados's *La maja y el ruiseñor* is comparatively voluptuous, but too often the singing is squally and uncomfortable. Turina's *Canto a Sevilla* is a song cycle framed by an orchestral introduction and epilogue, with a central interlude: these are omitted here. Lorengar sings vibrantly, but again her voice hardens to shrillness under pressure, and the bold vibrato means that the pitch is not always perfectly focused. However, lyrical charm is cer-

tainly present when Kiri Te Kanawa (partnered by Roger Vignoles) contributes Fernando Obradors's *5 Canciones clásicas españolas*.

But the highlight of the set comes on the second disc, with the vibrant mezzo of Marilyn Horne. She sings Falla's *7 Canciones populares españolas*, and *4 Villancicos españoles* of Joaquín Nin, with real flamenco fire, and yet can be just as lyrically appealing as Te Kanawa. Her accompanist, Martin Katz, gives strong support. Teresa Berganza (with Félix Lavilla at the piano) then charms the listener with two of Guridi's *Canciones castellanas*, including the tenderly sung *Mañanita de San Juan*, four of Lavilla's own charming *Canciones vascas*, and two memorably contrasted songs by Turina.

Nash, Heddle (tenor)

'Serenade': Arias from: BIZET: *The Fair Maid of Perth; The Pearl fishers.* ROSSINI: *The Barber of Seville.* MOZART: *Don Giovanni; Le nozze di Figaro* (both sung in Italian). BALFE: *The Bohemian Girl.* LEHAR: *Frederica.* OFFENBACH, arr. KORNGOLD: *La belle Hélène.* GOUNOD: *Faust.* DONIZETTI: *Elixir of love.* HANDEL: *Judas Maccabaeus.* MASSENET: *Manon.* Songs: TRAD.: *Annie Laurie* (all with orch.). BENEDICT: *Eily Mavoureen.* BISHOP: *The bloom is on the rye.* MORGAN: *My sweetheart when a boy.* MCGEOCH: *Two eyes of grey.* MACDOWELL: *To a wild rose.* WHITAKER: *Diaphenia.* DELIUS: *To the queen of my heart; Love's philosophy.* WHITE: *To Mary.* MOERAN: *Diaphenia; The sweet o' the year* (all with Gerald Moore).
(M) (**(*)) ASV mono CDAJA 5227 [id.].

Although there are a few (obvious) duplications, this ASV compilation nicely supplements the finer Dutton Lab. collection below. The transfers of the orchestral accompaniments, which often sound boxy and confined, are much less sophisticated, but the voice emerges naturally, even if it is projected with less uniform vividness. But there are genuine treasures here, not least the songs, with Gerald Moore, who is more faithfully caught. The delightful *To a wild rose*, the Delius and Moeran songs and the splendid excerpt from *Judas Maccabaeus* are among the highlights.

'The incomparable Heddle Nash': PUCCINI: *La Bohème,* Act IV (complete; with Lisa Perli, Brownlee, Alva, Andreva, LPO, Beecham). Arias from: MOZART: *Così fan tutte* (with Ina Souez); *Don Giovanni* (all in Italian). ROSSINI: *The Barber of Seville.* VERDI: *Rigoletto.* BIZET: *The Fair Maid of Perth.* Johann STRAUSS Jr: *Die Fledermaus* (with Dennis Noble) (all in English).
(M) (***) Dutton Lab. mono CDLX 7012 [id. full price].

Once again Dutton Laboratories provide incomparable transfers from 78s – of such quality that Beecham's extraordinarily theatrical (1935) Act IV of *La Bohème*, sung in Italian, communicates like a modern recording. Heddle Nash sings ardently, but Lisa Perli (Dora Labette) as Mimì is equally touching and, if the rest of the cast are less distinctive, Beecham's direction carries the day. Nash's four Mozart recordings (also sung in Italian) are included, notably the 1929 *Il mio tesoro*. Most cherishable of all is the *Serenade* from *The Fair Maid of Perth* from 1932, but there is some very striking Verdi in English, full of flair (in spite of awkward words), and a sparkling Johann Strauss duet with Dennis Noble. It seems carping to point out that, with only 69 minutes, there would have been room for more. But what there is is technically state of the art.

New College, Oxford, Choir, Higginbottom

'Carols from New College': O come, all ye faithful; The angel Gabriel; Ding dong! merrily on high; The holly and the ivy; I wonder as I wander; Sussex carol; This is the truth; A Virgin most pure; Rocking carol; Once in Royal David's city. ORD: *Adam lay y-bounden.* Richard Rodney BENNETT: *Out of your sleep.* HOWELLS: *A spotless rose; Here is the little door.* DARKE: *In the bleak midwinter.* MATHIAS: *A babe is born; Wassail carol.* WISHART: *Alleluya, A new work is come on hand.* LEIGHTON: *Lully, lulla, thou little tiny child.* JOUBERT: *There is no rose of such virtue.*

(M)*** CRD CRD 3443 [id.].

A beautiful Christmas record, the mood essentially serene and reflective. Both the Mathias settings are memorable and spark a lively response from the choir; Howells' *Here is the little door* is matched by Wishart's *Alleluya* and Kenneth Leighton's *Lully, lulla, thou little tiny child* in memorability. Fifteen of the twenty-one items here are sung unaccompanied, to maximum effect. The recording acoustic seems ideal and the balance is first class. The documentation, however, consists of just a list of titles and sources.

New Company, Harry Bicket

'Sacred voices': ALLEGRI: *Miserere.* LOBO: *Versa est in luctum.* PALESTRINA: *The Song of Solomon: Quae est ista; Descendit in hortum nocum; Quam pulchri sunt gressus tui; Duo ubera tue.* BYRD: *Haec dies.* PHILIPS: *Ascendit Deus.* MUNDY: *Vox Patris caelestis.* TALLIS: *Spem in alium* (40-part motet). DERING: *Factum est silentium.*

(M) *** Classic fm Dig. 75605 57029-2 [id.].

A splendid recording début for The New Company, a professional chamber choir of twelve, directed by Harry Bicket, which is expanded here to forty voices for a thrilling performance of Tallis's *Spem in alium*, one of the great masterpieces of Elizabethan music. The programme opens with a double choir version of Allegri's justly famous *Miserere*, with the second group atmospherically recessed alongside the confident soprano soloist, who soars up again and again to what the conductor calls that 'exquisitely floaty top C': and she hits the spot beautifully every time.

Then follows Lobo's hardly less ethereal *Versa est in luctum* and a characteristic sequence of four serenely flowing five-part motets from Palestrina's *Song of Solomon*, sensuously rich in harmonic implication, all written around 1583–4. Suddenly the mood changes and the pace quickens for William Byrd's *Haec dies*, with its joyful cross-rhythms and an exultant concluding *Alleluia*. Peter Philips's *Ascendit Deus* is similarly full of life and energy and it prepares the way for the contrasting three-part anthem by the lesser-known William Mundy. Its serene simplicity has great beauty, and it again offers a chance for a celestial soaring solo soprano.

After the climactic Tallis work, the programme ends with a short, but thrillingly jubilant, six-part Matins responsory by Richard Dering. The choir were recorded at Temple Church, London, the venue some ten decades earlier for one of the most famous choral recordings of all time: Mendelssohn's *Hear my Prayer*, with its famous solo from Master Ernest Lough, 'Oh for the wings of a dove'. The treble soloist here is a worthy successor.

New London Consort, Philip Pickett

'The Pilgrimage to Santiago' (21 cantigas from the collection of King Alfonso el Sabio).
*** O-L Dig. 433 148-2 (2) [id.].

Philip Pickett and his brilliant team of singers and players present what is described as 'a musical journey along the medieval pilgrim road to the shrine of St James at Santiago de Compostela'. The twenty-one pieces, lasting over two hours, together provide a mosaic of astonishing richness and vigour, directly related to the four main pilgrim routes to the shrine, via Navarre, Castile, Leon and Galicia.

Pickett argues the importance of the Islamic influence in Spain, with bells and percussion often added to the fiddles, lutes, tabors and other early instruments. So the long opening cantiga, *Quen a virgen ben servira*, begins with an instrumental introduction, where (echoing Islamic examples) the players attract attention with tuning-up and flourishes, before the singing begins. The main cantiga then punctuates the twelve narrative stanzas sung by the solo soprano with a catchy refrain, *Those who serve the virgin well will go to paradise.* Standing out among the singers is the soprano Catherine Bott, the soloist in most of the big cantigas, warm as well as pure-toned, negotiating the weird sliding portamentos that, following Islamic examples, decorate some of the vocal lines. Vivid sound, though the stereo spread of the chorus is limited.

Norman, Jessye (soprano)

'*Diva*': Arias from: WAGNER: *Tannhäuser; Der fliegende Holländer; Tristan und Isolde.* OFFENBACH: *Contes d'Hoffmann; La belle Hélène.* BERLIOZ: *Roméo et Juliette.*
(M) *** EMI (SIS) CDM5 65576-2 [id.].

This is a magnificent compilation, framed by four items from Jessye Norman's Wagner recital of 1987 with Klaus Tennstedt: Elisabeth's two arias from *Tannhäuser, Senta's Ballad* from *Der fliegende Holländer* and *Isolde's Liebestod*, all superb. Her formidable powers of characterization in tragedy and comedy alike are illustrated in the sequence of excerpts from Offenbach's *Contes d'Hoffmann* (four, including long-buried material from the Oeser Edition) and *La belle Hélène* (three), vocally flawless too. It is also good to have her Juliet represented, taken from Muti's otherwise flawed version of Berlioz's *Roméo et Juliette.* More than with most issues in this well-planned 'Diva' series, it is a snag to have no texts provided.

Lieder and songs: SCHUBERT: *Dem Unendlichen; Der Winterabend; Auflösung.* WAGNER: *Wesendonck Lieder.* POULENC: *Tu vois le feu du soir; La fraîcheur et le feu, Nos. 1–7* (all with Irwin Gage). RAVEL: *Chanson de rouet; Si morne* (with Dalton Baldwin). Arias from: WAGNER: *Tristan und Isolde; Tannhäuser; Die fliegende Holländer.* BRAHMS: *Ein deutsches Requiem* (with LPO, Tennstedt). BERLIOZ: *Roméo et Juliette* (with Philadelphia Orchestra, Muti). OFFENBACH: *Les contes d'Hoffmann* with Brussels Opera Orchestra, Cambreling).
(BB) *** Royal Classics Vocal Double Dig./ Analogue DCL 703952 (2).

One snag for the compilers of this EMI anthology is having only a limited range of recordings to draw from. But this selection is comprehensive enough, with the Wagner Tennstedt items plus the *Wesendonck Lieder* (with piano), songs by Schubert, Poulenc and Ravel, plus a curious mixture of Brahms (from the Tennstedt *German Requiem*), Berlioz (the usual Juliet aria) and an ongoing selection from Offenbach's *Contes d'Hoffmann*. There are genuine treasures here and this is more comprehensive than the 'Diva' compilation above and costs less, but again no texts are provided.

Oberlin, Russell (counter-tenor)

'*Troubadour and trouvère songs*', Volume 1 (with Seymour Barab, viol): BRULE: *Cil qui d'amor me conseille.* DE BORNEIL: *Reis glorios, verais lums e clartatz.* DANIEL: *Chanson do – Ih mot son plan e prim.* d'epinal: *Commensmens de dolce saison bele.* RIQUIER: *Ples de tristor, marritz e doloires;* DE VENTADOUR: *Can vei la lauzeta mover.*
*** Lyrichord LEMS 8001 [id.].

It is good to see the legendary Russell Oberlin return to the catalogue. Older readers will recall his Covent Garden appearance as Oberon in Britten's *Midsummer Night's Dream.* Unfortunately his concert career was cut short and he has since pursued a distinguished career as a scholar. This 1958 recital of 'Troubadour and trouvère songs' first appeared on the Experiences Anonymes label and, like so many of his all-too-few recordings (including an incredible Handel aria disc), has long been sought after. This voice was quite unique, a *real* counter-tenor of exquisite quality and, above all, artistry. The disc is expertly annotated and is of quite exceptional interest. LEMS stands for Lyrichord Early Music Series, and the discs we have heard so far are artistically impressive.

'*Las Cantigas de Santa Maria*' (with Joseph Iadone, lute): *Prologo; Cantigas Nos. 7, 36, 97, 111, 118, 160, 205, 261, 330, 340 & 364.*
✿ *** Lyrichord LEMS 8003 [id.].

The 400 *Cantigas de Santa Maria,* all of which have music, come from the time of Alfonso El Sabio, King of Spain (1221–84). He is credited with being their composer, but that seems unlikely since they are very diverse. The texts are in Galician, a language in general use in medieval Spain for literary and artistic purposes.

They are all concerned with miracles associated with the Virgin Mary, but the music itself has considerable variety and, while the basic style may come from European monodic chant, the melisma has a distinctly Spanish colouring, which in itself has Arab influences. The selection of a dozen items is very well made, for these simple strophic songs have an instant appeal when sung with such lyrical ease by the incomparable Russell Oberlin. The character of the *Cantigas* seems to suit his special timbre especially well, and he has made no finer record than this.

The recital opens with a Prologue in which the singer relates the qualities necessary to be a good troubadour and invokes the Virgin's acceptance of his skills with some confidence. Two of the settings are lively dance songs, Cantiga 36 telling how Mary appeared in the night on the mast of a ship journeying to Brittany and saved it from danger, and Cantiga 205 about the rescue of a Moorish woman with her child who were sitting on top of a tower which collapsed – yet neither she nor the child came to any harm. But it is the beauty of the lyrical music which is so striking, notably so in Cantigas 118 and 330, which are concerned with the restoration of a dead child to life and a simple song of praise for the Virgin herself. The recording is natural and vivid and, as with the other discs in this Series, the CD remastering by Nick Fritsch is first class. The content of this reissue is not generous in playing time, but it is of the very highest musical quality and interest.

'Troubadour and trouvère songs', Volume 5: English medieval songs (with Seymour Barab, viol): The St Godric songs. Worldes blis ne last no throwe. Bryd one breve; Man mei longe him liues wene; Stond wel moder under rode.
*** Lyrichord LEMS 8005 [id.].

The St Godric Songs are the earliest known songs in the English language. St Godric died in 1170, so they date from halfway through the twelfth century. The other items here belong to the latter part of the century. As with his first disc, above, Russell Oberlin is completely convincing in this repertoire, the purity of line and beauty of timbre consistently appealing. The accompanying viol is discreet and the sound is remarkably clear and vivid.

Opera choruses

'Grand opera choruses': VERDI: Nabucco: Va pensiero (Chorus of the Hebrew slaves). Il Trovatore: Vedi! le fosche (Anvil chorus). BEETHOVEN: Fidelio: O welche Lust (Prisoners' chorus) (Chicago Ch. & SO, Solti). BELLINI: Norma: Squilla il bronzo del dio! . . . Guerra, guerra! (Welsh Nat. Op. Ch. & O, Bonynge). WAGNER: Lohengrin: Prelude to Act III and Bridal chorus. Tannhäuser: Pilgrims' chorus (V. State Op. Konzertvereinigung or V. State Op. Ch., VPO, Solti). GOUNOD: Faust: Soldiers' chorus (Ambrosian Op. Ch., LSO, Bonynge). PUCCINI: Madama Butterfly: Humming chorus (V. State Op. Ch., VPO, Karajan). LEONCAVALLO: Pagliacci: I zampognari! . . . Don, din, don (Bell chorus) (Santa Cecilia, Rome, Ac. Ch. & O, Gardelli). BIZET: Carmen: Toreador chorus (John Alldis Ch., LPO, Solti). WEBER: Der Freischütz: Huntsmen's chorus. NICOLAI: Die lustigen Weiber von Windsor: O süsser Mond (Bav. R. Ch. & O, Kubelik). BERLIOZ: Les Troyens: Dieux protecteurs de la ville éternelle (Montreal Schubert Ch. & SO, Dutoit). MUSSORGSKY: Boris Godunov: Coronation scene (Ghiaurov, V. Boys' Ch., Sofia R. Ch., V. State Op. Ch., VPO, Karajan).
(M) *** Decca Dig./Analogue 458 205-2.

This 75-minute collection re-assembled for reissue in Decca's Opera Gala series is exceptional value

and offers vivid, and often demonstration-worthy, sound throughout. Most of the excerpts come from distinguished complete sets, notably the Pilgrims' chorus from Solti's Tannhäuser, which has a memorable sense of perspective, while the Lohengrin excerpt is hardly less impressive. However, that also means that they are not always cleanly tailored and sometimes there are soloists too.

A high proportion of the items are from Solti, but other highlights include Karajan's Humming chorus from Madama Butterfly, which is so warmly atmospheric, and the expansive Coronation scene from Boris Godunov. Bonynge conducts the War chorus from Norma and the Soldiers' chorus from Faust. Since the disc's previous issue additional items have been added, notably the excerpts from Der Freischütz and Nicolai's Merry Wives of Windsor (from Kubelik) and the Hymn of deliverance from Les Troyens (Dutoit). Good documentation and translations are provided, an exception rather than the rule for this kind of operatic collection.

Opera love songs

'Amor – Opera's great love songs': VERDI: Aida: Celeste Aida. Luisa Miller: Quando le sere al placido (Pavarotti). Rigoletto: Caro nome (Sutherland). PUCCINI: Gianni Schicchi: O mio babbino caro (Tebaldi). Manon Lescaut: Donna non vidi mai (Carreras). Tosca: Recondita armonia (Corelli); Vissi d'arte (Kiri Te Kanawa); E lucevan le stelle (Domingo). La Bohème: Musetta's waltz song (Elizabeth Harwood). Madama Butterfly: Un bel dì (Mirella Freni). Turandot: Signore ascolta! (Caballé); Nessun dorma (Pavarotti). DONIZETTI: La Favorita: O mio Fernando (Cossotto). L'elisir d'amore: Una furtiva lagrima. Fedora: Amor ti vieta. PONCHIELLI: La Gioconda: Cielo e mar. MASSENET: Werther: Pourquoi me réveiller (all Pavarotti). BIZET: Carmen: Habanera (Troyanos); Flower song (Domingo). MOZART: Nozze di Figaro: Voi che sapete (Frederica von Stade).
(M) *** Decca 458 201-2.

Brimming over with stellar performances, this generous (76-minute) collection is a true 'Opera gala'. Pavarotti dominates and seldom lets us down, and he ends the disc with a thrilling performance of his great showpiece, Nessun dorma, from his complete set conducted by Mehta. Many of the other excerpts too are drawn from outstanding sets, including Caballé's beautiful Signore ascolta! (taken from the same source), Freni's passionately expansive Un bel dì from Karajan's Madama Butterfly, Domingo's outstanding Flower song and Troyanos's Habanera, both from Solti's Carmen, and Frederica von Stade's delightful Voi che sapete, taken from the same conductor's highly successful Nozze di

Figaro. Tebaldi's ravishing *O mio babbino caro* dates from 1962 when the voice still had all its bloom, while Marilyn Horne's dark-voiced *Softly awakes my heart* comes from a 1967 recital. Nicely packaged in a slip case, the documentation includes full translations.

Oxford Camerata, Jeremy Summerly

'Lamentations': WHITE: *Lamentations.* TALLIS: *Lamentations, Sets I & II.* PALESTRINA: *Lesson I for Maundy Thursday.* LASSUS: *Lessons I & III for Maundy Thursday.* Estâvão DE BRITO: *Lesson I for Good Friday.*
🌑 (BB) *** Naxos Dig. 8.550572 [id.].

On the bargain Naxos label come nearly 70 minutes of sublime polyphony, beautifully sung by the fresh-toned Oxford Camerata under Jeremy Summerly. All these *Lamentations* (*Lessons* simply means collection of verses) are settings from the Old Testament book, *The Lamentations of Jeremiah*. They were intended for nocturnal use and are usually darkly intense in feeling. The English and Italian *Lamentations* have their own individuality, but the most striking of all is the *Good Friday Lesson* by the Portuguese composer Estâvão de Brito. This is very direct and strong in feeling for, as the anonymous insert-note writer points out, Portugal was under Spanish subjugation at the time and de Brito effectively uses dissonance at the words *non est lex* ('there is no law') to assert his nationalistic defiance. The recorded sound is vividly beautiful within an ideal ambience.

Palmer, Felicity (soprano), John Constable (piano)

'Love's old sweet song': Victorian and Edwardian ballads: SULLIVAN: *My dearest heart.* Haydn WOOD: *A Brown bird singing; Bird of love divine.* EDEN: *What's in the air today.* TRAVERS: *A Mood.* MOIR: *Down the vale.* SQUIRE: *If I might come to you.* BRAHE: *Two little words.* D'HARDELOT: *Three green bonnets.* EVERARD: *It's all right in the summertime.* MOLLOY: *Love's old sweet song.* SPEAKS: *Morning.* MURRAY: *I'll walk beside you.* SANDERSON: *The valley of laughter.* Lào SILESU: *Love, here is my heart.* LEHR: *Whatever is – is best.* BEHREND: *Daddy.*
(BB) *** Belart 461 490-2 [(M) id. import].

The ear-catching item here is Everard's *It's all right in the summertime*, which Felicity Palmer delivers in true music-hall style with a cor-blimey Cockney accent. Even if the piano postlude is also off-key (not matching the humour of the rest at all), the result is a glorious *tour de force* and sets the tone

for one of the most warmly characterful recitals of its kind. These were all drawing-room songs which for decades were despised; now, in performances like these, their overtly sentimental charm can be enjoyed afresh as a delightful period offering, superbly accompanied by John Constable. The acoustic is reverberant, not like a drawing-room at all, but the sound is full and vivid.

Paul Hofhaimer Consort, Salzburg, Michael Seywald

'Fedelta d'amore' (Music at the court of Salzburg): Motets, madrigals & dances by ANON.; GASTOLDI; SENFL; KOTTER; UNTERHOLZER; VECCHI; HOFHAIMER; PERKIN; BUCHNER; NEGRI.
(BB) *** Arte Nova Dig. 74321 61338-2 [id.].

Around 1600, the Archbishop's court in Salzburg was one of the great centres of European music, for which a range of composers, now half-forgotten, wrote not just religious but secular music like the twenty-one items here. Many are anonymous, with Paul Hofhaimer (1459–1537) providing five items and most of the others one each. Under Michael Seywald the talented group named after Hofhaimer give aptly vigorous, well-disciplined performances, with their impact heightened by the upfront sound, warm and intimate. An excellent bargain, offering one or two jewels like Ludwig Senfl's poignant lament, *Unsäglich Schmerz.*

Pavarotti, Luciano (tenor)

'Pavarotti's greatest hits': PUCCINI: *Turandot: Nessun dorma. Tosca: Recondita armonia; E lucevan le stelle. La Bohème: Che gelida manina.* DONIZETTI: *La fille du régiment: O mes amis . . . Pour mon âme. La Favorita: Spirito gentil. L'elisir d'amore: Una furtiva lagrima.* R. STRAUSS: *Der Rosenkavalier: Di rigori armato.* LEONCAVALLO: *Mattinata.* ROSSINI: *La Danza.* DE CURTIS: *Torna a Surriento.* BIZET: *Carmen: Flower song.* BELLINI: *I Puritani: A te o cara; Vanne, O rose fortunata.* VERDI: *Il Trovatore: Di qual tetra . . . Ah, si ben mio; Di quella pira. Rigoletto: La donna è mobile; Questa o quella. Requiem: Ingemisco. Aida: Celeste Aida.* FRANCK: *Panis angelicus.* GOUNOD: *Faust: Salut! Demeure.* SCHUBERT: *Ave Maria.* LEONCAVALLO: *I Pagliacci: Vesti la giubba.* PONCHIELLI: *La Gioconda: Cielo e mar.* DENZA: *Funiculì, funiculà.*
*** Decca (IMS) 417 011-2 (2) [id.].

This collection of 'greatest hits' can safely be recommended to all who have admired the golden beauty of Pavarotti's voice. Including as it does a fair proportion of earlier recordings, the two discs demonstrate the splendid consistency of his singing. Songs are included as well as excerpts from operas, including *Torna a Surriento, Funiculì, funiculà,* Leoncavallo's *Mattinata* and Rossini's *La Danza.* However, this is at premium price and there are plenty of less expensive collections.

'Tutto Pavarotti': VERDI: *Aida: Celeste Aida. Luisa Miller: Quando le sere al placido. La Traviata: De' miei bollenti spiriti. Il Trovatore: Ah si ben mio; Di quella pira. Rigoletto: La donna è mobile. Un ballo in maschera: La rivedrà nell'estasi.* DONIZETTI: *L'elisir d'amore: Una furtiva lagrima. Don Pasquale: Com'è gentil.* PONCHIELLI: *La Gioconda: Cielo e mar.* FLOTOW: *Martha: M'appari.* BIZET: *Carmen: Flower song.* MASSENET: *Werther: Pourquoi me réveiller.* MEYERBEER: *L'Africana: O paradiso.* BOITO: *Mefistofele: Dai campi, dai prati.* LEONCAVALLO: *Pagliacci: Vesti la giubba.* MASCAGNI: *Cavalleria rusticana: Addio alla madre.* GIORDANO: *Fedora: Amor ti vieta.* PUCCINI: *La Fanciulla del West: Ch'ella mi creda. Tosca: E lucevan le stelle. Manon Lescaut: Donna non vidi mai. La Bohème: Che gelida manina. Turandot: Nessun dorma.* ROSSINI: *Stabat Mater: Cuius animam.* BIZET: *Agnus Dei.* ADAM: *O holy night.* DI CAPUA: *O sole mio.* TOSTI: *A vucchella.* CARDILLO: *Core 'ngrato.* TAGLIAFERRI: *Passione.* CHERUBINI: *Mamma.* DALLA: *Caruso.*
(M) *** Decca 425 681-2 (2) [id.].

Opening with Dalla's *Caruso,* a popular song in the Neapolitan tradition, certainly effective, and no more vulgar than many earlier examples of the genre, this selection goes on through favourites like *O sole mio* and *Core 'ngrato* and one or two religious items, notably Adam's *Cantique de Noël,* to the hard core of operatic repertoire. Beginning with *Celeste Aida,* recorded in 1972, the selection of some twenty-two arias from complete sets covers Pavarotti's distinguished recording career with Decca from 1969 (*Cielo e mar* and the *Il Trovatore* excerpts) to 1985, although the opening song was, of course, recorded digitally in 1988. The rest is a mixture of brilliantly transferred analogue originals and a smaller number of digital masters, all or nearly all showing the great tenor in sparkling form. The records are at mid-price, but there are no translations or musical notes.

'The greatest ever Pavarotti' (with various orchestras and conductors): Arias from: VERDI: *Rigoletto; Il Trovatore; La Traviata; Aida.* PUCCINI: *La Bohème; Turandot; Tosca; Fanciulla del West; Manon Lescaut.* DONIZETTI: *L'elisir d'amore.* FLOTOW: *Martha.* BIZET: *Carmen.* LEONCAVALLO: *I Pagliacci.* GIORDANO: *Fedora.* MEYERBEER: *L'Africana.* MASSENET: *Werther.*

Songs: DALLA: *Caruso.* LEONCAVALLO: *Mattinata.* TOSTI: *Aprile; Marechiare; La Serenata.* CARDILLO: *Core 'ngrato.* ROSSINI: *La Danza.* MODUGNO: *Volare.* DENZA: *Funiculì, funiculà.* DE CURTIS: *Torna a Surriento.* DI CAPUA: *O sole mio!* SCHUBERT: *Ave Maria.* FRANCK: *Panis angelicus.* MANCINI: *In un palco della Scala* (with apologies to Pink Panther). GIORDANO: *Caro mio ben.* BIXIO: *Mamma.*
(M) *** Decca Analogue/Dig. 436 173-2 (2).

Such a collection as this is self-recommending and scarcely needs a review from us, merely a listing. The first disc opens with *La donna è mobile* (*Rigoletto*), *Che gelida manina* (*La Bohème*), *Nessun dorma* (*Turandot*), all taken from outstandingly successful complete recordings, and the rest of the programme, with many favourite lighter songs also given the golden touch, is hardly less appealing. The second CD includes Pavarotti's tribute to the Pink Panther and ends with a tingling live version of *Nessun dorma,* to compare with the studio version on disc one. Vivid, vintage Decca recording throughout.

'Grandi voci' (with Nat. PO, Chailly or Fabrittis): GIORDANO: *Fedora: Amor ti vieta. Andrea Chénier: Colpito qui m'avete . . . Un di all'azzuro spazio; Come un bel dì di maggio; Si, fui soldata.* BOITO: *Mefistofele: Dai campi, dai prati; Ogni mortal . . . Giunto sul passo estremo.* CILEA: *Adriana Lecouvreur: La dolcissima effigie; L'anima ho stanca.* MASCAGNI: *Iris: Apri la tua finestra!* MEYERBEER: *L'Africana: Mi batti il cor . . . O Paradiso.* MASSENET: *Werther: Pourquoi me réveiller.* PUCCINI: *La Fanciulla del West: Ch'ella mi creda. Manon Lescaut: Tra voi belle; Donna non vidi mai; Ah! non v'avvicinate! . . . No! No! pazzo son!* (with Howlett).
(M) **(*) Decca (IMS) Dig. 440 400-2 [id.].

This first digital recital record from Pavarotti had the voice more resplendent than ever. The passion with which he tackles Des Grieux's Act III plea from *Manon Lescaut* is devastating, and the big breast-beating numbers are all splendid, imaginative as well as heroic. But the slight pieces, Des Grieux's *Tra voi belle* and the *Iris Serenade,* could be lighter and more charming. The CD gives the voice even greater projection, with its full resonance and brilliance admirably caught, but it does also make the listener more aware of the occasional lack of subtlety of the presentation.

'Live': Recital 1 (with Mirella Freni): Arias and duets from: VERDI: *La Traviata; I vespri siciliani; Aida.* MASSENET: *Werther.* PONCHIELLI: *La Gioconda.* DONIZETTI: *La figlia del reggimento; L'elisir d'amore.* MEYERBEER: *L'Africana.* BOITO: *Mefistofele.* MASCAGNI: *L'amico Fritz.* PUCCINI: *Tosca.*

Recital 2 (with Katia Ricciarelli): Arias from:

VERDI: *La Traviata; Aida; Macbeth; La forza del destino; I Lombardi; Il Corsaro; Falstaff; Un ballo in maschera;* Duet from *Otello (Già nella notte densa).* Arias from PUCCINI: *Turandot.*
(B) **(*) Decca Double (IMS) 443 018-2 (2) [(M) id. import].

Here are two Pavarotti recitals for the price of one, although in the second, mainly a Verdi collection, Katia Ricciarelli, in splendid voice, gets the lion's share of the arias and she and Pavarotti join for only a single duet – from *Otello.* Pavarotti rounds off the programme as usual with *Nessun dorma,* to tumultuous applause. However, applause is not really a problem on the second disc, whereas it is often intrusive on the first. Artistically, however, the partnership of Pavarotti and Freni works well (as we know from their complete recordings). The *Werther* and *Africana* items were new to Pavarotti's repertory at the time; sweet singing from Freni, too, though her delivery at times could be more characterful. Vividly robust recording.

Pears, Sir Peter (tenor)

'The Land of lost content': Twentieth-century English songs (with (i) Benjamin Britten; (ii) Alan Bush; (iii) Viola Tunnard): (i) IRELAND: *The Land of lost content; The Trellis.* BRIDGE: *'Tis but a week; Goldenhair; When you are old; So perverse; Journey's end.* TIPPETT: *Songs for Ariel.* (ii) Alan BUSH: *Voices of the prophets.* (iii) DELIUS: *To daffodils.* MOERAN: *The merry month of May.* VAN DIEREN: *Dream pedlary; Take, o take those lips away.* WARLOCK: *Piggensie; Along the stream.* GRAINGER: *Bold William Taylor.* William BUSCH: *The echoing green; The Shepherd; If thou wilt ease thine heart; Come, o come, my life's delight.*
(BB) ** Belart 461 550-2 [(M) id. import].

This is a well-produced and interesting collection, but it contains little that is really memorable. Sir Michael Tippett's rhapsodical lyricism seems almost too free to pin down the words and Alan Bush's *Voices of the prophets,* for all its passion, is let down by the poem for the fourth section which sounds uncomfortably like Communist propaganda. The yearning quality of the idiom of the songs by William Busch is quite striking, especially coming after the pert Grainger folksong.

Pears, Peter (tenor), Julian Bream (lute)

Julian Bream Edition, Volume 19. Elizabethan lute songs: MORLEY: *Absence; It was a lover and his lass; Who is it?* ROSSETER: *What then is love?; If she forsake me; When Laura smiles.* DOWLAND: *I saw my lady weep; Dear, if you change; Stay,*

Time; Weep you no more; Shall I sue?; Sweet, stay awhile; Can she excuse?; Come, heavy sleep; Wilt thou unkind, thus leave me?; Sorrow stay; The lowest trees have tops; Time's eldest son, Old Age; In darkness let me dwell; Say, love, if ever thou didst find. FORD: *Come Phyllis; Fair, sweet, cruel.*
(M) *** BMG/RCA 09026 61609-2.

This vintage collection was recorded between 1963 and 1969 when Pears was at the peak of his form. The Dowland songs are particularly fine, sung with Pears's usual blend of intelligence and lyrical feeling, their nostalgic melancholy tenderly caught. Excellent, vivid, well-balanced recording, with Bream's expert accompaniments well in the picture. Most refreshing.

Pears, Peter (tenor), Benjamin Britten (piano)

Lieder: SCHUMANN: *Liederkreis, Op. 39;* FAURE: *La bonne chanson;* PURCELL: *5 songs;* SCHUBERT: *3 Songs;* BRITTEN: *4 Folksongs.*
(M) (***) BBC Music mono BBCB 8006-2 [id.].

Britten as pianist is, if anything, even more individual than Britten as conductor. With Pears in glowing voice (1958/9) he sparkles in his own realizations of Purcell songs and folksongs, while in Schumann's Eichendorff song cycle he makes the poetic piano-writing glow, as in *Frühlingsnacht* ('Spring night'), where the notes shimmer distinctively. The Fauré cycle too reminds one that as a fourteen-year-old Britten also set Verlaine's poetry. Clean focus in mono radio recording.

Polyphony, Stephen Layton

'O magnum mysterium' (A sequence of twentieth-century carols and Sarum chant):
Plainchant: *O radix lesse; O magnum mysterium; Puer natus est nobis; Reges Tharsis; Verbum caro factum est.* WISHART: *3 Carols, Op. 17, No. 3: Alleluya, A new work is come on hand.* HOWELLS: *3 Carol-anthems: Here is the little door; A spotless rose; Sing lullaby.* Richard Rodney BENNETT: *5 Carols: There is no rose; Out of your sleep; That younge child; Sweet was the song; Susanni.* Kenneth LEIGHTON: *Of a rose is my song; A Hymn of the Nativity; 3 Carols, Op. 25: The Star song; Lully lulla, thou little tiny child; An Ode on the birth of our Saviour.* WARLOCK: *As dew in Aprylle; Bethlehem Down; I saw a fair maiden; Benedicamus Domino; A Cornish Christmas carol.* BYRT: *All and some.* WALTON: *What cheer?*
*** Hyperion Dig. CDA 66925 [id.].

A gloriously sung collection in which (what Meurig

Bowen's extensive notes describe as) 'the magnificent corpus of British carols' is alive and still impressively expanding at the end of the twentieth century. The atmosphere is readily set by the opening plainchant, which frames and punctuates the concert with appropriate liturgical texts. Peter Wishart's exuberant *Alleluya* and the poignant *A spotless rose* immediately catch up the listener. This is the first of Howells's *Three Carol-anthems*, of which the others are equally lovely (especially the rocking *Sing lullaby*). The five Richard Rodney Bennett carols have their own particular brand of cool dissonance, with *There is no rose* and *Sweet was the song* particularly haunting.

But perhaps it is the series of beautiful Peter Warlock settings one remembers most for their ready melodic and harmonic memorability (notably *As dew in Aprylle*, the lovely *Bethlehem Down* and the serene *Lullaby my Jesus*) alongside the soaring music of Kenneth Leighton, helped in the ambitious *Nativity hymn* and the *Ode on the birth of our Saviour* by the rich, pure line of the soloist, Libby Crabtree, and in *Lully, lulla* by the equally ravishing contribution of Emma Preston-Dunlop. Walton's *What cheer?* brings an exuberant rhythmic spicing, but for the most part this programme captures the tranquil pastoral mood of Christmas Eve. The recording could hardly be bettered, clear yet with the most evocative ambience.

Popp, Lucia (soprano)

MOZART: *Exsultate jubilate.* SCHUBERT: *Die Forelle; Gretchen am Spinnrade; An Sylvia.* R. STRAUSS: *Zueignung; Wiegenlied.* Songs and arias from: LEHAR: *Die lustige Witwe.* J. STRAUSS Jr.: *Casanova; Die Fledermaus.* ZELLER: *Der Obersteiger.* ORFF: *Carmina burana.* MOZART: *Le nozze di Figaro; Così fan tutte; Die Entführung aus dem Serail; Die Zauberflöte.* GRIEG: *Peer Gynt.* PUCCINI: *La Bohème.* R. STRAUSS: *Vier letzte Lieder; Intermezzo.* DVORAK: *Rusalka.* TCHAIKOVSKY: *Eugene Onegin.* WAGNER: *Tannhäuser.* HANDEL: *Joshua.* ROSSINI: *Petite messe solennelle.* MAHLER: *Des Knaben Wunderhorn; Symphony No. 4.*

(BB)*** Royal Classics Vocal Double DCL 703932 (2).

Lucia Popp, Czechoslovakian born, finds an eastern-European lilt for the music of Lehár and sparkles in the other operetta items, takes just as readily to Mahler, and Richard Strauss, yet is a natural in Mozart, whether in the passion of *Come scoglio* or the mellow beauty of line of *Voi che sapete.* The two excerpts from Grieg's *Peer Gynt* are ravishingly sung. Throughout, Popp's musical imagination and concern for word meaning effectively counteract any feeling of sameness.

In Slavic repertoire, her portrayal of the water-

sprite in *Rusalka* is a highlight, but the one disappointment of the collection is the famous scena from *Eugene Onegin*; it opens well but later on Tatiana's outbursts sound rather constricted, and both singer and conductor do not let the music expand enough.

The second disc opens with *Dich teure Halle* from *Tannhäuser*, splendidly sung, with vibrant support from Haitink, and the five Lieder of Schubert and Strauss (accompanied by Sawallisch) are simply and appealingly sung, though not as memorable as the lovely excerpt from Strauss's *Intermezzo* and the Mahler items. The programme ends with the finale of Mahler's *Fourth Symphony*, for which Popp is ideally cast. The voice is often recorded rather close, which only occasionally exaggerates her tendency to squeeze salient notes. Good transfers, but no texts.

Prey, Hermann (baritone)

'*Bravo Figaro*': Arias and excerpts from: ROSSINI: *Il barbiere di Siviglia* (with Luigi Alva). MOZART: *Le nozze di Figaro* (with Edith Mathis); *Così fan tutte* (with Brigitte Fassbaender). WEBER: *Oberon* (with Judith Hamari). Johann STRAUSS Jr.: *Die Fledermaus* (with Julia Varady, Bernd Weikl). Lieder: MOZART: *Die Zufriedenheit; An die Freude* (with Bernhard Klee, piano). BRAHMS: *All'mein Gedanken; In stiller Nacht* (with Karl Engel, piano); *Volkslied* (with Leonard Hokanson, piano).

(BB) *** Belart 461 060-2 [id.].

This engaging collection is happily titled, for Hermann Prey was surely born to play Figaro, whether in Rossini's original (with Luiga Alva) or Mozart's sequel (with Edith Mathis). The excerpts from Kleiber's *Die Fledermaus* also scintillate, and the other Mozart and Weber excerpts, if not quite as distinctive, are all characterful. The Lieder are sung with a pleasing directness. A most winning recital.

Price, Leontyne (soprano)

'The essential Leontyne Price'

Discs 1–2: 'Her greatest opera roles': Arias from: VERDI: *Aida; Il Trovatore; Ernani; La forza del destino.* MOZART: *Così fan tutte; Don Giovanni.* PUCCINI: *Madama Butterfly; Tosca; Manon Lescaut; Turandot.* POULENC: *Dialogue des Carmélites.* R. STRAUSS: *Ariadne auf Naxos.* BARBER: *Antony and Cleopatra.*

Discs 3–4: 'Great opera scenes' from: VERDI: *Otello; Macbeth; Don Carlos; La Traviata.* BEETHOVEN: *Fidelio.* PUCCINI: *Suor Angelica; La Rondine; La Bohème.* BIZET: *Carmen.* MOZART: *Le nozze di Figaro.* R. STRAUSS: *Die ägyptische*

Helena; Salome; Die Frau ohne Schatten.
TCHAIKOVSKY: *Eugene Onegin.* BARBER:
Vanessa. MASSENET: *Manon.* PURCELL: *Dido and
Aeneas.*

Discs 5–6: *'Leontyne Price and friends':* Excerpts
from: VERDI: *Otello; Aida* (with Plácido
Domingo; Sherrill Milnes; Marilyn Horne); *Un
ballo in maschera; Ernani* (both with Carlo
Bergonzi); *Requiem* (with Janet Baker); *Il
Trovatore* (with Milnes). MOZART: *Così fan tutte*
(with Horne; Tatiana Troyanos). BELLINI: *Norma.*
PUCCINI: *Madama Butterfly* (both with Horne).
gershwin: *Porgy and Bess* (with William
Warfield). BIZET: *Carmen* (with Franco Corelli).

Discs 7–8: *'Leontyne Price in song':* BERLIOZ:
Les nuits d'été. R. STRAUSS: *Vier letzte Lieder.*
FAURE: *Clair de lune; Notre amour; Au cimetière;
Au bord de l'eau; Mandoline.* POULENC: *Main
dominée par le coeur. Miroirs brûlants: Je
nommerai ton front; Tu vois le feu du soir. Ce
doux petit visage.* BARBER: *Knoxville, Summer of
1915.* SCHUMANN: *Frauenliebe und -leben, Op.
42; Widmung (Myrthen); Mignon; Volksliedchen;
Schöne Wiege meiner Leiden; Er ist's; Heiss mich
nicht reden; Lust der Sturmnacht.* R. STRAUSS:
*Allerseelen; Schlagendes Herzen; Freundliche
Vision; Wie sollten wir geheim.* WOLF: *Der
Gärtner; Lebe wohl; Morgentau; Geh', Geliebter,
geh' jetzt.*

Discs 9–10: *'Spirituals, hymns & sacred songs':*
*Ev'ry time I feel the spirit; Let us break bread
together; His name so sweet; 'Round about de
mountain; Swing low, sweet chariot; Sit down,
servant; He's got the whole world in his hands;
Deep river; My soul's been anchored in de Lord;
On ma journey; A city called Heaven; Ride on,
King Jesus; I wish I knew how it would feel to be
free; Sinner, please don't let this harvest pass;
Sweet little Jesus boy; There is a Balm in Gilead;
Let us cheer the weary traveller; Ev'ry time I feel
the spirit; My way is cloudy; Nobody knows the
trouble I've seen; I couldn't hear nobody pray.*
DYKES: *Holy, holy, holy; Lead kindly light.*
KNAPP: *Blessed assurance.* SCHUBERT: *Ave
Maria.* CONVERSE: *What a friend we have in
Jesus.* TRAD.: *Amazing grace; Fairest Lord Jesus;
I wonder as I wander.* MALOTTE: *The Lord's
prayer.* DOANE: *Pass me not, O gentle Saviour.*
Samuel S. WESLEY: *The Church's one foundation.*
BRAHE: *Bless this house.* LOWRY: *I need Thee
every hour.* BACH/GOUNOD: *Ave Maria.*
GERSHWIN: *Porgy and Bess: Summertime.* WARD:
America the beautiful. JOHNSON: *Lift ev'ry voice
and sing.* LUTHER: *A mighty fortress is our God.* :
Battle hymn of the Republic.

Disc 11: *'In recital and Interview':* BRAHMS:
Zigeunerlieder, Op. 103. CILEA: *Adriana
Lecouvreur: Io son l'umile ancella.* TRAD.: *This*

little light of mine. Interview with John Pfeiffer
(recorded in April 1995).
(M) *** RCA 09026 68153-2 (11) [id.].

'The essential Leontyne Price': Arias and excerpts
from: VERDI: *La forza del destino; Il Trovatore;
Otello* (with Plácido Domingo). PUCCINI:
Madama Butterfly; La Rondine. Ç: *Carmen.*
MOZART: *Così fan tutte* (with Marilyn Horne).
Songs: BERLIOZ: *Les Nuits d'été: Absence.*
R. STRAUSS: *Vier letzte Lieder: Beim
Schlafengehen.* MALOTTE: *The Lord's prayer.*
GERSHWIN: *Porgy and Bess: Summertime.*
*Spiritual: Swing low, sweet chariot; Ride on, King
Jesus.*
(M) *** RCA 09026 68152-2 [id.].

To celebrate the seventieth birthday in February
1997 of this commanding American soprano, RCA
compiled this formidable collection of eleven discs,
presenting them in the most extravagant format,
with a fully bound, well-illustrated book – including
full texts – to match a substantial album in similar
format containing the discs. The presentation is
among the most impressive we have seen since the
coming of CD, and the choice of items lives up to
its lavishness, with the first two discs devoted to
Price's 'Greatest opera roles', mainly of Mozart,
Verdi, Puccini and Strauss, but also including the
role of the heroine in Barber's *Antony and Cleopatra*, specially written for her.

The next two discs, containing 'Great opera
scenes', range wider still, concentrating on the same
composers but also including unexpected items
from Purcell's *Dido and Aeneas* and Tchaikovsky's
Eugene Onegin. The two discs 'Price and friends'
have her in duet with such artists as Carlo Bergonzi,
Franco Corelli, Plácido Domingo, Dame Janet
Baker and her one-time husband, William Warfield.

The two discs of song then include such substantial items as Barber's *Knoxville* – one of her most
magical recordings – Schumann's *Frauenliebe*,
Strauss's *Four Last Songs* and Berlioz's *Les nuits
d'été*. Spirituals, hymns and sacred songs make up
the next two discs, leaving a final one of miscellaneous items, Brahms's *Zigeunerlieder*, and the
heroine's artistic credo from Cilea's *Adriana Lecouvreur*, all rounded off with an interview conducted by the late John Pfeiffer, who master-minded
the whole presentation just before he died.

What this rich collection repeatedly brings home
is the glorious consistency of Price in her singing
over the longest period, with barely any signs of
wear in the voice even in the later recordings, and
with every note firmly and surely in place, with her
golden tone pouring forth. There may be some
operatic roles which she personally did not enjoy –
Verdi's Lady Macbeth for one, as she makes clear
in her interview – but the quality of her singing was
seldom impaired. It is good too to have it brought
home how wide her sympathies have been, readily

encompassing such genres as German Lieder. A timely summary of a great career, with a well-chosen sampler disc for those not wanting to stretch to the whole survey. This single CD, however, does not include translations.

'Ultimate Collection': Arias from: BERLIOZ: *Les nuits d'été.* BIZET: *Carmen.* BARBER: *Antony and Cleopatra.* GERSHWIN: *Porgy and Bess.* MASSENET: *Manon.* MOZART: *Le nozze de Figaro; Il rè pastore.* PUCCINI: *Madama Butterfly; Manon Lescaut; La Rondine; Suor Angelica; Tosca; Turandot.* PURCELL: *Dido and Aeneas.* R. STRAUSS: *Im Abendrot (Vier letzte Lieder No. 1); Ariadne auf Naxos.* VERDI: *Aida; Un ballo in maschera; Don Carlos; La forza del destino; Il Trovatore.*
(M) **(*) RCA 74321 63463-2 [id.].

This CD may appeal to those who want some of Leontyne Price's most famous roles, or those who simply want a marvellously sung soprano operatic compilation. It is well programmed and includes some unlikely repertoire for Price (including Purcell), as well as many of the things you would expect. The recordings and performances are generally excellent, often brilliant. What is shabby about this release is that there is nothing in the documentation about the recordings, dates, conductors, orchestras, or the music. As for texts and translations, you must be joking.

Psalmody, Parley of Instruments, Peter Holman

'While shepherds watched' (Christmas music from English parish churches and chapels 1740–1830): BEESLY: *While shepherds watched.* ANON.: *Let an anthem of praise; Hark! how all the welkin rings.* J. C. SMITH: *While shepherds watched.* HELLENDAAL: *Concerto in E flat for strings, Op. 3/4: Pastorale.* KEY: *As shepherds watched their fleecy care.* ARNOLD: *Hark! the herald angels sing.* CLARK: *While shepherds watched.* HANDEL: *Hark! the herald angels sing; Hymning seraphs wake the morning.* JARMAN: *There were shepherds abiding in the field.* S. WESLEY: (Piano) *Rondo on 'God rest you merry, gentlemen'* (Timothy Roberts). MATTHEWS: *Angels from the realms of glory.* FOSTER: *While shepherds watched.*
*** Hyperion Dig. CDA 66924 [id.].

This is a Christmas collection of genuine novelty. None of the settings of *While shepherds watched* uses the familiar tune: the regal closing version from John Foster of Yorkshire is remarkably lively, as is the lighter variation from Joseph Key of Northampton, *As shepherds watched their fleecy care* with woodwind accompaniment. There are other

surprises too. Handel's *Hark! the herald angels* is neatly fitted to *See the conqu'ring hero comes,* and *Hymning seraphs* (presented as a tenor solo with fortepiano) turns out to be our old keyboard friend, 'The harmonious blacksmith'. Peiter Hellendaal's *Pastorale for strings* is in the best concerto grosso tradition, although Samuel Wesley's variations on *God rest you merry* are merely ingenious. Nevertheless the whole programme is presented with pleasing freshness and is very well sung, played and recorded.

Ramey, Samuel (bass)

'Grandi voci': Arias from: MOZART: *Le nozze di Figaro.* HANDEL: *Rodelinda.* DONIZETTI: *Anna Bolena.* VERDI: *I masnadieri; Macbeth.* BELLINI: *Norma.* STRAVINSKY: *The Rake's progress.* WEILL: *Street scene.* arr. COPLAND: *Old American songs – Set No. 1.*
(M) *** Decca (IMS) Dig. 448 251-2.

Instead of centring on a studio recital, Decca's *'Grandi Voci'* collection celebrating the achievement of Samuel Ramey selects excerpts from various complete recordings in which he has participated with distinction during the 1980s, beginning with excerpts from Solti's sparkling *Nozze di Figaro* (in which he took the name-role with distinction, making Figaro a more romantic figure than usual) and ending with his fine set of Copland's *Old American songs,* recorded with Warren Jones in 1990. With consistently vivid Decca sound, this gives a rounded picture of one of the finest basses of our time, whose range was remarkable.

Resnik, Regina (mezzo-soprano), Richard Woitach (piano)

Song recital: RAMEAU: *Le Grillon.* SPONTINI: *Les riens d'amour.* MARTINI: *Plaintes de Marie Stuart.* GAVEUX: *Dieu d'Israel.* TURINA: *Homenaje a Lope de Vega, Op. 90; Poema: Tu pupila es azul, Op. 81/2; Soneta: Vade retro!, Op. 54/2.* TCHAIKOVSKY: *At the ball; Can it be day?;* PROKOFIEV: *The grey-eyed king; Thoughts of the sunlight; Stolby.* MAHLER: *Des Knaben Wunderhorn: Das irdische Leben; Nicht wiedershen!; Lob des hohen Verstandes. Hans und Grete; Erinnerung.* MENOTTI: *The Medium: Afraid, am I afraid* (with Columbia Chamber Ensemble, Jorge Mester).
(M) *(*) Sony SMK 60784 [id.].

This recital was made just after Regina Resnik's début New York recital in 1967 and the first four French and Italian songs show her lack of experience in their lack of charm; they are further flawed by the quick vibrato, which the close microphones do not flatter. She is much more colloquially at home in the Spanish repertoire, and at her very best in the Russian songs. Here the vibrato is an asset, and the drama and dark melancholy are powerfully caught. The Mahler Lieder are more problematic. *Erinnerung* is all but ruined by the intrusive vibrato, and *Hans und Grete* is over-characterized, but the others are more successful. The excerpt from *The Medium* is splendidly histrionic. But this disc is only really recommendable to the singer's admirers.

Rolfe Johnson, Anthony (tenor), David Willison (piano)

English songs: VAUGHAN WILLIAMS: *Songs of travel.* G. BUTTERWORTH: *A Shropshire lad.* IRELAND: *The land of lost content.* GURNEY: *Down by the Salley Gardens; An Epitaph; Desire in spring; Black Stitchel.* WARLOCK: *My own country; Passing by; Pretty ring time.*

(B) *** Carlton 30367 02032 [(M) id. import].

It would be hard to design a better programme of twentieth-century English songs than this, providing one accepts the omission of Britten, and it is a surprise to discover that this nearly-70-minutes-long programme derives from two (Polygram) Polydor LPs from the mid-1970s. At that time this label was not exactly famous for this kind of repertoire but there is hidden treasure here. The performances of the Vaughan Williams and Butterworth cycles are full of life and colour (and are splendidly accompanied), and it is especially good to have the far lesser-known Gurney songs. The recordings have transferred well. A bargain.

Rouen Chambre Accentus Choir, Eric Ericson

ALFVEN: *Aftonen; Uti vår hage;* JERSILD: *Min yndlingsdal (My dear valley);* NYSTEDT: *O Crux;* SANDSTROM: *Two Poems;* STENHAMMAR: *Tre körvisor (Three choral pieces);* WERLE: *Canzone 126 del Petrarcha;* WIKANDER: *Kung Liljekonvalje (King of the Lily-of-the-valley); Förårskväll (Spring evening).*

**(*) Assai Dig. 207 182 [id.]

The Rouen-based Chœur de Chambre Accentus was founded in 1991 by Laurence Equilbey, herself an Ericson pupil, and they tackle this predominantly Swedish repertoire with complete sympathy. In the 1960s and '70s, Eric Ericson brought the Swedish Radio Choir to an unrivalled excellence (it was the Berlin Philharmonic of choirs). These French singers produce the beautifully blended and finely nuanced sound one associates with him. He has recorded Stenhammar's glorious choral songs to texts by the Danish poet, J. P. Jacobsen many times.

Wikander's *Kung Liljekonvalje (King of the Lily-of-the-Valley)* and Alfvén's *Aftonen (The Evening)* are affecting pieces and are beautifully done.

For most collectors the surprise will be *Min yndlingsdal (My dear valley)* by the Dane Jørgen Jersild, a contemporary of Vagn Holmboe, though less prolific. During the 1930s he studied with Roussel, and his writing has almost luminous quality. Jan Sandström is not to be confused with Sven David and is still in his mid-forties and these two pieces, *Anrop (Call)* and *Två japanska landskap (Two Japanese landscapes)*, date from his student years and are quite haunting. By its side Werle's Petrach setting seems more self-conscious. At less than 50 minutes this is short measure, but his repertoire is not widely known and is immensely rewarding.

Royal Liverpool Philharmonic Choir and Orchestra, St Ambrose R. C. Junior School Choir, Speake, Edmund Walters

'A Festival of Christmas' (with Jocelyn Bell, girl soprano): arr. WALTERS: *Ding dong! merrily on high; The boar's head; Buenos Reyes; Deck the hall.* arr. PETTMAN: *The Infant King.* WALTERS: *Where was Jesus born?; The carol singers; Dance little goatling; As Joseph was a-walking; Three little birdies; Little Robin redbreast; Hop-hop-hop; Little one sleep.* BYRD: *Cradle song.* BACH: *O little one sweet.* darke: *In the bleak midwinter.* GRUBER: *Silent night.* arr. WALLACE: *O come, all ye faithful.*

(M) *** Chandos Dig. CHAN 7111 [id.].

The introductory woodwind in the scoring of Edmund Walters's opening arrangement of *Ding dong! merrily on high*, and the light-hearted touches of syncopation, suggest that his approach to Christmas music has much in common with that of John Rutter. His own carols are jauntily engaging, helped by the freshness of the excellently trained St Ambrose Junior School Choir, who sing them with vigour and enthusiasm. *Little one sleep* (a treble solo) verges on sentimentality. But the Spanish carol *Buenos Reyes*, with its castanets, is most piquant and the two Basque carols *The Infant King* and *I saw a maiden* are most eloquently sung, as are the settings by Bach and Byrd. Fine recording too.

Russian opera: 'The splendours of Russian opera'

'The splendours of Russian opera': GLINKA: *Overture: Ruslan and Ludmilla.* BORODIN: *Prince Igor: Polovtsian dances* (with London Symphony

Chorus; both LSO, Solti); *Galitzky's aria.*
RIMSKY-KORSAKOV: *Sadko: Song of the Viking Guest.* RACHMANINOV: *Aleko: Aleko's cavatina* (all three, Nicolai Ghiaurov). TCHAIKOVSKY: *Eugene Onegin: Tatiana's letter scene* (Teresa Kubiak); *Entr'acte and Waltz scene* (Soloists, ROHCG Ch. & O, Solti). *The Maid of Orleans: Farewell to the forests* (Regina Resnik). MUSSORGSKY: *Boris Godunov: Coronation scene* (Ghiaurov, V. State Op. Ch., VPO, Karajan).
(M) **(*) Decca 458 216-2 [id.].

Issued at the same time as Decca's outstanding Baroque opera collection, this Russian compilation cannot match it, either in imaginative choice of items (here rather predictable) or in the consistent excellence of the performances. Solti opens the proceedings with his famous dashing account of the *Ruslan and Ludmilla overture* (although the transfer isn't very glamorous), and Ghiaurov's three arias certainly show the richness of his magnificent voice.

But it is Teresa Kubiak's memorable account of *Tatiana's letter scene* from *Eugene Onegin* that is the highlight of the concert, and this is neatly linked to the opera's *Waltz scene* by the *Entr'acte* based on Tatiana's music. It is good also to have Regina Resnik's fine *Farewell* aria from *The Maid of Orleans* (which musically has much in common with *Eugene Onegin*). But the present transfer of the choral *Coronation scene* from *Boris Godunov* seems to have lost some of the rich amplitude of Karajan's 1970 complete recording from which it is taken. As with the rest of Decca's current Opera Gala releases, the presentation is attractive, and full translations are included.

St George's Canzona, John Sothcott

Medieval songs and dances: Lamento di Tristano; L'autrier m'iere levaz; 4 Estampies real; Edi beo thu hevene quene; Eyns ne şoy ke plente fu; Tre fontane. PERRIN D'AGINCOURT: *Quant voi en la fin d'este.* Cantigas de Santa Maria: *Se ome fezer; Nas mentes semper teer; Como poden per sas culpas; Maravillosos et piadosos.*
(M)*** CRD CRD 3421 [id.].

As so often when early music is imaginatively re-created, one is astonished at the individuality of many of the ideas. This applies particularly to the second item in this collection, *Quant voi en la fin d'este,* attributed to the mid-thirteenth-century trouvère, Perrin d'Agincourt, but no less to the four Cantigas de Santa Maria. The instrumentation is at times suitably robust but does not eschew good intonation and subtle effects. The group is recorded vividly and the acoustics of St James, Clerkenwell, are never allowed to cloud detail. The sound is admirably firm and real in its CD format.

St John's College Choir, Cambridge, George Guest

'Christmas carols from St John's' (with Philip Kenyon, organ): TRAD.: *Unto us a boy is born; Ding dong! merrily on high; Good King Wenceslas; There is no rose.* arr. WALFORD DAVIES: *The holly and the ivy.* arr. WILLCOCKS: *Sussex carol; God rest you merry, gentlemen; O come, all ye faithful.* WARLOCK: *Balulalow.* HOLST: *In the bleak mid-winter.* HADLEY: *I sing of a maiden.* RUTTER: *Shepherd's pipe carol.* GRUBER: *Silent night.* MENDELSSOHN, arr. WILLCOCKS: *Hark! the herald angels sing.* arr. VAUGHAN WILLIAMS: *O little town of Bethlehem.* POSTON: *Jesus Christ the apple tree.* Raymond WILLIAMS: *2 Welsh carols.* KIRKPATRICK: *Away in a manger.*
(M) *** Chandos Dig. CHAN 7109 [id.].

An essentially traditional concert and none the worse for that when so beautifully sung and recorded. Among the more modern carols, Elizabeth Poston's beautiful *Jesus Christ the apple tree* stands out. Many of the arrangements are famous, notably the spectacular Willcocks versions of *Hark! the herald angels sing* and *O come, all ye faithful,* but some of the gentler, atmospheric items (*There is no rose*) are just as memorable. A most enjoyable hour of music.

Savall, Jordi (viola da gamba and conductor)

Jordi Savall Edition: Vocal recordings

Joan CEREROLS: *Missa de batalla; Missa pro defunctis* (with La Capella Reial).
(M) *** Audivis Astrée Dig. ES 9924 [id.].

Joan Cererols, Catalan by birth, spent his entire life at the monastery of Montserrat. His *Missa pro defunctis* is associated with the Plague, which was causing havoc in Barcelona in the mid seventeenth century. The Mass is written for two choirs, balancing low and high voices, alternating solemn, darker settings with music suggesting the divine light. The closing *Libera me* brings a profound feeling of acceptance and release. The shorter *Missa de batalla,* for three four-part 'choirs of glory', is outgoing and joyful, with plenty of rhythmic lift.

The Capella Reial is based on southern voices, which gives a striking authenticity of vocal colour. Instruments are also used in both works – wind, brass and strings – to add further richness to the sonority, and a military drum is added to the *Battle Mass* (without authority, but effectively) and is especially telling in the joyful *Agnus Dei.* A fascinating and rewarding listening experience, recommended to all. Texts but no translations are included.

Marc-Antoine CHARPENTIER: *Canticum in honorem Beatae Virginus Mariae (H.400); Litanies de la Vierge à 6 voix & 2 dessus de violes (H.83); Nativité de la Vierge (H.309); Magnificat (H.80) with Prélude pour le Magnificat à 4 voix (H.533); Pour la fête de l'Epiphanie (H.395); Prelude à 3 (H.509); Symphonie devant Regina: Pour la conception de la Vierge (H.313); Salve Regina a trois voix pareilles (H.23), with Prélude (H.23a); Stabat mater pour les religieuses (H.15)* (with Monserrat Figueras, Maria Cristina Kiehr, Arruaberrena, Lesne, Elwes, Cabré, Le Concert des Nations).
(M)*** Audivis Astrée Dig. ES 9929 [id.].

This imaginatively conceived collection gathers together some of the finest of Charpentier's shorter Marian settings. The opening *Canticum* is a non-liturgical dialogue celebration of the coming of Christ (including an angels' duet), the memorable *Salve Regina* for three parallel voices has some remarkable passing dissonances, *Pour la fête de l'Epiphanie*, a miniature oratorio, brings in Herod and the Magi, and the *Magnificat* rejoices in the Lord by richly alternating solo, duet and choral sections.

Then follows the shiningly beautiful *Stabat mater* led by the radiant singing of Maria Cristina Kiehr and finally an invocation (*Litanies*) to the Virgin, a passionate and touching extended prayer shared by six voices. With such a starry cast, the performances can hardly help being very distinguished (they combine robust fervour with the most delicate simplicity), and the recording is first class. An outstanding disc in every way with full translations included.

Juan del ENZINA: *Romances and Villancicos* (with Monserrat Figueras, Laurence Bonnal, Joan Cabero, Jordi Ricart, Daniele Carnovich, Hespèrion XX).
(M) *** Audivis Astrée Dig. ES 9925 [id.].

Juan del Enzina (1468–1529) was born in Salamanca and was much travelled, ending his life in Léon where he was Prior of the Cathedral. However, he is famous for secular music – villancicos and romances, and is as much a master of melancholy as of high spirits. His music here is presented with the kind of imaginative vitality and colour we used to associate especially with David Munrow, and the instrumental scoring, using drums and percussion, is piquant to match the vocal writing with its wide range of moods. Just try the *Cucú* song (track 8) and you will surely be won over to this highly infectious music-making.

MONTEVERDI: *Vespro della Beata Vergine (Vespers)* (with Monserrat Figueras, Marie

Cristina Kiehr, Picotti, Cota, Guy de Mey, Turk, Fagotto, Padova Centro Musica Antica Ch., La Capella Reial).
(M) **(*) Audivis Astrée Dig. ES 9936 (2) [id.].

Savall's spacious 1988 version of the Monteverdi *Vespers* may not be so vibrant as Gardiner's later DG Archive set, but as recorded in the expansive acoustics of the Santa Barbara Basilica in Mantua it has the fullness of sonority, both choral and instrumental, for which Savall's performances of early music are noted, and which are especially telling in the closing sections of the work, including the sonorous *Hymnus* and the *Magnificat*.

The solo team too are very impressive, both individually characterful and blending as a group, and the instrumental backing is first rate. There is certainly no lack of drama, but it is the lyrical richness and colour of Monteverdi's writing that are dominant. The recording is generally well focused and warmly atmospheric.

Cristóbal de MORALES: *Missa pro defunctis; Officium defunctorum* (with La Capella Reial de Catalunya, Hespèrion XX).
(M) *** Audivis Astrée Dig. ES 9926 [id.].

Cristóbal de Morales (whose dates, incidentally, are given wrongly in the documentation on the back of the disc as 1685–1759!) was born in Seville around 1500 and died in 1553. He was a highly influential composer of early sixteenth-century Spanish church music, writing much of it while spending the central ten years of his career from 1535 onward as an esteemed member of the Papal Choir in Rome, which at that time welcomed Spanish singers. He then returned to Spain as a rather unsuccessful maestro di capella at the cathedrals of Toledo and Málaga and proved unsuited to such organizational posts.

Yet the reputation of his music continued to grow after his death and it has since been described as the most important written by a Spanish composer in the papal chapel between Josquin and Palestrina. The five-part *Missa pro defunctis* dates from 1544 and its sombre progress has an impressive power. In each section, the opening chant is taken up by one of the voices, usually an upper part, like an ostinato, and the other four embroider the texture, which is gravely harmonic in feeling.

In the present performance an added underlying sonority is provided by sackbuts, adding weight to the opening *Introitus*, but especially effective in the *Sanctus*. In some ways the shorter *Officium defunctorum* is an even more impressive work. It has a simple structure with an Invitatory introducing and then alternating with verses of Psalm 94, followed by two *Nocturnes*, the first of which frames three Lessons from the Book of Job, and the second ending with the Responsory *Ne recorderis*. Savall and his singers and instrumentalists seem completely at one with this solemn writing, which is very like a vocal processional, and the austere harmonization gives an impression of profound beauty. The recording could hardly be bettered, but the documentation does not include translations.

SOR: *Italian arias, seguidillas and variaciones* (with Monserrat Figueras, José Miguel Moreno (guitar)).
(M) **(*) Audivis Astrée Dig. ES 9928 [id.].

Fernando Sor is mainly celebrated for his guitar music, and his vocal seguidillas are little known. The present collection was only recently discovered in London, brought back by travellers to southern Spain in the early nineteenth century. Also included are five Italian songs, actually published in London. All are sung with idiomatic charm and unexaggerated temperament by Monserrat Figueras, and interspersed by guitar pieces, of which the extended variations on the English air *Marlborough* are the most ambitious. These are evocatively played by José Moreno using a modern copy of a guitar made in Paris at the beginning of the nineteenth century. An attractive recital pleasingly recorded, but perhaps of specialist rather than general interest. Full translations are included.

ANON.: *Songs of old Catalonia: Laments and legends* (with Monserrat Figueras, Francesc Garrigosa, La Capella Reial de Catalunya).
⚫ (M) *** Audivis Astrée Dig. ES 9937 [id.].

This is rare repertoire, of appealing melodic simplicity and beauty. If you enjoy Canteloube's Auvergne settings, you might find this collection equally seductive. The Catalonian melodic line has distinctive rhythms and the underlying harmony alternates major and minor modes in the most disarming way.

The opening *Song of the King's son* (lute accompanied) is enchanting and after this instrumental and vocal numbers alternate. There are instrumental evocations of 'The spinner' (*Filadora*) and 'The teacher', and a sad evocation of *Mariagnetta* about a lover who cannot fulfil his desire with his beloved. The most familiar item (made famous by Casals) is *El cant deis ocells*, 'The song of the birds', a traditional Christmas lullaby heard here in Savall's arrangement for flute, harp and theorbo, supported by viols. Among the songs, *El Comte Arnau*, an extended narrative ballad, is most remarkable of all.

Its legend concerns the forbidden love affair between the Count and the Abbess of the Monastery of Sant Joan de les Abadesses and the nightly appearances of the condemned man to his wife. Its persistent melody is as haunting as the narrative, which is filled out with a spoken dialogue telling the story. The closing *Els sagadors* ('The reapers') is a majestic historical song with religious connections and alternates solo and choral verses.

In the solos the simple beauty of Montserrat Figueras's singing is matched by the delicacy of the accompaniments, which, like his scoring of the

instrumental pieces show Savall at his most felicitous. It is a great pity that only the Catalonian texts are included, without translations, but the documentation is otherwise splendid, as is the atmospheric quality of the recording.

ATT. SAVALL: *Jeanne La Pucelle (Joan of Arc, Maid of Orleans)*: incidental music for Jacques Rivette's film (with Soloists, La Capella Reial de Catalunya, Hespèrion XX).
(M) **(*) Audivis Astrée Dig. ES 9938 [id.].

Jordi Savall here proves equally impressive as composer and arranger as well as player and conductor in this brilliantly colourful film score, which integrates a great deal of music by Du Fay including romanticized excerpts from his mass *L'homme armé*. The score is in six sections, *Le Départ, Les Batailles* (where the trumpets of the opposing French and English armies are tuned a tone apart), *Le déliverance d'Orléans, Le chemin, Le sacre de Charles VIII* and the melancholy closing prison scene, where Savall's own piece, *Les Solitudes*, for solo harp, is particularly touching. The wide range of instrumentation, lutes, string, brass and vocal groupings, with the haunting use of tolling bells, continually tweaks the ear, and there is much here to relish, although for all Savall's skill it exists primarily as a film score, certainly most atmospherically recorded.

La Scala, Milan, Chorus and Orchestra, Arturo Toscanini

'The reopening of La Scala, 12 May 1946' (with soloists including Renata Tebaldi, Mafalda Favero and Tancredi Pasero): ROSSINI: *La gazza ladra: Overture. William Tell: Wedding chorus;* Act I: *Dance;* Act III: *Soldiers' dance. Mosè in Egitto: Prayer.* VERDI: *Nabucco: Overture & Chorus of Hebrew slaves. Overture: I vespri siciliani. Te Deum.* PUCCINI: *Manon Lescaut,* Act III (complete). BOITO: *Mefistofele: Prologue.*
(BB) (**(*)) Naxos mono 8.110821/22 (2).

The radio recording may be close, harsh and boxy, but it is firm and clear, so giving a vivid idea of one of the great musical events of post-war Europe. This marked Toscanini's return to the opera house where he had had his greatest triumphs. Each performance here is incandescent. The manner may often be uncomfortably taut, as it regularly was in his New York performances, but there is an extra warmth here too. Such items as the *Dance* from Rossini's *William Tell* are most delicately pointed, and the articulation throughout has a pin-point precision of a kind rarely heard from an Italian orchestra.

It is good too to hear the chosen soloists, with the emergent Renata Tebaldi shining alongside established colleagues like Mafalda Favero and Tancredi

Pasero. The short items by Rossini and Verdi on the first disc are then nicely contrasted against the three major items on the second. Toscanini's electrifying readings of Verdi's *Te Deum* and the *Prologue* from Boito's *Mefistofele* are both well known from RCA recordings, but it is especially good to have Act III of Puccini's *Manon Lescaut*, plainly a Toscanini favourite: uniquely powerful, this was the work which brought reconciliation between the conductor and composer after an estrangement.

Schock, Rudolf (tenor)

'Heroes': Arias and excerpts from: MOZART: *Die Entführung aus dem Serail; Die Zauberflöte.* WEBER: *Der Freischütz.* OFFENBACH: *Tales of Hoffmann.* ADAM: *The Postillion of Lonjumeau* (both sung in German). LEHAR: *Die lustige Witwe; Friederike; Das Land des Lächelns.* KUNNEKE: *Der Vetter aus Dingsda.* MASCAGNI: *L'amico Fritz.* GIORDANO: *Andrea Chénier* (both with Joan Hammond). PUCCINI: *Turandot.* WAGNER: *Die Meistersinger; Lohengrin* (with various artists).

(M) (***) EMI mono/stereo CDM5 66811-2.

In 1949 Rudolf Schock took over an Australian tour from Richard Tauber (who had died the previous year) and immediately established his operetta credentials. He confirms this experience here with winningly seductive versions of Tauber's famous hit songs from Lehár's *Die lustige Witwe, Friederike* and *Land des Lächelns*. But, as the arias from Mozart's *Die Entführung* and *Die Zauberflöte* suggest, there is also a certain vocal affinity with Fritz Wunderlich.

If Schock's vocal personality is not as striking as either of these two singers, he proves an ideally romantic Max in Weber's *Der Freischütz*. He brings real sparkle to the *Legend of Kleinzack* (it sounds remarkably effective in German), and is equally vivacious in Adam's *Postillion's song*. In the duets from Mascagni's *L'amico Fritz* and Giordano's *Andrea Chénier*, he is unexpectedly joined by Joan Hammond and together they charm the ear in the one, and generate a thrilling burst of passion in the other. The two arias from Kempe's 1953 *Lohengrin* and the ensemble from the 1956 *Die Meistersinger* make a good finale. All the recordings come from the 1950s Elektola catalogue and they are impressively remastered. Altogether this is a most enjoyable programme. (The disc has now been withdrawn in the UK just as we go to press, but is worth seeking out in the shops.)

The Scholars of London

French chansons: JOSQUIN: *Faute d'argent; Mille regretz.* JANNEQUIN: *Le chant des oiseaux; Or*

vien ça. SANDRIN: *Je ne le croy.* GOMBERT: *Aime qui vouldra; Quand je suis aupres.* SERMISY: *Tant que vivrai; Venez regrets; La, la, maistre Pierre.* ARCADELT: *En ce mois délicieux; Margot, labourez les vignes; Du temps que j'estois amoureux; Sa grand beauté.* TABOUROT: *Belle qui tiens ma vie.* vassal: *Vray Dieu.* CLEMENS: *Prière devant le repas; Action des Graces.* PASSEREAU: *Il est bel et bon.* LE JEUNE: *Ce n'est que fiel.* LASSUS: *Bonjour mon coeur; Si je suis brun; Beau le cristal; La nuit froide; Un jeune moine.* BERTRAND: *De nuit, le bien.* COSTELY: *Arrête un peu mon coeur.*

(BB) *** Naxos Dig. 8.550880 [id.].

This disc offers a representative selection from the thousands of sixteenth-century French polyphonic chansons, and ranges from the devotional to the amorous, the bawdy and the bucolic. It includes some of the best known, such as the ubiquitous Jannequin *Le chant des oiseaux*, and features such familiar masters as Josquin, Sermisy and Claude Le Jeune. It encompasses Flemish masters writing in the language such as Gombert and Lassus. The Scholars of London are expressive and persuasive guides in this repertoire and are decently recorded at St Silas the Martyr in Kentish Town. There is an all-too-short but thoughtful introduction, and the booklet then reproduces texts and translations. What more can you ask from a disc that would undoubtedly cost less than admission to a concert plus the programme?

Scholl, Andreas (counter-tenor)

'Heroes' (with Orchestra of the Age of Enlightenment, Sir Roger Norrington): Arias from HANDEL: *Giulio Cesare; Rodelinda; Saul; Semele; Serse.* HASSE: *Artaserse.* GLUCK: *Orfeo; Telemaco.* MOZART: *Ascanio in Alba; Mitridate.* *** Decca Dig. 466 196-2 [id.].

'There is more to heroism than winning fearlessly . . . My heroes have moments of weakness and must overcome their difficulties,' comments Andreas Scholl about the operatic characters represented in his Decca recital. Indeed it is the lovely tender singing in the lyrical arias that one remembers most, as in the familiar *Where'er you walk* and *Oh Lord whose mercies numberless* (from *Saul*, with its delicate closing harp solo from Frances Kelly), or *Con rauco mormorio* from *Rodelinda*.

In spite of the prevalence of Handel in the programme, Scholl overlaps with his Harmonia Mundi disc on only one aria, *Ombra mai fù*, just as characterful though less forwardly recorded. The other items range from Hasse (wonderfully light and nimble) to dramatic early Mozart. Altogether this is a formidable collection of arias designed originally for castrato, all performed characterfully with a firm, clear tone and virtuoso agility. *Che farò* from Gluck's *Orfeo* is on the slow side, but no less impressive for that. Clear, open sound, the voice caught brightly and naturally. Norrington's accompaniments are light-textured and fresh. But Scholl's earlier Harmonia Mundi Handel collection, including instrumental music also, is in many ways even more seductive – see above under Handel in the Composer index of our main volume.

Schwarzkopf, Dame Elisabeth

(soprano)

'*Diva*': Arias from: MOZART: *Le nozze di Figaro; Don Giovanni; Così fan tutte*. BEETHOVEN: *Fidelio*. WEBER: *Der Freischütz*. WAGNER: *Lohengrin*. SMETANA: *The Bartered Bride*. R. STRAUSS: *Der Rosenkavalier; Ariadne auf Naxos; Arabella*. HEUBERGER: *Der Opernball*. Johann STRAUSS Jr: *Die Fledermaus*.
(M) *** EMI stereo/mono CDM5 65577-2 [id.].

This single CD in EMI's 'Diva' series offers an excellent and shrewdly selected survey of Schwarzkopf's opera and operetta recordings. Mozart is very well represented, with Schwarzkopf as both Susanna and the Countess in *Figaro*, as Donna Elvira in *Don Giovanni* (from the masterly Giulini recording) and as Fiordiligi in *Così fan tutte* (commanding in *Come scoglio* under Boehm). From Richard Strauss there is not only the Marschallin's monologue (from the Karajan recording of *Rosenkavalier*) but also Ariadne's lament and Arabella's final solo, another of her most compelling Strauss performances. Immaculate accounts of Weber (Agathe's *Leise, leise* from *Freischütz*) and of Wagner (Elsa's Dream from *Lohengrin*) have been drawn from one of the finest of all her discs, with Heuberger's *Im chambre séparée* as an enchanting operetta tailpiece. Excellent transfers.

'*Elisabeth Schwarzkopf sings operetta*' (with Philharmonia Ch. and O, Ackermann): Excerpts from: HEUBERGER: *Der Opernball*. ZELLER: *Der Vogelhändler*. LEHAR: *Der Zarewitsch; Der Graf von Luxembourg; Giuditta*. J. STRAUSS JR: *Casanova*. MILLOCKER: *Die Dubarry*. SUPPE: *Boccaccio*. SIECZYNSKY: *Wien, du Stadt meiner Träume*.
🌑 (M) *** EMI CDM5 66989-2 [567004].

This is one of the most delectable recordings of operetta arias ever made, and it is here presented with excellent sound. Schwarzkopf's 'whoopsing' manner (as Philip Hope-Wallace called it) is irresistible, authentically catching the Viennese style, languor and sparkle combined. Try for example the exquisite *Im chambre séparée* or *Sei nicht bös*; but the whole programme is performed with supreme artistic command and ravishing tonal beauty. This outstanding example of the art of Elisabeth

Schwarzkopf at its most enchanting is a disc which ought to be in every collection. The CD transfer enhances the superbly balanced recording even further; it manages to cut out nearly all the background, gives the voice a natural presence and retains the orchestral bloom.

'*Unpublished recordings*' (with (i) Philh. O, Thurston Dart; (ii) Kathleen Ferrier, VPO, Karajan; (iii) Philh. O, Galliera; (iv) Walter Gieseking, Philh. O, Karajan): J. S. BACH: (i) *Cantata No. 199: Mein Herze schwimmt im Blut: Auf diese Schmerzens Reu; Doch Gott muss mir genädig sein; Mein Herze schwimmt im Blut*. (ii) *Mass in B min.: Christe eleison; Et in unum Dominum; Laudamus te*. (iii) MOZART: *Nehmt meinen Dank, K.383*. (iv) GIESEKING: *Kinderlieder*. R. STRAUSS: *4 Last songs*.
(M) (**(*)) EMI CDM7 63655-2.

Long-buried treasure here includes Bach duets with Kathleen Ferrier conducted by Karajan, a collection of charming children's songs by Gieseking, recorded almost impromptu, and, best of all, a live performance of Strauss's *Four Last songs* given under Karajan at the Festival Hall in 1956, a vintage year for Schwarzkopf. Sound quality varies, but the voice is gloriously caught.

'*Lieder recital*' (with Gerald Moore, piano): BACH: *Bist du bei mir*. PERGOLESI: *Se tu m'ami, se tu sospiri*. HANDEL: *Atalanta: Care selve*. GLUCK: *Die Pilger von Mekka: Einam Bach der fliesst*. BEETHOVEN: *Wonne de Wehmut*. SCHUBERT: *An Sylvia; Romanze aus Rosamunde; Die Vögel; Der Einsame; Vedi quanto adoro*. WOLF: *Kennst du das Land; Philine; Nachtzauber; Die Zigeunerin*. Richard STRAUSS: *Ruhe meine Seele; Wiegenlied; Schlechters Wetter; Hat gesagt, bleibt's nicht dabei*. Encores: MOZART: *Warnung*. SCHUMANN: *Der Nüssbaum*. SCHUBERT: *Ungeduld*.
(M) (**(*)) EMI mono CDH5 66084-2.

Schwarzkopf's 1956 Salzburg recital with Gerald Moore is the third to have appeared on CD, more varied than the earlier two, another great occasion caught on the wing. It ranges from Bach and Handel arias, expansive and poised, through a Schubert-like Gluck song and rare Beethoven to Schwarzkopf's regular repertory of Schubert, Wolf and Strauss, delectably done. Wolf's *Kennst du das Land*, greatest of all Lieder for a woman, here comes not as a climax but at the start of a group, building up with biting intensity. No texts are provided.

'*Schwarzkopf Songbook*' (with Gerald Moore, Geoffrey Parsons, Nicolas Medtner, Cyril Skalkiewicz (piano)): MOZART: *Warnung; Der Zauberer; Das Veilchen; Der Zauber*. SCHUBERT: *Ungeduld; Liebe schwärmt*. MENDELSSOHN: *Auf Flügeln des Gesanges*.

SCHUMANN: *6 Lieder from Liederkreis, Op. 39; Aufträge; Widmung.* LISZT: *Die drei Zigeuner.* BRAHMS: *Vergebliches Ständchen; Immer leiser; Wie Melodien; Der Jäger; Liebestreu; Vergebliches Ständchen.* JENSEN: *Murmeln des Lüftchen.* MAHLER: *Lob des hohen Verstandes.* R. STRAUSS: *Ach, was Kummer; Wer lieben will; 3 Ophelia Lieder.* WOLF: *25 Lieder from the Italienisches Liederbuch; 8 Goethe Lieder; 4 Mörike Lieder; Keine gleicht von allen Schönen; Wienlied (Im Sommer); Mausfallensprüchlein; In dem Schatten meiner Locken.* GRIEG: *Farmyard song; Ich liebe dich; Mit einer Wasserlilie; Letzter Frühling; Erstes Begegnen; Zu Rosenzeit; Mit einer Primula veris; Lauf der Welt.* DVORAK: *Songs my mother taught me.* TCHAIKOVSKY: *Nur wer die Sehnsucht kennt.* MUSSORGSKY: *In den Pilzen.* MEDTNER: *The muse; The rose; The waltz; When roses fade; 7 Goethe Lieder; Praeludium; Winternacht; Die Quelle.* SIBELIUS: *Die Echo-Nymph; Der Norden; Hundert Wege; Schiff, Schiff, säusle; Der Kuss; Der erste Kuss; War es ein Traum?; Schwarze Rosen.*

(M) *** EMI (SIS) mono/stereo CHS5 65860-2 (3) [CDHC 65860].

Issued to celebrate Schwarzkopf's eightieth birthday in December 1995, these three discs offer many rarities selected from many different periods in her career. So the second of the three, devoted entirely to Wolf, has twenty-five songs from the *Italian Songbook* in the mono recordings she made in 1959, four more than she contributed to the joint recording of that cycle, much better known, which she made with Fischer-Dieskau ten years later. These earlier examples are more intimate and often more intense.

The Mozart song recordings range from a girlish account of *Warnung*, recorded in 1947, and of *Der Zauberer*, recorded in 1951, to a 1970 recording of that second song, warmer, more positive and with more detail. Similarly in the Schumann selection, a 1951 recording of *Aufträge* is set against six songs from the Opus 39 *Liederkreis*, recorded as late as 1974. Brahms is generously represented, mainly from 1970 sessions, with an alternative version of *Vergebliches Ständchen* from 1954, lighter and fresher if less dramatic.

Liszt's *Three gypsies* prompt an aptly throaty tone, while a song by Adolf Jensen brings one of the loveliest performances of all. The first disc is rounded off with a Strauss group, including a previously unpublished radio recording of the Ophelia songs, compellingly characterized. The third disc is devoted to songs outside the German repertory, mainly done in German, as for example the eight Grieg songs. Medtner is the accompanist in eleven of his own tenderly lyrical songs, while the greatest treasure of all is the final group of eight Sibelius songs, recorded live in 1955 by Finnish

Radio in inspired performances, never previously published.

Unpublished recordings 1946–52 : BACH: *Cantata No. 51: Jauchzet Gott* (with Philh. O, Susskind). MOZART: *Exsultate jubilate, K.165; Das Veilchen. Die Zauberflöte:* excerpts (with piano); Schwarzkopf talks about the *Die Zauberflöte* recordings. Arias from VERDI: *La Traviata.* PUCCINI: *La Bohème.* BACH/GOUNOD: *Ave Maria.* ARNE: *When dasies pied.* MORLEY: *It was a lover and his lass.* schubert: *Gretchen am Spinnrade; Der Musensohn; Wiegenlied.* Richard STRAUSS: *Hat gesagt, bleibt's nicht dabei; Schlechtes Wetter.* WOLF: *Storchenbotschaft* (2 versions); *Epiphanias; Mein Liebster hat zu Tische; Du denkst mit einem Fädchen; Schweig'einmal still; Wer tat deinem Füsslein weh?; Bedeckt mich mit Blumen; Mögen alle bösen Zungen; Elfenlied; Nixe Binserfuss; Im Frühling; Die Spröde; Die Bekehrte; Mausfallen-sprüchlein; Wiegenlied in Sommer.*
🌑 *** Testament mono/stereo SBT 2172 (2) [id.].

Elisabeth Schwarzkopf, married to the recording producer and impresario Walter Legge, had a uniquely intensive recording career from the 1940s onwards. Here we have a magnificent store of the recordings made when her glorious voice was at its most radiant. For any lover of singing this is buried treasure when many of these items have an immediacy and freshness even more winning than later, published versions. Parallel versions of the jolly little Wolf song *Storchenbotschaft* demonstrate how rapid her development was between 1948 and 1951, leading to a whole collection of Wolf recorded in 1951, every one a jewel.

The three Schubert songs include *Der Musensohn*, joyfully buoyant, and *Gretchen am Spinnrade*, brighter and more passionate than in later recordings, with a little spontaneous gasp of emotion after the climax on *'sein Kuss!'*. Bach and Mozart too have an extra urgency compared with later, and Violetta's aria from Verdi's *La Traviata* is all the more intense, done in English. Most revealing of all is the private recording, some half-hour of music, made with piano accompaniment when Schwarzkopf was preparing to sing Pamina in English in a Covent Garden revival of Mozart's *Magic Flute*, a 'glimpse into the singer's workshop' centring on a ravishing account of *Ach ich fühls*.

Scotto, Renata (soprano)

Arias from: ROSSINI: *Il barbiere di Siviglia.* BELLINI: *I Puritani.* VERDI: *La Traviata; Nabucco.* PUCCINI: *La Bohème; Gianni Schicchi; Turandot; Madama Butterfly.* BOITO: *Mefistofele.* LEONCAVALLO: *Pagliacci.*

(BB) **(*) Royal Classics Vocal Double DCL 706632 (2).

This collection is based on a 1959 recital (with the Philharmonia Orchestra under Manno Wolf-Ferrari), early in Scotto's career. Although the CD transfers have a touch of shrillness, the widely ranging programme of arias has the voice at its freshest and most agile. There are four outstanding excerpts from the complete 1966 set of *Madama Butterfly* with Carlo Bergonzi, superbly conducted by Barbirolli the thrillingly wild arias from Muti's *Nabucco* (1978), and the same conductor's *La Traviata* (1982), where she is at her most moving, show how the voice has filled out, and spread above the stave. Yet her style has matured and become more forcefully dramatic, full of character. Altogether a fascinating portrait, even if the documentation is sparse.

Seefried, Irmgard (soprano), Erik Werba (piano)

Lieder: BRAHMS: *Es träumte mir; Nicht mehr zu dir zu gehen; Ständchen; Trost in Tränen; Unbewegte laue Luft; 6 Volkslieder: In stiller Nacht; Schwesterlein; Die Sonne scheint mehr; Die Trauernde; Der Versuchung; Volkslied.* SCHUBERT: *Mignon Lieder: Heiss mich nicht reden; Kennst du das Land; Nur wer die Sehnsucht kennt; So lasst mich scheinen.* WOLF: *Mignon Lieder I–IV: Heiss mich nicht reden; Kennst du das Land; Nur wer die Sehnsucht kennt; So lasst mich scheinen.* (Irmgard Seefried in conversation with John Amis).
(***) BBC Legends mono BBCL 4040-2 [id.].

Recorded by the BBC in the studio in January 1962, this recital brings out the open charm of Irmgard Seefried as a winning Lieder singer. Her Brahms group sets the pattern, bringing out the links with German folksong, fresh and tuneful. There is no lack of detail in her pointing of words, but she takes a direct view of even such a deeply meditative song as *In stiller Nacht*, singing with concentration but little mystery.

Such songs as *Schwesterlein* and *Ständchen* are given with such urgency that one holds one's breath, half expecting disaster. Seefried's forte is her full, strong creamy voice, here recorded rather close, so that Schubert's *Gretchen am Spinnrade* brings little build-up, and Wolf's supreme Lied, *Kennst du das Land*, remains fresh and forthright in its lyricism rather than offering darker emotions. The interview with John Amis, which comes as a delightful supplement, bears out the joyful enthusiasm of the singer, whose strength, beauty and openness defy any detailed reservations.

Shuard, Amy (soprano)

Recital (with Royal Opera House, Covent Garden Orchestra, Edward Downes or RPO, George Weldon): Arias from: VERDI: *Aida; Un ballo in maschera.* MASCAGNI: *Cavalleria rusticana.* PUCCINI: *Turandot; Gianni Schicchi; Turandot; Tosca; La Bohème.* GIORDANO: *Andrea Chénier.* TCHAIKOVSKY: *Eugene Onegin (Letter scene).*
(M) **(*) Dutton Lab. CDCLP 4006 [id.]

What this formidable aria collection triumphantly demonstrates is that Amy Shuard, for many years the leading soprano in the Covent Garden company, has been seriously underestimated. Her premature death at the age of 50 compounded what was already sadly evident, that this home-grown singer was not going to be fully appreciated. Even when originally issued on two LPs in the early 1960s, the recordings did not appear on a premium label, yet the singer, at once gloriously firm and strong, yet sensitively shaded and deeply expressive, whether as Aida, Turandot or Tatiana, can bear international comparison with other recording artists. The timbre may not have been of the most distinctive, but she amply compensated for the central strength and precision of everything she sang. There are few Turandots quite so incisive as this one. The Dutton transfer here is immaculate, with the voice vivid and clear.

Sinfonye, Stewart Wishart

'Gabriel's greeting' (Medieval carols) including: *Gabriel framevene king; Salva Virgo virginium; Ave Maria virgo virginium; Ther is no rose of swych vertu; Lolay, lolay; Nowell, nowell.*
**(*) Hyperion Dig. CDA 66685 [id.].

Unlike the Taverner Consort, who range over many centuries of music, Sinfonye concentrate on vocal and instrumental music from the thirteenth, fourteenth and fifteenth centuries, which usually consists of simple ostinato-like rhythmic ideas with a very distinctive melodic and harmonic character. These five singers and instrumentalists present their programme with spirit and vitality, but the range of the music is necessarily limited. Those who take to the repetitive medieval style will undoubtedly find this refreshing, and the recording is pleasingly live and atmospheric.

Soprano arias

'20 Great soprano arias' from: MOZART: *Le nozze di Figaro* (Kiri Te Kanawa; Ileana Cotrubas). *Die Entführung aus dem Serail* (Kathleen Battle). *Die Zauberflöte* (Sumi Jo). PUCCINI: *Madama Butterfly* (Régine Crespin). *Turandot* (Caballé; Virginia Zeani). *La Rondine* (Renata Tebaldi).

Tosca (Leontyne Price). *Gianni Schicchi* (Felicia Weathers). *La Bohème* (Mirella Freni; Elizabeth Harwood). VERDI: *I vespri siciliani* (Anita Cerquetti). *Un ballo in maschera* (Margaret Price). CATALANI: *La Wally* (Maria Chiara). PONCHIELLI: *La Gioconda* (Elena Souliotis). DONIZETTI: *La figlia del reggimento* (Graziella Sciutti). GOUNOD: *Faust* (Joan Sutherland). DVORAK: *Rusalka* (Pilar Lorengar). WAGNER: *Die Walküre* (Kirsten Flagstad).
(M) *** Decca 458 230-2 [id.].

Decca's collection of '20 Great soprano arias' is made the more interesting by its use of twenty different singers, and the choices are not always obvious ones; for instance Régine Crespin's very individual and very touching *Un bel dì* from *Madama Butterfly*, Elena Souliotis's searingly powerful *Suicido* from *La Gioconda* and the beautifully spun line of Maria Chiara's *Ne andrò lonata* from *La Wally*.

Opening with Kiri Te Kanawa's moving *Dove sono*, other highlights include Kathleen Battle's vivacious portrayal of Blonde in *Die Entführung*, Kirsten Flagstad as Sieglinde in *Die Walküre*, the charming Graziella Sciutti, in *La figlia del reggimento*, and Joan Sutherland's scintillating (1960) *Jewel song*. Both Margaret and Leontyne Price are included, and of course Freni.

Alongside these familiar names come rather less well-known singers, all in excellent voice (Anita Cerquetti in *I vespri siciliani*; Felicia Weathers as Lauretta in *Gianni Schicchi*; Pilar Lorengar no less striking in Rusalka's famous Moon invocation, and Virginia Zeani alongside Caballé – two very contrasted voices – as Liù in *Turandot*). The programme ends with Sumi Jo's sparklingly precise coloratura in the most familiar of the Queen of the Night's arias from *Die Zauberflöte*. This famous show-piece has never been better sung on record – it has drama as well as extraordinary bravura.

Souzay, Gérard (baritone), Dalton Baldwin (piano)

Mélodies françaises: FAURE: *Chanson du pêcheur; Poème d'un jour, Op. 21; Les berceaux; Le secret; Aurore; Fleur jetée; La rose; Madrigal; 5 Mélodies de Venise, Op. 58; La bonne chanson, Op. 61; Le parfum impérissable; Arpège; Prison; Soir; Dans la forêt de septembre; La fleur qui va sur l'eau; Le don silencieux; La chanson d'Eve, Op. 95, excerpts (Eau vivante; O mort, poussière d'étoiles). Le jardin clos, Op. 106, excerpts (Exaucement; Je me poserai sur ton coeur). Mirages, Op. 113; L'horizon chimérique, Op. 118.* POULENC: *Chansons villageoises; Calligrammes; Le travail du peintre; La fraîcheur et le feu; Airs chantés: Air vif. La grenouillère; Métamorphoses:*

Reine des mouettes. Priez pour paix. RAVEL: *5 Mélodies populaires grecques; Epigrammes de Clément Marot; Histoires naturelles; Chansons madécasses; 2 Mélodies hébraïques; Don Quichotte à Dulcinée; Les grands vents venus d'outre-mer; Sainte; Sur l'herbe.* LEGUERNEY: *20 Poèmes de la Pléiade, excerpts (Ma douce jouvence est passée; A son page).* HAHN: *L'heure exquise.* DUPARC: *L'invitation au voyage; Sérénade florentine; La vague et la cloche; Extase; Le manoir de Rosemonde; Lamento; La vie antérieure; Testament; Phidylé; Chanson triste; Elégie; Soupir.* GOUNOD: *L'absent; Sérénade.* CHABRIER: *Les cigales; Chanson pour Jeanne.* BIZET: *Chanson d'avril.* FRANCK: *Nocturne.* ROUSSEL: *Le jardin mouillé; Le bachelier de Salamanque.*
🌀 (M) *** Ph. 438 964-2 (4).

Now here is something to make the pulse quicken: Gérard Souzay recorded while still in his prime and in repertoire in which he was unmatched in his day. Only Bernac had as refined an interpretative intelligence and, of an older generation, only Panzera commanded an equal authority and tonal beauty. Souzay's 1963 recording of Fauré's *La bonne chanson* is one of the classics of the gramophone and has been extensively discussed in the *Stereo Record Guide* over the years. It was chosen by RL as one of his 'desert-island' discs in 'The Great Records' ('rich in artistry, imagination and insight').

The recording of the *Deux Mélodies hébraïques* is captivating, though Souzay made an even more haunting version for French EMI in the late 1950s; and one is hard pressed to choose between his *Don Quichotte à Dulcinée* and those of Panzera and Bernac. After Souzay's Philips disc with *La bonne chanson* came further recordings of Fauré, an anthology of other French mélodies and an LP of the Duparc songs, in every way superior to his later, EMI re-make in the early 1970s. This is treasure-trove which no lover of the French repertoire should be without. It is an essential acquisition for Souzay admirers. Not everyone can afford four CDs all at one go, even at mid-price, and Philips would be wise to re-package the Fauré songs as part of their bargain Duo series, and issue the Duparc separately as well.

Maria Stader (soprano)

'In memoriam': Arias from: BACH: *St. John's Passion; St Matthew Passion.* HANDEL: *Joshua; Messiah.* HAYDN: *The Creation; The Seasons.* MENDELSSOHN: *Elijah.* MOZART: *Die Entführung aus dem Serail; Don Giovanni; Le nozze di Figaro; Die Zauberflöte; Vesperae solennes de confessore.* Concert arias: *Un moto di gioia, K.579; A questo seno deh vieni, K.375; Exsultate,*

jubilate. MENDELSSOHN: songs: *Es weiss und röt es doch keiner; Nachtlied; Neue Liebe; Schilflied; Wanderlied.*

(B) ** DG Double Mono/Stereo 447 334–2 (2) [id.].

Although Maria Stader's reputation is in no doubt, this double-disc set is a mixed success. Perhaps best known as a Mozartian, some of her singing in this repertoire is a little variable: the *Entführung* aria, for example, sounds rather strained – the voice a bit shrill under pressure – though other examples show why her Mozart was so admired. In the oratorio extracts she is more secure, and there is also much to enjoy in the intimate Mendelssohn songs too. Whilst this set is not particularly recommendable to the general collector, admirers of this artist will be glad to have it, especially as some of the repertoire is available on CD for the first time. The recordings range from average to good, but the sleeve notes are restricted to biographical details only.

Stefano, Giuseppe di (tenor)

'Heroes': Arias and excerpts from: VERDI: *Rigoletto; Il Trovatore; La Traviata; Un ballo in maschera.* DONIZETTI: *Lucia di Lammermoor.* PUCCINI: *Manon Lescaut; La Bohème; Tosca; Madama Butterfly.* LEONCAVALLO: *Pagliacci.* MASCAGNI: *Cavalleria rusticana.*

(M) (***) EMI mono CDM5 66808-2.

Except for those demanding stereo, this is an outstanding demonstration of di Stefano's open-throated vocal ardour. The recordings date from between 1953 and 1956 when the voice was at its finest. Certainly the heroic side of his vocal personality comes over splendidly in Verdi (especially in *Di quella pira*) but he is at his finest and most responsive in the Puccini excerpts, the superb *Tosca* with de Sabata (1953), *Madama Butterfly* (1953), and *La Bohème* (1958). He is ideally cast as Turiddù, and his two arias from *Cavalleria rusticana*, which end the recital, are passionately moving, while the *Pagliacci Prologue* brings compellingly vibrant vocal histrionics. Excellent, vivid transfers which make one forget the age of the recordings.

Arias from: VERDI: *La Traviata; Un ballo in maschera; Rigoletto; Il Trovatore; La forza del destino.* PUCCINI: *La Bohème; Tosca; Manon Lescaut; Turandot; Madama Butterfly; La Fanciulla del West; Gianni Schicchi.* DONIZETTI: *Lucia di Lammermoor.* LEONCAVALLO: *Pagliacci.* MASCAGNI: *Cavalleria rusticana.* BIZET: *Les Pêcheurs de perles.* Songs: DI CAPUA: *O sole mio!* CARDILLO: *Core 'ngrato.* LEONCAVALLO: *Mattinata.* TOSTI: *La serenata.* DENZA: *Funiculì, funiculà.*

(BB) (***) Royal Classics Vocal Double mono/ stereo DCL 704822 (2).

Giuseppe di Stefano made his finest complete opera recordings for EMI at the end of the mono era, when he was usually partnered by Callas. Though he was not the subtlest of tenors, he was often in splendid voice and there is no doubting the visceral thrill of the key arias in the favourite Puccini roles, especially in *Manon Lescaut*, and the famous De Sabata *Tosca*, while he made a heroic figure of Pinkerton in *Butterfly* and he could be a tender Rodolfo in *La Bohème*. In Verdi he was both a crisply stylish Duke in *Rigoletto* and arresting as Manrico in *Il Trovatore*. Not everything here is equally distinctive, but he is obviously at home in the Neapolitan songs. The recording quality is variable but often the transfers are surprisingly successful.

'Torna a Surriento' (songs of Italy and Sicily): CD 1 (with New SO of London, Iller Pattacini): DE CURTIS: *Torna a Surriento; Tu ca' nun chiagne; Sonta chitarra!* BUONGIOVANNI: *Lacreme napulitane.* TAGLIAFERRI: *Napule canta; Pusilleco . . .* CALIFANO: *O 'surdato 'nnammurato.* CARDILLO: *Catari, Catari.* COSTA: *Era di maggio matenata; Scetate.* VALENTE: *Addio mia bella Napoli.* CD 2 (with Orchestra, Dino Olivieri): BIXIO: *Parlami d'amore Mariù.* BARBERIS: *Munasterio'e Santa-Chiara.* CESARINI: *Firenze sogna.* DE CURTIS: *Canta pe'me; 'A canzone'e Napule; Ti voglio tanto bene.* NARDELLA: *Che t'aggia di!* SIMI: *Come è bello far l'amore quanno è sera.* VANCHERI: *Sicilia bedda.* BUONGIOVANNI: *Fili d'oro.* DI LAZZARO: *Chitarra romana.* RIVI: *Addio, sogni di gloria.* TRAD., arr. FAVARA: *A la barcillunisi; Nota di li lavannari; A la vallelunghisa; Muttètti di lu pàliu; Chiovu 'aballati'; Cantu a timùni.*

(B) *** Decca Double 455 482-2 (2) [id.].

Giuseppe di Stefano was still in magnificent voice when, in the summer of 1964, he recorded the collection of popular Italian songs assembled on the first disc of this Decca Double. He projects the ardent numbers such as the title-song with characteristic lustiness but less subtlety; despite the inevitable touches of vulgarity, the singing is rich-toned and often charming, and a famous Neapolitan hit like *Catari, Catari* is winningly done. Pattacini's accompaniments are vividly idiomatic.

The second collection is even more generous, offering eighteen songs (against eleven on the first disc). This dates from 1958, when the voice was even more honeyed, so that Bixio's opening *Parlami d'amore Mariù* sounds almost like operetta and brings an engaging pianissimo ending. The luscious Mantovani-styled accompaniments are certainly seductive, and very well recorded, while in *Come è bello far l'amore quanno è sera* the use of the mandolin is particularly atmospheric.

Besides the popular Neapolitan numbers, there

are many comparative rarities here, often coming from Venice, Florence or Sicily, with their respective dialects. There are no translations, but none are really needed. As Frank Granville Barker observes in his note: 'Strong emotions are the concern of all these songs, expressed in no less straightforward melodies. The mood is intense, the singer declaring his devotion to his loved one, or despairing when it is not returned. Parting from home inspires as much anguish as parting from the loved one, as we hear in *Addio mia bella Napoli*.'

The group of six traditional songs arranged by Favara, which close the recital, are particularly fine; *Muttètti di lu pàliu* (introduced by a fine horn solo) is really memorable, with di Stefano responding to its plaintive melancholy with a very gentle closing cadence. He then follows with a sparkling tarantella, *Chiovu 'aballati'*. This is not a collection to play all at once (and memories of Gigli in this repertory are not vanquished), but in its field it is currently unsurpassed.

Streich, Rita (soprano)

'Waltzes and arias' (with Berlin RSO, RIAS Berlin, Kurt Gaebel): Johann STRAUSS Jr.: *Frühlingsstimmen; Draussen in Sievering*. SAINT-SAENS: *Le rossignol et la rose*. VERDI: *Lo spazzacamino*. ARDITI: *Parla waltz*. Josef STRAUSS: *Dorfschwalben aus Osterreich*. ALABIEV: *The Nightingale*. DELIBES: *Les filles de Cadiz*. CZERNIK: *Chi sa?* MARCHESI: *La folletta*. FLOTOW: *Last rose of summer*. DELL'ACQUA: *Villanelle*. ARDITI: *Il bacio*. Arias from: GODARD: *Jocelyn*. SUPPE: *Boccaccio*. DVORAK: *Rusalka*. MEYERBEER: *Dinorah*.

🎭 (M) *** DG mono/stereo 457 729-2 (2) [id.].

Possessing the prettiest coloratura soprano voice of the second half of the twentieth century (and she was hardly less attractive to look at!), Rita Streich measured up well to all the competition from the 'Golden Age'. It was a small voice but perfectly formed, and it recorded marvellously well. Many of the most memorable pieces included here come from a recital she recorded in 1958 in the Jesus Christus Kirche, Berlin.

Included were the Strauss waltzes, Dvořák's *Invocation to the moon*, the charming *Hab' ich nur deine Liebe* from *Boccaccio* and the equally delightful *Shadow song* from *Dinorah*. Godard's highly romantic *Berceuse* is the most famous item, but it is in the deliciously fragile Saint-Saëns vocalise, *Le rossignol et la rose*, and in Verdi's captivating song of the chimney sweep (*Lo spazzacamino*) that her magic sends a shiver of special pleasure to the nape of the neck. A worthy vocal addition for DG's series of 'Originals'.

'Folk songs and lullabies': Du, du liegst mir im Herzen; O du liabs Angeli; Frère Jacques; L'Amore de moi; Canto delle risaiole; Z'Lauterbach; Schlof sche, mein Vögele; Drink to me only with thine eyes; Nobody knows the trouble I've seen; Sakura, Sakura; Tschubtschik; Spi mladenez; In mezo al mar; Wenn ich ein Vöglein wär'; Der mond ist aufgegangen; Muss I denn zum Städtele 'maus; with Rudolf Lamy Choir and instrumental accompaniment, Michalski). Weisst Du, wieviel Sterne stehen; O wie wohl ist mir Abend; Wo e kleins Hüttle steht; All mein Gedanken; Glockenruf; Der Bürgermeister von Wesel; Der Wechsel der Jahreszeiten; Schlaf, Herzenssöhnchen; Schlafe, mein Prinzchen, schlaf ein; Sandmännchen; Der Kuckuck; Schwesterlein!; Ach Modr, ick will en Ding han; In der Fruah; Abendlied; Ave Maria (with Regenszburger Domspatzen, Bavarian Radio SO, Kurt Gaebel).

(M) *** DG 457 763–2 [id.]

This disc is a delight. Every song is most winning and it is difficult to say which is the more captivating, the Russian, French, English, or Swiss folk songs, all dressed up in freshly colourful orchestrations, and the delectable *Frère Jacques* presented in canon with the choir. Rita Streich sings with obvious affection, with her legendary creaminess of vocal timbre tickling the ear throughout the two collections, which were recorded in 1963 and 1964. Their remarkable variety, to say nothing of the vocal charm, prevents any sense that 79 minutes of folk-song is too much. It is regretted that DG, in these beautifully transferred recordings on their Originals label, has failed to provide any texts or translations. But this is still a reissue not to be missed.

Sutherland, Dame Joan (soprano)

'The Art of Joan Sutherland':

Volume 1: Arias from: HANDEL: *Alcina; Giulio Cesare; Samson*. MOZART: *Die Entführung; Il Re Pastore; Die Zauberflöte*.

Volume 2: Arias from French operas: OFFENBACH: *Le Grande-Duchesse de Gérolstein: Robinson Crusoé*. MEYERBEER: *Dinorah; Robert le Diable*. CHARPENTIER: *Louise*. AUBER: *Manon Lescaut*. BIZET: *Les Pêcheurs de Perles; Vasco de Gama*. MASSENET: *Cenrillon*. GOUNOD: *Faust; Mireille; Le Tribut de Zamora*. LECOCQ: *Le Coeur et la main*. MASSE: *Les Noces de Jeanette*.

Volume 3: 'Command Performance': WEBER: *Oberon*. MASSENET: *Le Cid*. MEYERBEER: *Dinorah; L'Étoile de Nord*. LEONCAVALLO: *Pagliacci*. VERDI: *I Masnadieri*. ROSSINI: *La cambiale di matrimonio*. BELLINI: *Beatrice di Tenda*. DONIZETTI: *La Fille du Regiment*.

OFFENBACH: *Countes d'Hoffman.* GOUNOD: *Faust.*

Volume 4: *'Rarities and surprises'*: Arias from: WAGNER: *Der fliegende Holländer; Lohengrin; Die Meistersinger; Rienzi; Tannhäuser; Tristan und Isolde; Die Walküre.* MOZART: *Le Nozze di Figaro:* arias. GLIERE: *Concerto for coloratura soprano.* STRAVINSKY: *Pastorale. Cui. Ici bas.* GRETCHANINOV: *Lullaby.*

Volume 5: *'Great Operatic Scenes'* from: MEYERBEER: *Les Huguenots.* BELLINI: *Norma.* DONIZETTI: *Lucia di Lammermoor.* VERDI: *Atilla; Ernani; I vespri siciliani; Traviata.* (B) *** Australian Decca 466 474–2 (5).

For Decca, Joan Sutherland was one of their most important recording artists, particularly during the analogue LP era. In return, often with the prompting, and careful and imaginative planning of her husband and musical partner Richard Bonynge, they provided an extraordinary wide-ranging discography over her remarkably long recording career. This bargain box from Decca's Australian branch is important for including many recordings not otherwise available on CD.

Volume 1 is a reminder of her excellent Handel performances, with the arias mainly taken from her complete opera recordings, although the ringing account of *Let the bright seraphim* is from *'The Art of the Prima Donna'*, as is the Mozart *Die Entführing* aria. The other Mozart items are from her 1979 Mozart LP: not one of her best discs, but one which Sutherland admirers will surely want.

The French arias on Volume 2 were recorded in 1968 and sound sparkingly vivid and fresh in this new transfer. This was one of her most successful and infectiously tuneful recital discs: highlights include swirling coloratura waltzes from *Robinson Crusoé* and *Mireille,* a sparkling bolero by Lecocq, and spectacular set-piece arias by Meyerbeer, Auber and Charpentier.

Volume 3, *'Command Performance'* is hardly less successful: the showy numbers of Meyerbeer, Donizetti and Offenbach display her virtuoso singing to the full, whilst her hauntingly exquisite bel canto in the Bellini item is another highlight.

Volume 4 includes her 1979 Wagner recital, and more items from the Mozart recital from the same year: this is not top-drawer Sutherland, but it is fascinating to hear (this is their CD debut); the Glière *Concerto for coloratura soprano* is quite superb.

The final volume, a collection of operatic scenes, includes the great 1959 Paris recording of the *Mad scene* from *Lucia,* as well as the arias from *Ernani* and the splendidly crisp bolera from *I vespri siciliani* from the same disc. All in all, a splendid collection of some great singing and interesting repertoire, with stylish orchestral contributions,

mainly from Richard Bonynge, and although no texts are provided, there are good sleeve notes and the set is offered at bargain price.

'Grandi voci': BELLINI: *Norma: Sediziose voci . . . Casta diva . . . Ah! bello a me ritorna. I Puritani: Qui la voce sua soave . . . Vien, diletto* (with ROHCG O, Molinari-Pradelli). VERDI: *Attila: Santo di patria . . . Allor che i forti corrono . . . Da te questo or m'è concesso* (with LSO, Bonynge); *Ernani: Surta è la notte . . . Ernani! Ernani, involami. I vespri siciliani: Mercè, dilette amiche (Boléro).* donizetti: *Lucia di Lammermoor: Ancor non giunse! . . . Regnava nel silenzio; Il dolce suono mi colpi di sua voce! . . . Ardon gl'incensi* (Mad scene). *Linda di Chamounix: Ah! tardai troppo . . . O luce di quest'anima.*
❀ (M) *** Decca 440 404-2 [id.].

Sutherland's *'Grandi voci'* disc is one of the most cherishable of all operatic recital records, bringing together the glorious, exuberant items from her very first recital disc, made within weeks of her first Covent Garden success in 1959, and – as a valuable supplement – the poised accounts of *Casta diva* and. *Vien, diletto* she recorded the following year as part of 'The Art of the prima donna'.

It was this 1959 recital which at once put Sutherland firmly on the map among the great recording artists of all time. Even she has never surpassed the freshness of these versions of the two big arias from *Lucia di Lammermoor,* sparkling in immaculate coloratura, while the lightness and point of the jaunty *Linda di Chamounix* aria and the *Boléro* from *I vespri siciliani* are just as winning. The aria from *Attila* comes from 'The age of bel canto' (1963). The sound is exceptionally vivid and immediate, though the accompaniments under Nello Santi are sometimes rough in ensemble.

'The age of bel canto' (with Marilyn Horne (mezzo-soprano), Richard Conrad (tenor), New SO of London, LSO and Chorus, Bonynge): PICCINNI: *La buona figliuola: Furia di donna irata.* HANDEL: *Atalanta: Care selve. Samson: With plaintive notes. Semele: Iris, hence away.* LAMPUGNANI: *Meraspe: Superbo di me stesso.* BONONCINI: *Astarto: Mio caro ben.* ARNE: *Artaxerxes: Oh! too lovely!* SHIELD: *Rosina: Light as thistledown; When William at eve.* MOZART: *Il rè pastore: Voi che fausti ognor donate. Die Zauberflöte: O zittre nicht. Die Entführung aus dem Serail: Ich baue ganz auf deine Stärke.* BOIELDIEU: *Angéla: Ma Fanchette est charmante.* ROSSINI: *Semiramide: Serbami ognor sì fido. Il barbiere di Siviglia: Ecco, ridente.* AUBER: *La Muette de Portici: Ferme tes yeux.* WEBER: *Der Freischütz: Und ob die Wolke sie verhülle.* BELLINI: *Beatrice di Tenda: Angiol di pace. La straniera: Un ritratto? . . . Sventurato il cor che*

fida. DONIZETTI: *Don Pasquale: Tornami a dir che m'ami. Lucrezia Borgia: Il segreto per esser felici*. VERDI: *Attila: Santo di patria . . . Allor che i forti corrono*. ARDITI: *Bolero*.
(M) *** Decca 448 594-2 (2) [id.].

For some reason this 1963 set has never been issued on CD before in its original complete form. Now it reappears in Decca's Classic Sound series. In this famous early recital Sutherland generously shared the honours with other singers who, like herself, have a deep concern for restoring the bel canto tradition. The tenor Richard Conrad sings far more tastefully than most of his tenor colleagues, with a pleasing lightness, but it is Marilyn Horne who firmly establishes her claim to stand beside Sutherland as a singer, often outshining her. It is enormously to Sutherland's credit that she welcomes such competition instead of trying to exaggerate her own merits by picking nonentities. Sutherland can easily afford such generosity, and the style of singing throughout the recital has a consistency obviously guided by Richard Bonynge. One may sometimes object to his insistence on a basically mannered style, but in this recital it is generally less obtrusive than hitherto. It is good to be reminded what a fine Mozartean Sutherland is, in the Queen of the Night's aria, and the delightful point of Shield's *Light as thistledown* is irresistible. Her *Semiramide* duet brings a performance of equal mastery. An essential set for all lovers of the art of singing. Full texts and translations are included.

'The art of the prima donna' (with ROHCG Ch. & O, Francesco Molinari-Pradelli): ARNE: *Artaxerxes: The soldier tir'd*. HANDEL: *Samson: Let the bright seraphim*. BELLINI: *Norma: Casta diva. I Puritani: Son vergin vezzosa; Qui la voce. La Sonnambula: Come per me sereno*. ROSSINI: *Semiramide: Bel raggio lusinghier*. GOUNOD: *Faust: Jewel song. Roméo et Juliette: Waltz song*. VERDI: *Otello: Willow song. Rigoletto: Caro nome. La Traviata: Ah fors' è lui; Sempre libera*. MOZART: *Die Entführung aus dem Serail: Marten aller Arten*. THOMAS: *Hamlet: Mad scene*. DELIBES: *Lakmé: Bell song*. MEYERBEER: *Les Huguenots: O beau pays*.
⚫ (M) *** Decca 452 298-2 (2) [id.].

This ambitious early two-disc recital (from 1960) has also now been reissued in Decca's Classic Sound series, for the recording on CD is amazingly full and realistic, far more believable than many new digital recordings. It remains one of Dame Joan Sutherland's outstanding gramophone achievements, and it is a matter of speculation whether even Melba or Tetrazzini in their heyday managed to provide sixteen consecutive recordings quite as dazzling as these performances. Indeed, it is the Golden Age that one naturally turns to rather than to current singers when making any comparisons.

Sutherland herself, by electing to sing each one of these fabulously difficult arias in tribute to a particular soprano of the past, from Mrs Billington in the eighteenth century, through Grisi, Malibran, Pasta and Jenny Lind in the nineteenth century, to Lilli Lehmann, Melba, Tetrazzini and Galli-Curci in this, is asking to be judged by the standards of the Golden Age.

On the basis of recorded reminders she comes out with flying colours, showing a greater consistency and certainly a wider range of sympathy than even the greatest Golden Agers possessed. The sparkle and delicacy of the *Puritani Polonaise*, the freshness and lightness of the Mad scene from Thomas's *Hamlet*, the commanding power of the *Entführung* aria and the breathtaking brilliance of the Queen's aria from *Les Huguenots* are all among the high spots here, while the arias which Sutherland later recorded in her complete opera sets regularly bring performances just as fine – and often finer – than the later versions.

'Love live forever (The Romance of musical comedy)' (with Ambrosian Light Opera Chorus, New Philharmonia Orchestra, Bonynge): Excerpts from: ROMBERG: *The Student prince; The Desert song*. RODGERS: *The Boys from Syracuse*. KERN: *Music in the air; Show Boat*. FRIML: *Rose Marie*. HERBERT: *The Only girl*. FRASER-SIMPSON: *The Maid of the Mountains*. GERMAN: *Tom Jones*. OFFENBACH: *La Périchole*. MASSENET: *Chérubin*. ZELLER: *Der Vogelhändler*. MILLOCKER: *The Dubarry*. FALL: *Die geschiedene Frau; Die spanische Nachtigall; Die Dollarprinzessin; Madame Pompadour; Die liebe Augustin*. LEHAR: *Eva; Die lustige Witwe; Paganini*. STRAUS: *Ein Walzertraum; The Chocolate soldier*. HEUBERGER: *Der Opernball*. J. STRAUSS Jr.: *Casanova*. KREISLER: *The King steps out*. POSFORD: *Balalaika*.
(B) *** Decca Double 452 955-2 (2) [id.].

Beginning with an exuberant account of the opening chorus from *The Student prince* and including a glorious performance of the title number from *The Desert song* (*Blue heaven*), this is a lilting, whooping recital to set against the superb Schwarzkopf record of operetta favourites which covers some of the same ground. Sutherland may not always match Schwarzkopf in the haunting Viennese quality which inhabits such an enchanting number as *Im chambre séparée*, but her range of repertoire here is far wider, including as it does a pair of Offenbach items, not to mention the songs from American and British musicals down to *The Boys from Syracuse*.

Above all it is the tune that counts and there are plenty of good ones, not least *Make believe* from *Show Boat* and the unforgettable *Love will find a way* from *The Maid of the Mountains*. Bonynge's sparkling selection ranges into the easily melodious world of Romberg and Friml, Fraser-Simpson and Oscar Straus, and most enterprisingly includes a pot-pourri from the German operettas of Leo Fall. What is immediately obvious is Sutherland's own delight in singing this music, with no apology whatever. Produced by Christopher Raeburn, the sumptuous Kingsway Hall recording catches the glory of Sutherland's voice (in the mid 1960s) to perfection against appropriately rich accompaniments all specially arranged by Douglas Gamley.

'Greatest hits': Excerpts from: HANDEL: *Samson.* PICCINNI: *La buona figliuola.* BELLINI: *Norma; I Puritani.* DONIZETTI: *La fille du régiment; Lucia di Lammermoor: Mad scene.* DELIBES: *Lakmé.* VERDI: *Rigoletto; La Traviata.* GOUNOD: *Faust.* OFFENBACH: *Contes d'Hoffmann.*
(M) *** Decca 458 209-2.

A 76-minute collection like this, well chosen to entertain, is self-recommending at mid-price. It has been nicely repackaged in a slip-case for this reissue in Decca's Opera Gala series, and translations are now included. The chosen recordings have been slightly amended since the previous issue but all come from the period when the voice was at its freshest: *Let the bright seraphim,* the delectable *Caro nome* and the vivacious *Jewel song* from *Faust* date from 1960, but here the justly famous 1959 Mad scene from *Lucia di Lammermoor* has been substituted for the performance in the complete set under Pritchard. The lively excerpt from *La fille du régiment* (1967) and the *Doll song* from *Contes d'Hoffmann* (1972) come from the complete sets, as does the famous Act I *La Traviata* scena (1962), which is now added. The sound is consistently vivid.

'Mad scenes' from: BELLINI: *I Puritani.* MEYERBEER: *Dinorah; L'Etoile du nord.* DONIZETTI: *Lucia di Lammermoor.* THOMAS: *Hamlet.*
(M) *** Decca 458 243–2 [id.]. Various orchestras, all cond. Bonynge.

No Sutherland 'mad scene' recital would be complete without her *Lucia* portrayal and here we have the 1971 version from the complete set. It is generally considered that her early 1959 Paris recording is her finest, but this one is equally compelling: her voice is richer, more characterful – and is better recorded and conducted. If it doesn't quite have the girlish quality which made the early one so remarkable, it makes up for it in maturity of interpretation.

The *Hamlet* scene is now a relative rarity: it is remarkably effective, with some particularly imaginative writing from Thomas: the humming chorus creates a haunting effect and the orchestration throughout is piquantly telling. As for Sutherland, it is remarkable how youthful she sounds. Considering that this digital recording was made

when she was in her fifties, her coloratura is still effortlessly beautiful.

The *Puritani* excerpt is taken from the 1973 complete recording – one of the most successful of all the Bonynge-Sutherland sets. The two Meyerbeer showpieces are as charming as they are brilliant, and complete this well-planned 'Opera Gala' compilation. Full texts and translations are included, which makes this especially recommendable among the current Sutherland single-disc anthologies.

Sutherland, Joan (soprano),
Marilyn Horne (mezzo-soprano),
Luciano Pavarotti (tenor)

'Live from the Lincoln Center, New York' (Duets and trios): VERDI: *Ernani: Solingo, errante e misero. Otello: Già nella notte densa. Il Trovatore: Madre non dormi?* BELLINI: *Norma: Adalgisa! . . . Oh! rimembranza! Ma di' . . . Oh non tremare.* PONCHIELLI: *La Gioconda: Ecco la barca . . . addio; Deh! non turbare.*
(M) *** Decca Dig. 458 207-2 [id.].

Not all gala concerts make good records, but this 1981 occasion is an exception; almost every item here puts an important gloss on the achievements of the three stars, not least in the concerted numbers which have been separated off for this single-disc reissue in Decca's Opera Gala series. It is good to have a sample not only of Sutherland's Desdemona, but also of Pavarotti's Otello (not at that time heard, either on stage or in the studio) in their account of the Act I duet. The final scene from *Il Trovatore* is more compelling here than on the complete set made by the same soloists five years earlier. At times the microphones catch a beat in the voices of both Sutherland and Horne, but not as obtrusively as on some studio discs. Lively accompaniments under Bonynge, bright, vivid, digital recording, but over-loud applause. The documentation includes full translations and a picture of the celebrated occasion.

Sutherland, Joan (soprano),
Luciano Pavarotti (tenor)

'Love duets' (with National PO, Richard Bonynge) from VERDI: *La Traviata; Otello; Aida* (with chorus). BELLINI: *La Sonnambula.* DONIZETTI: *Linda di Chamounix.*
(M) *** Decca 458 235-2 [id.].

This collection, recorded in the Kingsway Hall in 1976, offers a rare sample of Sutherland as *Aida* (*La fatale pietra . . . O terra, addio* from Act IV), a role she sang only once on stage, well before her international career began; and with this and her sensitive impersonations of Desdemona, Violetta (generously represented) and the Bellini and Donizetti heroines, Sutherland might have been expected to steal first honours here. In fact these are mainly duets to show off the tenor, and it is Pavarotti who runs away with the main glory, though both artists were plainly challenged to give their finest. The result, with excellent accompaniment, is among the most attractive and characterful duet recitals in the catalogue. The recording is admirably clear and well focused, and the sophistication of orchestral detail is striking in the *Otello* and *Aida* scenes which close the recital, with the singers given remarkable presence.

Tallis Scholars, Peter Phillips

'A Tudor collection': CORNYSH: *Salve regina; Ave Maria, mater Dei; Gaude virgo; Magnificat; Ah, Robin; Adieu, adieu, my heartes lust; Adieu, corage; Woefully arrayed; Stabat mater.* ANON..: *Westron wynde.* TAVERNER: *Western wynde Mass; Leroy kyrie; Missa gloria tibi trinitas; Dum transisset Sabbatum.* TALLIS: *If ye love me; Hear the voice and prayer; A New commandment; O Lord, give thy Holy Spirit; Purge me, O Lord; Verily, verily I say unto you; Remember not, O Lord God; Tunes for Archbishop Parker's Psalter; Out from the deep; O Lord, in thee is all my trust; Blessed are those that be undefiled; Spem in alium; Sancte Deus; Salvator mundi I & II; Gaude gloriosa; Miserere nostri; Loquebantur variis linguis.* BYRD: *Mass for five voices; Mass for four voices; Mass for three voices; Ave verum corpus; Infelix ego.*
(M) *** Gimell/Philips Dig. 454 895-2 (4).

This handsomely produced box collects together four of the CDs made by the Tallis Scholars between 1984 and 1988 when they were pioneering authentic performances of repertory which was later to be taken up by other groups. However, the excellence of their singing and the stylish expressiveness of their approach earned the group several *Gramophone* awards in the first few years of their recording career.

The nine Cornysh pieces issued here all derive from the Eton Choir Book and will surely come as a revelation to collectors unfamiliar with this period and a joy to those who are. Much of Cornysh's music has disappeared, including several Masses, and even the opening section of the *Stabat mater* lacks treble, counter-tenor and tenor parts (Peter Phillips uses Frank Lloyd Harrison's reconstruction). The music is quite unlike much other polyphony of the time and is florid, wild, complex and, at times, grave. The Tallis Scholars give magnificent, totally committed accounts of these glorious pieces – as usual their attack, ensemble and true

intonation and blend are remarkable. Excellent recording.

The Taverner six-part setting of the Mass, the *Missa gloria tibi trinitas*, is one of the great glories of Tudor music, richly varied in its invention (not least in rhythm) and expressive in a deeply personal way very rare for its period. Here it is given an intensely involving performance. Peter Phillips rejects all idea of reserve or cautiousness of expression; the result reflects the emotional basis of the inspiration the more compellingly. The motet *Dum transisset Sabbatum* is then presented more reflectively, another rich inspiration.

The Tallis disc collects the complete English anthems of the composer. Women's voices are used instead of boys', but the purity of the sound they produce is not in question, and the performances could hardly be more committed or more totally inside this repertoire. Peter Phillips is no less a master of the Byrd repertoire; undoubtedly these performances have great eloquence and variety of expression so that, when the drama is varied with a gentler mood, the contrast is the more striking. The sound made by the Scholars in Merton College Chapel is beautiful, both warm and fresh. The account of *Ave verum corpus* is movingly simple.

'Western Wind Masses': SHEPPARD: *Mass, The Western wynde.* TAVERNER: *Mass, Western Wynde.* TYE: *Mass, Western wind.*
*** Ph. Gimell Dig. 454 927-2 [id.].

It was a splendid idea for Gimell to gather together the three key Mass settings which use the well-known source theme, the *Western Wynde*. The performances are as eloquent as we would expect from this source and they are beautifully recorded. Taverner's setting emerges as the most imaginative, but Tye comes pretty close. A most enterprising issue which deserves support.

'Live in Oxford': OBRECHT: *Salve Regina.* JOSQUIN DESPREZ: *Gaude Virgo; Absalon fili mei.* TAVERNER: *Gaude plurium.* BYRD: *Tribus, Domine.* TALLIS: *O sacrum convivium.* MUNDY: *Adolescentulus sum ego; Vox Patris caelestis.*
*** Gimell/Ph. Dig. 454 998-2 [id.].

The fledgling Tallis Scholars gave their first concert, in 1973, in the Church of St Mary Magdalen, but have chosen the Chapel of Merton College for this, their twenty-fifth-anniversary programme. The beauty of its acoustic, resonant but unclouding, is ideal for their flowing style in this survey of fifteenth- and sixteenth-century masterpieces, ending with Mundy's spectacularly ambitious *Vox Patris caelestis*, with its vocal complexities confidently encompassed, especially by the soaring trebles.

'The spirit of the Renaissance': JOSQUIN DESPREZ: *Missa L'homme armé super voces musicales; Missa L'homme armé sexti toni.*

SHEPPARD: *Christe Redemptor omnium; In manus tuus I, II & III; Media vita; Regis Tharsis; Sacris solemnis; Verbum caro.* VICTORIA: *Tenebrae responsories.*

(B) **(*) Gimell/Ph. 462 846-2 (3) [id.].

This bargain box collects together in a slip case three CDs from the end of the 1980s when this fine group was earning international plaudits with almost every record they issued. Their flowing style has a special kind of serenity and this suits Josquin and Sheppard rather more than the *Tenebrae responsories* of Victoria, which call for rather more emotional surge. Each of the three discs is discussed separately in the Composer index in our main volume. The recording cannot be faulted.

'The best of the Renaissance': ALLEGRI: *Miserere.* BYRD: *Mass for five voices.* CARDOSO: *Magnificat.* DESPREZ: *Ave Maria; Missa 'Pange lingua'.* GESUALDO: *Tenebrae responsories for Holy Saturday.* LASSUS: *Osculetur me; Salve Regina.* LOBO: *Versa est in luctum.* PALESTRINA: *Missa Papae Marcelli.* TALLIS: *Spem in alium;* TAVERNER: *Dum transisset Sabbatum.*

❂ (B) *** Phil. Dig. Duo 462 862-2 (2) [id.].

This collection, recorded between 1980 and 1994 and originally released on Gimell Records, acts as a perfect summary of the Tallis Scholars' achievement. To mention just some of the highlights: Allegri's *Miserere* is given an ideal performance with the contrasting effects of the double choir, the soloists heard in the distance, stunningly conveyed – the effect is dramatic and effective. The solo treble is taken by a girl (Alison Stamp), whose contribution is superb, and this performance is justly famous.

The Tallis 40-part motet, *Spem in alium*, is no less brilliantly done: indeed, it is a thrilling performance in which the astonishingly complex polyphony is spaciously separated over a number of point sources, yet blends into a satisfying whole to reach a massive climax.

Byrd's *Mass for five voices* is a more dramatic performance than some rival versions, and the contrast between the drama and reflective passages is striking.

The *Tenebrae responsories for Holy Saturday* of Gesualdo are uncannily forward-looking: the remarkable dissonances and chromaticisms still have a sharp, refreshing impact on the modern ear, which recognizes the music leaping centuries.

The most celebrated of Palestrina's masses, the *Missa Papae Marcelli*, was recorded 'live' in Rome in 1990, and receives a perfectly judged, fluid performance in which the sense of movement never flags. Taverner's motet *Dum transisset Sabbatum*, a reflective work of rich inspiration, perfectly fits into the programme, and Cardoso's *Magnificat* makes a wonderfully rich end to a marvellous programme. The recordings are often in the demon-stration class and this is one of the great choral bargains in the catalogue.

Taverner Choir and Consort, Andrew Parrott

'The promise of ages': A Christmas collection (with members of New London Chamber Choir & Henrietta Barnett School Choir & (i) Frances Kelly, Welsh harp; (ii) Paul O'Shaughnessy, Irish fiddle): Charles BURNEY: *Hark! The herald angels sing.* arr. Edward JONES: (i) *Deck the hall.* NILES: (ii) *Lullay, thou tiny child; I wonder as I wander; Sing we the Virgin Mary.* TRAD.: *There is no rose of swych vertu; Lullay, lullow, I saw a swete semly syght; Song of the Nuns of Chester; Hayl, Mary, ful of grace; Hodie Christus natus est;* (ii) *The seven joys of Mary; Good people all, this Christmastide; Christmas eve.* HOLST: *I sing of a maiden; Jesu, thou the Virgin-born.* BRITTEN: (i) *Ceremony of carols: There is no rose; As dew in Aprille.* MAXWELL DAVIES: *O magnum mysterium; The Fader of heven.* WEIR: *Illuminare, Jerusalem.* VAUGHAN WILLIAMS: *In Bethlehem City.* MADAN: *Lo! he comes with clouds descending.*

*** Sony Dig. SK 60713 [id.].

Opening with an engagingly unfamiliar setting of *Hark! the herald angels sing* (perhaps by Charles Burney) this is an extraordinarily varied selection, ranging from very early carols and chants to striking modern settings from Holst, Britten, Maxwell Davies and Judith Weir. Further diversity is provided by delicate solo peformances on the Welsh harp (*Deck the hall*) and traditional Irish fiddle solos (*Good people all, this Chrismastide*). Indeed, this beautifully played, sung and recorded programme offers much pleasure from its very range and un-expected juxtapositions.

Many of the items are given as solos, while *There is no rose* is presented very touchingly as a vocal trio. Among the modern settings, *The Fader of heven* and *Illuminare, Jerusalem* stand out as haunt-ingly individual, but then so do the simpler medieval carols. The presentation in the resonant acoustic of St Jude-on-the-Hill, Hampstead Garden Suburb, could not be more evocative. Altogether this is a Christmas Eve entertainment of distinction, and it will give great pleasure.

Taverner Consort, Choir and Players, Andrew Parrott

'The Christmas Album' (Festive music from Europe and America): BILLINGS: *Methinks I see an heav'nly host; A virgin unspotted.* FOSTER: *While shepherds watched their flocks.* CEREROLS: *Serafin, quin con dulce harmonia.* Francisco de

VIDALES: *Los que fueren de buen gusto.*
PRAETORIUS: *Magnificat super Angelus ad pastores.* Marc-Antoine CHARPENTIER: *In nativitatem Domini nostri Jesu Christi canticum.* PASCHA: *Gloria.* arr. GREATOREX: *Adeste fidelis.*
(M) *** Virgin Veritas/EMI Dig. VC5 45155-2.

Another refreshing Christmas collection which treads much unfamiliar territory. Opening and closing with jolly carols that sound almost like rustic drinking songs, from the New England composer William Billings – with the chorus giving their pronunciation an appropriate transatlantic twang – the concert moves from a bright baroque setting of *While shepherds watched their flocks,* a new tune, with Bachian trumpets, by John Foster (1762–1822) to a haunting *Gloria* by Edmund Pascha. This represents Slovakia; from France there is a charming Christmas sequence by Marc-Antoine Charpentier.

In between comes a gloriously sonorous *Magnificat* by Michael Praetorius and, at last something familiar, *Adeste fidelis,* arranged by Thomas Greatorex in a choral concerto grosso style. Best of all are the *Villancicos,* one by Joan Cererols from Catalonia, one even jollier by the seventeenth-century Mexican Francisco de Vidales, which in their colour and vitality reflect the popular dance music of the time. Performances are as lively as they are stylish and the soloists are excellent. The 1991 recording, made at St John's at Hackney, London, has plenty of atmosphere and presence.

Tear, Robert (tenor)

'English baroque recital' (with Iona Brown, violin, Kenneth Heath, cello, Simon Preston and Colin Tilney, harpsichord continuo, ASMF, Marriner): HANDEL: *Look down, harmonious Saint; Meine Seele hört im Sehen; Süsse Stille.* ARNE: *Bacchus and Ariadne:* excerpts; *Fair Caelia love pretended:* excerpts. BOYCE: *Song of Momus to Mars.* James HOOK: *The Lass of Richmond Hill.*
(B) *** Decca Double 452 973-2 (2) [id.] (with HANDEL: *Acis and Galatea ***).

Robert Tear's 1969 recital offers a rare Handel cantata and two of his German songs, followed by an even rarer and certainly delightful collection of music by his English successors. This may in essence be a scholarly compilation, but it is one which imparts its learning in the most painless way, including as it does the vigorous Boyce song and the original, bouncing setting of *The Lass of Richmond Hill,* beautifully pointed. The *harmonious Saint* of the Handel cantata is of course St Cecilia, while Arne too is in Italianate mood in *Bacchus and Ariadne* – until he ends with a galumphing final number with ripe horn parts – very English. Robert

Tear is in excellent voice and the recording has all the atmospheric warmth one associates with Argo's recordings of the ASMF in St John's, Smith Square.

Tebaldi, Renata (soprano)

'Grandi voci': Arias and excerpts from: PUCCINI: *Madama Butterfly; La Bohème* (with Carlo Bergonzi); *Turandot* (with Mario del Monaco); *Tosca; Gianni Schicchi; Suor Angelica; La Fanciulla del West* (with Cornell MacNeil); *Manon Lescaut.* VERDI: *Aida; Otello* (with Luisa Ribacci); *La forza del destino.* CILEA: *Adriana Lecouvreur.* GIORDANO: *Andrea Chénier.* BOITO: *Mefistofele.* CATALANI: *La Wally.*
(M) *** Decca (IMS) 440 408-2 [id.].

Those wanting a single-disc, stereo representation of Tebaldi's vocal art could hardly do better than this. It is good that her early mono complete sets of *La Bohème* and *Madama Butterfly* are now again available, and the selection here rightly concentrates on her stereo remakes of the key Puccini operas in the late 1950s, when the voice was still creamily fresh. *Vissi d'arte* (1959) is particularly beautiful. She could be thrilling in Verdi too, as the splendid *Ritorna vincitor!* vibrantly demonstrates, taken from Karajan's complete *Aida,* made in the same year. With a playing time of 75 minutes, this recital should disappoint no one, for the Decca recordings come up as vividly as ever.

'A Tebaldi festival' (with (i) New Philh. O, cond. (ii) Anton Guadagno, or (iii) Richard Bonynge; (iv) Monte Carlo Op. O, Fausto Cleva): (i; ii) WAGNER: *Tannhäuser: Salve d'amor, recinto eletto! (Dich teure Halle); Elisabeth's prayer. Lohengrin: Elsa's dream. Tristan und Isolde: Liebestod.* BIZET: *Carmen: Habanera* (with Ambrosian Ch.)*; Card scene* (all sung in Italian). SAINT-SAENS: *Samson et Dalila: Amor! i mieie fini proteggi (Amor, viens m'aider); S'apre per te il mio cor (Mon coeur s'ouvre à ta voix).* MASSENET: *Manon: Addio, o nostro piccolo desco (Adieu, notre petite table); La tua non è mano che mi tocca? (N'est-ce plus ma main?).* (i; iii) VERDI: *Aida: Ritorna vincitor!* PUCCINI: *La Bohème: Musetta's waltz song.* (iv) BELLINI: *Norma: Sediziose voci . . . Casta diva* (with Alfredo Mariotti & Turin Ch.). *I Puritani: Qui la voce . . . Vien, diletto. La Sonnambula: Ah! non credea mirarti.* VERDI: *Nabucco: Ben io t'invenni . . . Salgo già del trono. Don Carlos: O don fatale.* Songs: ROSSINI: *Péchés de vieillesse: La regata veneziana (3 songs in Venetian dialect).* LARA: *Granada.* PONCE: *Estrellita.* CARDILLO: *Catari, Catari.* TOSTI: *'A vucchella.* DE CURTIS: *Non ti scordar di me.* RODGERS: *Carousel: If I loved you.*
(M) **(*) Decca (IMS) 452 456-2 (2) [id.].

What, Wagner in Italian! Tebaldi, for so long a

favourite diva, could apparently get away with almost anything during her vintage years with Decca, here displayed in a collection which ranges into unexpected corners. She amply justifies her choice of language in the rich lyricism of her Wagner, and it is good to hear such a ravishing account of *Musetta's waltz song*, a role she never assumed in the opera house. *Ritorna vincitor!*, too, is unforgettable, both commanding and richly secure – finer than her performance in her complete stereo set (under Karajan).

Plainly she has also chosen many of the other items out of sheer affection – the little songs of Lara, Ponce and Tosti – although the dialect songs of Rossini suit her less well. In those lighter items Douglas Gamley's lush arrangements and Bonynge's indulgent accompaniments add to the glamour of the presentation in the warm acoustics of Kingsway Hall. Though all this opening group was recorded as recently as 1969, the voice was still in fine condition, and anyone who has ever responded to the ripe, rich tone of this generous artist should revel in the sweetmeats presented here, not least the lovely melody from Rodgers's *Carousel*.

The closing group of Bellini and Verdi excerpts dates from the previous year and was produced by Christopher Raeburn in Monte Carlo. These items have never been issued before and presumably were not passed by Tebaldi herself. Although the two Verdi excerpts (from *Nabucco* and *Don Carlos*) are thrillingly dramatic and in Bellini the singing brings some glorious legato, cabalettas have moments of wildness and intonation is not always secure. Indeed, *Ah! non credea mirarti* should not have been issued, for it does the singer no justice. However, for the most part this is an endearing recital, and she is given consistently supportive accompaniments, while the voice never loses its bloom.

Songs and arias (with Giorgio Favaretto, piano): Recital I: Songs: ANON..: *Leggiadri occhi bello.* A. SCARLATTI: *Le violette.* ROSSINI: *Soirées musicales: La promessa.* BELLINI: *Dolente immagine di fille mia; Vanne, o rosa Fortunata.* MARTUCCI: *La canzone dei recordi (Al folto bosco; Cavanta il ruscello; Sul mar la navicella).* TRAD.., arr. FAVARA: *A la barcillunisa.* MASETTI: *Passo e non ti vedo.* TURINA: *Poema en forma de canciones: Cantares.* Arias: HANDEL: *Giulio Cesare: Piangerò la sorte mia.* SARTI: *Giulio Sabino: Lungi dal caro bene.*

Recital II: Songs: A. SCARLATTI: *Chi vuole innamorarsi.* ROSSINI: *Péchés de vieillesse: 3 Songs in Venetian dialect (Anzoleta avanti La Regata; Anzoleta co passa la Regata; Anzoleta dopo la Regata).* BELLINI: *Vaga luna che inargenti; Per pietà, bell'idol mio.* MASCAGNI: *M'ama . . . non m'ama.* RESPIGHI: *Notte.* TOSTI: *'A vucchella.* DAVICO: *O luna che fa lum.* Arias:

A. SCARLATTI: *Il Seddecia, Re di Gerusalemme: Caldo sangue.* HANDEL: *Amadigi di Gaula: Ah! spietato.* MOZART: *Ridente la calma, K.152; Un moto di gioia, K.579.*
(B) ** Decca Double 452 472-2 (2) [(M) id. import].

Here combined on a Decca Double are a pair of song recitals which Tebaldi recorded fairly early in her career, in 1956 and 1957 respectively, and which have been out of the catalogue for forty years, although four items – by Scarlatti, Rossini, Mozart and the charming Favara folksong arrangement – were put out on a stereo '45' disc at the beginning of the 1960s. The voice sounds young and fresh but, like many another Italian opera singer, Tebaldi proved hardly a stylist in eighteenth-century music, and the lighter songs do not always suit her big voice.

But when she comes to the arias it is a different matter. Cleopatra's lament from the third Act of Handel's *Giulio Cesare* brings a natural, flowing legato, and Sarti's *Lungi dal caro bene* is gently ravishing. The two Bellini ariettas are also appealingly sung, and Verdi's *Stornella* makes a lighthearted contrast, while the three excerpts from Martucci's seven-part mini-cycle about another forsaken maiden, sadly and affectionately remembering past times with her lover, produces a charming and touching response. The following Sicilian folksong, *A la barcillunisa*, soars like a Puccini aria, and the first disc ends seductively with Turina's *Cantares*.

The second recital opens with a vivacious canzonetta, nicely articulated, warning of the dangers of falling in love, and the following Scarlatti and Handel arias do not disappoint. Tebaldi obviously had a soft spot for Rossini's songs in Venetian dialect (which come from his 'Sins of my old age') and she sings them with a lighter touch here than in her later recording (see above).

Tebaldi's Mozart singing is freely peppered with intrusive aitches and occasional swerves, but she is back on form in the two Bellini songs and, after a rich-voiced if a very operatic version of Respighi's *Notte*, she finishes in lighter vein with a lilting Tosti favourite – another song she included in her later recital – and a meltingly affectionate account of a colloquial Tuscan song, arranged by Vincenzo Davico. Throughout, Giorgio Favaretto accompanies quite supportively, if without producing a distinctive personality, but the recording balance does not flatter him and the piano sounds rather withdrawn at times.

Terfel, Bryn (bass-baritone), Malcolm Martineau (piano)

'The vagabond and other English songs':
VAUGHAN WILLIAMS: Songs of travel (The vagabond; Let beauty awake; The roadside fire; Youth and love; In dreams; The infinite shining heavens; Whither must I wander; Bright in the ring of words; I have trod the upward and the downward slope). G. BUTTERWORTH: Bredon hill (Bredon hill; Oh fair enough; When the lad for longing sighs; On the idle hill of summer; With rue my heart is laden); The Shropshire lad (6 songs): Loveliest of trees; When I was one-and-twenty; Look not in my eyes; Think no more, lad; The lads in their hundreds; Is my team ploughing? FINZI: Let us garlands bring (Come away, death; Who is Silvia?; Fear no more the heat of the sun; O mistress mine; It was a lover and his lass). IRELAND: Sea fever; The vagabond; The bells of San Marie.

❀ *** DG Dig. 445 946-2 [id.].

No other collection of English songs has ever quite matched this one in its depth, intensity and sheer beauty. Terfel, the great Welsh singer of his generation, here shows his deep affinity with the English repertory, demonstrating triumphantly in each of the twenty-eight songs that this neglected genre deserves to be treated in terms similar to those of the German Lied and the French mélodie. The Vaughan Williams songs are perhaps the best known, nine sharply characterized settings of Robert Louis Stevenson which, thanks to Terfel's searching expressiveness matched by Martineau's inspired accompaniments, reveal depths of emotion hardly suspected.

The five Shakespeare settings by Finzi are just as memorable in their contrasted ways, five of the best-known lyrics from the plays that have been set countless times but which here are given new perspectives, thanks both to the composer and to the singer. The eleven Butterworth settings of Housman are among the finest inspirations of this short-lived composer, and it is good to have three sterling Ireland settings of Masefield, including the ever-popular Sea fever, which with Terfel emerges fresh and new. The singer's extreme range of tone and dynamic, down to the most delicate, firmly supported half-tones, is astonishing, adding intensity to one of the most felicitous song-recital records in years. The warm acoustic of the Henry Wood Hall gives a glow both to the voice and to the piano.

'Impressions' (with (i) E. Bar. Soloists, Gardiner; (ii) Malcolm Martineau, piano; (iii) Philh. O, Sinopoli; (iv) BPO, Abbado: (i) MOZART: Le nozze di Figaro: Se vuol ballare; Non più andrai; Aprite un po' quegli occhi. (ii) SCHUBERT: Litanei auf das Fest Allerseelen; Die Forelle; An die Musik; Erlkönig. (iii) MAHLER: Kindertotenlieder. (ii) VAUGHAN WILLIAMS: The vagabond; The roadside fire. (iv) WAGNER: Die Meistersinger: Wie duftet doch der Flieder. Tannhäuser: O! du mein holder Abendstern.

*** DG Dig. 449 190-2 [id.].

Ranging over the recordings made for DG up to his English song disc, this sampler gives a formidable idea of this brilliant young singer's powers, very well chosen not just from his solo discs but from complete opera sets and discs with orchestra.

'A night at the opera: Disc 1: Operatic arias (with Metropolitan Opera Orchestra, James Levine) from: MOZART: Le nozze di Figaro; Così fan tutte; Don Giovanni; Die Zauberflöte. WAGNER: Tannhäuser; Der fleigende Holländer. OFFENBACH: Contes d'Hoffmann. GOUNOD: Faust. BORODIN: Prince Igor. DONIZETTI: Don Pasquale. ROSSINI: La Cenerentola. VERDI: Macbeth; Falstaff.

Disc 2: Arias from: Handel (with Scottish Chamber Orchestra, Mackerras): Acis and Galatea; Alcina; Alexander's feast; Berenice; Dettingden Te Deum; Giulio Cesare; Judas Maccabaeus; Messiah; Orlando; Samson; Semele; Serse.

(M) *** DG Dig. 467 092–2 (2) [id.].

This two-disc compilation brings together without amendment Bryn Terfel's two impressive recital discs: the first of opera, from Mozart and Donizetti to Wagner, Verdi and Borodin, recorded in New York with James Levine conducting, and the second devoted to Handel, thirty-four arias in all. The miscellaneous recital, keenly enjoyable, offers, in Terfel's own words, 'a future diary of my opera plans' and demonstrates not just the warmth and musical imagination of this brilliant singer, but his range and power too.

The account of Non più andrai is weightier, maginally broader and even more characterful than the one he recorded as part of John Eliot Gardiner's complete set and that is typical of his development. Though Mozart is central to his repertory, it is striking that the most thrilling items of all are those which test him most severely, such as Igor's aria from Borodin's Prince Igor and the Dutchman's monologue. The Falstaff excerpt from Act I of Verdi's comic masterpiece similarly find him presenting a larger-than-life portrait with no holds barred over the widest dynamic range.

The Handel collection makes no distinction between those arias for oratorio or opera, both equally dramatic, particularly as Terfel interprets them. The range of expression is wide, with Terfel using a beautiful head-voice for such favourite lyrical arias as Ombra mai fù and Where'er you walk, both hushed and poised. More typical is his fire-snorting manner in such powerful arias as Revenge,

Timotheus cries from *Judas Maccabaeus*, and the three arias from *Messiah*, which with Terfel sound fresh and new. This is singing that is not just strong, varied and imaginative, but consistently beautiful too.

Vasari Singers, Jeremy Backhouse

'*Twentieth-century choral music*': PART: *Summa; The Beatitudes* (with John Keys, organ); 7 *Magnificat antiphons.* TAVERNER: *The Lamb; Funeral ikos; 2 Hymns to the Mother of God. Collegium Regale: Magnificat & Nunc dimittis.* RIDOUT: *Litany* (with Andrew Angus, bass). GORECKI: *Totus tuus.*

(B) *** CfP Dig. CD-CFP 6076 [(M) id. import].

This splendidly sung concert makes an ideal introduction to the admirable twentieth-century school of choral music, written by a group of composers who have not only returned to melody and tonality but have all linked their inspiration to the great ecclesiastical choral traditions of the past.

What is so readily demonstrated here is the musical common ground shared by all this vocal repertoire (written between 1977 and 1991). Here serenity and beauty are joined with lavishly blending sonorities and telling use of dynamic contrast. The Estonian composer Arvo Pärt's *Summa* (a fresh and carol-like setting of the Creed) is followed by John Taverner's justly famous and haunting carol, *The Lamb*, which Jeremy Backhouse enhances with an effective ritardando at the end of each verse. The music's serenity is interrupted by stabs of dissonance, a device Pärt uses even more readily in his set of *Beatitudes*, which ends dramatically with a powerful organ epilogue (John Keys).

Similarly, the melancholy simplicity of Taverner's *Funeral ikos* links to Alan Ridout's *Litany*, where a solo cantor alternates with bursts of richly harmonized choral tone. The ethereality of Taverner's two *Hymns to the Mother of God* then leads naturally into Pärt's brief but concentrated *Magnificat antiphons*, with the seventh the longest and most telling. Taverner's *Magnificat* not only brings an exotic oriental influence, but its rocking momentum makes a striking foil for the following more tranquil *Nunc dimittis.*

Finally, Górecki's exultant *Totus tuus*, written to celebrate the visit of Pope John Paul II to Poland in 1987, ends the programme with an exultant feeling, with the diminuendo on the repeated word *Maria* at the close of the piece wonderfully poignant. Indeed, the performances here of what is consistently inspired music could surely not be bettered, nor could the recording, atmospheric yet clear, made in the Church of St Giles, Cripplegate, London, in 1995, and superbly balanced by Mike Clements.

Von Otter, Anne Sofie (soprano)

'*Wings in the night*' (Swedish songs; with Bengt Forsberg, piano): PETERSON-BERGER: *Aspåkers-polska (Aspåker's polka); Aterkomst (Return); Böljeby-vals (Böljeby waltz); Like the stars in the sky (Som stjärnorna på himmeln); Marits visor (3 songs, Op. 12); Nothing is like the time of waiting (Intet är som väntanstider); When I walk by myself (När jag går för mig själv).* SJOGREN: *6 Songs from Julius Wolff's Tannhäuser.* Sigurd von KOCH: *In the month of Tjaitra (I månaden Tjaitra); Of lotus scent and moonshine (Af Lotusdoft och månens sken); The wild swans (De vilda svanarna) (3 songs).* STENHAMMAR: *Miss Blond and Miss Brunette (Jungfru blond och jungfru brunett); In the maple's shade (I lönnens skymning); Jutta comes to the Volkungs (Jutta kommer till Folkungarna); A seaside song (En strandvisa); A ship is sailing (Det far ett skepp); The wanderer (Vandraren).* RANGSTROM: *The farewell (Afskedet); Old Swedish (Gammalsvenskt); Melodi; Pan; Supplication to night (Bön till natten); Wings in the night (Vingar i natten).* ALFVEN: *The forest is asleep (Skogen sover); I kiss your white hand (Jag kysser din vita hand).*

⊙ *** DG Dig. 449 189-2 [id.].

So often Swedish singers, once they have made a name for themselves in the world, neglect their native repertoire in favour of Schumann, Brahms, Strauss and Wolf. Anne Sofie von Otter is an exception and, fresh from her recent successes in Scandinavian repertoire, above all her Grieg *Haugtussa* and her Sibelius recitals on BIS, she gives us a splendid anthology of Swedish songs. The disc takes its name from one of Ture Rangström's most haunting songs, *Vingar i natten* (*Wings in the night*), and, indeed, his are some of the loveliest songs in the Swedish *romans* repertoire. (*Romans* is the Nordic equivalent of *Lied*.) *Bön till natten* (*Supplication to the night*) is arguably the most beautiful of all Swedish songs and has the innocence and freshness of Grieg combined with a melancholy and purity that are totally individual.

Von Otter also includes songs by the composer-critic Wilhelm Peterson-Berger, whose criticism was much admired in his native Sweden and who was compared with Bernard Shaw (he is in fact an opinionated windbag) and whose songs have a certain wistful charm. The Stenhammar songs are among his finest, and von Otter adds some familiar Alfvén and less familiar repertoire by Emil Sjögren and Sigurd (not to be confused with Erland) von Koch. A disc to be treasured.

Vyvyan, Jennifer (soprano), Norma Procter (contralto)

'Songs of England': Jennifer Vyvyan (with Ernest Lush, piano): ANON., arr. DOLMETSCH: *Lye still my deare.* PURCELL: *Nymphs and shepherds; Fairest isle.* MORLEY: *Now is the month of Maying.* arr. VAUGHAN WILLIAMS: *I will give my love an apple.* ARNE: *Where the bee sucks; O ravishing delight.* arr. WHITTAKER: *Bobby Shaftoe.* arr. LEHMANN: *Cherry ripe.* arr. GRAINGER: *The sprig o'thyme.* arr. BRITTEN: *Sweet Polly Oliver.* HEAD: *Foxgloves.* HOWELLS: *Gavotte.* VAUGHAN WILLIAMS: *The new ghost.* HOPKINS: *Melancholy song.* QUILTER: *Love's philosophy.* Norma Procter (with Alec Redshaw, piano): TRAD.: *Lord Rendell; Soldier, soldier.* arr. SHARP: *I'm seventeen come Sunday; O no John!* arr. HUGHES: *How deep in love am I.* arr. BENJAMIN: *Jan.* arr. TAYLOR: *O can ye sew cushions?*

(BB) *** Belart 46 625-2 [id.].

Jennifer Vyvyan and Norma Procter were among the distinguished soloists in Boult's much admired mid 1950s Decca *Messiah* (see above), and here they delight us with a most attractive and wide-ranging collection of English songs. Both singers have a natural feeling for the folk material, and the recital opens with Vyvyan's glorious performance of the melancholy *Lye still my deare. Now is the month of Maying, I will give my love an apple* and *The sprig o'thyme* are equally lovely, while the livelier numbers, sung with superb diction, *Bobby Shaftoe* and Britten's arrangement of *Sweet Polly Oliver* are just as winning. Purcell's *Fairest isle* and Arne's *O ravishing delight* are well described by the latter title. Other highlights include Vaughan Williams's haunting *New ghost* and Quilter's lightly lilting *Love's philosophy.* When the rich-voiced Norma Procter takes over with *Lord Rendell*, the engaging *I'm seventeen come Sunday*, the emphatic *O no John!* and the superb *Soldier, soldier*, one thinks readily of Kathleen Ferrier's comparable affinity with this repertoire and there can be no higher praise. Benjamin's arrangement of *Jan* is very touching as is the closing *O can ye sew cushions?* The recording gives both singers splendid presence, but curiously the CD transfer of the earlier (1958) Procter sessions brings a slight loss of focus at times, and a hint of distortion. Never mind, this is still a delightful collection, and for once no texts are needed, for every word is clear. The piano accompaniments by Ernest Lush and Alec Redshaw are admirable.

Walker, Norman (bass)

'A portrait of Norman Walker': HANDEL: *Acis and Galatea: I rage, I melt, I burn . . . O ruddier than the cherry. Judas Maccabaeus: I feel the deity within . . . Arm, arm ye brave. Messiah: Why do the nations; The trumpet shall sound.* HAYDN: *The Creation: And God said; Now heav'n in fullest glory.* ELGAR: *Dream of Gerontius: Jesu by that shuddering dread.* HOLBROOKE: *Dylan: Sea King's song. The Children of Don: Noden's song.* GOUNOD: *Faust: Then leave her* (final trio; with Joan Cross, Webster Booth). MARCELLO: *Le quattro Stagioni: Dalle cime del'Api . . . Venti olà.* LANDI: *La morte d'Orfeo: Bevi, bevi.* PURCELL: *What can be done* (trio; with Alfred Deller, Richard Lewis). STORACE: *The pretty creature.* LANE WILSON: *False Phyllis.* HAYNES: *Off to Philadelphia.* CAPEL: *Love could I only tell thee!* MOZART: *The Magic Flute: O Isis and Osiris. The Abduction from the Seraglio: Ah, my pretty brace of fellows.*

✪ (M) (***) Dutton mono CDLX 7021 [id. full price].

Born in 1907, Norman Walker was by training one of the last of the great pre-war British basses, but his sense of style, his clean focus and his technical finesse gave him in many ways a linking role, ushering in a new generation of British singers. This splendid compilation, prepared in collaboration with Walker's record-archivist son, Malcolm, gives a vivid idea of a singer whose career was sadly cut short when he was still in his forties.

The earliest recording, never previously published, is of *O Isis and Osiris* from *The Magic Flute*, made when he was only twenty-one, with the voice already fully formed, but in an old-fashioned, rallentando style. Three of the recordings date from the 1930s – two excerpts from rare Holbrooke operas and the glorious *Trio* from Gounod's *Faust* with Joan Cross and Webster Booth – but most are from the early post-war period, when Walker contributed to such classic recordings as Sargent's pioneering version of Elgar's *Dream of Gerontius* (thrillingly represented here in one of the most vivid transfers) and both of his *Messiah* recordings, as well as the HMV 'History of Music in Sound'.

Full and dark as the voice is, Walker's agility in ornaments and rapid divisions is phenomenal, not least in another previously unpublished recording, a witty account of Osmin's aria from *The Seraglio*, done in English with Gerald Moore accompanying. What is remarkable is not only the charisma and vocal richness but also the clarity of the diction. The splendid Dutton transfers are among their finest yet, with plenty of body in the sound and the voice often given an extraordinarily real presence.

Walker, Sarah (mezzo-soprano)

'Blah, blah, blah' (with Roger Vignoles, piano, in cabaret at the Wigmore Hall): GERSHWIN: *Blah, blah, blah; They all laughed; Three times a day; Boy, what love has done to me.* PORTER: *Tale of the oyster; Where O where?.* BERNSTEIN: *Who am I?* NICHOLAS: *Place settings; Usherette's blues.* DRING: *Song of a nightclub proprietress.* BOLCOM: *Lime jello, marshmallow, cottage-cheese surprise.* FLANDERS AND SWANN: *A word on my ear.* LEHMANN: *There are fairies at the bottom of my garden.* WRIGHT: *Transatlantic lullaby.* BAKER: *Someone is sending me flowers.* SCHOENBERG: *3 Brettl Lieder.*
*** Hyp. Dig. CDA 66289 [id.].

Recorded live at the Wigmore Hall in London, Sarah Walker's recital of trifles is one of the happiest records you could wish to find, as well as one of the funniest. Her comic timing is masterly in such delectable revue numbers as Cole Porter's *Tale of the oyster* or William Bolcom's culinary patter-song, *Lime jello, marshmallow, cottage-cheese surprise.* Perhaps surprisingly, she does such a song as *There are fairies at the bottom of my garden* straight, restoring its touching quality in defiance of Beatrice Lillie's classic send-up.

Also, by treating a popular number such as *Transatlantic lullaby* as a serious song, she not only underlines purely musical qualities but touches a deeper vein than one might expect in a cabaret sequence. Three of Schoenberg's *Brettl Lieder*, in deft English translations by Michael Irwin, are sung just as delightfully – and more provocatively than the German versions which were recorded by Jill Gomez in her delectable 'Cabaret classics' recital.

The title, *Blah, blah, blah*, comes from the opening number, a witty concoction by George Gershwin with words by his brother, Ira, which reduces the popular love-song lyrics to the necessary – and predictable – rhymes. Roger Vignoles, always an understanding accompanist, here excels himself with playing of flair and brilliance, exuberantly encompassing every popular idiom in turn. The recording, unlike most made at the Wigmore Hall, captures some of the bloom of its acoustic; but that means that the voice is set slightly at a distance. Texts are provided but, with such clear diction from the singer, they are needed only occasionally.

Walker, Sarah (mezzo-soprano), Thomas Allen (baritone)

'Dreams and fancies' (Favourite English songs) with Roger Vignoles, piano: IRELAND: *If there were dreams to sell.* DELIUS: *Twilight fancies.* ARMSTRONG GIBBS: *Silver; Five eyes.* VAUGHAN WILLIAMS: *Silent noon; The water mill.* WARLOCK: *The fox; Jillian of Berry; The first mercy; The night.* SULLIVAN: *Orpheus with his lute.* HOWELLS: *King David; Gavotte; Come sing and dance; The little road to Bethlehem.* STANFORD: *The monkey's carol.* BRIDGE: *Isobel.* CLARKE: *The seal man; The aspidistra.* HAVELOCK NELSON: *Dirty work.* HOIBY: *Jabberwocky.* QUILTER: *Now sleeps the crimson petal.* GURNEY: *Sleep.* DUNHILL: *The cloths of heaven.*
(M)*** CRD Dig. CRD 3473 [id.].

A well-designed and delightful programme, and it is good to see the Roger Quilter favourite *Now sleeps the crimson petal* back in favour, alongside both the familiar and unfamilar items included here. Dunhill's *The cloths of heaven*, too, leaves the listener wanting more. The secret of a miscellaneous (72 minutes) recital like this is for each song to lead naturally into the next, and that is what happens here, while the listener relaxes and enjoys each contrasted setting as it Flows by. Sarah Walker is in inspired form and is very well accompanied.

'The Sea' (with Roger Vignoles, piano): IRELAND: *Sea fever.* HAYDN: *Mermaid's song; Sailor's song.* DIBDIN: *Tom Bowling.* WALTON: *Song for the Lord Mayor's table; Wapping Old Stairs.* WOLF: *Seemanns Abschied.* FAURE: *Les Berceaux; Au cimetière; L'horizon chimérique.* SCHUBERT: *Lied eines Schiffers an die Dioskuren.* BORODIN: *The Sea; The Sea Princess.* DEBUSSY: *Proses lyriques: De grêve.* IVES: *Swimmers.* SCHUMANN: *Die Meersee.* BERLIOZ: *Les nuits d'été: L'île inconnue.* MENDELSSOHN: *Wasserfahrt.* BRAHMS: *Die Meere.* TRAD., arr. Vignoles: *The Mermaid.* arr. BRITTEN: *Sail on, sail on.*
✪ *** Hyperion CDA 66165 [id.].

With Roger Vignoles as master of ceremonies in a brilliantly devised programme, ranging wide, this twin-headed recital celebrating 'The Sea' is a delight from beginning to end. Two outstandingly characterful singers are mutually challenged to their very finest form, whether in solo songs or duets. As sample, try the setting of the sea-song *The Mermaid*, brilliantly arranged by Vignoles, with hilarious key-switches on the comic quotations from *Rule, Britannia*. Excellent recording.

Wedding music

'The world of wedding music': WAGNER: *Lohengrin: Wedding march.* BACH: *Suite No. 3: Air* (Stephen Cleobury). CLARKE: *Prince of Denmark's march (Trumpet voluntary).* PURCELL: *Trumpet tune* (Simon Preston). BACHGOUNOD: *Ave Maria* (Kiri Te Kanawa). SCHUBERT: *Ave Maria.* MOZART: *Alleluja* (Leontyne Price). *Vespers: Laudate dominum* (Felicity Palmer).

KARG-ELERT: *Marche triomphale: Nun danket alle Gott.* BRAHMS: *Chorale prelude: Es ist ein Ros entsprungen.* WIDOR: *Symphony No. 5: Toccata.* MENDELSSOHN: *Midsummer Night's Dream: Wedding march* (Peter Hurford). WALFORD DAVIES: *God be in my head.* Hymn: *The Lord's my shepherd* (Huddersfield Choral Soc., Morris). STAINER: *Love divine.* Hymn: *Praise my soul, the King of heaven* (King's College Ch., Cleobury). bach: *Cantata No. 147: Jesu, joy of man's desiring.* Hymn: *Lead us, Heavenly Father, lead us* (St John's College Ch., Guest). HANDEL: *Samson: Let the bright seraphim* (Joan Sutherland).
(B) ** Decca 436 402-2 [(M) id. import].

An inexpensive present for any bride-to-be, with many traditional suggestions, well played and sung, though it would have been better to have omitted the Karg-Elert *Marche-triomphale* in favour of Handel's *Arrival of the Queen of Sheba,* to which many a contemporary bride trips down the aisle. Good sound.

Westminster Cathedral Choir, David Hill

'Treasures of the Spanish Renaissance': GUERRERO: *Surge propera amica mea; O altitudo divitiarum; O Domine Jesu Christe; O sacrum convivium; Ave, Virgo sanctissima; Regina coeli laetare.* LOBO: *Versa est in luctum; Ave Maria; O quam suavis es, Domine.* VIVANCO: *Magnificat octavi toni.*
*** Hyperion CDA 66168 [id.].

This immensely valuable collection reminds us vividly that Tomás Luis de Victoria was not the only master of church music in Renaissance Spain. Francisco Guerrero is generously represented here, and the spacious serenity of his polyphonic writing (for four, six and, in *Regina coeli laetare,* eight parts) creates the most beautiful sounds. A criticism might be made that tempi throughout this collection, which also includes fine music by Alonso Lobo and a superb eight-part *Magnificat* by Sebastian de Vivanco, are too measured, but the tension is held well, and David Hill is obviously concerned to convey the breadth of the writing. The singing is gloriously firm, with the long melismatic lines admirably controlled. Discreet accompaniments (using Renaissance double harp, bass dulcian and organ) do not affect the essentially a cappella nature of the performances. The Westminster Cathedral acoustic means the choral tone is richly upholstered, but the focus is always firm and clear.

Westminster Cathedral Choir, James O'Donnell

'Masterpieces of Mexican polyphony': FRANCO: *Salve regina.* PADILLA: *Deus in adiutorium; Mirabilia testimonium; Lamentation for Maundy Thursday; Salve Regina.* CAPILLAS: *Dis nobis, Maria; Magnificat.* SALAZAR: *O sacrum convivium.*
*** Hyperion Dig. CDA 66330 [id.].

The Westminster Choir under James O'Donnell are finding their way into hitherto unexplored Latin vocal repertoire – and what vocal impact it has! These musicians were employed in the new cathedrals when Spain colonized Mexico; only Capillas was native-born (though of Spanish descent). Padilla shows he had brought over a powerful Renaissance inheritance with him and uses double choir interplay to spectacularly resonant effect. Not all the other music is as ambitious as this, but there is a devotional concentration of feeling which illuminates even the simpler settings. The singing has the body and fervour this music needs, and the choir is splendidly recorded.

'Masterpieces of Portuguese polyphony': CARDOSO: *Lamentations for Maundy Thursday; Non mortui; Sitvit anima mea; Mulier quae erat; Tulerunt lapides; Nos autem gloriosi.* REBELO: *Panis angelicus.* DE CRISTO: *3 Christmas responsories; Magnificat a 8; Ave Maria a 8; Alma redemptoris mater; Ave maris stella; O crux venerabilis; Sanctissima quinque martires; Lachrimans sitivit; De profundis.*
*** Hyperion Dig. CDA 66512 [id.].

With the help of the Tallis Scholars we have already discovered Manuel Cardoso and the unique character of Portuguese Renaissance music. The present collection duplicates four of the motets on the Tallis Scholars' CD (see our main volume), but the Westminster performances are slightly more robust and add to their character. The *Lamentations for Maundy Thursday* show the composer at his most imaginatively expressive, 'a resplendent example of his chromatic serenity', as Ivan Moody, the writer of the excellent notes on this CD, aptly puts it.

The music of Cardoso's contemporary, Pedro de Cristo (c. 1550–1618) is hardly less individual. His *Magnificat a 8* for two choirs is particularly arresting, as is the much simpler *O magnum mysterium,* while the *Sanctissimi quinque martires* (celebrating five Franciscans who were killed in 1220 while attempting to convert Moroccan Moslems) has a radiant, flowing intensity. Rebelo's *Panis angelicus* is rich in its harmonic feeling, and Fernandez's *Alma redemptoris mater* ends the programme in a mood of quiet contemplation.

'Adeste fidelis' (with Ian Simcock): WADE: *O come, all ye faithful.* TRAD.: *Gabriel's message; O come, O come Emanuel; Ding dong! merrily on high; A maiden most gentle; I wonder as I wander; O little town of Bethlehem; In dulci jubilo; The holly and the ivy.* GAUNTLETT: *Once in Royal David's city.* DARKE: *In the bleak mid-winter.* CORNELIUS: *The three kings.* PETRUS: *Of the Father's love begotten.* KIRKPATRICK: *Away in a manger.* WARLOCK: *Bethlehem Down.* HADLEY: *I sing of a maiden.* GRUBER: *Silent night.* HOWELLS: *Sing lullaby.* TAVERNER: *The Lamb.* PARRY: *Welcome yule.* MENDELSSOHN: *Hark! the herald angels sing.*
*** Hyperion Dig. CDA 66668 [id.].

An extremely well-sung traditional carol collection. Although many of the arrangers are distinguished names, the arrangements of traditional carols are essentially simple, and the concert makes a great appeal by the quality of the singing and the beautiful digital recording, with the choir perfectly focused and realistically set back just at the right distance within the cathedral acoustic. The programme is spiced with one or two attractive modern settings, notably Patrick Hadley's ravishing *I sing of a maiden* and John Taverner's familiar and highly individual carol, *The Lamb.*

'Favourite motets from Westminster Cathedral': MENDELSSOHN: *Ave Maria; Hymn of Praise: I waited for the Lord.* BACH: *Cantata No. 147: Jesu, joy of man's desiring.* FRANCK: *Panis angelicus.* MAWBY: *Ave verum corpus.* ROSSINI: *O salutaris hostia.* HARRIS: *Faire is the heaven.* HOLST: *Ave Maria; Nunc dimittis.* GOUNOD: *Ave Maria.* FAURE: *Maria Mater gratiae.* ELGAR: *Ave verum corpus.* MOZART: *Ave verum corpus.* GRIEG: *Ave maris stella.* DE SEVERAC: *Tantum ergo.* VILLETTE: *Hymne à la Vierge.* SCHUBERT: *The Lord is my Shepherd.*
*** Hyperion Dig. CDA 66669 [id.].

The Westminster Cathedral Choir is a traditional men's and boys' choir of the highest calibre. The treble line is particularly rich, and this is essentially a satisfyingly full-throated concert, although there is no lack of dynamic nuance, and phrasing always flows naturally and musically. Franck's *Panis angelicus,* which gives the collection its sobriquet, is splendidly ripe, and other favourites like Bach's *Jesu, joy of man's desiring* and Mozart's *Ave verum* are most satisfyingly done.

Elgar's *Ave verum* too is a highlight, and Schubert's lovely setting of *The Lord is my Shepherd* is very successful in its English version. Among the novelties, De Séverac's *Tantum ergo* and the touching *Hymne à la Vierge* of Pierre Villette stand out, and the concert ends with a memorable account of Holst's setting of the *Nunc dimittis,* which opens ethereally and then soars into the heavens: the trebles are superbly ardent at the climax. The recording is outstandingly full and the cathedral ambience is caught without too much blurring.

Wunderlich, Fritz (tenor)

'Great voice': Arias and excerpts from: MOZART: *Die Zauberflöte; Die Entführung aus dem Serail.* VERDI: *La Traviata* (with Hilde Gueden); *Rigoletto* (with Erika Köth); *Don Carlos* (with Hermann Prey). TCHAIKOVSKY: *Eugene Onegin.* LORTZING: *Zar und Zimmermann; Der Waffenschmied.* ROSSINI: *Il barbiere di Siviglia.* PUCCINI: *La Bohème* (with Hermann Prey). *Tosca.* Lieder: SCHUBERT: *Heidenröslein.* BEETHOVEN: *Ich liebe dich.* TRAD.: *Funiculì funiculà; Ein Lied geht um die Welt* (with R. Lamy Ch.).
(B) *** DG Classikon 431 110-2 [(M) id. import].

Here is 70 minutes of gloriously heady tenor singing from one of the golden voices of the 1960s. Mozart's *Dies Bildnis* makes a ravishing opener, and *Hier soll ich dich denn sehen* from *Die Entführung* is equally beautiful. Then come two sparkling excerpts from *La Traviata* with Hilde Gueden and some memorable Tchaikovsky, like all the non-German repertoire, sung in German. The Rossini excerpt is wonderfully crisp and stylish.

Wunderlich is joined by the charming Erika Köth in *Rigoletto* and by the excellent Hermann Prey for the rousing *Don Carlos* duet (*Sie ist verloren . . . Er ist's! Carlos!*) and the excerpt from *Bohème.* Last in the operatic group comes the most famous *Tosca* aria, *Und es blitzen die Sterne* (not too difficult to identify in Italian), sung without excessive histrionics. The Schubert and Beethoven Lieder are lovely and, if the two final popular songs (with chorus) bring more fervour than they deserve, one can revel in everything else. Excellent recording throughout. It is a pity there are no translations or notes, but with singing like this one can manage without them. A splendid bargain.